Encyclopedia of

Library and Information Sciences, Fourth Edition

Volume 7

Encyclopedias from the Taylor & Francis Group

Print	Online

Agriculture

Encyclopedia of Agricultural, Food, and Biological Engineering, 2nd Ed.,
2 Vols. Pub'd. 10/21/10
K10554 (978-1-4398-1111-5)   K11382 (978-1-4398-2806-9)

Encyclopedia of Animal Science, 2nd Ed., 2 Vols.   Pub'd. 2/1/11
K10463 (978-1-4398-0932-7)   K10528 (978-0-415-80286-4)

Encyclopedia of Biotechnology in Agriculture and Food   Pub'd. 7/16/10
DK271X (978-0-8493-5027-6)   DKE5044 (978-0-8493-5044-3)

Business and Computer Science

Encyclopedia of Computer Science & Technology, 2nd Ed., 2 Vols.
Pub'd 12/21/2016
K21573 (978-1-4822-0819-1)   K21578 (978-1-4822-0822-1)

Encyclopedia of Information Assurance, 4 Vols.   Pub'd. 12/21/10
AU6620 (978-1-4200-6620-3)   AUE6620 (978-1-4200-6622-7)

Encyclopedia of Information Systems and Technology, 2 Vols.   Pub'd. 12/29/15
K15911 (978-1-4665-6077-2)   K21745 (978-1-4822-1432-1)

Encyclopedia of Library and Information Sciences, 4th Ed.   Publishing 2017
K15223 (978-1-4665-5259-3)   K15224 (978-1-4665-5260-9)

Encyclopedia of Software Engineering, 2 Vols.   Pub'd. 11/24/10
AU5977 (978-1-4200-5977-9)   AUE5977 (978-1-4200-5978-6)

Encyclopedia of Supply Chain Management, 2 Vols.   Pub'd. 12/21/11
K12842 (978-1-4398-6148-6)   K12843 (978-1-4398-6152-3)

Encyclopedia of U.S. Intelligence, 2 Vols.   Pub'd. 12/19/14
AU8957 (978-1-4200-8957-8)   AUE8957 (978-1-4200-8958-5)

Encyclopedia of Wireless and Mobile Communications, 2nd Ed., 3 Vols.
Pub'd. 12/18/12
K14731 (978-1-4665-0956-6)   KE16352 (978-1-4665-0969-6)

Chemistry, Materials and Chemical Engineering

Encyclopedia of Chemical Processing, 5 Vols.   Pub'd. 11/1/05
DK2243 (978-0-8247-5563-8)   DKE499X (978-0-8247-5499-0)

Encyclopedia of Chromatography, 3rd Ed.   Pub'd. 10/12/09
84593 (978-1-4200-8459-7)   84836 (978-1-4200-8483-2)

Encyclopedia of Iron, Steel, and Their Alloys, 5 Vols.   Pub'd. 1/6/16
K14814 (978-1-4665-1104-0)   K14815 (978-1-4665-1105-7)

Encyclopedia of Plasma Technology, 2 Vols.   Pub'd 12/12/2016
K14378 (978-1-4665-0059-4)   K21744 (978-1-4822-1431-4)

Encyclopedia of Supramolecular Chemistry, 2 Vols.   Pub'd. 5/5/04
DK056X (978-0-8247-5056-5)   DKE7259 (978-0-8247-4725-1)

Encyclopedia of Surface & Colloid Science, 3rd Ed., 10 Vols.   Pub'd. 8/27/15
K20465 (978-1-4665-9045-8)   K20478 (978-1-4665-9061-8)

Engineering

Dekker Encyclopedia of Nanoscience and Nanotechnology, 3rd Ed., 7 Vols.
Pub'd. 3/20/14
K14119 (978-1-4398-9134-6)   K14120 (978-1-4398-9135-3)

Encyclopedia of Energy Engineering and Technology, 2nd Ed., 4 Vols.
Pub'd. 12/1/14
K14633 (978-1-4665-0673-2)   KE16142 (978-1-4665-0674-9)

Encyclopedia of Optical and Photonic Engineering, 2nd Ed., 5 Vols.
Pub'd. 9/22/15
K12323 (978-1-4398-5097-8)   K12325 (978-1-4398-5099-2)

Environment

Encyclopedia of Environmental Management, 4 Vols.   Pub'd. 12/13/12
K11434 (978-1-4398-2927-1)   K11440 (978-1-4398-2933-2)

Encyclopedia of Environmental Science and Engineering, 6th Ed., 2 Vols.
Pub'd. 6/25/12
K10243 (978-1-4398-0442-1)   KE0278 (978-1-4398-0517-6)

Encyclopedia of Natural Resources, 2 Vols.   Pub'd. 7/23/14
K12418 (978-1-4398-5258-3)   K12420 (978-1-4398-5260-6)

Medicine

Encyclopedia of Biomaterials and Biomedical Engineering, 2nd Ed.
Pub'd. 5/28/08
H7802 (978-1-4200-7802-2)   HE7803 (978-1-4200-7803-9)

Encyclopedia of Biomedical Polymers and Polymeric Biomaterials, 11 Vols.
Pub'd. 4/2/15
K14324 (978-1-4398-9879-6)   K14404 (978-1-4665-0179-9)

Concise Encyclopedia of Biomedical Polymers and Polymeric Biomaterials,
2 Vols. Pub'd. 8/14/17
K14313 (978-1-4398-9855-0)   KE42253 (978-1-315-11644-0)

Encyclopedia of Biopharmaceutical Statistics, 3rd Ed.   Pub'd. 5/20/10
H100102 (978-1-4398-2245-6)   HE10326 (978-1-4398-2246-3)

Encyclopedia of Clinical Pharmacy   Pub'd. 11/14/02
DK7524 (978-0-8247-0752-1)   DKE6080 (978-0-8247-0608-1)

Encyclopedia of Dietary Supplements, 2nd Ed.   Pub'd. 6/25/10
H100094 (978-1-4398-1928-9)   HE10315 (978-1-4398-1929-6)

Encyclopedia of Medical Genomics and Proteomics, 2 Vols.   Pub'd. 12/29/04
DK2208 (978-0-8247-5564-5)   DK501X (978-0-8247-5501-0)

Encyclopedia of Pharmaceutical Science and Technology, 4th Ed., 6 Vols.
Pub'd. 7/1/13
H100233 (978-1-84184-819-8)   HE10420 (978-1-84184-820-4)

Routledge Encyclopedias

Encyclopedia of Public Administration and Public Policy, 3rd Ed., 5 Vols.
Pub'd. 11/6/15
K16418 (978-1-4665-6909-6)   K16434 (978-1-4665-6936-2)

Routledge Encyclopedia of Modernism   Pub'd 5/11/16
Y137844 (978-1-135-00035-6)

Routledge Encyclopedia of Philosophy Online   Pub'd. 11/1/00
RU22334 (978-0-415-24909-6)

Routledge Performance Archive   Pub'd. 11/12/12
Y148405 (978-0-203-77466-3)

Encyclopedia of

Library and Information Sciences, Fourth Edition

Volume 7

From: *Special Libraries* To: *Zoological Park and Aquarium Libraries and Archives*

Encyclopedia Edited By

John D. McDonald

and

Michael Levine-Clark

CRC Press
Taylor & Francis Group
Boca Raton London New York

CRC Press is an imprint of the
Taylor & Francis Group, an **informa** business

First published 2018 by CRC Press

Published 2019 by CRC Press
Taylor & Francis Group
6000 Broken Sound Parkway NW, Suite 300
Boca Raton, FL 33487-2742

© 2018 by Taylor & Francis Group, LLC
CRC Press is an imprint of the Taylor & Francis Group, an informa business

First issued in paperback 2020

No claim to original U.S. Government works

ISBN-13: 978-1-4665-5259-3 (HB Set)
ISBN-13: 978-0-8153-8634-6 (Vol. 7) (hbk)

ISBN-13: 978-0-3675-7010-1 (PB Set)
ISBN-13: 978-0-3675-7022-4 (Vol. 7) (pbk)

Visit the Taylor & Francis Web site at
http://www.taylorandfrancis.com

and the CRC Press Web site at
http://www.crcpress.com

Encyclopedia of Library and Information Sciences, Fourth Edition

Brief Contents

Volume I

Academic Libraries 1
Accessibility 14
Accreditation of Library and Information
    Studies Programs in the United States
    and Canada 18
Acquisitions Institute at Timberline Lodge ... 22
African Librarianship 33
Altmetrics 44
American Association of Law
    Libraries (AALL) 48
American Association of Museums (AAM) 56
American Association of School
    Librarians (AASL) 59
American Library Association (ALA) 67
American Medical Informatics
    Association (AMIA) 85
American National Standards
    Institute (ANSI) 87
American Society for Information Science
    and Technology (ASIST) 90
Approval Plans 96
Arab Federation for Libraries and
    Information (AFLI) 100
Archival Appraisal and Acquisition 105
Archival Arrangement and Description 115
Archival Documentation 127
Archival Finding Aids 133
Archival Management and Administration .. 141
Archival Reference and Access 149
Archival Science 166
Archives 179
Archivists and Collecting 195
Area and Interdisciplinary Studies
    Literatures and Their Users 209
ARMA International, Inc. 221
Armenia: Libraries, Archives, and
    Museums 228
Art Galleries 241
Art Librarianship 249
Art Museums 259
Artificial Intelligence 269
Artificial Neural Networks and Natural
    Language Processing 279
Arts Literatures and Their Users 293
ASLIB 301
Association for Information Science and
    Technology 311
Association for Information Systems (AIS) ... 318
Association for Library Collections and
    Technical Services 324
Association for Library Service to
    Children (ALSC) 333

Volume I (cont'd.)

Association of College and Research
    Libraries (ACRL) 338
Association of Library Trustees, Advocates,
    Friends and Foundations (ALTAFF) 361
Association of Research Libraries
    (ARL) 364
Association of Specialized and Cooperative
    Library Agencies (ASCLA) 376
Australia: Libraries, Archives, and
    Museums 379
Australian Library and Information
    Association (ALIA) 396
Authentication and Authorization 401
Automated Acquisitions 408
Automatic Abstracting and
    Summarization 418
Automatic Discourse Generation 430
Back-of-the-Book Indexing 440
Bibliographic Control *[ELIS Classic]* 447
Bibliographical Society (London) 456
Bibliographical Society of
    America (BSA) 463
Bibliography 468
Bibliometric Overview of Information
    Science 480
Bibliometric Research: History
    [ELIS Classic] 492
Bibliothèque Nationale de France 531
Binding *[ELIS Classic]* 538
Biological Information and Its Users 554
Blind and Physically Disabled: Library
    Services 563
Bliss Bibliographic Classification
    First Edition *[ELIS Classic]* 573
Bliss Bibliographic Classification
    Second Edition 581
Boolean Algebras *[ELIS Classic]* 591
Brazil: Library Science 597
Brazil: Library Science—Distance
    Education 603
Brazil: Museums 611
British Library 616
Business Informatics 630
Business Information and Its Users 635
Business Literature: History
    [ELIS Classic] 643
Canada: Libraries and Archives 654
Canadian Heritage Information
    Network (CHIN) 675
Canadian Library Association (CLA) 681
Careers and Education in Archives and
    Records Management 685

Volume I (cont'd.)

Careers and Education in Information
    Systems 693
Careers and Education in Library and
    Information Science 706
Careers and Education in Records and
    Information Management 715

Volume II

Cataloging 723
Cataloging Cultural Objects (CCO) 733
Catalogs and Cataloging: History
    [ELIS Classic] 743
Censorship and Content Regulation
    of the Internet 780
Center for Research Libraries 789
Charleston Conference 794
Chartered Institute of Library and
    Information Professionals (CILIP) 806
Chemistry Literature and Its Users
    [ELIS Classic] 814
Chemoinformatics 830
Children and Information Technology 839
Children's Literature 852
Children's Services in Libraries 876
China: Libraries, Archives, and Museums ... 886
Circulation Services 916
Citation Analysis 923
Citation Indexes and the *Web of Science* 940
Citer Motivations *[ELIS Classic]* 951
Classification Theory 958
Clinical Decision-Support Systems 974
College Libraries 983
Communication and Communication
    Studies 994
Communication Policy: United States 1007
Community Informatics 1027
Complexity and Self-Organization 1034
Computer-Mediated Communication
    (CMC) 1044
Computer-Supported Cooperative Work
    (CSCW) 1053
Conservation and Preservation of
    Museum Objects 1068
Controlled Vocabularies for Art,
    Architecture, and Material Culture ... 1076
Corporate Archives 1081
Corporate Art Collections 1086
Corporate Information Centers 1094
Corporate Records Management 1104

Volume II (cont'd.)

Credibility and Cognitive Authority of
    Information 1113
Croatia: Libraries, Archives, and
    Museums 1121
CrossRef Publisher Linking Network 1132
Cultural Memory 1139
Curating Archaeological Artifacts 1147
Curating Natural History Collections 1156
Custody and Chain of Custody 1164
Data and Data Quality 1171
Deaf and Hearing Impaired:
    Communication in Service
    Contexts *[ELIS Classic]* 1183
Decision Sciences 1192
Decision Support Systems 1200
Demand-Driven Acquisition/Patron-Driven
    Acquisition 1209
Denmark: Libraries, Archives, and
    Museums 1215
Descriptive Cataloging Principles 1229
Design Science in the Information
    Sciences 1242
Dewey Decimal Classification (DDC) 1256
Digital Content Licensing 1267
Digital Divide and Inclusion 1279
Digital Humanities 1286
Digital Humanities and Academic
    Libraries 1298
Digital Images 1307
Digital Millennium Copyright
    Act of 1998 1316
Digital Object Identifier (DOI®) System ... 1325
Digital Preservation 1332
Diplomatics 1338
Disaster Planning and Recovery for
    Cultural Institutions 1347
Document Information Systems 1360
Document Theory 1372
Document Type Definition (DTD) 1381
Dublin Core Metadata Initiative (DCMI):
    A Personal History 1390
Economics Literature: History
    [ELIS Classic] 1399
Electronic Records Preservation 1413
Electronic Resources & Libraries (ER&L) ... 1419
Encoded Archival Description 1423
Engineering Literatures and Their Users
    [ELIS Classic] 1433

Volume III

Epistemology 1455
Ethical and Legal Aspects of Archival
    Services 1463
Ethical Aspects of Library and
    Information Science 1469
Ethical Issues in Information Systems 1484
Ethiopia: Libraries, Archives, and
    Museums 1494
Everyday Life Information Seeking 1506
Evidence-Based Practice 1516
Exhibition Design 1523
Facet Analysis *[ELIS Classic]* 1534
Faceted Application of Subject
    Terminology (FAST) 1539
Federal Electronic Information in the
    United States 1549

Volume III (cont'd.)

Film and Broadcast Archives 1560
Film Archiving: History 1584
France: Archives, Museums, and
    Libraries 1589
Functional Requirements for Subject
    Authority Data (FRSAD):
    Conceptual Model 1606
Fuzzy Set Theory 1618
Games and Gaming 1636
Genealogical Literature and Its Users 1644
Genre Theory and Research 1662
Geographic Information Systems (GIS) 1671
Geographical Literature: History
    [ELIS Classic] 1683
Germany: Libraries, Archives, and
    Museums 1693
Global Open Knowledgebase 1710
Government Documents: Collection and
    Management 1715
Greece: Archives 1728
Greece: Libraries 1733
Greece: Museums 1741
Grey Literature *[ELIS Classic]* 1746
HathiTrust 1757
Health Science Professional Literatures
    and Their Users 1763
Historical and Archaeological Sites:
    Development and Preservation 1771
Historical Societies 1779
Historical Sources and Their Users 1786
History of Libraries 1796
History of Museums 1812
History of Paper 1824
History of Public Libraries
    [ELIS Classic] 1836
History of Records and Information
    Management 1850
History of the Book 1859
History: Three Basic Printing Processes 1865
Hospital Libraries 1870
Human–Computer Interaction Research
    in Information Retrieval 1895
Humanities Literatures and Their Users 1909
Hungary: Libraries, Archives, and
    Museums 1917
Hypertext and Hypercard: Early
    Development *[ELIS Classic]* 1935
Illumination *[ELIS Classic]* 1945
Impact Assessment of Cultural
    Institutions 1958
Incunabula *[ELIS Classic]* 1966
Indexing: History and Theory 1978
India: Libraries, Archives and Museums ... 1992
Indigenous Librarianship 2031
Information 2048
Information Arts 2064
Information Behavior 2074
Information Behavior Models 2086
Information Crises and Crisis Information ... 2094
Information Explosion 2101
Information Management 2106
Information Needs 2115
Information Needs and Behaviors of
    Diasporic Populations 2122
Information Needs and Behaviors of
    Populations in Less Developed
    Regions 2130
Information Policy: European Union 2138

Volume III (cont'd.)

Information Policy: United States 2147
Information Practice 2162
Information Retrieval Experimentation
    [ELIS Classic] 2172

Volume IV

Information Retrieval Protocols: Z39.50
    and Search and Retrieve via URL 2181
Information Retrieval Support
    Systems 2192
Information Retrieval Systems 2199
Information Scattering 2210
Information Science 2216
Information Search Process (ISP)
    Model 2232
Information Searching and Search
    Models 2239
Information Society 2253
Information Systems 2272
Information Systems Failure 2280
Information Technology Adoption 2290
Information Technology Literacy 2303
Information Technology Project
    Implementation in Developing
    Countries *[ELIS Classic]* 2312
Information Technology Standards for
    Libraries *[ELIS Classic]* 2341
Information Theory 2350
Information Use for Decision Making 2359
Informetrics 2367
Institutional Records and Archives 2377
Intellectual Freedom and the American
    Library Association (ALA): Historical
    Overview *[ELIS Classic]* 2387
Intelligence and Security Informatics 2398
International and Comparative
    Librarianship 2404
International Association of Sound and
    Audiovisual Archives (IASA) 2413
International Association of Technological
    University Libraries (IATUL) 2418
International Communication Association
    (ICA) 2421
International Council of Museums
    (ICOM) 2429
International Council on Archives (ICA) ... 2437
International Council on Knowledge
    Management (ICKM) 2445
International Federation of Library
    Associations and Institutions
    (IFLA) 2451
International Federation of Television
    Archives (FIAT/IFTA) 2465
International Organization for
    Standardization (ISO) 2470
International Records Management
    Standards ISO 15489 and 23081 2481
International Records Management Trust ... 2487
International Society for Knowledge
    Organization (ISKO) 2494
Internet Genres 2503
Internet Search Tools: History to 2000 2516
InterPARES 2526
iSchools 2536
Israel: Libraries, Archives, and
    Museums 2542

Volume IV (cont'd.)

Japan: Libraries, Archives, and
    Museums 2560
Kazakhstan: Libraries, Archives, and
    Museums 2578
Kenya: Libraries, Museums, and
    Archives 2592
Knowledge 2610
Knowledge Creation and Use in
    Organizations 2618
Knowledge Discovery in Data Streams 2626
Knowledge Management 2640
Knowledge Management Systems 2649
Knowledge Management: Early
    Development 2657
Knowledge Organization System
    Standards 2665
Knowledge: Tacit and Explicit 2677
Latent Semantic Indexing 2688
Latinos and U.S. Libraries: History 2698
Law Firm Librarianship 2705
Law Librarianship 2710
Law Literature and Its Users 2733
Learning and Information Seeking 2751
Libraries 2762
Library and Information Science 2768
Library and Information Technology
    Association (LITA) 2775
Library Anxiety 2782
Library Architecture and Design 2788
Library Architecture: History 2797
Library Automation: History 2810
Library Consortia in Europe 2822
Library Fundraising and Development 2832
Library Leadership and Management
    Association (LLAMA) 2841
Library of Congress Classification (LCC) 2847
Library of Congress Genre/Form Terms
    for Library and Archival Materials ... 2856
Library of Congress Subject Headings
    (LCSH) 2866
Library of Congress: History 2879
Library Portals and Gateways 2892
Library Publishing Initiatives:
    North America 2901

Volume V

Library Science in the United States:
    Early History 2909
Library Technical Services 2918
Linguistics and the Information Sciences 2927
Linked Data 2938
Lithuania: Libraries and Librarianship 2943
Louvre 2958
Machine Readable Cataloging (MARC):
    1961–1974 [ELIS Classic] 2963
Machine Readable Cataloging (MARC):
    1975–2007 2980
Makerspaces in Libraries 2990
Management of Very Large Distributed
    Shared Collections [ELIS Classic] 2997
Managing an Information Business 3004
Marketing Library and Information
    Services 3011
Mathematics Literature: History
    [ELIS Classic] 3019
Medical Library Association (MLA) 3033

Volume V (cont'd.)

Medical Literature: History
    [ELIS Classic] 3041
Metadata and Digital Information
    [ELIS Classic] 3058
Metamarkup Languages: SGML and
    XML 3072
Mexico: Libraries, Archives, and
    Museums 3082
Modeling Documents in Their Context 3105
Moldova: Archives, Museums, and
    Libraries 3117
Moving Image Indexing 3129
Multilingual Information Access 3140
Museum Accreditation Program 3146
Museum Architecture and Gallery Design ... 3148
Museum Collecting and Collections 3161
Museum Computer Network (MCN) 3170
Museum Informatics 3176
Museum Management 3185
Museum Registration and Documentation ... 3199
Museum Studies 3214
Museum Web Sites and Digital
    Collections 3222
Museums 3233
Museums and Community 3243
Museums and Their Visitors: Historic
    Relationship 3251
Museums as Place 3258
Music Information Retrieval 3267
Music Librarianship 3275
Name Authority Control 3288
National Archives 3298
National Biological Information
    Infrastructure (NBII) 3306
National Historical Publications and
    Records Commission (NHPRC) 3315
National Libraries 3320
National Library of Medicine 3334
Natural Language Processing for
    Information Retrieval 3346
Network Management 3356
Network of European Museum
    Organisations (NEMO) 3365
Networked Knowledge Organization
    Systems/Services (NKOS) 3366
New Zealand Aotearoa: Libraries 3371
Non-governmental Organizations and
    Information 3380
North American Serials Interest Group 3388
OCLC: A Worldwide Library
    Cooperative 3392
Older Adults' Information: Needs and
    Behavior 3406
One-Person Libraries 3413
Online Catalog Subject Searching 3422
Online Library Instruction 3432
Online Public Access Catalogs (OPACs)
    [ELIS Classic] 3450
Ontologies and Their Definition 3455
Open Access Scholarship and Publishing ... 3465
Open Archival Information System (OAIS)
    Reference Model 3477
Open Source Software 3488
Oral History in Libraries and Archives 3494
ORCID 3505
Organization Theories 3510
Organizational Culture 3520
Organizational Learning 3526

Volume V (cont'd.)

Organizational Memory 3534
Pacific Islands Association of Libraries
    and Archives (PIALA) 3541
Papyrology 3552
Patents and Patent Searching 3560
People with Disabilities 3573
Personal Information Management 3584
Peru: Libraries and Library Science 3606
Philosophy and the Information Sciences 3610
Philosophy of Science [ELIS Classic] 3623

Volume VI

Physical Sciences and Mathematics
    Literatures and Their Users 3637
Piracy in Digital Media 3649
Plagiarism of Print and Electronic
    Resources 3664
Poland: Libraries and Archives 3674
Politics of Representation in Museums 3688
Popular Literature Genres 3700
Precision and Recall [ELIS Classic] 3708
Presidential Libraries 3714
Primary Records: Future Prospects
    [ELIS Classic] 3719
Print on Demand 3733
Private Presses and Fine Printing
    [ELIS Classic] 3738
Provenance of Archival Materials 3746
Provenance of Museum Objects 3756
Provenance of Rare Books 3766
Public Librarianship [ELIS Classic] 3774
Public Libraries [ELIS Classic] 3781
Public Library Association (PLA) 3801
Qualitative Research Methods in Library
    and Information Science
    [ELIS Classic] 3806
Rare Book Collections 3820
Reading and Reading Acquisition 3830
Reading Disorders 3841
Reading Interests 3850
Recommender Systems and Expert
    Locators 3860
Records Compliance and Risk
    Management 3869
Records Continuum Model 3874
Records Organization and Access 3887
Records Retention Schedules 3892
Reference and Informational Genres 3897
Reference and User Services Association
    (RUSA) 3908
Reference Services 3912
Regional Library Networks:
    United States 3920
Relevance in Theory 3926
Relevance Judgments and Measurements 3940
Renaissance Libraries [ELIS Classic] 3948
Resource Description Framework (RDF) 3961
Saudi Arabia: Libraries, Archives, and
    Museums 3970
Scholarly and Trade Publishing
    [ELIS Classic] 3982
School Librarianship 3991
School Libraries 4000
Science and Engineering Librarianship 4008
Science and Technology Studies 4020
Search Engine Optimization 4029

Volume VI (cont'd.)

Search Engines 4046
Self-Publishing Online 4054
Semantic Interoperability 4062
Semantic Web 4080
Semiotics 4094
Senegal: Libraries, Archives, and
    Museums 4104
Sense-Making 4113
Serbia: Libraries, Archives, and
    Museums 4125
Serials Collection and Management
    [ELIS Classic] 4139
Serials Vendors [ELIS Classic] 4150
Shared Libraries 4158
Site Museums and Monuments 4164
Slovakia: Libraries, Archives, and
    Museums 4173
Smithsonian Institution 4188
Social Epistemology 4197
Social Influences on Classification 4204
Social Informatics 4212
Social Justice in Library and Information
    Science 4218
Social Networks and Information
    Transfer 4235
Social Science Literatures and Their
    Users [ELIS Classic] 4246
Social Science Professional Literatures
    and Their Users 4255
Society for Scholarly Publishing (SSP) 4262
Society for the History of Authorship,
    Reading and Publishing (SHARP) 4268
Society of American Archivists (SAA) 4271
Sociology of Reading 4279
Sociology of the Information Disciplines 4286
Software and Information Industry
    Association (SIIA) 4297
Sound and Audio Archives 4299
South Korea: Archives and Libraries 4307
Spain: Libraries, Archives, and Museums 4314
Special Collections 4335
Special Collections and Manuscripts 4343
Special Librarianship 4351

Volume VII

Special Libraries 4361
Special Libraries Association (SLA) 4370

Volume VII (cont'd.)

Specialty Museums 4379
State Archives 4384
State Libraries and State Library
    Agencies 4392
State-Sponsored Destruction of Books
    and Libraries 4400
Still Image Indexing 4407
Still Image Search and Retrieval 4417
Storytelling 4437
Strategic Planning in Academic Libraries 4447
Students' Information: Needs and
    Behavior 4459
Subject Cataloging Principles and
    Systems 4466
Subscription Libraries [ELIS Classic] 4478
Switzerland: Libraries, Archives, and
    Museums 4487
Tanzania: Libraries, Archives, Museums,
    and Information Systems 4497
Task-Based Information Searching:
    Research Methods 4526
Taxonomy 4537
Technical Writing 4547
Test Collections 4554
Text Encoding Initiative (TEI) 4559
Text REtrieval Conference (TREC) 4569
Theft, Vandalism, and Security in
    Libraries and Archives 4576
Theft, Vandalism, and Security in
    Museums 4593
Theological Librarianship 4604
Topic Maps 4611
Tunisia: Libraries, Archives, and
    Museums 4624
Ukraine: Libraries 4642
Undergraduate Library Collections
    [ELIS Classic] 4649
UNESCO: Communication and
    Information Sector 4656
Unicode Standard 4662
Unified Medical Language System®
    (UMLS®) Project 4672
Uniform Computer Information
    Transactions Act (UCITA) 4680
Unions in Public and Academic Libraries 4689
United Kingdom: Archives and
    Archival Science 4699
United Kingdom: Libraries and
    Librarianship 4707

Volume VII (cont'd.)

United Kingdom: Museums and
    Museology 4723
United States: Archives and
    Archival Science 4740
United States: Libraries and
    Librarianship in the 21st Century 4766
United States: Museums 4776
Universal Decimal Classification
    (UDC) 4783
University Archives 4791
Usability Testing of User Interfaces in
    Libraries 4797
User-Centered Design of Information
    Systems 4803
User-Centered Revolution: 1970–1995
    [ELIS Classic] 4812
User-Centered Revolution: 1995–2008 4847
User-Oriented and Cognitive Models of
    Information Retrieval 4872
Venezuela: Libraries and Librarianship 4886
Version Control 4896
Vietnam: Libraries, Archives, and
    Museums 4902
Visitor Studies 4917
Visual and Performing Arts Archives 4925
Visual Resources Association (VRA) 4933
Visual Resources Management in
    Cultural Institutions 4940
Volunteer Services in Cultural
    Institutions 4951
Wayfinding and Signage 4958
Web Scale Discovery Services 4978
Webometrics 4983
Word Processing: Early History
    [ELIS Classic] 4993
World Intellectual Property Organization
    (WIPO) 5000
World Summit on the Information
    Society (WSIS) 5012
World Wide Web (WWW) 5019
World Wide Web Consortium (W3C) 5034
XML Information Retrieval 5039
Young Adult Library Services Association
    (YALSA) 5052
Young Adult Services in Libraries 5058
Youth Information: Needs and
    Behavior 5067
Zoological Park and Aquarium Libraries
    and Archives 5077

Encyclopedia of Library and Information Sciences, Fourth Edition

Editors-in-Chief

John D. McDonald
Analytics and Assessment, EBSCO Information Services

Michael Levine-Clark
University of Denver Libraries, Denver, Colorado

Editorial Advisory Board

Contributors

June Abbas / *School of Library and Information Studies, University of Oklahoma, Norman, Oklahoma, U.S.A.*

Richard Abel / *Portland, Oregon, U.S.A.*

Eileen G. Abels / *College of Information Science and Technology, Drexel University, Philadelphia, Pennsylvania, U.S.A.*

Tia Abner / *American Medical Informatics Association (AMIA), Bethesda, Maryland, U.S.A.*

Donald C. Adcock / *Dominican University, River Forest, Illinois, U.S.A.*

Kendra S. Albright / *School of Library and Information Science, University of South Carolina, Columbia, South Carolina, U.S.A.*

Mikael Alexandersson / *University of Gothenburg, Gothenburg, Sweden*

Joan M. Aliprand / *Cupertino, California, U.S.A.*

Jacqueline Allen / *Dallas Museum of Art, Dallas, Texas, U.S.A.*

Romano Stephen Almagno / *International College of St. Bonaventure, Rome, Italy*

Connie J. Anderson-Cahoon / *Southern Oregon University Library, Ashland, Oregon, U.S.A.*

Karen Anderson / *Archives and Information Science, Mid Sweden University, ITM, Härnösand, Sweden*

Rick Anderson / *University of Utah, Salt Lake City, Utah, U.S.A.*

Silviu Andrieş-Tabac / *Institute of Cultural Heritage, Moldova Academy of Sciences, Chişinău, Republic of Moldova*

Peng Hwa Ang / *Wee Kim Wee School of Communication and Information, Nanyang Technological University, Singapore*

Hermina G.B. Anghelescu / *School of Library and Information Science, Wayne State University, Detroit, Michigan, U.S.A.*

Leah Arroyo / *American Association of Museums, Washington, District of Columbia, U.S.A.*

Terry Asla / *Senior Lifestyles Researcher, Seattle, U.S.A.*

Shiferaw Assefa / *University of Kansas, Lawrence, Kansas, U.S.A.*

Ilse Assmann / *Radio Broadcast Facilities, SABC, Johannesburg, South Africa*

Maija-Leena Aulikki Huotari / *University of Oulu, Oulu, Finland*

Henriette D. Avram / *Library of Congress, Washington, District of Columbia, U.S.A.*

Sven Axsäter / *Department of Industrial Management and Logistics, Lund University, Lund, Sweden*

Murtha Baca / *Getty Research Institute, Los Angeles, California, U.S.A.*

Roger S. Bagnall / *Institute for the Study of the Ancient World, New York University, New York, New York, U.S.A.*

Nestor Bamidis / *GSA-Archives of Macedonia, Thessaloniki, Greece*

Franz Barachini / *Business Innovation Consulting—Austria, Langenzersdorf, Austria*

Rebecca O. Barclay / *Rensselaer Polytechnic Institute, Troy, New York, U.S.A.*

Judit Bar-Ilan / *Department of Information Science, Bar-Ilan University, Ramat Gan, Israel*

Alex W. Barker / *Museum of Art and Archaeology, University of Missouri, Columbia, Missouri, U.S.A.*

John A. Bateman / *University of Bremen, Bremen, Germany*

Marcia J. Bates / *Department of Information Studies, Graduate School of Education and Information Studies, University of California, Los Angeles (UCLA), Los Angeles, California, U.S.A.*

Philippe Baumard / *School of Engineering, Stanford University, Stanford, California, U.S.A., and University Paul Cézanne, Aix-en-Provence, France*

David Bawden / *City, University of London, London, U.K.*

Jennifer Bawden / *Museum Studies Program, Faculty of Information Studies, University of Toronto, Toronto, Ontario, Canada*

David Bearman / *Archives & Museum Informatics, Toronto, Ontario, Canada*

William K. Beatty / *Northwestern University Medical School, Chicago, Illinois, U.S.A.*

A.R. Bednarek / *University of Florida, Gainesville, Florida, U.S.A.*

Clare Beghtol / *Faculty of Information Studies, University of Toronto, Toronto, Ontario, Canada*

Lori Bell / *Alliance Library System, East Peoria, Illinois, U.S.A.*

Danna Bell-Russel / *Library of Congress, Washington, District of Columbia, U.S.A.*

William Benedon / *Benedon & Associates, Encino, California, U.S.A.*

Anna Bergaliyeva / *Kazakhstan Institute of Management, Economics and Strategic Research (KIMEP), Almaty, Kazakhstan*

Sidney E. Berger / *Phillips Library, Peabody Essex Museum, Salem, Massachusetts, U.S.A.*

Andrew J. Berner / *University Club of New York, New York, New York, U.S.A.*

Sean F. Berrigan / *Policy, Library and Archives Canada, Ottawa, Ontario, Canada*

John W. Berry / *NILRC: Network of Illinois Learning Resources in Community Colleges, Dominican University, River Forest, Illinois, U.S.A.*

Michael W. Berry / *Department of Electrical Engineering and Computer Science, University of Tennessee, Knoxville, Tennessee, U.S.A.*

Suresh K. Bhavnani / *Center for Computational Medicine and Bioinformatics, University of Michigan, Ann Arbor, Michigan, U.S.A.*

Tamara Biggs / *Chicago History Museum, Chicago, Illinois, U.S.A.*

Frank Birkebæk / *Roskilde Museum, Roskilde, Denmark*

Ann P. Bishop / *Graduate School of Library and Information Science, University of Illinois at Urbana-Champaign, Urbana, Illinois, U.S.A.*

Julia Blixrud / *Association of Research Libraries, Washington, District of Columbia, U.S.A.*

Gloria Bordogna / *Italian National Research Council, Institute for the Dynamics of Environmental Processes, Dalmine, Italy*

Steve Bosch / *Administration Department, University of Arizona, Tucson, Arizona, U.S.A.*

Kimberly S. Bostwick / *Ecology and Evolutionary Biology, Cornell University Museum of Vertebrates, Ithaca, New York, U.S.A.*

Natalia T. Bowdoin / *University of South Carolina Aiken, Aiken, South Carolina, U.S.A.*

Patrick J. Boylan / *Department of Cultural Policy and Management, City University, London, U.K.*

Amy E. Brand / *CrossRef, Lynnfield, Massachusetts, U.S.A.*

Judy Brooker / *Australian Library and Information Association, Deakin, Australian Capital Territory, Australia*

Terrence Brooks / *iSchool, University of Washington, Seattle, Washington, U.S.A.*

Vanda Broughton / *School of Library, Archive and Information Studies, University College London, London, U.K.*

Cecelia Brown / *School of Library and Information Studies, University of Oklahoma, Norman, Oklahoma, U.S.A.*

Jos de Bruijn / *Digital Enterprise Research Institute, University of Innsbruck, Innsbruck, Austria*

Steve Bryant / *BFI National Archive, Herts, U.K.*

Alan Bryden / *International Organization for Standardization, Geneva, Switzerland*

Jeff E. Bullard / *Free Library of Philadelphia, Philadelphia, Pennsylvania, U.S.A.*

Kathleen Burns / *Beinecke Rare Book and Manuscript Library, Yale University, New Haven, Connecticut, U.S.A.*

Brenda A. Burton / *Library, Kirkland & Ellis LLP, Chicago, IL, U.S.A.*

E. Burton Swanson / *Anderson School of Management, University of California, Los Angeles, Los Angeles, California, U.S.A.*

Donald I. Butcher / *Canadian Library Association, Ottawa, Ontario, Canada*

Kevin Butterfield / *Wolf Law Library, College of William and Mary, Williamsburg, Virginia, U.S.A.*

Alex Byrne / *University of Technology, Sydney—Sydney, New South Wales, Australia*

Brian Byrne / *Discipline of Psychology, School of Behavioural, Cognitive and Social Sciences, University of New England, Armidale, New South Wales, Australia, Australian Research Council Centre of Excellence in Cognition and its Disorder, Australia, and National Health and Medical Research Council Centre of Research Excellence in Twin Research, Australia*

Bernadette G. Callery / *School of Information Sciences, University of Pittsburgh, Pittsburgh, Pennsylvania, U.S.A.*

Paul D. Callister / *Leon E. Bloch Law Library, University of Missouri-Kansas City School of Law, Kansas City, Missouri, U.S.A.*

Perrine Canavaggio / *International Council on Archives, Paris, France*

Sarah R. Canino / *Dickinson Music Library, Vassar College, Poughkeepsie, New York, U.S.A.*

Robert Capra / *School of Information and Library Science, University of North Carolina, Chapel Hill, North Carolina, U.S.A.*

Nicholas Carroll / *Hastings Research, Inc., Las Vegas, Nevada, U.S.A.*

Ben Carterette / *Department of Computer and Information Sciences, University of Delaware, Newark, Delaware, U.S.A.*

Vittorio Castelli / *T.J. Watson Research Center, IBM, Yorktown Heights, New York, U.S.A.*

Jane Rosetta Virginia Caulton / *Library of Congress, Washington, District of Columbia, U.S.A.*

Richard Cave / *Formerly at the Public Library of Science, San Francisco, California, U.S.A.*

Roderick Cave / *Loughborough University, Loughborough, U.K.*

Marcel Caya / *Department of History, University of Quebec at Montreal (UQAM), Montreal, Quebec, Canada*

Frank Cervone / *Purdue University Calumet, Hammond, Indiana, U.S.A.*

Leslie Champeny / *Alaska Resources Library and Information Services (ARLIS), Anchorage, Alaska, U.S.A.*

Lois Mai Chan / *School of Library and Information Science, University of Kentucky, Lexington, Kentucky, U.S.A.*

Sergio Chaparro-Univazo / *Graduate School of Library and Information Science, Simmons College, Boston, Massachusetts, U.S.A.*

Mary K. Chelton / *Graduate School of Library and Information Studies, Queens College Flushing, New York, U.S.A.*

Hsinchun Chen / *Department of Management Information Systems, University of Arizona, Tucson, Arizona, U.S.A.*

Jianhua Chen / *Computer Science Department, Louisiana State University, Baton Rouge, Louisiana, U.S.A.*

Eric R. Childress / *OCLC, Dublin, Ohio, U.S.A.*

Michael A. Chilton / *Department of Management, Kansas State University, Manhattan, Kansas, U.S.A.*

TzeHuey Chiou-Peng / *Spurlock Museum, University of Illinois at Urbana-Champaign, Urbana, Illinois, U.S.A.*

Hyun-Yang Cho / *Department of Library and Information Science, Kyonggi University, Suwon, South Korea*

Jae-Hwang Choi / *Department of Library and Information Science, Kyungpook National University, Daegu, South Korea*

Carol E.B. Choksy / *School of Library and Information Science, Indiana University, Bloomington, Indiana, U.S.A.*

Su Kim Chung / *University Libraries, University of Nevada–Las Vegas, Las Vegas, Nevada, U.S.A.*

James Church / *University Libraries, University of California, Berkeley, Berkeley, California, U.S.A.*

Barbara H. Clubb / *Ottawa Public Library, Ottawa, Ontario, Canada*

Arlene Cohen / *Pacific Islands Library Consultant, Seattle, Washington, U.S.A.*

Barbara Cohen-Stratyner / *New York Public Library for the Performing Arts, New York, U.S.A.*

Edward T. Cokely / *Center for Adaptive Behavior and Cognition, Max Planck Institute for Human Development, Berlin, Germany*

Arthur H. Cole / *Harvard University, Cambridge, Massachusetts, U.S.A.*

John Y. Cole / *Center for the Book, Library of Congress, Washington, District of Columbia, U.S.A.*

Patrick Tod Colegrove / *DeLaMare Science & Engineering Library, University Libraries, University of Nevada, Reno, Reno, Nevada, U.S.A.*

Edwin T. Coman, Jr. / *University of California, Riverside, California, U.S.A.*

Nora T. Corley / *Arctic Institute of North America, Montreal, Quebec, Canada*

Sheila Corrall / *Department of Information Studies, University of Sheffield, Sheffield, U.K.*

Erica Cosijn / *Department of Information Science, University of Pretoria, Pretoria, South Africa*

Richard J. Cox / *School of Computing and Information, University of Pittsburgh, Pittsburgh, Pennsylvania, U.S.A.*

Barbara M. Cross / *Records and Information Management, Sony Pictures Entertainment, Culver City, California, U.S.A.*

Kevin Crowston / *School of Information Studies, Syracuse University, Syracuse, New York, U.S.A.*

Adrian Cunningham / *National Archives of Australia (NAA), Canberra, Australian Capital Territory, Australia*

Judith N. Currano / *University of Pennsylvania, Philadelphia, Pennsylvania, U.S.A.*

Susan Curzon / *University Library, California State University–Northridge, Northridge, California, U.S.A.*

Ingetraut Dahlberg / *Bad Koenig, Germany*

Nan Christian Ploug Dahlkild / *Royal School of Library and Information Science, Copenhagen, Denmark*

Jay E. Daily / *University of Pittsburgh, Pittsburgh, Pennsylvania, U.S.A.*

Kimiz Dalkir / *Graduate School of Library and Information Studies, McGill University, Montreal, Quebec, Canada*

Prudence W. Dalrymple / *Drexel University College of Computing & Informatics, Philadelphia, Pennsylvania, U.S.A.*

Marcel Danesi / *Department of Anthropology, University of Toronto, Toronto, Ontario, Canada*

Xuan Hong Dang / *Computer Vision and Image Understanding, Institute for Infocomm, A* STAR, Singapore*

Yan Dang / *Department of Management Information Systems, University of Arizona, Tucson, Arizona, U.S.A.*

Evelyn Daniel / *School of Information and Library Science, University of North Carolina at Chapel Hill, Chapel Hill, North Carolina, U.S.A.*

Richard A. Danner / *School of Law, Duke University, Durham, North Carolina, U.S.A.*

Regina Dantas / *Museu Nacional, HCTE, Universidade Federal do Rio de Janeiro, Rio de Janeiro, Brazil*

Daniel C. Danzig / *Consultant, Pasadena, California, U.S.A.*

Robert Allen Daugherty / *University Library, University of Illinois at Chicago, Chicago, Illinois, U.S.A.*

Charles H. Davis / *Indiana University, Bloomington, IN, U.S.A., and School of Library and Information Science, Indiana University, Bloomington, Indiana, U.S.A.*

Gordon B. Davis / *Carlson School of Management, University of Minnesota, Minneapolis, Minnesota, U.S.A.*

Mary Ellen Davis / *American Library Association, Chicago, Illinois, U.S.A.*

Peter Davis / *International Centre for Cultural and Heritage Studies, Newcastle University, Newcastle upon Tyne, U.K.*

Sheryl Davis / *University Library, University of California, Riverside, Riverside, California, U.S.A.*

Ronald E. Day / *School of Library and Information Science, Indiana University, Bloomington, Indiana, U.S.A.*

Cheryl Dee / *School of Library and Information Science, University of South Florida, Tampa, Florida, U.S.A.*

Robert DeHart / *Department of History, Middle Tennessee State University, Murfreesboro, Tennessee, U.S.A.*

Brenda Dervin / *School of Communication, Ohio State University, Columbus, Ohio, U.S.A.*

Brian Detlor / *Information Systems, McMaster University, Hamilton, Ontario, Canada*

Don E. Detmer / *American Medical Informatics Association (AMIA), Bethesda, Maryland, U.S.A.*

Stella G. Dextre Clarke / *Information Consultant, Oxfordshire, U.K.*

Catherine Dhérent / *National Library of France, Paris, France*

Anne R. Diekema / *Gerald R. Sherratt Library, Southern Utah University, Cedar City, Utah, U.S.A.*

Susan S. DiMattia / *DiMattia Associates, Stamford, Connecticut, U.S.A.*

Gloria Dinerman / *The Library Co-Op, Inc., Edison, New Jersey, U.S.A.*

Jesse David Dinneen / *School of Information Studies, McGill University, Montreal, Quebec, Canada*

Bernard Dione / *School of Librarianship, Archivists Information Science (EBAD), Cheikh Anta Diop University, Dakar, Senegal*

Dieyi Diouf / *Central Library, Cheikh Anta Diop University of Dakar, Dakar, Senegal*

Keith Donohue / *National Historical Publications and Records Commission, Washington, District of Columbia, U.S.A.*

Ann Doyle / *X̲wi7x̲wa Library, First Nations House of Learning, University of British Columbia, Vancouver, British Columbia, Canada*

Carol D. Doyle / *Government Documents Department and Map Library, California State University, Fresno, California, U.S.A.*

Marek J. Druzdzel / *School of Information Sciences and Intelligent Systems Program, University of Pittsburgh, Pittsburgh, Pennsylvania, U.S.A., and Faculty of Computer Science, Bialystok Technical University, Bialystok, Poland*

Kathel Dunn / *National Library of Medicine, Bethesda, Maryland, U.S.A.*

Luciana Duranti / *School of Library, Archival and Information Studies, University of British Columbia, Vancouver, British Columbia, Canada*

Joan C. Durrance / *School of Information, University of Michigan, Ann Arbor, Michigan, U.S.A.*

Maria Economou / *Department of Communication and Cultural Technology, University of the Aegean, Mytilini, Greece*

Gary Edson / *Center for Advanced Study in Museum Science and Heritage Management, Museum of Texas Tech University, Lubbock, Texas, U.S.A.*

Mary B. Eggert / *Library, Kirkland & Ellis LLP, Chicago, IL, U.S.A.*

Daniel Eisenberg / *Florida State University, Tallahassee, Florida, U.S.A.*

Innocent I. Ekoja / *University Library, University of Abuja, Abuja, Nigeria*

Sarah Elliott / *International Centre for Cultural and Heritage Studies, Newcastle University, Newcastle upon Tyne, U.K.*

David Ellis / *Department of Information Studies, Aberystwyth University, Wales, U.K.*

Jill Emery / *Portland State University Library, Portland, Oregon, U.S.A.*

Zorana Ercegovac / *InfoEN Associates, Los Angeles, California, U.S.A.*

Timothy L. Ericson / *School of Information Science, University of Wisconsin-Milwaukee, Milwaukee, Wisconsin, U.S.A.*

Elena Escolano Rodríguez / *National Library of Spain, Madrid, Spain*

Leigh S. Estabrook / *Graduate School of Library and Information Science, University of Illinois at Urbana- / Champaign, Champaign, Illinois, U.S.A.*

Mark E. Estes / *Alameda County Law Library, Oakland, California, U.S.A.*

Beth Evans / *Library, Brooklyn College, City University of New York, Brooklyn, New York, U.S.A.*

Joanne Evans / *Centre for Organisational and Social Informatics, Monash University, Melbourne, Victoria, Australia*

Dominic J. Farace / *Grey Literature Network Service, TextRelease/GreyNet, Amsterdam, The Netherlands*

David Farneth / *Special Collections and Institutional Records, Getty Research Institute, Los Angeles, California, U.S.A.*

Sharon Fawcett / *Office of Presidential Libraries, National Archives and Records Administration, College Park, Maryland, U.S.A.*

Dieter Fensel / *Institute of Computer Science, University of Innsbruck, Innsbruck, Austria, and National University of Ireland, Galway, Galway, Ireland*

Thomas L. Findley / *Leo A. Daly/Architects & Engineers, Omaha, Nebraska, U.S.A.*

Karen E. Fisher / *Information School, University of Washington, Seattle, Washington, U.S.A.*

Nancy Fjällbrant / *Chalmers University of Technology Library, International Association of Technological University Libraries, Gothenburg, Sweden*

Julia Flanders / *Brown University, Providence, Rhode Island, U.S.A.*

Nancy Flury Carlson / *Westinghouse Electric Corporation, Pittsburgh, Pennsylvania, U.S.A.*

Roger R. Flynn / *School of Information Sciences and Intelligent Systems Program, University of Pittsburgh, Pittsburgh, Pennsylvania, U.S.A.*

Helen Forde / *Department of Information Studies, University College London, London, U.K.*

Douglas J. Foskett / *University of London, London, U.K.*

Susan Foutz / *Institute for Learning Innovation, Edgewater, Maryland, U.S.A.*

Christopher Fox / *Department of Computer Science, James Madison University, Harrisonburg, Virginia, U.S.A.*

Carl Franklin / *Consultant, Columbus, Ohio, U.S.A.*

Jonathan A. Franklin / *Gallagher Law Library, University of Washington, Seattle, Washington, U.S.A.*

Thomas J. Froehlich / *School of Library and Information Science, Kent State University, Kent, Ohio, U.S.A.*

Steve Fuller / *Department of Sociology, University of Warwick, Coventry, U.K.*

Crystal Fulton / *School of Information and Communication Studies, University College Dublin, Dublin, Ireland*

Carla J. Funk / *Medical Library Association, Chicago, Illinois, U.S.A.*

Jonathan Furner / *Department of Information Studies University of California, Los Angeles, Los Angeles, California, U.S.A.*

Dennis Galletta / *Katz Graduate School of Business, University of Pittsburgh, Pittsburgh, Pennsylvania, U.S.A.*

D. Linda Garcia / *Communication Culture and Technology, Georgetown University, Washington, District of Columbia, U.S.A.*

Holly Gardinier / *Honnold/Mudd Library, Libraries of The Claremont Colleges, Claremont, California, U.S.A.*

Sally Gardner Reed / *Association of Library Trustees, Advocates, Friends and Foundations (ALTAFF), Philadelphia, Pennsylvania, U.S.A.*

Janifer Gatenby / *Online Computer Library Center (OCLC), Leiden, The Netherlands*

Ramesh C. Gaur / *Kalanidhi Division, Indira Gandhi National Centre for the Arts (IGNCA), New Delhi, India*

Lee Anne George / *Association of Research Libraries, Washington, District of Columbia, U.S.A.*

David E. Gerard / *College of Librarianship Wales, Cardiganshire, Wales, U.K.*

Malcolm Getz / *Department of Economics, Vanderbilt University, Nashville, Tennessee, U.S.A.*

Mary W. Ghikas / *American Library Association, Chicago, Illinois, U.S.A.*

Nicholas Gibbins / *School of Electronics and Computer Science, University of Southampton, Southampton, U.K.*

Gerd Gigerenzer / *Center for Adaptive Behavior and Cognition, Max Planck Institute for Human Development, Berlin, Germany*

Tommaso Giordano / *Library, European University Institute, Florence, Italy*

Lilian Gisesa / *Kenya National Archives, Nairobi, Kenya*

Edward A. Goedeken / *Iowa State University, Ames, Iowa, U.S.A.*

Warren R. Goldmann / *National Technical Institute for the Deaf, Rochester Institute of Technology, Rochester, New York, U.S.A.*

David Gordon / *Milwaukee Art Museum, Milwaukee, Wisconsin, U.S.A.*

David B. Gracy II / *School of Information, University of Texas at Austin, Austin, Texas, U.S.A.*

Karen F. Gracy / *School of Library and Information Science, Kent State University, Kent, Ohio, U.S.A.*

Renny Granda / *Universidad Central de Venezuela, Caracas, Venezuela*

Paul Gray / *School of Information Systems and Technology, Claremont Graduate University, Claremont, California, U.S.A.*

Jane Greenberg / *Metadata Research Center, School of Information and Library Science, University of North Carolina at Chapel Hill, Chapel Hill, North Carolina, U.S.A.*

Karen Greenwood / *American Medical Informatics Association (AMIA), Bethesda, Maryland, U.S.A.*

Jill E. Grogg / *Libraries, University of Alabama, Tuscaloosa, Alabama, U.S.A.*

Melissa Gross / *School of Information, Florida State University, Tallahassee, Florida, U.S.A.*

Andrew Grove / *Guest Faculty, Information School, University of Washington, Seattle, Washington, U.S.A.*

Dinesh K. Gupta / *Department of Library and Information Science, Vardhaman Mahaveer Open University, 3 Kota, India*

Laurel L. Haak / *Open Researcher and Contributor ID, Inc. (ORCID), U.S.A.*

Kate Hagan / *American Association of Law Libraries, Chicago, Illinois, U.S.A.*

Kathleen Hall / *Leon E. Bloch Law Library, University of Missouri-Kansas City School of Law, Kansas City, Missouri, U.S.A.*

Virginia M.G. Hall / *Center for Educational Resources, The Sheridan Libraries, Johns Hopkins University, Baltimore, Maryland, U.S.A.*

Wendy Hall / *Intelligence, Agents, Multimedia Group, University of Southampton, Southampton, U.K.*

Stuart Hamilton / *International Federation of Library Associations and Institutions, The Hague, The Netherlands*

Maureen L. Hammer / *Knowledge Management, Batelle Memorial Institute, Charlottesville, Virginia, U.S.A.*

Jong-Yup Han / *Research Information Team, KORDI, Seoul, South Korea*

Debra Gold Hansen / *School of Library and Information Science, San Jose State University, Yorba Linda, California, U.S.A.*

Derek L. Hansen / *University of Maryland, College Park, Maryland, U.S.A.*

Eugene R. Hanson / *Shippensburg State College, Shippensburg, Pennsylvania, U.S.A.*

Jane Hardy / *Australian Library and Information Association, Deakin, Australian Capital Territory, Australia*

Julie Hart / *American Association of Museums, Washington, District of Columbia, U.S.A.*

Hiroyuki Hatano / *Surugadai University, Saitama, Japan*

Robert M. Hayes / *Department of Information Studies, University of California, Los Angeles, Los Angeles, California, U.S.A.*

Caroline Haythornthwaite / *Graduate School of Library and Information Science, University of Illinois at Urbana- / Champaign, Champaign, Illinois, U.S.A.*

Penny Hazelton / *Gallagher Law Library, University of Washington, Seattle, Washington, U.S.A.*

P. Bryan Heidorn / *Graduate School of Library and Information Science, University of Illinois at Urbana-Champaign, Champaign, Illinois, U.S.A.*

Helen Heinrich / *Collection Access and Management Services, California State University–Northridge, Northridge, California, U.S.A.*

Doris S. Helfer / *Collection Access and Management Services, California State University–Northridge, Northridge, California, U.S.A.*

Markus Helfert / *School of Computing, Dublin City University, Dublin, Ireland*

Jean Henefer / *School of Information and Communication Studies, University College Dublin, Dublin, Ireland*

Steven L. Hensen / *Rare Book, Manuscript and Special Collections Library, Duke University, Durham, North Carolina, U.S.A.*

Pamela M. Henson / *Archives, Smithsonian Institution, Washington, District of Columbia, U.S.A.*

Peter Hernon / *Graduate School of Library and Information Science, Simmons College, Boston, Massachusetts, U.S.A.*

Dorothy H. Hertzel / *Case Western Reserve University, Cleveland, Ohio, U.S.A.*

Francis Heylighen / *Free University of Brussels, Brussels, Belgium*

Randolph Hock / *Online Strategies, Annapolis, Maryland, U.S.A.*

Theodora L. Hodges / *Berkeley, California, U.S.A.*

Sara S. Hodson / *Huntington Library, San Marino, California, U.S.A.*

Judy C. Holoviak / *American Geophysical Union, Washington, District of Columbia, U.S.A.*

Aleksandra Horvat / *Faculty of Philosophy, University of Zagreb, Zagreb, Croatia*

Ali Houissa / *Olin Library, Cornell University, Ithaca, New York, U.S.A.*

Pamela Howard-Reguindin / *Library of Congress Office, Nairobi, Kenya*

Han-Yin Huang / *International Centre for Cultural and Heritage Studies, Newcastle University, Newcastle upon Tyne, U.K.*

Kathleen Hughes / *American Library Association, Chicago, Illinois, U.S.A.*

Betsy L. Humphreys / *National Library of Medicine, Bethesda, Maryland, U.S.A.*

Charlene S. Hurt / *University Library, Georgia State University, Atlanta, Georgia, U.S.A.*

Sue Hutley / *Australian Library and Information Association, Deakin, Australian Capital Territory, Australia*

John P. Immroth / *University of Pittsburgh, Pittsburgh, Pennsylvania, U.S.A.*

Peter Ingwersen / *Royal School of Library and Information Science, University of Copenhagen, Copenhagen, Denmark*

Vanessa Irvin / *Library and Information Science Program, Information and Computer Sciences Department, University of Hawaii at Mānoa, Honolulu, Hawaii, U.S.A.*

Karla Irwin / *University Libraries, University of Nevada–Las Vegas, Las Vegas, Nevada, U.S.A.*

October R. Ivins / *Ivins eContent Solutions, Sharon, Massachusetts, U.S.A.*

Kalervo Järvelin / *School of Information Science, University of Tampere, Tampere, Finland*

Jean Frédéric Jauslin / *Federal Department of Home Affairs (FDHA), Swiss Federal Office of Culture, Bern, Switzerland*

V. Jeyaraj / *Hepzibah Institute of Conversion, Chennai, India*

Scott Johnston / *McPherson Library, University of Victoria, Victoria, British Columbia, Canada*

Trevor Jones / *Mountain Heritage Center, Western Carolina University, Cullowhee, North Carolina, U.S.A.*

William Jones / *Information School, University of Washington, Seattle, Washington, U.S.A.*

Jay Jordan / *OCLC Online Computer Library Center, Inc., Dublin, Ohio, U.S.A.*

Corinne Jörgensen / *School of Information Studies, Florida State University, Tallahassee, Florida, U.S.A.*

Gene Joseph / *Aboriginal Library Consultant, Langley, British Columbia, Canada*

Daniel N. Joudrey / *School of Library and Information Science, Simmons College, Boston, Massachusetts, U.S.A.*

Heidi Julien / *Library and Information Studies, State University of New York–Buffalo, Buffalo, New York, U.S.A.*

Janet Kaaya / *Department of Information Studies, University of California, Los Angeles, California, U.S.A.*

Philomena Kagwiria Mwirigi / *Kenya National Library Service (KNLS), Nairobi, Kenya*

Athanase B. Kanamugire / *Library Consultant, Dhahran, Saudi Arabia*

Paul B. Kantor / *School of Communication and Information, Rutgers University, New Brunswick, New Jersey, U.S.A.*

Sofia Kapnisi / *International Federation of Library Associations and Institutions, The Hague, the Netherlands*

Nelson Otieno Karilus / *Kenya National Library Service (KNLS), Nairobi, Kenya*

Amy M. Kautzman / *University of California, Berkeley, Berkeley, California, U.S.A.*

Karalyn Kavanaugh / *Account Services Manager, EBSCO Information Services, Birmingham, Alabama, U.S.A.*

Caroline Kayoro / *Kenya National Library Service (KNLS), Nairobi, Kenya*

Andreas Kellerhals / *Federal Department of Home Affairs (FDHA), Swiss Federal Archives, Bern, Switzerland*

John M. Kennedy / *Indiana University, Bloomington, Indiana, U.S.A.*

Kristen Kern / *Portland State University, Portland, Oregon, U.S.A.*

Christopher S.G. Khoo / *School of Communication and Information, Nanyang Technological University, Singapore*

Tapan Khopkar / *University of Michigan, Ann Arbor, Michigan, U.S.A.*

Irene Muthoni Kibandi / *Kenya National Library Service (KNLS), Nairobi, Kenya*

Ruth E. Kifer / *Dr. Martin Luther King, Jr. Library, San Jose State University, San Jose, California, U.S.A.*

Seong Hee Kim / *Department of Library and Information Science, Chung-Ang University, Seoul, South Korea*

Pancras Kimaru / *Kenya National Library Service (KNLS), Nairobi, Kenya*

Karen E. King / *Washington, District of Columbia, U.S.A.*

William R. King / *University of Pittsburgh, Pittsburgh, Pennsylvania, U.S.A.*

Susan K. Kinnell / *Consultant, Santa Barbara, California, U.S.A.*

Laurence J. Kipp / *Harvard University, Cambridge, Massachusetts, U.S.A.*

Thomas G. Kirk, Jr. / *Earlham College Libraries, Earlham College, Richmond, Indiana, U.S.A.*

Breanne A. Kirsch / *Library, Emerging Technologies, University of South Carolina Upstate, Spartanburg, South Carolina, U.S.A.*

Vernon N. Kisling, Jr. / *Marston Science Library, University of Florida, Gainesville, Florida, U.S.A.*

Adam D. Knowles / *San Diego, California, U.S.A.*

Rebecca Knuth / *Library and Information Science Program, University of Hawaii, Honolulu, Hawaii, U.S.A.*

Michael Koenig / *College of Information and Computer Science, Long Island University, Brookville, New York, U.S.A.*

Jesse Koennecke / *Cornell University Library, Cornell University College of Arts and Sciences, Ithaca, New York, U.S.A.*

Jes Koepfler / *Museum Studies Program, Faculty of Information Studies, University of Toronto, Toronto, Ontario, Canada*

Amelia Koford / *Blumberg Memorial Library, Texas Lutheran University, Seguin, Texas, U.S.A.*

Toru Koizumi / *Library, Rikkyo University, Tokyo, Japan*

Josip Kolanović / *Croatian State Archives, Zagreb, Croatia*

Sjoerd Koopman / *International Federation of Library Associations and Institutions, The Hague, the Netherlands*

Donald Kraft / *Department of Computer Science, U.S. Air Force Academy, Colorado Springs, Colorado, U.S.A.*

Allison Krebs / *University of Arizona, Tucson, Arizona, U.S.A.*

Judith F. Krug / *Office for Intellectual Freedom, American Library Association, Chicago, Illinois, U.S.A.*

D.W. Krummel / *Emeritus, Graduate School of Library and Information Science, University of Illinois at Urbana-Champaign, Champaign, Illinois, U.S.A.*

Carol Collier Kuhlthau / *Department of Library and Information Science, Rutgers University, New Brunswick, New Jersey, U.S.A.*

Krishan Kumar / *Former Head, Department of Library and Information Science, University of Delhi, New Delhi, India*

Sanna Kumpulainen / *Library, Tampere University of Technology, Tampere, Finland*

Michael J. Kurtz / *National Archives at College Park, U.S. National Archives and Records Administration, College Park, Maryland, U.S.A.*

Zhenhua Lai / *Department of Management Information Systems, University of Arizona, Tucson, Arizona, U.S.A.*

Mounia Lalmas / *Department of Computing Science, University of Glasgow, Glasgow, U.K.*

Heather M. Lamond / *Massey University Library, Palmerston North, New Zealand*

F.W. Lancaster / *Graduate School of Library and Information Science, University of Illinois at Urbana-Champaign, Urbana, Illinois, U.S.A.*

Ronald L. Larsen / *School of Information Sciences, University of Pittsburgh, Pittsburgh, Pennsylvania, U.S.A.*

Ray R. Larson / *School of Information, University of California—Berkeley, Berkeley, California, U.S.A.*

Jesús Lau / *Library Services Unit USBI Veracruz (USBI VER), University of Veracruz, Veracruz, Mexico*

Judith V. Lechner / *Department of Educational Foundations, Leadership, and Technology, Auburn University, Auburn, Alabama, U.S.A.*

Christopher A. Lee / *School of Information and Library Science, University of North Carolina at Chapel Hill, Chapel Hill, North Carolina, U.S.A.*

Janet Lee / *University of Denver, Denver, Colorado, U.S.A, and Regis University, Denver, Colorado, U.S.A.*

Catherine Leekam / *Museum Studies Program, Faculty of Information Studies, University of Toronto, Toronto, Ontario, Canada*

Kjell Lemström / *Department of Computer Science, University of Helsinki, Helsinki, Finland*

Timothy F. Leslie / *Department of Geography and Geoinformation Science, George Mason University, Fairfax, Virginia, U.S.A.*

Noémie Lesquins / *Scientific Mission (DSR), National Library of France, Paris, France*

Rosalind K. Lett / *Information-2-Knowledge, Atlanta, Georgia, U.S.A.*

Allison V. Level / *Colorado State University, Fort Collins, Colorado, U.S.A.*

Michael Levine-Clark / *Penrose Library, University of Denver, Denver, Colorado, U.S.A.*

Anany Levitin / *Department of Computing Sciences, Villanova University, Villanova, Pennsylvania, U.S.A.*

Marjorie Lewis / *Canaan, New York, U.S.A.*

Elizabeth D. Liddy / *School of Information Studies, Syracuse University, Syracuse, New York, U.S.A.*

Silje C. Lier / *Software & Information Industry Association, Washington, District of Columbia, U.S.A.*

Jane E. Light / *Dr. Martin Luther King, Jr. Library, San Jose Public Library, San Jose, California, U.S.A.*

Paul M. Lima / *Canadian Heritage Information Network (CHIN), Gatineau, Quebec, Canada*

Louise Limberg / *Swedish School of Library and Information Science, University of Borås and University of Gothenburg, Borås, Sweden*

Shin-jeng Lin / *Department of Business Administration, Le Moyne College, Syracuse, New York, U.S.A.*

Sarah Lippincott / *Educopia Institute, Atlanta, Georgia, U.S.A.*

Peter Johan Lor / *School of Information Studies, University of Wisconsin-Milwaukee, Milwaukee, Wisconsin, U.S.A., and Department of Information Science, University of Pretoria, Pretoria, South Africa*

Beth Luey / *Fairhaven, Massachusetts, U.S.A.*

Joseph Luke / *Kazakhstan Institute of Management, Economics and Strategic Research (KIMEP), Almaty, Kazakhstan*

Claudia Lux / *Central and Regional Library of Berlin (ZLB), Berlin, Germany*

Marianne Lykke / *Information Interaction and Architecture, Royal School of Library and Information Science, Aalborg, Denmark*

Elena Macevičiūtė / *Faculty of Communication, Vilnius University, Vilnius, Lithuania, and Swedish School of Library and Information Science, University of Borås, Borås, Sweden*

Juan D. Machin-Mastromatteo / *Universidad Central de Venezuela, Caracas, Venezuela*

Barbara A. Macikas / *American Library Association, Chicago, Illinois, U.S.A.*

Leslie Madsen-Brooks / *Boise State University, Boise, Idaho, U.S.A.*

William J. Maher / *Archives, University of Illinois at Urbana-Champaign, Urbana, Illinois, U.S.A.*

Thomas Mann / *Library of Congress, Washington, District of Columbia, U.S.A.*

Sylva Natalie Manoogian / *Department of Information Studies, University of California, Los Angeles, Los Angeles, California, U.S.A.*

Daniel Marcu / *Information Sciences Institute, University of Southern California, Marina del Rey, California, U.S.A.*

James W. Marcum / *Fairleigh Dickinson University, Madison, New Jersey, U.S.A.*

Francesca Marini / *School of Library, Archival and Information Studies, University of British Columbia, Vancouver, British Columbia, Canada*

Johan Marklund / *Department of Industrial Management and Logistics, Lund University, Lund, Sweden*

Dian I. Martin / *Small Bear Technical Consulting, LLC, Thorn Hill, Tennessee, U.S.A.*

Susan K. Martin / *Lauinger Library, Georgetown University, Washington, District of Columbia, U.S.A.*

Paul F. Marty / *College of Communication and Information, Florida State University, Tallahassee, Florida, U.S.A.*

Dan Marwit / *Lee H. Skolnick Architecture + Design Partnership, New York, New York, U.S.A.*

Laura Matzer / *Arizona Museum for Youth, Mesa, Arizona, U.S.A.*

Robert L. Maxwell / *Special Collections and Metadata Catalog Department, Brigham Young University, Provo, Utah, U.S.A.*

Hope Mayo / *Houghton Library, Harvard University, Cambridge, Massachusetts, U.S.A.*

Sally H. McCallum / *Network Development and MARC Standards Office, Library of Congress, Washington, District of Columbia, U.S.A.*

Gavan McCarthy / *eScholarship Research Centre, University of Melbourne, Melbourne, Victoria, Australia*

Ian McGowan / *Former Librarian, National Library of Scotland, Edinburgh, U.K.*

Roger McHaney / *Department of Management, Kansas State University, Manhattan, Kansas, U.S.A.*

I.C. McIlwaine / *University College London, School of Library, Archive and Information Studies, London, U.K.*

Sue McKemmish / *Centre for Organisational and Social Informatics, Monash University, Melbourne, Victoria, Australia*

Marie E. McVeigh / *JCR and Bibliographic Policy, Thomson Reuters - Scientific, Philadelphia, Pennsylvania, U.S.A.*

Linda Mboya / *National Museums of Kenya, Nairobi, Kenya*

Judith Adams Meadows / *State Law Library of Montana, Helena, Montana, U.S.A.*

K. van der Meer / *Faculty of Electrical Engineering, Mathematics and Computer Science, Delft University, the Netherlands; Information and Library Science, IOIW, Antwerp University, Belgium; and D-CIS, Delft, The Netherlands*

Bharat Mehra / *School of Information Sciences, University of Tennessee, Knoxville, Tennessee, U.S.A.*

Margaret Ann Mellinger / *OSU Libraries & Press, Oregon State University, Corvallis, Oregon, U.S.A.*

Elizabeth E. Merritt / *American Association of Museums, Washington, District of Columbia, U.S.A.*

David Millman / *Academic Information Systems, Columbia University, New York, U.S.A.*

Jack Mills / *North-Western Polytechnic, London, U.K.*

Kevin L. Mills / *National Institute of Standards and Technology, Gaithersburg, Maryland, U.S.A.*

Staša Milojević / *Department of Information Studies, University of California, Los Angeles, Los Angeles, California, U.S.A.*

Marla Misunas / *Collections Information and Access, San Francisco Museum of Modern Art, San Francisco, California, U.S.A.*

Joan S. Mitchell / *OCLC Online Computer Library Center, Inc., Dublin, Ohio, U.S.A.*

Yoriko Miyabe / *Rikkyo University, Tokyo, Japan*

Diane Mizrachi / *University Libraries, University of California–Los Angeles, Los Angeles, California, U.S.A.*

William Moen / *Texas Center for Digital Knowledge, University of North Texas, Denton, Texas, U.S.A.*

Abdul Moid / *University of Karachi, Karachi, Pakistan*

Hermann Moisl / *Center for Research in Linguistics, University of Newcastle upon Tyne, Newcastle upon Tyne, U.K.*

Ole Magnus Mølbak Andersen / *Danish State Archives, Copenhagen, Denmark*

Mavis B. Molto / *Utah State University, Logan, Utah, U.S.A.*

Philip Mooney / *Heritage Communications, Coca-Cola Company, Atlanta, Georgia, U.S.A.*

Reagan W. Moore / *San Diego Supercomputer Center, University of North Carolina at Chapel Hill, Chapel Hill, North Carolina, U.S.A.*

Mersini Moreleli-Cacouris / *Department of Library Science and Information Systems, Technological Educational Institute (TEI) of Thessaloniki, Sindos, Greece*

Paul K. Moser / *Department of Philosophy, Loyola University Chicago, Chicago, Illinois, U.S.A.*

Clara C. Mosquera / *Library, Kirkland & Ellis LLP, Chicago, IL, U.S.A.*

David J. Muddiman / *Leeds Metropolitan University, Leeds, U.K.*

Nancy C. Mulvany / *Bayside Indexing Service, Fort Collins, Colorado, U.S.A.*

Sue Myburgh / *School of Communication, University of South Australia, Adelaide, South Australia, Australia*

Elli Mylonas / *Brown University, Providence, Rhode Island, U.S.A.*

Jeremy Myntti / *J. Willard Marriott Library, Salt Lake City, Utah, U.S.A.*

Jacob Nadal / *ReCAP: The Research Collections and Preservation Consortium, Princeton, New Jersey, U.S.A.*

Diane Nahl / *Information and Computer Sciences Department, University of Hawaii, Honolulu, Hawaii, U.S.A.*

Robert Nardini / *Vice President, Library Services, ProQuest Books, La Vergne, Tennessee, U.S.A.*

Arnold vander Nat / *Department of Philosophy, Loyola University Chicago, Chicago, Illinois, U.S.A.*

Charles M. Naumer / *Information School, University of Washington, Seattle, Washington, U.S.A.*

Sophie Ndegwa / *Kenya National Library Service (KNLS), Nairobi, Kenya*

Dixie Neilson / *University of Florida, Gainesville, Florida, U.S.A.*

Sarah Beth Nelson / *School of Information and Library Sciences, University of North Carolina at Chapel Hill, Chapel Hill, North Carolina, U.S.A.*

Stuart J. Nelson / *National Library of Medicine, Bethesda, Maryland, U.S.A.*

Stephanie Nemcsok / *Museum Studies Program, Faculty of Information Studies, University of Toronto, Toronto, Ontario, Canada*

Ken Neveroski / *College of Information and Computer Science, Long Island University, Brookville, New York, U.S.A.*

Jennifer Ng / *Museum Studies Program, Faculty of Information Studies, University of Toronto, Toronto, Ontario, Canada*

Melissa Niiya / *Portland Public Schools, Portland, Oregon, U.S.A.*

Angela Noseworthy / *Museum Studies Program, Faculty of Information Studies, University of Toronto, Toronto, Ontario, Canada*

Barbara E. Nye / *Ictus Consulting, LLC, Pasadena, California, U.S.A.*

Charles Nzivo / *Kenya National Library Service (KNLS), Nairobi, Kenya*

Dennis O'Brien / *Maps and Wayfinding, LLC, Mystic, Connecticut, U.S.A.*

Karen Lynn O'Brien / *American Library Association, Chicago, Illinois, U.S.A.*

Kieron O'Hara / *Intelligence, Agents, Multimedia Group, University of Southampton, Southampton, U.K.*

Elizabeth O'Keefe / *Morgan Library and Museum, New York, U.S.A.*

Denise I. O'Shea / *Fairleigh Dickinson University, Teaneck, New Jersey, U.S.A.*

Douglas W. Oard / *College of Information Studies, University of Maryland, College Park, Maryland, U.S.A.*

Maria Oldal / *Morgan Library and Museum, New York, U.S.A.*

Lorne Olfman / *School of Information Systems and Technology, Claremont Graduate University, Claremont, California, U.S.A.*

Bette W. Oliver / *Austin, Texas, U.S.A.*

Annette Olson / *Biological Resources Division, U.S. Geological Survey, Reston, Virginia, U.S.A.*

Hope A. Olson / *School of Information Studies, University of Wisconsin-Milwaukee, Milwaukee, Wisconsin, U.S.A.*

Lawrence J. Olszewski / *OCLC Library, Dublin, Ohio, U.S.A.*

Kok-Leong Ong / *School of Information Technology, Deakin University, Burwood, Victoria, Australia*

Tim Owen / *Chartered Institute of Library and Information Professionals (CILIP), London, U.K.*

John C. Paolillo / *School of Informatics and School of Library and Information Science, Indiana University, Bloomington, Indiana, U.S.A.*

Eun Bong Park / *Library Service Department, National Library of Korea, Seoul, South Korea*

Soyeon Park / *Department of Library and Information Science, Duksung Womens University, Seoul, South Korea*

Gabriella Pasi / *Department of Informatics, Systems and Communication, University of Studies of Milano Bicocca, Milan, Italy*

Norman Paskin / *Tertius Ltd., Oxford, U.K.*

Christiane Paul / *Whitney Museum of American Art, New York, U.S.A.*

Ellen Pearlstein / *Information Studies and UCLA / Getty Program in the Conservation of Ethnographic and Archaeological Materials, University of California, Los Angeles, Los Angeles, California, U.S.A.*

Kathleen de la Peña McCook / *School of Library and Information Science, University of South Florida, Tampa, Florida, U.S.A.*

Steve Pepper / *Department of Linguistics, University of Oslo, Oslo, Norway*

Manuel A. Pérez-Quiñones / *Department of Software and Information Systems, University of North Carolina, Charlotte, North Carolina, U.S.A.*

Paul Evan Peters / *University of Pittsburgh, Pittsburgh, Pennsylvania, U.S.A.*

Jakob Heide Petersen / *Danish Agency for Libraries and Media, Copenhagen, Denmark*

Mary Jane Petrowski / *American Library Association, Chicago, Illinois, U.S.A.*

Katharine J. Phenix / *Northglenn Branch, Rangeview Library District, Northglenn, Colorado, U.S.A.*

Robert B. Pickering / *Gilcrease Museum, and Museum Science and Management Program, University of Tulsa, Tulsa, Oklahoma, U.S.A.*

Janice T. Pilch / *Rutgers University Libraries, Rutgers University, New Brunswick, New Jersey, U.S.A.*

Thomas E. Pinelli / *Langley Research Center, National Aeronautics and Space Administration (NASA) Hampton, Virginia, U.S.A.*

Daniel Pitti / *Alderman Library, Institute for Advanced Technology in the Humanities, University of Virginia, Charlottesville, Virginia, U.S.A.*

Elena Ploşniţă / *Science Department, National Museum of Archaeology and History of Moldova, Chisinau, Republic of Moldova*

Gabriela Poduśelová / *Slovak National Museum, Bratislava, Slovak Republic*

Danny C.C. Poo / *School of Computing, Department of Information Systems, National University of Singapore, Singapore*

Martine Poulain / *Department of Libraries and Documentation, National Institute for the History of Art (INHA), Paris, France*

Tammy Powell / *National Library of Medicine, Bethesda, Maryland, U.S.A.*

Stephen Prine / *Library of Congress, Washington, District of Columbia, U.S.A.*

Mary Jo Pugh / *Editor, American Archivist, Walnut Creek, California, U.S.A.*

Ajit K. Pyati / *University of Western Ontario, London, Ontario, Canada*

Aimée C. Quinn / *Government Publications Services, Brooks Library, Central Washington University, Ellensburg, Washington, U.S.A.*

Jennie Quiñónez-Skinner / *University Library, California State University–Northridge, Northridge, California, U.S.A.*

Debbie Rabina / *School of Library and Information Science, Pratt Institute, New York, New York, U.S.A.*

Katalin Radics / *Research Library, University of California—Los Angeles, Los Angeles, California, U.S.A.*

Carl Rahkonen / *Harold S. Orendorff Music Library, Indiana University of Pennsylvania, Indiana, Pennsylvania, U.S.A.*

Jocelyn Rankin / *Centers for Disease Control and Prevention Library, Atlanta, Georgia, U.S.A.*

Samuel J. Redman / *Department of History, University of California, Berkeley, Berkeley, California, U.S.A.*

Thomas C. Redman / *Navesink Consulting Group, Little Silver, New Jersey, U.S.A.*

Barbara Reed / *Recordkeeping Innovation, Sydney, New South Wales, Australia*

Marcia Reed / *Getty Research Institute, Los Angeles, CA, U.S.A.*

CarrieLynn D. Reinhard / *Department of Communication, Business, and Information Technologies, Roskilde University, Roskilde, Denmark*

Harold C. Relyea / *Congressional Research Service, Library of Congress, Washington, District of Columbia, U.S.A.*

Steve Ricci / *Department of Information Studies/Film and Television, University of California–Los Angeles, Los Angeles, California, U.S.A.*

Ronald E. Rice / *Department of Communication, University of California–Santa Barbara, Santa Barbara, California, U.S.A.*

John V. Richardson, Jr. / *Department of Information Studies, University of California, Los Angeles, Los Angeles, California, U.S.A.*

Soo Young Rieh / *School of Information, University of Michigan, Ann Arbor, Michigan, U.S.A.*

Kevin S. Rioux / *Division of Library and Information Science, St. John's University, Queens, New York, U.S.A.*

Julian Roberts / *Wolfson College, University of Oxford, Oxford, U.K.*

Lyn Robinson / *City, University of London, London, U.K.*

Diane Robson / *University Libraries, Media Library, University of North Texas, Denton, Texas, U.S.A.*

Michael Rodriguez / *Michigan State University Libraries, East Lansin, Michigan, U.S.A.*

Juraj Roháč / *Department of Archival Science and Auxiliary Historical Sciences, Comenius University in, Bratislava, Slovak Republic*

Mark Roosa / *Pepperdine University, Malibu, California, U.S.A.*

Jonathan Rose / *Department of History, Drew University, Madison, New Jersey, U.S.A.*

Howard Rosenbaum / *School of Library and Information Science, Indiana University, Bloomington, Indiana, U.S.A.*

Catherine Sheldrick Ross / *Faculty of Information and Media Studies, University of Western Ontario, London, Ontario, Canada*

Shannon Ross / *Canadian Heritage Information Network (CHIN), Gatineau, Quebec, Canada*

Richard Rubin / *School of Library and Information Science, Kent State University, Kent, Ohio, U.S.A.*

Lynne M. Rudasill / *University of Illinois at Urbana-Champaign, Champaign, Illinois, U.S.A.*

Michael Rush / *Beinecke Rare Book and Manuscript Library, Yale University, New Haven, Connecticut, U.S.A.*

Mariza Russo / *Faculty of Administration and Accounting Sciences (FACC), Federal University of Rio de Janeiro, Rio de Janeiro, Brazil*

Athena Salaba / *Kent State University, Kent, Ohio, U.S.A.*

Romelia Salinas / *California State University, Los Angeles, Los Angeles, California, U.S.A.*

Airi Salminen / *Department of Computer Science and Information Systems, University of Jyväskylä, Jyväskylä, Finland*

Michael J. Salvo / *Department of English, Purdue University, West Lafayette, Indiana, U.S.A.*

Robert J. Sandusky / *University Library, University of Illinois at Chicago, Chicago, Illinois, U.S.A.*

Tefko Saracevic / *School of Communication and Information, Rutgers University, New Brunswick, New Jersey, U.S.A.*

Chris Sauer / *Said Business School, University of Oxford, Oxford, U.K.*

Rejéan Savard / *School of Library and Information Science, University of Montreal, Montreal, Quebec, Canada*

Reijo Savolainen / *School of Information Sciences, University of Tampere, Tampere, Finland*

Barbara Schaefer / *Geneseo, New York, U.S.A.*

Silvia Schenkolewski-Kroll / *Department of Information Science, Bar-Ilan University, Ramat Gan, Israel*

Lael J. Schooler / *Center for Adaptive Behavior and Cognition, Max Planck Institute for Human Development, Berlin, Germany*

Joachim Schöpfel / *Department of Library and Information Sciences (IDIST), GERiico Laboratory Charles de Gaulle University Lille 3, Villeneuve d'Ascq, France*

Catherine F. Schryer / *Department of English Language and Literature, University of Waterloo, Waterloo, Ontario, Canada*

Marjorie Schwarzer / *Museum Studies Department, John F. Kennedy University, Berkeley, California, U.S.A.*

Jo Ann Secor / *Lee H. Skolnick Architecture + Design Partnership, New York, New York, U.S.A.*

Sara Selwood / *Department of Cultural Policy and Management, City University, London, U.K.*

Frank B. Sessa / *University of Pittsburgh, Pittsburgh, Pennsylvania, U.S.A.*

Mark Sgambettera / *Bronx County Historical Society, Bronx, New York, U.S.A.*

Ayman Shabana / International Institute, University of California, Los Angeles, Los Angeles, California, U.S.A.

Nigel Shadbolt / *School of Electronics and Computer Science, University of Southampton, Southampton, U.K.*

Kalpana Shankar / *School of Informatics, Indiana University, Bloomington, Indiana, U.S.A.*

Debora Shaw / *School of Library and Information Science, Indiana University, Bloomington, Indiana, U.S.A.*

Conrad Shayo / *Department of Information and Decision Sciences, California State University—San Bernardino, San Bernardino, California, U.S.A.*

Elizabeth Shepherd / *Department of Information Studies, University College London, London, U.K.*

Beverly K. Sheppard / *Institute for Learning Innovation, Edgewater, Maryland, U.S.A.*

Ross Shimmon / *Faversham, U.K.*

Snunith Shoham / *Department of Information Science, Bar-Ilan University, Ramat Gan, Israel*

Lyudmila Shpilevaya / *New York Public Library, New York, New York, U.S.A.*

David Shumaker / *School of Library and Information Science, Catholic University of America, Washington, District of Columbia, U.S.A.*

Judith A. Siess / *Information Bridges International, Inc., Champaign, Illinois, U.S.A.*

John Edward Simmons / *Museologica, Bellefonte, Pennsylvania, U.S.A.*

Anestis Sitas / *Aristotle University of Thessaloniki, Thessaloniki, Greece*

Roswitha Skare / *Institute of Culture and Literature, UiT The Arctic University of Norway, Tromsø, Norway*

Katherine Skinner / *Educopia Institute, Atlanta, Georgia, U.S.A.*

Lee H. Skolnick / *Lee H. Skolnick Architecture + Design Partnership, New York, New York, U.S.A.*

Mette Skov / *Department of Communication and Psychology, Aalborg University, Aalborg, Denmark*

Bobby Smiley / *Vanderbilt University, Heard Libraries, Nashville, Tennessee, U.S.A.*

Linda C. Smith / *School of Information Sciences, University of Illinois at Urbana-Champaign, Champaign, Illinois, U.S.A.*

Lois Smith / *Human Factors and Ergonomics Society, Santa Monica, California, U.S.A.*

Lori Smith / *Linus A. Sims Memorial Library, Southeastern Louisiana University, Hammond, Louisiana, U.S.A.*

Patricia A. Smith / *Colorado State University, Fort Collins, Colorado, U.S.A.*

Scott A. Smith / *Langlois Public Library, Langlois, Oregon, U.S.A.*

A. Patricia Smith-Hunt / *Science Library, Preservation Services, University of California, Riverside, Riverside, California, U.S.A.*

Karen Smith-Yoshimura / *Online Computer Library Center (OCLC), San Mateo, California, U.S.A.*

Diane H. Sonnenwald / *University College Dublin, Dublin, Ireland*

Nour Soufi / *Library Cataloging and Metadata Center, University of California, Los Angeles, Los Angeles, California, U.S.A.*

Barbara M. Spiegelman / *Churchill Associates, Pittsburgh, Pennsylvania, U.S.A.*

Robert P. Spindler / *Department of Archives and Manuscripts, Arizona State University, Tempe, Arizona, U.S.A.*

Joie Springer / *Information Society Division, UNESCO, Paris, France*

Suresh Srinivasan / *National Library of Medicine, Bethesda, Maryland, U.S.A.*

Guy St. Clair / *Knowledge Management and Learning, SMR International, New York, New York, U.S.A.*

Cheryl L. Stadel-Bevans / *National Archives and Records Administration, College Park, Maryland, U.S.A.*

Jill Stein / *Institute for Learning Innovation, Edgewater, Maryland, U.S.A.*

Marcia K. Stein / *Museum of Fine Arts, Houston, Houston, Texas, U.S.A.*

Jela Steinerová / *Department of Library and Information Science, Comenius University in, Bratislava, Slovak Republic*

Dick Stenmark / *Department of Applied IT, IT University of Gothenburg, Gothenburg, Sweden*

Andy Stephens / *OBE, Board Secretary, Head of International Engagement, The British Library, London, U.K.*

Margaret Stieg Dalton / *School of Library and Information Studies, University of Alabama, Tuscaloosa, Alabama, U.S.A.*

Katina Strauch / *Addlestone Library, College of Charleston, Charleston, South Carolina, U.S.A.*

Robert D. Stueart / *Graduate School of Library and Information Science, Simmons College, Boston, Massachusetts, U.S.A.*

Paul F. Stuehrenberg / *Yale Divinity Library, New Haven, Connecticut, U.S.A.*

Brian William Sturm / *School of Information and Library Sciences, University of North Carolina at Chapel Hill, Chapel Hill, North Carolina, U.S.A.*

Anna Suorsa / *University of Oulu, Oulu, Finland*

Brett Sutton / *Aurora University, Aurora, Illinois, U.S.A.*

Sarah Sutton / *Mary and Jeff Bell Library, Texas A&M University-Corpus Christi, Corpus Christi, Texas, U.S.A.*

Destinee Kae Swanson / *Adams Museum & House, Inc., Deadwood, South Dakota, U.S.A.*

H.L. Swanson / *GSOE, University of California, Riverside, California, U.S.A.*

Miriam E. Sweeney / *School of Library and Information Studies, University of Alabama, Tuscaloosa, Alabama, U.S.A.*

Shelley Sweeney / *University of Manitoba, Winnipeg, Manitoba, Canada*

Jean Tague-Sutcliffe / *Graduate School of Library and Information Science, University of Western Ontario, London, Ontario, Canada*

Masaya Takayama / *National Archives of Japan, Tokyo, Japan*

Sanna Talja / *Department of Information Studies and Interactive Media, University of Tampere, Tampere, Finland*

G. Thomas Tanselle / *Vice President, John Simon Guggenheim Memorial Foundation, New York, New York, U.S.A.*

Ivan Tanzer / *Museum Studies Program, Faculty of Information Studies, University of Toronto, Toronto, Ontario, Canada*

Melissa Terras / *UCL Department of Information Studies, UCL Centre for Digital Humanities, University College London, London, U.K.*

Mike Thelwall / *School of Computing and Information Technology, University of Wolverhampton, Wolverhampton, U.K.*

Lynne M. Thomas / *Rare Books and Special Collections, Northern Illinois University, DeKalb, Illinois, U.S.A.*

Lawrence S. Thompson / *University of Kentucky, Lexington, Kentucky, U.S.A.*

Jens Thorhauge / *Danish Agency for Libraries and Media, Copenhagen, Denmark*

Anne Thurston / *International Records Management Trust, London, U.K.*

Michael Tiemann / *Open Source Initiative, Chapel Hill, North Carolina, U.S.A.*

Christinger Tomer / *School of Information Sciences, University of Pittsburgh, Pittsburgh, Pennsylvania, U.S.A.*

Elaine G. Toms / *Faculty of Management, Dalhousie University, Halifax, Nova Scotia, Canada*

Jack Toolin / *Whitney Museum of American Art, New York, U.S.A.*

Jennifer Trant / *Archives & Museum Informatics, Toronto, Ontario, Canada*

Barry Trott / *Williamsburg Regional Library, Williamsburg, Virginia, U.S.A.*

Alice Trussell / *Hale Library, Kansas State University, Manhattan, Kansas, U.S.A.*

John Mark Tucker / *Abilene Christian University, Abilene, Texas, U.S.A.*

James M. Turner / *School of Library and Information Sciences, University of Montreal, Montreal, Quebec, Canada*

Louise Tythacott / *Centre for Museology, University of Manchester, Manchester, U.K.*

George Tzanetakis / *Department of Computer Science, University of Victoria, Victoria, British Columbia, Canada*

Franklyn Herbert Upward / *Centre for Organisational and Social Informatics, Monash University, Melbourne, Victoria, Australia*

Richard Urban / *Graduate School of Library and Information Science, University of Illinois, Champaign, Illinois, U.S.A.*

Rachel E. Vacek / *University of Michigan, Ann Arbor, Michigan, U.S.A.*

Ron Van den Branden / *Centre for Scholarly Editing and Document Studies, Royal Academy of Dutch Language and Literature, Gent, Belgium*

Sydney C. Van Nort / *The City College of New York, The City University of New York, New York, U.S.A.*

Edward Vanhoutte / *Centre for Scholarly Editing and Document Studies, Royal Academy of Dutch Language and Literature, Gent, Belgium*

Rebecca Vargha / *Information and Library Science Library, University of North Carolina at Chapel Hill, Chapel Hill, North Carolina, U.S.A.*

Jana Varlejs / *School of Communication, Information and Library Studies, Rutgers University, New Brunswick, New Jersey, U.S.A.*

Jason Vaughan / *Library Technologies, University of Nevada, Las Vegas University Libraries, Las Vegas, Nevada, U.S.A.*

Dale J. Vidmar / *Southern Oregon University Library, Ashland, Oregon, U.S.A.*

Diane Vizine-Goetz / *OCLC Online Computer Library Center, Inc., Dublin, Ohio, U.S.A.*

Ellen M. Voorhees / *Information Technology Laboratory, National Institute of Standards and Technology, Gaithersburg, Maryland, U.S.A.*

Sharon L. Walbridge / *Libraries Washington State University, Pullman, Washington, U.S.A.*

Stephanie Walker / *Brooklyn College, City University of New York, Brooklyn, New York, U.S.A.*

Virginia A. Walter / *Department of Information Studies, University of California, Los Angeles, Los Angeles, California, U.S.A.*

Mark Warschauer / *School of Education, University of California, Irvine, CA, U.S.A.*

Nigel M. Waters / *Department of Geography and Geoinformation Science, George Mason University, Fairfax, Virginia, U.S.A.*

Kathryn M. Wayne / *Art History/Classics Library, University of California, Berkeley, California, U.S.A.*

Frank Webster / *City University, London, U.K.*

Jeff Weddle / *School of Library and Information Studies, University of Alabama, Tuscaloosa, Alabama, U.S.A.*

Judith Weedman / *School of Library and Information Science, San Jose State University, Fullerton, California, U.S.A.*

Stuart L. Weibel / *Office of Research and Special Projects, OCLC Research, Dublin, Ohio, U.S.A.*

Jennifer Weil Arns / *School of Library and Information Science, University of South Carolina, Columbia, South Carolina, U.S.A.*

Bella Hass Weinberg / *Division of Library and Information Science, St. John's University, Queens, New York, New York, U.S.A.*

Volker M. Welter / *Department of the History of Art and Architecture, University of California, Santa Barbara, Santa Barbara, California, U.S.A.*

Caryn Wesner-Early / *ASRC Aerospace & Defense, US Patent & Trademark Office, Alexandria, Virginia, U.S.A.*

Lynn Westbrook / *School of Information, University of Texas at Austin, Austin, Texas, U.S.A.*

Howard D. White / *College of Computing and Informatics, Drexel University, Philadelphia, PA, U.S.A., and College of Information Science and Technology, Drexel University, Philadelphia, Pennsylvania, U.S.A.*

Layna White / *San Francisco Museum of Modern Art, San Francisco, California, U.S.A.*

Michael J. White / *Engineering and Science Library, Queen's University, Kingston, Ontario, Canada*

Sarah K. Wiant / *School of Law, Washington and Lee University, Lexington, Virginia, U.S.A.*

Stephen E. Wiberley, Jr. / *University of Illinois at Chicago, Chicago, Illinois, U.S.A.*

Gunilla Widén-Wulff / *Information Studies, Åbo Akademi University, Åbo, Finland*

Bradley J. Wiles / *Hill Memorial Library, Louisiana State University, Baton Rouge, Louisiana, U.S.A.*

Mary I. Wilke / *Center for Research Libraries, Chicago, Illinois, U.S.A.*

Barratt Wilkins / *Retired State Librarian of Florida, Tallahassee, Florida, U.S.A.*

Peter Willett / *Department of Information Studies, University of Sheffield, Sheffield, U.K.*

Kate Williams / *University of Illinois at Urbana-Champaign, Champaign, Illinois, U.S.A.*

Kirsty Williamson / *Caulfield School of IT, Monash University, Caulfield, Victoria, Australia and School of Information Studies, Charles Sturt University, Wagga Wagga, New South Wales, Australia*

Concepción S. Wilson / *School of Information Systems, Technology and Management, University of New South Wales, Sydney, New South Wales, Australia*

Ian E. Wilson / *Librarian and Archivist of Canada 2004–2009, Ottawa, Ontario, Canada*

Kristen Wilson / *North Carolina State University Libraries, Raleigh, North Carolina, U.S.A.*

Thomas D. Wilson / *Publisher/Editor in Chief, Information Research, U.K.*

Catherine C. Wilt / *PALINET, Philadelphia, Pennsylvania, U.S.A.*

Charles Wilt / *Association for Library Collections and Technical Services (ALCTS), Chicago, Illinois, U.S.A.*

Niels Windfeld Lund / *Institute of Culture and Literature, UiT The Arctic University of Norway, Troms , Norway*

Michael F. Winter / *Shields Library, University of California, Davis, California, U.S.A.*

Erica Wiseman / *Graduate School of Library and Information Studies, McGill University, Montreal, Quebec, Canada*

Steve W. Witt / *University of Illinois at Urbana-Champaign, Champaign, Illinois, U.S.A.*

Blanche Woolls / *iSchool, San Jose State University, San Jose, California, U.S.A.*

Louisa Worthington / *Public Library Association, Chicago, Illinois, U.S.A.*

Jadwiga Woźniak-Kasperek / *Institute of Information and Book Studies, University of Warsaw, Warsaw, Poland*

Judith Wusteman / *School of Information and Communication Studies, University College Dublin, Dublin, Ireland*

Iris Xie / *School of Information Studies, University of Wisconsin–Milwaukee, Milwaukee, Wisconsin, U.S.A.*

Yiyu Yao / *Department of Computer Science, University of Regina, Regina, Saskatchewan, Canada, and International WIC Institute, Beijing University of Technology, Beijing, China*

Janis L. Young / *Library of Congress, Washington, District of Columbia, U.S.A.*

Priscilla C. Yu / *University Library, University of Illinois at Urbana-Champaign, Urbana, Illinois, U.S.A.*

Jana Zabinski / *American National Standards Institute, New York, New York, U.S.A.*

Lisl Zach / *iSchool, Drexel University, Philadelphia, Pennsylvania, U.S.A.*

Olga Zaitseva / *Kazakhstan Institute of Management, Economics and Strategic Research (KIMEP), Almaty, Kazakhstan*

Marcia Lei Zeng / *School of Library and Information Science, Kent State University, Kent, Ohio, U.S.A.*

Yi Zeng / *International WIC Institute, Beijing University of Technology, Beijing, China*

Višnja Zgaga / *Museum Documentation Center, Zagreb, Croatia*

Jun Zhang / *Pitney Bowes, Shelton, Connecticut, U.S.A.*

Yulei Zhang / *Department of Management Information Systems, University of Arizona, Tucson, Arizona, U.S.A.*

Kai Zheng / *Department of Health Management and Policy, University of Michigan, Ann Arbor, Michigan, U.S.A.*

Ning Zhong / *Department of Life Science and Informatics, Maebashi Institute of Technology, Maebashi-City, Japan, and International WIC Institute, Beijing University of Technology, Beijing, China*

Maja Žumer / *University of Ljubljana, Slovenia*

Vladimir Zwass / *Computer Science and Management Information Systems, Fairleigh Dickinson University, Teaneck, New Jersey, U.S.A.*

Encyclopedia of Library and Information Sciences, Fourth Edition

Contents

Volume I

Academic Libraries / *Susan Curzon and Jennie Quiñónez-Skinner* 1

Accessibility / *Lori Bell* 14

Accreditation of Library and Information Studies Programs in the United States and Canada /
    Karen Lynn O'Brien 18

Acquisitions Institute at Timberline Lodge / *Scott A. Smith* 22

African Librarianship / *Natalia T. Bowdoin and Janet Lee* 33

Altmetrics / *Richard Cave* 44

American Association of Law Libraries (AALL) / *Kate Hagan* 48

American Association of Museums (AAM) / *Elizabeth E. Merritt* 56

American Association of School Librarians (AASL) / *Donald C. Adcock* 59

American Library Association (ALA) / *Mary W. Ghikas* 67

American Medical Informatics Association (AMIA) / *Don E. Detmer, Tia Abner and Karen Greenwood* 85

American National Standards Institute (ANSI) / *Jana Zabinski* 87

American Society for Information Science and Technology (ASIST) / *Charles H. Davis and
    Debora Shaw* 90

Approval Plans / *Robert Nardini* 96

Arab Federation for Libraries and Information (AFLI) / *Nour Soufi* 100

Archival Appraisal and Acquisition / *Barbara Reed* 105

Archival Arrangement and Description / *Joanne Evans, Sue McKemmish and Barbara Reed* 115

Archival Documentation / *Gavan McCarthy and Joanne Evans* 127

Archival Finding Aids / *Su Kim Chung and Karla Irwin* 133

Archival Management and Administration / *Michael J. Kurtz* 141

Archival Reference and Access / *Mary Jo Pugh* 149

Archival Science / *Elizabeth Shepherd* 166

Archives / *Adrian Cunningham* 179

Archivists and Collecting / *Richard J. Cox* 195

Area and Interdisciplinary Studies Literatures and Their Users / *Lynn Westbrook* 209

ARMA International, Inc. / *Carol E. B. Choksy* 221

Armenia: Libraries, Archives, and Museums / *Sylva Natalie Manoogian* 228

Art Galleries / *Daniel C. Danzig* 241

Art Librarianship / *Kathryn M. Wayne* 249

Art Museums / *David Gordon* 259

Volume I (*cont'd.*)

Artificial Intelligence / *Jianhua Chen* 269

Artificial Neural Networks and Natural Language Processing / *Hermann Moisl* 279

Arts Literatures and Their Users / *Lisl Zach* 293

ASLIB / *David Bawden and Lyn Robinson* 301

Association for Information Science and Technology / *Diane H. Sonnenwald,*
Charles H. Davis and Debora Shaw 311

Association for Information Systems (AIS) / *William R. King and Dennis Galletta* 318

Association for Library Collections and Technical Services / *Charles Wilt* 324

Association for Library Service to Children (ALSC) / *Virginia A. Walter* 333

Association of College and Research Libraries (ACRL) / *Mary Ellen Davis and Mary Jane Petrowski* . . . 338

Association of Library Trustees, Advocates, Friends and Foundations (ALTAFF) / *Sally Gardner Reed* . . . 361

Association of Research Libraries (ARL) / *Lee Anne George and Julia Blixrud* 364

Association of Specialized and Cooperative Library Agencies (ASCLA) / *Barbara A. Macikas* 376

Australia: Libraries, Archives, and Museums / *Alex Byrne* 379

Australian Library and Information Association (ALIA) / *Sue Hutley, Jane Hardy and*
Judy Brooker 396

Authentication and Authorization / *David Millman* 401

Automated Acquisitions / *Patricia A. Smith and Allison V. Level* 408

Automatic Abstracting and Summarization / *Daniel Marcu* 418

Automatic Discourse Generation / *John A. Bateman* 430

Back-of-the-Book Indexing / *Nancy C. Mulvany* 440

Bibliographic Control *[ELIS Classic]* / *Robert L. Maxwell* 447

Bibliographical Society (London) / *Julian Roberts* 456

Bibliographical Society of America (BSA) / *Hope Mayo* 463

Bibliography / *D. W. Krummel* 468

Bibliometric Overview of Information Science / *Howard D. White* 480

Bibliometric Research: History *[ELIS Classic]* / *Dorothy H. Hertzel* 492

Bibliothèque Nationale de France / *Noémie Lesquins* 531

Binding *[ELIS Classic]* / *Lawrence S. Thompson* 538

Biological Information and Its Users / *Kalpana Shankar* 554

Blind and Physically Disabled: Library Services / *Jane Rosetta Virginia Caulton and Stephen Prine* 563

Bliss Bibliographic Classification First Edition *[ELIS Classic]* / *Jack Mills* 573

Bliss Bibliographic Classification Second Edition / *Vanda Broughton* 581

Boolean Algebras *[ELIS Classic]* / *A. R. Bednarek* 591

Brazil: Library Science / *Mariza Russo* 597

Brazil: Library Science—Distance Education / *Mariza Russo* 603

Brazil: Museums / *Regina Dantas and Pamela Howard-Reguindin* 611

British Library / *Andy Stephens* 616

Business Informatics / *Markus Helfert* 630

Business Information and Its Users / *Eileen G. Abels* 635

Business Literature: History *[ELIS Classic]* / *Edwin T. Coman, Jr.* 643

Canada: Libraries and Archives / *Ian E. Wilson and Sean F. Berrigan* 654

Canadian Heritage Information Network (CHIN) / *Shannon Ross and Paul M. Lima* 675

Canadian Library Association (CLA) / *Donald I. Butcher* 681

Careers and Education in Archives and Records Management / *Karen Anderson* 685

Careers and Education in Information Systems / *Paul Gray and Lorne Olfman* 693

Volume I (cont'd.)

Careers and Education in Library and Information Science / *Jana Varlejs* 706

Careers and Education in Records and Information Management / *Carol E. B. Choksy* 715

Volume II

Cataloging / *Daniel N. Joudrey* 723

Cataloging Cultural Objects (CCO) / *Elizabeth O'Keefe and Maria Oldal* 733

Catalogs and Cataloging: History *[ELIS Classic]* / *Eugene R. Hanson and Jay E. Daily* 743

Censorship and Content Regulation of the Internet / *Peng Hwa Ang* 780

Center for Research Libraries / *Mary I. Wilke* 789

Charleston Conference / *Katina Strauch* 794

Chartered Institute of Library and Information Professionals (CILIP) / *Tim Owen* 806

Chemistry Literature and Its Users *[ELIS Classic]* / *Judith N. Currano* 814

Chemoinformatics / *Peter Willett* 830

Children and Information Technology / *June Abbas* 839

Children's Literature / *Judith V. Lechner* 852

Children's Services in Libraries / *Virginia A. Walter and Melissa Gross* 876

China: Libraries, Archives, and Museums / *Priscilla C. Yu and TzeHuey Chiou-Peng* 886

Circulation Services / *Vanessa Irvin and Jeff E. Bullard* 916

Citation Analysis / *Howard D. White* 923

Citation Indexes and the *Web of Science* / *Marie E. McVeigh* 940

Citer Motivations *[ELIS Classic]* / *Terrence Brooks* 951

Classification Theory / *Clare Beghtol* 958

Clinical Decision-Support Systems / *Kai Zheng* 974

College Libraries / *Thomas G. Kirk, Jr.* 983

Communication and Communication Studies / *Brenda Dervin and CarrieLynn D. Reinhard* 994

Communication Policy: United States / *D. Linda Garcia* 1007

Community Informatics / *Kate Williams and Joan C. Durrance* 1027

Complexity and Self-Organization / *Francis Heylighen* 1034

Computer-Mediated Communication (CMC) / *Michael A. Chilton and Roger McHaney* 1044

Computer-Supported Cooperative Work (CSCW) / *Kevin L. Mills* 1053

Conservation and Preservation of Museum Objects / *Ellen Pearlstein* 1068

Controlled Vocabularies for Art, Architecture, and Material Culture / *Murtha Baca* 1076

Corporate Archives / *Philip Mooney* 1081

Corporate Art Collections / *Laura Matzer* 1086

Corporate Information Centers / *Barbara M. Spiegelman and Nancy Flury Carlson* 1094

Corporate Records Management / *Barbara M. Cross and Barbara E. Nye* 1104

Credibility and Cognitive Authority of Information / *Soo Young Rieh* 1113

Croatia: Libraries, Archives, and Museums / *Aleksandra Horvat, Josip Kolanović and Višnja Zgaga* . . . 1121

CrossRef Publisher Linking Network / *Amy E. Brand* 1132

Cultural Memory / *Robert DeHart* 1139

Curating Archaeological Artifacts / *Alex W. Barker* 1147

Curating Natural History Collections / *Kimberly S. Bostwick* 1156

Custody and Chain of Custody / *Bernadette G. Callery* 1164

Data and Data Quality / *Thomas C. Redman and Christopher Fox and Anany Levitin* 1171

Deaf and Hearing Impaired: Communication in Service Contexts *[ELIS Classic]* / *Warren R. Goldmann* . . . 1183

Volume II (*cont'd.*)

Decision Sciences / *Sven Axsäter and Johan Marklund* 1192

Decision Support Systems / *Marek J. Druzdzel and Roger R. Flynn* 1200

Demand-Driven Acquisition/Patron-Driven Acquisition / *Michael Levine-Clark* 1209

Denmark: Libraries, Archives, and Museums / *Jens Thorhauge, Jakob Heide Petersen and
    Ole Magnus Mølbak Andersen* 1215

Descriptive Cataloging Principles / *Elena Escolano Rodríguez* 1229

Design Science in the Information Sciences / *Judith Weedman* 1242

Dewey Decimal Classification (DDC) / *Joan S. Mitchell and Diane Vizine-Goetz* 1256

Digital Content Licensing / *Paul D. Callister and Kathleen Hall* 1267

Digital Divide and Inclusion / *Mark Warschauer and Melissa Niiya* 1279

Digital Humanities / *Julia Flanders and Elli Mylonas* 1286

Digital Humanities and Academic Libraries / *Bobby Smiley and Michael Rodriguez* 1298

Digital Images / *Melissa Terras* 1307

Digital Millennium Copyright Act of 1998 / *Jonathan A. Franklin* 1316

Digital Object Identifier (DOI®) System / *Norman Paskin* 1325

Digital Preservation / *Jacob Nadal* 1332

Diplomatics / *Luciana Duranti* 1338

Disaster Planning and Recovery for Cultural Institutions / *Sheryl Davis, A. Patricia Smith-Hunt and
    Kristen Kern* 1347

Document Information Systems / *K. van der Meer* 1360

Document Theory / *Niels Windfeld Lund and Roswitha Skare* 1372

Document Type Definition (DTD) / *Judith Wusteman* 1381

Dublin Core Metadata Initiative (DCMI): A Personal History / *Stuart L. Weibel* 1390

Economics Literature: History *[ELIS Classic]* / *Arthur H. Cole and Laurence J. Kipp* 1399

Electronic Records Preservation / *Robert P. Spindler* 1413

Electronic Resources & Libraries (ER&L) / *Jesse Koennecke* 1419

Encoded Archival Description / *Daniel Pitti and Michael Rush* 1423

Engineering Literatures and Their Users *[ELIS Classic]* / *Thomas E. Pinelli, Ann P. Bishop,
    Rebecca O. Barclay and John M. Kennedy* 1433

Volume III

Epistemology / *Paul K. Moser* 1455

Ethical and Legal Aspects of Archival Services / *Sara S. Hodson* 1463

Ethical Aspects of Library and Information Science / *Richard Rubin and Thomas J. Froehlich* . . 1469

Ethical Issues in Information Systems / *Vladimir Zwass* 1484

Ethiopia: Libraries, Archives, and Museums / *Shiferaw Assefa* 1494

Everyday Life Information Seeking / *Reijo Savolainen* 1506

Evidence-Based Practice / *Prudence W. Dalrymple* 1516

Exhibition Design / *Lee H. Skolnick, Dan Marwit and Jo Ann Secor* 1523

Facet Analysis *[ELIS Classic]* / *Douglas J. Foskett* 1534

Faceted Application of Subject Terminology (FAST) / *Eric R. Childress and Diane Vizine-Goetz* . . 1539

Federal Electronic Information in the United States / *Carol D. Doyle* 1549

Film and Broadcast Archives / *Karen F. Gracy and Karen E. King* 1560

Film Archiving: History / *Steve Ricci* 1584

France: Archives, Museums, and Libraries / *Martine Poulain* 1589

Volume III (*cont'd.*)

Functional Requirements for Subject Authority Data (FRSAD): Conceptual Model /
Marcia Lei Zeng, Athena Salaba and Maja Žumer 1606

Fuzzy Set Theory / *Donald Kraft, Gloria Bordogna and Gabriella Pasi* 1618

Games and Gaming / *Diane Robson and Breanne A. Kirsch* 1636

Genealogical Literature and Its Users / *Mavis B. Molto* 1644

Genre Theory and Research / *Catherine F. Schryer* 1662

Geographic Information Systems (GIS) / *Timothy F. Leslie and Nigel M. Waters* 1671

Geographical Literature: History [ELIS Classic] / *Nora T. Corley* 1683

Germany: Libraries, Archives, and Museums / *Claudia Lux* 1693

Global Open Knowledgebase / *Kristen Wilson* 1710

Government Documents: Collection and Management / *Aimée C. Quinn, Lori Smith and James Church* . . . 1715

Greece: Archives / *Nestor Bamidis* 1728

Greece: Libraries / *Anestis Sitas and Mersini Moreleli-Cacouris* 1733

Greece: Museums / *Maria Economou* 1741

Grey Literature [ELIS Classic] / *Joachim Schöpfel and Dominic J. Farace* 1746

HathiTrust / *Rick Anderson* 1757

Health Science Professional Literatures and Their Users / *Cheryl Dee and Jocelyn Rankin* 1763

Historical and Archaeological Sites: Development and Preservation / *Robert B. Pickering* 1771

Historical Societies / *Mark Sgambettera* 1779

Historical Sources and Their Users / *Margaret Stieg Dalton* 1786

History of Libraries / *John Mark Tucker and Edward A. Goedeken* 1796

History of Museums / *John Edward Simmons* 1812

History of Paper / *Sidney E. Berger* 1824

History of Public Libraries [ELIS Classic] / *Frank B. Sessa* 1836

History of Records and Information Management / *William Benedon* 1850

History of the Book / *Jonathan Rose* 1859

History: Three Basic Printing Processes / *Sidney E. Berger* 1865

Hospital Libraries / *Rosalind K. Lett* 1870

Human–Computer Interaction Research in Information Retrieval / *Shin-jeng Lin* 1895

Humanities Literatures and Their Users / *Stephen E. Wiberley, Jr.* 1909

Hungary: Libraries, Archives, and Museums / *Katalin Radics* 1917

Hypertext and Hypercard: Early Development [ELIS Classic] / *Susan K. Kinnell and Carl Franklin* . . . 1935

Illumination [ELIS Classic] / *Abdul Moid* 1945

Impact Assessment of Cultural Institutions / *Sara Selwood* 1958

Incunabula [ELIS Classic] / *John P. Immroth and Romano Stephen Almagno* 1966

Indexing: History and Theory / *Bella Hass Weinberg* 1978

India: Libraries, Archives and Museums / *Krishan Kumar, V. Jeyaraj and Ramesh C. Gaur* 1992

Indigenous Librarianship / *Kathleen Burns, Ann Doyle, Gene Joseph and Allison Krebs* 2031

Information / *Marcia J. Bates* 2048

Information Arts / *Christiane Paul and Jack Toolin* 2064

Information Behavior / *Marcia J. Bates* 2074

Information Behavior Models / *Thomas D. Wilson* 2086

Information Crises and Crisis Information / *Philippe Baumard* 2094

Information Explosion / *Ronald E. Day* 2101

Information Management / *Brian Detlor* 2106

Information Needs / *Charles M. Naumer and Karen E. Fisher* 2115

Volume III (*cont'd.*)

Information Needs and Behaviors of Diasporic Populations / *Ajit K. Pyati* 2122
Information Needs and Behaviors of Populations in Less Developed Regions / *Innocent I. Ekoja* 2130
Information Policy: European Union / *Debbie Rabina and Scott Johnston* 2138
Information Policy: United States / *Peter Hernon and Harold C. Relyea* 2147
Information Practice / *Crystal Fulton and Jean Henefer* 2162
Information Retrieval Experimentation *[ELIS Classic]* / *Jean Tague-Sutcliffe* 2172

Volume IV

Information Retrieval Protocols: Z39.50 and Search and Retrieve via URL / *William Moen* 2181
Information Retrieval Support Systems / *Yiyu Yao, Ning Zhong and Yi Zeng* 2192
Information Retrieval Systems / *Ray R. Larson* 2199
Information Scattering / *Suresh K. Bhavnani and Concepción S. Wilson* 2210
Information Science / *Tefko Saracevic* 2216
Information Search Process (ISP) Model / *Carol Collier Kuhlthau* 2232
Information Searching and Search Models / *Iris Xie* 2239
Information Society / *Frank Webster* 2253
Information Systems / *E. Burton Swanson* 2272
Information Systems Failure / *Chris Sauer and Gordon B. Davis* 2280
Information Technology Adoption / *Conrad Shayo* 2290
Information Technology Literacy / *James W. Marcum and Denise I. O'Shea* 2303
Information Technology Project Implementation in Developing Countries *[ELIS Classic]* /
    Athanase B. Kanamugire 2312
Information Technology Standards for Libraries *[ELIS Classic]* / *Christinger Tomer* 2341
Information Theory / *Paul B. Kantor* 2350
Information Use for Decision Making / *Edward T. Cokely, Lael J. Schooler and Gerd Gigerenzer* 2359
Informetrics / *Judit Bar-Ilan* 2367
Institutional Records and Archives / *David Farneth* 2377
Intellectual Freedom and the American Library Association (ALA):
    Historical Overview *[ELIS Classic]* / *Judith F. Krug* 2387
Intelligence and Security Informatics / *Hsinchun Chen, Zhenhua Lai, Yan Dang and Yulei Zhang* 2398
International and Comparative Librarianship / *Peter Johan Lor* 2404
International Association of Sound and Audiovisual Archives (IASA) / *Ilse Assmann* 2413
International Association of Technological University Libraries (IATUL) /
    Nancy Fjällbrant and Alice Trussell 2418
International Communication Association (ICA) / *Ronald E. Rice* 2421
International Council of Museums (ICOM) / *Patrick J. Boylan* 2429
International Council on Archives (ICA) / *Perrine Canavaggio and Marcel Caya* 2437
International Council on Knowledge Management (ICKM) / *Franz Barachini* 2445
International Federation of Library Associations and Institutions (IFLA) / *Ross Shimmon,*
    Peter Johan Lor, Sofia Kapnisi, Sjoerd Koopman and Stuart Hamilton 2451
International Federation of Television Archives (FIAT/IFTA) / *Steve Bryant* 2465
International Organization for Standardization (ISO) / *Alan Bryden and Catherine Dhérent* 2470
International Records Management Standards ISO 15489 and 23081 / *Barbara Reed* 2481

Volume IV (*cont'd.*)

International Records Management Trust / *Anne Thurston* 2487

International Society for Knowledge Organization (ISKO) / *Ingetraut Dahlberg* 2494

Internet Genres / *Kevin Crowston* 2503

Internet Search Tools: History to 2000 / *Dale J. Vidmar and Connie J. Anderson-Cahoon* 2516

InterPARES / *Luciana Duranti* 2526

iSchools / *Ronald L. Larsen* 2536

Israel: Libraries, Archives, and Museums / *Snunith Shoham and Silvia Schenkolewski-Kroll* 2542

Japan: Libraries, Archives, and Museums / *Masaya Takayama, Yoriko Miyabe,*
Toru Koizumi and Hiroyuki Hatano 2560

Kazakhstan: Libraries, Archives, and Museums / *Leslie Champeny, Joseph Luke,*
Anna Bergaliyeva and Olga Zaitseva 2578

Kenya: Libraries, Museums, and Archives / *Irene Muthoni Kibandi, Pancras Kimaru,*
Caroline Kayoro, Philomena Kagwiria Mwirigi, Sophie Ndegwa, Nelson Otieno Karilus,
Charles Nzivo, Linda Mboya and Lilian Gisesa 2592

Knowledge / *Paul K. Moser and Arnold vander Nat* 2610

Knowledge Creation and Use in Organizations / *Maija-Leena Aulikki Huotari and Anna Suorsa* 2618

Knowledge Discovery in Data Streams / *Xuan Hong Dang and Kok-Leong Ong* 2626

Knowledge Management / *Kimiz Dalkir* 2640

Knowledge Management Systems / *Dick Stenmark* 2649

Knowledge Management: Early Development / *Michael Koenig and Ken Neveroski* 2657

Knowledge Organization System Standards / *Stella G. Dextre Clarke* 2665

Knowledge: Tacit and Explicit / *Philippe Baumard* 2677

Latent Semantic Indexing / *Dian I. Martin and Michael W. Berry* 2688

Latinos and U.S. Libraries: History / *Romelia Salinas* 2698

Law Firm Librarianship / *Brenda A. Burton, Mary B. Eggert and Clara C. Mosquera* 2705

Law Librarianship / *Richard A. Danner, Mark E. Estes and Judith Adams Meadows* 2710

Law Literature and Its Users / *Penny Hazelton* 2733

Learning and Information Seeking / *Louise Limberg and Mikael Alexandersson* 2751

Libraries / *Jennifer Weil Arns* 2762

Library and Information Science / *Miriam E. Sweeney and Leigh S. Estabrook* 2768

Library and Information Technology Association (LITA) / *Rachel E. Vacek* 2775

Library Anxiety / *Diane Mizrachi* 2782

Library Architecture and Design / *Charlene S. Hurt and Thomas L. Findley* 2788

Library Architecture: History / *Nan Christian Ploug Dahlkild* 2797

Library Automation: History / *Robert M. Hayes* 2810

Library Consortia in Europe / *Tommaso Giordano* 2822

Library Fundraising and Development / *Susan K. Martin* 2832

Library Leadership and Management Association (LLAMA) / *Robert Allen Daugherty* 2841

Library of Congress Classification (LCC) / *Lois Mai Chan and Theodora L. Hodges* 2847

Library of Congress Genre/Form Terms for Library and Archival Materials /
Janis L. Young 2856

Library of Congress Subject Headings (LCSH) / *Janis L. Young* 2866

Library of Congress: History / *John Y. Cole* 2879

Library Portals and Gateways / *Frank Cervone* 2892

Library Publishing Initiatives: North America / *Katherine Skinner and Sarah Lippincott* 2901

Volume V

Library Science in the United States: Early History / *John V. Richardson, Jr.* 2909

Library Technical Services / *Doris S. Helfer and Helen Heinrich* 2918

Linguistics and the Information Sciences / *John C. Paolillo* 2927

Linked Data / *Jeremy Myntti* 2938

Lithuania: Libraries and Librarianship / *Elena Macevičiūtė* 2943

Louvre / *Bette W. Oliver* 2958

Machine Readable Cataloging (MARC): 1961–1974 *[ELIS Classic]* / *Henriette D. Avram* 2963

Machine Readable Cataloging (MARC): 1975–2007 / *Sally H. McCallum* 2980

Makerspaces in Libraries / *Patrick Tod Colegrove* 2990

Management of Very Large Distributed Shared Collections *[ELIS Classic]* / *Reagan W. Moore* 2997

Managing an Information Business / *Gloria Dinerman* 3004

Marketing Library and Information Services / *Dinesh K. Gupta and Réjean Savard* 3011

Mathematics Literature: History *[ELIS Classic]* / *Barbara Schaefer* 3019

Medical Library Association (MLA) / *Carla J. Funk* 3033

Medical Literature: History *[ELIS Classic]* / *William K. Beatty* 3041

Metadata and Digital Information *[ELIS Classic]* / *Jane Greenberg* 3058

Metamarkup Languages: SGML and XML / *Airi Salminen* 3072

Mexico: Libraries, Archives, and Museums / *Jesús Lau* 3082

Modeling Documents in Their Context / *Airi Salminen* 3105

Moldova: Archives, Museums, and Libraries / *Hermina G.B. Anghelescu,*
    Silviu Andrieş-Tabac and Elena Ploşniţă 3117

Moving Image Indexing / *James M. Turner* 3129

Multilingual Information Access / *Douglas W. Oard* 3140

Museum Accreditation Program / *Leah Arroyo and Julie Hart* 3146

Museum Architecture and Gallery Design / *Volker M. Welter* 3148

Museum Collecting and Collections / *Robert B. Pickering* 3161

Museum Computer Network (MCN) / *Marla Misunas and Richard Urban* 3170

Museum Informatics / *Paul F. Marty* 3176

Museum Management / *Gary Edson* 3185

Museum Registration and Documentation / *Dixie Neilson* 3199

Museum Studies / *Marjorie Schwarzer* 3214

Museum Web Sites and Digital Collections / *David Bearman and Jennifer Trant* 3222

Museums / *Leslie Madsen-Brooks* 3233

Museums and Community / *Tamara Biggs* 3243

Museums and Their Visitors: Historic Relationship / *Samuel J. Redman* 3251

Museums as Place / *Peter Davis and Han-Yin Huang* 3258

Music Information Retrieval / *Kjell Lemström and George Tzanetakis* 3267

Music Librarianship / *Holly Gardinier, Sarah R. Canino and Carl Rahkonen* 3275

Name Authority Control / *Janifer Gatenby and Karen Smith-Yoshimura* 3288

National Archives / *Helen Forde* 3298

National Biological Information Infrastructure (NBII) / *P. Bryan Heidorn and Annette Olson* 3306

National Historical Publications and Records Commission (NHPRC) / *Keith Donohue* 3315

National Libraries / *Ian McGowan* 3320

National Library of Medicine / *Kathel Dunn* 3334

Natural Language Processing for Information Retrieval / *Elizabeth D. Liddy* 3346

Network Management / *Robert J. Sandusky* 3356

Volume V (*cont'd.*)

Network of European Museum Organisations (NEMO) / *Frank Birkebæk* 3365

Networked Knowledge Organization Systems/Services (NKOS) / *Marianne Lykke* 3366

New Zealand Aotearoa: Libraries / *Heather M. Lamond* 3371

Non-governmental Organizations and Information / *Lynne M. Rudasill and Steve W. Witt* 3380

North American Serials Interest Group / *Jill Emery* 3388

OCLC: A Worldwide Library Cooperative / *Jay Jordan* 3392

Older Adults' Information: Needs and Behavior / *Kirsty Williamson and Terry Asla* 3406

One-Person Libraries / *Judith A. Siess* 3413

Online Catalog Subject Searching / *Danny C.C. Poo and Christopher S.G. Khoo* 3422

Online Library Instruction / *Beth Evans* 3432

Online Public Access Catalogs (OPACs) *[ELIS Classic]* / *Kevin Butterfield* 3450

Ontologies and Their Definition / *Jos de Bruijn and Dieter Fensel* 3455

Open Access Scholarship and Publishing / *Malcolm Getz* 3465

Open Archival Information System (OAIS) Reference Model / *Christopher A. Lee* 3477

Open Source Software / *Michael Tiemann* 3488

Oral History in Libraries and Archives / *Debra Gold Hansen* 3494

ORCID / *Laurel L. Haak* 3505

Organization Theories / *Evelyn Daniel* 3510

Organizational Culture / *Gunilla Widén-Wulff* 3520

Organizational Learning / *Erica Wiseman* 3526

Organizational Memory / *Maureen L. Hammer* 3534

Pacific Islands Association of Libraries and Archives (PIALA) / *Arlene Cohen* 3541

Papyrology / *Roger S. Bagnall* 3552

Patents and Patent Searching / *Michael J. White* 3560

People with Disabilities / *Amelia Koford* 3573

Personal Information Management / *William Jones, Jesse David Dinneen, Robert Capra,
Anne R. Diekema and Manuel A. Pérez-Quiñones* 3584

Peru: Libraries and Library Science / *Sergio Chaparro-Univazo* 3606

Philosophy and the Information Sciences / *Jonathan Furner* 3610

Philosophy of Science *[ELIS Classic]* / *Paul Evan Peters* 3623

Volume VI

Physical Sciences and Mathematics Literatures and Their Users / *Cecelia Brown* 3637

Piracy in Digital Media / *Stephanie Walker* 3649

Plagiarism of Print and Electronic Resources / *Zorana Ercegovac* 3664

Poland: Libraries and Archives / *Jadwiga Woźniak-Kasperek* 3674

Politics of Representation in Museums / *Louise Tythacott* 3688

Popular Literature Genres / *Barry Trott* 3700

Precision and Recall *[ELIS Classic]* / *F. W. Lancaster* 3708

Presidential Libraries / *Sharon Fawcett* 3714

Primary Records: Future Prospects *[ELIS Classic]* / *G. Thomas Tanselle* 3719

Print on Demand / *Steve Bosch* 3733

Private Presses and Fine Printing *[ELIS Classic]* / *Roderick Cave* 3738

Provenance of Archival Materials / *Shelley Sweeney* 3746

Provenance of Museum Objects / *Layna White* 3756

Volume VI (*cont'd.*)

Provenance of Rare Books / *Marcia Reed* 3766

Public Librarianship *[ELIS Classic]* / *Kathleen de la Peña McCook and Katharine J. Phenix* 3774

Public Libraries *[ELIS Classic]* / *Barbara H. Clubb* 3781

Public Library Association (PLA) / *Louisa Worthington and Kathleen Hughes* 3801

Qualitative Research Methods in Library and Information Science *[ELIS Classic]* / *Brett Sutton* 3806

Rare Book Collections / *Andrew J. Berner* 3820

Reading and Reading Acquisition / *Brian Byrne* 3830

Reading Disorders / *H.L. Swanson* 3841

Reading Interests / *Catherine Sheldrick Ross* 3850

Recommender Systems and Expert Locators / *Derek L. Hansen, Tapan Khopkar and Jun Zhang* 3860

Records Compliance and Risk Management / *Bradley J. Wiles* 3869

Records Continuum Model / *Sue McKemmish, Franklyn Herbert Upward and Barbara Reed* 3874

Records Organization and Access / *Sue Myburgh* 3887

Records Retention Schedules / *Barbara E. Nye* 3892

Reference and Informational Genres / *Thomas Mann* 3897

Reference and User Services Association (RUSA) / *Barbara A. Macikas* 3908

Reference Services / *Linda C. Smith* 3912

Regional Library Networks: United States / *Catherine C. Wilt* 3920

Relevance in Theory / *Howard D. White* 3926

Relevance Judgments and Measurements / *Erica Cosijn* 3940

Renaissance Libraries *[ELIS Classic]* / *Lawrence S. Thompson* 3948

Resource Description Framework (RDF) / *Nicholas Gibbins and Nigel Shadbolt* 3961

Saudi Arabia: Libraries, Archives, and Museums / *Ayman Shabana* 3970

Scholarly and Trade Publishing *[ELIS Classic]* / *Richard Abel* 3982

School Librarianship / *Blanche Woolls* 3991

School Libraries / *Blanche Woolls* 4000

Science and Engineering Librarianship / *Margaret Ann Mellinger* 4008

Science and Technology Studies / *Sanna Talja* 4020

Search Engine Optimization / *Nicholas Carroll* 4029

Search Engines / *Randolph Hock* 4046

Self-Publishing Online / *Caryn Wesner-Early* 4054

Semantic Interoperability / *Marcia Lei Zeng and Lois Mai Chan* 4062

Semantic Web / *Kieron O'Hara and Wendy Hall* 4080

Semiotics / *Marcel Danesi* 4094

Senegal: Libraries, Archives, and Museums / *Bernard Dione and Dieyi Diouf* 4104

Sense-Making / *Brenda Dervin and Charles M. Naumer* 4113

Serbia: Libraries, Archives, and Museums / *Staša Milojević* 4125

Serials Collection and Management *[ELIS Classic]* / *Sarah Sutton* 4139

Serials Vendors *[ELIS Classic]* / *Karalyn Kavanaugh* 4150

Shared Libraries / *Ruth E. Kifer and Jane E. Light* 4158

Site Museums and Monuments / *Destinee Kae Swanson* 4164

Slovakia: Libraries, Archives, and Museums / *Jela Steinerová, Juraj Roháč and Gabriela Podušelová* . . 4173

Smithsonian Institution / *Pamela M. Henson* 4188

Social Epistemology / *Steve Fuller* 4197

Social Influences on Classification / *Hope A. Olson* 4204

Social Informatics / *Howard Rosenbaum* 4212

Volume VI (*cont'd.*)

Social Justice in Library and Information Science / *Bharat Mehra, Kevin S. Rioux and Kendra S. Albright* 4218

Social Networks and Information Transfer / *Caroline Haythornthwaite* 4235

Social Science Literatures and Their Users *[ELIS Classic]* / *David Ellis* 4246

Social Science Professional Literatures and Their Users / *Lynn Westbrook* 4255

Society for Scholarly Publishing (SSP) / *Judy C. Holoviak, October R. Ivins and Lois Smith* 4262

Society for the History of Authorship, Reading and Publishing (SHARP) / *Beth Luey* 4268

Society of American Archivists (SAA) / *Timothy L. Ericson and Steven L. Hensen* 4271

Sociology of Reading / *Martine Poulain* 4279

Sociology of the Information Disciplines / *Michael F. Winter* 4286

Software and Information Industry Association (SIIA) / *Silje C. Lier* 4297

Sound and Audio Archives / *Mark Roosa* 4299

South Korea: Archives and Libraries / *Hyun-Yang Cho, Eun Bong Park, Soyeon Park, Jae-Hwang Choi, Seong Hee Kim and Jong-Yup Han* 4307

Spain: Libraries, Archives, and Museums / *Lawrence J. Olszewski* 4314

Special Collections / *Lynne M. Thomas* 4335

Special Collections and Manuscripts / *Lynne M. Thomas* 4343

Special Librarianship / *Susan S. DiMattia* 4351

Volume VII

Special Libraries / *David Shumaker* 4361

Special Libraries Association (SLA) / *Guy St. Clair, Andrew J. Berner and Rebecca Vargha* 4370

Specialty Museums / *Trevor Jones* 4379

State Archives / *David B. Gracy II and Adam D. Knowles* 4384

State Libraries and State Library Agencies / *Barratt Wilkins* 4392

State-Sponsored Destruction of Books and Libraries / *Rebecca Knuth* 4400

Still Image Indexing / *Corinne Jörgensen* 4407

Still Image Search and Retrieval / *Vittorio Castelli* 4417

Storytelling / *Sarah Beth Nelson and Brian William Sturm* 4437

Strategic Planning in Academic Libraries / *Sheila Corrall* 4447

Students' Information: Needs and Behavior / *Heidi Julien* 4459

Subject Cataloging Principles and Systems / *Theodora L. Hodges and Lois Mai Chan* 4466

Subscription Libraries *[ELIS Classic]* / *David E. Gerard* 4478

Switzerland: Libraries, Archives, and Museums / *Jean Frédéric Jauslin and Andreas Kellerhals* 4487

Tanzania: Libraries, Archives, Museums, and Information Systems / *Janet Kaaya* 4497

Task-Based Information Searching: Research Methods / *Sanna Kumpulainen* 4526

Taxonomy / *Andrew Grove* 4537

Technical Writing / *Michael J. Salvo* 4547

Test Collections / *Ben Carterette* 4554

Text Encoding Initiative (TEI) / *Edward Vanhoutte and Ron Van den Branden* 4559

Text REtrieval Conference (TREC) / *Ellen M. Voorhees* 4569

Theft, Vandalism, and Security in Libraries and Archives / *Sydney C. Van Nort* 4576

Theft, Vandalism, and Security in Museums / *Jes Koepfler, Ivan Tanzer, Stephanie Nemcsok, Jennifer Ng, Catherine Leekam, Angela Noseworthy and Jennifer Bawden* 4593

Theological Librarianship / *Paul F. Stuehrenberg* 4604

Volume VII (*cont'd.*)

Topic Maps / *Steve Pepper* 4611

Tunisia: Libraries, Archives, and Museums / *Ali Houissa* 4624

Ukraine: Libraries / *Lyudmila Shpilevaya* 4642

Undergraduate Library Collections *[ELIS Classic]* / *Amy M. Kautzman* 4649

UNESCO: Communication and Information Sector / *Joie Springer* 4656

Unicode Standard / *Joan M. Aliprand* 4662

Unified Medical Language System® (UMLS®) Project / *Stuart J. Nelson, Tammy Powell,*
Suresh Srinivasan and Betsy L. Humphreys 4672

Uniform Computer Information Transactions Act (UCITA) / *Sarah K. Wiant* 4680

Unions in Public and Academic Libraries / *Kathleen de la Peña McCook* 4689

United Kingdom: Archives and Archival Science / *Helen Forde* 4699

United Kingdom: Libraries and Librarianship / *David J. Muddiman* 4707

United Kingdom: Museums and Museology / *Sarah Elliott and Peter Davis* 4723

United States: Archives and Archival Science / *Cheryl L. Stadel-Bevans and Danna Bell-Russel* 4740

United States: Libraries and Librarianship in the 21st Century / *John W. Berry* 4766

United States: Museums / *Beverly K. Sheppard* 4776

Universal Decimal Classification (UDC) / *I. C. McIlwaine* 4783

University Archives / *William J. Maher* 4791

Usability Testing of User Interfaces in Libraries / *Sharon L. Walbridge* 4797

User-Centered Design of Information Systems / *Elaine G. Toms* 4803

User-Centered Revolution: 1970–1995 *[ELIS Classic]* / *Diane Nahl* 4812

User-Centered Revolution: 1995–2008 / *Diane Nahl* 4847

User-Oriented and Cognitive Models of Information Retrieval / *Mette Skov,*
Kalervo Järvelin and Peter Ingwersen 4872

Venezuela: Libraries and Librarianship / *Juan D. Machin-Mastromatteo and Renny Granda* 4886

Version Control / *Jill E. Grogg and Jeff Weddle* 4896

Vietnam: Libraries, Archives, and Museums / *Robert D. Stueart* 4902

Visitor Studies / *Susan Foutz and Jill Stein* 4917

Visual and Performing Arts Archives / *Francesca Marini* 4925

Visual Resources Association (VRA) / *Virginia M.G. Hall* 4933

Visual Resources Management in Cultural Institutions / *Jacqueline Allen and Marcia K. Stein* 4940

Volunteer Services in Cultural Institutions / *Barbara Cohen-Stratyner* 4951

Wayfinding and Signage / *Dennis O'Brien* 4958

Web Scale Discovery Services / *Jason Vaughan* 4978

Webometrics / *Mike Thelwall* 4983

Word Processing: Early History *[ELIS Classic]* / *Daniel Eisenberg* 4993

World Intellectual Property Organization (WIPO) / *Janice T. Pilch* 5000

World Summit on the Information Society (WSIS) / *Alex Byrne* 5012

World Wide Web (WWW) / *Christinger Tomer* 5019

World Wide Web Consortium (W3C) / *Terrence Brooks* 5034

XML Information Retrieval / *Mounia Lalmas* 5039

Young Adult Library Services Association (YALSA) / *Marjorie Lewis* 5052

Young Adult Services in Libraries / *Mary K. Chelton* 5058

Youth Information: Needs and Behavior / *Melissa Gross* 5067

Zoological Park and Aquarium Libraries and Archives / *Vernon N. Kisling, Jr.* 5077

Introduction to the Encyclopedia of Library and Information Sciences, Fourth Edition

How to Use This Encyclopedia

Entries are arranged alphabetically in this encyclopedia (see end papers for alphabetical list). The editors of this edition (ELIS-4) have decided to forego the Topical Table of Contents that was provided in ELIS-3 by editors Marcia Bates and Mary Niles Maack. At the time of publication of ELIS-3, the Topical TOC was crucial for readers to get a sense of how subjects were grouped and an understanding of the field or subfield through the clustering of categorical entries in the print edition. ELIS-4 is envisioned as a primarily online reference work where a Topical TOC does not serve the same purpose. The print edition is served well by the main TOC as well as the detailed index, while entries in the online version are easily discoverable through title, author, keyword, and full text searches.

In sum, relevant entries can be found by

1. Entry title (alphabetical arrangement of entries in the encyclopedia or listing in the end papers)
2. Specific name or keyword, including the index at the end of each volume

If the first name or keyword searched is not found, try several more variations—either different words or a different order of words. Most topics are described in several ways in the literature of a discipline, and the first term or phrase that comes to mind may not be the one used here.

Scope of the Encyclopedia

The title of the third edition, *Encyclopedia of Library and Information Sciences*, ended with the letter "s" because the encyclopedia was broadened to cover a spectrum of related and newly emerging information disciplines, including archival science, document theory, informatics, and records management, among others. The fourth edition continues this trend but with an extensive focus on the aspects of library and information sciences that have been heavily impacted by the adoption and reliance on online information distribution. This focus is reflected in the inclusion of numerous new entries such as digital preservation, altmetrics, web-scale discovery services, demand-driven acquisitions, and global open knowledgebases. Alongside these entries based on entirely new topics, the expanded use of the Internet for information has led to new treatment of traditional LIS topics such as resource description and access (RDA) that reflects the adoption of new standards for cataloging.

ELIS-4 also seeks to build upon the description of professional practice to round out the theoretical perspective that previous editions covered very well. Both current editors are academic research librarians and thus, focused heavily on addressing gaps in the encyclopedia related to academic research information while still relying heavily on the structure established by editors of ELIS-3. For example, ELIS-3 introduced country profiles and ELIS-4 builds upon that with new entries for New Zealand and a third on Brazil, in addition to revisions for Slovakia, Netherlands, Canada, Belarus, Kazakhstan, and Brazil among others. This edition also expands the number of entries for named cultural and information entities that did not appear in previous editions, such as the National Library of Medicine, North American Serials Interest Group (NASIG), the International Association of Scientific, Technical and Medical Publishers (STM), and ASLIB, as well as entities like the HathiTrust that have been established since the last edition was published. A number of new entries describing important information conferences such as the Acquisitions Institute at Timberline, the Charleston Conference, and Electronic Resources in Libraries (ER&L) also help round out the encyclopedia and further the description of the current state of academic research librarianship.

ELIS-4 also continues the tradition of designating important entries of historical or theoretical importance as "ELIS Classics." These are entries by major figures in the library and information sciences or those that describe core concepts in LIS theory, practice, or education that appeared in earlier editions of the encyclopedia. The current editors preserved the approximately 40 previous "ELIS Classics" and designated 13 previous entries as new "ELIS Classics."

There are more than 550 entries, of which more than 20 are new, another 93 are revisions to prior entries that have been brought up to date by their authors or by new authors, about 30 are ELIS Classics, and about 400 are reprinted from an earlier edition since they have remained relevant to the present. It is important to note that the editors also had to make some choices related to retiring entries that were no longer relevant—due to the passage of time and the development of the field, the technologies and theories described in those entries were deemed to be out of scope for the new edition and thus not revised or reprinted.

Encyclopedia Authors

As in past editions, the authors writing for the encyclopedia are major researchers, librarians and practitioners, and leaders in the fields and subfields in the disciplines in which they are writing. Noted scholars are well represented, and a number of authors are former leaders in LIS associations, including the American Library Association (ALA), the Association for College and Research Libraries (ACRL), the International Federation of Library Associations and Institutions (IFLA), the American Society for Information Science and Technology (ASIS&T), and the American Association of Library and Information Science Education (ALISE). In addition, there are many contributors who are current or former directors of major institutions. As in past editions, the editors are very proud of the range and diversity of authors who have written these entries for the encyclopedia and we thank them for sharing their expertise with the current and future readers and researchers in the field.

Finally, the editors for ELIS-4 have grappled with the challenges of entry generation that was noted by previous editors in nearly every edition: that not all ideas, topics, and potential entries were able to be completed for publication in this edition. While we made a valiant attempt to include entries identified by ELIS-3 editors but not secured for publication in that edition, we sometimes could not find authors willing to take those topics on. Similarly, we were sometimes unable to secure revisions to entries from new authors when previous authors were unable to perform that task. To the greatest extent possible, we endeavored to replace authors when entries were deemed important enough to appear in ELIS-4 but initial or previous authors had to decline or defaulted. No doubt, the editors of ELIS-5 will also pick up the mantle and attempt to round out the encyclopedia with entries for anything that ELIS-4 missed. As noted by editors Bates and Niles Maack in ELIS-3, this problem of missing topics was also acknowledged by Allen Kent, editor of the first edition of ELIS. Kent stated in 1973, "I have prepared this presentation to make sure the lessons of Diderot-d'Alembert are recalled in terms of encyclopedia-making as an exercise in the art of the possible."

Background and Development of the Encyclopedia

The first edition of ELIS, under the editorship principally of Allen Kent and Harold Lancour, was published between 1968 and 1982. The 33 volumes of the first edition were published in alphabetical sequence during those years. After the "Z" volume appeared in 1982, a number of supplements were published at roughly the rate of two per year, up to and including volume 73, which appeared in 2003. Miriam Drake was appointed editor for the second edition, which appeared in 2003, both online and in paper. The second edition came out at one time in four large-format volumes, with a supplement in 2005 [3]. Kent and Lancour covered a wide range of librarianship, information science, and some computer science topics. Drake, an academic library director, emphasized academic libraries, and the ELIS-2 volumes contained many profiles of major academic libraries and professional library associations.

The third edition, under the editorship of Marcia Bates and Mary Niles Maack, reflected a growing convergence among the several disciplines that concern themselves with information and the cultural record. As information science educators and noted researchers in the field, their focus was on growing the encyclopedia in the theoretical fields of information sciences as well as drawing together the associated information and cultural disciplines such as archival sciences and museum studies within the overall field of LIS.

For this edition, we have focused on developing the encyclopedia to reflect the changing nature of information production and consumption through online and digital forms. We have also endeavored to fill in gaps in the description of important people, places, and theories in the information sciences, and further enhanced the description of important concepts related to the provision of research information and the field's major institutions.

We continue to see the audience for the encyclopedia just as previous editors have: as principally consisting of 1) the educated lay person interested in one or more of its topics, 2) students learning about a topic, and 3) professionals and researchers in the several fields who want to learn about something new, or to be refreshed on a familiar topic.

We honored the previous editors by reengaging their superb Editorial Advisory Board with significant new additions of experts known to the current editors. (See listing in the front matter.) These leaders and experts from as many disciplines as are in the encyclopedia provided excellent guidance and feedback for the editors as they began the process of new topic generation, evaluation of previous entries, and offering to author or review numerous entries throughout the process of publication.

All new and revised entries were reviewed by one or more outside expert reviewer as well as one or more of the editors. Referees provided invaluable feedback to authors, including noting errors or omissions as well as making suggestions on additional aspects of the topic to cover. While we made every reasonable attempt through this process to check the accuracy of every entry and every fact, undoubtedly readers will find some topics explained more thoroughly or accurately than others. Indeed, due to the time frame from the beginning of the generation of the fourth edition and the time of publication, readers will reasonably note that some topics have been quickly superseded due to this passage of time, so the date of acceptance of the entry will be noted on each entry since several years may have passed since the writing of the entry and the publication of this edition.

Acknowledgments

This edition of the encyclopedia was possible only through the countless hours that the editors, John McDonald and Michael Levine-Clark, spent reviewing the previous encyclopedia entries, outlining the topics that were missing or that were newly emerging in the field, and identifying appropriate expert authors to write those new entries. In addition, the editors devoted extensive time to corresponding with previous authors encouraging them to revise their entries, and finding replacement authors for important entries that needed revisions but whose original authors were unavailable.

Both editors wish to acknowledge the expertise of each other and their knowledge of our field, their extensive network of contacts, and their ability to work closely together to ensure the success of this encyclopedia. Neither of them could have completed this project alone.

They acknowledge and thank the Taylor & Francis Group editors, Claire Miller and Rich O'Hanley, as well as Susan Lee, who passed away at the early stages of the preparation of this edition, and more recently, Alexandra Torres, who supported and kept the editors and authors on track over the course of the years of work on this edition of the encyclopedia.

The editors thank the authors who wrote and revised entries, and the huge number of reviewers who refereed the entries. Without their dedication, expertise, and willingness to share their knowledge with others, there would be no encyclopedia. They also wish to thank the Editorial Advisory Board for their advice, suggestions of topics and authors, their hours spent writing or reviewing for the final edition. They also wish to thank the previous editors, Marcia Bates and Mary Niles Maack, whose organization and structure for ELIS-3 provided an excellent blueprint for ELIS-4.

Encyclopedia of Library and Information Sciences, Fourth Edition

Volume 7

Pages 4361–5084

Special–Strategic

Student–Taxonomy

Technical–Topic

Tunisia–United Kingdom

United States–
User-Centered Design

User-Centered Revolution–
Version

Vietnam–Webometrics

Word–Zoological

Encyclopedia of Library
and Information Sciences,
Fourth Edition

Special Libraries

David Shumaker
School of Library and Information Science, Catholic University of America, Washington, District of Columbia, U.S.A.

Abstract

Special libraries are extremely diverse and are found in many different types of organizations, serving almost every conceivable discipline. With few exceptions, special libraries exist as units of larger organizations. Special libraries arose in the United States and Great Britain in the nineteenth century and have multiplied and spread worldwide throughout the twentieth. Despite their diversity, they have certain unifying characteristics. They acquire and maintain information resources in topics and areas of importance to a limited, well-defined customer base, and they offer a range of specialized and customized services to ensure that the right information reaches the right customers at the right time. They take their mission and goals from their parent organizations, and exist primarily to improve the ability of their customers to perform their tasks effectively. Recent advances in information technology and organizational development are changing the role of special libraries, bringing them both threats and broad new opportunities.

INTRODUCTION

This entry discusses the special library as a distinct type of library and a distinct entity that exists within many diverse types of organizations. It covers the definition and distinguishing characteristics of special libraries, their history, the services typically provided by special libraries, special considerations of professional ethics in special libraries, and important considerations in the management of the special library. This entry concludes with a review of current trends and the outlook for special library services and development.

DEFINITION

Special libraries are libraries that have one or more of the following attributes: a focus on specialized information resources, usually of a limited subject scope; a focus on a specialized and limited clientele; and the delivery of specialized services to that clientele. Some authorities add that a special library is one sponsored by a parent institution, such as "business and industrial firms, not-for-profit organizations, government agencies, and professional associations."[1]

Some of the prominent types of special libraries are medical libraries, law libraries, corporate libraries, libraries in legislative and executive agencies of government, music libraries, art libraries, engineering libraries, and libraries of trade and professional associations, to name a few. Many specialized libraries in institutions of higher education are also considered special libraries. For example, the library of a medical school, a law school, or a specialized research institute may be considered a special library.

Because special libraries are so diverse and may exist in many types of organizations, they may range in size from small operations administered by one person, to large institutions with their own buildings and hundreds of staff members. An example of the latter is the United States Congressional Research Service, a unit of the Library of Congress, which, while very broad in its subject interests, serves a very limited clientele—the members of the U.S. Congress and their staffs—and provides highly specialized services to its clients. The Congressional Research Services has nearly 700 staff.[2] A very different special library is the Linda Hall Library, which is open to the public, unlike most special libraries, but has a specialized focus on science and technology.[3]

An early definition (1914) focused on the nature of services provided as the differentiating characteristic of the special library:

> It may be said, of course, that every library is in a measure special, in its own field, and that state libraries, libraries of colleges and universities, of medicine, law, history, art and other subjects may be called special. But a special library, and the special departments of more general libraries-like the business branch in Newark - are the first and as yet almost the only print-administering institutions which professedly recognize the change in library method that the vast and swiftly mounting bulk of print is demanding; realize how ephemeral, and at the same time how exceedingly useful for the day and hour, is much of the present output of things-intended-to-be-read, and frankly adopt the new library creed as to print management, of careful selection, immediate use and ready rejection when usefulness is past.[4]

Encyclopedia of Library and Information Sciences, Fourth Edition DOI: 10.1081/E-ELIS4-120044555

The defining characteristic of special libraries was put more succinctly by John A. Lapp, who in 1918 wrote of the "...specialist's library and ... the problem of putting knowledge to work."[5] The phrase "Putting knowledge to work" has continued as a slogan of the Special Libraries Association to the present day.

This emphasis on special services as the characteristic of special libraries that sets them apart is also continued in contemporary librarianship by the International Federation of Library Associations and Institutions, Division of Special Libraries. It states that "The Division of Special Libraries is characterized by libraries with specific kinds of service functions and subject specialties.... These libraries vary in size but all provide specialized services to their clientele."[6]

Perhaps because of the diversity of institutions it covers, the term "special libraries" has always been something of a compromise. Dana, writing in 1914 of the founding of the Special Libraries Association, commented, "The name Special Libraries was chosen with some hesitation, and rather in default of a better; ..."[4] Writing 35 years later, S.R. Ranganathan echoed this hesitation, beginning an article with the sentence, "Special librarianship is a puzzling term."[7] The imprecision of the term "special library" continues to provoke discussions in the field and beyond.

HISTORY

Origins

Specialized libraries have existed from early times. Whether as personal libraries of the wealthy, libraries of religious institutions, or of scholarly societies, the idea of a shared collection of books for a special audience is nothing new. The Commercial Library at Hamburg, Germany, founded in the 1730s, is an early example of a special library established to support commerce and industry. The Pennsylvania Hospital started its medical library in 1763.[8] However, the idea of a "special library" as a distinct category only arose in Great Britain and the United States in the nineteenth century. In both countries, this emerging identity led to the formation of the first separate professional associations of those engaged in the operation and management of special libraries.

Twentieth Century to Present

In the United States, the rise of the library profession led to the formation of the American Library Association (ALA) in 1876. Not long afterward, continued growth in specialized libraries led to the establishment of associations for specialized libraries: the National Association of State Libraries in 1889, the Medical Library Association in 1898, and the American Association of Law Libraries in

1906. This continued growth then led to the formation of the Special Libraries Association in 1909, with 20 librarians participating. A directory of special libraries prepared by the Association in April, 1910, listed about 100 libraries.[9]

Events in Great Britain followed a similar course. During much of the latter half of the nineteenth and early twentieth centuries, the Library Association, founded in 1877, provided a home for all librarians, including those interested in special libraries.[10] In 1924, however, a group of these librarians formed Aslib, an association of special libraries.[8]

Public libraries played an important role in the early development of special libraries. A prime example was the public library of Newark, New Jersey, whose librarian, John Cotton Dana, established a commercial branch in the central business district in 1904. Dana also led the founding of the Special Libraries Association in 1909. Over time, however, specialized services in public library organizations have generally ceased to be thought of as special libraries, and their staff members are rarely involved in the special library professional groups.[8]

Over the course of the twentieth century, the number and distribution of special libraries continued to grow. Drawing on a series of published surveys and directories, Kruzas documented the increase in U.S. special libraries from 108 in 1910 to 975 in 1925 and 2480 in 1957.[11] The 60th edition of the *American Library Directory* (2007–2008) lists a total of 7881 special libraries in the United States, plus an additional 1300 when special libraries within public libraries, academic libraries, Armed Forces establishments, and other government libraries are included, for a total of 9181. It also lists 982 special libraries (including the above-mentioned categories) in Canada. In both countries, special libraries represent about 30% of the libraries listed.[12]

While not directly comparable, an analysis of data from the United States Bureau of Labor Statistics suggests that the proportion of library employment accounted for by special libraries is significantly lower: about 13%, or some 20,000 out of a total library employment of over 157,000.[13] This number excludes librarians who are working in educational institutions at all levels, or in local government, i.e., public libraries. It includes librarians in state and Federal government and in all nongovernment, noneducational organizations. In part this lower number may be due to the exclusion of special libraries within academic libraries, and in part it may be due to the smaller size of many special libraries.

Globalization

While special libraries arose as a distinct type of entity within North America and Great Britain, the concept soon spread globally. Professional groups for special libraries were established in Finland in 1929 and in Switzerland in

1939.[14] Special libraries arise in countries that undergo industrial and economic development, and are sustained in parallel with that development. By 1978, special libraries existed in many countries in all regions of the globe. The global spread of special libraries is now recognized by the existence of the Division of Special Libraries within the International Federation of Library Associations and Institutions (IFLA). The Division reported 508 members in 2002.[15]

SERVICES

The importance of specialized services in special libraries has been central from the early days of the profession. Dana, writing in 1914, described the work of the librarian in a special library in these terms:

> This librarian purchased periodicals, journals, proceedings of societies, leaflets, pamphlets, and books on the special field in which his employers were interested, studied them, indexed them, or tore up or clipped from them pertinent material and filed it under proper heading, and then either held himself in readiness to guide managers, foremen and others, directly to the latest information on any topics they might present, or compiled each week or each month a list of pertinent, classified references to the last words from all parts of the world on the fields covered by his organization's activities, and laid a copy of this list on the desk of every employe who could make good use of it.[4]

Dana's description continues to cover much of the service mix of special libraries almost 100 years later. Special libraries serve through focused collection development, customized organization of information, knowledgeable reference and research services, and proactive delivery of news updates. More recently, special libraries have developed new or enhanced services, such as information analysis and synthesis, competitive intelligence (CI), and knowledge management (KM).

Acquisitions and Collection Development

The essence of the special library is its focus on the specific interests of its user population. The special librarian restricts acquisitions to those materials of central interest to the sponsoring organization. The special library does not seek to duplicate the general information available through other accessible sources, such as local public and academic libraries.

As an extension of their collection development function, special libraries often become responsible for acquiring information resources that do not reside in the library, such as "desk copies" of texts, handbooks, and other publications. With the advent of the licensing of digital information resources, this function has in turn expanded into the role of contracting for, or licensing, access to digital collections on behalf of the members of the special library's parent organization. Where the parent organization is large and complex, this puts the special library squarely in the role of brokering access on behalf of the whole enterprise.

Organization of Information

Because the special library thus develops a very deep and narrow collection, the librarians often find that systems of organization developed for libraries of broader scope do not provide enough differentiation of highly detailed and technical subject matter to enable the librarian or the users to locate information effectively.

However, economic considerations lead special libraries to use general sources and systems of bibliographic description and organization, such as catalog records obtained from OCLC, Inc., containing Library of Congress and Dewey Decimal Classification numbers. Where resources are available, many of them augment the data from these sources with local subject headings and descriptors. Medical libraries make use of the specialized Medical Subject Headings (MeSH) of the U.S. National Library of Medicine. Further, the information required to meet the needs of many specialized customer groups is found not in the books typically covered by sources such as OCLC and the Library of Congress, but in specialized technical, professional, and trade serial publications. These publications are typically indexed by professional or commercial information services, using specialized thesauri. An example is the digital library service of the Association of Computing Machinery (ACM), which uses the Association's Computing Classification System to provide subject access.[16] In some fields, libraries collect other genres and forms of material such as technical reports. An example of a specialized information service of this type, with a custom thesaurus, is the U.S. Defense Technical Information Service.[17]

Reference and Research Center

The philosophy of the special library is to provide knowledgeable and responsive services. The emphasis on the knowledge of reference staff, and the expectation of in-depth research service, set the special library somewhat apart from its more generalized public and academic counterparts. The reference librarian in the special library is often expected to go beyond factual "ready reference" and advisory services, and to provide in-depth research services that may require a lengthy time commitment. To be effective in handling complex and sometimes technical questions, the staff must have relevant subject knowledge. For this reason, many special libraries require or prefer that their staff have relevant educational backgrounds. For example, staff members of law libraries often have law degrees in addition to degrees in library science. Those who do not possess the law degree generally take specialized courses in law librarianship and legal research in their library science programs. Similarly, medical and health sciences libraries seek to attract staff with graduate or undergraduate degrees in biology, chemistry, and similar disciplines. Staff of special libraries who lack relevant specialized education or experience find that they must learn their new field "on the job" in order to provide the knowledgeable, in-depth service expected of them.

The service philosophy of the special library differs from that of a generalized library in other important respects. In public libraries especially, there is often a presumption against the reference librarian asking a customer why information is being sought.[18] In the special library, it is often imperative for the librarian to understand the specific background of the request. Without this understanding, the librarian cannot focus the research and select the right information sensitively enough to be of real value to the customer. Thus the librarian commonly becomes privy to confidential and sensitive business information and is required to maintain confidentiality as a duty of employment. Along with the need for deep domain knowledge and specific understanding of the business need goes the need, for many requests, of responding very quickly. The nature of information requests in many organizational settings is that timeliness is as important as quality, and a "good enough" answer on time is valued, while a careful, detailed answer too late is not. Thus the special library staff members learn to move quickly and to "satisfice": provide information that is good enough, not perfect.

Finally, the special library often has a different philosophy with regard to the training or teaching role of the library reference staff than that of the public, school, or academic librarian. In those latter settings, a reference question is often viewed as a "teachable moment"—an opportunity for the librarian to show the customer how to carry out information seeking tasks. In the special library, staff members are often required to provide "the answer" and to do it quickly. In such circumstances, their function is to save the time of the customer and not to take up that time by engaging in an instructional encounter.

News Updating

Because special libraries typically serve a limited population, they come to know their customers, and their customers' ongoing information needs, quite well. As management authority Peter Drucker has said, "Librarians in a special library... can—and do—anticipate the customer's information needs. They can—and do—reach out to the customer and point him or her in the right information direction. They can—and do—know what new data is in their customer's field or sphere of interest."[19] Whether it is a medical specialist with an

ongoing interest in the research on a specific disease, or a business executive with an ongoing need for information about the company's competitors in a specific product line, many customers of special libraries have ongoing needs for updated information on a topic. For this reason, from the time of Dana's writing to the current time, special libraries have provided ongoing information services. These have gone under various names: Selective Dissemination of Information (SDI); Current Awareness, News Alerting, and specific brand names applied by specific special libraries. Whatever the name, the essence of these services includes: a subject scope narrowly defined and customized to meet the needs of a small audience; a publication coverage that may range from one source to a broad collection of sources; a frequency, again customized in collaboration with the customer, which may range from near instantaneous to daily, weekly, or monthly; and a format also customized to meet the audience's needs, ranging from very brief summaries of pertinent stories, to synthesized synopses of stories; or the full stories themselves.

Many tools are now available to provide current awareness services. They include news alert functions from the vendors of digital library resources; e-mail subscriptions, really simple syndication (RSS) feeds, and more. As these tools have evolved, the role of the special librarian has expanded to encompass facilitating customer awareness and access to these services, helping the customer set them up, and aggregating and selecting the results of disparate services to deliver a single integrated feed to the customer.

Trends in Special Library Services

Recent service trends in special libraries include the expansion of information analysis and synthesis, including CI, and the initiation of KM services. As digital information has become ubiquitous, the role of the physical library space as the repository of information, and the role of the librarian in maintaining the order and accessibility of the information resources, has been replaced by networked access from anywhere. As networked access has further opened the floodgates of the information stream, the employees of many organizations have struggled with the need to process, analyze, and synthesize it all. The staff of special libraries have been able to leverage their knowledge of sources, information retrieval methods, and knowledge of their customers' domains of interest to supply more sophisticated information analysis and retrieval than they could when they were preoccupied with the acquisition and maintenance of collections, and with the delivery of factual information.

Competitive intelligence is a special case of information analysis and synthesis. The practice of CI has arisen, first in for-profit corporations and more recently in non-profit and educational institutions, as organizational managers have become more attuned to the importance of understanding the marketplace and the competitive environment of the enterprise. CI calls for highly sophisticated collection and analysis of information bearing specifically on important decisions of the strategy and market development of the enterprise. Special libraries, because of their history of responsive collection and delivery of information, have become partners and leaders in many CI programs.

Likewise, KM has become established in many organizations. This is due to two factors: the increasing recognition of information and knowledge as sources of competitive advantage; and the awareness that much of what the organization needs to know is already known by someone in the organization. Thus, the challenge becomes to facilitate the sharing of what is known. Special libraries have become partners and leaders in KM for two fundamental reasons: they possess expertise in techniques of organizing and managing information that can be applied to internally generated as well as externally acquired information resources; and in many organizations they are one of the few entities that work on a substantive basis across a wide array of organizational units. One special library manager has referred to this as the library's mandate to "work across the white space" of the organization.[20]

ETHICS

The profession of librarianship has a strong concern with ethics. The Code of Ethics adopted by the ALA[21] and the codes of other professional organizations are evidence of this concern.[22,23] The application of professional ethics in a special library may be affected by its position as a unit of a larger organization. As Preer writes, "Special librarians have a dual identity arising from their work in libraries which support the goals of another profession or organization. They may find their professional values in conflict with institutional ones."[24]

With respect to the ALA code, there are two areas of primary interest. These are, "We provide the highest level of service to all library users…" (principle I.) and "We protect each library user's right to privacy and confidentiality with respect to information sought or received and resources consulted, borrowed, acquired or transmitted." (Principle III.)

The former principle conflicts with the special library's need to respect the power and authority structure of the organization, and to take its interests into account in service decisions. Consequently, as does any other organizational unit, the special library generally is obliged to respond first to the demands of its management sponsors, and to relegate the requests of other customers to a lower priority when conflicts arise. Similarly, the question of how much access and service to provide to those outside

the organization is heavily influenced by factors of competition and proprietary interest. While some special libraries are open to the public, many others provide restricted access, or none at all, to individuals who are not affiliated with the parent organization. Still others provide services through participation in interlibrary loan networks and other multitype library consortia, but do not deal directly with members of the public.[25]

In the latter principle, the ALA Code fails to take into account the lowered expectation of privacy that any individual has when acting as an employee and using systems and services furnished by the employer, in contrast to actions taken as a private citizen. The special librarian, on the other hand, as an employee of the enterprise, has an obligation to follow appropriate corporate policies that may provide for the disclosure of employee information pursuant to corporate policies, and with appropriate safeguards.

MANAGEMENT

Organizational Context

The unique aspects of managing a special library arise from its relationship to its parent organization. Whether it is a one-person information center serving a single unit like a marketing department or a research laboratory, or a complex library network serving an entire corporation, the special library occupies a distinctive position. Although it is often considered an administrative support function, like Human Resources or Fiscal Management, it differs from other support functions in that generally it has no mandate: no requirement that anyone use it. Therefore, the central task for the special library manager and staff is to align the library with the mission, vision, and strategy of the parent organization. The services of the special library must make a valuable contribution to the attainment of the parent organization's goals, and the special librarian must be able to articulate this contribution effectively to secure the support necessary for the library to thrive and to continue building and delivering its valuable services.

The organizational placement of the special library is critically important. Some libraries are set up to serve specific, relatively small, organizational units, such as a research and development group or a marketing department. In this case, the library takes its mission from that of the parent unit. Ideally, the library manager reports to the manager or director of the unit, and is thus able to learn about important developments within the unit, to adjust services as needed to respond to developments, and to make the accomplishments and value of the library visible to the senior manager and other managers in the unit.

When libraries serve a larger organizational unit or the entire corporation, the librarian rarely reports directly to the top manager. Libraries have been known to report to Facilities managers, Human Resource managers,

Information Technology managers, and Publications and Communications managers, to name a few. Debates continue about what is the "best" organizational placement for a special library. What seems clear is that the library manager needs a supervisor who understands the library's role, supports it, encourages its development, and is powerful enough within the organizational hierarchy to obtain the resources it needs.

In some organizations, all or some of the library functions are outsourced. This means that the organization contracts with another organization for the delivery of these functions. This may be limited to the contracting of specific tasks, such as acquisitions, cataloging, or shelving and filing, or it may encompass the contracting of the entire special library operation. Sometimes the decision to outsource is made as a cost-saving measure, and sometimes for strategic reasons. In the latter case, an organization may decide that library services are not one of its "core competencies" and take the library outsourcing action as part of a strategy of outsourcing all noncore functions. There is ongoing controversy in the profession about whether an outsourced library can deliver services as effectively as a library staffed and led by employees of the customer organization. Hill provides a case study of an outsourced library provider that recommended the customer organization take the library back as an in-house operation for this very reason.[26]

Planning and Budgeting

It is common for the special library to have a strategic plan, incorporating goals and multiyear action plans that are derived from the strategic plan of the parent organization. In this way, the library aligns with the parent organization.

Budgeting in the library should align in turn with the strategic plan. It has been said that "The budget is the true mission statement of an institution."[27] This presupposes that the library has a distinct budget, and that the library manager is responsible for preparing and defending it. The effective special librarian will adjust budget priorities to reflect the strategic priorities of the parent organization: requesting funds for staff, resources, systems, and other initiatives that are explicitly tied to the goals of both immediate and senior management.

Marketing

The need to deliver and articulate the value of the special library puts marketing at the center of its activities. The special library must identify, anticipate, and deliver services that fulfill the interests of multiple stakeholder groups in order to thrive in the organization. Key stakeholder groups include senior management of the library's parent organization; the immediate supervising managers of the library, the customers who use the library's services

and resources, and the managers of the customers. Each of these stakeholder groups has distinct interests that the special library must satisfy.

Because the customers and potential customers of most special libraries are limited to the members of the parent organization, marketing to this stakeholder group is relatively straightforward and often well developed. Special libraries use surveys, customer comment forms, focus groups, and other communications methods adopted from the marketing discipline to find out what their customers think about current services and resources, and what they want. A few special libraries have used the LibQual+ survey, administered by the Association of Research Libraries, for this purpose.[28,29] Similarly, there are generally well-understood media for promoting library services to the potential customer base. These include intranets, internal e-mail lists, printed employee magazines and newsletters, and exhibits in employee cafeterias and building common areas. Special libraries may also offer tours, programs, user-education sessions, and may volunteer to speak to employee groups and organizational meetings.

The fourth stakeholder group that the special library must include in its marketing and outreach is the group of managers of its customers. These mid-level managers may or may not be direct users of the library's services. In either case, they may be unaware of the full extent of the actual and potential value of the library to their employees, unless the library actively reaches out to them. And yet, their influence on the actions of their employees is enormous. If the manager encourages a new employee to explore the library and get to know the librarian, the employee is much more likely to do so. A desirable approach is that expressed by a technical manager at the MITRE Corporation in this quotation from MITRE's employee newsletter:

> When Omaha Site Leader Dave Poutre briefs new employees on their first day at work, he starts with what you'd expect: this is your badge, here's your timecard, and the restrooms are over there. Then he gets serious, because the most important part of his orientation is about the support provided by the Information Services team. "I consider Information Services an incredible technical resource," he says. "They're a true force multiplier. They have a lot of resources, a lot of databases, and are skilled at quickly and efficiently finding what I need. They know where to go for the right information and how to package it quickly. Tremendous time-savers? You bet!"[30]

Therefore, the special library must actively communicate both its actual value and its potential to add new value through service and resource enhancements.

Measuring and Communicating Value

The communication of value, both to customer management and through the special library's management chain from immediate supervisor to the executive level of the enterprise, presupposes that the library is able to articulate its value in the first place. Thus, the evaluation of library services is another critical element of managing a special library. There are several approaches to this task.

In for-profit corporations, units may be evaluated on their contribution to corporate sales and profits—the "top line" and the "bottom line." Their contributions may come in the form of increased sales and/or cost reductions. Special libraries may contribute in both ways. The marketing library that, through its research and analysis, contributes to a successful marketing campaign that increases sales, has contributed to the "top line." The research and development information center that negotiates a favorable license for critical technical content and extends it to cover all the research laboratories of the enterprise has contributed to cost savings both by reducing the overall cost associated with multiple uncoordinated, overlapping licenses, and by saving the time of the technical staff spent seeking the information they need to perform their work. The challenge is the actual measurement of both top line and bottom line contributions. Strouse provides a brief introduction to activity counts, the use of surveys, and the analysis of data to measure the return on investment in corporate special libraries. From his own research in a number of special libraries, he provides the following benchmark figures (in 2003 U.S. dollars):

- Time saved: $35 per library use
- Money saved: $42 per library use
- Revenue generated: $777 per library use[31]

Special libraries in government and the nonprofit sector have performed similar analyses, focused on cost savings rather than revenue generation. Tenopir and King provide a comprehensive review of the literature of these studies.[32]

OUTLOOK FOR SPECIAL LIBRARIES: BACK TO THE FUTURE?

The special library arose as a distinct type of library because organizations needed units to acquire the specialized information relevant to their activities, organize that information, and provide customized services to get it to the right people at the right time. The special library developed and prospered in proportion to its ability to deliver on this value proposition. In the past 20 years, however, advances in information technology and changes in the nature of work have altered this value proposition.

The fortunes of special libraries have always risen and fallen with those of their parent organizations, and in times of hardship for the enterprise, the library budget is an obvious target. However, indicators of a broad threat to special libraries date at least to the early 1990s. In two surveys taken five years apart, in 1990 and 1995, it was found that the number of libraries with over 20 employees had dropped from 11% to 6%.[33,34] An analysis performed in 2001 identified 33 closures of information services departments in businesses in a period of a few months.[35] In 2007, Matarazzo and Pearlstein estimated that the membership of the Special Libraries Association had declined by 20% in the preceding 10 years.[36]

Advances in information technology mean that digital information is now ubiquitous—available to the employees of the organization via computer network anywhere, any time. As the self-serve, interconnected digital information resource becomes a reality, employees no longer need to visit the library in person, nor to consult the librarian in person. In the aforementioned surveys (see notes above), Matarazzo found that corporate executives placed a declining value on the role of the librarian as expert searcher and information intermediary. If information is digital and distributed, the role of the special library as a central place in the organization where information may be found no longer has the value it once did. To the extent that customers can identify, locate, and retrieve information from a networked digital information store, the special library's role as gatekeeper is no longer needed.

Changes in the nature of work, both enabled and driven by the changes in information technology, place a premium on flexibility in the accomplishment of organizational goals. This flexibility takes the form of flexible teams, an increased emphasis on diverse skills, backgrounds, and viewpoints of team members, and in the demand for individuals to work anytime, anywhere, and collaborate virtually as well as face to face.

In harmony with these changes and the decline of their old value proposition, successful special libraries are now changing rapidly, and finding new ways of serving their customers. They are employing new technologies, offering new services, and developing new relationships. As this evolution takes place, the nature of the special library as a distinct organizational unit and as a physical space hangs in the balance. It may wither away, turn into a network rather than a unit, become exclusively digital, or emerge more robust than ever with both a physical and virtual presence, and new services that complement the old.

Writing in 1993, Davenport and Prusak noted the irony that as organizations have become more aware of the importance of information as a strategic asset, libraries have often played limited and even declining roles. Their call to "blow up the corporate library" meant not to do away with it, sweeping up the smithereens and carting them out with the corporate trash, but rather to turn the knowledge and expertise resident in the special library into itself a distributed, networked resource able to help the enterprise with one of its central needs and opportunities: to become a "learning organization."[37] This means the effective networking and distribution of information across the enterprise at the times and in the activities where it is needed.

Bauwens, writing in the same year as Davenport and Prusak, recounted his experiences as a solo librarian embedded in a functional team and collaborating remotely by the use of computers and networks. He envisioned the establishment of networks of information professionals throughout the enterprise, each serving a distinct customer group and all sharing professional insights with one another, to supplant the traditional special library.[38]

Many special libraries have been pursuing variations of the visions of Davenport, Prusak, and Bauwens. At the National Geographic Society, the library has taken as one of its missions to work across the "white space" of the organization: defined as "those places within the library and outside the library where no one else is working." As a result of this mission, the library has led or had an important role in developing for the Society "an intranet,... an internal university,... communities of practice" and more.[20] The library has been responsible for developing new products, such as a short history of the Society, and routinely contributes to the development of new product ideas—not just as a source of information.[39]

King, writing in 2004, focused on the role of digital technology in the distribution, use, and maintenance of information resources.[40] He predicted the continuance of journals and conference proceedings as forms of publication critical to many special libraries and their customers, but he also predicted that current publications of these types will be distributed predominantly in digital form. Digital collections have indeed become increasingly dominant, and with them have come customer expectations of anytime, anywhere, self-service access to them, with cross-links among related information objects, regardless of publisher or source. This digital future is now emerging in many special libraries.

Abram provides a summary of new service roles open to special libraries.[41] He sees the future in opportunities to partner with others across the organization and to form:

- Unified access points to information resources.
- Integration of information and learning services to strengthen the learning environment for each employee.
- Embedding librarians into organizational units and project teams to concentrate on all aspects of the information needs of the unit.
- Providing distance services and resources to an increasingly distributed and mobile workforce through mobile communications and virtual reality.
- Equipping customers to use information effectively in their work through customized information literacy training.

In this scenario, the special library becomes both a physical and a virtual presence. The physical space of the library changes from a reading room to a talking room: a space that enables face-to-face meetings and collaboration and the encounters with information and knowledge that lead to enhanced organizational performance, and may be mimicked in cyberspace by a virtual special library with all the same attributes.

This prospect for the evolving role of the special library has been summarized as "knowledge services": a "framework for management that embodies the highest objectives of knowledge management and combines them with the basic principles of the learning organization and the teaching organization."[42] In this framework, the special library takes responsibility for all the information and knowledge assets and processes of the organization. It integrates internal and external resources. It deals with recorded, recordable, and tacit knowledge, and enables connections among staff who know and those who need to know—as well as between staff of the organization and outsiders with important knowledge to share.

What seems certain is that many different organizations of different types will have an increasing need for effective management and delivery of information, and that those special libraries that continue to innovate and to "put knowledge to work" will have a bright future and an increasingly important role.

ACKNOWLEDGMENTS

The author wishes to thank Erin McKinney and Acacia Reed for their research assistance. The author is indebted to Susan Fifer Canby, Bruce Rosenstein, and Guy St. Clair for their professional insights and suggestions in the preparation of this entry.

REFERENCES

1. Mount, E. *Special Libraries and Information Centers: An Introductory Text*; Special Libraries Association: New York, 1983.
2. CRS. *About CRS*, http://www.loc.gov/crsinfo/whatscrs.html (accessed December 7, 2007).
3. *Linda Hall Library: Science, Engineering and Technology Information for the World*, 2006, http://www.lhl.lib.mo.us/about_lhl/index.shtml (accessed December 7, 2007).
4. Dana, J.C. The evolution of the special library. Spec. Libr. **1914**, *5* (5), 70–76.
5. Lapp, J.A. The growth of a big idea. Spec. Libr. **1918**, *9* (7/8), 157–159.
6. IFLA. *Division of Special Libraries*, October 2, 2007, http://www.ifla.org/VII/d2/dsl.htm (accessed December 7, 2007).
7. Ranganathan, S.R. Special librarianship—what it connotes. Spec. Libr. **1949**, 361–367.
8. Johns, A.W. *Special Libraries: Development of the Concept, Their Organizations, and Their Services*; Scarecrow Press: Metuchen, NJ, 1968.

9. Mitchill, A.C., Ed. *Special Libraries Association—Its First Fifty Years 1909–1959*; Special Libraries Association: New York, 1959.

10. CILIP. *How CILIP Was Formed*; August 5 2005, http://www.cilip.org.uk/aboutcilip/history/unification (accessed December 12, 2007).

11. Kruzas, A.T. *Business and Industrial Libraries in the United States, 1820–1940*; Special Libraries Association: New York, 1965.

12. *American Library Directory*, 60th Ed.; Information Today: Medford, NJ, 2007; Vol. 1.

13. BLS *National Employment Matrix, Employment by Industry, Occupation, and Percent Distribution, 2006 and Projected 2016: Librarians (25-4021)*, 2007, ftp://ftp.bls.gov/pub/special.requests/ep/ind-occ.matrix/occ_pdf/occ_25-4021.pdf (accessed December 27, 2007).

14. van Halm, J. *The Development of Special Libraries as an International Phenomenon*; Special Libraries Association State-of-the-Art Review, no. 4; Special Libraries Association: New York, 1978.

15. Campbell, H.C. IFLA: Library universality in a divided world. IFLA J. **2002**, *28* (3), 118–135.

16. ACM. *ACM Portal: The ACM Digital Library*, 2007, http://portal.acm.org/dl.cfm (accessed December 26, 2007).

17. DTIC. *Defense Technical Information Center: Information for the Defense Community*, December 2007, http://www.dtic.mil/dtic/index.html (accessed December 26, 2007).

18. Bopp, R.E.; Smith, L.C. *Reference and Information Services: An Introduction. Third ed*; Libraries Unlimited: Englewood, CO, 2001.

19. Rosenstein, B. Peter Drucker: A life of knowledge. Inform. Outlook **2005**, *9* (12), 32–33.

20. Fifer Canby, S. Strategies for climbing the corporate ladder. Inform. Outlook **2005**, *9* (5), 13–16.

21. ALA. *Code of Ethics of the American Library Association*, June 28 1995, http://www.ala.org/ala/oif/statementspols/codeofethics/codeethics.htm (accessed November 5, 2007).

22. ASIS&T. *ASIS&T Professional Guidelines*, 1995, http://www.asis.org/AboutASIS/professional-guidelines.html (accessed November 5, 2007).

23. SAA. *Code of Ethics for Archivists*, February 5, 2005, http://www.archivists.org/governance/handbook/app_ethics.asp (accessed December 26, 2007).

24. Preer, J. Special ethics for special librarians? Spec. Libr. **1991**, *82*, 12–18.

25. Strife, M.L. Special libraries and diversity: Ethical considerations. Ref. Libr. **1994**, *21* (45–46), 213–219.

26. Hill, C. Insourcing the outsourced library: The Sun story. Libr. J. **1998**, *123* (4), 46–48.

27. Sullivan, A. *Re: [DIG_REF] Shutting Down Chat*, 2003, http://finance.groups.yahoo.com/group/dig_ref/message/8060 (accessed December 23, 2007).

28. Nicula, J.G.; Laseter, S.B. *LibQUAL+TM and the Professional Military Library*. In *Special Libraries Association Annual Conference*; Special Libraries Association: Nashville, TN, 2004.

29. Shumaker, D.; Scheiberg, S. *The LibQual+ Survey in Special Libraries*. In *Special Libraries Association Annual Conference*; Special Libraries Association: Baltimore, MD, 2006.

30. Monaco, N. *MITRE's Information Sleuths: Let the Experts Do the Digging*, December 31, 2003, http://www.mitre.org/employment/trends_highlights/info_sleuths.html (accessed December 18, 2007).

31. Strouse, R. Demonstrating value and return on investment: The ongoing imperative. Inform. Outlook **2003**, *7* (3), 14–19.

32. Tenopir, C.; King, D.W. *Communication Patterns of Engineers*; IEEE Press: Piscataway, NJ, 2004.

33. Matarazzo, J.M.; Prusak, L.; Gauthier, M.R. *Valuing Corporate Libraries*; Special Libraries Association: Washington, DC, 1990.

34. Matarazzo, J.M.; Prusak, L. *The Value of Corporate Libraries*; Special Libraries Association: Washington, DC, 1995.

35. Musher, R. The changing role of the information professional. Online **2001**, *25* (5), 62–64.

36. Matarazzo, J.M.; Pearlstein, T. Corporate score: Marrying two expert tools will help you sustain your corporate library. Libr. J. **2007**, *132* (2), 42–43.

37. Davenport, T.H.; Prusak, L. Blow up the corporate library. Int. J. Inform. Manage. **1993**, *13*, 405–412.

38. Bauwens, M. *The Cybrarians Manifesto*, April 20, 1993, http://listserv.uh.edu/cgi-bin/wa?A2=ind9304C&L=PACS-L&P=R3879&I=-3 (accessed April 28, 2007).

39. Fifer Canby, S. *More Than Keeping Pace: Finding Your Competitive Edge, in Croatian Library Association*; Croatian Library Association: Zagreb, Croatia, 2006.

40. King, R.J. The future of the special library: In this librarian's view, the future will be more digital, more collaborative. Inform. Outlook **2004**, *8* (9), 10–16.

41. Abram, S. The future of reference in special libraries is what information pros can make it. Inform. Outlook **2007**, *11* (10), 35–37.

42. St. Clair, G.; Harriston, V.; Pellizzi, T.A. Toward world-class knowledge services: Emerging trends in specialized research libraries—Part two: The customer perspective. Inform. Outlook **2003**, *7*(7).

Special Libraries Association (SLA)

Guy St. Clair
Knowledge Management and Learning, SMR International, New York, New York, U.S.A.

Andrew J. Berner
University Club of New York, New York, New York, U.S.A.

Rebecca Vargha
Information and Library Science Library, University of North Carolina at Chapel Hill, Chapel Hill, North Carolina, U.S.A.

Abstract

Founded in 1909, the Special Libraries Association (SLA) serves the members of that branch of the library and information science professions generally thought of as "non-traditional." Special Libraries Association members work in corporate, research, scientific, institutional, and government libraries, as well as in other settings where their work is characteristically described as being in support of the organizational mission or enterprise of which their libraries are a part. With more than 10,000 members in 75 countries, SLA's role is to support professional knowledge workers in their work as they provide practical and utilitarian information, knowledge, and strategic learning to their identified knowledge customers and clients. The association has 58 regional chapters located throughout the world.

INTRODUCTION

Throughout its history, the Special Libraries Association (SLA) has served the members of that branch of the library and information science professions generally thought of as "non-traditional." To most people, librarianship refers to the profession which provides library services through public, academic, and school libraries. Thus the work of professional employees in specialized librarianship is best characterized as what it is "not": specialist librarians and the members of SLA do not usually work in public, academic, or school libraries (although some do, particularly in subject-specific departments in academic or public libraries). They work in corporate, research, scientific, institutional, and government libraries, as well as in other settings where their work is characteristically described as being in support of the organizational mission or enterprise of which their libraries are a part. As such, these organizational functional units are often not even referred to as "libraries" but are frequently described as "information centers," "knowledge centers," "research units," or by one of the myriad other designations that have come to be associated with specialized librarianship.

The Special Libraries Association was not the first organization to represent the unique interests of specialist librarians. There were already two such organizations in existence when SLA was founded in 1909. One was the Medical Library Association (originally the Association of Medical Librarians, founded in 1898) and the other was the American Association of Law Librarians, founded in 1906, but both were, obviously, specific to the subject

interests of their unique memberships. The situation was different when John Cotton Dana and his colleagues founded SLA, for they had recognized that a practical version of librarianship was required for any specialized library, regardless of its subject affiliation. Thus, while building on the concepts and methodologies of librarianship as then practiced, SLA was created and directed toward the particular and specific needs of those seeking information, knowledge, and strategic learning in pursuit of their practical goals. Today, while retaining its connection to the LIS profession through its name, SLA continues to support that pursuit, and the association's service sphere includes all specialist librarians, regardless of the subject specialty of the organizations where they are employed. Its Vision Statement was published in 2004, and it continues to state that case: "SLA is a non-profit global organization for innovative information professionals and their strategic partners."

With more than 10,000 members in 75 countries, SLA's role is to support professional knowledge workers in their work as they provide practical and utilitarian information, knowledge, and strategic learning to their identified knowledge customers and clients. The association has 58 regional chapters located throughout the world (although primarily in North America), 25 divisions representing subject interests, fields, or types of information-handling techniques, and 11 caucuses, informal groups of members who share a common interest not covered by any chapter, division, or committee. As a professional association, SLA promotes and strengthens its members through learning, advocacy, and networking

Encyclopedia of Library and Information Sciences, Fourth Edition DOI: 10.1081/E-ELIS4-120044968

initiatives, as outlined in its Mission Statement (also published in 2004). The association's core values are also available for public examination, and SLA's members take much pride in publishing the values that they bring to their work and expect from their colleagues in their unique branch of the library and information science professions:

Leadership Strengthening our roles as information leaders in our organizations and in our communities, including shaping information policy.

Service Responding to our clients' needs, adding qualitative and quantitative value to information services and products.

Innovation and Continuous Learning Embracing innovative solutions for the enhancement of services and intellectual advancement within the profession.

Results and Accountability Delivering measurable results in the information economy and our organizations. The Association and its members are expected to operate with the highest level of ethics and honesty.

Collaboration and Partnering Providing opportunities to meet, communicate, collaborate, and partner within the information industry and the business community.[1]

SPECIALIZED LIBRARIANSHIP AND THE ORIGINS OF SLA

The Special Libraries Association's origins are well-known within the LIS professions. and many of the association's members have over the years taken much pleasure in telling and re-telling the story. Historical information is based on that in SLA at 100: From Putting Knowledge to Work to Building the Knowledge Culture.[2] By the early twentieth century, John Cotton Dana—head of the Newark (NJ) Public Library and a notable leader in librarianship—had recognized that the distinctions between specialized librarianship and the broader profession were significant, even critical if service delivery in those organizations that required practical and utilitarian information was to meet the needs of the library's users. Firm in his belief that better service could be provided to library users when these distinctions are invoked, Dana began thinking about how specialized libraries are different, and how these differences might be exploited for the benefit of library users.

The differences were not always immediately apparent. As Dana recognized that changes were demanded in the management of libraries (what he referred to as "library method"), he was able also to recognize that the written word—the primary method for the formal delivery of information in his time—must not be available just for the student, or just for the casual reader. As he described the evolution of the specialized library in 1914, Dana

wrote that what is read "must also serve the industrialist, the investigator or scientist, and the social service worker." Even with his ability to recognize that change was taking place, though, and even with the association having been in existence for 5 years, Dana was not quite ready to specify what the change would be: "It is too soon," he wrote, "to say in just what manner this new form of service will be rendered."[3]

So while the needed changes were not particularly articulated at the time, SLA did indeed begin with a need for change, and the question of whether to change was not a consideration. It was to be major change, and it had even been anticipated before Dana and F. B. Deberard called a group of 20 librarians together on the verandah of the Mt. Washington Hotel in Bretton Woods, New Hampshire in 1909 to discuss the creation of the new organization. On the occasion of SLA's 50th anniversary in 1959, Elizabeth Ferguson described the meeting:

The participants in this "Verandah Conference," as it has come to be known, decided that the demands of their jobs had actually created a new kind of librarianship—that of library service geared to meet the needs of specialized situations. These librarians were breaking completely new ground. There were no patterns to follow. They had to play it by ear—a challenging but often difficult feat. They felt that they had everything to gain by forming their own working group to tackle their problems cooperatively.[4]

Dana served as SLA's first President, from 1909 to 1911, and early on, the cooperative focus was put forward as one of the group's specific attributes. The inclusiveness and diversity of SLA's membership was clearly established as a singular characteristic of the association, as is demonstrated in the association's Constitution (adopted at Bretton Woods on July 2, 1909):

The object of the Association is to promote the interests of the commercial, industrial, technical, civic, municipal, and legislative reference libraries, the special departments of the public libraries, universities, welfare associations, and business organizations.[5]

Dana made it clear at the time and in his later writings that the "special libraries movement" (as he and his colleagues called it) was in response to a need. The philosophy that guided general library practice in 1909 was not appropriate for meeting the demands of specific patrons who required information for totally practical—and not necessarily altruistic, intellectual, or recreational—purposes.

Nor should it be assumed that the "Verandah Conference" in New Hampshire was the only place where the necessity for addressing practical information needs had been discussed by librarians. Even Melvil Dewey had something to say in this matter. As libraries grew in numbers and, particularly, in size, more was required of librarians as information providers, and obviously a certain level of specialization would be brought forward. Dewey was aware of this trend, and even seemed to be leaning toward recognizing that some library patrons would require a different type and level of service delivery. As he put it: "Librarians are rapidly taking on their proper function as book experts for their various constituencies. But the librarian is rapidly outgrowing the idea that he is concerned with books alone. The public pays its money, not to dignify books as such, but because it wishes information...."[6] Thus even for Dewey the connection between libraries and practical information delivery was there. But Dewey, being a citizen of his times, and an active proponent of the "uplifting" role of libraries, naturally felt a connection between that role and the provision of materials for "inspiration" and "innocent recreation" also provided by libraries.

So a new "form" of library service, a new "library method" as it was called, was required, and Dana described it in his "evolution" article in 1914:

> The proper view of printed things is, that the stream thereof need not be anywhere completely stored behind the dykes and dams formed by the shelves of any library or of any group of libraries: but that from that stream as it rushes by, expert observers should select what is pertinent each to his own constituency, to his own organization, to his own community, hold it as long as it continues to have value to those for whom he selects it, make it easily accessible by some simple process, and then let it go.[3]

Dana then went on to elaborate, as was his very personal style, on how specialist librarians should carry out this charge by putting forth what he called "The New Library Creed".

> Select the best books, list them elaborately, save them forever—that was the sum of the librarians' creed of yesterday. Tomorrow it must be, select a few of the best books and keep them, as before, but also, select from the vast flood of print the things your constituency will find helpful, make them available with a minimum of expense, and discard them as soon as their usefulness is past.[3]

Despite their good intentions, Dana and the other founders of the association found that the new rule was difficult to put into practice. As they were quick to point out, this new type of librarianship was different, a field, as they put it, "not yet greatly cultivated," and from their perspective, it was the formation of SLA that would bring some sort of order from the chaos of early thinking about specialized librarianship. Through conversations, correspondence, and the conference of 1909, the effort began to take shape, but even as late as 1914, when he was writing 5 years after the association's founding, Dana described how he was disappointed that the "New Library Creed" had been as yet adopted by very few practicing librarians. He was also quick to state that

it is gaining followers, however, in the fields of research and industry whose leaders are rapidly and inevitably learning that only by having accessible all the records of experiment, exploration, and discovery pertaining to their own expertise, wherever made, can they hope to avoid mistakes, escape needless expenditures, and make profitable advances in any department of science or in any kind of industrial social work.[3]

From its earliest days, the name of the association and the type of professional services its members provided caused difficulty. While recognizing the "specialness" of what specialist librarians do, Dana was not shy about expressing some discomfort with the term:

> The name special libraries was chosen with some hesitation, and rather in default of a better; but it has seemed to fit the movement admirably. It may be said, of course, that every library is in a measure special, in its own field, and that state libraries, libraries of colleges and universities, of medicine, law, history, art and other subjects may be called special. But a special library, and the special departments of more general libraries—like the business branch at Newark—are the first and as yet almost the only print-administering institutions which professedly recognize the change in library method that the vast and swiftly mounting bulk of print is demanding; realize how ephemeral, and at the same time how exceedingly useful for the day and hour is much of the present output of things-intended-to-be-read, and frankly adopt the new library creed as to print management, of careful selection, immediate use, and ready rejection when usefulness is past.[3]

100 YEARS OF SPECIALIZED LIBRARIANSHIP

Celebrating its centenary in 2009, SLA as a professional association has made important contributions to the growth and development of information management, knowledge management, and strategic learning, the three disciplines that now converge into what is generally recognized in the larger management community as knowledge services. With its primary focus on the delivery of services in the corporate, research, scientific, and government fields, the association has been required to operate somewhat "outside" the usual LIS environment while attempting to continue its collaborative relationship with other library associations and working with them in an advocacy role for the larger LIS profession. From its earliest days, SLA was required to demonstrate to its members (and potential members) that their unique work placed particular and "special" requirements on the association.

By 1914, SLA had achieved remarkable success in meeting one of its goals, to serve as a clearinghouse of information. Today we would characterize this function as "knowledge sharing," and for the specialist librarians of

1914, it became tangible and practical when SLA was responsible for the creation of "PAIS", the Public Affairs Information Service (now "OCLC Public Affairs Information Service"), an effort undertaken to provide better access to the literature of public affairs. This work had been preceded by any number of published bibliographies, finding aids, and similar tools, all of which represent examples of the move in the direction of Dana's "practical and utilitarian" library services. As such, it represented—as Dr. John A. Lapp of the Indiana State Library (who had taken on the editorial responsibilities for *Special Libraries*, SLA's journal) said—one of the goals of the founders. These efforts at knowledge development and knowledge sharing inspired him to come up with a motto for specialist librarians, "putting knowledge to work" a motto which served as the association's tag-line for over 90 years.

The Great Depression brought major challenges, as did World War II. In both of these great national crises, specialist librarians and the association itself seemed to demonstrate the highest levels of commitment and service they were called upon to provide. As the 1930s began, there continued to be much enthusiasm among the association's members and its leaders about the "idea" of specialized librarianship, about how the specialized research library could be made a "profitable" department in the organization and function as a headquarters to which questions from throughout the entire organization could be referred, thus coordinating departmental activities and avoiding the duplication, delay, and expense of reproducing data already available and saving time and money. While not revenue-producing, these services were expected to be operated along with services that produce revenue for the host organizations, and included such activities as translation services, the producing of bibliographies, "literary researches," and the editing of technical manuscripts, tasks that could be undertaken, at a profit, by the staff of the specialized library.

The challenge during the years of the Great Depression built on the knowledge sharing that had been in evidence since the association's earliest days. Great efforts were made to ensure that all members were able to have "knowledge of the abilities of our entire membership," (some 1700 by 1935) as one president of SLA put it, thus providing another tangible and utilitarian benefit of membership and, hopefully, enabling the growth of the association. At the same time, this growth would result in one of the association's early leaders primary goals, the "development of a national viewpoint" about the values and benefits of specialized librarianship.

Yet these efforts at moving specialized librarianship forward were being undertaken in a society that was constantly being subjected to external forces that could not help but influence their success. That the Great Depression was occurring while the association's members and leadership were seeking to move specialized librarianship into the mainstream was a constant worry. The Special Libraries Association found itself involved in a variety of ways. Unemployment was the greatest fear, and SLA's Employment Committee was pressed into service "for the unemployed in our profession," but the committee cautioned, at the same time, that in its work it was obliged to "maintain its ideal of placing in a new position the best qualified special librarian, whether at the time employed or unemployed." Specialist librarians also needed to know just how they should react to the emergency situation they found themselves in, and it was not unusual for them to be offered in *Special Libraries*, encouraging and inspirational presentations about how they could get through the rough spots, with articles such as "Special Libraries in Time of Depression" being typical.

With World War II following immediately on and, in effect, ending the crisis of the Great Depression, specialist librarians found their professional skills in even more demand. One of the most impressive activities, undertaken shortly after the beginning of the war, was an effort to coordinate the services of the specialized libraries community. Recognizing that their first step was to gather data about what resources were available in the nation's specialized libraries, surveys were organized and distributed, and some 400 specialized libraries ("largely technical and business libraries") were contacted, with 150 reports quickly returned. These reports, "nearly all of them good, full reports which give an impressive picture of special library service and which, taken together, offer a unique tool for research," became a valuable resource for interlibrary cooperation among specialized libraries and led eventually to the development of a master file, sent to the Library of Congress, demonstrating which libraries specialize in which subject fields and what their specific strengths were. Thus the war emergency provided the opportunity for the first major analysis of research resources in specialized libraries in the United States, a goal that had often been discussed but which had never been attempted before.

That these efforts were vital to the war effort did not go unnoticed, even at the highest levels of government. President Franklin D. Roosevelt commended America's specialist librarians, calling them "the guardians of our technical knowledge," and noted that "through your special knowledge and through the quickness with which you work, you give to our business men and to our economists the data which they, too, need. You ask for no recognition. You work anonymously and unsung. But you are doing your job along with the army, the navy, and the air forces on America's front line." It was a great tribute to the members of the association, honoring them for the very skills and professional expertise that called them to their work.

It was important work. Of that there is no doubt. The war effort prompted an outpouring of professional expertise the likes of which had not been experienced before, and SLA as an organization was there to provide the support these specialist librarians needed. So their numbers grew, and by the end of the war, membership stood at 4300. For this remarkable growth to have occurred despite—perhaps because of—the war is equally remarkable.

With this new strength in numbers, as the war ended it became clear that the "special libraries movement" of SLA's founders was taking on new and ambitious goals. Throughout its history, public relations had always been part of SLA's service structure, and over the years many of its leaders and members had worked long and hard to ensure that the special libraries movement was duly put forward to those for whom it would provide benefit. But the universe of prospective users of practical information, knowledge, and learning was (and continues to be) a very large one, and no leader of the association has ever been satisfied that all that could be done in bringing the value of specialized librarianship to the attention of the decision makers in society has in fact been done. By the end of the 1940s, it was now clear that the promotion of specialized librarianship could be taken to a new level. For example, the development of an advisory service to business and industry was proposed. It would be a service that would involve the appointment of one or more specialists on the SLA staff with responsibility for consulting about the establishment of special libraries. Other responsibilities would include providing information services to specific groups and industries, the development of details and plans for the organization, equipment, and staffing of new specialized libraries, and reviewing the informational needs of all types of businesses and industries and of available reference tools in order to ascertain needed bibliographical aids and other reference publications which might be sponsored by the association.

The demand for expanded services from the association was there. Only forging the link between the potential users of specialized library services and the specialist librarians themselves remained to be accomplished, and in an historical essay on corporate and technology libraries, Edythe Moore painted a very clear picture of the opportunities:

> Just as had happened after WWI, there was tremendous growth in the numbers of corporate libraries, especially in scientific and technical areas, immediately following WWII. Established companies endeavored to catch up after giving their time and attention to the war effort, and new companies sprang into existence to take advantage of a whole array of sophisticated technologies developed for the military and which they now planned to use to provide products and services for civilian use.

> Not only did corporate libraries proliferate following the war, but they also rapidly expanded in size of collections, staff, and services offered. Burgeoning research and development, much of it sponsored by the U.S. Government, flooded the technical community with a growing

body of literature more interdisciplinary in nature than ever before and in new formats.[7]

Not surprisingly, this "growing body of literature" was soon perceived to be overwhelming, and leaders in the scientific and technical communities and in business management became almost desperate to find solutions to the problem. By 1955, it seemed clear that the documentation field—working alongside specialized librarianship—might provide the answers, and the association's leadership accepted a new definition for the discipline. Provided by SLA's Committee to Formulate Definitions on the Fundamental Characteristics of Special Librarianship, the work of specialist librarians was now defined: "The profession of special librarianship and documentation is the science of selecting, evaluating, organizing, and disseminating information in special fields of knowledge and the art of integrating and adapting information resources to the needs of a particular institution or clientele." It was a new way of describing the profession, and for the first time in SLA's ongoing efforts to define its discipline, the specific concept of documentation—the bringing together of useful information on a particular subject (i.e., documenting a subject) without regard to the form or format of that information—was attached to specialized librarianship.

In practice, the linking of specialized librarianship and documentation did not turn out to be a comfortable fit. Historian Robert V. Williams has written that "the term did not seem to appeal to special librarians and they continued to use special, despite their uneasiness with the word and despite the continuing need to reply to the general librarians retort that 'all libraries are special." Yet his case that specialist librarians were, even reluctantly, the first American documentalists is a good one: "It is quite clear from the variety of definitions offered, their explanations of what they were doing, and how they served their users, that they were the first American documentalists."[8]

Nevertheless, specialist librarians and documentalists could not come together. In 1971, a proposal was put forward to merge SLA and ASIS, the American Society for Information Science, and a Joint Merger Committee was appointed to study a possible merger. Brought forward to "seek areas of mutual interest and cooperation...based on the belief that our professional interests overlap or at least converge at some points with ASIS and can be furthered through such activities as joint meetings and projects at the Association level," the proposal did not make it past a questionnaire sent to the membership, for there was no clear mandate to continue the discussions.

One interesting development during this period was the growth of the membership and the role of SLA members as leaders. Their leadership role took on new challenges in the 1970s, particularly with issues having to do with copyright legislation. Indeed, copyright and the restructuring of copyright legislation became the defining focus of that decade. In the mid-years of the century, it had become clear to many in government that American copyright laws would require revision, and the U.S. Congress authorized the Copyright Office of the Library of Congress and an advisory group of specialists to conduct studies of the copyright law. By 1960, the first four studies, printed for the use of the Committee on the Judiciary, were made available through the Government Printing Office and announced in the library press, including in *Special Libraries*.

The association's position on copyright was put forward in testimony before the U.S. Congress. The statement included SLA's preference for the continuation of the "long recognized concept that the preparation of a single copy constitutes 'fair use.'" After referring to the difficulties—in a specialized library—of adhering to turn-around time requirements for seeking permission to make photocopies, the statement described four specific concerns, of which the most dangerous would be those that penalized for-profit organizations:

> The legislation to be enacted must not prevent or penalize the preparation of a photocopy for or by specialized libraries—particularly those in for-profit organizations. There will be immeasurable damage to the economy and the welfare of the nation if such intent is contained in the enacted version…or if such interpretation is possible after enactments of the law.

Finally, the association's testimony on this critically important issue made clear SLA's societal role: "The rapid transmission of man's knowledge—either to not-for-profit or to for-profit organizations—must not be impeded by law."

By 1976, the library photocopying sections of the new U.S. Copyright Law and pertinent portions of congressional reports had been mailed to all SLA members, and the next year the association published *Library Photocopying & the U.S. Copyright Law of 1976*, prepared under the supervision of the association's legal counsel by the SLA Special Committee on Copyright Law Practice and Implementation. The document, designed to assist members in understanding and complying with the new copyright law, and its distribution to the membership testified to the high level of interest SLA and its leadership had in the subject and their sense of obligation in providing direction for the association's members.

By the 1980s, this leadership role for SLA was being clearly recognized, yet there continued to be confusion about specialized librarianship and the role of specialized libraries in the organizations where they are part of the research structure. To clear the air, Past President Edward G. Strable bravely stepped forward to articulate the distinctions between specialized librarianship and other forms of professional practice within the LIS profession:

- Special libraries can be difficult to find—most are not visible to the general public.
- Most special libraries deal with a single subject or related group of subjects. The special library is the library of the organization, most often the only library, and serves all information needs.
- The scope of the special library's collection and service is determined by the objectives of the parent organization.
- Special libraries are usually found in organizations whose objectives are not primarily a library objective.
- Special libraries serve different kinds of clientele—almost never used by "everybody"—populated by user groups who have a work relationship with the organization which maintains the library.
- Special librarians—like their users—are frequently specialists.
- Special libraries tend to be comparatively small, often one-person. They also frequently have small user groups.
- A good number of special libraries are supported by private and not public funds. They spring from and are much a part of a competitive capitalistic system.
- Special libraries are characterized by risk—risk of failure is always present in business and industry, in associations and societies, and in the professions. Special libraries can be dissolved because they cost too much and don't bring in enough of a benefit to the sponsoring organization.[9]

Strable painted a very good picture of this branch of the profession, and his strong description seemed to match other forces that were coming into play. In that same year (1981), the great potential of electronic data processing and the value of the personal computer in business management was being clearly established (with *Time* magazine identifying the personal computer as the magazine's "Man of the Year" that year). With the strengths of information science now playing a major role in the management of research assets in many companies and organizations, SLA's leaders and members were quick to demonstrate that the association, as a professional, scientific, and educational organization, had an interest in playing a leading role as society transitioned into this new era of information, knowledge, and strategic learning. And for the most part, the members of the association—and certainly the leadership—understood that for themselves, as information professionals, leadership in information management was a natural role. Indeed, by 1983 SLA had published that "The mission of the Special Libraries Association is to advance the leadership role of its members in putting knowledge to work in the Information Society." Specialist librarians wanted and expected to participate in this era in which, as described often, the advantages of computerized information transfer would be available to and accessible by the greater lay public.

Knowledge workers, including specialist librarians, would be called upon to perform their professional roles in an environment in which important societal benefits, often forecast by idealists and futurists, would lead to the breaking down of societal boundaries, to an increased recognition of the value of diversity among the peoples of the world, and to the realization of social, economic, and cultural advantages through the transparent and non-hierarchical transfer of information.

Within a decade, the association began to look in yet another—and complementary—direction, with the identification, growth, and embrace by its members and leadership of knowledge management. In 1990, Microsoft Windows was introduced, and within 3 years, the U.S. Government officially went online, a fact that had serious implications for the association now that its headquarters had moved from New York City to Washington and its daily interactions necessarily coincided with those of the Federal government's information planning and service delivery. Two years later, e-commerce was introduced and by the end of the decade, some 90 million users in the United States and Canada were estimated to be "online," the descriptor which had now become standard in describing how people dealt with information transfer. Resonating strongly with SLA's membership—simply because of their role in the business and research environment—Thomas Stewart's seminal cover story about intellectual capital in the June 3, 1991 issue of *Fortune* set the stage for the transition from the focus on information in the information age to the coming focus on *managing* knowledge. "Intellectual capital," Stewart wrote, "[is] the sum of everything everybody in your company knows that gives you a competitive edge in the marketplace."[10] And who knew better in 1991 what everybody in their organizations knew, what they were working on? For specialist librarians, the promising framework for connecting information management, knowledge management, and strategic learning was being built. Special Libraries Association's members were ready to take on their leadership role in the process of delivering what would come to be known as knowledge services—the convergence of information management, knowledge management, and strategic learning—to their clients.

One approach was to take yet another look at the professional contributions specialist librarians bring to their employing organizations. In 1992, SLA's Presidential Commission on Professional Recruitment, Ethics, and Professional Standards, popularly known as "The PREPS Commission," had a specific charge, to focus on how the association and its members could encourage the best, the brightest, and most qualified people to enter the field of specialized librarianship. Emphasis was to be given to the unique role that specialist librarians play in information management, with the study commission looking at the issues of recruitment into specialized librarianship, ethics and the place of a code of ethics for specialized

librarianship, and standards and basic competencies for the discipline. The commission's work built on, as its chair Mary Dickerson described, "...the premise that special librarianship is a unique branch of the profession of librarianship; that despite the great diversity within special librarianship itself, special libraries nonetheless have different missions, focuses, and purposes than libraries in other branches of the profession."

The work and influence of the commission was a major step forward for the association, as it sought to codify some of the concerns associated with information services and the management and delivery of information by practitioners who had been educated as librarians. In identifying how SLA's members could recruit the brightest and best people into this branch of the profession, the PREPS Commission was also issuing a challenge, asking SLA's members to recognize that the difference between specialized librarianship and other types of librarianship was a very real difference, asking them to contemplate "if perhaps the time has not come to separate ourselves from others in the profession and promote that we are, in fact, an entirely different branch of the profession?" Of particular concern—as had been the case throughout SLA's history—was the fact that graduate programs in library and information studies did not provide sufficient particular attention to the skills and competencies required for success in specialized librarianship. In its findings, the commission noted that professional learning for specialist librarians could be expected to be provided in the future through another avenue, presumably through training, continuous education, and professional learning offered through professional organizations like SLA or through commercial learning providers.

Thus the face of specialized librarianship continued to change, and as it did, perceptions about this branch of the profession began to change as well. By the mid-1990s, it was clear that specialist librarians and information professionals—the very people who made up the membership of the association—were indeed thinking about themselves very differently than they had in earlier times. In fact, the focus shifted from themselves and their perceptions of themselves to the influence that they brought to their professional workplace, and it was time now to change the way management and organizational leaders thought about specialized librarianship and information management.

Following the work of the PREPS Commission, competencies became the subject of the association's next major effort, to devise and deliver to the business and research community a standardized framework for establishing criteria for successful performance in the information profession. The appointment of a Special Committee on Competencies for Special Librarians in 1994–1995 and the publication, in May 1996, of *Competencies for Special Librarians of the 21st Century*—which identified and described key competencies required for the successful management and delivery of excellent information services—might arguably be characterized as one of the most important events in the history of the association. For the first time, the emphasis was on the people who work as information professionals and not on facilities, collections, services, or products. Indeed, the significance of the work was well understood by all involved, including not just the special committee but the association's leaders, members, and many with whom they came in contact in the broader information management community.

These professional employees, now characterized as information professionals and not as special or specialist librarians, began to be further recognized as leaders in the management of information, knowledge, and strategic learning. Indeed, there was a strong movement within the association to move to the term, and despite a failure to change the name of the association in 2003, the characterization of its members as "information professionals" became the norm. The revised competencies statement of 2003[11] used the term instead of "special librarians," and the association's Web site added a page describing these knowledge workers and their contributions to their employing organizations:

About Information Professionals

An Information Professional ("IP") strategically uses information in his/her job to advance the mission of the organization. This is accomplished through the development, deployment, and management of information resources and services. The IP harnesses technology as a critical tool to accomplish goals. IPs include, but are not limited to, librarians, knowledge managers, chief information officers, web developers, information brokers, and consultants.

Information Professionals work for information organizations, which are defined as those entities that deliver information-based solutions to a given market. Some commonly used names for these organizations include libraries, information centers, competitive intelligence units, intranet departments, knowledge resource centers, content management organizations, and others.

The diverse responsibilities that Information Professionals may include:

- Developing and maintaining a portfolio of cost-effective, client-valued information services that are aligned with the strategic directions of the organization and client groups
- Building a dynamic collection of information resources based on a deep understanding of clients' information needs
- Gathering evidence to support decisions about the development of new services and products
- Maintaining current awareness of emerging technologies

- Assessing and communicating the value of the information organization, including information services, products and policies to senior management, key stakeholders and client groups
- Contributing effectively to senior management strategies and decisions regarding information applications, tools and technologies, and policies for the organization[12]

By the end of the twentieth century—90 years into SLA's history and in the very last month of the century—the distinctions between specialized librarianship and other kinds of library and information work were clearly identified by Professor Marion Paris. Addressing the practitioners themselves, Paris was very specific in describing how specialized librarianship is different from other types of library work and her description of specialized librarianship can almost be seen as an update of John Cotton Dana's "New Library Creed":

In searching for the technical, the obscure, the undocumented fugitive report, or the one final detail that will win a new client, special librarians have always been indifferent [to] walls and boundaries. Special librarians networked long before the noun underwent linguistic conversion into a verb.... Whether the context is a corporation or a museum or a military installation or a specialized academic collection or a research and development laboratory, the ethos of special librarianship veers sharply away [from that of other types of libraries].... According to the [American Library Association's] Library Bill of Rights special librarians are heretics. You practice censorship; you do not as a rule educate your customers; you do your clients' work for them, you acknowledge and admit that all customers of your libraries are not created equal. Summoning the totality of who you are (in possession of intelligence, education, experience, discernment and no small amount of cultivated prescience), you anticipate needs and cater to your customers. Moreover, it is essential to your credibility and to the continuing prosperity of your libraries that you make judgments about information sources and means of locating them. Means, by the way, that may be unconventional, but invariably their ends justify them. You create new information on demand. Knowledge management is merely a fresh take on your expertise: You collect information, organize it, store it, find it, and you repackage it.[13]

In the twenty-first century, the further evolution of this branch of the profession continues to take place with SLA taking the lead. In its Vision Statement of 2004, SLA identified networking, education, and advocacy as its core purposes. These are exemplified in the association's use of technology—unimaginable to the association's founders—to enhance globalization, professional development and learning, and communication (both between the association and its members, and among the membership itself). In SLA's second century, the foresight of John Cotton Dana and the association's other founders is evidenced by the fact that "putting knowledge to work" continues to be the overarching goal for the many information professionals who make up its membership.

REFERENCES

1. Inside SLA: Vision, mission, and core values statements. Available at http://www.sla.org/content/SLA/index.cfm.
2. St. Clair, G. *SLA at 100: From Putting Knowledge to Work to Building the Knowledge Culture*; SLA: Alexandria, VA, 2009.
3. Dana, J.C. The evolution of the special library. Spec. Libr. **1914**, *5*, 70–76 (Also published in *Librarian at Large*, Hanson, C.A., Ed.; Special Libraries Association: Washington, DC, 1991).
4. Ferguson, E. Association highlights. In *Special Libraries Association—Its First Fifty Years 1909–1959*; Mitchell, A.C., Ed.; Special Libraries Association: New York, 1959; 5.
5. Constitution of Special Libraries Association. Spec. Libr. **1910**, January *1*(1), 8.
6. Dewey, M. The future of the public librarian. *Public Libraries: A Monthly Review of Library Matters and Records*; Library Bureau: Chicago, IL, 1903; 8, 327 (quoted in Dickson, P. *The Library in America: A Celebration in Words and Pictures*; Facts on File: New York, 1986).
7. Moore, E. Corporate science and technology libraries: One hundred years of progress. In *One Hundred Years of Sci-Tech Libraries: A Brief History*; Mount, E., Ed.; The Haworth Press: New York, 1988.
8. Williams, R.V. The documentation and special libraries movements in the United States, 1910–1960. J. Am. Soc. Inform. Sci. **1997**, September *48*(9), 775–781.
9. Strable, E.G. Specialized libraries: How are they different?. Ill. Libr. **1980**, March *62*.
10. Stewart, T.A. Brainpower. Fortune **1991**, June 3, 45–60.
11. Competencies for Information Professionals of the 21st Century, Revised Edition, June 2003. Available at http://www.sla.org/content/learn/comp2003/index.cfm SLA.
12. SLA. About Information Professionals. Available at http://www.sla.org/content/SLA/professional/index.cfm.
13. Paris, M. Beyond competencies: A trendspotter's guide to library education. Inform. Outlook **1999**, December *2*(12).

Specialty Museums

Trevor Jones
Mountain Heritage Center, Western Carolina University, Cullowhee, North Carolina, U.S.A.

Abstract
The term "specialty museums" is broadly defined and difficult to classify. The term includes institutions that do not fit into the traditional museum categories of Art, History, and Science. Specialty museums lack a single organizing entity and determining the number of specialty museums presents serious challenges. Despite this, specialty museums have some unifying characteristics, albeit ones that raise important questions about the definition of museums as a whole.

INTRODUCTION

For the purposes of the Encyclopedia, this entry considers a number of different types of museums under a single entry. The term "specialty museum" is extremely broad and is often used as a catchall for any institution that does not fit into the traditional major museum categories of Art, History, and Science. Because of this, specialty museums run the gamut from sports halls of fame to stamp museums. The level of professionalism also varies widely, encompassing everything from multimillion dollar exhibits in state-of-the-art facilities, to one person's private passion run out of their basement. In both the United States and internationally, all museums, regardless of type, are often loosely organized even when they have much in common. Membership in museum associations tends to be voluntary and only rarely requires adherence to set standards of management or behavior. Due to the wide diversity of specialty museums, there is no single group or organization that unites them in a coherent whole.

Caveats aside, specialty museums share certain features that unify all museums. The first is the acquisition and care of collections. Although museums may define their collections in a dizzying variety of ways, most museums have the acquisition and care of physical artifacts as a core element of their mission.[1] A second, more recent development that unifies museums is a commitment to public service. Since the 1970s there has been an increasing emphasis on the service component of museums' missions. Today, all widely accepted listings of the defining characteristics of museums stress that institutions must not only collect but also work to provide a positive benefit to people and society.

The following sections detail the different types of specialty museums, the difficulties in categorizing and counting them, the changing definitions of museums, examples of some categories of specialty museums, and how specialty museums fit into current museum trends.

Types of Specialty Museums

The American Association of Museums (AAM) is the largest and most comprehensive museum organization in the United States. Every year, with AAM's guidance, National Register Publishing prints *The Official Museum Directory* which lists 38 separate categories for "Specialized Museums." The 38 categories of specialized museums recognized by AAM are[2]

- Agriculture Museums
- Antiques Museums
- Architecture Museums
- Audiovisual and Film Museums
- Circus Museums
- Comedy Museums
- Communications Museums
- Crime Museums
- Culturally Specific
- Electricity Museums
- Fire-Fighting Museums
- Forestry Museums
- Furniture Museums
- Gun Museums
- Hobby Museums
- Horological Museums
- Industrial Museums
- Lapidary Arts Museums
- Logging and Lumber Museums
- Mappariums
- Mining Museums
- Money and Numismatics Museums
- Musical Instruments Museums
- Philatelic Museums
- Photography Museums
- Religious Museums
- Scouting Museums
- Sports Museums
- Technology Museums

Encyclopedia of Library and Information Sciences, Fourth Edition DOI: 10.1081/E-ELIS4-120044548

- Typography Museums
- Village Museums
- Wax Museums
- Whaling Museums
- Woodcarving Museums

These categories are not exhaustive, and it is likely that many of them could also be classified in one or more of the traditional categories of Art, History, or Science also listed in *The Museum Directory*. For example, an Agriculture Museum could also be categorized as a History Museum if its main focus were the study of the history of agriculture. Indeed, *The Museum Directory* takes a mixed approach to the problem of defining museum categories. It separates museums mainly by the type of collections they hold (History, Art, Science, etc.) but also categorizes some institutions by their governance structure (such as College and University Museums).[2]

Organization of Specialty Museums

There is no single lobbying or professional group for specialty museums in the United States or internationally. None of the 26 Councils of Affiliates recognized by the American Association of Museums focuses on specialty museums as a separate entity, and it appears that most institutions categorized as specialty museums do not feel a strong affinity with other museums in their category.[3] There are, however, advocacy groups that represent subsets of the specialty museum category such as the Association of Railway Museums, the Council of American Jewish Museums, and the Council of American Maritime Museums. Although specialty museums can fit into a number of categories, and groups of specialty museums may band together to support mutual interests, specialty museums as a whole do not work as a unified advocacy group and do not necessarily even see themselves as distinct from other museum types.

Number of Specialty Museums in the United States and Internationally

The fragmented nature of specialty museums is a problem endemic to the museum community as a whole. With disparate missions, collecting interests, and governance structures, museums are loosely organized in the best of circumstances, and specialty museums are even more diffuse. There are no reliable data on the number of museums in the world and even less information on the number of specific types of museums. The American Association of Museums estimates that there are 17,500 museums in the United States alone, but only lists 9,500 of them in *The Official Museum Directory*.[4] Statistics on the number and type of international museums are even more challenging to determine with confidence. The United Kingdom's Art

Fund estimates that there are 2,500 museums in the United Kingdom and that 1,800 of these have earned accreditation. The Fund classifies these institutions by governance structure, not by type, so it is impossible to determine how many museums in the United Kingdom may fall into the specialty category.[5] On a broader scale, the International Council of Museums (ICOM) has assembled information from a number of countries and provides both the number of museums and their types, but this data is admittedly incomplete at best.[6]

Issues Surrounding the Definition of Specialty Museums as a Category

It is possible, but not entirely satisfying, to consider the problem of specialty museums by exploring how these institutions conform to accepted definitions of the term "museum." Museum themselves have long had difficulty precisely defining what is and what is not a museum, and these definitions have changed over time. While noting that museums are "infinitely diverse," the American Association of Museums' *Code of Ethics for Museums* notes that the common denominator for museums is making a "unique contribution to the public by collecting, preserving, and interpreting the things of this world."[7] The *Code* also acknowledges the wide variety of sizes and types of museums: "Their numbers include both governmental and private museums of anthropology, art history and natural history, aquariums, arboreta, art centers, botanical gardens, children's museums, historic sites, nature centers, planetariums, science and technology centers, and zoos."[7] The International Council of Museums offers an equally broad definition of a museum as "a non-profit making, permanent institution in the service of society and of its development, and open to the public, which acquires, conserves, researches, communicates and exhibits, for purposes of study, education and enjoyment, material evidence of people and their environment."[8] Finally, another widely accepted definition comes from the Museums Association of the United Kingdom which states: "A museum is an institution which collects, documents, preserves, exhibits and interprets material evidence and associated information for the public benefit."[9]

Museums are most commonly classified by their type of collection, but it is also possible to categorize them by

- The operating agency.
- The geographic area they serve.
- Their intended audience.
- The way in which they exhibit their collections.[10]

Although collection type remains the most common way to categorize museums, this method has been challenged in recent times (see section: "The Changing Face of Museums"). Museum theorist Stephen E. Weil in his classic book *Rethinking the Museum and Other Meditations*

(1990) advances the idea that the importance of museums is not how they accomplish their goals, but rather *why* they do it. Weil suggests that the core definition of museums hinges not on what they collect, but rather on how they serve the public and society.[11]

Expertise of Speciality Museums

Unlike more general museums which may hold collections from a wide variety of times and places, many specialty museums have the advantage of being able to concentrate in one area and develop specific expertise that may not be found in any other institution. A museum of railroading might well be expected to employ curators who are considered experts on both railroads and their construction, whereas a more general history museum might contain railroading artifacts, but lack in-depth expertise in interpreting them. In addition, many specialty museums also possess subject-focused libraries that may include rare books or manuscripts devoted to their specialized subject. These libraries typically serve as an institutional resource, and may only be accessible to museum staff and not the general public. In addition to research libraries, some specialty museums have also developed unique controlled vocabularies to describe their collections in more depth than seen in other museums. For example, many history museums in the United States use *The Revised Nomenclature for Museum Cataloging* (1995) to describe their collections. *Nomenclature* was developed to describe artifacts typically found in the collections of history museums, and many specialized museums find its standard vocabulary lacks the ability to adequately describe more comprehensive collections. For example, because *Nomenclature* only contains a few terms which describe Jewish religious artifacts, some museums specializing in Judaica have developed their own additional subject-specific controlled vocabularies in order to better describe these collections.

Examples of Specialty Museums

Specialty museums are nearly infinitely diverse, but most still conform to the standard definition of a museum as a place that collects, preserves, and interprets artifacts and information. At the Mütter Museum in Philadelphia, visitors can see sectioned pieces of human heads, conjoined twins, and thousands of specimens of human tissue showing the ravages of disease. Although it sounds like a freak show, the Mütter is a place of science. Founded in 1858 to "educate future doctors about anatomy and human medical anomalies," the Mütter's exhibits have a serious, educational focus, but also try to entertain (the museum's tagline is: "Disturbingly Informative!"). Although out of the mainstream and certainly a specialty museum, the Mütter does indeed collect, preserve, and interpret for the education and improvement of society.[12]

Not all specialty museums are so high-minded, however. The Museum of Bad Art (MOBA) in Dedham, MA was created in 1993 to exhibit the worst art its volunteer curators could find. The institution stages tongue-in-cheek exhibits that challenge the elitism the curators see as inherent in traditional art museums. Despite its low budget and nontraditional focus, however, MOBA's mission statement conforms perfectly to traditional definitions of what constitutes a museum: "The Museum of Bad Art (MOBA) is a community-based, private institution dedicated to the collection, preservation, exhibition and celebration of bad art in all its forms and in all its glory."[13] Although not a "serious" museum, MOBA does indeed perform a public service and is very popular with visitors!

Other specialized museums attempt to capture the essence of major discoveries or chart technological progress. The United Kingdom's National Museum of Computing has a mission "to collect and restore computer systems developed primarily in Britain and to enable people to explore that collection for inspiration, learning and enjoyment."[14] The National Museum of Computing's collection includes The Colossus, an early mainframe computer used by the British to break the German Lorenz cipher during World War II. In contrast to many other technological museums which display collections in a static state, the National Museum of Computing plans to restore every one of its artifacts to working order. The Museum has painstakingly rebuilt The Colossus to wartime specifications in order to evaluate and record the machine's ability to break German cipher texts from World War II. In a more traditional museum, the artifact would be exhibited, but not in working order. Another specialized computer museum, California's Computer History Museum, takes a more conventional approach to telling the history of technology. Although the museum has also restored some computers to working order, its exhibits consist of more familiar historical timelines and exhibits of advertising materials. The museum also possesses considerable staff expertise in its specialty area with an online searchable artifact catalog, an aggressive oral history program, and professional archival finding aids.[15]

In contrast to technological museums which chart the progress of a technology or invention, religious museums instead focus on communicating aspects of a specific faith. For example, the newly opened Sharjah Museum of Islamic Civilisation in the United Arab Emirates is housed in a traditional Middle Eastern *souq* or indoor market.[16] The museum displays over 5,000 artifacts in accordance with Islamic faith principles and celebrates the achievements of Muslims around the world. The museum boasts an Islamic Faith Gallery which describes key faith tenets, as well as a science and innovation gallery showing achievements by Muslim scientists. The Islamic Civilisation Museum attempts to convey Islamic history and culture around the world and also throughout all time periods. Thus, although the museum falls into the category of a specialized museum, it is in many ways a general museum of history and culture with a religious focus. Many other religious museums have a similar emphasis in conveying both the historical and cultural aspects of their faith, although most focus on the religion within a specified geographic region. The prominent Jewish Museum in New York City is "devoted exclusively to 4,000 years of art and Jewish culture." This Museum attempts to answer two fundamental questions: "How have the Jewish people been able to thrive for thousands of years, often in difficult and even tragic circumstances? [and] What constitutes the essence of Jewish identity?"[17] In addition this organization in New York, at least 13 other institutions worldwide also use the name "The Jewish Museum," and each also focuses on interpreting and preserving Jewish culture.

Some specialty museums target their appeal to a narrower field of subject enthusiasts or collectors, as does the Cody Firearms Museum in Cody, Wyoming. The Firearms Museum is part of the larger Buffalo Bill Historical Center, which houses five museums each examining some aspect of western art, history, culture, or the natural environment. The Firearms Museum "houses the most comprehensive assemblage of American firearms in the world" and is geared primarily to firearms collectors.[18] The museum's curatorial staff responds to all general questions for free but also conducts serial number research on Winchester, Marlin, and L.C. Smith firearms for a fee. The service provides a considerable and unusual income stream for the museum. The Firearms Museum also maintains an extensive library of books, articles, engineering drawings, and other documents related to the firearms industry. Although the Firearms Museum's exhibits do chart the technological development of firearms from their inception to the present, its displays are mostly of interest to collectors who want to see the subtle differences between every possible make and model of western firearm. The Cody Firearms Museum is a place of pilgrimage for many gun collectors, and articles written by the museum's staff are given extra credence in the collecting world due to the scope and depth of the institution's collections.

The Changing Face of Museums

Although statistical evidence is hard to find, it seems clear that much of the growth in the number of museums in recent years has been in the specialty category. Some authors have argued that specialization has become a trend because people are attempting to make a connection with something focused and definable in an increasingly diffuse and globalized world.[19]

As museums continue to change, it is debatable to what extent the current definitions of what a museum is will remain viable. Although museums are still traditionally categorized by the content of their collections, there has been an effort in recent years to modify museum definitions to "convey the fundamental character of the museum

rather than describe the variables."[20] These efforts have been spurred by the fact that there are an increasing number of idea-focused, rather than artifact-focused, museums. These new museums (most famously the Museum of Tolerance in Los Angeles, although there are many others) choose an issue common to all people and then ask visitors not to passively receive information, but instead mobilize them to take a stand and engage in political or social action.[21] These "idea museums" may collect, preserve, and interpret artifacts, but it is ideas-not things-that are at the core of their missions.

In the future, the museum community will also have to consider the role of virtual museums and how they fit into the traditional definition of museums. The Museum of Online Museums (MOOM) provides listings of dozens of online museums, some have physical sites, but most of which only exist virtually.[22] Certainly, the "World's Largest Webseum of Pocket Protectors" and the "Vintage Finnish Pulp Paperback Gallery" seem tailor-made for the specialty museums category, but what do institutions which exist only online share with more traditional brick and mortar museums? The museum community will continue to wrestle with these questions, and it is doubtful that any of the problems surrounding the classification and definition of what it means to be a museum will be resolved in the near future.

Conclusion

How do you categorize the unclassifiable? The term "specialty museum" remains nebulous with a nearly unimaginable diversity of museum types in 38 distinct categories. The definition of specialty museums is so broad that it is of limited use—except to categorize an institution as outside the three traditional categories of Art, History, or Science museums. The definition's usefulness is further hampered by the fact that specialty museums do not see themselves as members of a unified, distinct category. In addition, although specific subsets of specialty institutions may band together, they do not, as a rule, work cooperatively. However, specialty museums may be the fastest-growing category of museum in the United States and internationally. These institutions most commonly focus on traditional museum functions—the collection, preservation, and interpretation of artifacts, but the increasing numbers of museums that are focusing on ideas, not things, are changing the field. However they are classified, specialty museums range from the serious to the seriously wacky, and most do indeed benefit society and enrich the cultural fabric of the world.

REFERENCES

1. Dunn, H. Collection level description—The museum perspective. D-Lib Mag. **2000**, *6* (9), 1–8.

2. *The Official Museum Directory*; National Register Publishing: New Providence, NJ, 2007; Vol. 2.

3. *The Official Museum Directory*; National Register Publishing: New Providence, NJ; Vol. 1 A5.

4. http://www.aam-us.org/aboutmuseums/abc.cfm#how_many.

5. http://www.artfund.org/policyandcampaigns/faqs.html#6.

6. http://icom.museum/museum_directories.html.

7. http://www.aam-us.org/museumresources/ethics/coe.cfm.

8. http://icom.museum/definition.html.

9. Ambrose, T. Paine, C. *Museum Basics*; Routledge: New York, 1993; 8.

10. Ambrose, T. Paine, C. *Museum Basics*; Routledge: New York, 1993; 7.

11. Weil, S. *Rethinking the Museum and Other Meditations*; Smithsonian Institution Press: Washington and London, 1990; xvii.

12. http://www.collphyphil.org/mutter.asp.

13. http://www.museumofbadart.org/index.html.

14. http://www.tnmoc.org/.

15. http://www.computerhistory.org/explore/.

16. http://www.islamicmuseum.ae.

17. http://www.jewishmuseum.org/Directorsmessage.

18. http://www.bbhc.org/firearms/index.cfm.

19. Lord, B. The variety of participation and experiences in urban museum facilities. ICOM Brief **2005**, *25*, 16. Available at http://www.yppo.gr/0/ICAMT/Brief25.doc (accessed July 2008).

20. Edson, G. Quoted in Reevaluating the ICOM definition of the museum. Focus ICOM News **2004**, *2*, 4.

21. http://www.museumoftolerance.com/site/c.juLVJ8MRKtH/b.1452779/k.9172/Did_you_know.htm.

22. http://www.coudal.com/moom.

State Archives

David B. Gracy II
School of Information, University of Texas at Austin, Austin, Texas, U.S.A.

Adam D. Knowles
San Diego, California, U.S.A.

Abstract

State archives, as state agencies, perform an administrative role in state governments in the United States, managing the full life cycle of records produced in the conduct of state government. Records managers provide a system for managing records while the documentation is fulfilling the purpose for which it was created, while archivists manage that portion of records that has enduring value. Though records of state and equivalent levels of governments prior to the establishment of the United States were produced from the founding of the colonies, the first state archives was not created until 1779, the last almost two hundred years later. The history of state archives largely is a history written since 1901. Though interest in history motivated the increase in the number of state archival agencies in the first several decades of the twentieth century, administrative justification sustains them at the beginning of the twenty-first century.

INTRODUCTION

The term "state archives" designates: an *agency* of state government (and equivalent jurisdictions, as the District of Columbia and Territories such as Guam, the United States Virgin Islands, Northern Mariana Islands, American Samoa, and Puerto Rico, statistics for which, being not uniformly available, are excluded here), the *records* of entities of state government judged to have enduring value, and the *building* that houses the state archival agency and state archival records.

The mission of a state archives is the protection of the legal and economic rights and obligations of both state government and the citizens, former, present, and future, of the state by ensuring the integrity (validity and authenticity) of the records of government. The work of a state archives is identifying and securing state agency records of enduring value, preparing the records for use, ensuring their long-term preservation, and assisting those who come to use the records. Additionally, some state archives collect private archives of individuals and organizations for historical study.

Though the history of records of state governments (and their predecessors) dates from the establishment of European settlement in what is now the United States, the first state archives was not created until 1779, the last almost two hundred years later. The entry provides a history of U.S. state archives—both records and agencies.

NATURE AND FUNCTIONS

State archives are documents of every kind and sort—including hard copy and electronic; printed and manuscript; and promulgated documents, drafts, and notes—created in and used for conducting the business of state government. More specifically, state archives are the portion of those records that have enduring value and usefulness beyond the purpose for which they were created and initially used. This portion is estimated to be between 2% and 5% of the total. Before the establishment of the archival profession in the United States with the inauguration of the National Archives in 1935 and the founding of the Society of American Archivists (SAA) in 1936, the archival value of state records was judged primarily on a historical basis—the extent to which the information in the records contributed to knowledge of historical developments in the state. This view is predicated on the "Informational value" of records. Since the 1980s, however, the emphasis has fallen on the value of the records in documenting the activity of government, both for accountability and to ensure the authenticity of the documentation in relation to the activity in the conduct of which the records were created. This perspective prioritizes records' "Evidential value." Among the greatest challenges presently regarding state records is capturing the records of enduring value created in electronic form for preservation in or under the control of the state archival agency.

A state archives (which, in the singular, refers to the agency holding and managing the state archival records) performs an administrative service by documenting the functions and activities of state government. The mission of a state archives performing the archival and also the records management function designed to manage the accumulation of records in and the flow of records through office environments, is to protect the legal and economic rights and obligations of both state government and the citizens, former, present, and future of the state. The work

Encyclopedia of Library and Information Sciences, Fourth Edition DOI: 10.1081/E-ELIS4-120044426

of the state archives, coupled with the records management function for which state archives in all but 12 states in 2009 were responsible (excludes Arkansas and Minnesota that lacked functioning records management programs), is to identify and schedule agency records of archival value for eventual disposition in the state archives, to secure those records at the proper time, to ensure they are "arranged" (organized) as faithfully as possible in the files and order in which they were used while fulfilling the purpose for which they were created, to describe them so that users unfamiliar with the organization are able to locate the information they seek, to ensure preservation of the records to serve the information needs of state government and private citizens, and to assist those who come to use the records. Fundamental to the work is maintaining the integrity (validity and authenticity) of the documentation—that is, ensuring that the relationship of the records to the activities in the conduct of which they were created is undisturbed and clearly documented (Fig. 1).

Clear and explicit laws relating to the keeping and management of records are essential to the effective operation of a state archives program. A critically important element of such laws is defining the records for which the state archives has responsibility. Initially, to be encompassing in defining what is a state record, these statutes commonly borrowed from the 1943 Federal Records Act the phrase "regardless of physical form or characteristics." The growth of electronic records in the 1990s spurred state legislatures to refine and strengthen their definition of records to establish control over such records. The lawmakers, however, have yet to place in the state archivist the blanket, supreme authority both to determine in specific instances what is an archival state record and to secure that record for the state archives after it has fulfilled the purpose for which it was created. Similarly, while some states provide for the state archivist being a professional archivist, others assign the title to political positions.

Though all states have state archival agencies, only four (Vermont, 1779; California, 1850; Texas, 1876;

Fig. 1 Texas State Archives.
Source: Photograph taken by the author.

Massachusetts, 1896) established them before the twentieth century. Of the 50 state archival agencies in 2009, only seven (Alabama, Arkansas, Indiana, Maryland, Mississippi, New Mexico, and South Carolina) were independent agencies of government with a history or records management function, or both. The office of secretary of state, the office of record in state government, in 15 states continues to have direct responsibility for the state's archival records. State archives were discrete units of state historical societies in 11 states, of state libraries in nine states. (Precision in these numbers is difficult since in two states, the state archives is a unit under the state library, which in turn is a responsibility of the secretary of state.) The last states to create state archives as distinct agencies were Alaska, New York, North Dakota, and South Dakota, all of which did so between 1970 and 1977.

Appropriations to fund state archives vary from hundreds of thousands of dollars in small states to millions in large states. But, these appropriations are slim in relation to the size of the state budget and rarely have been commensurate with either (1) the potential disruptions to state government and citizen rights that would occur were use of the archival records to be compromised or lost or (2) the cost of recreating and validating the information in the affected records. Funding of the state archival agency commonly is less than one-tenth of 1% of the total state budget.

State archival agencies have two principal constituencies. One is state government employees needing to consult the records in the conduct of their work. The other is persons outside of government who need the information in the records. Among the most common nongovernment uses are: genealogy (predominant in 28 states), preparing for conducting business with a state agency, proving eligibility for a government service, legal and property research, and writing history. Since the 1980s, state archives recognizing the general unfamiliarity of the general public with archives have devoted attention specifically to promoting use of their holdings. The New York State Archives has led in developing programs to encourage teachers and students to use its holdings.

As use of the Internet for discovering and obtaining information has increased, so have demands for broader access to the holdings of archives of all sorts, and especially government archives. In response, state archival agencies have devoted substantial energy and resources to making finding aids (archival inventories of individual bodies of documentation, lists, and indexes) accessible electronically. Though in 2009, use of the extensive holdings of state archives continues to require in most cases that the user go to the repository to view the records, mounting of digital copies on the World Wide Web is proceeding at a rapid pace, especially of records sought by genealogists. The volume of state government records holdings in 2006 ranged from a total of 4600 cubic feet in

Vermont to 101,000 cubic feet in New York; the mean volume for the 50 states in 2006 was 37,100 cubic feet of state records, another 13,000 cubic feet of local records, and another 7000 cubic feet of private archives, for a total of 57,100 cubic feet (Fig. 2).

In addition to being responsible for the records of state government, 45 state archives have either advisory or custodial responsibility for records of local governments, though 10 of these states had no staff member assigned to local records.

Thirty-seven state archives fulfill an additional cultural role by collecting private archives—papers of individuals and records of organizations outside of state government—for the purpose of documenting and providing a resource for study of historical developments within the state. Only the state archives of Wisconsin (a unit of the Wisconsin Historical Society) has a greater volume of these holdings than of state records. How the state archives (both the records and the agency) are defined—whether as a cultural service or as an administrative service—is critical to the position of the agency within state government. Whereas an administrative role is essential to the functioning of government, the cultural service has been judged to be of secondary importance. In at least six states between 1933 and 2008 (Colorado, Florida, Maine, Michigan, Texas, and West Virginia), the governor or a legislative committee considered the state archives to be primarily a cultural service and proposed eliminating it, particularly by transferring its holdings and aspects of its work to a state university. None of the five initiatives succeeded.

HISTORY

The history of state archives can be divided into six periods:

Fig. 2 Entrance to California State Archives Search Room.
Source: Photograph taken by the author.

Period 1: Records before Agencies, Prior to 1901

Though officers of colonial government recognized the importance of using records in the conduct of the people's business, management of administrative records in the small government operations was left largely to their individual discretion, which often meant that the records were treated as personal property and carried home at the conclusion of a term of office. Some governors complained over the disappearance of needed records. Between this lack of institutional provision for archives and the many fires that occurred in those years, much was lost. The first building constructed to house the records of a colony was the Public Records Office in Williamsburg, Virginia, put up in the 1760s in response to a fire in the capitol.

Vermont in 1779 became the first state to make provision in law for management of state records by seating the responsibility with the secretary of state. A handful of states followed suit during the first half of the nineteenth century. Where they were worked on, "historical" state records commonly were reorganized into chronological order, rather than being maintained in files related to the business in the course of which they had been generated. Little attention was paid to contemporary records that by subsequent generations would be considered historical or archival. Richard Bartlett (1792–1837), Secretary of State of New Hampshire in 1836, harshly condemned this neglect. Succeeding generations of office holders and users of archives have echoed his condemnation as they have had to conduct affairs without the benefit of essential documentation.

In response to the 50th anniversary of the beginning of the American Revolution, many of the states with colonial histories spent large sums searching national archives (agencies) of European countries, especially Great Britain, and copying records relating to the state's colonial past. Since publication of these records provided both access to the records and preservation through multiplication of the texts, some states undertook ambitious programs of documentary publication. Though the work withered in the years leading up to and during the Civil War, the approach of the centennial of the Declaration of Independence revived concern for collecting and preserving local and state records.

The change in attitude toward the keeping of state archival records that resulted in the creation of formal repositories for them had its origin in the concern of historians for the availability of primary source materials (those created in the conduct of contemporary affairs or by participants recalling those affairs). Scientific historiography, which originated in Germany in the second half of the nineteenth century and took root in American graduate history programs in the final quarter of the century, required that practitioners conduct extensive research in archives. Few collecting archives (agencies) existed in the mold of the Massachusetts Historical Society, which in the last decade of the eighteenth century initiated the practice of collecting into a central repository the archives of individuals and organizations. For this reason primarily, the "scientific historians" focused on institutional (specifically government) history and sought access to state archives (records). In 1899, the American Historical Association (AHA) created the Public (meaning "government") Archives Commission (PAC) to survey and describe holdings of governmental records, including the condition in which they were found. Reporting in 1900 that the quantity and condition of records varied considerably from state to state, the commission advocated improvements in the care of state and local records.

Period 2: Founding of State Archives, 1901–1930s

The second period in the history of state archives began in 1901 with the founding of the Alabama Department of Archives and History as an independent agency of government. Spurred in part by the PACs work and under the direction of Thomas McAdory Owen, who had been instrumental in securing its creation and who served as the department's first and longtime head, the Alabama Department of Archives and History acquired not just government records but also a wide range of private archives, newspapers, and physical objects for exhibition.

During the first decade of the century, 16 states passed laws establishing state archives. One-third of the new state archives were established in the South (Alabama, Arkansas, Mississippi, North Carolina, Tennessee, and Virginia) and, as in Alabama, shared the common mission of the "diffusion of historical knowledge." That these state archives (agencies) arose in the South reflected a strong sense of regional identity and especially a concern with preserving records of Confederate military service. In the Midwest (Iowa, Ohio, and Wisconsin, led by Kansas and Nebraska in 1905), state archives were formed more commonly within historical societies. In a handful of states (Connecticut, Oklahoma, Tennessee, Texas, and Virginia) they were created as part of or moved into the state library. Though in many of the new state archives, years passed before resources and facilities were provided sufficient to accomplish the work prescribed to the state archival agency, state archivist Dunbar Rowland in Mississippi was able in 1914 to publish a guide to the state archives (records) that described all of the holdings of the agency; this guide was the first of its kind in the United States.

In 1909, under the leadership of Victor Paltsits of New York, the PAC organized a Conference of Archivists within the American Historical Association to provide a forum in which the historians who were accepting responsibility for or were taking jobs in state archives could meet and discuss issues common to their work. This was the first professional organization of archivists in the United States. At the same time, to help disseminate knowledge of best practices in the field, the National Association of State Libraries formed its own Committee on Public Archives. Starting in 1911, the committee published reports outlining developments in archival practice, and the progress of legislation relating to archival institutions and government records. Due substantially to the country's engagement in World War I, the Conference of Archivists failed in its attempt to produce a manual of practice. Cassius C. Stiles, the state archivist of Iowa, filled the void in 1928 when he published the first handbook widely consulted for their management, *Public Archives: A Manual for Their Administration in Iowa*. Before it ceased to exist, the AHAs PAC in 1932 published *The Preservation of Local Archives: A Guide for Public Officials*.

This founding period saw the establishment of state archives as agencies of government in two-thirds of the states to manage the historical records of the state, but few states drew on and profited from the experience of state archives in other states.

Period 3: Solidifying the Foundation, 1930s–1940s

Illinois state archivist Margaret Cross Norton opened a new period in the development of state archives. In 1929 at the annual meeting of the National Association of State Libraries, she read a paper titled "The Archives Department as an Administrative Unit of Government," in which she argued that state records are, first and foremost, legal and administrative documents of the state, the primary purpose of which is to fulfill not a historical, but an administrative role. Though the audience dominated by historians received her assertion in "stony silence," a half century later, Norton's view prevailed. Director of the Illinois State Archives for 35 years, 1922–1957, Norton became one of the most influential figures in the development of state archives. She fashioned an exemplary archival program, oversaw the construction of one of the first purpose-built archival repositories in the United States, passionately argued the value of archives, and published extensively on a wide range of archival issues.

Among the activities developed by the Works Progress Administration in 1934 in response to the Great Depression was the Historical Records Survey. While revealing the continuing negligence in the care of state and local records, it served as a training ground for state archivists and archival workers by exposing them to the volume of records that had accumulated, and the amount of work needed to establish effective control over them. Chief among the generation of state archivists who labored in the Survey were: Lester J. Cappon (Virginia), Christopher Crittenden (North Carolina), Milo M. Quaife (Michigan), William D. Overman (Ohio), and Morris L. Radoff (Maryland).

The first courses in archival administration were offered only at the end of the 1930s and beginning of the 1940s. The instructors had gained archival experience in public archives. Norton and Solon Buck, formerly with the Minnesota Historical Society, each taught for a period in the School of Library Service at Columbia University.

The founding of the SAA in 1936, the year after the new National Archives of the United States began operation, invigorated the state archival agencies. The archivists accepted Norton's views, and under the leadership of the SAAs first president, Albert Ray Newsome of North Carolina, who had been one of the proponents of the Historical Records Survey, agreed that the formulation of a model state archives law would be one of the first activities of the Society. Though the archivists achieved their goal in 1946, the model law was not widely adopted.

Period 4: Rise of Records Management, 1940s–1960s

During World War II, state archives began to apply the practices of the emerging field of records management, to control the growing mass of records created in the conduct of state business. Records management emerged independently and nearly simultaneously in the National Archives and in state archives (Texas, for one) in response to the dual needs to determine which among the millions of cubic feet of government records had enduring value without having to inspect each document and file, and to provide better access to the mountains of records for workers needing to use older files for the conduct of contemporary business. Archivists interested in records management, several of whom became the first generation of records managers, developed a system of functions designed to control the creation, flow, and disposition of the records in organizations. This allowed office workers to have at hand the records needed for the work they were doing and to avoid the uncontrolled accumulation of records that no longer served the needs of the worker.

With increasing frequency in the 1950s and 1960s the question arose whether responsibility for records management, including scheduling and destruction, should rest with the archival agency or other departments of government. No single answer emerged, though experience showed that administering the programs jointly improved the securing of archival records in the state archives and realized more efficient management of records throughout their life. By 2009, in 36 states the archival and records management programs were jointly administered. In the management of electronic records, this arrangement is proving to be especially advantageous.

Vigorous state archival programs under strong leaders at mid-twentieth century were Georgia under Mary Givens Bryan and Colorado under Dolores C. Renze.

Period 5: Building on Knowledge, 1960s–1980s

With funding from the private Council on Library Resources, Ernst Posner in 1962–1963 conducted the first in-depth study of state archival and records management programs. Published in 1964, his *American State Archives* recounted the history of state archives, described the program of each state, and offered standards for the organization of the archival service, the functions of state archives, and records management. The work showed that lethargy and neglect by state policy makers continued to characterize the archival and records functions of most states. Exceptions were Illinois under Norton and North Carolina under H. G. Jones.

A decade later, in 1974, to reunite archivists and records managers, who had lost their close association after the formation of professional associations for records managers, the leaders of state archival and records programs formed the National Association of State Archives and Records Administrators. In 1984, local and federal archivists and records managers were welcomed into the organization, and its name changed to National Association of Government Archives and Records Administrators.

In 1975, at the urging especially of South Carolina state archivist and former SAA President Charles E. Lee, Congress added the records program to the National Historical Publications Commission, thereby creating in the National Historical Publications and Records Commission (NHPRC), an office within the federal government giving grants to encourage archival work throughout the country. Orienting the program to the state level, the NHPRC required that grant requests from archives within a state be vetted by a State Historical Records Advisory Board (SHRAB) chaired by the head of the state archival program. This put the state archivist in a central position regarding archival development in the state. In the wake of President Ronald Reagan recommending elimination of the NHPRC as a money-saving measure, the NHPRC Records Program, at the initiative of director Larry J. Hackman (who subsequently became state archivist of New York and raised the New York program to national prominence) allocated what appeared to be the last NHPRC Records Program money for states to conduct surveys following on the example of Posner's work. The first 20 SHRAB studies formed the basis for the analysis *Documenting America: Assessing the Condition of Historical Records in the States* (1983), which showed a "cycle of poverty" of such magnitude that state archives collectively—and individually—were "unable to provide adequate care for their records." The hope that state legislatures, seeing the need, would take the responsibility they had long neglected for encouraging archival work within state government proved futile. Nevertheless, the structures set up in the states as a result of the NHPRC proved of sufficient value to the archival communities in the states that supporters successfully pressured Congress to save the NHPRC from elimination under Reagan and as requested consistently in the budgets of President George W. Bush. The SHRABs continued to function in 2008.

Period 6: Formalizing Standards, Pursuing Advocacy, and Grappling with Electronic Records, 1990s

Securing appropriate space in which to maintain state archives, for protection and to provide room in which to use them, has been difficult throughout the history of state archival agencies. Archival records, by their very nature being of enduring value, only and always increase in volume. Though half of the state archives occupy buildings constructed since the 1970s, the oldest facility was built in 1890. Twelve new facilities have been constructed since 1990, those of Arizona, Georgia, Mississippi, and Utah, since 2000, and plans are far along for construction or significant renovation of 27 more. Beyond providing for housing and use of the state archives (records), the new and renovated structures provide up-to-date environments for preservation, security, and fire suppression (Fig. 3).

The state archivists in 1989 created the Council of State Records Coordinators to formalize communication with and influence priorities of the NHPRC. Principal among the new initiatives were efforts to develop ways to manage electronic records. In forms that never existed before, combining text with sound and image, and incorporating hot links to other documents, records in electronic form presented new challenges. Among these were defining "the record" anew, determining the systems most appropriate for capturing bodies of documents of enduring value that have no physical manifestation (and for which any physical manifestation through printing robbed them of their unique qualities as electronic documents) and realizing methods for extending the life indefinitely of electronic records. The work continues.

In 2005, the Council of State Records Coordinators, having secured a staff through which to pursue the interests of state archivists as a group, especially the developing mission of advocating for state archival and records programs, reflected the new and growing emphasis by changing its name to Council of State Archivists. To provide the basis for its advocacy, the Council of State Archivists continued its predecessor's work of gathering and publishing documents [as *The State of State Records: A Status Report on State Archives and Records Management Programs in the United States* (2007)] compiling data from all the states for use by state archivists both in running their programs and in documenting the importance of archives to the public and to resource providers.

CONCLUSION

State archives (records) are essential to the functioning of state government and provision of services to the citizens entitled to those services. Once considered primarily a resource for historians, state archives (records) have come to be seen as primarily performing an essential administrative role within state government and for the citizens of the state. Though all states maintain state archives (both records and agencies), all but a handful of state archival agencies were established between 1901 and 1977. Only seven of these are independent agencies; the rest are units within larger offices and departments.

State archives (agencies) are at once similar in their archival functioning and as different in their operating environment as the governments they serve. In the colonial period when the volume of records produced in running government could be managed in offices, the history of state archives is one of the records themselves. In the twentieth century it is the history of both state records and state archival agencies. The dramatic increase in the volume of state records produced in the functioning of state government in the twentieth century led to formulation of techniques for managing records that were fulfilling the purpose for which they were created. Growing out of the archival function of controlling records of enduring value that had completed their initial use (archival enterprise), records management became separated from archival enterprise, but in the state government environment increasingly is being reunited. In the second half of the twentieth century, efforts expanded to include gathering information on all state archival programs, first by virtue of private funding of the Council on Library Resources, then at the initiative of the federal government through the National Historical Publications and Records Commission, and finally by the state archivists themselves organized in the Council of State Archivists. The information empowered state archivists to advocate for strengthening the archival programs of each and every state.

Fig. 3 Georgia Archives Building.
Source: Courtesy of Georgia Archives.

APPENDIX

Table A.1 Establishment and administrative location of state archival and records management programs February, 2009.

State	State archives established	Records management established	Program relationships	Archives parent agency	Records management parent agency (if separate)
Alabama	1901	1955	Joint	Independent	N/A
Alaska	1970	1955; Active 1968	Joint	State Library	N/A
Arizona	1937	1974	Joint	State Library	N/A
Arkansas	1905; Implemented 1911	authorized 1973; Currently suspended	Archives only	Independent	N/A
California	1850	1949	Separate	Secretary of State	General Services
Colorado	1951	1955	Joint	Administration	N/A
Connecticut	1909	1911	Joint	State Library	N/A
Delaware	1905	1977	Joint	Secretary of State	N/A
Florida	1967	1967	Joint	State Library	N/A
Georgia	1918	1971	Joint	Secretary of State	N/A
Hawaii	1905	1957–1958	Joint	General Services	N/A
Idaho	1947; full time archivist hired 1990	1998	Separate	State Historical Society	Administration
Illinois	1922	1979	Joint	Secretary of State	N/A
Indiana	1913	1979	Joint	Independent	N/A
Iowa	1906	1974	Joint	State Historical Society	N/A
Kansas	1905	1950s; funded 1992	Joint	State Historical Society	N/A
Kentucky	1958	1958	Joint	State Library	N/A
Louisiana	1956; implemented 1966	1956	Joint	Secretary of State	N/A
Maine	1965	1965	Joint	Secretary of State	N/A
Maryland	1935	1953	Separate	Independent	General Services
Massachusetts	1896	1976	Joint	Secretary of State	N/A
Michigan	1913	1952	Joint	Cultural Resources/ Affairs	N/A
Minnesota	1947	1963	Archives only	State Historical Society	N/A
Mississippi	1902	1981	Joint	Independent	N/A
Missouri	1965	1965	Joint	Secretary of State	N/A
Montana	1969	1977	Separate	State Historical Society	Secretary of State
Nebraska	1963	1969	Separate	State Historical Society	Secretary of State
Nevada	1965	1967	Joint	State Library	N/A
New Hampshire	1963; state archivist established 1979	1963	Joint	Secretary of State	N/A
New Jersey	1945	1953	Joint	Secretary of State	N/A
New Mexico	1959	unavailable	Joint	Independent	N/A
New York	authorized 1971; opened 1978	1950	Joint	Education	N/A
North Carolina	1903	1913	Joint	Cultural Resources/ Affairs	N/A
North Dakota	1977	1961	Separate	State Historical Society	Information Technology/ Management
Ohio	1927	1985	Separate	State Historical Society	General Services
Oklahoma	authorized 1939, 1947; staffed 1968	authorized 1961; staffed 1968	Joint	State Library	N/A
Oregon	1945	unavailable	Joint	Secretary of State	N/A
Pennsylvania	1903	1956	Separate	State Historical Society	Administration
Rhode Island	1930; in legislation 1989	1981	Joint	Secretary of State	N/A
South Carolina	1905; reorganized 1954	1966; in legislation 1973	Joint	Independent	N/A

(Continued)

Table A.1 Establishment and administrative location of state archival and records management programs February, 2009. *(Continued)*

State	State archives established	Records management established	Program relationships	Archives parent agency	Records management parent agency (if separate)
South Dakota	1975	1967	Separate	State Historical Society	Administration
Tennessee	1907	1957	Separate	State Library	General Services
Texas	1876	1947	Joint	State Library	N/A
Utah	1951	1970	Joint	Administration	N/A
Vermont	1779	1937	Joint	Secretary of State	N/A
Virginia	1902	Authorized 1942; established 1950	Joint	State Library	N/A
Washington	1909, fully functional 1957	1957	Joint	Secretary of State	N/A
West Virginia	1905	1961	Separate	Cultural Resources/ Affairs	Administration
Wisconsin	1907	1947	Separate	State Historical Society	Information Technology/ Management
Wyoming	1951	1959	Joint	Cultural Resources/ Affairs	N/A

Source: Courtesy of Council of State Archivists.

BIBLIOGRAPHY

1. Burnette, O. State and local archives in America. *Beneath the Footnote: A Guide to the Use and Preservation of American Historical Sources*, State Historical Society of Wisconsin: Madison, WI, 1969.
2. Council of State Archivists Website. Available at http://www.statearchivists.org/ (accessed September 2008).
3. In *Norton on Archives: The Writings of Margaret Cross Norton on Archival & Records Management*; Mitchell, T., Ed.; Southern Illinois University Press: Carbondale, IL, 1975.
4. Posner, E. *American State Archives*, University of Chicago Press: Chicago, IL, 1964.
5. State archival programs. Am. Archivist **2007**, *60* (2), Special Issue.
6. The State of State Records: A Status Report on State Archives and Records Management Programs in the United States; N.p.: Council of State Archivists, 2007. Available at http://www.statearchivists.org/reports/2007ARM report/ (accessed September 2008).
7. In *Documenting America: Assessing the Condition of Historical Records in the States*; Weber, L., Ed.; National Association of State Archives and Records Administrators: New York, 1983.

State Libraries and State Library Agencies

Barratt Wilkins
Retired State Librarian of Florida, Tallahassee, Florida, U.S.A.

Abstract

State Library agencies which vary from state-to-state as to history, role and scope, legal functions, personnel strength, and services, are reviewed. A book could be written about each of the fifty state library agencies and their impact on the development of libraries in their particular geographical area and nationwide. From little known agencies at the fringes of state government in the early nineteenth century to robust multipurpose agencies administering millions of state and federal dollars today, their growth has been most pointed in the past 55 years. This can be best viewed in the development of national standards for library functions at the state level, the introduction of federal aid in 1956 matched by hundreds of millions of dollars in state funds, the professionalization of state librarians and staff, and the broadening of state library functions and the accountability which follows.

INTRODUCTION

The literature about "state libraries" is not as robust as that of public, school, academic, and special libraries. This may be because of the relatively small number (less than 1%) of professional librarians working in state libraries, the relatively small number of scholars publishing in the field; and the specialized nature of use of state library collections. From the beginning of state libraries in the early nineteenth century, it took nearly 150 years of existence before these libraries began to become more than mere collections of books headed by a person with political connections. This entry seeks to inform the reader about early history and growth of state libraries and through change from an agrarian, oral-based culture to a culture based on the written word, it became possible to have establishment of national state library organizations for focused action, standards for library functions at the state level, professionalism of the state librarian and staff, and federal aid matched by millions of dollars from state and private sources. This entry also points to common characteristics and some notable examples of current state libraries.

DEFINITION

State library agencies are among the least understood and historically among the most obscure agencies in state government. The first elements of a commonly accepted definition of a state library agency were published in 1977 as a result of National Center for Education Statistics funded survey of the 50 states.[1],[2] The definition has been since codified both in federal law and The National Information Standards Organization, Z39.7-2004, 2.1.14.[3] and reads: "A State Library Agency is the official agency of a State

charged by the law of that State with the extension and development of public library services throughout the State, and has adequate authority under the law of the State to administer State plans in accordance with the provisions of Library Services and Technology Act (LSTA)." While this is the commonly accepted state library agency definition it does not cover the breadth of possible functions of such agencies as viewed in the twenty-first century. Such a definition would be hard to develop as there are only 10 state library agencies which manage the state archives of a state, 15 which offer preservation/conservation services, three which manage a state museum/art collection, 50 state library agencies which provide in some manner access to the Internet and World Wide Web, national and state databases, and interlibrary loan services, 27 which fund or host a State Center for the Book derived from the model at the Library of Congress, 19 which provide reference and loan materials directly to the public, 40 which provide support for literacy programs, and 22 which certify public librarians.[4]

No two state library agencies are the same in personnel strength, facilities, role and scope, legal foundation and authorizations, collections, services and activities, and history of development. There is no clear predetermined model for a state library agency although there are enough similarities to provide a historical overview, a discussion of trends, and brief overview of the leadership that has made state library agencies important during the years since the first federal aid act was signed into law in 1956.

"Successful state librarianship is a mixture of politics, personality, alliances, and position." The word "position" can be further defined as the socioeconomic trends and geographic history and place which establish the context for a state's government and functions. "How successful an agency is can be measured in how many lives are touched directly or indirectly by its services and

Encyclopedia of Library and Information Sciences, Fourth Edition DOI: 10.1081/E-ELIS4-120044853

activities." Thus state library leadership is paramount to success. Each state has developed differently based on its own politics, personalities, alliances, position and the socioeconomic trends, and geographical position in the United States.[5]

HISTORY

From the beginning of the nineteenth century, state libraries were largely insular institutions with the "state librarian" drawn from politicians, friends of politicians, and occasionally a learned man who had more than a passing interest in books. Because of their insularity as Dr. Wayne Wiegand has written, early state library agencies reveal the "staccato growth" characteristics of state funded programs on the margins of power.[6] This is what you would have found in the earliest territorial library in Florida where all materials were loosely packed into the offices of the Secretary of State who also served by law as ex-officio State Librarian. Except for a couple of appropriations in the 1850s prior to the United States Civil War, it was decades later that regular appropriation became available.

The states in the northeastern United States and those in the Far West benefited from more regular funding. The great federal survey of public libraries in United States published in the U.S. Centennial Year of 1876, provided a review of state and territorial libraries. It is interesting to note that all of the states at that time had a collection of books called a "state library" and all were legally established.[7] All of the state libraries listed in the 1876 survey were "traditional" state libraries—those units of state government which were formed to assemble the many volumes of books which were acquired from the federal government, exchanged with other libraries, or as a result of gifts, and needed some state government location overseen by an interested individual. Services were passive and the usage of materials was largely derived from visiting scholars and residents of a state, or by various officials of a state, like legislators, jurists, and government employees.

In 1893, historian Frederick Jackson Turner declared an end to the American frontier. A number of historians have pointed out that the growth of industrial power, coupled with heavy growth in cities and towns, populated with many new immigrants changed our culture from an agrarian oral tradition to a written tradition. Library leaders like Melvil Dewey in New York, C. B. Galbraith in Ohio, James L. Gillis in California, and Mary Spenner in Michigan brought traveling libraries to their states in the belief that states had a role in assisting in the education of their residents.

During the later part of the nineteenth century, a schism developed between traditional state library leaders and those who believed that states should bring books and reading to all areas of a state. State library commissions were established to develop the library extension movement and many of the leaders of this movement did not want the new service housed in the traditional state library. In fact, as late as 1937, James I. Wyer, State Librarian of New York, noted that of the 154 existing state libraries in the 48 U.S. states, a large majority did not support the library extension movement. One might ask why there were 154 "state libraries" instead of one per each of the 48 states in 1937. The main reason is that the existing national association of state libraries was made up of traditional state libraries, legislative reference bureaus, state historical societies, state archives, and several library extension agencies (see Appendix).

As the various state library commissions were established, states drew their statutory language from each other in defining the duties of the new agencies. Massachusetts, Wisconsin, North Carolina, Michigan, Maryland, Colorado, Indiana, Rhode Island, New Hampshire, and Pennsylvania were among examples of states which had both a state library and a newly formed state library commission, the latter charged with library extension.

During the ensuing decades between the World Wars, state government began to look at measures to streamline state government and looked for convenient ways to consolidate and merge agencies that seemed to have like functions, i.e., anything with the word "library." At this time a number of state library commissions and state libraries were merged under state departments of education.

In the southern part of the United States, traditional state libraries continued. When library commissions were established, these entities received poor public funding and received some grant funding from the private Carnegie Foundation or the Rosenwald Foundation. Fortunately, southeastern state library commission had leaders who influenced national library developments particularly in encouraging the first federal aid to libraries in the mid-1950s, and who established the first standards for library functions at the state level in 1963. Leaders included Essae Mae Culver (Louisiana), Estellene P. Walker (South Carolina), Lucille Nix (Georgia), Evelyn Day Mullen (Alabama), and Bessie B. Moore (Arkansas).

FEDERAL AID FROM CONGRESS

State Library Functions Development

There is little doubt, that the greatest impetus for the development of state library agencies as organizations of change and the growth of public library services came through passage of the initial federal Library Services Act in 1956.[8] Following this initial act, the Library Services and Construction Act was passed in 1966 adding federal aid for public library construction. In 1996, a rethinking of federal aid purposes brought changes in not only federal administration from the U.S. Department of Education to the new Institute of Museum and Library Services, but funds were increased for library networking and electronic communications and in providing assistance for all types of libraries.[9] Because of the 1956 legislation, at least two states established a state library administrative agency to administer the state's share of federal aid (Utah, South Dakota) and the last of the traditional state libraries merged with their state's library extension agencies and adopted the "State Library" name. Other significant changes included enactment of state aid to public library laws, establishments of library development units staffed with consultants to assist local government in establishing and developing public libraries, collecting and publishing library statistics, providing continuing education opportunities, summer reading support, and assisting in library planning, evaluation, and support. Other functions having grown out of federal aid, have been reference and referral services, statewide electronic database access coordination, and state-funded public library construction aid. And, finally as a result of other federal legislation, the state library administrative agencies were viewed in the 1990s as the natural lead agencies in coordinating e-rate, or reduced telecommunication rates for public libraries.

PROFESSIONAL ORGANIZATIONS

As with most like-minded groups of people who wish to share their experiences, state library leaders gathered at the national level to discuss issues, collections, standards, education, services to state employees, and legislatures. The National Association of State Librarians had an initial meeting in 1898 although there were earlier antecedents. Because of the makeup of this association with traditional state libraries, library extension commissions, legislative reference bureaus, and other agencies, nearly all attempts to develop national state library standards failed.[10] In 1936, the American Library Association published *The State Library Agencies; Its Functions And Organization*, which began to enumerate library functions of a state library agency. In 1950, the American Library Association established an Executive Board committee to study state library agencies as a basis of setting standards and strengthening services. (Information on early history of state library agency organization within American Library Association drawn from unpublished research by American Library Association, Research Library, Director, Karen Muller; Assistant Director, Valerie Hawkins; Intern, Elias Pera, November 2008.) However, it was not until 1963, under the American Association of State Libraries, a division of the American Library Association, that the first national standards for library functions at the state level were published.[11] A major revision was published

in 1970[12] and a 3rd edition was published in 1985.[13] These standards gave descriptions of what functions and services should be provided in a state library administrative agency but were constructed from inputs rather than empirical data about what works.

State library agencies have long been represented within the structure of the American Library Association, generally at the division level. This distinction is important because it has allowed the interests of state libraries to have a seat on the Council, the governing body of the American Library Association, to have representation on important national association committees and assembly's, authority to speak for state library interests on its own as if it had been issued by the American Library Association, and to develop and publish standards.

National names of professional organizations representing state libraries developed from the National Association of State Librarians (1898), the National Association of State Libraries (1904) (NASL), which were separate from the American Library Association. The latter merged with the newly formed State Library Agency Division of ALA in 1957. The result was the American Association of State Libraries (AASL) in 1957 which was shortened in 1971 to the Association of State Libraries Agencies (ASLA). In 1978, the Health and Rehabilitative Services Division merged with the ASLA to form the Association of Specialized and Cooperative Library Agencies (ASCLA). There is a State Library Agencies Section under the latter named ALA division.

CHIEF OFFICERS OF STATE LIBRARY AGENCES

With the growing influence of state library agencies in the planning and development of library services nationwide because of state administration of federal aid, a tension developed between the U.S. Department of Education and the 50 states. The U.S. Department of Education during the 1960s and 1970s had regional offices. Each regional office had a Federal Program Officer for administration of the Library Services and Construction Act and depending on each officer's interpretation of the law and administrative rules, were either relaxed or strict. The tension between state interpretation of a "state-based" program and federal interpretation of the law and rules, became so severe that the 50 state library chief officers decided to form an organization separate from the ALA to better represent their interest. Thus in 1973, the Chief Officers of State Library Agencies, Inc, (COSLA) was established. Its immediate goal was to speak with one voice to the U.S. Department of Education officials about federal administrative matters particularly concerning uniformity in interpretation of law and rules, and the second was to provide a unified voice to the Congress, the profession, and other national organizations and agencies on state library issues and programs.

Gradually some accommodation was reached with federal Education officials and it resulted in regional program officers being withdrawn from the regions and centralized in Washington, D.C. This resulted in coordination of responses to administrative questions from state library agencies.

Although the internal structure of COSLA has changed somewhat, its main organizational interests concern Legislation, Networking, Research and Statistics, Continuing Education, liaisons with various federal agencies including the Library of Congress, Institute of Museum and Library Services, National Library Service for the Blind and Physically Handicapped, and various national organizations including the American Library Association, International Federation of Library Associations and Institutions, Gates Foundation, E-Rate, Federation of State Humanities Councils, and various organizations representing the interest of archivists and government records managers. Two of these national organizations deserving special mention are the Gates Foundation and the E-rate program. These two national programs have provided millions of dollars, coordinated by state library agencies, to public libraries for linking to the Internet and helping make access to this international resource affordable to poorer residents of communities and for providing reduced rates to public library for linkages to the electronic networks.

COSLA Accomplishments

There is little doubt that one of the most significant accomplishments of COSLA has been its leadership in the conception, development, and passage of the federal Library Services and Technology Act in 1996 to replace the 40 year old Library Services and Construction Act and its antecedent. By the time of the 2nd White House Conference on Library and Information Services in 1991, Congress was asking the national library community for something new to replace the decades old federal aid program. The COSLA Legislation committee cochaired by Sara Parker(Pennsylvania) and Barratt Wilkins (Florida) outlined and developed what became a final draft of the new legislation. It called for consolidation of federal aid programs, a shift in federal administration from the U.S. Department of Education to the new Institute of Museum and Library Services and emphasized electronic linkages and networking among libraries, providing access to information, developing public and private partnerships, and targeting individuals who have difficulty using a library.

Among other accomplishments has been the work of members of the Research and Statistics Committee in helping design, formulate, and provide leadership in persuading the federal government to collect and disseminate national data on public (1990) and state (1993) libraries annually. The data has proved beneficial in establishing base line information about the development and growth

of public libraries and state library agencies nationwide. COSLA liaisons with the Gates Foundation and federal administration of the E-rate (reduced telecommunications rates) have been invaluable in advising and coordinating information between these organizations and the states thus ensuring that funds made available by private and public sources are expended as wisely as possible.

The work of COSLA and the expenditure of billions in federal dollars and the state dollars used to match those national funds, have caused the state library agencies to become more visible than they have ever been before. The funds have enabled the extension of library services to almost every citizen of the United States, it has helped equalize and provide for library service to the disabled and institutionalized, it has aided in the construction of a myriad of public library facilities, and it has developed strong public libraries in almost all areas of the country. Finally, these funds have provided assistance in developing multitype library cooperation, networks, and many of the statewide electronic libraries existing in the first decade of the twenty-first century.

STATE LIBRARY DEVELOPMENT ISSUES

Place in Government

A topic producing sharp differences of opinion and debate has been determining what is the best place for state library agencies in a state government structure. Fifty years ago as state policy makers began to move state library agencies from governance by gubernatorial-appointed commissions and boards to larger units of state government as in departments of education, departments of state, and departments of culture, Philip Moneypenny was finding other evidence to suggest that the strongest state libraries were independent state government agencies.[14] Seven years after Moneypenny's report in 1961, Douglas St. Angelo found that those state library agencies operated by public officials like state superintendents of schools, Governors, Secretaries of State were better in securing greater per capita support than those under independent board/commissions.[15]

A 1977 study found an almost even split between those state library agencies in state departments of education and those which were still under a gubernatorial-appointed commission or board. By 2000, the fifty-fifty split continued, but the number in each category declined as more state library agencies became parts of Departments of State, Departments of Cultural Resources, Cabinets concerned with Arts and Humanities, and other departments concerned with Children, Families, and Learning; Community and Economic Development: Administration; Information; and, the State Legislature. State library agencies in state education departments were more likely to be lost in comparisons with other larger components such as higher education, public schools, and vocational and technical education. State library agencies under an independent board/commission have been found to have the most discretion in policy and library development but are very dependent on the power and influence of their board members.

State Librarian Qualifications

The education and preparation for the position of state librarian and the political standing of the state librarian have been issues of discussion in states since Dr. James I. Wyer, New York State Librarian in 1937, pointed out that the position in many states was a political pawn and that a southern commonwealth had appointed a state beauty queen as State Librarian.[16] As noted in a 2000 article, "how the state librarian takes advantage of the appointed nature of the position is one of personal preference, politics, individual state experience, and the energy and practical intelligence of the individual."

Education of State Library Personnel

Library educators have not placed much emphasis on providing courses to prepare individuals for careers in state libraries or for state librarianship. Recently retired Florida State University Information Studies Dean Jane Robbins quoted an article by James Beasley in 1971, that "the state library is more an idealized form than a structure with a clear national identity." As there are no pure examples of a "state library" and that these agencies are so diverse in their structure and broad in their various missions, "that it has seemed more expedient to skim over them in educational programs." This has largely been the case in library education over the decades and it is even more so today as library education focuses on "information" rather than "libraries."[17]

As noted in 2000, some state librarians have used the position to make powerful differences in the development of library services in their states and in the nation. State librarians now serve generally from 4 to 8 years and some have been in office for less than four. The era of state librarians serving a quarter of a century or more in the state librarian's position appears to be over. Maine, Louisiana, Florida, Kentucky, and Indiana have all had recently retired examples of such long tenures.

Successful state librarians are not preoccupied by state issues and policies, nor do they indulge in insularity only focusing on in-state programs. For the State Librarian, that position's influence can be measured in what other state boards or commissions the individual serves on, the unfettered access to statewide elected officers, access to state legislators, staff and committee personnel, and involvement in regional and national level committees or professional organizations. As University of South Florida Distinguished Professor of Library and Information Science Kathleen de la Pena McCook has noted "librarians must be at every table."[18]

TRENDS AND ISSUES AFFECTING STATE LIBRARIES

Recent national trends being either influenced by state libraries or affecting state libraries include federal intrusion into the privacy of library users (USA Patriot Act); reduction in federal sources of information from changes in the U.S. Government Printing Office; withdrawal of previously available information from federal document depository libraries because of new sensitive or secret classifications; providing guidance to libraries and policy makers with the Children's Internet Protection Act (CIPA); expansion of state electronic libraries to include all types of libraries and funding to pay for the expanding access; the pressure to fund, digitize, and preserve more public and private information sources; pressure to increase state funding to aid local public library construction projects or to reinstitute federal construction aid withdrawn in 1996. Some recent state trends include reductions in state aid program appropriations because of shortfalls in state tax revenue; the loss of state personnel from downsizing; and state tax initiatives which threaten to reduce the amounts that local government can tax to provide local services.

STATE LIBRARY VITAL STATISTICS, FY 2006

All State Libraries, except Hawaii, offered public service hours from a high of 60 hr to a low of 32 hr. Total books and serial volumes were 23.4 million with two state libraries having collections exceeding 2 million books and serials. Of these two, the only Association of Research Libraries (ARL) member was the New York State Library. State libraries held 27.2 million uncataloged government documents. The State Libraries employed 3500 full-time equivalent (FTE) positions in FY 2006 of which approximately 1100 were professional librarians. State Libraries reported expenditures from all sources of $1.1 billion of which 82% was from state funds. State Librarian salaries ranged from $63,283 to $137,000 with an average of $92,404. Thirteen state librarians had salaries exceeding $100,000 in FY 2006.[19] For photographs of state library agency main buildings, go to http://www.cosla.org/, Image Gallery.

NOTABLE STATE LIBRARIES

Examples of notable state library agencies were drawn from either conversations with the chief officer of the state library agency, their agency's URL, or the Chief Officers of State

Fig. 1 Artist drawing of new entrance to the Archives Building of the Arizona Department of State Library, Archives, and Records Management, now under construction 2008–2009.

Library Agencies, Inc., URL All state library agencies have programs and services which stand out from time to time. The criteria for measurement are subject to debate as well as the standing of a state's library agency compared with others. For instance, the Arizona State Library, Archives and Public Records (Gladys Ann Wells, State Librarian, 1997–) agency is noted for its melding of the interests cited in its name into a strong service-oriented agency under the Arizona State Legislature—one of the two in the nation. A new multimillion dollar home for the State Archives unit of the agency is under construction. (Fig. 1)

Like Arizona, the Connecticut State Library (Kendall F. Wiggin, State Librarian, 1998–) is a large multipurpose agency. It is governed by a semiautonomous board comprising members from all three branches of government—the judiciary, the Legislature, and the Governor. Its units include history and genealogy, state archives, public records, library for the blind, museum of state history, law

and legislation, and government information. Successes include achieving funding for a state digital library, historic preservation funds, and state-funded library construction.

A notable example of a state library agency under a board of regents of a state university system, is the Georgia Public Library Service (Dr. Lamar Veatch, State Librarian, 2001–). In this "home" there is a high tolerance for independence and the agency benefits from not having legacy services like a state library collection and government documents. It operates a statewide library automation and lending network for public libraries, provides a robust program for local public library construction and major repair and renovation, and conducts an innovative program for identifying new leadership for librarianship. The GPLS recently won a second annual Mellon Award for Technology Coordination.

Because of its small scale, the Maine State Library (Gary Nichols, State Librarian, 1973–2008) program under a

Fig. 2 Artist drawing of lobby to Texas State Library and Archives Building, now under construction.
Source: Architect—Bailey Architects, Inc. Rendering by Don Oelfke.

Fig. 3 Artist drawing of new and enlarged Library of Virginia Building in Richmond, Virginia, 2009.

gubernatorial-appointed board, has more flexibility and it can act quickly. Perhaps its greatest accomplishment is having a seat on the board which governs the Maine Educational Technology Account. Moneys provided from this source underwrite a free-of-charge electronic network to over 1000 public and school library units.

One of the oldest state library agencies in existence is the New Jersey State Library (Norma Blake, State Librarian, 2001–) established in 1796. It is the only state library agency affiliated with a state college—the Thomas Edison State College. It has received national recognition for its Library Development program as one of the most exciting and dynamic in the nation. Its State Librarian Norma Blake was just named the 2008 Librarian of the Year by *Library Journal*.[20]

The Oregon State Library (James Sheppke, State Librarian, 1991–) is best known for its innovative state-funded program which aids public libraries in literacy for children (aged 0–5) and for children (aged 10–15)

The Texas State Library and Archives (Peggy Rudd, State Librarian, 1999–) is governed by a gubernatorial-appointed board. Its success and issues are large because of the state's geographical size. Successes include getting the Legislature to fund the first State Aid for public libraries in 2002 and in integrating medical libraries with public and academic libraries into its electronic library for resource sharing. The State Librarian is also noted for winning recognition for securing Governor's Office records and making them available for public use and access. (Fig. 2)

Fig. 3 provides an illustration of the new Library of Virginia building (which also houses the State Archives) in Richmond, Virginia.

CONCLUSION

This review of state library agencies has pointed out their slow development which did not gain national attention until after the Second World War. In the past 55 years

national standards for library functions at the state level were first published, the role and scope of state library agencies were first enumerated, the first federal funds for library development were made available by Congress, the professionalization of state librarians occurred, and national organizations of and for state librarians were established for joint action on issues and programs. In the future, more work will be done by scholars and state and federal agencies on the value of state libraries, measurements of impact, accountability, and efficiency and whether other forms of state coordination of library and information services will develop.

APPENDIX

Table A.1 State Library Establishment Dates.

State	City	Established
Alabama	Montgomery	1901
Alaska	Juneau	1957
Arizona	Phoenix	1864
Arkansas	Little Rock	1935
California	Sacramento	1850
Colorado	Denver	1876
Connecticut	Hartford	1854
Delaware	Dover	1901
Florida	Tallahassee	1845
Georgia	Atlanta	1897
Hawaii	Honolulu	1913
Idaho	Boise	1901
Illinois	Springfield	1839
Indiana	Indianapolis	1825
Iowa	Des Moines	1838
Kansas	Topeka	1855
Kentucky	Frankfort	1834
Louisiana	Baton Rouge	1925
Maine	Augusta	1839
Maryland	Baltimore	1886
Massachusetts	Boston	1826
Michigan	Lansing	1828
Minnesota	Roseville	1895

(Continued)

Table A.1 State Library Establishment Dates. *(Continued)*

State	City	Established
Mississippi	Jackson	1926
Missouri	Jefferson City	1907
Montana	Helena	1929
Nebraska	Lincoln	1854
Nevada	Carson City	1859
New Hampshire	Concord	1716
New Jersey	Trenton	1796
New Mexico	Santa Fe	1929
New York	Albany	1818
North Carolina	Raleigh	1812
North Dakota	Bismarck	1907
Ohio	Columbus	1817
Oklahoma	Oklahoma City	1890
Oregon	Salem	1905
Pennsylvania	Harrisburg	1745
Rhode Island	Providence	1852
South Carolina	Columbia	1943
South Dakota	Pierre	1913
Tennessee	Nashville	1854
Texas	Austin	1909
Utah	Salt Lake City	1957
Vermont	Montpelier	1825
Virginia	Richmond	1823
Washington	Olympia	1853
West Virginia	Charleston	1929
Wisconsin	Madison	1899
Wyoming	Cheyenne	1871

Source: Compiled by staff of Library, American Library Association, October 2008.

REFERENCES

1. Survey of State Library Agencies, University of Illinois Graduate School of Library Science: Urbana-Campaign, IL, 1979; 46; 1977 [funded by National Center for Education Statistics]. Occasional Papers Number 12.
2. Wilkins, B. State library agencies: Analysis of the NCES survey. In *Bowker Annual of Book Trade Almanac*; R. R. Bowker: New Providence, NJ, 1979; 287.
3. Public Law, 104-208; 20 USC Chapter 72; NISO Z39.7-2004, 2.1.14.
4. Institute of Museum and Library Services, *Library Statistics Program: State Library Agency Report for FY 2007*, Table 10A, 30-33. Available at http://harvester.census/imls/stlib.asp.
5. Wilkins, B. The art of state librarianship. In *The Functions and Roles of State Library Agencies*; American Library Association: Chicago, IL, 2000; 50–52.
6. Wiegand, W.A. The historical development of state library agencies. In *State Library Services and Issues; Facing Future Challenges*; Charles, R., Ed.; McClure Abelix Publishing Co: Norwood, NJ, 1986; 1.
7. Homes, H.A. State and territorial libraries. *Public Libraries in the United States of America, Their History, Condition, and Management*, 1876; 292–311 Special Report.
8. Holley, E.F.; Schremser, R.F. *The Library Service and Construction Act; an Historical Overview from the Viewpoint of Major Participants*; JAI Press: Greenwich, CT, 1983.
9. Kingma, B.; Shubert, J.F.; Yeoh, A. *The Impact of Federal Funding on State Library Agencies: The LSCA to LSTA Transition*; U.S. National Commission on Library and Information Science and the U.S. National Center for Education Statistics, May 2002. Available at http://www.nclis.gov/statsurv/surveys/stla/reports/StLA Policy Paper 2. 2002. pdf.
10. National Association of State Librarians, Libr. J. **1898**, December 23, 668–669.
11. *Standards for Library Functions at the State Level*; American Association State Libraries: Chicago, IL, 1963.
12. *Standards for Library Functions at the State Level*, 2nd Ed.; American Library Association: Chicago, IL, 1970.
13. *Standards for Library Functions at the State Level*, 3rd Ed.; American Library Association: Chicago, IL, 1985.
14. Moneypenny, P. *The Library Functions of the States*; American Library Association: Chicago, IL, 1966; 37.
15. Douglas, S.A.; Hartsfield, A.M.; Goldstein, H. *State Library Policy: Its Legislative and Environmental Contexts*; American Library Association: Chicago, IL, 1971; 66–67.
16. Wyer, J.I. State politics assailed in library posts. New York Times **1937**, June 22.
17. Carter, J.R. State librarianship: Challenging the enigma through library education. J. Educ. Librarianship **1980**, Spring *24*, 261–273.
18. McCook, K.P. *A Place at the Table: Participating in Community Building*; American Library Association Editions: Chicago, IL, 2000.
19. Institute of Museum and Library Services, *Library Statistics Program, State Library Agency Report for FY 2006*, 3–8. Available at http://harvester.census.gov/imls/stlib.asp.
20. Norma, B. Librarian of the Year. Libr. J. **2008**, January 15.

State-Sponsored Destruction of Books and Libraries

Rebecca Knuth
Library and Information Science Program, University of Hawaii, Honolulu, Hawaii, U.S.A.

Abstract
The circumstances and motivations for state-sponsored destruction of books and libraries are explored. Various historical examples are described, and commonalities across instances of "libricide" are drawn out of the histories. (Editor's abstract.)

The survival of books and libraries during war and political instability has always been problematic. Throughout history, as empires rose and fell, the circumstances surrounding the destruction of libraries typically followed one of three major patterns. Some libraries were lost as part of the ritualized ravaging of captured cities, palaces, and temples. As texts came to be seen as valuable property, a second pattern emerged: libraries and books became "loot" of war and were carried away at the prerogative of the victor. The removal of whole libraries demonstrated dominance in a new and different way from destroying them. At the same time as the conquered people were humiliated, the prestige and cultural patrimony of the conquering society was further enhanced. A third pattern evolved under ideological mandates (religious or political) that labeled certain materials offensive and called for censorship through violent purging or selective destruction. While all three patterns figured in the destruction of books and libraries in the twentieth century, permutations of the third pattern were the most significant; millions of books were sacrificed for extremist ideas.

These atrocities were but one type of loss in an extremely bloody century. Government-authorized mass murder of *civilians*—not soldiers—accounted for most deaths. Along with an increase in human casualties, state-sponsored destruction of culture rose dramatically. Two new terms, *genocide* and *ethnocide*, came into use to reflect a distinctly modern, analytical understanding of complex atrocities as phenomena with recognizable patterns. It was the truly unprecedented annihilation of 6 million Jews by the Nazis that led to the use of the term genocide, which combined the Greek *genos*, meaning "race" or "tribe," and *cide*, "killing." Coined in the 1930s by Raphael Lemkin, an émigré jurist, the term was institutionalized in a 1946 United Nations (U.N.) resolution (96-1) that condemned genocide and in a 1948 convention that banned it. In the next 50 years, researchers established a connection between modern genocide and ideology. In 1976 Irving Horowitz wrote of genocide as a policy, the "structural and systematic destruction of innocent people by a state bureaucratic apparatus" that sought to assure conformity with its ideology and model of society (p. 18).[1] Evidence of Communist genocides engineered by Stalin, Mao, and Pol Pot strengthened the theory of an ideological connection, and revealed a flaw in the U.N.'s definition: the omission of political groups as certifiable victims. Scholars then moved to address this issue. For example, in Frank Chalk and Kurt Jonassohn's 1990 study. *The History and Sociology of Genocide*, genocide is defined as "a form of one-sided mass killing in which a state or other authority intends to destroy a group, *as that group and membership in it are defined by the perpetrator*" (emphasis added) (p. 23).[2]

Because the U.N. definition of genocide emphasized bodily harm and physical circumstances and excluded attacks on a group's culture or institutions, a different term, *ethnocide*, was introduced to describe the organized commission of specific acts with intent to extinguish *culture*, utterly or in substantial part. This could include deprivation of the opportunity to use a language, to practice a religion, to create art in customary ways, to maintain basic social institutions, and to preserve memories and traditions.[3] Genocide, then, is the denial of the right of existence of entire human groups, as homicide is the denial of the right to live of individual human beings (General Assembly Resolution 96-1), while ethnocide is the destruction of a culture without necessarily killing its bearers.[4]

Recently a link has been established among genocide, ethnocide, and the destruction of texts.[5] A scholar in the history of books has introduced the word *libricide* (to date used only rarely in reference to the "murder" of a book) to delineate the destruction of texts as a pattern occurring within the larger context of ethnocide. Libricide is the state-sponsored and systematic destruction of books and libraries, and shares the same impulse toward negation as genocide and ethnocide. Libricide (like its parent phenomena) is *not* the sum of spontaneous crimes of passion committed by barbarians, as is commonly thought, but a method of problem solving that is deliberate, systematic, and violent. Books and libraries are targeted because of the functions they serve and the humanist values they support.

Encyclopedia of Library and Information Sciences, Fourth Edition DOI: 10.1081/E-ELIS4-120044806

Libraries organize knowledge and support structured religious and political perceptions that legitimize the governing power.[6] Michael Harris,[7] a prominent library historian, has posited that libraries are part of an ensemble of institutions dedicated to the creation, transmission, and reproduction of hegemonic ideology—that is, the guiding doctrine. In Western libraries in the twentieth century this doctrine was increasingly defined by humanism, a belief in intellectual freedom (the inalienable right to think, write, and read) and the ultimate authority of the mind in human living.[8] Humanism emphasizes individual intellectual and cultural achievement (as its Latin root, *humanus*, "centered on human beings," indicates) and looks upon books as tools for the acquisition of information and self-confidence and for the development of reason, understanding, and initiative. As the century progressed, humanism came to be associated with democratic societies, in which it took the form of generalized ideas and ideals such as equality, pluralism, individualism, and tolerance.

As extremist regimes arose and promulgated beliefs that were the antithesis of these values, the stage was set for intense conflict. Ideologues stressed orthodoxy, the subordination of the individual to the collective, and adherence to a single vision. Under highly nationalistic or revolutionary regimes, the dissemination of information was controlled, publications had to be ideologically correct, and library services were geared toward achieving ideological objectives. Books and libraries channeled the individual's development toward the goals of a utopian society, in which the "new man" replaces personal desires and aspirations with collective visions of a transformed society. In order to tether the individual in this way, extremist regimes had to mandate intolerance of opposing information and discourse, and target the material expression of humanism (unfettered books and libraries) with violence.

Books and libraries also, of course, hold historical records and support collective memory—the "stories" or myths that give meaning to the past, explain the present, and provide guidance for the future. In all cultures, these stories involve principles that help cultures organize their institutions, develop ideals, and find authority for their actions.[9] Democracies provide a fairly wide range of access to information and use records to support diversity. Ideologues exert greater control over written records in order to reconstruct history and foster myths of a glorious past, present victimization, and transcendent future, myths that will motivate followers to pursue extremist goals. The destruction of books and libraries belonging to enemies is a mechanism by which a regime and its followers, who are influenced by the emotional appeal of a distorted collective memory, seek to legitimize their domination of competing minorities or press claims to territory and resources. While emphasizing those written records that

support their claims, extremists may also seek to destroy any records that could compromise their position.

One might argue that the destruction of libraries is over-determined, because of the interplay of many contributing forces. Indeed, Indeed, the overlay of influencing factors and chaotic conditions often makes it difficult to determine whether acts of destruction are accidental or intentional. Libricide—systemic destruction—is usually intentional and relatively coordinated. Destruction can be internal—carried out within a nation and ranging from quiet deeds of censorship to aggressive acts of vandalism, terrorism, civil war, or genocide—or it can be external, a function of war or conquest. While small-scale destruction may occur during civil unrest, major internal destruction occurs when a change in the ruling regime initiates censorship and purging. This may extend to the annihilation of the materials of a particular despised group, often a religious, racial, or political group. In extreme cases, massive destruction is carried out by revolutionaries who view libraries as remnants of a pernicious social or political system; their anti-intellectual, antihumanist, and antihistorical attitudes make the censoring and restructuring of existing libraries imperative. Communism, a *revolutionary* ideology, has been heavily implicated in genocidal practices, as Stalin's devastation of the *kulaks* and Pol Pot's destruction of Cambodia's urban and educated population have clearly demonstrated.

Communism evolved from events that were rooted in great social distress: the French Revolution, which set the precedent of revolt against blatant economic and political inequality; and the Marxist movement, an intellectual response to the brutal working conditions and social disintegration brought about by industrialization. Marxism, as developed by German philosopher and economist Karl Marx in the 1800s, identified class struggle as the main agency of historical change and predicted the succession of capitalism by a socialist order—or classless society. Communism emerged after the Russian Revolution in 1917, when Marxist doctrines were adapted to Russian conditions, most profoundly by Lenin. Under Lenin and then Stalin, "socialism" became a facade for the pursuit of power, transforming Russian Communism into a fanatical ideology that justified the destruction of all human and institutional opponents. The Communists exported their revolution by making people aware of the possibility of other realities, and then posing Communism as the inevitable alternative to oppression. Communist doctrines would ultimately provide an ideological base for the overthrow of power structures in many countries.

A revolution has been defined as "political and/or social and/or economic and/or cultural upheaval which calls for a fundamental change in the existing order; it is relatively rapid and generally employs the use or threat of force" (p. 8).[10] J. W. Fulbright once observed, "A true revolution is almost always violent and usually it is extremely violent. Its essence is the destruction of the social fabric and institutions of a society, and an attempt, not necessarily successful, to create a new society with a new social fabric and new institutions" (p. 405).[11] Under Communism, the economic and political elite of the previous order, including intellectuals, were seen as recalcitrant reactionary counter-forces and thus became natural targets. Since libraries supported tradition and existing power structures, to the Communists they were the embodiment of cultural systems that assigned lower-status groups to varying degrees of cultural invisibility.[7] Communist genocide almost always extended to traditional cultural materials and institutions, and thus to books and libraries.

In China, party radicals viewed books as tools of the oppressors because they supported the skills, values, and way of life of the bourgeoisie. Books were vanities that, by perpetuating the past, became a hindrance to present and future revolution and to creativity and progress.[12] Marx[13] once wrote that the "tradition of all the dead generations weighs like a nightmare on the brain of the living" (p. 15). In the mid-1960s, years after the initial revolution, Mao Tse-tung led a "revolution of revitalization" against the four olds—old ideas, old cultures, old customs, and old habits—especially targeting China's intellectual and cultural structure: "For the modern utopian the destruction of the learning of the past, or its radical revision and reduction, represents the cessation of historical process and constitutes a basic precondition for happiness and justice" (p. 519).[12] Indeed, for revolutionary regimes, history begins with the revolution. Utopians (including the revolutionaries that adapted Marxism) harbored no doubts about their methods of selecting books for destruction or about the permanent implications of irrevocable destruction. Denying later generations the right of choosing what they would read ensured that the new order would remain forever.

By the twentieth century, libraries throughout the world had come to be associated with intellectuals, education, scholarship, history, tradition, democracy, and humanism. When these sociocultural structures and values were subjected to attack and modification by Communist revolutionaries, the fate of libraries as bastions of tradition and Western ideals became problematic. When, as in pre-*glasnost* Russia, the Communist leadership was striving for industrialization and technological superiority, libraries became essential in carrying out mandates for universal literacy and supporting scientific progress—within the constraints of ideology, thus at the same time as there was purging, censorship, and narrow restriction of selection policies, library systems that *supported* the revolution were expanded, an ethos of socialist librarianship was promoted, and a few specialized, closed libraries with foreign and scientific materials were quietly maintained by the government. On the other hand, when the Communist leadership vacillated between visions of industry (in which technological progress demanded access to information) and agriculture (in which sophisticated printed materials are irrelevant), libraries underwent cycles of growth and depletion. This was the case in China under Mao Tse-Tung. The massive destruction of books and libraries during China's Cultural Revolution (1965–1975) marked a retreat from industrialization and modernization into a peasant agrarian society. When the ultimate vision of a Communist regime is a radical agrarian society operating at an intellectual ground zero and when thus the ability to read and write is punishable by death, as it was in Cambodia under Pol Pot (1975–1979), libraries become superfluous.

Revolutionary ideologues, most notably the Communists, were not the sole agents of twentieth-century libricide. Virulent nationalists first purged their own libraries and then, through imperialism, the libraries of their enemies. While nationalists tend to be rightwing, as in the case of the Nazis (during World War II) and the Serbs (in the 1990s), leftist politicians have also expressed nationalistic tendencies and destroyed books and libraries when socialist doctrines have been compromised by imperialist impulses (the case with China and Tibet, e.g.). In struggles between competing nations, the destruction of libraries has always been justified as a wartime prerogative because these institutions contain materials that legitimize the competing power structure and express the enemy's national prestige and culture. When long-term occupation or annexation is envisioned, books are seized as loot, and information infrastructures are dismantled as part of initiatives to obliterate the identity and sovereignty of a defeated opponent and assume control of that nation's resources.

Destroying the enemy's intellectual and cultural institutions can break the will to resist; thus eliminating competition and neutralizing the threat that other creeds and values pose to one's own. In 1990 the Iraqis destroyed Kuwaiti libraries as part of a plan to reduce the country to a neutralized nineteenth colony, subject to the will of Iraqi nationalists—a pattern reminiscent of the Nazis' destruction of Poland. The Chinese destroyed Tibet's libraries because these institutions supported a separate Tibetan identity based on Buddhism, a creed antithetical to socialist transformation and Sinocization. The Serbs destroyed Muslim libraries because of the perceived imperatives of ethnic cleansing. When the goal of battle is the obliteration of a culture (as opposed to simply unseating a regime), the conquest of territories and their populations is accompanied by the destruction of libraries and any other institutions supporting memory or legitimizing past identities.[14]

From its roots in Europe, nationalism has grown to become the dominating political ideal of modern times. Nationalism is the identification of a people with a state formed around a specific geographical location. The identity of this "imagined community"[15] is forged within communal bonds of primordial identities shaped by common language, ethnicity, or religion. Loyalties once rooted in local familial or spiritual identities are channeled into a broader identity—nationalism—that derives its charismatic appeal from a combination of political legitimation and emotional power; that is, the power sensed from "belonging," from being assigned an esteemed identity. Nationalism carries the potential for polarization based on clear rules for inclusion and exclusion, however. In the hands of extremists, nationalism may be pitched at a virulent level, co-opted to rationalize violent policies, and developed as the ideological foundation for fanatic behavior. Nationalism has been, alternately, an integrative and a deconstructive force. Expressed as patriotism, a devotion and loyalty to one's own nation, it has supplied the foundation for modern political and organizational structure. It has also ignited vicious regional and global wars when patriotism has led to policies of militarism and imperialism.

Hans Kohn[16] describes nationalism as a political creed that inspires the supreme loyalty of the majority of people to the nation-state, and that serves as the indispensable framework for all social, cultural, and economic activities. Nationalism has various manifestations because it is conditioned by the social structure, the intellectual traditions and cultural history, and the geographic location of the society in which it is found. What is striking, however, is the basic similarity of the pattern that occurs when nationalism shifts from benign creed to toxic ideology: a progression of social disruption, grievance, and then receptivity to authoritarian leaders who espouse transformative solutions. As an ideology, nationalism "expresses the inflamed desire of the insufficiently regarded to count for something among the cultures of the world" (p. 261).[17]

In considering the destruction of texts, nationalism concerns us as an ideology; an encompassing, belief-driven sociopolitical program that provides systematic rules and seeks the ultimate transformation of society. Leaders such as Hitler, Milosevic, and Saddam Hussein have exploited the real grievances of their people by invoking great myths of national destiny and national persecution in order to marshal support for aggression and violence. The support of a critical mass of the population paves the way for scape-goating and the identification of the "enemy;" anyone who interferes in the realization of the idealized nation by rejecting its claims, occupying "national" territory, or otherwise blocking its aggrandizement. Because of the function of libraries as material and symbolic keepers of memory and of national and cultural identity, libraries provide stubborn witness against nationalistic claims, and thus come to be perceived as enemy forces.

Nationalism is often supported by militarism and a quasi-ideological policy, imperialism. Militarism is effectively established when a state's armed forces assume command of both military and civil affairs and unilaterally determine the nature of basic institutions, the choice of leaders, the allocation of resources, and the rights and duties of citizens.[18] Militarism adapts very well to extreme ideologies, because the very term military implies an acceptance of organized force as a legitimate means for realizing social objectives.[19] Militarists view that which is alien, foreign, or outside the frontier as barbarian, and hold other attitudes that lend themselves well to enforcing the values of imperialism and pursuit of national self-interest and manifest destiny. Militarism and imperialism rationalize war to the extent that it becomes imperative.[20]

Nationalism, militarism, and imperialism together form a lethal trinity, rendered even more toxic when prejudice reaches the point of racist policy—yet another level of paranoia that equates "otherness" with "enemy." Racism takes on ideological characteristics when extremist leaders seek to promote the superiority of their own race through official programs that deny simple rights to other races. It thrives when a society is disintegrating, when desperate populations will embrace what seems a simple, clear-cut solution to their plight, and a scapegoat provides a channel for their aggression. Tapping into a basic human fear of strangers, racist ideology can rapidly turn a majority against a subsection of the national populace simply by presenting the goals of the nation as dependent on race-linked attributes.

Germany's National Socialist doctrine (Nazism) stands as a prominent and infamous example of a racist ideology that resulted in genocide and libricide. Nazis constructed an image of the Jews as the "specter of an absolute menace" (p. 95)[21] and held Jewish blood responsible for contaminating and weakening the nation. Thus causing the loss of World War I and postwar depression and decline. According to the Nazis—a group that included many scholars and intellectuals—full realization of the preordained dominance of the Aryan race was dependent on extinguishing Judaism. Then, in an absolute, unapologetic commitment to racism—a concentrated effort to distinguish "us" from "them"—the Nazis moved beyond anti-Semitism to devise programs to deal with all "inferior" ethnic groups. For example, they moved quickly to destroy the Poles and Polish culture and killed 3 million non-Jewish Poles along with 3 million Polish Jews—22% of its total population.[22] Nazi programs demonstrated a totality of intention[20] that extended beyond the taking of lives to the dismantling of targeted groups' cultural artifacts and institutions: approximately 70% of all books in Poland were destroyed.

In Germany and Poland, synagogues were demolished and Jewish books and libraries were methodically burned, pulped, or confiscated for use in institutes devoted to addressing the "Jewish problem." Those institutes and any scholarship, whether "scientific" or "historical," that demonstrated the superiority of the Aryan race received generous funding. It is a common practice in extremist systems; all social and cultural institutions eventually become instruments of ideological promotion, and prejudice becomes intellectualized as fact.[20] Because cultural artifacts and institutions express identity in such a concrete fashion it becomes necessary to expunge from disputed territories any evidence of an opposing group. In Liberia, Burundi, and Rwanda, continuing racist acts of terrorism, ethnic cleansing, and related archival cleansing have almost completely destroyed all repositories and archives.[23]

"Ideology" can be defined broadly as any body of doctrine or thought. While sometimes used as a synonym for creeds and outlooks, twentieth-century historians and political scientists have increasingly leaned toward defining ideology as a *political* belief system that seeks the total reconstruction of society; it differs from creeds and outlooks in its greater explicitness, systematization, comprehensiveness, and urgency, as well as in the high intensity of concentration focused upon it.[24] To these scholars, ideology refers to an extremist sociopolitical program or philosophy constructed around a transforming idea. Political regimes use ideologies to organize beliefs and attitudes into a common, public, and broadly agreed-upon set of rules that help to regulate and control behavior in social and political contexts.[25] Ideologies replace traditional value systems, such as those based on religious or ethical principles.

In extremist political climates, both individual and cultural behavior must conform to the ideology. In the eyes of political extremists, for example, reading and research are political acts (their sole purpose being to further ideological goals) rather than inherently valuable activities that enrich the individual and advance the knowledge base of the human community. Citizens under an extremist regime need not—indeed, must not—have recourse to ideas that fall outside the ideological system of thought. A regime composed of ideologues does not regard "the disciplined pursuit of truth—by scientific procedures and in the mood characteristic of modern science—as part of its obligations" (p. 73).[24] The concepts of autonomous spheres of activity, an autonomous tradition of disciplined intellectual pursuits, and even the value of an individual's independent cognitive powers and strivings are alien to the orthodoxy demanded by an ideological orientation. Although strength appears to come from the unity of ideas, fear is the real source of power. Citizens fear their governments; ideologues fear books, any system in which information reaches the people, and unfettered scholarship and learning. Because ideologies thrive on intellectual closure, books and libraries fall under tremendous suspicion as entities that support both traditional systems and intellectual expansion and have the potential to influence individual perception and sow dissent.

In terms of psychological mechanisms, aggression against libraries can be seen as the result of a group's cultural predispositions that are activated—at least in part—by difficult conditions or "hard times." The psychological and cultural origins of mass killings (i.e., political violence) lie in responses to the social disintegration brought on by war and/or upheaval from rapid urbanization, secularization, and economic depression.[26] This same constellation of factors is also involved in violence to culture, the end product of a process set in motion by frustration, and an "underlying malaise in society that in

various ways blocks the paths to personal or collective fulfillment of basic human needs" (p. 4).[27] Populations most likely to turn to ideological solutions are those with inclinations toward authoritarian power structures and with established patterns of submission and conformity, punitive rejection of other groups, and a tendency to see the world in black and white.[25]

When individuals perceive security, well-being, self-concept, world view, and even life itself as threatened, and when cultural and social conditions create demands exceeding a people's resources to cope, then anger, resentment, and despair mount.[28] Traditional sociocultural and political patterns are discredited, and people turn to alternate visions—nationalism or Communism, for instance—that promise identity, hope, and control. In post-World War I Europe, the large and vague expectations on the part of millions of unemployed and uprooted peasants, war veterans, frontline heros, and dissatisfied students created a breeding ground for nationalism, which promised reassurance and novelty as well as shelter, food, stability, and jobs.[29] Nationalism subsequently took on fascist overtones and proffered the security of group identity, guidance, and structure. At the same time, in Russia Communism posed an alternate vision of an end to oppressive economic structures and the promise of an egalitarian and just society. In general, both fascist nationalism and Communism offered visions of a radically new and better world.

Political ideologies are particularly seductive in that they justify action in response to the victimization, frustration, and impotence brought on by hard times. Further, by identifying scapegoats, ideologies provide a channel for aggression stemming from this vulnerability. Identifying an enemy has beneficial psychological effects in times of chaos when there is no overt aggressor.[24] Any threat to well-being, safety, and survival can be construed as "the enemy," as when neighboring states or distant powers are seen as "thwarting" nationalist destiny, when other races "contaminate" bloodlines and prevent dominance by a master race, or when a class of society "sabotages" the revolution. Because any entity with this kind of potential is likely to have an institutionalized cultural framework that includes books and libraries, these material artifacts and institutions become targets.

Ideologies flourish under authoritarian regimes because they provide a philosophical basis for acquiescence and abandonment of the self, referred to by Erich Fromm[30] as "an escape from freedom." Under conditions of acute social stress, the freedom to claim privacy, to struggle with justice, injustice, and difficult life conditions, and to express ideas in a social context[25] is exchanged for the certainty and simplicity of ideology. Anxiety over basic needs and securities is exchanged for a closed intellectual system based on simple suppositions that explain and rationalize fate.[31] In a totalitarian system there is finally no separateness and no autonomous spheres, but also no authentic group life. Every facet of life is understood in terms of politics. The governing party demands total conformity and assumes an unchallengeable power to bind an entire people to its vision. Books are feared as an alternative voice—a voice not necessarily of dissent but of difference. When deified cult leaders and persuasive ideologies numb intellectual processes (not the least of which is doubt), citizens become agents of authority and suspend critical evaluation of the morality of an action. Both the leader and those followers who carry out acts of extreme violence share a psychological process that begins within fanaticism and progresses to antisocial behavior and then to an incapacity for empathy.[26] Neither human beings nor those cultural ideals (such as religious beliefs or humanism) or artifacts that were once held most dear are accorded value by the totalitarian government.

As the regime consolidates its power, ideology becomes a rationale for totalitarianism; ideological orthodoxy crowds out all dissent and difference, and conformity is imposed, if necessary, through violence. Because books and libraries preserve memory, provide witness, store evidence of the validity of a multitude of perspectives, facilitate intellectual freedom, and support group identity, they are carefully controlled, sanitized, and even extensively purged. When texts are too closely associated with an enemy, they are attacked along with the renegade group. When the human voice is extinguished, texts as the disembodied material expression of that voice are also destroyed.

During the twentieth century, post-Renaissance ideals of man using ideas to transform society and affect progress through reason took a toxic turn when ideologues redefined human advancement. Libraries became battlegrounds between humanists, for whom the destruction of books is the destruction of human potential—that which advances and uplifts individuals and society—and extremists for whom a specific instance of destruction is instrumental in bringing utopia and is thus a "liberating, redemptive act" for humanity (p. 30).[32] As we enter the twenty-first century, a humanism that accommodates pluralism and democracy will most likely remain on a collision course with ideologues, and the fate of books and libraries will remain problematic.

REFERENCES

1. Horowitz, I. *Genocide: State Power and Mass Miader.* Transaction: New Brunswick, NJ, 1976.
2. Chalk, F.; Jonassohn, K. *The History and Sociology of Genocide: Analyses and Case Studies*; Yale University Press: New Haven, CT, 1990.
3. Beardsley, M.C. Reflections on genocide and ethnocide. In *Genocide in Paraguay*; Arens, R., Ed.; Temple University Press: Philadelphia, PA, 1976; 85–101.
4. Kuper, L. *Genocide: Its Political Use in the Twentieth Century*; Yale University Press: New Haven, CT, 1981.
5. Knuth, R. *Libricide: The Violent Destruction of Books and Libraries in the 20th Century*; University of Toronto Press: Toronto, Canada (under contract).
6. Hobsbawm, E. Introduction: Inventing traditions. In *The Invention of Tradition*; Hobsbawm, E., Ranger, T., Eds.; Cambridge University Press: Cambridge, U.K., 1983; 1–14.
7. Harris, M.H. State, class, and cultural reproduction: Toward a theory of library science in the United states. In *Advances in Librarianship*; Simonton, W., Ed.; Academic: London, U.K., 1986; Vol. 14, 211–252.
8. MacLeish, A. Toward an intellectual offensive. ALA Bull. **1942**, *36* (6), 423–428.
9. Postman, N. *Technopoly: The Surrender of Culture to Technology*; Vintage: New York, 1992.
10. Blackey, R.; Paynton, R.; Paynton, C.T. *Revolution and the Revolutionary Ideal*; Schenkman: Cambridge, MA, 1976.
11. Blackey, R., Ed. *Revolutions and Revolutionists: A Comprehensive Guide to the Literature*; ABC-Clio: Santa Barbara, CA, 1982.
12. Thiem, J. The Great Library of Alexandria Burnt: Towards the history of a symbol. J. Hist. Ideas **1979**, *40* (4), 507–526.
13. Marx, K. *The 18th Brumaire of Louis Bonaparte*; International Publishers: New York, 1963.
14. Chapman, J. Destruction of a common heritage: The archaeology of war in Croatia, Bosnia and Hercegovina. Antiquity **1994**, *68* (258), 120–128.
15. Anderson, B. *Imagined Communities: Reflections on the Origin and the Spread of Nationalism*, rev. Ed.; Verso: New York, 1991.
16. Kohn, H. Nationalism. In *International Encyclopedia of the Social Sciences*; Sills, D.L., Ed.; MacMillan and Free Press: New York, 1968; Vol. 11, 63–69.
17. Berlin, I. *The Crooked Timber of Humanity: Chapters in the History of Ideas,* Hardy, H., Ed.; Knopf: New York, 1991.
18. Radway, L.I. Militarism. In *International Encyclopedia of the Social Sciences*; Sills, D.L., Ed.; Macmillan and Free Press: New York, 1968; Vol. 10, 300–305.
19. Lang, K. Military. In *International Encyclopedia of the Social Sciences*; Sills, D.L., Ed.; MacMillan and Free Press: New York, 1968; Vol. 11, 63–69.
20. Carlton, E. *War and Ideology*; Barnes & Noble: Savage, MD, 1990.
21. Gourevitch, P. *We Wish to Inform You That Tomorrow We Will Be Killed with Our Families: Stories From Rwanda*; Farrar Straus and Girous: New York, 1998.
22. Lukas, R.C. *The Forgotten Holocaust: The Poles Under Gernian Occupation, 1939–1944*; University Press of Kentucky: Lexington, KY, 1986.
23. UNESCO Memory of the World Program. In *Lost Memory: Libraries and Archives Destroyed in the Twentieth Century*; UNESCO: Paris, France, 1996.
24. Shils, E. The concept and function of ideology. In *Encyclopaedia of the Social Sciences*; Seligman, E., Ed.; Macmillan: New York, 1931; Vol. 7, 66–74.
25. Taylor, M. *The Fanatics: A Behavioural Approach to Political Violence*; Brassey's: London, U.K., 1991.

26. Staub, E. *Roots of Evil: The Origins of Genocide and Other Group Violence*; Cambridge University Press: Cambridge, U.K., 1989.

27. Lumsden, M. Sources of violence in the international system. In *International Violence*; Adeniran, T., Alexander, Y., Eds.; Praeger: New York, 1983; 3–19.

28. Marsella, A.J.; Yamada, A.M. Culture and mental health: An introduction and overview of foundations, concepts, and issues. In *The Handbook of Multicultural Mental Health: Assessment and Treatment of Diverse Populations*; Cuellar, I., Paniagua, F., Eds.; Academic: New York, 2000; 3–24.

29. Einaudi, M. Fascism. In *International Encyclopedia of the Social Sciences*; Sills, D.L., Ed.; Macmillan and Free Press: New York, 1968; Vol. 11, 334–341.

30. Fromm, E. *Escape from Freedom*; Holt, Rinehart & Winston: New York, 1941.

31. Bucheim, H. *Totalitarian Rule: It's Nature and Characteristics*; trans, by R. Heim, Wesleyan University Press: Middletown, CT, 1968.

32. Bartov, O. *Mirrors of Destruction: War, Genocide, and Modern Identity*; Oxford university Press: Oxford, U.K., 2000.

Still Image Indexing

Corinne Jörgensen
School of Information Studies, Florida State University, Tallahassee, Florida, U.S.A.

Abstract

General considerations in still image indexing are addressed, and theoretical foundations and major approaches to image indexing among several communities are explained. The most frequently used tools that support this endeavor are discussed. Newer approaches are considered, and major research topics for the future are presented.

INTRODUCTION

The topic of still image indexing has grown from a subject of interest primarily limited to a small community of professionals within libraries, archives, museums, and cultural heritage organizations, to a topic widely discussed not only in scholarly literature but also in the popular press. A major impetus for this expansion of interest has, without a doubt, been the rapid evolution of tools enabling the widespread creation of digital images, and the growth of networked collections of images available to ever-wider audiences through the Internet. Collections of images now range from groups of images posted by individuals on Web pages to shared collections such as those on the popular Flickr Web site to art and other museum exhibitions created and curated on Web sites or in virtual worlds such as Second Life. Finding images relevant not only to scholarly or professional interests but to a variety of personal interests is now a daily activity for millions of people across the world. This demand has stimulated the rapid expansion of commercial digital image services, and still image indexing is seen as an economic driver within the commercial sector, as well as an active area of scholarly research.

Still image indexing falls within the larger domain of visual information description and retrieval, that includes mechanisms for indexing and providing access to both still and moving images, as well as a variety of multimedia documents. For all these document types the single image (or frame for moving images) could be considered the most basic level of analysis. Therefore, the topic of still image indexing in this overview is referred to simply as "image indexing," with the understanding that this is referring to a fundamental and discrete unit of description of a single still image within a range of types of visual materials.

This entry covers general considerations in image indexing, theoretical foundations, and major approaches to image indexing among several communities, and the most frequently used tools that support this endeavor.

Newer approaches are considered, and major research topics for the future are presented.

CONSIDERATIONS IN IMAGE INDEXING

It should be noted that in the image indexing literature, "indexing," "classification," and "cataloging" may all be used informally to refer to the processes of assigning descriptors to images. Subject indexing is defined in a generalized sense, as "the indication of the theme or topic of any document, indeed any retrieval artifact, by any meaningful string of alphanumeric characters."[1] Kaiser takes the "reduction of literature to a smaller compass" as the common basis of these activities.[2] While the processes of reduction can differ (elimination, selection, concentration, recapitulation, and analysis), the goal remains the same, the creation of a succinct representation or surrogate for an item. It should also be noted, however, that in a continuum from subject cataloging to indexing, the general movement is toward increased term specificity and granularity of access.

Still image indexing is a process in which image features or attributes are selected for representation either by human indexers assigning textual descriptors or by a variety of digital methods, such as computer algorithms, that produce output representing features by text, numerals, mathematical formulas, or a combination of these. In the context of visual media, Medin and Barsalou propose a useful definition of an attribute: "any kind of feature, component, or property of a stimulus that can be represented by an information processing system." They continue: "We make no assumptions about the format of these representations... nor do we assume that the attributes correspond to innate detectors."[3] In this definition, "information processing system" includes both organizational and retrieval systems. An image attribute is therefore a feature, component, or property of a stimulus (an image) that can be represented by an information

Encyclopedia of Library and Information Sciences, Fourth Edition DOI: 10.1081/E-ELIS4-120044380

processing system. An image attribute is thus not limited to purely visual characteristics, but can include other cognitive, affective, or interpretive responses to the image such as those describing spatial, semantic, or emotional characteristics.

While there are a variety of issues associated with still image indexing, a major issue is the fact that still images by and large do not contain their own feature descriptors in a text format. A text document contains terms which themselves generally convey the subject or topic of a document, while an image may be "of" something but carry meanings that extend beyond the visual content, ranging from symbolic objects to abstract concepts. Bibliographic records associated with images typically give sparse, if any, visual content description. Visual percepts such as color and texture may also be difficult to describe with text, and many have commented on the inadequacy of language as a recording medium for describing image content that may essentially span several different domains. Image indexing languages, largely derived from traditional sources such as subject heading lists, often lack terminology that can convey either visual richness or symbolic, narrative, or affective aspects of an image, as these have been considered out of scope within standard indexing guidelines.

It is useful to employ several lenses through which to view progress in still image indexing. As noted above, the primary method of indexing images has been using text, placing it within the larger domains of document description and information retrieval research. Within the text domain, there has been a long-standing debate between proponents of free-text, or keyword, indexing vs. use of controlled vocabularies for document description. This debate extends back to the Cranfield II experiments that tested the retrieval capabilities of 33 indexing languages for text documents; this and subsequent studies found that a minimally controlled vocabulary (for instance, for word ending variants) performed as well as or better than a controlled vocabulary. (For a full discussion of controlled vocabularies, including their history, see Svenonius).[4] This debate continued through the rise of online subscription database indexing and searching services, the availability of full-text searchable databases, and continues today whenever discussions of the popular Web searching tool Google take place within the information industry. The more recent arrival of systems that allow end-users to "tag" items with descriptive terms has also created popular interest in what were once more esoteric discussions.

While this debate can be framed in terms of explicit questions concerning the functionality of these different types of access mechanisms, an implicit question also underlies this debate: the question of locus of authority. That is, which communities should be permitted to contribute to the mechanisms of document indexing, whether these be subject experts in museums or professional indexers developing controlled vocabularies, computer scientists who understand how to manipulate discrete packets of digital

information, or the end-user who knows what they want to call an object in an image, regardless of what others may select as an appropriate representation of it. This question has been brought to the forefront with systems that allow users to assign index terms, or "tags," to images and other documents. The development of image retrieval algorithms that operate directly on image components, bypassing text altogether, has also contributed to this debate.

This conflict between the desire for creating a perfect description and a user's simply finding the desired item still exists, while a middle ground is sought by institutions that grapple with it, and "it still remains to be seen if a middle ground between expert classification and no classification can be found in the process of determination of categories to enable users to browse image sets."[5] Others question the notion of "correct form" in relation to "findability," and suggest that limited time and resources would be better spent in putting in many words and phrases rather than laboring to produce "a few properly verified and expressed ones, particularly since so many of our potential users know little except the almost random nature of cyber searching."[6]

A variety of competing requirements and demands shape image indexing decisions within an organization. Among these are:

Collection considerations: These involve decisions such as whether to index the individual items within a collection or simply to provide a pointer to an entire collection. Granularity of indexing also becomes an issue as collections grow. Broad subject terms may be adequate for browsing and retrieval in a smaller collection, but do less to discriminate among images as their number increases. When cataloging is at the collection level, then providing links among related collections must be considered. Additionally, providing meaningful links among specific items within collections may also be desirable.

User considerations: User-centered indexing (as opposed to document-centered indexing) is considered by many to be basic to meeting users' information needs. Indexing can be oriented to the users of a specific collection [as has been done with the development of domain-specific thesauri such as the *Art & Architecture Thesaurus* (*AAT*)] or toward the needs of specific types of users, as has been done for stock photography collections with the addition of attributes of interest to graphic designers and other publication professionals (e.g., terms relating to image orientation or composition). However, determining the user group becomes more difficult in the digital environment, and images, with their various interpretations, can serve multiple user audiences and needs.

Vocabulary considerations: The decision as to which controlled vocabulary to use (if any) relates to both user and collection considerations. Choices include controlled vocabulary tools such as a thesaurus or subject headings, the use of free-text description in the form of keywords, or the use of associated texts such as captions, surrounding text, or literary works of critical analysis and interpretation. Each of these choices requires further decisions as to what kinds of structures should carry the indexing terms, or what kinds of tools are needed to enable selection of terms for indexing. While the type of collection and its typical users often determine the choice of vocabulary, there has been little empirical work testing the utility or the outcomes of these various vocabulary choices in relation to user needs. A more general image indexing vocabulary, to complement the domain- and collection-specific ones in existence, would also assist in indexing images across collections.

Image considerations: There are a number of decisions to be made concerning the access points provided for individual items. These relate to the scope of the indexing and whether indexing is limited to visual content such as the objects in an image, or will include higher-level semantic and interpretive aspects of images (symbolic meanings, aboutness), and image complexity. An additional consideration is whether to provide links among these multiple levels. These decisions obviously impact on the vocabulary considerations and should be contemplated in light of user and collection considerations as well.

Context considerations: These relate to information that is external to the image, such as the circumstances of production and the history of the item. Other factors (especially in the case of an image of an art object or cultural artifact) would be technique, medium, and other facets related to the production of the original item. Some recommend an archival perspective, speaking of what can be lost when cataloging or indexing of images takes place without regard to context. Standard access points such as country, ethnic group, content, source, and subject used in image collections are not enough to convey the larger value or meaning that an individual image may have as part of a larger collection. When an image is considered as an objective and independent entity, apart from other related works in a collection, the collection becomes an "infinite catalog of random observation."[7] Krause also argued early for providing additional indexing of the "soft" aspects of pictures, cultural, and historical meanings that may be clear such as "horrors of war," or "inner-city decay."[8] Of course, these meanings are also subject to change as history, cultures, and understandings and interpretations change.

As this brief overview reveals, the framework of image indexing decisions is complex and these decisions are not mutually exclusive of one another. Within these multiple

and sometimes conflicting perspectives this overview covers the theoretical foundations of image indexing, the tools and technologies typically employed in the process, and how the knowledge base underlying this activity is being impacted by advances in cognitive psychology, empirical research aimed at understanding users of image collections, and end-user image indexing behavior within individual and social contexts.

Frameworks for Image Indexing

A framework adopted by many authors for considering still image indexing utilizes two major indexing approaches, "concept based," and "content based," based upon the historical development of tools and technologies employed in the indexing process by two largely different communities.[9] Concept-based indexing refers to the use of text descriptors assigned to images by human indexers, whether these are selected from some type of controlled vocabulary or are natural language that is either assigned or drawn from accompanying text sources. Index terms cover the subject of the image and may include important people, events, objects, dates or time periods, locations, relationships, and meanings. Affective components or emotional impact of an image are usually considered out of scope. While this is the traditional approach most libraries, museums, and archives have adopted, indexing in this manner is time consuming and labor intensive, and thus expensive, and indexing consistency can vary greatly among indexers, collections, and institutions.

In contrast, the second approach, content-based indexing (usually referred to as content-based retrieval (CBR) because of its methods of implementation) uses image processing methods from computer science to "parse" images into mathematically describable components such as color, texture, shape, edges, and regions and assign labels or codes (that may or may not be human-readable) to these. This approach has the ability to process large numbers of images automatically and with some degree of consistency, but does not necessarily address features of interest to searchers.

While this framework provides a convenient starting point for discussing a variety of image indexing methods, tools, and technologies that have been researched and adopted, it does not directly address the underlying theories supporting each approach. Nor is the separation between the two approaches as distinct as this framework would suggest. In an "ideal" implementation, each approach aims for a complex and complete description of an image that will serve the retrieval needs of image searchers, and both draw upon theories that recognize the necessity for multiple levels of description. Each approach has evolved separately within different communities of practitioners and researchers and both approaches suffer from technical limitations. Content-based retrieval has focused primarily on the digital image, bypassing many of the other considerations surrounding indexing decisions, such as those discussed above. Concept-based retrieval, in contrast, has focused primarily on the users that particular institutions typically serve (as is appropriate) but have failed to recognize the power that an image gains when it becomes digital: the ability to reach a much larger audience and serve multiple purposes and needs. Many researchers are now recognizing that the most fruitful approach may be some combination of methods that utilizes the most powerful and appropriate aspects of several different approaches to the particular tasks at hand.

CONCEPT-BASED INDEXING

History

A number of communities have contributed to the development of concept-based image indexing methods. Historically, indexing of images has taken place largely within libraries, museums, and archives, where the need for access to and use of images is often immediate and tied to the particular tasks of a user community, such as teaching or research. Description has largely been accomplished through the use of some form of controlled vocabulary, considered a necessity as natural language lacks precision and order and can create many access problems in both physical and digital storage and retrieval systems. However, there is also an underlying tension existing in indexing of images or images of objects: the need to preserve the uniqueness of the object or image (especially as represented by written records of an art historical nature), while providing access to the object through some type of controlled vocabulary within an information retrieval system.

Although slide collections were in existence by the 1880s, the earliest slide and picture librarians had few resources to draw upon through the first half of the twentieth century. Broad subject access was provided through subject heading lists and reflected a practical orientation, responding both to user needs and a need to organize physical collections, yielding very limited multiple access points. Hierarchies were typically shallow, and the consistency, depth, and breadth varied considerably both within and across individual systems. (One of the earliest was The Picture Collection: Subject Headings, first published in 1910 as part of The Picture Collection by John Cotton Dana.[10] Current image indexing systems developed for specific collections still share a pragmatic, collection- and user-centered focus,[11] and these locally developed vocabularies often supplement more standard controlled vocabularies.[12]

The art history and museum communities have focused on images as objects in their own right (as cultural heritage) or as surrogates for art or museum objects. Art/museum image indexing serves a variety of purposes, such

as management of inventory, documentation of provenance, and preservation of fragile original materials, and distinguishing between the original and a surrogate are of particular concern. As museums are mostly concerned with unique items, more specialized terminology is desirable, and correct application of this terminology is paramount. Most art-oriented controlled vocabulary systems have followed a basic hierarchical structure starting with medium, and subdivided by period, country, geographical or cultural area, artist, and subject or type of object. Many of these have been developed in academic settings and are still in use today.

Theoretical Basis

Erwin Panofsky's discussion of the question of meaning in art[13,14] forms the basis for much of the theoretical work that has been done on the description and classification of images, including nonart images. Following initial visual perception of image fundamentals such as colors and shapes, Panofsky describes three successive levels of a viewer's understanding and interpretation, moving from the "of," or visual content of the image, to the "about," or the meaning of the image. The first level of pre-iconographical description requires only knowledge acquired from practical, everyday experience to interpret objects that primitives such as colors and shapes represent. Iconographical analysis draws upon literary and cultural sources for understanding aspects such as symbolism, and iconological interpretation may involve multiple subjective interpretations. Iconography is an important part of art historical description, but may also lead to information loss and increasing levels of subjectivity, as interpretive and symbolic meanings become the major access points and description of visual content is de-emphasized.

Given that one of the aims of indexing is to increase consistency in retrieval, consistency in indexing has been a prime goal of all indexing systems, and subjective aspects of images have generally been considered out of scope in most general indexing systems.

Shatford,[15] concerned with the lack of a theoretical basis for construction of subject-oriented organizational schemes for pictures, combined Panofsky's work with standard classification theory to provide an expanded basis for image classification. She proposes that a single image will have many meanings, from the specific object that the image represents (the Golden Gate Bridge) to generic or abstract words ("bridge" or "architecture"). She then extends the concept of "Generic Of" and "Specific Of," as well as the concept of "About," (derived from Panofsky's first and second levels) to a faceted classification system capable of answering a series of questions such as Who, What, When, and Where within each of these levels. She proposes that, as a minimum, an image should be indexed with both the "Generic Of" (skyscraper, office building) and "Specific Of" (Empire State Building).

The purpose of her system is to prevent possible useful subjects from being overlooked by those who are classifying or indexing these pictures. She cautions that any system for classification must be used within the context of the nature of a specific collection, and that until further research is done on types of user requests, the indexer should concentrate on the main subject of a picture within the framework of a special vs. a general collection. However, even determining the "main subject" of a picture can be complex, and depends upon the classifier's point of view. The main contribution this work makes to the image indexing community has been to emphasize the two major components to think about when indexing images, the "of" and the "about" of an image.

Tools

There are three major components of textual image description: 1) the terms used to describe the images, and the tools used to derive these image descriptors; 2) rules for when these terms or descriptors should be applied; and 3) a structure that stores and organizes the terms, such as fields in a database or metadata structures. More succinctly, these are often referred to as:

Data *value* tools provide values or terminology for representation

Data *content* tools provide guidelines for how terms are chosen and applied

Data *structure* tools organize and house the terms or values

Indexing and classification are processes in which images are described by employing data value tools and data content tools to determine and select terms appropriate to represent an image's features. Data structure tools organize these terms into a framework and may give them additional functionalities. An additional type of tool is a data "communication" tool, used for sharing information between data structures. While these tools are often discussed independently, their ability to facilitate image description is interdependent on all of them. A term for an image feature cannot be selected from a data value tool if there is no defined structure that will accept it, and likewise a data structure tool may be rich in what it can represent but values must be available to populate these structures. Tools such as these often develop into accepted standards.

Data value tools

Controlled vocabularies such as subject heading lists and thesauri are typical and widely used data value tools. Image indexing often relies on the use of a thesaurus rather than a list of subject headings for increased specificity in description. A thesaurus contains, in addition to controlled vocabulary terms, logical and semantic relationships among

terms. Svenonius notes that the language of art can be particularly problematic in creating controlled vocabularies for visual materials. It is rich in synonymy, shades of meaning are sometimes considered critical, and determining warrant for usage is complex; no one term may be dominant, and different specialties may prefer different terms, necessitating the incorporation of linguistic diversity.[16]

Another more serious problem for art thesaurus design concerns the description of objects of material culture, the objects and artifacts produced by a culture, including all those objects associated with their daily activities. When thesauri are constructed drawing upon frequently used terminology from the documents of a particular domain (a practice known as "literary warrant," where frequency of usage provides the authority for inclusion), the range of terms is limited to those occurring in the literature of that domain. However, in a thesaurus being used in museums for descriptions of objects of material culture as well as art, objects may go well beyond those normally considered within the literature of art history, and the number and type of objects needing description is potentially limitless. When object names are included in a thesaurus as compound terms (e.g., "iron hammer"), any frequently occurring term (e.g., the types of hammers and materials from which they are constructed) can cause an unacceptable burgeoning of the thesaurus. A faceted approach can limit the number of terms needed by allowing compound terms to be constructed from different facets (e.g., materials and types of tools), but limiting compound terms within a thesaurus can also constrain useful hierarchical structures that provide domain knowledge about how an item may be classified by a particular culture.

Two major data value tools are used in image indexing: the Library of Congress's *Thesaurus for Graphic Materials* (*TGM*) and the *AAT*. These two tools exemplify established approaches to the development of controlled vocabularies for image indexing and illustrate the issues associated with each approach. The main source of terminology for the first edition of the *TGM* was the *Library of Congress Subject Headings* (*LCSH*), itself drawn from subject matter within the collections of the Library of Congress, including the Library of Congress Prints and Photographs Division whose collections range from documentary photographs and architectural drawings to editorial cartoons and fine prints. The *TGM* was designed to provide "a substantial body of terms for subject indexing of pictures, particularly large general collections of historical images" through a controlled vocabulary "for describing a broad range of subjects, including activities, objects, and types of people, events, and places." Its historical focus extends to some abstract ideas found in allegorical prints and editorial cartoons.[17] New terms are added to the *TGM* as the topic is encountered in the course of cataloging and indexing. Cataloging projects (such as LC's American Memory project) and the disparate nature of indexing activities also give rise to variation in the selection and application of the indexing vocabulary. The TGM currently contains over 7000 terms.

The *AAT*, unlike the *TGM*, was constructed independently of the cataloging operations of any single institution.[18] It was designed to provide terminology for indexing the art, architecture, and material culture of the Western world from antiquity on, and it incorporates art historical and other highly specific concepts that relate to the creation, description, and appreciation of art and architecture. The *AAT* vocabulary was developed inductively using the concept of literary warrant and was developed to a high level of specificity in constructing the hierarchies that compose it. It is a compiled resource with contributors from outside institutions, as well as from internal Getty projects, and undergoes continuing scholarly review. The Getty is currently developing the Cultural Objects Name Authority, expected to join its other two name authority files (the *Union List of Artists Names*® or *ULAN*, and the Getty *Thesaurus of Geographic Names*® or TGN) in 2011. These vocabularies, available online, together comprise the Getty Vocabularies and are updated every month. The *AAT* contains about 34,000 concepts and 131,000 terms and is organized in over 30 hierarchies within its seven top-level facets: Associated Concepts; Physical Attributes; Styles and Periods; Agents; Activities; Materials; and Objects.

Neither of these two tools includes the more specialized iconographical terms found in *Iconclass*,[19] a hierarchically ordered collection of definitions of objects, persons, events, and abstract ideas that can be the subject of an image. It has 10 main divisions reflecting its primary concerns: subjects, themes, and the iconographical interpretation of images. The divisions consist of general areas such as religion and magic, nature, human beings, society and culture, and abstract ideas and concepts, and "special" topics such as history, the Bible, and mythology. *Iconclass* uses alphanumerical classification codes, and notations begin with a digit corresponding to one of its 10 main divisions. Every notation is part of a hierarchical structure and thus incorporates all of the iconographically broader terms in the hierarchy above it. This systematic classification has advantages over both uncontrolled and controlled vocabulary terms, as it can facilitate automatic searching up or down the hierarchy. For example, a search for paintings of flowers can return paintings of different kinds of flowers, without having to name each type individually. Additionally, the notational system is independent of language but can still be approached through natural language.

Issues with the *TGM* include a high degree of pre-coordination (compound terms formed from two terms that may be from different hierarchies, e.g., "straw hat" and "cowboy hat"), reflecting its origins in the *LCSH* and limiting the usefulness of much of the terminology (for instance, the ability to construct a term such as "straw cowboy hat"). It also lacks a true genus–species

relationship among many parent–child terms, contributing to an overall lack of specificity. In contrast, the *AAT* and *Iconclass* contain highly specialized or technical terms, often requiring indexers to consider terms appearing across several different facets and within a number of hierarchies. This, combined with the technical nature of these indexing languages results in the need for extensive training in their use and also in increased indexing time. These types of tools, by their nature, have more difficulty responding quickly to evolving patterns of usage.

Data content tools

Indexing should accomplish two goals: first, providing access to individual documents through specific attributes, and second, providing a means to form groups of like documents. Guidelines for terminology selection in the broad area of image indexing remain largely informal. Decisions as to depth of indexing are a consistent problem encountered across indexers and collections. Elings[20] describes the conflict:

> Subject indexing, depending on how it is applied, can offer the user broad or specific access to these collections. Broad subject indexing helps to unify collections by their content and can aid researchers at a higher level of information retrieval. Specific indexing can be time consuming for the cataloger but rewarding to the researcher. Too much specificity, however, can become an issue of indexing vs. analysis. In the end, the cataloger's task is to make the information broadly available and to provide some reasonable level of access. It is still up to the researcher to interpret the content and analyze the collection at a very specific level.

Shatford[15] proposes three questions to consider in relation to attributes to be indexed: which attributes need to be indexed, which can simply be noted in conjunction with the image, and which may be left to the searcher to perceive. These questions must be considered in relation to the type of collection and its users.

Several of the major data value tools for images provide general guidelines. The introduction to the *TGM* (http://www.loc.gov/rr/print/tgm1/iia.html) discusses some of the multiple aspects of pictures that catalogers should consider when trying to decide which subjects to index, such as historical significance or novel aspects of the subject matter, whether the subject is better represented elsewhere, the relationship of an item to other materials or collections, whether a particular point of view or message necessitates the indexing of the image's context, and image content that is unique primary evidence of a particular time and place.[21] The indexing should also provide both the specific (of) and generic (about) levels of access. These guidelines point to the particular emphasis of the *TGM* on historical and collection-level access. The *Thesaurus*

Iconographique, widely used in French museums, provides similar guidelines,[22] while the *AAT* provides more detailed instructions for use.

Until recently, there has not been a data content tool comparable to those data value tools available for unique art and material culture objects. The creation of *Cataloging Cultural Objects: A Guide to Describing Cultural Works and Their Images* (CCO) was designed to fill this gap.[23] While the primary focus of *CCO* is art and architecture, it also covers many other types of cultural works, including built works, installations, archaeological sites, artifacts, and functional objects from the realm of material culture. This tool is designed to provide guidance in structuring the elements of description and recommends the use of accepted data value tools, as well mapping to core data structure tools.

Data structure tools

Data structure tools, frequently developed as metadata frameworks, organize the terms representing image attributes. The need to share object and collection information in a networked environment has stimulated a number of recent metadata standardization efforts and exchange formats. A shared metadata structure enables interoperability and information exchange. This, coupled with the adoption of standardized sources for controlled vocabulary, can facilitate description consistency and shared cataloging efforts across multiple institutions.

The *Categories for the Description of Works of Art* (*CDWA*) was originally created by the Art Information Task Force and was intended to guide decisions about what information should be included in art information systems.[24] The need to "uniquely and unambiguously" identify particular art or museum objects or cultural artifacts guided the identification of core categories that can be modified according to local need and practice. Now part of the Getty Standards Program, it includes 512 categories and subcategories and can distinguish between information intrinsic to the work and information (related persons, places, and concepts) extrinsic to the work. Extrinsic information is stored in separate authorities that can then be reused. The *CDWA* also distinguishes between information for display (full descriptive texts) and information for retrieval, and for the latter recommends carefully chosen controlled vocabularies and authorities. A core set, designed to enhance accessibility across databases, includes Object/Work, Classification, Titles or Names, Creation, Measurements, Materials and Techniques, Subject Matter, Current Location, and Related Textual References, as well as core authorities: Person/Corporate Body, Place/Location, Generic Concept, and Subject.

Core categories for visual resources. Developed by the Visual Resources Association (VRA) Data Standards Committee, the *VRA Core* is an adaptation of the *CDWA* expanded to cover architecture and site-specific structures.[25] It provides metadata categories for the description of "works of visual culture as well as the images that document them" (VRA 2000). The Core is designed to facilitate sharing of information about visual works and is not intended as a complete set of elements; therefore, it can be extended by adding fields according to local needs. The latest version, *VRA Core 4.0*, contains changes that more easily enable its expression in XML.

Dublin core. The least-complex metadata structure discussed here is the Dublin Core (DC), which has been extended to accommodate visual materials. The "Simple Dublin Core" 15-element set is intended to facilitate discovery of resources in a networked environment. The *DC* has been developed through a series of workshops sponsored by Online Computer Library Center, Inc. (OCLC) and such cosponsors as the National Center for Supercomputing Applications, and the Coalition for Networked Information (CNI). The third workshop focused on description of visual resources of a particular kind, discrete images that can be identified as bounded or fixed (in the sense that the resource looks the same to all users). One conclusion of the workshop was that images and text are quite similar in their "discovery" requirements (CNI/OCLC Image Metadata Workshop, September 24–25, 1996, Dublin, Ohio). Thus, development of this metadata scheme has proceeded with the goal of formulating one structure for both images and text.[26] The Qualified DC includes three additional elements and has added qualifiers to support additional functionalities.

CONTENT-BASED INDEXING

Image indexing utilizing the techniques of computer processing of images is referred to as content-based indexing, or, more commonly CBR or content-based image retrieval. Images that are not "born digital" can be converted from an analog to a digital format, enabling automated feature extraction, computation, manipulation, and to some degree interpretation. Electronic images can be defined as "sets of data" and the term "pixel" refers to a single measurement within an image produced by this method. Image features such as color and texture are derived directly from the pixels in an image. A pixel, or group of pixels, while being a basic unit of measurement of the visual content of a digital image, will not necessarily map to what we would call an "indexing term."

Theories of Cognitive Processing

Much of the current work supporting machine processing of images comes from earlier research in artificial intelligence and machine vision, with the goal of recognition and automatic classification of objects (a useful introductory text is by R.C. Jain in Jain).[27] Research in cognitive science may be informative in several ways: for defining models of image similarity; for determining those image features having priority in the indexing process; and as models for machine processing of images. Evidence suggests that a number of different image attributes and relationships interact in the process of perceiving, understanding, and remembering an image. Many of the cognitive theories of perception have been used as models for complex methods of computer image processing that build from lower levels of color, texture, and shape to object recognition to object identification within limited domains.

Visual perception is thought to begin when an image or scene is decomposed into primitive elements such as color, motion, orientation, depth, contrast, and spatial resolution; shape and spatial relations are extracted and primitive features are assembled into larger objects and scenes. Elements that share the same information are grouped together perceptually, and grouping mechanisms override their individual constituents, whether of shape, size, color, or motion; an image, therefore, is perceived as a whole entity, or a "Gestalt," before its individual components are perceived. Contextual organizational principles known as the Gestalt principles[28] thus appear to organize parts of a picture into regions and objects that are perceived before the component parts are. This theory suggests an object or image in a Gestalt possesses features that are not inherent in the smaller features or regions from which the object or image is assembled. Gestalt theory holds that overall form, rather than lower level features, is the fundamental unit of perception, and perception of form is governed by cognitive rather than sensory processes. Eye-tracking experiments demonstrate that fixations occur in specific areas that correlate with both the Gestalt principles of "good form" (which describe perception of visual constructs such as texture, e.g., objects in proximity are perceived as a single entity) and experimental results in image memory: areas of detail; contrast, contours, and unfamiliar features considered to be of "low predictability." The Gestalt principles are today widely used in graphic design.

Other theories, such as *Recognition by Components*, suggest that an understanding of an object is facilitated by a process that assembles low-level features into larger understandable regions.[29] Physiological research demonstrating selective response of cells in the visual cortex to features in specific orientations supports these feature-based models. Even though patterns can vary, relationships among local features that are the most important to the pattern hold, thus allowing many varying images of an item to be recognized as a member of a class. While both the physical and semantic relations of objects in the visual field appear to affect interpretation and understanding, it is still not known exactly how these processes work, or if one takes precedence over the other at different points in the processing.

Tools

CBR

The analysis process for machine vision tries to determine the composition of complex objects in terms of simpler objects. Complex objects are defined using composition rules and constraints among the objects composing the complex object. Thus, machine processing of images proceeds by segmenting an image into processable units and performing some kind of analysis of these units in order to end up with a description in terms of specific features. Object recognition and image understanding involve moving from lower to higher levels of abstraction and require increasing levels of inference and reasoning. Lower level output of these processes can consist of color representations such as histograms, and an image composed of one or several such features is represented by fixed-length feature vectors with multiple real values. Higher level output can consist of either labeled graphic output or textual description. Such image processing involves both a loss of information at lower levels and computational complexity from increasing levels of inference and reasoning.

While machine vision has been an active field of research for several decades, CBR is a more recent application of these techniques. In the vocabulary of CBR, an image is represented by a "signature," composed of features such as color derived from its pixel values. Retrieval operates by defined rules for comparing features. Features may be either "global" or "local." A global feature represents the image in its entirety, such as the overall color distribution. Local features are determined by segmentation of the image into smaller regions using color, texture, and shape and can be used to identify objects within an image. From the perspective of CBR, image statistics produced by these methods could be sufficient for helping users find desired images, but in reality these methods are largely limited to searching for images with a similar distribution of image properties or features (color, texture, edges, and regions). While a wide range of features and query types is defined as being in the realm of CBR, in practice most research has focused on low-level features that can be extracted automatically.

Within computer science the lower syntactic levels have been extensively researched, producing multiple processing methods, and some systems operating on these principles are now in use. One early system, known as QBIC (for Query by Image Content, thus where the expression "CBR" comes from) was developed using IBM's technology. It utilizes a visual query constructed by a searcher as search input and matches this against stored image signatures representing features such as color, shape, and texture. This method is known as Query by Visual Example or QBVE. Some museums, most notably the State Hermitage Museum in St. Petersburg, Russia, have adopted this method as a search tool for their digital image collections.[30]

One difficulty with these systems has been the requirement that searchers construct an input image composed of primitives such as a round red object over a large blue area to represent a sunset over water; these searches are more useful when a searcher requires a specific layout, but less useful when a searcher wishes to search on concepts. Another difficulty is that multiple types of objects, for instance, pumpkins as well as sunsets, will be retrieved by the visual matching algorithms, confusing and frustrating searchers. Once a searcher finds an image similar to the one sought for, the searcher can then query the system to retrieve images that are visually similar.

The gap between what can be derived computationally and what a human might assign as an indexing term or use as a search term for an image has been referred to widely in the literature as the "semantic gap," or the gap between human similarity judgments that are based on multiple factors and visual similarity, based on a more constrained set of attributes. Current machine processing capabilities are limited in bridging computable low-level features and regions and higher inferential levels such as object identification, abstract concepts, symbols, and meanings. An early model attempting to bridge this gap and unify content and concept-based indexing is a 10 level "pyramid" that builds from syntactic features to interpretive levels of generic, specific, and abstract object understanding and meaning.[31] Efforts to build semantic retrieval systems rely on methods of machine learning (derived from neural network models) using a set of labeled or captioned images as input to develop models of common semantic concepts. However, these systems are limited in that the system has no way to learn concepts that are not labeled. This method is further extended by the Query by Semantic Example method that uses an input image rather than a text query.[32] This input image can be translated into an internal semantic representation expanding the range of possibilities among image features that may be matched. While success is still limited, this approach is showing more promise than just matching on visual features that possess limited similarity value in the context of many image queries.

IMAGE TAGGING SYSTEMS

Within image indexing, the issue of "locus of authority" comes into play at the level of the semantic gap (while the term "semantic gap" came into existence in the context of content-based retrieval, many would argue that it also applies to differences in image description between communities of scholars and end-searcher communities who may have very different needs), and most notably in discussion of workflow considerations in organizations doing image indexing. The volume of visual materials needing access points is overtaking the ability of standard processes to handle them in the controlled way seen necessary for bibliographic description. At the same time, systems that allow users to view and share items are also providing means for those same users to describe these items, through an informal process of assigning natural language terms, or tags, to items. While the phenomenon of social tagging is beyond this discussion, museums, libraries, and archives with visual collections (as well as commercial sites such as Flickr) are leading the way in providing tagging utilities for their users. Tagging is seen as a low-cost, if somewhat uncontrolled, method of providing multiple access points for these visual documents. There are currently several projects undertaking evaluation of tags supplied for image collections, the most notable being the steve project (http://www.steve.museum) that has a number of museums implementing tagging of their digital images and an active research community around these efforts. The appropriateness of tagging for these collections and the role that tagging will play in increasing access to image collections remains to be seen, but early results are demonstrating value in the increased number of access points being provided. There are a number of interesting questions remaining, such as how tags can best interface with existing descriptions, and what additional sources, such as associated texts, could supply tags.

CONCLUSION

A great many tools have been developed for still image indexing in the past several decades. There is an evolving consensus that both controlled vocabularies and natural language descriptions are useful, depending upon the information exposed to the search tool, the mode of searching (browsing versus known-item search), and whether precision or recall is more important to the task. We have reached the point where more empirical research is needed to establish within what contexts searchers gain the greatest utility from the variety of tools available. There is much fascinating research remaining to be done in the area of still image indexing and in visual retrieval in general. Standardized test beds for different methods remain lacking, as do easily used integrated indexing records (that can accommodate data in a variety of formats), and studies of end-user image searching remain scarce. Indeed, decisions as to what to index are complex, knowledge about image searching is incomplete, guidelines and tools are plentiful but evaluations of these are scarce as well, and many valuable access points are potentially lost in the indexing process unless a variety of searchers and needs are taken into consideration.

REFERENCES

1. Chan, L.M.; Richmond, P.A.; Svenonius, E., Eds. *Theory of Subject Analysis: A Sourcebook*; Libraries Unlimited: Littleton, CO, 1985; xii–xiv.

2. Kaiser, J.O. Systematic indexing. In *Theory of Subject Analysis*; Chan, L.M.; Richmond, P.A.; Svenonius, E., Eds.; Libraries Unlimited: Littleton, CO, 1985; 305. (Note: This is a reprint of an article originally published in 1911).

3. Medin, D.L.; Barsalou, L.W. Categorization processes and categorical perception. In *Categorical Perception*; Harnad, S., Ed.; Cambridge University Press: New York, 1987, 485.

4. Svenonius, E. Design of controlled vocabularies. In *Encyclopedia of Library and Information Science*; Drake, M., Ed.; CRC Press: New York, 2003; Vol. 2, 822–838.

5. Frost, C.O. The University of Michigan School of Information Art Image Browser: Designing and testing a model for image retrieval. In *Knowledge Organization and Change*; Green, R., Ed.; Indeks Verlag: Frankfurt/Main, Germany, 1996; Vol. 5, 187.

6. Fry, E. Image access and cyber searching: The Philadelphia experiment. Art Doc. **1998**, *17* (2), 52.

7. Ohrn, S.G. *Cataloguing in Context: The African Studies Program Slide Archives*; African Studies Program, Indiana University: Bloomington, IN, 1975; 16–20.

8. Krause, M.G. Intellectual problems of indexing picture collections. Audiov. Libr. **1988**, *14* (2), 73–81.

9. Enser, P.G.B. Visual image retrieval: Seeking the alliance of concept-based and content-based paradigms. J. Inf. Sci. **2000**, *26* (4), 199–210.

10. Dane, W.J. The Picture Collection, 6th Ed.; Shoe String Press: Hamden, CT, 1968.

11. Schroeder, K.A. Layered indexing of images at the General Motors Media Archives. The Indexer **1998**, *21* (1), 11–14. (See also Australian Pictorial Thesaurus, http://www.picturethesaurus.gov.au/) (accessed October 4, 2008).

12. Graham, M.E. *The Description and Indexing of Images: Report of a Survey of ARLIS Members, 1998/99*; University of Northumbria: Newcastle, U.K., 1999.

13. Panofsky, E. *Meaning in the Visual Arts: Papers in and on Art History*; Doubleday Anchor Books: Garden City, NY, 1955.

14. Panofsky, E. Studies in Iconology, Reprint Ed.; Harper & Row: New York, 1962.

15. Shatford, S. Analyzing the subject of a picture: A theoretical approach. Catalog. Classif. Quart. **1986**, *6* (3), 39–62.

16. Svenonius, E. Thesauri. In *Automatic Processing of Art History Data and Documents*; Corti, L., Schmitt, M., Eds.; J. Paul Getty Trust: Los Angeles, CA, 1984; 33–48.

17. Parker, E.B. *LC Thesaurus for Graphic Materials: Topical Terms for Subject Access*; With an introduction by Jackie, M. Dooley. Library of Congress: Washington, DC, 1987, viii, http://www.loc.gov/rr/print/tgm1/

18. http://www.getty.edu/research/conducting_research/vocabularies/ (accessed October 4, 2008).

19. http://www.iconclass.nl/ (accessed October 4, 2008).

20. Elings, M.W. Pictorial archives and EAD: Indexing collections for online access. Art Doc. **2000**, *19* (2), 13.

21. Parker, E.B. *LC Thesaurus for Graphic Materials: Topical Terms for Subject Access*; With an introduction by Jackie M. Dooley. Library of Congress: Washington, DC, 1987; xiv–xv.

22. Garnier, F. *Thesaurus Iconographique, système descriptif des représentations*; Le Leopold d'Or: Paris, France, 1984; 17–29.

23. http://www.vrafoundation.org/ccoweb/cco/about.html (accessed October 4, 2008).

24. http://www.getty.edu/research/conducting_research/standards/cdwa/index.html (accessed October 4, 2008).

25. http://www.vraweb.org/projects/vracore4/index.html (accessed October 4, 2008).

26. Weibel, S.L.; Koch, T. The Dublin Core Metadata Initiative: Mission, current activities, and future directions. D-Lib. Mag. **2000**, *6*(12). http://www.dlib.org/dlib/december00/weibel/12weibel.html.

27. Jain, R.C.; Kasturi, R.; Schunck, B.G. *Machine Vision*, McGraw-Hill Series in Computer Science, Liu, C.L., Ed.; McGraw-Hill: New York, 1995.

28. Wertheimer, M. Principles of perceptual organization. In *Readings in Perception*; Beardslee, D.C., Wertheimer, M., Eds.; D. Van Nostrand Company: Princeton, NJ, 1958; 115–135.

29. Biederman, I. Recognition-by-components: A theory of human image understanding. Psychol. Rev. **1987**, *94* (2), 115–147.

30. http://www.hermitagemuseum.org/fcgi-bin/db2www/qbicSearch.mac/qbic?selLang = English (accessed October 4, 2008).

31. Jaimes, A.; Chang, S.-F. *A Conceptual Framework for Indexing Visual Information at Multiple Levels*. A paper delivered at the Internet Imaging conference, San Jose, CA, January 2000.

32. Vasconcelos, N. From pixels to semantic spaces: Advances in content-based image retrieval. IEEE Comput. **2007**, *40* (7), 20–26.

BIBLIOGRAPHY

Many of these topics and sources are discussed in much further detail in the following items:

1. An overview of the Gestalt principles and their application in design may be found in the paper "Identifying Commonly-Used Gestalt Principles as a Design Framework for Multi-Sensory Displays," by Chang and Nesbitt in *Systems, Man and Cybernetics 2006*. SMC '06, 3: 2452–2457.

2. For more details of human visual processes, the reader is referred to books such as Gregory's *Eye and Brain* and Hendee's *The Perception of Visual Information* (Gregory, 1997; Hendee and Wells, 1997). A good nontechnical introduction can also be found in Hoffman's *Visual Intelligence* (Hoffman, 2000).

3. For more detailed information on visual perception, the reader is referred to the excellent chapter for the lay reader, "Light, Color, and Shape: The Science of Vision," *In the Eye of the Beholder* (Bruce and Young, 1998).

4. Jörgensen, C. *Image Retrieval: Theory and Research*; Scarecrow Press: Latham, MD, 2003.

Still Image Search and Retrieval

Vittorio Castelli
T.J. Watson Research Center, IBM, Yorktown Heights, New York, U.S.A.

Abstract

We describe approaches and techniques for indexing and retrieving still images from multimedia databases. We specifically emphasize content-based image retrieval (CBIR), a class of techniques where the user composes queries that specify the content of the desired images. After a brief overview of digital image formats, we analyze different approaches to content specification: in terms of low-level visual features, of objects, and of metadata. We then describe a general progressive framework that combines these approaches. We finally conclude the entry with an overview of common applications of image repositories and digital libraries, such as medical imaging, remote-sensing imaging, and data for the oil industry.

INTRODUCTION

During the first decade of the twenty-first century digital images have rapidly supplanted traditional film-based images in many application areas. The most visible example is consumer photography, where, due to technological advancements, the digital medium has overtaken the traditional film. Digital cameras with high-quality optics and high-resolution sensors are much smaller than old 35 mm cameras. Cellular phones often have built-in digital cameras with resolutions that match that of a typical mid-range computer monitor. External USB hard disks with 1 Tb of capacity or more are available at a fraction of the cost of a personal computer, allowing consumers to store large numbers of digital pictures. Distributing digital images is also very easy: telecommunication companies offer services to share images acquired via cellular phone cameras, while social networking sites provide intuitive interfaces for posting personal photographs on the Internet. Accessing images over the Web has become almost instantaneous, thanks to the widespread availability of broadband connectivity for home use, over the phone lines (using DSL, i.e., Digital Subscriber Line, technology), or over the cable-television networks.

Digital imagery has quickly supplanted traditional imagery in scientific fields, particularly in radiology. Several types of radiological images have always been acquired through electronic sensors—magnetic resonance imaging (MRI), TAC, and Positron emission tomography (PET), for example. The availability of high-resolution sensors and especially of high-resolution, high-contrast computer displays has made it possible in many cases to replace traditional, film-based x-ray imagery with digital images. Technological advances are making digital radiography appealing even in applications where high-resolution images are required, such as for mammography.

Advances in imaging techniques have also enabled the reproduction of precious documents, historical artifacts, and figurative art masterpieces with sufficient wealth of details to be usable not only by the general public, but even by scholars. This trend was pioneered in the mid-1990s, for example, by the Vatican Digital Library initiative;[1] more recent development include the digital rendering of Michelangelo's David statue.[2]

Quite interestingly, techniques for *retrieving* digital images from large collections or from the Internet have only partially kept up with the pace of the digital imagery explosion. The most widely used search engines can retrieve images through keyword-based searches and build image indexes based on the HTML tags of the images and on keywords that appear in the text in the proximity of the images. Specific scientific fields have developed metadata standards to describe information on how images are acquired and on their content. However, the ultimate goal, the ability of retrieving images by specifying the desired content, is still a research topic and, despite the numerous advances in the field, has proven, so far, to be an elusive achievement.

In this entry, we provide an overview of still-image retrieval by content. We start section "Introduction" by discussing how images are represented in digital format. In section "Image Formats and Data Compression" we introduce the concept of content-based retrieval of still-image data (CBIR, for content-based image retrieval). Section "Query Specification" introduces the definition of *objects* as the building blocks for content representation within an image. In section "Content Representation and Objects" we identify different abstraction levels at which objects can be specified. We discuss how simple objects can be defined as connected regions that are homogeneous with respect to pixel-level, feature-level, semantic-level, and metadata-level characteristics. We describe how

Encyclopedia of Library and Information Sciences, Fourth Edition DOI: 10.1081/E-ELIS4-120044400

information can be efficiently represented at these different levels, how a user can specify content, and what mechanisms can be used to perform the search. Simple objects can also be defined simultaneously at multiple abstraction levels, and aggregated to form composite objects. The semantics of both types of objects, and the techniques required to search for them are the subject of section "Defining Content at Multiple Abstraction Levels."

In section "Progressive Search at Multiple Abstraction Levels" we briefly introduce a different perspective on image retrieval, affective image retrieval, where the image is treated as a signifier and the user specifies the desired signified. For example, a user could ask the system to retrieve images that convey "happiness," that describe "democracy," or that illustrate "Memorial Day."

In section "Effective Image Retrieval" we then discuss specific applications of the techniques described in the entry to Digital Libraries. We analyze specific examples of digital libraries of scientific data: medical image databases, repositories of remotely sensed images, and databases used by the oil industry.

IMAGE FORMATS AND DATA COMPRESSION

Data compression techniques are commonly used in image databases to reduce the required storage space. As we shall see in later sections it is sometimes possible to use properties of the compression algorithms for indexing and retrieval purposes. Hence, we briefly review some fundamental concepts of image compression.

The goal of source coding (data compression) is to produce a representation of the original signal which requires fewer bits. Compression is accomplished by reducing the redundancy present in the original data, and possibly by selectively discarding some information. Methods that discard information are called *lossy*, and the remaining ones are called *lossless*. In (gray scale) images, there are two main sources of redundancy: the similarity of spatially close pixels, and the nonuniformity in the overall intensity distribution.

Neighboring pixels commonly have similar brightness (intensity), and it is often possible to rather accurately estimate a pixel value from those of the surrounding ones. Hence, only the difference between the predicted and the original values needs to be encoded, and this difference in general can be represented by fewer bits than the original grayscale value. Two main classes of approaches exist to reduce spatial redundancy. The first operates in the *spatial domain*, by exploiting local redundancy. A typical example is the lossless mode of JPEG standard: here, the image is scanned line by line from left to right, the value of each pixel is predicted using the values of the closest previously scanned pixels and the difference between predicted and actual values is computed (this approach is also known as predictive coding). The second class of approaches

operates in a *transform domain*. Natural images have higher energy in the lower frequencies of the spatial spectrum, that describe slower intensity variations, than in the higher frequencies. The *two-dimensional Fourier transform* [3, Chapter 8] hence concentrates most of the image energy in a few low-frequency coefficients. Each Fourier coefficient is generated from the entire image, and is not easily predicted from neighboring coefficients, hence the transform effectively reduces spatial redundancy. The *two-dimensional block discrete cosine transform* (DCT), used in the JPEG standard[4] is closely related to the Fourier transform, but is more local in nature: the image is first blocked into 8×8 squares, and each block is transformed separately. Again, most of the energy is concentrated in a small subset of coefficients, and coefficients cannot be effectively predicted from the values of their neighbors because their statistical dependence is weak. The *wavelet transform*,[5] used in the JPEG2000 standard,[6] relies on a high-pass filter (H) and a low-pass filter (L). The image rows are filtered separately, and the result is filtered column by column. This operation produces a subband, which is commonly identified by the used filters: for instance, if rows are filtered with the high-pass filter and the columns with the low-pass filter, the resulting subband is denoted by HL. Hence, there are four possible subbands, LL, HL, LH, and HH, depicted in Fig. 1. Subbands are downsampled by retaining each other row and each other column. A ℓ level wavelet transform repeats the described operation on the LL subband $\ell - 1$ times. The transform yields both spatial and spectral information. The lower-frequency subband (LL at level ℓ) is well localized in frequency and each coefficient depends on a large number of image pixels. The higher-frequency subband (HH at level 1) is well localized in space, but contains information on roughly the top half of the frequency spectrum. Most transform coefficients at the higher levels have values close to zero, while most of the energy is in the lower-frequency subbands. Fig. 1 illustrates this concept. The LL subband is a smaller version of the original image, the LH subband captures edges aligned with the horizontal axis, the LH subband captures edges aligned with the vertical axis, and the HH subband captures diagonal edges.

From both wavelet transform and block DCT it is easy to obtain a multiresolution representation of the image, that is, a sequence of increasingly smaller and coarser approximations to the original. As we shall see in subsequent entries, this property can be advantageously used during search.

The second cause of redundancy is present in most images: some of the intensity values are more common than others, and data compression can be achieved by encoding them with shorter codewords. Numerous techniques exist to accomplish this task, such as Shannon coding, Huffman coding, Arithmetic coding, and Lempel-Ziv-like codes, etc. An introduction can be found in Cover.[7] In general, higher intensity redundancy results in better compression. Spatial redundancy reduction almost

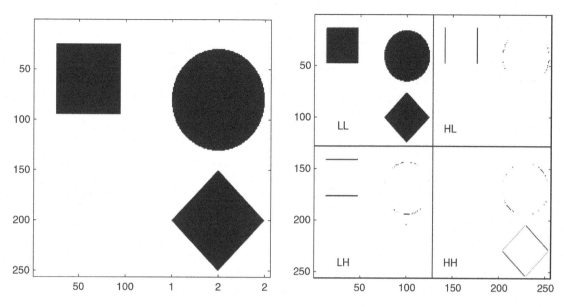

Fig. 1   A simple image (left) and its two-dimensional wavelet transform (right).

invariably yields a significant increase in the intensity redundancy, and for this reason favors compressibility.

With lossless techniques, images typically compress by a factor of 2–3. If higher compression ratios are desired, information must be selectively discarded to improve compressibility. Two mechanisms are available, thresholding and quantizing,[8] which are usually applied after the spatial redundancy reduction and always before the intensity redundancy reduction. Thresholding changes to zero all values that are close to it. For example, in predictive coding, all small prediction errors could be set to zero. Quantizing (via *scalar quantization*, SQ) means reducing the number of allowed intensity values, by partitioning the intensity scale into regions (bins), assigning a representative intensity value to each bin, and changing each pixel to the representative value of the bin into which it falls. Both thresholding and quantization can be used simultaneously.

A substantial amount of research has been devoted to a general class of quantization schemes, called *vector quantization* (VQ).[8,9] VQ has its root in the well-known result in Information Theory that states that quantizing *independent* Gaussian random variables together yields lower distortion at the same rate than quantizing them separately (see, e.g., Problem 13.1 in Cover and Thomas[10]). Further improvements can be achieved if the random variables are not independent, as it is typically the case for neighboring image pixels. VQ compression of an image consists of: tessellating the image into groups of neighboring pixels having the same size, say d (e.g., dividing the image into 2×2 pixel regions); partitioning the d-dimensional space of pixel groups into bins; selecting a representative group of d pixels for each bin; and mapping each group of pixels from the image to the representative group of the bin into which it falls.

If thresholding, VQ, or SQ are used, either on the image or on its transform,[11,12] it is generally not possible to recover the original data from its compressed version. To select the thresholding and quantization parameters, often a measure of similarity between the original and reconstructed image is used, such as the mean squared error. Compression ratios of 10 to 1 or better are possible with lossy schemes, without appreciable deterioration of the image quality. However, since these techniques nevertheless introduce visual artifacts, their application to scientific data is rare, and essentially limited to remote browsing of the images over slow networks. By combining a lossy scheme with lossless encoding of the difference between the original and reconstructed image, it is possible to obtain a lossless scheme which can also be used for image retrieval.

SEARCHING IMAGE REPOSITORIES BY CONTENT

In traditional relational databases, queries are expressed using a highly structured language, such as SQL. This is possible because the information managed by the database is itself highly structured and can be stored, for instance, in one or more tables. Images, like many other types of multimedia data, are by nature unstructured. Therefore, they are difficult to organize using relational or object-relational databases and to retrieve using a structured query language. No universal solution exists to the problem of organizing and searching data in image databases: information retrieval from image repositories is a field of research that is currently in the process of reaching maturity.

Ideally, multimedia repositories should be searched by allowing the user to specify the desired content of the data to be retrieved. However, the old proverb "a picture is worth a thousand words" describes well the difficulties that a user encounters when attempting to specify exactly what the retrieved images should contain. The almost universal approach to overcome this difficulty is to rely on similarity-based search. The large class of heterogeneous methodologies developed for searching multimedia databases is commonly known in the field as *content-based retrieval* (CBR).[13] The main challenges posed by content-based search are automatic extraction and indexing of the content (to which this entry is devoted), query specification, and display of the results. In practice, however, the problem is very hard. In particular, a chasm exists between what search features can be extracted by existing systems from the user's query, and what content the user is actually interested in. This is called *semantic gap*,[14] and was well characterized by Smeulders et al.,[15] as the "lack of coincidence between the information that one can extract from the visual data and the interpretation that the same data have for a user in a given situation." Most of the research in CBR has been devoted to map information that can be extracted automatically from images, from associated metadata, and from context information (such as text near images embedded into documents) to user's semantic.

QUERY SPECIFICATION

There are numerous query specifications styles that are appropriate for image databases. The early CBR systems, such as QBIC,[13] VisualSeek,[16] and Virage,[17] used an example-based interface where the user would construct queries by supplying one or more examples. Graphical Query Languages offer an appealing alternative; however they have a steep learning curve and limited support for multimedia datatypes and relationships. A drag-and-drop interface supporting a quasinatural query language that combines English-like sentences with multimedia data, such as images, has been proposed in Bergman et al.[18] and used in conjunction with the SPIRE system[19] in a variety of application scenarios. This interface supports the composition of the type of queries described in this entry. Intelligent user interfaces for CBIR are described in Vermilyer.[20]

Many CBR systems rely on a paradigm for interaction with the user called *Relevance Feedback*.[21] In relevance feedback, the user issues a query and, upon receiving a set of results, inspects them, selects those that are most relevant and submits them to the system. The system appropriately modifies the query based on the user's feedback. The turn-taking dialog between user and system continues until the user is satisfied with the results.

CONTENT REPRESENTATION AND OBJECTS

In this entry, we define the content of images in terms of *objects*. We distinguish between simple objects, which can be thought as the building blocks of an image, and composite objects, collections of simple objects grouped by spatial (or temporal) relations. Therefore, we will not distinguish between a "scene" and the image of a complex object with multiple parts: our concept of composite object encompasses both.

Simple Objects and Attributes

A *simple object* is a connected region of an image which is homogeneous with respect to some specific characteristics. An entire image and any connected portion of an image are therefore simple objects, defined by constraints on pixel locations.

Objects have *attributes*. We distinguish *defining* attributes, that are used in the definition of a particular type of object, from *non-defining* attributes, that do not characterize the type of object. For example, a forested area can be defined as a region of a remotely sensed image having specific spectral reflectance and textural characteristics: in this case texture and spectral reflectance are defining attributes, while the location of the forest and its size in pixels are not.

Attributes can be *numerical* or *categorical*. Surface area and location are examples of numerical attributes. The type of a lesion observed in a MRI scan of the brain is a categorical attribute. Categorical attributes can be further characterized as *sharp* or *fuzzy*. An attribute of a geological stratum in a formation microscanner imager (FMI) is its thickness. Thickness can be defined as a sharp attribute, and measured for instance in feet, or as a fuzzy attribute, taking fuzzy values such as "thin," "medium," and "thick." A stratum 4 ft thick could also be characterized by membership values of .6 to the "thin" category, .4 to the "medium" category and 0 to the "thick" category. Attributes can also be either *deterministic* or *probabilistic*. Consider measuring the area of a lake in square meters (thus, we define it as a numerical, sharp attribute) using a remotely sensed image: while some pixels clearly fall entirely within the lake, some contain both dry land and water. Hence, the lake surface cannot be measured exactly, and only an estimate can be produced. This estimate can be treated as a random variable, and confidence intervals can be constructed from the image, for example by counting the number of pixels containing both water and dry land. Similarly, consider classifying automatically a forested area using a remotely sensed image, and assume that the statistical classifier decides that with probability .9 the forest is an evergreen forest, and with probability .1 is deciduous. Here the class label (a categorical attribute) is probabilistic rather than deterministic.

It is important to note the distinction between fuzzy attributes and probabilistic attributes. In the forest example, the classifier is telling us that of all forested areas looking like the one being analyzed, 90% are evergreen forests, and 10% are deciduous forests. This is different from saying that 90% of the trees in the patch of vegetation are evergreen and the remaining 10% are deciduous. The former characterization is probabilistic, the latter is fuzzy.

Finally, we note that attributes can be either *scalar* or *vector-valued*. The size (in number of pixels) of an object is an example of scalar attribute, its color histogram (section "Color Descriptors and Color Matching") is a vector-valued attribute.

Composite Objects

Simple objects are not sufficient to characterize the content of images. A *composite object* or *compound object* is a collection of simple objects that satisfy a set of spatial or temporal relations. A river delta as seen in a FMI image can be defined as a group of well-defined strata, arranged in a specific order.

Like attributes, spatial and temporal relations can themselves be sharp (for instance, "within n pixels") or fuzzy (for instance, "near"). Composite objects provide a powerful paradigm for specifying the content of images, especially those used in scientific applications.

Examples of object-based image representations are the paradigm adopted in SPIRE,[19,22] described in this entry, the *blobworld* representation,[23,24] and the framework used in VisualSEEk.[16] The blobworld approach, based on segmenting images with an Expectation-Maximization (EM) algorithm[25] applied to combined color and texture features, is well-tailored toward identifying objects in photographic images, provided that they stand out from the background. Each object is efficiently represented by replacing it with a "blob"—an ellipse identified by its centroid and its scatter matrix. In VisualSEEk, the query is specified in terms of color regions and their spatial organization.

DEFINING CONTENT AT MULTIPLE ABSTRACTION LEVELS

Attributes of image objects, or, more generally, of multimedia data, can be represented, described and searched at different levels of abstraction. We can readily identify four such levels, namely raw-data, feature, semantic, and metadata level. Simple objects can be defined at each level, or simultaneously at multiple levels.

Searching Images at the Raw Data Level

Digital images are two-dimensional arrays of pixels. Each pixel is represented as one or more numeric values denoting the intensities in different bands of the electromagnetic spectrum at its specific location. A pixel-level object can be defined as a connected portion of an image. Two pixel-level objects are equal if they have the same size and shape, and if the pixels in the corresponding positions have identical values.

Similarity between two pixel-levels objects having the same size and shape is defined in terms of similarity between the values of the pixels in corresponding positions. A pixel-level object having n pixels can be represented as a n-dimensional point, by making each pixel correspond to a different coordinate. The difference between two pixel-level objects can then be defined in terms of the Euclidean distance between the corresponding points. Alternatively, a pixel-level object can be represented as an n-dimensional vector, starting at the origin and ending at the above defined n-dimensional point. In this case, the similarity between two objects can be defined using their inner product.

The SPIRE system[19] supports image search at the numerous levels, including the raw-data level.

Progressive pixel-level retrieval

Computing the Euclidean distance (or the inner product) between a query object and all the subsets having identical shape and size, of all the images in the database, is a very expensive operation. Matching can be based on cross-correlation, or the correlation coefficient. [3, Chapter 20] Here, image representation can significantly reduce the computational complexity. Cross-correlation is still an expensive operation in the pixel domain. However, multiplying the Fourier transforms of two images (a much faster operation) is equivalent to computing the cross-correlation in the pixel domain. In Vaidyanathan,[26] the author notices that cross-correlating the corresponding subbands of two images and adding the results produces a subsampled version of the cross-correlation. By noticing that the wavelet transform concentrates most of the energy in the lower-frequency subbands, and that a similar property holds for the low-frequency components of block-DCT, Li, Turek and Feig[27] and Castelli et al.[28] concluded that the results of Vaidyanathan,[26] can be well approximated by just considering the cross-convolution of the lower-frequency subbands (or DCT coefficients). Local maxima in this approximation suggest possible location of matches. Once candidate locations are identified, the search can be refined by computing and adding contributions from higher-frequency subbands. Large computational savings are achieved by refining the search only around candidate matches rather than on the entire image.

Rather than being a general mechanism, raw-level search has specific applications. It is extremely useful to identify distinctive objects across a time series of images or of images acquired from different instruments, hence it is useful for coregistration purposes. For example, remotely sensed images of the same region acquired by the same instrument vary over time because of slight differences in the orbit, altitude, and orientation of the platform. To coregister the images, ground control points are identified, using pixel-level techniques, and their positions used to compute the warping mapping between the images. Analogously, in medical imaging, distinctive anatomical features must be precisely identified to compute the exact position of the tissues or organs of interest.

Features

The term *feature* denotes an aspect of an image that can be captured by a numeric or, more rarely, categorical quantity (called a descriptor) computed from the raw data. By definition, features do not have an immediate semantic meaning. In the literature, the term feature is often used to denote the descriptor.

Typical image features describe color, texture, and spatial properties, such as shape. We distinguish between *global features*, that represent an image in its entirety, and *local features* that capture localized properties. Global feature descriptors are often used for photographic images, but have in general poor retrieval qualities. It is likely that the use of global features originated with one of the early CBR systems, QBIC,[13] which represented each image with a color feature vector, a texture feature vector, and a shape feature vector. In reality, when a new image is ingested in QBIC, the operator is supposed to manually outline a region of interest, from which the feature descriptors are extracted, and that becomes the subject of the image. Local feature descriptors are much more useful for indexing purposes. They are either extracted by first segmenting the image into homogeneous regions and computing features for each region (as in the blobworld,) or by dividing the image into a large number of small, overlapping windows (e.g., overlapping), and computing features for each window.[28] The advantages of the first approach are that it produces a smaller data volume, and that an appropriate segmentation scheme often produces results that are acceptable from the viewpoint of the user. The advantage of the second approach is the increased flexibility, since objects are not predefined and can be extracted to better match the query.

We now discuss two of the most commonly encountered classes of features in image databases: color and texture. In each subsection, we briefly describe how the category is used, what descriptors are commonly used and how similarity is captured. We conclude each subsection with remarks on specific applications, and, when appropriate, on how to speed up the search by relying on properties of image compression schemes.

Color Features

The use of color for retrieval

Color is commonly used to index images,[29] and is one of the main features used in early CBIR systems, such as QBIC[13] and Virage.[17] It is a very important feature for photographic images and works of art, and histological images. It has limited applicability to radiological imaging, which is almost universally displayed in gray scale (and only rarely using false-colors, which are not useful in indexing), in oil-exploration imagery (where, again, false coloring is used), and in satellite imagery, where the multispectral information is used to extract semantics and not used directly as a low-level property.

Color descriptors and color matching

Color features for similarity retrieval are usually variations of the color histogram. The first step in the feature computation is a selection of the color space. For typical digital photographs, where each pixel is represented as the superposition of three basic colors, red, green, and blue, the RGB space is the most natural choice. Here, each pixel value corresponds to a point in a three-dimensional space, whose coordinates are the red, green, and blue intensity. Pixels of images compressed with the JPEG image compression standard can be immediately represented in the YCrCb space. The natural color space for television data (such as newscasts, sport events, movies, etc.) depends on the standard: NTSC uses the YIQ space, PAL and SECAM use the YUV standard. None of the mentioned color spaces is perceptually uniform, in the sense that Euclidean distances between points in the color space do not capture well the subjective similarity between colors. Hence, numerous other color spaces have been used with moderate success by different authors, such as the hue-saturation-value (HSV) space,[29] the Munsell color space,[30] the opponent-axis space,[31] or the CIE-LUV space.[32]

The second step in the color histogram computation is quantization: the color space is subdivided into cells, a representative color is selected for each cell, and all the pixel values falling in a specific cell are replaced by the representative value. The quantized color space usually contains anywhere from 64 to 4096 different colors.

The color histogram of an image is finally computed by counting how many pixels fall in each cell of the quantized color space. The counts can be normalized (divided by the size of the image), in which case they sum to 1. A non-normalized color histogram having b bins can be represented as a point in a b-dimensional space, the ith coordinate of which is equal to the number of counts in the ith bin. If the color histogram is normalized, it lies on a b-dimensional simplex, which is a $(b - 1)$-dimensional surface.

Different functions on the color histogram spaces have been proposed to capture similarity between images. These functions are usually distances between the points representing the histograms. While the choice of the color space and of the number of quantization bins appear to affect the quality of the retrieval, the choice of the similarity function is less important, and most commonly used ones are essentially interchangeable.

Image representation can be combined with color feature extraction. For instance, research has been done on how to approximate the histograms of images compressed with the JPEG standard with the color histogram of the DC components.[33]

Further Uses of Color

Color is a powerful means for conveying meaning and emotions. Itten[34] codified a psychological theory on the use of the color in art to convey semantics. It is unsurprising, then, that color has been used to retrieve images of paintings from collections of art works. Colombo, Del Bimbo, and Pala[35] analyze the color content of photographs of paintings, and derive measures of harmonic accordance, contrast of luminance, contrast of saturation, and contrast of warmth. As a response to a query, the system returns the most similar paintings with respect to one or more of the listed color quantities. Del Bimbo et al.[36] extract color and shape using a multiresolution representation of the image. By using a low-resolution approximation (which can be easily obtained from the wavelet transform or the block-DCT), the system can make judgments about the overall color composition of the painting and use them during retrieval.

Texture Features

Definition and use

Texture describes the local intensity variations in an image. In natural images, texture is a property of individual surfaces, and is an important visual cue especially for categorizing materials and substances: water, wood, grass, snow, cloth, fur, brick walls, sand, etc. are just few examples of entities that humans can identify even in black and white pictures based on texture.

Texture is extremely important in scientific imagery, where commonly expert use textural characteristics to interpret the data. For example, in remotely sensed images, erosion patterns, types of tree associations, and types of crops can be analyzed in terms of texture. In well-bore and core images, the stratigraphical analysis is exquisitely textural in nature. In some types of medical images, such as mammograms, texture is a powerful indicator of pathology.

Texture descriptors

Texture descriptors are generally extracted from gray-scale images. For color images, descriptors are computed from the overall intensity map (computed by adding the square of the pixel values in each color band), from each individual color band, or from selected color bands. Color textures have been the subject of rather few studies.[37–39]

There are three main classes of texture descriptors.

Spatial-domain descriptors are computed directly from the image (or the intensity map). Several feature sets belong to this class, and here we describe the most common ones.

The *gray-level differences histogram*[40] counts how many times the differences between pixel values in a window and the value at the center occur within an image or a region. Statistical properties of the histogram, such as its mean, variance, central moments, entropy, etc., are used to represent texture properties, such as overall brilliance, intensity variations, etc.

The *co-occurrence matrix* counts how many times a pair of intensity values occurs in pixels having a fixed distance in a predefined direction. Corresponding texture descriptors[41–43] are derived properties of the matrix, such as the entropy or the moments, and have been related to visual properties, such as regularity, homogeneity, directionality, and periodicity of the texture.

Tamura's features[44] were selected to capture specific characteristics of the human visual system, and describe texture in terms of coarseness, directionality, roughness, regularity, contrast, and line-likeness. Studies show that, in practice, coarseness, contrast, and directionality alone yield most of the discriminatory ability of the feature set, and that adding the remaining three features improves retrieval results only marginally. Tamura's features capture very well high-level characteristics of texture, but fail to provide fine-level discrimination.

Transform-domain descriptors are computed from a transform of the image. When an image is compressed with a transform-based method, the corresponding texture descriptors can be obtained at a very moderate computational cost.

Wavelet-based descriptors[45] capture the local spatial frequency content of the image. $2^k \times 2^k$ portion of an image is described to a good degree of approximation by $3d + 1$ subblocks of a d-levels wavelet transform: one in each of the three high-frequency subbands (HL, LH, HH) at each level, and one in the low frequency subbands at level d. A block at level ℓ has size $2^{k-\ell} \times 2^{k-\ell}$. Smith and Chang[45] suggest computing the wavelet transform of the image, conceptually dividing the image into nonoverlapping square blocks, and considering for each block the corresponding $3d + 1$ portions of the transform. The mean value and the variance of the coefficients within each transform portion are then computed, and concatenated to produce a texture feature vector. The authors also suggest an algorithm for merging adjacent image blocks to segment the image into regions of homogeneous texture.

Gabor-based features[46] are among the most discriminating texture descriptors available. The (even, symmetric) Gabor filters are uncorrelated Gaussians with variances σ_x and σ_y in the x- and y-directions, modulated by a sinusoid of frequency ϕ varying along the x-axis, and rotated by an angle θ, hence they are defined by four parameters. In the spatial frequency domain, they correspond to two Gaussians having variances $1/(2\pi\sigma_x)$ and $1/(2\pi\sigma_y)$, centered at ϕ and $-\phi$ respectively, in a reference frame rotated by θ. Their main property is that they trade off optimally localization in the spatial domain and in the frequency/orientation domain. Hence, the magnitudes of the Gabor coefficients give a good indication of directionality and periodicity of the texture. A texture feature vector is constructed by selecting a group of filters at various orientations, scale (variances), and frequencies, computing the corresponding Gabor coefficients, and concatenating them. Experiments show that Gabor features are competitive with other texture descriptor sets in a wide variety of application domains,[45,47,48] and have been successfully used for texture discrimination and classification[49] and image segmentation.[50]

Random-field models describe texture as a spatial stochastic process. Technically, in this context a spatial stochastic process is a probability measure on the collection of possible images.[51] Practically, a random field is a probability distribution over sets of neighboring pixels. Markov random fields (MRF) are a special class of processes specified through the conditional distribution of the value of a pixel given the values of specific neighbors. Due to their effectiveness, they have been used for a long time for description and representation,[52–54] classification,[55–57] synthesis,[58,59] compression,[59] and segmentation of texture.[60–64] Gaussian MRF are particularly appealing, due to the simplicity of the model: here pixel values can be written as the sum of a linear combinations of the values of their neighbors and of a correlated Gaussian noise. Simultaneous autoregressive models (SAM), where the Gaussian noise is white (i.e., uncorrelated), are even simpler, and have been widely used for image retrieval field. Typical texture features obtained from random field models are the parameters of the model itself: for example, a SAM texture descriptor would consist of the vector of coefficients used in the linear combination and of the variance of the white Gaussian noise. It is also possible to simultaneously fit different models to the data (characterized, for instance, by different neighborhoods), and use the index selected model a further descriptor.

Texture Similarity and Texture-Based Retrieval

Similarity (or better, dissimilarity) between texture feature vectors is usually measured by means of a distance function. Let $\mathbf{x}$ and $\mathbf{y}$ denote two such vectors. The most commonly used metric is the Euclidean distance, defined as

$$D^{(2)}(\mathbf{x}, \mathbf{y}) = \sqrt{\sum_{i=1}^{d} (\mathbf{x}[i] - \mathbf{y}[i])^2}$$

It is rotationally invariant and weights all the features equally. This last property is undesirable when the ranges of the different feature descriptors vary significantly. For example, the variance of the gray scale difference histogram is often much larger than the mean, and would have a significantly bigger effect in determining similarity. Furthermore, additional flexibility is required when the system is allowed to learn the relative importance of different features from the user input and feedback. Metrics that can be used to satisfy both requirements are the weighted Minkowsky distances and the generalized Euclidean distance. The former is defined as

$$D^p(\mathbf{x}, \mathbf{y}) = \left[\sum_{i=1}^{d} w_i |\mathbf{x}[i] - \mathbf{y}[i]|^p \right]^{1/p}$$

where

p is a positive number
w_i are weights
d is the length of the feature vector
The latter is defined as

$$D(\mathbf{x}, \mathbf{y}) = [(\mathbf{x} - \mathbf{y})^{\mathrm{T}} \mathbf{K}(\mathbf{x} - \mathbf{y})]^{1/2}$$

where $\mathbf{K}$ is a positive definite matrix having determinant equal to 1. Further details on similarity measures for retrieval can be found in Santini and Jain.[65]

Progressive texture retrieval

As previously described, several texture features can be extracted from image transforms, and therefore are easily computed when the images are compressed using a transform-based scheme. Texture features extracted from different levels of the multiresolution pyramid can also be used to speed up search.[40] Here, an optimal starting level in the pyramid is identified using the examples provided with the query. Pruning of the search space is then performed by texture matching at this starting level: note that higher starting levels are characterized by fewer homogeneous regions within images, and hence yield faster matching. However, a higher starting level introduces a larger approximation in the matching, as details are lost, and therefore the selectivity threshold for the pruning must be relaxed accordingly. Since the two effects are contrasting, there is always an optimum starting level from the speed viewpoint. Only the regions that pass the pruning stage are retained and further analyzed at the immediately finer level of the multiresolution pyramid. The process is repeated until the full-resolution level is reached. Tenfold increase in retrieval speed have been observed with this technique.

Shape Features

At a first glance, searching images repositories by specifying the shape of desired contained objects appears to be a natural and intuitive approach to CBR. In reality, however, it is a problematic endeavor at best. First, most animate objects are not rigid and their shapes can vary substantially as they move. Even for rigid objects, perspective and angle of view can radically change the shapes recorded in an image. Additionally, shape is not invariant with respect to rotations of the image. In spite of these difficulties, shape-based image retrieval has been an active and often successful field of investigation. Another difficulty with shape features is that they rely heavily on accurate images segmentation, which is largely unsolved. If objects cannot be precisely segmented, shape features can be misleading or even meaningless. In contrast, color or texture features are not so sensitive to inaccurate segmentation. For example, if an object is segmented into two pieces, the colors from the two pieces still reflect the object, but the partial shapes can be arbitrary and dramatically different from the true shape.

Indexing images by shape requires solving three separate classes of problems. The first is *shape extraction*: images must be analyzed to extract shapes of objects. The literature in this field is very large, and image retrieval has borrowed techniques from other disciplines, such as robotic vision. The wide spectrum of approaches to shape extraction range from accurate segmentation, to approximate representation of shape regions, to extraction of low-level features that capture aspects of shape, such as edges.

The second problem is *shape representation*: the shape must be described by numeric quantities that can be used for retrieval. Numerous descriptors have been proposed in the literature, which can be classified along several dimensions. A first distinction is between *global* and *local* descriptors. Global descriptors capture properties of the shape as a whole, for example its elongation or the overall smoothness of the contour. Local descriptor capture properties of selected regions of the shape, for example, the presence of sharp angles in the contour. A second distinction is between *complete* and *partial* descriptors. Complete descriptors attempt to retain all properties of the shape, while partial descriptor capture only characteristics that are deemed salient for retrieval. A third distinction is between *interior* and *boundary* representations. Interior methods describe a shape, for example, by means of approximations or using a sequence of approximations. Boundary methods describe properties of the contour line, for example, by

means of piecewise polynomial lines. Other dimensions distinguish between *rotationally invariant* and *rotationally variant* features, *single-scale* and *multi-scale* features, *composition-of-part* and *deformation* methods.

The third problem is *shape matching*. This is typically accomplished by means of an appropriate distance function. Unfortunately, there is no universal shape similarity metric: different feature are matched with different, specific similarity functions. A detailed discussion of these metrics, a more in-depth view of the categorization reported in this section can be found in Kimia,[66] which is an excellent introduction to shape-based retrieval.

Shape-based techniques have had only limited application in photographic image retrieval, where often segmented shapes are associated with texture- and color-based representations of the interior.[67] In contrast, shape has been successfully used in several specialized application areas, such as medical imaging;[68] biometric identification;[69] and retrieval of logos, trademarks, and watermarks.[70] A survey on recent advances in CBR of three-dimensional shapes can be found in Icke.[71]

Searching Images at the Semantic Level

Semantic content characterization

Searching images at the semantic level is one of the most difficult tasks faced by CBIR systems. The main challenges are representing semantics, extracting it automatically from the images, and indexing it. These problems are particularly severe in databases of photographic image, where the subjectivity of the user perception plays a major role. For example, a specific image could be described as "an outdoors scene," "a picture from an outdoors sport event," "a picture from a golf tournament," or "a picture of the 18th hole at the St. Andrews golf club in the year 2000, taken while Tiger Woods is putting to win the tournament and the golf grand slam." Scientific data, however, is often more amenable to automatic extraction of semantic content. We first discuss photographic images, and later scientific imagery.

Jaimes and Chang[72] proposed a scheme to represent multimedia content which uses 10 abstraction levels, divided into two groups. The first group contains levels related to percept, corresponds to the pixel and feature levels, and divides into different levels global and local content. The second group, containing six levels (generic object, generic scene, specific object, specific scene, abstract object, abstract scene,) provides a very good framework for describing semantic content in photographic images and video, and can be successfully used as guideline for constructing indexes. Referring to the example of the previous paragraph, the first two descriptions would be indexed at the generic scene, while the last belongs to the specific scene level.

Semantic content extraction

While researchers have proposed solutions on how to organize semantic content for search purposes, the automatic extraction of semantic content from photographic images and video is still an unsolved problem and will remain such at least for the next few years. Some of the difficulties encountered are very similar to those raised by the automatic object recognition problem, to which the computer vision discipline has devoted decades of efforts. Specific algorithms exist to identify particular classes of objects within images, such as deciduous trees,[73] naked people and horses;[74] specific types of scenes, such as sunsets, outdoors, and indoors images;[75] and some very high level semantics such as warmth, and harmony of a painting.[35] Automatic image annotation is a form of semantic context extraction: Li and Wang[76,77] propose methods for automatically associating a collection of labels to images.[78]

Still-image retrieval at the semantic level can pose challenges beyond those related to object recognition: users, for example, might look for images with a specific purpose in mind, for example, to evoke desired emotions (e.g., images that evoke sadness, images with dramatic effect, etc.), which is discussed in the section "Affective Image Retrieval."

Following Liu et al.,[79] we classify the technical approaches to semantic content extraction into five categories:

1. *Defining high-level concepts through object ontology*. Methods of this class rely on small-size vocabularies of simple descriptors and a mechanism for mapping low-level features extracted from the image into the vocabulary. An example of such descriptor could be "bright-green region." High-level semantic concepts are expressed in terms of the descriptors: a "lawn" could be described as a "bright-green region located in the bottom half of a photograph." The main limitation of the approach lies in how to appropriately design ontologies for specific tasks.

2. *Using supervised or unsupervised learning*. In the case of supervised learning, a training set consisting of examples labeled with high-level semantic labels is used to train a classifier. The classifier learns to associate low-level features with semantic concepts. In unsupervised learning, the low-level features representations of a large collection of images are partitioned into similar groups, and groups are associated to semantic concepts. The similarity measure is defined on the feature space, or on the space of probability distributions over the feature space, such as in Li and Wang.[77]

    The main limitation of supervised learning methods is their reliance on large manually labeled training sets. The main limitation of unsupervised learning methods is that the correspondence between groups and semantic concepts is incidental.

3. *Interacting with the user via relevance feedback*. Semantic concepts are learned on the fly by a classifier through an iterative refinement process. During a turn of the iterative refinement process, the user is shown candidate examples picked by the classifier, marks some as positive (in some cases, as negative); the classifier then updates its internal model using the user feedback. The main limitation of the approach lies in the limited number of examples that a user can reasonably label.

4. *Matching content through semantic templates*. A semantic template is the "signature" of a semantic concept extracted from a collection of representative images. Unlike when using supervised learning, the designer of semantic concepts must often have a good understanding of the underlying features.

5. *Combining image features and features from surrounding text*. This approach is well suited for retrieval of images from the World Wide Web, which are embedded within HTML pages. Currently, the analysis of the surrounding text is often limited to keyword selection, but advances in natural language processing make the approach increasingly appealing. An important challenge arises from the difficulty of determining whether the surrounding text is actually descriptive of the image content.

Scientific data offers numerous opportunities for automatic semantic content extraction. Experts often interpret the imagery by relying on low-level visual cues, which might be captured by a computer. Additionally, a great deal of the semantic content can be described in terms of objects and their spatial relations, there are no scenes, and the abstract levels of Jaimes and Chang are irrelevant. We briefly discuss three cases: remotely sensed images, oil well-bore images, and medical images.

One of the main uses of multispectral remotely sensed images is to identify and distinguish different types of land cover. The applications are numerous: from management of forestry to the identification of diseases in crops, to crop yield prediction, to environmental monitoring. Different types of land cover have different spectral reflectance: for instance, vegetation reflects in the green part of the spectrum, absorbs in the red (hence, leaves and grass look green), and is highly reflective in the near infrared; barren terrain, on the other hand, has moderate to high reflectance in all the visible and near-infrared spectrum. Automatic classifiers can be constructed to label the individual pixels, identify connected regions and produce semantic objects such as "forests," "urban areas," "bodies of water," etc. These classifiers are usually specific to an instrument, a particular geographical region and a given time of the year.

Well bore data for the oil industry contain both image-like information (acquired, for instance, by the FMI instrument) and one-dimensional data, acquired by appropriate log instruments. Bulk lithology (the type of rock) can be inferred from the log data, and classifiers can automate the task. The well can then be partitioned into labeled strata and rock formations, defined as associations of strata satisfying relative position constraints, can easily be searched.

Radiological imagery has recently received substantial attention as a prime candidate for automatic extraction of semantic content. In addition to the data acquired by the medical instrument, each image is analyzed by a trained radiologist, who produces a reading containing semantic information. This reading is then stored in the medical information system and linked to the image, together with additional metadata, as mandated by the standards with which the repository complies. An ontology based approach for retrieving semantic content from medical image repositories is reported in by Wei and Barnaghi,[80] while Lehmann et al.[81] describes a strategy for automatic image categorization according to a large number of semantic classes. An overview of recent results related to CBIR from medical images can be found in Müller et al.[82]

Progressive semantic retrieval

Progressive techniques that rely on properties of compression schemes exist to speed up the daunting task of labeling the tens of gigabytes produced daily by an instrument. Progressive classification[83] analyzes the multiresolution pyramid. It uses a different classifier for each level of the pyramid. Starting from an appropriate level, the appropriate classifier decides whether each pixel corresponds to a semantically homogeneous region at full resolution, in which case it labels the entire region, or not, in which case it marks the pixel. The marked pixels are then analyzed at the immediately finer resolution level, using an analogous classifier. The process terminates when the full-resolution level is reached and all marked pixels are labeled. This approach is not only several times faster than pixel-wise classification, but, under general condition, it is also more accurate.

Metadata

Metadata is the highest content abstraction level. It corresponds to information that cannot be inferred or extracted from the image itself, or that is associated to the image in a manual fashion. The date and time of a photographic image, the names of the people appearing in it, the author of a painting and his biography, the location of a well, the name and medical history of a patient, the satellite used to acquire an image are examples of metadata.

Metadata is either structured, and is characterized by the presence of predefined fields whose values have well-specified types, or unstructured, for example textual captions of images. Standards exist or are emerging to regulate structured metadata. They are always specific to a particular application domain, such as medicine, geographical information, remotely sensed data, etc.

Structured metadata is amenable to management using a traditional database. Unstructured metadata can be indexed using information retrieval methodologies. Both cases are beyond the scope of this entry.

PROGRESSIVE SEARCH AT MULTIPLE ABSTRACTION LEVELS

Only the simplest multimedia queries are expressed in terms of a single attribute. These queries are called *atomic* by Fagin.[84] They retrieve the simplest simple objects. For example, one could ask a photographic database for pictures of the current president of the United States (semantic query), a museum digital catalog for paintings by Renoir (metadata query), a fashion archive for fabric having a certain mix of colors (feature-level query). The repository would probably answer the query by returning a large number of results. More specific queries that return a smaller, better defined set of images, are expressed in terms of multiple attributes. For instance, the user might want to retrieve images of paintings by Renoir having as subject scenes from "la Grenouillère," or images of a tumor (metadata-level) having specific size and contour characteristics (feature level).

To support multiple-attribute queries, an image repository has to solve several problems, related to both the semantics of the query and its execution. In this section we discuss these classes of problems and describe solutions proposed in the literature.

The Semantics of Combining Multiple Attributes

Image and multimedia databases must support approximate queries: the user can only provide an approximate description of the desired content, and ask the repository to return the images that best match the specification. It is acceptable to ask for images of gray cars, and have the system return a ranked list of three images, containing respectively a gray sedan, a "metallic silver" convertible and a "silver frost" SUV. The similarity search paradigm yields a significant amount of flexibility, but at the same time complicates the interpretation of queries. Consider asking a photographic image database for pictures of "red cars." In a traditional database, this query would be expressed in SQL as `select image_id where subject='car' and color='gray'`, and the result would be a list of image identifiers containing gray cars. In the example, only the gray sedan would be returned.

In a multimedia database, the equalities in the constraints are substituted by similarity functions, and the "and" connective becomes a function that combines the similarity values of the two constraints. Early CBIR systems, such as QBIC, allowed the user to combine similarities with respect to color, texture, and shape. The user selects the importance of the three features using a graphical user interface, the similarity of images to the query is then computed separately for each feature, and the three resulting scores are combined by means of a weighted average with coefficients proportional to the importance of the features. This approach is simple, but lacks flexibility.

The query framework implemented in the Garlic system[85,86] solves the problem by treating similarity scores as fuzzy membership functions.[84,89] Scores obtained from matching individual constraints are normalized between 0 (no match) and 1 (perfect match), and combined using fuzzy Boolean connectives. The simplest forms of fuzzy AND and OR are respectively, the minimum and the maximum of the connected scores, while the negation (NOT) corresponds to subtracting the score from 1. Hence, if the color "silver frost" matches gray with a score of .8 and an SUV matches a car with a score of .9, the silver frost SUV matches the query for a gray car with an overall score of .8, the minimum of the two.

This framework can conceptually be extended to composite objects,[90] by noting that relations between simple objects produce sharp or fuzzy scores that can be treated in the same way as the object attribute scores.

Searching at Multiple Levels of Abstractions

Fagin[84,89] proposes an algorithm that executes queries containing m constraints on attributes. The algorithm assumes that the search engine can return the top k results in response to atomic queries, and that can compute the score of a database item with respect to an atomic query. The algorithm first evaluates in parallel the m atomic queries, returning for each the smallest set of top results such that there are k distinct database items that appear in each result set. Clearly, when the atomic queries are combined with the minimum function, or with a function which is monotonic in the scores, these k database items constitute the result set L. The algorithm then combines, for each item of L, the scores of the individual atomic query, to produce its score. The scored results are finally sorted in decreasing order and returned to the user.

A sequential processing algorithm for retrieving composite objects is described by Li et al.,[90] and consists of three procedures. The first procedure consists of linearizing the description of a composite object into a set of subgoals. The ordering is a function of the dependence between simple objects and of the availability of precomputed indexes for executing atomic queries. The result of the step is a chain of subtasks. The second procedure manages the computation of sets of L results from each subtask. The first time the procedure is invoked on a subtask, it produces the best L matches, the second time it produces the next best L matches, etc. The third procedure

controls the execution flow in a dynamic programming fashion: it starts from the first task in the chain, and retrieves the best k matches (out of the block of L items retrieved by the second procedure), then it executes the second task, and retrieves the best k matches for the subproblem consisting of the first and second task. The computation continues by subsequently adding tasks, and keeping track of the scores of the individual subtasks and of the current set of results. It is possible that the score of the kth partial result be smaller than the scores of the worst result currently produced by a particular subtask: if this is the case, the algorithm might be ignoring relevant database items, and a backtracking is invoked, that retrieves further objects from the offending subtask.

Further enhancements of the algorithm are presented in by Li et al.[91] where several fuzzy relations are discussed, and details are given on the execution flow control.

When ordering the subtasks, it pays to consider the abstraction level at which they operate. Metadata atomic queries are usually faster to execute and more restrictive than queries at any other level. They are in general followed by semantic queries, feature-level queries, and raw-data queries in the order. Further optimization can be performed in a query-dependent fashion: the system can collect statistics on how effective different types of queries are at pruning the search space, and use the information while staging the query execution.[92]

AFFECTIVE IMAGE RETRIEVAL

Up to this point, we have concerned ourselves with the problem of describing the visual content of images for the purpose of search and retrieval. However, since the early days of mankind, imagery has been used as a powerful way of describing concepts that transcend the pictorial representation. The image acts as a signifier and refers to a signified which could be an emotion (e.g., sadness, tranquility, etc.), an abstract concept (e.g., portrait paintings often convey information on the personality of the sitter), an event or a recurrence (e.g., the Vietnam War, the Declaration of Independence, etc.). Paintings have also been used to convey philosophical or theological teaching (e.g., the background of the Mona Lisa captures Leonardo's view of a dynamic, ever changing nature, and contains clear references to the author's fascination with hydrodynamics and hydraulics). Affective image indexing and retrieval is a discipline that lies at the intersection of affective computing[93] and CBIR; its goal is to support queries containing the specification of the emotions evoked by the desired images.

Most approaches to affective image indexing and retrieval rely on the correlation between low-level perceptual cues and the emotions they cause.[35] For example Li et al.,[94] map texture features to a thesaurus of affective concepts; Wu et al.[95] analyze the usefulness of color, text, shape, and their combination for affective image retrieval, while Bianchi-Berthouze and Kato[96] describe a system that interactively creates a Kansei user model based on low-level features extracted from Web images.

IMAGE REPOSITORIES AND DIGITAL LIBRARIES

Early research in still-image retrieval was often pursued in connection with the field of *multimedia digital libraries*. Digital libraries are organized collections of multimedia data, providing storage, retrieval, and transmission functionalities. They are used to manage text,[97] music and audio,[98] images,[30] video,[99] and other forms of electronic content. During their development, early digital libraries posed numerous challenges in all fields of computer science. At the hardware and system software levels, new computer architectures have been invented to efficiently store and transmit large amount of data; requirements have been imposed on operating systems to provide the desired quality of service and data integrity; and new assumptions on how data is accessed and modified have guided the design of file systems that efficiently manage multimedia files. At the application level, new systems for acquiring digital content have been developed; novel content representation models have been devised; algorithms for efficiently searching large collections of data have been explored; and simple, yet powerful user interfaces have been investigated to specify the desired content and to represent the returned results.

In recent years, efforts have been pursued in different directions that often depend on the application field. For example, in remote sensing the focus has shifted from creating large repositories containing data from a large variety of sources to supporting federations of data as service providers. For example, the Federation of Earth Science Information Partners, or ESIP—http://www. esipfed.org/—, originated from a NASA grant, is composed of distributors of satellite and ground-based data sets, providers of data products and technologies, organizations that develop tools for Earth Science, and strategic funding partners. As a consequence, problems of metadata standardization and of interoperability of data sets and data products derived from the data sets have taken the precedence over the original still-image retrieval problems. Other fields of investigation include collaborative learning,[100] data fusion, digital library federation, leveraging new computation paradigms such as grid computing,[101] supporting e-Science,[102] all of which are beyond the scope of this entry. The present section contains an overview of the early work in the area of digital libraries for image data, where a substantial emphasis was devoted to image retrieval.

The ground work in the general area of digital libraries was sponsored by the Digital Libraries Initiative (DLI).

The first studies were conducted at Carnegie Mellon,[99] U.C. Berkeley,[103] U.C. Santa Barbara,[104] University of Illinois at Urbana-Champaign,[97] University of Michigan,[105] and Stanford University.[106] The field of research has since seen a proliferation of projects. Early image digital libraries organized photographic images, catalogs of museums and art galleries,[107] fingerprints,[69] medical data,[108,109] geographically referenced data,[104] satellite images,[28] etc. We briefly review some of these applications.

Medical Image Databases

Medical imaging[110] is one of the most powerful diagnostic tools available. X-ray radiographs are essentially the only radiological images acquired using film, in analog format: most other modalities acquire data in digital format, hence can be managed by a digital library. Digital radiography and digital mammography are becoming increasingly popular, and we will see in the near future filmless radiology departments. Enabling technologies in digital radiology include: advances in sensor quality (resolution, signal-to-noise ratio), which make the quality of digital images comparable to that of film-based images; improvements in high-resolution, high-contrast flat-panel displays, which increase the productivity of radiologist; and high-speed connections to the Internet, that enable teleradiology, whereby a specialist can diagnose images acquired in multiple hospitals or imaging clinics.

Medical imaging is characterized by a variety of modalities, which are suited to investigating different types of properties, and yield data in different formats. Anatomy, physiology, biochemistry, and spatial properties of the body and its organs can be studied with appropriate radiological instruments.

X-ray radiography is the most common form of medical imaging. It directly measures the opacity of the body or of contrast media to electromagnetic radiation having wavelengths in the 100 to 0.01 Å range. The part of the body to be imaged is placed between a source that produces a large, non-diverging beam of x-rays and a sensor array, which records the intensity of the transmitted radiation. A digital radiograph is large: for example, a digital mammogram is a gray-scale image whose typical size is 4000×4000 pixels, and where each pixel is represented as a 12 or 14 bit number: hence, a single mammogram corresponds to 32 megabytes of data.

Computed tomography (CT) produces indirectly images of slices of the body. A series of digital radiographs of the same thin area of the body are acquired from different angles. The resulting set of projection is then analyzed by a computer which reconstructs a slice, whose typical size is 512×512 pixels, each represented by 2 bytes. During an examination, several slices are acquired, and about 20 megabytes of data are generated.

MRI measures the amount of water present in tissues, by aligning the spins of the hydrogen atoms in a thin slice of the body to a strong magnetic field, tilting them, and measuring the variations in magnetic field while the spins realign. A computer analyzes the signal and produces a 256×256 pixels image, where each pixel requires one or two bytes. Numerous slices are typically acquired during a single examination, and 10–20 megabytes of data are generated. Functional MRI is a novel technique that measures activity of organs, typically the brain. Angiographic MRI is used to image blood vessels. Diffusion MRI images the diffusion of liquids in tissues, and is used in the diagnosis of ischemic strokes.

PET measures positrons emitted by radioactive dies which are injected in the body and distribute themselves within the target organ in proportion to the physiological activity of its various parts. PET therefore measures the distribution of the source of radiation within the body.

Ultrasounds are extremely useful for imaging soft tissues, but cannot penetrate bones. Their use is mostly limited to the abdomen and the heart. During an ultrasound examination, the apparatus measures the reflectance (rather than the transparency) of the tissues to the ultrasounds emitted by a source. Doppler ultrasound is a special technique that allows to measure the blood flow within desired organs, such as the liver, and is the only type of medical image to be displayed in color for diagnostic purposes.

Several other diagnostic imaging techniques exist, including single photon emission computed tomography (SPECT), magnetic source imaging (MSI), digital subtraction angiography (DSA), electrical impedance tomography (EIT), electrical source imaging (ESI), etc.

A typical radiology department can easily generate several gigabytes of data a day. The data is heterogeneous in nature: even within the same modality, scanners produced by different manufacturers generate data with different characteristics and formats. The two main problems in this field are dealing with the large number of different equipment types (from scanners, to display workstations, to communication networks, large storage subsystems, database management systems, etc.) that form a picture archiving and communication system (PACS), and managing the sheer volume and the different formats of the data. Recently the ARC-NEMA Digital Imaging and Communications in Medicine (DICOM) standard has specified a non-proprietary digital image format, a specific data file structure and protocols for the interchange of biomedical images and associated medical information.

Medical image databases have an incredible potential in diagnostic medicine, in medical research, and in education; however, their use in such applications is still limited. For example, we can envision that future medical image databases will be powerful differential diagnosis tools: the radiologist, facing an unclear case, will be able to retrieve and consult all the images containing a similar lesion stored in the data repository, but there still are no commercial systems supporting this capability. In medical research, we auspicate that image features will be widely included in clinical studies. Education is probably the application where image databases are starting to realize their potential: for example, the Uniformed Service University of Health Sciences, the U.S. federal government health sciences university, operates an online medical image database called MedPix™, which incorporates peer-reviewed radiological teaching files. MedPix contains images with associated textual information and provides image and textual search tools. MedPix is a prominent example of the radiological resources available on the World Wide Web. A survey of these Web-based resources can be found in Schiller and Fink.[111]

Query-by-content from medical image databases has mostly relied on metadata, texture, and shape features, since most medical images are typically in gray scale. In a recent study,[81] the authors investigate the use of the combination of texture features with scaled representation of the images to categorize medical images for CBR purpose. They report that, even with global features and with a large number of categories,[81] they were able to achieve 85% classification accuracy and the correct class was within the top ten guesses in 98% of the cases. Specialized applications of texture in the medical domain include the analysis and enhancement of mammograms. A mammogram is essentially a texture image that rarely contains objects with a well-defined contour. Digital enhancement of mammographical images should increase the visual difference between normal tissue and abnormalities,[112] and filters that match the specific texture of abnormalities should be used.[113] Similarly, texture features are extremely valuable inputs to automatic classifiers of medical images.[114] We conclude this section by directing the reader interested in CBIR in the medical domain to Müller et al.,[82] which contains a broad overview of the topic as well as an extensive bibliography.

Remotely Sensed Image Databases

Remotely sensed images provides us with a wealth of information that find applications in meteorology, earth sciences, environmental studies, urban planning, forestry management, agriculture, education, and, of course, law enforcement and defense.[115]

Instruments are carried on satellites (platforms) that orbit the earth. Often several instruments are carried on a single platform. Geostationary satellites are on an equatorial orbit, while lower-altitude platforms are usually on a quasipolar orbit. An instrument consists of one or a few parallel rows of sensors. Each row contains from a few dozens to a few tens of thousands sensors, each of which acquires a pixel of data, requiring one or two bytes. For polar-orbiting satellites, the rows are parallel to the surface of the earth and perpendicular to the direction of motion of the platform. At predefined intervals, each row of sensors acquires data from a long and narrow strip of the surface of the earth, and produces a line in the image. Between intervals, the platform moves along its orbit, and at different acquisition times the field of view of the instrument covers a different strip. The imaging process is therefore somewhat analogous to that of a desktop scanner.

Satellite images represent different quantities. Most instruments acquire data reflected data in one or more spectral bands. Instrument having long sensor rows usually acquire data in few spectral bands. The LANDSAT Thematic Mapper (TM), for example, acquires data in 6 spectral bands from blue to mid-infrared and in one thermal band, at 30 m resolution, and has more than 6000 pixels per line. Spectrometers, on the other hand, acquire data simultaneously in hundreds of narrow spectral bands, but typically have shorter sensor rows. For example, the CASI instrument has 288 spectral channels and 512 pixels per line.

Few instruments image emissions in the far infrared portion of the electromagnetic spectrum, and essentially measure the temperature of the surface of the earth, of the oceans, or of strata in the atmosphere. Synthetic aperture radars (SARs) measure the reflectance of the surface to microwave or short wave emissions generated on the satellite, as well as the distance between the surface and the satellite, and they yield images that can be used to produce elevation maps or to study certain types of land covers, such as ice.

Satellite instruments image the surface at a wide variety of resolutions. In some meteorological satellites, a pixel corresponds to several square miles on the surface. The NOAA AVHRR instrument acquires data having resolution of about 1 km. The LANDSAT Multi-Spectral Scanner is a medium resolution instrument with resolution of 79 m on the ground. The French SPOT 1 and 2 have resolutions of 10 m. Until recently, satellites capable of acquiring high-resolution images have had only military applications. More recent commercial satellites can acquire images with impressive details: for example the QuickBird satellite owned by DigitalGlobe is capable of 60 cm (roughly 2 ft) resolution in panchromatic mode and of 240 cm in multispectral mode. Images from QuickBird form part of the high-resolution images available via the popular Web-based application Google Earth mapping service. Some images from the Google Earth mapping service have an even higher resolution; at the time of this writing these images are actually aerial photos, rather than satellite images.

Numerous properties of satellite imagery pose challenges to the image database technology. Orbiting instruments generate data at an impressive rate: for example, the Earth Observing System satellites produce about 300 gigabytes a day. The data is collected at few sites, and its distribution in electronic format is difficult due to its sheer volume. The image content is extremely dense, and different information is useful in different application fields: hence satellite data management requires powerful indexing methodologies.

Image Databases for the Oil Industry

The oil industry is a major producer and user of image and volumetric data. Using seismic techniques, large three-dimensional models of geological formations are constructed. From the types of strata and their formations, it is possible to infer the presence of oil, the extension of the reservoir, and to determine the best strategies for drilling. The resolution of such three-dimensional data is in the order of meters or of tens of meters, and each model corresponds to a surface area of tens or hundreds of square km, and to depths of several km.

The relatively poor resolution of such data makes it inadequate for fine-tuning the drilling process. In some occasions, the stratum containing oil is only a few feet deep, and the drill has to be steered right into the stratum. Different types of images are used for this purpose. During the drilling process, it is possible to extract portions of the core, which are then cut, polished, and photographed. Similarly, packs of instruments are lowered to the bottom of the well and slowly retrieved. Some of the instruments measure global properties of the surrounding strata every few feet, such as the gamma ray emission, while others have arrays of sensors that are pressed against the walls of the well, and produce high-resolution measurements of properties such as electric conductivity. The formation FMI has 196 such sensors that measure the electrical resistivity along the circumference of the bore at depth intervals of 0.1 in. FMI data is usually represented as a false-color image having 196 columns and tens of thousands (or more) rows.

In some cases, microphotographs of core samples are used to assess the yield potentials of an oil field.

Besides the large amount of data, image databases for the oil industry face the challenge of data fusion: three-dimensional data, well-bore images, and microphotographs are often used in conjunction to make operative decisions. Powerful indexing techniques are also needed: for example, when combining three-dimensional seismic data (which provides a global, low-resolution view of the oil field) with images from the different well bores (which provide a sparse, highly localized, and high-resolution characterization), the analyst is often interested in determining the exact depths of specific geological formations at all well locations, to improve the accuracy of the model. This is currently a slow, labor-intensive process that requires manually matching hard copies of FMI images, tens of meters long. Automatic extraction and indexing of the data can substantially simplify the task.[48,116]

CONCLUSIONS

We have defined a framework for defining, representing, and searching the content of image repositories at different abstraction levels. We have discussed how raw-data, feature, and semantic level descriptions can be extracted from the images and automatically indexed. We have noted how the combination of image representation (compression) and processing yield significant speedups in content extraction at each abstraction level.

Simple objects, defined as connected image regions which are homogeneous with respect to specific characteristics, form the atomic unit of content retrieval. They can be defined and searched at one or more abstraction levels. Composite objects are sets of simple objects satisfying spatial or temporal constraints. We have discussed the semantics of simple and composite objects and described appropriate retrieval methodologies.

There are numerous open problems in the field. The automatic extraction of semantic content from photographic images is probably the most complex. The investigation of new high-dimensional indexing structures supporting flexible metrics is also an open area of research. Improvements in the interaction between the user and the system where the system learns how individual users tend to formulate queries are needed to make large digital libraries easier to use. Standards need to be defined, to allow a search engine to simultaneously query multiple repositories, and combine the contained information. Finally, a better infrastructure, with faster communication lines, is needed to remotely query large image repository.

ACKNOWLEDGMENTS

The author would like to thank Dr. Chung-Sheng Li, Dr. Lawrence D. Bergman, Dr. Yuan-Chi Chang, Dr. John R. Smith, and Dr. John J. Turek for the years of cooperation that led to the development of the SPIRE system, Dr. Ian Bryant, Dr. Peter Tilke, Dr. Barbara Thompson, Dr. Loey Knapp, and Dr. Nand Lal, for their comments and suggestions, and for defining applications scenarios for our technology.

REFERENCES

1. Mintzer, F. et al. Toward on-line, worldwide access to Vatican library materials. IBM J. Res. Dev. **1996**, *40* (2), 139–162.
2. Koller, D. et al. Protected interactive 3D graphics via remote rendering. In *Proceedings of the 31st International Conference on Computer Graphics and Interactive Techniques, SIGGRAPH2004*, New York, ACM Press: New York, 2004; 695–703.
3. Pratt, W.K. *Digital Image Processing*, 2nd Ed.; John Wiley & Sons: New York, 1991.
4. Pennebaker, W.; Mitchell, J.L. *JPEG Still Image Data Compression Standard*; Van Nostrand Reinhold: New York, 1993.
5. Shensa, M.J. The discrete wavelet transform: Wedding the Á trous and Mallat algorithms. IEEE Trans. Sig. Proc. **1992**, *40* (10), 2110–2130.
6. Lee, D.T. JPEG 2000: Retrospective and new developments. Proc. IEEE **2005**, *93* (1), 32–41.
7. Cover, T.J.; Thomas, J.A. *Elements of Information Theory*, 2nd Ed.; John Wiley & Sons: New York, 2006.
8. Gray, R.M.; Neuhoff, D.L. Quantization. *IEEE Trans. Info. Theory Commemorative Issue*. October **1998**, *44* (5), 2325–2383.
9. Gersho, A.; Gray, R.M. *Vector Quantization and Signal Compression*; Kluwer: Boston, MA, 1992.
10. Cover, T.J.; Thomas, J.A. *Elements of Information Theory*; John Wiley & Sons: New York, 1991.
11. Cosman, P.; Gray, R.M.; Vetterli, M. Vector quantization of image subbands: A survey. IEEE Trans. Image Process. **1996**, *5* (2), 202–225.
12. Shapiro, J.M. Embedded image coding using zerotrees of wavelet coefficients. IEEE Trans. Signal Process. **1993**, *41* (12), 3445–3462.
13. Niblack, W. et al. The QBIC project: Querying images by content using color texture, and shape. In *Proceedings of the SPIE—The International Society for Optical Engineering, Storage and Retrieval for Image and Video Databases*, 1993; Vol. 1908, 173–187.
14. Hare, J.S. et al. Bridging the semantic gap in multimedia information retrieval: Top-down and bottom-up approaches. In *Mastering the Gap: From Information Extraction to Semantic Representation*, 3rd European Semantic Web Conference, Bouquet, P.; Brunelli, R.; Chanod, J.-P.; Niederée, C.; Stoermer, H., Eds.; ["lib/utils: month1_12737" not defined] 2006.
15. Smeulders, A. et al. Content-based image retrieval at the end of the early years. IEEE Trans. Pattern Anal. Mach. Intell. **2000**, *22* (12), 1449–1380.
16. Smith, J.R.; Chang, S.-F. VisualSeek: A fully automated content-based image query system. In *Proceedings of the ACM Multimedia '96*, Boston, MA, November, 18–22, 1996. 87–98.
17. Bach, J.R. et al. The Virage image search engine: An open framework for image management. In *Storage and Retrieval for Still Image Video Databases*, Proceedings of the SPIE—The International Society for Optical Engineering, 1996; Vol. 2670, 76–87.
18. Bergman, L.D. et al. Drag-and-drop multimedia: An interface framework for digital libraries. IJODL **1999**, *2* (2/3), 170–177, (Special Issue on User Interfaces for Digital Libraries).
19. Bergman, L.D. et al. SPIRE, a digital library for scientific information. IJODL **2000**, *3* (1), 85–99, (Special Issue on Tradition of Alexandrian Scholars).
20. Vermilyer, R. Intelligent user interface agents in content-based image retrieval. In *Proceedings of the 2006 IEEE SoutheastCon*, Memphis, TN, 2006. 136–142.
21. Zhou, X.S.; Huang, T.S. Relevance feedback in image retrieval: A comprehensive review. Multimedia Syst.

2003, *8* (3), 536–544 (Special Issue on Content-Based Image Retrieval).

22. Castelli, V. et al. Search and progressive information retrieval from distributed image/video databases: The SPIRE project. In *Proceedings of the ECDL '98*, Crete, Greece, September, 1998.

23. Belongie, S. et al. Color- and texture-based image segmentation using EM and its application to content-based image retrieval. In *Proceedings of the Sixth International Conference on Computer Vision*, January 1998.

24. Carson, C. et al. Region-based image query. In *Proceedings of the IEEE CVPR '97 Workshop on Content-Based Access of Image and Video Libraries*, Santa Barbara, CA, 1997.

25. Dempster, A.P.; Laird, N.M.; Rubin, D.B. Maximum likelihood from incomplete data via the EM algorithm. J. Roy. Stat. Soc. B **1977**, *39* (1), 1–38.

26. Vaidyanathan, P.P. Orthonormal and biorthonormal filter banks as convolvers, and convolutional coding gain. IEEE Trans. Signal Process. **1993**, *41* (6), 2110–2130.

27. Li, C.-S.; Turek, J.J.; Feig, E. Progressive template matching for content-based retrieval in earth observing satellite image databases. Proc. SPIE Photonic East **1995**, *2606*, 134–144.

28. Castelli, V. et al. Progressive search and retrieval in large image archives. IBM J. Res. Dev. March **1998**, *42* (2), 253–268.

29. Smith, J.R.; Chang, S.-F. Tools and techniques for color image retrieval. In *Proceedings of the SPIE Storage and Retrieval for Still Image Video Databases*, San Jose, CA, February, 1996; Vol. 2670, 426–637.

30. Niblack, W. et al. The QBIC project: Querying images by content using color texture, and shape. IBM Res. J. **1993**, *9203* (81511).

31. Swain, M.J.; Ballard, D.H. Color indexing. Int. J. Comput. Vis. **1991**, *7*(1).

32. Gray, R.S. Content-based image retrieval: color and edges; Technical Report 95-252. Department of Computer Science, Dartmouth University: Dartmouth, MA, 1995.

33. Feig, E.; Li, C.-S. Computing image histograms from compressed data. In *Proceedings of the SPIE Electronic Imaging and Multimedia Systems*, Beijing, China, 1996; Vol. 2898, 118–124.

34. Itten, J. *Kunst der Farbe*; Otto Maier Verlag: Ravensburg, Germany, 1961 (in German).

35. Colombo, C.; Del Bimbo, A.; Pala, P. Semantics in visual information retrieval. IEEE Multimedia **1999**, *6* (3), 38–53.

36. Del Bimbo, A. et al. Visual querying by color perceptive regions. Pattern Recogn. **1998**, *31* (9), 1241–1253.

37. Gagalowicz, A.; Ma, S.D.; Tournier-Lasserve, C. Efficient models for color textures. In *Proceedings of the IEEE International Conference on Pattern Recognition, ICPR '86*, 1986; 412–414.

38. Hernandez, O.J.; Khotanzad, A. An image retrieval system using multispectral random field models, color, and geometric features. In *Proceedings of the 33rd Applied Imagery Pattern Recognition Workshop*, October, 2004; 251–256.

39. Yu, H.; Li, M.; Zhang, H.; Feng, J. Color texture moment for content-based image retrieval. In *Proceedings of the IEEE Int. Conf. Image Processing, ICIP '02*, Rochester, NY, June, 2002; 929–932.

40. Li, C.-S.; Chen, M.-S. Progressive texture matching for earth observing satellite image databases. In *Proceedings of the SPIE on Multimedia Storage and Archiving Systems*, Boston, MA, November, 18–19, 1996; Vol. 2916, 150–161.

41. Davis, L.S.; Johns, S.; Aggarwal, J.K. Texture analysis using generalized co-occurrence matrices. IEEE Trans, Pattern Anal. Mach. Intell. July **1979**, *1* (3), 251–259.

42. Haralick, R.M.; Shanmugam, K.; Dinstein, I. Texture features for image classification. IEEE Trans. Syst. Man. Cybernet. **1973**, *3*, 610–621.

43. Parkkinen, J.; Selkainaho, K.; Oja, E. Detecting texture periodicity from the co-occurrence matrix. Pattern Recogn. Lett. **1990**, *11*, 43–50.

44. Tamura, H.; Mori, S.; Yamawaki, T. Texture features corresponding to visual perception. IEEE Trans. Syst. Man. Cybern. **1978**, *8* (6), 460–473.

45. Smith, J.R.; Chang, S.-F. Quad-tree segmentation for texture-based image query. In *Proceedings of the ACM Multimedia '94, San Francisco, CA*, October, 15–20, 1994; 279–286.

46. Jain, A.K.; Farrokhnia, F. Unsupervised texture segmentation using Gabor filters. Pattern Recogn. **1991**, *24* (12), 1167–1186.

47. Li, C.-S.; Castelli, V. Deriving texture feature set for content-based retrieval of satellite image database. In *Proceedings of the IEEE International Conference on Image Processing, ICIP '97*, Santa Barbara, CA, October, 26–29, 1997; 567–579.

48. Li, C.-S. et al., Comparing texture feature sets for retrieving core images in petroleum applications. In *Proceedings of the SPIE Storage and Retrieval for Image and Video Databases VII*, San Jose, CA January 1999; Vol. 3656, 2–11.

49. Ma, W.Y.; Manjunath, B.S. Texture features and learning similarity. In *Proceedings of the IEEE Computer Vision and Pattern Recognition, CVPR '96*, San Francisco, CA, June, 18–20, 1996; 425–430.

50. Ma, W.Y.; Manjunath, B.S. Edge flow: A framework of boundary detection and image segmentation. In *Proceedings of the IEEE Computer Vision and Pattern Recognition, CVPR '97*, 1997; 744–749.

51. Guyon, X. *Random Fields on a Network: Modeling, Statistics, and Applications*; Springer Verlag: New York, 1995.

52. Chen, C.C.; Dubes, R.C. Experiments in fitting discrete Markov random fields to textures. In *Proceedings of the IEEE Computer Vision and Pattern Recognition, CVPR '89*, 1989; 298–303.

53. Hassner, M.; Sklansky, J. Markov random field models of digitized image texture. In *Proceedings of the IEEE International Conference on Pattern Recognition, ICPR '78*, 1978; 538–540.

54. Hassner, M.; Sklansky, J. The use of Markov random fields as models of texture. Comput. Graphics Image Process. **1980**, *12*, 357–370.

55. Chellappa, R.; Chatterjee, S. Classification of textures using Gaussian Markov random fields. IEEE Trans. Acoust. Speech Signal Process **1985**, *33*, 959–963.

56. Cohen, F.S.; Fan, Z.; Attali, S. Automated inspection of textile fabrics using textural models. IEEE Trans. Pattern Anal. Mach. Intell. **1991**, *13* (8), 803–808.

57. Solberg, A.H.S.; Taxt, T.; Jain, A.K. A Markov random field model for classification of multisource satellite imagery. IEEE Trans. Geosci. Remote Sens. **1996**, *34* (1), 100–113.

58. Chellappa, R.; Chatterjee, S.; Bagdazian, R. Texture synthesis and compression using Gaussian-Markov random field models. IEEE Trans. Syst. Man Cybernet. March **1985**, *15* (2), 298–303.

59. Chellappa, R.; Kashyap, R.L. Texture synthesis using 2-D noncausal autoregressive models. IEEE Trans. Acoust. Speech Signal Process. **1985**. 33, 194–203.

60. Bouman, C.A.; Shapiro, M. A multiscale random field model for Bayesian image segmentation. IEEE Trans. Image Process. March **1994**, *3* (2), 162–177.

61. Chen, J.L.; Kunda, A. Automatic unsupervised texture segmentation using Hidden Markov Model. In *Proceedings of the IEEE ICASSP '93*, 1993; 21–24.

62. Goktepe, M.; Yalabik, N.; Atalay, V. Unsupervised segmentation of gray level Markov model textures with hierarchical self organizing maps. In *Proceedings of the IEEE International Conference on Pattern Recognition, ICPR '96*, Vienna, Austria, 1996; D7M.3.

63. Hansen, F.R.; Elliott, H. Image segmentation using simple Markov field models. Comput. Graphics Image Process. **1982**, *20*, 101–132.

64. Noda, H.; Shirazi, M.N.; Kawaguchi, E. A MRF model-based method for unsupervised textured image segmentation. In *Proceedings of the IEEE International Conference on Pattern Recognition, ICPR '96*, 1996; B94.2.

65. Santini, S.; Jain, R. Similarity measures. IEEE Trans. Pattern Anal. Mach. Intell. **1999**, *21* (9), 871–883.

66. Kimia, B.B. Shape representation for image retrieval. In *Image Databases, Search and Retrieval of Digital Imagery*; Castelli, V., Bergman, L.D., Eds.; John Wiley & Sons: New York, 2002; Chap. 13, 345–372.

67. Carson, C. et al. Blobworld: A system for region-based image indexing and retrieval (long version); Technical report UCB/CSD-99-1041; EECS Department, University of California: Berkeley, CA, 1999.

68. Antani, S.; Lee, D.J.; Longa, L.R.; Thoma, G.R. Evaluation of shape similarity measurement methods for spine x-ray images. J. Vis. Commun. Image Repres. September **2004**, *15* (3), 285–302.

69. Jain, A.; Lin, H.; Bolle, R. On-line fingerprint verification. IEEE Trans. Pattern Anal. Mach. Intell. **1997**, *19* (4), 302–314.

70. Eakins, J.P.; Boardman, J.M.; Shields, K. Retrieval of trade mark images by shape feature-the ARTISAN project. In *Proceedings of the IEE Colloquium on Intelligent Image Databases*, May, 1996; 1–6.

71. Icke, I. Content based 3d shape retrieval a survey of state of the art. Pattern Recognition Laboratory, The Graduate Center, City University of New York (http://www.cs.gc.cuny.edu/icke/academic/2ndexam.pdf), November 2004.

72. Jaimes, A.; Chang, S.-F. A conceptual framework for indexing visual information at multiple levels. In *Proceedings of the SPIE—The International Society for Optical Engineering, Internet Imaging*, San Jose, CA, January, 2000; Vol. 3964, 2–15.

73. Haering, N.; da Vitoria Lobo, N. Features and classification methods to locate deciduous trees in images. Comput. Vis. Image Und. July/August **1999**, *75* (1/2), 133–149.

74. Forsyth, D.A.; Fleck, M.M. Body plans. In *Proceedings of the IEEE Computer Vision and Pattern Recognition, CVPR '97*, 1997.

75. Vailaya, A. et al. Content-based hierarchical classification of vacation images. In *Proceedings of the IEEE International Conference on Multimedia Computing and Systems*, Florence, Italy, June, 7–11, 1999; 518–523.

76. Li, J.; Wang, J.Z. Automatic linguistic indexing of pictures by a statistical modeling approach. IEEE Trans. Pattern Anal. Mach. Intell. **2003**, *25* (9), 1075–1088.

77. Li, J.; Wang, J.Z. Real-time computerized annotation of pictures. IEEE Trans. Pattern Anal. Mach. Intell. **2008**, *30* (6), 985–1002.

78. Li, J.; Wang, J.Z. Alpir™ automatic photo tagging and visual image search. Online Demo.

79. Liu, Y. et al. A survey of content-based image retrieval with high-level semantics. Pattern Recogn. **2007**, *40* (1), 262–282.

80. Wei, W.; Barnaghi, P.M. Semantic support for medical image search and retrieval. In *BIEN'07: Proceeding of the Fifth IASTED International Conference*, Anaheim, CA, 2007. ACTA Press: Anaheim, CA, 2007; 315–319.

81. Lehmann, T. et al. Automatic categorization of medical images for content-based retrieval and data mining. Comput. Med. Imag. Grap. **2005**, *29* (2–3), 143–155.

82. Müller, H. et al. A review of content-based image retrieval systems in medical applications—Clinical benefits and future directions. Int. J. Med. Inform. **2003**, *73* (1), 1–23.

83. Castelli, V. et al. Progressive classification in the compressed domain for large EOS satellite databases. In *Proceedings of the IEEE ICASSP '96*, May, 1996; Vol. 4, 2201–2204.

84. Fagin, R. Fuzzy queries in multimedia database systems. In *Proceedings of the 17th ACM Symposium on Principles of Database Systems, PODS '98*, Seattle, WA, June, 1–3, 1998; ACM Press: New York, 1998; 1–10.

85. Carey, M.J. et al. Towards heterogeneous multimedia information systems: The Garlic approach. In *Proceedings of the Fifth International Workshop on Research Issues in Data Engineering: Distributed Object Management*, 1995; 124–131.

86. Cody, W. et al. Querying multimedia data from multiple repositories by content, the Garlic project. In *Proceedings of the Third Working Conference on Visual Database Systems*, 1995.

87. Kilr, G.J.; Yuan, B. *Fuzzy Sets and Fuzzy Logic, Theory and Applications*; Prentice Hall: Upper Saddle River, NJ, 1995.

88. Zadeh, L.A. Fuzzy sets. Inform. Control **1965**, *8* (3), 338–353.

89. Fagin, R. Combining fuzzy information from multiple systems. In *Proceedings of the 15th ACM Symposium on Principles of Database Systems, PODS '96*, Montreal, Quebec, Canada, June, 3–5, 1996; ACM Press: New York, 1996; 216–226.

90. Li, C.-S. et al. Sequential processing for content-based retrieval of composite objects. In *Proceedings of the SPIE Storage and Retrieval for Image and Video Databases VI*, San Jose, CA, January, 24–30, 1998; Vol. 3312, 2–13.

91. Li, C.-S. et al. Framework for efficient processing of content-based fuzzy Cartesian queries. In *Proceedings of*

the *SPIE Storage and Retrieval for Media Databases*, 2000; Vol. 3972, 64–75. Also available as IBM Research Report RC21640, January 11, 2000.

92. Li, C.-S. et al. Progressive content-based retrieval of image and video with adaptive and iterative refinement. U.S. Patent 05,734,893, March 31, 1998.

93. Tao, J.; Tan, T. Affective computing: A review. In *Affective Computing and Intelligent Interaction, Lecture Notes in Computer Science*; Springer, Berlin/Heidelberg, 2005; Vol. 3784, 239–247.

94. Li, H.; Li, J.; Song, J.; Chen, J. Fuzzy mapping from image texture to affective thesaurus. In *Bio-Inspired Computational Intelligence and Applications, Lecture Notes in Computer Science*, Springer: Berlin/Heidelberg, 2007; Vol. 4688, 357–367.

95. Wu, Q.; Zhou, C.; Wang, C. Content-based affective image classification and retrieval using support vector machines. In *Affective Computing and Intelligent Interaction, Lecture Notes in Computer Science*, Springer: Berlin/Heidelberg, 2005; Vol. 3784, 239–247.

96. Bianchi-Berthouze, N.; Kato, T. K-dime: An adaptive system to retrieve images from the web using subjective criteria. In *DNIS '00: Proceedings of the International Workshop on Databases in Networked Information Systems*, London, U.K., Springer-Verlag, 2000; 157–172.

97. Schatz, B. et al. Federating diverse collections of scientific literature. IEEE Comput. Mag. **1996**, *29* (5), 28–36.

98. Li, V.O.K.; Wanjiun, L. Distributed multimedia systems. Proc. IEEE **1997**, *85* (7), 1063–1108.

99. Wactlar, H.D.; Kanade, T.; Smith, M.A.; Stevens, S.M. Intelligent access to digital video: Informedia project. IEEE, Comput. Mag. **1996**, *29* (5), 46–52.

100. Collins, L.M. et al. Collaborative eScience libraries. Int. J. Digit. Libr. **2007**, *7* (1), 31–33.

101. Candela, L. et al. Diligent: Integrating digital library and grid technologies for a new Earth observation research infrastructure. Int. J. Digit. Libr. **2007**, *7* (1), 59–80.

102. Digital Library Goes e-Science (DLSci06). Workshop Held in Conjunction with ECDL 2006, Alicante, Spain, September, 17–22, 2006.

103. Wilensky, R. Towards work-centered digital information services. IEEE Comput. Mag. **1996**, *29* (5), 37–43.

104. Smith, T.R. A digital library for geographically referenced materials. IEEE Comput. Mag. **1996**, *29* (5), 54–60.

105. Atkins, D.E. et al. Toward inquiry-based education through interacting software agents. IEEE Comput. Mag. May **1996**, *29* (5), 69–76.

106. Paepcke, A. et al. Using distributed objects for digital library interoperability. IEEE Comput. Mag. **1996**, *29* (5), 61–68.

107. Mintzer, F. Developing digital libraries of cultural content for internet access. IEEE Commun. Mag. **1999**, *37* (1), 72–78.

108. D'Alessandro, M.P. et al. The Iowa Health Book: Creating, organizing and distributing a digital medical library of multimedia consumer health information on the internet to improve rural health care by increasing rural patient access to information. In *Proceedings of the Third Forum on Research and Technology Advances in Digital Libraries ADL '96*, 1996. 28–34.

109. Lowe, H.J. et al. The image engine HPCC project, a medical digital library system using agent-based technology to create an integrated view of the electronic medical record. In *Proceedings of the 3rd Forum on Research and Technology Advances in Digital Libraries, ADL '96*, Washington, DC, May, 1996; 45–56.

110. Macowsky, A. *Medical Imaging Systems*; Prentice Hall: Englewood Cliffs, NJ, 1983.

111. Schiller, A.; Fink, G. Radiology resources on the net: So many images, so little time. Emerg. Med. News **2004**, *26* (3), 38–40.

112. Petrick, N. et al. An adaptive density-weighted contrast enhancement filter for mammographic breast mass detection. IEEE Trans. Med. Imaging **1996**, *15* (1), 59–67.

113. Strickland, R.N.; Han, H. Wavelet transform matched filters for the detection and classification of microcalcifications in mammography. In *Proceedings of the IEEE International Conference on Image Processing, ICIP '95*, Washington, DC, October, 23–26, 1995; Vol. 1, 422–425.

114. Christoyianni, I.; Dermatas, E.; Kokkinakis, G. Neural classification of abnormal tissue in digital mammography using statistical features of the texture. In *Proceedings of the Sixth IEEE International Conference on Electronics, Circuits and Systems, ICECS '99*, September, 1999; 117–120.

115. Richards, J.A. *Remote Sensing Digital Image Analysis, an Introduction*, 2nd Ed.; Springer-Verlag: New York, 1993.

116. Bergman, L.D. et al. PetroSPIRE: A multi-modal content-based retrieval system for petroleum applications. Multimedia Storage and Archiving System, Boston, MA, 1999; Vol. 3846.

117. Castelli, V.; Bergman, L.D., Eds. *Image Databases, Search and Retrieval of Digital Imagery*; John Wiley & Sons: New York, 2002.

118. Chen, Y.; Li, J.; Wang, J.Z. *Machine Learning and Statistical Modeling Approaches to Image Retrieval*; Springer 2004.

119. Feng, D.D.; Siu, W.C.; Zhang, H., Eds. Multimedia Information Retrieval and Management; Springer: Berlin, 2003.

120. Marques, O.; Furht, B. *Content-Based Image and Video Retrieval (Multimedia Systems and Applications)*; Springer: Berlin, 2002.

121. Wilhelmus, A.; Smeulders, M.; Jain, R., Eds. *Image Databases and Multi-media Search*; World Scientific: Singapore, 1997.

122. Sagarmay, D., Ed. *Multimedia Systems and Content-Based Image Retrieval*; Idea Group, Inc., 2004.

123. Eakins, J.; Graham, M. Content-based image retrieval. http://www.jisc.ac.uk/publications/publications/contentimagefinalreport.aspx 39, JISC (October 1999).

124. Datta, R.; Joshi, D.; Li, J.; Wang, J.Z. Image retrieval: Ideas, influences, and trends of the new age. ACM Comput. Surv. April **2008**, *40* (2), 1–60.

125. Venters, C.C.; Cooper, M.A review of content-based image retrieval systems. http://www.jisc.ac.uk/publications/publications/contentreviewfinalreport.aspx, JISC, June 2000.

126. Kherfi, M.L.; Ziou, D.; Bernardi, A. Image retrieval from the World Wide Web: Issues, techniques, and systems. ACM Comput. Surv. **2004**, *36* (1), 35–67.

BIBLIOGRAPHY

We conclude this entry by listing additional resources for the interested readers. In recent years, several books have been published on the topic of still-image repositories, search, and retrieval. A general introduction can be found in Chen,[117] while Feng[118] describes a Machine Learning approach to CBIR. Numerous books on multimedia repositories contain sections on image collections, including Marques[119] and Wilhelmus.[120] In addition to these publications, which can be used as introductions to the topic or as textbooks, several collections of selected papers have appeared in the literature.[121,122] Numerous articles review current results in CBIR,[123,124] CBIR systems,[125] shape-based retrieval,[71] semantic-level retrieval,[79] as well as for applications such as CBIR for medical imaging[82] and retrieval from the World Wide Web.[126]

Storytelling

Sarah Beth Nelson
Brian William Sturm
School of Information and Library Sciences, University of North Carolina at Chapel Hill,
Chapel Hill, North Carolina, U.S.A.

Abstract

Storytelling is an increasingly ubiquitous term applied in various fields with markedly different meanings. This article addresses the meanings of the term, the kinds of stories and storytelling, a brief overview of the history of storytelling, some advice for practicing storytellers, and a discussion of the myriad contexts in which storytelling occurs today.

INTRODUCTION AND SCOPE

As the contexts of information work expand beyond the traditional walls of the library, so too have the uses of the word "storytelling." Indeed, "storytelling" is currently so fashionable in so many contexts that it is becoming somewhat hackneyed and cliché. Most anything can be considered storytelling. Marketing professionals use it to describe strategies for establishing an organization's brand identity. Advertising executives espouse its power to sell products. Corporate managers employ it in conflict resolution, and fiction writers and video game designers claim it as fundamental to their art. Storytelling is perhaps so pervasive because—some scholars argue—humans actually *think* in story format,[1] and story forms the basis for human communication. Etymologically, the English word "story" evolved from the Old French *estoire*, and earlier still, from the Latin *historia*.[2] The word "tell" evolved from the Old High German word *zählen*, meaning to count or reckon.[3] Thus, to tell stories was to recount life histories.

Whereas all of these uses of the term are powerful, storytelling in information and library science contexts has traditionally meant face-to-face, oral performance of folk literature for children in a special "storytime" setting, and its use in this entry emphasizes—yet extends—these traditional roots. It is the face-to-face, synchronous communication of narrative that separates (and, hence, defines) storytelling from its other contexts and from related performance arts such as traditional theater or reading books aloud. What makes storytelling unique is that the storyteller(s) and the listener(s) create the storylistening experience together as the story unfolds because the storyteller changes the developing narrative in response to an audience's feedback.

KINDS OF STORIES AND STORYTELLING

Because stories are so pervasive and cross disciplinary boundaries, there is no definitive typology for the various kinds of stories and storytelling. As folklore scholar William Bascom explained many years ago, "Definitions and classifications are neither particularly interesting nor necessarily fruitful, but if any field of study needs clarification of its basic terminology, it is clearly folklore, which has so long been plagued by inconsistent and contradictory definitions."[4]

Librarians, for example, might divide "story" into fiction and nonfiction, and then subdivide the former by genre and the latter by content. Later library storytelling manuals, such as Caroline Feller Bauer's 1977 classic *Handbook for Storytellers*, organize stories into such categories as folktales, literary tales, fables, myths, epics, legends, and religious stories.[5]

An early manual of storytelling (1925) for the child education community by William Forbush divides the world of story into six categories: primitive stories (stories of the forest and animal world), myths, fairy stories, epic stories, biography and purposive stories, and storytelling poems.[6] Polish-American educator Anne Pellowski's more recent and scholarly overview, *The World of Storytelling*, categorizes storytelling both by function and by context: Bardic, Religious, Folk, Theatrical, Library & Institutional, Camp/Park/Playground, and Hygienic/Therapeutic.[7]

In folklore, *Funk & Wagnalls Standard Dictionary of Folklore, Mythology, and Legend* proposes the division of stories into prose narrative, speech, proverb, and riddle.[8] Prose narrative is further subdivided into "myth," "legend," and "tale," a fairly common approach, but not entirely agreed upon. Under the entry entitled "folktale," the editors include legends and traditions, fairy tales, animal tales, and myths.[9] For prose narratives, Bascom has proposed the distinction between myth, legend, and folktale such that, *"folktales are prose narratives which are regarded as fiction…myths are prose narratives which, in the society in which they are told, are considered to be truthful accounts of what happened in the remote past…[and] legends are prose narratives which, like myths, are regarded as true by the narrator and his audience, but they are set in a period considered less remote, when the world was much as it is today."*(italics in original).[10] More recent scholars agree that "most [folklore] genres are not well defined, and researchers currently use crude heuristics or intuition to assign the genres";[11] however, Nguyen and her colleagues still propose their own set of narrative genre categories, including fairy tales, legends, saint's legends, urban legends, personal narratives, riddles, situation puzzles, jokes, and songs.

HISTORY

The Origins of Storytelling

The very earliest storytelling may have been poetry. Strabo tells us, "Ornate poetry was the first to make its appearance, and was well received." The words "rhapsody," "comedy," and "tragedy," he points out, are all derived from "ode." (This is more apparent in the ancient Greek: Ode = ᾠδή. Rhapsody = ῥαψῳδία. Comedy = κωμῳδία. Tragedy = τραγῳδία.)[12]

It makes sense that early performative speech would be in the form of poetry because the poetic form lends itself to being remembered. In the absence of writing, one must, as Walter Ong puts it, "Think memorable thoughts." He specifically mentions the following mnemonic devices: rhythm, pattern, repetition, antitheses, alliteration, assonance, epithets, and formulae.[13] These are typical characteristics of poetry. Poetic speech is deeply intertwined with orality.

Johan Huizinga, writing on human play, also argues for poetry as the progenitor of performative speech. He identifies "[t]he true appellation of the archaic poet" as *"vates, the possessed, the God-smitten, the raving one."* He says that the "poet-seer splits up into the figures of the prophet, the priest, the soothsayer, the mystagogue and the poet as we know him; even the philosopher, the legislator, the orator, the demagogue, the sophist and the rhetor spring from that primordial composite type, the *vates*."[14] From poetry comes all performative speaking and writing. From the *vates* comes, among the others mentioned, the storyteller.

The oldest known story, Lugalbanda, comes from Sumeria. It was written down as two poems on clay tablets and had been passed down orally before that. Gilgamesh,

which was believed to be the oldest story for some time, references the story of Lugalbanda, who was Gilgamesh's father.[15]

Before the invention of writing, narrative storytelling, did much more than entertain. Narratives were the libraries of a culture, preserving information about the cultural group, and their way of life. Ong states, "Most, if not all, oral cultures generate quite substantial narratives or series of narratives, such as the stories of the Trojan wars among the ancient Greeks, the coyote stories among various Native American populations, the Anansi (spider) stories in Belize and other Caribbean cultures with some African heritage, the Sunjata stories of old Mali, the Mwindo stories among the Nyaga, and so on."[16] The narrative form holds information together, makes it more memorable, and more easily transferable.

Following are brief descriptions of the use of oral narrative in a variety of cultures. The list is not exhaustive, but highlights some notable examples.

Storytelling was a fine art in early Iceland and many people told their own sagas. This, then, evolved into Icelanders telling stories they heard as well as lived. We know from Ari, who wrote a history of Iceland (*Íslendingabók*), not only many of the sagas, but also their provenance. "Ari was born about 1067, and his chief source of information was his foster-father Hallr, an old man and famous for his wisdom, who in early life had been acquainted with St Olaf. Among his other informants are mentioned Teitr, another foster-son of Hallr, and grandson of Gizurr the White; Oddr, a grandson of Hallr á Síðu; and Thuríðr, a daughter of Snorri Goði. Gizurr, Hallr á Síðu, and Snori Goði are among the most prominent characters who figure in sagas relating to the beginning of the eleventh century."[17] Before Ari recorded these sagas, the lives of generations were preserved through oral narrative.

As stated above, Ong specifically mentions the cultural significance of the Coyote narratives. Karl Kroeber says of the Native American trickster, "Nothing more upsets conventional Western logicians than this buffoonish embodiment of self-destructive greed - who simultaneously is the creator of culture."[18] Coyote does not just preserve culture, he makes it. Gerald Vizenor says Coyote is "not a neutral instrument that reveals codes and structural harmonies in tribal cultures."[19] Coyote stories help the listeners make sense of their world and understand how to interact with it.

Other cultures also preserved sacred knowledge through narrative. Nora and Munro Chadwick, in their analysis of the Old Testament, state, "It is apparently the prevailing opinion now among Hebrew scholars that the early narrative texts were largely derived from saga."[20] The stories in the Old Testament are oral narratives transferred to text.

The Chadwicks write of some of the Turkish peoples, "In the art of extemporisation especially the Tatars are past masters." And "the powers of memory were highly valued and cultivated among these people."[21] Storytelling for them could be an improvised performance or a faithful rendering of a traditional tale. In Islam, as in other religions, the main repository of sacred knowledge, for some time, was not texts, but people. The Chadwicks describe a "custom among the richer chiefs, notably those of the Kirghiz and the Turkomans, of keeping a mullah, or educated Mohammedan scholar, in their camps."[22] This person, among other things, was a storyteller.

The Polynesians were also very concerned with memory. Their sagas and poetry have preserved historical events that occurred as far back as 20 generations in their past. Chronology of this area is accepted as relatively accurate dating back to 1300 (European discovery of Polynesia was in the late 1500s) due to oral histories and genealogies. Social standing was inherited, so perfect accuracy, at least in one's own genealogy and family stories was a necessity. Some of the ancient poetry can no longer be fully translated because it contains obsolete words.[23]

Stories told today in Sudan still maintain the memory of the culture. In the introduction to *The Clever Sheikh of the Butana*, Stephen Howard talks of Ali Lutfi Abdallah listening to stories as a child. "The old women of the community were the lending libraries for these stories, remembering and embellishing as their energy permitted or as the children's restlessness demanded. . . .But as is characteristic of an oral society, their memories served to preserve ancient traditions. Older women are often a conservative force in this culture as well, in that they conserve the values which they were taught as girls."[24] The power of the oral narrative is not lost in the presence of writing, but the place of storytelling has changed in the modern world.

Recent History

Organized storytelling in the United States has its roots in the kindergarten movement established by educator Friedrich Froebel in Germany in 1837. German immigrants brought with them Froebel's belief that storytelling should be part of the kindergarten program, and they included it when the first kindergarten was incorporated into a U.S. public school in 1873. Soon after the American Library Association was founded in 1876, storytelling began to appear in public libraries across the nation. The rise of storytelling in libraries is often credited to a national tour by acclaimed English storyteller Marie Shedlock in 1900–1901, though several years earlier public libraries had experimented with the art form and established "story hours" for children. Children's librarians were captivated by Shedlock's performances, and they soon made storytelling a major part of children's story hours. Kindergarten teacher Sara Cone Bryant's *How to Tell Stories to Children* was the first American publication (1905) to

address the practice of storytelling, and it started a wave of storytelling manuals written by educators and librarians.[25]

The early 1900s was a volatile growth period for storytelling. Children's librarians used their performances to help indoctrinate immigrant children to American values and ideals. The rise of the library "branch" movement in the 1920s allowed storytelling to reach more children, and in the 1930s churches and public parks began offering regular storytelling experiences. Schools other than kindergartens began to emphasize storytelling in the classroom, and an explosion of "how-to" manuals helped spur its distribution. The new medium of FM radio (1933) brought even greater dissemination of stories, though it changed the experience dramatically. The rise of preschools in the 1940s with their concomitant emphasis on reading and literacy began a decline in storytelling in favor of reading books aloud. The growth of the picture book format in children's literature and developments in color printing quality throughout the first half of the twentieth century augmented this decline, and the introduction of the color television in the 1950s and 1960s so captivated the population, that by the late 1960s, storytelling was no longer an emphasis, though it was still widely practiced.[26]

Then in 1975, a new organization was founded in the United States—The National Association for the Preservation and Perpetuation of Storytelling (now the National Storytelling Network)—that began to promote storytelling in the United States as a professional career.[27] Other organizations soon followed, including the Story Circle Network, helping women share the stories of their lives and raising public awareness of the importance of women's personal histories;[28] the National Association of Black Storytellers;[29] the California Indian Storytelling Association;[30] the League for the Advancement of New England Storytelling;[31] the Northlands Storytelling Network;[32] the Jewish Storytelling Coalition;[33] the Network of Biblical Storytellers;[34] Spellbinders, training retirees as volunteer storytellers in schools;[35] and many state and local associations or guilds that sponsor festivals, workshops, and other storytelling events.

The 1980s and 1990s saw a rise in professional storytellers in the United States, and many children's librarians began to hire professional performers instead of learning the art themselves. Storytelling in library education also began to wane as the field of librarianship expanded into the vast, new information economy. In the early decades of the twenty-first century, we see the field of storytelling continuing to expand and change. The prevalence of video and audio recordings of modern storytelling create new ties to the library world through the need for curation and dissemination.

The Moth, a New York storytelling show, consists of novice performers sharing brief, true, personal stories. The show has gained an enormous following, creating tours, spinoff shows, radio hours, and podcasts that reach across the globe.[36]

StoryCorps, although not live storytelling, has brought attention to the need to preserve our personal and family stories. Individuals record their stories in an interview, directly to a digital format, and all the stories are archived by the American Folklife Center at the Library of Congress in Washington, DC. There are community archive centers in various locations throughout the country and interviews produced for national broadcast are available on the Web.[37]

Contemporary storytelling is not exclusively personal. Members of the Society for Creative Anachronism meet informally in Bardic Circles to share stories and songs.[38] Mythology story slams following the Myth-Off format occur internationally.[39] There are also events, like the Going Deep retreat, during which performers share long-form traditional stories.[40]

Storytelling remains vital around the world. The Storytellers of Canada, "connects storytellers across Canada through its publications, Web site, annual conference and ongoing advocacy to form a nationwide community of storytelling," and there are many regional associations and guilds.[41] The Storytelling Guild of Australia is a national network of storytellers, librarians, educators, and therapists whose objective is to "promote the craft and skills of storytelling; offer opportunities, resources, workshops, coaching, [and] accreditation for storytellers; [and] provide a forum for storytellers to share skills."[42] The website is hosted by the National Library of Australia. The New Zealand Guild of Storytellers, founded by a librarian, "is dedicated to preserving, practicing and promoting the art of Storytelling."[43] The Scottish Storytelling Center and Network's purpose "is the support and development of storytelling in all sectors of society, in all parts of Scotland, and in international contexts."[44] Similar work is done in the United Kingdom by the Society for Storytelling.[45]

In other parts of the world, storytelling efforts are supported by associations connected with reading, communication, theatrical arts, language and literacy, museums, and other cultural heritage organizations. The Indian Storytelling Network "draws upon many ancient Indian traditions regarding developing ways of using Stories and Storytelling for Education, Therapy, and Coaching."[46] The Asian Storytelling Network "offers storytelling programmes for every occasion and venue."[47] Storymoja, an African publishing company, collaborates with international partners to produce a storytelling festival in Nairobi annually[48] and the Kanoon Institute for the Intellectual Development of Children & Young Adults hosts a festival in Iran.[49] The Norwegian Storytelling Forum's members work in educational, health, and business contexts to promote storytelling and storytellers.[50] Rumah Dongeng Indonesia provides a similar set of services for storytellers across Indonesia,[51] and the Storytelling Association does

so for Singapore.[52] The International Storytelling Network, based in Spain, "is a site of storytellers open to spreading Storytelling, Promote reading, Literary creation, and Performing arts."[53]

FINDING STORIES

Storytellers search many sources to find appropriate stories to add to their repertoires. Traditional stories in collections, picture books, audiobooks, and e-books provide a wealth of opportunities to read and hear stories, and the Internet is replete with full-text story websites. Some of these provide access to specific types of stories, like Snopes.com[54] for contemporary legends or Aesopfables.com[55] for Aesop's fables. Some provide a variety of different story types, such as Americanfolklore.net,[56] with categories for spooky stories; tall tales; myths and legends; urban legends; folk tales; fables and fairy tales; campfire stories; children's stories; animal stories; and jokes, riddles, and tongue twisters. This site also has broad geographic and ethnic subcategories. The folklore and mythology electronic texts archive created by the University of Pittsburgh[57] is another excellent source of full-text stories. The Perseus database, run by Tufts,[58] contains numerous Greek and Roman myths in their original language and in translation. The Project Gutenberg site[59] has access to many public domain collections of folktales.

There is more to finding a good story, however, than stumbling upon it during exploratory reading. Folklorists have devised two principal indexing strategies to facilitate access to world folktales: the type index and the motif index.

Type indices treat stories as a unit, drawing very similar stories together for comparative analysis. Each story type is assigned a number and letter (i.e., 510A Cinderella) based upon the classification system designed by Antti Aarne and Stith Thompson in 1961, called *The Types of the Folktale*: *A Classification and Bibliography*.[60] The bulk of the index is the type classification system with associated short, story descriptions and keyword bibliographic references to the source texts. It is a superb, scholarly work that indexes academic and abstruse sources, and is, therefore, best used by folklore scholars who have access to such erudite material. For those needing access to more readily available sources, D. L. Ashliman's *A Guide to Folktales in the English Language* is an easier source to use, with more complete story annotations and a layout that makes tracking specific stories down much simpler, but it lacks the motif analysis included in the Aarne document.[61]

Motif indices, on the other hand, break stories down into component parts and then index those story "pieces." Any particular folktale may have as many as 20 or 30 motifs present (i.e., the Cinderella tale includes motifs: S31: Cruel stepmother; D315.1: Transformation: rat to person; R221: Heroine's threefold flight from the ball; and H36.1: Slipper test, among many others).[62] Stith Thompson is, perhaps, the name most often associated with folklore motif indexing as his classification scheme *The Motif Index of Folk Literature* in 1960 became a standard for other indexers of folktales. Many other scholars have pursued similar structuralist objectives, resulting in myriad motif indices emphasizing particular cultures or audiences that broaden the coverage of folklore and deepen and extend the original classification scheme Thompson envisioned. A sampling of these indices includes Hireko Ikeda's *A Type and Motif Index of Japanese Folk-Literature* (1971),[63] B.F. Kirtley's *A Motif Index of Polynesian, Melanesian and Micronesian Narratives* (1980),[64] Helen Flowers' *A Classification of the Folktale of the West Indies by Types and Motifs* (1952),[65] Lena Neuland's *Motif-Index of Latvian Folktales and Legends* (1981),[66] Hasan El-Shamy's *Folk Traditions of the Arab World: A Guide to Motif Classification* (1995),[67] and Margaret Read MacDonald and Brian W. Sturm's *Storyteller's Sourcebook: A Subject, Title, and Motif Index to Folklore Collections for Children, 1983–1999* (2001),[68] as well as Margaret Read MacDonald's earlier work, *The Storyteller's Sourcebook* (1982).[69]

LEARNING STORIES

How to learn a story for performance depends on many factors, including personal preferences, cultural storytelling traditions, and the social and political context of the storytelling experience. Some cultures are conservative and require storytellers to learn and perform stories verbatim in order to preserve traditional performance styles and keep the content of stories accurate and culturally authentic. Others adopt a liberal approach that provides storytellers more creative license to adapt and alter their stories. While the former leads to more choreographed and memorized story learning, the latter demands more improvisational skill from the performer. Some cultures merge the memorized with the extemporaneous in performance, as documented by Albert Lord in his analysis of singers of Slavic oral epics (byliny); Lord found that these performers had vast repertoires of stock formulae and phrases that could be combined, repeated, and interspersed throughout their impromptu compositions.[70]

Modern storytelling manuals offer many suggestions for how to learn a story for performance; the most common is to visualize the story so that the storyteller can "see" the tale like a movie or series of pictures that unfold in the mind's eye as the story proceeds. Storytellers then improvise the words to match the pictures they see, often incorporating memorized words or phrases that augment the cultural authenticity or ethnic "flavor" of the story. There are, however, myriad other techniques to aid in learning a story, from storyboarding (creating a series of illustrations that outline the plot), "scening" (using short phrases that divide the story into chunks or scenes), outlining (creating a detailed overview of the plot), and scripting (adding staging and performance notes to an outline), to writing out the entire plot for memorization (for people who are word-learners).

PERFORMING STORIES

There are several key points that most manuals of storytelling address in their attempt to help novices master the art of story performance. First, the story is carried on the breath, so storytellers must explore the full potential of their voices: volume (loud or soft), pitch (high or low), emphasis, emotional tone, rate (fast or slow), rhythm, enunciation, and silence. Second, effective communication involves the body: facial expressions, gestures, posture, muscle tension, proximity to audience, eye contact, and the use of physical contact. Third, appearance also influences a performance, including clothing, hair styles, color choices, and adornment. Fourth, storytellers must determine the relative merits of accessories or props such as musical instruments, puppets, magic, noisemakers, pictures, string figures, balloon animals, paper cutouts, or projected images.

At each moment of the performance, many of these elements are at play, and the storyteller must constantly adjust each of them to maximize the impact of the story for the audience. In short, so long as each element of the performance improves the *story* and the immersion of the audience in the story world, the storyteller is performing well. Common advice from storytellers and storytelling manuals includes

- Only tell stories you love as your enthusiasm for the story is *very* contagious.
- Recall the mood of the story and open with that mood.
- Use large gestures at the beginning of the story if appropriate to relieve nervousness.
- Pause after the introduction to "signal" the story's beginning.
- Watch the audience for feedback and change the story to increase its impact.
- Speak slowly and clearly as the audience only gets one chance to hear the story's message.
- Vary the rhythm and pacing to create an "ebb and flow" in the story's intensity.
- Practice, practice, practice.
- Know how long your story is and how to adjust the length during the performance if necessary.
- Prepare for your storytelling environment: microphone, large or small space, indoors or outdoors, ambient noise.

STORYTELLING IN CONTEXT

Storytelling in Business

Storytelling is currently used in many areas of the business world. Annett Simmons lists the following story types organizational leaders and salespeople use to inspire trust:

1. "Who I Am" stories
2. "Why I Am Here" stories
3. "The Vision" story
4. "Teaching" stories
5. "Values-in-Action" stories
6. "I Know What You Are Thinking" stories[71]

Stories are also used to create a brand and advertise products. Employees at all levels share stories in order to better understand their role in an organization and communicate their experiences. Stories preserve institutional knowledge. Storytelling can also be a part of organizational analysis and strategic planning.[72] Some companies even ask customers "to tell personal stories about their consumer experiences."[73] These stories influence how the company moves forward.

Storytelling in Education

"All over the world and in all races, listening to stories has. . .always been to children one of the most effective doorways unto life and knowledge." Storytelling "is of great value in training the memory"; it increases vocabulary, "awakens and educates real and natural feelings," and assists in "the development of character."[74] Whereas these claims by Forbush are undocumented, Kendall Haven has collected much of the research on storytelling and its power in his book *Story Proof*, which documents the value of storytelling in such areas as text comprehension, logical thinking, meaning-making, motivation for learning, community-building, language mastery, writing success, and memory.[75]

Hamilton and Weiss state that storytelling has value for children in schools because hearing stories: stimulates the imagination; instills in children a love of language and motivates them to read; improves listening skills; improves such language skills as vocabulary, comprehension, sequencing, and story recall; encourages creative writing; and gives children a common set of words and ideas that help create the classroom culture.[76]

Collins and Cooper concur and extend these ideas, stating that storytelling: enhances imagination and visualization, develops appreciation of the beauty and rhythm of language, increases vocabulary, refines speaking skills, improves listening skills, allows students to interact with adults on a personal level, enhances writing skills, develops reading skills and sparks interest in reading, enhances critical and creative thinking skills, nourishes students' intuitive side, helps students see literature as a mirror of human experience, and helps students understand their own and others' cultural heritage.[77]

There is also value in students as storytellers. They use storytelling to communicate things they have learned and to begin to impose a narrative structure on personal accounts. Storytelling helps students work through difficult situations and emotions. It teaches empathy by allowing them to live briefly in another person's world. Retelling stories they have read encourages students to engage more fully with the text, imagining what characters felt, how they spoke, and what they did with their bodies. Most importantly, storytelling, like other arts, increases students', "self-observation, standard setting, self-reaction, and self-efficacy."[78] It helps students learn how to learn.

Storytelling teaching artists visit schools to entertain, and to inspire teachers and students. Teaching artists offer residencies (instruction over a period of time) in areas such as storytelling, literacy development, writing, digital storytelling, improvisation, bullying prevention and self-respect, cultural enrichment, and storytelling arts-integration with any curriculum subject.[79–81]

Healing Storytelling

Folktales and storytelling are valuable on psychological and therapeutic levels. Child psychologist, Bruno Bettleheim's seminal work, *The Uses of Enchantment*, explores how folktales resonate with archetypal images and scenarios that help children cope with the emotional challenges of growing up.[82] Similar work has been done for adults by Marie-Louise von Franz, Robert Bly, Allan Chinen, and Clarissa Pinkola Estés, among others.

Storytelling focuses the attention, allowing listeners to become "completely immersed in the present"; it "charms the mind, rests the perturbed spirit and even helps prepare the body either for sleep or for renewed activity"; it aids in "broadening social imagination and thus developing the spirit of generosity"[83] Listening to stories can make one calm, collected, and maybe even a better person.

Telling stories is therapeutic for the performers as well. Veterans, former addicts, survivors of various traumas, and even those just making their way through the typical challenges of everyday life, find peace in telling their stories. The Administration for Native Americans, in their page on Native American Veterans and storytelling for healing, says healing stories contain important values that include, "acceptance, courage, truth, and spirituality. When these are in place, some individuals can begin to make meaning of their experiences."[84] Listeners gain understanding, and if they are in a similar situation, take comfort in knowing they are not alone.

Stories heal communities. Jo Carson, storyteller, playwright, and one of the founders of Alternate ROOTS, worked with communities across the country to tell their most important stories through plays.[85] She collected oral histories from the community and turned them into plays that were performed by members of the community. These plays consisted of more storytelling than dialog. The communities often chose the theme themselves. Stories might center on a past traumatic event or episodes from the community's history that spoke to current challenges. In her book, *Spider Speculations*, Carson says projects like these "change people's perceptions of their place and their community so that it somehow becomes a place worth keeping," or restore the soul and keep alive the feeling of community.[86]

There is some interest in the power of words to heal physical ailments through such techniques as neurolinguistic programming. NLP involves understanding another person's preferred way of sensing the world, and communicating with them using this mode. However, at this time there is not sufficient evidence to indicate that these techniques have a significant effect on physical health outcomes.[87]

Religious Storytelling

Although the sacred texts of many of the world's religions have long since been immortalized in writing, telling the stories aloud is understood to have a continuing inherent value. "For centuries the meaning of the stories of scripture lay in the *experience* of hearing them. The faithful located their own experience within the framework of that overarching story."[88] Hearing religious stories told aloud allows the listener to better relate the story to his or her own life.

Yitzak Buxbaum tells a story about religious storytelling: "[T]he famous hasidic leader, the Seer of Lublin, told how he once passed by a synagogue from which shone a supernal light." He thought, "Certainly, there are great scholars inside, studying the Torah in holiness." But when he entered, he saw two ordinary hasidim, not studying Torah but sitting and conversing. He asked them, "Friends, what are you talking about?" The hasidim answered, "We are telling stories about the deeds of the tzaddikim." "When he heard that, the Seer was very moved, for he realized that their storytelling produced the same divine light and illumination as does Torah study."[89] Telling religious stories here is equated not with reading the Torah, but studying it. Storytelling enables deeper understanding.

For these reasons, a number of individuals and organizations participate in religious storytelling. The Network of Biblical Storytellers, for example, supports performances based on the Christian scriptures through their organization, website, yearly festival gathering, and magazine.[34] The Jewish Storytelling Coalition similarly connects Jewish storytellers.[33] Traditional Japanese storytelling is being used to share the teachings of Buddhism.[90] Harikatha, a form of storytelling in South India, is based on religious texts and incorporates music and dance.[91] Storytelling continues to be a main method for transferring religious knowledge.

Storytelling in Libraries

Librarians tell stories alongside the reading of books during story hours and other library programs. These stories often have a literary connection, allowing the librarians to suggest books children might like to read if they enjoyed the story. Libraries also hire professional tellers to perform, usually for child audiences, but occasionally for teen or adult audiences. Professional tellers may or may not make a direct connection between their stories and books in the library as they often tell these same stories in other venues as well. However, storytellers and other performers are most sought-after during the summer reading program, so they will often tailor these performances to the summer reading theme.

As keepers of the printed, digital, and spoken word, libraries are also beginning to consider the challenges surrounding the preservation of oral narrative. After speaking with several First Nations elders, Charles Maina writes of some of the complexities libraries face when collecting traditional knowledge. He mentions the loss of context when an oral performance is fixed in a medium, issues of ownership, and the difficulties of classifying holistic wisdom.[92] The digital medium has encouraged a general attitude that almost anything and everything can be preserved; however, digital files do deteriorate, and the devices used to read them can become obsolete. Even after oral knowledge has been respectfully collected, actually preserving it as audio or video in a long-term archive takes careful planning.

Storytelling in Arts and Cultural Institutions

Museums, historical centers, parks, and other cultural institutions use the power of story to share information in a meaningful and memorable way. Historic Philadelphia's Once Upon a Nation program, for example, shares stories that "cover a wealth of topics and span time from the seventeenth century through today and share American history with 21st-century flair."[93] Many parks, similarly, have performers tell the stories of their place throughout time. The Milwaukee Public Museum has "Museum Storytelling" once a month, often based around exhibits, like the Hebior mammoth and Egyptian artifacts.[94] Storytelling brings to life the information these institutions have to share.

Storytelling Events

Finally, storytelling also happens just for the sake of storytelling. The National Storytelling Festival in Jonesborough, Tennessee, was first held in 1973, and "sparked a renaissance of storytelling."[95] Other festivals now occur throughout the United States every year, such as the Timpanogos Storytelling Festival in Orem, Utah,[96] The Texas Storytelling Festival in Denton,[97] and the Peach State Storytelling Festival in Atlanta, Georgia.[98] At these festivals, paid tellers take the stage before an audience that has come for stories. Often, the day is broken up with workshops, open mic sessions, story slams, or simply different genres of storytelling.

Dedicated storytelling performances have also moved off the festival stage. At The Moth and events inspired by The Moth, amateur tellers perform for crowds assembled in bars. Unlike festivals, which feature all kinds of storytelling, Moth events contain exclusively true, personal stories.[36]

Story slams are sometimes held as a portion of a larger event, like a festival or as stand-alone events. Slams are competitions, with each teller being awarded points in categories such as artistry, adherence to a theme, staying within a time limit, etc. At the end of the slam, winners are recognized. Some slams feature personal stories, like Connecticut's Campus Slammer,[99] and others like MythOff[100] feature traditional stories.

CONCLUSION

Storytelling grew out of a need to preserve and transmit the wisdom and values of a culture. In spite of the ever-changing and growing field of communication technology, storytelling continues to be culturally significant. It still teaches, still heals, still connects human beings in a way nothing else can. Storytelling embraces technology: books, radio, television, the Internet, and beyond. These things add to the transmission of stories, but do not replace face to face oral transmission. Even the so-called "digital natives" are gathering to share and listen to stories. Some of the venues have changed. The styles have changed. But people young and old see the value in getting together, breathing the same air, and telling their stories.

REFERENCES

1. Fuller, R. The Primacy of Story. Context **1991**, 27, 26–28.
2. Oxford University Press. Story. 2016. http://www.oed.com/view/Entry/190981?rskey=C5H8c9&result=1&isAdvanced=false#eid (accessed November 2014).
3. Harper, D. Tell. 2016. http://www.etymonline.com/index.php?term=tell (accessed November 2014).
4. Bascom, W. The forms of folklore: prose narratives. J. Am. Folk.**1965**, 78(307), 3.
5. Bauer, C.F. Handbook for Storytellers; American Library Association: Chicago, IL, 1977; viii.
6. Forbush, W.B. A Manual of stories; American Institute of Child Life: Philadelphia, PA, 1925; 17–20.
7. Pellowski, A. The World of Storytelling; H.W. Wilson: New York, 1990; v–vii.
8. Leach, M.; Fried, J. Funk and Wagnalls Standard Dictionary of Folklore, Mythology, and Legend. Harper & Row: New York, 1984; 1139.
9. Leach, M.; Fried, J. Funk and Wagnalls Standard Dictionary of Folklore, Mythology, and Legend. Harper & Row: New York, 1984; 408–409.
10. Bascom, W. The forms of folklore: prose narratives. J. Am. Folk. **1965**, 78(307), 4.
11. Nguyen, D.; Trieschnigg, D.; Meder, T.; Theune, M. Automatic classification of folk narrative genres. *Empirical Methods in Natural Language Processing, Proceedings of the Conference on Natural Language Processing, Vienna, Austria, September 21, 2012*, Jancsary, J. Ögai. Vienna, Austria, 2012; 378. http://depot.knaw.nl/13065/1/56_nguyen12w.pdf (accessed November 2014).
12. Hamilton, H.C.; Falconer, W., Trans. *The Geography of Strabo*; George Bell & Sons: London, U.K., 1903, Book 1, Chapter 2, Section 6. http://www.perseus.tufts.edu/hopper/text?doc=Perseus%3Atext%3A1999.01.0239%3Abook%3D1%3Achapter%3D2%3Asection%3D6 (accessed November 2014).
13. Ong, W. *Orality and Literacy: The Technologizing of the Word*; Routledge: New York, 2002; 34.
14. Huizinga, J. *Homo Ludens: A Study of the Play-Element in Culture*; Beacon Press: Boston, MA, 1955; 120–121.
15. Henderson, K. *Lugalbanda: The Boy Who Got Caught Up in a War*; Candlewick Press: Cambridge, MA, 2006; 10–11.
16. Ong, W. *Orality and Literacy: The Technologizing of the Word*; Routledge: New York, 2002; 137.
17. Chadwick, H.M.; Chadwick, N.K. *The Growth of Literature*; Cambridge University Press: Cambridge, U.K., 1940, Vol. I, 582.
18. Kroeber, K. *Artistry in Native American Myths*; University of Nebraska Press: Lincoln, NE, 1998; 224–226.
19. Vizenor, G.R. *Narrative Chance: Postmodern Discourse on Native American Indian Literatures*; University of Oklahoma Press: Norman, OK, 1993; 194.
20. Chadwick, H.M.; Chadwick, N.K. *The Growth of Literature*; Cambridge University Press: Cambridge, U.K., 1940, Vol. II, 642.
21. Chadwick, H.M.; Chadwick, N.K. *The Growth of Literature*; Cambridge University Press: Cambridge, U.K., 1940, Vol. III, 14–15.
22. Chadwick, H.M.; Chadwick, N.K. *The Growth of Literature*; Cambridge University Press: Cambridge, U.K., 1940, Vol. III, 13.
23. Chadwick, H.M.; Chadwick, N.K. *The Growth of Literature*; Cambridge University Press: Cambridge, U.K., 1940, Vol. III, 234–238.
24. Howard, W.S. Introduction. In *The Clever Sheikh of the Butana and Other Stories*; Abdallah, A.L., Ed.; Interlink Books: New York, 1999; xi.
25. Alvey, R.G. *The Historical Development of Organized Storytelling to Children in the United States*; PhD dissertation; University of Pennsylvania: Philadelphia, PA, 1974; 10. http://libproxy.lib.unc.edu/login?url=http://search.proquest.com/docview/302724154?accountid=14244 (accessed November 2014).
26. Alvey, R.G. *The Historical Development of Organized Storytelling to Children in the United States*; PhD dissertation; University of Pennsylvania: Philadelphia, PA, 1974. http://

libproxy.lib.unc.edu/login?url=http://search.proquest.com/docview/302724154?accountid=14244 (accessed November 2014).

27. National Storytelling Network. *National Storytelling Network*, 2016. http://www.storynet.org/ (accessed October 2014).

28. Story Circle Network, Inc. *Story Circle Network*, 2016. http://www.storycircle.org/ (accessed October 2014).

29. National Association of Black Storytellers, Inc. *National Association of Black Storytellers*, n.d., http://www.nabsinc.org/ (accessed October 2014).

30. California Indian Storytelling Association. *California Indian Storytelling Association*, n.d., http://www.cistory.org/ (accessed October 2014).

31. League for the Advancement of New England Storytelling. *League for the Advancement of New England Storytelling*, 2015. http://lanes.org/ (accessed November 2014).

32. Northlands Storytelling Network. *Northlands Storytelling Network*, 2016. http://www.northlands.net/ (accessed November 2014).

33. Jewish Storytelling Coalition. *Jewish Storytelling Coalition*, 2014. http://www.jewishstorytelling.org/ (accessed October 2014).

34. Network of Biblical Storytellers International. *Network of Biblical Storytellers International*, 2010. http://www.nbsint.org/ (accessed October 2014).

35. Spellbinders. *Spellbinders*, 2015. http://www.spellbinders.org/ (accessed November 2014).

36. The Moth. *The Moth*, n.d. http://themoth.org/ (accessed October 2014).

37. Story Corps, Inc. *Story Corps*, 2016. http://storycorps.org/ (accessed October 2014).

38. Society for Creative Anachronism, Inc. *Jargon*, 2016. http://www.sca.org/officers/chatelain/pdf/jargon.pdf (accessed October 2014).

39. Mythoff. *Mythoff*, 2016. https://www.facebook.com/mythoff (accessed October 2014).

40. Going Deep. Going Deep, *Long Traditional Stories Retreat*, 2015. https://www.facebook.com/groups/221772087868063/ (accessed October 2014).

41. Storytellers of Canada. *Storytellers of Canada*, 2016. http://www.storytellers-conteurs.ca/ (accessed October 2014).

42. Australian Storytelling. Australian Storytelling, 2016. http://www.australianstorytelling.org.au/ (accessed October 2014).

43. NZ Guild of Storytellers. *The New Zealand Guild of Storytellers*, 2016. http://storytelling.org.nz/ (accessed October 2014).

44. Traditional Arts and Culture Scotland. *Traditional Arts & Culture Scotland*, 2016. http://www.scottishstorytellingcentre.co.uk/ (accessed October 2014).

45. The Society for Storytelling. *Society for Storytelling*, 2016. http://www.sfs.org.uk/ (accessed October 2014).

46. Indian Storytelling Network. *Indian Storytelling Network*, n.d. http://www.indianstorytellingnetwork.org/ (accessed October 2014).

47. Asian Storytelling Network. *Asian Storytelling Network*, n.d. http://www.asianstorytellingnetwork.com/ (accessed October 2014).

48. Storymoja Festival. *Storymoja Festival*, 2014. http://storymojafestival.com/about-the-festival/ (accessed November 2014).

49. Kanoon International Affairs. *The 17th International Storytelling Festival*, 2016. http://www.kanoonintl.com/?p=8888 (accessed November 2014).

50. Norsk Fortellerforum. *Norsk Fortellerforum*, 2015. http://www.norskfortellerforum.no/ (accessed November 2014).

51. Rumah Dongeng Indonesia. *Rumah Dongeng Indonesia*, 2011. http://lembagarumahdongengindonesia.wordpress.com/ (accessed November 2014).

52. Storytelling Association (Singapore). *Storytelling Association (Singapore)*, 2016. http://storytellingsingapore.com/ (accessed November 2014).

53. Red Internacional de Cuentacuentos. *International Storytelling Network*, n.d. http://www.cuentacuentos.eu/ (accessed October 2014).

54. Snopes.com. *Snopes.com*, 2016. http://snopes.com (accessed November 2014).

55. Long, J.R. *Aesop's Fables Online Collection*, 2014. http://www.aesopfables.com (accessed November 2014).

56. Schlosser, S.E. *American Folklore*, 2015. http://americanfolklore.net (accessed November 2014).

57. Ashliman, D.L. *Folklore and Mythology Electronic Texts*, 2016. http://www.pitt.edu/~dash/folktexts.html (accessed November 2014).

58. Crane, G.R. *Perseus Digital Library*, n.d. http://www.perseus.tufts.edu/hopper/collections (accessed November 2014).

59. Project Gutenberg. *Project Gutenberg*, 2016. http://www.gutenberg.org (accessed November 2014).

60. Aarne, A. *The Types of Folktale: A Classification and Bibliography*; Thompson, S., Ed.; Academia Scientarum Fennica: Helsinki, Finland, 1961.

61. Ashliman, D.L. *A Guide to Folktales in the English Language: Based on the Aarne-Thompson Classification System*; Greenwood Press: New York, 1987.

62. Thompson, S. *Motif-Index of Folk-Literature: A Classification of Narrative Elements in Folktales, Ballads, Myths, Fables, Mediaeval Romances, Exampla, Fabliaux*; Indiana University Press: Bloomington, IN, 1960.

63. Ikeda, H. *A Type and Motif Index of Japanese Folk-Literature*; Suomalainen Tiedeakatemia: Helsinki, Finland, 1971.

64. Kirtley, B.F. *A Motif-Index of Polynesian, Melanesian, and Micronesian Narratives*; Arno Press: New York, 1980.

65. Flowers, H.L. *A Classification of the Folktale of the West Indies by Types and Motifs*; PhD dissertation; Indiana University: Bloomington, IN, 1952.

66. Neuland, L. *Motif-index of Latvian Folktales and Legends*; Suomalainen Tiedeakatemia: Helsinki, Finland, 1981.

67. El-Shamy, H.M. *Folk Traditions of the Arab World: A Guide to Motif Classification*; Indiana University Press: Bloomington, IN, 1995.

68. MacDonald, M.R.; Sturm, B. *The Storyteller's Sourcebook: A Subject, Title, and Motif Index to Folklore Collections for Children, 1983–1999*; Gale Group: Detroit, MI, 2001.

69. MacDonald, M.R. *The Storyteller's Sourcebook: A Subject, Title, and Motif Index to Folklore Collections for Children*; Neal-Schuman: Detroit, MI, 1982.

70. Lord, A.B. *The Singer of Tales*; Harvard University Press: Cambridge, MA, 1960.

71. Simmons, A. *The Story Factor: Inspiration, Influence, and Persuasion Through the Art of Storytelling*; Basic Books: New York, 2001.

72. Storytelling in Organizations. *Storytelling in Organizations*, 2016. http://storytellinginorganizations.com/ (accessed October 2014).

73. Nussbaum, B. The power of design. *Business Week*; 2004, May 17; p. 4.

74. Forbush, W.B. *A Manual of Stories*; American Institute of Child Life: Philadelphia, PA, 1925; 3–9.

75. Haven, K. *Story Proof: The Science Behind the Startling Power of Story*; Libraries Unlimited: Westport, CT, 2007.

76. Hamilton, M.; Weiss, M. *Children Tell Stories: A Teaching Guide*; Richard C. Owen: Katonah, NY, 1990; 3–7.

77. Collins, R.; Cooper, P.J. *The Power of Story: Teaching Through Storytelling*; Waveland Press: Long Grove, IL, 1997; 11–17.

78. Baum, S.; Owen, S.; Oreck, B. Transferring individual self-regulation processes from arts to academics. Arts Educ. Policy Rev. **1997**, *98*(4), 33.

79. Knutson, K. *Rippling Stories*, n.d., http://www.ripplingstories.com/Rippling_Stories_-_Storyteller_Katie_Knutson/Residencies.html (accessed October 2014).

80. Sue Black, *Sue Black*, 2013. http://www.sue-black.com/studentworkshops.html (accessed October 2014).

81. Suzi Whaples, Suzi "Mama" Whaples, n.d. http://suziwhaples.com/programs-and-workshops/ (accessed October 2014).

82. Bettleheim, B. *The Uses of Enchantment: The Meaning and Importance of Fairy Tales*; Vintage Books: New York, 1977.

83. Forbush, W.B *A Manual of stories*; American Institute of Child Life: Philadelphia, PA, 1925; 4–5.

84. Crane, G.R. *Perseus Digital Library*, n.d. http://www.acf.hhs.gov/programs/ana/resource/native-american-veterans-storytelling-for-healing-0?page=2 (accessed October 2014).

85. Lisa Mount, *About Jo*, n.d. http://jocarson.net/?page_id=13 (accessed November 2014).

86. Carson, J. *Spider Speculations*; Theatre Communications Group: New York, 2008.

87. Sturt, J.; Ali, S.; Robertson, W. Neurolinguistic programming: a systematic review of the effects on health outcomes. Br. J. Gen. Pract. **November 2012**, e757–e764.

88. Dewey, D. *Biblical Storytelling as Spiritual Discipline Grounded in Scholarship*, 2011. http://www.nbsint.org/assets/1408/8-22-2011_biblicalstorytellingspirituality scholarship.pdf (accessed November 2014).

89. Buxbaum, Y., *Storytelling and Spirituality in Judaism*, 2003. http://www.hasidicstories.com/Articles/Hasidic_Theories/spirit.html (accessed November 2014).

90. Nishide, T., *Spreading Buddhism via old-style storytelling*, 2014. http://www.japantimes.co.jp/news/2014/02/06/national/spreading-buddhism-via-old-style-storytelling/#.VEaCX2TF9hw (accessed October 2014).

91. Carnatica. *Harikatha*, n.d. http://www.carnatica.net/harikatha-main.htm (accessed October 2014).

92. Maina, C.K. Traditional knowledge management and preservation: intersections with library and information science. Int. Inf. Libr. Rev. **2012**, *44*, 17.

93. Historyic Philadelphia. *Why Storytelling?* 2014. http://historicphiladelphia.org/uploads/pdf/Press%20Materials/2014%20/Storytelling%20Backgrounder%202014.pdf (accessed October 2014).

94. Milwaukee Public Museum. *Programs, Events, and Exhibitions*, 2016. http://www.mpm.edu/plan-visit/calendar/museum-storytelling (accessed October 2014).

95. International Storytelling Center. *National Storytelling Festival*, 2016. http://www.storytellingcenter.net/festival/history/ (accessed October 2014).

96. Timpanogos Storytelling Institute. *Timpanogos Storytelling Festival*, 2016. http://timpfest.org/ (accessed October 2014).

97. Tejas Storytelling Association. *Texas Storytelling Festival*, 2016. http://www.tejasstorytelling.com/festival/ (accessed October 2014).

98. Southern Order of Storytellers. *Peach State Storytelling Festival*, 2016. http://southernorderofstorytellers.org/events/sos-storytelling-events/sos-festival/ (accessed October 2014).

99. Connecticut Storytelling Center, *Campus Slammer*, n.d., http://www.connstorycenter.org/campusslammer.htm (accessed October 2014).

100. Mythoff. *Mythoff*, 2016. https://www.facebook.com/mythoff (accessed October 2012).

BIBLIOGRAPHY

1. Bly, J. *Iron John: A Book About Men*; Da Capo Press: Cambridge, MA, 2004.

2. Chinen, A.B. *Once Upon a Midlife*; Xlibris: Bloomington, IN, 2003.

3. de Vos, G. *Storytelling for Young Adults: a Guide to Tales for Teens*, 2nd Ed.; Libraries Unlimited: Westport, CT, 2003.

4. de Vos, G.; Harris, M. *Telling Tales: Storytelling in the Family*; Dragon Hill Publishing: Edmonton, AB, 1995.

5. Estés, C.P. *Women Who Run With the Wolves: Myths and Stories of the Wild Woman Archetype*; Ballantine Books: New York, 1996.

6. Greene, E.; Del Negro, J.M. *Storytelling: Art and Technique*, 4th Ed.; Libraries Unlimited: Santa Barbara, CA, 2010.

7. Lipman, D. *The Storytelling Coach: How to Listen, Praise, and Bring Out People's Best*; August House: Little Rock, AR, 1995.

8. MacDonald, M.R.; Whitman, J.M.; Whitman, N.F. *Teaching with Story: Classroom Connections to Storytelling*; August House: Little Rock, AR, 2013.

9. Pellowski, A. *Drawing Stories from Around the World and a Sampling of European Handkerchief Stories*; Libraries Unlimited: Westport, CT, 2005.

10. Sawyer, R. *The Way of the Storyteller*; Viking: New York, 1942.

11. Shedlock, M. *The Art of the Storyteller*; Dover: New York, 1951.

12. Von Franz, M.L. *Archetypal Patterns in Fairy Tales*; Inner City Books: Toronto, Ontario, Canada, 1997.

Strategic Planning in Academic Libraries

Sheila Corrall
Department of Information Studies, University of Sheffield, Sheffield, U.K.

Abstract

The core concept of strategic planning is addressed, as well as the historical context of its development in academic libraries, and contemporary approaches to library strategic management. It reviews published literature and current practice, concentrating on planning processes, strategy documents and key elements of strategic planning.

INTRODUCTION

Strategic planning is essentially about deciding and refining organizational objectives and working consistently and persistently to translate those objectives into actions and outcomes. It requires insight and foresight to interpret past events and present trends to determine future directions. Strategic planners need to have eclectic interests, a flexible mindset, and an inclusive style that involves people in envisaging change, developing strategies, and making plans.

Planning is often a formal requirement, but in any case it is good management practice and has several potential benefits, particularly when carried out in a participative style with stakeholder involvement. For example:

- It brings new perspectives and insights to service development by posing unusual questions and forcing consideration of options.
- It strengthens the case for funding and provides the necessary context for both the annual budget round and special funding bids.
- It enables delegated decisions and quick flexible responses on the front line, improving satisfaction for customers and staff.
- It inspires confidence in the service by demonstrating an understanding of the key issues and showing how they will be addressed.
- It creates a shared view of the future and commitment to doing new things, facilitating change by giving people a sense of ownership.

Strategic planning has various functions: to clarify organizational purpose and objectives; to establish corporate directions and priorities; to assess environmental drivers and constraints; to identify critical issues and pressures; to determine resource allocation and utilization; to improve internal coherence and coordination; and to inform operational decisions and actions.

This article covers the core concepts of strategic planning, the historical context of its development in academic libraries, and contemporary approaches to library strategy. It reviews published literature and current practice, concentrating on planning processes, strategy documents and key elements of strategic planning.

CORE CONCEPTS

Effective strategic planning involves understanding the business arena, assessing your resource base and creating a shared view of the future, by asking fundamental questions such as:

- Why do we exist? What business are we in? (mission)
- Where are we now? How did we get here? (situation audit)
- What factors will impact our future? (environmental appraisal)
- What do we want to be? Where do we want to go? (vision and goals)
- How can we get there? What are the implications? (strategic options)
- What needs to be done? Who will do it? When? (action plans)
- How will we track progress? (performance indicators)

The terminology of strategy and planning is confusing. There is no standard usage; the same terms are used in different ways, and they can have different meanings according to context. People often confuse "policy" and "strategy" and find it difficult to differentiate "mission" and "vision." Commentators often conceptualize aims, directions, goals, objectives, strategies, and targets as a hierarchy of objectives (using "objective" as a generic term) but may place these terms in different orders; the choice of term at successive levels in the hierarchy is not significant, but it is important to have consistency of usage

Encyclopedia of Library and Information Sciences, Fourth Edition DOI: 10.1081/E-ELIS4-120008654

within an organization to aid communication and avoid confusion.

The word "strategy" is used at one level to denote overall direction, as indicated by Johnson and Scholes, "Strategy is the *direction* and *scope* of an organization over the *long term*: which achieves *advantage* for the organization through its configuration of *resources* within a changing *environment*, to meet the needs of *markets* and to fulfil *stakeholder* expectations."[1]

However, as well as representing the overall objective for an organization or what it aims to do, "strategy" is also used to describe how an organization will achieve its objective or aim. At this level, strategies are defined sets or emerging patterns of actions and tasks taking the organization toward its goals and targets. Drucker accordingly describes "strategy" as "a company's basic approach to achieving its overall objectives" and defines "strategic planning" as: "the planning for a company's long-term future that includes the setting of major overall objectives, the determination of the basic approaches to be used in pursuing these objectives, and the means to be used in obtaining the necessary resources to be employed."[2]

Despite differences in terminology and presentation, literature and practice point to general consensus about what constitutes strategic planning or "strategic management" (the term often preferred now to emphasize the iterative nature and comprehensive scope of the strategy process). There are four main aspects, that can be seen as a set of interlocking components: environmental appraisal, strategic profiling, strategy development, and program management.

Environmental Appraisal

This aspect covers researching and analyzing the forces of the external world, including your own industry/sector and its marketplace, as well as reviewing and auditing the internal situation, especially your performance and resources. The tools used include environmental scanning, PEST/STEP analysis, stakeholder mapping, competitive benchmarking, SWOT, and cross-impact analysis. The typical output is a set of formal planning assumptions to inform other aspects of the planning process.

Strategic Profiling

This involves discussing and agreeing fundamental issues, such as the scope, purpose, and functions of your organization; its guiding principles and philosophies; your desired future situation and the direction required to get there. Tools used include: mission, positioning, vision, and values statements; key result areas; critical success factors; goals; and targets. The typical output is a series of related objectives statements to inform the development and evaluation of strategies.

Strategy Development

This requires the formation and adoption of strategies, action programs, and resource plans, by identifying and evaluating options and sensitivities, considering supporting strategies and contingency plans, and specifying performance indicators. Tools used include generic strategy models, portfolio matrices, and cost-benefit analysis. The typical output is a formal strategy document or plan to inform operational/project planning and funding bids.

Program Management

This aspect includes taking actions and monitoring progress, reviewing objectives and refining plans, elaborating tasks and incorporating targets into annual budgets and operational plans. Tools used include gantt charts, milestone plans, responsibility charts, risk analysis, and performance measurement. Typical outputs are project plans, operational plans, budget projections, risk registers, progress reports, financial reports, and other monitoring statements.

There is considerable overlap between corporate/business strategy and marketing strategy, and many of the models and tools used in strategic planning are concerned with marketing variables. However, strategic planning is essentially about defining the business (or businesses) of the organization and setting overall business objectives, whereas marketing plans elaborate strategies to achieve these objectives; market research is an essential aspect of the environmental analysis that underpins strategic planning.

HISTORICAL CONTEXT

Strategic planning originated in the United States during the 1960s and spread to Europe and beyond in the 1970s and 1980s, becoming an accepted part of managerial thinking and practice in the business world and the public sector. It is distinguished from other types of planning by its focus on environmental trends and concern with fundamental questions about where an organization is going and how it will get there. Although long–range planning is associated with incremental growth and evolutionary change, strategic planning is particularly associated with revolutionary change or even total reconception.

The adoption of strategic planning concepts and techniques by library and information service managers has followed the general trend, with American libraries acting as pioneers from the 1970s onward, and libraries in other countries gradually following their lead. In the United States, many university libraries engaged in planning as part of an institutionwide activity, but in the United

Kingdom, they often became involved in strategic planning ahead of their parent bodies.

The Association of Research Libraries (ARL) has played a significant part in the development of strategic planning in academic libraries through its Office of Management Studies, which carries out consultancy and training for its members[3–5] and has published several collections of library planning documents.[6–8] In the United Kingdom, the Society of College, National and University Libraries (SCONUL) has worked with the Universities and Colleges Information Systems Association and the Higher Education Staff Development Agency to develop strategic management capability in the sector, by offering a strategic management program for service directors and including strategic planning and scenario development in a course for service managers.[9]

Funding pressures in the higher education sector over the last two decades have made strategic planning a managerial necessity, and many institutions now have elaborate and sophisticated systems to meet internal needs and external requirements. In the United Kingdom, funding bodies have formally required institutions to submit both general (corporate) plans and more specific strategies as a condition for the release of funds. Library planning, therefore, needs to be linked to and integrated with an array of institutional, functional, and departmental strategies and plans, in a complex system, which is best seen as a network or web of strategies, rather than the traditional conception as a hierarchy of plans. This issue was highlighted by the Ellard report on performance indicators for academic libraries in 1995, which included "the cohesiveness between the mission, aims and objectives and strategic plan of the institution and those of its library" as an indicator of integration.[10]

PUBLISHED LITERATURE

There are numerous publications on business planning and corporate strategy but relatively few titles on strategic planning for academic institutions and their libraries. Most of the literature on strategic management in higher education is based on practical case studies, with some authors offering a more objective or theoretical perspective. Academic library strategists have accordingly drawn on models outside higher education as well as learning from professional colleagues.

Academic Strategy

Among the many strategy writers cited, Chandler,[11] Bryson,[12] and Steiner[13] have been particularly influential, in addition to marketing guru Kotler[14] and the higher education specialists, Cope[15] and Keller.[16] Although American writers have led the field, contributors from other countries have emerged more recently with Meade's

account of strategic reorientation at the University of Otago[17] and Watson's reflections on strategic management in contemporary England, which draw on the remodeling of the corporate and strategic plans of the University of Brighton.[18]

The central place of strategic planning in higher education is further evidenced by more specific and practical publications issued in the last few years. Berge and Schrum describe how the development and implementation of technology-enhanced distance learning programs need to be integrated into institutional strategic planning (and budgeting).[19] At a more general level, Lerner's "strategic planning primer for higher education" takes readers through the key steps and alerts them to potential pitfalls. She also explains the distinctive features of university planning and highlights business models that have proved useful in the sector, providing links to the California State University Northridge strategic planning site.[20] In England, the Higher Education Funding Council has issued a 44-page guide for heads of institutions, senior managers and governing bodies, based on consultation and case studies across the sector.[21]

Library Planning

Textbooks on library planning began to appear in the 1980s. The pioneering 1984 volume by Riggs, *Strategic Planning for Library Managers*, looks somewhat dated now, but it made a significant contribution in introducing business concepts and techniques to the library community.[22] McKee's 1989 book, *Planning Library Service*, ranged more broadly across the whole field of management and was the first British treatment of the topic.[23] More practical guidance on strategic planning was provided in Jacob's *How-To-Do-It Manual*[24] and Corrall's *Know How Guide*.[25] The latter was subsequently revised and expanded into a much more comprehensive handbook, *Strategic Management of Information Services*, which includes many examples from the literature and practice of academic librarianship.[26] Other books have concentrated on particular aspects of or approaches to library strategy: Giesecke introduces the theory and practice of scenario planning;[27] Weingand explains how futuring methods can be used with conventional marketing/planning techniques;[28] and Gorman discusses the core values of libraries and librarianship.[29]

Articles on academic library planning can be traced back to the same era. Although the concept of strategic planning is not mentioned and the term "strategies" is only used in passing, McClure's 1978 contribution to *College & Research Libraries* is in practice an early discussion of the benefits of a formal approach to strategy with practical suggestions about how to do it.[30] Davis (writing from the perspective of a sympathetic bystander) similarly advocates a proactive approach to planning, with staff participation and stakeholder involvement.[31]

Case studies

With the exception of the monographs by Biddle[32] and Hayes,[33] much of the literature on academic library planning consists of journal articles describing and evaluating the planning processes used at particular institutions. Thus, Ensor details the data-gathering methods used at Indiana State University,[34] Baker describes the top-down process adopted at Massachusetts Institute of Technology,[35] Brindley outlines the more participative style used at Aston University,[36] Gratch and Wood discuss the approach taken to implementation at Bowling Green State University,[37] Butler and Davis reflect on their respective experiences at Michigan State University and the State University of New York at Albany,[38] Lee identifies factors determining success at Harvard College,[39] Blunden-Ellis elaborates the key issues addressed in planning the Consortium of Academic Libraries in Manchester,[40] and Shoaf describes the proactive and highly participative approach used at Brown University.[41]

In contrast to these relatively brief accounts, Lynch provides an in-depth case study with extensive insights into the planning issues facing the University of Illinois at Chicago Library. This volume contains eight chapters from colleagues involved in the planning process, reflecting their different views on the library and its environment. The book also reproduces the strategic plan eventually developed by the library.[42] Another distinctive collection is the volume edited by Williams containing 14 articles offering multiple perspectives on the planning processes at 12 U.S. institutions. The authors include college and university presidents, provosts, and planners as well as librarians.[43] Among these is an early appraisal of how strategic planning can facilitate the convergence of a library with cognate services: Watson argues that the cooperation required to develop a unitwide plan helped managers "gain a broader perspective of the roles of each of the components and envision new ways in which the components might interact in support of each other."[44]

Specific aspects

Other authors focus on specific dimensions of strategic planning. Wilson[45] and Brophy[46] both discuss the mission of the academic library; Forsman suggests how organizational values can be used in planning;[47] Birdsall and Hersley present a planning model emphasizing stakeholder involvement;[48] Michalak considers the strategic planning of library facilities;[49] Hewison describes a participative approach to vision statements;[50] Tuck considers the use of surveys and evaluation in implementing and monitoring a strategic plan;[51] Bevan and Dolphin describe the incorporation of an IT strategy into a library plan;[52] Birdsall revisits stakeholder engagement and

explores the political dimensions of strategic planning;[53] Corrall and Brewerton report on the use of scenarios in strategic visioning and space planning;[54,55] and Feinman shows how library staff can contribute to and influence university strategic planning.[56]

PLANNING PROCESSES

Both planning horizons (time spans covered by plans) and planning time lines (time devoted to the process) have shortened significantly in recent years. In past decades, long-range plans covered 5, 10, or even 20 yr, but today organizations generally opt for no more than 5 yr—often only 3—and the same pattern is evident in academic libraries. Irrespective of the period covered, strategic plans are usually reviewed annually to inform yearly budgets and operational plans and sometimes "rolled forward" by dropping the first year and adding another at the end. (This practice of edging forward incrementally is quite different from the sort of fundamental review that strategic planning requires and, therefore, should only be seen as an interim exercise limited to no more than two or three iterations.)

In the 1980s, it was quite common for first iterations of strategic planning to be conducted over a period of 12 months or longer, with some reported instances of exercises taking 18 months to 2 yr—notably, the University of Illinois at Chicago.[42] Today, the period of any formally defined process is more likely to be 6 months or less, because the pace of change is so fast that a longer gestation period makes little sense. This compression of the formal strategic planning process into a matter of months makes the requirement for library managers to engage staff continuously in less formal strategic thinking and environmental scanning even more important.

One of the trends evident in both library planning and business strategy processes is the move to a more participative and inclusive style, with more extensive involvement of staff, customers, and other stakeholders. Another tendency is for managers to acknowledge "real-time strategy" as a continuous (learning) process instead of seeing it as a "one-off" exercise or part of an annual ritual. The formal or organized planning process has thus become more concerned with capturing information and decisions rather than initiating environmental scans, competitive benchmarking, customer surveys, etc. because the latter are now ongoing activities in many academic libraries.

Strategic planning has been conceptualized as a series of fundamental questions and a set of interlocking components. It can also be seen in more practical terms as a sequence of iterative steps. Models for operationalizing the strategic planning process vary and need to be considered in relation to the size and type of organization and the scope and purpose of the plan. Library managers have learned over the years that planning processes (whatever their scale) need to be properly managed and carefully planned. The key tasks involved can be summarized as follows:

- Defining the project.
- Auditing the situation.
- Setting strategic objectives.
- Identifying different strategies.
- Evaluating the alternatives.
- Preparing budget estimates.
- Formulating the plan.
- Initiating action programs.
- Monitoring strategy progress.
- Reviewing the plan.

These tasks can be interpreted at various levels. For example, "setting strategic objectives" could include a full review of organizational values, purpose, and functions, and the development of a strategic vision, or it might be confined to determining or just confirming strategic directions and goals for the next year or two. Apart from the crucial first step of defining the task ("planning to plan"), the ordering of tasks is largely a matter of personal (or organizational) choice, so that some people like to start with strategic objectives (including mission and vision), whereas others prefer to begin with situation analysis. The last three tasks move beyond planning to implementation, but often information obtained and insights gained here will prompt revision and rethinking of earlier work, demonstrating that the process needs to be seen as iterative and interactive, rather than linear.

Practical Examples

Academic libraries use a variety of planning models and methods, but some common themes are evident from their websites and documents, such as the use of steering committees, management retreats, facilitated workshops, and focus groups. New Mexico State University Library designed a planning process around five special committees,[57] whereas the University of Memphis Libraries worked through a Strategic Plan Team and five Goal Teams, with Objective Teams to oversee implementation.[58]

The University of Queensland Library sees strategic planning as a dynamic activity involving all staff and has used an "appreciative inquiry process" (discover, dream, design, deliver) since 1998.[59] Curtin Library and Information Service followed the University's strategic planning framework, based on Kaplan and Norton's Balanced Scorecard,[60,61] and the University of Arizona Library works through a team structure using tools and techniques based on the Japanese concept of Hoshin planning to focus on "a few breakthrough goals that are vital to the Library's success."[62]

Textbooks and case studies point to the pitfalls of planning exercises. Common mistakes include: allowing some managers to opt out; assigning responsibilities to committees rather than individuals; confusing strategic planning with operational planning; constructing overelaborate systems and procedures; generating long lists of unprioritized initiatives; ignoring resource implications and funding issues; and not following through from strategy to action.

STRATEGY DOCUMENTS

Many critics argue that it is not worth bothering with formal plans because they become out-of-date almost as soon as they are written. This view assumes that strategy documents are static entities, but a sensible process makes provision for refining and updating both the plans of an organization and the assumptions on which they are based. Mount Holyoke College Library, Information, and Technology Services explicitly describe their plan as "a continually evolving document whose evolution is very dependent upon feedback from the community."[63]

Many academic libraries are actually required to submit some form of plan as part of an institutional planning and budgeting cycle, but in any case there are sound reasons for documenting plans in print or electronically.

1. The process of writing and editing a strategy documents forces people to think through their goals and objectives and serves as a double check on overall consistency, organizational capacity, and other critical issues.
2. Written plans provide a visual medium of communication for both internal and external audiences and make it easier to convey a consistent message to staff and others in different places at different times.
3. A formal record of intended activities provides a vital mechanism for control, enabling regular and ad hoc monitoring of whether specified actions have been carried out and underlying assumptions have proved correct.

The level of detail included in a plan will be influenced by formal requirements, personal preferences, and specific decisions on whether to develop a hierarchy or family of plans presenting successively more detailed elaborations of strategies, actions, and timetables. The plan needs to state what you intend to do and why, how you will do it and when, with enough information on background and resources to convince readers. It is essential to define the scope of the plan, particularly the period covered and the services included (e.g., library services only or library, IT, and educational media provision). It is desirable to provide a contents list and an executive summary if the document runs to more than five pages.

Contemporary academic library planning statements vary significantly in length, format, and contents. The trend is toward more concise documents, covering shorter time spans, with a sharper focus on intended results. Lengthy descriptions of service characteristics have generally been replaced with brief summaries of strategic issues, proposed approaches, and performance indicators. Vision statements have become more prominent, often forming the main narrative section of the plan and sometimes comprising a set of alternative scenarios representing different planning assumptions. Many elements previously included (such as SWOT analyses and statistical data) are now relegated to appendices or excluded altogether.

Practical Examples

Most plans today cover 5–10 pages, although there are a few examples of much longer documents—notably, the plans of Monash, Rutgers, and Syracuse universities, which all contain around 25–30 pages.[64–66] The first library plans produced in the 1980s ranged from basic typescripts for internal use only to glossy publications made available to all. Many libraries now publish their plans via their websites, often offering several formats (typically, HTML and PDF or Word).

The style of presentation is generally quite simple, but some libraries have been more creative in their use of layout and design: Macquarie University Library makes use of blocks and columns of text in double-page spreads to convey "where we want to be," "desired outcomes," and "how we will do it" in relation to teaching partnerships, research partnerships, and community outreach.[67] Other university libraries have given their plans meaningful titles to reinforce the key messages of their documents (e.g., Rutgers: "A bridge to the future;"[65] Syracuse: "Targets for transformation;"[66] and the University of Sheffield: "New worlds of information."[68]

More significantly, there is a trend toward using websites to make the planning process more transparent and participative. The strategic planning home page of the University of Arizona Library provides links to extensive documentation, such as the "team charge" and other descriptions of the planning process, in addition to end products from that process (including a 17-page Current Situation Analysis).[69] The University Libraries at Virginia Tech have a web page devoted to Library Strategic Plan Steps 2000–2001, which lists their Steering Committee and Coordinators and then describes the process, with links to working papers, workshop outputs, and draft plans.[70] The website for the Syracuse plan provides links to progress reports, invites questions about the plan, and allows library staff to express their interest, suggest an initiative, or submit a report. The introductory part of the plan provides an explanation of the process and a glossary of planning terminology; definitions of terms (such as "mission statement" and "planning themes") are also repeated at the relevant points in the text.[66]

In summary, contemporary planning statements generally have three main components:

- An introductory section, which sets the context of the document, covering both the external factors and institutional issues.
- The overall strategy, which states the ambitions of the service, expressed in its vision, mission, values, and goals.
- The forward plan, which lays out the intentions for the period, elaborated as strategies and actions with responsibilities and timescales.

The latter may form a separate document, and additional information may be included as appendices (e.g., the remit and/or membership of the planning team, the results of customer surveys, risk analyses, and contingency plans). The introduction may be prefaced by a foreword (from the director or dean).

KEY ELEMENTS

Irrespective of whether their strategy is formally presented in a single strategic plan or as separate statements, academic libraries typically consider the following areas as part of their planning activities: their mission or purpose; their values and beliefs; their view of the future, expressed in a single vision or multiple scenarios; their directions and goals; their plans for actions and the financial resources required.

Library Missions

Most academic libraries include a formal statement of their fundamental purpose or mission in their strategy documents. The terms "mission" and "purpose" are generally used interchangeably, but some institutions distinguish between purpose as a timeless expression of an organization's reason for existence and mission as a more time-specific concept relating the enduring purpose to current directions and goals. Others see mission as a comprehensive construct embracing not only purpose and function but also values and culture, so that it covers behavioral aspects as well as business focus. The length and format of such statements also varies from a few lines to several paragraphs or a full page, and academic library examples reflect this full spectrum.

A common model is to begin with a sentence or paragraph summarizing the overall role and then supplement this with a set of bullet points or sentences, highlighting key functions or activities. New Mexico State University Library provides a short statement of this type.[57] Sheffield uses a longer version, starting with three sentences that relate its mission to that of the university, locate the library within the institutional structure, and state its leadership role, before listing nine principal objectives or functions.[68]

Although the purpose of an academic library has not changed fundamentally, the shifts of emphasis from holdings to access, from print to electronic and from mediation to self-service have led to changes in the phrasing of mission statements to reflect more accurately the customer focus and networked environment of contemporary services; thus, the Mission of the University of Washington Libraries refers to "connecting people with knowledge."[71] Some libraries have also used their mission statements to differentiate themselves from their peers, by highlighting distinctive aspects—exemplified by Birkbeck College Library's Mission to "develop and maintain services which especially suit the needs of students who are in employment."[72]

Service Values

The production of formal statements of the beliefs or principles that underpin organizational or professional philosophies has become more common over the past decade, and this is reflected in the prominence given to values in current academic library plans. Values statements can be seen as a part of the framework that guides discretionary decision making, along with vision and direction statements. Such statements can be particularly useful at times of rapid change as a means of reassuring people that underlying values remain constant when other things are altering radically. Values statements can also be used to support cultural change by asserting new values seen as critical to success in the future (in conjunction with old ones).

Values statements in library plans typically take the form of a set of words or phrases as headlines, which are then elaborated in a longer phrase or sentence. Libraries have traditionally concentrated on values associated with our professional mission, such as the preservation of our cultural heritage, promotion of information literacy, and protection of intellectual freedom, but they have often also incorporated into their statements references to more general humanistic values, such as democracy, diversity, equity, integrity, literacy, and privacy. Contemporary examples still reflect these important concerns but tend to give more prominence to modes of working and styles of delivery thought necessary for success in the changing environment around us, notably collaboration and partnership, flexibility and responsiveness, initiative and innovation.

Formulating a values statement is a challenging task as the final choice of concepts selected for emphasis inevitably raises questions about points considered but not included in the end product. However, most libraries restrict their statements to around half a page, accepting that it is hard to make key messages stand out in a lengthier presentation. The statement of the University of Western Australia Library is a typical example, built around the values of responsiveness, innovation, collaboration, and commitment to quality.[73] In contrast to American and Australian practice, few British academic libraries include values statements in their strategy documents.

Strategic Visioning

Visioning is now a frequent activity in all types of organizations, as an integral part of strategic planning and management, particularly associated with radical organizational change. Visioning exercises and vision statements are seen as an effective way to capture ideas about the future and to communicate the scale of the transformation envisaged to stakeholders. The content and length of vision statements vary, but most commentators agree that visions need to be both aspirational and inspirational, which means that style and tone are critical factors. Visioning has connotations of a "best," "desirable," or "ideal" future, but there has been a noticeable shift recently from "soft" statements to harder, more realistic, and specific descriptions that contain "actionable" concepts or components. The challenge is to manage the inherent tension between ambition and capability by striking the right balance between idealism and realism.

Library vision statements are mostly around one or two pages long, but published examples range from a few paragraphs to several pages. Purdue University Libraries have used visioning to plan shorter-term changes and also for team building at branch or department level.[50] At the other end of the scale, SCONUL has conducted two visioning exercises to produce a shared national view of academic information services in the future, which have provided guidance and stimulus to members developing their institutional strategies and plans, as well as supporting the work of SCONUL in dealing with other bodies. The resulting statements (which also include planning assumptions) have been used as reference documents, lobbying materials, educational aids, and communication tools at local, regional, national, and international levels.[74,75]

Edinburgh University Library exemplifies the trend toward more realistic and specific vision statements that emphasize capability and actionability. Its strategic vision runs to two pages and contains six key messages, each supported by one or two paragraphs explaining the situation envisaged in more detail. This vision also gains immediacy and power by using the present tense to describe the future.[76] Other academic libraries have chosen to present their visions much more succinctly in a short paragraph or even just a single sentence. Short statements run the risk of blandness and require careful drafting (and redrafting) to ensure that they have real meaning and sufficient focus to distinguish the service from its peers. The University of Washington Libraries have succeeded in outlining several dimensions of their service in only three sentences: "The University of Washington Libraries will anticipate and meet the needs of our communities in their search for knowledge. We will do this at any time and any place. We will use our extraordinary staff and our world-class portal to resources and services in creating a model information literate community."[71]

In a slightly longer statement, the Virginia Tech Libraries concentrate on only two key aspects—collaborative partnership and support in any location—preferring instead to emphasize the library's task as supporting the business of the university:

> We will be collaborative partners with members of the university community as we collectively work to position the university as a top-tier research institution. Wherever they are located, members of the Virginia Tech community will be supported by the library as they engage in research, as they share in quality learning experiences at the undergraduate and graduate levels, and as they work in transferring knowledge and expertise between the university and society.[77]

Macquarie University Library similarly promotes the aspiration of success through partnership in a very short "vision": "To be an indispensable partner in the provision of quality education and research at Macquarie University."[67]

Shorter forms of vision statements such as the above are often referred to more accurately as "positioning statements" or statements of "strategic intent," particularly when they are used alongside longer descriptions of an organization's desired future.

Scenario Development

Scenarios are simplified descriptions of multiple futures—alternative visions—and are particularly useful when there is concern about the uncertainty of critical planning assumptions. Scenario development involves identifying a range of possible outcomes for key environmental influences and then selecting combinations of these alternative states to articulate different but plausible futures. Properly done, it combines environmental scanning with strategic visioning, using both facts and perceptions—hard and soft inputs—to illuminate the dynamics, cross-impacts, and cause-and-effect relationships of external and internal forces potentially affecting an organization. The scale and pace of change over the last decade has led to renewed interest in scenario development and new publications on the subject, which have been cited and used by library managers.[30][78,79]

Scenarios are often used to convey the impact and implications of technology on organizations, and this has been a common theme in library scenarios. In 1984, ARL designed four scenarios to use in planning library staff needs for the next decade.[80] In 1996, to stimulate thinking about a future network-based scholarly communication system, Peters similarly formulated four scenarios written from the perspective of higher education institutions and their libraries: "Another marketplace for global enterprise"; "Mass customisation for and by individuals"; "Knowledge guilds reign supreme;" and "Ivory towers in cyberspace."[81]

Another common use is the production of "resource scenarios" to illustrate the implications of budget adjustments (usually cuts) for organizations. For example, Shapiro describes how administrators at Michigan State University were asked to prepare three brief scenarios showing how their unit would look if its base budget were reduced by 5, 10, 15%.[82] More positively, Dewey refers to a request for the University of Iowa Libraries to add three scenarios to their plan, showing what they could accomplish with a 15% increase, 5% increase, and 5% decrease in their budget.[3]

Scenarios (like visions) can be used at various levels (e.g., the organization as a whole, a particular department, or a specific project) and for a variety of purposes. They have proved popular and effective in library space planning, enabling more dramatic presentation of the potential impact of a new building on the local learning environment than a conventional proposal. At Reading University Library, alternative scenarios were successfully used in 1997 to communicate the different service implications of building an extension and remodeling existing space.[54] Significantly, the second scenario was not intended to be a "doomsday" vision: it represented a genuine attempt to remodel existing accommodation to meet future needs, but its logic showed the spiraling knock-on effects of space constraints.[83] In 1998, a more structured approach to scenario development was used at the University's Bulmershe Library, in a highly participative exercise involving a wide range of stakeholders.[55]

At the University of Arizona Library, the Branches Libraries Space Planning Team developed four divergent scenarios—"Book truckin," "Tomorrowland," "Full stop," and "Future on the cheap"—which were summarized as bullet points on a matrix diagram and then described in more detail with current situational abstracts for each one.[84] Staff used a 12-step methodology adapted from established models, covering the whole planning process from identifying the critical decision issue to producing a facilities master plan.[85]

Other organizations have developed scenarios for strategic plans or reports purely as illustrative material showing how the same future might look from different perspectives (rather than describing different futures based on varying interpretations of the environment). For example, in 1993 the Follett report offered three "sketches" to illustrate some of the possibilities opened up by the technology of the "virtual library," written from the perspectives of an undergraduate, an academic, and a "virtual librarian."[86] Similarly, Rutgers included five "Scenarios of the future" in their 1999 plan explaining how a professor, an undergraduate, a graduate student, and researchers might find and locate information resources if the proposed Digital Library Initiative became a reality.[65]

Examples of this type are more accurately described as "sketches" or "scenes" (rather than "scenarios") in the context of strategic planning.

Goal Statements

Strategic goals (also known as strategic objectives) are direction statements that indicate the movement or improvement needed to achieve the desired future state (as expressed in the vision). Effective goals are expressed in action-oriented terms that are capable of conversion into specific targets enabling managers to plan tasks and measure performance. Libraries usually group their goals/objectives and targets under broad headings, variously described as "strategic directions," "strategic issues," "strategic priorities," or "strategic thrusts"; "key action areas," "key performance areas," or "key result areas"; "planning imperatives" or "planning themes." For example, Purdue's *Plan 2004: A Framework for Action* groups its goals under four strategic directions: The Learning Library, Scholarly Communication, User-Centered Services, and Infrastructure.[87]

Alternatively, people sometimes just use the term "goal" to denote broad areas that provide a framework for organizing initiatives and actions in groups that have some coherence but not necessarily reflecting day-to-day organizational boundaries. The goal translation process, whereby each top-level "goal," "objective," or "strategy" is converted from a general statement of what you want to achieve to a more specific description of how it will be done, is the key to successful strategy implementation. Moreover, this "what/how" translation process needs to take place at successive levels in the organization, so that institutional goals are converted into library goals and high-level librarywide goals are translated into lower-level goals for library sites or teams.

The University of Sydney Library offers two views of the relationship between University Goals and Library Strategies by ordering things differently in its 5-yr Strategic Plan and annual Key Results document. In the former, Library Strategies are grouped as a bullet-point listing under each major University Goal; in the latter, the Strategies (together with details of Actions, Resources, Responsibility, Target Dates, and Performance Indicators) are grouped under 10 Key Result statements, with one or more Associated University Goals listed under each Key Result area. In this way, the library not only shows how it proposes to support each university goal but also explains how the actions taken in a particular year relate to those goals.[88]

Goals specify the key directions for an organization or service over the planning period, but they cannot be finally confirmed until strategies have been properly developed to the point where the resource implications and organizational dependencies of the actions required can be assessed. Strategy development needs both analytical and creative inputs; many libraries have found it useful to follow a systematic process. For example, the six-step STRIDE model takes planners through a series of questions:

- Situation: What is the current position of the service, product(s), or facilities?
- Targets: What is the overall goal and what are the intermediate objective(s) or milestone(s)?
- Restraints: Are there constraints on progress, such as policies or resources?
- Insights: What information and ideas are needed for a workable strategy?
- Delivery: What exactly needs to be done, by whom, and when?
- Evaluation: How will success be judged and performance measured?[26]

Action Planning

It is debatable how far strategic plans should be developed into action plans, and there is significant variation in practice, with some organizations expressing their strategies in rather general terms, whereas others include quite specific objectives (with numbers attached). There are trends in both directions, with many managers favoring broad-brush statements to give them some flexibility if circumstances change suddenly, but also more organizations requiring identifiable outcomes and making managers formally accountable for the results specified in their plans.

The plan of the University of Washington Libraries is an example of the former type: each Key Action Area is defined by four or five sentences indicating some of the underlying issues, but any statements of intent are at a very general level.[71] Plans of this type, where there are few measurable outcomes specified, could more accurately be described as policy statements in this context. Others state explicitly in the introductory sections of their strategic plans that action planning is separately documented; thus, Sheffield states that "the Library compiles annual Operational Objectives on a rolling three-year basis to enable the plan to be implemented effectively."[68]

There is considerable variation in the detail provided in strategic action plans, ranging from simple lists showing completion dates and persons responsible against the required tasks or desired results to elaborate formulations of initiatives and actions incorporating priority rankings and status reports as well as showing the people involved and the planned timetable. The plan of Birkbeck College Library is at one end of the spectrum, with sets of one-line actions, responsible people, and target dates grouped under eight headings.[72] At the other extreme, for each of its 17 goals, Syracuse University Library provides information on their priority and feasibility (ranked as high/medium/low), the rationale, success indicators, and specific initiatives, and then details the project manager, action team leader, start date, and timescale (short/mid/

long-range) for each initiative. Further details are recorded in Action Plan Progress Reports, including action team members, actions to date, modifications to the plan and/or team, obstacles or barriers to progress, and timetable for completion.[66]

It is clear that many academic libraries have learned from experience that if they do not develop tightly specified action plans to support their strategies, the desired service developments will just not happen, because of the continuing pressure of day-to-day service delivery. Managers also need to think about the extent to which their plans depend on actions and resources from other parts of the organization and take that into account in their planning. Irrespective of whether action plans are included in the strategy document, action planning needs to be seen as part of the planning process.

Financial Commentary

There is evidently much pressure on academic libraries to identify outcomes and justify expenditure, so it is quite surprising that resourcing and funding issues do not feature more prominently in their strategic plans. Although managers may regard budget reports and projections as confidential or sensitive information, some mention at least of the financial implications or feasibility of their strategies might be expected. Some libraries have at least flagged resourcing as an issue, albeit in fairly general terms. For example, Sheffield draws attention to "the declining purchasing power of its present budget" in the introduction to its plan and also has a specific section on resources reinforcing this point after reference to other funding issues.[68]

Others make explicit statements about the funding required to implement their strategies comprehensively. In the Memphis plan, the objectives listed under each major goal are subdivided into those "that can be met with existing resources" and those "that require new/additional resources beyond what the unit is able to generate through restructuring and internal reallocation."[58] The Rutgers plan has a substantial appendix entitled "Budgetary Overview," which sets the goal of parity with the top quartile of AAU universities (in line with institutional aims) and outlines several funding strategies.[65] Edinburgh gives even more prominence to expenditure requirements and income streams, placing "Funding" and "Cost Recovery and Income Generation" first and second of its eight strategic goals, setting targets under both headings and similarly proposing benchmarking against comparators.[76]

CONCLUSION

Strategic planning in academic libraries has evolved over the past three decades from a management concept to established practice. Planning frameworks and strategy processes in higher education have grown in line with administrative changes and external demands. Convergence of library and computing services is taking place at several levels (operational, tactical/developmental, and strategic), and this is reflected in the changing scope of library and information service plans and the development of comprehensive information strategies.

The proliferation of strategies is shifting the focus of attention from the production and implementation of plans to the linking and integration of a "strategy web." Academic libraries have generally seen their strategic plans as both supporting and influencing the higher-level strategies of the institution, but libraries that seize the opportunities offered by creative partnerships to develop joined-up (or joint) plans with related services may see this balance alter and their influence increase. Strategic planning has served us well in the past, and if we continue to adapt and refine our systems and processes, it will help us to create a better future.

REFERENCES

1. Johnson, G.; Scholes, K. *Corporate Strategy*, 5th Ed.; Prentice Hall: London, U.K., 1999.
2. Drucker, P.F. *Management*; Butterworth-Heinemann: Oxford, U.K., 1974(1988).
3. Dewey, B.I. The University of Iowa Libraries' Strategic Plan. In *Strategic Planning in Higher Education: Implementing New Roles for the Academic Library*; WilliamsII, J.F., Ed.; Haworth Press: New York, 1991; 99–112.
4. Mulhare, E.M. The library long-range planning process at Wayne State. In *Strategic Planning in Higher Education: Implementing New Roles for the Academic Library*; Williams, J.F., Ed.; Haworth Press: New York, 1991; 113–129.
5. Cain, L.J.; Louden, W.F. University Libraries and Academic Strategic Planning at the University of Cincinnati. In *Strategic Planning in Higher Education: Implementing New Roles for the Academic Library*; Williams, J.F., Ed.; Haworth Press: New York, 1991; 167–179.
6. Association of Research Libraries, Office of Management Services, Systems and Procedures Exchange Center *Strategic Planning in ARL Libraries*, SPEC Kit 108; ARL: Washington, DC, 1984.
7. Association of Research Libraries, Office of Management Services, Systems and Procedures Exchange Center *Strategic Plans in ARL Libraries*; SPEC Kit 158; ARL: Washington, DC, 1989.
8. Association of Research Libraries, Office of Management Services, Systems and Procedures Exchange Center, *Strategic Planning in ARL Libraries*; SPEC Kit 210; ARL: Washington, DC, 1995.
9. Higher Education Staff Development Agency, Making management work: A course for practising managers. http://www.hesda.org.uk/events/making.htm (accessed October 2001).
10. Joint Funding Councils' Ad Hoc Group on Performance Indicators for Libraries, *The Effective Academic Library:*

A Framework for Evaluating the Performance of UK Academic Libraries: A Consultative Report to the HEFCE, SHEFC, HEFCW, and DENI; The Councils: Bristol, UK, 1995. Chairman: Kevin Ellard.

11. Chandler, A.D. Strategy and Structure: Chapters in the History of the Industrial Enterprise; MIT Press: Cambridge, MA, 1962.

12. Bryson, J.M. Strategic Planning for Public and Nonprofit Organizations: A Guide to Strengthening and Sustaining Organizational Achievement; Jossey-Bass: San Francisco, CA, 1988.

13. Steiner, G.A. Strategic Planning: What Every Manager Must Know; Free Press: New York, 1997.

14. Kotler, P.; Murray, P.E. Strategic planning for higher education. J. High. Educ. 1981, 52 (5), 470–489.

15. Cope, R.G. Strategic Policy Planning: A Guide for College and University Administrators; Ireland Educational Corporation: Littleton, CO, 1978.

16. Keller, G. Academic Strategy: The Management Revolution in American Higher Education; Johns Hopkins University Press: Baltimore, MA, 1983.

17. Meade, P.H. Challenges Facing Universities: Quality, Leadership and the Management of Change; University of Otago: Dunedin, New Zealand, 1997.

18. Watson, D. Managing Strategy; Open University Press: Buckingham, U.K., 2000.

19. Berge, Z.L.; Schrum, L. Linking strategic planning with program implementation for distance education. Cause/Eff. 1998, 21 (3), 31–38. http://www.educause.edu/ir/library/html/cem9836.html (accessed October 2001).

20. Lerner, A.L. A strategic planning primer for higher education. 1999. http://www.des.calstate.edu/strategic.html (accessed October 2001).

21. Higher Education Funding Council for England. Strategic Planning in Higher Education: A Guide for Heads of Institutions, Senior Managers, and Members of Governing Bodies; The Council: Bristol, U.K., 2000. http://www.hefce.ac.uk/Pubs/HEFCE/2000/00_24.htm (accessed October 2001).

22. Riggs, D.E. Strategic Planning for Library Managers; Oryx Press: Phoenix, AZ, 1984.

23. McKee, B. Planning Library Service; Clive Bingley: London, U.K., 1989.

24. Jacob, M.E.L. Strategic Planning: A How-To-Do-It Manual for Librarians; Neal-Schuman: New York, 1990.

25. Corrall, S. Strategic Planning for Library and Information Services, Aslib Know How Guide; Aslib: London, U.K., 1994.

26. Corrall, S. Strategic Management of Information Services: A Planning Handbook; Aslib/IMI: London, U.K., 2000.

27. Scenario Planning for Libraries; Giesecke, J., Ed.; Scenario Planning for Libraries; American Library Association: Chicago, IL, 1998.

28. Weingand, D.E. Future-Driven Library Marketing; American Library Association: Chicago, IL, 1998.

29. Gorman, M. Our Enduring Values: Librarianship in the 21st Century; American Library Association: Chicago, IL, 2000.

30. McClure, C. The planning process: Strategies for action. Coll. Res. Libr. 1978, 39 (6), 456–466.

31. Davis, P. Libraries at the turning point: Issues in proactive planning. J. Libr. Adm. 1980, 1, 11–24.

32. Biddle, S.F. Planning in the University Library; Greenwood Press: Westport, CT, 1992.

33. Hayes, R.M. Strategic Management for Academic Libraries: A Handbook; Greenwood Press: Westport, CT, 1993.

34. Ensor, P. Strategic planning in an academic library. Libr. Admin. Manage. 1988, 2 (3), 145–150.

35. Baker, S.M. Strategic planning for libraries in the electronic age. IATUL Q. 1989, 3 (4), 200–206.

36. Brindley, L.J. Library development plans—A case study: Aston university library and information services. Br. J. Acad. Librariansh. 1990, 5 (3), 155–158.

37. Gratch, B.; Wood, E. Strategic planning: Implementation and first-year appraisal. J. Acad. Librariansh. 1991, 17 (1), 10–15.

38. Butler, M.; Davis, H. Strategic planning as a catalyst for change in the 1990s. Coll. Res. Libr. 1992, 53 (5), 393–403.

39. Lee, S. Organizational change in the Harvard College Library: A continued struggle for redefinition and renewal. J. Acad. Librariansh. 1993, 19 (4), 225–230.

40. Blunden-Ellis, J. The Consortium of Academic Libraries in Manchester (CALIM): Strategic and Development Planning for a New Consortium. In Resource Sharing: New Technologies as a Must for Universal Availability of Information; Helal, A.H., Weiss, J.W., Eds.; Universitatsbibliothek Essen: Essen, Germany, 1994; 99–114.

41. Shoaf, E.C. Fifteen months in the planning trenches: Strategically positioning the research library for the new century. Libr. Admin. Manage. 2001, 15 (1), 4–13.

42. The Academic Library in Transition: Planning for the 1990s; Lynch, B.P., Ed. Neal Schuman Publishers: New York, 1989.

43. Strategic Planning in Higher Education: Implementing New Roles for the Academic Library; Williams, J.F., Ed. Haworth Press: New York, 1991.

44. Watson, E.I. Transforming the Library: Strategic Planning at Bradley University—The Library Perspective. In Strategic Planning in Higher Education: Implementing New Roles for the Academic Library; Williams, J.F., Ed.; Haworth Press: New York, 1991; 137–145.

45. Wilson, P. Mission and information: What business are we in?. J. Acad. Librariansh. 1988, 14 (2), 82–86.

46. Brophy, P. The mission of the academic library. Br. J. Acad. Librariansh. 1991, 6 (3), 135–147.

47. Forsman, R. Incorporating organizational values into the strategic planning process. J. Acad. Librariansh. 1990, 16 (3), 150–153.

48. Birdsall, D.G.; Hensley, O.D. A new strategic planning model for academic libraries. Coll. Res. Libr. 1994, 55 (2), 149–159.

49. Michalak, S. Planning academic library facilities: The library will have walls. J. Libr. Adm. 1994, 20 (2), 93–114.

50. Hewison, N.S. Achieving change in libraries: Vision at the department, branch and team levels. Libr. Adm. Manage. 1995, 9 (3), 153–158.

51. Tuck, J. Operational planning and performance measurement in the John Rylands university library of Manchester. New Rev. Acad. Librariansh. 1995, 1, 15–31.

52. Bevan, N.; Dolphin, P. Preparing an IT strategy. SCONUL Newsl. 1997, 12, 16–21.

53. Birdsall, D.G. Strategic Planning in Academic Libraries: A Political Perspective. In Restructuring Academic Libraries:

Organizational Development in the Wake of Technological Change; Schwartz, C.A., Ed.; Association of College and Research Libraries: Chicago, IL, 1997; 253–261.

54. Corrall, S. Scenario planning: A strategic management tool for the future. Manag. Inf. **1998**, *5* (9), 34–37.

55. Brewerton, A. First, find some visionaries. Libr. Assoc. Rec. **1999**, *101* (6), 354–356.

56. Feinman, V.J. Five steps toward planning today for tomorrow's needs. Comput. Libr. **1999**, *19* (1), 18–21. http://www.infotoday.com/cilmag/jan99/story1.htm (accessed October 2001).

57. New Mexico State University Library Strategic plan 1997– 2002. http://lib.nmsu.edu/aboutlib/straplan.html (accessed October 2001).

58. The University of Memphis Libraries Strategic plan 1998– 2003. http://www.lib.memphis.edu/stratgic.htm (accessed October 2001).

59. The University of Queensland Library Profile and operational plan 2001–2004. http://www.library.uq.edu.au/ about/ (accessed October 2001).

60. Curtin University of Technology. Library and Information Service LIS Plan 2000–2005. http://lisweb.curtin.edu.au/ organization/documents/stratplan2000.html (accessed October 2001).

61. Kaplan, R.S.; Norton, D.P. The balanced scorecard— Measures that drive performance. Harvard Bus. Rev. **1992**, *70* (1), 71–79.

62. University of Arizona Library Strategic Long Range Planning Team charge. http://dizzy.library.arizona.edu/library/ teams/slrp/SLRPCharge.html (accessed October 2001).

63. Mount Holyoke College. Library, Information and Technology Services Strategic plan. http://www.mtholyoke.edu/ lits/about/plan/index.shtml (accessed October 2001).

64. Monash University Library Operational plan, 2000–2004. http://www.lib.monash.edu.au/OPlans/2000/2000-4intro. html (accessed October 2001).

65. Rutgers University Libraries A bridge to the future: The Rutgers Digital Library Initiative. 1999, http://www.libraries.rutgers.edu/rul/about/long_range_plan.shtml (accessed October 2001).

66. Syracuse University Library Strategic plan. http://libwww. syr.edu/information/strategicplan/index.html (accessed October 2001).

67. Macquarie University Library Strategic plan 1999. http:// www.lib.mq.edu.au/resources/staffpublications/strategic/ index.html (accessed October 2001).

68. The University of Sheffield Library New worlds of information: The library strategic plan 2001/2001–2003/2004. Mission statement and objectives. http://www.shef.ac.uk/ library/libdocs/indexsp.html (accessed October 2001).

69. University of Arizona Library Strategic Long Range Planning Team home page. http://dizzy.library.arizona.edu/ library/teams/slrp/frameref.html (accessed October 2001).

70. Virginia Polytechnic Institute and State University. Virginia Tech University Libraries Library strategic plan steps 2000–2001. http://www.lib.vt.edu/info/stratplan/overview. html (accessed October 2001).

71. University of Washington. University Libraries 2001 Strategic plan. Mission. http://www.lib.washington.edu/about/ StrategicPlan2001.html (accessed October 2001).

72. Birkbeck College Library, Mission statement and strategic plan. http://www.bbk.ac.uk/lib/STRATPLN.PDF (accessed October 2001).

73. University of Western Australia Library Strategic plan 1999–2001. http://www.library.uwa.edu.au/publications/ plan/strategic_plan_1999.html (accessed October 2001).

74. Standing Conference of National and University Libraries, *The SCONUL Vision: The Academic Library in the Year 2002*; SCONUL Briefing Paper; SCONUL: London, 1998 http://www.sconul.ac.uk/vision.htm (accessed October 2001).

75. Standing Conference of National and University Libraries, *The SCONUL Vision: Academic Information Services in the Year 2005*; SCONUL Briefing Paper; SCONUL: London, 2001. http://www.sconul.ac.uk/vision2005.htm (accessed October 2001).

76. University of Edinburgh, Library strategy 1999–2002. http://www.lib.ed.ac.uk/lib/about/policy/strategy.shtml (accessed October 2001).

77. Virginia Polytechnic Institute and State University. University Libraries at Virginia Tech A research library for a major university: The strategic plan for the Virginia tech libraries. [Draft]. http://www.lib.vt.edu/info/stratplan/overview.html (accessed October 2001).

78. Schwartz, P. *The Art of the Long View*; Doubleday: New York, 1991.

79. van der Heijden, K. *Scenarios: The Art of Strategic Conversation*; John Wiley: Chichester, U.K., 1996.

80. Jurow, S.; Webster, D. Building new futures for research libraries. J. Libr. Adm. **1991**, *14* (2), 5–19.

81. Peters, P.E. From serial publications to document delivery to knowledge management: Our fascinating journey, just begun. Ser. Libr. **1996**, *28* (1/2), 37–55.

82. Shapiro, B.J. Refocusing, Rebalancing, and Refining (R^3): The Libraries' Role in Strategic Long-Range Planning at Michigan State University. In *Strategic Planning in Higher Education: Implementing New Roles for the Academic Library*; Williams, J.F., Ed.; Haworth Press: New York, 1991; 79–98.

83. Corrall, S. University library: Visions of the future. Univ. Read. Bull. **1997**, 313, 6–7. See also http://www.rdg.ac.uk/ libweb/Lib/Report/scenarios.html (accessed October 2001).

84. University of Arizona Library Scenarios main page http:// www.library.arizona.edu/library/teams/space9798/branches/ scenario/scenario.htm (accessed October 2001).

85. University of Arizona Library Scenario planning process. [Working draft] http://www.library.arizona.edu/library/ teams/space9798/branches/overview/process1.htr (accessed October 2001).

86. Joint Funding Councils' Libraries Review Group *Report*; The Councils: Bristol, UK, 1993(Chairman: Professor Sir Brian Follett). http://www.ukoln.ac.uk/services/papers/ follett/report/ch7.html (accessed October 2001).

87. Purdue University Libraries Plan 2004: A framework for action http://www.lib.purdue.edu/plan2004/framework_ for_action.html (accessed October 2001).

88. University of Sydney Library Planning documents, Strategic plan 1999–2004; Key results 2000 http://www.library. usyd.edu.au/staff/plan/ accessed October 2001).

Students' Information: Needs and Behavior

Heidi Julien
Library and Information Studies, State University of New York–Buffalo, Buffalo, New York, U.S.A.

Abstract

Students' information behavior is affected by their physical and cognitive developmental stage. Current students are widely understood to be experienced and confident in using online information and communication technologies, although their skill levels commonly are considered to be insufficient. Significant opportunity exists to develop more sophisticated searching skills, as well as ability to critically evaluate information. Information literacy instruction is key to developing these skills. Library use mostly occurs virtually, for both on campus and distance students, and students strongly prefer information available online in full text.

INTRODUCTION

This entry describes current understanding of students' information needs and behavior, based on recent research in library and information science. Students are defined as people at secondary and postsecondary school age (including high school, college, and university students); young children are therefore not included. In addition, students are not necessarily homogeneous in their age groupings. For purposes of this entry, student age groups are assumed to be generally homogeneous; that is, high school students are assumed to be in their mid to late adolescence (e.g., 15–18 years of age), undergraduates or college students are assumed to be in late adolescence and early adulthood (e.g., 18–23 years of age), and graduate students are in early adulthood (e.g., 21–25 years old).

In addition, this entry focuses on young people in their role as students, rather than in any other everyday life role (e.g., employee, family member, leisure group member); the context of interest is the school or academic context. It is important to keep in mind, however, that often these life roles intermingle, so clear separation of information behavior in terms of the student role may not always be differentiated clearly from a person's role as a friend or family member. Information behavior is defined broadly and holistically as including cognitive, behavioral, and affective aspects of active and passive information seeking and information use. The entry makes generalizations about students' information behavior. Clearly, some students will not think and behave in ways that are typical for their age group.

DEVELOPMENTAL CHARACTERISTICS

Because the group of people under consideration in this entry are mid- to late adolescents and young adults, developmental issues are relevant to understanding their information behavior. Students are in the process of developing their reasoning skills; some are able to think more abstractly, logically, and rationally than others. Some are able to consider multiple possibilities and consider the world hypothetically. The ability to "think about thinking" or to think "meta-cognitively" is also developmental; students will have varying abilities to reflect on their feelings, and their thinking. These abilities typically improve as students grow older. Biologically, the brain's frontal lobe development is not complete until people are in their 20s; this part of the brain is responsible for planning and judgment. Thus, age-related physical development also will affect information behaviors.

Developmental approaches to cognition recognize that thinking develops from a stage where relying on received authority is typical, to more active meaning-making and conscious decision-making among many possible alternatives. Implications for information behavior may include passive acceptance of online information as inherently authoritative at earlier cognitive stages, with increased ability for critical evaluative analysis of information at later stages. Therefore, high school students may uncritically rely on information found on the open web through general search engines to a greater degree than more experienced, and developmentally more mature, graduate students. It is also commonly accepted that as people develop they become more cognitively flexible and reflective. These changes may lead older students to greater openness toward new information, and motivate more active information searching, as well as reflection about the credibility and value of information that is found. It is quite possible that a wide range of cognitive ability and flexibility, tendency toward reflection, and epistemological orientation will exist among any group of high school or postsecondary students, making it unwise to draw strict conclusions about cognitive developmental stage.

Encyclopedia of Library and Information Sciences, Fourth Edition DOI: 10.1081/E-EISA-120053111

However, it is prudent to recognize that among students as a group a wide range of cognitive characteristics will exist, including thinking that is not as advanced developmentally as many adults' thinking. And, ability to think and plan will necessarily and profoundly affect information behavior.[1]

THE NET GENERATION

Currently, it is widely recognized that most students in North America belong to a generation variously labeled as the "net" generation, or as "millennial" generation. While this label undoubtedly generalizes, an understanding of how it may describe many students can be helpful in developing appropriate information services for this user group. The "net" generation label connotes a number of attributes, many of which relate directly to information behavior. Most basically, the vast majority of students use the Internet regularly, and the majority report that they access the Internet in their school setting, in addition to home or other access.[2] In the United States, as of 2014, 97% of 18–29-year-old people used the Internet; the largest proportions are white and urban or suburban, and enjoy higher-income levels.[3] Net generation students are flexible with respect to media format; they are open to seeking and receiving information in a variety of formats, although they express a clear preference for electronic formats, such as the Internet, the web, and cell phone technology. Instant messaging is preferred over email, and multimedia social computing software such as Facebook is very popular. There is significant confidence in using electronic technologies, although for complex information searching situations, there may be a large gap between confidence and actual skill level. Indeed, testing for search skills and ability to evaluate credibility of information reveals these gaps and is generating widespread concern about general skill levels among student populations. This concern relates to students' actual ability to locate and evaluate information appropriate for academic purposes, but also relates to information sought and used for personal decision-making (e.g., for sexual health). Students' weaknesses when judging credibility may relate to a drop in respect for authority, perceived by some observers, along with increased emphasis on social computing and democratic principles of collective effort, so that "authority" of information may be less important for this generation than was the case for older generations. The well-known popularity of democratic information sources such as Wikipedia is a good example.

Another common trait among the net generation is little tolerance for print formats, which may be viewed as old-fashioned, unwieldy, and too slow; timely information retrieval is of the essence. There is also a preference for multimedia, so there is a predilection for information contextualized by music and images. These students are purported to be skilled multitaskers, apparently able to simultaneously attend to multiple sources of information; whether that is truly the case is uncertain. Their preferred learning style is experiential, so that active and enjoyable and entertaining methods of learning are favored over reading print or listening to lecture material alone. An inclination for collaborative learning also affects information behavior, increasing a focus on group information sharing. Speed and convenience, as well as habitual use of the web for information seeking in general, are key variables in information source preference. Thus, quick, and very possibly relatively ineffective, general web searches (e.g., using Google) often suffice to provide information for many purposes, including school assignments. Libraries and librarians may be viewed as associated with a dated institution, and there is often little understanding that academic databases used to complete assignments are likely provided by libraries rather than simply existing on the open web.

This set of generational characteristics presents a multitude of challenges for information service providers, in terms of meeting expectations and preferences for information format, and in communicating with students whose learning styles and communication preferences differ substantially from those of service providers who identify with an older generation.

INFORMATION SEARCHING BEHAVIOR

Information searching specifically means the active, typically online, searching for information that students do as they seek to fulfill assignment requirements. One of the most influential theories of information searching by students, which is user-centered and has proven to be very robust, is the Information Search Process (ISP), developed by Carol Kuhlthau.[4] The ISP is based on the principle of uncertainty and assumes that students search for information in order to make meaning. The ISP describes information searching along three continuums: thoughts, feelings, and actions; thus, it is holistic in its approach and is particularly noted for including affect or emotion as integral to information behavior. According to the ISP, students progress relatively predictably through a series of stages in their information searching, beginning with initiation, moving to selection, exploration, formulation, collection, and presentation. Each of these stages is characterized by affective experiences (such as relative anxiety or confidence), thoughts (e.g., vague or interested), and physical actions. Each stage is associated with a particular goal related to the ISP, and specific tasks related to achieving that goal. Understanding where a particular student might be on this continuum can help information services providers to give assistance appropriate to the stage. In addition, when students themselves understand that information searching is a process, and that their feelings and experiences are shared by others, anxiety can be reduced and search effectiveness can be improved.

Like most searchers, students' searching behavior is constrained by time limits (especially when meeting assignment deadlines) and information overload. Many students make choices about what information to use based on expedience, or convenience, which is a "satisficing"[5] approach. Convenience supersedes quality as a criterion for information source selection. Timeliness is a key factor for information selection; students prefer information that can be found quickly. One result is that when quickly identified information is found, searching may be brought to a premature close, with the result that better quality, more detailed, or more topically relevant information may not be found. This focus on convenience, including time-savings, ease of access, and ease of use, can be explained by gratification theory and rational choice theory.[6] Students primarily focus on the product of their information seeking, rather than the process.[7] However, students can be taught to consider information seeking as a process and to appreciate the skill set (information literacy) involved in information seeking. Unfortunately, students who demonstrate relatively low levels of information literacy tend to overestimate their information literacy expertise.[8] Research across many institutions, with students of a wide age range and who are studying in a variety of disciplines, consistently demonstrates that students generally are challenged by selecting appropriate databases, constructing effective search strategies, and evaluating information found. Search strategies are often ad hoc and incoherent, and identifying keywords and terms is a significant challenge.[9] There also is a tendency to believe that all online information is equally valuable. More sophisticated searching is observed from students with greater domain knowledge; thus, students who are more experienced with subject content (e.g., graduate students) will be more sophisticated searchers than novices. Improved searching skills demonstrated by more senior students also results from greater experience and from more information literacy skills training. In general, the open web is much preferred over formal online sources such as databases or specialized portals. Google is the most used Internet search engine and is favored because it is perceived as easy to use. In addition, many students use it out of habit because it is the search engine of choice for personal information needs. Naturally, that habit develops because these users experience success; that is, they find information that, in their judgment, satisfies their needs. Other search engines, such as Yahoo!, are used far less frequently than Google, and library catalogs are used very little, even for school assignments. Wikipedia is often used at the beginning of the search process to locate background or summary information; students like Wikipedia for its coverage, currency, comprehensibility, and convenience.[10] Students with relatively low information skills tend to have learned their skills from friends and family.

Students who can demonstrate higher skill levels have often learned these skills from professionals such as teachers and librarians. Interestingly, many students view information literacy skills as relatively easy to acquire and prefer to learn this skill set from other people rather than an online training tool.[7]

Students experience information overload and are frustrated by the challenges of starting information searches. They are also frustrated by the need to sift through unwanted search results, including outdated information. Students also are often confused by library classification practices and by unusual information sources, such as statistics. Students often lack the context needed to conduct efficient and effective searches, such as understanding appropriate steps in a search for academic information, understanding terminology and key terms for an unfamiliar topic, and setting boundaries on a search. Wikipedia can be helpful to address these specific issues.[11] Students often turn first to course readings and materials, but they also appreciate the databases provided by libraries, even if the range of databases searched is narrow. However, students tend not to make use of the expertise and support that librarians can provide.[12]

Among the personality characteristics that affect approach to searching behavior is self-efficacy or the belief that one can achieve one's goals. Self-efficacy is related to confidence, but is a distinct trait that is open to development. When students feel self-efficacy about their searching skills, or even computer use in general, they are more likely to explore unfamiliar territory and to search more deeply. Self-efficacy also has been positively correlated with library use.[13] A range of other personality characteristics, such as extroversion, neuroticism, and level of engagement (motivation), have been found to affect searching behavior, but the practical implications of this understanding for information providers are not yet clear. For example, the depth with which information searching occurs may be related more to personality than to discipline of study.[14] Other individual differences, such as gender and cognitive style, may be relevant to searching effectiveness.[15] External factors such as group dynamics may also affect information seeking as young persons are often significantly influenced by their peers.

LIBRARY USE

In the student role, young people frequently are expected by their instructors to make use of libraries for research. Even if libraries are significantly less preferred than the web, and even when students do not realize that access to proprietary databases is provided as a library service, libraries do play a role in students' information behavior. For most students in most educational settings, little use is made of in-person reference services and virtual reference services are not popular, although students prefer online chat over other forms of reference service.[16] In addition, because most students prefer to use online information sources, in-person searching for information, and use of print materials are significantly less important for this user group. Efficiency and predictability are the principles guiding students' academic research.[17] Most freshmen are challenged by searching academic library portals, with reading scholarly materials, and with effective database searching and library use in general.[18] Indeed, many students actively avoid using the library as a physical space for information searching, although that space may be sought out for studying or socializing purposes. Many students also actively avoid consulting library staff because staff expertise is not well understood and sometimes because of negative experiences with library staff who lack understanding of the developmental and affective aspects of information seeking. Library anxiety is a phenomenon affecting many students; they are intimidated by the library and lack confidence in their ability to successfully negotiate its intricate and complex systems. Library anxiety is also characterized by a fear of asking for help. International students with additional language barriers may be particularly affected by library anxiety. Interestingly, and for unknown reasons, African-American graduate students appear to experience less library anxiety than do their white peers; differences among different student groups have not been fully explored, however.[19] Students are largely unaware of the materials and services that libraries offer; for example, they often do not know that libraries can provide access to databases containing information directly relevant to school assignments. This points to a significant need for greater assistance to students, online and in person, as well as more training opportunities (see section "Information Literacy").

Attempts to increase library use, or at least help students to appreciate library services, such as knowing about licensed online databases, requires a marketing orientation informed by understanding students as a user group (see "Net Generation"). There are some libraries that are central to the information seeking of their students, and the research literature does provide examples where library staff have worked closely with teachers to meet students' needs effectively. In particular, when library websites can meet students' preferences for convenient, effective access to quality online information, those libraries are valued by their student users. One of the challenges facing students who use library websites is the jargon that is understood by librarians but not by users. Another challenge is that, due to students' emphasis on convenience, full-text information is greatly preferred over information that must be located via a multiple-step process (e.g., locating print sources on the basis of citations). Thus, information that is not made available online in full text may be underused or never used at all.

INFORMATION LITERACY

Information research requires a skill set commonly referred to as "information literacy." These skills include the ability to recognize information needs, to efficiently and effectively search for information required, and to use information ethically (e.g., to avoid plagiarism and to cite references appropriately). Information literacy includes cognitive understandings (e.g., understanding Boolean logic), behavioral skills (e.g., keyboarding), affective attributes (e.g., confidence to use databases), and attitudes such as respect for intellectual property. Relational models of information literacy emphasize information literacy as a process and as knowledge-building. Whether conceived a list of skills or as a more complex set of concepts, there is little disagreement about the need to develop information literacy. As a group, students particularly require information literacy skills to conduct the research required to complete assignments. These skills are not innate, nor are they developed through experience alone. Explicit instruction is required in order to learn sophisticated, efficient, and effective skills to find and evaluate information. There is ample evidence that teaching information literacy skills results in increased skill level, increased confidence in using libraries and in information seeking, improvements to learning outcomes, and increased program retention rates. Indeed, college students who have graduated from high schools with librarians and library programs perform significantly better in their academics at the postsecondary level. In addition, students are able to apply information literacy skills learned in a library context to other areas of their lives, improving their information search and evaluation skills for information seeking and decision-making in personal situations.

There is disparity in the training that students receive at the high school level. Training opportunities at the postsecondary level vary as well. At some educational institutions, mandatory information literacy skills training ensures minimal exposure to search skills and critical evaluation skills. However, many colleges and universities do not require information literacy training for students. Most institutions offer some training opportunities, however. These range from introductory orientations and library tours, to 1-hour focused workshops, to course-integrated workshops. Logical sequences of skills training opportunities also are available at many institutions, while others offer elective credit-bearing information literacy courses. Because of this diversity of opportunity, many students receive little or no formal training in information literacy skills. In addition, many students do not feel confident to ask for help in person, or by other means, often because they are concerned about appearing stupid. If students enter a physical library, they often receive informal at-need specific instruction if they ask library staff for help. This may take the form of quick database searching tips, for instance. In addition, libraries typically provide online information literacy skills training through their websites. This ranges from online "pathfinders" to interactive tutorials focusing on how to search particular databases or skill sets (e.g., how to avoid plagiarism or how to accurately cite source material). A minority of students receive training in how to use the Internet, which is the most significant information source for this user group.

Teaching methods appropriate to students will vary with the specific group, but high school students may be particularly motivated by methods that incorporate contemporary themes and pop culture references. In addition, active learning methods, such as hands-on instruction in a laboratory environment, are generally more effective than more passive methods, such as lecturing. Information literacy skills are best taught in a context of close collaboration between librarians and teachers or faculty, within the context of the curriculum. Thus, the timing of development of specific skills correlates with what students are learning and with the assignments they are working on. Students learning within a problem-based curriculum, as is often the case in health-related disciplines, tend to develop more sophisticated information literacy skills because these skills are critical to find the research- or evidence-based information for successful learning.

Despite the apparent need to develop information literacy among students, significant barriers exist for librarians who wish to undertake this work. These barriers include negative or ambivalent student attitudes toward libraries and lack of understanding of librarians' expertise. Institutional barriers such as complex librarian–faculty relationships, which hinder collaboration on information literacy initiatives, ambivalence on the part of library administrators, and lack of funding for staff and teaching resources, are also challenging. In addition, some librarians are uncomfortable with the teaching role, and many librarians who are tasked with providing information literacy instruction are relatively unprepared for that work.

SPECIFIC STUDENT GROUPS

Some differences in information behavior are discernable between different subgroups of students. It has already been noted that search skills and ability to critically evaluate information appears to improve over time, so older students (e.g., graduate students) are likely to be more efficient and successful information searchers than high school students. In part, this is due to increased domain knowledge as disciplinary specialization deepens, but is undoubtedly also due to biological maturation. As the brain reaches developmental maturity, judgment and planning ability improve.

Disciplinary differences among students are not as sharp as those observed among different disciplinary groupings of scholars and scientists; students in different disciplines behave far more alike than they do differently.

Standard conceptions about the preferences by humanities scholars for browsing, for instance, are not necessarily applicable to students studying in those disciplines, particularly at the undergraduate level. This is the case despite the strong influence of educators, who presumably are disciplinary experts, on the information-seeking behaviors of their students (especially in recommending specific databases). Thus, the typical behaviors described earlier apply to students across areas of study. One analysis of students grouped by broad disciplinary characteristics found that undergraduates in "soft," "pure," and "life" disciplines are more active information seekers than their peers in "hard," "applied," and "nonlife" disciplines. "Hard" disciplines included engineering and physical sciences, while the "soft" label was applied to humanities and social sciences. "Pure" referred to physical sciences, humanities, and social sciences, while engineering, business, and education were considered to be "applied." Social sciences and education were considered to be "life" disciplines; the others were labeled "nonlife."[20] At best, these kinds of differences suggest that focusing library and instructional services on those students who are the least active information seekers might increase their information searching activity. However, curricular imperatives, assignment structures, and instructor expectations will all play significant roles in mediating students' information behavior.

Some groups of students encounter additional barriers to their information seeking. International students are a group worthy of special attention by information services providers. Language and cultural barriers often combine to make information searching and library use particularly challenging for these students, and database searching can be especially difficult for students whose first language is not English.[21] Library anxiety may be especially acute, and lack of confidence may stand in the way of seeking much needed help. In addition, unfamiliar and complex library systems and organization, including confusing library jargon and alien physical arrangements such as open stacks, may increase anxiety. There is little doubt that providing focused information literacy and library use instruction for international students is critical to ensure effective information access. In addition, African-American students may face barriers due to actual or perceived impacts of racism because many academic libraries are largely white (majority) environments.[22]

CONCLUSIONS

As a user group, today's students present information service providers with a variety of opportunities and challenges. Students' information-seeking habits in their academic contexts appear to be less rational and are less effective than information experts would like. Partly motivated by developmental stage, and partly by their unique experiences as the "net" generation, students are focused on finding full-text online information as conveniently and quickly as possible. Sophisticated search strategies, critical evaluation of information, and appreciation for intellectual property are skills and attitudes that require development. Information literacy instruction is critical if students in general are to become skilled information seekers and ethical information users. Experience using computers and general web search engines is insufficient. More likely, experience engenders confidence, which is unmatched by demonstrable skill. This situation provides librarians with significant opportunity to reimagine their services and to fill an important instructional role. Librarians alone have the expertise required to guide students to sophisticated information-seeking strategies. Students have much to gain from that expertise. The challenge will be to meet these opportunities with conviction, resources, and a clear understanding of the preferences and habits of this user group.

ACKNOWLEDGMENTS

This entry is a revision of a previous entry with the same title published in the *Encyclopedia of Information Science*. The author sincerely appreciates the invaluable research assistance of Shelagh Genuis.

REFERENCES

1. Whitmire, E. The relationship between undergraduates' epistemological beliefs, reflective judgment, and their information-seeking behavior. Inf. Process. Manag. **2004**, *40* (1), 97–111.
2. Rainie, L.; Hitlin, P. The internet at school. Pew Internet and American Life Project 2005. http://www.pewinternet. org/2005/08/02/the-internet-at-school/ (accessed August 2014).
3. Pew Research Internet Project. http://www.pewinternet. org/data-trend/internet-use/latest-stats/ (accessed September 2014).
4. Kuhlthau, C.C. *Seeking Meaning: A Process Approach to Library and Information Services*, 2nd Ed.; Libraries Unlimited: Westport, CT, 2004.
5. Simon, H. *The Sciences of the Artificial*, 2nd Ed.; MIT Press: Cambridge, MA, 1981.
6. Connaway, L.S.; Dickey, T.J; Radford, M.L. 'If it is too inconvenient, i'm not going after it.:' convenience as a critical factor in information-seeking behaviors. Libr. Inf. Sci. Res. **2011**, *33* (3), 179–190.
7. Gross, M.; Latham, D. Experiences with and perceptions of information: a phenomenographic study of first-year college students. Libr. Q. **2011**, *81* (2), 161–186.
8. Latham, D.; Gross, M. Enhancing skills, effecting change: evaluating an intervention for students with below-proficient information literacy skills. Can. J. Inf. Libr. Sci. **2011**, *35* (4), 367–383.
9. Duncan, V.; Holtslander, L. Utilizing grounded theory to explore the information-seeking behavior of senior nursing students. J. Med. Libr. Assoc. **2012**, *100* (1), 20–27.
10. Head, A.J.; Eisenberg, M.B. How today's college students use Wikipedia for course-related research. First Monday **2010**, *15* (3).
11. Head, A.J.; Eisenberg, M.B. Finding context: what today's college students say about conducting research in the digital age, Project Information Literacy Progress Report. February 4, 2009. http://projectinfolit.org/images/pdfs/ pil_progressreport_2_2009.pdf (accessed August 2014).
12. Head, A.J.; Eisenberg, M.B. Lessons learned: how college students seek information in the digital age, Project Information Literacy First Year Report with Student Survey Findings. December 1, 2009. http://projectinfolit.org/images/ pdfs/pil_fall2009_finalv_yr1_12_2009v2.pdf (accessed August 2014).
13. Fields, A.M. Self-efficacy and the first-year university student's authority of knowledge: an exploratory study. J. Acad. Librariansh. **2005**, *31* (6), 539–545.
14. Heinström, J. Fast surfing, broad scanning and deep diving: the influence of personality and study approach on students' information-seeking behavior. J. Doc. **2005**, *61* (2), 228–247.
15. Ford, N.; Miller, D.; Moss, N. The role of individual differences in internet searching: an empirical study. J. Am. Soc. Inf. Sci. Technol. **2001**, *52* (12), 1049–1066.
16. Chow, A.; Croxton, R. Information-seeking behavior and reference medium preferences. Ref. User Serv. Q. **2012**, *51* (3), 246–262.
17. Head, A.J.; Eisenberg, M.B. Truth be told: how college students evaluate and use information in the digital age, Project Information Literacy Progress Report. November 1, 2010. http://projectinfolit.org/images/pdfs/pil_fall2010_ survey_fullreport1.pdf (accessed August 2014).
18. Head, A.J. Learning the ropes: how freshmen conduct course research once they enter college, Project Information Literacy Research Report. December 4, 2013. http:// projectinfolit.org/images/pdfs/pil_2013_freshmenstudy_ fullreport.pdf (accessed August 2014).
19. Jiao, Q.G.; Onwuegbuzie, A.J.; Bostick, S.L. Racial differences in library anxiety among graduate students. Libr. Rev. **2004**, *53* (4), 228–235.
20. Whitmire, E. Disciplinary differences and undergraduates' information-seeking behavior. J. Am. Soc. Inf. Sci. Technol. **2002**, *53* (8), 631–638.
21. Vanopstal, K.; Stichele, R.; Laureys, G.; Buysschaert, J. PubMed searches by Dutch-speaking nursing students: the impact of language and system experience. J. Am. Soc. Inf. Sci. Technol. **2012**, *63* (8), 1538–1552.
22. Katopol, P. Information anxiety and African-American students in a graduate education program. Educ. Libr. **2012**, *35* (1–2), 5–14.

BIBLIOGRAPHY

1. Al-Muomen, N.; Morris, A.; Maynard, S. Modelling information-seeking behaviour of graduate students at Kuwait University. J. Doc. **2012**, *68* (4), 430–459.

2. Badke, W. The path of least resistance. Online Search. **2013**, *37* (1), 65–67.

3. Beheshti, J.; Large, A., Eds. *The Information Behavior of a New Generation: Children and Teens in the 21st Century*; The Scarecrow Press: Lanham, MD, 2013.

4. Blummer, B.; Watulak, S.; Kenton, J. The research experience for education graduate students: a phenomenographic study. Internet Ref. Serv. Q. **2012**, *17* (3/4), 117–146.

5. Bronstein, J. The role of perceived self-efficacy in the information seeking behavior of library and information science students. J. Acad. Librariansh. **2014**, *40* (2), 101–106.

6. Case, Donald O. *Looking for Information: A Survey of Research on Information Seeking, Needs, and Behavior*, 3rd Ed.; Emerald Publishing Group: Bingley, U.K., 2012.

7. Catalano, A. Patterns of graduate students' information seeking behavior: a meta-synthesis of the literature. J. Doc. **2013**, *69* (2), 243–274.

8. Chelton, M.K.; Cool, C., Eds. *Youth Information-seeking Behavior II: Theories, Models, and Issues*; The Scarecrow Press: Lanham, MD, 2007.

9. Daly, E. College libraries and student culture: what we now know. Portal: Libr. Acad. **2012**, *12* (2), 223–224.

10. Dhillon, M.K. Online information seeking and higher education students. In *Youth Information-seeking Behavior II: Context, Theories, Models, and Issues*; Chelton, M.K., Cool, C., Eds.; The Scarecrow Press, Inc.: Lanham, MD, 2007; 165–205.

11. Diehm, R.; Lupton, M. Approaches to learning information literacy: a phenomenographic study. J. Acad. Librariansh. **2012**, *38* (4), 217–225.

12. Ferran-Ferrer, N.; Minguillón, J.; Pérez-Montoro, M. Key factors in the transfer of information-related competencies between academic, workplace, and daily life contexts. J. Am. Soc. Inf. Sci. Technol. **2013**, *64* (6), 1112–1121.

13. Gross, M.; Latham, D. Undergraduate perceptions of information literacy: defining, attaining, and self-assessing skills. Coll. Res. Libr. **2009**, *70* (4), 336–350.

14. Hess, D.; Rainie, L.; Kalehoff, M. College students and the web: a Pew Internet data memo. Pew Internet and American Life Project 2002. http://www.pewinternet.org/2002/09/15/college-students-and-the-web/ (accessed August, 2014).

15. Jordan, J. Meta-synthesis of the research on information seeking behaviour of graduate students highlights different library resource needs across disciplines and cultures. Evid. Based Libr. Inf. Pract. **2013**, *8* (4), 132–135.

16. Mbabu, L.; Bertram, A.; Varnum, K. Patterns of undergraduates' use of scholarly databases in a large research university. J. Acad. Librariansh. **2013**, *39* (2), 189–193.

17. Mizrachi, D.; Bates, M. Undergraduates' personal academic information management and the consideration of time and task-urgency. J. Am. Soc. Inf. Sci. Technol. **2013**, *64* (8), 1590–1607.

18. Rempel, H.; Buck, S.; Deitering, A. Examining student research choices and processes in a disintermediated searching environment. Portal: Libr. Acad. **2013**, *13* (4), 363–384.

19. Rowley, J.; Urquhart, C. Understanding student information behavior in relation to electronic information services: lessons from longitudinal monitoring and evaluation, Part 1. J. Am. Soc. Inf. Sci. Technol. **2007**, *58* (8), 1162–1174.

20. Sloan, M.; McPhee, K. Information seeking in context: results of graduate student interviews. Partnership: Can. J. Libr. Inf. Pract. Res. **2013**, *8* (1), 1–18.

21. Smith, A.; Rainie, L.; Zickuhr, K. College students and technology, 2010. http://www.pewinternet.org/2011/07/19/college-students-and-technology/ (accessed August 2014).

22. Urquhart, C.; Rowley, J. Understanding student information behavior in relation to electronic information services: lessons from longitudinal monitoring and evaluation, Part 2. J. Am. Soc. Inf. Sci. Technol. **2007**, *58* (8), 1188–1197.

Student–Taxonomy

Subject Cataloging Principles and Systems

Theodora L. Hodges
Berkeley, California, U.S.A.

Lois Mai Chan
School of Library and Information Science, University of Kentucky, Lexington, Kentucky, U.S.A.

Abstract

After an introduction that addresses the means people use to search for information, this entry articulates the principles underlying various subject access options, including both controlled vocabulary systems and classification. It begins with a brief history of subject access provisions, including an account of the impact of automation, and goes on to discuss in some detail the principles underlying American library practice in respect to subject access. It then, briefly, describes selected subject-access schemes (including both subject heading lists and classification systems) in terms of how they reflect the principles presented, and how well they fulfill their stated functions.

INTRODUCTION

Ever since libraries have existed, those in charge of them have tried to make it possible for the people who use them to select and retrieve from their collections items that are relevant to their queries. Apparently, this was true even over 2000 years ago, for the hundreds of thousands of papyrus scrolls in the ancient Alexandrian library—although no index still exists.[1] As of this writing, October 2008, there is much discussion in the library profession about whether traditional thinking about subject access is still relevant to existing conditions. This entry takes the position that it is, that subject cataloging—a term that embraces both subject heading assignment and classification—may even play an increasingly significant role in the information retrieval world of the future.

APPROACHES TO SEARCHING

For many years now, there have been three approaches to searching by subject: through controlled vocabulary, through full-text or keywords, and, less so than the others, through classification.

Controlled Vocabulary Searching

Controlled vocabulary searches are usually made on library catalogs and indexes consisting of document surrogates (*document surrogates* is the current terminological usage for what have traditionally been called bibliographic or catalog records and, more recently, metadata records). Controlled vocabulary access depends on two circumstances: 1) the existence of a controlled vocabulary,

i.e., a list of preferred terms—called a subject heading list or thesaurus—of which *Library of Congress Subject Headings* (LCSH)[2] is the best known in the English-speaking world; and 2) the assignment of terms from the list to the documents in a collection or database. (Assigning subject terms to documents is called subject indexing or subject cataloging.) In library classification, the counterpart to subject indexing from a term list, the same requirements prevail: the existence of a classification scheme (such as the *Library of Congress Classification* [LCC][3] or the *Dewey Decimal Classification* [DDC]),[4] and the assignment of class numbers from the chosen scheme to documents. "Numbers" is used here to reflect common usage in respect to classification-based notation. Notation used for extant classification systems varies from one scheme to another: DDC's notation is almost fully numerical; LCC's is alpha-numerical; and both the Colon Classification (CC) and the Universal Decimal Classification (UDC) include punctuation marks in their notation.

In controlled vocabulary or classification number searching, users input query terms or class numbers, and the system delivers material tagged with those terms or numbers. The fact that the term *subject cataloging* is sometimes used for both subject heading and classification number assignment reflects the parallelism between the two operations.

Controlled vocabulary lists

In a controlled vocabulary list, one term among synonyms is chosen as the preferred term (called subject heading or descriptor): the others are included in the list as lead-in terms with SEE or USE references that direct searchers to the preferred term. Other cross-references are given under

Encyclopedia of Library and Information Sciences, Fourth Edition DOI: 10.1081/E-ELIS4-120043713

the preferred term, directing users to broader, narrower, and related terms. Such sets of references, with their associated preferred terms, are referred to as a list's *reference structure*, and are an essential part of controlled vocabulary lists. A controlled vocabulary search delivers a high proportion of material in the database searched that pertains to the topic indicated by a user's query term, and reports very little else. A means of searching that is akin to controlled vocabulary searching is searching by assigned classification numbers. The numbers representing class positions in a classification scheme can also be considered controlled, in the sense that much thought has gone into both designing the scheme and assigning the numbers to documents.

Authority control

An important point regarding controlled vocabulary lists is that, for each preferred term, a record must be created that shows what preferred-term decisions were made, what the bases for such decisions were, and what cross-references are associated with the term. Such a record is called a subject authority record, and a collected set of all authority records is called a subject authority file. System managers try to keep such files meticulously up to date because authority records are essential to the management of any controlled vocabulary system, whatever its venue or setting.

Keyword and Full-Text Searching

Keyword or full-text searching is most commonly done through the Internet, with its vast, hardly imaginable, store of resources. In keyword searching, users submit query terms that are then matched against the full texts of items in the database of the system offering the search service used. One advantage of keyword searching is that information is retrieved on the authors' own words, which often reflect the most current terminology in a particular subject field. Others are that keyword searching is fast and easy, and many are satisfied with its search results. A major drawback, however, is that if searchers want to retrieve all information, or as much information as possible, on a given subject, they must search on all the synonyms for that subject. A second problem is that most keyword searches pull up an overwhelming number of items. In the interests of improved efficiency and effectiveness, therefore, many search services have taken to partitioning their databases. There are now several Googles, for instance, including Google Earth, Google Travel, and Google Scholar.[5]

Searching by Classification Numbers

The last subject-search practice to be discussed is classification. For generations, people roamed library stacks to find material of interest. When they found something promising, they often found neighboring materials of interest as well. This is because traditional classification schemes group similar materials together and arrange them hierarchically.

Shelf browsing may be losing its attraction as people turn more and more to online searching. However, some online public access catalogs (OPACs) allow the option of displaying catalog records in class number order. (Looking through a list of classification numbers online recreates, without the ambience, an experience similar to browsing in library stacks.) Furthermore, it is possible that future programs may be developed that preserve and enhance the benefits of shelf browsing by mapping classification and controlled subject terms one against the other.[6] Such mapped systems could become powerful retrieval tools.

HISTORY OF SUBJECT ACCESS IN LIBRARY CATALOGS

Early library catalogs were primarily finding-lists providing both author entries and catchword title entries for each item along with a symbol or number indicating its location in the collection. A catchword was the leading word in a title if it expressed subject content, but in cases like *An Introduction to Physics*, "physics" would be used as the entry word. This practice indicated that, by 1850 or so, librarians had begun to be aware of the significance of the subject approach to library material.[7]

During the 1800s many libraries had what were called classed catalogs, with subject headings in the form: *Plants—Trees—Evergreens—Pines—Southern pines*. Such a catalog required an index to use effectively. A catalog assigning *Southern pines*, or *Pines, Southern* for the same book was called a dictionary or alphabetical-specific catalog. By 1900, almost all American library catalogs were in dictionary form.

Early Standard Subject Lists

Before there was a standard list for subject headings, catalogers in individual libraries assigned subject headings as they saw fit. The advantages of having a standard list had become apparent by the early 1890s, probably due to the increase in interlibrary loan operations and the introduction of centralized cataloging.

In 1895, the first standard list for subject headings appeared: the *List of Subject Headings for Use in Dictionary Catalogs* (commonly called the ALA List), produced by an American Library Association (ALA) committee.[8] It was discontinued after 1914 when the Library of Congress (LC) began publishing its own list, now titled *Library of Congress Subject Headings*[2] and referred to as LCSH.

After LC started distributing printed catalog cards at the beginning of the twentieth century, the Library's descriptive and subject cataloging practices gradually became the de facto standard for American libraries. However, LCSH and its predecessors were designed for, and reflect the practice of, large research collections. They have never been ideally suitable for medium-sized or small collections. Early on, the gap was filled by a list compiled by Minnie Earl Sears and first published in 1923 under the title *Subject Headings for Small Libraries*. This list was based on LCSH, and so is compatible with it. It was later renamed *Sears List of Subject Headings*, with the nineteenth edition appearing in 2007.[9] Despite the ease of using the LC subject headings that appear in cataloging copy, (i.e., records prepared by other agencies that can be downloaded for use in one's own system), the *Sears* list is still favored by many American school libraries and small or medium-sized public libraries. (This list is discussed in somewhat more detail later in this entry.)

Later and a book about FAST is in publication many lists of subject headings were developed for special fields and applications. Probably the best known among these is *Medical Subject Headings* (MeSH). In recent times, an interesting system is under development, (FAST), *Faceted Application of Subject Terminology* a subject headings list based on LCSH vocabulary used under highly simplified application rules. FAST began as an attempt to make the richness of LCSH vocabulary available for tagging Internet resources, and is now (fall 2008) in the testing stage. (FAST is described in more detail later in this entry).[10]

Impact of Automation

The impact of automation on library-based subject access over the last several decades has been immeasurable. In the late 1950s, when it was clear that the computer was becoming an important player in all phases of American life, LC took steps toward automating its operations. An important element in its automation drive was the development of *Machine Readable Cataloging* (MARC), an encoding language now known as MARC 21 Formats.[11] In October 1966, LC began trial distribution of MARC tapes containing cataloging records with MARC codes. Not long after, LC and many libraries nation-wide began work on converting all their records to machine-readable form. With general catalog conversion, the long-familiar banks of wooden catalog-drawer cases began disappearing, to be replaced by computer terminals, many accompanied by printers. These terminals were off-line tools at first. By the 1980s, many library catalogs were online and were known as OPACs Online Public Access Catalogs. By then, the Internet had become a factor to be reckoned with, the first appearance of the term *Internet* having been in 1974. And during 1989, a new system was in development at the Center for European Nuclear Research (CERN) in Switzerland; it combined hypertext and Internet technologies and

was called the *World Wide Web*.[12] CERN released the Web in 1991, to enthusiastic popular acclaim. OPACs made considerable gains in sophistication during the 1990s and later, offering not only Internet access but highly refined search options. Many now refer to them as WebPACs. Furthermore, libraries have provided access to more and more online resources through their portals. Some of these resources are cataloged and incorporated into local OPACs.

PRINCIPLES GOVERNING CONTROLLED VOCABULARIES

The discussion turns now to the principles underlying the design and construction of controlled vocabulary systems. Early on, theorists and practitioners realized that retrieval effectiveness was increased if certain principles were followed in designing their systems, and so moved toward standardization. Among the early writers on the topic was Charles Ammi Cutter. Perhaps ironically, because of how early he was active, it was Cutter who articulated the basic principles of effective subject cataloging in his 1876 *Rules for a Dictionary Catalog*.[13] What he said has been much discussed ever since, but never significantly improved upon. Among Cutter's statements were two objectives, much quoted even now: 1) to enable a person to find a book of which the subject is known; and 2) to show what the library has on a given subject. The first addresses the need to locate individual items, the second the need to collocate materials on the same subject.

Most of the principles governing current thought and practice on subject access vocabulary either spring directly from Cutter's work or reflect his thinking to a considerable degree. The terms used for various aspects of such vocabulary are discussed below. These are 1) convenience of the public; 2) uniform and unique headings; 3) specific and direct entry; 4) consistency and currency in terminology; and 5) provision of cross-references. All of these apply just as forcefully to nonlibrary surrogate systems as they do to library practice.

Convenience of the Public

For Cutter, the most important consideration in the cataloging of library materials was "the best interest of the user." He called this principle "the convenience of the public." He felt that catalogers should be concerned with "the public's habitual way of looking at things" and that such habits should not be ignored even if they occasionally demand a sacrifice of logic and simplicity. It is worth noting here that the library user population in Cutter's day was probably more homogeneous than it is in this century. Cutter's *common usage* principle, though unassailable in intent, is the hardest of his recommendations to implement effectively today because of the wide spectrum of information needs in the population now using libraries and other information services. One approach to solving the user-variability problem is to try to develop a system that adheres to strictly formed principles, on the assumption that a logical and consistent system can be learned by its users. When one looks beyond Cutter's insistence on reflecting general usage, one finds that his early rules went a long way toward laying the groundwork for a logical and consistent subject access apparatus.

Uniform and Unique Headings

In order to show what a collection or a database has on a given subject, its subject access system must adopt a principle of uniform headings, that is, all material on a given subject must be tagged with the same heading. If a subject has more than one name ("ascorbic acid" and "Vitamin C," for instance) one must be chosen as the valid or authorized heading, with *SEE* or *USE* references from alternate terms. In general, it is hoped that the term chosen is unambiguous and familiar to all users of the catalog. The converse of the principle of uniform headings is that of unique headings, a principle that requires that the same term should not be used to represent more than one subject. If the same term must be used in more than one sense, as is often the case when different disciplines or fields of knowledge are involved, some qualification or clarification must be added so that it will be clear to the user which meaning is intended, for instance, "iris (eye)" and "iris (plant)."

Direct and Specific Entry

The rule for direct entry was set forth by Cutter in his *Rules for a Dictionary Catalog*: "Enter a work under its subject headings, not under the heading of a class which includes that subject…."[13] The principle of *direct entry* applies to how headings are formulated: the heading *Monkeys* is direct; the heading *Mammals—Primates—Monkeys* is indirect, although they are both just as specific. The principle of *specific entry* governs how headings are assigned to documents, and calls for as close a match as possible—in terms of generality or specificity—between the heading used and the material being cataloged. In other words, a chosen heading should be neither broader nor narrower than the topic it is intended to cover. In recent years there has been much theoretical discussion on just what *specificity* means in the context of subject indexing.[14] It is doubtful the question was problematic for Cutter, as one of his concerns at the time was presumably to counteract the then prevalent tendency of catalogers to think in classed-entry terms. An informative discussion of specific and direct entry may be found in *Library of Congress Subject Headings: Principles and Application*.[15]

Consistent and Current Terminology

It follows from what has been said above, particularly regarding the justifications for uniform headings, that heading terminology should be both consistent and current. So should the terminology in classification schemes. Two elements are particularly important in this respect: synonymy and changing usage. Choices among synonymous terms may require difficult decisions. By principle, common usage prevails when it can be determined. However, the more specialized a library's collection and clientele, the more specialized its indexing terminology should be; special libraries, therefore, often develop their own controlled vocabularies or make extensive modifications in standard lists. A change in usage should be reflected in terminology, but there is often an unavoidable delay because, for emerging subjects, it takes time for terminology to crystallize. Controlled vocabulary lists, including subject heading lists, thesauri, and classification provisions, must therefore undergo constant revision to be maximally effective. The goal is to reflect new terminology as soon as it is stabilized, and to replace obsolete terms as soon as they are recognized as being out-of-date. Revision is a job that posed a serious workload problem in manual environments and is not trivial even in the online environment.

Design Factors

The factors discussed just above focused on terminology. Two other factors are of equal importance: cross-reference structure and whether the system is enumerative or faceted.

Provision of cross-references

In any catalog or information service product using subject tags from a controlled-vocabulary list, cross-references are essential at least from lead-in terms to the relevant preferred terms. Modern systems also offer references to broader terms, narrower terms, and related terms. Cross-references have been a desirable feature in library catalogs ever since Cutter's time, and have been an essential factor in user success in controlled vocabulary searches in both manual and online environments. (They are also important to subject catalogers in both subject heading and classification number assignment.)

Enumeration versus faceting

In a fully enumerative system all headings, including main-heading/subdivision strings, appear in full in the list. In a faceted system, terms are listed in separate groups, each group representing a facet that contains terms which share the same characteristic, such as concept, object, time, place, language, genre, and so on.

An alternative approach which is exemplified by LCSH and Sears is a system containing a primary term list of main headings, with subsidiary or auxiliary lists of terms that may be assigned as subdivisions or additional headings whenever they are appropriate for works in hand. Another practice lying between enumeration and faceting is the use of "pattern" or "key" headings. In this practice, the subdivisions under main headings that represent a category may be used as a guide under other main headings in the same category. For example, Shakespeare is a key heading for authors in Sears. A third practice, exemplified in LCSH, is to issue lists of "free-floating" subdivisions, i.e., subdivisions that are listed separately and may be attached to main headings where appropriate. An example of such lists is *Free-Floating Subdivisions: An Alphabetical Index*, issued by the Library of Congress.[16]

Precoordination versus postcoordination

Enumerative systems are by nature precoordinate systems; faceted systems, on the other hand, can be used either precoordinately or postcoordinately, depending on whether the combination or synthesis takes place at the cataloging stage or at the point of retrieval. In a precoordinate system, single-concept terms may be precombined to represent multiple-concept topics during the creation of the vocabulary list (i.e., by the creator of the list) or during the assignment of the complex term or heading to a particular document (i.e., by the indexer or the cataloger), both resulting in the presence of complex subject heading strings in the bibliographic record. In a postcoordinate system, on the other hand, single-concept terms are listed separately both in the vocabulary list and in the bibliographic record, and the combination takes place at the point of retrieval (i.e., by the searcher). In other words, in postcoordinate systems end users infer document content from the sum of assigned terms.

Summary: Controlled Vocabulary Principles

In sum, the topic of subject access through controlled vocabulary lists can be considered in the following way. On choice of terminology, the same principles have governed practice since Charles Ammi Cutter articulated them in 1876: convenience of the public, common usage, uniform and unique headings, and generous cross-references. Within these boundaries, lists may be either enumerative or faceted, or lie somewhere in between.

PRINCIPLES GOVERNING CLASSIFICATION SYSTEMS

Classification Theory

Classification, broadly defined, is the process of organizing knowledge into some systematic order. It has been considered the most fundamental activity of the human mind. The essential act of classification is the multistage process of deciding on a property or characteristic of interest, distinguishing things or objects that possess that property from those that lack it, and grouping things or objects that share a common property or characteristic into a class. Other essential aspects of classification are establishing relationships among classes and making distinctions within classes to arrive at broader and finer divisions. Those who devise and use library classification schemes do much the same thing. The classification of library materials can thus be seen as a special application of a much more general human intellectual activity.

Traditional classification theory

The traditional ideas of library classification were borrowed from the logical or philosophical principles of classification. Early classificationists began with the universe of knowledge as a whole and divided it into successive stages of classes and subclasses, with a chosen characteristic, also called *facet*, as the basis for each stage. In classical systems, for a broad subject area called a main class, such a progression is from general to specific, forming a hierarchical or "tree" structure in which each class is a *species* of the class on the preceding level and a *genus* to the one below it. The "array" of classes on each level, ideally mutually exclusive and totally exhaustive categories, forms a coordinate relationship from one to another: in other words, progressive subclasses on different levels in each hierarchy form a "chain" reflecting superordinate and subordinate relationships.

Modern classification theory

One of the approaches of modern classification theory, instead of cleaving to strict hierarchical principles, is to start with specifics, identifying the basic components of subjects and listing under each discipline, or main class, the elements or aspects that are topically important within that class. The same operation can be thought of as the *analysis* (or breaking up) of a subject into its component parts and the *synthesis* (or reassembling) of those parts as required for the purpose at hand. Most major subjects or disciplines have their own class-specific *facets*: for instance, a discipline such as Education might have a facet for Persons Taught, a facet for Subjects Taught, a facet for Educators, a facet for Methods of Instruction, a facet for Educational Institutions, and so on. In her *The Intellectual Foundation of Information Organization*,[17] Elaine Svenonius defines "facets" in part in the following terms: "Facets are groupings of terms obtained by the first division of a subject discipline into homogeneous categories. To characterize a facet as semantically cohesive is to say that the terms in it have similar referents. For instance, terms in one facet may all refer to processes, like mining, building, or cataloging; in another they may refer to concrete objects, like coal, houses, or books."

In addition, recurring or common facets, such as form divisions, geographical divisions, and chronological divisions, are usually listed separately for application to all classes. In cataloging with such a scheme, the act of classification essentially consists of identifying appropriate component facets and combining them according to a predetermined *citation formula*. Such a classification is called a faceted classification. An example is Ranganathan's *Colon Classification*, primarily important today because it brought the idea of faceted classification to the attention of the Western world.[18] The brief description of the Universal Decimal Classification (UDC) at the end of this entry presents a hierarchical system with many provisions for synthesis by facets.[19–21]

Library classification

Traditionally, library classification has involved labeling materials in a collection according to the provisions of an inclusive, usually hierarchically arranged, grouping scheme. The labels, called notation, usually in the form of numerals or letters or a combination of both, serve a dual function: to arrange items in a logical order on library shelves, and to provide a systematic display of bibliographic entries in printed catalogs, bibliographies, and indexes. In any grouping operation, the basis for grouping must be determined. In library classification, it is subject. In biological taxonomy, on the other hand, it is ontogeny, the development of life forms.

The two major library-oriented classification systems in the United States today, DDC and LCC, are both large fully developed hierarchical systems that are general in scope.[3,4] Both are considered only briefly at the end of this entry, because they are the main foci of systems described and analyzed in other entries in this ELIS edition.

Classification according to such hierarchical principles, with biological taxonomy as the prevailing model, was in a particularly active stage of development during the latter part of the nineteenth century. DDC and LCC both originated at that time and still, to an increasingly limited degree, reflect the general intellectual climate of that era. Each would be seriously out of date by now were it not for the fact that each responsible organization, OCLC's Dewey Services and LC's Policy and Standards Division, is conscientious about undertaking revisions and issuing updates.

Design and application principles

The parallel between classification and controlled vocabulary as avenues to effective information retrieval continues to hold both for the design of classification systems and for using them to assign class numbers to physical items or to organize lists of bibliographic items. Space limits prevent thorough analysis here; the following list of considerations presents an overview.

Scope: The system should cover the range of material of interest to the persons expected to use the collections for which the classification scheme is being built.

Literary warrant: The system should accommodate new concepts showing up in material being cataloged, and should, in general, offer provisions (classification positions) that mirror the information environment in which the system is used.

Terminology: Wording within the system should be uniform, unique, current in respect to subject matter covered, and in line with the usage of those for whom the scheme was developed.

User aids: Explanatory notes, cross-references, and indexes should be generously provided, with end-users as well as catalogers in mind.

Application guidelines for subject analysis: All possible aids, some in addition to those just noted, should be available to catalogers, to help them determine the best fit between the subject matter of the piece in hand and the provisions of the classification scheme being used.

Revision: Constant revision is needed, to keep the scheme as hospitable, as responsive, and as up-to-date as possible.

Summary

In the online age, the idea of subject access through traditional classification schemes does not come readily to mind. Yet such an approach has been used by generations of searchers who realized that if they knew of one work that gave them helpful information they were likely to find other helpful items if they looked before and after the shelf placement of the one they started with. That is because classification brings similar works together in an order that proceeds from the most general to the most specific, an array that many searchers find more helpful than tools that point them directly to a specific subject. With many classification schemes now available in full online, some of the advantages of shelf browsing are now available from desktops. Furthermore, tools taking full advantage of computer potential could be devised—indeed have been proposed—that would play classification and controlled vocabulary terms against each other to result in a very powerful search tool.[6]

SUBJECT ACCESS SYSTEMS: CONTROLLED VOCABULARIES AND CLASSIFICATION

We now turn to a consideration of subject access systems, reporting on how they reflect the principles described above, and noting the extent to which they carry out the functions for which they were designed. We begin with the controlled term lists LCSH, FAST (Faceted Application of Subject Technologies), Sears List of Subject Headings, and MeSH. We continue with the classification schemes Bibliographic Classification (BC), Colon Classification (CC), DDC, LCC, National Library of Medicine (NLM) Classification, and UDC. However, CC, DDC, LCC, LCSH, and UDC are represented by other entries in this ELIS edition, and so are treated here only in respect to the aspects noted above: reflection of principles and functional performance.

LCSH

LCSH is the most widely used system of its kind in the world. It is also the largest controlled vocabulary in English. In 1999, an ALA committee on subject access stated that LCSH offers many advantages as a means for subject access.[22] Among them are that it is a rich vocabulary of very wide scope, with synonym and homograph control and generous cross-references, and that it is a dependable scheme, continuously updated, with the support of the US Library of Congress behind it.

An important consideration is that LC pays attention to the needs of other cataloging agencies that use LCSH, and provides frequent notifications of additions and changes as well as ample instructional materials (particularly the *Subject Cataloging Manual: Subject Headings* and the Library's *Weekly Lists*).[23,24]

A study of LCSH shows that it reflects the general principles of controlled vocabulary construction detailed above, and that it fills the need for which it was first undertaken. In addition, the system has gone beyond its early warrant to cooperate with the whole library community, in America and abroad.

FAST (Faceted Application of Subject Terminology)

In 1998, the Online Computer Library Center (OCLC) began exploring a new approach to subject vocabulary while it was in the process of searching for a subject access system that would optimize the use of technology for Dublin Core (DC) metadata records.[24] In keeping with DC premises, it was determined that a subject vocabulary suitable for the Web environment should be 1) simple; 2) easy for catalogers to assign and maintain; 3) easy for searchers to understand and search on; and 5) flexible enough for use across disciplines and in various knowledge discovery and access environments—not the least of which is the OPAC.

In creating a new subject schema, decisions must be made on both vocabulary (semantics) and on whether the system will be enumerative or faceted. Regarding semantics, OCLC decided to retain the vocabulary of LCSH for the following reasons:

1. It is a comprehensive list.
2. It is well supplied with cross-references.
3. A system based on it would be compatible with LCSH proper and with MARC-coded records.
4. An automatic conversion of LCSH headings would be possible.
5. There would be cost benefits from the fact that many of the changes to LCSH can be incorporated into the new schema, thus minimizing maintenance.

A drawback to the use of LCSH as it stands was found to be its complex set of application rules, so complex that only professionally trained catalogers can apply LCSH effectively. For this reason, OCLC decided to devise a simplified syntax for governing how subject headings would be applied. Such a change would not only make the system easier at the tagging end but would also allow computer technology to be used to greater advantage in thesaurus maintenance and subject authority control. Work proceeded on those premises. The result of these considerations was the design of a schema called FAST.[10]

The FAST schema

As its name implies, the FAST system consists of separate elements. These elements comprise eight facets: seven subject facets and a form/genre facet. Headings in the subject facets reflect what the work being cataloged or indexed is *about*; form/genre headings, on the other hand, represent what the work *is*, for example, "dictionary." Subject facets include Topic, Place, Time, Person, Corporate body, Event, and Title of works. All FAST headings are fully established and appear in the FAST authority system as such, even those which in LCSH were constructed using pattern headings or free-floating subdivisions. In other words, FAST is an enumerated system with very few decisions required of those who use it.

FAST headings look very much like those in LCSH, the salient difference being in subdivisions. In FAST, all the terms in a subject string must come from the same facet. The following example shows the difference between LCSH and FAST subject headings for a work on alcohol and aging.

LC subject headings:

> **Older people—Alcohol use—United States**
> **Alcoholism—United States**
> **Aging—United States—Psychological aspects**
> **Aging—United States**

FAST headings:

> **Alcoholism** (Topic facet)
> **Older people—Alcohol use** (Topic/subdivision facet)
> **Aging—Psychological aspects** (Topic/subdivision facet)
> **United States** (Place facet)

The above examples illustrate the fact that FAST terms that belong to different facets are listed on documents separately, with end users inferring meaning from the sum of assigned terms. This fact brings FAST in, line with the basic principles of the Dublin Core,[25] one of the initial aims of the project. However, some complex terms within a given facet may be listed in precombined form, that is, as term strings. Alcoholism—Psychological aspects and Older people—Alcohol use are both examples of precombined FAST terms. Note that for each combination, both words belong in the same facet; otherwise precombination would not be possible.

FAST name headings

FAST geographic headings containing jurisdictional names are derived from the Name Authority File maintained by the LC (LC/NAF), and those containing non-jurisdictional headings from LCSH. The structure of FAST geographic headings is based on the MARC Code List for Geographic Areas.[26] Local places are represented in the indirect form, for example, **France—Paris**. FAST headings for other types of proper names (including persons, corporate bodies, events, and uniform titles) that have been used as subject headings are also based on the LC/NAF or extracted from the LCSH list and LC headings on MARC records in OCLC's WorldCat.

FAST authority files

The FAST authority files are built from LCSH headings and LC/NAF and subject headings extracted from MARC records in OCLC's WorldCat. Multiterm Readings are broken into FAST facets by means of a computer-based deconstruction program. For example, the LCSH heading **France—History—Wars of the Huguenots, 1562–1598—Pamphlets** results in the following FAST headings:

Topical:	**Wars of the Huguenots**
Geographic:	**France**
Period	**1562–1598**
Form:	**History**
	Pamphlets

Because of its wide acceptance, the MARC 21 format for authority data[27] was adopted for the creation of FAST authority records.

At this writing, fall 2008, work on the FAST authority files is near completion. The FAST authority records will be extensively tested and evaluated, and the evaluation will determine if the FAST team has achieved its goal of creating a new subject schema for metadata that retains the rich vocabulary of LCSH while being easy to apply and use.

Summary

In sum, FAST is a system which is

1. Based on the LCSH vocabulary.
2. Designed for the electronic environment.
3. A faceted vocabulary.
4. Usable by people with minimal training and experience.
5. Amenable to automated authority control.

Because tests of the FAST system are still in progress, one cannot yet judge whether it will perform as it was designed to do. If successful, the effort will not only have helped the whole information community, but will have demonstrated that much can be gained by maintaining the essence of a time-tested system and only changing application rules that may have facilitated searches in manual systems but have no role to play in the online environment.

Sears List of Subject Headings

Background

The Sears list of Subject Headings[9] was created in the early 1920s because LCSH, which was designed for large academic and research libraries, was not a good fit for the access needs of small and medium-sized general libraries. It was a cataloger named Minnie Earl Sears who decided to make a list to fill the gap. After studying usage patterns in many small libraries, she chose, for her list, to follow the underlying principles and patterns of the LCSH system, with adaptations to meet the particular needs of small libraries. Her adaptations were, in the main, reduction in scope and simpler vocabulary.

Features

Therefore, although the Sears list is not an abridgment of LCSH, it is similar in principle, format, and structure. It is a list of preferred terms and lead-in terms, with generous cross-references. Like LCSH, it is a partially enumerative system, with *key headings* analogous to LCSH pattern headings, and with considerable freedom (following guidelines) given to its catalogers to use terms not in the list. An interesting feature of Sears is that, its headings are followed by classification numbers taken from the *Abridged Dewey Decimal Classification*.[28] There have been many editions of *List of Subject Headings for Small Libraries* since the first appeared in 1923, the most recent being the nineteenth, in 2007, under the title *Sears List of Subject Headings*.[9]

Summary

Today, in America, the Sears list is used widely by school libraries and most public libraries. And, because it parallels

LCSH fairly closely, it exemplifies the principles, articulated earlier in this entry, on which LCSH is based. Managers of the Sears list deserve professional support and acclaim because they serve a population that is not adequately served in other information retrieval situations.

The foregoing description of the Sears list has been necessarily terse. Readers who want or need more information are directed to the preface to the latest edition of Sears.

MeSH

LCSH and *Sears List of Subject Headings* are not the only controlled vocabulary systems used in American libraries and information agencies. Most of the others are designed for special subject fields. The discussion now turns to MeSH as an example of a specialized controlled vocabulary. MeSH is the system designed and used by the NLM for assigning indexing terms to books and journal articles in the biomedical sciences. It has gained considerable acceptance outside of NLM and is now widely used by biomedical and health sciences libraries and by the abstracting and indexing services that serve the field. MeSH now exists in an online version, accessible on the NLM Web site and available for downloading in several data formats (including XML, ASCII MeSH, and MeSH/MARC).[29]

MeSH structure

MeSH was originally based on LCSH but has departed considerably from it as, over the years, MeSH has become an increasingly faceted postcoordinate system.

MeSH tree structures

The most striking feature of MeSH is its categorized system of descriptors (called "tree structures") that show hierarchical relationships among terms. *Tree Structures*[30] consists of 15 categories in which each heading is placed in relationship to other headings that represent similar areas and concepts. A system of "tree numbers" (each consisting of a capital letter followed by one or more digits) reflects the hierarchies. Each category is subdivided into one or more subcategories, with headings arranged hierarchically in each, and each heading is accompanied by the full tree number giving the location of the heading in the "tree." If a topic represented by a given heading belongs to more than one subcategory, that heading may appear in several places in the *tree structures*. When a concept appears in more than one hierarchy, it is assigned multiple tree numbers. The tree structures provide a classificatory approach to medical subjects,[31] manifesting hierarchical principles and providing a logical basis for the cross-references. In online retrieval, the tree numbers, also called descriptor codes, can be used to search for related

subjects. MeSH contains the following types of terms: Descriptors (main headings), Qualifiers, Publication Types, Geographics, and References. Descriptors, also called main headings, represent main topics, usually in the form of single words or phrases, the latter sometimes inverted.

MeSH qualifiers

A *qualifier*, formerly called a *subheading*, is used to refine the meaning of a main heading by specifying one of its aspects. Qualifiers are used with descriptors to collocate those documents concerned with a particular aspect of a subject. Because not every qualifier is suitable for use with every main heading, there is a list of "Qualifiers by Allowable Category"[32] which contains 62 subject categories and their associated qualifiers. There are two types of qualifiers: topical and publication type. An example of a publication type qualifier is "Abstracts [publication type]." MeSH also includes geographic headings, which include the names of continents, regions, countries, states, and other geographic entities. These are listed in category Z of the tree structures but do not appear in the alphabetical list.

Cross-references

MeSH makes full use of cross-references, and is particularly generous with nonpreferred entry terms with their associated *see references*.[33] In types, MeSH references are similar to those in other controlled-vocabulary systems.

Summary

The brief account above should demonstrate that those in a special field can construct a controlled vocabulary system that will encompass all the terms and relationship-indicators they need to represent adequately the subject content of materials in their collections without losing compatibility (in other words, interoperability) with other systems. There are many special-purpose systems, and, as complexity increases in all endeavors, there are likely to be many more. For some, especially those dealing with materials not in written form, special markups or coding languages have been devised. These are described in chapter 4 of *Cataloging and Classification*.[34]

MAJOR CLASSIFICATION SCHEMES

In American libraries, the two major classification systems in use today are the Dewey Decimal System (DDC) and the Library of Congress Classification (LCC).[3,4] Both are basically enumerative hierarchical systems, reflecting traditional classification principles and departing from a strict enumerative pattern only through their use of auxiliary tables. Both systems are obviously successful, as evidenced by their strong influence on classification systems elsewhere in the world. Both, also, are covered by other entries in this ELIS edition and so receive little more than a mention here.

However, there are other classification systems that are particularly worthy of notice. One is a special system devised by the NLM in cooperation with the Library of Congress (LC), which is described below.

Another is the Colon Classification (CC),[18] important primarily because it has contributed so much to modern classification theory: it is the grandfather of the principle of creating a classification built on individually listed terms representing aspects of topics, in other words, built on facets. The *CC* is covered in a separate ELIS entry and so is not discussed further here.

A third is the Bibliographic Classification (BC), a well-thought-out scheme developed by an American librarian named Henry Evelyn Bliss.[35] This classification was not adopted by many American libraries, but received considerably more attention in the United Kingdom. It is particularly interesting at the present time because of its long list of auxiliaries; in other words, BC has now moved a long way in the direction of faceted classification. (J. D. Anderson points out the potential of BC facets in his current ELIS entry on LCSH.)

A fourth system is the Universal Decimal Classification (UDC),[19–21] important because it has moved so far toward faceting and, like the *BC*, embodies powerful features that designers of new classification systems might find beneficial if incorporated into the schemes under development.

An account of the *NLM Classification* follows, and a brief account of the *UDC* (also the subject of a separate ELIS entry) follows in turn.

NLM Classification

The *NLM Classification*[36] is an example of a special-subject classification system that was expressly designed to be fully compatible with an extensive, existing general classification system. In this case the general system is the *LCC*.[3] What the original designers of the NLM Classification proposed was a classification scheme that would (first) follow LCC in both style of classification and general pattern of notation; (second) develop its own classification scheme for medicine and related subjects, fitting it into LCC's vacant class W; and (third) develop its own scheme for the preclinical sciences, using LCC's vacant subclasses QS through QZ (in LCC main class Q for science). In response, the LC agreed with NLM that the main class W and subclasses QS to QZ would be permanently excluded from LCC. For any material in its collection that does not fall within either medicine or the preclinical sciences, NLM uses LCC as it stands.

The resulting NLM classification system has many advantages for a specialized medical library such as

NLM. The organization and development of the subject matter that is its primary concern is fully under its control, while provisions for peripheral subjects are developed and kept up to date by outside specialists, in this case the LC staff. Yet the two parts of the system are fully compatible. One especially useful feature of the system is its detailed index, which contains terms chosen to conform to those in MeSH and follows each major term or sub-term with a class number or range of numbers, including numbers from LCC.

UDC

The UDC is discussed here because it is such an interesting example of how a classification system can develop. UDC began as an adaptation of the Dewey system to make it useful for compiling a universal bibliography and indexing the journal articles the bibliography would cover. Considerably more detailed provisions are required for journal indexing than for book cataloging, and perhaps for this reason the UDC designers turned more readily toward modern classification theory than did either of the two major American classification systems. As UDC grew, it incorporated many of the features of a faceted scheme, providing for a considerable degree of synthesis, or number building, through combining concepts by means of auxiliary devices. An especially interesting feature is the use of punctuation marks or other symbols to indicate the relationships of the parts of a built number: a colon for simple relationship, equal sign for language of work, quotation marks for time or period, and so on.

In sum, UDC is a powerful system, one that is particularly suited to the machine environment: relatively simple retrieval algorithms can be written that can refine or expand searches simply through operations on its class numbers. UDC deserves attention from retrieval theorists in the English-speaking world. It has a lot to offer.

More information on UDC can be found in *The Universal Decimal Classification: A Guide to its Use*,[19] at UDC online,[20] and at (http://www.udcc.org/about.htm).[21]

CONCLUDING SUMMARY: SUBJECT ACCESS SYSTEMS

This entry began with an account of twenty-first century provisions and practices in regard to subject access, as they stand in the early fall of 2008. It did not address any omens of future change to be found in current happenings and current literature. Suffice it to say that large changes seem to be in the air.

What the entry did attempt was to present the theoretical foundations of currently functioning subject access systems in the hope of illuminating the factors that must be considered in developing new or improved subject access systems. To this end, it described the advantages and drawbacks to both controlled vocabulary and full-text searching, and went on to mention the particular (though not often used) benefits of searching by classification arrays.

On controlled vocabulary searching, it made the point that if appropriate search terms are submitted, controlled-vocabulary searches deliver a high fraction of available material of likely use to a searcher, and very little else. On full-text searching, it acknowledged that such searching is fast and easy, and that user satisfaction with that approach is usually high; it went on, however, to point out that the lists of found items are often of overwhelming length, and that searchers must submit multiple synonyms of query terms to have a hope of attaining a representative sample of potentially helpful material.

The discussion then turned to the principles governing the construction of extant subject access systems. Those used by search engines are proprietary, and not available to outsiders; they are therefore beyond discussion. Those on which controlled vocabulary and classification systems are built are well known and much studied: both were discussed at some length in the body of the entry. The piece finished with brief analyses of how well prominent systems exemplify the principles discussed, and how well they appear to be serving the target populations for which they were designed. The controlled-vocabulary systems covered in some detail are FAST, MeSH, and Sears; the only classification system given more than cursory attention is the *NLM Classification*. *LCSH* figures in the discussion when it is particularly relevant, but only in brief because it is the main focus of another entry in this ELIS edition. The same is true for *LCC* and *DDC*. The entry closes with a short section on *UDC*, even though it is the focus of another ELIS entry. Its inclusion here stems from the authors' desire to point out how very well the system is suited to the online age. Its schedule captions and particularly its notation could well serve as the base for powerful search algorithms.

BIBLIOGRAPHICAL NOTE

Much of the material in this entry mirrors, in greatly reduced detail, information and analyses which appear in the third edition of Lois Mai Chan's *Cataloging and Classification* (The Scarecrow Press, Inc.: Lanham, Maryland, Toronto, Plymouth, U.K., 2007.)

REFERENCES

1. Egyptology Online, Alexandria: [section, The Royal Library of Alexandria]. Available at http://egyptologyonline.com/alexandria.
2. *Library of Congress Subject Headings*; Library of Congress: Washington, DC, 1975–.
3. *Library of Congress Classification: A–Z*, Library of Congress: Washington, DC, 1904–.
4. Dewey, M. *Dewey Decimal Classification and Relative Index*, 22nd Ed.; Mitchell, J.S., Beale, J., Martin, G., Matthews, W.E., Jr., New, G.R., Eds.; OCLC Online Computer Library Center, Inc.: Dublin, OH, 2003.
5. http://www.google.com/corporate/history.html [About Google].
6. Chan, L.M. Exploiting LCSH, LCC, and DDC to retrieve networked resources: Issues and challenges Proceedings of the Bicentennial Conference on Bibliographic Control for the New Millennium: Confronting the Challenges of Networked Resources and the Web Washington, DC, November, 15–17, 2000; Sandberg-Fox, A.M., Ed.; Library of Congress, Cataloging Distribution Service: Washington, DC, 2001; 159–178 Sponsored by the Library of Congress Directorate.
7. Pettee, J. *Subject Headings: The History and Theory of the Alphabetical Subject Approach to Books*; H. W. Wilson Company: New York, 1947; 151.
8. American Library Association. *List of Subject Headings for Use in Dictionary Catalogs*, Boston, MA, 1895; Prepared by a Committee of the American Library Association; Published for the ALA Publishing Section of the Library Bureau: 2nd revised edition, 1878; revised edition 1911.
9. *Sears List of Subject Headings*, 19th Ed.; Miller, J., Ed.; H.W. Wilson Company: New York, 2007; Bristow, B.A., Eds.
10. Chan, L.M.; Childress, E.; Dean, R.; O'Neill, E.; Visine-Goetz, D. A faceted approach to subject data in the Dublin core metadata record. J. Intern. Catalog. **2001**, *4*(1/2), 35–47.
11. *MARC 21 Format for Bibliographic Data: Including Guidelines for Content Designation*, Cataloging Distribution Service; Library of Congress: Washington, DC, 1999.
12. World Wide Web. In *A Brief History of the Internet*; Available at http://www.isoc.org/internet/history//brief.shtml.
13. Cutter, C. *Rules for a Dictionary Catalog*, 4th Ed. Government Printing Office: Washington, DC, 1904; 6ff rewritten.
14. Svenonius, E. LCSH: Semantics, syntax, and specificity. In *The LCSH Century: One Hundred Years with the Library of Congress Subject Headings System*; Stone, A., Ed.; Haworth Information Press: New York, 2000; 17–30.
15. Chan, L.M. *Library of Congress Subject Headings: Principles and Application*, 4th Ed.; Libraries Unlimited: Westport, CT, London, 2005; 27–28.
16. *Free-Floating Subdivisions: An Alphabetical Index*; Library of Congress, Cataloging Distribution Service: Washington, DC, 1989.
17. Svenonius, E. *The Intellectual Foundation of Information Organization*; The MIT Press: Cambridge, MA, 2000; 139.
18. Ranganathan, S. *Colon Classification*, 7th Ed.; Gopinath, M.A., Ed.; Sarada Ranganathan Endowment for Library Science: Bangalore, 1987.
19. McIlwaine, I. *The Universal Decimal Classification: A Guide to Its Use*; UDC Consortium: The Hague, 2000.
20. UDC Online, 2005. http://www.udconline.net.
21. http://www.udcc.org/about.htm.
22. Association for Library Collections & Technical Services, Cataloging and Classification Section, Subject Analysis Committee, Subcommittee on Metadata and Subject Analysis. Subject Data in the Metadata Record: Recommendations

and Rationale: A Report from the ALCTS/CCS/SAC/ Subcommittee on Metadata and Subject Analysis, 1999. Available at http://www.ala.org/acts/organization/ccs/sac/ metarpt2.html.

23. Library of Congress, Cataloging Policy and Support Office, *Subject Cataloging Manual: Subject Headings*, 5th Ed.; Library of Congress: Washington, DC, 1996.

24. Subject Cataloging Division. Library of Congress Subject Headings, 8th Ed.; Cataloging Distribution Service; Library of Congress: Washington, 1975. Published annually, with weekly updates: Weekly Lists. http://www.loc. gov/aba/cataloging/subject/weeklylists/ [Weekly Lists] Library of Congress.

25. *Dublin Core Metadata Element Set, 2007*, NISO Standard Z39.85–2007; NISO Press: Bethesda, MD, 2007; Available at http://www.niso.org/standards/resources/z39.85–2007. pdf (accessed August 2008).

26. *MARC Code List for Geographic Areas*. http://www.loc. gov/marc/geoareas/gacshome.html.

27. *MARC 21 Format for Authority Data: Including Guidelines for Content Designation*, Prepared by Network Development and MARC Standards Office, Library of Congress, in cooperation with Standards and Support, National Library of Canada. Library of Congress, Cataloging Distribution Service: Washington; National Library of Canada: Ottawa, ON, 1999.

28. Dewey, M. *Abridged Dewey Decimal Classification and Relative Index;* Ed. 14 OCLC Online Computer Library Center, Inc.: Dublin OH, 2004; Mitchell, J.S., Editor in Chief; Beale, J., Martin, G., Matthews, Jr., W.E., New, G.R., Assistant Editors.

29. *Medical Subject Headings*, 1st Ed.; U.S. Department of Health and Human Services, Public Health Service, National Institutes of Health, National Library of Medicine: Bethesda, MD, 2003. Available at http://www.nlm. nih.gov/mesh/.

30. National Library of Medicine. *Medical Subject Headings: Features of the MeSH Vocabulary*. http://www.nlm.nih. gov/mesh/intro_features.html.

31. Gullion, S. Cataloging and classification: Classification and subject cataloging. In *Handbook of Medical Library Practice*, 4th Ed.; Darling, L., Bishop, D., Colaianni, L., Eds.; Medical Library Association: Chicago IL, 1983; 269.

32. National Library of Medicine. *Medical Subject Headings: Qualifiers by Allowable Category*. http://www.nlm.nih. gov/mesh/topcat2007.html.

33. National Library of Medicine. *Medical Subject Headings: Entry Vocabulary*. http://www.nlm.nih.gov/ mesh/intro_entry2007.html.mtml.

34. Chan, L.M. *Cataloging and Classification*, 3rd Ed.; The Scarecrow Press, Inc.: Lanham, Maryland, Toronto, Plymouth, U.K., 2007; 213–223.

35. Bliss, H. *Bibliographic Classification,* 2nd Ed.; Butterworths: London, 1977.

36. *National Library of Medicine Classification*, 5th Ed. National Library of Medicine: Bethesda, MD, 1999; NIH Publication, no. 00-1535; http://www.nlm.nih.gov/class/ (accessed October 2007).

BIBLIOGRAPHY

1. Bates, M. Fundamental forms of information. JASIS **2007**, *57*(8), 1033–1045.

2. Chan, L.M. *Cataloging and Classification: An Introduction*, 3rd Ed.; Scarecrow Press: Lanham, MD, 2007.

3. Chan, L.M. *A Guide to the Library of Congress Classification*, 5th Ed.; Libraries Unlimited: Littleton, CO, 1999.

4. Chan, L.M. *Library of Congress Subject Headings: Principles and Application*, 4th Ed.; Libraries Unlimited: Westport, CT, 2005.

5. In *Theory of Subject Analysis: A Sourcebook*; Chan, L.M., Richmond, P.A., Svenonius, E., Eds.; Libraries Unlimited: Littleton, CO, 1985.

6. Miksa, F.L. *The Subject in the Dictionary Catalog from Cutter to The Present*; American Library Association: Chicago, IL, 1983.

7. Svenonius, E. *The Intellectual Foundation of Information Organization*; The MIT Press: Cambridge, MA, 2000.

8. Taylor, A. *Introduction to Cataloging and Classification*, 10th Ed. Libraries Unlimited: Westport, CN, 2006.

9. Wilson, P. *Two Kinds of Power: An Essay on Bibliographical Control*; University of California Press: Berkeley, CA, 1968.

Subscription Libraries *[ELIS Classic]*

David E. Gerard
College of Librarianship Wales, Cardiganshire, Wales, U.K.

Abstract
The author's survey of subscription libraries includes discussion of both libraries owned by subscribers, and libraries that are commercial lending libraries, otherwise known as *circulating libraries*. The primary emphasis is on libraries in the United Kingdom.

—*ELIS Classic*, *from 1980*

INTRODUCTION

The term *subscription library* is used here to denote two main categories of library:

1. Collections founded and administered out of funds drawn from a membership in the form of subscriptions and entrance fees, the library being the property of the entire membership and managed by a committee of trustees elected by and from the members.
2. Commercial lending libraries, usually called *circulating libraries*; these derived their income from the loan of books to borrowers, who paid a periodic subscription and/or a small fee for each volume borrowed.

Libraries in the first category tended to become permanent collections; the latter were often dependent on the prosperity of individual booksellers from whose premises they were usually managed. There were variations within each of the two kinds, but it is on the libraries' significance rather than on the descriptive details that this article dwells.

HISTORY

In whatever form, the subscription library was an eighteenth-century phenomenon. However, traces of them are observable from the seventeenth century and even earlier, and many survived into the twentieth century; some are still active in Great Britain today. They were a product of that kind of social enterprise—one might almost say code—characteristic of the Augustan Age, which was at its most representative in the club, the salon, and the conversazione, those focal points of civilized discourse patronized by the rising middle class of business and professional men in London and in the country at large. The rise of cultural manifestations of the kind we are about to survey is explained by the advancement of science and the diffusion of a humane culture beyond the narrow confines of theology so typical of earlier generations and by the expanding economy and its concomitant, surplus wealth for the trading classes. The indulgence of a proper curiosity about a world that was impinging upon insular British society more and more, and the intellectual cultivation of subjects whose range increased every year, rested largely with an elite that used the word *gentlemen* to describe itself. It is the word most fitting as a description of the class and the culture that founded the libraries of the period. Those perceptible changes in the economic and social structure of the nation after the accession of Queen Anne (1702) brought with them a secularization in learning and, more gradually, in politics; and the complexion of libraries began to change. The collections of ecclesiastical learning—of Greek, Latin, and Hebrew synonymous with the great public and private libraries of the sixteenth and seventeenth centuries (the Bodleian, Sion College, Lambeth Palace, and the parish libraries throughout Britain)—served a traditional clerical readership, the custodians of scholarship.

With the Hanoverian monarchs came changes, the most instrumental of which were the stagecoach, the newspaper, and the political coffee house, securing a wider reading public and a general increase in communication and sophistication; in short, the *literate* reader began to replace the *learned* reader. Amused and instructed by such new and palpably untheological papers as the *Tatler* (1709–1711) and the *Spectator* (1711–1713), and later still by the wholly successful *Gentleman's Magazine* (1731; whose title identifies the new readership and a new kind of journal), the man of affairs was fed with new worlds of information on a regular basis. His expectations and his attention were redirected. Books and pamphlets designed for a public with a devouring interest in current affairs began to multiply. The first great journalist, Daniel Defoe, busily supplied the needs of the new readership, and many lesser figures followed his example. Emphasis on the contingent and the contemporary encourage a climate in which the novel flourished, itself a derivative of a vigorous newspaper and periodical press. Translations of French and Italian prose romances and new realist narratives

Encyclopedia of Library and Information Sciences, Fourth Edition DOI: 10.1081/E-ELIS4-120008959

offered surcease from the strain of business or, for the wives of the new merchant aristocracy, surcease from ennui. They provided the imaginative stimulus of the new age for the leisured classes. Yet the book trade, that most conservative of institutions, kept prices high, and the limited technical resources of the hand printing press restricted the size of editions. Hence, it is no surprise to find that ingenious means were devised to circumvent high prices and make books more available at lower cost to interested readers. What the book trade could not or would not supply cheaply, mutual cooperation would provide. Quite simply, the idea of subscription (already familiar to authors and booksellers as a publishing device by which to share production costs) was applied to the purchase of books that could be enjoyed by a wide circle of readers willing to pay a relatively small annual sum for borrowing privileges. The purpose of such mutual aid is succinctly stated in the prospectus issued by the projectors of the Liverpool Library in 1757, the library claimed as the first public subscription library in Europe: "With a view to furnishing an ample fund of amusement and improvement at the easiest expense."

The book clubs and reading societies that flourished from the early years of the eighteenth century usually comprised a small, restricted membership. They supported a small, transient collection of books, and their function was social as well as intellectual. Although secular in character, they modeled themselves on the informal groups of clergy that had met in earlier days to enjoy each other's company and that often had combined to create a private collection of books to provide subjects for discussion. The Society of the Clergy of Doncaster (1714) is an example of this kind of clerical-professional group; but their aim was explicitly "the improvement of Christian knowledge," and they met, as was customary, in each other's houses. The Gentlemen's Society of Spalding was formed in 1710 (and survives to this day), to read and circulate new publications. They met in a coffee house, a typical venue, and offered each other enlightenment by giving papers on a variety of subjects (antiquities, natural history, topography, improvements in applied sciences) and through literary conversation. Such public—yet private—assembly was typical of the age, and the fact that the intellectual activity was book-based stimulated a natural desire for more reading matter and so helped promote the market for books. The book club may fairly claim to be the prototype not only of the subscription library for the middle class but also of the early nineteenth-century working-class reading clubs and, by a natural extension, of the Mechanics' Institute libraries. From the privileged to the less privileged, from the few to the many, habits are thus diffused. As Frank Beckwith put it:

> in the book club lies the germ of the proprietary library; the latter is only an extension of the former, and differs in degree not kind.[1]

The reading society of the early eighteenth century provided the model for the future shape of libraries as a means of mutual aid in the acquisition and circulation of books. Money for purchases came from the joint subscriptions of members, and a steady supply of serious, contemporary publications was assured, ready to be discussed in an agreeable environment, whether tavern, coffee house, or private house. When interest in the books flagged, they were sold to members, or auctioned, or divided up by lot. Later in the century, against the background of political revolution in France and the newly emergent United States, book clubs acquired a radical tinge and tended to be associated with extremist political sects. Many reading rooms and clubs opened to support and debate republican issues; they often operated on the fringes of legality and specialized in collections of pamphlets and periodicals rather than full-length books. Whichever section of society they served, book clubs and reading groups were always the most economical form of library provision, requiring no large book stock or paid librarian and no elaborate premises beyond a few shelves in a corner, or perhaps a modest room at most.

SUBSCRIPTION LIBRARIES

The permanent subscription library may therefore be described as a lineal descendant of the book club and the learned society library that had been a feature of London life since the founding of the Royal Society in 1662. In an age when personal patronage was on the decline and municipal or state aid not yet conceived, collective private enterprise was the only source of book supply other than by private purchase. The value of a permanent library, properly housed and administered, must have been obvious to the gentlemen—most of them prominent citizens—who had begun to assemble the informal collections in coffee house and home, in the larger towns and cities. An amenity of this kind must have seemed desirable as a matter of civic pride. Development proceeded toward the first "public" library, albeit limited to the purses that could afford the subscription. In the nature of things, readership was bound to be confined to the educated, professional classes; yet the objective, a permanent repository of the best books of the day, was creditable in any community, and it would lead to unforeseen consequences. Once made, the transition—from an ephemeral collection of interest to a small circle of readers, to a consciously selected, cumulative collection for the use of any who could afford it—was irreversible and it was an incentive to change in the political and intellectual life of the nation.

It is vain to argue the case for the "first" subscription library. Like so many other social phenomena, it appeared quite suddenly within a short space of time in sundry places. As so often in the field of education (formal and informal), Scotland appeared as the pioneer, and pride of place as the first permanent subscription library is usually accorded to the lead miners of Leadhills, Lanarkshire, who founded what they called a Reading Society in 1741, though its book collection was clearly to be permanent. The first gentlemen's subscription libraries also seem to have been Scottish: the Society Library of Dumfries was founded in 1745, and what was significantly described as the Public Library of Kelso, in 1751. In England, in 1757 Liverpool founded the first public subscription library from two reading societies, part of an energetic local renaissance of culture founded on mercantile prosperity. The mode by which the new subscription library evolved from the simpler organism may be illustrated by the Liverpool example. The two reading societies were the Coffee House Club, which met at the Merchants' Coffee House, and the Talbot, which met at a tavern of that name. The members of both clubs inserted an advertisement in the *Williamson's Liverpool Advertiser* of February 10, 1758:

> To all gentlemen and ladies who desire to encourage the progress of useful knowledge, to procure themselves a rational entertainment, and do a great deal of good at small expense, the following scheme is proposed. The two reading societies who meet at the Merchants' Coffee House (Dale St) and the Talbot (Water St) being willing to make their plans as extremely useful as possible, and sensible how much some public provision of this kind is wante, here mutually propose to throw their present stock of books together and thereby lay the foundations of a public library. The manner of which will be determined by a Committee, to be chosen out of both clubs.

That is a material illustration of the evolutionary process from club to permanent institution.

The organization of a typical subscription library was essentially simple. An entrance fee was charged, which usually entitled the member to a share, making him a proprietor; hence the term *proprietary library* often used of these institutions. Together with an annual subscription, such fees provided the income that paid for the books and running costs. The committee of members, chaired by a president, was the responsible body, and they appointed the librarian, who was their servant, not their equal.

Fees ranged from one guinea to five guineas a year, and membership varied from perhaps a score in a village to the 450-strong Leeds Library in 1791. The managing committee, the president, and the secretary were annually elected at the annual general meeting, the real power being in the secretary's hands. The librarian held office indefinitely, once appointed. He was usually ill-paid, the mere custodian of the books with no personal power of book selection or policy; his function was solely to carry out the wishes of his committee, and his duties were strictly defined and often menial. But the novelty of this emergent

species of library lies in the fact that for the first time in library history, a permanent body of management and officers worked in concert. Their continuity was guaranteed so long as a membership could be recruited, a pattern that remedied the weakness of earlier attempts at library organization: chronic instability.

The new structure promoted efficient management: proper records were kept, library routines were laid down, and technical expertise in cataloging, classification, and library administration began to develop. The result was a consciously created organism made visible on the shelves, in commodious premises furnished for use, rather than in a room haphazardly fitted. The library was more than a club; it was a monument to local pride, a public conservatory of knowledge and information (though of a traditional kind), and a symbol of the eighteenth-century oligarchic conception of society. Because the book stock was the sole and undivided property of the whole society, permanence was a condition implicit in the organization. This was an incentive to the creation of a balanced, judiciously chosen collection—one strongest in the humanities, since education in that age pivoted upon study of the *literae humaniores*. Sectarian or learned bias was avoided (as befitted the true English gentlemen); above all, partisanship (political and denominational) was eschewed.

In the largest cities, the proprietary library soon became identified with the place itself; Birmingham Library and Leeds Library meant the subscription libraries. In most towns, however, the library's aims, like its premises, were much more modest. Experience in the administration of libraries grew gradually but noticeably; the regulations served as models to later generations of librarians concerned about the day-to-day governance of their collections and readers. Terms of loan, action with defaulters, care of books, and the organization of knowledge became more systematic in this more secure environment; in a word, a *professional* ethos was created in the best libraries. Their survival over so many years in an unaltered form is a tribute to their essential soundness. While librarians' salaries were meager, at least the practice of budgeting for annual growth on a practicable basis was possible. Though practice varied, usually about one-third of the income was devoted to the purchase of books and the librarian's salary, and the remaining two-thirds was spent on rent and rates of buildings, printing, stationery, candles, and other vital provisions.

London was not well served by proprietary libraries. A London Library and a Westminster Library existed in the late eighteenth century, and they amalgamated in the early nineteenth century. However, this institution soon failed, and the barrenness of library provision in the capital city was not remedied until 1841, when Thomas Carlyle and others created the London Library we know today. It became the largest of all in due course—it has a stock now formidable in range and depth, it still serves London and country subscribers, and its printed catalogs and subject indexes are models of bibliographical accuracy and valuable sources of reference.

The decline of the provincial subscription libraries dates from the mid-nineteenth century. Library provision was developing from other quarters. As reading habits permeated more social levels, so did book supply. Working men's clubs began subscription libraries for their members from about 1820, the earliest trade union libraries date from 1832, Chartist libraries are known in 1839, Robert Owen's Halls of Science contained libraries, and even some factories operated "libraries" of a kind for use by the workers in the 1830s. Most important of all, the Mechanics' Institutes were founded in 1823. These were financed on the same principle as the gentlemen's libraries, by entrance fee and subscription suited to the pockets of the superior artisans. But, few records remain of the attempts by the working class to organize their own subscription libraries, though their existence argues a vigorous attempt to engage with the political and social problems of the day. After 1850, the first rate-supported, and therefore truly public, libraries became a reality, and they must have drawn many upper-working-class readers to them, wretchedly inadequate though they were. Slowly, then, but inevitably, changes brought about the closure of the proprietary libraries: competition from the new public libraries and the success of commercial circulating libraries. The poor financing of the public libraries delayed their effects on the subscription libraries until the twentieth century, by which time only the largest cities could support both. It is interesting to note the attempts made by the latter to retain their members by intensified purchases of current literature and an emphasis on recreational reading. However, in the efficient supply of such publications, they could not compete with the highly organized network of shops and other agencies provided by the new library phenomena of the age: W.H. Smith in his railway book-stalls and Charles Edward Mudie from his enormous circulating library in New Oxford Street, each supplying a host of readers throughout the kingdom with their leisure reading. The fate of the subscription libraries was sealed. Some surrendered their collections to the local public or university library; in Liverpool, for instance, the Lyceum continued as a club in its splendid building erected in 1801, but its collections were handed over to the Liverpool public libraries in 1942. There are some notable survivors that offer the quiet atmosphere of a club, reasonably good service in contemporary literature, and strong and unrivaled collections of eighteenth- and nineteenth-century materials: Birmingham, Nottingham, Leeds, and Manchester are examples of extant veterans, though their financial situation is precarious.

In sum, the proprietary subscription library was a substantial part of the intellectual history of Great Britain from 1750 to 1900. As institutions, they could never have served more than a privileged fraction of the whole reading community, but they were entitled to bear the label "public," even if in a restricted sense. They served an affluent minority, but their example supplied the humbler reaches of society with an incentive to establish libraries for their own political and educational needs. The educated classes secured entrance by the purse and as part of the traditions of their class; it was a matter of prestige. Within these limits, the libraries served their purpose as fully as possible, though their claims to be all things to all men were abridged by the intrinsic nature of their allegiance and structure. Their purposes did not include the supply of thorough information on great questions of public and national interests. Nevertheless, they were the bridge between the older, exclusive world of theological learning and the modern world of almost universal book provision from public funds. And the tradesmen's libraries and working men's libraries of the early nineteenth century, short-lived though they were, at least made reading accessible for a modest fee and so formed habits of discussion that assisted the education of political leaders in the second half of the nineteenth century.

CIRCULATING LIBRARIES

Like the proprietary library, the circulating library was a response to a social need in an age of increasing leisure. There were two characteristics common to these libraries: they lacked (whether justified or not) the image of a serious readership, and, as a branch of the book trade, they appeared early. In the late seventeenth century books could be borrowed for a few pence per week from some booksellers' establishments, as we know from surviving advertisements. This promoted business in a small world of readers. Since that time the slow process of democratizing the reading public has continued, with consequent effects on standards of taste that are debated with unflagging zeal to this day.

Although the term *circulating library* was sometimes employed by subscription libraries, it is convenient to apply it solely to that class of library organized for profit by booksellers. The formal literature associated with learned society libraries made little provision for the emotional as distinct from the intellectual life of the average reader, particularly the growing numbers of women readers. Hence, the history of circulating libraries may be said to be coeval with the history of popular taste during the period when leisure reading was emergent; that is, the period of the rise of the novel, somewhere between the time of Aphra Behn (ca. 1680) and Henry Fielding (1750). French romances translated into English coincided with the provision by the first women novelists of a steady supply of fiction to suit the appetites of a growing leisured class (many of whom were presumed to be female, though there is little firm evidence to support that assumption). Eliza Heywood (1693–1756) was the first woman to earn her living from her pen and is representative of the new class of writer. Journalism catered to the contemporary taste for realism, combining topicality, adventure, and piety in an irresistible blend. This was the age of the first daily paper, the *Daily Courant* (1702), and its many imitators; and of the first elegant essay serials, emblematized in the *Tatler* (1709–1711) and *Spectator* (1711–1713). Novels like *Love in Excess* reached six editions between 1719 and 1725. Booksellers were quick to discern a new market as a means to extend business, and, without doubt, the idea of the circulating library conferred economic benefits on both borrowers and lenders. Thus, a new leisure industry was created; it was significantly present in resorts and spa towns, and in the centers of fashion: Hastings, Bath, Cheltenham, and Leamington. Not only booksellers but other tradesmen reaped extra rewards if they included a lending library among their stock-in-trade; notably, milliners, haberdashers, and tobacconists.

The few notices that tell us of the existence of a rudimentary lending system in the late seventeenth-century book trade are found in contemporary newspapers and booksellers' advertisements. Francis Kirkman, a stationer, offered some of his stock in 1661 "lent to read," and a certain Widow Page in 1674 offered "all sorts of histories to buy or let out to read." When Benjamin Franklin was working as a printer in 1725, he made a private arrangement with a London bookseller under which he hired books for home reading, which testifies to the practice. Allan Ramsay, the Edinburgh bookseller and man of letters, is usually credited with the first organized circulating library in Great Britain; it was a lucrative part of his bookselling business. In 1728, one Thomas Sendall opened a library in Bristol, and, very soon, the new habit was part of the social scene. The main period of growth was 1740–1800. London is alleged to have had nine circulating libraries by 1740, but the first names of which anything is known are those of T. Wright, William Bathoe, and Samuel Fancourt. While the actual priority is in dispute, there is no doubt that Samuel Fancourt's establishment at Crane Court, off Fleet Street, opened in 1742, quickly became preeminent, and seems to have been the first known library to have used the term *circulating* to describe itself. In fact, his enterprise was a mixture of commercial circulating library and nonproprietary subscription library; that is, its subscribers were in no sense proprietors owning shares, but they could elect a committee of members who acted as trustees under the controlling direction of the benevolent Mr. Fancourt, the real proprietor. Samuel Fancourt was the librarian and the business was conducted for his profit. His bulky catalog, an *Alphabetical Catalogue of Books and Pamphlets Belonging to the Circulating Library in Crane Court* (2 vols., 1748), reveals that a high proportion of his stock was theological. In general, the range was wide and the books of substantial merit and seriousness; there is little here to support any charge of frivolity. The fact that Fancourt was a Dissenting minister perhaps makes his case unusual, but the plan

he outlined in his catalog and the details of his organization were those of the classic circulating library. He was declared bankrupt in 1759, despite initial success, and disappeared into history—not before he hinted at the key to a prosperous lending business, which, he said, was the subscription, "the active and vivifying principle." Another pioneer was Francis Noble, who started his Large Library of Useful and Entertaining Books in 1746.

Prerequisites of success were business efficiency, reliable methods of dealing with the routines of stock acquisition and lending procedures, and the publication of catalogs, which were used by the customers for selection. As in proprietary libraries, early procedures in circulating libraries prefigured later developments in library economy. Fixed subscription rates, loan periods, borrowers' registers, accession books, accounts, tickets, labels, and library stamps—all the paraphernalia associated with library work even today in the age of computerized issue systems and catalogs—had to be created with little precedent. As book stocks grew larger, separate premises were opened as complete libraries in themselves, and the most successful became household names: Wright, Bathoe, Bell, William Lane, Day (the last named persisting until 1957 when it was absorbed into Harrod's, the London department store, as part of their circulating library). Many went bankrupt—bookselling and lending was an unpredictable form of commerce—and a bankruptcy attracted rival firms avid for stock at cheap rates to replenish their shelves. In fashionable towns like Bath competition was fierce.

Borrowers paid their subscriptions by the month, the quarter, half year, or year; and rates varied from 5 shillings for the season to the standard 1 guinea per annum. The device of classed subscriptions allowed the new publications to be reserved for those able to pay the higher fees or permitted more books to be issued at one time (up to six volumes instead of the customary two). Nonsubscribers were allowed to borrow books for a lending fee of a few pence per volume and were obliged to leave a deposit equal to the value of the book borrowed. Printed catalogs sold at 6 pence or 1 shilling, and the readers ordered their titles from them. Although direct access to the shelves was not unknown, a clerk normally served as intermediary. Time allowed for reading varied from two days to one month, depending on the recency of the books, and books could be changed on the same day they were issued. Fines were charged for overdue books, and books lost or damaged had to be paid for in full. Delivery to local and country subscribers was prompt; they were sent by carriage and this service cost more. Shelf arrangement was probably by size, as the catalogs were usually so arranged: duodecimo, octavo, quarto, folio, with separate shelving for pamphlets. Popular works were bought in multiples, especially novels, and the majority of the duodecimo works (in which format most three-volume novels appeared) were bound in quarter leather with marbled boards. In the most flourishing agencies, book stocks must have accumulated quickly; Bell's British Library in the Strand, for instance, claimed to have 100,000 volumes in 1787.

As to the perennial question on the proportion of fiction in the stock of circulating libraries, the difficulty is lack of evidence. Despite their notoriety as warehouses of worthless romances, the evidence we have is inconclusive simply because neither business records nor catalogs have survived in sufficient quantities to warrant irrefutable deductions. Surviving records indicate an average fiction percentage of 20%, which hardly suggests drug shops; but this evidence comes from the larger, better-known establishments with a varied clientele, chiefly those in London. The many small businesses that were the backbone of the trade throughout the country have left no trace, and it is in their shops that we might suspect a high proportion of fiction and light literature, as in the tobacconists' libraries of the twentieth century. Indeed, a pamphlet published in 1797 (*The Use of Circulating Libraries Considered; with Instructions for Opening and Conducting a Library upon a Small Plan*) is explicit on the point: it recommends a stock comprising 80% fiction for the best returns! The borrowers' registers that survive are scanty, and there are only two catalogs from the earlier period: Samuel Fancourt's, already mentioned, and William Bathoe's (1760). From them we can deduce that not only novels, but also sermons and pamphlets were among the most popular reading matter. The only eighteenth-century list of subscribers to survive is that of Marshall's of Bath (fl. 1793–1796); it shows twice as many men as women readers, a fact that does not support the popular picture of readers as being overwhelmingly female, and there is no reason to assume that Marshall's was an unusual case.

There is little doubt that the libraries must have changed the habits of the semieducated readers, particularly women. The growing numbers and efficiency of the libraries, the corresponding growth in demand, the whole machinery of loans, and the rise in the leisured reading public suggest some degree of cause and effect, if studied against the kinds of best-selling fiction of the period 1750–1770 and of the later period, 1770–1780. There was a progressive decline in quality—a narrowing of range and an increased superficiality—as if novelists were supplying material to assuage a prodigious appetite rather than an educated sensibility. After Smollett's death in 1771, the decline accelerated and the quantity of prose fiction of inferior type is manifest. The reputation of the libraries as purveyors of worthless literature had begun. Smollett was followed by Mrs. Radcliffe; Sterne, by Henry Mackenzie; and Samuel Richardson, by Mrs. Sheridan. The number of novels printed between 1750 and 1770 was about 600; in the period 1770–1780, it was 1,400, of a standard so trivial that magazines scarcely reviewed them. These factors

probably accounted for the correlation in most critics' minds between the circulating libraries and bad fiction. The oft-quoted remark of Sir Anthony Absolute in Sheridan's play *The Rivals* (1774) confirms the current view:

> A circulating library in a town is an evergreen tree of diabolical knowledge. It blossoms through the year. And depend on it, Mrs Malaprop, that they who are so fond of handling the leaves will long for the fruit at last (Act 1, Scene 2).

Others deplored the commercial atmosphere and compared the novels to factory-produced printed cloth. And, in the *Gentleman's Magazine* of 1805, we read:

> The circulating libraries and reading rooms in every market town degrade us by the impertinence and abuse of curiosity. They poison our leisure hours without improving them, and introduce negligent systems of religion compared to which the formal systems of antiquity, whether Papist or Puritan, were the strictest care of religious parents.

Yet they were not without supporters; Southey said of Bull's circulating library at Bath:

> It was then to me what the Bodleian would be now.[2]

In the *Monthly Magazine* (1821), an anonymous contributor wrote:

> It is computed that there are in the United Kingdom at least 1500 circulating libraries, each supported by an average of 70 subscribers.

Further confirmation of the fashion is given in J. Britton's *Picture of London* (24th ed., 1826), which indicates that there was a circulating library in nearly every small town. In general, their influence was thought by orthodox spokesmen to be pernicious, a view summed up neatly in the *Quarterly Review*:

> The Circulating Library has been the chief hotbed for forcing a crop of writers without talent and readers without discrimination.[3]

The most enterprising library of the late eighteenth century was William Lane's Minerva Library (fl. 1790–1820), a by-product of Lane's "fiction factory," which produced the "Minerva novels" around the turn of the century. The name became synonymous with light fiction of the emptiest kind, and as both publisher and disseminator, Lane exercised a virtual monopoly in this profitable field. He would furnish lending libraries and classified catalogs to shops anywhere in London or the provinces; by the year 1795, he was publishing more novels than all the other 25 London publishers combined. The vacuous romance and the sensational gothic tale were his stock-in-trade, and he created a fortune for himself by concentrating his product on a specific class of reader, women of the middle class in town and country. How far his control of this medium affected the fortunes of the novel and the standards of future popular novelists is an interesting question, which would be worth investigation if space allowed. By sustained advertising and shrewd promotion, he won a faithful clientele with this kind of publicity:

> The Historian is furnished with Remarks; the Gay and Volatile with Amusement; the Sedate with a useful Friend for Solitary Hours; Theatrical Amateurs with an Agreeable Companion. In every point of view Institutions of this Kind must be forcibly Convenient to all Classes of People, of General Service and Utility.[4]

Observe the emphasis on utility in an age when that principle was at the heart of the latest philosophical system.

The history of the circulating library in the nineteenth century is the history of its growing complexity and concentration in fewer hands. Two names are eponymous in the field: Charles Edward Mudie and W.H. Smith. Both started business life as news agents, and by observing the habits of customers and their taste for unexceptionable novels, they built their respective empires. Improved transport (especially rail), after 1840, was a major factor in the speed and efficiency of supply, and so in the expansion of a business. W.H. Smith opened his first bookstall in 1848, and he promptly applied for the monopoly of news agencies and bookstalls in the railway stations serving London and the northwestern regions, an enterprise that became wholly his when Mudie refused to collaborate. He controlled the railway reading public as Mudie did the residential borrowers, and he operated on the same principles of selection, earning himself the nickname "The North Western Missionary." In 1852, Mudie opened his purpose-built premises in New Oxford Street and was soon a national institution serving thousands of customers in London and the country. His publishing orders were so huge that he was a guarantee against failure but also a force to be reckoned with when criteria for selection were in question. The relation between Mudie's overt control of the fiction market and the type of novel published is fairly plain: any work that transgressed canons of Victorian orthodox morality was excluded as "pernicious." Circulating libraries, publishers, and authors combined to produce an acceptable commodity for the mass middle-class market. The typical Mudie's reader would approve Mrs. Henry Wood's fiction, Martin Tupper's verse, and *Eliza Cook's Journal*. The subscription of 1 guinea a year per volume meant that a novel in three volumes brought in more revenue, so that the continued life of the three-decker novel was assured until the 1890s despite its high price of 31/6. At the time of his death in 1890, Mudie's

business was supported by 25,000 patrons. Speedy supply of new books and concentration on works of transient appeal meant a conditioning of taste with implications for the developing, newly emancipated reading public that came into being after the Education Act of 1870 and also for the sophisticated printing technology of the late nineteenth century.

By the end of World War I, other agencies were supplying books to a much enlarged readership; most notable were the public libraries, which became financially respectable after the removal of the penny rate limitation in 1919. Their books began to compare more favorably with what was offered by the commercial agencies. Increased public finance, more public library branches, and the newly founded County Library Service ushered in the final phase in the life of the commercial lending libraries. When a public service demonstrates its capacity to provide not only collections of depth and variety but also current material—and with specialized attention to the needs of children, students, and professional people—then the recreational circulating library cannot long compete. In their efforts to survive, their provision grew shallower and soon they were extinct. The commercial book club was the natural successor to the circulating library, and if Mudie were alive today, he would be running a book club. Mudie's closed its doors in 1937. The era of the chain-store lending libraries—Boots Cash Chemists "Booklovers Library" (1900), W. H. Smith's bookshop libraries (1906), the Times Book Club (1905)—ended in the 1960s. Boots issued one million books in 1930 from its 450 branches. Smith's administered 690 branches with their concomitant libraries, but financial difficulties forced them to operate at a loss as an inducement to customers until the losses could no longer be sustained. Smith's closed its service in 1961; Boots, in 1966; and the Times Book Club, in 1962. The many rental agencies in tobacconists and other retail shops that loaned books at 2d per volume were a common sight in the suburbs before World War II, their stock-in-trade consisting entirely of superficial escapist literature. By the 1960s, they, too (like the chain-store prototypes) disappeared. A phenomenon that had endured as part of the social scene for over 200 years, serving a reading public by purely private enterprise on strict market principles, had become extinct.

REFERENCES

1. Beckwith, F.J. Doc. **1947**, *3* (2), 83.
2. Southey, R. *Life and Correspondence of the Late Robert Southey*, Southey, C.C., Ed.; Vol. 1. Entry for January 19, 1823.
3. Friswell, J.H. Circulating libraries: Their contents and their readers. London Society December **1871**, 20, 515–524 .
4. Advertisement, *Leeds Intelligencer*, May 1, 1787.

BIBLIOGRAPHY

Books

1. *Account of the Rise and Progress of the Subscription Library, Kingston-upon-Hull*; Kingston-upon-Hull, 1810.
2. Altick, R. *The English Common Reader*; University of Chicago Press: Chicago, IL, 1957.
3. Anderson, J. *History of the Belfast Library, Known as the Linen Hall Library*; Belfast, Northern Island, 1888.
4. Blakey, D. *The Minerva Press, 1790–1820*; Oxford University Press, for the Bibliographical Society: Oxford, U.K., 1939.
5. *Carlyle and the London Library*; Christie, M., Ed.; Chapman and Hall: London, U.K., 1907.
6. Chapman, R.W. Authors and Booksellers. In *Johnson's England*; Turbeville, A.S., Ed.; Clarendon Press: Oxford, U.K., 1933; 310–330.
7. Colman, G. *Polly Honeycombe*; 1760 (one-act play satirizing circulating library novels).
8. Crawford, J.C. *Wanlockhead Miners' Library: A Guide Book*; Wanlockhead Museum Trust, 1978.
9. Cruse, A. *The Englishman and His Books in the Early Nineteenth Century*; Harrap: London, U.K., 1930.
10. Cruse, A. *The Victorians and Their Books*; Allen and Unwin: London, U.K., 1935, reprinted 1968.
11. *Dictionary of National Biography*, consult entries under Samuel Fancourt and Charles Edward Mudie.
12. Donne-Smith, B. Commercial Libraries. In *Book World*; Hampden, J., Ed.; Allen and Unwin: London, U.K., 1957; 180–186.
13. Fancourt, S. *Alphabetical Catalogue of Books and Pamphlets Belonging to the Circulating Library in Crane Court*; 1748, 2 vols.
14. Fancourt, S. *The Narrative*; 1747.
15. Griest, G.L. *Mudie's Circulating Library and the Victorian Novel*; David and Charles: Newton Abbot, 1970.
16. Hull Subscription Library. *History of the Subscription Library at Kingston-upon-Hull*; Kirk: Hull, 1876.
17. Joy, T. *The Right Way to Run a Library Business*; Right Way Books: Kingswood, 1949.
18. Kaufman, P. *Borrowings from the Bristol Library, 1773–1784*; Bibliographical Society of Virginia: Charlottesville, 1960.
19. Kaufman, P. *Libraries and Their Users*; Library Association: London, U.K., 1969.
20. Kelly, T. *Early Public Libraries*; Library Association: London, U.K., 1966.
21. Kelly, T. *History of Public Libraries in Great Britain, 1845–1965*; Library Association: London, U.K., 1973.
22. Lackington, J. *Memoirs of the First Forty-Five Years of the Life of James Lackington, Bookseller*; Garland: New York, 1974; 1794; facsimile reprint.
23. *Leeds Library, 1768–1968*; The Library: Leeds, 1968.
24. Mangin, E. *An Essay on Light Reading*; 1808.
25. Moore, G. *Literature at Nurse*; Vizetelly, 1885 (an attack on Mudie's Library).
26. Nichols, J. *Literary Anecdotes of the Eighteenth Century*; 1812, 6 vols.; reprint, Kraus, New York, 1966; Vol. 6, Part 1: "The Gentlemen's Society of Spalding."
27. Noall, C. *The Penzance Library, 1818–1968*; Penzance Library, 1968.
28. Ollé, J.G. Subscription Libraries. In *Library History: An Examination Guidebook*; 2nd Ed.; Bingley: London, U.K., 1971; 51–61.
29. Parish, C. *History of the Birmingham Library*; Library Association: London, U.K., 1966.
30. Plomer, H.R. Index of Circulating Libraries in England and Scotland. In *Dictionary of the Printers and Booksellers Who Were at Work in England, Scotland, and Ireland, 1726–1775*; 431–432.
31. Pratt, T. *The Portico Library, Manchester: Its History and Associations 1802–1922*; Sherratt and Hughes: Manchester, 1922.
32. Preston, W.C. *Mudie's Library*; Ballantyne: Hanson, 1894.
33. *Queens of the Circulating Library*; Walbank, F.A., Ed.; Evans: London, U.K., 1950.
34. Richardson, F.R. The Circulating Library. In *The Book World*; Hampden, J., Ed.; Nelson: London, 1935; 195–202.
35. Russell, J. *A History of the Nottingham Subscription Library*; Nottingham: Derry, 1916.
36. Simpkin Marshall Ltd. *The Lending Library: How to Run It for Profit*, 2nd Ed.; Simpkin Marshall, 1930.
37. Society of Bookmen, *Report on the Commercial Circulating Libraries and the Price of Books*; 1928. Privately Printed.
38. Stephen, L. *English Literature and Society in the Eighteenth Century*; Duckworth: London, U.K., 1904, reprinted 1965.
39. Summers, M. The Publishers and the Circulating Libraries. In *The Gothic Quest*; Fortune Press: London, U.K., 1938; 60–105.
40. Taylor, J.T. The Circulating Library. In *Early Opposition to the English Novel*; King's Crown Press: Morningside Heights, NY, 1943; 21–51.
41. Timmins, S. *Centenary of the Birmingham Library, 1779–1879*; Birmingham, 1879.
42. Tovey, C. *A Free Library for Bristol*; Bristol, 1853.
43. *The London Library*; Grindea, M., Ed.; Boydell Press, 1978 (an anthology of tributes from contemporary writers, originally published as a special number of *Adam*, the international literary review, in 1977).
44. *The Use of Circulating Libraries Considered; with Instructions for Opening and Conducting a Library*; 1797.
45. Varma, D.P. *The Evergreen Tree of Diabolical Knowledge*; Consortium Press: Washington, D.C., 1972 (includes "An Inventory of Circulating Libraries in London, Provincial Towns, Watering Places and Spas," Appendix 4; and the text of *The Use of Circulating Libraries Considered*, 1797, Appendix 5).
46. Ward, T.A. *A Short Account of the Sheffield Library*; Sheffield, 1825.
47. Wilson, T. *The Use of Circulating Libraries Considered*; 1797.
48. Wright, C.T.H. *The London Library*; London Library: London, U.K., 1926.

Theses

This is a representative selection of individual library histories (all have been reproduced by University Microfilms, Ann Arbor, Mich.).

1. Davis, S.W. *The Founding of the Portico Library (Manchester)*; 1969.
2. Hitch, A. *Books in Bury: A History of Libraries in Bury, Lancashire, to 1900*; 1974.
3. Hooton, J.F. *Libraries in Hull in the 19th Century*; 1967.
4. Kite, V.J. *Libraries in Bath, 1618–1964*; 1970.
5. Morley, J. *Libraries of Newark-on-Trent, 1698–1960*; 1970.
6. Varley, A. *A History of Libraries in Cheltenham, 1780–1905*; 1970.
7. Wilson, R. *A History of King's Lynn Libraries, 1797–1905*; 1972.

Periodical Articles

Files of the major periodicals relating to librarianship are worth consultation since much relevant material may be found therin; viz., *The Library History, Journal of Library History, Library Quarterly, Library Review, Libri, Library Association Record*, and *Library World*.

1. Axon, W.E.A. A London circulating library of 1743. Library, 2nd ser. **1900**, *1* (4), 377–378.
2. Beckwith, F. The Beginnings of the Leeds Library. In *Thoresby Society, Publications*, Miscellanies; Vol. 11, 145–165. No. 37.
3. Beckwith, F. The eighteenth century proprietary library in England. J. Doc. **1947**, *3* (2), 81–98.
4. Clarke, A. The reputed first circulating library in London. Library, 2nd ser. **1900**, *1* (3), 274–289.
5. Collar, H. An 18th century book society. Essex Rev. **1935**, *44*, 109–112.
6. Country book clubs 50 years ago. Gentleman's Mag. **1852**, *37*, 571–572. n.s.
7. Crawford, J.C. Two miners' libraries in the '70s. Lib. Rev. **1971**, *23*, 14–17 (Wanlockhead and Leadhills Reading Societies).
8. Fawcett, T. The founding of the Norfolk and Norwich literary institution. Libr. Hist. **1967**, *1* (2), 46–53.
9. Friswell, J.H. Circulating libraries: Their contents and their readers. London Society **1871**, *20*, 515–524.
10. Gillam, S. 125 years of the London library. Prog. Libr. Sci. 1966; 162–173.
11. Hamlyn, H. Eighteenth Century Circulating Libraries in England. Library, 5th ser. **1947**, *1* (4), 197–222.
12. Hepworth, P. Norfolk and Norwich Subscription Library. East Anglian Rev. **1955**, *14*, 575–579.
13. Hints of a Plan for a Book Club. Oeconomist **1799**, 350–357.
14. Joynes, S.E. The Sheffield library, 1771–1907. Libr. Hist. **1971**, *2* (3), 91–116.
15. Kaufman, P. The eighteenth century London and Westminster library societies. Library, 5th ser. **1970**, *25* (3), 237–247.
16. Kaufman, P. Library news from Kelso. Libr. Rev. **1960**, *17* (135), 486–489.
17. Kaufman, P. The rise of community libraries in Scotland. Pap. Bibliogr. Soc. Am. **1965**, *59* (3), 233–294.
18. Keating, P. A miners' library. Times Lit. Suppl. 6 **1978**; 16–17 (Wanlockhead Library and Reading Society, 1756–1946).
19. Keith, S. Mudie's circulating library. Ninet.-Century Fict. *11*, 156–157.
20. Kelly, T. Norwich, pioneer of public libraries. Norfolk Archaeol. **1969**, *34*, 215–222.
21. Knott, J. Circulating libraries in newcastle-upon-Tyne in the 18th and 19th centuries. Libr. Hist. **1972**, *2* (6), 227–249.
22. London circulating libraries. The Times 2, **1913**, 3.
23. Lough, J.; Lough, M. Aberdeen circulating libraries in the eighteenth century. Aberd. Univ. Rev. **1945–1946**, *35*, 17–23.
24. McDonald, W.R. Circulating libraries in the north east of Scotland in the eighteenth century. Bibliothek **1968**, *5* (4), 119–137.
25. McGill, E. The evergreen tree of diabolical knowledge. Bookman **1931**, *80*, 267–272.
26. McKillop, A.D. English circulating libraries, 1725–1750. Library, 4th ser. **1934**, *14* (4), 477–485.
27. Macintyre, P. Historical Sketch of the Liverpool Library. Trans. Hist. Soc. Lancs. Ches. **1856–1857**, *9*, 236–244.
28. Milne, J. A great circulating library. Cornhill Mag. **1935**, *78*, 449–457 (on W.H. Smith's Lending Libraries).
29. Milne, J. A library of today. Cornhill Mag. **1934**, *77*, 444–449 (on the Boots Booklovers' Library).
30. Monster-misery of literature. Blackwood's Mag. **1844**, *55*, 557–560 (a sharp attack on circulating libraries).
31. Morley, J. Newark book society, 1777–1872. Libr. Hist. **1968**, *1* (3), 77–86.
32. Ollé, J.G. The lost libraries. Libr. Rev. **1966**, *20* (159), 452–456. (on Boots, W.H. Smith's, and other commercial lending libraries).
33. Pollard, A.W. Commercial circulating libraries and the price of books. Library **1929**, *9* (4), 411–416.
34. Russell, H.W. A plan for a public library at Church-Langton, Leicestershire, 1760. Libr. Hist. **1968**, *1* (3), 68–76.
35. Scott, W. George Colman's Polly Honeycombe and circulating library fiction in 1760. Notes & Queries **1968**, *15*, 465–467. n.s.
36. Thompson, A.R. The use of libraries by the working class in Scotland in the early nineteenth century. Scott. Hist. Rev. **1963**, *42*, 21–29.
37. Walton, J. An eighteenth century village library (Luddenden, Yorkshire). Librarian Book World **1939**, *28* (12), 329–331.
38. Wright, C.T.H. The soul's dispensary. Ninet. Century **1922**, *91*, 533–544.

Switzerland: Libraries, Archives, and Museums

Jean Frédéric Jauslin
Federal Department of Home Affairs (FDHA), Swiss Federal Office of Culture, Bern, Switzerland

Andreas Kellerhals
Federal Department of Home Affairs (FDHA), Swiss Federal Archives, Bern, Switzerland

Abstract

This entry offers a brief history of libraries, archives, and museums in Switzerland, a federal republic with 26 cantons. The authors focus on contemporary developments including the creation of consortia, professional education, digital libraries and virtual archives.

INTRODUCTION

Brief Historical, Geographical, Economic, and Sociocultural Context

Switzerland is a multiethnic, multilingual, and multiconfessional nation held together by the desire of its people to be united. It has been a federal State since 1848—one of 23 in the world and the second oldest after the United States. Switzerland has a federal structure with three different political levels: Confederation, cantons, and communes. The Confederation is the term used in Switzerland to describe the State. The Confederation has authority in all areas in which it is empowered by the Federal Constitution, such as in foreign and security policy, customs and monetary affairs, nationally applicable legislation and defense. Tasks which do not expressly fall within the domain of the Confederation are matters for the cantons, which are the next level down. According to the Federal Constitution culture is above all under the authority of the cantons. The Confederation may only act in this field as far as questions of national importance are concerned. Switzerland has 26 cantons. All the cantons are divided into communes, of which there are currently over 2700. Their number is in decline as a result of amalgamations.

Switzerland is bordered by Germany to the north, Austria and the Principality of Liechtenstein to the east, Italy to the south and France to the west. Switzerland is a small, mountainous country, extending over a part of the central Alps and the northern pre-Alps. With its mountains and hills, rivers, and lakes, Switzerland boasts a diverse landscape despite measuring only 220 km (137 mi) from north to south and 348 km (217 mi) from west to east (Fig. 1).

The population of Switzerland is 7,581,520 (July 2008 est.) and its people speak three official languages: German 63.7%, French 20.4%, Italian 6.5%. The Swiss economy is mainly geared towards the provision of services. While in the 1960s half of all employees were still working in the industrial sector, at the beginning of the twenty-first century this proportion had sunk to around 25%. At the same time, the proportion of workers in the service sector grew from 39% to over 70%, while less than 4% gained their income from agriculture. The proportion of exports in Switzerland's Gross Domestic Product (GDP) is high compared to other nations. A first rate educational system is one of the foundations of Switzerland's economic competitiveness.

Switzerland's culture is influenced by its geography and multilingualism. Its central position between three major European cultural areas (the German speaking area, France, and Italy) and its own linguistic division have led to great diversity in its literature, art, architecture, music, and customs. Each linguistic region has its own radio programs and numerous newspapers. Famous music and film festivals, art exhibitions, a large number of museums and numerous traditional customs attract large numbers of foreign visitors.

LIBRARY AND INFORMATION PROFESSIONS

Systems and Services

Brief overview of legislation and types of libraries

In line with Swiss federal structure, legislation for libraries in Switzerland is not enacted at a national (federal) level but at a state (cantonal) or local (communal) level. Only three publicly accessible libraries are financed at the federal level (though restricted-access libraries are also funded federally): the Swiss National Library (NL) and two libraries of the Swiss Federal Institute of Technology (Ecole polytechnique fédérale de Lausanne, Eidgenössische Technische Hochschule Zürich). The latter functions as the Swiss Center for Information on Science and Technology.

Encyclopedia of Library and Information Sciences, Fourth Edition DOI: 10.1081/E-ELIS4-120043842

Student–Taxonomy

Fig. 1 Map of Switzerland.
Source: CIA *The World Factbook*.https://www.cia.gov/library/publications/the-world-factbook/geos/sz.html.

This structure gives rise to a wide variety of policies and in addition makes it difficult to calculate the number of libraries in the country. It has been estimated that there are around 6000, ranging in size from very small volunteer libraries up to the NL, and including the libraries of the international organizations. However, this figure cannot be confirmed.[1,2] The most reliable and up-to-date figures about the range of public and scientific libraries in Switzerland are available from the Swiss Federal Statistical Office. They categorize libraries as follows:

- National
- University
- Networks of university libraries
- Networks of specialized further education libraries
- Public libraries
- Special libraries

School libraries are not included in the statistics. The analysis of any figures is complicated by the fact that many university libraries are also cantonal or even municipal libraries (or vice versa) and are open to the general public. Cantonal libraries may have a dual role of collecting the cultural heritage of a canton and also providing public library services.

National library and information services

In 1894 the federal parliament established the first federal decree concerning the establishment of a Swiss NL, fixing its location (Bern) and its cultural goals: the mandate of the Swiss NL, then as now, is to collect Helvetica (a new law in 1992 specified all formats on- and off-line, print,

and digital) published since 1848, the founding of the Swiss Confederation.[3] The term Helvetica covers all works by Swiss authors (fiction and nonfiction); publications translated in Switzerland or by Swiss authors; works published abroad concerning a topic or a Swiss public figure. It also covers all newspapers and serials published and/or printed in Switzerland; associations' publications, timetables, telephone directories, theses, official publications, maps and atlases, and musical scores. It should be noted that there is no legal deposit at a national level in Switzerland, though it exists at the cantonal level for Vaud, Geneva, and Valais. Consequently, the Swiss NL has to negotiate with publishers to acquire material through voluntary deposit. Helvetica produced before 1848 are located in state and university libraries across the country. In addition to collecting, cataloging, and preserving its collection, the NL is unusual compared to other national libraries in that it is also mandated to lend material to the general public as well as researchers, both in reading rooms and in users' homes or offices. [The Swiss National Library is mandated to collect, catalog, preserve, and make available all information either printed or on other media, having a link with Switzerland (Art. 2, alinea 1, Federal law on the Swiss National Library 1992).]

Despite the lack of legislation concerning national projects or cooperation, the NL has a tradition of working with other libraries in Switzerland and abroad as the following examples illustrate.

The NL maintains the Swiss Union Catalogue (CCS/GK) which serves all Swiss libraries and documentation and information centers. It contains the Union Catalogue of monographs: a microfilmed card catalog listing foreign publications as well as Swiss publications from before

1900 but reported before the end of 2002 by libraries in the Swiss interlibrary loan network. Initially set up in 1928, it manages a catalog of more than 5 million titles and remains an important research tool for foreign collections held in Swiss libraries up to the end of the twentieth century. Post-1900 publications are listed in the online catalog Helveticat. It is complemented by the Swiss Virtual catalog[4] a meta-catalog that searches simultaneously in 18 catalogs of libraries and networks in Switzerland and in Liechtenstein, and by the Swiss Gateway to periodicals (SZP/PSP) which gives access to serial titles in the main catalogs of Swiss libraries.[5]

The NL cooperates in "BibliOpass" a network of almost 600 Swiss university and cantonal libraries. A user card from one of the libraries enables a user—without any additional fees—to register in all the network's libraries and to consult their collections and borrow documents.[6]

In the online environment, the NL has launched the project E-Helvetica which covers the collection and archiving of e-publications.[7] The project began in 2001 under the leadership of the NL which cooperates on it with cantonal and university libraries as well as commercial publishers (Karger and Stämpfli) and noncommercial publishers. The goal is to create the environment and conditions that will enable the collection, description, dissemination, and long-term conservation of Helvetica in electronic form and to develop an archival system for electronic publications. Projects within this initiative include archiving of online theses, of journals and of Web pages.

In 2006, the NL launched a survey into digitization activities in Swiss cantonal libraries with a view to coordinating activities and avoiding duplicate effort. As a result of the study, the creation of a site bringing together digitization efforts was evaluated in 2007. Here again, lack of legislation means that all such cooperation is voluntary but Swiss libraries are aware of the need to pool resources. This can also be seen in the work to create the Swiss poster collection, a cooperative digitized poster collection bringing together museums and libraries.[8]

Internationally, the NL is a founding member and partner of the European Library a portal for the 45 European national libraries and their resources (digital and print).[9] This service was launched by the CENL (Conference of European National Librarians) of which the NL is an active member.[10]

In the field of bibliographic control, the NL manages the Swiss ISSN centre which assigns ISSNs on request from the publishers and also retrospectively for earlier titles of a publication. Titles are entered in Helveticat, the NL online catalog, then sent to the ISSN register which cooperates with all the national centers worldwide. The NL is also a training library, providing training for those entering the information and documentation schools; apprenticeships for LIS assistants and training for graduate librarians.

Academic and research libraries—very brief overview

As indicated above, academic and research libraries may have a dual function as cantonal or public libraries. Many of them date back to the sixteenth to eighteenth centuries and supplement the cultural heritage collections of the NL. They are funded by the cantons or in some case are managed as foundations. As stated earlier, the two libraries of the Swiss Federal Institute of Technology in Zurich and Lausanne are funded centrally. University and research libraries have a long tradition of cooperation, exemplified by the library networks that have been developed in the past years, for example RERO, the Library Network of Western Switzerland,[11] IDS, the German-Swiss Network[12] the Consortium of Swiss Academic Libraries[13] and the Swissbib project launched in 2007.[14]

Digital library collections and services—a few examples

There are no nationally funded programs for the creation of digital library collections or digitization. As previously indicated, there are plans to harvest Web sites in cooperation between cantonal libraries and the NL. Some central financing was made available to launch the Swiss Consortium for licensing electronic publications. Otherwise, libraries and other institutions must finance their projects, though some assistance is available through the auspices of MEMORIAV a foundation for the preservation of the Swiss audiovisual heritage (e.g., Swiss posters).[15] In addition to the initiatives mentioned under the Swiss NL, activities of note include the RERO DOC digital library[16] containing books, theses, and dissertations, the digitization of the Journal de Genève (600,000 pages, a cooperative effort of the Swiss NL, the Bibliothèque de Genève and the publisher Le Temps), and the digitization of 100,000 books from the University Library of Lausanne in cooperation with Google.

Education for LIS: examinations, certification, university level programs and continuing education (information provided by Ms Yolande Estermann on the Swiss-lib list, June 29, 2007).

In Switzerland, LIS training is organized in two main areas:

- Basic training
- Continuing education

Basic training may be in a field of technical competence, or general or senior management.

It is organized according to the training scheme managed by the Federal office for professional Education and technology.[17] The following routes to the profession are available:

Vocational training through an apprenticeship following the end of obligatory school education. The official title of this is: CFC d'assistant en information documentaire. This federally recognized certificate in LIS is carried out in an accredited institution and supplemented by classes. More details may be found at the Web site of the Association of Information and Documentation Assistants.[18]

Following this, the holder of a CFC in AID may take what further examinations to enter a HES (specialized high school). Additionally, a holder of what is in Switzerland termed a "maturité gymnasiale" (high school diploma) may also enroll in the HES program without having followed the CFC AID on condition that he or she has professional experience of 40 weeks in a LIS service.

The HES studies may be carried out in Geneva (in French) or Chur (in German) and are aligned to the Bologna system i.e.,

- A Baccalaureate in LIS of 180 ECTS (European Credit Transfer and Accumulation System), after 3 years of full time study. This Baccalaureate has been accredited by the Federal government and allows the schools to deliver the degree "Bachelor of science HES en information documentaire."

This level of training aims to allow recipients to carry out the following professions: librarian, researcher, archivist, documentalist, records manager, and manage small units of up to 10 people.[19,20]

In addition, the two schools have submitted a request for accreditation for a Masters program (90 ECTS). In Geneva, this takes the form of a 50/50 cooperation with the School of Library and Information Science of the University of Montreal. Students (Canadian and Swiss) will follow one year of study in Montreal and one in Geneva, concentrating on areas such as strategic management with a goal to working within large private companies, international organizations, networks, or major libraries.

The second area of training concerns continuing education and is aimed at those who have already acquired basic training in LIS or in another field. It comprises Certificates of Advanced Studies (around 10 ECTS, available at Bern University, Fribourg, Zurich, and Luzern), Diplomas of Advanced Studies (around 30 ECTS, available at Geneva and Zurich) and Masters of Advanced Studies (around 60 ECTS, available at Chur, Geneva, and Zurich).

There is no tradition in Switzerland of recognition of experience as a substitute for study as is the case in France, but this approach will be studied.

The multiplicity of routes to diplomas and the current restructuring still underway (a new law is planned for 2011) mean that it is difficult for employers at present to understand the structure of higher education in Switzerland, and the requirements for different categories of employment but the alignment with Bologna should in the long term facilitate exchange and mobility.

Professional associations: History, membership, and major achievements

The Swiss Library Association (Association des Bibliothèques et Bibliothécaires Suisses (BBS) is the national association for libraries and information centers and serves as an umbrella for a variety of sub-groups and working parties (see Web site for details).[21] There are around 300 institutional members and 1450 individual members (2007) covering all sectors of libraries and information centers, national, regional, local, public, private, specialized. The goals of the BBS are as follows:

- To represent its members in discussion with the political public arena
- To lobby the political and cultural decision makers to encourage and support the development of libraries, copyright matters, education, and training
- To network, exchange information and professional experience nationally and internationally
- To support LIS training and continuing education, including the organization of training for its members
- To give information to members on current areas of interest for the profession
- To support the development of the Information society in Switzerland, including activities within the World Summit on the Information Society (WSIS)

These are carried out through its Web site, journal, training programs, conference, and publications. National partners include: The Swiss Documentalists Association (Association suisse de documentation (ASD)), the Association of Swiss Archivists (Association des archivistes suisses (AAS)), the Working community of Swiss public libraries (Communauté de travail des bibliothèques suisses de lecture publique (CLP)), the Swiss-French Documentation group (Groupe romand de documentation (GRD)), different interest groups, working groups, committees.

Internationally, the BBS is a member of the following organizations:

- International Federation of Library Associations and Institutions (IFLA)
- European Bureau of Library, Information and Documentation Associations (EBLIDA)
- Fédération des utilisateurs de droits d'auteurs et voisins (DUN)

The BBS was founded in 1897 with the name d'Association des bibliothécaires suisses (ABS) and along with the associations of the United States (1876), Great Britain (1877), and Austria (1896), is one of the oldest library associations in the world. In 1927, the ABS was one of the founding members of IFLA. Between 1937 and 1998 the Association was in charge of the librarian diploma, replaced in 1998 by the AID (see above) and Information specialist diploma. The Association changed its name to become BBS in 1992. In August 2007 members of BBS and ASD will vote on a proposal to merge the two associations to become the Swiss Information Association (official name still to be determined).[22]

ARCHIVES

Legislation

The Federal Act on Archiving (Archiving Act, BGA, 1998) regulates archiving at the federal level and requires all federal authorities and all private institutions and individuals carrying out federal functions to archive their records. It also stipulates the duties and responsibilities of the Swiss Federal Archives (SFA) and the right of access, free of charge, to federal fonds. Cantonal laws or regulations constitute the legal basis for archiving at cantonal and communal (local) level and are entirely independent of federal legislation. Communal archives are covered by cantonal archives.

There is no real legal obligation for private institutions to archive their records for the long term. However, the code of obligations and other (international) liability regulations may require private institutions to archive at least part of their records independently though there is no requirement to grant public access.

The Swiss Federal Archives and Archival Services

The SFA is located in Bern, the capital of Switzerland. It was founded in 1798 under the Helvetic Republic and is now attached to the Federal Department of Home Affairs. It houses the archives from the time of the Helvetic Republic (1798–1803), the mediation (1803–1813), the Tagsatzung [assembly of envoys from all over Switzerland] period (1814–1848) and the Federal State (1848 to present). The archives include documents from the Federal Parliament (legislative), the government and the federal administration (executive). The Federal Courts (judicial) are responsible for their own archiving in accordance with the principles of the Federal Archiving Act; so, too, are the Swiss National Bank and various autonomous federal institutions (e.g., ETH Zurich/EPF Lausanne, Swiss Post, the federal railways). The SFA also keeps over 550 private archives of people and organizations with a close link to the federal state. Information on access to the Federal Archives can be found on the Federal Archives' Web site: http://www.bar.admin.ch.

The SFA is the Confederation's service center for sustainable records management. It advises the administrative offices on their records management, assesses documents together with them, accepting and preserving any documents worth archiving; it allows interested parties access,

free of charge, to the archives once the protection periods have expired (normally 30 years). In this way the state's accountability is ensured. Archives also serve as a source for historically orientated research.

The SFA is the largest public archive in Switzerland in terms of the size of the archival records (50 lkm, 12 TB) and the number of employees (around 50 staff). Even without formal authority over the cantonal and communal archives, it plays a leading role and is often at the cutting edge of further specialist developments (e.g., digital archiving). It also represents Switzerland abroad and is a point of contact for foreign archive agencies.

Apart from the SFA, the Swiss Film Archive, the Swiss National Sound Archives and other institutions such as the Swiss Social Archives and the Swiss Business Archives also have archiving tasks or manage collections of national importance.

Cantonal and Local Archives

Each of the 26 cantons manages its own archives, the size of which varies enormously (from archives with one or two people to archives with 25 employees). They mostly come under the cantonal government's staff office or the Department of Education and Culture, or very occasionally the Department of Home Affairs or the Department of Justice. These archives have kept records from the early Middle Ages, and in some instances also contain church records, which were taken over by the state from the time of the reformation until the nineteenth century.

The Conference of Archives Directors acts as a consulting and discussion forum for archiving matters at cantonal and federal levels. Out of some 3000 political communes, it is mainly the larger towns that have professional archives which are subordinated to the appropriate cantonal archive. They often contain also parish archives. The civil status registers (formerly known as baptism, marriage, and death registers) are only found at communal or cantonal level. Their records are in high demand at the local and regional levels.

Some cantons are the successors of large city states (Bern, Zurich). In the nineteenth century the archives were separated (canton or city records, sometimes even the "Burgergemeinde"). The separation of archives was also necessary for new cantons such as Aargau and Vaud which had been independent cantons since 1803 (separation of the archives of the city state of Bern); in 1972 the same separation had to be made owing to the creation of the canton of Jura.[23] An overview of all cantonal and communal archives can be found at http://www.vsa-aas.org/Archivadressen.241.0.html.

University Archives

The Federal Institutes of Technology also manage their own archives as laid down in the Federal Act on

Archiving. The cantonal universities have their own archives which are supervised by the cantonal archives; some of these were only created recently.

Film and Audiovisual Archives

The two important institutions for film and sound are the Swiss Film Archive in Lausanne and the Swiss National Sound Archives in Lugano. The former is a private foundation that is two-thirds subsidized by the private sector. The organization, which was founded in 1948 and restructured in 1981, is responsible for preserving and making accessible (screening) films that were either made in Switzerland, about Switzerland or by Swiss. It also preserves foreign films that were shown in Switzerland and film posters and photographs (http://www.cinematheque. ch). The Swiss National Sound Archives in Lugano is financed by a private foundation set up in 1987. It is responsible for collecting and cataloging any recordings that make a reference to Swiss history or culture and making them available. It carries out this task in collaboration with the Swiss NL in Bern. The National Sound Archives collaborates with the Swiss Broadcasting Corporation (SRG SSR idée suisse) to digitalize and archive historic radio broadcasts. The National Sound Archives also collects all recordings by SUISA (Swiss Authors Copyright Society) that it receives in connection with the administration of authors' and reproduction rights (http:// www.fonoteca.ch).

In the area of photography there are several nationally important institutions in Switzerland such as the Photography Foundation in Winterthur (http://www.fotostiftung. ch), the Musée de l'Elysée in Lausanne (http://www. elysee.ch) or the Photography Museum in Vevey (http:// www.cameramuseum.ch/d_basis.php).

Even at the regional level there are specialized institutions such as the La-Chaux-de-Fonds library with its film documentation center which collects and conserves audiovisual and iconographic sources of regional significance. Other examples are Lausanne's city archives or the new media libraries in Valais. Many archives, libraries, or museums have major photograph collections (e.g., Basel-Stadt's state archive and Bern's Burgerbibliothek).

Memoriav,[15] the association for conserving audiovisual cultural heritage in Switzerland, organizes a network for these institutions. It was set up by the Swiss NL, the SFA, the Swiss Film Archive, the Swiss National Sound Archives, the Federal Office of Communications (OFCOM) (supervisory authority of the SBC) and the Swiss Broadcasting Corporation (SRG SSR idée Suisse) and now numbers around 160 members. With a budget of just under CHF 3 million per annum, the association promotes restoration measures, cataloging work and communication activities such as exhibitions, film screenings, etc.

Other Archives

In addition to Switzerland's state sector archives there is a rich archiving landscape including institutions of international, nationwide, regional, or local importance. The archives of international organizations are mostly located in Geneva, e.g., the headquarters of the ICRC, of the League of Nations and the United Nation's European office. The archives of the ICRC and of the League of Nation, in particular, are of international importance, whereas archiving at the United Nation organizations (e.g., UNHCR, ILO, WTO, ITU, WHO, WIPO, Human Rights Commission) is difficult to gauge as the level of professionalism varies considerably. Interestingly, the WSIS took place in Geneva, which was of great importance for archiving worldwide. The Human Rights Commission is also interested in archives as institutions of democracy and the rule of law. Also housed in Geneva are the World Council of Churches' archives (since 1948).

Lausanne is home to the archives (and museum) of the International Olympic Committee (set up in 1993). These archives contain many collections of photographs and documents in addition to the traditional archives. Given that environment, other sports associations such as the International Cyclists' Union (UCI, since 2002) or UEFA and FIFA (Zurich, 1932) also set up their headquarters in Switzerland. Many of these archives are open to the general public.

Other institutions of national importance are the Swiss Social Archive, the Archives of Contemporary History in Zurich and the Swiss Business Archive in Basel. The Social Archive (set up in 1906 by pastor and social democrat, Paul Pflüger) combines a library, a comprehensive collection of literature on the social history of Switzerland and the archives of persons and institutions involved in workers', women's, or youth movements (e.g., trade unions) (http://www.sozialarchiv.ch). The Swiss Business Archive (founded in 1910 by Rudolf Wackernagel, the state archivist of Basel-Stadt) documents industrial and business history and holds the archives of companies that have been liquidated; it is affiliated to the Basel University library. It plays a key role in the Private Business Archive working group of the Association of Swiss Archivists (ASA) and operates the Web site http://www.arCHeco.ch that lists all the business archives accessible for research purposes (http://www.ub.unibas.ch/wwz/wwzprosp.htm).

The Archives of Contemporary History (set up in 1974) is affiliated to the Institute of History at the Federal Institute of Technology in Zurich (ETH Zurich) and collects the archives of private individuals and associations (e.g., the archives of the Swiss Trade and Industry Association) and documents contemporary history from the First World War up to the present day (http://www.afz.ethz.ch).

In the last decades of the twentieth century the number of specialized archives increased dramatically. Notable examples include the Gosteli Foundation, an archive on the Swiss women's movement, located in Worblaufen (Bern), the "Associazione Archivi Riuniti delle Donne Ticino" in Melano, the "Archive de la Construction moderne" at the Federal Institute of Technology in Lausanne (EPFL), ETH Zurich's gta (Geschichte und Theorie der Architektur [history and theory of architecture]) archive and the "Archivio del Moderno," which is part of the "Accademia di architettura di Mendrisio."

There is currently a tendency for all these institutions to combine their functions as a repository and documentation center and to open their archives to the public, while at the same time assuring the protection of private data. The Swiss NL also comes under this category. Since 1991 it extended its standard collection with the creation of a Swiss literature archive and collects the "fonds" of writers that they have endowed, bequeathed, or sold to the Confederation.

At the regional level private archives focusing on local history emerged. Examples are the "Archives de la vie privée" in Geneva (created in 1994) or the "Archives de la vie ordinaire" in Neuchâtel (set up in 2003). Finally, special collections with a specific theme also exist such as the Max Frisch Archive and the Thomas Mann Archive in Zurich, not to mention botanical archives, music archives etc.

A new phenomenon has emerged since the end of the twentieth century: virtual archives. These are often run by interest groups that define themselves either through specific media carriers or a specific subject. These groups conserve and catalog documents but, rather than physically conserving them themselves, they pass on such fonds to existing (public) archives. The "Archiv für Agrargeschichte" [agricultural history archive] for instance, established in 2002, first cataloged the archives of 13 semi-state organizations of national importance in the field of agriculture and afterwards passed them on to the SFA in 2004.

The number of professional company archives is still small and the number of enterprise archives open to the public even smaller. Apart from the requirement under the Swiss Code of Obligations to conserve company books and papers there is no formal requirement in Switzerland to keep archives as such. Nevertheless, some of the large internationally active banks, insurance companies and industrial firms (e.g., pharmaceuticals or food sectors, machine industry) have very well maintained archives which, building on professionally organized records management, have become an essential management tool. Another group of companies with often professional archives are traditional (family) enterprises such as private banks or watch manufacturers (e.g., Patek Philippe SA in Geneva, Jaeger-Le Coultre, au Le Sentier). However, most of them are rather inaccessible to the general public; only the "Independent Experts Commission: Switzerland—Second World War," established by parliament in 1996, had unrestricted access to these archives for 5 years.

The situation with associations, unions, political parties, trade unions, etc. is not much better. Some have, nonetheless, deposited their archives with public institutions (e.g., the Social Democratic Party and some trade unions have deposited their archives in the Swiss Social Archive).

The Private Business Archive working group of the ASA brings together historians and archivists from private companies and public institutions with a view to raising companies' awareness of their responsibility to archive and to create an overview of existing company archives.

The oldest archives in Switzerland are those of the Roman Catholic Church. They comprise archives from dioceses, parishes, orders, and religious congregations (such as the Swiss Capuchins in Lucerne) and abbeys (such as St. Gallen, St. Maurice, Einsiedeln, Engelberg, and Disentis).

Added to that, there are the archives of missionary societies.

The Protestant church is organized at cantonal level and its archives are closely linked to Switzerland's political structure. The ASA's "spiritual archives" working group plays a role in coordinating, supporting, and sensitizing. Furthermore it also keeps track of the "fonds" of spiritual institutions and is now trying to involve other important denominations.[24]

Digital Archival Collections

There are already several fonds available in digital format, but the main challenge lies in creating archival systems capable of archiving digitally produced documents, deeds, and data. The SFA plays a key role here. At federal level, this task is one of the government's key projects for the transition to the information society and the establishment and extension of eGovernment/eAdministration structures, which should allow barrier-free contact and exchange among authorities, and between the authorities and the business world and private citizens (http://www.bar.admin.ch/themen/00532/00536/index.html?lang=de).

Some of the items available in digital format include the federal government's official publications (the Federal Gazette, http://www.amtsdruckschriften.bar.admin.ch); others are yet to be digitalized. Selected documents on foreign policy from 1848 to 1961 are also available from the Swiss Diplomatic Documents project (DoDiS, DDS: http://www.dodis.ch/d/home.asp). The Archives of Contemporary History operates a virtual reading room (http://www.afz.ethz.ch and http://onlinearchives.ethz.ch). Since 2005 the Basel-Stadt state archive has been gradually making its collection of photographs accessible online (http://www.staatsarchiv.bs.ch). Memoriav offers access through its Memobase online database to various collections of photographs, sound and film documents, partly with direct access to the documents themselves (http://www.memobase.ch).

Archival Science in Switzerland and Archivist Education

For a long time there was no actual professional training in Switzerland to become an archivist. The professional association has offered in-service introduction courses and further training events. Since 1998, however, there has been I+D (Information and Documentation) training, I+D university of applied sciences syllabuses, and since 2002 a university-level certificate course called archiving and information science, which in 2006 became the Master of Advanced Studies in Archival and Information Science (http://www.unibe.ch). The I+D training courses now incorporate the former vocational training courses for librarians, archivists, and documentalists. The I+D training delegation was formed jointly in 1994 by the Swiss Association of Libraries and Librarians (BBS), the Swiss Documentation Association (SVD), and the ASA and aims to coordinate these training courses (http://www.bda-aid. ch/delegation.html).

Professional Associations

As a professional association the ASA attends to the interests of its members, is committed to further training of the archival community and to raising awareness of the importance of archives for society (http://www.vsa-aas.org).

In addition, at the conference of leading archivists at cantonal and federal levels and from the Principality of Liechtenstein, archival concerns are discussed at national level, joint projects initiated and carried out and information policy conducted. The conference is currently concentrating on finding solutions to digital archiving.

Electronic Records

One of the key projects in the Swiss government's strategy for an information society (1998) is the establishment of an electronic archive. Strategic planning and work began in 2000, and the first prototype applications have been developed, tested, and put into operation with the appropriate infrastructure. These are being developed further so that they can be rolled out for general use.

In 2006 the Federal Council also commissioned SFA to draw up a plan of action for the uniform and standardized use of electronic data and documents in the federal administration. This essentially consists of managing the information lifecycle of digital information and streamlining the federal administration's heterogeneous information systems.

The federal government, 18 cantons and the Principality of Liechtenstein have also created a coordination office for the sustainable archiving of electronic documents in order to give an incentive to and coordinate troubleshooting within the federal structures (http://www.kost-ceco.ch).

The ASA's eCommittee working group is concerned with digital archiving at association level. The committee manages its own projects but supports third party projects with a focus on education. It also promotes awareness of problems and increases understanding for all aspects of digital archiving.

Preservation

The job of maintaining the fonds is based on several principles and does not necessarily mean preserving fonds in their original form. The main problem is the lack of quality of industrially produced paper. The Federal Archives together with the Swiss NL is operating a mass neutralizing procedure to remove the acid from this paper and make it more durable. A new challenge is posed by the variety of information carriers and the conservation of audiovisual and electronic documents. In the audiovisual area particularly the Memoriav association focuses on methodology and project financing. Basically, the aim is to preempt any problems in order to keep restoration work to a minimum. This means that the purchase and use of information carriers suitable for archiving is an important part of prevention.

MUSEUMS AND MUSEOLOGY

Some Statistics

Switzerland has a total of more than 948 museums (as of 2006). This corresponds roughly to one museum per 8000 residents and is therefore the highest museum density in the world. The Swiss museum landscape is characterized by remarkable recent growth. In 1960, Switzerland had just 274 museums; in 1980, 508 and by 2000 there were already 923 museums. There are numerous reasons for this enormous growth (conserving the identity at the local, regional, and national levels; private collection activities, tourism, etc.). Swiss museums are well attended. Art museums (25%) and zoos (24%) accounted for a quarter each of all visitors. 26 Swiss museums (3% of all museums) had more than 100,000 visitors in 2006. Additional statistical data is available on the homepage for Association of Swiss Museum (http://www.vms-ams.ch).

National Museums

The federal government itself has only seven museums due to the federal character of Switzerland and the associated cultural primacy of the Cantons. Three cultural-historical museums are housed under "The Swiss National Museum" brand. The museum group possesses the most important cultural-historical collection in Switzerland encompassing some 1 million objects of national significance. The three museums forming the Swiss National Museum group provide a national and international looking glass into the culture and history of the Swiss living area. As museums for cultural history, the exhibitions, special exhibits and events focus on developments within the area referred to today as Switzerland; from prehistoric to early history up to the present day. They are dedicated to a broad meaning of the word culture that endeavors to merge history, applied and visual arts as well as historical settings into a comprehensive cultural-historical viewpoint. Details on the other Federal Museums are available on the homepage of the Swiss Federal Office of Culture (http://www.bak.admin.ch).

Major Museums at the Subnational Level

There are another 933 museums in addition to the federally-owned museums. Museums with national and to some extent even internationally acclaim include, among others: *Major art museums*:

- Foundation Beyeler
- Kunsthaus Zurich
- Kunstmuseum Basle
- Zentrum Paul Klee, Berne
- Museum of Fine Arts, Berne

Science and natural history museums:

- Museum of Transport, Lucerne
- Technorama, Winterthur
- Museum of Natural History of Geneva

Historical museums:

- Historical Museum Basle
- Historical Museum Bern

Zoos and botanical gardens:

- Zurich Zoo
- Basle Zoo
- Botanical gardens, Geneva

Digital Museum Exhibits and Services

Seventeen percent of Swiss museums have digitally recorded a significant portion of their collections. Only a few museums have, however, an Internet presence including a presentation platform for their collections.

Museology and Education

Basic and continuing education courses in museology are rather modest: for a number of years now, the Association of Swiss Museums (ASM) has offered a basic training course in museology in cooperation with the International Council of Museums, Swiss branch (ICOM) as well as various continuing education courses. At the university

level, the Universities of Neuenburg, Geneva, Lausanne, and Fribourg will begin offering a masters program in museology starting in the winter semester 2007/2008.

Professional Associations

The following larger associations are active in museums in Switzerland:

- Association of Swiss Museums (http://www.vms-ams.ch)
- International Council of Museums, Swiss branch (http://www.icom-suisse.ch)
- Swiss Association of museum cultural mediators (http://www.mediamus.ch)
- Swiss Association of Museologists (http://www.museologie.ch)
- Swiss Association for conservation and restoration (http://www.skr.ch)

Key Contemporary Issues

The key contemporary issues for museums include:

- Problems with financing due to a decline in public funding.
- Higher internal financing causing neglect in preservation activities of collections.
- High competitive pressure among museums compared to other leisure activities.

CONCLUSIONS

Switzerland's numerous museums, archives, and libraries are a visible sign of its concern to preserve its heritage and pass it on to future generations. The principal role of these institutions in showcasing a society and its culture is filled at the federal level by the Museums of the Confederation, the Federal Archives and the NL, but also as through the monetary support of the Federal Office of Culture (OFC). This office has the job of fomenting culture in all its diversity and making sure it can develop in complete independence. It supports creation in the fields of cinema, art, and design. Moreover, it promotes and encourages training for young Swiss people from abroad, and projects of the diverse linguistic and cultural communities. The OFC also oversees the conservation of the architectural heritage, monuments, and archeological sites which allow the passing on of knowledge from one generation to the next.

Culture may go on for ever, but it is far from being immutable. It evolves with the passing of time, through cross-fertilization and encounters made along the way. Like mankind, it can progress and develop. But it is vital to remember that every cultural manifestation owes its existence to what went before. Just as the values of the

Switzerland: Libraries, Archives, and Museums

past help us in our understanding of those of our everyday life, they need to be flaunted, exhibited, and studied. We need to preserve these treasures, both material and immaterial, if we are to ensure the survival of cultural values from before our time.

In terms of culture, the legacies of history are cataloged, preserved, and made as accessible to the public as possible by the museums, archives, and libraries. All citizens should understand the cultural universe in which they move, and should therefore have access to the subjects, the studies and the research which others before them have approached and gone into in depth. The places and institutions where these testimonies are preserved give an idea of humankind's incredible ingenuity. They display human creativity and fertile imagination. They demonstrate that when an artist creates a finished product to transcend, challenge, or discuss the original from which inspiration was drawn, something undeniably positive has taken place.

By definition, museums, archives, and libraries are vast sources and fascinating inventories of this variable but ongoing phenomenon we call culture. They are the custodians of the past, and by the same token the vectors of the future.

REFERENCES

1. For list of libraries accessible on-line see. http://www. switch.ch/libraries/.
2. http://www.ichschweiz.ch/bibliotheken.asp?lang=en.
3. http://www.nb.admin.ch.
4. http://www.chvk.ch/.
5. http://ead.nb.admin.ch/web/swiss-serials/psp_de.html.
6. BibliOpass—An Open Library Network in Switzerland/A. Rivier, J.-M. Rod Liber Quarterly,—The Journal of European Research Libraries vol. 16 (2006), no 1 Liber Quarterly.
7. http://www.nb.admin.ch/slb/slb_professionnel/ projektarbeit/00719/index.html?lang=fr.
8. http://www.nb.admin.ch/posters.
9. http://www.theeuropeanlibrary.org.
10. http://www.cenl.org.
11. http://www.rero.ch.
12. http://www.informationsverbund.ch/.
13. http://lib.consortium.ch.
14. http://www.swissbib.org.
15. http://en.memoriav.ch/.
16. http://doc.rero.ch/?ln=en.
17. http://www.bbt.admin.ch/index.html?lang=en.
18. http://www.aaid.ch/.
19. http://www.hesge.ch/heg/metiers_formations/form_hes_ bachelor/form_id.asp and http://www.fh-htwchur.ch/Informations-wissenschaft.17.0.html http://doc.rero.ch/?ln=en.
20. http://www.fh-htwchur.ch/Informations-wissenschaft.17.0. html.
21. http://www.bbs.ch.
22. http://www.bbs.ch/documents/BBS-SVD_Fusionsvertrag. pdf1182862246741.pdf.
23. Santschi, C. Archive, ch. 2.2: Gemeindearchive [communal records], in the Historic Dictionary of Switzerland (HLS), 11.02.2005 version, (translated from French). Available at http://www.hls-dhs-dss.ch/textes/d/D12820-3-2.php.) (accessed September 24, 2007).
24. Santschi, C. Archive, chap. 3: Privatarchive, in Historical Dictionary of Switzerland (HLS), Version dated 11.02.2005, (translated from French). Available at http:// www.hls-dhs-dss.ch/textes/d/D12820-1-2.php. (accessed September 24, 2007).

BIBLIOGRAPHY

1. Bodmer, J.-P. Zurich Central Library. In *Internatioal Dictionary of Library Histories*; Stam, D.H., Ed.; Fitzroy Dearborn: London, U.K, 2001; Vol. 2.
2. Coutaz, G.; Huber, R.; Kellerhals, A.; Pfiffner, A.; Roth-Lochner, B. *Archivpraxis in der Schweiz/Pratiques archivistiques en Suisses*, Heirt+Jetzt-Verlag, Baden, 2007.
3. Luck, R. Swiss National Library. In *International Dictionary of Library Histories*; Stam, D.H., Ed.; Fitzroy Dearborn: London, U.K., 2001; Vol. 2.

Student–Taxonomy

Tanzania: Libraries, Archives, Museums, and Information Systems

Janet Kaaya
Department of Information Studies, University of California, Los Angeles, California, U.S.A.

Abstract

This entry outlines the historical development and current status of library and information systems and services in Tanzania. It places emphasis on the Tanzania Library Services Board, which includes the National Central Library and which constitutes a hub of the library system in the country, and its key players in that evolution. It also covers academic libraries; school and children's libraries; special libraries and specialized information services and agencies; archival systems; museums; botanical gardens, zoos and herbaria; professional development and associations; and scholarly publishing. Finally, the entry touches on policy initiatives related to information and communications technology-enhanced information services and learning for national development. The majority of libraries in Tanzania were created immediately after that country's independence in 1961, with the exception of a few libraries that were established and run by private bodies or by colonial government-sponsored associations to cater to their members. Therefore, most of the existing libraries developed out of not only the Government's need to exercise its responsibility for developing a literate society but also its recognition of the fact that libraries and similar institutions are important elements of a nation's cultural heritage. It is because of this that libraries and other agencies covered in this entry were created as central institutions for preserving and disseminating information resources and providing information systems to support learning and research for national development. The Tanzanian government and its agencies provide funds for most library and related operations.

INTRODUCTION

Tanzania (also known as the United Republic of Tanzania) is located in East Africa, bordering the Indian Ocean to the east; Kenya and Uganda to the north; Burundi, Congo DR and Rwanda to the west; and Malawi, Mozambique, and Zambia to the south. The country occupies a total of 364,900 sq. mi (945,087 sq. km) of which 22,799 sq. mi (59,050 sq. km) constitute water bodies. The climate varies from tropical along the Indian Ocean coast, semi-arid in the central parts to temperate in the highlands (lowest elevation is 0—sea level—and the highest elevation is 19,340 ft or 5895 m—Mt. Kilimanjaro). The estimated population as of July 2007 is 39,384,223 with the annual growth rate of 2.1%[1] and, according to 2002 census, the adult literacy rate was estimated at 69.4%. Kiswahili/Swahili is the national language while both Swahili and English are official languages. English is primarily the language of commerce, administration, and higher education. There are about 120 ethnic groups each with its own language plus several dialects in each group; however, Swahili is a common language spoken by everybody and as a medium of instruction in all public primary schools (most private primary schools use English as a medium of instruction). The official capital of Tanzania is Dodoma, but most government business and commercial activity is conducted in Dar es Salaam. The government is gradually moving to Dodoma (all parliamentary sessions are held there).

Historically, the country was colonized by Germans in the late nineteenth century. After World War I, it was under British administration (it was then called Tanganyika). It became independent on December 9, 1961 and united with Zanzibar in 1964 to become what is now known as Tanzania. The country is divided into 21 administrative regions on the mainland (former Tanganyika) and 5 in Zanzibar (Fig. 1). Zanzibar has its own government and a parliament while the union government administers the mainland part of the country along with such key union government ministries as foreign affairs, national security, and defense.

Tanzania's economy is still dependent on agriculture, accounting for about 40% of the country's Gross Domestic Product (GDP); other sectors are industry (18% GDP) and services (39% GDP). The country's current GDP's real growth rate stands at about 7% and the estimated GDP per capita is $1300.[1]

In terms of indicators for information and communications technologies (ICTs) and associated services, the capacity of existing networks is generally low but with

Encyclopedia of Library and Information Sciences, Fourth Edition DOI: 10.1081/E-ELIS4-120043540

Fig. 1 Map of Tanzania showing administrative regions: 1) Currently, there are branch TLSB libraries (regional libraries) in all but two mainland regions (Manyara and Singida); 2) Zanzibar (Unguja and Pemba) has five regions—Pemba North (Wete), Pemba South (Mkoani), Zanzibar Central/South (Koani), Zanzibar North (Mkokotoni), and Zanzibar Urban/West (Zanzibar); 3) Map reproduced with owner's permission.

great potential for expanding digital mobile capacity. While there are only 240,000 estimated subscribers of landline telephones (0.58% penetration), there are nearly 9.5 million subscribers of cell phone services which is about 24% penetration. There are about 20,800 Internet hosts in Tanzania providing services to some 400,000 users according to 2007 estimates.[1,2] However, it is difficult to estimate the number of Internet users in Tanzania as well as in most other African countries since most Internet users get the service through public access points (such as Internet cafes, schools, libraries, offices, etc, even via a neighbor's computer) rather than individual ownership of access terminals. For more indicators, see Table 1.

The country has a network of libraries and information centers which include the Tanzania Library Services Board's National Central Library (NCL) with its branches in 19 regions, special libraries that also include those under different government departments, academic libraries [the major ones being those of the University of Dar es Salaam (UDSM) and Sokoine University of Agriculture (SUA)], school libraries, and several libraries or information centers under nongovernmental organizations (NGOs) and international cultural relations agencies. In addition, there are specialized information services—with or without library support—that take advantage of evolving ICTs to provide services to users. This entry describes these libraries and information centers, along with existing records administration and archival systems; museums; botanical gardens, herbaria and zoos; scholarly publishing situation; professional development in library and information sciences; professional associations; and an outline of key policy initiatives that advocate the role of ICTs in national development. There are parallel services in Zanzibar, mostly under the Zanzibar Central Library and the Department of Archives, Museums, and Antiquities.[7]

Table 1 Tanzania: Country characteristics and key ICT/development indicators.

Country name	Tanzania (or United Republic of Tanzania)
Region	East Africa
Size	364,900 sq. mi (945,087 sq. km)
Capital	Dodoma [pop. 324,347]; Major city: Dar es Salaam [pop. 2,497,940] (2002 census);
Population	34,569,232 (2002 census); 39,384,223 (2007 est.)
Independence	December 9, 1961
Legal system	Founded on English common law
Governance	Executive branch (President, Vice President); legislative branch (National Assembly); judicial branch (Chief Justice)
Languages	Swahili (national; official; primary education); English (official; commercial; higher education); more than 120 indigenous languages and dialects
Adult literacy rate	69.4% [male 77.5%; female 62.2%] (2002 census)
Combined primary, secondary, and tertiary gross enrolment ratio	50.4% [global average: 67.8] (2005 est.)
Life expectancy at birth	51.5 years (2007 est.)
People living with HIV/AIDS	6.5% of the population (2005 est.)
GDP contribution by sector	42.8% agriculture; 38.7% service; 18.4% industry (2007 est.)
GDP growth rate	7.3% (2007 est.)
Inflation rate	7% (2007 est)
GDP per capita	US$ 1,300 (2007 est.)
Currency	Tanzanian Shilling, TSh (1 TSh = 100 cents
Human development index value	0.467 [global average: 0.743] (2005 est.)
Internet hosts	20,757 (2007 est.)
Internet users	400,000 [1% pop.] (2007 est.)
Telephone subscribers	Landlines: 236,500 [0.58% pop]; Cell phones: 9,358,000 [23.8% pop.] (2007 est.)
Number of radio stations	47 (year 2006)
Number of TV Stations	29 (year 2006)
Number of newspapers distributed nationwide	42 (2005 est.)

Source: Adapted from CIA,[1] Internet World Stats,[2] UNAIDS/WHO,[3] UNDP,[4] ITU,[5] and TCRA.[6]

LIBRARY AND INFORMATION SYSTEMS AND SERVICES

Public Libraries (see Appendix A—Chronology)

Pre-independence synopsis

It has been well established that certain kinds of written materials in the form of book or manuscript collections were in existence during precolonial period in Tanzania. There are Swahili manuscripts dating back to the 1790s (see Swahili Manuscripts Database from the School of Tropical and Oriental Studies' Web site at http://www.swahilimanuscripts.soas.ac.uk/, accessed August 20, 2008). Also, there are indications that there likely existed a library within the ancient city of Kilwa Kisiwani along the East African coast of present southern Tanzania[8] characterized by current medieval ruins in Kilwa (For pictures of the ruins see http://en.wikipedia.org/wiki/Kilwa_Kisiwani or http://www.utalii.com/Off_the_normal_ path/kilwa.htm or http://www.umiacs.umd.edu/~yaser/AFRICA06/kilwa.html, accessed February 28, 2008). However, the history of modern library services in Tanzania is relatively short and most of the current network of libraries for public access in the country was developed after independence in 1961. Prior to that, library services were tied to those of the other two East African countries (Kenya and Uganda) which—like Tanzania—were under the British colonial administration until early 1960s. Further, like in many other African countries such as Nigeria,[9] the first modern libraries to be established in Tanzania were special libraries that aimed to serve specific information needs of colonial rulers and their interests, thus not accessible to general public. As Olden[10] states:

> Libraries were the tool of the colonial state in the sense that the earliest collections had been built up around agricultural and mining research institutes, which were concerned with maximizing cash crops of value to the imperial power or with the exploitation of mineral resources and with the running of government secretariats and law courts [69]. But, as has been shown, library provision in Tanganyika at the time of independence was meager indeed (p. 440).

Therefore, at independence, there were three broad categories of libraries in Tanzania:[11,12]

- Libraries with restricted access such as those run by colleges, schools, various government agencies clubs, and other voluntary agencies;
- Subscription libraries—open to people who could afford a fee, such as King George VI Memorial Library in Tanga, Ismailia Community libraries and the libraries under the East African Literature Bureau (EALB);
- Freely accessible libraries, only two—the British Council Library/British Information Service and the United States Information Services.

Early pre-independence efforts

In 1944, the East African governments decided to commission an expert, E. Huxley, to conduct a survey on the state of library and literature services, and to suggest best ways to develop library services in East Africa. He submitted his report to the three governments in 1945.

Subsequently, the EALB was founded in 1948 as a constituent component of the East African High Commission (EAHC) which was also created in the same year to "administer services common to Tanganyika, Zanzibar, Kenya, and Uganda" (p. 423).[10] The first EALB librarian was George Annesley, and the funding for establishing the Bureau was made available through the colonial Development and Welfare Fund. The Bureau's main objective was to address an ever-increasing demand for documents among Africans. Annesley studied Huxley's report and prepared another report that centered on implementing Huxley's 1945 recommendations. Prior to that, according to Ilomo[11] "the first library legislation of its kind in the history of Tanzania, the Municipalities Ordinance, was enacted in 1946" (p. 99) to empower town and municipal entities to build and run libraries for their constituents. However, the Ordinance didn't work because it lacked strategies for resource allocations. The EALB started a library service in Tanganyika in 1951, based in Dar es Salaam. The library also maintained book collections in 76 centers around the country and provided services through postal services for users not served through the established centers.

In 1953, the Bureau Librarian attended a United Nations Educational, Scientific, and Cultural Organization (UNESCO) seminar (For more details about the seminar see: UNESCO. *Development of Public Libraries in Africa: The Ibadan Seminar*; UNESCO Public Library Manuals, No. 6; UNESCO: Paris, 1954; 1–153.) on public libraries in Ibadan-Nigeria. Thereafter, he visited Ghana, whose Library Board was already well established and considered a good example of library systems for Africa (it seems several African countries later decided to adopt the Ghanaian model of national library services). Meanwhile, the British Government had adopted a policy of developing library services in East Africa. Thus in 1959 the Colonial Secretary, Sir Alan Lennox Boyd, sent a dispatch No. 932 dated August 27, 1959 to the EAHC's Administrator, regarding the British Government's proposal to finance library development in East Africa via the British Council.[13] As a result, the Colonial Office approved the appointment of S.W. Hockey as the libraries organizer in East Africa under the British Council, owing to his previous 15 years of similar experience in the British West Indies.[13] Hockey conducted a survey of then existing library facilities and prepared a report on the development of library services in East Africa; this was later submitted to East African governments. He recommended the following: 1) appointment of a library board; 2) establishment of a pilot library project, followed by construction of a central library; 3) progressive establishment of regional branch libraries around the country plus mobile libraries; 4) development of a school library service; and 5) coordination of government library resources.

Postindependence developments

By early 1961, Tanganyika which had already been given internal self-government by Britain, was preparing for its Independence Day and was the first East African country to accept the Hockey Report.[13,14] Furthermore, in July 1961, the Government of Tanganyika adopted a postindependence 3-year Development Plan 1961/1962–1963/1964 that also comprised strategies for library development. The plan included a proposal to build a new NCL that could serve as: 1) a public library service from the City of Dar es Salaam; 2) a national library to house all printed items received under legal deposit; and 3) the administrative head office for nationwide public and school library systems. It was not possible to implement the plan because the anticipated director did not arrive early. The government created a library planning committee to recommend ways of implementing the plan.

Tanganyika became independent on December 9, 1961 and the following year the government enacted the Libraries (Deposit of Books) Act 1962. The Act required that each Tanganyikan publisher would give a copy of each of their books(s) to the University College of Dar es Salaam—later the University of Dar es Salaam.[11] In October 1962, the Library Planning Committee met and decided that the anticipated national library service be called the Tanganyika Library Services (TLS), and necessary legislation to that effect was developed. Mr. Hockey, in consultation with the EALB director, was responsible for drafting that legislation.[11–13] On July 11, 1963, President J.K. Nyerere assented to the TLS Board Act (see http://www.parliament.go.tz/Polis/PAMS/Docs/39-1963.pdf). This was amended by an Act of Parliament No. 6 of 1975 (http://www.parliament.go.tz/Polis/PAMS/Docs/6-1975.pdf) to replace the name "Tanganyika" with "Tanzania" and to broaden the functions of TLSB (accessed September 2, 2008 from the Tanzania Parliament's Web site http://www.parliament.go.tz/) of 1963 with the objectives to: promote, establish, equip, manage, maintain, and develop libraries in Tanganyika (followed the Ghanaian model of national library services).

In August 1963, Edward Maxwell Broome arrived in Tanganyika to take up his responsibility as the first Director of Library Services (there was no single trained local librarian at the time). He immediately started necessary consultations with the architects for a new NCL. The TLS Board was appointed on November 1, 1963 and commenced its work immediately. Between November 1, 1963 and March 31, 1964, TLS operated under the auspices of the EALB from which it inherited books, equipment, funds, and staff. The library started with an initial collection of 30,000 volumes inherited from EALB plus 20,000 volumes donated to Tanganyika by the British Council (very few of the books were cataloged). The library had one full time librarian, the director, and one part time staff. The library lacked effective services to open to public until early 1965. According to Kaungamno and Ilomo:[12]

> the Pilot Library earlier envisaged by the Hockey Report was opened to the residents of Dar es Salaam in a make-shift building along Suleiman Street, later renamed as Mkwepu Street. Response to this new service was considerable. In fact it was an overwhelming success although some people seemed to be satisfying their personal curiosity and therefore did not register for membership. The greatest response came from school children and students who have since formed the backbone of users of TLS libraries. As far as adults were concerned, the majority who visited the libraries were foreigners. This is understandable because they came from countries where libraries had long been established and assimilated into their culture and social structure. The number of African adults was quite substantial and [they] used the library for study and reference purposes (p. 94).

Generally, for the new director, it was challenging, but he experienced a smooth start because he enjoyed an especially favorable political environment provided by a new nationalist government; and, as such, he was able to carry out his duties effectively. The new institution was created on a firm foundation.[12]

To make provision for the depository status to TLS, Libraries (Deposit of Books) Order 1963 was enacted to amend the Libraries (Deposit of Books) Act 1962. Further development led to the rebirth of TLS as a semiautonomous body (a parastatal organization) under the Ministry of Education, with its head office in Dar es Salaam. In the same year, TLS opened its first branch in Iringa Town (southern Tanzania) with its library located in a makeshift building. On July 1, 1964, the government adopted the TLS Board's Library Development Plan and incorporated it into the National Five-Year Plan 1964–1969. In 1965, the King George VI Memorial Library in Tanga and the Kilimanjaro Native Cooperative Union Library in Moshi were absorbed into TLS, abolishing the subscription system.[14]

President J.K. Nyerere opened the new building of the NCL on December 9, 1967 to mark 6 years of independence. In his address he said:[11,14]

> When I formally open this building today on the sixth anniversary of our independence, we shall be taking a further step towards the fulfilment of the goals we set ourselves in 1954, at the beginning of TANU. For we shall be marking the beginning of another opportunity for self-improvement and dignified enjoyment, by the citizens of our free country. ...books are very important way to knowledge and to self-improvement; from them we can learn ideas, new techniques of working and new methods. We can learn about the development of man and all its different aspects; we can broaden our understanding of other people, and even of ourselves. All experiences of mankind, all his discoveries and his inventions, can be

> learned about through reading....the real importance to our nation of this Central Library derives from the fact that it is the hub of the wheel from which spokes will reach out to towns and villages throughout mainland Tanzania....would like to give everyone an assurance that the Tanzania Government will continue to give to the work you have started all support which is within its power.

In its effort to spread library services throughout the country, the TLS opened two branch libraries in 1968; one in Mwanza (south of Lake Victoria) and another in a permanent building in Iringa. Other branches followed suit, including Bukoba (west of Lake Victoria, 1969); Arusha and Moshi (northern highlands, 1970), Kibaha (about 20 mi west of Dar es Salaam, 1970); Morogoro (about 120 mi west of Dar es Salaam, 1974); Tabora (western Tanzania, 1976); Mbeya (southern highlands); Mtwara (south-eastern); Musoma in Mara (east of Lake Victoria, 1979); Sumbawanga in Rukwa (south-western Tanzania, 1983); Dodoma (central Tanzania and the new capital, 1997); and Lindi (south-eastern Tanzania, 1998). Apart from its own funds, the Government received foreign support to construct branch libraries; for instance Denmark funded nine libraries, the United Kingdom (one library), other Nordic countries (one), and one was acquired from the King George VI Memorial Trust. As early as 1964, the TLS Board started to locate and acquire suitable sites, particularly in the hearts of major shopping, trading and employment centers, for its network of libraries with full support from the newly independent government. Later, new regional libraries were opened in Kigoma, Mtwara, Ruvuma, and Shinyanga, plus several district and divisional libraries (For more details about TLS and a list of regional and district libraries visit the TLS' Web site at http://www.tlsb.or.tz/default.asp, accessed August 20, 2008).

Libraries and literacy education

On July 1, 1969, the Government of Tanzania adopted the Second Library Plan and incorporated it into the Second National Five-Year Development Plan 1969–1974.[15] The plan placed emphasis on extending library services to rural areas using both fixed and mobile libraries; building six branch libraries; and establishing a school library service. Later in the year, a UNESCO-supported project for rural library service was inaugurated. This literacy enhancement-oriented project started in Mwanza Region. While addressing the nation for the New Year on December 31, 1969, President Nyerere declared 1970 as an adult education year. He said:[14,16]

> We all have to be students, that is, we all have to be willing to learn, and anxious to use every method of learning that is available to us ... we have to be willing to teach whatever skills we have by whatever method we can—by

demonstration and example, by discussion, by answering questions or by formal classroom work. If we play our part, both as students and teachers, we shall really make some progress ... the importance of adult education both for our country and every individual cannot be over emphasized.

Libraries, through TLS, were instrumental in the successful implementation of adult education campaign,[17–22] complemented by the use of Swahili as a universal language in Tanzania and the enforcement of universal primary education. One of the functions bestowed to Tanzania Library Services Board (TLSB), in the Act of Parliament that established it, states: "to initiate, sponsor, participate in, finance, and assist in campaigns for the eradication of illiteracy" [See Appendix B,[4] (1f)]. The TLS took part in the establishment of about 3000 village/rural libraries, coordinated bookmobile service in rural areas, and a book lending program by mail for library users from remote parts of the country. These mobile library services were also extended to secondary schools and colleges.[23] However, the mobile library services were later disbanded in the mid-1980s due to economic constraints. In addition, radio and cinema programs were widely used in that campaign, and rural newspapers were as important as books. Dahlgren[18] notes that, in implementing the national literacy campaign, the government of Tanzania:

> recognized the need for printed materials to eradicate illiteracy. So in 1974 Unesco [UNESCO] and a Norwegian agency funded a monthly rural newspaper called *Elimu haina mwisho* (*Education has no end*) and experienced instant success. It has a standard format of four pages: national news, local news, miscellany, and practical matters; and has a circulation of about 100,000 (p. 4).

Clearly, pre-independence colonial government in Tanzania did not give due priority to literacy education; for instance, at the time of independence in 1961 the adult literacy rate was mere 15%.[24] When J.K. Nyerere launched literacy campaign on December 31, 1969, the literacy rate was nearly 24% (his aim was to eradicate illiteracy by 1975). By the mid-1980s when he retired, the adult literacy rate had surpassed 90%,[19,24–28] but it has now gone down to around 69%. Many development scholars blame "side-effects" of the Structural Adjustment programs of the 1990s for this dismal reverse of illiteracy in Africa and other related regions.[28,29] However, the government is currently implementing several programs to improve the situation, including reemphasizing universal primary education, adult education, and vocational training, as well as improving library services.[24,30]

Bibliographic Control

In April 1975, the Parliament enacted the Tanzania Library Services Board Act 1975 that repealed the 1963 Library Act and widened the Board's functions, responsibilities, and powers relating to, for example, documentation services, professional training, promoting literacy education, and advocating development of indigenous literature (For details, see http://www.parliament.go.tz/Polis/PAMS/Docs/6-1975.pdf, accessed August 20, 2008). Subsequently, TLS established the Tanzania National Documentation Centre to disseminate information via such services as bibliographic, referral, reference, document delivery, and current awareness—especially in key sectors of agriculture, industry, health, and education.

Also, the National Bibliographic Agency was founded in 1983 "to collect, record, and conserve the national literacy output for current use and for posterity,"[12] and one of its products was the Tanzania National Bibliography. In the same year, the African Standing Conference on Bibliographic Control was held in Tanzania. At that meeting, UNESCO pledged to supply a microcomputer to facilitate processing and storage of information; to that end, TLS received the package in 1985. Subsequently, TLS created a national bibliographic database using UNESCO-supplied CDS-ISIS program (does not require software-license fee). Minja[31] reports that TLSB implemented the Windows version of CDS-ISIS, WINSIS, to facilitate the production of the *Tanzania National Bibliography* (TNB). Apart from producing TNB, the Agency administers allocation of ISBNs and ISSNs in Tanzania on behalf of the International ISBN Agency (London) and the Centre International de l'ISSN (Paris). In doing so, the agency promotes standardization of bibliographic records in Tanzania.[32]

Shifts in institutional structures and policies

In a major shift in the development of library services in Tanzania, TLS introduced user registration fees in 1996. This turn of events has since been received with skepticism, because it seems to contradict various national policies and priorities of ridding Tanzania of poverty and illiteracy.[8,33–35] Many government-run functional literacy campaigns (including those related to preventive medicine and modern farming) need to go hand in hand with free access to and use of library services. Matovelo and Lwehabura[8] have explored and discussed wider implications of users fees for socioeconomic development of Tanzania and other developing countries, noting,

> Discouraging a fee for basic library services for the time being may have a positive impact on the long-term social and economic development. For libraries in economically less developed countries, this time should be considered as the time for investing in the value information and expansion as well as creation of public library clientele [and] library services demand. It should be a period of advocacy rather than [a period of] restrictions and barriers to the service (p. 26).

Also, Malmgren[35] reports the introduction of user registration fees at Arusha Regional Library led to decreased library use by women. Malmgren notes "One conclusion that is possible to draw from this is that one of the greatest effects of introducing membership fees was that adult women stopped coming to the library while the share of adult men increased." (p. 31) However, other observers looked at this development from a different angle. For instance, Mlaki[36] reported initial success: "The new procedure for membership enrolment is proving successful. Actually it has reduced the congestion of users and many library users are now feeling responsible for the library facilities" (p. 171).

Other developments that might have affected the structure and functions of TLS include local government reform measures that were introduced in the mid-1990s. Under these measures, the local governments would take up some role in running public libraries in their constituencies; as such TLS is gradually decentralizing many of its functions and responsibilities. Consequently, local government library boards were established in 1997.[36] Currently, TLS and regional or local authorities have established a partnership in which these authorities cover construction costs for new library buildings while TLS provides furniture, equipment, reading materials, and expertise. In view of these developments and other challenges facing TLS, the TLSB launched the institution's five-year strategic plan (1999–2004) in November 1999 which addressed the following issues as the Board's key development components:[37,38] fund raising, decentralization of regional libraries, rehabilitation of library buildings, human resources development, establishment of regional libraries, collection development, strengthening extension services, and strengthening the School of Library, Archives and Documentation Studies (SLADS), increased automation of TLS information systems, marketing of library services, introduction of civic education in regional libraries, revival of the printing unit, professional support, and staff development.

The current organizational structure of TLSB comprises the Board Chairperson who is appointed by the President of Tanzania and 10 board members appointed by the minister responsible for education, plus the Director General of TLS as the Board's secretary (ex-officio). The Board is responsible for policy formulation and implementation. Even though the main library building in Dar es Salaam is popularly known as the NCL, there is no mention of a national library in the Act that established the TLS Board (1975) or its 1963 predecessor. Kaungamno (the former director) and Ilomo (the former chief librarian) contend that,[12]

> It would seem that the Government feared that if the NCL were designated as a NL for Tanzania, TLS would probably be unable to perform adequately the proper functions of a NL and those of a public library network. In the

1970s, the government decided to establish a NL in Dodoma (sic!). It would also seem that the idea was born after the new capital city planners had visited capital cities in the world. Indeed national libraries are prestigious institutions. They optimize the cultures and intellectualism of the countries which have them. As a progressive country, Tanzania would not wish to lag behind in this respect. In mooting the idea of a NL, librarians were not consulted. It was an independent decision... (p. 133).

The TLS collection includes about 802,834 book volumes and 900 titles of periodicals (456,002 pieces) including newspapers.[31,39] It is estimated that the system acquires about 20,750 volumes of books annually (via purchase, exchange programs, and donations) and employs about 80 professionals, 60 paraprofessionals, and around 215 support staff.[31] In addition, TLS currently maintains a total of 143,340 registered users and about 13,762,083 occasional users.[39] Public access to the Internet at NCL is based on a cybercafé layout operated by the library; that is, users pay to use library computers.[40]

Cultural–educational relations and NGO libraries/information centers

The history of library development in Tanzania is also associated with the existence of several libraries or information centers that were established by foreign nations with bilateral relations with Tanzania to foster mutual cultural understandings. In addition, there are libraries or information centers operated by local and international NGOs and intergovernmental organizations. Almost all of them are based in Dar es Salaam. Notable examples include the Thomas R. Pickering Information Resource Center which is "a research and reference service of the U.S. Department of State, specializing in current U.S. Policy, Democratization, Rule of Law and Human Rights, Trade Liberalization, and Media. It promotes understanding between Tanzanians and Americans by providing information on topics important to our bilateral relationship" (For details on the services offered, visit http://tanzania.usembassy.gov/irc.html, accessed September 1, 2008 from the Embassy of the United States in Tanzania Web site, http://tanzania.usembassy.gov/index.html). The British Council and its library have for years been a destination for students and other users for information resources. (For details, visit the British Council Information Services Web site at http://www.britishcouncil.org/tanzania-information-services.htm, accessed September 1, 2008.) Others include the Alliance Francaise (for details see Alliance Francaise Dar es Salaam Web site at http://www.ambafrance-tz.org/rubrique.php3?id_rubrique=54, accessed August 20, 2008), the Russian Tanzanian Cultural Centre, Iranian Cultural Centre, Korean Cultural Centre, and Libyan Cultural Centre.

Like other similar centers worldwide, the United Nations Information Center in Dar es Salaam (see http://www.unic.undp.org/, accessed September 1, 2008) informs the public of the aims and activities of the United Nation. It is therefore a

unique source for UN documents, reports, and public information materials, including complete coverage of the proceedings of UN conferences; sessions of the General Assembly; Security Council; Economic and Social Council; and other UN bodies dealing with such issues as peacekeeping, peacemaking, human rights, disarmament, economic and social development, environment, disaster relief, refugees, and election monitoring.[41]

Another important UN agency, the International Criminal Tribunal for Rwanda (ICTR), maintains a specialized library (for details, visit the ICTR's Library homepage at http://69.94.11.53/default.htm, accessed September 20, 2008) on international criminal law. Based in Arusha, the library also maintains databases and other resources on international criminal law, and "Given its location in the East African region, which is increasingly sought after for information searches by law societies, legal institutions and universities of the host country and its neighbours, the ICTR library is rapidly establishing itself as the Legal Reference Library in the subregion."[42]

One notable example of NGO libraries is the African Medical Foundation's Information Centre and its Online Resource Centre (for details visit AMREF's Web site at http://www.amref.org/info-centre/online-resource-centre/our-services/, accessed August 21, 2008) that provides such services as reference, document lending, and online access to full-text resources. Membership registration at a fee is required.

Academic Libraries

UDSM and academic libraries

The academic library system in Tanzania has for years been associated with the country's main institution of higher learning, the UDSM. This university was established in 1970 following a decision by three East African nations of Kenya, Tanzania, and Uganda to elevate three constituent colleges of the University of East Africa to create three independent universities for each country: Makerere University (Uganda), UDSM (Tanzania), and the University of Nairobi (Kenya). The University College of Dar es Salaam itself dates back to 1961 along with the existence of its library under Harold Holdsworth as its first librarian.[10] All other Tanzanian universities are relatively recent and the second largest one, SUA, was UDSM's faculty of agriculture until it became a full-fledged university in 1984. Moreover, the university

library at SUA serves as the National Agricultural Library (this was established the Sokoine National Agricultural Library Act, 1991, (see http://www.parliament.go.tz/Polis/PAMS/Docs/21-1991.pdf, accessed from the Parliament of Tanzania's Web site) and a legal deposit center for related publications in Tanzania. Similarly, the Muhimbili University of Health and Allied Medicine (MUHAS), as well as Ardhi University (lands and architectural studies) were until 2007 the constituent colleges of UDSM. The library at MUHAS maintains the largest collection of medical-related information resources in the country.

The UDSM has seven faculties (equivalent to schools in the U.S. universities), three constituent colleges and eight institutes and centers (for details visit UDSM's Web site at http://www.udsm.ac.tz/, for academic units, see http://www.udsm.ac.tz/academic_units/academic.html). Its student population is about 13,000 and still growing (see http://www.library.udsm.ac.tz/about_us/index.php, accessed February 20, 2008 from the University of Dar es Salaam's Library and Information Services Web site) plus about 800 faculty members.[43] As noted above, the development and status of academic libraries in Tanzania essentially reflect those of UDSM and, like UDSM, they face increasing student enrollment challenges. Some students from these other universities have sought to use UDSM library facilities[44,45] under informal or formal arrangements. This library maintains substantial volumes of monographs, journal subscriptions, newspaper collection, maps, government publications, the East Africana collection, manuscripts, and other specialized collections. (For details see the UDSM-Library's Web site at http://www.library.udsm.ac.tz/index.php and its guide at http://www.library.udsm.ac.tz/about_us/Library_giude.php, accessed August 20, 2008.) These are searched via the Library's online public access catalog as well as its backup manual catalog. The library maintains its own IT unit for coordinating automation of services, ensuring their quality control, and for providing digital resources and corresponding information literacy training to the academic community. The law library at UDSM maintains the largest collection of legal materials in East Africa[44] and it is included in the university-wide public online catalog.

Policy shifts and expansion of institutions of higher learning in the 1990s

Until around mid-1990s the national education policy stipulated that higher learning education should be under government control and public funded. As Kiondo[46] puts it,

These universities were fully financed by public funds as part of the Tanzanian policy that major socio economic and political activities were strictly under government control. In the late 1980s and 1990s the burden of strict control of educational and other sectors was too heavy for the government to bear. Under strict austerity measures the capacity of the universities to fulfil the key mission and run its activities was severely affected ...At another level, the pressure of globalisation and the need for socio-economic and political reform as a way forward for sustainable development have had tremendous impact on Tanzanian society. One of [the] significant impacts has been the dramatic shift in the management of national affairs through a liberalisation policy [that] has led major reforms in almost every sector including the education sector. Under the Education sector reform, privately funded Universities were for the first time established. At the same time, there was a dire need to expand access to higher education in state owned Universities by increasing enrolment and to transform them to modern universities of the 21st century.

Therefore, both government and the private sector—including NGOs—established new universities and the Government started to expand existing public universities.

Thus, additional institutions include the Open University of Tanzania (public, distance learning, founded in 1992; with branches in all regions); Tumaini University (private, established in 1996 under the Lutheran Church in Tanzania) with four constituent colleges; St. Augustine University of Tanzania (private, established in 1998 under the Catholic Church) with three constituent colleges; Mt. Meru University (private, accredited in 2005, founded and managed by the Baptist Churches of East Africa and the Southern Baptist Convention of the United States); The Hubert Kairuki Memorial University (private; established 1997, accredited in 2000); the International Medical and Technological University, Dar es Salaam (private; established 1995); the Dar es Salaam Institute of Technology (public, established 1997); The University of Arusha (private, formerly Tanzania Adventist College under the Seventh-Day Adventist Church); and Mzumbe University (public, established in 2001). Others are the University of Dodoma (abbreviated UDOM, public, established 2007. This is the newest public university that is "designed to be a comprehensive university, which will train and produce human capital in the major professions for economic development. UDOM will enrol 40,000 students when fully operational," (http://www.udom.ac.tz/the%20University.html, accessed September 1, 2008); Saint John's University of Tanzania (private, established in 2007 under the Anglican Church of Tanzania); Stefano Moshi Memorial University College (private, established in 2007 under the Lutheran Church in Tanzania); the Aga Khan University—Tanzania Institute of Higher Education (private, under the Aga Khan Foundation); Teofilo Kisanji University (private, established in 1996 under the Moravian Church in Tanzania); and Muslim University of Morogoro (private, established in 2004 under the Muslim Development Foundation).

In Zanzibar, there are three universities: State University of Zanzibar (public, established in 2002), Zanzibar University (private, under the Darul Iman Charitable Association, opened in 1998), and Zanzibar/Chukwani College of Education (private, under the International University of Africa, Khartoum). For the status of libraries and related information services of these institutions see their URLs in Appendix C and click their library links.

Changing roles and challenges

Like other academic libraries all over the world, academic libraries in Tanzania are responding to many challenges of the twenty-first century that have prompted their universities to undergo major transformations.[47] These universities and other institutions of higher learning have to design market-driven academic and research programs and to increase enrollments in both the traditional and new programs, coupled with improvement of overall university infrastructure in order to meet national manpower demands. Correspondingly, academic libraries are challenged to support their institutions to meet their academic and research missions in an ever-changing environment of information-resource landscape. To that end, Nkhoma-Wamunza[45] observes (p. 37):

> the role and survival of academic and research libraries depends largely on their ability to satisfy and meet user needs from a wide range of disciplines, and the extent to which they have effectively integrated library and IT resources to support teaching, learning and research and service to the community as well as their ability to build comprehensive and balanced collections.

These challenges are even more important in many developing country academic libraries where their nations are striving to increase human resources capacity to meet the needs of developing economies. In that connection, Kiondo[46] underscores the role of university libraries in the context of Tanzania (p. 2):

> In the process of transforming Tanzanian [u]niversities into modern [u]niversities, libraries have been part and parcel of the process by undertaking several innovative activities. These include applying Information Technology in organisation and management of information services, imparting new skills to staff, building databases and providing electronic information services.

To that end, one of the initiatives that UDSM Library has taken is to forge special arrangements with other institutions and organizations, such as the International Network for the Availability of Scientific Publications (INASP), to ensure access to information resources in various forms and means,[45] including the Programme for the Enhancement of Research Information. (For details see http://www.inasp.info/file/104/peri-programme-for-the-enhancement-of-research-information.html, accessed September 20, 2008.) This goes hand in hand with staff and user training and retraining on new information services and their applications especially in utilizing electronic resources and embracing the whole concept of "digital libraries" and its implication in the LIS school curricula.[43,48] Also, in collaboration with the Norwegian International Development Agency, UDSM Library microfilmed its East Africana (apart from its notable manuscript collection, the East Africana Collection includes government publications, United Nations documents, maps, theses and the liberation movement materials. The Tanzanian legal deposit materials are kept in this section) manuscripts as well as its newspaper collection for improved access and preservation; and it contributes to the Database of African Theses and Dissertations under the Association of African Universities. The UDSM participates in the African Virtual University, "a technology-enhanced learning network to increase access to quality higher education for those living in sub-Saharan African countries." (For details visit http://www.avu-lc.udsm.ac.tz/index.html and http://www.distancelearning-tz.org/, accessed September 20, 2008.)

School Libraries and Library Services for Children

School libraries

School libraries cater to thousands of primary and secondary schools in Tanzania. In 2008, 8,410,094 pupils were enrolled in about 15,673 primary schools; most of the schools (more than 14,440) were government schools.[30,48,49] The enrollment in secondary schools was 1,222,403 in 3798 schools.[49] The net enrollment ratio for primary school was equivalent to 96.1% in 2006; however, on average, each required text book was shared by three pupils[49] underlining the importance of school libraries to fill the gap and to provide other information resources to school communities. To that end, postindependent development of library services went hand in hand with concerted efforts to develop school libraries in the country. For example, in 1965, Mary Tizzard, then Head of Schools and Children's Services at TLS, conducted a survey of school libraries and produced a report which would have set a foundation for improving school libraries in the country.[11,14] However, her report was never published or implemented due to ensuing events. For example, in that year (i.e. 1965), Tanzania broke diplomatic relations with Britain following Ian Smith's unilateral declaration of independence in Rhodesia (now Zimbabwe). As a result, the TLS Board lost £250,000 library development fund which was enough to build 17 branch (regional) libraries in the country. In the 1970s, the government, through the Tanzania Library Services' committee on services to school libraries, adopted a "model system"[11,50] because, given limited resources, it was not possible to cover all

schools at once. Under that system, a few well-equipped libraries were developed in different parts of the country as a first step toward expanding the service to other schools. The implementation of this project started with three secondary schools:[51] Mzumbe (Morogoro), Mazengo (Dodoma), and Iringa Girls School (Iringa), and the project received financial support from UNESCO. This was a successful approach as it also involved training of teacher–librarians, and it is reported that two associations of teacher–librarians were formed to share their experiences in running school libraries and to help spread the approach to other schools.

Even though school libraries are not under the auspices of TLS, they still depend on it for professional expertise; also, secondary and primary school students constitute the largest user-group of TLSB libraries owing to resource-constraint nature of school libraries. Moreover, the TLS services are highly skewed in favor of urban area,[34,52] largely because during postindependence evolution of library services, TLSB chose to establish libraries in the following order of priority:[36] Regional→District→Division→Village. So far, judging from the list of libraries given in the TLSB's current Web site, 19 of 21 regions have regional libraries while there are about only a dozen district libraries in 125 districts. (For more details about TLS and a list of regional and district libraries, visit the TLS' Web site at http://www.tlsb.or.tz/default.asp, accessed August 20, 2008.) One of the ongoing Government's strategies to redress the shortcoming is to improve access to information resources through ICT-enhanced projects and to improve general infrastructure in rural areas (see the sections on "The Role of Information Technology in Teaching and Learning" and "A Note on Key Policy Initiatives").

Library services for children

Over the years, library services for children have been part and parcel of TLS operations through its children's library at the NCL; these include such services as reference, lending, story-telling, and access to audiovisual materials. Moreover, the inauguration of the Children's Multimedia Resource Centre in 1999 at the NCL's children's library was a milestone in these services. The center exposes various computer-based tools—such as games/video/audio objects—to children. The Center is intended to achieve the following objectives (extracted from the TLSB's Web site at http://www.tlsb.or.tz/projects.asp, accessed August 20, 2008):

- To stimulate children and youth minds and (to) enable them (to) get easy access to the library's collection of audio and visual materials.
- To attract more children/youth to join the library, hence develop a reading habit and love of books.

- To expose the children/youth to the use of latest information and communication technology in computerization and related facilities.
- To enable children/youth to get access to information in various forms such as textual, sound, still, and moving pictures.
- Enable children/youth to see the library as a place for adventure, filled with stories, facts, pictures, and music.
- To create interest in creative activities and prepare them to become good future citizens.
- To make the centre a cultural and a social meeting place for children and youth.

Apart from library services, the Government and a group of foreign donors initiated the Children's Book Project in 1991 to produce and distribute reading materials for children. (For details visit the Children's Book Project's Web site at http://www.cbp.or.tz/default.asp, accessed September 20, 2008.) The project also advocates supporting indigenous authors of children's books and other materials.

The role of information technology in teaching and learning

The Government of Tanzania recognizes the fact that advances in information and communication technologies have the potential for enhancing teaching and learning processes. In 2007, the Ministry of Education and Vocational Training (MoEVT) inaugurated the ICT Policy for Basic Education[30] along the lines of the Tanzania National ICT Policy of 2003.[53] This is based on the MoEVT's conviction that "the use of ICT in teaching and learning as well as administration and management represents a powerful tool with which to achieve educational and national development objectives."[30]

According to MoEVT, the basic education entities that this new policy encompasses include preschool, primary, secondary/high school, teacher education, and nonformal and adult (literary) education. The policy's phased implementation strategy accords priority to teacher education—both preservice and in-service—followed by secondary education, primary education, and an education management information system. It also exploits other national initiatives (e.g., see the section on "A Note on Key Policy Initiatives") to support areas that are not in the initial phases of implementation and complementing priority areas. Examples of complementary initiatives include community telecenters that avail their services to neighboring primary and secondary schools, NGOs that donate refurbished computers, the ICT for Rural Development Pilot Project, and university-based (especially the University of Dar es Salaam and the Open University of Tanzania) ICT tools to facilitate learners and trainers with

disabilities. As such, the policy's implementation strategy takes a holistic approach. Currently, very few primary schools have access to Internet (or computers for that matter). Radio is the most commonly used media to support learning in both primary and secondary schools through nationally-broadcast programs; also, almost all of these schools have radios while only some of them have TVs.

Special Libraries and Specialized Information Services

The emergence of special libraries

As noted before, special libraries predate all other libraries in Tanzania owing to the fact that they have served special interest and professional groups over the years. According to Dahlgren,[18] there were 120 special libraries in 1922. We can include libraries of different government agencies in this group of libraries such as those of the Ministry of Agriculture and of its network of research stations scattered all over the country, the ministries or agencies responsible for lands, minerals, planning, finance, environment, science and technology, transport, communication, and so on. Just to give an example of one area of specialized libraries in Tanzania—law libraries—to see their composition, as enumerated by Msuya;[44] these include the Attorney General Chambers libraries in Dar es Salaam and Zanzibar, the Tanzania Legal Corporation library in Dar es Salaam with its branch libraries in Arusha and Mwanza, the National Assembly Library in Dodoma and its branch in Dar es Salaam, the Law Reform Commission of Tanzanian library in Dar es Salaam, and small libraries related to human-rights NGOs. The materials held in these libraries comprise those related to pre- and postindependence legislation (such as acts of parliament), the Tanzania Law Reports (formerly the Tanganyika Law Reports and included in the former East African Law Reports). A series of these reports are available in CD-ROMs. The National Bureau of Statistics has a statistical library that acts as a reference center for statistical information including national economic trends, population census and demographic data, and sector-related surveys. (For details visit the National Bureau of Statistics Tanzania Web site at http://www.nbs.go.tz/, accessed September 24, 2008.)

Specialized information services

Specialized information services that also employ information technology tools have recently evolved out of various specialized libraries or agencies to improve the provision of specialized information resources to their users. Notable examples include the Parliamentary Online Information Service, POLIS (see what constitutes POLIS at http://www.parliament.go.tz/polis/Bunge/Polis.asp?Menu=0, accessed September 3, 2008 from the Parliament of Tanzania's Web site at http://www.parliament.go.tz/), that was inaugurated in 2004 to help members of Tanzania's Parliament gain access to "information on members, legislation, bills, budget, Hansard (the record of debates), committees, and elections."[54] There are also several management information systems and centers such as the Tanzania Development Information Center (for details and important links see the Tanzania Development Information Center's Web site at http://www.tdic.or.tz/, accessed September 2, 2008), the Tanzania Global Development Learning Centre (http://www.tgdlc.go.tz/, accessed September 1, 2008), the Integrated Financial Management System,[55,56] e-procurement,[55] (see also the Public Procurement Regulatory Authority's Web site at http://www.ppra.go.tz/, accessed September 2, 2008), Health Management Information Systems,[55] the Education Information Management System,[55] the Tanzania Education Network,[55,57] as well as the proposed sustainable land management information system.[58] One information service that was created in the 1970s is the Tanzania National Research Information Service under the auspices of the Commission for Science and Technology, COSTECH (for details and links related to COSTECH, including an Act of Parliament that established it visit its Web site at http://www.costech.or.tz/, accessed August 20, 2008), which functions as a government agency for monitoring and coordinating scientific research and technology development in and about the country. The COSTECH also coordinates community-based telecenters in the country.

Many government agencies upload current information related to their areas on their Web sites. (Most of them have PDF links; see for example the Web site of the Law Reform Commission of Tanzania at http://www.lrct.or.tz/acts_page.php where recent acts of parliament are listed and available for downloading.) Furthermore, the official online government portal (http://www.tanzania.go.tz/) provides links to information and documents related to different government agents. Online access to government documents is a milestone in Tanzania since there have been delays in publishing important information by the sole publisher of government publications—the Government Printer—due to resource constraints; sometimes, even when these documents are released the number of copies has not satisfied local demand. For example, Msuya[44] reports on the situation regarding legislation materials (p. 54):

> Since independence, the Government has passed new laws and amended out-dated ones. However, there are major delays from the time the laws are passed by Parliament to the time they are printed by Government Printer, due to the relatively out-dated technology used and frequent machine breakdowns. As a result, the Government Printer does not have the ability to produce sufficient copies to meet the demand.

While researchers, educators, libraries, and a few citizens are able to access these documents online, the majority of other citizens—particularly the rural population—have no access since the Internet connections have not spread to many rural areas. This is an important challenge to developing nations along with addressing the issue of archiving electronic resources.

ARCHIVES AND ARCHIVAL SYSTEM

Record Management Structures

Like the development and status of library system, the existing system of record management is relatively recent in Tanzania even though Karugila[59] reports that "[A] properly organized government registry was functioning by 1891" (p. 14) under the administration of German Imperial Government. Postindependence record management system in Tanzania has been under the Tanzania National Archives (TNA) which was established by an act of parliament of 1965, amended in 1979, and then repealed through the Records and Archives Management Act of 2002. (For details of the Records and Archives Management Act, visit http://www.parliament.go.tz/Polis/PAMS/Docs/3-2002.pdf, accessed September 2, 2008 from the Tanzania Parliament's Web site http://www.parliament.go.tz/.) These were preceded by the Records Disposal Ordinance Cap 9 of 1931 under British colonial administration. Prior to the enactment of the 2002 Act, it was believed that previous legislation had many inadequacies in providing sound direction for efficient records management.[60] The Records and Archives Management Act of 2002 established the Records and Archives Management Department (RAMD) to "provide for the proper administration and better management of public records and archives throughout their life cycle, to repeal the Records (Disposal) Ordinance, 1931, and the National Archives Act, 1965, and for connected matters." (For details of the Records and Archives Management Act, visit http://www.parliament.go.tz/Polis/PAMS/Docs/3-2002.pdf, accessed September 2, 2008 from the Tanzania Parliament's Web site http://www.parliament.go.tz/.) Like TLS, the RAMD is based in Dar es Salaam; in addition, it administers six branches (regional offices) in Arusha, Dodoma, Mbeya, Mwanza, Singida, and Tanga.

Schneider[61] outlines the composition of the materials held in the national archives of Tanzania; this also reflects the country's history of government administration (p. 447):

> The three major groups of materials retained within the TNA system are records from German colonial times (pre-1916/17), the British records (pre-1962), and records from various levels of government and administration of post-independence documents that originate from central

government and ministerial headquarters. A considerable number of post-1962 records originating from local level government and administration have been moved to Dar es Salaam. However, the regional branch offices also house such materials in collections of varying sizes. As a rule of thumb, the majority of those local files that had been closed by 1968, and that have been brought into archives system, are in Dar es Salaam. Much of the recent material that has found its way into the TNA system is retained by the regional branches.

Zanzibar has its own national archives under the Zanzibar National Archives in the Department of Archives, Museums, and Antiquities. (For details and the history, structure as well as the list, and description of collections under the auspices of the Zanzibar National Archives, visit its homepage at http://www.zanzibarheritage.go.tz/Archives.htm, accessed September 20, 2008.)

Status and Downside

Records and the information these records hold as evidence of various decisions and actions are invaluable resources for current and future functions and decision-making processes of government and organizational entities.

> Without reliable records, government cannot administer justice and cannot manage the state's resources, its revenue, or its civil service. It cannot deliver services such as education and health care. Without accurate and reliable records, and effective systems to manage them, governments cannot be held accountable for their decisions and actions, and the rights and obligations of citizens and corporate bodies cannot be upheld.[62]

Therefore, the importance of managing and preserving records cannot be overemphasized. Schneider[61] observes that the records in the national archives of Tanzania in Dar es Salaam are generally poorly organized which makes it difficult for researchers to locate materials. In addition, according to Schneider, the system lacks comprehensive assessment of what materials have been made available to TNA over years, and, on the whole, many records seem to have been lost during different transitions between three major administrative periods (Germans/British/postindependence). Still, Schneider contends that many colonial records made their way to the TNA while hardly a handful of them still exist outside of TNA with the exception of the two former colonial authority nations and the archives of their allies such as Belgium (who colonized Congo DR and whose troops temporarily occupied western Tanzania when German troops were defeated at the conclusion of World War I). Karugila[59] reports that most of the German colonial records prior to 1890 are maintained by the Zanzibar national archives (the capital of German colonial government—German East Africa—moved from Zanzibar to Dar es Salaam in January 1891).

As Schneider observes above, the problem of poor record management in Tanzania affects not only their access by researchers but also makes it difficult to track the nation's past experience to gain better informed knowledge for purposes of current and future development programs. Nyirenda[63] has discussed a number of factors that might contribute to the situation including colonial legacy (colonial governments sent important records to Europe for preservation and took no effort in developing viable record management systems in Africa; as such, newly independent nations had to start from scratch). Also, Nyirenda pinpoints ineffective postindependence legislation related to record management as the issue of records management program was not explicitly defined in the substantive law; instead, it was redefined through government circulars that were not observed all the time. Katundu[60] addresses this deficiency as well, noting

> A good example here has been the absence of legal provisions in the 1965 National Archives Act as regards the management of current and semi-current records in most public agencies. The act has been silent on this and implicitly it was left to the creators of these records to determine their management. This can create an environment conducive to poor accountability, corruption, fraud and maladministration (p. 78.)

Other factors noted by Nyirenda are resource constraints (human, physical, and financial) and general administrative incompetence coupled with weaknesses in adhering to standards and regulations in record management which in turn affected administration of national archives. The Act of 2002 was intended to address some of these deficiencies; for instance, Katundu[60] remarks (p. 76):

> The Act is primarily the most significant change in the way record keeping is to be coordinated by public offices for a number of reasons. Firstly, it legally lays the foundations of effective records and archives management in relation to legislation, ... Secondly, the Act is crucial as it intends to resuscitate achievements in records and archives administration recorded between 1965 and 1969 when deterioration and collapse of records management and archives administration systems began. ... Thirdly, through its various provisions specifically on structural mechanism of managing records, the Act tries to provide and facilitate a unified records management structure both at central and local government levels. The act has therefore come at the right moment in trying to create the basis for facilitating the maintenance of good record keeping systems which is of particular significance specifically now when vital records are needed in response to the public sector reform currently underway in the country.

Despite the above developments, Katundu, in providing a critical analysis of the Act, decries its deficiencies in the sense that it lacks necessary provisions for making available adequate resources for manpower training and, especially, for management of electronic records. Accordingly, the Act only defines electronic records as types of records but it lacks a guiding principle for their management. Katundu also notes that the Act vests too much power to the Director of Records and Archives Management in the President's Office. Other observers[62] note that the current legislation is not explicit on the management of electronic records "because the supporting legislation, referring specifically to electronic records as evidence, had yet to be defined. Records and Archives Management Department has sent several staff for introductory training in electronic records management and is developing an electronic records management policy" (p. 5).

The shortcomings surrounding record management systems are not only confined to government departments. Wema[64] discusses the shortcomings in the management of university records at the UDSM and proposes an efficient program for managing those records, while Mnjama[65] talks of the problems still facing the management of records a regional body that preceded the current East African Community.

MUSEUMS

National Museum System

There are several museums in Tanzania even though many people think of the museum building in Dar es Salaam as a sole representative of the historical artifacts of the country. Historically, the main National Museum in Dar es Salaam can be traced back to 1934 when the then Governor of Tanganyika Territory Sir Harold Mac Michael initiated the idea of creating a museum for Dar es Salaam.[66] Following the death of King George V in 1936, it was decided that his Memorial Museum be built, and it was later opened to the public in 1940. The location has since remained along Shaaban Robert Street and the museum includes such exhibition halls (for details see http://www. houseofculture.or.tz/exhibitions.htm, accessed August 20, 2008) as the Hall of Man (cultural and biological evolution), the Biology Hall (Tanzania's biodiversity), the History Gallery (history of Tanzania through exhibitions of objects, manuscripts, photographs, and other thematic illustrations), and the Ethnographic Hall (Tanzania's cultural diversity). One of the historical treasures displayed at the National Museum is a skull of the first human, *Australopithecus boisei* (this was discovered by Dr. Leakey in 1959 at Olduvai Gorge in Arusha, northern Tanzania), as well as related foot prints. The Museum also displays many antique artifacts from various ethnic groups in Tanzania, as well as several memorabilia from World War I. It is a clear destination for researchers, students, tourists, and for general public enjoyment; it also organizes educational programs and tours for adults, children, students, and teachers.

The main National Museum (renamed "Museum and House of Culture" in 2003) (see http://www.houseofculture. or.tz/house_of_culture.htm, accessed August 20, 2008] in 2003) is part of a body corporate—the National Museum of Tanzania—that was established by an Act of Parliament (http://www.parliament.go.tz/Polis/PAMS/Docs/7-1980. pdf, accessed August 21, 2008) of 1980 which repealed the National Museum Act, 1962. Accordingly, the National Museum of Tanzania is "a scientific educational and cultural institution charged with the duties of collecting, conserving, displaying, and researching on all materials relating to Tanzanian's cultural and natural heritage."[66]

Apart from the main Museum, the present National Museum of Tanzania incorporates the Village Museum (for example, see pictures at http://www.houseofculture. or.tz/village_museum.htm, accessed August 20, 2008) in Dar es Salaam (on-site collection of traditional houses from various ethnic groups and places in Tanzania); the Natural History Museum (see http://www.houseofculture. or.tz/natural_history_museum.htm, accessed August 20, 2008) in Arusha; the Arusha Declaration Museum (see http://www.arushamuseum.ac.tz/, accessed August 20, 2008) in Arusha with its exhibition depicting "the development of Tanzanian societies from precolonial period to present with particular emphasis on the political and economic changes"[67] and the Mwl. J.K. Nyerere Museum in Butiama, Musoma (birth- and burial-place of the First President of Tanzania (the Father of the Nation), Julius K. Nyerere.

In Zanzibar, the museums are under the jurisdiction of the Department of Archives, Museums, and Antiquities. Zanzibar has a substantially rich and long cultural history as reflected in previous archaeological investigations.[68,69] However, until as recently as the 1990s, the postrevolution government in Zanzibar did not promote most of its historical artifacts since the Island's history was also marred by such bitter memories as slavery and colonialism.[70] A new museum building is currently under construction at Unguja Ukuu Archaeological site where an ancient town (500–900 A.D.) was based in Zanzibar.[71]

Private Museums

Apart from government-sponsored museums described above, there are private or community museums that aim to promote specific cultural traditions. For instance, the Sukuma Museum in Mwanza is "a community based organization that promotes and celebrates the traditional and contemporary arts of the Sukuma culture" (For details and online galleries visit the museum's Web site at http:// philip.greenspun.com/sukuma/, accessed August 20, 2008). Bagamoyo Museum is located in the historical town of Bagamoyo (the first capital of German East Africa), about 45 mi north of Dar es Salaam. Its exhibitions depict the town's history and its direct past connection to outside world, namely Arab and Indian traders, European explorers, and European Christian missionaries. The exhibitions include documents, a few artifacts from slave trade and old photographs. In northern Tanzania, the Maasai Cultural Museum[72] depicts the Maasai people and their culture. It is located about 15 mi west of Arusha Town, within the Meserani Snake Park.[73] The Mkwawa Memorial Museum in Kalenga-Iringa, exhibits the skull of Mkwawa, the Hehe Chief. The skull was repatriated from Germany in 1954 (for details see http://community.iexplore. com/planning/journalEntryFreeForm.asp?journalID=2533 6&entryID=13769&n=Mkwawa+Museum and http://www. mkwawa.com/day4kalenga.asp; accessed February 3, 2009). The newest museum, the Museum of Tanzanite, was recently opened in Arusha to display the Tanzanite gemstone and its vestiges. This museum will be known as the "Tanzanite Experience Museum" (see media reports at http://www.ippmedia.com/ipp/guardian/2008/08/21/ 120977.html and http://www.safarilands.org/index.php/ technology/more/worlds_first_tanzanite_museum_opens_ in_arusha_tanzania/, accessed September 25, 2008).

Private Art Galleries

There are several private art galleries in Dar es Salaam and other major cities that attract tourists, scholars, and other visitors. They usually exhibit paintings, traditional wooden carvings, do performances and related displays that depict Tanzanian or East African contemporary art. These include La Petite Galerie (Oysterbay), Nyerere Cultural Centre, Raza Art Gallery, Tinga Tinga Art Center (see for examples http://www.africanstudies.uct.ac.za/ postamble/tingatinga.pdf for background information, and http://www.africanstudies.uct.ac.za/postamble/pernille.php, accessed September 1, 2008), Color Center, Mandawa Studio, Twiga Art Gallery, African Art and Tanzanite; all in Dar es Salaam. The African Art and Tanzanite displays masks, ebony, Masai collection, bone work, leather articles, wildlife products, Zanzibar furniture, and antiques (see http://www.africaart.co.tz/, accessed August 20, 2008).

Antiquities

Both the museums and the antiquities in Tanzania are under the Tanzania Museums and Antiquities Agency within the auspices of the Ministry of Natural Resources and Tourism. The Antiquities Division itself is entrusted with ensuring the sustainable preservation of nation's cultural heritage in the form of historical sites, monuments, and relics such as:[74,75]

- any building, fortification, interment, midden, dam or any structure erected built or formed by human agency in Tanganyika before the year 1863;

- any rock painting or any immovable object painted, sculptured, carved, incised or modified by human agency in Tanganyika before the year 1863;
- any earthwork, trench, edit, well, cave, tunnel or other modification of the soil or rock dug, excavated or otherwise engineered by human agency in Tanganyika before the year 1861;
- any ethnographical object or any wooden door or door frame carved in Tanganyika in any African or oriental style before the year 1940;
- any object declared to be a protected heritage by the minister responsible for the Antiquities Department.

These are just examples of the antiquities as defined in the principal legislation, the Antiquities Act of 1964, as amended through the Antiquities (Amendment) Act of 1979.[74] The Antiquities Act of 1964 repealed previous legislation, the Monuments Preservation Ordinance of 1939/1949, to broaden the coverage of the heritage objects earmarked for conservation such as any ethnographic objects. Some of the cultural heritage sites include Kilwa Kisiwani and Songo Mnara islands in Indian Ocean (about 175 mi south of Dar es Salaam) which contain ruins of such historical monuments as the twelfth-century mosques, a palace, a prison, and urban structures. Similar structures and early Swahili settlements can be found in Bagamoyo and Zanzibar. Also, there palaeoanthropological and archeological sites such as the Olduvai Gorge; Ismila Middle Stone Age (Iringa); Laetoli Footprints (about 28 mi south of Olduvai Gorge, estimated to be 3.5 million years old); prehistoric burial site in the Ngorongoro Crater; Kiara rock-shelter paintings (Bukoba); Kwihara Tembe-Kigoma (Dr. David Livingstone's anti slavery "museum"); several German era buildings of architectural importance in various towns; Amboni caves (Tanga); Mbozi Meteorite, Mbeya (weighs about 25 metric tons); Kondoa-Irangi Rock Paintings-Dodoma (some of them 30,000 years old); ruins of an ancient (fifteenth century) irrigation site in Engaruka, and so on. Some of these sites and monuments—such as Kilwa Kisiwani and Songo Mnara, have been incorporated into the UNESCO's World Heritage List.[76]

In Zanzibar, the conservation of historical sites is under the Department of Archives, Museums, and Antiquities. The Zanzibar's Old Town is of particular interest to tourists and researchers alike. (For details see http://www. zanzibarheritage.go.tz/Antiquities.htm, accessed September 20, 2008.)

BOTANICAL GARDENS, HERBARIA, AND ZOOS

Botanical Gardens

The Dar es Salaam Botanical Gardens (adjacent to the main Museum building) were established in 1893 under the first Director of Agriculture, Dr. Franz Stuhlmann, of

German East Africa (Tanganyika) administration. It became fully operational in 1906. Comprising mostly indigenous plants and a few exotic species, the gardens offer relaxing as well as educational experience to visitors as noted in the following statements:

> offer the perfect place to enjoy some peace and quiet and to examine the country's colourful native flora. Wander among purple bougainvillea, blue jacaranda, scarlet flame trees and red hibiscus. As well as the indigenous plants and flowers, this is one of the few places in the world where you can see the coco-de-mer palm tree, native to the Seychelles.[77]

> These lovely gardens are a remnant of the German era in Tanzania. Beautiful palms and many types of ferns grow here. Majestic peacocks can be spotted walking around the gardens. The gardens offer a haven of peace and tranquility in the midst of Dar es Salaam's chaotic city life.[78]

The Germans also set up another botanical garden in Amani, Tanga (north-eastern Tanzania) in 1893. This was later developed into an agricultural institute—Biological-Agricultural Institute of Amani— that became operational in 1902 with resident and visiting scientists, and with such facilities and functions as "botanical, zoological, and chemical laboratories performing soil analyses, disease, fertilizer, and other basic biological research, and by 1907 a total of 650 'useful plants' were cultivated there."[79] After World War I, the British administration renamed the institute "East African Agricultural Research Station" and some of its facilities were transferred to Kenya (see the section on "Herbaria"). Most initial plantations of the Amani Botanical Gardens now are incorporated into the Amani Nature Reserve in the East Usambara Mountains. The Reserve was legally established by a declaration order in 1997 through the Gazette of the United Republic of Tanzania No. 19 Vol. 78.[80] According to the Tropical Biology Association, the Reserve is "globally recognized centre of biodiversity and one of the most valuable conservation areas in Africa ...It is likely that the Amani Botanical Garden still contains one of the largest collections of exotic plants in Africa. It is estimated that about 600 different taxa were planted with about 460 still surviving."[81]

Herbaria

The National Herbarium of Tanzania (NHT) is based at the Tropical Pesticides Research Institute (TPRI), Arusha, and was instituted through an Act of Parliament of 1979 that established TPRI. The NHT's mandate in centered around "cataloging the entire flora of Tanzania and recording the resultant information for easy access by the general public and other institutions,"[82] and to carry out taxonomic research.[83] The herbarium also maintains a database of indigenous plants of Tanzania and its repository contains over 65,000 specimens.[84]

Other key herbaria in Tanzania include the UDSM Herbarium under the Department of Botany (120,000 specimens), mainly used for training purposes. Others are under the Tanzania Forestry Research Institute (60,000) and the College of African Wildlife Management ($\sim$5,000), all these ranging from 27 to 104 years old.[84] The largest collection of herbarium materials in the country was established at Amani, alongside the Amani Botanical Garden during German administration; in 1948 the herbarium was relocated to Nairobi-Kenya (see http://www.bgci.org/garden.php?id=1335&ftrCountry=TZ&ftrKeyword=&ftrBGCImem=&ftrIAReg=, accessed September 1, 2008) as part of the East African Herbarium.

Zoos

Zoos are not very popular in Tanzania probably because of the country's rich natural wildlife parks and virgin forests; thus potential investments in zoos seem not to have received noticeable priority from either government or private agencies. There is one small zoo in Usa River, a small town about 15 mi east of Arusha. It was established initially as a game sanctuary for orphaned and ill wild animals. In addition, it "has a pond with flamingos, pelicans and gardens grazed by eland and zebra—a good place for lazy Sunday afternoon with the kids."[85] Other popular zoos include the Saa Nane Island Game Reserve in Mwanza, north-western Tanzania around Lake Victoria[85] and the Meserani Snake Park in Arusha.[73] The snake park displays different varieties of snakes "common in Eastern and Southern Africa from the Black Mamba to the Black and Red spitting Cobras and the African Python."[72] The park also contains such other reptiles as crocodiles, lizards, and tortoises, and it serves as a sanctuary for injured or orphaned birds.

SCHOLARLY PUBLISHING

Situation Analysis

As in many other African countries, Tanzania's publishing industry is generally marginal in terms of its contribution to the global publishing market. It tends to concentrate on the production of text books for primary and secondary schools[86] while scholarly publishing is generally minimal despite postindependence efforts to promote scholarly publishing through establishment of the Dar es Salaam University Press (DUP) (for details, see http://www.dup.co.tz/, accessed September 1, 2008) and other publishing houses. Bgoya[86] suggests possible reasons for the marginalized situation, including lack of interest in African-generated scholarly materials by international book market (booksellers, buyers, and librarians). But, Bgoya also argues that African governments have not given due priorities—in terms of allocation of resources—to their universities or even to provide incentives to their own scholars (including those based in Europe and North America) to enhance local scholarly publishing. According to Bgoya, the university presses in Africa have deteriorated, thus negatively affecting the quantity and quality of scholarly publishing outputs that would better compete in international markets and contribute to the global knowledge pool. However, he takes notes of gradual recoveries brought about by different initiatives that publishers are taking to ensure and sustain their survival.

Apart from DUP, other key publishers that also produce scholarly publications include the Tanzania Publishing House, Mkuki na Nyota Publishers (for details, visit http://www.mkukinanyota.com/home.html, accessed September 1, 2008), and Oxford University Press, Dar es Salaam. Moreover, the first printing presses in Tanzania were established by early Christian missionaries to publish religious and school materials, especially in local languages. Most of these presses still exist and have evolved into full-fledged publishing houses, such as Vuga Press (see http://www.elct-ned.org/index.php/newsclips/2198-vuga-press-is-also-a-publishing-house, accessed September 1, 2008) (Soni–Lushoto, Tanga, north-eastern Tanzania), Benedictine Publications and Peramiho Printing Press (Songea, southern Tanzania), the Ndanda Mission Press (see http://www.ndanda.org/, accessed September 1, 2008) (Mtwara, south-eastern Tanzania), the Tanganyika Mission Press and Publication (Tabora, western Tanzania), and the Catholic Publishers Limited (Dar es Salaam).

Current initiatives

Tanzania's major publishers participate in various initiatives to facilitate publication and distribution of locally-created scholarly materials. These include

- The African Publishers Network—founded in 1992 "to promote indigenous publishing throughout Africa."[87] It is based in Abidjan Cote d'Ivoire.
- The African Books Collective (for details see http://www.africanbookscollective.com/, accessed September 1, 2008)—founded in 1989 and representing member publishers to distribute African literature in the English-language in Europe, North America, and in Commonwealth countries outside Africa. It is coordinated from Oxford, United Kingdom.
- The Book Development Council of Tanzania—an NGO, was founded in 1999 to "coordinate and stimulate the activities of public and private sector agencies in the book industry of Tanzania so that more and better books of all kinds may be made available to the readers of all kinds…of all ages throughout Tanzania" (for details see http://www.bamvita.or.tz/default.asp, accessed August 21, 2008).

- Exploring Electronic Publishing Opportunities.[86,88]
- Initiatives from the INASP—such as improving journal quality, publishing, publicity, and access; electronic journal publishing and dissemination such as the African Journals Online (for details see http://www.inasp.info/file/121/, accessed August 21, 2008).
- Promoting Scholarly Publishing in African Languages.[86,89]

Various professional associations in Tanzania and East Africa as a whole play a key role in promoting scholarly publishing through their variety of activities including journal publications (for example, some of the selected scholarly journals listed in Table 2 are published by professional associations).

INTELLECTUAL PROPERTY REGULATIONS

Pre-independence regulations and related legislation on intellectual property rights were basically meant to protect the interests of colonial powers and their allies, and their subjects who came to settle in Tanganyika.[90] Such regulations were governed through the Trade Marks Ordinance of 1922, the Copyright Ordinance of 1924 and the Patents Ordinance of 1924. Some authors still take these pre-independence regulations with skepticism, noting that they "were promulgated to inhibit innovative activities among the indigenous Tanzanians."[90] Accordingly, the newly independent nation of Tanzania was somewhat silent on intellectual property regulations until 1966 when the new Copyright Act repealed the Copyright Ordinance of 1924. Likewise, the Trade and Service Marks Act of 1986 repealed the Trade Marks Ordinance of 1922, and the Patents Act of 1987 repealed the Patents Ordinance of 1924. The significance of these new legislations was that they removed a precondition for granting intellectual property rights in the United Kingdom before they were made effective in Tanzania through registration; in other words, the intellectual property rights-granting agencies in Tanzania were given powers to grant rights to deserved authors of creative works or innovators.

The latest legislation that is relevant to the scope of this entry is the Copyright and Neighboring Rights Act No. 7 of 1999 that repealed the Copyright Act of 1966. This new legislation is intended to "make better provisions for protection of copyright and neighbouring rights in literary, artistic works and folklore, and for related matters" (for details see http://www.parliament.go.tz/Polis/PAMS/Docs/7-1999.pdf, accessed September 20, 2008).

In order to administer the economic and moral rights of copyright owners, the Copyright and Neighboring Rights Act of 1999 established the Copyright Society of Tanzania (COSOTA) under the Ministry of Industry and Trade. Specific functions of COSOTA include the following

Table 2 Selected key scholarly journals published in Tanzania.

Africa Theological Journal (Makumira University College)

African Journal of Finance and Management (Institute of Finance Management)

The African Review Journal (University of Dar es Salaam)

East African Journal of Public Health (East African Public Health Association)

Eastern Africa Law Review (University of Dar es Salaam)

Huria: Journal of the Open University of Tanzania (Open University of Tanzania)

Journal of Building and Land Development (Ardhi University)

Journal of Development Studies (University of Dar es Salaam)

Journal of Population Studies and Development (University of Dar es Salaam)

Journal of the Geographical Association of Tanzania (Geographical Association of Tanzania)

Kioo cha Lugha: Journal of Kiswahili Department (University of Dar es Salaam)

Mulika: *Journal of the Institute of Kiswahili Research* (University of Dar es Salaam)

Papers in Education and Development: Journal of the Faculty of Education (University of Dar es Salaam)

Tanzania Dental Journal (Tanzania Dental Association)

Tanzania Journal of Forestry and Nature Conservation (Faculty of Forestry and Nature Conservation, Sokoine University of Agriculture)

Tanzania Journal of Health Research (National Institute for Medical Research)

Tanzania Journal of Science (Faculty of Science, University of Dar es Salaam)

Tanzania Medical Journal (Medical Association of Tanzania)

Tanzania Veterinary Journal [The Tropical Veterinarian] (Tanzania Veterinary Association and Faculty of Veterinary Medicine of Sokoine University of Agriculture)

Tanzania Zamani (Historical Association of Tanzania)

Tanzanian Economic Trends (TET) Journal (University of Dar es Salaam)

Tanzanian Mathematical Bulletin (Mathematical Association of Tanzania)

UHANDISI Journal (University of Dar es Salaam—engineering colleges)

University of Dar es Salaam Library Journal (University of Dar es Salaam Library)

UONGOZI Journal of Management and Development Dynamics (Mzumbe University)

UTAFITI: *Journal of the Faculty of Arts and Social Sciences* (University of Dar es Salaam)

Western Indian Ocean Journal of Marine Science (Western Indian Ocean Marine Science Association)

(for details see http://www.parliament.go.tz/Polis/PAMS/Docs/7-1999.pdf, accessed September 20, 2008; see also COSOTA's Web site at http://www.cosota-tz.org/frameset-t5.html, accessed September 20, 2008):

- To promote and protect the interests of authors, performers, translators, and publishers;
- To collect and distribute royalties of the copyright owners;

- To maintain registers of works, authors, performers, translators, producers, and other copyright owners;
- To identify and publicize the rights of owners; and in case of a dispute or an infringement, to provide necessary evidence;
- To advise the responsible minister on all matters related to this copyright law.

Certain observers have reported a lack of effective enforcement of intellectual property laws in Tanzania. They note, for example, that "despite the recent legislation, enforcement of intellectual property rights remains ineffective. Violations are not seriously investigated, and the courts lack experience and training in IPR issues" (see http://www.state.gov/e/eeb/ifd/2006/62039.htm, accessed September 20, 2008). To that end, a group of authors established the Tanzania Writers Association in 1978 to—among other objectives, safeguard the interests and rights of creative writers in the country. There is a parallel association for music performers and producers, the Tanzania Dance Music Association.

On the international scene, Tanzania is a founding member of the African Regional Intellectual Property Organization (ARIPO)—established in 1976, based in Harare-Zimbabwe—and a party to ARIPO's protocols on patents and trade marks. Also, since 1963, Tanzania has been a party to the Berne Convention (relating to the protection of literary and artistic works) and the Paris Convention (relating to the protection of industrial property: patents, trademarks and industrial designs), both of which are administered by the World Intellectual Property Organization (WIPO) of the United Nations. Tanzania joined WIPO in 1983. Likewise, since 1999 Tanzania has been a contracting nation to the Nice Agreement Concerning the International Classification of Goods and Services for the Purposes of Registration of Marks, and the world-wide Patent Cooperation Treaty.

PROFESSIONAL DEVELOPMENT

Post-independence Challenges and Remedies

As noted before, like many other newly-independent African nations, Tanzania lacked sufficient trained librarians, information specialists, and related professionals, and had to rely on expatriates (mainly from the United Kingdom, United States of America, Canada, Australia, and Scandinavian countries), technical advisers from UN agencies (especially the UNESCO) and volunteers (Peace Corps, VSO [Volunteer Service Overseas (of UK)], etc. In 1971, the first Director of Library Services, E.M. Broome, returned to the United Kingdom and a Tanzanian, Ezekiel Kaungamno, assumed the position. According to Kaungamno and Ilomo, at the time of

Mr. Broome's departure, TLS had become steadily-established and of some standing among library professional circles.[14]

To alleviate shortages of trained professionals and to meet manpower demands of a growing network of libraries in Tanzania, the Government through TLS embarked on a vigorous professional training program.[11–14] The goal was to develop a cadre of library and information professionals of TLS and its branch libraries, and to support other (non-TLSB) libraries. Subsequently, in 1972 the government established the National Library Assistant's Certificate course at Dar es Salaam Teacher's College; this was transferred to the NCL's building in 1974. The program still provides basic training for library paraprofessionals. In the same year, the TLS Board adopted the Staff Development Program for senior staff, leading to substantial enrollments in various library schools abroad. In addition, several mid-level staff went to the East African School of Librarianship (Makerere University) in Uganda, where they pursued professional training at "diploma" and, in later years, degree levels. In addition, the TLS Board thought that there was a need to establish a locally-based school to train mid-level staff in librarianship and archival studies, hence the founding of the School of Librarianship and Archives and Documentation Studies in 1989. At the same time, many more graduate level staff went to the School of Information Studies for Africa, Addis Ababa University, Ethiopia, for master's level studies. Many others went to universities in Europe, North America and Australia for graduate (M.A./M.Sc., Ph.D.) degrees. Most of those who went abroad received fellowships from Government (of Tanzania and such foreign and international agencies as the British Council and the International Development Research Center of Canada. These and other donors and NGOs have also sponsored students to attend local schools; for example, the Norwegian Agency for International Development has supported students to attend a 2 year diploma program at School of Librarianship and Archives and Documentation Studies. (See the Tanzania Library Association's Chairman's report at SCECSAL conference at http://www.scecsal.org/stlacr06.html, accessed August 21, 2008.)

Apart from attending long-term programs, information professionals in Tanzania have benefited from short courses, mostly through partnerships among national and international institutions such as the Tanzania Library Association (TLA), INASP, the Center for Agricultural and Rural Development, The British Council, The World Bank, UN agencies, Association for Strengthening Agricultural Research in Eastern and Central Africa, Southern African Center for Cooperation in Agricultural and Natural Resources Research and Training, NGOs (e.g., Libraries without borders), and several international and bilateral donor agencies. Some of these donors, such as the Swedish International Development Cooperation Agency and its Department for Research Cooperation, have played key roles in supporting capacity-building projects of local institutions to develop ICT-enhanced training.

Training Institutions in Tanzania

Reflecting on locally-available resources for professional training in the field, basic professional training in library and information sciences is provided by TLS through its national library assistants' course. Mid-level "diploma" training is available from SLADS, while higher level training programs (first degree, masters, Ph.D.) are obtained from the UDSM (Department of Information Studies) and from a number of the newly-established public and private universities. Table 3 provides a summary of institutions that provide information/library-related training programs and the programs they offer.

PROFESSIONAL ASSOCIATIONS

The TLA is the main professional association in the field. It was initially affiliated with the East African Library Association (EALA) until its formal establishment in 1973 following the dissolution of EALA. It promotes the profession through such activities as workshops, short courses, formal talks, conferences, online discussion groups, film programs, and publication of a newsletter. (For details, see http://www.tla.or.tz/index.htm, accessed August 20, 2008.) The TLA is also affiliated to the Standing Conference of Eastern, Central, and Southern African Library and Information Associations (SCECSAL) (for details about SCECSAL, a list of current member countries and its conferences visit its Web site at http://www.scecsal.org/, accessed August 20, 2008) which stemmed from the EALA's former members' decision to retain their biennial conference and decided to invite other countries in the region. There are also proposals to transform SCECSAL into a regional federation of library and information associations. In addition, TLA is affiliated with the International Federation of Library Associations and Institutions as a member along with other several individual institutions in Tanzania. In addition, many information professionals in Tanzania who went to foreign countries for graduate studies joined professional associations in those countries and retained their memberships after their return to Tanzania. In doing so, they have helped to strengthen their local institutions through transfer and diffusion of innovations from other countries.

The book publishing industry has its own association, The East African Book Development Association, which is a registered society in Tanzania, Kenya, and Uganda. Its motto is "Enhancing Literacy for Poverty Eradication" and its vision is "A literate and enriched people through the promotion of books and reading," while its mission is to "support development of all functions of the book sector in the East African region and to enhance cross-border

Table 3 Institutions that provide information/library-related training programs in Tanzania.

Institution	Department/school/faculty	Location	Programs (and year started)	Outputs
UDSM	Faculty of Arts and Social Sciences, Department of Information Studies	Dar es Salaam (DSM)	Information Studies, 1997	Master of Arts in Information Studies; Ph.D. in Information Studies
UDSM	Department of Computer Science	DSM	Information Systems; Computer Science; CISCO Program	B.Sc./M.Sc. in Computer Science; B.Sc. with Computer Science; Diploma in Computer Science
UDSM	UDSM Computing Centre (Business entity of the University to meet market demand for skills in ICT applications)	DSM	Computing and Information Technology; Various professional courses (for details see http://www.ucc.co.tz/services/training/courses.php)	Certificate and Diploma in Computing and Information Technology; Various course certificates
St. Augustine University of Tanzania	Ruaha University College, Faculty of ICT	Iringa (southern Tanzania)	Information and Communication Technology (ICT), 2005	Bachelor of ICT (Information Systems); Bachelor of Computer Science; Diploma in Computer Science
Tumaini University	Tumaini University Dar es Salaam College (former Waldorf College-Tanzania)	DSM	Library and Information Services, 2003; Mass Communication, 2003	Bachelor of Arts in Library and Information Studies; Bachelor of Arts in Mass Communication
TLSB	School of Library, Archives and Documentation Studies	Bagamoyo	Library and Information Science, 1989	Diploma in Librarianship; Certificate in Librarianship
TLSB	Tanzania Library Services	DSM	National Library Assistants Certificate Course, 1972	Certificate in Librarianship
University of Dodoma	College of Informatics and Virtual Education.	Dodoma	IC, 2007	Bachelor of Science in Information Systems
Institute of Finance Management	—	DSM	Information Technology and Management	Master of Information Technology and Management; Advanced Diploma in Information Technology; Certificate in Information Technology
Tanzania Public Service College	(http://www.tpsc.go.tz)	DSM	Record Management, 1997	Certificate in Record Management
Mzumbe University	Faculty of Science and Technology, Department of ICT	Morogoro	ICT Management (ICTM), 2003/2004	B.Sc. in ICTM; Certificate in ICT
College of Business Education	—	DSM and Dodoma	ICT	Certificate in ICT
Institute of Accountancy Arusha	Department of Information Technology	Arusha	Computer Science and IT, 2001	Certificate and Advanced Diploma in IT/Computer Science

trade in books" (For details and for the objectives of EABDA, visit its homepage at http://www.eabda.com/home.php?LinkID=0c3c8322b833376d737f14a98a77d998, accessed September 20, 2008). Likewise, the Tanzania Writers Association brings authors together to promote creative writing.

As noted before, Tanzania is also witnessing exponential growth of its universities; as well as several individual institutional strategies to employ ICT-enhanced library and information services aimed to improve access to information resources by academic communities. Their libraries want to bring their efforts together through the proposed Tanzanian Academic and Research Libraries Association. This might lead to establishing formal networks that will promote sharing of meager resources through, for example, coordinated acquisition of library materials and subscriptions of licensed electronic resources.

Student–Taxonomy

A NOTE ON KEY POLICY INITIATIVES

Apart from the National and MoEVT ICT policy plans,[30,53] Tanzania is implementing a number of national initiatives and participating in related international agendas that take into account, among other things; the need to enhance citizen-centered development of information-based society that benefits from potentials of ICTs in achieving national development goals. These include the following:[30,53,91,92]

- The Tanzania Development Vision 2025—envisioning high-quality livelihood, peace, good governance and well-educated and learning society.
- The National Strategy for Growth and Reduction of Poverty, Tanzania—envisioning empowered citizens with more access to information and related ICTs for better decisions in individual income-generating activities that lead to better life and poverty reduction.
- The Millennium Development Goals, Tanzania— envisioning a universal primary education, redressing gender disparities in education and advocating global partnerships for development and ultimate poverty reduction.
- Education and Training Policy of 1995, Tanzania—recognizing the importance of computer training in enhancing scientific technological development in Tanzania; thus incorporating computer studies in school curricula.
- The Education Sector Development Programme, Tanzania (primary and secondary education)—striving to improve enrollment, quality teacher education, and employing ICT-enhanced education and training.
- Education Sector Review, Tanzania—increasing the use of ICTs to improve education quality.
- National ICT Backbone Infrastructure Initiative, Tanzania—developing a vibrant and sustainable national ICT infrastructure to support economic development.
- National e-Government Strategy, Tanzania—employing ICTs to improve delivery of and access to government services.
- Rural Telecommunications ICT Fund and Universal Communication Access Fund, Tanzania—through the Universal Communication Access Act of 2006, a fund was established "for enabling accessibility and participation by communication operators in the provision of communication services, with a view to promoting social, education, and economic development of the rural and urban under-served areas; to provide for availability of communication services by establishing a legal framework for universal service providers to meet the communication needs of consumers and to provide for related matters." (For details see http://www.tcra.go.tz/policy/ucsa.pdf, accessed September 24, 2008.) It thus entails building an ICT infrastructure backbone linking all district and regional headquarters by 2010 using fiber optic technology.

- Local Government Reform Programme, Tanzania— including implementation of management information systems to improve planning, budgeting, and reporting processes.
- Rural Electrification Programme, Tanzania.
- The World Summit on the Information Society (WSIS)—aiming to create citizen- and development-centered information society, focusing on integrating ICTs into all levels of education and domestic policies through implementing the WSIS Declaration of Principles and Action Plan (Tanzania is a signatory to this declaration)
- Various sector policy documents and strategies. (Visit the official online gateway of the Government of Tanzania at http://www.tanzania.go.tz/ for links to various sectors, accessed August 20, 2008.)

CONCLUSIONS AND CHALLENGES AHEAD

The foregoing sections describe the historical development and current status of library and information systems and services in Tanzania, focusing on the postindependence situation and also touching on pre-independence evolution. Most of the library and information systems came into fruition after independence in 1961, with the exception of a few special libraries. The public library system under the auspices of the Tanzania Library Services Board constitutes the hub of the library system in the country, including the NCL, 19 branch libraries spread over 19 of 21 regions of Mainland Tanzania and several district libraries. There is a long way to go to spread libraries in rural areas and there are strategies to improve communications infrastructure in those areas including initiating ICT-enhanced teaching and learning strategies in secondary and primary schools.[30,93] Also, the TLSB is coordinating efforts to expand its network of libraries in partnership with local governments throughout the country. Zanzibar maintains its public library services under the Zanzibar Central Library.

There are around 50 institutions of higher learning— both public and private—in Tanzania, with varying levels of library holdings; however, the UDSM Library is the largest academic library in the country. Recent years have seen a sharp growth of universities as a result of Government's policy of encouraging the private sector to enhance its participation in promoting education for national development while the government itself is expanding public universities to increase student enrollments. As a result, these institutions are facing challenges of meeting the information needs of the expanded academic communities with meager resources—including skilled staff—by employing ICT-enhanced strategies aimed to improve access to information resources. Several observers in the profession have suggested strategies to address impending twenty-first century challenges to developing-countries academic libraries and their institutions, other libraries, and information centers. The strategies include open access initiatives;[93,94] revisiting library collection development policies taking into consideration the balance between print and electronic resources;[95] enhancing information literacy and e-learning programs;[93,96,97] augmenting training in electronic information management (including electronic records); digital networking and audiovisual archiving for improved preservation and shared access;[43,48,62,64,95] and exploring the potential of cell phones as a tool for accessing information resources and learning.[30,98]

The entry also describes school libraries, information services for children, as well as special libraries and specialized information services; focusing especially on ongoing national initiatives to utilize potentials of information technology to facilitate teaching and learning, and access to information resources. To that end, the entry highlights the situation of professional development efforts, scholarly publishing and professional associations and their contributions in addressing the impending challenges. In addition, the entry outlines the structures of the archival system, museums, botanical gardens, zoos, and herbaria in Tanzania, citing how researchers have reported the difficulties in accessing records in the national archives of Tanzania and how the legislation on archives is not explicit on electronic records management. Finally, the entry goes further to outline broader national policy initiatives that aim to address broader socioeconomic challenges and the role of ICTs in that endeavor.

Generally, much of the progress thus far in terms of library development, literacy education, and overall learning achievements in the Tanzanian society have been achieved over a brief four-decade span of independence. In particular, the first president, Julius K. Nyerere, was instrumental in advocating the development of a literate society in Tanzania by committing government resources to develop libraries, schools, and adult learning programs. These were supported by different legislations that have been mentioned in this entry and listed in the chronology (Appendix 1). All these were implemented by a dedicated team of local pioneers in the field, including the first TLS director, Ezekiel Kaungamno.

ACKNOWLEDGMENTS

I wish to acknowledge the help of Sara McGah and Ken Roehrs in editing this work. Many thanks go to ELIS-3 and Taylor & Francis editors for their guidance and cooperation; and to anonymous reviewers for their useful comments that have enhanced the quality this work. I am very grateful to Mike Shand of the University of Glasgow for graciously letting me make use of his up-to-date administrative map of Tanzania for this entry.

APPENDIX A

Table A Chronology of library and information system development in Tanzania.

1944	Representatives of the East African governments met and decided to commission an expert who would survey the state of library and literature provision and make recommendations for their improvement. E. Huxley was commissioned to undertake the survey.
1945	E. Huxley submits a report on literature and library provision to East African governments.
1946	Municipalities Ordinance 1946 as subsequently amended empowered councils to establish, erect and construct, acquire, maintain, assist, promote and control *inter alia* public libraries either within, or with the consent of the Minister without the geographical limits of the Municipality.
1948	Founding of the East African High Commission (EAHC). Founding of The East African Literature Bureau as a branch of the EAHC. George Annesley, ALA, arrives in E.A. as the first Bureau Librarian. Publication of the Annesley Report on the implementation of the Huxley Report.
1951	The East African Literature Bureau started a library service in Tanganyika.
1953	George Annesley, the Bureau Librarian attended the Ibadan UNESCO Seminar on Public Libraries; thereafter, he visited the Ghana Library Board which had already made progress and considered a model public library system for the rest of Africa to emulate.
1946	Colonial Secretary Sir Alan Lennox Boyd sent dispatch No. 932 of August 27, 1959 to the Administrator, EAHC, on British Government's proposal to finance library development in East Africa through the British Council.
1947	Colonial Office approved the appointment of S. W. Hockey, MBE, FLA, as a British Council Libraries Organizer in East Africa. He had been on a successful similar assignment for 15 years in the British West Indies. Mr. S.W. Hockey surveyed existing library facilities and submitted a report to 3 East African governments on the development of library services in East Africa.
1961	The Tanganyika Government accepted the Hockey Report—the first East African country to do so. In July, the Tanganyika Government adopted post-independence Three-Year Development Plan 1961/62–1963/64. The plan included a proposal to construct the National Central Library which would be related to the territorial expansion of libraries. December 9, 1961: Tanganyika became independent.
1962	Enactment of the Libraries (Deposit of Books) Act 1962. It provided for one perfect copy of every book printed in Tanganyika to the

(Continued)

Table A Chronology of library and information system development in Tanzania. *(Continued)*

University College of Dar es Salaam. October: A Library Planning Committee resolved that the national library service to be established should be called the **Tanganyika Library Services (TLS)**. The National Museum Act 1962, enacted.

1963   July 11: President J.K. Nyerere assented to the Tanganyika Library Services Board Act 1963. August: E.M. Broome Esq. FLA arrived in Tanganyika to take up his responsibility as first Director of Library services. November 1: The Tanganyika Library Services Board was appointed and commenced its work. Libraries (Deposit of Books) order 1963 made under the Libraries (Deposit of Books) Act 1962. Between November 1, 1963 and March 31 1964 TLS operated under the canopy of the East African Literature Bureau from which it inherited books, equipment, funds and staff.

1964   April 1: The Tanganyika Library Service was born as a parastatal organization under the Ministry of Education. Opening of Iringa Library in a makeshift building July 1: Adoption of the TLS Board's Library Development Plan and its incorporation into the National Five-Year Plan 1964–69. The Antiquities Act, 1964, enacted.

1965   Absorption of King George VI Memorial Library, Tanga and the Kilimanjaro Native Cooperative Union Library into TLS. Miss Mary Tizzard, Head of Schools and Children's services at TLS HQ surveyed school libraries and produced a report that would form a basis for improving school libraries in the country (it remained unpublished/unimplemented). Tanzania broke diplomatic relations with Britain following Ian Smith's unilateral declaration of independence of Rhodesia/Zimbabwe. As a result the TLS Board lost £250,000 that had been earmarked by the British Government to support library development in Tanzania.

1965   National Archives Act, 1965 enacted.

1966   Survey of government libraries leading to the F. N. Fogg Report, recommending the integration of all types of libraries into a single national library service with TLS as its nucleus and playing a leading role. The Copyright Act, 1966, enacted. The Act repealed the Copyright Ordinance of 1924.

1967   December 9: The National Central Library building was opened Mwl. J.K. Nyerere, first President of the United Republic of Tanzania. Opening of Iringa and Mwanza branch libraries.

1968/9   Survey of school libraries and the establishment of 3 model secondary school libraries by Emma Frost, a UNESCO expert.

1969   February 7: Opening of Bukoba Branch Library. July 1: Adoption of the Second Library Plan; this was incorporated into the National Five-Year

(Continued)

Table A Chronology of library and information system development in Tanzania. *(Continued)*

Development Plan 1969–74. Inauguration of rural library services through the support from UNESCO's literary work-oriented project, Mwanza. December 31: President Nyerere declared 1970 as an adult education year. TLS fully involved.

1970   Opening of Arusha, Kibaha and Moshi branch libraries.

1971   Inauguration of a School Mobile Library Service for secondary schools in several regions. The first Director of Library Services, E.M. Broome, Esq. FLA, returned to the United Kingdom; a Tanzanian, Ezekiel Kaungamno took over.

1972   Establishment of the National Library Assistants Certificate Course at the Dar es Salaam Teacher's College.

1974   July 1: The National Library Assistants Certificate Course was transferred to the National Central Library. Morogoro branch library opened. Charles P. Bourne surveyed Tanzania's library and information services and produced a report "Planning for a National Information Research Centre." He carried out this work on behalf of UNESCO. Adoption of the TLS Board's Staff Development Program for senior staff.

1975   April: Enactment of the Tanzania Library Services Board Act 1975. The Act repealed the 1963 Library Act and widened the Board's functions, responsibilities and powers. Opening of Mbeya and Mtwara branch libraries. Planning for the Tanzania National Documentation Centre began followed by the arrival of Mr. Kulkarni, an Indian expert recruited from the Commonwealth Secretariat by the Tanzania Government as a TLS's adviser on the subject. K. Samaha, a UNESCO consultant visited Tanzania at the request of the Government and produced a report on the Establishment of a National Focal Point for Scientific and Technological Information. A proposal for establishing a library school was submitted to the government for the first time.

1976   R.F. Munn from Morgantown, Virginia, United States undertook an assignment at the invitation of the government of Tanzania and produced a report, "Improving Agricultural Library Services in Tanzania." Opening of Tabora branch library.

1978   The TLSB submitted to the Ministry of Education a detailed document on the proposed library school.

1979   TLSB was given the responsibility to plan, build and manage a national library to be built in Dodoma, the new capital (not implemented as of September 2008). February: Opening of Mara regional library in Musoma. The National Archives (Amendment) Act, 1979 (Act No. 6/79) to amend the National Archives Act, 1965. The

(Continued)

Table A Chronology of library and information system development in Tanzania. *(Continued)*

	Antiquities (Amendment) Act, 1979, enacted (amending the Antiquities Act of 1964). The Tropical Pesticide Research Institute Act, 1979, enacted. The Act also established the National Herbarium of Tanzania.
1980	The National Museum of Tanzania Act of 1980 enacted; the National Museum Act of 1962 repealed. Construction starts of TLS printing and binding unit building in Dar es Salaam.
1981	Economic crisis led to massive cancellation of journal and book subscriptions.
1983	January: National Bibliographic Agency (NBA) founded to collect, record and conserve the national literacy output for current use and for posterity. February 16: Opening of Rukwa regional library in Sumbawanga. TLS submitted to the Ministry of Education a national library policy proposal. African Standing Conference on Bibliographic Control was held in Tanzania. The National Bibliographic Agency (NBA) was founded at TLS.
1985	International conference on resource sharing within southern African countries was held in Tanzania.
1986	The TLS received a microcomputer and accessories for computerizing the NBA database. The Trade and Service Marks Act, 1986, enacted. The Act repeals the Trade Marks Ordinance of 1922.
1987	The Patents Act, 1987, enacted. The Act repeals the Patents Ordinance of 1924.
1988	The TLS launched a diploma course at the School of Library, Archives and Documentation Studies in Bagamoyo.
1993	Tanzania Broadcasting Services Act of 1993 [for details see http://www.tcra.go.tz/policy/Tanzania%20broadcasting%20Act%206%20of%201993.pdf (accessed September 24, 2008).] enacted.
1996	Library user registration fees introduced. Local government reform measures introduced. These would result in the decentralization of TLS functions and responsibilities.
1997	National Telecommunications Policy of 1997 [for details see http://www.tcra.go.tz/policy/NTP1997.pdf (accessed September 24, 2008).] launched. Declaration order to establish the Amani Nature Reserve in the East Usambara Mountains (the Amani Botanical Gardens based in this reserve).
1997/8	Regional libraries opened in Dodoma and Lindi.
1999	The TLS' five-year strategic plan 1999–2004 launched. Inauguration of a multimedia centre in the Children's Library at the National Central Library, Dar es Salaam. The Copyright and Neighboring Rights Act No. 7 of 1999 enacted. The Act repealed the Copyright Act of 1966.
2002	Enactment of the Records and Archives Management Act [for details of the Records and Archives Management Act, visit http://www.parliament.go.tz/Polis/PAMS/Docs/3-2002.pdf (accessed September 2, 2008 from the Tanzania Parliament's Web site http://www.parliament.go.tz/).] of 2002 [repeals the Records (Disposal) Ordinance of 1931 and

(Continued)

Table A Chronology of library and information system development in Tanzania. *(Continued)*

	the National Archives Act, 1965; establishes the Records and Archives Management Department]
2003	National Postal Policy of 2003 [for details see http://www.tcra.go.tz/policy/NATIONALPOSTALPOLICY.pdf (accessed September 24, 2008).] inaugurated. Tanzania Communications Act of 1993 [for details see http://www.tcra.go.tz/policy/Tanzania%20Communications%20Act%2018%201993.pdf (accessed September 24, 2008).] enacted. Tanzania Communications Regulatory Authority Act of 2003 enacted "for the purpose of regulation of telecommunications, broadcasting, postal services; to provide for allocation and management of radio spectrum, covering electronic technologies and other Information and Communication Technologies (ICT) applications and to provide for its operation in place of former authorities and for related matters" [for details see http://www.tcra.go.tz/policy/Tanzania%20Communications%20Regulatory%20Act-2003.pdf (accessed September 24, 2008).]. National ICT Policy of 2003 launched[53] National Museum building renamed "Museum and House of Culture"
2006	The Universal Communications Service Access Act of 2006 [for details see http://www.tcra.go.tz/policy/ucsa.pdf (accessed September 24, 2008).] enacted.
2008	An Act No. 7 of 2008 to provide for the establishment of the UNESCO National Commission and to provide for related matters (http://www.parliament.go.tz/Polis/PAMS/Docs/7-2008.pdf).

See the section on "Academic Libraries" for the years of establishment of various academic institutions in Tanzania (by implication, their libraries were set up when these institutions were established).
Source: Adapted from Kaungamno and Ilomo[12] plus scores of other sources with amendments/updates by the author.

APPENDIX B

Table B Functions and powers of the TLSB.

Functions
4.
1. The functions of the Board shall be:
a. to promote, establish, equip, manage, maintain, and develop libraries in the United Republic;
b. to set up, establish, equip, manage, maintain and develop documentation centers and to provide documentation services;
c. to provide facilities for the study of, and for training in, the principles, procedure, and techniques of librarianship, and such other related subjects as the Board may from time to time decide;
d. to conduct examinations and to grant diplomas, certificates and other awards of the Board;
e. to sponsor, arrange and provide facilities for conferences and seminars for discussion of matters relating to library and documentation services;
f. to initiate, sponsor, participate in, finance and assist in campaigns for the eradication of illiteracy;

(Continued)

Table B Functions and powers of the TLSB. *(Continued)*

Functions

g. to provide an efficient library service both in the urban and rural areas and to stimulate public interest in literature generally and in Tanzania literature in particular;

h. to sponsor, promote, assist and engage in the production of books and other literary works;

i. to assume responsibility for the revival, production and preservation of indigenous and traditional literary works;

j. to plan and coordinate library and documentation services in the United Republic;

k. to advise the Government and parastatal institutions on all matters relating to the production of books and other literary works;

l. to advise the Government and parastatal institutions on all matters relating to library and documentation services;

m. to provide advisory services and financial technical assistance necessary for or incidental to the proper and efficient development of enterprises engaged in the production of books and other literary works;

n. to carry out research in the development of library and documentation services and the production and marketing of books and other literary works;

o. to do all such acts and things, as in the opinion of the Board may be necessary to uphold and support, the credit of the Board and to obtain and justify public confidence, and to avert and minimize any loss to the Board;

p. to do anything or enter into any transaction, which in the opinion of the Board, is calculated to: facilitate the proper and efficient exercise by the Board of its functions under this Act, including:

   (i) the carrying on of any of the activities of the Board in participation with any other person;

   (ii) the acquisition, by agreement, of interests in enterprises engaged in activities in which the Board may lawfully be engaged under this Act, and the management of the affairs or the continuance of the business of such enterprises;

   (iii) the establishment of branches within the United Republic or elsewhere.

Powers in relation to libraries

5(1) The Board may, with the consent of the Minister, make by-laws:

a. requiring all or any category of public libraries in Tanganyika to be registered with the Board and providing for the form of and the fee for such registration;

b. prohibiting employment of any person as a librarian of any public library unless such person holds a degree, diploma or other award specified in such by-laws;

c. requiring such schools and other educational institutions, including institutes of higher education, as may be specified in the by-laws to establish and maintain libraries in such manner and of such standard as may be prescribed;

d. requiring public libraries registered with it to comply with such requirements as to the maintenance of

(Continued)

Table B Functions and powers of the TLSB. *(Continued)*

Powers in relation to libraries

indexes, the preparation of registers of members, the submission of financial and other returns and such other matter as may be prescribed.

(2) It shall be the duty of every person who prints or produces or causes to be printed or produced in Tanganyika any book or other literary work intended for sale or public distribution or exhibition, whether in consideration of any fee or otherwise, to supply the Board, free of charge, not less than two copies of such book or other literary work: Provided that in the case of any of any gramophone record, film or other book, not being a printed material, the Board may direct that the person producing the same shall supply the Board with one copy only.

(3) It shall be lawful for the Board by notice in writing, to require the person responsible for the management of any public library registered with it to make available in or to remove from any library such books and other literary works as the Board may in such notice specify.

(4) Any person who contravenes any by-law made under subsection (1) or fails to comply with the requirement of subsection (2) or with any notice given under subsection (3) shall be guilty of an offence and shall be liable on conviction to a fine not exceeding twenty thousand shillings or to imprisonment for a term not exceeding three years or to both such fine and imprisonment.

Source: Adapted from United Republic of Tanzania. *Tanzania Library Services Board Act No. 6 of 1975*; Dar es Salaam, Tanzania, 1975; Sections 4(1) a–p, 5(1–4); pp. 42–43 (see also http://www.parliament.go.tz/Polis/PAMS/Docs/6-1975.pdf).

APPENDIX C

Table C Major higher learning institutions in Tanzania and their URLs.

1. University of Dar es Salaam (UDSM)—http://www.udsm.ac.tz (Dar es Salaam)
   - Dar es Salaam University College of Education—http://duce.ac.tz/ (Dar es Salaam)
   - Mkwawa University College of Education—http://muce.ac.tz/ (Iringa)
   - The Institute of Journalism and Mass Communication—http://www.ijmc.udsm.ac.tz/ (Dar es Salaam)
2. Sokoine University of Agriculture (SUA)—http://www.suanet.ac.tz (Morogoro)
   - Moshi University College of Cooperative and Business Studies—http://www.muccobs.ac.tz/ (Moshi)
3. Muhimbili University of Health and Allied Sciences (formerly Muhimbili University College of Health Sciences, MUCHS, of UDSM)—http://www.muchs.ac.tz (Dar es Salaam)
4. Ardhi University (formerly University College of Lands and Architectural Studies, UCLAS, of UDSM)—http://www.uclas.ac.tz (Dar es Salaam)
5. Open University of Tanzania (OUT)—http://www.tanzania.go.tz/out.htm (Dar es Salaam)

(Continued)

Table C Major higher learning institutions in Tanzania and their URLs. (Continued)

6. Mzumbe University (MU)—http://www.mzumbe.ac.tz/ (Morogoro)
7. State University of Zanzibar—http://www.suza.ac.tz/ (Zanzibar)
8. Tumaini University—http://www.elct.org/tumaini.html
   - Makumira University College—http://www.makumira.ac.tz/ (Arusha)
   - Kilimanjaro Christian Medical College—http://www.kcmc.ac.tz/KCM%20College.htm (Moshi)
   - Iringa University College—http://www.elct.org/iringa.html (Iringa)
   - Dar es Salaam College—http://www.tumainidsm.ac.tz/ (Dar es Salaam; formerly Waldorf College Tanzania)
9. St. Augustine University of Tanzania—http://www.saut.ac.tz/ (Mwanza)
   - Bugando University College of Health Sciences—http://www.bugando.ac.tz/ (Mwanza)
   - Mwenge University College of Education—http://www.mwuce.org/ (Moshi)
   - Ruaha University College, a Constituent College of Law and Technological Sciences—http://www.ruco.ac.tz/ (Iringa)
10. Mount Meru University—http://www.mmu.ac.tz/ (Arusha)
11. The University of Arusha—http://www.universityofarusha.ac.tz/ (Arusha)
12. The Hubert Kairuki Memorial University—http://www.hkmu.ac.tz/ (Dar es Salaam)
13. International Medical and Technological University—http://www.imtu.edu/pou.htm (Dar es Salaam)
14. Zanzibar University—http://www.zanvarsity.ac.tz/ (Zanzibar)
15. Zanzibar/Chukwani College of Education—(Zanzibar)
16. University of Dodoma—http://www.udom.ac.tz/ (Dodoma)
   - College of Education
   - College of Humanities and Social Sciences
   - College of Information and Virtual Education
   - School of Life Sciences
   - School of Health and Allied Sciences
17. Saint John's University of Tanzania—http://www.sjut.ac.tz/ (Dodoma)
18. Stefano Moshi Memorial University College—http://mwikacollege.com/ (Moshi)
19. The Aga Khan University—Tanzania Institute of Higher Education—(http://www.aku.edu/)
20. Teofilo Kisanji University—http://teku.ac.tz/ (Mbeya)
21. Muslim University of Morogoro—http://www.mum.ac.tz/ (Morogoro)
22. Dar es Salaam Institute of Technology (DIT)—http://www.dit.ac.tz (Dar es Salaam)
23. Technical College Arusha (TCA)—http://tca.habari.co.tz
24. Mbeya Institute of Science and Technology (MIST)
25. Institute of Finance Management—http://www.ifm.ac.tz/ (Dar es Salaam)
26. The DMI-St. Joseph Group of institutions—http://stjoseph-tanzania.com/index1.html
   - St. Joseph College of Engineering and Technology (SJCET), Dar es salaam
   - St. Joseph Institute of Information Technology (SJIIT), Songea

(Continued)

Table C Major higher learning institutions in Tanzania and their URLs. (Continued)

   - Tanzania Institute of Management(TIM), Dar es salaam
27. College of Business Education (Dar es Salaam and Dodoma campuses)—http://www.cbe.ac.tz/
28. Institute of Accountancy Arusha—http://www.iaa.ac.tz/08/
29. Eastern and Southern Africa Management Institute (ESAMI), Arusha—http://www.esami-africa.org/ (regional institution)
30. College of African Wildlife Management, Mweka-Moshi—http://www.mwekawildlife.org/

REFERENCES

1. CIA. *The 2008 World Factbook.* Available at https://www.cia.gov/library/publications/the-world-factbook/index.html (accessed August 8, 2008).
2. Internet World Stats. *Usage and Population Statistics 2008.* Available at http://www.internetworldstats.com/ (accessed September 20, 2008).
3. UNAIDS/WHO. *Sub-Saharan Africa AIDS Epidemic Update: Regional Summary*, 2008. Joint United Nations Programme on HIV/AIDS (UNAIDS) and World Health Organization (WHO). Available at http://data.unaids.org/pub/Report/2008/jc1526_epibriefs_ssafrica_en.pdf (accessed September 20, 2008).
4. UNDP. *Human Development Report 2007/8—Fighting Climate Change: Human Solidarity in a Divided World.* Available at http://hdr.undp.org/hdr2007–2008/ (accessed September 20, 2008).
5. International Telecommunication Union. *ITU/ICT Statistics 2008.* Available at http://www.itu.int/ITU-D/ict/statistics/ (accessed September 20, 2008).
6. TCRA. *TCRA Statistics: Broadcasting Services 2000–2006.* Available at http://www.tcra.go.tz/publications/broadcast.html (accessed September 20, 2008).
7. Zanzibar Department of Archives Museums and Antiquities. Available at http://www.zanzibarheritage.go.tz/.
8. Matovelo, D.S.; Lwehabura, M.J.F. User fee in public libraries: perspectives, opportunities and challenges in Tanzania's libraries. Univ. Dar es Salaam Libr. J. **2004**, *6* (2), 13–31.
9. Aguolu, C. *Libraries of learning and research in Nigeria higher education: emergence, roles and responsibilities*, Ph.D. Dissertation Library Science; University of California: Berkeley, CA, 1977; 692.
10. Olden, A. "For poor nations a library service is vital": establishing a national public library service in Tanzania in the 1960s. Libr. Quart. **2005**, *75*(4), 421–445.
11. Ilomo, C.S. The history and work of Tanzania Library Service 1963–80. In *Aspects of African Librarianship: A Collection of Writings*; Wise, M., Ed.; Mansell Publishing Limited: London, U.K., 1985; 98–153.
12. Kaungamno, E.E.; Ilomo, C.S. *Libraries: Vital Factors in Development (TLS Silver Jubilee 1964–1989)*; Education Services Centre: Dar es Salaam, Tanzania, 1989.
13. Kaungamno, E.E.; Ilomo, C.S. Library services in West and East Africa. In *Books Build Nations*; TransAfrica/TLS: Dar es Salaam, Tanzania, 1979; Vol. 1, 66–137.

14. Kaungamno, E.E.; Ilomo, C.S. Library services in Tanzania. In *Books Build Nations*; TransAfrica/TLS: Dar es Salaam, Tanzania, 1979; Vol. 2, 1–237.

15. *Five Year Development Plan, 1964–69*, Government Printer: Dar es Salaam, Tanzania, 1964; United Republic of Tanzania.

16. Stabler, E. Kenya and Tanzania: strategies and realities in education and development. Afr. Affairs **1979**, *78*(310), 33–56.

17. Arunsi, N.O. The library and adult education in Tanzania: a survey. In *Libraries in East Africa*; Wallenius, A-B., Ed.; The Scandinavian Institute of African Studies: Uppsala, Sweden, 1971; 83–124.

18. Dahlgren, C. The Tanzania Library Service: a review of recent literature. World Libr. **1994**, *5*(1). Available at http://www.worlib.org/vol05no1/dahlgren_v05n1.shtml (accessed August 20, 2008).

19. Malekani, A.W. Problems affecting the promotion of literacy in Tanzania and the role of Library and Information Science (LIS) profession in alleviating the situation. Univ. Dar es Salaam Libr. J. **2005**, *7*(1), 57–70.

20. Mpogolo, Z.J. Post-literacy and continuing education in Tanzania. Int. Rev. Educ. **1984**, *30*(3), 351–358.

21. Newa, J. Libraries in national literary education programmes in Africa south of the Sahara: the state-of-the-art. Int. Libr. Rev. **1990**, *22*, 73–94.

22. Nilsson, T. The library and adult education in Tanzania: a discussion. In *Libraries in East Africa*; Wallenius, A-B., Ed.; The Scandinavian Institute of African Studies: Uppsala, Sweden, 1971; 53–82.

23. Adi, H.; Sherwood, M. *Pan-African History: Political Figures from Africa and the Diaspora Since 1787*; Routledge: New York, 2003; 147–151.

24. Bhalalusesa, E.P. Education for all in Tanzania: rhetoric or reality? Adult Basic Educ. **2005**, *15*(2), 67–83.

25. Moore, D. *Reaching the Villages: Radio in Tanzania*, 2000. Available at http://www.pateplumaradio.com/genbroad/tanzania.html (accessed August 20, 2008).

26. O'Connor, A. The changing geography of eastern Africa. In *The Changing Geography of Africa and the Middle East*; Chapman, G.P., Baker, K.M., Eds.; Routledge: New York, 1993; 114–138.

27. Mpogolo, Z.J. *A Nationwide Literacy Campaign: The Tanzanian Experience. Literacy Lessons*; International Bureau of Education: Geneva, Switzerland, 1990; 1–17 Report: ED321048.

28. Brock-Utne, B. Peace education in postcolonial Africa. Peabody J. Educ. **1996**, *71*(3), 170–190.

29. Anup. Structural Adjustment—a Major Cause Poverty. Available at http://www.globalissues.org/article/3/structural-adjustment-a-major-cause-of-poverty Shah.

30. *Information & Communication Technology (ICT) Policy for Basic Education*; Ministry of Education and Vocational Training: Dar es Salaam, Tanzania, 2007; United Republic of Tanzania. Available at http://www.moe.go.tz/pdf/ICT%20Policy%20for%20Basic%20Education.pdf (accessed September 1, 2008).

31. Minja, I.U.B. Tanzania: Tanzania Library Services Board. In *The Use of ICTs in African Public Libraries: A Survey of Ten Countries in Anglophone Africa*; Chisenga, J., Ed.; International Network for the Availability of Scientific Publications (INASP): Oxford, U.K., 2004; 104–107.

32. Mlaki, T.E. The national bibliographic agency of Tanzania. IFLA J. **1986**, *12*, 352–355.

33. Marandu, A.A.M. *The Impact of Charging for Services in Public Libraries in Tanzania (Elective paper)*; School of Library, Archives and Documentation Studies: Bagamoyo, Tanzania, 1993; 1–28.

34. Issak, A. Public libraries in Africa: a synthesis report on the literature cited in the bibliography and the country reports. In *Public Libraries in Africa: A Report and Annotated Bibliography*; Issak, A., Ed.; International Network for the Availability of Scientific Publications (INASP): Oxford, U.K., 2000; 8 Comp.

35. Malmgren, P. *Surviving—Not Living: A Study of a Library and Its Users in Northern Tanzania,* Master's thesis; Swedish School of Library and Information Studies, Borås University College: Borås, Sweden, 1999.

36. Mlaki, T.E. Public libraries in Tanzania. In *Public Libraries in Africa: A Report and Annotated Bibliography*; Issak, A., Ed.; International Network for the Availability of Scientific Publications (INASP): Oxford, U.K., 2000; 165–171.

37. Tanzania Library Services Board. *Five-Year Strategic Work Plan. 1999–2004*; TLSB: Dar es Salaam, Tanzania, 1999; 1–50.

38. Tanzania Library Services Board. *A Profile*; TLSB: Dar es Salaam, Tanzania, December 2000.

39. Tanzania Library Services Board (TLSB). Available at http://www.tlsb.or.tz/default.asp.

40. Chisenga, J. Part one: Survey of the status and use of ICTs in public libraries in sub-Saharan Africa. In *The Use of ICTs in African Public Libraries: A Survey of Ten Countries in Anglophone Africa*; Chisenga, J., Ed.; International Network for the Availability of Scientific Publications (INASP): Oxford, U.K., 2004; 3–19.

41. United Nations Information Centres. Available at http://www.un-ngls.org/documents/pdf/ngo.guide/7unics.pdf.

42. International Criminal Tribunal for Rwanda. Available at http://69.94.11.53/default.htm.

43. Msuya, J. The information studies program of the University of Dar es Salaam: perceptions of stakeholders. Inform. Dev. **2005**, *21*(3), 209–217.

44. Msuya, J. The distribution of law libraries in Tanzania and availability of primary sources of legal information. Univ. Dar es Salaam Libr. J. **2002**, *3*(1–2), 51–59.

45. Nkhoma-Wamunza, A.G. Re-thinking changing roles of academic and research librarians in Tanzania: reflections, prospects and challenges. Univ. Dar es Salaam Libr. J. **2003**, *5*(2), 35–46.

46. Kiondo, E. Towards building modern universities in Tanzania: the role of electronic resource sharing networks in teaching, learning and research. Univ. Dar es Salaam Libr. J. **2003**, *5*(1), 1–12.

47. Mwakilana, P.; Nawe, J. The role of academic libraries in facilitating institutional transformation programmes: the case of two constitutional [constituent] colleges of the University of Dar es Salaam. Univ. Dar es Salaam Libr. J. **2005**, *7*(2), 84–97.

48. Rosenberg, D. *Towards the Digital Library: Findings of an Investigation to Establish the Current Status of University Libraries in Africa*; International Network for the Availability of Scientific Publications (INASP): Oxford, U.K., 2005; 1–36. Available at http://www.inasp.info/uploaded/

documents/digital-libr-final-format-web.pdf (accessed September 25, 2008).

49. United Republic of Tanzania. *Hotuba ya Waziri wa Elimu na Mafunzo ya Ufundi Mhe. Profesa Jumanne A. Maghembe (Mb), kuhusu Makadirio ya Matumizi ya Fedha kwa Mwaka 2008/2009*; Ministry of Education and Vocational Training: Dar es Salaam, Tanzania, 2008. Available at http://www.moe.go.tz/pdf/HOTUBA%20YA%20WEMU% 202008~2009.pdf (accessed September 1, 2008).

50. Kaungamno, E.E. *School Libraries as a Basic Tool for Teaching;* Tanzania Library Services Board: Dar es Salaam, Tanzania, 1973; Occasional papers (Tanzania Library Service) No. 25.

51. Frost, K.E. *Tanzania School Libraries, May 1968-December 1970, UNESCO Document 2374/RMS.RS/DBA*; UNESCO: Paris, France, 1971; 1–23.

52. Oketch, M.; Rolleston, C. Policies on free primary and secondary education in East Africa: retrospect and prospect. Rev. Res. Educ. **2007**, *31*, 131–158.

53. The United Republic of Tanzania. *National Information and Communications Technologies Policy 2003*; Ministry of Communications and Transport: Dar es Salaam, Tanzania, 2003. Available at http://www.tcra.go.tz/policy/ Nationa%20ICT%20Policy%20of%202003.pdf (accessed September 24, 2008).

54. http://unpan1.un.org/intradoc/groups/public/documents/ Other/UNPAN025361.pdf [see also http://news.bbc.co.uk/ 2/hi/technology/3673431.stm].

55. http://www.itu.int/wsis/docs2/pc1/contributions/tanzania.doc.

56. http://unpan1.un.org/intradoc/groups/public/documents/ cafrad/unpan006453.pdf.

57. http://www.tenmet.org/.

58. http://ces.iisc.ernet.in/energy/HC270799/LM/SUSLUP/ Thema3/356/356.pdf.

59. Karugila, J.M. German records in Tanzania. Afr. Res. Doc. **1989**, *50*, 12–18.

60. Katundu, D.R.M. Tanzania's 2002 records and archives management act: a critical appraisal. Univ. Dar es Salaam Libr. J. **2002**, *4*(1 and 2), 75–89.

61. Schneider, L. The Tanzania national archives. Hist. Afr. **2003**, *30*, 447–454.

62. World Bank/International Records Management Trust. *Evidence-Based Governance in the Electronic Age: Case Study Financial Records and Information Systems in Tanzania*; World Bank/International Records Management Trust: London, U.K., 2002; 1–32.

63. Nyirenda, H.D. Archives administration in Tanzania: Quo vadis?. Afr. J. Libr. Inform. Sci. **1994**, *4*(2), 107–116.

64. Wema, E. Problems of managing semi-active records in institutions of higher learning: the case of University of Dar Es Salaam. Univ. Dar es Salaam Libr. J. **2003**, *5*(1), 46–56.

65. Mnjama, N. The records of the East African Community. Afr. Res. Doc. **2000**, *82*, 3–12.

66. http://www.museum.or.tz/.

67. http://www.arushamuseum.ac.tz/index.htm.

68. Croucher, S.K. Clove plantations on nineteenth-century Zanzibar—possibilities for gender archaeology in Africa. J. Soc. Archaeol. **2007**, *7*(3), 302–324.

69. Kessy, E.T. Iron age settlement patterns and economic change on Zanzibar and Pemba islands. In *East African Archaeology: Foragers, Potters, Smiths, and Traders*;

Kusimba, C.M., Kusimba, S.B., Eds.; University of Pennsylvania Museum of Archaeology and Anthropology: Philadelphia, PA, 2003; 117–131.

70. http://www.zanzibarheritage.go.tz/museums.htm.

71. http://www.zanzibarheritage.go.tz/Unguja%20Ukuu% 20Site%20Museum.htm.

72. http://www.meseranisnakepark.com/maasai-cultural-museum.html.

73. http://www.meseranisnakepark.com/.

74. http://www.parliament.go.tz/Polis/PAMS/Docs/22–1979. pdf.

75. Msuya, C.S. *Cultural heritage in Tanzania*; Division of Antiquities, Tanzania: Dar es Salaam, Tanzania 1–41 slide presentation. Available at http://ts-den.aluka.org/fsi/img/ misc/pdf/CHWorkshop/ChedielSimonMsuya.pdf (accessed September 25, 2008).

76. http://www.international.icomos.org/risk/2001/tanz2001. htm#.

77. http://www.tanserve.com/trivia/index_files/places.htm.

78. http://www.tour-tanzania.com/destination_guide.

79. Doody, K.Z., Howell, K.M., Fanning, E., Eds. *Amani Nature Reserve: A Biodiversity Survey*; Frontier Tanzania; Forestry and Beekeeping Division and Metsähallitus Consulting: Dar es Salaam, Tanzania and Vantaa, Finland, 2001; East Usambara Conservation Area Management Programme Technical Paper No. 52. Available at http:// veli.pohjonen.org/usambara/tecpap52.pdf (accessed August 20, 2008).

80. http://www.easternarc.org/eucamp/amanigazetted.html.

81. http://www.tropical-biology.org/research/dip/amani.htm.

82. http://www.aluka.org/page/about/partners/tanzania_nht.jsp.

83. United Republic of Tanzania. *The Tropical Pesticide Research Institute Act, 1979 (Act No. 18)*; Government Printer: Dar es Salaam, Tanzania, 1979. Available at http://www.parliament.go.tz/Polis/PAMS/Docs/18–1979. pdf (accessed September 1, 2008). For some amendments see http://www.kilimo.go.tz/Regulations/The%20Tropical %20Pesticides%20Research%20Institute%20Act,% 201979.doc (accessed September 1, 2008).

84. Kabuye, C.S. Assessment of status of Herbaria and capabilities in taxonomy and systematics for natural resources inventory in sub-Saharan Africa. Syst. Geogr. Plants **2001**, *71*(2), 237–245.

85. Finke, J. *Tanzania*, 1st Ed.; Rough Guides: London, U.K., 2003; 407–481.

86. Bgoya, W. Introduction—scholarly publishing in Africa: an overview. In *African Scholarly Publishing Essays*; Mlambo, A., Ed.; African Books Collective Ltd: Oxford, U.K., 2007; 1–10, the Dag Hammarskjöld Foundation: Uppsala, Sweden; International Network for the Availability of Scientific Publications: Oxford, UK.

87. http://www.freewebs.com/africanpublishers/index.htm.

88. Aina, L.O.; Mutula, S.M. Opportunities for electronic publishing in Africa. In *African Scholarly Publishing Essays*; Mlambo, A., Ed.; African Books Collective Ltd: Oxford, U.K., 2007; 193–200 the Dag Hammarskjöld Foundation: Uppsala, Sweden; International Network for the Availability of Scientific Publications: Oxford, U.K.

89. Mulokozi, M.M. Scholarly writing and publishing in African languages—with emphasis on Kiswahili: problems and challenges. In *African Scholarly Publishing Essays*;

Mlambo, A., Ed.; African Books Collective Ltd: Oxford, U.K., 2007; 104–111, the Dag Hammarskjöld Foundation: Uppsala, Sweden; International Network for the Availability of Scientific Publications: Oxford, U.K.

90. Mahingila, E. *Intellectual Property Landscape in Tanzania: The Emerging Role of the Business Registration and Licensing Agency (BRELA) in Assisting Small/Medium Enterprises...*, WIPO/TCCIA: Dar es Salaam, Tanzania, 2005; 1–6. Available at http://www.wipo.int/edocs/mdocs/sme/en/wipo_ip_dar_05/wipo_ip_dar_05_www_78437.pdf (accessed September 20, 2008).

91. http://www.poralg.go.tz/mis/index.php.

92. http://www.moneybiz.co.za/african_business_and_technology/african_business_and_technology.asp?african_business_and_technology = 31.

93. Lujara, S.K.; Kissaka, M.M.; Trojer, L.; Mvungi, N.H. Introduction of open-source e-learning environment and resources: a novel approach for secondary schools in Tanzania. Int. J. Soc. Sci. **2006**, *1*(4), 237–241.

94. Christian, G.E. Open access initiative and the developing world. Afr. J. Libr. Arch. Inf. Sci. **2008**, *18*(1), 1–10.

95. Kiondo, E. The University of Dar es Salaam Library: collection development in the electronic information environment. Libr. Hi Tech News **2004**, *6*, 19–24.

96. Manda, P.A. Electronic resources usage in academic and research institutions in Tanzania. Inf. Dev. **2005**, *21*(4), 269–282.

97. http://www.ics.heacademy.ac.uk/italics/vol5–1/pdf/hepworth-evans-final.pdf.

98. http://www.cellular-news.com/story/27024.php.

Task-Based Information Searching: Research Methods

Sanna Kumpulainen
Library, Tampere University of Technology, Tampere, Finland

Abstract
It is widely agreed that searching is part of a larger task performance and that it should be studied in this context. To be able to reveal the process nature of searching, a task-based approach can be used. This entry discusses task-based approach and its use as a framework for field studies, discusses relevant task features, and presents some of the typical methods for studying task-based information interaction in the real-world context.

INTRODUCTION

This entry provides an overview for studying task-based information searching in the real-world context. In order to understand which methods to use in a task-based field study, one has to consider several aspects of the complex task-based setting. Since so little is known about the relations of searching and the underlying tasks, the study of information-intensive task performance requires research methods that are mostly exploratory and descriptive real-world studies. This allows reporting actual behavior with the contextual aspect. By using a task-based approach, the actions of the searcher with both the cognitive and affective aspects can be studied.

People search for information in order to better accomplish tasks at hand.[1] Task trigger information needs,[2] or anomalous state of knowledge (ASK),[3] that lead to various information interactions, including searching. Task-based information searching entails a task that is conducted. When people perform information-intensive tasks, they tend to use the whole information environment available, including various types of information, search tools, and data repositories. During task performance processes, people use several tools in an integrated way to access various types of information. Typically, information-searching studies view at a small piece of the process at time or use only one search tool in a test situation, which lead to narrow understanding of the holistic process of searching. By using too narrow research setting, it is not possible to study the heterogeneous nature of the information source use or the task-related characteristics that affect the search situation. This complexity and the process nature of searching necessitate task-based fieldwork studies in real-life context.

Task-based information searching is a complex phenomenon influenced by contextual characteristics, searcher's personal traits, and the prevailing information environment.[1] Contextual characteristics include the organization, its culture, and its information environment; the task performer's traits, searcher's previous knowledge, experience with similar tasks. One should not forget the varying tasks themselves that affect information behavior. Learning from the experiences of the searchers requires data collection based on multiple methods and triangulation of the findings because no single method is reliable and sufficient in order to study the complexity of real-world searching. Further, there is not a common understanding what are the characteristics of tasks that actually affect the searching. If we understood better the tasks and their intrinsic search tasks, it would not only increase understanding of this important area but also bring more power to experimental test design or even user simulations.

This entry provides a short background, discusses tasks, task complexity and task-based approach, and lastly, gives an overview of some research methods, such as questionnaires, interviews, and shadowing, which are used in fieldwork in task-based information searching.

BACKGROUND

Nowadays, information access is ubiquitous and happens continuously—inseparable from the work task in many cases. In a matter of fact, information is searched in order to fulfill an information need, which is triggered by problems, situations, and daily activities people are in.[1,4–7] Information searching does not occur in a vacuum but is an inseparable part of the surrounding activities, situations, and contexts.[8] The situations people are in may call just some very timely information—such as a bus schedule—or aimlessly passing time, or they may require learning of new skills and knowledge creation in order to accomplish a larger goal. One way to frame the situations for research purposes is to use the task-based approach. Instead of looking at search tasks—querying one information system—task-based approach to information searching is taking the underlying larger task as a starting

Encyclopedia of Library and Information Sciences, Fourth Edition DOI: 10.1081/E-EISA-120053108

point to examine information searching. During task performance, people may need some additional information that cannot be remembered or created with the existing knowledge. This need, which is also called anomalous state of knowledge,[9] prompts information seeking. This might include asking a colleague, checking one's own notes, or searching an information repository.

Since the information searching occurs during a task, the searching should be studied, and evaluated, in relation to the task performance process.[7,10,11] The focus is on the information interaction that happens during that process. A related term, information retrieval, has been defined as the study of how the system replies to a request, or as how humans interact with a system. The task-based approach adopts the latter view, but in a larger context. There has been a turn in information interaction studies from a search task setting into a wider perspective, taking the whole work task as a context of searching. In studying the searching in the context of a task, task-based information searching takes a cognitive viewpoint on information retrieval and human information activities.[1] This viewpoint entails the idea that personal information needs should be treated as potentially dynamic contrary to the static view in traditional information retrieval research.

Searching, even when studied during work task performance, is tightly coupled with the use of information systems or search tools. These tools are used in order to get to the contents, not just to interact with the system interface. Information searching entails the whole cycle from the searcher's cognitive state to the representation of the information itself. While much is known about how systems work in retrieving documents, there is lack of knowledge on the user side and of how searching relates to task performance, how people use the information tools available to them, and where the tools fail to meet their needs.[12,13] Understanding and exploiting contextual information may transform how people perform information discovery, analysis, and synthesis tasks.[1] In order to build better tools, our understanding about searchers, underlying information environments and tasks, and their interrelations is crucial. In case of studying interactive information systems, in order to know the "goodness" of a system, their ability to advance the underlying task should be tested.[10]

Information searching has been both studied with experimental settings in laboratory conditions and as natural settings in the real world. These branches of research differ from their research goals and methods.

Both are needed and the first approach seems more common at this point of time.[11] Although these branches have different goals, there are some connections in between: real-world studies may reveal something that can be further tested in laboratory conditions. In order to test something relevant, one should know first what to test. This knowledge is gathered by field work in real-life situations and exploratory and descriptive studies of this kind

may inform hypothesis formation to be further tested in controlled experimental settings.

Experimental settings usually entail researcher involvement and controlled environments and report quantitative results. Some of these elements may be included in field studies as well, but usually fieldwork occurs in natural environments without any excessive researcher involvement. Moreover, usually in experimental interactive information retrieval and search studies tasks are seen as a vehicle for research,[14] whereas in fieldwork tasks are regarded as inherent part of human daily performance. In controlled settings, it is very demanding to create long-lasting task processes with assigned tasks and therefore experimental studies commonly use more limited search tasks.

Fieldwork studies are intended to observe how real people search in order to complete real tasks. However, experimental studies in information searching are intended to study particular effects of the selected variables on human or system behaviors. This requires control over the situation. In experimental research designs, assigned tasks help with controlling the setting. Assigned tasks are hard to design and they may lack contextual features or personal aspects such as motivational or affective triggers that, in the real world, are present in search processes. Borlund[15] and Wildemuth and Freund[16] provide recommendations on how to design assigned tasks. Despite the challenges in designing tasks, there are experimental studies that have incorporated exquisitely real-world features.[17,18] In these studies, assigned tasks are designed to reflect real-world situations.

The present entry focuses on fieldwork methods. The aims of fieldwork lie on understanding how people behave with the tools they are used to work with and during the tasks they are doing. Nevertheless, for those more interested in experimental settings, Kelly[14] provides a broad overview on how to study interactive information retrieval and evaluate systems with users, Kelly and Sugimoto,[19] a recent review on interactive evaluation research, and Wildemuth et al.,[20] a review on assigned task difficulty and complexity in experimental settings.

TASKS IN TASK-BASED INFORMATION SEARCHING

A task is an activity to be performed in order to accomplish a goal.[6] Task-based information searching is interested in the information interaction related to the task performance. A task at hand may be either a leisure or work-related task. It is seen as a triggering force behind the information needs,[21] or ASK,[9] possibly leading to information searching. According to Järvelin and others,[11] it is a part of a larger task performance process, which can be cut down into activities, searching being one of them. Searching is one small part of the larger task, among other activities, that are all aiming at task fulfillment.[11,22]

Task Granularity

Human task performance and searching may be examined in different context and on different levels of abstraction.[1] Tasks are interpreted at multiple levels of granularity, and this is related to one's understanding about the task.[22] Task doer needs to understand the preconditions and goals for performance. As her understanding about the task increases, and if the focus is formulated, she is more capable of decomposing the task into smaller pieces. These pieces are conceptualized as stages,[23,24] during which the cognitive and affective states evolve, or as successive subtasks or actions,[11] which advance the fulfillment of the task.

Byström and Hansen[22] look at the task granularity as a hierarchical structure, where information-seeking tasks are part of a larger (work) task, and search tasks are part of an information-seeking task. They also discuss information use as an essential part of a larger task and as a contributing factor in task accomplishment. Järvelin and others[11] decompose a (learning) task into five cognitive and behavioral activities, which are task planning, searching information items, selecting between them, working with them, and synthesizing and reporting.

Similarly to Byströms and Hansen's levels in their task hierarchy, Kekäläinen and Järvelin[25] present a nested model of context to evaluate information searching.[1,25] They separated sociocultural, organizational, the work task, the information-seeking task, and the information retrieval levels. Tasks may be analyzed on these levels as task descriptions or goals. All these levels are present in a task performance process and the phenomena during task performance may belong to varying contextual levels.[26] The contextual levels also outline the methods and the participants in the study to some extent. On the socio-organizational level, research interest may lie on decomposing networked phenomena and identifying its actors.[27,28] On the organizational level, one may be interested in task flows in the organization and of division of labor, etc.,[29] or studying on the high-level task context in collaborative information searching during team-work.[30,31] This entry, however, takes the view of studying one individual at time, but similar settings may also be applicable to groups of people.

Typically studies on information searching take the search task level as a starting point. However, in real world the goals and constraints of the tasks are derived from higher-level tasks.[1,24,32] Taking the higher-level context into account, the missing links between larger tasks and search tasks may be found. The larger, motivating task is binding the subactions together, which might seem atomistic if separated from each other. If just the single search task is taken as a starting point, one system

setting might seem reasonable. However, if the scope is broadened toward a larger task, one may have to accept the whole information environment composed of multiple types of information systems providing heterogeneous data or information, such as audio, pictorial, numerical, or text data. The actual information is created during the process, collected piece by piece from various sources and finally interpreted and used in knowledge creation.[33] The task has several features additional to the granularity one being the task complexity, which is discussed next.

Task Complexity

Task complexity and difficulty are very commonly integrated in information searching research.[20] Research in information searching has discussed task complexity from both objective and subjective perspectives. These two perspectives have different background. Objective task complexity supposes "an objective task external to and independent on task performers."[34] In the objective task complexity, the structure of the task and aspects related to the task are used in assessing the task complexity. The increasing number of choices (paths) leading to the desired outcome increases task complexity. Objective task complexity is the complexity of the prescribed task seen by the person prescribing the task, and subjective task complexity is the complexity of the actual task for the task performer executing it.[34]

Tasks may be difficult to perform by many factors; for example, there might be too many alternatives to consider, imprecise or missing raw data, a great deal of irrelevant information, lack of ideas, or insufficient methods.[1,35] This characterization, which considers the features of the task, treats complexity as a function of objective task characteristics.[36]

Further, Campbell[36] and Liu and Li[34] consider task complexity as composed of number of subtasks. Albertson and Meadows[37] use similar construction: complex search tasks contain multiple subtopics. Objective task complexity may be defined also as the number of steps required in order to reach the completion. Li and Belkin's[38] comprehensive task categorization uses both objective and subjective characteristics. It is based on earlier categorizations in information research literature and includes a number of dimensions, which may be divided into objective and subjective parts. Objectivity here means the number of paths between which the task performer has to choose during the task. The subjective aspect in the categorization is called difficulty.

An example of more subjective approach is a priori task complexity. Byström and Järvelin's[39] approach to task complexity is an intersection between the task and actor characteristics: it evaluates task complexity on the basis of the actor's a priori understanding about the features of tasks—namely the information needed, the process, and the outcome. If all the aspects are known, the task is routine, and if none, the task is considered as complex.[39,40] There are different levels in between. In complex tasks, the actor lacks a mental model sufficient for enabling him or her to assess what needs to be done. The a priori task complexity has been used in field studies because it does not require subject expertise. In a priori task complexity, the task performer's previous knowledge on similar tasks affects the complexity assessment, because the more experience the person has with similar tasks, the more focused the conceptual structure of the task.[41] Byström and Järvelin's[39] a priori task complexity has been applied also to some extent by Bell and Ruthven,[42] Kumpulainen,[40,43] and Kumpulainen and Järvelin.[26,33]

Both objective and subjective views on task complexity may be employed in fieldwork. However, if a person does not know what the outcome is or cannot describe the possible paths, it is very hard to count or consider the different aspects or the paths to the completion. In fieldwork, the task complexity can be assessed only after the task performance, when all the queries and needed steps or subtasks are already conducted.

However, researchers cannot be sure during fieldwork that the participant is actually going to end the task during the research time period. Therefore, the a priori task complexity may be more useful in real-life studies. This way, a task complexity assessment can be collected for all task performance sequences even if the task processes do not reach the completion. One should keep in mind that natural research settings include always some compromises and instability. Therefore, because of the (possibly) uncompleted and incomplete tasks, it is hard to compare different task performance sessions with another ones if one uses the objective complexity and the numbers of subtask constructs, or the total number of paths, are needed.

Whether the task is self-formulated or assigned, it is the perceived task that is performed after all. The perceived task is the task performer's current understanding about the task goals and the suitable path(s) leading to that goal. This means that people who have the same assigned task treat it according to their understanding. This perception may change during the task performance due to learning about the task itself. Perception of the task and possible solutions are evolving and getting clearer toward the end of the process. One critical point is the focus formulation phase, during which the actor creates a clear understanding what the task is about.[23,41] Focus formulation allows the searcher to make pertinent judgments about the retrieved items. Without this formulation, a task can be performed, but the outcome might not be good.[44]

The Process Nature of Searching

Task performance and searching are evolving, iterative processes. According to Toms,[32] the process of achieving

the task outcome determines the success in task performance. Therefore, tasks and search tasks internal to them should be studied as processes. The processes may be decomposed into smaller events. There are models that look task performance in stages,[23,24] and models that decompose tasks into subtasks, which are performed as series of actions.[11,43,45,46]

One of the early stage models was the Kuhlthau's ISP model.[23] The ISP model consists of six stages, during which the information search process evolves, and the searcher formulates a focused understanding about the topic. According to the model, this point is critical since the focus formulation enables the searcher to assess the relevance of information items. Kuhlthau's model examines the searching process at levels of physical actions, cognitive and affective aspect, and it was developed to inform librarians. Vakkari's[24] task-based information search model was based on the ISP, and it consisted of three stages. Both models used stages, and the searcher moved from a stage to another in the course of searching. Models in information searching research that decompose task processes into subtasks are not very common. A very recent model of Järvelin and colleagues[11] decomposes a learning task into five subtasks and discusses program theories[47] of these subtasks as a tool for information retrieval evaluation.

The berry-picking model by Bates was one of the first models that described searching and exploration task performance as a process.[48] It was developed in an OPAC (online public access catalog) environment, which included references to full texts. Bates' berry-picking model is based on the idea that pieces of information are collected from separate documents or information objects during the search, and the understanding about the task was created during the berry-picking episodes. This is a natural way humans explore their information environments, and this applies also to web environment.

The study of task-based searching as a process entails that the subtasks, the search stage, or phase should be taken into account. The process of searching affects the searchers' understanding about the task itself, the perceived utility of information, and what will be the next step in the process. Together with the procedural approach, task features such as complexity and granularity are worth consideration in research setting. Due to their complexity, these task-related phenomena often require multimethod research. In the next section, we discuss some of the methods that may be used in task-based field studies.

STUDYING TASK-BASED INFORMATION SEARCHING IN THE FIELD

Due to the complexities of studying information searching during tasks in their context, it requires multiple and often tedious means of data collection. The traditional means of data collection for studying human actions include questionnaires, interviews, diaries, and observation.[1] The quality of results obtained from field research depends greatly on the data gathered in the field.

There are some field studies that relate searching to larger tasks. Typically, the type of task-based research uses multiple methods. To review a few, Byström and Järvelin[39] studied information seeking related to tasks in municipal administration through diaries and questionnaires. Saastamoinen and others[49] revisited this study and studied how task complexity was related to the information types in municipal administration by using task shadowing and questionnaires. Kumpulainen and colleagues,[33,40,50] Huuskonen and Vakkari,[51,52] Freund and colleagues,[53] and Markkula and Sormunen[54] used shadowing combined with some other method. Kumpulainen and colleagues[33,40,50] examined how query types and the use of various systems varied according to task complexity in molecular medicine. They used shadowing, interviews, logging, and photographs. Huuskonen and Vakkari[51] studied by using worksite observations and interviews, how social workers record and use information in a client information system during various tasks. Freund and colleagues[53] used a multimethod approach using focus groups, interviews, shadowing, and resource audits in their study on software engineers' task-based information behavior. Markkula and Sormunen[54] used interviews and task observations to study the work processes of journalists, which included various stages, and these stages shaped information access and interaction.

Attfield and Dowell also studied journalists, but they used interviews and grounded theory for analysis.[55] Bartlett and Toms[56] also used interviews as a data collection method in their study of biotechnology experts work tasks and made a detailed task analysis showing each subtask in the workflow. Vakkari and Huuskonen[44] used questionnaires, search logs, and expert outcome evaluations in their study, which analyzed which aspects of search process and search output were associated with the task outcome in medical students essay writing assignment.

Consequently, it seems that multiple methods are used in studying task-based information searching. In the following, we discuss the typical methods used and data triangulation, which facilitates the in-depth study of complex task performance sessions.

Questionnaires

Questionnaires are a very economic way to collect data and are typically used to study topics that are already known to some extent. However, like all the methods represented in the entry, questionnaires can be used in different types of research settings.[57] Firstly, exploratory research questionnaires benefit from open-ended questions, which allow deep understanding and some unexpected findings. Second type is descriptive survey, which may be used, for example, in collecting opinions about some issue, and typically includes multiple choices and predefined categories. This type is considered as conclusive due to its quantitative nature. Thirdly, one may use questionnaires in explanatory studies in order to study the causality. In explanatory research, careful preplanning of the questions is required. The aim is to explain the cause and effect relationship between variables. Causality may be studied to reveal which variables are the cause and which are the effect and to study what is the type of the relationship between the causal variables and the effect to be predicted.

Questionnaires are usually understood as a means of quantitative research, but they can be also used as a qualitative manner with open-ended questions in an exploratory research setting. The questionnaires in information searching and seeking studies are typically circulated among some social group or staff in an organization, so everyone in the target group is included. Therefore, no actual sampling method is used.

The value of collected data completely depends upon how well respondents answer on questionnaires, and, on the other hand, how good the wording in the questionnaire is. Usually, an explanatory survey is based on a theory from which a hypothesis is derived and the concepts are operationalized. However, in task-based approaches one useful way is just to survey in an exploratory or descriptive manner, for example, what is the perceived information environment like, what are the populations preferences for suitable information tools and to survey what kinds of tasks they perceive doing.[58,59] This kind of research is typical of task-based searching studies. There is no attempt to explore why a phenomenon occurs, but just to state that it does. This is the case if very little is known about, for example, the tools people use in their daily activities. However, since the control over how people respond to a questionnaire is low, questionnaires also benefit if used in combination with some other methods.

Nowadays, questionnaire studies are typically published in web form and a link to the form is distributed via web home page or email. Via web questionnaires, researchers are able to reach large groups of people quickly and simultaneously, they are easy to handle, and the data are already structured in suitable form for further analysis (e.g., a spreadsheet form). However, web questionnaires may be subject to a bias toward certain groups (active, willing to answer, tech savvy, etc.), and they typically suffer from low response rates. Web questionnaires also suffer from the same deficiencies as the paper form questionnaires: it is hard to capture the meaningful aspects of human actions and to place the actions or phenomena that are captured in any context in which they occur—not to mention the process nature of searching. Further, questionnaires have been criticized to block creative thinking and imagination beyond the research setting.[60] However, despite the criticism, open-ended qualitative–style questionnaire studies are very useful in the case the researcher does not know much about the field and needs to get a quick overview of the information environment the people are engaged with and their opinions about it.

Interviews

Interview is one of the major approaches of data collection in qualitative research. Interviews are the best way to collect in depth data on how people understand or feel about phenomena in their everyday lives.[51] It is a means to uncover their experiences and the meaning of these experiences. Interviewing is a good method of studying the "why" questions, and interviewing is focused in comparison with shadowing; one does not have to see everything. During the interview, the researcher creates a personal contact but access to the field is easier than when observing.[50]

Maybe the most used type of interview in task-based studies is a semistructured interview. In this type of interview, the interviewer has broad themes and topics, which are discussed, and the interviewer steers the situation toward the central topics. Preparation is important to be able to steer, and the interviewer should make an interview guide, which includes all the topics that should be covered. In semistructured interviews, the interview guide keeps one on track but still allows her to collect unlimited qualitative data.

There should be a clear purpose for the interview. During the whole interview, the interviewee must feel confident to talk freely. The flow of conversation should be kept going and the interviewer should listen actively and keep the questions simple. However, interviews are open to bias and problems. Opinions regarding behavior are not the same as actual behavior, and the respondents may not correctly remember the answers to questions or they might be unwilling to tell the flow of actual events. People are not good in recalling simple tasks that are executed on a routine basis or exact protocols they follow. More precise accounts of actual behavior are collected by observation, but interviews are very useful when collecting data about people's interpretations about their tasks (e.g., perceived difficulty) or opinions about the search tools they use.

Critical Incident Technique

The critical incident technique is a set of procedures used for collecting the observations of human activity and behaviors.[61] Typically, the participants are asked to recall a recent incident that has relevance to the research questions, and it is used as a vehicle for interviews. The participants may answer the interview questions by reflecting their actions related to that recalled incident or demonstrate their behavior during that recent incident.

This helps the participants to anchor their thoughts and behaviors to a certain incident, and may introduce some reality to basic interview settings. Critical incident technique is suitable for collecting data in the field and in more controlled environments. Critical incident technique is a very flexible method and helps to bind the findings to practical real-world tasks. In task-based information searching, the participants are asked to recall a recent task that included any information-searching episodes. Then, they are interviewed about the causes, descriptions, and outcomes of the task. The actors' feelings and perceptions of the situation are collected and the actions taken during the task are either interviewed or demonstrated. These scenarios can be presented as narratives, visualized in diagrams, or as a causal model. Examples of use of the critical incident method are research by Zach,[62] Auster and Choo,[63] and Roos and others.[58]

Critical incident method can be used also as a vehicle for observational research.[51] The participants are asked to recall a recent situation or a task and to perform the task. Task may be observed at the participants' work place, home, or any other place or environment where the critical incident task has been previously conducted. Also, making people recall a recent task is a good way to bring naturalistic tasks into experimental settings.

This method is very flexible and suitable for studying everyday problem solving, but its challenges lie already in the remembering of the task. The tasks that are recalled tend to be rather simple, and the participants may remember the actual behaviors imprecisely and present idealized workflows. This method, however, helps to bind the searching activities and the underlying task together and it may help in revealing the procedural nature of task performance.

Diaries

Diaries are a good way to collect data on participants' recollections of transactions, such as tasks and used information systems. Usually, diaries are collected with structured forms and diaries are filled after a workday or task performance. People are asked to describe relevant actions and, for example, information sources they used during particular task performance processes. There might be questions about reflecting the events or their features, which relate to the research questions. Therefore, in addition to just collecting the events, diaries provide clues to the importance of events for the participants and their attitudes about those events. Diaries also provide data in textual form, which is easy to analyze compared with voice recordings, for instance, or video diaries. Diaries may be collected via web forms, so that makes the data even easier to handle. Diaries can be a useful strategy for data collection when periods of prolonged participant observation are not practical. This might be the case in order to have a rich source of data of reflections that communicate the stories of their daily lives.

Usually in task-based studies diaries are used in combination with some other data collection method. Byström,[39,64] Hansen,[65] and Saastamoinen and colleagues[49] used diaries in their studies and triangulated the data collection with some other type of data, such as interviews and shadowing. They collected information about the participants' reflections on the task complexity and the use of various information resources, among other things. However, despite the usefulness of diaries in some occasions, participants may find filling in the diaries time consuming and cumbersome. If the diaries are not collected during observations, the researchers cannot know how long after the event the diary was actually made and, consequently, the events might be not remembered correctly. Processes may be collected with diaries, but as discussed previously, they are a means of collecting recollections. People do not describe sequences of actions precisely and sometimes they even tidy up their descriptions of performance. Instead, they tend to describe idealized procedures leaving out some workarounds or problems.

Shadowing

Shadowing is a qualitative method, which involves a researcher closely following people over a period of time to uncover the real-time actions performed in some context.[66,67] It enables the study of information searching in context of real everyday practices and situations and reveals such barriers and routine like workflows that people are not actually aware of. Shadowing facilitates the study of complex tasks and task processes as they are and it is a very agile method. As it is known, people are not good in describing what really happens, but they describe their ideal ideas how things go. This is not necessarily what actually happened. Shadowing can be done over long periods of time or applied more rapidly to gain a quick understanding about a problem.

Before starting the shadowing, it is important to get to know both the organizational environment and the information environment they work with in case of studying information searching. Without knowing what the participants refer to makes it very hard to follow the flow of actions at the start of shadowing. Also, taking some time to carefully select the participants and the venue is important: participants need to take the actions that contribute to the research questions. It is of high importance to carefully select suitable participants for the study. The investigator should be aware of the current tasks the participants are going to conduct, and the shadowing sessions should be arranged so that the kinds of actions, for example, searching, really occur during the shadowing. One practical way is just to simply ask the participants that when they have planned to do some searching and arrive at that point of time to collect the data.

The shadowing method does not require undistorted situations. The participants certainly are aware of being shadowed, and this may have an effect on their behavior and task performance. However, nearly all participants usually become comfortable with the situation after a short while. The method is about gaining an "inside view" of the research questions. Throughout the shadowing period, be it few hours or several months, the researcher asks questions, which will prompt a commentary from the participant. Some questions will be for clarification, other questions to reveal a purpose of actions. During the shadowing, the researcher will write a continuous set of field notes. Shadowing yields data that is more detailed than data gathered through many other data collection methods. Shadowing does not collect the accounts of participants' opinions but observes it directly and gives the researcher first-hand detailed data both on aspects that are habitual or mundane, and the problematic to express, which may be otherwise difficult to collect.

A task is performed in task sessions. These task sessions are observed. During a task performance session, a person is working on a particular task. There might be several ongoing tasks over time, but just one session at the time is performed. Multitasking or parallel task performance means that people switch between the tasks. An actor starts at some point, for example, in the morning when she comes at the working place, or just stops the previous task and changes to another. There might be interruptions during the task, but the task session may continue after the break.

One important aspect in shadowing is to build trust. If the participant does not feel comfortable, critical information could be missed. The researcher must continually work on the personal relationship throughout the shadowing period. By providing information on what purposes the collected data is used and to allow participants to discuss the suitable shadowing times might help the participants to feel they have some control. The agreement that the shadowing may be stopped or paused at any time if it gets too distressing also eases the participants' situation.

Shadowing produces a massive detailed data set that is rich and thick in every aspect. Also, shadowing is a physically and cognitively burdening method for the researcher. It is not easy to follow people around day after day and still trying to stay focused. One of the questions that are of main importance is to keep the research questions in mind all the time, and not "going-native," which means adopting the views and opinions of the research participants. One of the biggest challenges in shadowing is the data handling.[66] The researcher should already before the fieldwork plan how to collect the data and how to analyze it. This also brings more focus to the fieldwork. For collecting the notes, a pen and a hardback notebook are the best. The data handling might be assisted by the use of smart pens or other devises. With the handwritten notes, the researcher already creates a focused view on actions, and so a part of the first-round analysis is already done. Video recordings of several hours are hardly usable, but it can be used if one needs detailed data on a short occasion.

Transaction Logs

A transaction log is "an electronic record of interactions that have occurred between a system and users of that system."[68] There are basically two ways to collect transaction log data, namely client-side or server-side log data. Client-side data collection may be more intrusive than server-side, but it is more accurate and can reveal participant's interactions with the whole information environment via varying channels[33] while server-side logs reveal the interactions with materials on one server. Both have their advantages providing detailed data on user behavior, and they allow studying the process nature of searching. However, the log data lacks depth and are ineffective as a methods of gaining an understanding of the underlying motivations, affective characteristics, cognitive factors, and contextual aspects that influence task-based information searching.[68] User intent analysis based solely on transaction logs has been described as guessing.[69] This is because similar queries are used for quite different search goals. Even an obvious known item search (e.g., for a homepage) may in fact be an unknown fact search (for an email address). However, this method is very valuable if used in a concerted way with some other (qualitative) method, such as shadowing or questionnaires. Despite its benefits, the biggest obstacle to successfully use client-side logging is that organizations or participants may prohibit any data collection on their computers.

Triangulation

Triangulation means the use of two or more methods of data collection in the study of some aspect(s) of human behavior.[70] In other words, it refers to a multimethod research. Although triangulation may be of combining theories, methods, data sets, and investigators in the study of the same object,[70] in this entry, however, the focus is on triangulating the methods. Triangulation advances the study of circumstances when a complex phenomenon requires analysis when some controversial aspects needs studying or when an established approach provides a limited and perhaps distorted picture and where a researcher is engaged in a case study. These all are conditions for a task-based information searching study.

Triangulation of methods raises the research above the possible biases related to the personality of the researcher that stem from a use of a single method.[70] Using more than one method to examine the same research question enables the strengthening of the validity and confidence of the findings. However, sometimes research methods may

show opposite or discrepant events. In this case, the researcher should interpret why this happened and maybe use just one source of data in the analysis. However, there should be an understanding, which is the main data and use that in the interpretation of analysis. By the use of data triangulation, qualitative information can be added to flat quantitative data, such as questionnaire or log data, and more accurate quantitative data may increase the validity of the qualitative data.

Even before the data collection, the researcher should have some understanding about how the analysis will be done. After the triangulated data collection, data need to be merged. By collecting various types of data during the information intensive tasks, researchers should find a way to ensure that they know which data are connected to which task in possibly separate data sets (e.g., time stamps and personal account on log data). In the task-based studies, the point of departure for analysis is the task as a unit of analysis.[64] One way to study the processes of tasks is to analyze the data as task performance sessions. A task performance session is the period of time, during which the participants are conducting a particular task; if the task is ended or changed, the session ends. This can be done by merging all data about each task performance session and then analyzed it together.

Fig. 1 depicts an approach to frame a task session. It has been used in Kumpulainen's[31] studies in task-based information searching in the biotechnology domain. In the procedure, every time a participant starts a task session, the participant is interviewed about what is the aim of the task, how well the participant is able to describe the task content, what information and which sources are to be used, and with which procedures the task is to be performed. These questions aim at assessing the a priori task complexity. During the task performance, field notes and interaction logs were collected. When the participant indicates that the task session might be at the end, some questions take place that ensure the ending of the session. Participants may switch to another task, stop working, or just have a break and continue after a while.

After framing the task sessions, other aspects related to research questions, such as task complexity, type, or stage, can be analyzed. Data may be analyzed using qualitative methods, for example, by classifying, the grounded theory

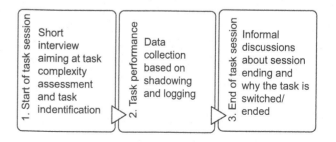

Fig. 1 Task session procedure for triangulation of interview data, transaction logs, and shadowing field notes.

approach, content analysis, visualizations, etc., or by quantifying it. One option to analyze the data is task analysis, which is a way to do detailed task decomposition.[56,71] If task analysis is too fine graded, processes may be studied also by event analysis.[72]

Ethical Concerns

Always, when using humans in research, an informed consent is needed. The researcher needs to think about the confidentiality and protect the identity of the participants. Participants should be informed about the purpose of the investigation and the main features of the research design. There might be some confidential material that the researcher is exposed to during the research, and the way shown to address this kind of material should be agreed in advance. The researcher should cause as little harm to the participants and their organizations or social environments as possible.

CONCLUSION

Real-world information searching is a combination of inquiry, discovery, and serendipity. It is nonlinear and iterative and entails the use of various heterogeneous information types from wide ranges of sources. By task-based studies, we are able to more realistically describe the human behavior during a task performance process, and by this inform not only system design, but also other highly controlled research settings such as simulation studies. On the downside, field studies focus on a specific organizational setting or a specific domain, where limited number and type of tools and data are used in tasks typical to that domain. The specific findings cannot be generalized to other contexts. However, it is not yet clear how the searcher should be modeled or simulated, so there is a world still to discover. Fieldwork remains under pressure due to costs and resource demands, but it still is an invaluable way to study how things really happen.

The existing models of task-based information searching suggest that task performance and information searching are processes that should be studied longitudinally over several work task performance sessions and search sessions. The task-based research is still uncommon, and there is still a need for investigating how and what features of tasks affect the searching. Therefore, the task-based approach provides a useful framework to study complex situations during information intensive work tasks, and further, a means to reveal the procedural nature of searching.

ACKNOWLEDGMENTS

Support during the writing from the Netherlands Organization for Scientific Research (NWO project # 640.005.001; WebART) at the University of Amsterdam, the Netherlands, is acknowledged.

REFERENCES

1. Ingwersen, P.; Järvelin, K. *The Turn: Integration of Information Seeking and Retrieval in Context*; The Information Retrieval Series; Springer-Verlag New York, Inc: Secaucus, NJ, 2005.
2. Taylor, R.S. Question-negotiation and information seeking in libraries. Coll. Res. Libr. **1968**, *29* (3), 178–194.
3. Belkin, N.J.; Oddy, R.N.; Brooks, H.M. ASK for information retrieval. J. Doc. **1993**, *38* (2), 61–71. 1982.
4. Belkin, N.J.; Seeger, T.; Wersig, G. Distributed expert problem treatment as a model for information system analysis and design. J. Inf. Sci. **1982**, *5* (5), 153–167.
5. Belkin, N.J. The cognitive viewpoint in information science. J. Inf. Sci. **1990**, *16* (1), 11–15.
6. Vakkari, P. Task-based information searching. Annu. Rev. Inf. Sci. Technol. (ARIST) **2003**, *37*, 413–464.
7. Wersig, G. *Informationssoziologie: Hinweise Zu Einem Informationswissenschaftlichen Teilbereich*; Athenäum: Frankfurt am Main, Germany, 1973.
8. Blandford, A.; Attfield, S.J. *Interacting with Information*; Morgan & Claypool Publishers: San Rafael, CA, 2010.
9. Belkin, N.J.; Oddy, R.N.; Brooks, H.M. Ask for information retrieval: Part I. Background and theory. J. Doc. **1982**, *38* (2), 61–71.
10. Belkin, N.J. On the evaluation of interactive information retrieval systems. In *The Janus Faced Scholar: A Festschrift in Honour of Peter Ingwersen*; Royal School of Library and Information Science: Copenhagen, Denmark, 2010; 13–21.
11. Järvelin, K.; Vakkari, P.; Arvola, P.; Baskaya, F.; Järvelin, A.; Kekäläinen, J.; Keskustalo, H.; Kumpulainen, S.; Saastamoinen, M.; Savolainen, R. Task-based information interaction evaluation: the viewpoint of program theory. ACM Trans. Inf. Syst. (TOIS) **2015**, *33* (1), 3.
12. Callan, J.; Allan, J.; Clarke, C.L.A.; Dumais, S.; Evans, D.A.; Sanderson, M.; Zhai, C. Meeting of the MINDS: an information retrieval research agenda. SIGIR Forum **2007**, *41* (2), 25–34.
13. Kelly, D.; Arguello, J.; Capra, R. NSF workshop on task-based information search systems. SIGIR Forum **2013**, *47* (2), 116–127.
14. Kelly, D. Methods for evaluating interactive information retrieval systems with users. Found. Trends Inf. Retriev. **2009**, *3* (1–2), 1–224.
15. Borlund, P. *Evaluation of Interactive Information Retrieval Systems*; Åbo Akademi University Press: Åbo, Finland, 2000.
16. Wildemuth, B.M.; Freund, L. Assigning search tasks designed to elicit exploratory search behaviors. In *Proceedings of the Symposium on Human-Computer Interaction and Information Retrieval*, Anonymous; ACM: New York, 2012; 4.
17. Bron, M.; Van Gorp, J.; Nack, F.; de Rijke, M.; Vishneuski, A.; de Leeuw, S. A subjunctive exploratory search interface to support media studies researchers. In *Proceedings of the*

35th International ACM SIGIR Conference on Research and Development in Information Retrieval, Anonymous; ACM: New York, 2012; 425–434.

18. Liu, J.; Belkin, N.J. Personalizing information retrieval for multi-session tasks: examining the roles of task stage, task type, and topic knowledge on the interpretation of dwell time as an indicator of document usefulness. J. Am. Soc. Inf. Sci. Technol. **2015**, *66* (1), 58–81.

19. Kelly, D.; Sugimoto, C.R. A systematic review of interactive information retrieval evaluation studies, 1967–2006. J. Am. Soc. Inf. Sci. Technol. **2013**, *64* (4), 745–770.

20. Wildemuth, B.; Freund, L.; Toms, E.G. Untangling search task complexity and difficulty in the context of interactive information retrieval studies. J. Doc. **2014**, *70* (6), 1118–1140.

21. Taylor, R.S. The process of asking questions. Am. Doc. **1962**, *13* (4), 391–396.

22. Byström, K.; Hansen, P. Conceptual framework for tasks in information studies. J. Am. Soc. Inf. Sci. Technol. **2005**, *56* (10), 1050–1061.

23. Kuhlthau, C.C. Seeking meaning: a process approach to library and information services. In *Information Management, Policy, and Services*; Ablex: Norwood, NJ, 1993.

24. Vakkari, P. A theory of the task-based information retrieval process: a summary and generalisation of a longitudinal study. J. Doc. **2001**, *57* (1), 44–60.

25. Kekäläinen, J.; Järvelin, K. Evaluating information retrieval systems under the challenges of interaction and multidimensional dynamic relevance. In *The Fourth International Conference on Conceptions of Library and Information Science COLIS4*, Seattle, WA July 21–25, 2002; 253–270.

26. Kumpulainen, S.; Järvelin, K. Barriers to task-based information access in molecular medicine. J. Am. Soc. Inf. Sci. Technol. **2012**, *63* (1), 86–97.

27. Law, J.; Hassard, J. *Actor Network Theory and After*; Blackwell: Oxford, U.K., 1999.

28. Latour, B. *Reassembling the Social-an Introduction to Actor-Network-Theory: Reassembling the Social-An Introduction to Actor-Network-Theory*; Oxford University Press: New York, 2005.

29. *Engeström, Y. Activity theory as a framework for analyzing and redesigning work. Ergonomics 2000, 43* (7), 960–974.

30. Foster, J. Collaborative information seeking and retrieval. Annu. Rev. Inf. Sci. Technol. **2006**, *40* (1), 329–356.

31. Shah, C. Collaborative information seeking. J. Assoc. Inf. Sci. Technol. **2014**, *65* (2), 215–236.

32. Toms, E.G. Task-based information searching and retrieval. In *Interactive Information Seeking, Behaviour and Retrieval*; Ruthven, I., Kelly, D., Eds.; Facet Publishing: London, U.K., 2011; 43–75.

33. Kumpulainen, S.; Järvelin, K. Information interaction in molecular medicine: integrated use of multiple channels. In *Proceeding of the Third Symposium on Information Interaction in Context*, ACM: New York/New Brunswick, NJ, 2010; 95–104.

34. Liu, P.; Li, Z. Task complexity: a review and conceptualization framework. Int. J. Ind. Ergonomics **2012**, *42* (6), 553–568.

35. March, J.G.; Simon, H.A.; Guetzkow, H. *Organizations*; Wiley: New York, 1964.

36. Campbell, D.J. Task complexity: a review and analysis. Acad. Manage. Rev. **1988**, *13* (1), 40–52.

37. Albertson, D.; Meadows, C. Situated topic complexity in interactive video retrieval. J. Am. Soc. Inf. Sci. Technol. **2011**, *62* (9), 1676–1695.

38. Li, Y.; Belkin, N.J. A faceted approach to conceptualizing tasks in information seeking. Inf. Process. Manag. **2008**, *44* (6), 1822–1837.

39. Byström, K.; Järvelin, K. Task complexity affects information seeking and use. Inf. Process. Manag. **1995**, *31* (2), 191–213.

40. Kumpulainen, S. *Task-based information access in molecular medicine: task performance, barriers, and searching within a heterogeneous information environment*, Acta Electronica Universitatis Tamperensis, 1360; Tampere University Press: Tampere, Finland, 2013.

41. Vakkari, P. Exploratory searching as conceptual exploration. Proceedings of HCIR, New Brunswick, NJ, August 22, 2010, 24–27.

42. Bell, D.; Ruthven, I. Searcher's assessments of task complexity for web searching. In *Advances in Information Retrieval (Vol. 2997 of the Series Lecture Notes in Computer Sciences)*; McDonald, S., Tait, J., Eds.; Springer: Berlin/Heidelberg, Germany, 2004; Vol. 2997, 57–71.

43. Kumpulainen, S. Trails across the heterogeneous information environment: manual integration patterns of search systems in molecular medicine. J. Doc. **2014**, *70* (5), 8–8.

44. Vakkari, P.; Huuskonen, S. Search effort degrades search output but improves task outcome. J. Am. Soc. Inf. Sci. Technol. **2012**, *63* (4), 657–670.

45. Lin, S.; Belkin, N.J. Modeling multiple information seeking episodes. Proc. ASIS Annu. Meet. **2000**, *37*, 133–147.

46. Marchionini, G. *Information Seeking in Electronic Environments*, Cambridge Series on Human-Computer Interaction; 9; Cambridge University Press: Cambridge, U.K., 1995.

47. Rossi, P.H.; Lipsey, M.W.; Freeman, H.E. *Evaluation: A Systematic Approach*; Sage publications: Thousand Oaks, CA, 2003.

48. Bates, M.J. The design of browsing and berrypicking techniques for the online search interface. Online Inf. Rev. **1993**, *13* (5), 407–424.

49. Saastamoinen, M.; Kumpulainen, S.; Järvelin, K. Task complexity and information searching in administrative tasks revisited. In *Proceedings of the Fourth Information Interaction in Context Symposium*, Nijmegen, The Netherlands, Anonymous; ACM: New York, 2012; 204–213.

50. Kumpulainen, S.; Järvelin, K.; Serola, S.; Doherty, A.; Byrne, D.; Smeaton, A.F.; Jones, G.F.J. Data collection methods for task-based information access in molecular medicine. In *Mobilizing Health Information to Support Healthcare-Related Knowledge Work: Proceedings of the 1st International Workshop on Mobilizing Health Information to Support Healthcare-Related Knowledge Work*, Martins, H.M.G., Ed.; INSTICC Press: Setubal, Portugal, 2009; 49–58.

51. Huuskonen, S.; Vakkari, P. I did it my way: social workers as secondary designers of a client information system. Inf. Process. Manag. **2013**, *49* (1), 380–391.

52. Huuskonen, S.; Vakkari, P. Client information system as an everyday information tool in child protection work. In

Proceedings of the Third Symposium on Information Interaction in Context, Anonymous; ACM: New York, 2010; 3–12.

53. Freund, L.; Toms, E.G.; Clarke, C.L. Modeling task-genre relationships for IR in the workplace. In *Proceedings of the 28th Annual International ACM SIGIR Conference on Research and Development in Information Retrieval*, Anonymous; ACM: New York, 2005; 441–448.

54. Markkula, M.; Sormunen, E. Video needs at the different stages of television program making process. In *Proceedings of the First International Conference on Information Interaction in Context*, Anonymous; ACM: New York, 2006; 111–118.

55. Attfield, S.; Dowell, J. Information seeking and use by newspaper journalists. J. Doc. **2003**, *59* (2), 187–204.

56. Bartlett, J.C.; Toms, E.G. Developing a protocol for bioinformatics analysis: an integrated information behavior and task analysis approach. J. Am. Soc. Inf. Sci. Technol. **2005**, *56* (5), 469–482.

57. Sue, V.M.; Ritter, L.A. *Conducting Online Surveys*; Sage: Thousand Oaks, CA, 2012.

58. Roos, A.; Kumpulainen, S.; Järvelin, K.; Hedlund, T. The information environment of researchers in molecular medicine. Inf. Res. **2009**, *13* (3), paper 353.

59. Bartlett, J.C.; Ishimura, Y.; Kloda, L.A. Scientists' preferences for bioinformatics tools: the selection of information retrieval systems. In *Proceedings of the Fourth Information Interaction in Context Symposium, Nijmegen*, The Netherlands, ACM: New York, 2012; 224–233.

60. De Vaus, D.A. *Surveys in Social Research*; Routledge: London, U.K., 2002.

61. Flanagan, J.C. The critical incident technique. Psychol. Bull. **1954**, *51*, 327–358.

62. Zach, L. When is "enough" enough? Modeling the information-seeking and stopping behavior of senior arts administrators. J. Am. Soc. Inf. Sci. Technol. **2005**, *56* (1), 23–35.

63. Auster, E.; Choo, C.W. How senior managers acquire and use information in environmental scanning. Inf. Process. Manag. **1994**, *30* (5), 607–618.

64. Byström, K. Information and information sources in tasks of varying complexity. J. Am. Soc. Inf. Sci. Technol. **2002**, *53* (7), 581–591.

65. Hansen, P. Task-Based Information Seeking and Retrieval in the Patent Domain: Processes and Relationships, Acta Universitatis Tamperensis; 1631. Tampere University Press: Tampere, Finland, 2011.

66. McDonald, S. Studying actions in context: a qualitative shadowing method for organizational research. Qual. Res. **2005**, *5* (4), 455–473.

67. Czarniawska, B. *Shadowing and Other Techniques for Doing Fieldwork in Modern Societies*; Liber: Malmö, Sweden, 2007.

68. Jansen, B.J.; Spink, A.; Taksa, I. *Handbook of Research on Web Log Analysis*; Hershey: New York, 2009. Information Science Reference.

69. Broder, A. A taxonomy of web search. SIGIR Forum **2002**, *36* (2), 3–10.

70. Denzin, N.K. *The Research Act: A Theoretical Introduction to Sociological Methods*; Aldine Publishing: Chicago, IL, 1970.

71. Vicente, K.J. *Cognitive Work Analysis: Toward Safe, Productive, and Healthy Computer-Based Work*; Lawrence Erlbaum Associates: Mahwah, NJ, 1999.

72. Miles, M.B.; Huberman, A.M. *Qualitative Data Analysis: An Expanded Sourcebook*; Sage: Thousand Oaks, CA, 1994.

Taxonomy

Andrew Grove
Guest Faculty, Information School, University of Washington, Seattle, Washington, U.S.A.

Abstract

Taxonomy reflects the human instinct to organize. Once limited in Western culture to certain natural sciences, in the early twenty-first century, it has expanded to many domains, practices, and uses. Domains now include almost anything of interest, but particularly those motivated by business needs. Practices and uses include description, analysis, prediction, mapping terminology, information access, representation of knowledge, and tool-building. For information science, taxonomy is a powerful tool for connecting information content with information consumers effectively and efficiently.

INTRODUCTION

The practice of taxonomy reflects the human instinct to organize our experiences and perceptions of the world. Many organisms categorize objects: the practice is essential to survival, if only to classify possible food sources as edible or inedible, situations as safe or dangerous, environments as habitable or inhabitable, and so forth. Once such classifications are made, new experiences, objects, and situations may be placed in them, thus simplifying mental processes and interaction with the environment. Humans have developed this instinct to a high degree of sophistication, possibly because of the ability to perceive and process a great many details about the physical world they inhabit. But for people, organization goes far beyond survival needs. It inhabits the very core of human understanding and knowledge. With organization, facts and data become information and eventually knowledge, a rich source of philosophical discourse. Even for those not philosophically inclined, organization of information is an essential part of truly understanding and knowing a topic. According to cognitive psychology, all humans classify; the associations formed by classifying afford economy of thought for understanding the world.

Furthermore, classification may be the earliest technique of scholarship, and classifications provide building blocks with which to construct understandings.[1,2] Many teachers believe that thoroughly understanding the terminology of a discipline is at least half the task of learning it; using taxonomy is one very effective path to such learning. Classification enables children to identify objects correctly, and they use it extensively.[3] Organizing and classification is a useful vehicle for communication; if several parties agree on organization, they have a solid foundation for agreement on meaning, and therefore, mutual understanding. Finally, organizing things is one component of manipulating the environment; for humans, that is an essential

survival mechanism. Thus, even at its most abstract, organization has roots in the continuation of life. That makes it a deeply seated, perhaps essential, part of living.

Given the universal practice of organizing things, it is remarkable that only in the most recent 2500 years of human history has attention been paid to the principles and practice of categorization, classification, and taxonomy. Once almost exclusively the domain and practice of the natural sciences, taxonomy is now practiced in many other disciplines and venues, including the social sciences, computer science, information science, linguistics, cognitive science, and Internet site design and construction. Within these fields, taxonomy has acquired a wide range of meanings no longer restricted to the classical understanding of biology.[4–6] Taxonomy is now applying its early sense of organizing things in accord with particular principles ("taxis": arrangement; "nomos": law) to a broader range of domains after several centuries of limitation to biology and other natural sciences. In the 1990s, taxonomy was redefined as any semantically significant, systematic organization of content[7,8] or as the process of developing such organization.[9] This definition sometimes includes any collection whose individual elements have been assigned to various nodes of a classification system. Thus, taxonomy is sometimes considered the process of matching collection items with predefined labels, and sometimes it is the creation and arrangement, as well as the resulting product, of the classification system itself.

A much overlooked and seldom discussed motivation for taxonomy is the desire of humans to communicate. Understandings of meaning contribute significantly to the human experience; shared and mutually agreeable understandings facilitate communication and connection, a fundamental goal of humans (and possibly other creatures); differences often generate undesired outcomes. Taxonomy, because it organizes entities using representations

Encyclopedia of Library and Information Sciences, Fourth Edition DOI: 10.1081/E-ELIS4-120044405

of them (usually words), creates and facilitates language agreement; users of any particular taxonomy implicitly (and sometimes explicitly) agree upon the organization represented and, equally important, the terminology and semantics.

Taxonomy, in and of itself, through the process of organization and creating (or making explicit) agreement of language, performs an important and valuable role—describing the human experiences and perceptions of the world. When integrated with tools and processes for further exploration and discovery, dialogue and communication, taxonomy can perform a role central to the success (or failure) of such tools and processes; and, through them, the fundamental motivations for their existence and operation: making sense and communicating.

HISTORY OF TAXONOMY

Although Aristotle receives credit for setting out principles of biological taxonomy, one of the earliest recorded taxonomic structures is from the Book of Genesis, "These are the sons of Ham: Cush, Mizraim, Put, and Canaan. The sons of Cush: Seba, Havilah, Sabtah, Raamah, and Sabtecha..."[10] a genealogy of the descendents of Ham (and, by extension, Adam), which predates Aristotle by many centuries. The *Historia Animalium* by Aristotle (384–322 B.C.E.) based taxonomy on the concept of grouping entities because of inherent properties, which collectively define similarities and differences. Properties are determined empirically, by examining many specimens for such characteristics and is an inductive process from observed examples, resulting in a lexical definition.[11] According to Aristotle, important properties included mode of reproduction and habitat, as well as form.[12] Aristotle's basic methodology is still in use, although with some refinement. Linnaeus (1701–1778) introduced the practice of deriving the various levels of a taxonomy from the properties of the organisms or objects in the entire collection. With this development, he prepared the way for later scientific work involving the collection and examination of minute details of many specimens. His procedure contrasted with the practice established by Aristotle and is now commonly called bottom-up classification. By the time Darwin (1809–1882) wrote *The Origin of Species* in 1859, enough data had collected that additional principles of grouping division were necessary. He proposed that evolutionary lineage be considered as one criteria for the classification of species. Thus began the transition of biological taxonomy from a phenetic (observable characteristics, such as form) basis to a phylogenetic (evolutionary history of genetically related groups) basis. This eventually resulted in the ongoing debate whether evolutionary history is a necessary and sufficient criteria or only one of several to consider for accurate classification.

TAXONOMY

Classical Taxonomy

Taxonomy, as developed by Aristotle and refined by Gessner, Ray, Lamarck, Linnaeus, and Darwin, is a form of classification in which objects in a collection are grouped into nested subcollections based on observed similarities and differences. Such analysis has the goal of systematically organizing information and knowledge of organisms.[13] In this sense of the word, taxonomy, as applied in biology, has been called systematics. Although different methodologies have been practiced, the basic principle has remained the same: entities are classed on the basis of inherent properties.

In biology, taxonomy is used to develop classifications of living organisms according to characteristics of form and evolutionary history and to assign newly discovered organisms to existing classifications. These classifications have developed into hierarchical systems composed of lineages, or branches, progressing with increasing specificity from common origins to increasingly divergent specializations, or species. At the top of the hierarchy are five kingdoms: animals, plants, fungi, protista (predominately single-celled organisms), and monera (bacteria). Under these kingdoms, organisms are arranged into at least six ranks, each more specialized than the preceding: phylum, class, order, family, genus, and species. An organism is always classed at least as specific as the species, and possibly more specifically if it is identified as a subspecies, a varietal, or a hybrid. Although most taxonomists are in general agreement concerning the assignment of various species to particular genera, wide disagreement can exist for assignment of genera to family and even more so respecting family membership in particular orders. For some kingdoms, there is dispute whether some of the categories actually have meaning or useful purpose, or whether they are not finely enough defined. One outcome is a set of intermediate classes, such as subkingdom, subphylum, superclass, subclass, infraclass, cohort, and tribe.

Three major strands of thought prevail in biological taxonomy: the phenetic, which considers physical characteristics only; the phyletic (cladistic), which considers evolutionary lineage only; and evolutionary taxonomy, which uses observed similarities and differences, as well as evolutionary history. Because knowledge of evolutionary descent is determined by meticulously examining all characteristics of form, such as the macrolevel of skeletal fossils or the microlevel of molecular biology, the reality is the phenetic and the phyletic tend toward convergence. If the fossil record for any group were complete and taxonomy completely established, phenetic and phyletic arrangements would be identical.[11]

Chemistry and physics provide a well-known example of a classification, which is seldom labeled a taxonomy but most certainly represents one: the periodic table of the elements, in which chemical elements are arranged in a highly structured format according to inherent properties. One measure of the validity and usefulness of the periodic table is its power to predict new elements, a function at which it excels. Another measure of its strength is its descriptive power. The taxonomy structure of the periodic table represents very detailed knowledge about any given element, and the ability to read the table enables one to learn much about elements and their relationships to each other.

As scientists extend human senses with ever more detailed examination of basic units of matter, such as DNA and subatomic particles, definition and classification of common taxonomic subjects continues to shift. A case in point is that of wolves, illustrating ongoing debate over defining a species.[14]

Numerical Taxonomy

The advent of molecular biology—with modern research instruments and methodologies, massive numbers of data points, and corresponding quantities of data values—has prompted the development of new techniques for discerning similarities and differences in organisms. A strictly phenetic approach, numerical taxonomy (also known as taximetrics) is the application of multivariate analysis to measurable features. By using quantitative methods to manipulate large amounts of data and numbers of specimens, numerical taxonomy derives classes and populates them on the basis of inherent properties. Depending on the techniques used, numerical taxonomy either clusters organisms directly, on the basis of similarities (correlation) or indirectly by virtue of differences (distance). In cluster analysis, correlation and distance measures are the inverse of each other.

Many measures of correlation exist, but it is often computed using the Pearson product–moment correlation:

$$r = \sum (x_1 - m_x)(y_1 - m_y)/(n-1)s_x s_y$$

where

r is the product–moment correlation coefficient

x_1 and y_1 are the x and y values for one member of a population

m_x and m_y are the mean of x and y, respectively

s_1 and s_2 are the standard deviations of x and y, respectively

n is the number of measurements

The value of r varies from -1 to 1, with the strength of correlation expressed by the distance from 0, giving an r value for either positive or negative correlations. Assuming two variables with normal distribution, r is a reasonable correlation measure to use. If the distributions deviate widely from normal, or the sample is not large, other correlation measures are more appropriate.[15] Because the correlation and distance measures are inverse, one might think that measuring dissimilarity would simply involve taking the inverse of r. Although that is possible, a more direct approach is to compute the Euclidean, or Pythagorean distance, d, between pairs of values. The equation is expressed in many forms:[16]

$$d = \sqrt{((x_1 - x_2)^2 (y_1 - y_2)^2 + \cdots + (x_{1n} - y_{1n}))}$$

where

x_1 and x_2 are the x and y values for one member of a population

y_1 and y_2 are the x and y values for another member

n is the number of measurements

For the purposes of numerical taxonomy, strong correlations (or, correspondingly small distances) are taken as indications of similarity.

Numerical taxonomy is not without criticism. It has not been adequately considered whether the mathematical and statistical techniques involved are appropriate for taxonomy.[11] Furthermore, there is some risk of selecting irrelevant observations as variables; a trivial example would be to calculate r for species and habitat (to say several organisms are similar because they live in the same vicinity would be erroneous).[12] A more serious risk is that of grouping things based on the absence of a particular feature (many men are balding, and balding is a genetic trait; nevertheless, not all balding men are related).

Contemporary Taxonomy

It is no longer possible to think of taxonomy as process and practice and taxonomies as products in two or three closely related senses only; the terms have acquired a variety of widely disparate meanings, depending on discipline, domain, and application. Interest in and practice of taxonomy has exploded in the early years of the twenty-first century, with Google Scholar returning over 880,000 search results for "taxonomy" in free text and over 825,000 in the title in mid-July, 2008. Noteworthy is the large proportion of results categorized as from the domain of social sciences, arts, and humanities, 16%; and 11.5% from engineering, computer science, and mathematics. Considering that information science overlaps the two categories, it seems reasonable to posit that taxonomy has recently attained considerable status as a research topic outside its traditional sphere of the natural sciences (46.5%). Thus, the proper field of discussion is classifications that have taxonomic characteristics, known as taxonomic classificatory structures, or simply, taxonomic structures. Such constructs can describe abstract concepts, such as opinions, thoughts, behaviors, intentions, emotions, ideals, mores, and beliefs, as well as physical objects that exist independently of human thought.

Whether abstract concepts can have inherent and immutable properties is open to debate. Nevertheless, organization of them seems amenable to certain taxonomic principles, and useful classifications are possible. In this entry, taxonomies and taxonomic structures are used somewhat interchangeably, although taxonomy often refers to process and practice, as well.

Many disciplines, such as biology, physics, astronomy, psychology, and linguistics, generate taxonomies of a classical nature and use them primarily for descriptive purposes. In some cases, classifications are used as research instruments, in which their predictive powers provide a means for testing hypotheses. A different application is the use of taxonomic structures for their ability to affect, wholly or in part, computer and information operations: artificial intelligence (AI), information science, and object-oriented programming (OOP). Artificial intelligence and information science both construct taxonomic structures to deal with massive amounts of information, whereas OOP uses them as integral parts of its methodology and computer programs.

Ontologies in AI

Taxonomic structures in AI are more commonly known as ontologies. Because AI draws heavily from deductive logic, which depends heavily on assertions and facts, AI developers compile facts and data about the objects within particular domains of interest. These compilations are called knowledge bases, and ontologies are an essential tool for managing them. As used in AI, an ontology is more closely akin to kinds of abstract entities to be admitted to a language system. Such concepts are organized generally in a manner that permits sharing and reuse.[17] Ontology and taxonomy often have the same sense: a classification of categories or kinds of concepts, maintained in a knowledge base.[8] In AI, the term ontology has several senses. Some researchers in the AI community consider an ontology to be an abstraction, without realization in concrete form—the conceptual and logical mental construct that forms the basis of a knowledge base—the design, which may be either explicitly formalized or implicitly assumed. Others consider an ontology to be some explicit terminological or semantic structure that captures and expresses the abstract logical design.[18] It is the latter sense that more closely fits the notion of taxonomic structures.

Object-oriented programming

An object-oriented program has many of the characteristics of a taxonomic structure. Essential to OOP are the notions of class and inheritance, both essential components of a taxonomy. Class, in OOP, refers to the concepts of object type (which enables reuse based on type) and modular program structures. For the purposes of understanding an object-oriented program as a taxonomic structure, classes can be thought of as software concepts that are instantiated with programming objects. Classes (thus, objects) have degrees of similarity and dissimilarity, characteristics that enable relating them to each other in hierarchical structures. Because computers require explicit instructions to function, OOP has developed very explicit rules for construction of classes and development of inheritance. Classes may be variants of other classes; a subclass will have all the properties and methods of its superclass, plus some additional characteristic, and they may be combinations of other classes, again with all the features of their ancestors; the intersection of features sets them apart from their ancestors. It is the two qualities of defining program elements in terms of other elements and relationships (particularly hierarchical ones) between the elements that define object-oriented programs as taxonomic structures.

Information access systems

Although taxonomic structures of several types have been essential components of information access systems for many years, the rapid growth and development of the World Wide Web, as well as various intranets that use technologies developed for the Web, have prompted renewed research and development. Indeed, as the distribution of Google Scholar search results for the social sciences, arts, and humanities topic area (19%), plus engineering, computer science, and mathematics (14%) indicates, the information industry has fueled the expansion of taxonomy more than any other factor. At the opening of the 1990s, taxonomy, with few exceptions, meant the descriptive arrangement of organisms and objects in the natural sciences. Scholars often developed small, very limited, highly specialized taxonomies as instruments for research in psychology and the social sciences. The principles of taxonomy were also receiving close scrutiny by computer scientists in AI and OOP. That was the extent of interest in taxonomy. By the end of the twentieth century, however, taxonomy had become a phrase to describe almost any information access system that attempted to match an information user's terminology with the terminology in a system. Given almost another decade, the label "taxonomy" has been applied to such wide variety of language and terminology compilations as to severely dilute the original meaning of the term in common parlance. "Taxonomic structure" represents an attempt to more systematically define the discipline. Exponential growth in the volume of information on both the Web and various intranets has highlighted the need for such terminology control.[27]

Researchers and practitioners continue pursuing taxonomic structures as a means of providing useful and reasonably sized search results from Internet catalogs containing several million sites. The explosion of information available over the Internet and private intranets has exceeded the ability of simple keyword searches to retrieve information; as a result many sites have turned to classification schemes, often called taxonomies, to help users find information.[28] Some system builders use techniques from natural language processing (NLP) to generate classification of key words and phrases from text. These classifications can be combined into a single, virtual taxonomy for retrieving information from the Web. The primary purpose of these taxonomies is to resolve ambiguity and duplication in language.[19] Although many of these classifications are not taxonomies by classical definition (especially internal ones for nonpublic use), research and development continue in the theory and practice of constructing effective taxonomic structures. At the same time, development and use of more traditional taxonomic structures continues. The following systems are particularly important, being almost alone among taxonomic structures in information access systems as having been developed according to widely accepted practices and standards: hierarchically arranged subject heading lists (Library of Congress Subject Headings), geographic place names (Thesaurus of Geographic Names), traditional classifications (Library of Congress Classification and Dewey Decimal Classification), and various indexing languages and thesauri [Art and Architecture Thesaurus, INSPEC Thesaurus, (ERIC) Thesaurus of ERIC Descriptors, to name a few]. The accepted standards for developing thesauri and indexing languages are: Guidelines for the Construction, Format, and Management of Monolingual Thesauri, ANSI Standard Z39.19-2003; Guidelines for the Establishment and Development of Monolingual Thesauri, ISO 2788; Guidelines for the Establishment and Development of Multilingual Thesauri, ISO 5964; Guidelines for the Establishment and Development of Monolingual Thesauri, BS 5723; and Guidelines for the Establishment and Development of Multilingual Thesauri, BS 6723.

THEORY AND PRINCIPLES OF TAXONOMY

Taxonomy has legitimate roots in the natural sciences, logic, linguistics, semantics, and the cognitive sciences; collectively, these contribute to a body of theories and principles that provide rigorous guidance to the construction of taxonomies. Taxonomy is also pragmatic; a taxonomic structure must serve at least one useful purpose or be discarded, no matter how carefully and correctly constructed. Because of this dual nature, one must sometimes turn to the practice of taxonomy to discern theory and principles, and other times study theory and principles to establish practice, which is well illustrated in the earliest taxonomies. Aristotle established the practice of observing characteristics of form, habits, and habitats of plants and animals, using these properties to identify and define the organisms. In doing this, he also explicated certain principles and established an early theory of

taxonomy. Aristotle's categorization of organisms was well grounded in the philosophy of logic, particularly deduction. Theory posits as an axiom that organisms sharing certain characteristics are related to one another. In fact, if they share enough particular characteristics, they are separate instances (members) of the same category. Empirical observation notes that certain organisms share certain characteristics. Logic deduces the organisms are related. The circularity of this argument, based as it is on an accepted axiom, does not detract from utilitarian practicality of the resulting categories. Thus, theory and practice have collaborated to produce a useful outcome. To be correct, of course, the syllogistic argument must be logically correct (i.e., the axiom properties pair must entail the conclusion). In other words, the axiomatic properties must establish necessary and sufficient criteria for membership in the category. Therein lay the difficulty, unaddressed for many hundreds of years: how many and which properties are necessary and sufficient? Furthermore, what degree of difference or similarity must be present to class something in one class or another? Pragmatism states that utilitarian practicality is the final arbiter.

Hierarchically arranging structures of knowledge is another important principle and practice of taxonomy, sitting solidly in the pragmatic camp as a means of representing knowledge. Although organizing and categorizing things, information, and concepts are instinctive and practiced by all humans, arranging categories hierarchically seems to be a learned behavior and is possibly not practiced by all cultures. In Western tradition, hierarchical classification [i.e., representations which graphically display similar entities (in clusters) and dissimilar entities (as apart or separate from each other)] did not arise until the work of Andrea Cesalpino, with his De plantis (1583), a systematic taxonomy of plants. Empirical attention to inherent characteristics does not proceed for long without the observation that not only are some specimens more alike than others, but some groups of specimens are more alike than others. It makes sense to cluster groups and to cluster those clusters repeatedly until all clusters are gathered into one. This methodology, building ever-larger groups with a process of gathering like items together, did not prevail prior to Linnaeus. Until his time, the standard practice was a combination of empirical observation, which identified specimens as members of a species, and successive division of a large class into ever-smaller groups until suitable categories were found for the species. Often the intermediate groups were created by examining habitats (shore birds, alpine flowers, desert shrubs, etc.), modes of locomotion (wading birds), or function (hunting dogs, draft horses, aromatic plants, medicinal plants). In some cases, groupings created on the basis of observation of action (perching birds) coincided with orders defined on the basis of inherent properties (Passeriformes); but the overlap was accidental, not based on a rigorous principle of grouping organisms because of common inherent structural qualities (e.g., the shape of certain birds' feet). Linnaeus applied the principle of inherent properties to the higher categories (taxa), which is still in use. Darwin considered evolutionary lineage as a characteristic to include when developing hierarchical categories. In this he introduced the new principle of developmental stages as a method of hierarchical arrangement. Although the use of evolutionary history applies, strictly speaking, only to biological organisms, the principle of arranging taxonomic structures according to lines of ancestry and descent has broader application. A common example is a genealogy or family tree. Other examples include a series of product lines, the history of inventions, and the growth of ideas; all of which are topics amenable to classifying with hierarchical taxonomic structures along evolutionary, or developmental lines.

With widespread adoption of these five principles of logical entailment, empirical observation, hierarchical arrangements based on similar inherent properties, evolutionary history (or developmental stages), and pragmatic utility, taxonomy has a solid foundation. Understanding gained in the twentieth century from linguistics, semantics, and cognitive psychology has added new theoretical principles and refined existing ones. The very strict requirements of programming computers for AI, NLP, OOP, and information access have renewed attention to understanding language and how the mind works. A significant contribution from linguistics is understanding of the relationships between words. Semantics focuses on the words used for labeling the concepts classified in taxonomic structures. From cognitive psychology comes awareness of how the mind organizes thoughts and processes language, especially for different purposes, such as determining relevance, generality, or subsumption. Purposes in classification are accomplished by using language, and evaluating terms for appropriate use seems to be driven by mental constructs, which may be called principles.[20] The relationship between a concept and a lexical unit (lexeme) represents a binding function in language; various relationships connect thoughts, meaning, ideas, objects, anything about which communication is possible. Certain relationships are particularly important: generic (a.k.a. genus–species, kind-of, IsA or Is A), meronomy (partitive, or whole-part), genealogical (ancestor–descendent), membership, equivalence, association, causality, and temporal precedence. Many relationships are hierarchical in nature, but the associative relationship has received increased attention in recent years.[21] The generic relationship, which is hierarchical, is equivalent to logical entailment: concept A, represented by term A, has all the characteristics necessary for concept B, represented by term B, to be a "kind of" A. In this the relationship is not only logical but also definitional (semantic). Definitions determine subsumption, which is similar to the logic involved in entailment. Entailment, or subsumption, may be used to test the equivalence of

definitions; the absence of equivalence can be interpreted as the presence of subsumption.[22] The meaning of a concept, or lexeme, determines logical relationship among concepts and lexemes.

Careful attention must be given to the words used for labeling concepts in taxonomic structures, the "nomenclature." Classical taxonomy has developed rules for naming nodes at each level of a taxonomic tree. At the species level, for instance, plants and animals have a binomial name consisting of the genera and a differentia, a term setting one species apart from all others in the same genera. Indexing languages (thesauri) following standard guidelines cast most concept labels in the form of plural nouns, which reduces ambiguity in cases where the singular form could be any of several distinct lexemes, each with its own sense of meaning. For example, "map" without a definite article might be a verb or a noun. "Maps," isolated from a sentence, is more likely understood as a plural noun. In cases of nouns alone, having no possible confusion with verbs of the same form, the singular always refers to one of something, whereas the plural refers to many, which constitutes a class or group of things. Classes are the fundamental elements of classification and taxonomy. Use of the plural form reduces confusion as to whether the referent is a concept, or an instance or exemplar of the concept. Lexemes may be single, compound, or multiword. As compound and multiword terms, they frequently serve to subdivide classes of things. For example, the class of tools called *saws* may be divided into cross-cut saws, rip saws, and coping saws, or chainsaws, electric saws, and gas-driven saws, respectively. Clearly, the form of a lexeme serves to create an implicit placement in a hierarchical taxonomic structure.

The particular example of saws illustrates two principles of classification: by use or application (cutting across the grain, cutting with the grain, making small, curving cuts), and by inherent property (saws with teeth fastened to a chain, saws driven by electricity or power). Seemingly trivial in this example, classification by external attributes, such as activity, habitat, diet, clothing, or associations, has rationalized oppression for millennia. Taxonomy, poorly done, runs the risk of incompletely and inaccurately describing human experience, perception, and beliefs, with consequent detrimental outcomes.

Cognitive psychology provides insight into classification as mental process, giving strong support to incorporating hierarchy into taxonomic structures and establishing guidelines regarding terminology choice and form. Organizing perceptions, data, information, and thoughts is an important part of acquiring information, making sense of that information, and problem solving. With classification, people develop mental pictures of topics and problems, which may be divided and subdivided, thus simplifying the learning of complex knowledge. Classification is also useful for developing inferences or expectations directed at achieving specific goals. Classification and taxonomy are fundamental components of learning, communication, and comprehension.[3] The importance of hierarchy as a feature of taxonomic structures cannot be overstated. Several studies support the notion that hierarchical structures are a fundamental and essential component of memory.[23] Word association tests elicit information, not only about the test words but also about the classes that contain them. Other studies indicate a mental transformation of nonhierarchical statements into hierarchical form, possibly in an effort to place new perceptions into some familiar context. Grouping of concepts that seem similar is thus a means of generalization and simplification.[23] Taxonomic structures provide efficient storage mechanisms for data and information; if such structures accurately model internal mental constructs, they are more likely to be useful. Classification enables people to deal with categories and groups, rather than individual instances, thus enabling more efficient use of memory and cognitive processes.[1]

METHODOLOGY AND PRACTICES

Methodologies

    Systematic
    Organic

Practices and uses

    Description
    Prediction
    Language mapping
    Information finding

Classification can mean either assigning entities to existing classes or creating classes by clustering existing entities. Taxonomy means both: classing entities and creating new classes. Collections of entities are examined to create a taxonomic structure and individual entities are assigned to the classes (taxa) created. Once the initial collection is classified, new specimens, or entities, are assigned to existing taxa; the structure is dynamic and, if necessary, new taxa may be created. An example of this is the recent creation of two biological superkingdoms to reflect fundamental differences in cell structure.

 Discussion of taxonomy methodologies and uses may, itself, be organized into a simple taxonomy, illustrated here in an indented outline:

Methodologies
    Systematic
        Manual
        Automated
            Numerical
        Semiautomated

        Organic
Uses
    Descriptions
        Abstract pattern visibility
    Analysis
        Visible patterns clarify further direction
        Visible patterns expose gaps
        Visible patterns expose overlaps
    Predictions
    Language maps
        Structures
            Hierarchical—existential relationships
            Synonymy—semantic relationships of equivalence
            Associative—situational and/or contextual
                relationships important to communities of
                interest and practice; e.g.:
                    Process—product
                    Geographic location—governing entity
                    Object—purpose
                    Event—unit of time
    Information retrieval systems

Use of this outline to discuss methodologies, practices, and uses, will illustrate some of the power of taxonomy for organization and communication.

Systematic taxonomy follows, as one might expect, rigorous processes and policies, which have themselves been through several cycles of development, test, revision, and adoption; they have, in other words, withstood the tests of time and pragmatic utility. In manual taxonomy construction, a collection of elements is examined carefully, and inherent properties are listed. Through an iterative process, the properties, and thus the elements, are grouped into taxa of similar entities, which, in turn, are grouped into a hierarchy of increasing specialization. Automated taxonomy has a similar goal but attempts to attain it in different ways. In numerical taxonomy, mathematical techniques of cluster analysis are applied to listings of inherent characteristics. The same techniques are also applied in domains with inadequate inherent features. One solution is to use the technique of content analysis to evaluate data from various sources such as questionnaire responses, interviews, and usability studies. One school of practice attempts to extract taxonomies from text based on linguistic features: notably, word and phrase frequencies, cooccurrence, part-of-speech, and proximity. Many variations of this approach exist, but the basic theme is that literature about similar topics will use similar language, and such similarities can be discovered and revealed by using mathematical techniques. One of the variations involves a simple raw processing of text, accepting the results. Most efforts, however, "train" computer programs with manually constructed taxonomies and carefully selected corpora of text, a process in which the program "learns" which word and phrase patterns are significant within chosen design criteria. The program is then used to analyze a much larger body of text. In many respects, this procedure is only the classing, or indexing, half of the taxonomy process; it makes no pretense of generating taxonomic structures from scratch. A semiautomated process would be that in which mathematical techniques generate a suggested taxonomy, which is then subjected to a manual review and edit process, producing the final taxonomic structure.

Organic taxonomy, in the form of "folksonomies," and other "social" phenomenon, represent the human desire for involvement and autonomy in the very fundamental acts of sense-making and communicating as simultaneous social and individual behaviors. Folksonomies and other shared tags created by end-users, rather than authors or professional intermediaries, have received a great deal of attention in recent years.[24–26] Although they do not represent formal taxonomy, they serve similar pragmatic purposes and address some of the issues plaguing taxonomy; notably the problems of scale, complex rule sets, and arriving at consensus for agreement about language. Noteworthy characteristics of folksonomies include: flat lists of terms (keywords), multiple meanings for identical terms (homography), and multiple terms for one concept (synonymy). At best, the three features alone maintain the ambiguity inherent in natural language (particularly when out of context). At worst, they increase ambiguity. Folksonomies by themselves do little to facilitate agreement about meaning, nor do they serve well as classifications. Without reasonably disciplined and systematic attention to the principles and practices of taxonomy, folksonomies are informal categories at best.[25] Nonetheless, folksonomies provide valuable insight into the thinking, behaviors, needs and desires, and properties of many more people and information entities than might otherwise be possible. They offer potential as useful additions to the taxonomy toolbox.

In the absence of reasonably defined and desired purposes, taxonomy has little value other than satisfying individual interests and motivations. More communal uses include description, analysis, prediction, language agreement, and retrieving information, as outlined above.

At its most basic, taxonomy has descriptive power; if any given taxonomy, particularly its structure, does not describe the covered domain, identification of it as a taxonomy comes into question. At best, the structure might be a collection of loosely related categories. Description sets baselines, provides foundations, creates common starting points for extending taxonomy to other purposes. Following description, taxonomy facilitates information and knowledge analysis. It reveals patterns which help clarify possible future actions; it exposes gaps and overlaps in representations of knowledge. Such exposures, in turn, identify other possible actions. Highly structured and richly detailed taxonomic structures, such as the periodic table of the elements and evolutionary trees, predict the existence of yet-undiscovered elements and prehistoric organisms.

In information science, taxonomy performs the very useful function of mapping language. When integrated into information systems, particularly for browse and search, taxonomic structures serve many purposes, all working together toward both high recall and accurate precision, an elusive goal for many decades. Simply listed, taxonomy functions in information systems to

Represent communally accepted language.
Promote shared use of language.
Provide clear paths into detailed levels of specificity.
Enable aggregated retrieval of selected specific concepts using a broader collective label.
Convert end-user search terminology to that developed by communities of practice.
Use that terminology for search, both metadata enabled and free-text.
Suggest related avenues of exploration and search.
Programmatically deliver information of possible interest to select individuals and communities based on inherent and situational characteristics of them.
Facilitate reporting and analysis of end-users, content, content creators and providers, and storage and delivery systems.
Enforce regulatory compliance.

This list does not exhaust the possibilities. In short, taxonomy connects the dots, closes the loops, and provides the linguistic and semantic backbones necessary to complete information transactions.

After years of research and development, integration of taxonomy with information systems has still not expanded much beyond relatively small academic pilots and applications in private industry or large government agencies. Obstacles to adoption include scalability, funding, and, often, misunderstanding regarding the value of such systems.

SUMMARY AND CONCLUSION

From its beginning as a process and system for organizing plants and animals, taxonomy has developed into a widely varied collection of classification schemes and practices applied in many disparate disciplines. In various natural sciences, particularly biology, astronomy, and geology, taxonomy continues as an important practice within each discipline. In the twentieth century, new techniques using statistical analysis and computers came into use for classifying natural objects and organisms on the basis of inherent properties that were previously unavailable for study. This is particularly the case in microbiology where numerical taxonomy creates clusters of organisms having similar genetic properties. Numerical taxonomy has also been applied in the social sciences and information access applications, although the validity of the clusterings as accurate representations on inherent similarities in those disciplines is open to question. Taxonomies are an important part of systems developed for exploring AI. There, they take the form of ontologies, highly structured compilations of data, information, and knowledge that are used to support the logical reasoning attempted by AI. The computer science practice of OOP also incorporates taxonomy in the sense that object-oriented programs can be categorized as taxonomies. They have the features of class and inheritance, which correspond to the taxonomic features of taxa and relationships of entailment, expressed in hierarchical structures. Information access systems utilize taxonomies for navigation of Web sites and to aid searching for information on the Internet. In the context of electronic online information, taxonomies support retrieval of as many relevant information items as possible and retrieval of highly specific items. An essential contribution of taxonomy to such systems is their ability to disambiguate terminology by representing the relationships between concepts and thus providing context in which to understand and use domain-specific vocabularies. Having begun in the study of biology, taxonomy has developed a solid structure of theory and principles that guide methodology and development of taxonomic structures, with application and use far removed from taxonomy.

Beginning with the collection and study of inherent characteristics of many members of a domain of interest, taxonomy uses principles of logic and linguistic entailment, semantics, and meaning, plus insight into human mental activity to create taxonomic structures with practical utility. Regardless of where practices or with what final purpose, taxonomy utilizes of the common methodology of examining many specimens of examples of things to be classified into a taxonomic structure. Such examination may be manual, automated, or semiautomated. Each emphasizes different principles of taxonomy theory, with manual being the most comprehensive and semiautomated attempting to use automation to handle large amounts of data needing human interpretation. Automated methods include clustering algorithms and various techniques from NLP.

Regardless of the methodology and techniques used to develop taxonomic structures, in the final analysis, they are utilitarian objects, whether they serve academic research and descriptive purposes or more commonplace information retrieval from the Internet and other information systems. Well-designed and constructed taxonomic structures have descriptive, predictive, and analytical powers, which make them essential components of many information science endeavors. Integrating taxonomy with information systems can enhance end-user experiences and retrieval of desired information in many ways, all part of a chain of transactions, characterized as "connecting the dots."

REFERENCES

1. Stefik, M. *Introduction to Knowledge Systems*; Morgan Kaufmann: San Francisco, CA, 1995; 543, 604.
2. Saracevic, T.; Kantor, P.B. Studying the value of library and information services. Part II. Methodology and taxonomy. J. Am. Soc. Inform. Sci. **1997**, *48* (6), 543–563.
3. Maity, R.; Bhattacharya, S.; Ghosh, A.; Ghosal, T.K. Teaching non-hierarchical classification. Comput. Educ. **1992**, *18* (4), 319–328.
4. Simpson, J.A.; Weiner, E.S.C., Eds. *Oxford English Dictionary*, 2nd Ed.; Oxford University Press: Oxford, U.K., 1989.
5. Simpson, J.; Weiner, E.; Proffitt, M., Eds. *Oxford English Dictionary Addtions*; Oxford University Press: Oxford, U.K., 1993–1997.
6. Simpson, J., Ed.; *OED Online*, 3rd Ed.; Oxford University Press: Oxford, U.K., March 2009, in progress; http://www.oed.com (accessed December 2000).
7. Sliwa, C. Intranet users tackle chaos. Comput. World **2000**, *34* (30), 85.
8. Sowa, J.F., Ed. *Principles of Semantic Networks: Explorations in the Representation of Knowledge*; Morgan Kaufmann: San Mateo, CA, 1991; 3, 4.
9. Smith, L.C.; Warner, A.J. A taxonomy of representations in information retrieval system design. J. Inform. Sci. **1984**, *8* (3), 113.
10. Genesis 10:1-7ff. *New English Bible*.
11. *Encyclopaedia Britannica CD 99*, Multimedia Edition; 1994–1999.
12. Meyer, B. *Object-Oriented Software Construction*, 2nd Ed.; Prentice Hall PTR: Upper Saddle River, NJ, 1997; 866.
13. Jacob, E.K. Classification and categorization: Drawing the line. In *Proceedings of the 2nd ASIS SIG/CR Classification Research Workshop*, Washington, DC, October, 27, 1991; 78.
14. Zimmer, C. What is a species? Sci. Am. **2008**, June, 72.
15. Kachigan, S.K. *Statistical Analysis: An Interdisciplinary Introduction to Univariate and Multivariate Methods*; Radius: New York, 1986; 208.
16. Kaufman, L.; Rousseeuw, P.J. *Finding Groups in Data: An Introduction to Cluster Analysis*; Wiley: New York, 1990; 11.
17. Moens, M.-F. *Automatic Indexing and Abstraction of Document Texts*; Kluwer: Boston, MA, 2000; 106.
18. Guarino, N.; Giaretta, P. Ontologies and knowledge bases: Towards a terminological clarification. In *Towards Very Large Knowledge Bases: Knowledge Building & Knowledge Sharing*; Mars, N.J.I., Ed.; IOS Press: Amsterdam, 1995; 23.
19. Woods, W.A. Finding information on the Web: A knowledge representation approach; http://www.ai.mit.edu/projects/iiip/conferences/www95/woods.html (accessed December 2000).
20. McCaffrey, A. Applied cladistics: New methodologies for information classification research. In *Proceedings of the 2nd ASIS SIG/CR Classification Research Workshop*, Washington, DC, October 27, 1991; 96.
21. Molholt, P. A model for standardization in the definition and for of associative, interconcept links. Thesis, Graduate Faculty of Rensselaer Polytechnic Institute, Troy, NY, 1996.

22. Doyle, J.; Patil, R.S. Two these of knowledge representation: Language restrictions, taxonomic classification, and the utility of representation services. Artif. Intell. **1991**, *48* (3), 261–197.

23. Fernadez, M.M.; Eastman, C.M. Basic taxonomic structures and levels of abstraction. In *Advances of Classification Research*, Proceedings of the 1st ASIS SIG/CR Classification Research Workshop, Toronto, ON, November 4, 1990; Humphry, S.M., Kwasnik, B.H., Eds.; Learned Information: Medford NJ, 1990; 61.

24. Christiaens, S. Metadata mechanisms: From ontology to folksonomy… and back. In *OTM Workshops*; Meersman, R., Tari, Z., Herrero, P., et al., Eds.; Springer-Verlag: Berlin, 2006; 199–207.

25. Mathes, A. Folsonomies—Cooperative classification and communication through shared metadata, 2004; http://adammathes.com/academic/computer-mediated-communication/folksonomies.pdf (accessed June, 2008).

26. Vander Wal, T.Folksonomy definition and Wikipedia, 2005; http://vanderwal.net/folksonomy.html (accessed July, 2008).

27. Borck, J.R. Beyond the hype, what will an EIP do for you? InfoWorld **2000**, *22* (28), 49.

28. Vogel, C.; Powers, J. Quality metrics: How to ensure quality taxonomies. In *National Online Meeting Proceedings*; Williams, M.E., Ed.; Information Today: Medford, NJ, 2000; 433.

Technical Writing

Michael J. Salvo
Department of English, Purdue University, West Lafayette, Indiana, U.S.A.

Abstract

Technical writing conveys practical information for readers to put to use. Technical writing is done in most workplaces by a variety of professionals whose interest in writing is secondary to their primary work function, while specialists in technical communication concentrate on the processes of effective writing and knowledge creation. Professional and technical writers research and articulate solutions for professionals who need to write effectively. Therefore, technical writers construct and manage others' writing environments, and are responsible for managing documents, knowledge, and information flow in organizations. Technical writing is writing with a purpose in an organization, and so is distinguished from creative writing and academic writing in its purpose, scope, and audience.

INTRODUCTION

Defined narrowly, technical writing articulates process, procedural, and practical information both for specialized and general audiences. Technical writers interpret complex technical concepts and articulate ideas in accessible language to enable users to accomplish their goals. To present appropriate content, writers must understand the audience who will use the document and their purpose in using it. Audience analysis is a key feature of technical writing. Technical writing is writing with a specific purpose, intended to convey information from producer to consumer in the clearest and most effective way possible. Technical writers work with a variety of genres: they inform their organizations by preparing whitepapers and research reports, support decision-making with recommendation reports, and support organizational knowledge by writing procedural manuals, writing and maintaining policy, and managing collections of internal documentation. Common forms of technical writing include procedure guides and how-to manuals for household appliances and electronics. As an academic field of study, technical writing expanded in the late twentieth century as personal computers became ubiquitous and Internet connections common. Indeed, as computers moved from desktop publishing to network communication devices, digital Web-based new media have redefined the boundaries of a field once limited to written communication. In the late twentieth century, technical writing grew to include a wide variety of communication media, and hence expanded to the more expansive moniker of technical communication. Today, technical communicators work under a variety of professional titles. The list, of course, includes technical writer, but new titles are as varied as copywriter, content manager, user-experience designer, information architect, information designer, and document manager. Technical communication specialists continue to advise organizations on effective communication practices.

The rise of technical and professional writing in America is closely tied to the development of the Morrill Land Grant Colleges in the twentieth century. Indeed, the location of these programs, their names, and specialties are very much a product of local conditions and traditions. Technical writing is most closely tied with a tradition of nonacademic writing that supported writing instruction for engineers and scientists. Professional and business writing often accompany writing instruction in business schools. Recently, more programs have taken on the name technical communication to reflect the expanded role in speech and multimedia presentation. In the middle to late twentieth century, the growth and expansion of technical communication as a field in its own right is closely tied to the expansion of personal computing technology and, at the turn of the millennium, the growth in popular use of the World Wide Web. Recent interests in information design and information architecture closely link the research being produced in technical communication programs to the research being undertaken by researchers in library and information science, creating opportunities for collaboration and hybridization between the two fields. Technical writing is complex, dynamic, and expanding, technologically sophisticated, and concerned with the role of users in producing, accessing, storing, retrieving, and perhaps most importantly, understanding and putting to use the information stored in texts written to support high technology. Both technical communication and information science share an interest in innovation and expansion into the growing culture of new media and the storage and retrieval of human knowledge through the World Wide Web. There are analogous, if sometimes competing, definitions of technical writing, often quibbling over the scope of the term and asserting differences: that professional communication contains technical and business writing

Encyclopedia of Library and Information Sciences, Fourth Edition DOI: 10.1081/E-ELIS4-120043421

rather than technical communication serving as the larger term. Such taxonomic distinctions are important to specialists in the field, often revealing institutional as well as historical lineage as well as political and cultural sympathies of various departments and programs within higher education. Technical writers emerge from the study of rhetoric and rhetorical theory, and technical writing provides the nonacademic counterpoint to the large field of academic writing often called composition, which focuses on the first year as well as upper-level academic writing in postsecondary institutions of higher learning. Rhetoric and writing programs are gaining recognition, and increasingly are being titled "writing studies." This entry discusses the long history of technical writing with particular attention to the post-World War II era through the late twentieth century. The late twentieth and early twenty-first century development of technical writing is closely associated with personal computing and the World Wide Web, and the entry concludes with discussion of emerging digital media, with special attention to developments in information design and architecture.

RECENT RESEARCH

Recent research in technical writing has moved beyond the 1990s concern with professional recognition and legitimation. The field's preoccupation with its own status is exemplified, and seems to have concluded, with publication of the two-volume collection *Power and Legitimacy in Technical Communication* edited by Teresa Kynell-Hunt and Gerald Savage.[1,2] Recently, activity theory has emerged as a viable foundation for grounding technical writing research, exemplified by Clay Spinuzzi's 2003 *Tracing Genres Through Organizations*.[3] Spinuzzi's book historicizes genre, encourages teachers to include history and rhetoric in technical writing pedagogy, and connects present research to the constructivist tradition, such as Joann Yates' *Control Through Communication*,[4] an example of cultural history tracing the development of business and technical writing through the nineteenth century. Recent books, such as the edited collection *Critical Power Tools*,[5] have articulated the relationship between technical writing and cultural studies and the role of new media, as with Carol Lipson and Michael Day's *Technical Communication and the World Wide Web*.[6] Methodology in technical writing research has been a perennial concern; emerging from a humanities perspective, scientific methods have sometimes been mismatched with the goals of technical writing. Some of this uneasiness seems inevitable as technical writers often represent the needs of nonspecialists to scientists and engineers. The history of rhetoric is older than that of scientific inquiry, and measuring effective communication in context is a qualitative rather than quantitative endeavor. In response, some researchers have used rhetoric's uneasy relationship with

empirical methodology as a strength, opening spaces for critical, reflective research.[7] Johndan Johnson-Eilola and Stuart Selber's *Central Readings in Technical Communication*[8] collect landmark essays in the twentieth century while also asserting the centrality of journal articles to the development of the field: the development of technical communication research has been driven by articles in a healthy number of scholarly and professional journals such as (alphabetically listed) *Business Communication Quarterly*; *IEEE Transactions on Professional Communication*; *Information Design Journal* (*Document Design* recently merged with *IDJ*); *Journal of Business Communication*; *Journal of Business and Technical Communication*; *Journal Of Computer-Mediated Communication*; *Journal of Computer-Supported Cooperative Work*; *Journal of Technical Writing and Communication*, *Kairos: A Journal of Rhetoric, Technology, and Pedagogy*; *Management Communication Quarterly*; *Written Communication*; *Technical Communication*; and *Technical Communication Quarterly*. Technical writing research has for the most part left concerns of the field's legitimacy behind in the late twentieth century [1,2] and much recent research has been articulating what Bruno Latour[9] calls the parliament of people, texts, and technology.

TECHNICAL WRITING AS A FIELD OF STUDY

Technical writing as a profession was boosted in the late twentieth century with the widespread adoption of personal computing technology in the workplace and for home use. There was a need, within the hardware producers and programming organizations, as well as among independent writers, to clearly document and guide growing numbers of users through the process of effectively utilizing digital computers on the job and in the home. In the early twenty-first century, as more documentation is available online, there is less need for print-based documentation separate from the program as many new applications integrate guidance within the programs themselves.

Technical writing can no longer, if it could ever accurately, be defined simply in functional terms or limited to the scientistic need to write with clarity, brevity, and specificity. This is, in the early twenty-first century, considered a limited and antagonistic definition (referred to as the "CBS" school) that arises out of a history of technical writing's uneasy placement within the humanities. In higher education institutions, most often located in departments of English, technical writing was often discounted as service primarily presented to programs in engineering and business schools. English departments eschewed their service roles in preference for literary study through the twentieth century. Late in the twentieth century and continuing to the present, growing numbers of writing programs are emerging with concentrations in both academic writing, or composition, and nonacademic writing. While technical communication is predominantly taught in English departments located in colleges of humanities, specialized programs exist in engineering and business as well as journalism schools in addition to dedicated rhetoric and writing studies programs.

The rapid expansion of technical writing in the late twentieth century to meet the demand for documentation of personal computers created opportunities for writers without formal training in technical writing. Practitioners of technical writing have a wide range of training and experience, and with writing programs offering more and better workplace and professional writing curricula, researchers have noted generational tensions in the workplace between those professionals with coursework in rhetoric, project management, and usability and those with more traditional English coursework.

Early History

Earl Morrogh[10] takes a long view of the history of technical writing, tracing its emergence as prior to and part of the inspiration for written literacy. Opening with clay tablets to the emergence of the alphabet to Roman military texts, this perspective is consistent with mid-twentieth century scholars' attention to literate representations for specific commercial purposes. Walter Ong[11,12] traces the emergence of literacy back to cuneiform clay tablets used to account for trade in the eastern Mediterranean. These prealphabetic texts were technical in nature, counting the numbers of vessels of goods held in the holds of ships plying the calm waters of the ancient Mediterranean sea before even the Egyptians were building pyramids. These earliest texts were technical in their functional interest and attempt to record wealth, trade value, and to account for decisions made in foreign ports by agents of newly centralizing power. That is to say, technical communication is synonymous with the invention of centralized human society and cocreative of the modern human mind. Ong asserts that the Semitic alphabet was the first of its kind, replacing both the cuneiform tablet writing and pictographic representation of the Egyptians and that all subsequent alphabets are at least inspired by if not derived directly from the ancient Hebrew.

Similarly, Earl Morrogh asserts a very long lineage for what he titles information architecture, which he defines broadly as the struggle "to create, communicate, manage, and preserve information" (p. 3).[10] Following Morrogh, technical communicators often define themselves in terms of the first two elements of the definition: creation and communication of information, while library and information scientists are concerned with the second two elements, management and preservation of information that others have authored. In the age of computers, ubiquitous access, and information overload, both technical communicators and library and information scientists find

themselves concerned with effective information storage and retrieval. Morrogh narrates a number of moments in the long history of human development in which information production outstripped contemporary technologies for storage and retrieval, and our current age of Information Anxiety[13] is only the latest in a long series of epochal change: from speech to text to print, and the technologization of the word from telegraph, telephone, radio, and television, to our own information age augmented by the World Wide Web. Information architecture, then, is the field of inquiry where technical communicators and library and information scientists find their interests most closely aligned.

From Roman military manuals to the mining books of secrets written by Agricola, powerful and valuable technical knowledge was stored in written form. These texts, as described by Bernadette Longo,[14] were both powerful and valuable, and as such were often written in code or the information was purposely misreported in order to keep the uninitiated in ignorance. Often, these how-to texts were both encoded and contained misleading information: acting as pneumonic devices, the books of secrets would unlock the magic of metallurgy, or of medicine, or of civil administration only if one had a guide to the books. These manuals were not intended for everyone: they were reminders to the initiated—memory books—and instruction manuals for the aspiring metallurgist, civil servant, or soldier, and reading would be accompanied by a learned guide during the period of apprenticeship.

The nineteenth century rise of mass culture and urbanization was accompanied by the rise of the corporation and genres of business communication that we recognize today. Memos, reports for decision-making, research and technology, and technical illustrations, as well as patent applications became common forms of intra- and interorganization communication. This is also roughly when card catalogs and written collection inventories, which become library holding databases, become common elements of both corporate and public library collections, information storage and retrieval processes that became part and representative of industrial age information storage and retrieval from the civil war through World War I.[4]

Twentieth Century

Robert R. Johnson[15] and Robert Connors[16] locate the next major turning point in technical communication at the massive scientific and administrative expansion necessary to administer the movement of people and equipment in World WarII. Accompanying the administrative and material challenges were the increasingly technical weapons and tools employed around the globe, from radar to mobile weapons and, in the increasingly swift processes of recursive design, upgrades to these systems on the battlefield. It became necessary to document new designs—improvements—so that soldiers in the field could, with their existing literacy skills, open a weapon's packing crate, read the instructions, and successfully assemble and deploy new weapons. Robert R. Johnson reports that the first attempts at such user-centered design were disasters, resulting in mechanical malfunction, misfires, and bodily injury and even occasionally in an operator's death. Often these so-called accidents were attributed to operator (human) error; however, on closer reflection, it appears that there were, in the words of Donald Norman,[17] "Gulfs of Evaluation and of Execution between the designer and user of the technologies." To solve this problem with human error (and the dangers of industrial accidents), designers had to consider the design not from their own but from the users' perspectives. Technology could be designed not merely for esthetic or functional ends but for easier, safer operation and the design of technologies could aid in their ease of use and adoption into the users' working lives. This realization leads, in Johnson's argument, to the rise of *user-centered design*.

After World War II, accompanying the expansion of need for technical expertise among soldiers on the line was the massive rise in technical consumer goods purchased for use in the increasingly popular suburban tract house. Everything from washing machines to refrigerators to, later, televisions were finding their way into the living rooms, garages, utility rooms, and basements of these single-family, lower-density houses. Lower-density neighborhoods encouraged greater reliance on automobiles. Automobiles required technical manuals to support regular maintenance, as America became a mobile, suburban culture in the middle twentieth century. These developments also resulted in expanding the vision of technical communication to include household technologies, as Katherine Durak[18] argued, asserting "the household as a setting of consequence." From Agricola's books of mining secrets to the post-World War II suburbanization of American culture, technical communication has participated and expanded upon the spread of literacy to an increasingly high percentage of people, beginning with the preliterate need for accuracy in trade, expanded through the advent of the printing press, providing for the informational needs of an increasingly technological culture. Technical communication followed need into technical and engineering universities, exemplified by American land grant public institutions of higher learning, and into suburban homes with the adoption of domestic technologies from sewing and washing machines to refrigerators and later entertainment devices like radios and televisions. At the end of the twentieth century, technical communication became increasingly user-centered as the personal computer required precise task-oriented documentation and guidance. Online, the Web has many guides and documents showing how users can put their technological investments to better use. The widespread use of these many kinds of texts supported the dissemination and spread of the technological information these documents contained, paving the way from what some critics have called a democratization of technology.[19]

The postwar period of industrial expansion chugged along, building wealth and expanding the cold-war period of Pax-Americana, leading to the multiplication of access and complexity resulting in the dawn of the information age as exemplified first by the early adoption of personal computers in the form of hobbyists followed by the more robust and culturally significant spread of computer use with the commercialization of the World Wide Web (Web) and electronic mail. Personal computing further lowered the obstacles to the tools of printing and dissemination of texts. Even before the Web, do-it-yourself desktop publishing made it possible to produce many paper copies of documents. Document design[20] became a concern of writers, further lowering the financial barriers to disseminating printed work. With the growth of personal computing, the need for clear, end-user-centered documentation increased, and programmers could no longer assume that their user had a similar level of technical preparation. Especially with the move from computer operating systems that ran on command line interfaces (CLI) to graphic user interfaces (GUI), many more citizens were able to purchase and put to use respectably powered computing devices in their homes and offices. And all this was possible before the advent of the Web.

Through the late 1990s, the Web created a cottage industry of secondary market how-to books for personal computing. Even before the Web, many technical writers found a thriving market in teaching new users how to take advantage of productivity software, digital tax and financial tools, databases, and word processing and desktop publishing applications. Bookstores reflected this expanding need for documentation that was better than the manuals produced by large programming organizations, eventually resulting in the humorously titled "Dummies" and "Idiots" guides to just about everything. These books are the result of the realization that we are a nation of experts who have deep expertise in a very narrow set of specialized knowledge. For the vast majority of high-technology situations, we are novices, or in the unfortunate construction of these books, we are geniuses in our specialties but idiots and dummies in everything else.

Understanding the user as human being is at the heart of user-centered and human-centered design that works to present a technology interface that effectively presents the power of the technology to the user, in a human scale and task-oriented perspective. Users need not understand the underlying technology represented by the interface but rather see how the tool lying behind the interface can fulfill their needs. Indeed, the interface is the face the tool presents to users. The shift from system to user-centered recognizes the widespread dissemination of high-technology digital tools throughout culture, the democratization of access in which all have a printing press, radio, and television receiver as well as broadcast capability, and the PC moved from being seen primarily as a personal *computing* device and becomes a personal *communication* device. Technical writers filled a need by documenting and presenting information for effectively using these communication devices by people who had no interest in knowing how or why the technology works.

The New Millennium

The shift from computing to communication is a shift from, in Richard Lanham's[21] words, looking at technology to looking through technology. For many, their personal computers have become their promised video phones, and although the travel is virtual, they are likewise personal transporters, allowing users to transport their vision, their gaze, across the globe and, through NASA's rovers and telescopic devices—our virtual eyes—out into space and to the very edges of the solar system.

The cost of entry was vastly reduced: no longer was it necessary to train—to become expert—in the use of computers. What followed was the need to increasingly redesign the interface and the procedures to get online and participate on the Web so that the greatest number of users could become self-sufficient online, getting connected to the internet at speeds that made new online media viable. YouTube is the latest example of an organization that learned how to better deliver video. By creating generally understood accessible standards for video upload, conversion, and distribution, almost all Web users have access to acceptable quality video—if users can access youtube.com, they have access to content. In this way, YouTube is a victory for participation and access, even if the content leaves many scratching their heads and wondering what value the content may have to culture. In sum, users get to participate in the creation of Web content and also access what has been posted, without regard for the meaning or value of what has been posted. Users accessing YouTube are not thinking about search algorithms, taxonomic structures, or about how the videos are encoded and made available online. However, each of these elements is of importance to the new generation of technical communicators who take very seriously design, placement, and accessibility of digital video: the very things that make YouTube an enjoyable rather than frustrating experience.

Accompanying the expansion of access for posting and viewing is an expansion to access to the organization of content. So-called folksonomies, which are augmenting more centrally controlled taxonomies, represent a new level of user-participation, actually labeling content with searchable metadata, so that users become organizers and archivists as well as end-users. This control not just of the content but of the organization and navigability of content—or its findability, to borrow a phrase from Peter Morville—is a hallmark of what has been called the second wave of internet entrepreneurship, commonly referred

to as Web 2.0. Folksonomies may seem to challenge the accustomed control and authority of the information organization professionals: that is, of information and library scientists. And perhaps from certain perspectives, it does. However, opportunities exist to invent, support, and change with evermore creative means of opening information up to user labeling and organization. Recent books like *The Wisdom of Crowds*,[22] *Glut*,[23] *and Everything is Miscellaneous*[24] all assert a new and interesting role of information and library science, but this role is different from traditional librarianship, and shares much in common with recent research in technical writing.

Brenton Faber[25,26] argues that "change" is both a powerful trope and new constant in the information organization. Libraries, traditionally described as beginning in the United States with Benjamin Franklin's subscription group through Carnegie-funded public lending libraries, have traditionally been seen as a site for access to printed material. However, just as railroads and shipping companies had to rethink their identities at the dawn of the information age, so too do libraries find themselves rethinking identities and embracing change, seeing themselves not strictly as providers of access to books. Rather, libraries are redefining themselves as providers of access to information, which also requires developing a critical sense of information valuation, so that library patrons can become increasingly effective users of information resources. However, the Internet age has given individual users much greater access to information. Likewise, librarians and information science professionals are encountering similar change and some have begun to reimagine their profession and responsibilities in terms of teaching library patrons effective and critical information assessment and retrieval, both online and in print. It is also ripe for deeper collaboration with technical writing as well as with closely and further flung specialties. Culture is and will continue to reconsider the definition of deeply held values, such as literacy, and information professionals are well-placed to not only participate but to create innovative practices in collaboration with professionals in related fields, like technical writers who also see the challenges of information architecture and user-integration as central to the challenges of this current wave of technological and cultural change.

This current age of change, seen from the perspective of technical writing and communication, has to do with the changing nature of expertise. Experts are expected to help guide nonexperts, what this entry refers to as end-users, or simply users, to accomplish what they want. Balanced with the challenges of user-centered design is awareness of experts, or stakeholders, who have responsibilities to the local institution, the national and international standards of professional conduct, and to historical identity. The rise of do-it-yourself culture is exemplified by the hobbyist programmer, seen as an information

Technical–Topic

seeker who challenges traditional modes of patron behavior in the library. Effectively preparing for Web-savvy internet users further complicates librarianship. Like librarians rethinking their role in an age of information, technical writers are redefining their professional responsibilities to take advantage of opportunities made possible with digitization of information, like findability, critical information assessment, and user-centered design. These skills are needed *in addition to* traditional professional responsibilities. And it is no easy task to develop whole new arenas of expertise and responsibility.

Jay David Bolter and David Gruisin,[27] writing about new media, coined the term *remediation* to describe the process of new media's impact on old. Radio impacted fictional novels. Television changes radio. And all have been affected by the massive and incredibly fast adoption of digital computing technology—specifically the world-wide expansion of use of the Web. It is important, as Bolter and Gruisin explain, to remember that radio didn't simply disappear when NBC, CBS, and ABC started broadcasting. So too, the three networks didn't cease their broadcasts when cable became another common way of accessing televisual media. Mentioned above, railroad executives—or managers of old transportation media—who saw themselves as operating engines and cars on rails, soon found themselves at a distinct professional and cultural disadvantage to those visionaries who saw trains as part of a network that transported goods around the world. These postindustrial workers engineered better systems for transporting these manufactured goods and raw materials between cargo ships, trains, and trucks—an arm of business management now known as logistics—found themselves in widespread demand and valuable members of the team of symbolic analysts who support the postindustrial global economy. So too, technical writers who see their profession in limited ways as creating static documents for packaged software systems with long development lives and slow redesign cycles have witnessed reduced opportunity and less prestige, while those who have ventured into Web-based delivery, experimented with new software models like open source and usable systems, have found themselves in increasing demand for their expertise. As Faber argues, change has become the one constant.

FUTURE OF TECHNICAL WRITING

Technical writing sees one of its future directions of growth and development in information architecture, of creating structures users can participate in and better take advantage of greater access to information resources. Technical communicators see information scientists and librarians as potential partners rather than rivals with whom the future of information architecture and design can be invented and communicated. Whereas technical

communicators emphasize the creation of content, effective writing and reading, and writing texts that help readers comprehend and put information to use, information science professionals emphasize storage and retrieval of that information. Opportunities for hybridization, cross-fertilization, and cooperation in understanding and innovating in an era of great technological and cultural change exist. Technical writers look towards a future integrating processes of information design and information architecture into their traditional roles of writing effectively to be read, as information scientists learn how to better support the challenges of user-initiated search, and accommodate the expansion of access to information through the Web, as the definition of librarian changes to include emerging responsibilities of information scientists.

CONCLUSION

In the early twenty-first century, technical writing is in a state of transition and flux. Like so many professions with roots in the expansion of industrial post-World War II American culture, technical writing is struggling to rearticulate its expertise in the postindustrial, global, and digital age of information. Research in the field of rhetoric and writing studies has articulated numerous directions for technical writing to take in its twenty-first century redesign. Most promising among these are information design and architecture, which rearticulates technical writing expertise in terms of Robert Reich's symbolic analytical work, redefining work as symbolic manipulation, a definition much in synch with earlier twentieth century rhetorical articulations of humans as "symbol-using animals," as Kenneth Burke has asserted. Technical writing, with its dual histories as both writing for specific purposes and as nonacademic writing, asserts an identity separate from the academic study of writing and pedagogy in the first year composition class, yet shares much of the same rhetorical basis and intellectual history. Two threads characterize this identity of professional and technical communication. The first larger group is comprised for the most part of professionals working in a variety of fields, from doctors to lawyers to engineers, programmers, and managers, all of whom spend a sizeable amount of their working time writing. These are the professionals writing who need the support of the second, smaller group of professional technical writing researchers who can articulate best practices and research-based solutions to problems shared by a variety of professionals who need to write effectively. This second group of professional writers, technical communication scholars, and rhetoric researchers will also find themselves increasingly called upon to solve challenging communication problems faced by professionals from various fields of postindustrial work as new media and new economy challenges require innovative solutions.

REFERENCES

1. Kynell-Hunt, T.; Savage, G.J. *Power and Legitimacy in Technical Communication: The Historical and Contemporary Struggle for Professional Status*; Baywood's Technical Communication Series; Baywood Publishing Company: Amityville, NY, 2003; Vol. I.

2. Kynell-Hunt, T.; Savage, G.J. *Power and Legitimacy in Technical Communication: Strategies for Professional Status*; Baywood's Technical Communication Series; Baywood Publishing Company: Amityville, NY, 2004; Vol. II.

3. Spinuzzi, C. *Tracing Genres Through Organizations: A Sociocultural Approach to Information Design*; MIT Press: Cambridge, MA, 2003.

4. Yates, J. *Control Through Communication: The Rise of System in American Management*; Johns Hopkins University Press, 1989; paperback edition, 1993.

5. Scott, B.; Longo, B.; Katherine, V.W. *Critical Power Tools*; SUNY Press: Albany, NY, 2006.

6. Lipson, C.; Michael, J.D., Eds. *Technical Communication and the World Wide Web*; Lawrence Erlbaum and Associates: Mahwah, NJ, 2005.

7. Sullivan, P.; James, E.P. *Opening Spaces: Writing Technologies and Critical Research Practices*; Ablex and Computers and Composition/New Directions in Computers and Composition Studies: Greenwich, CT, 1997.

8. Johnson-Eilola, J.; Selber, S.A., Eds. *Central Works in Technical Communication*; Oxford University Press: Oxford, NY, 2004.

9. Latour, B. *We Have Never Been Modern*; Harvester Wheatsheaf: Hemel Hempstead, 1993.

10. Morrogh, E. *Information Architecture: An Emerging 21st Century Profession*; Prentice Hall: Upper Saddle River, NJ, 2003.

11. Ong, W.J. The writer's audience is always a fiction. PMLA **1975**, January *90*, 9–21.

12. Ong, Walter J. *Orality and Literacy: The Technologizing of the Word*, 1st Ed.; Methuen: New York, 1982; 2nd Ed.; Routledge: New York, 2002.

13. Wurman, R.S. *Information Anxiety*, 1st Ed.; Doubleday: New York, 1989.

14. Longo, B. *Spurious Coin: A History of Science. Management, and Technical Writing*; SUNY Press: Albany, NY, May 20, 2000.

15. Johnson, R.R. *User-Centered Technology: A Rhetorical Theory for Computers and Other Mundane Artifacts*; SUNY Press: Albany, NY, 1998.

16. Connors, R. The rise of technical writing instruction in America. J. Tech. Writ. Commun. **1982**, *12*, 329–352.

17. Norman, D. *The Design of Everyday Things*, 2nd Ed.; Continuum Press: New York, 1988; Basic Books, 2002.

18. Durack, K.T. Gender, technology, and the history of technical communication. Tech. Commun. Quart. Summer **1997**, *6* (3), 249–260.

19. Feenberg, A. *Critical Theory of Technology*; Oxford University Press: Oxford, NY, 1991.

20. Schriver, K. *Dynamics in Document Design*; Wiley: New York, 1997.

21. Lanham, R.A. *The Electronic Word: Democracy, Technology, and the Arts*; University of Chicago Press: Chicago, IL, 1993.

22. Surowiecki, J. *The Wisdom of Crowds: Why the Many Are Smarter Than the Few*; Anchor Publishing: Port Moody, BC, 2005.

23. Wright, A. *Glut: Mastering Information Through the Ages*; Joseph Henry Press: Washington, DC, July 2007.

24. Weinberger, D. *Everything Is Miscellaneous: The Power of the New Digital Disorder*; Times Books: New York, 2007.

25. Faber, B. *Discourse, Technology & Change*; Continuum: New York & London, 2007.

26. Faber, B. *Community Action and Organizational Change: Image, Narrative, Identity*; Southern Illinois University Press: Carbondale, IL, 2002.

27. Bolter, J.D.; Richard, G. *Remediation: Understanding New Media*; The MIT Press: Cambridge, MA, 2000.

Technical–Topic

Test Collections

Ben Carterette
Department of Computer and Information Sciences, University of Delaware, Newark, Delaware, U.S.A.

Abstract
Research and development of search engines and other information retrieval (IR) systems proceeds by a cycle of design, implementation, and experimentation, with the results of each experiment influencing design decisions in the next iteration of the cycle. Batch experiments on *test collections* help ensure that this process goes as smoothly and as quickly as possible. A test collection comprises a collection of documents, a set of information needs, and judgments of the relevance of documents to those needs.

INTRODUCTION

In the early 1960s, a librarian employed by Cranfield Aeronautics was working on search systems to help aeronautical engineers locate research papers relevant to particular engineering questions. His systems involved combinations of cataloging and labeling methods called "precision devices"—those designed to increase the proportion of matching material that was relevant—and "recall devices"—those designed to increase the proportion of relevant material that was found.[1] Between these two broad classes of devices, many permutations and variations were possible. He needed a way to measure the utility of one precision device over another, one recall device over another, or a precision device versus a recall device. In other words, he needed to be able to *evaluate* the devices' performance and compare them to one another.

A straightforward way to go about this is to bring in actual users of the system, have them interact with it for a while, and measure how well and how fast they are able to complete certain tasks. Today this is called a "user-based evaluation." While user-based evaluations are invaluable for measuring certain aspects of retrieval systems, they are also slow, expensive, and inefficient: each iteration of the design cycle requires a new study with new users, who must be compensated for their time. Meanwhile, differences between systems commingle with the abilities and preferences of the users, limiting conclusions that can be drawn about the systems independent of the particular users in the study. Finally, the data the users generate is not reusable; once a design cycle starts anew, the entire process must be started from scratch. Comparing a wide variety of systems with different (and sometimes very subtle) combinations of precision and recall devices made this process far too inefficient.

Instead, the librarian—Cyril Cleverdon—hit upon an idea that would allow them to *automatically* differentiate between the performance of different devices. He in effect reverse engineered a user study. He assembled a collection of research papers and contacted their authors, asking them to provide the research questions that had inspired the paper. He then asked the authors to rate each of the cited references on a scale of 1–5 with regard to how relevant it was to each of the research questions. This produced data by which he could simulate a user study: the author-provided research questions were a set of information needs that would be similar to those of the system's users, and the judgments of relevance told him which articles would be better to retrieve. The same data could be used again and again, under the assumption that the ability to answer that particular set of research questions better would generalize to the wider space of research questions that users would want to ask.

This basic method (and indeed the documents, questions, and judgments themselves) was picked up by Professor Gerard Salton of Cornell for the evaluation of his highly influential automatic text indexing and retrieval system SMART.[2] As a result, it is now the de facto approach to evaluating automatic retrieval system performance, and it is referred to as the "Cranfield paradigm." Evaluations within this paradigm are called "system-based evaluations." The key component to a system-based evaluation is a *test collection*: a set of documents or other objects that will be indexed and searched, a set of information needs that are representative of the needs of typical users, and judgments of the relevance of indexed objects to those information needs.

The test collection resulting from the above study—the Cranfield collection of aeronautical engineering abstracts—consisted of 1400 documents, 225 information needs, and roughly 1800 relevance judgments, on average eight per information need. Those that were not provided by the authors were filled in by students later on. Since then, test collections have grown with the size and complexity of organization and retrieval problems. Modern

Encyclopedia of Library and Information Sciences, Fourth Edition DOI: 10.1081/E-ELIS4-120044382

test collections in information retrieval (IR) research consist of millions of full-text documents, and in development of Web search engines, tens of billions of Web pages and other information.

This entry is about the components of a test collection, how test collections are assembled, and particular test collections used in current research and development. Before getting to that, it is important to understand how a test collection reflects a particular retrieval task and a definition of relevance.

RETRIEVAL TASKS AND RELEVANCE

People use search engines for many different reasons: library catalog search, Web search, literature search; routing and filtering; known-item search, novel-item search, passage search; question answering, summarization, media search, and so on. Each of these is a different *retrieval task*, and a test collection built to study one task is not necessarily the right collection for studying another. Each task suggests a different definition of *relevance*; since the definition of relevance affects every judgment to every document in the test collection, the use of a particular test collection entails the use of a particular definition of relevance designed to handle a particular retrieval task.

The prototypical task is called ad hoc retrieval: a user enters an arbitrary query and the engine returns a ranked list of documents that "match" the query according to some model. The query is considered a one-time event, with the corpus unchanging from the time the query is entered to the time the results are returned. This contrasts with tasks such as routing or filtering, in which the corpus changes over time and new documents are constantly checked for relevance against "standing" queries, or question answering, in which the query is a natural-language question and the ranked list consists of natural-language answers that are not necessarily literally attested in any document in the corpus. Tasks such as known-item retrieval,[3] home page finding,[4] and topic distillation[5] are similar to ad hoc retrieval in the basic framework, but differ in that users performing one of these tasks is looking for something more specific than information about a topic; they are looking for (respectively) a particular document, a home page, or pages that are entries into hyperlinked sites of dispersed but relevant material. Novel-item retrieval has the goal of retrieving things—often passages rather than documents—that have *not* been seen before[6] (where "before" is generally taken to mean "higher in a ranked list").

More than any other factor, the retrieval task dictates the definition of relevance that is used when judging documents. In IR broadly defined, relevance is considered to be a semantic or pragmatic property of documents and queries. It is not syntactic, as in database systems: a

document cannot be considered relevant only by virtue of containing the query terms, nor can it be considered nonrelevant only because it lacks some or all query terms. Because words can have multiple meanings and concepts can be represented by words that the user has not thought of, it is always possible that a document is relevant despite containing none of the query terms (or, similarly, that a document is nonrelevant despite containing all of the query terms). The relevance of a document must therefore be assessed independently of the query and the system that retrieved it, but with respect to the retrieval task and the full information need.

To see the influence of task on relevance, consider the criteria for relevance under different tasks. In tasks like ad hoc and routing, a document is typically considered relevant if it contains any information about the topic. Known-item retrieval and home page finding require only one relevant document (or a very small set). For the topic distillation task, relevant pages may contain no information about the topic at all; it is sufficient that they be a gateway to a site about the topic. Determining whether pages are "novel" depends on knowing what has been ranked above them,[7] or possibly on what a user has seen in the past.

Even within the domain of a particular task, relevance can be difficult to define precisely.[8–10] Befitting the concept of system-based evaluation, the most widely used notion of relevance is *system-oriented*, in which the relevance of a document to a query is dependent only on the representations of the document and query, and not on any "external" features of the user that submitted the query, the state of the corpus, other documents in a ranking, and so on.[11] This sort of definition clearly facilitates repeatable system-based evaluations, though other definitions by which relevance is ranking-dependent or corpus-dependent certainly do not make such evaluations impossible. Definitions of relevance that are conditioned to a greater degree on the user result in experiments that are not as easily repeatable, as a user's needs can evolve in time even as the corpus is considered static.

There is also the question of whether relevance should be measured on a binary, graded, or continuous scale, or whether it is better treated as a preferential judgment between two or more documents.[12] Topical relevance is typically defined on a binary scale: a document is either relevant (on-topic) or it is not. On the Web, where queries are very short, often ambiguous, and users tend not to look past the top 10 documents retrieved, relevance on a 3- or 5-point graded scale has become standard (cf. Burges, Shaked, et al.[13] and Carterette and Jones[14] for Web-inspired work on ranking and evaluating using graded judgments). Rorvig proposed that relevance be assessed as a relative property between two documents, which could translate into a continuous measure of utility.[12] These decisions depend to a large extent on the task as well.

TEST COLLECTION CONSTRUCTION

Putting together a test collection that is interesting for IR research is a difficult task.[15] The documents should be heterogeneous enough that one can expect performance to generalize to other collections, but homogeneous enough that query samples will cover a fair amount of the possible space of information needs. The information needs should be representative of the space of needs users of the corpus will have, and large enough that statistically significant conclusions about systems can be reached. They should not be too easy for the systems (i.e., an untuned system should not be able to find all of the relevant documents), but they should not be too hard either (an untuned system should be able to find at least a few relevant documents). Queries that are too easy or too hard are not the ones that one can expect to achieve gains on through research and development, and thus are not ideal for testing. It should be noted that *some* easy and hard queries should be interspersed in the set. If a system cannot answer the easiest query, it is clearly a poor system; further testing is not required.

Tague-Sutcliffe explicates some of the particular considerations in the construction of a test collection.[16] In assembling a corpus, one must consider "size, concentration, form, medium, subject coverage, and warrant or expected use of the database," which in turn refer to the number of documents, the degree of homogeneity among them, the "completeness of the representation" (short citation, abstract, full-text), the "communication medium" (text, sound, video). All of these are to some extent influenced by the task (the expected use of the database). As for queries, it is preferable that they come from real users of the system, but, as Tague-Sutcliffe says, this is often more difficult and expensive than one might think, particularly when it comes to vetting their queries for coherence and ease. Artificial queries can be generated from the documents (for example, by using words in document titles), or the researcher/developer can "backfit" queries to fit a particular set of documents.

Then there is the issue of relevance judgments. Since these are semantic (or pragmatic) judgments, they require some human input. Typically they are made by assessors hired expressly for the purpose of making relevance judgments. Sometimes these assessors may provide information needs and queries as well; it stands to reason that the person best equipped to judge a document is the one who came up with the information need that retrieved it. The standard way to collect relevance judgments is by *system pooling*:[17] the set of test queries is run through the set of systems to be compared, and the top N results from each system for each query are pooled. This entire pool is then judged for relevance. This focuses the judging effort on those documents least likely to be nonrelevant, and allows exact understanding of precision (the proportion of retrieved documents that are relevant) up to rank N. It

leaves some uncertainty in recall (the proportion of relevant documents that were retrieved), since there may be relevant documents that were not retrieved by any system and thus unjudged by any assessor.

In practice, a retrieval system developer may have a corpus ready to be searched, for example an intranet, a large database of short texts, or a collection of books, and a set of information needs that can be sampled. The problem is not in finding a corpus or information needs, but in acquiring enough relevance judgments that will allow them to have confidence in the evaluation.

Repeatability and Reusability

In an ideal setting, system-based evaluations over test collections are *repeatable*: the same experimental environment produces the same results every time. This means that published results can be verified by other researchers and developers, and results can be directly compared across developers and over time. Additionally, an ideal test collection is *reusable*: though its relevance judgments may have been collected from a particular set of systems, they should be complete enough that they can reliably evaluate new systems with properties that are as yet unknown. This way, new systems can be reliably compared to old; as well, the high cost of collecting judgments can be amortized over many experiments.

If a test collection contains a relevance judgment of every document to every query, it goes without saying that the test collection is reusable. Test collections constructed using the pooling method are not so complete, which raises the question of whether they are reusable. This was answered in the positive for a class of collections (the *TREC collections*; see below) by Zobel;[18] while pooling failed to find up to 50% of the relevant documents for some of the test queries, these missing judgments did not seriously affect comparisons between systems. It is likely that pooling requires some degree of diversity among systems that has not been measured, and in a setting in which such diversity is not available, test collections may be less reusable.

Assessor Agreement

The system-oriented notion of relevance treats it as a *semantic* property, concerned with the meaning of the query and the document. User-oriented approaches are *pragmatic*, concerned more with what is needed by the user at the time the query was entered. In either case, relevance judgments are subject to disagreement among assessors.

The effect of disagreement on system-based evaluations is an important one and deserving of study. Cormack et al. proposed a method for acquiring relevance judgments called "Interactive Searching and Judging" (ISJ), by which assessors submit a query to a retrieval engine, judge retrieved documents, and then reformulate the query based on what they have learned in making those judgments.[19] Using this method to acquire judgments for a particular widely disseminated set of information needs produced a set of judgments that overlapped only 33% with the provided judgments. Despite this, the evaluation of systems over those topics did not substantially change; other studies have independently reached the same conclusion.[20,21] This suggests that evaluations are rather robust to disagreement between assessors. Presumably there is much greater agreement on some documents than others, and those documents that assessors agree highly on tend to be the ones that are most useful for differentiating between systems.

AVAILABLE TEST COLLECTIONS

Some of the test collections that have appeared most frequently in the literature are the Cranfield collection of aerodynamics technical papers, the OHSUMED corpus of medical abstracts, the CACM corpus of abstracts from *Communications of the ACM*, the INSPEC corpus, the Text REtrieval Conference (TREC) news corpora, consisting of articles from the *New York Times*, *Wall Street Journal*, *Associated Press*, and more, and the TREC GOV corpora, consisting of millions of Web pages in the .gov domain. The first four of these contain fewer than 30,000 documents; it is only in the last 20 years that large test collections have become widely available for IR research.[22] Each of these has an associated set of information needs either taken from actual needs of users of the corpus or developed for the express purpose of retrieval research.

In 1980, a corpus of 11,000 documents was considered "unusually large" (q.v. Robertson et al.[23]). Part of the reason is the computational power available at the time, of course, but by 1990 corpus sizes had not grown significantly larger.[22] I have not found any paper before 1992 using a collection of more than 30,000 documents. Tague-Sutcliffe and Hawking have both observed that the limited size of these test collections limits the conclusions that can be drawn about system performance; as a result, small collections like Cranfield, CACM, OHSUMED, and INSPEC are no longer in wide use.

IR research has been a fast-moving field, and as a result, in its early days small collections that had been developed for one task were often coerced into use for another. This was partially due to the cost of constructing a test collection: though cheaper than a series of user studies, there is still a significant startup cost that a small research group cannot necessarily afford. This was one of the motivating factors for the TREC, which began in 1992.[22,24] The first large-scale test collections for general research purposes came out of TREC: Where previous collections had been no more than several megabytes of short text articles, the new TIPSTER collection was about 3 GB and consisted of over a million full-text documents from the Associated Press, Wall Street Journal, and Federal Register, along with abstracts from the Department of Energy.[24] The sets of information needs were smaller (50 topics rather than the several hundred queries in previous collections), but more tightly focused, well-defined, and assembled with greater quality control.[22] This collection was developed for the standard ad hoc task, and in the intervening time more documents and queries have been added, new domains sampled, and new tasks represented. Today there are research test collections with up to 25 million documents and tens of thousands of queries (though the relevance judgments are very sparse). There are test collections designed for many different tasks, including routing and filtering, home-page finding, known-item finding, topic distillation, question answering, expert finding, patent search, and many more.

The collections produced by TREC, which are available from TREC's Web site (http://trec.nist.gov) are now standard and ubiquitous in IR research. Similar evaluation conferences such as NTCIR (NII Test Collections for IR Systems; http://research.nii.ac.jp/ntcir) and CLEF (Cross-Language Evaluation Forum; http://clef-campaign.org) have emerged to provide a greater breadth of data for retrieval in other languages and for other tasks (such as patent retrieval, image retrieval, and video retrieval) as the field has grown substantially over the last decade.

CONCLUSION

A test collection comprises a set of documents, a set of information needs or queries, and a set of judgments of relevance of documents to those information needs. They enable rapid IR research and development through batch evaluations of system performance.

REFERENCES

1. Cleverdon, C.W.; Mills, J. The testing of index language devices. In *Readings in Information Retrieval*; Spärck Jones, K., Willett, P., Eds.; Morgan Kaufmann Publishers: San Francisco, CA, 1997; 98–110.

2. Salton, G.; Lesk, M.E. Computer evaluation of indexing and text processing. In *Readings in Information Retrieval*; Spärck Jones, K., Willett, P., Eds.; Morgan Kaufmann Publishers: San Francisco, CA, 1997; 60–84.

3. Beitzel, S.M.; Jensen, E.C.; Chowdhury, A.; Grossman, D.; Frieder, O. Using manually-built web directories for automatic evaluation of known-item retrieval SIGIR'03: Proceedings of the 26th Annual International ACM SIGIR Conference on Research and Development in Information Retrieval Toronto, ON, Canada July 28–August, 1, 2003; Callan, J., Hawking, D., Smeaton, A., Eds.; ACM: New York, NY, 2003; 373–374.

Technical–Topic

4. Hawking, D.; Craswell, N. Overview of the TREC-2001 Web track Proceedings of the 10th Text Retrieval Conference (TREC 2001) Gaithersburg, MD November, 2001; Voorhees, E., Ed.; NIST: Gaithersburg, MD, 2001; 61–67.

5. Craswell, N. Hawking, D. Overview of the TREC-2002 Web track Proceedings of the 11th Text REtrieval Conference (TREC 2002) Gaithersburg, MD November, 2002; Voorhees, E., Ed.; NIST: Gaithersburg, MD, 2002; 86–95.

6. Harman, D. Overview of the TREC 2002 Novelty track Proceedings of the 11th Text REtrieval Conference (TREC 2002) Gaithersburg, MD November, 2002; Voorhees, E., Ed.; NIST: Gaithersburg, MD, 2002 46–55.

7. Carbonell, J.; Goldstein, J. The use of MMR, diversity-based reranking for reordering documents and producing summaries SIGIR '98: Proceedings of the 21st Annual International ACM SIGIR Conference on Research and Development in Information Retrieval Melbourne, Australia August, 24–28, 1998; Croft, W.B., Moffat, A., van Rijsbergen, C.J., Wilkinson, R., Zobel, J., Eds.; ACM: New York, NY, 1998; 335–336.

8. Mizzaro, S. Relevance: The whole history. JASIS **1997**, *48*(9), 810–832.

9. Belkin, N.J. Ineffable concepts in information retrieval. In *Readings in Information Retrieval*; Spärck Jones, K., Willett, P., Eds.; Morgan Kaufmann Publishers: San Francisco, CA, 1997; 44–58.

10. Saracevic, T.; Kantor, P.; Chamis, A.Y.; Trivison, D. A study of information seeking and retrieving. In *Readings in Information Retrieval*; Spärck Jones, K., Willett, P., Eds.; Morgan Kaufmann Publishers: San Francisco, CA, 1997; 175–190.

11. Lavrenko, V. *A generative theory of relevance*, University of Massachusetts: Amherst, MA, 2004; Ph.D. thesis.

12. Rorvig, M.E. The simple scalability of documents. JASIS **1990**, *41*(8), 590–598.

13. Burges, C.; Shaked, T.; Renshaw, E.; Lazier, A.; Deeds, M.; Hamilton, N.; Hullender, G. Learning to rank using gradient descent ICML '05: Proceedings of the 22nd International Conference on Machine Learning Bonn, Germany August, 7–11, 2005; Raedt, L.D., Wrobel, S., Eds.; ACM: New York, NY, 2005; Vol. 119, 89–96.

14. Carterette, B.; Jones, R. Evaluating search engines by modeling the relationship between relevance and clicks Advances in Neural Information Processing Systems Vancouver, Canada December, 2008; Platt, J.C., Koller, D., Singer, Y., Roweis, S., Eds.; MIT Press: Cambridge, MA, 2008; Vol. 20, 217–224.

15. Tague, J. The pragmatics of information retrieval evaluation. In *Information Retrieval Experiment*; Spärck Jones, K., Ed.; Buttersworth: London, U.K., 1981; 59–102.

16. Tague-Sutcliffe, J. The pragmatics of information retrieval evaluation revisited. In *Readings in Information Retrieval*; Spärck Jones, K., Willett, P., Eds.; Morgan Kaufmann Publishers: San Francisco, CA, 1997; 205–216.

17. Spärck Jones, K.; van Rijsbergen, C.J. Information retrieval test collections. J. Doc. **1976**, *32*(1), 59–75.

18. Zobel, J. How reliable are the results of large-scale information retrieval experiments SIGIR '98: Proceedings of the 21st Annual International ACM SIGIR Conference on Research and Development in Information Retrieval Melbourne, Australia Aug, 24–28, 1998; Croft, W.B., Moffat, A., van Rijsbergen, C.J., Wilkinson, R., Zobel, J., Eds.; ACM: New York, NY 307–314.

19. Cormack, G.V.; Palmer, C.R. Clarke, C.L. Efficient construction of large test collections SIGIR '98: Proceedings of the 21st Annual International ACM SIGIR Conference on Research and Development in Information Retrieval Melbourne, Australia August, 24–28, 1998; Croft, W.B., Moffat, A., van Rijsbergen, C.J., Wilkinson, R., Zobel, J., Eds.; ACM: New York, NY, 1998; 282–289.

20. Voorhees, E. Variations in relevance judgments and the measurement of retrieval effectiveness SIGIR '98: Proceedings of the 21st Annual International ACM SIGIR Conference on Research and Development in Information Retrieval Melbourne, Australia Aug, 24–28, 1998; Croft, W.B., Moffat, A., van Rijsbergen, C.J., Wilkinson, R., Zobel, J., Eds.; ACM: New York, NY 315–323.

21. Harter, S.P. Variations in relevance assessments and the measurement of retrieval effectiveness. JASIS **1996**, *47*(1), 37–49.

22. Voorhees, E.M.; Harman, D.K. *TREC: Experiment and Evaluation in Information Retrieval*, MIT Press: Cambridge, MA, 2005.

23. Robertson, S.E.; van Rijsbergen, C.J.; Porter, M.F. Probabilistic models of indexing and searching Proceedings of the Third Annual ACM Conference on Research and Development in Information Retrieval Cambridge, England June, 23–27, 1980; van Rijsbergen, C.J., Ed.; Butterworth & Co.: Kent, U.K. 35–56.

24. Harman, D. The TREC conferences. In *Readings in Information Retrieval*; Spärck Jones, K., Willett, P., Eds.; Morgan Kaufmann Publishers: San Francisco, CA, 1997; 247–256.

Technical-Topic

Text Encoding Initiative (TEI)

Edward Vanhoutte
Ron Van den Branden
Centre for Scholarly Editing and Document Studies, Royal Academy of Dutch Language and Literature, Gent, Belgium

Abstract

The result of community efforts among computing humanists, the Text Encoding Initiative or TEI is the *de facto* standard for the encoding of texts in the humanities. This entry explains the historical context of the TEI, its fundamental principles, history, and organization.

INTRODUCTION

Computers can only process texts whose characters are represented by a system that relates to the binary system computers can interpret. This is called character encoding. One such character encoding scheme based on the English alphabet is ASCII (American Standard Code for Information Interchange). Character encoding facilitates the storage of text in computers and the transmission of text through telecommunication networks. Character encoding, however, does not say anything about the semantics, interpretation, or structure of a text. Such information on a text is called meta-information. If we want to add any meta-information to a text so that it can be processed by computers, we need to encode or markup texts. We can do this by inserting natural language expressions (or codes representing them) in the text with the same character encoding the text is using, but separated from the text by specific markers. One such expression, we call a tag. All of the tags used to encode a text together constitute a markup language. The application of a markup language to a text, we call text encoding.

The Text Encoding Initiative (TEI) is a standard for the representation of textual material in digital form through the means of text encoding. This standard is the collaborative product of a community of scholars, chiefly from the humanities, social sciences, and linguistics who are organized in the TEI Consortium (TEI-C http://www.tei-c.org). The TEI Consortium is a nonprofit membership organization and governs a wide variety of activities such as the development, publication, and maintenance of the text encoding standard documented in the *TEI Guidelines*, the discussion and development of the standard on the TEI mailing list (TEI-L) and in Special Interest Groups (SIG), the gathering of the TEI community on yearly members meetings, and the promotion of the standard in publications, on workshops, training courses, colloquia, and conferences. These activities are generally open to nonmembers as well.

By "TEI Guidelines" one may refer both to the markup language and tag set proposed by the TEI Consortium and to its documentation online or in print. Informally "TEI Guidelines" is often abbreviated to "TEI." In this entry "TEI Guidelines" is used as the general term for the encoding standard. The *TEI Guidelines* are widely used by libraries, museums, publishers, and individual scholars to present texts for online research, teaching, and preservation. Since the TEI is expressed in terms of the eXtensible Markup Language (XML) and since it provides procedures and mechanics to adapt to one's own project needs, the *TEI Guidelines* define an open standard that is generally applicable to any text and purpose.

The entry first introduces the concepts of text encoding and markup languages in the humanities and then introduces the TEI encoding principles. Next, the article provides a brief historical survey of the TEI Guidelines and ends with a presentation of the Consortium's organization.

TEXT ENCODING IN THE HUMANITIES

Since the earliest uses of computers and computational techniques in the humanities at the end of the 1940s, scholars, projects, and research groups had to look for systems that could provide *representations* of data which the computer could process. Computers, as Michael Sperberg-McQueen has reminded us are binary machines that "can contain and operate on patterns of electronic charges, but they cannot contain numbers, which are abstract mathematical objects not electronic charges, nor texts, which are complex, abstract cultural and linguistic objects" (p. 34).[1] This is clearly seen in the mechanics of early input devices such as punched cards where a hole at a certain coordinate actually meant a 1 or 0 (true or false) for the character or numerical represented by this coordinate according to the specific character set of the computer

Encyclopedia of Library and Information Sciences, Fourth Edition DOI: 10.1081/E-ELIS4-120043748

Technical–Topic

used. Because different computers used different character sets with a different number of characters, texts first had to be transcribed into that character set. All characters, punctuation marks, diacritics, and significant changes of type style had to be encoded with an inadequate budget of characters. This resulted in a complex of "flags" for distinguishing uppercase and lowercase letters, for coding accented characters, the start of a new chapter, paragraph, sentence, or word. These "flags" were also used for adding analytical information to the text such as word classes, morphological, syntactic, and lexical information. Ideally, each project used its own set of conventions consistently throughout. Since this set of conventions was usually designed on the basis of an analysis of the textual material to be transcribed to machine-readable text, another corpus of textual material would possibly need another set of conventions. The design of these sets of conventions was also heavily dependent on the nature and infrastructure of the project, such as the type of computers, software, and devices such as magnetic tapes of a certain kind that were available.

Although several projects were able to produce meaningful scholarly results with this internally consistent approach, the particular nature of each set of conventions or encoding scheme had lots of disadvantages. Texts prepared in such a proprietary scheme by one project could not readily be used by other projects; software developed for the analysis of such texts could hence not be used outside the project due to an incompatibility of encoding schemes and nonstandardization of hardware. However, with the increase of texts being prepared in machine-readable format, the call for an economic use of resources increased as well. Already in 1967, Michael Kay argued in favor of a "standard code in which any text received from an outside source can be assumed to be" (p. 171).[2] This code would behave as an exchange format which allowed the users to use their own conventions at output and at input (p. 172).[2]

MARKUP LANGUAGES IN THE HUMANITIES

Procedural and Descriptive Markup

When human beings read texts, they perceive both the information stored in the linguistic code of the text and the meta-information which is inferred from the appearance and interpretation of the text. By convention, italics are, for instance, used as a code signaling a title of a book, play, or movie; a foreign word or phrase; or emphatic use of the language. Through their cognitive abilities, readers usually have no problems selecting the most appropriate interpretation of an italic string of text. Computers, however, need to be informed about these issues in order to be able to process them. This can be done by way of a markup language that

provides rules to formally separate information (the text in a document) from meta-information (information *about* the text in a document).Whereas markup languages in use in the typesetting community were mainly of a procedural nature, that is, they indicate procedures that a particular application should follow (e.g., printing a string of text in italics), the humanities were also and mainly considered with descriptive markup that identifies the entity type of tokens (e.g., identifying that a string of text is a title of a book or a foreign word). Unlike procedural or presentational markup, descriptive markup establishes a one to one mapping between logical elements in the text and their markup. In order to achieve this, descriptive markup languages tend to formally separate information (the text in a document) from meta-information (information *about* the text in a document).

Early Attempts

Some sort of standardization of text encoding for the encoding and analysis of literary texts was reached by the COCOA encoding scheme originally developed for the COCOA program in the 1960s and 1970s,[3] but used as an input standard by the Oxford Concordance Program (OCP) in the 1980s[4] and by the Textual Analysis Computing Tools (TACT) in the 1990s.[5] For the transcription and encoding of classical Greek texts, the beta-transcription/encoding system reached some level of standardized use.[6]

The Standard Generalized Markup Language (SGML)

The call for a markup language that could guarantee reusability, interchange, system and software independence, portability, and collaboration in the humanities was answered by the publication of the Standard Generalized Markup Language (SGML) as an ISO standard in 1986 (ISO 8879:1986).[7] Based on IBM's *Document Composition Facility Generalized Markup Language*, SGML was developed mainly by Charles Goldfarb as a metalanguage for the description of markup schemes that satisfied at least seven requirements for an encoding standard (pp. 28–29):[8]

1. The requirement of comprehensiveness.
2. The requirement of simplicity.
3. The requirement that documents be processable by software of moderate complexity.
4. The requirement that the standard not be dependent on any particular characteristic set or text-entry device.
5. The requirement that the standard not be geared to any particular analytic program or printing system.

6. The requirement that the standard should describe text in editable form.

7. The requirement that the standard allow the interchange of encoded texts across communication networks.

In order to achieve universal exchangeability and software and platform independence, SGML made use exclusively of the ASCII codes. As mentioned above, SGML is not a markup language itself, but a metalanguage by which one can create separate markup languages for separate purposes. This means that SGML defines the rules and procedures to specify the vocabulary and the syntax of a markup language in a formal Document Type Definition (DTD). Such a DTD is a formal description of, for instance, names for all elements, names and default values for their attributes, rules about how elements can nest and how often they can occur, and names for reusable pieces of data (entities). The DTD enables full control, parsing, and validation of SGML-encoded documents. By and large the most popular SGML DTD is the Hypertext Markup Language (HTML) developed for the exchange of graphical documents over the Internet.

A markup scheme with all these qualities was exactly what the humanities were looking for in their quest for a descriptive encoding standard for the preparation and interchange of electronic texts for scholarly research. There was a strong consensus among the computing humanists that SGML offered a better foundation for research-oriented text encoding than other such schemes.[8,9] From the beginning, however, SGML was also criticized for at least two problematic matters: SGML's hierarchical perspective on text, i.e., the representation of text as a hierarchical tree structure, and SGML's verbose markup system.[9] These two issues have since been central to the theoretical and educational debates on markup languages in the humanities.

The eXtensible Markup Language (XML)

The publication of the eXtensible Markup Language (XML) 1.0 as a W3C recommendation in 1998[10] brought together the best features of SGML and HTML and soon achieved huge popularity. Among the strengths XML borrowed from SGML are the explicitness of descriptive markup, the expressive power of hierarchic models, the extensibility of markup languages, and the possibility to validate a document against a DTD. From HTML it borrowed simplicity and the possibility to work without a DTD. Technically speaking, XML is a subset of SGML and the recommendation was developed by a group of people with a long standing experience in SGML, many of whom were members of the TEI community.

For example, a simple two-paragraph document could be encoded as follows in XML:

```
<?xml version="1.0" encoding="UTF-8"?>
<document>
    <!-- paragraphs go here -->
    <paragraph number="1">Paragraph one of
        <title>an XML example</title>.</paragraph>
    <paragraph number="2">Paragraph two of this
        example.</paragraph>
</document>
```

This is an example of an XML document, representing both information and meta-information. Information (plain text) is contained in *XML elements*, delimited by *start tags* (e.g., <document>) and *end tags* (e.g., </document>). Additional information to these XML elements can be given in *attributes*, consisting of a name (e.g., number) and a value (e.g., [1]). *XML comments* are delimited by start markers (<!--) and end markers (-->). This particular example illustrates how XML enables semantically transparent encoding of a document (<document>), which consists of two paragraphs (<paragraph>), the first of which contains text identified as a title (<title>). By providing facilities to define own tags and attributes, XML allows encoders to devise their own markup languages for their document (types).

Among more technical ones, Steven DeRose pointed out substantial advantages of XML to the TEI community: by allowing for more flexible automatic parsing strategies and easy delivery of electronic documents with cheap ubiquitous tools such as Web browsers, XML could spread the notion of descriptive markup to a wide audience that will thus be acquainted with the concepts articulated in the TEI Guidelines (p. 19).[11] Because of its advantages and widespread popularity, XML became the metalanguage of choice for expressing the rules for descriptive text encoding in TEI.

TEI: GROUND RULES

Guidelines

The conclusions and the work of the TEI community are formulated as guidelines, rules, and recommendations rather than standards, because it is acknowledged that each scholar must have the freedom of expressing their own theory of text by encoding the features they think important in the text. A wide array of possible solutions to encoding matters is demonstrated in the TEI Guidelines which therefore should be considered a reference manual rather than a tutorial. Mastering the complete TEI encoding scheme implies a steep learning curve, but few projects require a complete knowledge of the TEI. Therefore, a manageable subset of the full TEI encoding scheme was published as TEI Lite, currently describing 145 elements.[12] Originally intended as an introduction and a didactic stepping stone to the full recommendations, TEI

Lite has, since its publication in 1995, become one of the most popular TEI customizations and proves to meet the needs of 90% of the TEI community, 90% of the time.

The ground rules discussed in this section apply to the most recent version of the TEI at the time of writing, i.e., TEI P5. See the section on TEI: History for more details about P5 and previous versions of the TEI Guidelines.

Text Structure

The TEI Guidelines[13] define a set of rules to mark up the phenomena in a wide range of texts in a descriptive fashion. This means that, for example, encoders can (and should) not just indicate *that* a bit of text is printed in italics, but *why* this is the case: either because it appears to be a title in a bibliographical reference, or a technical term, a foreign word, a regular word with rhetorical emphasis, and so on. Texts that are enriched with intelligible meta-information not only can be preserved and reused more easily by humans, but also can be processed more intelligently by computers.

The TEI guarantees this potential by imposing a common structure on texts:

```
<TEI xmlns="http://www.tei-c.org/ns/1.0">
  <teiHeader>
    <fileDesc>
      <titleStmt>
        <title><!- -Title- -></title>
      </titleStmt>
      <publicationStmt>
        <p><!- -Publication Information- -></p>
      </publicationStmt>
      <sourceDesc>
        <p><!- -Information about the source- -></p>
      </sourceDesc>
    </fileDesc>
  </teiHeader>
  <text>
    <body>
      <p n="1">Paragraph one of <title>an
        XML example</title>.</p>
      <p n="2">Paragraph two of this
        example.</p>
    </body>
  </text>
</TEI>
```

This example, as any TEI text, is recognizable as a TEI text by the outermost *<TEI>* element, which is declared in the dedicated TEI namespace (http://www.tei-c.org/ns/1.0). The TEI considers texts units of information that are composed of two mandatory parts:

- A header (*<teiHeader>*) containing descriptive meta-information. This should minimally document following aspects of the electronic file itself (*<fileDesc>*):
  - The title statement (*<titleStmt>*), providing information about the title, author, and others responsible for the electronic text.
  - The publication statement (*<publicationStmt>*), providing publication details about the electronic text.
  - A description of the source (*<sourceDesc>*), documenting bibliographic details about the electronic text's material source (if any).
- the actual text (*<text>*) containing meta-information about the text's structure and the actual text. This should minimally contain a text body (*<body>*). The body contains lower-level text structures like paragraphs (*<p>*), or different structures for text genres other than prose: lines for poetry, speeches for drama.

Apart from simple texts, TEI provides means to encode composite texts, either by grouping structurally related texts in a *<group>* element inside *<text>*, or treating them as a corpus of diverse texts, using *<teiCorpus>* as the outermost element.

TEI Modules

As illustrated by this example, a significant part of the rules in the TEI Guidelines apply to the expression of descriptive and structural meta-information about the text. Yet, the TEI defines concepts to represent a much wider array of textual phenomena, amounting to a total of 503 elements and 210 attributes. These are organized into 21 modules, grouping related elements and attributes:

1. The TEI Infrastructure
   Definition of common datatypes and modular class structures used to define the elements and attributes in the other modules.
2. The TEI Header
   Definition of the elements that make up the header section of TEI documents. Its major parts provide elements to encode detailed metadata about bibliographic aspects of electronic texts, their relationship with the source materials from which they may have been derived, nonbibliographic details, and a complete revision history.
3. Elements Available in All TEI Documents
   Definition of elements and attributes that may occur in any TEI text, of whatever genre. These elements cover textual phenomena like paragraphs, highlighting and quotation, editorial changes (marking of errors, regularizations, additions), data-like structures (names, addresses, dates, numbers, abbreviations),

cross-reference mechanisms, lists, notes, graphical elements, bibliographic references, and passages of verse or drama.

4. Default Text Structure

Definition of elements and attributes that describe the structure of TEI texts, like front matter and title pages, text body, and back matter. These may contain further divisions, possibly introduced by headings, salutations, opening formulae, and/or concluded by closing formulae, closing salutations, trailing material, and postscripts.

5. Representation of Nonstandard Characters and Glyphs

Definition of specific provisions for representing characters for which no standardized representation (such as defined by the *Unicode Consortium*http://www.unicode.org/) exists.

6. Verse

Definition of specific elements and attributes for dedicated analysis of verse materials, such as caesurae, metrical systems, rhyme schemes, and enjambments.

7. Performance Texts

Definition of specific elements and attributes for dedicated analysis of drama materials. These include provisions for encoding specific phenomena in front matter and back matter, like details about performances, prologues, epilogues, the dramatic setting, and cast lists. Other drama-specific structures include speeches and stage directions. For multimedia performances, elements for the description of screen contents, camera angles, captions, and sound are provided.

8. Transcriptions of Speech

Definition of elements and attributes for (general purpose) transcription of different kinds of spoken material. These cover phenomena like utterances, pauses, nonlexical sounds, gestures, and shifts in vocal quality. Besides this, specific header elements for describing the vocal source of the transcription are provided.

9. Dictionaries

Definition of elements and attributes for representing dictionaries, with provisions for unstructured and structured dictionary entries (possibly grouped). Dictionary entries may be structured with a number of specific elements indicating homonyms, sense, word form, grammatical information, definitions, citations, usage, and etymology.

10. Manuscript Description

Definition of specific header and structural elements and attributes for the encoding of manuscript sources. Header elements include provisions for detailed documentation of a manuscript's or manuscript part's identification, heading information, contents, physical description, history, and additional information. Dedicated text elements cover phenomena like catchwords, dimensions, heraldry, watermarks, and so on.

11. Representation of Primary Sources

Definition of elements and attributes for detailed transcription of primary sources. Phenomena covered are facsimiles, more complex additions, deletions, substitutions and restorations, document hands, damage to the source material, and illegibility of the text.

12. Critical Apparatus

Definition of elements and attributes for the representation of (different versions of texts as) scholarly editions, listing all variation between the versions in a variant apparatus.

13. Names, Dates, People, and Places

Definition of elements and attributes for more detailed analysis of names of persons, organizations, and places, their referents (persons, organizations, and places), and aspects of temporal analyses.

14. Tables, Formulae and Graphics

Definition of specific elements and attributes for detailed representation of graphical elements in texts, like tables, formulae, and images.

15. Language Corpora

Definition of elements and attributes for the encoding of corpora of texts that have been collected according to specific criteria. Most of these elements apply to the documentation of these sampling criteria, and contextual information about the texts, participants, and their communicative setting.

16. Linking, Segmentation, and Alignment

Definition of elements and attributes for representing complex systems of cross-references between identified anchor places in TEI texts. Recommendations are given for either in-line or stand-off reference mechanisms.

17. Simple Analytic Mechanisms

Definition of elements and attributes that allow the association of simple analyses and interpretations with text elements. Mechanisms for the representation of both generic and particular linguistic analyses are discussed.

18. Feature Structures

Definition of elements and attributes for constructing complex analytical frameworks that can be used to represent specific analyses in TEI texts.

19. Graphs, Networks, and Trees

Definition of elements and attributes for the analytical representation of schematic relationships between nodes in graphs and charts.

20. Certainty and Responsibility

Definition of elements for detailed attribution of certainty for the encoding in a TEI text, as well as the identification of the responsibility for these encodings.

Technical–Topic

21. Documentation Elements

Definition of elements and attributes for the documentation of the encoding scheme used in TEI texts. This module provides means to define elements, attributes, element and attribute classes, either by changing existing definitions or by creating new ones.

Each of these modules and the use of the elements they define are discussed extensively in a dedicated chapter of the TEI Guidelines.

Using TEI

In order to use TEI for the encoding of texts, users must make sure that their texts belong to the TEI namespace (http://www.tei-c.org/ns/1.0) and adhere to the requirements of the text model proposed by the TEI. In order to facilitate this conformance, it is possible (and strongly suggested) to associate TEI texts with formal representations of this text model. These formal *structural grammars* of a TEI compatible model of the text can be expressed in a number of ways, commonly referred to as a *TEI schema*. Technically, a TEI schema can be expressed in a variety of formal languages such as *Document Type Definition* (http://www.w3.org/TR/REC-xml/#dt-doctype), *W3C XML Schema* (http://www.w3.org/XML/Schema), or the *RELAX NG* schema language (http://www.relaxng.org/). It is important to notice that no such thing as "the TEI schema" exists. Rather, users are expected to select their desired TEI elements and attributes from the TEI modules, possibly with alterations or extensions where required. In this way, TEI offers a stable base with unambiguous means for the representation of basic textual phenomena, while providing standardized mechanisms for user customization for uncovered features. It is a particular feature of TEI that these abstract text models themselves can be expressed as TEI texts, using the documentation elements defined in the dedicated module *Documentation Elements*. A minimal TEI customization file looks as follows:

```
<TEI xmlns="http://www.tei-c.org/ns/1.0" xml:lang="en">
<teiHeader>
  <fileDesc>
    <titleStmt>
      <title>A TEI customization</title>
      <author>generated by Roma</author>
    </titleStmt>
    <publicationStmt>
      <p>for use by whoever wants it</p>
    </publicationStmt>
    <sourceDesc>
      <p>created on Thursday 24th July 2008
         10:20:17 AM by the form at
         http://www.tei-c.org.uk/Roma/</p>
```

```
    </sourceDesc>
  </fileDesc>
</teiHeader>
<text>
  <front>
    <divGen type="toc"/>
  </front>
  <body>
   <p>My TEI Customization starts with modules tei,
   core, header, and textstructure</p>
   <schemaSpec ident="TBEcustom" docLang="en"
   xml:lang="en" prefix=" ">
     <moduleRef key="tei"/>
     <moduleRef key="header"/>
     <moduleRef key="core"/>
     <moduleRef key="textstructure"/>
   </schemaSpec>
  </body>
</text>
</TEI>
```

Besides the common minimal TEI structure (<teiHeader> and <text>), a TEI customization file has one specific element which defines the TEI schema (<schemaSpec>). A TEI schema must minimally include the modules which define the minimal TEI text structure: the *TEI infrastructure* module, the *core* module with all common TEI elements, the *header* module defining all teiHeader elements, and the *textstructure* module defining the elements representing the minimal structure of TEI texts.

In the vein of *Literary Programming* (http://www.literateprogramming.com/), a TEI customization file not only contains the formal declaration of TEI elements inside <schemaSpec>, but may also contain prose documentation of the TEI encoding scheme it defines. Consequently, TEI customization files are commonly called *ODD files* (One Document Does it all), because they serve as a source for the derivation of

- A formal TEI schema (either as a DTD, W3C XML Schema, or RELAX NG schema).
- Human-friendly documentation of the TEI encoding scheme (in HTML, PDF, or XML).

In order to accommodate the process of creating customized TEI schemas and prose documentation, the TEI has developed a dedicated piece of software called *Roma* http://www.tei-c.org/Roma/. This is an ODD processor, offering an intuitive Web-based interface for the creation and basic editing of ODD files, generation of according TEI schemas and prose documentation in a number of presentation formats.

A TEI schema, stating all structural conditions and restraints for the elements and attributes in TEI texts can then be used to automatically validate actual TEI documents with an XML parser. Consider, for example, following fragments:

[A]

```
<TEI xmlns="http://www.tei-c.org/ns/1.0">
    <teiHeader>
      <fileDesc>
        <titleStmt>
          <title>A sample TEI document</title>
        </titleStmt>
        <publicationStmt>
          <publisher>
            Taylor & Francis
          </publisher>
          <pubPlace>London</pubPlace>
          <date when="2008"/>
        </publicationStmt>
        <sourceDesc>
          <p>No source, born digital</p>
        </sourceDesc>
      </fileDesc>
    </teiHeader>
    <text>
      <body>
        <p>This is a sample paragraph, illustrating a
        <name type="organization">TEI</name>
        document. </p>
      </body>
    </text>
</TEI>
```

[B]

```
<TEI xmlns="http://www.tei-c.org/ns/1.0">
  <text>
    <body>
      <p>This is a sample paragraph, illustrating a
      <orgName>TEI</orgName> document.</p>
    </body>
  </text>
</TEI>
```

When validated against a TEI schema derived from the previous ODD file, file [A] will be recognized as a valid TEI document, while file [B] will not:

- The TEI prescribes that the <teiHeader> *must* be present in each document, and that it precede the <text> part.
- The minimal set of TEI modules does not include the specialized <orgName> element. Although it is a TEI element, using it requires selection of the appropriate TEI module in the ODD file (in this case, the module for *Names, Dates, People, and Places*).

TEI: HISTORY

After the concise overview of the most recent version of TEI (P5) in the preceding section, this section explains the historical development of the TEI Guidelines.

Poughkeepsie Principles

Shortly after the publication of the SGML specification as an ISO Standard, a diverse group of 32 humanities computing scholars gathered at Vassar College in Poughkeepsie, New York in a 2-day meeting (November 11 and 12, 1987) called for by the Association for Computers and the Humanities (ACH, http://www.ach.org), funded by the National Endowment for the Humanities (NEH), and convened by Nancy Ide and Michael Sperberg McQueen. The main topic of the meeting was the question how and whether an encoding standard for machine-readable texts intended for scholarly research should be developed. Among the delegates were representatives from the main European text archives and from important North American academic and commercial research centers. Contrary to the disappointing outcomes of other such meetings in San Diego in 1977 or in Pisa in 1980, this meeting did reach its goal with the formulation and the agreement on the following set of methodological principles—the so-called *Poughkeepsie Principles*—for the preparation of text encoding guidelines for literary, linguistic, and historical research (pp. 132–133),[14] (p. E.6-4),[15] (p. 6.):[16]

1. The guidelines are intended to provide a standard format for data interchange in humanities research.
2. The guidelines are also intended to suggest principles for the encoding of texts in the same format.
3. The guidelines should
   a. Define a recommended syntax for the format
   b. Define a metalanguage for the description of text-encoding schemes
   c. Describe the new format and representative existing schemes both in that metalanguage and in prose.
4. The guidelines should propose sets of coding conventions suited for various applications.
5. The guidelines should include a minimal set of conventions for encoding new texts in the format.
6. The guidelines are to be drafted by committees on
   a. Text documentation
   b. Text representation
   c. Text interpretation and analysis
   d. Metalanguage definition and description of existing and proposed schemes coordinated by a steering committee of representatives of the principal sponsoring organizations.
7. Compatibility with existing standards will be maintained as far as possible.
8. A number of large text archives have agreed in principle to support the guidelines in their function as an interchange format. We encourage funding agencies to support development of tools to facilitate this interchange.
9. Conversion of existing machine-readable texts to the new format involves the translation of their conventions into the syntax of the new format. No

requirements will be made for the addition of information not already coded in the texts.

For the implementation of these principles the ACH was joined by the Association for Literary and Linguistic Computing (ALLC, http://www.allc.org) and the Association for Computational Linguistics (ACL, http://www.aclweb.org/). Together they established the Text Encoding Initiative (TEI) whose mission it was to develop the *Poughkeepsie Principles* into workable text encoding guidelines. The Text Encoding Initiative very soon came to adopt SGML, published a year before as ISO standard, as its framework. Initial funding was provided by the US National Endowment for the Humanities, Directorate General XIII of the Commission of the European Communities, the Canadian Social Science and Humanities Research Council, and the Andrew W. Mellon Foundation.

TEI P1 and TEI P2

From the Poughkeepsie Principles the TEI concluded that the TEI Guidelines should

- Provide a standard format for data interchange.
- Provide guidance for encoding of texts in this format.
- Support the encoding of all kinds of features of all kinds of texts studied by researchers.
- Allow the rigorous definition and efficient processing of texts.
- Provide for user-defined extensions.
- Be application independent.
- Be simple, clear, and concrete.
- Be simple for researchers to use without specialized software.

A Steering Committee consisting of representatives of the ACH, the ACL, and the ALLC appointed Michael Sperberg-McQueen as editor-in-chief and Lou Burnard as European editor of the Guidelines.

The first public proposal for the TEI Guidelines was published in July 1990 under the title *Guidelines for the Encoding and Interchange of Machine-Readable Texts* with the TEI document number TEI P1 (for Proposal 1). This version was reprinted with minor changes and corrections, as version 1.1 in November 1990.[17] Further development of the TEI Guidelines was done by four Working Committees (Text Documentation, Text Representation, Text Analysis and Interpretation, and Metalanguage and Syntax) and a number of specialist Working Groups among which groups on character sets, text criticism, hypertext and hypermedia, formulae, tables, figures, and graphics, language corpora, manuscripts and codicology, verse, drama and performance texts, literary prose, linguistic description, spoken text, literary studies,

historical studies, print dictionaries, machine lexica, and terminological data. The extensions and revisions resulting from this work, together with extensive public comment resulted in the drafting of a revised version, TEI P2, that was released chapter by chapter between March 1992 and the end of 1993[18] and that included substantial amounts of new material.

TEI P3

The following step was the publication of the TEI P3 *Guidelines for Electronic Text Encoding and Interchange* in 1994[19] that presented a further revision of all chapters published under the document number TEI P2, and the addition of further chapters. A final revised edition of these P3 Guidelines correcting several typographic and other errors, and introducing one new element was published in 1999.[20] The publication of this 1292 page documentation of the definitive guidelines defining some 439 elements marked the conclusion of the initial development work. With this work, the Poughkeepsie Guidelines were met by providing a framework for the encoding of texts in any natural language, of any date, in any literary genre or text type, without restriction on form or content and treating both continuous materials ("running text") and discontinuous materials such as dictionaries and linguistic corpora.

TEI P4

Recognizing the benefits for the TEI community, the P4 revision of the TEI Guidelines[21] was published in 2002 by the newly formed TEI Consortium in order to provide equal support for XML and SGML applications using the TEI scheme. The chief objective of this revision was to implement proper XML support in the Guidelines, while ensuring that documents produced to earlier TEI specifications remained usable with the new version. The XML support was realized by the expression of the TEI Guidelines in XML and the conformation to a TEI conformant XML DTD. The TEI P4 generated a set of DTD fragments that could be combined together to form either SGML or XML DTDs and thus achieved backward compatibility with TEI P3 encoded texts. In other words, any document conforming to the TEI P3 SGML DTD was guaranteed to conform to the TEI P4 XML version of it. This "double awareness" of the TEI P4 is the reason why this version was called an "XML-compatible edition" rather than an "XML edition." This was achieved by restricting the revisions needed to make the P4 version with its 441 elements to error correction only. During this process of revision, however, many possibilities for other, more fundamental changes had been identified, which led to the current TEI P5 version of the Guidelines.

TEI P5

In 2003 the TEI Consortium asked their membership to convene Special Interest Groups (SIGs) whose aim could be to advise revision of certain chapters of the Guidelines and suggest changes and improvements in view of the P5. With the establishment of the new TEI Council, which superintends the technical work of the TEI Consortium, it became possible to agree on an agenda to enhance and modify the Guidelines more fundamentally which resulted in a full revision of the Guidelines published as TEI P5.[13] TEI P5 contains a full XML expression of the TEI Guidelines and introduces new elements, revises content models, and reorganizes elements in a modular class system that facilitates flexible adaptations to users' needs. Contrary to its predecessor, TEI P5 does not offer backward compatibility with previous versions of the TEI. The TEI Consortium will, however, maintain and error correct the P4 Guidelines. This means that users still have the option between P4 and P5.

TEI: ORGANIZATION

The TEI Consortium was established in 2000 as a not-for-profit membership organization to sustain and develop the Text Encoding Initiative (TEI). The Consortium is supported by a number of host institutions. It is managed by a Board of Directors, and its technical work is overseen by an elected technical Council who take responsibility over the content of the TEI Guidelines.

The TEI charter outlines the consortium's goals and fundamental principles. Its goals are

1. To establish and maintain a home for the Text Encoding Initiative (TEI) in the form of a permanent organizational structure.
2. To ensure the continued funding of TEI-C activities, for example: editorial maintenance and development of the TEI Guidelines and DTD/Schema training and outreach activities, and services to members.
3. To create and maintain a governance structure for the TEI-C with broad representation of TEI user-communities.

The Consortium honors four fundamental principles:

1. The TEI Guidelines, other documentation, and DTD/Schema should be free to users.
2. Participation in TEI-C activities should be open (even to nonmembers) at all levels.
3. The TEI-C should be internationally and interdisciplinarily representative.
4. No role with respect to the TEI-C should be without term.

Involvement in the consortium is possible in three categories: voting membership which is open to individuals, institutions, or projects; nonvoting subscription, which is open to personal individuals only; and sponsorship, which is open to individual or corporate sponsors. Only members have the right to vote on consortium issues and in elections to the Board and the Council, have access to a restricted Web site with prerelease drafts of Consortium working documents and technical reports, announcements and news, and a database of members, sponsors, and subscribers, with contact information, and benefit from discounts on training, consulting, and certification. The Consortium members meet annually at a Members' Meeting where current critical issues in text encoding are discussed, and members of the Council and members of the Board of Directors are elected. The membership fee payable varies depending on the kind of project or institution and its location depending on where the economy of the member's country falls in the four-part listing of Low, Lower-Middle, Middle-Upper, and High Income Economies, as defined by the World Bank.

CONCLUSIONS

Computers can only deal with explicit data. The function of markup is to represent textual material into digital form through the explicating act of text encoding. Descriptive markup reveals what the encoder thinks to be implicit or hidden aspects of a text, and is thus an interpretive medium which often documents scholarly research next to structural information about the text. In order for this research to be exchangeable, analyzable, reusable, and preservable, texts in the field of the humanities should be encoded according to a standard which defines a common vocabulary, grammar, and syntax, while leaving the implementation of the standard up to the encoder. A result of communal efforts among computing humanists, the Text Encoding Initiative documents such a standard in the TEI Guidelines. These guidelines are fully adaptable and customizable to one's specific project while enhancing this project's compatibility with other projects employing the TEI. For over two decades, the TEI has been used extensively in projects from different disciplines, fields, and subjects internationally. The ongoing engagements of a broad user community through the organization of the TEI Consortium consolidates the importance of the text encoding standard and informs its continuous development and maintenance.

REFERENCES

1. Sperberg-McQueen, C.M. Text in the electronic age: Textual study and text encoding with examples from Medieval texts. Literary Linguist. Comput. **1991**, *6* (1), 34–46.

2. Kay, M. Standards for encoding data in a natural language. Comput. Humanit. **1967**, *1* (5), 170–177.

3. Russel, D.B. *COCOA: A Word Count and Concordance Generator for Atlas*; Atlas Computer Laboratory: Chilton, U.K., 1967.

4. Hockey, S. *Oxford Concordance Program Users' Manual*; Oxford University Computing Service: Oxford, U.K., 1980.

5. Lancashire, I.; Bradley, J.; McCarty, W.; Stairs, M.; Woolridge, T.R. *Using TACT with Electronic Texts*; Modern Language Association of America: New York, 1996.

6. Berkowitz, L.; Squiter, K.A. *Thesaurus Linguae Graecae, Canon of Greek Authors and Works*; Oxford University Press: New York/Oxford, 1986.

7. Goldfarb, C.E. *The SGML Handbook*; Clarendon Press: Oxford, U.K., 1990.

8. Barnard, D.T.; Fraser, C.A.; Logan, G.M. Generalized markup for literary texts. Literary Linguist. Comput. **1988**, *3* (1), 26–31.

9. Barnard, D.T.; Hayter, R.; Karababa, M.; Logan, G.; McFadden, J. SGML-based markup for literary texts: Two problems and some solutions. Comput. Humanit. **1988**, *22* (4), 265–276.

10. Bray, T.; Paoli, J.; Sperberg-McQueen, C.M. *Extensible Markup Language (XML) 1.0.*; W3C Recommendation February 10, 1998 http://www.w3.org/TR/1998/REC-xml-19980210 (accessed September 2008).

11. DeRose, S.J. XML and the TEI. Comput. Humanit. **1999**, *33* (1–2), 11–30.

12. Burnard, L.; Sperberg-McQueen, C.M. TEI Lite: Encoding for interchange: An introduction to the TEI Revised for TEI P5 release; February 2006. http://www.tei-c.org/release/doc/tei-p5-exemplars/html/teilite.doc.html.

13. TEI Consortium, Ed.; *TEI P5: Guidelines for Electronic Text Encoding and Interchange*, Text Encoding Initiative Consortium, http://www.tei-c.org/Guidelines/P5/ (accessed October 2008).

14. Burnard, L. Report of Workshop on Text Encoding Guidelines. Literary Linguist. Comput. **1988**, *3* (2), 131–133.

15. Ide, N.M.; Sperberg-McQueen, C.M. Development of a Standard for Encoding Literary and Linguistic Materials. In *Cologne Computer Conference 1988. Uses of the Computer in the Humanities and Social Sciences*, Volume of Abstracts. Cologne, Germany, September 7–10, 1988; E6-3-4.

16. Ide, N.; Sperberg-McQueen, C.M. The TEI: History, goals, and future. Comput. Humanit. **1995**, *29* (1), 5–15.

17. Sperberg-McQueen, M.; Burnard, L., Eds. *TEI P1: Guidelines for the Encoding and Interchange of Machine Readable Texts*; ACH-ALLC-ACL Text Encoding Initiative: Chicago/Oxford, 1990. http://www.tei-c.org.uk/Vault/Vault-GL.html (accessed October 2008).

18. Sperberg-McQueen, M.; Burnard, L., Eds. *TEI P2 Guidelines for the Encoding and Interchange of Machine Readable Texts Draft P2 (published serially 1992–1993)*; Draft Version 2 of April 1993, 19 chapters. http://www.tei-c.org.uk/Vault/Vault-GL.html (accessed October 2008).

19. Sperberg-McQueen, C.M.; Burnard, L., Eds. *Guidelines for Electronic Text Encoding and Interchange. TEI P3*; Text Encoding Initiative: Oxford, Providence, Charlottesville, Bergen, 1994.

20. Sperberg-McQueen, C.M.; Burnard, L., Eds. *Guidelines for Electronic Text Encoding and Interchange. TEI P3*; Revised reprint. Text Encoding Initiative: Oxford, Providence, Charlottesville, Bergen, 1999.

21. Sperberg-McQueen, C.M.; Burnard, L., Eds. *TEI P4: Guidelines for Electronic Text Encoding and Interchange, XML-compatible edition*; XML conversion by Bauman, S., Burnard, L., DeRose, S., and Rahtz, S.; Text Encoding Initiative Consortium: Oxford, Providence, Charlottesville, Bergen, 2002. http://www.tei-c.org.uk/P4X/ (accessed October 2008).

BIBLIOGRAPHY

1. Burnard, L.; O'Brien O'Keeffe, K.; Unsworth, J., Eds. *Electronic Textual Editing*; MLA: New York, 2006. http://www.tei-c.org/About/Archive_new/ETE/ (accessed October 2008).

2. Cummings, J. The text encoding initiative and the study of literature. In *A Companion to Digital Literary Studies*; Siemens, R., Schreibman, S., Eds.; Blackwell Publishing: Malden, MA, Oxford, 2007; 451–476. http://www.digitalhumanities.org/companionDLS/ (accessed October 2008).

3. Ide, N.; Véronis, J., Eds. *Text Encoding Initiative: Background and Context*; Kluwer Academic Publishers: Dordrecht, 1995. Reprinted from Comput. Humanit. **1995**, *29*.

4. Mylonas, E.; Renear, A., Eds. Special issue: Selected papers from TEI 10: Celebrating the tenth anniversary of the text encoding initiative. Comput. Humanit **1999**, *33*(1–2).

5. Schreibman, S.; Rahts, S., Eds. Special Issue: TEI at 20. LLC. J. Digit. Scholarsh. Humanit. **2009**, *24*.

6. Van den Branden, R.; Vanhoutte, E.; Terras, M. *TEI By Example*; http://www.teibyexample.org (accessed October 2008).

Technical–Topic

Text REtrieval Conference (TREC)

Ellen M. Voorhees
*Information Technology Laboratory, National Institute of Standards and Technology,
Gaithersburg, Maryland, U.S.A.*

Abstract

This entry summarizes the history, results, and impact of the Text REtrieval Conference (TREC), a
workshop series designed to support the information retrieval community by building the infrastructure
necessary for large-scale evaluation of retrieval technology.

Technical–Topic

INTRODUCTION

The Text REtrieval Conference (TREC) is a series of
annual workshops designed to support the information
retrieval community by building the infrastructure necessary for large-scale evaluation of retrieval technology.
The conference series is organized by the U.S. National
Institute of Standards and Technology (NIST) with financial support from the U.S. defense and intelligence community. The first workshop was held in November, 1992
and there has been a workshop each year since then.
Text REtrieval Conference participants are researchers
in text retrieval and related natural language processing
fields representing academic, commercial, and government organizations. Almost 300 organizations from six
continents have participated in some TREC.

The Text REtrieval Conference is a modern example of
the Cranfield tradition in which retrieval system effectiveness is evaluated through test collections. Test collections
are abstractions of real user information-seeking tasks that
allow researchers to quickly and inexpensively compare
the relative effectiveness of competing retrieval technologies. They support tight development cycles leading to
improved effectiveness in shorter development time. The
Text REtrieval Conference has created a variety of publicly available test collections, has standardized the experimental methodology for using test collections, and has
demonstrated the validity and efficacy of the methodology
for the typical ad hoc retrieval task. In addition, TREC has
extended use of the test collection methodology to new
tasks. The results have been significant. Retrieval effectiveness for the ad hoc task approximately doubled in the
first six years of TREC, and the retrieval techniques used
for the ad hoc task have been demonstrated to be effective
for other tasks as well.

This entry summarizes the history, results, and impact of
TREC. The next section places TREC in the historical context that led to its inception and outlines the mechanics of
how TREC works. The following section reviews what has
been learned about text collection evaluation methodology

from TREC. The final main section of this entry provides an
overview of the variety of different tasks that have been
examined in TREC and highlights the retrieval results that
have been demonstrated in those tasks.

HISTORICAL CONTEXT

Test collections were introduced in the 1960s by Cyril
Cleverdon and his colleagues in the Cranfield tests, a
series of experiments designed to identify appropriate
indexing languages for document retrieval.[1] A test collection consists of a set of documents; a set of information
need statements, called topics in TREC; and a list of
which documents in the collection should be retrieved for
which need, called relevance judgments. While the use of
a static set of relevance judgments to represent the user in
a retrieval experiment was controversial, other researchers
started using the Cranfield collection to perform different
experiments. Over the course of the following 20 years,
many experiments were performed and additional test
collections were built. But by 1990 there was growing
dissatisfaction with the methodology such that even some
experimenters were questioning its usefulness.[2] There
were two main problems. First, the available test collections were small, containing at most several thousand
documents and a few tens of topics. Operators of the
commercial retrieval systems of the day were not con-
vinced that techniques demonstrated on small test collections would transfer to their much larger environments.
Second, there was no concerted effort on the part of different research groups to use the same data or evaluation
measures. As a result, the experimental findings from different groups were usually incomparable and it was not
possible to build on one another's work.

In 1991, NIST was asked to build a large test collection
for use in evaluating text retrieval technology developed
as part of the Defense Advanced Research Projects
Agency's (DARPA) Tipster project. The National Institute
of Standards and Technology agreed, and proposed that in

Encyclopedia of Library and Information Sciences, Fourth Edition DOI: 10.1081/E-ELIS4-120044470

addition to building a large test collection, it would also organize a workshop to investigate the larger issues surrounding test collection use.

The first two TRECs had two tasks, the ad hoc task and the routing task. The ad hoc task is the prototypical retrieval task such as a researcher doing a literature search in a library. In this environment, the system knows the set of documents to be searched (the library's holdings), but cannot anticipate the particular topic that will be investigated. In contrast, the routing task assumes the topics are static but need to be matched to a stream of new documents. The routing task is similar to the task performed by a news clipping service or a library profiling system.

The National Institute of Standards and Technology supplied a common set of test documents and a set of 50 topic statements for each task. The format of the topic statements varied over the years, but generally consisted of at least a brief natural language statement of the information desired (e.g., *Document will discuss how MCI has been doing since the Bell System breakup.*). Participants used their systems to run the topics against the document collection, and returned to NIST a list of the top-ranked documents for each topic.

Since the document sets used in the first TRECs contained between 800,000 and 1,000,000 documents, they were too large for each document to be judged for each topic. Instead, TREC implemented a technique called pooling that had been suggested by Karen Spärck Jones and Keith van Rijsbergen as a way to build relevance judgments for large collections.[3] As used in TREC, a pool for a topic consists of the union of the top X (usually 100) documents across runs submitted to that task. The documents in a pool are then viewed by a human and judged as to whether they are relevant to the topic. Documents that do not get added to the pool (because no system retrieved them at high enough ranks) are not judged but are assumed to be not relevant.

Once all the relevance judgments for all of the topics in the test set were complete, NIST evaluated the retrieval runs on the basis of the relevance judgments and returned the evaluation results to the participants. A little more than a month later, researchers who had submitted runs gathered for a workshop to discuss the results and share their experiences.

Starting in TREC-3 (1994), additional tasks, called tracks, were added to TREC, and today TREC is comprised of a constantly evolving set of tracks. The tracks serve several purposes. First, tracks act as incubators for new research areas: the first running of a track often defines what the problem *really* is, and a track creates the necessary infrastructure (test collections, evaluation methodology, etc.) to support research on its task. The tracks also demonstrate the robustness of core retrieval technology in that the same techniques are frequently appropriate for a variety of tasks. Finally, the tracks make TREC attractive to a broader community by providing tasks that match the research interests of more groups.

In addition to the variety of TREC tracks, TREC has inspired other evaluation projects that are based on the TREC model. These projects include the Japanese National Institute of Information Test Collection for IR Systems project (NTCIR, http://research.nii.ac.jp/ntcir/), the Cross Language Evaluation Forum (CLEF, http://www.clef-campaign.org/), and the Initiative for the Evaluation of XML Retrieval (INEX, http://inex.is.informatik.uni-duisburg.de).

TEST COLLECTION EVALUATION METHODOLOGY

One of the motivating goals for TREC was to establish a common evaluation methodology for retrieval from realistically sized collections. The goal of having experimenters report the same evaluation measures was largely met by introducing trec_eval, an evaluation program that provides a common implementation for over 100 different evaluation measures. A much smaller set of measures, including the recall-precision graph, mean average precision, and precision at ten documents retrieved, has become the de facto standard by which retrieval effectiveness is characterized. But TREC has done more than provide a standard scoring routine and common data sets. The Text REtrieval Conference's scale—both the size of the test collections and the number of retrieval results—has provided an unique opportunity for validating the use of test collections and exploring the limits of the evaluation methodology. This section summarizes the findings of three such investigations: examining the effect of changes in relevance judgments, examining the effect of judging only a subset of the document collection, and examining the soundness of the conclusions reached in test collection experiments.

Consistency

One objection to test collections that dates back to the Cranfield tests is the use of relevance judgments as the basis for evaluation. Relevance is known to be very idiosyncratic,[4] and critics question how an evaluation methodology can be based on such an unstable foundation. An experiment using the TREC-4 and TREC-6 retrieval results investigated the effect of changing relevance assessors on system comparisons.[5] The experiment demonstrated that the absolute scores for evaluation measures did change when different relevance assessors were used, but the relative scores between runs did not change. That is, if system A evaluated as better than system B using one set of judgments, then system A almost always evaluated as better than system B using a second set of judgments (the exception was in the case where the two runs evaluated as so similar to one another that they should be deemed equivalent). The stable comparisons result held for different evaluation measures and for different kinds of assessors, and was independent of whether a judgment was based on a single assessor's opinion or was the consensus opinion of a majority of assessors.

Completeness

An important criterion for test collections is that they be reusable, that is, they can be used to compare not only the original result sets that contributed to the pools but also subsequent result sets produced using the same topic and document sets. The use of pooling where only some documents are judged for a topic caused people to question whether TREC collections were reusable since they believed runs that had not contributed to the pools would be unfairly penalized. Examination of larger pools did confirm one aspect of the critics' fears: there are unjudged documents remaining in the collections that would have been judged relevant had they made it into the pools.[6] Further, the quality of the final test collection does depend on the diversity of the runs that contribute to the pools and the number of documents selected from each run.[7] But tests also showed that the TREC collections are not biased against unjudged runs. In these tests, the documents uniquely retrieved by a TREC run are treated as not relevant when that run is evaluated. The difference in the evaluation results for runs evaluated both with and without their own uniquely retrieved relevant documents has until recently been smaller than the difference produced by changing relevance assessors.[8]

Repeating the uniquely retrieved relevant test on the very latest collections built from millions of Web pages suggests that pooling has a size dependency that prevents it from producing reusable test collections for arbitrarily large document sets.[9] Devising new techniques for building massive test collections is thus an area of active research.

Soundness

Retrieval effectiveness is reported as an average over a set of topics because retrieval system performance is known to vary widely depending on the topic. An analysis of variance model fitted to the TREC-3 results demonstrated that the topic and system effects, as well as the interaction between topic and system, were all highly significant, with the topic effect the largest.[10] This variability in topic performance has a profound effect on retrieval system evaluation because it is difficult to isolate the relatively small differences in performance that can be attributed to retrieval system differences.

The repository of runs that have been submitted to TREC made it possible to empirically determine the relationship between the number of topics in a test collection, the observed difference in evaluation scores (*delta*), and the likelihood that a single comparison of two retrieval runs will lead to the correct conclusion.[11] Once the relationship was established, it was used to derive the minimum difference in scores required for a certain level of confidence in the results given the number of topics used in the comparison. As expected, the likelihood of an erroneous comparison decreases as the number of topics used increases. The likelihood of an error also decreases as the size of *delta* increases, though requiring large differences in scores before deciding two runs are different decreases the power of the experiment. However, the percentage difference in retrieval scores required for confidence in the conclusion for 50 topics (the number of topics in a typical TREC test collection) was larger than has generally been used to signify meaningful differences in the IR literature.

This conclusion that a comparatively large difference in scores is required to have confidence that a single comparison correctly indicates the better system does not invalidate the usefulness of test collections. The primary use of test collections is not cross-system comparison but optimizing the effectiveness of a single system. Experiments with variants of a single system require much smaller absolute differences in scores to yield meaningful results because most of the variance due to system–topic interaction is controlled. In addition, the confidence in a cross-system comparison can be significantly increased by repeating the comparison using multiple collections. Even a very small difference that is consistently present in multiple collections is likely to represent a true difference among systems.

THE TRACKS

The TREC track structure enables TREC to extend the test collection paradigm to tasks other than ad hoc retrieval. The set of tracks run in any particular TREC depends on the interests of the participants and sponsors, as well as on the suitability of the problem to the TREC environment. The decision of which tracks to include is made by the TREC program committee, a group of academic, industrial, and government researchers who have the responsibility for oversight of TREC. Tracks are discontinued when the goals of the track are met, or when there are diminishing returns on what can be learned about the area in TREC. Some tracks run for many years but change focus in different years.

Fig. 1 shows many of the tracks that were run in the different years of TREC, grouping the tracks by the aspect that differentiates them from one another. The aspects, listed on the left of the figure show the breadth of the problems that TREC has addressed, while the individual tracks listed on the right show the progression of tasks within the given problem area. This section provides a

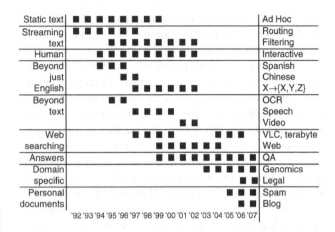

Fig. 1 A subset of the TREC tracks and the years in which they were held. The track name is given on the right while the distinguishing focus of the track is given on the left.

recap of the main lessons learned about the various tasks and aspects.

Static Text

The main task in TREC for the first eight years was the ad hoc task, a task in which systems rank the documents in a known document set against not previously seen topics. The eight years of the task produced eight test collections, each consisting of a document set, a set of 50 topics, and a set of pooled relevance judgments. The document sets consist of full-text documents, mostly news articles with some government documents and a small amount of other types of documents also included. The final three years of the task (TRECs 6–8) used the same document set, so the combination of the topics and relevance judgments from those years represents a test collection with 150 topics.

Improvement in retrieval effectiveness cannot be determined simply by looking at TREC scores from year to year. It is invalid to compare the results from one year of TREC to the results of another year since any differences are likely to be caused by the different test collections in use. However, developers of the SMART retrieval system kept a frozen copy of the system they used to participate in each of the eight TREC ad hoc tasks.[12] After every TREC, they ran each system on each test collection. For every test collection, the later versions of the SMART system were much more effective than the earlier versions of the SMART system, with the later scores approximately twice that of the earlier scores. While this is evidence for only one system, the SMART system results consistently tracked with the other systems' results in each TREC, and thus the SMART results can be considered representative of the state of the art at that time. The improvement was evident for all evaluation scores that were examined, including mean average precision and precision and recall at various cutoff levels.

The results from the top-performing systems in the ad hoc task suggest the increased effectiveness arose from improvements in two general areas, query expansion, and indexing of full-text documents. The most common way of expanding the query is to use pseudorelevance (or blind) feedback: retrieve a first set of documents using the original query; assume the first X documents are relevant; perform relevance feedback with that set of documents to create a new query (usually including both new terms and refined query weights); and return the results of searching with the new query to the user. Doing a similar type of expansion but using a document set other than the target collection has also been effective. For document indexing, the following best practices emerged from the ad hoc task results:

- Tokenization that regularizes word forms is generally helpful. The most common form of regularization is stemming, but normalizing proper nouns to a standard format can also be helpful.
- Simple "phrasing" techniques are generally helpful. The most helpful part of phrasing is the identification of common collocations that are then treated as a single unit. More elaborate schemes have shown little benefit.
- Appropriate weighting of terms is critical. The best weighting schemes reflect the discrimination power of a term in the corpus and control for document length. There are several different weighting schemes that achieve these goals and are equivalently effective. Language modeling techniques are both effective and provide a theoretical justification for the weights assigned.

Streaming Text

The second task in the first TRECs was the routing task. In the routing task, systems used old topics with known relevance judgments to produce queries that were then used to rank a new document set. A more realistic formulation of this task emerged several years later as the filtering track. In a filtering task a system makes a binary decision for each document in a document stream whether to retrieve that document in response to a standing query. There are different variants of the task depending on the timing and amount of feedback (relevance information) the system is given. Effectiveness in the filtering track was generally evaluated using a utility measure in which the system gained one amount of points for correctly retrieving a relevant document and lost a lesser amount of points for incorrectly retrieving a nonrelevant document. Comparison between routing and filtering results from the same systems demonstrated that forcing a binary retrieval decision is a much more difficult problem than simply ranking documents since the former requires setting a retrieval threshold.

Human in the Loop

The interactive track was one of the first tracks to be added to TREC. The goal of the interactive track was to study text retrieval systems in interaction with users, where both the process and the final search outcome are of interest. A main difficulty of studying the interactive behavior of retrieval systems is that searchers and topics generally have a much larger effect on search results than does the retrieval system used.

The experimental design of the TREC-6 interactive track included the use of a common baseline system.[13] The particular retrieval system used at a site (an experimental system) was compared to the common control system that was also run at each site. The direct comparison between the experimental and control systems was used to derive a measure of how much better the experimental system was than the control, independent of topic, searcher, and any other site-specific effects. The expectation was that different experimental systems could then be indirectly compared across sites relative to the common control. Unfortunately, analysis of the track results could neither confirm nor refute the equivalence of the direct and indirect comparison of systems, and without clear positive evidence for the usefulness of the control system it was difficult to justify the cost of adding another system to an experimental design.

Beyond English

Another of the early tracks to be introduced into TREC was the Spanish track. The task in the Spanish track was a basic ad hoc retrieval task except the topics and documents were written in Spanish rather than English. The track was discontinued when the results demonstrated that retrieval systems could retrieve Spanish documents as effectively as English documents. Another single language track, this time using Chinese as a language with a very different structure than that of English, was introduced next. Again, systems were able to effectively retrieve Chinese documents using Chinese topics.

A successor to the single language tracks was the cross-language track. A cross-language retrieval system uses topics written in one language to retrieve documents written in one of a variety of languages. In the first TREC cross-language track participants searched for documents in one target language using topics written in a different language. Later versions of the track had participants search for documents using topics in one language against the entire combined document collection; still later versions of the track used more disparate languages (English topics against either Chinese or Arabic document sets). One of the unexpected results of the cross-language track was the demonstration that cross-language retrieval can be more effective than the corresponding monolingual search due to the expansion that results from translating the query.

Beyond Text

In addition to testing the ability of retrieval systems to retrieve text written in languages other than English, TREC contained a series of three tracks designed to test the ability of systems to retrieve information encoded in media other than electronic text. In the confusion track, systems retrieved documents that were the output of an OCR process. In the spoken document retrieval track, systems retrieved documents that were the output of speech recognition systems. In both tracks, the goal was to measure the effect of mistakes in the text (i.e., corrupted text) on retrieval effectiveness. The results in both tracks suggested that natural language is sufficiently redundant that error-filled text can be retrieved as effectively as clean texts for error rates likely to be seen in real-life applications. For speech recognition output, the worst effect on retrieval effectiveness was out of vocabulary (OOV) words. Participants compensated for OOV words by using adaptive language models to limit the number of OOV words encountered, and by expanding recognized text by related clean texts to include OOV words in the documents.

The video track focused on retrieving information recorded in digital videos. A document in the track was defined as a video shot, and ad hoc search topics were expressed as textual statements of information need, possibly including a still or video image as an example of the type of information sought. Unlike OCR and speech recognition output, there is no obvious way of reducing video to a set of words. As a result, there is little overlap in the techniques used to retrieve text documents versus video documents. The video track was spun off from TREC as its own TRECVid evaluation workshop in 2003 (see http://trecvid.nist.gov) and continues to date.

The Web and Size

While two gigabytes of text was a large amount of text when TREC began, it was soon eclipsed by the ever-growing stores of information commercial retrieval engines were searching, especially with the advent of the World Wide Web. A series of tracks explored the related issues of Web search and retrieval efficiency in the context of document collections much larger than the TREC ad hoc collections.

The first of these tracks was the very large corpus (VLC) track. The track used a 100 gigabyte static subset of the Web as its test set and evaluated systems on both precision of the top 20 documents retrieved and speed at which the results could be assembled. This naturally led to a Web track to investigate information-seeking tasks on the Web. Web search is different from searching other large data sets in several important ways, including the massive link structure, the lack of editorial control, the different uses of search on the Web (finding information, locating services, navigating the link structure), and the use of active content. The main results of the Web track were to demonstrate that the different search tasks require different strategies for best effectiveness. Traditional retrieval methods based on page content generally worked well for information-seeking topics, for example, whereas navigational queries such as finding a home page required making use of the link structure (such as using anchor text or link counts). The terabyte track (which actually used a 426 gigabyte crawl of the .gov domain) returned to the search efficiency focus while also exploring the question of how best to build reusable test collections for massive data sets. Getting an unbiased judgment set through traditional pooling for document sets of this scale is too expensive because too many documents must be judged. Alternative sampling strategies have been suggested but remain to be adequately vetted.

Question Answering

While a list of on-topic documents is undoubtedly useful, even that can be more information than a user wants to examine. The TREC question answering track was introduced in 1999 to focus attention on the problem of returning exactly the answer in response to a question. The initial question answering tracks focused on factoid questions such as "Where is the Taj Mahal?". Later tracks have incorporated more difficult question types such as list questions (a question whose answer is a distinct set of instances of the type requested such as "What actors have played Tevye in "Fiddler on the Roof?") and definition/biographical questions (such as "What is a golden parachute?" or "Who is Vlad the Impaler?").

The question answering track was the first large-scale evaluation of open-domain question answering systems, and it has brought the benefits of test collection evaluation observed in other parts of TREC to bear on the question answering task. The track established a common task for the retrieval and natural language processing research communities, creating a renaissance in question answering research. This wave of research has created significant progress in automatic natural language understanding as researchers have successfully incorporated sophisticated language processing into their question answering systems.

Domain-Specific Retrieval

Domain-specific retrieval tasks look to exploit knowledge about the subject area to improve retrieval effectiveness. Implementing domain-specific evaluation tasks requires people with expertise in the domain to create topics and perform relevance judgments.

The first domain-specific track in TREC was the genomics track. The scenario assumed in the track was that of a biological researcher (that is, someone who already has considerable domain knowledge) confronted with the need to learn about a new gene very quickly. The track included a number of different types of tasks in the different years it

was run including ad hoc document retrieval, passage retrieval, document classification, and aspect retrieval. Topic development and relevance judgments were made by people with a background in biology; in several years the topics were derived from information needs solicited from practicing biologists. Results of the track showed that careful use of domain resources could improve retrieval effectiveness, though good generic retrieval technology was surprisingly competitive.

The legal track is focused on a specific aspect of retrieval in the legal domain, that of meeting the needs of lawyers to engage in effective discovery of digital documents. Currently, it is common for the two sides involved in litigation to negotiate a Boolean expression that defines the set of documents that are then examined by humans to determine which are responsive to a discovery request. The goal of the track is to evaluate the effectiveness of this and other search technologies in facilitating the discovery process. The track uses hypothetical complaints and corresponding requests to produce documents developed by practicing lawyers as topics. Relevance judgments are made by legal professionals who follow their typical work practices in reviewing the documents. The track is relatively new having started in 2006. Results to date have demonstrated that several different techniques including the Boolean query produce document sets that have similar numbers of responsive documents yet retrieve only some responsive documents in common. This is an important finding since high recall (the need to find most of the responsive documents) is a requirement of the real-world task.

Personal Documents

The final two tracks are distinguished by the personal nature of the documents used in the track. In the spam track the document set is an e-mail stream; in the blog track the document set is a large collection of blog pages.

The goal in the spam track was to evaluate how well systems are able to separate spam and ham (non-spam) when given an e-mail sequence. The primary difficulty in performing such an evaluation is getting appropriate corpora to use in a public test. Making real e-mail streams public is not possible due to privacy concerns, but artificially generated streams and privacy-protecting modifications to real streams tend to compromise the information used by classifiers to distinguish spam and ham. The track solved this problem by requiring filters to conform to the interface defined by a software jig and having participants submit filters to be run on the sequestered private e-mail stream. The overall results of the spam track were consistent across the three years in which it was run. Detecting spam is easier when feedback is frequent and plentiful, but even in the more difficult cases filters were able to detect the vast majority of spam with high accuracy. There was no indication that more recent spam was any harder to detect than earlier spam, though the total amount of spam included in the private stream (which included all of the mail sent to a single individual in three distinct time periods corresponding to the different years of the track) increased significantly over the years while the amount of ham stayed roughly constant.

Blog pages are personal in that they are often used to express an opinion of the author. They are also interesting as retrieval test documents because language use within blog pages tends to be more informal than in other types of documents. The main task within the blog track has been to find documents that contain an opinion about the target cited in the topic statement. Results of the track to date show that the effectiveness of finding opinion documents is strongly dominated by a system's ability to find topically relevant documents.

CONCLUSION

When TREC began, there was real doubt as to whether the statistical systems that had been developed in the research labs (as opposed to the operational systems that used Boolean searches on manually indexed collections) could effectively retrieve documents from "large" collections. Text REtrieval Conference has shown not only that the retrieval engines of the early 1990s did scale to large collections, but that those engines have improved since then. This effectiveness has been demonstrated both in the laboratory on TREC test collections, and by today's operational systems that incorporate the techniques. Further, the techniques are routinely used on collections far larger than what was considered large in 1992. Web search engines are a prime example of the power of the statistical techniques: the ability of search engines to point users to the information they seek has been fundamental to the success of the Web.

At the time of this writing TREC 2007, the 16th TREC workshop, has just concluded. Plans are underway for TREC 2008, and it is expected that TREC will continue for the foreseeable future. The TREC Web site, http://trec.nist.gov, contains a wealth of information about TREC including the full proceedings for each of the workshop (in the Publications section) and details regarding how to obtain the test collections (in the Data section). The call for participation in TREC is issued each December and is posted on the main page of the TREC Web site while it is active.

REFERENCES

1. Cleverdon, C.W. The Cranfield tests on index language devices. Aslib Proc. **1967**, *19*, 173–192 Reprinted in *Readings in Information Retrieval*; Spärck-Jones, K., Willett, P., Eds.; Morgan Kaufmann: San Francisco, CA, 1997.
2. Robertson, S.E.; Hancock-Beaulieu, M.M. On the evaluation of IR systems. Inform. Process. Manage. **1992**, *28*(4), 457–466.
3. Sparck Jones, K.; van Rijsbergen, C. Computer Laboratory, University of Cambridge: Cambridge, 1975; Report on the need for and provision of an "ideal" information retrieval test collection. British Library Research and Development Report 5266.
4. Schamber, L. Relevance and information behavior. Annu. Rev. Inform. Sci. Technol. **1994**, *29*, 3–48.
5. Voorhees, E.M. Variations in relevance judgments and the measurement of retrieval effectiveness. Inform. Process. Manage. **2000**, *36*, 697–716.
6. Harman, D. Overview of the fourth Text REtrieval Conference (TREC-4) Proceedings of the Fourth Text REtrieval Conference (TREC-4); Harman, D.K., Ed.; 1996; October 1–23 NIST Special Publication 500-236.
7. Zobel, J. How reliable are the results of large-scale information retrieval experiments? Proceedings of the 21st Annual International ACM SIGIR Conference on Research and Development in Information Retrieval Melbourne, Australia August, 1998; Croft, W.B., Moffat, A., van Rijsbergen, C.J., Wilkinson, R., Zobel, J., Eds.; ACM Press: New York 307–314.
8. Voorhees, E.M.; Harman, D. *Overview of the eighth Text REtrieval Conference (TREC-8) Proceedings of the Eighth Text REtrieval Conference (TREC-8),* Voorhees, E.M., Harman, D.K., Eds.; 2000; 1–24 NIST Special Publication 500-246.
9. Buckley, C.; Dimmick, D.; Soboroff, I.; Voorhees, E. Bias and the limits of pooling Proceedings of the Twenty-Ninth Annual International ACM SIGIR Conference on Research and Development in Information Retrieval, 2006; 619–620.
10. Banks, D.; Over, P.; Zhang, N.-F. Blind men and elephants: six approaches to TREC data. Inform. Retriev. **1999**, *1*, 7–34.
11. Voorhees, E.M.; Buckley, C. The effect of topic set size on retrieval experiment error Proceedings of the 25th Annual International ACM SIGIR Conference on Research and Development in Information Retrieval, 2002; 316–323.
12. Buckley, C.; Walz, J. SMART in TREC 8 Proceedings of the Eighth Text REtrieval Conference (TREC-8); Voorhees, E.M., Harman, D.K., Eds.; 2000; 577–582 NIST Special Publication 500-246.
13. Lagergren, E.; Over, P. Comparing interactive information retrieval systems across sites: The TREC-6 interactive track matrix experiment Proceedings of the 21st Annual International ACM SIGIR Conference on Research and Development in Information Retrieval Melbourne, Australia August, 1998; Croft, W.B., Moffat, A., van Rijsbergen, C.J., Wilkinson, R., Zobel, J., Eds.; ACM Press: New York 164–172.

BIBLIOGRAPHY

This entry is based largely on the introductory and evaluation chapters of the TREC book and summary articles that have appeared in the American Society for Information Science and Technology's *Bulletin* and the *Communications of the ACM* publications. As noted above, the TREC Web site contains a wide variety of information about TREC.

1. Voorhees, E.M., Harman, D.K., Eds. *TREC: Experiment and Evaluation in Information Retrieval*; MIT Press: Cambridge, MA, 2005.
2. Voorhees, E.M. TREC: Improving information access through evaluation. ASIST Bull. **2005**, *32*(1), 16–21.
3. Voorhees, E.M. TREC: Continuing information retrieval's tradition of experimentation. Commun. ACM **2007**, *50*(11), 51–54.

Technical–Topic

Theft, Vandalism, and Security in Libraries and Archives

Sydney C. Van Nort
The City College of New York, The City University of New York, New York, U.S.A.

Abstract

The scope of library theft is difficult to determine because accurate statistical data regarding annual losses of library materials in the United States are not available. Possibly over $25 million worth of library materials continue to come up missing from American library shelves, and the unauthorized accessing, and possible tampering, with digital collections or administrative records can be a problem as well. Book dealers can be effective allies in combating library theft, whether the perpetrator is a patron or a staff member. The notorious cases of theft by Daniel Spiegelman from the Columbia University Rare Book and Manuscript Library collections and of Stephen Carrie Blumberg, whose collecting mania spurred him to help himself to items from 327 libraries, are summarized. These cases illustrate the difficulties of detection or deterrence without the effective application of legal statutes and sentencing. The importance of the implementation of consistent security measures, whether it is the installation of security systems or policies as a planning process for the prevention of this type of disaster, is stated. Some suggested measures for theft prevention mentioned here are the installation of alarm systems, video surveillance, patron searching upon exiting, materials marking, and the use of colored photocopy paper. The need for effective communication among librarians and book dealers for the reporting and possible prevention of theft losses is noted.

SCOPE OF THE PROBLEM

When I first approached this topic in 1992, I discovered that there was very little accurate data that had been compiled indicating losses due to thefts or attrition of library materials. The best figures that were available were estimates, which was astonishing for a profession that prides itself on collecting such accurate data regarding circulation figures and the number of volumes and journals that are collected. (These are used as one measure of comparison among libraries for ranking their collections.) Katherine Keyes Leab was the administrator of formerly the only computerized database of reports of missing library items operating in the United States, Bookline Alert: Missing Books and Manuscripts (BAMBAM). As she expressed it, "one of the problems is that there are no numbers. That in itself is significant."[1] Unfortunately, she has discontinued it for lack of financial support.[2] Others in the profession agree. Ronald Lieberman, former chair of the Security Committee of the Antiquarian Booksellers' Association of America (ABAA), concurred that there is "no good substantial statistical information available at this time."[3]

The International League of Antiquarian Booksellers has established a database for compiling reports of stolen books since June 15, 2010, and the Antiquarian Booksellers Association encourages the reporting of thefts on The New Antiquarian—a blog on the security section. These two sources can provide current data regarding the problem. The Antiquarian Booksellers blog includes postings regarding security issues, with a minority actually reporting a specific theft. There were nineteen thefts reported from libraries in 2013 to the International League of Antiquarian Booksellers database, and sixteen thefts were reported from libraries in 2014 (only one of those was from an American library), and the majority of the reports posted during both years were primarily from book dealers and book collectors.[4]

The Rare Book and Manuscript Section of the Association of College and Research Libraries (ACRL), affiliated with the American Library Association (ALA), has a blog for the posting of thefts. For the year 2013, there are ten thefts reported, four from U.S. libraries, one from Canadian institutions, and five from foreign libraries. During 2014 six American libraries and institutions reported thefts.[5]

One estimate from Alice Harrison Bahr in 1978 stated that

> In the United States, where the nation's libraries contain an estimated 1.5 billion volumes, a loss of even 1% annually amounts to some 15 million books. Again, using an average cost of $15 to replace a missing book, the total amount replacement cost would be $225 million. This is more than 10% of what libraries spend annually. The 15 million volumes are almost 16% of the 95 million volumes added annually by the nation's libraries.[6]

And many of the items stolen from libraries are worth far more than $15. Rare books and manuscripts present an especially inviting target. A well-known book theft

Encyclopedia of Library and Information Sciences, Fourth Edition DOI: 10.1081/E-ELIS4-120053499

scholar, Lawrence S. Thompson, noted the increasing activity of professional thieves which has made "the record of major thefts in the last 15 years … little short of appalling." Current reports back him up.

Whether spurred on by love or greed, book theft has become a serious, costly problem and one that is not easily solved. Studies indicate that electronic security systems can be effective book theft deterrents, but alternative theft prevention programs have also been successful. Evaluation of theft control programs is in a state of flux. The only program librarians unanimously find unworkable is the honor system. In 1968 the Tarlton Law Library in Texas left legal treatises on open shelves to test the honor system. At the end of one year over $4000 worth of material had been lost.[7]

Another factor that contributed to the problem being underreported and neglected is that in the past it was more common for an institution not to report the theft than to report it. This was usually due to concerns about offending or driving away potential donors. Sometimes elaborate measures have been taken to recover the stolen items, even going so far as to buy them back at auction rather than explaining to the dealer before the sale and presenting proof of ownership to be awarded custody of the items through replevin.

Communication among librarians and with book and manuscript dealers is the best defense against this sort of criminal activity. For the most part, book dealers are honest; they will post notices in their trade newsletters regarding any unscrupulous dealer activity and warn their colleagues not to deal with him or her for the next five years. This type of crime needs to be taken more seriously. Art theft, which includes book theft, is the second most prevalent type of crime after narcotics activity internationally. It affects a similar percentage of victims, including institutions.[8]

Data regarding cases of art theft have been compiled for the United States by the Federal Bureau of Investigation (FBI) and by the International Foundation for Art Research (IFAR) in New York. Even so, firm statistics regarding the recovery rate of these stolen items do not exist either; only estimates can be made. According to Constance Lowenthal of the IFAR, the recovery rate of stolen art items is about 10%. (Less than 14% of art stolen internationally is ever recovered and returned to its rightful owner.) This is not a firm statistic because the owners of the items do not always report the recovery of their items to the authorities that were notified at the time of the theft. For famous works of art, the recovery rate is closer to 50%, but this is also an estimated figure, and these figures are not linked to whether the thefts were initially made public or not.[9] The motive for such crime is clearly monetary gain since the average art theft broken down statistically nets the thief approximately $25,000 per item or $50,000 per incident. This is in contrast to the average bank robbery that only nets the thief approximately $1400 in cash per incident.[10]

The FBI has been primarily involved in the investigation of theft and recovery of other types of property in the United States, that is, other than books and library materials, although they have investigated thefts of large numbers of library materials stolen, often reported as missing from more than one institution. One major focus of their investigation has been into art thefts, and as an aid in this matter, they created the National Stolen Art File (NASF) in May of 1979. This database includes information on approximately 5000 paintings, prints, and sculptures valued at $2000 or more that have been reported as stolen. The database is updated annually, and when a stolen art object is reported as having been recovered, the report is removed from NASF. Although this database primarily records data concerning stolen art items, valuable manuscript items are also included.[11]

The problem of library and archival theft has not been at the forefront of institutional concerns, but estimated losses such as these suggested by Alice Harrison Bahr indicate that perhaps they should be. Many institutions have been more occupied with budgetary planning and the constraints placed on them by lack of sufficient funds and the subsequent impact on the level of staffing or on collection maintenance, development, or expansion. Libraries have to assess the rate of depletion of materials in their collections because in order to maintain services for their users, materials that are not returned or recovered will have to be replaced. The problem of theft of materials, either in their entirety or partially by the mutilation of certain pages from a volume, should receive greater attention because when materials are missing from a collection, it not only detracts from the integrity of that collection, but it detracts from the collective cultural heritage.[12] This was acknowledged in the sentencing of Daniel Spiegelman by Judge Lewis Kaplan for the theft of forty items from Columbia University.[13] Replacement of stolen or mutilated library books is sometimes an option because duplicates can be purchased, either in reprint or in a microfilm of the volume that may be available, but archival materials are unique, and when they are gone it is very difficult to obtain another item of comparable value to the collection, either from the same record-creator or concerning the same subject matter from the same time period.

The topic of library theft has not gone unnoticed in the library profession. The published literature in the librarianship and archival journals discuss incidents of theft of materials from institutions that are open to the public where presumably some of their visitors have helped themselves to the books and manuscripts from those collections and kept them.[14] Sometimes they attempt to sell the materials to book and manuscript dealers or sometimes to a librarian, which can lead to their arrest.[15]

Alerting these or any other organizations that might be appropriate that materials are missing from the collection is only the first step. An accurate inventory of which items have been determined to be missing should be drawn up listing the appraised value of the items and describing them in as much detail as possible, mentioning if they are marked items (and if so, where the markings appear) and if they have any other distinguishing markings or evidence of any repair work. The investigation of the theft can take a long period of time, so a chronology of all events related to the investigation should be compiled from the day the theft is reported until the materials are recovered and/or a suspect in the theft is prosecuted and, hopefully, convicted.[16]

Two of these organizations (BAMBAM and the FBI) established a national database for logging the reports of stolen or missing items, and the third (ABAA) has a network for dissemination of this information. ABAA, due to its close links with the book dealer trade in America, has traditionally been in a good position to get the word out to book dealers that certain items have been reported as stolen through a regular column in Antiquarian Bookman that circulates widely in the trade. Daniel Leab and Katharine Keyes Leab, as the editors of American Book Prices Current, founded BAMBAM in 1981 as a nonprofit database whereby libraries could log onto their system directly and record the information regarding lost and stolen items. This system did not usually operate in this manner, since more frequently the reporting officer for the library telephoned Katharine Leab and report the information to her to be entered into the system.[17] However, the entry of data into this system was not organized into a standardized format, such as the machine-readable or MARC format used by other data systems, which made it difficult to search efficiently because the data was sometimes entered by library staff members and sometimes by staff members at BAMBAM. When an item was reported as having been recovered, the record was deleted from BAMBAM's database. The lack of standardization meant that the compilation of accurate statistical information about the thefts reported on the database could not be compiled. A plan to incorporate the reporting features of BAMBAM with the MARC format was formulated. Katharine Leab coordinated BAMBAM for fourteen years, and negotiations fell through to get the Online Computer Library Center (OCLC) to administer it instead and standardize the data into MARC format in conjunction with ABAA and the Rare Book and Manuscript Security Committee Section of ALA,[18] and as mentioned earlier, it has been terminated.

As of May 1992, there were 1400 records in the BAMBAM database, but not all of those records were for individual items; some of them represented entire archives.[19] In July of 1984, 118 items were listed in BAMBAM[20] and in the summer of 1987, 77 items were listed.[21] With sporadic figures such as these, it is impossible to determine overall annual trends. Hopefully, according to Ronald Lieberman, the OCLC database would have been a useful tool for providing this type of information and to help determine the patterns of losses.[22] Susan Allen, of the Special Collections Department at the Claremont Colleges and former chair of the Rare Book and Manuscript Section of the ALA, is presently also attempting to gather statistical data on library thefts. During the week of April 20–24, 1992, she sent an electronic mail message to various colleagues at other libraries in the United States to ask if anyone had compiled figures of such reports and to ask for their help in such an effort. Since 1987 she has compiled the reports of items reported missing throughout the country that she has become aware of and has kept a narrative list.[23]

These databases have also been created in response to a rising crime rate in the United States as a whole, which has included crimes in libraries, archives, and art museums. Evidence of this problem has been compiled by Alan Jay Lincoln, who served as the editor of a special issue of Library Trends, "Protecting the Library."[24] Trends in library crimes, which include thefts of library, patron, and staff property as well as assaults of patrons and staff members are reported in Crime in the Library: A Study of Patterns, Impact and Security[25] and in Library Crime and Security, which was coauthored by Carol Zall Lincoln and appeared in Library and Archival Security.[26] Alan Jay Lincoln does not only report the problem of library crime, he also includes suggestions for combating the problem, including the installation of security systems and the implementation of new procedures.

In his introduction to the special issue on Protecting the Library, Lincoln states that the range of problems of crime and disruption affecting libraries has become greater, and the impact of crime in and against libraries more widespread.[27] He continues by stating

Perhaps the oldest problem, ... is the theft of books. The problem continues today and in many libraries is considered a major operating cost. This involves the theft of rare books by profit-oriented thieves as well as the theft of expensive but commonplace volumes by "ordinary" patrons, students, and faculty. Unlike the professional thief, others steal for selfish motives; they "need" the book, they "like" the book, they "can't find the book anyplace else," and so on. In academic libraries, the perceived competition for scare resources entices students and faculty to take what they "must have." Of course, taking a popular volume not only improves one's own chances of success, but simultaneously reduces others' chances.

As libraries continue to develop their nonbook resources, these materials become increasingly popular targets of thieves. Episodes of theft are not confined to books. Records, tapes, software and hardware have become favored targets in some libraries. At times, these items -

as well as books - are not stolen but are mutilated, reducing both the value and usefulness of the materials. Mutilation may be in the form of slashing needed pages from journals or books. In terms of motivation, this action may be more similar to vandalism in that the perpetrator's goal is to obtain some desired material rather than destroy it. We were told of one episode of valuable information stored on computer discs being thrown in toilets by intruders. Acts of property destruction also occur with alarming regularity. Buildings are defaced and occasionally burned, equipment is damaged, and files are destroyed. Libraries also are likely to be targets for the so-called "white collar" crimes of false billing and other fraud, counterfeit money exchange, and theft by employees. The theft of personal items belonging to staff and patrons also may be a problem in some areas. As we shall demonstrate later, it is the unusual library that is free of all crime and disruption.

While property crimes against the library are the most common types of offenses, they may not be the most feared. Crimes against persons evoke strong reactions from those involved or concerned. Even when a library is free from personal crimes, the anticipation of a possible episode can be devastating to employee and patron morale.[28]

Alan Jay Lincoln presents the results of the Library Crime Research Project in his article *Patterns and Costs of Crime*.[29] This was a three-year study of the crime and disruption patterns in public libraries in all fifty states. It was a broad study designed not only to assess problems of crime and disruption but also to identify many of the conditions that facilitate or help to control these problems. The survey questions covered a variety of topics including 1) characteristics of the library and community; 2) descriptions of patrons and patron use patterns; 3) experiences with eighteen different types of crime and disruption; and 4) direct and indirect costs of crime including the use of security equipment and procedures. A total of 2,920 surveys were distributed to a sampling of the public libraries listed in the *American Library Directory*, and the 1647 surveys that had been returned by August 1983 were analyzed.[30] In regard to theft of library materials, four kinds of theft were measured. These were book theft, which was the most common offense reported, reference material theft, theft of equipment, and other theft. Eighty percent of the responding participants reported at least one episode of book theft, and the majority of these involved six episodes.[31] The results of this survey are outlined in the tables compiled from this study. (See Leab and Leab, Table 1, p. 71; Table 2, p. 73; Table 3, p. 74.)

The prevailing attitude in the past was that a theft should not be publicized to any outside authorities. This practice is no longer seen as ethical in the professional or library world. Virtually all institutions, large and small, have experienced theft problems.[32] Efforts to keep thefts quiet sometimes led some institutions to take peculiar

measures to recover their stolen items, such as buying back at public auction the letters and other documents that had been stolen from them previously, rather than approaching the auction house and proving their ownership of the documents and requesting their return.

Instances of library theft continue to be reported by libraries throughout America, whether it is committed by staff members or visitors. Staff members have been reported to removing not only collection materials from the premises, items that have been accessioned and catalogued, and items that have not been fully accessioned and processed such as books, compact discs (CDs), and DVDs but also cash from fines collected or benefit book sales and office supplies.[33] An instance of theft by a visitor includes the case of E. Forbes Smiley III, a map dealer and collector who was sentenced to 42 mo in prison by U.S. District Judge Bond Arterton on September 27, 2006, and was instructed to make a payment of $1.9 million in restitution to the antiquarian booksellers and collectors he defrauded.[34] Mr. Smiley had admitted to purloining 97 maps over an eight-year period from various libraries including the New York and Boston public libraries, Chicago's Newberry Library, Yale University, Harvard University, and the British Library.[35] Mr. Smiley was attributed with stealing 108 maps, but the total number of missing maps from those institutions is 256. Mr. Smiley was sentenced to forty-two months and he served three years and six days. He officially earned parole on January 17, 2010.[36]

The Wisconsin Historical Society was the site of a brash break-in when Matthew Brooke smashed the glass bookcase containing the bound volume of the *Pennsylvania Evening Post* containing issues dating to January to April 1777. Although the volume is valued at $3000–$5000, the explanation for the crime offered to the court by Mr. Brooke when he was charged in September of 2005 was that he wished to read an article about a historical figure named William Hill, not to profit from the sale of the item.[37] Digital recordings are also of interest to library patrons as well as library staffers, as illustrated by the case of Binh Huu Hoang who pled guilty to first-degree theft for stealing $3000 worth of CDs and DVDs from the Multnomah County Library (Oregon). Mr. Hoang was banned from the library and sentenced on July 28, 2005, to three days in jail, three years of probation, and 160 hr of community service.[38]

Electronic articles available from libraries by purchase or subscription and personal data are targeted by cyber criminals around the world. The National Terrorism Advisory Board reported that Chinese hackers claimed to have exploited the City College of New York Library Proxy Server, downloading 25,000 e-mails and passwords. This incident occurred on September 16, 2013, and was reported to the City College of the New York Information Technology Department on September 30, 2013. The Information Technology Department subsequently shut down the City College of New York Library Proxy Server without notifying either the chief librarian or the library computing manager. This server facilitates off-campus access for members of the City College of New York community to electronic material including database subscription articles and electronic books. There was no evidence that the Library Proxy Server was compromised. Proxy Server access was subsequently restored.[39]

These and other motivations for library theft have been noted in the past and continue to be reported. The reasons for library theft listed in the 1971 doctoral thesis by Stephen Glen Poland, "Characteristics, Behaviors and Attitudes of Male College Students who have Committed Theft," were

1. Acquisitive vandalism
2. Tactical vandalism
3. Ideological vandalism
4. Play vandalism

An instance of tactical vandalism is presented as a case study by Bruce Shuman where the perpetrator, a law student, tried to borrow a reference work *Black's Law Dictionary* only until the end of the term from a public library branch because the competition for access to this work was so great among his classmates that he felt he needed his own copy because he was determined not to fail law school.[40] An instance of ideological vandalism was reported by the San Francisco Public Library.[41] An instance of vindictive vandalism, not to a library's physical assets, but to its financial assets, was perpetrated by a former employee, the information systems manager, whose actions were all the more insidious because this individual entrusted with access to the computing systems and network, the detection of the implanted program was all the more difficult to detect prior to the creation of the damage to the personnel, payroll, vendor, and circulation records. This computer programmer was convicted in Fort Worth, Texas, in 1998 of inserting a computer virus into his former employee's system that wiped out 168,000 records. The virus activated two days after he was fired, similar to a time bomb waiting to perpetuate the sabotage.[42] An instance of play vandalism by several teenagers was reported by the Pennsauken Free Public Library (New Jersey) when they threw books and began yelling, creating a chaotic scene for fifteen to twenty minutes while there was a power failure. Order was restored after the emergency lighting activated and police arrived on the scene.[43]

Libraries that have been perceived in the past as safe places to work or study have become sites for crimes of assault, equipment theft, and electronic data tampering or deletion, as mentioned earlier. Some of these assaults have included instances of rape[44] or other bodily harm causing death.[45] The murder of a librarian in Georgia brought home the issues of workplace safety. The victim was working alone in a small-town library in 1993. The 16-yrs-old youth arrested for the crime stated that the motive for the crime was the desire to obtain the staff member's expensive jewelry.[46]

Other threats to library property and visitors have been reported, demonstrating that libraries are not isolated from these dangers that are present in the current environment. Bomb threats[47] and the concerns left in the wake of the shootings at the Virginia Tech on April 16, 2007,[48] have left library managers considering installing metal detectors or instituting patron searches as they enter the library to prevent the admission of weapons into the facility in addition to the search of patrons or their belongings as they leave the library to prevent the unauthorized removal of materials.

With regard to the safekeeping of digitized information, librarians have to countermand intrusion from two constituencies, the government and criminals that might be computer crackers or hackers. With regard to the former, in the wake of the Patriot Act, patron records regarding activity and circulation have to be reprogrammed in order to prevent unnecessary inspection of such records. The massive flow of partially encrypted data across networks designed to allow for the unhindered flow of digital information potentially enables the criminal element access to data in order to perpetuate identity or financial theft.[49]

By following the guidelines mentioned earlier, and implementing the sound security practices they advocate, hopefully thefts of library materials will be prevented by all but the most determined professional criminals. Good basic security and preservation policies should be practiced, such as marking valuable materials so that proof of ownership can be established if they are stolen, maintaining accurate cataloguing and inventory records so that an accurate report of what has been determined to be missing can be filed in case they are stolen, and keeping copies of those records that can be made available in order to prove ownership. Only by continual maintenance of accurate inventory, cataloging, and shelf list records can the theft of materials be determined with precision, whether it was by a patron or a staff member. Accurate record keeping is especially important for archival repositories, which include the maintenance of accurate inventory records, particularly the calendars of papers for the sets of papers in the collection, retention of the paging call slips with the name of each patron who requests materials, and of the registration forms filled out by the researchers. The paging slips are useful when items are discovered to be missing, and it can be determined more easily who may be the culprit. It has been suggested that each folder should be inspected or weighed by a staff member before archival materials are turned over to a patron in order to prevent the patron from being able to claim that those materials were not in the folder when it was given to them for use and that they are not responsible for any missing items.

In order for the library and archival profession to assess the problem of the theft of materials, to prevent further thefts, and to recover their materials, the scope of this problem must be determined accurately. A standardized computerized national database, such as the one that had been proposed by OCLC was a first step. Only with accurate reporting can overall annual or regional trends be determined. Institutions might be able to take preventive measures based on the emerging pattern, perhaps microfilming their collections of letters by Franklin Roosevelt if they seem to be the target for possible theft or placing volumes of illustrated botanical texts in closed stack areas if they are being mutilated in libraries in other parts of the country. Greater efforts to microfilm or digitize as much manuscript material in archival collections as possible should be undertaken because the replacement film copy reduces wear on the originals and provides documentation of proof of ownership if they are stolen, and if the master microfilm is stored off-site, the film can be a substitute for the originals if they are permanently lost or destroyed due to fire or flood.

IMPORTANCE OF GOOD COMMUNICATION WITH BOOK DEALERS

Open links of communication to the community of book dealers have been instrumental in the recovery of several of the items stolen from the Columbia University Rare Book and Manuscript Library. This theft was first discovered on July 5, 1994. The next day, on July 6th a list was compiled that went out on *ex libris*, to the ABAA network, to *AB Bookman*, and to the art theft networks. This list was subsequently updated to include the twenty-two items finally posted, valued at $350,000. Descriptions and photographs of some of the stolen items were published in *IFAR Reports* over the next several months. In June of 1995, Jean Ashton, the director of the department, was about to send the list to the book dealers in the secondary market when they got a break in the case with an arrest.[50]

When the theft of the seventeen rare manuscripts was originally discovered in July 1994, it had been speculated that it had to be an inside job. However, when the Dutch police arrested a suspect in Amsterdam on June 7, 1996, they found a convicted forger from Yonkers with two fake passports and a fake Columbia University identification, according to Federal agents.[51]

The arrest, prosecution, and subsequent sentencing of Mr. Daniel Spiegelman (aka Mr. Kikabidze) brought a certain sense of relief, particularly since he subsequently told the authorities where some of the stolen items were stored, in safety deposit boxes in various locations in New York City and State. The items that were recovered—including two fifteenth-century *Books of Hours*, the historical chronicle from Caesar to Charles VI, a nineteenth-century Koran, a papal letter written in 1202, and documents bearing

signatures that appeared to be those of George Washington and John Adams—were all intact. There were seventeen codices taken, including European manuscripts produced in Europe from the thirteenth to the sixteenth centuries, and eight of these have not yet been recovered. There were twenty-three document sets taken and seven of those have still not been recovered. Some of the outstanding documents include two boxes of papers from the Thomas Alva Edison collection. The removal of leaves or miniatures by the thief for separate sale was the greatest fear of Jean Ashton and of those investigating this case. This fear was realized when the nine-volume Blaeu atlas was recovered, and it was determined that more than 250 maps had been cut out of the atlas set. As Jean Ashton explained at the Fatico Hearing for *United States vs. Spiegelman* on March 20, 1998, there was a five-year loss from 1993 to 1998 of scholarship, while the students of Columbia University would not have had the opportunity to be exposed to the materials that had been stolen by Mr. Spiegelman. The complete experience of intellectual examination continues to be curtailed because not all of the items have been recovered and sixteen of the stolen items may never be recovered such as the copy of the *Nuremberg Chronicles* that Mr. Spiegelman admitted to selling in Europe. This loss to scholarship is incalculable.[52] The felon never named any accomplice.[53]

Mr. Spiegelman was extradited to the United States. Law enforcement officials theorized that he tried to hold some bargaining chips to better his position since he must have realized that it is not good to go to prison for a long time. The authorities had him extradited to the United States for prosecution (something that Mr. Spiegelman tried to prevent; attorneys from the U.S. Attorney's office traveled to the Netherlands to argue for his extradition, which was scheduled for December 21, 1995), particularly since any statements he made in Holland where he was held were not valid in U.S. courts. In November 1997, Mr. Spiegelman was in custody awaiting trial. A prior plea bargain was retracted. The defendant gave information relative to his selling of maps and books in Paris. This information was forwarded to the French authorities who were unable or unwilling to further the investigation or recovery of the items.[54]

He was turned in to the authorities and to Jean Ashton by three book dealers in Germany, Switzerland, and the Netherlands who called her and Detective Kalafus to notify them that the pieces had appeared on the market. Detective R.J. Kalafus was a 30-yr veteran of the New York City police force assigned to the 26th Precinct, who investigated cases of theft from three of the Columbia University Libraries. The dealers told Jean Ashton that a man calling himself William Taylor offered to sell a set of rare manuscripts that contained several pieces missing from the Columbia University Libraries collection. The suspect showed the dealers photographs of one of the *Book of Hours* and of another manuscript he also offered for sale for 70,000 Dutch Guilders (about $44,500). One of the dealers in Amsterdam agreed to pay 60,000 guilders. When the man returned with the merchandise, he was arrested because the authorities had been contacted in the interim.

Judge Lewis Kaplan sentenced Daniel Spiegelman in April of 1998 to 60 mo in prison, 3 yrs of supervised release, 300 hr of community service, and restitution of $314,150 for the theft of works valued at $1.3 million. Judge Kaplan imposed a lengthier sentence because the magnitude of the crime meant the deprivation "of a generation of scholars and students of the irreplaceable raw materials by which they seek to discern the lessons of the past and help us to avoid repeating it. That's what differentiates [this] offense from a simple theft of money or other easily replaceable property."[55]

Mr. Spiegelman's activities did not end there. In October 1999, Jean Aston received a call from an autograph dealer in Greenwich, Connecticut, Basil Panagopolous, because he had been offered some papers of Thomas A. Edison and Presidents Thomas Jefferson and James Monroe that Mr. Panagopolous suspected were from the Columbia University Libraries collection. Apparently Mr. Spiegelman had escaped from his work release program in Manhattan, retrieved the materials from an unknown location, and crossed state lines in an attempt to sell them. The alertness of the manuscript dealer lead to Mr. Spiegelman's rearrest and an additional twenty-four-month sentence. This sentence was imposed by Judge Loretta Preska on May 24, 2000, followed by an additional three years of probation. It is clear that Mr. Spiegelman is still aware of the location of materials taken from the Columbia University Rare Book and Manuscript Library that have never been recovered.[56] Mr. Spiegelman served his sentence of a little more than six years in custody and was released on July 19, 2001.[57]

This type of crime should be taken more seriously as the Stephen Blumberg case, in which thousands of volumes were eventually recovered, illustrates. Valued at a total of $5.3 million, the materials were taken from 327 public, private, and university libraries in 45 states over a 20-yr period. This case and others highlight the value of the materials that were stolen. Stephen Carrie Blumberg, born in 1951, was arrested on March 20, 1990, and sentenced to 5 yrs in prison. He was released on December 29, 1995, after serving his term. He was not fulfilling the terms of his supervised release or parole and subsequently surrendered to authorities and was rearrested on January 5, 1996. He was subsequently held in a federal prison hospital mental health facility in Rochester, Minnesota, for psychiatric evaluation and released in June 1997.[58] His bibliokleptomania led him to accumulate 11,000 books, letters, and manuscripts, which filled his house in Ottumwa, Iowa.[59] His obsession with books grew out of his earlier collecting manias for doorknobs and other such hardware items.

As a notorious recent case, it dramatizes the problem of library theft for the library community,[60] as do others. The library community was aware of the activities of Stephen Blumberg prior to his arrest, but due to poor communication among libraries, he eluded apprehension until an informant helped the federal authorities. Stephen Blumberg obtained false identification and passed himself off as Professor Matt McGue, a faculty member of the University of Minnesota. Although he was arrested and convicted of trespass at the University of California-Riverside library and of possession of burglary tools under this identity, he apparently continued his activities until his subsequent arrest even though a report of this incident had been published in *Library & Archival Security*.[61] The search of his premises by the FBI revealed materials reported missing from more than 327 institutions in 45 states and Canada. He was convicted on January 31, 1991, in U.S. District Court of all the felony counts with which he had been charged, including conspiracy to transport stolen property across state lines, two counts of transportation of stolen property, and one count of possession of stolen property. He had pleaded insanity to the charges.[62] Although he had been arrested previously for pilfering materials from a library under an assumed name, the pattern of his activities was not revealed to the library community as a whole until his arrest, trial, and conviction. This case has underscored the need for an accurate national database to record missing materials from libraries so that if a pattern of these activities is present it can be revealed sooner and librarians can be alerted to the possible danger to materials in their collections.

As various libraries began to discover that books were missing due to Mr. Blumberg's activities, the ACRL Rare Book and Manuscript Section Security Committee began in 1987 to gather a single listing of library thefts, the "Incidence of Theft." A member of the committee volunteered to keep it up to date and to issue a revised version prior to each annual ALA meeting. A document of one page in length grew to 22 pages by 1995, highlighting the problem and the exchange of information among libraries.[63]

TREASURES MISSING FROM THE LIBRARY OF CONGRESS

The Library of Congress, the de facto national research library, has been plagued with problems of theft and mutilation of their materials since 1992.[64] As a response to this problem, procedures were into place at that time, including closing the stacks whereby the library beefed up security by barring all but essential personnel from the collections and an agreement that it would notify both the U.S. Attorney's office and the FBI of any "property offenses." Despite the assurances of James Billington, the Librarian of Congress, when he stated in October 1994 that security was "one of the three top institutional priorities of the library," Deborah Maceda contended that the ransacking of the library's collection continued unchecked. Deborah Maceda was the library's Protective Services Office staff member who was removed from office on July 12 for submitting notification of missing materials. She compiled a list in June 1995 of mutilated documents that filled 68 pages, showing that 26,985 plates are known to be missing from publications valued at a total of $1.75 million. Former Senator Connie Mack called for a General Accountability Office investigation into security lapses and the magnitude of the losses. Senator Mack, Florida Republican, as former chair of the Appropriations Subcommittee that oversees the library, had the authority to call for such an investigation, especially after receiving memos and reports of these losses from Deborah Maceda. An aide to Senator Mack said other committees with jurisdiction over the library were notified.[65] Hearings investigating these allegations were held before the Joint Committee on the Library of Congress and the Appropriations Committee on November 29, 1995.[66]

Sometimes cases of theft can even lead to murder. A robbery of 89 ancient manuscripts from the Russian National Library in St. Petersburg dating from the thirteenth to the eighteenth centuries was posted on the ABAA Stolen Book List by Vladimir Zaitsev, the library director. Dmitry Yakubovskiy, a controversial lawyer and alleged former KGB agent with the nickname "General Dima," was arrested after being detained on December 20, 1994, on suspicion of complicity in the theft of those eighty-nine manuscripts worth about $100 million from St. Petersburg's National Library. He had emigrated to Canada and then returned to Russia prior to his arrest. According to reports, Mr. Yakubovskiy had very good relations with many top Russian officials. Yevgeny Melnitsky joined the team to defend Mr. Yakubovskiy in August 1995. The attorney, Yevgeny Melnitsky, 49, was found by his driver in his apartment on September 25, 1995, with his throat cut and his head bludgeoned, according to police detective Marina Gurina.[67] Authorities said they found no sign of forced entry or evidence of anything having been taken from the apartment. Police said they were investigating a potential link to his work in defending the controversial lawyer Dmitry Yakubovskiy. Mr. Melnitsky had important documents related to the case that were "dangerous to some people," one of the other Yakubovskiy defense lawyers said, on condition of anonymity.[68] On September 20, Melnitsky had been elected chairman of a District Electoral Commission. The Electoral Commission does not believe that his murder has anything to do with these activities, but rather with the legal case.[69]

REPLEVIN

As mentioned earlier, sometimes libraries have taken elaborate measures to recover their stolen items. In the case of

the documents that were stolen from three Texan institutions, proving their prior ownership to the satisfaction of the Parke-Bernet Galleries would have been relatively easy since these letters had been referred to in publications concerning early Texas history, and the source for these documents had been cited as these respective repositories. Members of the staff at the Texas State Library did not exercise their right of replevin or recovery by a person or institution of goods claimed to belong to them, on the promise to test the matter in court and give the goods up again, if defeated. Cataloging records alone formulates a weak case; other documentation should be produced to prove ownership definitively in court, such as microfilm of the manuscript items, a citation in an exhibit catalog, or credit to a repository in the publication of a set of papers. Forty-two items among the lots sold in an auction held at Parke-Bernet Galleries on November 21, 1967, belonged to the Texas State Library, the University of Texas, or Rosenberg Library in Galveston. Representatives for the University of Texas were present at the sale and bought back many of these items, which were returned to the Texas State Library, having been "recovered" in New York.[70]

SUGGESTIONS FOR PREVENTION

Spend the Money on Security Systems and Trust No One

Detective R.J. Kalafus, as mentioned earlier, has investigated cases of theft from three of the Columbia University Libraries, and he offers two main points for the prevention of this type of crime: spend the money on security systems and trust no one. Spending the money for security systems, whether they be alarm systems or video surveillance, may be difficult in this time of budget cuts, but the consequences may be more costly. When choosing a security system, it would be wise to consult with a law enforcement agent to get a recommendation. Something else to keep in mind is to limit the number of keys issued to staff for access to secure areas. Only a limited number of those keys should be issued to authorized personnel.

In the course of his investigation of the theft from the Columbia University Rare Book and Manuscript Department, following the initial report of the theft, Detective Kalafus visited the department to survey their security system and arrangements. He assessed their alarm system to be fairly good, and any loud noise will set it off, even the sound of a closing elevator door. To help him with his inquiry, he was given six book storage boxes by staff members to take with him for examination. He found it ironic that as he was leaving with these boxes, no one stopped him or questioned him regarding what he was doing with them, it was not until he stopped to light a cigarette that half a dozen people suddenly appeared to tell him to put it out. He has determined that there were too many keys issued to various staff members.

Another thing to remember is trust no one. When security procedures are implemented, they should be applied consistently. As mentioned earlier, the Library of Congress implemented new procedures in 1992 which were not followed, resulting in very little change in the numbers of mutilated volumes on the shelves.

Use Consistent Security Procedures: Search Everyone

When security procedures are implemented, they should be followed consistently. At the very least, everyone should pass through a security checkpoint upon exiting. If it is determined that someone should be subject to a search, which may be objectionable, it should be explained gently but firmly that this is for everyone's benefit, since whenever any materials are permanently removed from a library collection, it detracts from the overall integrity of that collection and diminishes our overall cultural heritage.

Of course, no alarm system designed to alert one to an outside break-in can protect the collection from an inside theft. Terry Belanger, speaking at the 1983 Oberlin Conference on Theft reported in *Library Journal*, estimated that "25% of the thefts are inside jobs committed by students, professors, librarians, staff members, and janitors, rather than professional criminals."[71] Ronald Lieberman, former chair of the Security Committee of the ABAA confirmed that "insider theft is a problem."[72]

Two cases of insider theft that have come to light occurred at the University of Georgia library in Athens and at the Rosenbach Museum and Library in Philadelphia. Materials belonging to the rare book collection including more than a thousand rare maps, manuscripts, and folio places, estimated as being worth over $1 million, were discovered to have been stolen over a period of several years. The theft was discovered when it was determined that items were missing from the map collection in June of 1986. During a subsequent inventory of the collection, the list of missing items was expanded to include a 1776 British atlas, and a set of nineteenth-century botanical folio prints, *Les Liliacees* published in eight volumes, and duplicate copies of various items in the map collection. Thomas E. Camden, the head of the Hargrett Rare Book and Manuscripts Collection, noted that their "biggest problem is trying to identify the materials as ours once they have been located," since many of the items were not marked.[73] A former employee, Robert "Skeet" Willingham Jr., resigned on October 15, 1986, after an investigation into the suspected thefts had already begun in June of 1986. He became the prime suspect for these thefts after his home had been searched four separate times by campus police who found materials that could have come from the library in the course of those searches.

The campus police filed an affidavit in connection with these searchers and stating that "It is known that [Willingham] has sold property belonging to the University of Georgia."[74] Thomas Camden, commenting on this insider theft problem, noted that the University of Georgia library with closed stacks has had few problems with theft by patrons, but added that "I don't know of any system that will protect a library from within."[75]

The case of the missing materials at Rosenbach Museum and Library in Philadelphia was more insidious because in the course of their investigation it was revealed that inventory records had been purposely altered by the perpetrator of the thefts to cover up the fact that he was pilfering documents from their collection and selling them through book and manuscript dealers. When Ellen Dunlap took over as director of the Rosenbach Museum and Library in 1983, she had no idea that she would inherit a serious problem as a result of the activities of the former director, Clive Driver. Not only had he worked there for twenty years and served as director since 1965, he had actually been allowed to live on the premises.[76] When Dunlap took over as director in 1983, an investigation of a file marked "Missing Items" was inconclusive. A more serious problem emerged when the Rosenbach was contacted by telephone on February 26, 1987, by Mary Jo Kline of Sotheby's inquiring about a 1790 John Adams letter to John Trumbull that was about to be consigned to auction. The staff of the Rosenbach were unable to establish if the Rosenbach had ownership of this document or not, particularly since the inventory book had been emended in blue pencil, creating doubt as to whether it had be deaccessioned after 1959. During the course of the continuing investigation into this mystery, Mary Jo Kline revealed that the current holder of the letter was a Massachusetts dealer, Paul Richards. Paul Richards in turn identified the person who had sold him this document as Clive Driver, who had recently retired nearby.

When this revelation was made, the alarm bells went off and Ellen Dunlap had to go into action. After conferring with their lawyer and members of the board, changing the locks, and contacting the insurance agent, she filed a civil suit in federal court to seek return of the Rosenbach's property.[77] In November of 1989 the civil suit was settled with a provision for the return to the Rosenbach of fifty-eight documents disseminated by Clive Driver. Criminal charges were also filed against Driver who was convicted on felony charges and sentenced to pay a $50,000 fine and serve 3 years of probation that includes 2,000 hr of community service for the interstate transportation of an historical document.[78]

The case of the materials stolen from the Rosenbach Museum and Library by Clive Driver that were sold to the Massachusetts dealer, Paul Richards, and the case of the materials stolen from the Columbia University Rare Book and Manuscript Department by Mr. Spiegelman both illustrate the point that the staff of libraries and archival institutions should foster good relations with book and document dealers so that they will be more likely to notify the authorities and those institutions known to them as collecting books or documents concerning a particular subject category when they are offered materials for sale that are related to that topic. This would not only help in the recovery of stolen materials but also could be a means of increasing the holdings in a collection within a certain subject area since the institution could consider purchasing the material from the dealer. Reporting missing items to ABAA and getting it listed in the column published in *Antiquarian Bookman* is only part of the recovery process, and staff members at institutions should make direct contact with those dealers who specialize in materials relevant to their collections. Also, the curator of a special collection or rare books collection in a library should be familiar with the current market value of materials in the collection by consulting dealer catalogues and listings of prices paid in an auction house sale of items comparable to those in the collection.[79]

Microfilming

Mimi Bowling, former curator of the Manuscript Department at the New York Public Library, suggests another approach—microfilming. Microfilming manuscripts reduces the wear on the originals while providing an acceptable substitute for most researchers. As she explains it, "Good security measures are good preservation practice for anything valuable. Be sure not to [have it] handled more than [it] needs to be, limit [the] use to film [as] one solution."[80]

Also, in keeping with the idea of limiting the number of keys that are issued, at the New York Public Library Manuscript Department, only a few members of the staff have been issued electronic key cards that open the containerized steel shelf units, and the system records the key code used to operate it and the time that the shelves were opened. Since the key codes are each linked to a specific staff member, the access to these stacks can be monitored.[81] Although it is possible to withdraw materials from one area of the stacks and place them in another stack area, if accurate shelf lists are maintained, it should be quickly apparent that the materials are out of place.

Mark Materials and Use Colored Photocopy Paper

The practice of marking manuscripts and other library materials has been the subject of controversy within the library profession. Each set of guidelines promoted by the RBMS Security Committee give specific instructions as to how to mark these materials in such a fashion that they will not be disfigured to such an extent that they will be unusable by researchers or prohibit them from being exhibited by the institution that owns the material. The Library of Congress recommends the marking of paper

manuscripts with a proof of ownership and will even provide upon request bottles of ink that can be transferred by means of a five-point ownership stamp. This ink has been tested for its resistance to removal by application of solvents or bleaches and for its slightly alkaline pH of 7.0 to 7.5, and it is nonmigrating to other pages and nondestructive to the paper.[82] At the Oberlin Conference on Theft in 1983, Katherine Leab of BAMBAM recommended the establishment of a national registry of library markings.[82] The importance of marking archival materials with a distinctive stamp denoting ownership and keeping track of the different designs for these ownership marks used by the institution was emphasized again by Katherine Leab.[84] Ronald Lieberman, the former chair of the Security Committee of ABAA, also recommends the use of marking library materials as an aid in proving ownership and for deterring theft.[85] However, he does not neglect to mention that cancellation of these ownership marks is equally important and marking the materials as "WITHDRAWN" or indicating that they were deaccessioned in some fashion. Of course, the cataloging and inventory records should also indicate if certain items were deaccessioned.[86] Lieberman also mentioned that accurate inventory records are important because then one can be more "aware [of] what is in the collection so that it will be more apparent that [any materials are] missing."[87] Those inventory records are vital for proving ownership and are an aid in recovery as well.

These guidelines regarding the marking of library materials for security reasons state that all materials should be marked. This includes Medieval and Renaissance manuscripts, incunabula and early printed books, single-leaf manuscripts, broadsides, prints, maps, and printed books. The process of adding an ownership mark to library materials at the time of acquisition could be incorporated into the initial processing of materials, but the retrospective marking of a large collection is a difficult undertaking. Such a project has to be planned carefully so that it is implemented in an orderly way to make the best use of staff resources and time and of money from the budget.[88] Considering the constraints placed on most institutions by limited budgets, it is unrealistic to expect that most of them will undertake such a procedure. It is unlikely that institutions will try to mark the contents of their entire collection; therefore efforts should probably be directed at those items that have been appraised to have a high value because they are likely to be targeted by thieves. The marking of library materials either with an inked stamp, a perforated pattern, or an embossed pattern also violates one of the principles of conservation, not to carry out any procedure on library materials, which is irreversible. Even though this may be the case and such marking can detract from the aesthetic or exhibition value of the materials, Katherine Leab believes that archivists should spend more of their time marking the manuscripts in their care. Katherine Leab has also suggested for manuscript collections that make photocopies of their materials available to researchers on demand should make the photocopy on colored paper so that the patron cannot substitute the copy for the original document when the folder is returned. The copy should also be clearly marked as such by the institution.[89]

The preparation of manuscript or other library materials for microfilming would take about the same amount of time as retrospectively marking them, because in each case the materials have to be physically handled by staff members for a period of time to carry out either procedure. Since microfilming is usually not destructive to the original materials and does not detract from their aesthetic value nor is it an irreversible procedure, it is a better security option. In addition, the microfilm and the records stating that the materials were scheduled for microfilming are additional documentation that can prove ownership if the originals are stolen.

BETTER AWARENESS: LOBBY STATE LEGISLATURES

Another program that can be undertaken by institutions to help prevent library theft is to lobby for stronger statutes for the conviction and prosecution of library crimes. Hopefully, if criminals are aware that they will be prosecuted under strict legal codes if they are caught, they will think twice before perpetrating such crimes. The Society of American Archivists sponsored the drafting of model legislation in 1975 and lobbied the law enforcement community to enact the proposed legislation. A law passed in Virginia that contains provisions that can be effectively be enforced served as the model. This legislation (Virginia Code SS42.1-72/1.74.1) defines the crime of mutilation of library materials as a class I misdemeanor. The concealment of a book or other library material while still on the premises of the library or removing it in a concealed fashion is defined as larceny. This is highly significant because it prevents a prospective thief from claiming that he forgot to return the manuscript or book or that he meant to have the material charged out. This legislation also grants the archivist or librarian immunity from civil liability for actions arising out of the detention of a suspect. However, if a patron is detained due to suspected activity that may constitute theft, the library staff should handle the situation carefully. The person can be detained on the library premises preferably by two staff members, one of them can be a member of the institution's security force, and no action should be taken until municipal law enforcement officials arrive.[90]

How seriously a municipality takes library theft can be reflected by the punishments allowed under local laws. Massachusetts passed a law in 1990 allowing for fines of up to $25,000 and 5 yrs in jail for stealing library materials. The need for such a strict measure was demonstrated

by one small-town library serving a population of 23,000 was losing $12,000 worth of books each year. It was estimated that throughout this Commonwealth, public libraries had material losses of $1.1 million yearly.[91] It is amazing that it took so long for such a statue to be enacted. During the 1930s a ring of book thieves visited libraries throughout Massachusetts and other eastern states by either simply taking volumes off the shelves and hiding them in their overcoats or checked them out as library patrons under an alias and never returned them. They removed or disguised any library ownership marks and sold them to secondhand book dealers on Fourth Avenue in New York.[92]

Some locations abroad, such as Nigeria, take a rather serious view of such infractions. A conviction of theft of library property can earn the perpetrator up to seven years in prison, if the magistrate sees fit to impose such a sentence.[93]

SECURITY DEVICES

One widely utilized prevention measure that has been taken by libraries throughout the United States is the installation of electronic and other mechanical security devices. Some of these security devices detect intrusions on the premises when they are closed for operation to personnel and the public. They can also detect intrusion into secured areas while the institution is open for normal operations. These magnetic sensors, pressure sensitive mats or sensors, and photoelectric or ultrasonic beams can all activate an alarm system when they are triggered, either an alarm audible on the premises that can frighten away the intruder or an alarm that is silent at the premises but that activates a signal at another location, such as a nearby police station or at the office of a contracted security service.

A security system that has been installed in libraries throughout the country since the 1970s is the security system that electronically surveys patrons as they exit to detect if they have any improperly charged out library materials. For these systems to work, treated detector tags must be placed in each material in the library collection, and when these tags are taken past the sensing screens, usually located near the circulation desk or at the exit point for the library premises, an alarm will sound if the materials are not charged out properly. These detection tags are placed in the library materials when they are initially processed at the time of acquisition.[94] Such systems are not foolproof in this age of ever more sophisticated technology. Tattle tags can be silenced with a device that could be purchased for $17.99 at Radio Shack.[95] A tattle-tape system is difficult to implement in archives in any case because the materials are often single leaves that make it more difficult to attach the tags to the leaves than it would be to attach them to bound volumes. The number of single-leaf items in an archive poses a similar problem to that of marking manuscripts, and it is very difficult for an institution to allocate the amount of staff time that would be needed either to attach the special tags or to mark the individual leaves. Also archival materials never circulate, so it would be better for the institution to direct their resources to monitoring the use of the materials on the premises.

The recently introduced technology for the library security market, radio-frequency identification, offers an alternative to magnetic strip tattle tags and barcode identification tags. The smaller tag size makes it possible to attach them more easily to individual document items. However, the greater cost per unit, around $0.65–$0.75 each, versus about $0.02 for barcode tags has prevented a large penetration into the library market. In addition, the feature allowing for more universal tracking of the item and potentially of the user who has the item in his or her possession has raised questions regarding privacy invasion of the user. Until the privacy issues and cost factors regarding the per unit cost and the cost of interfacing the technology with circulation transactions can be standardized, many libraries are likely to remain with barcode identification systems.[96]

Careful planning and layout of the reading room where archival materials are used can aid the staff members to accurately monitor how materials are being used and if they might be concealed by a patron. What is of primary importance is to have at least one staff member present at all times. The desk area where the staff member is positioned should be elevated and have a clear line of sight to all work areas at the reading tables. If additional staff members have offices located nearby, glass walls can be installed so that they can periodically assist in the monitoring effort. Strategic placement of two-way mirrors and of closed circuit television cameras can be included to aid the staff member in surveying the activities in the reading room (see illustration on page 5 in Timothy Walsh, *Archives and Manuscripts: Security*. Chicago: Society of American Archivists, 1977). Although it is difficult for the staff member to observe the closed circuit monitor and the patrons in the reading room and it may be too expensive to assign a member of the institutional security force to constantly watch the monitor, the presence of an active camera can be a deterrent to a thief, and the videotape is important evidence for the eventual prosecution of the perpetrator.[97]

When someone is convicted of this type of theft, stronger sentencing should be implemented. As illustrated by the examples of the cases mentioned earlier, Stephen Blumberg, who has served his five-year term, and Clive Driver, who was sentenced to three years probation, including 2,000 hours of community service with a $50,000 fine illustrate, this type of crime is not taken seriously enough. In yet another case of insider theft, Carol Ann Van Swearingen, a former librarian at Tremont

Road library in Upper Arlington, pled guilty to one count of theft for having nearly 6000 books and other materials in her home without library permission. For this crime she has been given two years of probation whereby she must seek counseling for her obsession with books, perform 160 hr of community service, and pay a $2500 fine.[98] However, some public libraries are adopting "get tough" attitude and are calling for help from their local police. The Rolling Meadows Library in Illinois now asks for police help when a patron has kept materials worth $250 or more for a period of 60 days. A uniformed police officer pays a call on the recalcitrant patron and requests the missing materials and instructs them that they have to appear before a judge. This kind of enforcement of the Illinois law against library theft is getting results; about $4000 worth of materials have been recovered.[99]

COMMUNICATION AMONG LIBRARIANS ABOUT THIS PROBLEM

Members of the library and archival profession have also discussed the problem of what to do about missing library materials in meetings such as the one convened at Oberlin College in 1983 to discuss the problem of library theft in the wake of the thefts by James R. Shinn, who was apprehended in April 1981 by William A. Moffett, director of the libraries at Oberlin College. James Shinn was linked to the theft of $750,000 worth of valuable books from the open stacks of some 40 libraries throughout the country.[100] The Society of American Archivists has periodically sponsored discussion of this issue at a conference held in Detroit in 1979[101] and at their annual meeting in September 1991, which included a panel discussion of insider theft of archival materials in the program. The panelists included Ellen Dunlap formerly of the Rosenbach Museum and Library; Daniel Traister of Special Collections at the Van Pelt Library, the University of Pennsylvania; and Robert Bazin from the Philadelphia office of the FBI.[102] A Preconference Workshop on "Security in Archives and Manuscripts Repositories" was scheduled on September 12, 1992, as one of the activities associated with the annual meeting in September 1992 of the Society of American Archivists held in Montreal. Mimi Bowling, curator of manuscripts at the New York Public Library, and Richard Strassberg of Cornell University were going to lead the discussion. It was canceled due to lack of enrollment.

The various public and private libraries that have the responsibility for the safekeeping of materials for the public trust and to make them available for scholarship have formulated guidelines through professional associations as to what measures to take to prevent the loss of the materials in their possession and what to do in the event that any materials are discovered to be in fact missing and possibly stolen. The ACRL and the ALA have been

Technical–Topic

particularly active in this area. The Society of American Archivists sponsored the publication in 1977 of *Archives and Manuscripts: Security* by Timothy Walch that engendered discussion of the issue of library security within the archival and library professions by suggesting a basic checklist system approach for planning a security program.[103] The ACRL approved a set of "Guidelines Regarding Thefts in Libraries" in 1988.[104] The set of "Guidelines for the Security of Rare Book, Manuscript, and Other Special Collections" drafted by the ACRL Rare Book and Manuscript Section's Security Committee in 1982 and approved in June of 1990 are of particular interest to the archival profession.[105]

These sets of guidelines suggest that a security officer should be appointed from among the staff members who will act as a liaison with the institution's legal counsel and security force as well as with the Security Committee, Rare Book and Manuscript Section, ACRL, and ALA. The security officer will coordinate the steps to be taken regarding the notification of outside organizations that materials have been discovered to be missing. The major reporting organizations for library thefts are the ABAA, BAMBAM, and the FBI if the value of the stolen materials is greater than $5000, and there is reason to believe the items could be transported across state lines.[106] Local and state police authorities should be notified in the event there is any criminal activity in a library, whether it is the theft of library materials or of cash from the fines box or in potentially serious cases when a patron is assaulted by another patron.[107]

CONCLUSION

What can I say in conclusion? Take steps to plan for such a disaster just as for a fire or flood beforehand. Install security devices and implement consistent security procedures. Mark or microfilm or digitize the materials in your collection, especially manuscript materials. Foster good relations with law enforcement agents and book dealers; they are your best allies for turning in a suspect in case of a theft. Also, it is the responsibility of the director of any manuscript department to keep track of the market and have a sense of the value of the items in his or her care. If a theft does happen in your institution, the first thing you as a staff member in authority should do is to start a log of events, starting from the first day the theft is detected. Such a log may become useful for building the case against any suspects. Hopefully if perpetrators are caught and prosecuted under existing statutes and receive sentences that are more strenuous than community service, they will realize that the personal or monetary gain is not worth the risk, and libraries can turn their efforts to other areas, possibly promoting programs to serve their users and their community.

REFERENCES

1. Telephone conversation with Katherine Keyes Leab formerly of BAMBAM, May 4, 1992.
2. Greve, F. Culture vultures valuable books, illustrations looted from libraries to feed black market" The Denver Post, Knight-Ridder News Service, Aug 30, 1995.
3. Telephone conversation with Ronald Lieberman, former chair of the Security of ABAA, May 5, 1992.
4. ILAB Committee. *ILAB Stolen Book Database*; Thefts of Collections, 2014, www.stolen-book.org/eng/presentation.html.
5. Healey, E. RBMS Web Editor. *Theft Report Updates*, 2014, rbms.info/thefts-reports.
6. Bahr, A.H. *Book Theft and Library Security Systems, 1978–79*; Knowledge Industry Publications: White Plains, NY, 1978; 3–4.
7. Bahr, p. 4.
8. Art theft Investigation facts sent via fax. Conversation with Detectives Kalafus and Henriquez, 26th Precinct, October 4, 1995, Oct 9, 1995.
9. Telephone conversation with Constance Lowenthal, International Foundation for Art Research, Mar 11, 1992.
10. Fax from R.J. Kalafus, Oct 9, 1995.
11. Cole, A.C. The FBI's National Stolen Art File. FBI Law Enforc. Bull. May 1989; 11–12.
12. Library thieves take all but the covers. *The New York Times*, Apr 7, 1992; A18.
13. McDade, T. *The Book Thief: The True Crimes of Daniel Spiegelman*; 2006, Praeger Publishers: Westport, CT, 159.
14. Bahr, p. 4.
15. Wagner, A. Archival security and insecurity. Colo. Libr. Sept **1985**, *11*, 11.
16. Allen, S.M. Theft in Libraries or Archives. College & Research Libraries News **November 1990**; *51* (10), 940–943.
17. Telephone conversation with Katherine Keyes Leab formerly of BAMBAM, Feb 28, 1992.
18. Telephone conversation with Katherine Keyes Leab formerly of BAMBAM, Feb 28, 1992; telephone conversation with Ronald Lieberman, former chair of the Security of ABAA, Apr 3, 1992.
19. Telephone conversation with Katherine Keyes Leab formerly of BAMBAM, May 28, 1992.
20. Leab, K.K.; Leab, D. BAMBAM update, current as of July 1984. Libr. Arch. Secur. **Summer 1984**, *16* (4), 67–107.
21. Leab, K.K.; Leab, D. BAMBAM update, Summer 1987. Libr. Arch. Secur. **Summer 1987**, *7* (2), 59–130.
22. Telephone conversation with Ronald Lieberman, former chair of the Security of ABAA, May 5, 1992.
23. Telephone conversation with Susan Allen, former chair of the Rare Books and Manuscripts Section, ALA, Apr 24, 1992.
24. Lincoln, A.J. Protecting the library, Special issue. Libr. Trends **Summer 1984**, *33*.
25. Lincoln, A.J. *Crime in the Library: A Study of Patterns, Impact and Security*; R.R. Bowker Company: New York, 1984.
26. Lincoln, A.J.; Lincoln, C.Z. Library crime and security. Libr. Arch. Secur. Spring–Summer **1986**, *8*.

27. Lincoln, A.J. Introduction, Special issue. Libr. Trends **Summer 1984**, *33*, 3.

28. Lincoln, A.J. Introduction. Libr. Trends **Summer 1984**, *33*, 4–5.

29. Lincoln, A.J. Patterns and costs of crime. Libr. Trends **Summer 1984**, *33*, 69–76.

30. Lincoln, A.J. Patterns and costs of crime. Libr. Trends **Summer 1984**, *33*, 69.

31. Lincoln, A.J. Patterns and costs of crime. Libr. Trends **Summer 1984**, *33*, 70.

32. Allen, p. 940.

33. Holt, G.E. Theft by library staff. Bottom Line **2007**, *20* (2), 85–93.

34. Map thief gets three-and-a-half years. Am. Libr. **2006**, *37* (10), 12.

35. Map dealer now admits library theft. Am. Libr. **2006**, *36* (8), 18.

36. Blanding, M. *The Map Thief: The Gripping Story of an Esteemed Map Dealer Who Made Millions Stealing Priceless Maps*; Gotham Books: New York, 2014; 210.

37. Man charged in rare book theft. Am. Libr. **2005**, *36* (10), 28–29.

38. Multnomah thief banned. Am. Libr. **2005**, *36* (8), 25.

39. Minutes of the First Stated Meeting of the Library Department Faculty, Oct 2, 2013, p. 1.

40. Shuman, B.A. *Borrowing privileges*. Case Studies in Library Security, Libraries Unlimited: Westport, CT, 2002; 21–29.

41. Gay book slasher sentenced. Am. Libr. **2002**, *33*(10).

42. Shuman, B.A. *Library Security and Safety Handbook: Prevention, Policies, and Procedures*; American Library Association: Chicago, IL, 1999.

43. Rowdy teens blamed in blackout free-for-all. Am. Libr. **1998**, *29* (5), 23–25.

44. Krist, C. Rape of teenager raises security issues. Am. Libr. **1996**, *27*, 15–16.

45. Gunman kills two at mormon library. Am. Libr. **1999**, *30* (6), 28.

46. Shuman, Library Security and Safety Handbook. 70.

47. Bomb threat evacuates Brigham Young University. Am. Libr. **1999**, *30* (9), 25.

48. Library security threats follow Virginia tech shootings. Am. Libr. **2007**, *38*(6).

49. Fox, R. Vandals at the gates. OCLC Syst. Serv. **2006**, *22* (4), 249–255.

50. Conversation with Jean Ashton, Aug 2, 1995.

51. Sullivan, J. Dutch arrest man in theft at Columbia. *The New York Times* Jun 17, 1995; *17*.

52. McDade, *The Book Thief*, pp. 147–148.

53. Sullivan, J. Dutch arrest man in theft at Columbia. *The New York Times*, Jun 17, 1995; 17.

54. Fax from R.J. Kalafus, Nov 12, 1997.

55. Weiser, B. *The New York Times*; Apr 25, 1998; 3.

56. Ashton, J. Picking up the pieces: The lengthy saga of a library theft. In *The Strategic Stewardship of Cultural Resources: To Preserve and Protect*; Merrill, A.T., Ed.; The Haworth Press: New York, 2003; 94.

57. McDade, *The Book Thief*, p. 176.

58. Telephone Conversation with Al Overbaugh; Public Relations Office, Federal Court: Des Moines, IA, Feb 21, 1996.

59. Shhhh. Quiet thieves stealing book treasures from libraries. The Orlando Sentinel, Knight-Ridder Newspapers, Sept 10, 1995.

60. Return of Rare Books May Face Lengthy Delay. United Press International, Mar 27, 1990.

61. Steve Huntsberry, J. Forged identification: A key to library archives. Libr. Arch. Secur. **1989**, *9* (3–4), 69–74.

62. Book thief convicted. College and Research Libraries News, Apr 1991; 234.

63. Shuman *Library Security and Safety Handbook*, 43.

64. Library Thieves Take All but the Covers. *The New York Times*, Apr 7, 1992; A18.

65. Larson, R., Library of Congress upgrades probe of thefts, mutilations. *The Washington Times*, Aug 18, 1995; Gleick, E. An embattled library of congress copes with a whistle blower's account of lost and mutilated books. *Time*, Sept 25, 1995.

66. Eilperin, J. Inspectors fault library management structure. Roll Call, Nov 30, 1995.

67. Murder in Russia raises concern. *The Dayton Daily News*, Sept 29, 1995.

68. Defense Lawyer Found Slain in His Apartment. The Record; Bergen Record Corp., Sept 29, 1995.

69. Notorious Lawyer's Solicitor Murdered in St. Petersburg, The Russian Information Agency ITAR-TASS, Sept 27, 1995.

70. Taylor, W.T. Chapter 3: Looting Texas Libraries. In *Texfake: An Account of the Theft and Forgery of Early Texas Printed Documents*; W. Thomas Taylor: Austin, TX, 1991; 30–31.

71. Oberlin Conference on Theft Calls for Action. Libr. J. **Nov 15, 1983**, *108* (20), 2118.

72. Telephone conversation with Ronald Lieberman, former chair of the Security of ABAA, Apr 3, 1992.

73. Ex-staffer suspected in theft of major library treasures. A. Libr. **Apr 1987**, *18*, 242.

74. Scandal at University of Georgia over theft of rare items. Libr. J. **Apr 1, 1987**, *112*, 15.

75. Ex-staffer suspected in theft of major library treasures, p. 242.

76. Dunlap, E.S. Draft of Remarks. SAA Annual Meeting, Philadelphia, PA, 1991, Panel on insider theft (with Bob Bazin and Dan Traister),1–2.

77. Dunlap, E.S. Administrative Concerns. In *Forged Documents*, Proceedings of the 1989 Houston Conference; Bozeman, Pat1990. Oak Knoll Books: New Castle, Delaware, 26–28.

78. Miller, E.S.Driver Gets Probation, $50,000 fine, Community Service.

79. Telephone conversation with Katherine Keyes Leab formerly of BAMBAM, February 28, 1992.

80. Telephone conversation with Mimi Bowling, Manuscripts Librarian of the New York Public Library, Rare Books and Manuscripts Department, Mar 17, 1992.

81. Telephone conversation with Mimi Bowling, Manuscripts Librarian of the New York Public Library, Rare Books and Manuscripts Department, March 17, 1992.

82. Marking Paper Manuscripts. National Preservation Program Publication, Library of Congress, Preservation Leaflet No. 4, p. 2.

83. Korey, M.E. *The Oberlin Conference on Theft*; Schreyer, A., Ed.; Rare Books, 1983–1984; 132.

84. Telephone conversation with Katherine Keyes Leab formerly of BAMBAM, May 28, 1992.

85. Telephone conversation with Ronald Lieberman, former chair of the Security of ABAA, Apr 3, 1992. Lieberman, R. Security Concerns for Archival Collections. AB Bookman's Weekly Oct 14, 1991, *88* (16), 1440.

86. Lieberman, R. Security concerns for archival collections. *AB Bookman's Weekly*, 88, No. 16 (October 14, 1991). p. 1440.

87. Telephone conversation with Ronald Lieberman, former chair of the Security of ABAA, April 3, 1992.

88. Allen, p. 943.

89. Telephone conversation with Katherine Keyes Leab formerly of BAMBAM, February 28, 1992.

90. Welch, pp. 19–20, Parker, P.J. Statutory protection of library materials. Libr. Trends **Summer 1984**, *33*, 77–85.

91. Shuman, *Library Security and Safety Handbook*, 21–62.

92. McDade, T. *The Thieves of Book Row: New York's Most Notorious Rare Book Ring and the Man Who Stopped It*; Oxford University Press: New York, 2013; 47.

93. Shuman, *Library Security and Safety Handbook*, 21.

94. Bahr, pp. 33–35.

95. Greve, F. Culture vultures: Valuable books. illustrations looted from libraries to feed black market, The Denver Post, Knight-Ridder News Service, Aug 30, 1995.

96. Technology observations from the big easy.

97. Bahr, pp. 105–106.

98. Cadwallader, B. No jail for book thief. Dispatch Courts Reporter, The Columbus Dispatch, Aug 1, 1995.

99. Winter, C. Libraries call out the police to make patrons pay notice. Chicago Tribune, Sept 13, 1995.

100. Korey, M.E. *The Oberlin Conference on Theft*; Schreyer, A., Ed.; Rare Books, 1983–1984, 130.

101. Korey, p. 129.

102. Enscoe, D. *Archivists: We're Our Own Worst Enemy*. United Press International, Sept 26, 1991, *26*.

103. Walch, T. *Archives and Manuscripts: Security*; Society of American Archivists: Chicago, IL, 1977.

104. RBMS Security Committee, Guidelines regarding thefts in libraries. College Res. Libr. News **Mar 1988**, *49* (3), 159–162.

105. Jenkins, J.H. Guidelines for the security of rare book, manuscript, and other special collections. In *Rare Books and Manuscript Thefts: A Security System for Librarians, Booksellers, and Collectors*; Antiquarian Booksellers Association of American: New York, 1982; 12–16; ACRL guidelines for the security of rare book, manuscript, and other special collections. College Res. Libr. News **Mar 1990**, *51* (3), 240–244, ALA Standards Committee at the 1990 Annual Conference, Jun 1990.

106. Jenkins, J.H. Guidelines for the security of rare book, manuscript, and other special collections. *Rare Books and Manuscript Thefts: A Security System for Librarians, Booksellers, and Collectors*; Antiquarian Booksellers Association of American: New York, 1982; 5–11.

107. Lincoln, A.J. *Crime in the Library: A Study of Patterns, Impact and Security*; R.R. Bowker Company: New York, 1984; 132–154.

BIBLIOGRAPHY

1. ACRL offers assistance to FBI in rare book recovery ($20 million recovered in Iowa raid). College Res. Libr. News **May 1990**, *5*, 408.

2. Allen, S.M. Book thief convicted (he had pleaded insanity). College Res. Libr. News **Apr 1991**, *4*, 234.

3. Allen, S.M. The Blumberg Case: A Costly Lesson for Librarians Presented at the Rare Books and Manuscripts Preconference in Chapel Hill, North Carolina. *AB Bookmans Weekly* Sept 2, 1991, *88*, 769–773.

4. Allen, S.M. Theft in libraries or archives. College Res. Libr. News **Nov 1991**, *51* (10), 939–943.

5. Alley, B. The high cost of locking barn doors (microcomputer security devices). Technicalities **Sept 1987**, *7*, 1.

6. Almagro, B.R. The curse-a-book security system. Libr. Arch. Secur. **Fall–Winter 1987**, *7*, 49–53.

7. Arndt, D.A. Jr. Problem patrons and library security. *Emerging Solutions in Reference Services: Implications for Libraries in the New Millennium*; Edwards, J.D., Ed.; The Haworth Information Press: New York, 2001; 19–40.

8. Ashe, M. Collection management: A delicate balance (security concerns; report of a session at the 1991 ARLIS/NA conference. Art Doc. **Summer 1987**, *10*, 79–81.

9. Bahr, A.H. *Book Theft and Library Security Systems, 1978–79*; Knowledge Industry Publications: White Plains, NY, 1978.

10. Bahr, A.H. The thief in our midst (internal theft). Libr. Arch. Secur. **1989**, *9* (3–4), 77–81.

11. Basbanes, N.A. *A Gentle Madness: Bibliophiles, Bibliomanes, and the Eternal Passion for Books*; Henry Holt and Company: New York, 1995.

12. Battles, M. *Library: An Unquiet History*; W.W. Norton & Company: New York, 2003.

13. Berger, S.H. What is so rare…: issues in rare book librarianship. Libr. Trends. **Summer 1987**, *30*(1).

14. Blanding, M. *The Map Thief: The Gripping Story of an Esteemed Rare-Map Dealer Who Made Millions Stealing Priceless Maps*; Gotham Books: New York, 2014.

15. Bomb threat evacuates Brigham Young University. Am. Libr. **1999**, *30* (9), 25.

16. Bozeman, P.; *Forged Documents: Proceedings of the 1989 Houston Conference*; Oak Knoll Books: New Castle, Delaware, 1990.

17. Bradsher, J.G. *Managing Archives and Archival Institutions*; University of Chicago Press: Chicago, IL, 1989.

18. Burnett, C. Analysis of inventory losses from long beach public library. Libr. Arch. Secur. *10*(1).

19. Burnham, B. Cultural vultures. Saturday Review, Sept 1, 1979; 36–37.

20. Brand, M. *Security for Libraries: People, Buildings, Collections*; American Library Association: Chicago, IL, 1984.

21. Cadwallader, B. No jail for book thief. Dispatch Courts Reporter, The Columbus Dispatch, Aug 1, 1995.

22. Campbell, B.R. Rare Government Documents: Identification and Protection (1988 ALA Conference Session). *Conservation Administration News*, Jul 1990, *42*, 10–11.

23. Cocks, Fraser *Old Oregon*; Summer 1991; 12–16.

24. Cole, A.C. The FBI's national stolen art file. FBI Law Enforc. Bull. May 1989.

25. Deadline for book return (October 18, 1991 is deadline for filing claims for materials stolen by stephen blumberg and confiscated by the FBI). Libr. J. **Sept 15, 1991**, *116*, 25.

26. Defense lawyer found slain in his apartment. The Record; Bergen Record Corp, Sept 29, 1995.

27. Enscoe, D. Archivists: We're our own worst enemy. United Press International, Sept 26, 1991.

28. Eilperin, J. Inspectors fault library management structure. Roll Call, Nov 30, 1995.

29. Ex-staffer suspected in theft of major library treasures. Am. Libr. **Apr 1987**, *18*, 242.

30. Former University of Georgia librarian convicted on theft charge. Libr. J. **Oct 15, 1988**, *113*, 18.

31. Fox, R. Vandals at the gates. OCLC Syst. Serv. **2006**, *22* (4), 249–255.

32. Gandert, S.R. Protecting your collection: A handbook survey and guide for the security of rare books, manuscripts, archives and works of art. Libr. Arch. Secur. **1982**, *4*(1–2).

33. Gaughan, T.M. 15-year jail sentence for georgia rare book thief. Am. Libr. **Nov 1988**, *19*, 840.

34. Gaughan, T.M. Cache of stolen rare books said to number some 30,000 (found March 20 in an Ottumwa, Iowa, House). Am. Libr. **May 1990**, *21*, 231.

35. Gaughan, T.M. Insanity plea fails; book thief convicted in Iowa. Am. Libr. **Mar 1991**, *22*, 198.

36. Gaughan, T.M. Oscar nominee-book thief pleads no contest (to possession of stolen property). Am. Libr. **Jan 1989**, *20*, 7–8.

37. Gatewood, D. Technology bound to keep books where they belong. Newsday, Jan 20, 1992.

38. Gay book slasher sentenced. Am. Libr. **2002**, *33*(10).

39. Gleick, E. An embattled library of congress copes with a whistle blower's account of lost and mutilated books. *Time* Sept 25, 1995, *25*.

40. Greve, F. Culture vultures valuable books, illustrations looted from libraries to feed black market. The Denver Post, Knight-Ridder News Service, Aug 30, 1995.

41. Gunman kills two at mormon library. Am. Libr., **1999**, *30* (6), 28.

42. Gurnsey wartime documents vanish. *The Times*, Dec 19, 1991.

43. Hanson, C.Z. Electronic security has put a spotlight on theft. Libr. Arch. Secur. **1989**, *9* (3–4), 63–68.

44. Harvey, M. *The Island of Lost Maps: A True Story of Cartographic Crime*; Random House: New York, 2000.

45. Huntsberry, J.S. Forged identification: A key to library archives. Libr. Arch. Secur. **1989**, *9* (3–4), 69–74.

46. Janjigian, A.S. Intrusion detection systems for residence, libraries, small museums, and art galleries. *Museum, Archive, and Library Security*; Fennelly, L.J., Ed.; Butterworths: Boston, MA, 1983.

47. Jenkins, J.H. *Rare Books and Manuscript Thefts: A Security System for Librarians, Booksellers, and Collectors*; Antiquarian Booksellers Association of American: New York, 1982.

48. Korey, M.E. *The Oberlin Conference on Theft*; Schreyer, A., Ed.; 1983–1984.

49. Krist, C. Rape of teenager raises security issues. Am. Libr. **1996**, *27*, 5–16.

50. Larson, R. Library of Congress Upgrades probe of thefts, mutilations. *The Washington Times*, Aug 18, 1995.

51. Leab, K.K.; Leab D.J. BAMBAM update (current as of March 1987. Libr. Arch. Secur., **Summer 1987**, *7* (2), 59–130.

52. Leab, K.K.; Leab, D.J. BAMBAM update, current as of July 1984. Libr. Arch. Secur. **Summer 1984**, *16* (4), 67–107.

53. Leab, K.K. *Bookline Alert: Missing Books and Manuscripts*; American Books Prices Current: New York, 1982.

54. Librarian charged in theft (Boston college library). AB Bookmans Weekly **Nov 3, 1986**, *78*, 746–747.

55. Library thief found guilty: Case proves library security network effective in tracing stolen books. Libr. J. **Mar 1, 1991**, *116*, 19.

56. Library thief sentenced (convicted of stealing rare books and other items. Am. Libr. **Oct 1991**, *22*, 839.

57. Library thieves take all but the covers. *The New York Times*, Apr 7, 1992.

58. Lieberman, R. Security concerns for archival collections. AB Bookman's Weekly **Oct 14, 1991**, *88* (16), 1440–1444.

59. Lincoln, A.J. Library legislation related to crime and security (excerpts from the codes of ten states). Libr. Arch. Secur. **1990**, *10* (2), 77–101.

60. Lincoln, A.J. *Crime in the Library: A Study of Patterns, Impact and Security*; R.R. Bowker Company: New York, 1984.

61. Lincoln, A.J. Protecting the library. Libr. Trends, **Summer 1984**, *33*.

62. Lincoln, A.J.; Lincoln, C.Z. Library crime and security. Libr. Arch. Secur. **Spring–Summer 1986**, *8*.

63. Man arrested as suspect in thefts of rare materials. College Res. Libr. News **Jun 1988**, *6*, 358.

64. Man charged in rare book theft. Am. Libr. **2005**, *36* (10), 28–29.

65. Manges, G.L. Security of rare book, manuscripts and special collections. PNLA Q. **Winter 1989**, *53*, 18.

66. Map dealer now admits library theft. Am. Libr. **2006**, *36* (8), 18.

67. Map thief gets three-and-a-half years. Am. Libr. **2006**, *37* (10), 12.

68. Marking Paper Manuscripts. National Preservation Program Publication, Library of Congress, Preservation Leaflet No. 4 (Mar 1983).

69. McDade, T. *Thieves of Book Row: New York's Most Notorious Rare Book Ring and the Man Who Stopped It*; Oxford University Press: New York, 2013.

70. McDade, T. *The Book Thief: The True Crimes of Daniel Spiegelman*; Praeger: Westport, CT, 2006.

71. Merrill, A.T. *The Strategic Stewardship of Cultural Resources: To Preserve and Protect*; The Haworth Press: New York, 2003.

72. Miller, M. Driver gets probation, $50,000 fine, community service. Hartford Courant, Oct 16, 1991; 6.

73. Moon, M.J. Library security: Protecting the investment. Colo. Libr. (Special issue) **Sept 1985**, *11*, 6–17.

74. Multnomah thief banned. Am. Libr. **2005**, *36* (8), 25.

75. Murder In Russia Raises Concern. The Dayton Daily News, Sept 29, 1995.

76. National Centre for Library and Archive Security National preservation office extending its role. State Libr. **Nov 1988**, *36*, 36.

77. Notorious Lawyer's Solicitor Murdered in St. Petersburg. The Russian Information Agency ITAR-TASS (Sept 27, 1995).

78. Oberlin conference on theft calls for action. Libr. J. **Nov 15, 1983**, *108* (20), 2118.

79. OCLC helps the fbi track stolen books; retrospective conversion staffers and 40 librarians help fbi find rightful

Technical–Topic

owners of 30,000 rare books. Libr. J. **Oct 15, 1990**, *115*, 30.

80. Ocmulgee director sentenced. Am. Libr. **Sept 2006**, *37* (8), 22–23.

81. Oscar nominee-book thief pleads no contest. Am. Libr. Jan 1989; 7–8.

82. Otness, H.M. "Going Plating": Stealing maps from libraries. Inform. Bull. Presented at WAML Spring Meeting, Pasadena, CA, **1987**, *19*, 206–210.

83. Pearson, L.R. And the winner is not … police seek oscar nominee over library cache in locker. Am. Libr. **May 1988**, *19*, 333–334.

84. Pinzelik, B.P. Monitoring book losses in an academic library. Libr. Arch. Secur. **Winter 1984**, *6*, 1–12.

85. Bahr, A.H. *Book Theft and Library Security Systems, 1978–79*; Knowledge Industry Publications: White Plains, NY, 1978; 34–35.

86. Police seek oscar nominee over library cache in locker. Am. Libr. May 1988; 333–336.

87. RBMS Ad Hoc Committee for Developing Transfer Guidelines, Guidelines on the selection of general collection materials for transfer to special collections. College Res. Libr. News **Jul/Aug 1958**, *46* (7), 349–352.

88. RBMS Ethical Standards Review Committee, Standards for ethical conduct for rare book, manuscript, and special collections librarians. College Res. Libr. News **Dec 1991**, *52* (11), 721–729.

89. RBMS Security Committee. ACRL guidelines for the security of rare book, manuscript, and other special collections. College Res. Libr. News **Mar 1990**, *51* (3), 240–244.

90. RBMS Security Committee, Guidelines regarding thefts in libraries. College Res. Libr. News **Mar 1988**, *49* (3), 159–162.

91. Rare items missing from UGA libraries. The Georgia Librarian **Feb 1978**, *24*, 5.

92. Reducing theft, mutilation, and defacement of library materials. Conservation Administration News **Apr 1984**, *17*, 1–4.

93. Return of rare books may face lengthy delay. United Press International 1990, BC Cycle (Mar 27, 1990).

94. Rowdy teens blamed in blackout free-for-all. Am. Libr. **1998**, *29* (5), 23–25.

95. SAA code of ethics for archivists. Am. Arch. **Summer 1980**, *43* (3), 414–418.

96. Sable, M.H. *The Protection of the Library and Archive: An International Bibliography*; The Haworth Press: New York, 1984.

97. Samuelson, T.; Laura, S.; Catherine, C. Unusual suspects: The case of insider theft in research libraries and special collections. College Res. Libr. News, **Nov 2012**, *3* (6), 556–568.

98. Scandal at University of Georgia over theft of rare items. Libr. J. **Apr 1, 1987**, *112*, 15.

99. Shhhh: Quiet thieves stealing book treasures from libraries. The Orlando Sentinel, Knight-Ridder Newspapers, Sept 10, 1988.

100. Shuman, B.A. *Case Studies in Library Security*; Libraries Unlimited: Westport, CT, 2002.

101. Shuman, B.A. *Library Security and Safety Handbook: Prevention, Policies, and Procedures*; American Library Association: Chicago, IL, 1999.

102. Smith, F.E. Questionable strategies in library security studies. Libr. Arch. Secur. **Winter 1988**, *6*, 43–53.

103. Stolen and strayed. IFAR Rep. **Sept 1988**, *9*(9).

104. Sullivan, J. Dutch arrest man in theft at Columbia. *The New York Times*, Jun 17, 1995, 23.

105. Switzer, T.R. *Safe at Work? Library Security and Safety Issues*; The Scarecrow Press, Inc.: Lanham, MD, 1999.

106. Taylor, W. *Thomas. Texfake: An Account of the Theft and Forgery of Early Texas Printed Documents*; W. Thomas Taylor: Austin, TX, 1991.

107. Holt, G.E. Theft by library staff. Bottom Line **2007**, *20* (2), 85–93.

108. Towner, L.W. An end to innocence (the rise of thefts in libraries). Am. Libr. **March 1988**, *19*, 210–213.

109. Treadwell, J. Determining a fair price for lost books: A case study. Libr. Arch. Secur. **1989**, *9*(1).

110. Trinkaus-Randall, G. Preserving special collections through internal security. Coll. Res. Libr. **July 1989**, *50*, 448–454.

111. Two get prison in Wisconsin in historical society thefts. Chicago Tribune, Jun 6, 1991.

112. Tyron, J.S. Premises liability for librarians. Libr. Arch. Secur. **Summer 1998**, *10* (2), 3–21.

113. Calvin, R. USPS, AAP try scanning to recover lost books (efforts to avoid auctioning). Publishers Weekly **Aug 17, 1990**, *237*, 10.

114. Wall, C. Inventory: What you might expect to be missing. Libr. Arch. Secur. **Summer 1998**, *7*, 27–31.

115. Walch, T. Archives and Manuscripts: Security; Society of American Archivists: Chicago, IL, 1977.

116. Weiser, B. Sentence by judge reflects historic documents' value. *The New York Times*; Apr. 25, 1998; 3.

117. Weissman, D. Treasures of New Jersey history are missing from state's archives. The Star-Ledger, Dec 7, 1987.

118. Winter, C. Libraries call out the police to make patrons pay notice. Chicago Tribune, Sept 9, 1991.

119. Yanez, L. Court searches for missing morrison papers; bail bond sheet sold at auction. Fort Lauderdale News & Sun-Sentinel, Dec 9, 1991.

Theft, Vandalism, and Security in Museums

Jes Koepfler
Ivan Tanzer
Stephanie Nemcsok
Jennifer Ng
Catherine Leekam
Angela Noseworthy
Jennifer Bawden
Museum Studies Program, Faculty of Information Studies, University of Toronto, Toronto, Ontario, Canada

Abstract

Theft and vandalism are two criminal acts that occur within museums and other cultural heritage institutions. This entry provides a historical context for art theft with an international scope, and highlights such famous examples as the thefts of the *Mona Lisa*, two versions of *The Scream*, and multiple masterworks stolen from the Isabella Stewart Gardner Museum in Boston, Massachusetts. Next, the complex definitions of vandalism, citing case study examples of Mary Richardson's attack on the *Rokeby Venus*, and Yuan Chai's and Jian Jun Xi's actions on Tracey Emin's work, *My Bed*. Finally, a discussion of museum responses to incidences such as these highlights the preventative measures and security devices that cultural heritage institutions employ to deter potential wrong-doers and protect the objects they hold in the public trust.

INTRODUCTION

As public institutions, museums, art galleries, and historic sites are professionally and ethically bound to protect and conserve their collections from all forms of deterioration, damage, and loss. The theft or destruction of any artwork or artifact is a collective loss for society, and as caretakers of these material goods, museums have an essential role to prevent these crimes from occurring. The International Council of Museums (ICOM) Code of Ethics describes the primary responsibility of museums "to protect and promote this heritage as well as the human, physical, and financial resources made available for that purpose."[1] Museum stewardship includes intrinsic notions of "rightful ownership, permanence, documentation, accessibility, and responsible disposal."[2] In short, they ideally ensure that all objects in their collections will survive for the benefit of present and future generations. Acts of theft and vandalism, therefore, pose very real threats to the proper functioning of all cultural heritage institutions.

Famous examples of theft provide a historical context for this type of crime on an international scale, and include such examples as the thefts of the *Mona Lisa* from the Musée du Louvre in Paris, France (created 1502; stolen 1911); two versions of *The Scream* from the Norwegian National Gallery and the Munch Museum in Oslo, Norway (created 1893; stolen 1994 and 2004, respectively); and multiple masterworks stolen from the Isabella Stewart Gardner Museum in Boston, Massachusetts (multiple

dates; stolen 1990). Vandalism varies more considerably in its levels of criminality, depending upon the intent of the action, and case study examples of Mary Richardson's attack on the *Rokeby Venus* (created ca. 1640s–1650s; vandalized 1914); and the instance when Yuan Chai and Jian Jun Xi jumped onto Tracey Emin's work, *My Bed* (created 1998; vandalized 1999), serve to illuminate the political and artistic motivations behind this behavior. Incidences such as these and many others have prompted museums to develop preventative measures and security devices to deter potential wrong-doers and protect the objects that they hold in the public trust. In addition, a host of international government and professional organizations designed to track stolen and affected cultural property have evolved, including the International Foundation for Art Research (IFAR) New York, International Committee on Museum Security (ICOM-ICMS) Paris, the Federal Bureau of Investigation (FBI) Art Crime Team Washington, the Metropolitan Police Arts and Antiques Unit London, the Interpol Art Theft Division Lyon, and others.

THEFT

Definitions of Theft

A variety of definitions are associated with theft, including moral, legal, and popularized types. In a moral sense, theft

Encyclopedia of Library and Information Sciences, Fourth Edition DOI: 10.1081/E-ELIS4-120044736

is defined as the act of stealing; the unlawful or wrongful taking of property with intent to deprive the owner of his or her possession.[3]

In a literal, legal sense the Criminal Code of Canada states that "An act of theft is committed by taking or converting anything, whether animate or inanimate, with intent to deprive, temporarily or absolutely, the owner of it, or a person who has a special property or interest in it. This also includes transformations to anything in such a manner that it cannot be restored in the condition in which it was at the time it was taken or converted."[4]

The U.S. Criminal Code specifically articulates a definition of theft in the context of museums: "Theft of a major artwork" refers to a person who

> steals or obtains by fraud from the care, custody, or control of a museum any object of cultural heritage; or knowing that an object of cultural heritage has been stolen or obtained by fraud, if in fact the object was stolen or obtained from the care, custody, or control of a museum (whether or not that fact is known to the person), receives, conceals, exhibits, or disposes of the object.[5]

In this description, theft is distinguished from acts of vandalism and forgery. Theft is usually intentional, with the criminal's intent to take an object for trade, bargaining, or selling outright. The most common motive for theft from museums and cultural heritage institutions is financial gain. Whether sold illegally on the black-market, or used as ransom or leverage, art theft is a $6 billion industry.[6]

A Brief History of Theft in Museums

The history of art is laden with examples of objects changing hands under questionable circumstances. Issues such as wartime looting and the many problematic examples of repatriation are but two of a vast list of potential starting points for the study of such crimes; these particular issues are addressed in other entry (see entry on "Art Looting and Trafficking," p. 272 for more information). A brief historical introduction here provides information on two key individuals inextricably linked with the history of art crime.

Adam Worth (1844–1902) is known as "the Napoleon of the criminal world."[7] He is most famously remembered for stealing a portrait of the Duchess of Devonshire by Thomas Gainsborough from the Thomas Agnew & Sons gallery in London, England (created 1787; stolen 1876). With the help of his accomplices, Worth stole the painting, which at the time had been sold at auction for 10,000 guineas, and was then the most expensive work of art in the world. Worth held onto the painting until just before his death in 1902, when he was forced to relinquish it due to financial reasons.[8]

Author Simon Houpt frames Joseph Duveen (1869–1939) as a master opportunist, and one of the most successful art dealers of all time. Duveen, who is best known

for saying that "Europe has a great deal of art, and America has a great deal of money," was a British-born entrepreneur who made his fortune by purchasing the collections of failing European aristocrats and facilitating their reselling to American industrialists seeking a means of class distinction. Although his methods were sometimes described as unscrupulous, Duveen nonetheless contributed greatly to the development of North American collections as well as the museum system in England, funding wings at both the Tate and National galleries.[9]

Famous Cases of Theft in Museums

Although art crimes continue to occur at an alarming rate around the world, there are certain examples which illustrate the unfortunate history of events that mark the past. Three of the most recognizable instances of theft occurred in Paris, Oslo, and Boston in 1911, 1994/2004, and 1990, respectively. The thefts of the *Mona Lisa*, two versions of *The Scream*, and the masterworks stolen from the Isabella Stewart Gardner Museum, constitute ample illustrations for a succinct study of art theft from the last century.

The *Mona Lisa* was stolen from the Musée du Louvre in August 1911 by Vincenzo Peruggia, an employee of the museum. Peruggia, a carpenter by trade, had been hired to install protective glass cases around certain works, including the *Mona Lisa*, as a result of recent attacks by vandals to the museum. Peruggia removed the painting from its wall hanging after quietly emerging from a storage closet that he had hidden in overnight. He then proceeded to separate the work from its frame in a stairwell, placed the painting inside his coat, and walked out of the museum, which was closed that day. Peruggia kept the work in his apartment in Paris for 2 years, but was caught by police when he tried to sell it to the Uffizi in Florence, for the price of 500,000 lira. He was eventually convicted in court and served a sentence of 7 months and 9.[10]

As a result of its disappearance, the *Mona Lisa* gained immense popularity and is recognized worldwide. Darian Leader, an author and psychoanalyst, postulated that Leonardo da Vinci's *Mona Lisa* really only became famous after it was stolen. In his publication, *Stealing the Mona Lisa: What Art Stops Us from Seeing*, Leader states that "in the ensuing months [after the theft] composers wrote tunes about the Mona Lisa and its subject's beauty; editorial cartoonists mocked police efforts to find her. …."[11] Peruggia's motives for the theft are not wholly clear, however during his trial he claimed that he had acted as a patriot, endeavoring to return an important piece of cultural property to its native Italy.[12] His efforts to sell the *Mona Lisa* suggest that monetary gain was a motivating factor in the theft. Another theory proposes that Peruggia had been hired by Eduardo de Valfierno, an Argentine con man, to steal the work, and that Valfierno had planned to make forgeries of the artwork and sell them across the globe to buyers who thought that they were acquiring the authentic *Mona Lisa*.[13]

In a second, equally brazen theft, four men broke into the Norwegian National Gallery on February 12, 1994, and stole one of Edvard Munch's iconic versions of *The Scream* (1893), leaving behind a card upon which was written "thanks for the poor security."[14] Prior to its theft, the painting had been moved to the ground floor of the gallery as part of the festivities surrounding the XVII Olympic Winter Games in Lillehammer (1994). Following a coordinated sting operation orchestrated by the J. Paul Getty Museum (Los Angeles, California) and the Metropolitan Police (Scotland Yard, London, England), the painting was recovered without significant damage on May 7 of the same year. Ten years later a second version of *The Scream*, as well as a *Madonna* also painted by Munch, was stolen from the Munch Museum on August 22, 2004, by masked gunmen. The City Government of Oslo offered a reward of 2 million kroner (approximately $368,000) for the recovery of the painting, and, after a lengthy search, it was recovered on August 31, 2006. Of six original suspects, three were eventually convicted for the crime. Police disclosed no details surrounding the recovery operation, but both paintings are undergoing conservation for damage they suffered while out of the museum's care. Further to these restoration activities, the museum itself closed its doors for a period of 10 mo, during which time it underwent a $5 million security overhaul, and upon reopening was dubbed by Norwegian journalists, "Fortress Munch."[15]

A third example of a significant theft occurred at the Isabella Stewart Gardner Museum on March 18, 1990, and remains to this day the largest art theft committed in the United States in terms of value and number of works stolen. Disguised as Boston police officers, thieves entered the museum and stole 13 works by such distinguished artists as Johannes Vermeer, Rembrandt Harmenszoon van Rijn, Éduoard Manet, and Edgar Degas along with French and Chinese artifacts. The significance of this crime lies not only in the number of works stolen, but also in their collective worth, which is estimated at upwards of $500 million.[16]

To this day the case remains unsolved. Due to the strict stipulations outlined in Isabella Gardner's will, the collection must remain on display permanently, forcing the museum to exhibit the empty frames of the stolen paintings in their original locations. A $5 million reward for information or assistance in solving the crime has attracted numerous investigators and art theft institutions, however none have been able to successfully track down even one of the stolen works.[17] Harold J. Smith, an iconic private art investigator, is immortalized in Rebecca Dreyfus' documentary of 2005, *Stolen*, which examines the theft at the Gardner and provides insight into the workings of art crime and the people and organizations that combat its continual spread. Until his death in 2005, Smith made cracking the Gardner theft his top priority.

Museum Responses to Theft

In the past, cases of theft have depended on the efforts of police officers and specialist art hunters, who have pursued museum objects as they would other types of stolen goods. In part, the search for these objects has been successful, because of the difficulties inherent in the disposal of well-known artifacts for criminals. It is challenging to sell recognized pieces on the open market unless a buyer is already arranged, since the fame of the object alone provokes a great deal of attention from members of the general public and the antiquities market, as well as legal authorities. For these reasons FBI Special Agent Robert Wittman noted that "the real art in art theft is not stealing, but selling."[18]

There are a number of databases and search engines on the Internet today dedicated to tracking and locating stolen material. They allow for the systematic cataloging and access of stolen materials from around the world. The purpose of these types of research tools is to allow for the identification of stolen items before a purchase is made by an institution or individual, and also increase intelligence on illicit trade and sale. The Art Loss Register is the world's largest private online database of lost and stolen art, antiquities, and collectibles, listing approximately 170,000 items in 2006. It was created in London in 1991 as a result of the need for stakeholders in businesses, insurance companies, and associated art industries to minimize and deter art crimes, as well as facilitate the recovery of lost or stolen works.[19] Many countries have created comparable databases; one American example is the National Stolen Art File used by the FBI Art Crime Team.[20] Other organizations, such as the Association for Research into Crimes against Art (ARCA) and IFAR, have focused on the study of the motivations behind vandalism, theft, and even forgery, acting as consultants on protection and recovery issues.[21,22] In addition to databases and think tanks, international police forces and investigation teams have made significant progress in deterring, recovering, and solving crimes by collaborating over a vast and complicated worldwide network of agencies. The three most established forces are those of the FBI Art Crime Team, the Metropolitan Police Art and Antiques Unit, and the Interpol Art Theft Division, which facilitate the sharing of information among different police departments.[23–25]

Despite the sophistication of the international art tracking network, Julian Radcliffe, the Chairman of the Art Loss Register, has argued that art theft has remained a low priority for most of the world's police forces and governments.[26] It is condemned by law throughout the world in the form of National Protective Laws on art and cultural property,[27] and there is an increasing need for legitimate provenance, or history of the object, in the art and antiquities market; however few governments are willing to provide the funds or resources necessary to adequately hunt for lost art and artifacts. Italy is one of the few countries to implement a strong political policy on this issue, including funding for specialized police forces that are equipped with hundreds of personnel, who specialize in crimes against cultural property.[28] These groups include the Tutela Partimonio Culturale, which protects Italy's cultural heritage, and the Nucleo Tutela Patrimonio Artistico, which specializes in the protection of artwork and in the recovery of stolen paintings.[29]

Museums assist in counteracting weaknesses in art trade regulation and law enforcement by helping to publicize cases of theft in the media. The Art Gallery of Ontario issued news releases immediately following the theft of five ivory reliefs in 2004, which alerted the general public and art dealers to the crime, and made the pieces far more difficult to sell. The gallery also offered a $120,000 Canadian reward for the return of the ivories, and a week after the theft, they were returned through an intermediary.[30–32] The Isabella Stewart Gardner Museum has not yet recovered any of its stolen masterworks despite the $5 million reward, but on the 15th anniversary of the theft, the museum issued a press release pleading for the proper maintenance of the works.[33]

Unfortunately, some institutions have been tempted to minimize the situation in order to avoid negative publicity. One particularly dangerous and costly habit is the payment of ransom to thieves in return for stolen material. The Tate gallery in London, England, won back two J.M.W. Turner paintings that were stolen while on loan to the Schirn gallery in Frankfurt, Germany, in 1994 after paying over £6 million in ransom over many years. The J. Paul Getty Museum was also instrumental in the reclamation of Munch's *The Scream* in 1994 (mentioned earlier), on behalf of the Norwegian government.[34] Responses like these may lead to the successful recovery of a prized artwork, but few organizations have the funds necessary for successful ransom payment, and there is concern that compliance with ransom demands may perpetuate the problem.

VANDALISM

Definitions of Vandalism

Unlike the more straightforward examples of theft, there is no singular, shared definition of vandalism within and among law, academia, and cultural heritage institutions. The disparity centers on questions of motivation and purpose, since "not all destruction is perceived as deliberate, but an event can be considered intentional or unintentional according to one's conception of nature or agency, and according to one's specific intentions in speaking of the damage."[35,36] Due to its sometimes ambiguous nature, few criminal codes even mention vandalism. The Criminal Code of Canada Section 430 refers to vandalism instead as "mischief" and describes it as willful destruction or damage of property that hinders the use, enjoyment, or

operation of the property for others.[37] In the United States, the FBI Art Crime Team in Washington, DC, defines vandalism as an act with the intent "to willfully or maliciously destroy, injure, disfigure, or deface any public or private property, real or personal, without the consent of the owner or person having custody or control by cutting, tearing, breaking, marking, painting, drawing, covering with filth, or any other such means as may be specified by local law."[38] There are many other identified forms of vandalism, including burning, melting down, and decapitation, dismemberment, burying, and others.[39] The tools vandals use to commit their crimes range from paint, lipstick, nail files, and gum to more violent devices, such as knives and acid.[40]

Most of the academic definitions of vandalism come from the field of psychology. In *The Psychology of Vandalism*, Arnold P. Goldstein summarizes various definitions for vandalism and points out that they "collectively highlighted intentionality, destructiveness, and property ownership as the central features...of vandalism...[It] is an intentional act of destruction or defacement of property not one's own."[41] Many scholars have also proposed typologies and theories to explain vandalism and motivations for the act. Three theories in particular are most relevant to the discussion of vandalism in museums: Czikszenmihalyi and Larsen's "Enjoyment Theory," which suggests that vandalism happens when intrinsic rewards from acts of destruction overpower the punitive effects of its consequences; Allen and Greenberger's "Aesthetic Theory," which proposes that an interest in the appearance of an object after being vandalized could be an eliciting stimuli for vandalism; and Fisher and Baron's "Equity-Control Theory," which offers that vandalistic behavior is a means to correct situations perceived to be wrong.[42]

As art critic Michael Kimmelman noted, "it's tempting to look for a grand, unified theory of vandalism, but the specific motivations of the people who attack art are...as diverse as the objects they choose to hurt. More often it's not pranksters who slash art but self-promoters with a supposed cause."[43] It is, however, useful to have certain parameters to qualify cases of vandalism as art or crime, especially when debates between the two remain inconclusive and the boundaries between art and crime continue to blur.

A Brief History of Vandalism in Museums

The origin of the word vandalism comes from the Vandals, a Germanic tribe that invaded Western Europe in the fourth and fifth centuries A.D. Destroying Roman buildings and cultural artifacts, their actions were described as "barbaric ignorance, [with a] lack of taste and sensibility."[44,45] The association of their actions with art and culture ties the original meaning of "vandal" to the destruction and damage of cultural heritage. The term vandalism was officially coined in 1794, when participants of the French Revolution destroyed art and monuments throughout the country,[46] reinforcing the historic link between culture and the political acts of vandals.

Statistics show that public property is more often the target of vandalism than private property, due to the seemingly anonymous nature of both the owner of the object and the crime itself.[47] Public sculptures are particularly vulnerable, pointed to by the theft and subsequent destruction of Henry Moore's *Reclining Figure* (created 1969–1970; vandalized 2006) from the Henry Moore Foundation in Hertfordshire, England, which was believed to have been melted down for the value of its bronze.[48] In addition, the act of publicly assigning value to works of art and reinforcing perceptions of museums as "temples of fame" contribute publicity to the perceived benefits of vandalizing cultural heritage objects.[49]

Some argue that destruction is an intrinsic aspect of culture as "the destruction of objects produces new meanings and practices, and damaged things may become more valuable than previous."[50] This phenomenon has even inspired new design aesthetics. The initial connection between vandalism and the accepted aesthetic is rooted in the Dada art movement with Marcel Duchamp and many other artists creating "non-art" in protest of society's bourgeois indulgence. Initially, the work focused on attacking imagery, such as Duchamp's work of art entitled *L.H.O.O. Q.* (1920), which involved vandalizing the cultural icon of the *Mona Lisa* with a drawn-on mustache and goatee applied to a reproduction of the famous painting.[51] While the original work itself was not vandalized, Duchamp invoked its destruction by defacing the copy. Other inspired aesthetics progressed even further including "vandalizable sculpture" and auto-destructive art, developed by William Turnbull and Gustav Metzger, respectively, in the 1960s, as well as graffiti art made famous by Robert "Banksy" Banks, selling his works for over half a million dollars in the 1980s.[52,53] Indeed, "the vandalism of the last century becomes today's tourist attraction" and institutions that argue against such forms of modern art may be interpreted as attacking "artistic innovation."[54,55] These forms of art that incorporate vandalism, as well as manifestations of performance art, challenge the status quo by forcing a duality of both condemning vandalism as a crime and inviting works of art rooted in vandalism into museum collections.

The historic role of the museum has also been in question regarding the acquisition, interpretation, and preservation of collections. When an artifact was removed from its original location, the link between the object and its ritual context changed, ultimately altering its appearance, value, and meaning, which were redefined through the representation and interpretation of that object in the institutional setting.[56] In addition, material culture conservation sought to improve upon the past by altering its relics, revealing that "not even the most painstaking renovation conformed with original work."[57] The ethics of

conservation practice have since sought less intrusive treatments that are reversible. The reality that the work of conservators is not seen as vandalism illustrates the important role that societal perceptions and intentionality play in understanding vandalism within the museum context today.

Famous Cases of Vandalism in Museums

When Mary Richardson attacked Diego Rodríguez de Silva y Velázquez' *Rokeby Venus* on March 10, 1914, at the National Gallery in London,[58] she demonstrated an instance in contemporary history of a case of vandalism that was clearly criminal. Richardson smashed the protective glass around the painting and cut the canvas seven times with a meat cleaver that she had concealed in her jacket.[59] After attacking the painting, she was arrested at the museum. Despite her political motives to support the suffragette movement,[59] Richardson's intentions in this case of ideological vandalism were to cause damage to the masterpiece. This political motivation drew attention to her specific cause through the destruction of cultural property.[60] Richardson knew that she had no rights to, or ownership of, the painting, and she was aware that slashing the canvas would destroy it completely. In her statement to the Women's Social and Political Union she wrote, "I have tried to destroy the picture of the most beautiful woman in mythological history as a protest against the Government for destroying Mrs. Pankhurst, who is the most beautiful character in modern history."[58]

Vandalism also occurs when performance artists damage artifacts or works of art in order to make an artistic statement. In these cases of aesthetic vandalism, the artists' behaviors are no less vandalistic and illegal than the previous example, but the criminality is debatable in terms of artistic discourse, considering the underlying intention to create new art. On October 24, 1999, two art students, Yuan Chai and Jian Jun Xi, jumped onto Tracey Emin's work, *My Bed*, at the Tate gallery, and named the action *Two Naked Men Jump Into Tracey's Bed*.[61] The pair was seminaked and staged a pillow fight on the bed, then attempted to drink from one of the vodka bottles on display.[62] Security guards took them away before they could finish the rest of their performance plans, including touching the bed, smelling it, and performing "critical sex," all of which they felt were necessary responses to the piece.[61,62] Chai and Xi had slogans written on their bodies in English and Chinese that they claim were statements to "make the public think about what is good art."[61] They were detained at the police station, but ultimately were not charged, in accordance with the wishes of the artist and the museum.[61,62]

As acts of vandalism are brought into public discourse, some forms, such as graffiti (mentioned earlier) eventually become recognized and legitimized as art. It was once seen as a form of "subversive public communication,"[63] but now is considered an art form from certain perspectives. In the process of creating graffiti, public property is defaced and therefore considered an illegal act of vandalism. However, the artistic quality of many graffiti paintings on buildings and moving subway cars attracted the attention of art collectors and entered the world of museums and art galleries in the form of large canvasses or pieces of paper in the late twentieth and early twenty-first centuries.[63] For instance, from June 30 to September 3, 2006, the Brooklyn Museum presented an exhibition, titled *Graffiti*, which displayed 20 large-scale graffiti paintings from multiple artists.[63] Such exhibitions blur the boundaries of graffiti's status as both a form of art and an accusable crime. Although the gallery graffiti pieces involved a change of medium from public property surfaces to canvasses or paper, the legitimization of graffiti as an art form extends from within the gallery or museum into the public sphere.

Museum Responses to Vandalism

Vandalism presents another serious threat to the ethical and professional responsibilities of museums and galleries. As with theft, the best responses are preventative measures that protect collections on display and prevent damage from occurring. Once vandalism has happened, museum responses are influenced by the severity of the damage and the value of the work that is affected.

The most passive response is no response, to the point where no legal action or claims for damages are made at all. This strategy might be explained by the belief that great publicity of a sensational crime only encourages the perpetrator and inspires other vandals, since ideological vandalism, for example, relies on publicity for the transmission of the message to a wider audience.[64] The attack on the *Rokeby Venus* was impossible to hide in this manner, since the crime and political cause was so highly contentious. The gallery was closed temporarily, but women who attempted to visit it unaccompanied were denied admission for a longer period of time. More recently in 1999, Lars Kiel Bertelsen and Klaus Christensen were not permitted access to any archive files on the case in the National Gallery, London, and the writers argue that this refusal is symptomatic of the institutional repression of such acts of vandalism, even when the act itself was impossible to repress at the time.[58]

While some museums have suppressed the effects of vandalism, others have attempted to harness the violence and chaos inherent in such acts in the name of creative expression. The Detroit Museum of New Art's (MONA) *kaBOOM!* program in 2002 is an example of a gallery show that encouraged visitors to participate in the creation and manipulation of art through its destruction. MONA announced that over the course of the exhibition, visitors would be invited "to smash, drop, throw, and slash artworks…" as an expression of the chaotic, violent

nature of modern life.[65] The show was inspired by the work of the Dadaists, which rejected the traditional standards of aesthetics and intellectualism by embracing chaos, irrationality, and surrealism in literature, theater, and the visual arts. These artists also attempted to provoke violent visitor participation, as with the 1920 *Dada Spring Awakening* show, which included a large sculpture of the Dadaist, Max Ernst, with an axe beside it, along with an invitation to smash anything in the gallery.[66] Both *kaBOOM!* and *Dada Spring Awakening* investigated the relationship between the artist and the visitor. Although the question remains as to whether permitted defacement can actually be defined as vandalism, by allowing visitors to demolish or alter works of art, these shows also transform the relationship that exists between the public and otherwise untouchable museum or gallery pieces. In this context vandalism is no longer a crime, but a positive, creative act that connects museums to their visitors.

An artifact or a work of art that has been vandalized requires some form of treatment to minimize the damage and prevent any further deterioration of the piece. Instances of smeared lipstick or smudged ink are relatively easy to treat while more serious cases, such as cuts in a canvas or cracks in a sculpture, require treatments that are more costly and time-consuming, and may even raise ethical issues for the museum because the restoration of an object automatically alters its original state. For example, Rembrandt's *Danae* (created 1636; vandalized 1985), which is held at the State Hermitage Museum in St. Petersburg, Russia, was slashed with a knife, and poured over with approximately 1 L of sulfuric acid. The attack occurred on a Saturday afternoon when the museum's director and members of the restoration department were off site. Since no immediate professional assistance was on hand, the damage to the painting was considerable. The first direct action taken to salvage the work was suggested by two professors from the St. Petersburg State Institute of Technology nearby, who arrived on the scene about an hour after the event and advised that the picture be kept upright and rinsed with water in order to minimize the destruction until the return of properly trained staff. Afterward, the work was painstakingly inspected by professional conservators, and over the next 12 years restorers at the Hermitage worked over the canvas with microscopes and specialized equipment, using a full-sized reproduction as a mapping guide. The process was extremely difficult, and the use of water has since been critiqued on the grounds that the extra liquid facilitated the spread of the acid, highlighting the many challenges museums face in responding to acts of vandalism.[67]

PREVENTION OF THEFT AND VANDALISM IN MUSEUMS

As repositories for cultural property, museums have a public responsibility not only to respond to acts of theft and vandalism appropriately, but also to protect the collections in their care. In 1974 ICOM established ICMS to publish a compilation of security recommendations, titled *Museum Security* (1977, 1993), for cultural heritage institutions worldwide. This was followed by the *Museum Security Survey* (1981), a companion book in the form of a detailed questionnaire designed to identify security risks in cultural facilities.[68] Two principles that these books advocate are that every individual is responsible for the protection of cultural heritage, and that preventing crime in the museum means keeping the building secure 24 hr a day, every day of the year.[69]

Security policies and procedures are an important aspect of museum protection. They allow staff to identify security goals and objectives, and to implement them in an institution-wide effort. Policies designate levels of responsibility and authority while setting out the existence of procedures, including key control, locks, access, property control, investigative services, security surveys, artifact escort, alarms, guards, exhibit security requirements, and storage security requirements. Both staff members and volunteers alike use procedures and regulations such as these when working in museums, which help to ensure a high standard of care for their respective collections.[70]

From the building's exterior perimeter to the galleries' display cases, numerous low-tech measures are taken to prevent theft and vandalism in museums. Objects are separated, and thus protected, from visitors through the use of glass encasements, velvet ropes, metal bars, and raised platforms. To prevent theft, security hardware for cases and frames are used, such as specialized fasteners, screws, and hooks.[70] To deter unwanted graffiti and some forms of play vandalism on art, ink- and scratch-resistant coatings are available for use on durable material types.[71] To prevent damage, many museums establish rules of behavior for their galleries and require that large groups are chaperoned.[72] Most institutions provide some form of a complimentary coat-check service so that visitors do not take bulky garments or oversized bags into the museum, because both of these could be used to smuggle tools into the galleries or sneak stolen objects out. Museums attempt to prevent theft and vandalism in the off-hours by locking all doors and windows and using exterior lighting as a deterrent for potential predators. Whenever possible, security systems ranging from alarms to on-duty security guards or regular police patrols are used to protect the museum and its collections.[73]

In addition to these security measures, many museums are adopting a technological approach to protecting their objects within galleries and storage spaces, typically through alarms and surveillance. Equipment used to monitor a space includes closed-circuit television (CCTV) cameras as well as electromagnetic locks and key cards. CCTV cameras are installed in public spaces, while the image feeds to a central station, contacting security guards in the event of a suspicious incident. The systems may range from elaborate color cameras with the ability to pan and tilt, to simpler cameras that provide black and white, static images.[74]

Internal security is an extremely important measure for preventing theft and vandalism from occurring within gallery spaces. Limiting and tracking access to collections minimizes the risk of theft from storage areas. Few employees should have keys to a storage room, and in some cases, an identification check with a security guard is required prior to entry.[75] Damage or theft can also occur when visitors gain access to these areas. A collections access policy is used to determine procedures, supervision, and levels of permission for visitors. Study areas, learning centers, visible storage, online catalogs, and photographs are all used to provide access to the collection without admittance to secure storage areas. Visitor screening is a common practice with permission given only to genuine researchers or students. In some cases, institutions require access request letters or forms, including institutional affiliation, purpose, duration of the study, proposed use of the information, and references. Vigilant record keeping discourages potential thieves and vandals as periodic inventories identify and potentially halt such acts.[76]

Mechanisms to detect theft or vandalism can encompass an entire building or focus on a single artifact. Regardless of the area or object being protected, alarms consist of a sensor to identify a problem, a method of communicating and announcing the problem, and a response.[74] There are a number of different types of sensors that are used to activate an alarm, including those triggered by vibration, motion, pressure, or disruption of an electric current. Exhibit cases carry such alarms, using sensors that activate when the glass is broken. Motion detectors are also useful in exhibits where artifacts or artworks are not contained within a case. If a visitor wanders too close, the alarm will chirp alerting both the individual and security personnel. Magnetic detectors are more suitable as general intrusion alarms around perimeter windows and exterior doors.

Traveling exhibitions and outgoing artifact loans are another security risk for museums. Formal loan agreements detail artifact inventories, conditions, insurance, and security procedures. A common practice is to use a designated courier whose responsibility it is to ensure the safety of the objects at all times.[77] Transportation details are usually undisclosed, in the sense that travel routes, dates, and times are maintained on a need-to-know basis.[78] Fine art transportation is a lucrative business worldwide with 79 independent firms belonging to the International Convention of Exhibition and Fine Art Transporters, where members meet annually to develop professional standards for the care and transport of art and antiquities.[79]

Outdoor sites are more vulnerable to theft and vandalism because these spaces are not easily enclosed and are rarely guarded 24 hr a day. In many countries, laws exist to deter theft by establishing such sites as protected and the artifacts as national property, prohibiting their collection, trade, or export. In 1970, in response to market demands for cultural property, the United Nations Educational, Scientific and Cultural Organization held the Convention on the Means of Prohibiting and Preventing the Illicit Import, Export, and Transfer of Ownership of Cultural Property;[80] it is ratified by 102 countries to date.[81] In many countries, however, this does not eliminate cultural theft, since most artifacts from outdoor sites are not documented, and are either indiscoverable as protected objects or are inadequate evidence in court.[82] The prevention of theft and vandalism to these types of public spaces is a continuing struggle facing professionals in the cultural heritage field today.

CONCLUSION

Accounts of theft and vandalism in museums and other public spaces highlights the value that society places on its collective heritage, and blurs the definitional lines between what is considered crime and what is considered art. In each instance, the motivations behind the action and the value of the art or artifact involved determine how the museum or public will respond to its loss or desecration. Theft presents a clear example of crime in museums, which may serve to increase both the monetary and emotional value of the object with its disappearance, as described in the case study of the theft of the *Mona Lisa*. While vandalism has traditionally been associated with some of the worst examples of museum crime, it has also acted as a powerful tool of self-expression and inspired art movements, pointed to by the discussion of the Dadaists and graffiti artists. The introduction of new technologies and systems in today's cultural heritage institutions allows for increased security and prevention against these and other criminal acts, as well as the shared knowledge and international effort toward the recovery of stolen goods. With these organizations and institutions working together, along with increased public awareness and societal responsibility, museums will ensure that all objects in their collections survive for the benefit of future generations.

KEY INDIVIDUALS AND ORGANIZATIONS

Art Loss Register: The world's largest private database of lost and stolen art, antiquities, and collectibles, created in London in 1991 to minimize and deter art crimes, as well as facilitate the recovery of lost or stolen works (http://www.artloss.com).

Association for Research into Crimes against Art (ARCA): Focuses on the motivations behind art vandalism and theft, as well as forgery, acting as consultants on art protection and recovery issues (http://www.artcrime.info).

Federal Bureau of Investigation Art Crime Team: The FBI established its Art Crime Team in 2004, composed of 12 Special Agents, each responsible for addressing art and cultural property crime cases in an assigned geographic region. The team is coordinated through the FBI's Art Theft Program in Washington, DC (http://www.fbi.gov).

International Convention of Exhibition and Fine Art Transporters (ICEFAT): A worldwide democratic organization of independent art transporters dedicated to promoting the highest standards of professionalism in the field of museum and gallery shipping (http://www.icefat.org).

International Council of Museums (ICOM): An international network of museum professionals, institutions, and committees held to their own Code of Ethics in museums (http://icom.museum).

International Committee on Museum Security (ICOM-ICMS): A committee formed by ICOM to represent and support their aims and objectives with reference to museum security by providing advice, programs, and forums for museum professionals.

International Foundation for Art Research (IFAR): This organization offers information on authenticity, ownership, theft, and legal and ethical issues related to stolen objects, including issues of looting followed by repatriation, and scholarly information related to ownership and law (http://www.ifar.org).

Interpol Art Theft Division: A division of the U.K. police force, which facilitates the sharing of information related to the theft and disappearance of art and artifacts among different police departments in the effort of recovery (http://www.interpol.int).

Metropolitan Police Art and Antiques Unit: This unit is responsible for the collation and dissemination of intelligence pertaining to art crime and continues to run and update the London Stolen Art Database (http://www.met.police.uk/artandantiques/).

Museum Security Network (MSN): This organization provides a listserv for museum professionals, providing current events related to security and crime in cultural heritage institutions (http://www.museum-security.org).

National Stolen Art File: An American register used by the FBI Art Crime Team to minimize and deter art crimes, as well as facilitate the recovery of lost or stolen works (http://www.fbi.gov).

United Nations Educational, Scientific and Cultural Organization (UNESCO): A United Nations agency that promotes international cooperation in the fields of education, science, culture, and communication (http://www.unesco.org).

ACKNOWLEDGMENTS

The authors of this entry would like to extend their thanks to Dr. Carl Benn, Ph.D., Chief Curator, City of Toronto Museums and Heritage Services, for his assistance and support, and acknowledge David Bearman, President, Archives & Museum Informatics LLC, for suggesting the authors to the encyclopedia editor.

REFERENCES

1. *ICOM Code of Ethics for Museums*, 2006, 5. http://icom. museum/code2006_eng.pdf (accessed January 2008).
2. *ICOM Code of Ethics for Museums,* 2006, 6. http://icom. museum/code2006_eng.pdf (accessed January 2008).
3. Larceny, *Compact Oxford English Dictionary.* http://www. askoxford.com/concise_oed/larceny?view=uk (accessed January 2008).
4. Criminal Code of Canada, Section 322. Theft. http://laws. justice.gc.ca/en/showdoc/cs/C-46/bo-ga:l_IX-gb:s_322// en#anchorbo-ga:l_IX-gb:s_322 (accessed January 2008).
5. United States Criminal Code, Section 668. Theft of major artwork. http://frwebgate.access.gpo.gov/cgi-bin/getdoc. cgi?dbname=browse_usc&docid=Cite:+18USC668 (accessed January 2008).
6. Federal Bureau of Investigation Art Crimes Team. http:// www.fbi.gov/hq/cid/arttheft/arttheft.htm (accessed January 2008).
7. Macintyre, B. *The Napoleon of Crime*; Harper Collins: London, U.K., 1997; 7.
8. Houpt, S. *Museum of the Missing*; Key Porter Books: Toronto, ON, 2006; 75.
9. Houpt, S. *Museum of the Missing*; Key Porter Books: Toronto, ON, 2006; 27.
10. Faltermayer, C.; Lopez, S. The Great Art Caper. Time Nov. 17, **1997**. http://www.time.com/time/magazine/ article/0,9171,987372,00.html and http://www.artphile. com (accessed January 2008).
11. Houpt, S. *Museum of the Missing*; Key Porter Books: Toronto, ON, 2006; 135.
12. Houpt, S. *Museum of the Missing*; Key Porter Books: Toronto, ON, 2006; 83.
13. Houpt, S. *Museum of the Missing*; Key Porter Books: Toronto, ON, 2006; 84–85.
14. Associated Press. World News Briefs: 4 Norwegians Guilty in Theft of 'The Scream'. New York Times Archive, January 18, **1996**. http://query.nytimes.com/gst/fullpage.html? res=9A06E6DF1E39F93BA25752C0A960958260 (accessed January 2008).
15. Houpt, S. *Museum of the Missing*; Key Porter Books: Toronto, ON, 2006; 133.
16. Boser, U. *The Isabella Stewart Gardner Heist.* http://www. boser.org/Site/Gardner.html (accessed January 2008).
17. Houpt, S. *Museum of the Missing*; Key Porter Books: Toronto, ON, 2006; 124.
18. Houpt, S. *Museum of the Missing*; Key Porter Books: Toronto, ON, 2006; 105–108.
19. Art Loss Register. http://www.artloss.com (accessed February 2008).
20. National Stolen Art File. http://www.fbi.gov/hq/cid/artheft/ nationalstolen.htm (accessed February 2008).
21. Association for Research into Crimes against Art. http:// www.artcrime.info (accessed February 2008).
22. International Foundation for Art Research. http://www.ifar. org (accessed February 2008).
23. Federal Bureau of Investigation Art Crime Team. http:// www.fbi.gov/hq/cid/arttheft/arttheft.htm (accessed February 2008).
24. Metropolitan Police Art and Antiques Unit. http://www. met.police.uk/crimeprevention/art.htm (accessed January 2008).
25. Interpol Art Theft Division. http://www.interpol.com/Public/WorkOfArt/Default.asp (accessed January 2008).
26. Radcliffe, J. Foreward. In *Museum of the Missing*; Houpt, S., Ed.; Key Porter Books: Toronto, ON, 2006; 7.
27. Meyer, K.E. Appendix B: Table of National Protective Laws. In *The Plundered Past;* Atheneum: New York, 1973; 240.
28. Houpt, S. *Museum of the Missing*; Key Porter Books: Toronto, ON, 2006; 126.
29. Carabinieri. http://www.carabinieri.it/Internet/Cittadino/ Informazioni/Tutela/Patrimonio+Culturale/ (accessed February 2008).
30. AXA Art Insurance. Art Insurer in Dash to Assist Canadian Theft Investigation. http://www.axaart.co.uk/press/ releases/ivories_stolen.html (accessed January 2008).
31. CPProt.net Selected Reports. Art hunt 'A matter of pride'. http://cpprot.te.verweg.com/2004-January/000352.html (accessed January 2008).
32. Ellwand, G. Toronto lawyer tight-lipped about return of ivory sculptures. Canadian Broadcasting Corporation News Online February 2, **2004**. http://www.cbc.ca/arts/story/ 2004/02/02/agorecoverylaw020204.html (accessed January 2008).
33. Houpt, S. *Museum of the Missing*; Key Porter Books: Toronto, ON, 2006; 88.
34. Houpt, S. *Museum of the Missing*; Key Porter Books: Toronto, ON, 2006; 120–121.
35. Lévy-Leboyer, C. Introduction: Vandalism and the social sciences. In *Vandalism: Behavior and Motivations*; Lévy-Leboyer, C., Ed.; North-Holland: Amsterdam, the Netherlands, 1984; 3.
36. Rambelli, F.; Reinders, E. What does iconoclasm create? What does preservation destroy?Reflections on iconoclasm in East Asia. In *Iconoclasm: Contested Objects, Contested Terms*; Boldrick, S., Clay, R., Eds.; Ashgate: Aldershot, 2007; 19.
37. Criminal Code of Canada, Section 430. Mischief. http:// laws.justice.gc.ca/en/ShowDoc/cs/C-46/bo-ga:l_X::bo-a: l_XI/en?page=7&isPrinting=false (accessed February 2008).
38. Federal Bureau of Investigation. Offense Definitions. *Crime in the United States 2005.* (accessed February 2008). Released September 2006. http://www.fbi.gov/ucr/05cius/ about/offense_definitions.html (accessed February 2008).
39. Ford, C. Iconoclasm, the commodity, and the art of painting. In *Iconoclasm: Contested Objects, Contested Terms*; Boldrick, S., Clay, R., Eds.; Ashgate: Aldershot, England, 2007; 77.
40. Gamboni, D. *The Destruction of Art: Iconoclasm and Vandalism Since the French Revolution*; Reaktion Books: London, U.K., 1997; 192.
41. Goldstein, A.P. *The Psychology of Vandalism*; Plenum Press: New York, 1996; 20.
42. Goldstein, A.P. *The Psychology of Vandalism*; Plenum Press: New York, 1996; 39–45.

Technical–Topic

43. Kimmelman, M. Art as a target for vandals. International Herald Tribune October 16, **2007**. http://www.iht.com/articles/2007/10/15/arts/vandals.php?page=1 (accessed January 2008).

44. Goldstein, A.P. *The Psychology of Vandalism*; Plenum Press: New York, 1996; 17.

45. Cohen, S. Property destruction: Motives and meanings. In *Vandalism*; Ward, C., Ed.; Architectural Press: London, U.K., 1973; 33–34.

46. Cohen, S. Property destruction: Motives and meanings. In *Vandalism*; Ward, C., Ed.; Architectural Press: London, U.K., 1973; 34.

47. Lévy-Leboyer, C. Introduction: Vandalism and the social sciences. In *Vandalism: Behavior and Motivations*; Lévy-Leboyer, C., Ed.; North-Holland: Amsterdam, the Netherlands, 1984; 6–10.

48. Lyall, S. Thieves fond of heavy lifting are making off with England's Bronze Sculptures. New York Times, January 26, 2006. E7.

49. Gamboni, D. *The Destruction of Art: Iconoclasm and Vandalism Since the French Revolution*; Reaktion Books: London, U.K., 1997; 191.

50. Rambelli, F.; Reinders, E. What does iconoclasm create? What does preservation destroy? Reflections on iconoclasm in East Asia. In *Iconoclasm: Contested Objects, Contested Terms*; Boldrick, S., Clay, R., Eds.; Ashgate: Aldershot, England, 2007; 17–18.

51. Ganz Blythe, S.; Powers, E.D. *Looking at Dada*; Museum of Modern Art: New York, 2007; 48–49.

52. Gamboni, D. *The Destruction of Art: Iconoclasm and Vandalism Since the French Revolution*; Reaktion Books: London, U.K., 1997; 275.

53. Basquiat did it first. The Art Newspaper, January 7, **2007** (182). http://www.theartnewspaper.com/ (accessed January 2008).

54. Coffield, F. *Vandalism & Graffiti: The State of the Art*; Calouste Gulbenkian Foundation: London, U.K., 1991; 28.

55. Gamboni, D. *The Destruction of Art: Iconoclasm and Vandalism Since the French Revolution*; Reaktion Books: London, U.K., 1997; 206.

56. Rambelli, F.; Reinders, E. What does iconoclasm create? What does preservation destroy? Reflections on iconoclasm in East Asia. In *Iconoclasm: Contested Objects, Contested Terms*; Boldrick, S., Clay, R., Eds.; Ashgate: Aldershot, England, 2007; 26.

57. Loventhal, D. *The Past is a Foreign Country*; Cambridge University Press: Cambridge, U.K., 1985; 278.

58. Bertelsen, L.K.; Christensen, K. Political vandalism, art, and gender. ARK **1999**. http://www.kvinfo.dk/side/563/article/282/ (accessed January 2008).

59. McKim-Smith, G. The rhetoric of rape, the language of vandalism. Woman's Art J. **2002**, (Spring/Summer), 31.

60. Cohen, S. Property destruction: Motives and meanings. In *Vandalism*; Ward, C., Ed.; Architectural Press: London, U.K., 1973; 43.

61. Feathers fly at art show. BBC News October 24, **1999**. http://news.bbc.co.uk/2/hi/uk_news/484393.stm (accessed January 2008).

62. Gibbons, F. Satirists jump into Tracey's bed. Guardian Unlimited October 25, **1999**. http://www.guardian.co.uk/turner1999/Story/0,12119,201733,00.html (accessed January 2008).

63. Brooklyn Museum. *Exhibitions: Graffiti*. http://www.brooklynmuseum.org/exhibitions/graffiti/ (accessed January 2008).

64. Gamboni, D. *The Destruction of Art: Iconoclasm and Vandalism Since the French Revolution*; Reaktion Books: London, U.K., 1997; 191–193.

65. Detroit Museum of New Art. *kaBOOM!* March 9–April 28, 2002. http://www.detroitmona.com/kaboom.htm (accessed January 2008).

66. Church, T. *Max Ernst 1891–1976*. http://www.konstbolaget.se/artist/149 (accessed February 2008).

67. Russell, J. Healing a disfigured Rembrandt's wounds. New York Times August 31, 1997.

68. ICOM and the International Committee on Museum Security Preface. In *Museum Security and Protection*; Liston, D., Ed.; Routledge: London, U.K., 1993; xi.

69. ICOM and the International Committee on Museum Security, Cultural protection duties and responsibilities. In *Museum Security and Protection*; Liston, D., Ed.; Routledge: London, U.K., 1993; 40–51.

70. Howard, R.F. Museum security. The American Association of Museums (AAM) Publications **1958**, *18*, 1–12.

71. Tillotson, R.A. Damage. In *Museum Security*; Menkes, D. D., Ed.; ICOM: Paris, France, 1977; 146–148.

72. ICOM and the International Committee on Museum Security, Vigilance and guard services. In *Museum Security and Protection*; Liston, D., Ed.; Routledge: London, U.K., 1993; 72.

73. Chapman, J. Physical security. In *Primer on Museum Security*; New York State Historical Association: Cooperstown, NY, 1966; 4–6.

74. ICOM and the International Committee on Museum Security, Electronic building protection. In *Museum Security and Protection*; Liston, D., Ed.; Routledge: London, U.K., 1993; 178–195.

75. Hilberry, J.D.; Weinberg, S.K. Museum collections storage. In *Care of Collections*; Knell, S., Ed.; Routledge: London, U.K., 1994; 159–160.

76. Richoux, J.A.; Serota-Braden, J.; Demyttenaere, N. A policy for collections access. In *Care of Collections*; Knell, S., Ed.; Routledge: London, U.K., 1994; 179–185.

77. Mervin, R. Role of the courier. In *Art in Transit: Handbook for Packing and Transporting Paintings*; Richard, M., Mecklenburg, M.F., Merrill, R.M., Eds.; National Gallery of Art: Washington, DC, 1991; 3.

78. ICOM and the International Committee on Museum Security, Non-building cultural property protection. In *Museum Security and Protection*; Liston, D., Ed.; Routledge: London, U.K., 1993; 257–258.

79. International Convention of Exhibition and Fine Art Transporters. http://www.icefat.org/about.html (accessed January 2008).

80. Gerstenblith, P. Controlling the international market in antiquities: Reducing the harm, preserving the past. Chicago J. Int. Law **2007**, *8* (1), 176.

81. United Nations Educational, Scientific and Cultural Organization. http://www.unesco.org/culture/laws/1970/html_eng/page3.shtml (accessed January 2008).

82. Gerstenblith, P. Controlling the international market in antiquities: Reducing the harm, preserving the past. Chicago J. In. Law **2007**, *8* (1), 177–179.

BIBLIOGRAPHY

1. Behrman, S.N. *Duveen: The Story of the Most Spectacular Art Dealer of All Time*; The Little Bookroom: New York, 2002.
2. Dolnick, E. *The Rescue Artist: A True Story of Art, Thieves, and the Hunt for a Missing Masterpiece*; Harper Collins: New York, 2006.
3. Fennelly, L.J. *Museum, Archive, and Library Security*; Butterworths: Boston, MA, 1983.
4. Gamboni, D. *The Destruction of Art: Iconoclasm and Vandalism Since the French Revolution*; Reaktion Books: London, U.K., 1997.
5. Hart, M. *The Irish Game: A True Story of Crime*; Penguin Group: New York, 2005.
6. Leader, D. *Stealing the Mona Lisa: What Art Stops Us from Seeing*; Shoemaker & Hoard: Berkeley, CA, 2004.
7. McShane, T. *Stolen Masterpiece Tracker*; Barricade Books, Inc.: Fort Lee, NJ, 2006.

Technical–Topic

Theological Librarianship

Paul F. Stuehrenberg
Yale Divinity Library, New Haven, Connecticut, U.S.A.

Abstract

Christian theological libraries trace their origins to the early church. Early centers included Jerusalem, Alexandria, and, most famously, Caesarea, where the library supported the work of such scholars as Origin, Eusebius, and Jerome. The Vivarium, a religious community founded by Cassiodorus, provided a model for medieval monastic libraries. At the close of the Middle Ages faculties of theology developed libraries that continue to this day. In North America independent seminaries and schools of theology appeared in the early nineteenth century in response to the rise of Unitarianism. The American Theological Library Association was founded in 1947 in part to improve standards for theological libraries. It has played a leadership role in the professional development of theological librarians, and the indexing and preservation of theological literature. Theological libraries range in size from small operations supporting the curriculum to comprehensive research institutions. Many theological libraries remain small and underfunded.

When you come, bring the cloak I left with Carpus at Troas, also the books, and above all the parchments (2 Tim.4:13).

Theology is a text-based discipline. From their beginnings, Christians used books. For Christian theology those texts begin with the Bible, originally the Hebrew Bible, or Old Testament, and its Greek translation, the Septuagint. Then, early in its history, Christians adopted selected apostolic writings as the New Testament. There were also other, noncanonical writings, both Christian and Jewish, almost from the beginning, some of which no longer survive. Other early Christian literature includes sermons, letters, and, increasingly as time went by, polemical and apologetic treatises. The growth of the literature of theology led to the creation of libraries.

ORIGINS

There were three types of early Christian libraries: congregational, larger libraries in Christian centers, and monastic. Even small communities built libraries that served their liturgical, catechetical, and archival needs. The libraries established at larger centers helped to support scholarship, often with the support of the local bishop.[1] Early centers included Jerusalem, Alexandria, and, most famously, Caesarea.

The library at Caesarea is a model for how Christian libraries were created and how they were supported during the first centuries after Christ. Origen (ca. 185-ca. 254) moved from Alexandria to Caesarea, bringing with him his personal library, which included Biblical texts, commentaries, and technical works. Origen used his library as the basis for a prolific output of commentaries, homilies, and other works of scholarship. His most notable work was the Hexapla, which included the Hebrew and Greek texts of the Old Testament in parallel columns. Late in the third century, a wealthy Christian presbyter, Pamphilus (d. 310), settled in Caesarea and began to accumulate a library of sacred works, the core of which came from Origen's library. The collection that he built became so famous in latter antiquity that it was described, with some exaggeration, as the Christian equivalent of the library of Alexandria. Like the library of Alexandria, this was no mere collection of books, but a place where books were copied, emended, and produced. Eusebius (260–339), Pamphilus' student and the eventual bishop of the city, continued to expand the library and based his scholarship upon it. Jerome notes that Euzoios, bishop of Caesarea from ca. 376 to ca. 379, set out to restore the library by having its holdings copied from papyrus scrolls onto parchment codices.[2]

Christians were early adopters of the codex. By the end of the first century the codex became the standard format used by Christians, while others in the ancient world continued to use the papyrus scroll. The advantages of the codex include economy (writing on both sides of paper), compactness, comprehensiveness (collected editions), convenience of use (it can be read using one hand rather than two), and ease of reference.[3]

One of the best documented monastic libraries was that founded by Cassiodorus (ca. 487–ca. 580). After a distinguished political career, Cassiodorus founded a monastic community called the Vivarium. Here he brought together a large library of Christian and classical texts for the

Encyclopedia of Library and Information Sciences, Fourth Edition DOI: 10.1081/E-ELIS4-120043860

education of the community of monks, as described in his *Institutiones divinarum et saecularium litterarum.* The community was not only to study the books he gathered, but was also charged with producing copies.[4] The Vivarium came to serve as a model that was followed by monastic communities during the Middle Ages. Indeed, it is due in no small part to these monastic communities that the literature of antiquity, both Christian and secular, survived. An example of the use to which such a library could be made is provided by the Venerable Bede (673–735), who, working independently, but with access to a good library at the monastery at Jarrow, produced impressive works of scholarship that were highly valued throughout the Middle Ages. The library upon which he relied was destroyed by Viking raiders in about 860.

EUROPEAN THEOLOGICAL LIBRARIES

Effective as they were at preserving the literature of antiquity, monasteries were not learned academies, but rather, "schools for the practice of virtue."[5] While Roman civilization remained alive in isolated communities, there was a general decline in learning after the fall of the Roman Empire. This was arrested for a time by the Carolingians, who aimed for nothing less than the reform of society through education, especially in the language arts, with the goal of establishing a Christian civilization. Their essential contribution was that they established a minimal standard of literacy to be promoted "by *every* bishop and *every* abbot," and that the enterprise was to be underwritten by the consistent and generous patronage of the state.[6] The result was a sustained period of creativity. Scholars emended ancient texts and wrote new works designed to undergird the study of the liberal arts and sacred texts. Teams of scribes toiled in scriptoria to produce manuscripts both for their own use and for distribution.[7] Indeed, very little literature survives from the ancient world, sacred or profane, that was not copied during the Carolingian era. To train the scribes, religious leaders, and government officials necessary to support their empire and its programs, the Carolingians established schools that were supported by the public authority. Associated with the better schools were libraries. Laon stands as one example of the cathedral library.[8]

By the twelfth century the cathedral and monastic schools began to give way to a new way of studying of theology. Up to this point scholars had worked largely independently, despite the advances made under the Carolingians. In the twelfth century for the first time there was a large enough community of teaching masters and an environment in which they and their pupils could meet freely for it to be possible to speak of a general revision of educational methods and purposes.[9] In this context the study of theology as an academic discipline evolved. Bernard of Chartres described himself and his twelfth-century

contemporaries as "dwarfs standing on the shoulders of giants."[10] The masters of the twelfth-century were not, for the most part, great men, but the schools they set up were for the first time recognizably "academic" in the modern sense, in that they were characterized by a steady aggregation of small changes. The schools that grew up in the twelfth century prepared the way for the development of the university in the thirteenth. The books that were to become the basic theological textbooks for the remainder of the Middle Ages were written during the twelfth century, including the *Glossa ordinaria*, a compilation of patristic commentary on the Biblical text, the *Historia scholastica* of Peter Comestor, an aid for understanding the literal sense of the Bible, and, most important, the *Sentences* of Peter Lombard, which might be characterized as the first systematic theology textbook. These textbooks were a new kind of book—not meant to be read straight through, but rather to serve as references, complete with such apparatuses as indexes, running heads, and marginal notations.[11]

The educational model that developed was for basic education to take place in the grammar school, then the study of the seven liberal arts in an academy or Latin school, followed by the study of theology in a university faculty of theology.[12] As the schools developed, they gathered libraries to support their teaching. The pattern remained much the same following the Reformation, with the exception that the faculties of theology would be either Protestant or Roman Catholic.

THE NORTH AMERICAN EXPERIENCE

From colonial times Protestants in North America adopted the English model for training clergy. Colleges were established for the training of leaders for "church and civil state," in the words of Yale's charter. For most clergy in colonial times the bachelor's degree provided sufficient training. A minority might choose to read theology with a college professor or with a local clergyman. This practice increased somewhat after the Great Awakening, so much so that some senior clergy became what might be called "one-teacher schools," with several students in residence at any given time.[13] The rise of Unitarianism in the beginning of the nineteenth century led to the perceived need to have better trained clergy, which led to the creation of theological seminaries, beginning with Andover in 1808. Within the next two decades the number of theological seminaries and divinity schools mushroomed. Many of the smaller seminaries were "poorly endowed, inadequately staffed and under-enrolled." There are three indicators of the relative strength of the schools: the size of faculty, the number of students enrolled, and the size of library. "Although the number of books in the library was not an absolute guide to the quality of education, a rough correlation existed between library acquisitions and educational standards," for the availability of an adequate library was the major factor supporting the professional development of faculty.[14]

Standards for theological seminaries remained problematic throughout the nineteenth century and into the twentieth. The Conference of Theological Schools was created in 1920 to help the schools address this problem. This organization was restructured in 1936 as an accrediting agency, the American Association of Theological Schools (AATS). Of the 46 schools accredited in its first year, all but 11 had notations for lack of adherence to standards. One initiative the AATS (later, ATS) undertook to improve the libraries of its member institutions was to help to found the American Theological Library Association (ATLA) in 1947. Yet, even though each successive version of the AATS standards would raise the bar for seminary libraries, especially for professional staff, many seminary libraries have remained small and poorly financed.[15]

THE ATLA

The first meeting of what was to become the ATLA took place June 23–24, 1947, at Louisville Presbyterian Seminary. For a fuller account of the first 50 years of the American Theological Library Association, see O'Brien and O'Brien.[16] AATS invited 110 institutions to the meeting. Fifty librarians, one seminary president, and one dean attended. From the outset they faced daunting problems, and set about immediately to address them. At the very first conference a committee was appointed to look into the indexing of theological journals. By 1952 the committee had devised a plan whereby staff at 20 institutions would share responsibility for indexing, under the leadership of Stillson Judah. The result was the *Index to religious periodical literature*. The 1949 conference appointed a Committee on Microphotography. Initially the purpose of its program was to reproduce the literature of theology so that the texts could be distributed to member institutions. In 1951 a committee on cataloging and classification was appointed. One of the problems they faced was that theological libraries at the time were using at least three different classification systems: the Dewey Decimal System, the Library of Congress classification system, and the system devised by Julia Pettee at Union Theological Seminary in New York. For more on her remarkable career, see Spoor.[17] In 1952 there was a joint ATLA/AATS committee on accreditation standards. The new standards shifted the emphasis on adequacy away from quantitative measurement to a focus on the educational process.

The importance of ATLA's efforts was recognized within a decade of its founding by the awarding of several grants. In 1956 the Sealantic Fund gave ATLA a grant of $110,000: $80,000 for microtext and $30,000 for indexing. To oversee the expenditure of these funds, the following year the Board of Microtext was organized, with Raymond P. Morris as chair (he served until his retirement in 1972). That same year the Board on Religious Periodical Literature was established with Jannette E. Newhall as chair and Lucy Markley as editor. In 1960 Calvin Schmitt was appointed chair (he retired in 1979) and G. Fay Dickerson as indexer (she retired in 1984). The experiment of having volunteers prepare the index came to an end.

In the 1960s ATLA received a series of grants from the Lilly Endowment and the Sealantic Fund for the training of theological librarians. The normal pattern up to that time was that schools would appoint a faculty member as the librarian, who would oversee a staff with training in library science, but no background in theology. The programs developed with this funding were sufficiently successful that a decade later the norm became that library staff would have training in both library science and theology.

Another transformative grant was received in 1961: the Sealantic Fund gave $875,000 to support the Library Development Program. The primary objective of the Program was to increase book purchases, thereby strengthening the libraries' collections. The Program was designed in such a way that participating libraries would also have to increase staffing levels to participate. By the third year of the grant, all 85 eligible AATS institutions participated in the Program either fully or in part. Library expenditures rose in those three years from $2.8 million to more than $3.877 million. For more on the Library Development Program, see Stuehrenberg.[18]

By the 1970s there was a growing recognition of the need for preservation of microfilming. Charles Willard and Andrew Scrimgeour conducted a study that led to the creation for preservation microfilming program for monographs. In September 1985 Robert P. Markham was hired as the Director of Programs for the preservation effort. ATLA became a significant participant in national efforts to reformat brittle books. Over the period of 1987–1992, ATLA received nine National Endowment for the Humanities (NEH) grants totaling $1,524,330 and filmed 19,000 titles. ATLA continued an active preservation program into the new millennium. Recent microfilming projects receiving NEH funding include Christianity and the Encounter with World Religions, 1850–1950, African American Religious Serials, 1850–1950, and Religious Periodical Literature of the Hispanic and Indigenous People of the Americas, 1850–1985.

In 1976 the *Index to religious periodical literature* was renamed *Religion index one*, and ATLA began the publication of *Religion index two: multiauthor works*. This was followed in 1980 by a volume indexing *Festschriften, 1960–1969*, which was prepared by Betty and Elmer O'Brien. In 1982 a retrospective project, *Religion index two: multiauthor works, 1970–1975*, filled in the gaps between the two publications. The last print volume of *Religion index two* appeared in 1999.

The *ATLA religion database*, incorporating both *Religion index one* (periodicals) and *Religion index two* (multiauthor works) first appeared on CD-Rom in 1989. Initially it was published and distributed by H.W. Wilson. That arrangement ceased in February 1993, when ATLA first produced its own disc. For an account of the birth of the ATLA religion database on CD-Rom, see Moore.[19] In 2008 ATLA discontinued all CD-Rom products, with the database now available online.

The *Ethics index* was conceived of as a way for ATLA to broaden its presence in the electronic reference marketplace and to serve as a source of additional revenues during a period of institutional downsizing and scarcity of funds among theological libraries. It first appeared in February 1994. However, the anticipated expanded market did not materialize, and the ATLA budget was in deficit for two years in a row. ATLA abandoned the project, with the last CD-Rom appearing in June 1996. ATLA was forced to reduce staff in order not to go bankrupt, and then began rebuilding.

In 1997 ATLA signed contracts with SilverPlatter and FirstSearch to distribute the *ATLA religion database*, followed in 1999 with Ebsco. These agreements paved the way for a dramatic increase in ATLA's revenues, a phenomenon that has continued to this day. The *ATLA religion database* is now accepted as the standard index for religious periodical literature in the academic marketplace.

In 2001 ATLA undertook the Retrospective Indexing Project, which consisted of the indexing of pre-1949 volumes of titles included in the *Index to religious periodical literature*. More than 100 institutional members pledged support. Originally 134 titles were on the list for retrospective indexing. The project ended in August 2005 with 40,000 index records for 47 periodical titles.

In 1999 ATLA announced the coming of ATLAS (ATLA serials), with a promise to supply full-text electronic access to 50 years of 50 journals. The project was launched on January 31, 2001, with a $3.94 million grant from the Lilly Endowment. As of August 2006 there were 86 journal titles in ATLAS and 192,768 articles.

Also in 1999 ATLA completed the conversion of the back file of *Old Testament abstracts* and signed an agreement to produce an electronic edition of *Catholic periodical and literature index*. In 2004 *New Testament abstracts* was added to its electronic publications.

From 1985 to 1991 ATLA underwent a thorough restructuring of its governance, programs, finances, and staffing. The restructuring followed a financial management study by Peat, Marwick funded by a $25,000 Lilly Endowment grant. Previously ATLA's management structure was thoroughly decentralized, with operations dispersed between such places as Chicago, Princeton, and St. Meinrad, with bank accounts in Fort Worth,

incorporation in Delaware, and executive responsibility changing location each year to wherever the president might be located. The reorganization merged ATLA's two semiautonomous program boards (Preservation and Indexing) with the Board of Directors, resulting in one Board with the power to define the association's mission and to set policy. By appointing an executive director as the chief executive officer, bringing all staff together at a headquarters location, adopting a unified budget, and following accepted accounting procedures, ATLA was able to use its resources more effectively.[20]

In the reorganization, ATLA adopted the Carver Policy Governance model (http://www.carvergovernance.com/model.htm), under which the Board of Directors sets policies and charges the Executive Director with carrying them out within certain executive limitations. The mission of ATLA is currently defined as fostering the study of theology and religion by enhancing the development of theological and religious libraries and librarianship. In pursuit of that mission ATLA (http://www.atla.com/about/html) has four organizational ends:

1. To foster the professional growth of its members, and to enhance their ability to serve their constituencies as administrators and librarians.
2. To advance the profession of theological librarianship, and to assist theological librarians in defining and interpreting the proper role and function of libraries in theological education.
3. To promote quality library and information services in support of teaching, learning, and research in theology, religion, and related disciplines, and to create such tools and aids as may be helpful in accomplishing this.
4. To stimulate purposeful collaboration among librarians of theological libraries and religious studies collections; and to develop programmatic solutions to information-related problems common to those librarians and collections.

The membership elects the Board of Directors, who have "moral ownership" of the Association. The structure of the annual conference was changed from having standing committees to the establishment of "Interest Groups," which are created by the membership. The current interest groups include Collection Evaluation and Development, College and University, Judaica, Lesbian and Gay, Public Services, Special Collections, Technical Services, World Christianity, and World Religions. Denominational groups also meet at the annual conference.

Since the Executive Director is responsible for carrying out policies established by the Board of Directors, the Executive Director appoints advisory committees that help the Executive Director to understand the interests of the membership. Current advisory committees include the Professional Development Committee and the

Technical–Topic

Publications Committee. The Executive Director also appoints the Annual Conference Committee and the Education Committee, which is responsible for continuing education at the annual conference. Standing committees of the Board of Directors include the Endowment Committee and the Nominating Committee. The Special Committee of the Association for International Collaboration coordinates the Association's activities regarding international theological librarianship, supports efforts of individual libraries and librarians to participate in international theological librarianship activities, and plans annual conference activities relating to international theological librarianship.

Before the reorganization members volunteered hundreds of hours each year to running the projects, programs, boards, and committees of the Association. With the reorganization members now rely on professional staff to manage the Association's affairs, leaving the members free to focus on furthering the professional ends of theological librarianship.

Begun as an association of Protestant theological libraries from North America, ATLA now is the premier professional association for theological libraries for all branches of Christianity, Protestant, Roman Catholic, and Eastern Orthodox. While member libraries are still primarily from North America, ATLA has a growing number of international library institutional and individual members, as well. Individual and institutional members are listed in the annual *Summary of Proceedings*.

OTHER PROFESSIONAL ASSOCIATIONS SUPPORTING THE WORK OF THEOLOGICAL LIBRARIES

The Association of Christian Librarians (http://www.acl.org/) was established in 1957, and today has more than 500 individual and nearly 150 institutional members representing a wide spectrum of denominations. Members work in a variety of libraries, including Bible colleges, seminaries, colleges, and universities. Members are asked to subscribe to a statement of faith. They publish the periodical the *Christian librarian*, and print and online versions of the *Christian periodical index*, the leading guide to periodical literature from the evangelical perspective.

The Association of Jewish Libraries (AJL) (http://www.jewishlibraries.org/ajlweb/index.htm) promotes Jewish literacy through enhancement of libraries and library resources and through leadership for the profession and practitioners of Judaica librarianship. AJL was created in 1965 as a result of the merger of two organizations: the Jewish Librarians Association (founded in 1946), which concerned itself with collections of Judaica in academic, archival, or research institutions and the Jewish Library Association (founded in 1962), which concerned itself

with collections in synagogue, school, and community center libraries, as well as other smaller libraries and media centers. They publish a quarterly newsletter, convention proceedings, and an annual scholarly publication, *Judaica librarianship*.

Established in 1921, the Catholic Library Association (CLA) (http://www.cathla.org/index.php) is an international membership organization, providing its members professional development through educational and networking experiences, publications, scholarships, and other services. CLA coordinates the exchange of ideas, provides a source of inspirational support and guidance in ethical issues related to librarianship, and offers fellowship for those who seek, serve, preserve, and share the word in all its forms. Members come from a variety of institutions, from primary schools and congregational libraries to universities and seminaries. CLA publishes a quarterly journal, the *Catholic library world*, and the *Catholic periodical and literature index* (now distributed in electronic form in partnership with ATLA).

INTERNATIONAL THEOLOGICAL LIBRARY ASSOCIATIONS

Australian and New Zealand Theological Library Association (ANZTLA) (http://www.anztla.org/), founded in 1985, is an association of both individual and institutional members. It maintains the *Australasian religion index online* (formerly published as a print index since 1989) and the *Australasian union list of serials in theological collections online* and an online *Newsletter*.

The Forum of Asian Theological Librarians (ForATL) (http://www.foratl.org/index.htm) traces its origins to the Consultation of Asian Theological Librarians held in May 1991 in Chiang Mai, Thailand, under the sponsorship of the Programme for Theology and Cultures in Asia. It has institutional and individual members from throughout Asia. Membership is chiefly from Protestant institutions. It sponsors periodic consultations and has published a directory of Asian theological libraries.

Bibliothèques Européenes de Théologie (BETH) (http://www.theo.kuleuven.be/beth/) was founded in 1954 under the auspices of UNESCO as the International Association of Theological Libraries. Today BETH is an ecumenical association of the national theological library associations in Europe, with additional members gathered from among the various individual theological libraries that are recognized as extraordinary in their scope, either from their collections or from their influence in the international sphere. For an account of the founding of BETH, see Geuns and Wolf-Dahm.[21]

Red Latinoamericana de Información (RLIT; formerly the Latin American Theological Information Network, http://www.ibiblio.org/rlit/) was founded in 1994 and has members from throughout Central and South America. It is open to all theological libraries, but membership is predominantly Protestant.

In addition, there are national theological library associations in many countries.

THEOLOGICAL LIBRARIES TODAY

Theological libraries today are a diverse group of institutions, ranging from one-person operations to denominational seminary libraries to university-related divinity libraries. Theological libraries can be divided into four categories. The first two types have collections that essentially support the curriculum in the broader sense; that is, besides the curriculum proper, they provide access to the Christian heritage reflected in the curriculum. The first type collects materials almost exclusively North American publications, with only a minimum of foreign materials. This type of library likely acquires between 800 and 1200 volumes per year and not more than 200–300 journals. Type two libraries would acquire additional foreign materials and their acquisitions programs might double that of type one libraries. A type three library also gathers documentary literature, understood as a broad segment of non-scholarly religious literature, such as the literature produced by a denomination. Type four libraries are research institutions. They seek to acquire the scholarly literature essential to the history and development of all branches of Christian thought without regard to language, date, country of origin, and theological perspective. The focus is not on being exhaustive, but on acquiring the scholarly literature that has defined and is shaping Christian thought.[22]

In the 1970s ATS encouraged theological schools to merge their libraries to make it possible to build larger, more efficient libraries. The Graduate Theological Union in Berkeley, CA, is one of the more successful examples. Nine schools went together to create what instantly became one of the largest theological libraries in the country. Their cooperation also enabled them to create a graduate program that none of them could have accomplished on their own. Another example is the JKM Library in Chicago, which now serves the Lutheran School of Theology at Chicago and McCormick Theological Seminary. Both institutions, while maintaining their separate identity, are now located in the same complex with a common library. The three seminaries of the Eastern Cluster of Lutheran Seminaries (located in Columbia, SC; Gettysburg; and Philadelphia, PA) have undertaken the experiment of having one library in three locations, with a common collection development policy. Books remain in the physical location where they last circulated. Many other seminaries have developed distance education sites, or satellite campuses, requiring them to find creative ways of providing library services.

The world of theological librarianship is relatively small. In 2005 ATLA had 492 individual members and 265 institutional members. That means that there are relatively few positions open at any given time. But when a position does come open, qualified candidates are highly sought after. Theological libraries in North America today tend to prefer candidates for professional positions who have at least masters' degrees in both library science and theology (or a related discipline). For training in library science, most candidates follow the academic librarianship track in ALA-accredited schools. ATLA now sponsors a course in theological librarianship offered through the University of Illinois that can be taken by students at other institutions as a part of their program. Postings for some directorships require a doctorate, usually in one of the disciplines of theology. Many institutions outside of North America tend to require less theological training for library staff, often assigning some professional activity, such as book selection, to faculty.

In a recent survey two-thirds of the theological librarians responding considered theological librarianship to be a ministry, while the other third considered themselves to be in an occupation that happened to be at a theological institution.[23] Many theological librarians, especially those in denominational seminary libraries, may also be ordained clergy. Many theological librarians have faculty status, especially for the director, sometimes for other professional staff as well. Theologically trained librarians also work in other types of libraries, as well, especially college and university libraries, doing a variety of tasks, such as subject bibliographers, general reference, and cataloging of humanities resources.

As is the case with librarianship in general, technology is changing theological librarianship. While an increasing number of theological journals are available electronically, many are still available only in print, and likely will be for some time. In part this is because most religion periodicals are published by organizations that issue one or two journals. As already noted, ATLA is one of the major providers of electronic periodicals through ATLAS. On the other hand, since theology is a text-based discipline, there is an increasing corpus of theological texts available electronically. Several publishers provide packages of Biblical texts and reference works, including Logos Bible Software and BibleWorks. Patristic and medieval authors are covered by the electronic editions of *Patrologia Latina*, *Patrologia Graeca*, and *Corpus Christianorum*. *Past Masters* provides critical texts for selected philosophers and theologians. And there are electronic texts available for an increasing number of theologians, including such figures as Thomas Aquinas, Martin Luther, and Karl Barth.

What of the future of theological libraries? According to Dan Aleshire, Executive Director of ATS, they will be with us for the foreseeable future. The purpose of the academic library has been to provide access to trustworthy, authoritative knowledge. The library has historically controlled for "authoritative and trustworthy" through its collection development policies, and controlled for "access" through its organizing, cataloging, and circulating.[24] While the manner in which libraries deliver those services in the future may vary, teaching and research will continue to have need of those services.

REFERENCES

1. Gamble, H.Y. *Books and Readers in the Early Church*; Yale University Press: New Haven, CT, 1995; 144.

2. Grafton, A.; Williams, M. *Christianity and the Transformation of the Book: Origen, Eusebius, and the Library of Caesarea*; The Belknap Press of Harvard University Press: Cambridge, MA, 2006.

3. Roberts, C.H.; Skeat, T.C. *The Birth of the Codex*; Published for the British Academy by the Oxford University Press: London, U.K., 1983; 45–53.

4. Gamble, H.Y. *Books and Readers in the Early Church*; Yale University Press: New Haven, CT, 1995; 198–200.

5. Contreni, J.J. *Carolingian Learning, Masters and Manuscripts*; Variorum: Hampshire, U.K., 1992; I.4.

6. Contreni, J.J. *Carolingian Learning, Masters and Manuscripts*; Variorum: Hampshire, U.K., 1992; I.10. Emphasis by Contreni.

7. Contreni, J.J. *Carolingian Learning, Masters and Manuscripts*; Variorum: Hampshire, U.K., 1992; III.65. Originally published: *Renaissances before the Renaissance: Cultural Revivals of Late Antiquity and the Middle Ages*; Warren, T., Ed.; Stanford University Press: Stanford, CA, 1984; 59–74.

8. Contreni, J.J. *Carolingian Learning, Masters and Manuscripts*; Variorum: Hampshire, U.K., 1992; XIII. Originally published as The formation of Laon's cathedral library in the ninth century. Studi Medievali **1972**, *13*, 919–939.

9. Evans, G.R. *Old Arts and New Theology: The Beginnings of Theology as an Academic Discipline*; Clarendon Press: Oxford, U.K., 1980; 3.

10. Evans, G.R. *Old Arts and New Theology: The Beginnings of Theology as an Academic Discipline*; Clarendon Press: Oxford, U.K., 1980; v.

11. Lesley, S. *Masters of the Sacred Page: Manuscripts of Theology in the Latin West to 1274*; University of Notre Dame Press: Notre Dame, IN, 2001. especially 33.

12. Miller, G.T. *Piety and Intellect: The Aims and Purposes of Ante-Bellum Theological Education*; Scholars Press: Atlanta, GA, 1990; 14.

13. Miller, G.T. *Piety and Intellect: The Aims and Purposes of Ante-Bellum Theological Education*; Scholars Press: Atlanta, GA, 1990; 55.

14. Miller, G.T. *Piety and Intellect: The Aims and Purposes of Ante-Bellum Theological Education*; Scholars Press: Atlanta, GA, 1990; 200–201.

15. Miller, G.T. *Piety and Profession: American Protestant Theological Education, 1870–1970*; Eerdmans: Grand Rapids, MI, 2007; 466.

16. O'Brien, E.J.; O'Brien, B.A. From volunteerism to corporate professionalism: A historical sketch of the American Theological Library Association. In *The American Theological Library Association: Essays in Celebration of the First Fifty Years*; Graham, M.P., Hotchkiss, V.R., Rowe, K.E., Eds.; American Theological Library Association: Evanston, IL, 1996; 3–24.

17. Spoor, R.D. Julia Pettee and her contribution to theological librarianship. In *The American Theological Library Association: Essays in Celebration of the First Fifty Years*; 183–195.

18. Stuehrenberg, P.F. A giant step forward: The Sealantic Fund and the American Theological Library Association Library Development Fund. In *The American Theological Library Association: Essays in Celebration of the First Fifty Years*; 60–70.

19. Moore, M.E. The ATLA religion database on CD-Rom: its first year. J. Relig. Theol. Inform. **1994**, *2* (1), 115–135.

20. Bollier, J.A. The internationalization of the American Theological Library Association. In *The American Theological Library Association: Essays in Celebration of the First Fifty Years*; 33.

21. Geuns, A.J.; Wolf-Dahm, B. Theological libraries: An overview on history and present activities of the International Council of Associations of Theological Libraries. INSPEL **1998**, *32* (3), 139–158.

22. Peterson, S.L. Collection development in theological libraries: A new model, a new hope. *Essays on Theological Librarianship Presented to Calvin Henry Schmitt*; de Klerk, P., Hilgert, E., Eds.; American Theological Library Association: Philadelphia, PA, 1980; 143–162.

23. Keck, A.J. Information or divine access: Theological librarianship within the context of a ministry. In *The American Theological Library Association: Essays in Celebration of the First Fifty Years*; 172–182.

24. Aleshire, D. Librarianship is a noun: Speculation about the future of theological librarianship. In *Summary of Proceedings, American Theological Library Association Annual Conference*, Chicago, IL, 2006; Vol. 60, 90.

Topic Maps

Steve Pepper
Department of Linguistics, University of Oslo, Oslo, Norway

Abstract

Topic Maps is an international standard technology for describing knowledge structures and using them to improve the findability of information. It is based on a formal model that subsumes those of traditional finding aids such as indexes, glossaries, and thesauri, and extends them to cater for the additional complexities of digital information. Topic Maps is increasingly used in enterprise information integration, knowledge management, e-learning, and digital libraries, and as the foundation for Web-based information delivery solutions. This entry provides a comprehensive treatment of the core concepts, as well as describing the background and current status of the standard and its relationship to traditional knowledge organization techniques.

INTRODUCTION

Topic Maps is a standard technology for describing knowledge structures and using them to improve the findability of information. It is based on a formal model that subsumes those of traditional finding aids, such as indexes, glossaries, and thesauri, and caters for the additional complexities of digital information. The model is defined in an ISO standard (ISO 13250), along with interchange syntaxes, a formal semantics, and a graphical notation. Ancillary standards define a Topic Maps Query Language (TMQL), a Topic Maps Constraint Language (TMCL), and mappings to other knowledge organization specifications, such as Dublin Core. Since its initial standardization in 2000, Topic Maps is finding increasing application as the foundation for Web sites and portals, as well as in knowledge management (KM), e-learning, and more.

This entry provides a comprehensive treatment of the core concepts, in addition to the background and current status of the standard, its relationship to traditional knowledge organization techniques, and examples of the kinds of applications for which it is being used. This entry follows the established convention of using initial capitals ("Topic Maps") when referring to the standard itself or the technology in general, and lower case ("topic maps") when referring to the document-like artifacts created through the application of that technology.

BACKGROUND AND HISTORY

Origin and Development

The concepts of Topic Maps originated in the context of the Davenport Group, during the development of the DocBook application, as an answer to the problem of how to automate the merging of (digital) back-of-book indexes. The key insight, due to Dr. Steven R. Newcomb, was that such indexes are in fact models of knowledge. Their digital encoding is based on their surface appearance, but they actually have an implicit, underlying structure. If that structure could be represented formally, it would be possible to automate the merging process.

An initial model was defined in 1992 using the concepts of the HyTime standard, of which Dr. Newcomb was coeditor, under the auspices of a project called the Conventions for the Application of HyTime (CApH), sponsored by the Graphics Communications Association Research Institute (GCARI). After a number of iterations, during which the model was gradually refined, the work was brought into ISO, and went through further revision cycles before being adopted as ISO 13250:2000 under the editorship of Newcomb and coeditors Dr. Michel Biezunski and Martin Bryan. Responsibility was given to Working Group 3 of the subcommittee ISO/IEC JTC 1/SC 34.

The standard was originally defined in terms of an SGML DTD. In fact, it was defined in terms of a "meta-DTD" according to the SGML Architecture facility offered by the draft HyTime standard. Although never finally standardized, the concepts inherent in meta-DTDs found their way into DITA, XML namespaces, and HTML "microformats." By the time it was published, Extensible Markup Language (XML) was replacing SGML, especially on the Web. In order to create an XML-based version of the specification an ad hoc working group called TopicMaps.Org was formed by Newcomb and Biezunski and this resulted in the publication in March 2001 of *XML Topic Maps (XTM) 1.0*,[1] edited by Steve Pepper and Graham Moore.

In addition to defining a new, XML-compatible DTD for representing topic maps, the new specification removed the dependence on HyTime, clarified some of the terminology, and simplified parts of the model. XTM gained immediate recognition and has to all intents and

Encyclopedia of Library and Information Sciences, Fourth Edition DOI: 10.1081/E-ELIS4-120044331

purposes replaced the original version. In 2003, the XTM DTD was folded back into the second edition of the ISO standard[2] and from that point on stewardship of the standard passed back to the ISO committee.

Current Status

In 2003 a road map was devised for the further development of the standard, to include a data model, reference model, query language, and constraint language. As of the present writing (late 2008), the Topic Maps family of ISO specifications is as follows:

- ISO/IEC 13250: Information Technology—Topic Maps—
  — Part 1: Overview and basic concepts[3]
  — Part 2: Data model[4]
  — Part 3: XML syntax[5]
  — Part 4: Canonicalization[6]
  — Part 5: Reference model[7]
  — Part 6: Compact syntax[8]
  — Part 7: Graphical notation[9]
- ISO/IEC 18048: Information Technology—TQML[10]
- ISO/IEC 19076: Information Technology—TMCL[11]
- ISO/IEC TR 29111: Information Technology—Topic Maps—Expressing Dublin Core Metadata using Topic Maps[12]

Parts 2 and 3 were published in 2007. Most of the remainder exist as stable drafts and are expected to be published in 2009. Work continues in SC 34/WG 3 and interested parties are encouraged to attend meetings and participate through their national standards bodies. For further information, see the SC 34 Web site at http://www.jtc1sc34.org and the WG 3 Web site at http://www.isotopicmaps.org.

CORE CONCEPTS

This section presents the core concepts of the Topic Maps paradigm. The back-of-book index is used throughout as a familiar point of reference for illustrative purposes. In line with long-established tradition in the Topic Maps community, this entry will use the domain of opera for its examples, based on the *Italian Opera Topic Map*.[13]

Subjects

The core concepts of Topic Maps are relatively few and for the most part easily grasped. They are often referred to as the "TAO of Topic Maps," after the eponymous paper which has served as a basic introduction since it was first published in 2000.[14] However, even more fundamental than the TAO is the emphasis on *subjects*.

In the Topic Maps world view, the most essential property of information is not where it resides (the document-centric view) or which application was used to create it (the application-centric view), but its *aboutness*, i.e., the subject (or subjects) that it is about. This subject-centric view lies at the very heart of the Topic Maps paradigm.

There are many reasons for insisting on the primacy of subjects: the starting point for most acts of information retrieval (e.g., searches on the Web) is one or more subjects; in the aggregation of information and knowledge, subjects usually constitute the most useful collation points; in fact, the whole purpose of creating information can be viewed as capturing knowledge *about certain subjects* in order that it can be shared and reused. While other forms of metadata such as author, publisher, and creation date are important for certain information management tasks, for the key end-user task of information retrieval, aboutness is most critical. Since the purpose of Topic Maps is to alleviate infoglut and improve the findability of information, subject-centricity is the central feature.

Subjects and topics

The concept of "subject" is defined by ISO/IEC 13250:2006[4] as follows:

3.14 **subject**

anything whatsoever, regardless of whether it exists or has any other specific characteristics, about which anything whatsoever may be asserted by any means whatsoever

A subject, in other words, is literally anything about which the author of a topic map wishes to make assertions. Typical subjects in the domain of opera might be the composer Giacomo Puccini; his operas, including *Tosca* and *Madama Butterfly*; Lucca, the city where Puccini was born; and Teatro Costanzi, where *Tosca* was first performed. These are also the kind of subjects one would expect to find in the index of a book on opera.

The Topic Maps data model (TMDM)[4] defines a model for representing subjects such as these, and assertions about them, within an information system. The Topic Maps Reference Model (TMRM),[7] which offers a more abstract and low-level model, is described below. In order to represent a subject a proxy is required, and this is called a "topic." A topic is thus the (symbolic) representation of a (nonsymbolic) referent, i.e., the subject. In the words of the standard:

3.18 **topic**

symbol used within a topic map to represent one, and only one, subject, in order to allow statements to be made about the subject

A topic map covering the domain of opera will thus include topics that represent subjects such as Puccini, *Tosca*, and Lucca.

The collocation objective

Topic Maps employs the nearly synonymous words "topic" and "subject" as very precise terms for the two components of a representation relationship: symbol and referent (Fig. 1).

There is a one-to-one relationship between topics and subjects in the sense that each topic, by definition, represents one and only one subject. Because of this, the terms "topic" and "subject" are often used interchangeably in informal discourse about Topic Maps. The goal of any Topic Maps application is to ensure that each subject is represented by one, and only one, topic. Once this goal (referred to as the "collocation objective") is achieved, everything that is known (within a given system) about a particular subject becomes accessible from a single point, via the one and only topic representing that subject, and thus the problem of information retrieval is in principle solved.

The means by which the collocation objective is achieved within a system relies heavily on the Topic Maps concept of "identity," which can also be applied across systems, and thus provides the foundation for "global knowledge interchange"—the potentially unrestricted collation of knowledge from disparate sources. The term "global knowledge interchange" is due to Steve Newcomb.[15]

Identity

The fundamental issue in achieving the collocation objective is to know when two topics represent the same subject, a situation that can often arise when merging topic maps. When this is the case, the two topics in question must be merged into a single topic that has the union of the characteristics (i.e., names, occurrences, and associations) of the original topics. Once the two topics have been merged, order will have been restored and collocation will once more obtain.

Since the merging of topic maps is intended to be an automated process, the key question is, how can a machine "know" when two topics represent the same subject? The solution adopted in the TMDM is to use explicit, globally unique identifiers. If two topics share an identifier they are deemed to represent the same subject and merging occurs. Identifiers usually take the form of Uniform Resource Identifiers (URIs) and these come in two flavors: "subject identifiers" and "subject locators." The TMDM actually allows any kind of "locator notation" to be used, but the interchange syntax (XTM) only supports Internationalized Resource Identifiers (IRIs), an extended form of URIs which permits international characters. A third kind of identifier, item identifiers, are only of interest to implementors of Topic Maps systems. Subject locators were called subject addresses in the first version of the standard.

Subject locators, as their name suggests, are URIs that identify subjects via their location. They can therefore only be used with subjects that have a specific location that can be expressed using a URI—in other words, network-addressable information resources, such as documents (in the broadest sense), newsfeeds, and other data that can be retrieved via Web-based queries. Subjects like this can be identified *directly* via their network addresses.

Most subjects, like Puccini, *Tosca*, and Lucca, do not fall into this category. They reside outside any computer system and are thus in some sense "ineffable"; there is a chasm between the "outside world" in which they exist and the computer system in which they are represented, and this chasm can ultimately only be bridged by human intellect. This is achieved in the Topic Maps paradigm through *indirect* identification using subject identifiers.

A subject identifier is (also) a URI, but it does not address the subject directly; rather it addresses it indirectly, via a "subject descriptor," which the TMDM defines as an "information resource that is referred to from a topic map in an attempt to unambiguously identify the subject represented by a topic to a human being." Subject descriptor is sometimes also termed "subject indicator."

Fig. 2 shows how an ineffable (or "non-addressable") subject, such as Puccini, can be identified indirectly via a subject descriptor, whose address (http://psi.ontopedia.net/Puccini) functions as a subject identifier.

The distinction between direct and indirect identification, which is supported in both the TMDM and the interchanges syntaxes, provides a solution to what has been widely referred to as the "identity crisis" that has caused concern in the Semantic Web community over a number of years.[16] At the same time, the duality of subject identifier and subject descriptor neatly reflects the dichotomy of the human/computer relationship. Subject identifiers are for use by computers in ascertaining whether or not two topics represent the same subject: if two topics have an identifier in common, they are simply merged; computers have no need to resolve the URI to ascertain exactly what the subject is. Humans, on the other hand, need to be able to do this, because it is they who are ultimately responsible for assigning identifiers; the subject descriptor provides them with an "indication" (through a description, definition, illustration, or whatever) of the subject in question.

Topics are surrogates, or "proxies" (inside the computer) for the ineffable *subjects* that you might want to talk about, such as Puccini, love, or the second law of thermodynamics

A *subject* in the real world

A *topic* in the computer domain

Fig. 1 Subjects and topics.

Technical–Topic

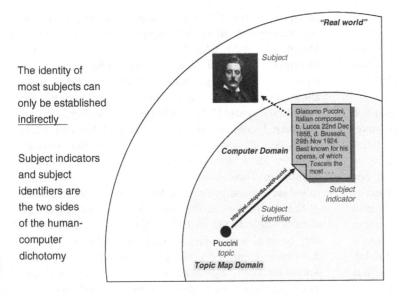

The identity of
most subjects can
only be established
indirectly

Subject indicators
and subject
identifiers are
the two sides
of the human-
computer
dichotomy

Fig. 2   Subject identifiers.

The concepts of indirect identification using subject identifiers and subject descriptors has been extended into a whole paradigm, known as "published subjects" that seeks to provide an open, distributed solution to the problem of defining and discovering globally unique subject identifiers.[17]

The TAO of Topic Maps

Having covered the essentials of subjects and how they are represented by topics, we now turn to assertions about subjects.

A topic map is a representation of a set of assertions about one or more subjects. The TMDM defines three kinds of assertion—or "statement"—that can be made about a subject: "names," "occurrences," and "associations" (Fig. 3). Associations represent general relationships between subjects; occurrences represent a particular form of "aboutness" relationship in which the participants are an information resource and a subject that the resource is "about"; and names represent relationships between subjects and the labels used by humans to refer to them.

Topics represent
subjects

Associations represent
relationships

Occurrences link
resources to topics

Each of these can
be typed

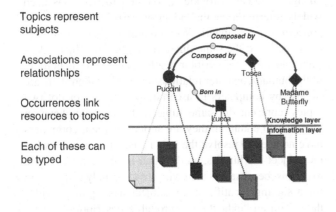

Fig. 3   The TAO model.

The following section describes each of these in more detail.

Associations and roles

Associations express relationships among subjects, for example between Puccini and *Tosca*, or between Puccini and Lucca. They correspond to *See also* entries in a back-of-book index and serve a similar navigational purpose. But there is an important difference in that associations permit the nature of each relationship to be made explicit using "association types": thus, the relationship between Puccini and *Tosca* can be stated to be of type "composed by," whereas that between Puccini and Lucca is of type "born in." The ability to distinguish association types adds precision, provides more information to the user, and improves findability. Association types are themselves subjects and are therefore represented as topics.

A single association may involve any number of subjects. Binary associations (involving two subjects, as in the examples given so far) are by far the most common, and also the easiest to process; they correspond somewhat to transitive verbal constructs in natural language, such as "*Puccini* composed *Tosca*." Ternary associations (involving three subjects), while less common, can be useful for relationships that in English might be expressed using a ditransitive verb or an additional thematic role ("*Tosca* kills *Scarpia* with a *knife*"). Associations of higher arity are infrequent; the relationships they might be used to represent (such as that between an opera and multiple librettists) are usually better expressed using multiple binary associations. Unary associations (involving a single subject) are also possible; they often correspond to intransitive verbs and can be used to represent "relationships" that in other modeling paradigms might be expressed using Boolean properties (e.g., "*Turandot* was unfinished").

Describing a relationship in natural language can give a false impression of directionality: there is no difference, in terms of the basic relationship being described, between the statements "*Tosca* was composed by Puccini" and "Puccini composed *Tosca*." The difference is rather one of focus. This situation is reflected in Topic Maps by the absence of any formal notion of direction in associations. The order in which topics are specified has no significance; instead, the nature of the subject's involvement in the relationship is expressed through the concept of "association role." Each participant in an association is deemed to play a "role" of a certain type. In order to clarify the respective roles of the participants in the example above (and avoid the possible interpretation of Puccini having been composed by *Tosca* instead of vice versa), it must be explicitly stated that Puccini plays the role of (say) "composer," and that *Tosca* plays the role of (say) "work." In more precise Topic Maps terminology, "composer" and "work" are "association role *types*" and, like association types, they are represented by topics (Fig. 4). Exactly what constitutes the roles in this relationship (as opposed to the role types) is less immediately intuitive; one approach is to think in terms of Puccini qua composer of Tosca (as opposed to Puccini qua composer of Madama Butterfly—or indeed qua husband of Elvira or qua pupil of Ponchielli).

Association types (and role types) are defined by the topic map author according to the requirements of the information, the knowledge it embodies, and the application for which it is intended. There is thus no limit to the kinds of relationship that may be expressed in Topic Maps. However, because of their ubiquity (and utility) in knowledge modeling, two association types are given special status. These are "type-instance" and "supertype–subtype" which carry particular semantics defined in terms of membership of sets of topics called "topic types." Their special status consists in the following: 1) the standard defines identifiers for these association types (and their corresponding role types) in the TMDM; 2) special syntax is available for type-instance in XTM and Compact Topic Maps Syntax (CTM); and 3) they invoke the application of

inheritance mechanisms in certain forms of processing in the query and constraint languages.

Topic types constitute a built-in mechanism for classifying topics and for building a certain kind of hierarchy. That is, type hierarchies–not subject hierarchies of the kind used in subject classification systems, where the subjects do not necessarily (or usually) constitute sets or classes, and the transitivity of type hierarchies does not hold. These can be represented in Topic Maps (as discussed below) but not by using the predefined association types. Topic types for the example topics mentioned so far might be "composer" (for Puccini), "opera" (*Tosca*), and "city" (Lucca). These might in turn be defined as subtypes of "person," "musical work," and "place," respectively.

It is important not to conflate the concepts of topic type and association role type. The former classifies a subject in terms of its "essential being," whereas the latter merely describes the role it plays in a particular relationship. Sometimes, however, the same topic is used as both a topic type and an association role type. This is because the essential being of a subject is often defined in terms of some kind of relationship: it is precisely because Puccini composed *Tosca* (and many other operas) that he is today regarded first and foremost as a composer; he both *plays the role of* "composer" (in the relationship with *Tosca*, etc.) and at the same time *is a* "composer." On the other hand, the roles he plays in his relationships with his teacher Ponchielli, his wife Elvira, and his birthplace Lucca, are of different types, namely "pupil," "husband," and "person" (Fig. 5). Note that there is almost always an implicit supertype -subtype relationship between the role type and the type of the role playing topic, but there is no general rule for which is which.

Occurrences

Occurrences represent a particular kind of relationship—that of "aboutness" between an information resource and a subject. The resource in question may be very small, such as a string representing a date, in which case it is normally

Technical–Topic

Composer   City

Role types (here, person, and place) characterize the nature of the subject's involvement in the relationship

Fig. 4 Anatomy of an association.

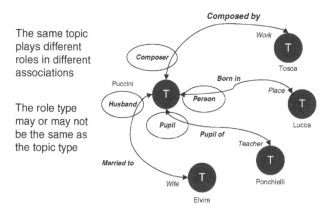

Fig. 5 Role type and topic type.

included in the topic map and known as an "internal occurrence." Or else it may be stored externally, because of its size, notation, provenance, or whatever, and referenced via a locator—normally a URL—which corresponds to a page number in a back-of-index (itself a locator for some piece of information relevant to the subject in question). In the latest version of the Topic Maps standard, support is included for specifying the data type (i.e., notation or format) of an occurrence.

Like associations (and association roles), occurrences may be classified by type; typical "occurrence types" in the domain of opera might be "biography" and "date of birth" (for topics of type "composer"); "synopsis" and "premiere date" (for topics of type "opera"); and "map" (for topics of type "city"). Occurrence types provide more information to the user about the nature of the related resource (in contrast to an unqualified list of page numbers in a typical back-of-book index).

Finally, occurrence types—like association types and role types—may be freely defined (again, as topics) to suit the needs of users and applications; there are no predefined types.

Names

Because of their importance in providing labels by means of which humans can refer to and discourse about subjects, names are given privileged status in the Topic Maps model. They may be regarded as a special type of occurrence that carries naming semantics. Like occurrences, names may be typed (and once again, name types are represented as topics), but unlike occurrences they are restricted to a single data type, "string," in order to ensure that they can always be processed by any system.

It is also possible to specify "variants" of a name, and this facility is widely used to represent sort keys, alternative orthographies, transliterations, misspellings, and so on.

In order to cater for synonyms, the model allows multiple names for the same subject. Distinctions such as language, preferred status, and context of use may be indicated using name types or the concept of "scope" (discussed below).

There is no specific facility in the model for handling homonyms because there is no need: there are no restrictions on what names a subject can have, nor on whether two (or more) subjects have the same name, so homonymy is not an issue as far as the model is concerned. It is left to the application to provide disambiguation based on contextual information available in the topic map: the first line of disambiguation is usually the topic type ("Tosca the opera" as opposed to "Tosca the character"); when this does not suffice, some other association can be used, as with "Puccini's *Bohème*" (i.e., the *La Bohème composed by* Puccini) as opposed to "Catalani's *Bohème*," or "the Paris *located in* France" as opposed to "the Paris *located in* Texas."

Fig. 3 illustrates the basic TAO model and depicts an information layer (below), containing information resources of any and every shape and form, and a knowledge layer (above). The latter consists of (typed) topics and associations, and is connected to the information layer via (typed) occurrences. Identity, scope, and reification (described below) are not depicted.

Ontologies

The term "typing topic" is used informally to refer to any topic that is used (or intended to be used) to type some other construct, whether it be a topic, association, association role, occurrence, or name. Taken together, the set of typing topics in a topic map constitutes a description of the kind of "things" (i.e., subjects) and the kind of relationships that exist in the domain in question (e.g., opera). Viewed in this way, the typing topics can be said to represent the "ontology" of the topic map and the topic map to contain its own ontology. There is no single, broadly accepted definition of the term "ontology" in the information sciences, nor is it defined in the Topic Maps standard, but the informal usage adopted here corresponds very closely to that of John Sowa who defines ontology as a "classification of the types and subtypes of concepts and relations necessary to describe everything in the application domain."[18]

Constraints on the types (or classes) that constitute an ontology are defined using TMCL, discussed below.

Additional Concepts

The basic model of (typed) topics that can have names and occurrences and play roles in associations with other topics is very simple and yet powerful enough to express a broad range of knowledge structures—in fact, to make any kind of assertion about any kind of subject—and many current applications of Topic Maps use no more than this core functionality. Additional concepts that provide further expressivity are "scope" (for qualifying assertions in terms of their contextual validity) and "reification" (for making assertions about assertions).

Scope

Knowledge that is aggregated from different sources through the merging of topic maps is likely to contain contradictory statements or have varying relevance in different contexts. For this reason, Topic Maps includes a built-in mechanism called "scope" for expressing the contextual validity of any assertion. Scope is expressed as a set of topics which qualify a statement (i.e., a name, occurrence, or association) and indicate the context in which the assertion represented by the statement may be considered valid. If no scope is explicitly specified, the scope is said to be "unconstrained."

The interpretation of what it means to be "valid," and precisely how the scoping topics "indicate" context, is left to the application and as a result the interoperability of scope is limited. However, usage conventions emerging among users of Topic Maps are resulting in increased interoperability. These include specifying the historical applicability or natural language of names and expressing the provenance of occurrences and associations.

Examples of the use of scope in the *Italian Opera Topic Map* include:

- English names of certain operas.
- Provenance of conflicting assertions (e.g., whether the opera *Isabeau* was first performed at the Teatro Colon or the Teatro Coliseo).
- Source of multiple synopses of the same opera (e.g., from Arizona Opera and Opera News).
- Context in which a character has a certain voice type (e.g., Musetta, a soprano in Puccini's *La Bohème* and a mezzo in Leoncavallo's).

Reification

Scope can be regarded as a special case (asserting the *contextual validity* of an assertion) of a more general capability (asserting *anything* about an assertion). Assertions represent relationships between subjects, but a relationship can be regarded as a subject in its own right, about which one might want to make further assertions. One way to do this is to represent the relationship as a topic from the outset; another is to "reify" the name, occurrence, or association in question.

Reification (literally "thingification") in the Topic Maps sense of the term is defined as "making a topic represent the subject of another topic map construct," in other words, turning a name, occurrence, association role (or even the topic map itself) into a topic in order to make assertions about the thing it represents. This is equivalent to nominalization in natural language, as in "Reagan met Gorbachev in ReykjavıÇk. The meeting took place in October 1986." In the *Italian Opera Topic Map* the relationship between *Tosca* and Rome (where the opera takes place), is reified as a "The setting of Tosca in Rome" in order to provide an appropriate subject for classifying Susan Nicassio's book *Tosca's Rome*.

The most widespread use of reification is to reify the topic map itself, thereby creating a topic that can be used for specifying metadata about the topic map (for example, using Dublin Core as discussed below).

THE TOPIC MAPS FAMILY OF STANDARDS

The model described in the preceding sections is specified in detail in the TMDM, which is Part 2 of the ISO standard.[4] This section provides a brief overview of the remaining parts (excluding Part 1, which is merely a nonnormative introduction), along with short descriptions of two related standards, ISO 18048 (TQML) and ISO 19756 (TMCL), and a technical report, ISO TR 29111 (Expressing Dublin Core Metadata in Topic Maps).

Syntaxes and Notations

Part 3 of ISO 13250[5] specifies an XML-based syntax called XTM whose purpose is to enable topic maps to be interchanged between systems. This is the core interchange syntax; it is defined in terms of a mapping to the TMDM and all conforming Topic Maps systems are expected to support it. The original HyTime-based syntax (HyTM) is no longer part of the standard and most tools do not support it. However, because it is rather verbose, XTM is not generally considered suitable for hand-editing, and for that reason other, nonstandard syntaxes were devised (Fig. 6). The most widely used of these are LTM[19] and AsTMa,[20] both of which offer compact, text-based notations. A standard text-based notation called CTM[8] has been defined more recently; a visual notation called Graphical Topic Maps Notation (GTM)[9] provides a common way of visualizing topic maps and their ontologies, and a canonicalization syntax (CXTM)[6] supports conformance testing of Topic Maps systems.

The Reference Model

Part 5 of ISO 13250[7] defines a low-level model called the TMRM which is more abstract and has fewer ontological commitments than the TMDM. Its purpose is to serve as a minimal, conceptual foundation for subject-centric data models such as the TMDM, and to supply ontologically neutral terminology for their disclosure. It defines what is required to enable mapping between different subject-centric data models in order to meet the overall goal of the Topic Maps standards, that each subject has a single location for all the information about it.

The TMRM is defined in terms of proxies consisting of properties which themselves are key/value pairs; the only ontological commitments are two types of relationship: *sub* (subclass of) and *isa* (instance of). In addition to requirements on constraint languages and merging operations, the TMRM includes a path expression language and a mapping to the TMDM, and thereby provides a formal semantics for the latter. It also provides a formal foundation for the related standards TQML and TMCL.

The Query Language

Topic Maps Query Language[10] provides a standard way of accessing Topic Maps-based information, just as Structured Query Language (SQL) does for relational data and XQuery does for XML data. The initial version provides

```
<topic id="la-boheme">
  <instanceOf><topicRef xlink:href="#opera"/></instanceOf>
  <baseName>
    <baseNameString>La Bohème</baseNameString>
    <variant>
      <parameters>
        <subjectIndicatorRef
          xlink:href="http://www.topicmaps.org/xtm/1.0/core.xtm#sort"/>
      </parameters>
      <variantName><resourceData>Boheme, La</resourceData></variantName>
    </variant>
  </baseName>
  <occurrence>
    <instanceOf><topicRef xlink:href="#homepage"/></instanceOf>
    <resourceRef
       xlink:href="http://www.opera.it/Opere/La-Boheme/La-Boheme.html"/>
  </occurrence>
  <occurrence>
    <instanceOf><topicRef xlink:href="#premiere-date"/></instanceOf>
    <resourceData>1896-02-01</resourceData>
  </occurrence>
</topic>
```

Fig. 6 XTM 1.0 syntax.

access functionality only; later versions are expected to also cover updates. The language currently offers three very powerful and isomorphic ways to express queries:

- SELECT expressions, with FROM, WHERE, ORDER BY, UNIQUE, OFFSET, and LIMIT clauses.
- FLWR expressions, with FOR, WHERE, ORDER BY, and RETURN clauses.
- Path expressions, similar in flavor to Xpath, which can be used alone or in combination with the foregoing.

All three types of expression can return results in tabular form; FLWR expressions can additionally generate XML and Topic Maps output.

The Constraint Language

Topic Maps Constraint Language[11] defines a language for expressing ontology-based constraints that a class of topic maps is expected to follow, thus ensuring greater consistency and more predictable results for both users and applications.

Typical constraints on the *Italian Opera Topic Map* might be as follows:

- All topics of type "composer" must play the role of "composer" in at least one "composed-by" association.
- Every "composed-by" relationship must involve exactly two topics of types "composer" and "opera," playing the roles "composer" and "work," respectively.

TMCL defines constraint types and an interpretation of instances of those types. The interpretation indicates what it means for an instance of a given constraint type to be evaluated in the context of a TMDM instance, with the result of the evaluation being either true or false. Constraint types are defined in terms of the TMDM and their formal interpretation in terms of TQML.

KNOWLEDGE ORGANIZATION

One of the most important aspects of Topic Maps is the ability of the model to represent virtually any kind of knowledge structure or data model. It is this capability— coupled with the ability to merge arbitrary topic maps— that underlies its value proposition: improved information management and enhanced findability through connecting disparate systems and collating information and knowledge from different sources.

Given that the original impetus for the development of the Topic Maps paradigm came from the requirement to be able to merge back-of-book indexes, it is only to be expected that the model should handle every feature of indexes. But the model was also constructed in such a way that it extends to every other known form of knowledge organization, including thesauri, bibliographic records, glossaries, and subject classification systems[21]—and can also subsume hierarchical, relational, and associative data models in general. This section explains how such structures are mapped to the Topic Maps model.

Indexes

Most back-of-book indexes consist of a set of *entries*, arranged alphabetically by *main heading* (sometimes called an "access point" or "subject heading") and containing zero or more *subentries* (or "subheadings"), *reference locators*, and *cross-references*.[22]

In Topic Maps terms, every *entry* (except those that only consist of a *See* cross-reference, discussed below) corresponds to a topic and its *main heading* corresponds to a topic name. *Subentries* are named topics that are related to the topic of the main entry by an association of type "subentry of" (with the role types "main entry" and "subentry"). *Reference locators* equate to the locators of (external) occurrences, which would normally take the form of URIs rather than page numbers. *See also* references correspond to generic associations (of type "see also," or simply "related to") between topics that represent the respective entries. Finally, *See* references indicate alternate labels for the topics represented by the referenced entries and thus correspond to additional names (of type "alternate name") for the topics representing those entries.

In some indexes the typeface used for main headings may vary (usually italic in addition to roman, sometimes also boldface). This is a simple form of classification by topic type. Similarly, the use of a different typeface for a reference locator (i.e., page number) is a simple form of classification by occurrence type. Finally, some books contain multiple indexes (e.g., people, places, subjects), which again corresponds to the use of topic types.

Glossaries

A glossary is a list of terms in a particular domain of knowledge along with their definitions. Like indexes, glossaries consist of a set of alphabetically arranged entries, each of which is the equivalent of a main heading. Subentries are not usual, but *See* and *See also* cross-references may occur. Most importantly, each glossary entry contains a definition instead of reference locators.

Using Topic Maps a glossary can be modeled exactly like an index, except that instead of multiple external occurrences, the topic corresponding to each glossary entry will have a single internal occurrence of type "definition." Thus multiple indexes and glossaries can all be represented within a single topic map.

Thesauri

A thesaurus consists of a set of *terms* and *scope notes*, organized through three kinds of semantic relationship: *equivalence*, *hierarchy*, and *association*. Terms are the names of concepts and thus correspond to topic names; scope notes consist of information pertinent to the topic and therefore correspond to occurrences of type "scope note."

The equivalence relationship handles synonyms and thus corresponds to topics with multiple names; a USE relation would indicate the default (preferred) topic name, while a USED FOR relation would indicate a name of type "non-preferred" or "alternate."

Hierarchy relationships are created by pointing to *broader terms* (BT) and *narrower terms* (NT). Since these are the inverse of each other, they correspond to associations of a single type ("broader/narrower") which link topics representing broader concepts (e.g., "opera") to topics representing narrower concepts (e.g., "aria"). In some thesauri other, more semantically explicit kinds of hierarchical relationship are used (e.g., generic and partitive). These can be represented using more specific association types. Note that the BT/NT relationship, despite being hierarchical, is not the same as the supertype/subtype relationship defined in the Topic Maps standard.

Finally, associative relationships (indicated using *related terms*, RT) equate to *See also* references in back-of-book indexes: they are (nonhierarchical) relationships of no specific type and thus correspond to associations of type "related to."

Since indexes, glossaries, and thesauri can all be represented by the same model, they can be combined in a single topic map, thus removing potential redundancy. In fact, if the topics that represent index and glossary entries are arranged hierarchically, using associations of type "broader/narrower," the result *is* a thesaurus—or possibly multiple thesauri, depending on the number of hierarchies involved. Individual documents or information resources are classified against such a thesaurus by making them occurrences of one or more thesaurus topics.

Taxonomies and subject classification systems are similar to thesauri; they are often somewhat simpler, and they may be more constrained (for example, some taxonomies allow only a strict-type hierarchy based on the generic supertype/subtype relationship), but their representation as topic maps and their practical application is essentially the same.

Faceted Classification

A faceted classification system can be viewed as a set of classification subjects that are grouped along axes called facets. In a topic map this is represented as a set of topics, each of which is related via an association to a topic that represents a facet, and some of which may be organized hierarchically via additional associations.

Bibliographic Records

Bibliographic records are descriptions of information entities, which may be abstract (works) or concrete (documents).[23] They employ bibliographic languages to describe the attributes of those entities, ranging from the properties of *works* (e.g., author, title, subject), to the properties of *expressions* (translator, editor, language), *manifestations* (publisher, ISBN, format), and *items* (location, call number, condition). Attributes are described as property/value pairs in which the value can be a string, date, integer, or some other data type; or else the name of another entity (such as the author or publisher).

Bibliographic records based on languages of this kind can be represented as topic maps by creating topics to represent each information entity and using statements (names, occurrences, or associations, as appropriate) to represent the attributes. Those attributes with naming semantics (e.g., title) become topic names; attributes that name other entities (e.g., author, publisher), or that represent terms in an authority file (e.g., a predefined set of media types) become associations and give rise to topics that represent the entities or terms in question; other attributes are represented as either internal or (occasionally) external occurrences.

One widely used bibliographic language is the Dublin Core Metadata Set[24] which defines a basic set of 15 abstract "elements," along with a number of "other elements and element refinements," a set of encoding schemes, and a (media) type vocabulary. An ISO Technical Report[12] describes how to represent Dublin Core descriptions using Topic Maps.[25] A similar approach can be used with MARC-21.

In the FRBR (Functional Requirements for Bibliographic Records) model, relationships between works and expressions are represented by an association, as are relationships between expressions and manifestations, and between manifestations and items. Entities of all kinds (including groups 2 and 3) are represented as topics.[26]

Other Data Models

In addition to the knowledge models described above, most forms of structured data can be represented as topic maps through some kind of schema-dependent mapping. This section looks briefly at how this works with XML (hierarchical), RDBMS (relational database management system), and Resource Description Framework (RDF) (associative) data, respectively.

XML allows the structure of information to be represented in a hierarchy of elements and subelements, with some annotation of elements (via attributes), including linking across (and beyond) the element hierarchy. The semantics of the element and attribute types are vocabulary dependent, but they can be extracted and represented as a topic map using techniques described by Pepper and Garshol[27] and Garshol and Bogachev.[28]

In the entity–relation (ER) model, entities equate to topic types and relations to association types, while attributes correspond to names, occurrences, and identifiers (Fig. 7). When mapping relational data to a topic map, each row in an entity table (for example, "Organizations") gives rise to a topic of the corresponding type (in this case, "organization"); each column can result in an identifier, name, occurrence, or association, depending on whether the data is an ID, a string with naming semantics, some other kind of string data, or a foreign key reference, respectively. Each row in a relation table (for example, "Employment") results in an association of the given type (here, "employed by") whose role players are found via the foreign key references.

The associative (graph-based) model of the RDF is much closer to the Topic Maps model than XML or ER, and this means that RDF data can be used in Topic Maps systems with almost no mapping.[29,30] It has also been demonstrated that data conforming to EXPRESS data models can be transformed to Topic Maps with relative ease, although this work has not yet been published. The EXPRESS modeling language is part of the product data standard STEP (ISO 10303).

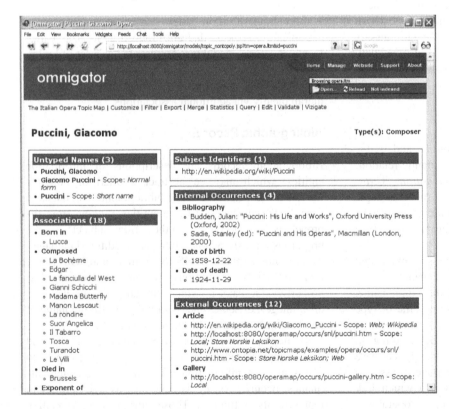

Fig. 7 A topic page in the Omnigator.

AREAS OF APPLICATION

As the preceding section has shown, virtually any form of structured data, information, or knowledge can be represented as a topic map. This is not to suggest that all information should be maintained directly in Topic Maps form. A more common scenario is to use Topic Maps as a meta-model for integrating portions of data that originate from different systems (some of which may be Topic Maps-based). The procedure is to generate multiple topic maps from disparate sources and then merge them to provide a unified view of the information gestalt.

It is the flexibility of the Topic Maps model and the robustness of the identity paradigm on which merging is based that provide the clue to identifying application scenarios in which the technology can excel. Another quality of Topic Maps is its intuitiveness: experience shows that the TAO model is very easy for users to grasp, presumably because it derives from artifacts, such as indexes, that humans have used for centuries to locate and manage information. The associative nature of the model is also a factor in this, reflecting as it does how people think, learn, and store information in their own "semantic memories."

Most applications of Topic Maps fall into four broad categories: enterprise information integration (EII), KM, e-learning, and Web publishing.

From the EII perspective, Topic Maps offers an out-of-the-box "meta-model" for integrating information, and a powerful identity mechanism for enabling subject-based merging. A topic map can provide an aggregation layer on top of existing information systems, or function as a hub for transferring data between systems, or both. Either way, Topic Maps removes the need for costly point-to-point system integration.

From the KM perspective, Topic Maps provides—arguably for the first time—the ability to really capture and manage some degree of *human knowledge*—not just information—in a standards-based form, enabling it to be shared and reused across departments, organizations, and systems. The topic/association layer constitutes a distributable and queryable knowledge base, which can be tightly coupled with content management systems via the occurrence axis.

In the domain of e-learning, Topic Maps has particular relevance, not just because of its strengths as a content management technology, but because it bridges the gap between information and knowledge.[31] In Norway, successful experiments have been conducted in which school students are encouraged to create topic maps to record what they have learned, and the National School Curriculum itself now has its definitive expression in the form of a topic map.[32]

One application whose potential is as yet largely untapped is the use of Topic Maps as the foundation for digital libraries. At its most basic, a digital library can be defined as digital content that is organized along bibliographic principles. It requires technology of a new kind that is attuned to the needs of digital information while at the same time supporting bibliographic principles and practices. Topic Maps is just that. An early example of the application of Topic Maps to this purpose is the award-winning New Zealand Electronic Text Centre (Fig. 8).[33]

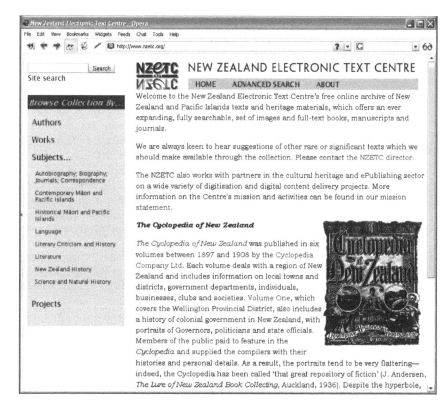

Fig. 8 A Topic Maps-based digital library.
Source: http://www.nzetc.org.[33]

Technical–Topic

In all of these applications, and many others besides, the World Wide Web provides the most important channel for disseminating information, via Web sites, portals, and intranets. Despite in some ways predating the Web, Topic Maps has proven to be well-suited to this form of publishing: the TAO model offers a readymade "information architecture" in which each page is devoted to a single well-defined topic and contains information collated from the names and occurrences of that topic, with intuitive navigation paths between pages generated from associations between topics. An increasing number of second and third generation Web sites are currently reorganizing their content into topic maps, and a product such as the *Omnigator*,[34] which is a Web-based browser for topic maps (Fig. 7), is essentially a tool for creating "instant Web sites": when it loads a topic map, the result is a bare-bones, out-of-the-box Web site.

CONCLUSION

Topic Maps is a paradigm-shifting technology. Through its emphasis on the centrality of subjects, rather than documents or applications, it presages a radically new way of using computers to manage information and knowledge, dubbed subject-centric computing.

The key strengths of Topic Maps are a flexible model that can represent any kind of data structure; a robust model of identity; the ability to merge arbitrary topic maps; a well-defined syntax for exchanging topic maps between systems; status as an ISO-approved international standard; and a vibrant and committed user community. Witness the annual user's conference in Oslo, the annual academic conference (Topic Maps Research and Applications, TMRA) in Leipzig, the Web site http://www.topicmaps.com, various mailing lists, etc.

Topic Maps is particularly well-suited for integrating information from disparate sources, bridging the gap between information and knowledge, and acting as an information architecture for Web-based information delivery.

REFERENCES

1. Pepper, S.; Moore, G., Eds. *XML Topic Maps (XTM) 1.0*; TopicMaps.Org 2001, Available at http://www.topicmaps.org/xtm/1.0/ (accessed November 15, 2008).
2. *ISO/IEC 13250:2003 Information Technology—SGML Applications—Topic Maps*, 2nd Ed. International Organization for Standardization: Geneva, Switzerland, 2003.
3. *ISO/IEC 13250 Information Technology—Topic Maps—Part 1: Overview and Basic Concepts*, Available at http://www.jtc1sc34.org/repository/0877.zip (accessed November 15, 2008).
4. *ISO/IEC 13250:2006 Information Technology—Topic Maps—Part 2: Data Model*, Available at http://www.isotopicmaps.org/sam/sam-model/ (accessed November 15, 2008).
5. *ISO/IEC 13250:2007 Information Technology—Topic Maps—Part 3: XML Syntax*, Available at http://www.isotopicmaps.org/sam/sam-xtm/ (accessed November 15, 2008).
6. *ISO/IEC 13250 Information Technology—Topic Maps—Part 4: Canonical Syntax*, Available at http://www.isotopicmaps.org/cxtm/ (accessed November 15, 2008).
7. *ISO/IEC 13250 Information Technology—Topic Maps—Part 5: Reference Model*, Available at http://www.isotopicmaps.org/tmrm/ (accessed November 15, 2008).
8. *ISO/IEC 13250 Information Technology—Topic Maps—Part 6: Compact Syntax*, Available at http://www.isotopicmaps.org/ctm/ (accessed November 15, 2008).
9. *ISO/IEC 13250 Information Technology—Topic Maps—Part 7: Graphical Notation*, Available at http://www.isotopicmaps.org/gtm/ (accessed November 15, 2008).
10. *ISO/IEC CD 18048: Information Technology—Topic Maps—Query Language (TQML)*, International Organization for Standardization: Geneva, Switzerland, 2007; Available at http://www.isotopicmaps.org/tmql/ (accessed November 15, 2008).
11. *ISO/IEC CD 18048: Information Technology—Topic Maps—Constraint Language (TMCL)*, International Organization for Standardization: Geneva, Switzerland, 2007; Available at http://www.isotopicmaps.org/tmcl/ (accessed November 15, 2008).
12. *ISO/IEC TR 29111 Information Technology—Topic Maps—Expressing Dublin Core Metadata Using Topic Maps*, International Organization for Standardization: Geneva, Switzerland, 2007; Available at http://www.jtc1sc34.org/repository/0884.htm (accessed November 15, 2008).
13. Pepper, S. *The Italian Opera Topic Map*, Available at http://www.ontopedia.net/omnigator/ (accessed November 15, 2008).
14. Pepper, S. *The TAO of Topic Maps*, Ontopia, 2002; Available at http://www.ontopia.net/topicmaps/materials/tao.html (accessed November 15, 2008).
15. Newcomb, S.R. A perspective on the quest for global knowledge interchange. In *XML Topic Maps: Creating and Using Topic Maps for the Web*; Park, J., Hunting, S., Eds.; Addison-Wesley: Boston, MA, 2003; Available at http://www.pearsonhighered.com/samplechapter/0201749602.pdf (accessed November 15, 2008).
16. Pepper, S.; Schwab, S. *Curing the Web's Identity Crisis: Subject Indicators for RDF*, Ontopia, 2003; Available at http://www.ontopia.net/topicmaps/materials/identitycrisis.html (accessed November 15, 2008).
17. Pepper, S. *The Case for Published Subjects*, Ontopia, 2006; Available at http://www.ontopia.net/topicmaps/materials/The_Case_for_Published_Subjects.pdf (accessed November 15, 2008).
18. Sowa, J.F. *Knowledge Representation: Logical, Philosophical and Computational Foundations*; Brooks/Cole: Pacific Grove, CA, 2000.
19. Garshol, L.M. *The Linear Topic Map Notation v 1.3*, Ontopia, 2006; Available at http://www.ontopia.net/download/ltm.html (accessed November 15, 2008).

20. Barta, R. Heuer, L. *AsTMa = 2.0 Language Definition*, Available at http://astma.it.bond.edu.au/astma = -spec-2.0r1.0.dbk (accessed November 15, 2008).

21. Garshol, L.M. *Metadata? Thesauri? Taxonomies? Topic Maps!*, Ontopia, 2004; Available at http://www.ontopia.net/topicmaps/materials/tm-vs-thesauri.html (accessed November 15, 2008).

22. Mulvany, N.C. *Indexing Books*; University of Chicago Press: Chicago, IL, 1994.

23. Svenonius, E. *The Intellectual Foundations of Information Organization*; MIT Press: Cambridge, MA, 2000.

24. DCMI Usage Board, *DCMI Metadata Terms*, Available at http://dublincore.org/documents/dcmi-terms/ (accessed November 15, 2008).

25. Pepper, S. Expressing dublin core in topic maps. *Scaling Topic Maps*, Available at http://www.springerlink.com/content/94u5130537r38172/ (accessed November 15, 2008).

26. Oh, S.G. *MARC, FRBR and RDA: Topic Maps Perspective*, Topic Maps 2008, Available at http://www.topicmaps.com/tm2008/oh.ppt (accessed November 15, 2008).

27. Pepper, S. Garshol, L.M. *The XML Papers*, Ontopia, 2002; Available at http://www.ontopia.net/topicmaps/materials/xmlconf.html (accessed November 15, 2008).

28. Garshol, L.M. Bogachev, D. TM/XML—Topic maps fragments in XML. *Charting the Topic Maps Research and Applications Landscape*, Available at http://www.springerlink.com/content/m376708254802517/ (accessed November 15, 2008). See also http://www.ontopia.net/topicmaps/tmxml.html (accessed November 15, 2008).

29. In *A Survey of RDF/Topic Maps Interoperability Proposals*; Pepper, S., Vitali, F., Garshol, L.M., Gessa, N., Presutti, V., Eds.; 2006; February 10 http://www.w3.org/TR/rdftm-survey W3C Working Group Note: (accessed November 15, 2008).

30. Pepper, S., Presutti, V., Garshol, L.M., Vitali, F., Eds. *Guidelines for RDF/Topic Maps Interoperability*; 2006; June 30, Available at http://www.w3.org/2001/sw/Best Practices/RDFTM/guidelines-20060630.html W3C Editor's Draft: (accessed November 15, 2008).

31. Lavik, S.; Meløy, J.R.; Nordeng, T.W. BrainBank learning—building personal topic maps as a strategy for learning. *Proceedings of XML 2004*, Washington, DC, Available at http://www.idealliance.org/proceedings/xml04/papers/21/brainbank.pdf (accessed November 15, 2008).

32. Lavik, S.; Nordeng, T.W.; Meløy, J.R.; Hoel, T. Remote topic maps in learning. *Leveraging the Semantics of Topic Maps*, Available at http://www.springerlink.com/content/g56x15p381uh32k9/ (accessed November 15, 2008).

33. *New Zealand Electronic Text Centre*, Available at http://www.nzetc.org (accessed November 15, 2008).

34. *Omnigator*, Ontopia, 2001–2006; Available at http://www.ontopia.net/omnigator Ontopia (accessed November 15, 2008).

BIBLIOGRAPHY

1. Maicher, L., Garshol, L.M., Eds. Scaling Topic Maps Third International Conference on Topic Maps Research and Applications, TMRA 2007 Leipzig, Germany October, 2007; Springer-Verlag: Berlin, Heidelberg, 2008; October.

2. Maicher, L., Park, J., Eds. Charting the Topic Maps Research and Applications Landscape First International Workshop on Topic Maps Research and Applications, TMRA 2005 Leipzig, Germany October, 2005; Springer-Verlag: Berlin, Heidelberg, 2006.

3. Maicher, L., Sigel, A., Garshol, L.M., Eds. Leveraging the Semantics of Topic Maps Second International Conference on Topic Maps Research and Applications, TMRA 2006 Leipzig, Germany October, 2006; Springer-Verlag: Berlin, Heidelberg, 2007.

Technical–Topic

Tunisia: Libraries, Archives, and Museums

Ali Houissa
Olin Library, Cornell University, Ithaca, New York, U.S.A.

Abstract

This entry provides factual data and background on the development and current state of libraries, archives, and museums in Tunisia. Emphasis is on the more-significant components of these sectors historically and culturally. The development of cultural institutions since Tunisia became independent and important legislation concerning these institutions are addressed in some detail. The conclusions point out that despite considerable investment in cultural and information infrastructure and services, there remain considerable hurdles to overcome for this emerging albeit studious country.

INTRODUCTION

Tunisia is a compact but kaleidoscopic North African country of 10 million located on the southern shore of the Mediterranean Sea, wedged between Algeria and Libya. Its strategic position and climate have made it a coveted land since ancient times. Vestiges of past civilizations remain visible testimony to the country's rich and diverse history, stretching back 3000 years. Culturally, modern Tunisia represents a rich admixture of native and foreign influences. While predominately Arab and Muslim these days, the country has been deeply imbued with diverse civilizations, including Berber, Phoenecian, Roman, Arab, Ottoman, and European. Contemporary Tunisia retains numerous traces of its long and diverse past. From the flourishing Roman era that lasted six centuries and witnessed the advent of Christianity, some of the best Roman mosaics in the world still survive. Rich Islamic architectural patchwork coexists with vestiges of French colonial influence. As a token of the country's rich patrimony, Tunisia is home to at least seven monuments and sites on the UNESCO World Heritage list. Rivalries between European interests over Tunisia in more-recent centuries culminated in a French invasion in 1881 and the establishment of a protectorate regime that lasted until 1956 (Fig. 1).

The newly independent republic has since pursued modernizing social policies, giving high priority to universal education and establishing rights for women unmatched by neighboring nations. As the Arab country that most wants to be seen as modern, Tunisia has taken a moderate stance domestically as well as in its foreign relations and is now among the region's emerging countries being the one with the fastest economic growth. More than 20% of the Tunisian government's annual budget goes to education and cultural institutions such as libraries, archives, museums, and arts centers. The following sections highlight Tunisia's most significant achievements and infrastructures in the fields of library and information science, archival systems, and museology.

LIBRARY AND INFORMATION PROFESSIONS, SYSTEMS, AND SERVICES

Historic Background

Libraries and books in preindependent Tunisia

Perhaps the oldest, continually existing library in Tunisia is that of the Grand Mosque of Qayrawan (also spelled Kairouan) and its attendant, now defunct, university, which is considered "amongst the first universities throughout history."[1] Tunisia is practically a bilingual country; French is widely used in daily life besides Arabic. In this study, transcription and romanization of Arabic is based largely on the ALA-LC Romanization Tables: Transliteration schemes for non-Roman scripts (http://www.loc.gov/catdir/cpso/romanization/arabic.pdf). As the country's holy Muslim city and the site of the oldest religious shrine in western Islam, Qayrawan was founded in 670 A.D. and had developed into a great center of learning. By the tenth century its religious, cultural, and scholastic influences reached parts of Africa, Europe, and Asia, attracting students and scholars from afar. The Grand Mosque has preserved some of the remnants of its great intellectual apogee and memory of its scholars through books and documents they wrote or assigned others to write. Many of these unique documents were part of the curriculum taught then and were considered "the largest and best known collection in the Arab Islamic world."[2] The Grand Mosque's library included mostly religious manuscripts and Korans written in large part on parchment. Following the sack of the city in the eleventh century, much of the library's collection was lost. Many of the surviving works are now preserved at the National Library

Encyclopedia of Library and Information Sciences, Fourth Edition DOI: 10.1081/E-ELIS4-120043623

Fig. 1   Map of Tunisia.

contemporaneous development tightly linked to books and knowledge diffusion that should be mentioned is papermaking and the establishment of paper mills all over the Islamic provinces by the eleventh and twelfth centuries. In North Africa the work of eleventh century Prince al-Mu'izz ibn Badīs al-Zīrī, a patron of the arts, included a brief account of medieval papermaking in his treatise 'Umdat al-Kuttab (Staff of the Scribes and Implements of the Discerning, or, The Pillar for Penmen), the only medieval Arabic work on the art of the book to survive.[6]

Other Tunisian cities' grand mosques also had library collections, the remnants of which can still be found today. The Zaytūnah Mosque, in Tunis, which was once also one of the oldest universities, has a considerable library.[7] Large numbers of its manuscripts and books were housed in the Zaytūnah's al-Abdalīyah Library. Although not the oldest of the country's libraries, it was possibly the richest of all. It had several collections totaling in the tens of thousands. Most rulers of the Hafsid dynasty of the thirteenth to sixteenth centuries in Tunis vied with each other for the prestige associated with building the collection, which at some point exceeded an estimated 100,000 volumes, including rare manuscripts.[8] When Spanish troops invaded and occupied Tunis between 1534 and 1574, many of the precious books and manuscripts in its libraries were looted or destroyed. The succession of Turkish dynasties that subsequently expelled the Spanish restored and expanded the Zaytūnah Grand Mosque and its affiliated libraries.[9] The nineteenth century country's ruler, the bey of Tunis, Ahmad Pasha I, was the patron and promoter of the Ahmadīyah Library and added large numbers of books to its collection.[10]

Independent Tunisia

Tunisia had generally enjoyed a period of relative political and social stability from the late sixteenth century until the establishment of the French Protectorate in 1881. That was also an era of idle cultural, intellectual, and scientific life. French colonial rule shook the country and brought many important social and political changes. Not long after the end of the World War II, France felt compelled to make some concessions to Tunisia, a process that culminated in the end of French colonial rule in 1956 and the establishment of a republican-presidential style regime. The French legacy, however, endures to date and is visible in many aspects of daily life. Since the earlier years of independence, the new regime's top priorities have been to reform education and encourage culture, and it has set aside a sizable portion of its operating budget for that purpose. Schooling became compulsory, free, and state-guaranteed between the ages of 6 and 16. By the 2006 school year, primary, secondary, technical, and vocational schools had a total enrollment of close to 2.5 million. The number of institutions of higher education increased from a couple at independence to 178 in 2006 with an estimated

in Tunis. A handwritten catalog containing a quite detailed description of the contents of the Grand Mosque's library, compiled in 1293 A.D., was uncovered in the mid-twentieth century (Fig. 2).[3]

Another cultural and learning hub in Qayrawan was Bayt al-Hikmah (House of Wisdom, or House of Knowledge), a pioneering gathering of scholars-cum-translators whose principal role was to render into Arabic what had survived of the mathematical, scientific, and philosophical legacy of the ancient world[4] that had been lost to medieval Europe. Established at the end of the ninth century, Bayt al-Hikmah of Qayrawan rivaled its famous counterpart in Baghdad in the study of medicine, astronomy, engineering, grammar, and translation.[5] A crucial

Fig. 2 The seventh century Qayrawan Grand Mosque.

enrollment of 365,000 students, 56% of whom were female students.[11] The constitution of the new republic provides for freedom of the press and of speech. The Tunisian press began publishing in the second half of the nineteenth century and flourished under colonial rule. It followed the French model, by which newspapers were highly editorialized and represented the official position of the government. That tradition has continued in independent Tunisia. The country now has 22 daily newspapers for an aggregate circulation of 375,000 copies, over 210 national weeklies and monthlies with a circulation close to 900,000, and more than 700 foreign magazines and newspapers.[12] The Internet reaches over 953,800 subscribers, a tenth of the population in 2005.[13] Tunisian book publishing, generally divided between Arabic and French, is a relatively small industry of approximately 125 publishers.[14] Book production has been on the increase over the years, from just a handful of titles published in the early years of independence to about 1500 in 2006. However, for 65% of those titles, print runs rarely surpass 500 copies.[14] Tunisia's most prestigious literary distinction is the "Comar d'Or" (Golden Comar)—from the name of a Tunisian philanthropic insurance agency that organizes and funds the event every year. The country's library system is diversified and relatively well established compared to other Arab and African nations. Overall, its information and cultural infrastructures, as spotlighted in the following sections, are impressive for a country of this size.

National Library and Information Services

Dār al-Kutub al-Waṭanīyah (Bibliothèque nationale, http://www.bibliotheque.nat.tn/)

The National Library of Tunisia (Fig. 3) is an administrative public establishment under the Ministry of Culture and Safeguard of Patrimony. Its origins as a national repository go back to 1885, when it was the Bibliothèque française, (also Bibliothèque française de Tunis and Bibliothèque générale). Its first holdings consisted mainly of the private collection of Charles Tissot, a French diplomatic officer and researcher in Tunis at the time. They were gradually enriched with thousands of Arabic books and manuscripts transferred from the Grand Mosque of Tunis and other madrassa schools. In 1910 the library was relocated to a building in a sector of the old city called al-ʻAṭṭarīn, which served since 1813 as one of five military barracks in the capital. Later, under French rule, it was used as headquarters of the Antiquities Administration (Direction des antiquités). It became known then as the Bibliothèque française de Tunis. Upon independence in 1956, the library started to function as the de facto national library. Its mission was to build collections in all formats, especially of works published in Tunisia, which

Fig. 3 The new building of the Tunisian National Library.

must by law be deposited there; conserve them; and make them available to the public. It functioned as a research library with a strong focus on the humanities. The introduction of mandatory legal deposit in 1956 required commercial publishers to provide copies of all published books to the National Library. In 1967 and by virtue of a government decree, all "public manuscripts" held in public libraries, mosques, and zawiyahs (religious shrines) were ordered to be transferred to the National Library.[15] The library currently has over 2 million monographs, 40,000 manuscripts, 13,000 periodicals (titles), and 5000 maps.[16]

The library's main publications are two annuals: al-Kitāb al-Tūnisī: al-Bībliyūghrāfiyā al-Waṭanīyah Waaṭanīyah = Bibliographie nationale tunisienne = Le Livre tunisien and al-Fihris al-'Âmm lil-Makhaṭuaṭat = Catalogue général des manuscrits. It also issues an annual bibliographic list of university theses and dissertations and occasionally puts out special bibliographies. Its online catalog is actually the previously mentioned Tunisian National Bibliography and is searchable in Arabic and Latin characters for titles published in 1997 and later. Bibliographies of the years 1997–2002 are now accessible online (http://www.bibliotheque.nat.tn/asp/index_ar.htm). Tunisiana, a Latin-script-only database, gives access to entries for documents published in Tunisia prior to 1966. There are several projects under way concerning the conversion into PDF of the full text of periodicals and serials (examples: al-'Alam al-Adabī; Shabab; al- Mabahaith; al-Ra'id al-Tunisī) as well as a number of manuscripts and original legal texts (Tunsian Constitution, the Personnel Status Code). The National Library, which began the automation of its bibliographic data in 1997, has undertaken the retrospective conversion of the old catalogs and files dating back to the end of the nineteenth century. Its multilingual catalog includes books published between 1500 and 1830. An in-house facility for retrospective conversion was set up in 2002. The ISBD and UNIMARC standard formats for recording bibliographic data were introduced in the 1980s. Bibliographic databases have been established using:

- UNESCO's common communication format (CCF), a standard for creating bibliographic cataloging records developed by UNESCO in 1984 for nonlibrary agencies. Common communication format offers a simple platform for machine-readable bibliographic data for the benefit of developing nations. Unlike MARC, CCF specifies no rules for description, permitting minimal records and groups of fields called record segments that allow for relationships between fields and records.
- UNESCO's CDS/ISIS, a bibliographic information management software to develop catalogs of manuscripts and old documents. This free library information storage and retrieval software for microcomputers was introduced in 1985.

- MINISIS, an integrated multiplatform software, for information production and management in a variety of languages and character sets.

By the mid-1990s the National Library started considering the acquisition of a MARC-format-compliant, multiscript-capable, integrated library system (ILS). In 2005 the Horizon integrated library system, developed by Ameritech Library Services and Arabized by a Saudi Arabian company, was chosen as the ILS system. The National Library has adhered to the ISBN system since 1988. It started using the CDS-ISIS bibliographic software in 1991 to catalog legal deposit items to be listed in the Tunisian National Bibliography. For all ongoing retrospective conversion projects, UNIMARC is the format used. The old Roman script catalog (up to 1966) with 200,000 bibliographic records was converted between 2001 and 2005; the old Arabic manuscripts catalogs were automated in 2005. The conversion of the more-recent Roman script catalog (1966–1998) started in 2006.[17] To complete the picture, a national authority file using UNIMARC Authority format was planned for 2006. In its effort to build what is hoped will be the national virtual library, the National Library embarked on digitizing first the "main national heritage works," such as manuscripts and older print documents, books, periodicals, and bibliographies, many of which are also being made available as CD-ROMs. The National Library opened to the public in February 2005 in a new location in downtown Tunis. The new building covers 35,000 m^2 of space and includes a spacious room for reading documents, a conference room, a laboratory, an exhibition hall, a visitors' gallery, a restaurant, and a 10,300 m^2 parking lot.

Legislation Concerning Libraries

Legal deposit and copyright

Modern Tunisia inherited from its former French colonial occupier (1881–1956) a political structure and a cultural environment that are still visible everywhere. The French instituted the first press and publishing codes during colonial rule, and after independence in 1956, the government enacted legislation related to media and cultural institutions, many of which were drafted on the basis of the French "Depot Legal" system. Embedded in the Tunisian Press Code,[18] the system of legal deposit impacts all sorts of publications. Publishers, distributors and printers, public agencies, and university institutions must submit copies of all printed material to the Ministry of Culture, the National Library, the Ministry of the Interior, and the Public Prosecutor's Office. The categories of documents subject to legal deposit include official and unofficial publications as well as academic publications. Upon deposit of the copies, a receipt (récépissé) is issued by the Ministry of the Interior; only then can the publications be produced and distributed. Foreign publications must get clearance from the Ministry of the Interior before distribution in the country. The Press Code was amended in 1988, 1993, and 2001. The more-recent amendments removed punitive measures that had included prison sentences and payment of fines for publishing without a legal permit. In theory, by virtue of these amendments, no newspaper can be suspended without a court decision. A 2005 amendment to the Press Law abolished the legal deposit process altogether, including related sanctions and punitive measures.[19] Some jurists and observers have questioned such legislation and the sincerity of the recent reforms to abolish the legal submission process.[20]

Tunisian law provides for intellectual property rights and copyright protection, including publication procedures, the transfer of rights and permission to photocopy.[21] But, as elsewhere, enforcement is an ongoing problem.

Statutes and legislation concerning libraries and librarianship

Since independence, administrative oversight of Tunisian libraries has shifted several times among government agencies and ministries. Libraries and library staff and professionals are largely part of the public service, and their status is covered by provisions of legislation governing Tunisia's public administration. Laws addressing specific library entities, the jurisdictions they fall under, their funding, organization, and governance have been enacted and amended over the years. The following decrees and laws are the more significant:

- Decree no. 92-1353, July 20, 1992. Fixing the conditions and requirements governing nominations of library directors at universities and institutions of higher education and research. The law covers compensation, benefits, indemnities, and advantages accorded to appointees.[22]
- Decree no. 94-559, March 15, 1994. Concerning structure and organization of the National Library and outlining its areas of responsibility.[23]
- Decree no. 99-2762, December 6, 1999. Addressing the particular status of all personnel working in libraries and documentation centers that are part of the public administration.[24]
- Decree no. 79-756, August 1979. Concerning mission, description, and organization of the National Library.[25]
- Decree no. 79-698, August 1979. Regarding creation and transfer of positions at the National Library.[26]
- Decree no. 75-254, April 1975. Addressing the status of management staff (cadres) of libraries, documentation centers, and archives.[27]

All statutes and decrees consulted for this study were published in French in the official *Tunsian Gazette, Journal fficiel*, and are available in digitized format in the online database of the Centre national universitaire de documentation scientifique et technique: http://www.cnudst.rnrt.tn/wwwisis/jort.06/form.htm.

Academic Libraries

There are currently 178 institutions of higher education, among them 13 universities (Ezzitouna Islamic University, Manouba University, Tunis University, Tunis El Manar University, University of 7 November at Carthage, Jendouba University, Sousse University, Sfax University, Gabes University, Kairouan University, Monastir University, Gafsa University, and the Virtual University), in addition to the 24 Higher Institutes of Technological Studies (ISETs), 6 Higher Institutes of Teacher Training (ISFMs), and about 20 licensed private higher education institutions.[28] One hundred fifty-five institutions are under the supervision of the Ministry of Higher Education, and 23 others come under shared supervision of that and other ministries (Communication and Technologies; Youth, Agriculture, Social Affairs, etc.).[29] The student population in 2006 was estimated at 430,000.[30]

Each university has a central library, bibliothèque universitaire centrale (BUC), responsible for all institutional information needs. All central libraries are part of a national electronic library network of BUCs in the country.[31] The total university libraries holdings is estimated at over a million titles, not including 100,000 published and unpublished theses and dissertations.[30]

The National University Network, Réseau national universitaire (RNU), is a project to create an online academic network connecting all institutions of higher education and research establishments in Tunisia to each other and to the Internet. By 2007 the number of RNU users was estimated at 221,924. The computer center al-Khawarizmī (Centre de calcul el Khawarizmi, CCK) was designated the Internet service provider for all institutions of higher learning in 1997. Included among its services are Web hosting, electronic mail, file transfer, database development and management, faculty training, and hosting of the university library system union catalog, BIRUNI (Bibliothèque Informatisée pour la Rénovation UNIversitaires, previously known also as BIbliothèque des Ressources UNIversitaires). It was initially launched in 1996 and was envisioned as a virtual library project using VIRTUA, the ILS by VTLS. The BIRUNI union catalog's main page functions as a gateway for searching all university catalogs. It also provides clustered links to Tunisia's university library catalogs by region: "Catalog of the North" "Catalog of the Center" "Catalog of the South." Although the site lists the categories "electronic periodicals" and "online theses," at the time of this writing the links to them are not active. Access to fee-based electronic resources and online databases is through the National Academic Center for Scientific and Technical

Information (Centre national universitaire de documentation scientifique et technique, CNUDST).

Centre national universitaire de documentation scientifique et technique (CNUDST, http://www.cnudst.rnrt.tn)

The center was created in 1979 as a unit of the Ministry of Higher Education with the broad mandate to support the acquisition of, and access to, scientific and technical information for the Tunisian research community (law No. 78-59 of December 29, 1978, and Decree No. 99-2241 of October 11, 1999).[32] Centre national universitaire de documentation scientifique et technique holds the legal deposit right to receive one copy of every publication issued by institutions of higher education and scientific research in the country and is responsible for acquiring all such scientific documents by Tunisians in French universities. It houses the "virtual library of research" and provides gateway access to electronic resources consisting of subscriptions to databases and full-text online scientific periodicals. Centre national universitaire de documentation scientifique et technique negotiates database licenses on behalf of higher education and research establishments. Moreover, the center has developed, on its own, four freely accessible, online bibliographic databases:

- TUNIDOC. Lists documents, monographs, theses, articles, etc. relating to Tunisia or written by Tunisians. There were 37,129 multilingual, multidisciplinary entries as of April 2007.
- TUNIPER. A union catalog of serials and periodicals available in 130 Tunisian institutions. As of February 2007, 17,739 titles were listed.
- *JORT [Journal officiel de la république tunisienne]*. A bibliographic and full-text, online database of most laws, legislation, and other legal statutes published in the Official Journal of the Republic of Tunisia since January 1, 1956. As of March 2007 it contains 55,235 entries in Arabic and French.
- BDRGI (Base de donneés des ressources gratuites sur Internet). A selected online guide to electronic resources available on the Internet.

EUMEDCONNECT

This is a project funded by the European Commission to provide dedicated Internet connections between the research and educational communities of the Mediterranean region. It will link the national research and education networks of Algeria, Cyprus, Egypt, Israel, Jordan, Lebanon, Malta, Morocco, the Palestinian Authority, Syria, Tunisia, and Turkey to Europe through the pan-European research and education network called GÉANT. The potential benefit from this initiative for Tunisia's research and education sector is dedicated connectivity to research in state-of-the-art research information databases and facilities in European research institutions. DANTE, the "Delivery of Advanced Network Technology to Europe," runs the circuit that links Tunisia to the network through Italy in coordination with Réseau fédéré de la recherche (RFR), managed by the Tunisian Secretary of State for Scientific Research and Technology.

Public Libraries

There are about 380 public libraries throughout the country,[33] supervised by the Ministry of Culture (Ministère de la culture et de la sauvegarde du patrimoine). The Public Libraries Service (Direction de la lecture publique) in that ministry, founded in 1965, administers almost all public Tunisian libraries and publishes an annual Bulletin. Estimated total library holdings as of 2005 were about 5 million books, but only 60,000 of them are unique titles. Libraries are divided as follows:

- 311 public libraries, of which 305 have children's branches.
- 24 regional libraries and 28 mobile libraries.

In 2004 there were 5,230,179 public library visitors, almost half of them children and young adults. Of that number only 167,000 were registered users, who checked out 3,760,059 books.[34] Public libraries charge an annual fee, the equivalent of U.S. $1 for adults and half of that for youths, for use of all library services including the Internet.

Most public libraries that have been using card catalogs and traditional methods to manage their collections are becoming automated. Increasingly, modern information technologies, such as integrated library systems, computer catalogs, and library networks, are being introduced. In 1998 a pilot public library, the Médiathèque Ariana, went live with a biscript (Roman–Arabic) ILS based on UNIMARC. In 2004 the French government funded a project to promote public reading and the public library sector. One of its aims was to computerize the Ministry of Culture's Public Reading Service (Direction de la lecture publique) as a first step toward full automation and networking of the public libraries countrywide. The funding also includes acquisitions of book materials, especially for youth, and covers staff education and training at the Tunisian Higher Institute for Documentation (Institut supérieur de documentation) and in France.

There remains room for improvement when it comes to the role public libraries play in most people's lives; there is a lack of well-established reading habits, and books continue to be viewed outside school curriculums as unaffordable luxury items. But a vast action-program launched in 1997 with the aim of gradually connecting public libraries to the Internet has been a promising development.

School Libraries

Despite limited resources, the Tunisian government has allocated, in the decades since independence, about 7% of the gross national product (GNP) to education, one of the higher such ratios in the world. In 1991 a new education-system reform law[35] was passed instituting compulsory and free schooling for children up to the age of 16 and stipulating that public education of all children of school age is a "right" and an "obligation." As a result, enrollment reached over 99% among 6-year-olds. It is worth noting that, based on the available government statistics, regional disparities of access to schools persist: coastal and north-eastern regions continue to achieve the best schooling rates compared to rural areas in the northwest and southwest.[36]

The rate of enrollment in primary education for children 6 to 11 years old was 98% during the 2005/2006 school year, for a total of 1,120,424 pupils in the primary cycle of public schools ("Premier cycle de l' enseignement de base," 6 years) and 571,986 in the second cycle ("Deuxième cycle de l' enseignement de base," 3 years). Enrollment in secondary public schools (enseignement secondaire) during the same year was 503,531.[37] Tunisian primary and secondary schools have strong language programs, allocating more time to foreign language instruction than most European countries (29% of total instruction time in Tunisia in contrast to 10% in Europe). French is introduced at age 8, English at age 10, and a third language in secondary school.[38] All school libraries in primary through preparatory and secondary schools are, in terms of human resources, administration, and funding, under the purview and centralized supervision of the Ministry of Education and Vocational Training, Service of Means and School Libraries (Ministère de l'éducation et de la formation, Service des moyens et des bibliothèques scolaires.[39] The ministry acquires books through group purchases, a centralized process established in 1991.[40] There are no available surveys of school library holdings. Secondary schools tend to have more libraries than primary schools; the concept of library in the latter category, if it ever applies, should be used loosely. School directors have small discretionary budgets for incidental expenses, including book purchases, and many accept additional supplies from other community sources. Other than textbooks, most titles, for the use of students and teachers, are in Arabic and French and cover literature, philosophy, science, technology, and economics. School libraries are not well funded and are rarely considered the focal point for learning in Tunisian schools. As a consequence, they are not well stocked. The limited commitment to school library service reflects a salient lack of learning opportunities outside the formal classroom, attributed quite often to limited funding. When it comes to the extras outside the classroom programs, however, libraries compete with sports, music, etc. for time and funds. Moreover, the textbook is perceived as a complete book—other classroom teaching materials complete the picture.

The advent of the Internet, its spread throughout educational institutions, and its general popularity has been a mixed blessing for libraries and reading. In fact, school libraries (and all kinds of public libraries) are increasingly called "médiathèques," that is, basically media centers offering a range of learning resources from textbooks, dictionaries, and encyclopedias to media materials, audiovisual aids, and increasingly the Internet—hardware and connection offered for free to all schools, courtesy of the government and the Ministry of Education.

The Tunisian government has invested heavily in computer training, technology, and online services and has succeeded in providing all secondary schools and tertiary institutions with computers, IT laboratories, and Internet connections. It has been working on a program that will bring all primary schools technologically up to speed by 2006. In addition, the Education Ministry has established a Virtual School to support distance learning and has set up EduNet (http://www.evt.edunet.tn/indexan.htm), an educational gateway and network linking Tunisian elementary and secondary schools to the Internet. EduNet provides a variety of Web services such as general information, e-learning sites, e-mail, databases, etc. By the late 1990s, EduNet had connected almost 500 primary, all 400 secondary, and over 50 technical schools.

In 2002 the ministry launched the Educational Virtual Library (Bibliothèque virtuelle éducative (BVE), presented as a tool linking the education community to online resources useful for information research and supplementing what is available in print, including: JSTOR Journal Storage, *Blackwell Synergy*, IEEE's *POP ALL*, Proquest's *ABI/INFORM Global*, Elsevier's *Scopus*, and Thomson ISI's *Web of Science*. The system's gateway (http://www.bve.edunet.tn/fr/index.php) is bilingual, French and Arabic, and allows online searching by Dewey classification numbers.

Outside the Tunisian school system there are a number of international schools, often affiliated with foreign organizations or countries and their cultural missions. Worth mentioning is the American Cooperative School of Tunis (ACST) which, since 1959, provides elementary, middle, and high school American education. The school offers a curriculum that essentially follows the guidelines of U.S. public schools adapted to the needs of international students and a program leading to a U.S. academic diploma and the International Baccalaureate diploma. At the beginning of the 2006/2007 school year, enrollment was 494 (pre-K to grade 5: 264; grades 6–8: 114; and grades 9–12: 116). The 10-acre campus includes an administrative preschool building containing an elementary library with an amphitheater and elementary computer lab. For the upper school there are computer labs, art rooms, and the main library with more than 12,000 volumes and a computer research area. The ACST Middle and High School Library sets up monthly displays of books, artifacts, and interactive materials surrounding a current topic.

Special Libraries

Tunisia has a number of wide-ranging special libraries maintained by associations, government departments and services, research institutions outside universities, learned societies, NGOs, etc. Their collections are, as is usually the case for this type, in a specific field such as agriculture, law, social sciences, medicine, economics, and engineering. Collections and services are for the most part designed to provide for the information needs of their primary users and other specialists in the respective field and to a lesser extent the needs of members of the public at large. Some of the largest special libraries are those under the jurisdiction and direct supervision of government ministries.

In 1977, a national commission for documentation and information (Commission nationale de documentation, CND) was charged with developing a plan for setting up a national information system network structured by sector (libraries, documentation centers, archives, etc.) and connected to international information networks. Each component of that system was to be called a Centre national pilote sectoriel, CNPS (national specialized pilot center). Each of the resulting 12 CNPSs is assigned to build a network in its respective sector of specialty. Together, all the CNPSs form Réseau national d'information et de documentation (RNID), the national information and documentation network.

Generally, technical and scientific information and documentation is the responsibility of three main bodies: Centre de documentation nationale (CDN); Centre national universitaire de documentation scientifique et technique (CNUDST), described in a previous section; and Centre national de documentation agricole (CNDA).

Centre de documentation nationale (CDN)

The National Documentation Center collects and preserves all documents and information on cultural, political, social, or economic issues available anywhere and directly relating to Tunisia. Created in 1966, the status of the CDN is defined and governed by a 1982 Presidential Decree[41] as the cornerstone of the national information network. It currently has a library of about 8,000 monographs, 2,400 periodicals, 10,000 press documents ("dossiers de presse"), and 50,000 photographs,[42] most of them accessed through the center's computerized database, TANIT. It has developed a guide to information services in Tunisia and created a number of databases including ITARAT, on governmental structures and related information, and ASSO, on associations. The CDN is an IIP focal point for UNESCO (Intergovernmental Informatics Program). The CDN is also the subregional focal point for the Francophone database Banque

internationale d'information sur les états francophones (BIEF), and its program named "La Francophonie," a network of focal points in 52 Francophone member states.

Centre national de documentation agricole (CNDA)

The National Center for Agricultural Documentation was conceived under the Ministry of Agriculture as a central hub for collection and dissemination of current and retrospective agricultural information and data. It publishes TUNAGRI, the national agricultural bibliography, and CARIST, a quarterly bulletin that covers current research information, reference documents, and agricultural facts and figures, as well as places, names of agricultural scientists in the country, and other online resources (market research, agricultural politics, etc.). It also has a legal resources database, JORTAGRI, for texts of legislation, laws, decrees, etc. relating to agriculture (http://www.onagri.nat.tn/Default.htm). The center also provides gateway access to automated agricultural databases. The AGRINET, managed by the Institut de la recherche et de l'enseignement supérieur agricole (IRESA), connects 14 institutions of higher education in agriculture as well as 7 regional research centers. It also connects the various departments of the Agriculture Ministry as well as its regional representations (Commissariats régionaux) throughout the country. The CNDA is affiliated with the international agriculture system, AGRIS, the international information system for the agricultural sciences and technology created by the Food and Agriculture Organization (FAO) of the United Nations.

Réseau national de santé (RNS)

In the medical and health fields, the National Health Network provides connectivity to 84 hospitals, including all the 20 university hospital centers and 44 regional hospitals and 23 regional branches of the heath Ministry (Directions régionales de la santé). It is managed by the Ministry's Centre informatique du ministère de la santé publique (CIMSP), providing distance information services, "télémedicine," to doctors in remote regions of the country and services to health centers far from large population areas.

Library, Information Science, and Archival Education and Training

Specialized training and education in librarianship and information sciences in Tunisia has developed very slowly, arduously, and sometimes erratically. After several years of being scattered among a few institutions it became, in the last couple of decades, centralized at one institute. Historically, formal professional training for librarians and archivists started in 1964 at the Institut Ali Bash Hamba, a public institution initially set up with assistance from the German foundation Friedrich Naumann Stiftung several years after the country gained independence. Its main and somehow vaguely defined goal was the development and dissemination of cultural, economic, social, and technical information in Tunisia. Between 1966 and 1971 it offered training sessions lasting six months each, conducted by a corps of international instructors dispatched by the International Federation for Information and Documentation (Fédération internationale d'information et de documentation, FID). This college-level training program attracted students and professionals from French-speaking countries in Africa; about 100 of them graduated with degrees in documentation. In 1965 the Tunisian Ministry of Cultural Affairs was prompted to start a course specifically for librarians at the National Library. Although it did not last very long, the program graduated two groups of assistant librarians and four groups of library assistants at the end of four years. By the early 1970s, training of librarians was transferred to the National School of Administration (Ecole nationale d'administration, ENA). This is the school, similar to its famous French counterpart, where government officials and functionaries are trained under the jurisdiction of the Prime Ministry. The Friedrich Naumann Stiftung again provided financial support, including scholarships and recruitment of foreign lecturers. The curriculum was organized into three training cycles, each lasting two years. By 1979 library science and archival training was moved to the Institute of Journalism and Information Sciences (Institut de presse et des sciences de l'information, IPSI) under the purview of the Ministry of Higher Education, Scientific Research and Technology. It was first planned as a four-year undergraduate-level program. However, that program in turn was scrapped and replaced by another two-year professional program in library science; candidates for admission were required to take an entrance exam. A two-year graduate-level program was introduced in 1984–1985 at IPSI that accepted students with the equivalent of a bachelor's degree in any subject. Lacking in experienced faculty and relying mainly on professional librarians as part-time lecturers, that program was also cancelled a few years later despite attracting about 100 students a year. A major improvement started in the mid-1980s, when the Institut supérieur de documentation (ISD) (http://www.isd.rnu.tn/en/default.asp), took responsibility for developing a full-fledged undergraduate program in librarianship and archival sciences. According to its founding law,[43] ISD is a public institution of higher education and research that provides training for managerial and professional staff in library sciences, documentation, and archives. It is part of the University of Manouba, Tunis, under the Ministry of Higher Education, Scientific Research and Technology. The ISD's original course of studies consists of a two-year training cycle for three categories of students:

- 1st category:
  Beginners holding new high school finishing diploma (Baccalauréat) who plan to graduate as library assistants after a two-year program.
- 2nd category:
  Graduates in other specialties planning to become librarians, documentalists, or archivists after undertaking an additional two-year training.
- 3rd category:
  Holders of an undergraduate degree (four years) in other disciplines, especially humanities, who plan to be curators (conservateurs) in libraries and other resource centers.

Since 1988, ISD has offered a four-year specialized program leading to a full university degree (Maîtrise: four years). More recently it set up a graduate-level program, "Diplôme d'Etudes Supérieures Spécialisées (DESS)," roughly the equivalent of a master's degree. Admission to the program is subject to a competitive entrance examination. The Institut supérieur de documentation is currently the only university-level institution that is dedicated to providing specialized training in the field of library, information, and archival science. As of the 2006–2007 academic year, total enrollment at ISD was 1466 students: 363 in the 1st category mentioned above, 289 in the 2nd, and 814 in the 3rd; it also has 74 teaching faculty and staff. Graduates of ISD programs can apply to, and be recruited by, the National Archives, the National Library, public libraries, university libraries, resource centers and archives units (in ministries and public administrations), and private firms and companies.

Library, information science, and the archival profession

L'Association Tunisienne des bibliothécaires, documentalistes et archivistes (ATDBA), is the only professional association for librarians, archivists, and researchers in the field of information science. It was founded in 1965 and currently has 250 active members. Its main publication is RASSID: Revue de l'Association tunisienne des documentalistes, bibliothecaires et archivistes pour l'information documentaire, a multilingual journal issued four times a year.

ARCHIVES AND ARCHIVAL SCIENCE

The Superior Council of Archives, Conseil supérieur des archives, is the official governing and advisory board responsible for setting national archival policy. It is under the jurisdiction of the Prime Ministry and presided over by the prime minister. Established by virtue of Decree no. 94-1618 of 26 July 1994,[44] the council is made up of

10 ministers and government secretaries as well as a Technical Committee charged with compiling materials to be considered and approved by the full council. The Technical Committee includes professionals and researchers in the archival field, the general director of the National Archives, representatives of the association of archivists, and archives users.

Legislation Concerning Archives and Records Keeping

- Decree no. 70-118 of April 11, 1970, concerning the reorganization of all government services under the Prime Ministry, including archives administration, which was renamed "Division des archives générales."[45]
- Decrees no. 88-1979 and 88-1981 of December 13, 1988, concerning the general organization, structure, and management of the national archives; fixing procedures of handling and disposition of archival records.[46]
- Decree no. 389 of February 21, 1997, containing general provisions regarding the organization and management of the National Archives that include the definition of its structure, administrative hierarchy, budget, financial arrangements, and contracts. (Decree no. 389 repeals the Decrees of December 13, 1979 and December 1988). Accordingly, public services and state bodies in Tunisia are required to elaborate, in collaboration with the National Archives, a program for the management of their records and to agree on procedures and work out methods of handling archival records throughout their lifecycle. The program should cover all functions meant to ensure proper handling of records in terms of appraisal, inventory, and classification.[47]

The National Archives

al-Arshīf al-Waaṭanī al-Tunisī (Archives nationales tunisiennes, http://www.archives.nat.tn/)

The founding of the Tunisian National Archives (Fig. 4) dates back to 1874, when a small archival section was created within the Grand Ministry (Prime Ministry). It was initially named Centre des correspondences de l'état, or State Correspondence Center, and designated a repository of public and official records that were transferred from such locations as the royal Bardo Palace and various other document-producing sources of the civil service and state institutions. During the French colonial period (1881–1956), the Tunisian staff and administration of the center was maintained but it came under the supervision of a French senior official, secrétaire général du gouvernement, and its functions were restricted to internal affairs that were directly linked to the "indigenous" Tunisian population only, such as regional and local administration, justice, religion and worship, endowments, etc. At that time, the French "resident general" (high commissioner) exclusively ran the important ministries of war and foreign affairs. In 1883 the Archives générales du gouvernement (State General Archives) was established as the repository of all official documents under the secretary general of government. Records collected by the services directly relevant to the French resident general in Tunisia were transferred to France. Since 1983, Tunisia has actively proceeded with microfilming or obtaining copies of these records. When the country became independent, the Archives générales du gouvernement took the name Archives générales. In 1967 the archives administration became known as the Division des archives générales et de la documentation (General Archives and Documentation Division). Its task was to collect and preserve the state's general archives. By 1970, it was again renamed Division des archives générales.

With a current staff of 56, including 24 professional archivists and conservation specialists, the National Archives, a financially autonomous institution that, under the oversight of the Prime Ministry, is responsible for collecting, preserving, and making accessible all archival resources, including those available abroad and deemed relevant to Tunisia. The National Archives works in close collaboration with record-producing bodies and institutions such as government ministries and public departments, institutions, and services. These bodies are required by law to develop specific methods and schedules for appraisal and management of their records. The Common records appraisal schedule, established by a prime minister in 2000 is a management tool completely integrated into the administrative processes of all government and public bodies. It fixes for each type of record the period for which it is to be preserved and made available, the period for which it is preserved as a semicurrent record, and the destination of a record or file following the expiry of its retention period, which is often disposed

Fig. 4 New building of the Tunisian National Archives.

of or transferred to the National Archives. On a local level, for regional entities such as municipalities that are outside the direct purview of the central government, the system for archival records communication and management is still in development.

The most ancient preserved record available at the National Archives dates back to 1582 A.D., although the bulk of the archives concerns mainly the period from the seventeenth century to the present and is divided into the following major groups:

- The Ottoman Period
- The Colonial Period
- Independent Tunisia
- Documentary Holdings (mostly printed monographs, periodicals, and newspapers)

The National Archives' "historical library" includes more than 6000 monographs, mainly in Arabic and French, in addition to manuscripts in Arabic, Turkish, French, Italian, and English dating back several centuries. There are also an estimated 725 periodicals and historical newspaper titles in Arabic, French, Italian, and Hebrew.

The best organized and maintained records and holdings are from the Ottoman period in Tunisia, with particularly rich holdings covering the Husaynite dynasty (1705–1881) and French colonial Tunisia, from 1881 to 1956. Most of the documents and texts concern the Tunisian state and reflect essential aspects of the political and administrative organization of the country, as well as its economic and social and cultural changes for a good part of three centuries.

Access to records is available on site at the National Archives and is strictly regulated according to type and age. "Current" official records are practically inaccessible to the general public. For noncurrent records, the periods after which public access becomes possible are according to the following categories:

- 30 years beginning with the date of the public record's creation.
- 60 years for records that:
  - Are a threat to the private life of individuals or related to national security matters
  - Contain personal information or relate to private life and behavior
  - Relate to legal matters
- 100 years for
  - Civil registers and similar official records
  - Records comprising of personal medical information and personal files

Clearance to consult records for research purposes prior to the expiration of the specified retention periods is given only if the user can provide written approval from a research institution and agrees to undergo a background check to establish that the information wanted is not a threat to individual safety and public order.

Public access to records and use of the National Archives' reading rooms requires a small one-time fee to obtain a reader's card. Foreign nationals are allowed access provided that they display a pass approved in advance by the director of the National Archives.

Photocopying is authorized for a fee in conformity with internal Archives regulations.

Records and record groups are cataloged according to a hierarchical classification system using common characteristics such as similarity of function, subject, and type. The system, consisting of several levels of grouping, proceeds from the "general" to the "specific" and is presented in a hierarchical form with each level (class, subclass, division, and subdivision) indicated by a heading and a classification index:

- *Class:* 3000 Financial resources management
  - *Subclass:* 3100 Budget elaboration
    - *Division:* 3170 Budget change
      - *Subdivision:* 3171 Application for extra credits

Descriptors, accompanied by a classification index, are arranged alphabetically with cross-references and associated terms.

Two databases are used as the National Archives' online catalog:

- Kitāb
  For preserved works such as monographs, documents, and periodicals in Arabic or other languages available at the National Archives. The number of records is estimated at about 10,000 with a 5–10% annual increase.
- Dhākrah
  For records, official documents, and treaties and comprising about 75,000 entries (with a 5–10% annual increase).

ISAD (G) (General International Standard Archival Description, 2nd edition), is the standard followed for archival description in this database.

The National Archives publishes finding aids, studies, research papers, and pedagogical tools. Its official publication is "Inventaires des documents d'archives conservés."

In 2004 Tunisia established a National Archives Day, which is celebrated every February 26th "to focus attention on archives. . .as a key to national memory and as a source for study and research." (Fig. 5)

It is important to point out that, other than the National Archives, several local and foreign institutions hold important records relating to the modern and contemporary history of Tunisia. The most important ones are

Fig. 5 Poster celebrating Tunisia's first National Archives Day.

- The Higher Institute for the National Movement History, at Mannouba campus, holding microfilm records of the French colonial "Résidence générale."
- The Ministry of the State Property, Department of Documentation and Archives, holding historical documents of the Endowments Administration, "Jam'īyah des Habous."
- Municipalities responsible for the preservation of records relating to the civil register acts (birth, marriage, and death certificates) and those concerned with city planning.
- Courts in charge of holding and safeguarding the documents they produce.
- The Archbishopric of Tunis, holding all records relating to the Catholic population that lived in Tunis during the French colonial rule.
- The French Consulate in Tunis, holding all records relating to the civil register acts (birth, marriage, and death) of French nationals who lived in Tunisia during the Colonial Period after 1914.

Foreign-based repositories of documents that are relevant to Tunisia include notably:

- Direction des Archives du ministère des affaires étrangères (Department of the Archives of the Ministry of Foreign Affairs), Centre Parisien 37, Quai d'Orsey, 75007, Paris, holds civil register acts of the European community in Tunisia prior to 1914 and the diplomatic correspondence of the Ministry of Foreign Affairs.
- Archives nationales, in Paris, previously named Centre historique des archives nationales de France.
- Centre des archives d'outre-mer, Aix-en-Provence, France.
- The diplomatic archives of several countries, namely, England, Italy, Germany, United States, Sweden, and Norway, have records relating to the history of modern Tunisia.

Archival education and the profession

Training and education for archivist at the university level is at the Institute of Information Science (ISD), described in a previous section. The main professional association is also the Tunisian Association of Documentalists, Librarians, and Archivists (ATDBA), established in the mid-1960s.

Finally, it should be mentioned that in 2005 the International Association of Francophone Archives launched its International Francophone Archival Portal (PIAF) (http://www.piaf-archives.org) as a clearinghouse offering training for archivists of the Francophone community. International Francophone Archival Portal offers free online basic training on records and archives management focusing on the continuing education needs of archival technicians and professionals, but it does not result in a diploma.

MUSEUMS AND MUSEOLOGY

General Background

There are two leading bodies in the area of museology, historic preservation, and cultural heritage in Tunisia:

1. The Agency for Heritage Development and Cultural Promotion, Agence de mise en valeur du patrimoine et de promotion culturelle (AMVPPC) (http://www.igm.com.tn/amvppc/eng/accueil.php), is a national agency established in 1988 under the authority of the Ministry of Culture and Heritage Conservation to restore and manage the country's historical and archeological heritage.[48] Its mission is to implement government policy in various fields related to the restoration, preservation, management, and promotion of the country's archaeological and historical heritage at about 60 sites, monuments, and museums. It is the body in charge of delivering authorization required for any activities taking place within the confines of sites under its responsibility. Agence de mise en valeur du patrimoine et de promotion culturelle is headed by a director general and has seven departments: Technical, Cultural Promotion, Management, Production and

Organization, Study and Programming, Administration and Finance, and Coordination and Follow-Up. The agency undertook the rehabilitation of older museums such as the National Bardo Museum, and the museums of Enfidha, Nabeul, and El Jem, as well as the Popular Arts and Traditions museums of Monastir and Houmt-Souk. It created new museums as well in Moknine, Chemtou, and Mahdia and the Sahara museum in Douz and also participated in the creation and design of museums for other parties: the National Military Museum (Qasr al-Wardah), the Mareth Line Museum, the National Guard Museum, and the Film Museum. As a promoter of cultural tourism, it played a central role in the creation of the Carthage-Sidi Bou Said Archaeological Park; the refurbishment of the Baron d'Erlanger's palace in Sidi Bou Said, housing the Center of Arab and Mediterranean Music; the Archaeological Park of Dougga; and the Sbeitla-Kasserine Archaeological Park. In 2002, in an effort to modernize the country's cultural infrastructure, the Tunisian government launched, with support from the World Bank, a multiyear project that would improve the sector through strengthening the legal and institutional framework, encouraging cultural tourism, and refurbishing six selected sites: Ancient Carthage, Bardo Museum, Sousse Museum, the Medina Old City of Qayrawan, the archaeological site of Oudna, and the island of Jerbah. A unit operating within the AMVPPC is responsible for the project's implementation.

2. The National Institute for Cultural Heritage, Institut national du patrimoine (INP) (http://www.inp.rnrt.tn/), was founded in 1957 as the Institut national d'archéologie et d'art, before changing its name in 1993. It is a technical and scientific institution under the Ministry of Culture in charge of preserving, studying, and making the cultural, archeological, historic, and artistic heritage of the country accessible to the public. The institute has various technical facilities, such as a central laboratory, a center for the restoration of Qayrawan manuscripts (Centre de restauration des manuscrits de Kairouan), a center for calligraphy (Centre national de la calligraphie), and an education center (Cours de Tunis) for training Tunisian and North African architects in different conservation specialties. Its publications include

- Africa: journal for research and excavations in prehistoric and Islamic antiquities in Tunisia, 1966–
- Reppal: research journal for Phoenician, Punic, and Lybico-Berber antiquities
- La Revue des arts des traditions populaires, specializing in folklore and popular cultural monuments, objects, traditions, rituals, and beliefs
- Bulletin du CEDAC: annual information letter published by the Centre d'etudes et de documentation archeologique de Carthage, an affiliate

institution of INP, reporting on archeological digs and excavation results at the Carthage site.

Tunisia's cultural assets include many archaeological sites, parks, and historical settlements, several of which are listed as World Heritage Sites under the international convention administered by UNESCO. There are numerous museums located throughout the country, varying widely in significance from the national and prestigious to the smaller and pedestrian. Among the 18 historical and archaeological sites in Tunisia that receive visitors and the 27 museums, "antiquariums," and archaeological, historical, and natural parks, the following are particularly noteworthy.

Museums

Musée national du Bardo(http://www.di.com.tn/museebardo/)

The Bardo National Museum (Fig. 6) houses the largest—and arguably the finest—collection of Roman mosaics in the world. Situated in Bardo, a near suburb of Tunis, the museum building was originally a residence/palace that had been restored and expanded over the centuries before being dedicated first in 1882 as a museum, namely, al-Mathaaf al-'Alawī: Le Musée Alaoui. In 1899 a second extension space, called the small palace, was added to it to house collections of Islamic arts and artifacts. In 1956, at Tunisia's independence, it officially became the National Museum in Bardo.

Bardo Museum is spread over approximately $11,000 \text{ m}^2$. The exhibits represent vast collections of relics from every period of Tunisia's past, and collections are presented by department-era: Prehistory, Punic, Roman, Christian, Arab-Moslem, Bronze and Greek marbles, etc. Many of

Fig. 6 Bardo National Museum main entrance, on the right, as seen in the summer of 2007 prior to renovation work.

the exhibits are impressive from an archaeological point of view, as well as compelling and beautiful, although the premises, the labyrinthine ground plan, and exhibition rooms have been in need of renovation for many years. Work on the renovation and alteration of the building has been contracted to the French architectural agency Codou Hindley and is expected to last 27 months. It will enlarge the museum by doubling the existing space. The planned modernization will add new, handicapped-accessible structures and underground spaces for public displays in addition to an auditorium, a laboratory, a cafeteria, and a restaurant.

Musée national de Carthage

Carthage National Museum, also known as the National Archeological Museum, is located on the hill of Byrsa in close proximity to the ancient city of Carthage and to several important excavation sites. Officially founded in 1964, it is a repository of numerous antiquities and the product of archaeological excavations since the nineteenth century. It has a great mosaics collection and other archeological materials. Exhibits include information about the course of the different excavation campaigns, a small scale model of Punic Carthage, the Capitol built by the Romans on the ruins of Punic Carthage, tophets used for child sacrifice, Punic and early Christian antiquities, mosaics, jewelry and ornaments, everyday objects, clay masks, funerary stelae and sarcophagi, etc. The two-story museum itself is relatively small but is incorporated into an area of another seven sites, or the museum gardens, where a variety of ancient remains are on display, including a 10 f high marble statue commemorating Louis IX's crusade to Tunis (1270)—though the statue is in fact a likeness of Emperor Charles V. The museum is the official center for all research activities, preservation, and administration of the Carthage site, where the Centre d' etudes et de documentation archeologique de Carthage is located (see Bulletin du CEDAC). It is therefore a first stop immediately before exploring the ruins of Carthage itself, a UNESCO World Heritage site.

Musée national d'Utique (http://www.inp.rnrt.tn/Museeutique.htm)

Commonly known as the first colony founded by the Phoenicians in North Africa, Utica was originally founded around the eighth century B.C. as a port north of Carthage on the trade route of the Phoenicians to the western Mediterranean. Excavations at the site have yielded two Punic cemeteries and Roman ruins, including baths and a villa with mosaics. The two-room museum is located on the site and contains Punic and area exhibits going back to the seventh century B.C.

Musée archéologique de Chimtou (http://www.chimtou.com/)

The museum and ancient site at Chimtou, the country's site museum, is an archeological complex of 10,000 m^2 developed under the authority of the Tunisian Institute of National Heritage with assistance from the German Archaeological Institute in Rome.

The museum contains four exhibit rooms in three wings—more than 16,145 ft^2 displaying the results of over 25 years of excavations at the ancient quarries and the site of Chimtou. Chimtou's famous golden marble was first quarried under the Numidians (149–118 B.C.). Under Roman rule, the marble served as decoration in public buildings all over the empire, including in Rome. The site offers a number of finds from various historic eras, including pagan temples, Numidian tombs, the remnants of a fifth century Christian church, a Roman way, marble quarries, and a turbine-driven grain mill. At the beginning of the twentieth century the marble yard was restored to working condition. The museum itself houses, in addition to an information space and lecture theatre, an exceptional treasure of 1647 gold coins and stresses the Numidian civilization and the extraction of marble by the Romans. The exhibits are arranged by topic:

- Protohistoric Simitthu 500–100 B.C.
- The Royal Numidian Altar
- Marmor Numidicum
- The Ancient Marble of Simitthus
- Roman Town Colonia Iulia Augusta Numidica Simitthensium
- Funeral Monuments

Musée des arts islamiques de Rakkada

The Raqqada Museum, created in 1986 and housed in a former presidential palace near the city of Qayrawan, has the country's largest collection of Islamic art, in particular, manuscripts of the Koran from the Great Mosque of Qayrawan, famously called the Blue Koran. It also has an interesting collection of ceramics, glass, and bronze objects and numerous coins from various medieval periods.

Musée de Sidi Kasim al-Jalizi (Ceramic Museum)

Located in the mausoleum of Sīdī Qāsim al-Jalīzī, a famous saint and ceramist of Andalusian origin, in the western part of the old city in Tunis. It is a small museum featuring old ceramics. The fifteenth century mausoleum is an homage to this saint, whose history reports that he was a manufacturer of ceramic squares, hence its name (ceramic squares in the North African dialect are called *jalīzi* or *zalīž*). Since 1981 this restored building has sheltered an old ceramics collection (thirteenth to sixteenth centuries) and an epigraphic collection of old funerary steles.

Musée des arts et traditions populaires

The Museum of Popular Art and Tradition, also known as Musée Dar Ben Abdallah and as Musée du patrimoine traditionnel de la ville de Tunis, was inaugurated in 1978 and housed in an eighteenth century bourgeois residence in the center of the Medina (old city) of Tunis. It has two sections, one for family life, customs, and rites and the other for public life in the city. On display are various collections of traditional Tunisian domestic objects, costumes, jewelry, and old furniture. There is a display room reserved for the horse and the rider and their gear and ornaments.

Musée Dar Cherait (http://www.darcherait.com.tn/)

This is the first private and possibly the best "living museum" in the country. Founded in 1990 in Tozeur, a southern desert oasis town that for centuries served as a caravan station, it contains art objects depicting the lifestyle in bygone times of a well-to-do middle-class Tunisian family, complete with reconstructed rooms, scenes of daily life, and samples of pottery, utensils, and antiques. There are also replicas of the bedroom of the last *bey* (Tunisia's monarch), a palace scene, and a Bedouin tent. The private collection contains good examples of centuries-old Tunisian artifacts. The museum building, part of the Dar Cherait Complex, is housed in a restored mansion and a Bedouin tent.

Musée Sidi Zitouni

This popular art and traditions museum was set up in 1968 in the shrine of the saint Sīdī Zitounī, located in Ḥaawmat al-Suq, on the southern island of Jerbah. Its unique collections depict traditional daily life in several adjacent towns and villages and include formal Jewish and Moslem clothing as well as samples of silver jewelry that was the specialty of local Jewish artisans; a reconstruction of a pottery workshop; and a display of utensils, pottery, and old furniture.

Additionally, there are other important historical and archeological museums throughout the country that should be mentioned: Musée du site de Bulla Regia, Musée du site de Makthar, Musée archéologique d'Enfidha, Musée archéologique de Sousse, Musée archéologique de Nabeul, Musée du site de Kerkouane, Musée archéologique de Sbeïtla, Musée archéologique de Chimtou, Musée archéologique de Lamta, Musée archéologique de Salakta, Musée archéologique d'El Jem, Musée archéologique de Gafsa, and Musée archéologique de Sfax.

The World Heritage Committee has inscribed on its World Heritage List for cultural values the following Tunisian Cultural Properties: amphitheater of El Jem, in 1979; site of the ancient city of Carthage, in 1979; the Medina (old city) of Tunis, in 1979; Punic town of Kerkuane and its necropolis, in 1985; Medina of Sousse, in 1988; the old city of Kairouan, in 1988; Dougga/Thugga archeological site, in 1997; and the nature preserve Ichkeul National Park, in 1980.

Education and the profession in museology

Training and education in archaeology, museology, ethnography, protection, and evaluation of the national heritage is done mostly within the INP. For many decades curators and cadres in the field have also been graduates of L'école du Louvre à Paris en muséologie in France. The country's quasi-professional association is the Comité national des musées, founded in 1961 and currently headquartered at the Bardo Museum.

National Parks

Natural parks and sites

Ichkeul National Park. Of Tunisia's six national parks, the most significant is the one around the lake, Ichkeul, in the north. Officially designated as a Wetland World Heritage Site, it is one of only two water-based, UNESCO-protected biosphere reserves in the world—the other is the Florida Everglades. It is the best vintage point from which to watch Tunisia's most colorful birds. As a bird sanctuary, the park is best visited between October and February, when it becomes a hugely populated stopping point for waterfowl and game birds migrating between Africa and Europe. Among other animal species there are water buffalo, wild boar, jackals, mongoose, and European genets as well as a limited number of crested porcupines. Djebel Ichkeul (Ichkeul massif) was originally acquired by the state in 1891; until that date the lake surrounding Djebel Ichkeul had been used as a hunting reserve. The creation of the national park was ratified by Presidential Decree No. 80-1608, of December 18, 1980.[49]

Belvedère Park and zoological gardens

Established in 1892 on a hill near the center of Tunis, Belvedère was designed by Joseph Lafacade, chief gardner of the city of Paris, France, and first opened to the public in 1910. Today the park is the largest urban park in the country, covering 110 ha. At its center is a sixteenth century Qubbah, a pavilion that provides an excellent view of the city and an example of neo-Moorish-inspired Tunisian architecture. Beside the park there is a zoo, Parc Zoologique de la Ville de Tunis, featuring African fauna, including 61 mammal, 94 bird, and 5 reptile species.

It was set up in 1963 with German assistance and covers 15 hectares.

Musée océanographique de Salammbô "Dar el Hout" (http://www.mes.tn/instm/fr/infrastructure/musee.html)

The national maritime and oceanography museum was built in 1924 during the French era in Tunisia in Salambo, not far from ancient Carthage, on a site called Palais des Suffétes de la Mer. Today, after a number of restructuring improvements, the museum has, in addition to a laboratory, a library, and a conference room, eleven display rooms, or "salles," that include aquariums:

Salle 1: La Tunisie pays marin
Salle 2: La Tunisie et la Méditerranée
Salle 3: Les aquariums d'eau douce
Salle 4: Les lagunes Tunisiennes
Salle 5: Migration de l'anguille
Salle 6: Les îles et les espèces protégées
Salle 7: Le littoral
Salle 8: La communauté d'oiseaux
Salle 9: Les techniques de pêche
Salle 10: Les poissons
Salle 11: Les aquariums d'eau de mer

Cultural and Arts Centers

Maison des arts "Dar el founoun"

As the preeminent national center for cultural and musical activities and art exhibitions affiliated with the Ministry of Culture, the center's original mission was to encourage and showcase plastic arts by Tunisian and foreign painters. Its activities revolve mainly around free exhibitions and occasional conferences. It has a 6000-volumes library and publishes monographs, catalogs, and brochures on a small scale. The site is close to the Belvédère garden in Tunis and existed as a cultural center long before it gained its new name and vocation in 1992.

Centre d'arts vivants de la ville de Radès

In 1982, the Ministry of Culture created the center as an education and training academy for student artists and professionals in the arts field. In addition to courses, it organizes exhibitions, conferences, and workshops for new and established artists. It also functions as a fine arts academy, accepting applications for artist-in-residence positions that last three to six months. It is open to the public and periodically organizes special workshop sessions for youth.

Centre culturel international d'Hammamet

Located in a villa built in 1927 in the north-eastern resort town of Ḥaammamat by a wealthy Romanian named George Sebastian, the International Cultural Center was founded in 1962. It includes an open arena and theater stage built in 1964 based on Greek and Roman models. It is the setting of an international festival of music and drama that takes place in July and August each year. Described by Frank Lloyd Wright as the most beautiful villa in the world, Sebastian's house and surrounding gardens with over 300 species of plants was a destination of prominent personalities such as Winston Churchill, Anthony Eden, and Field Marshall Erwin Rommel and a variety of artists who came to visit and create. It continues to function as an international artists' retreat.

CONCLUSION

Since the country gained independence, successive Tunisian governments have pursued reformist and modernist policies, especially in the cultural and educational spheres. While well aware of its millennia-old cultural roots and being custodian of vestiges that are considered important World Heritage sites, this emerging country faces a number of challenges. In spite of Tunisia's economic and social successes, its cultural scene is still in need of realizing full potential. The state remains the dominating sponsor and patron of culture and the arts. In this respect, it has succeeded in developing a considerable cultural infrastructure throughout the country. It has also built an adequate statutory framework consisting of legislation related to cultural matters that is designed to ensure, for instance, the protection of intellectual and artistic property, the preservation of the country's heritage, and guaranteed freedom of information and the media. In reality, however, the country still faces a long road ahead with regard to all of these issues. Moreover, despite concerted efforts over the decades since independence, there is a manifest lack of interest in books and reading among a large swath of the population, and publishing levels outside official and educational institutions continue to be low. Critics also see serious shortcomings in the areas of artistic creation and theatrical and cinematographic productions. Tunisia's rich cultural heritage and assets are underappreciated, and the various concerted measures undertaken by the government authorities in recent years to encourage, for instance, cultural tourism were mainly geared toward foreign visitors. There is arguably looming danger to many historical sites as a consequence of the conflicting pressures on land use from urban, agricultural, and tourism expansion. Some historical sites are deteriorating due to aging and weathering or inadequate maintenance. Finally, it must be pointed out that in the area of information and communication technologies, the Tunisian government has invested heavily in online services, computer training, and hardware acquisition so much that the World Economic Forum recently designated the country as first in Africa for network readiness.

REFERENCES

1. Mackensen, R.S. Four great libraries of medieval Baghdad. Libr. Quart. July **1932**, *2*, 279–299.

2. al-Rammah, M. The ancient library of Kairaouan and its methods of conservation. In T*he Conservation and Preservation of Islamic Manuscripts*, Proceedings of the Third Conference of Al-Furqan Islamic Heritage Foundation; Al-Furqan Islamic Heritage Foundation: London, U.K., 1995; 31–32.

3. Shabbuh, I. Sijil qadim li-Maktabat Jami'al-Qayrawan. Majallat Ma'had al-Makhtutat al-'Arabiya November **1956**, *2*, 339–372.

4. 'Abd al-Wahhab, H.H. Bayt al-Hikmah al-Tunisi. Bahth tarikhi fi awwal m'uasaasah 'ilmiyah jam'iyah fi al-bilad al-Ifriqiyah. Majallat Majma al-Lughah al-Arabiyah **1963–1964**, *30*, 128.

5. al-Rammah, M. The Ancient Library of Kairaouan and its methods of conservation. In *The Conservation and Preservation of Islamic Manuscripts*, Proceedings of the Third Conference of Al-Furqan Islamic Heritage Foundation; Al-Furqan Islamic Heritage Foundation: London, U.K., 1995; 29.

6. al-Mu'izz ibn Bādīs, Emir of Ifrīqiyah. *Mediaeval Arabic Bookmaking and Its Relation to Early Chemistry and Pharmacology*; American Philosophical Society: Philadelphia, PA, 1962; 13–50 (Translation of Umdat al-Kuttab Wa'uddat Dhawi al-Albab, by Martin Levey).

7. Pedersen, J. *The Arabic Book*; Princeton University Press: Princeton, NJ, 1984; 129.

8. Abd al-Qadir, A.M. Al-Maktabah al-Tuniusiyah wa-Inayatuha bi-Almakhtut al-Arabi. Majallat Mahad al-Makhtutat al-Arabyiah May **1971**, *17*, 179–187.

9. Deeb, M.J. Al-Zaytuna. *The Oxford Encyclopedia of the Modern Islamic World*; Oxford University Press: New York, 1995; Vol. 4, 374.

10. Sibai, M. *Mosque Libraries: An Historical Study*; Mansell Publishing Limited: London and New York, 1987; 92.

11. http://www.tunisiaonline.com/map.html.

12. La Press Reference, Tunisia. Available at http://www.pressreference.com/Sw-Ur/Tunisia.html.

13. Central Intelligence Agency (CIA). *World Factbook*. Available at https://www.cia.gov/library/publications/the-world-factbook/print/ts.html (accessed July 2007).

14. La Presse. Available at http://www.nytimes.com/.

15. Ministry of Culture and Preservation of Patrimony. Available at http://www.culture.tn/culture/HTML/institutions/bn.htm.

16. Ministry of Culture and Preservation of Patrimony. Bibliothèque nationale. Available at http://www.culture.tn/culture/HTML/institutions/bn.htm.

17. The National Library of Tunisia & UNIMARC. Available at http://unimarc.bn.pt/a_u_g/annick-bernard_tunisie.pdf.

18. *Code de la Presse*; Imprimerie officielle de la République tunisienne: Tunis, Tunisia, 1977.

19. Tunisiaonline. Available at http://www.tunisiaonline.com/government/government1.html .

20. International Freedom of Expression eXchange (IFEX). Tunisia Monitoring Group. *Report of the Tunisia Monitoring Group*. Available at http://campaigns.ifex.org/tmg/IFEXTMGreport_April2007.doc.

21. http://www.wipo.int/about-ip/en/ipworldwide/pdf/tn.pdf.

22. Tunisia. *Journal officiel de la République tunisienne = al-Ra'id al-Rasm lil-Jumhuriyah al-Tunisiyah*; al-Maṭba'ah al-Rasmīyah lil-Jumhūrīyah al-Tūnisīyah, Tūnis August **1992**, *51*, 986 (French).

23. Tunisia. *Journal officiel de la République tunisienne = al-Ra'id al-Rasmi lil-Jumhuriyah al-Tunisiyah*; al-Maṭba'ah al-Rasmīyah lil-Jumhūrīyah al-Tūnisīyah, Tūnis March **1994**, *23*, 503 (French).

24. Tunisia. *Journal officiel de la République tunisienne = al-Ra'id al-Rasmi lil-Jumhuriyah al-Tunisiyah*; al-Maṭba'ah al-Rasmīyah lil-Jumhūrīyah al-Tūnisīyah, Tūnis December **1999**, *101*, 2638 (French).

25. Tunisia. *Journal officiel de la République tunisienne = al-Ra'id al-Rasmi lil-Jumhuriyah al-Tunisiyah*; al-Maṭba'ah al-Rasmīyah lil-Jumhūrīyah al-Tūnisīyah, Tūnis August **1979**, *51*, 2330 (French).

26. Tunisia. *Journal officiel de la République tunisienne = al-Ra'id al-Rasmi lil-Jumhuriyah al-Tunisiyah*; al-Rasmīyah lil-Jumhūrīyah al-Tūnisīyah, Tūnis August **1979**, *48*, 2198 (French).

27. Tunisia. *Journal officiel de la République tunisienne = al-Ra'id al-Rasmi lil-Jumhuriyah al-Tunisiyah*; al-Maṭba'ah al-Rasmīyah lil-Jumhūrīyah al-Tūnisīyah, Tūnis April **1975**, *29*, 852 (French).

28. Tunisia. Directory of Higher Education Institutions. Available at http://www.mes.tn/annuaire_ang.pdf.

29. Higher Education and Scientific Research in Tunisia. Available at http://www.universites.tn/anglais/index.htm.

30. Ksibi, A. University libraries in the south: from virtual to real. Inform. Dev. **2006**, *22* (4), 252–262. Available at http://www.ifla.org/IV/ifla72/papers/072_Ksibi_trans-en.pdf (accessed May 2007).

31. Portail des Professionels de Bibliothèques Universitaires. Available at http://www.cck.rnu.tn/biruni/reseau/reseaux.htm.

32. Tunisia. *Journal officiel de la République tunisienne = al-Ra'id al-Rasmi lil-Jumhuriyah al-Tunisiyah*; al-Maṭba'ah al-Rasmīyah lil-Jumhūrīyah al-Tūnisīyah, Tūnis December **1978**, *87*, 3777 Modified: October **1999**, *85*, 2016 (French).

33. *Report on IFEX—TMG Mission to Tunis*, 2005. Available at http://www.ifla.org/faife/faife/tunis-report2005.htm (accessed July 2007).

34. *al-Sabah* (newspaper, Web edition). Available at http://www.assabah.com.tn/.

35. Tunisia. *Journal officiel de la République tunisienne = al-Ra'id al-Rasmi lil-Jumhuriyah al-Tunisiyah*; al-Maṭba'ah al-Rasmīyah lil-Jumhūrīyah al-Tūnisīyah, Tūnis August **1991**, *55*, 1398 (French).

36. *Education pour tous: Bilan à l'an 2000. Rapport final*, Coordinateur du bilan national: Fatma Tarhouni, Inspectrice Générale de l'Education, Ministere de l'Education. Available at http://www.unesco.org/education/wef/countryreports/tunesia/contents.html#cont (accessed March 2007).

37. Ministère de l'Education et de la Formation. Etablissements, élèves et enseignants 2006 online statistics. Available at http://www.education.tn/fr/statistiques/education/etab_eleves_ensig.htm.

38. L'évaluation de l'éducation pour tous à l'an 2000: Rapport des pays. Tunisie. Available at http://www.unesco.org/education/wef/countryreports/tunesia/rapport_1_.html.

39. http://www.education.tn/en/ministere/mef_dgpfc.htm.

40. International Bureau of Education = Bureau de l'Education International: Tunisia (UNESCO, Geneva, Switzerland) Le développement de l'éducation en Tunisie, 1996–2000, septembre 2001 (Tunisia, Ministère de l'Education. 46th Session of the International Conference on Education, Geneva, September 5–8, 2001). Documents et ressources sur la République tunisienne (rapports et statistiques), 34. Available at http://www.ibe.unesco.org/International/ICE/natrap/Tunisia_Fr.pdf.

41. Tunisia. *Journal officiel de la République tunisienne = al-Ra'id al-Rasmi lil-Jumhuriyah al-Tunisiyah*; al-Maṭbaʻah al-Rasmīyah lil-Jumhūrīyah al-Tūnisīyah, Tūnis August **1982**, *61*, 1990 (French).

42. *The world of learning online*, 2007. Available at http://www.worldoflearning.com/views/entry/TN/3/1/4 (accessed August 2007).

43. Tunisia. *Journal officiel de la République tunisienne = al-Ra'id al-Rasmi lil-Jumhuriyah al-Tunisiyah*; al-Maṭbaʻah al-Rasmīyah lil-Jumhūrīyah al-Tūnisīyah, Tūnis July **1981**, *48*, 1664 (French).

44. Tunisia. *Journal officiel de la République tunisienne = al-Ra'id al-Rasmi lil-Jumhuriyah al-Tunisiyah*; al-Maṭbaʻah al-Rasmīyah lil-Jumhūrīyah al-Tūnisīyah, Tūnis July **1994**, *62*, 1296 (French).

45. Tunisia. *Journal officiel de la République tunisienne = al-Ra'id al-Rasmi lil-Jumhuriyah al-Tunisiyah*; al-Maṭbaʻah al-Rasmīyah lil-Jumhūrīyah al-Tūnisīyah, Tūnis July **1970**, *19*, 386 (French).

46. Tunisia. *Journal officiel de la République tunisienne = al-Ra'id al-Rasmi lil-Jumhuriyah al-Tunisiyah*; al-Maṭbaʻah al-Rasmīyah lil-Jumhūrīyah al-Tūnisīyah, Tūnis July **1988**, *85*, 1747–1749 (French).

47. Tunisia. *Journal officiel de la République tunisienne = al-Ra'id al-Rasmi lil-Jumhuriyah al-Tunisiyah*; al-Maṭbaʻah al-Rasmīyah lil-Jumhūrīyah al-Tūnisīyah, Tūnis July **1997**, *17*, 356 (French).

48. Tunisia. *Journal officiel de la République tunisienne = al-Ra'id al-Rasmi lil-Jumhuriyah al-Tunisiyah*; al-Maṭbaʻah al-Rasmīyah lil-Jumhūrīyah al-Tūnisīyah, Tūnis March **1997**, *19*, 387 (French).

49. Tunisia. *Journal officiel de la République tunisienne = al-Ra'id al-Rasmi lil-Jumhuriyah al-Tunisiyah*; al-Maṭbaʻah al-Rasmīyah lil-Jumhūrīyah al-Tūnisīyah, Tūnis December **1980**, *77*, 3328 (French).

Ukraine: Libraries

Lyudmila Shpilevaya
New York Public Library, New York, New York, U.S.A.

Abstract

The geopolitical location of Ukraine in Central-Eastern Europe has significantly influenced the historical and present development of the country and its libraries. The Ukraine became a fully sovereign state in 1991, after long periods of successive domination by Poland-Lithuania, Russia, and the Soviet Union. Since Ukraine became independent libraries have been rethinking their role in society, considering different goals and facing new challenges. Those challenges are closely linked to democratic changes occurring in Ukraine during the last decade. This entry gives a brief history of libraries in Ukraine, reviews conditions and development of Ukrainian libraries, and discusses new trends in their activities. It also contains basic information about some of the major libraries in Ukraine.

INTRODUCTION

Ukraine is located in Central-Eastern Europe (see Fig. 1). The geopolitical location of Ukraine has significantly influenced the historical and present development of the country. Ukraine is the second largest country in Europe. The Ukrainian culture and dramatic history goes back to the 5th century, when Kyiv (the capital of Ukraine) was founded. The Ukrainian Parliament passed a declaration of sovereignty in July 1990 and, in August 1991, declared Ukraine independent of the Union of Soviet Socialist Republics (USSR).

Libraries and librarianship in Ukraine reflect the history and development of the country and its people. Because Ukraine became an independent sovereign state, the libraries have been rethinking their role in society, considering different goals and facing new challenges. Those challenges are closely linked to democratic changes occurring in Ukraine during the last decade. This entry gives a brief history of libraries in Ukraine, reviews conditions and development of Ukrainian libraries, and discusses new trends in their activities. It also contains basic information about some of the major libraries in Ukraine.

HISTORY OF LIBRARIES IN UKRAINE

Earliest chronicles of libraries in Ukraine date from the 11th century (the Library of Saint Sophia's Cathedral, also known as "The Prince of Kyiv Rus Yaroslav's the Wise Library" and "The Library of the Kyiv-Pechers'ka Lavra").[1] "At the beginning of the 14th century a large collection (215 manuscripts and books) was housed at Supral' Monastery; there were smaller ones at Sluc'k (founded 1494), L'viv (founded 1579), and elsewhere."[2] There were well-known libraries located in monasteries and private libraries owned by famous clergymen and Cossack's nobility during the 16th–18th centuries. Examples of these are the libraries of L'viv Stavropygian Brotherhood (16th century); Petro Mohyla (1596–1647), later donated to the Kyiv Academy; Dmytro Tuptalo; Feofan Prokopovych (1681–1736), containing 3000 volumes; and Lazar Baranovych.[2]

During the 19th century, many academic and public libraries were founded. Some of them are the libraries in Kharkiv (1805), Odesa (1829), and the Library of Kyiv University (1834).[3]

There was a short period when Ukraine attempted to establish itself as an independent state (1918–1921). At that time, the National Library of the Ukrainian State was established (1918). However, Ukraine lost its own state system and became a part of the USSR in 1922. During the World War II, German troops occupied Ukrainian territory (1941–1944). This war brought great losses to the libraries. Before the beginning of the Second World War, there were 44,662 libraries with total book collections amounting to 102 million items.[1] The official estimates of losses say that more than 40,000 libraries were ruined or damaged and about 80 million books were destroyed or stolen. Nevertheless, the library network in Ukraine was basically restored by 1950.[1] Under the Soviet regime, the libraries had a strict centralized administration ensuring strong censorship and dictating communist ideology. The Soviet Union had proclaimed a new "nationality," "the Soviet human being," which meant the erasure of individual national and ethnic identities. The libraries were an important instrument toward the achievement of that goal. The libraries of the Soviet republics were deprived of their individual identities. They were all headed by the Moscow library administration, and they served Moscow politics and ideologies.

Encyclopedia of Library and Information Sciences, Fourth Edition DOI: 10.1081/E-ELIS4-120024122

Fig. 1 Map of Ukraine.
Source: CIA World Factbook https://www.cia.gov/library/publications/the-world-factbook/goes/up.html.

CONTEMPORARY LIBRARY SYSTEM IN UKRAINE

Most of the modern library network in Ukraine had been formed during the Soviet era (1920–1991). Since 1991, when Ukraine achieved its desired independence and became a sovereign state, the libraries have been rethinking their role in the society, considering different goals and facing new challenges. The library community is currently working toward "new library policies in Ukraine based on free access to ideas, library materials and services. Intellectual freedom issues are the basis of contemporary library and information policies in Ukraine."[4] Intellectual freedom is closely connected to important issues such as open and free access to information and resistance to censorship. Successful achievement of these goals is highly contingent on changes in the librarians' attitudes and training.

The information technologies that have changed the missions, goals, and functions of world libraries during the last 10 years have become a part of library practice in Ukraine. Users of the Internet in Ukraine in 1999 have increased 3 times (from 0.5 million at the beginning of the year to 1.5 million at the end), and the user growth rate was the highest among all the European countries.[5] The impact of computerization has significantly changed the tradition functions of library services. Now Ukrainian librarians, along with their traditional services, are providing virtual services such as e-mailed reference, electronic catalogs, and Internet access. Most librarians welcome technological changes but also see the value in their historical function of assisting people to find information—whether digitized or between the covers of a book. They understand that for success, the professional librarian needs a combination of communication and computer skills. When the computerization of libraries is

successfully completed and a general unified network is created, the new information technologies will ease the tasks related to bibliographic and authority control.

Another important task for libraries is the creation of a national bibliography "Ukrainica," which will accumulate all publications published in Ukraine, all publications in Ukrainian language, irrespective of place of publication, and all publications linked to Ukraine irrespective of language. Three libraries, the Vernadsky National Library, the National Parliament Library, and the Stefanyk Lviv Scientific Library, are at the head of this undertaking. The Vernadsky National Library has already published the fifth volume of the "National Bibliography of Ukraine."

> The decade has not been easy for the Ukrainian people as they strive to create a democratic state, a free-market economy, and a civil society. This transition period has been extremely difficult for libraries and librarians who now have far less financial support from the government than during the Soviet period.[6]

In recent years, there has been positive movement in the state library politics. Important documents such as "The Law of Ukraine on Libraries and Librarianship" (1995), "The Program on the Preservation of Library and Archival Collections, 2000–2005" (approved by the Cabinet of Ministries of Ukraine, 1999), "The Program of Libraries' Acquisitions for the Period up to 2005" (approved by the Cabinet of Ministries of Ukraine, 2002), and two Presidential Decrees, "Establishment of the All-Ukrainian Day of Librarians—September, 30th" (1998) and "Urgent Measures toward Development of Libraries of Ukraine" (2000), have been signed.[7] Those documents increase the prestige of the libraries and give them new parameters for improved and increased operations. Although Ukraine has affirmed these documents, they

Tunisia–United Kingdom

have not been followed by either sufficient funding or support to meet the libraries' growth and development needs.

Ukrainian libraries are striving to integrate into the international library society. They are working on extending their international contacts, seeking international partnerships and funding, and participating in international associations and programs. One of the results of such partnerships is the bilingual (Ukrainian/English) Internet reference site, "Ukrainian Library World Gateway."[8] This Web-based directory has been developed by the British Council in Ukraine, the Ukrainian Library Association, and the Library of the National University "Kyiv-Mohyla Academy." It is a centralized source of information regarding to Ukrainian libraries and professional information for Ukrainian librarians.

The present library network of Ukraine consists of public, academic, school, university, and special libraries (Fig. 2). The greatest problems facing Ukrainian libraries of all types are insufficient budgets for collections and general operating expenses, substandard salaries for librarians, and low levels of computerization and Internet access for both library professionals and users.

Ukrainian librarians have two professional associations: The Association of Ukrainian Libraries (ABU) and The Ukrainian Library Association (UBA). Membership in both associations is open to individual librarians as well as for the libraries. The Association of Ukrainian Libraries (ABU), founded in 1991, unites mostly academic, medical, agricultural, technical, and some university libraries. Information on this organization can be founded on its Web site.[9] The Ukrainian Library Association (UBA) was founded in 1995. The Web site for this organization provides practical information for professionals in the field.[10]

There are two levels of professional library education: "medium" that is the equivalent of 2-year college program and "high" level of professional education that requires completion of a 4-year program at an accredited college or university. Three academic institutions in Ukraine currently certify the librarians with "high" qualification: The Kyiv National University of Culture and Arts,[11] The Kharkiv State Academy of Culture,[12] and The Rivne State Institute of Culture.

Public Libraries

Public libraries are the most extended library system under the patronage of the Ministry of Culture and Arts of Ukraine. According to the Ministry statistics, there are almost 20,000 public libraries in Ukraine. The complete book collections of them amount to 302 million issues. On average, a public library contains 16,000 publications; a village library contains 10,000. The book supply, per capita, is about 6 issues in municipal libraries and 10 issues per capita in village libraries. These numbers are relatively high in comparison to the IFLA standards, which recommend sustaining collections based on a count of three books per capita in small towns and villages and two books per capita in more populated areas. The book supply in Ukrainian village libraries is three times larger than world standards. It is estimated that there are 17 million users of the public libraries in Ukraine. However, the amount of new acquisitions in recent years is three times less than the International Federation of Library Associations and Institutions (IFLA) standard, 70 publications per 1000 people.[13] Compared to other types of libraries, the public libraries are funded better, their collections are more or less updated, and more and more regional libraries are opening their own Web sites. An important role in solving the problem of public libraries' computerizations belongs to the Library Electronic Access Project (LEAP). This is a project of the Public Affairs Section of the U.S. Embassy. It helps to create free Internet centers in public libraries and to provide an open exchange of information and communication. Public libraries have received grants up to $24,000 for computer equipment, software, Internet access, and training. In the last 2 years, 71 Internet centers have been opened in public libraries throughout Ukraine.[14]

The National Parliamentary Library of Ukraine

Founded in 1866, as a public library, this library became the State Library of Ukraine in 1957. In 1994, the status of national library was conferred and it was renamed "The National Parliamentary Library of Ukraine" (NPLU). This library is the main library of the Ministry of Culture and Arts of Ukraine, and it is the central library of the Ukrainian public library system. The NPLU is a research institution in library science and bibliography. It serves as a national depository for all Ukrainian publications and is a center for international book exchange. Its collection is universal in character and amounts to more than 4 million issues, including rare Old-Slavonic books of the 16th–18th centuries.[15] NPLU considers formation of an electronic

Type of Libraries	Amount of libraries	Amount of collection (million)	Amount of readers (million)	Use of library materials (million)	Amount of library staff (thousand)
Public	20.000	350	17	350	36
Libraries of educational institutions, including schools	20.800	8	1,6	10	18,7
University libraries	267	106	1,5	102	6,5
Technical/Industry	2.500	156	0,75	10	3,5
Medical	1.033	30	0,77	25,3	2,2
Agricultural	275	21	3	20	2
Academic	96	29	0,37	8	1
Total	**45.000**	**700**	**25**	**500**	**70**

Fig. 2 Libraries in Ukraine statistics.

database, including the establishment of electronic catalogs linking them to other library and research institutions around the world, as its primary goal. At present, the library has established an electronic catalog of new acquisitions (containing more than 209,000 bibliographic records) and an electronic catalog of articles from Ukrainian and Russian research publications (more than 200,000 bibliographic records). The creation of the information system and expanded access to world information resources is growing through grants and aid from international charitable foundations and International Research & Exchanges Board (IREX).[16]

Korolenko State Scientific Library in Kharkiv

One of the oldest and largest libraries in Ukraine was founded in 1886 as a public library. A significant role in the development of the library was played by notable figures in Ukrainian history and culture; among them are professors Bahalii and Sumtsov and librarian Khavkina. At the beginning of the 20th century, many foreign libraries contributed to the development of the unique collection of the library, including The New York Public Library, The Library of Congress, and The National Library of France.[3] In 1921, the library acquired the designation of state library and became a national depository. The collections of the library run to more than 6 million items, including 50,000 in the rare book collection, more than 600,000 Ukrainian language publications, and a unique collection of musical scores (104,000 items). Like other Ukrainian libraries, this one is working toward the automation and computerization of library processes. The library is also a research center in the field of library science. Each year, it publishes approximately 30 titles of bibliographies and books on librarianship.[15]

The State Library of Ukraine for Children

Founded in 1967, it is the primary children's library in Ukraine and the national depository of children's literature. It is also the research, reference-bibliographic, and consulting center for more than 1000 children's libraries and about 22,000 school libraries in Ukraine. Its collections run to 440,000 books, magazines, audio recordings, videos, and CDs. Each year, about 18,000 users visit the library. The library hosts many different activities and events for children at the library. Examples include a puppet theater, theater studio "Ovation" and a club of connoisseurs of Ukrainian arts, and circles of soft toys "Fantastic Needle." The library publishes the bibliographies of recommended reading for different age groups (also available online), some topical bibliographies, and method materials for teachers and children's librarians. The library Web site and online catalog are also available.[17]

Academic Libraries

The network of academic libraries in Ukraine consists of The Vernadsky National Library, The Stefanyk Library of the National Academy of Sciences of Ukraine, and 96 other libraries of the scientific-research institutions of the National Academy of Sciences of Ukraine. The complete academic library network's collections amount to 26 million items of materials, including about 6 million in foreign languages. These collections serve as a document base for scientific research and experiments in different areas of humanities, social sciences, engineering and technology, business, sciences, and arts. Annually, the academic libraries of Ukraine serve more than 208,000 users.[18]

The Vernadsky National Library of Ukraine

The Vernadsky National Library of Ukraine is the largest library in Ukraine. Founded in 1918, as the National Library of the Ukrainian State, it changed its functions several times as well as its name. In 1996, the library received the status of the National Library and its contemporary name and designation. The library contains many distinctive collections that are universal in scope and range from the 3rd century BC to contemporary foreign and Ukrainian publications. A fire in May 1964 inflicted significant damage on the collections of the library.[19] In October 2002, more than 200,000 books, magazines, and newspapers were heavily damaged by water, steam, and humidity when a pipeline in the library's central heating system began leaking.[20]

There are more than 14 million items in the library holdings. Annually, the library receives 140,000–160,000 documents (books, magazines, newspapers, etc.). Each year, about 250,000 readers use the library resources and receive 3.5 to 4 million documents.[21] Since 1969, the library has developed a large collection of publications of the United Nations (UN) and its specialized bodies. Every year, it receives more than 15,000 UN documents. The library maintains an international book exchange with more than 1400 academic foreign institutes and libraries participating. There are more than 30 catalogs and card files and a specialized collection of 160,000 reference and bibliographical publications, including one of the few sets in Eastern Europe of the printed catalog of the New York Public Library in 800 volumes.[19] The Vernadsky National Library has more than 250 computers in use for creating the National Electronic Library of Ukraine and to serve readers by providing electronic information resources. The library has about 40 departments, staffed by 900 employees.[21]

The Lviv Stefanyk Scientific Library

The Stefanyk Library of the National Academy of Sciences of Ukraine is one of the largest libraries of Ukraine.

It was founded in 1940, based on the collections of several private and institutional libraries, including the libraries of the Ossolineum, The Shevchenko Scientific Society, and The Lviv National Home. In 1989, the library acquired the status of an official research institute. The sole Research Center of Periodicals in Ukraine functions in this library. The Lviv Stefanyk Scientific Library's research priorities include the following: "Documental Memory" of Ukraine, bibliography and librarianship, and rare books collection. The library personnel numbers about 300 employees. The library collections have more than 7 million items, including the remarkable collection of Ukrainian periodicals of the 19th–20th centuries, rare books (250,000 items), and manuscript holdings of more than 120,000 units from the 13th to 20th centuries. These collections make The Lviv Stefanyk Scientific Library the second richest library in Ukraine.[22]

The University Libraries

The Maksymovych Scientific Library of the National Shevchenko University

The library was founded in 1834, at the same time as the university. Its collection was based on the library of the Kremenets Lyceum holdings. Now the library collection counts more than 3.5 million items including more than 16,000 titles of periodicals. Among these are rare books of the 15th–19th centuries in Old-Slavonic, Ukrainian, Russian, Polish, German, French, Italian, and English, the works by University professors from 1837 until present, and books (with autographs) of famous figures in the fields of science and arts. Annually, more than 72,000 readers are served in 32 reading rooms and 13 circulation divisions. The library provides different activities such as authors' readings, literature debates, and book exhibitions. The library is a research center that coordinates and consults with more than 150 other university and college libraries in Ukraine.[15]

Scientific Library of the National University "Kyiv-Mohyla Academy"

This library is one of the newest research libraries in Ukraine. It is an important part of the university education and creative laboratory. This library began in 1992, with one book and two librarians. Ten years later, at the beginning of 2002, its collections consisted of 300,000 volumes/80,000 titles. The library provides services for students and professors based on its own collections and database as well as utilizing the resources of other Ukrainian libraries. The library introduced methods such as barcoding in circulation and checkpoint monitoring systems. This library is one of the very few libraries that uses international standards such as Anglo-American cataloging rules (AACR-2), U.S. machine readable cataloging

(USMARC) format for bibliographic and authority data, and the Library of Congress Subject Headings. The library has received financial support and grants from International Renaissance Foundation (IRF), the America House, International Research & Exchanges Board (IREX), the German Library Institute, Lange & Springer, McArthur Foundation, and others. The library has an electronic catalog and database.[23]

Special Libraries

Special libraries include a wide range of libraries that belong to different businesses and organizations. They incorporate medical, technical, and agricultural libraries as well as libraries of different ministries and governmental organizations. The libraries for the blind also belong in this category.

The State Scientific Medical Library of Ukraine

The State Scientific Medical Library of the Healthcare Ministry of Ukraine, founded in 1930, is one of the largest medical libraries in Europe. It is a research, consulting, and administrative center for 998 medical libraries in Ukraine. It is also a national depository of publications on medicine and related fields. Its complete book collection amounts to 1.3 million items, dating from the 16th century to current editions.[15] The library also maintains the largest department of patents and normative technical documentations in medicine in the country. The library has official exchange partners in 32 countries that allow improvement and development of the library collection. There are a few card catalogs, including alphabetical, systematical/topical, and subject catalogs. Since 1993, the library has generated electronic catalog of books and dissertations, and since 1998—electronic catalog of articles. The library Web site (only in Ukrainian) gives information about the library, its facilities, reference sources, and links to other medical libraries.[24]

Agricultural Libraries

In the category of special libraries, the agricultural libraries play a very important role in agrarian Ukraine. The network of agricultural libraries consists of 273 libraries, including 20 libraries of agricultural universities, 77 libraries of agricultural research institutes and their branches, 61 libraries of research-experimental stations, and 115 libraries of agricultural colleges. They have concentrated about 20 million of items of general and specific information resources of agriculture and related fields. Annually, more than 700,000 users visit the agricultural libraries and borrow 19 million documents, including books, magazines, newspapers, and patents.[25]

The Scientific Agricultural Library of the National Agricultural University

Founded in 1921, the library is the main research, consulting, and interlibrary loan center of the agricultural libraries network. It is also the national depository of agricultural publications. The library collection runs to more than 1 million books, magazines, and dissertations in Ukrainian, Russian, and other languages. Annually, the library receives more than 30,000 books and 600 periodical titles, including foreign publications.[15] The special collection of rare books includes the works by famous agricultural scientists Dokuchaev, Vavilov, Chaianov, and Williams. The library contains valuable Russian periodicals of the 19th century, e.g., "Trudy Volnogo Ekonomicheskogo Obshchestva" and "Selskii khoziain" (1888–1917). The library has Yearbooks of the Department of Agriculture of the United States dating from 1896.[3] The library activities are not limited to collection development and public service. They include research and consultation services on the specifics of agriculture libraries, and they provide continuing education for agricultural network librarians. The library also publishes information relevant to both the fields of agriculture and agriculture librarianship. The library has developed and begun to create an "Electronic Agricultural Library." They organize seminars, workshops, and conferences for librarians. On the pages of the Library's Bulletin (first published in 2001), readers can find reviews of the practices of agricultural libraries and exchange information and experiences in that field.[25] Besides the bulletin, the library publishes monthly lists of new agricultural publications and some topical bibliographies.

The State Scientific Technical Library of Ukraine

Founded in 1935, the library is the primary and the largest technical library in Ukraine. It is a national depository of technical publications. Its collections consist of 20 million items, including books, magazines, dissertations, Ukrainian and foreign standards, technical specifications, and special catalogs of Ukrainian- and foreign-manufactured products. One of the most important and popular departments among users part of the library is its patent department. There are approximately 18 million documents acquired from 57 countries in the patent department. There is a complex of different catalogs, card files, and electronic databases that allow retrieval of information.[26]

The Central Library of the Ukrainian Association of the Blind

Founded in 1936, the library is an important educational and cultural center for visually impaired people.[15] The library collection consists of about 170,000 items, including talking books, Braille books, Ukrainian and Russian audio periodicals (Gorizont, Obrii, Zdorov'ia, Svit liudyny), CDs, and descriptive videos. It includes materials in Ukrainian, Russian, Polish, Romanian, Bulgarian, and Esperanto, among other languages. The library provides reference and information services for users.[3] The Central Library for the Blind has, for many years, been the distributor of Ukrainian and Russian Braille Bible excerpts to sight-impaired people all over Ukraine. The library sends Bible Portions to 78 other libraries for the blind throughout the country.[27] Annually, the libraries for the blind serve 40,000 readers.[15]

CONCLUSION

The libraries have always played an important role in the history and culture of Ukraine. They have preserved the rich Ukrainian heritage and have served as the frontline resource in education and as the heralds of new ideas. Recent changes in political situations have greatly affected Ukrainian society and libraries. The libraries of Ukraine are now active participants in the international library society and are becoming a contributing part of the world information force. Now Ukrainian librarians can discover the accomplishments of their colleagues abroad and share their own experiences in the field of library science.

ACKNOWLEDGMENTS

I would like to thank my colleagues from the Vinnytsia Regional Scientific Library (Ukraine), Tetiana Yaroshenko from the Library of the National University "Kyiv-Mohyla Academy," and Valentyna Pashkova from the Ukrainian Library Association for sharing information. My special thanks to my friend, Michael Wood, for all her help and support.

REFERENCES

1. Holdenberg, L.I. Biblioteky. *Radianska Entsyklopediia Istorii Ukrainy*; Holovna Redaktsiia URE: Kyiv, 1969; Vol. 1, 139–140.
2. Wynar, B. Libraries. In *Encyclopedia of Ukraine*; Husar Struk, D., Ed.; University of Toronto Press, Inc.: Toronto, ON, 1993; Vol. 3, 115–119.
3. *Ukraina Bibliotechna*; Polihrafknyha: Kyiv, 1992; Ref. [4].
4. *Libraries and Intellectual Freedom: Ukraine. FAIFE World Report.* Available at http://www.ifla.org/fafe/report/ukrairne.htm (accessed July 2003).
5. Lysenko, V. Vykorystannia suchasnykh informatsiinykh tekhnolohii zadlia rozvytku hromadianskoho suspilstva. Available at http://www.irex.kiev.ua/newtechnology.html (accessed August 2003).
6. Schaffner, B.L. Libraries in Ukraine: a decade of independence. Int. Leads **2002**, *16*(1), 1–2, 8.

7. Normatyvni akty Ukrainy v bibliotechnii i sumizhnykh haluziakh. Available at http://nbuv.gov.ua/law (accessed August 2003).

8. Ukrainian Library World Gateway. Available at http://www.ukrlibworld.kiev.ua (accessed August 2003).

9. Asotsiatsiia Bibliotek Ukrainy. Available at http://www.nbuv.gov.ua/abu/ (accessed August 2003).

10. Ukrainian Library Association. Available at http://www.uba.org.ua/ (accessed August 2003).

11. Kyivskyi Natsionalnyi Universytet Kultury I mystetstv. Available at http://www.knukim-edu.kiev.ua/ (accessed August 2003).

12. Kharkivska Derzhavna Akademiia Kultury. Available at http://www.ic.ac.kharkov.ua/ (accessed August 2003).

13. Prokosheva, T.M. Stan bibliotechnoi spravy v Ukraini. Perspektyvy rozvytku bibliotek. *Profesiinyi Bibliotechnyi Rukh: Nazustrich Zminam Bibliotechno-Informatsiinoho Seredovyshcha Kyiv*, 2001; 4–8.

14. LEAP (Library Electronic Access Project). Available at http://www.usinfo.usemb.kiev.ua/irc_leap_eng.html (accessed August 2003).

15. *Bibliotechna Ukraina: Dovidnyk*, Abrys: Kyiv, 1996.

16. Kornienko, A. Vyvazheno, osmysleno pratsiuemo dlia suspilstva. Bibl. Planet. **2003**, (1), 4–5.

17. State Library of Ukraine for Children. Available at http://www.chl.kiev.ua/ENG/Chl_me_e.htm (accessed July 2003).

18. Biblioteky Natsionalnoi Akademii Nauk Ukrainy: Dovidnyk. Available at http://www.nbuv.gov.ua/books/19/96saaanu.html (accessed July 2003).

19. Shpilevaya, L.; Kasinec, E. National Library of Ukraine Vernads'kyi, V. I. In *International Dictionary of Library Histories*; Stam, D.H., Ed.; Fitzroy Dearborn Publishers: Chicago, IL, 2001; Vol. 2, 593–594.

20. Ukraine National Library Suffers Water Damage. Available at http://www.ala.org/PrinterTemplat (accessed August 2003).

21. The Vernadsky National Library. Available at http://www.nbuv.gov.ua (accessed July 2003).

22. Lvivska Naukova Biblioteka imeni Stefanyka NAN Ukrainy. Available at http://www.lsl.lviv.ua/aboutu.htm (accessed August 2003).

23. Scientific Library NaUKMA. Available at http://www.library.ukma.kiev.ua/collections/English/ (accessed July 2003).

24. Derzhavna Naukova Medychna Biblioteka Ukrainy. Available at http://www.ukrlibworld.kiev.ua/med/start.htm (accessed August 2003).

25. Serikova, N.N. Naukovo-metodychne zabezpechennia diialnosti silskohospodarskykh bibliotek Ukrainy. *Profesiinyi Bibliotechnyi Rukh: Nazustrich Zminam Bibliotechno-Informatsiinoho Seredovyshcha*, Kyiv, 2001; 41–44.

26. Gosudarstvennaia Nauchno-Tekhnicheskaia Biblioteka Ukrainy. Available at http://www.gntb.n-t.org/ob.htm (accessed August 2003).

27. Benediktovich, M. Bible library for the blind. Available at http://www.biblesociety.org/wr_359/359_15.htm (accessed August 2003).

Undergraduate Library Collections *[ELIS Classic]*

Amy M. Kautzman
University of California, Berkeley, Berkeley, California, U.S.A.

Abstract
The undergraduate library is a collection specifically set aside to serve the research needs of undergraduate students. Generally, it is in a building separate from the main research collection. Historically, it is a recent phenomenon, located primarily in the United States within the past 50 years. This entry will examine the reasons why this special collection is desired and developed, and continues to be useful in today's hyper-information-rich culture; and will look at the history, architecture, collections, and services of undergraduate libraries.

BACKGROUND

An undergraduate library's purpose is to serve expressly the needs of students in their first 4 years of college. Although the collection is not limited to resources that are required for an undergraduate education, it is expected that the majority of the student's research needs will be met with finely tuned holdings. Undergraduate libraries are most often found at large research institutions where there are multiple libraries, many of which are highly specialized. In effect, undergraduate libraries are designed to help the inexperienced student researcher find a way through too many research options. According to the American Library Association (ALA), "as a group, most first-year students share the following characteristics:

1. They do not yet have the sophisticated research skills needed to exploit the research library's potential.
2. They are intimidated by the complexity and size of a large library system.
3. They are often reluctant to ask for assistance in the use of a library.
4. They are unaware of the many services and resources that are available in university libraries."[1]

Many undergraduates lack research experience and sophistication. Although a small college library is better able to direct users to materials, universities the size of University of California at Berkeley, Michigan, or Harvard are frustrating mazes of multiple libraries that confuse and discourage novice researchers. The undergraduate library makes space for young researchers in a complicated library system.

HISTORY

The yearning for a specialized library serving the undergraduate population is neither original nor recent. In 1601,

at the University of Uppsala, Olef Rudbeck proposed a duplicate library for undergraduates. He felt that it "should be set up in the main building for students who may always use them (the books) there.[2]" Not long after, in 1602, the Bodley Library (precursor to the Bodleian) opened. As early as 1608, the new librarian, Thomas James, inquired into building a special collection to better serve his young clientele. He received this response from Sir Thomas Bodley:

> Your deuise for a Libarie for the yonguer sort will haue many great exceptions, and one special force. That there must be an other keeper ordeined for that place. And where yow mention the yonguer sort, I knowe what books should be bought for them, but the elder as well [as] the yonguer, may hae often occasion to looke vpon them: and if there were any suche, they can not require so great a rowme. In effect, to my understanding, there is muche to be saied against it, as vndoubtedly your self will readily finde, vpon further consideration. (Wagmen.[3])

It is fascinating and telling to realize that the issues of staffing and audience were readily invoked in the nascent history of library management, in the end trumping public service for the presumed lack of funding.

In spite of Thomas James' request for a special collection, early library collections were not concerned with undergraduates. With nowhere near the number of publications that libraries now offer, books were rare, valuable, and not readily available. It was difficult to make books accessible to students, much less have duplicate collections, when folios were chained to the wall to discourage theft. In addition, the pedagogy of the day relied on rote memorization that did not require the use of a large number of books. The emergence of the research university model revolutionized old disciplines. Two countries, Scotland and Germany, developed the single-discipline professorial model we know so well. The advent of an industrial society, from around 1789 to 1939, transformed education.

Encyclopedia of Library and Information Sciences, Fourth Edition DOI: 10.1081/E-ELIS4-120020354

Just as the division of labor segmented the work environment, so it came to effect the educational system. According to Harold Perkin, most universities were envisioned as seminaries, with a few other disciplines also taught. Schools had ignored the need for technically trained students, even as "the applied science and technology needed for the new manufacturing, mining, and transport industries had to be taught in new institutions".[4] Along with the expansion of disciplines in higher education came changes to the library's collections. Although the early university libraries had strong "divinity" collections, along with law and science, the new education model, with its stress on research, emphasized growth in the subjects of literature, political thought, and natural sciences. As libraries collected more titles, the use of monographs went up accordingly.

The expanding curriculum did not immediately change undergraduate education. But over time, students began to desire access to the stacks and to a greater variety of titles. One solution was for student societies and student libraries to purchase and manage a selection of basic texts. Person[2] notes that "student-owned libraries were particularly strong at Yale, Princeton, Columbia, and Dartmouth, and in some cases surpasse(d) the college libraries themselves in holdings." Harvard and others used a model of "house," or dorm, libraries where each house owned a working library of titles necessary for research.

In 1857, Harvard students proposed a separate collection of books specifically for their needs. They pointed out the "utter inadequacy of the College library to meet the wants of undergraduates in their last two years."[5] In 1907, Columbia College, just down the road in New York City, listened to the students and developed the Columbia College Study, which became the first special library service directed toward undergraduates. Although the Columbia College Study was a step in the right direction, it did little more than highlight a service dilemma: How is a library to serve the deep research needs of graduate students and faculty while also supporting the very general needs of a large, inexperienced group of undergraduates?

Further complicating the issue, President Franklin D. Roosevelt signed into law the Servicemen's Readjustment Act of 1944. Also known as the GI Bill, this law helped millions of veterans reacclimate to civilian and academic life. From 1946 to 1948, returning veterans made up almost 50% of all students. This influx of students overburdened libraries and universities, and caused a flurry of building and expansion matching the growth of the student body.

Widener Library (Harvard's primary research library in the humanities and social sciences), always tight on space, became more crowded. How do we serve both the faculty and the growing number of undergraduate researchers? The answer came from Harvard in 1949 when Lamont Library, the first undergraduate library, opened to great anticipation. Keyes D. Metcalf, the Director of the

Harvard University Library at the time of Lamont's completion, had strong objectives in mind for Lamont. These objectives, one could say, can still be applied to any successful undergraduate library, as follows:

1. To concentrate as far as practicable the library service for undergraduates in a central location;
2. To make the books readily accessible to the students;
3. To encourage general and recreational, as well as assigned and collateral reading.[6]

The opening day collection of 39,000 titles (over 80,000 volumes) was a great success—unless you were a student from Radcliffe. Although students from both Harvard and its sister school, Radcliffe, were now allowed into the Widener stacks with a pass, it took until 1967 for women to be allowed into Lamont. Female students were barred from Lamont Library for fear that making the secluded stacks coed might distract students from their studies and encourage romantic trysts. Today, there are few limitations on which campus users can enter into an undergraduate library, with many faculty and graduate students enamored with the ease of use and open stacks.

ARCHITECTURE

Undergraduate libraries have many physical commonalties. Most have a modern architectural sensibility that comes from both a recent history and an embracing of the contemporary aesthetic of function over ornate form. The Lamont Library, for example, was the first modern building built on the Harvard campus to break from the neo-Georgian brick tradition. It has smooth lines, an abundance of large windows, burnished woodwork, and natural light in the tradition of mid 20th century architecture. Although nobody will deny that it is much easier to use than the Widener Library, Lamont did have detractors. An article in the *Harvard Crimson* pointed out that,

> in the past five years, some of the enthusiasm for blonde wood and plate glass has evaporated, and unfortunately for Lamont, its machine-like, often submarine atmosphere has proved the main deterrent to its complete popularity. Nevertheless, by and large, the story of these five years is a success story.[7]

The Moffitt Library, at University of California at Berkeley, also incorporates a contemporary design. The modernist concrete frame building is meant to suggest a Japanese garden pavilion but has instead been nicknamed the "parking garage." Critics aside, the radical way in which undergraduate libraries simplified research encouraged a whole new approach to the library as a "place."

A successful undergraduate library will be located smack dab on undergraduate traffic routes. The University of Texas at Austin did a fabulous job in locating its undergraduate library between the student union building and the main library. Such libraries should be easily accessible with the open stacks and materials arranged with user ease in mind. Library services, such as reserve reading, a circulation desk, and a welcoming reference desk, are designed to be front and center on entering the building. Seating and study space is more important in a library where students gather for long periods of time. Crowded dorms, lack of quiet study space, and the desire to be near friends usually guarantee that the undergraduate library is a popular destination. Other special resources such as media and computer centers as well as group study rooms are incorporated into the design. Undergraduates use these services more heavily than senior researchers; thus it makes sense to place them in an easily accessible location. It is also true that undergraduates incorporate new technologies into their lives more readily. Therefore many undergraduate libraries are the first to add cutting-edge technologies and new media into their services.

When Harry H. Ransom (Main University Vice President and Provost, at the University of Texas at Austin) conceived of the undergraduate library, he understood the contemporary reasons for building a specialized collection. However, he also understood the shifting nature of academics when he outright acknowledged the need for an undergraduate program to mutate.

> Its (the library's) planners have resisted all influences to make the place a mausoleum of dead ideas attended by the undertakers of polite scholarship. No amount of planning can anticipate the opportunities and obligations that a dynamic educational program will produce from year to future year. Equally important inhabitants of the mere building, of course, will be both the immortal words and the growing, mortal minds. Therefore the really significant changes that lie ahead will be mental rather than architectural.[8]

Ransom is an example of the forward thinking that allowed University of Texas at Austin to develop innovative partnerships with campus computing, resulting in its highly successful web-based library education site, TILT.[9]

It is not an overstatement to emphasize the importance of the library to the undergraduate. As a sense of place, it defines the learning experience, the socializing of students, and the exploration of new subjects. In many institutions, the undergraduate library is the central academic experience. What we do not know is how future library use and technology will affect the infrastructure of the library. Seers have been announcing the end of brick-and-mortar libraries for over a decade. And although building and collection use has changed phenomenally, the desire on the part of faculty and students for a place to be surrounded by books (and computers) is unabated.

COLLECTION DEVELOPMENT

The onus of an undergraduate collection is to reflect and support the institution's curriculum. The collection is seen as an ever-changing reflection of classic readings and current topics. In general, undergraduate titles circulate for a shorter period of time, reflecting the tighter schedule and general nature of their scholarship. The need for weeding is ongoing, and it is the mission of the selector to keep abreast of new classes and departments. Being that it was first, the Lamont Library card file became the standard that latter undergraduate collections were built on. The University of Michigan's Shapiro Undergraduate Library holdings were also referred to as a supreme example of a public university's undergraduate collection. Static lists of titles, in the long run, were not very useful in building dynamic collections. In 1964, the ALA and the Association of College and Research Libraries began to publish *Choice: Current Reviews for Academic Libraries. Choice's* purpose was to provide reviews of recently published books that best fit in an undergraduate collection. *Choice* subject editors choose a limited number of titles that are then reviewed by librarians. As the *Choice* web site says, their reviewers are

> selected for their subject expertise, their active involvement with undergraduate students and curricula, their diverse viewpoints and backgrounds, and their sensitivity to scholarly trends. Reference publications are reviewed by practicing academic librarians, many of whom are subject specialists with advanced degrees.[10]

In today's collection climate, approval plans are often the default for building undergraduate collections. A librarian with a solid understanding of a user's needs and the ability to fine-tune an approval plan can receive shelf-ready books more quickly than ever.

When building or maintaining an undergraduate collection, ALA encourages a well-thought-out collection policy that considers the following:

1. Because many undergraduate courses require large numbers of students to use the same library materials, direct curriculum support will be provided through reserve collections and through purchase of multiple copies of items with high demand.
2. Undergraduate libraries provide effective access to information resources through reference sources in a variety of formats. Reference collections in undergraduate libraries should concentrate on the more standard and interdisciplinary indexes and sources. Periodical collections should emphasize the titles covered by these indexes.
3. Subject coverage of collections in undergraduate libraries encompasses a broad range of disciplines that offer the information needed for papers, speeches, and projects required in the wide variety of courses taken

by undergraduates. More specialized and advanced needs will be met by specific referral to other library sources on campus.

4. The library experience of undergraduates should encourage them to seek information of personal interest. Collection policies should include access to information on current events, cultural interests, careers, and recreational reading, among others, to encourage exploration of information resources as a part of everyday life. Because of the special nature of undergraduate libraries, collection policies should include withdrawal practices. Collections should be dynamic and responsive to the needs of a changing curriculum and clientele.[11]

The joy of a well-developed undergraduate library is that it informs and serves all university researchers while staying current and useful. For upper-level undergraduates as well as professors and graduate students, the undergraduate library is an excellent starting place. For deeper information needs, there is always the option of visiting the research library.

CONSTANTLY MUTATING PURPOSE

Throughout the decades, the expansion of undergraduate libraries continued, peaking with 30 undergraduate-specific libraries being added from 1960 to 1970.[12] The increase of undergraduate libraries matched the growing number of students enrolled in college. However, the 1970s saw a decline in the number of undergraduate libraries as missions changed, space was reallocated, and libraries were merged or shut down. Henry W. Wingate, author of *The Undergraduate Library: Is It Obsolete?* claimed,

> The reasons for the disenchantment with the undergraduate library concept can be traced to 1) changes in curriculum and teaching methods, and 2) tighter library budgets that preclude the extensive duplication of books and services required, and, perhaps most importantly, the realization that a separate facility works to deprive the undergraduate of a learning experience that only a large research library can offer.[13]

Undergraduate libraries succeeded when they developed a well-thought-out mission that supported a user-centric focus. In Irene Braden's 1970 book, *The Undergraduate Library*, she lists six categories in which undergraduate libraries differ from research libraries, as follows:

1. Providing open access to the collection to avoid the difficulties of the closed stack system;
2. Centralizing and simplifying services to the undergraduate;

3. Providing a collection of carefully selected books, containing the titles all undergraduates should be exposed to for their liberal education, as well as incorporating the reserved book collection;
4. Attempting to make the library an instructional tool by planning it as a center for instruction in library use, to prepare undergraduates for using larger collections, and to staff it with librarians interested in teaching the undergraduates the resources of a library and the means of tapping those resources;
5. Providing services additional to those given by the research collection;
6. Constructing a building with the undergraduates' habits of use in mind.[8]

In effect, Braden took the physical qualities of the earliest undergraduate libraries (a distinct building and collection) and added a pedagogical purpose that would build critical learning skills into library research. Braden was a harbinger of the importance of instruction in undergraduate libraries—a trend that has yet to slow down.

Libraries have become more complicated as online resources multiply and universities develop multiple catalogs to handle their metadata. The need for understanding how information is researched, published, and made available is one of the most important tools we can pass on to our students. Critical thinking skills—the ability to develop, question, test, and prove one's own as well as another's hypothesis—are the basic purpose of undergraduate education. The undergraduate library is often the locus of discovery. Paula Kaufman (Librarian, University of Illinois, Urbana-Champaign) states, "There is a renewed interest in undergraduate teaching in research universities. Also we feel acutely the need to provide a different kind of instruction to our students, most of whom are undergraduate students."[14]

Many of our students feel they are competent online researchers. They troll the Internet, find full-text articles, and link to sites that fulfill their curiosity. The reality is that they do find information, just as students were able to find titles in the research library, when allowed access. The question asked by instruction librarians throughout the 1980s and 1990s is broader: Now that you have found information, do you know how to evaluate it, then find even more that is on target for your research and ever-growing information needs?

UNDERGRADUATE LIBRARIES TODAY

The 1990s were a time of refocusing on the undergraduate library's purpose, as well as questioning the purpose of all libraries. As the Internet and online resources threatened funding and a lessening of faculty support, innovative libraries looked to transform how they were viewed and used.

One unusual example is the David Adamany Undergraduate Library at Wayne State University. Built in 1997, it is the newest undergraduate library in the nation. The rethinking of a library for undergraduates culminated in a building with 500 computer workstations providing access to electronic resources and a media collection of videos, DVDs, laser discs, and audiotapes. A one-stop service, the undergraduate library also provides students with information on careers and student survival skills. And yes, it still holds books and periodicals.

UWired, at the University of Washington, is the perfect example of the library collaborating with the Office of Undergraduate Education and Computing and Communications. This amalgam promoted "broad-based discussions, experimentation, and analysis about the following areas:

- Innovation in teaching and learning with technology tools;
- Fluency in information technology;
- New ways for students and faculty to access technology-enabled tools and resources."[15]

Those three points could not be more different, and yet similar, to the reasons for constructing the Lamont Library more than 50 years ago.

In their article, "One Size Doesn't Fit All: Designing Scaleable, Client-Centered Support for Technology in Teaching," Mark Donovan and Scott Macklin explain that,

> though UWired began as an initiative to support student uses of technology, the UWired partners understood that parallel efforts aimed at supporting teachers were a necessity. UWired's efforts to support faculty were initially confined to workshops and faculty showcases. These early efforts were driven by the energies of those faculty who were pioneering educational uses of then-new technologies such as email and the Web.[16]

Working in space donated by the undergraduate library, UWired became highly lauded as a model of instruction/library/technology partnership.

Information commons and information gateways are two other terms that have gained relevancy. The term *commons* refers back to community, a collective entity. It is the library trying to recreate a sense of place, shared community, and information sharing. The gateway concept relates to the opening of an access point, perhaps to the commons. Interestingly enough, the physical undergraduate collections at the University of Washington are kept in the Odegaard Undergraduate Library and Computing Commons, whereas the University of Indiana has the Information Commons/Undergraduate Services. The traits shared by information commons and gateways are not unlike those shared by the earliest undergraduate libraries.

For many libraries, the collection focus has changed to a combination of virtual and physical resources—relying heavily on computers and wireless access. Yet the sense of purpose continues with the focus on undergraduate-specific collections as well as common study space and furniture appropriate for lounging. In addition, most libraries now incorporate a café and/or coffee shop. The café is a certain moneymaker, replacing the once-golden copy center. But more than that, it is a social center that is yet another hook for pulling in users. In the past, smoking was the number one social consideration when designing an undergraduate space. Today, it is coffee.

UNDERGRADUATE LIBRARY ORGANIZATIONS

The ALA's subgroup, the Association of College and Research Libraries, sponsors the Undergraduate Librarians Discussion Group.[17] Known as UGLI, they are the primary group for conversation on subjects of interest to the operation of undergraduate libraries. They support a basic web site and list of active undergraduate libraries. The endnotes from previous citations refer to the ALA web site where two important undergraduate library documents are located. *The Mission of a University Undergraduate Library: Model Statement* and the *Guidelines for University Undergraduate Libraries* are useful reads for any library that serves undergraduates, even if undergraduates are not the primary audience of collection. Directly below is a list of self-designated undergraduate libraries. Although the numbers are down from the peak in the 1970s, it is still an impressive list of institutions that have made a symbolic, budgetary, and pedagogical priority of our "yonguer sort."

CURRENT UNDERGRADUATE LIBRARIES

Columbia University (New York, NY)
  Philip L. Milstein Family College Library
Cornell University (Ithaca, NY)
  Uris Library
George Mason University (Fairfax, VA)
  Johnson Center Library
Harvard University (Cambridge, MA)
  Lamont, Harvard College Library
Indiana University-Bloomington (Bloomington, IN)
  Undergraduate Library Services
Purdue University (West Lafayette, IN)
  John W. Hicks Undergraduate Library
Southern Illinois University at Carbondale (Carbondale, IL)
  Undergraduate Library Division (in Morris)
Stanford University (Stanford, CA)
  Meyer Library
State University of New York at Buffalo (Buffalo, NY)
  Oscar A. Silverman Undergraduate Library
University of Arizona (Tucson, AZ)
  Integrated Learning Center

University of California at Berkeley (Berkeley, CA)
Moffitt Undergraduate Library
University of California at Los Angeles (Los Angeles, CA)
College Library
University of California at San Diego (San Diego, CA)
Center for Library and Instructional Computing Services (CLICS)
University of Chicago (Chicago, IL)
Harper Library
University of Illinois at Urbana-Champaign (Urbana, IL)
Undergraduate Library
University of Michigan (Ann Arbor, MI)
Shapiro Undergraduate Library
University of North Carolina at Chapel Hill (Chapel Hill, NC)
R. B. House Undergraduate Library
University of Southern California (Los Angeles, CA)
Thomas and Dorothy Leavey Library
University of Texas at Austin (Austin, TX)
Undergraduate Library
University of Virginia (Charlottesville, VA)
Clemons Library
University of Washington (Seattle, WA)
Odegaard Undergraduate Library
University of Wisconsin-Madison (Madison, WI)
Helen C. White College Library
Wayne State University (Detroit, MI)
David Adamany Undergraduate Library[18]

CONCLUSION

The one constant in the half century since Lamont was built is its focus on undergraduates and their research needs. It is important that developing scholars have a safe place in which to learn how to use the multitude of research options available to them. The building design is as important as the selection of the collection and the service configurations that help acquaint users with the tools. As libraries become ever more complicated and as students are faced with a growing number of full-text resources, students will need guidance in formulating their research strategies and selecting appropriate and trustworthy artifacts (physical or not).

Although many libraries have changed how they serve undergraduates, there will most certainly be a number of large research libraries that will continue to support their undergraduate libraries as part of their research and library mission.

REFERENCES

1. The mission of a university undergraduate library: Model statement. http://www.ala.org/ala/acrl/acrlstandards/missionuniversity.htm (accessed May 2004).

2. Person, R.C. *A New Path: Undergraduate Libraries at United States and Canadian Universities, 1949–1987*; Greenwood Press: New York, 1988; 3.

3. Wagman, F.H. The Case for the Undergraduate Library. In *Reader in Undergraduate Libraries*; Wilkinson, B.R., Ed.; Information Handling Services: Englewood, CO, 1978; 109.

4. Perkin, H. History of Universities. In *International Higher Education: An Encyclopedia*; Altbach, P.G., Ed.; Garland Publ., Inc.: New York, 1991; 169–204.

5. *Reader in Undergraduate Libraries*, Wilkinson, B.R. Ed.: Information Handling Services: Englewood, CO, 1978, 5.

6. Metcalf, K.D.; Shepley, H.R. The Lamont Library. Harv. Libr. Bull. **1949**, *3* (1), 5–30. (offprint).

7. Pope, J.A. Harvard Crimson. Wednesday, January 20, **1954**. http://www.thecrimson.com/article.aspx?ref=486745 (accessed May 2004).

8. Braden, I. *The Undergraduate Library* ACRL Monograph; ALA: Chicago, 1970; Vol. 31, 2, 117.

9. http://tilt.lib.utsystem.edu/faq/ (accessed May 2004).

10. http://www.ala.org/ala/acrl/acrlpubs/choice/selectionpolicy/selectionpolicy.htm (accessed May 2004).

11. http://www.ala.org/ala/acrl/acrlstandards/guidelinesuniversity.htm. (accessed May 2004).

12. Person, R.C. Table 4: United States and Canadian Universities Having Undergraduate Libraries, by Year of Founding and (in Parenthesis) by Year of Closing. In *A New Path: Undergraduate Libraries at United States and Canadian Universities, 1949–1987;* Greenwood Press: New York, 1988; 54.

13. Wingate, H.R. The undergraduate library: Is it obsolete? Coll. Res. Libr. January, **1978**, *3*, 29–33.

14. The fate of the undergraduate library. Libr. J. November, **2000**, *125* (18), 1.

15. http://www.washington.edu/uwired/about/index.shtml (accessed May 2004).

16. Donovan, M.; Macklin, S. One Size Doesn't Fit All: Designing Scaleable, Client-Centered Support for Technology in Teaching. In *CAUSE98: The Networked Academy, An EDUCAUSE Conference on Information Technology in Higher Education*, Washington State Convention and Trade Center, Seattle, WA, December, 8–11, 1998. http://www.educause.edu/ir/library/html/cnc9846/cnc9846.html (accessed May 2004).

17. http://www.lib.utexas.edu/ugli/ (accessed May 2004).

18. http://www.lib.utexas.edu/ugli/directory.html. (accessed May 2004).

BIBLIOGRAPHY

1. Engle, M.O. Forty-five years after Lamont: The university undergraduate library in the 1990s. Libr. Trends Fall, **1995**,*44* (2), 368.

2. Haak, J.R. Goal Determination and the Undergraduate Library. Paper prepared for the Institute on Training for Service in Undergraduate Libraries, University of California Library, San Diego, CA, August 17–21, 1970. ERIC doc. ED 42474.

3. Hardesty, L. *Faculty and the Library: The Undergraduate Experience;* Ablex Publ. Corp.: Norwood, NJ, 1991.

4. Jackson, S.L. *Libraries and Librarianship in the West*; McGraw-Hill Book Co.: San Francisco, 1974.

5. Knapp, P. *The Academic Library Response to New Directions in Undergraduate Education;* ERIC Clearinghouse for Library and Information Sciences, Review Series No. 2; April, 1970. Mpls; ERIC doc. ED 39390.

6. Kuhn, W.B. Planning the Undergraduate Library. Paper prepared for the Institute on Training for Service in Undergraduate Libraries; University of California Library, San Diego, CA, August 17–21, 1970.

7. Person, R.C. *The Role of the Undergraduate Library in United States and Canadian Universities;* Southern Illinois University at Carbondale: Illinois, 1983.

8. Voigt, M.J. The Undergraduate Library: The Collection and Its Selection. Paper prepared for the Institute on Training for Service in Undergraduate Libraries; University of California Library, San Diego, CA, August 17–21, 1970. ERIC doc. ED 42477.

9. Wilkinson, B.R. The Undergraduate Library's Public Service Record: Reference Services. Paper prepared for the Institute on Training for Service in Undergraduate Libraries; University of California Library, San Diego, CA, August 17–21, 1970. ERIC doc. ED 42473.

10. Wilkinson, B.R. *Reference Services for Undergraduate Students: Four Case Studies;* The Scarecrow Press, Inc.: Metuchen, NJ, 1972.

UNESCO: Communication and Information Sector

Joie Springer
Information Society Division, UNESCO, Paris, France

Abstract
This entry presents a brief overview of UNESCO and the activities implemented by its Information Society Division in pursuit of its overall mandate to promote the free flow of ideas and universal access to information. It looks at the origins of the program, its current strategic objectives, and some of its activities, especially those relating to libraries and archives, which are designed to meet the development needs of the world's population.

INTRODUCTION

For 60 years, the United Nations Educational, Scientific and Cultural Organization (UNESCO) has had the responsibility of ensuring the spread of knowledge through improved access to printed and published materials. Much of this is available in libraries and archives, which are the traditional caretakers of knowledge. This entry is intended to provide an understanding and appreciation of the work of UNESCO in the development of libraries and archives and the new thrusts in information management in the cyberspace age.

UNESCO was founded in the aftermath of the Second World War as a specialized agency with lofty ideals of creating and maintaining a culture of peace, by changing mentalities. To achieve this goal, it has sought to promote dialog based upon mutual respect and dignity of different cultures by maintaining, increasing, and diffusing knowledge as decreed, in part, in its constitution, by assuring the conservation and protection of the world's inheritance of books and monuments of history and science, as well as by encouraging cooperation among nations in all branches of intellectual activity, including the exchange of publications, objects of artistic and scientific interest, and other materials of information.

Policy and direction are approved sexennially (Medium-Term Strategy) by the General Conference of Member States and are concretized in its biennial programs and budgets, which focus on development priorities. Currently, the major emphasis is on attaining the United Nations Millennium Development Goals which, inter alia, target the reduction of global levels of extreme poverty, attaining universal primary education, elimination of gender disparity, and development of strategies for sustainable development.

These ambitious goals are achieved through a pragmatic approach covering the five Program Sectors of UNESCO (Education, Natural Sciences, Social and Human Sciences, Culture, Communication, and Information). UNESCO's current *Medium Term Strategy for 2008–2013* (http://unesdoc.unesco.org/images/0014/001499/149999e.pdf) proposes that the Organization adopt a bolder policy with respect to national development priorities, including, in the information field, for it to assume a stronger leadership role in the provision of universal access to knowledge. To this end, it has set "building inclusive knowledge societies through information and communication" as one of its overarching objectives.

Consequently, the priority of promoting the free flow of ideas and universal access to information is high among the principal strategic objectives of the Communication and Information Sector; the others being promoting the expression of pluralism and cultural diversity in the media and world information networks as well as promoting access for all to information and communication technologies (ICTs). The sector is composed of three divisions, namely

- The Communication Development Division
- The Division for Freedom of Expression, Democracy, and Peace
- The Information Society Division

The Information Society Division has been assigned the responsibility of steering policies for universal access to information, which includes the formulation of national information policy frameworks; the preservation of documentary information in all its forms; building information literacy capacities; encouraging the development of knowledge societies and fostering ethical considerations for the information society.

The Division was established at the start of the twenty-first century to lead information developments and respond to the challenges of the third millennium. It was born of a merger of the former General Information Program (PGI) and the Intergovernmental Informatics Program (IIP). PGI had in turn been established in 1977 in response to the convergence between scientific and

Tunisia–United Kingdom

technological information (UNISIST) and documentation, libraries, and archives (NATIS) whereas IIP had been set up in 1985 to develop and implement concrete projects in the field of informatics.

UNESCO's Department of Documentation, Libraries and Archives (DBA) created in 1966 dealt with the development of information infrastructures while the UNISIST program had been established in 1972 as an intergovernmental program to coordinate cooperation in the field of scientific and technical information. However, the recommendations of the Intergovernmental Conference on the Planning of National Documentation, Library and Archive Infrastructures (NATIS) organized by DBA in 1974 revealed overlaps with those formulated by the 1971 UNISIST Conference. Duplication in the Programs led to proposals for a merger of the two as the PGI under an Intergovernmental Council that would be responsible "for guiding the conception and planning of the program, in particular by making recommendations on the content of the biennial programs and budgets and the Medium-Term Plans, reviewing the results achieved, recommending priorities, and encouraging the participation of Member States in the implementation of the program."

The retention of the name "UNISIST" was recommended by UNESCO's General Conference "for appropriate use" and can still be found on a number of documents produced by the Information Society Division, but although documentation, library, and archives infrastructures remain integral to the Program, the acronym "NATIS" was dropped from UNESCO usage.

The information program has always been both interdisciplinary and intersectoral with applications for all branches of knowledge and sectors of human activity even though structures, lines of emphasis, and approaches have been modified over the years as philosophies and technologies evolved. An evaluation of the Program (http://unesdoc.unesco.org/images/0008/000805/080582eb.pdf) provides more in-depth information on the history, activities, and accomplishments of PGI during its first 10 years.

IIP, on the other hand was established in order to "strengthen international cooperation and national efforts devoted to the training of specialists, the development of infrastructure, the definition of national policies, and the better recognition of the role of informatics."

With the information revolution, an increasing overlap of the two programs was perceived, as both were progressively concentrating their activities on two main areas: content for the information society, and building "infostructure" through training, the establishment of information policies, and the promotion of networking. UNESCO's Director-General therefore suggested in 1996 that they would be best served by a single secretariat and that a new program should be designed to meet the needs of the information age.

Following a wide consultative process guided by an Ad Hoc Working Group, the Information for All Program (IFAP) was created as a platform for global discussion on information access, enabling participation of all in the global information society, and on ethical, legal, and societal consequences of the use of ICTs. IFAP provides a framework for international cooperation and partnerships in the information field by developing strategies and tools to narrow the digital divides of the information society. It is guided by an Intergovernmental Council composed of 26 members representing all geographic regions of the world. Its secretariat is assured by the Information Society Division.

An evaluation in 2006 concluded that IFAP had achieved limited success only as the scope of its action had, to a large extent, been overtaken by the World Summit on the Information Society (WSIS) process and this action is now being implemented by other stakeholders. To maintain its relevance in the information age, IFAP's program has been reviewed, and it has been tasked to attain five main strategic targets: information for development, information accessibility, information literacy, information ethics, and information preservation with libraries and archives playing a major contributory role in achieving each of these objectives.

While other bodies and organizations have concentrated on providing digital connectivity as well as the technology to help leapfrog into the information age, UNESCO has tended to place more emphasis on its concept of Knowledge Societies, that is, facilitating access to content and building capacities to make effective use of information. In this regard, it has identified four anchors on which to ground its principles of inclusion and pluralism that are based on human needs and rights. These are knowledge creation, knowledge preservation, knowledge dissemination, and knowledge utilization.

Our organization has been working on a wide variety of approaches and actions to help build national and regional capabilities and its contribution to the WSIS succeeded in broadening the debate to the point where the final Declaration of Principles and the Plan of Action of the Summit entrenched the four principles espoused by the organization, namely freedom of expression; universal access to information; the promotion of cultural diversity, multilingualism, and local content; and equal access to education. The Action Plan reflects UNESCO's belief in the importance of "democratization of access" and focuses on the ability to use technology rather than on technology itself. This means that in capitalizing on the opportunities offered by ICTs, greater attention is being paid to capacity building in support of societal transformation and on the adoption of best practices in e-governance services, with particular focus on addressing the obstacles to progress, especially in developing countries.

The role of information in addressing development issues has not always been fully understood by some governments or countries. Knowledge-based and knowledge-led development has the potential to achieve many of the targets set under the Millennium Development Goals especially those relating to universal primary education and sustainability, on condition that there is equitable access to and use of requisite information and expertise. For this reason, emphasis is being given to *information for development* as a strategic goal of the IFAP and the Information Society Division, and a major focus of UNESCO's policy is to contribute to the formulation of national information policies and laws that reinforce the position of libraries, archives, and other knowledge institutions to fully accomplish their function as content providers contributing to continued access to recorded information.

This is particularly applicable in developing countries, which face problems caused by globalization and its impact on their societies. Globalization is largely driven by ICTs, which are radically transforming societies, both modern and traditional, and shaping patterns of growth, and wealth creation. They can provide for the expansion of home-based job opportunities and offer potential benefits to all of humanity. But sadly, in many regions of the world, this is still an unrealized dream. So, while information or knowledge has become a principal force of social transformation, much of it still remains out of the reach of those for whom it is absolutely indispensable to revolutionize their lives in order to rise from the misery of poverty. Countries that are technologically equipped to maximize the advantages of the information society are speeding along the information highway, while others that need to invest much more in human resources or infrastructure development are mere hitchhikers. However, inequitable access plagues all countries, not just the poorer ones, and increases the divide within, and among, nations.

It is therefore incumbent on governments and local authorities to reduce these divides, and as information is largely channelled by libraries and archives, they can have a key role to play in enabling all sectors of society to receive, generate, and/or disseminate information on all areas of interest, in addition to being a facilitator between the policies of, and services provided by, local and national government and the community or nation they serve. The challenge for these institutions is to provide access to content in support of a greater social qualitative change while respecting their individual charters. By promoting empowerment and participation through equitable access and sharing of knowledge, community information points contribute fundamentally to development.

For an information component to be successfully integrated into development plans, the capacity to access and use information is a prerequisite. While access to ICTs can enable greater participation in the benefits of knowledge societies, people must be adept not only in their use, but, as defined in the Alexandria Proclamation which was adopted by the High Level Colloquium on Information Literacy and Lifelong Learning in Egypt in November 2005, they must also have the ability to "seek, evaluate, use, and create information effectively to achieve their personal, social, occupational, and educational goals." In other words, they must be information literate.

All libraries, especially public and community libraries, must be able to contribute to achieving *information literacy* and part of UNESCO's main strategy in this area consists of awareness-raising about the importance of information literacy at all levels of the educational process and of establishing guidelines for incorporating information literacy issues in curricula. A key plank in this strategy is the integration of libraries into information literacy programs as they provide resources and services in an environment that fosters free and open inquiry and serve as catalysts for the interpretation and application of knowledge in all fields of learning. UNESCO is therefore developing a conceptual framework whose objectives, strategies, and actions will contribute to both critical understanding and active participation by enabling the interpretation of data and making of informed judgments by users of information sources.

To this end, the Organization has conducted international meetings, funded projects, published guides, and created an Internet portal to sensitize those interested in learning about the concept and its applications. A number of workshops across the globe have provided trainers with the basic skills required to transmit to others how to effectively access and assess information from different sources. Much of its work in the field of information literacy is being conducted in cooperation with the International Federation of Library Associations and Institutions (IFLA). This includes the creation of an international directory database (http://www.infolitglobal.info), in English and Spanish, of information literacy resources. These resources can be adapted or be used as examples in building new information literacy applications or to assess achievements and plan future policies.

As mentioned earlier, technological advances have given rise to new opportunities, but they have also led to concerns about the use of information, especially digital information, which can be easily manipulated. UNESCO has consequently initiated an international debate on *information ethics* (infoethics) to examine the ethical, legal, and societal aspects of the application of ICTs. While acknowledging the right to freedom of expression, universal access to information, especially public domain information and the right to education as being of primary importance, other rights including the right to privacy and proprietary rights must also be respected.

The challenges and opportunities presented by ICTs require that appropriate mechanisms and safeguards are in place to guide development and enable policy makers to explore benefits and risks especially for the protection of the more vulnerable members of their community, as well as striking the balance between intellectual property rights and the rights of users to access information. One option that is being explored is the possible establishment of a national advisory body composed of all stakeholders to address ethical issues such as peace, upholding fundamental values of freedom, equality, tolerance, shared responsibility, and respect for nature in order to establish a national framework.

IFAP's strategic objective of *information accessibility* takes into account the wide range of factors that can block access to sources of information with a consequent impact on development. ICTs have transformed, for better and for worse, traditional practices that provided access to information needed for development or to address areas of concern. Issues related to copyright, piracy, and protection of data have led to the impositions of conditions that restrict access to sources of information and knowledge, which used to be easily available in the past. At the same time, the Internet has opened up new and broader opportunities with the potential to allow unprecedented numbers of people to share and obtain information from wider sources and in their own language. Admittedly, a huge percentage of the world's population has yet to publish content in native languages but the expansion of digital services and connectivity should lead to an evolution of this situation. Furthermore, the incremental growth in the use of cell phones is viewed as an exciting possibility for the transmission and reception of information in local languages in future.

UNESCO's *Recommendation concerning the Promotion and Use of Multilingualism and Universal Access to Cyberspace*, which was adopted in 2003, has been important in this regard as it has opened new vistas promoting multilingualism and multilingual search tools on the Internet with a corresponding increase in linguistic diversity on the Internet. This is an important step in protecting some of the world's endangered languages. UNESCO is further encouraging research to assess the extent of progress in achieving a multilingual cyberspace so as to adjust its area of focus as required. Emphasis is currently being given to activities that will lead to the inclusion of additional languages and the dissemination of more local content in cyberspace, as well as to the development of Internationalized Domain Names (IDNs).

Accessibility to information is also boosted by UNESCO's promotion of Free and Open Source Software (FOSS), Open Educational Resources (OER), and its Open Training Platform (OTP) while contributing to building capacities in their use. It has focussed on the development of open information processing tools, interoperability standards, metadata, and more, that permit equitable access to the use of ICTs. These can also be particularly beneficial to the approximately one-third of the world's population, which is affected by disability or reduced mobility by removing their isolation from the outside world and aiding their social and economic participation in society. UNESCO's program helps to promote the rights and needs of people with disabilities, including increasing awareness of accessible technologies and supporting their development as well as publishing

accessibility guidelines for community information centers to cater to people with disabilities.

Much of constructing knowledge societies relates to ensuring adequate access to information. However, the flip side of the coin, or *information preservation*, is of equal, if not more, concern to UNESCO since the disappearance of information leads to an impoverishment of humanity.

From the founding of UNESCO, its documentary heritage program, whether as an independent unit or as a Division attached to a Program Sector, has always had one constant goal, that of enabling access to the knowledge, and information produced anywhere in the world, and ensuring its continued availability through preservative actions. In fact, UNESCO's first budget made provision for the reconstruction of libraries; and libraries and archives continue to be among its priorities some 60 years later, even as their form and role have changed in response to technological progress or societal transformations.

Training and capacity building for information personnel have been traditionally supported by UNESCO since its creation. In addition to sponsoring workshops, training courses and symposia, the Organization has set up two information portals: the *UNESCO Libraries Portal* (http://www.unesco.org/webworld/portal_bib) and the *UNESCO Archives Portal* (http://www.unesco.org/webworld/portal_archives) as a public service access to online resources related to, or to issues affecting, the information profession. They include institutional Web sites, training, and job opportunities as well as other resources related to information management and to international cooperation in these fields.

Since 1946, the Organization has been involved in the construction, or reconstitution, of some of the major libraries of the world, including the Bibliotheca Alexandrina in Egypt, the National Library of Latvia, and the rebuilding of the National and University Library of Bosnia and Herzegovina following its destruction in 1992. It has also contributed to establishing library expertise in most countries of the world; provided assistance in the move from traditional to electronic information management; and advised on coping with technological obsolescence, among other activities, in enabling libraries to contribute to lifelong learning, economic, and personal development as well as promote preservation of heritage.

Apart from serving as physical or virtual information access points, libraries have a social responsibility to eliminate barriers to knowledge, to constructive participation, and the development of democracy. The enormous potential of libraries is still largely untapped but their mix of resources and services provide for equal and democratic access to information.

In 1979, UNESCO created its Records and Archives Management Program (RAMP) in cooperation with the International Council on Archives (ICA) to support national development, archival training, and protect archival heritage. This was extended in 1980 to audiovisual archives with the adoption of the *Recommendation for the Safeguarding and Preservation of Moving Images*. To preserve this heritage, UNESCO works closely with a group of NGOs under an umbrella structure better known as Coordinating Council of Audiovisual Archives Associations (CCAAA) (http://www.ccaaa.org) composed of AMIA, IASA, ICA, IFLA, FIAF, FIAT/IFTA, and SEAPAVAA whose main objective is to cooperate on influencing the development of public policy on issues of importance to professional audiovisual archivists.

UNESCO's archives programs have achieved significant gains through tangible outcomes such as the publication of model legal guidelines for the establishment of archives or the organization of the highly successful Joint Technical Symposia (JTS). Other projects include promoting the creation of human rights archives particularly in countries in the process of transition to democracy. These archives are of fundamental importance as evidence supporting victims' rights for reparation.

Yet, despite all efforts to protect and safeguard documentary heritage, threats to its existence continue to be a cause of alarm as natural disasters, chemical decomposition, wars, negligence, deliberate destruction, ignorance, and obsolescence contribute to losses with drastic consequences, as millions of items have either disappeared, or are on the verge of doing so. Conservative estimates are that more than 80% of the early films have been deliberately destroyed or have otherwise been lost. A graphic picture is painted in "Lost Memory: Libraries and Archives destroyed in the Twentieth Century" which was commissioned by UNESCO to obtain accurate information on the losses that occurred in the twentieth century alone.

This dramatic situation called for an urgent response and in 1992, UNESCO created the *Memory of the World Programme* (http://www.unesco.org/webworld/en/mow) as its flagship project to protect and promote the documentary heritage. The objectives of the Program are

1. To facilitate preservation, by the most appropriate techniques, of the world's documentary heritage.
2. To assist universal access to documentary heritage by encouraging the digitization of access copies of items while respecting legislative, cultural sensitivities, and other limitations to access.
3. To increase awareness worldwide of the existence and significance of documentary heritage, especially through the Memory of the World registers.

Four main strategic actions form the pillars of UNESCO's action to accomplish these goals and they can be summarized as

Identification of documentary heritage: This involves identifying documentary and assessing its impact for the country concerned. If it is determined that its influence has been felt beyond national borders, or that the rest of the world would benefit from greater knowledge of the content, it could be listed on a Memory of the World register.

Raising awareness: This is especially important in regions where documentary heritage is endangered or awareness is low. Emphasis is given to preservation techniques and cooperation with professional bodies and associations.

Preservation: This is the main focus of the Program with particular attention accorded to heritage listed on a Memory of the World register. While the original document may be important as an object in itself, the content that resides on the carrier is the main focus of the program.

Access: Permanent access is the fourth goal of the Program as everyone has the right of access to their documentary heritage, the right to know it exists, and where to find it.

An International Advisory Committee of 14 members is appointed by the Director-General of UNESCO in their personal capacity to guide the planning and implementation of the Program and make recommendations concerning the inscription of nominations on the International Register, as well as the award of the UNESCO/Jikji Memory of the World Prize in recognition of outstanding preservation work.

Public impact and education are crucial in raising awareness of the vulnerability of information and the Memory of the World Register (http://www.unesco.org/webworld/en/mow-register) is the main component in this strategy. Currently there are 193 items from 80 different countries, 3 International Organization and 1 private foundation, and items cover all types of information carriers whether these are films or rock inscriptions, sound recordings or photographs, and tapestries or printed pages. Some are as recent as the 1986 Radio Broadcast of the Philippine People Power Revolution or as old as the Hittite cuneiform tablets from Turkey that date from the 2nd millennium B.C. Age is not a deciding factor; what matters is that the item is considered significant for the whole of humanity.

Paradoxically, modern documents are more endangered than older ones. The increase in digital materials and their short life expectancy have given rise to concerns about long-term preservation. Furthermore, as audiovisual and electronic documents are machine readable only, they need specific equipment and/or software to be retrieved. But playback equipment rapidly becomes obsolete resulting in the inability to access the content. Therefore, timely migration to newer technologies, operating systems, and software platforms must be factored into digital preservation policies and plans. Traditional preservation policies are irrelevant where digital materials are concerned.

Digital preservation, which is closely related to the strategic priorities for *information development* and *information accessibility*, is a key component of the Memory of the World Program. Management of digital information has its own specific problems, added to which is the fact that it is still not yet universally known that the costs of systematically preserving digital information is higher in the long term than those required to preserve traditional analog documents.

UNESCO has developed a strategy for digital preservation, which is built on raising global awareness of the dangers facing digital heritage through its *Charter on the Preservation of Digital Heritage*, disseminating technical guidelines and capacity building in association with governments, policy makers, information producers, heritage institutions, and experts as well as the software industry and standard-setting organizations.

One recent initiative is the creation of a World Digital Library (http://www.wdl.org) being set up in collaboration with the Library of Congress in the United States. This project is designed to foster intercultural dialogue and understanding, preserve heritage, and facilitate greater access to knowledge. It is being implemented as part of the Memory of the World Program and a prototype, developed by the Library of Congress and UNESCO with partner institutions (Bibliotheca Alexandrina, the National Library of Egypt, the National Library of Brazil, the National Library of Russia, and the Russian State Library) was demonstrated in October 2007 ahead of a formal launch which took place on 21 April 2009 at UNESCO's Headquarters in Paris. It currently functions in Arabic, Chinese, English, French, Portuguese, Russian, and Spanish and libraries and archives around the world are encouraged to be part of this global endeavor.

CONCLUSION

This description of the major areas of the work of the Information Society Division relating to information management and building knowledge societies covers but a small part of UNESCO's vast programs in education and learning, sciences, culture, communication, and information. Through its action and flagship projects, UNESCO has been able to contribute to achieving global development objectives such as those outlined in the WSIS's Plan of Action, or the Millennium Development Goals. This focus on creating "infostructures" and equipping all peoples, including disadvantaged, marginalized, and vulnerable groups, with the capacities to benefit from access to information and knowledge, remains true to its own constitutional mandate of spreading access to, and protecting, the world's sources of knowledge.

BIBLIOGRAPHY

1. Intergovernmental Council for the General Information Programme (PGI). *Basic Texts and Statistics*, Article 4. (PGI 94/COUNCIL/INF. 1).
2. Kenneth, H.R. *Review of the General Information Programme, 1977–1987: A Compilation of Information on Its Characteristics, Activities and Accomplishments*; UNESCO: Paris, 1988 (PGI-88/WS/19).
3. *Lost Memory—Libraries and Archives Destroyed in the Twentieth Century (CII-96/WS/1)*; UNESCO: Paris, 1996.
4. *Memory of the World—General Guidelines to Safeguard Documentary Heritage (CII-95/WS-11)*; UNESCO: Paris, 1995.
5. *Statutes of the Intergovernmental Committee for the Intergovernmental Informatics Programme*, Article 6 (CII 96/WS/5).
6. *Strategic Plan for the Information for All Programme (2008–2013)*; UNESCO: Paris, 2008.
7. Towards Knowledge Societies. *UNESCO World Report*, UNESCO Publishing: Paris, 2005.
8. *Understanding Information Literacy: A Primer*; UNESCO: Paris, 2007 (CI-2007/WS/18 – CLD 3008.7).

Unicode Standard

Joan M. Aliprand
Cupertino, California, U.S.A.

Abstract

The Unicode Standard is the single, universal character standard for all text, covering all of the world's writing systems, modern and ancient, as well as other elements of text such as technical symbols. Unicode provides the basis for the processing, storage, and interchange of textual data worldwide; it is fundamental to modern software and information technology protocols, and provides the character infrastructure of the World Wide Web. Unicode underlies modern systems and software products for libraries. Use of Unicode is explicitly included in the specifications for MARC 21 and UNIMARC records, and Z39.50 information retrieval, and is implicit in library standards and protocols based on Extensible Markup Language (XML) or Hypertext Markup Language (HTML).

INTRODUCTION

The Unicode Standard is the universal character encoding for the world's writing systems, and is fundamental to information technology worldwide. The first half of this entry covers key features of the Unicode Standard as well as the rationale for its development. The second half describes use of the Unicode Standard, with particular emphasis on library standards and protocols.

THE UNICODE STANDARD IN GENERAL

The Unicode Standard provides a uniform, universal architecture and encoding for all languages of the world, with over 100,000 characters currently encoded. Supporting the needs of all types of users, its coverage includes minority and historical scripts as well as those in common use. In addition, the Unicode Standard contains the largest set of characters for mathematical and technical publishing in existence, and an extensive set of musical symbols.[1]

The Unicode Standard is the basis for the processing, storage, and seamless interchange of textual data worldwide. Unicode underlies modern software and Internet protocols, and provides the character infrastructure of the World Wide Web.[2]

Much more than just a large character set, the Unicode Standard also defines how characters function. The extensive set of character attributes and the implementation algorithms specified in the Unicode Standard exist to ensure interoperability among implementations.

There are three constituent parts to the Unicode Standard: the book *The Unicode Standard*, the Unicode Character Database (UCD), and the Unicode Standard Annexes (UAXs). (All three constituent parts are available online;

The Unicode Standard is also available as a book. All updates to the constituent parts are published online.)

The Unicode Character Database (UCD) is a collection of data files that

- Contain the Unicode character code points and character names.
- Specify properties assigned to Unicode characters.
- Provide certain mappings between Unicode characters (e.g., 1:1 case mappings).

The UCD also contains explanatory documentation on UCD file formats and data in the files.[3]

The 12 Unicode Standard Annexes (UAXs) cover significant features of the Unicode Standard in detail. Some UAXs, such as the Unicode Bidirectional Algorithm and the Unicode Line Breaking Algorithm, provide specifications for particular programming tasks.

DEVELOPMENT OF THE UNICODE STANDARD

By the late twentieth century, many different international, national, and corporate coded character sets had been developed for the processing, storage, and exchange of the characters of writing systems.[4] Multilingual software applications had to deal with two serious problems: the same code value used to represent different characters, and different codes for a particular character encoded in multiple character sets.

When several character sets are used together in computer data, International Standard ISO/IEC 2022 provides a technique to distinguish them.[5] Data in a particular character set is identified by means of a preceding "announcer," the *escape sequence*, so called because it begins with the control character *Escape* (1B hexadecimal).[6] The International Organization for Standardization (ISO) administers

Encyclopedia of Library and Information Sciences, Fourth Edition DOI: 10.1081/E-ELIS4-120044843

a registry that assigns a specific escape sequence to each character set submitted for registration. The problem with the ISO/IEC 2022 technique is that it is "stateful." As a result, if identification of the applicable character sets is missing, correct interpretation and presentation of the coded data is not possible.

Both the MARC 21 and the UNIMARC formats permit use of multiple character sets, and specify the ISO/IEC 2022 technique of escape sequences to identify character sets.[7–9] The problems described above may occur in library data encoded using multiple character sets.

MARC 21 and UNIMARC character sets both exhibit use of the same code value to represent different characters. In the individual MARC 21 character sets, for example, the value 66 (hexadecimal) represents five different letters: *Latin small letter f*, *Arabic letter noon*, *Cyrillic capital letter ef*, *Greek small letter epsilon*, and *Hebrew letter zayin*. The value 66 can also occur in 3-byte encodings of the East Asian Character Code (EACC).[10]

Use of different codes for the same character is seen in the Extended Latin character sets of MARC 21 and UNIMARC: MARC 21 Extended Latin (a superset of ANSEL), and International Standard ISO 5426, respectively.[11–13] The two character sets have 52 characters in common, but only one character has the same encoding. For example, the lowercase form of *Latin letter o with stroke* is encoded as 32 (hexadecimal) in MARC 21 Extended Latin but 79 (hexadecimal) in ISO 5426.

For over two decades, EACC was used in MARC 21 records for Chinese, Japanese, and Korean (CJK) data. Libraries in Asia, however, used either a national standard character set or an industry set such as Big-5. While many ideographs occur in all of these character sets, the various character sets encode the ideographs differently.[14]

The primary goal in developing the Unicode Standard was to remedy the chaotic situation in multilingual software. The developers of the Unicode Standard envisioned a uniform method of character identification that would be a paradigm shift in multilingual computing. Unicode was designed to be universal, unambiguous, and efficient.

The Unicode Standard, Version 1.0 was published in 1991. There have been five major versions to date. The number of graphic characters in the Unicode Standard has grown from 28,282 in Version 1.0 to 100,507 in Version 5.1. Unicode is fundamental to modern information technology worldwide, and is used in all types of applications, from hand-held devices to massive databases.

THE UNICODE STANDARD AND ISO/IEC 10646

The Unicode Standard is code-for-code identical to International Standard ISO/IEC 10646, the *Universal Multiple-Octet Coded Character Set*, also known as the Universal Character Set (UCS).[15] The Unicode Standard is the official way to implement ISO/IEC 10646.

The ongoing development of ISO/IEC 10646 is the responsibility of Working Group WG 2 of ISO/IEC JTC 1/SC 2, the subcommittee responsible for international standards for coded character sets. ISO/IEC JTC 1 is the Joint Technical Committee on information technology standardization of ISO and the International Electrotechnical Commission (IEC).

The Unicode Consortium and ISO/IEC JTC 1/SC 2 and its WG 2 have had a formal liaison relationship since 1992, and work closely together to coordinate and synchronize all additions to either standard, thus maintaining exactly the same character names and code points in both. Version 5.1 of the Unicode Standard is synchronized with ISO/IEC 10646:2003 plus its Amendments 1 through 4.

An implementation that is conformant to Unicode is also conformant to ISO/IEC 10646, but the reverse is not necessarily true because the Unicode Standard also specifies character properties and implementation algorithms.

DESIGN PRINCIPLES OF THE UNICODE STANDARD

The Unicode Standard is based on a set of 10 design principles: universality, efficiency, characters (not glyphs), semantics, plain text, logical order, unification, dynamic composition, stability, and convertibility. Except for a library-related comment on dynamic composition, this section is a condensation of Section 2.2 "Unicode Design Principles" from *The Unicode Standard, Version 5.0*.[16]

Universality

The character repertoire of the Unicode Standard is intended to be universal in coverage, containing all the characters for textual representation in all modern writing systems and in most historic writing systems, as well as symbols used in plain text.

Efficiency

To keep character coding simple and efficient, the Unicode Standard assigns each character a unique numeric value and name. This unique identification of each character eliminates the need for cumbersome escape sequences and shift states. All of the Unicode encoding forms (described below) are self-synchronizing and nonoverlapping, facilitating access and searching within streams of characters.

Characters, Not Glyphs

Characters are abstract representations of the smallest components of written language that have semantic value.

Tunisia–United Kingdom

Glyphs	Unicode Characters
A ɪ A A A A A A	U+0041 LATIN CAPITAL LETTER A
a a a a a a a a	U+0061 LATIN SMALL LETTER A
п n ū	U+043F CYRILLIC SMALL LETTER PE
ه ه ه ه	U+0647 ARABIC LETTER HEH
fi fi	U+0066 LATIN SMALL LETTER F + U+0069 LATIN SMALL LETTER I

Fig. 1 Characters versus glyphs.
Source: *The Unicode Standard, Version 5.0*, Fig 2-2, p. 15. [16]
Copyright © 1991–2007 Unicode, Inc. All rights reserved.

Examples of such components are the letters, punctuation, digits, and other signs comprising natural language text and technical notation. The Unicode Standard encodes the character, not the various ways it can be visually represented.

Glyphs are the visual representations of characters as they are written or displayed, and can have various forms or shapes. Some writing systems require the use of particular glyphic forms. The form that the character takes when it is displayed (e.g., on a computer screen) is determined by text rendering software and the font currently in use.

Figure 1 shows the distinction between characters and glyphs. The illustration includes two examples of customary use: the positional forms for the Arabic letter *heh*, and the Cyrillic small letter *pe* with the italic alternatives used in Russia and Serbia, respectively.

Semantics

The Unicode Standard views character semantics as inherent to the definition of a character. A character's semantics are determined by its identity, normative properties, and behavior. The Unicode Standard defines more than 50 different character attributes, called properties. The Unicode Character Database, an integral part of the Unicode Standard, provides machine-readable character property tables for use in implementations.

Examples of character properties are

- The name that formally and uniquely identifies the character.
- The script of the character.
- The general category of the character (letter, punctuation, symbol, white space, etc.).
- The numeric value when the character is a digit.
- Casing (upper, lower, title, and folding).
- Sequences of characters that are equivalent.
- Whether the characters may be used in program-language identifiers.
- How the character behaves in text with mixed directions, such as Arabic or Hebrew with English.

- Properties related to text boundaries, such as word breaks and line breaks.

Many of the properties assigned to characters are needed for algorithms that make use of them to produce expected results; for example, the Unicode Collation Algorithm, that specifies the default sorting behavior of text.[17]

Plain Text

Plain text represents the basic, interchangeable content of text, not its appearance. Plain text contains enough information to permit the text to be rendered legibly, and nothing more. Additional formatting that affects the appearance of text (for example, language identification, font size, color, or hypertext links) is determined by higher level protocols and is not specified by the Unicode Standard.

Logical Order

Unicode characters are stored in logical order from first to last in the representation of text in computer memory. This approximates the order in which the characters are typed on a keyboard. When Unicode data is displayed, the text rendering process needs to recognize the directionality of each character and display text correctly for reading.

In some writing systems, such as Arabic and Hebrew, text is written and read from right to left. Text rendering becomes complicated when a document contains text in different directions (e.g., text in Arabic and English). The Unicode Bidirectional Algorithm specifies how mixed left-to-right and right-to-left horizontal text can be displayed in proper reading order.[18]

Unification

The Unicode Standard avoids duplicate encoding of characters by unifying them within scripts across languages: characters that are equivalent are given a single code. Common letters, punctuation marks, symbols, and diacritics are given one code each, regardless of language, as are common East Asian ideographs (used to write Chinese, Japanese, Korean, and historical Vietnamese).

Dynamic Composition

Dynamic composition is the rendition of composite textual elements, such as accented letters or modern Korean Hangul syllables, from a sequence of characters. In other standards that cover accented letters or modern Korean Hangul, the accented letters or the Hangul syllables are usually encoded as single characters (i.e., as a static *precomposed* form of the textual element).

Librarians are familiar with the concept of dynamic composition; the use of separate diacritical marks with the letters of the English alphabet dates from MARC's beginning.[19] EACC, in contrast, contains over 2,000 characters that are precomposed Hangul syllables.

Some text elements can be encoded either as static precomposed forms or by dynamic composition. For static precomposed forms (included for compatibility with certain standards), the Unicode Standard provides a mapping to the equivalent dynamically composed sequence of characters. Neither of these alternatives is prescribed as the "correct" one; each is merely equivalent to the other.

Stability

Certain aspects of the Unicode Standard must be absolutely stable across successive versions, so that implementers and users can be guaranteed that text data, once encoded, retains the same meaning. Most importantly, this means that once Unicode characters are assigned, their code point assignments cannot be changed, nor can characters be removed. Unicode character names are also never changed, so that they can be used as identifiers that are valid across versions. Stability guarantees also apply to certain important character properties.

Convertibility

For particular national, international, and corporate standards, character identity is retained for interchange of data between Unicode and these other standards. When a variant form or even character duplication exists in one of these standards, these characters are kept separate in the Unicode Standard instead of being unified. This guarantees accurate convertibility between the specified standards and Unicode.

UNICODE CHARACTERS AND ENCODING FORMS

This section presents an overview of the character content of the Unicode Standard, followed by a summary description of the three Unicode encoding forms (including UTF-8, which is specified for MARC 21 use). It condenses information from several sections of *The Unicode Standard, Version 5.0* (identified in the references).

Allocation of Unicode Characters

In computer processing, characters are represented as numbers. The *codespace* is the range of numbers available to code characters. A particular number in this range is called a *code point*. Each code point can be assigned to a character or designated for another use. The entire codespace of the Unicode Standard contains 1,114,112

unique code points which is more than sufficient for all known requirements.[20]

It is convenient to think of the Unicode codespace as being divided into planes, with each plane containing 65,536 (64K) code points. The first 64K code points of the Unicode codespace are designated as the Basic Multilingual Plane (BMP); also called Plane 0. To date, only 6 of the 17 planes (0–2, 14–16) have defined uses.[21]

The BMP contains all the common-use characters for all the modern scripts of the world, as well as many historical and rare characters. There are 53,333 characters allocated to the BMP (as of Version 5.1). Figure 2 shows the allocation areas on the BMP, with the General Scripts area shown in more detail on the right. The numbers to the left of each shaded bar are code point values in hexadecimal notation.[6]

The General Scripts area encodes many of the scripts in modern use, such as Latin, Greek, and Cyrillic. The first 128 characters in the Unicode Standard (beginning the Latin block) are exactly compatible with those of the ASCII standard and ISO/IEC 646, the International Reference Version of ASCII.[22],[23] The first 256 characters are exactly compatible with International Standard ISO/IEC 8859-1, also known as Latin-1.[24] Additional scripts are encoded in the Supplementary General Scripts area, after the Symbols area.

The CJK Miscellaneous area includes Hiragana and Katakana for Japanese, punctuation for East Asian scripts, and a large number of East Asian compatibility characters. The CJKV Ideographic area occupies a large part of the BMP. It contains unified Han ideographs for Chinese, Japanese, Korean, and historical Vietnamese, divided into two blocks: the Unified Repertoire and Ordering (20,924 characters), and Extension A (6,582 characters). The Asian Scripts area contains 11,172 Hangul syllables for Korean, plus several other Asian scripts.

The Surrogates area contains only surrogate code points used in the UTF-16 encoding form. The Private Use area contains 6,400 code points whose use can be defined by private agreements among cooperating users. The Compatibility and Specials area contains many compatibility variants of characters from widely used corporate and national standards that have other representations in the Unicode Standard.

Version 3.1 saw the first use of the supplementary planes with the addition of 44,946 characters including CJK Unified Ideographs Extension B on Plane 2. Version 3.2 added 1016 characters including a large set of symbols, which benefit mathematical and technical publishing. A large number of additional minority and historic scripts and various symbols and punctuation marks were added in Versions 4.0 through 5.1.

Unicode Encoding Forms

The Unicode Standard defines three encoding forms that allow the same data to be transmitted in a byte, word or

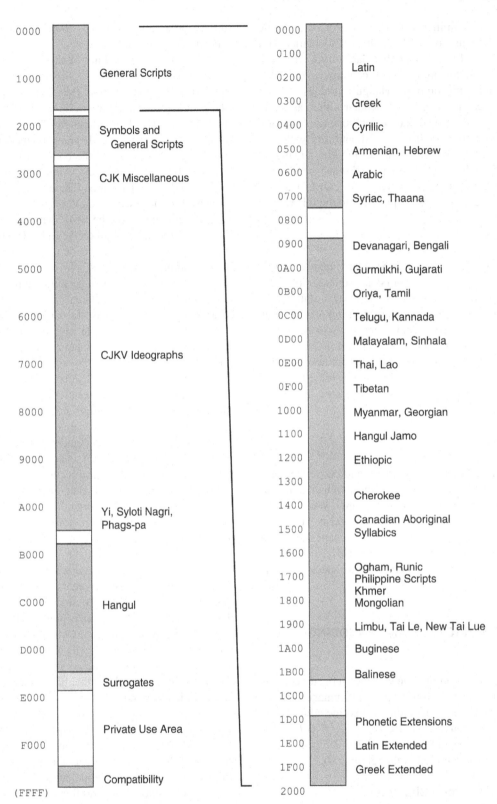

Fig. 2 Allocation on the Basic Multilingual Plane (BMP).
Source: *The Unicode Standard, Version 5.0*, Figure 2-14, p. 44.[21]
Copyright © 1991–2007 Unicode, Inc. All rights reserved.

double word oriented format (i.e., in 8, 16, or 32 bits per code unit).[25] All three encoding forms encode the *same* common character repertoire and can be efficiently transformed into one another without loss of data. All three encoding forms need at most 4 bytes (or 32 bits) of data for each character. The Unicode Consortium fully endorses the use of any of these encoding forms as a conformant way of implementing the Unicode Standard.

UTF-8 is a way of transforming all Unicode characters into a variable length encoding of bytes. UTF-8 has these advantages:

- The Unicode characters corresponding to those of ASCII have the same byte values as ASCII.
- Unicode characters transformed into UTF-8 can be used with much existing byte-oriented software without extensive software rewrites.

The MARC 21 Specifications stipulate that when exchange records are encoded in Unicode, UTF-8 must be used.[26]

UTF-16 is reasonably compact and all the heavily used characters fit into a single 16 bit code unit, while all other characters are accessible via pairs of 16 bit code units (*surrogate pairs*). UTF-16 is popular in many environments that need to balance efficient access to characters with economical use of storage.

UTF-32: Each Unicode character is encoded in a single 32 bit code unit when using UTF-32. UTF-32 is popular where memory space is no concern, but fixed-width, single code unit access to characters is desired.

The Unicode encoding forms correspond exactly to forms of use and transformation formats defined in ISO/IEC 10646. UTF-32 corresponds to the international standard's four-octet form UCS-4; UTF-8 and UTF-16 are defined in annexes of ISO/IEC 10646.

THE UNICODE CONSORTIUM

The Unicode Consortium was incorporated in 1991 as a nonprofit organization under the name Unicode, Inc.[27] The Consortium's purpose is to develop, extend, and promote use of the Unicode Standard and other standards related to internationalization technologies.

Unicode Consortium members associated with academia and libraries include (as of October 2008): The University of California at Berkeley (Institutional Member), and Bibliothèque universitaire des langues et civilisations (BULAC). Columbia University, Ex Libris, Getty Trust Information Technology Services, Innovative Interfaces, LIB-IT, OCLC, SIL International, Utilika Foundation, VTLS, and the Wenlin Institute (all Associate Members).

Liaison Membership in the Unicode Consortium is offered by invitation only to standards organizations that have interests in common with the Consortium, particularly in technical areas. Liaison members associated with academia and libraries include (as of October 2008) Linguistic Society of America (LSA), National Endowment for the Humanities (NEH), National Information Standards Organization (NISO), Research Institute for Languages and Cultures of Asia and Africa (ILCAA) at the Tokyo University of Foreign Studies, Research Institute for the Languages of Finland (RILF), Special Libraries

Association (SLA), and United Nations Group of Experts on Geographical Names (UNGEGN).

The Unicode Consortium and ISO 15924

International Standard ISO 15924, *Information and Documentation—Codes for the Representation of Names of Scripts* was developed by the ISO technical committee TC 46 (Information and documentation) following on earlier work by ISO/TC 37 (Terminology and other language and content resources).[28] The script codes created under the provisions of ISO 15924 are "devised for use in terminology, lexicography, bibliography, and linguistics, but they may be used for any application requiring the expression of scripts in coded form."

ISO appointed the Unicode Consortium as the Registration Authority for ISO 15924.[29] The Registration Authority is responsible for maintenance of the script codes, including evaluation of proposals for additional codes. It is advised by a Joint Advisory Committee (JAC); members of the JAC represent the Registration Authority and other relevant ISO technical committees and agencies.

UNICODE IN COMPUTERS AND ON THE WEB

Microsoft's Windows NT 3.1, released in 1993, was the first major operating system to support Unicode.[30] Today, the Unicode Standard provides the foundation for an increasingly global information technology industry based on the World Wide Web and XML (Extensible Markup Language).

The World Wide Web Consortium (W3C) has developed two syntaxes for Web documents—HTML (Hypertext Markup Language) and XML—both of which allow use of Unicode. *Unicode in XML and Other Markup Languages* has been published jointly by W3C and the Unicode Consortium.[31]

HTML allows use of various character sets, including Unicode (as its International Standard counterpart, ISO/IEC 10646). Unicode was adopted as the document character set for HTML in HTML 4.01.[32] Specifically, section 5.1 *The Document Character Set* states: "The ASCII character set is not sufficient for a global information system such as the Web, so HTML uses the much more complete character set called the *Universal Character Set* (*UCS*), defined in [ISO10646]. This standard defines a repertoire of thousands of characters used by communities all over the world." and "The character set defined in [ISO10646] is character-by-character equivalent to Unicode ([UNICODE])."

XML, developed initially for electronic publishing, is increasingly used for data storage and exchange.[33] Unicode is XML's default character set. In *Extensible Markup Language (XML) 1.0*, Section 2.2 "Characters" states: "Legal characters are tab, carriage return, line feed, and the legal characters of Unicode and ISO/IEC 10646." Section 4.3.3 "Character Encoding in Entities" requires "All XML processors MUST accept the UTF-8 and UTF-16 encodings of Unicode 3.1."

The *Character Model for the World Wide Web 1.0: Fundamentals*, approved as a W3C Recommendation in 2005, provides "a common reference for consistent, interoperable text manipulation on the World Wide Web" and builds on "the Universal Character Set, defined jointly by the Unicode Standard and ISO/IEC 10646."[2] It discusses the concepts *character*, *encoding*, and *string*, as well as processing issues such as string indexing.

The *Character Model for the World Wide Web 1.0: Normalization* is currently at the Working Draft stage.[34] The *Character Model for the World Wide Web 1.0: Resource Identifiers*, currently at the W3C Candidate Recommendation stage, addresses character encoding of resource identifiers, "a compact string of characters for identifying an abstract or physical resource."[35]

UNICODE AND LIBRARIES

In libraries, the predominant interest in Unicode has been its potential to improve access to material written in non-Latin scripts that were not covered by MARC 21 or UNIMARC, but this is only one of the benefits of using Unicode for library data.

The overall benefit is that use of Unicode eliminates the isolation of libraries from mainstream information technology. Because Unicode supports the needs of all types of users, including libraries, there is no longer any need for library-specific character sets. All modern software and protocols utilize Unicode, so commercially available software and fonts can be more easily used in library applications.

In 2007, the MARC 21 specifications were amended to remove the restriction permitting use of only a subset of Unicode characters.[36] A much-desired benefit of this amendment is the ability to include additional non-Latin scripts in MARC 21 exchange records.

For scripts that have always been permitted in MARC 21 records, the benefit of this change is that additional elements of text may now be transcribed directly, instead of being represented via a cataloging convention (such as a description enclosed in brackets) or in romanization. Examples of characters that may now be used in MARC 21 records include

- For Latin script, additional letters include those such as *B with hook*, needed to write certain African languages, and the letters *yogh* and *wynn* of archaic English.
- Five times as many East Asian ideographs in the Unicode Standard as in EACC: over 70,000 compared

to over 13,000.[37,10] National and industry character sets of East Asia were important sources for the ideographic content of Unicode.

- An extensive repertoire of mathematical, technical, and musical symbols.

Libraries are making increasing use of general information technology standards, XML in particular. Because Unicode is fundamental to modern information technology, new protocols and products for libraries are making increasing use of Unicode, if only through using a particular methodology that, in turn, relies on Unicode. Unicode is specified as the default character set of XML, so a library application based on XML uses Unicode, unless an alternative encoding is explicitly declared.

The remainder of this section discusses use of Unicode in those library technology specifications that originated before HTML and XML were available: MARC 21, UNIMARC, and Z39.50.

Unicode and MARC 21

Prior to the development of the Unicode Standard, MARC 21 specified 12 individual character sets, (sometimes referred to as "MARC-8" because of their use in an 8-bit environment).[38] Five of the character sets—Basic Latin (equivalent to ASCII), Extended Latin (a superset of ANSEL), superscripts, subscripts, and Greek symbols—were used in records in any of the MARC 21 formats.[22,12] The other seven—Basic Hebrew, Basic Cyrillic, Extended Cyrillic, Basic Arabic, Extended Arabic, Greek, and EACC—were used only in bibliographic records.

For records encoded with the MARC-8 character sets, the default character sets are Basic Latin and Extended Latin.[39,11] In many systems used by libraries, the five character sets common to all MARC 21 records were implemented as a single "Latin" or "Roman" character set.

Use of Unicode in MARC 21 records was approved in 1998 with acceptance of MARBI Proposal 98-18.[40] MARC 21 records must be encoded either in the Unicode encoding form UTF-8 or in the older individual character sets. The Library of Congress has published mappings from the characters of the individual MARC 21 character sets to Unicode equivalents (expressed as UTF-8 byte sequences).[41] Initial use of Unicode in MARC 21 records was limited use to a specified subset of writing systems, corresponding to the scope of the individual MARC 21 character sets; the restriction was lifted in 2007.[36]

Use of Unicode in MARC 21 affects the order of combining characters relative to the base letter. (*Combining characters* is the term used in MARC 21 documentation for what are called *diacritics*, *non-spacing graphic characters* or *character modifiers* in other library contexts.) With the introduction of Unicode as an encoding option for MARC 21 exchange records, the position of the base letter relative to combining characters now depends on the encoding being used. When data is encoded in UTF-8, the Unicode convention of base letter first is followed. When data is encoded in the MARC 21 character sets, the original MARC convention of base letter after the combining character(s) applies.

In 2007, the Library of Congress announced that non-Latin characters were to be allowed in references in name authority records.[42] Initially, the character content of the records is limited to the repertoire of the MARC-8 character sets. Authority records exchanged between NACO nodes are encoded in UTF-8. (NACO is the Name Authority Cooperative Program of the Program for Cooperative Cataloging.) Cataloging Distribution Service subscribers may choose MARC 21 authority records in either UTF-8 or the MARC-8 character sets.

Because some older library systems may still be limited to the individual MARC-8 character sets, two methods have been defined for representation of Unicode characters that cannot be mapped to any of the characters in these sets.[43] One method, which substitutes the vertical bar character (ASCII hexadecimal 7C) as a placeholder for the unmappable character, is *lossy*, that is, destructive because the identity of the unmappable character is lost. The alternative method is *lossless* because the character that could not be converted is explicitly identified by a numeric character reference (NCR), modeled on character entity references in HTML.

Unicode and UNIMARC

UNIMARC, published by the International Federation of Library Associations and Institutions (IFLA) is the other international exchange format for MARC records.[8] Manuals have been published for the bibliographic, authorities, and holdings formats; the classification format is under development.

Like MARC 21, UNIMARC specifies use of individual character sets, nine published by ISO, and one (Basic Cyrillic) registered with ISO. When individual character sets are used in a UNIMARC record, the default character set is ISO/IEC 646, the International Reference Version (IRV) of ASCII.[23]

UNIMARC also specifies "ISO 10646 Level 3 (Unicode, UTF-8)" as a valid character set. No other character sets are used in this case. "Level 3" is a feature of ISO/IEC 10646 to designate data that may include combining characters.

A unique feature of UNIMARC is the ability to include coded information about use of scripts in a record. UNIMARC specifies 16 two-letter codes, rather than using the codes defined in ISO 15924.[28] Additional codes indicate the reading direction of the script; left to right, or right to left. These script and direction codes are used in the *General Processing Data* field (tag 100) and in subfield 7 that conveys script information for specific fields.

Unicode and Z39.50

Z39.50 is the original cross-system search and retrieve protocol developed for library use.[44] Version 3 was updated in April 2002 to add the "10,646 character set" to the character set choices for character set and language negotiation.[45] Supplementary choices cover *collection*, *implementation level*, and *syntax*.

Using this terminology derived from International Standard ISO/IEC 10646, Unicode data has these features: collection designation to identify which version of the Unicode Standard is used, implementation level 3, and one of the syntax choices UTF-8, UTF-16, and UCS-4 (=UTF-32).[46]

LIBRARY SYSTEMS

Surveys conducted in 2002 and 2006 of providers of library systems and services showed that most integrated library systems already utilized Unicode internally to some extent.[47,48] The earlier study by Tull identified two record storage situations: use of UTF-8, and storage in the MARC-8 character sets with conversion to UTF-8 for browser display. With the removal of the restriction on data content of MARC 21 records in 2007, any integrated library system that does not utilize Unicode end-to-end will soon do so.

The MARC 21 restriction applied only to the exchange of data. Some libraries and organizations began to use additional scripts within their own system before the restriction was removed e.g., OCLC introduced support for Tamil and Thai in 2006; Bengali and Devanagari were subsequently added.[49,50]

Changes to the MARC 21 formats (e.g., the changes related to Unicode use introduced in 2007) are not always implemented in library software products. The ALCTS (Association for Library Collections and Technical Services) Task Force on Non-English Access received comments pointing out that products supporting interlibrary loan, bibliographic citations, and federated searching do not support non-Latin script data adequately; the cause is undetermined.[51,52]

CONCLUSION

The development of the Unicode Standard is one of the most significant events in information technology. Unicode is fundamental to the worldwide exchange and display of textual information in multiple languages and scripts. Its use is now well established in all types of systems, software, and standards.

In the library community, Unicode has been viewed as the solution to the lack of support for non-Latin scripts in library systems, but it is far more than that. Finally, libraries and the information industry are using the same method to encode data, which means that mainstream technology can be brought into libraries with considerably less effort. The enormous increase in the repertoire of available characters allows for more the accurate description of library resources. The need for romanization is greatly reduced, significantly improving access to library resources, particularly for those who use non-Latin writing systems. The Unicode Standard brings major benefits to libraries and their users worldwide.

ACKNOWLEDGMENTS

Laura Tull was the author of the first version of this entry published in 2004.

Material from *The Unicode Standard, Version 5.0* and other publications of the Unicode Consortium is copyright © 1991–2010 Unicode, Inc. All rights reserved. Used with permission.

The Unicode® Consortium is a registered trademark, and Unicode™ is a trademark of Unicode, Inc. (http://www.unicode.org).

REFERENCES

1. The Unicode Consortium, *About the Unicode Standard*, Available at http://www.unicode.org/standard/standard.html (accessed October 14, 2008).
2. World Wide Web Consortium, *Character Model for the World Wide Web 1.0: Fundamentals*, 2005; W3C Recommendation, Available at http://www.w3.org/TR/charmod/ (accessed October 14, 2008).
3. Davis, M.; Whistler, K. *Unicode Character Database*, 2008; Unicode Standard Annex 44, Available at http://www.unicode.org/reports/tr44/ (accessed October 14, 2008).
4. Gillam, R. A brief history of character encoding. *Unicode Demystified: A Practical Programmers Guide to the Encoding Standard*, Addison-Wesley: Boston, MA, 2003; 25–59.
5. International Organization for Standardization, *Information Technology: Character Code Structure and Extension Techniques*; ISO/IEC 2022: Geneva, 1994.
6. Hexadecimal is the base 16 numbering system. Hexadecimal digits are written either as the numbers 0 through 15, or using the digits 0–9 and the letters A–F. The value used here can be written either as 1/11 or as 1B.
7. Library of Congress. Network Development and MARC Standards Office, *MARC 21 Specifications for Record Structure, Character Sets, and Exchange Media*, 2007; Updated Available at http://www.loc.gov/marc/specifications/spechome.html (accessed October 14, 2008).
8. International Federation of Library Associations and Institutions, *UNIMARC Formats and Related Documentation*, Available at http://www.ifla.org/VI/8/unimarc-publist.htm (accessed October 14, 2008).
9. Aliprand, J.M. Nonroman scripts in the bibliographic environment. In *Encyclopedia of Library and Information Science*, 1st Ed.; Kent, A., Hall, C.M., Eds.; Marcel Dekker, Inc.: New York, 1995; Vol. 56, 260–283.
10. National Information Standards Organization, *East Asian Character Code for Bibliographic Use; ANSI/NISO Z39.64-1989*; NISO Press: Bethesda, MD, 1989.
11. Library of Congress. Network Development and MARC Standards Office, Code table extended Latin (ANSEL). *MARC 21 Specifications for Record Structure, Character Sets, and Exchange Media*, 2007; Updated Available at http://lcweb2.loc.gov/diglib/codetables/45.html (accessed October 14, 2008).
12. National Information Standards Organization, *Extended Latin Alphabet Coded Character Set for Bibliographic Use*; NISO Press: Bethesda, MD, 1993; ANSI/NISO Z39.47-1993;.
13. International Organization for Standardization, *Extension of the Latin Alphabet Coded Character Set for Bibliographic Information Interchange*; ISO 5426: Geneva, 1983.
14. *The Chinese Character Code for Information Interchange, developed in Taiwan, was the model for the East Asian Character Code for Bibliographic Use* (EACC), so these two character sets do have many encodings in common.
15. International Organization for Standardization, *Information Technology—Universal Multiple-Octet Coded Character Set (UCS), augmented by Amendments 1–4*; ISO/IEC 10646: Geneva, 2003, 2003.
16. The Unicode Consortium, 2.2 Unicode design principles. *The Unicode Standard, Version 5.0*; Addison-Wesley: Upper Saddle River, NJ, 2007; 13–23.
17. Davis, M.; Whistler, K. *Unicode Collation Algorithm*, 2008; Unicode Technical Standard 10; Available at http://www.unicode.org/reports/tr10/ (accessed October 14, 2008).
18. Davis, M. *Unicode Bidirectional Algorithm*, 2008; Unicode Standard Annex 9; Available at http://www.unicode.org/reports/tr9/ (accessed October 14, 2008).
19. Rather, L.J. Special characters and diacritical marks used in roman alphabets. Libr. Resour. Tech. Ser. **1968**, *12*(3), 285–294.
20. The Unicode Consortium, 2.4 Code points and characters. *The Unicode Standard, Version 5.0*; Addison-Wesley: Upper Saddle River, NJ, 2007; 25–8.
21. The Unicode Consortium, 2.8 Unicode allocation and 2.9 Details of allocation. *The Unicode Standard, Version 5.0*; Addison-Wesley: Upper Saddle River, NJ, 2007; 38–46.
22. American National Standards Institute, *Information Systems—Coded Character Set—7-Bit American National Standard Code for Information Interchange (7-bit ASCII)*; New York, 1986; ANSI/INCITS 4-1986.
23. International Organization for Standardization, *Information Technology—ISO 7-Bit Coded Character Set for Information Interchange*; ISO/IEC 646: Geneva, 1991, 1991.
24. International Organization for Standardization, *Latin Alphabet No. 1, Part 1, Information Processing—8-Bit Single-Byte Coded Graphic Character Sets*; ISO/IEC 8859-1: Geneva, 1998.

25. The Unicode Consortium, 2.5 Encoding forms. *The Unicode Standard, Version 5.0*; Addison-Wesley: Upper Saddle River, NJ, 2007; 28–35.

26. Library of Congress. Network Development and MARC Standards Office, Implementation: UTF-8 encoding form. *MARC 21 Specifications for Record Structure, Character Sets, and Exchange Media*, 2007; Updated Available at http://www.loc.gov/marc/specifications/speccharucs.html# implementation (accessed October 14, 2008).

27. The Unicode Consortium. http://www.unicode.org/.

28. International Organization for Standardization, *Information and Documentation—Codes for the Representation of Names of Scripts*; ISO 15924: Geneva, 2004, 2004.

29. ISO 15924 Registration Authority. http://www.unicode.org/iso15924/.

30. *Developing International Software*, Microsoft Press: Redmond, WA, 2003; 63 Dr. International.

31. World Wide Web Consortium; Unicode Consortium, *Unicode in XML and other Markup Languages*; 2007; W3C Working Group Note; Unicode Technical Report 20. Available at http://www.unicode.org/reports/tr20/ and http://www.w3.org/TR/unicode-xml/ (both accessed October 14, 2008).

32. World Wide Web Consortium, *HTML 4.01 Specification*, 1999; W3C Recommendation; Available at http://www.w3.org/TR/html401/ (accessed October 14, 2008).

33. World Wide Web Consortium, *Extensible Markup Language (XML) 1.0*, 4th Ed., 2006; W3C Recommendation; Available at http://www.w3.org/TR/xml/ (accessed October 14, 2008).

34. World Wide Web Consortium, *Character Model for the World Wide Web 1.0: Normalization*, 2005; W3C Working Draft; Available at http://www.w3.org/TR/charmod-norm/ (accessed October 14, 2008).

35. World Wide Web Consortium, *Character Model for the World Wide Web 1.0: Resource Identifiers*, 2004; W3C Candidate Recommendation; Available at http://www.w3.org/TR/charmod-resid/ (accessed October 14, 2008).

36. Library of Congress. Network Development and MARC Standards Office, Unicode encoding environment. *MARC 21 Specifications for Record Structure, Character Sets, and Exchange Media*, 2007; Updated Available at http://www.loc.gov/marc/specifications/speccharucs.html (accessed October 14, 2008).

37. The Unicode Consortium, 12.1 Han: CJK standards. *The Unicode Standard, Version 5.0*; Addison-Wesley: Upper Saddle River, NJ, 2007; 409–411.

38. Library of Congress. Network Development and MARC Standards Office, MARC-8 encoding environment. *MARC 21 Specifications for Record Structure, Character Sets, and Exchange Media*, 2007; Updated Available at http://www.loc.gov/marc/specifications/speccharmarc8.html (accessed October 14, 2008).

39. Library of Congress. Network Development and MARC Standards Office, Code table basic Latin (ASCII). *MARC 21 Specifications for Record Structure, Character Sets, and Exchange Media*, 2007; Updated Available at http://lcweb2.loc.gov/diglib/codetables/42.html (accessed October 14, 2008).

40. MARBI Unicode Encoding and Recognition Technical Issues Task Force, *Unicode Identification and Encoding in USMARC Records; Proposal 98–18*, 1998; Library of Congress, Network Development and MARC Standards Office Available at http://www.loc.gov/marc/marbi/1998/98-18.html (accessed October 14, 2008).

41. Library of Congress. Network Development and MARC Standards Office, MARC-8 code tables. *MARC 21 Specifications for Record Structure, Character Sets, and Exchange Media*, 2007; Updated Available at http://www.loc.gov/marc/specifications/specchartables.html (accessed October 14, 2008).

42. Library of Congress. Acquisitions and Bibliographic Access Directorate, *Announcement on Non-Latin Script References in Authority Records*, 2007; Available at http://www.loc.gov/catdir/cpso/nonroman_announce.pdf (accessed October 14, 2008).

43. Library of Congress. Network Development and MARC Standards Office, Issues specific to converting Unicode to MARC-8. *MARC 21 Specifications for Record Structure, Character Sets, and Exchange Media*, 2007; Updated Available at http://www.loc.gov/marc/specifications/speccharconversion.html (accessed October 14, 2008).

44. National Information Standards Organization, *Information Retrieval (Z39.50): Application Service Definition and Protocol Specification*; NISO Press: Bethesda, MD, 2003; ANSI/NISO Z39.50-2003.

45. Z39.50 Implementors Group, *Character Set and Language Negotiation (4)*; Library of Congress, Network Development and MARC Standards Office, 2002; Available at http://www.loc.gov/z3950/agency/defns/charneg-4.html (accessed October 14, 2008).

46. The Unicode Consortium, C.5 Identification of features for the Unicode Standard. *The Unicode Standard, Version 5.0*; Addison-Wesley: Upper Saddle River, NJ, 2007; 1097–8.

47. Tull, L. Library systems and Unicode: a review of the current state of development. Inform. Technol. Libr. **2002**, *21*(4), 181–185.

48. Appendix J.: ILS vendors/local systems (compiled by Joan M. Aliprand), and Appendix K: Authority control vendors (compiled by Kristin Lindlan). In ALCTS Task Force on Non-English Access. *Report*; Rev.; Association for Library Collections & Technical Services, 2007; 34–38. http://www.ala.org/ala/mgrps/divs/alcts/ianda/nonenglish/07marchrpt.pdf.

49. Patton, G. OCLC. *ALCTS Task Force on Non-English Access. Report*, Association for Library Collections & Technical Services, 2007; 30 Rev.; Available at http://www.ala.org/ala/mgrps/divs/alcts/ianda/nonenglish/07marchrpt.pdf (accessed October 14, 2008).

50. OCLC. WorldCat: a Global Catalog. http://www.oclc.org/us/en/worldcat/catalog/default.htm.

51. ALCTS Task Force on Non-English Access, *Comments Received and Their Disposition*, Association for Library Collections & Technical Services, 2007; Available at http://www.ala.org/ala/mgrps/divs/alcts/ianda/nonenglish/07rptcomments.pdf (accessed October 14, 2008).

52. ALCTS, pronounced uh-lex, is the Association for Library Collections & Technical Services, a division of the American Library Association.

Unified Medical Language System® (UMLS®) Project

Stuart J. Nelson
Tammy Powell
Suresh Srinivasan
Betsy L. Humphreys
National Library of Medicine, Bethesda, Maryland, U.S.A.

Abstract

The Unified Medical Language System (UMLS) is a long-term research and development effort of the National Library of Medicine, aimed at assisting users in finding information from multiple sources without understanding the intricacies of each particular source. Consisting of three major knowledge sources, a Metathesaurus, a Semantic Network, and a set of lexical processing tools, the UMLS is produced and released twice yearly. Recent efforts have been aimed at expanding coverage in genetics and in clinical vocabularies designed for use in medical record systems. RxNorm, produced and released on a monthly basis, with weekly updates, is an outgrowth of the UMLS, focusing on medication terminology.

INTRODUCTION

In 1986, Donald A. B. Lindberg, M.D., Director of the National Library of Medicine (NLM), initiated a long-term research and development effort known as the Unified Medical Language System. Anticipating increasing amounts of biomedical information available in electronic form, he believed that NLM should facilitate the development of advanced information systems that could retrieve and integrate information from a variety of disparate information sources, including bibliographic databases, patient record systems, factual databanks, and knowledge bases. He recognized that a major barrier to effective retrieval and integration of information from multiple sources was the "naming problem," the variety of different ways that the same concepts are expressed in different information sources and by different information seekers.

To address the complex problems of relating user inquiries to the content of biomedical information sources and of aggregating comparable data derived from disparate databases, the NLM assembled a multidisciplinary in-house research group and also awarded a series of research contracts to a number of primarily academic investigators. The first several years of UMLS research were devoted to studying user needs, developing research tools, identifying required capabilities, exploring alternative methods for delivering these capabilities, and defining in general terms the new knowledge sources that would be needed to support integrated use of information from disparate electronic biomedical sources. Based on the results of this early work, the conception of UMLS components as "middleware" designed for use by system developers emerged. Rather than build a single vocabulary based on classical approaches, a methodology of integrating the disparate terminologies was designed. Since 1990, NLM has issued regular editions of UMLS Knowledge Sources and associated lexical programs, at least annually. The current frequency of releases is two times per year.

Over the past 18 years, the UMLS resources have grown and developed, the methodology for creating them has matured, and their utility has been demonstrated in many different information systems. Today more than 3000 individuals and institutions worldwide license the UMLS resources, which are free-of-charge. The majority of the licensees use one or more of the UMLS components in information systems, often in creative and innovative undertakings. The NLM itself uses UMLS components to enhance retrieval from a number of its information services, including the MEDLINE database available via PubMed, the ClinicalTrials.gov database of ongoing clinical trials sponsored by the National Institutes of Health and other organizations, and the NLM Gateway, which provides a single point of entry to a number of different NLM databases. The Library also relies heavily on the UMLS resources to aid its high volume indexing and cataloging operations and in its natural language processing and digital library research programs.

Subsequent sections of this entry describe: 1) UMLS Knowledge Sources in general, 2) key characteristics of the Metathesaurus and the Semantic Network, 3) the production of the Metathesaurus and the distribution mechanisms for the UMLS resources, 4) MetamorphoSys, a utility program that assists UMLS users in unpacking new releases and customizing the Metathesaurus for particular applications, and 5) RxNorm, a standardized nomenclature for clinical drugs, that addresses special requirements for linking medication vocabularies that were not amenable to Metathesaurus construction techniques.

Encyclopedia of Library and Information Sciences, Fourth Edition DOI: 10.1081/E-ELIS4-120043969

THE KNOWLEDGE SOURCES

There are three major UMLS knowledge sources: a large Metathesaurus® of concepts and terms from many biomedical vocabularies and classifications; a Semantic Network of sensible relationships among the broad semantic types or categories to which all Metathesaurus concepts are assigned; and the SPECIALIST Lexicon which contains syntactic, morphological, and orthographic information for biomedical and common words in the English language. The Lexicon and its associated lexical resources are used to generate the indexes to the Metathesaurus and also have wide applicability in natural language processing applications in the biomedical domain. From 1991 to 1998, the NLM also produced a fourth UMLS Knowledge Source, an Information Sources Map that described the scope, content, and access conditions for many publicly available biomedical databases. The development of the World Wide Web offered other promising approaches to addressing the problem of determining which of many information sources contain content relevant to a particular inquiry.

The Metathesaurus and the Semantic Network will be discussed in this entry. Those interested in the SPECIALIST lexicon and its related natural language processing resources should consult the Bibliography at the end of this entry.

The Metathesaurus

The Metathesaurus is the central vocabulary component of the UMLS. The term Metathesaurus draws on Webster's Dictionary third definition for the prefix "Meta," i.e., "more comprehensive, transcending." In a sense, the Metathesaurus transcends the specific vocabularies and classifications it encompasses.

The Metathesaurus is a database of information on concepts whose names appear in one or more of a number of different controlled vocabularies and classifications used in the field of biomedicine. In general, the scope of the Metathesaurus is determined by the combined scope of its source vocabularies. The Metathesaurus preserves the meanings, hierarchical connections, and other relationships between terms present in its source vocabularies, while adding certain basic information about each of its concepts and establishing new relationships between concepts and terms from different source vocabularies.

The Metathesaurus contains concepts and concept names from more than 145 vocabularies and classifications, some in multiple editions. The April 2008 release of the Metathesaurus (2008AA) includes approximately 1.55 million concepts and 7.78 million concept names. Most of the source vocabularies are included in their entirety. Some material from the UMLS Metathesaurus is from copyrighted sources.

Of particular note are two collections of source vocabularies relating to important areas in modern biomedicine. The inclusion of major genomics vocabularies—the Gene Ontology, the Human Genome Organization (HUGO) Gene Nomenclature, and the names of clinical genetic syndromes from Online Mendelian Inheritance of Man (OMIM)—makes the UMLS Metathesaurus a useful tool in mining the genomics literature for data and in linking genomic and clinical information together.

The UMLS Metathesaurus also includes standard vocabularies believed useful in building, indexing, and aggregating electronic health records and in enabling sophisticated clinical decision support at the point of care. As the central coordinating body for standard clinical terminologies within the Department of Health and Human Services, NLM plays a leading role in making key clinical terminologies freely available within the United States and in mapping them to administrative coding systems, used in health statistics and health care billing. Since 1999, NLM has funded the ongoing development and free dissemination of Logical Observations Identifiers Names and Codes (LOINC), a standard nomenclature for laboratory tests and other clinical measurements. In 2003, the Library negotiated an innovative U.S.-wide license for the Systematized Nomenclature of Medicine—Clinical Terms (SNOMED CT) to make this vocabulary available for U.S.-wide use. NLM also assisted the formation of the International Health Terminology Standards Development Organisation, which purchased SNOMED CT from the College of American Pathologists in 2007. NLM is the U.S. member of this new international organization. The Library itself produces the RxNorm clinical drug terminology (see below). The UMLS Metathesaurus is one of the dissemination vehicles for these standard clinical terminologies and for the mappings from them to administrative classification and coding systems, such as the International Classification of Diseases, Current Procedural Terminology, and the Healthcare Common Procedure Coding System.

Organization of the Metathesaurus

I. A. Richards, in his introduction to Roget's Pocket Thesaurus, described a thesaurus as the opposite of a dictionary, where you go to look up a word when you know the meaning. By this definition, a thesaurus is organized by the principle of semantic locality. That is, words and phrases close to one another in meaning can be found in the same area. A review of the first thesaurus in the English language, which was designed by Roget, illustrates that principle. Organized in general categories, then into more specific ones, are lists of words and phrases close in meaning to one another.

The Metathesaurus is organized according to this broad principle. All words and phrases that mean the same thing form a distinct concept or synonym class in the

Metathesaurus. Each separate meaning appears as its own concept, together with links (represented relationships) to other concepts in the Metathesaurus. These relationships to the other concepts serve to define the semantic neighborhood of the concept. A user of the Metathesaurus, whether human or program, can navigate within this semantic neighborhood to find the names for the concept sought.

Multiple meanings of the same term are dealt with by separating the meanings and presenting them in different semantic neighborhoods. If you look up the word "tree" in a dictionary you will see one entry with multiple definitions. If you search for "tree" in the Metathesaurus you will find that it names two separate concepts. One concept is the plant and the other one means hierarchy. Each of these meanings has differing relationships within the Metathesaurus.

Although the Metathesaurus can be usefully compared with Roget's thesaurus, it does not fit the common information science definition of "thesaurus" as a list of preferred subject headings or descriptors, often with a cross-reference structure, created for use in the organization and retrieval of documents within some domain. This definition of thesaurus applies to some of the source vocabularies within the Metathesaurus, but not to the Metathesaurus itself, which necessarily encompasses vocabularies with a wide range of different purposes and semantic and structural properties.

Concept structure

The first step in organizing the Metathesaurus is to connect the alternative names for the same concept. Each concept record contains the strings of alphanumeric characters and terms that express the meaning of the concept. Strings that are lexical variants of each other (that is, identical after a series of well-defined manipulations that can be done computationally, e.g., making all characters lower case, putting all words in a defined order, and changing all plural forms to singular) are grouped together as a single term. One string is designated, by convention, as the preferred form of that term. Table 1 illustrates the terms for one meaning of, "Milk Hypersensitivity." In Table 1, "Milk Hypersensitivity" and "Hypersensitivity, Milk" are lexical variants. Also in Table 1, the ten terms all have the same meaning. They are therefore linked together as alternate names of the same concept, with one term designated as the preferred name of the concept. The designation of preferred forms and preferred names is done by algorithm based on an order of precedence among source vocabularies. Because this is done by an arbitrary convention, any user can change and select their own order of precedence among vocabularies using their own tools or MetamorphoSys (see below).

Each concept in the Metathesaurus has a unique concept identifier (CUI), which itself has no intrinsic

Table 1 Synonymous terms and their sources.

Term	Source/term type/code
Milk hypersensitivity	MSH2008_2008_02_04/MH/D016269
Milk hypersensitivity	NDFRT_2004_01/DI/C6882
Hypersensitivity, milk	MSH2008_2008_02_04/EP/D016269
Hypersensitivities, milk	MSH2008_2008_02_04/PM/D016269
Milk hypersensitivities	MSH2008_2008_02_04/PM/D016269
Allergy, milk	MSH2008_2008_02_04/EP/D016269
Milk allergy	MSH2008_2008_02_04/EN/D016269
Milk allergy	MEDLINEPLUS_20040814/ET/T1256
Milk allergy	MDR11_0/PT/10027633
Milk allergy	MDR11_0/LT/10027633
Allergies, milk	MSH2008_2008_02_04/PM/D016269
Milk allergies	MSH2008_2008_02_04/PM/D016269
Food allergy to milk	CCPSS99/PT/0006002
Food allergy to milk product	CCPSS99/PT/0026295
Hipersensibilidad a la Leche	MSHSPA2008/MH/D016269
Alergia a la Leche	MSHSPA2008/EP/D016269
Alergia a la leche	MDRSPA10_1/PT/10027633
Alergia a la leche	MDRSPA10_1/LT/10027633

The meaning of the Source Abbreviations and Term Types can be obtained by reviewing the UMLS documentation.
Source: Material drawn from the 2008 UMLS Metathesaurus.

meaning. This unique identifier is represented in the Metathesaurus by the letter C followed by one or more digits (i.e., C0010028). This identifier remains the same across versions of the Metathesaurus, irrespective of the term designated as the preferred name of the concept. This facilitates file maintenance and management, as well as tracking the meanings assigned to a given term changes over time. It is "the name [of a concept] that never changes."

Relationships

The Metathesaurus also represents relationships between different concepts. Many relationships are derived directly from the source vocabularies. For example, the fact that there is a relationship between "Opium" and "Plant Extracts" is derived from the hierarchical tree structures in the Medical Subject Headings (MeSH) vocabulary. The exact nature of the relationship may or may not be represented in the source vocabulary, although the contextual and hierarchical relationships are identified as such. Relationships between concepts from different source

Table 2 Relationships within the UMLS Metathesaurus.

Relationship	Definition
Broader (RB)	Has a meaning which includes that of the concept.
Narrower (RN)	Has a meaning which is included in that of the concept.
Other related (RO)	Has a relationship other than synonymous, narrower, or broader.
LIKE (RL)	The two concepts are similar or "alike." In the current edition of the Metathesaurus, most relationships with this attribute link MeSH supplementary concepts which are largely chemicals. Many of the concepts linked by this relationship may be synonymous and will be in a single concept identifier in future editions of the Metathesaurus. Source-specific mappings from one vocabulary to another also have this relationship, along with the label for the relationship attribute of "mapped_to."
Parent (PAR)	Is a parent in a hierarchy of a Metathesaurus source vocabulary.
Child (CHD)	Is a child in a hierarchy of a Metathesaurus source vocabulary.
Sibling (SIB)	Shares a parent in a hierarchy in a Metathesaurus source vocabulary.
AQ	Is an allowed qualifier for a concept in a Metathesaurus source vocabulary.
QB	Can be qualified by a concept in a Metathesaurus source vocabulary.

vocabularies are also, on occasion, created during Metathesaurus construction. For example, the MediSpan (MDDB) concept "Infant Foods Powder" is identified in the Metathesaurus as having a narrower-than relationship to "Infant Food," a concept that is present in MeSH, SNOMED, and others.

Nine types of relationships exist in the Metathesaurus. They are listed in Table 2. Relationships are reciprocal, so that, for example, where one concept is broader than another, the other is noted as being narrower than the first. Relationship attributes, describing the exact nature of a relationship, may be assigned to a given relationship. These attributes include the set of permissible relationships within the Semantic Network (discussed below), with additional relationships, including that of "mapped_to." Other relationship attributes originate from the source vocabularies.

Many of the source vocabularies included in the Metathesaurus place the concepts they include in some context. These contexts are in general hierarchical arrangements, for some organizational or classification purpose. NLM endeavors to preserve all of these different contexts in the Metathesaurus, so a single concept in the Metathesaurus can appear in multiple different hierarchies. As an example, several of the contexts in which the concept "fruit" appears are shown in Table 3. There is no

attempt to merge or combine the different contextual views into one coherent hierarchical arrangement for the Metathesaurus. Given the different perspectives and purposes of the many UMLS source vocabularies, this would be an essentially impossible task.

Semantic types

Each Metathesaurus concept is assigned at least one semantic type. The types are drawn from the Semantic Network (see below). The types provide a general categorization of the concept, and allow some reasoning about the possible meaning of the concept. In all cases, the most specific semantic type available in the hierarchy is assigned to the concept. For example, the concept "Macaca" receives the semantic type "Mammal" because there is not a more specific type, e.g., "Primate," available in the Network.

Additional attributes

Within each concept, there are many data elements provided both by the sources and created by NLM. There are over 110 attributes and data elements in the Metathesaurus. Each attribute in the Metathesaurus is labeled with the source, which asserted that attribute.

Of particular note is that there may be narrative description(s) of the meaning of the concept. The majority of these definitions come from MeSH and National Cancer Institute (NCI) Thesaurus, but there are also definitions from a number of other sources. A few definitions are created specifically for the Metathesaurus when they are needed to distinguish among different meanings of the same string.

The Semantic Network

The Semantic Network is tied very closely to the content of the Metathesaurus. In general, semantic networks attempt to impart common sense knowledge to computers, allowing them to "reason" and draw conclusions about entities by virtue of the categories to which they have been assigned. The semantic links provide the structure for the network and represent important relationships in the domain. The UMLS Semantic Network consists of 135 semantic types, broad categories intended to indicate the general area of meaning of a Metathesaurus concept, together with 54 relationships or semantic links.

The Semantic Network can be visualized as a diagram where the types make up nodes within a network. The top of the network has two nodes, "Entity" and "Event." The remaining types each appear only in one location within the network. Figure 1 includes a portion of the UMLS Semantic Network.

The primary link between the nodes is the "isa" link. This establishes the hierarchy of types within the Network

Table 3 Representative hierarchical contexts for the concept "fruit".

Alcohol and other drug thesaurus
Technology, safety, and accidents
Technology, manufacturing, and agriculture
Food product
Beverage +
Chocolate
Dietary fiber +
Fish, shellfish, other seafood
Food-product ingredient
Fruits
Grain, cereal +
Junk food
Meat and dairy products +
Nut, seed
Pastry, sweets
Vegetables
Vitamin supplement
SNOMED CT
Substance +
Dietary substance +
Foods +
Fruit nuts and seeds +
Fruit
MeSH
Organisms (MeSH Category)
Plants
Plant components
Plant components, aerial
Flowering tops +
Fruit
Nuts
Seeds +
Plant epidermis +
Plant leaves +
Plant shoots +
Plant stems +
Technology, food and beverages (MeSH category)
Technology, industry, agriculture (MeSH category)
Food and beverages
Food
Bread
Candy +
Cereals +
Condiments +
Crops, agricultural +
Dairy products +
Dietary carbohydrates +
Dietary fats +
Dietary fiber
Dietary proteins +
Dietary supplements +
Eggs +
Flour
Food additives +
Food, genetically modified
Foods, specialized +
Fruit
Honey

(Continued)

Table 3 Representative hierarchical contexts for the concept "fruit". *(Continued)*

Meat +
Micronutrients +
Molasses
Nuts
Seeds
Vegetables +

Concept name bolded for readability.
+Indicates has children not shown.
Source: Contexts drawn from 2008 UMLS Metathesaurus.

and is used for deciding on the most specific semantic type available for assignment to a Metathesaurus concept. In addition, a set of nonhierarchical relations between the types has been identified. These are grouped into five major categories, which are themselves relations: "physically related to," "spatially related to," "temporally related to," "functionally related to," and "conceptually related to."

The relations are stated between semantic types and do not necessarily apply to all instances of concepts that have been assigned to those semantic types. That is, the relation may or may not hold between any particular pair of concepts. So, although "treats" is one of several valid relations between the semantic types "Pharmacologic Substance" and "Disease or Syndrome," a particular pharmacologic substance (e.g., penicillin) may not treat a particular disease (e.g., AIDS).

PRODUCTION AND DISTRIBUTION OF THE UMLS

Making the Metathesaurus

To understand the process of making the Metathesaurus, it is helpful to review the steps taken in adding a new vocabulary to the Metathesaurus. (Adding an update to a vocabulary already present in the Metathesaurus is quite similar.) The NLM begins by acquiring the rights to incorporate a vocabulary into the Metathesaurus. The rights include permission to include and represent the vocabulary in this form, and to distribute the vocabulary to UMLS licensees. However, a UMLS license alone does not permit a licensee to use every source vocabulary for any purpose. For some applications of some source vocabularies, the user must also establish a separate agreement with the individual vocabulary producer. The UMLS license describes when this is necessary.

Once a machine-readable version of a vocabulary is made available to the NLM it is converted into a "normal" or canonical form. This "inversion" process requires careful consideration of how the source represents its meanings and attempts to make all of this representation explicit. Depending on the vocabulary and the context of

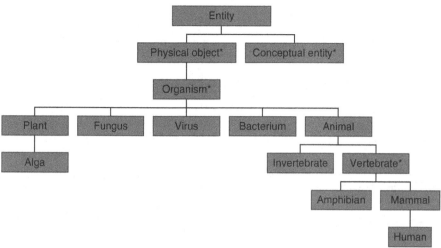

Fig. 1 A portion of the UMLS semantic network.

* Additional children not shown

a given term, the meaning of that term, what is being named by it, can differ from the same term in other vocabularies. Each source is then added to the existing Metathesaurus. Terms from different sources which are lexically similar to each other or to existing terms in the Metathesaurus, or which appear from other indications to be semantically identical to concepts in the Metathesaurus, are brought together (merged) as proposed synonyms located in a single Metathesaurus concept.

After this merging, the results are reviewed by editors, largely to assess if the proposed concept merge is appropriate. This human step, which requires understanding of the meaning of a term in the source is the key to successful linking of that term to different terms from different source vocabularies. Contextual information about what is being named can be almost entirely implicit (e.g., a vocabulary describing medical procedures with a drug term name may really mean the procedure of administering that drug), or represented more explicitly. Judging whether or not the same referent is being named can be difficult. Practical decisions of what constitutes synonymy are dominated by the consideration of what an expert in the area might discern as a notable difference in meaning. Editors also may add information such as additional relationships and semantic types. This human review is expedited by computational assistance, as is the quality assurance that takes place after the editing.

In categorizing the concepts, editors are encouraged to consider the most specific semantic type available. If the concept is broad or not represented by a more specific type, a broad category in the semantic type hierarchy is used. For example, a sub-tree under the node "Physical Object" is "Manufactured Object." It has three nodes, "Medical Device," "Drug Delivery Device," and "Research Device." It is clear that there are manufactured objects other than medical devices, drug delivery devices, or research devices. Rather than proliferate the number of semantic types to encompass multiple additional

subcategories for these objects, concepts that are neither medical devices nor research devices are simply assigned the more general semantic type "Manufactured Object."

Periodically various types of quality assurance efforts are performed. The most important of these are efforts to ensure that there is no missed synonymy, i.e., no terms meaning exactly the same thing in different concepts. Another important effort is made to ensure that every concept is linked to others by some relationship.

In preparation for releasing of the next version of the Metathesaurus, all new releasable concepts are assigned CUIs, while concepts previously present in the Metathesaurus retain their CUIs. The Metathesaurus is released as a set of relational tables. Each term in a source is identified with its own unique identifier, and a group of terms judged synonymous share the same CUI.

Licensing and Distribution of the UMLS

The UMLS is available free of charge to anyone who wishes to license it. The license agreement, available at http://www.nlm.nih.gov/research/umls/, must be completed and signed electronically. As noted above, UMLS licensees may also have to enter into separate license agreements with the producers of specific vocabularies present in the Metathesaurus. No additional agreements are required for use of the other UMLS components.

Licensed users may ftp the UMLS Knowledge Sources or access them interactively from the UMLS Knowledge Source Server. On request, DVDs are provided to users who do not have adequate connectivity to ftp the large files.

MetamorphoSys

As the Metathesaurus has grown in size, dealing with the file sizes and the many constituent vocabularies has introduced new challenges, requiring custom compression techniques for the packaging and distribution of the content. This has consequently created the need for a tool to allow users to unpack the data at their local installations. Furthermore, due to the different needs of the users, the entire content of the Metathesaurus is rarely needed or wanted for any specific application. Some content may actually be harmful to particular applications, or users may not have the additional licenses required for some uses of some source vocabularies. Thus, the need arises to create useful, user-definable subsets of the Metathesaurus with all the data and referential integrities present in the full release. This, in general, is a nontrivial task beyond the scope of many users.

MetamorphoSys is a utility program designed to meet these and other needs. An early version for subsetting was first introduced in 1999 and has since then grown into its current form as an installation, subsetting, and browsing tool for the UMLS Metathesaurus. It is implemented as a platform-independent Java application freely distributed with the UMLS data on the DVD or available as an Internet download.

MetamorphoSys is first an installation program for the UMLS. It is required to unpack the UMLS knowledge sources from the internal, compressed distribution format. It allows customization on a variety of axes: inclusion/exclusion by source and term type, semantic type, language, content view, etc. It permits reorganizing the ranking precedence of the different sources that contribute meaning to concepts. Users can also modify the suppressibility of concept names that might not be useful, or even harmful, in their applications. It comes with input and output handlers for a variety of formats. It provides load scripts to allow the Metathesaurus and Semantic Network data for subsets to be loaded into a database management system. It is designed with an open, extensible architecture so users can define custom filters to include or exclude either whole concepts or constituent elements of concepts in predictable ways.

Included as part of MetamorphoSys is a browser application that can be used to browse the custom subsets of the Metathesaurus created. The browser can display reports for concepts searched for in a variety of ways: by concept unique identifier, by code, or by words in the concept names. Both the search and display can be constrained by source, semantic type, and content view. There is an integrated tree browser that allows users to navigate the hierarchies of all sources that provide contexts.

RxNorm

RxNorm is a standardized nomenclature for clinical drugs. RxNorm, and its associated contributing vocabularies, address an important issue in supporting interoperability that could not be addressed by the traditional means of building the Metathesaurus. Unlike other portions of the Metathesaurus, RxNorm deals with the problem of unrecognized synonymy by establishing standard, normalized, names for the clinical drugs, defined as ingredients and strengths provided in a dosage form. Each drug has a name created using a standard methodology, with controlled segments, and with defined relationships to other concepts in RxNorm. The names are created by reviewing the names within one of the source vocabularies, and then using the information in that name and source to create the standard name, asserting synonymy between that source vocabulary name and the created name.

In response to the perceived need for frequent updates to clinical drug information, RxNorm provides monthly releases of all of its source vocabularies, together with the standard names created in the RxNorm system, with more frequent releases of new additions. The file formats are essentially identical to that of the Metathesaurus. Identifiers from the Metathesaurus are consistent with the identifiers in the current extant version of the Metathesaurus. At the time of release of the Metathesaurus, the next (usually simultaneous) release of RxNorm is consistent with the new release.

CONCLUSION

The NLM produces and distributes the UMLS, consisting of multipurpose, electronic Knowledge Sources and associated software tools for system developers and researchers in the fields of biomedicine and health. The unique characteristics, large scale, and regular update schedule of the UMLS resources have promoted their heavy use in wide range of information retrieval, natural language processing, data creation, and decision support applications.

BIBLIOGRAPHY

1. Additional information and documentation may be found. Available at http://umls.nlm.nih.gov.

GENERAL BACKGROUND

1. Bodenreider, O. The Unified Medical Language System (UMLS): Integrating biomedical terminology. Nucleic Acids Res. **2004**, January 1 *32*, D267–D270 (Database issue).
2. Campbell, K.E.; Oliver, D.E.; Spackman, K.A.; Shortliffe, E.H. Representing thoughts, words, and things in the UMLS. J. Am. Med. Inform. Assoc. **1998**, September–October *5* (5), 421–431.
3. Humphreys, B.L.; Lindberg, D.A.; Schoolman, H.M.; Barnett, G.O. The Unified Medical Language System: An informatics research collaboration. J. Am. Med. Inform. Assoc. **1998**, January–February *5*(1), 1–11.

4. Lindberg, D.A.; Humphreys, B.L.; McCray, A.T. The unified medical language system. Methods Inf. Med. **1993**, August *32*(4), 281–91.

5. McCray, A.T.; Razi, A.M.; Bangalore, A.K.; Browne, A.C.; Stavri, P.Z. The UMLS Knowledge Source Server: A versatile Internet-based research tool. Proc. AMIA Annu. Fall Symp. **1996**, 164–168.

THE SPECIALIST LEXICON AND NATURAL LANGUAGE PROCESSING

1. Browne, A.C.; Divita, G.; Aronson, A.R.; McCray, A.T. UMLS language and vocabulary tools. AMIA Annu. Symp. Proc. **2003**, 798.

2. Divita, G.; Browne, A.C.; Rindflesch, T.C. Evaluating lexical variant generation to improve information retrieval. Proc. AMIA Annu. Fall Symp. **1998**, 775–779.

3. McCray, A.T. The nature of lexical knowledge. Methods Inf. Med. **1998**, November *37*(4–5), 353–360.

4. McCray, A.T.; Browne, A.C. Discovering the modifiers in a terminology data set. Proc. AMIA Annu Fall Symp. **1998**, 780–784.

5. McCray, A.T.; Srinivasan, S.; Browne, A.C. Lexical methods for managing variation in biomedical terminologies. Proc. Annu. Symp. Comput. Appl. Med. Care **1994**, 235–239.

6. McCray, A.T.; Loane, R.F.; Browne, A.C.; Bangalore, A.K. Terminology issues in user access to Web-based medical information. Proc AMIA Annu. Fall Symp. **1999**, 107–111.

SEMANTICS OF THE METATHESAURUS

1. Hole, W.T.; Srinivasan, S. Discovery of missed synonymy in a large concept-oriented Metathesaurus. Proc. AMIA Annu. Fall Symp. **2000**, 354–358.

2. McCray, A.T.; Nelson, S.J. The representation of meaning in the UMLS. Methods Inf. Med **1995**, March *34*(1–2), 193–201.

3. Nelson, S.J.; Tuttle, M.S.; Cole, W.G.; Sherertz, D.D.; Sperzel, W.D.; Erlbaum, M.S.; Fuller, L.L.; Olson, N.E. From meaning to term: Semantic locality in the UMLS Metathesaurus. Proc. Annu. Symp. Comput. Appl. Med. Care **1991**, 209–213.

4. Tuttle, M.S.; Cole, W.G.; Sherertz, D.D.; Nelson, S.J. Navigating to knowledge. Methods Inf. Med **1995**, March *34*(1–2), 214–31.

THE SEMANTIC NETWORK

1. McCray, A.T. UMLS semantic network. Proc. Annu. Symp. Comput. Appl. Med. Care **1989**, 503–507.

2. McCray, A.T.; Hole, W.T. The scope and structure of the first version of the UMLS semantic network. Proc. Annu. Symp. Comput. Appl. Med. Care **1990**, 126–133.

3. Tuttle, M.S.; Nelson, S.J.; Fuller, L.F.; Sherertz, D.D.; Erlbaum, M.S.; Sperzel, W.D.; Olson, N.E.; Suarez-Munist, O.N. The semantic foundations of the UMLS Metathesaurus. Medinfo **1992**, 1506–1511.

RxNorm

1. Nelson, S.J. Drug Information at the National Library of Medicine 43rd Annual Meeting of Drug Information Association Atlanta, GA June, 19, 2007. Available at http://www.nlm.nih.gov/mesh/presentations/DIA2007_drug_information/index.htm.

2. Nelson, S.J.; Brown, S.H.; Erlbaum, M.S.; Olson, N.; Powell, T.; Carlsen, Brian Carter, John Tuttle, M.S.; Hole, W.T. A semantic normal form for clinical drugs in the UMLS: Early experiences with the VANDF*Bio*Medical Informatics: One Discipline*, Proceedings of the Annual Symposium of the American Medical Informatics Association San Antonio, TX November, 9–13, 2002; Kohane, I.S., Ed.; Hanley & Belfus, Inc.: Philadelphia, PA, 2002; 557–561.

Uniform Computer Information Transactions Act (UCITA)

Sarah K. Wiant
School of Law, Washington and Lee University, Lexington, Virginia, U.S.A.

Abstract

The Uniform Computer Information Transactions Act (UCITA) is an attempt to conform state law relating to software and information licensing to a uniform national standard. UCITA began as a proposed revision to the Uniform Commercial Code (UCC). For more than 10 years the National Conference of Commissioners on Uniform State Laws (NCCUSL) and the American Law Institute (ALI) debated the merits of various proposals to cover the licensing of software and information, including the proposal UCC 2B, but were unable to agree on a solution. In May 1999, the ALI withdrew its support after concluding that the UCC 2B approach was flawed. Despite opposition from the ALI and dozens of educational, library, and consumer groups, NCCUSL ratified the model legislation in July of 1999, renamed it UCITA, and sent it to the states for enactment without either the endorsement of the ALI or a review by the American Bar Association. UCITA enjoys strong support among the high-technology community including large software companies like Microsoft and Internet companies like AOL. UCITA has also met with stiff opposition throughout its 10 years history. Critics have expressed concerns about its wide-reaching scope, its effect on existing copyright and consumer protection laws, and its questionable fit with the First Amendment. These and other issues, such as its favorable treatment of choice of law and forum clauses and the difficulty of meeting its standard of unconscionability, have resulted in its failure to gain acceptance in most states. Courts are still trying to resolve many of these issues today. The overall trend appears to be toward enforcement of shrink-wrap license agreements when the licensee has an opportunity to review the terms and accept or reject them. Thus, in spite of NCCUSL's failure to gain wide acceptance of UCITA, decisions by the courts could ultimately have a similar impact on the way information transactions are viewed.

INTRODUCTION

The Uniform Computer Information Transactions Act (UCITA) is an attempt to conform state law relating to software and information licensing to a uniform national standard. Specifically, the legislation was drafted to address the problem of "shrink-wrap" software licenses, which bind consumers to their tenets as a condition of use. Often this term generically encompasses "click-through," "active click wrap," and "browse-wrap" licenses, which accompany much of the information found online. Unlike shrink-wrap licenses, which take their name from the plastic they are often printed on, click-through, active click wrap, and browse-wrap licenses exist only electronically. They typically appear on the monitor as a condition of accessing information or installing software. Most users agree to these conditions as a matter of course, without stopping to read or consider their restrictions. Although licenses such as these have become commonplace, some courts have hesitated to enforce them. Disparate judicial treatment of these agreements led to an attempt to standardize the law relating to them.

HISTORY

UCITA[1] began as a proposed revision to the Uniform Commercial Code (UCC). Most states have adopted the UCC or some version of it, and it is generally considered the most influential source of contract law in the United States. It is drafted by two groups, the American Law Institute (ALI)[2] composed of some 3000 elected judges, law professors, and lawyers and the National Conference of Commissioners on Uniform State Laws (NCCUSL),[3] an organization comprised of approximately 300 lawyers, judges, and law professors appointed by states as commissioners. If both organizations approve a revision, it is then generally reviewed by the American Bar Association (ABA) before being submitted to each state government for adoption. Each state then enacts the proposed section or selected provisions, and those enactments become the law of that state.

For more than 10 years the two groups debated the merits of various proposals to cover the licensing of software and information, including the proposal UCC 2B, but were unable to agree on a solution. Current law is based on transactions of tangible goods. Both sides saw a need for

Encyclopedia of Library and Information Sciences, Fourth Edition DOI: 10.1081/E-ELIS4-120043970

consistent and clear uniform rules for transactions involving software and information. In May 1999, the ALI withdrew its support after concluding that the UCC 2B approach was flawed.[4] Despite opposition from the ALI and dozens of educational, library, and consumer groups, NCCUSL ratified the model legislation in July of 1999, renamed it UCITA, and sent it to the states for enactment without either the endorsement of the ALI or a review by the ABA.

The model legislation has been studied by or introduced to at least 27 state legislatures, but only Virginia and Maryland have enacted it. Although Virginia, in 2000, was first to enact this legislation, a compromise was struck by the General Assembly that delayed the effective date of UCITA in Virginia until July 1, 2001, allowing for a year of study and amendment.[5] Maryland, the only other state to enact this legislation, set an effective date of October 1, 2000.[6]

UCITA enjoys strong support among the high-technology community including large software companies like Microsoft and Internet companies like AOL. They support a free market where the parties choose models that support their transactions. It is opposed, however, by diverse groups, such as the Americans for Fair Electronic Commerce (AFFECT) which includes a coalition of library associations, newspaper and magazine publishers, insurance companies, and small engineering and software companies.[7] A number of state Attorneys General signed a letter to NCCUSL expressing reservations about the proposed legislation.[8]

Because of the controversial nature of the model legislation and the hearings and debates by numerous states, the matter was brought to the ABA. At its 2001 annual meeting, the ABA appointed a task force comprised of representatives from both sides of the debate to study further UCITA. On January 31, 2002, the ABA published a report of its findings on UCITA.[9] Although the ABA acknowledged that UCITA is a worthy goal, and some measure of uniform regulations are needed for computer transactions, the ABA believed UCITA to be inadequate and too convoluted.[10] NCCUSL responded with several amendments in 2002, however, these amendments failed to adopt some key ABA recommendations, including a requirement for pretransaction disclosure of terms.[11] Anticipating rejection of these amendments, in February 2003 NCCUSL withdrew its resolution before it was voted on by the ABA House of Delegates.[12] Without ABA support, in August of 2003 NCCUSL discharged the UCITA Standby Committee and announced that no further resources would be expended to promote UCITA.[13] The debate has been spirited on both sides.

UCITA CONCERNS

UCITA has met with stiff opposition throughout its 10 years history. Critics have expressed concerns about its wide-reaching scope, its effect on existing copyright and consumer protection laws, and its questionable fit with the First Amendment. These and other issues, such as its favorable treatment of choice of law and forum clauses and the difficulty of meeting its standard of unconscionability, have resulted in its failure to gain acceptance in most states. Courts are still trying to resolve many of these issues today.

Scope

This controversial legislation would have a profound effect on library operations because the definitions of information and computer information in UCITA cover just about everything. Information is defined as "data, text, images, sounds, mask works or computer programs, including collections and compilations of them."[14] Computer information is defined as information in an electronic form which is obtained from or through the use of a computer or which is in a form capable of being processed by a computer. The term includes a copy of the information and any documentation package associated with the copy.[15] These definitions include most information a library acquires, although UCITA excludes traditional written forms such as books. Only software and information in electronic format is covered, so a book on CD-ROM would be covered.

Two types of licenses are considered: mass-market licenses and specific one-on-one licenses. Mass-market licenses are those such as general retail or consumer licenses. They are nonnegotiated licenses. The specific one-on-one contracts are usually aimed at industry and are also covered. UCITA is the default when contracts are nonnegotiated or fail to address an issue. A UCITA license could allow content providers to bypass many of the protections traditionally afforded by the public law of copyright, and will likely replace it with the private law of contracts, becoming the central body of law governing information transactions. It gives greater power to copyright holders to write agreements restricting the use of their products.

Copyright and Software Licenses

Public policy

The Copyright Act of 1976 struck a careful balance, granting protection to authors in exchange for certain public uses of their works.[16] Authors and other content providers are enabled by UCITA to contract around the important public uses guaranteed by copyright law. The statute would validate shrink-wrap and click-through licenses that would restrict uses by libraries allowed by federal copyright law. Libraries most rely on the following sections of the Copyright Act to carry on their day-to-day activities: section 109 of the Copyright Act establishes the first sale doctrine as a result of which libraries can lend, sell, or otherwise distribute materials they have purchased; section 107 permits fair use on which libraries rely to make and distribute certain copies; and, section 108—the exemptions for libraries and archives—provides for preservation, lending, and interlibrary loan.

The first sale doctrine, set out in section 109 of the Copyright Act of 1976, terminates the rights of the author in the work after its initial sale, and allows the new owner, such as a library, to resell, dispose of, display, and make use of newly purchased content. Many functions, such as lending, browsing, and resale are triggered by the first sale of the work. More specifically, section 109 permits a nonprofit library or a nonprofit educational institution to lend software for nonprofit purposes.[17] Because UCITA allows authors and publishers to license their works instead of selling them, no sale occurs, and the protections afforded under the first sale doctrine never ripen. Critics of UCITA argue that it limits rights of users to sell or transfer licensed software effectively overturning the Copyright Act's first sale doctrine.

In the absence of a sale, the right to sell or transfer licensed information remains with the author or his designee. The author of the work may impose restrictions on lending or reselling the information. Additionally, licenses last only for a finite period, driving costs higher as libraries repeatedly pay for access to the same information. The archival function of libraries could be severely curtailed: the expiration of the license may terminate access to the information, and any right to make archival copies could be limited by the terms of the license.

Even core values such as fair use are threatened by UCITA. Shrink-wrap and click-through licenses allow vendors to condition access to information on acceptance of the terms of an agreement. To access information, end users may have to agree to not reproduce the material. The fair use exemption on which educators rely for classroom[18] and reserve[19] copying may be in jeopardy. Moreover, copying done by individuals for purposes allowed under fair use of the Copyright Act[20] such as copying for research and criticism also may be limited by shrink-wrap and click-through licenses. Although fair use would remain a defense to any copyright claim, the publisher could prevail on any claim based on the contract, rendering the copyright defense moot.

Libraries and archives fear that clauses in a UCITA contract would allow vendors to dictate limitations on rights otherwise available to them to conduct business. For example, without negotiation, interlibrary loans could be prohibited and remote access to information by students, faculty, and researchers could be limited by license terms. Such limitations would be particularly aggravating when the supplemental information to a book is supplied on a CD that may be loaned under section 108 of the Copyright Act,[21] but may not be loaned with its companion book under a clause pursuant to UCITA.[22] A license

could also limit copying to preclude the copies allowed for preservation purposes or even backup.

The Copyright Act exemptions allow users and libraries to make copies under restricted conditions without seeking permission and/or without paying royalties. These limitations were carved out of the copyright holder's exclusive rights based on public policies to encourage creativity. State laws like UCITA supplement federal intellectual property laws and policies, but in many ways they may impose new business models. The issue is the extent to which federal preemption controls.

The relationship between preemption under the federal copyright act of a state law that is equivalent to a right granted under copyright law and state contract law, which varies the effect of section 301 of the Copyright Act, is unclear.[23] The legal issues are extremely complicated and are unresolved. Section 105 of UCITA speaks of the relation to federal law and fundamental public policy:

§ 105 Relation to Federal Law; Fundamental Public Policy; Transactions Subject to Other State Law.

(a) A provision of this [Act] which is preempted by federal law is unenforceable to the extent of the preemption.

(b) If a term of a contract violates a fundamental public policy, the court may refuse to enforce the contract, enforce the remainder of the contract without the impermissible term, or limit the application of the impermissible term so as to avoid a result contrary to public policy, in each case to the extent that the interest in enforcement is clearly outweighed by a public policy against enforcement of the term...[24]

As written, UCITA provides that if a federal law invalidates a state contract law or contract term, federal law controls. Section 105(a) refers to preemption but no general preemption of contracting issues arises under the copyright law.[25] The model legislation does not specify when federal preemption may occur. Under section 105 of UCITA a court may refuse to enforce a contract if it violates fundamental public policy.[26]

The commentary accompanying UCITA addresses the complexity of the problem, however, it leaves the broader issue to be resolved by a different body.[27] Courts may follow the analysis set out in the commentary but are not required to do so. A contract may, however, be unenforceable because of federal preemption based on public policy. The issue is whether courts will consider fair use a fundamental public policy.

Public policies attempt to balance competing interests and define the allocation of risks between parties to prevent undesirable results that occur due to unequal bargaining power and strengths between parties. For example, the copyright law gives a creator a limited exclusive right to control the work for a finite term of protection and an incentive to create it.[28] Society gains the benefit of using the work after the limitation expires and the work becomes part of the public domain. The public also gains restricted access during the term of protection through exemptions to the exclusive rights based on public policy. Public policies apply to everyone. In contrast, contract law often allows the contracting parties to circumvent the balance stuck by public policies. This competing value is known as "freedom of contract."[29]

While there are circumstances in which contracting around a public policy results in a socially and economically desirable result, when the circumstance does not permit negotiation, such as with a standard form contract, it is of substantial concern. Transactions costs may be minimized, but the end result for the nondrafting party may be a waiver of rights. Licensing terms for mass-market retail or online information products such as those used by libraries can "limit access to and use of electronic materials, prohibit making copies of materials for archiving or preservation or prevent interlibrary loan, or prohibit the transfer or donation of electronic products."[30]

National library amendment

Library groups in opposition offered an amendment that would replace existing section 105(b) with proposed 105 (b)(1) and (2). The proposed amendment would allow parties to contract around public policies in a negotiated contract, facilitating commerce in the way that the drafters of UCITA envisioned, but would prevent the drafting party from imposing overreaching licenses in a standard form contract that favor the drafter, thus maintaining the benefit of public policies when the licensee has virtually no negotiating power. In some instances, a party might be willing to give up fair use rights. The proposed language, however, would have limited the broader effect of standard form contracts that might severely limit the ability to cite, criticize, reverse engineer, or otherwise use these works to society's benefit.[31] The proposed amendment attempted to balance the laissez-faire drafters, who would permit a new business model to try anything, with a certainty of social benefits to protect weaker parties. Unfortunately, none of these proposed changes have been adopted.

Some authorities in attempting to redress the imbalance between the freedom of contract of private property rights and the public good uses of information propose strict scrutiny of socially questionable terms and offer a doctrine of "public-interest unconscionability."[32] Undoubtedly, the enforcement of negotiated contractual agreements is a "fundamental public policy." The question is how to handle agreements that arise from standard form contracts of adhesion. One way is to respect the traditional balance of public/private interests; the other way is to submit standard form contracts to a high level of scrutiny proposed by the public-interest unconscionability doctrine.[33]

Virginia libraries amendment

During the year of study between the enactment and the effective date of UCITA in Virginia, the Virginia Library Association, concerned that UCITA would preclude the lending of a CD-ROM of information, perhaps even the supplement to a companion book, persuaded the General Assembly to amend the legislation to allow nonprofit libraries and archives to lend tangible copies (CD-ROMs) under restrictive conditions.[34] NCCUSL met with members of the library community in the hope that language could be negotiated to become an amendment to the model version of UCITA that could be submitted to other states.

The statute permits a qualified library or institution to make a tangible copy available to users for course reserves or ordinary lending, including interlibrary loan; to copy for archival and preservation purposes; and to make use of the copy for classroom purposes.[35] The amendment applies to conduct that is "not otherwise unlawful or restricted under the Copyright Act..." This arguably includes any act undertaken by a library under fair use or any other exemption that allows libraries, archives, and nonprofit educational institutions to carry out their missions; all of these exemptions are restrictions under the Copyright Act. Next, the statute provides that the standard form contract covers the use of a tangible copy of information content to a licensee. The question is whether a user must first determine if the shrink-wrap or the click-through license is a standard form contract. The benefit of this exemption is surprisingly not limited to a nonprofit library or archive or a nonprofit educational institution. Initially, the drafts included a very restrictive definition of libraries that would not include museums or government agency or court libraries, but after much debate between NCCUSL representatives and members of the library community, a clause was added to clarify that the "terms nonprofit library, archive or educational institution have the same meaning as used in section 108, 109, 110 of the Copyright Act, 17 U.S.C. §§ 108, 109, and 110."[36]

Much of the library community viewed the Virginia amendment as too restrictive and withdrew their support as a national amendment.[37] The Virginia Association of Law Libraries (VALL) had several problems with the language offered to libraries, but because of the concern that opposition might affect funding for public libraries and other institutions it remained neutral during the legislative session.[38] VALL, in particular, objected to the amendment's narrow application to only tangible copies obtained by libraries, such as CD-ROMs, at a time when publishers are moving away from tangible products towards the online environment. It does not apply to online databases or to other content distributed directly over the Internet, therefore, providing only a short-term benefit, if any.[39] Worse, it could be read to restrict further rights that otherwise are available under copyright law. By specifying which uses can be made of tangible copies, the statute could be read to prohibit all other uses.

The amendment permits the copyright holder to vary the terms of the license providing that the change in terms is conspicuous, that the library manifests assent to the changes, or that the library knew or had reason to know that the terms would follow when it ordered a copy.[40] There are numerous problems with this part of the statute. There is no definition of conspicuous. Although authorities have debated manifestation of assent, there is generally no accepted definition for behavior that would constitute assent. Because staff, who may have little or no training in issues of intellectual property law, open most material received by libraries, by opening the package their behavior may constitute assent. Moreover, the software often must be loaded and run before the terms can even be reviewed. Loading software may or may not be a sufficient manifestation of assent. Any action taken by staff, regardless of their authority to bind the organization to an acquisition in an online environment, may authorize the license. Must the terms appear on the home page of a site or is it legally adequate to post a button on the page that would take the user to a screen with terms and conditions for use? Must a user click "I agree" in order to manifest assent? Most authorities recommend that the user be required to agree to the terms and conditions by taking some type of formal step such as clicking "I agree" before being bound by them. Again, staff who are unaware of the legal consequences may undertake the initial step of adding material to the collection by using the site, by bypassing the click button, or even by clicking "I agree."

The library has a right to return the software in the same manner that a library could return a book that upon inspection was found inappropriate for the collection.

Finally, the Virginia statute does not alter the general burden of proof in an infringement, contract, or other action. The Virginia library amendment does nothing to clarify the relationship between a contract that violates a public policy, including whether such policy is under the federal copyright law, and one that does not.[41]

Consumer Protection and Warranties

A UCITA license will affect more than copyright law. It will fundamentally change the way consumers interact with software and information vendors. Because libraries are among the largest consumers of software and digital information, the language in licenses is critical to users. Several provisions of UCITA illustrate how this legislation reshapes the relationship between information consumers and information vendors. Some of these sections create doubts about whether software transactions are covered by consumer protection laws.

Despite the lack of opportunity to review the terms of a license, a licensee may be bound by "manifesting assent" to the terms. Section 112 defines how a person or an electronic agent manifests assent and includes formation of a contract by double-clicking after payment and delivery.[42] This section coupled with Section 208, which provides that the terms of a record become the terms of the contract if the party manifests assent[43] to the terms, permits vendors to impose potentially restrictive terms on use of information postpurchase or to impose additional costs by requiring return of goods rather than preacquisition presentation of terms. There are no presale reviews of the product.

Under a shrink-wrap or click-through license subject to this legislation, vendors could unilaterally modify the terms of a contract during its operation.[44] Such a modification could be viewed as accepted by the licensee by their continued use of the software or information. Courts likely will enforce the modified contract unless it is "manifestly unreasonable." This is one of the most pernicious part of the model legislation and opponents view it as the worst kind of bait and switch to lure consumers to the product. In the context of mass-market sales of software in a box in a store, it is not feasible to disclose the entire license prior to the sale of the software; however, it makes no sense to permit postassent contractual modifications to a click-through license.

In spite of the 2002 amendments, which provide that state consumer protection laws apply when a license is otherwise silent on the matter, UCITA permits copyright holders to include clauses in their licenses that disclaim warranties and liabilities. The model legislation immunizes software and information providers from liability when the software they provide is "flawed" or "buggy." Vendors are afforded similar protection when the documentation is inadequate or incorrect. The provision allows a vendor to sell "as is" even when the vendor knows of the defects and fails to disclose the problem to the user.[45] A licensee will have the benefit of an implied license only when it undertakes a reasonable inspection that fails to reveal the defect. Moreover, the Virginia version of UCITA states that the occasional failure to provide service does not constitute a breach of contract.[46] This leaves libraries and other subscribers to online databases without a remedy when online services are inaccessible to their patrons.

A self-help provision[47] that allowed software or content providers to remotely disable software if they had reason to believe that a licensee was in violation of its license agreement was particularly controversial. Late payments or perceived misuse of a product were deemed just cause to trigger the self-help provisions. A vendor could disable the software even for an unknowing and minor infraction of the license. The model legislation was redrafted to require reasonable notice before this remedy could be effected.[48] Although the 2002 Amendments banned "electronic self-help," the problem still exists because the statute permits "electronic regulation of performance," which is essentially the same thing. These measures could further complicate the mission of libraries because electronic products may disappear at the expiration of the term of the license. The disappearance of information without notice could hamper preservation activities.

Finally, UCITA legitimizes e-mail, recognizing communications by this method for the purposes of contracting and legal notice.[49] While this is a laudable goal, the statute falls short by failing to require that the addressee actually read the message. Electronic mail notification is recognized if the message is properly addressed and received. Messages thwarted by full in-boxes or buggy e-mail are just as effective as messages properly delivered.

First Amendment Issues

Even traditional First Amendment principles such as fair comment are called into question by the UCITA statute. Access to software or information may be conditioned on a licensed agreement that says the software package or information cannot be reviewed or critiqued by a magazine or newspaper without the permission of the vendor. This would allow a vendor to preclude public comment or criticism of the product by preventing negative reviews from appearing in print to the detriment of users and potential purchasers of the information or software; however, in July 2002, NCCUSL amended this section so that vendors will no longer be able to silence critics through contract.[50] Provisions that prohibit users, in most cases, from reverse engineering a product are permitted by UCITA. Users may be allowed to reverse engineer for interoperability.

Choice of Forum/Choice of Law

Under a UCITA contract the licensor may designate the forum, generally the state in which the software producer is located, in which any issues would be litigated, making it inconvenient if not impossible for the licensee to resolve the issue. In other cases, the licensor may not designate the state where the issues will be litigated, but may designate instead the body of law that the court must consider.[51] It is likely that such licenses will designate a body of state law that includes UCITA with its clauses favorable to the producers. Venue and choice of law clauses may render some state contracts unenforceable. For the resolution of conflicts between state institutions such as colleges and universities or public libraries and licensors, jurisdiction must be within the state. Typically a state agent authorized to bind the state cannot enter into a contract that specifies the law of another state as controlling. For others, these sections continue to present significant issues.

Some states that considered the enactment of UCITA found these provisions particularly objectionable and passed "bomb-shelter" legislation to protect the residents of their state. For example, North Carolina legislators passed language that provides.

§ 66-329 Choice of Law in Computer Information Agreement.

A choice of law provision in a computer information agreement which provides that the contract is to be interpreted pursuant to the laws of a state that has enacted the UCITA, as proposed by the NCCUSL, or any substantially similar law, is voidable and the agreement shall be interpreted pursuant to the laws of this state if the party against whom enforcement of the choice of law provisions is sought is a resident of this state or has its principal place of business located in this state. For purposes of this section, a "computer information agreement" means an agreement that would be governed by the UCITA or substantially similar law as enacted in the state specified in the choice of law provisions if that state's law were applied to the agreement. This section may not be varied by agreement of the parties. This section shall remain in force until such time as the North Carolina General Assembly enacts the UCITA or any substantially similar law and that law becomes effective.[52]

This poison-pill type of legislation has been passed or considered by states that do not have to appease technology industries.[53] It protects the interests of the citizens of the state while giving UCITA time to prove that it is working in Virginia and Maryland.

Although support for UCITA has declined, narrower efforts at reform have simultaneously been underway. One such effort resulted in recent amendments to UCC Article 1 regarding, among other things, choice of law.[54] Previously, contracts containing choice of law provisions had to bear a "reasonable relation" to the designated state whose law would govern.[55] The revision, however, gives greater autonomy to the parties by providing that choice of law clauses can be upheld "whether or not the transaction bears a relation to the State designated…."[56] Because courts currently rely on the UCC for transactions in computer information, if adopted by the states, this change could have a similar impact as that proposed by UCITA. Of the 28 states that have adopted the Article 1 amendments, however, all have rejected this particular change and have chosen to use alternate wording which maintains some form of the "reasonable relation" requirement.

Unreasonable Standard Amendment

The standard for unconscionability proposed by the drafters of UCITA in Section 111 requires that a term must "shock the conscience" to be void on any ground other than public policy under section 105. This is a very high legal standard. AFFECT proposed a change from an unconscionable standard to an unconscionable or unexpected standard for determining whether a term within a standard form contract is valid.

Section 111. Unconscionable or Unexpected Contract or Term

(a) If a court as a matter of law finds a contract or a term thereof to have been unconscionable or to have frustrated the reasonable expectations of the nondrafting party at the time it was made, the court may refuse to enforce the contract, enforce the remainder of the contract without the unconscionable or unexpected term, or limit the application of the unconscionable or unexpected term so as to avoid an unconscionable or unexpected result.

(b) If it is claimed or appears to the court that a contract or term thereof may be unconscionable or unexpected, the parties must be afforded a reasonable opportunity to present evidence as to its commercial setting, purpose, and effect to aid the court in making the determination.[57]

A standard form contract under UCITA, however, may include a surprising term that does not reach the level of a public policy concern. The statute as drafted does not address this situation. The reasonable expectations standard is more appropriate than the unconscionability standard in a standard form contract under UCITA because it facilitates evaluation of the term from the perspective of the nondrafting party. The term does not necessarily need to "shock the conscience." The library community believes that many, if not all, unconscionable terms, by definition, would frustrate the reasonable expectations of the nondrafting party.[58]

COURTS AND RELATED LEGISLATION

Fear of the unknown causes publishers to include restrictive language. The last thing either side wants is litigation. UCITA offers a new legal framework by which libraries and educational institutions would acquire and use information, and which would affect the ability of these organizations to carry out their missions. However, because of the many controversial and unresolved issues surrounding UCITA, it has been enacted in only two states.

In the absence of a legal template such as UCITA, courts have relied on existing copyright and intellectual property law, industry norms, and the UCC in dealing with computer information transactions. Although the United States Supreme Court has yet to provide any definitive ruling, several lower courts have heard cases arising from shrink-wrap or click-wrap license agreements. These cases present two central issues. First, whether shrink-wrap and click-wrap licenses are enforceable generally or, alternatively, should be treated as unenforceable contracts of adhesion. Second, if licenses are found to be enforceable, whether particular terms of the license which override traditional copyright exemptions, such as the

doctrines of fair use and first sale, are enforceable. Courts remain divided on the first issue of general enforceability. Some decisions, such as *Meridian Project Systems, Inc. v. Hardin Construction Company, LLC*, 426 F. Supp. 2d 1101 (E.D. Cal. 2006), uphold licenses.[59] Others, such as *Wachter Management Company v. Dexter & Chaney, Inc.*, 144 P.3d 747 (Kan. 2006), find such licenses to be unenforceable under the UCC.[60]

Two early decisions from the U.S. Court of Appeals for the Fifth and Seventh Circuits take opposing positions with regard to the second issue. In *Vault Corporation v. Quaid Software Ltd.*, 847 F.2d 255 (5th Cir. 1988), the court determined that shrink-wrap license terms which prohibited the copying of a computer software program were preempted by a Copyright Act limitation on the exclusive rights of the program's creator.[61] In *ProDC, Inc. v. Zeidenberg*, 86 F.3d 1447 (7th Cir. 1996), however, the court concluded that the agreed-to terms of a shrink-wrap license under state law are not preempted by federal copyright law.[62] In recent years, in cases where the license is held to be enforceable generally, courts are usually in agreement with *ProCD* regarding preemption. The overall trend appears to be toward enforcement of shrink-wrap license agreements when, whether made available before or after purchase, the licensee has an opportunity to review the terms and accept or reject them. Thus, in spite of NCCUSL's failure to gain wide acceptance of UCITA, decisions by the courts could ultimately have a similar impact on the way information transactions are viewed.

A recent amendment to the UCC adds to the difficulty courts face. Traditionally, courts have applied UCC standards to transactions that involve a mix of goods and information and, in some instances, those that deal solely with information. This is because the UCC is well established and, for the most part, consistent across all states. In 2004, however, NCCUSL and ALI amended UCC Article 2 to explicitly exclude information from the definition of "goods" covered by the UCC.[63] Such a change could be problematic because it directs courts to discontinue application of the UCC in pure information transactions, and creates doubt about its applicability in mixed transactions, without providing a framework to replace it. Because most states have not yet adopted this change, its full impact remains to be seen. Currently, most courts continue to interpret the UCC with enough flexibility to govern software and other information-related transactions.[64]

CONCLUSION

The trend is no longer the acquisition of physical copies of information but rather the access to information in a digital format. Libraries are seeing increased use of click-through licenses and shrink-wrap licenses as they acquire digital supplements to traditional products, receive updates to online products, and gain access to new sources. Limiting rights which are otherwise available to libraries and users under the Copyright Act is generally not an issue when such limitations are the result of negotiation between the parties. The problem with UCITA, however, is that it allows for these rights to be limited without notice or agreement by the consumer.

Whatever the direction this area of the law takes, it is clear that librarians and information specialists must learn as much as possible about the issues and be watchful of restrictions applicable to their users and institutions. Users should expect nothing less in a license agreement than rights librarians are urged to ensure in a negotiated agreement.[65] Understanding and complying with licenses will be a cost of doing business. Look to your licenses, print copies of them, and date them. Educate staff and users about terms of use recognizing the copyrights of the licensor and your rights as licensee. Like risk management decisions in determining whether a particular use of a copy is a fair use, reviewing licenses and determining the extent to which you can use the information is a cost of business.

ACKNOWLEDGMENTS

The author wishes to thank her research assistant, Spencer Jarvis, and the Frances Lewis Law Center for its support.

REFERENCES

1. Uniform Computer Information Transactions Act, http://www.law.upenn.edu/bll/archives/ulc/ucita/2002.htm (accessed January 2009).
2. American Law Institute, http://www.ali.org (accessed January 2009).
3. National Commissioners of Uniform State Laws, http://www.nccusl.org/Update/ (accessed January 2009).
4. American Library Association, UCITA History, http://www.ala.org/ala/aboutala/official/wo/woissues/copyright/nata/nata.cfm/ucitaa/05.cfm (accessed January 2009).
5. 2000 Va. Acts chs. 101 and 996.
6. 2000 Md. Laws ch. 11.
7. Americans for Fair Electronic Commercial Transactions, http://www.ucita.com (accessed January 2009).
8. Letter from 13 Attorneys General to NCCUSL Opposing UCITA, http://jamesshuggins.com/h/tek1/ucita_ags_1999 0723_letter.htm and Second letter from 11 more Attorneys General to NCCUSL opposing UCITA, http://www.jamesshuggins.com/h/tek1/ucita_ags_19990728_letter.htm (accessed January 2009).
9. American Bar Association working group report on UCITA, January 31, 2002, http://www.abanet.org/ucita/report_on_ucita.pdf (accessed January 2009).
10. Americans for Fair Electronic Commercial Transactions, *supra* note 7.
11. Amendments to Uniform Information Computer Transactions Act, passed by NCCUSL at its annual meeting in Tucson, AZ between July 26–August 2, 2002. http://www.law.upenn.edu/bll/ulc/ucita/2002act.htm (accessed January 2009).
12. AFFECT celebrates withdrawal of UCITA from ABA consideration http://www.ucita.com/pdf/PressReleasefeb03.pdf (accessed January 2009).
13. UCITA Committee is discharged http://www.nccusl.org/nccusl/DesktopModules/NewsDisplay.aspx?ItemID = 56 (accessed January 2009).
14. Uniform Computer Information Transactions Act § 102 (35), *supra* note 1.
15. Uniform Computer Information Transactions Act § 102 (10), *supra* note 1.
16. 17 U.S.C. §§ 101–1332 (2006).
17. 17 U.S.C. § 109(b)(1)(A) (2006).
18. *Agreement on Guidelines for Classroom Copying in Not-For-Profit Educational Institutions With Respect to Books and Periodicals, H.R. Rep. No. 1476, 94th Cong., 2nd Sess*—reprinted in 17 Omnibus Copyright Revision Legislative History 68–71 (1977).
19. *Library Reserve Guidelines, ALA Model Policy Concerning College and University Photocopying for Classroom Research and Library Reserve Use (1982)*—reprinted in Laura N. Gasaway and Sarah K. Wiant, Libraries and copyright: A guide to copyright law in the 1990's 241 (1994).
20. 17 U.S.C. § 107 (2006).
21. 17 U.S.C. § 108(b) (2006).
22. Uniform Computer Information Transactions Act § 102 Comment 39, *supra* note 1.
23. 17 U.S.C. § 301 (2006).
24. Uniform Computer Information Transactions Act § 105, *supra* note 1.
25. *Nat'l Car Rental Sys., Inc. v. Computer Assocs. Int'l., 991 F.2d 426* (8th Cir. 1993).
26. Uniform Computer Information Transactions Act § 105(b), *supra* note 1.
27. Uniform Computer Information Transactions Act, *supra* note 1.
28. Americans for Fair Electronic Commercial Transactions, *supra* note 7.
29. Id.
30. Id.
31. Id.
32. Reichman, J.H.; Franklin, J.A. Privately legislated intellectual property rights: Reconciling freedom of contract with public good uses of information. Univ. Penn. Law Rev. 1999, *147*, 875. 929–930, 961–964.
33. Id, at 961–964.
34. Virginia Uniform Computer Information Transactions Act, Va. Code Ann. § 59.1–503.10 (2006).
35. Va. Code Ann. § 59.1–503.10(a) (2006).
36. Va. Code Ann. § 59.1–503.10(d) (2006).
37. UCITA on a Fast-Track. Washington Brief, American Association of Law Libraries, February, 2001. http://www.aallnet.org/aallwash/lu022001.asp (accessed January 2009).
38. Virginia Association of Law Libraries, Statement on the "Library Amendment" to Virginia UCITA, March, 2001.

http://aallnet.org/chapter/vall/vallucita.htm (accessed January 2009).

39. Id.

40. Va. Code Ann. § 59.1–503.10(b) (2006).

41. Va. Code Ann. § 59.1–503.10(c) (2006).

42. Uniform Computer Information Transactions Act § 112, *supra* note 1.

43. Uniform Computer Information Transactions Act § 208, *supra* note 1.

44. Uniform Computer Information Transactions Act § 304, *supra* note 1.

45. Uniform Computer Information Transactions Act § 403, *supra* note 1.

46. Va. Code Ann. § 59.1–506.11(b) (2006).

47. Uniform Computer Information Transactions Act § 605, *supra* note 1.

48. Uniform Computer Information Transactions Act § 617, *supra* note 1.

49. Uniform Computer Information Transactions Act § 102 Comment 47, *supra* note 1.

50. Uniform Computer Information Transactions Act § 105, *supra* note 1.

51. Uniform Computer Information Transactions Act § 109, *supra* note 1.

52. N.C. Gen. Stat. § 66–329 (2006).

53. McDonald, B.D. The Uniform Computer Information Transactions Act. Berkeley Tech. L.J. 2001, *16*, 461.

54. Americans for Fair Electronic Commerce Transactions, Proposed Amendment to UCC Article 1-Section 301: Choice of Law. http://www.ucita.com/Legislation.htm#one (accessed January 2009).

55. U.C.C. § 1-105 (2001).

56. U.C.C. § 1-301 (2007).

57. Americans for Fair Electronic Commercial Transactions, *supra* note 7.

58. Id.

59. *Meridian Project Sys., Inc. v. Hardin Constr. Co., LLC,* 426 F. Supp. 2d 1101, 1107 (E.D. Cal. 2006).

60. *Wachter Mgmt. Co. v. Dexter & Chaney, Inc.,* 144 P.3d 747, 751 (Kan. 2006).

61. *Vault Corp. v. Quaid Software Ltd.,* 847 F.2d 255, 261 (5th Cir. 1988).

62. *ProDC, Inc. v. Zeidenberg,* 86 F.3d 1447, 1455 (7th Cir. 1996).

63. U.C.C. § 2-103 (2007).

64. *See, e.g., Wachter Mgmt. Co. v. Dexter & Chaney, Inc.,* 144 P.3d 747, 750 (Kan. 2006) (holding that services provided by vendor were incidental to buyer's purchase of software, and therefore software qualified as "goods" under UCC).

65. Principles of licensing electronic resources. http://www.arl.org/sc/marketplace/license/liprinciples.html (accessed January 2009).

Unions in Public and Academic Libraries

Kathleen de la Peña McCook
School of Library and Information Science, University of South Florida, Tampa, Florida, U.S.A.

Abstract
The role of unions and collective bargaining in U.S. public and academic libraries is stated with a summary of historical development. After noting the lack of national association attention to unionization, the evolution of the American Library Association-Allied Professional Association (ALA-APA) is described. The connection between human rights and unions is discussed. Appendices with URLS of public and academic library worker unions in the United States and Canada as compiled by the author are included.

INTRODUCTION

Unions contribute to a stable, productive workforce—where workers have a say in improving their jobs. Library workers in public, academic, and school libraries have organized in unions for better wages, working conditions, and benefits. In 2006 taken as a whole, U.S. union library workers earned almost 21% more than their nonunion counterparts.[1,2] A stratified sample of 3418 public and academic libraries found the union advantage extends across all library sizes and types. Union membership varied by region from a high of 15.9% in the North Atlantic to a low of 1.9% in the Southeast. This clearly demonstrates the power of unions to raise salaries in the predominantly female, underpaid library world. If wages and salaries are so much higher among unionized library workers, why is union membership—overall, less than 20% of the workforce? There is no simple answer. The field is not monolithic. Academic librarians function in educational settings tied to the fortunes of their colleges or universities and usually—when collective bargaining is in place—to a faculty union. Public librarians work in the public sector in a variety of governmental structures—city, county, district. The professional associations have not placed the betterment of library workers at the center of their agendas as have the American Federation of Teachers (AFT) or the National Education Association (NEA), but have focused on the development of the institution. The largest association in the United States is the American Library Association (ALA), not the American Librarian Association. Nevertheless, many librarians have organized in unions or as part of larger unions. While these may not account for the majority of librarians, they do account for a large number and collective bargaining is an important aspect of the structure of the field's human resource component.

PUBLIC LIBRARIES

The first public library unions were affiliated with the American Federation of Labor (AFL): New York Public Library and the Library of Congress formed in 1917; Boston Public Library and the District of Columbia Public Library formed in 1918 and the Philadelphia Free Library formed in 1919.[3] Bernard Berelson has examined the historical context of these first public library unions and their dissolution. All but the Library of Congress union disbanded by 1929 due to the overwhelming strength of the opposition or poor leadership.[4] Of special note is the debate that took place about the status of women as articulated by union organizer/suffragist Maud Malone of the New York Public Library Employees Union.[5]

In his overview of unionism written for *Library Trends*, "Employee Organization and Collective Bargaining in Libraries," (1976) Herbert Biblo characterized the years 1934–1949 as the second wave of public library unionism.[6,7] The passage of the National Labor Relations Act, (also known as the Wagner Act) in 1935 and the creation of the National Labor Relations Board to regulate collective bargaining fostered organizing. The Cleveland Public Library Employees Union was organized as part of the American Federation of State, County, and Municipal Employees (AFSCME, AFL) in 1937, but became part of the State, County, and Municipal Workers of American (SCMWA, CIO) later that year.

Joyce M. Latham has tracked the State County and Municipal Workers of America, a white-collar CIO union, and in particular the development of the Chicago Public Library's Local 88 (1937)—one of "several unions which emerged as a response to the failure of middle class structures in the face of the economic challenges of the Depression." Latham's work is especially recommended as a thorough and extensive analysis of the origins of public librarians' engagement in challenges to dominant social

Encyclopedia of Library and Information Sciences, Fourth Edition DOI: 10.1081/E-ELIS4-120043805

and cultural constructs during the period of the late 1930s–1940s.[8] Other public library unions founded during this period include Milwaukee, Grand Rapids, Detroit, Minneapolis, Atlanta, Newark, Boston, and Wayne County. Biblo notes that these unions came and went with Atlanta and Grand Rapids never reemerging after their initial organization.

During the 1950s no new public library unions emerged, but in the 1960s a new wave of unionization began with locals formed in Philadelphia, Milwaukee, Boston, Chicago, Cleveland, Detroit, Brooklyn, Buffalo and Erie, Washington, DC, Enoch Pratt, Contra Costa, Los Angeles, New York, Queens, Santa Monica, Youngstown, Oshkosh, Berkeley, Bloomfield, Enfield, Morris County, Newark, Oakland, and San Francisco. Additionally, John F. Kennedy's Executive Order of January 17, 1962 on Employee-management cooperation in the Federal service set the tone for increased labor organizing in governments. At the state level some enacted laws like California's Meyers-Milias-Brown Act passed in 1968 to govern labor relations in local governments. Librarian unionism was documented by Melvin S. Goldstein in his 1968 report on collective bargaining efforts on behalf of professional librarians in the United States which included digests of collective bargaining agreements currently then in force as well as the status of negotiations.[9]

At the 1975 watershed conference, "Collective Bargaining in Libraries," Don Wasserman of AFSCME, presented the context for increased bargaining activity in the public sector and noted that bargaining entered more readily into "mission of the agency," than had blue-collar workers.[10] In his 1975 monograph, *Unionization: The Viewpoint of Librarians*, Theodore Guyton accounted for the emergence of library labor unions, their goals, and their patterns of growth. His study provides a solid overview of unionization grounded in labor history and theory and includes a survey of librarians' attitudes toward unionization.[3]

The high-water mark of library union literature came in 1981 with the publication of *Librarians and Labor Relations* which assessed economics, politics, and history in light of new laws, court decisions, and changing personnel trends. The volume examined librarian-management relations and placed library worker unionizing in the larger context of the labor movement.[11] Doreen Lilore, a former president of a public library local and staff member at AFSCME, wrote an exceptional study of the state of public library unions in 1984 with attention to negotiating the labor agreement, contract administration, analysis of grievance procedures, and a content analysis of public library labor agreements. Her review of the external interaction between the local and management is a major contribution to the history of public library unionism[12] and built on the earlier analysis by Joseph Vignone.[13]

However, after the 1980s the literature and reporting of public library unionism declined. Public sector unions came under much duress after the Professional Air Traffic Controllers Organization (PATCO) strike in 1981 and the Reagan testing of the strength of the labor movement.[14] The ALA focused on issues of pay equity and comparable worth during the 1980s and 1990s, but did not provide a forum for ongoing discussion of labor issues or unions within the association.

Public library workers' unionization issues are very situational and differ greatly from library to library. Much depends on the larger context of unionization in a government jurisdiction. If there is an overall organizing unit of government employees—AFSCME or Service Employees International Union (SEIU)—then library workers might be a part of the larger union. In other cases librarians organize as locals of larger units. While one library might divide workers between librarians and clerical and support workers, another might combine them into one local. Weber's 1992 article on support staff unions in Ohio demonstrates the need for unions to reflect local and state situations. For example, at the time of his article the Toledo-Lucas County Public Library had two unions. Office, clerical, and maintenance employees were represented by the Communication Workers of American and the librarian local under the Marine Engineers Beneficial Association.[15]

In 2002 the journal, *Public Libraries*, published a forum on unions, edited by Hampton (Skip) Auld. The discussion was spurred by the support of some ALA members for striking Marriott hotel workers during the Association's 2001 conference.[16] Ann Sparanese, a public library shop steward and her local's delegate to the County Labor Council, expressed her opinion: "I do think the union helps ensure fairness and respect on the job and is a powerful shield for all employees against a management that would like to act against an employee without doing the necessary homework."[17]

The longest strike in the history of public librarianship—89 days—by the 800 members of CUPE (Canadian Union of Public Employees) 391 of the Vancouver Public Library in summer 2007 was documented in an extensive essay by Anita Galanopoulos. The CUPE 391 strike was for pay equity, improved benefits, rights for part-time and auxiliary workers and better job security/technological change protection. The "Bargaining and Strike Chronology" included on her essay provides a detailed look at the blueprint of a strike.[18]

See Appendix I. for a list of public library unions in the United States and Canada.

ACADEMIC UNIONS

Academic library workers, unlike public library workers, almost never organize as a local within a larger union. Herbert Biblo noted that the Librarian Shop, Howard University, Local 10 UFWA, CIO seems to have been the first collective bargaining agreement to cover an academic library staff in the United States (1945).[6] However, since the beginning of formal collective bargaining involving college faculty academic librarians have participated in faculty bargaining units based on a community of interest.

The three unions that account for the majority of unionized academic librarians are the American Association of University Professors (AAUP), the AFT, and the NEA. Those wishing a foundational study of the growth of the AFT and the NEA should refer to *Blackboard Unions*.[19]

The literature of academic library unionism is scant. Weatherford's 1976 Council on Library Resources study, *Collective Bargaining and the Academic Librarian*, places library bargaining in the context of the national organizations as he summarized the commingled history of academic librarians and classroom faculty. He also underscored the role of faculty status for librarians vis-à-vis the librarians' participation in the bargaining unit.[20,21] In the literature of academic librarianship continued concern over faculty status has seemed to override discussion of collective bargaining issues.[22,23]

At the national level the Association of College and Research Libraries (ACRL) intertwines issues of faculty status and collective bargaining. The policy regarding collective bargaining current as of 2008 is that "academic librarians shall be included on the same basis as their faculty colleagues in units for collective bargaining. Such units shall be guided by the standards and guidelines of ACRL pertaining to faculty and academic status."[24,25]

The most comprehensive source for unionization information about higher education is *The Directory of Faculty Contracts and Bargaining Agents in Institutions of Higher Education* a compilation of every collective bargaining relationship covering faculty in the United States. As of January 2006, over 375,000 faculties had union representation in the United States organized into 575 separate bargaining units and distributed across 491 institutions or systems of higher education with 1125 campuses.[26]

A state of the art of support staff unionization in 1986 and a literature review: *Unions for Academic Library Support Staff* examined unionization at 176 academic libraries.[27] There is no single list of support staff unions in academic libraries. Collective bargaining generally encompasses multiple job classifications on a campus such as AFSCME or SEIU.

The literature of academic librarianship has few discussions of faculty unionism. However, one recent essay, "Librarians as Key Players in Faculty Unions," that describes the role of library faculty at Eastern Washington University provides insight into the articulation of faculty status for librarians and collective bargaining. The essay demonstrates the collegiality developed through teaching and library faculty working toward common goals.[28] More articles that provide a functional analysis of the role of unionism in faculty worklife would contribute to better

understanding of the importance of unions to academic librarians.

A rare program at a national conference sponsored by the American Library Association-Allied Professional Association (ALA-APA) at the ALA Conference in New Orleans on June 25, 2006 addressed the role of unions in academic libraries. John Buschman, one of the presenters, summarized: "unionized library faculty have both rights and responsibilities to the library and its services as a whole, and their sponsoring institution. If the status is meaningful beyond a mere title, then librarians must take the responsibilities and the power they have seriously and utilize them judiciously, and this means going well beyond pleasing the boss."[29]

See Appendix II. For a list of academic library unions in the United States and Canada.

Unions and the ALA

The lack of ALA's focus on unions has been noted by many researchers. After a short-lived Library Union Round Table that existed from 1938 until the 1950s there was no formal entity in the national association that addressed union concern. The ALA's Office for Library Personnel Resources did develop and distribute a packet on Unionization and Collective Bargaining in 1982 as part of that Office's overall commitment to library personnel issues under the stewardship of Margaret Myers.[30] A search of the ALA's archives turns up very little information about library unions and collective bargaining.

The election of Maurice J. Freedman as president of the ALA in 2001 saw a new focus on library worklife. Freedman established a Special Presidential Task Force on Better Salaries and Pay Equity. As part of this initiative the Task Force published the "Advocating for Better Salaries and Pay Equity Toolkit" coordinated by Margaret Myers, retired director of ALA's Office for Library Personnel Resources that included contact information for and links to unions, FAQs on unions in libraries, and a sample neutrality agreement.[31] This work led to the formation of the Library Advisory Committee to the AFSCME and a Library Workers Caucus. The union working group also connected with SEIU, which reported on the relative pay and benefits of union and nonunion library workers.[32]

With the ALA climate for considering library worklife issues changing in the twenty-first century the ALA-APA was established in June 2001 as a companion organization to the ALA. The ALA-APA is a nonprofit organization for the purpose of promoting "the mutual professional interests of librarians and other library workers." It enables certification of individuals in specializations beyond the initial professional degree and also has the charge of advocacy for the "mutual professional interests of librarians and other library workers."

The union subcommittee of ALA-APA is charged: 1) to investigate the extent of the presence and role of unions among library workers; 2) to report findings to the ALA-APA Standing Committee on the Salaries and Status of Library Workers; 3) to work towards the initiation of a relationship and dialogue among ALA, ALA-APA, and national unions representing library workers, in order to improve their salaries, working conditions and status; 4) to encourage ongoing research and publishing on unionization in libraries; 5) to develop union support and advocacy materials for the Better Salaries Task Force Tool Kit; and 6) to be the permanent interest group within ALA-APA that would serve as a resource for both active and developing unions of library workers.[33]

Unions Today

There is no single source that lists all unions in which library workers participate. The author has created a list of public and academic unions with links to Web sites as appendices to this entry. These lists were put together by numerous searches state by state and may not be comprehensive, but they are the single most complete source of union information at this writing. They will be updated at the *Union Librarian* blog.[34] Readers should be aware that there is some fluidity to unions across the United States and Canada and some data may have changed since this entry was submitted. Library workers belong to a variety of unions including, but not limited to the AAUP, the AFT, AFSCME, National Association of Government Employees, SEIU, United Autoworkers, United Service and Allied Workers of RI, United Public Employees of California (UPEC), United Service and Allied Workers of RI.

Unions and Human Rights

In 2008 the world celebrated the 60th anniversary of the Universal Declaration of Human Rights (UDHR). During the drafting of the Declaration there had been tension between the World Federation of Trade and the International Labor Organization about the inclusion of union rights. Mrs. Roosevelt "explained that the United States delegation considered that the right to form and join trade unions was an essential element of freedom."[35] Unionization as a human right was included in the UDHR as Article 23.

Article 23.

1. Everyone has the right to work, to free choice of employment, to just and favorable conditions of work and to protection against unemployment.
2. Everyone, without any discrimination, has the right to equal pay for equal work.
3. Everyone who works has the right to just and favorable remuneration ensuring for himself and his family an existence worthy of human dignity, and supplemented, if necessary, by other means of social protection.

4. Everyone has the right to form and to join trade unions for the protection of his interests.[36]

Sixty years later, unions continue to be viewed as fundamental to democracy. Elaine Bernard wrote in 2008: "Unions are the premier institution of a free, democratic society, promoting democracy in the workplace, as well as economic and social justice, and equality. They have this role because they are instruments of transformation of members and of society at large. In this wonderful transformation rests the real power of unions."[37]

The democratic victories in the 2008 general U.S. elections had enthusiastic support from unions. Unions to which the majority of library workers belong (AFSCME, AFT, NEA, SEIU) contributed funds and volunteers to get out the vote. It remains to be seen as the Democratic Party holds power in the federal government if the more positive climate for unionization provides an opportunity for unions to grow among library workers in the public and educational sectors.[38]

APPENDIX I: PUBLIC LIBRARY UNIONS

Canada
Canadian Union of Public Employees, http://cupe.ca/
Le Syndicat canadien de la fonction publique (SCFP), http://scfp.ca/about?slashSess=199b096f1f24b748eb866bb05e396ae6

Alberta
Calgary Public Library (CUPE 1169), http://www.1169.cupe.ca/

British Columbia
Canadian Union of Public Employees BC Division (CUPE BC), http://www.cupe.bc.ca/
CUPE BC Library Committee, http://www.cupe.bc.ca/405
CUPE Local 391 (Vancouver Public Library and Gibsons and District Public Library Workers), http://www.cupe391.ca/index.html
Gibsons District Public Library, http://gibsons.bclibrary.ca/ *
British Columbia Government and Service Employees' Union. Component 6. Social, Educational and Health Services, http://www.bcgeu.ca/C6_Social_Information_and_Health *
Vancouver, http://www.cupe391.ca/index.html

Quebec
Montreal
Syndicat des professionnelles et professionnels municipaux de Montréal, http://www.sppmm.org/index.html

United States
California
Los Angeles County Librarians. SEIU Local 660, http://www.seiu721.org/Default.aspx

Los Angeles Public Library. Local 2626 of AFSCME, http://www.librariansguild.org/

San Francisco Public Library. SEIU Local 790, http://www.seiu1021.org/

San Jose, http://www.afscme-mef.org/mission.html

Shasta County. United Public Employees of California (UPEC), http://www.upec792.org/

Connecticut

Cheshire (CT) Public Library, http://www.cheshirelib.org/

District of Columbia

Library of Congress Professional Guild, AFSCME Local 2910, representing over 1600 employees at the Library of Congress, http://www.guild2910.org/

Florida

Broward County—[Collective Bargaining Agreement between the Board of County Commissioners Broward County, Florida and the Government Supervisors Association of Florida Opeiu, Afl-cio, Local 100 Broward County Supervisory unit October 1, 2002, to September 30, 2005], http://www.broward.org/humanresources/hui02836.pdf

Jacksonville, http://cwa3106.org/ *

Orange County Library System SEIU local 8, http://www.seiuflpublicservicesunion.org/

Massachusetts

Boston Public Library, http://www.bpl.org/

Massachusetts Library Staff Association, http://www.mlsa-4928.org/

Includes:

Abington Public Library
Attleboro Public Library
Braintree: Thayer Public Library
Bridgewater Public Library
Cambridge Public Library
Everett: Parlin Memorial Library
Foxborough: Boyden Library
Franklin Public Library
Holbrook Public Library
Hull Public Library
Lexington: Cary Memorial Library
Lynnfield
Medford Public Library
Middleborough Public Library
Milford Town Library
Milton Public Library
North Reading: Flint Memorial Library
Pepperell: The Lawrence Library
Quincy: Thomas Crane Public Library
Stoneham Public Library
Stoughton Public Library
Wakefield Public Library
Wayland Free Public Library
Weston Public Library
Weymouth Public Libraries
West Springfield Public Library

Winthrop Public Library & Museum
Woburn Public Library

Worcester Public Librarians part of National Association of Government Employees.

Local 495, http://www.worcpublib.org/index.html

Michigan

Detroit Public Library UAW 2200, http://www.uaw.org/about/localunions.html

Minnesota

Hennepin County. AFSCME Local 2864 (Professional Employees, including HCL Librarians), http://www.afscmelocal34.org/

Support staff are Local 2822 AFSCME

New Hampshire

Nashua Public Library Employees Local 4831.

New Jersey

Ocean County Library, http://www.unitedworkersunion.org

New York

Brooklyn Public Library, http://www.local1482.org/index.html

Buffalo and Erie County Public Library, http://www.buffalolib.org/employment/

Librarians, http://labecpl.bfn.org/

Civil Service Employee Association (CSEA)

American Federation of State, County and Municipal Employees (AFSCME)

New York Public Library, http://www.local1930.org/

Queens Public Library, http://www.local1321.org/

Tompkins County Public Library [NY], http://uaw2300.clarityconnect.com/ *

Ohio

Cincinnati (Public Library of Cincinnati and Hamilton County), http://www.seiu1199.org/plch.cfm

Cleveland Public Library, http://www.seiu1199.org/docUploads/ClevelandPublicLibraryContract.pdf

Hamilton County (Public Library of Cincinnati and Hamilton County), http://www.seiu1199.org/plch.cfm

Lucas County—Toledo—Lucas County Public Library Association of Public Library, http://www.seiu1199.org/plch.cfm

Employees. APLE. UAW Local 5242, http://www.orgsites.com/oh/aple/index.html

Stark County Library District (Canton), http://www.seiu1199.org/plch.cfm

Toledo—Lucas County Public Library (Association of Public Library Employees. APLE. UAW Local 5242), http://www.orgsites.com/oh/aple/index.html

Pennsylvania

Philadelphia Free Library, http://www.library.phila.gov/

Rhode Island

Providence Public Library. United Service and Allied Workers of Rhode Island. (USAW- RI).

Washington (State)

Council 2, http://www.council2.com/

THE WASHINGTON State Council of County and City Employees, (WSCCCE) AFSCME, AFL-CIO represents more than 16,000 employees who provide services to the citizens of Washington state. It is a democratic union providing a real voice for its members through active participation and professional representation. The Union works to preserve and enhance workers' compensation and benefits. It also promotes job security and improves other employment conditions.

King County Public Library [WA], http://www.kclsvoice.org/ *

Wisconsin

Milwaukee Public Library, http://www.afscme48.org/local426.html

Wisconsin Council AFSCME 40, http://www.afscmecouncil40.org/units.htm

Source: McCook, Kathleen de la Peña. *Union Librarian*, http://unionlibrarian.blogspot.com/.[34]

APPENDIX II: ACADEMIC LIBRARY UNIONS

Canada

Acadia University Faculty Association, http://www.caut.ca/aufa/

L'Association des Professeur(e)s de Bishop's University, http://www.caut.ca/apbu/index.htm

Athabasca University Faculty Association, http://aufa.ab.ca/

Bishop's University, http://www.caut.ca/apbu/index.htm

Brandon University, http://www.bufa.org/index.asp

Brock University, http://www.bufaweb.com/

Canadian Association of University Teachers, http://www.caut.ca/en/links/index.asp

Cape Breton University, http://www.cbufa.ca/main/

Carleton University, http://www.caut.ca/cuasa/

Concordia University, http://alcor.concordia.ca/%7Ecufa/

Dalhousie University, http://www.dfa.ns.ca/

Lakehead University, http://www.lufa.org/

Laurentian University, http://www.lufapul.ca/

McGill University, http://maut.mcgill.ca/

Non-Academic Certified Association (MUNACA), http://www.munaca.com/eng/

McMaster University, http://www.mcmaster.ca/mufa/

Memorial University of New Foundland, http://www.mun.ca/munfa/

Mount Allison, http://www.mafa.ca/press.htm

Mount Saint Vincent University, http://www3.ns.sympatico.ca/msvufa/

Nipissing University, http://www.nipissingu.ca/nufa/

Northern Ontario School of Medicine, http://www.nosmfa.ca/

Ontario Public Service Employees Union, http://www.opseu.org/caat/colleges.htm

Queen's University, http://www.qufa.ca/

Ryerson University, http://www.ryerson.ca/~rfa/

St. Francis Xavier University, http://www.stfx.ca/stfxaut/Main.html

Saint Mary's University. Halifax, http://www.smufu.org/

Saint Thomas More College, http://www.stmcollege.ca/facultyunion/index.html

Simon Fraser University, http://www.sfufa.ca/

Trent University, http://www.trentu.ca/org/tufa/

University of Alberta, http://www.uofaweb.ualberta.ca/aasua/

University of British Columbia, http://www.facultyassoc.ubc.ca/

University of Calgary, http://www.ucalgary.ca/UofC/departments/TUCFA/

University of Guelph (Ontario), http://www.caut.ca/ugfa/

University of Lethbridge, http://www.uleth.ca/ulfa/

University of Manitoba Faculty Association, http://www.umfa.ca/

Université Université de Moncton, http://www3.umoncton.ca/templates/udem2/udem02.cfm?CFID=475205&CFTOKEN=11554667&user_id=369&page=11231&template=35&resultat=0&order_num=&mot_recherche=&write=0&student_id=0&debut=0&curr_page=1#session.addtoken

University of New Brunswick, http://www.unb.ca/AUNBT/

University of Ottawa, http://www.apuo.uottawa.ca/

University of Prince Edward Island, http://www.upeifa.org/

University of Regina, http://www.urfa.uregina.ca/

University of St. Thomas, http://www.caut.ca/faust/

University of Saskatchewan, http://www.usaskfaculty.ca/

University of Toronto, http://www.utfa.org/

University of Victoria, http://web.uvic.ca/facassn/

University of Waterloo, http://www.fauw.uwaterloo.ca/

University of Western Ontario, http://www.uwofa.ca/

University of Windsor, http://athena.uwindsor.ca/wufa

University of Winnipeg, http://uwfa.ca/

Wilfrid Laurier University, http://www.wlufa.ca/index.html

York University, http://www.yufa.org/

United States

Alaska

University of Alaska. United Academics, http://www.unitedacademics.net/

California

California Faculty Association, http://www.calfac.org/

California State University Bakersfield

California State University Channel Islands

California State University Chico

California State University Dominguez Hills

California State University East Bay

California State University Fresno

California State University Fullerton

Humboldt State University

California State University Long Beach

California State University Los Angeles
California Maritime Academy
California State University Monterey Bay
California State University Northridge
California State Polytechnic University, Pomona
California State University Sacramento
California State University San Bernardino
San Diego State University
San Francisco State University
San Jose State University
California Polytechnic State University, San Luis Obispo
California State University San Marcos
Sonoma State University
California State University Stanislaus

Los Angeles College Faculty Guild, http://www.aft1521.org/

City College
East L.A. College
Harbor College
Mission College
Pierce College
Southwest College
Trade Tech College
Valley College
West L.A. College

San Francisco Art Institute, http://www.aaup-ca.org/
sfai_home.html

University of California, http://www.cft.org/councils/
uc/index.html

The University Council-AFT is the governance body of the eight campus locals of lecturers and librarians employed by the UC system. UC-AFT is the bargaining agent for units 17 and 18 systemwide, http://www.cft.org/councils/uc/History.html

UC-AFT Librarians Contract, http://www.cft.org/councils/uc/lib.contract.html

University of California Berkeley. UC-AFT BERKELEY-SAN FRANCISCO LOCAL 1474, http://berkeleyaft.org/

Yuba College, http://www.yubacollegefaculty.com/

Colorado

Regis University, http://www.regis.edu/regis.asp?sctn=facst&p1=res&p2=rc&p3=aaup

Connecticut

Connecticut State University, http://www.ccsu.edu/aaup/csu/Default.htm

University of Connecticut, http://www.ucpea.org/

Florida

United Faculty of Florida, http://www.unitedfacultyofflorida.org/ Includes:

Broward Community College
Florida A&M University
Florida Atlantic University
Fla. Comm. College at Jacksonville

Florida Gulf Coast University
Florida International University
Florida State University
Hillsborough Community College
New College of Florida
University of Central Florida
University of Florida
University of North Florida
University of South Florida
University of West Florida

Hawaii

University of Hawaii Professional Assembly, http://www.uhpa.org/

Illinois

Chicago State University, http://www.upilocal4100.org/text/csuIndex.htm

College of DuPage, http://codfaculty.org/

Eastern Illinois University, http://www.eiu.edu/%7EEiuUpi/

Governor's State University, http://www.upigsu.org/index2.htm

Illinois Education Association, http://www.ieanea.org/

Northeastern Illinois University, http://www.upi4100.org/neiu/index.htm

Northern Illinois University Instructors, http://www.upi4100.org/niu/

University of Illinois at Springfield, http://www.upilocal4100.org/text/WhoStuff/CampusChapters.html

University Professionals of Illinois, http://www.upilocal4100.org/

We stand 2700 strong. The University Professionals of Illinois, Local 4100, IFT, AFT, AFL-CIO, Is the recognized leader in academic bargaining for higher education in Illinois, representing seven of the 12 Illinois public universities at the bargaining table.

Western Illinois University, http://www.wiu.edu/UPI/

Iowa

University of Northern Iowa, http://www.uni.edu/unitedfaculty/

Kansas

Fort Hays University, http://www.fhsu-aaup.com/

Maine

Universities of Maine-Professional Staff Association, http://umpsa.maine.edu/index.html

University of Maine at Augusta
University of Maine at Farmington
University of Maine at Fort Kent
University of Maine at Machias
University of Maine
University of Maine at Presque Isle
University of Southern Maine

Maryland

MONTGOMERY COLLEGE, http://www.fhsu-aaup.com/

Massachusetts

Emerson College-Adjunct Faculty, http://www.emersonafec.com/

Suffolk University-Adjunct Faculty, http://www.saf-aaup.org/

University of Massachusetts, Massachusetts Society of Professors, http://umassmsp.org/

Michigan

Eastern Michigan University, http://www.emu-aaup.org/

Michigan Education Association, http://www.mea.org/Design.cfm?p=5573

Michigan Technological University, http://webpages.charter.net/mtu_aaup/

Northern Michigan University, http://myweb.nmu.edu/~aaup/

Oakland University, http://www.oaklandaaup.org/default.asp

Wayne State University, http://wayne.edu/

Western Michigan University, http://www.wmich.edu/aaup/index.php

Minnesota

Minnesota State College Faculty (MSCF), http://mscf.educationminnesota.org/

Nebraska

University of Nebraska-Omaha, http://www.unomaha.edu/aaup/

Nevada

Truckee Meadows Community College, http://www.unr.edu/nfa/tmcc.htm

New Hampshire

University of New Hampshire, http://chaucer.unh.edu/aaup/

New Jersey

LIBRARIANS COMMITTEE of the Council of New Jersey State College Locals http://www.cnjscl.org/lib_committee.htm

Council of New Jersey State College Locals, AFT, AFL-CIO which represents over 8,000 faculty, adjunct faculty, librarians and professional staff at the following institutions of higher education: http://www.cnjscl.org/

The College of New Jersey http://www.tcnj.edu/~aft/aft.htm

Kean University http://www.kft2187.org/

Montclair State University http://aftlocal1904.org/

New Jersey Institute of Technology

New Jersey City University http://aftlocal1839.org/

Ramapo College of New Jersey http://ramapoaft.org/

Richard Stockton College http://intraweb.stockton.edu/eyos/page.cfm?siteID=147&pageID=1

Rider University AAUP http://www-usr.rider.edu/~aaup/

Rowan University http://nj.aft.org/023730/

Rutgers, The State University of New Jersey http://www.rutgersaaup.com/about.htm

The College of New Jersey http://www.tcnj.edu/~aft/aft.htm

Union of Rutgers Administrators, AFT Local 1766, represents Administrative Assistants, Library supervisors and Library Associates at all three campuses of Rutgers University and a few other titles such as Digital Resources coordinator, Media coordinator, Graphics coordinator. http://www.ura-aft.org/

Union County College http://www.ucc-aaup.org/

University of Medicine and Dentistry of New Jersey (UMDNJ)[includes University Libraries] http://www.aaupumdnj.org/

William Paterson University http://www.aft-local-1796.org/

New York

Adelphi University, http://www.aaupadelphi.org/

City University of New York-Professional Staff Congress, http://www.psc-cuny.org/

D'Youville College, http://ddl.dyc.edu/%7Eaaup/

Hofstra University, http://www.aaup-hofstra.org/

New York Institute of Technology, http://www.aaupatnyit.org/

United University Professions, http://www.uupinfo.org/

United University Professions (UUP) is the union representing more than 31,000 academic and professional faculties on 29 State University of New York campuses, plus System Administration, Empire State College, and the New York State Theatre Institute. UUP is affiliated with the New York State United Teachers and the American Federation of Teachers, AFL-CIO.

With some 800 job titles included in the bargaining unit, UUP reflects the diversity of the State University. Members include Librarians.

Albany

Alfred, http://web.alfredstate.edu/uup/

Binghamton, http://www.uupbinghamton.org/

Brockport, http://www.uuphost.org/brockport/

Brooklyn Health Science Center

Buffalo Center, http://wings.buffalo.edu/uup/

Buffalo Health Science Center

Buffalo State, http://www.buffalostate.edu/orgs/uup/

Canton, http://www.canton.edu/

Cobleskill

Cortland, http://www.uuphost.org/cortland/

Delhi

Empire State

Environmental Science and Forestry, http://www.esf.edu/la/

Farmingdale, http://snyfarvc.cc.farmingdale.edu/~uup/

Fredonia, http://www.fredonia.edu/uup/

Geneseo

Maritime

Morrisville

New Paltz, http://www.uuphost.org/newpaltz/

New York State Theatre Institute

Old Westbury

Oneonta, http://organizations.oneonta.edu/uup/

Optometry, http://www.uuphost.org/optometry/

Oswego

Plattsburgh

Potsdam

Purchase, http://fafner.openlib.org/~purchaseuup/index.html

Stony Brook Center, http://www.uuphost.org/sbwest/

Stony Brook Health Sciences Center, http://www.uuphost.org/stonybrookhsc/index.html

System Administration, http://www.uupsysadm.org/

Upstate Medical University, Syracuse, http://www.uupinfosyr.org/

Utica/Rome

Ohio

Cincinnati State Technical & Community College, http://www.cinstateaaup.org/

Cleveland State University, http://aaupuc.org/

Cuyahoga Community College, http://www.ccc-aaup.org/

Kent State University, http://www.aaupksu.org/

University of Akron, http://www.akronaaup.org/

University of Cincinnati, http://aaupuc.org/

University of Toledo, http://www.utaaup.com/splash.shtml

Wright State University, http://www.wright.edu/admin/aaup/aaup.html

Oregon

Oregon University System-Collective Bargaining Units, http://www.ous.edu/hr/labor/

Eastern Oregon University, http://www2.eou.edu/~repres/

Portland State University, http://www.pdx.edu/oaa/documents/AAUP.pdf

Portland State University—Part-Time Faculty, http://www.pdx.edu/oaa/documents/AFT.pdf

Southern Oregon University, http://www.sou.edu/apsou/contracts/2005-2007/05-07%20Final%20Agreement.pdf

Western Oregon University Federation of Teachers, http://www.wouft.org/us.html

Pennsylvania

Allegheny, Community College of. CCAC/AFT LOCAL 2067, http://www.ccac.edu/default.aspx?id=138130

Association of Pennsylvania State College and University Faculties, http://www.apscuf.com/

Bloomsburg University, http://www.apscuf.com/bloomsburg/index.html

California University, http://www.apscuf.com/california/contact.html

Cheyney University, http://www.apscuf.com/cheyney/news.html

Clarion University, http://www.apscuf.com/clarion/index.html

East Stroudsburg University, http://www.esu.edu/apscuf/

Edinboro University, http://www.apscuf.com/edinboro/index.html

Kutztown University, http://www.apscuf.com/kutztown/index.html

Lock Haven University, http://www.lhup.edu/apscuf/

Mansfield University, http://www.apscuf.com/mansfield/index.html

Millersville University, http://www.apscuf.com/millersville/index.html

Shippensburg University, http://www.apscuf.com/shippensburg/index.html

Slippery Rock University, http://www.apscuf.com/slipperyrock/index.html

West Chester University, http://www.apscufwcu.com/

Philadelphia Faculty and Staff Federation of Community College of Philadelphia (FSFCCP), http://www.aft2026.org/

Texas

Texas A&M System, http://www.tamus.edu/

Many A&M System employees participate in collective bargaining contracts with labor organizations for issues regarding wages, hours of employment, or work conditions?

A: No. Any such collective bargaining contract is void under Texas law. Additionally, labor organizations may not be recognized as bargaining agents for a group of public employees.

Vermont

University of Vermont, http://www.unitedacademics.org/

Washington

University of Washington-AAUP-Advocacy Chapter-not union, http://depts.washington.edu/uwaaup/

Washington State, United Faculty of, http://www.ufws.org/

Central Washington University, http://ufcentral.org/

Eastern Washington University, http://www.ufws.org/eastern/index.html

Western Washington University, http://www.ufww.org/

Source: McCook, Kathleen de la Peña. *Union Librarian*, http://unionlibrarian.blogspot.com/.[34]

REFERENCES

1. AFL-CIO, Department of Professional Employees. The union difference for library employees: Wage and salary differences between union and non-union library workers, based on the American Library Association-Allied Professional Association Salary Survey, 2006. Prog. Libr. **2008**, *31*, 75–103.

2. Grady, J. Davis, D. *ALA-APA Salary Survey: Non-MLS—Public and Academic*, American Library Association-Allied Professional Association, American Library Association Office for Research and Statistics: Chicago, IL, 2006.

3. Guyton, T.L. *Unionization: The Viewpoint of Librarians*, American Library Association: Chicago, IL, 1975; 11–12.

4. Berelson, B. Library unionization. Libr. Quart. **1939**, *9*, 497–498.

5. Milden, J.W. Women, public libraries, and library unions: The formative years. J. Libr. Hist. **1977**, *12*, 150–58.

6. Biblo, H. Librarians and trade unionism. Libr. Trends *25*, 423–433 (October 25).

7. Library Unions Round Table, ALA Bulletin 34 (August, 1940): 154; 35 (September, 1941): 119–123; 36 (September 15, 1942): 104–108; 38 (September, 1944): 366–367; 40 September 15, 1946): 102–107; 41 (September 15, 1947) 77–81; 42 (September 15, 1948): 74–76; 44 (May, 1950): 193; 45 (December, 1951): 406; 46 (December 1952): 411; 47 (December 1953): 573.

8. Latham, J.M. *White collar read: The American Public Library and the left led CIO: A case study of the Chicago Public Library, 1929–1952*, University of Illinois: IL, 2007; Ph.D. dissertation Urbana-Champaign.

9. Goldstein, M.S. *Collective bargaining in the field of librarianship*, Library Personnel Relations, Pratt Institute: Brooklyn, NY, 1968; December 16 Submitted as a Term Paper for LS 53.

10. Wasserman, D. Unionization of library personnel: Where we stand today. In *Collective Bargaining in Libraries*; Schlipf, F.A., Ed.; University of Illinois: Urbana-Champaign, IL, 1975; 28.

11. O'Reilly, R.C.; O'Reilly, M.I. *Librarians and Labor Relations*, Greenwood Press: Westport, CT, 1981.

12. Lilore, D. *The Local Union in Public Libraries*, Library Professional Publications: Hamden, CT, 1984.

13. Vignone, J.A. *Collective Bargaining Procedures for Public Library Employees: An Inquiry into the Opinions and Attitudes of Public Librarians, Directors and Board Members*, Scarecrow Press: Metuchen, NJ, 1971.

14. Hurd, R. Reflections on PATCO's legacy: Labor's challenges persist. Emp. Respons. Rights J. **2006**, *18*, 207–214.

15. Weber, M. Support staff unions in academic and public libraries: Some suggestions for mangers with reference to the Ohio experience, 1984–1990. J. Libr. Admin. **1992**, *17*, 65–86.

16. Hampton, (Skip) A., Ed. The benefits and deficiencies of unions in public libraries. Publ. Libr. **2002**, *41*(3), 135–142.

17. Sparanese, A.C. Unions in libraries: A positive view. Publ. Libr. **2002**, *41*, 140.

18. Galanopoulos, A. et al. An indomitable spirit: The eight hundred of CUPE 391. Prog. Libr. **2007–2008**, *30*, 38–69.

19. Murphy, M. *Blackboard Unions: The AFT and the NEA 1900–1980*, Cornell University Press: Ithaca, NY, 1990.

20. Weatherford, J.W. *Collective Bargaining and the Academic Librarian*, Scarecrow Press: Metuchen, NJ, 1976; 15.

21. Weatherford, J.W. *Librarians' Agreements: Bargaining for a Heterogeneous Profession*, Scarecrow Press: Metuchen, NJ, 1988.

22. Mary, K.; Bolin, M.K. Librarian status at US Research Universities: Extending the typology. J. Acad. Librar. **2008**, *34*, 416–424.

23. Hovekamp, T.M. Unionization and job satisfaction among professional library employees in academic research institutions. Coll. Res. Libr. **1995**, *56*, 341–350.

24. Association of College & Research Libraries, *Guideline on Collective Bargaining*, Approved by the ACRL Academic Status Committee and approved by the ACRL Board of Directors and the ALA Standards Committee at the 1993 Midwinter Meeting. In 2000, the ACRL Committee on the Status of Academic Librarians reviewed the guideline as requested by ACRL and no changes to the current text were recommended. The ACRL Board of Directors reaffirmed the guideline at the 2008 Annual Conference. Available at http://www.ala.org/ala/mgrps/divs/acrl/standards/guidelinecollective.cfm.

25. Association of College & Research Libraries, *Guidelines for Academic Status for College and University Librarians*, Revised by the ACRL Committee on the Status of Academic Librarians and approved by the ACRL Board of Directors on January 23, 2007. Available at http://www.ala.org/ala/mgrps/divs/acrl/standards/guidelinesacademic.cfm.

26. *The 2006 Directory of Faculty Contracts and Bargaining Agents in Institutions of Higher Education*, National Center for the Study of Collective Bargaining in Higher Education and the Professions (NCSCBHEP): New York, 2006. Available at http://www.hunter.cuny.edu/ncscbhep/index.shtml.

27. Kusack, J.M. *Unions for Academic Library Support Staff: Impact on Workers and the Workplace*, Greenwood: New York, 1986.

28. Milton, S. Librarians: Key players in faculty unions. Alki **2005**, *21*, 5–7.

29. Buschman, J. et al. Ignored too long: The benefits of managing a library with a union [adapted from a program sponsored by American Library Association-Allied Professional Association (ALA-APA) at the American Library Association Annual Conference in New Orleans on June 25, 2006] Libr. Worklife **2007**, *4*. Available at http://www.ala-apa.org/newsletter/vol4no01/spotlight.htm.

30. American Library Association, *Office for Library Personnel Resources. The T.I.P. (Topics in Personnel) Kits information series #1—Unionization and Collective Bargaining*, Chicago, 1982.

31. Freedman, M.J. Now is the time for better salaries. Am. Libr. **2002**, *33*, 7.

32. Leber, M. Putting pay first. Libr. J. **2003**, *128*, 43–44, 46–47.

33. ALA-APA (American Library Association-Allied Professional Association), *Union Subcommittee*. Available at http://www.ala-apa.org/salaries/union.html.

34. In *Union Librarian*; McCook, Kathleen de la Peña, Ed. Available at http://unionlibrarian.blogspot.com/.

35. Morsink, J. *The Socialist Shape of Work-Related Rights. The Universal Declaration of Human Rights: Origins, Drafting & Intent*, University of Pennsylvania Press: Philadelphia, PA, 1999; 157–190.

36. http://www.un.org/Overview/rights.html Universal Declaration of Human Rights, 1948.

37. Bernard, E. State of US labor & building union power. Democratic Left **2008**, *36*, 6.

38. McCook, Kathleen de la Peña There is power in a union. Annual since 2006. Prog. Libr. Winter issues.

United Kingdom: Archives and Archival Science

Helen Forde
Department of Information Studies, University College London, London, U.K.

Abstract

This entry traces the development of record keeping and archives services in the United Kingdom, highlighting the differences between the constituent home countries, local authority responsibilities, and the diversity of business, religious and community archives. It looks at the development of the archive profession and training, and suggests that information management may become the way the profession develops in an electronic age. The role of the main professional organizations and societies relating to archives and records management is outlined, with an emphasis on the crucial advocacy role they play in ensuring that the importance of the records, in whatever format, is not overlooked.

INTRODUCTION

Archives and records in the United Kingdom are an unrivaled source of historical information with some of the main series of national archives surviving in an unbroken tradition from the twelfth century. As the United Kingdom embraces four different home countries, the arrangements for the records and archives vary in each. This is further complicated by the different legislative systems in Scotland and by the devolution of Scotland and Wales in the recent past. Other archives of businesses, religions, local authorities, and communities also differ in their arrangements for records management and permanent preservation with globalization resulting in additional complexities.

LEGISLATION AND ACCOMMODATION FOR ARCHIVES AND RECORDS

England and Wales

The Public Record Office (PRO) Act 1838 was the first legislation for archival material in England and Wales, bringing together the records of the ancient departments of state, in particular, the Exchequer, Chancery and Courts of Law in a government department, the PRO headed by the Master of the Rolls. It did not cover papers held in government departments, though these were often transferred once the PRO, as a repository in Chancery Lane in central London, became a place of safekeeping. An Order in Council of 1852 regularized the existing situation by extending the remit of the Master of the Rolls, but the PRO staff had no control over selection in departments nor was there any provision for the destruction of unwanted material. Access issues were not addressed, although search rooms were provided in the late

nineteenth century additions to the PRO building in Chancery Lane.

In 1869, the Royal Commission on Historical Manuscripts was created to locate and provide access to records held in private collections. It published reports on them, providing details on the type of information contained in the manuscripts and where they were located. It continued this work on the premises of, and in conjunction with the staff at the PRO but in 1959 it received a further royal warrant and moved to new accommodation in Quality Court, Chancery Lane. By this time, it was in charge of the National Register of Archives (created in 1945), a project that was deliberately focused on nongovernmental archives and which was the forerunner of the more ambitious and all-embracing electronic databases that are now current.

Sir Hilary Jenkinson (1882–1961) was one of the dominant figures in the early twentieth century as a shaper of British archival theory. This was to become the basis of practice both at home and in many of the then colonies. He worked at the PRO, eventually becoming Deputy Keeper (effective head) in 1947, and it was here that he developed the concepts which were outlined in his book. *A Manual of Archive Administration* (Oxford: Clarendon Press, 1922). He used his experiences to direct and guide the emerging profession to ensure that modern records, as well as those of greater age, were catered for adequately and many of his innovations, such as The National Register of Archives, survived well after his death.

After the Second World War, concern over the uncoordinated accumulation of records led to the publication of a report by the Grigg Committee (Command Paper 9163) in 1954 recommending

- Clear reviewing procedures for selection by the department.
- The appointment of departmental record officers.

Encyclopedia of Library and Information Sciences, Fourth Edition DOI: 10.1081/E-ELIS4-120044855

- An advisory role for the PRO and the appointment of a records administration officer and staff to oversee the new procedures.
- The transfer of responsibility for the PRO from the Master of the Rolls to a minister.
- Access provision to material held by the PRO for material over 50 years old unless there were special considerations.
- The inclusion of cinematograph film, photographs, and sound recordings as public records where appropriate.

These provisions were incorporated into the Public Records Act 1958, which was followed by a further Act in 1968 to reduce the closure period to 30 years. Concern that records of the Second World War should be released en bloc, apart from those of service personnel, led to their release in 1972, following the precedent of the release of those of the First World War.

By 1976, pressure on the space required to store the increasing volume of national archives resulted in the opening of a new facility at Kew, in south west London, to which the nineteenth and twentieth century holdings were transferred. The latter was extended in 1996 to house the entire archive and the central London repository was closed apart from a Family Record Centre for genealogists, run jointly with the Office of National Statistics. This closed in 2008 due, in part, to the increasing number of archival resources available online.

Access provisions were changed by the Freedom of Information Act, which came into force in 2005 guaranteeing a general right of access to information held by public authorities subject to certain provisions about public interest. A Code of Practice was issued from the Lord Chancellor's Office to guide departments in carrying out the Act. Further consultation is currently (2008) being conducted into the feasibility of a reduction of the 30 year rule. An Access to environmental information is regulated by the EU Directive 2003/2004 EC, replacing the 1992 Environmental Information Regulations. This ensures the right of access to environmental information held by public bodies.

Data Protection legislation, initially (1984) referring only to data held on individuals electronically, was revised by the Data Protection Act passed in 1998 to cover the protection of data on individuals in all formats, while permitting the legitimate collection of such data by organizations that require access for research purposes.

The partnership established in 2003 between the Royal Commission on Historical Manuscripts (HMC) and the then PRO vested the responsibilities of the Commissioners in the Keeper of Public Records, who was thereafter known as the Chief Executive of The National Archives (TNA). This enabled TNA to advise about the location and the condition of private papers and manuscripts, in addition to managing public records. The TNA now comprises the former PRO, the Royal Commission on Historical Manuscripts, the Office of Public Sector Information, and Her Majesty's Stationery Office.

Despite the remit of the PRO as the government archive, some private collections have been deposited with the public records since, at the time of transfer, the record office was regarded as the most appropriate location. These include some Church of England material, notably the probate records for the Archdiocese of Canterbury. These records are among the most regularly consulted since they cover the testamentary records of many famous, and not so famous, people up to 1858. Together with other records of interest to genealogists these are now online.

Records designated as public records on account of their enduring value are mainly kept at TNA but a significant minority are kept in over 200 other repositories, many of them are local record offices. These are known as Places of Deposit, and the public archives held in each are subject to the same regulation as those held centrally. The National Advisory Service (the merger of the Royal Commission on Historical Manuscripts and the Archive Inspection Unit of the former PRO) has published *The National Archives Standard for Record Repositories* setting out best practice for archive provision. It is supported by a Framework of Standards, covering a wider range of best practice to cater for the equally wide range of repositories. The governing bodies of those holding public records are asked to subscribe to the Standard, and those attaining the essential requirements are approved by TNA.

Scotland

Responsibility for the archives in Scotland is vested in the Keeper of Records and legislation consequently relates to this post. The Public Records (Scotland) Act 1937 was largely concerned with the transfer to the Keeper of the records of the central and local courts of law as well as government departments, agencies, nondepartmental public bodies, statutory bodies corporate, and local authorities. In 1937, the Keeper also had the responsibility for the creation and maintenance of the Register of Saisines (Seisins [The instrument [in Scotland] by which the possession of feudal property is proved. (*Oxford English Dictionary*)]), but that function was split by the Public Registers and Records (Scotland) Act 1948 as a recognition of the difference between the two activities. The U.K. wide Public Records Act 1958 (see above) enabled the transfer of records of public bodies operating partly or wholly in Scotland to the National Archives of Scotland (NAS), and provisions similar to those outlined in the 1958 Act for selection, transfer, and preservation of the records were adopted by the Scottish Office in 1962 for public bodies in Scotland; at the same time similar access provisions were adopted together with the reduction to a 30 year limit in 1967.

The Keeper has also been able to take in private records, following an amendment to the Act in 1985, in which procedures for disposal were set out and the Scottish Advisory Council was established. Data Protection provisions for Scotland are in line with those for England and Wales; similarly, the Freedom of Information Act (Scotland) 2002 covers public bodies in Scotland. Currently (2008), a review of legislation on government records in Scotland is being carried out to ensure that they are appropriate and accessible; this follows the recommendation of the Shaw report (2007) (http://www.scotland.gov.uk/Publications/2007/11/20104729/). The NAS is situated on three sites in Edinburgh, two of which are open to the public, General Register House and West Register House. In addition, Thomas Thomson House, in the west of Edinburgh is its main repository and also houses the conservation department and offices.

Northern Ireland

The Public Records Act (Northern Ireland) 1923 established the Public Record Office of Northern Ireland (PRONI) shortly after the destruction of many of the Irish public records in the fire in the Four Courts, Dublin in 1922. The Act stipulated that it was legal for PRONI to bring in records, which were not expressly created by government as a deliberate attempt to ensure that as many documents as possible were retained to compensate for the very serious loss in Dublin. Private records, in particular, were targeted for collection, safekeeping, and public access. After the Second World War, the pressure on storage space increased and the Northern Ireland government followed the recommendations of the 1954 Grigg report (see above) to introduce regular reviews of material in government departments and disposal schedules. In 1976, in accordance with the practice elsewhere in the United Kingdom, the 30 year rule was introduced.

The Public Record Office of Northern Ireland has moved to different parts of the government of Northern Ireland being part of the Department of Finance from 1924 to 1984; part of the Department of the Environment until it changed to become an executive agency in 1995; and finally part of the Department of Culture, Arts and Leisure (DCAL) in 1999. Following the review of Public Administration in 2006, it ceased to be an agency and its status is now as a division of DCAL. The frequent changes have been due, in part, to the recent troubled history of devolved government in Northern Ireland. In response to demand from government departments, PRONI drew up the Northern Ireland Record Management Standard (NIRMS) in 2002.

Wales

Welsh public records are governed by the same provisions as those in England; they were moved to the PRO in the mid-nineteenth century but requests for a specific record office for Wales were being made in a bill introduced to Parliament as early as 1913. No further progress was made until the Public Records Act 1958 nominated repositories in Wales as suitable Places of Deposit for public records (see above) and also authorized the return of the bulk of the Welsh records to the National Library of Wales.

The Government of Wales Act 1997 made provision for the concept of Welsh Public Records, which, in the following Government of Wales Act 2006, included a list of bodies whose records were to be accorded that status. The U.K. Public Records Acts 1958 and 1967 remain in force until provisions are established.

Local Records in England and Wales

No specific legislation relates to local administrative records or the provision of county or borough archive services. The Local Government (Records) Act 1962 conferred discretionary powers on local authorities (now including all county councils, London boroughs, metropolitan districts, and unitary councils) to provide a limited archive service relating to the acquisition of and access to archival material, not restricted to official material. Stewardship and wider advisory powers were not included. The Local Government Act 1972 (s224) required local authorities to make proper arrangements for archives belonging to, or in the custody of, officers of the council; this was followed in 1999 by guidance on "proper arrangements," issued by the department then responsible, the Department of the Environment, Transport, and the Regions. It refers to the management of records, in whatever format and the historical records that should be kept by an established archive.

Manorial records, held in local record offices are nominally under the custodianship of the Master of the Rolls and come under special protection due to the enduring legal position of many of the properties mentioned in the records. All pre-1925 manorial documents, except deeds and other evidence of title, are protected under the regulations published in the 1924 amendment to the Law of Property Act 1922, (s122A). Original responsibility for maintaining the register of manorial property was undertaken by the PRO on behalf of the Master of the Rolls, then by the Royal Commission on Historical Manuscripts following the Public Records Act 1958, and subsequently by TNA; Historical Manuscripts Commission when the two combined in 2003. The rules prevent the removal of manorial documents from England and Wales without the permission of the Master of the Rolls, require ownership details, or changes, to be registered, require custodians to provide safe and appropriate storage conditions and permit the removal of any documents to a more appropriate place of deposit if necessary.

Responsibility for documents relating to tithes paid to the Church of England is also held by the Master of the

Tunisia–United Kingdom

Rolls and also exercised by TNA: Historical Manuscripts Commission. The original tithe apportionment maps and schedules, created as a result of the Tithe Apportionment Act 1838 (6&7 Will.IV, c.7) are held at TNA, and the two copies are held locally, often by now in the appropriate county record office. Rules have been issued relating to the care and custody of the records.

The Parochial Records and Registers Measure, passed by the General Synod of the Church of England in 1978, was a recognition of the public interest in these records and the need to ensure their security and preservation as well as providing access. Diocesan record offices had been established by the Parochial Records and Registers Measure 1929 but in practice, the spread of local record offices has resulted in many being designated as diocesan repositories. The principal duties imposed by the measure include the deposit of all noncurrent records and registers over 100 years old in the appointed diocesan office with reasonable access during working hours and regular inspection of the conditions provided for those which are retained.

The Local Government (Wales) Act 1994 required all new unitary authorities to provide plans to the Secretary of State for proposed archive delivery services. These were to include all records belonging to the local authority or of which they had custody.

ARCHIVE SERVICES

The functions of TNA in all three home countries are broadly similar; the main principles remain the provision of selection, preservation, and access services, together with advisory services especially on electronic materials.

In England and Wales, TNA offers services to the records management community and all custodians of records with the responsibility for caring for records, including private owners. The National Advisory Services offer advice and guidance on the creation, management, care, and use of records and archives by

- Setting standards and outlining best practice.
- Advising archive professionals using *The National Archives' Standard for Record Repositories*.
- Advising private owners and organizations on archive issues.
- Developing guidance and policies on electronic records management for government.
- Providing advice and guidance for statutory Places of Deposit to ensure the maintenance of high standards of care and access to public records.
- Promoting good records management and the cultural and historical importance of archives for evidence of good governance; this includes business archives and religious archives.

In England, services to users include the provision of resources on-site at the record office in Kew, in south west London. The service varies between the traditional advice to readers delivered in person by knowledgeable staff, to the recent *Your Archives* wiki, a Web site designed to allow users to contribute their knowledge of archival sources held by TNA and other U.K. archives. Development of the TNA web site has also enabled TNA to put its own catalog online for users to consult prior to a visit and to participate with others in the English strand of the beginnings of a virtual national archives catalog for the United Kingdom, *Access to Archives* (A2A). Gradually this objective is being achieved through the Global Search function on the TNA Web site where it is now (2008) possible to access information on collections held both at TNA and elsewhere.

Research services also include corporate research, TNA having been given Independent Research Organization status in 2005. This is frequently undertaken in partnership with university departments whose staff have specialized knowledge of TNA collections but also in the form of applied research in conservation science, information, records and archives management, digital preservation, and the provision of public sector information. It is intended to support decision making in TNA and by extension to the wider archive and library community.

Access services have changed considerably in the recent past, leading to a much wider audience through electronic means. Investment in developing these services has been high, particularly in the digitization of archival material. Access to the basic information remains free but charges are levied for copies of material, which has been downloaded, ensuring continuing income for further investment. Information on the records available in this format is on the relevant Web sites and catalogs. Partnerships, with private genealogical services in particular, have resulted in the management of such digital resources to be undertaken out of the public sector.

Access hours at Kew have increased as a result of the wider focus on citizens' rights. Regular surveys are made by the Public Services Quality Group (PSQG) to measure the satisfaction of users with services and offer users the chance to suggest improvements. These have resulted in changes to improving access and to developing a dialogue with the users.

Scotland, Wales, and Northern Ireland

Like its counterpart in England, NAS offers advice to government departments on all aspects of records management, to public and private owners of historical material and to the general public on using the records in its care. Similarly, it works in partnership with other organizations to promote Scottish archival interests, and it has been to the fore in developing online services, particularly for genealogists.

In Wales, the National Library manages the Welsh archival material deposited there that includes both public records and private transfers. Services are broadly similar to those offered in England and Scotland. The Welsh Assembly has the responsibility for records management services to Assembly departments.

In Northern Ireland, PRONI has the same responsibilities for the Northern Ireland Civil Service records management and the services to users of the record office as the TNA in the other countries.

Local Archives Services

Local authorities in England and Wales manage their own archive services while those that are designated as Places of Deposit for public records (see above) have to comply with the relevant regulations for their safekeeping and access. Most countries and some metropolitan areas have archive services though some combine them with local history centres (e.g., Surrey) or libraries (e.g., Birmingham). A noticeable trend in the last 20 years has been the reduction in the number of county archivists, the posts being either downgraded or being merged with that of those responsible for History Services or Local Studies.

Changes in local government organization and geographical boundaries have resulted in some amalgamations of historic collections or joint services with several contributing partners. The results of the 2007 self-assessment exercise (Nicholas Kingsley' Self assessment of local authority archives 2007: the results revealed' *Record Keeping*, Winter 2008, pp. 10–15) (see above) suggests that size matters; larger organizations are better able to provide a wider range of services to a higher quality than small organizations which struggle with limited resources. This suggests that further amalgamation may be the only way in which to maintain high service standards.

Local authority archives keep not only the records of that organization covering a wide range of materials including those relating to the Poor Law, health, and education but also many records donated or deposited by the community. These can include solicitors' and estate agents' papers, transport records, business and industrial records, antiquarian material, voluntary organizations' records including those of charitable bodies, local societies and clubs, literary archives, diocesan material (see below) including parish registers, estate and family archives including manorial records, and many other types of archival material local in nature. Court records from the Quarter and Petty Sessions often survive locally, and many hospitals and national health organizations deposit their material with local authority record offices.

The emphasis on delivery for archives, both local and public in the early twenty-first century is on the contribution that the services can make to government initiatives such as education, health care, and citizenship as well as the insights into historic information that have been the traditional services offered.

ARCHIVES OF HIGHER EDUCATION ORGANIZATIONS

College and university archives are maintained by their institutions, often in conjunction with manuscript and other collections. They vary from the medieval college foundations of Oxford and Cambridge universities to the modern collections of, for example the University of Warwick where many contemporary political and trade union records are kept. Notable alumni of universities often donate their papers to these institutions in later life; these are kept as appropriate but if the content is more applicable to another organization the authors are often advised on which is the more appropriate repository.

Services to readers vary according to institution but the central point of access to descriptions of archives held in higher education organizations is the online *Archives Hub* (http://www.archiveshub.ac.uk); this is progressively adding information at collections level and increasingly to complete catalog descriptions. Another higher education cataloging project is AIM25 (http://www.aim25.ac.uk/), an organization which provides electronic access to collection level descriptions of the archives of over 90 higher education institutions and learned societies within the greater London area, the name signifying that they are within the orbit of the London ring road, the M25.

BUSINESS ARCHIVES

Many businesses in the United Kingdom hold their own archives, including those which relate to enterprises in both the United Kingdom and abroad. These range from major international companies such as BP, Diageo or Marks and Spencer, banks including the Bank of England and major mining and excavation companies to smaller local organizations. Local record offices frequently aim to retain material where the original business is no longer trading, though it is often in the way of a rescue operation; recently the records of a paper manufacturer, William Sommerville and Son Ltd., a major nineteenth century employer in Midlothian, Scotland were deposited with the Midlothian Local Studies and Archive Service having been salvaged from a skip and this is not at all unusual.

While business archives are private, and therefore not subject to government regulation apart from the requirements for retaining certain financial records, many participate in wider activities to promote education or encourage genealogists to use their resources. The services they offer may be curtailed due to commercial needs and confidentiality agreements but where necessary these are managed sensitively. Initiatives among the larger organizations include the digitization of N.M. Rothschild & Sons' records relating to the involvement of the banking firm in nineteenth century Brazil and the development of a museum by another banking firm, HBOS, in Edinburgh with a particular remit to promote financial education among schoolchildren. Local businesses may well be associated with other activities in local study centers, contributing photographic and other material to displays. In some areas, communities have come together to ensure the survival of personal and community archives that record past local employment opportunities and businesses (see below).

Business archives are promoted by the Business Archives Council established in 1934 to encourage the preservation of British business records, and to advise on their administration and management. The Council is acutely aware that the continuing existence and accessibility of business archives is closely linked to the fortunes of their owners, and of the need to strengthen rescue activities and respond to collections at risk. Consequently, it keeps in close touch with record offices and local study centers to advise them of opportunities and to encourage the deposit of materials at risk.

FILM AND AUDIOVISUAL ARCHIVES

The British Film Archive was founded in 1935 as a part of the remit of the British Film Institute "to maintain a national repository of films of permanent value." It is recognized internationally as one of the four founders of the International Federation of Film Archives (FIAF). It collects U.K. film of all kinds as well as material produced overseas, and currently (2008) holds over 7 million stills, 1 million transparencies, and 20,000 posters. The collecting policy is wide, including feature films, professional and amateur films, documentaries, propaganda films, and television programs. It is also the official repository for video recordings of Parliamentary proceedings and government films selected for permanent preservation by TNA. The services include involvement in film festivals, regular release of material to be seen at local cinemas, and the release of film and television programs on DVD. The preservation section is housed in premises funded by the late John Paul Getty and the staff work on the restoration of degraded materials with a view to enabling screening. Highly flammable nitrate film is housed separately.

Twelve public sector film archives are established in different parts of the U.K. forming the U.K. film archive forum. The English regional film archives have a remit to collect moving image material of relevance to their region. This includes audiovisual material made either in or by people from each region. Some operate within a record office, such as the Wessex Film Archive at the Hampshire Record Office, others within universities, such as the Media Archive for Central England (MACE) at Leicester University or the East Anglia Film Archive at the University of East Anglia. Wales and Scotland have their own film archives held in both cases in their respective national libraries, with the same regional emphasis. No dedicated archive exists for Northern Ireland but some film material is available in the Ulster Folk and Transport Museum. The services offered vary according to funding arrangements but often include local screenings, talks to interested groups, and retrieval of material for individual and commercial use.

Specialist film archives include the extensive collections held by the Imperial War Museum, which is dedicated to film and video related to twentieth century conflict involving British and Commonwealth forces. The British Broadcasting Company (BBC) holds about 4 million items from radio and television as well as collections of sheet music and press cuttings. Material is made available both to the BBC and to individuals, and much use is made of the Web site to promote film and sound recordings of notable events and anniversaries.

The British Sound Archive is maintained by the British Library, and it holds over a million discs, 185,000 tapes, and many other sound and video recordings from all over the world, covering the entire range of recorded sound from music, drama, and literature, to oral history and wildlife sounds. The archives range from cylinders made in the late nineteenth century to the latest CD, DVD, and minidisk recordings. It includes copies of commercial recordings issued in the United Kingdom, together with selected commercial recordings from overseas, radio broadcasts and many privately made recordings. Increasingly these are being made available online.

Film and video material held in higher education organizations is promoted by the British Universities Film and Video Council (BUFVC) through its library and viewing and editing facilities.

RELIGIOUS ARCHIVES

Religious archives, other than those of the Church of England (see above), are normally kept either by the denomination in question, in a special library or in local record offices. Although each faith has different arrangements for deposit and access most have Web sites from which it is possible to ascertain opening hours. Dr. Williams' Library in Gordon Square, London is a rich source for a wide variety of both manuscript and printed sources for the history of nonconformity in the United Kingdom. More information is available from the Religious Archives Group of the Society of Archivists and a recent report on the state of religious archives in the United Kingdom (http://www.nationalarchives.gov.uk/archives/advice-corporate.html).

The Roman Catholic Church in England maintains diocesan records, some (e.g., in Birmingham) dating back to the seventeenth century although the Roman Catholic church was not officially recognized in England until 1850. The Scottish Catholic Archives are currently (2008) maintained in Edinburgh; many of the archives date back before 1878 when the Hierarchy was re-established in Scotland.

The central archives of the Religious Society of Friends (Quakers) are held in Friends House Library, London though local records, as for other nonconformist groups, are often found in the relevant record office.

The national Baptist archives are held in the Angus Library at Regent's Park College in Oxford and include the records of some local Baptist churches from the seventeenth century, though these are also found in local record offices.

The central archives of the Congregational Union of England and Wales are held in Dr. Williams' Library (see above).

Jewish archives in England are scattered between different synagogues and university deposits, including those of prominent Jews. In Scotland, the Scottish Jewish Archive in Glasgow has been established to collect a wide range of materials to document the history of the Jewish diaspora in Scotland since the eighteenth century.

COMMUNITY ARCHIVES

Community archives have developed during the past 10 years largely as unofficial records of communities where information about earlier activities, including industry, are in the danger of being forgotten. The definition of the term is still being debated but in essence, it is agreed that a community archive should be a collection that includes primary sources, in whatever format, rather than a series of articles. All groups, of whatever origin, are encouraged to contribute to the growing corpus of information held online by CommunityArchives.org.uk as well as collecting their own materials. Typically, they are based on location but can also include literature and arts archives. The movement is supported by the National Council on Archives Community Advisory Group.

RARE MANUSCRIPT LIBRARIES

Many libraries in the United Kingdom hold rare manuscripts including the National Libraries of Scotland and Wales and the British Library in London. The university libraries have major collections and in many cases, individual colleges, especially at the older universities also hold important materials. Professional bodies frequently own library and archival collections donated by former members.

ARCHIVAL PROFESSION

The archival profession in the United Kingdom grew up in the middle of the twentieth century, successor to a long line of record keepers, librarians, and antiquarians who were charged with the care of archival and historical materials. The development of a separate profession after the Second World War was due, at least in part, to the increasing number of archives deposited in local authority care.

Postgraduate courses were originally established at the School of Library, Archive, and Information Studies at University College London (SLAIS), at Liverpool University, and at the University of Wales at Bangor and Aberystwyth. In-house training was provided by some of the larger institutions such as the then PRO (now TNA) and the Bodleian Library in Oxford. Sixty years later the number of courses has risen to reflect the changes in need and the technological advances that make physical presence at a course less necessary. The archive and records management course at SLAIS continues to offer programs to both home and overseas students, and it has developed a research center, ICARUS. Liverpool University Centre for Archive Studies (LUCAS) also undertakes research as well as offering archive and records management courses at both postgraduate and undergraduate levels both on-site and for distance learners, and Aberystwyth University uses the advantage of collaboration with the History and Welsh History Department for the Information Studies programs. The latter offers distance learning options as does the Centre for Archive and Information Studies (CAIS) at the University of Dundee where the centre also caters for family and local historians. The University of Northumbria offers a distance-learning course in records management.

Information management has increasingly been the focus of many of these courses with the development of electronic communications, not the least at Glasgow University where the Humanities Advanced Technology and Information Institute (HATII) was formed in 1997, bringing together expertise in Information Communication and Technology (ICT) in the heritage sector. It offers an MSc in Information Management and Preservation (Digital) and has an extensive research program.

An important link between the universities and the profession is maintained by the accreditation of courses by the Society of Archivists (see below), which also offers additional training and short courses for professional development.

PROFESSIONAL SOCIETIES AND ORGANIZATIONS

The Society of Archivists (http://www.archives.org.uk/) was founded in 1947 as the first professional organization for archivists, and it has grown to include conservators, records managers, and institutional affiliates. It exists to promote the care and preservation of archives and the better administration of archive repositories, to advance the training of its members, and to encourage relevant research and publications. It has a range of benefits for its members, now (2008) nearly 2000, and plays an important role in relation to professional qualifications (see above). It holds an annual conference, has regional representation, and works with other related bodies in promoting archives. Many special interest groups operate under the umbrella of the Society.

The Records Management Society (http://www.rms-gb. org.uk/) launched in 1983, recognized the needs of an ever-increasing number of people working in the fields of records and information management, including those who wish to develop new management systems. It supports professionals through sharing expertise and knowledge.

The Institute for Conservation (ICON) (http://www. icon.org.uk/) was formed in 2005 from several groups of conservators in all disciplines, including archive conservation. It is the lead body for conservation in the United Kingdom and provides guidance, advocacy, training, and education opportunities, uniting the conservation profession and the wider heritage community.

The National Council on Archives (NCA) (http://www. ncaonline.org.uk/) was established in 1988 to bring together the major bodies and organizations, including service providers, users, depositors, and policy makers, across the United Kingdom concerned with archives and their use. It aims to develop consensus on matters of mutual concern and provide an authoritative common voice for the archival community. It encourages and assists the education of the public about archives, and some of its objectives are delivered through the PSQG and the Community Archives Development Group (see above).

The Museums, Libraries and Archives Council (MLA) (http://www.mla.gov.uk/) is the designated nondepartmental public body with a responsibility for strategic work to promote the role of museums, libraries, and

archives in the United Kingdom and within government programs. It has an importance in bringing the different parts of the heritage sector together to work in partnership rather than in isolation, emphasizing the value of coordination.

CONCLUSION

The twentieth century witnessed the development of the professional care for archives in the United Kingdom, and archive and records management services relevant to communities and individuals. The profession has progressed from one dominated by antiquarians to one which seeks to offer services to users of all kinds, based on the belief of the fundamental right to information. Management of that information is becoming the dominant theme in training archivists and records managers, together with partnership with libraries and museums to provide a stronger and wider platform for the heritage sector. The development of electronic communications will continue to challenge the profession, testing long held principles and offering new ways of delivering services.

FURTHER READING AND INFORMATION

All the organizations mentioned above have Web sites with additional and up-to-date information. In addition, Janet Foster and Julia Sheppard (eds.) *British Archives; A Guide to Archive Resources in the United Kingdom* 4th ed. (Palgrave, 2002) gives useful information about over 1000 archives in the United Kingdom, though current arrangements for access should be checked online or by phone. Online resources for this include the TNA Archon Directory (http://www.nationalarchives.gov.uk/archon/). *The Public Record Office 1838–1958* (HMSO 1991) and its subsequent volume *The Public Record Office 1959–1969* (Public Record Office 2000) give extensive details on the organization and its development.

United Kingdom: Libraries and Librarianship

David J. Muddiman
Leeds Metropolitan University, Leeds, U.K.

Abstract

This entry provides an overview of contemporary libraries and librarianship in the United Kingdom. After an introduction which identifies some of the key phases and determinants of library development, separate sections are included which discuss national libraries; public libraries; academic (university) libraries; school and college libraries; special libraries. In each case a basic structural and statistical description is provided, the history of the sector is presented in outline, and current policy issues and concerns are discussed. The entry concludes with an examination of United Kingdom librarianship, its professional associations, and library education and research.

INTRODUCTION

The United Kingdom of Great Britain and Northern Ireland (U.K.) is a parliamentary democracy and constitutional monarchy of, in mid-2007, an estimated 60.95 million people.[1] The United Kingdom is a permanent member of the UN Security Council; a founding member of NATO and of the (British) Commonwealth; and since 1973 a member of the European Union, although not its economic and monetary union. The centralized governance of the United Kingdom has been recently modified by constitutional reform, which, in 1999, created devolved administration of domestic affairs (including libraries) in Scotland, Wales, and Northern Ireland. The U.K. economy is now overwhelmingly postindustrial with an estimated 80.4% of the labor force employed in services; 18.2% in industry and 1.4% in agriculture. In comparative global terms, the United Kingdom is a prosperous and advanced capitalist democracy with a per capita GDP of $35,300 in 2007.[2] However, significantly for libraries, higher level literacy rates in the United Kingdom are relatively low compared with other advanced economies: 16% of adults over 16 years of age have literacy levels equivalent only to those expected in children of 11 years or less.[3] Also of importance for libraries is the multicultural character of U.K. society. In the 2001 population census 7.9% of Britons described themselves as of minority ethnicity (that is, a category other than "White British" in census returns). London is the most ethnically diverse city in the United Kingdom, with 40% of Londoners belonging to a minority ethnic group.[4]

The modern history of the United Kingdom is underpinned, on the one hand, by its rise to preeminence as the "first industrial nation" and, on the other, by its maritime dominance which, by the late nineteenth century, had created an empire which covered one-quarter of the Earth's surface. Since then, two narratives of British twentieth century history have competed for the attention of historians. The first, an epic chronicle of two world wars and decline of empire, is at first sight of little relevance to libraries—although see the counterarguments made, for example, by G.K. Peatling.[5] The second—which charts the evolution of modern British society, its transformations of class and culture and the rise and decline of its social institutions—has provided a much firmer context for the historical analysis of library and information services. In particular, the history of the British welfare state, the scrutiny of its character and limitations, and the examination of its more recent partial dismantling provide arguably the most appropriate framework and chronology for understanding modern U.K. library and information services.

This is not to say, however, that the development of libraries in the United Kingdom was entirely dependent on the state. Before the mid-nineteenth century a diverse range of libraries had flowered in Britain in response to the demands of an increasingly literate society, financed by private contributions, subscriptions, and endowments. Libraries of colleges and the ancient universities; religious libraries; scientific and philosophical society libraries; circulating and subscription libraries; mechanics institutes; the library of the British Museum itself (founded in 1753)—all of these amounted to an arguably impressive aggregation which catered for many diverse and specialized needs. However, by 1850 the limitations of these libraries had become clear. On the one hand, they offered uneven and unsystematic provision of knowledge, increasingly inadequate in a modern industrial state becoming conscious of its utility and value. On the other hand, these libraries, in the main, limited their provision to specific client groups or those with the capacity to pay—a situation which became gradually recognized as untenable in a society where universal education, numeracy, and literacy were becoming utilitarian, moral, and spiritual goals.

Encyclopedia of Library and Information Sciences, Fourth Edition DOI: 10.1081/E-ELIS4-120044909

As a result, the passage of an act enabling the establishment of taxpayer funded public libraries in 1850 (1853 in Scotland and Ireland) was as significant for its symbolic as well as its practical consequences. Between 1850 and 1914, library expansion as a whole in the United Kingdom became more and more dependent on public support, either from local ratepayers (in the case of public libraries) or through central government grants. These years saw the foundation of over 500 public library authorities; the expansion of existing university libraries and six new ones in "civic" universities; a hugely expanded British Museum Library which evolved into a "national" library; and the establishment of the National Library of Wales. Important as such expansion was, it remained however partial and uneven, reflecting local and sectional interests, legislation which was permissive rather than mandatory and in some cases, still, the generosity of benefactors such as Carnegie and Passmore Edwards. Only after the shock of the First World War did the construction of library systems become a truly organized state project; the Kenyon Report of 1927 encouraging their development as an "engine of great potentiality for state welfare."[6] Over the next 50 years or so, the United Kingdom, with a great deal of success, attempted to develop comprehensive networks of national, public, academic, and specialist libraries. These were usually locally managed but were often co-ordinated by focused policy networks comprising government advisors and powerful professional groupings such as the Library Association (founded in 1877); Aslib (the Association of Special Libraries and Information Bureaux, founded in 1924), and SCONUL (the Standing Conference on National and University Libraries, founded in 1956). Such governance crystallized in influential policy reports such as those by McColvin on public libraries (1942),[7] Dainton on national libraries (1969),[8] and Parry on university libraries (1967),[9] which determined strategic direction and state funding priorities. These were sometimes linked to formal legislation such as the 1964 Public Libraries Act and the 1972 Act which established the British Library.

By 1979, U.K. library provision was widely admired throughout the world not least because it seemed to combine secure financial support from a social democratic state with a relative autonomy of governance and ethics which minimized direct political interference. However, this U.K. model was not without its critics. Some claimed that U.K. information services were disorganized and uneven, compared, for example with the seemingly comprehensive state scientific and industrial services provided in the USSR.[10] United Kingdom public library services, others argued, were limited and conservative, focusing on a middle-class clientele and neglecting outreach and other service models which might attract disadvantaged users.[11] However, since the mid-1980s, critiques such as these have been largely superseded by arguments more sympathetic to Conservative Prime Minister Margaret

Fig. 1 The United Kingdom.
Source: https://www.cia.gov/library/publications/the-world-fact book/geos/uk.html (accessed December 31, 2008).

Thatcher's project of rolling back the U.K. welfare state. The U.K. library sector has become, it is claimed, largely unresponsive to the demands of a dynamic free-market economy which is now linked to the fast developing "information" revolution.[12] As a consequence, libraries in Britain have been exhorted simultaneously to commercialize their management and marketing and to informatise their services and provision, replacing books and documents with electronic networks and products. United Kingdom public, academic, national, and special libraries have, as we show in subsequent sections, responded to these pressures with differing strategies and with varying levels of success.

NATIONAL LIBRARIES

The United Kingdom is perhaps unique in possessing three "national' libraries": the British Library (BL); the National Library of Scotland (NLS); and the National Library of Wales (NLW). The British Library is, of course, preeminent among these and is the subject of a separate entry in this encyclopedia (see the entry, "British Library," p. 677). The library can trace its origins back to 1753 when a library was established in the British Museum based on the bequeathed collections of Sir Hans Sloane; the library subsequently expanded exponentially in Victorian times, especially under the tenure of librarian Antonio Panizzi (Keeper of Printed Books 1837–1856 and Principal Librarian and Director 1856–1866) who oversaw the development of its Bloomsbury site and the famous round reading room. Subsequent developments in the later nineteenth and twentieth centuries saw the foundation of a series of "national" libraries: the Patent Office Library (from 1854); the Science Museum Science Library (from 1883); the Central Library for Students (from 1916 to 1931, after 1931 the National Central Library); and the National Lending Library for Science and Technology (from 1957). The British Library Act of 1972, which created the modern-day BL, effectively unified this by then unwieldy number of national services and collections in science, commerce, reference and interlending. Subsequently the library has rationalized its operations around two locations: its public face at the St Pancras Building in North London, opened in 1998; and its back office and collection storage facilities at Boston Spa, West Yorkshire. The library employs an estimated 2000 staff who operate on resources of approximately £120 million per annum (2007). It maintains collections of approximately 14 million monographs and 880,000 serial titles as well as numerous manuscript, audiovisual and, increasingly, digital sources. (For more detailed statistical information see the separate entry *British Library*.) It is one of six legal deposit libraries in Britain and Ireland (others being the NLS; the NLW; the Bodleian, Oxford University; and Cambridge University Library and Trinity College, Dublin) and is entitled, under the terms of the Legal Deposit Libraries Act (2003) to receive copies of all U.K. publications including, now, certain forms of electronically published material. In line with this, the contemporary BL is strategically committed to expanding its digital presence—in terms of collecting electronic publications; electronic catalogs and access; and digital conservation. In the era of the World Wide Web, it aims to be a "national library which serves the world."

The National Libraries of Scotland and Wales might reasonably be said to have less ambitious goals: most significantly since the advent of devolved government in the United Kingdom in 1999 they have become focused on their public role as a focus of Scottish and Welsh national culture. Historically, NLS has a longer lineage: its origins can be traced to the Edinburgh Advocates Library founded in 1682 which in 1709 was given the privilege of legal deposit. Throughout the eighteenth and nineteenth centuries this library was regarded as a national library in all but name—eventually it became one by Act of Parliament in 1925. The modern library is now located in its George IV Bridge Building in Edinburgh with a second site, completed in 1995, at Causewayside, further from the city centre. NLW is, by contrast, a mainly twentieth century institution: it was created by Royal Charter in 1907 and sited, despite opposition from Cardiff, in Aberystwyth, geographically central in Wales but away from its most populous cities. The library is housed in an imposing neo-classical building above the town which was eventually completed in 1965. Like the NLS, it benefited from extensive refurbishment in the 1990s.

Functionally, both libraries are similar in many respects: both are U.K. legal deposit libraries; they have collections of a comparable size (circa 6 million monographs in Wales, 8 million in Scotland); they employ similar numbers of staff (265 in Scotland; 300 in Wales); they operate on comparable budgets—total operating incomes of £13 million in Wales (2006/2007); £12 million in Scotland (2004/2005).[13,14] Both effectively serve as hybrid regional research and national libraries, balancing the general needs of researchers with a growing awareness of their public function as centers of the printed word in Scotland and Wales. Since 1999, when oversight and funding of each library was transferred to the Scottish and Welsh Executives, respectively, both have adopted strategic plans which highlight this latter role and which stress the promotion of national heritage, languages. and culture.

PUBLIC LIBRARIES

United Kingdom public libraries currently constitute a network of 4657 static and mobile service points, administered by 208 local authorities who are responsible for library provision. The largest public library ranked by book issues is now the Norwich and Norfolk Millennium Library which lends 1.157 million books per year; the busiest library in terms of visits is Birmingham Central Library with 1.564 million visitors. In total, U.K. public libraries issue 315 million books per year (2006/7), a decline of 61 million since 2001/2002; although children's book issues have remained static over the same period at 90 million per annum. To some extent this decline has been counterbalanced by an increase in library visits to 337 million per year—a 6% increase on 2001/2002. Many of these extra visitors have undoubtedly been attracted by the establishment of a "People's Network" of (in the main) free to use Internet points in libraries comprising 41,000 workstations by 2006/2007. Expenditure on public libraries currently amounts to £1157 million per annum and this, despite the People's Network, has remained largely stable since the advent of the Labour government in 1997. Fifty-five percent of this sum is spent on staff; 12% on books and materials and 33% on buildings, equipment, and other items.[15] The comparatively low expenditure on books and materials has attracted vociferous criticism in recent years.[16]

Public libraries in England and Wales are managed within the framework of the 1964 Public Library and Museums Act, which requires that each local library authority provide a "comprehensive and efficient service." (Scotland has its own public library legislation, most recently the Public Libraries Act (Scotland), 1955). In England, the central government Department for Culture Media and Sport (DCMS) is responsible for ensuring the implementation of the act and through its agency the Museums, Libraries and Archives Council (MLA) it coordinates policy and strategic direction; the Scottish, Welsh and Northern Ireland devolved executives now exercise similar functions in these regions. In recent years DCMS and MLA have tried to bring a degree of consistency to uneven local library services through the introduction of public library standards in 2001. However, these have been subsequently diluted, not least because of lack of clarity regarding the consequences of non-compliance. Perhaps more important has been the policy document *Framework for the Future* (2003) which DCMS heralded as a "long term strategic vision for the public library."[17] This tried to resolve, albeit with a mixed degree of success, some of the dilemmas facing the public library in an advanced "information" society (see discussion below).

The history of the U.K. public library movement is now well documented and the facts of public library development are clear enough. The basic picture is one of enabling acts of parliament supported by government enquiries and reports leading to gradual long-term expansion and improvement, albeit punctuated by alternate periods of inertia and reform. The initial public library act of 1850 was sponsored by the utilitarian radical Liverpool MP William Ewart and supported by evidence gathered by Edward Edwards, a British Museum library assistant later to become City Librarian of Manchester. The act permitted any municipal borough with a population above 10,000 to establish a "free" library provided two-thirds of ratepayers supported one, setting a limit on the local tax which could be raised. The first local borough to adopt the act was the city of Norwich (in 1850); although the most important early civic library to be opened was Manchester in 1852, at a ceremony attended

by Dickens, Thackeray, and other distinguished Victorians. Until the 1880s further expansion was slow—by 1886 only 125 authorities had established libraries. After amending legislation in 1886, however, which relaxed the conditions for adoption, new libraries burgeoned, encouraged also by endowments from philanthropists such as Scots-American steel magnate Andrew Carnegie and journal publisher John Passmore Edwards. By 1918, 561 municipal boroughs—the majority—had established libraries, some with a fairly large network of branches.[18] Subsequent periods of expansion included the 1920s and 1930s, after a 1919 act which enabled rural counties to operate as library authorities and finally the 1960s, when the integrated national library system recommended in the famous McColvin Report of 1942 finally reached near fruition. Arguably the "golden age" of the U.K. public library, the 1960s saw a doubling of real expenditure on the service; the construction of many modern library buildings; the expansion of information, children's and outreach services, and a rationalization of administration through the creation of larger authorities in England and Wales in a Local Government Act of 1972. Since the 1980s, however, fortunes have been rather more mixed: in common with much of the U.K. welfare state, public libraries have faced expenditure cutbacks, decreasing professional staff numbers and a worrying fall, since the 1990s, in adult (although not children's) book loans. Nevertheless, public librarians have attempted to innovate through community librarianship and "outreach" initiatives; improving "customer" responsiveness; implementing the aforementioned "People's Network" and opening some impressive new library buildings— aptly at Norwich, the first U.K. public library authority and more recently in award-winning buildings at Peckham, South London, and Brighton.

Beyond this relatively straightforward narrative of growth and development, however, U.K. public library history is undoubtedly more complex than it first appears. In contrast to its steady material progress, the underlying philosophy and rationale of the public library has always been contested, and an analysis of over 150 years of debate about the purpose and societal impact of the service reveals a series of unresolved tensions at the heart of the public library idea. Perhaps the most fundamental of these were the differences between Benthamite liberals, such as Ewart, who saw libraries primarily as a vehicle for *individual* self-improvement and opportunity, and late Victorian idealists, socialists and even some nationalist conservatives, who emphasized the benefits of the library for *communities* and society as a whole. Many subsequent public library policy debates can be traced back to these differences: the legitimacy of libraries' leisure role and specifically the "great fiction question" (regarding provision of leisure reading) which surfaced in the 1890s; the debates over provision to, and expenditure on, reluctant, "disadvantaged" and mainly working-class library clients which began in the 1930s; conflict between "localism" and the perceived need for national structures and standards; tensions, especially from the 1960s onwards, between stock provision driven by reader demand and more culturally conservative collection management policies. Most of these issues have never really been resolved: instead, in the mid-twentieth century years of plenty, public libraries attempted arguably to be all things to all people. Questions of fundamental purpose were certainly sidelined in favor of a functional consensus of "public service," typified by the 1971 statement of *Public Library Aims and Objectives*, produced by the Public Library Research Group.[19] This defined public libraries as a "multipurpose information-education-culture agency" and enumerated their objectives under the headings of education; information; culture, and leisure. Most subsequent government policy documents—including the recent *Framework for the Future*[17] have continued this all inclusive public service convention.

Partly as a consequence of this legacy, twenty-first century public library policy tends to be hampered by unresolved problems of purpose and rationale. These are complicated still further by the onset of the "information" society which has brought with it the informatisation and networking of libraries; new business-led managerial practices; and market-oriented "retail" models of service. Initially, from its inception in the mid-1990s until its near completion in 2004, the key library informatization project—the People's Network—was heralded optimistically as a "turning point" for the U.K. public library, marking, perhaps, a reconstitution of the "public sphere" in the information society. More latterly, however, and despite the network's undoubted initial success, such optimism has been replaced by a realization that wiring up the library is perhaps not the panacea it once seemed—especially as home Internet access becomes cheaper and more universal in the United Kingdom (in 2006, 57% of U.K. households had home Internet access).[20] The focus on the network has consequently dissipated and been superseded by an eclectic mix of ideas and blueprints for the public library's future. These include the initiatives of radical and "community" librarians who advocate refocusing the service around literacy, community engagement and social inclusion; the visions of "modernizers" who want to reinvent public libraries as centers of new digital technologies and rebrand them as "Idea Stores" or "Discovery Centers"; and the arguments of traditionalists who favor a "back to basics" approach of restoring expenditure on books and a return to the core purpose of book provision, linked usually to a retail led strategy of improved marketing and promotion. The impact of such competing ideas—none of them dominant—is difficult to gauge. However, in a climate of financial pressures, falling book issues and the disaggregation of U.K. local government, the clamor for urgent and sometimes contradictory action has undoubtedly engendered a sense

of uncertainty and insecurity in public library circles. Perhaps it is finally the case that the public service consensus, which has sustained British public libraries over the last century or so, is beginning to dissolve.

ACADEMIC LIBRARIES

In the United Kingdom, libraries in universities and colleges of higher education (commonly known as "academic" libraries) now operate within a unified framework of state higher education created in Education Reform Acts of 1988 and 1992. (In the United Kingdom "higher" education is defined as degree or diploma level education targeted at students of 18 years old or over.) They are funded in the main through their parent universities or colleges, which receive most of their income in turn from block grants made by regional funding councils (for England, Wales, Scotland, and Northern Ireland) and student tuition fees. Academic libraries provide services in a total of 168 higher education institutions, 106 of them universities and the remainder colleges of higher education. They serve an estimated total of 2.34 million students (1.79 million undergraduates, the remainder postgraduate) and 165,000 academic staff; total higher education library expenditure amounted to £561million in academic year 2005–2006. Within these institutions there are a total of 864 separate academic library service points employing in 2007 10,565 staff, 3979 of them professional, the majority of the latter being members of CILIP.[15],[21] Collectively, U.K. academic libraries are represented by the Society of College, National and University Libraries (SCONUL) which serves as a forum and lobbying body for the whole sector. In addition, Research Libraries UK (formerly CURL, the Consortium of University Research Libraries) performs a similar function reflecting the interests of 25 leading university research libraries, together with Britain's national libraries and the Victoria and Albert Museum.

United Kingdom academic libraries have, of course, a long heritage dating back to the foundation of the medieval universities in the late thirteenth and fourteenth centuries. Recognizable university libraries were established at Oxford in 1412; Cambridge in 1424; St Andrews in 1411, and Glasgow in 1451, although collections of donated books in particular colleges predate these. Subsequent development of university libraries progressed unevenly, although major advances paralleled the proliferation of the printed book in the late Tudor period and saw the expansion of Cambridge University Library, the establishment of Edinburgh (1580) and the foundation of the Bodleian Library at Oxford (1602). It was not, however, until after 1750 that these libraries really began to resemble the familiar institutions of today: the century after that date witnessed, often for the first time, reader access to shelves; transparent catalogs, and skilled librarians. By 1849 the

Bodleian, for example, comprised 220,000 printed volumes and 21,000 manuscripts compared with only 30,000 volumes and 6000 manuscripts, respectively, in 1714.[22] By then, moreover, the medieval universities had been joined by new universities in London and Durham each of which began to develop library systems. Perhaps even more significantly, by the end of the nineteenth century, libraries were being established at several new "civic" universities and colleges in Britain's major cities, many of them with a scientific and technical bias. By 1925, 13 such institutions were operating, most of them funded by the British state, which had established a University Grants Committee (UGC) in 1919.

Between 1930 and 1960 academic library development continued piecemeal, although some impressive buildings, such as the Brotherton Library at Leeds (see Fig. 2) date from this time. Although library services gradually became professionalized (SCONUL was founded in 1956) and libraries were developed as the number of colleges and universities grew, there was little uniformity in the resources which parent institutions granted to libraries, or in the services and priorities of the libraries themselves. Two key developments of the 1960s changed matters. The first, a report for the UGC subsequently known as The Parry Report (1967), recommended a number of minimum standards for academic libraries including the principle that universities should devote "about six percent" of their budget to library provision, and these were broadly accepted. The second, the creation first of a group of new elite universities and, more widely, of a large number of vocationally oriented "polytechnics" with degree awarding powers, spawned the development of a large number of new libraries in higher education, establishing the service structures still in place today. Library development between 1970 and 1992 subsequently coalesced around two broad models:

- An academic/research model which prioritized collection development and management and was mainly adopted by larger, older, and elite universities with substantial research resources (many of these libraries founded CURL in 1983).

- A teaching and learning library model which focused on currency of resources and renewal of stock together with undergraduate student needs and user education. This model was largely adopted in polytechnics, colleges of higher education, and some smaller "modern" universities.

In many ways, of course, contemporary adaptations of these models of academic library provision still persist. However, arguably since 1992 when the United Kingdom moved to a uniform system of HE, the direction of academic library policy has been instead dictated by a new educational paradigm of massified, and more latterly networked, higher education. In 1988/1989 U.K. universities enrolled 517,000 undergraduate students. By 2005/ 2006 this figure was 1.79 million.[21] The Universities Funding Council commissioned Follett Report (1993) heralded a period of unprecedented change for academic libraries as they adapted, in the main very positively, to this new environment. Following Follett, the new post-1992 Higher Education Funding Councils (for England,

Fig. 2 The magnificent interior of the Brotherton Library, University of Leeds. Opened in 1936, the central rotunda consciously imitates the famous British Museum Library reading room.
Source: University of Leeds.

Scotland, Wales, and Northern Ireland) together provided over £140 million which was spent on over 100 new building developments. Even more significantly for the future, through the Funding Councils' Joint Information Systems Committee (JISC, established in 1993), Follett inaugurated the so-called E-Lib program in which a £15 million budget contributed to over 60 developmental ICT projects in fields such as electronic journals; digitization of catalogs and source material; online publishing and electronic document delivery.

After the completion of E-Lib in 2001 and the concurrent stabilization of networked technologies around the World Wide Web, many U.K. academic libraries moved rapidly to a "hybrid library" model of complementary electronic and print-on-paper services. Such moves were often accelerated by the convergence of library management with that of ICT and media resources across whole institutions, together with, since 2003/2004 the adoption by many universities of virtual learning systems such as WebCT or Blackboard. Spurred on by these developments, some academic librarians have become especially focused upon the theory and practice of information literacy, SCONUL itself developing the now ubiquitous "seven pillars" approach to student information skills. According to SCONUL, U.K. academic libraries over the next 10 years are likely to become increasingly personalized and customer focused and be characterized by "complex blended systems" and multiuse, multipurpose buildings.[23] While many influential U.K. academic librarians actively embrace this vision of flux and change, others urge caution at such "postmodern" approaches, worrying openly about the custodial and collection management role of the university library, the decline of scholarly research and authoritative published knowledge.[24] Such tensions, perhaps, together with the consolidation of interest groupings such as Research Libraries UK, suggest that the character of U.K. academic libraries (like higher education itself) may become increasingly heterogeneous and diverse.

SCHOOLS, COLLEGES, AND SERVICES TO CHILDREN

Colleges of Further Education

Although many of the United Kingdom's universities have now developed a focus on technical and vocational qualifications, the bedrock of U.K. provision in this field is a network of 495 Further Education (FE) Colleges. These colleges offer a range of subdegree qualifications to students aged 16 years and over; a few also offer higher level qualifications such as "Foundation" degrees in collaboration with local universities. Most of the colleges were established in the 1950s and 1960s: initially they were administered by local education authorities; however,

following the reorganization of the sector in 1992 they are now corporate bodies overseen and funded by a Learning and Skills Council (in England) and similar bodies in the rest of the United Kingdom. All of the colleges have developed libraries serving the needs of staff and students but these vary considerably from college to college: there are no statutory requirements regarding service levels, although colleges are subject to an inspection regime overseen by OFSTED (the U.K. Office for Standards in Education) which includes scrutiny of learning resource standards. Consequently, some colleges and their librarians have developed innovative, well resourced learning resource centers which characteristically locate the library at the center of the college managed and virtual learning environment. At the other extreme, however, some college library services are undoubtedly under-resourced, marginalized and lacking in professional library staff. The most recent CILIP survey in 2003[25] found, for example, that only 7.2% of college libraries received over 1% of the college budget and that several small colleges (those with less than 8000 students) were operating without qualified library staff. The median number of professional staff in these small colleges was one; in medium colleges (8000–18,000 students) it was two and in large colleges of over 18,000 students, four. Notwithstanding such problems, however, many U.K. FE college librarians maintain a vigorous commitment to modernizing and improving services in the field. They are represented by the CoFHE group of CILIP (which produces important guidance on standards and good practice)[26] and the Council for Learning Resources in Colleges (CoLRiC) which acts as a lobby group for the enhancement and improvement of services.

School Libraries

Libraries in U.K. schools have, of course, a much longer heritage than those in FE colleges. Some English grammar schools began to develop systematic collections of books in the sixteenth century and by the late seventeenth century several of these schools had relatively large libraries of a few hundred books or more with written rules and designated masters in charge.[27] However, it was not until the early twentieth century that school libraries began to appear in publicly funded schools: in 1906 the U.K. Board of Education stipulated that every new secondary school (for pupils aged 11 and over) should keep a library. Subsequent progress was slow—in 1936 the Carnegie United Kingdom Trust reported uneven and largely poor school library provision, a situation that only gradually improved before the 1970s. By then, school libraries had become almost universal in secondary schools and most local education authorities (LEAs) in addition funded school library support services which provided materials and professional advice for libraries in both secondary and primary (elementary) schools. By this time also, school librarianship in the United Kingdom had become organized professionally, the Library Association maintaining a specialist School Libraries Group and a separate School Library Association (SLA—founded in 1937) attracting the support of interested teachers and teacher-librarians. Both of these organizations acted as foci for progress and innovation, producing journals which disseminated good practice together with standards and guidelines. Spurred on by such activity, the 1970s and 1980s were, by and large, decades of expansion and improvement in school library services, especially through the development of integrated school resource centers and quality provision of book stock. Some local education authorities, such as Nottinghamshire and the Inner London Education Authority (both of which appointed qualified librarians in all secondary schools), were at the forefront of these innovations.

Since 1990, however, it is generally the case that the progress made toward universal high quality school library provision has been complicated if not reversed. In spite of pressure from the LA (more latterly CILIP) and the SLA, and in part because of continuing tensions between them, the issue of professional staffing in school libraries has never been resolved: the most recent survey by CILIP (2002) estimates that only 30% of the 4000 or so secondary school libraries in the United Kingdom are managed by a chartered librarian; 20% are run by teachers or teacher librarians; and the remaining 50% by library assistants or others.[28] Moreover, local management of school budgets, introduced in 1990, has severely affected the stability and effectiveness of LEA school library support services: these services no longer receive direct funding from LEAs but instead enter into contractual agreements with individual schools who "purchase" their services and are no longer required to use them. Some schools have consequently opted out of this provision—the most recent figures estimate that 15/193 LEA support services have been forced to close since 2000–2001 and that they now serve only 82% of primary school children compared with 90% at that time.[15] In spite of these difficulties, however, expenditure on school library services as a whole has been maintained roughly in line with inflation (a total spend of £39 million or £1.85 per pupil in 2005/2006) and U.K. school librarianship as a professional activity continues to thrive. Many schools have developed model services and initiatives in fields such as reading and literacy; information skills; materials selection; special needs provision; and children's access to and use of the World Wide Web. Many of these new developments are embedded in CILIP's *Guidelines for Secondary School Libraries* (2004) and *The Primary School Library Guidelines* (2002).[29,30]

Public Library Services to Children

Closely linked to school library support services in many areas of the United Kingdom are children's departments of public libraries: both are operated by local authorities and often share a number of professional and administrative functions. Unlike schools, however, public libraries are legally obliged to provide children's services by the 1964 Public Libraries Act. As on March 31, 2006 they held 25.3 million children's books, equivalent to 2.3 per child, and they spent approximately £50 million per annum on the service. United Kingdom public libraries are estimated as employing approximately 600 FTE professional children's librarians, with a further 100 employed in shared posts with schools services. In 2005/2006 they loaned approximately 90 million books, a figure which, unlike its adult counterpart, is rising again at a rate of 4% per annum after falls in the 1980s and 1990s. An estimated 55% of U.K. children aged 0–14 are registered members of public libraries.[31]

Children's public libraries in the United Kingdom date back almost to the inception of the public library itself—Manchester Public Library opened a separate room (for boys) in 1861 and in 1871 Birmingham Public Library recorded a collection of 456 books for children.[32] However, subsequent development of children's services was uneven, although the decade before World War I (when many separate children's collections were first established) and 1925–1939 (when children's librarianship as a distinct profession emerged) marked significant advances. It was not until the late 1960s and 1970s, however, that services experienced major advance. Underpinned by the statutory force of the 1964 Act, fueled by a quantum leap in both the quantity and quality of children's books and inspired by classic professional texts such as Janet Hill's *Children are People* (1973),[33] children's librarianship became arguably the most proactive, creative, and successful component of U.K. public library provision. Since then children's librarians have played a leading part in developments such as outreach, services to teenagers, ethnic minorities, and children with special needs; they have engaged in literacy and more latterly information literacy work—the latter especially in conjunction with the establishment since 2000 of the "People's Network" in the public library. Since 1997 children's libraries have also become important in a number of the Labour government's multiagency "social inclusion" initiatives—the most significant of these perhaps being "Bookstart" (and its successor "Surestart"), a literacy and social care initiative targeted at children under 5 years of age and offered now in 85% of U.K. local authorities. In part because of work such as this, children's services tend to have avoided much of the uncertainty of purpose which has dogged the rest of the U.K. public library movement. Despite recurring problems of funding, management, and inconsistency in service levels, children's services in general enjoy the rhetorical support of policymakers because of their clear educational focus and relevance to literacy. There is, moreover, general professional agreement on a strategy for developing children's libraries—embodied in the policy document *Start with the Child* (2002) this proposes a program of innovation and diversification of provision in response to new media and the changing culture and needs of children.[34] Access to resources to fully implement such plans, however, continues to be problematic.

SPECIAL LIBRARIES

Specialist information provision in the United Kingdom is now, as one would anticipate in any advanced post-industrial society, kaleidoscopic in its subject range and heterogeneous in its institutional arrangements. The current *ASLIB Directory of Information Sources in the United Kingdom* lists over 10,700 organizational repositories of information: only a minority of these are obviously libraries.[35] However, special *libraries*, in the sense of collections and services in limited subject fields, and more especially "workplace" libraries, serving distinct groups of occupational and institutional users, clearly still constitute an important subsection of this specialist information landscape. Some of these employ large numbers of people in complex organizational settings—the BBC Information and Archives Department, for example, having a staff of over 600[36]—whereas many services in small companies and voluntary organizations are operated by lone librarians. The extent of special library provision is, of course, notoriously difficult to map, but the most recent reliable U.K. survey data, recorded in 1998–2002 suggests a distribution by sector as in Table 1.

Significant specialist areas absent from this survey include libraries in the National Health Service (an estimated 375 libraries in 2002);[38] news, media, and publishing (an estimated 80 media organizations with libraries in 2008);[39] and industrial sectors beyond energy and pharmaceuticals. All in all, an informed estimate would probably gauge that around 5000 specialist information units which are recognizable as libraries currently operate in the United Kingdom: this figure roughly tallies with CILIP estimates of approximately 4000 professional members working in the special libraries sector (see section "U.K. Library and Information Profession"). However, as we

shall see, some sectors, such as commercial, industrial, and media libraries, have been subject in the past few years to closure, contraction, or drastic organizational change, whereas others, such as libraries in health and other government services, appear to be consolidating around new "hybrid" models of service provision.

The first genuine examples of specialist library provision in the United Kingdom are generally held to have been founded in the early modern period, although arguably some collections (such as, for example, those of medieval monasteries) predate these. The institutions of the traditional professions—medicine, law, and the church—tended to develop libraries from the mid-sixteenth century onward, such as those in the Royal College of Physicians and the Inns of Court in London. The scientific revolution of the seventeenth and eighteenth centuries subsequently underpinned the foundation of important libraries such as those of the Royal Society (1666) and a number of provincial and specialist scientific societies; the increasing reliance of government on knowledge and information also began to be acknowledged through the creation of the Foreign Office Library (1801) and the House of Commons Library (1818). However, it was not until the second part of the nineteenth century that special libraries began to noticeably proliferate in significant numbers. Impelled by a cluster of societal forces linked to accelerating modernity—the increasing specialization of knowledge; the diffusion of knowledge reliant industries; the rise of professional occupations; the expansion of the state and its bureaucracy; the invention of new information and communication technologies—libraries and information or "intelligence" bureaux of diverse kinds began to penetrate the United Kingdom's governance and economy. By the 1920s, large industrial concerns such as Metropolitan Vickers in Manchester and Rowntree in York had established libraries linked to sophisticated research and intelligence centers; the state itself also began to fund technical libraries in "Research Associations" linked to specialist industrial sectors. In 1924 a grouping of 84 such public and private sector concerns organized themselves in ASLIB—the Association of Special Libraries and Information Bureaux—an umbrella group which acted less as a professional association than a "clearing house" for an envisaged national network of specialized information services. From 1944 ASLIB attracted state funding to further this goal; by 1960 it had 2500 corporate members, processed a workload of 35,000 enquires per annum; employed over 40 staff and supported a prestigious research department.[40] By this time, specialized library and information networks in most of the sectors enumerated above had been established along lines that are recognizable today: central government libraries expanded enormously in the three decades after World War II (for example, the Board of Trade Library in 1950 had a staff of 40 with one professional librarian; by 1976 this had grown to 147 staff with 46 librarians[41]) and, by

Table 1 Distribution of U.K. special libraries by workplace sector (1998).

Sector	Number of libraries
Government departments	60
Other government organizations	379
Voluntary agencies	1390
Professional societies, etc.	210
Legal	1400
Commercial; financial	211
Energy	83
Pharmaceuticals	93
Management/information consultants	200

Source: From LISU, *Library and Information Statistics Tables*, LISU, Loughborough University, U.K.[37]

1972, a survey estimated that 1182 industrial and commercial libraries were operating in Britain.[42] Most of these libraries by the 1970s offered a proactive information service to their users. This generally included the use of the techniques of documentation pioneered in Britain by S.C. Bradford and others in the mid-twentieth century, and it supplemented the traditional librarian's function of the collection and organization of information with techniques of analysis and dissemination. Some of this work became professionally recognized as "information science" in the 1960s and 1970s, specifically through the foundation (in 1958) of the Institute of Information Scientists (IIS), an organization which had 750 members by 1970.[40] By comparison, "special librarianship" in Britain, in contrast to the United States, never convincingly evolved as a specialist profession, although the U.K. Library Association did set up a rather poorly supported Reference, Special and Information Section in 1949.

All in all, by the mid-1970s, the United Kingdom could boast a relatively well-developed and well-organized network of specialist library and information provision, in part supported by the state through ASLIB grants and other mechanisms of arms-length subsidy. Over the next 30 years, however, this system of state-sponsored pluralism would in large part fragment as a result of the economic, technological, and political transformations linked to postindustrialism. In the commercial and industrial sectors, many hitherto site-specific libraries, especially those in large companies, were restructured or downsized as a result of accelerating globalization and corporate realignment. In the public (state) sector similar upheavals were experienced in the wake of the privatization, between 1979 and 1997, of large state utilities such as energy, water, coal, steel, telecoms, and railways. Even libraries in government departments themselves, and those in state-funded services such as health, underwent a commercialization of sorts through the introduction of private sector management regimes such as cost-benefit analysis; market testing and performance measurement—procedures which became ubiquitous in all United Kingdom special libraries by the end of the century. Linked to, and facilitating, many of these trends was the information technology revolution: especially the advent of organizational intranets from the late 1980s and the Internet from the late 1990s onward. These technical changes heralded a major transformation of the structures, functions and scope of United Kingdom special library and information services. On the one hand, they seemed to promise a prominent role for library and information services in the exploitation of a newly recognized and valued commodity; on the other, they threatened the potential extinction of the "library" and the special librarian and their replacement by the database, the World Wide Web and the intelligent network.

At the present time many of these transformations are still incomplete; however, what is clear is that the shift to a postindustrial political economy has had an uneven impact on the United Kingdom's special library networks. ASLIB has contracted, losing its government funding in the late 1970s and transforming itself into a commercially focused "Association for Information Management" in 1983, offering information consultancy services, training and publishing to an international market. (ASLIB finally abandoned its charitable status in 2004 and now operates on full commercial lines. It currently has a corporate membership of approximately 380 members.[43]) Some special library sectors have similarly suffered: in news and media provision an almost complete revolution appears to have been effected since 1998 with the traditional "cuttings" service being completely replaced by digital systems where editorial staff have direct access to electronic data and records.[36] Other service sectors, however, such as health, legal information, and voluntary agencies have witnessed a proliferation of small library and information units as the importance of information has come to be acknowledged in, for example, medium-sized law firms and headquarters of charities. More traditionally run library services, such as those in central government and professional and learned bodies, have typically contracted in size and been forced to change, but they have in the main retained their institutional integrity. Even in these cases, however, a constant theme—not unique to the United Kingdom—has been modernization: the challenge faced by specialist librarians to establish a new role for themselves and their libraries in the face of constant organizational and technical change. Consequently, most special libraries in the United Kingdom now transparently operate in a "hybrid" library environment, coupling traditional elements of document based provision—needs assessment; current awareness; collection management; enquiry work—with an increasing focus on the creation, organization, and accessing of digital resources and the "digital consumer." As their parent organizations inexorably move toward an integrated digital environment it seems likely that the specialist information professionals of the future will gradually supplant their traditional "intermediary" role with a broader remit for organizational information resources, encompassing new functions such as internal records management, digital archiving, information auditing, and knowledge capture. Whether or not this new aggregation of professional work—variously labeled "information"; "knowledge" or "records" management—will result in the salvation or the demise of the special library, remains, of course, to be seen.

THE U.K. LIBRARY AND INFORMATION PROFESSIONS

The Workforce

According to the most authoritative current estimate, the total U.K. library and information workforce comprises

61,230 employees as at mid-2005.[44] Fifty-eight percent of these employees are estimated to be female, 42% male; 52% work full-time, 48% part-time. These figures include 21,691 full-time equivalent posts in public libraries, 9470 in academic and school libraries, and 2252 in the British Library and other national libraries. In public libraries an estimated 23% of posts are of professional level; in academic libraries the proportion is a predictably higher one of 34% and in national libraries 41%. Recent trends indicate a marked decline by 5% since the year 2000 of professional posts in public libraries; however, this is counterbalanced by a similar rise in the professionalized workforce in academic libraries. The extent of professionalization in the wider information sector—business, industrial, voluntary, and other specialized information services is unclear. However, CILIP (see below) in 2003 reported 1737 members working in industry and commerce; 746 in medicine and health; 1066 in specialist government libraries; and 288 as independent consultants.[45] This amounts to a total of approximately 4000 members, or 25% of the institute's membership.

CILIP

CILIP, the Chartered Institute of Information and Library Professionals, is the main U.K. body representing this librarianship and information science (LIS) workforce. CILIP was inaugurated only relatively recently on April 1, 2002 as the result of a merger between the former Library Association and the Institute of Information Scientists. It is governed on democratic principles with an elected President and Council of Trustees, although in practice the permanent Chief Executive (currently Bob McKee) is perhaps the most influential figure in its management and strategic direction. CILIP is organized into 12 regional branches including CILIP in Scotland (Slainte), Wales, and Ireland—entities which effectively superseded partly autonomous library associations there. Its membership currently stands at 21,000[46] and is drawn almost equally from public libraries (24%) academic and school libraries (24%) and specialist information services (25%); the remainder comprising members in national libraries (3%) and overseas, retired, and student members.[45] The main level of membership within the Institute is that of chartered member (MCLIP) which is the basic professional credential in U.K. information work. Through CILIP's recently approved Framework of Qualifications this is now complemented by the award of fellow (FCLIP) for excellence in professional achievement and certified affiliate (ACLIP), an award which accredits achievement and experience among paraprofessional workers.

In addition to these core membership functions, CILIP undertakes a very wide range of activities which belie its relatively small size and resources. As well as the aforementioned regional branches, the Institute supports 29 specialist interest groups which range across the spectra of library and information science and management, and many of these groups sponsor world class journals, conferences, and professional training. CILIP maintains a publishing arm (Facet Publications) which produces leading research monographs, textbooks, and handbooks. It also publishes *Library and Information Update*, the key monthly newsletter and review of the U.K. library and information community and it organizes a regular program of training, conferences, and professional development events. CILIP's work in policy and advocacy (see also below) is also becoming increasingly important, focusing currently on aspects of information society policy such as copyright and legal matters; social inclusion; information literacy; equal opportunities; and economic development. Some of this policy work can be seen to be of international significance: CILIP's *Ethical Principles and Code of Professional Practice*, for example, serving as a model for many LIS organizations worldwide. International work more generally continues through CILIP's numerous links with IFLA and its efforts to bring an LIS professional influence to bear on global informational developments, for example through input to the UNESCO World Summit on the Information Society.

History of the Library and Information Professions

The professionalization of library and information work in the United Kingdom is linked to the establishment and evolution of a number of professional groupings in the century between 1870 and 1970. Although most of these groupings are now unified under the umbrella of CILIP, this has not always been the case. The largest and most important of these, the Library Association (LA), was founded in 1877, one year after its American equivalent and arguably as a direct consequence of the impact of the latter's inaugural meeting. Although the LA's initial objectives were impressively broad—"to unite all persons engaged in or interested in library work for the purpose of promoting the best possible administration of existing libraries and the formation of new ones where desirable"—during its first 50 years the association proved itself rather exclusive. True, it was in 1898 granted a Royal Charter and the right to award professional qualifications. By 1899 it had also created what proved to be the seminal journal in early twentieth century librarianship—the *Library Association Record*. However, its leaders—initially until 1895 a group of eminent bookmen and bibliographers, and after that a succession of leading public librarians such as Duff Brown, Jast, and Berwick Sayers—were arguably overly concerned with status, professional standards, and policy lobbying. Membership matters were certainly neglected. Little was done to encourage the bulk of library staff—library assistants—to support the association; they formed a separate Library Assistants' Association (LAA) in 1895. Moreover, the perceived public library bias of the LA deterred potential members in universities and special libraries. By 1928 membership stood at a disappointing 897 members, a situation which set limits on both the influence and range of activities of the association.[47]

During the 1930s, however, reforms largely associated with Ernest A. Savage (Hon. Secretary of the LA, 1928–1934) and Lionel R. McColvin (Hon. Secretary 1934–51) expanded both the LA's membership base and its range of professional activities. The Association of Assistant Librarians (formerly the LAA) became a section of the LA in 1930 and some formerly independent regional groupings became branches. A logically planned structure of specialist interest sections and regional branches was established. Money was obtained from the Carnegie United Kingdom Trust and the Rockefeller Foundation to establish a professionally staffed headquarters and information service. A public profile, typified by the inauguration of awards like the Carnegie Medal for Children's Literature in 1936, was established. By 1939, membership had risen to over 6000 and although World War II brought a pause, expansion resumed in the 1950s and 1960s. The establishment of permanent schools of librarianship in Colleges of Advanced Education and later universities, together with the reform and streamlining of the LA's own associateship regulations and examinations, ensured a steady supply of new members. The proliferation of public, academic, and public sector specialist libraries, in what would prove to be the heyday of the British welfare state, provided ready employment for them. By 1965, LA membership exceeded 15,000; by 1980, 3 years after its centenary year, it had reached 25,000, its historic peak.[48] By this time the LA had become a sophisticated, multifaceted modern bureaucracy which, despite periodic complaints of members, operated effectively and by and large on democratic lines. Its range of functions—course accreditation; conferences; training; publishing; professional advice; international work; policy development and lobbying; continuing professional development—typified those of a progressive professional body. Most would be familiar to observers of post-2002 CILIP.

Despite these advances, the impression (some would argue misplaced) that the LA was, at root, a public library association continued to persist. Although academic and school librarians did join in increasing numbers after 1950, and although specialist LA interest groups were formed, these specialisms in the end found it necessary to organize professionally outside the association in the guise of the School Library Association (formed in 1937) and SCONUL (formed in 1956—see the sections on School Libraries and Academic Libraries). More importantly still, despite the creation of successive Reference, Special and Information Sections from the 1950s onward, the LA continued to find it difficult to recruit members from industrial, technical, and commercial libraries. In part this was due to the continuing growth of ASLIB (see section

"Special Libraries"), which despite its corporate membership structure in effect functioned very much as a professional forum for these librarians until the 1970s. In part also, this schism was based on the developing contention in the 1940s and 1950s that "documentation" and, more latterly, "information science" was a distinct and arguably more sophisticated occupation than librarianship. Such ideas were to result in 1958 in the foundation of the U.K. Institute of Information Scientists (IIS) by a group of scientific and industrial information officers led by Jason Farradane, a Scientific Information Officer then employed by the Tate and Lyle Sugar Company. Led by Farradane (who moved on to an academic career) the Institute successfully sponsored the development of a number of degree courses in Information Science in the late 1960s and 1970s. This academic ethos subsequently attracted a good number of intellectuals and researchers in information related fields to its ranks, ensuring that it attained a certain prestige and influence, especially in professional education and publication (see also below). It never, however, became a mass membership association, even after the perceived expansion of information work as an occupation in the 1980s. In 1970 it had 750 members;[40] at its dissolution in 2002 this figure was 2200.[49]

Since 1980, the steady growth of the U.K. library and information profession has given way to a more turbulent environment associated with the so-called "information revolution." Although some commentators conjectured that librarianship would prosper in emerging information-work employment markets, it quickly became apparent that the challenges of a shifting "postprofessional" information landscape potentially outweighed the benefits. Some traditional librarianship tasks, and posts, were rendered obsolete by technical change. Cutbacks in (especially professional) posts in the U.K. public sector, especially during the tenure of the Conservative government of 1979–1997, eroded the LA's core employee base; moreover some employers in public and academic libraries began to question the need for professional librarianship credentials and "open up" library posts to applicants with generic IT; management, and business skills. In specialist and commercial fields, new competitors (computer professionals; systems specialists; information and knowledge managers) emerged to claim that they, and not librarians or information scientists, were experts in the handling of information. As a result of these pressures, LA membership fell into gentle, although not catastrophic, decline; IIS membership stalled, failing to grasp the potential (as some saw it) of the proliferation of "information" work.

The U.K. library and information profession's response to this was, as we have seen above, one of rationalization, merger, and the formation of CILIP in 2002. Such a merger had been mooted since the mid-1980s by influential establishment figures such as Wilfred Saunders, who in his *Towards a Unified Professional Organisation for Library and Information Science and Services* (1989) argued for a federation of the LA, the IIS, and ASLIB as the most effective strategy of competing in the new professional environment. Most commentators, and indeed association members, accepted such rationalization as sensible and inevitable, although in the event ASLIB remained outside the arrangement, pursuing a path of corporate consultancy, publication and training and commercial governance (see section "Special Libraries"). In the 6 years since its creation CILIP, as we have seen, has undoubtedly consolidated its respected public profile as the United Kingdom's leading information work (as opposed to information technology) professional grouping, although its influence with government, and more especially the private sector, remains uneven. Tensions, too, persist between its disparate occupational sections and, perhaps more significantly, between its professional traditions of rigorous accreditation and occupational control and the need now to compete for members in a fluid and deregulated neo-liberal occupational environment. The ability of CILIP to successfully resolve some of these issues will, to a large degree, determine the nature and extent of professionalization in the United Kingdom library and information workforce in the decades to come.

LIBRARIANSHIP AND INFORMATION SCIENCE—EDUCATION, TRAINING, AND RESEARCH

Closely linked to the evolution of U.K. professional associations was the development of training and education for the nascent U.K. library occupations. Between 1898, when it received its Royal Charter, and 1939, the LA laid down and incrementally improved an examination system linked to a register of professional members. This established the basic standards and structure of professional librarianship in the United Kingdom, comprising "associates" and "fellows" who were both classed as chartered LA members. Students prepared themselves for these examinations through a mixture of part-time classes, summer schools, and a correspondence course operated from the 1920s onward by the Library Assistants' Association. Examination syllabi consisted largely of "practical" topics: library administration; bibliography; cataloging, and classification, but knowledge of (initially) English literature was tested. (Eventually this was replaced by a paper allowing candidates to specialize in a choice of "information sources" options.) University College London School of Librarianship, founded in 1919, constituted the one exception to this professional monopoly of library education: by the 1930s, under its charismatic head E. A. Baker, it offered a 2 year diploma and 1 year postgraduate course as an alternative to LA examinations. Both of these were broader in scope and more critical and theoretical than the LA scheme.

By 1945, however, it had become clear that the prewar system of professional preparation was inadequate in meeting the needs of an expanding labor market: although the LA had 6510 members by then only 1617 of these were qualified/chartered.[50] Consequently, in the wake of recommendations in the McColvin Report, the United Kingdom finally embarked upon establishing a national system of library education based in universities and colleges. At first, between 1945 and 1955, schools of librarianship were created in nine technical and commercial colleges in major British cities; these schools prepared students for a reformed LA diploma, and after 1966 for degrees awarded by the Council for National Academic Awards (CNAA). In the 1960s, they were joined by six university departments offering degrees and postgraduate diplomas validated and examined internally. Traditional LA examinations continued throughout this time, but they gradually diminished in popularity and were discontinued in 1985. The LA, by now joined by the IIS, gradually became in effect an accrediting body for courses rather than an examining body. However, in membership terms it reaped the reward of this expanded system: by 1972 its chartered members numbered 12,988.[50] By 1980, the first edition of the student guide *Which Library School* listed 16 U.K. schools of library and information studies providing 24 undergraduate degrees and 17 postgraduate diplomas and masters' awards. Librarians and information scientists were finally becoming a graduate profession.

One major consequence of this expanded system of training and education was blossoming in the United Kingdom of the academic disciplines of librarianship and, a little later, information science. Before 1939, theoretical writing and research activities in the library and documentation fields had been limited to intellectual "scholar" librarians such as Duff Brown; Jast; Baker, and Bradford. However, with the advent in the 1950s and 1960s of full-time professional employment in library education, the main dimensions of a British interpretation of both librarianship and information science began to be laid down. Raymond Irwin, head of the UCL school, set out the main features of U.K. "librarianship" (which he contrasted to U.S. "library science") in his *Librarianship: Essays in Applied Bibliography* (1949); Bradford did the same in his *Documentation* (1948). Gradually, in the 1950s and 1960s, an accepted "core" librarianship curriculum emerged comprising applied bibliography; cataloging and indexing; library management; libraries in society: a subject structure reflected in the revised Library Association examination syllabus of 1964. Farradane, Saunders, Vickery, and other information scientists developed an "information science" variant of this in the late 1960s and 1970s, codified in the *Criteria for Courses in Information Science* approved by the IIS. Academic journals, such as the *Journal of Documentation* (established 1945) and the *Journal of Librarianship* (1969), further underpinned these developing disciplines and in the 1960s LIS education began to be supplemented by consistent and professional research activity in the field. Some schools of LIS, such as the postgraduate school at Sheffield and the large department at the Polytechnic of North London developed a major research focus, although they never attained a monopoly of LIS research: important centers elsewhere in the professional LIS community, such as the ASLIB Research Department, saw to that. Nevertheless, research in the field had become sufficiently legitimized for funding to be provided between 1964 and 1973 by the U.K. government Office of Scientific and Technical Information (OSTI) and after that, with an expanded remit, by the British Library Research and Development Department (BLRDD). The era of the BLRDD (1974–1999), a government agency with dedicated research funding for libraries, had few parallels elsewhere. In 1975–1976, its most generously funded year, BLRRD distributed £1.1 million in LIS research funding and, although its inflation adjusted grant declined after that, it still accounted for 46% of total LIS research funding in 1985. It supported a very wide range of projects ranging from information storage and retrieval through to public, academic, and school libraries and professional education itself. Overall, between 1975 and 1988 BLRDD funded 712 LIS research projects, 29% of them based in schools of LIS.[51] This represented arguably a golden age in U.K. LIS research.

By 1980, LIS and its associated education and training programs in the United Kingdom arguably constituted a classic public service formation—comprising the state as educator and main employer; the professional bodies and the academy. Over the next 25 years, however, the "information revolution," in tandem with the contraction of the British welfare state, would herald major change, creating a less uniform, more flexible, and disorganized educational system which some would argue marks the beginnings of decline. Core LIS curricula laid down in the 1960s and 1970s have been superseded by a range of information-related courses, beginning in the late 1980s with "information studies" programs and subsequently shifting in the 1990s to "information management" curricula constructed around new management studies approaches to information resource management (IRM). More latterly, a good number of LIS schools have experimented (not totally successfully) with fashionable "niche" offerings such as Knowledge Management; Health Informatics; Web Information Management; and so on. Flexible modes of study such as distance and "blended" learning have also become popular: Aberystwyth University and Robert Gordon University, Aberdeen currently offering successful distance degree programs. (CILIP provides a list of currently accredited courses).[52] An alternative mechanism for demonstrating professional competence (and route to CILIP membership) has also been created through the establishment of a state regulated National Vocational Qualification (NVQ) in Information and Library Work—a program which ironically echoes much of the apprenticeship culture dominant in U.K. librarianship before the "academic drift" of the

1960s. CILIP, and most of the U.K. LIS community, have welcomed these developments, pointing to the expansion of LIS into new fields such as knowledge management and its responsiveness to a flexible, postindustrial labor market. However, these changes have also been accompanied by institutional retrenchment in the schools and departments of LIS. Undergraduate degrees in librarianship and information science have declined in popularity—only 13 of these were offered in 2007 compared with 24 in 2000.[53] Library schools themselves have been forced to cut back their staff numbers, and the majority, especially those in the new universities (former "polytechnics"), have lost their autonomy being absorbed into computing, information technology or business schools and faculties. Two universities, Queen's University Belfast and Birmingham City University (formerly Birmingham Polytechnic), no longer offer accredited courses in LIS.

The permanent impact of these developments on the future of the LIS disciplines in the United Kingdom is still uncertain. On the positive side, however, it is clear over the last decade that, despite the retrenchments noted above, and despite the final demise of BLRDD in 1999, research in the LIS field has recovered and in some areas flourished. British Library Research and Development Department has been replaced by a multiplicity of research funders—the European Commission (which made 89 awards in 2003); the U.K. Joint Information Systems Committee (74); the Arts and Humanities Research Council (AHRC) (31); and the Museums Libraries and Archives Council (10) being the largest sources of support.[54] This devolution of funding has undoubtedly resulted in a broadening of the scope of research compared with the BLRDD era: LIS research has more or less effectively expanded into fields such as information policy; European research; information resource management; and information and library history. Moreover, the interest of some new funders in supporting highly applied, developmental, "evidence-based" and contract-driven projects has cemented the involvement in the field of research consultancies such as Electronic Publishing Services Ltd; TFPL; TALIS; and Information Management Associates.

Despite this competition, most academic schools of LIS have managed to expand their research activities. Research "centers," such as CERLIM at Manchester Metropolitan University and CIBER at City University (more recently UCL) have fostered research cultures and focused research interests, and the majority of LIS schools have increased their throughput of doctoral students. Librarianship and information science departments have also taken the lion's share of "academic" research funding allocated to the discipline by the AHRC. Most important, however, has been the impact of the Higher Education Funding Council's Research Assessment Exercise (RAE), a periodic review of research performance in U.K. universities which began in 1992 and was repeated in 1996, 2001, and 2007. (See Nicholas[54] for the 2001 RAE tables and ratings of schools and departments. The 2007 Research Assessment Exercise is still underway at the time of writing this entry, July 2008). Library and Information Management effectively established itself as a separate "unit of assessment" for these exercises, and this has enabled research intensive schools (such as those at Sheffield University, Loughborough University, and City University— all awarded a top 5 or 5* rating in 2001) together with groupings of successful LIS researchers elsewhere to showcase their activities in the eyes of their parent institutions, the wider academic community and the funding bodies. In this way, visibly successful research has, over the last 10 years, to some degree compensated for the problems faced by U.K. schools of LIS with issues such as curriculum offerings, student recruitment, and institutional restructuring. Whether or not LIS researchers and academics will be able to consolidate this position—and maintain library and information science as a distinct "discipline" in British universities in the twenty-first century— will depend not only on the quality of their research and teaching but, ultimately, upon the future resilience (and influence) of the U.K. library and information community itself.

REFERENCES

1. National Statistics, *Population Estimates*; Available at http://www.statistics.gov.uk (accessed November 2008).
2. Central Intelligence Agency, *The World Factbook 2008*. Available at http://cia.gov/library/publications/the-world-factbook/geos/uk.htm (accessed May 2008).
3. National Literacy Trust, *Adult Literacy Levels*; Available at http://www.literacytrust.org.uk.Database/stats/adultstats.html (accessed May 2008).
4. Commission for Racial Equality, *Ethnic Minorities in Britain*; CRE: London, U.K., 2007; 8.
5. Peatling, G.K. Public libraries and national identity in Britain, 1850–1919. Libr. Hist. **2004**, *20* (1), 33–47.
6. Board of Education, Public Libraries Committee, *Report on Public Libraries in England and Wales*; Board of Education: London, U.K., 1927.
7. McColvin, L.R. *The Public Library System of Great Britain: A Report on Its Present Condition with Proposals for Post-War Re-Organisation*; Library Association: London, U.K., 1942.
8. *Report of the National Libraries Committee*; HMSO: London, U.K., 1969; [The Dainton Report].
9. University Grants Committee, *Report of the Committee on Libraries*; UGC: London, U.K., 1967; [The Parry Report].
10. Lamb, J.P. *Commercial and Technical Libraries*; Allen and Unwin: London, U.K., 1955; 284.
11. Coleman, P. *Whose Problem? The Public Library and the Disadvantaged*; Association of Assistant Librarians: Newcastle-under-Lyme, 1981.
12. Cronin, B.; Davenport, E. *Post Professionalism: Transforming the Information Heartland*; Taylor Graham: London, U.K., 1988.
13. National Library of Scotland, 2005; *Annual Report and Accounts for the Year Ended 31st March*. Available at http://www.nls.uk/about/publications (accessed September 2008).
14. Green, A.M. *The National Library of Wales—a Ten Minute Tour*. Available at http://www.llgc.org.uk/fileadmin/documents (accessed September 2008).
15. LISU, *Libraries, Museums and Publishing Online Statistics Tables*. Available at http://www.lboro.ac.uk/departments/ls/lisu/lampost.html (accessed June 2008).
16. Coates, T. *Who's in Charge? Responsibility for the Public Library*; Libri: London, U.K., 2003.
17. Department of, Culture, Media and Sport, *Framework for the Future. Libraries, Learning and Information in the Next Decade*; DCMS: London, U.K., 2003.
18. Black, A. The people's university: Models of public library history. In *The Cambridge History of Libraries in Britain and Ireland Vol.III*; Black, A., Hoare, P., Eds.; Cambridge University Press: Cambridge, U.K., 2006; 24–39.
19. Public Library Research Group, Public library aims and objectives. Libr. Assoc. Record **1971**, *73* (12), 233–234.
20. National Statistics. *Internet Access: Households and Individuals*; Available at http://www.statistics.gov.uk/pdfdir/inta0806/pdf (accessed July 2008).
21. Universities, U.K. *Higher Education in Facts and Figures*; Universities U.K.: London, 2007.
22. Freshwater, P. Books and universities. In *The Cambridge History of Libraries in Britain and Ireland Vol. II*; Mandelbrote, G., Manley, K., Eds.; Cambridge University Press: Cambridge, U.K., 2006; 347.
23. SCONUL, *SCONUL Vision 2010*; Available at http://www.sconul.ac.uk/publications/pubs/vision2010 (accessed July 2008).
24. Carr, R. *The Academic Research Library in a Decade of Change*; Chandos Press: Oxford, U.K., 2007.
25. CILIP, *UK Survey of Library and Learning Resource Provision in Further Education Colleges*; CILIP: London, U.K., 2003.
26. Enyon, A. *Guidelines for Colleges: Recommendations for Learning Resources*; Facet Publishing: London, U.K., 2005.
27. Barker, W. School libraries c.1540 to 1640. In *The Cambridge History of Libraries in Britain and Ireland Vol.1*; Leedham-Green, E., Webber, T., Eds.; Cambridge University Press: Cambridge, U.K., 2006; 435–447.
28. CILIP, *Survey of Secondary School Libraries*; CILIP: London, 2002; http://www.cilip.org.uk/specialinterestgroups/bysubject/youth/publications/youngpeople/secondaryschoollibraries.htm (accessed July 2008).
29. Barrett, L.; Douglas, J. Eds.; *CILIP Guidelines for Secondary School Libraries*; 2nd Ed.; CILIP: London, U.K., 2004.
30. CILIP, *The Primary School Library Guidelines*; CILIP: London, U.K., 2002.
31. Creaser, C.; Maynard, S. *A Survey of Library Services to Schools and Children in the UK 2005–6*; LISU: Loughborough University, U.K., 2006; 1–2.
32. Denham, D. Public library services to children. In *The Cambridge History of Libraries in Britain and Ireland Vol.III*; Black, A., Hoare, P., Eds.; Cambridge University Press: Cambridge, U.K., 2006; 92–109.
33. Hill, J. *Children are People: The Librarian in the Community*; Hamish Hamilton: London, U.K., 1973.

34. CILIP, *Start with the Child: Report of the CILIP Working Group on Services to Children and Young People*; CILIP: London, U.K., 2002.

35. *The ASLIB Directory of Information Sources in the United Kingdom*, 14th Ed. Europa Publications: London, U.K., 2006.

36. Schopflin, K.; Nelsson, R.In *Media Libraries. In British Librarianship and Information Work 2001–2005*; Bowman, J.H., Ed.; Ashgate: Aldershot, U.K., 2007; 198–213.

37. LISU. *Library and Information Statistics Tables*; LISU: Loughborough University, United Kingdom, 1998.

38. LISU. *Library and Information Statistics Tables*; LISU: Loughborough University, U.K., 2002.

39. Association of UK Media Librarians. *Organisations*; http://www.aukml.org.uk (accessed August 2008).

40. Black, A.; Muddiman, D.; Plant, H. *The Early Information Society: Information Management in Britain before the Computer*; Ashgate: Aldershot, U.K., 2007.

41. Murphy, C. Government and parliamentary libraries. In *The Cambridge History of Libraries in Britain and Ireland Vol. III*; Black, A., Hoare, P., Eds.; Cambridge University Press: Cambridge, U.K., 2006; 483.

42. Sherwell, J. Industrial and commercial libraries. In *British Librarianship and Information Work 1981–5*; Bromley, D., Allott, A., Eds.; Library Association: London, U.K., 1986; 54.

43. ASLIB. Membership. http://www.aslib.co.uk (accessed August 2008).

44. LISU. *Annual Digest of Statistics*; LISU: Loughborough University, U.K., 2006.

45. LISU, *Library and Information Statistics Tables for the United Kingdom*; LISU: Loughborough University, U.K., 2004; 3.

46. CILIP, *About CILIP*. Available at http://www.cilip.org.uk/aboutcilip (accessed July 2008).

47. Munford, W.A. *A History of the Library Association 1877–1977*; Library Association: London, U.K., 1976.

48. Harrison, K.C. Library Association. In *International Encyclopaedia of Library and Information Services*; Wedgeworth, R., Ed.; ALA: Chicago, IL, 1993; 465–470.

49. CILIP, *How CILIP was Formed*. Available at http://www.cilip.org.uk/aboutcilip/history (accessed April 2008).

50. Haslam, D.D. A short history of the Library Association. J. Librarianship **1974**, *6* (3), 152.

51. Meadows, J. *Innovation in Information: Twenty Years of the British Library Research and Development Department*; Bowker-Saur: London, U.K., 1994; 146–153.

52. CILIP, *Courses in Library and Information Studies Currently Accredited by CILIP*. Available at http://www.cilip.org.uk/qualificationschartership/wheretostudy (accessed April 2008).

53. Huckle, M.; Watson, M. Education and training. In *British Librarianship and Information Work 2001–2005*; Bowman, J.H., Ed.; Ashgate: Aldershot, U.K., 2007; 354.

54. Nicholas, D. Research. In *British Librarianship and Information Work 2001–2005*; Bowman, J.H., Ed.; Ashgate: Aldershot, U.K., 2007; 362–365.

BIBLIOGRAPHY

1. Black, A. *The Public Library in Britain 1914–2000*; The British Library: London, U.K., 2000.

2. Bowman, J.H., Ed. In *British Librarianship and Information Work 1991–2000*; Ashgate: Aldershot, U.K., 2006.

3. Bowman, J.H., Ed. In *British Librarianship and Information Work 2001–2005*; Ashgate: Aldershot, U.K., 2007.

4. Hoare, P., Ed. In *The Cambridge History of Libraries in Britain and Ireland [in 3 vols]*; Cambridge University Press: Cambridge, U.K., 2006.

United Kingdom: Museums and Museology

Sarah Elliott
Peter Davis
International Centre for Cultural and Heritage Studies, Newcastle University, Newcastle upon Tyne, U.K.

Abstract

This entry attempts to capture the rich diversity of museums in the United Kingdom. Following a discussion of the evolution of British museums in their historical context from the private collecting through the profound impact of global exploration the authors examine major changes in the museum sector in the latter part of the twentieth century. Because discussion on types of museum organized according to discipline is rendered problematic by the frequent occurrence of multidisciplinarity in U.K. collections, this entry uses a framework of organization and funding to identify seven types of institutions: 1) national; 2) university; 3) armed services; 4) local authority; 5) independent; 6) English Heritage; 7) the National Trust; and 8) the living collections of zoos and botanical gardens.

INTRODUCTION

The museums scene in the United Kingdom has been described as "fascinatingly variegated" and "idiosyncratic," a state of affairs resulting from a history of perpetual development linked to an engagement with shifting social needs but without a strategic framework.[1] This entry attempts to capture this arguably unique diversity, first locating the museums of the United Kingdom in their historical context—from the private collecting for founding collections that enabled their establishment in the country, through the profound impact of global exploration, trade and empire, the significance of national societies and local literary and philosophical societies, and the effects of the Museums Act (1845) and other Acts of Parliament in the mid-1800s, to the major changes in the sector in the latter part of the twentieth century.

An overview of museum provision is then presented. Discussion on types of museum organized according to discipline is rendered problematic by the frequent occurrence of multidisciplinarity in U.K. collections, thus they are articulated here according to frameworks of organization and funding—national, university, armed services, local authority, and independent—with additional classifications for English Heritage, the arguably statutorily anomalous National Trust, and the living collections of zoos and botanical gardens. The record reveals that the United Kingdom was in the vanguard of public museum provision, but as understanding of the factors that lead to *effective* provision has advanced, so the significance of the integrated museum profession, and the mix of skills, knowledge, and attitudes of those engaged in museum work, has become clear. An outline of the museum workforce and museum work follows, together with a brief account of the professional associations, specialist groups and museum training courses that underpin them.

Currently, the museums of the United Kingdom are seen as a public service, redefined and moved beyond their traditional cultural role into coordinates for change in society. They have undergone a remarkable renaissance over recent years with important funding strands coming online, but the sector is still seen as fragile and a formal national structure, anchoring museums' support within government, remains a cultural policy challenge.

A BRIEF HISTORY OF MUSEUMS IN THE UNITED KINGDOM

The history of U.K. museums has been exceptionally well-documented, with publications devoted to the histories of individual national museums,[2] individual provincial museums,[3] regional museum provision,[4] and university collections.[5] Early phases of collecting have been described by MacGregor[6] and Hunter,[7] amongst others. Academics have also addressed issues such as the history of museum architecture,[8] collecting,[9,10] and exhibitions.[11,12] Although Alexander[13] provides interesting insights on museum development in the United Kingdom, arguably the most comprehensive account has been provided by Lewis;[14] much of the following is based on this.

Early private collections were formed in Britain in the early seventeenth century. Sir Robert Cotton (1571–1631), best known for his library, also collected coins, medals, and antiquities, and his friend Sir Walter Cope (d. 1614) traveled widely and amassed a variety of natural and cultural objects. John Tradescant I (1570–1638) knew Cope and had seen his museum, and it may be that the nature of

"Tradescant's Ark" at Lambeth, London was influenced by Cope's collection. Tradescant visited mainland Europe, Norway, and Algiers and used his contacts to develop his museum; when he died his son John II (1608–1662) took over the collection, adding to it during three visits to Virginia. In 1656, a catalog of the collection—*Museum Tradescantianum*—was published, "the first recorded use of the word 'museum' in England in its currently accepted form."[15] The collection eventually passed to Elias Ashmole (1617–1692), who in turn gave it to Oxford University; the building which housed the collection in Oxford, with its associated laboratory and teaching facilities, eventually became known as the Ashmolean Museum.[16]

Although the Tradescants are well known, there were rivals to the "Ark," including the museum belonging to Robert Hubert (Forges) near St. Paul's; Hubert was an entrepreneur, inviting the nobility and academics to see his collections, so giving them additional status. He created special exhibitions, held private views and could give guided tours in four languages. Other collectors from the same period include John Bargrave (1610–1680) and Sir James Balfour (1600–1657). Later in the century, collectors such as James Petiver (1663–1718) were beginning to take a different approach to their collections, publishing catalogs of them, and actively promoting scientific and rational collecting. Petiver's collections were acquired by Sir Hans Sloane (1660–1753), whose museum became the foundation of the British Museum.

The Enlightenment witnessed the creation of an international scientific network. Diderot (1713–1784) produced his *Encyclopedie* (1751–1777); people began to question the nature of fossils and geological time, Lamarck (1744–1829) and Erasmus Darwin (1731–1802) pondered the nature of evolution. There was a growing interest in other cultures and in world geography and from about 1750 there was new emphasis on aesthetics, sentiment, and common virtues which were expressed in poetry, fashion, and art. There was increasing access to information and free speech, and above all the use of reason to understand the world. These changes had a profound effect on collecting and the establishment of museums in Britain and elsewhere in Europe. At the forefront were national societies, especially the Royal Society (founded 1660), but local societies such as the Manchester Literary and Philosophical Society (1781), the Birmingham Lunar Society (1766), and the Philosophical Society of Edinburgh (1732), all developed major collections. The end result of this intellectual activity was the establishment of the first public museums—for example in Britain the Ashmolean Museum (1683), the Sedgwick Museum, Cambridge (1728), and the British Museum (1759). Meanwhile the private museums developed by Sir Ashton Lever (1774) and William Bullock (1795) were also extremely popular with the public, using novel methods of display such as habitat groups of animals.

The nineteenth century was a time of massive social change, a drift to urban living began, as did the generation of wealth which allowed some people a degree of leisure time. It was a time of educational reforms and the founding of learned organizations such as the Belfast Natural History Society (1821), Leeds Literary and Philosophical Society (1821), Manchester Natural History Society (1821), and the Newcastle upon Tyne Literary and Philosophical Society (1793). Brears and Davies[4] have discussed the significance of the Literary and Philosophical Societies in the formation of provincial museums in Britain. Other bodies played a vital role in promoting local museum collections which were made accessible to the public—especially Naturalists' Field Clubs and Mechanics Institutes. The former encouraged active field work, the formation of local collections, and the dissemination of knowledge in local specialist journals.

Urbanization and industrialization created cities of great economic strength and power; they were frequently centers of trade with the rest of the world, at a time when Britain was developing its Empire and exploring all corners of the world. Cities such as Liverpool, Bristol, Glasgow, and Newcastle had access to new cultures, new environments. The combination of growing wealth, civic pride, and fashionable learned societies, aided by the Victorian ethic for self-improvement, led to collection-building on a grand scale. Many of Britain's great museum buildings were established at this time, including the British Museum (1823), the National Gallery (1838), the Fitzwilliam Museum, Cambridge (1816), and the Hunterian Museum, Glasgow (1807).

Many of the collections formed by the learned societies and private individuals were transferred to local governmental authorities following the passing of the Museums Act in 1845 which enabled local authorities to levy a 1/2 penny rate if the population exceeded 10,000. Lewis[17] notes the museums were to be provided "for instruction and recreation." Sunderland Museum is notable as the first ever municipal museum (1846), its founding collections made by a late eighteenth-century scientific society; Canterbury (1847) and Warrington (1848) followed, again utilizing collections made by local learned societies. Other Acts of Parliament followed, including the Public Libraries and Museums Acts of 1850 and 1855; from this time Libraries were mandatory functions of local authorities, whereas museums remained a discretionary service. The Acts had an immediate effect; by 1860 there were some 90 museums in Britain; when the British Association reported on museums in 1887 this figure had grown to 217.[18] This growth in the number of municipal museums led to a call for increasing professionalism; consequently the Museums Association was inaugurated at York in June 1889 to represent not only curators but also representatives from museum committees. The educational potential of museums began to be more widely recognized about this time, with Liverpool organizing loan collections for use in schools from 1884.

Lewis[19] regards the period between the two World Wars as a time of "reassessment and consolidation," and describes in detail the various reports aided by the Carnegie United Kingdom Trust, the Museums Association and the Standing Commission on Museums and Galleries. The Miers Report (1929) is regarded as particularly influential in changing conventional practices in museums, encouraging them to relate more closely to their local communities, promote educational activities, and provide better training for museum staff. The years following World War II, a period of severe financial restraint, saw little investment in museums; despite this a survey of provincial museums carried out in 1963 recorded some 876 sites with collections and open to the public. The period up until 1975 was one of even more rapid growth and diversity in the museum sector; site museums, community involvement, industrial museums, interpretive centers, and an emphasis on the conservation of natural and cultural areas flourished against a backdrop of the growing environmental movement. New museums were opened, including the Museum of London and branch museums of the Science Museum in York and Bradford; by 1987 the Museums Association estimated that the total number of museums in the United Kingdom had reached 2131.

The latter part of the twentieth century witnessed major changes in the museums sector in the United Kingdom. Concerns about minimum professional standards led to the Museum Association's "Accreditation" guidelines, and then to the Museum and Galleries Commission's "Registration" scheme. Museums entered the digital age, with the initial emphasis being on the ways new technologies could assist with collections documentation; support and the setting of documentation standards was aided by the Museums Documentation Association from 1977. Arguably the main impact on museums from the 1980s onwards was reduced levels of government funding; in order to deal with financial strictures museums had either to cut costs—usually through voluntary and forced redundancies or reductions in activities—or seek new ways of raising money. Museums increasingly had to demonstrate they were using funds wisely; such accountability also meant a significant change in the staff structures of museums as specialist curatorial posts were reduced to make way for marketing and promotional staff or those delivering public oriented projects. There were major changes in management style in museums as they became more business oriented; strategic planning, marketing, corporate sponsorship, business development, and project planning became techniques employed by all museums. Priorities were re-assessed and financial targets considered against the growing demands on museums to not only conserve the nation's heritage but also to play a major social role, contributing to education, the economy, and quality of life. These multiple pressures on museums have continued to grow in the twenty-first century and are discussed further below.

MUSEUM PROVISION IN THE UNITED KINGDOM: MUSEUM TYPES

The distinctiveness of museums in the United Kingdom can be observed in terms of their disciplinarity and frequently their multidisciplinarity, but also in the ways they are organized and funded.[20] Although there is merit in describing the U.K. museum scene by focusing on the museums' raison d'être—their collections, their arguably unparalleled diversity makes such classification problematic. The scene, comprising some 2500 museums,[21] can be more usefully articulated through an engagement with governance. Through this, they can be categorized into five main groupings, namely national, university, armed services, local authority, and independent, with an additional classification for those museums owned and managed by the National Trust and by English Heritage. The Museums and Galleries Commission's DOMUS database categorized museums in this way.[22] Differentiated by exhibiting living objects (examples of natural history)[23] but sharing many common features in performing scientific, educational and recreational roles, zoos, botanical gardens, and aquaria are *forms* of museum[24] and are included here.

National Museums

In the United Kingdom, there is no statutory definition of National Museums, their authority residing in miscellaneous acts, charters, and Treasury minutes.[25] However, those institutions recognized as such can be defined in practice by their direct or core government funding, their administration by Boards of Trustees on the nation's behalf, and the national significance of their collections.[26] The Museums, Libraries and Archives Council's *List of Museums with Full Registration or Accreditation: July 2008* records a total of 53 individual museums within its National Museums section.

The National Museums are based in London, Liverpool, Edinburgh, Cardiff, and Belfast, and most have branches in other cities or operate from several sites. The British Museum in London, established by an Act of Parliament in 1753 around a collection bequeathed by the physician, naturalist, and collector Sir Hans Sloane, is the oldest and largest. Other prominent London Nationals include the Victoria and Albert Museum (art and design), the Natural History Museum, and the Science Museum, all arrayed on a tract of land established in South Kensington as a cultural and educational district after the Great Exhibition of 1851. The National Gallery, housing one of the world's greatest collections of Western European paintings, and the Tate, a family of four galleries (two in London) holding British Art from 1500 and international modern art, complete the "big six" of the 13 based in the capital. On Merseyside, National Museums Liverpool is a varied grouping of eight museums made public following the abolition of Merseyside County Council in 1986. Amgueddfa Cymru/National Museum Wales is a network of seven museums, with the National Museum Cardiff, opened to the public in 1927, at its heart. In Scotland, the National Galleries of Scotland has branches in Edinburgh, while National Museums Scotland operates sites both within the capital and further south near Dumfries (National Museum of Costume) and in East Kilbride (Museum of Rural Life). More recently, the National Museums and Galleries of Northern Ireland was established under the Museums and Galleries (Northern Ireland) Order of 1998.

Between them, the National Museums receive approximately 35 million visits a year (figures for 2005/6 from a National Museums Directors' Conference brief after Department for Culture Media and Sport data, see the National Museums Directors' Conference),[27] and in 2005–2006 were allocated some £300 million in grants-in-aid with just over £22 million capital grants-in-aid from central government.[28] Income is also generated by the National Lottery, donations and sponsorship, and trading. The overall economic impact of the National Museums is hugely significant, at approximately £1.5 billion per annum.[29]

University Museums

The genealogy of museums in the United Kingdom is intimately linked to its universities.[30] The oldest public museum in the country, and arguably the world, is the Ashmolean Museum of the University of Oxford. Its founding collections, based on the miscellaneous curiosities of the Tradescant Ark (see history section above), emerged in the public domain within a purpose-built museum in 1683. Other donations to higher education institutions were recorded much earlier, but the subsequent development of systematic collections in scientific disciplines facilitated the emergence of several great teaching and research museums.[30] Cambridge University, for example, developed a substantial new museum of geology, zoology, and archaeology. The Sedgwick Museum was founded by the bequest of Dr John Woodward (1665–1728) on his death in 1728. In 1842 Woodward's collection (then the "Woodwardian Museum," comprising four cabinets of minerals, rocks and fossils), was moved to the new Cockerell building, its first permanent home. After the extensive collecting of Professor Adam Sedgwick (1785–1873), the Museum moved again in 1904 to the present Sedgwick Museum building (for more on the founding collection, see Price).[31] Elsewhere, Glasgow University was bequeathed the anatomical collection of John Hunter and opened the Hunterian Museum (1807), while Owens College (later Manchester University) took over the long-established collections of the local Natural History Society to create

the Manchester Museum (1888). Numerous other smaller departmental collections also emerged.

The importance of the major university museums is signaled today by the Department for Culture, Media, and Sport (DCMS) identification of their collections as being of national or international significance ("Designation"); there are currently around 400 higher education museums, galleries and collections, together comprising 4% of the United Kingdom's museum sector,[32] but they are keepers of 30% of all Designated collections in the country.[32] Along with the Ashmolean, the Sedgwick, and the Manchester Museums, other holders of Designated collections include the Fitzwilliam Museum (Cambridge University) together with the more constrained but comparable institutions of the Whitworth Art Gallery (Manchester University), the Courtauld Institute Gallery (University of London), the Barber Institute of Fine Arts and the Lapworth Museum (Birmingham University), and the Pitt Rivers Museum and the Museum of Natural History at Oxford University. These great institutions are among the hundred or so higher education museums open on a regular basis, and among the 38 that receive core funding from the Arts and Humanities Research Council (AHRC) in England and the Scottish Higher Education Funding Council (SHEFC).[32] The AHRC/SHEFC-funded museums deliver beyond their traditional commitment to academic audiences, maintaining a range of public services, education, and exhibition programs comparable to those of regional and national museums. Attracting some 2 million visitors a year (2002 figures), they have a good track record of wider social engagement, and thus are increasingly important in advancing the cultural contribution of their parent institutions. The vast majority of higher education museums, galleries and collections, however, are little known. Buried within their departments and institutions, they "are solely dependent on the very modest resources available to them from higher education teaching and research budgets, generally under the auspices of their academic department." [30] According to a recent report, many have deteriorating physical infrastructure, and are suffering from decreasing revenue funding and a consequent erosion of their intellectual and heritage capital.[33]

Armed Services Museums

A third category of museums that are mainly or partly funded by central government is that of the approximately 200 museums of the armed services.[34] The long and rich tradition of the British armed forces (the Royal Navy has been extant for 450 years, the British Army's history spans over three centuries, and the Royal Air Force has been in operation since 1918), and particularly the stable units of the army with set depots in which historical artefacts could accumulate and the strong county connection of the regiments, account for this unusually high number of museums dealing with some aspect of military history or containing military collections.[35] Of these military museums, four Nationals have a direct armed services remit: the National Army Museum, the Royal Air Force Museum, the Imperial War Museum, and the National War Museum of Scotland (part of National Museums Scotland).

The National Army Museum, established by Royal Charter in 1960 and now sited in Chelsea, is a repository of the history and heritage of the Regular and Auxiliary forces of the British Army and of the Commonwealth. Through its collections of uniforms, weapons, medals, paintings, drawings, archives, and transport, a narrative from Agincourt in the early fifteenth century to peacekeeping in the twenty-first is presented. The Museum also has a role "supporting the Defence Purpose through its contribution to the Army's image in society; to the remembrance of those who have served, and to the education of Servicemen and Servicewomen,"[36] and is committed to broader societal learning output. The Royal Air Force Museum was founded 3 years later, with collections held in Hendon (London) and at its outstation in Cosford, Shropshire comprising materials recording the history of the Royal Air Force and its relationship with aviation generally. It was World War I, however, that stimulated the formation of an all-service national museum dedicated to all aspects of armed conflicts involving Britain and the Commonwealth since 1914. The Imperial War Museum's original intent to comprehensively record and commemorate the Great War effected an encyclopedic coverage of that conflict, but its terms of reference were soon extended, initially to World War II and then to British military actions up to the present day. In Scotland, the National War Museum (formerly the Scottish United Services Museum) sited in Edinburgh Castle also has the combined services in its mandate (albeit within the Scottish context) and was created in 1930 to commemorate the sacrifice made by Scotland in World War I.[37] Portrayal of the Royal Navy is not undertaken by a single museum, "its essential story being told by the National Maritime Museum and the four designated but non-national museums: The Royal Navy Museum Portsmouth, The Royal Marines Museum in Southsea, The Royal Navy Submarine Museum in Gosport, [and] The Fleet Air Arm Museum in Yeovilton."[38]

Other Nationals, namely the Royal Armouries (1680s) and the Science Museum (1857), have collections related to the history of defence, but "the depiction of war through museums exhibitions (in the United Kingdom) is most likely to be found in regimental museums"[39] and those allied to the corps of the British Army. Over 130 exist,[40] including strong regimental museum provision in Scotland and Wales, and five in Northern Ireland. (Those in Northern Ireland are: Royal Irish Fusiliers Regimental Museum, Armagh; Royal Ulster Rifles Museum, Belfast; North Irish Horse Regimental Collection [temporarily closed to the public], Belfast; Royal Irish Regiment Museum, Ballymena [closed pending relocation]; Royal Inniskilling Fusiliers Regimental Museum, Enniskillen, see Army Museums).[41] Formed not to present war per se, but "for the specific purpose of instilling and fostering in the regiment the *esprit de corps* which enables it to fight more effectively,"[39] regimental museums have strong territorial links—regionalism and the military being a binary notion forged by King George III, "who first realized the importance of fostering regional loyalties and attitudes for soldiers serving together."[42] Despite the amalgamations of many regiments in the 1960s, longstanding local links have enabled many collections to be assimilated into local authority museums. Indeed, the Museums and Galleries Commission report of 1990 on armed services museums noted that nearly 40 were managed within local authority museums.[43] Notable regimental and corps museums include those among the first to be formed (often museums of technology as well as military)—the Royal Artillery Regiment Museums in Woolwich (1778) and the Royal Engineers Museum in Chatham (1875) have collections based on the models and exhibits used at their training establishments—and the Tank Museum at Bovington.

Almost all regimental and corps museums are instituted as charitable trusts, most receive support from the Ministry of Defence (MOD) (grant-in-aid funding of about £4.8 million to the National Army Museum, and £4–5 million to 69 others, see Stephens)[44] and just under half still occupy MOD property.[45] Their development today is also aided to a considerable degree by the Army Museums Ogilby Trust, a charity set up in 1954 to assist the museums with funds, advocacy, information, and advice.

Local Authority Museums

Prior to any direct reference to local authority museums, some explication is pertinent of the rather arcane local government environment within which they operate. Indeed, a greatly-increased complexity has characterized this environment over the last decade, with devolved governments in Edinburgh, Cardiff, and Belfast adding a further layer of complication.[46] Babbidge[47] provides a good overview of the local authority sector in Britain and its interface with museums, but its structure can be briefly drawn here. The architecture of local government in the United Kingdom is, as noted, complex, its history one of gradual evolution and change since the Middle Ages. The historic counties, established in England for Norman administration and based on earlier Anglo-Saxon kingdoms and shires, however, acted as agencies of the state for several hundred years and continue to form (albeit with altered boundaries) the basis of modern local government. In Wales, Henry VIII (r.1509–1547) imposed an administrative structure on that country with the Act of Union (1536), and the names and boundaries remained virtually the same until reorganization in 1974. In Scotland, the royal free burghs (a "burgh" is a Scots term for a town or municipality) were highly autonomous units of local government from the twelfth century, developing provision of basic services for local people until their abolition in 1975; current arrangements for Scotland and Wales, however, date from the mid-1990s with the creation of 32 all-purpose unitary councils in the former and 22 in the latter. The 1970s also ushered change in Northern Ireland, when the present pattern of local government with 26 councils was established. The single tier all-purpose council, also found in parts of England and including the City of London, 32 London Boroughs, 36 Metropolitan and 47 Shire Unitary, is responsible for all local authority functions. In 2000 a new Greater London Authority was created (directly-elected Mayor and separately elected Assembly) with responsibility for four functional bodies—the Metropolitan Police Authority, the London Fire and Emergency Planning Authority, Transport for London and the London Development Agency. The London Borough Councils, however, essentially perform the same functions as any single tier authority. The remainder of England has a two tier system, in which two separate councils divide responsibilities—county councils (the upper tier) are mandated core functions and district councils (the lower tier) deliver more local services. Across Britain, the bottom tier of local government comprises Town, Parish, and Community Councils.

Most councils (around 75% of the 442 first and second tier local authorities in Britain) operate some form of museum service (Babbidge describes how the councils use one, or a mix of some, or all, of the following means of provision: "193 (44%) make direct museum provision; around 25 have devolved management of their museum services to a specially-created charity; approximately 50 participate in joint arrangements with other local authorities; one-third core-fund independent museums, whether in their localities, or occasionally, outside their administrative areas"),[48] although the museums under their (direct or indirect) authority vary considerably in size, quality, and importance. Many of the major regional museums were founded in the nineteenth century with encyclopedic collections (see history section above) and are housed in elegant civic buildings. Examples include museums and galleries at Birmingham and Bristol. Birmingham Museum and Art Gallery, opened in purpose-built accommodation by the Prince of Wales (later King Edward VII) in 1885, originally represented the desire of prominent citizens to improve manufacturing quality in the "City of a Thousand Trades" as well as to better the lot of the working man through exposure to art and natural history.[49] It drew on contributions and donations from the Birmingham glass manufacturer Thomas Clarkson Osler, the great industrialist Richard Tangye, the glass-worker Thomas Collier Barnes, and the proprietor of the Birmingham Daily Post, John Feeny. Today, the institution's collections cover fine and applied arts, archeology

and ethnography, natural history and social history. In Bristol, the City Museum and Art Gallery's origins lie in the foundation of the Bristol Institution for the Advancement of Science and Art (1823) and the slightly older Bristol Literary and Philosophical Society, and it benefitted from the donations of the tobacco baron Sir William Henry Wills (1830–1911). In Scotland, the first municipal authority to consider museum provision was Glasgow, and when the coachbuilder and art collector Archibald McLellan (1796–1854) bequeathed a collection of 400 paintings, the core of the city's Old Master collection was laid down. Museum provision of other local authorities in Scotland around the time included Paisley (1870) and Dundee (1873), the latter founded on the collections of the Watt Institution.[50]

Outwith the large conurbations a huge number of smaller, district authority museums perform an important and active role as "interpreters of local history, and as biological, geological and archaeological record centres," all maintaining a commitment to local education and community service.[51] The Central Museum at Southend on Sea, for example, covers geology, archeology, social and local history, local wildlife, and the industrial history of South East Essex.[52] Smaller independent museums are also supported by many local authorities in whose areas they operate.

Local authorities form a significant museum provider in the United Kingdom, with the 22 largest local authority services attracting some 12 million visitors annually.[53] Lawley[53] notes that 40% of Registered museums in the United Kingdom are operated by local councils. Overall, however, regional provision is variable, a characteristic rooted in recent years in unreliable revenue funding, and historically in piecemeal development *sans* clear legislative frameworks.[54] In England and Wales, the nature and extent of provision is articulated by the Public Libraries and Museums Act 1964, which gives county and district councils *discretionary* powers to "provide and maintain museums and art galleries within their administrative area or elsewhere in England and Wales and do all such things are as necessary or expedient for or in connection with the provision and maintenance of those museums," and in Scotland by the Local Government and Planning (Scotland) Act 1982 (as amended), which places upon local authorities a duty to "ensure that there is adequate provision of facilities for the inhabitants of their area for recreational, sporting, cultural, and social activities."

A much stronger strategic and operational framework for museums and galleries in England was envisaged with the publication of the Resource report *Renaissance in the Regions* (2001). Produced by a task force convened at the behest of Chris Smith, then Secretary of State for Culture, Media, and Sport, to review the state of the nation's network of regional museums, the report identified problems including inconsistent provision, sectoral fragmentation, and a failure to sustainably deliver government policy (e.g. education, creativity, and social inclusion), and recommended a major redefinition of museum structural interfaces and cooperative practice. It proposed a transformational initiative that sought to make museums fit for the twenty-first century. With the uptake of Renaissance, years of under-investment have been reversed, with nearly £150 million allocated to regional museums between 2002 and 2008, and a new structure—"a "hub" for each of the nine regions made up of a group of the largest museums, funded by central government and working together to improve museums across the whole region"[55]—put in place. The achievements of Renaissance, however, have not reduced the vulnerability of nonstatutory services. In 2005/2006, council spending on museums and galleries in Britain amounted to just over £320 million, or 0.19% of total local authority net expenditure,[56] and cuts and closures in London[57] and a funding crisis in Wales, where "there is nothing like the investment of Renaissance,"[58] remain major concerns.

Independent Museums

A substantial number of museums in the United Kingdom are managed outside the traditional frameworks of central or local government. In the nomenclature of recent years they are known as "independent" museums. Defined by the Association of Independent Museums (AIM) as having "a board of trustees or other policy making body which are not directly controlled by or the direct responsibility of any central government department or local or regional authority or similar political subdivision," they comprise museums with charitable status (and therefore within the public sector) and those that operate for commercial gain.[59] Some have considerable public authority financial support, and others receive little or none.[60] In 2000, there were thought to be approximately 1215 such museums in the United Kingdom, with around half of a specialist nature.[61]

Although the majority have been created since the mid-1960s in a flurry of growth, the first generation of independent museums in the United Kingdom is arguably those with roots in the activities of societies, clubs, or other groups of interested people. As Cossons[60] points out,

> many of the great collections now held by public authorities, and some of the buildings that house them, have their origins in the activities of...societies, and gentlemen's clubs, which if they were still being run in this way today, would certainly place them in the category of independent museums.

Despite local authority accession of numerous collections and buildings, some societies' museums, such as that of the Sussex Archaeological Society at Lewes (1846), still exist in their original forms, and others retain an independent identity with a governing body replete with society members.[60] Overall, however, the decline of society museums—run as originally established—was effected by monetary constraints. Holding to principles of free admission, they were sustained by membership subscription and endowments, a funding pattern that collapsed after the first generation of members disappeared. Rising operating and care costs compounded the issue and necessitated a linkage with local authorities.[62] Cossons[62] notes that four decades ago it would have been a rational assumption that "these early society museums formed part of the transitional, formative phase of museum development in this country, a phase that had been superseded by a more formalized Local Authority based structure of museums" delivering a service to people in their locality. In the 1970s, however, shifts in public attitudes toward the material traditionally held in museums, increased affluence, leisure and mobility, a new popular awareness and sensitivity toward the environment and place, and a keenly felt need to record the changing industrial landscape coalesced and catalyzed a new breed of museum.

The independent museums that emerged swept away the "dull and dusty" image projected by local authority museums[63] at the time and could be characterized by "a pioneering spirit, a can-do attitude and an innovative, entrepreneurial approach."[64] Established by community or industry groups and covering areas previously generally unrepresented in the traditional museums milieu—industrial archeology, transport history, vernacular architecture, and building preservation (often *in situ*)—they operated as charitable trusts and raised their revenue from admission fees and commercial activities. As well as the world renowned Ironbridge, now a collection of 10 museums, they included the Weald and Downland Open Air Museum in West Sussex, the National Motor Museum at Beaulieu in Hampshire, the Bass Museum in Burton upon Trent (latterly the Coors Visitor Centre), and the Gladstone Working Pottery Museum in Stoke-on-Trent.[63] Ironbridge and the Gladstone Working Pottery Museum typify the important strain of new museums created as a direct result of the changes in the industrial landscape, where the unattractive relics of past industrial activity—evidence of an important cultural phenomenon of world significance—were being rapidly eliminated. The former was established in 1967 to preserve and interpret the remains of the Industrial Revolution around the gorge spanned by world's first cast iron bridge at Coalbrookdale. The latter, centered on bottle ovens typical of hundreds that dominated the Stoke skyline in the nineteenth and early twentieth centuries, opened in 1974 as a result of an eleventh hour reprieve from demolition after local people mobilized to save the site. Other smaller independent museums have been initiated by local communities and embrace all subjects within a locality, tapping into a local scale desire to see evidence of communities' own history collected, and preserved in their own local museum.[65]

The independent museum constituency continued to grow in the decades following the 1970s, and its total income is now approximately £300 million, a quarter of the total museums economy.[59] Their influence on the wider museum world in the United Kingdom has been strong, especially their entrepreneurism and commercial attitude; running shops, events, cafes, and visitor attractions have been widely adopted as mainstream museums accept the notion of social entrepreneurship.[63] Many of the display and interpretation techniques employed by independent museums have also been embraced by the public sector.[66] More recently, it is "The Trust model popularized by independents [that] is now heading for the mainstream as a growing number of local authorities explore the advantages of converting their museum services to (semi) independent charities."[67] The management of Glasgow's museums and galleries, for example, has been entrusted to a charitable company—the Culture and Sport Glasgow Trust—in a move to facilitate greater financial flexibility and tap into Lottery and other funds. While other museum services, such as Sheffield and York, are also now run by charitable trusts, in Glasgow the new company will be responsible for the city's entire cultural division.[68]

NATIONAL TRUST AND ENGLISH HERITAGE

National Trust

Although for many years the National Trust ethos held that it did *not* operate museums,[69] it is now widely recognized that the organization's "entire ensemble of objects, buildings, gardens, landscapes and the cultural networks they are part of constitute a very live and relevant museum holding."[70] This museum holding is considerable. In 2006, the Trust became the largest accredited museum authority in the United Kingdom, with 149 properties registered as museums, or almost 10% of the national constituency of registered museums.[71] Its land holdings comprise over 600,000 acres and 700 miles of coastline in a broad geographical spread over England, Wales, and Northern Ireland (Many National Trust properties house important collections of furniture, fine and decorative art, costumes, and antiquities. In the mid-1990s, the Museums and Galleries Registration Scheme was extended to include such collections. The National Trust's land holdings, however, cannot be registered as museums, see Resource).[72] The Trust is a charity completely independent of government, managed since 2005 by a Council and Board of Trustees, and relies on income through the fees of its 3.5 million subscribing members, donations and legacies, and revenue raised from commercial operations.[73] Over 12 million visitors are attracted annually to the Trust's charging properties, while over 50 million visit its open air holdings (Figures given

are for 2007, see National Trust).[74] In Scotland, the National Trust for Scotland—founded in 1931 at the initiative of Rural Scotland—has similar statutory powers as the National Trust, but operates with an entirely independent constitution. Around 188,000 acres of countryside are in its care together with 128 properties, holdings that are supported by a membership of almost 300,000 and attract some 1.25 million visitors annually.[75]

The National Trust was founded as a result of the vision and mobilizing activities of three Victorian philanthropists—Octavia Hill (1838–1912), a social reformer active in improving housing for the urban poor, Sir Robert Hunter (1844–1913), a solicitor involved with the Commons Preservation Society (founded in 1865 by John Ruskin, John Stuart Mill, William Morris and others to help protect the remaining communally held lands against enclosure), and Canon Hardwicke Rawnsley (1851–1920), a Lake District clergyman and poet—who recognized the need for an organization to act as a guardian of the nation's natural and cultural heritage at a time of increasing threat from uncontrolled development and industrialization. The catalyst that led to the idea was the threat to a garden in Deptford, east London. The garden was Sayes Court, created by the seventeenth century diarist John Evelyn, whose "original plan of 1653 shows what must have been one of the finest gardens of the time."[76] In 1884 an Evelyn family scion approached Octavia Hill with a view to its safeguarding for the enjoyment of the public, but no organization was extant that had the legal power to hold property for preservation in perpetuity. She decided to engage with the ideas laid out in a paper sent to the National Association for the Promotion of Social Science by Robert Hunter in which he posited the notion of a "land company," formed "with a view to the protection of public interests in the open spaces of the country."[77] The idea had come too late to secure Sayes Court,[78] but some ten years later, in January 1895, the "National Trust" was formally constituted as a public, nonprofit organization, vested with the power to:

> promote the permanent preservation for the benefit of the nation of lands and tenements, including buildings, of beauty or historic interest, and as regards lands for the preservation, so far as practicable, of their natural aspect, features and animal and plant life (National Trust Act 1907).

The first building acquired by the Trust was the fourteenth century half-timbered Clergy House at Alfriston, Sussex, in 1896, but soon Barras Head, overlooking the rocky outcrop associated with King Arthur on the Cornish coast, the sixteenth century Joiners' Hall in Salisbury and a small part of Wicken Fen near Cambridge (the Trust's first nature reserve) were acquired, and the small but dedicated membership went on to amass more scenic lands and grand historic buildings. By 1900, Trust membership stood at approximately 250 members and 180 properties, including the Farne Islands, large stretches of the Lake District, Bodium and Tattershall castles, Chedworth Roman villa and the Elizabethan manor house Barrington Court, came under Trust ownership.[79] The year Barrington Court was purchased, the National Trust Act (1907) reached the Statute Book, conferring on the Trust the power to declare property inalienable. Today, the majority of Trust properties are protected in this way, securing their future in perpetuity.

English Heritage

English Heritage (officially the Historic Buildings and Monuments Commission for England) is a national agency with a broad remit of managing the historic environment in England. As an executive nondepartmental public body sponsored by the DCMS, it is the government's statutory adviser and works in partnership with central government departments, voluntary organizations and the private sector to "conserve and enhance the historic environment, broaden public access to the heritage (and) increase people's understanding of the past."[80] These responsibilities are articulated in the National Heritage Act (1983) and are met by the organization in multiple ways, including championing the heritage nationally and internationally, conservation grant-giving, provision of preservation advice, and registering, protecting, and promoting significant historic buildings, monuments, and landscapes.[80] English Heritage also maintains a public archive, the National Monuments Record, but is arguably most widely known for its care of Stonehenge and over 400 other historic properties on behalf of the nation. Although English Heritage receives grant-in-aid from the government (£129.4 million in 2007/2008), these historic properties generate valuable revenue (£11.4 million in admissions and a further £9.9 million from retail and catering in 2007/2008) through visitor numbers exceeding 5 million.[81] They also provide the milieu for a membership of some 665,000.[81] Similar bodies operate in Wales (Cadw), Scotland (Historic Scotland), and in Northern Ireland (the Environment and Heritage Service Northern Ireland).

ZOOS AND BOTANICAL GARDENS

Zoos

The pursuit of looking at wild animals has always been popular in Britain,[82] with the first exotic specimen—a walrus—purportedly being exhibited in England during the reign of Alfred the Great (r. 871–899).[82] There are accounts of the Norse explorer Othere, whose voyages in the northern seas was incorporated by King Alfred into an Anglos-Saxon translation of Orosius' universal history,

presenting the king with walrus tusks. Indeed, King Alfred's reign saw an influx of walrus ivory into England.[83] Collections of exotic animals were exhibited in traveling fairs from Elizabethan times into the twentieth century, their acquisition facilitated by the great discoveries of the fifteenth and sixteenth centuries and access to a global mercantile shipping trade, but the first permanent zoological collection—comprising lions, lynx, leopards, camels, porcupines, and an owl[82]— in the country was the result of a diplomatic gesture in the form of a ceremonial gift from William of Montpellier to King Henry 1 (r. 1100–1135). Another gift, this time of three leopards from the Holy Roman Emperor Frederick II to King Henry III (r. 1216–1272), led to the establishment of a menagerie in the Tower of London,[82] some animals of which (including an elephant) could be viewed by the public.[84]

From the late Middle Ages, the practice of keeping wild animals was still the province of the nobility and wealthy, and nonsystematically organized private collections in castles and estates across Britain proliferated, both conferring power and status on their owners and gratifying curiosity. At the beginning of the nineteenth century, however, serendipity (although still rife in determining the composition of many menageries of the era including the popular, arcade-like Exeter Exchange on London's Strand) was abandoned when the first zoological collection to be specifically founded for scientific purposes was established, that of the Zoological Society of London.

In a climate of colonial expansion, imperialism, and nationalism, Sir Stamford Raffles, a former colonial administrator in the East Indies, began the Zoological Society of London in 1826, its stated rationale being "the advancement of Zoology and Animal Physiology and the introduction of new and curious subjects of the Animal Kingdom"; The conferring of power enabled by the practice of keeping wild animals had now shifted to the nation, as "the rhetorical goal implicitly shared by Raffles and the other founders of the Zoological Society (was) to acquire, maintain and display representatives of the animal kingdom in a way that echoed and emphasized British preeminence."[85] Two years later, the London Zoological Gardens opened in Regent's Park to fellows of the society and in 1846, to the public. The emphasis of policy and investigations carried out in the zoo at the time was shaped by landowners within the society, who promulgated domestication and acclimatization (a breeding farm was established at Kingston Hill to this end), and the naturalists, who "wished the zoo to stock exotic animals of taxonomic interest, without regard for their attractiveness, edibility, or other usefulness,"[86] and focus on comparative anatomy and pathology. Today, the opportunities for scientific research are much broader, and the remit of the Zoological Society's research division (the Institute of Zoology, now in a strategic partnership with Cambridge University) spans evolutionary biology, genetics, ecology, reproductive biology, and wildlife epidemiology.[87]

London Zoo, then *primus inter pare*, continues to be one of the world's greatest with excellent research and a mission that privileges the conservation of wild animals and their natural habitats.

The conservation message at London Zoo is explicit and reflects a sea-change in U.K. zoos in recent years as they have reconsidered their roles, often in light of "dwindling attendances and budget shortfalls."[88] Change has also been forced by the environmental lobby (as concern escalates for the preservation of wild stocks of animals), and shaped by the debate (triggered in the United Kingdom by the critical financial problems of London Zoo in the early 1990s) on the ethics of keeping wild animals and the need for "clarity about captivity (that is) essential to the humane transformation of zoos."[89] Furthermore, U.K. zoos are now regulated through the Zoo Licensing Act 1981 (as amended) under which they must meet minimum standards in *inter alia* animal husbandry and are obliged to participate in conservation and to promote public education and awareness of biodiversity conservation.[90] Today, Holtorf[91] notes, "Zoos are the most frequently visited types of museum in the world." Despite an overall decrease in U.K. zoo attendance in the 40 years prior to 1998,[92] shifts in zoo dynamics heavily promoting conservation as a key objective and the transformation of zoo environments (with commensurate enhancement of their credibility among the public) have arguably resulted in a gradual increase in zoo visits over the last 20 years in the kingdom.[92,93] Indeed, Mackay[94] has indicated that zoos generate some 7 million visits a year. This popularity has been crucial as many U.K. zoos operate under charitable status and "Visitors and their gate receipts, on-site expenditure and animal sponsorship are the lifeline for zoos, representing the major funding source for the majority of zoos in the United Kingdom."[95]

A large number of establishments display wild animals to the public in the United Kingdom—*The International Zoo Yearbook*[96] lists 65 zoos and aquariums "together with a number of institutions with important animal collections, such as primate research centers, universities, and bird parks," while the Department for the Environment, Food, and Rural Affairs' list of licensed zoos operating in England alone in 2007 was much larger at 270 establishments.[97] The Born Free Foundation's 2000–2004 survey listed approximately 479 establishments displaying wild animals to the public for seven or more days a year in Britain;[98] The Foundation's latest estimate for the United Kingdom is over 530.[99] London Zoo aside, at the developmental and attendance vanguard, some are particularly notable. Chester Zoo, generally acknowledged as the largest conventional U.K. zoo at 110 acres,[100] was founded in the early 1930s by George Mottershead with a collection of animals from an earlier zoo at Shavington, near Crewe. Mottershead's original desire to have a "zoo without bars" perhaps explains the zoo's international renown today for innovative enclosure

designs. It is also known for its breeding successes and involvement in cooperative breeding programs, and plays an important role in developing conservation outreach, research, education, and marketing strategies. In 2007 visitor attendance was approximately 1.3 million, making the zoo the United Kingdom's leading wildlife attraction and fourth in the kingdom's most visited overall attractions.[101] Edinburgh Zoo is also a highly successful visitor attraction (the second most visited charging attraction in Scotland), with 650,000 visitors recorded in 2006.[96] The Royal Zoological Society of Scotland, founded in 1909, opened the zoo in 1913 and today it occupies 82 acres of parkland and is a leading center of conservation, education, and research.[102] Recognizing the educational potential of defragmenting the exhibits and making reference to the "vital and multitudinous interfaces between plants and animals,"[103] the zoo has adopted a holistic approach to habitat creation and plans to redevelop the entire site around four complex biotic communities, or biomes. (The four biomes are: Oceans and Wetlands, Tropical Forests, Woodlands, and Grasslands. The society is also creating two biomes at the Highland Wildlife Park, with Mountain and Tundra species.)[104] Zoogeographic display is also a feature of Paignton Zoo in Devon after its £6 million transformation into an environmental park in 1996.[105]

Botanical Gardens

At the turn of the new millennium a project described as "a showcase for economic botany and ethnobotany" constructed in the moon-like space of an exhausted china clay quarry in Cornwall attracted some 2 million visitors in its first full operating year, and through visitor spending brought £155 million into the economy of the county.[106] The Eden Project, although differing from a traditional botanic garden in that its primary purpose is to draw a broad public contingent, interest them in plants and demonstrate human dependence on plants,[107] is a hugely popular recent addition to the long and distinguished history of the maintenance of plant collections for scientific study and educational purposes in the United Kingdom.

Although the garden of John Gerrard in Holborn (1575) had botanical aspects and the formal gardens attributed to Dr. William Turner at the Duke of Somerset's Syon House are linked to the naturalist's *Names of Herbes* (1548),[108] the earliest botanic garden in Britain was established with the benefaction of Sir Henry Danvers, first Earl of Danby, in 1621 by the University of Oxford as a physic garden, growing plants for medicinal research. Its "Nursery of Simples," and plants in a conservatory "heated by a four-wheel fire basket of burning charcoal hauled back and forth by a gardener," allowed students to learn their *materia medica* at a time when "the development of other sciences was being hampered by medieval tradition."[109] Contemporaneous with Oxford was the private garden (c. 1630) of John Tradescant (1570–1668) in South

Lambeth, (although Allen[110] notes that he was more concerned with flowers that exhibited size, color, and strangeness, and fruits of succulence, than with the value of simples), and in 1673 the Chelsea Physic Garden was formed by the Society of Apothecaries. Scotland's first physic garden dates back to 1670 when a small plot of land at St. Anne's Yards adjacent to Holyrood Palace in Edinburgh was laid out by Dr. Robert Sibbald (later first Professor of Medicine at Edinburgh University) and Dr. Andrew Balfour.[111] Although relocated in 1763 to a "green field" site on the ancient high road to Leith,[111] the garden now known as the Royal Botanic Garden Edinburgh has unbroken lineage, an aspect shared with the Chelsea and Oxford gardens.

British botanic gardens morphed in the seventeenth and eighteenth centuries into colonial tropes of expansion and commercial development (Calcutta, Pamplemousse in Mauritious), and in the nineteenth century into civic gardens, established by "enlightened local government authorities (Sheffield, Glasgow)…as havens of green space in industrial cities"[112] and advancing the horticultural aspects of their living collections. Today, the notion of a botanical garden as a sanctuary has emerged,[113] responding (like zoos) to the demands of the conservation movement and taking "much of the responsibility for the genetic protection of threatened species, along with *ex situ* protection of plants with economic and ecological importance."[113] Although Davis[114] has argued that the influence of environmentalism on botanical gardens in the United Kingdom has been less evident than in other countries—especially the United States of America—there are some notable exceptions. The Royal Botanic Gardens Kew, is an iconic example.

The Royal Botanic Gardens, Kew is broadly recognized as one of the foremost centers for counsel, assistance, and action on plant and fungus conservation in the world, increasingly contributing to the development of international conservation strategies. Its programs engage with myriad endangered and threatened plants and their ecologically connected plant communities, and employ an advanced array of techniques (storage and cryopreservation of seeds, embryos and pollen, and micropropagation) to support *ex situ* and *in situ* conservation projects.[115] The eminence and global influence of Kew, inscribed on the list of World Heritage Sites in 2003, has been constructed over centuries. From 1752, when Princess Augusta assisted by the keen botanist the third Earl of Bute and the architect Sir William Chambers began to develop her ten acres at Kew House, the Royal Botanic Gardens has functioned as a ferme ornée (an "ornamental farm" — a country estate laid out for profit [through gardening] and pleasure [by using aesthetic principles]) for King George III; the hub of botanical collecting and exchange (where economic botany had a direct practical relevance to both Britain and her colonies) under the "superintendence" of the king's chief botanic advisor Sir

Joseph Banks and similarly later under Dr. Joseph Dalton Hooker; a nursery for botanists and gardeners; and currently, in an age of ecological crisis, as a global leader in ecological stewardship.

Kew is a major visitor attraction. In 2007/2008, Kew and its sister garden at Wakehurst Place, West Sussex achieved just over 1.9 million visits.[116] It is an executive nondepartmental public body (created by the National Heritage Act 1983) governed by a Board of Trustees and sponsored by the Department for the Environment, Food, and Rural Affairs, receiving £25.2 million grants-in-aid, with additional visitor income, investment income and fundraising totalling £30.8 million.[116]

MUSEOLOGY AND FUTURE TRENDS

The Museum Profession

The (numerical) growth of the museum workforce in the United Kingdom has been considerable over the last 50 years, reflecting a major expansion in museum numbers (almost three new museums a week were opening in the 1980s) and the wider role of museums' approved missions within their communities and regions.[117] The Digest of Museum Statistics analysis of 1999[118] provides an indication of museum employment numbers across the then 1300 registered museums in the United Kingdom: 15,365 FTE (full-time equivalent) paid staff, of which 12,590 were in "permanent" positions, 2275 held temporary contracts, and 744 were employed as freelance specialists. However, the paid staff were considerably outnumbered by a volunteer workforce of approximately 25,206 FTE individuals. The survey revealed the national museums (6065), local authority museums (4799) and independent museums (3307) to be employers of the majority of paid staff, while the latter's utilization of some 15,786 volunteers placed it substantially ahead in unpaid staff numbers. In recent years, shifts in the U.K. labor market toward greater flexibility have been reflected in museums as "far higher levels of consultant and temporary or short-term contract staffing" have become evident.[119] While the gender diversity of the museum workforce is generally good (51% of all curatorial and managerial positions in local authority sector and 46% for the nationals and independents)[120]—indeed in some areas of museum practice (e.g. development) women dominate in numbers and seniority[121]—there are still few women in the top museum posts.[121] The ethnic diversity of the museum workforce, however, does not mirror the plurality of society (see issues section below).

Museum work has traditionally been associated with the curator, "an academic specializing in a specific collection-related field who can perform all the tasks necessary to the museums,"[122] and in many parts of the world museums continue to function with a narrow range of staff mainly consisting of "scholar-curators" at the professional level.[123] In the United Kingdom, although the curator is still pivotal, Parr's[124] observation that museums "encompass a plurality of professions" is pertinent. The workforce comprises a variety of specialists in both subject and service fields, a result of the increasingly complex nature of museums and a more sophisticated understanding of all the factors that lead to effective provision. As Kavanagh[122] notes:

> In the larger museums teams of people work side by side: curators, education officers, conservators, exhibition technicians, designers, registrars, gallery assistants and attendants, outreach workers, audience advocates, writers, marketing specialists, security experts and managers. In smaller museums, curators, trained to have a high level of awareness and a good degree of competence in these skill areas, operate to the limits of their own versatility. They often work with freelance specialists.

The increasing prevalence of museum studies courses in the United Kingdom and frequent reference to a "museum profession" might suggest the homogenization of museum careers and a unitary profession,[124] but the diversity in knowledge and skills noted above required *within* museums, and the diversity *among* museums in type, collections, and audience expectations, render this notion nugatory. As Kavanagh[125] points out, "uniformity within the profession can be found more in a jointly held, but broad philosophy about the value of museums" and "an overarching sense of social and educational purpose" than in specific sets of skills and tasks. There is evidence of "a shared identity of museum professionalism,"[125] and an understanding of professionalism not as an end in itself but as a "spiritual behaviour through which we seek to accomplish larger purposes."[126]

In Britain, momentum for the professionalization of museums and museum work began apace at the end of the nineteenth century, part of the growth in the new social phenomenon of professionalization that had seen many groups of workers—outwith the traditional learned professions of theology, medicine and law—seek status and recognition of their vocational endeavors through the constitution of distinct "professions." This movement among museum workers, stressing the notion that the multiple museum types faced many of the same practical problems, effected the creation of the first museum association in the world (1889), and the earliest production of museological literature.[127] Today, the Museums Association is the "single authoritative voice for the whole museum community,"[128] disseminating information through *Museums Journal* (1901) and other print and Web-based output, lobbying government and setting ethical standards, engaging its members (5000 individual, 600 institutional and 250 corporate) in events around museum issues (including an annual conference) and furthering the position and qualification of museum staff.[129]

Other professional associations operating at a national level include ICOM-UK, ICON (Institute of Conservation, the lead voice for the conservation of cultural heritage in the United Kingdom), the Museum Professionals Group (exists to provide a forum for its constituency of new museum professionals), the National Museum Directors' Conference (founded in 1929 and funded by the participating institutions, provides a discussion and collaboration platform for its membership, also represents the interests of national museums to government and other stakeholders), the AIM (Association of Independent Museums), and the University Museums Group U.K. Museums in the United Kingdom also have a remarkable contingent of support and advocacy at national level in the form of specialist groups whose remit embraces a facet of museum function or issues allied to the subject of museum collections. The earliest of these is the Group for Education in Museums (1948), but their real growth came in the 1970s[130] and relatively recent counts list more than 20 such groups.[131] The specialist groups include: Natural Sciences Collections Association (NatSCA), Geological Curators Group (GCG), Dress and Textile Specialists (DATS), Association for Cultural Enterprises (ACE), Museum Ethnographers Group (MEG), Social History Curators Group (SHCG), Society of Museum Archaeologists (SMA), Touring Exhibitions Group, Visual Arts and Galleries Association, Museums and Galleries History Group), although today there are many more. Subject specialist networks were a key element of the *Renaissance in the Regions* report (2001), and consequently over £500,000 of Renaissance funding has been invested in existing and new specialist groups.[132] At a regional level, professional groups exist in a country-wide network of federations. The regional federations include: South Western Federation of Museums and Art Galleries, Midlands Federation of Museums and Art Galleries, South Midlands Museums Federation, North West Federation of Museums and Art Galleries, Scottish Museums Federation, and Federation of Museums and Art Galleries of Wales.[133]

Recognition of the need for specialized training in museum work has been extant in the United Kingdom for many years, with early initiatives following a Royal Commission investigation into the problems of the national museums and galleries between 1927 and 1930.[134] The Museums Association took the lead in 1930 with the establishment of its Museums Diploma training, operated on a voluntary basis by experienced staff in leading national and local museums, and the first one week training course was run that year in London. In 1980, the Association released the formal teaching elements of the Diploma to the University of Leicester. Today, the Association retains control of admission to the successor to the original Diploma, the Associateship of the Association, but the future nature of this professional qualification is currently under review. The first full-time postgraduate diplomas—now Masters degrees—in Museum Studies were introduced by the University of Leicester (1966) and then by the University of Manchester (1971), with curricula and aims based on the Museums Association's Diploma program. Nowadays many courses are offered in Museum Studies and related subjects at universities throughout the United Kingdom, and other recent initiatives by the Museums, Libraries and Archives Council have been established to encourage new entry routes into the sector.

Key Contemporary Issues

Museums have been part of the fabric of society for some considerable time in the United Kingdom, shifting to serve different generations and to satisfy the agendas of the day. The last 10 years have been particularly notable for the policy discourses of the Labour government (elected in 1997) that have "continuously layered ever greater and ever more diverse expectations onto the museum sector and museum professionals."[135] These expectations are centered on the redefinition of museums as a public service, moving them beyond their traditional cultural role to one in which they become coordinates for change in society, resolving problems such as social exclusion (defined by the government's Social Exclusion Unit in 1997 as "a shorthand label for what happens when individuals or areas suffer from a combination of linked problems such as unemployment, poor skills, low incomes, poor housing, high crime environments, bad health and family breakdown") and orientating their work toward lifelong learning, identity and community building, public health, and economic and social integration. Initial formal articulation of the government's social inclusion expectations of museums appeared in the 1999 document *Museums for the Many*[136] with its focus on widening access, but the broader agenda was signaled by the publication of *Centres for Social Change*.[137] While many academics/ practitioners[138–140] find the proactive use of museums' potential to address social problems justifiable, the coherence and feasibility of this "partly reimagined museum" have been questioned by others.[141]

Requirements for U.K. museums to assume new roles as agents of social inclusion have rendered workforce diversity increasingly important to the sector. Although there was "explicit recognition in the early 1980s that the profession...was insufficiently diverse,"[142] a 2006 survey by the Museums Association into the cultural diversity of staff (the Museums Libraries and Archives Council defines cultural diversity as "diversity based around ethnicity and race,"[143] at hub museums across England identified the percentage of staff from black and minority ethnic (BME) backgrounds as 2.49%, compared with 8% of the population total, with severe under-representation in educational, interpretation and curatorial positions.[144] These results echoed the imbalance found in an earlier report into cultural diversity at national museums by the National Museums Directors' Conference.[145] Sandell[142] has cited outdated workplace cultures and structures as contributory and

perpetuating factors, including a passive response to the problem, whereby under-representation is attributed to the demographic profile of a region and a lack of BME candidates for jobs ("museums do not operate discriminatory practices and...responsibility for change lies, therefore, not with the museum, but with people from ethnic minority communities, their attitudes and aspirations"),[146] and the exclusionary corporate culture of "homosocial reproduction" (a tendency to recruit to an implicit model that reflects the existing demographics of the profession). Within the context of strategic imperatives for museums to consider diversity issues, however, recent initiatives have emerged (see, for example, the Museums Association workforce development agenda), many of which can be characterized by the use of "positive action."

Overall, the last decade has been notable for the remarkable renaissance of museums in the United Kingdom, largely made possible for English regional museums with *Renaissance* funding (see local authority museums above), and for all museum types with the financial support of the Heritage Lottery Fund (HLF). The creation of a National Lottery in 1993 and the decision not to use the principle of additionality (i.e., replace existing government spending) with the profits, but to benefit "good causes" (arts; charities; health, education and the environment; heritage, sports), has generated enormous sums of money for those causes. The good cause that has principally benefited museums is Heritage, and the HLF is the distributing body, operating across England, Scotland, Wales, and Northern Ireland. Since 1994, the Fund has awarded £4 billion to more than 26,000 projects,[147] from tiny community events to multimillion pound capital schemes. Brown[148] provides examples of nonnational museum beneficiaries—the Horniman Museum and the Dulwich Picture Gallery in south London, the New Art Gallery in Walsall, and the Ashmolean in Oxford, but the bold and costly national museum projects—the Tate Modern (the transformation of a disused power station on London's South Bank) and the British Museum (the iconic dome over the Museum's inner courtyard)—are perhaps the most well-known.

CONCLUSION

Guarantees about the future of U.K. museums, however, are not possible. In developing a national strategy for museums in England, Swain[149] has emphasized that the sector is fragile and at a tipping point. Continued investment and development is seen as crucial to make a long term beneficial difference to all society. In Europe, recent trends have been for nations to reexamine their cultural legislation and strengthen legislative structures for their national heritage, in the case of museums, often creating linkages between national museums and designated regional and local institutions, articulating measures for constructive protection and guaranteeing public access.[150] As Babbidge[151] notes, in the United Kingdom, *Renaissance* has begun to deliver a comparable framework for English museums but,

> What is lacking is a formal status that cements the system, so that it has a long-term purpose rather than becoming another short-term initiative. It could also provide an opportunity to define a national structure that takes National museums into account, builds bridges with other parts of the heritage, and defines the core legal requirements for being a 21st century museum.

There can be no doubt that U.K. museums have made remarkable strides through free entry to the nationals, *Renaissance*, the HLF, and new methods of engagement, but long-term, joined-up, sustainable (economic and environmental) processes and vision will safeguard the nation's diverse and great cultural assets—some of the finest museums in the world.

REFERENCES

1. Lewis, G. Introduction. In *The Manual of Curatorship*; Thompson, J., Ed.; Butterworth-Heinemann: Oxford, U.K., 1992; 3–4.

2. Stearn, W.T. *The Natural History Museum at South Kensington: A History of the British Museum (Natural History) 1753–1980*; Heinemann: London, U.K., 1981.

3. Jessop, L.; Sinclair, N. *Sunderland Museum: The People's Palace in the Park*; Sunderland Museum and Art Gallery: Sunderland, U.K., 1996.

4. Brears, P.; Davies, S. *Treasures for the People: The Story of Museums and Art Galleries in Yorkshire and Humberside*; Yorkshire and Humberside Museums Council: Leeds, U.K., 1989.

5. Taub, L.; Willmoth, F. *The Whipple Museum of the History of Science: Instruments and Interpretations, to Celebrate the 60th Anniversary of R. S. Whipple's Gift to the University of Cambridge*; Cambridge University Press: Cambridge, U.K., 2006.

6. MacGregor, A. The cabinet of curiosities in seventeenth century Britain. In *The Origins of Museums: The Cabinet of Curiosities in Sixteenth- and Seventeenth-Century Europe*; Impey, O.R., MacGregor, A., Eds.; Clarenden Press: Oxford, U.K., 1985.

7. Hunter, M. The cabinet institutionalized: The Royal Society's 'Repository' and its background. In *The Origins of Museums: The Cabinet of Curiosities in Sixteenth- and Seventeenth-Century Europe*; Impey, O.R., MacGregor, A., Eds.; Clarenden Press: Oxford, U.K., 1985.

8. Yanni, C. *Nature's Museums: Victorian Science and the Architecture of Display*; Althone Press: London, U.K., 1999.

9. Elsner, J., Cardinal, R., Eds. *The Cultures of Collecting*; London, U.K., 1994; Reaktion Books.

10. Pearce, S.M. *On Collecting: An Investigation into Collecting in the European Tradition*; Routledge: London, U.K., New York, 1995.

11. Black, B.J. *On Exhibit: Victorians and their Museums*; University Press of Virginia: Charlottesville, VA, 2000.

12. MacDonald, S. *The Politics of Display: Museums, Science, Culture*; Routledge: London and New York, 1998.

13. Alexander, E.P. *Museums in Motion: An Introduction to the History and Functions of Museums*; American Association for State and Local History: Nashville, TN, 1979.

14. Lewis, G. Museums in Britain: A historical survey. In *The Manual of Curatorship*; Thompson, J., Ed.; Butterworth-Heinemann: Oxford, U.K., 1992; 22–46.

15. Lewis, G. Museums in Britain: A historical survey. In *The Manual of Curatorship*; Thompson, J., Ed.; Butterworth-Heinemann: Oxford, U.K., 1992; 23.

16. MacGregor, A. The cabinet of curiosities in seventeenth century Britain. In *The Origins of Museums: The Cabinet of Curiosities in Sixteenth- and Seventeenth-Century Europe*; Impey, O.R., MacGregor, A., Eds.; Clarenden Press: Oxford, U.K., 1985.

17. Lewis, G. Museums in Britain: A historical survey. In *The Manual of Curatorship*; Thompson, J., Ed.; Butterworth-Heinemann: Oxford, U.K., 1992; 27.

18. Lewis, G. Museums in Britain: A historical survey. In *The Manual of Curatorship*; Thompson, J., Ed.; Butterworth-Heinemann: Oxford, U.K., 1992; 30.

19. Lewis, G. Museums in Britain: A historical survey. In *The Manual of Curatorship*; Thompson, J., Ed.; Butterworth-Heinemann: Oxford, U.K., 1992.

20. Kavanagh, G., Ed. *Museum Provision and Professionalism*; Routledge: London, U.K., 1994.

21. http://www.mla.gov.uk/about/work_with/mla/museums Museums, Libraries and Archives Council. About Museums.

22. Carter, S.; Hurst, B.; Kerr, R.H.; Taylor, E.; Winsor, P. *Museum Focus. Facts and Figures on Museums in the UK,*; Museums and Galleries Commission: London, U.K., 1999; Issue 2.

23. Mason, P. Zoos as heritage tourism attractions: A neglected area of research?. Int. J. Heritage Stud. **1999**, *5*(3, 4), 193–202.

24. Alexander, E.P.; Alexander, M. *Museums in Motion: An Introduction to the History and Functions of Museums*; 2nd Ed. Altamira Press: Lanham, MD; New York, 2008; Toronto, ON, Canada; Plymouth, U.K.

25. The Burlington Magazine. The National Museums defined and defended. Burlington. Mag. **1988**, *130*(1023), 411.

26. Museums and Galleries Commission. *Museum Matter*; HMSO: London, 1992; 13–21.

27. National Museums Directors' Conference. *National Collections: An NMDC Brief, June 2007*; http://www.nationalmuseums.org.uk/images/publications/nmdc_national_collections_brief_jun07.pdf.

28. Travers, T. *Museums and Galleries in Britain: Economic, Social and Creative Impacts*; London School of Economics: London, U.K., 2006; 26–27.

29. National Museums Directors' Conference. *National Collections: An NMDC Brief, June 2007*; http://www.nationalmuseums.org.uk/images/publications/nmdc_national_collections_brief_jun07.pdf .

30. Arnold-Forster, K. A developing sense of crisis: a new look at university collections in the United Kingdom. Museum. Int. **2000**, *52*(3), 10–14.

31. Price, D. John Woodward and a surviving British geological collection from the early eighteenth century. J. Hist. Coll. **1989**, *1*(1), 79–95.

32. University Museums Group. *University Museums in the United Kingdom*; University Museums Group: Norwich, London, U.K., 2004.

33. University Museums Group. *University Museums in the United Kingdom*; University Museums Group: Norwich, London, U.K., 2004; 27.

34. Museums and Galleries Commission. *The Museums of the Armed Forces. Report by a Working Party*; HMSO: London, U.K., 1990; 9.

35. Thwaites, P. *Presenting Arms. Museum Representation of British Military History, 1660–1900*; Leicester University Press: London, U.K., New York, 1996; 7.

36. National Army Museum. *National Army Museum Annual Report and Accounts 2006/2007*; National Army Museum: London, 2007; 5 Available at http://www.national-army-museum.ac.uk/aboutUs/files/0607accounts.pdf. (accessed June 2008).

37. National Museums Scotland. *National War Museum*; http://www.nms.ac.uk/w m-planyourvisit.aspx.

38. Museums and Galleries Commission. *The Museums of the Armed Forces. Report by a Working Party*; HMSO: London, U.K., 1990; 16.

39. Jones, S. Making histories of wars. In *Making Histories in Museums*; Kavanagh, G., Ed.; Leicester University Press: London, U.K., New York, 1996; 152.

40. Army Museums Ogilby Trust. *Army Museums Ogilby Trust*, Available at http://www.army museums.org.uk/trust.htm (accessed June 2008).

41. http://www.armymuseums.co.uk/amot-search/default.asp? Category=AMOT&Service=Museum-Display&region=NorthernIreland.

42. Newton, P. Military museums and the Army Museums Ogilby Trust. Museums. J. **1987**, *87*(2), 67.

43. Museums and Galleries Commission. *The Museums of the Armed Forces*; HMSO: London, U.K., 1990; 23 Report by a working Party.

44. Stephens, S. National Service. Museums. J. **2006**, *106*(7), 26–29.

45. Museums and Galleries Commission. *The Museums of the Armed Forces. Report by a Working Party*; HMSO: London, U.K., 1990.

46. Babbidge, A. *Local Authorities and Independent Museums: A Research Study*; Association of Independent Museums: London, U.K., 2007; 6.

47. Babbidge, A. *Local Authorities and Independent Museums: A Research Study*; Association of Independent Museums: London, U.K., 2007; 8–26.

48. Babbidge, A. *Local Authorities and Independent Museums: A Research Study*; Association of Independent Museums: London, U.K., 2007; 21.

49. Birmingham City Council. The History of Birmingham's Museum and Art Gallery. http://www.birmingham.gov.uk/GenerateContent?CONTENT_ITEM_ID=2680&CONTENT_ITEM_TYPE=0&MENU_ID=1761.

50. Blair, J.A., Ed.. *100 Years of Dundee Museums and Art Galleries, 1873–1973*; Dundee Museums and Art Galleries: Dundee, U.K., 1973.

51. Museums and Galleries Commission. The museum scene. In *Museum Provision and Professionalism*; Kavanagh, G., Ed.; Routledge: London, U.K., 1994; 99.

52. Audit Commission. *The Road to Wigan Pier? Managing Local Authority Museums and Art Galleries*; HMSO:

London, U.K., 1991; 9 Audit Commission Local Government Report No. 3.

53. Lawley, I. Local authority museums and the modernizing government agenda in England. Museum. Soc. **2003**, *1*(2), 75–86.

54. Resource. In *Renaissance in the Regions: A New Vision for England's Museums*, Resource, The Council for Museums, Archives and Libraries: London, U.K., 2001; 18.

55. Museums Association. *Renaissance in the Regions: England's Regional Museums*, Available at http://www.museumsassociation.org/ma/8121 (accessed June 2008).

56. Babbidge, A. *Local Authorities and Independent Museums: A Research Study*; Association of Independent Museums: London, U.K., 2007; 22.

57. Heal, S. Are London's local authority museums heading for crisis. Museums. J. **2007**, *107*(10), 17.

58. Steel, P. Wales hit by funding crisis. Museums. J. **2008**, *108*(5), 11.

59. Babbidge, A. *Local Authorities and Independent Museums: A Research Study*; Association of Independent Museums: London, U.K., 2007; 27.

60. Cossons, N. Independent museums. In *Manual of Curatorship, A Guide to Museum Practice*, 2nd Ed.; Thompson, J., Ed.; Butterworth-Heinemann Ltd.: Oxford, U.K., 1992; 112.

61. Babbidge, A. *Local Authorities and Independent Museums: A Research Study*; Association of Independent Museums: London, U.K., 2007; 27, 29.

62. Cossons, N. Independent museums. In *Manual of Curatorship, A Guide to Museum Practice*, 2nd Ed.; Thompson, J., Ed.; Butterworth-Heinemann Ltd.: Oxford, U.K., 1992; 113.

63. Nightingale, J. Independence day. Museums. J. **2007**, *107*(6), 24–27.

64. Nightingale, J. Independence day. Museums. J. **2007**, *107*(6), 24.

65. Cossons, N. Independent museums. *Manual of Curatorship, A Guide to Museum Practice*, 2nd Ed.; Thompson, J., Ed.; Butterworth-Heinemann Ltd.: Oxford, U.K., 1992; 114.

66. Middleton, V.T.C. Purpose of museums and special characteristics of independents. In *Museum Provision and Professionalism*; Kavanagh, G., Ed.; Routledge: London, U.K., 1994; 112–115.

67. Nightingale, J. Independence day. Museums. J. **2007**, *107*(6), 27.

68. Nightingale, J. Trust or bust. Museums. J. **2007**, *107*(5), 26–29.

69. Pugh, C. Building trust. Museums. J. **2006**, *106*(12), 16–17.

70. Pugh, C. Building trust. Museums. J. **2006**, *106*(12), 16.

71. National Trust. Trust gains prestigious new status as an accredited museum authority. Art. Buil. Coll. Bull. **2006**, (Spring), 1–2.

72. *Renaissance in the Regions: A New Vision for England's Museums*, Resource, The Council for Museums, Archives and Libraries: London, U.K., 2001; 26 Resource.

73. National Trust. *History of the Trust: 1884–1912*, Available at http://www.nationaltrust.org.uk/main/w-trust/w-thecharity/w-thecharity_our-past/w-history_trust/w-history_trust-1884_1912.htm (accessed January 2009).

74. National Trust. *Facts about the Trust*; http://www.nationaltrust.org.uk/main/w-trust/w-thecharity/w-what_we_do/w-factsabouttrust.htm.

75. National Trust for Scotland. *Your Trust in Scotland, Annual Review for 2006–2007*; National Trust for Scotland: Edinburgh, 2007.

76. Leith-Ross, P. The garden of John Evelyn at Deptford. Garden. Hist. **1997**, *25*(2), 138–152.

77. Fedden, R. *The Continuing Purpose: A History of the National Trust, Its Aims and Work*; Longmans: London, U.K., 1968; 3.

78. Murphy, G. *Founders of the National Trust*; National Trust (Enterprises) Ltd.: Swindon, U.K., 2002.

79. Barthel, D. Historic preservation: a comparative analysis. Sociol. Forum. **1989**, *4*(1), 90.

80. English Heritage. *Who we are*. http://www.english-heritage.org.uk/server/show/nav.1665.

81. *English Heritage Annual Report and Accounts, 2007/08*, HMSO: London, U.K., 2008; English Heritage.

82. Keeling, C. Zoological gardens of Great Britain. In *Zoo and Aquarium History: Ancient Animal Collections to Zoological Gardens*; Kisling, V., Ed.; CRC Press: Boca Raton, London, 2001; 49 New York; Washington DC.

83. Graham-Campbell, J.; Batey, C. *Vikings in Scotland: An Archaeological Survey*; Edinburgh University Press: Edinburgh, U.K., 1998.

84. Hoage, R.J.; Roskell, A.; Mansour, J. Menageries and Zoos to 1900. In *New Animals, New Worlds. From Menageries to Zoological Park in the Nineteenth Century*; Hoage, R.J., Deiss, W.A., Eds.; The John Hopkins University Press: Baltimore, London, U.K., 1996; 13.

85. Ritvo, H. The order of nature, constructing the collections of Victorian zoos. In *New Animals, New Worlds. From Menageries to Zoological Park in the Nineteenth Century*; Hoage, R.J., Deiss, W.A., Eds.; The John Hopkins University Press: Baltimore, London, U.K., 1996; 46.

86. Ritvo, H. The order of nature, constructing the collections of Victorian zoos. In *New Animals, New Worlds. From Menageries to Zoological Park in the Nineteenth Century*; Hoage, R.J., Deiss, W.A., Eds.; The John Hopkins University Press: Baltimore, London, U.K., 1996; 45.

87. Zoological Society of London. *About the Institute of Zoology*, Available at http://www.zoo.cam.ac.uk/ioz/aboutioz.htm (accessed June 2008).

88. Davis, P. *Museums and the Natural Environment. The Role of Natural History Museums in Biological Conservation*; Leicester University Press: London, U.K., New York, 1996; 213.

89. Denning, K. Regarding the zoo: on the deployment of a metaphor. Int. J. Heritage. Stud. **2008**, *14*(1), 60–73.

90. U.K. Department for Environment, Food and Rural Affairs. Zoos Forum Handbook. http://www.defra.gov.uk/wildlife-countryside/protection/zoo/zf-handbook.htm.

91. Holtorf, C. Zoos as heritage: an archaeological perspective. Int. J. Heritage Stud. **2008**, *14*(1), 3.

92. Davey, G. An analysis of country, socio-economic and time factors on world-wide zoo attendance during a 40 year period. Int. Zoo. Yearbook. **2007**, *41*, 217–225.

93. Turley, S.K. Exploring the future of the traditional U.K. zoo. J. Vacation. Marketing. **1999**, *5*(4), 340–355.

94. Mackay, A. Beyond attendance Figures. Zoo. Federation News **1994**, (Spring), 40–46.

95. Turley, S.K. Exploring the future of the traditional U.K. zoo. J. Vacation Marketing **1999**, *5*(4), 349.

96. Zoological Society of London. Zoos and aquariums of the world. Int. Zoo Yearbook **2008**, *42*, 225–393.

97. U.K. Department for the Environment, Food and Rural Affairs. *Defra List of Zoos Operating in England (November 2007)*. http://www.defra.gov.uk/wildlife-countryside/pdf/protection/zoos-list.pdf.

98. Born Free Foundation. *Captive Wild Animals in Britain: Public Display and Zoo Licensing*. http://www.apgaw.org/userimages/APGAW%20zoo%20licensing%20report_1.pdf.

99. Born Free Foundation. *Zoos in the U.K.* http://www.bornfree.org.uk/campaigns/zoo-check/zoos/zoos-in-the-uk/.

100. Turley, S.K. Exploring the future of the traditional U.K. zoo. J. Vacation Marketing **1999**, *5*(4), 340.

101. North of England Zoological Society. *Sharing our Vision, 2007 Annual Report of the North of England Zoological Society*. http://www.chesterzoo.org/sitecore/shell/Controls/Rich%20Text%20Editor/~/media/8F9AA2DEF67641F88FF03A8897FC139F.ashx.

102. Royal Zoological Society of Scotland. *Annual review 2007*. http://www.edinburghzoo.org.uk/export/sites/default/common/documents/annual-report/2007/RZSS_Annualreview07.pdf.

103. Robinson, M.H. The zoo that is not: education for conservation. Conserv. Biol **1989**, *3*, 214.

104. Royal Zoological Society of Scotland. *Annual Review 2007*. http://www.edinburghzoo.org.uk/export/sites/default/common/documents/annualreport/2007/RZSS_Annualreview07.pdf.

105. Turley, S.K. Exploring the future of the traditional U.K. zoo. J. Vacation Marketing **1999**, *5*(4), 340–355 Paignton Zoo. *Animals*. Available at http://www.paigntonzoo.org.uk/anim als.php (accessed January 2009).

106. Prance, G. A paradise for economic botanists: the Eden Project. Econ. Bot. **2002**, *56*(3), 230.

107. Prance, G. A paradise for economic botanists: the Eden Project. Econ. Bot. **2002**, *56*(3), 226–230.

108. Reynolds, S. Heston and Isleworth: Syon House. In *A History of the County of Middlesex*, 1st Ed.; Reynolds, S., Ed.; Oxford University Press for the Institute of Historical Research: London, U.K., 1962; Vol. 3, 97–100.

109. Alexander, E.P.; Alexander, M. *Museums in Motion: An Introduction to the History and Functions of Museums*; 2nd Ed. Altamira Press: Lanham MD, New York, 2008; 142 Toronto ON, Canada; Plymouth, U.K.

110. Allen, M. *The Tradescants: Their Plants, Gardens and Museum 1570–1762*; Michael Joseph: London, U.K., 1964.

111. Royal Botanic Garden Edinburgh. *History of the Botanics*. http://www.rbge.org.uk/about-us/history.

112. Davis, P. *Museums and the Natural Environment. The Role of Natural History Museums in Biological Conservation*; Leicester University Press: London, U.K., New York, 1996; 230.

113. Rinker, H.B. *The Weight of a Petal: The Value of Botanical Gardens*; American Institute of Biological Sciences: Washington, DC, 2002; Available at http://www.actionbioscience.org/biodiversity/rinker2.html (accessed June 2008).

114. Davis, P. *Museums and the Natural Environment. The Role of Natural History Museums in Biological Conservation*; Leicester University Press: London U.K., New York, 1996.

115. Royal Botanic Gardens, Kew. *Conservation and Wildlife: Conservation and Sustainable Use.* http://www.kew.org/conservation/index.html.

116. Royal Botanic Gardens, Kew. *Annual Report and Accounts for the Year Ended 31 March 2008*, TSO: London, U.K., 2008.

117. Boylan, P. The Museum Profession. In *A Companion to Museum Studies*; Macdonald, S., Ed.; Blackwell Publishing: Malden, MA, USA, 2006; 415–430 Oxford, U.K.; Carlton (Victoria), Australia.

118. Carter, S.; Hurst, B.; Kerr, R.H.; Taylor, E.; Winsor, P. *Museum Focus. Facts and Figures on Museums in the UK*; Museums and Galleries Commission: London, U.K., 1999; Issue 2.

119. Boylan, P. The Museum Profession. In *A Companion to Museum Studies*; Macdonald, S., Ed.; Blackwell Publishing: Malden, MA, 2006; 417 Oxford, U.K.; Carlton (Victoria), Australia.

120. Klemm, M.; Wilson, N.; Scott, M. Museum sector workforce survey: An analysis of the workforce in the museum, gallery and heritage sector in the United Kingdom. In *Museum Provision and Professionalism*; Kavanagh, G., Ed.; Routledge: London, U.K., 1994; 164–171.

121. Austwick, D. Leading questions. Museums. J. **2006**, *106*(11), 18–19.

122. Introduction. In *Museum Provision and Professionalism*; Kavanagh, G., Ed.; Routledge: London, U.K., 1994; 7.

123. Boylan, P. The Museum Profession. In *A Companion to Museum Studies*; Macdonald, S., Ed.; Blackwell Publishing: Malden, MA, 2006; 419 Oxford, U.K.; Carlton (Victoria), Australia.

124. Parr, A. A plurality of professions. Curator **1964**, *7*, 287–295.

125. Curatorial identity. In *Museum Provision and Professionalism*; Kavanagh, G., Ed.; Routledge: London, U.K., 1994; 127–128.

126. Weil, S. The ongoing pursuit of professional status. In *Museum Provision and Professionalism*; Kavanagh, G., Ed.; Routledge: London, U.K., 1994; 252.

127. Glaser, A.; Zenetou, A. *Museums: A Place to Work. Planning Museum Careers*; Routledge (in association with The Smithsonian Institution): London U.K., New York, 1996.

128. Resource. *Renaissance in the Regions: A New Vision for England's Museums*; Resource, The Council for Museums, Archives and Libraries: London, U.K., 2001; 74.

129. Museums Association. *History.* http://www.museumsassociation.org/ma/9783.

130. Lewis, G. The organization of museums. In *The Manual of Curatorship*; Thompson, J., Ed.; Butterworth-Heinemann: Oxford, U.K., 1992; 54.

131. Woodhead, P.; Stansfield, G. *Keyguide to Information Sources in Museum Studies*, 2nd Ed.; Mansell: London U.K, Chicago, IL, 1994; 20.

132. Museums, Libraries and Archives Council. *Subject Specialist Networks.* http://www.mla.gov.uk/what/programmes/renaissance/ssns.

133. http://www.collectionslink.org.uk/find_a_network/regional_networks.

134. Boylan, P. The Museum Profession. In *A Companion to Museum Studies*; Macdonald, S., Ed.; Blackwell Publishing: Malden, MA, USA, 2006; 424 Oxford; U.K.; Carlton (Victoria), Australia.

135. Tlili, A.; Gerwirtz, S.; Cribb, A. New Labour's Socially Responsible Museum. Roles, functions and greater expectations. Policy. Stud. **2007**, *28*(3), 269–289.

136. Department for Culture, Media and Sport. *Museums for the Many–Standards for Museums and Galleries to Use when Developing Access Policies*; Department for Culture, Media and Sport: London, U.K., 1999.

137. Department for Culture, Media and Sport. *Centres for Social Change: Museums, Galleries and Archives for All. Policy Guidance on Social Inclusion for DCMS funded and Local Authority Museums, Libraries and Archives in England*; Department for Culture, Media and Sport: London, U.K., 2000.

138. Abram, R.J. Harnessing the power of history. In *Museums, Society, Inequality*; Sandell, R., Ed.; Routledge: London, U.K., 2002; 125–141.

139. Flemming, D. The regeneration game. Museums J. **1997**, *97*(4), 32–33.

140. Sandell, R. Museums and the combating of social inequality. In *Museums, Society, Inequality*; Sandell, R., Ed.; Routledge: London, U.K., 2002; 3–23.

141. Newman, A.; McLean, F. Presumption, policy and practice: the use of museums and galleries as agents of social inclusion in Great Britain. Int. J. Cult. Policy. **2004**, *10*(2), 167–181.

142. Sandell, R. The strategic significance of workforce diversity in museums. Int. J. Heritage. Stud. **2000**, *6*(3), 213–230.

143. Museums, Libraries and Archives Council. *Cultural Diversity: Ethnicity and Race.* Online. Available: http://mlac.gov.uk/policy/Diversity/Black_And_Minority_Ethnic_Communities.

144. Steel, P. MA poll finds regional museums lack diversity. Museums. J. **2006**, *106*(7), 11.

145. National Museums Directors' Conference*National Museums Directors' Conference, Cultural Diversity, Final Report and Recommendations*, National Museums Directors' Conference London, U.K. 2006 http://www.nationalmuseums.org.uk/images/publications/cultural_diversity_final_report.pdf (accessed January 2009).

146. Sandell, R. The strategic significance of workforce diversity in museums. Int. J. Heritage Stud. **2000**, *6*(3), 216.

147. Heritage Lottery Fund. *Who are we?*, Available at http://www.hlf.org.uk/English/AboutUs/ (accessed January 2009).

148. Brown, C. The renaissance of museums in Britain. Eur. Rev. **2005**, *13*(4), 617–636.

149. Swain, H. Developing a National Strategy for Museums in England Presentation made at the Museums Association Annual Conference Glasgow, U.K., Oct, 22–24, 2007.

150. Babbidge, A. Forty Years On. Cultural. Trend. **2005**, *14*(1), 3–66 No.53, 152.

151. Babbidge, A. Forty Years On. Cultural. Trend. **2005**, *14*(1), 46 No.53.

United States: Archives and Archival Science

Cheryl L. Stadel-Bevans
National Archives and Records Administration, College Park, Maryland, U.S.A.

Danna Bell-Russel
Library of Congress, Washington, District of Columbia, U.S.A.

Abstract

The archival tradition in the United States of America consists of two components, a public records tradition and a personal papers or historical manuscript tradition. This entry will explore both traditions and their effects on the archival profession over time. It will also discuss professional development and professional organizations for American archives. It includes profiles of significant archival repositories.

INTRODUCTION

Early American colonists brought with them the habit of keeping public records from Europe. The founding generation added a strong personal papers component. These two traditions intertwined to form contemporary American archival theory and practices.

This entry will explore the history of archives in America as it descended from the English tradition; developments in the practice of archives and records management; the types of materials kept; the types of repositories that exist; professional development and training; and recent developments in the archival field.

EARLY HISTORY

Recordkeeping has long been vital to society. Knowing who was born when or who owns certain property allows for a civil society. When the European colonists came to America, they brought with them their traditions of public recordkeeping. These records would be filed with the local government or churches. They were not necessarily at that time managed as archival records, and there were no archivists *per se*. Clerks and administrators cared for the records created and filed.

The colonists who broke with England and became the founding generation of American citizens were well aware of the importance of keeping records. Their inability to access records was one of the grievances listed against King George in the Declaration of Independence.[1] When they wrote the Constitution, they required the Congress to maintain journals. They also codified in the Fourth Amendment the right of citizens to protect their personal papers from unreasonable search and seizures.[2] Unfortunately, this awareness did not lead them to establish proper archives or to take adequate preservation measures for government records, and many records were lost or destroyed over time due to neglect and disasters, both natural and man-made. One exception to this is Vermont, where, in 1779, the recordkeeping responsibility was enumerated as a function of the Office of the Secretary of State.

These early Americans were also very aware of their own role in the making of the country and founded some of the earliest historical societies in the country to preserve their legacy. The earliest was the Massachusetts Historical Society, founded in 1791. Others soon followed, including the New-York Historical Society in 1804, and the American Antiquarian Society in 1812.

This began the duality of the American archival tradition wherein public records were maintained by governments and sometimes churches, while personal papers and other historical manuscripts were preserved by historical associations. From the beginning, the traditions served two fundamentally different purposes. The public records captured transactions and served a legal and administrative function. The manuscript tradition primarily served history and historians and was meant to record the achievements of a particular person or group of persons. However, at times, historical societies would also accept deposits of government records in the absence of any other formal programs for managing them.

Because historical societies saw themselves as serving history, they focused more on collecting and preserving the documents and other items that would add to the collective knowledge. Preservation and access, at least access for scholars, were key components. Early "archivists" in the historical societies were usually trained as historians.

These practices remained the same until the end of the nineteenth century. After the Civil War, the volume of records being produced greatly expanded, a pattern that would be repeated after World War II. The U.S. Congress passed the first records disposal legislation in 1889 in response. It met with limited success as agencies remained reluctant to part with their records. This was followed in

Encyclopedia of Library and Information Sciences, Fourth Edition DOI: 10.1081/E-ELIS4-120044026

1903 with legislation to allow agencies to transfer their records to the Library of Congress (Fig. 1). Among the records transferred were those from the Continental Congress.[3]

At the same time, the movement to establish formal state archives programs began. This was primarily led by the Southern states to preserve the Confederate legacy of the Civil War. The Alabama State Archives was founded in 1901 and was followed quickly by Mississippi in 1902. Throughout the first decade of the 1900s, many other states would also establish archives. Even Hawaii, as a territory, established its archives in 1906. New York was the most recent state to establish a program, in 1971. It is, unusually, a program of the State Education Department. It is also worth noting here that the bulk of New York's early records were destroyed in a fire in 1911.

Meanwhile, the 1880s and 1890s saw an increased emphasis on the use of primary sources in historical scholarship. To aid these efforts, many historical societies published collected works of their materials to provide for both access and a certain level of preservation of the contents through duplication. The American Historical Association (AHA) was founded in 1884 and quickly initiated several studies and committees on archives. These efforts eventually led to the establishment of the Public Archives Commission within the AHA in 1899, followed by the first Conference of Archivists held in 1909. These were formed in part to address the AHA's need to better understand and access primary source materials for historical scholarship. Also, increasingly, there was a need felt within the AHA to incorporate federal records into historical research.

Additionally, fires, always a hazard, continued to plague government agencies and their records storage. In 1877 and again in 1896, the U.S. Congress began

exploring the idea of building a Hall of Records for the storage of inactive agency records. Competing interests prevented authorization of the planning and funding for such a building until 1904. Even with funding, efforts to build a Hall of Records would again be delayed, because advocates were instead supporting the movement to build a proper National Archives for the long-term preservation and public access to records. Chief among them was J. Franklin Jameson, who would pursue this ideal until the National Archives were established.[3]

THE MODERN ERA

The fight to establish the U.S. National Archives was a long one. The AHA created a committee on the National Archives in 1908. Authorization for the building finally came in March 1913, at the very end of Taft's administration. Unfortunately, the authorization did not include funding.[3] During World War I, efforts and funds were directed elsewhere and no progress was made towards establishing the Archives. Once the conflict ended, congressmen wanted federal buildings located in their districts and kept resisting the building of new structures in DC without corresponding new buildings in their districts. The impasse broke in May 1926, with an omnibus buildings law that came complete with funding. It would take another 12 years before the building was finished and opened for research (Fig. 2). In 1934, the National Archives Act authorized the creation of the new executive agency to protect the records of the federal government.[3]

In a parallel development, the Conference of Archives within the AHA continued to grow throughout the 1910s and 1920s, moving away from the historian/scholar model and more toward a true archivist model. These archivists

Fig. 1 The first Manuscript Division Reading Room, Thomas Jefferson Building, ca. 1920s. Photograph courtesy of the Manuscript Division, Library of Congress.

Fig. 2 National Archives Building, Washington, D.C.
Source: Photograph courtesy of the National Archives
and Records Administration.

began to feel the need for their own association, separate
from the AHA. In December of 1936, the Conference met
separately for the first time, and the Society of American
Archivists (SAA) was launched. SAA has held an annual
meeting every year since 1937 and has published the
American Archivist since 1938. From the beginning, it
has been open for membership to archivists, rather than
institutions, and during its first year had 124 members.
Today, SAA has over 4000 individual members.

A third development during the 1930s was the beginning of the implementation of formal archival methods.
Public records organizations, particularly the National
Archives with its brand-new staff, needed better ways in
which to proceed to organize the records they held.

Once again, Americans looked to the Europeans.
English, Dutch, and German theories and practices were
studied. As the European tradition was primarily related to
public records, these newly imported methods mostly
applied to government and organizational records and not
to manuscript collections. Early proponents of this
approach included Margaret Cross Norton, State Archivist
of Illinois, and Theodore R. Schellenberg and Oliver
Wendell Holmes, two prominent historians who became
National Archives staff members.

Part of the appeal of the European approach for government archivists is that it brought a "scientific" methodology to the organization of records. This approach
introduced the concepts of provenance and original order,
which drew upon the administrative history of the records.
The manuscripts tradition continued to emphasize the
uniqueness of the materials and organized them by subject
classification, more like library classification, to suit historical scholarship needs (Fig. 3).

The European approach also brought with it some efficiency, in particular, being able to work the records in

groups rather than at the item level. This efficiency
became especially important during the 1940s. During
World War II, there was an increase in the number of
federal agencies as well as a quite rapid expansion in the
volume of records being produced. This led Schellenberg
and Holmes at the National Archives to develop the twin
concepts of record group and record series. These two
concepts, based on the principle of provenance, allow
archivists to organize collections of records according to
the administrative structures that created them. This
approach had an immediate impact on government and
other institutional records repositories, but it would not be
adopted for use in historical societies and other manuscript
collections until more than a decade later.

The World War II boom in records production was
not limited to the federal government. State governments

Fig. 3 Archivist Harry Heiss and archives technician Scott
McLemee processing the Victor Gruen Papers.
Source: Photograph courtesy of the Manuscript Division,
Library of Congress.

also saw an increase in volume and many collecting repositories had increased donations or started collecting manuscripts in new areas. For example, the Sophia Smith Collection at Smith College (Fig. 4) began collecting materials related to women's history in 1942 and what is now the Schlesinger Library at Harvard University followed suit a year later.

In the post-war era, the seed of records management that began in the 1930s and grew during the 1940s came to fruition in the 1950s. By this time, records management—the systematic control of an organization's records from the records' creation through their final disposition—was seen as a discipline separate from archives, which focused only on managing permanent records. Also introduced during this time was the new field of study, information science, which used computers for collecting, storing, classifying, retrieving, manipulating, and disseminating information.

One unfortunate consequence of the focus on records management and administrative efficiency was that the National Archives was too successful at promoting it and lost its status as an independent federal agency.[4] In 1949, the National Archives became the National Archives and Records Service, a division of the General Services Administration, the administrative agency of the federal government. It would take until 1985 for the National Archives to regain its independent status and another new name, National Archives and Records Administration.[5]

While the 1940s and 1950s saw an increase in the growth of state archival programs, the 1960s and 1970s witnessed a rapid increase in nongovernmental archival institutions. These new institutions were primarily academic and cultural repositories. They added a new element to the archival mix, as they combined both the tradition of public recordkeeping in the form of maintaining institutional history and organizational records and the historical manuscripts traditions as they collected materials from their communities and in support of their academic research goals.

PROFESSIONAL SOCIETIES AND PROFESSIONALISM

At various times during its history, SAA has been perceived as not meeting the needs of all archivists, and this has led to the formation of other archival associations. As records managers felt that they were focused on different tasks and duties—primarily those of current records rather than historical records—from archivists, they chose to form the American Records Management Association (ARMA) in 1955. It is now known just as "ARMA International" and consists of approximately 11,000 members.

Also in 1955, the Rare Books Section was established with the American Library Association (ALA). Its membership was drawn primarily from academic institutions. It became the Rare Books and Manuscripts Section in 1967 under guidance of Richard Berner and Arline Custer.[6]

The 1960s witnessed the founding of the National Endowment for the Humanities (NEH) in 1965 and the establishment of the grants program of the National Historical Publications and Records Commission (NHPRC) in 1964. Since its creation as part of National Archives in 1934, the NHPRC focused on producing scholarly editions of the papers of the founding fathers. The new grants program greatly increased this work. In 1975, the NHPRC's role expanded to protect records at risk and establish archival programs. As part of this expansion, it also required the establishment of State Historical Records Advisory Boards (SHRABs). The directors of the SHRABs eventually organized into a group, one that is now known as the Council of State Archivists. Additionally, the NHPRC funded publication of SAA's first set of basic archival manuals in 1977.[4]

United States–
User-Centered Design

Fig. 4 Gymnastic exercises in Alumnae Gymnasium, 1904. The space shown now houses the reading room for the Smith College Archives and Sophia Smith Collection.
Source: Photograph by katherine E. McClellan, used with permission of the Smith College Archives, Northampton, Massachusetts.

The rapid growth of nongovernmental archival institutions led to many changes within the archival profession during the early 1970s. The focus of the profession shifted from managing buildings and institutions to maintaining professional identity.[7] SAA grew larger and changed its focus, as academic archivists joined the Society and began to have a greater role in its governance. This led to some more groups splitting away. In 1972, the National Association of Government Archives and Records Administrators (NAGARA) was formed to concentrate on the issues related to governmental materials. Many regional archival associations also began during this time. These had the benefit of being smaller and local, providing more opportunities for contact within the profession. The two largest of these, the Mid-Atlantic Regional Archives Conference (MARAC) and the Midwest Archives Conference (MAC), were both established in 1972.

Until the 1970s, there was little formal academic training available for archivists. The earliest archivists would have been either historians or clerk/administrators whose responsibilities happened to include caring for records and manuscripts, and all training was done on the job. While many historians began to see the need and advocate for more formal approaches to archives management during the late 1800s and early 1900s, no formal training emerged.

It was not until the founding of the National Archives, with its immediate need for a full staff, that the awareness of the lack of training programs became more acute. The number of archivists needed prior to this was fairly small and could be drawn from the historian and librarian communities. The Archives need could not be filled by drawing on those who had already become archivists. Due, however, to the Great Depression occurring in the United States at that time, many historians and librarians were out of work, and the Archives was able to employ many of these people to create its initial staff. At the same time, the Works Progress Administration (WPA), a federal project during the Great Depression for employing the unemployed to work on public projects, hired many historians for its historical records survey. The WPA trained these people to conduct inventories of records. They looked primarily at records being produced at the state and local government level, but also included some private collections and other records. Some of the WPA-trained people would come to work for the National Archives later. Therefore, as had happened previously, most training continued to be postemployment.

Several efforts examined the training issue from different angles. Both the ALA and SAA established committees to study the educational needs of archivists. Both advocated some level of training in library methods as well as history. A few programs adopted this approach. The first academic program for archivists was established in the renowned library program at Columbia University in 1938, where a series of courses were offered.

The following year, Ernst Posner arrived from Germany and began teaching in the history department at American University. His classes, which were offered in conjunction with the National Archives, became the standard training for Archives employees for many, many years. This derailed many other needs for more formal training of archivists elsewhere. The next archival training program to be instituted in a history department would not appear until Wayne State University began offering archives classes in 1962.

Most training for archivists remained on-the-job or through an apprenticeship program. Then, in the 1970s, the number of academic programs began to expand. This paralleled the growth in awareness over professional identity within the greater community of archivists. These courses were offered in both history and library science departments, primarily at the graduate level, and were primarily taught by practicing archivists serving as adjunct faculty. During this time, the first dual degree program in both subject areas was offered by Case Western University. Unfortunately, this program no longer exists. As did many other institutions during the 1980s and 1990s, including Columbia University, Case Western University chose to eliminate its library science program.

SAA also developed its first set of guidelines on graduate archival education, which were issued in 1977. As Richard Berner points out,

> While the SAA's committee [on education and training] continued its work in developing specifications for formal archival education as a subfield of an established academic discipline such as librarianship or history, the committee also addressed the well-known fact that most practicing archivists had been self-taught. Consequently, it promoted post-employment training programs.[6]

Another important development during these decades was the recognition of the need for standardization. It began with the publication of the *National Union Catalog of Manuscript Collections (NUCMC)* in the 1950s, which "...attempted to gather standard information about archival collections from widely differing repositories and to reduce that information to a uniform catalog card format."[4] This raised the question of how to create standards for materials that were unique and reemphasized the differences between public records and manuscript collections.

While each repository would continue to implement their own way of managing their collections, they began to use common means for description. Description standards became and continue be an important component of the professional discourse. In addition to the *NUCMC*, archivists developed the SPINDEX system for preparing and indexing archival finding aids in the 1960s, the Machine Readable Cataloging–Archival and Manuscripts Control (MARC-AMC) format for use in library cataloging systems in the 1980s, and Encoded Archival Description (EAD) for use on the Internet in the 1990s. In 2004, SAA released *Describing Archives: A Content Standard (DACS)*.

Much of the focus on description standards came from the availability of technology to be used as a tool in doing this work. The technology also added a new component to the archival landscape—that of electronic records. While machine-readable records had started with the first IBM punch cards, their importance as archival materials was not seen until the 1960s. The Inter-University Consortium for Political and Social Research (ICPSR) was established in 1962 to provide an archives for data users. In 1970, the National Archives accessioned its first electronic records. A conference on data archives at the 8th World Congress of Sociology in 1974 led to the founding of the professional association for data librarians and archivists, the International Association for Social Science Information Service and Technology (IASSIST). SAA offered numerous workshops on managing electronic records during the 1980s and 1990s, and these workshops continue to be in high demand today. In the 1990s, the NHPRC once again expanded its focus and established the electronic records research agenda.

During the last quarter of the twentieth century, the debate over education and qualifications for archivists continued. The need for a common professional identity in a field which did not have one path for careers, especially since SAA was not in a position to manage the accreditation of graduate archival programs, led to the founding of the Academy of Certified Archivists in 1988. Not all agreed as many archivists saw certification as a move toward a preference for technical training over a liberal arts education.[7] SAA also updated its guidelines for graduate archival education twice during this time, in 1988 and 1994, and yet another version was released in 2002. The related guidelines for archival continuing education were adopted in 1997 and revised significantly in 2006.[8,9]

Today, archivists continue to enter the profession from many different directions, as shown by the results of the 2005 SAA archival census.[10] Some have received formal academic training, some participate in apprenticeship programs, others take short courses, and still others receive no formal training at all. Most archival professional associations continue to offer postemployment workshops and training to aid archivists in acquiring the skills they need for their positions.

In the 2000s, the two areas of widespread focus were digitizing materials and reducing the amount of materials in the processing backlog. The NHPRC revised its guidelines for the scope of electronic records projects; allowed for funds to be used for digitization projects; and promoted the publication of electronic editions. The federal government expanded its requirements for hiring archivists to allow archival science classes to meet the necessary education requirements. (Prior to the change, the Office of Personnel Management's Individual Occupational Requirements for the Archivist job series only allowed classes in history, American civilization, economics, political science, public administration, and government to be counted toward the educational requirements.) There was a growing interest in the archival field as the SAA student chapters increased to 28 in number. Academic programs also began to offer online classes, and professional organizations offered online workshops.

CONCLUSION

Since the founding of the nation, archives in America have had a bifurcated nature. The first citizens kept both public records and historical manuscripts of the events occurring. These two traditions have been maintained over the intervening years, sometimes focusing on their differences and at other times embracing their similarities. Even groups that have split apart have occasionally rejoined forces, such as with the joint meeting of SAA, NAGARA, and the Council of State Archivists in 2005.

Currently the divide is most apparent in the argument over which is a better educational path to a career in archives—an advanced degree in history or library science, with a couple of institutions establishing programs that lead to an advanced degree in archival science. Some even argue that no degree is needed at all. Most agree, in very basic terms, that it is a combination of the skills one learns while doing the work and learning a certain level of archival theory that makes one trained as an archivist.

As recently as 2008, the president of the Society of American Archives questioned "whether [archivists] are a united profession" or a group divided by its distinctions. He reiterates the thought that all who "preserve the primary documentation that sustains cultural and institutional memory" should be considered part of the profession.[11] The similarities of what archivists do should outweigh the differences.

PROFILES OF ARCHIVAL REPOSITORIES

This section provides information about many archival institutions, representing the diverse nature of archives in the United States. The repositories were chosen for a variety of reasons, including the prominence of the institution, the significance of the founding of the institution, the programmatic activities of the institution, the activities of the staff within national or regional professional associations, or the authors' familiarity of the programs. The profiles are not provided as a comprehensive or definitive list, but merely as a means to convey the breadth of diversity. Many of the institutions listed could have been placed easily into another category.

The information provided in the profiles comes directly from the Web sites of the institutions themselves. In some cases, the information has been edited for brevity and style.

National Archives and Records Administration

The U.S. National Archives was established by Congress in 1934 as an independent executive branch agency of the federal government. In 1949, it became a division of the General Services Administration and was renamed the National Archives and Records Service (NARS). In 1985, it again gained independent status and another new name, the National Archives and Records Administration (NARA).

NARA collects all of the permanent records of the federal government. It is the keeper of the Declaration of Independence, the Constitution of the United States, and the Bill of Rights. Additionally, there are at present approximately 9 billion pages of textual records; 7.2 million maps, charts, and architectural drawings; more than 20 million still photographs; over 3 million data files; and more than 365,000 reels of film and 110,000 videotapes.

At first housed in a single building in Washington, DC, NARA now has 38 facilities across the United States including 14 regional repositories and 13 presidential libraries. For fiscal year 2008, NARA had 138,167 in-person daily researchers; 377,040 public program attendees; 3,046,809 exhibit and museum visitors; and 37,806,682 online visitors. That same year, NARA received 1,221,858 written reference requests, of which 1,148,870 pertained to records at the National Personnel Records Center in St. Louis, Missouri.[12]

NARA also provides for the management of records created by all three branches of the United States federal government—executive, legislative, and judicial. It runs a government-wide records management program that identifies records of permanent value, assures the timely destruction of temporary records, and provides federal agencies with guidance on managing their current records. The regulations for federal agencies are codified in 36 CFR §§1220-1239. Links to all of NARA's regulations may be found at http://www.archives.gov/about/regulations/index.html.

NARA also administers the Federal Register (FR) and the National Historic Records and Publications Commission (NHPRC). The FR is the daily newspaper of the federal government. It provides legal notice of administrative rules and notices and Presidential documents in a comprehensive, uniform manner. The NHPRC supports a wide range of activities to preserve, publish, and encourage the use of documentary sources through grants and other activities.[13]

State and Local Government Archives

The phrase "state or local government archives" generally refers to records of permanent value created by state or local governments, the agency that preserves those records, and the buildings in which the records are housed. While NARA is responsible for federal records management programs and archives, there is no national guidance for state, city, county, or other local government archival programs. Each state has its own regulations for programs, and local governments may institute their own additional measures.

All 50 States and the District of Columbia have archival programs. Some are managed as historical societies, some as archives, and some as divisions within other branches of state government, such as the Office of the Secretary of State or Education.

The entry on State Archives elsewhere in this volume provides more detail on these programs. The profiles below detail examples of local government archives.

Multnomah County (Oregon) Archives

The Multnomah County Archives contains records documenting county activities from its formation in 1854 until the present. Given the County's history, the bulk of the records represent the actions of the Board of County Commissioners and, after 1967, the County Chair's Office. But most departments, offices, and programs have at least some representation in the county's archival record. The archives contains roughly 950 cubic feet of records, 18,200 maps and drawings (both flat and rolled), 500 volumes, 800 recorded discs, 4750 cassette tapes, and 13,000 reels of original microfilm.[14]

New Orleans Notorial Archives

Founded in 1867, this repository holds over 40,000,000 pages of signed acts compiled by the notaries of New Orleans, Louisiana, over three centuries. The only repository dedicated to notorial records in the United States, the materials within this repository include information on land purchases, loans, contracts, and surveys. One unique aspect of this repository is that all of the records are bound in volumes to ensure arrangement and proper housing of the records. The collections are microfilmed and the microfilm is housed at the Louisiana State archives.[15]

San Antonio Municipal Archives Program

The San Antonio Municipal Archives Program was begun in February 2007 under the Office of the City Clerk, and in partnership with the San Antonio Public Library's Texana/Genealogy department, and the San Antonio Public Library Foundation. Prior to this date, there was no formal program or policies in place for the preservation of historical documents created by City departments. Located in the Municipal Records Facility, the program aims to appropriately house, organize, and make available for research the history of the City of San Antonio. Historical records, aerial photographs of the city, a mayoral collection and other valuable items can be found in the City's first ever San Antonio Archives Program. The program, envisioned to possibly become a model for other municipal governments, is intended to preserve the City's historical findings.

Currently, the collection includes archived City Council minutes, ordinances, aerial photographs of the city, maps from the City Engineer and historical items such as letters from Mexican General Santa Anna.[16,17]

Academic Repositories and Digital Projects

Archival programs in academic settings frequently include both the formal institutional archives as well as many "special collections," i.e., manuscript collections in particular subject areas as well as personal paper collections from faculty and other community members. While there are some national rules for recordkeeping based on protecting student privacy, most private academic archival programs are not regulated. Public colleges and universities must follow the requirements of their governing jurisdictions, which are usually state-issued regulations.

While government archivists have frequently been at the forefront of electronic records management, academic archivists have led efforts in digitalizing archival and library materials. They have been instrumental in creating digital libraries and digital institutional repositories.

Cornell University

Officially established in 1951, the original purpose of the Cornell archives was to document everyday life in upstate New York. This changed in 1945, when the repository acquired the Ezra Cornell Papers. These materials documented the founding of Cornell University and its establishment through the sale of Western lands. In subsequent years, the papers of the early presidents and trustees were added as were the personal and professional papers of individual faculty members.

Currently, the Archives collect and preserve records of historical, legal, fiscal, and/or administrative value to Cornell University. Holdings include official records and reports of the university, its officers, and component parts; private papers of faculty, students, staff, and alumni; official and student publications; maps and architectural records; audiovisual materials including still photographs and negatives, motion picture film, oral history interviews, and audio and video tapes; and artifacts and ephemera documenting Cornell's history.

The Cornell University Archives is part of the Division of Rare and Manuscript Collections. The Division holds 400,000 printed volumes, more than 70 million manuscripts, a million photographs, paintings, prints, and other visual media. These include collections in East Asian

history and culture, sexuality and gender, travel and tourism, and science and technology.

Cornell has also been at the forefront of developing digital collections. They have worked to provide digital surrogates of their collections and have also been involved with a number of collaborative projects with institutions such as the National Agricultural Library, the National Science Foundation, and the Massachusetts Institute of Technology to create digital collections. It is also one of the partners in the Making of America project, which is described later in this entry.

Cornell staff has also been involved with creating several programs such as the Digital Imaging Tutorial and the Digital Preservation Management Workshop and tutorial to help train archivists in how to create and preserve digital content. Cornell University staff have also written and presented extensively on digital library issues.[18–20]

The University of Michigan

The Bentley Historical Library at the University of Michigan was established in 1935 by the University Regents to carry out two functions: to serve as the official archives of the University and to document the history of the state of Michigan and the activities of its people, organizations, and voluntary associations. The library has extensive holdings on the history of the state and the university, including more than 30,000 linear feet of archives and manuscripts, 57,000 printed volumes, 1.5 million photographs and other visual materials, and over 10,000 maps.

Collections include the Michigan Historical Collection, which documents the history of Michigan from the days of exploration to the present and the archives of the University of Michigan. The Bentley is also home to several archival training programs, which have helped shaped many leaders of the archival profession. It is also of interest that one of the former heads of the Bentley, Robert Warner, was the guiding force behind the National Archives and Records Administration becoming an independent government agency.

Moreover, in 1993, the University of Michigan library launched its first digital project. In addition to working to bring over 200 collections online, staff have helped created OAIster, a union catalog for digital collections, and the Digital Library eXtension Service, which provides the foundation and the framework for educational and nonprofit institutions to fully develop their digital library collections, as well as many other projects to develop standards and provide support for digital programs. It is also one of the partners in the Making of America project.[21,22]

Making of America

A collaboration between the Cornell University Library, the University of Michigan, and the Library of Congress, the Making of America project provides access to digitized copies of books and periodicals from all three institutes. The initial project was a collaboration between Michigan and Cornell in the hopes of developing a collection of materials that would serve both campuses and would also document American social history in the last half of the nineteenth century. In 1999, the Library of Congress joined the project by providing access to the periodical *Garden and Forest*.

At present, Michigan has contributed 10,000 books and 50,000 journal articles with nineteenth century imprints. Cornell has contributed 267 books and 955 serial volumes. The collection is particularly strong in the subject areas of education, psychology, American history, sociology, religion, and science and technology.[23,24]

California Digital Library

The California Digital Library, established in 1997, supports the assembly and creative use of the world's digital scholarship and knowledge. In addition, they work to improve the development and management of digital collections, innovation in scholarly publishing, and the long-term preservation of digital information. They work to improve Web capture technology; provide access to primary sources through the Calisphere project, the Mark Twain project, and the online archive of California; and to insure preservation to digital content.[25]

Duke University

The Digital Collections Program at Duke focuses on digitizing and making available the manuscripts, rare books, documentary photographs, historic advertisements, popular music, and other materials found within the Duke Library collections. Collections include historic sheet music from the late nineteenth to the early twentieth century, historical medical images, extensive photograph collections, and material on the history of Duke University and the town of Durham, North Carolina.[26]

Massachusetts Institute of Technology and DSpace

The archives at the Massachusetts Institute of Technology (MIT) houses the documents that tell the history of the institution, the papers of noted professors and students, books written by MIT staff and students, and oral histories of members of the MIT community. They also manage the institutions records management activities.

MIT is also the home of DSpace. DSpace was created in collaboration with Hewlett Packard so that MIT could save, share, and search its digital research materials. Released in 2002, DSpace was created as Open Source Software. It stores data in a nonproprietary format, which allows for access by users even if the original software used for the creation of the document disappears. This allows users to customize DSpace to meet their institution needs. DSpace can capture, store, index, preserve, and redistribute the material created by scholars in digital format. It allows access to scholarly documents that have been created only in digital form and creates a searchable digital archive with documents using a variety of formats including text, images, audio and video items, and databases. It also allows for flexibility in the use of metadata, allowing users to customize DSpace to work with the policies and procedures already in place at their institutions.

The DSpace Foundation was created with other repositories around the world to study how DSpace is being used and to provide support to smaller repositories using DSpace. It also provides leadership for the DSpace community and also works to encourage wider use of the DSpace software.[27,28]

Stanford University

Stanford University's digital collections include material drawn from throughout its collections. Included are covers from dime novel and penny dreadfuls, maps, material from the Stanford Geological Survey, correspondence from Athanasius Kircher, and the records of the General Agreement on Tariffs and Trade. Stanford has also been at the forefront of the digital library movement helping to develop standards and supporting documentation to help in the creation and support of digital collections. One of the major initiatives is the LOCKSS (Lots of Copies Keep Stuff Safe), which provides open source software to help repositories keep their digital collections safe.[29,30]

University of Chicago

The manuscript holdings of the Special Collections Research Center of the University of Chicago Library measure 6055 linear feet and span the period from the second century A.D. to the present. Collections held by the University include the Berlin Collection acquired by William Rainey Harper in 1891; the manuscript collection of the John Crerar Library, which focuses on science and medicine; late medieval and Renaissance secular and religious texts; and commonplace books, musical scores, sermons, papal dispatches, poetry, and letters. Among the more important of the modern manuscript collections are the editorial files of *Poetry* Magazine, which contain letters and manuscripts of many leading American and English poets of the first half of the twentieth century, including T. S. Eliot, Robert Frost, Amy Lowell, Marianne Moore, Ezra Pound, Wallace Stevens, Sara Teasdale, William Carlos Williams, and William Butler Yeats; the personal papers of Poetry's editor, Harriet Monroe; and the papers of Morton D. Zabel and others associated with the publication of modern poetry, especially in Chicago.

The collections also include the papers of Stephen A. Douglass, Saul Bellow, Ida B. Wells, Julius Rosenwald, the Chicago Jazz Archive, the Illinois chapter of the American Civil Liberties Union collections, the American Association for Public Opinion Research, and the Adlai Stevenson Institute of International Affairs.[31]

The University of North Carolina at Chapel Hill

The University of North Carolina at Chapel Hill has been at the forefront of digitizing collections focusing on North Carolina and the American South. One of their major projects has been the Documenting the American South collection. This collection provides Internet access to texts, images, and audio files related to southern history, literature, and culture. Currently, Documenting the American South includes 12 thematic collections of books, diaries, posters, artifacts, letters, oral history interviews, and songs.[32]

Yale University

The resources held by Manuscripts and Archives include over 1700 collections of personal and family papers and organizational records that document a variety of areas, and the Yale University Archives. Originally established in 1938, the Historical Manuscripts Room served as a place to hold historical collections that did not have a home of their own.

The Yale Archives began 1906 when the staff of the Yale Memorabilia Room began to collect publications, records, and objects, particularly those related to Yale College classes. A curator for this collection was appointed in 1918, and the first university archivist was appointed in 1958. In 1961, the library established the combined position of university archivist and curator of historical manuscripts that, along with the building of the Beinecke Rare Book and Manuscript Library, led to eventual consolidation of the Memorabilia collection, the Yale Archives, historical manuscripts, and the House collections. Collection strengths include public policy and administration; diplomacy and international affairs; political and social thought and commentary; science, medicine, and the environment; legal and judicial history; the visual and performing arts; urban planning and architecture; environmental policy and affairs; psychology and psychiatry; and lesbian, gay, bisexual, and transgender history and culture. In addition, the department has extensive holdings on New Haven, Connecticut, and New England history. A recent acquisition is the Fortunoff Video Archive for Holocaust Testimonies, which holds more than 4300 testimonies providing firsthand experience of the holocaust.[33]

Manuscript Repositories and Historical Societies

A manuscript repository is an institution that collects historical materials from people or organizations other than itself. A historical society is a manuscript repository that focuses its collecting on a specific topic, such as a geographical area or a particular event.

The entry on Historical Societies elsewhere in this volume provides more detail on those institutions, particularly State Historical Societies. The profiles below detail examples of other types of historical societies and manuscript repositories.

Library of Congress

The Manuscript Division was one of several "departments" established in 1897 when the Library of Congress moved from the United States Capitol to a separate building nearby. In 1903, by an act of Congress and an executive order, the State Department began transferring historical papers, including several presidential collections, which had been acquired by the federal government, to the Manuscript Division.

The Manuscript Division broadly collects materials relating to political history, cultural history, and the history of science, and materials from nongovernmental organizations. At present the Division holds nearly 60 million items contained in 11,000 separate collections (Fig. 5).

The Library holds papers from 23 presidents starting with George Washington and ending with Calvin Coolidge. Some presidential papers such as the John and John Quincy Adams papers are held in repositories near their homes. Later presidential papers are held in presidential libraries overseen by the National Archives and Records Administration. The Library also holds papers of other notable governmental officials and leaders such as John Paul Jones, George S. Patton, Alexander Haig, Daniel Patrick Moynihan, and Thurgood Marshall.

The Manuscript Division serves as the archival repository for a number of nongovernmental organizations, which have significantly affected American life, including the National Association for the Advancement of Colored People, National Urban League, National American Woman Suffrage Association, National Woman's Party, and Brotherhood of Sleeping Car Porters. Other large organizational collections include the records of the League of Women Voters and the American Colonization Society.

Additional notable collections include the papers of Susan B. Anthony, Frederick Douglass, Margaret Sanger, Luther Burbank, J. Robert Oppenheimer, Groucho Marx, Lillian Gish, Jessica Tandy, Hume Cronyn, Frederick Law Olmsted, and Ludwig Mies van der Rohe.

Though the Manuscript Division has the largest number of manuscript collections, the Performing Arts Reading Room and the American Folklife Center also hold manuscript collections.

Begun as a pilot project in 1990 to digitize materials and make them available on CD-ROM, in 1994, the Library of Congress launched the American Memory

Fig. 5 The current Manuscript Division Reading Room, Madison Building.
Source: Photograph courtesy of the Manuscript Division, Library of Congress.

historical collections as the flagship of the National Digital Library Program—a pioneering systematic effort to digitize some of the foremost historical treasures in the Library and other major research archives and make them readily available on the Web to Congress, scholars, educators, students, the general public, and the global Internet community.[34,35]

American Philosophical Society

The American Philosophical Society was created by Benjamin Franklin in 1769 to help "improve the common stock of knowledge." Early members included doctors, lawyers, clergymen, and merchants interested in science, and also many learned artisans and tradesmen like Franklin. The Society served as the prototype for a number of other learned societies and also provided space for the University of Pennsylvania. It has provided grant funds to encourage scientific research, given awards to honor outstanding work in the sciences, and developed publications to encourage researchers to share their knowledge.

The Society houses over 7 million manuscripts within hundreds of collections of personal papers and archival materials. Collections include the papers of Benjamin Franklin, Charles Darwin, Charles Willson Peale, and Franz Boas. The collections range from the mid-eighteenth century to the present, with an emphasis on documenting anthropology and its subfields (ethnology, biological anthropology, linguistics, and archaeology), the mathematical and physical sciences, the earth sciences, and the life sciences (evolutionary theory, genetics, eugenics, biochemistry, molecular biology, and paleontology). The repository also houses over 200,000 volumes and bound periodicals and thousands of maps and prints. Many of its long series of American and foreign scientific publications are not easily available elsewhere. Rare books include first editions of Newton's *Principia*,

Franklin's *Experiments and Observations*, and Darwin's *Origin of Species*.[36]

Chicago History Museum

The Chicago History Museum is a privately endowed, independent institution devoted to collecting, interpreting, and presenting the rich multicultural history of Chicago and Illinois, as well as other aspects of American history. The Museum has over 22 million artifacts and documents. The Archives and Manuscript Division holds collections that document life in the region from 1683 to the present day, focusing on topics such the Chicago area's early history, social conditions and problems, twentieth-century neighborhood life, community organizations, African American history, ethnic history, women's history, civil liberties and civil rights, politics, religious-centered social action, labor unions, environmental concerns, teachers, and school reformers. Also of interest to users will be the Studs Terkel/WFMT Oral history archives, which include audio recordings of interviews, readings, and musical programs aired during Studs Terkel's tenure at WFMT Radio from the early 1950s through 1999. People heard on the recordings include Mahalia Jackson, Louis Armstrong, Carl Sandburg, Ralph Ellison, Dorothy Parker, and Mike Royko.[37]

Urban Archives at Temple University

The Urban Archives was established in 1967 to document the social, economic, and physical development of the Philadelphia area from the mid-nineteenth century to the present. The Archives functions as a repository for organizational records and related materials, and as a research facility for those interested in urban studies. The Archives collections are particularly strong in areas involving social service organizations, unions, housing development, community organizations, and contain many records from organizations involved with African Americans, education, and crime.[38]

Military Archives

Military archives are historical societies that focus on the history of military service.

Air Force Historical Research Center

The Air Force Historical Research Agency is the repository for Air Force historical documents. It consists today of over 70,000,000 pages devoted to the history of the service, and represents the world's largest and most valuable organized collection of documents on U.S. military aviation. Included within the collection are unit histories, the papers of retired general officers and other Air Force personnel, documents from various military actions, and oral histories.[39]

Center for Military History

The Center of Military History is responsible for the appropriate use of history throughout the U.S. Army. The Center records the history of the Army during peace and wartime. Officially this section dates back to the creation of the historical branch in 1943 and its work to preserve the history of World War II. Their work includes creating documents studying the activities of the Army, maintaining the organizational history of Army units, preserving the history of significant units during reorganizations, and providing an annual history of the Department of the Army.

The Center for Military History serves as a clearinghouse for oral history programs and also maintains its own oral history collections including end of tour interviews for staff. The Center also manages a system of 59 Army museums and 176 other holdings, encompassing some 500,000 artifacts and over 15,000 works of military art.[40]

Naval Historical Center

As the official history program of the United States Navy, the Naval Historical Center manages the Navy Department Library, 12 Navy museums, art collections, archives, and an underwater archaeology program. The Center prepares and publishes reference, documentary, analytical, and narrative works on the history of the U.S. Navy.[41]

Religious Archives

Religious archives are archival repositories that collect materials pertaining to religion and spirituality. These archives may be the institutional archives for a particular religious organization or group or a manuscript repository that collects material pertaining to the religious life.

American Jewish Historical Society

Founded in 1892, the American Jewish Historical Society's holdings include 20 million documents, 50,000 books, paintings, and other objects that document the contributions of the American Jewish community to life in the Americas from the sixteenth century to the present. Included within the collections are the first American book published in Hebrew and the handwritten original of Emma Lazarus' *The New Colossus*, which graces the Statue of Liberty.

The American Jewish Historical Society houses approximately 1000 archival collections, comprising 10,000 linear feet. Notable personal collections include the papers of Haym Salomon, Emma Lazarus, Henry Roth, and Stephen Wise. Organizational collections include the papers of the Council of Jewish Federations and Welfare Funds (now called United Jewish Communities); the American Jewish Congress; the National Jewish Welfare Board, the Jewish Reconstructionist Federation; Congregation Shearith Israel, New York; the Graduate School for Jewish Social Work, New York; the National Association of Hillel Directors; and the Grand Street Boy's Association.

The American Jewish Historical Society also holds photographic collections that depict the efforts of immigrant aid organizations and Jewish businesses throughout the United States. There are also images of Jewish chaplains and soldiers who served during World War I and World War II, Jewish community centers, orphanages, and synagogues.[42]

American Jewish Archives

The American Jewish Archives, which is housed at the Hebrew Union College in Cincinnati, Ohio, holds nearly 800 major manuscript collections and over 16,000 smaller collections. The repository holds over 13,000 images. Originally founded by Jacob Rader Marcus in 1947, its goal is to provide a documentary heritage of the religious, organizational, economic, cultural, personal, social, and family life of the American Jewish community. Included within the collection are the papers of several noted rabbis, information on women within the Jewish community, and material on noted Jewish organizations and on the Holocaust.[43]

Archdiocese of Chicago

The Archdiocese of Chicago's Joseph Cardinal Bernardin Archives & Records Center is the official repository for the records of the Roman Catholic Archdiocese of Chicago. This collection was started in 1966 by then Archbishop John Cody. The Archives has more than 8000 cubic feet of materials, making it one of the world's largest repositories of Archdiocesan Archives. Most of the material is from the twentieth century. Materials included within this collection include the papers and photographs of former ordinaries (Cardinals: Mundelein, Stritch, Meyer, Cody, and Bernardin), auxiliary bishops, chancellors, vicar general, and the administrative records of various Archdiocesan agencies and programs. Also included are organizational papers for the Chicago House of the Order of the Poor Clares, the St. Vincent de Paul Society, the Catholic Action Federation, and the Catholic Youth Organization. The Archives houses the oral history projects for Rev. Steven Avella and Michael Hartnett.

The Archives also maintains collections of sacramental registers (pre-1916 available on microfilm), student transcripts, yearbooks, class photographs, parish annual reports, liturgical and devotional materials, cemetery records, diocesan deceased priest files, *New World* obituaries, deed and construction files, orphanage records, and architectural drawings from Archdiocesan institutions. Commemorative books are available for parishes, religious orders, diocesan clergy, and institutions.[44]

Archives of the Episcopal Church U.S.A.

The Archives of the Episcopal Church U.S.A. is the official repository for the records of the Episcopal Church. The Archives also gathers the records of national Church bodies, the various offices of missionary program and administrative support of the Episcopal Church Center, affiliated Episcopal organizations, and the personal papers of prominent lay and ordained leaders. The Archives of the Episcopal Church is the official repository for records of the Church's General Convention, its committees, boards and agencies, and the corporate body of the national Church, the Domestic and Foreign Missionary Society of the Protestant Episcopal Church in the United States of America. Included in these umbrella bodies are the various program and administrative offices of the Episcopal Church Center in New York City. The official papers of the Primate and the Office of the Presiding Bishop are also located in the Archives. The Archives also holds the records for other churches that may no longer exist to ensure that these materials are available for future researchers.[45]

Billy Graham Center Archives at Wheaton College

The focus of the Billy Graham Center Archives is to gather, preserve, and make available materials on the history of North American nondenominational Protestant efforts to spread the Christian Gospel. These collections include private papers of individuals, records of organizations, and hundreds of oral history interviews. These collections include the papers of the Billy Graham and the Billy Graham Evangelistic Association (BGEA) and other groups working to spread the word of the gospel around the world.[46]

Family History Center of the Church of Jesus Christ of Latter-Day Saints

The Family History Library has the largest collection of genealogical materials in the world. Most of the records are on microfilm; other formats include microfiche, books, maps, charts, and CD-ROMs. Most of the records of the collection date from 1550 to 1920. The Family History Library had its beginnings in 1894, with the founding of the Genealogical Society of Utah. Leaders of The Church of Jesus Christ of Latter-Day Saints organized the society to assist Church members with their family history and genealogical research. Its extensive record collection is available to professional genealogists and amateur researchers alike.[47,48]

United Methodist Church

The Archives and History Center of the United Methodist Church was officially opened on October 2, 1982, and is housed on the campus of Drew University in Madison, New Jersey. It contains a museum, a large collection of books, documents, records, photographs, and artifacts relating to United Methodist History. The purpose of the Center is "to gather, preserve, hold title to, and disseminate materials on the history of The United Methodist Church and its antecedents." The collections include the papers of some of the notable leaders of the Methodist Church and of some of churches within the denomination. Also included are recording from radio programs documenting items of interest to the community.[49]

Business Archives

Business archives house the corporate records of the parent organization or, in some cases, are historical societies that focus on the acquisition of corporate records. The entry on Business Archives in North America elsewhere in this volume provides more detail on the history of those programs. Also included in this category are organizations that are in the business of managing archives for institutions that do not have an archival staff in-house to work with collections.

Coca-Cola

The collections of the Coca-Cola Company run from 1880 to the present day and measure approximately 2000 linear feet. At present, nearly 1200 items from the archives are on display in the World of Coca-Cola exhibit which is seen by nearly a million visitors a year. In addition to the memorabilia that is on display, the Coca-Cola Archives has administrative, financial, legal, and marketing materials.[50]

Ford Motor Company

The Ford Motor Company Archives, which was established in 1951, is one of the oldest and most comprehensive corporate archives in the United States. The company archives contains more than 13,000 boxes of company records. The archives was started as part of the Ford Motor Company's 50th anniversary celebration. Dr. Robert Bahmer, then Assistant Archivist of the United States, developed the proposal for the archives indicating the benefits of maintaining archives to the Ford Motor Company leadership. After a very active start after the celebration of the anniversary, the Archives faced major budget cuts and was deemed not to be important. It was also suggested that material be destroyed or sent to other repositories. Though the archives did continue with limited support until the mid-1990s, it took another anniversary celebration to again focus interest on the archival collections. At that point, a professional archivist was brought on-board and work was done to help show the importance of the archives to the organization. Thanks to the work of the archivist, the Ford Motor Company began again to recognize how the archives could assist not only with anniversary celebrations but also with issues relating to many aspects of the organization including design, marketing, and legal support.[51,52]

Levi Strauss

The Levi Strauss historical collections of documents, clothing, photographs, films, posters, advertising materials, and artifacts dates back to the mid-1800s and includes items such as the 1974 Levi's® edition of the Gremlin automobile. There are 400 linear feet of documents, including letters from Cary Grant, Henry Kissinger, Lady Bird Johnson, and Clint Eastwood; 4500 photographs; 5000 garments including the oldest pair of 501 jeans from 1879; and marketing materials including posters and different artifacts.[53]

History Associates

History Associates Incorporated was started in 1981 when two of the founders were commissioned to write a book about the U.S. Department of Energy's response to the Three Mile Island disaster. They along with two other colleagues realized that they could help business and government leaders realize the importance of the historical materials they held. The company provides historical research and writing of company histories and other documents, managing historical records and providing records management support, and a place to store important historical records off-site.[54]

History Factory

The History Factory started in 1979 as Informative Design Group, Inc. Originally the company planned to merge historical research with graphic design to inform and educate members of the company and the general public. This mix of archives and marketing was appealing to clients and helped them to realize the importance of their historical collections. They asked the company for assistance in preserving their historical materials.

In 1989, the company changed its name to the History Factory and in addition to the marketing work it had done in the past they began to offer archives management support and support for oral history programs. They continue to work to supply support for corporate anniversary programming, corporate history books, and heritage-based marketing and communications initiatives as well as supplying archival support and storage for their clients.[55]

Data and Electronic Records Archives

Data archives are repositories that preserve databases and other records in electronic form that were created in a format that only a computer can process. Traditionally they have been focused on collecting data files in the social sciences and providing services that promote the secondary use of the data. More recently, electronic records archives have expanded to collect other digital formats, such as text documents and Web pages.

Inter-university Consortium for Political and Social Research (ICPSR)

Established in 1962, Inter-University Consortium for Political and Social Research (ICPSR) at the University of Michigan is the world's largest archive of digital social science data. ICPSR provides leadership and training in data access, curation, and methods of analysis for a diverse and expanding social science research community. One of ICPSR's primary activities is to provide raw data for analysis. They collect data from a variety of resources and make it available for users.

In addition to their work to provide access to data, they are also at the forefront of activities to ensure long-term access to digital data. They host the Digital Preservation Management tutorial, which helps users learn about issues involved in digital preservation and ways to deal with some of these issues, as well as hosting workshops on digital preservation.

ICPSR is also one of the leaders of the Data Preservation Alliance for the Social Sciences (Data-PASS). Data-PASS is a broad-based partnership devoted to identifying, acquiring, and preserving data at-risk of being lost to the social science research community. Examples of at-risk data include opinion polls, voting records, large-scale surveys on family growth and income, and many other social science studies. The other leaders in the partnership are the Roper Center for Public Opinion Research at the University of Connecticut, the Howard W. Odum Institute at the University of North Carolina-Chapel Hill, the Henry A. Murray Research Archive (a member of the Institute for Quantitative Social Science at Harvard University), the National Archives and Records Administration, and the Harvard-MIT Data Center (also a member of the Institute for Quantitative Social Science at Harvard University). The project is supported by an award from the Library of Congress through its National Digital Information Infrastructure and Preservation Program (NDIIPP).[56]

Electronic and Special Media Records Services Division, NARA

The Electronic and Special Media Records Services Division—The National Archives and Records Administration (NARA) custodial program for electronic records—began as the Data Archives Staff in 1968. The Division accessions, preserves, and provides access to electronic records of continuing value created by the U.S. Congress, the courts, the Executive Office of the President, numerous Presidential Commissions, and nearly 100 bureaus, departments, and other components of executive branch agencies and their contractors. Through these activities, NARA enables researchers to gain access to federal records designed for computer processing that federal agencies have transferred to archival custody. The holdings are as diverse as the activities and interests of the federal government and consist of more than 3 million unique files. The records may be from any type of computer applications, such as database management systems, word processing, computer modeling, or geographic information systems. The records may concern virtually any area or subject in which the Federal Government is involved, including: agricultural; attitudinal; demographic; economic and financial statistics; education; environmental; health and social services; international; military; and scientific data.[57]

Electronic Records Archives, NARA

In the late 1990s, the National Archives and Records Administration (NARA) began work to deal with the changing nature of electronic records that were arriving from federal government agencies. NARA needed to figure out how to best manage born digital records that were not databases, including determining how best to acquire, appraise, preserve, and provide access to these materials and help government agencies learn how to deal with the lifecycle of electronic records.

In 1998, NARA began working on the Electronic Records Archives (ERA) project, with the goal of being able to authentically preserve and provide access to electronic records created anywhere in the federal government, free from dependence on any specific hardware or software, and enabling NARA to carry out its mission into the future. After several years of conducting research in collaboration with other state and federal government agencies, computer scientists, and others to determine the problems involved with handling electronic records and to consider solutions, NARA launched the first phase of the ERA information technology system in 2008.[58]

Minerva/Library of Congress Web Archives

The Library of Congress Web Archives (LCWA) is composed of collections of archived Web sites selected by subject specialists to represent Web-based information on a designated topic. It is part of a continuing effort by the Library to evaluate, select, collect, catalog, provide access to, and preserve digital materials for future generations of researchers. This project, originally called MINERVA, started in 2000 by collecting Web sites relating to the 2000 elections. Staff members reviewed ways to select, collect, and provide access to these Web sites. Later staff worked to capture Web sites that documented the 2002, 2004, 2006, and 2008 elections; the Iraq war; the events of September 11, 2001; the reaction to Hurricane Katrina; and the Papal transition.[59]

Museum Archives

Archives within museums "...document the history and development of the museum, its collections, exhibitions, and programs as well as the contributions of individuals and groups associated with the museum."[60]

Smithsonian Institution

The Smithsonian Institution Archives started in 1891. It collects the papers of the Smithsonian and of people associated with the Smithsonian. The most recent guide to the collections notes that there over 1100 record units comprising more than 15,500 cubic feet of archival material. In addition to the institutional archives of the Smithsonian, several of the museums have their own archives.[61]

The Air and Space Museum archival collection contains approximately 10,000 cubic feet of material including an estimated 1.7 million photographs, 700,000 feet of motion picture film, and 2 million technical drawings which span the history of flight from ancient times to the present day.[62]

The National Anthropological Archives and Human Studies Film Archives collect and preserve historical and contemporary anthropological materials that document the world's cultures and the history of anthropology. The collections include the Smithsonian's earliest attempts to document North American Indian culture, the diaries of

John Wesley Powell, and the ethnographic and linguistic research of Franz Boas, Frances Densmore, Alice Cunningham Fletcher, Albert S. Gatschet, John Peabody Harrington, and J. N. B. Hewitt. They also include early 635,000 ethnological and archaeological photographs (including some of the earliest images of indigenous people worldwide); 20,000 works of native art (mainly North American, Asian, and Oceanic); 11,400 sound recordings; and more than 8 million ft of original film and video materials.[63]

The Archives Center of the National Museum of American History holds more than 1000 collections. They include material on advertising, music, and technology. These include original television scripts, sheet music, advertising campaign literature, and personal paper collections including Henry Tupper, the creator of Tupperware.[64]

The Archives of American Art, open since 1954, has collected roughly 16 million letters, photographs, diaries, oral history interviews, sketches, scrapbooks, business records, and other documents that support the study of the history of the visual arts in America.[65]

Getty Museum

The Getty Research Institute is dedicated to furthering knowledge and advancing understanding of the visual arts. The library holds over 190 collections of letters and other materials from artists and scholars such as Man Ray, Beaumont and Nancy Newhall, Paul Outerbridge, and E. Maurice Bloch.[66]

United States Holocaust Museum

The United States Holocaust Museum, which opened in 1993, has one of the largest and most comprehensive collections of Holocaust-related materials in the world. The collections include material on Jewish life in Europe before the Holocaust; the rise of the Nazi movement; their persecution of various groups including homosexuals, Roma and Sinti (Gypsies), Jehovah's Witnesses and political dissidents; information on ghettos, concentration camps and killing centers; the liberation of Europe and the war crimes trials; and the various Holocaust memorials and commemorations around the world.

The Archives branch consists of nearly 42 million pages of records including personal papers, memoirs and testimonies of Holocaust survivors and victims, oral histories, photographs, and microfilm copies of material from countries around the world on the Holocaust. In addition, there is over 1000 hr of historical films and film clips documenting the Holocaust and World War II.[67]

Warhol Museum

The Warhol Museum and Archives documents the work of noted artist Andy Warhol. The collection currently consists of over 8000 cubic feet of material. This collection includes scrapbooks of press clippings related to Warhol's work and his private and public life; art supplies and materials used by Warhol; posters publicizing his exhibitions and films; over 4000 audio tapes featuring interviews and conversations between Warhol and his friends and associates; thousands of documentary photographs; an entire run of *Interview* magazine, which Warhol founded in 1969; his extensive library of books and periodicals; hundreds of decorative art objects; many personal items such as clothing; and over 30 of the silver-white wigs that became one of Warhol's defining features.[68]

Audiovisual Archives

Audiovisual archives are collections that contain photographs, art, maps, technical drawings, sound recordings, sheet music, film, and other types of records that are primarily not textual. Detailed articles on Sound and Audio Archives and Film and Broadcast Archives may be found elsewhere in this encyclopedia.

Museum archives frequently have extensive visual materials, such as with the Smithsonian's various archives. The National Archives' Special Media Archives Division holds an estimated 8 million photographs and graphic images; over 15 million maps, charts, aerial photographs, architectural drawings, patents, and ships plans; nearly 300,000 reels of motion picture film; and more than 200,000 sound and video recordings. The Library of Congress Prints and Photographs Division has more than 13 million images, including photographs, fine and popular prints and drawings, posters, and architectural and engineering drawings.[69]

Performing Arts Archives

A special type of audiovisual archives is the performing arts archives, which documents theatre, dance, music, and other types of performances.

Center for Black Music Research

The Center for Black Music Research at Columbia College Chicago was founded in 1983 and is the only organization of its kind. The Library and Archives of the center includes the personal papers and music manuscripts of many composers and musicians including William Grant Still, Robert Leigh Morris, and Guido Sinclair. It also includes scores donated by musicians, and the papers of the National Association of Negro Musicians and the Society of Black Composers. The collection also includes recordings covering the 1900s to the present with a focus on vernacular and popular music focus on the United States, Caribbean, South Africa, Central Africa, and Central America.[70]

Folger Shakespeare Library

The Folger Shakespeare Library has the world's largest collection of Shakespeare materials and major collections of other rare Renaissance books, manuscripts, and works of art. The Folger opened in 1932 as a gift to the American nation from Henry Clay Folger and his wife Emily Jordan Folger. The library houses more than 256,000 books; 60,000 manuscripts; 250,000 playbills; 200 oil paintings; some 50,000 drawings, watercolors, prints, and photographs; and a variety of other materials, including musical instruments, costumes, and films.

The Folger's collection of 60,000 manuscripts range in date from the late thirteenth century to the present day, and offer a wealth of unique material relating to Shakespeare, the theater, or the early modern period. Included in the collection are letters written by the poet John Donne, prompt books for Shakespearian productions, papers of noted actor and theater owner David Garrick, and papers that document the lives of those living in the sixteenth and seventeenth centuries.[71]

New York Public Library for the Performing Arts

The New York Public Library for the Performing Arts houses one of the world's most extensive collection of circulating, reference, and rare archival collections in its field. The music and dance collections were merged together in 1965 at the Lincoln Center. Included within the collections are historic recordings, videotapes, manuscripts, sheet music, set, light and costume designs, posters, programs, and photographs. The Dance Collection has over 1 million manuscript items documenting all forms of dance and includes the personal papers of Merce Cunningham, Vaslav Nijinsky, Rudolf Nureyev, Agnes de Mille, and Jerome Robbins. The Music Collections includes original manuscripts by Bach, Mozart, Beethoven, and Wagner as well as material from contemporary composers such as Charles Tomlinson Griffes, Louis Moreau Gottschalk, Leo Smit, Ray Green, and Andre Singer.

In addition to these collections, the repository also holds the Rodgers and Hammerstein Archives of Recorded Sound. This collection holds a variety of sound recordings from symphonic work to presidential speeches and works to ensure the preservation of recorded sound.

The Billy Rose Theatre Collection of The New York Public Library is one of the largest and most comprehensive archives devoted to the theatrical arts. Within the collections, users can find a 1767 program for a performance of Romeo and Juliet in Philadelphia, read a letter from Edwin Booth to his daughter, review the working script for Orson Welles African-American Macbeth, study costume designs from the film Anna and the King of Siam, analyze a videotape of A Chorus Line, or read scripts from current television hits. In recent years, the Theatre

Collection acquired the archives of famed theatrical producer Joseph Papp and theatre and screen star Lillian Gish. Also included within this collection is the Theatre on Film and Tape Archive, which is authorized by all of America's theatrical guilds and unions to videotape live theatre performances from across the United States. More than 4500 tapes include Broadway, Off-Broadway, and regional theatre productions; theatre-related television programs, films, and documentaries; and interviews with distinguished theatre professionals.[72]

Popular Culture Archives

Popular culture archives document a wide range of hobbies, entertainment, and special interests in the United States.

Baseball Hall of Fame

The A. Bartlett Giamatti Research Center holds a large collection of baseball books, magazines, newspaper clippings, and archival material on baseball and related topics. The collections include historic newspapers, baseball guides, clipping files, publications created by baseball teams, contract cards for the players and archival collections including the Doubleday papers, the Mills Commission papers, the Roger Angell collection, the Garry Herrmann papers, and the Landis papers. The collections also include over 500,000 images of players, teams, stadiums, events and miscellaneous subjects and over 12,000 hours of moving image and sound recordings. The collection includes interviews, game highlights, television and radio broadcasts, animation, and music.[73]

Brown Popular Culture Library at Bowling Green University

The Brown Popular Culture Library was founded in 1969 and is dedicated to the acquisition and preservation of research materials on American popular culture created after 1876. It is the most comprehensive repository of its kind in the United States. The manuscript collections support and complement existing print collections in the areas of popular fiction, popular entertainment, and the graphic arts. Many of the manuscripts also document the history of popular culture and pioneers in the field. These manuscript collections include literary manuscripts; movie and television scripts; dime novels; storypapers and nickel weeklies; pulp magazines; fanzines and other amateur publications; comic books and graphic novels; and posters, postcards, greeting cards, and mail-order catalogs.[74]

Cultural Heritage Archives

The collections in cultural heritage archives illustrate the diversity of personal experiences in the United States. They document the history of ethnic and racial communities.

American Folklife Center

Originally created as the Archive of Folk Song in 1928, the American Folklife Center is one of the largest repositories of traditional life in the world. It includes over 3 million photographs, manuscripts, audio recordings, and moving images that document traditional culture from all around the world. Started by Robert Gordon, it was eventually taken over by John Lomax who traveled throughout the United States eventually with his son Alan to collect folk music. Eventually the focus of the Center expanded to include the collection of folk stories, verbal arts, and oral history. The 1976 legislation that established the American Folklife Center directs it to "preserve and present American folklife" through programs of research, scholarship, training, live performances, exhibits, publications, and preservation. The Center is involved in the Save Our Sounds project to preserve historic sound recordings and the Veterans History Project, which works to obtain firsthand account of war time experiences of veterans and those actively supporting war efforts from World War I to the present Afghanistan and Iraq conflicts. They also sponsor regular performances from groups providing traditional music and dance performances and lectures from those working to learn more about and preserve traditional folkways.

Also of note, the American Folklife Center is the custodian for the September 11 Digital Archive. This collection uses electronic media to collect, preserve, and present the history of September 11, 2001, and its aftermath. The Archive contains more than 150,000 digital items, a tally that includes more than 40,000 e-mails and other electronic communications, more than 40,000 firsthand stories, and more than 15,000 digital images. In September 2003, the Library of Congress accepted the Archive into its collections, an event that both ensured the Archive's long-term preservation and marked the library's first major digital acquisition.[75]

American Heritage Center

The mission of the American Heritage Center is to preserve a clearly defined set of primary sources and rare books—reflecting the written, image, and audio history of Wyoming, the Rocky Mountain Region, and select aspects of the American past—and to make those sources accessible to all. The major collecting areas include Wyoming and the American West, the mining and petroleum industries, U.S. politics and world affairs, environment and natural resources, journalism, transportation, the history of books, and twentieth century entertainment such as popular music, radio, television, and film.

The American Heritage Center was officially established in 1945. The manuscript collections have nearly 90,000 cubic feet of historically important documents and artifacts.[76]

Amistad Center

As the nation's largest independent archives specializing in the history of African Americans and other ethnic groups, the Amistad Research Center is dedicated to preserving America's ethnic heritage. The collection contains approximately 250,000 photographs dating from 1859. Literary manuscript holdings contain letters and original manuscripts from prominent Harlem Renaissance writers and poets. The manuscript collections contain over 15 million documents that record the efforts of those who have charted African American history and race relations. While about 90% of the holdings document African American history, 10% document other ethnic groups such as Appalachian whites, Asian Americans, and Native Americans.[77]

Balch Institute, Historical Society of Pennsylvania

The Balch Institute was incorporated on April 12, 1971. The Institute collections included material documenting the immigration of southern and eastern Europeans; the records of the Atlantis, the first successful Greek newspaper in the United States; materials documenting Puerto Rican immigration to Harlem; the American Friends Service Committee; and the Anthracite Region Ethnic Archives Project, which started by documenting the miners especially those immigrants from the eastern and southern parts of Europe living in the Anthracite region and later expanded to include the various organizations supporting ethnic groups within the community.

As of January 2002, the Balch Institute merged with the Historical Society of Pennsylvania, and the mission and collections of the Balch have been fully integrated into the Society.[78]

Centro de Estudios Puertorriqueños, Hunter College, City University of New York

The Centro Library and Archives is devoted to collecting, preserving, and providing access to resources documenting the history and culture of Puerto Ricans. Established in 1973 as a component of the Center for Puerto Rican Studies, the Centro Library and Archives was dedicated to activist and educator, Evelina López Antonetty in 1986. The Centro Archives, known as the Archives of the Puerto Rican Diaspora, were formally established in 1989. The collections include books, newspapers, periodicals, audio, films and videos, manuscripts, photographs, prints, and recorded music. The holdings include personal papers, records of organizations and institutions, photographic collections, broadsides, programs, and ephemera.[79]

Clark Atlanta University

The Robert W. Woodruff Library of the Atlanta University Center, Inc., is an independent entity organized and operating to provide an academic library for the exclusive benefit of its member institutions—Clark Atlanta University, the Interdenominational Theological Center, Morehouse College, and Spelman College. The Archives and Special Collections department houses over 7000 linear feet of manuscript collections and organizational records, and over 35,000 books, pamphlets, and other printed materials. The core of the manuscript holdings is built upon the Atlanta University Trevor Arnett Library's Negro Collection. The collections document civil rights, race relations, education, literature, visual and performing arts, religion, politics, and social work. They include the Countee Cullen/Harold Jackman Memorial Collection, and papers of Hoyt Fuller and Wayman Carver that focus on black contributions to literature, music, performing and visual arts; personal papers of scholars C. Eric Lincoln and Walter Rodney, and religious leaders Harry V. Richardson and Edler G. Hawkins; records of civil rights organizations such as the Commission on Interracial Cooperation, Southern Regional Council, and Southern Conference for Human Welfare; files documenting African American education such as the Freedmen's Aid Society, Southern Education Foundation, and United Negro College Fund.

The Atlanta University Center entered the forefront of the African-American archives with the 2006 acquisition of a historic collection of writings, sermons, and other items representing the life and work of Dr. Martin Luther King Jr. by King's alma mater, Morehouse College. The Robert W. Woodruff Library of the Atlanta University Center was designated as "custodian" of the Morehouse College Martin Luther King Jr. Collection, and charged with housing and overseeing the security and preservation of the collection. The approximately 10,000 items within this collection cover much of King's life and work between the years 1944 and 1968.[80,81]

Heard Museum Archives

The Archives of the Heard Museum includes a wide range of materials that document Native American history, culture, and art. The materials cover all indigenous peoples of the Americas. The majority of the holdings date from the mid-nineteenth century to present. The collections emphasize Native American artists and provide context for the understanding of the museum's ethnographic and fine art collections.

The Archival materials reflect a broad spectrum of relationships and activities with Native Americans, including more than 300,000 historic and contemporary photographs. Major collections include the Fred Harvey Company photographs and papers, the R. Brownell McGrew photographs and papers, the Barry Goldwater color photography collection, American Indian Boarding School Collection, and the collections of Native American artists Pop Chalee and Joe Baker. The Archives hold approximately 300 linear feet of manuscripts, personal collections, and other cultural

materials, including more than 150 linear feet of institutional records from the Heard.[82]

Japanese American History Archives

The Japanese American History Archives is an extensive collection of books, periodicals, documents, maps, photographs, art, and film relating to the Japanese experience in the United States from the mid-1800s to the present. Created in 1977, it provides a strong collection of material documenting the Japanese–American experience but also assists many other institutions by translating documents from Japanese to English and English to Japanese.[83]

Moorland-Spingarn Research Center at Howard

The Moorland-Spingarn Research Center at Howard University is recognized as one of the world's largest and most comprehensive repositories for the documentation of the history and culture of people of African descent in Africa, the Americas, and other parts of the world. Its collections include more than 175,000 bound volumes and tens of thousands of journals, periodicals, and newspapers; more than 17,000 feet of manuscript and archival collections; nearly 1000 audio tapes; hundreds of artifacts; 100,000 prints, photographs, maps, and other graphic items.

The foundation of this collection was a gift from the Reverend Jesse E. Moorland who donated over 3000 books, pamphlets, and other historical materials to the University in 1914. Another major landmark was the 1946 purchase of the private library of Arthur Barnette Spingarn, who chaired the NAACP's legal committee and also served as its president. The work of developing the research center continued under the watchful eye of Dorothy Porter Wesley, the first African American woman to get a masters degree in Library Science from Columbia University. She worked for the next 43 years on the research center and the annual lecture series given at the Center now bears her name.

By 1957, the collection had added a number of collections including the papers of Alain Locke, the Joel Spingarn Papers, photographs by Carl Van Vechten, and the Oswald Garrison Villard collection of Anti-Slavery papers. Starting in 1974 work again continued to develop archival collections and the papers of Paul Robeson, Vernon Jordan, Charles Diggs, Jr., Benjamin Mayes, Charles H. Houston, and Rayford Logan were added to a growing number of collections being donated to the Center. At present, there are over 190 manuscript collections available.[84]

Museum of Chinese in the Americas

Founded in 1980, the Museum of Chinese in America is dedicated to preserving and presenting the history, heritage, culture, and diverse experiences of people of Chinese descent in the United States. One of the Museum's major goals is to make Chinese American history accessible to the general public, ranging from scholars to young children, from community members to international tourists.

Some of the manuscript collections include paper sculptures created by passengers of the ship Golden Venture while they waited in detention to find out their immigration status, material from the Chinese Musical and Theatrical Association that document the activities of the Cantonese opera clubs that flourished in North American Chinatowns from the 1930s to the present, materials documenting the life of an immigrant family who eventually created a number of major business in New York's Chinatown, and the papers of Hazel Ying Lee, a noted Chinese American woman aviator during the 1930s and 1940s.[85]

Schomburg Center for Black Culture

The Schomburg Center for Research in Black Culture is one of the world's leading research facilities devoted to the preservation of materials on the global African and African diasporan experiences. Today, the Schomburg Center contains over 10,000,000 items and provides services and programs for constituents from the United States and abroad.

The Manuscripts, Archives, and Rare Books Division collection has grown through the years, beginning with the rare treasures from Arturo Alfonso Schomburg's personal holdings. Today, it contains more than 3900 rare books, 580 manuscript collections, and 15,000 pieces of sheet music and rare printed materials. These include the original manuscript of Richard Wright's *Native Son*; the papers of Dr. Robert Weaver, the first black U. S. cabinet officer; Gustavus Vassa's autobiography, which provides evidence for Granville Sharp's attack on slavery in the British colonies in 1796; and records of the Civil Rights Congress.

Also included within the Schomburg's collections are images from mid-eighteenth century graphics to contemporary documentary and art photographs. The more than 500,000 items include portraits of many prominent nineteenth- and twentieth-century black artists, political figures, actors, musicians, athletes, and social activists. The collection also documents black life throughout the world, including scenes from Africa and the slave era through the twentieth century Americas. Among the photographers represented are James VanDerZee, Gordon Parks, Edward Steichen, Coreen Simpson, Bert Andrews, and Chester Higgins.

The Schomburg also has a large collection of audiovisual documentation of black culture including music, oral history recordings, motion pictures, and videotapes. Included are early radio broadcasts and recordings of

statements by celebrated personalities such as Marcus Garvey, Booker T. Washington, and George Washington Carver. Musical documentation ranges from African chants to American jazz. Of special interest is the Oral History/Video Documentation Project, which videotapes interviews with historically or culturally significant figures. It offers over 5000 hours of oral history recordings and more than 5000 motion pictures and videotapes.[86]

Women's History Archives

Women's history archives collect materials that record the contributions women have made to society. Often begun because traditional repositories only inadequately captured the efforts of women, these archives continue to focus their efforts on documenting underrepresented populations.

Sophia Smith Collection

The Sophia Smith Collection at Smith College was founded in 1942. Named for the founder of Smith College, it collections includes 585 collections of manuscripts, archives, photographs, oral histories, and other primary sources documenting women's history from the colonial era to the present.

Subject strengths include birth control and reproductive rights, women's rights, suffrage, the contemporary women's movement, U.S. women working abroad, the arts (especially theatre), the professions (especially journalism and social work), and middle-class family life in nineteenth- and twentieth-century New England. Of special interest is the YWCA archives, which includes 800 boxes documenting the history of this important organization and its role in assisting racial and ethnic minorities, immigrants, and working class women.[87]

Schlesinger Library at Radcliffe College of Harvard University

The library's origins date back to the gift of Maud Wood Park, a leader in the suffrage movement, who in 1943 donated her collection of books, papers, and memorabilia on women reformers. To honor Harvard University historian Arthur M. Schlesinger and his wife Elizabeth Bancroft Schlesinger, who were strong supporters of the mission of the women's rights collection, the library was renamed in 1965.

The library's principal holdings date from the founding of the United States to the present and include materials on the women's rights movements, feminism, health, social reform, education, professional life, volunteer and civic efforts, family relationships, and travel. Collections include the archives of Radcliffe College, the papers of Charlotte Perkins Gilman, Dorothy West, June Jordan and Pauli Murray and the records of the National Organization for Women, 9 to 5: National Association of Working Women, the Boston's Women's Health Book Collective, and the National Association of Women Judges. The archival collections also include material focusing on the culinary arts, including the papers of Julia Child and M. F. K. Fisher.

The collections also include over 90,000 photographs, ranging from casual snapshots to the works of professional photographers as well as audiotapes, videotapes and oral history tapes, and transcripts.[88]

Sallie Bingham Center for Women's History and Culture

The Sallie Bingham Center for Women's History and Culture in Duke's Special Collection Library acquires preserves and makes available to a large population of researchers published and unpublished materials that reflect the public and private lives of women, past and present. Collecting areas of interest include the lives of southern women, girl culture, women's sexuality and gender expressions, lay and ordained church women, and the history of feminist theory and activitism.[89]

Iowa Women's Archives

The Iowa Women's Archives holds more than 1100 manuscript collections that chronicle the lives and work of Iowa women, their families, and their communities. These personal papers and organizational records date from the nineteenth century to the present. Together with oral histories, they document the activities of Iowa women throughout the state and beyond its borders. Subjects covered include suffrage, women and sports, and the lives of women in rural communities.

Of special interest is the Mujeres Latinas project that works to preserve the history of Latina women living in Iowa. This collection includes oral histories and manuscript collections documenting those women who came to Iowa to assist with the harvest and decided to stay in the community.[90]

Gender and Sexuality Archives

Gender and sexuality archives promote the study of human sexuality, gender identification, and reproduction.

Cornell Human Sexuality Project

In 1988, the Mariposa Education and Research Foundation donated its accumulated archive to Cornell, which formed the basis of the Human Sexuality Collection. The principal emphases of the collection are lesbian, bisexual, gay and transgendered lives, and the politics of sex.

The Human Sexuality Collection contains a wealth of information that documents women's lives, including the emergence of the American lesbian and gay rights movement and different perspectives on the pornography business. Notable collections include the National Gay and Lesbian Task Force papers; documentation of lesbian publishing including lesbian and feminist periodicals from the 1950s to the present from across the United States, lesbian pulp novels, and contemporary lesbian erotica; oral history projects; and photographs of leaders of the gay rights movement.[91]

GBLT Historical Society

The Gay, Lesbian, Bisexual Transgender (GLBT) Historical Society collects, preserves, and interprets the history of GLBT people and the communities that support them. The Archives and Manuscripts collection are focused on gay, lesbian, bisexual, transgender, and queer life in the wider San Francisco Bay area and Northern California. The organization works to document the tremendous diversity of GLBT life, its sexual, social, political, economic, cultural, religious, and spiritual dimensions focusing not only the lives of GLBT leaders, but also ordinary people, organizations, and informal groups.[92]

Kinsey Institute

The Kinsey Institute at Indiana University promotes interdisciplinary research and scholarship in the fields of human sexuality, gender, and reproduction. The Institute was founded in 1947, just before the publication of *Sexual Behavior in the Human Male* in 1948. The Kinsey Institute houses extensive archival collections, including the papers of Dr. Alfred Kinsey, the records of the Institute and materials of other research scholars such as Alex Comfort, Havelock Ellis, and Albert Ellis, and organizations such as Sexual Freedom League and Society for the Scientific Study of Sexuality.[93]

Lesbian Herstory Archives

The Lesbian Herstory Archives is home to the world's largest collection of materials by and about lesbians and their communities. Started in 1972 to ensure the preservation of lesbian culture the collection includes an extensive collection of books, newsletter and periodicals, photographs, films, diaries, posters, and oral histories. Archival collections of note include material from the Black Lesbian Study Group of New York, the Lesbian Resource Center of Seattle, and the Lesbian Avengers.[94]

National Gay and Lesbian Archives

The ONE National Gay & Lesbian Archives honors the past, celebrates the present, and enriches the future of all lesbian, gay, bisexual, and transgender people by supporting education and research. ONE is dedicated to collecting, preserving, documenting, studying, and communicating the history, challenges, and aspirations of gay, lesbian, bisexual, and transgender community. They collect manuscripts, photographs, memorabilia, graphics, ephemera, and other historically significant materials.[95]

Labor Archives

A late twentieth-century phenomenon, labor archives in the United States seek to document unions and the labor movement.

George Meany Memorial Archives

The American Federation of Labor-Congress of Industrial Organizations (AFL-CIO) established the George Meany Memorial Archives in 1980 to honor the memory of its first president, and to provide a program to preserve its historical records and make them available for research. The George Meany Memorial Archives holds the records of the AFL-CIO, including administrative and staff departments, constitutional trade departments, and some federation-sponsored programs. Dating from the earliest days of the American Federation of Labor (1881), but offering almost complete records from the founding of the AFL-CIO (1955), the collections provide rich resources for historians, political scientists, trade union activists, and undergraduate and graduate students who want to examine a wide range of twentieth-century American political and social issues.[96]

Kheel Center at Cornell University

The Kheel Center for Labor-Management Documentation & Archives was founded in 1949 as the Labor-Management Documentation Center. Its purpose is the preservation of original source materials relevant to the history of American labor unions, management theory as it applies to labor and industrial relations, and the history of employees at the workplace. The collections include 350,000 images documenting the labor movement in the twentieth century. It also includes over 19,000 linear feet of manuscript letters and documents. Included are the papers of the Amalgamated Clothing Workers of America, the International Ladies' Garment Workers' Union, the Brotherhood of Railroad Trainmen, and the National Consumers' League.[97]

Reuther Library, Wayne State University

The Walter P. Reuther Library of Labor and Urban Affairs is the largest labor archive in North America. Its mission is to collect, preserve, and provide access to the documentary and visual heritage of the American labor movement, related reform movements, and individual participants. The collection also includes records related to urban affairs, with emphasis on the history of metropolitan Detroit.

The Reuther holds more than 2000 collections related to such topics as union history and working class organizations, African Americans and women in the labor movement, as well as radical, social, and political reform movements. Collections also focus on the history of twentieth century Detroit, including such topics as social welfare, health care, politics, civil rights, women's rights, and metropolitan Detroit social communities. The Reuther also houses the archives of Wayne State University. The collection traces Wayne State's growth from the Detroit Medical College in 1868 to its emergence as a world-class research university.[98]

Tamiment Library and Wagner Archives, New York University

The Tamiment Library and Robert F. Wagner Labor Archives at New York University provide extensive research collections for scholarly research on Labor and the Left. The primary focus is the complex relationship between trade unionism and progressive politics and how this evolved over time. Archival, print, photograph, film, and oral history collections describe the history of the labor movement and how it related to the broader struggle for economic, social, and political change.

Tamiment/Wagner holds more than 400 manuscript collections, a total of more than 15,000 feet of original papers and records. Some of the collections include material from various locals of the Communications Workers of America, the papers of Eugene V. Debs, Elinor Ferry, Nelson Frank, and recordings of songs by Joe Glazer. It is also the repository for the Archives of Irish America, the Abraham Lincoln Brigade Archives, and a growing Asian American labor collection. The library also holds has more than 500,000 photographs documenting a wide range of subjects including: union organizing, the changing nature of work, strikes, rallies, demonstrations, progressive political campaigns, socialists, communists, anarchists, and members of other leftist organizations. They also depict working class resorts, summer camps, New York City street scenes, and architecture.[99]

Science, Technology, and Health Care Archives

Science, technology, and health care archives collect materials relating to the natural, physical, and social sciences; engineering; technology; medicine; and health care.

Alan Mason Chesney Archives, Johns Hopkins Medical School

The Alan Mason Chesney Medical Archives is the official archival repository of the Johns Hopkins Medical Institutions. Holdings include materials from the Johns Hopkins Hospital and from the health divisions of the Johns Hopkins University (Bloomberg School of Public Health,

School of Medicine, and School of Nursing). The collections include the records of the Johns Hopkins Medical Institutions and over 200 collections of personal papers covering the years of 1900 to the present. Some of the papers include laboratory notebooks, research data, and personal diaries. Notable collections include the papers of Alfred Blalock, who pioneered the "blue baby" operation; Alan Mason Chesney, who served as dean of the medical school; W. Horsley Gantt, who explored the relationship between physiological functions and behavior; and William Osler, who established the training program used by medical students in the United States.[100]

California Academy of Sciences

The California Academy of Science has over 400 archive and manuscript collections, and over 300,000 images. The archives includes material on the history of the Academy, research on the Galapagos Island, the Elkus Indians papers that documents Indian Affairs from 1922 to 1963, the paper of C. Templeton Crocker, Benjamin Draper, Frank Talbot, and John McCosker.[101]

California Institute of Technology

The Institute Archives preserves the papers, documents, artifacts, and pictorial materials that tell the school's history, from 1891 to the present. The Archives houses close to 200 manuscript collections, the majority of which are the papers of Caltech's faculty and administrative officers. These include the papers of Lee A. DuBridge, Richard Feynman, George Ellery Hale, Theodore von Kármán, and Robert A. Millikan. Since 1978 the Archives has conducted an oral history program centered on the Caltech community which includes more than 150 interviews.[102]

Charles Babbage Center

The Charles Babbage Institute is dedicated to preserving the history of information technology and promoting and conducting research in the field. The archives collects, preserves, and provides access archival collections and rare publications documenting the history of technology. Collections include the papers of the Association for Women in Computing, Edmund C. Berkeley, Martin A. Goetz, and Curt A. Monash. The Institute is also home to the historical archives of the Burroughs Corporation, once the nation's largest manufacturer of adding machines and, later, a major computer company. The collection includes over 100,000 photographs depicting the entire visual history of Burroughs from its origin as the American Arithmometer Corporation in 1886 to its merger with the Sperry Corporation to form the Unisys Corporation in 1986.[103]

Claude Moore Library at University of Virginia

The Historical Collections and Services division of the Claude Moore Library is dedicated to the preservation and presentation of the history of the health sciences at the University of Virginia and around the world. The collection includes a large number of rare books including a collection of books on optics gathered by Adolph Lomb of the Bausch and Lomb Optical Company. Archival collections include the Philip S. Hench Walter Reed Yellow Fever Collection, which documents the work of Reed's and others to stop the spread of Yellow Fever; the papers of Henry Rose Carter, who eventually became Assistant Surgeon General of the United States; the papers of Wade Hampton Frost, who studied water pollution and established epidemiology as a field of medical research; and documents from the Blue Ridge Sanatorium, which worked to prevent and eradicate tuberculosis.[104]

David Sarnoff Library

The David Sarnoff Library documents David Sarnoff's life; the history of radio, television, electronics, and communications; and the history of the Radio Corporation of America (RCA). Built in 1967 by RCA, the David Sarnoff Library contains a museum, the archives, and a library. Besides Mr. Sarnoff's papers and memorabilia, the Library's holdings include 25,000 photographs and thousands of notebooks, reports, publications, and artifacts related to the histories of RCA Laboratories and RCA.[105]

Linda Hall Library

The Linda Hall Library is the largest privately funded library of science, engineering, and technology in the world open to the public. The Library has acquired several strong collections over the years including the collection of the American Academy of Arts and Sciences, founded in 1780, portions of the Franklin Institute's library, the notebooks of A. B. Nichols, who worked as an engineer on the Panama Canal, and the collections of the Engineering Societies Library.[106]

National Agriculture Library

The National Agricultural Library Special Collection division houses rare books, manuscript collections, nursery and seed trade catalogs, photographs, and posters from the 1500s to the present. Materials cover a variety of agricultural subjects including horticulture, entomology, poultry sciences, natural history, and are not limited to domestic publications.

The Library's Special Collections houses over 300 manuscript and archival collections containing materials from the nineteenth through the twenty-first centuries.

Manuscript collections include papers of individuals who worked for or were associated with the U.S. Department of Agriculture or who were involved in agricultural activities. These collections include the papers of Charles Valentine Riley, John Wyss, and Layne R Beaty, and a small collection of Jefferson manuscripts focusing on his farming activities.[107]

National Library of Medicine

The National Library of Medicine houses a large collection of archives and manuscripts related the history of medicine. Most of the archival and manuscript material dates from the seventeenth century and includes approximately 10,000 linear feet of material. The Library also owns about 200 pre-1601 Western and Islamic manuscripts. Significant modern collections include the papers of U.S. Surgeons General, including C. Everett Koop, and the papers of Nobel Prize-winning scientists, particularly those connected with NIH.[108]

Niels Bohr Library and Archives and Center for History of Physics, American Institute of Physics

The Niels Bohr Library & Archives and the Center for History of Physics work to help preserve and make known the history of modern physics and allied sciences. They collect a wide variety of materials including photographs, oral histories, books, AIP, and Member Society archives. Photograph collections include portraits and snapshots primarily of modern American physicists, astronomers, and geophysicists but includes many other scientists, as well as photos and illustrations of laboratories, telescopes, accelerators and other instruments, objects, and places. There are over a thousand tape-recorded oral histories that provide information on the lives and work of noted scientists. Manuscript collections include the records of the American Institute of Physics as well as the personal papers of Samuel A. Goudsmit, Robert W. Wood, John Van Vleck, and Lew Kowarski.[109]

REFERENCES

1. The Declaration of Independence, paragraph 6.
2. The Constitution of the United States, Amendment IV.
3. McCoy, D.R. The struggle to establish a national archives in the United States. In *Guardian of Heritage: Essays on the History of the National Archives*; Walch, T., Ed.; National Archives and Records Administration: Washington, 1985; 1–15.
4. O'Toole, J.M.; Cox, R.J. *Understanding Archives & Manuscripts; Archival Fundamental Series II*; Society of American Archivists: Chicago, IL, 2006.
5. http://www.archives.gov/about/history/milestones.html.
6. Berner, R.C. *Archival Theory and Practice in the United States: A Historical Analysis*; University of Washington Press: Seattle, WA, 1983.
7. Gilliland-Swetland, L.J. The provenance of a profession: The permanence of the public archives and historical manuscript traditions in American Archival Theory. Am. Archivist **1991**, *54*, 160–173 Reprinted in *American Archival Studies: Readings in Theory and Practice*; Jimerson, R.C., Ed.; The Society of American Archivists: Chicago, 2000; 123–141.
8. http://www.archivists.org/prof-education/ed_guidelines.asp.
9. http://www.archivists.org/prof-education/ace.asp.
10. Walch, V.I. A*CENSUS: A closer look. Am. Arch. **2006**, *69*, 327–348 http://www.archivists.org/a-census/ACensus-Part3-Expanded.pdf (accessed January 2009).
11. Greene, M.A. E Pluribus Unum. Arch. Outlook **2008**, January/February *3*, 24.
12. http://www.archives.gov/about/plans-reports/performance-accountability/2008/index.pdf.
13. http://www.archives.gov/publications/general-info-leaflets/1.html.
14. http://www2.co.multnomah.or.us/Public/EntryPoint?ch=7941581427967010VgnVCM1000003bc614acRCRD.
15. http://www.notarialarchives.org/history.htm.
16. http://www.sanantonio.gov/clerk/Records/Archivist/Index.asp.
17. http://www.sanantonio.gov/news/NewsReleases/nr07ArchivesProgram.asp?res=1280&ver=true.
18. http://rmc.library.cornell.edu/collections/cuhist.html.
19. http://campusgw.library.cornell.edu/about/digital.html.
20. http://www.library.cornell.edu/about/digital_projects.html.
21. http://bentley.umich.edu/ http://www.lib.umich.edu/lit/dlps/featured.html.
22. http://www.lib.umich.edu/lit/dlps/projects.html.
23. http://memory.loc.gov/ammem/ndlpcoop/moahtml/ncpcollab.html.
24. http://quod.lib.umich.edu/m/moagrp/ and http://cdl.library.cornell.edu/moa/.
25. http://www.cdlib.org/.
26. http://library.duke.edu/digitalcollections/.
27. http://libraries.mit.edu/archives/about/what-is-archives.html.
28. http://www.dspace.org.
29. http://library.stanford.edu/depts/hasrg/hdis/.
30. http://library.stanford.edu/depts/diroff/biennial/Digital_Library_ Program/digital_library_program.html.
31. http://www.lib.uchicago.edu/e/spcl/.
32. http://www.lib.unc.edu/digitalprojects.html.
33. http://www.yale.edu/collections_collaborative/primarysources/overview.html.
34. http://www.loc.gov/rr/mss/mss_abt.html http://www.loc.gov/rr/mss/guide/.
35. http://memory.loc.gov/ammem/about/index.html.
36. http://www.amphilsoc.org/library/manuscri.htm.
37. http://chicagohistory.org/.
38. http://library.temple.edu/collections/urbana/;jsessionid=B86FF0E0EBE5B254633D24010855D25A?bhcp=1.
39. http://www.au.af.mil/au/afhra/.
40. http://www.history.army.mil/.
41. http://www.history.navy.mil/.
42. http://www.ajhs.org/reference/.

43. http://www.americanjewisharchives.org/.
44. http://archives.archchicago.org/.
45. http://episcopalarchives.org/index.html.
46. http://www.wheaton.edu/bgc/archives/archhp1.html.
47. http://www.familysearch.org/eng/library/FHL/frameset_library.asp.
48. http://www.familysearch.org/eng/library/fhl/frameset_library.asp?PAGE=library_history.asp.
49. http://www.gcah.org/site/c.ghKJI0PHIoE/b.2858857/k.BF4D/Home.htm.
50. http://www.coca-colaconversations.com/ and http://www.thecoca-colacompany.com/heritage/mooney.html.
51. http://bentley.umich.edu/academic/practicum/docs/ford history.doc.
52. http://www.archivists.org/archivesmonth/AAM2008/Ford MotorAAM2008.pdf.
53. http://www.levistrauss.com/Heritage/OurArchives.aspx.
54. http://www.historyassociates.com/about/index.htm.
55. http://www.historyfactory.com/.
56. http://www.icpsr.umich.edu/ and http://www.icpsr.umich.edu/DATAPASS/.
57. http://www.archives.gov/research/electronic-records/.
58. http://www.archives.gov/era/.
59. http://lcweb2.loc.gov/diglib/lcwa/html/lcwa-home.html.
60. http://www.archivists.org/governance/guidelines/museum_guidelines.asp.
61. http://siarchives.si.edu/.
62. http://www.nasm.si.edu/research/arch/.
63. http://www.nmnh.si.edu/naa/about.htm.
64. http://americanhistory.si.edu/archives/b-1.htm.
65. http://www.aaa.si.edu/.
66. http://www.getty.edu/research/institute/.
67. http://www.ushmm.org/.
68. http://www.warhol.org/collections/archives.html.
69. http://www.archives.gov/research/formats/ and http://www.loc.gov/rr/print/.
70. http://www.colum.edu/cbmr/.
71. http://www.folger.edu/index.cfm.
72. http://www.nypl.org/research/lpa/lpa.html.
73. http://web.baseballhalloffame.org/index.jsp.
74. http://www.bgsu.edu/colleges/library/pcl/.
75. http://www.loc.gov/folklife/archive.html and http://911digitalarchive.org/.
76. http://ahc.uwyo.edu/default.htm.
77. http://www.amistadresearchcenter.org/.
78. http://www.hsp.org/.
79. http://www.centropr.org/.
80. http://www.auctr.edu/collections/archives-collections.asp.
81. http://www.auctr.edu/mlkcollection/history-exhibit.asp.
82. http://www.heard.org/Page.aspx?pid=223.
83. http://amacord.com/fillmore/museum/jt/jaha/jaha.html.
84. http://www.founders.howard.edu/moorland-spingarn/.
85. http://www.mocanyc.org/collections.
86. http://www.nypl.org/research/sc/sc.html.
87. http://www.smith.edu/libraries/libs/ssc/.
88. http://www.radcliffe.edu/schlesinger_library.aspx.
89. http://library.duke.edu/specialcollections/bingham/index.html.
90. http://www.lib.uiowa.edu/iwa/.
91. http://rmc.library.cornell.edu/collections/sexandgender.html.
92. http://www.glbthistory.org/.
93. http://www.kinseyinstitute.org/about/index.html.
94. http://www.lesbianherstoryarchives.org/.
95. http://www.onearchives.org/collections/new.
96. http://www.georgemeany.org/archives/home.html.
97. http://www.ilr.cornell.edu/library/kheel/.
98. http://www.reuther.wayne.edu/.
99. http://www.nyu.edu/library/bobst/research/tam/index.html.
100. http://www.medicalarchives.jhmi.edu/aboutamc.htm.
101. http://research.calacademy.org/research/library/special/.
102. http://archives.caltech.edu//.
103. http://www.cbi.umn.edu/.
104. http://www.hsl.virginia.edu/historical/index.cfm.
105. http://www.davidsarnoff.org/.
106. http://www.lindahall.org/.
107. http://riley.nal.usda.gov/nal_display/index.php?info_center=8&tax_level=1&tax_subject=158.
108. http://www.nlm.nih.gov/hmd/collections/archives/index.html.
109. http://www.aip.org/history/nbl/index.html.

BIBLIOGRAPHY

Monographs

1. In *Thirty Years of Electronic Records*; Ambacher, B.I., Ed.; The Scarecrow Press, Inc.: Lanham, MD, 2003.
2. Cox, R.J. *Closing an Era: Historical Perspectives on Modern Archives and Records Management*, Greenwood Press: Westport, CT, 2000.
3. In *A Modern Archives Reader: Basic Readings on Archival Theory and Practice*; Daniels, M.F., Walch, T., Eds.; National Archives and Records Service: Washington, DC, 1984.
4. Gondos, V., Jr. *J. Franklin Jameson and the Birth of the National Archives, 1906–1926*, University of Pennsylvania Press: Philadelphia, PA, 1981.
5. In *American Archival Studies: Readings in Theory and Practice*; Jimerson, R.C., Ed.; The Society of American Archivists: Chicago, IL, 2000; 143–173.
6. Mitchell, T.W. *Norton on Archives: The Writings of Margaret Cross Norton on Archival and Records Management*, Society of American Archivists: Chicago, IL, 2003; with a foreword by Ernst M Posner and a new introduction by Randall Jimerson; SAA Archival Classics Series.
7. Posner, E. *American State Archives*, University of Chicago Press: Chicago, IL, 1964.
8. Posner, E. *Archives in the Ancient World*, Harvard University Press: Cambridge, MA, 1972.
9. Schellenberg, T.R. *Modern Archives: Principles and Techniques*, University of Chicago Press: Chicago, IL, 1956.

Journals

10. American Archivist (Journal of the Society of American Archivists). Available at http://www.archivists.org/periodicals/aa.asp.

11. Archival Issues: The Journal of the Midwest Archives Conference. Available at http://www.midwestarchives.org/archivalissues.asp.
12. IASSIST Quarterly (Journal of the International Association for Social Science Information Service and Technology). Available at http://www.iassistdata.org/publications/iq/.
13. Information Management (Journal of ARMA). Available at http://www.arma.org/imj/index.cfm.
14. Journal of Archival Organization Haworth Press, Inc Publisher. Available at http://www.haworthpressinc.com/store/product.asp?sku=J201.
15. Provenance (Journal of the Society of Georgia Archivists). Available at http://soga.org/pubs/prov/provenance.php.

United States: Libraries and Librarianship in the 21st Century

John W. Berry
NILRC: Network of Illinois Learning Resources in Community Colleges, Dominican University, River Forest, Illinois, U.S.A.

Abstract
This entry gives an overview of libraries and librarianship in the United States and explores several trends that will continue to have an impact on American libraries for the foreseeable future. These trends include: network neutrality and digital rights management; recruitment and diversity of library workers; the continuing development of the Internet; Library 2.0 and beyond (blogs, podcasts and wikis); libraries and the gaming phenomenon; librarian and library worker salaries; and library advocacy and funding.

Editor's Note: We have commissioned John Berry, an eminent library leader and former president of ALA, to contribute an entry that provides a general overview of the status of American libraries followed by a discussion of trends, issues, and technologies that impact American libraries and librarians in the first decade of the twenty-first century. His approach differs from that taken in our county entries because American libraries and library history are well represented in other entries in ELIS-3, and because most of the major library associations headquartered in the United States are covered by individual entries. Because American museums and archives are less fully covered by ELIS-3 entries, those two sections provide more historical background and discuss differences among various types of archives and museums. Beverly Sheppard, former head of Institute of Museum and Library Services, has contributed the section on Museums in the United States. The section on American Archives was prepared by Cheryl Stadel-Bevans formerly with the National Archives and Records Service and by Danna Bell-Russel with the Library of Congress. Each of the three sections has its own abstract, keywords, and reference list.

FACTS ABOUT LIBRARIES IN THE UNITED STATES

The American Library Association (ALA) estimates there are 123,291 libraries of all types in the United States in 2008 (see Table 1). No single annual survey provides exact statistics on all types of library spaces. The public, academic, and school library statistics below come from four surveys by the *National Center for Education Statistics (NCES): Public Libraries in the United States: Fiscal Year 2005; Academic Libraries: 2004 (2006); A Brief Profile of America's Public Schools (2007)* for the number of school library media centers in public schools and BIA (Bureau of Indian Affairs) schools; and the *Schools and Staffing Survey, 1999–2000 (2002)* for the number of school library media centers in private schools. Figures for special libraries, armed forces libraries, and government libraries are from the American Library Directory 2007–2008 (Fig. 1).

ALA also reports that operating budgets in all libraries are increasing at 3–4% each year, mostly going to staff salaries, but services and collections in libraries are also increasing. Public library visits are rising, and circulation of audio and video materials have risen by 14% annually from FY 2003 through FY 2006 even as book circulations have declined substantially. http://www.ala.org/ala/aboutala/hqops/library/libraryfactsheet/alalibrary factsheet4.cfm

The State of America's Libraries: A Report from the American Library Association

In April 2007, a report called *The State of America's Libraries*, published by the American Library Association found that

> Public, school and university libraries are flourishing, both in traditional ways and in the still-exploding universe of the Internet. Library use is up nationwide among all types of library users, continuing a decade-long trend. Almost 1.8 billion visitors checked out more than 2 billion items last year at everything from one-room rural libraries to spectacular facilities such as Seattle's Central Library which opened in 2004.[1]

ALA also found that the number of visits to public libraries in the United States increased 61% between 1994 and 2004.

Investment in e-books at academic and research libraries rose by 68% from 2002 to 2004, the most recent year for which federal data are available. Electronic serials expenditure has also increased at major research libraries

Encyclopedia of Library and Information Sciences, Fourth Edition DOI: 10.1081/E-ELIS4-120043450

Table 1.

Public libraries (administrative units)		9,208
Centrals[a]	9,050	
Branches	7,542	
Buildings	16,592	
Academic Libraries		**3,617**
Less than four year	1,334	
Four year and above	2,283	
Total	3,617	
School Libraries		**99,783**
Public schools	82,569	
Private schools	17,054	
BIA (Bureau of Indian Affairs)	160	
Total	99,783	
Special Libraries[b]		**9,066**
Armed Forces Libraries		**296**
Government Libraries		**1,159**
Total		**123,129**

[a] The number of central buildings is different from the number of public libraries because some public library systems have no central building and some have more than one.
[b] Special libraries include Corporate, Medical, Law, Religious, etc.
Source: ALA Fact Sheet 1, http://www.ala.org/ala/aboutala/offices/library/libraryfactsheet/alalibraryfactsheet1.cfm#[2]

and usage of electronic materials has skyrocketed. At the same time, circulation has declined slightly and reference services have declined more steeply.[3],[4]

Public libraries are on the forefront in delivering new programs to their users while still providing the traditional services that people expect from their libraries—the tools to conduct a job search, write a résumé, and learn new work skills. Despite a growing body of research that links school libraries and positive student achievement, school library media centers have been hard hit by funding cuts in recent years.

The American library community continues its work to defend the First Amendment rights of library users against secret government surveillance, including the USA PATRIOT Act passed in October 2001. Librarians also continued their efforts to oppose censorship challenges that restrict the free flow of information and ideas to both adults and children.

From Awareness to Funding: A Study of Library Support in America (2008)

In July 2008, OCLC, the world's largest bibliographic records utility, with the private market research firm Leo Burnett, published a new study of U.S. public libraries called: *From Awareness to Funding: A Study of Library Support in America* by DeRosa and Johnson.[5]

The following are the key findings of this study:

- The American public's awareness of libraries is based on yesterday.
- The research provides important insights into what U.S. voters and their elected officials know, and what they do not know, about public libraries and public library funding.
- Most U.S. residents are aware of the traditional "informational" library services, such as books, newspapers, magazines, and Internet access.
- Far fewer know about the many value-added and "transformational" services provided by their libraries, such as teen programs, computer training, and "English as a second language" (ESL) classes.
- Support for library funding comes from those who believe libraries transform lives, and not necessarily from those who use the library.

Many American public libraries have responded by launching marketing campaigns focused on increasing

Fig. 1 Fleet library at the Rhode Island School of Design.(2007 winner American Institute of Architects/American Library Association Library Buildings Awards Program).
Source: Renovation by: office dA, Boston, MA. Photograph by: John Horner Photography, Somerville, MA.

awareness of the library and its services. Despite numerous marketing and communications efforts across the country, the perception of the library as "a physical place offering traditional information services (books and information)" remains well entrenched in the minds of library users.

And while the perceptions of the library may remain fixed, the information landscape is changing rapidly. The knowledge landscape is expanding and the library's once unique position as the "place that provides books and information" is increasingly crowded. Powerful rivals with deeper pockets such as Google and Barnes & Noble are able to fund stronger marketing initiatives to reach information consumers and are redefining user expectations of information access. Without action, the survey argues, it is almost certain that the library's brand will continue to be seen as a *legacy* service, a "nice to have" but not critical institution, more relevant in the past than for the future.

This OCLC sponsored advocacy research identified that residents are not aware that libraries are under financial stress. Most residents do not realize that libraries—maybe even their local library—have cut services, reduced hours or limited new material acquisitions due to reductions in their operating budgets or increases in operating costs, such as health care, collections, and utilities. On the other hand, elected officials are generally supportive and aware of the financial needs of their libraries. Those surveyed report that they are aware of the varied and important services offered by their libraries and recognize their importance to their communities. But the research also revealed that despite their appreciation for the library, local elected officials are not typically inclined to increase library funding. The majority felt that their libraries have sufficient operating funds.

If, despite the efforts of existing marketing campaigns, the library brand is still about "books and information," the survey asks how the library can be positioned as a "transformational force" in the minds of more users and voters? If current library marketing campaigns are focused mainly on driving usage of libraries and awareness of their services, what is needed to increase library funding to inspire, and activate, residents and local elected officials to increase funding for libraries the survey asks.

Not all residents in a community are equal when marketing or advocating for increased funding for libraries. This inequality is not unexpected or unusual.[14] As described by OCLC's market research partner, Leo Burnett:

Not everyone is alike and different people want different things from the category. They evaluate, perceive and use brands differently.[14] No brand has "universal appeal" and the more brands there are in a category, the more this is true. "For every brand, there is a greater chance to build business [funding] among some segments of consumers than others. If these segments can be identified, the brand

has a 'roadmap for growth' and can customize marketing efforts to the most likely prospects."[4]

The Library Supporter Segmentation Pyramid for this research identified four public library market tiers: 1) residents who are not registered or do not typically vote in elections (Chronic Nonvoters); 2) voters with high barriers to supporting the library (Barriers to Support); 3) voters who are probable library funding supporters (Probable Supporters); and 4) voters who are definite library funding supporters (Super Supporters). Within these four overarching market tiers the study made an additional 10 distinct market segments, named to reflect their distinctive characteristics: 1) Chronic Nonvoters; 2) Financially Strapped; 3) Detached; 4) The Web Wins; 5) Just for Fun; 6) Kid Driven; 7) Library as Office; 8) Look to Librarians; 9) Greater Good; and 10) Super Supporters.

The OCLC research identified several important shared values and beliefs across the target market segments, the Probable Supporters and the Super Supporters:

- They are involved in their communities.
- They recognize the library's importance to the community and to a child's education.
- They are not always heavy users of the library, but believe the library is a noble place, important and relevant to the community.
- They recognize the value of a "passionate librarian" as a true advocate for lifelong learning.
- They see the library as a vital community resource like public schools, fire, and police, and are willing to increase their taxes to support the library.[5]

The survey concludes that awakening and reinforcing the transformational value of the library is the most important factor in increasing library funding support.

A successful library funding support campaign must

- Make the library relevant for the twenty-first century.
- Instill a sense of urgency by putting the library in a competitive context for funding, alongside the public schools, fire department, and police department.
- Activate conversations about the library's importance in community infrastructure and its role in the community's future.[18] "To thrive tomorrow, libraries must translate belief to awareness, and awareness to action."[5]

Key Issues for Academic Libraries and Librarians

In its Environmental Scan 2007 (2008), The Association of College and Research Libraries (ACRL) identified the "Top Ten Assumptions for the Future of Academic Libraries and Librarians"[6] and they include

1. There will be an increased emphasis on digitizing collections, preserving digital archives, and improving

methods of data storage, retrieval, curation, and service.

2. The skill set for librarians will continue to evolve in response to the changing needs and expectations of the populations they serve, and the professional background of library staff will become increasingly diverse in support of expanded service programs and administrative needs.

3. Students and faculty will continue to demand increasing access to library resources and services, and to expect to find a rich digital library presence both in enterprise academic systems and as a feature of social computing.

4. Debates about intellectual property will become increasingly common in higher education, and resources and educational programming related to intellectual property management will become an important part of library service to the academic community.

5. The evolution of information technology will shape both the practice of scholarly inquiry and the daily routine of students and faculty, and demands for technology-related services and technology-rich user environments will continue to grow and will require additional funding.

6. Higher education will be increasingly viewed as a business, and calls for accountability and for quantitative measures of library contributions to the research, teaching, and service missions of the institution will shape library assessment programs and approaches to the allocation of institutional resources.

7. As part of the "business of higher education," students will increasingly view themselves as "customers" of the academic library and will demand high-quality facilities, resources, and services attuned to their needs and concerns.

8. Online learning will continue to expand as an option for students and faculty—both on campus and off—and libraries will gear resources and services for delivery to a distributed academic community.

9. Demands for free, public access to data collected, and research completed, as part of publicly funded research programs will continue to grow.

10. The protection of privacy and support for intellectual freedom will continue to be defining issues for academic libraries and librarians.[7]

In addition, the ACRL Research Committee identified several "emerging issues" that are already of considerable local significance in academic libraries and will likely grow in importance in years to come.

- There will be broader collaboration between academic, public, special, and school librarians on topics of common concern, e.g., public engagement, information, and media literacy.
- Pressure to make library facilities "greener" will increase. Developments in this area will likely take place as part of broader institutional efforts.
- Library facilities and services will become increasingly integrated with research, teaching, and learning programs across campus, including those housed in information technology programs and student services program.
- The library's print materials will be moved from prime library space and relocated to off-site locations; space currently housing collections will be repurposed to support collaborative learning, new modes of research support, and interactive learning areas.
- Tensions will continue to grow each year as decisions are made that determine what portion of the budget will be used to purchase digital collections as opposed to will be used to preserve and provide access to unique collections held by the library.
- Library patrons will use semantic Web search techniques to locate information resources. The need to meet the needs of e-science and e-scholarship in the social sciences and the humanities will increase and require new approaches to the design and delivery of core library services.
- Collaboration between academic libraries and university publication programs will increase as their roles become increasingly complementary.
- The focus for academic libraries will shift from the creation and management of large, on-site library collections to the design and delivery of library services.
- Regional and professional accrediting bodies will require greater accountability using a wide range of assessment techniques.
- A crisis will occur in Library and Information Science (LIS) education as schools prepare students to assume new roles in academic libraries and as contributors to campus programs.
- Interdisciplinary studies, new models of undergraduate and graduate education, and newly developed areas of inquiry will stretch library resources and service model. The tools and techniques of social computing will provide new opportunities for the design and delivery of library resources and services, but will also make increasing demands on library staff and systems.

Librarians and Library Salaries

ALA estimates that the total number of professional librarians working in the United States is approximately 150,000 (see Table 2). The ALA Library Fact Sheet 2 notes that "the library work force includes librarians and other professionals, paraprofessionals, clerical and technical personnel."[7] The fact sheet summarizes the latest

Table 2 Librarian and library employees in the United States.

	Librarians	Other paid staff	Total paid staff
Academic Libraries	26,469	67,121	93,590
Public libraries	45,354	92,501	137,855
Public school libraries	50,553	30,785	81,338
Private school libraries	11,060	3,360	14,420
BIA school libraries	88	63	151
Total	133,524	193,830	327,354

Source: ALA Fact Sheet 2, http://www.ala.org/ala/aboutala/hqops/library/libraryfactsheet/alalibraryfactsheet2.cfm.[7]

available statistics on the two major categories—librarians and other professionals, and other paid staff—in the three types of libraries for which reliable national figures are available from National Center for Education Statistics (NCES) and the Institute of Museum and Library Services (IMLS).

The ALA fact sheet also notes that firm numbers for those employed in special libraries (e.g., libraries serving businesses, scientific agencies, hospitals, law firms, and nonprofit organizations) are not available. However, based on information available from several related associations (such as the Special Libraries Association), ALA estimates that in 2001 approximately 15,307 librarians were employed in special libraries.

Salaries paid to librarians vary by type of library and by region of the country, and are also affected by other factors; for example salaries are usually lower in rural areas and highest in major cities. Results of the annual ALA-APA (Allied Professional Association) Salary Surveys in 2007 offer hope for advocates of higher salaries for library workers. According to the surveys, the mean salary of librarians rose faster than most estimates of inflation.

Six-figure salaries were reported for several non-MLS positions. Two surveys: *ALA-APA Salary Survey: Librarian—Public and Academic* (*Librarian Salary Survey*) and *ALA-APA Salary Survey: Non-MLS—Public and Academic* (*Non-MLS Salary Survey*) are highlighted below.

- According to *ALA-APA Salary Survey: Librarian—Public and Academic* (*Librarian Salary Survey*), the mean librarian salary rose to $57,809, an increase of $1550 from 2006.
- Significantly, this increase of 2.8% was higher than the Consumer Price Index of 2.4% for the same time period (February 2007). The U.S. Bureau of Labor Statistics' Employment Cost Index (ECI), another measure of inflation, was between 2.4% and 3.1% for 2005, the latest figures available.[9]

Non-MLS salary survey

The scope of the 2007 survey was expanded to include positions not requiring an ALA-accredited MLS to assess salaries of other professionals working in libraries, including accountants, human resource professionals, grant writers, and information technology staff. This data will allow for comparisons of their salaries in the external market. Salary data are from the 2006 and 2007 *Librarian Salary Survey* and *Non-MLS Salary Survey*.[10]

RECRUITMENT AND DIVERSITY

The U.S. Census Bureau, based on definitions from the Bureau of Labor Statistics, distinguishes between "credentialed" and "noncredentialed" librarians. Credentialed librarians are defined as librarians who report that they have completed a master's degree or another degree higher than a master's. The area of study is not asked in the census, hence it is inferred that librarians with a master's degree have completed their degree in library science.[11]

Noncredentialed librarians are all other persons whose occupation is listed as librarian but who have not completed a master's degree. Similar degree-based distinctions are not made for library assistants or clerks.

Credentialed and noncredentialed librarians, as well as library technicians and assistants, are predominantly female, white, and are not limited by disability. This finding held true in both the 1990 and 2000 decennial census data.

Credentialed librarians are predominantly women, aged 45–54 years, and white. They are not limited by disability and work full-time (40+ hr per week). Noncredentialed librarians represent approximately 43% of those reporting for the industry "library" and have a slightly more balanced ethnic and racial distribution than do credentialed librarians. Sixteen-point-eight percent (16.8%) of noncredentialed librarians selected nonwhite race/ethnicity categories, whereas only 11% of credentialed librarians did so. Three[4] percent more Latinos reported holding noncredentialed librarian positions, and 2% more African Americans. Other distribution differences were less than 1%. Type of library employed varies little from credentialed to noncredentialed librarians.

Library assistants are even more predominantly female than librarians, are more likely to be 35 years of age or under, and white. They, too, are not limited by disability. Unlike their librarian counterparts, they almost equally work full- and part-time weekly schedules. Type of library employed largely mirrors that reported by credentialed and noncredentialed librarians, except that higher education/academic was the second largest employer of non-MLS staff.

As American communities, urban, suburban, or rural, become more diverse in nearly every dimension, the profession of librarianship has placed more emphasis on ensuring that libraries remain in touch with the communities they serve. The ALA data suggests that libraries strategically plan around human resource development and succession planning. The persistent lag in diversity in library education programs, the number of librarians and library assistants leaving the profession prematurely, the aging and retirement of racial and ethnic minority library workers, and the continued under-representation of workers with disabilities, suggests a proportionally less diverse library workforce in the future.

Finally, the diversity study suggests that diversity should not be seen as a separate programmatic effort, but as a central framework of twenty-first century library and information science practice. "The very existence of libraries rests on our ability to create institutions and resource centers where would-be users see their information needs and themselves reflected."[11]

KEY ISSUES FOR ALL AMERICAN LIBRARIES

Network Neutrality and Digital Rights Management

Network neutrality (also called net neutrality, Internet neutrality, or simply NN) is a principle that is applied to residential broadband networks and potentially to all networks. A neutral broadband network is characterized by being free of restrictions on the kinds of equipment that may be attached to it, on the modes of communication allowed, it does not restrict content, sites, or platforms, and communication is not unreasonably degraded by other communication streams.

The American library community believes that intellectual freedom is critical to our democracy, because the nation relies on people's ability to inform themselves. The growth of the Internet connecting people of diverse geographical, political, and ideological backgrounds, has greatly enhanced everyone's ability to share and to inform both themselves and others. The American Library Association and allied associations have taken the position on network neutrality that owners and managers of the information "pipelines" should not be able to control the content nor switch some information providers to slower "lanes." While many states are addressing this issue, there is likely to be another effort at the federal level by allied associations on one hand and the broad providers and other telecommunications service on the other.

In the context of the net neutrality debate, it is equally important that the freedom of libraries and librarians to provide innovative new kinds of information services will be central to the growth and development of a democratic culture. A world in which librarians and other noncommercial enterprises are, of necessity, limited to the Internet's "slow lanes" while high-definition movies receive preferential treatment is counter to a central tenet in a democratic society—the necessity of enabling educators, librarians, and, in fact, all citizens to inform themselves and each other just as much as the major commercial and media interests can inform them. The ability of the Internet to spread and share ideas is increasing rapidly. With cutting-edge technology, individuals and small groups can produce rich audio and video resources that used to be the exclusive domain of large corporations. ALA continues to support effective network neutrality policies that assure freedom of expression on the Internet and equity for all types of information providers. It is hoped that future discussions on network neutrality will be less polarized and able to reach consensus on this difficult and divisive issue. Consensus would ensure a fair distribution of Internet connectivity and speed that enables rather than restricts citizen access to the global Internet.

Digital Rights Management: A Brief Introduction

Digital Rights Management (DRM) is a term used for technologies that control how digital content is used. While copyright holders have exclusive rights of copyright—such as the right to make a copy or the right to distribute a work to the public—to date, they have not had the right to control how works are used (the right to see a work, for example, or to read a work). In addition, fair use, a statutory exemption to the copyright law, allows users to exercise a copyright under certain conditions.[12]

Depending on the outlook of the individual or group defining the term, it can have a number of connotations including the following:

- "Digital rights management technologies are aimed at increasing the kinds and/or scope of control that rightsholders can assert over their intellectual property assets."—*Electronic Frontier Foundation*
- "DRM must be about the 'digital management of rights' not the 'management of digital rights.'"—*W3C Workshop Report on DRM for the Web*
- "The purpose of DRM technology is to control access to, track and limit uses of digital works."—The American Library Association
- "DRM are the technologies, tools, and processes that protect intellectual property during digital content commerce..." —Publishers' Requirements for DRM, *W3C Workshop Report on DRM for the Web*
- "DRM systems restrict the use of digital files in order to protect the interests of copyright holders."—*Electronic Privacy Information Center*[13]

The well-established user privileges in the analog environment are generally seen as threatened by DRM in the American community. Copyright owners have acted in response to the proliferation of digital content, where the 1000th copy is identical to the first. In terms of distribution, the Internet now enables instantaneous distribution of digital content across a global network moving content owners and users into a new arena where each is adjusting to ensure, assert, and in some cases, enhance their rights. Content owners are looking to DRM technologies as a means to control the use of their content. Many public interest organizations, including the leading U.S. library associations, fear that DRM technologies will be "used by copyright owners to erode capabilities that had previously been permitted to the public by copyright law under the 'fair use' doctrine (or its cousins, such as first sale or limited term)."[14]

DRM technologies can also be used for unethical and illegal activities including infringing on privacy, personal profiling, and price discrimination based on personally identifiable information and obstructing the development of open source software. For libraries, DRM technologies can additionally impact first-sale, preservation activities, and institute pay-per-use pricing.

The entertainment industry, led primarily by the Motion Picture Association of America (MPAA) and the Recording Industry Association of America (RIAA), is actively pursuing DRM-friendly policy initiatives through federal legislation and regulations, the courts, and standards organizations. The consumer electronics and the information technology industries are also joining the debate because their products would need to be redesigned to meet entertainment industry needs. Profits, business models, and the implications of technology mandates are driving this part of the debate. Meanwhile, libraries, educational institutions (K-12 and higher education), and consumers will be heavily affected by any decisions made by the federal government, courts, and standards bodies. Public advocacy groups have broadened the policy debate to include user rights such as privacy, fair use, first-sale, and preservation.

Gaming in Libraries

The library field is seeing all types of libraries adding the phrase "gaming and libraries" to their array of services.

A 2007 issue of *Library Technology Reports* examined the growing, and increasingly visible, intersections the library profession has with the gaming phenomenon.

Historically, gaming and games have been central to leisure and learning activities in societies since ancient times. Sumerian games, ancient Egyptian games, medieval games, turn-of-the-century games, and contemporary games all have threads in common:

- Games test problem-solving skills.
- Games are inclusive.
- Games create community.
- Games facilitate learning.

- Games provide fields for practice of leadership and team skills.
- Games develop identity.[14]

Since the beginning of the twenty-first century, college and university courses, departments, and academic fields have been formed to study video games, and educators and librarians, and health care professionals are examining ways to incorporate these threads into schools, universities, hospitals, and nursing homes. A growing contingent of librarians are creating new intersections of services, where libraries can meet and serve gamers.

In mid-2008, the American Library Association launched an innovative project to track and measure the impact of gaming on literacy skills and build a model for library gaming that can be used nationally. Funding for the project is a $1 million grant from the Verizon Foundation, justifying such a project by that: "Gaming is a magnet that attracts library users of all types and, beyond its entertainment value, has proven to be a powerful tool for literacy and learning,"[15]

As part of the grant, ALA will work directly with 12 leading gaming experts to document the use of gaming as a literacy tool and monitor the results of gaming initiatives. The information will be used to build "The Librarians' Guide to Gaming," a comprehensive, online literacy and gaming toolbox, which will then be field-tested by several libraries.

The experts creating the best practices during the initial phase of the project are from 14 libraries across the United States.

Web 2.0 and Library 2.0

Web 2.0 is a term used to denote several different concepts:

- Web sites based on a particular set of technologies such as AJAX(Asynchronous JavaScript and XML).
- Web sites which incorporate a strong social component, involving user profiles, friend links.
- Web sites which encourage user-generated content in the form of text, video, and photo postings along with comments, tags, and ratings.

Some sites are easy to classify: social networking sites such as Facebook and MySpace are often held up as prototypical examples of Web 2.0, primarily due to their social networking aspects which include the user as a first-class object, but also due to their use of new user interface technologies (Facebook in particular). Other sites are resolutely Web 1 in their approach: Craigslist, for example, emulates an e-mail list server, and has no public user profiles, or fancy dynamic pages.

The term Web 2.0 was coined in 2004, and many of the first truly Web 2.0 sites began emerging in late 2003 and early 2004. A definition of Web 2.0 by O'Reilly (2005) emphasizes viewing the Web as a platform. Some of the important features that mark out a Web 2.0 site include:

- Users as first class entities in the system, with prominent profile pages, including such features as age, sex, location, testimonials, or comments about the user by other users.
- The ability to form connections between users, via links to other users who are "friends," membership in "groups" of various kinds, and subscriptions or RSS feeds of "updates" from other users.
- The ability to post content in many forms: photos, videos, blogs, comments, and ratings on other users' content, tagging of own or others' content, and some ability to control privacy and sharing.
- Other more technical features, including a public API to allow third-party enhancements and "mashups," and embedding of various rich content types (e.g., Flash videos), and communication with other users through internal email or IM systems.[16]

Library 2.0 Defined

The term Library 2.0 was coined by Michael Casey on his blog LibraryCrunch as a direct spin-off of the terms Business 2.0 and Web 2.0. Casey suggested that libraries, especially public libraries, were at a crossroads where many of the elements of Web 2.0 had applicable value within the library community, both in technology-driven services and in nontechnology-based services. In particular, he described the need for libraries to adopt a strategy for constant change while promoting a participatory role for library users.[17],[18]

Library 2.0 made its conference debut at Internet Librarian 2005 when Michael Stephens, then of Saint Joseph County Public Library (IN) addressed the idea in relation to the typical library Web site. With Library 2.0, library services are frequently evaluated and updated to meet the changing needs of library users. Library 2.0 also calls for libraries to encourage user participation and feedback in the development and maintaining of library services.

The active and empowered library user is a significant component of Library 2.0. With information and ideas flowing in both directions—from the library to the user and from the user to the library—library services have the ability to evolve and improve on a constant and rapid basis. The user is participant, cocreator, builder, and consultant—whether the product is virtual or physical. Library 2.0 has been a source of debate in the blogosphere. Some librarian bloggers have argued that these key principles are not new and have been part of the service philosophies of many library reformers since the nineteenth century. Others are calling for more concrete examples of how libraries can get to Library 2.0.

Proponents of Library 2.0, such as Stephen Abram, Michael Stephens, Paul Miller and others, have spoken to these criticisms, arguing that while individual pieces of Library 2.0 may not be entirely new, the convergence of these service goals and ideas with many new Web 2.0 technologies has led to a new generation of library service.

Libraries are exploring ways to meet the rapidly changing needs of users by using Web 2.0 technology. Some of the aspects of Library 2.0 include commenting, tagging, bookmarking, discussions, using social networking software, plug-ins, and widgets. Inspired by Web 2.0, it is an attempt to make the library a more user-driven institution.

Blogs and Blogging

A blog (a shortened form of "Web log") is a Web site, typically maintained by an individual, with regular entries of commentary, descriptions of events, or other material such as graphics or video. Entries are commonly displayed in reverse-chronological order. Blog can also be used as a verb, meaning to maintain or add content to a blog.

Many blogs, including several in library and information sciences, provide commentary or news on a particular subject; others function as more personal journals or diaries. Blogs combine text, images, and links to other blogs, Web pages, and other media related to its topic. The ability for readers to leave comments in an interactive format is an important part of many blogs and what makes them part of Web and Library 2.0. In December 2007, the blog search engine *Technorati* was tracking more than 112 million blogs worldwide.[19]

Podcasts

A podcast is a series of digital media files distributed over the Internet using syndication feeds for playback on computers and portable media players. The term podcast, like broadcast, can refer either to the series of content itself or to the method by which it is syndicated; the latter is also called podcasting.

Though podcasters' Web sites may also offer direct download or streaming of their content, a podcast is distinguished from other digital media formats by its ability to be syndicated, subscribed to, and downloaded automatically when new content is added, using an aggregator or feed reader capable of reading feed formats such as RSS (Really Simple Syndication).[20]

Wikis

A *wiki* is a collection of Web pages designed to enable anyone who accesses it to contribute or modify content, using a simplified markup language. Wikis are often used to create collaborative Web sites and to power community Web sites. The collaborative encyclopedia, Wikipedia, is one of the best-known wikis. Wikis are used in business to provide intranets and Knowledge Management Systems "Wiki" (/wiki/) is originally a Hawaiian word for "fast."[20]

Taken together, blogs, podcasts, and wikis, along with social networking sites, make up the digital framework for Library 2.0.

Library 2.0 Debates

Although many libraries are adopting features of the new social networking of Web 2.0, it is not yet clear how these new features will be incorporated into existing library services. In a program preceding the 2008 American Library Association Annual Conference, the Urban Libraries Council (ULC) brought together library directors, managers, and young librarians to consider transformational trends in learning and social networking that demand faster library innovation. "In an era of Google, what do libraries become?" asked ULC's "virtual" scholar Jeff Garreau, a scenario planner and author of *Radical Evolution*.

John Seely Brown, author of *The Social Life of Information*, discussed the notion of twenty-first century literacy— "that technologies are central to success"—and the shift from "I think therefore I am" to "We participate, therefore we are" and "I am what I produce and other people build on." Two other invited panelists who had been expected to endorse those ideas challenged Brown's social learning construct. Owen Wasow, cofounder of BlackPlanet.com, contradicted Brown, saying that core skills—reading, writing, math—are key to success. "Technology should be subservient to higher goals," he said. J.C. Herz, *Joystick Nation* author and founder, emphasized libraries as "the social space around content," especially books, and urged librarians to be "the network (or community) around books."

A third panelist, Joe Janes, University of Washington I School Associate Dean, said that "digital neighborhoods are bereft of the services and resources we represent. How do you provide that service?" One answer might be in the new values for the profession Janes proposed: "collaboration, participation, interaction, creativity, connectivity and connectedness, openness, vision, reflection, and play."[21]

CONCLUSION

Libraries and librarianship in the United States have an exciting and challenging future—a future that is driven both by traditional collections and services and by an expanding array of new, largely technology-based materials and services. The fundamental nature of the library and information space in this century will continue to be influenced by the global Internet, savvy technology companies with deep financial resources, and agendas for continuing growth and expansion. Web 2.0, Library 2.0, and their future iterations will also determine, in large part, what future libraries will be.

Funding is a central issue for all types of libraries, especially those in the public sector. Library supporters will need to use sophisticated advocacy and marketing strategies to maintain and increase support from government officials and community leaders and build partnerships and collaborative relationships with the private sector.

The possibilities of libraries being widely perceived as a nonessential legacy service are very real. Dynamic and creative leadership by the next generation of library leaders is essential to ensure that libraries will not only serve users for the foreseeable future, but also increase their role in the education of users with skill sets appropriate to twenty-first century global citizens.

REFERENCES

1. American Library Association, *The State of America's Libraries: A Report From the American Library Association*. American Library Association: Chicago, IL, 2007.
2. ALA Fact Sheet 1, http://www.ala.org/ala/aboutala/hqops/library/libraryfactsheet/alalibraryfactsheet1.cfm#.
3. Martell, C. The absent user: Physical use of academic library collections and services continues to decline 1995–2006. J. Acad. Librarian. **2008**, September *34*(5), 400–407.
4. Martell, C. The elusive user: Changing use patterns in academic libraries 1995 to 2004. Coll. Res. Libr. **2007**, September *68*(5), 435–444.
5. DeRosa, C.; Johnson, J. *From Awareness to Funding: A Study of Library Support in America*; OCLC: Dublin, OH, 2008.
6. *Environmental Scan 2007*; Association of College & Research Libraries: Chicago, IL, 2008.
7. Berners-Lee, T., http://dig.csail.mit.edu/breadcrumbs/node/144.
8. ALA Fact Sheet 2, http://www.ala.org/ala/aboutala/hqops/library/libraryfactsheet/alalibraryfactsheet2.cfm.
9. Grady, J.; Davis, D.; Bragg, J. *Library Staff Salaries 2007: Librarian Salaries Increase 2.08 Percent; Some Non-MLS Salaries in the Six-Figures*; ALA-APA: Chicago, IL, 2008.
10. ALA-APA Library Salary Database a subscription-based tool, http://cs.ala.org/websurvey/salarysurvey/salarysurveyform/form.cf.
11. Davis, D.; Hall, T. *Diversity Counts*; Office for Research and Statistics and Office for Diversity, American Library Association, 2007; January 3 Revised.
12. ALA Washington Office, http://www.ala.org/ala/aboutala/offices/wo/woissues/copyrightb/digitalrights/digitalrightsmanagement.cfm.
13. ALA Washington Office, http://www.ala.org/ala/washoff/woissues/copyrightb/digitalrights/digitalrightsmanagement.cfm.
14. Levine, J. Gaming and libraries: Intersection of services. ALA TechSource, Libr. Technol. Rep. **2007**, *42*(5).
15. Library 2.0 Defined, http://www.ala.org/ala/pressreleases2008/june2008/verizon08.cfm.
16. Cormode, G.; Krishnamurthy, B. Key differences between Web 1.0 and Web 2.0. First Monday. **2008**, June *13*(6).

17. Casey, M. Library/crunch, http://librarycrunch.com/?page_id=27.
18. Library 2.0 Defined, http://en.wikipedia.org/wiki/Library_2.0.
19. Blogs and Bloggings, http://en.wikipedia.org/wiki/Blog.
20. Podcasts, http://en.wikipedia.org/wiki/Podcast.
21. Library 2.0 Debates, http://www.libraryjournal.com/article/CA6574094.html.

BIBLIOGRAPHY

Directories of Libraries

1. UNESCO Libraries Portal—over 14,000 links worldwide: http://www.unesco.org/webworld/portal_bib.
2. LibLinks—Directory of library resource links organized by U.S. states: http://www.liblinks.org/.
3. lib-web-cats: A directory of over 34,000 worldwide libraries spanning 118 countries: http://www.librarytechnology.org/libwebcats/.
4. Libraries of the World and their Catalogs: http://www.sylviamilne.co.uk/libcats.htm (compiled by a retired librarian).
5. Wikisource, The Free Library: http://en.wikisource.org/wiki/.
6. International Federation of Library Associations and Institutions: http://www.ifla.org/.
7. Professional Library Associations from Jenkins Law Library: http://www.jenkinslaw.org/researchlinks/index.php?rl=207.
8. "The Infinite Library," Technology Review article on the Google Library Project: http://www.technologyreview.com/InfoTech/wtr_14408,308,p1.html.
9. Librariansworld.com @ the Librarians Networking Site: http://www.librariansworld.com/.
10. "The Deserted Library: As Students Work Online, Reading Rooms Empty Out—Leading Some Campuses to Add Starbucks": http://chronicle.com/free/v48/i12/12a03501.htm (from The Chronicle of Higher Education).
11. "Thoughtful Design Keeps New Libraries Relevant": http://chronicle.com/weekly/v52/i06/06b00101.htm (from The Chronicle of Higher Education).

Other Organizations

1. Electronic Frontier Foundation (EFF): http://www.eff.org.
2. Electronic Privacy Information Center (EPIC): http://www.epic.org.
3. Motion Picture Association of America (MPAA): http://www.mpaa.org/home.htm.
4. Recording Industry Association of America (RIAA): http://www.riaa.org/.
5. World Wide Web Consortium (W3C): http://www.w3.org.

Library Lists

1. Lists of Libraries: http://www.ala.org/library/fact3.html (mailing lists).
2. The Nation's Largest Libraries: http://www.ala.org/ala/aboutala/offices/library/libraryfactsheet/alalibraryfactsheet22.cfm (A Listing by Volumes Held).

Advocacy and Net Neutrality

1. http://www.ala.org/issues&advocacy.
2. http://www.ala.org/ala/issues/issuesadvocacy.cfm (net neutrality).
3. http://www.ala.org/ala/oif/ifissues/netnuetrality.cfm.

Diversity

1. http://www.ala.org/ala/ors/diversitycounts/diversitycounts_rev0.pdf.

United States–
User-Centered Design

United States: Museums

Beverly K. Sheppard
Institute for Learning Innovation, Edgewater, Maryland, U.S.A.

Abstract

America's museums are among the nation's most important cultural assets. These museums are remarkably diverse in size and discipline and increasingly reflect the issues, diversity, and complexity of their communities. American museums are highly professionalized, working within well-defined standards with well-trained, specialized staff. National leadership and support for museums comes through the American Association of Museums, the Institute of Museum and Library Services and numerous discipline-based professional associations. The museum field today works more closely with the public and communities than ever before, reflecting a trend toward accountability, collaboration, and the creation of public value.

INTRODUCTION

America's museums are among the nation's most important cultural assets. Although no current census of museums exists, the American Association of Museums (AAM) estimates approximately 17,500 museums are located across the country, in communities of all sizes.[1] These institutions are both collecting and non-collecting institutions that share a common mission of service to the public. The majority of American museums are nongovernmental (privately operated) organizations, governed by boards of trustees, incorporated within their states of residence and operation, and given exemption from payment of federal taxes, with approval from the Internal Revenue Service. There are also a number of museums that are supported at least in part by municipal, state, or federal entities.

America's best known museums are its large urban institutions, such as the Metropolitan Museum of Art and Museum of Modern Art in New York City, the Field Museum and Art Institute in Chicago, and the Getty Museum in Los Angeles. The Smithsonian Institution in Washington, D.C. is a full campus of world class museums, and many other cities, such as Baltimore, Atlanta, Philadelphia, and Boston offer urban aquariums, zoos, science centers, history museums, art museums, and children's museums as part of their rich assemblage of distinguished museums. Small museums, located in America's small towns and rural areas make up as many as 75% of the nation's museums.[1] Their collections often represent local and regional history.

American museums are remarkably diverse. They include art museums, history museums and historic sites, children's museums, museums committed to science and technology, natural history museums, zoos, aquariums, botanical gardens, and arboreta. The increasing number of ethnically specific museums—museums focusing on the history of such groups as African Americans, Latinos, and Asian Americans—demonstrates America's current interest in building museums to preserve and share diverse cultural developments and contributions.

DEFINITIONS

The *Code of Ethics for Museums*,[2] written by the AAM identifies the common denominator of all types of museums as making a "unique contribution to the public by collecting, preserving, and interpreting the things of this world." Recent publications, such as AAMs *Excellence and Equity*,[3] further stress the importance of the educational purpose of museums, asserting that education should be specifically identified in every museum's mission statement.

The federal government, in the Museum and Library Services Act,[4] defines a museum as, "A public or private nonprofit agency or institution organized on a permanent basis for essentially education or aesthetic purposes, which, utilizing a professional staff, owns or utilizes tangible objects, cares for them, and exhibits them to the public on a regular basis." This definition provides the criteria for federal funding to museums as administered by the Institute of Museum and Library Services (IMLS).

Further criteria for federal funding require that a museum must:

- Be organized as a public or private nonprofit institution that exists on a permanent basis for essentially educational or aesthetic reasons.
- Care for and own or use tangible objects, whether animate or inanimate, and exhibit these objects on a regular basis through facilities that it owns or operates.
- Have at least one professional staff member or the full-time equivalent, whether paid or unpaid, whose

primary responsibility is the acquisition, care, or exhibition of the public objects owned or used by the museum.
- Be open and provide museum services to the general public for at least 120 days a year.

BRIEF HISTORY

Charles Wilson Peale founded America's first museum in 1786. Peale, an artist, scientist, and Revolutionary War officer and patriot, opened his eclectic museum in Philadelphia. Its contents included living species of toads, lizards, snakes, and other amphibians, along with his collection of stuffed and mounted animals. He eventually included the entire skeleton of a mastodon which he helped excavate from a farmer's field in upper New York State. Peale exhibited his natural and scientific curiosities and collections alongside many of his own paintings, including an extensive collection of miniatures of Revolutionary War officers. Peale's painting, *The Artist in his Museum*, completed in 1822, is a self-portrait of Peale lifting a heavy velvet curtain to reveal the wonders exhibited inside. In 1806, Peale also founded the Pennsylvania Academy of Fine Arts, the nation's first art school. His emphasis on education, both in the museum and the art school, may have set in motion the educational role that museums continue to pay today.

The nineteenth century was America's first great era of museum building. Museums became the handsome symbols of a growing civic pride. Historical societies opened in large and small towns, celebrating their community's founders and collecting icons of local accomplishment. The Smithsonian Institution, dedicated to "the increase and diffusion of knowledge," was founded in 1846 and became an integral part of the nation's capitol. The first American zoo opened in Philadelphia in 1854, the first botanical garden in Washington, D.C. in 1850, and the first children's museum in Brooklyn in 1899. Museums created after the Civil War quickly developed into models of professional museums—with their objects displayed in an orderly and purposeful manner. Private collections became public, and art collections, housed in magnificent urban temples, proved that American cities could compete as world-class cultural centers. Individuals such as Henry Frick and Isabella Stewart Gardner provided the contents of their homes to be converted into museums for the public. The 1870s also witnessed the founding of such great institutions as the Museum of Fine Arts in Boston, the Metropolitan Museum of Art, and the Philadelphia Museum of Art. The power and wealth of their benefactors could be seen in every aspect of their majestic facades and their world famous collections.

The work of these early museums focused on collections, scholarship and cultural authority, developing world standards in collecting, researching, conserving, and managing collections. An educational mission was also present early on, and the school field trip became a core practice, acknowledging museums as places that could open new worlds to all who visited. Throughout this early era, enormous personal philanthropy built America's great collections and museums. Even today, individual and foundation giving remains the cornerstone of museum finances. An array of government entities, including such national agencies as the IMLS, the National Science Foundation, the National Endowment for the Arts, and the National Endowment for the Humanities, provide some funding in support of museum programs, exhibits, conservation, and research. However, most museums rely far more substantially on private funding and earned income.

Museum building continued during the twentieth century. Indeed, as many as half of the nation's museums have been started since 1960. Many of the country's small historical societies developed in response to the bicentennial celebrations in the 1970s when American history took center stage. Science centers and children's museums have shown considerable growth in recent years, providing new ideas about interactive and experience-based learning. They parallel a contemporary interest in and concern about science literacy, early learning opportunities and learning outside the classroom. As noted, many special interest and special purpose museums, such as those chronicling Native American, African American, and gay and lesbian history and culture have contributed in recent years to the diversity of American museums. Such great variety of museums suggests that Americans see museums as places that offer significant ways of encountering and understanding a complex world.

During this same period, many American museums took on broader social responsibilities. Zoos, for example, quickly changed from "menageries" to educational displays of animals in natural habitats. In the last 40 years, they have become centers of learning, promoting conservation, and education about all forms of animal life. Similarly, botanical gardens have expanded their missions—building campuses of public gardens, classrooms, and research facilities to share issues of biodiversity and a threatened natural world.

Children's museums and science and technology centers have been clear about their educational mission from their beginnings. Just as Americans delighted in their discoveries of scientific wonders and technology at the Philadelphia Centennial Exposition of 1876, they quickly became captured by such major institutions as the Museum of Science and Industry in Chicago and the National Air and Space Museum in Washington, D.C. Science and technology centers have become increasingly prominent across the country and are among the most interactive of America's museums, inviting learning in a direct and engaging manner. More than 100 science museums opened their doors in the 1990s. With a similarly direct educational mission, children's museums also are now the fastest-growing sector of the museum community.

American museums were seeing unparalleled attendance and growth in the late twentieth century. Numerous studies in the late 1990s depicted a lively and prosperous time for museums. Statistics gathered by the AAM[5] suggested that American museums welcomed approximately 865 million visits a year, a total that reflected a 50% increase over the previous decade. Thirty-six percent of travelers surveyed noted that their travels would include a museum destination. In addition to providing exhibits and programs for general visitors, museums were also increasing their school services. A study from the IMLS determined that 88% of museums actively provided programs for students from kindergarten through the 12th grade, and many of those also provided specific educational offerings for teachers.[6]

The optimism of the twentieth century, however, was decidedly interrupted by the events of September 11, 2001, and the subsequent financial downturns that rocked the nation and the world. The bright museum reports of the 1990s have been replaced in recent years with serious reports of increasing debt, declining attendance, critically deferred maintenance, and overstretched government and private funding sources. The events of a dramatically changed era are also changing museums and forcing renewed thinking about museum missions and purposes in an altered world. As a result, new attention is being given to such topics as community collaboration, renewed educational emphasis, new approaches to the use of technology, and the role of museums in creating public value.

HOW MUSEUMS OPERATE

Museums may be public or private, university-owned or controlled, owned by a government entity, such as a city or country, or organized as part of a larger cultural complex. The majority of museums are not-for-profit entities. Their business models are structured to provide public services and benefits, rather than to make financial gains for their shareholders. They require Boards of Trustees or Directors who maintain the financial oversight as well as responsibility for establishing the policies that guide the institutions.

Day-to-day operations are managed by professional museum staff, trained to manage finances, maintain collections, undertake research, develop exhibits, plan educational programs, and communicate with the public. Staff positions may include administrative and financial personnel, curators and registrars, conservators, scholars, educators, exhibit designers, and an array of support personnel. Museums are guided in their work by institutional mission statements. Museum missions generally speak to collecting, preserving, exhibiting, and interpreting with a focus on providing value for the public.

Museum directors are their institution's chief executives. The director manages the day-to-day operations of the museum, sets operational goals and objectives, oversees personnel and reports to a Board of Directors. Directors may come from many different backgrounds. Increasingly, directors are stepping into their leadership roles from the world of business rather than scholarship. While for many years, directors exhibited strong academic backgrounds in the subject areas of their institutions, such as art history, zoology, botany, or history, Boards of Trustees, responsible for hiring the chief executive, have begun to look outside of academic disciplines, seeking administrative and financial experience.

Recently, the director's role has become more heavily focused on fundraising and financial management. Some institutions, such as the Philadelphia Museum of Art, have experimented with dividing the leadership roles between an artistic director and a business administrator. Others now routinely hire a Chief Operating Officer (COO), taking another model from the business sector. The COO manages the day-to-day operations while the Director focuses on fundraising and key policy issues.

The decade of the 1990s and the early twenty-first century, has been a time of great change in museums, leading them increasingly toward greater self-sufficiency as business enterprises. The museum director in this changed environment now needs to demonstrate a breadth of leadership skills, not unlike those found in the for-profit business world. Financial and marketing acuity are essential to make certain that the museum survives in a new, competitive, and global marketplace.

The curatorial positions in a museum are highly specialized. They require significant subject matter scholarship, as well as deep knowledge of issues related to the care of collections. In an art museum, for example, there may be a curator of twentieth century art, of prints and drawings, of European art, Asian art, etc. The largest of museums will have many different curators, each responsible for specific collections. It is not uncommon for a small museum, however, to have a single curator, who oversees all collection functions.

Curators, registrars, and conservators share important responsibilities for the management of collections. Curators are generally responsible for undertaking collection research and acquisition, developing object provenance, maintaining collection records, and making certain collections are properly cared for and preserved. Registrars are highly specialized members of the curatorial staff who oversee all aspects of record keeping and collection management. Conservators assess, maintain, and repair artifacts of all kinds. They are the museum's specialists in advising on and establishing the optimal conditions for collection storage.

Curators are often the primary exhibit developers. Their knowledge of subject matter and objects within a collection is the creative force behind most museum exhibitions—the primary educational vehicles that enlighten visitors with fresh information and insights related to a central theme and illustrated through objects and text. Thus, the curators are often the creative "authors" of the exhibit content.

In most museums today, however, curators do not work alone on the design and development of exhibits. Many museums routinely work in exhibit teams, groups of staff that represent the various perspectives that connect the exhibition to its audience. The exhibit team will often include members of the museum education staff, marketing staff, exhibit designers, and evaluators, each of whom brings a specific expertise to the process. Museum educators, for example, are becoming increasingly important in museums, charged with the primary responsibility of understanding how people learn in informal settings and representing the public perspective throughout the exhibit development process.

The educational role of American museums took on new importance with the 1992 report *Excellence and Equity: The Public Dimension of Museums*, published by the AAM.[3] This landmark report stressed the educational dimension of every area of a museum's practice, encouraging all museums to integrate their educational purpose in their mission statements, and to enhance their ability to reach diverse audiences with rich opportunities for lifelong learning. With this report, the role of museum educators grew dramatically in importance.

Museum educators specialize in understanding how people learn in informal settings. Their responsibilities are to ensure that exhibit design, way-finding, programs, and special activities incorporate current educational theories and optimal learning experiences. Educators may specialize in student audiences, working closely with schools, or they may focus on adult or family learning, program development or the development of teaching materials. Museum educators are expected to be deeply knowledgeable about both content and theory and should oversee their applications within the museum setting.

Other departments within museums include:

- Public information offices, responsible for marketing and public relations and frequently publications.
- Development or advancement offices, charged with the primary goal of raising funds through such activities as membership, grants writing, and fundraising campaigns.
- Facilities and grounds, maintaining all aspects of the museum site.
- Security personnel, responsible for human safety as well as disaster planning and mitigation.
- Librarian and/or archivist, organizing and maintaining scholarly materials and archival collections.
- Adjunct business personnel, such as museum shops and food service, all designed to add earned revenue to the financial mix.

In addition to the above, museums are employing greater use of technology in all of their functions. Information and technology specialists are essential to maintain technology equipment and connections and to advise and develop many new tools and learning applications. Many museums are experimenting with handheld devices, powered by wireless technology, as educational aids and visitor guides. Interactive computers, videos, and large-screen theaters also require major growth and specialty within a museum's technical staff.

Most American museums are highly professionalized. Access to professional standards is widely available through the many associations that serve museums and through numerous publications, conferences, and workshops. Since 1970, the AAM has set and promoted standards and best practices through its Accreditation Program. Museum associations, such as the American Association for State and Local History, have also developed standards that are specifically applicable to small museums, including those that are managed by small paid staff or are fully operated by volunteers. Other specialized associations, such as the Association of Zoos and Aquariums offer their own, more highly focused, accreditation programs. These programs reflect the changes over the years in traditional museum practices, expanding to embrace evolving roles and issues in collecting, educating, and serving the public. They include an emphasis on museum ethics and address such emerging issues as collections related to Nazi-era provenance and Native American repatriation.

The AAM is the overarching professional association serving the nation's museums. However, a number of affiliate organizations, who work collaboratively with AAM in professional deliberations, exist to meet the specialized needs of the diverse museum types. These affiliates include:

- American Association of Museum Volunteers.
- American Association for State and Local History.
- American Federation of the Arts.
- The American Institute for Conservation of Historic and Artistic Works.
- American Public Gardens Association.
- American Zoo and Aquarium Association.
- Association for Living History, Farm, and Agricultural Museums.
- Association of African American Museums.
- Association of Art Museum Directors.
- Association of Children's Museums.
- Association of College and University Museums and Galleries.
- Association of Railway Museums, Inc.
- Association of Science Museum Directors.
- Association of Science-Technology Centers Incorporated.
- College Art Association.
- Council for Museum Anthropology.
- Council of American Jewish Museums.

- International Association of Museum Facility Administrators.
- International Museum Theatre Alliance.
- Museum Computer Network.
- Museum Store Association.
- Museum Trustee Association.
- National Science Collections Alliance.

In addition to these associations, museums are also served by six regional associations and a number of professional interest committees.

Museums also have representation at the federal government level. The IMLS, established by the Museum and Library Services Act of 1996 and its subsequent reauthorization, is the federal agency with primary responsibility for government funding in support of both museums and libraries. The Act authorizes the agency to undertake the following leadership roles:

- To encourage and support museums in carrying out their public service roles of connecting the whole of society to cultural, artistic, historic, natural, and scientific understandings that constitute our heritage.
- To encourage and support museums in carrying out their educational role, as core providers of learning and in conjunction with schools, families, and communities.
- To encourage leadership, innovation, and applications of the most current technologies and practices to enhance museum services.
- To assist, encourage, and support museums in carrying out their stewardship responsibilities to achieve the highest standards in conservation and care of the cultural, historic, natural, and scientific heritage of the United States to benefit future generations.
- To assist, encourage, and support museums in achieving the highest standards of management and service to the public, and to ease the financial burden borne by museums as a result of their increasing use by the public.
- To support resource sharing and partnerships among museums, libraries, schools, and other community organizations.[7]

Each year, Congress and the Executive Office determine the amount of support allocated to these purposes within the federal budget. In 2007, the support for museums was approximately $32 million.

Additional grant support for museum programs and services may also come through the National Science Foundation, the National Endowment for the Arts, the National Endowment for the Humanities, and the National Institutes for Health. Occasional funding is sometimes related to special initiatives of other federal agencies as well.

STEWARDSHIP OF COLLECTIONS

The core activities of most museums are found within their mission statements and are generally identified as collecting, preserving, researching, exhibiting, and interpreting. Each activity is undertaken as part of the public trust, which assigns the care and conservation of collections to the museum in return for learning more about these collections and their role and relationship to the human experience.

Collections are at the core of the museum experience and are often cited as what differentiates the museum experience from other similar experiences. Museums offer the opportunity to learn from authentic objects. Museum collections have had many sources. They may have been amassed by a private collector, by such an institution as the Catholic Church and its leadership, through the spoils of war, by a civic enterprise seeking to preserve its history, a university, a scientific expedition, or perhaps an informal association bound to a common preservation goal. Many large urban museums set on a course of assembling great collections as a source of civic pride. Many small institutions exist to share the quirky interests of a single, dedicated collector. Scientific and natural history collections have often been acquired by subject specialists interested in studying specific species or scientific phenomenon. Whatever the source, collections become a centerpiece of museum activity and require significant care and organization.

Frequently, as much as 80–90% of a museum's collection is not on public view at any given time. Stored collections must be carefully housed in conditions that provide appropriate temperature and humidity controls. Further, they must be kept safe from pest damage or other environmental factors that can erode their physical integrity and must be kept secure from theft. They must be protected from light as well, and often kept in mini environments designed specifically to preserve their unique materials and constructions. Providing such a safe environment and proper care is a fundamental responsibility of all museums. It is, however, very expensive and often requires highly skilled personnel.

The best of museums do provide such adequate care, but a recent survey undertaken by Heritage Preservation and funded by the IMLS, found extensive risk to the nation's collections, largely the result of inadequate funding. The report, known as the Heritage Health Index,[8] states that over 4.8 billion artifacts are held in trust by more than 30,000 archives, historical societies, libraries, museums, scientific research collections, and archaeological repositories across the United States. Among the artifacts described as at risk are 4.7 million works of art; 13.5 million historic artifacts, such as flags, quilts, pottery, and Presidential memorabilia; 153 million photographs; 189 million natural science specimens, and as many as 270 million rare and unique books, periodicals, and scrapbooks. Clearly, the care of collections, considered an essential responsibility of all of those institutions charged with preserving our heritage, is a massive undertaking.

Environmental controls, security, and disaster planning are needed to preserve collections, Also necessary, and frequently part of the museum's activities, are conservation practices that can repair and stabilize collections. The conservation of the enormous American flag at the National Museum of American History of the Smithsonian Institution drew national attention to the art of conservation. Conservation practices are always critical following such natural disasters as the Hurricane Katrina and many lesser but highly damaging events such as fires, floods, leaks, and insect damage. These efforts are a much underfunded aspect of many museums' essential work.

The acquisition and disposal of collections is generally governed by a Trustee-approved collections' plan that adheres to profession-wide policies. Deaccessioning policies, governing the sale of collections, have become increasingly controversial. Most museum associations have policies requiring that proceeds from such sales be used solely to support future acquisitions or serious conservation needs. Recently, some museums have challenged these restrictions, citing the need to use deaccessioning revenue to relieve severe financial stress. The topic is under review by several associations.

CURRENT TRENDS IN MUSEUMS

The late 1990s and early twenty-first century may be described as an era of accountability, particularly among government agencies and the foundation world. The focus on the tools of accountability, such as benchmarks, standards, and performance indicators, has had a profound impact on the nation's nonprofit organizations. The new and sweeping interest in quantitative and qualitative measures of success are leading to a new discipline within museum practice, that of audience research and evaluation.

The tightening of funding at all levels, including government sources and private foundations, has increased the scrutiny over the uses and impacts of such funding. Reporting requirements have changed. Emphasis has shifted from a reporting of project "outputs"—such as, the number of people served, lists of programs and events, descriptions of exhibits, types of activities—to "outcomes"—evidence of how these activities have benefited audiences and communities.

In 1993, the Government Performance and Results Act[9] required that all federal funding agencies begin to gather objective evidence of the public good accomplished through such funding. Similar patterns and interest are now common among private foundations that support the work of nonprofit institutions of all kinds. Museums

and other cultural institutions have had to create and apply new measurements to their work, to capture both the quantitative and the qualitative impact of their programs and exhibits. Research and evaluation in museums is now receiving strong interest, both to meet the needs of these funding sources, as well as to provide essential feedback to museum practitioners.

The increased interest in obtaining evidence of impact is presently leading to consistent use of such techniques as audience surveys, focus groups, online questionnaires, and on-site interviews. Museums are hiring consultants and new staff to conduct evaluations of exhibits and programs at all stages of development, testing concepts before they are fully developed, trying out new exhibit models, and undertaking extensive summative evaluations to learn from each experience. The audience voice has never been so keenly sought in the history of American museums.

The accountability standards are just one aspect of a current museum trend to look toward the for-profit world for business models. Just as museum directors are frequently coming from the business world, boards of directors are exploring how new management techniques might apply to the operation of museums. The early years of this new century are filled with apprehension about the fiscal stability of many not-for-profit institutions, including museums. This concern emerges from changes in philanthropy and ongoing debates about the role of government in funding America's cultural organizations. Museums in most European countries, and indeed in many nations, enjoy much stronger, centralized support for their museums. The history of this country, however, and its support of entrepreneurship and private enterprise have created a much different model. America's museums are deeply engaged at this time in considering how best to achieve sustainability into the future. As in the past, much of the support for these institutions comes from individuals in the private sector. Competition for such dollars runs high, and museum boards and administration continue to explore new models consistent with the social and economic changes around them.

One such exploration has been in building closer and more direct relationships between museums and their publics. The enhanced role of audience feedback noted in the trend toward audience evaluation and research is also a significant factor in creating active communication between museums and their publics. The expectation that museums will serve broad public needs continues to expand. The last three decades have witnessed a growing trend for museums to shift their primary activity from the internal functions of collections care and exhibit development to an external interest in putting museum assets to work for the public good.

The image of a museum as a center for debate and discussion, controversy and convening is quite a different image from the museum as a treasure house of beautiful objects. However, the contemporary world of museums and museum associations is advocating for a stronger public role for their institutions. The enormous collections of museums have the capacity to connect to current public issues in numerous ways. Children's museums, seen as trusted environments for young children and their parents, are using their popularity to address issues of concern to American families. Science museums are exploring such critical issues as global warming and other assaults on the environment, using the visual impact of their collections and trust in their scholarship to encourage their visitors to take action. Zoos and aquariums have long understood the public's affection for animals, dolphins, whales, and many kinds of living creatures. This understanding allows these institutions to use this positive response as a springboard to lessons in conservation. History museums, likewise, recognize the opportunity to present historic events that strongly echo current issues to enable visitors to link the lessons of the past to contemporary concerns.

Other forms of creating social value are also more commonplace in today's museums. In recent years many science-based institutions have created programs for underserved audiences. Science museums, for example, seeking to overcome gender bias have added numerous programs to attract girls to careers in science. Youth and teens have been given new voice in museum settings through programs focusing on building self esteem and social skills. Museums of all disciplines have showcased the achievements of diverse nationalities and races, serving as a catalyst for tolerance and cultural understanding. Following the events of September 11, 2001, for example, museums mounted exhibitions on Islamic art, science, and religion to present a more enlightened view of Islamic culture than what many Americans held. The rise of ethnically specific museums, such as African American and Native American museums, reflects the need to hear the silent voices of the nation's past and celebrate the contributions of these societies and groups to American life. Recent years have witnessed the development of gay–lesbian–transsexual museums as well, also noting the degree to which American museums reflect and respond to current social concerns. Following challenges to the teaching of evolution, for example, some religious groups developed biblical museums to provide alternative points of view.

The dynamic history and development of America's museums, their breadth of collections and scholarly expertise, their educational impact and their deeper integration into the nation's communities are all challenging old images of stuffiness or pretension or exclusivity. These institutions are evolving with society and the idea of the American museum as a public forum is clearly a growing phenomenon.

REFERENCES

1. http://www.aam-us.org/aboutmuseums/abc.cfh#how-many.
2. http://www.aam-us.org/museumresources/ethics/coe.cfm.
3. American Association of Museums, *Excellence and Equity: Education and the Public Dimension of Museums*, American Association of Museums: Washington, DC, 1992.
4. http://www.imls.gov/gov/about/20usc.shtm.
5. http://www.aam-us.org/aboutmuseums/abc.cfm#how-many.
6. Institute of Museum and Library Services, *True Needs/True Partners: Museums Serving Schools, Survey Highlights*, Institute of Museum and Library Services: Washington, DC, 1998.
7. http://www.imls.gov/about/aboutshtm.
8. http://www.heritagehealthindex.org.
9. http://www.whitehouse.gov/omb/mgmt-gpra/gplaw2m.htm/.

Universal Decimal Classification (UDC)

I. C. McIlwaine
University College London, School of Library, Archive and Information Studies, London, U.K.

Abstract

This entry outlines the history, application, and nature of the Universal Decimal Classification (UDC). It explains its structure, management, revision, and the many changes that have taken place since the Task Force for UDC Development reported in 1990, and the UDC Consortium was formed. This led to the creation of the machine-readable database, or Master Reference File (MRF), consisting of some 66,000 terms, which forms the basis of all published editions and is revised and updated annually. Revision procedures and applications in an online environment are noted and the potential for future development discussed.

INTRODUCTION

The Universal Decimal Classification (UDC) is one of the major general classification schemes available for the organization of information. In many ways, it was the forerunner of later developments since, although it is based on the Dewey Decimal Classification (DDC), from the outset it included a number of auxiliary tables for the expression of recurring concepts, such as forms, languages, places, dates, the majority of which were not incorporated into the DDC parent scheme until well into the twentieth century. It is translated into a number of different languages, issued in a range of sizes and formats and now is controlled at the UDC headquarters in The Hague. An outline of the history, content, application, and potential together with the management that controls it is provided below.

HISTORY

The UDC has its origins in the project conceived by two Belgian lawyers, Paul Otlet and Henri La Fontaine at the end of the nineteenth century. They embarked on an ambitious enterprise to create a comprehensive listing of everything that had been written since the invention of printing, a *Répertoire bibliographique universel*. They decided to organize this information systematically in a vast card index and therefore sought an appropriate method for the arrangement. They were attracted to Dewey's *Decimal Classification* which, in 1895, had recently reached its fifth edition, so they entered into an agreement with Dewey to use his classification, with certain clearly defined modifications and expansions. At that time the scheme had only a few thousand subdivisions but its notation had great potential for universal usage because of the wider application of Arabic numerals than any other notational system. Otlet and La Fontaine expanded Dewey's scheme to suit their requirements and added a number of synthetic devices and

auxiliary tables which in due course turned the enumerative structure of the original into the much more flexible and detailed *Universal Decimal Classification*. The first edition of this expansion was published between 1905 and 1907 as *Manuel du Répertoire bibliographique universel*.[1] It consisted of some 33,000 subdivisions and had an index of ca. 38,000 entries.

It became widely used in Europe in a range of different libraries, but World War I and the resultant shortage of funds led to the abandonment of the major bibliographical endeavor. The classification, however, survived and a much expanded second edition in French, now entitled *Classification décimale universelle*[2] was published in four volumes between 1927 and 1934. This second edition, together with later expansions and additions was used as the basis of all future editions for many years. Work began on editions in German and in English in the early 1930s, but again war interrupted work and the German edition was not completed until 1953[3] and the full English edition was never completed.

The originators set up an organization to take responsibility for their work and to publish the accompanying classification, the Institut International de Bibliographie (IIB) also known as the Brussels Institute, after its original location. In 1931 the organization's name was changed to the International Institute of Documentation (IID) and as the result of increasing Dutch influence, largely emanating from Frits Donker Duyvis who had been an active participant in work on the scheme throughout the 1920s, its headquarters was moved to Deventer in the Netherlands and in 1937 it was moved once again to The Hague and its name was changed yet again, to the Féderation Internationale de Documentation (FID). Donker Duyvis's control of the scheme became absolute after the outbreak of World War II, and the deaths of La Fontaine in 1943 and of Otlet in 1944.[4]

Editions of varying fullness have been published throughout the whole history of the scheme and by the

Encyclopedia of Library and Information Sciences, Fourth Edition DOI: 10.1081/E-ELIS4-120043532

United States– User-Centered Design

1980s it had been published in many languages and formats. The full edition consisted of over 200,000 classes at this date and it was supported by the worldwide network of FID's membership which consisted of around 100 countries. It has been calculated that it is used in approximately 111 countries[5] and is available in some 38 different languages. It is frequently thought that its use is principally by specialized and in particular scientific and technical institutions. This is certainly true in the English-speaking world, and to a certain extent in Russia and the former members of the Soviet Union where its use was obligatory in such institutions. But it is widely used in libraries of all types in Spanish-speaking countries, in Portugal, and in many countries of Eastern Europe, ranging from children's libraries to large public and university libraries.

Historically, it was developed to three different levels, the full edition, medium editions (which became particularly popular from the 1970s onwards, thanks partly to the impetus from a three-language edition in French, German, and English envisaged as part of the celebrations for the centenary of Dewey's *Decimal Classification* in 1976) and abridged editions. It was also published in "special subject editions," with the major discipline(s) given the full expansion while other parts of the scheme which were the "fringe topics" to the principal interest but were needed for the organization of a specialist collection were outlined in an abbreviated form. Such editions include the *ABC Abridged Building Classification*[6] and the *Universal Decimal Classification for Polar Libraries*.[7] The most up-to-date such version is the *Global Forest Decimal Classification*[8] which in 2006 is being revised and converted into an online version.[9]

For many years, until the 1990s, the maintenance of the classification was undertaken in The Hague by the editor. This was originally under the supervision of Donker Duyvis and latterly in the charge of Geoffrey Lloyd and his staff together with the Secretary General of FID and a Central Classification Committee. This Committee was made up of representatives of the various language editions of the classification, together with representatives from the national committees responsible locally for the scheme. All changes had to be approved by this body and were circulated for approval prior to implementation. There was also at that time what was known as a "starvation policy" whereby no number could be reused with a different meaning for a period of 10 years. This revision method was an extremely slow and time-consuming exercise, especially the requirement to gain the approval of all the national committees prior to implementation. By the end of the 1980s FID found it was no longer in a position to maintain the classification at the level of development achieved in the past and that it was becoming both too expensive and too outdated in parts to be a manageable undertaking for the organization.[10] It set up an international Task Force to investigate the viability of the classification and to recommend a policy for the future.[11]

This body reported in 1990 and recommended among other improvements, the setting up of a Consortium of publishers to manage the classification and the creation of a machine-readable Master File of a maintainable size, approximately the size of that which had previously been known as a Medium Edition (ca. 60,000 + entries). This Consortium is known as the UDC Consortium (UDCC) and is managed by an Executive Committee, together with an Editor-in-chief and an Editorial Board, set up in 1994, who take care of the development of the classification. The "ten-year starvation rule" was also abolished at this time, permitting greater flexibility and the ability to incorporate new expansions and revisions in their logical place more speedily. The headquarters remain in the Koninklijke Bibliotheek in The Hague, and until its demise in 2000 FID was a member of the Consortium. Other members are the publishers of major language editions, such as English, French, Spanish, and Russian. Editions in other languages are produced by national publishers under license in a variety of formats and sizes. The office in The Hague is managed by the UDC Director who is responsible for issuing licenses, organizing subscriptions, and the day-to-day running of the business.

The machine-readable master file, known as the Master Reference File (MRF) is maintained in The Hague and is updated annually on January 1st, after the publication of the annual *Extensions and corrections to the UDC* in the preceding November. The original version of the Master File was based on the English Medium Edition of the Classification (BS 1000M: 1985) together with subsequent revisions and amendments up to 1992 as that material was already available in a machine-readable format. Most editions of the classification published since 1992 are the size of the MRF, approximately 66,000 entries in "standard" editions, or smaller editions, some as abbreviated as 4000 entries. It is issued in a range of different formats such as on CD-ROM or online as in the British Standards Institution's UDC Online, as well as in hard copy. The MRF is the authorized text and any developments that exceed its content are not authorized by the UDCC. The MRF exists in English only, but there is scope for expansion to include a range of other languages and proposals for a multilingual edition have been made. There are editions in French, Spanish, and Czech of similar size to the English master text which could form the basis of such an undertaking, but many published editions of the scheme are based on different stages of development and revision depending on the year when the translation began, and this creates obvious editorial problems for coordination.

STRUCTURE OF THE CLASSIFICATION

The outline of the main classes corresponds broadly to its parent, with the exception of class 4 which was vacated in the 1960s and has not been used since that date. But unlike the original, there is no three figure base and each number is treated as if it were a decimal:

0	Generalities (including computer science, management)
1	Philosophy. Psychology
2	Religion. Theology
3	Social sciences (including gender studies, demography, sociology, politics, economics, law, public administration, and education)
4	Vacant
5	Mathematics and natural sciences (including environmental studies)
6	Applied sciences (including biotechnology, medicine, agriculture, transport, and technologies)
7	Fine arts. Applied arts. Entertainment. Games. Sport
8	Language. Linguistics. Literature (including philology)
9	Archaeology. Geography. Biography. History

NOTATION

In addition to its prime function of mechanizing the order, the UDC notation aims at expressiveness. Frequently the addition of a digit symbolizes a subdivision on a hierarchical basis:

597/599	Vertebrata
599	Mammalia. Mammals
599.8	Primates
599.88	Hylobatidae and Pongidae. Anthropoid apes
599.883	Pongidae
599.883.1	Orang utan
599.883.4	Chimpanzees
599.883.6	Gorilla

The notation makes two distinct uses of the numerals that are available; firstly, they are used as main numbers 1–9, expanded as required, and secondly as auxiliary numbers. The latter are numbers added to the main numbers to express additional facets of a subject, such as physical forms, geographic areas, chronological subdivisions, commonly recurring properties, etc., each with a distinct facet indicator.

Each digit should be regarded as a decimal fraction, less than unity. For ease of reading a point, which has no mathematical significance, is introduced and a long number broken up, normally after every third digit:

6	Applied sciences
62	Engineering
622	Mining
622.2	Mining operations
622.23	Excavation
622.233	Drilling for blasting
622.233.4	Hammer drills and drilling

AUXILIARY TABLES

The auxiliary tables are of two kinds, common auxiliaries which express generally recurrent characteristics and special auxiliaries which denote locally recurrent characteristics. The common auxiliary subdivisions consist of numeric tables together with certain linking symbols used to join any concept in the main tables to any other. Each table has a distinctive piece of notation:

1a	Co-ordination. Extension	
	+, /	
1b	Relation. Subgrouping. Order fixing	
	:, [...], ::	
1c	Language	
	= ...	
1d	Form	
	(0/09)	
1e	Place	
	(1/9)	
1f	Race, ethnic grouping and nationality	
	(=...)	
1g	Time	
	"..."	
1h	Subject specification by notations from non-UDC sources, e.g., A/Z	
1k	General characteristics	
	-02 Properties	
	-03 Materials	
	-04 Relations, Processes, and Operations	
	-05 Persons	

In addition to these commonly applicable auxiliaries constantly recurring concepts within a limited subject field may be expressed by the use of special auxiliaries. Unlike the common auxiliaries the same notation may be used with a different meaning in the special auxiliaries occurring in different parts of the main tables. Three kinds of notation are used in special auxiliary tables: the hyphen series -1/-9 [but not -0 which is used for the common auxiliaries of general characteristics (Table 1k)] employed principally for an analytical or differentiative function, e.g., 82-1/-9 to denote literary form, etc.; the point-nought series, covering aspect studies, specialized activities, and operations, etc., e.g., in class 7 to denote styles and specialized principles, techniques, etc. in the Arts; and the apostrophe series which are usually more specific and are often synthetic in function, e.g., in 547—Organic Chemistry for chemical compounds.

Special auxiliaries may be used both to amplify the common auxiliaries, e.g., in the Area Table (1e) to express such concepts as the points of the compass:

(1-11)	East. Eastern
(4-11)	Eastern Europe
(44-11)	Eastern France
(443.61-11)	Eastern Paris

and to express particular concepts recurring throughout a single discipline or group of disciplines

7.079	Arts festivals
791.65.079	Film festivals
82:7.079	Literature festivals

Full details of the content and application of the main tables and the auxiliaries are set out in the introduction to the classification and in *The Universal Decimal Classification: A Guide to its Use* published by the UDCC.[12]

THEORETICAL BASIS

Unlike its contemporaries at the end of the nineteenth century, the UDC incorporated a number of devices to make it more flexible and better to provide for the detailed specification essential for the bibliographic undertaking for which it was originally planned. It was the first truly analytico-synthetic classification, enabling any one concept to be linked notationally to another. In this way it foreshadowed the fully faceted schemes developed originally by Ranganathan some 35 years later, and followed especially by the Classification Research Group in the United Kingdom for the development of special classifications and indexing systems such as PRECIS in the years following World War II. It permits synthesis in several ways. Classes that have been developed or revised since the 1980s are all fully faceted. Examples include Class 2—Religion, Class 8—Literature and Language, and Class 93/94—History. This is implemented through the use of the colon and the other connecting symbols outlined above to join together two or more concepts. This facility makes it possible to express compound topics and to develop the classification to accommodate new topics which frequently have their roots in previously existing disciplines. Classes that have been developed by means of this device include 502/504—Environmental Science and 60—Biotechnology, where much of the detail is gained through the use of the colon, e.g.:

502.3.272:531.62	Energy conservation
502.3:551.510.534:502.12	Ozone layer depletion
602.6:599.323MUS	Creation of transgenetic mice
602.643:54-126	Polymers as vectors
602.72:612.646:602.9	Cloning of human embryos for stem cell research

The array of common auxiliaries also makes for considerable flexibility, as does the facility for intercalation of those which have a clearly marked beginning and end, such as the notations in Tables 1e and 1f for Area and Time, respectively. Intercalation provides the means of changing the citation order to suit individual needs. Class 34—Law provides an example of this, where the main schedule for Law is divided first by legal topic, but it may be found more convenient to have an arrangement of Legal system—legal subject, e.g.:

347(410.5).23 Scotland—Property law

rather than

347.23(410.5) Property law—Scotland

This flexibility has been greatly enhanced by the development of Table 1k, especially the concepts listed at -02—Common auxiliaries of Properties and -04—Common auxiliaries of Relations, Processes, and Operations.

All revisions which have taken place since the 1980s have been fully faceted and have a notation that reflects the hierarchical position of each concept, to aid machine-searching, so that it is possible to search up and down a hierarchy by truncating or extending the notation. Class 2—Religion provides an excellent example of this approach. This classification was introduced in 2000 and is the first attempt by a general scheme of classification to present an unbiased approach to the discipline.[13] The class is arranged so that each religion is listed and accompanied by a series of auxiliary tables enabling the enumeration of appropriate concepts. The classification therefore provides a listing of faiths and the notation used for listing those faiths is simply an ordering device, and in no way implies any subordination of one to another, because of the problem of enumerating so large a number. The religions are arranged according to their historical origin, beginning with prehistoric and primitive religions. The "big five" faiths, Hinduism, Buddhism, Judaism, Christianity, and Islam are all allocated a two-digit number, the remainder in some cases have longer notations. Moving on from the enumeration of the various faiths and religions, the principal facets (in inverted order, following the principle adopted in all recent revisions) are as follows:

Religion	
(Theory and philosophy)	Religious concepts and ideas
(Evidences of religion)	Sacred books. Scriptures
(Agents)	Persons in the subject
(Operations)	Social and ritual practice and observance
(Processes)	Development, decline, interfaith relations
(Parts)	Religious organizations, associations, orders, sects, and movements
(Kinds)	Religions by various characteristics e.g., Orthodox, Liberal, monotheistic
(Entities, Systems)	Specific religions and faiths

CITATION ORDER

There is no official introduction to UDC editions and the many editions of the classification usually include their own introductions, frequently copied (with or without permission) from other editions. Instructions on usage appear in the various guides issued in a range of languages, the most recent being translations of *The UDC: A Guide to its Use*[14] but notable for its clarity and authority is Jack Mills' Guide of 1963 authorized by the British Standards Institution (BS1000C: 1963).[15] A fixed, obligatory citation order raises problems with so flexible and adaptable a classification. International exchange of bibliographic information requires a standard order but this can conflict with maximum expressiveness and the flexibility of the scheme appeals to many of its users who can adapt it to suit their own circumstances. Nowhere is there laid down a standard, compulsory order, but the MRF provides instructions on citation order in a number of places, particularly in the instructions for the application of the Common Auxiliaries, especially those in Table 1k the Common Auxiliaries of Properties, Materials, Relations, Processes and Operations, and Persons which may not be used independently or cited first in a compound notation. The current MRF is far from uniform in its recommendations in this matter but the default citation order, which follows the principle of inversion, works well in the majority of cases where there is no specialist requirement. As at present constituted, it would be exceedingly difficult to impose a rigid citation order and it is most unlikely that it would be followed by users who are accustomed to adapting the classification to their specialized requirements.[16]

FILING ORDER

Unlike citation order, which depends to a certain extent upon the needs of individual circumstances, a fixed filing order is laid down for the arrangement of the various codes which represent concepts in the UDC. There is a fixed order for the filing of the various symbols so that a user should be able to anticipate the arrangement when consulting a UDC file.

The filing order in the UDC is based on the principle of proceeding from the general to the particular and is demonstrated below:

Symbol		Example
Independent auxiliaries		
=	=112.2	German language (i.e., documents in German)
(0...)	(0.035.22)	Microfilmed documents
(1/9)	(430)	Germany
(=...)	(=1.410)	British nationals
"..."	"19"	Twentieth century
+	622.341.1+669.1	Iron-ore mining and ferrous metallurgy

/	622.341.1/.2	Mining of iron ores and manganese ores
Simple number		
	622.341.1	Iron-ore mining
Auxiliaries as suffixes		
:	622.341.1:338.124.4	Economic crises in iron-ore mining (*may be reversed* to form 338.124.4:622.341.1)
::	622.341.1::338.124.4	Economic crises in iron-ore mining (*may not be reversed*)
=	622.341.1=112.2	Documents in German about iron-ore mining
(0...)	622.341.1(0.035.22)	Microfilmed documents about iron-ore mining
(1/9)	622.341.1(430)	Iron-ore mining in Germany
(=...)	622.341.1(=411.21)	Iron-ore mining amongst Arabs
"..."	622.341.1"19"	Iron-ore mining in the twentieth century
*	622.341.1*Fe2O3	Mining of red haematite (Fe^2O^3)
A/Z	622.341.1GOE	Named iron ores: Goethite
-0	622.341.1-057.2	Manual workers in iron-ore mining
-1/-9	622.341.1-78	Protective devices and measures in iron-ore mining
.0	622.341.1.03	Geological character of iron-ore deposits
'	622.341.1'17	Wastes, residues from iron-ore mining
Next simple number		
622.341.11		Mining magnetite–haematite ores

The filing order, by and large, follows the principles implicit in the standard citation order whereby within any given class mark subject concepts precede forms and place and time come last in the subject sequence. The use of the colon, however, may result in a more specific concept filing ahead of a general one, for example:

622.341.1:338.124.4   Economic crises in iron-oremining

is much more specific than

622.341.1(0.035.22)   Microfilmed documents about iron-ore mining

MAIN CLASSES

Although in broad outline, the classification resembles the DDC, there are many places where the two schemes diverge in detail. This is particularly true in classes 5 and 6 where different standard classifications for the sciences have been followed. In the future, the detail of these classes may be altered to use the currently vacant class 4 to extend such disciplines as Medicine and its related sciences of Psychology, Biochemistry, etc. Class 0 has also been developed to incorporate Computer Science at 004 and Management at 005, since both are seen as being generally applicable. Both classes are fully faceted and contain concepts that will be needed throughout the classification, e.g.:

004.78:336.717	Online computing systems for banking transactions
005.521:330.133.1	Value analysis
005.912:656.874	Use of courier services

One development in 2006 which is noteworthy is collaboration of the UDC with its parent scheme. The DDC has been investigating the possibilities of adapting the new classification of class 2 for the creation of a less biased approach to religion. A project has been undertaken to map the UDC scheme onto the Dewey Class 200 and to convert the classification into a Dewey-like notation in order to improve the unbiased approach that Dewey has been attempting to achieve in recent editions. A pilot study mapping UDC 24—Buddhism to Dewey's 194 class has been conducted and the conclusion has been reached that the more profitable approach is to use the UDC base with a revised DDC notation. Because the UDC is a fully faceted schedule and DDC's auxiliaries differ considerably from those of UDC, mappings will be developed at the facet level for topics within the Religion schedule of both schemes. UDC has more detail than DDC and it is not intended to expand DDC to the same level of detail. The revised schedule for DDC is intended to be issued as an alternative in the first instance.[17]

AUTOMATION AND THE UDC

The UDC was one of the earliest of the general schemes to be explored for its possibilities for mechanized retrieval. M. Rigby[18] prepared a report in 1981 and subsequent research has resulted in the scheme's application in a number of automated systems ranging from KWIC (Key Word in Context) indexes to the computerization of classified catalogs. The classification is particularly suited to machine searching. Its hierarchical structure facilitates searching up and down for more specific or more general concepts. The meaning of a number remains constant and therefore it is easy to retrieve concepts that have been expressed precoordinately in a postcoordinate manner.

A long-standing problem with the scheme has been the use of the colon to express relationships of all kinds, without distinction. Perrault,[19] as long ago as 1968, published a "schema" of relators to clarify the ambiguities inherent in the use of the colon. This was a lengthy

schedule with an alphabetical notation identifying a large number of different types of relationship. It was circulated by FID in the previous year but was not received with much enthusiasm and was never incorporated into the structure of the classification. Another proposal along similar lines was made by Caless as the result of work at the VELA Seismic Information Analysis Center of the University of Michigan.[20] This also, was never incorporated into the scheme. However, the introduction of Table 1k-04—Table of Common Relations, Processes, and Operations in 2003 has resulted in the ability to express 11 different phase relations, such as bias phase, association, dependence, complementarity, etc., thereby greatly improving expressiveness and addressing the problems identified half a century previously.

One of the earliest projects with machine-retrieval was Automatic Direct Access to information with Online UDC System (AUDACIOUS) undertaken by Freeman and Atherton in 1967–1968 at the American Institute of Physics.[21] This was a command-driven, interactive system which used the nuclear science sections of the UDC schedules with English descriptions. It provided remote direct access to files containing 2330 items from Nuclear Science Abstracts which were indexed by UDC and was part of a larger project which provided machine-readable files of UDC, automatic typesetting, composition of UDC schedules, and a statistical evaluation of the classification as a retrieval tool. The resultant conclusions had considerable influence on future applications. Throughout the late 1960s and early 1970s a series of conferences was held to examine the possibilities of the UDC as a retrieval tool.[22–24] The impetus faded, however, with the financial problems of FID during the 1980s and it was not until a decade later that much interest was demonstrated in the use of UDC in a networked environment. Buxton[25] in 1990 examined the feasibility of using the scheme in these circumstances, drawing attention to examples of automated usage and also highlighting the shortcomings of the scheme for such application, such as the tendency to repeat the same concept in different parts of the schedule, due to the dependence of the classification on "aspect." This is a problem that recent revisions have taken note of and continue to address and correct. There are many concepts scattered throughout the schedules, as in the following example of "alcohol":

Practical laboratory chemistry	542.423	Heating by alcohol
Analytical chemistry	543.632.532	Hydroxyl groups, free alcohols
Organic chemistry	547.26	Saturated monohydric alcohols
Medicine	613.81	Alcoholic drinks
Engineering	62-631.4	Alcohol
Chemical technology	661.72	Alcohols and their derivatives
Industry	678.744.7	Polyvinyl alcohol

There are, however, bonuses to this apparent scattering, as if one wishes to contextualize a search and focus on browsing to improve precision, the aspect element of the classification is a considerable advantage, since it is possible, for example, to retrieve everything concerning medical aspects of alcohol and exclude all other contexts by simply using the 613.81 notation rather than searching on words. Recall is improved further in systems where it is possible to use words in combination with UDC numbers.

The advent of the Online Public Access Catalog (OPAC) presented opportunities for exploiting the facility for searching, browsing, and displaying classification data that the UDC offers, and which traditional classified catalogs had used to advantage for decades. By and large, this feature of the classification has not been realized. Where its potential has been implemented in an OPAC it is by libraries which purchased specially designed systems such as ETHICS at the Eidgenössischen Hochschule in Zurich[26] and the MUSCAT system used by the Scott Polar Library in Cambridge (U.K.).[27] For the UDC to be effectively applied in an OPAC it is essential to have an automated classification schedule, an authority file for the classification, and an interface which permits the display and browsing of hierarchies and provide both simple and postcoordinate search facilities that use both classmarks and natural language.

The use of classification on the Internet has resulted in a number of research projects such as DESIRE, NORDIC, SCORPION, and CORC, and these have demonstrated that classification can play a significant role in improving searchability. The full potential of library classification in general and of UDC in particular has yet to be realized. The classification is, however, used to provide quality information via certain services which attempt to create directories by analyzing and classifying resources intellectually and employ programs for the automatic harvesting and classification of resources. Automatic classification of Internet resources becomes all the more urgent as their growth makes any manual classification unmanageable. Services classified by UDC include SOSIG and NISS. SOSIG—Social Science Information Gateway (http:// sosig.ac.uk) has over 50,000 social sciences Web pages stored in the database which is regularly updated. In 2006 it incorporated Law and was relaunched as INTUTE (http:// www.ukcle.ac.uk/directions/previous/issue4/sosig.html). NISS—National Information on Software and Services) Information Gateway (http://niss.ac.uk) is a U.K. national information service for the education community which is part of HERO (Higher Education and Research Opportunities in the United Kingdom) (http://www.hero.ac.uk). Both services are based on very broad headings from UDC and on out-of-date versions of the scheme, though they may incorporate more recent amendments. This cannot be discerned as they do not display the UDC structure on the interface or UDC numbers in the metadata.[28]

Automatic classification using UDC should ideally make provision for creating both simple and compound numbers, using vocabulary built up in an authority file. A more rigorous approach to defining the content of Web documents has been detected in Web sites which integrate UDC into their operation.[29] The synthetic approach of UDC means that concepts are expressed by a notation that is built up during the process of classification, rather than appearing readymade in the schedules. Hence the necessity for an authority list which must be accompanied by an index to the scheme enhanced by natural language terms that may occur in a full-text database. This is not an easy task to create, and the majority of existing automatic classification systems tend to extract terms from the schedules and to limit their selection to simple numbers. Examples of services which have experimented with automatic classification include WWW Subject Tree of WAIS (Wide Area Information Server) Databases. This gateway is part of the Nordic WAIS/World Wide Web Project (http:// www.ub2.lu.se/autpo_new/UDC.html).[30]

Another project using UDC for automatic classification was GERHARD (German Harvest automated Retrieval and Directory (http://www.gerhard.de/) which was focused on the classifying and indexing of German Web pages. It integrated both searching and browsing facilities. The researchers used a trilingual version of UDC comprising 60,000 entries, and 15 different relations are possible. Each entry includes a UDC notation and a natural language description with synonyms in German, English, and French. The objective was to convert the classification to a lexicon that mapped classification entries to the codes in the scheme. Natural language expressions of the documents were matched with the UDC entries using linguistic classification. GERHARD demonstrates the advantages of having a classification as the backbone of the retrieval system. The number of documents assigned to a given category is clear, as is the number of documents in displayed subcategories. It is easy to move through the hierarchy of categories and the system is user-friendly. Until 2006, when it ceased to be available, it was the most sophisticated application of the UDC for the purpose of Internet resource discovery.

CONCLUSION

The UDC is a classification that is widely used in the non-English speaking world, both for the traditional purpose of arranging books on shelves and for application in more sophisticated retrieval systems. It has great potential for application in a networked world since it is possible to create a system that permits searching on each separate element in a classmark and to combine words and numbers for the purposes of searching. Recent revision work has concentrated on increasing the basis of facet analysis throughout the scheme and on eliminating places where the same concept is repeated in a different context, in order to improve the structure for machine searching. The use of a sophisticated system such as this is very expensive and the full potential of UDC has yet to be realized in the modern environment.

REFERENCES

1. *Manuel du Répertoire Bibliographique Universel*; Institut International de Bibliographie: Brussels, 1907.
2. *Classification Décimale Universelle*; Institut International de Bibliographie: Brussels, 1927–1933; (FID 151).
3. *Dezimal-Klassifikation (Deutsche Gesamtausgabe)*; Beuth-Vertrieb GmbH: Berlin/Köln, 1934–1953; 3te Internationale Ausgabe; (FID 196).
4. Rayward, W.B. *The Universe of Information*; VINITI: Moscow, 1975; (FID 520).
5. Slavic, A. UDC translations: A 2004 survey report and bibliography. Ext. Corr. UDC **2004**, *26*, 58–80.
6. *ABC Abridged Building Classification for Architects, Builders, Civil Engineers 1981*; An Foras Forbartha: Dublin, 1983; (FID 596).
7. *Universal Decimal Classification for Polar Libraries*; 4th Ed.; Scott Polar Research Institute: Cambridge, 1994.
8. *Global Forest Decimal Classification (GFDC)*; IUFRO: Vienna, 2006; Bilingual English/German edition.
9. Holder, B. Updating the global forest decimal classification (GFDC). Ext. Corr. UDC **2004**, *26*, 42–43.
10. McIlwaine, I.C. The universal decimal classification: Some factors concerning its origins, development and influence. In *Historical Studies in Information Science*; Bellardo Hahn, T., Buckland, M., Eds.; Information Today: Medford, NJ, 1998; 94–106.
11. Gilchrist, A.; Strachan, D., Eds. *The UDC: Essays for a New Decade*; Aslib: London, 1990.
12. McIlwaine, I.C. *The Universal Decimal Classification: a Guide to its Use*; 2nd Ed. UDC Consortium: The Hague, 2007.
13. Broughton, V. *A New Classification for the Literature of Religion*. Available at http://www.ifla.org/IV/ifla66/papers/034-130e.htm.
14. *BS 1000C: 1963 Guide to the Universal Decimal Classification (UDC)*; BSI: London, 1963; (FID No. 345).
15. Robinson, G. Citation order in UDC. Ext. Corr. UDC **2003**, *25*, 19–27.

16. McIlwaine, I.C.; Mitchell, J.S. The New Ecumenism: Exploration of a DDC/UDC View of religion Knowledge Organization for a Global Learning Society: Proceedings of the 9th International ISKO Conference Vienna, Austria July, 4–7, 2006; Budin, G., Swertz, C., Mitgusch, K., Eds.; Ergon: Würzburg, 2006; 323–330 (Advances in Knowledge Organization, 10).
17. Rigby, M. *Automation and the UDC*; FID: The Hague, 1981; (FID 565).
18. Perrault, J.M. *Towards a Theory for UDC*; Clive Bingley: London, 1969.
19. Caless, T.W.; Kirk, D.B. An application of UDC to machine searching. J. Doc. **1967**, *23*, 208–215.
20. Freeman, R.; Atherton, P. *AUDACIOUS: An Experiment with an On-line, Interactive Retrieval System Using the Universal Decimal Classification as the Index Language in the Field of Nuclear Science*; American Institute of Physics: New York, 1968; (AIP/UDC-7).
21. Mölgaard-Hansen, R.; Rigby, M., Eds. In *Seminar on UDC in a Mechanized Retrieval System, Copenhagen, 2–6 September, 1968: Proceedings*; Danish Centre for Documentation: Copenhagen, 1969; (FID/CR report no. 9).
22. In *Seminar on UDC and Mechanized Information Systems, Frankfurt, 1–5 June 1970: Proceedings*; Mölgaard-Hansen, R., Westring-Nielsen, M., Eds.; Danish Centre for Documentation: Copenhagen, 1971; (FID/CR report no. 11).
23. *International Symposium: UDC in Relation to Other Indexing Languages, Herceg Novi, Yugoslavia, 28 June–1 July 1971: Proceedings*, Yugoslav Center for Technical and Scientific Documentation: Belgrade, 1972.
24. Buxton, A.B. Computer searching of UDC numbers. J. Doc. **1990**, *46*, 193–217 Updated version published in *Encyclopedia of Library and Information Science*; Kent, A., Lancour, H., Eds.; Marcel Dekker: New York, 1993; Vol. 51, 132–151.
25. Loth, K.; Funk, H. Subject search in ETHICS on the basis of the UDC. In *The UDC: Essays for a New Decade*; Gilchrist, A., Strachan, D., Eds.; Aslib: London, 1990; 35–46.
26. Porter, M.; Galpin, V. Relevance feedback in a public access catalogue for a research library: Muscat at the Scott Polar Institute. Program **1988**, *22*, 1–20.
27. Slavic, A. UDC in subject gateways: Experiment or opportunity?. Knowl. Organ. **2006**, *33*(2), 67–85.
28. Toth, E. Innovative solutions in automatic classification: A brief summary. Libri. **2002**, *52*, 48–53.
29. Ardö, A. Improving resource discovery and retrieval on the Internet: The NORDIC WAIS/World Wide Web Project. NORDINFO Nytt. **1994**, *17*, 13–28 Summary report.

University Archives

William J. Maher

Archives, University of Illinois at Urbana-Champaign, Urbana, Illinois, U.S.A.

Abstract

Universities, colleges, polytechnic institutes, arts academies, and other postsecondary institutions have established archival programs to hold and make accessible the documentary heritage of those institutions in order to protect individual and institutional rights and to provide a cultural context for understanding of the institution's past. University archives are managed by professional archivists following best practices of the archival field, but they are reflective of the distinctive history of the particular institution.

EMERGENCE AND DEVELOPMENT OF UNIVERSITY ARCHIVES

The post-World War II era's great expansion in higher education has supported an equally dramatic growth in the establishment and scope of university archival programs. After many years largely in the shadow of governmental archives and private historical societies, academic archives have finally come into their own, and many academic archivists have assumed leadership positions in the international community of archivists. Indeed, the archives now found in the world's universities, colleges, and other institutions of postsecondary education contain some of the most important materials for understanding culture and society. Over the same period, while historically a discipline separate from library and information science, archives have grown closer to library practices. Although manuscripts and special collections have been part of academic libraries for decades, they were often relegated to the periphery, and a typical approach was to apply item-level cataloging and subject-oriented description rather than archival methodology. During the more general broadening of librarianship's scope starting in the early 1990s, archivists in academic libraries have experienced a greater acceptance of their need for autonomy to follow archival methodology at the same time that archival approaches have shown their usefulness for expanding areas of library materials.

Advances in technology for both the control of information materials and the very materials themselves have enabled a convergence of library and archives practices for capturing, preserving, and making accessible diverse information resources. However, there are enduring characteristics of archives that differentiate archivists from librarians: 1) archival materials are treated as aggregates; 2) the materials are viewed as organic or naturally occurring as the result of administrative action rather than as synthetically and retrospectively created; and 3) their nature inherently varies greatly from institution to institution, thus making standardization difficult.[1,2]

The variety among higher education archives renders generalizations difficult because, when examined closely, any generalized picture may not fit well with the characteristics of a given archives, its parent institution, or even the overall type of educational institution to which an archives belongs. Still an overview is enormously useful as an introduction, as a way of assessing relative practices, and as groundwork for the identification of norms for future development.

DEFINITIONS

Some definitions are needed to frame the discussion of the scope, contents, and functioning of university archives. For the purpose of this entry, archives may be defined as the organized noncurrent records of an institution, organization, family, or individual deemed to have enduring value and retained for administrative or research use. The purposes of archives include accountability, preservation of heritage, and services as a laboratory for educational programs. Archives also refers to the formal program that manages records of enduring value, the physical place occupied by the program, and to the materials held in such repositories. Additionally, in common professional parlance, "archives" is used to describe a wide variety of documentary forms from institutional and private sources, whether created formally as part of a systematic records system or as the result of private collecting of material based on its subject content.[3]

Nevertheless, there is value in understanding the differences among three related categories of archival materials: traditional records created by official institutional transactions; privately generated or "personal archives;" and "manuscript collections"—materials synthetically collected and retained for their subject matter pertinence. The distinction of archives from manuscripts is a particularly relevant in regard to university archives because of the tendencies of academic libraries to focus on subject

Encyclopedia of Library and Information Sciences, Fourth Edition DOI: 10.1081/E-ELIS4-120043652

United States—
User-Centered Design

matter pertinence and item-level control even when dealing with manuscripts. Although the methodologies and resources needed for archives, private papers, and manuscript collections vary, university archival programs frequently contain all three categories, because all three often have a bearing on the fundamental university archival responsibility of providing accountability and preserving heritage. However, to understand the core of university archives worldwide, it may be best to focus only on the basic institutional records program, along with that limited body of private papers bearing directly on the institution, such as faculty papers. In this context, the core would not include the unrelated "manuscript" gatherings that have become so popular in U.S. colleges and universities.[4]

Equally important for this entry is a definition of "university." University archives occur in all types of postsecondary educational institutions, whether they are polytechnic institutes, 2 or 4 year programs, graduate research universities, specialized professional colleges (such as law or medicine), or arts and music schools. Further diversity is introduced by the matter of sponsorship or affiliation: universities may be official organs of a governmental authority or privately supported by tuition funds and endowments. In addition, one particular type of private institution—the religiously affiliated—will also result in significant differences, depending on denominational or doctrinal connection and institutional mission (general education vs. training of clergy for religious service).

VARIABLES AFFECTING THE NATURE OF UNIVERSITY ARCHIVES

There are additional typologies which can have significant bearing on university archives' holdings and user constituencies. For example, in a general research university with both graduate and undergraduate programs in the arts and sciences, the archives can serve as a research laboratory where undergraduate and graduate students in disciplines such as history, anthropology, and languages may exploit the university's past as a means of learning how to do research or narrative writing. In a university that is predominately a professional school (e.g., law, medicine, or engineering), connecting students with the university's past through archivally based assignments may be less possible, and the archives may find that a proportionately greater part of its users are the alumni and fund-raising offices. Schools of art, music, dance, and theatre are similar in many respects to the professional and technical schools, but they may place greater emphasis on non-textual records. At nonresidential 4-year undergraduate and 2-year "junior" colleges, the archives' challenge may be to connect with the students when their time on campus is far more limited, necessitating a more active outreach

program so those archivists may engage their student clientele.

All of these variations can come together to have an important influence on what kinds of records and manuscripts are available to the archives. While certain core administrative records (e.g., catalogs, faculty minutes, executive officers' reports, correspondence, and policy documents) will be fundamental to any kind of university, the variety and scope of faculty personal papers may be far greater in a general university with strong social science programs than in, for example, an engineering institute or music academy where the disciplines themselves are much less focused on textual studies and textual production. Of course, this is not to say that the papers of engineers and musicians are any less valuable; rather, documenting the careers of such faculty may be a greater archival challenge.

Two other environmental variables can have further significant effect on the nature of the university archives: country/national traditions and age of institution. Country of origin, national traditions, or other governmental mandates can dictate much of the character of a university. Beyond the clear effect that national public-records laws have on the archivist's authority to control what does and does not come to the archives and on what is mandated for public access, national traditions can effect the character of universities and thus their archives. For example, a postcolonial public university in an African or South Asian country may well be focused on technical training, technological advancement, and the development of a national literature. In a European postcommunist country, traditions of centralized control may still persist, making it possible for its archivist to apply administrative mandates for the management of records. By contrast, in the United States, the fierce tradition of state-by-state independence and distrust of central government authority makes it difficult to develop consistent archival policies for the routine systematic transfer of records to university archives.

While there are a number of important universities well-known for their great age, e.g., Bologna, Paris, Oxford, and Harvard, the inescapable fact is that worldwide, the majority of institutions date from the twentieth century. Universities of significant antiquity face challenges in balancing attention to very old documents (with almost relic status) against modern items that by comparison to medieval papal bulls or princely commissions with wax seals can seem quite mundane. On the other hand, newer universities do have an opportunity to apply the most modern professional archival standards to their heritage but with the proximity of their own past and their urgent need to establish their authenticity, their relatively young age may lead such universities to discount their past so much that archives are at the bottom of their priority lists for financial and policy resources.

NATURE OF A UNIVERSITY ARCHIVES AND DOMAINS OF ARCHIVAL WORK

Recognizing the limits of generalizations, we can still define a university archives as a formally authorized and professionally managed program for the selection, accessioning, arrangement, description, preservation, and use of the official records, personal archives, and private manuscripts of enduring value for telling the story of the university, its programs, people, and place. An archives exists to support accountability and documentation of institutional and personal rights, and to enrich the university and its people by the preservation and presentation of its cultural heritage.

Professional management of the university archives consists of systematic practices in seven distinct archival domains:

Effective authorization of the archives by the parent institutions allows the program to ensure the retention, preservation, and utilization of archival holdings.

Authentication of documentary information through the analysis of its content and evidence obtained during the process of its accession or through a systematic records management program ensures the integrity of the archival record.

Appraisal of documents for their value as evidence and information on the basis of anticipated use in relation to the costs of description and retention ensures the selection of the smallest and best body of records.

Arrangement of information according to source and original order to sustain the integrity the documents had while in active use, following the related principles of *respect des fonds*, provenance, and sanctity of the original order guarantee that the archival holdings reflect their original meaning and relationships.

Description of documents, according to best practices and standards, via finding aids, guides, and inventories enables long-term access to their informational contents and ongoing administrative control of the holdings.

Preservation or physical protection ensures the future availability of documents in a safe environment and on physical media that will remain accessible, renewable, or convertible for the period of expected use.

Archivists promote and facilitate the use of documents to explain the past, provide guidance in the present, and accountability to the future.

In the three common understandings of the word "archives"—as documentary material, as a physical place, and as a program that manages these materials—it is the documentary content which has the greatest visibility to the program's parent institution and constituencies. Archival material can come in all physical formats including stone, cloth, parchment, paper, glass, plastics, and electronic media. Likewise, archival information can be recorded as words, numbers, codes, images, sounds, and moving images. To achieve its purpose, the university archives must be all-inclusive of physical media and recording structures.

HOLDINGS OF A UNIVERSITY ARCHIVES

Regardless of physical materials or record formats, an overarching typology of the holdings needed in a university archives consists of the following: official or office records (correspondence, reports, minutes, images, etc.) created by university officers and staff to complete their individual mandates; publications (documents produced by the institution in multiple print copies or via broadcast/posting on the Internet) whether of a bureaucratic, promotional, scientific, or cultural nature; and personal papers (material in all physical formats created and retained by individual students, faculty, and alumni reflecting their professional and private lives as members of the social community of the institution). Adequate documentation of the university requires attention to all three of these categories, although those archives maintained primarily for administrative purposes may emphasize official records and publications at the expense of the more personal, human, and diffuse picture that is drawn by personal papers.

Some professional literature has attempted to list the variety of specific records that should be part of a university archives.[5] These inventories proceed on a hierarchical structural analysis mentioning such items as catalogs, graduation lists, policies and regulations, minutes, reports and correspondence of the board of control, chief executive officers, academic officers (provosts, rectors, and deans), faculty assemblies, and student affairs administration, and facilities managers. Such lists are useful points of reference, but a functional rather than structural analysis may provide a more strategically useful typology.[6] True, one might end up identifying such a broad array of documentation for the archivist to manage that it may seem to offer little advantage over the more traditional structural and hierarchical model, but the functional approach is an efficient way to strategically sequence decisions centered on the context of the records. The functional analysis approach should help archivists at different types of institutions to de-emphasize some areas when they are not relevant to that type of institution. For example, at a 2-year or 4-year undergraduate college, the archivist might make the strategic decision to de-emphasize the function of the creation of new knowledge while an archivist at a general university with a strong research emphasis may make the strategic choice of de-emphasizing efforts to accessions of materials on primary- and secondary-school teacher training.

CORE UNIVERSITY FUNCTIONS TO BE DOCUMENTED

In general, the core functions of a university to consider in relation to a university archives are:

Establish and sustain functions are those legal and administrative activities that create and support the continued existence of the university. This area includes not just charters and legislative mandates, but also records of financial administration, fund-raising, property acquisition, physical plant planning and development, employment management, and institutional reporting.

Educate. While many universities have been particularly wily in taking on multiple personae, by definition their signature function is to educate students. Important documentation of this function may include course catalogs, syllabi, grade records, Web course sequences, and student notebooks, exams, and papers. Operating strategically, a university archives may elect to limit accessions for the educate function to just course descriptions and grade records, or if funded sufficiently, it might decide to document the learning process by capturing Web course content, class blogs, and student essays.

Creation of knowledge. Universities, especially those with postbaccalaureate programs put a great emphasis on having faculty and advanced students engaged in the discovery of new knowledge, the writing of scientific research studies, and the making and performance of cultural and artistic works. Inevitably, documentation of this function requires attention to the personal papers of faculty and sometimes students through materials such as laboratory notebooks, manuscript drafts, or audio, and video recordings of performances, but it also requires administrative office records on the management of research laboratories, research funding grants and contracts, performing arts facilities, and cultural and scientific museums.

Socialization. Whether one regards higher education as an authoritarian effort to restrain the excesses of post-adolescent youth or merely confine them until the hormones settle, the fact is that universities bring together large numbers of maturing individuals who quickly form social networks through educational and extracurricular activities. Not only is the place of the university in the former student's life very much defined by the socialization that occurs there, but the university itself is also defined by its student and faculty life. Socialization can be one of the most important educational functions of the university. By its very nature as a matter of intangible personal interactions, the socialization function is difficult to document. Clearly, personal papers, (such as diaries, scrapbooks, blogs, MySpace® sites, photo albums, and correspondence) will be essential for documentation of this function in any depth. Because such materials can be complicated to acquire, describe, and preserve, some university archives may choose to limit their work in this area to keeping only the official records and publications pertaining to the institutional structures in which the socialization occurs, such as housing regulations, programs for intramural clubs and athletics, student newspapers, and organization Web sites, although broader coverage may provide for a very lively archival program of appeal to many extra-institutional researchers.

Public engagement. An enduring function of universities is the broad range of activities by which the institution interacts with the general populace as a whole. These activities include continuing education and extension programs whereby the knowledge of the university's specialized disciplines is distributed to the public as applied services and thus can range from agricultural information bulletins, medical services, and veterinary clinics to evening and distance-learning classes. Public engagement activities can also include music extension courses, art exhibitions, musical and dramatic performances, and public athletic events. The popularity of some of these activities can often mean that the university has great public visibility and that the archives receives many reference requests for historical information about these engagement programs. Thus, even though some such activities (e.g., "big time" intercollegiate athletics) at first might not seem to be central to the mission of higher education, failing to document them, even if only at the strategically limited level of maintaining a record set of event programs, will deprive the archives of an opportunity to connect with a nonspecialist public audience.

PROGRAMMATIC ACTIVITIES OF A UNIVERSITY ARCHIVES

A successful university archives is certainly more than a gathering of interesting and important historical records. It needs to incorporate a number of programmatic activities beyond those identified as the seven core domains noted above. Although not every archives can be deeply engaged in each, attention to a healthy mix is important. These programs can include oral history to capture the memories and character of members of the university community, and to fill-in gaps in the "written" record.[7] Exhibits and other outreach programs, such as concerts, open houses, exhibitions, lectures, performances, history contests, media appearances, curricular presentations or instructional programs to the campus and community schools, publications, etc., are important for ensuring a steady flow of research users to the archives and to counteract the false impression that archives are merely dusty obscure documents of little relevance to today's public. Limited by the strictures of intellectual property law, digitization projects that result in Internet posting of historical documents of interest to the general public (e.g., genealogical information) can be an effective way of engaging the public in the archives' mission while also enhancing the university's reputation.[8] Records and information management services, while related to the core ability to document the university, can also be built as a supplemental program to extend beyond mere records disposition scheduling to include a full suite of records and information services (e.g., files management, scanning and imaging services, or vital records protection) and can help the archives expand its campus credibility while also improving the overall quality of university information.

CONSTITUENCIES SERVED

As evidenced by both the basic services to be offered and expanded programmatic activities, university archives have multiple and sometimes divergent constituencies. Its value to each will likely be rooted in different, if sometimes conflicting interests and expectations. For example, legal affairs and core administrative units rely on the archives to supply as complete a record as possible when the university needs to ensure that its actions are free of liabilities. Likewise, archives are needed in instances when the university must respond to claims against it. Alumni affairs and campus fund-raising offices may be most interested in the archives for historical narratives that enable them to connect the university's past with donors able to fund future developments. Faculty may look to the archives as a laboratory-like setting where their students can go to write research papers and speeches. Faculty also see archives as places where they can go to deposit collections of relevance to their own disciplines. For example, the archives may be asked by a faculty geographer to take on the records of a regional environmental action council that just succeeded in blocking a river damming project. Students are also an important, though highly divergent, archival constituency. On the one hand, the archives may be simply the place they go to learn how to use primary sources or to look up some historical fact in fulfillment of a class assignment. On the other hand, the archives may contain historical background on a club or activity they are seeking to join or revive. In less common, but not unheard of circumstances, students may come to the archives to absorb everything possible about the institution as they discover how compelling the past of something familiar can be. Similarly, for alumni, the archives is an ideal resource from which they can recreate those days of fond and intense memories. In addition, there are important external constituencies, including graduate students and scholars from other universities, local school groups, and news media writers and researchers. Understanding the different interests and needs of each constituency can be a challenge for the archivist, although the archivist should be careful not to cater so exclusively to any single constituency that it is defined primarily by that group. In fact, failing to cultivate multiple constituencies will jeopardize the success and even survival of the archives when resources become short, when administrations change, or when one particular constituency becomes alienated or weakened.

THE ARCHIVIST'S CHARACTERISTICS AND PROFESSIONAL BACKGROUND

As suggested by the breadth and depth of responsibilities, holdings, programs, and constituencies, the university archivist must perform quite a juggling act. University archival work requires strong written and oral communication skills, an interest in and patience for research, and a general tenacity. While such general management skills are absolutely essential, the archives clearly needs persons with training not only in historical methods but also in archival theory and methodology. Exact training options will vary from region to region and country to country, but they generally include course work and internships in archival studies presented in postbaccalaureate programs in history or library-science schools, or sometimes in national archival agencies. Regardless of preappointment training, it is important for the university archivist to be actively engaged in archival professional associations. On a regional, national, and international basis, such organizations offer continuing education opportunities, standards development, public policy advocacy, professional literature, and social networking through which university archivists can share problems and develop solutions.[9],[10] Most importantly, they offer the challenge of a framework in which the university archivist examines his or her own problems and solutions in the context of practices and professional standards elsewhere, as well as in relation to archivists in other kinds of institutions such as governments, businesses, and religious bodies. At the same time, some of the general archival organizations often include subgroups just for university archives, such as the International Council on Archives' Section on University and Research Institution Archives (http://www.library. uiuc.edu/ica-suv/), the Society of American Archivists' College and University Archives Section (http://www.archi-vists.org/saagroups/cnu/index.asp), the Australian Society of Archivists' University Archives Special Interest Group (http://www.archivists.org.au/structure.html#uni), the Association of Canadian Archivists' University and College Archives Special Interest Section (http://archivists.ca/ special_interest/university.aspx), or the Society of Archivists (U.K.) Archives for Education and Learning Group (http://www.archives.org.uk/content.asp?id = 148). It is through such bodies that the profession has been defined and by which the advances of university archives will be measured.

REFERENCES

1. Burckel, N. Academic archives: retrospect and prospect. In *College and University Archives: Readings in Theory and Practice*; Prom, C., Swain, E.D., Eds.; Society of American Archivists: Chicago, IL, 2008.
2. Schina, B.; Wells, G. University archives and records programs in the United States and Canada. Archiv. Issues **2002**, *27* (1), 35–51.

United States– User-Centered Design

3. Richard, P.M. *A Glossary of Archival and Records Terminology (Archival Fundamentals Series II)*; Society of American Archivists: Chicago, IL, 2005.

4. Maher, W.J. *The Management of College and University Archives*; Society of American Archivists: Chicago, IL, 1992; and Scarecrow Press: Metuchen, NJ.

5. Society of American Archivists, College and University Archives Section. *Guidelines for College and University Archives*. Available at http://www.archivists.org/governance/guidelines/cu_guidelines.asp.

6. Samuels, H.W. *Varsity Letters: Documenting Modern Colleges and Universities*; Society of American Archivists: Chicago, IL, 1992; and Scarecrow Press: Metuchen, NJ.

7. Swain, E.D. Remembering alma mater: oral history and the documentation of student culture. Archiv. Issues **2002**, *26* (2), 129–143.

8. Chute, T. Selling the college and university archives: current outreach perspectives. Archiv. Issues **2001**, *25* (1&2), 31–46.

9. Society of American Archivists. *College and University Archives: Selected Readings*, Society of American Archivists: Chicago, IL, 1979.

10. Prom, C., Swain, E.D., Eds. *College and University Archives: Readings in Theory and Practice*; Society of American Archivists: Chicago, IL, 2008.

Usability Testing of User Interfaces in Libraries

Sharon L. Walbridge
Libraries Washington State University, Pullman, Washington, U.S.A.

Abstract

As libraries face increasing competition in providing information, we must insure that our library systems are usable, effective, efficient, and perhaps even enticing. How do librarians know that systems give users what they need and want? One way is usability testing. Usability testing has been around the computer industry for at least a decade, but library use of the method is relatively new. It has been a common perception that library systems were designed for librarians. Even if the user was considered, it was from the perspective of librarians who worked with the user. Those perceptions were anecdotal, and librarians frequently disagreed with one another about user behavior and knowledge.

WHAT IS USABILITY TESTING?

Usability testing is the process of actually observing users working on a system or product, taking the information gained in that process, and making changes in the system under test, then testing again to see if the changes improved the system for users. It is not a formal research process, as a limited number of people are tested. It is not based on statistics, but on observation. What is proven again and again is that a small number of users, anywhere from three to eight, will yield 80% of the problems people will have with the system. In fact, in testing eight people, observers will begin to see patterns of problems after seeing four or five test participants.

WHY DO TESTING?

Rather than spending hours in committee meetings discussing effective system design, creating a system and then testing it will save time and energy. The order of buttons, how much information to include, whether a help function is usable, whether terminology is understandable, whether navigation paths are understood, where people will expect to find information, etc.—all of these aspects of systems can be evaluated via usability testing. The predictability of effective use of a library's online catalog or a website can be enhanced through such testing. Endless hours spent with programmers tfocan be avoided. Results of usability testing can be used with system vendors to provide input on system upgrades. In fact, if system vendors do their own usability testing, their own design processes will be more efficient. Why should every library that buys a system have to go through time-consuming implementation to find errors that could have been caught early in the vendor's design process? As systems vendors offer more custom options, there are more choices

that need to be made. The best way to determine the effectiveness of choices is to ask the user.

Usability testing does not necessarily have to be a major time or effort commitment. It is better to test in small "chunks" rather than all-encompassing efforts. Common wisdom is to test small and often. For example, rather than test all aspects of the online catalog, focus on serials.

HOW DOES USABILITY TESTING DIFFER FROM BETA TESTING?

System vendors beta test to see if their systems work before delivery to customers. Beta testing differs from usability testing. While systems may work technically, they need to work effectively and efficiently and be understood by users. A system can be sophisticated in terms of having "bells and whistles," but users may not understand when to use those capabilities. Terminology and navigation may create inadvertent barriers to the usability of the system.

What are the various methods that can be used to test usability? In addition to formal usability testing, there are other ways to gain important input into user's perceptions and experience with the system. These include the following:

- Formal usability testing—actual users are observed using a system performing a list of predetermined tasks. Participants are asked to "think aloud," and observers record what is said and what is done.
- Card sort—used to gain information on the structure of a system or web page, index cards representing individual concepts are given to participants who arrange them in a structure that makes sense to them.
- Category membership—tests participants' understanding of various categories, including what they think should be in each category and what the category should be named.

Encyclopedia of Library and Information Sciences, Fourth Edition DOI: 10.1081/E-ELIS4-120008712

- Focus group—small groups of people share their opinions and ideas on the system.
- Field study—users are observed in their natural environment as they carry out normal tasks.
- Automated testing—an automated form of usability testing that uses software to conduct test sessions and collect data.
- Walk-up kiosk—may be used in combination with automated testing, a booth with a computer allows users to interact with a system.
- Cognitive walkthrough—designers of the system try to predict users' actions by doing actual tasks themselves.
- Questionnaire—a set of questions is designed to collect responses and opinions of users regarding the system.
- Site usage log—server logs collect user transactions and movements and actions, and these are subsequently analyzed.
- Heuristic evaluation—a system interface is analyzed by evaluators using a set of usability principles.
- Interview—a semistructured conversation is held between individual users and information gatherers about the system being tested.
- Opinion poll—questions are asked of system users to get feedback on specific topics related to the system.

For more information on these various techniques, see http://www.vancouver.wsu.edu/fac/campbell/usability/acrl.

Usability testing can provide valuable feedback regarding on-line catalogs, web pages, and user guides—anything that is designed for users to find information, use information, etc. Signage, handouts, stack labels, stack arrangement, almost anything in the library that is designed to help users, can be evaluated and made more effective with usability testing.

DOING USABILITY TESTING

The following is a guide for libraries interested in doing usability testing. Start by doing some reading on the subject (http://www.vancouver.wsu.edu/fac/diller/usability/usebib.htm). There are several good books about usability testing and good websites. Jeffrey Rubins' *Handbook of Usability Testing* is a particularly good source for process and practical advice that can easily be adapted for library use.

PREPARE FOR TESTING

For an outline of formal usability test procedures, see http://www.vancouver.wsu.edu/fac/campbell/usability/acrl. For examples of all of the materials needed for usability testing, see http://www.vancouver.wsu.edu/fac/diller/usability/contents.htm.

Preparation for testing includes complying with institutional policies related to the use of human subjects, constructing a timetable, and formulating a purpose statement, problem statement, and task list.

While most universities have policies and procedures for testing human subjects, it may not be clear if usability testing is covered by these policies. The kind of human subject testing covered by institutional policy is usually physical or psychological. The university compliance office or institutional review board can determine if the library's testing is covered. Appropriate forms should be submitted for the project to the institutional review board or compliance officer.

A timetable is a guiding document and is essential in setting up tests and implementing them. The timetable specifies expectations, tasks, and all of the steps necessary to design and complete the testing. In libraries, it is often the case that those doing the testing have other responsibilities. The timetable lets everyone involved know what needs to be done and when tasks need to be completed.

The purpose statement is the key to a successful usability test. It answers the question of why testing is being carried out and helps to ensure that testing is directed to the processes for which user feedback is essential. For example, if the online catalog is being tested, the goal is to test people's ability to use that tool, not what is in the catalog, circulation policies, collection development effectiveness, etc.

The problems to be investigated relate to the purpose statement. Adherence to the purpose statement ensures that the problems relate specifically to the purpose of the project. The task list builds from the problem statements, as the problem statements build from the purpose statement, going from general to specific. Each step should help in refining the next, but care must be taken to make sure that each truly relates to and focuses on the next step.

The task list includes questions that comprise the actual test. Depending on the purpose and scope of the project, the test can vary from a few questions to many. Experts counsel that more focused tests and testing more often are more effective. Even if the test is fairly wide in scope, the test session should not exceed 1 hr, and 30 to 40 min is preferable. After a full hour, the participant and the observers will likely be tired.

How much to cover in any given usability test is an open issue. The number of questions to be included in an hour session can vary depending on the complexity of questions and tasks. Experience will likely indicate that shorter sessions with focused questions are better than longer sessions. This strategy will enable more effective smaller scope tests rather than comprehensive ones.

PREPARE MATERIALS

Materials to be prepared include introductory script, human subject consent forms, documents related to any financial reimbursement, and data input sheets. Any equipment to be used in the test should be tested in advance to ensure a smooth test.

The introductory script is read to test participants to give them a uniform platform of understanding. It sets the tone for the session and helps to make the participant comfortable. The introduction should contain information on why the library is doing usability testing; the goals of the test; how results will be collected and used; and expression of gratitude for the persons' participation.

The human subject form needs to be explained to test participants and that institutional policy requires that they sign the form to indicate their consent. It is important that participants understand that the usability test is not an invasive one.

If a financial incentive is being offered, paperwork needs to be completed to make sure reimbursement occurs through the library or institution business office. Participants need to know that if their check is not received in a timely manner, they should check back with one of the observers.

Data input sheets are used to record whether or not the participant successfully completes the task; the time taken to complete the task; whether or not there were false starts; the steps taken to complete the task; and all comments made by the participant during the process of completing the task.

Equipment needed for the test will include, at minimum, a tape recorder, cassettes, a computer, and a clock. Participants need to know that they are not being tested, it is the system that is being tested. This message needs to be reemphasized to reassure the participant, especially if the person is having difficulty with the tasks during the session. Participants need to know that failure is as instructive as successful completion of tasks, because observers need to know the aspects of the system that work and those that do not work.

Self-confidence is important. Observers and test conductors will gain confidence as tasks are completed. Test participants will pick up observers' tension or lack of confidence. Careful and complete preparation increases confidence with the purposes and tasks of the test. Usability testing is serious business, but it can be fun for participants and observers.

TEST PARTICIPANTS

There are many ways to recruit volunteers for usability testing—flyers in the library, ads in campus or community newspapers, website notices, personal contacts at library service desks, etc. If demographics are important, it is advisable to use a screening questionnaire. For example, if a college, university, or public library is interested in testing the usability of its online catalog or website among its diverse community, each client segment can be tested

or a larger sample of people can be recruited. In a sample size of eight participants, an academic library could have three undergraduate students, three graduate students, and two faculty. Within that group, one would want a mix of males and females, traditional age students, and older students, etc. The screening questionnaire can help in choosing the volunteers. Questionnaires should identify status (undergraduate, graduate student, or faculty), age, sex, computer literacy, library use and knowledge, etc.

Librarians who have done usability testing report varying experiences in recruiting test participants. For some, it is easy to collect a pool of interested people, but for others, the process has been more difficult. Incentives help in either case. Whether the incentive is money, copy cards, gift certificates to the campus bookstore, etc., offering them lends a touch of credibility to the process. A little extra cash always appeals to students. Some universities may have policies against paying faculty for activities such as usability testing and faculty may participate as a symbol of support for the library.

In the case of universities, at least three communities of users—undergraduates, graduate students, and faculty—use the library and need to be tested. One of the obvious solutions is a two level interface—one for novices and one for the sophisticated user. It may be that this is not possible for system design or financial reasons. Regardless of whether there is one interface or two, the system still needs to be tested for usability. In the case of the website, there likely will be only one approach. In testing, one could have one group of test participants representing a demographic sampling of users, or one could have three groups of three representing the three primary user groups (undergraduates, graduate students, and faculty).

Pretesting the test questions helps to ensure that participants understand them. Are the tasks doable? Is the terminology easily understood? In a dynamic environment such as a website, are the test questions still appropriate or have changes been made that make the question no longer relevant?

Observers should actually take the test themselves so they have a sense of what steps will be necessary to complete the task. This testing will help observers follow test participants actions and judge whether or not their courses of action are legitimate, efficient, and effective. There may be several ways to get to an answer, but there is likely to be one "best way." Whether or not that is obvious to the user may be important.

In preparing for test sessions, tasks should be assigned to observers in advance. Who will meet the test participant and guide them to the test site? Who will read the introductory information? Who will ensure data sheets are in the room? Who will be responsible for seeing that the equipment is there in place and operating correctly? Who is activating the tape recorder? (If a video camera is being used, a third person should run it, but a tape recorder can be operated by one of the observers.) Who will give the participant the summary general impression debriefing sheet? By deciding these questions in advance of the session, the test will run smoothly and appear to be more professional.

Some universities have invested in usability laboratories that enable them to use two video cameras and a separate observation room. OCLC Online Computer Library Center has three rooms—a control room, a test room, and a closed-circuit observation room. It is feasible for libraries to do a distinctly low-tech operation. A meeting room or office with a computer can be used as a bare-bones test facility. While it is beneficial to have at least one video camera trained on the screen, it is possible to use a cassette recorder to capture the test participants' comments. The audiocassette will enable observers to go back to check any comments that might have been missed or reconcile the observers notes on the comments. If an office or meeting room is used for testing, the environment needs to be uncluttered so that the atmosphere is conducive to concentration.

A clock should be available to test the time taken for each question comprising the test. The time taken is important, even if the tasks are completed successfully. If it takes more than a minute or two to answer straightforward questions in the test, the system needs to be examined in terms of efficiency.

Define success—there may be numerous ways to get the answer to a question. Is there one efficient and effective path or are there several? The answers need to be decided before administration of the test, so that the observers will agree as to whether or not a question has been successfully completed.

THE TEST SESSION

Meeting test participants and escorting them to the test facility will let users know their participation is valued. This time can be used to thank the person for volunteering and to begin to put the person at ease with small talk. In the test room, the participant should be introduced to observers and others in the room. The introductory script should be read by the designated observer, institutional policies regarding human subjects should be explained, and the participant should be asked to sign consent forms. Ask the person if there are any questions. Start the test.

During the test, the observers need to be alert and follow everything that is done and said. Once each task is completed, or the person has become hopelessly stuck and is ready to give up, observers should indicate that it is all right to move to the next task. If additional time is needed to complete recording of tasks and comments, ask the person to wait until the observers are caught up. Observers should ask the participant any questions they have about the process used or comments made before moving on to the next task.

One of the most difficult aspects of the process is having test participants verbalize what they are thinking and doing. This aspect of the test process is important, as it will offer clues and important information on how information is being interpreted, the logic of steps taken, and the understandability of terminology, content, etc. Recording ensures that nothing important is missed in the comments. It is beneficial to have the session videotaped, as the comments can relate more clearly to what is happening at the keyboard and on the screen.

The timing and content of observers' dialog with the participants is a difficult aspect of the process, as it is tempting to jump in to help, especially if the person appears to be lost. Experienced observers will gain confidence in their ability to talk with participants without unduly interfering, adding to a person's knowledge and therefore potentially "corrupting" the results. Periods of silence while the person struggles can be uncomfortable for all involved, but observers need to err to the side of caution to allow the test participant time to struggle through as they would in a real-life situation, where they needed information and were on their own with the library system.

AFTER THE TEST

Post-test activities consist of debriefing participants and observers and determining if changes need to be made in the system or if problems can be solved by instruction or online help.

The importance of debriefing after each test session cannot be overestimated. Debriefing the participant will give the person a chance to relax and to chat about the test experience. One of the most important aspects of this debriefing is the opportunity to do a little library instruction. Telling people what went wrong if they had problems with a particular task will enable them to immediately use the system more effectively. It is not unusual for participants to leave the test session with benefits in terms of things they did not know that they could immediately put into practice. This learning serves as another benefit of participation.

One of the elements involved in the debriefing can be a "general impression" questionnaire that gives participants the opportunity to make general comments about the system and to rate the system in general terms.

Debriefing the observers also is important. It is critical to do this debriefing in a timely fashion, preferably right after each session. Observers should go over the data input sheet and note any discrepancies in impressions of the results. Is there agreement on whether each task was completed successfully? What happened that was surprising or particularly interesting? As sessions proceed, are there common patterns or themes?

In analyzing test results, the goal is to decide what is needed to improve the problem areas. As soon as possible after a round of testing, data should be collected in terms of identification of problems areas—places where failures in completing tasks successfully occurred or the participants took too long in completing tasks or there were false starts, even if the tasks were accomplished successfully.

Given what was learned in the usability test, careful consideration should be made as to how the system can be improved. This may require some intensive thought and discussion, as the solutions to problems may not be obvious or simple. It is best not to put any constraints on thinking about how the changes can be implemented. Changes in the system are later steps in the process. Solutions may be two pronged—changes in system design as well as emphasis in library instruction. Who needs to be involved in making the changes? Is there a team that oversees changes to the website, or does a technical services unit (acquisitions, cataloging or serials processing) need to be approached to determine the feasibility of changes in the way information appears in the online catalog?

After initial evaluation of test results, the responsibility for making changes needs to be determined. Is the system customizable so that changes can be done in-house? If the answer is theoretically yes, are there resources to do it? If the answer is no, can the system vendor can be contacted directly, or is it necessary to go through a user group/enhancement process? Can the system be improved by education or instruction; can effectiveness be improved through by bibliographic instruction sessions? Would more online help in some form improve the system?

Retesting should be done every time changes are made in the system, whether those changes come about through usability testing or they are incorporated in a normal new release of software. If the changes have come about through usability testing, care should be taken to make sure the retest is similar to the initial test, to see whether the changes have actually helped the user in the identified problem areas. Ideally, the same questions should be asked again.

OUTCOMES

What Have Librarians Learned Through Usability Testing?

Users do not have a great deal of trouble navigating through systems. They become quickly frustrated and disenchanted with multiple layers.

Users do not understand normal library terms such as serial, monograph, volume, etc. There are a number of ways to deal with this problem, although none of them are guaranteed. Online glossaries, emphasis in library instruction sessions, use of standard terminology (not library jargon), and mouse-overs all may work to help the

situation. Users do not understand concepts such as the difference in content between the online catalog and full-text indexes. If they are asked to find a journal citation, more likely than not, they will look in the online catalog rather than full-text indexes. Again, the solution to this may be to attack the problem on as many fronts as possible, library instruction, mouse-overs, etc.

Users expect consistency. All of the students on a large university campus use the same catalog, and they may well use more than one library on campus. The library's website needs to contain the same information for each library on campus, preferably in the same place. If the libraries are decentralized, this can be problematic, but testing will prove that users expect consistency. As education becomes more and more interdisciplinary, the need for consistency will increase.

More and more library users access library systems from their dorm rooms, apartments, offices, computer labs, etc. Remote users should have as easy a time using the library's systems as do in-library users. Remote access impacts system design in relationship to images, etc. Even if systems are readily accessible from remote locations, different computer capabilities may exist for distance education students, disabled students, and others.

CONCLUSION

Librarians who have done usability testing quickly become advocates for the technique. Testing can yield quick results that can lead to increasing the effectiveness of the library's online catalog or the website. As outlined above, the process need not be expensive in terms of economics or effort. Although the first test experience may be more time consuming, the experience will make each successive test easier. Lessons learned in each process will bring efficiency to further testing. Usability testing is a rewarding way to bring accountability to critical library tools and to improve library operations.

BIBLIOGRAPHY

1. Campbell, N.; Diller, K.; Chisman, J. Learning from our users: Usability testing of WebPacs and Web sites. In Proceedings of Internet Librarian International 2000; Information Today: Medford, NJ, 30–35.
2. Chisman, J.; Diller, K.; Walbridge, S. Usability testing: A case study. Coll. Res. Libr. November **1999**, *60.6*, 552–569.
3. Corry, M.D.; Frick, T.W.; Hansen, L. User-centered design and usability testing of a web site: An illustrative case study. Educ. Technol. Res. Dev. **1997**, *45.4*, 65–76.
4. Dickstein, R.; Mills, V. Usability testing at the University of Arizona Library: How to let the users in on the design. Infor. Technol. Libr. September **2000**, *19.3*, 144–151.
5. Dumas, J.; Redish, J. *A Practical Guide to Usability Testing*; Ablex: Norwood, NJ, 1993.

6. Falks, A.; Hyland, N. Gaining user insight: A case study illustrating the card sort technique. Coll. Res. Libr. July **2000**, *61.4*, 349–357.

7. Glitz, B. The focus group technique in library research: An introduction. Bull. Med. Libr. Assoc. October **1997**, *85.4*, 385–390.

8. Hughes, M. Rigor in usability testing. Tech. Commun. **1999**, *Fourth Quarter*, 488–494.

9. McGillis, L.; Toms, E.G. Usability of the academic library web site: Implications for design. Coll. Res. Libr. July **2001**, *62.4*, 355–367.

10. Murphy, B. Usability testing. OCLC Newsl. September/October **1997**, *229*, 21–23.

11. Nielsen, J. *Usability Engineering*; Academic Press: Boston, MA, 1993.

12. Nielsen, J. *Designing Web Usability*; New Riders Publishing: Indianapolis, IN, 2000.

13. Pearrow, M. *The Web Site Usability Handbook*; Charles River Media: Rockland, MA, 2000.

14. Rubin, J. *Handbook of Usability Testing: How to Plan, Design and Conduct Effective Tests*; John Wiley & Sons, Inc.: New York, 1994.

15. Silipigni Connaway, L.; et al. Online catalogs from the user's perspective: The use of focus group interviews. Coll. Res. Libr. September **1997**, *58.5*, 403–420.

16. Spool, J.M. *Web Site Usability: A Designer's Guide*; Morgan Kaufmann Publishers: San Francisco, CA, 1999.

17. Travis, T.A.; Norlin, E. Testing the competition: Usability of commercial information sites compared with academic library web sites. Coll. Res. Libr. September **2002**, *63.5*, 433–448.

18. Usability testing started in OCLC Office of Research. OCLC Newsl. September/October **1997**, *229*, 24–25.

19. Veldof, J.R.; Prasse, M.J.; Mills, V. Chauffeured by the user: Usability in the electronic library. J. Libr. Adm. **1999**, *26.3–4*, 115–140.

20. Wilson, B.F.; Palmer, M. Usability testing of a Website and a Web user survey. In *Proceedings of the Section on Survey Research Methods, American Statistical Association 1997*; American Statistical Association: Washington, DC, 1997; 1069–1073.

21. Yoakam, L. Writers test documentation to determine users' needs. OCLC Newsl. September/October **1997**, *229*, 27.

User-Centered Design of Information Systems

Elaine G. Toms
Faculty of Management, Dalhousie University, Halifax, Nova Scotia, Canada

Abstract

User-centered design (UCD) emerged a couple of decades ago because people had difficulties in using systems. It is founded on the principle that users need to be involved in the design and development process for systems to be truly usable—efficient, effective, and satisfying. This entry provides an account of the background—the technological and social forces that affect the evolution of systems development, an explanation of the theoretical foundation on which UCD is build, and a description of a typical UCD process.

INTRODUCTION

Rationale, Definition, and Scope

User-Centered Design (UCD) was founded on the premise that knowledge of users and their participation in the way systems are designed is essential.[1] User-centered design is a "multidisciplinary design approach based on the active involvement of users to improve the understanding of user and task requirements, and the interaction of user design and evaluation."[2] The emphasis is on "quality in use," the ultimate goal of a UCD process. This is not merely about pandering to the wants of the consumer (i.e., developing what sells), as the marketplace is littered with market flops; it is about understanding and uncovering the current and prospective needs of the user, and developing solutions that do not "frustrate, cost, confuse, irritate, and kill us."[3] It is not to be confused with making products "user friendly," a phrase that conjures up a rather pedantic notion of design, while at the same time making an implicit assessment about the "unfriendliness" of early systems.[4] The UCD approach was intended to make systems that are "easy to buy, easy to unpack, easy to set up, easy to upgrade, easy to learn, easy to use, engaging, intuitive, and integrated.[5]

As a result of this human-machine mix, UCD is inherently inter- and multidisciplinary, drawing from a blend of psychology, computer science, artificial intelligence, linguistics, anthropology, and sociology,[6] and in recent years particularly with web developments, graphic design, and animation as well as information science and business.

This entry first provides background on the genesis of UCD, following by a section on the philosophy and theoretical underpinnings of UCD, and then a description of the method as it is generally practiced.

Foundations

Traditionally systems design and development followed a system-centered, expert-driven methodology in which a set of requirements were defined at the beginning of a project, and the development process unfolded in a linear fashion from the list of specifications (i.e., what the system is supposed to be able to do) to the final product. This was adequate while systems were used by experts. With the emergence of end-user computing, users—the average people on the street—were unable to use products that resulted from such a process. The problems lay in the design of the user-interface, that part of the system that is visible to the user and with which the user interacts with the system. Users made mistakes, did not understand how to proceed, and could not figure out how to complete a task. The final assessment was that insufficient effort had been placed in understanding how users typically behave and perform the tasks for which the product was designed. In short, users were too much of an afterthought in the design process.

One of the earliest advocates of a focus on people first was Don Norman, a cognitive psychologist, who observed how people used many products including refrigerators, stoves, teapots, and doors as well as all sorts of electronic and digital devices.[7] Norman noted the mismatch between what the system expected the user to do, and what users typically do when faced with possible choices. Sometimes the product lacked an appropriate affordance, the property of a product which suggests what to do with it (compare a door knob which suggests twisting, with a lever-style handle). Sometimes there were no visible cues as to what to do next or a mismatch between what the user expected to do, and what appeared to be available (consider even today's cell phones in which some phones are turned on by pressing "end," or turned off by pressing "start").

Sometimes the system provided no feedback as to whether anything had occurred when a user pressed a button, clicked on a menu choice, or issued a command (the "loading page" feedback mechanism within today's web browsers show the extent to which the browser has loaded the page). In those early days (and to a certain extent today), the user's conceptual model of the system, that is the user's notion of how the system should work, did not match how the system actually functioned. Emerging out of this understanding was the need for more UCDs. "Know thy user"[8] became the mantra, and often appended is the phrase "for they are not you," a statement directed at system developers.

User-centered design can be traced back to the 1960s when human factors started to address the way that scientists and engineers interacted with costly large mainframe computer systems; this was primarily but not solely related to the ergonomics of the hardware. The concept of the interface was limited in scope, as the interface was solely for command-line interaction, in which the system provided a prompt, and the user entered a response or command; the cost was strictly in programmers' time which was inexpensive when compared with the cost of the technology.

By the late 1970s to early 1980s, personal computers made word processing, spreadsheet manipulation, and simple graphics creation accessible to the person on the street. In 1981 IBM introduced its personal computer for home and small business users who had knowledge of the application domain, but no interest in the internal workings of the computer, unlike the typical computer users of the previous era. The concept of the graphical user interface or GUI (as in "gooey" as it was fondly called), emerged and, and with it, the demand for more user centered technologies.

The need to support the end user brought an increased awareness of the need to understand simply how people function: their cognitive processes, including motor learning, problem solving, semantic memory, and perception, and how these processes affect peoples' use of technologies. Human–computer interaction (HCI) emerged as a discipline and the Association of Computing Machinery established the Special Interest Group on Computer-Human Interaction (SIGCHI) devoted to promoting human factors in the human–computer interaction process. UCD and HCI are sometimes used interchangeably, but UCD is a methodology of HCI.

Two core publications of the mid-1980s focused attention on the UCD problem. Norman and Draper's[6] edited monograph, *User Centered Systems Design* emerged out of a workshop at the University of California, San Diego in 1984 (and included a blue ribbon group of human–computer interaction pioneers). In the introduction, the two editors expressed their goals for the book, which have become the underlying foundation of UCD:

We wish to…ask what the goals and needs of the users are, what tools they need, what kind of tasks they wish to perform, and what methods they would prefer to use. We would like to start with the users and to work from there.[9]

This was, at the time, a novel idea; but this book was the first consolidated synthesis to an emerging concept. At about the same time, Gould and Lewis outlined three core principles for design that included a focus on users, empirical measurement, and iterative design.[10] These have stood the test of time, and today serve as the basis for much of UCD practice. Emerging from this work was the concept of usability, and as already stated was not to be confused with user friendly. Making systems usable is a more complex construct that includes learnability, efficiency, memorability, being error-free, and subjectively pleasing.[11]

The 1980s also saw the emergence of a new type of information system for the information consumer. With the introduction of CD-ROM technology, large bibliographic databases which were formerly only accessible to expert intermediaries and domain experts willing to learn a cryptic code were now reachable by working domain professionals (e.g., scientists, lawyers, doctors, journalists) who had limited computer expertise within months, the former databases that contained abstracts and bibliographic citations to published newspaper, journals, and technical publications evolved into full-text systems, also available initially on CD ROMs and later on mainframe systems with client-side graphical user interfaces.

At about the same time, how society, organizations, and culture shape the use of technology was being noticed. This introduced the importance of context: the situation in which the technology is being used affects that use and must be attended to within the design process. Suchman's ground-breaking study of the lowly photocopier identified how situatedness affected human social behavior in the context of technology use.[12] As a result, the need to integrate those influences called for more social and organizational analyses to be included in the design process. The concept of user incorporated more that the qualities of the individual.

By the 1990s, technology was not solely about transactional based technologies with structured data (e.g., numbers, codes) as its core; the emergence of the Internet and Web "informational" systems provided access to unstructured information (think text rather than numbers) that included ordinary homepages, newspapers, and the complete contents of books, journals, and videos. This placed new design needs on the concept of the user, the user's task, and the environment in which the user was situated. With the emergence of the Web, the custodians of information—from publishers to libraries, from government to the not-for-profit sector and e-commerce—had to re-think and transform their existing approaches to systems development.

Surprisingly, early technological developments did not match expectations in terms of increased productivity. Landauer claimed that the problem lay with inadequate engineering design for application software which was due to the lack of systematic testing of technologies in terms of their actual utility.[13] Instead he asserted that too much attention was focused on characteristics such as the speed of technology, its data storage capacity, the flawless operation of the technology, the number of features implemented, and its graphics quality. He argued for more testing of the ability of the technology to assist people in doing the work they needed to do. Despite the plethora of usability testing that was emerging at this time, Landauer claimed that too much of that testing was being devoted to aspects of the interface that would affect sales such as color and gadgetry, rather than addressing the formal functionality and usability of the system. Even today, customer satisfaction is considered the core success factor in assessing UCD processes internally.[14]

By the twenty-first century, the focus was all about the user or customer, as e-commerce entered the arena; the economic consequences of non-user oriented technologies now had a direct effect on a firm's economic survival. Users now "marched" with their mice from one non-usable Web site or e-commerce storefront to another. With the emergence of the Web, social computing enabled users to not just march with their mice, but also to complain, comment, and compliment technologies and services in listservs, blogs, wikis, and consumer-oriented Web sites.

Companies and organizations could no longer hide behind a poor technology. Today UCD is practiced by a range of systems developers including IBM, Microsoft, Google, Apple, and SAP. It has been a cornerstone of operations within IBM.[15] Within the information world, and libraries in particular, the concept of UCD came late, since most of the systems used by this group are produced by third-party vendors who have a limited marketplace for their products, and thus limited resources to apply to UCD. For example, it was not until 1990 that OCLC created its Usability Lab.

Emerging from this history was UCD as both a philosophy and a process. As a basic principle, UCD places the person—the user, and not the system at the center of systems development.

It is a process that considers cognitive factors (such as perception, memory, learning, problem-solving, etc.) as a core influence on a person's interaction with an object. This concept is as relevant to the design of teapots as it is to the computer mouse, word processors, search engines, and webcasting systems, and to the myriad of information appliances that are emerging in the marketplace.

PHILOSOPHY

Central to UCD is the conceptual foundation on which it is built. In this section, the three core concepts: information system, design, and user referenced by UCD, are defined, and then integrated into the core theoretical perspective that underpins UCD.

Information System

Information system is a complex term. It is an application of computing and information technology developed to meet a defined need or purpose. The term is used to include the database and application programs as well as the procedures used to manipulate the database in concert with the application programs, and the hardware (e.g., computers, printers, telecommunication devices, and networks) used for processing data and information.

Information system is often identified with business applications, in particular, transaction processing systems such as payroll, book lending, and interlibrary loan systems. These could be classed as operational systems intended for planning and control within an organization. But the term information system is also used and continues to be used for both tactical and strategic information systems such as decision-support systems, executive information systems, and financial systems.

With the emergence of the Web in particular, information system is now used not just to reference transaction-based systems that manipulate structured data. When technology enabled mass storage and the ability to completely represent and present an information object (rather than just to access to its metadata), information systems enabled and facilitated many human information processes: finding, reading, synthesizing, evaluating, and so on of unstructured information. Now the range of tasks supported by information systems spans routine operations of, for example, automatic bank machines, to complex decision-making and problem-solving systems that require extensive backtracking and digressions.

This description above specifies the entire system, from a UCD perspective, the system begins with that aspect seen by the user—the user interface.

Design

User-centered design, as a philosophy, has its roots in industrial and architectural design. Design emerged around the fourteenth to fifteenth centuries, although there is no specific event to which this concept is attached.[16] Design arose with "the separation of thinking and doing"[16] after the work of master craftsmen, for example, was divided into architects and builders, and today that distinction can be used to separate designers from programmers in systems development.

The word design may be interpreted in multiple ways: on the one hand it specifies the process used, while on the other it references the arrangement of all of the components contained in the design. Design is imposed, and "only when the constituent parts of a whole have the unique end of contributing to the consummation of a conscious experience, do design and shape lose superimposed character and become form."[17] Dewey was talking about art, but the same sentiment is true of systems design. Eames took a more pragmatic approach in referring to design as "a plan for arranging elements in such a way as to best accomplish a particular purpose."[18] The end product of a design is not purely a visual object, but a complex artifact that may support one or all of the senses depending on its purpose. From a systems design perspective, when all of the elements, procedures, and objects work in harmony, the system almost "disappears" as the user is "one" with the visible components.

In practice systems design stems from industrial design with a focus on the action and activities that define the purpose of the product. As such design involves a two-stage process: the first is a conceptual process to identify what the product is expected to do and how the action will unfold; and the second is the physical where the conceptual elements are rendered into real-world objects, such as layout, menu labels, icons, and buttons. The lines between the conceptual and physical are blurred in UCD.

User

Early users of information systems were experts who performed often routine and predictable actions with applications. They were technically trained and technically oriented, and more than willing to learn the arcane commands or procedures required to use an application. Over time, the user became anyone who applied a set of actions to a computing device, and the designer of a system was no longer comparable to the person who would subsequently use the application.

User as a concept has met with considerable discussion. Bannon pointed out very early in the development of UCD that a user was not necessarily a person who makes only casual use of a system.[19] A novice or naïve computer user may be an expert in the application domain, for example, accounting, medicine; and, sometimes a novice in the application domain may be an expert computer user.

Instead, the word, user, is a generic concept that is intended to be replaced with a specific "job" or task function as in lawyers when speaking of legal information systems, or accountants when speaking of accounting systems. But a system might also have multiple levels of expertise as a citizen, mayor, or property inspector for municipal information systems. A typical user may be classed according to many attributes such as skill level (naïve vs. expert, e.g., a law student vs. a partner, a history undergraduate student vs. a history professor); and by nature of use (ad hoc or daily). Nielsen characterizes users along three dimensions: computer expertise, computer experience, and knowledge about the task domain.[11] As a result, the concept of user is more complex than one

imagines which somewhat explains the nature of UCD methodology (discussed later on).

Particularly within the engineering community, the term "stakeholders" is preferred to reflect the broader group from implicit to explicit consumers of the system. Lodge,[20,21] classed stakeholders into six types of users: governing body, sponsor, user specified, end user, input generator (the person who will enter data into a system) and the output receiver. This nomenclature tends not to be used within the human–computer interaction and information science communities.

Conceptual foundation of UCD

How design, user and information system are blended is reflected in the early thinkers of UCD. In what is now considered a seminal work, Moran posited that "to design the user interface of a system is to design the user's model. The designer needs to understand...what knowledge goes into the user's conceptual model"[22] so that ultimately the user should not have to struggle to figure out what the designer intended. This led to thinking about how users act, behave, and perceive.

Card and colleagues[23,24] proposed a "model human processor" that could be used by the designer in contemplating how a person interacts with a computer at the interface. The model included three human systems, each with its own memories and processes: 1) a perceptual system that connects a person's sensations from the physical work to internal representations in the mind; 2) a motor system that translates human thought into physical actions; and 3) a cognitive system that retrieves facts, solved problems, and selects a suitable course of actions. Notably, for some tasks, the human behaves as a serial processor (clicking on a button in response to a display), while in others, the action requires integrated, parallel operations that engage the three human systems at once (reading from and selecting from, and finally resolving the information contained on a single webpage). In addition to describing how complex and dynamic a human is, Card and colleagues specified both the typical and range of values that could be expected in human performance. In doing so they provided a standard for the measurement concerns of Gould and Lewis.[10]

At about the same time, Norman described a "theory of action" to assist in understanding how users use systems[25] as illustrated in Fig. 1. In general, a user approaches a system with a goal likely dictated by the task to be accomplished, but personal to the individual. The goal is converted into an intention which is acted upon, and subsequently executed using the system. The system is in a certain state of readiness; imagine a computer that has just been turned on. The user perceives, interprets, and evaluates the response from the system. Norman claimed that the users' goals and the perceived state of the system had to traverse two "gulfs" before users could make use of

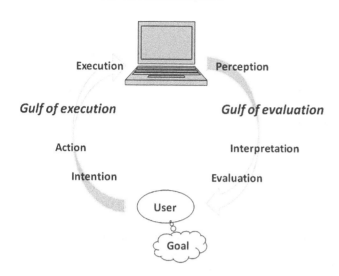

Fig. 1 Norman's "Gulfs" embedded in his "theory of action" to describe how people interact with systems.[26]

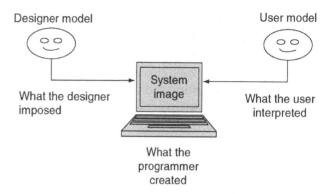

Fig. 2 Designer, user, and programmers perspectives of the user.[29]

the system to achieve their goals. Thus, when the user approaches the system, the first challenge is what action can be taken to "bridge" the Gulf of Execution. When the system responds to a user's action, the user must now interpret that response to cross the Gulf of Evaluation. In using any system, this pairing of action and evaluation is a constant and continuous process.

Design needs to account for that process as the most elegantly designed systems fail when the user is uncertain about which action to take, or the system responds with a non-interpretable reply. At the beginning of a project (see Fig. 2), a designer envisions a conceptualization of the system, called the Designer Model, which is imposed on the system and is reflected in the System Image that is represented in the physical world by the user interface and represents the programmer's implementation of the designer's specifications.[27] The user approaches the user interface with a preconceived notion of what to expect; we consider this the User Model. Designers' models consist of the ideas that the designers attempt to embody in a system; the users' conceptual model is a mental representation that is formed by experience—experience with older technology, the physical world, related applications, and so on.[28,29] If the user's conceptual model is in line with the designer's model of the system, then the user is able to perform actions, and interpret responses made by the system. But when the two models are mismatched, the user is unable to bridge the Gulfs illustrated in Fig. 1. The degree of discontinuity is directly related to how well the designer's model and the programmer's rendering of it actually match the user's model of the system. The user interface serves as the "bridge" between these two conceptual models. In general, when the designer fails to take user needs and requirements into account in the design process, the system is unlikely to succeed.

User-centered design emerged from this awareness of the tension between the designer's view of the world and

the user's and is fundamentally the foundation for UCD practice. Over time, the focus on the user model morphed into the need for a full understanding of user in context—environmentally, socially, physically.[12] In more recent years, affect, the user's emotional response to systems has also emerged as a core factor in design; it is no longer sufficient for a system to be fully functional, but now needs to be "attractive" and perceived by its users as attractive as well.[29]

PROCESS

In addition to having a strong conceptual foundation, UCD defines a process—a practice or procedure—for the design of information systems. Back in 1985, Gould and Lewis[10] identified three principles that would lead to a UCD system:

1. Focus on users and their tasks early in the design phase.
2. Assess and evaluate through the design/development process.
3. Use an iterative design process so that the result can be improved over the developmental life cycle.

These have been modified and augmented over the years, and Shneiderman's principles[30] illustrated in Fig. 3 is one of the most parsimonious examples of these.

What is believed to be the first example of UCD in practice is the 1984 Olympic Messaging System designed to provide voicemail and communication support for athletes at the Games.[31] The following brief synopsis of that work serves to illustrate the UCD process in practice.

At the beginning, an initial analysis of requirements was prepared and commented on by designers, managers, and prospective users. From this assessment, a number of functions that the system was expected to enable were modified, and some were removed. Simulations of these functions were tested and evaluated by the intended user

1. Strive for consistency.
2. Enable frequent users to use shortcuts.
3. Offer informative feedback.
4. Design dialogs to yield closure.
5. Offer error prevention and simple error handling.
6. Permit easy reversal of actions.
7. Support internal locus of control.
8. Reduce short-term memory load.

Fig. 3 Shneiderman's principles of UCD.[30]

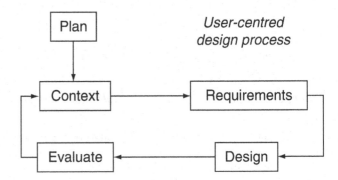

Fig. 4 UCD process as described by ISO 13497.

groups: athletes and their friends and families. In addition, site visits to the Olympic village and interviews with those involved with the Olympics brought new information and data. Finally a prototype was build and tested with a wide range of people. Over the course of its development from the initial concept to the first prototype (and subsequently the final product), the design followed the three principles developed by Gould and Lewis.[10]

The UCD Process

Although practices may vary from organization to organization and from text to text, the International Standards Organization's standard, "Human-Centered Design Processes for Interactive Systems,"[32] describes the core elements. Written at a high conceptual level, the standard is not prescriptive, but provides guidance in the form of a five-stage model illustrated in Fig. 4.

Plan the human centered process

As suggested by the title, the intent of this stage is the development of a plan for the succeeding stages, and for how the UCD process fits within the entire systems development project. This is a living document that is updated over the life of the project.

The complexity of the plan will depend on whether the system is an innovation (i.e., nothing currently exists), replacement technologies for an existing product (e.g., word processor replaced the typewriter, and the online catalog replaced the card catalog), or a new version of an existing digital product. Thus, in some situations, the knowledge of users and their context may already be known, or the existing technology may place constraints on the design such as an application that works in a Windows environment rather than a Macintosh, or a technology that will be an added component to an existing application.

Understand and specify the context of use

In this stage, understanding users and their tasks as well as the organizational and physical environment in which the

system will be used are the core components. These will subsequently guide design rationale and additionally prescribe how evaluation—success of the product—will be measured. The context of use is described in terms of:

1. Who the users are and what special characteristics they have.
2. What work tasks users will need to perform, and how those tasks are interrelated, including the allocation of human and technological resources needed to complete a task.
3. The matrix of user and task characteristics, so that specific scenarios of use can be described.
4. The context or specific environment (including physical and social characteristics) in which the system will be used.
5. The benchmarks that will be used to define both minimal and optimal requirements.[32]

This stage identifies the range of intended users, the scope of their tasks and the contextual environment in which they operate. Central to this is an understanding of what the work is supposed to achieve; this is not about what the computer system is supposed to do, rather an explanation of the work task in isolation from the technology.

Specify user and organizational requirements

At this stage, the functional requirements of the system are specified with respect to users and the organization. What must the system do for it to be considered successful? This will describe:

1. Required performance of the new system with respect to operational and financial objectives, and to relevant statutory or legislative requirements (including safety and health).
2. Task performance and its integration with work design and organization.
3. Operations and maintenance feasibility.[32]

This stage will document the design goals, guidelines and constraints, identify the priorities, and provide measurable criteria for testing the design, including usability criteria (e.g., efficiency, effectiveness, and satisfaction levels).

Produce design solutions

This stage includes devising the rough concept through to sketching and developing a complete design. This requires integrating existing knowledge and technological capability with knowledge of users and the context. It may include visual design, information architecture, and interaction design. Potential designs are:

1. Created using existing standards, best practices, accepted guidelines and examples of other systems etc.) to develop a proposed design solution.
2. Rendered using simulations, low-fidelity prototypes, mock-ups, etc.
3. Evaluated by users who are observed performing specified tasks, with or without the assistance of evaluators, and modified from feedback.
4. Modified until design objectives (including usability objectives) are met.[32]

This stage involves building a range of prototypes from low-fidelity paper prototypes, to high-fidelity prototypes that simulate the activity of the system.

Evaluate designs against user requirements

This stage evaluates the design with the user community using the application in a realistic environment. Depending on the number of iterations, this stage may be a formative evaluation intended to provide feedback to improve the design, or it may be summative to determine how well the system meets the criteria set out in the original plan.

These five stages are intended to be repeated as often as is required over the life of the project. Iteration and evaluation are considered critical to the success. In addition to the ISO approach, other variations have been well documented.[33–35]

Each of these five stages uses a variety of methodologies to collect the essential data required to fulfill the requirements of that particular stage. For example, in understanding context (Stage 2), a collection of formal and information techniques are used to find out what the system is intended to do. This stage usually involves a visit to the workplace and an observation of how things are currently being done, as the way work is performed is often not like the way that procedural manuals stipulate. Observation and interviewing (formal and informal) together with careful note taking and sometimes videotaping provides a wealth of data from which to identify the issues. Stage 5, the evaluation component, uses a variety of techniques depending on how many iterations of the process have been completed. Early evaluation

techniques are more likely to be done with cognitive walkthroughs, and heuristic evaluation; later stages will do user testing with real users performing real tasks.

STANDARDS, PRINCIPLES, RULES, AND STYLE GUIDES

An international standard for UCD (previously discussed) specifies the design and development process, but is not the only standard relevant to UCD. ISO 16982 specifies usability methods that support "human"-centered design and is complementary to ISO9241-11, *Guidance on Usability* which identifies how usability can be evaluated in terms of user performance (efficiency and effectiveness) and satisfaction. This is somewhat related to ISO 9126 which defines six categories related to software quality for the software engineering community: functionality, reliability, usability, efficiency, maintainability, and portability, as well as the overall goal of achieving quality in use. Other related standards recommend specifications for usability of consumer products (ISO 20282), icon symbols and functions (ISO 11581), pen-based interfaces (ISO 14754), mobile—PDAs—tools (ISO 18021), multimedia user interfaces (ISO 14915) (55) and documentation (ISO 15910) and a format for writing reports of usability test results (ISO 25062).

In addition to standards, a variety of principles such as the ones mentioned earlier are used. In the actual conduct of design, a number of rules or heuristics are applied such as number of items to use in menus, color and font combinations, and layout. In addition, individual organizations have developed "style guides" to prescribe how design is accomplished for products developed by that group. IBM, Microsoft, and Apple all have developed style guides for the development of software. As a result, UCD has some consistencies in practice, but could not be considered a standardized methodology.

USE AND VALUE OF UCD

The term UCD is not exclusive; some groups refer to it as customer-centered design, experience design, or usage-centered design. Raskin[36] distinguished between human centered and user-centered design. He claims a two-level design process in which the first stage is to ensure that the design relates to universal psychological attributes common to all humans, such as visibility of interface objects, amount of memorization that is acceptable, and human use of graphical elements. Once a system meets normal human physiological and psychological constraints, then the designers should attend to the task requirements of that particular user group. Raskin alleged that designers hand over responsibility for the human element to industry who is not always attuned to human capabilities.

United States—
User-Centered Design

The value of UCD is not universally understood or accepted. In a snapshot of UCD penetration among experienced practitioners, nearly three-quarters of respondents reported that UCD affected development within their organization and improved the usability of the final product.[37] But, it also provided a picture of a methodology that was not universally adopted. Often cited as a barrier to UCD practices are resources and organizational resistance, because there are no clear metrics about how to assess a UCD process. These findings result from a survey distributed in 2000 and 2001.[14] Undoubtedly with the growth in consumer digital products and the web, UCD now has greater penetration in organizations that produce consumer products. Ease of use for example, has been touted as the top factor contributing to conversion rates for Web sites, that is, getting customers to translate their visits into actions, or, in other words, purchases. Clearly in order to actually do that, one needs to adapt a UCD approach.

CONCLUSION

User-centered design is a process based on a strong conceptual foundation embedded in understanding how people function as human beings, and within the particular job function that a technology is intended to facilitate. The end product of such a process will provide a good fit between the user and the tasks that the user needs to accomplish, and the system that is intended to facilitate that activity. This is tightly integrated to a particular context that has social, political, and legal implications.

REFERENCES

1. Preece, J.; Rogers, Y.; Sharp, H.; Benyon, D.; Holland, S.; Carey, T. *Human-Computer Interaction: Concepts and Design*; Addison-Wesley: Wokingham, U.K., 1994.
2. Mao, J.-Y.; Vredenburg, K.; Smith, P.W.; Carey, T. The state of user-centered design practice. Commun. ACM **2005**, *48* (3), 105.
3. Cooper, A. *The Inmates are Running the Asylum*; SAMS: Indianapolis, IN, 1999; 17.
4. Winograd, T.; Flores, F. *Understanding Computers and Cognition: A New Foundation for Design*; Addison-Wesley: Reading, MA, 1987.
5. Vredenburg, K. Increasing ease of use. Commun. ACM **1999**, *42* (5), 67.
6. Norman, D.A.; Draper, S.W. (Eds.). *User Centered System Design: New Perspectives on Human-Computer-Interaction*; Erlbaum: Hillsdale, NJ, 1986.
7. Norman, D.A. *The Psychology of Everyday Things*; Doubleday: New York, 1988.
8. Hansen, W.J. User engineering principles for interactive systems. In Proceedings of the May 16–18, 1972, Spring Joint Computer Conference, Atlantic City, NJ, May 16–18, 1972, AFIPS '72; ACM: New York, 523–532.
9. Norman, D.A.; Draper, S.W. (Eds.). *User Centered System Design: New Perspectives on Human-Computer-Interaction*; Erlbaum: Hillsdale, NJ, 1986, 2.
10. Gould, J.D.; Lewis, C. Designing for usability: Key principles and what designers think. Commun. ACM **1985**, *28* (3), 300–311.
11. Nielsen, J. *Usability Engineering*; Academic Press: Boston, MA, 1993.
12. Suchman, L. *Plans and Situated Actions: The Problem of Human Machine Communication*; Cambridge University Press: Cambridge, U.K., 1987.
13. Landauer, T.K. *The Trouble with Computers: Usefulness, Usability and Productivity*; MIT Press: Cambridge, MA, 1996.
14. Vredenburg, K.; Mao, J.-K.; Smith, P.W.; Carey, T. A survey of user-centered design practice. In Proceedings of the SIGCHI Conference on Human Factors in Computing Systems: Changing Our World, Changing Ourselves, Minneapolis, MN, April, 20–25, 2002, CHI '02; ACM: New York, 471–478.
15. Vredenburg, K. Increasing ease of use. Commun. ACM **1999**, *42* (5), 67–71.
16. Cooley, M. Human-centered design. In *Information Design*; Jacobson, R., Ed.; MIT Press: Cambridge, MA, 2000; 59–81.
17. Dewey, J. *Art as Experience*; Penguin: New York, 1934, reprinted 2005; 122.
18. Eames, C. *Design Q&A*; (Color film directed by Charles Eames), 1972.
19. Bannon, L. From human factors to human actors: The role of psychology and human–computer interaction studies in systems design. In *Design at Work: Cooperative Design of Computer Systems*; Greenbaum, J., Kyng, M., Eds.; Lawrence Erlbaum Associates: Hillsdale, NJ, 1990; 25–44.
20. Lodge, L. A user led model of systems development. In *Participation in Systems Development*; Knight, K., Ed.; UNICOM Applied IT Reports, Kogan Page: London, U.K., 1989.
21. Smith, A. *Human Computer Factors: A Study of Users and Information Systems*; McGraw Hill: London, U.K., 1997.
22. Moran, T.P. The command language grammar: A representation for the use interface of interactive computer systems. Int. J. Man-Machine Stud. **1981**, *15*, 3–50.
23. Card, S.K.; Moran, T.P.; Newell, A. *The Psychology of Human-Computer Interaction*; Lawrence Erlbaum Associates: Hillsdale, NJ, 1983.
24. Newell, A.; Card, S.K. The prospects for psychological science in human–computer interaction. Hum-Comp. Interact. **1985**, *1* (3), 209–242.
25. Norman, D.A. Cognitive engineering. In *User Centered System Design: New Perspectives on Human-Computer-Interaction*; Norman, D.A., Draper, S.W., Eds.; Erlbaum: Hillsdale, NJ, 1986; 31–61.
26. Norman, D.A. Cognitive engineering. In *User Centered System Design: New Perspectives on Human-Computer-Interaction*; Norman, D.A., Draper, S.W., Eds.; Erlbaum: Hillsdale, NJ, 1986; 39, 40, 42.
27. Norman, D.A. Cognitive engineering. In *User Centered System Design: New Perspectives on Human-Computer-Interaction*; Norman, D.A., Draper, S.W., Eds.; Erlbaum: Hillsdale, NJ, 1986; 46.

28. Carroll, J.M. Mental Models and Software human factors: an overview. Yorktown, NY: IBM Watson Research Centre, Research Report RC 10616, 1984.

29. Norman, D.A. *Emotional Design: Why We Love (or Hate) Everyday Things*; Basic Books: New York, 2004.

30. Shneiderman, B. *Designing the User Interface: Strategies for Effective Human-Computer Interaction*, 3rd Ed.; Addison Wesley: Menlo Park, CA, 1997.

31. Gould, J.D.; Boies, S.J.; Levy, S.; Richards, J.T.; Schoonard, J. The 1984 Olympic message system: A test of behavioral principle of system design. Commun. ACM **1987**, *30* (9), 758–769.

32. ISO/IEC. 13407, Human-centred design processes for interactive systems, ISO/IEC 13407 1999.

33. Vredenburg, K.; Isensee, S.; Righi, C. *User-Centered Design: An Integrated Approach*; Prentice Hall: Upper Saddle River, NJ, 2002.

34. Rosson, M.B.; Carroll, J.M. *Usability Engineering. Scenario-Based Development of Human- Computer Interaction*; Academic Press: San Diego, CA, 2002.

35. Mayhew, D.J. *The Usability Engineering Lifecycle: A Practitioner's Handbook for User Interface Design*; Morgan Kaufman: San Francisco, CA, 1999.

36. Raskin, J. *The Humane Interface: New Directions for Designing Interactive Systems*; Addison-Wesley: Boston, MA, 2000.

37. Mao, J-Y.; Vredenburg, K.; Smith, P.W.; Carey, T. The state of user-centered design practice. Commun. ACM **2005**, *48* (3), 105–109.

User-Centered Revolution: 1970–1995 *[ELIS Classic]*

Diane Nahl
Information and Computer Sciences Department, University of Hawaii, Honolulu, Hawaii, U.S.A.

Abstract
Nahl traces the increasing emphasis on an orientation to the user as central to information service design, information system design, and library education for professionals and end users.

—ELIS Classic, from 1992

THE NEW PARADIGM ESTABLISHES ITSELF

The user-centered revolution in library and information science was generated by the general availability of search technology for novice and users who rapidly outnumbered experts and intermediaries. The needs of this new class of searchers have changed the priorities in the information environment. In response, researchers have developed new types of data that more closely represent users' actual experience with systems. This interest led to an evolution in the methodologies applied to user studies over the past twenty-five years, from survey questionnaires and feedback forms to interviews, journals, logs, and case histories. The development in methodology represents a shift in focus from gathering anonymous, statistical data on users to individualizing users through ethnographic and psychological approaches.

With technology came transaction logs, a new online, real-time data-gathering method that records every keystroke of every user. Such logs have become a unique source of detailed information on what people do when they search. However, even this level of detail was not sufficient to understand why people make particular command choices and errors. Systematic self-reporting methods were introduced to obtain cognitive and affective data on reasonings, reactions, and decisions. Ethnographic studies using personal journals, protocol analyses, and self-witnessing methods uncovered the overwhelming quality of feelings in the research process. This new knowledge about users is driving the development of new systems and interfaces designed around user-centered principles. However, there was some resistance among designers, administrators, and librarians to the idea of taking care of novices' feelings.

User-Centered Versus System-Centered Approaches

The term user-centered arose in the minds of librarians and information specialists who wanted more services for end users, patrons, clients, students, and the public at large

within the information environment. They saw the status quo as "system-centered"; that is, insufficiently responsive to user needs and realities. One early observer notes the "growing movement" at the time for *user-oriented* systems to shift from "source-controlled" to "receiver-controlled".[1] The expression user-centered has become a maxim—a principle—and represents a new paradigm for defining, measuring, and explaining the behavior of library users, database searchers, and Internet navigators. A search of the literature of the past two decades yields dozens of articles and some books bearing in their title or abstract one of the following expressions of this new orientation:

- User-centered
- User-friendly
- User-based
- User-oriented
- User-responsive
- Client-centered
- Human-centered
- People-centered

Two themes emerged in reviewing literature with a conscious user-centered focus: (1) methods of application that seek to alleviate specific user needs and (2) the integration of theoretical justifications and accounts that researchers have proposed for transforming the information environment through user-centered interventions.

It is worth noting at the outset that the system-centered approach in the design of information facilities routinely advises a testing procedure with actual users within the design process before features are finalized. However, this technique has proved to be inadequate, primarily because user categories have been based on designers' intuitions rather than on research about how users actually perceive, think, and organize and what their intentions are during the information-seeking process. As pointed out by Walther and O'Neil in the early days of online users, "Intuition and good judgment on the part of the designer seem insufficient for specifying the features which an

Encyclopedia of Library and Information Sciences, Fourth Edition DOI: 10.1081/E-ELIS4-120044792

interface should possess" (p. 115).[2] Despite this attempt to give users a greater weight in the interface design equation, system-centeredness has remained essentially the same. The reason for this is clarified in the discussion of the advent of the user-centered paradigm and its essential characteristics. In speaking of this basic shift, one commentator points to a distinction between the concept of information as "like a brick," whereas users are like "empty buckets into which [information] bricks can be thrown" (p. 160).[3] According to Dervin, the invalidity of this metaphor is shown by two outcomes; the "nonuse of information" by both professionals and the general public, and the user-oriented case studies of how people acquire and assimilate information in their daily lives and occupations. Reviewing the data, Dervin concludes

> The important point here is, when it comes to understanding how and why and with what effect human beings pay attention to, process, and use something that an outside observer calls information, we must start by understanding what the user (or potential user) calls information. Information processing and use are, within the context of relativistic assumptions about information, sense-making activities. The emphasis here is on the word "making" for it denotes that the perceiver of the information is not an empty bucket but is actively making sense (pp. 164–165).[3]

Information as an "observer construct" has had to give way to information as a "user construct" because the "empty bucket has evolved into a thinking, self-controlling human being" and "information changes from brick to clay, moved and shaped in unique ways by each perceiver" (p. 169).[3] Because making sense of the world is part of the human condition, knowledge building is therefore a "personal information-seeking" activity.

> Questions asked have dealt with locating self and other (Where am I? Where are they?), with finding possibilities (What can I do?) and evaluating possibilities (Will it work?), and with assessing aloneness (Is anyone listening? Doesn't anyone else agree? Am I the only one?). Perhaps the most important aspect of the findings to date is that they support the premise that looking for information relativistically is a more powerful entry for understanding information needs and use (p. 170).[3]

Looking at information seeking relatively requires one to recognize that situation-specific factors are more important to users than general considerations. For example, users' interests and involvement ("issue oriented") are better predictors of information-seeking activity than users' education or experience. When individuals see their situation as giving them options for decision or movement, they are more likely to engage in information seeking than when they see themselves under total constraint (pp. 171–172).[3] Another reason that information is "relativistic" is that "the effect of the information received is the use created for it by the user." In other words, the situation-specific,

momentary information need determines what information will have impact at that time. Research in this new "relativistic information framework" can help systems designers make the shift to this user-centered orientation.

Replacing the Centrality of the System

In the early days of the new paradigm, there was not yet a full appreciation of the need to remove the centrality of the system. User-centered consciousness was not fully awakened until one saw the necessity of designing systems through understanding users. The following is an example of an early attempt to promote "an empirical approach to user-centered design."

> The problems which accrue to the human user by virtue of being made a component of the system—of the *user* actually being placed on-line to the computer—were largely ignored until very recently. A user protest led to calls for a shift of emphasis from the elegance of algorithms and computational efficiency to the discovery of ways to make the on-line user interface more acceptable to the user (p. 114).[2]

As it turned out, more than "a shift of emphasis" was required. For instance, Walther and O'Neil define the flexibility of an interface as "the factors inherent in the interface program which would make it easier or more convenient for the user to express his commands, given that the commands had to follow a specific syntax" (p. 116);[2] however, this orientation remains part of the system-centered paradigm because it passively accepts the priority or fixity of the system, although it recognizes that acceptability and convenience to users is to be taken into account. Another example is in the earlier attempts to use empirical or objective measures of *user satisfaction*. Researchers often turned to existing "attitude measures" such as the semantic differential,[4] which provides subjects with a series of bipolar scales on which to rate their attitude toward aspects of the system.

> The results indicate that the users of the flexible version [of the online editor], irrespective of any other factors, rated their version as more tolerant, more flexible, more like a person, more friendly, and more pleasant than the inflexible version (p. 117).[2]

Future development of the user-centered paradigm will view such attempts as insufficient. Attitude scales have the following three inherent weaknesses relating to the object being rated, the timing of the rating, and its content. These problems need to be remedied by utilizing different techniques that avoid them.

First, the *object to be rated* by the user needs to be the user's experience, not the system. Thus, *not* "On a scale of 1 to 7, how easy is this editor to use?" but rather, "On a scale of 1 to 7, how much confusion did you experience with this editor?" Second, the *act of rating* needs to be in proximity to where the activity occurs, not at the end of a session, or even later, but concurrently, during the activity itself. Thus, more than a single probe is necessary, as a user's experience may vary greatly from one minute to the next, depending on various difficulties. Third, the *content of the rating* category must originate from the user's mental structure rather than the experimenter's, otherwise measures such as attitude scales, survey questions, census data, and personality tests represent system-centered accommodations to user protests of user-unfriendly systems.

More recent statements of user-centered system evaluation and design continue to promote the centrality of users[5], but there is a shift in emphasis away from treating users as a method of determining baseline measures for design standards, toward "application-based evaluation procedures." This represents an orientation toward operational effectiveness rather than design efficiency. In this view, system redesign can be motivated by how inconvenient it is to learn rather than how effectively it can perform under ideal conditions.

Criteria for User-Friendliness

Wallace has proposed a framework for evaluating the user-friendliness of a system.[6] The list includes the following types of measures:

- Users must be given options for preferences.
- Online system operation and assistance should be available at beginner and more advanced levels.
- System behavior has to be transparent to users.
- Warning messages must be benign or lighthearted.
- System design must take into account the physical and psychological needs of users.
- System use should require no special skills.
- The general language of novices and their routine level of communicative skills should not be surpassed in instructions or explanations.
- The system should behave in a uniform way to allow users to anticipate functions.
- A variety of types of problem solving should be available for particular operations.
- Learning by doing should be the preferred mode of instruction and presentation.

One project that implemented these and additional user-friendly features is known as ELSA, "an intelligent electronic library search assistant."[7] Four design concepts guided the development of ELSA.

- Using labels that are transparent to users (e.g., buttons with the names "run search," "new search," and "show full list")
- Providing assistance with controlled vocabulary (e.g., a synonyms list)

- Actively helping users explore topic areas (e.g., providing suggestions for narrower topics and screening out more distantly related items)
- Accommodating different styles of interaction (e.g., an option to type in search items or select them with the mouse from a list)

Another historical example is the user-centered redesign of the MELVYL system in response to empirically discovering the answer to the question, "What do users really want?" According to Farley,[8] the process of collecting and maintaining a comment database optional to users has uncovered bugs in the system as well as numerous user-unfriendly features that could form the basis for redesign. Today, with Internet networking of libraries, MELVYL has learned to "compete in attractiveness" to users who are more sophisticated and computer literate, although still novice searchers.

The development of intelligent search assistants such as ELSA would not have occurred without the climate created by the user-centered revolution that gave it scientific legitimacy and made research grants available for user studies. The first phase of the transformation concluded when *user-friendliness* became a legitimate scientific research issue. An important thrust came from the human-computer interaction field populated by engineers, programmers, and applied psychologists.

Toward Human-Centered Design

In a whimsical mood, one of the architects of the user-centered revolution in the area of systems design and technology describes a still common attitude regarding the introduction of new technology.

> One of the things that stands out when talking to long-term users of poorly designed systems is that these people take great pride in their skills. They had to go through great difficulties to master the system, and they are rightfully proud of having done so. . . . Rather than ease the situation for those who follow, it becomes a sort of initiation rite. The hardy survivors of the experience claim to share a common bond and look with disdain upon those who have not been through the same rites. They share horror stories with one another (p. 176).[9]

Norman reveals that he "got attacked by hundreds of professional programmers across the country" when he wrote an article criticizing the UNIX system as user-unfriendly: "If I didn't approve of UNIX, they told me, I had no business using it. Besides, who was I anyway to criticize computer software? In other words, you weren't allowed to criticize unless you were a professional. Being a mere user of the stuff didn't qualify" (p. 177).[9] However, a new paradigm was in the ascendancy, and it is achieving full victory. The user-centered revolution not only gives users more clout in the design equation but works to make users the *central* point of focus and interest for planners, backers, designers, engineers, and trainers of information systems.

Understandability and usability are two principles that apply equally to design and documentation issues. According to proponents of "cognitive engineering."[10] Understandability of instructions depends on providing a good conceptual model of the task or system. Good models are those that allow users to predict the effects of their actions. Users will invent false models when the appearance of some system features (the visible setup) does not match the functions desired (p. 16).[10] The designer's model is formalized by the design process itself. The user's model evolves through interaction with the system. The system image consists of the visible structure or appearance of the interface (control, keys, instructions, labels, visualization aids or interface metaphor, etc.). All communication between designer and user takes place through the system image. If the system image does not make the design model clear, users end up with a wrong mental model as evidenced by symptoms such as an inability to predict, difficulty in using, a shallow understanding, and an inability to solve problems. One of the key factors in helping users develop an accurate conceptual model is to provide immediate feedback for every action or choice made.

User Errors

By studying the psychology of everyday actions, cognitive engineers have discovered many reasons why people make errors. First, one should note that people blame themselves for errors: "It is as if they take perverse pride in thinking of themselves as mechanically [or technologically] incompetent" (p. 35).[10] Second, experience has shown that good system interfaces can be designed that make errors easy to detect and easy to reverse or, if not, have minimal consequences. Good designers heed the maxim: If an error is possible, someone will make it. One common source of errors is inadequate mapping, where users develop misconceptions in their mental models of the system. The existence of conflictual habits is another source of error (e.g., frequently hitting the wrong key for a particular operation). Users are reassured when they are reminded that making errors is routine in everyday automated activities such as keyboarding. Natural situations allow for routine correction of errors, such as retyping or abandoning a sentence midway and beginning a new sentence. This explains why error recovery procedures have become essential in designing computer systems in the user-centered era.

Norman (p. 107)[10] has identified several types of user errors. *Capture errors* occur when a frequently performed activity suddenly takes charge instead of the intended one (e.g., hitting the wrong function key; hitting return instead of an F key; waiting while staring at the screen without having entered the command). *Description errors* result from performing a correct action but on the wrong object, which occur when we are distracted, bored, or fatigued. *Data-driven errors* occur when the sight of some object or information intrudes into an action sequence (e.g., typing the wrong information on a line; choosing an unintended menu item). *Associated activation errors* occur when an association of ideas or thoughts triggers a nonrelevant action (e.g., typing an incorrect subject heading phrase). *Loss of activation errors* occur when the goal of an action is momentarily forgotten or when part of a sequence is temporarily inhibited. *Mode errors* occur when users forget what mode they are in when there are several (e.g., typing a command appropriate to another mode). Inherent in creating a user-friendly information environment is the requirement to discover what errors users routinely make, to expect them, and to provide accessible remedies for them.

> For the first time in history, we are truly free to make machines that fit human needs, independent of mechanical constraints. New information technologies can enhance the power of human thinking, for machine plus person can do more than either alone, but only if the technology complements human abilities. We need more information-processing tools that complement our thinking, reasoning, and memory skills as comfortably as the calculator enhances our arithmetic skills. We can transform the hard technology of computers and information processing into soft technology suitable for people if we start with the needs of the human users, not with the requirements of the technology (pp. 52–53).[11]

At this stage, according to one commentator, designers of information systems are now committed to a "user-centered design philosophy," and have begun implementing interfaces that take into account "end-user information seeking needs."[12]

User-centered online design philosophy

Marchionini makes three assumptions about the characteristics of end users in electronic environments.[12] First, end users are not interested in system characteristics such as design, elegance, or data structure. Instead, they want to get to the end of their work; they want answers, not pointers; they want document delivery, not information retrieval. A second assumption is that "end-users want to achieve their goals with a minimum of cognitive load and a maximum of enjoyment" (p. 156).[12] This assumption echoes the law of least effort.

> Moreover humans seek the path of least cognitive resistance and prefer recognition tasks to recall tasks; most people will trade time to minimize complexity. Finally, humans will perform better and continue to use systems that are pleasureful or interesting (pp. 157–158).[12]

Computer-augmented information seeking can create a more relaxed, less stressful, more pleasant search environment. In other words, if it is user-centered, it is affectively more benign. In the past, attempts at designing more user-friendly information systems have led to software interfaces known as "metaphors," such as the Desk Top metaphor for the operating system on Macintosh computers, and its competitor, the Windows metaphor. This approach has been applied more recently to developing alternatives to traditional command language interfaces. For example, Borgman and colleagues developed the "library metaphor" for an Online Public Access Catalog (OPAC) interface in an elementary school that uses the Dewey system and allows students to browse hierarchical graphic bookshelves (pp. 55–68).[13] Some of the more recent search support innovations include the following, according to Mar-chionini's review:

- Query-by-example[14]
- Spatial database representations[15]
- Online thesauri tied into the search command sequence[16]
- Interfaces that offer suggestions to users, including dynamic queries that evolve as part of the interaction with the system[17]
- Problem articulation as pruning (where users begin with all items in the database selected and each query results in a subset; e.g., computer library CD-ROM)
- Problem articulation "on the fly" through active browsing and judicious navigation in hypertext systems[18]

Other developments include the addition of alternate input devices such as data gloves, gesture recognizers, speech recognizers, and eye trackers (p. 160).[12] Marchionini quotes Gauch, saying that, "In electronic environments, the IR problem is not finding information, it is filtering information" (p. 161).[12] This comment reflects a fundamental dilemma of end users in today's information environment. However, novice users still do have great difficulties finding information because of their inadequate knowledge of search logic and vocabulary selection difficulties. Marchionini concludes that user-centered interfaces should accommodate individual differences, cultural diversity of individuals, and users' affective and cognitive characteristics.

Writing Affective Point-of-use Instructions

The potential importance of help instructions in influencing the user's affective information environment was demonstrated in an experimental study. Nahl showed that the stress and anxiety routinely experienced by novice searchers can be alleviated by adding a distinctly affective component to the instructions, consisting of providing additional orientation, advice, and reassurance.[19] The importance of psychological factors in searching was examined by asking subjects to indicate on a self-efficacy scale how confident they were in their ability to achieve a successful search outcome. Subjects who felt more optimistic in predicting a positive outcome has significantly better outcome scores than those who predicted low success for their searches. This suggests that optimism and self-confidence as a searcher empower users to better cope with the information environment. For instance, they found the instructions more helpful and comprehensible, they expressed more satisfaction with search results, and they spent less time per search. By contrast, searchers who expected low success expressed more frustration during the search activity, tried out a greater number of unsuccessful strategies, found the instructions less helpful, and spent more time per search. Fortunately, the pessimistic user self-orientation appears to be modifiable.

> Optimism in searching is a learnable affective skill that involves generating positive self-regulatory sentences throughout the searching process. Point-of-use instructions and online Help facilities can either ignore this aspect of the user's environment, or they can attempt to deal with explicitly. Future research will have to discover the specific verbalizations that need to be added in the form of elaborations to the instructions so that searchers will come to expect probable success rather than probable failure. One approach might be to identify what verbalizations are used by novice searchers who operate under a positive role model through think-aloud protocols, and then to incorporate these sentences in point-of-use instructions (p. 187).[20]

Because the affective information environment is dynamic and challenging, users need to be taught coping skills that reduce stress and errors.

Written point-of-use instructions and online help screens provide good opportunities for user-centered interfaces to deliver both cognitive and affective information services. As reviewed by Nahl,[20] user-centered consciousness in the area of software documentation and help instructions first took the form of "minimalist," advancing the principle that verbose text is tedious, confusing, and repelling to users in general. Shorter, well-organized, and indexed manuals are not only preferred by users but are also less costly to produce. This tend was beneficial, as it enabled systems professionals to focus on what users prefer in terms of length or detail and easy-to-understand language.

A sample of written point-of-use instructions for CD-ROM database searching typical of university library handouts was analyzed and found to be minimalist in both cognitive and affective information, but especially the latter.[20] Breaking minimalist principles in user instructions, Nahl edited and lengthened an existing point-of-use instruction sheet by adding sentences that served as "affective speech acts," providing users with extra orientation, extra advice, and plenty of reassurances. The elaborated version was three times longer than the former but was rated significantly more helpful and comprehensible to subjects in a controlled experiment.

Perceived Self-Efficacy as a Searcher

An interesting and unexpected finding from the preceding experiment was that novice users enter the search situation with definite beliefs about their probable success. Subjects were asked to review five search tasks they were about to perform and predict their probable success. The group was then divided for analysis into two subgroups, namely the upper and lower halves in terms of self-confidence as searchers. The results showed significant differences in all of the dependent measures of user behavior, despite the fact that the students in the two subgroups did not differ in searching or computing experience. Novice users who had higher expectations of search success also had higher retrieval scores, expressed greater satisfaction with results, felt less frustrated during the searching, were more effective in their search strategies, and were more efficient. Rather than viewing these features as permanent psychological or demographic differences, Nahl sees a searcher's self-efficacy beliefs as a learned mental habit that, with effort and instruction, can be further developed.

Nahl relates these findings to prior research and theory on *self-efficacy beliefs*[21,22] and *speech act theory*.[23–25] As users engage in the act of searching, a continuous stream of silent verbalizations is produced as a means of making things understandable, and as a by-product of their affective involvement, by taking charge, users can consciously manage these sentences and use them to regulate their behavior.

One method of self-control involves the use of self-regulatory sentences thought to oneself. *Self-regulatory sentences*, viewed as habitual speech acts of users in a learning setting, can be witnessed and deliberately changed in self-modification attempts. "Learned optimism"[26] is an affective habit some users evolve by acquiring an "optimistic" style of talking to themselves during searching by expressing greater self-confidence in a successful search outcome. "Learned pessimism," on the other hand, is a habit of "helplessness" in the face of challenge and apparent constraint. Users who have low self-efficacy beliefs as searchers have acquired "pessimistic" habits of thinking and express lower self-confidence in their search success. Because habits can be retrained, Nahl suggests that instructions and help assistance contain advice and reassurance that counteract negative self-talk and help users establish more adaptive self-regulatory speech acts while operating in the information environment.

Boolean Pitfalls

One of the stumbling blocks for novice users of online systems such as CD-ROM bibliographic and full-text databases is that search principles operate by Boolean logic, which at first may seem counterintuitive. For example, in ordinary language, a query problem may state "Search for articles on the dangers and risks of caffeine and caffeine products to pregnant women." One possible solution might be the search statement:

(danger OR risk) AND caffeine AND pregnant women

Note that in Boolean logic, the *and* between "dangers and risks" requires a transformation to the OR operator. In "caffeine and caffeine products," the words *and products* should be ignored. Transforming that AND to OR would not be a fatal search logic error, but in ordinary language, it appears to novices as if the search statement should read as follows:

dangers AND risks AND caffeine AND caffeine products AND pregnant women

In the words of one novice attempting to think in Boolean: "You need to find out about both caffeine and caffeine products, so you need to put AND between them." However, this search statement is not likely to produce the expected results.

There is evidence of the occurrence of a leakage between the semantic and the logical features of Boolean cognitions. Semantically, both caffeine and other caffeine-related products are of interest here, and it is true; however, the operational logic of searching requires the OR operator if either subject is wanted. In order to block semantic leakage from influencing the logical requirement, a cognitive transition must take place in which the primary focus is on searching the text of records rather than on the semantic features of the topic. This semantic to search logic transition may at first seem contrary to ordinary thinking.

As pointed out by Nahl,[27] composing valid Boolean search statements depends on an accurate understanding of both the semantic and logical features of the operation. Searchers must learn to keep intact the boundary between these two aspects. There must not be any leakage in the rational "membrane" that separates the semantic from the logical functions. The following example shows how one novice searcher, after reading the instructions, did not separate the semantic aspects from the purely logical features of a Boolean search statement. The task was to:

Circle the concept(s) that must appear in every article retrieved by this strategy: (driving behavior OR drivers) AND risk-taking

The subject inaccurately circled "driving behavior" and wrote the following explanation:

Because the interest is in driving and correlation to behavior, style, motive, etc., I feel that the circled concept must be in every article.

In operation here is the act of reasoning by similarity instead of reasoning by search probability logic. The problem should have been solved purely from the perspective of formal Boolean logic [i.e., (A OR B) AND C, requiring that concept C appear in each of the retrieved records]. Instead, *semantic leakage* form the topic "driving" led this novice to ignore the necessary logical implications of the Boolean connector. Data such as these indicate which aspects of Boolean reasoning need to be specifically explained and taught.

User-centered online design philosophy must take into account several dynamic factors. Some researchers point to the need for accommodating individual differences, cultural diversity, and affective and cognitive characteristics. Novices need different types of elaborations in oral and written instructions for using systems, especially those that provide orientation, advice, and reassurance. Even the self-confidence of novice searchers plays an influential role in their style, success, and satisfaction. Avoiding Boolean pitfalls and understanding search logic cannot be left to self-instruction. The recognition that users require training that incorporates all of these dynamics has led to a change in public awareness.

THE PUBLIC SECTOR

In the area of library management, one study refers to "a user-oriented approach" when priorities for library services are set through the use of survey data[28] comparing the budgets and opinions of three special library directors with the research staffs of three organizations as to their attitudes and priorities. Surveying users to get data relevant for planning information services is a response by the system to calls for becoming more user-centered. An early expression of the user-centered paradigm is found in the work of Parks,[29] who focused on information needs in the public library sector for the handicapped and the elderly. Parks identifies the passage of Titles IV-A and IV-B of the Library Services and Construction Act as marking the beginning of a new community attitude and practice toward the institutionalized and the challenged in our society. This trend has seeped into the *physical* environment of libraries (e.g., signs, central floor plan, electric-eye doors, color, plants, fish tanks) the *organizational* environment (e.g., hours, formal teaching, special programs), and the *human* environment (e.g., social climate, group rituals, flexibility, individualized response, initiative, poise). The passage of the Americans with Disabilities Act continues to deepen this trend.

The Role of Technology

Two factors seem to drive the movement of the user-centered paradigm shift: the rapidly increasing number of novice end users and changing technology. These two factors are interrelated. An increasing population of novice users and greater technological complexity combine to exert social pressure on the managers of information environments. The role of technology was described this way by a library educator.

> In short, this is an era of stressful change brought on by convulsive waves of shifting values on every front. Change is not new to libraries, of course, but what is new is the collapsed time-scale of change. In the past change was faced as it happened, but lately social and technological alternatives have occurred at so great a rate that change must be dealt with continuously. The order of change is entirely different from anything which came before. Whether one calls this change revolutionary or evolutionary hardly matters; what counts is the degree to which such change will affect the library's role in society. As one librarian put it recently, "the trouble with our times is that the future is not what it used to be" (p. 409).[30]

A recent review of Ranganathan's 1928 "Five Laws of Library Science" shows where these principles operate today within the new information technology. According to Sharma's analysis, new technology "is enabling the realization of Ranganathan's vision of user-centered, user-friendly information service implied in his Five Laws" (p. 258).[31]

1. Books are for use.
2. Every reader his book.
3. Every book its reader.
4. Save the time of the reader.
5. The library is a growing organism.

The *open access* technology has enabled realization of the first law as embodied, for example, in online catalogs that "show whether a document is on the shelves of the library or not; and if charged out, when it is due back in the library" (p. 260).[31] *Resource sharing* and networking have helped validate the second law, and the third law is facilitated by cross-references and keyword search modes in online databases. Finding information in the shortest possible time with online searching, full-text, and CD-ROM technology serve the fourth law; planning and organization of libraries can promote the fifth law. Realistically, these laws are potentiated by new technology, but technology must assist users in more significant ways before these laws can be attained.

With the new networking technology, "information space" has become so vast that new methods have been invented to allow users to "navigate cyberspace." Various "browsers" introduce their own problems in usability. Old skills for reading paper formats and sequential paging habits have to be modified and applied to screen-presented text, scrolling, and hypertext linking within and across documents. Text formatting, color, highlighting, and speed of access have become important user-related considerations that influence the quality and success of "surfing sessions" on the Internet.

Futures Planning

Those who plan for library services for the next century have adopted a clear user-centered focus. For example, Shapiro and Long (p. 286)[32] advocate the "reengineering" of user services in academic libraries by spelling out a number of principles.

- Recognizing and dealing with the whole range of user needs (i.e., reference service, telecommunications software assistance, and searching difficulties).
- Transforming services staff into information "caseworkers" so that librarians try to maintain postconsultation follow-up procedures to track what happens to users after they have been referred to other specialists.
- Process or procedures must be developed to suit users rather than organizational structure, and continuous change based on feedback or evaluation is essential for effectiveness of information delivery.
- Information technology must not be used merely to provide access through automation but to assist users, such as automated problem-tracking systems and information desks or kiosks.
- Collaboration across the campus with faculty groups and the computing center is essential in producing "symbiotic" operations in support of users.

One study investigated what users of a university library think libraries of the future should be like. The most frequently cited "critical" use of the ideal library of the future was "speedy retrieval and simplicity of use" (p. 307)[33] Other desired uses included computerized catalog, online searching of databases, full-text retrieval, wide availability of terminals, remote access, twenty-four-hour availability, and personal library assistance services. Another commentator on types of services that would be offered in "user-responsive research libraries" warns that

Some futurists foresee them becoming outmoded storehouses of printed materials, repositories that lie outside of the mainstream of academic life. Others predict that they will become vital information centers, growing more central to research and teaching as the information world becomes even more complex. A cogent case can be argued for either of these opposing extremes, but the final outcome is still beyond our field of vision (p. 59).[34]

To ensure a positive final outcome to the user-centered revolution, the following system features are recommended for the electronic information environment:

- It should be more access-oriented, less size-oriented.
- There should be universal adaptation to the technology by the entire library staff.
- Personnel should give up the myth that researchers and scholars are skilled users.

Dougherty calls for "a significant overhaul of the duties of most reference librarians and bibliographers" to assist them in developing a better understanding of faculty information needs, their information-gathering habits, and their service preferences.

Customer Service Philosophy

The knowledge needed by information workers to deliver adequate services has become quite broad, according to a recent textbook that addresses "customer service in the information environment."

It is Mr. St Clair's premise that the information services practitioner must be broadly defined to include persons engaged in every aspect of information service from records management to technology-based information transfer. The connecting link in all of this information work and the basis for this book is that user needs determine the nature of the information service and that the user's knowledge of the subject area is a critical component in determining how the information services practitioner will organize the information and make it accessible in the most efficient manner possible, (from the foreword by John Ganly).[35]

The recognition that information systems should represent how users think rather than how librarians organize information has become the cornerstone of the new paradigm. The "new philosophy of service" aims for "the provision of quality information to its customers," including such customer service mottoes as the following:

1. People come first.
2. We give accurate and reliable information.
3. We are serious about our high level of service.
4. We cannot afford to give one wrong answer.
5. We are accessible and easy to approach.
6. We are doers—we work hard.
7. We are often pleased but never satisfied.
8. We want our staff to be happy working for us.
9. Service is a state of mind. People must care and have a desire to do it right and to do it now.
10. The client is always right.
11. Everyone must be thinking about how to do his or her job better and more effectively.
12. Enthusiasm and faith are necessary to remove barriers and increase productivity and decrease costs (pp. 5–6,[35] attributed to Meg Paul).

This new philosophy of information service strikes some librarians as a model more appropriate for commercial settings than academic and public libraries.[36] This conflict illustrates how the new user-centered paradigm is being extended. It appears that new technology, in such forms as the Internet and World Wide Web, has deepened the connection between marketing principles and library and information services. This shift is reflected in the historical sequence of designations referring to recipients of library and information services: readers, patrons, clients, end users, and customers. "Customer" service in the information environment brings marketing principles to librarians and information specialists.

Central to the new marketing attitude of information provision, whether for the corporate library or public school multimedia lab, is the "information audit" or user survey. Needs analysis identifies the character of the constituent user groups. Focus groups can help determine what kind of information delivery users prefer. Test runs reveal which procedures users resist or are reluctant to follow, or that produce errors. User surveys elicit responses and comments by potential users. In considering the question of why the wishes of the information consumers have not been better taken care of in the past, St Clair points out that

> We have been remarkably successful in using technology in the organization of information, and we are justifiably proud of our long history is using information technology in creating information products and services *for our customers*. What we haven't done is to use the same technology for creating programs to help us learn more *about* our customers. We haven't taken the time because we've been so busy developing the information products that we forgot who we were developing the products for (p. 93).[35]

"User-oriented evaluation" (UOE) has been promoted as *action research* "carried out with the aim of generating information which may be used, in some way, to improve information systems and services" (p. 93).[37] UOE methods include test searches, user attitudes, failure analysis, case study, microevaluation, and other forms of situation-specific qualitative and quantitative analyses. The complexities of studying the user in the information environment require new and more intensive methods.[38]

The user-centered trend is creating a basic revision of library management and operation in the form of incorporating user input at various levels as a structural component of the management process. One expert advises a phasing-in process starting with the creation of a collection development committee with liaisons to faculty and jointly established written procedures.[39] Collection vendors would be invited to receive input from the joint committee. Similarly, faculty would serve on a serials development committee and initiate procedures for campuswide departmental input. The structural integration of users into the management fabric itself creates the "client-centered library" (p. 351).[39]

The Role of Legislation

Legislation and community attitude are important influencing factors in shaping information institutions to their users. In 1979, the board of the Association of American Library Schools set up a task force to examine the implications of the White House Conference on Library and Information Services,[40] in which the principal theme was a reaffirmation of free and full access for all citizens. Although the members of the task force recognized this thrust and supported it, they felt that even more needs to be done, such as "recruiting to the profession representatives from the information impoverished, who may have the advantage of instant credibility with their constituencies" (p. 250).[40] At least one of the "elements of a comprehensive national library and information services program" was explicitly from a user-centered point of view, recognizing the idea that *access* includes *education*.

A-5. *Access to Library and Information Services*

That institutions educating library and informational services practitioners assume responsibility to address the need of said consumers through their training and education, and that guidelines by appropriate governmental leaders establish standards of in-service training and that training standards for library professionals be implemented without delay

In other words, librarians need to be educated in how to instruct users to gain access to filter and evaluate information.

Educating Information Specialists

The education of future librarians to function in technologically reengineered library settings is addressed in a study describing "a model of how academic libraries and schools of library and information studies (LIS) may collaborate to provide useful education experiences to LIS students and reliable reference services to library users."[41] Students study and apply information-retrieval principles and reference interview theory, as well as "role playing, analysis of frequently asked questions, and philosophy of information service" (p. 292).[41] The emphasis is on the case-study approach, as students were required to follow up on the advice and instruction they gave to library users, to test its efficacy, and to study the entire information-retrieval cycle.

In both the courses and the fieldwork, students were urged to accept a client-centered philosophy of reference librarianship and to view library users and librarians as linked in the research process. Students were encouraged to be approachable at the information desk, to look out for people who might need information, to ask follow-up questions in reference interviews, to encourage people to return to the desk to go to another service point for further assistance, and to express a variety of user-centered values and attitudes while at the information desk.

This reference fieldwork allowed LIS students to gain experience in answering online catalog and directional questions at one of the library's busiest information service points. The experience enabled LIS students to make the immediate connection between the theoretical content of the course and the actual experience of reference work in a large academic library. The students consistently expressed their appreciation of this integration of theory and practice that allows them to try out various principles in vivo and receive immediate feedback from library users.

The two factors driving the user-centered movement are the increase in the number of novice end users and the rapid change in technology. Future planning in library services for the next century supports a clear user-centered focus. The customer service philosophy, although not acceptable to everyone, nevertheless points to the recognition that information systems should represent how users think rather than solely how librarians organize information. Legislation, community attitude, and education of information specialists are moving toward a client-centered philosophy of reference librarianship. The increasing social consciousness of the importance of the user cannot by itself create an intellectual revolution unless supporting scientific theory evolves along with it.

COMMUNICATION THEORY

Sense Making

One of the earliest statements defining the concept of user-centeredness is attributed to the critique of Zweizig and Dervin, whose approach is based in American communication research.

> Since the 1970s, critical attitudes toward the narrow conceptions germane to a system-centered approach were evinced. Institutions such as libraries distributing information were seen as instruments serving information seeking and use, not as an end. The critique was made explicit by Douglas Zweizig and Brenda Dervin, precursors of the *user-centered approach* to information seeking and use. They proposed that instead of asking who is using the library or how much is the library used, the question should be for what purpose was the library used and how did it help? Thus the important question would be not library use, not library users, but library uses.[42] Since the late 1970s, suggestions for a refocus of research on the individual actors seeking and using information in practical social and cultural contexts have become more frequent [see, e.g., 43–45]. Today we see that these efforts have been successful—the user-centered approach is about to offer the traditional intermediary-centered approach a serious paradigmatic alternative (p. 14).[46]

Sense-making research investigates behavior, both internal (i.e., cognitive) and external (i.e., procedural), allowing individuals to construct and design their movement through time-space. Sense-making behavior is thus

communication behavior. Information is the sense that is created at a specific moment by an individual. Information does not exist apart from the subjective, constructive process. The central activities of sense making are information seeking, processing, creating, and using. Sense making is a process; sense is the product of this process. According to Dervin, "sense" includes "knowledge," but also a host of other subjective factors that reflect an individual's interpretations of a situation, including "intuitions, opinions hunches, effective responses, evaluations, questions, etc." (p. 16).[46] Thinking and perceiving are referred to as "moving forward in the cognitive terrain." When there is a lack of relevant information or there is confusion and uncertainty, routine thinking no longer works effectively, and a situation called "gap-facing" arises and elicits "gap-defining" and "gap-bridging" activities. People evaluate their gaps differently; "optimists" may see no problem where "pessimists" are stumped. They may differ in "rigidity" or "flexibility" in their gap-bridging.

Dervin's sense-making concept, defined as the "movement of thoughts and questions through cognitive time-space," is explained by another commentator as follows:

> In this sense, one may be said to move through a series of thoughts and experiences, to encounter "barriers" to one's progress, to "lose" one's way, etc. In either case, any given movement can be interrupted when an individual is confronted by the need for some form of guidance; that is, when they need to know something. Based on the work of Carter,[47] such conditions are considered cognitive "gaps," and may be exemplified in their most general form by the need for street directions or instructions on the use of Boolean connectors, depending on the behavior context. Information seeking is defined within this framework as "gap bridging." Gap bridging can be accomplished by thinking up an answer, asking for help, looking for useful information, or by any other functional method that enables the individual to continue moving. These gap-bridging attempts are operationalized as "questioning," whether spoken by individuals or unspoken (p. 649).[48]

In an attempt to apply Dervin's sense-making theory to the day-to-day operation of a library, Morris asks such basic questions as, "What does it mean to have a user-centered reference service?" or "What should a user-centered approach to cataloging entail?" (p. 20).[49] User-centered in this theoretical context means viewing information as something "construed by users" and designing systems and services that are tailored to how humans think and feel when processing information to meet a need. This is in contrast to the traditional system-oriented definition based on the work of Shannon and Weaver[50] that views information as having an objective existence outside the individual.

> When we seek information through the traditional paradigm, our goal is to find the external "information reality"

that corresponds to our internal need. As Dervin points out, we don't talk as if we hold this traditional view of information. On the contrary, we admit that knowledge isn't absolute, that what really matters are people, that people change, and that a message sent doesn't equal a message received (p. 21).[49]

In the sense-making model, information becomes "whatever an individual finds 'informing'" (p. 22).[51] Information triggers changes in the user's perceptions, which alter how the information is perceived. The user is seen not as a passive receptacle but as an active participant in a constructive process of information processing. Although users are unique individuals, there is a common or universal process through which all users pass in adaptation to a particular information activity. Addressing user-centered services to these commonalities requires scientific knowledge about the actions, thoughts, and feelings that constitute the experience of being a novice user.

According to Morris, a primary goal of information professionals should be "understanding and clarifying ambiguous information needs" (p. 25).[49] Ambiguity and uncertainty can be unpleasant and stressful feelings; hence, library services such as reference interviews need to be negotiated by librarians with a view to "intervening" in the person's state of information challenge. Vague requests, or those that are too broad or too narrow, may require probing with open questions, addressing the need behind the demand rather than the want or demand as first formulated by the user. An interesting point raised by Morris is that users tend to operate under the system-centered paradigm in their own views of what information is or what the process of finding it is like. The self-contradictory nature of users is captured vividly in the following description:

> The picture of the individual that emerges from these studies in psychology holds complex implications for a user-centered, constructivist model of information. Humans are, by their nature, contradictory: drawn to make quick decisions that reduce uncertainty but struggling to understand clearly enough to make a good decision; striving for order, but enjoying the intellectual challenge of disorderly facts and unconventional ideas; needing the familiar, but craving the risk of the unknown; unable to express what is needed, but nonetheless perpetually asking questions; highly knowledgeable, but unable to transfer that knowledge. This is the user whom we wish to serve (p. 29).[49]

In a radical proposal, Dervin[52] urges that we abandon the traditional system-centered categories of users such as demography (age, race, education, gender), personality (cognitive styles and preferences), ability or literacy levels (language, computer, knowledge), purpose for using the system (information, entertainment, research), and user-satisfaction ratings. Such categories, Dervin argues, "lead us to a view of communication systems that makes haves and have-nots inevitable" (p. 217).[52] The "haves" are those who successfully use the system, whereas the "have-nots must somehow get more of what they lack—education, money, literacy, motivation to read news, computer skill, cognitive complexity, etc.—so that they can become like the haves" (p. 217).[52]

Revising User Categories

Dervin proposes a radical redesign of the information world based on a deliberate refocusing of the nature of user categories.

The actor's situation. This category of user behavior identifies "why in a given situation a person tries to use an information or communication system" (p. 225).[52] How complex is the situation? Is it a piece of a larger project? Under what constraints is the user operating? What barriers does the user perceive?

Gaps in sense making. A query points to some gap in information and the outcome of a search yields a message that can help close the gap by constructing new meaning or new understanding. An information gap is not to be defined by topical categories or subjects, as in the system-centered orientation. Instead, gaps are "gaps regarding the characteristics, aspects, or dimensions of self, others, objects, events, timing, spacing, causes, consequences, and what-ifs" (p. 225).[52]

Actor-defined purpose. System-defined purposes for "looking for information" traditionally include such broad categories as information, entertainment, social, cultural, and escape. User-centered purposes are more situationally specific, such as "getting pictures (cognitions), finding direction, gaining skills, getting motivation, avoiding bad places, getting out of bad places, getting support, getting connected, achieving goals, getting happiness, getting rest" (p. 225).[52]

Information-Using Strategies, Values, and Traits

User strategies are adaptive mechanisms that people employ in searching for and using information. These include "browsing, formatting, grouping, highlighting, indexing, citing, digesting, abstracting, formulating, transmitting, interpreting, connecting, and skimming" (p. 225).[52] "Actors" (i.e., searchers) evaluate information in terms of its meaning to them; that is, its "timeliness, breadth, adaptability, accuracy, specificity, touchability, moveability, and newsiness" (p. 225).[52] The term "information traits" covers "the specific characteristics of how the user would like the information presented," such as quantitative data versus qualitative assessment, precedence setting versus futures planning, hard facts versus opinion, single point versus options, and clinical observation versus census.

When comparing traditional user categories with these user-centered dimensions, a clearer view emerges of how the information world needs to be redesigned to make it more serviceable to users in terms of instruction, assistance, and organization (cataloging and indexing). In terms of *user assistance*, build a focus on user categories. Under what constraints is the user operating? Is the user more interested in gaining an understanding of something specific or exploring without a fixed goal? At what stage of the seeking process is the user at this time? Does the user want to take the information home? Does the user want to see hard facts only or is there an interest in clinical studies also?

In terms of user-centered *information organization*, the focus is on indexing content in terms that users can recognize in relation to their momentary and variable intentions and motives. How do I just browse? How do I reformat this text? Where do I find a citation for this? What would help reformulate this? Where can I find a digest of this? I need to see an interpretation of this (and so forth). A user-friendly environment anticipates and accommodates, facilitates, reassures, and above all, delivers and satisfies. To achieve the goals, information professionals have developed methods for identifying and measuring users' behaviors—their actions, thoughts, and feelings during the information-seeking or knowledge acquisition process.

MODIFYING USER BEHAVIOR

Learning Principles for Searcher Self-Modification

A number of writers in the field of library science have urged the application of learning theory principles to library instruction and services.[53–55] The field of psychology has broadly discussed the "conditions of learning" that need to be present when acquiring new habits, and some of these were summarized for the narrower field of acquiring information retrieval skills.[55]

Sufficient motivation for learning

Search behavior is goal-directed behavior hierarchically organized so that subgoals constitute larger goals. For instance, looking up a word or entry in an index is a subskill within the larger skill of locating a document. The subskill requires the searcher to inspect the list, look up and down, page through, select terms, and so on. This subskill has its own goal and motivation. If the searcher lacks sufficient motivation to persist in the look-up operation, the subactivity will be prematurely abandoned, with negative consequences to the overall search effort. A single global assessment or rating of a user's motivation or interest in completing a task is thus unlikely to predict accurately a person's multiple motivational requirements with all the subtasks. The information environment needs

to be designed to encourage and facilitate the emergence of sufficient motivation at multiple levels of administration and instruction.[56]

Active responding

Instruction must provide for some form of responding or active participation from the user. In the sensorimotor domain, locating an item on a computer screen is a prerequisite skill that needs to be practiced beyond some minimum level before one can expect users to have success in finding information. In the cognitive domain, users need to be given learning opportunities to rehearse reasoning sequences such as "What would happen if I do X?" or how to redirect a search strategy that is not effective. In the affective domain, novices need to be given the experience of overcoming an information challenge by helping them complete a task or operation successfully.

Providing reinforcement

In the educational and clinical psychology literature, a "reinforcing stimulus" is an incentive that works; that is, if that reward is systematically applied in a teaching context, learners will acquire that target habit more quickly. Of course, some incentives do not work. One guiding principle is to discover what users find relevant and rewarding in specific information situations. Although it is universally recognized that rewarded repetitions lead to learning new skills, given the hierarchical organization of information skills, global rewards are not always sufficient to maintain consistent reinforcement. Sometimes too much emphasis may be given by users and professionals alike to the end result or to overall search success. If this is unsatisfactory, a general negative pall is cast over the entire information-seeking enterprise. Instead, users can be *taught to appreciate* the little successes within the overall (temporary) impasse.

Reinforcement strengthens the behavior to which it is applied. The repetition and rehearsal that occur with hands-on experience become opportunities for applying reinforcement and evolving a routine habit. These experiences need to be instructionally managed to provide sufficient success for subactivities. Both external and internal levels need to be considered by information professionals. Special attention must be given to *self-reinforcement* activities by searchers, as explained in this description.

> Search behavior continuously operates to overcome the aversive stimulus of unfulfilled information needs. Every subactivity is accompanied by affective and cognitive reactions. Success builds self-esteem; failure engenders depression. Part of BI [bibliographic instruction] might be teaching patrons how to "self-reinforce" during searching. Many patrons are ill-equipped to deal with the emotions that are aroused during searching. They may engage in

damaging self-talk, making self-accusations such as: "You stupid fool. Why did you forget to write that down?" or "I'll never get this done in time." BI could therefore include the teaching of appropriate self-talk such as; "It is normal to feel confused in the beginning of a search" or "Other people make the same mistakes." Teaching students to use self-reinforcing "speech acts" while searching is part of encouraging independent learning skills; the librarian's words, if not the librarian, are present to guide and regulate search behavior (pp. 79–80).[55]

Broadening user instruction to include motivational skills and self-regulatory speech acts may appear to some information professionals as too personal or even invasive. However, from a user-centered perspective, the new inner focus on users is both legitimate and beneficial to their needs, preferences, and growth potential in life long holistic information activities.

Search Behavior as Problem Solving

There are three broad components of information seeking (p. 402);[57] information need, search strategy, and execution of strategy. Search behavior is redefined as "a problem-solving activity in which subskills are organized and retrieved according to the individual's perception of a current information need" (p. 403).[57] conducting a search is a broader unit within which are embedded hierarchical subskills, one of which might be the strategy of using periodical indexes. Similarly, this subskill has other organized subskills within it, such as deciding on search terms, selecting the right index, looking up the subject in the index with the most current date first, and so forth. Each subskill is itself composed of other hierarchically organized skills. Search behavior is thus "goal-directed problem solving" (p. 403).[57] User-centered instruction takes this into account: "Library use is an activity of one mind seeking contact with other minds. The study of the cognitive processes of library users allows librarians to develop a new focus on the inner microenvironment of information seekers" (p. 407).[57]

Indexing is the language chosen by information specialists to reflect the "about-ness" or content of documents. "User-centered indexing," according to Fidel (p. 572),[58] "cannot be developed before searching behavior is understood better." A number of issues that guide the practice of indexers are related to users. One is the issue of user language; that is, the level and specificity of the index terms. Another is the exhaustiveness or comprehensiveness (i.e., what to cover and what to leave out). In the older paradigm, also known as "the document-oriented approach" (p. 573),[58] "indexing can be done with no knowledge or consideration of users or their needs," but in the new paradigm, "request-oriented indexing" acknowledges the centrality of users. One example cited

by Fidel is a study in which a "filtering" technique is employed to check each descriptor chosen by the indexer: "Would any one of our users who is interested in the content of this document use this descriptor as part of the query formulation?" (p. 574).[58] Request-oriented indexing depends on the indexer's ability to anticipate user requests. Each document is represented in the database by a list of anticipated requests, and these elements form the index language.

Automated indexing has grown in the past thirty years, and its developers claim that retrieval performance is at least as good as systems that use intellectual indexing (p. 575).[58] Several reasons are given in favor of the user-friendliness of automated indexing. One is that search requests expressed in natural language are accepted and Boolean query formulation is not required. A second advantage cited is the provision for relevance feedback based on user ratings of retrievals and how these can improve the search. Other advantages mentioned are ranked output of retrievals in terms of relevance and the capability of automatic query expansion. Thus, on the one hand, automated indexing provides advantages in flexibility, dynamism, and control. On the other hand, its terms are limited to the language of the text itself, as no descriptors or keywords are employed.

An experimental study attempted to implement a user-responsive search system that allowed people to "add keywords to the indexing of an online retrieval system based on their use of the documents in the system" (p. 153).[59] A dynamic system that adapts to the needs of users is indeed a user-centered feature, although we still lack the practical knowledge for implementing such a system. In this case, the system had difficulty dealing with user language and error control. Variant spellings, errors in spelling, and terms that are too broad need more complex expert systems than are now routinely available. In an attempt to remedy this insufficiency, Denning and Smith[7] tested ELSA, an intermediary system that features the capability of "intelligent search functions" that solve some of the problems associated with user spelling and language. For example, when users are not familiar with the syntax of a system, they may type in "Search James, William" which does not work, as the system expects "aut/James, William." ELSA helps with this problem by accepting variant forms for author searches and by making lists of available concepts as well as lists containing synonyms that trigger available concepts.

There has always been the recognition among indexers that indexing and searching are related, but now the powerful tools of automation are providing new user-centered capabilities. The trend is not to choose one system over another, but to make all systems available simultaneously in the service of accommodating user styles, needs, and backgrounds. This is especially desirable because there is "little agreement in the names people use and the names recommended for use by LC [Library of Congress Subject

Headings], implying that retrieval systems should do more to accommodate common naming behavior" (p. 116).[60]

Types of Moves in Searching

To understand the user's perspective, Fidel[61–63] has studied how users make decisions by observing their "moves" within a search activity. Examples of moves made by searchers include any activity that allows them to continue progressing, such as the following:

- Using help files
- Reading the screen
- Issuing commands
- Guessing
- Rereading the screen
- Asking questions of themselves or others
- Consulting documentation
- Trying to get to a menu
- Trying to get out of a menu
- Trying to figure out where they are
- Modifying a search string
- Displaying a record

Fidel has studied several aspects of online searching behavior, including (1) choosing databases, (2) choosing search terms; (3) conducting the search, (4) reviewing results (feedback review), (5) making new decisions in response to the evaluation of results, and (6) terminating the search and getting a printout.[61–63] Her approach consists in identifying incidents in which a search key was selected, and then fitting each incident into a decision tree, resulting in a catalog of criteria for decisions. For instance, during the process of choosing search terms, the first decision point is to determine whether a "single-meaning term" (which is good for free-text searching) is wanted or a "common term (broad and fuzzy meaning with too many contextual variations)" (p. 493).[61] In case it is a single-meaning term, the next decision point is to map the term to a descriptor. For example, the topic "Anxiety about using computers" is matched to descriptors such as TECHNOPHOBIA (narrower) or ANXIETY (broader). This matching process involves a semantic content (or the concept) and the system language (controlled vocabulary). If no exact match is found, then a partial match may work in conjunction with text words (key terms) for an inclusive search. If no match is found, text words can be used to probe indexing further. This case-history approach demonstrates that searchers use intuitive as well as explicit "rules" for decisions.

Descriptive efforts on how users make decisions in an information retrieval situation produce knowledge engineering trees that can help in the design of intermediary

systems that assist the searcher through "dialog box" inquiriers about the user's purpose and scope of the search as well as requesting evaluation of sample retrievals. According to Fidel

> Understanding how searchers of all types look for information, and how they interact with existing systems, can provide guidelines for searchers' training and assistance (p. 501).[62]

It is evident that decisions during searching are guided by users' *perceptions*. These can be identified by asking them to state the reason for a particular decision. These reasons or perceptions can often be validated by objectively observable evidence such as transaction logs that record what keys have actually been pressed in sequence. Another method of validation consists in examining frequency distributions and correlations across several searchers for a single search, or across several searches for one individual. Other variations include the number of databases, different subject areas, type of information venue (research, industry, other), and the number of moves required (task complexity). Having conducted research with these variations, in her conclusions Fidel emphasizes the finding that search decisions and strategy are heavily determined by system features, especially the structure of controlled vocabulary and the availability of effective online thesauri.

> Thus, research should be carried out to discover which features of databases and their thesauri can be standardized without affecting retrieval quality. The role of intermediary expert systems will then be to bridge the necessary differences, employing switching languages and other terminological and semantic networks (p. 514).[62]

Fidel analyzed the verbal and search protocols of forty-seven professionals in the hope of discovering "what characteristics of searching behavior constitute a searching style" and "in what way one individual searcher is different from another, all external conditions being equal" (p. 515).[63] Fidel, citing Fenichel,[64] estimates that research on online search behavior has declined recently because prior experiments have failed to provide conclusive results on such individual differences as experience, cognitive attributes,[65] personality traits,[66] and type of request.[67]

A common explanation given for these partly negative results is that "individual search styles override most measured attributes of searching behavior" (p. 515).[63] Fidel thinks that this attitude is premature because we do not yet understand the specifics of search styles. She analyzed data on verbal protocols of thought processes, both while searching and from interviews with searchers to determine reasons for their search key selections. Fidel built a two-layered model to represent the derivation of six types of moves. A move is defined as any modification in search strategy aimed at improving results. Operational moves do not change the meaning of a request, whereas conceptual moves do. For instance, type 2 moves are operational moves aimed at increasing precision. Other examples of moves include the following:

Type 1
- Intersect free-text terms to occur in a predetermined field
- Limit time (by date)

Type 3
- Add synonyms and variant spellings
- Eliminate restrictions previously imposed

Type 4
- Intersect a set with a set representing another query component
- Select a narrower concept

Type 6
- Enter a broader descriptor or term
- Group together search terms to broaden the meaning of a set

Of the 1244 moves made by the forty-seven professionals in their 281 searches, 60 percent were operational and 40 percent were conceptual. The number of moves to increase recall was about double the number of moves to increase precision. Fidel takes this as a sign of "the difficulty in achieving satisfactory recall in the databases currently available" (p. 518).[63] Operational moves are used to improve precision or to reduce a set, whereas conceptual moves are used to improve both precision and recall. The average number of moves per search was five, with a range of one to eighteen. It is of interest that these professional searchers only used 25 percent of the available moves, indicating that "search systems should remind searchers of the complete array of moves possible in online searching" (p. 519).[63] Interactivity (number of moves) was not related to purpose, concern with recall, or subject area. It thus appears to be an element of search style.

In conclusion. Fidel uncovered three search style characteristics of professionals that were not related to results or success.

1. Level of interaction or number of moves
2. Preference for operational versus conceptual moves
3. Preference for using text words versus descriptors

Nahl believes that these search style measures can be influenced by the speech act content of instructions, as well as by other searcher characteristics such as success,

satisfaction, self-confidence, and frustration.[20] Because both the cognitive and affective domains of the user's world must be addressed, it is clear that the new user-centered perspective needs to focus on a broader spectrum of the user's involvement in the search process.

Reformulations

According to Dalrymple, "the user-centered approach derives its questions and methodology from the behavioral sciences" (p. 272).[68] In her study, subjects were assigned search problems, and their cognitive processes were studied by having them think aloud while searching. Of special interest were the "reformulations," an expression that refers to the attempt to refine the terms of a query.

Reformulations are assumed to be cognitive processes that interact with searchers' long-term memory retrieval operations and may be conceptually similar to database access and retrieval operations. "Presearch reformulations" transform the language of the information need into terminology that initiates the search. "Search reformulations" are modifications of search terms during the search. For example, the statement, "I'm looking for books about women writers in twentieth century German literature" needs to be translated into the form, "Feminist writers," This presearch reformulation may be modified later during the search by adding, "Feminist writers German literature." Dalrymple found that a significantly greater number of reformulations were made when subjects searched an online catalog as opposed to a card catalog. She calls for additional investigations on reformulation to determine whether or not it can be taught, how it is affected by the urgency of the information need or by individual differences in search style, and whether or not it functions as a request for feedback from the system.

Transaction-Log Analysis

The need to study more closely the cognitive processes of searchers was aided by software capabilities that permit a detailed approach to the study of online search behavior known as transaction-log analysis. The authors of a "manifesto regarding the future of transaction log analysis," Sandore and colleagues,[69] urge the development of unobtrusive measures for expanding the information base librarians have about users' style and pattern of information seeking, including searching, browsing habits, circulation activities, and evaluating and digesting information. Such expanded "tracking" will allow the resolution of the fundamental question "whether it is the system or the user that requires improvements" (p. 106).[69] The authors suggest that

It is possible to conceive of an IR system that was so adaptable that it could make searches successful when conducted by someone with a totally misguided mental model of the search process. If we design systems that are "idiot proof," are we encouraging mediocrity by not attempting to educate users with feedback from their searching mistakes (p. 106)[69]?

These researchers advocate helping users become proficient searchers, and to accomplish this, one needs a research program using transaction-log analysis to advance the knowledge base that information professionals have available about users. Transaction-log analysis "provides a glimpse of the world of user searching that is otherwise inaccessible" (p. 106).[69] The sequence of cognitive activity is captured in the verbatim record of keystrokes of a searcher, representing decisions made throughout the search. Common strategies, varieties of errors, predominant search modes, and the like are revealed, providing heretofore unavailable information on how users adapt to the system.

User-centered design in the 1990s dovetails with the area of human-computer interaction (HCI), incorporating cognitive engineering, software engineering, and usability engineering, including artificial intelligence (AI).[70] There is a new awareness and concern about the need to "overcome the gulf that exists between system designers and users" (p. 438).[70] There is a new desire to deal with users' psychological blocks and frustrations by building systems that accommodate the various levels of skills and try to eliminate unnatural human-computer exchanges such as having to wait for the execution of a command without knowing how long it will take or even if it is processing the command. Currently, more information-retrieval software designers are providing transaction-log utilities that can aid in studying the local use of systems. Transaction logs do not capture the thoughts and feelings of searchers and thus cannot provide insight as to why search decisions were made. To achieve a fuller description of an individual's search process, a complementary methodology is required to supplement the transaction-log data.

The Affective-Cognitive Connection

The desire to assist novice users in learning to operate unfamiliar information systems has naturally focused on what knowledge needs to be imparted to allow users to become independent explorers. However, working with novices within an educational setting made it clear to several researchers[19,56,60,71,72] that dealing with cognitive issues is not sufficient. The affective domain in learning is equally important and possibly more fundamental. Without the desire and continuous motivation to learn, few novices would become independent searchers and cyberspace navigators. There is a significant dimension of *resistance* to information seeking that reflects feelings of technophobia, information shock, and depression commonly experienced by novices within a bewilderingly complex information world.

There has been a lack of integration of cognitive and affective functions in the user as illustrated in an experimental study on 120 sixth graders comparing their recall scores on entries from Compton's Multimedia Encyclopedia on CD-ROM.[73] The research question was whether multimedia presentations were more effective than simple text on screen. No significant main effects were found, and the authors conclude that "it is not sufficient to add animation to text in order automatically to enhance children's learning" (p. 527).[73] Although this conclusion is qualified in some ways, it appears that the system's assessment is based on the children's performance on cognitive skills alone (recall and inference). The authors report that "reactions to the CD-ROM were almost uniformly very positive" and that students "found the animation sequences appealing," but still conclude that "its effectiveness as a means to improved learning is dependent on a number of factors such as text, text type, and media integration" (p. 527).[73] It is clear that the affective aspect is given no weight in the assessment of improved *learning*. The tendency to use comprehension measures without integrating them with affective measures is a characteristic feature of user studies in the older paradigm.

The following is an example of an experimental study that does not integrate the affective and the cognitive domains, but gives equal weight to them in systematic contrasts and evaluation. Seventy graduate students in LIS were introduced to HyperLynx, a hypertext bibliographic information retrieval system.[74] They were given five search queries, one of which was "to find documents that discuss information retrieval effectiveness." Search success varied with the query; some were more difficult than others. In the cognitive domain, knowledge of hypertext systems was assessed in interviews, and it was found that this variable had no effect on ability to search or success. In fact, the knowledge differential was small because few students had more than a slight reading knowledge of what hypertext is. In the affective domain, users were asked to compare the hypertext system with the Boolean-based systems they had experienced previously. There was generally favorable response to the hypertext system by the majority, but at the same time, all subjects expressed frustration at not being able to use Boolean searching with the full-text documents. It is concluded that user "preference for string searching for particular search tasks such as authors and very specific content suggests the need for a hybrid system with both string and hypertext search capabilities" (p. 27).[74] In this study the cognitive and the affective domains were equally addressed, to the greater benefit of users as they struggle to operate in fluid information environments.

An explicit attempt to integrate the affective and cognitive domains of information behavior is found in a study by Metoyer-Duran (p. 320).[75] She was interested in how information in a community is diffused by "information gatekeepers," or "persons who help individuals gain access to resources needed to solve problems." Information providers and librarians are information gatekeepers by profession, but many people in a community act as agents of information diffusion, for example, housewives who attempt to alter the family's eating habits and present them with a new dietary philosophy for which they rely on new information. She presents a taxonomic framework with three interacting domains: (1) *cognitive skills*, specifying the conceptual knowledge needed for information literacy, including terminology and logical reasoning strategy; (2) *technological skills*, referring to the operational literacy of information systems and data structures; and (3) *affective skills*, referring to the gatekeeper's "innovation diffusion and learning behavior" (p. 332),[75] including resisting or impeding the flow of information or absorbing information selectively and distributing it to others.

The importance of connecting affective and cognitive functions is well known in theory, although considered difficult to apply in practice. Two comments by psychologists illustrate this emphasis: the first goes back to the first modern behaviorist (i.e., after Descartes) and the second is a current research report sponsored by the Air Force Human Resources Lab.

> Man has two faculties; will and understanding. When the understanding is governed by the will they together constitute one mind, and thus one life, for then what the man wills and does he also thinks and intends (no. 35).[76]

> These two parts, the will and the understanding, are most distinct from each other, and for this reason, as before said, the human brain is divided into two parts, called hemispheres. To its left hemisphere pertain the intellectual faculties, and to the right those of the will (nos. 45 and 644).[76]

> All activities are changes of state and variations of form, and the latter are from the former. By state in man his love is meant, and by changes of state the affections of love; by form in man his intelligence is meant, and by variations of form his thoughts; and thoughts are from affections (no. 1146).[77]

> It is simply not possible to design either cognitive or psychomotor instruction without including some affective component. The very act of establishing an instructional goal implies some value to the person, organization, or society in its achievement. The motivation to learn may already exist in the student before instruction, or it may need to be generated or enhanced by the instructional program. It is precisely because the affective is so entwined with the cognitive and psychomotor learning achievements that it needs careful attention during the design and development of instruction (p. 18).[78]

The ACS information unit

In the filed of LIS, Kuhlthau has consistently called attention to the neglect of the affective domain.

> While information seeking is recognized as a cognitive process, the affective process is rarely considered as interacting with the cognitive as part of a whole experience. Incorporation of the affective ... is essential for fully understanding the experience of information seeking, but it has not yet occurred on any significant scale... There is much we do not know about how individuals construe and reconstrue during information seeking. These studies do indicate, however, that the process is not purely cognitive. Feelings of anxiety are prevalent early in the search, and levels of confidence increase considerably during the process. . . . While it may not be necessary to dwell on feelings in information-seeking situations, it is necessary to incorporate an awareness of affect into our professional construct of information seeking. Until the triad of thinking, feeling, and acting is fully accepted as the nature of information seeking, mediation [i.e., instructional intervention] is likely to be fragmented and limited (pp. 112, 117, and 127).[72]

Kuhlthau astutely points to the need for information professionals to become more systematic and more holistic in their approach to instructing users by addressing affective and cognitive domains.

To this must be added attention to the sensorimotor domain of hand-eye coordination and action. In an effort to express this connectivity of function among the three behavioral domains, a three-dimensional model of learning information structure was proposed by Jakobovits and Nahl-Jakobovits[79] emphasing the principle that every information skill from the smallest to the most general is constructed from affective, cognitive, and sensorimotor behaviors acting together as a unit within a hierarchical behavioral system.

> The instructional significance of the Affective Cognitive Sensorimotor (ACS) information unit is that teaching people to become searchers, or helping searchers to be better searchers, involves the management of three different types of human memory—affective, cognitive, and sensorimotor. Affective memory is required for acquiring affective information skills, just as cognitive memory is required for learning cognitive information skills. The same is true for sensorimotor memory. Advances in research and practice will reveal the characteristics of each memory and how these may be applied to curriculum design (p. 460).[79]

The suggestion that information teaching and services adopt a behaviorally integrated design broadens and deepens the user-centered consciousness of information professionals because it involves a holistic orientation toward users. *Holistic user-centeredness* provides "a unifying framework for preparing curricula in any subject" and "represents a shift from impressionistic instruction that is based on expert knowledge alone to an approach based on both formal analysis of learner needs and expert knowledge" (p. 74).[80] The permanence of the user-centered revolution may depend on productive research and development of a comprehensive theory of user behavior in the information environment.

Longitudinal Study of Information Seekers

In a series of studies on information seeking from the user's perspective, Kuhlthau[81] explored the cognitive and affective aspects of users' experiences in information-seeking situations. She points to a gap between how searchers think and feel, on the one hand, and how information providers think and organize information on the other. At one end of the spectrum, the system's pattern is based on certainty and order; at the other, the user's pattern is based on uncertainty and confusion. Thus, information has a mechanistic as well as a human dimension. Users assimilate information from various sources and transform it into meaning by constructing a personal point of view and creating new knowledge that is sharable with others (p. 361).[81] Her review of the research on information seeking from the user's perspective includes the following highlights:

1. Most studies conducted in the past are from the perspective of the system.[82]
2. There is a new interest in moving away from system-oriented research toward a focus on users of information, especially on their problem-solving and decision-making behaviors.[83]
3. A fresh approach provides a cognitive science point of view that takes into account the user's thinking processes and evaluations of the information retrieved.[84]
4. Users interpret information in terms of personal life characteristics and these are likely to be as important as system considerations in information retrieval.[85,86]
5. To understand how people find and use information, we need to combine their cognitive maps of the searching environment with a model of the system's design features.[87]
6. The users' ability to articulate requests to the information system depends on their levels of understanding their problems. Because their level of awareness of their information need may be initially low, they may have little success in specifying what is needed.[87]
7. Users' queries involve at least four levels of awareness of information need: "visceral" (below the threshold of awareness), "conscious" (aware of the need but not yet formulated in specific terms), "formalized" (explicitly expressed), and "compromised" (translated into the terms of the system).[88]

Kuhlthau emphasizes that an information search "is a process of construction which involves the whole experience of the person, feelings as well as thoughts and actions" (p. 362).[81] To put it more specifically,

> A model representing the user's sense-making process of information seeking ought to incorporate three realms of activity: physical, actual actions taken; affective, feelings experienced; and cognitive, thoughts concerned both process and content… While purely cognitive conceptions of information need are adequate for some research purposes, consideration of the affective dimension of users' problems is necessary to address a wider, holistic view of information use (p. 362).[81]

Kuhlthau argues for a new "dynamic" perspective on the searcher's world. An information need becomes "the gap between the user's knowledge about the problem or topic and what the user needs to know to solve the problem" (p. 362).[81] She argues her perspective through "personal construct theory," originated by personality theorist George Kelly.[89] This cognitive approach describes how new information is assimilated, beginning with "confusion" brought about by "inconsistences and incompatibilities" between the new information and currently held constructs. Doubting the validity of the information may follow confusion, and experienced threat may lead one to discard the new information. Alternately, users may attempt to incorporate new information by constructing new hypotheses that allow a more inclusive construct system.

Kuhlthau's focus on longitudinal studies represents an interest in the dynamic evolution of an information-seeking problem within the personality parameters of a user. To obtain data on this private arena of the searcher's world, Kuhlthau's subjects kept written records of their feelings, thoughts, and actions about their library research project. They also kept logs in which they recorded the sources they used, the procedures they went through in finding sources, and their evaluation of their usefulness. In addition, they filled out a questionnaire that asked about their perceptions in six areas of library activity: topic selection, research assignments, focus formulation, procedures for gathering information, frequency of library use, and role of mediators. Taped interviews were conducted in which students drew flowcharts describing the process they followed.

With this intensive and longitudinal data on twenty college students, Kuhlthau developed a six-stage model of the research process. The model was verified with 385 college students at eleven universities with three temporal data points; initiation of the research assignment, its midpoint, and its closure. Her observations draw an affective progression in the search process, from initial states of uncertainty with vagueness to later stages of optimism, confidence, and satisfaction with more narrowed, focused, and synthesized information (p. 367).[81] Kuhlthau notes three broad psychological effects; (1) interest in a topic increases as a search progresses; (2) the topic changes as information is gathered; and (3) a central theme evolves as information is gathered. Her conclusion on the importance of the affective component is explicit.

> By neglecting to address affective aspects, information specialists are overlooking one of the main elements driving information use (p. 370).[81]

The primacy of affect has been known in education and psychology, and only recently has come under consideration in information environments.

The Taxonomic Model

The taxonomic model has been applied by Metoyer-Duran to form three-dimensional profiles to idealized types of information gatekeepers;[75] for example the "broker profile," the "information professional profile," or the "unaffiliated gatekeeper profile." This last refers to individuals who think of themselves as ordinary people rather than innovators, yet they respond out of "personal conscience, or a sense of social obligation, to community members who turn to them for information or referral to help resolve basic problems" (p. 336).[75] The information behaviors that occur within the unaffiliated profile are ranked at a low level in all three information domains in comparison to the professional profile. In the affective domain, information professionals and managers have a facilitating function, whereas conservative community members are seen as having an impeding function because they tend to express opposition to innovation. Metoyer-Duran's analysis is of interest to the user-centered paradigm because it encourages a view of information-seeking behavior as culturally influenced and interprets it within a social and communicative perspective.

Another attempt at integrating the cognitive and affective domains of users is the taxonomic approach to information-seeking behavior representing Nahl's research.[20,71,79,90] The level of integration of the three behavioral domains may be seen in the following example (p. 75):[80]

> These three behavioral domains are interdependent, so that every *affective* behavior is accompanied by related *cognitive* and *sensorimotor* behavior. For example, a student who gets an assignment from a professor suddenly has a new *goal*; to get the assignment done by the due date. Then the student must cognitively *plan* how to accomplish it. And finally *execute* the required steps. Within this global process, many sub-goals and intermediate plans and acts occur. For example, "Search PsycLIT

> for journal articles on the topic" is a sub-goal. Within this, there are sub-sub-goals of selecting search terms, planning search statements, and entering them on the keyboard.

This approach contrasts with the profile model used by Metoyer-Duran,[75] primarily in the specificity with which the information behaviors are identified. The affective-cognitive integration needs to be applied at both the general level (as in Metoyer-Duran[75] and the microdescriptive level, as in the following illustrations (p. 7):[91]

1. In the *affective* domain; feeling excitement at a discovery; experiencing stress from doubt; being disappointed after a search; persisting in an effort; taking care to be thorough; being pleased with a quotation; sticking to a plain; overcoming technophobia
2. In the *cognitive* domain; devising a search protocol; deciding to retain a title; summarizing an article; noting a connection; evaluating relevance; rank-ordered preferences; thinking of a productive keyword; using correct command statements
3. In the *sensorimotor* domain; walking to locations; discriminating between symbols; hand-eye coordination; taking notes; noticing presence or absence; copying precisely; operating a terminal; following a map; alphabetizing; following range numbers and guide words; finding information on screen displays

An integrated approach in the user-centered paradigm involves all three behavioral domains at the general and specific levels.

The Novice Searcher's World

The taxonomic cataloging of user behaviors in information environments, also referred to as the "matrix approach,"[92] promotes the user-centered paradigm by facilitating the identification of skills and errors that populate the searcher's world. In a detailed study of some of the psychological factors that are presented in the searcher's dynamic world[19,20] seven environmental layers were identified. Fig. 1 illustrates the complex information retrieval environment of the novice; first, the *search query*, which provides an overall context because it is the ultimate goal that motivates the beginning and end of a search effort; second, the *subject headings* and indexes, which limit the universe of searchable topics; third, the search *software*, which imposes particular requirements for operation; fourth, the point-of-use *instructions* and online help, which provide suggestions and examples to facilitate problem solving or troubleshooting; fifth, the *sensorimotor* environment, which determines how users interact with the screen and the keyboard; sixth, the *cognitive* environment of users' reasoning processes and the formulation of search strategies;

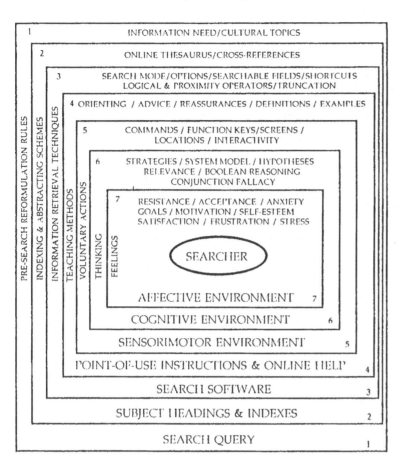

Fig. 1 The searcher's dynamic world.

and seventh, the central *affective* environment populated by users' emotions and motives.

These seven environmental layers envelop searchers and create a dynamic world that the user-centered approach needs to address, individually as well as globally. For example, an attempt was made to address the affective and cognitive environment of searchers through point-of-use instructions that were specifically written to anticipate common problems experienced by novice searchers using a CD-ROM database.[20] As a guide to developing the language of the instructions, an affective taxonomy was used that lists instructional speech acts at three levels. First, the *orienting* level is intended "to reduce anger and maintain reality check"; for example, "telling what is reasonable to expect" affects whether a searcher is being realistic or is disappointed, and "telling how long it takes (seconds or minutes)" helps alleviate impatience due to unfamiliarity. Second, the *advising* level "counteracts anxiety and builds positive attitudes"; for example, "giving feedback (what will happen if...)" helps alleviate anxiety and builds confidence, and "rank-ordering options or strategies" reduces fear of failure and builds feelings of trust. Third, the *reassuring* level is

intended "to overcome resistance and encourage acceptance"; for example, "affirming principle that users are never at fault" eases acceptance by reducing resistance, and "reinforcing user's perceived self-efficacy" helps users overcome feelings of helplessness and leaves them feeling empowered. Taking care to orient, advise, and reassure novice users helps reduce the psychological cost or operating in challenging information environments.

Affective Management Principles

Other features of the information environment have been identified in support of the affective needs of users. In one study, four principles are stated. First, *affective knowing* asserts that "a procedure is not fully understood until it is performed for some desired goal" (p. 25).[56] In other words, users learn most when given the freedom to practice searching for topics in which they have some interest. Second, *social facilitation* refers to the strengthening of motivation and persistence when the search is performed jointly with a peer or within a small group. Third, *affective feedback* calls for "manifesting the affective reactions of individuals to themselves" through an attitude scale that visibly shows where the raters are in relation to their own ideal. This activity "clarifies for them the distance they need to cover to master target skills" (p. 27).[56] Another method is to help learners correct their errors in feedback sessions to facilitate their continuous striving for improvement. Fourth, *validation* is the process of orienting, advising, and reassuring users so that they can more easily cope with the challenges of the information environment.

Questioning Behavior of Novice Searchers

In the information retrieval literature, user questions are considered to be equivalent to topical information needs or research queries.[3,93,94] However, the search process plunges users into another parallel domain of information needs (i.e., they need information about searching itself): "The basic underlying assumptions... are that question generation arises from an information need and that questioning is a behavioral act to satisfy that need" (p. 95).[86]

An interesting finding about the needs of searchers was reported by Nahl and Tenopir[90] who tape-recorded and analyzed every question that seven novice searchers asked a human monitor during five one-hour sessions while searching a full-text database for information on their own topics. More than 1000 questions were asked at an average of one per minute. One-third of these user questions were in the category *seeking confirmation*, defined as a question that contains the answer, so that the monitor always responds affirmatively (e.g., "Is it 3 comma k?" or "So now I want to combine both of them?"). In other words, searchers knew the answers but needed confirmation in order to proceed comfortably. As the authors point out,

> From a system-centered point of view it might appear that seeking confirmation questions are superfluous, since no new cognitive information is provided. However, from a user-centered view-point it is assumed that confirmation questions are essential to help searchers persevere instead of quitting prematurely. Searchers need continuous motivation to keep postponing quitting. Confirmation seeking is simply a method for providing searchers with this continuous motivation. It is thus affectively essential, even if cognitively superfluous (p. 282).[90]

Other types of questions included *formatting input* (e.g., "So what do I press?" or "Do I have to leave a space?"), *search strategy* (e.g., "Is this something I'd want to truncate?" or "What if I just want a picture and this database doesn't have pictures?" and *personal chat* (e.g., "Do most people try to keep up with reading all of the [full text]?" or "Can you imagine a bookless library?"). The authors point out that

> Some affective system functions now exist in the form of confirmation requests presented by the system after a command is given, e.g., after issuing a quit application command, the system may present a question. "Really quit? No [Yes]." Others include notifying searchers of what the system is doing during processing time, e.g., "Searching ..." and "Please be patient, this takes awhile' and "I'm reversing the order of your search terms for a faster search"; and warnings about the possible negative consequences of a search act, e.g., "EDUCATION is a long search" (p. 285).[90]

In this study, users spontaneously asked a long series of questions throughout their searches that pertained to many aspects of navigating in the system environment. The importance of feelings in the search process became evident when the transcripts of the search session were analyzed.

> The analysis of these naturally occurring questions reveals not only the reasoning process of these novice searchers but also the dynamics of feelings, which indexes the users' hesitations, desire for confirmation, avoidances, fears, and the like. These interact with the user's knowledge and reasoning to determine the outcome of their external actions. For example, novices sometimes quit a search prematurely without obtaining needed information, when it is easily obtainable through a simple modification in strategy. The present data reveal that *information need* is not unitary: instead, there exists a stream of hierarchically organized information needs (p. 281).[90]

Affectively oriented questions primarily dealt with the users' need for continuing motivation to carry out their intentions in the moment-by-moment decision making that constitutes a search. If this motivation wanes, users terminate searches. The human monitor's response provided the reassurance that searchers were interpreting the situation correctly and performing the right move. *Cognitively oriented questions* dealt with the users' need to understand results and select search steps. Sensorimotor questions dealt primarily with the users' need to format input with the correct search syntax and grammar. In both cases, the monitor's answers supplied the missing information to enable searchers to progress. Nahl and Tenopir call for the development of "affectively oriented system functions" that are more responsive to users in the area of their greatest needs. An awareness of this principle may already be observed in many systems for novice end users, such as the following:

- Providing an option for confirmation request (e.g., "Really quit? No [Yes]", or "Delete file xx N [Y]")
- Notifying searchers of what the system is doing during processing time (e.g., "Searching..." or "Connecting... Waiting for reply... Transferring data... 23K out of 35K read ... 12 secs. remaining")
- Warning about the possible consequences of a search act (e.g., "HISTORY is a long search! DO you wish to specify further?")

As research on users accumulates, a professional knowledge base will be developed for understanding and serving people's information needs.

Providing a user-centered environment requires an understanding of how users learn and acquire proficiency in information seeking. Three factors have been identified from learning theory that ensure the orderly acquisition of affective, cognitive, and sensorimotor skills, namely, "sufficient motivation, active responding, and reinforcement."[55] According to this view, information seeking is a complex behavior that is acquired to some extent through the laws of conditioning. Good decisions are automatically reinforced because they lead to positive outcomes. Thus, the sequence of actions that led to the results is strengthened (i.e., it has been added to the learner's repertoire of search behavior skills and is therefore more likely to be repeated as a habit). Positive consequences improve skills, whereas failures weaken the behavior. The information environment needs to address user failure: "The remedy for negative consequences in online searching is to have workable alternatives to continue the search in a new direction. Bibliographic Instruction (BI) can facilitate this by teaching users how to respond to system error messages, too few or too many "hits,' and other searching problems" (p. 77).[55]

Uncertainty and Zones of Intervention

As discussed previously, the importance of the affective information environment is fully recognized and addressed in the work of Kuhlthau (p. 187),[72] who recommends the counseling approach to library services.

> The mission of the 1980s was to automate and to network library and information services. Access has been dramatically expanded by automation, networking collections, and databases. Operations for providing information and resources have been streamlined by technological applications. While automating and networking continue to be a priority, the mission of the 1990s, and beyond, calls for services that promote the understanding of ever-increasing amounts of information. A mission of library and information services of the 1990s is to counsel people in the use of resources and information for learning, working, and living. It is no longer sufficient for library and information services merely to provide resources and to offer assistance in the location of materials and information. In the technological age, people require services that counsel them in understanding information and guide them in the process of seeking meaning.

Kuhlthau's central thesis is that vast information pools coupled with rapid technological change engenders unpredictability: "Uncertainty is pervasive in the seemingly certain technological environment. The confrontation between the uncertain person and the certain system requires professional intervention. There is a critical need

for professional counseling in seeking meaning and understanding information" (p. 187).[72] As pointed out by Morris (p. 230),[49] Kuhlthau's method is close to Dervin's sense-making approach reviewed above in viewing information seeking as the construction of personal meaning. Cognitive enrichment is preceded by affective uncertainty and followed by affective satisfaction.

Relying on the writings of George Kelly, Jerome Bruner, and S. Vygotsky, Kuhlthau attempts to locate the information search activity within the basic personality structure of the individual. Although Kuhlthau does not use the following specific descriptions, her approach is consistent with this type of behavioral model.

The affective domain drives the information search process through one's awareness of an information need. A person is "driven" to seek answers, and when information is perceived as personally relevant, it is seized upon by the cognitive domain and thus acquired as one's own. The person is now changed because different thoughts and feelings occur. One's conclusions are different (or reconfirmed and strengthened) and one's outlook or mood has changed. This process of personality involvement with new information includes certain feelings and thoughts that are common or universal as psychological processes. These include feelings of uncertainty, confused thoughts, resistance to new information, anxiety, and depression. Individual differences exist in how intense or enduring these processes are, and how well the individual is equipped to cope with challenge and stress.

Kuhlthau recommends various strategies for implementing "a process approach" to information counseling. One important step at the beginning is to help users become aware of the stages of information seeking, especially the reality of uncertainty, confusion, stress, and discouragement. The strategy of "charting" helps users visualize the entire research process, thus making expectations more objective. Seeking meaning is a "constructive process," and ignorance of this process frequently limits the choices people make. This fits with the idea that helplessness is a learned habit, or that self-efficacy beliefs are based on habitual modes of explanations in one's thinking and coping strategies. Kuhlthau emphasizes the importance of "conversing" or discussing with users their research steps throughout the process and not just during an initial consultation period.

Kuhlthau's proposals reinforce Nahl's description of the novice searcher's world as dynamic in both the affective and cognitive domains of behavior. An information need creates a gap between what the user knows and what information is needed to solve a problem,[96] and as the information-gathering process unfolds, the user's state of mind changes, cognitively and affectively. It is a unique experience in which "the choices along the way are dependent on personal constructs rather than on one universal predictable search for everyone" (p. 9).[72] To be valid, user-centered approaches must allow for individualization.

Self-Witnessing Methodology

Nahl's taxonomic model, especially its structural integration of levels and domains of user behaviors, is compatible with Dervin's sense-making theory and Kuhlthau's counseling approach to the information search process. These three orientations converge on placing the user at the center and employing scientific techniques for discovering the details of the user's live experience in the information environment. Self-witnessing methodology emerges as a common tool serving objectivity, empiricism, and a theoretical framework, even if still in development. There are three basic characteristics to this behavioral methodology; concurrent self-reports, authentic self-descriptions, and integrated probing.

Concurrent self-reports

A major problem with system-centered "user-centeredness" is that it is insufficiently objective, despite the use of summative rating scales and survey data. It uses categories of measurements intuitively selected by the experimenter in order to obtain global, summarative, and *retrospective* judgments from users. In a major scholarly effort, Ericsson and Simon[97] fully establish the superiority of *concurrent* reports obtained throughout the time user activity and experience are occurring. *Protocol analysis* involves tape-recording users saying aloud the thoughts and feelings they experience during the task, transcribing the audio, and analyzing it to reveal thought sequences, decisions points, intentions, and reactions. The categories that emerge from such analysis are thoroughly user-grounded, with minimal imposition by the experimenter. They are objective because users are the only source of data for their thoughts, reasons, and perceptions. Reporting on such data as they occur is a natural process of language activity and does not depend on special abilities or training, as illustrated in another major study.[98]

Authentic self-descriptions

Two reasons may be stated why self-witnessing data are more authentic and useful than data based on summative rating scales or surveys. First, they use natural language expressions, which are more accurate and specific. Second, they are spontaneous responses to the ongoing mental activity and state. However, intermittent probing by the experimenter is necessary in order to ensure relevance and completeness of information obtained.

Integrated probing

Research on the self-witnessing method[24,97–99] indicates that although the user's self-reports are spontaneous and natural, they are incomplete unless the experimenter provides adequate prompts. What constitutes adequacy in prompting varies with the theoretical justification of the study. In the taxonomic approach, probes are defined by level and domain, especially the latter. For instance, cognitive prompts elicit rationales for decisions, whereas affective prompts call forth motives and intentions that seek fulfillment from cognitive rationales through sensorimotor executions.

User-Based Behavioral Objectives for Bibliographic Instruction

Within the bibliographic instruction field, the most recent version of the model formulated by the profession is user-oriented in its purpose, attempting to incorporate and "outline the pertinent processes individuals use when gathering information" (p. 257).[100] However, the model statement of educational objectives for user instruction remains at a broad level of description, in the form of general and terminal objectives. From a user-centered perspective, the model statement needs to evolve toward specifying the actual behaviors performed by users during an information-seeking or -processing activity at the level of enabling objectives. The authors of the objectives recommend that instructors select terminal objectives from the model statement and create necessary enabling objectives specific to local needs. A step toward this elaboration was proposed and involves content analysis of user self-reports (or "structured diaries") that describe one's feelings, thoughts, and actions while engaged in searching.

> The self-reports of library users provide access to relevant information about their mental processes as they pursue an assignment. We obtained information on inaccurate assumptions and other errors, on skills learned during the assignment, and on how to improve assignment instructions. Self-reports indicate part of what students feel, think, and do in carrying out an assignment. Such information may be helpful in understanding the nature of library users' feelings, thoughts, and actions. It is an advantage to be able to correctly anticipate user behavior and to communicate adequately with users, accommodating our suggestions to their level and pace (p. 6).[91]

Nahl-Jakobovits and Jakobovits present a "taxonomy of library speech acts" in the affective, cognitive, and sensorimotor domains to help information specialists develop empirical, user-based enabling objectives in the planning of instruction. The deepening of user-centered consciousness is possible when the information skills of the users are defined as "integrated behavioral objectives."

> Bibliographic Instructional Design (BID) represents the new paradigm in BI, a shift from a tool-based library instruction approach to an interactive, access-based approach focused on active learning and critical thinking. BID places an emphasis on the needs and behaviors of

information seekers in complex information environments. B1 librarians have accepted the vital role of teaching people how to interact with information systems, how to evaluate output, and how to gain control of the information environments (p. 73).[80]

The authors propose a taxonomy of terminal objectives for information literacy that is organized in a matrix of three levels and three behavioral domains. Information literacy begins with *critical thinking skills* (level 1), proceeds to *information retrieval skills* (level 2), and matures in lifelong *learning to learn skills* (level 3). Each level includes affective, cognitive, and sensorimotor learning objectives. For example, affective skills at the critical thinking level (A1) involve "becoming sensitive to the need to evaluate information." Cognitive skills at the information retrieval level (C2) involve "formulating a question and planning a search strategy. Sensorimotor skills at the learning to learn level (S3) involve "facilitating one's life through lifelong information seeking and enjoying its rich benefits."[80] Similarly, using the matrix definition, all nine zones of instructional objectives are defined. Information specialists can use this taxonomy to plan instruction and assistance that is *integrated*, so that the objectives address the affective, the cognitive, and the sensorimotor domains of user behavior.

From the perspective of user-based design or planning of instruction and assistance, objectives are laid out in a synthetic or developmental order; from over-all goals to general objectives, terminal objectives, and enabling behavioral objectives. For example, a decision to provide an Internet connection in an academic library might lead a committee to decide to provide instruction in how to conduct Veronica searches of Gopher menus. This is a *general* objective. A subcommittee might then consult with other experts and draw up a list of terminal objectives that might include navigating menus, formulating queries, applying Boolean operators, and saving documents to users' disks. The list of *terminal* objectives would then be assigned to instructional staff to work for locating Internet documents through Veronica searches. *Enabling* objectives at the behavioral level normally require demonstrations, supervised search practice, handouts, charts, the user of online help, and other learning activities. Enabling objectives guide instructional procedures and need to be very specific and detailed. For example

General objectives: Teaching new Internet users to conduct Veronica searches and save retrieved documents to their disks
Terminal objectives: Accessing the Gopher menu: accessing the Veronica screen; formulating queries; using Boolean operations; saving a document
Enabling objectives: Locating Gopher; highlighting Gopher indexes; using line numbers on Gopher menus; canceling a request; selecting possible Gopher titles for various topics of interest; beginning a Veronica search; devising search terms; using Boolean operators; using bookmarks; using the history function; using commands for saving and printing options; inserting and ejecting disks; and so forth.

Note that as we descend the synthetic tree from general to specific, there is a need to include greater detail. However, from the user's perspective, the order of learning and understanding is exactly reversed. Users begin with an ability to understand at the level of the enabling objectives. How do I get out of this screen? How do I get there directly? Where did I go before this? What's the save command? These are their immediate problems and their total focus. The solution to a lack of enabling skills is provided at the next level up, where terminal objectives organize individual skills into the ability to execute complex goal-related tasks. At the third level, users begin to acquire self-confidence in their general ability as an information-literate person capable of sitting down at a terminal and figuring out how to search the Internet. Users thus see *analytically* (from frustrating detail to general know-how), whereas instructors see *synthetically* (from general goals to specific objectives).

Research on the modification of users' behavior with systems highlights the complexity of the user's involvement in the information environment. Some researchers perceive the need to consider the whole user and have proposed holistic theories to help safeguard user-centered consciousness in the applied world of system design and user access.

Constructing a Scientific Basis for User-Centeredness

The past two decades have brought user-centered consciousness to the fore; the next few years should yield greater theoretical sophistication and efficiency. Theoretical integration with psychology, education, sociology, and communication is already visible. Table 1 is a summary of the work to date of three researchers who have independently evolved a scientific and empirical orientation toward user-centeredness. The list is not meant to be exhaustive, and other researchers could be included whose work and ideas are compatible.[12,58,94,96,101,102]

Although distinctly different in procedure and disciplinary grounding, the writings of Brenda Dervin, Carol Collier Kuhlthau, and Diane Nahl together encompass a broad section of scientific research and method giving credence to the expectation of a new user-centered paradigm, effective enough to produce a permanent change in how the information world continues to develop.

The three approaches listed in Table 1 taken together cover the entire spectrum of the user's universe.

Table 1   Dervin, Kuhlthau, and Nahl: Key Concepts of Three Complementary User-Centered Methodologies

The topic		
Dervin's sense-making Communication Theory	Kuhlthau's diagnosis—intervention orientation	Nahl's self-witnessing behavior model
The main question		
How users assimilate information and apply it to their life situation	What stages users go through and how to assist them in the information-seeking process	What users feel, think, and do during an information-seeking session or task
The main answer		
Empowering users by facilitating information transfer within society	Diagnosing user problems and intervening with particular information services at the appropriate stage	Instructing lifelong novices to acquire integrated behavioral self-modification habits
Key concepts		
<ul><li>Constructivism</li><li>Information as clay versus brick</li><li>Observer versus user constructs</li><li>User-based user categories</li><li>Relativistic information framework</li><li>Searching filling an information gap</li><li>Knowledge as information transfer</li><li>Information exchange as a communicative act</li></ul>	<ul><li>Constructivist personality theory</li><li>Searching is seeking meaning</li><li>Longitudinal stages in the information search process</li><li>Attention to affective and cognitive needs</li><li>Overcoming uncertainty and information anxiety</li><li>Zones of intervention for information services</li><li>Information counseling</li></ul>	<ul><li>Integrated ACS information unit</li><li>Self-witnessing method</li><li>Affective micro-information skills</li><li>Teaching self-regulatory information speech acts</li><li>Modifying self-efficacy beliefs of searchers</li><li>Planning user-based behavioral objectives</li><li>Lifelong novicehood and information literate novices</li></ul>

Dervin: How users assimilate information in reaction to their life situation

Kuhlthau: What challenges users go through in the information search process and how to assist them in lifelong information seeking

Nahl: What users feel, think, and perform during information sessions or tasks.

Dervin's conceptual basis lies in the mechanisms that tie the social setting to the individual's mental framework. Information is not so much a fixed resource or product as a social occasion for communicative exchanges between author-producer and user-consumer. Information is what consumers use to alter their life situation. Affective needs reveal cognitive gaps that propel the person to seek, whereupon one seizes what seems relevant and meaningful; that is, what will make a difference in one's situation. This difference translates into acquiring understanding, changing attitudes, solving problems, constructing interpretations, or becoming more persuasive with friends or employees. Dervin's descriptions of the information user or consumer make it clear that we are all information seekers and consumers. Being a user or a novice is not a demographic category or personality factor, it is a continuous lifelong process, a state of operating that we all must regularly assume as part of our societal functioning.

Kuhlthau's conceptual basis is grounded in a psychological maxim. People seek meaning in life, and information seeking is driven by this deep need to make sense out of reality, to attribute causes to events, to hypothesize about what might be. But there is a turmoil associated with this reality construction because events change or new forces and constraints come into being. With mounting pressure to know, analyze, and decide, one is thrown into states of confusion and uncertainty, sometimes with such intensity that the individual may withdraw or resist further information seeking. The syndromes of technophobia, infoshock, and avoidance can be scientifically studied and cataloged. With knowledge of the stages that users go through, information professionals can provide effective assistance by accurately diagnosing the stage a user is in and intervening with appropriate affective and cognitive facilitation procedures.

Nahl's taxonomic self-witnessing contributes two basic ideas from behaviorism: first, that thoughts and feelings are behaviors like motor actions; and second, that the three domains (affective, cognitive, sensorimotor) are exhaustive and integrated categories of human behavior. During a search session or activity, users produce a continuous stream of goal-motives, reasonings, and coordinated sensorimotor executions. This stream of behavior is hierarchically organized with goal-feelings directing cognitive sequences that explode into overt decision and action. Behaviors are organized into habits that serve goals and situational demands. They can also be changed by using appropriate behavioral modification techniques such as modeling, imitation, role taking, self-witnessing, instruction, and communication.

User-centered instruction and management needs to view the target behaviors of users guided by bibliographic instruction design that addresses all three domains of human endeavor. Being optimistic about search outcomes and feeling enthusiasm for one's successes are *affective skills* that can be targeted as behavioral objectives in instruction and measurement. Doubting oneself, avoiding technology, and feeling depressed or overwhelmed in an information crisis are routine affections, cognitions, and acts that respond well to self-modification attempts through self-regulatory speech acts and social support. Higher motives have a controlling influence on lower motives, and users can be given self-witnessing tools to help them become aware of the negative and positive learning contingencies in their information environment. Such tools include inventories of the skills and errors users frequently make in specific situations, along with taxonomic descriptions of information states, stages, and processes.

THE FUTURE OF USER-CENTERED APPROACHES

User-centeredness became visible with policy, was advanced through methodology, and eventuated in a new theory, a new view of the global dimensions that impinge upon users. As policy, user-centeredness continues as an organized affirmative-action-like program attempting to reverse the user-*un* friendly atmosphere of the system-centered information environment. This includes the sphere of legislation, planning of services, and the education of professionals. As methodology, user-centeredness has evolved a wide range of measures for user factors in the information equation. Three degrees of shifts have occurred. Nearest to the system-centered orientation are user data obtained through rating forms, survey questionnaires, and interviews. Further along, and closer to users' search activities, are transaction logs, journals or diaries, and longitudinal case histories. Closest to user-centeredness are concurrent think-aloud protocols and directed self-witnessing reports, including rating scales, if used concurrently, about one's actions, thoughts, and feelings throughout the search process.

As theory, user-centeredness has evolved an entirely new range of explanations of what it is like to be users and how to manage their needs. Cognitive science, communication theory, and educational psychology each play visible roles in the development of the user-centered paradigm. The *cognitive science* influence is a source of knowledge for understanding how users think within the information sphere, including how they solve problems, how they make decisions, how they represent systems conceptually to themselves, how they deal with special terminology, and what errors they are prone to make. Influence from *communication theory* continues to evolve a transactional perspective on information as a subjective, creative, or constructivist accomplishment. The information gap that users face with disturbing feelings of uncertainty demands an existential confrontation with oneself and the world of

information. Managing this world for users is unavoidably involving to information professionals, demanding an activist mind-set that pursues, probes, and guides users through various types of interventions.

The influence on user-centered consciousness from *educational psychology* may be seen in the *taxonomic* approach that relies on behaviorism as a means for studying thoughts and feelings in an objectified manner. The matrix approach attempts to identify the simpler components that make up the complex. It relies on two basic concepts known to educators and psychologists, namely, *levels of development* and *domains of behavior*.

User-Centered Principles

Summarizing the trend of the past two decades, the following user-centered principles have emerged.

1. *Counseling interventions.* Information professionals can operate more effectively as information counselors than simply as information providers.

   Acknowledging the wholeness and integrity of users as human persons consists of providing affective support within cognitive information transfer.

   Understanding users consists of recognizing the common experience of a *predictable cyclic process* feeling challenged, reacting with infoshock and resistance, accepting assistance and redirection, viewing one's progress with satisfaction, and feeling restored and empowered. This up-and-down cycle recurs many times within a search effort, and managing its natural evolution with every user is the routine business of information professionals in the new paradigm.

2. *Role taking.* Information professionals can gain a more developed consciousness of user-centeredness by role taking, or putting themselves in the place of users.

   Role taking is a major concept in social psychology and communication. Taking the steps that users go through, coming up against the same barriers users must cope with, overcoming blocks, feeling overwhelmed by too much or too little information—these are useful experiences that may help information professionals tune in to user perceptions. One approach is to search for information that is personally relevant and observe the process from beginning to its resolution, if ever. Information professionals need to be users and searchers on a continuous and lifelong basis. Another approach is to participate in a group exercise of role taking in which one professional assumes the role of user, a second takes the role of the librarian, and the third acts as an observer who provides feedback afterward for a discussion of the interaction. The three then exchange roles.

3. *Discourse management skills.* Information professionals can be more serviceable by acquiring

discourse management skills such as interviewing, negotiating, counseling, and reformulating.

Examples include the use of open questions to avoid premature closure, to personalize the topic, to ask follow-up questions, to identify where the user is in the information search process, and to identify the user's area and level of information need.

4. *Follow-up services.* Information professionals are user-centered when they follow up on user activities in an attempt to establish closure.

Following up on searchers completes the cycle of assistance. It is the recognition that users are real people who need to go through actual steps. Creating a link back to the information professional may be critical to ensure accuracy, success, and satisfaction for users.

A deeper understanding of user-centered consciousness may be gained by applying humanistic principles to the design of the information world. A well-known approach is that of Carl Rogers, a founder of the humanistic psychology movement.[103,104] A basic tenet of this approach is that humans have an inborn need for *positive regard*, which is to receive sympathy, care, and acceptance from relevant sources. Out of this need to receive positive regard from others, we evolve the need for *positive self-regard*, which manifests itself as holding favorable self-perceptions. A problem arises when the positive regard others give us is constrained by *conditions of worth*. For example, children learn that they can have their parents' love and respect only if they behave in accordance with their parents' wishes. This conditional acceptance helps develop the children's conscience. At the same time, however, it leads to internalization of unfavorable self-assessment. One's perception of self-worth suffers and frequently leads to maladjustment such as alienation, anxiety, denial, and self-blame.

Rogerian therapy attempts to remedy this state of mind by giving clients *unconditional positive regard* so that they might experience positive self-regard even in failure. To reflect this orientation and commitment to the client. Rogers termed the approach *"client-centered* therapy," also referred to as *nondirective therapy* because it encourages clients to solve their own problems within a proper atmosphere. It involves the attempt to understand clients' *internal frame of reference*, which includes their thoughts and feelings in their struggle to cope. If we substitute "searchers" for clients, and "librarians" for therapists, we can summarize the Rogerian form of user-centered instructions in the following five additional principles.

5. *Affective contact.* Information professionals and users must be in affective contact; that is, they must express to each other the relevant feelings that the search environment evokes in both. Instructing must therefore

have an affective component explicitly dealing with the feelings engendered by the search environment.

6. *Incongruence or uncertainty.* Information professionals can gain a deeper understanding of searchers when they perceive them as being in a state of incongruence or uncertainty, needing to succeed while lacking sufficient knowledge.

User-oriented management of the affective information environment will take steps to legitimize the searcher's negative or stressful psychological state by presenting it as an ordinary problem created by the setting requirements rather than by the searcher's deficits.

7. State *of congruence with users.* Information professionals are in a state of congruency in relation to searchers when they accept searchers' weaknesses and ineptitudes and at the same time desire to help searchers acquire positive self-regard.

To be "accepting" simply means to acknowledge such insufficiencies as normal at the beginning, with routine remedies in the form of assistance, exploration, and instruction.

8. *Emphatic understanding of users.* Information professionals can acquire an empathic understanding of searchers' internal frame of reference.

User-centered instruction or assistance takes the point of view of the searcher instead of the system. To do this adequately, research will have to discover empirically what users' cognitive and affective needs are while searching and build responses to these into systems.

The dynamic pace of change in the information world has spawned a new status for those who actively strive to work within information structures, that of the "perpetual novice."[105]

9. *Lifelong novicehood.* The greening of the information world will have arrived when information professionals fully acknowledge the primary reality of the information environment i.e., novices will always be with us.

The recognition of this reality does not come easily, even for sophisticated observers. For example, Morris[49] analyzes the role of expertise in the process of knowledge transfer, and refers to a study by Kaplan et. al.[106] that tries to identify the differences between experts and novices in various disciplines. A major conclusion is that "experts are not experts by virtue of some generic problem-solving skill, but only in their knowledge of a particular content domain" and that "the way in which experts initially *perceived* a problem is what distinguishes them from novices; how they proceed after the problem has been set up was not significant" (p. 29).[49] There is a general tendency on the part of information specialists to assume that the quicker we get rid of novices in the information world the better it will be, as if novicehood were a temporary state to be ended upon the completion of the instruction. In addition, many believe that as computer literacy becomes more widespread, very little instruction in system use will be needed. There is as yet an insufficient consciousness among many professionals of the reality that *novicehood* in the information world never ceases.

In the mid-1970s, librarians were discussing whether or not patrons and researchers would want to do their own searching on the commercial information-retrieval systems and whether that would be a good idea. The end-user revolution is now behind us, and its character is beginning to unfold as an unprecedented number of people are attempting to operate on a daily basis within a rapidly evolving technological environment—so rapid that a new social phenomenon is occurring; we find that even as information professionals we are all novices all of the time, struggling (intellectually and emotionally) to learn, keep up with, and operate the latest versions of multiple systems, continuously adding new systems to our repertoire.

We need to understand this organic change in our information environments. What does it mean for a person to forever be a novice, to never know a system completely, to discover after months of use that an unknown easy shortcut could have saved much effort, to be deprived of support in acquiring system skills? Who does not feel this on a regular basis, whether it is students learning to search online catalogs and databases or librarians exploring Internet search engines? Are hackers and computing facility administrators exempt from "the state of novicedom?"

Information-literate novices

The information age has created a new status for users that may be referred to as "lifelong novicehood," an expression that represents the reality for most people who are intermittent yet steady users of the information superhighway. The kaleidoscope of networked information systems requires novices or intermittent users to actively participate in the successful operation of these evolving systems. This interactivity requires *information literacy* because it involves a variety of information-management skills, including the following:

- Figuring out screen instructions and command option lines
- Understanding the notion of canceling a command
- Constructing a viable cognitive map of the system
- Maintaining routinized checking procedures for typing accuracy
- Paying close attention to command structure, spacing, and shortcuts
- Keeping notes that are retrievable when needed
- Retrying operations with slight modifications and refinements until they succeed

Before the advent of user-centered consciousness, the idea of "being information literate" and the idea of "being a novice" appeared contradictory or mutually exclusive. However, although we see ourselves forced to assume lifelong novicehood, there is no substitute for information literacy, and this has rightly assumed a topic of importance among bibliographic instruction specialists.[80] As the user-centered revolution passes the point of no return, the information world is endeavoring to restructure in order to create a user-friendly environment for information-literate novices. Without information literacy, novices cannot function.

The Perpetual Novice

Currently, in libraries, campus computer labs, and computing center units we can observe confusion, inexplicable technical delays, and intractable passing of the buck regarding who is supposed to know what. This reflects the reality that technical and administrative experts in the information world normally operate in a mode that appears very much like the way novice users operate. This is because the hardware and software they get used to are frequently updated and made compatible with new hardware and software. Experts in the computer world can never stop having to learn a new system, thus being a novice user of it. The challenge of working out compatibility in each unit or location is intense, as is evident from newsgroups for systems directors and information professionals. The principle that novices will always be with us is thus an outcome that is a feature of the structure of the information world rather than of the mental state of users. The information world has the inherent character of changing at a rate faster than users can assimilate. They are thus in a perpetual state of information shock. User-centered consciousness can come of age by promoting an information environment that is designed for "the perpetual novice."

> Novices may take two paths one of which—if carried to its logical extreme—may lead to a "happy hacker" mentality; while the other path may lead to a state of being which I call "the perpetual novice." In effect, I am saying that regardless of "how" you classify yourself when you first begin to learn the technology, some of you may overcome whatever reluctance you may have had initially to become enthusiastic users of these services, while others of you will begin to (or continue to) show some reluctance about this mode of communication in perpetuity. Ultimately, the latter group may turn into "perpetual novices" who "must" use the system for work and will do so, while still keeping empathy with the newbies. You may find yourself in that position because of your job requirements or social requirements or even an internal driving force that keeps you wanting to learn about new technologies though you know you will never grasp it all. Many things in this field (specifically speaking about telecom) and in our society are rapidly changing and one can find it difficult if not impossible to keep up with everything. I find the term "perpetual novice" or "perpetual newbie" very applicable

to myself. Partially due to my job, mostly due to my own curiosity. I am always finding myself in a game of catch up, even when teaching others my new "discoveries."[105]

A GRADUATE STUDENT WROTE

I think I approach anything computer-related from the perspective of "goodie, here's a new challenge!" I always like playing or working on computers. Basically, the more "user-friendly" the computer is, the more I hate it!! I like the old low-level archaic systems. For example. I like MS-DOS. Unix shell, and OS/2's shell. I hate Macs... I think part of this comes from a "hacker mentality," whereby you think you are doing some wickedly complex scheming quite easily. Others get the impression that you are some kind of "wizard." The whole thing comes back to bravado. I get really excited when I get far into a system, especially if I think I'm not supposed to be that far under the system.[105]

In the last analysis, it seems, hackers and novices differ only in self-image. There is no big mystery about the expert and the computer hacker—they just never give up! Lifelong novicehood creates new kinds of challenges for information professionals because nothing can be taken for granted about what particular users may already know. An illuminating expression of this dilemma was posted to the bibliographic instruction listserv Bibliographic Instruction List (BI-L) by Rick Newell of Washington Library Network (WLN) in the fall of 1994.

This is going to sound like a very strange question: Do any of you ever give instruction on how to press keys on a computer keyboard? I do training for library staff (including clerks, paraprofessionals, and librarians) on Internet, online searching, etc. I just assume that everyone knows how to press keys, but I'm starting to conclude that this isn't true. Sometimes people will hold a key down too long (especially the "enter" key), and of course the function of that key repeats, and they get unexpected results. Or when I tell someone to press "Control-C", they don't always know that means to hold "Control" and press "C". Some people don't know that F1 is function key 1, not "F" followed by "1". I've always said I would like to quickly move beyond teaching "which key to press" and talk about more interesting things like search strategies, but I'm starting to think that perhaps more instruction is needed in the mechanics. I could point out all these "which keys to press," and "how to press them" things at the beginning of each class, but I'm afraid that people who are already experienced computer users will be offended. Probably most BI-L subscribers teach college students who already are familiar with computers. Any comments??

There exists a wide range of experiences and skills across user populations; still, the majority of novice searchers are also novice computer users.

Surfing Versus Searching

We can gain a deeper understanding of what is user-centered by studying the growth of the Internet as a natural or cultural phenomenon. The spontaneous development of homepage architecture on the World Wide Web is an expression of the user-centered revolution. Through its worldwide telecommunications network, the information superhighway functions as a physical scaffolding for virtual cyberspace. Users are now *navigators*, and "cybernauts," a status equivalent to the *information literate novice*. It is now expected that an information-literate user can approach a terminal, launch an application such as Netscape, and begin exploring the multimedia global network of the World Wide Web. Visible command buttons on the screen and standardized pulldown menus allow the first-time information-literate user to surf around in cyberspace, traversing time and geography, hopping from hypertext links placed there by other cybernauts eager to serve as travel guides and commentators. The term surfing expresses a certain freedom in navigating or gliding around at will, deciding to follow a link purely on the basis of a momentary attraction or curiosity, and backing out of it, retracing steps, or going on to new places. Although traditional search functions are available, browsing is the primary method of navigation on the Web.

Electronic Bookmarks

A truly user-centered feature of cyberspace is the universal availability of navigation *browsers* with hypertext capability that have two basic functions. One allows users to *navigate* by hopping from link to link at will, and the other allows users to retrace their steps in a variety of convenient ways. For instance, the bookmarks facility in many multimedia browsers on the Internet permits users to save any address of any location they travel to by creating a permanent personal address list that they can activate at any time and search, thus providing a permanent record of one's travels through cyberspace. The bookmarks list is "hot" in the sense that one can select and click any item and be taken to that address location again almost instantaneously. This function is user-friendly and allows serendipitous browsing and collecting of links to be revisited and explored more fully at other times. In effect, the bookmarks facility for hypertext networks such as the World Wide Web permits users to create personalized indexes, catalogs, and personal information retrieval systems almost effortlessly and without advance technical skills.

Clearly, the next stage for end users is creating individualized information-retrieval and delivery systems on the Net. Many end users are already providing information services for themselves and interested others on the Web in the homepage format. Homepages permit end users to design information presentation, retrieval, and delivery systems tailored to the owner's expertise and topical interests.

In cyberspace, everyone is an expert in self-defined specializations. "Websters" create personalized calling cards, resumes, family histories; they impart their knowledge on subjects, point visitors to other related or interesting sites, or provide a service of some kind that visitors may request. For example, Tony's Bad Style homepage presents his evaluation of homepages that he visits. He makes it his business to travel the Web, critiquing homepages because he is interested in developing acceptable quality control standards for homepage structure and content and hopes to influence others with his prescriptive analyses. Some other examples include homepages dealing with selling products and services (e.g., magazines, advertise their print versions; record companies display pictures and bios of artists and you can hear part of a song; and shopping malls of various types are advertised), emotional support, searchable directories of visual artists with pictures of their works, gardening advice, home-buying advice, confessions, and a catalog of useless sites (like litter on the information highway). End users may also receive mail from visitors and have them fill out questionnaires directly on their homepage.

Navigation history

History is another user-friendly function of hypertext browsers that keeps track of every document one has accessed and highlights that link in a special color, irrespective of where the link occurs. World Wide Web indexes and documents each have unique access locations known as URL (uniform resource locator) addresses. When browsers click on a hot link that appears on a Web "page" (or screen), the client browser (e.g., Netscape) accesses that URL location through live telecommunications lines (telnet, FTP, etc.). The same URL address on a link can appear anywhere on anyone's homepage or document. In addition, when one creates a link, one can choose any title or description for it as long as the URL address is the same, in other words, the same document or index page appears under many different titles or descriptive annotations throughout cyberspace. The history function shows users what pages or documents they have already seen at least once, even though the link names or titles are variable or entirely different. This is user-friendly because it allows greater control over navigation and helps users avoid endlessly reviewing the same material. With the history feature, the same document or file has a variety of different names, but this is an advantage, because it allows multiple independent access to the same information, not unlike cross-references in thesauri and subject indexes.

Personalized subject indexes

Another user-friendly feature of Web browsers allows novices to instantly construct individualized subject indexes on any desired topic or activity. Standardized subject indexes are easily accessed by clicking a link and are maintained and updated as a free service from many sources on the Web—academic, commercial, and individual (e.g., Yahoo, Whole Earth Catalog, InfoSeek). These are user-friendly and contribute to more orderliness on the Internet. First-time users may also click on Netscape's search button and type topics in natural language (e.g., automobiles, skin care, cats, museums, or Hawaii). Within seconds, a new document appears on the screen as a subject index containing hot links to addresses that relate to the specified topic. This list can be saved as a permanent file and one can collect as many as desired. Within minutes, a first-time user can create an individualized database on a topic for personal use or for the use of others.

Forces Against the User-Centered Revolution

It may be surprising to have to raise this issue, and yet familiarity with the information world today reveals the existence of social forces that act to divert or retard the user-centered revolution. Four such counterproductive influences follow.

Technophobia

It is ironic that many people experience an aversion to or fear of computers, because the user-centered revolution is taking place in an electronic information environment. Although unpleasant, this is nevertheless a normal affective response in human–machine interaction in the early stages of becoming information literate. The ability or skill to overcome technophobia is part of the repertoire of the lifelong novice. There may, however, be large individual differences in the time it takes to acquire self-confidence as a searcher or navigator, and there are conflictual and emotionally challenging intermediate states. User-friendly systems and affectively oriented instructions can ease the transition; yet being lifelong novices, people may regularly regress into technophobia when the old repertoire does not work with a new system. The kindly management of generalized technophobia remains a central goal of the user-centered paradigm as more and more novices of all ages and backgrounds begin to participate in the cyberspace world.

Information shock

A second counteracting force is *infoshock* or the emotional reactions of feeling overwhelmed by unfamiliar and complex information. Experience in an academic setting shows that students learning to use the Internet as a course-integrated assignment go through weeks of frustration, anxiety, and even depression. These are their reactions to being pressured by course deadlines while being challenged by what seem to be information deadends. Research is needed to discover effective techniques for managing users' experience of information shock in the electronic environment.

Information illiteracy

If lifelong novicehood is to be endured by users, they need to be given *metatools* that empower them to operate by systematic trial and error instead of semirandomly or illogically. Information literacy skills provide users with the prerequisites of how to read instructions, evolve mental maps of systems, keep notes that are needed later, check one's typing, retrieve, filter, and evaluate information, and retrace one's electronic steps. Lacking these skills, information-*illiterate* users may be overcome by technophobia, discouragement, and avoidance. Information illiteracy creates an insurmountable barrier, defeating the gains of the user-centered revolution.

Maintenance cost

As the Internet grows, the cost of running it and keeping it user-friendly becomes a potential threat to the user-centered revolution. For instance, nonacademic users pay a monthly access fee and cumulative connect time. The latter cost can exert a prohibitive pressure that interferes with the convenience of browsing freely without undue concern for how long one can stay on a screen. In addition, millions of users have already moved past the navigation state to full-fledged membership as World Wide Web homepage owners. Millions more will follow. This means that one must rent disk space on a Web server. The space issue becomes potentially prohibitive even with academic and professional users who receive Internet services as part of their job setting. As more people begin to own virtual real estate in cyberland, space and traffic becomes forces that threaten users' ability to explore and build the virtual information world.

User-Centered Consciousness in Cyberspace

The rapid development of the Internet would not have been possible in the absence of the user-centered revolution of the past twenty-five years. Driving the mass explosion of the information world are entertainment technologies and information services. There is a sensitivity to "customer needs-based networking," as described by one commentator.

> The newest mandate for the online information networks is to develop applications for the general public. This is the message conveyed by the feverish superhighway activity in Washington, DC, by the new commercialism cropping up everywhere on the existing networks, and, forcefully, by the joint venture takeover frenzy in the cable, broadcast, entertainment and general communications industries. The new dawning is focused on the great masses of potential general users, who so far never have experienced the joys of telnet, and perhaps never will have sufficient time, energy or interest to appreciate its more arcane beauties (p. 12).[107]

Because "the new dawning is focused on the masses," it is thoroughly steeped in user-centered consciousness. But note a certain pessimism about users who "never will... appreciate its more arcane beauties." It may be better to work with an orientation that strives to eliminate arcane beauties and make them openly accessible to all novices. As more novice users join in, there is a growing need to demystify the Internet.

The cyberspace of the Internet has the potential to empower users by providing a public platform for individuals to display and share their expertise in a wide variety of areas (e.g., dog care, computer systems, racing cars, emotional support, poetry, and recipes). This explosion in self-publishing permits unprecedented self-expression and creativity, and mirrors the exponential growth of end-user computing. In these early days in the cyberspace community, a characteristic phenomenon is the willingness of so many people to post detailed answers to strangers' questions on electronic bulletin boards and discussion groups. One may wonder what motivates this kind of public spirited, "gift giving" effort. One webmaster who was asked this question said that he responds out of a sense of mutuality and identification with other webmasters who are stumped by some technical problem to which someone else may have found a solution. "The whole thing would stop working if we didn't come to each other's rescue," he insisted.

We are at the threshold of achieving universal access to the global Internet infrastructure. It is an exciting historical time when cyberspace communities on the World Wide Web are being founded in all departments of societal information activities—educational, scientific, governmental, cultural, commercial, artistic, and personal. Homepages of all types and functions spring up literally by the hour! There is a frontier spirit of pioneering and innovation that parallels population forces that brought immigrants to the new World and adventurers out West. The new attitude is thoroughly steeped in user-centered consciousness because *the cyberspace revolution is the user's revolution.* Hackers, net potatoes, scholars, students, marketers, consumers, publishers, public officials—these and others make up the Internet. They have all unwittingly taken on a new status, that of lifelong novicedom.

Community-Building Forces in Cyberspace

Just as there are social forces that counteract the user-centered revolution, those that operate in the progressive direction are no less vigorous and impressive. Two are mentioned here.

Cybersocialization forces

It is remarkable to observe the positive social forces that operate within the user-centered electronic revolution. *Cybercommunities* are virtual in the sense that they are independent of place, geography, and even demographic variable. One may wonder what motivates thousands of people to build up the virtual architecture of cyberspace. Professional and commercial motives have not been among the principal initiating forces in the evolution of networking.[108] Today, a search on "homepage" yields many more individuals, families, and membership clubs than businesses or institutions. We are currently on the threshold of an explosion in homepages and homepage development services. One educator has created a "generational homepage" involving new students every semester in a virtual learning community that produces an unending virtual superdocument on the topics of the courses.[109] It is easy to imagine families producing and maintaining elaborate generational genealogical homepage multimedia scrapbooks on the Web, complete with home videos and family travelogues.

The homepage phenomenon can be seen as an expression in cyberspace of the spirit of frontier development. Librarians and information professionals will no doubt become involved in working with individuals, faculty, students, and community members to develop their own homepages for presenting and retrieving online information. This is a natural outgrowth of the traditional reader service, as homepages are personalized information delivery systems with resources collected by and for the individual. For example, faculty members may ask librarians to assist them in creating homepages for particular courses that include useful Internet addresses, the full text of course materials and lecture notes, and model student assignments.

Freedom

Surfing the net has become a technological expression of an individual's inalienable right to pursue happiness. Internet technology allows one to pursue only what one desires. Attraction is the decision point for traversing a path (or not). Just as people loved the advent of highways that allowed them to take off to wherever they pleased, today the information superhighway provides people with the new freedom of browsing where they will. Furthermore, social contacts in virtual reality take on new dimensions of freedom previously unattainable in human experience. *Cyberpersonalities* and "virtual selves" allow users to strip themselves of their regular identities and perhaps shed some inhibitions in the process. In cyberspace, everyone is an actor who can play different roles of choice and even become famous. This tendency to develop anonymous personas has been the focus of a warning cry in political places with the consequent promotion of regulation and legislative oversight of the Internet.

Roles of Information Professionals

Some in the field see that user-based methodologies can create new forms of data on library use that provide

opportunities "to redesign libraries in fundamental ways" (p. 301).[110,111] The end-user revolution has engendered new roles for information professionals that place them directly within the sphere of user concerns. The trends toward creating information that exists only online, creating machine-readable text of older books, articles, and images, and providing online access to current text and information services, along with the online self-publishing explosion establish the new technological milieu for information professionals. With the advent of new research methods, the knowledge base on end users has grown and has focused on their inner world, establishing the new psycho-social milieu. The evolution in user methodologies represents a graphic shift in perspective on users from the retrospective, summative, distal data of surveys, to the concurrent, formative, proximal data of ethnographic methods. At this stage, theoretical integration of these approaches will promote a holistic approach in the further creation of the information environment.

REFERENCES

1. Brittain, J.M. *Information and Its Users: A Review with Special Reference to Social Sciences*; Bath University Press: Bath, U.K., 1970.
2. Walther, G.H.; O'NeilJr., H.F. The user-computer interface in an information utility delivery system: An empirical approach to user-centered design. In Proceedings of the American Society for Information Science, Annual Meeting, Atlanta, Georgia Knowledge Industry Publications: White Plains, NY, 1974; 114–119.
3. Dervin, B. Information as a user-construct: The relevance of perceived information needs to synthesis and interpretation. In *Knowledge Structure and Use: Implications for Synthesis and Interpretation*; Ward, S.; Reed, L.J., Eds.; Temple University Press: Philadelphia, PA, 1983; 154–183.
4. Osgood, C.E.; Suci, G.J.; Tannenbaum, P.H. *The Measurement of Meaning*; University of Illinois Press: Urbana, IL, 1957.
5. Nilan, M.S.; Hert, C.A. Incorporating the User in System Evaluation and Design. In 13th National Online Meeting Proceedings—1992; Williams, M.E., Ed.; Learned Information: Medford, NJ, 1992; 217–223.
6. Wallace, D.P. *The User-Friendliness of the Library Catalog*, vol. 163, W. C. Allen, Ed.; University of Illinois Graduate School of Library and Information Science: Urbana-Champaign, IL, 1984, 42.
7. Denning, R.; Smith, P.J. Interface design concepts in the development of ELSA, an intelligent electronic library search assistant. Inform. Tech. Libr. **1994**, *43* (13), 133–147.
8. Farley, L. The evaluation of a user-oriented system: The MELVYL system's many designs. Inform. Tech. Libr. **1992**, *11* (2), 163–168.
9. Norman, D.A. *Turn Signals Are the Facial Expressions of Automobiles*; Addison-Wesley: Reading: MA, 1992.

10. Norman, D.A. *The Psychology of Everyday Things*; Basic Books: New York, 1988.

11. Norman, D.A. Toward human-centered design. Tech. Rev. **1993**, *96* (July), 47–53.

12. Marchionini, G. Interfaces for end-user information seeking. JASIS **1992**, *43*, 156–163.

13. Borgman, C.L.; Gallagher, A.L.; Krieger, D.; Bower, J. Children's use of an interactive catalog of science materials. In Proceedings of the 53rd ASIS Annual Meeting. Henderson, D., Ed.; Learned Information, Medford, NJ, 1990; 55–68.

14. Zloof, M.M. Query-by-example: A database language. IBM Syst. J. **1977**, *16*, 324–343.

15. Herot, C.E. Spatial Management of Data. ACM Trans., Database Syst. **1980**, *5*, 493–514.

16. Chen, H.; Dhar, V. A knowledge-based approach to the design of document-based retrieval systems. In Proceedings of the Conference on Office Information Systems, Lochovsky, F.H., Allen, R.B., Eds.; ACM: New York, 1990; 281–290.

17. Meadow, C.T. OAKDEC: A program for studying the effects on users of a procedural expert system for database searching. Inform. Proc. Mgmt. **1988**, *24*, 449–457.

18. Frisse, M.E.; Cousins, S.B. Information retrieval from hypertext: Update on the dynamic medical handbook project. In Hypertext '89 Proceedings; ACM: New York, 1989; 199–212.

19. Nahl, D. The novice searcher's world: Instructions, self-confidence, and success, unpublished manuscript.

20. Nahl, D. CD-ROM point-of-use instructions for novice searchers: A comparison of user-centered affectively elaborated and system-centered unelaborated text. Unpublished Ph.D. dissertation, University of Hawaii: Honolulu, 1993.

21. Bandura, A. Human agency in social cognitive theory. Am. Psychol. **1989**, *44*, 1175–1193.

22. Bandura, A.; Adams, N.E. Analysis of self-efficacy theory of behavioral change. Cog. Ther. Res. **1977**, *1*, 287–310.

23. Searle, J.R. *Speech Acts: An Essay in the Philosophy of Language*; Cambridge University Press: London, U.K., 1969.

24. Labov, W.; Fanshel, D. *Therapeutic Discourse: Psychotherapy as Conversation*; Academic Press: New York, 1977.

25. Habermas, J. *The Theory of Communicative Action: Reason and the Rationalization of Society*; Beacon Press: Boston, MA, 1984; vol. 1.

26. Seligman, M.E.P. *Learned Optimism*; Knopf: New York, 1990.

27. Nahl, D. Affective elaborations of Boolean search instructions for novices: Effects on comprehension, self-confidence, and error type. In Proceedings of the 58th Annual Meeting; Information Today: Medford, NJ, 1995.

28. Robertson, W.D. A user-oriented approach to setting priorities for library services. Special Libr. **1980**, *71* (8), 345–353.

29. Parks, L. The Library in the institution. Libr. Trends **1978**, *26* (3), 319–340.

30. Becker, J. Libraries, society, and technological change. Libr. Trends **1978**, *27* (3), 409–416.

31. Sharma, R.N. Ranganathan's impact on international librarianship through tnformation technology. Libr **1992**, *42* (3), 258–267.

32. Shapiro, B.J.; Long, K.B. Just say yes: Reengineering library user services for the 21st century. J. Acad. Libr. **1994**, *20* (5/6), 285–294.

33. Berger, K.W.; Hines, R.W. What does the user really want? The library user survey project at Duke University. J. Acad. Libr. **1994**, *20* (5/6), 306–309.

34. Dougherty, R.M. Needed: User-responsive research libraries. Libr. J. **1991**, *116* (Jan.), 59–62.

35. St Clair, G. *Customer Service in the Information Environment*; Bowker-Saur: London, U.K., 1993.

36. Hoadley, I.B. Customer service? Not really. College Res. Libr. News **1995**, *56* (3), 175–176.

37. Bawden, D. *User-oriented Evaluation of Information Systems and Services*; Gower: Brookfield, VT, 1990.

38. Hancock-Beaulieu, M.E. *Information Systems for End-Users: Research and Development Issues*; Taylor Graham: London, U.K., 1992.

39. Harloe, B. Achieving client-centered collection development in small and medium-sized academic libraries. College Res. Libr. **1989**, *50* (3), 344–353.

40. Association of Library Schools Task Force Implications of the White House conference on library and information services for library education. J. Educ. Libr. **1981**, *21* (3), 246–262.

41. Nahl, D.; Coder, A.; Black, J.; Smith, M. Effectiveness of fieldwork at the information desk: A prototype for academic library-library school collaboration. J. Acad. Libr. **1994**, *20* (5,6), 291–294.

42. Zweizig, D.; Dervin, B. Public library use, users, uses: advances in knowledge of the characteristics and needs of the adult clientele of American public libraries. In *Advances in Librarianship*; Voigt, M.J., Harris, M.K., Eds.; Academic Press: New York, 1977; 231–255.

43. Wersig, G.; Windel, G. Information science needs a theory of 'information actions.'. Soc. Sci. Inform. Stud. **1985**, *5* (1), 11–23.

44. Wilson, T.D. The cognitive approach to information-seeking behavior and information use. Soc. Sci. Inform. Stud. **1984**, *4* (2–3), 197–204.

45. Wilson, T.D. On user studies and information needs. J. Doc. **1981**, *37* (March), 3–15.

46. Savolainen, R. The sense-making theory; Reviewing the interests of a user-centered approach to information seeking and use. Inform. Proc. Mgmt. **1993**, *29* (1), 13–28.

47. Carter, R. Discontinuity and communication. In East-West Center Conference on Communication Theory; East-West Center: Honolulu, 1980.

48. Jacobson, T.L. Sense-making in a database environment. Inform. Pro. Mgmt. **1991**, *27*, 647–657.

49. Morris, R.C.T. Toward a user-centered information service. JASIS **1994**, *45* (1), 20–30.

50. Shannon, C.E.; Weaver, W. *The Mathematical Theory of Communication*; University of Illinois Press: Urbana, IL, 1949.

51. Dervin, B. Useful theory for librarianship: Communication, not information. Drexel Libr. Q. **1977**, *13*, 16–32.

52. Dervin, B. Users as research inventions: How research categories perpetuate inequalities. J. Commun. **1989**, *39* (3), 216–233.

53. Aluri, R. Application of learning theories to library-use instruction. Libri **1981**, *31* (Aug), 140–152.

54. Tucket, H.W.; Stoffle, C.J. Learning theory and the self-reliant library user. RQ **1984**, *24*, 58–66.

55. Nahl-Jakobovits, D.; Jakobovits, L. Learning principles and the library environment. Res. Strat. **1990**, *8* (2), 74–81.

56. Nahl-Jakobovits, D.; Jakobovits, L.A. Managing the affective micro-information environment. Res. Strat. **1985**, *3* (1), 17–28.

57. Nahl-Jakobovits, D. Problem solving, creative librarianship, and search behavior. College Res. Libr. **1988**, *49* (5), 400–408.

58. Fidel, R. User-centered indexing. JASIS **1994**, *45* (8), 572–576.

59. Tague, J.M. User-responsive subject control in bibliographic retrieval systems. Inform. Proc. Mgmt. **1981**, *17*, 149–159.

60. Mellon, C. Library anxiety: A grounded theory and its development. College Res. Libr. **1986**, *47*, 160–165.

61. Fidel, R. Searcher's selection of search keys: 1. The selection routine. JASIS **1991**, *42* (7), 490–500.

62. Fidel, R. Searcher's selection of search keys: II. Controlled vocabulary of free-text searching. JASIS **1991**, *42* (7), 501–514.

63. Fidel, R. Searcher's selection of search keys: III. Searching styles. JASIS **1991**, *42* (7), 515–527.

64. Fenichel, C.H. "Online searching: Measures that discriminate among users with different types of experience." JASIS **1981**, *32*, 23–32.

65. Woelfle, N.N. Individual differences in online search behavior: The effect of learning styles and cognitive abilities on process and outcome Ph.D. dissertation, Case Western Reserve University, Cleveland, 1984.

66. Bellardo, T. An investigation of online searcher traits and their relationship to search outcomes. JASIS **1985**, *36*, 241–250.

67. Saracevic, T.; Kantor, P. A study of information seeking and retrieving: III. Searchers, searches, and overlap. JASIS **1988**, *39*, 197–216.

68. Dalrymple, P.W. Retrieval by reformulation in two library catalogs: Toward a cognitive model of searching behavior. JASIS **1990**, *41*, 272–281.

69. Sandore, B.; Flaherty, P.; Kaske, N.K.; Kurth, M.; Peters, T. A manifesto regarding the future of transaction log analysis. Libr. Hi Tech. **1993**, *11* (2), 105–106.

70. Wang, P. Janseen Research Foundation's adverse experience literature database: A user-centered design for human-computer interaction. Drug Inform. J. **1993**, *27*, 437–446.

71. Jakobovits, L.A.; Nahl-Jakobovits, D. Learning the library: Taxonomy of skills and errors. College Res. Libr. **1987**, *48* (3), 203–214.

72. Kuhlthau, C.C. *Seeking Meaning: A Process Approach to Library and Information Services*; Ablex Publishing: Norwood, NJ, 1993, 199.

73. Large, A.; Behesti, J.; Bruleux, A.; Renaud, A. Multimedia and comprehension: A cognitive study. JASIS **1994**, *45* (7), 515–528.

74. Dimetroff, A.; Wolfram, D. Searcher response in a hypertext-based bibliographic retrieval system. JASIS **1995**, *46* (1), 22–29.

75. Metoyer-Duran, C. Information-seeking behavior of gatekeepers in ethnolinguistic communities: Overview of a taxonomy. Libr. Inform. Sci. Res. **1991**, *13*, 319–346.

76. Swedenborg, E. *Arcana Coelestia*, 1837 ed., vol. 1 (1749), Swedenborg Foundation: New York, 1978, 253.

77. Swedenborg, E. *Apocalypse Explained*, 1785 ed.; Potts, J. F., Ed.; Swedenborg Foundation: New York, 1976.

78. Main, R.G. *Integrating the Affective Domain into the Instructional Design Process;* California State University; Chico College of Communication: Chico, CA, 1992.

79. Jakobovits, L.A.; Nahl-Jakobovits, D. Measuring information searching competence. College Res. Libr. **1990**, *51* (5), 448–462.

80. Nahl-Jakobovits, D.; Jakobovits, L.A. Bibliographic instructional design for information literacy: Integrating affective and cognitive objectives. Res. Strat. **1993**, *11* (2), 73–88.

81. Kuhlthau, C.C. Inside the search process: Information seeking from the user's perspective. JASIS **1991**, *42* (5), 361–371.

82. Dervin, B.; Nilan, M. Information needs and uses. In *Annual Review of Information Science and Technology (ARIST)*; Williams, M.E., Ed.; Knowledge Industry Publications: White Plains, NY, 1986; 3–33.

83. Borgman, C. Psychological research in human-computer interaction. In *Annual Review of Information Science and Technology (ARIST)*; Williams, M.E., Ed.; 1984; 33–64.

84. Ingwersen, P. Search procedures in the library analyzed from the cognitive point of view. J. Doc. **1982**, *38*, 165–191.

85. James, R. Libraries in the mind: How can we see users' perceptions of libraries. J. Libr. **1983**, *15*, 19–28.

86. Hollnagel, E.; Woods, D.D. Cognitive systems engineering: New wine in new bottles. Int. J. Man-Mach. Stud. **1983**, *18*, 583–600.

87. Belkin, N.J. Cognitive models and information transfer. Soc. Sci. Inform. Stud. **1984**, *4*, 111–113.

88. Taylor, R.S. *Value-Added Processes in Information Systems*; Ablex Publishing: Norwood, NJ, 1986.

89. Kelly, G.A. *A Theory of Personality: They Psychology of Personal Constructs*; W. W. Norton: New York, 1963.

90. Nahl, D.; Tenopir, C. Affective and cognitive searching behavior of novice end-users of a full text database. JASIS **1996**, *47*, 276–286.

91. Nahl-Jakobovits, D.; Jakobovits, L.A. A content analysis method for developing user-based objectives. Res. Strat. **1992**, *10* (1), 4–16.

92. Wright, C.; Larsen, M.E. Basic information access skills: Curriculum design using a matrix approach. Res. Strat. Summer **1990**, *8*, 104–115.

93. Saracevic, T.; Kantor, P.; Chamis, A.Y.; Trivison, D. A study of information seeking and retrieving: I. Background and methodology. JASIS **1988**, *39*, 161–175.

94. Saracevic, T.; Mokros, H.; Su, L. Nature of interaction between users and intermediaries in online searching: A qualitative analysis. In Proceedings of the 54rd American Society for Information Science Annual Meeting. Learned Information: Medford, NJ, 1990; vol. 27; 47–54.

95. Horne, E.E. An investigation into self-questioning behavior during problem-solving. In Proceedings of the 53rd American Society for Information Science Annual Meeting, Information Today: Medford, NJ, 1990; vol. 27, 86–97.

96. Belkin, N.J.; Brooks, H.M.; Oddy, R.N. ASK for information retrieval. J. Doc. **1982**, *38*, 61–71.

97. Ericsson, K.A.; Simon, H.A. *Protocol Analysis: Verbal Reports as Data*; MIT Press: Cambridge, MA, 1993.

98. Hurlburt, R.T. *Sampling Normal and Schizophrenic Inner Experience*; Plenum Press: New York, 1990.

99. Tenopir, C.; Nahl-Jakobovits, D.; Howard, D. Strategies and assessment online: Novices' experience. Libr. Inform. Sci. Res. July–September **1991**, *13* (3), 227–266.

100. Dusenbury, C., Ed. *Read This First: An Owner's Guide to the New Model Statement of Objectives for Academic Bibliographic Instruction*; ACRL/ALA: Chicago, IL, 1991.

101. Fidel, R.; Soergel, D. Factors affecting online bibliographic retrieval: A conceptual framework for research. JASIS **1983**, *34*, 163–180.

102. Bates, M.J. Information search tactics. JASIS **1979**, *30*, 205–214.

103. Rogers, C.R. *Client-Centered Therapy: Its Current Practice. Implications, and Theory*; Houghton Mifflin: Boston, MA, 1951.

104. Rogers, C.R. Client-centered therapy. In *American Handbook of Psychiatry*; Arieti, S., Ed.; Basic Books: New York, 1966; 183–200.

105. Davis, D. The perpetual novice, Guest lecture, School of Library and Information Studies; University of Hawaii: Honolulu, HI, March 1995.

106. Kaplan, S.; Gruppen, L.D.; Leventhal, L.M.; Board, F. The components of expertise: A cross-disciplinary review. Technical report 89-NOV-01. Department of Computer Science, Bowling Green State University: Bowling Green, OH, 1989.

107. Kessler, J. International entertainment on the internet: Customer needs-based-networking. Bull. Am. Soc. Inform. Sci. **1994**, *21* (1), 12–14.

108. Jacobsen, K. Time to put the internet in perspective. College Res. Libr. News **1995**, *56* (3), 144–147.

109. James, L.; Bogan, K. Analyzing linkage structure in a course-integrated virtual learning community on the World Wide Web. In *INET '95*: Internet Society, Honolulu, 1995.

110. Wilson, L.A. Building the user-centered library. RQ **1995**, *34* (3), 297–301.

111. Martell, C. *The Client-Centered Academic Library: An Organizational Model*; Greenwood: Westport, CT, 1983.

User-Centered Revolution: 1995–2008

Diane Nahl
Information and Computer Sciences Department, University of Hawaii, Honolulu, Hawaii, U.S.A.

Abstract
This entry reviews a sample of current research on information behavior (IB), examines recent research on online IB and use of electronic resources offered in libraries, describes the state of user-centered design, provides evidence of a commitment to the user-centered paradigm in library and information science research and education, and presents the response to the unprecedented rise of online participatory culture.

INTRODUCTION

In the past two decades, the field of library and information science (LIS) has become increasingly multidisciplinary in theory building, research focus, methodological sophistication, and praxis. Library and information science programs have diversified their faculty, programs continuously update and create innovative curricula and degree offerings, and researchers collaborate with and borrow from communication, anthropology, cognitive science, and computer science among other disciplines. A "user-centered" individual, organization, business, locale, or system must focus on discovering and responding to actual wants and needs of the people determined to be the users. To that end, researchers and system designers have developed and adapted methods to obtain relevant details of user behavior in order to improve systems and services. A previous entry, "The user-centered revolution: 1970–1995," traces the origins of the user-centered focus to a shift in clientele from experts to novice end users:[1]

> The user-centered revolution in library and information science was generated by the general availability of search technology for novice end-users who rapidly out-numbered experts and intermediaries. The needs of this new class of searchers have changed the priorities in the information environment. In response, researchers have developed new types of data that more closely represent users' actual experience with systems. This interest led to an evolution in the methodologies applied to user studies over the past 25 years [1970–1995], from survey questionnaires and feedback forms, to interviews, journals, logs, and case histories. The development in methodology represents a shift in focus from gathering anonymous, statistical data on users, to individualizing users through ethnographic and psychological approaches.

The present entry reviews a sample of the LIS literature that treats user issues since 1995, with emphasis on topics concerning the emergence, rapid expansion, and full integration of the World Wide Web into social life and work. This brief period has experienced unprecedented penetration of the user-centered paradigm. The literature reveals that by 2001 the user-oriented perspective had entered every LIS subarea.

The trend toward user-centeredness is termed "revolution" because software engineers and interface designers produced applications and systems experienced as hostile by many users. The computer revolution was brought about by technologists, however, as computer use expanded to the population at large, an increasing proportion of users found themselves in frustrating states of mind marked by puzzlement, anger, phobia, and helplessness. The computer engineering field was slow to address these user reactions and concerns. The general attitude toward "end users" was that improving their computer literacy skills would solve their problems. While the software and interface environment was experienced as psychologically hostile and unfriendly to millions of users, it was not recognized that systems were responsible for user-problems. By the time the Internet became popular in the mid-1990s "usability testing" had become a standard subject in interface design courses and texts. When software engineering adopted the human factors maxim of fitting technology to people instead of requiring people to adjust to technology, the burden of making systems work for people shifted to the designers and the user-centered revolution was underway. One indication of the deepening of the user-centered revolution is the dramatic upsurge in user-centered language in disciplinary databases and on the Web.

User-Centered Language

Earlier reviews of the print and online literature concerning the user-centered revolution covered material containing a variety of user-focused terminology.[1] Table 1 shows that since 1970 the internalization of a

Encyclopedia of Library and Information Sciences, Fourth Edition DOI: 10.1081/E-ELIS4-120044680

user-centered philosophy has given rise to continuously expanding user-oriented concepts that highlight the activities of interacting, experiencing, and participating online. Google searches were conducted on the terms used in the earlier print and online literature concepts and some related terms. Table 1 supports the conclusion that user-centeredness has become an essential concern to system architects in every content area.

Terms relating to user factors continue to proliferate, with 19 new terms added for the period 2001–2008 to the original set of eight terms in Table 1. In 7 years occurrence of the term "user friendly" increased from nearly 1.5 million to nearly 28 million postings, while "user centered" also grew from 33,000 to nearly a million by the end of 2008. Other terms with very large postings include usability (23 million), user experience (11 million), user defined (8 million), user generated (6.5 million), user created (5.6 million), customer experience (4.5 million), user contributed (4.5 million), and user input (2.8 million). On

http://www.amazon.com, 2051 titles appeared under the subject "Web usability" in December 2008, more than 30 times the 67 "usability" titles offered in 2001. The term "user-centered" retrieved 2569 titles in December 2008. The list in Table 1 is not exhaustive, and while search results are dynamic the increasing trend continues. A full analysis would yield many more related terms that emphasize a user orientation, and a requirement to pay attention to what people actually do while using systems and operating within information environments (IEs) in order to support, augment, and enhance their activities.

This entry reviews a sample of current research on information behavior (IB), examines recent research on online IB and use of electronic resources offered in libraries, describes the state of user-centered design (UCD), provides evidence of a commitment to the user-centered paradigm in LIS research and education and in libraries, and presents the response to the unprecedented rise of online participatory culture.

Table 1 User-centered terms: A comparison of early print literature and the Web

Print literature 1970–1995	Google.com September 2001	Terms searched within quotes	Google.com December 2008
user-centered	33,000	user centered	909,000
user-friendly	1,400,000	user friendly	27,700,000
user-based	34,000	user based	743,000
user-oriented	32,000	user oriented	435,000
user-responsive	800	user responsive	855,000
client-centered	22,000	client centered	828,000
human-centered	18,000	human centered	409,000
people-centered	13,000	people centered	189,000
	570,000	human centered	111,000
	251,000	user defined	8,000,000
	41,000	user needs	2,230,000
	595,000	user perspective	1,060,000
	39,000	usability	22,900,000
	18,000	usability testing	803,000
	6,000	user testing	962,000
	8,300	user evaluation	90,900
	16,000	usability evaluation	154,000
		usability engineering	223,000
		user centric	404,000
		user driven	626,000
		user created	5,660,000
		user generated	6,500,000
		user contributed	4,560,000
		user input	2,830,000
		user determined	83,800
		patron driven	6,290
		user experience	11,300,000
		customer experience	4,540,000
		user interactions	443,000
		interaction design	1,930,000
		user experience design	283,000
		user centered design	406,000
		user centered web design	6,250
		participatory design	172,000

DESIGNING HUMAN-CENTERED IES

Several large studies have produced findings to guide the continuing design of the IE. The IE includes all physical and online settings where people are engaged in the perusal and/or exchange of data, images, text, information, or knowledge, including details about anything in life such as work, events, beliefs, imaginings, relationships, health, entertainment, etc. An IE may be grounded in technological affordances such as computers and other telecommunications devices, or a self-contained setting such as home, library, school, home improvement center, physician's office, hair salon, neighborhood coffee house, or any community setting. The studies reported in this section reveal major trends in IB made visible through enormous and mushrooming public use of the World Wide Web over the past 15 years. The following top trends for libraries emerged in recent studies of user behavior, including users of public libraries, academic libraries, school libraries, government sites, etc.:

1. Increasing use of electronic resources in libraries
2. Search engine (SE) supremacy
3. Web 2.0 interactivity and participation
4. Difficulties with academic electronic resources

For most public and academic library users the convenience of full-text electronic resources makes them preferable to print material. People of all generations love SEs more than any other information retrieval mode, and libraries are responding with "next generation" online catalogs that resemble familiar SEs. The interactive applications introduced by Web 2.0 have sparked the public's imagination, and have increased the appetite for interactivity and establishing connections with others online. As a result, libraries have implemented a variety of Web 2.0 interactive services dubbed as Library 2.0 (see the section "Information is personal"). The escalating preference for a Web-style information seeking experience is evident in data from several studies where people report that the formality and structure of academic databases requires more effort, more time, and more technical vocabulary in queries.

Carol Tenopir's meta-analysis of over 200 research studies on users and uses of electronic resources provided in libraries yields a rich set of findings on user behavior and makes several user-centered recommendations. Tenopir found "Both faculty and students use and like electronic resources and most readily adopt them if the sources are perceived as convenient, relevant, and time saving to their natural workflow" and "Experts in different subject disciplines (work fields) have different usage patterns and preferences for print or electronic. There is no one right solution for services or system design for every subject discipline."[2] The wide variety of differences in undergraduate, graduate, faculty, and researcher uses of electronic databases challenge providers and libraries to

meet needs on many levels. Tenopir's review shows "The concept of a single typical 'user' of information systems is clearly a fallacy." Some of the user-centered recommendations include

- Allow users to customize and personalize electronic resource pages.
- Publishers create products that better support the workflow of users.
- Recommend electronic resources to users to increase awareness of relevant material.
- Teach students how to evaluate found material and help them with search strategy.
- Develop virtual reference services to support increasing electronic resource use.
- Provide both "viewer-friendly" (html) and "printer-friendly" (pdf) full-text formats.

Tenopir's report provides a plethora of data illustrating the diversity of users and uses of electronic resources and the inherent complexity of the IE.

A 2007 Pew study, Information Searches that Solve Problems, found libraries performed well when people face personal problems that require obtaining information for decision-making:[3]

> Library help is effective. Among those who received help at the library, 88% say they found a lot or some of what they were seeking, including 38% who say a lot. By contrast, among those who did not seek help at the library, only 53% found a lot or some of what they were seeking, including 29% who say a lot.

Though in some studies Generation Y users (ages 18–29) report avoiding the library, Estabrook, Witt, and Rainie found that young adults in the Pew study are the heaviest users when it comes to looking for information about personal matters or anything else, and that they valued library resources and access to technology.[4] One of the main user-centered findings from the Institute of Museum and Library Services (IMLS) Museums and Libraries Engaging America's Youth study encourages librarians to "substantively involve youth in program design and decision making" and recommends "Programs should strongly align institutional focus and audience needs, especially by performing needs assessments to inform program selection or design."[5] In November 2007, Library Trends issued a Call for Papers for a special issue devoted to exploring the current use of Web 2.0 technologies in libraries that serve teens, and how future services might be developed to better meet the needs of Web 2.0 savvy young adults. The issue focuses on the following user-centered areas:

- MySpace, Facebook, and other social networking sites
- Use of blogs
- Security and safety

- Getting staff and managers onboard
- Gaming—does it have a place in libraries?
- Online reading groups
- Podcasting—library tours and other uses
- Web 2.0 approaches to information skills
- Wikis and online communities

Involving tweens and teens in the design of Web 2.0 services is consistent with the deepening user-centered participatory trend.

The 2007 Association for College and Research Libraries (ACRL) Environmental Scan produced a set of Top 10 Assumptions about users of college and university information services.[6] The research found that demand for online library services will continue to strengthen (p. 13):

> Students and faculty will continue to demand increasing access to library resources and services, and to expect to find a rich digital library presence both in enterprise academic systems and as a feature of social computing.

The 2007 Scan also highlights the significant changes brought about by Web 2.0 and subsequent challenges of implementing Library 2.0 for improving infrastructure, contributing and creating content, and designing and delivering interactive services. Recent research in the application of user-centered social media in libraries is examined in the report; however, the area is nascent, rapidly evolving, and the professional literature continues to expand.

The Joint Information Systems Committee (JISC) study of college students and researchers in Britain, found they have become "information consumers" comfortable using commercial SEs, online library services and databases, wikis, social networking, and other forms of information access.[7] Ian Rowlands describes "horizontal" information seeking behavior characterized by "bouncing, checking and viewing…." calling users "promiscuous, diverse and volatile."[7] Users in this study spent an average of 4–8 min on e-book sites, but did more navigating than reading, and exhibited "squirreling behaviour" in gathering information in case it might be needed in the future.[8] As for online abilities,[9]

> Digital literacies and information literacies do not go hand in hand. A careful look at the literature over the past 25 years finds no improvement (or deterioration) in young people's information skills.

However, a majority of students in the 2007 Educause study of Undergraduates and Information Technology reported that they use and are skilled with a wide variety of technologies, and only 26% indicated they wanted more technology training.[10] Carol Tenopir uncovered evidence in the findings of a meta-analysis of 200 studies between 1995 and 2003 that these trends have been developing since the early Web began attracting users. For example,

"Most high school and undergraduate students turn first to the Internet for class assignments and feel they are expert searchers" and "Younger users rely on electronic resources more heavily and rate themselves more expert in using them than do older users."[2]

Eszter Hargittai studied the digital fluency of 1160 first year students at Princeton including their perceptions of their online skills as well as their understanding of online concepts.[11] This wired generation reported high confidence in their digital abilities, "52.2 percent claimed to be fairly skilled, 33.0 percent believed themselves to be very skilled and the remaining 8.5 percent thought of themselves as experts" (p. 10). Hargittai had students rank their level of understanding to explore perceived knowledge of the online concepts, "frames, preference settings, pdf, spam, jpg, bookmark, newsgroup, mp3, and browser" and the more recent Web terms "bookmarklet, feed reader, malware, mashup, phishing, podcasting, real simple syndication (RSS), social bookmarking, tabbed browsing, torrent, tagging, Web feeds, widget, and wiki" (pp. 12–13).[12] The *Oxford English Dictionary* defines mash-up as "a mixture or fusion of disparate elements" and *MSN Encarta* defines it as a "digitally created mix of songs: a song in digital format created by combining parts of different songs, for example the music track of one song and the vocal track of another." While the majority of students gave high ratings on the basic concepts, on the more recent terms most reported low levels of understanding. Hargittai proposes 11 user-centered areas of skill that need greater attention in research and teaching (pp. 13–14):

1. Effective and safe ways of communicating with others.
2. Knowledge of how to contribute to group discussions and share content.
3. Knowledge about and use of tools.
4. Knowledge of what is available.
5. Ability to find content.
6. Efficiency in Web navigation.
7. Ability to assess source and message credibility.
8. Understanding of privacy issues.
9. Understanding of security issues.
10. Knowledge of where and how to seek assistance with questions.
11. Customization.

Taken together, these studies identify the IB of the Net Generation of college students as driver of the expansion in the use of interactive technology in society, particularly on campus. These digital natives were born into technology and will continue to drive its social uses; however, they need to deepen their understanding of and abilities with new forms of content provision.

> In the space of one school day, 21st-century children might converse with their friends using instant messaging,

watch webcams of live events happening anywhere in the world, read e-books that contain links to relevant information, use videoconferencing to share ideas with students at schools in other states or on other continents, and use the Internet to access databases and websites containing information on a topic of choice.[13]

Net Gen search behavior emphasizes speed, simplicity in concept, interface and database, full gratification in answers, and ease.[14]

Still, the international 2005 OCLC Perceptions of Libraries and Information Resources study found that most people are not aware of online library services:[15]

> The findings indicate that information consumers view libraries as places to borrow print books, but they are unaware of the rich electronic content they can access through libraries.

The vast majority (84%) found information using a SE and were very satisfied with results (93%), claiming that the quality and quantity of information provided is higher than from libraries. These user assessments are based primarily on the generally high confidence users express in their abilities to evaluate the quality and trustworthiness of retrieved information (86%). Other studies of the predominance of SE use among college students found that Google was used 45% and library catalogs used 10%.[16]

- Students prefer to locate information or resources via a SE above all other options, and Google is the SE of choice.
- Students' use of academic resources is low.
- Students find it difficult to locate information and resources.
- Students may trade quality of results for effort and time spent searching.
- Students' use of SEs now influences their perception and expectations of other electronic resources.

Frequently cited reasons given for low use of academic electronic resources are the need to find, choose, and search different databases; hierarchical arrangement, complexity, and differing interfaces; the lack of total full-text retrieval; and the technicality of academic vocabulary combined with less full-text makes it difficult to retrieve relevant material.

The perceived difficulty of online catalogs and subscription databases, the need to justify their escalating cost, and the development of the SE, the greatest technology trend of the Internet age, has stimulated universities to create novel user-centered approaches to win back students to their resources. Indiana University has an agreement with SE ChaCha, touting its "Human Guide" component that allows online catalog users to link to a librarian for assistance during a search session.[17] ChaCha

maintains a knowledgebase of vetted answers, so as it is used could become more valuable to the university community. The interface is similar to the sparse Google search page with a Guide button on the results page, and ubiquitous Google Ads, revealing that online catalogs, like other SEs, can be accepted as revenue-producing entities. Trend watchers point out that user-centeredness is key to successful catalog improvement:[18]

> The most significant difference between traditional library catalogs and the "next generation" library catalog lies in: 1) the enhancement of the discovery process and 2) providing services against the collection beyond simple identify. Putting the users' needs and characteristics at the center of the query process will greatly enhance the discovery process.

The broader interface design community has come to a similar conclusion.

Centrality of Users in Design

It is recognized that interfaces have physical, social, cognitive, and affective aspects.[19–24] A central concern of human-computer interaction (HCI) research has been to determine the effects of human physical, cognitive, and affective characteristics on the interactions between users and computers for specific tasks. As HCI researchers from a variety of disciplines developed models of human activity and used these models to design new interfaces, it became evident that a new design protocol must include a variety of interactive process and social approaches.

The UCD movement in computer science, particularly the area of HCI, has transformed a field which has shifted orientation, has redefined its scope, and has adopted a process approach that emphasizes the user experience, not only in interaction with information technology, but interaction with information in any form, in any setting, and in collaboration with others. In the second edition of *Interaction Design*, Helen Sharp, Yvonne Rogers and Jenny Preece describe the new user-centered process approach as "… creating user experiences that enhance and augment the way people work, communicate, and interact."[25] The four main principles of interaction design may be applied in any discipline or setting and are not limited to computer interface design or telecommunications technology design:[26]

1. Identifying needs and establishing requirements of the user experience.
2. Developing alternative designs that meet those requirements.
3. Building interactive versions of the designs so that they can be communicated and assessed.
4. Evaluating what is being built throughout the process and the user experience it offers.

Inherent in each of these activities is the focus on the agency of individuals and groups in their use of information systems. Interaction design seeks to discover user priorities and desires in order to facilitate and accommodate those goals in interactive environments. To that end "user experience architects" (UX) utilize a variety of process and ethnographic methodologies to gather user data throughout the stages of design. "Experience designers" seek feedback on thoughts, feelings, impressions, and preferences through observing users engaged in natural settings, interviews, questionnaires, performance tests in the lab, having users interact with prototypes, having users think aloud during activities, biometric measurement during activities, having users participate in and contribute to design sessions, and other process methods.

These user experience design principles are expressed in greater detail through design principles that have evolved within the HCI field:[27,28]

- Visibility
- Feedback
- Constraints
- Consistency
- Affordance

In practice these five principles interact, creating complex dynamics that must be worked out with users within the design process. Affordance is a key concept that helps users notice what they can do at any given point in use or on a given screen, for example, a visible link invites (affords) clicking.[29]

The marked shift in orientation from an exclusive focus on "system" to "user and system" to the "user experience in interaction with systems of any type" profoundly influences the design process. Sharp et al. distinguish between "usability goals" and "user experience goals" and emphasize that each design must address both types of user goals with different approaches and analyses. Traditional usability goals inherited from the field of human factors include the following quality components:[30]

- Effectiveness
- Efficiency
- Safety
- Utility
- Learnability
- Memorability

Some usability goals include specific attention to identifying errors and how satisfied users are with the design.

User experience goals constitute a different, highly affective set of positive and negative qualities, feelings, and preferences. For example, designers elicit user responses regarding whether an experience is:[31]

- Satisfying
- Engaging
- Entertaining
- Helpful
- Motivating
- Pleasurable
- Provocative
- Challenging
- Frustrating
- Boring
- Annoying

User experience goals are often said to be subjective while usability goals are considered objective. However, researchers find great value in open-ended responses offering rich, spontaneous user discourse that reveals the centrality of affect in information reception and use. Capurro and Hjorland make the point that "Meaning is, however, determined in social and cultural contexts."[32] Individual interpretive responses, therefore, reflect the community practices that enable designers to create supportive and symbiotic systems.[33]

Participatory design, also termed cooperative design or contextual design, is a user-centered approach that integrates users throughout the process as design partners.[34–36] This design philosophy is deeper than UCD, which includes user input at various points throughout design, while participatory design makes users codesigners. For example, the International Children's Digital Library (ICDL) project of the Human-Computer Interaction Laboratory at the University of Maryland hired several children of varying ages to work with researchers in the Lab designing the site for children.[37] Researchers involve children from many different countries and regions of the world who contribute in a meaningful way to the site's design as well as to the growing content it offers. Children contribute to design elements, help select books to add to the international online collection, and write reviews of their favorite books for other children.[38] International Children's Digital Library researchers study the children's response to reading e-books as well as to reading other children's online reviews, finding that children incorporate novel expressions describing how a book made them feel. Their affective language is added to metadata to help kids in searching the collection because it reflects their own way of thinking. For example, ICDL added several affective search terms contributed by kids, including happy, sad, scared, and funny, among others.

Divergently, user-centered pioneer Jakob Nielsen cautions that designers should not rely on what users say about an interface because their descriptions may be neither accurate nor reliable. To design an easy-to-use interface, he recommends paying attention to what users do and not what they say, because users tend to base their evaluation of a product on surface features, which are often quite different from reports based on actual use[39]:

Another example is the drop-down menu. Users always love the idea: finally a standard user interface widget that they understand and that stays the same on every page. However, while they offer users a sense of power over the design, drop-down menus often have low usability and either confuse users or lead them to unintended parts of the site.

Yet despite such problems, the drop down menu is present in most interactive systems. Nielsen warns that focus groups can give mixed results.[39] When discussing past behavior, users self-reported data is typically three steps removed from reality. This is because users cannot remember specific details of complex processes and tend to fill-in memory gaps with what seems plausible. Second, people construct things or speculate about what might be easier or harder for them rather than rely on actual recalled aspects. Concurrent data gathering methods such as observing users interacting with a system or recording think aloud protocols can provide more accurate data on what users actually experience in a process.

Designing for Diversity

Global computing has necessarily strengthened the fundamental user-centered concern for how to accommodate the diversity of users, which shows itself in individual differences in perceptual and motor capacity, in cognitive ability and intellectual skills, in emotional coping skills, in handling complexity, as well as in personality, cultural background, and expectations. Computer literacy depends on memory for detail and order and the ability to solve problems to make appropriate decisions. Since these cognitive abilities are normally distributed in a diverse population, half of the users of a system will have below average intellectual skills, yet many interfaces must accommodate the wide range of skill in the entire population.

The design community has responded to people with diverse physical challenges by creating adaptive hardware and software. These efforts are aided by the mandates of equality of accessibility in the Americans with Disabilities Act.[40–43] People also differ in perceptual skills such as time perception and scanning ability to locate information on screen displays. There are both individual and culturally based orienting habits and mindsets that the computing environment must accommodate.[44] Affective habits also vary in a diverse population, for example, moods or motivational states of users vary from hour to hour, day to day. Some respond to lower levels of frustration while others tolerate a bit of anxiety and uncertainty. Illness or injury, drugs or medication, sleep deprivation, and emotional distress affect perceptual and cognitive abilities. Eventually, such diverse conditions must be anticipated and provided for by system designers.[45,46]

Cognitive problems of users involve difficulties in acquiring progressive computer literacy skills for many whose educational background has not prepared them adequately with basic skills. They are overwhelmed by the bewildering complexity of software and hardware options in an era when designers still believe that simplicity is a sacrifice rather than a desired feature. Libraries have created many new services to bridge the digital divide, for example by engaging tech-savvy teens to teach senior citizens computer, networking, and gaming skills that help people overcome limitations, understand technology, and increase their participation in the life of the community and their families.[47,48]

Standardizing UCD Principles

Inspection of design Web sites demonstrates a strengthened advocacy for users and a high degree of agreement concerning what constitutes good UCD. One example is the updated and expanded IBM design specifications:

> In the following four sections, this site addresses the challenge of creating great user experiences through the discipline of User Engineering, supported by design guidelines, tools and other relevant materials.[49,50]

The shift in terminology to the more encompassing "user engineering" that incorporates UCD, illustrates the deepening of the trend toward holistic design, and the opening of the design process to include frequent and systematic feedback from potential and future users. The previous 2001 IBM document pointed out that the Web connects everybody to everything with a single interface but cautioned that there is a difference between physical access and functional use since numerous people who may be connected are nevertheless incapable of using many of the available systems.

> Many people acknowledge and accept the standards for such things as power voltage, power plugs, and even e-mail headers, but deny the need for standardizing user interfaces. They argue that users are intelligent and instinctive individuals and can adapt to any given design. It is true that users can adapt to almost anything. They surely had to do so in the past. Why should users have to adapt to machines? Do they voluntarily or involuntarily adapt to machines? Research on human factors in human-computer interaction shows that users of a new interface demonstrate a consistent desire to get started right away... This distinct desire or preference forces them to figure out...the interface without the benefits of a user-friendly design.[49,50]

Despite the humanizing shift in design philosophy, it is common to struggle with technology and design during routine information tasks. For example, a study of 50 state health department sites reported that universally they are deemed not user friendly.[51] People are supposed to be able to conduct a variety of medical information tasks using these sites such as filing medical claims, comparing health care providers, determining eligibility for assistance programs, and becoming aware of and informed about services. Two-thirds of the sites had a reading level too difficult for an average person, many did not provide for non-English speakers, and more than half "did not meet the minimum recommended accessibility standards..."[51]

In addition, as desktop and laptop systems have become more powerful, operating systems and applications have become more complex. Both affective load and cognitive load rise with uncertainty, and the frequent transitions to upgrades or new software makes it increasingly difficult for an ordinary user to install a system and its components. Replacing its focus in 2001 on standardization and universality of interfaces to solve ease of use problems, IBM's 2008 design site content emphasizes value, diversity, personalization, and collaboration.[49] Eleven design principles are provided and the fourth is Users:

Principle: Users

Description: Each group of users must be identified and characterized. This includes identifying the user goals and how they are measured. This is critical data for the Business Model work product and for tracking progress during the design process. The total user experience must be defined for each user group. Those aspects addressed by the project are identified, consistent with the business goals. Details of the tasks performed by each user group must be recorded, together with all important measures. In addition, information must be collected on how users wish to perform their tasks.

Purpose: Provide a clear understanding of the users' world and what it will take to satisfy their expectations.

User eXperience Research gathers and records all user requirements including who they are (roles), what they want to achieve (goals), how they wish to do it (tasks), and their success criteria (measures & targets).

Ideally, typical or target users are incorporated into the design process to test the design until it is accepted. IBM invites visitors to its Web site to volunteer for user experience design studies.[52] As the Web grows, usability becomes more important because users are often lost or get stuck, not knowing what to do next.

Jakob Nielsen discusses Web usability principles and what to avoid.[53,54] Nielsen's annual Top 10 Mistakes in Web Design essays document numerous ongoing follies of design and the consequences in lost productivity, and lost revenue due to user frustration and loss of customers, including not answering users' questions, inconsistency, user-hostile messages, obtuse page titles, animations,

pop-ups, advertisements, and more.[53,54] Still, the ubiquitous and obtuse "404 Not Found" Web error message continues to plague users:

We understand what 404 means: Page Not Found. But the average internet user has no idea what 404 means or what to do about it. To them, it's yet another unintelligible error message from the computer. Most 404 pages are unvarnished geek-speak.[55]

The Department of Health and Human Services has produced a set of extensive usability guidelines based on research intended to "...reflect HHS' commitment to identifying innovative, research-based approaches that result in highly responsive and easy-to-use Web sites for the public."[56] The current set of *Guidelines* increased by 10% to 209 items, demonstrating the growing complexity of creating usable and acceptable sites. Chapter two of the Guidelines is devoted to Users, Chapter 17 covers Search, and Chapter 18 is devoted to Usability. Search includes the following user-oriented *Guidelines* to support term discovery:[57]

Guideline: Construct a Web site's search engine to respond to users' terminology. Keep in mind that designers' preferred keywords may not match users' preferred keywords, and content writers may overestimate the specialized vocabulary of their audience. (p. 5)

Guideline: Provide templates to facilitate the use of search engines. Templates are predefined sets of keywords that help users select relevant vocabulary for their search topic. (p. 9)

The *Guidelines* recommend arranging topics in hierarchies. Similarly, the usability chapter reports that[58]:

Inspection methods, such as heuristic evaluations or expert reviews, tend to generate large numbers of potential usability' problems' that never turn out to be actual usability problems. (p. 1)

Guideline: Solicit usability testing participants' comments either during or after the performance of tasks. (p. 3)

Therefore, system-centered usability testing that employs inspection evaluation is inefficient in comparison to user-centered testing that isolates germane problems sooner. The *Guidelines* recommend the use of think aloud or retrospective critical incident methods to ensure discovery of the most salient user requirements. The goal of universal usability and ease of use will continue to be a challenge to the design community into the distant future because the diversity of users and uses ensures that one size cannot fit all.

One of the underlying forces working against user-friendly software, hardware, databases, digital libraries, and content-laden Web sites was termed "infomania" in

2005 by Edwin Hallowell, also referred to as information overload or Attention Deficit Trait (ADT):

> Infomania is the mental state of continuous stress and distraction caused by the combination of queued messaging overload and incessant interruptions.[59]

Zeldes, Sward, and Louchheim report that knowledge workers typically accomplish a mere three minutes of uninterrupted work during a task. Sources of distraction include "e-mail, instant messages, phone calls, text messages, and coworkers" among others.[59] Incessant incoming information accumulates and pressures people to attend to it, process it, file it, make decisions with it, organize it, store it, and delete it. This situation creates stress as people experience frequent frustration in information-intensive environments, and the resulting losses in productivity can soar to billions annually.

SPREAD OF THE USER-CENTERED PARADIGM IN LIS

Researchers in virtually all subareas of LIS have adopted a user-centered perspective in their investigations. While many cite Dervin and Nilan's 1986 *ARIST* review article as the inception of the user-centered turn in LIS, some prominent researchers have published historical reviews tracing its origins to the 1950s and 1960s studies of information practices of scientists in particular disciplines as well as other groups.[60–63] Marcia Bates credits the work of Stanford communications professor William Paisley who focused on behavioral aspects of information use.[61,64,65]

Current areas of special interest include: user generated content, IB models, emotional aspects of information seeking and use, information architecture, building community networks, Web 2.0 social software, open digital content, virtual services, and gaming, among others.[66] Mike Eisenberg encourages libraries to lead in the rapidly evolving technological environment, where social media dominate in a "parallel information universe," where content is delivered and users are interactively engaged through a variety of online devices, applications, and services.[67] Inspection of recent conference programs in information science and technology shows a prevailing user-centered concentration in research.

Professional Conferences with a User Focus

American Library Association's (ALA) Office for Information Technology Policy (OITP) and the Association for Library and Information Science Education (ALISE) jointly sponsored a 2008 session on "Participatory

Librarianship and Web 2.0 in the Curriculum." The call for participation reflects a sense of urgency to integrate new user-oriented services into LIS curricula to ensure that graduates are prepared to enter a more user-defined IE:

> The library landscape is constantly in flux. New technologies, new practices, and new theories are the sign of an active field. However, these dynamic forces also lead to confusion and conflict. It also leads to a spate of new services and functions that are sometimes awkward to integrate into existing research, operations and curricula. In today's world of Web 2.0, Library 2.0, social networks, blogs and wiki's what concepts are durable and what is new that must be imparted to the next generation of professionals?[68]

The variety of Web 2.0 applications continues to swell so that a critical process for adoption must be developed to equip graduates with adequate tools for making new service decisions. For example, the 2007 ACRL New York Annual Symposium, "Library 2.0 a New Social Model" illustrates the demand for instruction in the application of social media. It offered practitioners three sessions that covered "Social Software in Academic Libraries," "Technical Services 2.0: "Mashing up" Traditional and New Services," and "Library 2.0 and Web 2.0, Changing the Face of Professional Development."[69]

The Computers in Libraries 2008 program lists sessions on SecondLife, YouTube, and other Web 2.0 topics:[66]

- Social software
- Communities and collaboration
- User generated content
- Engaging the audience
- Gaming and learning
- Open source

The user-centered focus was evident at the American Society for Information Science and Technology (ASIST) 2007 themed, "Joining Research and Practice: Social Computing and Information Science," including presentations on

- Social information architecture
- Participation behavior
- Social tagging
- Folksonomies
- Social computing
- Online communities
- Blogs and wikis for scholarly communication
- End-user collection building
- Digital natives

The ASIST 2008 annual conference program "People Transforming Information—Information Transforming People" continues the strong focus on social interaction:[70]

- Individual identities and how they are transformed by the impact of information technologies.
- The societal archive—is it disappearing and/or being marginalized?
- Societal attentions and how emphasis on information technology either allows or hinders these.
- Openness, access, and privacy issues.
- Generational, economic, and sociocultural dimensions of impact of information on people's lives.
- Cognitive and emotional aspects of interactions with information.
- Reshaping the boundary between personal and public information space.
- The effect of collective information creation on authority and trust.
- Information by the people for the people.
- The role of information in connecting people and community building.
- How well is current technology meeting human needs, and what should future technology research and development involve to better meet our needs?

The American Society for Information Science and Technology (ASIST) held its first Social Computing Summit in 2008, to focus on "Social networking services, data portability, open social networks, mobile services, social computing and politics, global voices, social computing and the enterprise, and youth social computing."[71]

The Annual Research Symposium of the Special Interest Group on Information Needs, Seeking and Use (SIG USE) takes an inherently situated, social, constructivist, relational, interactive, and holistic approach to the study of IB.[72,73] Special Interest Group on Information Needs, Seeking and Use is the leading ASIST SIG for user studies and has published two edited volumes of IB research and theory.[24,74] The 2006 Symposium focused on emotional design and affect in IB, and the 2007 Symposium featured research on the use of mobile devices during a wide variety of user-driven information-intensive activities:

- Searching WebMD
- Checking stock portfolios
- Meeting up through dodgeball.com
- Chatting with friends on MySpace
- Playing online games
- Sharing photos
- Making plane reservations
- Paying bills and shopping

The Information Seeking in Context (ISIC) conference that originated in 1996 is entirely devoted to the study of situated IB, examining an ever-widening variety of particular user groups in specific information contexts and settings.[75,76] A sample of the ISIC 2006 conference program presentations illustrates the current trend in diversification of the user-centered paradigm in user group, methodology, and granularity of analysis:

- Uncertainty
- Interpersonal information seeking
- Information sharing
- Personal information seeking
- Motivation and information seeking

Investigations of everyday information seeking is a burgeoning area that has attracted experienced information retrieval researchers who have turned their attention to the micro level to study the information needs and uses of particular user groups within social contexts. These efforts to further specify levels in the human aspects of IB will continue to extend to narrower domains and into deeper layers of thinking, perceiving, learning, valuing, and accepting information. The Second International Symposium on Information Interaction in Context (IIiX) exemplifies this user-centered thrust:[77]

- Case studies, field experiments, simulations, etc. of context-sensitive information seeking and retrieval.
- Context-aware retrieval models.
- Relevance feedback—implicit and explicit—and query modification issues for capturing context.
- Other approaches to eliciting, identifying, and expressing/capturing contextual information.[78]
- Task-based interactive information retrieval and seeking behavior.
- The effect of genre, media, language, modality, and structure on context.
- Personalized and collaborative information access in context.
- Contextual information interaction theory.
- Interactive information retrieval and interface issues.
- Nature of relevance in contexts.
- Measures of performance in context and situation-sensitive information access.
- Test collections for context-sensitive research.

There was some focus on user perspective at the IA Summit 2007, themed "Enriching Information Architecture," but one year later at IA Summit 2008 the theme "Experiencing Information" focused entirely on the user experience:[79,80]

- Information quantity and the experience of choice
- The timing of information encounters and information use
- The subconscious consumption of information
- Rapid or intuitive processing of information
- The social and participatory aspects of information and information communities
- The wide range of information media: the Web, virtual worlds, ubiquitous computing, mobile technology, physical spaces

The Association for Computing Machinery (ACM) Computer/Human Interaction 2007 Conference, CHI 2007, highlighted the continuing efforts of the HCI community to humanize the interface and to design for interaction and the user experience:

- Beyond usability: Social, situational, and contextual factors
- Rethinking humans, computers, interaction and design
- People looking at people
- Emotion and empathy
- Programming by and with end-users
- Ethnography
- Capturing Life Experiences

These conferences and a growing group of others demonstrate that information science and computer science research has taken the user-centered turn. It follows that degree programs preparing information professionals and information scientists have altered and enhanced curriculum to support users in the IE.

The Rise of Informatics and Participatory Culture

A study of 26 LIS programs was conducted between 1998 and 2000 in the Kellogg-ALISE Information Professions and Education Reform project known as KALIPER. The results of this detailed case study analysis revealed six trends affecting curricular change.[81,82] The second trend that emerged from an analysis of program mission statements, course descriptions, course titles and syllabi revealed a predominant focus on the social and cognitive aspects of information, information systems, and information use.[84] The programs emphasize user constructs and dynamics that permeate their core and elective curricula in the areas of information seeking, user behavior, user needs, user-centered information services, and user engagement practices.[85] Markey warns programs to look beyond the user-centered paradigm to prepare future information professionals because, due to the spread of information and communication technology (ICT), disintermediation will likely displace libraries in that domain. She recommends, "Instead, programs should stake out unclaimed or disputed areas such as the organization of information, content creation, authoritative information, and/or collection preservation." Informatics has emerged within several disciplines as a user-oriented specialty.[86–92]

Informatics refers to the study of information systems, particularly the relationships among people, information, and information technology. Undergraduate and graduate programs in informatics offer a definitively human-centered approach to the study of information systems and technology. Students completing these degrees develop conceptual understandings of information and technology, a variety of technical skills, a human-centered perspective in designing, implementing and evaluating information

system use, engagement with communities of practice to foster networking, they share tools and resources, and work with open source "communityware" information and content management systems that are designed for public use. Ann Bishop and colleagues in the University of Illinois Community Informatics Initiative[93,94] focus on understanding the social context that has led to the digital divide, and work to develop models for public libraries to collaborate with underserved groups in the creation of innovative technology-based information services relevant to people's everyday lives.[95]

> The core of the CII is community inquiry: collaborative action to create knowledge and technology connected to people's values, history, and lived experiences; the development of models of engagement that are just, democratic, participatory, and open-ended; and the integration of theory and practice in an experimental and critical manner.

As further evidence of the social participation trend in curricula, the theme for the 2008 meeting of the ALISE was Community Engagement: Integrating Learning, Research, and Practice. American Library Association's OITP published the Participatory Librarianship Starter Kit[96] that encourages creating participatory networks, and enhancing material offered to users by linking topics to a variety of resources (conversations) from the library, the Web, the community, and beyond, including existing sets of "answers":

> Simply put participatory librarianship recasts library and library practice using the fundamental concept that knowledge is created through conversation. Libraries are in the knowledge business, therefore libraries are in the conversation business. Participatory librarians approach their work as facilitators of conversation. Be it in practice, policies, programs and/or tools, participatory librarians seek to enrich, capture, store and disseminate the conversations of their communities.

For example, virtual reference service aims to "look at the core of the reference process as a conversation between a librarian and a patron."[97,98] Reference conversations proceed through exchanging understandings and "are ultimately a learning act." The focus on human interaction, participation, and the value of acting together to change lives for the better, orients information professionals to maximizing the social utility of technology and content or expression by gaining technical skills, networking skills, engagement skills, and needs assessment skills.

Some refer to this human-centered activism as evidence of a Copernican paradigm shift from a primary focus on libraries and librarianship to a focus on information, from organizing information containers to understanding the role of information in people's lives and helping them make productive uses.[99,100] This change in locus was first seen in the flurry of programs adding information to their names, missions, goals, and objectives, and course titles, and in user studies applying qualitative and ethnographic social science methods to investigate the human experience in needing, accessing, and using information. The impetus for understanding users' IB can be traced to the increasing pressure of an intensifying societal expectation that people become informed in every aspect of life including health, legal, insurance, personal finance, consumer product, and environmental knowledge, as well as interpersonal competencies or emotional intelligence.[101] A responsible person can no longer simply rely on professionals to advise and recommend, instead, one must become informed through personal research and obtain second opinions to make intelligent choices about available opportunities, options, or treatments, and one must use information to help avoid disease, disability, penalties, fines, or unfavorable judgments, and to make informed decisions.

> By "life information" is meant information needed for successful living. The area of need ranges all the way from sheer survival (stay away from dogs that walk funny and foam from the mouth) to the most advanced forms of self-realization (where can I study ceramics or transcendental meditation?). The scope of information falling under this rubric is greater than may at first appear. It includes vast amounts of information about how to do many different things in one's culture that will be acceptable and lead to one's survival and emotional satisfaction.[102]

The information age provides abundant information to those who are connected to the networks, nevertheless, one must make the necessary effort to value, notice, identify, locate, obtain, store, evaluate, and utilize information; determine its ultimate effectiveness; and often, report the results to others (family, physicians, friends, fellow students and teachers, employers or coworkers, etc.) and find it again at a later time on a different occasion. In addition, there is the ever-expanding information universe of work that continuously pushes people to update and upgrade their knowledge and skills within an IE that demands lifelong learning. Informatics research will continue to gather importance because of the trend toward a continuously enlarging responsibility to obtain and manage personal information.

Multidisciplinary Influences in LIS Curriculum

The field of HCI has been at the forefront of the UCD, interaction design, and user experience design movement.[103] Library and information science programs and I-Schools have developed curricula based in the computer science design philosophy, which has become increasingly multidisciplinary through integrating psychological, sociological, and anthropological theory and methods. As

evidence of the expansion of the trend to incorporate users in interface design, usability assessment texts have emerged that treat the needs of information-intensive, content rich Web sites produced and maintained by librarians for their user communities.[104–108] Stephen Bell advocates applying design thinking "to help users accomplish their work by removing barriers or inefficiencies..." and introduces the user-centered IDEO design method and the Designing Better Libraries blog.[109–111]

Courses offered in information programs have diversified from the single usability or UCD course to include varied offerings and tracks. Some examples include

- Usability Analysis
- Information Users in the Knowledge Society
- Information Behavior
- Seminar in Information Use and Users in Context
- Information Architecture
- Communities of Practice
- Assessing Information Needs
- Human Dimension in Information Systems
- Interface and Interaction Design

In 2008, the University of Michigan School of Information (SI) launched six new specializations, including four user-centered tracks[112–115]:

- Social Computing
- Incentive-Centered Design
- Community Informatics
- Information Analysis and Retrieval

The courses in these areas integrate such user factors as design ethics, psychological principles, interaction principles, social network analysis, online communities, computer-supported cooperative work, public goods, personalization, information use in communities, and user contributed content, among others.

The San Jose State University School of Library and Information Science (SLIS) was first to create a Second Life portal to deliver courses in the virtual world that allow students to create services, build information service environments, and conduct research in the SLIS virtual information space.[116] Courses for practitioners in the Virtual Worlds CE Series were offered for the first time in 2007 at the University of Illinois Graduate School of Library and Information Science:

- Second Life 101
- Introduction to Virtual World Librarianship
- Survey of Librarianship in Virtual Worlds
- Technical Skills for the Virtual World Librarian
- Intermediate Virtual World Librarianship—Programming and Planning
- Libraries and Immersive Learning in 3D Virtual Environments

- Working with a Class in Second Life
- Setting Up an Educational Presence in Second Life

The I-School at the University of Washington began offering a Certificate in Virtual Worlds for professionals seeking advancement in the following new skill areas:[117]

- Design virtual worlds, including multimedia
- Build in and account for human interaction
- Program and integrate with databases
- Evaluate the effectiveness of virtual worlds

The strong multidisciplinary user-centered trend in LIS curriculum development will continue and widen beyond system design and use into traditional areas of the field including archives, preservation, serials, acquisitions, information organization, reference services, and information access.

Information Literacy Mandates

Information literacy (IL) is an area of curriculum development that has lagged behind the profession. Heidi Julien analyzed the curricula of 93 LIS programs worldwide and determined that most programs did not have a course that prepares graduates to take on responsibilities for managing existing IL, digital literacy, and information fluency programs, including designing, planning, and teaching sessions, workshops, and full courses that are predominant in libraries around the globe.[118] In academic libraries, IL librarians must provide leadership in campus efforts to integrate IL components in General Education reform, and in school libraries developing IL skills is fundamental to every grade level. Julien argues for curriculum development to address this neglected core competency.

Information literacy, media literacy, digital literacy, and technological literacy coalesce in the online environment. In the past two decades, IL programs, user instruction services, instructional Web sites, and interactive online tutorials have proliferated in libraries worldwide. Information fluency has become a strong movement, evidenced in the mission and goal statements of academic, public, and school libraries which commonly cite endeavors to teach users to become independent, critical, and ethical information seekers and information users. The annual survey of freshmen in 700 American colleges by the University of California at Los Angeles (UCLA) provides a representative picture of the IL skills of entering students.[119] The survey reports that 76% used the Internet for assignments but only 35% said they critically evaluated information found in Internet searches.[120] In the past decade, accrediting bodies began mandating IL instruction in higher education. Outcomes assessment of IL competencies has gained momentum driven by the mandates from accrediting bodies, that is, schools must

demonstrate that graduates are information literate.[121] Standard 2 states: "Baccalaureate programs engage students in an integrated course of study... to prepare them for work, citizenship, and a fulfilling life. These programs also ensure the development of core learning abilities and competencies including... Information literacy..." Other accrediting bodies have similar requirements. The outcomes assessment model fits within data-driven strategic planning models that predominate in libraries. Professional associations have developed IL standards, competencies, and curricula to assist information professionals in measuring gains in skills.[122–126] The Reference and User Services (RUSA) division of ALA published six Guidelines for the Introduction of Electronic Information Resources to Users, of which the fourth is devoted to user-centered instruction. Guideline 4.3 addresses individual user factors:[127]

4. User Education/Instruction

4.1 Determine the appropriate type and level of instruction for a new electronic information resource.

4.2 Determine the extent to which the service should be incorporated into existing user instruction and the extent to which new instructional sessions or methods would be helpful.

4.3 Design user instruction to accommodate various learning styles and experience levels and include a combination of point of use instruction for individuals, group instruction, peer assistance (both user-user and instructor-instructor), tutorials, documentation, and/or signage.

The American Association of School Librarians (AASL) Standards for the twenty-first Century Learner overlap significantly with the ACRL Competencies while acknowledging that "Learning has a social context." In addition to acquiring critical thinking and evaluation skills,

The Standards describe how learners use skills, resources, and tools to

3. share knowledge and participate ethically and productively as members of our democratic society;

4. pursue personal and aesthetic growth.[128]

The AASL Standards' emphasis on the social aspects of learning, the ethical use of resources, and the value of self-improvement reflects the user-centered active learning movement in education that integrates learning community, collaborative learning, reflective learning, service learning, problem-based learning, inquiry learning, and informal learning models. These relational approaches continue to rise in prominence in higher education, particularly with the influx of social media and gaming models in learning, and will likely influence the future revision of the ACRL Competencies.

Originating in 1990, the Instruction Section of the International Federation of Library Associations (IFLA) has worked to promote IL skills in libraries worldwide. The 2006 Guidelines set international standards for global citizens:[129,130]

> Information skills are vital to the success of lifelong learning, employment, and daily interpersonal communication of any citizen, such as when a person needs information about health services for someone in his/her care, or a student requires specific information to complete an assessment.

The IFLA Guidelines take a constructivist approach to lifelong learning of IL skills, and overlap with the ACRL and AASL standards, with a strong emphasis on ethical use of information systems and resources. The IFLA Guidelines do not mention other social aspects present in the AASL standards, such as the social nature of learning and aesthetic values of learners. IL standards for these professional groups will evolve to address social learning and personal values as the user focus continues to strengthen.

INFORMATION IS PERSONAL

As a result of the societal forces of participation and community engagement, theory building has been developing at the intersection of the fields of communication, anthropology, sociology, and the psychology of information retrieval. The "sense making" approach was formulated by Brenda Dervin whose model is thoroughly user-centered, and grounded in constructivist assumptions about information seekers and users.[131,132] In this view, information is defined in terms of people's attention, processing, seeking, and use. Dervin's approach to user-centeredness complements Carol Kuhlthau's constructivist approach to information problem solving and information counseling, Marcia Bates' cognitive-behavioral approach to understanding searching, and Paul Solomon's approach to situated information discovery.[133–135] These person-centric approaches view the IE of systems and interfaces in terms of users' behavior. Information behavior is defined as what users do when they handle information and adjust to it.[136] "Information behavior…encompasses information seeking as well as the totality of other *unintentional* or *passive* behaviors (such as glimpsing or encountering information), as well as purposive behaviors that do not involve seeking, such as actively *avoiding* information." Salient user factors include: what they do and see, what they think or know, and what people feel that motivates them to continue or quit, to be satisfied or to continue searching, to strive to comprehend or

remain bewildered, to continue as a novice or strive to become an advanced daily user. In the purest sense in this approach there is no information, only situated IB, that is, information is embodied in IB.

The study of IB in a rapidly evolving technological society demands close attention to a full range of broad and specific user dynamics.[24,74,137] The multidisciplinary theoretical approaches in IB research acknowledge the centrality of the user's values, feelings, and perceptions in the information reception and use process. Each approach focuses on how the perspective of users determines their IB. Findings from IB research show that users are highly interactive, with dynamic motives and intentions. As goal-directed sense-makers, users are seeking meaning, bridging information gaps, dealing with uncertainty and anomalous states of knowledge, translating their own ideas into system terms, actively updating personal frames of reference, filtering both information and feelings, and applying personal constructs in the information seeking, reception, use, sharing, and creation process.[24] The users have become the creators, producers, and disseminators of content, therefore information retrieval systems and environments must concretely incorporate this reality into design to achieve the user-friendly systems that people need.[45,138]

In 2003 nearly half of all Internet users had added online content through file sharing, building or posting to Web sites and blogs, or posting content for businesses and organizations.[139] According to Henry Jenkins, director of MIT's Comparative Media Studies Program,

> …a participatory culture is a culture with relatively low barriers to artistic expression and civic engagement, strong support for creating and sharing one's creations, and some type of informal mentorship whereby what is known by the most experienced is passed along to novices.[140]

The forms of participatory culture include memberships in online communities (*Friendster*, *Facebook*, *MySpace*, *Twitter* and other more specialized online communities such as *LinkedIn*), metagaming, producing digital sampling, "skinning" and "modding," videomaking, fiction writing, zines, "mash-ups," working in teams to complete tasks and develop new knowledge (e.g., *Wikipedia*), and shaping the flow of media (podcasting, blogging).[141–145]

Wikipedia defines metagaming as "a broad term usually used to define any strategy, action or method used in a game which transcends a prescribed ruleset, uses external factors to affect the game, or goes beyond the supposed limits or environment set by the game." MSN Encarta defines "digital sampling" as an "electronic process used in telecommunications for transforming a constantly varying (analog) signal into one composed of discrete units, a digital signal" and one definition for "skinning" is "to change the appearance of images produced by existing software, without changing their function." A description of modding via Technology Source is, "Many of today's games—especially the first-person perspective, three-dimensional world games—are "open" to mods (modifications) of an enormous number of their features, including the environment, the characters, and the game play. Through modding, it is even possible to construct an entirely new game."

A user-centered emphasis enhances access to the full range of information activities, and advocates integrating the individual via engagement and involvement into the ongoing social practices of the community, so that technology works synergistically in the user's daily life of activities.[146] Library 2.0 pioneers advocate a major shift in perspective from "library functions and resources" to customer and user goals, interests, and desires for simplicity and ease of use. The digital user's focus is on participation, collaboration, membership, social networking, teamwork, task optimization, and successful completion. Self-expression is thus performed within intersubjective environments of communities of practice, and libraries are uniquely well placed to establish and foster active user communities by utilizing the new social media.[147]

Web 2.0, Library 2.0, User 2.0: The Social Software Revolution

After the total acceptance of SEs, User Generated Content (UGC) is the biggest user-centered trend affecting libraries, publishing, and news media. User Generated Content involves the use of social networking, folksonomies, blogs, wikis, and other interactive online facilities that allow self-expression. User Generated Content, also called user defined content or user contributed content, has surged as people flock to online sites to ask questions and seek answers, deposit their thoughts, musings, views, strong opinions, knowledge, evaluations and reviews, images, activity status updates, creativity, and vision for others to read or ignore, perhaps to attract comment and interact in an exchange of ideas or strong disagreements and agreements. The social software movement has sparked controversy over the traditional top-down prescriptive model of information standards and authority and the disintermediating, bottom-up inductive dynamic of social media. Professional news organizations now provide e-mail and blogs welcoming user input, and regular segments are devoted to "news" reported by "citizen journalists" who log in to leave information, including e-mail, voicemail, photos, and video. For example, the major cable networks have instituted the user-centered i-Report, U-Report, and News to Me segments, and viewers are implored to take polls on questions of the day and post comments and questions on the network's Facebook, MY Space, and Twitter pages. Some consider this

democratizing trend to be positive, persistent, and highly collaborative, while others deplore its baseness, lack of authority, anonymity, irresponsible demagoguery, and other cultural offenses.[148,149] As the lively debate evolves, the newly empowered authors and content creators will continue to find their voice and to prevail in Web 2.0 territory and beyond. Library users have begun to interact and provide input using the Library 2.0 participatory services designed and implemented by tech-savvy Librarian 2.0 information professionals.[150–161] Authors will write regularly updated reports about their initiatives for at least two years on a wiki hosted by the Association for College & Research Libraries (ACRL).

Library 2.0 represents the library that immerses itself in the advanced functionality of Web 2.0 technology to benefit the user experience by providing access to content through a personalized and co-constructed infosphere. According to Habib,

> The term Library 2.0 was introduced by Michael Casey in September 2005. ... The term was exposed to a wider audience when Michael Stephens discussed Library 2.0 on the ALA's Techsource Blog.[162]

The "Librarian 2.0" according to Stephen Abram,

> understands his or her users at a deep level – not just as pointers and clickers. Librarian 2.0 understands end users deeply in terms of their goals and aspirations, workflows, social and content needs, and more. Librarian 2.0 is where the user is, when the user is there. This is an immersion environment that librarians are eminently qualified to contribute to.[163]

Social software for library-related interaction and services incorporates blogs and RSS feeds to involve users in participatory exchanges that link comments, chat rooms, online discussions, blogs, wikis, photo and video sharing sites, podcasts with streaming media, e-mail, and Instant Messaging (IM).[164] Through these recent technological developments librarians have become involved in creating conversations, connections, and community within their user populations.[158] According to Abram "we are entering a period of enormous change - far greater than what we've ever experienced in our lives to date."[163] The new global transformation in the infosphere is powered by interactivity on an unprecedented scale. Social collaboration is as old as community and society, however the social-technological environment has become organic and symbiotic.[23] Despite the digital divide, human–machine symbiosis encompasses daily life for greater numbers of people, such that there is hardly a portion of the day that people are not connected to some technological device, creating and exploring intersubjective communication spaces in which our daily life of thinking, feeling, and sensing is shared virtually and co-experienced with many others.

The early Web environment also offered new ways for people to connect, including e-mail, Usenet groups, hyperlinks, directories, surfing, SEs, online shopping, and e-Bay bidding.[165] Beyond connectivity and access to vast information, Web 2.0 provides the living thrill of participatory culture where people take a personal hand in co-constructing a dynamic information world of *intersubjectivity*.[166–168] Social theorists and researchers use the term intersubjectivity to refer to use of the shared knowledge of jointly accepted group practices when people interact. Individual values, meanings, information, and knowledge are shared and dynamically created in social interaction, hence "Knowledge and knowledge structures are neither objective nor subjective, but intersubjective, produced within a shared system of meanings."[168] Social networking magnifies the intersubjective sphere, rendering the former Web paradigm limited, formal, and impersonal. Today's Web "page" is dynamic as the screen explodes in striking visuals and sounds, streaming video, sidebars with animated ads and polls, RSS content updated to the moment, and with deep level inserts like content filters, cookies, notebooks, dictionaries, SEs, polls, maps, fill forms, interactive graphics, widgets, customization and personalization, user tags and metadata, archived discussions, user reviews, ratings, and comments. Social technology has become an organic component of community life, a transformative user-generated trend in computing and communication.

Technology users today are empowered and enhanced because people can do more, see more, hear more, network more, enjoy more, and create more of what they want together. The meaning of technology has shifted from "computation" and "connection," to collaboration, co-construction, community, continuity, and co-presence in real time and in virtual senses.[169] Web 2.0 is explosively producing global intersubjectivity within an infosphere that is organized in channels defined by what people do, think, and feel on the daily round.[170] Floridi defines the infosphere as "the whole informational environment constituted by all informational entities (thus including informational agents as well), their properties, interactions, processes and mutual relations. It is an environment comparable to, but different from cyberspace (which is only one of its sub-regions, as it were), since it also includes off-line and analogue spaces of information. We shall see that it is also an environment (and hence a concept) that is rapidly evolving." Web portals and user gathering places are organized by special interests, niche topics, and targeted activities. Originally information space was organized by topic or subject matter, but the new social information dynamic has added a layer of content that is organized by activity. People go to sites to do things: to shop, transfer funds and pay bills, meet with online friends, send e-cards, trade stocks, find map directions or an address, order pizza, play online games with avatars, contribute to collaborative wikis, consult live online reference librarians, attend classes in immersive learning environments, see and contribute to the latest postings on blogs of interest, view and respond to updates on friend's activities, upload and download songs, videos, photographs, ringtones, resumes, and tax forms, etc. In social media users define the uses.

Stephen Abram provides a list of the technologies that "serve as the emerging foundation for Web. 2.0":[163]

* Really simple syndication (RSS)
* Wikis
* New and revised programming approaches like AJAX and APIs
* Blogs and blogging
* Commentary and comments functionality
* Personalization and "My Profile" features
* Personal media such as Podcasting and MP3 files
* Streaming media audio and video formats
* Reviews and user driven ratings
* Personalized Alerts
* Web Services (e.g., virtual reference service)
* Instant messaging and virtual reference including co-browsing
* Folksonomies, tagging, and tag clouds
* Photo and video sites (e.g., Flickr, Picasa, YouTube)
* Social networking software
* Open Access, Open Source, Open Content
* Socially driven content
* Social bookmarking (such as Delic.io.us)

Michael Stephens also identifies the following:[159]

* Building a community Web site with a blog
* Libraries and social sites like MySpace, Facebook, YouTube
* Messaging in a 2.0 World: Twitter & SMS
* Podcasting

A survey of public libraries in South Carolina confirms that social technologies are quickly transforming public libraries into participatory gathering places.[171] Services offered include instant messaging for reference services (30%), photo sharing accounts (23%), library blog (40%), and wiki (10%). More than half of the librarians have an instant messaging account, and one in three have a personal blog and participate in adding content to a library wiki. Libraries are also experimenting with building online communities, online library book clubs, user forums, offering library news using RSS, hosting webcasts and webinars, providing widgets for building personal digital collections[172–175] and digital DVD downloads, among many other user-centered interactive services. Some librarians caution that simply adding interactive services does not guarantee that people will use them or provide input, and that needs assessment, active participation of librarians and continuous evaluation are necessary to success.[176]

Benefits of Tagging and Social Bookmarking

The 2008 Library of Congress report on the Future of Bibliographic Control opened the gates to UGC in stating "User-contributed data, such as reviews or rankings, can help other users identify resources of possible interest to them."[177] In an unprecedented agreement with the image-tagging site Flickr.com, the Library posted large collections of digital photographs with a request for input, "You're invited to help describe photographs in the Library of Congress' collection on Flickr, by adding tags or leaving comments."[178] The Library intends to harness "key caption information" from masses of people viewing the images on the Flickr Commons site, effectively making indexers of users.

For libraries, "Tagging, as with del.icio.us and other social bookmarking tools, lets libraries label books in ways that make more sense to patrons than traditional subject headings."[179] Sites such as LibraryThing and Shelfari provide libraries with a user-centered approach to reducing barriers to participation, enabling users to post reviews, ratings, and tags to ease retrieval for other users.[172] The marvel is that people are keen to descriptively tag items, to comment on their usefulness, and to receive recommendations based on similarly tagged items. Users also want to build online collections using widgets that post book jacket images for new books with certain tags, or random books, or favorite books read by friends, or books one has read in one's lifetime, or books one plans to read, or the ICDL Children's Book of the Day, etc. The same holds good for music and video. Users love to arrange and organize information. The next generation online catalogs incorporate tagging and other social software features, but also promise "opportunities to get away from the OPAC and focus resources on new areas, such as 3-D information visualization, mass digitization, Library 2.0, and metadata related to digital resources."[180,181]

Second Life Immersive Social Learning Environment

It is often claimed that Generations X and Y have been brought up in a world of videogames that have become more complex and graphically elaborate since their inception in the 1970s with the simple yet fascinating Pong computer game. Web 2.0 librarians, young adult librarians, and instruction librarians see an opportunity in designing user-centered services involving games, gaming, and gamers. Libraries that offer ludic programming have instituted videogame tournaments and have created IL instruction using gaming formats.[182–185] Sharon Stoerger notes that participatory information technology is habit forming to the "Net Generation or Millenials" who have been raised on games and the Internet.[186] The teaching approach of lecture, textbook, and report assignment that has served previous generations now seems insipid, dry, and staid. Today's young adults are enlivened by participation and engagement, from which comes involvement and excitement. There is less value attached to merely new information if it is not optimized by participatory experience in an interactive media-rich virtual environment. This social reality laid the foundation for adapting a virtual world gaming environment to provide library services. In the Second Life virtual environment thousands of patrons visit Second Life Libraries every day, experiencing in world reference services from the main teleport landing on Info Island I.[187] Volunteer avatar librarians serve the many virtual reference stations through the Alliance Library System.

According to technology forecasters, "By the end of 2011, 80 percent of active Internet users (and Fortune 500 enterprises) will have a second life."[188] In 2007 more than eight million people had "resident accounts" in the collaborative virtual world of Second Life, one of dozens of virtual environments specialized for children, tweens, teens, or adults.[189] In April 2006, the Alliance Library System began work in the 3-D multiuser virtual environment (MUVE) of Second Life, helping to develop in-world libraries, collections, and immersive reference services.[190] What began as a single library, in less than two years grew to 43 islands of the Info Archipelago where over 1000 avatar librarians provide in-world reference service, create and provide virtual spaces for students and educators for classes and collaborative projects, create teleport boards linking the libraries and collections, market and hold events to support literacy, reading, authors, artists, and technology development for libraries, and develop collaborative projects with colleagues, students, and others.[191] Avatar librarians also provide course and research support to educators teaching in-world, and offer orientation classes and professional development programs for librarians and LIS graduate students who wish to explore work in Second Life.[192] The myriad advantages of 3-D virtuality for avatar librarians include flying, teleporting, automatic language translation in reference and other collaborations, serving a global clientele and new forms of diversity in user avatars, collaborating with colleagues worldwide, enhanced social and professional networking via affinity groups and friending, enhanced social presence for distance communication, virtual building, scripting, filming, and creating innovative interactive information affordances. The constructivist virtual environment stimulates imagination and feeds innovation in developing new library and information services. Second Life offers a complete research environment for avatar information studies, information seeking in virtual worlds, virtual IL, embodied distance learning, HCI interface studies, AI, and other areas.[193] In 2008 the American Library Association opened a virtual Washington Office in Second Life's Cybrary City on InfoIsland.[194]

The wildly popular social networking sites have sparked another user-revolution that is inherent in the new "participatory culture" consciousness.[195,196]

The Second Life browser software comes equipped with build-tools, group options, communication tools such as chat and instant messenger, and a menu-driven video capture tool for users to record "machinima" of their experiences, simulations or live events. Machinima is familiar to millions of gamers around the world and is defined as "animated filmmaking within a real-time virtual 3D environment.[189]

Librarians also create "story-based *machinima* instruction series" that combine filmmaking, animation, and 3-D video-gaming for instructional delivery. In the machinima (machine-cinema) environment, avatar actors and events in the virtual world are controlled by scripts chosen by users. Some avatar librarians create machinima to document and archive informational, cultural, and educational events in Second Life.[197] On video-sharing sites, collaborative software allows users to edit or piece together a multimedia film from the raw footage of video uploaded by other users, enabling group editing and storyboarding for joint media productions and community information sharing with collaborative content creation.

Library and information science programs have begun to offer courses and workshops on social computing and the immersive learning environment Second Life that focus on how to make use of the game-based, virtual environment created by the engaging online Second Life world for instruction and self-development. The University of Illinois GSLIS wants to "take the library forward to its future incarnations" beyond the "traditional read-lecture-and-discuss format," making use of the new game-based immersive learning technology that can provide new ways of library instruction and reference services.[198] In 2009, the University of Washington I-School began a three-course Certificate Program in Virtual Worlds designed to prepare professionals for work in virtual environments.[117] A *YouTube* video shows how the San Jose State University School of Library and Information Science is integrating Second Life into its graduate teaching and research program.[199] The eLearning virtual campus contains classrooms, individual computer workstations, buildings, faculty offices, walkways on grassy paths, and an eCafe used as a social gathering place. The virtual version of the San Jose LIS School sits on a virtual island surrounded by other islands that house libraries and projects by other institutions. Lili Luo and Jeremy Kemp's research on early adopters among LIS educators found that Second Life is considered a viable instructional platform for 85% ($n = 20$) of respondents.[200] In the broader context, the 2008 JISC *Serious Virtual Worlds* report provides a review of the use of virtual worlds to support learning and training, including a review of the field and

case study examples, a typology and a list of virtual worlds, and a prediction that future education will take place within virtual worlds.[201]

Although virtual worlds have been around for over 20 years, it is only really in the last five years that the real potential for virtual worlds has been recognised, and the next 20 years could bring about a virtual world revolution that has the capability to radical (sic) shift how we learn. To ensure that this revolution is successful at engaging students and supporting the development of higher order thinking skills it is vital that we work together as a community and integrate our plans so that the learners of the future have an educational system that gives them an enriched learning experience, does not suppress creativity and helps to create a cohesive community that works together for the greater good.

To ensure that this happens, we need to monitor closely what the exact implications will be of virtual self-organised communities, we need to refocus our educational practices upon the key aims and objectives of our society and we need to find ways to promote excellence in cross-disciplinary research and methodologies.

Learners are fast becoming co-creators of their learning experiences, and virtual worlds and Web 2.0 offer the most constructivist platforms for those activities. The Web 2.0 and 3D infosphere is not merely a more complex information platform for providing users with interactive Web applications. Abram sees the evolving interactive technology as a vehicle for providing "deeper user experiences." The Internet is thus not merely more collaborative, but transformational. Collaborative constructions are not merely social, but a new way of creating content, meaning, and value.[202] Open communication, decentralization of authority, and disintermediation of specialty are producing a new intersubjectivity whose content is a living expression of humanity, diversity, and inventiveness.

Information Ethics

As vast numbers of people have entered the online domain they have created new uses and abuses of its systems and content. An ethics vocabulary is emerging with terms users need to understand such as cyberethics, computer ethics, information technology ethics, global information ethics, Internet ethics, content filtering, digital rights, acceptable use policies, electronic privacy, and netiquette.[203–208] The ethical implications of online use are central to increased legislation and social debate over proper and improper or illegal use of online systems. There is much for users to be concerned about in the online environment, including: e-mail scams, phishing, pharming, and spam, spy software, information security, identity theft, cyber-stalking, griefing, unobtrusive monitoring, information warfare, firewalls, reliability, privacy policies, and Web spoofing, as well as defense against virus, destructive worms, Trojan horse, denial of service, and other malicious code attacks. All creators of information products and artistic content must be concerned about the ease of online copyright violations, censorship, identity, and intellectual property theft.

A user-centered discipline has emerged in response to a phenomenon that challenges privacy and security of personal information. "Exoinformation" refers to the electronic trail left behind when people are active online: accessing a Web site, sending e-mail, participating in chat rooms, shopping online, filling in registration forms or applications, entering a search query, checking a stock quote, clicking a link, time spent on a page, and many other forms of information left behind through use. With the onset of ubiquitous, integrated, global computing, the sheer amount of exoinformation about ourselves that we leave behind is enormous: what route we take to work at what speed, what we bought at the supermarket, who left a message on our voicemail, what documents we accessed in an electronic library, which news we read daily, when our parents passed on and from what cause, who our online friends are, our favorite books, music and DVDs, what groups we belong to, and so on. According to Benjamin Brunk "an entire industry devoted to collecting and making sense of exoinformation already thrives."[209] This naturally raises concerns among users and watchdog groups over misuse, abuse, and criminal activities involved in stealing, manipulating, and profiting from such information. System design and information policy has been evolving a user-centered focus to protect people online; however, such efforts add significantly to the information management work for each individual, as passwords and privacy policies accumulate in an overwhelming barrage of new data to track and keep. In addition, fears are sparked routinely with pop-up warnings and alerts threatening dire consequences if a user ignores the interruption.

CONCLUSION

Complexity is continuously increasing in the IE and human complexity remains a vast domain to explore. It is early in the development of widely used online systems, and there is too little research on interface use and design in LIS and in HCI, particularly with new Web 2.0 applications and virtual platforms. Originally LIS studies concentrated on subject experts and expert searchers, and few in HCI have studied large information systems and their users. Even the rising tide of LIS and HCI Web studies is too small to predict a universal simplified system, and findings about user diversity from the past decade suggest that is a false goal. The rise of virtual environments as immersive learning and work platforms portends greater change and innovation for the information professions. It is clear that user-oriented research will continue to evolve in many fields of study where

understanding IB is considered important to facilitating progress. The LIS field is the most advanced discipline in user-centered focus, theory, methodology, and application. Multidisciplinarity has enhanced the field's ability to diversify and extend the user-centered paradigm. This continued evolution has the potential to inform other disciplines concerned with understanding IB. Just as twentieth century general systems theory revolutionized thinking and research across disciplines, twenty-first century user-centered research will revolutionize theory and praxis applicable to diverse settings, industries, disciplines, communities, and groups. The user-centered trend led by LIS has become as pervasive as ubiquitous computing and is fast becoming user-driven.

This total involvement or "immersion" in the ecology of information technology has become the new basis for learning. Technological affordances are synergistically linked to sensory organs and motor output, mediated by cognitive and affective procedures that validate belongingness and self-confidence.[23] Sensory-motor engagement with technological affordances is critical to the process, but it is not the primary motive for the experience or participation. The value and motive for interacting with technology centers on users' feelings in conjunction with their thoughts, which are necessarily grounded in social group practices. From this arises an intention to interact with a technological affordance. People are motivated to optimize information by engaging with it through their collaborative goals and plans. Recent research and praxis show that people have a strong desire to create and publish content, to write and publish reviews of content, to index and tag content, and to organize and arrange content, and this for individual as well as altruistic uses. The increasing democratization of the IE has engendered new roles for information professionals. In the current and evolving IE, people are free to engage systems to communicate, design, and create. Blending games, community, and learning produces engagement, interactivity and fun, and that core of the user experience will continue to drive the development of user-centered systems and services in the twenty-first century IE. It is clear that user-centeredness will be implicit in all systems.

REFERENCES

1. Nahl, D. The user-centered revolution: 1970–1995. In *Encyclopedia of Microcomputers*, 1st Ed.; Kent, A., Ed.; Marcel Dekker: New York, 1997; Vol. 19, 143–199. http://www2.hawaii.edu/~nahl/articles/user/user1toend_toc.html (accessed December 2008).
2. Tenopir, C.; Hitchcock, B.; Pillow, S.A. *Use and Users of Electronic Library Resources: An Overview and Analysis of Recent Research Studies*; Council on Library and Information Resources: Washington, DC, 2003. http://bibpurl.oclc.org/web/5394 (accessed December 2008).
3. Estabrook, L.; Witt, E.; Rainie, L. *Information Searches That Solve Problems: How People Use the Internet, Libraries, and Government Agencies When They Need*

Help; Pew Internet & American Life Project: Washington, DC, 2007; 21. http://www.pewinternet.org/pdfs/Pew_UI_LibrariesReport.pdf (accessed December 2008).

4. Estabrook, L.; Witt, E.; Rainie, L. *Information Searches That Solve Problems: How People Use the Internet, Libraries, and Government Agencies When They Need Help*; Pew Internet & American Life Project: Washington, DC, 2007; iii. http://www.pewinternet.org/pdfs/Pew_UI_LibrariesReport.pdf (accessed December 2008).

5. Koke, J.; Dierking, L. *Museums and Libraries Engaging America's Youth: Final Report of a Study of IMLS Youth Programs, 1998–2003*; Institute of Museum and Library Services: Washington, DC, 2007; 9. http://www.imls.gov/pdf/YouthReport.pdf (accessed December 2008).

6. Association of College and Research Libraries *Environmental Scan 2007*. ACRL, American Library Association: Chicago, 2008; 13. http://www.ala.org/ala/mgrps/divs/acrl/publications/whitepapers/Environmental_Scan_2.pdf (accessed December 2008).

7. University College, London; British Library; Joint Information Systems Committee. *Information Behaviour of the Researcher of the Future*; UCL: London, U.K., 2008; 8. http://www.jisc.ac.uk/media/documents/programmes/reppres/gg_final_keynote_11012008.pdf (accessed December 2008).

8. University College, London; British Library; Joint Information Systems Committee *Information Behaviour of the Researcher of the Future*; UCL: London, U.K., 2008; 10. http://www.jisc.ac.uk/media/documents/programmes/reppres/gg_final_keynote_11012008.pdf (accessed December 2008).

9. University College, London; British Library; Joint Information Systems Committee *Information Behaviour of the Researcher of the Future*; UCL: London, U.K., 2008; 20. http://www.jisc.ac.uk/media/documents/programmes/reppres/gg_final_keynote_11012008.pdf (accessed December 2008).

10. Salaway, G.; Caruso, J.B.; Nelson, M.R. The ECAR study of undergraduate students and information technology. Educause **2007**, *6*, 35–55. http://www.educause.edu/ers0706 (accessed December 2008).

11. Hargittai, E. A framework for studying differences in people's digital media uses. In *Cyberworld Unlimited*; Kutscher, N., Otto, H., Eds.; VS Verlag für Sozialwissenschaften/GWV Fachverlage GmbH, 2007; 121–137. http://eszter.com/research/c10-digitalmediausesframework.html (accessed December 2008).

12. http://encarta.msn.com/dictionary_/mashup.html (accessed December 2008).

13. Small, R.V. Surviving in the information age. Threshold **2008**, (Winter), 24. http://www.ciconline.org/threshold winter08; http://www.ciconline.org/c/document_library/get_file?folderId=105&name=THWinter08SurvivingintheInformationAge.pdf (accessed December 2008).

14. Lippincott, J. Net generation students and libraries. Educause Rev. **2006**, (March/April), 57. http://www.educause.edu/Resources/EducatingtheNetGeneration/NetGenerationStudentsandLibrar/6067 (accessed December 2008).

15. De Rosa, C. *Perceptions of Libraries and Information Resources: A Report to the OCLC Membership*; Online Computer Library Center (OCLC): Dublin, OH, 2005. http://www.oclc.org/reports/2005perceptions.htm (accessed December 2008).

16. Griffiths, J.R.; Brophy, P. Student searching behavior and the Web: Use of academic resources and Google. Libr. Trends **2005**, *53* (4), 539–554.

17. Briggs, L.L. Inside Indiana U's Move to ChaCha: University to bolster research with guided search functionality. Campus Technol. **2007**. http://campustechnology.com/articles/49582/ (accessed December 2008).

18. Morgan, E.L. Today's digital information landscape. 2007. http://infomotions.com/musings/digital-landscape/ (accessed December 2008).

19. Norman, D.A. *Emotional Design: Why We Love (Or Hate) Everyday Things*; Basic Books: New York, 2004.

20. Picard, R.W. *Affective Computing*; MIT Press: Boston, MA, 1997.

21. Sharp, H.; Rogers, Y.; Preece, J. Affective aspects. In *Interaction Design: Beyond Human-Computer Interaction*, 2nd Ed.; Wiley: Chichester, U.K., 2007; 181–215.

22. Rogers, Y. New theoretical approaches for human-computer interaction. In *Annual Review of Information Science and Technology*; Cronin, B., Ed.; Information Today, Inc.: Medford, NJ, 2004; Vol. 38, 87–143.

23. Nahl, D. Social-biological information technology: An integrated conceptual framework. J. Am. Soc. Inform. Sci. Technol. **2007**, *58* (13), 2021–2046.

24. Nahl, D.; Bilal, D., Eds. *Information and Emotion: The Emergent Affective Paradigm in Information Behavior Research and Theory*; Information Today: Medford, NJ, 2007.

25. Sharp, H.; Rogers, Y.; Preece, J. *Interaction Design: Beyond Human-Computer Interaction*, 2nd Ed.; Wiley: Chichester, U.K., 2007; 9.

26. Sharp, H.; Rogers, Y.; Preece, J. *Interaction Design: Beyond Human-Computer Interaction*, 2nd Ed.; Wiley: Chichester, U.K., 2007; 17.

27. Shneiderman, B.; Plaisant, C. *Designing the User Interface: Strategies for Effective Human-Computer Interaction*, 4th Ed.; Pearson/Addison Wesley: Boston, MA, 2004.

28. Norman, D.A. *The Design of Everyday Things*; Doubleday: New York, 1990.

29. Sharp, H.; Rogers, Y.; Preece, J. *Interaction Design: Beyond Human-Computer Interaction*, 2nd Ed.; Wiley: Chichester, U.K., 2007; 16.

30. Sharp, H.; Rogers, Y.; Preece, J. *Interaction Design: Beyond Human-Computer Interaction*, 2nd Ed.; Wiley: Chichester, U.K., 2007; 20.

31. Sharp, H.; Rogers, Y.; Preece, J. *Interaction Design: Beyond Human-Computer Interaction*, 2nd Ed.; Wiley: Chichester, U.K., 2007; 26.

32. Capurro, R.; Hjorland, B. The concept of information. ARIST **2003**, *37*, 397.

33. Nahl, D. Domain interaction discourse analysis: A technique for charting the flow of micro-information behavior. J. Doc. **2007**, *63* (3), 323–339.

34. Schuler, D.; Namioka, A. *Participatory Design: Principles and Practices*; L. Erlbaum Associates: New Jersey, 1993.

35. Muller, M.J.; Haslwanter, J.H.; Dayton, T. Participatory practices in the software lifecycle. In *Handbook of Human-Computer Interaction*; 2nd Ed.; Helander, M.,

Landauer, T.K., Prabhu, P.V., Eds.; Elsevier: Amsterdam, 1997; 255–297.

36. Button, G. Studies of work in human-computer action. In *HCI Models, Theories, and Frameworks: Toward a Multidisciplinary Science*; Carroll, J.M., Ed.; The Morgan Kaufmann series in interactive technologies; Morgan Kaufmann: San Francisco, CA, 2003; 359.

37. International Children's Digital Library. http://www.icdlbooks.org/ (accessed December 2008).

38. Massey, S.A.; Druin, A.; Weeks, A.C. Emotion, response and recommendation: The role of affect in children's book reviews in a digital library. In *Information and Emotion: The Emergent Affective Paradigm in Information Behavior Research and Theory*; Nahl, D., Bilal, D., Eds.; Information Today: Medford, NJ, 2007; 135–160.

39. Nielsen, J. First rule of usability? Don't listen to users. Alertbox **2001**. http://www.useit.com/alertbox/20010805.html (accessed December 2008).

40. U.S. Department of Justice. ADA Home Page. http://www.ada.gov/ (accessed December 2008).

41. Job Accommodation Network. ADA Library. http://www.jan.wvu.edu/links/adalinks.htm (accessed December 2008).

42. IBM. Rational Policy Tester Accessibility Edition. http://www-306.ibm.com/software/awdtools/tester/policy/accessibility/ (accessed December 2008).

43. IBM. Human Ability and Accessibility Center. http://www-03.ibm.com/able/ (accessed December 2008).

44. Sternberg, R.J.; Ben-Zeev, T. *Complex Cognition: The Psychology of Human Thought*; Oxford University Press: Oxford, U.K., 2001.

45. Picard, R.W. *Affective Computing*; MIT Press: Cambridge, MA, 1997.

46. Picard, R.W. *Affective Computing*; MIT Press: Boston, 2000.

47. Thompson, L. Tech-savvy teens teach computer skills at library. *The Seattle Times* December **2007**. http://seattletimes.nwsource.com/html/snohomishcountynews/2004065990_techteens12n.html (accessed December 2008).

48. Senior Friendly Libraries: Resources and discussion about library services to older adults Successful Wii Gaming Program at Old Bridge Public Library. http://seniorfriendlylibraries.blogspot.com/2007/11/successful-wii-gaming-program-at-old.html (accessed December 2008).

49. Design @ IBM. http://www-03.ibm.com/easy/page/558 (accessed December 2008).

50. Ominsky, M.; Stern, K.R.; Rudd, J.R. User-Centered Design at IBM Consulting. Int. J. Hum. Comput. Interact. **2002**, *14* (3&4), 349–368. http://www-935.ibm.com/services/us/index.wss/summary/igs/a1024123; http://www-935.ibm.com/services/us/igs/pdf/ucd-at-ibm-consulting.pdf (accessed December 2008).

51. State health department Web sites are not user-friendly. AORN J. **2006**. http://findarticles.com/p/articles/mi_m0FSL/is_4_84_ai_n16818862 (accessed April 2009).

52. Register to volunteer for an IBM user experience study. https://www-01.ibm.com/software/ucd/register.html (accessed December 2008).

53. Nielsen, J. Usability 101: Introduction to usability. Alertbox **2003**. http://www.useit.com/alertbox/20030825.html (accessed December 2008).

54. Nielsen, J. Top ten mistakes in Web design. Alertbox **2007**. http://www.useit.com/alertbox/9605.html (accessed December 2008).

55. Atwood, J. Coding Horror: Programming and human factors. http://www.codinghorror.com/blog/archives/000819.html (accessed December 2008).

56. U.S. Department of Health and Human Services. *Research-Based Web Design & Usability Guidelines*; U.S. Government Printing Office: Washington, DC, 2006; ii. http://www.usability.gov/pdfs/foreword.pdf (accessed December 2008).

57. U.S. Department of Health and Human. Services. *Research-Based Web Design & Usability Guidelines*; U.S. Government Printing Office: Washington, DC, 2006; 5–9. http://www.usability.gov/pdfs/chapter17.pdf (accessed December 2008).

58. U.S. Department of Health and Human Services. *Research-Based Web Design & Usability Guidelines*; U.S. Government Printing Office: Washington, DC, 2006; 1–3http://www.usability.gov/pdfs/chapter18.pdf (accessed December 2008).

59. Zeldes, N.; Sward, D.; Louchheim, S. Infomania: Why we can't afford to ignore it any longer. First Monday **2007**, *12*(8), http://firstmonday.org/htbin/cgiwrap/bin/ojs/index.php/fm/article/view/1973/1848 (accessed December 2008).

60. Dervin, B.; Nilan, M. Information needs and uses. In *Annual Review of Information Science and Technology*; Williams, M.E., Ed.; Knowledge Industry Publications, Inc. for American Society for Information Science: White Plains, NY, 1986; Vol. 21.

61. Bates, M.J. Information science at the University of California at Berkeley in the 1960s: A memoir of student days. Libr. Trends **2004**, *52* (4), 683–701.

62. Dalrymple, P.W. A quarter century of user-centered study: The impact of Zweizig and Dervin on LIS research. Libr. Inform. Sci. Res. **2001**, *23* (2), 155–165.

63. Talja, S.; Hartel, J. Revisiting the user-centred turn in information science research: an intellectual history perspective. Inform. Res. **2007**, *12*(4), paper colis04, http://InformationR.net/ir/12-4/colis/colis04.html (accessed December 2008).

64. Paisley, W.J.; Parker, E.B. Information retrieval as a receiver-controlled communication system. In Proceedings of the Symposium on Education for Information Science, Warrenton, Virginia, September 7–10, 1965, Heilprin, L.B., Markuson, B.E., Goodman, F.L., Eds.; Symposium on Education for Information Science; Spartan Books: Washington, DC, 1965; 23–31.

65. Paisley, W.J. Information needs and uses. In *Annual Review of Information Science and Technology*; Cuadra, C.A., Ed.; Encyclopaedia Britannica: Chicago, IL, 1968; Vol. 3, 1–30.

66. Information Today, Inc. 23rd Annual Computers in Libraries 2008. http://www.infotoday.com/cil2008/ (accessed December 2008).

67. Eisenberg, M. The parallel information universe: What's out there and what it means for libraries. Libr. J. **2008**. http://www.libraryjournal.com/article/CA6551184.html (accessed December 2008).

68. ALA's Office for Information Technology Policy; Association of Library and Information Science Education

(ALISE). Participatory Librarianship and Web 2.0 in the Curriculum; **2008**. http://quartz.syr.edu/rdlankes/Presentations/2008/ALISE.pdf (accessed December 2008).

69. Library 2.0. A New Social Model. ACRL/NY Annual Symposium 2007. http://www.acrlny.org/symp2007/program.html (accessed December 2008).

70. ASIS&T. People Transforming Information—Information Transforming People, October 24–29, 2008, Columbus, OH. http://www.asis.org/Conferences/AM08/am08cfp.html (accessed December 2008).

71. ASIS&T. ASIS&T Social Computing Summit. http://www.asis.org/Conferences/SCS08/SCS08.html (accessed December 2008).

72. ASIS&T. SIG USE 6th Annual Research Symposium at ASIS&T 2006: Information Realities: Exploring Affective and Emotional Aspects in Information Seeking and Use. http://www.asis.org/Conferences/AM06/siguse.html (accessed December 2008).

73. ASIS&T. 7th Annual Research Symposium of the Special Interest Group on Information Needs, Seeking and Use (SIG/USE). Mobility and Social Networks in Information Behavior. http://www.asis.org/Conferences/AM07/use.html (accessed December 2008).

74. Fisher, K.E.; Erdelez, S.; McKechnie, L., Eds.; *Theories of Information Behavior*, ASIST Monograph Series. Published for the American Society for Information Science and Technology by Information Today: Medford, NJ, 2005.

75. ISIC 2006. Information Seeking In Context. http://www.hss.uts.edu.au/isic2006/conferenceprog/index.html (accessed December 2008).

76. Information Research. In *Papers presented at ISIC 2006: the 6th Information Seeking in Context Conference*, Sydney, Australia, July, 19–21, 2006. Part I. http://informationr.net/ir/11-4/infres114.html (accessed December 2008).

77. Information Interaction in Context, October 14–17, 2008, London, U.K. http://irsg.bcs.org/iiix2008/ (accessed December 2008).

78. CHI 2007, April 28-May 3, 2007, San Jose, CA. Welcome to the Computer/Human Interaction 2007 Conference Site. http://www.chi2007.org/ (accessed December 2008).

79. IA Summit 2007. http://www.iasummit.org/2007/program.htm (accessed December 2008).

80. IA Summit 2008. http://www.iasummit.org/2008/ (accessed December 2008).

81. Pettigrew, K.E.; Durrance, J.C. KALIPER project: Final report—KALIPER: Introduction and overview of results. JELIS **2001**, *42* (3), 170–180.

82. Callison, D.; Tilley, C.L. Descriptive impressions of the library and information education evolution of 1988–1998 as reflected in job announcements, ALISE descriptors, and new course titles. JELIS **2001**, *42* (3), 181–199.

83. Sutton, S.A. Trends, trend projections, and crystal ball gazing. JELIS **2001**, *42* (3), 241–247.

84. Pettigrew, K.E.; Durrance, J.C. KALIPER project: Final report—KALIPER: Introduction and overview of results. JELIS **2001**, *42* (3), 175.

85. Markey, K. Current educational trends in the information and library science curriculum. JELIS **2004**, *45* (4), 317–339.

86. Hinson, C.L. Legal informatics: Opportunities for information science. JELIS **2005**, *46* (2), 134–153.

87. Ford, N. *Web-Based Learning Through Educational Informatics: Information Science Meets Educational Computing*; Information Science Pub: Hershey, PA, 2008.

88. Marty, P.F.; Rayward, W.B.; Twidale, M.B. Museum informatics. ARIST **2003**, *37*, 259–294.

89. Russell, M.; Brittain, J.M. Health informatics. ARIST **2002**, *36*, 591–628.

90. Sawyer, S.; Eschenfelder, K.R. Social informatics: Perspectives, examples and trends. ARIST **2002**, *36*, 427–466.

91. Kling, R.; Crawford, H.; Rosenbaum, H.; Sawyer, S.; Weisband, S. *Learning from Social Informatics: Information and Communication Technologies in Human Contexts*; The Center for Social Informatics: Bloomington, IN, 2000. http://uainfo.arizona.edu/~weisband/site-PDFs/SI_report_Aug_14.pdf (accessed December 2008).

92. Erdelez, S.; O'Hare, S. Legal informatics: Application of information technology in law. ARIST **1997**, *32*, 367–402.

93. Bishop, A.P.; Van House, N.A.; Buttenfield, B.P., Eds. *Digital Library Use: Social Practice in Design and Evaluation*; Digital libraries and electronic publishing; MIT Press: Cambridge, MA, 2003.

94. Community Informatics Initiative. http://www.cii.uiuc.edu/ (accessed December 2008).

95. Nelson, V.; Bishop, A. The community is the curriculum. In *4th Prato International Community Informatics Conference, Community Informatics—Prospects for Communities and Action*, Prato, Italy, November 5–7, 2007. http://www.ccnr.net/prato2007/archive/papers.htm; http://www.ccnr.net/prato2007/archive/nelsonbishopfinal.pdf (accessed December 2008).

96. The Information Institute of Syracuse & ALA's OITP Present The Participatory Librarianship Starter Kit. http://ptbed.org/ (accessed December 2008).

97. Lankes, R.D. Virtual reference to participatory librarianship: Expanding the conversation. Bull. Am. Soc. Inform. Sci. Technol. **2008**, *34* (2), 13.

98. https://www.asis.org/Bulletin/Dec-07/Bulletin_DecJan08.pdf (accessed December 2008).

99. Van House, N.; Sutton, S.A. The Panda syndrome: An ecology of LIS education. JELIS **1996**, *37* (2), 131–147.

100. Sutton, S.A. Trends, trend projections, and crystal ball gazing. JELIS **2001**, *42* (3), 244–245.

101. Hernon, P.; Giesecke, J.; Alire, C.A. *Academic Librarians as Emotionally Intelligent Leaders*; Libraries Unlimited: Westport, CT, 2007.

102. Bates, M.J. Speculations on the sociocultural context of public information provision in the seventies and beyond. In *Library and Information Service Needs of the Nation; Proceedings of a Conference on the Needs of Occupational, Ethnic, and Other Groups in the United States*; Cuadra, C.A., Bates, M.J., Eds.; For sale by the Supt. of Docs., U.S. Govt. Print. Off.: Washington, DC, 1974; 51–76.

103. Sharp, H.; Rogers, Y.; Preece, J. *Interaction Design: Beyond Human-Computer Interaction*, 2nd Ed. Wiley: Chichester, U.K., 2007.

104. Lehman, T.; Nikkel, T. *Making Library Web Sites Usable: A LITA Guide*; Neal-Schuman Publishers: New York, 2008.

User-Centered Revolution–
Version

105. Campbell, N. *Usability Assessment of Library-Related Web Sites: Methods and Case Studies*; Library and Information Technology Association, American Library Association: Chicago, IL, 2001.

106. Garlock, K.L.; Piontek, S. *Designing Web Interfaces to Library Services and Resources*; American Library Association: Chicago, IL, 1999.

107. Caswell, J.V. Building an integrated user interface to electronic resources. Inform. Technol. Libr. **1997**, *16* (2), 63–72.

108. Abels, E.G.; White, M.D.; Hahn, K. Identifying user-based criteria for Web pages. Internet Res.—Westport Bradford **1997**, *7* (4), 252–262.

109. Bell, S.J. Design thinking: A design approach to the delivery of outstanding service can help put the user experience first. Am. Libr. **2008**, *39* (1), 44–49.

110. Bell, S.J.; Shank, J.D. *Academic Librarianship by Design: A Blended Librarian's Guide to the Tools and Techniques*; American Library Association: Chicago, IL, 2007.

111. Steven Bell's Resource Center. http://stevenbell.info/design.htm (accessed December 2008).

112. University of Michigan School of Information, Social Computing (SC) Specialization. http://www.si.umich.edu/msi/sc.htm (accessed December 2008).

113. University of Michigan School of Information, Incentive-Centered Design (ICD) Specialization. http://www.si.umich.edu/msi/icd.htm (accessed December 2008).

114. University of Michigan School of Information, Community Informatics (CI) Specialization. http://www.si.umich.edu/msi/ci.htm (accessed December 2008).

115. University of Michigan School of Information, Information Analysis and Retrieval (IAR) Specialization. http://www.si.umich.edu/msi/iar.htm (accessed December 2008).

116. SJSU's School of Library & Information Science Second Life portal. http://slisweb.sjsu.edu/sl/index.php/Main_Page (accessed December 2008).

117. UW Extension Certificate Program in Virtual Worlds (online). http://extension.washington.edu/ext/certificates/vir/vir_gen.asp (accessed December 2008).

118. Julien, H. Education for information literacy instruction: A global perspective. JELIS **2005**, *46* (2), 210–216.

119. UCLA Graduate School of Education & Information Studies, Higher Education Research Institute, The Freshman Survey. http://www.gseis.ucla.edu/heri/cirpoverview.php (accessed December 2008).

120. UCLA Newsroom. http://newsroom.ucla.edu/portal/ucla/xx-42995.aspx (accessed December 2008).

121. Western Association of Schools and Colleges (U.S.) Standard 2 achieving educational objectives through core functions. In *Handbook of Accreditation Standards, Institutional Review Process, Policies and Practices: Addressing Core Commitments to Institutional Capacity and Educational Effectiveness*; WASC: Alameda, CA, 2001; 34–37.

122. Association of College & Research Libraries, a Division of the American Library Association (ACRL). Objectives for Information Literacy Instruction: A Model Statement for Academic Librarians. http://www.ala.org/ala/mgrps/divs/acrl/standards/objectivesinformation.cfm (accessed December 2008).

123. Bruce, C. *The Seven Faces of Information Literacy*; Auslib Press: Adelaide, South Australia, Australia, 1997.

124. Daugherty, A.; Russo, M.F. *Information Literacy Programs in the Digital Age: Educating College and University Students Online*; Association of College and Research Libraries: Chicago, IL, 2007.

125. Small, R.V. Surviving in the information age. Threshold **2008**, Winter, 23–27. http://www.ciconline.org/threshold winter08; http://www.ciconline.org/c/document_library/get_file?folderId=105&name=THWinter08Survivinginthe InformationAge.pdf (accessed December 2008).

126. National Research Council (U.S.), *Being Fluent with Information Technology*; National Academy Press: Washington, DC, 1999. http://www.nap.edu/books/030906399X/html/ (accessed December 2008).

127. Reference and User Services Association (RUSA). RUSA Reference Guidelines, Guidelines for the Introduction of Electronic Information Resources to Users. http://www.ala.org/ala/mgrps/divs/rusa/resources/guidelines/guidelinesintroduction.cfm (accessed December 2008).

128. American Association of School Librarians (AASL), AASL Standards for the 21st-Century Learner. http://www.ala.org/ala/aasl/aaslproftools/learningstandards/standards.cfm (accessed December 2008).

129. IFLA. Information Literacy Section. Lau, J. Guidelines on Information Literacy for Lifelong Learning. http://www.ifla.org/VII/s42/index.htm (accessed December 2008).

130. Lau, J., Ed. *Information Literacy: International Perspectives*; K G Saur: S.I., 2008. http://www.ifla.org/V/pr/saur131.htm (accessed December 2008).

131. Dervin, B.; Foreman-Wernet, L.; Lauterbach, E. *Sense-Making Methodology Reader: Selected Writings of Brenda Dervin*; Hampton Press: Cresskill, NJ, 2003.

132. Dervin, B. Information and democracy: An examination of underlying assumptions. JASIS **1994**, *45* (6), 369–385.

133. Kuhlthau, C.C. *Seeking Meaning: A Process Approach to Library and Information Services*, 2nd Ed.; Libraries Unlimited: Westport, CT, 2004.

134. Bates, M.J. What is browsing—really? A model drawing from behavioural science research. Inform. Res. **2007**, *12*(4) paper 330. http://InformationR.net/ir/12-4/paper330.html (accessed December 2008).

135. Solomon, P. Discovering information in context. ARIST **2002**, *36*, 229–264.

136. Case, D.O. *Looking for Information: A Survey of Research on Information Seeking, Needs, and Behavior*, 2nd Ed.; Elsevier: Burlington, MA, 2007; 5.

137. Nahl, D. A conceptual framework for defining information behavior. SIMILE: Stud. Media Inform. Lit. Educ. **2001**, *1* (2), 1–16. http://utpjournals.metapress.com/content/f695043tk142qh56/?p=8887ec59edeb466fa94d19b89 fe2c957&pi=0 (accessed December 2008).

138. Suoranta, J.; Vadén, T. *Wikiworld: Political Economy and the Promise of Participatory Media*; Wordpress.com: s.l., 2008. http://wikiworld.wordpress.com/ (accessed December 2008).

139. Lenhart, A.; Horrigan, J.; Fallows, D. *Content Creation Online: 44% of U.S. Internet Users Have Contributed Their Thoughts and Their Files to the Online World*; Pew Internet & American Life Project: Washington, DC, 2004.

http://www.pewinternet.org/pdfs/PIP_Content_Creation_Report.pdf (accessed December 2008).

140. Jenkins, H. *Convergence Culture: Where Old and New Media Collide*; New York University Press: New York, 2006.

141. http://en.wikipedia.org/wiki/Metagame (accessed December 2008).

142. http://encarta.msn.com/encyclopedia_762505442/digital_sampling.html (accessed December 2008).

143. http://encarta.msn.com/dictionary_/skinning.html (accessed December 2008).

144. http://technologysource.org/extra/231/definition/5/ (accessed December 2008).

145. OED susbscription. http://dictionary.oed.com.eres.library.manoa.hawaii.edu/cgi/entry/50291914?single=1&query_type=word&queryword=mashup&first=1&max_to_show=10 (accessed December 2008).

146. Liu, S. Engaging users: The future of academic library Web sites. Coll. Res. Libr. **2008**, *69* (1), 6–15.

147. Wenger, E. *Communities of Practice: Learning, Meaning, and Identity*; Learning in doing; Cambridge University Press: Cambridge, U.K., 1998.

148. Keen, A. *The Cult of the Amateur: How Today's Internet Is Killing Our Culture*; Doubleday/Currency: New York, 2007.

149. Manjoo, F. *True Enough: Learning to Live in a Post-Fact Society*; Wiley: Hoboken, NJ, 2008.

150. Casey, M.E.; Savastinuk, L.C. *Library 2.0: A Guide to Participatory Library Service*; Information Today: Medford, NJ, 2007.

151. Cohen, L.B. *Library 2.0 Initiatives in Academic Libraries*; Association of College and Research Libraries: Chicago, IL, 2008.

152. Farkas, M.G. *Social Software in Libraries: Building Collaboration, Communication, and Community Online*; Information Today: Medford, NJ, 2007.

153. Coombs, K.A.; Griffey, J. *Library Blogging*; Linworth Pub: Columbus, OH, 2008.

154. Crawford, W. *Public Library Blogs: 252 Examples*; Cites & Insights: Mountain View, CA, 2007.

155. Crawford, W. *Academic Library Blogs: 231 Examples*; Cites & Insights: Mountain View, CA, 2008.

156. Fichter, D. Using Wikis to support online collaboration in libraries. Inform. Outlook **2006**, *10* (1), 30–31.

157. Bar-Ilan, J. The use of Weblogs (blogs) by librarians and libraries to disseminate information. Inform. Res. **2007**, *12*(4). paper 323. http://InformationR.net/ir/12-4/paper323.html (accessed December 2008).

158. Stephens, M. Web 2.0 and libraries: Best practices for social software. Libr. Technol. Rep. **2006**, *42*(4). http://www.techsource.ala.org/ltr/web-20-and-libraries-best-practices-for-social-software.html (accessed December 2008).

159. Stephens, M. Web 2.0 & libraries, Part 2: Trends and technologies. Libr. Technol. Rep. **2007**, *43*(5). http://www.techsource.ala.org/ltr/web-20-libraries-part-2-trends-and-technologies.html (accessed December 2008).

160. Sauers, M.P. *Blogging and RSS: A Librarian's Guide*; Information Today: Medford, NJ, 2006.

161. http://acrl.ala.org/L2Initiatives (accessed December 2008).

162. Habib, M.C. Toward Academic Library 2.0: Development and application of a Library 2.0 methodology. School of Information and Library Science, University of North Carolina at Chapel Hill, 2006. http://etd.ils.unc.edu/dspace/bitstream/1901/356/1/michaelhabib.pdf (accessed June 2008). http://mchabib.com/2006/11/22/toward-academic-library-20-development-and-application-of-a-library-20-methodology-my-masters-paper/ (accessed December 2008).

163. Abram, S. Web 2.0, Library 2.0, and Librarian 2.0: Preparing for the 2.0 World. SirsiDynix OneSource **2006**, *2*(1), http://www.imakenews.com/sirsi/e_article000505688.cfm (accessed December 2008).

164. Gibbons, S. *The Academic Library and the Net Gen Student: Making the Connections*; American Library Association: Chicago, IL, 2007.

165. Cormode, G.; Balachander, K. Key differences between Web 1.0 and Web 2.0. First Monday June **2008**, *13*(6). http://www.uic.edu/htbin/cgiwrap/bin/ojs/index.php/fm/article/viewArticle/2125/1972 (accessed June 2008).

166. Habermas, J. *The Theory of Communicative Action*; Beacon Press: Boston, MA, 1984; Vol. 1, 50.

167. Suthers, D.D. Technology affordances for intersubjective meaning-making: A research agenda for CSCL. Int. J. Comput. Support. Collab. Learn. **2006**, *1*(2). http://lilt.ics.hawaii.edu/lilt/papers/2006/Suthers-ijCSCL-2006.pdf (accessed December 2008).

168. Talja, S. Constituting "information"and "user" as research objects: A theory of knowledge formations as an alternative to the information man-theory. In *Information Seeking in Context, Proceedings of an International Conference on Information Seeking in Context*, Tampere, Finland, August 14–16, 1996; Vakkari, P., Savolainen, R., Dervin, B., Eds.; Taylor Graham Publishing: London, U.K., 1997; 67–80.

169. Gordon, R.S., Eds. *Information Tomorrow: Reflections on Technology and the Future of Public and Academic Libraries*; Information Today: Medford, NJ, 2007.

170. Floridi, L. A look into the future impact of ICT on our lives. Inform. Soc. **2007**, *23* (1), 59–64.

171. South Carolina State Library. Emerging Technology Use in SC Public Libraries Report, July 2007. http://www.statelibrary.sc.gov/docs/statistics/tech_express_survey.pdf (accessed December 2008).

172. Tomaiuolo, N.; Quint, B. *The Web Library: Building a World Class Personal Library with Free Web Resources*; Information Today: Medford, NJ, 2004.

173. Library Thing. http://www.librarything.com/ (accessed December 2008).

174. Shelfari. http://www.shelfari.com/ (accessed December 2008).

175. My Library. http://books.google.com/ (accessed December 2008).

176. Litwin, R. Annotated list of things not to forget (in the 2.0 craze). http://libraryjuicepress.com/blog/?p=353 (accessed December 2008).

177. Library of Congress. On the Record Report of The Library of Congress Working Group on the Future of Bibliographic Control; Library of Congress: Washington, DC, 2008; 10. http://www.loc.gov/bibliographic-future/

178. news/lcwg-ontherecord-jan08-final.pdf (accessed December 2008).

178. The Commons on Flickr. http://www.flickr.com/commons (accessed December 2008).

179. Rethlefsen, M.L. Tags help make libraries Del.icio.us: Social bookmarking and tagging boost participation. Libr. J. **2007**. http://www.libraryjournal.com/article/CA6476403.html (accessed December 2008).

180. Eden, B. Information organization future for libraries. Libr. Technol. Rep. **2007**, *43*(6), http://www.techsource.ala.org/ltr/information-organization-future-for-libraries.html (accessed December 2008).

181. Breeding, M. Next-generation library catalogs. Libr. Technol. Rep. **2007**, *43*(4). http://www.techsource.ala.org/ltr/next-generation-library-catalogs.html (accessed December 2008).

182. Neiburger, E. *Gamers…in the Library?!: The Why, What, and How of Videogame Tournaments for All Ages*; American Library Association: Chicago, IL, 2007.

183. Levine, J. Gaming and libraries: Intersection of services. Libr. Technol. Rep. **2006**, *42*(5). http://www.techsource.ala.org/ltr/gaming-and-libraries-intersection-of-services.html (accessed December 2008).

184. Levine, J. Gaming and libraries update: Broadening the intersections. Libr. Technol. Rep. **2008**, *44*(3). http://www.techsource.ala.org/ltr/gaming-and-libraries-update.html (accessed December 2008).

185. Burek Pierce, J. *Sex, Brains, and Video Games: A Librarian's Guide to Teens in the Twenty-first Century*; American Library Association: Chicago, IL, 2007.

186. Stoerger, S. It's not whether you win or lose, but how you play the game: The role of virtual worlds in education, annotated bibliography. School of Library and Information Science, Indiana University. http://ella.slis.indiana.edu/~sstoerge/virtualworlds.htm (accessed December 2008).

187. iLibrarian. A Quick Guide to Second Life for Librarians. http://oedb.org/blogs/ilibrarian/2007/a-quick-guide-to-second-life-for-librarians/ (accessed December 2008).

188. Trzeciak, J. McMaster University Library, Archive for the 'Teaching and Learning' Category. http://ulatmac.wordpress.com/category/teaching-and-learning/ (accessed December 2008).

189. Swanson, B.D. Second Life *Machinima* for Libraries: The intersection of instruction, outreach and marketing in a virtual world. In World Library and Information Congress: 73rd IFLA General Conference and Council, Durban, South Africa, August 19–23, 2007; 133.

190. *Virtual Worlds, Real Libraries: Librarians and Educators in Second Life and Other Multi-User Virtual Environments*; Bell, L.; Trueman, R.B., Eds.; Information Today: Medford, NJ, 2008; xvii.

191. Peters, T. Librarianship in virtual worlds. Libr. Technol. Rep. **2008**, *44* (7), 5–32.

192. http://www.alliancelibrarysystem.com/pdf08/TrendsReport2008.pdf (accessed December 2008).

193. Ostrander, M. Talking, looking, flying, searching: information seeking behaviour in Second Life. Libr. Hi Tech **2008**, *26* (4), 512–524.

194. Second Life Library. http://infoisland.org/ (accessed December 2008).

195. Jenkins, H. *Convergence Culture: Where Old and New Media Collide*; University Press: New York, 2006; 152.

196. Jenkins, H.; Purushotma, R.; Clinton, K.; Weigel, M.; Robinson, A.J. *Confronting the Challenges of Participatory Culture: Media Education for the 21st Century*; MacArthur Foundation: Chicago, IL, 2006. http://digitallearning.macfound.org/atf/cf/%7B7E45C7E0-A3E0-4B89-AC9C-E807E1B0AE4E%7D/JENKINS_WHITE_PAPER.PDF (accessed December 2008).

197. Silverstar, HVX (Bernadette Swanson). Machinima From the Very Beautiful Second Life. http://www.youtube.com/user/HVXSilverstar (accessed December 2008).

198. Lynn, A. GSLIS to Lead Team that will Preserve Virtual Worlds. Graduate School of Library and Information Science, University of Illinois at Urbana-Champaign, **2007**. http://www.lis.uiuc.edu/oc/news/displaynews.html?source=Fd6K1gvuPtiviGHOhd7Wgw==&year=Tpfh-axYyS2d3HIF5XQQxw== (accessed December 2008).

199. San Jose State University, School of Library and Information Science. YouTube Video. http://www.youtube.com/watch?v=j-9zt3Sd7oc (accessed December 2008).

200. Luo, L.; Kemp, J. Second life: Exploring the immersive instructional venue for library and information science education. J. Educ. Libr. Inform. Sci. **2008**, *49* (3), 147–166.

201. de Freitas, S. *Serious Virtual Worlds: A Scoping Study*; Joint Information Systems Committee (JISC): London, U.K., **2008**, 37. http://www.jisc.ac.uk/media/documents/publications/seriousvirtualworldsv1.pdf (accessed December 2008).

202. Center for Collective Intelligence. The Developmental Arc of Participation of Massive Voluntary Collaboration, K. Crowston. http://cci.mit.edu/crowston.html (accessed December 2008).

203. Froehlich, T. A brief history of information ethics. Textos universitaris de biblioteconomia i documentació **2004**, 13. http://www.ub.es/bid/13froel2.htm (accessed December 2008).

204. Frohmann, B. Cyber ethics: Bodies or bytes? Int. Inform. Libr. Rev. **2000**, *32*, 423–436.

205. Moore, A.D., Eds. *Information Ethics: Privacy, Property, and Power*; University of Washington Press: Seattle, WA, 2005.

206. Quigley, M. *Encyclopedia of Information Ethics and Security*; Information Science Reference: Hershey, PA, 2007.

207. Woodward, J.A. *What Every Librarian Should Know About Electronic Privacy*; Libraries Unlimited: Westport, CT, 2007.

208. De Rosa, C.; Cantrell, J.; Havens, A.; Hawk, J.; Jenkins, L.; Gauder, B.; Limes, R.; Cellentani, D. *Sharing, Privacy and Trust in Our Networked World: A Report to the OCLC Membership*; OCLC: Dublin, OH, 2008. http://www.oclc.org/reports (accessed December 2008).

209. Brunk, B. Cover story—Exoinformation & interface design. Bull. Am. Soc. Inform. Sci. **2001**, *27* (6), 11–13.

User-Oriented and Cognitive Models of Information Retrieval

Mette Skov
Department of Communication and Psychology, Aalborg University, Aalborg, Denmark

Kalervo Järvelin
School of Information Science, University of Tampere, Tampere, Finland

Peter Ingwersen
Royal School of Library and Information Science, University of Copenhagen, Copenhagen, Denmark

Abstract

The domain of user-oriented and cognitive information retrieval (IR) is first discussed, followed by a discussion on the dimensions and types of models one may build for the domain. The focus of the present entry is on the models of user-oriented and cognitive IR, not on their empirical applications. Several models with different emphases on user-oriented and cognitive IR are presented—ranging from overall approaches and relevance models to procedural models, cognitive models, and task-based models. The present entry does not discuss empirical findings based on the models.

INTRODUCTION

The Cranfield model of information retrieval (IR) has dominated IR research until recently—up to 2005. Currently, user-oriented research is popular but theoretical development is quite scarce. The focus of system-driven research is IR algorithms and their evaluation. Algorithms are evaluated for their capability of finding topically relevant documents.

Laboratory IR has recently been challenged by progress in the research into *relevance*, *interactive IR*, and *information seeking*. Recent work in analyzing the concept of relevance has resulted in identifying higher-order relevances, such as cognitive relevance and situational relevance, in addition to algorithmic and topical relevance. Real human users of IR systems introduce nonbinary, subjective, and dynamic relevance judgments into interactive IR processes. Moreover, recent theoretical and empirical work in information seeking suggests that IR is but one means of information seeking, which takes place in a context determined by, for example, a person's task, its phase, and situation. For larger tasks, one may identify multiple stages, strategies, tactics or modes of information access, and dynamic relevance. IR strategies, tactics, and relevance assessments are therefore affected by the stages of task performance.

Because of these empirical findings and theoretical arguments, the traditional Cranfield model of IR evaluation was challenged for its (lack of) realism. It has therefore been suggested that the developers of IR algorithms should consider how the algorithms are to be evaluated—in which frameworks and how to guarantee validity. Ingwersen and Järvelin[1] discuss the limitations of, and challenges to, the system-driven laboratory IR.

User-oriented research on the IR phenomena was (and is) not necessarily based on any specific epistemological perspective. It might be practice related or very pragmatic in scope. On the other hand, since its start in 1977, the cognitive approach to IR could briefly be characterized as user and intermediary oriented, with an explicit epistemic approach underlying its scope. Since mid-1990s the approach has gained momentum and turned into a holistic view of *all* the interactive communication processes that occur during information transfer—including those associated with the retrieval engine. Simultaneously, a user-centered IR research shifted focus from exploring traditional (scholarly) online interaction with the human intermediary as a central actor to web-based IR with the end user as the player.

A cognitive turn took place in IR in the early 1990s. Robertson and Hancock-Beaulieu[2] see this turn to consist of three facets (or revolutions) that are crucial to understand in order to proceed toward a more integrated (holistic) theory of IR: the cognitive, the relevance, and the interactive revolutions. The cognitive and interactive revolutions combined entail the ideas that personal information needs ought to be treated as potentially dynamic, not static. They may change over time—probably due to learning and *cognition* in context during IR interaction. Relevance assessments, hence, also become dynamic and may take place in a variety of dimensions, so that the traditional topicality as a measure of relevance does not stand alone.

The present entry first discusses the domain of, and the kinds of models one may build for, user-oriented and cognitive IR. The focus of the entry is on the models, not on their empirical applications, and therefore we present

Encyclopedia of Library and Information Sciences, Fourth Edition DOI: 10.1081/E-ELIS4-120053496

several models with different emphases on user-oriented and cognitive IR—ranging from overall approaches and relevance models to procedural models, task-based models, and cognitive models. Due to space limitations, we had to choose between candidate models to present, and therefore some excellent models had to be excluded.

THE DOMAIN OF USER-ORIENTED AND COGNITIVE IR

When the system-driven IR research could be seen to neglect information seekers in its modeling and experimentation, user-oriented IR research focused precisely on them. The complementary nature of these two areas may be seen in the light of Fig. 1.

The system-driven IR research focused on the left side of the figure, on authors' texts, their representation, queries, and retrieval. Text includes all kinds of signs included in documents, such as video, photos, and sound. The user-oriented and initial cognitive IR research focused on the right side, on users' problem space, information problems, requests, interaction with intermediaries, interface design, and query formulation but hardly on analyzing authors' texts, their representation, queries, or IR techniques. With the turn into a holistic view in the 1990s of *all* the interactive communication processes that occur during information transfer, the cognitive approach finally encompassed all the components of Fig. 1—including the algorithmic and document areas. The cognitive and user-oriented approaches were compared to the systems-driven one in several respects (Ingwersen and Järvelin,[1] pp. 192–194). Salient among the former are:

- *Task dependency*: The perceived work task (or non-job-related daily-life task or interest) situation is seen as the underlying reason for information need development.

- *Role of intermediary*: The role of human intermediaries was originally much in focus but has declined in and after the 1990s; likewise, automatic intermediary systems were in focus in the 1980s, but this focus faded away in the 1990s; currently, end-user behavior and interaction is in focus.
- *Interaction*: This is seen as the central process for cognitive IR; interaction has the purpose to benefit from the cognitive differences between various actors in the IR process; harmonizing such differences is regarded futile.
- *Relevance*: This is seen as objective and subjective, multidimensional, dynamic, and of nonbinary nature.
- *Context*: IR is placed in context in a holistic way: all components/cognitive actors and structures of information seeking and IR are contextual to one another.

CONCEPTUAL MODELS IN INFORMATION RETRIEVAL

There are several different types of models in user-oriented and cognitive IR research. The terminology in the area varies—scholars discuss various models, paradigms, metatheories, etc.—while often meaning the same or a very similar notion: socially shared *ontological* (what is out there to investigate?), *conceptual* (how to name that?), *factual* (what to take as givens?), *epistemological* (how can we possibly know about it?), and *methodological* (how can we learn about it?) assumptions in a research area. The present entry discusses them as *conceptual* models (Ingwersen and Järvelin,[1] p. 12).

Functions of Conceptual Models

Conceptual models provide the conceptual and methodological tools for formulating hypotheses and theories. Thus, they are, in fact, broader and more fundamental than

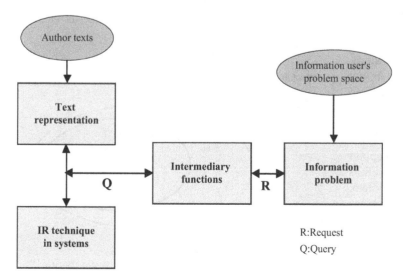

Fig. 1 IR research areas.
Source: From Ingwersen and Wormell.[1]

R:Request
Q:Query

scientific theories in that they set the preconditions of theory formulation. When they are also seen to represent schools of thought, chronological continuity, or principles, beliefs, and values of the research community, they become paradigms.

The conceptual model of a research area is always constructed—it does not simply lie somewhere out there waiting for discovery. The construction of conceptual models in a research area often requires conceptual and terminological development. This may involve defining concepts better—regarding preciseness, accuracy, simplicity, generality, and suitability for expressing propositions. Moreover, good concepts represent essential features (objects, relationships, events) and classify central phenomena in ways that lead to interesting hypotheses. This means that the concepts should relate to each other explicitly and in systematic and fruitful ways (Ingwersen and Järvelin,[1] pp. 11–13).

In the following, models are grouped into generic models and relevance models ("Generic Models" and "Relevance Models" sections), process models ("Online Interaction–Process Models" section), models on cognitive structures and actors ("Cognitive Structures and Actors" section), and task-based models ("Task-Based Models" section).

MODELS OF USER-ORIENTED AND COGNITIVE IR

Generic Models

To map out a research area, one needs a model of a broad scope. Often such models are, in addition to being broad, also generic summary models over a large domain. The Ingwersen–Wormell model and Wilson's model, discussed in the following text, are such examples.

The Ingwersen–Wormell model

The interaction model by Ingwersen and Wormell[3] (Fig. 1) represents the components and the interactive processes in IR. The right-hand side presents the user's (or actor's) problem space, for example, as part of a process of interest fulfillment or problem solving. If not solved by the actor alone, this "problem space" may lead to an information problem or need that results in a request for information, often formulated for an IR system.

In the middle, the intermediary functions consist of the entire system's capacity to understand and support the information problem of the current actor, as well as the search possibilities and logic of the source system. These functions form part of the professional knowledge of the human intermediary (librarian/information specialist) or may be skillfully adapted to a front end to the system as a search interface, in order to support retrieval. On the left side, components consist of author texts to be represented through indexing and of IR techniques that determine the behavior of the IR system.

Interaction takes place between an intermediary and an actor having a desire for information, whereby request formulation and reformulation (R) may occur. The query denotes reformulation or transformations (Q) of the request(s) for information, in the form required by the actual IR technique. At search time, the IR technique and actor's request and query (re)formulation interact.

The model reflects the typical pre-web and pre-PC research situation strongly involving a human intermediary or an interface construct consisting of intermediary knowledge and functionalities—see also the MONSTRAT and Mediator models ("Cognitive Structures and Actors" section). The model points to a number of central variables involved in IR interaction, most of which were studied intensively. The text representation component and processes were the least investigated—yet note the Anomalous State of Knowledge (ASK)-based studies ("Cognitive Structures and Actors" section) and the THOMAS system,[4] which early on included this aspect.

Wilson's model

Wilson[5] summarized the central user-oriented or cognitive research models associated with information behavior studies, including interactive IR. His overall model (Fig. 2) demonstrates the nesting of the central concepts, hereby also showing their contextual nature.

The central idea in Wilson's model is that interactive IR always takes place in the context of information seeking that again constitutes one of several information behavioral activities. As Wilson saw it, many IR models were basically confined to IR (the Cranfield model of IR) or interactive information retrieval (IIR)—not covering the information-seeking process. A limitation of such models would be—as they contain strong elements of IR systems—that they do not explicitly point to softer seeking processes *not* involving formal information channels. The model points to ideas about which kind of behavioral processes are distinctively

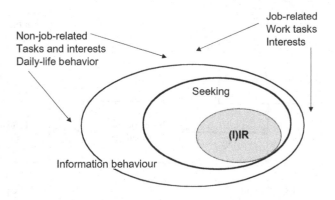

Fig. 2 A nested model of information behavior.
Sources: Modified from Wilson[5]; Ingwersen and Järvelin.[1]

not seeking processes, as, for instance, communication and generation. Wilson's model depicted in Fig. 2 contains, as an added feature, also the underlying situational reasons for information (seeking and IIR) behavior: the notions of "daily-life interests" and "work task."

Relevance Models

The concept of relevance has been a difficult issue in information science and IR through the years. It received a lot of attention in the 1960s and 1970s—as reflected in Saracevic's[6] review. The main orientations in the notion of relevance were found early: on one hand, one may speak about topical relevance and on the other hand, about user-oriented relevance. After a decline of interest in relevance in the 1970s–1980s, there was a revival of interest in the 1990s, producing several models of relevance based on a dynamic, multidimensional, and multigraded view of relevance. Here the models by Saracevic, Cosijn, Wang and Soergel, and Borlund are discussed.

Saracevic's stratified model

Saracevic's stratified model of interaction levels[7] was inspired by the idea of actors placed in a context—called the "environment." The model (Table 1) served dual purposes: it pointed to three communication levels and led to a revised view of the types of relevance involved in IR. The communication levels consisted of a *surface processing stratum* (light gray) dealing with data processing between sources and interface—based on a query; this stratum is hence concerned with morpholexical and syntactic levels of information processing. The second stratum is the *interactive cognitive communication level* (gray) embracing the processes of perceiving information during human–machine interaction in relation to the perceived need for information. The third stratum is called "situational" (dark gray) and refers to information use with respect to a perceived work task in context. The latter

Table 1 The Saracevic stratified model in tabular form

Interaction	Layer	Adaptation	Information use
Interaction Levels/strata	Environment		Information use
	Situation	Adaptation	
	User knowledge, tasks, etc.		
	Query characteristics		
	Interface	Adaptation	
	Computational resources		
	Informational resources		

Source: Adapted from Saracevic,[7] p. 218.

two strata also rely on semantic and pragmatic levels of information processing.

Saracevic proposed a range of relevance types in IR interaction,[7] suggesting five increasingly subjective types of relevance: 1) "algorithmic" relevance, which is the basis for the ranked output by the search engine and refers to the statistical and morpholexical relationships between request (or query) and retrieved objects; 2) "topicality" relevance, basically dealing with the aboutness relationship between document contents retrieved and request, as assessed by a person [owing to the human assessment (interpretation), this type of relevance is not objective but rather of subjective, emotional, and intellectual nature]; 3) "pertinence" relevance, which is associated between the nature of retrieved objects and the information need as perceived by the actor at a given point in time; 4) "situational" relevance, corresponding to the relation between the retrieved objects and the work task (or daily-life) situation as perceived by the individual actor; and 5) "emotional/intentional" relevance. This stratified model became later extended to include graded relevance as an additional dimension by Spink, Greisdorf, and Bateman.[8]

The Cosijn model

Cosijn and Ingwersen[11] further developed the Saracevic's model. They saw the emotional/intentional type as forming a natural part of *all* the subjective relevance categories;[2–4] they also replaced it by a "socio-cognitive" relevance category referring to domain, context, and collective situational preferences. The socio-cognitive relevance by Cosijn and Ingwersen is objective and tangible. It signifies situational relevance assessments and interpretations made by *several* cognitive actors, simultaneously (like in a team or program committee) and/or temporally (citations, in links).

Fig. 3 integrates relevance types with the stages of an interactive IR process. Moving from the lower right-hand corner upward signifies awareness and perception of the work task context that influences the information-seeking processes turning into IR interaction and finally algorithmic IR. The opposite move implies feedback from the system and possible request and need modification, as well as the use of information for task performance, influenced by the simultaneous relevance judgments. Automatic query modification takes place in the upper left corner, based on algorithmic relevance assessment. This model suggests hypotheses on relationships between relevance types and criteria, and information-seeking, and retrieval processes and actions.

The Wang–Soergel model

Moving into the details of using information resulting from IIR, Wang and Soergel produced their document

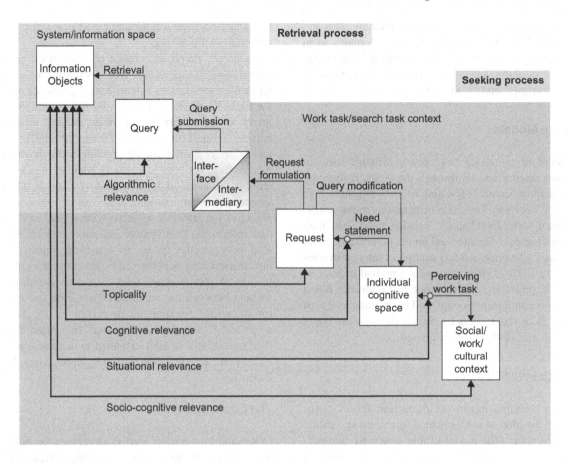

Fig. 3 Integrating relevance types with the process stages of interactive IR.
Sources: From Cosijn.[9,10]

selection framework.[12] It was based on a longitudinal empirical study of 25 self-selected faculty and graduate students in Agricultural Economics. The framework, Table 2, was also a stage model. It presents in great detail the decision stages by applying 11 relevance criteria and five document value dimensions for the decision to select (and potentially later to use) retrieved documents. In addition, it succeeds in combining the criteria, values, and decisions with so-called document information elements, that is, author-generated document structures and data elements, as well as significant data connected to the "isness" of information objects. These are representations of additional cognitive actors responsible for the being of documents. It supplies highly interesting and novel possibilities of hypothesis generation on relationships between *structured* document *features*, actor knowledge, multiple relevance criteria, *and* perceived value(s) of documents. It supplements the Cosijn model pinpointing to assessment variables at each point of subjective relevance judgment.

The Borlund model

Borlund summarized and discussed relevance research.[13] Her model seeks to cover all the relevance types discussed

earlier in an analytical manner, taking into account the temporal dimension too (Fig. 4).

The double circle signifies that more than one actor (assessor or user) may be influenced by the same work task situation, also over time, and thus produce socio-cognitive relevance assessments.[11] Each actor may dynamically over time perceive the work task differently (CW–CW^n) and thus produce new versions of the actor's information need (N–N^n). Algorithmic relevance (A) takes place in the real world and is objective, whereas intellectual topicality (IT), as Borlund calls "topicality," and pertinence (P) are seen as subjective manifestations of relevance. IT curves into the actor to signify interpretation activities. The model may in addition point to other relationships and comparisons, for instance, between the real work task and formulated requests and queries or between the task, its fulfillment, and the retrieved objects.

Online Interaction–Process Models

A number of models describe and analyze online searching, mainly in a Boolean real-life searching environment. Models by Fidel and Bates, discussed here, are representative and, owing to their generic nature, also still highly useful in the web IR context. Further, a model by

Table 2 A tabular representation of Wang–Soergel document selection decision stages

Process				
	Knowledge of		**Decision rules**	
	Topic		Elimination	
	Person		Multiple criteria	
	Organization		Dominance	
	Journal		Scarcity	
	Document type		Satisfice	
			Chain	
Document → Components	DIEs →	Criteria →	Values →	Decision
	Title	Topicality	Epistemic	Acceptance
	Author	Orientation	Functional	Maybe
	Abstract	Quality	Conditional	Rejection
	Journal	Novelty	Social	
	Series	Availability	Emotional	
	Date	Authority		
	Type	Relation		

DIEs, document information elements; values, document values/worth.
Source: Adapted from Wang and Soergel,[12] p. 118.

Kumpulainen is presented as it includes dimensions of searching patterns in heterogeneous information environments. The models focus on the actor's behavior in online interaction, especially on the acts (at various levels of conceptualization) that the actor may choose to implement.

Fidel's models

Fidel and Soergel[15] developed a comprehensive model on factors affecting online bibliographic retrieval. They classified hundreds of searching variables into seven categories such as the *retrieval setting* (the organization, the status of online searching within it, the actor group), the *actor* (e.g., personality, education, and experience), the *request* (e.g., domain, complexity, and specificity), the *database(s)* used for searching (like coverage, structure, and cost), the *search system* (e.g., searching aids and output formats), the *search process* (e.g., interaction with the actor and query formulation), and *search outcome* (recall, precision, and other measures). This model suggests a large number of variables and their possible relationships. The authors also noted that, taken individually, the variables seem to have little influence on the search outcome. This model is abstract and analyzes to some degree the relationships of categories and their proposed variables. It is a specific model for all online (bibliographic) IR—but can easily be usable in web IR environments.

In a range of empirical studies, Fidel investigated the basic dimensions of online searching.[16–21] She first observed online searchers doing their regular job-related searches. This led to a characterization of *operationalist*

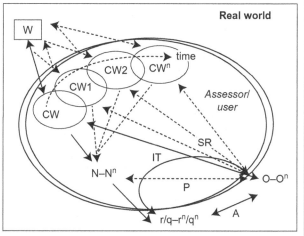
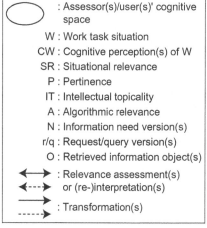

Fig. 4 Types of relevance in a temporal setting.
Sources: Modified from Ingwersen and Järvelin[1]; Borlund.[14]

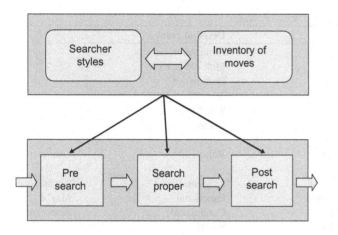

Fig. 5 A simplified view of Fidel's model.
Source: From Fidel and Soergel.[15]

and *conceptualist searchers* at pre-search, search proper, and post-search stages (Fig. 5). The former tended to use a large range of IR system capabilities in interaction (operational moves), focus on precision, but tended not to modify the specific meaning of requests. On the contrary, the latter tended to map requests into a faceted structure, focus on recall, and to use conceptual moves and thus modify the specific meaning of requests.

Subsequently she analyzed the searchers' moves in interaction that are used to cut down or enlarge, or to move, a search to better target it. Eighteen operational moves and a dozen conceptual moves were identified. The former keep the meaning of a search formulation intact but affect the result size or target, for example, by limiting a search key to an index term field, adding a synonym, or limiting by year of publication or language. The latter changes the conceptual content of a search formulation, for example, by intersecting the formulation with a new conceptual facet and by using broader or narrower index terms.

Finally, Fidel analyzed the searcher's selection of search keys and searching styles during operational online IR. Searching style was found to have a primary effect on retrieval behavior over three dimensions: 1) level of interaction; 2) preference for operational or conceptual moves; and 3) preference for text words or index terms. The *operationalist searcher* prefers to employ operational moves and is less concerned with recall than the *conceptualist* counterpart. The *free-text searcher* prefers to apply text keys and avoids consulting a thesauri. In effect, Fidel's model is a model on the interaction process stages, possible moves, search key selection, and the searching actor's styles.

Bates' berrypicking

Bates[22,23] classified information search and idea tactics, which were intended for use in teaching and facilitating searching—seen as an interactive process using a (Boolean) IR system. In all, 29 search tactics in four categories and 17 idea tactics were proposed. The tactics can be used to analyze what happens in a search process and to facilitate further steps in an ongoing process—related to Fidel's moves. The tactics themselves do not contain factors that would connect the search process to its context—for analysis and explanation.

Later, Bates[24] criticizes the narrow view of IR (traditional online and laboratory noninteractive) as searching based on a stable topical need. To Bates, real-life IIR was exploratory like *berry picking*. She developed berry picking as a principle for actor behavior that became very influential during the 1990s. The principle entails that each new piece of information that the actors encounter provides them potentially with new ideas and direction to follow through interaction, and consequently a new conception of their information need. At each stage of the search, the actor may identify useful information items leading the actor onward. Therefore the actor's requests and queries have several versions, which may change owing to the system feedback and actor's interpretation. Thus, we may here not simply talk of alternative versions of the request but also of more profound modifications. During the process, the actor may also repeat a query or revisit some earlier retrieved objects due to knowledge processes and cognition. Bates called this mode of retrieval an "evolving search." The information need situation is hence not satisfied by a single final retrieved set, but by a series of selections on the road, so to speak, of individual (elements of) information objects. Bates suggested several capabilities that might support the actors better in their various information-seeking strategies than the IR systems of that time. In effect, Bates' model is an abstract descriptive model of IR interaction.

Search trails

Kumpulainen[25] presented a task-based approach to model search behavior patterns. Influenced by earlier search process models reflecting people's real-world search behavior (e.g., Fidel,[18] Bates),[22] Kumpulainen's model targets a need to understand search behavior across several search systems. Search patterns across information systems are named "trails" and defined as follows: "A trail is a manual integration pattern, which includes one or more sequences of queries, and which may spread over several search systems containing heterogeneous information types" (Kumpulainen,[25] p. 857). Based on a qualitative study within the domain of molecular medicine, Kumpulainen empirically identified and modeled five different trail types: 1) *single* trails where only one query and one system is involved; 2) a *list* formed by similar types of queries submitted into a single system; 3) a *chain* formed by searches to several systems in a chain-like manner; 4) a *branch* formed by a search to several systems, which can

Table 3 The communication system of information science

Linguistic level of the system		
Generators	$\rightarrow$ Texts	$\leftrightarrow$ Recipients
Cognitive level of the system		
States of knowledge	$\rightarrow$ Information	$\leftrightarrow$ ASK

Single-headed arrows ($\rightarrow$) denote transformations and double-headed arrows ($\leftrightarrow$) interaction.
Source: Adapted from Belkin[26]

be concurrent and are unordered; and 5) a *berry-picking* trail formed by an exploratory search behavior and a dynamic information need. The strength of the modeled trail types is that they reflect a real-world heterogeneous information environment where actors might submit several queries across different search systems.

Cognitive Structures and Actors

The cognitive approach to IR produced several models of cognitive structures and actors and their interaction. The seminal ASK model by Belkin and colleagues and the MONSTRAT and Mediator models by Belkin and colleagues and Ingwersen are discussed in the following text. The latter were part of the active development of intelligent intermediary systems for IR in the 1980s and early 1990s.

The ASK model

Belkin[26–28] developed the ASK hypothesis and a concept of information for information science. The model in Table 3 is very general and abstract. Initially, it signified the cognitive communication system of information science;[26] later on, it mapped the IR interaction at the two most important levels of cognition: 1) the cognitive and 2) the linguistic (surface) levels of communication.[27] In contrast to earlier and contemporary common beliefs in user studies and laboratory IR that an information need "jumps out of the blue"—and is context free—the ASK hypothesis attempted to explain *why* information need situations occur. The fundamental reason behind an ASK was the problematic situation the actor was facing if the actor could not manage to fulfill an issue or solve a problem at hand. In addition, ASK implies that the ensuing information (search) situation is dynamic, and needs and requests may change with variation in cognition over retrieval session time. At the surface level of a message, we have the texts (signs), with which the recipient interacts. If the recipient perceives the signs, information is communicated at the cognitive level, and the ASK is thus under change. This model led to more detailed cognitive communication models for information transfer, for example, by Ingwersen,[29] p. 33, and further to the "bag" models for interaction (Ingwersen and Järvelin,[1] p. 33, p. 50). Also, the ASK model led, through several empirical studies, to the MONSTRAT model by Belkin, Seeger, and Wersig.[30]

Table 4 Functions of the MONSTRAT model

Name of function	Description
Dialogue mode (DM)	Determine appropriate dialogue type for situation, e.g., natural language, menu, form-based
Problem state (PS)	Determine position of user in problem treatment process, e.g., formulating problem for a paper (student)
Problem mode (PM)	Determine appropriate mechanism capability, e.g., reference IR or referral to institutions and persons
User model (UM)	Generate description of user type, goals, beliefs, e.g., graduate student, thesis or paper, R&D person, etc.
Problem description (PD)	Generate description of problem type, tonic, structure, environment, wanted attributes in texts (doc.type)
Retrieval strategy (RS)	Choose and apply appropriate retrieval strategies to knowledge resource, e.g., exact match, extended Boolean
Response generator (RG)	Determine propositional structure of response to user appropriate to situation, e.g., list document titles
Input analyst (IA)	Convert input from user into structures usable by functional experts, e.g., parce NL request text, note option selection
Output generator (OG)	Convert propositional response to form appropriate to user and situation, e.g., display new menu, rank titles
Explanation (EX)	Describe mechanism operation, capabilities, etc. to user as appropriate

Source: Adapted from Belkin et al.,[31] p. 399.

The MONSTRAT and Mediator models

Belkin and colleagues followed up the work on the ASK hypothesis by a functional discourse analysis of pre-search client–librarian interactions. This led to an analysis scheme consisting of 10 categories and a number of sub-categories (Table 4). The metacategories of the scheme correspond to the intermediary functions that constitute the analytic MONSTRAT Model (*mo*dular functions based on *n*atural information processes for *strat*egic problem treatments) developed by Belkin, Seeger, and Wersig,[30] which, again, was the basis of the active development of intelligent intermediary systems in the 1980s.[31]

Probably owing to its foundation in the analysis of search interviews, the model encompasses the functionality of an interface for interactive IR but emphasizes strongly the human actor side. Only the retrieval strategy (RS), response generator (RG), and the output generator (OG) functionalities are associated with underlying IR engines and/or information sources. Hence, intelligent systems built on MONSTRAT (and similar expert system architectures) become stand-alone systems. The underlying document collection and the retrieval engine is integrated with the interface and hence not really modeled by MONSTRAT. This led Ingwersen to propose an extension to MONSTRAT, the Mediator model.[29] That model is based on 13 major functionalities and more than 50 minor ones. A rather symmetric cognitive view of the information transfer processes and knowledge types involved is reflected in the principle of the model. According to the Mediator model, an intermediary mechanism must possess knowledge of the underlying *system setting*, including knowledge of documents, representation algorithms, and database structures, and the *IR processes*, that is, source selection and strategies. Symmetrically, it should contain knowledge of users (human actors) and their potential preferences and expectations, IR knowhow, and domain knowledge (a preconditioned *user model*) and be able to carry out *actual user and request model building* during retrieval, based on the user model. In order to be operational, it must consist of knowledge concerned with *domains and domain tasks* (emotional/ conceptual structures) and have *intentionality*, that is, means to store and use expectations based on past experiences and are able to plan its actions. Bates[32] discusses critically the desirable level of automatic support in IR interfaces.

Ingwersen's interactive IR model

A more symmetric perspective of IR interaction and transfer in general, centering on the interface–actor interaction, is observable in the contextual models by Ingwersen (Ingwersen;[29] extended in),[33] which further explore the IR processes and components originally depicted in Fig. 1. Ingwersen[29,33] modeled IR interaction by incorporating the socio-organizational environment (context) of the current actor. That context includes the scientific or professional domain(s) with information preferences, strategies, and work tasks that influence the perception of the actor. The model also emphasized polyrepresentation in documents, in search engines, and in the cognitive space of searchers at any point in time. Further, the model introduced the influence of context on the information and system spaces and the social interaction between socio-organizational factors and actors. It is in this model that cognitive actors appear for the first time, signified by the notion of "models" in each component. However, the model did not explicitly demonstrate the relevance and information use dimensions of interactive IR. The principle of polyrepresentation is derived from the cognitive models and is further analyzed.[34]

Task-Based Models

Toward the end of the 1990s, the cognitive models of IR increasingly developed into explicitly task-based models. Vakkari[35,36] extended the Kuhlthau model of information seeking into the field of task-based IR. Ingwersen

and Järvelin[1] further developed Ingwersen's model ("Cognitive Structures and Actors" section) into a genuine multidimensional research framework for IR and seeking studies, Xie's model[37] suggested how to integrate macro- and microlevels of interactive IR, and finally, Järvelin and colleagues[38] proposed and modeled an evaluation framework encompassing the complexity of task-based information interaction in practice.

Vakkari's model

Vakkari[35,36] extended the Kuhlthau model of information seeking[39] in the field of task-based IR, based on a series of longitudinal empirical studies (Fig. 6). His model explicates the relationships of task performance stages, kinds of information sought and its potential contribution, factors related to searching, and relevance assessments and information use. In addition to the analysis explicated by the model, Vakkari showed that phases in task performance were systematically connected to the information searched for, and the search tactics and usefulness of the information retrieved.

The strengths of the model include the following: 1) There is a clear-cut and necessary distinction between domain knowledge associated with (work) task performance, and IR knowledge. 2) Work task stages and the use of information in work task performance are clearly separated from search task execution. The end product of the search task that of relevance assessments bridges back to the use of information in task execution. 3) There exists the concept of "expected contribution," which refers to the experience gained by the actor in temporal sense.

The Ingwersen–Järvelin integrated model

Ingwersen and Järvelin,[1] (p. 261, 274) further developed and extended the cognitive and task-based IR models to a comprehensive model of information seeking and retrieval (IS&R) (Fig. 7). Numbers on the model basically deal with processes of interaction (1–4) such as social interaction (1) or refer to different kinds of generation and transformation of cognition or cognitive influence (5–8). They are explained in the following text in more detail.

The model (Fig. 7) emphasizes the information processes that are executed during IS&R in context over time: First, processes of social interaction (1) are found between the actor(s) and their past and present sociocultural or organizational context. Social interaction may instigate IS&R activities, but may also form part of their fulfillment. Second, information interaction also takes place between the cognitive actor(s) and the cognitive manifestations embedded in the IT, and the existing information objects via interfaces (2/3). The latter two components interact vertically (4) and constitute the core of an information system. This interaction only takes place at the linguistic sign level. Third, cognitive and emotional

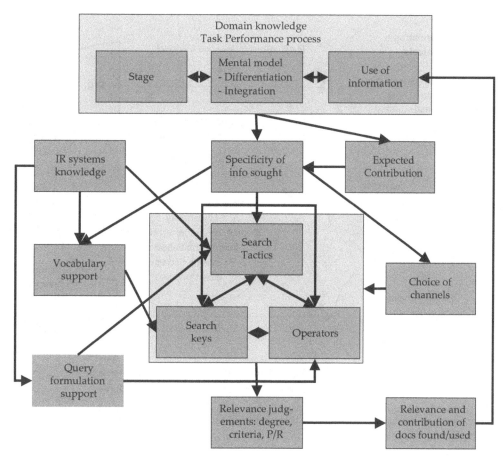

Fig. 6 Stages in work and search task performance. Arrows represent the direction of impact.
Source: Vakkari.[36]

transformations and generation of potential information may occur as required by the individual actor (5/7), as well as from the social, cultural, or organizational context toward the IT and information object components (6/8) *over time*. This implies a steady influence on the information behavior of other actors—and hence on the cognitive–emotional structures representing them. The impact entails that actors may collaborate in teams—like in collaborative IR(CIR)—and collectively adapt to their surroundings.

The model emphasizes that all the participating cognitive structures are in context of all other cognitive components of the model. Hence, there exists a mutual dependency of context and actor or component, including intracomponent structures. For instance, images in objects naturally act as context for the surrounding text—and *vice versa*. At a more detailed level, depicted inside the nodes, the model develops further into the complexity of cognitive structures associated with its five components. Each structure may take a different form depending on the type of information objects, media, and domain.

The framework suggests *empirical variables* that can be combined for research, and from which one may make hypotheses and predictions of potential solutions, for instance, for IR systems development or evaluation

(Ingwersen and Järvelin,[1] pp. 274–275). A more complete set of research variables categorized into nine dimensions extracted from this model, as well as suggestions for research designs, are discussed in Ingwersen and Järvelin,[1] pp. 313–376.

Xie's planned-situational interactive IR model

With an aim to integrate macro- and microlevels of interactive IR, Xie[37] proposed in 2008 the planned-situational interactive IR model (Fig. 8). The model builds on earlier interactive IR models, empirical research, the planned model approach from cognitive science, and theory of situated action derived from social science. At the microlevel, the model illustrates the determining factors of information-seeking strategies. Thus, it presents the relationship between 1) levels of actor goals and tasks including dimensions of work/search tasks, 2) actor's personal information infrastructure, and 3) information-seeking strategies constituted by interactive intentions and retrieval tactics. Further, the model illustrates how plans and situations codetermine interactive intentions and retrieval tactics in the information-seeking process (Xie,[37] p. 236) and thus argues that information-seeking

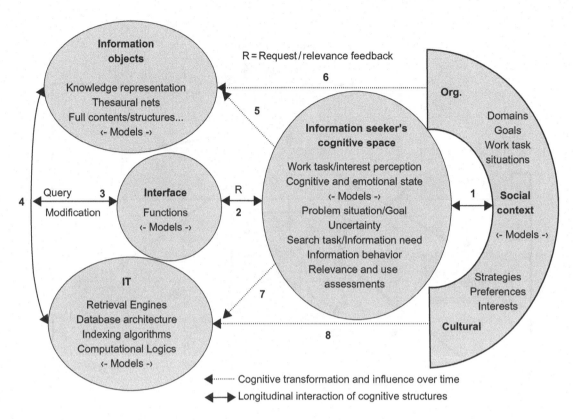

Fig. 7   Cognitive framework of interactive information seeking, retrieval, and behavioral processes.
Source: Ingwersen and Järvelin.[1]

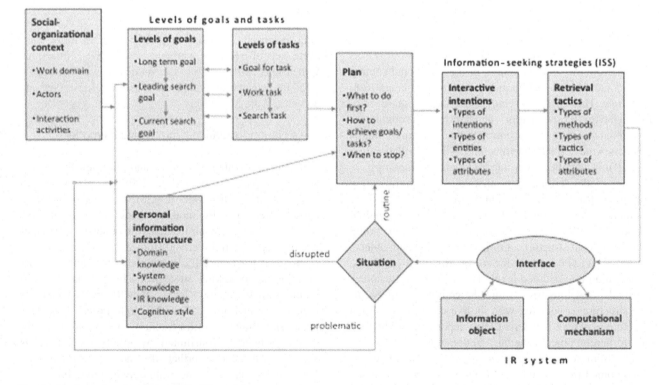

Fig. 8   Planned-situational interactive IR model.
Source: From Xie.[37]

strategies can be seen as a product of plans and situations. In contrast to earlier models by Xie, the planned-situational interactive IR model includes the social–organizational context and actor–system interaction at the macrolevel. The model can therefore be seen as a further development of the Ingwersen–Järvelin integrated model[1] illustrating how to integrate microlevel elements of interactive IR process to the macrolevel processes. This is the main strength of the model in combination with the comprehensive explanation of how the model relates to and builds upon earlier user-oriented and cognitive IR models (Ingwersen and Järvelin,[1] Bates,[22,23] Vakkari,[35] Kuhlthau,[39] Ellis[46]).

Task-based information interaction evaluation framework

Järvelin and colleagues[38] pointed to the need for a comprehensive and systematic evaluation framework encompassing the complexity of task-based information interaction in practice, that is, involving actors, contextual factors, and highly interactive search situations and focusing on how interactive IR improves human task performance—in contrast to taking a traditional IR approach measuring ranking of relevant documents. Accordingly, the authors modeled an overall evaluation framework illustrating the components in a task-based information interaction (Fig. 9). Building on program theory,[40] the evaluation framework aims to generate program theories upon which task-based information interaction evaluation can be built. The evaluation framework consists of 1) *inputs* of contextual factors, perceived task, and actor; 2) *activities* undertaken during the process, namely, task planning and assessment, searching information items, selecting items, working with items, and synthesizing and reporting; 3) immediate *outputs* such as documents or presentations; and 4) possible *outcomes* measuring learning or task outcomes. Järvelin and colleagues describe in detail how the framework supports the evaluation of each of the individual activities using their specific program theories. A main strength of the evaluation framework is

that it focuses on explaining causal relationships between program components *and* explaining how components are related to each other. Accordingly, evaluation is not limited to, for example, performance of the individual tool, but aims to encompass the complexity of humans performing tasks with tools in contexts.

CONCLUSION

In contrast to the Cranfield model of IR, there must exist several models for information seeking and interactive IR that complement one another. Which one to use is dependent on the kind of IS&R processes one wishes to study, in particular when involving seeking actors. The latter models constitute a form and level of complexity not dealt with in system-driven information research and models.

The future may see the development of models and frameworks that increasingly encompass (task-based) context. Here it seems important to stress not only that socio-cultural and organizational contexts are central to information interaction but that the system, network, and information space—the systemic context—are vital for understanding such processes. Even relevant infrastructural features, like bandwidth or legislation, may necessarily form part of such contextual models.

FURTHER READING

Ingwersen and Willett[41] is an introduction to systems-oriented and cognitive approaches to IR. In addition, there are early ARIST reviews on search techniques,[42] cognitive research,[43] and the user-oriented perspectives of IR research and analysis methods.[44] Further reviews and discussions of the cognitive approach to IR during the 1980s can be found in Belkin's overview,[45] in Ellis's[46,47] critical essays on the cognitive paradigm, and in Ingwersen's,[29] monograph. Belkin outlined the major contributions of analytic and empirical nature that have been rather explicitly based on the cognitive approach. The latest

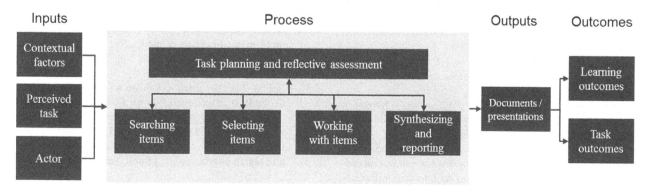

Fig. 9 Overall task-based interactive information evaluation framework based on program theory and five activity types.
Source: From Järvelin et al.[38]

period sees the review on relevance research by Schamber,[48] while Efthimiadis[49] and Spink and Losee[50] provide in-depth discussions of models and empirical results of (human) query expansion and feedback issues, respectively. Harter and Hert[51] review the approaches and methods for the evaluation of IR systems, also of relevance to user-oriented evaluations. In addition, Kelly and Sugimoto[52] present a systematic review of 40 yrs of interactive IR evaluation studies. Vakkari reviews the issues addressed in research on task-based information searching.[53] Web searching studies during the period and comparisons to more traditional (I) IR studies are reviewed by Jansen and Pooch.[54] Studies of the reading and use of academic literature is discussed by King and Tenopir[55] Further reviews and discussions of the cognitive approach to IR during the 1990s can be found in Ingwersen's[56] ARIST chapter, and Ingwersen[57] discusses the user's role in interactive IR evaluation studies. Ingwersen and Järvelin[1] develop a synthesis of laboratory and cognitive approaches to information seeking and retrieval.

REFERENCES

1. Ingwersen, P.; Järvelin, K. *The Turn: Integration of Information Seeking and Retrieval in Context*; Springer: Dortrecht, the Netherlands, 2005.
2. Robertson, S.E.; Hancock-Beaulieu, M. On the evaluation of IR systems. Inform. Process. Manage. **1992**, *28* (4), 457–466.
3. Ingwersen, P.; Wormell, I. Means to improved subject access and representation in modern information retrieval. Libr **1988**, *38* (2), 94–119.
4. Oddy, R.N. Retrieving references by dialogue rather than by query formulation. J. Inform. Sci. **1977**, *1*, 37–53.
5. Wilson, T.D. Models in information behavior research. J. Doc. **1999**, *55* (3), 249–270.
6. Saracevic, T. Relevance: A review of and framework for the thinking on the notion in information science. J. Am. Soc. Inform. Sci. **1975**, *26* (6), 321–343.
7. Saracevic, T. Relevance reconsidered. In *Information Science: Integration in Perspective*, Proceedings of the Second International Conference on Conceptions of Library and Information Science (CoLIS 2), Copenhagen, Denmark, Oct 13–16, 1996; Ingwersen, P., Pors, N.O., Eds.; Royal School of Librarianship: Copenhagen, Denmark, 1996; 201–218.
8. Spink, A.; Greisdorf, H.; Bateman, J. From highly relevant to not relevant: Examining different regions of relevance. Inform. Process. Manage. **1998**, *34* (5), 599–621.
9. Cosijn, E. *Relevance Judgements in Information Retrieval*. PhD thesis, Department of Information Science, University of Pretoria: Pretoria, South Africa, 2003.
10. Cosijn, E. Relevance judgements within the context of work tasks. In *Information Interaction in Context*, Proceedings of the First IIiX Symposium on Information Interaction in Context, Copenhagen, Denmark, Oct 18–20, 2006; Ruthven, I.; et al. Eds.; Royal School of Librarianship: Copenhagen, Denmark, 2006; 20–29.
11. Cosijn, E.; Ingwersen, P. Dimensions of relevance. Inform. Process. Manage. **2000**, *36*, 533–550.
12. Wang, P.; Soergel, D. A cognitive model of document use during a research project: Study I: Document selection. J. Am. Soc. Inform. Sci. **1998**, *49* (2), 115–133.
13. Borlund, P. The concept of relevance in IR. J. Am. Soc. Inform. Sci. Technol. **2003**, *54* (10), 913–925.
14. Borlund, P. Experimental components for the evaluation of interactive information retrieval systems. J. Doc. **2000**, *56* (1), 71–90.
15. Fidel, R.; Soergel, D. Factors affecting online bibliographic retrieval: A conceptual framework for research. J. Am. Soc. Inform. Sci. **1983**, *34* (3), 163–180.
16. Fidel, R. Online searching styles: A case-study-based model of searching behavior. J. Am. Soc. Inform. Sci. **1984a**, *35* (4), 211–221.
17. Fidel, R. The case study method: A case study. Libr. Inform. Sci. Res. **1984**, *6* (3), 273–288.
18. Fidel, R. Moves in online searching. Online Rev. **1985**, *9* (1), 61–74.
19. Fidel, R. Searchers' selection of search keys, I: The selection routine. J. Am. Soc. Inform. Sci. **1991c**, *42* (7), 490–500.
20. Fidel, R. Searchers' selection of search keys, II: Controlled vocabulary or free-text searching. J. Am. Soc. Inform. Sci. **1991b**, *42* (7), 501–514.
21. Fidel, R. Searchers' selection of search keys, III: Searching styles. J. Am. Soc. Inform. Sci. **1991c**, *42* (7), 515–527.
22. Bates, M.J. Information search tactics. J. Am. Soc. Inform. Sci. **1979a**, *30* (4), 205–214.
23. Bates, M.J. Idea tactics. J. Am. Soc. Inform. Sci. **1979b**, *30* (5), 280–289.
24. Bates, M.J. The design of browsing and berrypicking techniques for the online search interface. Online Rev. **1989**, *13* (5), 407–424.
25. Kumpulainen, S. Trails across the heterogeneous information environment: manual integration patterns of search systems in molecular medicine. J. Doc. **2014**, *70* (5), 856–877.
26. Belkin, N.J. Information concepts for information science. J. Doc. **1978**, *34* (1), 55–85.
27. Belkin, N.J.; Oddy, R.N.; Brooks, H.M. Ask for information retrieval: Part 1. J. Doc. **1982a**, *38* (2), 61–71.
28. Belkin, N.J.; Oddy, R.N.; Brooks, H. ASK for information retrieval: Part 2. J. Doc. **1982b**, *38* (3), 145–164.
29. Ingwersen, P. *Information Retrieval Interaction*; Taylor Graham: London, U.K., 1992.
30. Belkin, N.J.; Seeger, T.; Wersig, G. Distributed expert problem treatment as a model for information systems analysis and design. J. Inform. Sci.: Princ. Pract. **1983**, *5*, 153–167.
31. Belkin, N.J.; Borgman, C.L.; Brooks, H.M.; Bylander, T.; Croft, W.B.; Daniels, P.J. et al. Distributed expert-based information systems: An interdisciplinary approach. Inform. Process. Manage. **1987**, *23* (5), 395–409.
32. Bates, M. Where should the person stop and the information search interface start? Inform. Process. Manage. **1990**, *26* (5), 575–591.
33. Ingwersen, P. Cognitive perspectives of information retrieval interaction: Elements of a cognitive IR theory. J. Doc. **1996**, *52* (1), 3–50.

34. Ingwersen, P. *Scientometric Indicators and Webometrics and the Polyrepresentation Principle in Information Retrieval*; Ess Publications: New Delhi, India, 2012, Sarada Ranganathan Endowment Lectures, 28.

35. Vakkari, P. A theory of the task-based information retrieval process: A summary and generalization of a longitudinal study. J. Doc. **2001a**, *57* (1), 44–60.

36. Vakkari, P. Changes in search tactics and relevance judgments in preparing a research proposal: A summary of findings of a longitudinal study. Inform. Retr. **2001b**, *4* (3/4), 295–310.

37. Xie, I. *Interactive Information Retrieval in Digital Environments*; IGI Publishing: Hershey, PA, 2008.

38. Järvelin, K.; Vakkari, P.; Arvola, P.; Baskaya, F.; Järvelin, A.; Kekäläinen, J.; et al. Task-based information interaction evaluation: The viewpoint of program theory. ACM Trans. Inform. Syst. **2015**, *33*(1), 1–30.

39. Kuhlthau, C.C. *Seeking Meaning*; Ablex: Norwood, NY, 1993.

40. Rossi, P.H.; Lipsey, M.W.; Freeman, H. *Evaluation: A Systematic Approach*; Sage: Thousand Oaks, CA, 2004.

41. Ingwersen, P.; Willett, P. An introduction to algorithmic and cognitive approaches for information retrieval. Libri **1995**, *45* (3/4), 160–177.

42. Bates, M.J. Search tactics. In *Annual Review of Information Science and Technology*; Williams, M.E., Ed.; Learned Information: Medford, NJ, 1981; Vol. 16, 139–169.

43. Allen, B.L. Cognitive research in information science: Implications for design. In *Annual Review of Information Science and Technology*; Williams, M.E., Ed.; Learned Information: Medford, NJ, 1991; Vol. 26, 3–37.

44. Sugar, W. User-centered perspective of information retrieval research and analysis methods. In *Annual Review of Information Science and Technology*; Williams, M.E., Ed.; Information Today: Medford, NJ, 1995; Vol. 30, 77–109.

45. Belkin, N.J. The cognitive viewpoint in information science. J. Inform. Sci.: Princ. Pract. **1990**, *16* (1), 11–15.

46. Ellis, D. A behavioural approach to information retrieval design. J. Doc. **1989**, *45* (3), 171–212.

47. Ellis, D. The physical and cognitive paradigms in information retrieval research. J. Doc. **1992**, *48* (1), 45–64.

48. Schamber, L. Relevance and information behavior. In *Annual Review of Information Science and Technology*; Williams, M.E., Ed.; Learned Information: Medford, NJ, 1994; Vol. 29, 3–48.

49. Efthimiadis, E.N. Query expansion. In *Annual Review of Information Science and Technology*; Williams, M.E., Ed.; Information Today: Medford, NJ, 1996; Vol. 31, 121–187.

50. Spink, A.; Losee, R.M. Feedback in information retrieval. In *Annual Review of Information Science and Technology*; Williams, M.E., Ed.; Information Today: Medford, NJ, 1996; Vol. 31, 33–78.

51. Harter, S.P.; Hert, C.A. Evaluation of information retrieval systems: Approaches, issues, and methods. In *Annual Review of Information Science and Technology*; Williams, M.E., Ed.; Information Today: Medford, NJ, 1997; Vol. 32, 3–94.

52. Kelly, D.; Sugimoto, C.R. A systematic review of interactive information retrieval evaluation studies, 1967–2006. J. Am. Soc. Inform. Sci. Technol. **2013**, *64* (4), 745–770.

53. Vakkari, P. Task based information searching. In *Annual Review of Information Science and Technology*; Cronin, B., Ed.; Information Today: Medford, NJ, 2003; Vol. 37, 413–464.

54. Jansen, B.J.; Pooch, U. A review of Web searching studies and a framework for future research. J. Am. Soc. Inform. Sci. **2001**, *52* (3), 235–246.

55. King, D.W.; Tenopir, C. Using and reading scholarly literature. In *Annual Review of Information Science and Technology*; Williams, M.E., Ed.; Information Today: Medford, NJ, 2001; Vol. 34, 423–477.

56. Ingwersen, P. Cognitive information retrieval. In *Annual Review of Information Science and Technology*; Williams, M.E., Ed.; Information Today: Medford, NJ, 2001; Vol. 34, 3–52.

57. Ingwersen, P. The user in interactive information retrieval evaluation. In *Advanced Topics in Information Retrieval*; Melucci, M., Yeates, B., Eds.; Springer: New York, 2011; Vol. 33, 91–118.

Venezuela: Libraries and Librarianship

Juan D. Machin-Mastromatteo
Renny Granda
Universidad Central de Venezuela, Caracas, Venezuela

Abstract
This entry presents a general, brief, and nonexhaustive overview on the origin, development, and the crises of Venezuelan libraries and librarianship. The first section offers an historical background on the first Venezuelan libraries, highlighting the origin of the National Library, together with some of the most important characters of this early history. Moreover, it narrates milestones such as the first Law of Libraries of the country, the celebration of librarian's day, and the *Caracas Declaration*. The second section briefly presents some current types and examples of Venezuelan libraries, such as academic, public, special, digital, and repositories. The third section discusses the development of Venezuelan librarianship, the related professional degree and professional education, including the main schools, programs, and curricula. The fourth section summarizes the current crisis faced by libraries and the profession itself. Finally, some brief comments are offered as a conclusion.

The university cannot be neutral in the historical debate between democracy and dictatorship.
—*Rómulo Betancourt (1959)*

A National Information Policy has more possibilities of receiving significant government attention if it were supported by information professionals.
—*Iraset Páez Urdaneta, In Information for the development of Latin America (1990)*

Manuel Segundo Sánchez showed, in his patient and quiet labor, that there was a liberating force of the spirit, that there was an escape and an alibi to arm the resistance, which was no other than mankind's culture, in front of which dictators and warlords in power would never understand their unassailable argument.
—*Karl Krispin (2007)*

INTRODUCTION

The topic of libraries and librarianship in Venezuela is challenging. Over the last years, this sector has had the same results as any aspect of national life: fragmented, dispersed, confused, hermetic, and uncertain. In this Latin American country, librarianship is an undervalued profession; it is not taken into account, even by the academia. Only two universities offer undergraduate programs on librarianship, and they keep a technical paradigm tied to archival science. In general, library infrastructure is scarce given the national population of over 30 million inhabitants. The development of school libraries is practically inexistent, the National System of

Public Libraries (NSPL) was established between 1970 and 1980, and the base of the pyramid is comprised by the academic libraries, which are located throughout the main cities of the country. Some special and institutional libraries are noteworthy, but they are isolated cases. The National Library (NL) is the main library institution in the country; public policies of the sector and the planning of the NSPL stem from it. However, this institutional figure has not been enough to carry out large projects and a responsible and stable professional scholarship. Within a complex political, social, economic, and cultural context, Venezuelan libraries claim to be vindicated.

HISTORICAL BACKGROUND

Historians set the arrival of books to Venezuela between the sixteenth and seventeenth centuries. From 1600, the presence of books starts to be notorious in colonial time cities.[1] Books arriving from Spain made possible to start developing the first libraries with these manuscripts or printed books, from approximates of 25–500 volumes, and in no way they represented the ideal institutions for the custody, preservation, and classification of collections, which started to appear from the nineteenth century.[1] This section summarizes the first Venezuelan libraries, the first printed publications, the origin of the NL, as well as the most important figures of this early stage of Venezuelan libraries and librarianship, such as the first bibliographers and the leading roles of Rómulo and Virginia Betancourt. Moreover, some notable developments are presented, such as the first and only law of libraries in the country, the events leading to the commemoration of the librarian and archivist day, and the *Caracas Declaration*.

First Steps and the Establishing of the National Library

The first known colonial library belonged to the Convent of Our Lady of Salceda in St. Anne of Coro, it was established by the end of the sixteenth century, and according to chroniclers, historians, and librarians, it comprised 300 volumes which were sometimes lent to the city's inhabitants.[2] Libraries from the seventeenth and eighteenth centuries were mainly private and belonged to national aristocrats, destined to family use, as well as those belonging to the clergy.[1]

In 1691, there was a notable decree by the provincial of the Franciscan order, Diego de Hoces, which indicated how convent libraries should function and it called for the appointment of a librarian to be in charge of the loan service for 2 hours each day and to maintain a written log for this service. This is the earliest registered presence of a librarian in Venezuela. A century later, in 1790, the first known librarian appeared: Father Cristóbal de Quesada, who also taught Latin and grammar to Andrés Bello, and worked at the library of the Convent of the Mercy in Caracas.[1] At the time of the Independence (nineteenth century), there were two key moments: the first Venezuelan periodical, the weekly *Gazette of Caracas*, was printed in 1808; and in 1810, the first book was printed, the Manual Calendar and Universal Guide of Foreigners in Venezuela for the year of 1810. Both publications were prepared in the press owned by Gallagher and Lamb.[2] Furthermore, the idea of a new type of library which would allow readers access emerges: the public library (PL). Its role was also intended as a tool for public instruction after the date of the Declaration of Independence, on April 19, 1810.[1] This idea was published in a printed sheet that began to circulate by the beginning of 1811, *Thinking of a public library in Caracas*, signed by Juan Germán Roscio and possibly written by Francisco Javier Ustáriz,[1,2] both signatories of the *Declaration of Independence*. It was the first intention of a project to create a public library, which was deferred by the Independence War. Even so, during the period of the *War till Death* (1814), the Liberator Simón Bolívar commissioned the collecting of books and ordered the formation of a public library.[2]

From 1830, the idea of creating a NL appears. Particularly in 1831, the Interior Secretary Antonio Leocadio Guzmán manifested the need of merging the convent libraries and books dispersed throughout government offices.[1] Diverse decrees with the intention of creating the NL were issued in the subsequent years, but these initiatives were not so successful. Some of such decrees were 1) by president José Antonio Páez in 1833, pointed out by some scholars as the date of the foundation of the NL;[3,4] 2) by president José Tadeo Monagas in 1850; 3) a decree from 1852, which also assigned a budget to the NL; 4) by president Julián Castro in 1858, which appointed several directors and organizational changes; and 5) by president José Ruperto Monagas, in 1869, which presented improvements for the NL in areas such as staff salary and service regulations. Finally, in 1870, it was during the government of the president Antonio Guzmán Blanco that a solid base for the functioning of the NL was established.[1] The first statistical report of the NL collection appeared in 1873, being comprised by 5862 volumes. In 1874, Guzmán stipulated that the collections of the convent libraries were to be delivered to the Universidad Central de Venezuela (UCV), the first and largest public university. These collections were to be incorporated to the NL, which was located at the time in the university campus. In 1875, Adolfo Enrns publishes the *Catalog of the Library of the University of Caracas*, the first printed catalog of the NL and of Venezuelan bibliography. Ernst directed the NL from 1876 to 1889. In 1892, the library separated from the UCV and in the following year it was moved to another location through a decree by the president Joaquín Crespo.[1]

At the beginning of the twentieth century, the situation of the country was critical due to the Civil War. When Juan Vicente Gómez got into power in 1908, he decided to appoint the construction of a dedicated headquarter for the NL, so in 1910, he commissioned architect Alejandro Chataing with this construction. This new headquarter was built next to the UCV and it was inaugurated in 1911, coinciding with the commemoration of the Centennial of the Independence. In 1937, after the end of the dictatorship, a stage of modernization of the NL was started by its director Enrique Planchart. From 1950 toward the end of the twentieth century, the library had five directors; the most important of them took office in 1974 and transformed the institution into an autonomous organization, among other improvements. In 1960, the Book Bank was created as a nonprofit organization, thereby starting a new vision of library services. In 1974, Venezuela became the first Latin American country to have policies for the creation of the NSPL.[1] The current headquarter of the NL, designed by José Tomás Sanabria, consists of a building with a total size of 80,000 m^2, which was constructed from 1981 and began to function in 1989.[2]

The First Bibliographers

In this brief historical journey, it is relevant to mention the first characters that conducted activities related to this discipline. In the first place, there were the fathers of Venezuelan bibliography, Arístides Rojas, Adolfo Ernst, Juan Piñango Ordoñez, Adolfo Fryndesberg, and Manuel Segundo Sánchez. The latter was a true pioneer in setting the bases of Venezuelan bibliographic research, by establishing the foundations for the development of this discipline in Venezuela, and from 1913 to 1920 he directed the NL. Among his most important works were *Venezuelan Bibliography* (1914), which includes nearly 1500 records and until now it is considered the only work of its kind; the *Venezuelan Library* (1917), *Bibliographic Yearbook* (1917), which the NL took as a model from 1942 in order to systematically compile its own yearbooks; and the *Bibliography of Bibliographic Indexes Related to Venezuela* (1939). He also conducted research on the printing press in Venezuela and created the denomination of *Venezuelan incunabula* for every Venezuelan publication printed from 1808 (year of the first printed publication) and 1821 (Battle of Carabobo). Curiously, Walter Lichtenstein acquired the private library of Sánchez and his books ended up in universities of the United States such as Harvard, Northwestern, and the University of Chicago. Finally, there is the figure of Pedro Grases, compiler of the fundamental writings of Venezuelan intellectuals and statesmen. His most important works are related to the history of the printing press in Venezuela, an inventory of printings of the period between 1808 and 1812, the trajectory of the *Gazette of Caracas* from 1808 to 1822, the Angostura printings of 1817–1822, the *Venezuelan Constitution* of 1811, his bibliographic research on various subjects and profound reflections on Venezuelan bibliographic research.[5]

Rómulo and Virginia Betancourt

Rómulo Betancourt was the first president of the Venezuelan democracy (1959–1964), he belonged to the Generation of 1928, a group of student leaders which organized the first popular manifestation against the dictatorship of Juan Vicente Gómez (1908–1935). Being a strong opponent of the Gómez regime, he lived a part of those years in exile. Between 1931 and 1935 he lived in Costa Rica, where he started his ideological journeys throughout Latin America. In those years, he worked at the National Library of Costa Rica, taking advantage for advancing and deepening his reading of works such as the 15 volumes of the *Contemporary History of Venezuela* by González Guinán, resulting in his writing of a magnificent summary.[6] Betancourt was a militant in diverse clandestine political organizations such as the Venezuelan Communist Party and the National Democratic Party. The latter was the predecessor of the political party Democratic Action (AD), founded in 1941 by Betancourt and other Venezuelan left-wing leaders. Betancourt converted a country of warlords and militaries into one of a civil society and republican institutions.[7] Because of his political views, he was eternally pursued, but despite this persecution and his strong dissident activities he never stopped reading, studying, writing, and publishing journalistic articles, booklets, and books.[6] His daughter, Virginia Betancourt, will always be appreciated by the educated and democratic Venezuela for her efforts as the director of the NL

between 1974 and 1999, her contribution in the founding of the Book Bank in 1960, and her labor in preserving and classifying her father's personal archive.[6] During her administration of the NL, he was responsible for establishing the autonomous character of the institution, creating the NSPL, and promoting the Law of Libraries of 1977. Additionally, she encouraged professional meetings and of Latin American integration, such as the one which originated the *Caracas Declaration*. She also participated in the creation of the Association of Ibero-American National Libraries (ABINIA) and her labor made her worthy of the International Federation of Library Associations and Institutions (IFLA) Medal in 2005.

Law of Libraries (1977)

The National Library Autonomous Institute and Library Services (NLAILS) Law[8] created the figure of the NLAILS from the NL and was the basis for the creation of the NSPL. It was during the era of the discourses about systems, networks, and library management, besides the modernization and transformation of the NL. Legislators and leaders took the advantage of this opportunity to start building the library network throughout the country. With this law, Venezuela stepped forward into the vanguard of the library movement in Latin America, being the third country of the region to create a law of this kind,[9] which was even considered a model for some library movements in Latin America.[10]

The NLAILS Law is still in effect, as no new legislation has been passed, despite the fact that it is obsolete and it does not develop the particular area of public libraries. The law is now obsolete because it is antiquated and inadequate given the current circumstances it must govern. It was passed more than 30 years ago, when another constitution ruled the country's destiny, thus overpassing the limits of Venezuela's legal reality. The current constitution of 1999 brought significant changes in every institutional area, mainly materialized through different legal reforms made by the new parliament and especially with legislation through presidential decrees. The NLAILS Law is a *survivor* of that time of major legal reforms. In consequence of the mentioned changes, this Law stopped being useful in its area of application, and nowadays it is officially mentioned exclusively when the president makes changes in the direction of the NL.

Librarian and Archivist's Day, One Date and Three Motives (1982)

The National Librarian and Archivist's Day is celebrated every July 27. This date was chosen as the most iconic for the profession for three reasons. First, July 27, 1945 is recorded as the date of death of Manuel Segundo Sánchez. Second, July 27, 1950 corresponds to the graduation of the first cohort of library and archives professionals from the UCV. The third event happened on July 27, 1977 with the enactment of the *NLAILS Law*.[8] Considering these events, on July 23, 1982 the Presidential Decree N° 1.564 was published in the Official Gazette of the Republic of Venezuela N° 32,522, declaring July 27 as the *National Librarian and Archivist's Day*. The document states:

the activities of Library and Archives professionals constitute factors of progress and development for the country, because they fulfill support to education, research, and to the development of science and technology through libraries, archives and information and documentation centers, hence it is fair to recognize their function within the Venezuelan society (p. 245827).[11]

Caracas Declaration (1982)

The *Caracas Declaration for the Public Library as a factor of development and instrument of social change in Latin America and the Caribbean* was the product of the consensus between experts from 30 countries, that was reached during the *Regional Meeting on the Current State and Development Strategies for the Development Public Library Services in Latin America and the Caribbean*, during October 25–29, 1982. *The Declaration* is the first and most important technical-normative document on PL of the region because it allowed pushing the library movement in Latin America and the Caribbean (LAC).

The Declaration was a regional agreement celebrated in the Venezuelan capital and supported by the United Nations Educational, Scientific and Cultural Organization (UNESCO), the Regional Center for the Promotion of the Book in Latin America and the Caribbean (CERLALC), IFLA, and the Venezuelan NLAILS. *The Declaration* contains the shared visions of the region's professionals at an historical moment: one which opened the door to wider views of social reality, democratic life, and regional integration. Hence, one of the first aspects it mentions is the support to the main principles stated in the UNESCO Public Library Manifesto of 1972. From these principles, the main needs of the region were compared and they were adapted to LAC reality in order to adopt them.

The first part of *The Declaration* enumerates eight principles for a PL of the region, in order to assume the commitment toward development, democracy, and social change in LAC. These principles "express the will of a library majority on what the public library should be in our countries."[12] These are summarized as follows:

1. Ensure free access to information which must be broad, current, and representative of the sum of different thoughts, in various formats.
2. Stimulate people's participation in national life, enhancing the role of the library as a facilitator of social change and participation in democratic life.
3. Promote the understanding, dissemination, and defense of national indigenous and minority culture to assert

cultural identity and the recognition and respect toward other cultures.
4. Promote the formation of critical, selective, and creative readers through reading, thus training each individual to play an active role in society.
5. Support lifelong learning, eradicating illiteracy, and supporting services for children, teenagers, neo-readers, and disabled readers, both socially and physically.
6. Serve as information and communication centers for the community.
7. Develop national library services.
8. Support an economically strong and culturally independent national and regional editorial industry.[13]

The second part refers to the basic conditions for the development of PL in LAC, conforming a vision closer and more real regarding the state of the LAC library, stating the true needs or shortcomings, mainly institutional, which prevented (and in some cases, still prevent) the improvement of services in the region. *The Declaration* states the need of a legal framework to regulate the functions of the PL, contemplating State obligation to offer library services, a national coordination, a system of services, normalization of technical processes, strategies to train human resources, and the sustainable endowment of services. It highlights the role of the State "regarding its functioning and development, and emphasizing the need of the libraries to be included in the development plans of each country, in pointing the State obligation to offer public library services and assigning them sufficient yearly budget for their development" (p. 17).[14] Moreover, issues such as "to stimulate citizen participation in democratic life" (p. 16)[10] started to be taken into account.

VENEZUELAN LIBRARIES

The national library infrastructure is currently scarce, given a population of over 30 million inhabitants. Regardless, this section mentions the main libraries: academic, including university and school libraries; the dense network of public libraries and their variations; special libraries supporting the labor of both the private and public sectors; institutional and governmental libraries; and lastly some experiences in digital libraries and repositories.

Academic Libraries

Venezuelan academic libraries include university and school libraries. In public and private universities, there are libraries which fundamentally support professional development and research. The most relevant from public universities are those of Universidad Central de Venezuela, Universidad Simón Bolívar, Universidad de Los

Andes, Universidad de Carabobo, Universidad del Zulia, Universidad de Oriente, and Universidad Nacional Abierta. The most relevant from private universities are those of Universidad Católica Andrés Bello, Universidad Metropolitana, and Universidad Santa María. The main national universities also count with specialized academic libraries according to the faculty or field of knowledge to which they dedicate. School libraries can be found in private institutions but especially in public schools. The responsibility of the State in the conformation of a public school library system rests in the Ministry of Education. In the mid-1980s, there were nearly 1700 school libraries dependent from the mentioned governmental office.[1]

Public Libraries

The NLAILS is the governing body of the NSPL, and it was inspired by both the *UNESCO Public Library Manifesto* and the *Caracas Declaration*.[4] The system is comprised by 727 libraries nationwide, organized in 24 state library networks with a total capacity for approximately 38,229 readers, 3687 of them are located in the capital city of Caracas.[15] Despite these figures, some of its weaknesses are related to the lack of clear policies, technological infrastructure, and an inadequate library staff selection, which in general is neither professional nor trained for such functions.[4] Regarding statistics, 88% of PL users are students, with an average age of 20 years, and 71% of them study in public institutions. Only 12% of the total users do not study and their average age is 37 years, from this percentage 75% of them are employed.[15] Part of the explanation behind these figures is that in many cases PLs fulfill the roles or alleviate the lack of school libraries in many sectors throughout the country.

Among the PL, one of the most emblematic is the Book Bank because it was established in 1960, before the NLAILS Law was even drafted, but still it started to provide the basic framework to start developing a network of school and public libraries, first in Caracas and then in other regions of the country. The Book Bank is the "depositary of a valuable collection comprised by books for children and teenagers, specialized literature on these literary genres, documental records, periodicals, and texts related to the book and reading promotion" (p. 25).[3] The Book Bank researches, experiments, innovates, and proposes guidelines for reading promotion and also carries out diverse cultural activities that are not necessarily related to reading.

Special Libraries

The Marcel Roche Library of the Venezuelan Institute of Scientific Research (IVIC) might be the most relevant special library of the country and because it is subordinated to the Ministry of Science, Technology and Innovation, it is one of the few libraries that can afford and acquire academic databases and scientific journals, given the currency exchange control imposed by the government since 2003. Other notable special libraries are those from each of the National Academies: Language, History, Medicine, Political, Economic, and Social Sciences; Physical, Natural and Mathematical Sciences; as well as the Ernesto Peltzer Library of the Central Bank; the libraries of the Supreme Court of Justice, National Assembly, Attorney General; those in the museums of Natural Sciences, Fine Arts, and Contemporary Arts; the library of the Rómulo Gallegos Center of Latin-American Studies; and those within some foundations, such as the *Rojas Astudillo, Pedro Manuel Arcaya, John Boulton, Vicente Lecuna, Humboldt, La Salle, Centro Venezolano Americano*, among many others.[1]

Digital Libraries and Repositories

Regarding digital libraries, the Venezuelan experiences have been incipient. The closest related cases are repertories of specialized information, such as the *Scientific, Humanistic and Technological Information System* of the UCV, university digital journals and some repositories such as: *National Repository of Open Source Software, Intellectual Production Repository Universidad Centrocidental Lisandro Alvarado, SABER UCV, SABER Universidad de los Andes* (ULA), *Institutional Repository Universidad de Oriente, Institutional Repository Universidad Pedagógica Experimental Libertador*, and *Intellectual Production Universidad Simón Bolívar*. Finally, there is the repository *Metadatum*, which aims to group all the academic repositories of the country that are using the OAI-PMH protocol, and to serve as a metasearch engine.

Although there are many repositories in the country's main universities, the first and only institutional open access mandate dates from 2009 and corresponds to the ULA. This consists in preserving the following documents in institutional repositories: 1) theses, 2) research products funded by the Scientific, Humanistic and Technological Development Council, and 3) all University publications.[16] Despite this scenario, it is important to point out that Venezuela has the sixth place in number of publications indexed in the Network of Scientific Journals from Latin America and the Caribbean, Spain and Portugal (Redalyc), with a total of 54 quality scientific journals, in open access.[17]

VENEZUELAN LIBRARIANSHIP

There are two Venezuelan traditional Library schools: the Schools of Libraries and Archives of the Universidad Central de Venezuela (EBA-UCV) and its counterpart in the Universidad del Zulia (EBA-LUZ). The UCV is located in Caracas, the capital city. It was founded in 1721, and it is among the oldest universities in the occidental hemisphere. This university has been the alma mater of many notable Venezuelan scientists, humanists, intellectuals, and presidents. Its current location, the University City of Caracas was built between 1940 and 1960, it was designed by Carlos Raúl Villanueva, with the collaborations of avant-garde artists from the era, and in 2000 it was declared a World Heritage Site by the UNESCO. The EBA-UCV was founded in 1948, and it offers two 5-year bachelor programs, one in library science and the other in archival science. It also offers two master programs: *Management of Information Networks* and *Information and Communication for Development*.

The EBA-LUZ was created in 1962, and it offers the same bachelor programs together with a master in *Information Sciences*. Other universities with more recent academic options are the Universidad de Carabobo, centering on documental certification courses and bachelors; the Universidad Católica Andrés Bello, with a master on *Information Systems*; and the Universidad Yacambú, with a bachelor in *Information and Documentation*. Sadly, there are no doctoral options in the field, resulting in a few doctors with LIS PhDs obtained in other countries and the majority of doctors with a LIS background have obtained PhDs in education, sociology, social sciences, among other disciplines. For the year 2001, there were a total of 3490 LIS professionals registered in the country, nearly 1900 of them were women.[18]

Origin of the Professional Degree (1950)

The period between February and July 1950 saw the definition of the university degree conferred on the first library and archives professionals of the country. The first director of the EBA-UCV, José Fabbiani Ruiz, manifested his unrest on the matter on February 4, proposing the title of *cataloger-librarian*. Just a month before the graduation of the first cohort of students, in the Assembly on June 26, Fabbiani argued that even if the previously mentioned title was approved in a previous session, the students, director, and teachers of the School thought that the alternative title of *librarianship technician* was more adequate. That was mainly because the title of *catalogers* would presumably prevent them from directing a library, being necessary to obtain a more general and positive title, one that would be a promise and not a menace, according to Fabbiani. The ensuing discussion had interventions from professors Acosta Saignes, Olivares Figueroa, Oliver, Rosenblat, Granell, the Faculty Dean Casanovas, and Fabbiani himself. Finally, several titles were proposed: *library technician*, *library technique graduate*, *library assistant*, *library auxiliary*, and *librarianship technician*. After some deliberations a voting took place, the winning alternative was the one proposed by the School. Hence, on July 27, 1950,

the first *Librarianship Technicians* of the country had their graduation.[19]

Professional Education

Venezuelan librarianship professional formation was in part caused and inspired by the seminal speech that José Ortega y Gasset delivered in the Second IFLA International Congress, in the Universidad de Madrid, on May 20, 1935. The mentioned discourse was published as the book titled Librarian's Mission, which was the way these ideas were disseminated in Venezuela, before there were professional education schools. The mentioned ideas made people start to realize that the profession was a collective need and it was socially indispensable, thus making vital to professionalize a traditionally empirical occupation.[20] Some of Ortega y Gasset's ideas that are inherent to the essence of Venezuelan information professionals and the early curriculum designs are 1) a concern with enabling access to information as a human right, either for the purpose of scientific and financial advancement as well as for communication and recreation; and 2) the idea that the right to information is the means that ensures the scientific, humanistic, technological, and social progress of the country and the world.[20]

Moreover, from the cited ideas, library, and archives, schools are responsible of developing professionals who may contribute in part to their profession, through teaching and research; and also to society, being aware of social, financial, and scientific development at a global level and to answer any need of information, science, and culture that society may have. The national professional training has seven bases that were stated from the beginning as different skills: basic, administrative, technical processing, information sources, documentation and information, research, and understanding of human nature.[20] These bases have been kept until today, adding additional facets such as to have historical and social consciousness of the objects and areas of study, as well as topics of social relevance such as user formation, reading promotion programs, and information literacy. Moreover, there are the technological facets, of information policies, and of informetrics. All these facets are not necessarily integrated in the compulsory curriculum, but they may be developed by the student through elective courses or as transversal axes in the curriculum design. Regarding their attitudes, the ideal professional must be competent, critical, reflexive, and participant in the issues of their context. Additionally, good Venezuelan librarians are characterized for their service vocation, constancy, professionalism, their lifelong learning, and for pushing to the limit the resources and possibilities at their disposal for providing their services and fulfilling their mission.

It is complicated to summarize the current state, the challenges, and opportunities of Venezuelan professional training, because every institution has their characteristics and circumstances. In the frame of developing some contributions to the curricular change, three stages of the curricular evolution in the EBA-UCV have been defined: technical, disciplinary, and transdisciplinary, indicating that the revision and updating of the curriculum and the naming of the professional studies in the field have been deferred.[21] The transition in the EBA-LUZ has passed from a theoretical and technical formation, then reinforcing management and technological areas, and finally it has diminished the general formation, enhancing professional and research courses.[21,22] In both cases, the main considerations behind the initiatives of curricular change have been driven by academic and employment dynamics, both nationally and internationally, which are also what informs the construction of the professional profile. In the country, there have been curricular evaluations in the EBA-LUZ[22] as well as comparative evaluations between the Venezuelan curricula. The latter have set the bases for developing guidelines and methodologies to guarantee aspects such as quality assurance, pertinence of formation, the degree to which formation answers the needs of the discipline and society, the possibility of national and international accreditation, and internationalization.[23] Regarding the comparative study of Venezuelan curricula, it turns out that both are academicist, humanistic, and sociological, but the elements to revise in national curriculum design are teleological, axiological, transdisciplinar, cooperation, and interchange fundaments, as well as to develop market studies to achieve an empirical and common grounding for curricula design, being aware of the local and global relationship, to strengthen the construction of a pedagogical theory, and encourage the configuration of knowledge, learning, and research networks.[24] Finally, the need of introducing the competency-based curriculum has been stressed, and it is something that the EBA-LUZ has already tried.[25]

Apart from the cited experiences that improve the curricula, some authors highlight the dubious need of framing the curriculum to the initiatives of the current Venezuelan government administration (1999–2014), thus presenting the Information Sciences Formation Program.[26] This program, given its definition and except for its ideological fixation, results redundant when considering the already established learning options, as it indicates that it is innovative simply because it seeks to overcome anachronisms that sadly are grounded in the general perception that people have about the information professional but that the mentioned traditional university formation already takes into account. These perceptions are the exclusive role of a custodian, to grant access to information to the communities, and to improve means and devices for information handling. In conclusion, this tends to erroneously insinuate that the established formation programs do not take into account the needs of the society as well as those from public and private institutions.

CURRENT STATE

The Venezuelan situation has become more complicated during the last 22 years, with events that have resulted in the current and never before seen financial, political, and social crisis, such as the Black Friday, the Caracazo, failed coups d'état, trials to government officers for corruption charges, a new Constitution, devaluations and currency exchange controls, a new political class in power, the enterprise and oil strikes, instability, an unsafe country, as well as polarization and confrontation. It is only to be expected that Venezuelan libraries and librarianship are outside of these issues and like it has happened with other sectors, they have suffered the ideological and polarizing onslaughts that have been occurring during current government administration (1999–2014).

Libraries and Their Public

For 1999, Venezuela had already shown a high literacy rate, with approximately 92.3% of the population of over 15 years.[27] However, it seems that in Venezuela, the discussions on libraries have been put aside, because of the country's situation, of society, and librarians themselves, of the development of information and communication technologies (ICTs) or because the Internet has displaced reference librarians and now everyone searches independently for information, for better or worse. Moreover, libraries have not been given their place, importance, and the fundamental value they deserve, thus there is a general lack of interest in them. The figures confirm it, 80% of the population recognizes that they do not go to a library, barely a 9.1% visits a public library, and an ephemeral 1.2% goes to the NL for information and education needs.[28] Officially, it has been reported as a significant achievement that in 2012, the NL had attended more than 11 million users (p. 414).[29] Furthermore, the paradox of a raising number of readers but not of books sold is starting to be envisaged. The main cause of this phenomenon can be found in the infamous currency exchange control, which is described in the following section.

Financial Issues

In order to discuss the financial issues of Venezuela, it is necessary to take into account the presence of a set of complex rules that have regulated a governmental currency exchange control during the past 12 years. These rules have contributed to a massive inflation, costs speculation, and innumerable challenges for any person or institution intending to travel or acquire imported products or services. This currency control was established in 2003, it is based on official exchange rates for US Dollars (USD) and Euros, and it is still in place with complementary or alternative currency exchange systems. These schemes complicate the financial situation, because they started with an exchange rate of 1.60 Bolívares Fuertes (BsF) for each USD, then BsF 1.92/USD in 2004, and BsF 6.30/USD in 2013.

Today, the currency control is based on a new scheme of three values, one fixed to 6.30/USD for "prioritary" sectors and the other two are "complementary": the first starts at BsF 11.36/USD, but with high fluctuations, and the second is an alternative system that seeks to eliminate the alternative black market, by fluctuating according to supply and demand, and starting at BsF 51.86/USD. This control, together with the currency reconversion of 2008, which eliminated 3 zeroes to the national currency and the calculation of the National Budget according to the prices of the oil barrel, has resulted in the creation of development funds that are discretionally managed by the government and has cast serious doubts about their transparency. Academic libraries have felt the most direct impact of the currency exchange control, because for them it is very hard, if not impossible, to receive the foreign currency needed to subscribe academic databases and import library materials that are not manufactured in the country. This makes the IVIC library, because of its subordination to the State, one of the few libraries of the country that can currently count with these resources.

The current main economic activity of the country is the oil exploitation, between 2000 and 2008 there was a spectacular rise in oil barrel prices, from 20 to more than a 100 USD. Despite its condition of being a single product economy, Venezuela has been privileged because of the volatility of prices and the immediate liquidity of oil sales in the international market. According to the National Institute of Statistics, between 2003 and 2012, the government made a social inversion (SI) of 772,000 million USD, mainly through the so-called Social Missions. The SI for the period 1999–2011 represented around 60% of the State's income.[30] Moreover, between 2008 and 2012, the State oil company Petróleos de Venezuela (PDVSA) received a total income of 520,000 million USD (p. 156).[31] It has been calculated that the revenue for 2013 was between 82,000 and 85,000 million USD.[32]

Between 2004 and 2009, Venezuelan SI was directed firstly toward education, then social security, health, housing and services, social development, and participation.[33] However, the investments made in culture, communication, and science and technology occupy a precarious space in the assignment of public expenditures. Considering the magnitude of the SI, it is valid to ask how much have been invested in Venezuelan libraries. Sadly, it is difficult to offer a detailed scenario with the scarce statistical data offered by the NLAILS; moreover, on its website there are no data available on any library indicator. Furthermore, the available statistics go only as far as 2005, and except for the *Cultural Statistical Yearbook, 1990–2003: Venezuelan Book's and Libraries' numbers*;[15]

one copy of the *2007 Statistical Yearbook of the NL* and the *Annual Reports and Accounts of the Ministry of Culture* (MCMPPC),[34] there are not enough pertinent data sources. Through the study of the different editions of this last source, it is possible to calculate that the total inversion dedicated to the NLAILS and hence to our libraries between 2005 and 2013 was of 1169.9 million BsF, or 315.9 million USD. During this period, NLAILS has directed its plans through projects which essentially reiterate every year the reinforcement and push of the NLAILS and the NSPL. This indicates that this goal has not being achieved or not completed. It also means that the majority of the resources should have been directed to invest and develop the NSPL.[34] In order to put the previously mentioned amount in perspective, we can take into account that PDVSA's income between 2008 and 2012 was over 520,000 million USD. Then, the resources transferred to the NLAILS in the same period were of 186.4 million USD. This means that the SI directed to the PL sector in Venezuela represents 0.03% of the total revenue generated by the sales of oil. Thus, a great deal of the issues of the NSPL is originated by budget problems.

The obstacles highlighted in NLAILS report during the execution of the mentioned projects are insufficiency of financial resources, insufficient assignation provided by the *Law of Budget*, suspension of the Information System *Northwestern Online Total Integrated System* (NOTIS), noncompliance of the *Law of Legal Deposit*, cuts in the planned investments for the acquisition of collections, deterioration of infrastructures, lack of preventive and corrective maintenance of the public libraries, obsolescence of computer equipment, obsolescence of collections, lack of resources for the paper edition and dissemination of technical documents for librarians, difficulties for compiling statistics, lack of imported resources and materials which affect the activities of preservation and conservation, lack of capable and specialized professionals, among others.[15,34] Moreover, the lines of action of recent projects start to contain an ideological charge, by talking of concepts such as the *First Socialist Plan*.

Most of the challenges academic libraries and the NLAILS are reporting and facing are related to financial issues, which are aggravated by the currency control. The main problem for libraries is that very few of the resources they must acquire are currently manufactured or sold within the country. Hence, the resources that can be imported imply extra charges over the product's cost, which are derived from the currency control itself, the speculation of costs, and disproportionate import duties and taxes from the State. This situation is further complicated for public libraries, from the NLAILS to the smallest ones, because budget allocations are marginal. The currency control and the scarce financial resources are part of a vicious circle, because with the limited budgets libraries can acquire less resources every year due to the fluctuation of exchange rates, together with inflation, speculation, and State taxes that do not forgive even books.

Legal Issues

NLAILS' administrative activities face different lingering challenges; the majority of them are caused by budget insufficiency, which raises some doubts about the legal bases supporting our libraries, the convenience of institutionalism, centralization, decentralization, or administrative de-concentration. Libraries' public service character is mandated by the Constitution of the Bolivarian Republic of Venezuela (CBRV),[35] but the question is: how we can socially transform libraries in order to fulfill this constitutional mandate that would be their raison d'être? Article 108 is the only part of the CBRV where the word "library" appears, it states:

"Media, both public and private, must contribute to citizen formation. The State will guarantee public services of radio, television, and library and computer networks, with the purpose of allowing universal access to information. Educational centers must incorporate the knowledge and application of new technologies, their innovations, according to the requirements established by law" (p. 23).[35]

Apart from the first and only *NLAILS Law*,[8] other two legal instruments have supported libraries: 1) *Legal Deposit Law* of 1993, which compels the editorial sector to send a copy of all publications produced in the country to the NL; and 2) *Organic Municipal Regime Law* of 1989, which mandated the existence of municipal PL according to the amount of inhabitants or population, but such disposition is nowhere to be found in the new *Organic Public Municipal Power Law* of 2010, which replaced the previously mentioned legislation. CERLALC points out that Venezuela does not offer data regarding reading and library indicators (p. 5),[36] specifically the number of PL for every 100,000 inhabitants. This is due in part to the elimination from the current legislation of the requirement of offering municipal library services. However, recently the NLAILS Press Department declared that a new NL Law is being drafted, announcing the "discussion" of a project. It draws attention to the fact that this notice seems to be a reaction in front of the controversial *Organic Culture Law*, approved in August 2013 and also that the promoters of the so-called library constituent are conducting the "debate and analysis" of the future legal text behind closed doors, when what would be required is a broad, open, diverse, and inclusive consultation, which is characteristic of the participative democracy advocated by the CBRV.[35] This consultation should count not only with working groups in the NL, but it should also take into account what the traditional library schools might have to say, as well as the professional associations (despite their dispersion), the national library workers, cultural promoters, and citizens.

CONCLUSION

This is the moment to vindicate Venezuelan libraries, to restore their fundamental value, and teach their usefulness to the nation's development. Information professionals and librarians have the responsibility of demonstrating the vital importance of libraries to political leaders, and to make sure their constitutional provision is assumed on the basis of human rights. National library schools must include in their curricular design a much broader and less rigid social vision of libraries, which allow for the identification of the professional role in front of society and diverse communities. Research and comparative librarianship are essential to entrepreneurship, innovation, and competitiveness in a world that is increasingly an information society.

Venezuela faces one of the most difficult times of its history. Libraries as institutions and librarianship as profession are instruments for social change and the strengthening of democracy. It is fundamental, now more than ever, to make Venezuelans understand that without information, education, and culture there would never be a "powerful country," much less a "motherland." Before extracting all oil reserves, we must learn to read, and to think in a free, critical, and selective way. Moreover, we have to see our fellowmen as just one more person in the construction of great deeds and not as an adversary that must be ignored because of their political affiliation or their ideology. Finally, before building bridges, highways, schools, hospitals, or even large libraries, first we must build citizenship together. Being citizens is what will open us the way toward development.

REFERENCES

1. Pérez, O.A. Bibliotecas. In *Diccionario de Historia de Venezuela*, 2nd Ed.; Fundación Polar: Caracas, Venezuela, 1997; 441–448.
2. Himiob, S. *Historia de la Biblioteca Nacional de Venezuela*; Instituto Autónomo Biblioteca Nacional y de Servicios de Bibliotecas: Caracas, Venezuela, 2008; 1–180.
3. Diaz, E. Criterios metodológicos para la formulación de planes de fomento de la lectura desde la biblioteca pública, Thesis (BA), Universidad Central de Venezuela, Caracas, Venezuela, 2007; 1–161.
4. Alvarado, A. La función social de la biblioteca pública vista a través de cuatro expertos. Thesis (BA), Universidad Central de Venezuela, Caracas, Venezuela, 2008.
5. Méndez, I. Pedro Grases y la historia de la cultura en Venezuela. El Nacional, September 12, 2009, http://venezuelaysuhistoria.blogspot.com/2009/09/la-gran-obra-de-don-pedro-grases.html (accessed January 2015).
6. Aizpúrua, J. *Rómulo Betancourt, padre de la democracia venezolana* [Audiobook]; Sophia Producciones: Caracas, Venezuela, 2011.
7. Ulacio, S. Hay que erradicar la represión salvaje. Versión Final, September 27, 2009, p.6.
8. Congreso de la República de Venezuela. *Ley del Instituto Autónomo Biblioteca Nacional y de Servicios de Bibliotecas*, *Gaceta Oficial Nro. 31284*; Congreso Nacional: Caracas, Venezuela, 1977; 235799–235806, http://www.cerlalc.org/

leytipo/Bibliotecas/Venezuela/Ley_insti_autonomo.pdf (accessed January 2015).

9. Flores, C.; Gómez, R.; Soto, M. Legislación de bibliotecas públicas de América Latina: Análisis comparativo. In *XVI Conferencia Internacional de Bibliotecología*, Santiago, Chile, November 2–3, 2011. http://eprints.rclis.org/17502/ (accessed January 2015).

10. Rodríguez, G. *La biblioteca pública: análisis a manifiestos y directrices*; Fondo Editorial COMFENALCO: Antioquia, Colombia, 2007; 1–68.

11. Herrera, L. *Decreto N° 1.564 – 22 de julio de 1982*, Gaceta Oficial N° 32.522; Procuraduría General de la República: Caracas, Venezuela, 1982; 245823–245827, http://www.pgr.gob.ve/dmdocuments/1982/32522.pdf (accessed January 2015).

12. Córdoba, S. La cooperación regional para el desarrollo social, cultural y bibliotecario. In *60th IFLA General Conference*, Havana, Cuba, August 21–27, 1994. http://www.ifla.org/IV/ifla60/60-cors.htm (accessed January 2015).

13. UNESCO; CERLALC; IFLA; IABNSB. *Declaración de Caracas. En Reunión Regional sobre el Estado Actual y las Estrategias para el Desarrollo de los Servicios de Bibliotecas Públicas en América Latina y el Caribe*; Informe Final: Caracas, Venezuela, October 25–29, 1982; 12–17. http://unesdoc.unesco.org/images/0005/000525/052531sb.pdf (accessed January 2015).

14. Jaramillo, O.; Álvarez, D.; Moncada, D. Políticas públicas para bibliotecas públicas: Una propuesta de soluciones locales a problemas globales. Investigación Bibliotecológica, **2005**, *19*(39), http://www.ejournal.unam.mx/ibi/vol19-39/IBIO3902.pdf (accessed January 2015).

15. Guzmán, C. *Anuario estadístico cultural, 1990-2003: Las cifras del libro y las bibliotecas en Venezuela*; Fundación Polar: Caracas, Venezuela, 2004; 1–203.

16. ROARMAP. About the repository [Universidad de los Andes], 2009, http://roarmap.eprints.org/631/ (accessed January 2015).

17. Redalyc. Red de Revistas Científicas de América Latina y el Caribe, España y Portugal, 2014, http://www.redalyc.org/home.oa (accessed January 2015).

18. Instituto Nacional de Estadística. *Censo de población y vivienda 2001, cuadros estadísticos*; INE: Caracas, Venezuela, 2005; Vol. I, 1–489.

19. Mastromatteo, E. Una anécdota. Nihiloteca, *2010, http://nihiloteca.blogspot.com/2010_07_01_archive.html (accessed January 2015).*

20. Vicentelli, H. Formación del bibliotecario y archivólogo en Venezuela. Transinformação. **1989**, *1*(2), 187–94.

21. Mastromatteo, E. Bases, fundamentos y perfil profesional: Aporte para el cambio curricular de la EBA-UCV. Thesis (MSc), Universidad Central de Venezuela, Caracas, Venezuela, 2005; 1–182, http://eprints.rclis.org/7672/ (accessed January 2015).

22. Pirela, J. Desarrollo curricular de la Escuela de Bibliotecología y Archivología de la Universidad del Zulia. In *V Encuentro de Educadores e Investigadores de Bibliotecología, Archivología y Ciencia de la Información de Iberoamérica y el Caribe*, Maracaibo, Venezuela, 1998.

23. Pirela, J.; Portillo, L. La evaluación de planes de estudio en Bibliotecología, Archivología y Ciencia de la Información: Enfoques y metodologías. *Revista de Artes y Humanidades UNICA*. **2009**, *10*(3), 256–274.

24. Pirela, J.; Peña, T. La formación del profesional de la información en Venezuela: Una mirada comparativa desde sus diseños curriculares. *Educere*. **2006**, *10*(32), 131–138.

25. Pirela, J.; Portillo, L. Construyendo el perfil por competencias del profesional de la información a partir de un dialogo permanente con la sociedad. In *IV Encontro Ibérico EDIBCIC*, Coimbra, Portugal, November 18–20, 2009, http://eprints.rclis.org/23020/ (accessed January 2015).

26. Montilla, L.; Pérez, G. Ciencias de la Información: Formación, retos y nueva propuesta desde Venezuela. Biblios. **2012**, *46*, 33–9.

27. Ministerio de Educación, Cultura y Deportes. *Plan Nacional de Lectura (2002–2012): Todos por la lectura*; El Ministerio: Caracas, Venezuela, 2002; 6.

28. CENAL. *Estudio del Comportamiento Lector, Acceso al Libro y la Lectura en Venezuela*; Centro Nacional del Libro: Caracas, Venezuela, 2012; 1–118, http://www.distribuidoradellibro.gob.ve/ESTUDIO-CENAL-COMPORTAMIENTO-LECTOR.pdf (accessed January 2015).

29. Ministerio del Poder Popular para la Cultura. *Memorias y cuentas del Ministerio del Poder Popular para la Cultura*; El Ministerio: Caracas, Venezuela, 2013.

30. Agencia Venezolana de Noticias. Gobierno venezolano ha invertido $772 mil millones en área social, April, 2012, http://www.avn.info.ve/contenido/gobierno-bolivariano-ha-invertido-772-mil-millones-%C3%A1rea-social (accessed January 2015).

31. Petróleos de Venezuela. *Informe de Gestión Anual 2012*; PDVSA: Caracas, Venezuela, 2012; 1–174, http://www.pdvsa.com/interface.sp/database/fichero/free/8010/1625.PDF (accessed January 2015).

32. Yapur, N. Manejo discrecional de renta petrolera impide atender demanda de divisas. El Nacional, February 16, 2014, http://www.el-nacional.com/economia/divisas-alcanzan-manejo-renta-petrolera_0_355764629.html, (accessed January 2015).

33. Aponte, C. El gasto público social durante los períodos presidenciales de Hugo Chávez: 1999–2009. Cuadernos del CENDES. **2010**, *27*(73), 31–70, http://www.scielo.org.ve/pdf/cdc/v27n73/art03.pdf (accessed January 2015).

34. Ministerio del Poder Popular para la Cultura. *Memorias y cuentas del Ministerio del Poder Popular para la Cultura*; El Ministerio: Caracas, Venezuela, 2006; 2007; 2008; 2009; 2010; 2011; 2012; 2013.

35. Asamblea Nacional de la República Bolivariana de Venezuela. *Constitución Nacional de la República Bolivariana de Venezuela*, Gaceta Oficial Extraordinaria N° 5.453; Asamblea Nacional: Caracas, Venezuela, 1999; 1–45, https://www.oas.org/dil/esp/Constitucion_Venezuela.pdf (accessed June 2014).

36. CERLALC-UNESCO. El libro en cifras. *Boletín estadístico del libro en Iberoamérica*. **2012**, *1*(1), 1–16, http://cerlalc.org/wp-content/uploads/2013/03/LEC_I_Def.pdf (accessed January 2015).

Version Control

Jill E. Grogg
Libraries, University of Alabama, Tuscaloosa, Alabama, U.S.A.

Jeff Weddle
School of Library and Information Studies, University of Alabama, Tuscaloosa, Alabama, U.S.A.

Abstract

Broadly, version control is the attempt to define the relationships among multiple iterations of a scholarly text, particularly journal articles. Version control existed in the print world, but the electronic environment has exacerbated the matter due to a number of varied factors, including the ease with which digital scholarship can be distributed and adapted. Political and technological issues also affect the problem of version control. Because any given article may have a preprint, a postprint, a version in the official journal, and a version in an institutional repository, among other copies, some mechanism must exist to relate and explain the relationships among these manifestations. Several current initiatives are underway within the information industry to address the problem of version control.

INTRODUCTION

For library and information science, version control is the activity of identifying and managing iterations of a document for archival and retrieval purposes. While version control can be problematic for documents and information objects of all types and formats, it is especially so for scholarly communication—particularly journal articles—distributed in electronic formats.

In all the many unforeseen challenges that electronic publishing has unleashed for the information profession, there exist two principle elements: political and technical. Version control is no exception. Many stakeholders in the information industry are shaping the version control discussion, and these discussions have resulted in recommended solutions and directions.

In 2002, a research team headed by Raymond Siemens produced a report entitled "The Credibility of Electronic Publishing" for the Humanities and Social Sciences Federation of Canada (HSSFC). This report attempted to define and assess the current state of affairs for scholarly electronic publishing as well as provide some recommendations for future action.[1] One of the sections of the report, "Archiving and Text Fluidity/Version Control," specifically addresses the unique situation that electronic publishing presents for text alteration. In this section, members of the HSSFC-appointed research team note:

> Texts can be adapted, abstracted, translated, edited, condensed, corrected, marked up, transcribed, annotated, amended, paraphrased, transliterated, illustrated, indexed, or abridged. They can be commented upon or referenced by other texts. They can be analysed or synthesized. These modifications, and any others that might be considered, produce distinct versions, all related to the original text.[2]

Indeed, what is important to note is that any alteration(s) to an original text produces a distinct version. Therefore, versions of a text need to be uniquely identifiable while simultaneously containing information that describes the relationships among the various versions. Version control, then, is the effort to "name the versions of the text" and to specify "the differences between the revision and the original text."[2] Moreover, version control endeavors to define what is meant by the original and authoritative text.

In 2005, the U.S. Government Printing Office (GPO) prepared a white paper on version control of documents within the purview of the Federal Depository Library Program. The GPO was particularly concerned with electronically disseminated documents. Government Printing Office concerns fall into seven broad categories. These include version definition, or "unique manifestation of a publication"; version control, which includes "acquiring, cataloging, storing, preserving, and retrieving different versions of publications"; version triggers, which are changes that exceed agreed upon limits; version detection, which deals with identifying and detecting alternate versions; version identifiers, which are metadata tags; version crosswalks, which are a subset of version identifiers and provide links to all other versions; and depository library responsibilities for superseded versions. While it focuses on government documents, the GPO report is extensible in that it offers parameters that can be applied to any discussion of version control.[3]

In April 2008, the National Information Standards Organization (NISO), in partnership with the Association of Learned and Professional Society Publishers (ALPSP), released a report that defines specific stages or iterations of a journal article. Similar to the GPO's seven broad categories, the NISO/ALPSP Journal Article Versions (JAV) Technical Working Group identified seven terms, or stages, of an article's development. According to members of the JAV Technical Working Group, the report is meant to offer recommended practices for the scholarly publishing community. The report summarizes the issue:

> Researchers, their institutions, and journal publishers are rapidly moving on from using static, single copies of research papers that are essentially "images" of a printed document. Changes in the way we create, edit, circulate, validate, publish, find, use, and update articles are producing multiple versions whose status and provenance is often unclear. Online searching now allows multiple versions to be found but rarely makes clear the relationships between them.[4]

Specific recommendations of the group are discussed in subsequent sections.

SCOPE AND HISTORY

Standards, rules, local practices, terminology, and definitions evolved over many years to ensure version control of printed matter. Even so, it has always been problematic to ensure that a published text is in complete agreement with all other versions of that text. Pirated or plagiarized editions, misreadings of manuscripts, and other issues have long clouded issues of text authenticity and authority. With the emergence of electronic publications, these rules, practices, and so forth face much greater challenges. Contemporary efforts to address long-standing problems of unique manuscript identification are addressed by Matthew J. Driscoll in "The MASTER Project: Defining Standards for Electronic Manuscript Catalog Records." The international Manuscript Access through Standards for Electronic Records (MASTER) Project's "document type definition" (DTD) standards and application of the closely associated Text Encoding Initiative's (TEI) *Guidelines for Electronic Text Encoding and Interchange* are applied to archived medieval manuscripts. TEI guidelines allow for description along several broad and flexible categories, including its physical location; title, place of origin, and language(s); contents; physical description; history; and administrative issues such as availability and custodial history.[5]

The shift from printed manuscripts to electronic documents greatly accelerated the appearance of document iteration. This acceleration becomes problematic when coupled with the fact that gate-keeping functions traditionally associated with scholarly and commercial publishing diminish when authors, or any other person, can, in some cases, disregard copyright law and change a text at will, store it on a server, and disseminate it via whatever scheme he or she chooses. Copyright becomes a tangled Web when one considers that the author may no longer hold copyright to his or her own work if he or she has agreed to transfer copyright to the publisher for a limited or unlimited amount of time. Therefore, he or she may not possess the legal permission to post particular versions—especially the final "published" version—of his or her own work by self-archiving on a personal Web site or in an institutional repository.

Self-archiving is usually the process of an author maintaining a document copy in electronic format. This electronic document may be made available to the author or anyone else designated by the author. The clear benefit of self-archiving is easy access and information dissemination within the scholarly community. One potentially negative consequence is that variant versions of a particular document may circulate in this way. An institutional repository is "defined to be a Web-based database (repository) of scholarly material which is institutionally defined (as opposed to a subject-based repository)"[6]

Issues of copyright and permission to disseminate work are usually negotiated between the author and the publisher at the time of publication; many publishers have specific policies and guidelines regarding how an author may alter and/or disseminate versions of his or her work after publication. For instance, some publishers allow authors to retain copyright to their work but negotiate from the author the one-time rights, exclusive for a given amount of time (e.g., 90 days), to be the first publisher of the work, and the right to distribute the work exclusively for a given amount of time (e.g., 90 days) after publication. After this predetermined period (e.g., 90 days), the author may distribute, reprint, etc., as he or she pleases. On the other end of the spectrum, some publishers have much stricter and more limited agreements with authors wherein the author transfers copyright to the publisher in perpetuity.

Regardless of the copyright issues involved and the myriad possibilities for agreements between the publisher and the author, it remains that many different versions of any given article do and can exist. To focus on the journal article for purposes of explication, one journal article can exist in multiple electronic versions. In 2005, Sally Morris offered a partial list of possible versions of one journal article:

1. Privately circulated early draft (could be >1 iteration).
2. Version presented at public event (again, could be >1).
3. Pre-submission version(s).
4. Version as submitted to journal x (may differ when resubmitted to journal y).
5. Version amended after peer review (may go through >1 round of amendment).

6. Version as accepted by journal x.

7. Accepted version, with substantive editing by journal editor and/or publisher (again, may be multiple iterations).

8. Accepted version, with substantive editing and copyediting—ready for publication.

9. Publication version (as above, formatted and paginated)—proof.

10. Publication version corrected and passed for publication.

11. Published version, not on publisher's site (e.g., PDF), thus potentially lacking some functionality.

12. Published version (on publisher's site, with full functionality).

13. Post-publication version with errata/addenda (maybe on publisher's site, with functionality) or elsewhere without it.[7]

VERSION OF RECORD AND OPEN ACCESS

While it is beyond the scope of this entry to explore the complicated world of open access (OA), it is impossible to discuss version control without addressing some of the major features of OA. Broadly, OA is the movement to make scholarly literature "digital, online, free of charge, and free of most copyright and licensing restrictions."[8] Morris does not explicitly refer to any particular publishing models in her list; she does not overtly refer to OA or toll-based models because version control issues prevail in both worlds. Indeed, journal articles published in the more traditional toll-based scholarly literature, or journal articles published in OA journals can be versions of record.

The NISO/ALPSP JAV Technical Working Group defines version of record (VoR): "a fixed version of a journal article that has been made available by any organization that acts as a publisher by formally and exclusively declaring the article 'published.'"[4] Furthermore, the notes to the VoR definition explain:

> The VoR may exist in more than one location (e.g., a publisher's Web site, an aggregator site, and one or more repositories). That is, there may be more than one *copy* of a VoR but there is only one *version* of a VoR. In Functional Requirements for Bibliographic Records (FRBR) terms, there may be more than one *manifestation* or *instance* of a VoR, but there is only one *expression* of it.[4]

In other words, VoR transcends notions of multiple copies. Yet, the increasing prevalence OA archives and repositories have ultimately complicated the issue of version control for the scholarly community. The mere existence of such OA material (and other toll-based copies such as those that exist in aggregator databases) requires the reliance on FRBR differentiation between manifestation and expression.

Version control faces two distinct sets of challenges: political and technological. OA itself is an increasingly

political movement, especially in light of the Consolidated Appropriations Act, 2008, which includes a provision directing the National Institutes of Health (NIH) to require "scientists to submit final peer-reviewed journal manuscripts that arise from NIH funds to the digital archive PubMed Central upon acceptance for publication."[9] This Act was signed into law despite lobbying efforts of the Partnership for Research Integrity in Science and Medicine (http://www.prismcoalition.org), which is a coalition that has the support of the Professional and Scholarly Publishing Division of the Association of American Publishing.

In addition to the complexities that OA introduces, version control often resembles a Gordian knot because divergent groups have a vested interest in insuring that their voices are heard in any effort to create standardized solutions. Publishers, authors, researchers, vendors, aggregators, subscription agents, OA advocates, universities and other research centers, librarians, standards organizations—while there is some consensus of opinion among this variegated list, each group nonetheless represents a particular constituency with unique goals and interests. The JAV Technical Working Group's report lists the following stakeholders as important variables in identifying the dimensions of an article version: author, editor, referee, publisher, librarian, reader, and funder. Other dimensions articulated by the JAV Technical Working Group are time, added value, manifestation, and siblings.[4]

PEER REVIEW

In 2000, a working group of publishers acknowledged one outcome of the version control problem as changing the context within which peer-reviewed articles are perceived: "The peer-reviewed article will continue to play a crucial part in the certification, communication, and recording of scientific research. However, in the electronic environment it represents one point on a potential continuum of communication."[10] Peer review—in one form or another—has represented the bedrock of reputable scholarly output since at least the beginning of modern science in the seventeenth century, and any discussion of a potential change in its role in scholarly communication is significant.

The issue of peer review as it relates to OA and thus version control is a volatile one, with information industry stakeholders arguing many sides of this complicated issue. Some say that peer review in OA scholarly output is as rigorous and honest as it is within conventional toll-based publishing; others argue that peer review and thus quality of scholarship suffers in the face of OA. In her 2005 article, "Version Control of Journal Articles," Morris noted the emerging problem of definitive or authoritative versions of documents verses "good enough" versions and its implications for scholars. The problem, as described by Morris, is pernicious. As listed earlier, she identifies 13 basic variants, from privately circulated early drafts, through post-publication versions with errata and addenda and argues that a reader cannot easily discern differences between these versions.[11]

Steven Harnad addresses the worries of researchers, university administrators, and librarians in terms of version control and peer review. He notes that there is no need to be concerned about self-archiving because:

> There will be self-archived preprints, revised drafts, final accepted, published drafts (postprints), updated, corrected post-postprints, peer comments, author replies, revised second editions. OAI-compliant Eprint Archives will tag each version with a unique identifier. All versions will be retrieved by a cross-archive OAI search, and the 'hits' can then be identified and compared by the user to select the most recent, official or definitive draft, exactly as if they had all been found in the same index catalog.[12]

OAI is the Open Archives Initiative, and it "develops and promotes interoperability standards that aim to facilitate the efficient dissemination of content."[13]

APPROPRIATE COPY AND OpenURL

In addition to the implications for readers, Morris observed that version control is of great concern to libraries, which are faced with the multifaceted problems of tight budgets; appropriate copies based upon institutional affiliation; multiple, free online versions; and versions which are either self-archived or archived by independent institutions or other repositories. In response to some of these issues, libraries point users to their appropriate copy via link resolvers and the OpenURL framework. It is important to distinguish between the version control and the appropriate copy problem. The appropriate copy problem has two equal dimensions: 1) the multiple availability of any given resource from a variety of sources and 2) the subsequent challenge of pointing the reader to the copy of this resource appropriate for him or her, usually by virtue of his or her institutional affiliations.

If restricted to the toll-based universe, a given journal article might be available from the publisher or from a number of secondary aggregators (e.g., EBSCO, ProQuest, Gale). A researcher at a university may have access to only some of these article copies, and the library or information center wants to insure that the researcher reaches those copies which are appropriate for him or her. If expanded to include the OA universe of materials, the phrase "appropriate copy" then comes to "denote the copy of a resource to which a user has rightful access, usually by virtue of his or her institutional affiliations but perhaps also by virtue of an information object being *open access*."[14]

The OpenURL framework was developed to address the appropriate copy problem, and it is now a NISO

standard, Z39.88, OpenURL v. 1.0. Via link resolvers, the OpenURL framework is widely used to point users to their appropriate copies. The appropriate copy problem and its solution in OpenURL/link resolvers primarily address a problem of access; version control, on the other hand encompasses issues of authority and management as well as defining the stages in the life cycle of an article. OpenURL also primarily focuses on pointing users to versions of record, which, again, can be in multiple locations. The other versions of an article—such as more ephemeral ones kept in an author's institutional repository, for example—are currently outside the technical capability of the OpenURL/link resolvers. With version control, many technological hurdles remain, including: a standardized schema to identify the VoR or authoritative version as well as an extensible model to identify and explain the relationships among the different iterations of a document.

TECHNOLOGICAL INITIATIVES

One such effort to clearly articulate the different stages in the life of an article as well as the relationships among those stages was released in an April 2008 report by a joint partnership between NISO and ALPSP, the JAV Technical Working Group. Perhaps the most definitive work to date on the issue of version control, the recommended practices released by the JAV Technical Working Group attempts to "provide a simple, practical way of describing the versions of scholarly journal articles that typically appear online before, during and after formal journal publication."[4] The working group builds upon earlier, previously mentioned efforts.

In September 2005, NISO and ALPSP charged the group with creating a plan that included:

1. Creation of use cases to identify the most common journal article life cycles.
2. Analysis of use cases to determine common life cycle stages.
3. Selection of preferred vocabulary for the most common life cycle stages.
4. Development of appropriate metadata to identify each variant version and its relationship to other versions, in particular the definitive, fully functional published version.
5. Establishment of practical systems for ensuring that the metadata is applied by authors or repository managers and publishers.[15]

Cliff Morgan, Vice President, Planning and Development and Director, John Wiley & Sons, Ltd., was the chair of the joint NISO/ALPSP working group. In an August 2007 interview, Morgan noted: "In the digital world, multiple versions of journal articles are often available online. This can cause confusion because there is no way of identifying the various versions by either a common terminology or identification scheme." Morgan went on to explain that the working group "will recommend terms and definitions for journal article versions and define the relationships between these versions. We're focusing on key stages rather than every possible iteration of an article from origination to publication."[16]

Critical to the working group's efforts is the notion that the group focuses on "key stages" of the version continuum rather than "every possible iteration." The group considered a variety of attributes in order to describe different versions: "Ownership, bibliographic context, identifiers [e.g., digital object identifier (DOI)], relationships, fixity, and peer review are explicitly stated in the terms and definitions that we recommend. They can be described by the article version names and some are already covered by standard metadata elements (e.g., bibliographic reference, date, and DOI)."[4] Of particular note is the attention paid to the version of record. Morgan elucidated the importance of this stage:

> The VoR constitutes the 'minutes of science'—the formally certified record of a research project. It is this version that has been peer-reviewed, edited, composed, and verified by the author; it is this version that benefits from publisher investment in managing the above process, building the journal brand, and adding functionality such as linking and e-alerts, and for which the publisher takes legal responsibility. This is also the version that is most likely to be cited by other researchers.[16]

If the VoR is easily identifiable, then the problem of researchers questioning which version is the final, authoritative one is solved.

The seven stages identified by the working group are:

1. Author's Original.
2. Submitted Manuscript Under Review.
3. Accepted Manuscript.
4. Proof.
5. Version of Record.
6. Corrected Version of Record.
7. Enhanced Version of Record.

Each stage is accompanied by a full definition and note. Also included in the report are graphical representations of the relationships among formal and gray literature as well as a number of "use cases" to provide a clearer picture of how the recommended terms would apply in real-world situations.

What remains to be seen is to what extent the recommendations in the report will be implemented by publishers and other stakeholders in the information industry. Version control is still very much an issue in flux, and thus it presents interested parties with a moving target. Some publishers have already created and maintained internal practices for version control that may or may not be consistent with the group's recommended practices. If a publisher has invested significant capital in creating and maintaining an internal schema, then only time will tell if the said publisher will implement the NISO/ALPSP recommendations. Additionally, while the report explains some relationships among formal and gray literature, the group primarily concerned itself with a fairly narrow scope: journal articles. The continued evolution of the formally published journal article itself presents problems. If the electronic version with an assigned DOI is the version of record, then it begs the question about the necessity of assigning volume, issue, and page numbers for a journal article version of record. Questions of version control for other formal literature—book chapters, proceedings, etc.—remain. Moreover, an ocean of gray literature exists. With the advent of electronic publishing, gray literature and other informal publishing enjoy unprecedented accessibility. Such accessibility arguably leads to formerly "hidden" scholarship now occupying a more prominent place in our intellectual space and community of scholarship. Ultimately, many questions remain and while the group's work is essential, it is only one step toward an unknown future.

Version control is an international issue and as such, there are multiple initiatives underway to address its unique challenges. Two other programs created to study version control are the United Kingdom-based Joint Information Systems Committee Validating Repository Content project (VALREC, http://www.jisc.ac.uk/whatwedo/programmes/programme_rep_pres/tools/valrec.aspx and http://valrec.eprints.org/) and the London School of Economics VERSIONS Project (http://www.lse.ac.uk/library/versions/).

CONCLUSION

Version control remains a thorny issue with many technological and political barriers. The very nature of electronic information allows for an ease of replication and adaptation heretofore unheard of in scholarly communication. However, information industry stakeholders have recognized the issue and have formed a variety of international projects to study and recommend standardized solutions for identifying and managing iterations of a document for archival and retrieval purposes.

REFERENCES

1. Siemens, R.; Best, M.; Burk, A.; Grove-White, E.; Gue'don, J.-C.; Kerr, J.; Pope, A.; Rockwell, G.; Siemens, L. The Credibility of Electronic Publishing: A Report to the Humanities and Social Sciences Federation of Canada.

2002, http://web.mala.bc.ca/hssfc/Final/Credibility.htm (accessed December 2007).

2. Burk, A.; Kerr, J.; Pope, A. Section 4: Archiving and text fluidity/version control. In The Credibility of Electronic Publishing: A Report to the Humanities and Social Sciences Federation of Canada. 2002, http://web.mala.bc.ca/hssfc/Final/Archiving.htm (accessed December 2007).

3. United States Government Printing Office. Office of Information Dissemination, Program Development Service; Version control: Draft. 2005, http://www.access.gpo.gov/su_docs/fdlp/pubs/proceedings/05spring/cdqa/version_control_white_paper.pdf (accessed December 2007).

4. National Information Standards Organization/Association of Learned and Professional Society Publishers, Journal Article Versions Technical Working Group. Journal Article Versions (JAV): Recommendations of te NISO/ALPSP JAV Technical Working Group. April 2008. http://www.niso.org/publications/rp/RP-8—2008.pdf (accessed November 2008).

5. Driscoll, M.J. The MASTER project: Defining standards for electronic manuscript catalogue records. In Care and Conservation of Manuscripts 6, Proceedings of the Sixth International Seminar, Royal Library, Copenhagen, Denmark, October 19–20, 2000; Fellows-Jensen, G.; Springborg, P., Eds.; Museum Tusculanum Press: Copenhagen, Denmark, 2002, http://books.google.com/books?hl = en&id = iz17G5pKB1AC&dq = care + and + conservation + of + manuscripts + 6&printsec = frontcover&source = web&ots = G8zvpZ8zW0&sig = oI8B6q7UHIYC0p45QkN1FYU4C7w#PPP1,M1 (accessed December 2007).

6. Bailey, C.W., Jr. Institutional repositories, Tout de suite; 2008, http://www.digital-scholarship.org/ts/irtoutsuite.pdf (accessed January 2008).

7. Grogg, J.E. Linking users to open access. Searcher **2005**, *13* (4), 52–56.

8. Suber, P. Open access overview; 2007. http://www.earlham.edu/~peters/fos/overview.htm (accessed January 2008).

9. U.S. Department of Health and Human Services. National Institutes of Health Public Access. http://publicaccess.nih.gov/ (accessed November 2008).

10. Antelman, K. Self-archiving practice and the influence of publisher policies in the social sciences. Learn. Publ. **2006**, *19* (2), 85–95.

11. Morris, S. Version control of journal articles; 2005. http://www.niso.org/workrooms/jav/Morris.pdf (accessed November 2008).

12. Harnad, S. Open Access to peer-reviewed research through author/institution self-archiving. In *Digital Libraries*; Andrews, J., Law, D., Eds.; Ashgate: Hants, U.K., 2004; 63–98.

13. Open archives initiative. http://www.openarchives.org/ (accessed January 2008).

14. Grogg, J.E. Introduction linking and the OpenURL. Libr. Technol. Rep. **2006**, *42* (1), 5–7.

15. National Information Standards Organization. NISO/ALPSP Working Group on Versions of Journal Articles. http://www.niso.org/workrooms/jav (accessed November 2008).

16. Library Connect, Editorial Office. Five quick questions with Cliff Morgan. Elsevier Libr. Connect Newsl. **2007**, *5* (3), 9. http://libraryconnect.elsevier.com/lcn/0503/lcn0503.pdf (accessed January 2008).

Vietnam: Libraries, Archives, and Museums

Robert D. Stueart
Graduate School of Library and Information Science, Simmons College, Boston, Massachusetts, U.S.A.

Abstract

Vietnam has a long and illustrious history of information services development - from the introduction of printing in the 14th Century, through the French influence in the 19th Century when many valuable collections and guidelines for libraries were developed, to the modern advances information services development, with some state-of-the-art information centers and services. The richness of the culture and the development of the society is reflected in the valuable collections and services currently offered in it's libraries, information centers, museums and archives.

SOCIALIST REPUBLIC OF VIETNAM (CONG HOA XA HOI CHU NGHIA VIETNAM)

VIETNAM

Vietnam, a 1500 km narrow stretch of land, is located in Southeast Asia, bordered by the Gulf of Tonkin and the South China Sea to the east, China to the north, Laos and Cambodia to the west, and the Gulf of Thailand to the south (see Fig. 1). Diacritical Vietnamese language marks have not been used in this entry, to simplify printing.

History

The modern-day history of Vietnam dates back to the tenth century—during the time that the Ngo (939–965), Dinh (968–80), and Pre-Le (980–1009) dynasties began to consolidate and defend an independent country. Previous to that Vietnam had been conquered by China in 207 B.C. and dominated by Han until the 111 B.C. In the fifteenth century, China made its final attempt to dominate Vietnam but was defeated.

Commencing in the mid-nineteenth century, the country came under the dominance of France when Indochina, consisting of Vietnam, Cambodia, and Laos, was established under a French decree of 1857. Vietnam declared independence from Japan and France on September 2, 1945. However, it remained under French control until the communist Viet Minh defeated French forces at Dien Bien Phu on May 5, 1954.

The Vietnamese trace the origins of their culture and nation to the fertile plains of the Red River Delta in northern Vietnam. After centuries of developing a civilization and economy based on the cultivation of irrigated rice, the Vietnamese, in the tenth century, began expanding southward in search of new rice lands. Until the mid-nineteenth century, the Vietnamese gradually moved down the narrow coastal plain of the Indochina Peninsula, ultimately extending their reach into the broad Mekong River Delta.

The conquest of Vietnam by France began in 1858 and was completed by 1884. It became part of French Indochina in 1887. Vietnam declared independence after World War II, but France continued to rule until its 1954 defeat by Communist forces under Ho Chi Minh. Under the Geneva Accords of 1954, Vietnam was temporarily divided at the 17th parallel when North Vietnam was reconstructed as the Democratic Republic of Vietnam. South Vietnam struggled another 20 years for independence against U.S. forces and Saigon's government until the Paris Agreements of 1973 when U.S. troops withdrew. In 1975, Ho Chi Minh and his forces overthrew the Saigon Government and unified the country as the Socialist Republic of Vietnam, with Hanoi being declared the capitol. As of 2005, a three-person collective leadership has been responsible for governing Vietnam. This triumvirate consists of the Vietnam Communist Party, VCP General Secretary, the Prime Minister and the President.

Vietnam's history is a story of struggle to develop a sense of nationhood and to maintain that against internal and external pressures.

Population

Vietnam's population is over 84 million, and is growing at a rate of about 1.2% each year.[1] Recent estimates put Vietnam's age distribution as follows: 0–14 years of age, 29.4%; 15– 64, 65%; and 65 and older, 5.6%.

Vietnamese, or "Viets," also known as Kinhs, are the predominant ethnic group, constituting about 86% of the population. Chinese account for 3% of the population, while the remaining numbers are of other ethnic backgrounds—estimated at around 54 groups—the largest being the Hmong, Thai, Khmer, Cham, and Montagnards.

Fig. 1 Map of Vietnam.
Source: CIA *The World Factbook.*

Most of these indigenous live in the Central Highlands and extreme northern Vietnam.

Vietnamese is the official language of Vietnam, with English increasing in popularity as a second language. French remains a language of record for many historical documents, and some Russian documents are of note. With 7.6 million followers, Buddhism is the most popular religion. The second most popular religion is Roman Catholicism, with 6 million adherents.

Vietnam's literacy rate is about 94%, including 95.8% for men and 92.3% for women. Educational attainment is less impressive. Although, 5 years of primary school education is compulsory, and about 92% of eligible children are enrolled in primary school, only about two-thirds of them complete the fifth grade.

Economy

Although Vietnam's economy, which continues to expand at an annual rate in excess of 7%, is one of the fastest growing in the world, that economy is growing from a low base. It still reflects the crippling effect of the Second Indochina War (1954–1975) and the repressive economic measures introduced in its aftermath.[2]

LIBRARIES

Libraries and information centers in Vietnam can be categorized in two groups: 1) a network of scientific libraries (National System of Scientific and Technological Information—NSSTI) and 2) a network of public libraries, including central, city and provincial, district and children's libraries.

History

The introduction of printing, using wooden blocks and boards, has been dated sometime after the fourteenth century. However, manuscripts, dating before that time, formed the first collections of "library" materials. Much of the collections developed before the time of the Nguyen dynasties in Hue (1802–1945) have been lost or destroyed due to civil wars and invasions and only about a fourth of the Nguyen collections survived the wars of the twentieth century.[3] Many of those surviving Han-Nom writings (combining the classical Chinese characters of Han with Nom, the Vietnamese language style) are now located in the Vietnam Academy of Social Sciences—Institute of Han-Nom Studies in Hanoi which has a large number of ancient texts on Confucianism in VietNam.[4] During the second part of the nineteenth century, French colonization of Vietnam brought the development of a number of libraries, including libraries of the Société des Etudes Indochinoises and the École Française d'Extrême Orient (EFEO). Most of those early collections belonged to learned societies or the government under French direction.

In 1917 a Frenchman, Paul Bourdet, arrived in Vietnam and immediately introduced the idea of development of a Direction des Archives et des Bibliothèques de l'Indochine[5] in order to:

* Establish a central library and archive in Hanoi, with branches in Saigon, Hue, and Hai Phong (this latter one

never materialized), as well as Phnom Penh in Cambodia and Vientiane in Laos

• Develop and institute legal deposit laws
• Initiate cooperative assistance to other libraries and archives in existence[6]

The library in Saigon became the Bibliothèque Central Cochinchine and adopted the role of that earlier Library and Archives (BCC). In 1919, the Bibliothèque Centrale Hanoi (BCH) was created with legal depository rights for all of Indochina.

In the first half of the twentieth century, several major collections were developed in libraries, particularly in Hanoi and Saigon. However, in 1945, with the commencement of military conflicts with Japan many resources were damaged and some were moved to France in the early 1950s. With internal conflict came a move to relocate some resources, including books, journals and archives, from the Bibliothèque Central Hanoi (BCH) in Hanoi to Saigon. In 1959, the Directorate of National Archives and Libraries (DNAL) was established in South Vietnam with the aim of creating a national library with resources from the old BCC and those materials brought south, while some were removed to France. The resources of this new unit became what was called the General Library [now the General Science Library, the major public library—other than the National Library of Vietnam (NLV)] which was named the National Library of South Vietnam in 1971 when a new library building was opened. Three years later the DNAL was disbanded. The library holdings are a part of the General Science library in Ho Chi Minh City. Earlier, in the 1960s, public libraries began to establish a network of town and district public libraries.

Years of turmoil in the country have taken a toll on the development of information services, and many segments of the system of information services are attempting rapid recovery. This recovery is being aided by a number of international organizations working with various information services institutions. Those international efforts include UNESCO, International Federation of Library Associations and Institutions (IFLA), and other who have contributed substantially by advising and encouraging an efficient library and information services infrastructure in Vietnam. Vietnamese librarians are becoming more involved in international professional activities, including those of IFLA, the Congress of Southeast Asian Libraries, UNESCO, and other. In addition, philanthropic organizations have supported both the development of libraries and the education of librarians, primarily Atlantic Philanthropies which has contributed in the form of financing the development of state-of-the-art Learning Resource Centers (LRCs) in major universities in the country (Can Tho, Da Nang, Hue, and Thai Nguyen). They, along with Harvard Yenching Foundation, and others have supported the graduate education of over 50 master's degree students at Simmons College in Boston, United States of America—under the educational direction of Dr. Patricia Oyler—and of other programs at the University of New Zealand in Wellington. Many of those graduated librarians are now in leadership positions in academic libraries and information center throughout the country. Dr. Oyler has been recognized by the Vietnamese government, as has Mr. Michael Robinson, formerly of Atlantic Philanthropies, as international colleagues who have made significant contributions to library and information services in the country. Librarians have also received archival and librarianship training in several other countries—Australia, Japan, Great Britain, and France among them. UNESCO has been supportive of many preservation efforts in the library community.

Several library organizations are involved in digitization projects, including: the National Library (digitization of abstracts of thesis), National Center for Scientific and Technological Information (NACESTI) (digitization of technical reports); Han-Nom Institute (digitization of paper rubbings of Han Nom steles); Vietnam National University (VNU) (digitization of course packs for students), Natural Sciences Library, Ho Chi Minh City (sponsored translation of Greenstone software into Vietnamese); and General Sciences Library (GSL) (digitization of SaiGon-HCMC Collection).

Today, all libraries and information centers in Vietnam operate under the Ordinance on Libraries, the highest legislation on library and information services passed in 2001 by the National Assembly of Vietnam with the intent to develop library resources and to increase state management efficiency in library activities. Another piece of legislation affecting information services, augmenting the 2001 ordinance, was passed by the Vietnamese National Assembly on November 20, 2005. That law relates to intellectual property for noncommercial purposes—including cultural exchanges or propaganda—indicating the fact that permission need not be obtained from creators/owners or royalties paid. This enhanced information services provided by nonprofit libraries and information centers. It addresses rights and responsibilities of organizations and individuals in library activities; library organization and operation; library investment and development; state management on library development; reward and handling violation in library activities; and implementation provisions.

Libraries are organized by category and/or type and are the responsibility of four different government ministries. Academic libraries and school libraries are discussed under one topic, since they are both under the supervision of the Ministry of Education.

The four categories are: public, academic, school and special

Public Libraries

The current public libraries system was set up in 1954, after the Indochina War. The system includes not only the National Library, but also provincial libraries located in capitals of the provinces, district libraries located in capitals of the districts, and village libraries. The public library system supports many literacy efforts through the development of programs—children's art exhibits, book exhibitions, reading classes, story-telling, lectures on important topics, and mobile services to remote areas of the country.

The Public Library System, administratively under the Ministry of Culture and Information, now the Ministry of Culture, Sports, and Tourism, is organized at four levels, correlating to levels of government. They include:

- NLV
- 64 provincial libraries of the 64 province administrative units
- 589 district libraries within the 633 district administrative units
- 8677 ward and commune libraries, including Reading Rooms for Children and Village libraries or book cabinets[7]

The NLV

The primary public library unit in the country is the NLV.[8] The impetus for a National Library, as indicated above, was establishment, by the General Governors of Indochina on November 29, 1917, of the Central Library, located in Saigon. The National Library in Hanoi was named NLV by the Provisional Revolutionary Government of the Democratic Republic of Vietnam on October 22, 1945. However, it was not until the 1960s that Vietnam began further development of the central collections of the NLV in Hanoi. The Library has the statute at the Department level within the Ministry of Culture and Information, now renamed the Ministry of Culture, Sports, and Tourism. The NLV is now organized and operated in accordance with the Government's Resolution No. 401/Ttg dated September 9, 1976 on the Library's Functions, Targets, and Missions. This Ordinance was amended by the National Assembly in 2001. Its adoption of the intellectual property law went into effect on July 1, 2006. A new library building was completed in 2001, adding to the infrastructure of the Library.

The National Library serves as the primary depository of the nation's recorded history. Its charges include:

- Compiling and publishing the national bibliographies of Vietnam
- Developing and preserving a national Vietnamese collection by deposit of domestic publications, doctoral thesis, and patents
- Collecting relevant foreign materials of different forms, on Vietnam and works of Vietnamese living abroad, as well as manuscripts of famous Vietnamese writers through purchase and exchange
- Organizing materials and developing an information reference system to serve readers as the nation's information centre for culture and arts

- Publishing monthly and annually national bibliographies of Vietnam
- Maintaining an awareness of new developments in order to provide professional guidance to the public library community nationwide
- Providing professional guidance to all library systems nationwide; especially the public library system through the establishment and administration of the Local Area Networks and the Wide Area Networks (WANs) of the public library system, and carry out R & D projects on library and information sciences
- Coordinating library activities such as acquisition on foreign periodicals and books, union catalogs, and carry out interlibrary loan[9]

In 2005, NLV completed the national project "Building the National Electronic/Digital Library in the NLV" which was begun in 2001 and most major public and academic libraries and information centers have now joined that Integrated Library System.

The *National Bibliography of Vietnam* has been a production of the Library since 1955 and compiled monthly and annually. Since 1997, the NLV has been developing and maintaining a WAN system for public libraries in accordance with Resolution No. 579 by Ministry of Culture and Information. It has adopted and adapted MARC21 for its own use and that of the public library system. In 2006, under contract with OCLC (Online Computer Library Center), the NLV began, and has now completed, translating the Dewey Decimal Classification, Abridged Edition 14 into Vietnamese for use by libraries in the country. It provides some computers with peripheral equipment and photocopy machines for each provincial library. The National Library is also supporting an international effort to develop the Vietnam Union Catalog in an effort to create an international union list of Vietnamese *quoc ngu* titles held in Vietnam's major libraries.

The National Library maintains several databases, including:

- The book (SACH) database, which contains records of books in Vietnamese and Latin languages from 1950 to the present time, as well as some books in Cyrillic, Chinese, and Japanese script.
- The serial publications database (JM) which includes records of serial publications, acquired by NLV since its establishment to the present. This database contains newspapers and magazines in Vietnamese and foreign language, including serial publications in Cyrillic characters.
- The thesis database (LA) which contains records of over 5500 doctoral dissertations by Vietnamese citizens in Vietnam and abroad. This database contains half of the total number of thesis stored in the NLV.
- The newspaper and periodicals of Indochina database (NCUU) which includes about 1700 titles.

GSL

The GSL in Ho Chi Minh City, formerly Saigon, is the other major public library in Vietnam and is the geneses of the original national library established by France in the nineteenth century. The term "general sciences" is a misnomer in the library's title, since the library serves the primary role of an open public library with extensive services to the general public, to schools and to other public libraries in the area. In addition, it is an important preservation center, including archives and preservation facilities. Founded over one hundred years ago as the Library of the Admirals and Governors, the library was later recognized as the National Library of South Vietnam. It now possesses over 1.5 million books.

In the international arena, the library acts as a deposit library for UNESCO, World Bank, the Food and Agricultural Organization and the International Atomic Energy Agency. It is responsible for collecting and maintaining materials of all kinds published inside and outside the country. The library, under the former dynamic leadership of Ms. Nguyen Thi Bac, now reaches over 150,000 users yearly. Ms. Bac, a Simmons graduate of 1994, took early retirement in 2008, to work with several Scandinavian NGOs and is now country director for the Right to Read Foundation.

In addition, the library supervises 24 district libraries in the city and provides professional support to 21 provincial libraries. With Ho Chi Minh City being the country's center of business and commerce, no other public library in the country has as much activity, including an extensive exchange program with international agencies, overseas acquisitions, and constant use of the collection by scholars from abroad. It publishes the journal *Library Information Bulletin of South Vietnam*.

General Sciences Library has a unique and extensive collection of Vietnamese materials from 1954 to 1975 and the Library is working with theNLV, the legal depository, to include those holdings in the database of Vietnamese publications. Notable special collections of over 400,000 volumes include seventeenth and eighteenth century French/European and Indochinois materials. Notable services include model programs for the visually impaired, titled "Library for the Blind" project, and a state-of-the-art digitizing and microfilming services, as well as archives and preservation center.

Other Public Libraries

Other large libraries include those in Hanoi and Hue. In recent years, more than 1500 new public libraries have been created—as Cultural Village Bookcases, Pagoda Libraries, Bookcases of Commune Cultural Post Offices, etc. More than 150 mobile libraries have been developed within the last few years, as well as such activities as Libraries on Boats, Book Bags for Border Guards, Bookcases in Communes, Cultural Post Offices, etc. This is in support of promoting culture and information in remote and rural regions.

Academic Libraries

The administration of both university and general educational/school libraries is under the jurisdiction of the Ministry of Education and Training. There are 45 academic libraries in Vietnam under the Ministry of Education and Training. In addition, there are a number of international universities, such as the RMIT (Royal Melbourne Institute of Technology) National University Vietnam, located in Ho Chi Minh City, whose libraries are under the regulations of those international governments or organizations.

All academic libraries are administratively under the Ministry of Education and Training. Several digital library projects are in the planning stages or being implemented, including the e-Book project at the VNU, Hanoi, Library and the use of the Greenstone Digital Library open source software at the VNU, Ho Chi Minh City University of Natural Sciences Library. Integrated library management systems have been or are being implemented in many of the academic libraries.

There are two academic library associations: NALA— The Northern Academic Library Association of Universities and Colleges (Hanoi) and FESAL—The Federation of Southern Academic Libraries (Ho Chi Minh City).

On February 12th, 2001, Decision No. 15/2001/QĐ-TTg reorganized the two national universities in the country: they are each amalgamations of 10 previously existing higher education institutions. Libraries within those amalgamated universities are:

VNU Hanoi Library and Information Center

Vietnam National University now provides information services for all colleges and member units within its system. The university, itself, has had several name changes over the years: the University of Indochina (established in 1906); VNU (Dai hoc Dong Duong, established November 1945); the University of Hanoi (Dai hoc Tong hop Ha Noi, June 1956). This University's unified Library and Information Center was established in 1997 on the basis of amalgamating the libraries of the University of Hanoi (previously named the College of Social Science and Humanities), the College of Natural Science, and the former Hanoi Foreign Language Teachers' Training College, currently named the College of Foreign Languages.

VNU Ho Chi Minh City Central Library

Vietnam National University Ho Chi Minh City was founded in 1995 by a government decree 16/CP and now consists of five universities and one faculty. The library system of the VNU Ho Chi Minh City consists of the Central University and one library in each of the universities which make-up the system.

Other Academic Libraries in Vietnam

Several universities have been provided with new library buildings called LRCs have been provided with new library buildings, with a substantial information infrastructure, including technology and access to on-line resources, through grants from Atlantic Foundation. Those LRCs are located in: Can Tho University, Da Nang University, Hue University, and Thai Nguyen University. These projects of developing state of the art academic resource centers have been implemented through contracts with RMIT in Australia, and the professional staffs have been educated with master's degrees in library and information science, primarily through contracts with Simmons College in Boston, Massachusetts, United States of America.

School Libraries

Some 17,000 school libraries about half of the secondary schools have libraries, with an equal number in elementary schools. Organizations, such as Room to Read, are working with local area residents to create school libraries in villages. Over 160 such libraries have been created in Vietnam.[10]

Scientific, Technological and Other Special Libraries and Information Systems

Most special scientific and technical libraries are under the Ministry of Science, Technology, and Environment. There are approximately 60 research libraries run by research institutes and 218 other special libraries. Other special information centers are under various ministries or other governmental agencies.

National Agency for Science and Technology Information of Vietnam

According to the Government Degree number 28/2008/ND-CP, dated March 14, 2008, on the functions, responsibilities, authorities, and organizational structure of the Ministry of Science and Technology in Vietnam, what was formerly known as NACESTI has been changed to the National Agency for Science and Technology Information of Vietnam, NASTIV, with added responsibilities. The organization was originally established in accordance with the Decision No. 497/TCCB dated September, the 24th, 1990 by the Chairman of the State Committee for Science on the basis of merging two former organizations: the Central Library on Science and Technology (Founded in 1960) and the Central Institute for Scientific and

Technical Information (founded in 1972). Under Dr. Ta Ba Hung's leadership NASTIV is the primary force in the development of scientific and technological information services in the country. One activity of particular importance for information services is that both MARC21-VN and AACR2 were translated by NASTIV Added responsibilities, under the new designation, include:

- Management of Science and Technology Information Network in Vietnam
- Management and implementation statistical data on Science and Technology
- Management and operation of Vietnam Research and Education Network (VinaREN)

Its primary role is to manage and coordinate scientific and technological library activities in the whole country and formulate national S & T information and Documentation Policy. National Agency for Science and Technology Information of Vietnam serves as the leading center of the national information system on scientific and technological information and documentation and has responsibility for managing overall scientific, technological, and environmental information and documentation activities in Vietnam. It, therefore, has a twofold mission: management of S & T information activity and serving as the national information center for science and technology[11] by providing traditional and electronic library services to readers.

Since 2001, NASTIVs Library has subscribed to hundreds of online e-journals in the applied sciences, business, and management. In order to facilitate information sources sharing, NASTIV established VISTA (Vietnam Information for Science and Technology Advance)[12] in 1997. This is a nationwide information network that is playing an important role in resource sharing and meeting the information requirements of scholars and the SME community in Vietnam. Through VISTA various types of information, collected, or produced by NASTIV, are distributed to those who can access the Internet. Through VISTA, all 61 provinces are interconnected for sharing information on science and technology by leased lines or by dial-up through the public telephone lines.

National Agency for Science and Technology Information of Vietnam has been a leader in digital library development as a major trend in library and information services development in Vietnam. This is an approach strongly supported by both high-ranking policy-makers and library communities. In 2007, it hosted—along with the NLV, General Science Library of Ho Chi Minh City (GSL), the Library & Information Center of the VNU Hanoi (LIC/VNUH), Hanoi University of Technology, Vietnam Association on Scientific and Technological Information & Documentation (VASTID), Vietnam Library Association (VLA), Vietnam Association for Information Processing—the 10th International Conference on Asian Digital Libraries with the theme "Asian Digital libraries."

In order to meet the urgent needs of Internet users for digital information in the Vietnamese language and in English, NASTIV publishes a number of electronics bulletins and e-journals that are accessible over the Internet. National Agency for Science and Technology Information of Vietnam's major databases include: the Central Library for Science & Technology Catalog, a multidisciplinary database that reflects a rich Vietnam collection of monographs on science and technology; SCITEC, a foreign multidisciplinary scientific and technological documents database covering journal articles and conference proceedings; KQNC, a domestic R & D projects reports database that reflects completed R & D projects financed by the government budget; STD, a comprehensive multidisciplinary database on science and technology that covers domestic periodicals' articles, conference proceedings; and VNDOC, the Vietnam Science and Technology Abstracts (in English); as well as a. Foreign Periodicals Union Catalogue Database, covering the holding information on about 6000 foreign periodicals titles available in about 40 leading information centers and libraries in the country.

The National Center for Social Science and Humanities Library

The National Center for Social Sciences and Humanities of Vietnam, was originally set up in 1975 with the mandate to develop and maintain a collection of research materials. In 2004, it was renamed the Vietnamese Academy of Social Sciences (VASS). Within VASS there are roughly twenty seven institutes and centers. This main library is located at the Institute of Social Science Information. Each institute, likewise, has its own library. Today that library has the largest collection in. the country of social sciences and humanities materials. It preserves many valuable documents, including ancient books, handwritten documents, very precious photographic materials, etc. It is a leader in library and information activities of the social sciences and humanities. The Center itself serves 16 institutes, seven research centers, a museum of ethnology, and various research support offices.

The Central Institute for Medical Information and Libraries

The Ministry of Health Library was set up in 1979 on the foundations of the former Central Medical Library. The Institute's library is the leading medical-pharmaceutical information institution in Vietnam responsible for using information technologies in providing medical library and information services; providing the health and medical information; training and guiding the library and information in the medical library and information system throughout the country. It is also the national focal point

for international relationships in the medical library and information area.

The Military Library System

Section 4 of Article 19 of the government's Ordinance on Libraries[13] states that "Libraries of the people's armed force units" are established to serve the demands of officers and men with such units, and may serve other subjects according to such libraries' regulations. The system of military libraries is under the Ministry of Defense and includes some 1500 libraries and mobile unit libraries. Of them there are 54 main libraries, each with a collection of from 200,000 to 300,000 volumes.

LIBRARY AND INFORMATION SCIENCE EDUCATION AND TRAINING

Education and training of information and library services staff is promulgated at several levels:

- Certificate of Library Technician, awarded to those who have completed secondary vocational school.
- Bachelor of Library Science, Bachelor of Information, Library and Computer Science: for undergraduates who have successfully completed university. A diploma for "Scientific and Technological Information Engineers" is under consideration.
- Master of Library Science awarded to graduates who have completed the post-graduate requirements.

Master of Library and Information Science programs are offered at some universities. Most universities or colleges now offer the bachelor's degree, the basic educational degree for librarians in Vietnam. Some offer diplomas. Five higher education institutions offering library and information science programs are:

VNU Hanoi, University of Social Sciences and Humanities

Faculty of Library and Information Science

The newly designated faculty was established in 2004. However, the program continues a tradition of education and scientific research first developed by the Department of Library Science which belonged to the Faculty of History—Hanoi University, established in 1973, and later designated as the Department of Library and Information Science—University of Social Sciences and Humanities (USSH), VNU in 1996. Since that earlier time the University has been training undergraduate students at this Hanoi campus. The primary goal of the faculty is one of educating both undergraduate and postgraduate students and developing their professional skills and theoretical knowledge relating to library and information science. Currently both graduate and doctoral programs provide deeper insights, methodologies, and analytical skills in library and information science.

The Hanoi University of Culture

The Hanoi University of Culture was established in 1961 as the Cultural College of Hanoi on the foundations of the former Cultural, Theoretic, and Professional School. From its beginning it has trained library technicians and undergraduates who received a diploma, and since 1991, the University has offered the master's degree in Library Science. Unlike other higher education institutions the cultural university reports to the formerly named Ministry of Culture and Information, now the Ministry of Culture, Sports, and Tourism, and is responsible for training vocational students as well as undergraduates in areas that include culture, library science, and museology.

VNU Ho Chi Minh City USSH

School of Library and Information Science

The unit was established in 1976, from the former Saigon University of Sciences. The Faculty of Library Science was set up in 1986–1987 to offer a Bachelor of Library Science program for the Southern provinces. The School now prepares students for three degrees: technician, undergraduate, and postgraduate.

The Ho Chi Minh City College of Culture

The College was established in 1976 to train secondary vocational level students in the cultural professions. This College, as with the Hanoi University of Culture, reports directly reports to the Ministry of Culture, Sports, and Tourism. Since its establishment, it has trained library technicians. In 1985, it has been allowed by the Ministry to enroll students for short-term courses to train librarians for Southern provinces. It also offers a certificate program.

Can Tho University Learning Resources Center

Library and Information Management Program

This new program, established in 2006, is an undergraduate program educating library and information science students, particularly from the Mekong Delta area.

Several other organizations, including the National Library, NACESTI School of Central Archives and the Army Libraries, offer training programs on topics of importance in educating professionals responsible for providing information services.

THE VLA

The original VLA (Hoi Vien VietNam) was founded in 1959 but was in existence only a couple of years. It was reestablished in 1968 and was in existence until 1975.

The recently reinstituted VLA, the nationwide grouping of Vietnamese librarians, was officially founded on October 22, 2006 with more than 300 librarians and information professionals representing all types of library systems in the country. According to the Association's Charter, the VLA has the objectives to: Advance and strengthen Vietnamese librarianship; enhance the roles and positions of librarians and library institutions in the Vietnamese people's social and cultural life; make positive contributions to the economic, social, and cultural development of the country. Vietnam Library Association also strives to:

- Establish, maintain and strengthen networks, partnerships and linkages among Vietnamese and foreign librarians, libraries, library schools, and library associations and related organizations in order to share and improve professional knowledge; foster the development and international integration of Vietnamese librarians and library institutions.
- Serve as a national forum for library professionals, library related people and library friends to share experience, to promote mutual understanding, and to unite their intellectual power to solve major issues of the Vietnamese library professions.

Vietnamese Library and Information Science Journals

Two primary journals relating to library and information services in the country are:

- *Vietnam Library Journal* (Tap chi Thu Vien VietNam), revival of the previously published *Library Bulletin (Tap San Thu Vien)* National Library of Vietnam, Hanoi, Quarterly, 2007.
- *Journal of Information and Documentation (*Tap San Thong Tin Va Tu Lieu*)* NACESTI, under the Ministry of Science, Technology and Environment, in Hanoi. Quarterly, 1990—This journal is in Vietnamese with abstracts in English. It is also published online. (http://www.vjol.info/).

Other journals and newsletters include:

Southern Library and Information Newsletter (Thong tin & Th vien phia Nam). General Sciences Library Association for Library Information Science & Documentation.-Ho Chi Minh City, semi-annual; 1993–

Library-Information Technology Newsletter (Ban tin Cong nghe Thong tin Th vien): University of Natural Sciences.– Ho Chi Minh City. Monthly 1998–(http://www.glib.hcmuns.edu.vn).

National Technology and Science—Information and Documentation Center Newsletter (Ban tin Trung tam Thong tin—T lieu Khoa học va Cong nghe Quoc gia) Ministry of Science Technology and Environment.— Hanoi, Quarterly, (http://www.vista.gov.vn)

*Newsletter of Pedagogical College of Ho Chi (*Minh City Ban tin th vien), Monthly; 2002–

ARCHIVES

Manuscripts formed the basis for the first archival collections and have existed since the Ly dynasty in the eleventh century. An exact date has not been determined for the introduction of printing, the use of wooden blocks and boards, began sometime after the beginning of the twelfth century. During the twelfth to seventeenth centuries there was development of archival collections, primarily under the Tong (1460–1497) dynasty. However, official archives had been kept from the early days of the kings of Dai Viet, so that by the time of that Nguyen Dynasties (1802–1945) a substantial repository for official documents existed under the administrative control of a state office for libraries and archives. This repository housed both manuscripts and printed materials in cur Han (classical Chinese, the official language of the court until the early years of the twentieth century) and later the ideographic *chu nom* and romanized *quoc ngu* scripts, including land records and official court documents known collectively as *chau ban*. This was a substantial repository for official documents under the administrative control of a full-blown state office for libraries and archives. Most of those materials have not survived and, indeed, only about 5% of pre-1802 Nguyen dynasty (1802–1945) materials have survived. Approximately three-quarters of all Nguyen dynasty court records were destroyed during the First Indochina War of 1946–1954. Those which survived and are still in the country are in the National Archives Center #1, National Archives Centre #2, and the Institute of Han-Nom Studies Library in Hanoi.

Record keeping, of a more western approach, was introduced in the 1860s by French colonial authorities who enacted legislation to archive documents of national importance. During the early years of the colonial period, French government documents were stored in a variety of different government offices throughout the country. However, following the decree of the Indochinese General Governor, the Central Archives, and Library of Indochina was set up in Hanoi in 1917, with satellite archives in Saigon and Hue. Some few wood-block printed editions,

of earlier Buddhist texts, dating from the 1650s, are now in the National Archives in Hanoi. The majority of those surviving documents date from 1802, when the last ruling dynasty, the Nguyen (1802–1945), was in power. After 1954, the depositories in Hanoi and Saigon, respectively, housed the state archives of North and South Vietnam.

The current system of state archives dates from September 8, 1945 when the Provisional Government of the Democratic Republic of Vietnam issued a Decree establishing a National Service of Archives, Official Documents, and Libraries under the Ministry of Education. Shortly thereafter, on January 3, 1946 President Ho Chí Minh signed Circular 1C-VP, which emphasized the special values of archival materials in the task of national reconstruction. That decree prohibited destruction of any official record without the consent of competent authority.

Prior to 1962, the northern archives operated as a branch of the National Library, but Decree 102/CP of that year set up a separate National Archives Department within the Prime Minister's Office. Following Reunification in 1975 the public records office in Ho Chi Minh City became National Archives Centre 2. Today all of the older holdings of the Vietnamese National Archives are stored in these two repositories. A state-of-the-art new repository— National Archives Center 3 was opened in April 2002 to house the records of national, regional, and interregional agencies and institutions of the Democratic Republic of Vietnam (1945–1976) and the Socialist Republic of Vietnam (1976–present).

In 2003, the National Archives Department was renamed the State Records and Archives Department of Vietnam.

The northern archives operated as a branch of the National Library until 1962 when Decree 102/CP set up a separate National Archives Department within the Prime Minister's Office. At that time the old colonial records office on the grounds of the National Library became an annex known as National Archives Center #1. Following Reunification in 1975, the public records office in Ho Chi Minh City became National Archives Center #2. Today all of the older holdings of the Vietnamese National Archives are stored in these two repositories. A new state-of-the-art repository, the National Archives Center #3, was opened in April 2002 to house the records of national, regional and interregional agencies and institutions of the Democratic Republic of Vietnam (1945–1976) and the Socialist Republic of Vietnam (1976–present).

State Records and Archives Department of Vietnam

On January 25, 1991 Decision 24-CT of the President of the Council of Ministers made the Archives State Department responsible for the management of archives activities in the country and in 1992 the State Archives was placed under the Government Committee on Organization and Personnel, Ministry of Home Affairs. On April 4,

2001, the National Assembly's Standing Committee passed the Ordinance on National Archives. Cultural Heritage Law and in 2003 the National Archives Department was renamed the State Records and Archives Department of Vietnam.

The State Records and Archives Department of Vietnam consists of a network of some 70 provincial and municipal archives which are responsible for keeping, caring for and making accessible records of the events and decisions that shaped the nation, including central and local records of the Viet kings, the French colonial government, the US-backed Government of South Vietnam, the Democratic Republic of Vietnam, and the Socialist Republic of Vietnam.

However, the most important archival and printed texts, under public control, are held in those repositories in Vietnam including the National Archives centers, two in Hanoi and one in Ho Chi Minh City, and the three research institutes in Hanoi, under the control of the National Center for Social Sciences and Humanities, those being: the Sino Nom Research Institute; the Historical Institute; and the Social Sciences Information Institute.

Other major collections, as previously mentioned, are in the National Library in Hanoi and the GSL in Ho Chi Minh City. Some materials also can be found in several other archives and libraries, including the Archives of the Central Committee of the Communist Party, the Army Library, the former library of the Pasteur Institute, and several provincial repositories[14] as well as archives in various ministries, however declassified noncurrent records of the Ministries of Foreign Affairs, Defense, and Public Security are transferred to the National Archives Centers after 30 years. Other government organizations also maintain some archival records as do some provincial archives centers, and some professional organizations, as well as academic units within universities. For instance, special archives include the Institute of Music Sound Archive, the cinematic archives of the Vietnam Film Institute, and archives of the Vietnam Buddhist Association and the Catholic Church in Vietnam.

The State Records Management and Archives Department of Vietnam is responsible for, among other things:

- Developing long-term and short-term plans for archives development on a country-wide basis, as well as directing and controlling their implementation.
- Directing research work and application of scientific and technological advancements into archival work.
- Conducting training and retraining for records management and archival work personnel; regulating emulation and rewards in archival activities.[15]

In order to preserve safely and make full use of archives, one of the primary measures directed by the SADV (State Archives Department of Vietnam) is to reinforce the application of information technology in archives work. It has established databases to serve the management, multiuser access and security preservation of some valuable Chauban (Emperor's records), Mocban (Woodblock records) of Nguyen Dynasty, and sound recordings, on CD-ROM.

The National Archives

The National Archives operates as the chief agency of the archives sector in Vietnam with the mission of carrying out the unified and centralized administration of archival work and archival national records at the nationwide level, including the task of applying information technology in the archives domain. It is responsible for organizing, guiding, and inspecting the implementation of government regulations on archives and records management. With that responsibility it manages the holdings of the State Records and Archives Department, including (instructing, selecting, preserving, and utilizing records at the National Archives Center as well as historical archives and at archives of all government agencies.[16] The three centers are:

National Archives Center #1 in Hanoi is responsible for collecting, acquiring, preserving, and making effective use of archival records of national significance from feudal times (with the exception of woodblock records), including the French colonial period. It includes 60 archive collections and records groups, plus a range of books and materials dating from 1488 to 1945, including: Han-Nom (Chinese and Sino-transcribed Vietnamese) records produced by the feudal dynasties of Vietnam, principally royal records (and land records of the Nguyen kings and records of the Royal Viceroy in Tonkin and what is now Hanoi from 1802 to 1945; Records of the French colonial administration from 1858 to 1945, and records produced by the French-backed administrations in the north of Vietnam between 1945 and 1954 and historical books, periodicals, reviews, and official gazettes published prior to 1945.

National Archives Center #2 in Ho Chí Minh City is responsible for collecting, acquiring, preserving, and making effective use of archival records of national significance from the feudal period and from the French colonial territories of Annam and Cochin–china, the southern region of Vietnam including 55 archival collections and records groups, disks, sound recordings, and photographs and negatives dating from 1802 to the present, including: administrative records produced by the Governors General of Cochin–china, the Governors of Annam, the U.S.-backed Government of South Vietnam and various revolutionary organizations established in the south after 1975. It also houses scientific and technological records such as maps and atlases dating from 1862 to 1975; audiovisual records, photographs, films, newsreels, and sound recordings produced before 1975; woodblock records of various books and bibliographies produced by the Nguyen dynasty (1802–1945), and a collection in Han-Nom (Chinese and Sino-transcribed Vietnamese.

National Archives Center #3, opened in 2002) in Hanoi, is responsible for collecting, acquiring, preserving, and making effective use of archival records of national significance created by central, regional and interregional agencies, and institutions of the Democratic Republic of Vietnam (1945–1976) and the Socialist Republic of Vietnam (1976-present). which includes administrative records produced by state central agencies and institutions such as the National Assembly, Government, Ministries, and regional and interregional committees from 1945 to the present; scientific and technological records, including records of the design and construction of important national works such as the Ho Chi Minh Mausoleum, videotapes and documentary and newsreel films of historical value; and personal papers and records, including personal papers, manuscripts of creative works by famous scientists, writers, artists, and political figures.

Besides those three archive centers, the Department also operates a Center for Scientific Research, an Information Technology Center, a Center for the Secure Preservation of National Archives and two secondary level training schools—the Central Secondary School of Records Management and Archives in Hanoi and the Central Secondary School of Records Management and Archives in Hồ Chí Minh City.

Those centers house only limited materials of potential significance for Cold War scholars.[17] The post-1945 section of the National Archives in Hanoi contains documents generated prior to 1975.[18,19] The National Library houses the primary collection of materials relating to the records of war in the country, which were produced in various resistance zones from 1946 through 1954.

Center for Conservation and Restoration of Archive Materials

The Center[20] was established in 1993 to function as a repair and restoration center for the records of the national archive centers and various other institutions. Its primary responsibilities are: preparing and implementing long-term and short-term plans for the restoration, disinfection, fumigation, and deacidification of national archive records; coordinating with other organizations and individuals in identifying records and archives in need of conservation measures; receiving materials and undertake the necessary conservation and restoration work, ensuring that works are safeguarded during the process; and participating in studies toward and applications of scientific and technological advances in the conservation and restoration of archives. UNESCO has worked with colleagues at the center, and others in Southeast Asia, to address primary issues, including "Cultural Heritage Management."

Institute for International Affairs

This Institute in the Ministry of Foreign Affairs maintains the archival materials of the Cold War period, but those materials remain primarily inaccessible to both Vietnamese and foreign researchers. Collections of materials for that period are in the Foreign Ministry, Communist Party, and Army collections and have not been deposited into the National Archives.[21]

Vietnamese Record and Archives Association

The Association was founded under Decision 28/2001-QD-TCCBCP issued on May 23, 2001 by Minister-Chairman of Government Committee of Organization and Personnel as a social/professional organization representing Vietnamese individuals and organizations engaged in the archives profession and other concerned branches.[22] It is chaired by the Director General of the Department. The Association's aims are to:

- Assemble and unify members for exchange and dissemination of professional knowledge and experience.
- Enhance professional capacity.
- Coordinate with institutions and organizations engaged in archival profession to contribute to the development of Vietnamese archives in order to preserve safely and make effective use of national archival records for the national construction and defense of the Socialist Republic of Vietnam.

Archival Journals

Vietnam Records and Archives Review is published bimonthly by the Vietnam Record and Archives Association as a forum for research, instruction, guidance, and the exchange of information and experience on records management, archival, and office work.

Vietnam Records and Archives Magazine is published bimonthly by the State Records and Archives Department of Vietnam. The journal is similar to *The American Archivist* in that it contains articles on archival theory and practice, and also highlights specific projects in state archives centers around Vietnam. The journal publishes, among other topics, articles describing current practices and trends in archival science, including digital access and preservation of electronic records.

Archival Studies Education

In 1968, an archives education program was begun within the history department of Hanoi University, to train archivists at the tertiary level. In 1996, it became a separate "Faculty of Archival Studies and Office Management" in the University of Social Sciences and Humanities within the VNU complex. Both a 4 year BA and a 2 year MA program are offered.

In 1974, the Archives Department of Vietnam founded a secondary school in Hanoi—the Central Secondary School of Archives and Office Skills 1—to train records and archives staff at intermediate level. A second school was opened in Ho Chi Minh City—as the Central Secondary School of Archives and Office Skills 2—in 1979. They both offered Secondary Certificates in Records and Archives Management. The one located in Hanoi was upgraded in June 2005 to a college level degree. In addition, the State Records and Archives Department of Vietnam and the Association of Vietnam Archives also provide regularly the short-term intensive training courses in archives.[23]

MUSEUMS

History

The concept of the museum in Vietnam was introduced by the French who founded the Mission *archéologique d'Indochine* in Saigon (now Ho Chi Minh City); in 1901. It later moved to Hanoi and became the EFEO, with the aim of describing the archaeology of French Indochina, conserving its monuments, collecting its manuscripts, and undertaking research into the region's linguistic heritage. The first museum was developed in Hanoi in 1910 to display archaeological and ethnological artifacts, and paraphernalia from the Nguyen kings, including particularly royal regalia.[24] The scholarly work of the EFEO provided the groundwork for the establishment of the Cham Sculpture Museum (1915–1916) in DaNang; the Musée Louis Finôt (1926), now the Vietnam History Museum in Hanoi and the Musée Blanchard de la Brosse (1927), now the Vietnam History Museum in Ho Chí Minh City. After 1954, the *Musée Blanchard de la Brosse* in Saigon became the National Museum of South Vietnam, but prior to 1975 no other museums were constructed by the South Vietnamese authorities.

During this same period in the north the Musée Louis Finôt became the Vietnam History Museum and a number of new museums were established—the Museum of the Vietnamese Revolution (1959), the Vietnam Military History Museum (1959), the Vietnam Fine Art Museum (1966), the Museum of the Viet Bac Autonomous Region (1959)—now the Museum of Ethnology in Thai Nguyen—and the Hai Phong City Museum (1959).

Ministry of Culture and Information, through its National Cultural Heritage Department, formerly the Museums and Conservation Department, is assigned responsibility for managing the five national museums as well as for providing general professional guidance in the fields of conservation and museology at the national level. It is the governmental agency responsible for managing cultural

activities throughout the country, including museums, preservation of cultural heritage and libraries.[25]

On June 29, 2001, the National Assembly adopted the current *Law on Cultural Heritage*, which acknowledges that cultural heritage plays a significant role in the continuing national development and preservation of the culture of Vietnamese people. The law states that "The State's policies shall encourage work to collect, compile, translate, inventory, classify, and preserve works of literature, art, science, oral tradition, and folklore of the multiethnic Vietnamese community."[26]

In 1954, a separate Preservation and Conservation Department had been established and this unit became a Division of the Department of Cultural Heritage, following the introduction of a new law enacted in July 2003. This mandate was enacted in order to fulfill the objectives of preserving and promoting the country's cultural heritage. The information technology section and information on archives section of the Department of Cultural Heritage are now integrated as an Office of Information and Documentation, with the future goal of providing an information system repository on national relics, using modern information technology. Several "virtual museums" are directed by another unit, the Division of Relic Management which administers five heritage sites that have been recognized by UNESCO as world heritage sites (Hoi An's Ancient Town, My Son Sanctuary, Ha Long Bay, Hue, and Phong Nha Ke Bang Caves).

Vietnam currently has over 120 major museum institutions in which to date some 4 million objects have been inventoried and preserved. Five of these institutions are National Museums managed by the Ministry of Culture and Information. Some 30 others fall under the management of various other government offices, mass media organizations and agencies, including the Ministry of Defense (People's Army of Vietnam), the Ministry of Industry, the Vietnam Academy of Social Sciences, the Vietnamese Women's Association, the Pasteur Institute, the Oceanographic Institute, the Hoi An Centre for Monuments Management and Preservation, the Hue Historic Monuments Conservation Centre, and various tertiary training colleges. However, by far the greatest number of Vietnam's museums—more than 90 in number — fall under the direct management of the country's 63 provincial and municipal authorities.[24] The overall system of Vietnam museums includes several categories, including national, provincial, and city museums; as well as those nongovernmental specific museums, and museums belongs to the armed forces.

Museology Education

A 4-year graduate training program in conservation and museology was initiated by the Faculty of History at the Hanoi National University during the 1970s. In the late 1980s, the program was transferred to the University of Culture in Hanoi as a Faculty of Conservation and

Museum Studies (*Trng Đại học Văn hóa Hà Nội*). The Hanoi University of Culture also has a training program on "Cultural Management."

National Museums of Vietnam

National Museums under the Ministry of Culture and information. The National Museums are responsible for collecting, preserving, and exhibiting artifacts about the nation's history and culture. Five of these institutions are National Museums managed by the Ministry of Culture and Information.

Ho Chi Minh City Museum (Bao Tang Ho Chi Minh)

Located in a beautiful building was constructed in 1885–1890 by a French architect as a museum but became the Cochin–china Governor's residence. The Museum was opened on May 19, 1990, President Ho Chi Minh's birthday. Housed in a four-storey building designed in the shape of a lotus, the museum depicts the life and times of Ho Chi Minh and his major contribution to the founding of the Socialist Republic of Vietnam. The main showroom exhibits more than 2000 documents, articles, pictures, and exhibits illustrating not only President Ho Chi Minh's achievements but also the most important contemporaneous events that occurred throughout the rest of the world during his lifetime. The museum also incorporates a library and research rooms.

National Museum of Vietnamese Revolution (Hanoi) (Bao Tang Cach Mang)

As regulated in the Decision 37/2004/QD-BVHTT dated June 28, 2004 of the Ministry of Culture and Information, Originally established in January 1959, the Museum of the Vietnamese Revolution is housed in an elegant two-storey building formerly used by the Trade Department. It has been renovated and redesigned into 30 exhibition rooms which contain more than 80,000 historical artifacts. The first room presents Vietnam and the Vietnamese. The exhibition continues with exhibits on the national liberation movements of Vietnam against the French before the establishment of the Communist Party (1858–1930); the struggle for independence under the leadership of the Communist Party (1930–1975); and the construction and defense of the Socialist Republic of Vietnam (1976–1994).

Vietnam Fine Arts Museum (Hanoi) (Bao Tang My Thuat)

As regulated in the Decision 37/2004/QD-BVHTT dated June 28, 2004 of the Ministry of Culture and Information, Vietnam Fine Arts Museum has the responsibility of conserving, exhibiting typical art work, materials, and objects of Vietnam. It was built in the 1930s by the French, and reserved for the French colonial rulers' daughters throughout the Indochina who came to Hanoi to study. In 1962, the government requested the Ministry of Culture to transform the building from the western architecture into a Vietnamese appearance with ornamental details from the traditional architecture of communal house and fit for exhibiting works of fine arts. On June 26, 1966 Vietnam Fine Arts Museum was officially inaugurated. Throughout 40 years, the Vietnam Fine Arts Museum has been the center for fine arts and culture study, contributing to the preservation and promotion of the nation's cultural heritage. It is an information services organization, directly affiliated to the Ministry of Culture and Information, whose role is one of conserving, exhibiting typical art work, materials, and objects of Vietnam. Objects and artworks date back to prehistoric times.

Museum of Vietnam History (Ho Chi Minh) (Bao Tang Lich Su)

The museum was originally established in the 1920s as the *Musée Louis Finot* and housed in a building which typifies the hybrid "Indochinese style" of architecture. The archeological collection includes relics from the Hung era and Neolithic graves, Bronze age implements, bronze drums from Ngoc Lai and Mieu Mon, Chom relics, stele, statues, ceramics. This museum traces the history of the Vietnamese people from the earliest times to the present day using displays of cultural and ethnological significance. Exhibits are displayed on two floors which cover an area of more than 2000 m.

Vietnam Museum of Ethnology (Hanoi) (Bao Tang Dan Ltoc Hoc)

This is both a research center and a public museum exhibiting the ethnic groups of Vietnam. Proposal for the Vietnam Museum of Ethnology was officially approved on December 14, 1987. On October 24, 1995, the Prime Minister made the decision on establishment of the Vietnam Museum of Ethnology, under National Centre for Social Sciences and Humanities. The Museum opened in 1997. The mission of the Museum is scientific research, collection, documentation, conservation, exhibition, and preserving the cultural and historic patrimony of the nation's different ethnic groups. The museum also serves to guide research, conservation, and technology that are specific to the work of an ethnographic museum. It is a vital museum in maintaining and promoting the treasure of cultural, artistic heritages of Vietnamese ethnic communities. As a center for ethnographic research the museum employing many experts on the different ethnic groups, located in Thai Nguyen.[27]

Other Major Museums

Vietnamese Women's Museum (Hanoi)

Was dedicated on October 20, 1995, the 65th anniversary of the Vietnamese Women's Association, in honor of the brave Vietnamese women who had played an integral part in the social and political scenario of Vietnam. It honors the involvement of Vietnamese women in the fight for national independence and national construction. The Vietnamese woman is expressed through their struggle to liberate women, as well as exhibiting traditional handicrafts and costumes of the 54 Vietnamese ethnic groups.

Vietnam Military History Museum (Hanoi)

Military history from King An Duong era to the present day. Vietnamese victory of Dien Bien Phu showed the accomplishment of the Vietnamese people and army's protracted struggle against the French. On October 10, 1954, the Vietnamese army took Hanoi. In celebration, on July 17, 1956, an official decision was taken to form a board in charge of building the Army Museum. When war spread over the country, the Museum changed its direction corresponding to wartime, strengthening scientific research, preserving and protecting objects, collecting artifacts at battlefield. On December 12, 1959, President Ho Chi Minh, State and Party leaders came and inspected the exhibition then permitted holding the museum's opening ceremony on December 22, 1959 on the occasion of the 15th anniversary of founding the Vietnam People's Army. In 2002, the Army museum changed its name into the Vietnam Military History Museum.[28] Its exhibitions present the Vietnamese military history from the first period of founding the country to the Ho Chi Minh era.

Geological Museum of Vietnam (Hanoi)

Geological Museum of VN now is an official member of the International Council of Museum, belongs to the Natural Scientific Museum system in VN. It is a leading national office, which conserves geological-mineral specimens. After the establishment of Geological Survey of Indochina in 1898, the two French geologists Lantenois and Mansuy received the task of building up the Geological Museum. In 1997, the Geological Museum was unified with the Institute for Geological Information and Documentation to form the Institute of Geological Information, Archives, and Museum, but in 2003 the Geological Museum was again separated from the Institute of Geological Information, Archives, and Museum.

ACKNOWLEDGMENTS

I would like to thank some of my former students, all of whom now occupy leading positions in the library and information services professions in Vietnam. They include, particularly: Quan Mai Binh, Nguyen Huy Chuong, Nguyen Thi Bac, Dang Thi Mai, and Tran Thu Lan.

REFERENCES

1. http://en.wikipedia.org/wiki/Demographics_of_Vietnam (accessed October 28, 2007).
2. Library of Congress—Federal Research Division, Country Profile: Vietnam. Available at lcweb2.loc.gov/frd/cs/profiles/Vietnam.
3. Macmillan, S. Vietnam: Libraries and information services. In *Encyclopedia of Library and Information Science*; CRC Press: Boca Raton, FL; Vol. 45, Suppl. 10, 363.
4. Institute of Han Nom Studies. Available at http://www.harvard-yenching.org/HYI_-_NhogiaoTMTE07.pdf.
5. Marr, D.G.M. *(Compiler, with the assistance of Alilunas-Rodgers, K.). Vietnam; World Bibliographical Series*; Clio Press: Oxford, U.K., 1992; Vol. 147.
6. Vietnam: Libraries and information services. In *Encyclopedia of Library and Information Science*; CRC Press: Boca Raton, FL, Vol. 43, Suppl. 8, 365.
7. Vietnam: Social/cultural/ICT4D/public libraries/other service models: Phase 2 Report, March 2007, Prepared for Global Libraries, Bill & Melinda Gates Foundation.
8. National Assembly of Vietnam. Ordinance on Libraries, April 2001.
9. Government of Vietnam. Available at http://www.nlv.gov.vn (accessed October 28, 2007).
10. Room to Read, "Libraries". Available at http://roomtoread.org/programs/libraries.html.
11. Hung, T.B. Digital library development in Vietnam. Available at http://pnclink.org/annual/annual2002/pdf/0922/12/d221204.pdf.
12. Vietnam Information for Science and Technology Advance. Available at http://www.vista.gov.vn.
13. Vietnam Government, Regulation No 31/2000/PL-UBTVQH 10 of December 28, 2000.
14. Henchey, J. *Preservation and Archives in Vietnam*; Council on Library Resources: Washington, DC, 1998.
15. State Records and Management Department of Vietnam. Available at http://www.archives.gov.vn/gioi_thieu_chung/ab_chucnang_nv/index_html (accessed October 28, 2007).
16. Vietnam Cultural Profile: Archives. Available at http://www.vatrial.librios.net/Viet%5FNam/Directories/Vi_ACYAIw-7879_ADs-t_Nam_Cultural_Profile/-3495.html.
17. Henchey, J. Excerpts from Report of a libraries research trip to Vietnam, July–August 1990. CORMOSEA Bull. 19.2 June **1991**, 2–5.
18. Woodrow Wilson International Center for Scholars. Vietnam archives and scholarship on the Cole War period. Available at http://www.wilsoncenter.org/topics/pubs/ACFB79.pdf.
19. Marr, D. The national archives of Vietnam. CORMOSEA Bull. 19.1 June **1990**, 8–16.
20. Duong, Van Kham. Information technology for preservation and providing access to the archives of Vietnam.

Available at http://pnclink.org/annual/annual2002/pdf/0922/8/m220803.pdf (accessed November 10, 2007).

21. Woodrow Wilson International Center for Scholars. Available at http://www.wilsoncenter.org/topics/pubs/ACFB79.pdf (accessed November 10, 2007).

22. Government of Vietnam, Archives. Available at http://www.archives.gov.vn/tin_tuc/.

23. Hoang, T. Archival education in Vietnam. Available at http://www.nijl.ac.jp/~apcae2nd/S104.htm.

24. Cultural Profile, Vietnam. Available at http://www.culturalprofiles.org.uk/Vietnam/Directories/Vi_ACYAw-7879_ADst_Nam_Cultural_Profile/-3583.html (accessed November 10, 2007).

25. Vietnamese Government. Decree No. 15/CP dated March 2, 1993.

26. Ministry of Culture and Information. *Laws and Regulations*, Chapter III, Article 23.

27. Vietnam Museum of Ethnology. Available at http://www.vme.org.vn/aboutus.history.asp (accessed November 10, 2007).

28. Vietnam Military History Museum. Available at http://www.btlsqsvn.org.vn (accessed November 10, 2007).

Visitor Studies

Susan Foutz
Jill Stein
Institute for Learning Innovation, Edgewater, Maryland, U.S.A.

Abstract
The field of visitor studies seeks to document and understand the experiences and outcomes of visitors to museums and other informal educational settings. Both research and evaluation studies help to inform what we know about visitors to these settings and the impacts of their visits. This entry explores the theoretical foundations, goals and objectives of the field, commonly used research methodologies, and what we have learned about visitors in museum-like settings.

INTRODUCTION

The field of visitor studies is grounded in the context of museums and other informal learning environments, such as science and nature centers, zoos, aquariums, gardens, national parks, IMAX movie theaters, planetariums, or libraries. The main objective of visitor studies is to understand how people benefit from and utilize these settings, and to help inform institutions in the development of exhibitions, programming, and other public education activities. In contrast to marketing research, visitor studies focuses on institutions and experiences that have a learning agenda or educational mission. This "learning" is defined broadly within visitor studies to encompass all levels of cognition, affect, skill development, and personal growth. Researchers in the field focus on the experience and impacts on the "whole person," not just the learning of facts.

While educational theorists and other scholars began to study the visitor experience in museums in the early part of the twentieth century,[1–4] visitor studies did not fully emerge as a recognized discipline until the 1980s, roughly coinciding with the founding of the U.S.-based Visitor Studies Association (VSA) and its initial publications. This period also saw a substantial increase in the number of research studies related to visitor learning in museums and other informal contexts.[5] These efforts to understand the impacts of museum programs and exhibits on visitors were driven largely by mandates from federal funding agencies to show accountability for grants received, but also out of recognizing the value of incorporating the "visitor's voice" into museum exhibition and programmatic planning.

While requirements from funders still drive many studies, the field has continued to expand in the past several decades and many institutions now utilize visitor studies to help establish mission and goals, align programs and exhibits with mission, develop and refine visitor experiences, and better meet the needs and interests of a diverse range of audiences. The field of visitor studies has addressed such issues as motivation for visitation, socially mediated learning, family learning, personal meaning-making, cultural relevance, the role of identity and memory in museum learning, and long-term impacts of museum experiences. In this entry, we will address the definition of visitor studies, the key theoretical foundations that underlie the field, goals and objectives of the field, commonly used research designs and methods, what we have learned about visitors in museum-like settings, and current trends in visitor studies research.

WHAT IS VISITOR STUDIES?

Visitor studies takes place within multiple disciplines, including museum studies, leisure and tourism studies, interpretation, informal science education, and environmental and conservation education, though it is considered by many an academic and professional discipline in its own right. In contrast to marketing, visitor studies provides the voice of the visitor, while marketing research aims to provide the visitor with what the visitor wants or expects. Visitor studies, however, allows for audience input into a system that is also driven by other criteria, such as curatorial and educator input, or alignment with the institution's mission and goals. It is also important to note that visitor studies extends beyond actual visitors to a museum or museum-like setting, and can include the perspectives of potential visitors, non-visitors, or even a community as a whole.

The field of visitor studies is often divided into two key activities: 1) research and 2) evaluation, or applied research. While both research and evaluation use similar approaches and methods, they differ in their questions, goals, and applications. Basic research in visitor studies, as in any discipline, seeks to expand the knowledge of the

Encyclopedia of Library and Information Sciences, Fourth Edition DOI: 10.1081/E-ELIS4-120044034

Vietnam–Webometrics

field and provide generalizable data—that is, knowledge that is not bound by one specific context or situation. This research can be hypothesis-driven (deductive) or emergent (inductive). Evaluation, on the other hand, seeks to answer specific questions about a particular population's experience of a specific exhibit, program, or other informal learning activity. The results of evaluation are not intended to be generalizable beyond the specific circumstances in which the study was carried out.

Evaluation is divided into three main stages: 1) Front-end evaluation, which is conducted in the early stages of planning and development, is designed to assess the needs, interests, and perceptions of potential visitors and non-visitors as a means to inform the planning process, test assumptions, and reveal visitors' awareness, knowledge, and understanding about a specific topic or idea; 2) Formative evaluation, which takes place during the development of an exhibition or program, when changes are still possible, aims to change or improve the exhibit or program based on visitors' responses, reactions, and behaviors (when a program or exhibit is completed and tested in full and in situ, the evaluation is referred to as "remedial" evaluation); and 3) Summative evaluation, which is carried out after an exhibit or program is considered complete, is designed to assess the effectiveness of the exhibit or program in reaching its intended goals and outcomes for visitors.

It is important to note that while visitor studies and evaluation are often thought of as synonymous, museum evaluation in itself does not necessarily include the visitor voice—it is only within the context of visitor studies that evaluation becomes visitor-centered. Evaluation is also a much larger field of study, reaching beyond museums, to focus on diverse educational and social enterprises. The American Evaluation Association (AES) defines evaluation as "assessing the strengths and weaknesses of programs, policies, personnel, products, and organizations to improve their effectiveness."[6] Indeed this is the role evaluation plays within visitor studies, but visitor studies is commonly thought of as being somewhat different from evaluation.

Multiple terms have been used to define the type of learning studied by visitor studies. One is "informal" learning, meaning learning that takes place outside a formal, structured environment such as school. Another commonly used term is "free-choice learning," which emphasizes the idea that individuals are generally choosing to spend time at places like museums, zoos, science centers, and gardens—or, even if they are taken there by someone else, such as a parent or grandparent, they make choices about where they go and what they do. In a free-choice learning environment, no curriculum guides the learning and visitors attend to what is interesting to them. Other terms commonly used in visitor studies are "non-formal learning" which is often used in environmental education to distinguish visitors who take part in defined

programming from those who self-explore, who are called informal learners; and "lifelong learning," which is used to emphasize this type of learning as taking place in informal settings across one's lifespan.

It should be noted that "informal" learning is referred to in other disciplines, such as sociology, as learning that takes place when sender and receiver of information have no learning or teaching agenda—for example, when people exchange information in conversations or through observing others in their daily life. Visitor studies looks at this particular aspect of learning only as it occurs within the walls of the institutions we study.

Another key component of this type of learning is that it is not measured or assessed through testing, as in formal education, and allows for multiple experiences and outcomes. Informal or free-choice learning is not entirely predetermined by the institution staff, but rather influenced by the environment that is created. This type of learning also differs from formal education as it occurs throughout one's lifetime in a variety of contexts. While visitor studies is focused on "learning" in informal contexts, the field defines learning in broad terms to include outcomes related to personal and social growth, building awareness, shifting attitudes, and affective or emotional responses—not just the cognition of "facts." The field recognizes that experiences in museum-like settings provide individuals with more than just the opportunity to learn new facts, but to make connections to themselves and to others, reinforce or challenge knowledge and ideas they already had, or to inspire curiosity or interest in new topics.

THEORETICAL FOUNDATIONS OF VISITOR STUDIES

Visitor studies has naturally drawn a great deal of its theoretical foundation from education and learning theory, as well as cognitive psychology and human development. We will briefly describe some of the key theoretical foundations here. The basis of all theories of knowledge and learning is the field of *epistemology*, which asks "What is knowledge?"[7] Epistemological theories generally lie on a spectrum between two extremes: realism, which purports that there are objective truths in the world that can be known or learned by individuals; and idealism, which states that knowledge exists only in the minds of individuals and that there is no objective truth. Most theories of learning reside somewhere in between these two extremes.

One framework that has informed visitor studies is *behaviorism*. Descriptions of behaviorism focus on attempts to understand people's actions through observable behaviors in response to stimuli without regard to internal processes or mental states. In some visitor studies circles, this has led to the linking of behaviorism with the "transmission–absorption model" of communication, whereby it is assumed that a fact or concept, if communicated well, will be understood by a target audience. Within visitor studies, behaviorism has influenced the development of methods designed to use observable behaviors as indicators for learning and other processes. A more commonly used framework in visitor studies is *constructivism*, which posits that learning occurs through the active participation of the learner, who "constructs" or makes meaning as they explore and discover.[8] In other words, learning is highly personal, internally constructed, and based more in the process than in outcomes. Another key foundational theory used in visitor studies is *socioculturalism*, which asserts that an individual's social world plays a significant role in how that individual interprets what they see, experience, and learn.[9] In this perspective, it is crucial to examine the social and cultural context in which learning takes place in order to fully understand the processes and impacts of such learning.

More recently, researchers have explored learning theories such as social learning, in which learning is viewed as a social process where individuals build or "scaffold" on each other—rather than an individual pursuit. Often this social learning is explored through the analysis of conversations that groups have during museum visits.[10] Within this realm, some researchers have focused specifically on family learning,[11] or how intergenerational groups connect, interact, and learn from and about one another in informal learning contexts. Some researchers have focused specifically on youth learning, sometimes drawing upon *positive youth development* frameworks to understand the broader impacts of programs on the development of youth in relation to areas such as self image, confidence, social skills, compassion, empowerment, and civic engagement.[12]

Researchers in visitor studies have also explored how identity and motivation might relate to learning, or to what degree and in what ways an individual's "entry narrative" (or prior knowledge, perspectives, interests, and motivations for visiting) impact what and how they learn, and the degree to which identity plays into the experience of learning itself.[13–16] Other theoretical pursuits include the role of memory as a precursor to impacts; that is, the role of the museum in the construction of the self and "possible selves" (who one can become, both personally and professionally) over the course of one's lifetime.[17] Another lens recently used by researchers in visitor studies is that of long-term impacts, or how experiences in informal learning contexts may affect an individual over time. The idea behind this perspective is that the impacts of a museum visit do not all occur during or immediately after the experience, but may develop and shift for days, weeks, months, or years beyond it.

At the applied level, visitor studies often uses program theory to structure experiences that align goals and objectives with activities, in order to achieve specific outcomes. A process of *logic or program modeling* is used to help institutions plan or reflect upon the ways in which their mission is reflected in their outputs (or activities and products) and, ultimately, in visitor outcomes. Drawn from the field of program evaluation, this technique helps the researcher and the program staff to verify that the program accomplished what it sets out to do. Program modeling helps institutions understand to what degree activities and actions provided are linked to visitor outcomes.

GOALS AND OBJECTIVES OF VISITOR STUDIES

The overarching goal of visitor studies is to bring the "visitor voice" to the table when it would not otherwise be present. That is, as museums and other informal learning institutions engage in planning, development, and alignment of their mission with outputs and activities, visitor studies allows these institutions to incorporate the perspective of current and potential visitors, as well as non-visitors, into these processes. It is important to recognize that the work of visitor studies is not prescriptive; it does not tell institutions what to do or how to do it, but serves as a tool by which to inform them of how visitors and non-visitors think and feel about a given experience (e.g., exhibit or program), concept, topic, or even the museum as a whole, as well as to measure the effectiveness of an exhibit or program, and underlying mechanisms that support or hinder visitor engagement.

Visitor studies can be viewed as supporting four main, though not necessarily distinct, objectives: 1) providing valuable information on the effectiveness or impacts of a specific exhibition or program; 2) supporting visitor learning more broadly, including a wide range of audiences based on type of group (e.g., families or intergenerational, school groups, the elderly), cultural background, personal interests, prior knowledge, or identity; 3) informing strategic and interpretive planning for informal learning organizations; and 4) increasing our knowledge of how, where, what, and why people choose to learn in their spare time across their lifespan.

One of the most basic objectives of visitor studies is to provide feedback, from the visitors' perspective, on specific museum experiences, most often an exhibition, exhibit component, interpretive strategy, or program. In this way, visitor studies supports informal learning institutions in creating accessible, relevant, and valuable experiences that align with institutional goals and mission. Essentially, visitor studies can be used in very specific, targeted ways to assess the nature or impacts of a particular experience.

Another primary goal of visitor studies is to more broadly support the needs and interests of a wide range of visitors. Museums were historically designed and developed as collecting institutions and were not concerned with the value of those collections vis-à-vis the general public. Even as museums became more aware of themselves as important learning institutions in the first half of the twentieth century, exhibits and programs were largely created from the curatorial perspective with little understanding of visitors' wants, needs, or prior knowledge related to a given topic. In more recent years, visitor studies has been recognized as an essential practice in understanding and supporting the broad range of needs, interests, and learning styles of museum visitors and visiting groups.

Through the accumulation of knowledge about the visitor experience in museums, professionals engaged in visitor studies have increasingly served the role of informing institution-wide strategic and/or interpretive planning efforts. Often focusing on more than one specific exhibition or program, the objective of these efforts is to help institutions think more broadly about the audiences they serve, approaches to engaging new audiences, and how to integrate visitor perspectives throughout all levels of the institution. In this capacity, visitor studies provides empirically based knowledge (through research, evaluation, and/or literature reviews) that supports informal learning institutions in making crucial decisions about exhibition design, interpretive approaches, and public outreach and education strategies.

Finally, one of the underlying objectives of visitor studies is to increase our general knowledge of how people learn, what motivates them to learn, the types of factors that influence learning (such as an individual's "entry narrative"—which includes prior knowledge, experience, attitudes, and reasons for visiting), and the role of the sociocultural context in which learning takes place. This knowledge adds to our understanding of the significant role that museums and museum-like settings can play in people's lives across their lifespan.

VISITOR STUDIES AS A PROFESSION

Visitor studies as a profession in its own right emerged in the 1970s and 1980s. One of the early visitor studies-focused publications, *Visitor Behavior*, was first published in 1986. The journal exemplified the need for those already engaged in visitor studies to create a space for communicating findings and supporting professional practice.[18] Two years later, in 1988, VSA was founded and held its first conference.[19] At this first conference, a major goal was to identify indicators that visitor studies had emerged as a distinct field, including a critical mass of professionals involved in visitor studies, institutional commitment to the field, and a literature base.[20] VSA became the publishing organization for *Visitor Behavior*, the full archives of which can be accessed through the VSA Web site (http://www.visitorstudies.org). Concurrently, the field of evaluation also coalesced into a recognized discipline, as exemplified by the first annual conference of the AEA in 1986.[21]

Since the 1980s the field of visitor studies has become increasingly professionalized and academically minded. Developments include the creation of the Committee on Audience Research and Evaluation (CARE) within the American Association of Museums (AAM) and the committee's authoring of professional standards of "competent and responsible support and practice of visitor studies."[22] A continuing concern facing the field is supporting and ensuring professional practice by identifying key competencies and hosting professional development workshops. In another parallel with the broader evaluation field, visitor studies professionals and organizations have pushed for a formalized system of credentialing professionals. Unlike evaluation or museum studies, which are degree granting fields taught at universities, visitor studies as such has no degree program at this time. However, there are advanced degree programs in informal learning, such as through the Center for Informal Learning and Schools, a partnership of the Exploratorium, King's College London, and UC Santa Cruz (http://cils.exploratorium.edu), University of Pittsburgh's Center for Learning in Out of School Environments (http://upclose.lrdc.pitt.edu/), and the program in Free-Choice Learning at Oregon State University (http://seagrant.oregonstate.edu/freechoice/index.html).

Major associations and conferences that present visitor studies and support the profession include VSA, AAM, the Association of Science-Technology Centers (ASTC), the Association of Zoos and Aquariums (AZA), American Educational Research Association (AERA). Journals that publish visitor studies include *Visitor Studies* (published by VSA), *Curator, Science Education, The Journal of Museum Education, Informal Learning Review, Environmental Education Research*, and *Museums & Social Issues*.

RESEARCH DESIGN AND METHODOLOGY

As is typical in social science-based research and evaluation, visitor studies may use quantitative or qualitative research designs or use a mixed-method approach. A review of the literature is recommended before the study is begun to ground the study in what is already known about the subject. Given the interdisciplinary nature of visitor studies, researchers tend to review literature from a wide range of disciplines for any one study they undertake. Theories from the social sciences may inform the lens the researcher uses to frame their investigation (e.g., behaviorism, constructivism, socioculturalisim), to provide focus to the subject of the investigation or to interpret the data.

While research designs can be broadly categorized as quantitative, qualitative, or mixed, it is important to note that specific methods used to gather data (such as surveys, interviews, and observations) are not for the most part tied to being quantitative or qualitative, and can be analyzed through either lens, depending on the nature of the research or evaluation questions.

Quantitative Research Designs

Quantitative research designs are commonly used in visitor studies. These studies may use experimental, quasiexperimental, or nonexperimental designs. Experimental designs usually compare two different treatments based on random assignment to the treatments. This design is more likely to be used in a laboratory-type setting, rather than on the museum floor, because it allows for greater control of the experience by the researcher. An example of an experimental design could be asking two or more groups to complete the same task but some element of the experience is varied, like the signage, for each group. Quasiexperimental designs also use two or more treatments, but the treatments are not based upon individual random assignment. Instead, a matched-sampling technique may be used, as is common in studies of school groups where two similar classrooms or schools are matched together, each receiving a different treatment. Nonexperimental quantitative designs use no comparison groups or multiple treatment types. This design is commonly used in surveying visitors as they complete an exhibition or program. The sampling technique used may or may not be random, depending on the nature of the research question(s) being asked.

Quantitative research designs use methods that allow for statistical analysis and the reporting of numerical data. Surveys, interviews, observing visitor behavior, and visitor tracking are used to gather quantitative data about visitor's knowledge, attitudes, and behaviors. SPSS and SAS are social science software packages designed for the analysis of quantitative data, although Microsoft Office applications may also be used.

Qualitative Research Designs

Qualitative research designs are commonly used in visitor studies. Qualitative research designs are used to uncover the meanings behind events, gather perspectives from participants, and find out how or why something occurred. Qualitative designs are intended to contextualize events, people, and behaviors. All qualitative study designs have in common the use of techniques which generate word-based descriptions that attempt to capture "thick descriptions" of people, events, or phenomena.[23] While multiple types of qualitative methodologies have been identified,[24] case studies and ethnography are used most frequently.

Qualitative methods include interviews, observations, focus groups, and other methods to generate textual data that is not analyzed numerically. These data may be analyzed using techniques of pattern, theme, and content analysis.[25] Specifically designed software such as Atlas. ti, HyperRESEARCH, NUD*IST and NVivo are becoming more common tools for qualitative data analysis as the capabilities of the software improve.

Mixed Method Research Designs

Mixed method studies use both qualitative and quantitative methods within a single study. Methods may be combined to use the strengths of both quantitative and qualitative approaches or for triangulation of data. For example, both tracking and interviews may be combined in an attempt to understand how visitors utilize an exhibition, with one set of data confirming, supporting, or enriching the other. Mixed method studies are often nested or iterative, meaning the project is multistage and one study builds upon another. A good example of this would be using an open-ended interview to explore an idea with a limited number of visitors and then a close-ended survey to gather more generalizable data, or using a survey with visitors as they leave an exhibition and following up months later with an open-ended telephone interview.[26]

WHAT WE KNOW ABOUT VISITORS

Who Visits and Why Do They Visit

Other than the number of tickets sold on an annual basis, museums often have very little detailed information about their visitors. In the United States, organizations such as AAM, AZA, and ASTC annually survey their member institutions. This information adds to our knowledge about who visits these institutions, as well as field-wide differences. For example, zoos commonly have higher attendance than other types of museums and attract a larger number of families.

Over the last 30 years, statistics have shown that museum visitors are well-educated, have relatively high incomes compared to the rest of the population, and are usually White/Caucasian. According to the National Science Board, roughly 60% of the population averages three visits a year to museums.[27] These trends in attendance are relatively stable over time and across multiple countries. A study comparing Southern Californian museum visitation in 1984 and 2005 found that despite the increasing percentage of Latinos in the general population, museum visitors were no more likely to be Latino; instead Caucasians made up the majority of museum visitors in both 1984 and 2005.[28] However, a critical factor that is more relevant in predicting who will visit is childhood visitation. Regardless of education or income, visiting museums as a child with one's family has a positive correlation with visitation as an adult. Note that school visitation as a child does not have the same impact on adult museum-going habits as visiting with one's family.

Marilyn Hood undertook some of the field's original studies into who visits museums, who does not, and why. Non-visitors do not visit because the message or value of the museum has not been communicated to them.[29] In a study of visitors, occasional visitors, and non-visitors in the Toledo, Ohio, area, Hood found that non-visitors valued leisure experiences that allowed for social interaction, active participation, and feeling comfortable in their surroundings, and did not visit museums because they felt museums did not encompass these attributes.[30] Recent studies have shown that non-visitors perceive specific museums as not being culturally relevant and also hold negative preconceptions about museums in general.[31]

Visitors come to museums and museum-like institutions for a range of reasons. While museum professionals often think of their institutions primarily in terms of the educational mission, visitors think of much more than education. Museums are seen as a place for entertainment, spending quality time with family and friends, a "must-see" destination, or even a place to go to get out of the rain or the summer heat. The field of social psychology has much to share with researchers investigating visitor motivations. Underlying these reasons for visiting a museum are issues of self-determination, self-fulfillment, and intrinsic motivation.[32,33] People visit museums because they find something appealing or rewarding in the visit. Visiting is an intentional behavior that allows for the fulfillment of desires or perceived needs, all within an enjoyable setting.

What Are the Outcomes of the Visit

Just as a range of reasons for visiting have been identified, a range of outcomes have also been identified by the field of visitor studies. These outcomes are grouped under the heading of "learning" and include knowledge, affective responses, and behaviors. Visitor studies traditionally emphasized the knowledge-based or cognitive outcomes from a visit. Museum practitioners wanted to know how much of the main message or big idea of the exhibition or program visitors could express at the end of their visit. Visitor studies supplied the data that allowed designers to see how many visitors "got" the exhibition.

As the field grew, researchers pushed the boundaries of what counted as "learning" in or from an experience. Books like *Family Learning in Museums* and *Learning Conversations in Museums* and the Contextual Model of Learning posited by Falk and Dierking embraced the idea that visits do more than impart factual knowledge to visitors.[34–36] Recent discussions in publications like *Informal Learning Review*, *Science Education*, and *Environmental Education Research* broadened the perspective of possible and desirable outcomes further.[37–39]

Learning during and after a visit is embedded in the social and physical contexts of the visitor. With this broadened view of what learning is and how it occurs,

researchers began to look more broadly at learning outcomes from a visit. Current studies are just as likely to investigate emotional or affective responses as cognitive gains. Affective responses include attitudes and perceptions towards an exhibition itself or the content. How did a visitor feel about modern art before, and after, an exhibit?

Visitor studies research also investigates visitor behaviors during and after the visit. Behavior change is an important facet of many conservation-focused institutions such as zoos or aquariums. These organizations have a strong interest in teaching their visitors about the wildlife in their collections, and how human activity impacts the ecosystems of these organisms in the wild. These institutions, however, commonly attempt to leverage this knowledge of nature and ecosystems to have their visitors make a change in their behavior: recycle, use less water and energy, donate to WWF, or write their congressperson. The field of visitor studies is just beginning to tap into the wealth of knowledge on behavior change from other fields. Drawing from fields such as health, psychology, and environmental education, the interdisciplinary nature of visitor studies allows researchers to seek out theories that have been formulated in other fields and apply them to visitor studies.

One can state that most experiences that are researched by visitor studies are of relatively short duration, and hence the relative intensity of individual impacts is sometimes rather small: latent knowledge is brought to the fore, awareness is raised, emotional connections are made, enjoyment and fulfillment is reached, a sense of belonging is rekindled, or quality family time is spent. In contrast to school assessment, visitor studies often deals with small changes on the individual level that, aggregated over many visitors, amount to considerable benefits to society. Few experiences that visitor studies concerns itself with are transformative for individuals alone, and those tend to come from programming that is longer-lasting and more involved, like volunteering as an interpreter in a museum or taking part in a citizen-science project. A new field in visitor studies is focusing on the value of entire institutions to their community and on the relative contribution of individual experiences within a stream of lifelong engagement in leisure-time learning. It is within these contexts that the field of visitor studies is able to document the benefits of lifelong, informal, or free-choice learning.

CURRENT RESEARCH TRENDS IN VISITOR STUDIES

As more is learned about visitors and why they come, we realize how much there is that we do not know. The boundaries of the field have been sketched and now there is a real push to add to the depth of knowledge. Researchers have been pushing for more longitudinal studies, more investigations into the role of social groups in learning, and personal factors such as motivations and identity. This is not to say that researchers have overlooked these issues, only that the field as a whole needs to know more about the role of these factors in visitation and the impacts of visitation.

Longitudinal studies allow researchers to learn more about aspects having to do with on-going behaviors or outcomes of a visit. For example, a study conducted six months after a visit to an aquarium allows researchers to ask questions about whether behavior change *actually happened*, whereas at the time of the visit only a visitor's *intention* to change can be documented.[40] A recent review of long-term visitor studies pointed out, however, that there are few such studies and most look at a relatively short length of time (i.e., a year or less).[41] The field needs to undertake more longitudinal studies and studies of greater temporal length. These types of studies will allow the field to say with more certainty what the impacts of visitation really are and how museum visits fit into the fabric of a person's life.

Likewise, more research is needed on how the outcomes of a visit are mediated by the social group with which one visits. Both what and how people learn is impacted by the social setting in which the learning takes place. People within groups talk about their own experiences in relation to what they are seeing, they draw upon the skills and memories of others, and the act of visiting creates another shared experience among the group. In light of the fact that most museum visitors come to the museum as part of a social group, visitor studies research has only just begun to touch upon the social aspects of visiting, learning, and visit outcomes.

Greater investigation into personal aspects such as motivations and identity are also needed in the field of visitor studies. Recent studies and discussion in the field have described motivations for visiting in terms of the enacted or situated identity of the visitor. In one recent study, researchers grouped zoo and aquarium visitors into five identity-related motivations (explorer, facilitator, experience seeker, professional/hobbyist, and spiritual pilgrim) and found that slightly more than half (55%) of those interviewed had a single strong motivating factor for their visit.[42] These conversations hearken back to the reason why people choose to visit in the first place. What do we really know about how a museum visit supports a person's view of themselves? By continuing to draw from the theories and results of diverse disciplines, researchers will add to our knowledge of what drives visits to museums.

The field of visitor studies also is under increasing pressures from forces outside the field. Funding agencies such as the National Science Foundation and the National Institutes of Health play a role in shaping the practices of the field, both the questions that are asked and the way the research is conducted. Recent trends include the push for rigorous studies as defined by the U.S. Department of Education Report of the Academic Competitiveness Council from May 2007 (mostly experimental or quasiexperimental research designs), and the enforcement of federal regulations guiding the protection of human subjects in research in educational settings that had previously not focused on these issues (NSF-ISE, NIH-SEPA).[43] Professional associations like VSA and AEA are working to actively shape policy and let funding agencies know how these changes effect how visitor studies are conducted.

CONCLUSION

Visitor studies have impacted the way museum practitioners view their visitors and, therefore, the types of experiences that are created. Whether through evaluation or basic research, visitor studies pushes the museum field to learn more about why visitors come to these institutions and what happens during and after the visit. Visitor studies are increasingly being used to frame the importance of learning throughout the lifespan.

REFERENCES

1. Coleman, L.V. *The Museum in America: A Critical Study*, American Association of Museums: Washington, DC, 1939.
2. Dewey, J. *Experience and Education*, Macmillan: New York, 1938.
3. Gilman, B.I. Museum fatigue. Sci. Mon. **1916**, *12*, 62–74.
4. Wittlin, A.S. *The Museum, its History and its Tasks in Education*, Routledge & Kegan Paul: London, 1949.
5. http://www.eval.org/aboutus/organization/aboutus.asp American Evaluation Association.
6. Bitgood, S. Visitor studies: Coming of age. Visit. Behav. **1988**, *3*(3), 3.
7. Hein, G. *Learning in the Museum*, Routledge: New York, 1998.
8. Piaget, J. *The Child's Concept of the World*, Routeledge & Kegan Paul: London, 1929.
9. Vygotsky, L. *Mind in Society: The Development of Higher Psychological Processes*, Harvard University Press: Cambridge, MA, 1978.
10. In *Learning Conversations in Museums*; Leinhardt, G.; Crowley, K.; Knutson, K.; Eds.; Lawrence Erlbaum Associates: Mahwah, NJ, 2002.
11. Ellenbogen, K.M.; Luke, J.J.; Dierking, L.D. Family learning research in museums: An emerging disciplinary matrix. Sci. Educ. **2004**, *88*(S1), 48–58.
12. Eccles, J.S.; Gootman, J.A. *Community Programs to Promote Youth Development*, National Academy Press: Washington, DC, 2002.
13. Doering, Z.D.; Pekarik, A.J. Questioning the entrance narrative. J. Mus. Educ. **1996**, *21*(3), 20–25.

14. Falk, J.H. An identity-centered approach to understanding museum learning. Curator **2006**, *49*(2), 151–166.

15. Packer, J.; Ballantyne, R. Motivational factors and the visitor experience: A comparison of three sites. Curator **2002**, *45*(3), 183–198.

16. Rounds, J. Doing identity work in museums. Curator **2006**, *49*(2), 133–150.

17. Anderson, D. Visitors' long-term memories of World Expositions. Curator **2003**, *46*(4), 400–420.

18. Bitgood, S. Editorial note. Visit. Behav. **1986**, *1*(1), 1.

19. Our history. Available at http://www.visitorstudies.org/index.php?page=about Visitor Studies Association. About VSA:.

20. Bitgood, S. Introduction: Visitor studies—1988. In *Visitor Studies: Theory, Research and Practice*; Bitgood, S., Ed.; Visitor Studies Association: Columbus, OH, 1989; Vol. 1, 5–10.

21. Annual conference history. Available at http://www.eval.org/Training/conferencehistory.asp American Evaluation Association.

22. Resources. Available at http://www.care-aam.org/Resources/default.aspx Committee on Audience Research and Evaluation.

23. Geertz, C. *The Interpretation of Cultures*, Basic Books: New York, 1973.

24. Creswell, J.W. *Qualitative Inquiry and Research Design: Choosing among Five Traditions*, Sage Publications: Thousand Oaks, CA, 1998; 1–12.

25. Patton, M.Q. *Qualitative Research & Evaluation Methods*, 3rd Ed. Sage Publications: Thousand Oaks, CA, 2002; 431–534.

26. Creswell, J.W. *Research Design: Qualitative, Quantitative, and Mixed Method Approaches*, 2nd Ed. Sage Publications: Thousand Oaks, CA, 2003.

27. National Science Board. *Science and Engineering Indicators 2008*, National Science Foundation: Arlington, VA, 2008.

28. Haselhoff, K. Ong, P.M. Issue 7: Museum Attendance, Population Shifts, and Changing Tastes. *The Ralph and Goldy Lewis Center for Regional Policy Studies*, Southern California Survey: Los Angeles, 2005,; http://repositories.cdlib.org/lewis/scs/Vol1_No7/(accessed March 2008).

29. Hood, M.G. After 70 years of audience research, what have we learned?. Visi. Stud. **1993**, *5*(1), 16–27.

30. Hood, M.G. Staying away: Why people choose to not visit museums. Mus. News **1983**, *61*(4), 50–57.

31. Steiner, K. Researching non-visiting groups 20th Annual Visitor Studies Association Conference, Ottawa, Ontario, Canada Visitor Studies Association: Columbus, OH, 2007; July 17–21.

32. Deci, E.L.; Ryan, R.M. *Intrinsic Motivation and Self-Determination in Human Behavior*, Plenum Press: New York, 1985.

33. Eisenberger, R. The Museum goer's motives: The social and the sublime. Visit. Stud. Today **1999**, *11*(3), 1–4.

34. Borun, M. Dritsas, J. Johnson, J. Peter, N.E. Wagner, K. Fadigan, K. Jangaard, A. Stroup, E. Wenger, A. *Family Learning in Museums: The PISEC Perspective*, The Franklin Institute: Philadelphia, PA, 1998.

35. In *Learning Conversations in Museums*; Leinhardt, G., Crowley, K.; Knutson, K.; Eds.; Lawrence Erlbaum Associates: Mahwah, NJ, 2002.

36. Falk, J.H.; Deirking, L.D. *Learning from Museums: Visitor Experiences and the Making of Meaning*, AltaMira Press: Walnut Creek, CA, 2000.

37. Dierking, L.D.; Cohen Jones, M.; Wadman, M.; Falk, J.H.; Storksdieck, M.; Ellenbogen, K. Broadening our notions of the impact of free-choice learning experiences. Inform. Learn. Rev. **2002**, *55*(July–August), 4–7 1.

38. Rennie, L.J.; Johnston, D.J. The nature of learning and its implications for research on learning from museums. Sci. Educ. **2004**, *88*(S1), 4–16.

39. Storksdieck, M.; Ellenbogen, K.; Heimlich, J.E. Changing minds? Factors that influence free-choice learning about environmental conservation. Environ. Educ. Res. **2005**, *11*(3), 353–369.

40. Adelman, L.M.; Falk, J.H.; James, S. Impact of National Aquarium in Baltimore on visitor's conservation attitudes, behavior, and knowledge. Curator **2000**, *43*(1), 33–61.

41. Anderson, D. Storksdieck, M. Spock, M. Understanding the long-term impacts of museum experiences. In *In Principle, In Practice: Museums a Learning Institutions*; Falk, J.H., Deirking, L.D., Foutz, S., Eds.; AltaMira Press: Lanham, MD, 2007; 197–215.

42. Falk, J.H.; Heimlich, J.E.; Bronnenkant, K. Using identity-related visit motivations as a tool for understanding adult zoo and aquarium visitors' meaning-making. Curator **2008**, *51*(1), 55–79.

43. U.S. Department of Education, *Report of the Academic Competitiveness Council*, U.S. Department of Education: Washington DC, 2007; May.

Visual and Performing Arts Archives

Francesca Marini
School of Library, Archival and Information Studies, University of British Columbia,
Vancouver, British Columbia, Canada

Abstract

This entry offers a brief introduction to visual and performing arts archives. It discusses some of the main issues concerning the creation, archiving, and management of visual arts and performing arts materials, it lists examples of materials and of repositories in which they are held, and it points to professional associations and resources in these fields.

INTRODUCTION

Visual arts may be defined as "the arts created primarily for visual perception, as drawing, graphics, painting, sculpture, and the decorative arts" (s.v. "visual arts").[1] The performing arts may be defined as "arts or skills that require public performance, as acting, singing and dancing" (s.v. "performing arts").[1] These simple definitions are appropriate for the purpose of this entry, although they might be greatly broadened and made more articulate, according to the very complex discussions and competing points of view that exist in the visual and performing arts worlds. A full list of visual arts is almost impossible to compile. Other examples that may be added to the ones above include architecture, photography, design, illustration, installation, video art, digital art, cartooning, and comic art. The notion of performing arts expands to include live events such as theatre, dance, music, opera, musical theatre, pantomime, puppetry, circus, and fairs, and events that imply recording, such as film and broadcast. Live and recorded elements of course may merge in the same event, as it happens, for example, in multimedia theatre and digital performance. Canadian performance scholar Catherine Graham writes that nowadays the boundaries "between theatre and other art forms, between recorded and live…forms of dramatic performance are increasingly blurred, both in practice and in theory" (p. 3).[2] Performance art is considered one of the visual arts (s.v. "visual arts"),[3] but has also a key place in the larger world of performance.[4] Film may be considered part of both the visual and the performing arts. The various activities carried out in the visual and the performing arts produce materials with different functions and in different formats. Many of these materials end up in archives. Archives preserve memory and the records "created and received in the course of individual or institutional activity and set aside (preserved) as evidence of that activity" (s.v. "record"),[5] as well as "for action or reference" (s.v. "record").[6] The word "archives" may designate: the

whole of the holdings, and be therefore used as a plural with a singular article ("an archives"); the institution that manages the holdings (e.g., The U.S. National Archives and Records Administration); the physical space in which the holdings are kept (see Pearce-Moses,[5] s.v. "archives"). The goal of this entry is to offer a brief introduction to issues concerning the archiving and management of visual arts and performing arts materials, to list examples of materials and of repositories in which they are held, and to point to professional associations and resources in these fields. The entry opens with a brief discussion of how visual and performing arts materials come into being, and it presents examples of materials and of repositories in which they may be held ("Visual and Performing Arts Materials: Creation, Types and Repositories"); it then briefly discusses some key issues in relation to the archiving and management of visual and performing arts materials ("Archiving and Managing Visual and Performing Arts Materials: Selected Issues"). Finally, it summarizes the main issues ("Conclusion"), and points to selected references cited in the text or recommended for further reading.

VISUAL AND PERFORMING ARTS MATERIALS: CREATION, TYPES, AND REPOSITORIES

In archival theory and practice it is key to understand the context of the materials (s.v. "context").[5] For example: who created them, how, and why; what their original use was; how they were organized; what relationships exist among the materials originating from the same individual or institution; what happened to the materials over time; and more. Many people and institutions are involved in the creation; for example, artists, directors, theatre companies, film studios, galleries, managers and impresarios, costume and set designers, lighting designers, technical staff, marketing staff, the audience, and more. Visual and performing arts materials are born from both individual

Encyclopedia of Library and Information Sciences, Fourth Edition DOI: 10.1081/E-ELIS4-120043465

Vietnam–Webometrics

and collaborative efforts; collaboration is an essential aspect of the performing arts, and is also a strong element in the visual arts. Materials may relate directly to a specific outcome or event (such as a visual art creation or a theatre performance); to a specific creator (such as a painter or an actor, or a company/studio/gallery); or to several events and creators at once. Materials may therefore relate to specific individuals, institutions, outcomes or events, or to a combination of all these. Materials may remain with their original creator or they may be transferred elsewhere; they may have a very complex life, existing in different places and with different purposes at different points in time. Some examples:

- American theatre artist Robert Wilson maintains his own archive, The Robert Wilson Archive at the Byrd Hoffman Water Mill Foundation; he has also donated videos of his performances to the Theatre on Film and Tape Archive of the New York Public Library for the Performing Arts and part of his papers to the Columbia University Rare Book and Manuscripts Library.[7]
- A substantial part of the personal papers of Austrian-born actor and director Eric von Stroheim first stayed with him and then with his family for decades, until the family donated them to The Margaret Herrick Library of The Academy of Motion Picture Arts and Sciences in Los Angeles in 2002.[8]
- American artist Romare Bearden donated his papers to the Smithsonian Institution Archives of American Art between 1977 and 1983.[9]

Visual and performing arts materials originate from a complex process. Australian performing arts librarian Richard Stone writes that:

> Common to all the performing arts is a progression from creative impulses and inspiration, to preparation and execution, to the ultimate performance/s before an audience. At any point of this process objects, documents and publications are generated. All of them are potential for heritage consideration, for being collected and preserved. (p. 31)[10]

With a slight modification, the above paragraph may also be applied to the visual arts. The process of creation is of course not necessarily linear and sequential in time, and the stages described above should be seen as possibly recurring and overlapping. Many materials originate from the creative and technical processes that ultimately lead to visual art creations and to performances. The process is as important as the final product, therefore all materials are potentially relevant for preservation in archives, and archivists need to thoroughly understand the process in order to acquire and manage the materials.[11] The final outcome is not always fixed in form: for example, a live performance such as a concert, a ballet, or a spoken-word show is never exactly the same in its different instantiations; a digital

performance may change depending on technical considerations; and an installation may adapt to different environments. The final outcome may or may not be in the archives. For example, a painting might be in a private home, a gallery, or a museum, although some paintings end up in archives. Live performances cannot be in an archives, because they do not survive in their entirety after being performed, although recordings of them often exist in archives. Digital performances may sometimes be preserved, although with difficulty; in these cases, they may be held in archives. Film and broadcasts are usually held in archives. In terms of types and formats of materials, archivists need a broad understanding of: the materials generated in the course of the creation process (e.g., sketches of a painting or of the costumes for a show); the final outcomes of the process (e.g., a painting, or costumes for a show); and the entire variety of materials related to the final outcomes (e.g., the correspondence of a painter, a contract with a costume designer, posters advertising a show). Different types of repositories may hold different materials.

To try and visualize how materials are created and where they are kept, we can make a couple of hypothetical examples. An artist may create a painting in his studio having his wife as a model; the artist may be part of a movement or a creative group; the painting may be commissioned by a gallery, shown in an exhibition and then sold to an art collector; when the collector dies, his family may decide to donate the painting to a museum. Besides the work of art in itself, many other materials are created through time in the course of this process. Some examples may be: sketches of the painting; diaries by the painter or his wife discussing the experience; photographs of the wife posing as a model for the painting; correspondence with other artists who are part of the same movement or group; legal correspondence with the gallery that commissioned the work; documentation of the exhibition, in form of photographs, newspaper accounts and critic reviews, advertising materials such as posters and promotional postcards, and more; contracts and papers detailing the sale of the work to a collector; papers regarding the donation of the work from the collector's family to a museum, and more. These are only a few examples of materials related to the creation and life of a specific work of art, which may end up in archives. The sketches, diaries, photographs and correspondence would be part of the artist and artist's wife archives; copies of the legal correspondence with the gallery and documentation of the exhibition might exist in both the gallery's and the artist's archives; copies of papers concerning the sale of the work to a collector would exist in both the collector's and the gallery's archives; copies of papers regarding the donation to a museum would exist in both the collector's family archives and the museum archives; and so on. Of course, the artist's/gallery's/collector's papers could eventually be acquired by the museum that ultimately got the work, or by another archives, institution, or foundation. Archives in the strict sense of the term, made only of materials preserved because of their enduring value (s.v. "archives"),[5] will not exist in every case; individuals and institutions sometimes keep too much or too little. A theatrical production may produce a great deal of materials. For example: A playwright writes a play; the play is based on personal experience and on research, of which a documentation is kept; several drafts of the play are composed before getting to the final version; the play has been commissioned by a theatre. The theatre produces the play for its new season; the theatre is of course a very complex organization, with a structure encompassing administrative, legal, financial, artistic, technical, educational, marketing, and publicity requirements and activities. Among those specifically employed in the production there are actors and dancers, the director, the dramaturg (who is not the author of the play, but the one who analyzes and explains a play in view of its staging), the playwright, the costume designer, the set designer, the lighting designer, the composer, the production manager, and more. In different degrees, all of these people base their work on research and preparatory work, which produces documentation; they then create materials in the course of the production (annotated scripts and promptbooks, notes, videos of rehearsal, sketches, charts, scores, props, costumes, and more). The production is of course supported by all of the theatre's administrative, management, and technical staff, with all the materials that this entails. Among the many activities, it is advertised (with posters, news releases, photographs, and more) and explained to the audience (e.g., in the programs, in summaries and analyses posted on the theatre's Web site, and more). Once the production opens, it is video-recorded and photographed (in the course of a regular performance in front of the audience, or during a performance staged just for this purpose); it is reviewed by critics; it is discussed by the audience; it tours in different cities and countries, maybe with changes in cast, or in other aspects, such as the costumes; and more. Performances in a production are not identical and differ from one another, according to several factors (performers, audience's reactions, and more). Once a production is over, some of the materials created in relation to it are re-used, while others are discarded. For example, set designs may be used in another show, as they are or with some alterations; or they may simply be discarded. The same thing may happen with costumes. In some productions costumes and sets are especially created, while in others they are simply rented. Advertising materials such as posters and programs may easily disappear. As in the first example discussed above, the materials are many and complex, and may belong to different archives at different stages. The playwright's drafts, notes, research materials, and copies of the correspondence with the theatre will initially stay with her, and may later be donated to an archives. The materials related to the production and chosen for long-term preservation will stay in the theatre's archives, if the theatre has one, or will go to another archives (e.g., a city archives) once they have served their initial purpose. Costume and set designers' sketches will stay with the theatre if theirs was a work for hire, or will stay with the designers. Some of the actors' and director's notes and papers will likely stay with them initially, and so on.

Visual and performing arts materials, of both local and international relevance, will therefore be part of a variety of archives, including personal archives, in-house archives (such as the archives of theatres and galleries), archives of art and research institutions, archives of foundations, university archives, municipal archives, national archives, and more. Visual and performing arts materials will also be present in a variety of special collections in libraries. The next section presents some examples of repositories.

Examples of Repositories

Among national repositories, examples are

- The U.S. National Archives and Records Administration (NARA) (http://www.archives.gov/; accessed August 12, 2008) has several relevant holdings, including: Motion Picture Films and Sound and Video Recordings (http://www.archives.gov/research/formats/film-sound-video.html; accessed August 12, 2008); Cartographic and Architectural Records (http://www.archives.gov/research/formats/cartographic.html; accessed August 12, 2008); Photographs and Graphic Works (http://www.archives.gov/research/formats/photographs-dc.html; accessed August 12, 2008).
- Library and Archives Canada (LAC)/Bibliothèque et Archives Canada (BAC) (http://www.lac-bac.ca/; accessed August 12, 2008) has many relevant holdings, including: moving image; architectural records; photographs; sound recordings; music documentation; works of art; and personal papers.[12]
- The Library of Congress (http://www.loc.gov/index.html; accessed August 12, 2008) has several relevant departments, including: The American Folklife Center (http://www.loc.gov/folklife/; accessed August 12, 2008); the Motion Picture, Broadcasting and Recorded Sound Division (http://www.loc.gov/rr/mopic/; accessed August 12, 2008); the Music Division (http://www.loc.gov/rr/perform/; accessed August 12, 2008); and the Prints and Photographs Division (http://www.loc.gov/rr/print/; accessed August 12, 2008).
- The Smithsonian Institution in Washington, District of Columbia, encompasses several research units, including: the Archives of American Art (http://www.aaa.si.edu/; accessed August 12, 2008); the Smithsonian Institution Archives (http://www.siarchives.si.edu/; accessed August 12, 2008); the Smithsonian Institution Libraries (http://www.sil.si.edu/; accessed August 12, 2008); and the Ralph Rinzler Folklife Archives and Collections,

part of the Smithsonian Center for Folklife and Cultural Heritage (http://www.folklife.si.edu/center/archives. html; accessed August 12, 2008). The Smithsonian also houses extremely large photography collections (http:// photography.si.edu/; accessed August 12, 2008).

- The British Library's (http://www.bl.uk/; accessed August 12, 2008) relevant departments include the Music Collections (http://www.bl.uk/reshelp/bldept/ music/index.html; accessed March 26, 2009), and the British Library Sound Archive (http://www.bl.uk/nsa; accessed March 26, 2009).
- La Bibliothèque nationale de France (BnF) (http:// www.bnf.fr/default.htm; accessed August 12, 2008) has many relevant collections and departments, including: the Département des Arts du Spectacle, the Département de la Musique, the Département de l'Audiovisuel, le Département des Estampes et de la photographie, and the Bibliothèque-Musée de l'Opéra (http://www.bnf.fr/pages/zNavigat/frame/collections. htm?ancre=arts.htm; accessed August 12, 2008).

Among dedicated repositories, examples are

- The Research Institute of The Getty in Los Angeles (http://www.getty.edu/research/; accessed August 12, 2008); its Research Library holds general library collections, special collections, and a Photo Study Collection, with a focus on "the history of art, architecture, and archaeology with relevant materials in the humanities and social sciences"[13] (http://www.getty. edu/research/conducting_research/library/index.html; accessed August 12, 2008).
- The Museum Archives (http://moma.org/learn/ resources/archives; accessed March 15, 2009) of the Museum of Modern Art (MoMA) in New York City (http://moma.org/; accessed August 12, 2008) holds documentation on the Museum's activities, and on aspects of modern and contemporary art. There are also several study_centers at MoMA; they include the Lily Auchincloss Study Center for Architecture and Design, The Drawings Study Center, the Joseph and Sylvia Slifka Painting and Sculpture Study Center, Erna and Victor Hasselblad Photography Study Center, The Abby Aldrich Rockefeller Print Room, the Celeste Bartos International Film Study Center, as well as The Celeste Bartos Film Preservation Center in Hamlin, Pennsylvania (http://moma.org/learn/resources/study_ centers; accessed March 15, 2008).
- The Academy Film Archive (http://www.oscars.org/ filmarchive/index.html; accessed August 12, 2008) and The Margaret Herrick Library (http://www.oscars. org/library/index.html; accessed August 12, 2008) of The Academy of Motion Picture Arts and Sciences in Los Angeles (http://www.oscars.org/; accessed August 12, 2008) are, together with MoMA, among the largest film repositories in the world.

- The George Eastman House International Museum of Photography and Film (http://www.eastmanhouse.org/; accessed August 12, 2008) promotes many activities and has a world-famous museum of photography and film archives (http://www.eastmanhouse.org/inc/ the_museum/welcome.php; accessed August 12, 2008). Its collections include photography (http:// www.eastmanhouse.org/inc/collections/photography. php; accessed August 12, 2008), motion picture (http://www.eastmanhouse.org/inc/collections/ motion_picture.php; accessed August 12, 2008), and photographic and cinematographic equipment (http:// www.eastmanhouse.org/inc/collections/technology. php; accessed August 12, 2008). The Richard and Ronay Menschel Library is part of The George Eastman House and focuses on photography and motion picture (http://www.eastmanhouse.org/inc/collections/ library.php; accessed August 12, 2008).
- The New York Public Library for the Performing Arts (http://www.nypl.org/research/lpa/lpa.html; accessed August 12, 2008) "houses the world's most extensive combination of circulating and non-circulating reference and research materials on music, dance, theatre, recorded sound, and other performing arts."[14] The Circulating Collections include: Arts Administration; Dance; Drama; Music; the Orchestra Collection; Recorded Sound and Moving Image.[15] The Research Collections include: the Jerome Robbins Dance Division; the Music Division; the Rodgers and Hammerstein Archives of Recorded Sound; and the Billy Rose Theatre Collection.[15] The Theatre on Film and Tape Archive (TOFT), championed by Betty Corwin, is part of the Billy Rose Theatre Collection and, since 1970, "has been engaged in a unique documentation effort"[16] recording theatre productions and documenting theatre personalities.
- The Metropolitan Opera (The Met) Archives in New York City (http://www.metoperafamily.org/metopera/ history/; accessed August 12, 2008) are "devoted mainly to Met history and the holdings consist of written record, photographs, costumes, art works and related material."[17]
- The Harvard Theatre Collection (http://hcl.harvard. edu/libraries/houghton/collections/htc.html; accessed August 12, 2008) is part of the Houghton Library at Harvard University in Cambridge, Massachusetts, and documents the history of the performing arts. The Harvard Theatre Collection is considered "the oldest major theatre collection in the world."[18]
- The National Theatre Archive (http://www. nationaltheatre.org.uk/?lid=7058; accessed August 12, 2008) "is the repository for the administrative and technical records of the National Theatre" in London, United Kingdom.[19] The National Theatre has developed a Web site about its productions and educational activities, Stagework (http://www.stagework.org/ stageworks/index.html; accessed August 12, 2008).

- La Bibliothèque-musée de la Comédie-Française in Paris, France (http://www.comedie-francaise.fr/dev/institution_bibliotheque-musee-infos.php; accessed August 12, 2008) houses archives, iconographic materials, publications, artworks, and three-dimensional objects related to the history and activities of the Comédie-Française.
- The Biblioteca e Raccolta Teatrale del Burcardo (Burcardo Library and Theatre Collection) in Rome, Italy (http://www.burcardo.org/english/index.htm; accessed August 12, 2008) is "an office of the Italian Society of Authors and Publishers - SIAE"[20] and houses special collections, a library, and a museum, as well as the SIAE Historical Archives. Its holdings are among the largest in Italy.

There are several portals, lists, and directories that point users to visual and performing arts archives and special collections. One example is the *SIBMAS International Directory of Performing Arts Collections and Institutions*, available through the SIBMAS Web site (http://www.sibmas.org/; accessed August 12, 2008).

Many archives also digitize some of their materials and make them available as online collections. Archives and institutions often develop online exhibitions, too. Some archives and institutions also use theirs and other materials to develop projects and Web sites for education and outreach.

ARCHIVING AND MANAGING VISUAL AND PERFORMING ARTS MATERIALS: SELECTED ISSUES

Archivists working with visual and performing arts materials follow the general principles and practices of their profession, but also need to tailor them to the specificity of the materials. This section will briefly address some key aspects of visual and performing arts archivists' work. For a more complete discussion, readers may refer to the works cited in the references and bibliography sections, as well as to the Web sites of institutions and associations mentioned in this entry.

How do you document the visual and performing arts? Their complexity and dynamic characteristics make it in most cases impossible to thoroughly document all of their aspects. Especially the live components of a performance or dynamic art event can never be adequately captured. The intention of many artists is actually to create something that cannot be fixed. Some artists and theorists question and investigate the attempt to create a record of the visual and performing arts.[21–23] Many artists, companies and institutions are involved in documentation efforts, though. This is done for many reasons: reflecting on the work done; making it available for future reference and inspiration; producing materials that can be used for

publicity and outreach; preserving the artistic and cultural heritage; and more. Video-recording, photography, and many other means are used in documentation efforts; all of them have both advantages and limitations, and there exist a strong debate on why and how to use them in both the traditional and the digital environment.[24] Many archivists become directly involved in the documentation process, especially, but not only, when they work in in-house archives such as archives of theatres and galleries. Archivists may promote and/or help coordinate the documentation efforts, according to internal policies and existing guidelines, when in place. The people who are part of the visual and performing arts are essential sources, with their minds and bodies, for transmitting and perpetuating knowledge; interviews and oral histories, among other methods, are therefore important to documentation efforts.

Given that the visual and performing arts are dynamic and happen through time, archivists need to be proactive in acquiring existing documentation or in actually promoting the creation of new documentation; this active engagement makes visual and performing arts archivists different from more traditional archivists.[11]

In order to communicate with artists and to acquire/create documentation in a timely manner, visual and performing arts archivists need to thoroughly understand visual and performing arts practice. As described earlier, the process through which materials are created is very complex and multifaceted, and often as important as the final outcome; materials go through a very complex life. Archivists need to understand this complexity and the reasons why materials were created in the first place. Archivists acquire this knowledge by staying in close contact with practice, and by sometimes taking part in it; many visual and performing arts archivists are actually artists and performers.[11] An understanding of practice also implies acquiring the technical knowledge necessary to manage the materials. Archivists need to be knowledgeable of the wide range and complexity of formats (audio, video, digital and more), techniques and skills used in the visual and performing arts, in order to correctly manage, preserve, and make available the materials. Given the proliferation of formats and media, and many other considerations, preservation is an extremely difficult endeavor in these fields. Understanding the materials is essential for arranging and describing them, too, especially since existing standards and guidelines generally need to be adjusted and tailored when applied in the fields of visual and performing arts. All of these skills are also necessary when providing service to users and explaining the materials to them. Archivists in these fields are very close to the users, who come from a wide range of areas and have different purposes (p. 14).[11] Archivists often serve the creators directly, as it happens in in-house archives, and are very active in supporting creativity and promoting use through a variety of activities and initiatives.[11] Even more than other types of archives, visual and performing arts archives are there to be actively used, for practical needs, creativity, inspiration, research, and more. In managing visual and performing arts materials, issues of copyright, intellectual property and privacy are crucial. Archivists need to consider artistic and commercial needs, and privacy issues that may arise from managing sensitive and controversial materials, which are very common in the visual and performing arts. Archivists also face ethical issues related to the overall process of documentation and to the nature of the materials. Given the complexity of their work, visual and performing arts archivists need the full support and expertise of their professional communities. Being actively part of professional associations is therefore essential; the next section highlights some relevant associations.

Visual and Performing Arts Professional Associations

Professional associations support the work of those who manage visual and performing arts materials, and also provide useful help to the creators and users of the materials. Professionals are usually part of more than one association. Broad-interest associations include the Society of American Archivists (SAA; http://www.archivists.org; accessed: August 12, 2008) and the Association of Canadian Archivists (ACA; http://www.archivists.ca; accessed: August 12, 2008). The following are examples of professional associations and groups that specifically focus on issues relevant to visual and performing arts archives:

- The Visual Resources Association (VRA), the international association of image media professionals established in 1982 (http://www.vraweb.org/; accessed August 12, 2008).
- The Art Libraries Society UK & Ireland (ARLIS/UK & Ireland) established in 1969, which supports professionals involved in the documentation of the visual arts, including architecture and design (http://www.arlis.org.uk/; accessed August 12, 2008).
- The Art Libraries Society of North America (ARLIS/NA), established in 1972 (http://www.arlisna.org/; accessed: August 12, 2008), and other affiliated organizations (http://www.arlisna.org/about/affiliates.html; accessed August 12, 2008).
- The International Federation of Library Associations and Institutions (IFLA) Art Libraries Section, which is "concerned with all formats of textual and visual documentation for the visual arts"[25] (http://www.ifla.org/VII/s30/index.htm; accessed August 12, 2008).
- The Society of American Archivists' Visual Materials Section Cataloging and Access Roundtable (VMCAR), established in 1990, which supports archivists and other professionals working with visual materials (http://www.lib.lsu.edu/SAA/vmcar.html; and http://

www.lib.lsu.edu/SAA/VMhome.html; accessed August 12, 2008).
- The International Council of Museums/Conseil international des musées (ICOM), established in 1946, is an international organization of museums and museum professionals, and it maintains formal relations with UNESCO[26] (http://icom.museum/; accessed August 12, 2008).
- The Association of Moving Image Archivists (AMIA), established in 1990, which supports professionals working with moving images (http://www.amianet.org/; accessed August 12, 2008).
- The Fédération Internationale des Archives du Film/International Federation of Film Archives/Federación Internacional de Archivos Fílmicos (FIAF), established in 1938, "is a collaborative association of the world's leading film archives"[27] (http://www.fiafnet.org/; accessed August 12, 2008).
- The Fédération Internationale des Archives de Télévision/International Federation of Television Archives (FIAT/IFTA), established in 1977 (http://www.fiatifta.org/; accessed August 12, 2008).
- The Association for Recorded Sound Collections (ARSC), established in 1966, is an international organization that focuses on all aspects of recordings and recorded sound (http://www.arsc-audio.org/; accessed August 12, 2008).
- The International Association of Sound and Audiovisual Archives (IASA), established in1969 (http://www.iasa-web.org/; accessed August 12, 2008).
- The Music Library Association (MLA), established in 1931 in the United States (http://www.musiclibraryassoc.org/; accessed August 12, 2008).
- The International Association of Music Libraries Archives and Documentation Centres (IAML), established in 1951 (http://www.iaml.info/; accessed August 12, 2008).
- The Canadian Association of Music Libraries, Archives, and Documentation Centres (CAML)/Association canadienne des bibliothèques, archives et centres de documentation musicaux (ACBM), established in 1971 (http://www.yorku.ca/caml/; accessed August 12, 2008).
- The Dance Heritage Coalition (DHC), established in 1992 in the United States, "is a national alliance of institutions holding significant collections of materials documenting the history of dance"[28] (http://www.danceheritage.org/; accessed August 12, 2008).
- The Société Internationale des Bibliothèques et des Musées des Arts du Spectacle/International Association of Libraries and Museums of the Performing Arts (SIBMAS) was established in 1954 (http://www.sibmas.org/; accessed August 12, 2008).
- The Theatre Information Group (TIG), which "originated as Theatre Information Group London in 1979 and is the U.K. affiliate of SIBMAS."[29]

- The Theatre Library Association (TLA) was established in 1937 in the United States (http://tla.library.unt.edu/; accessed August 12, 2008).
- The Society of American Archivists' Performing Arts Roundtable (PAR) was established in 1986 (http://www.archivists.org/saagroups/performart/index.html; accessed August 12, 2008).
- The Performing Arts Heritage Special Interest Group of Museums Australia (PASIG) was established in the early 1990s (http://www.museumsaustralia.org.au/site/page78.php and http://amol.org.au/pasig/; accessed March 4, 2009).

The above-mentioned associations also work together with other associations of scholars and practitioners such as the International Federation for Theatre Research (IFTR)/ Fédération internationale pour la recherche théâtrale (FIRT) (http://www.firt-iftr.org/firt/home.jsp; accessed August 12, 2008) and the College Art Association (http://www.collegeart.org/; accessed August 12, 2008).

CONCLUSION

This entry has provided a brief introduction to visual and performing arts archives, which are extremely dynamic, complex and fascinating for both archivists and users. Materials originate from a multitude of interrelated and often collaborative activities, present a great variety of formats, and are kept in different types of repositories. Since the visual and performing arts are very alive and always experimenting with the new, archivists need to be in close contact with artistic practice, and need to be proactive in their work. Archivists need to always be aware of the big picture, in order to encourage creativity, promote use, and address the ethical and practical issues that arise from archiving and managing visual and performing arts materials. This entry hopes to serve as a useful introduction to those who work in the visual and performing arts, to the archivists who work with visual and performing arts materials, and to the users who are interested in accessing them. The arts are a vital part of life and there are different ways of engaging in them and supporting them; working with visual and performing arts archives is one way to do this.

REFERENCES

1. Random House *Random House Webster's College Dictionary*; Random House: New York, 1996.
2. Graham, C. Liveness and mediatized performance: Beyond contradiction. Can. Theatre Rev. **2006**, *127* (Summer), 3–5.
3. The J. Paul Getty Trust *The Getty Art & Architecture Thesaurus® Online*; The J. Paul Getty Trust: Los Angeles, 2000. http://www.getty.edu/research/conducting_research/vocabularies/aat/ (accessed August 12, 2008).
4. Carlson, M. *Performance: A Critical Introduction*, 2nd Ed.; Routledge: New York and London, 2004.
5. Pearce-Moses, R. *A Glossary of Archival and Records Terminology*; The Society of American Archivists: Chicago, IL, 2005.
6. The InterPARES 2 Project. *Terminology Database-Glossary*. http://www.interpares.org/ip2/ip2_terminology_db.cfm (accessed August 12, 2008).
7. The Robert Wilson Archive. http://www.robertwilson.com/archive/overview.php (accessed August 12, 2008).
8. Schmidlin, R. My Saga of the newly discovered estate of Erich von Stroheim. Moving Image **2006**, *6* (2), 101–109.
9. Aikens, B. Provenance. In *Romare Bearden: A Finding Aid to the Romare Bearden Papers, 1937–1982, in the Archives of American Art*; Smithsonian Archives of American Art: Washington, DC, 2003. http://www.aaa.si.edu/collectionsonline/bearroma/overview.htm (accessed March 4, 2009).
10. Stone, R. The show goes on! Preserving performing arts ephemera, or the power of the program. Arts Libr. J. **2000**, *25* (2), 31–35.
11. Marini, F. Archivists, librarians, and theatre research. Archivaria **2007**, *63* (Spring), 7–33.
12. Library and Archives Canada (LAC). In our collection: Overview. http://www.lac-bac.ca/collection/003-300-e.html (accessed August 12, 2008).
13. The Getty Research Institute. Research library overview. http://www.getty.edu/research/conducting_research/library/index.html (accessed August 12, 2008).
14. The New York Public Library for the Performing Arts. About the library. http://www.nypl.org/research/lpa/general/ (accessed August 12, 2008).
15. The New York Public Library for the Performing Arts. Collections. http://www.nypl.org/research/lpa/collections/ (accessed August 12, 2008).
16. The New York Public Library for the Performing Arts, Billy Rose Theatre Collection. Special features: Supporting the vitality of theatre. http://www.nypl.org/research/lpa/the/the.specfea.html#toft (accessed August 12, 2008).
17. Pennino, J. Electronic mail message to author, July 17, 2007.
18. Harvard Theatre Collection. About the collection-history. http://hcl.harvard.edu/libraries/houghton/collections/htc.html (accessed August 12, 2008).
19. The National Theatre. Archive. http://www.nationaltheatre.org.uk/?lid=7058 (accessed August 12, 2008).
20. Biblioteca e Raccolta Teatrale del Burcardo (Burcardo Library and Theatre Collection). General information. http://www.burcardo.org/english/info.html (accessed August 12, 2008).
21. Merewether, C., Ed. *The Archive*; MIT Press: London and Cambridge, MA, 2006.
22. Phelan, P. *Unmarked: The Politics of Performance*; Routledge: London and New York, 1993.
23. Taylor, D. *The Archive and the Repertoire: Performing Cultural Memory in the Americas*; Duke University Press: Durham, NC, and London, 2003; reprint, 2005.
24. Schlesinger, K.; Bloom, P.; Ferguson, A., Eds. *Performance Documentation and Preservation in an Online Environment*; Theatre Library Association: New York, 2004.

25. International Federation of Library Associations and Institutions (IFLA) Art Libraries Section. Scope. http://www.ifla.org/VII/s30/index.htm (accessed August 12, 2008).

26. International Council of Museums/Conseil international des musées (ICOM). ICOM mission. http://icom.museum/mission.html (accessed August 12, 2008).

27. The International Federation of Film Archives (FIAF). What is FIAF? http://www.fiafnet.org/uk/ (accessed August 12, 2008).

28. Dance Heritage Coalition (DHC). Mission statement. http://www.danceheritage.org/about/mission.html (accessed August 12, 2008).

29. Baxter, G. Electronic mail message to author, July 10, 2007.

BIBLIOGRAPHY

1. Bergeron, R. Archiving moving-image and audio-cultural works in Canada. Archivaria **2007**, *63* (Spring), 55–74.

2. Blouin, F.X., Jr.; Rosenberg, W.G., Eds. *Archives, Documentation, and Institutions of Social Memory: Essays From the Sawyer Seminar*; University of Michigan Press: Ann Arbor, MI, 2006.

3. Bowser, E.; Magliozzi, R.S. Film archiving as a profession: An interview with Eileen Bowser. Moving Image **2003**, *3* (1), 132–146.

4. Carter, R.G.S. Tainted archives: Art, archives, and authenticity. Archivaria **2007**, *63* (Spring), 75–86.

5. Couch, N.; Allen, N., Eds. *The Humanities and the Library*, 2nd Ed.; American Library Association: Chicago, IL and London, 1993.

6. Dircks, P.T., Ed. *American Puppetry: Collections, History and Performance*; McFarland & Company: Jefferson, NC, 2004. London, England.

7. Dixon, S. *Digital Performance: A History of New Media in Theater, Dance, Performance Art, and Installation*; The MIT Press: Cambridge, MA, 2007. London, England.

8. Harvey, K.; Moosberger, M. Theatre archives' outreach and core archival functions. Archivaria **2007**, *63* (Spring), 35–54.

9. Lavédrine, B. *A Guide to the Preventive Conservation of Photograph Collections*; The Getty Conservation Institute: Los Angeles, 2003. Translated by Sharon Grevet.

10. Lowell, W.; Nelb, T.R. *Architectural Records: Managing Design and Construction Records*; Society of American Archivists: Chicago, IL, 2006.

11. Murphy, P. Documentation of performance art. Coll. Res. Libr **1992**, News 53 (April), 246–248.

12. National Film Preservation Foundation, *The Film Preservation Guide: The Basics for Archives, Libraries, and Museums*; National Film Preservation Foundation: San Francisco, 2004. http://www.filmpreservation.org/preservation/film_guide.html (accessed August 12, 2008).

13. Ney, D. Let's go to the videotape. Lincoln Center paves the way for archival video, and three cities follow suit. Am. Theatre **1999**, *16* (4), 47–48.

14. Preziosi, D. Seeing through art history. In *Knowledges: Historical and Critical Studies in Disciplinarity*; Messer-Davidow, E., Shumway, D.R., Sylvan, D.J., Eds.; University Press of Virginia: Charlottesville, VA, 1993; 215–231.

15. Schaffner, I.; Winzen, M., Eds. *Deep Storage: Collecting, Storing and Archiving in Art*; Prestel: Munich, New York, 1998.

16. Taylor, H.A. Documentary art and the role of the archivist. Am.Arch. **1979**, *42* (4), 417–428.

17. Ritzenthaler, M.L.; Vogt-O'Connor, D.; Zinkham, H.; Carnell, B.; Peterson, K., Eds. *Photographs: Archival Care and Management*; The Society of American Archivists: Chicago, IL, 2006.

18. Ullman West, M. Dancers as living archives. Chronicle of Higher Education **2006**, *52* (31), B14–B17.

19. Varney, D.; Fensham, R. More-and-less-than: Liveness, video recording, and the future of performance. New Theatre Quart. **2000**, *XVI* (1), 88–96.

20. Winkler, K., Ed. *Their Championship Season: Acquiring, Processing and Using Performing Arts Archives*; Theatre Library Association: New York, 2001.

21. Wythe, D., Ed. *Museum Archives: An Introduction*, 2nd Ed.; The Society of American Archivists: Chicago, IL, 2004.

Visual Resources Association (VRA)

Virginia M.G. Hall
Center for Educational Resources, The Sheridan Libraries, Johns Hopkins University, Baltimore, Maryland, U.S.A.

Abstract

This entry provides an overview of the Visual Resources Association (VRA), an international organization for image media professionals. Beginning with an introduction to the organization and its mission, the entry then provides a history of VRA, including events leading up to its founding in 1982, and gives the background for its importance in the field of information sciences today. Following is an explanation of the organizational structure, a description of the VRA Foundation, and information on the regional chapters, appointments, and standing committees. Two important data standard initiatives, VRA Core and *Cataloging Cultural Objects* (CCO), are described. The entry also provides information on the publications and communications of VRA, the annual conferences, the jointly sponsored (with the Art Libraries Society of North America) Summer Educational Institute for Visual Resources and Image Management (SEI), and VRA's affiliates.

INTRODUCTION

The Visual Resources Association (VRA) is a multidisciplinary organization dedicated to furthering research and education in the field of media management within the educational, cultural heritage, and commercial environments. The Association is committed to providing leadership in the visual resources field, developing and advocating standards, and offering educational tools and opportunities for the benefit of the community at large. VRA implements these goals through publication programs and educational activities. The Association offers a forum for issues of vital concern to the field, including preservation of and access to media documenting visual culture, cataloging and classification standards and practices, integration of technology-based instruction and research, digital humanities, intellectual property policy, visual literacy, and other topics of interest to the field. Through collaboration, partnership, and outreach with the broader information management, educational, and scholarly communities, the Association actively supports the primacy of visual information in documenting and understanding humanity's shared cultural experience.

The international membership includes information specialists; digital image specialists; archivists; art, architecture, film, video, metadata, and digital librarians; museum professionals; architectural firms; galleries; publishers; vendors; rights and reproductions officials; photographers; art historians; artists; scientists; and academic technologists.

Information for this section was culled from a number of Association documents and the VRA website. Many of these sources are anonymously written and reflect an accumulation of information over a period of years by different writers and editors including known contributors: Kathe Hicks Albrecht, Heather Cleary, Lise Hawkos, Benjamin Kessler, Elisa Lanzi, and Elaine Paul.

VRA HISTORY

From as early as 1968, visual resources curators had been meeting during the annual College Art Association (CAA) conferences. The curatorship of slide and photograph collections required special skills and techniques that were not generally available in established curriculums and could be gained only through experience. For the earliest practitioners in the field, who were often isolated within their respective institutions, this knowledge was hard earned and therefore of great value when they had occasion to meet and share information. During these sessions, curators discussed issues of particular interest to CAA members whose work involved the management of art slide collections. Given the success of these meetings, during the next several years, attempts were made to formalize the relationship of these curators with the larger CAA, yet the group remained essentially an ad hoc committee of visual resources curators for some years.

In 1972, the Art Libraries Society of North America (ARLIS/NA) was founded. Visual resources curators comprised a significant special interest group whose purpose was to provide support and development for those members of ARLIS/NA involved in visual resources management.

By the late 1970s, both regional activity and international activity were under way. Comité International d'Histoire de l'Art (CIHA) recognized the visual resources subgroup as an important part of the international association. Visual

Encyclopedia of Library and Information Sciences, Fourth Edition DOI: 10.1081/E-ELIS4-120053509

resources sessions were provided during the *CIHA conference* in Bologna in 1979. On the regional level, in 1972, curators began meeting at annual conferences held by the Mid-America College Art Association (MACAA) and in 1976 at the *Southeastern College Art Conference* (SECAC) meetings.

While this range of meeting venues encouraged participation, it also meant that visual resources remained an adjunct to larger concerns and that affiliation along professional lines was episodic and impermanent. An attempt to organize visual resources curators more formally as a subgroup within the CAA in 1973 was rebuffed by that organization's executive board over the technicality that the only level of suborganization allowed by bylaws was that of a committee.

During this time, a number of educational initiatives, including seminars, workshops, and college courses, were developed for slide and photograph collection curators. A short-lived master's program, called "Curatorial Science for Slide Collections and Photographic Archives," was inaugurated in 1969 at the Allen R. Hite Art Institute of the University of Louisville. Sustained largely by the efforts of dedicated individuals in the visual resources field, some of these early initiatives faltered for lack of institutional support.

One particularly dedicated individual was Nancy DeLaurier, Curator of Slides and Photographs at the University of Missouri, Kansas City. Under her leadership, the MACAA visual resources group began to meet independently, creating workshops and sessions on various aspects of visual resources management. In 1976, DeLaurier began conducting a summer workshop offering fundamentals of collection administration for slide curators. The workshop, "Basic Training for Slide Curators," was held in Kansas City from 1976 to1983. From 1984 to1997, the summer workshop was continued and expanded at the University of Texas at Austin, primarily led by Nancy Schuller (University of Texas at Austin) and Christine Sundt (University of Oregon).

For the workshops, members developed several kits for the benefit of attending visual resources curators. These kits included information on slide room organization, standards of visual resources management, and other practical aspects of the visual resources profession. These eventually evolved into guides published by MACAA, which, in turn, gave rise to what would later become VRA *Special Bulletins*. This group also began regular publication of the *Slides and Photographs Newsletter*, which for a number of years was the main conduit of information for the visual resources community. The *Slides and Photographs Newsletter* was published under the sponsorship of the CAA from 1972 to 1974 and from 1974 to 1979 under the sponsorship of the MACAA. This newsletter eventually became known as the *International Bulletin for Photographic Documentation of the Visual Arts*. DeLaurier was also responsible for the publication

of the first edition of the *Slide Buyers' Guide* (University of Missouri, Kansas City, 1972).

Parallel to these developments, in 1974, Betty Jo Irvine, then head of the Fine Arts Library at Indiana University, published her monograph *Slide Libraries: A Guide for Academic Institutions and Museums* (Libraries Unlimited for Art Libraries Society). After surveying over one hundred visual resources collections, Irvine presented the first comprehensive, scholarly overview of the field. Irvine treated visual resources as a special, if idiosyncratic, branch of librarianship, and thus governable by general principles of librarianship at large. To this end, she emphasized the value of library education and methodology, in contrast to the extensive subject knowledge and more empirical on-the-job training advocated by DeLaurier, Schuller, and other authorities. Schuller's *Guide for the Management of Visual Resources Collections* was published by the MACAA Visual Resources Committee in 1979.

Visual resources literature in the 1970s addressed a wide variety of topics, including classification, copy photography, slide vendors, equipment, and conservation. However, a round of surveys confirmed that the most pressing issue of the day was professional status, as of then not yet truly conferred by any authoritative body. While both CAA and ARLIS/NA agreed in principle on the need for professional recognition of visual resources curators, the requirement of some measure of library education, favored by ARLIS/NA, proved to be a subject of disagreement within the profession. A sequence of committee deliberations resulted in a statement supporting professional status that, while an important first step, lacked definitive standards.

In 1980, the *Slides and Photographs Newsletter* was renamed the *International Bulletin for Photographic Documentation of the Visual Arts* and soon was independently supported by subscription. With the new decade, it was clear that the profession was ready to form its own organization. Discussions were held, and in 1982 a survey measuring organizational preferences was made of curators in ARLIS/NA, CAA, MACAA, and SECAC. While this survey had inconclusive results, it gave rise to a more pointed referendum that offered four choices: 1) maintain the status quo; 2) make an existing group such as ARLIS/NA or the Special Libraries Association the focus for all national visual resources activities; 3) form an information clearinghouse to coordinate the visual resources activities of other organizations; or 4) form a new and separate visual resources organization.

Although only forty-two people voted, a clear majority favored the creation of a new organization. It was on this basis that the VRA was incorporated as a nonprofit organization in Kansas City, Missouri, in August 1982. From a legal standpoint, VRA was a self-chartered continuation of the CAA committee. Temporary officers were Christine Sundt (chair), Nancy Schuller (vice chair), and Nancy DeLaurier (secretary/treasurer). Bylaws were drawn up and the first official meeting was held during the annual CAA meeting in Philadelphia in February 1983. Membership was extended to those curators who subscribed to the *International Bulletin for Photographic Documentation of the Visual Arts*. In Philadelphia, officers were elected. They included Christine Sundt, president; Suzanne Babineau-Simenauer, vice president; Helen McGinnis, secretary; Nancy Schuller, treasurer; and Nancy DeLaurier, former president.

The new organization thrived, growing in membership, providing professional support, and continuing to develop a strong publications program. The latter included the publication of a scholarly journal independent of the *International Bulletin for Photographic Documentation of the Visual Arts* entitled *VRA Bulletin.*

The 1990s brought the development and rapid explosion of the Internet and the subsequent expansion of the visual resources field to include managing digital media. During this time it became clear that VRA no longer served just its membership, but played a new and significant role educating the public and contributing research to the broader field of library and information science and instructional technology. The organization led in the effort to develop public understanding of issues on copyright and intellectual property rights, protocols for dissemination of digital materials, standards of cataloging, and the importance of providing a broad public access to cultural information in the digital age.

The organization was invited to send a representative to the Conference on Fair Use (CONFU), which was convened in September of 1994 under the auspices of the United States Patent and Trademark Office and the United States Copyright Office. Attending the conference were representatives from more than sixty different commercial, public, and educational interest groups. CONFU representatives met monthly through 1997 in an attempt to develop fair use guidelines for use of digital and electronic media in image archives, multimedia, interlibrary loan services, electronic reserves, and distance learning initiatives. Despite the fact that the process did not yield workable guidelines, it was an important forum for VRA as it gave the organization recognition on the national scene as a significant contributor on issues of intellectual property rights in the digital age. The VRA was asked to participate in a series of public forums on copyright that were organized by the National Initiative for a Networked Cultural Heritage (NINCH). These Copyright Town Meetings were held in venues across the country between 1997 and 2003 and were open to the public for discussion and debate.

In other developments during the 1990s, VRA annual conferences began attracting a growing number of non-members interested in learning about visual resources; VRA-L, the Association's listserv, became a dynamic resource for members; and the VRA website evolved into an important source of information for students, professionals, freelance photographers, and intellectual property

rights managers in the image media world. Members of the VRA began to educate the larger community on issues such as copyright, image management, technical digital image issues, data standards, cataloging standards, and other emerging issues of importance. At the turn of the millennium, data standards came to the forefront with the Cataloguing Cultural Objects project (CCO) and the introduction of VRA Core. *Cataloging Cultural Objects: A Guide to Describing Cultural Works and Their Images*, published by the American Library Association in 2006, gained national recognition by standardizing the cataloging of visual information, and CCO sponsored workshops, the CCO website, and other outreach efforts began educating a broad audience. VRA Core, based on Dublin Core, grew from a list of elements to describe art and architectural images into a recognized data standard, with an XML schema to promote the sharing of records describing images of cultural heritage materials.

VRA Education Committee began to sponsor conference workshops on important topics of broad interest and offering these workshops and sessions at VRA and other professional conferences. *The Digital Scene*, later called *Image Stuff* and then *Images*, was featured on the VRA website. It was used to disseminate information on collaborative projects, new standards in imaging and metadata, digital preservation issues, consortial projects, training opportunities, and reports from the field. In 2004 VRA, in conjunction with the ARLIS/NA, began offering the Summer Educational Institute for Visual Resources and Image Management (SEI) to provide in-depth educational opportunities to new and seasoned professionals in the field.

Standards for the profession have remained an important consideration. In 1995, ARLIS/NA and VRA adopted *The Criteria for the Hiring and Retention of Visual Resources Professionals*, a set of guidelines for visual resources professionals. This document was revised in 2002 and is currently undergoing a further update. The division within the profession on the desirability of formal library training versus an advanced degree in a content area was resolved by recognizing that different degrees would be applicable to varying situations (academic institutions, research collections, museums, historical societies, archives, public libraries, governmental agencies, and corporations). And, as a variety of media types may be found in a visual resources collection, the electronic management of those materials has become a primary consideration for the profession.

The combined effects of rapid technological change and the financial crisis of 2008 resulted in the elimination of numerous visual resources positions and facilities. VRA convened a White Paper Task Force to respond to these measures, which in 2009 produced the white paper entitled "Advocating for Visual Resources Management in Educational and Cultural Institutions." The paper asserts the continuing importance of visual resources to teaching, learning, and institutional identity. Arguing that administrative responses to budgetary crises at this time were often shortsighted, the paper identifies six strategic areas for consideration in planning for the future: 1) multiple sources for images; 2) ways of integrating personal and institutional collections; 3) social computing and collaborative projects; 4) the life-cycle continuum of image assets and their description; 5) rights and copyright compliance; and 6) visual literacy.

Several years later, the visual resources profession remains in a state of transition, with many positions' duties attending to image-related tasks beyond curating collections, such as providing instruction in digital imaging and image research, specialization and support in instructional technology, and facilitating various types of digital scholarship. In response to these transformations, VRA charged a Professional Status Task Force with investigating current professional status issues within the field of image and media management. A final report was submitted in June 2016.

Since 1988 the VRA has honored an individual who has made an outstanding career contribution to the field of visual resources and image management with an annual Distinguished Service Award. Nominees must have achieved a level of distinction in the field either through leadership, research, or service to the profession. The Nancy DeLaurier Award, named for one of the pioneers of the visual resources profession, annually honors a visual resources professional for distinguished achievement in the field. Originally conceived in 1997 as a writing award, to be presented in recognition of a published paper, the Nancy DeLaurier Award now recognizes other forms of achievement in the field, as measured by immediate impact, and may take the form of published work, oral presentation, project management, software development, technology application, website creation, or other outstanding effort.

Today VRA is a firmly established international association with hundreds of active members. The association provides its members wide-ranging benefits. VRA is now a leader in developing public awareness on copyright and intellectual property rights, establishing protocols for the dissemination of digital materials, recommending cataloging standards, and promoting broad public access to cultural information in the digital age.

ORGANIZATIONAL STRUCTURE

VRA is governed by an executive board comprised of five regular officers serving two year terms plus an officer who serves one year as president-elect and then two years as president. The other officers are the secretary, treasurer, vice president for conference arrangements, vice president for conference program, and the public relations and communications officer. The former president serves 1 year in a non-board advisory capacity. Officers are nominated by a committee and elected in balloting by eligible VRA

members. The board makes appointments, oversees standing committees and task forces, and approves the organization of regional chapters.

VRA FOUNDATION

In 2004 a task force was appointed by the VRA board to investigate the tax status situation of VRA and to make recommendations. The VRA was incorporated in 1982 as a 501(c) 6 organization, a trade association. Although a trade association is nonprofit, it is an organization established solely to provide direct services to its members. VRA is a fine example of a well-functioning and significant 501(c) 6 organization. As it has grown, the Association's importance has come to extend beyond its member services. Yet, due to the U.S. Internal Revenue Service tax status limitations, VRA, as a 501(c) 6 trade association, has not been able to pursue major grants to engage in research or other educational endeavors.

The Association's educational and research components are now important assets and major resources for the general public and the field of information management. After a year of studying the issues, the task force recommended that from an organizational standpoint, a separate 501(c) 3 VRA Foundation offered a way to most efficiently oversee and extend these significant and influential educational and research efforts.

In July 2007, the VRA Foundation was incorporated in the state of Delaware, and in September 2007 the Internal Revenue Service granted the Foundation 501(c) 3 tax status. The purpose of the VRA Foundation is to develop and expand educational and research opportunities in the public interest; establish standards for emerging electronic media; manage grants and develop programs to improve the visual resources field; conduct and/or sponsor research in the information sciences and educational technology; publish informative articles, guidelines, and online resources; and complement the work of VRA by providing educational, literary, and scientific outreach to the larger community and general public. Through the VRA Foundation, VRA furthers its significant and growing educational and research efforts. Accordingly, the VRA Foundation has assumed responsibility for the Summer Educational Institute and Cataloguing Cultural Objects.

The VRA Foundation board is comprised of seven directors serving two-year terms. Four of the directors are appointed by the VRA board, and three by the Foundation board. Three officers—a chair, treasurer, and secretary—are selected by the directors from their ranks.

REGIONAL CHAPTERS

VRA has fourteen active regional chapters. The Chapter program was developed to extend VRA outreach and professional support to the local level. Attending chapter meetings provides opportunities to make professional contacts, share knowledge and expertise with colleagues, and benefit from continuing education events. The following regions are represented: Canada, Great Lakes, Greater New York, Mid-Atlantic, Midwest, New England, Northern California, Pacific Rim, Southeast, Southern California, Texas, Upstate New York, the Wild West (Mountains and Plains states), and an International Chapter with members from various countries across the globe.

APPOINTMENTS

The VRA board appoints both individuals and task forces to undertake short- or long-term projects, investigations, initiatives, or service. Current appointees include the editors of Association publications and website, a Communications Technology Advisor, a Social Networking Contributor, a VRA Archivist, a representative to the Picture Licensing Universal System Coalition (PLUS) Board of Directors, Affiliate Representatives who liaise with VRA's affiliated organizations, and several working task forces. Appointed independent contractor positions include a membership services coordinator, an accountant, and a bookkeeper.

STANDING COMMITTEES

VRA maintains a number of standing committees to work on Association projects, initiatives, and outreach. Standing committees include Awards, Data Standards, Development, Education, Financial Advisory, Intellectual Property Rights, Membership, Nominating, Travel Awards, and VRA Core Oversight.

PUBLICATIONS AND COMMUNICATIONS

The VRA Bulletin

The *VRA Bulletin* is published twice a year by the Association. A journal of professional practice and the flagship publication of the Association, it features articles on important professional issues ranging from cataloging, copy photography procedures, image and data standards, and collection management and administration. Also included in the *VRA Bulletin* are reviews of recent publications, and updates on commercial image sources.

VRAweb.org

The VRA website, located at the URL http://www.vraweb. org, has both public- and members-only sections. The home page features a dynamic News section that provides current updates on Association activities and events. Other

sections of the publicly accessible site contain the VRA Constitution and Bylaws; Association history and mission; listings of current executive board members, appointees, chapters, and committees; information about VRA affiliates, past and future conferences, membership benefits, the awards program, employment opportunities, the Mentor Program, and special interest groups; as well as links to numerous VRA documents and initiatives.

The members-only section of the site includes the member directory, as well as business meeting minutes, annual reports, financial statements, strategic plans, outreach materials, and forms and documents used for leadership and management purposes.

VRA Listserv

The VRA Listserv, VRA-L, is intended to expedite communication among VRA members on important issues related to the Association, to visual resource curatorship, to related technologies, and to the profession. Appropriate postings forwarded from VRA nonmembers are welcome. Subscription to VRA-L is restricted to VRA members or paid subscribers to VRA-L. VRA-L was started in 1991 and has been an active Listserv serving as a vital communication tool for its members.

Social Media

VRA's appointed Social Networking Contributor coordinates VRA's communications via social media. Current accounts include Facebook, LinkedIn, and Twitter.

Special Bulletins

The *Special Bulletins* are occasional publications, each on a different, specific subject. While *Special Bulletins* are no longer being published in favor of disseminating content in the *VRA Bulletin* and on the VRA website, many of the *Special Bulletins* are still in print and available through the Association. Selected titles are also available for downloading as electronic documents. The publications include guides to cataloging Asian and Chinese Art, subject classifications for image collections, standards for photograph and slide conservation, a guide to copy photography, disaster planning for visual resources collections, a description of iconographic contents and diagrams for cataloging complex works of art, and, most recently, strategies for transition to the use of digital media.

DATA STANDARDS

Cataloging Cultural Objects (CCO)

Cataloging Cultural Objects: A Guide to Describing Cultural Works and Their Images (CCO) is a data content standard for the description of art and cultural objects and their visual surrogates, sponsored by VRA, and published in 2006 by the American Library Association (ALA). CCO was developed by the VRA to provide guidance to visual resources curators, museum documentation specialists, librarians, archivists, and others engaged in describing works of art and architecture, objects of material culture, and their images. Oversight of CCO has been assumed by the VRA Foundation.

VRA Core Categories

Since the 1980s, VRA has worked on creating standards to describe images. As every visual resources collection uses different and variant standards, the Association has worked toward creating a usable and common standard. VRA Core 4.0 is a data standard for the cultural heritage community that was developed by the VRA's Data Standards Committee. It consists of a metadata element set (units of information such as title, location, date) as well as an initial blueprint for how those elements can be hierarchically structured. The element set provides a categorical organization for the description of works of visual culture as well as the images that document them.

The Metadata Encoding and Transmission Standard (METS) Editorial Board officially endorsed VRA Core 4.0 schemas (release version April 9, 2007). This endorsement confirms VRA Core 4.0 schemas (both restricted and unrestricted) are in line with nationally recognized metadata standards and will work well as an extension schema for any METS objects that contain images of cultural heritage resources.

Based on the Dublin Core model, VRA Core has grown from a list of elements to describe art and architectural images to a data standard, with an XML schema to promote the sharing of records, for describing images of cultural heritage.

Five versions of VRA Core have been released:

1. VRA Core 1.0—published in 1996
2. VRA Core 2.0—published in 1998
3. VRA Core 3.0—published in 2002
4. VRA Core 4.0 beta—published in 2005
5. VRA Core 4.0—published in 2007

ANNUAL CONFERENCE

VRA conducts an annual conference, held in a different city each year. This event provides workshops, sessions, and seminars on issues of interest, a chance to meet colleagues both formally and informally, and the opportunity to view current commercial products. VRA members and nonmembers alike attend the VRA annual conferences to learn about the profession and network with colleagues in the field.

SUMMER EDUCATIONAL INSTITUTE FOR VISUAL RESOURCES AND IMAGE MANAGEMENT

The SEI began as a joint VRA and ARLIS/NA project in 2004. Now administered for VRA by the VRA Foundation (VRAF), the Institute provides a standardized and sustainable program for training in image collection management, with a focus on issues related to the transition from analog to digital collections. SEI is held in diverse geographical locations in order to encourage broad participation by professionals seeking standardized training.

Professionals in the field of visual resources currently have to master several different sets of knowledge/expertise to successfully administer existing resources, preserve unique collections within those resources, and engage in the process of converting analog resources to digital modes of presentation. In addition, they have to be conversant with national and international standards, organizations, metadata initiatives, and online resources. As most library and information science programs do not address the needs of image collection professionals, the jointly sponsored ARLIS/NA–VRA Summer Educational Institute is intended to provide a standardized and sustainable program for visual resources training, with a focus on issues related to the transition from analog to digital collections.

As an ongoing endeavor, SEI changes in focus and emphasis each year to meet the needs of new professionals and of institutions facing the demanding metamorphosis from analog slide collections into digital image resources.

SEI is open to professionals, paraprofessionals, and graduate level students in visual resources, library science, the fine arts, related humanities fields, and other image information disciplines. Anyone with a need to learn about managing image collections is encouraged to participate. SEI is designed to serve various levels of expertise including individuals new to the profession, librarians or other information professionals with new responsibilities to oversee and manage image collections, and visual resources managers and art librarians who wish to update their knowledge of current practices.

AFFILIATES

VRA seeks mutually beneficial affiliations in support of its mission, with the goal of facilitating steady communications, collaborative opportunities, and participation in the events and activities of like-minded organizations. Current VRA affiliates are the Art Libraries Society of North America (ARLIS/NA), the College Art Association (CAA), the Society of Architectural Historians (SAH), and the *Southeastern College Art Conference* (SECAC). Other like-minded organizations are listed on VRA's website.

CONCLUSION

The VRA, an international organization, has an active membership of professionals in the image management field from educational, cultural heritage, and commercial environments. The Association was formed in 1983 by slide and photograph curators from institutions of higher learning and museums who supported the teaching and research of art and architectural and art historians. It has grown to include a wide range of specialists supporting image collections and other image- and media-related endeavors. Educational and informational outreach is provided through annual conferences, the SEI, the *VRA Bulletin*, and the VRA website. VRA has been a leader in educating the larger community on copyright and fair use issues, image management, digital image technology, data standards, and cataloging standards.

Visual Resources Management in Cultural Institutions

Jacqueline Allen
Dallas Museum of Art, Dallas, Texas, U.S.A.

Marcia K. Stein
Museum of Fine Arts, Houston, Houston, Texas, U.S.A.

Abstract

Visual resources collections play a vital, yet virtually invisible, role in the life of a museum. They exist to support the mission of their institution through dissemination of the accurate reproduction of works in the collection as well as being the central repository for images acquired for publications and exhibitions. This entry will primarily discuss the history, collections, organization, and professional protocols of art museum visual resources collections in the United States, realizing that the scope of collections and activities of those entrusted with them can be generalized to any cultural institution's needs. It seeks to highlight how collections are built from various sources and the skills and knowledge a manager of those collections must possess to effectively carry out their duties. An extensive recommended reading list is included to point the reader to standard literature for a deeper understanding of important aspects of managing visual collections. An emphasis is placed on understanding issues with digital image formats, rather than film, since most collections are shifting workflows and staffing to accommodate digital formats. Issues surrounding the preservation and dispersal of film-based collections will also be addressed.

INTRODUCTION

Museums are institutions that collect, preserve, and interpret all manner of things, from masterpieces of art to the most common of utilitarian objects (http://icom.museum/the-vision/museum-definition/). By creating and maintaining the visual record of museum objects and events, visual resources collections play a vital, yet virtually invisible, role in the life of a museum. Visual resources collections may contain any of a number of different types of photographic formats from glass-plate negatives to high-resolution, direct-capture digital images, all with the purpose of documenting the history of the cultural institution, the objects in the collection, the way in which they are exhibited, and the role of the object in history. This entry will primarily discuss the history, collections, organization, and professional protocols of art museum visual resources collections in the United States, realizing that the scope of collections and activities of those entrusted with them can be generalized to any cultural institution's needs. This is due to the authors' affiliation and the wide range of documentation relating to art museum collections; however, collection stewardship guidelines and issues surrounding management of digital collections can be applied to visual resources collections within any cultural institution.

Various names are assigned to the department that acquires, organizes, and distributes images. Traditionally, it had been called the visual resources library—a name that reflects the content—a library of images used for publications, programs, and teaching. With the introduction of digital formats came a natural progression of new responsibilities based on the ease of reproducibility and repurposing of images in-house, followed by a name more descriptive of the function rather than the content. Several art museum collections have changed department names to reflect broader imaging functions. In 2002, the department of Photographic Services, once a separate department at the Museum of Fine Arts, Houston, was moved to the Image Library and renamed the Photographic and Imaging Services Department when it was recognized that the functions of both departments were intertwined. The Dallas Museum of Art's visual resources library was renamed Imaging Services, has also included the photographers and rights management since 2002, and in 2014 moved all non-object photography to the institutional archives, with imaging staff reporting to information technology (IT) and digital media. Other museums have formed departments based on the digital format such as the Brooklyn Museum of Art's department, Digital Collections and Services, formed in 2005 that includes the photo studio, scan lab, rights-related activities, and digital asset management. For this entry, we will refer to the activities of acquiring, organizing, and distributing images, as visual resources management.

HISTORIC CONTEXT

The reproduction of works of art by artists, collectors, and, later, museums is well documented in the history of art. Painted copies and drawings after original works created a precedent for later mechanical reproductions, such as printed copies that could be made in great numbers, not only to grace the walls of humbler owners but also to disseminate information about new and important objects. The photographic reproduction of art objects was a natural result, and museums were quick to embrace the new medium as early as the 1850s. The history of visual resources collections in museums dates back almost to the beginning of photography itself. Museums hired photographers to document their objects and events to promote not only scholarship but also the museums themselves. Museums have always taken advantage of the newest photographic formats available, moving from glass negatives and salt prints in the mid-nineteenth century to film and now to digital. For the majority of the twentieth century, museum visual resources collections housed extensive libraries of black-and-white negatives and prints, color transparencies in various sizes (120 mm, 4×5 in., 8×10 in., with 4×5's being the standard), and 35 mm color slides. With the introduction of direct digital capture, the standard format of the early twenty-first century has moved to high-resolution digital images captured on high-end DSLR cameras and professional digital camera systems. A chronology of the "slide library" can be found online at http://en.wikipedia.org/wiki/Slide_library.

Although the professional standards for visual resources managers are the same for collections in universities and museums, the roles played by the collections are much different. This is evident especially in the way that the museum visual resources collection supports traditional noneducational activities. Visual resources collections in universities exist primarily to support the teaching curriculum of the university or department. Museum visual resources collections often function in this way, but it is just one of the many functions of the department. A major role of many visual resources collections is to promote the museum and its collections through the dissemination of high-quality reproduction images. In the case of art museum collections, the responsibility of providing high-quality images is extremely important since a poor reproduction of a great painting could be seen as a reflection on the quality of the art collection itself.

BUILDING COLLECTIONS

The content of visual resources collections varies according to the needs of the institution and constituency that they serve. Some purely consist of photography relating directly to the objects in their own collection. Others include noncollection materials that provide historical or subject context in which the museum's objects can be understood. The collections may either be available for public use or have access restrictions limiting patronage to staff and/or volunteers. For example, the American Museum of Natural History's Photographic Collection in New York City dates back to the Museum's beginnings.

Albert Bickmore, founder of the Museum, who became superintendent of public education, gave lantern slide lectures to school teachers. A lantern slide lending library was formed under the auspices of the department of public education. Meanwhile, Museum scientists were traveling the globe and returning with negatives. Prints were often pasted into scrapbooks in the science departments; and the negatives and scrapbooks were later deposited in the Museum's education department. The Museum Library's Special Collections is now in charge of virtually all of the negatives in the institution, and most of the prints, as well as many of the historic lantern slides. The collection as it is known today is supervised by the museum archivist and head of Library Special Collections.

The origin of the content, whether physical film or digital image, will depend on whether the image originates with the institution or if it is documenting an exterior event or object, in which case a third-party provider will need to be consulted for terms of use. For institutional images and event or program documentation, the institution may have staff photographers or photographers that are hired for a specific project. Many museums require that non-staff photographers sign "work for hire" contracts that relinquish the copyright of their photography to the museum, thereby granting full ownership of the photography to the museum. Consultation with museum counsel is necessary when contracts such as these are drafted. Cataloging and stewardship of those images may reside with staff in the visual resources library or be the responsibility of another department, such as the archives. There are instances where photography is created for a specified purpose. Images that document a work's condition or complex installation procedure could be created by the museum's photographer or a conservator, but may not be housed in the visual resources library due to confidentiality. Those images may be linked directly to object documentation, but access would be limited to specific staff.

Other Content Sources

Reference images, those images whose content is owned by a third party, can come from a variety of sources. Reference images might be used for study purposes by staff, illustrations for a lecture, reproductions in an exhibition catalogue, or didactic materials in an exhibition. Ideally, the images would be obtained from the source that created the image; however, that is not always practical, or necessary. Third-party providers can fill most needs for teaching images and related uses, but not all. Those images will be subscribed to or purchased for educational use and will have use restrictions. In some cases, for example, with ARTstor, museums are both contributors and subscribers to third-party content. ARTstor is a subscription service that provides remote access to a growing database of images for teaching (http://www.artstor.org/). While not generally needed for educational use, at times, visual resources managers may need to license images from stock photo collections such as Getty Images or Art Resource. Frequently, images for teaching are scanned from previously published sources in the tradition of copy-photography. This content source should only be utilized within the parameters of copyright laws in the region, such as Fair Use in the United States. Several organizations have published Fair Use Statements in recent years and they are listed in the "Visual Resources Management Resources" section.

An Ever-Changing Landscape

Storage issues have always been a major concern for visual resources managers. In the past, physical storage of photographic negatives and positives has posed interesting and sometimes dangerous problems. Some materials require cold storage (color positives), while others do best in dark, dry, temperature-neutral environments (black-and-white negatives). In an extreme case, nitrate negative films must be housed in secure, cold, pressurized containers to prevent explosive reactions with air. The common thread for these types of materials, however, is the need for physical space for storage. Storage rooms and sometimes even whole floors are necessary to provide the physical storage space for photographic materials. Visual resources managers must also be knowledgeable in the conservation requirements for each type of material in their collection and make suitable arrangements for the storage and housing of each type of material.

Digital storage may not require the physical space of earlier materials, but it is no less important for the viability of any visual resources collection. The actual footprint of storage space can be reduced drastically if the digital files are stored entirely on local or cloud-based servers. The decision to keep all files on servers requires that server technology is kept up to date, and data migration policies are implemented. As technology changes and new digital file formats are developed, migration policies must be in place to ensure that files created today will be able to be accessed in the future. The information contained in a digital image file is dependent on the format chosen. File formats become obsolete as newer formats are developed, so institutions have to make a commitment to migrate data files to current formats. The use of compressed file formats or proprietary formats is discouraged. Compressed files, most notably "lossy"-type formats, cannot be depended upon for future accuracy of information. Proprietary formats are often the first types of files to become obsolete and therefore very difficult to access in the future. Digital files may also be stored off-line on media such as magnetic tape, optical drives, and CD/DVD media. This method is not recommended and the choice to save files on such media presents its own preservation issues that involve the obsolescence of the physical media as well as the computer hardware to access it. The visual resources

manager must weigh the benefits of storing files off-line, which may be less expensive in the short term in terms of network storage costs, against the costs of physical storage space for the media and the staff time and expense of migrating both media and file data. Off-line storage also makes retrieval and distribution difficult.

Working in conjunction with institutional IT staff, visual resources managers must plan for scalable solutions that will protect the digital collections they have toiled to create. In managing collection documentation, especially of art objects, image file sizes can become huge and inefficient to store in-house. Cloud-based storage services are being used for management of large collections and can be useful if a reliable and secure service is selected. The choice to outsource file storage can eliminate the need to increase back-up storage solutions to meet demands for preservation and retrieval if a server fails in-house.

The downside of having virtual assets rather than physical ones, however, is that access and retrieval are now totally dependent on computer searches, making proper and often complex cataloging systems necessary. In the past, many museums did not see the need to undertake extensive cataloging initiatives for their film-based visual resources collections, relying instead on a physical filing system for retrieval. Larger museums, with larger collections of images such as Harvard University's Fogg Museum of Art, invested in cataloging systems and became the prototype for others. With the advent of digital collections, even the smallest museum is now having to deal with retrieval issues making database and system decisions important. While some museums have chosen to create their own databases in software applications such as FileMakerPro or Microsoft Access, it is recommended that visual resources collections employ specialized digital asset management systems (DAMS), which combine sophisticated cataloging data with retrieval and distribution functionality. DAMS that also include elements of digital rights management are preferred, but are currently difficult to obtain and require much customization.

Best Practices

The digital revolution has affected every aspect of our daily and professional lives. To that end, sustainability is a concern for many and research is ongoing at universities and coalitions of organizations to create best practices for those working in the field. Through the advice of these organizations, the field of visual resources management is becoming more standardized, and museums are embracing the idea that sustainable image collections are important in intellectual and fiscal terms. By following the basic guidelines outlined by these best practices, museums have a means of creating and caring for collections that will provide rich resources for scholars and museumgoers now and in the future.

Issues have come to pass with the establishment of digital imaging that visual resources collections did not have to deal with previously. When photographic collections were film-based, many visual resources collections had limited technology concerns beyond transparency viewing. For some institutions, common office supplies and furniture sufficed for the care of collections, while others employed state-of-the-art conservation supplies for housing materials, the choice of which was often based on funding and how each museum administrator viewed the importance of the collection. Typewriters and, later, word processors and computers were used to create labels for the materials. With the advent of digital collections, however, the visual resources collection may be the department with the most sophisticated computer equipment in the entire museum.

With digital formats come a new set of variables to manage when providing images for users. Current equipment and software are as important for efficient processing of requests as is knowledgeable staff. Visual resources managers work in a fast-paced environment where requestors expect to be able to access images without delay. There is a perception that digital image creation is faster than traditional photography. While that is not completely true, managers who can integrate the processes of image capture (whether directly from the object or scanned from existing photography), image manipulation, cataloging, and reliable delivery systems will encounter the least number of problems when delivering a requested set of images. Settling on standard image formats and consistent workflows ensures delivery of high-quality images.

Color management is one of the most important aspects of digital quality control and must be integrated into all visual resources activities. It involves a wide range of processes including matching digital images to displays and prints, calibrating printers, and using color management tools. At the very least, digital systems require a basic knowledge of how to synchronize monitors throughout the lab to ensure a consistent image output for users. Art museums spend a great amount of time working with printing presses to ensure color fidelity for images of their objects. The Universal Photographic Digital Imaging Guidelines, which promotes color sustainability from the viewpoint of the museum photographer, is one such resource for best practices (http://www.updig.org/index. html).

The use of digital systems requires that visual resources staff maintain a close working relationship with IT staff. In a film-based collection, interaction with the IT department was only necessary to provide support for word-processing programs, database application issues, or e-mail problems. Now, the department head must communicate a variety of requirements such as the need for and issues about image manipulation software, color management tools, servers to store images, fast connections to the

server to transfer images, and outsourced storage for large files, just to name a few.

Although collections may be acquiring images and filling requests in strictly digital formats, issues surrounding film storage and production continue to be relevant to the visual resources manager. As long as collections house or produce film or prints, best practices for processing, duplication, and especially storage must be maintained. For example, the Library of Congress includes collection care guidelines on their website http://www.loc.gov/preservation/care/photo.html.

Visual resources managers are routinely entrusted with digital conversion projects. This is where knowledge of film formats and capabilities of those formats are invaluable. Whether converted on a case-by-case basis or en masse, unique collections are being converted to digital formats for ease of distribution or presentation online. For example, when cultural institutions work with partners on a project, as in the case of a catalog related to a traveling exhibition, one partner might only have images on film for an object. In order for these images to be distributed to the publisher, the film has to be converted to a standard digital format.

Archival Images

If an institutional archive has not been established in a cultural institution, then master images taken of events, exhibition installations, and personnel are most effectively managed by centralizing them in the visual resources collection. Exhibition installation images are critical to documenting one of the most important activities of the museum and are requested frequently for publication, especially for reproduction within an artist monograph. Acquisitions for the permanent collection and the display or exhibition of those and other works is a primary activity for cultural institutions, and one for which a careful record must be maintained. For any event that takes place at a museum, there is the possibility that a photographic record will be created. Program documentation includes photography of speakers at a lecture, dance performers, school groups, family activities, or exhibition openings. Additions or changes to the public spaces, building exterior, object storage, or landscape are important historic records and are of interest as documents showing changes that have taken place over time. If staff portraits are taken and archived, the visual resources collection may be the repository for these images.

The nature of documentation images makes them a prime candidate for transfer from film formats to digital. Digitization allows for effective distribution (of copies) and preservation (of the original) because the documented event, now passed, is not available to reshoot with direct digital capture. The library at the American Museum of Natural History is systematically scanning its rare book illustrations as well as extensive documentary image

Vietnam—Webometrics

collections estimated to contain over 1 million images between negative, print, large format transparency, lantern slide, and 35 mm slide collections. After completing a pilot project for digitization and online access, Picturing the Museum: Education and Exhibition at the American Museum of Natural History (http://images.library.amnh.org/photos), the AMNH Research Library established Digital Special Collections (http://lbry-web-007.amnh.org/digital/), supervised by the museum archivist and carried out by the visual resources librarian with assistance from project managers, lab managers, and volunteers. In addition to building collections, the new visual resources team also works with museum departments and researchers to provide data and images for special events, exhibition needs, and publications. Through conversion to digital formats, the vast photographic collections at the AMNH Library can be accessed by researchers and the public for a fascinating glimpse into the past.

Object photography occasionally requires updates due to changes in the physical state of an object, changing tastes in three-dimensional object backgrounds, or the need for an image taken from a different angle. Previous versions of object photography might be retained for documentation of an object's condition over time.

To simplify the discussion of archival documentation, only photographic images were addressed here in detail; however, the ability to create audio and video documentation of the subjects noted is becoming commonplace and carries its own set of issues for storage and distribution. Since these files are also moving to direct digital capture, visual resources managers have needs in common with creators of that content and might even collaborate on finding solutions for the institution.

COLLECTION ACCESS

User Services

Visual resources staff need to be effective teachers. They have to communicate instructions on many levels that range with the patron's familiarity of the image collections. Staff new to the museum will need to be trained in the scope of the content and services as well as basic methods for making requests. When film was the primary delivery format, the choices were limited, and requests could be filled by sending film to a professional photography laboratory that employed standard formats for development or duplication. With digital images, and the variety of possible end-user formats, an initial in-person interview setting is generally the most efficient way to arrive at the final format necessary to fill a request.

Imaging staff become well versed in the activities of the institution as a whole while filling image requests. Making formats available, appropriate to the end use, is important to being able to fill the requestor's needs. Staff involved in

museum activities other than curatorial and education will primarily need access to digital images from one of three categories: the permanent collection, recent events, or upcoming exhibitions. The staff who are in charge of interpreting and exhibiting the collection will require a wholly other set of images to study, teach about, and interpret objects in their care. The ability to effectively communicate with scholars on a full range of topics is a unique and valued quality of the museum visual resources professional.

There are several levels of collection sharing that either originate with or are facilitated by staff in imaging. The most basic level of service is filling requests for in-house uses that can either be for a program taking place at the institution, a staff person who is asked to speak on the collection elsewhere, or via printed materials that are produced about exhibitions or programs. A fast-growing resource for learning about all aspects of a cultural institution is their website where users expect to see images of the collection, details about upcoming programs, and a variety of educational materials. The visual resources staff is central to this primary communication vehicle since many images that appear online are delivered directly or indirectly through the visual resources department.

Virtual Organization

In digital collections where a DAMS has not been implemented, images may be organized in a variety of ways and may or may not be available for browsing, and staff intervention is frequently necessary if the correct images are to be found. Object collection photography is filed or stored on a server according to the object's accession number or some close variation of that. Events are generally described according to the department of origin and the date the event took place. Exhibition images are generally organized by the exhibition title and selected by the organizers to represent the overall theme. They are used in print or website advertising, on invitations, or as illustrations for articles and reviews in newspapers or journals.

Images that originate on film are converted to a digital format before printing. In many cases, scanned images are produced in-house, and central scanning services have been integrated into the workflow of the imaging department. The more that staff in visual resources know about digital formats for printing and online use, the more relevant the department will be to filling institutional needs now and in the future. When preparing a digital image for any request, the most important question to ask is, "How will the image be used?" The ability to deliver correct formats for an end use is a critical function of visual resources.

Collection Preservation and Dispersal

Images produced by direct digital capture, and permanent retention of the resulting digital files, have resulted in many print and film-based collections being disposed of, downsized, or ceased and physically moved to special collections or archives departments. When this is the case, staff find that the format of the image drives departmental priorities to shift and emphasize management of and access to the digital files using multiple computer systems. In cases where the image format has dictated reporting structure, organizations are actively seeking staff skilled in technology applications and well-developed metadata management and database skills. Deep subject knowledge is required as an educational foundation, but technical expertise and experience has become a deciding factor for many new hires. Distribution of digital content relies heavily on consistent metadata application and efficient workflow management. This transition of focus has been prompted in many cases by an increased emphasis on online access, with image collections as a central audience draw.

Dispersal of collections has prompted much discussion among professionals, and in 2014 the Visual Resources Association's Slide and Transitional Media Task Force published *Guidelines for the Evaluation, Retention, and Deaccessioning of 35 mm Slide Collections in Educational and Cultural Institutions*. Emphasis is placed on retaining unique collections, which in some cases results in simply downsizing teaching collections to retain only one copy of an image, or transferring documentation image management to institutional archives collections.

At the Dallas Museum of Art, an administrative reorganization led to legacy image collections in several formats being physically moved to the department of archives. Images included exhibition and permanent collection gallery installations, events, building and construction documentation, and portraits or informal images of people. Formats included black and white prints, color prints, 35 mm slides, 35 mm negatives, 4×5 negatives, 4×5 transparencies, and images on optical disk (if digital files were removed from the media and cataloged in the digital asset management system, the disks were discarded). In terms of organization, for ease of access and reference purposes, the transferred prints, negatives, slides, and disks were added to existing collections of permanent print photography and each collection was simultaneously reprocessed. In this case, slides have been removed from cabinets and sleeved during reprocessing, though one could choose to process slides as a separate series and store them in boxes or drawers. The analog photography collection at the Dallas Museum of Art is considered closed since the museum is no longer producing print or film-based image records.

Cataloging and Standards

Images need descriptive cataloging for intellectual control and to create paths for access to images for a particular use. Terms need to be assigned consistently and stored relative to the image or with a path to the location of an image. To facilitate image sharing, standards for data fields, such as Categories for the Description of Works of Art, and content creation, such as Cataloging Cultural Objects, were introduced that are now becoming sophisticated and essential to managing digital collections. Without good cataloging, standard image naming, and reliable storage systems, a growing digital collection can become useless in a very short amount of time. See "Visual Resources Management Resources" for relevant cataloging content and data standards. For examples of online museum image collections, see the British Museum http://www.britishmuseum.org/, or the Metropolitan Museum of Art http://www.metmuseum.org/.

Digital Asset Management Systems and Digital Rights Management Systems

Content management systems (CMS), including DAMS, are integrated computer systems used to manage, distribute, and store digital files. The term DAMS most often refers to such systems that manage only nontextual files such as image, video, audio, and gaming-related formats. DAMS allow for the ingestion of master files and accompanying metadata, the ability to search for specific files meeting specific search criteria, the creation of derivative files from the master for a variety of uses, the storage of the master files, and in some cases active file preservation and migration platforms.

Digital rights management systems (DRMS) are systems designed to manage the usage rights for digital files. While many CMS and DAMS include some digital rights management services, the two types of systems are not identical, and care must be taken by visual resources management professionals to ensure which institutional solutions are chosen that balance the need for access against the intellectual property rights afforded to the creators of digital materials.

The need for sophisticated computer systems to manage digital assets and digital rights arrives at different times at different institutions. In some institutions, DAMS and DRMS implementations are part of a larger institution-wide initiative to gain control of digital assets ranging from text documents to video footage. At others, the decision to implement these systems happen at a departmental level, focusing on only one type of digital asset, such as still photographic images. Implementation of DAMS often occurs when the number of redundant files becomes so confusing on shared network servers that questions arise concerning authoritative data and file accuracy.

Data linkage between a museum's collection management system and its DAMS should exist for images of works from a museum's collection to promote consistency across museum departments when releasing information to the public. The combination of data found in the collection management system with the descriptive cataloging data often employed in the visual resources collection provides a very sound basis for searching collection objects by patrons from the most dedicated university scholar to the occasional museum visitor.

Rights and Reproductions

A function that might be assumed by the visual resources collection in a museum is the acquisition and granting of reproduction rights, especially when the visual resources department houses the photography or images in question. Museums are often asked by outside parties for permission to reproduce images of objects from their collection. Some museums see this function as a revenue-generating activity and set monetary goals that the department must meet. Others see this function as a way to expand knowledge about the museums' collections, so they take a less profit-driven approach. A growing number of museums have separated commercial from scholarly requests and have begun to grant free access to images for scholarly publications through services such as ARTstor's Images for Academic Publishing (http://www.artstor.org/content/collaborations) or added features to their own site, such as the Open Access for Scholarly Content option at the Metropolitan Museum of Art. Most museums continue to charge reproduction and/or image usage fees for nonscholarly or commercial reproduction requests.

Copyright

Staff members that work with or are in the position to distribute visual collections to users and potential publishers need to be aware of intellectual property law and guidelines. This is essential in any collection where unique intellectual content is being recorded and distributed. In the United States, an understanding of the Fair Use Doctrine of U.S. Copyright Law is also a necessity since misunderstandings of this doctrine are rampant at nonprofit institutions. A common statement heard in visual resources collections is, "My use is educational; therefore my use falls under Fair Use." Use must meet certain requirements to be seen as Fair Use, so it is incumbent on visual resources professionals to fully understand the parameters of laws in the region in which they work. In the United States, see http://www.copyright.gov/fls/fl102.html.

Museums, like most libraries and archives, are in the position of owning objects for which they do not own the copyrights. In order to publish catalogs, produce retail objects, and even post images of art objects on their own institution's websites, museums must often negotiate with individual rights holders or clearing houses. American visual artists might choose to outsource requests for reproduction of their work to clearing houses such as Artists Rights Society (ARS) (http://www.arsny.com/) or Visual

Artists and Galleries Association (http://vagarights.com/), which are based in the United States. A list of organizations outside the United States is summarized on the ARS website.

VISUAL RESOURCES STAFF

Visual resources professionals from both museums and universities began meeting at academic conferences in the 1960s to discuss common issues and solutions to caring for art history slide collections. Since that time, the profession has evolved to include members from a wide variety of institutions that care for images in all formats on a variety of topics. Organizations such as the Art Libraries Society of North America and the Visual Resources Association have developed and advocated professional competencies for members of the field, and these have become more widely adopted by museums over the past decade.

Levels of staffing will vary with the type of activities performed. Depending on how many image functions have been centralized in an institution, the size of the staff can vary. For example, in an art museum, there might be a department head, a cataloger, a database specialist, a rights and reproductions manager, an administrative assistant, and/or photographers.

In terms of organizational structure, visual resources collections are administratively aligned with a wide variety of areas including the museum library, archives and special collections, registrar, education, collections and curatorial, IT, and academic deans in the case of collections affiliated with a university. Visual resources management has been performed by both professional and volunteer staff, depending on the institution. With the advent of digital technologies, especially the Internet and museums' presence on the World Wide Web, professional staffs and sophisticated data management practices are becoming the norm at even the smallest institutions.

Competencies

The competencies listed here outline the primary abilities needed to perform a range of tasks or functions within visual resources management. They can be used to assess a level of excellence for the visual resources manager or as a basis for training staff to perform a specific role in the image library. The professional organizations, VRA and ARLIS/NA, have published detailed studies and articles on the topic, which are listed in the "Visual Resources Management Resources" section.

Visual resources managers should have both broad and specialized subject knowledge in a field appropriate to the type of institution and/or library and information science. A minimum educational requirement for professional staff includes a postbaccalaureate degree in either area with broad coursework or comprehensive on-the-job experience in the other area.

Managers and staff should access, use, and distribute information ethically and legally with attention to copyright guidelines and demonstrate a cooperative attitude, initiative, self-motivation, and the ability to advocate for and motivate others.

Managers should be effective instructors, capable of self-management and the management of others. They should help shape the future of their institution or organization and their profession. Successful managers will plan and manage projects, set and attain goals, establish workflows, and delegate tasks effectively. To keep staff informed and current, managers must have a broad understanding of technology issues and working knowledge of best practices in the areas of usability, interoperability, and digital preservation.

All visual resources staff should have the following skills and abilities for successful execution of their duties:

Organizational and time-management skills for priority setting, and setting and meeting deadlines

Financial management skills including basic accounting, record-keeping, and reporting

The skills necessary to ensure quality access, presentation, and preservation of digital image collections

Flexibility in adapting to frequent changes in IT formats and methods of delivery

The ability to select appropriate technological tools and apply them effectively, particularly those tools that are vital to caring for cultural collections, such as DAMS, DRMS, and photographic equipment

---

The Role of Professional Organizations

Attendance at professional meetings serves multiple purposes, but primarily extends training to include current issues. Several organizations offer one-day or longer workshops, sessions, meetings, and opportunities to get involved in the community and contribute to the shaping of this profession.

Further educational opportunities are available through annual workshops offered such as The Summer Educational Institute (SEI). The SEI is a joint VRA–ARLIS/NA program that provides a standardized and sustainable curriculum for training in image collection management. Each year, the focus on issues related to the transition from analog to digital collections becomes more relevant. The curriculum includes focused study on intellectual property rights, metadata, digital imaging, and discussions on current issues and expanding the role of the image management professional. Notification of like opportunities for specialized or in-depth investigation of a topic can be found by joining one or more professional organizations and subscribing to their listserv. There are multiple

opportunities every year to attend local and national meetings. For collections with limited budgets for professional travel, some have awards that are offered by application on a competitive basis.

Involvement is also considered a competency for effective management of visual collections. Contribution to the advancement of the visual resources profession involves knowledge sharing that includes publication and presentation of research findings and professional practices. Networking activities and participation in lifelong learning and professional development opportunities that build on existing knowledge and experience are also encouraged and necessary to remain current with the ever-changing landscape.

Planning and Administration

Whether a one-person department or the leader of a team of staff, a visual resources collection manager has a responsibility to plan for the future at all times. Departmental budgets and future planning are inextricably intertwined. Providing that the IT department absorbs costs related to software and asset management systems, specialized imaging equipment and qualified personnel are the primary expenditures when managing a VR collection, and the manager must communicate that essential need to budget preparers to meet user expectations over time. Equipment upgrade schedules (generally a two-year rotation) need to be communicated to and understood by the institution's IT department; in fact it is most effective if a VR staff person is assigned to keeping an equipment "wish list" current so that when budgets are prepared the most current needs can be addressed.

In the case of a larger staff, there are more management responsibilities. The department head must contribute to the recruitment, orientation, training, supervision, and evaluation of their staff. Securing and retaining qualified personnel is an ongoing concern. The skills necessary to providing seamless service are the direct result of appropriate levels of expertise and ongoing training. A good manager can contribute to the success of everyone on the team by advocating for further education and encouraging staff to stay current with best practices and to upgrade skills as opportunities become available. Staff training is continuous since new techniques and approaches are constantly being developed. Staff members must be good communicators with knowledge of the subject matter at hand and have a baseline expertise in software programs. For example, to work in an art museum, a fine art or art history background is expected in addition to technical competencies specific to their job.

The manager also sets the tone for open communication, cooperation, and team building, which is essential in an environment where deadlines are ever present and the needs of various departments will eventually overlap. Marketing key services of the department to staff is one way to create departmental support. Marketing can include collaboration with other departments on institution-wide projects (such as a publication) or simply helping new staff to understand the role of visual resources within the institution. It is sometimes necessary for visual resources staff to willingly take on new responsibilities to grow with the needs of the institution. The manager sets the tone for the department's success.

CONCLUSION

Visual resources staffs play a vital role in the life of a cultural institution. The proliferation of images, in their various formats and for numerous uses, requires the attention of a professional manager to effectively acquire, manage, and circulate the collections. Guidelines for housing, cataloging, preserving, and distributing images are evolving at a rapid rate, especially since the introduction of digital formats in the mid-1990s. Since then, the focus on creating and distributing best practice guidelines has dominated the field and highlighted standards for quality that can be controlled and effected at the institutional level. Visual resources professionals are being acknowledged for their expertise in project management, copyright issues, digital technologies, and image creation and reuse.

Advances in digital imaging technology and image sharing methods are driving professional conference program content and conversations. Each year, new ideas about fair use of images, copyright interpretation, cataloging guidelines, image formats, and software advances are being published and presented at conferences. Digital formats and a variety of asset management systems have brought new scenarios for the profession and future generations of image users.

VISUAL RESOURCES MANAGEMENT RESOURCES

Assessing Copyright Status

Young, A.M., Ed. *Rights & Reproductions: The Handbook for Cultural Institutions*; Indianapolis Museum of Art: Indianapolis, IN; Washington, DC: American Alliance of Museums, 2015.

Lawson, R. Copyright and fair use in the art museum library: An overview. In *Art Museum Libraries and Librarianship*; Benedetti, J.M. Ed.; Scarecrow Press:Lanham, MD, 2007; 53–60.
    A good summary of the issues and related legislation.

The Digital Image Rights Computator (DIRC), http://dirc.vraweb.org/
    This program is intended to assist the user in assessing the intellectual property status of an object.

Copyright term and the public domain in the United States, https://copyright.cornell.edu/resources/publicdomain.cfm
    An annually updated chart.

WIPO guide on managing intellectual property for museums, http://www.wipo.int/copyright/en/museums_ip/
    Assists museums in learning to use the intellectual property (IP) system to improve the management of their collections in the digital environment.

Aufderheide, P. *Copyright, Permissions, and Fair Use among Visual Artists and the Academic and Museum Visual Arts Communities: An Issues Report*; College Art Association: New York, 2014.
    http://www.collegeart.org/pdf/FairUseIssuesReport.pdf
    The fair use issues report completed the initial phase of a multi year project to develop CAA's *Code of Best Practices in Fair Use for the Visual Arts* in 2015.

Code of Best Practices in Fair Use for the Visual Arts; College Art Association: New York, 2015. http://www.collegeart.org/pdf/fair-use/best-practices-fair-use-visual-arts.pdf

Statement on the Fair Use of Images for Teaching, Research, and Study. Visual Resources Association, June 2013. http://vraweb.org/wp-content/uploads/2011/01/VRA_FairUse_Statement_Pages_Links.pdf
    This statement was drafted by members of the VRA's Intellectual Property Rights Committee and draws on expertise of members as well as existing documentation surrounding the longstanding practices of image use in educational contexts.

Guidelines for the Use of Copyrighted Materials and Works of Art by Art Museums; Association of Art Museum Directors: New York and Washington DC, 2017. https://aamd.org/sites/default/files/document/AAMD_Fair%20Use_%20FINAL%20203_24_17%20-%20Guidelines%20for%20Copyrighted%20Materials%20and%20Works%20of%20Art.pdf

Transition to Digital Formats

Hamma, K. Public domain art in an age of easier mechanical reproducibility, *11* (11), http://www.dlib.org/dlib/november05/hamma/11hamma.html (November 2005).

RLGDigiNews Special issue: Introduction: Managing digital assets in US museums, *10* (6), http://worldcat.org/arcviewer/1/OCC/2007/07/10/0000068924/viewer/file1.html (December 15, 2006).

Waibel, G. From hand-crafted to mass-digitized. http://hangingtogether.org/?p=256 (August 29, 2007).

Organizations and Sources for Project Reports and White Papers

Note: Useful and timely resources will be linked to the appropriate menu item on each organization's website; serial publications are noted where available.

ARLIS/NA (*Art Documentation*, ISSN 0730-7187), http://www.arlisna.org/

ARLIS/UK and Ireland (*Art Libraries Journal*, ISSN 0307-4722), http://www.arlis.org.uk/

College Art Association, http://www.collegeart.org
    See Image Resource Directory, http://www.collegeart.org/ip/ip_image.
    See CAA Committee on Intellectual Property, http://www.collegeart.org/ip/.

Getty Research Institute, http://www.getty.edu/research/publications/electronic_publications/index.html
The Institute publishes numerous professional resources and makes them freely available online and available for purchase in print.
Library of Congress—Standards, http://www.loc.gov/standards/
Museum Computer Network, http://www.mcn.edu/
NINCH Guide to Good Practice, http://www.ninch.org/programs/practice/ includes sections on Metadata and Digital Asset Management.
OCLC Research Reports, http://www.oclc.org/research/publications/reports.html
Society of American Archivists (*American Archivist*, ISSN 0360-9081), http://www2.archivists.org/
See Visual Materials Section, http://www2.archivists.org/groups/visual-materials-section.
Visual Resources: An International Journal of Documentation; Taylor & Francis. ISSN 0197-3762 (Print), ISSN 1477-2809 (Online)
Visual Resources Association (*Visual Resources Association Bulletin*, ISSN 1046-9001), http://vraweb.org/
Additional professional organizations are listed at http://vraweb.org/about/affiliations/.
VRA-L is a membership-based listserv that is widely considered essential reading for visual resources professionals.

Cataloging

Baca, M., Ed. *Introduction to Art Image Access: Issues, Tools, Standards, Strategies.* Getty Research Institute: Los Angeles, CA, 2002, http://www.getty.edu/research/publications/electronic_publications/intro_aia/index.html

Authorities

Union List of Artist Names (ULAN), Cultural Objects Name Authority (CONA), Library of Congress Name Authority Files (LCNAF), Library of Congress Subject Headings (LCSH).

Vocabularies

Art & Architecture Thesaurus (AAT), Thesaurus for Graphic Materials - Library of Congress (TGM), the Getty Thesaurus of Geographic Names (TGN).

Content

Baca, M. *Cataloging Cultural Objects: A Guide to Describing Cultural Works and Their Images*; American Library Association: Chicago, IL, 2006. ISBN 778-0-83:9:5-64.4, http://cco.vrafoundation.org/index.php/toolkit/cco_pdf_version/. See also the CCO Commons for practical application, http://cco.vrafoundation.org/.
Provides guidelines for selecting, ordering, and formatting data used to populate catalog records based on core [data standards] categories in CDWA and VRA Core.

Describing Archives: a Content Standard.; 2nd Ed.; Society of American Archivists: Chicago, IL, 2013. (DACS) ISBN 978-1-931666-08-4. http://files.archivists.org/pubs/DACS2E-2013_v0315.pdf
Content standard for writing consistent archival descriptions.

Data Standards and Guidelines

Introduction to Metadata, http://www.getty.edu/research/publications/electronic_publications/intrometadata
Metadata Standards Crosswalk, http://www.getty.edu/research/conducting_research/standards/intrometadata/crosswalks.html
Categories for the Description of Works of Art (CDWA), http://www.getty.edu/research/publications/electronic_publications/cdwa
Dublin Core Metadata Initiative (DCMI), http://dublincore.org/
Machine-Readable Cataloging (MARC), http://www.loc.gov/marc/
VRA Core 4.0, http://www.loc.gov/standards/vracore/schemas.html

Staffing and Advocacy

Advocating for Visual Resources Management in Educational and Cultural Institutions. October 2009. Visual Resources Association White Paper. http://vraweb.org/wp-content/uploads/2013/02/vra_white_paper.pdf
Ball, H. et al. *Core Competencies and Core Curricula for the Art Library and Visual Resources Professions*; Art Libraries Society of North America: Calgary, Alberta, Canada, 2006. (Occasional Paper No. 15) ISBN 0-942740-21-1. See also ARLIS NA Core Competencies for Art Information Professionals, https://arlisna.org/publications/arlis-na-research-reports/435-arlis-na-core-competencies-for-art-information-professionals
The criteria for hiring and retention of visual resources professionals. In *Guidelines for the Visual Resources Profession*; Kopatz, K., Ed.; Joint publication of the Art Libraries Society of North America and the Visual Resources Association: Laguna Beach, CA, 2000; 1–5. Updated 2002. http://vrawebor.ipower.com/resources/general/criteria.html and http://www.collegeart.org/standards-and-guidelines/guidelines/hiring-visual-resources-professionals; under revision 2017.
Iyer, H. Core Competencies for Visual Resources Management. http://vraweb.org/wp-content/uploads/2016/09/iyer_core_competencies.pdf
Iyer, H. (2009). A profession in transition: towards development and implementation of standards for visual resources management. Part A—The organization's perspective. *Information Research, 14* (3), 412. [Available from September 9, 2009 at http://InformationR.net/ir/14-3/paper412.html
Iyer, H. (2009). A profession in transition: towards development and implementation of standards for visual resources management. Part B - the professional's perspective and beyond. *Information Research, 14* (4), 413. [Available from November 3, 2009 at http://InformationR.net/ir/14-4/paper413.html]

Collections

Whiteside, A.B. et al. *Collection Development Policies for Libraries and Visual Collections in the Arts*; Art Libraries Society of North America: Calgary, Alberta, Canada, 2000. (Occasional Paper No. 12) ISBN 978-0-942740-17-2.

Wythe, D., Ed. *Museum Archives: An Introduction*; Society of American Archivists: Chicago, IL, 2004. ISBN 1-931666-06-7.

Includes chapters on photographs and audiovisual materials.

Software Selection

Digital Asset Management and Museums—An Introduction. Canadian Heritage Information Network (CHIN). http://www.rcip-chin.gc.ca/contenu_numerique-digital_content/fiches_techniques-tip_sheets/gestion_contenus_numeriques-digital_assets_management-eng.jsp

Digital Image Database Standards: A checklist that highlights issues and functionality to consider when choosing a database for image management and distribution.
http://www.arlisna.org/images/researchreports/pubsarchive/didsc.pdf

The DAM Maturity Model http://dammaturitymodel.org/

The DAM Maturity Model (DAM-MM) identifies four categories within the digital asset management ecosystem: People, Information, Systems, and Processes. The DAM-MM can be used to assess the level at which an organization has successfully implemented digital asset management and can help identify areas to prioritize for improvement.

Museum Computer Network, Digital Asset Management (DAM) SIG.

The DAM SIG is one of several MCN special interest groups that may be of interest to visual resources professionals. Its focus is to share information regarding digital asset management strategies for the cultural sector.

Volunteer Services in Cultural Institutions

Barbara Cohen-Stratyner
New York Public Library for the Performing Arts, New York, U.S.A.

Abstract
This entry offers a brief introduction to volunteerism in museums, science centers, historical societies and sites, and related mission-driven cultural institutions. It discusses the primary models and categories of public and institutional service to these cultural institutions, in common with and distinct from libraries. It points to the ways in which trends in population impact and change volunteerism and provides a guide to the growing bibliography and professional literature concerned with volunteerism and volunteer management.

INTRODUCTION

Museums and related institutions have a long tradition of volunteer participation. Many art museums and historical societies or sites were founded by their original volunteer corps. The primary mission of most institutions, "to collect and interpret" artifacts, generally relies on individuals presenting information to the public. That function is often shared among staff and different groups of volunteers. Volunteers serve many functions behind the scenes in institutions.

The contemporary movement to transform museums, like libraries, into culturally competent services also relates to volunteerism. The professional organizations in both fields recommend expanding the recruitment and use of volunteers from different age groups, from adolescence to senior citizens, and from the full range of communities and populations served (or targeted) by the institutions. Volunteers are seen more and more as change agents. Concurrently, the field of volunteer management has developed into a professional offshoot of nonprofit management.

HISTORY AND TRADITIONS OF VOLUNTEERISM

Volunteerism is considered a quintessential value in American culture. It has been linked to most political and social movements of the last three centuries and the literature that documents them. Volunteerism is an inherent factor in the social mission of museums and related institutions, that philosophy which distinguishes a museum from a collection. There are hundreds of definitions of volunteering, as that word is used in different contexts (see the Map of the Volunteer World on the Energize. com Web site). The social sciences study volunteering as it reflects and impacts on American life.[1] The phrase "museums and related institutions" refers to museums,

historical societies and sites, parks, botanical gardens or arboreta, zoos and aquariums, children's museums, and science and technology centers, as well as similar mission-driven organizations that display, preserve, and interpret artifacts or sites.

SERVICES TO PUBLIC

"Smile Desks"

The most common, traditional volunteer service is in orientation and greeting. There are "smile desks" at the entrances to most museums, in common with hospitals, libraries, public buildings, and many performing arts nonprofits. Typical statements of responsibilities include "welcome and directing the public, hand out support materials and answer questions about the grounds, programs, history and facilities."[2] As audiences change, "smile desks" are frequently staffed with volunteers able to answer questions and distribute information in multiple languages, learning modes, and such responses to Americans with Disabilities Act accommodations as Braille and large-print publications.

Many of the efforts to expand visitorship result in a parallel expansion of service points and hours. Museums with large education programs may have separate entrances for class visits. Free nights and concerts designed to attract young adults, "Gen-X and -Yers," require additional "smile desks" and the volunteers to staff them.

In some institutions, the "smile desk" also serves as an admission desk or shop, which can require volunteers to handle funds. Responsibilities may also include institutional development services, such as selling memberships and donation forms. Other public service points that may require volunteers to handle identification documents or cash equivalents (credit cards, etc.) are distribution points

Encyclopedia of Library and Information Sciences, Fourth Edition DOI: 10.1081/E-ELIS4-120044113

Vietnam–Webometrics

for the various forms of audio guides. This contentious issue may become moot if museums switch to audio content for visitors' own electronic equipment (cell phones, PDAs, etc.).

SERVICES SPECIFIC TO MUSEUMS

In general, docents are volunteers who have been trained by the museum professional staff to give tours of exhibitions, permanent galleries, or sites. A typical statement of the rewards of docent service can be found on the Oakland Museum site's volunteer page: "It's the excitement that comes with learning from top professionals in your chosen field. It's the opportunity to make new friends with people who have similar interests. It's being part of a great institution. Most of all, it's helping to ignite a spark in a young person's imagination, or the pleasure of leading visitors toward making discoveries that bring new insights about life in our great state."[3]

Docents in Art and History Museums

Docents are required to obtain extensive training in the content and context of the collections, exhibitions and gallery artifacts, and in the educational philosophy of the institution. For example, the information for prospective docents in the Bruce Museum (Fairfield, Connecticut) Web site specifies that they be "interested in giving tours that generate conversations with their audience through questions (inquiry-based)," as well as being "the Museum's ambassador to the public [and] leading groups of children, teens, and/or adults."[4] Training schedules vary, but generally include 1 year of intensive classes and observation, with required continuing education and curatorial talks.

Gallery Interpreters in Science Museums

In addition to docents, who are trained by the institution, science museums and centers often use young or retired scientists as gallery interpreters for specific exhibitions or projects that relate to the docents' academic field. They generally receive orientation to the exhibit or gallery and training in the educational style preferred by the institution, but not the general classes required by art and history museums.

Volunteers in Historical Societies

One set of functions that are associated with historical societies, houses, and sites are the use of large numbers of volunteers as costumed interpreters and reenactors. Their participation is vital since they provide not only large numbers, but also the range in ages needed to duplicate the extended families in historical populations. Institutions that recreate communities at specific periods in history engage both paid staff and volunteers to serve

specific roles or trades and seek out community members who know and can demonstrate those processes in the appropriate period manner. Connections are made through the modern-day equivalent, whether nonprofit based, such as 4-H Club members serving as farmers, or commercial, such as a knitting store or class providing spinning or knitting demonstrators. They are then trained in historical methods of production and in museum theater techniques of maintaining character.

Historical sites which are associated with battlegrounds or specific events require large number of volunteers as reenactors. Although they can also provide regularly scheduled services, they are most in demand at annual festivals and commemorations. The American Association for State and Local History's Technical Leaflet on *Planning Commemorations*[5] credits volunteers as the "most important source of extra labor," providing reenactors and interpreters, but also law enforcement, medical staff, and support services. The authors, Andrew Duppstadt, Rob Boyette, and Sgt. Damian J.M. Smith, recommend partnering with local military organizations, ROTC programs, and local civic groups to obtain the volunteers.

Botanical Gardens

Botanical gardens frequently use volunteers as on-site demonstrators, modeling correct methods of garden preparation and maintenance or woodland rehabilitation, as appropriate to their sites. These institutions have also partnered with related local organizations, such as parks conservancies and outreach programs, to work with community gardening programs, *casitas* farming, or park restoration. A library of model volunteer manuals and application forms can be found on the Web site of the professional organization, http://www.publicgardens.org. In many urban centers, these projects serve as community access points (see below).[6]

Additional Public Services

As nonprofit institutions increase partnering to improve community service, more opportunities are made available to volunteers that do not specifically relate to museum functions. These "floating" services with partnership cultural institutions generally focus on mentoring or enriched reading, literacy, and other forms of homework assistance, often involving before- or after-school programs. These services are discussed further in the section on community access.

INTERNAL SERVICES

Institutional Advancement

Volunteers also support the institutional advancement functions of institutions. They assist in fundraising activities through event planning, invitation addressing, and acquisition of in-kind donations for events, especially auctions. In smaller institutions, they often manage membership services and communication. The cyclical relationship between volunteerism and membership is analyzed in the AASLH Technical Leaflet #237, "Membership Matters: Establishing a Vital Membership Program in Your Museum" (2007).[7] Members become volunteers and provide contact information and service for membership drives. The required skills range from attractive handwriting to knowledge of computer hardware and software. As more volunteer applications are available online, institutions are increasing the detail provided for volunteering opportunities and the skills that are required. The Wave Hill application, for example, offers garden-specific and "indoors" opportunities and differentiates among a gallery attendant, business office assistant, development and membership assistant, family art project assistant, public program administrative assistant, public program assistant, public relations assistant, [and] shop attendant."[1] Additional paraprofessional service can range from carpentry and embroidery, for a historic house, to gardening.

Museum Professionals as Volunteers

As the impact of the 2005 hurricane season on New Orleans and the area became known, the museum community itself organized corps of professionals giving volunteers service. Museums Helping Museums: A National Relief Effort for the Gulf Region linked the American Association of Museums (AAM) with affiliated and regional organizations of museums. A related effort was made by the American Association for State and Local History and American Institute for Conservation to form the History Emergency Assistance Recovery Team project. Together, these professional organizations, as well as Heritage Preservation, rescued artifacts, buildings, and staff in the impacted areas and provided models and professional education for disaster planning and recovery for the field.[8,9] Many regional museum associations and related organizations have annual volunteering projects connected to their annual meetings, such as the Mid-Atlantic Association of Museum's "White Glove Gang," which sends registrars, conservators, and collections management staff to local small or understaffed museums for 2 days of service.

THE CHANGING FACE OF VOLUNTEERS

"Women's lib," the migration of women into professional careers, was considered a seismological sociological shift which resulted in studies of volunteers and their motivations. Challenging the widely held assumption that young adult women volunteered because it was expected of them

has resulted in literature which focused on volunteering as a means to serve self-expression and self-esteem (as discussed in Susan J. Ellis, *The Volunteer Recruitment and Membership Development Book*, 1996).[10] More recently, studies of volunteerism have developed in parallel to visitor studies, resulting in empirical evaluations of volunteer expectations and motivations across gender[11] and age categories.[12] While very important in understanding volunteerism in American society, they have not specified museum service at all, but are more likely to lump it under "other." In addition, those studies that differentiate between "community action" and "civic engagement" do not specify into which category museum service falls.

FUTURE TRENDS

The Corporation for National and Community Service, in partnership with the Bureau of Labor Statistics and the U.S. Census Bureau, produces "a detailed breakdown of America's volunteering habits and patterns..." in *Volunteering in American: 2007 State Trends and Rankings in Civic Life*.[13] In this most recent edition, the authors identify three age groups driving the growth in volunteering from 1974 to 2006: young adults, midlife adults, and older adults. (Introduction, pp. 3–4).

Young Adult Volunteers

The use of young adults as service providers has grown in libraries and cultural institutions. Many now put in hours of community volunteering for service organizations, such as the National Honor Society, graduation requirements, or such cultural coming-of-age traditions as B'nai Mitzvah programs. Museums and related institutions currently make up a very small percentage of teen volunteering opportunities.[14] However, museums have developed and documented many creative programs to target and facilitate service by young adults. An early model for programs was provided by YouthALIVE (Youth Achievement through Learning, Involvement, Volunteering, and Employment), a 1991–1999 initiative of the Association of Science and Technology Centers (ASTC) with support from the Wallace-Reader's Digest Fund. Recognizing the participants in youth programs "develop intellectually ... gain social competence ... and learn about the world of work," ASTC institutions were urged to develop programs with adolescents. They were trained for visible volunteering positions, which included explainers/interpreters, who work in the galleries "involving visitors more directly with the exhibit by discussing concepts, answering questions, and providing assistance with the operation of exhibit" and demonstrators, who "work with mobile carts of stations in public areas where they lead activities."[15]

Professional periodicals in both the library and museum fields have actively promoted the use of adolescents as volunteers in a variety of roles. The most reported in libraries and organizations that partner with libraries have been literacy and homework help programs that target adolescents to work with their peers and younger children. The American Library Association's guide to *Creating a full-service homework center in your library* (Cindy Mediavilla, 2001) described model programs in Minnesota, Queens, New York, and California, which use high school and college students provided with pay, no pay, and service learning credits. Elizabeth Lai wrote about the Toronto Public Library's model program for teens as successful literacy volunteers for reluctant readers in "The Buddy System" in *Children and Libraries*.[16]

High school students are also now found in advisory councils for art and history museums and related institutions and serve in educational roles in galleries. In *Museum News* (September/October 2005), Deborah Schwartz analyzed programs in art and science museums across the country.[17] The teenagers' roles in the museums include gallery explainers, peer docents, and advisory councils, as well as virtual volunteering (see below) in technologically advanced institutions. She points out that museums can attract adolescents with authentic experiences coupled with flexible informal learning opportunities, but that staff must be prepared and committed to the projects. The article, which was based on a panel presented at the 2005 AAM annual meeting, provides a list of 18 model programs across a range of institutions.

Midlife Adults

The Corporation for National and Community Service tracked a 30 year rise in volunteering by midlife adults (which they defined as 45–64 years old) and credited it to Baby Boomers. An analysis of this report published in *New York Nonprofit Press* (April 2007, p. 14) credited Boomers' education level and propensity to have children later in life. "Once their children leave, Baby Boomers could maintain relatively high volunteer rates because of the higher education levels and expectations that they will work later in life than previous generations."[18] The highest retention rates were for volunteers who perform management activities ("such as strategic planning, volunteer management and coordination, and marketing"), rather than active public service, such as tutoring, mentoring, and coaching. The report recommended matching volunteers with appropriate and challenging assignments and provided professional development opportunities for volunteers … to increase and sustain volunteer participation." These factors favor museum volunteer docent programs, which tend to require continuous training.

This population also gained from the rising trend in corporate support for cultural and service nonprofits— providing support for active volunteering, rather than, or as well as, funding. This trend grew from practices in specific industries, such as telecommunications and Silicon Valley, and has become widespread. Some firms target individual institutions or providers and design team-building volunteer activities for their staff. Others provide work-release, flex time, or annual leave programs for an employee's own choice of institutions or providers.[19] Midlife adults also provide services through "virtual volunteering" (see below).

Older Populations

Volunteering in America 2007 notes that the volunteer rate for older adults (65 and older) increased over the last three decades. Volunteering offers social contact and a community of respect for older adults without impacting on pension or Social Security income. Longer life expectancy is expected to add to this trend, although it may be balanced by delays in retirement ages.

It is necessary to pay attention to services and access issues for volunteers as well as visitors. Age-related changes in vision, hearing, and mobility could have precluded older populations from volunteering, but museums now have much more information and access to services to provide accommodations that facilitate their continuing participation. Since museums and related institutions have 10 years of experience developing accommodations for visitors covered by the Americans with Disabilities Act, they can serve in leadership roles in working with volunteers with late life and ADA challenges.

VOLUNTEERS AND COMMUNITY ACCESS

Over the last decade, the progressive library literature has focused on public libraries as points of entry for new users, new immigrants, and new populations into their communities. Camilia Alire and Orlando Archibeque's *Serving Latino Communities: A How-To-Do-It Manual for Librarians*, 1998, exemplifies guidebooks for this movement toward culturally competent institutions. As they pointed out, institutions are expected to provide services that had previously been supported by other nonprofit or governmental entities, among them, English as a Second Language, adult literacy, citizenship and GED training, as well as immigrant law advisories. They provide a list of tips for recruiting Latino volunteers which can serve as a model for all volunteer managers in a much wider range of institutions. It begins "check out your current staff," to which we can include current volunteers; enlist the help of formal and informal community leaders; work with other institutions, from senior citizen centers to recreation centers; and ends "invest in your young adults."[20]

Through partnerships, museums and, especially, urban historical societies have joined or supported libraries and immigrant-specific programs. Institutions and staff who had committed themselves to creating dialogic museums and the goals of civic engagement had long been promoting community advisory groups for facilities, interpretation, and exhibition planning. The 2002 issue of the *Journal of Museum Education* (volume 27, nos. 2&3), for example, focused entirely on community liaisons, community involvement, and off-site community programs. In AAM staff members Kim Igoe and Alexandra Marmion Roosa's report on the AAM's Museums and Community Initiative, they referred to volunteering in the "limitations of museum" section, citing complaints about "a homogenous staff and volunteers" (p. 19).[21] In response, museums have adopted from public libraries the important role of community connectors—advising the institutions to the community's needs and notifying community members of the institutions' willingness to serve. Most institutions use volunteers in these roles, but are, whenever possible, guiding them into professional training.[22]

VOLUNTEER MANAGEMENT

The field of volunteer management itself has grown concurrent both with the changes in the volunteering population and the rise of academic study of nonprofit management. James Fisher's *Leadership and Management of Volunteer Programs* (San Francisco: Jossey-Bass, 1993) cites S. J. Ellis and K. H. Noyes' description of the three "historical categories of volunteer leadership: first, the member of a volunteer groups selected to be the leader...; second, the paid staff person who supervises volunteers as a secondary responsibility...; third, the staff person, full or part-time, paid or unpaid, whose primary function is to coordinate the work of volunteers."[23]

The rising number of volunteers who have or had had substantive professional careers is believed to have pushed the professionalism of management. The field mirrors most of the concerns of management and administration, including policies, risks, job or task descriptions, screening and selecting volunteers, supervision, assessment and ethics. Fisher, Ellis, and Noyes (now Noyes-Campbell) have written extensively on the field of volunteer administrators for publishers and imprints devoted to nonprofit management. Many of their examples relate to medical and community-based organizations, not museums. The American Council for the Arts and the AAM Volunteers published a standard text, a handbook for volunteer program administration specific to museums and related institutions in 1993. The AAM has updated it as *Transforming Museum Volunteering*: *A Practical Guide for Engaging 21st Century Volunteers*, by Ellen Hirzy. Online resource libraries of special value to the field of volunteer management can be found on http://www.energizeinc.com and http://www.managementhelp.org.

IMPACT OF THE INTERNET

The Internet is changing the way people use libraries and museums. But the ways that institutional Web sites can be used to prepare for visits has not resulted in less need for volunteers. It has augmented and facilitated volunteer management. In her "Volunteer Line" column, Bonnie McCrae wrote on using the Internet for recruitment and training of volunteers, citing many resources for management, free technical support, and training.[24]

The Internet has spawned a new group of volunteers available to cultural institutions. An additional change facilitated by the Internet lies in the growth of referring organizational sites that offer potential volunteers with a menu of opportunities for single-time or long-term commitments. In some areas, they are independent screening sites; in others, they are services of municipalities or nonprofits with wide-ranging projects. In the online version of *Library Journal*, the WebWatch section provides descriptions of three kinds of Internet-based services for volunteerism—general Web sites for nonprofit management that provides information for potential volunteers and sites that target specific age groups or professions.[25]

"Virtual volunteerism" began in the IT field as programmers and other professionals donated their services to cultural and community nonprofits for the development of data bases, systems, and Web sites through TechSoup.com, NetAid.org, serviceleader.org, and similar projects. The term also now includes the virtual community that assists institutions through less specifically technological skills, such as researching and database preparation. Conhaim points out that these people can include "nontraditional" volunteers, who "travel too much ..., have conditions that interfere with their mobility, [and] have unusual work schedules."[26] Jayne Craven has emphasized the value of virtual volunteers to institutions with her columns on Coyote Communications and TechSoup.[27]

RESOURCES

The following institutional Web sites can provide helpful information, models for programming, and additional links.

General organizations for museum service:

American Association of Museums (http://www.aam-us.org)

Standing Professional Committee on Diversity in Museums (http://www.aamdivcom.org)

Vietnam–Webometrics

Affiliate organizations:

American Association for Museum Volunteers (http://www.aamv.org)

American Association for State and Local History (http://www.aaslh.org)

American Public Gardens Association (http://www.publicgardens.org)

American Zoo and Aquarium Association (http://www.aza.org)

Association for Living History, Farm and Agricultural Museums (http://www.alhfam.org)

Association of African American Museums (http://www.blackmuseums.org)

Association of Art Museum Directors (http://www.aamd.org)

Association of Children's Museums (http://www.childrensmuseum.org)

Association of College and University Museums and Galleries (http://www.acumg.org)

Association of Railway Museums, Inc. (http://www.railwaymuseums.org)

Association of Science and Technology Centers (http://www.astc.org/resource/youth)

International Museum Theatre Alliance (http://www.imtal.org)

Museum Trustee Association (http://www.mta.org)

Organizations for volunteers:

Action Without Borders/Idealist.org (http://www.idealist.org)

Network for Good (http://www.networkforgood.org)

Senior Corps (http://www.seniorcorps.org)

USA Freedom Corps (http://www.freedomcorps.gov)

Organizations for volunteer management and/or training:

Association for Volunteer Administration (http://www.avaintl.org)

Energizeinc (http://www.energizeinc.com)

Information Today (http://www.Infotoday.com/linkup)

National Docent Symposium Council (http://www.docents.net)

(http://www.Philanthropy.com)

Volunteer Management Resource Library (http://www.managementhelp.org/staffing/)

CONCLUSIONS

Cultural institutions are increasingly reliant on volunteers to serve the public, serve the institution, and present the institution and its mission to the public. Volunteerism provides institutions with their most immediate response to societies' trends. Museums and other cultural institutions are developing an independent literature on volunteering and volunteer management, but the specific needs and opportunities of cultural volunteering have not yet been the focus on empirical studies. It remains a challenge to define institutions relationships with their volunteers, communities, and stakeholders.

REFERENCES

1. Wilson, J. Volunteering. Ann. Rev. Sociol. **2000**, August *26*, 215–240.
2. Wave, H. *Volunteer Application*; Wave Hill: New York, 2007.
3. Oakland Museum of California; Oakland Museum of California: Oakland, CA, 2005. Available at http://www.museumca.org/about/volunteer.html (accessed May 11, 2008).
4. Bruce Museum; Bruce Museum: Greenwich, CT, 2004–2008. Available at http://www.brucemuseum.org/aboutus/volunteer.php (accessed May 11, 2008).
5. American Association of State and Local History, *Planning Commemorations, AASLH Technical Leaflet 241*; AASLH: Nashville, TN, 2008.
6. American Public Gardens Association; APGA: Wilmington, DE. Available at http://www.publicgardens.org/ (accessed February 13, 2008).
7. American Association of State and Local History, *Membership Matters: Establishing a Vital Membership Program in Your Museum*; AASLH: Nashville, TN, 2007; AASLH Technical Leaflet 237.
8. American Association of Museums, *Earlier Projects*; AAM: Washington, DC, 1999. Available at http://www.aam-us.org/sp/earlier.cfm (accessed February 14, 2008).
9. Nicholson, K. Special report: Recovering from disaster. Hist. News **2006**, Spring (Spring), 7 within entire issue dedicated to Recovering from Disaster.
10. Ellis, S.J. *The Volunteer Recruitment and Membership Development Book*; Energize, Inc.: Philadelphia, PA, 1996; 21–29.
11. Taniguchi, H. Men and women volunteering: Gender differences in the effects of employment and family characteristics. Nonprofit Voluntary Sector Quart. **2006**, *35*(1), 83–101.
12. Rotolo, T.; Wilson, J. What happened to the 'long civic generation?:' Explaining cohort differences in volunteerism. Social Forces **2004**, *82*(3), 1091–1121.
13. The Corporation for National and Community Service, *Volunteering in America: 2007 State Trends and Rankings*.
14. Mark Hugo Lopez and Karlo Barrios Marcelo, "Volunteering among young people," Fact sheet update, April 2007. Available at http://www.servicelearning.org/instant_info/links_collection/index.php?pop-up_id=516.
15. Association of Science-Technology Centers, 3. http://www.astc.org/resource/youth/index.htm (accessed May 11, 2008).
16. Lai, E. The buddy system. Children Libr. **2006**, Spring, 21–23.

17. Schwartz, D.F. Dude, where's my museum? Inviting teens to transform museums. Museum News **2005**, September/ October, 36–41.

18. *Baby boomers are boost to volunteers*, New York Nonprofit Press, 2007; April 14.

19. Stannard-Friel, J. How employee volunteers multiply your community impact, posted December 2, 2005 on OnPhilanthropy.com) (accessed February 11, 2008).

20. Alire, C.; Orlando, A. *Serving Latino Communities: A How-To-Do-It Manual for Librarians*; Neal-Schuman Publishers, Inc.: New York, 1998; 142–147.

21. Igoe, K.; Alexandra, M.R. Listening to the voices in our communities. J. Museum Educ. **2002**, *27*(2&3), 19.

22. Cuban, S. *Serving New Immigrant Communities in the Library*; Libraries Unlimited: Westport, CT, 2007; 92.

23. Ellis, S.J.; Noyes, K.H. *By the People: A History of Americans as Volunteers*, Rev. Ed.; Jossey-Bass: San Francisco, CA, 1990; 3.

24. McCrae, B. "Volunteer Line" column. Colorado Libr. J. **2004**, Spring, 48–49.

25. Hillson, B. "Web Watch" column. Libr. J. **2003**, March *4*, 30–32.

26. Conhaim, W.W. Virtual volunteering. Inform. Today **2003**, March 27.

27. Craven, J. Myths about online volunteering, July 26, 2007, consulted on TechSoup.com (accessed February 13, 2008).

Wayfinding and Signage

Dennis O'Brien
Maps and Wayfinding, LLC, Mystic, Connecticut, U.S.A.

Abstract
The mental processes, physical elements, and materials involved in wayfinding and wayfinding signage are explored. Wayfinding is defined, and thematic and physical wayfinding are distinguished. The professions doing wayfinding design are described; copious examples of such design are provided. The importance and character of signage are developed, and the histories of both wayfinding and signage are briefly described. Detailed information on common types of substrates and additives for both fixed-content and nonelectric changeable-content signs is provided in tabular form.

INTRODUCTION

There are an estimated 117,000 libraries and 17,500 museums of all kinds in the United States today.[1] Through all those public institutions, and so many others, there is a steady stream of visitors, some of whom have no idea how to get where they are going, or how they will find what they want when they get there. Resolving these shortcomings is the job of wayfinding and signage. Wayfinding is a research, design, manufacturing, and installation discipline practiced mostly by professionals for the benefit of all people who need to move around in the digital and real-worlds.

In its practical application, wayfinding is a coordinated program. This program includes how people think about their institution and its visitors, what programs and information are made available to those visitors, and what physical spaces and objects are provided for visitors' wayfinding use. Signage of all types is an important part of any wayfinding program.

WAYFINDING

Definition and Types

Wayfinding should be thought of as a coordinated plan of policies, physical elements, and programs designed to make that facility's form, structure, contents, amenities, and offerings recognizable and accessible—or "transparent"—to the visitors. It can welcome visitors, ease their new-space anxieties, tell them where they are, guide them to where they are going, and, most important, remove any barriers that might get in the way of visitors' receptivity, involvement, enjoyment, and learning.

Two forms of wayfinding are "Thematic" and "Physical." Thematic wayfinding deals with why a person is in a place, and what that person might expect. In a museum, the use of color, lighting, and type styles might set the theme for an exhibit, separating it from other spaces and uses. In a library the themes of the spaces are more straightforward.

Physical wayfinding deals with a person's understanding of, orientation to, and navigation and movement through a space. This entry will deal with physical wayfinding, primarily in libraries and museums, calling it, simply wayfinding. Many of the concepts and principals discussed can be applied to thematic wayfinding as well.

In short, wayfinding can allow an institution to present a welcoming attitude toward its visitors. This is referred to as an institution's visitability. *Visitability* encompasses every aspect of an institution's amenities, offerings, and creature comforts no matter how small or large, and addresses whether or not they are sufficient and of high enough quality for all visitors.

Wayfinding can be defined as the *mental processes* and *physical elements* needed for people to recognize and understand an environment, orient themselves, and move around.

Mental processes

Research in neuroscience beginning in the early 1990s has allowed researchers to pinpoint which areas of the brain are functioning during various wayfinding activities. Using functional magnetic resonance imaging (fMRI) and positron emission tomography (PET) scanning techniques, researchers are able to "see" brain function in real time as test subjects perform recognition, orientation, and navigation tasks in both familiar and unfamiliar virtual environments.[2,3] For example, it was found that the right hippocampus and right caudate nucleus areas of the brain are associated, respectively, with knowing and navigating place locations accurately, and doing so quickly.[4]

The wayfinding process is different for different people. All humans, however, use their senses and various parts of their brains to follow two broad patterns while

Encyclopedia of Library and Information Sciences, Fourth Edition DOI: 10.1081/E-ELIS4-120044069

wayfinding through a space. The first is recollection of other experiences. The second, called topology, is a recognition and use of enclosure, order, proximity, and separation in spatial relationships.[5] Along with these patterns, wayfinding in general has two parts: making decisions, and moving. Decisions on how to move are based on the mode of movement to use, time constraints, movement speed and direction, and what route to follow.[6]

Within these patterns and parts, the five steps in the wayfinding process could be listed as follows:

1. Recognition. What is this place? What's familiar? What's unfamiliar?
2. Orientation. Where am I? Where am I going?
3. Understanding. Why am I here? What will I do here?
4. Navigation. How will I get there? How will I move next? How will I get back?
5. Debriefing. What has been the outcome of my visit? Would I recommend it or do it again?

The sequence from 1 to 3 has a thematic component, and can sometimes proceed in another order. Some of these processes occur remotely, before a visitor ever leaves home. The acronym created by the first letters of the five wayfinding processes is R-O-U-N-D. This is a useful way to remember that any visit involves not only the whole of each visitor's abilities, but also starts and ends in the same place.

Museum visitors practice recreational wayfinding,[7] which may include specific objectives or destinations, but is primarily to explore and enjoy a setting. Library visitors are much more likely to practice directed or goal-oriented wayfinding activities combined with occasional explorations.[8] During any activity, people sort out their surroundings by forming cognitive maps.

The Cognitive Map. The most important mental process practiced by humans while interacting with spaces is cognitive mapping, described as "…the process by which an organism makes representations of its environment in its brain."[9] All people form "maps" in their minds of the environments they experience. When visiting a familiar place, people form cognitive maps before they begin. In unfamiliar spaces, maps can only be formed on the go.[10] These "maps" have an enormous impact on any visitor's behavior. The formation process has two parts: the person's background knowledge and his or her experience of the environment.

Background knowledge refers to information, experiences, and skills people carry with them. These include the following categories common to all humans:

1. Biological. Bilateral symmetry (the two sides of our bodies are more or less mirrors of one-another); two distinct genders—with differences in wayfinding strategies;[6] balance; major sensory organs except touch located in our heads; and bodily functions.

2. Environmental. Spatial and aesthetic sensibilities; and the human conditions that new spaces cause anxiety, and order is comfortable while disorder is not.[11]
3. Cultural. Conventions and ethics; language; behavior; and architectural shapes and landmark recognition.
4. Personal. Level of education; degree of interest in a subject; physical and mental abilities; social skills; and age.

Each person's mental map is unique based on his or her abilities of sight, hearing, smell, taste, touch, reasoning, and sense of time; and each map serves the orientation and navigation needs of its creator. Therefore, mental maps do not necessarily resemble conventional maps. A mental "picture" of a place created by a person who is blind, for example, would be far different from one created by a sighted person.

Physical elements

The physical elements available to a visitor for purposes of wayfinding can be grouped into four general categories: spaces, structures, objects, and content. They are hardly ever used in isolation, one from another, nor are they necessarily encountered in that order.

Properly designed and sequenced, physical elements allow visitors to undertake their own personal mental processes, and progress from introduction to decisions to action in a smooth continuum. To facilitate these activities, spaces, structures, objects, and wayfinding content must be "legible." Legibility means presented clearly and plainly, and able to be read. Since physical elements are meant to be accessed, approached, entered, moved throughout, and exited, it is necessary that they possess unmistakable *positive attributes* in order to function well.

Positive attributes of physical elements in alphabetical order, with examples:

1. Circulation. Logic of flow plays an important part in visitors' comfort, understanding, and use of space, and any institution's visitability and marketing effort. Circulation necessarily proceeds from the macro (airports, highways, parking lots) to the micro (exhibits, rest rooms, benches) by way of:
   a. Paths. The routes available for movement.
   b. Edges. The boundaries or barriers between regions or elements.
   c. Districts. Identifiable regions into which, and out of which, visitors can move.
   d. Nodes. Locations on which visitors can focus and into which they can enter. They may be intersections, activity centers, or convergences of paths.
   e. Landmarks. Points of focus, like nodes, but primarily important to visitors at a distance for direction or orientation.[12]

2. Clarity. Understanding of the form and function of practical elements should be easy to acquire: Information should be presented in languages or symbols understandable by the majority of visitors.

3. Cleanliness. Clutter and dirt can be disorienting, unappealing, or dangerous: Clean rest rooms, for example, are essential for visitors' well-being, and are an important part of an institution's marketing and visitability.

4. Clues. Functioning parts need to have their operation apparent in their design: It should be obvious from the look and feel of a door's handle, for example, whether it is meant to be pushed, pulled, or turned.

5. Comfort. An environment should be psychologically and physically easy to use, and provide creature comforts: Low sound levels usually calm and soothe people, and contribute to a facility's marketing and visitability.

6. Communication. Physical elements can be designed and located in order to telegraph their functions: Large ornate centrally located doorways say "grand entrance."

7. Community. Environments should be designed with an overall sense of inclusion: Physical features designed to accommodate visitors with disabilities commonly function better for all visitors. This is the basis of *Universal Design*, defined as: Physical sites, systems, and attitudes that are designed and built to accommodate as wide a range of people as possible with the fewest exceptions or special cases.

8. Completeness. If a facility needs something that is not there, it is incomplete: Providing staff members for wayfinding assistance is fairly common, but if the personnel are not properly trained, supported, equipped, dressed, and positioned for the task, there presence and function are incomplete.

9. Composition. Environmental elements should be shaped, sized, scaled, colored, positioned, oriented, and related to one another in ways that enhance visitors' awareness and improve visitor movement: Any given wall can be an impediment to movement, or a channel for it.

10. Concept. Having a general theme for a physical place enhances the visitor experience and an institutions' mission and visitability: During the nineteenth century, the concepts of "library" and "museum" were imprinted on the conscience of Americans using imposing architecture.

11. Conciseness. An environment should include all the information needed but no more: Simpler is better.

12. Conservation. Physical elements can be installed to increase public awareness of existing problems; to prevent environmental degradation of sensitive areas by visitors; and, by using sustainable and nontoxic materials, as ecological solutions in themselves.

13. Consistency. Once an element is presented in a certain way, that presentation should remain the same throughout all uses: Identical waste receptacles placed on the right side of each public door would be an example of a constant.

14. Conspicuousness. Elements should be sized and placed according to their use: Interior spaces intended as gathering areas should be large, centrally located, and easily accessed by multiple routes; restrooms can be "tucked away" as long as paths to them are clear.

15. Contrast. Elements with different functions should be distinguishable as such: A glass door should not look like a glass window; light gray words do not show up on white backgrounds.

16. Control. Periodic evaluation of a facility is necessary to stay informed about subjects such as safety, security, cleanliness, and relevance to visitors: Evaluation must be accompanied by a willingness to update obsolete or dysfunctional elements as needed.

17. Conventions. Conventions are commonly agreed upon standards or rules: Using yellow as a warning color is an example of a convention.

18. Correctness: Elements should be as accurate as possible: The phrase "visitor services" has come to mean information available about attractions outside a facility. It is used incorrectly, then, on signage to refer to amenities inside a facility, such as a food service or restroom.

19. Correlation. Wayfinding visuals should agree with the facility they represent in overall layout and in their details: A 45° left turn would not correlate with a sign arrow pointing 90° left.

20. Creativity. A pretty, innovative, or engaging environment will enhance visitor appeal, prolong involvement, and stimulate absorption: A willingness to break new ground in design approach, materials, and function is important.

21. Current. Environments should be kept up to date: Evolving, repairing, and improving might all be needed to meet the needs of visitors and maintain an institution's visitability.[13]

These positive attributes should be incorporated into the four general categories of *Physical Elements*:

Physical Elements categories in order from the macro to the micro:

Spaces. We humans have a long background of relating our location to that of the sun, moon, and stars. In outdoor settings that relationship is used, sometimes unconsciously, for orientation. On a more regional scale, landmarks such as mountains, hills, and rivers offer the same opportunities. Locally, visual recognition of landmarks and vistas can impact how a visitor recognizes a place, chooses a direction, or follows a route.

Structures. Built environments fall into only a few broad categories of usage: residential, commercial, industrial, recreational, educational, medical, and governmental.Generic elements used to sculpt structures for wayfinding include spaces, shapes, relative scale, colors, paths, textures, boundaries, sight lines, lighting, sound, and temperatures. These qualities are embodied in specific elements such as doors, windows, walls, or stairs. To the largest extent possible, these elements should be designed and constructed as part of a master wayfinding program, adhere to the qualities of "legibility," be aesthetically pleasing, and be composed of sustainable and nontoxic materials.

Objects. Objects refers to any built or manufactured element smaller than a structure. This could include something as large as an information desk or as small as a doorknob. This also includes signs and printed materials of all kinds. As with structures, all objects should be designed, installed, and operated as part of a master wayfinding program, adhere to the qualities of "legibility," be attractive, and be made of sustainable and nontoxic materials whenever possible.

Content. In order to function for wayfinding, spaces, structures, and objects need content. Beside the general elements of color, shape, etc., content also refers to more explicit components in the environment as well as on published pieces and the Web. Virtually all content is rendered in digital form at some point before being used in its final form. There are five general categories of content:

1. Graphics. Drawings, diagrams, schematics, and other representations are more commonly used for exhibits and displays, but occasionally come in handy for wayfinding.

    A map is the most common nonsymbol graphic used for wayfinding. It is also the most popular wayfinding tool sought by visitors after a knowledgeable staff member.[14] Map design and illustration should conform to the 21 positive attributes listed above. There are only two basic illustration styles for all maps: a plan view from directly overhead and one of a variety of bird's-eye-views from some side angle. Varieties of these two styles is common. See Fig. 1 for an example of a combination view map. An attractive map also works well as a branding and marketing tool and enhances an institution's visitability.

2. Images. Photographs, videos, scale models, and reenactments are popular for printed pieces, computer installations, kiosks, and introductory theater presentations. They are used less for non-electronic wayfinding signage, but are used extensively in interpretive installations. See Fig. 2 for a scale model.

3. People. A knowledgeable staff member, properly trained and located, can be the most successful component in an institution's wayfinding program, and is the source of information most sought after by visitors to museums and libraries.[14]

4. Symbols. Recognized standard colors and graphic symbols for accessibility, activities, direction, lodging, services, transportation, and warning are essential for legible communication, and particularly for comprehension by people who do not read the written language in any given location.[15],[16] Institutional logos or corporate marks can also serve as devices for identity, branding, promotion, marketing, and enhancing visitability. See Figs. 3–5.

5. Text. The written word constitutes the bulk of content when signage, printed media, and electronic devices are considered. The use of text on wayfinding signs is usually minimal and in large sizes. Several requirements for appropriate type styles, contrast with background, height-to-width ratio, stroke width-to-height ratio, and height-to-viewing distance are set down in the Americans with Disabilities Act (ADA) of 1991, and other sources.[17]

People and Wayfinding

Who needs wayfinding?

Anyone who moves about by any means in an unfamiliar environment needs wayfinding assistance, each according to his or her reasons for visiting, mental processes, and physical abilities.

It is important to emphasize that "visitors" does not just mean the customers who walk through the front door of a facility. Visitors must also include staff, volunteers, and service or materials suppliers. Due to their specific service and wayfinding needs, these various categories of people must sometimes share space congenially and safely, but are sometimes intentionally kept separate. All their wayfinding needs must therefore be successfully addressed. It is not good planning, for example, to provide wheelchair access at the front door, only to neglect an efficient means of refuse removal out back. All functions of a facility directly or indirectly impact visitors' uses of that facility.

Who designs wayfinding?

Several professional disciplines have responsibility for understanding wayfinding behavior—vital for providing wayfinding programs and signage systems—and creating and installing spaces, structures, objects, and content suitable for use by visitors. Wayfinding is interdisciplinary, and these professionals often work in concert. These are

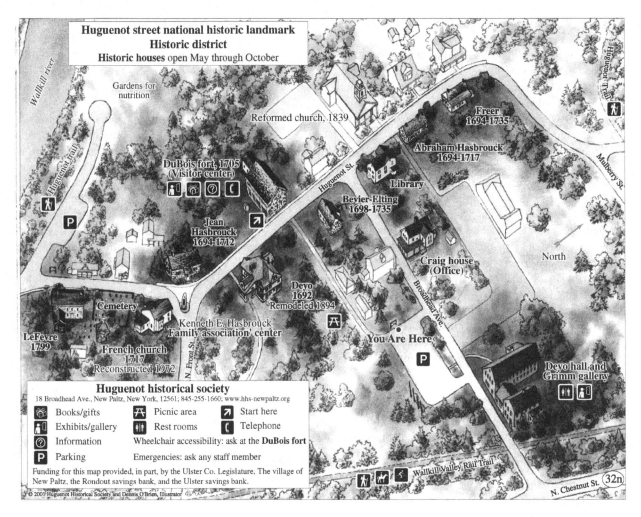

Fig. 1 You-Are-Here map of Huguenot Historical Society, New Paltz, New York. The layout is a plan view of the property, while the buildings are illustrated in a bird's-eye-view. Design by the author.

the most common professions, in broad categories, listed alphabetically:

1. Architects. People who are responsible for planning, designing, and constructing buildings, their mechanical systems, and their attending environs. Architects must be familiar with building materials, local and federal regulations governing all aspects of structures, use of space, and aesthetics.

2. Consultants. People called in to advise on a project due to their skill or knowledge in a specific

Fig. 2 The three-dimensional tactile map of the U.S. Capital area used for orientation in the Capital Building, Washington, D.C.
Source: Photograph by the author.

Fig. 3 The four accessibility symbols required by the Americans with Disability Act of 1991(4). From left to right they are the international symbols of Accessibility, Access for Hearing Loss, Telecommunications Device for the Deaf (TDD), and Volume Control. There are thousands of other "standard" symbols available, worldwide.

discipline or area of expertise. Anyone involved in a project for an institution who is not employed there can be considered a consultant.

3. Contractors. People responsible for constructing a facility. They must have knowledge of materials, building practices, and regulations. The discipline can include carpenters, steel workers, plumbers, electricians, masons, or construction managers.

4. Designers. Plan and create spaces, structures, objects, or content in a specific discipline or area of specialization. Their output is, in turn, used by fabricators and contractors to build and install the designed elements. Designers can work in areas such as graphics, industrial products and processes, wayfinding, computers, fashion, lighting, sound, or automobiles.

5. Engineers. Responsible for the detailed structure, fabrication, and operation of any technologically complex object, environment, or process. They can work in disciplines such as aerospace, chemistry, communications, computers, construction, the environment, fluids, light, and sound.

6. Fabricators. Build and install components of facilities such as signage, exhibits, furniture, or cabinetry, rather than the whole facility. Fabricators must be

familiar with the materials and manufacturing processes of their discipline, and often have design experience as well.

7. Landscape architects. Concentrate primarily on everything outside of structures. This discipline does not concern itself only with land and plants, but can include creating all manner of outdoor facilities such as paths, walls, out-buildings, patios, and installations involving water.

8. Planners. Formulate strategies for short- or long-term change or growth in an area or institution, often incorporating programs, policies, and development as well as structures and other physical elements.

9. Psychologists. Study issues relating to the function of the human mind. They can operate in many disciplines. The most important for wayfinding is environmental psychology, which is focused on the relationship between humans and the physical world.

10. Sociologists. Study issues of human associations in groups such as societies and cultures. They, too, can function in one of several sub-disciplines, and as such, can contribute valuable insights into human relations with specific categories of public institutions.

History of Wayfinding

The many elements contained in modern wayfinding were not all developed simultaneously. Some, not surprising, are far older than others.

Maps. Maps are the oldest form of wayfinding communication, preceding both written and numeric language in the upper Paleolithic.[18]

One of the earliest graphics that is clearly a map came from Nuzi in northeast Iraq, and dates to 2500–2300 B.C.[19] Egyptians, too, developed a sophisticated tradition of measured mapping by 2000 B.C.

Fig. 4 A highway sign in Vermont showing international standard and locally relevant symbols and non-standard colors used together.
Source: Photograph by the author.

Vietnam–Webometrics

Fig. 5 The business logo for Atlantic Merchants, Mystic, Connecticut. This symbol was used much like most logos, on outdoor signage, stationary, bumper stickers, self-stick labels, and other uses.
Source: Design by the author.

Very little evidence exists that the Greeks, centuries later, had much time to advance the art of map-making on a local level, or contemplate itineraries, the forerunners to guidebooks and road maps.[20]

The Imperial Romans were avid travelers, and, unlike the Greeks, had detailed *Itinerarium* (guide books) and to-scale you-are-here maps to assist them on their journeys. Caesar Augustus had a large version of a map of the entire Roman Empire produced by Agrippa around 19 B.C. engraved in marble in 7 B.C., and installed near the Pantheon. It is quite possible that this map and its copies throughout the Empire were the prototypes on which the first Roman *itinerarium* were based.[21] By A.D. 200, *itinerarium* were produced on papyrus and leather-bound.[22]

Two types of *itinerarium* existed in Imperial Rome. Of the first type, written guidebooks without maps, the best known is probably *Guide Book of Greece*, written between A.D. 160 and A.D. 180 by Pausanias.[23] Pausanias was so thorough that his guidebook was still popular among nineteenth century travelers, and can be considered the direct precursor of the *Guide Bleus* and the guidebooks of Karl Baedeker.[24]

Of the second type of *itineriarium*, maps with scant text, the lone existing example is an eleventh- or twelfth-century copy of a third-century original known as the Peutinger Map (*Tabula Peutingeriana*), named after Konrad Peutinger who discovered it. The map covers the Roman Empire from India to Britain. It was designed and constructed to fold and fit into a carrying case.[25,26] The

Peutinger Map included accurate road distances, illustrated symbols representing different size cities, temples, lighthouses, spas, bathing facilities, forts, imperial residences, way-stations, and sketches of trees representing the forest regions of Germany and Syria.[26]

Advancements in the skill of map-making all but ceased during the period from about 500–1000 A.D. For the period referred to as the Middle Ages, the Christian Church promulgated its own theories about the world, subjecting virtually every human endeavor, including representing the physical world, to its mindset. During this period, countless works of geography and cartography were suppressed or destroyed by church officials.[27–31]

The tradition of the measured survey that had been almost lost in Western cultures since the fall of Imperial Rome reappeared in Europe between the ninth and twelfth centuries with the copying of the Roman treatises on estate surveying.[32] The *Chronica majora* (1253) was an update of the Roman itinerary designed and illustrated by the English Benedictine monk Matthew Paris. At the same time this type of "strip map" was a more sophisticated version of the Peutinger Map style of illustration, it was the beginning of the future of European cartography.[33,34]

Not long after, and continuing up to the present day, maps improved in accuracy, and depicted closer relationships to the world they represented. Thus, the strip map, as useful as it had proved for so long, gave way to a map style showing a truer network of roads. This tradition, of course, corresponded with the ever more complex matrix of roads available for travel throughout most of the world.[35]

Wayfinding devices. The first known appearance of the wheel was around 3500 B.C. in Mesopotamia, with roads, bridges, way-markers, and road maps following shortly thereafter.[36] There were also post stations at intervals manned by grooms, and containing itineraries—papyrus maps—showing distances between posts.[37]

Like the Persian roads, Egyptian roads were dotted with posts to assist travelers.[37] The Egyptian desert roads were marked with "stone cairns and also, it is suggested, by an occasional glyph that gave directions or distance."[38]

The Greeks employed a more rudimentary system of marking distances on their roads from that of the Egyptians by placing simple piles of stones, and, later, *hermae*—square stone pillars with busts of Mercury on top—in towns.[39]

Traveling for pleasure and culture started in earnest with the Imperial Romans. As a result, wayfinding, including well-made roads, directional signage, mile markers, inns, guidebooks, "fast food," and guides, were firmly established by the second century A.D.[40] The Roman Miliaria, or milestones, are of particular importance as the grand ancestors of wayfinding objects. They were huge cylindrical columns of stone, usually over six feet high and weighing two tons or more, positioned on all Roman roads every 1000 paces (a Roman mile) after 123 B.C. They contained a wealth of information often including the distance from the town where the road originated, the name and titles of the originating emperor, and sometimes the builders' names and completion dates.[36]

As an important component of wayfinding, tourist guides in the ancient world were quite common.[41,42] The Greek Herodotus (ca. 424 B.C.), for example, traveled extensively and relied on priests and locals everywhere he went for information.[43] In another example, the city of Pompeii, when unearthed from its volcanic grave of A.D. 79, was found to be primarily a seaside resort town specializing in tourists and soldiers on leave.[44] Under those circumstances, it can be assumed that there were ample guides on hand for all manner of assistance.[45]

From approximately A.D. 500 to A.D. 1000, travel in the Western world was both sparse and hazardous: "Where the barbarians had passed, the roads, communication systems and inns that the Romans had built fell apart."[46]

From around 1000 A.D. to the middle of the thirteenth century, travel for the benefits of pilgrimage steadily increased. By the fifteenth century travel for pursuits religious and secular were on the rise all over Europe and the Middle East. These travelers enjoyed businesses providing nearly all the wayfinding amenities of today's tourism: assistance bureaus, beggars, guidebooks, inns, outdoor signage, promotional literature, roadside fast food stands, digestive problems, travel agencies, and travel books.[47,48]

Another way in which tourism and accompanying wayfinding evolved slowly during the eighteenth century, and more rapidly during the nineteenth, was in the number and relative affluence of the travelers. Also, during the eighteenth century, museums, zoos, and botanical gardens began opening to the public, while public libraries mushroomed in number and popularity during the nineteenth century.

SIGNAGE

Definition

The definition of "sign" is any object containing graphic displays of text and/or visuals intended to communicate information. This is a broad definition, and includes, in practical installations, a necessarily diverse array of stationary, mobile, non-electric, and electric objects.

See Table 1 for a listing of the most common signage substrate materials for fixed or changeable signs, content materials applied to substrates, and nonelectric changeable sign types.[49] See Table 2 for expected outcomes of a successful wayfinding and signage program.

Two general design principals

Two overarching design principals guide the creation of wayfinding signage programs:

1. A system of wayfinding signs must have a consistent look throughout. This refers to structure, content, and placement. See Fig. 6 for an example of a signage program for the interior of a library.

   Repetition and consistency of look and usage throughout a signage program is key to successfully funneling visitors in toward a facility, and guiding them through it. Imagery should be recognizable as visually and thematically consistent every time it is used, including a Web site, building graphics and signs, handout maps and brochures, and ID badges. To compliment any branding or marketing program this repetition and consistency should be incorporated into non-wayfinding uses.

   Federal, state, and local regulations often dictate the size, design, and placement parameters within which a signage program is achieved, in whole or in part. Working within regulations requires familiarity with personnel and regulations, patience, flexibility, and innovation.

2. A wayfinding signage program should have elements that are plain, simple, uncluttered, and stylistically distinct from all other visuals throughout a facility. Complying with the regulations for proper use of signage set down in the Americans with Disabilities Act[17] will go a long way toward achieving this.

History of Signage

Evidence for signs communicating specific information such as advertising a shop's wares seems meager until Dynastic Egypt. Egyptian shops did, on occasion, have signs advertising their products or services with inscriptions and visuals.[50] The prolific Greek signage primarily took the shape of carved or painted images affixed to the outsides of various establishments. The images were designed and rendered to represent the wares or services offered within, and thus became the historic precedent for shingle signs as well as trademarks.[51] See Fig. 7 for a modern example of both in one sign.

By the time of Imperial Rome, there existed about the same level of signage as a typical contemporary American shopping mall. Business identification, advertising signs, political and opinion placards, billboards, sporting marquees, graffiti, and banners competed for the attention of the public.[52,53] Written and pictorial street signs were also common, but more often they were made of stone or terra-cotta relief and "let into the pilasters at the side of the open shop-fronts." Some streets even derived their names from signs of businesses displayed along them.[50] This is very well documented because of the approximately 900 shop signs unearthed from the volcanic ruins of Pompeii and Herculaneum.[52,53]

After 1000 A.D. The Roman pictorial tradition in signs had evolved in two ways. First, the relief and painted signs

Table 1 Most commonly used sign materials.

Category/ brand	Material contents	Strength	Durability	Look/sizes	Formation process	Compatible materials	Installation locations	Relative cost	Uses
Substrates[a]									
A. *Paper, Illustration Board, Posterboard, Cardboard*	*Paper, wood, cloth; sometimes recycled, sometimes plasticized.*	*Low*	*Short term*	*Matte, glossy, smooth, or rough depending on process. Paper: all colors Boards: most colors. Various sizes.*	*Water squeezed out of pulp mat with a binder rolled or pressed.*	*Wet or dry traditional media. Glued 2D/3D objects. Digital inks.[b] Self-stick products.*	*Interior mostly.*	*Low*	*Professional and amateur posters, notices, signs, announcements. Hung or folded self-standing. Recyclable.*
B. Foam board	Polystyrene foam core, clay-coat paper.	Medium	Long term. Easily dented.	Matte surfaces. White, black, gray, several colors. Self-stick surfaces available. 4' × 8' sheets 1/8"–1" thick	Extruded polystyrene core. Laminated both sides with high-quality clay-coated paper.	Wet or dry traditional media. Glued 2D/3D objects.[b] Self-stick products.	Interior mostly.	Low	Professional and amateur posters, notices, signs, announcements. Hung or folded self-standing. Recyclable. Cuttable, foldable for model making and display. Archival, flame retardant, and memory foam available.
C. Medium density overlay (MDO)	Exterior-grade plywood with high resin solid overlays. Phenolic on both sides, UV curing available.	Very high	Very-long term	Smooth surfaces Minimum grain. Wood color. 4' (w). 8', 10', or 12' (l). 5/16"–3/4" thick	Multiple wood layers glued under pressure. Coated.	Paint, coatings, self-sticks. Can be nailed, sawed, routed, and glued.	Exterior	Medium to high	For permanent installations.
D. Alucobond	*Polyethylene core. Aluminum faces (85% recycled aluminum)*	*High*	*Very-long term*	*Virtually any color or finish; 4'2 × 14'2" sheets. 5'2" × 164" sheets. 3, 4, or 6 mm thick*	*Solid polyethylene core bonded to 2.02" sheets of Kynar system painted aluminum.*	*Can be folded, bent, cut, painted, or printed.*	*Interior or exterior*	*High*	*Architecture, display, signs, cladding.*
E. Coroplast [*Cloraplast*]	Corrugated plastic	Low to medium	Long term	Varied surfaces; many colors; additives: anti-UV, flame retardant, anti-static/	High impact polypropylene copolymer extruded twin-wall corrugated sheets [*recycled material*]	Screen printing, paint, self-sticks. Can be die cut, cut, hot air/sonic welded, and glued into custom shapes/packaging.	Interior or exterior	Low	Packaging, display, signs.

Material	Type	Rating	Durability	Dimensions/description	Composition	Finishing	Location	Cost	Applications
F. Banner Vinyl/ nylon [Nylon]	Organic ethenyl (Combination) [Polyamide]	High	Long term to medium term (exterior use)	corrosion, custom colors, etc.; Widths to 106". 2–10 mm thick. Gloss/semi finish (Matte finish, woven look) [Woven, "rip-stop"]. Any color; Standard/custom sizes—16' width, any length.	Extruded strands woven to cloth.	Print inks, paints, self-sticks, appliqués.	Interior or exterior	Medium	Signs, displays, flags, backdrops. Flame retardant.
G. Sintra, Komatex, Celtec	PVC plastic	Low to high (depending on thickness)	Long term	Matte surfaces, 12 homogeneous colors; 4' × 8', 5' × 10' sheets. 1, 2, 3, 4, 5, 6, 10, 13, or 19 mm thick	Closed-cell high-density expanded polyvinyl chloride sheets.	Can be heat/vacuum formed, bent, sawed, cut (to 3 mm). Print, paint (in some, products), self-stick, glued, screwed, riveted.	Interior or exterior	High	Signs, display, shapes, 3D products.
H. High impact styrene (Styrofoam)	Thermoplastic	High (Low)	Long term	Glossy surfaces. Clear, many colors; 4' × 8' sheets. 0.02", 0.03", 0.04", 0.06", 0.08", 0.1", 0.125", or 0.187" (Expandable foam) thick	Petroleum based polymer. (Expanded polystyrene)	Paint, self-sticks, sawed, cut, drilled, sheared, punched, heat/vacuum formed. (Molded)	Interior or exterior	Medium	Signs, esp. ADA, displays, 3D products (Insulation, packaging)
I. Uvex, Gemex	*Cellulose, acetate, butyrate.*	*High*	*Long term*	*High-glossy faces, UV resistant; 4' × 8' sheets, 0.06"—0.25" thick. Film rolls: 0.003–0.03"*	*Cellulose modified by butyric and acetic acids. Non-petroleum, renewable resource.*	*Inks, paints, self-sticks, colorants.*	*Interior or exterior*	*Medium*	*For signs, displays, individual letters. As panels for illuminated signs.*

(Continued)

Table 1 Most commonly used sign materials. *(Continued)*

Category/brand	Material contents	Strength	Durability	Look/sizes	Formation process	Compatible materials	Installation locations	Relative cost	Uses
J. Wood	Pine, Cedar [Redwood]	Medium to high	Long to medium term (exterior use)	Coated/finished to any luster; To 12″ w × 6″ thick 16″ l	Cut, milled, cured trees. Sometimes coated or impregnated.	Self-sticks, ink, paint. Can be sawed, cut, sandblasted, etc.	Interior or exterior. Coatings extend life.	Low to medium	Signs, displays, 3D products, letters. Easy to work. [Used less frequently] Recyclable.
K. Metal	Bronze, brass, aluminum. [Steel]	High	Long term	Glossy, matte, brushed, textured surfaces; Shapes and sizes: standard/custom by manufacturer.	Molded/cast formed from raw/recycled materials.	Paint, self-sticks, printed, cut, drilled, sheared, punched, bent, sand/water blasted, molded.	Interior or exterior	High	For signs, displays, architectural/3D elements, bases for other materials, letters. [Magnetic]
L. X-board	97% postconsumer paper waste, organic adhesives.	High and crush resistant.	Long term (Interior)	Matte to glossy. White surfaces; 1200 (w) × 2440 or 2900 mm. 10, 12, 16, 20, or 32 mm thick.	Stiff paper surfaces bonded to a honeycomb interior.	Self-sticks, paint, print, laminated with veneers. Can be cut, sawed, and miter folded.	Interior	Medium	Signs, walls, 3D products, furniture. Recyclable.
M. Paperstone	100% FSC certified recycled paper, water-based phenolic resin with cashew nut shell binder, pigments.	High	Long	Grainless panels: 60″ × 144″. ¾″, 1″, and 1¼″. 6 standard edges Custom by manufacturer.	Heat and pressure. Can be pressure "embossed" for signage.	Paints, coatings. Can be worked like hardwood.	Interior or exterior	Medium	Signs, esp. ADA. Counter tops and other architectural uses.
N. Medium-density fiberboard (MDF, MDFB, Customwood, Craftwood) [Particle board]	Soft wood fibers, binders, resins. Sometimes scrap/waste wood, bamboo, glass, steel, recycled paper. [Larger particles, different glues]	High	Long term interior use, exterior when sealed	Grainless various surfaces or Green: moisture resistant. Red: fire retardant. 2.5–30 mm thick. Sizes standard/custom by manufacturer.	Fibered materials combined with resins under heat and pressure.	Paints, inks, self-sticks, veneers. Can be sawed, cut, routed, etc., like plywood.	Primarily interior. [Not good with water/humidity]	Lower than wood	Architectural/3D products, furniture. Signs, displays. Can be made from recycled materials and also be recyclable.

Surface additives

Type	Composition	Cost	Durability	Appearance	Process/Ingredients	Surfaces	Location		Application
A. Adhesive vinyl	Polyvinyl chloride (PVC), plasticizers. Additives such as colors, UV absorbers, stabilizers, fillers.[a] Single adhesive surface. Comes without adhesive.	High	Long term (interior use). Medium (exterior use)	Matte to glossy. Dozens of colors, clear, metallic, transparent, translucent; 2–7 mm thick. Rolls 15″–48″ (w) × 5, 10, 50 yards (l).	Cast formulation mixed/poured onto a sheet and moved through a series of ovens. Calendered: No solvents. "Dough" is extruded/ squeezed between rollers.	Can be printed or cut by hand or CNC machine, and applied to most surfaces. Comes with backing paper.	Interior or exterior	Medium	Letters, logos, shapes, large surfaces, windows (forward or backward) back lit surfaces
B. Ink/paint #1[c] (Solvent-based)	Various petroleum-based vehicles. Pigments. High VOC, 4-butyrolacto cyclohexanone.	High	Long term	Matte to glossy, depending on additives. Unlimited colors. Cartridge or bulk.	Solvents, dyes, pigments, resins, lubricants, etc.[c]	Most surfaces porous or nonporous. Dries fast. Cures slowly.	Interior or exterior	Medium to high depending on additives	Apply images/text to almost any surface.[c] High-color brilliance. Toxic fumes and nonbiodegradable.
C. Ink/paint #2 (Low-solvent based)	Diethylene glycol. Diethyl ether. Tetraethylene glycol. Pigments. Medium to low VOC	High	Long term	Matte to glossy, depending on additives. Unlimited colors. Cartridge or bulk.	Solvents, dyes, pigments, resins, lubricants, etc.[c]	Most porous surfaces. Dries fast.	Interior or sometimes exterior	Low	Apply images/text to almost any surface. High-color brilliance. Low-toxic fumes. Nonbiodegradable.
D. Ink/paint #3 (oil-based)	Mineral oil. Pigments.	Medium to low	Medium (interior use). Low (exterior use).	Matte to glossy, depend on additives. Unlimited colors; Cartridge or bulk.	Mineral oil, dyes, pigments, etc. Lengthens print-head life.	Most porous surfaces.[c] Dries fast. Cures fast.	Interior or sometimes exterior	Low	Apply images/text to almost any surface. High-color brilliance. Low-toxic fumes. Nonbiodegradable.
E Ink/paint #4 (water-based). [Aqueous]	Latex/acetylene glycol/pigment. [Ethylene oxide surfactant/wetting agent/penetrating agent/pigment/ water]	Low	Long term (interior use). Short term (exterior use).	Matte to glossy, depending on additives. Unlimited colors; Cartridge or bulk. Dyes, pigments, etc. Sometimes drying inhibitors.	Water solvent	Most porous surfaces.[c] Dries fast.	Interior or sometimes exterior	Low	Paper surfaces. Nontoxic fumes. Nonbiodegradable.

(Continued)

Table 1 Most commonly used sign materials. (*Continued*)

Category/brand	Material contents	Strength	Durability	Look/sizes	Formation process	Compatible materials	Installation locations	Relative cost	Uses
F. Ink/paint #5 (*Eco-solvent based*)	*Various vegetable solvents: soy, corn. Binders: Cotton wood pulp.*	*Medium to low*	*Long term (interior use), short term (exterior use)*	*Matte Unlimited color. High-color brilliance.*	*Lighter solvent. Less pigment needed.*	*Most porous surfaces. Dries slower.*	*Interior or sometimes exterior*	*High initially but low ultimately*	*Apply to most porous materials. Nontoxic. Mostly biodegradable.*

Non-electric changeable signs[a]

Category/brand	Material contents	Flexibility	Look/sizes	Formation process	Compatible materials	Installation locations	Relative cost[d]	Uses
A. "Menu Boards"	Frame of plastic, wood, bronze, or aluminum. Grooved felt board. Plastic letters inserted into the grooves with pegs on back.	Individual letters inserted in felt grooves form lines of words. Some lighted. Some covered with acrylic. Some boards switch with cork boards.	Frame colors by material. 12″ × 18″–96″ × 48″. Felt in several colors. Letters black/white. 5/16″–2″ height. Wall mounts. 1 or 2 pedestal styles.	Extruded metal/plastic frame. Rigid felt board in frame. Molded acrylic letters.	Symbols, arrows available with letters.	Interior. Exterior with cover or under shelter	Low	Churches, schools, restaurants, any place with constantly changing messages on signs.
B. "Slider" add-ons	Frames of aluminum, bronze, wood PVC, acrylic, etc. Text strips of acrylic, paper, vinyl, metal.	Text strips slide in channels from the side. Some covered. Some lighted.	Frame colors by material. Standard/custom sizes. Text strips in standard/custom sizes/colors/typestyles/materials.	Extruded metal/plastic frames. Text strip channels integral with frame or inserted in frame. Text strips printed, routed, etched depending on material	Larger custom panels available: maps, graphics, phrases, logos.	Interior. Exterior with cover or under shelter	Medium to high depending on material	Directories, room door, or function identifiers. Any place needing semipermanent text/graphics, or an expanding list. Some include Braille. Some permanent.
C. "Face" add-ons	Frames/panels of bronze, wood, PVC, metals, acrylic, etc. Attachments of various	Attachments onto backing by clips, clip channels, magnets, screws, pressure, velcro, glue.	Frame/panel colors by materials. Standard/custom sizes/shapes. Attachments in standard/custom sizes/colors/	Extruded frames. Panels manufactured by material. Attachment strips extruded/cast. Other shapes manufactured by	Larger custom panels available: maps, graphics, phrases, logos.	Interior. Exterior with cover or under shelter	Medium to high depending on material.	Directories, room door, or function identifiers. Any place needing semipermanent text/graphics, or an expanding list. Some include Braille. Donor

Sign type	Materials[a]	Features	Shapes/styles	How made	Interior/exterior	Cost[d]	Application
	woods, plastics, metals cast stone, depending on use.	Some covered. Some lighted.	typestyles. Shapes: strips or standard/ custom ovals, rectangles, tree "leaves," etc.	material, printed, routed, etched, etc.			recognition. Some permanent.
D. Pedestal frames: "A" frame with wheels. [Dry-erase.] Chalkboard. {Snap frame} Channel frames	Frames of chrome, bronze, acrylic, wood, baked enamel steel, enamel steel depending on style. Inserts are paper, any printable poster/information material, depending on use. [Melamine, polyester coated steel, enameled steel (magnetic)]. Some with felt boards.	Frames take a poster or board for temporary use. Poster slides in a channel or {frame "snaps" apart/together} depending on style. Boards in frame take [makers], chalk, press-in letters in felt. Some covered. "A" frame is 2-sided easel.	Frame/pedestal colors by material. 1 or 2 pedestals. Some clamp/slat-wall/ magnetized. Frames take various sizes rectangles, [precut arrow]. Frame atop pedestal. Straight or angled. 48″–60″ h. Clamp, slat-wall, magnetized. Table styles are 8″–11″ h.	Extruded frames/ pedestal posts. Some frames molded. Wood/ pedestal bases/ other styles manufactured according to material/use.	Interior mostly. Plastic styles exterior. Posters in slots can be of any material that fits, contain any message.	{Low} to high depending on materials/styles/sizes.	Any installation needing temporary to semipermanent information free-standing and/or movable. Some clamp to shelf/ table.

For a more complete table of sign materials, see http://www.mapsandwayfinding.com;Underlined and Italic text denotes environmentally responsible processes or recyclable materials, in whole or in part. ADA, Americans with Disabilities Act; FSC, Forest Stewardship Council; CNC, Computer Numerical Control; VOC, Volatile Organic Compound.

a Specifications are for most commonly available materials.
b Must be able to fit substrate through printer.
c All printing inks and paints must be matched with appropriate substrates for compatibility.
d Compared with other changeable sign types.

Table 2 Outcomes an institution can expect from a successful wayfinding and signage program.

A. Compliance with local, state, and federal regulations.
B. Removal of physical and cognitive barriers for all visitors.
C. Enhancement of visitability.
D. Benefits for visitors, staff, volunteers, and suppliers of goods and services.
E. Savings of staff time and money.
F. Clarity and focus of brand recognition.
G. Improvement of "good neighbor" standing.
H. Recognition by the community, colleagues, and industry organizations.
I. Contributions to environmental efforts.
J. Upturn in visitors' word-of-mouth enthusiasm.
K. Opportunities for new visitor niche markets.
L. Options for new advertising directions.
M. Increase in revenue.

Fig. 7 A men's room sign in the Honolulu airport, Hawaii: an example of a shingle sign with standard international symbols with English and Chinese text.
Source: Photograph by the author.

Fig. 6 A signage program containing international standard and proprietary symbols, standard colors, and uniform sizes and shapes. Pine Point School Library and Information Center, Stonington, Connecticut.
Source: Designs by the author.

Fig. 8 A free-standing frame sign with proprietary logo, colors, text font, and sign design. Westerly Land Trust, Westerly, Rhode Island.
Source: Design and photograph by the author.

had been supplanted more typically by shingle signs. Second, the images had become more sophisticated and specialized, not only depicting services within, but in the case of inns and taverns, displaying images or icons designed to attract specific groups of travelers. Thus a cross might be used to attract the Christian traveler, a star or moon used for the pagan, or a sword advertising a place catering to a military traveler.[54]

By the end of the fourteenth century, every conceivable type of wayfinding signage in existence today was already in place. The primary difference between then and now was in sophistication, use of electricity, and ever-increases in size.

During the seventeenth century German Inns displayed heraldic symbols by their front doors as testimony to their acceptability to visiting nobles. As with the modern custom of displaying a window full of chamber of commerce, Triple A, or assorted endorsement stickers, the more symbols displayed, the better the establishment.[55] This technique was a boon to both the travelers and the inns.

Types of Signs and Materials

General types or functions

Wayfinding signage can be classified in five major message groups.

1. Directional. Point the way to a location or function. They usually contain a combination of an arrow and text or symbol.
2. Identification. Name a location or a facility at a location. Street addresses and names of buildings are examples.

Fig. 9 Three types of wayfinding information: a city parking regulations sign, a warning printed on a sidewalk, and a mirror positioned so a truck driver can "see around a corner". New Orleans, Louisiana.
Source: Photograph by the author.

Fig. 10 An interpretive sign made of an imbedded thermosetting resin on aluminum post legs. Westerly Land Trust, Westerly, Rhode Island. **Source:** Design and photograph by the author.

3. Information. Explain, describe, or list data for a location. Building directories, hours, or stationery maps are examples.
4. Regulatory. Communicate special uses or instructions. "Do Not Enter" or "Private" are examples.
5. Warning. Communicates a danger or hazard. "Watch out for poison ivy" or "Danger, High Voltage" are examples.[56]

Specific types

The following are more specific types of signs listed by installation styles, uses, and materials used for signs and content. There are hundreds of materials used in the sign industry, each formulated for its most appropriate use in regard to strength, durability, look, formation processes,

compatibility with other materials, installation location, intended audience, and cost.

Fixed content signs. These are "carrying" surfaces, called substrates, with accompanying content that do not change once they are manufactured. Some are meant to be temporary, others are not meant to be removed or replaced easily. These can be single installations or separate letters on a surface, and lighted in a variety of ways, including from inside the sign or letters.

1. Temporary signs can be posters, banners, or signs usually made with less expensive materials.
2. Permanent signs can be installed indoors or outdoors, and include street signs, building identification, room and restroom signs, most vehicle graphics, most You-Are-Here information, and advertising. These signs

Fig. 11 Changeable electric sign: a pedestrian crossing light with speakers installed on top to send audible signals to people who are blind, Albany, New York. Streetlights, crosswalk lines, curb cuts, under-foot texture changes, open vistas, and important building landmarks are also wayfinding elements. **Source:** Photograph by the author.

Fig. 12 Changeable electric sign: Backlit and LED matrix flight information sign, Copenhagen Airport. Design by Mollerup Designlab, Copenhagen, Denmark.
Source: Photograph by the author.

can be walls with painted or attached content, panels attached to a wall or hanging from it at 90°, "shingle" style, free standing panels in frames, or on poles, "A" frame stands with panels and content on both sides. See Figs. 8–10.

Changeable content signs. These signs can have permanently attached or portable substrate, with changeable or programmable content. Uses include announcement boards, warnings or advisories, identification of temporary locations, crowd control, interpretation information, or advertising.

1. Nonelectric types have letters or lines of text, images, etc., that can be applied and changed mechanically. The most common examples are menu boards and directories.
2. Electric styles have content that can be changed by electric and/or digital means. They can range in size and use from huge animated outdoor advertising to handheld interactive computers.

See Figs. 11 and 12 for two types of changeable signs.

CONCLUSION

Wayfinding and signs have been a part of Western culture for thousands of years, coming to a developed level during the height of the Roman Empire, by which time all today's basic types of wayfinding elements, maps, and signage had come into being. Today, the materials involved in wayfinding have gotten more sophisticated, immediate, and interactive, owing to a long history of advances in concepts, principals, and materials.

The charge of wayfinding is that people of all types and abilities be afforded the chance to move around freely and find what they need wherever they go with a minimum of confusion or barriers. There is a vast discipline of professionals, and an impressive number of materials and processes available to insure that this charge is accomplished as often as possible in an attractive, straightforward, and environmentally sound fashion.

Human behavior, thought processes, design principals, positive attributes of elements, people, and categories of uses and materials all contribute to the creative mix known as wayfinding and signage.

ACKNOWLEDGMENTS

Authors, specialists, and resources cited in this entry were very generous with their experience and insights. I would like to thank my wife, Deborah M. O'Brien for her assistance and patience during the writing. As helpful as these people have been, no one but the author is responsible for the contents.

REFERENCES

1. http://www.ala.org/ala/alalibrary/libraryfactsheet/alalibraryfactsheet1.cfm. and http://www.aam-us.org/aboutmuseums/abc.cfm#how-many (accessed September 8, 2007).
2. Maguire, E.A.; Burgess, N.; Donnett, J.G.; Frackowiak, R. S.J.; Frith, C.D.; O'Keefe, J. Knowing where and getting there: a human navigation network. Science **1998**, *280* (5365), 921–922.
3. Burgess, N. Spatial cognition and the brain. The year in cognitive neuroscience. Ann. NY Acad. Sci. **2008**, *1124*, 77.

4. Maguire, E.A.; Burgess, N.; Donnett, J.G.; Frackowiak, R. S.J.; Frith, C.D.; O'Keefe, J. Knowing where and getting there: a human navigation network. Science **1998**, *280* (5365), 921.

5. Xia, J. (Cecilia); Arrowsmith, C.; Jackson, M.; Cartwright, W. The wayfinding process relationships between decision-making and landmark utility. Tourism Manage **2008**, *29*, 445.

6. Xia, J. (Cecilia); Arrowsmith, C.; Jackson, M.; Cartwright, W. The wayfinding process relationships between decision-making and landmark utility. Tourism Manage **2008**, *29*, 446.

7. Arthur, P. Passini, R. *Wayfinding: People, Signs, and Architecture*; Mcgraw-Hill: New York, 1992; v.

8. Case, J. Director, Mystic and Noank Library. *Personal communication*, 2006.

9. In *The Evolution of Cognitive Maps*; Laszlo, E., Masulli, I., Eds.; Gordon and Breach Scientific Publications: Yverdon, Switzerland, 1993; 1.

10. Xia, J. (Cecilia); Arrowsmith, C.; Jackson, M.; Cartwright, W. The wayfinding process relationships between decision-making and landmark utility. Tourism Manage **2008**, *29*, 447–450.

11. Baskaya, A.; Wilson, C.; Ozcan, Y.Z. Wayfinding in an unfamiliar environment: different spatial settings of two polyclinics. Environ. Behav. **2004**, *36*(6), 840–841.

12. Lynch, K. *Image of the City*; MIT Press: Cambridge, MA, 1960; 47–48.

13. O'Brien, D. *Wayfinding and the Illustrated Handout Map in American Village Museums*, 1998; 95–143 Thesis. Syracuse, U. This is a summary of the list that was an expansion of the first list that appeared in the Thesis.

14. Deasy, C.M. *Designing Places for People*; Watson-Guptill: New York, 1985; 35.

15. Dreyfuss, H. *Symbol Sourcebook*; McGraw-Hill: New York, 1972; 16.

16. AIGA, *Symbol Signs*, 2nd Ed.; American Institute of Graphic Arts: New York, 1993; 8–10.

17. Society for Environmental Graphic Design (SEGD), *The Americans with Disabilities Act White Paper: SEGD's Clarification and Interpretation of the ADA Signage Requirements*, 2nd edition SEGD: Cambridge, MA, 1993; Department of Justice. "The Americans with Disabilities Act." Federal Register, 28 CFR Part 36, Title III. DOJ, July 26, 1991. A facsimile is available at: Uniform Federal Accessibility Standards (UFAS): http://www.access-board. gov/ufas/ufas-html/ufas./htm#9. Or at: ADA Accessibility Guidelines (ADAAG): http://www.access-board.gov/ adaag/html/adaag.htm.

18. Harley, J.B., Woodward, D., Eds. *The History of Cartography*; University of Chicago Press: Chicago, IL, 1987; Vol. 1, 1–50.

19. Harvey, P.D.A. *The History of Topographical Maps*; Thames and Hudson: New York, 1980; 49.

20. Wilford, J.N. *The Mapmakers*; Knopf: New York, 1980; 12.

21. Mooney, W.W. *Ancient Romans*; Gorham Press: Boston, MA, 1920; 45.

22. Feifer, M. *Tourism in History*; Stein and Day: New York, 1985; 16.

23. Casson, L. *Travel in the Ancient World*; Hakkert: Toronto, ON, 1974; 292.

24. Casson, L. *Travel in the Ancient World*; Hakkert: Toronto, ON, 1974; 299.

25. Von Hagan, V.M. *The Roads that Led to Rome*; World Publishing: Cleveland, OH, 1967; 10.

26. Wilford, J.N. *The Mapmakers*; Knopf: New York, 1980; 48.

27. Neal, H.E. *Of Maps and Men*; Funk and Wagnalls: New York, 1970; 30–32.

28. Burkhart, A.J. Medlik, S. *Tourism*; Heinemann: London, U. K., 1974; 3.

29. Michael, S.; Southworth, S. *Maps: A Visual Survey and Design Guide*; Little Brown and Company: Boston, MA, 1982; 26.

30. Feifer, M. *Tourism in History*; Stein and Day: New York, 1985; 25–28.

31. Wagner, C.L.H. *The Story of Signs*; Arthur MacGibbon: Boston, MA, 1954; 4.

32. Elliot, J. *The City in Maps*; British Library: London, U.K., 1987; 11.

33. Labarge, M.W. *Medieval Travellers*; W. W. Norton: New York, 1982; 11.

34. Vaughan, R., Ed. *The Illustrated Chronicles of Matthew Paris*; Alan Sutton and Corpus Christi College: Cambridge, U.K., 1993; vii–xi.

35. Harvey, P.D.A. *The History of Topographical Maps*; Thames and Hudson: New York, 1980; 142–143.

36. Von Hagan, V.M. *The Roads that Led to Rome*; World Publishing: Cleveland, OH, 1967; 20.

37. Von Hagan, V.M. *The Roads that Led to Rome*; World Publishing: Cleveland, OH, 1967; 21.

38. Von Hagan, V.M. *The Roads that Led to Rome*; World Publishing: Cleveland, OH, 1967; 50.

39. Von Hagan, V.M. *The Roads that Led to Rome*; World Publishing, 1967; 21–50.

40. Feifer, M. *Tourism in History*; Stein and Day: New York, 1985; 2, 10–12 23.

41. Feifer, M. *Tourism in History*; Stein and Day: New York, 1985; 21–22.

42. Casson, L. *Travel in the Ancient World*; Hakkert: Toronto, ON, 1974; 298.

43. Herodotus. *An Account of Egypt*, P. F. Collier & Son: New York, 1910; 6–7 76–77 Trans. Macaulay, G.C. *Voyages and Travels*;.

44. Kirkpatrick, P.R. *Pompeiian Graffiti*; University of Massachusetts: Amherst, MA, 1980; 5.

45. O'Brien, D. *Wayfinding and the Illustrated Handout Map in American Village Museums*, 1998; 20 Thesis. Syracuse, U.

46. Feifer, M. *Tourism in History*; Stein and Day: New York, 1985; 25.

47. Feifer, M. *Tourism in History*; Stein and Day: New York, 1985; 28–31.

48. Wagner, C.L.H. *The Story of Signs*; Arthur MacGibbon: Boston, MA, 1954; 5–6.

49. http://www.mapsandwayfinding.com For a more detailed table listing sign materials, see.

50. Larwood, J. Hotten, J.C. *English Inn Signs: A Revised and Modernized Version of The History of Signboards*; Arco Publishing: New York, 1985; 1.

51. Wagner, C.L.H. *The Story of Signs*; Arthur MacGibbon: Boston, MA, 1954; 3.

Vietnam–Webometrics

52. Brion, M. *Pompeii and Herculaneum*; Paul Elik: London, U.K., 1960; 129–130.
53. Schwartzman, A. *Designage: The Art of the Decorative Sign*; Chronicle Books: San Francisco, CA, 1998; 8.
54. Larwood, J. Hotten, J.C. *English Inn Signs: A Revised and Modernized Version of The History of Signboards*; Arco Publishing: New York, 1985; 2.
55. Feifer, M. *Tourism in History*; Stein and Day: New York, 1985; 72.
56. Mollerup, P. *Wayshowing*; Lars Müller: Baden, Switzerland, 2005; 103–126.

BIBLIOGRAPHY

Wayfinding behavior

1. Downs, R.M.; David, S. *Image & Environment: Cognitive Mapping and Spatial Behavior*; Aldine Transactions: New Brunswick, NJ, 2005; [Transaction Publishing, 1973]).
2. In *Wayfinding Behavior: Cognitive Mapping and Other Spatial Processes*; Golledge, R.G., Ed.; The Johns Hopkins University Press: Baltimore, MD, 1999.
3. Jonsson, E. *Inner Navigation: Why We Get Lost and How We Find Our Way*; Scribner: New York, NY, 2002.

Principles of design and graphic communication

1. Carpman, J.R.; Myron, A.G. *Design That Cares: Planning Health Facilities for Patients and Visitors*, 2nd Ed.; Jossey-Bass: San Francisco, CA, 1993.
2. Lidwell, W.; Kritina, H.; Jill, B. *Universal Principles of Design*; Rockport Publishing: Gloucester, MA, 2003.
3. Tufte, E.R. *The Visual Display of Quantitative Information*, 2nd Ed.; Graphics Press: Cheshire, CT, 2001.
4. Wurman, R.S. *Information Architects*; Graphis Press: Zurich, Switzerland, 1996.

Signage and wayfinding design

1. Berger, C.M. *Wayfinding: Designing and Implementing Graphic Navigation Systems*; RotoVision: Mies, Switzerland, 2005.
2. Calori, C. *Signage and Wayfinding Design;* John Wiley & Sons: Hoboken, NJ, 2007.
3. Smitshuijzen, E. *Signage Design Manual*; Lars Müller Publishing: Baden, Switzerland, 2007.
4. Uebele, A. *Signage Systems & Information Graphics: A Professional Sourcebook*; Thames & Hudson: New York, NY, 2007.

Web Scale Discovery Services

Jason Vaughan
Library Technologies, University of Nevada, Las Vegas University Libraries, Las Vegas, Nevada, U.S.A

Abstract

Web scale discovery services facilitate a streamlined discovery and delivery environment for end users. These services began gaining traction in the library marketplace around 2010, as multiple services from various vendors entered general release into general release. These services consist of a modern web interface used to search and retrieve results from a large preaggregated and optimized central index hosted and maintained by a discovery service vendor. Compared to earlier library search tools, web scale discovery services offer a single search box approach, with queries returning results to a much greater level of granularity than the traditional library online public access catalog (OPAC) (such as returning results indexed at the individual article level). Web scale discovery services search a greater pool of content, sourced from both local library repositories (e.g., OPAC holdings, digital collection holdings) and remotely licensed sources (e.g., publisher or aggregator provided electronic journal content). Web scale discovery services can be compared to an earlier predecessor, "federated search." A primary differentiator with web scale discovery resides in the fact that a pre aggregated and optimized central index is searched, as opposed to a real-time search of multiple, disparate targets. Compared to earlier library search technologies, web scale discovery services offer the promise of quickly returning results at a granular level, typically ranked by relevancy. Web scale discovery services are at an early stage of development, with some noted concerns, which may be addressed in the future as the product space matures.

INTRODUCTION AND DEFINITION

Compared to earlier search and retrieval tools, web scale discovery services offer a more expansive and responsive search across library owned and licensed content. Relative to older technologies such as the library OPAC (online public access catalog), web scale discovery services are in an earlier stage of maturation. This entry seeks to provide a definition, note several precursor search technologies, and briefly discuss the interface, content, and technical infrastructure typically associated with this services. The conclusion provides a brief mention of some current noted challenges, initiatives, and potential future developments.

"Web scale," as noted by Breeding, can be characterized as "Large-scale technology platforms; applications delivered through multitenant software as a service; massively aggregated approaches to data; highly cooperative arrangements among participating libraries."[1] Web scale discovery services can be considered a growing and important component of the library information management/discovery/delivery ecosystem. As noted by Hoeppner, web scale discovery can be considered "a preharvested central index coupled with a richly featured discovery layer that provides a single search across a library's local, open access, and subscription collections."[2] The National Federation of Advanced Information Services (NFAIS) notes,

"A Discovery Service can be broadly defined as a link between the information User and the Platform on or location at which the information resides . . . a Discovery Service is defined as one that provides a 'single search box' to access a central index of pre-indexed metadata and/or full text. The content that is pre-indexed is harvested from both remotely and locally held repositories to create a searchable broad central index of robust metadata. This is done via agreements with Content Owners who may license access to their metadata and/or full text for indexing purposes directly or through a Content Aggregator, via access to open collections and repositories, and via agreements to access local library resources and special collections. The central index allows for rapid search and retrieval of information resources to which a library has right of access within their own holdings or through shared/open resources and interlibrary loan and is integral to the discovery service infrastructure."[3]

As noted by Vaughan,[4] "Web scale discovery can be considered a service capable of searching across a vast range of preharvested and indexed content quickly and seamlessly." Components typically include a cloud hosted search service (allowing the end user to perform searches against indexed content stored a large, centralized, pre-indexed database of metadata encompassing a variety of local and remote content. "Web scale" can connote the size of the index and expansiveness of search. Development and adoption of web scale discovery services involve several chief stakeholders, including libraries and their users, content providers, and vendors creating, hosting, and evolving the interface and indexing infrastructure for

Encyclopedia of Library and Information Sciences, Fourth Edition DOI: 10.1081/E-ELIS4-120049504

the services. Web scale discovery services include a technological component (front-end search interface, back-end index) and a content component (metadata and/or full text associated with local holdings and remotely licensed content). Together, a modern user interface provides a mechanism to initiate a search against a unified, pre-aggregated index, with results returned at a more precise, granular level than previously realized with earlier library tailored discovery tools.

Web-scale discovery services have involved arrangements encompassing multiple, and sometimes overlapping, stakeholders. As noted by NFAIS, there are multiple participants at some level or another associated with the provisioning and utilization of web-scale discovery services. These include the original content owner, the platform hosting the content, the discovery service itself, the discovery service subscriber (such as an academic library) and the user (such as a faculty member or student).

PRECEDENTS AND HISTORY

In the networked library environment, precedents of web scale discovery services include the OPAC and federated search discovery tools. The OPAC, with development dating back to the late 1970s and which ultimately largely replaced hardcopy card catalogs services, provides an electronic interface enabling search and retrieval functions against a database of content normally tied to a local library's collection and normally indexed to the bibliographic / item level of granularity (e.g., monographs, e-books, etc., but not, for example, individual journal articles). OPACs gradually evolved from a text-based to a graphical user interface accessible via a web browser, and eventually allowed for inclusion of hyperlinks to hosted content beyond the local library. Later, "next-generation" OPACs, introduced in the early twenty-first century (and still in use by some libraries at present), added additional features such as faceted searching (allowing users to narrow down an initial retrieved list of results on factors such as publication date, material type, etc.) and the ability to include harvested content from other, usually local, repositories (e.g., such as content found in asset management systems or other institutional repositories). The OPAC traditionally included only local content, and typically only fielded metadata was searched (though, as products evolved, search capabilities grew to include advanced keyword searching, and search of richer content such as tables of contents).

Beginning in the 1990s, the advent and growth of remotely hosted, often subscription based electronic databases (providing abstracting and indexing information, and, in some instances, native full text) contributed toward what became known as a "siloed" information environment. A large number of search interfaces and content pools associated with a multitude of databases and online journals contributed toward a disjointed discovery

environment. Adequate awareness, skill, and time were necessary to perform comprehensive and encompassing information searches. Federated search tools, first debuting in the late 1990s, provided a web-based single search box, and represented an early attempt to ease the fragmented search environment. Users typed in their search term(s), which were then broadcast simultaneously in real time to preconfigured targets (resources searched). This often included both local targets, such as the OPAC index, and remotely hosted targets, such as abstracting and indexing (A&I) and/or full-text databases of remotely hosted content licensed by the library. As such, federated search provided access to a larger set of content than usually contained in an OPAC alone. Frequently noted limitations of federated search included slow performance, poor presentation of returned results, challenges in deduplication of results, and providing effective relevancy ranking across the set of returned results (e.g., such as the tendency to provide results from the first, not necessarily best, remote database to respond to the search query).

Google Scholar, a search tool debuting in 2004 from Google, Inc., has many features similar to web scale discovery services developed later, specifically tailored toward the library environment. Google Scholar provides a web-based search interface, returning ranked results from a pre-aggregated index of content including journal articles, books, and other content types. Content within the index can include repositories outside the library (e.g., academic publishers, etc.), and, through leveraging additional services (via local library link resolvers and OCLC's Open WorldCat service), can optionally provide greater end-user awareness of local library content. Google Scholar differed from earlier federated search tools by having a pre-aggregated index, capable of quickly returning results ranked by relevancy.

In the library environment, use of the label "web scale discovery services" often refers to the commercial products debuting around late 2007, specifically tailored toward the library environment. These products are normally marketed as "services," given that there is ongoing work by the vendor (interface development content additions to the index, etc.), and, consequently, an annual service cost to libraries subscribing to the service. Examples of current services include OCLC WorldCat Local (introduced in 2007), Serials Solutions Summon (2009), Ebsco Discovery Service (2010), and Ex Libris Primo Central (2010). Visioned as a whole, the evolution of these services signifies an evolving end user search environment, from an earlier one often geared toward known-item search, to one which has a larger serendipitous, interdisciplinary discovery aspect.

CHARACTERISTICS: CONTENT

Relative to earlier indexes associated with library content, indexes associated with web scale discovery services are large in size and broad in depth of included content types. Depending on vendor, the reported size of individual records associated with web scale discovery indexes range from hundreds of millions of item to over one billion. Items are indexed to a more granular level than traditional OPAC systems, a level such as individual journal articles, discrete photographic images within a digital collection, etc. Content can include both locally hosted content as well as remotely hosted/licensed content which is often matched against licensed / paid content subscribed to by the library, from a variety of. Content, regardless of source, is typically ingested into a large, centralized prebuilt and normalized index. Typical examples of locally hosted content can include records associated with locally held books, digital collections, and other materials found in institutional repositories. Examples of remotely hosted content types include scholarly journal articles, consumer magazine articles, newspapers, conference proceedings, abstract and index records, and electronic books. Leveraging a discovery and delivery ecosystem also comprised of technologies such as knowledgebases and link resolvers, the Such content can include licensed/paid content (matched against library subscriptions in the overall discovery and delivery ecosystem)) as well as free, open access content. For indexing purposes, content providers may provide item fulltext, standard fielded metadata (title, author, publication date, etc.), and/or value-added metadata (such as keywords, abstracts, subject headings). External content providers can include the original primary publisher of the content, producers of abstracting and indexing data, and other content aggregators. A chief way library-tailored web scale discovery services differ from a general web search engine is that the index is comprised of content that could be considered at least somewhat vetted by the library, in the sense it's comprised of content with some level of collection oversight— content which is often owned, licensed, or otherwise at least minimally selected by the library.

CHARACTERISTICS: INTERFACE AND TECHNICAL INFRASTRUCTURE

Web scale discovery services are accessed via a web browser and include features, which, in the library environment, were often initially introduced in late-generation library OPACs. This includes a (default) single search box (alleviating the need to choose a specific index such as author, title, etc.), with an option for a more tailored, often fielded search via an advanced search option. The interface includes faceted search, allowing users to refine a set of returned results on parameters such as publication date range, material type, or location (dependent on the particular vendor). Richer evaluative record content may be included, such as monograph cover images, reviews, and summaries, and web 2.0 social community reviews or

recommender services. Other elements include "did you mean," type prediction, spell checking, rich export, and automated citation management functionality. By default, results are normally returned ranked by relevancy, determined by factors such as publication date, appearance of the search term in particular metadata fields, and proximity of search terms relative to each other. Alternate presentation orders can be selected, such as most recently published items first. Compared to predecessors such as earlier OPACs and legacy federated search tools, and facilitated by central hosted by the vendor, enhancements for web scale discovery services normally follow a rapid development cycle, which can include rapidly expanding indexes and evolving interfaces.

Content metadata associated with a discovery service's centralized index can be sourced (harvested) from many providers, both locally and remotely hosted. Metadata associated with this content is typically normalized to the discovery vendor's particular record schema. The centralized index may grow over time as new content is ingested and incorporated into the index. This approach differs to earlier federated search tools, which searched multiple dispersed indexes (often with different record schemas) in real time. In the case of more modern web scale discovery services, the user searches a massive, uniform, single index, allowing for results returned more rapidly. This approach also facilitates the return of results ranked according to the discovery service's algorithm (or sorted, often at the end-user's discretion, by parameters such as newest items first. Depending on the particular vendor's implementation, records of the same discrete item sourced from different providers (e.g. a particular journal article) received from different content may be deduped or merged into a single record.

In the content delivery ecosystem, web scale discovery services typically utilize an OpenURL link resolver to facilitate resolution to the final item a user hopes to retrieve (e.g., such as a fulltext article hosted by the original publisher). Vendors may provide APIs allowing local customers to enhance or develop alternate search and retrieval interfaces that still search the centralized hosted index.

The discovery index and search interface are typically hosted by the discovery service vendor, in a software as a service (Saas) context, in a cloud-based infrastructure. Competing web scale discovery services vary in the degree their search services are curtailed or restricted for nonauthenticated users; in some products, the full index may not be open for search (let alone full content retrieval/ view) for unauthenticated users. Web scale discovery services may tailor or scope results to each individual library customer, with the goal that returned results match subscription holdings, locally hosted content, and open access content, all materials which the library user should have legitimate access to. In some services, the index may be open to search by the local library user as well as those not affiliated with that particular library (i.e., all users can search, but authorization credentials may be requested at the time they tried to retrieve the licensed full text).

Discovery services may make underlying service calls to other repositories for real-time information (such as availability status for a monograph owned by the library, or to place a hold on a locally owned item). To present the final resolution content, such as a full-text journal article, the user may be taken out of the immediate discovery service context, (e.g. such as taken to a different website through a new browser window or tab). Given the number of different associated components in the information discovery and delivery ecosystem, some components of which may come from disparate vendors, there exists the chance of failure in the user seamlessly retrieving the full content associated with an item.

As noted above, web scale discovery services are normally marketed as a subscription service, with the maintenance, hosting, development, and backup handled by the vendor.

Responsibilities of the local library can include initial metadata field mapping of local content to the vendor's record schema, as well as sending local repository record loads to the vendor (e.g., such as bibliographic records from the library's local catalog). This can include an initial load to initiate the service with local materials, and incremental loads that reflect local content additions, deletions, or changes. The local library may also have some capacity to determine if certain interface features are activated and available in their instance for their particular end user clientele.

INITIAL CHALLENGES/AREAS OF FUTURE DEVELOPMENT

Web scale discovery services for libraries are at maturing but still relatively an early stage of development, and some initial challenges have been evidenced. Some of these are reflective of the complex array of stakeholders involved in the provisioning and usage of web scale discovery services. Content providers, content aggregators, and librarians each have unique concerns and perspectives, and interests they wish to advocate and emphasize. A chief issue is librarians' contention that discovery service vendors have lacked transparency in stating precisely what content is included in the searchable index, which in turn makes it difficult to educate end users as to whether a particular set of content (e.g., a particular journal title important to their discipline or research interest) is included. Content coverage comparisons between current vendor services are hard to conduct. Size of index is only one consideration in comparing products, and, while index size was an early differentiator among products, this has lessened over time as each major index now contains a large amount of content. Some vendors can conduct at

least a partial content overlap analysis (e.g., for serial titles held/subscribed to by the library) to help the library determine what portion of their content is included and indexed by their discovery tool.

Another observed challenge relates to how content is indexed. As noted above, different vendors, for the exact same item, may index a different amount of associated data related to that precise item. In building their service's index, vendors may have one data source for a particular item, or multiple data sources. Source data may include a citation, an abstract, the full text, particular metadata fields, or a combination. The vendors may themselves provide additional enhancement services against the metadata after receipt by the original content provider, such as the addition of subject headings. Such distinctions are important, in that the depth of indexing for an item can positively or negatively impact the relevancy of returned results for a search. This becomes increasingly significant when considering the sheer size of the index being searched, as relevancy can be harder to tune as an index grows in size. In the future, vendors may look to incorporate additional factors to help determine relevancy, such as better understanding the user's context, research interests, or previous search queries.

Another challenge revolves around the concept of vendor neutrality. Several discovery service vendors are associated with parent companies whose other responsibilities include native content provisioning. Concerns have been raised by librarians (and competing vendors) that this could compromise the ability to remain content provider neutral (i.e., the possibility exists to promote content from the service's parent company above content sourced from other providers). Similarly, concerns have been raised that some vendors may be entering into exclusive agreements with some publishers, hindering such content from being included in the indexes of other services.

A NFAIS report mentions additional challenges, such as diminishment of content owner or aggregator brand awareness, potentially negative alterations in usage patterns / counts experienced by content providers, and a lack of transparency related to search algorithms used to determine relevancy.

Web scale discovery services provide a more streamlined discovery and delivery environment than earlier tools. While the single search box and optimizations in full text delivery have perceived advantages (the search experience is more "Google-like"), it also represents change for librarians in how they inform, educate, and provide assistance to library end users seeking information. As they presently exist, web-scale discovery services may be ideally suited to a particular user or particular type of research need. Efforts may be needed to educate users that library web scale discovery services do not include ALL content, acknowledging that other resources, depending on the research need, may still need to be consulted should a user wish to conduct a truly comprehensive search. This can be challenging as it competes against a "need-it-now" search environment, with many users looking for easy, rapid returns for a search query. Similarly, some content by its specialized nature may be better attuned to different indexing schema or presentation of results, and such search and retrieval flexibility may not exist with a standard web scale discovery index or interface.

Two significant initiatives which worked to synthesize and provide recommendations for some observed concerns related to web scale discovery services included one sponsored by NISO and another sponsored by NFAIS. NISO established an Open Discovery Initiative, which released a recommended practice entitled "Open Discovery Initiative: Promoting Transparency in Discovery" (NISO, Open Discovery Initiative: Promoting Transparency in Discovery. 2014; http://www.niso.org/workrooms/odi/publications/rp/rp-19-2014 [accessed August 8, 2017]). NFAIS released a report entitled "Recommended Practices: Discovery Services" (NFAIS, Recommended Practices: Discovery Services. 2013; https://nfais.memberclicks.net/assets/docs/BestPractices/recommended_practices_final_aug_2013.pdf [accessed August 8, 2017]). These initiatives sought to synthesize and provide recommendations related to several observed concerns associated to web scale discovery services.

CONCLUSION

Libraries are increasingly adopting web scale discovery services, as vendor offerings mature and libraries dedicate budgets toward web scale discovery service subscriptions. Searching across a wide body of scholarly content has been a goal for libraries for some time, as evidenced by the earlier development of the Z39.50 protocol and the later advent of traditional, first-generation federated search products. The centralized pre-indexed database associated with modern web scale discovery services mitigates several noted problems of earlier search technologies and offers a more streamlined discovery and delivery environment for a significant cross section of end users.

Various avenues of potential development may be pursued in the future, perhaps to help address challenges noted above. Several discovery service vendors have released modern "library services platforms," targeted to replace the traditional "integrated library system," utilizing new information architectures geared toward more efficient management of electronic content and based on a more open data foundation. In the future, discovery services associated with a particular vendor may increasingly be integrated into the particular library service platform offered by the same vendor. Relevancy ranking will continue to be honed and discovery services may become more aware of "where the user is," perhaps evidenced by deeper integration in social media as well as greater responsiveness or dedicated applications (e.g. mobile access). As discovery services evolve, the traditional discovery portal of libraries, the OPAC, will increasingly be relegated to a shrinking, supporting role in the discovery ecosystem.

REFERENCES

1. Breeding, M. The systems librarian: Library web-scale. Comput. Libr. **2012**, *32* (1), 19–21.
2. Hoeppner, A. The ins and outs of evaluating web-scale discovery services. Comput. Libr. **2012**, *32*(3), 6–10 and 38–40.
3. NFAIS, Recommended Practices: Discovery Services. August 2013; 2, https://nfais.memberclicks.net/assets/docs/BestPractices/recommended_practices_final_aug_2013.pdf (accessed August 2017).
4. Vaughan, J. Library web scale discovery services. Web scale discovery: What and why? Libr. Technol. Rep. American Library Association: Chicago **2011**, *47* (1), 5–11.

Webometrics

Mike Thelwall

School of Computing and Information Technology, University of Wolverhampton, Wolverhampton, U.K.

Abstract

Webometrics is an information science field concerned with measuring aspects of the World Wide Web (WWW) for a variety of information science research goals. It came into existence about five years after the Web was formed and has since grown to become a significant aspect of information science, at least in terms of published research. Although some webometrics research has focused on the structure or evolution of the Web itself or the performance of commercial search engines, most has used data from the Web to shed light on information provision or online communication in various contexts. Most prominently, techniques have been developed to track, map, and assess Web-based informal scholarly communication, for example, in terms of the hyperlinks between academic Web sites or the online impact of digital repositories. In addition, a range of nonacademic issues and groups of Web users have also been analyzed.

INTRODUCTION

Webometrics, which has been described as one of the dominating forces in library and information science research at the start of the twenty-first century,[1] is "the study of the quantitative aspects of the construction and use of information resources, structures, and technologies on the WWW drawing on bibliometric and informetric approaches."[2] This definition emphasizes a heritage in the information science field of informetrics, in addition to the scope of studies (the Web) and their methodological orientation (quantitative). Webometrics is sometimes given other interpretations; the widest is simply quantitative studies of Web-related information—which is similar to computer science Web metrics/dynamics.[3,4] A closely related term is cybermetrics, which is quantitative research into all aspects of the Internet, including e-mail and network traffic. Much information science webometrics research has been concerned with link analysis or search engine evaluation. In fact, individual researchers and articles have often investigated both because search engines have often been used to gather raw data for link analysis. Other webometrics topics include online citation analysis, analysis of the online profiles of individuals, longitudinal studies of Web change, and investigations of the online spread of issues. After an overview of the history of webometrics, an introduction will be given to the main topic areas.

HISTORY

The term webometrics was coined in an early article of Almind and Ingwersen,[5] and by the end of 1997 a number of quantitative Web studies had been published, some by information scientists. One prominent study was Ray Larson's conference paper: *Bibliometrics of the World Wide Web: An Exploratory Analysis of the Intellectual Structure of Cyberspace*. The idea of using Web page hyperlinks to extract relationships from the Web emerged within information science at this time, in parallel with the invention of the influential link ranking algorithm PageRank for Google, which had its intellectual roots in bibliometrics.[6]

The first information scientist to publish a discussion of the potential for transferring information science techniques to the Internet was the Brazilian Marcia J. Bossy,[7] with an article in a French online and print journal. Larson[8] published the earliest "bibliometrics of the Web" study of real data, seeking link-based methods for identifying topic organization on the Web. Rodriguez i Garin[9] and Almind and Ingwersen[5] simultaneously identified the ability of advanced search engine interfaces to deliver powerful statistics about Web pages and links. At the time AltaVista was the most potent instrument for this kind of research. Rousseau[10] took a more mathematical approach, identifying Zipf's law on the Web and predating the later more famous statistical physics discoveries of power laws in the Web. Essentially, a power law indicates a highly skewed distribution. For example, a few Web pages attract an enormous number of links whereas most Web pages attract only a few. Another important milestone was Aguillo's[11] claim that new indicators for research and development could be constructed from the Web. This helped to trigger European funding for Web indicator research. In terms of meetings, webometrics has been most associated with scientometrics and has been well represented in all recent International Society for Scientometrics and Informetrics conferences.

Encyclopedia of Library and Information Sciences, Fourth Edition DOI: 10.1081/E-ELIS4-120044480

The first webometrics journal special issue was published in a 2001 volume of the journal *Scientometrics*, with van Raan[12] predicting—accurately so far—that the potential uses of the Web for research would not threaten the status of high quality peer-reviewed journals, and that traditional bibliometrics would therefore continue to be important. The special issue served as a warning for information scientists of the dangers of uncritical acceptance of Web data from search engines and of drawing unjustified conclusions from hyperlink data in particular.[13,14] Subsequent research, reported below, including some in a 2004 *Journal of the American Society for Information Science and Technology* special issue, has shown that the problems identified are not insurmountable.

SCHOLARLY COMMUNICATION

Although there has been some webometric link analysis research on nonacademic domains,[15] it has been in a minority so far, and so this review will be dominated by the academic link analysis tradition. Much information science research into scholarly communication has focused on extracting information from documents, such as journal articles, produced by scholars. A natural question to ask about the Web, therefore, is whether academic Web pages could yield useful new information about scholarly communication. This has led to different lines of enquiry, for instance concerning e-journals or university Web sites. Most research has focused on hyperlinks as potential indicators of impact through analogies with citations.[16,17] Background information about the link structure of the Web can be found in two popular science books.[18,19]

Journals

Journal articles form a key component of research in most disciplines and have traditionally been central to bibliometric research into scholarly communication. Journal impact factors, calculated by Thomson Reuters (formerly Thomson Scientific, and the Institute for Scientific Information or ISI), are influential estimates of the average impact of the articles published by a journal. They are the average number of citations that articles from a 2 years period (e.g., 2003–2004) receive from articles published the following year (e.g., 2005).[20,21] The citations used in the calculation come from the documents (mainly academic journals) indexed by the ISI.

Webometric studies have calculated online versions of these impact factors by replacing citations with one of the following types of interdocument connection.

- Counts of hyperlinks to journal articles or whole journal Web sites.
- Counts of online citations, i.e., traditional citations in Web pages.

- Counts of citations of the URLs of online articles: "URL citations."
- Counts of either of the two above: "Web/URL citations."
- Counts of citations in Google Scholar or in online digital libraries.

Calculations are typically not time-constrained in the way that journal impact factors are. In other words, counts are performed irrespective of the age of the source or target document. A number of studies have assessed whether link calculations can give useful results. A standard technique has been to correlate ISI impact factors with online versions, looking for statistically significant similarities between them.[22,23] Although early findings were inconclusive, later research did find significant correlations, as summarized below.

- Links to journal Web sites correlate with journal impact factors, provided that a single discipline is analyzed.[24,25] Nevertheless, different fields show a different ratio of Web site inlinks to ISI citations, and factors that contribute to higher inlink counts for a journal Web site include the site age and the quantity of information hosted.[26]
- Web citations, URL citations and Google Scholar citations of journal articles correlate significantly with print citations for most journals and across a range of science and social science disciplines.[27–29]
- About 25–30% of Web citations of journal articles represent intellectual impact, and this figure is quite stable across a range of journals.[28,30] There are typically more Web citations for a journal article than ISI citations.
- There are significant disciplinary differences in the extent to which articles are cited on the Web, at least for open access articles.[29]

Despite the significant correlations found, a practical problem for using Web links/citations as a replacement for journal impact factors is that they can originate in large replicated or automatically generated pages. These include online library catalogs and journal publishers' digital libraries. A promising approach, however, is the calculation of online statistics from large quality-controlled collections of articles online. Two examples are the CiteSeer computer science public Web library[31,32] and arXiv.org, a self-publishing archive,[33] but these currently represent field-specific possibilities.[34]

Log Analysis of Journal Usage

Web log analysis is different from most webometrics because log file data is about the Web rather than being part of the Web itself. Nevertheless, research into the use of digital libraries is directly relevant to other webometrics research into scholarly communication. Indeed, since log files can give direct evidence of the usage of articles, including some user demographics,[35] and publishers like Elsevier now provide their editors with summary statistics about the number of online accesses of individual articles, it seems that this kind of data may significantly supplement or replace citations for evaluation purposes.[36] The main drawback is that log file statistics are dependant upon the organization of the digital library Web site and some technical decisions about how to track users and so are not directly comparable, unless a standardization initiative can circumvent this problem. This is a sensitive issue since journals can be compared and ranked based upon usage statistics.[37] In addition this data is of commercial value to the publishers and so may not be made available for research and evaluation without specific authorization.

An early Web log study used an individual open access online journal, First Monday, and defined "classic articles" as those that were downloaded most frequently.[36] When analyzing individual open access journals, there is a need to "clean" the log files from automated download requests, such as from search engine crawlers. An early large-scale analysis of a publisher's digital library was that of Elsevier in Taiwan, which was able to count instances of browsing and downloading journals and use them, amongst other things, to identify the most popular subjects and journals. Interestingly, the list of the top downloaded journals was significantly different from the top browsed journals and so future research should be careful not to use browsing statistics as a proxy for downloads.[37] An investigation into open access publishing in arXiv.org found a significant but fairly moderate Pearson correlation between the natural logarithms of downloads and citations for articles in four different disciplines, including mathematics (0.347) and physics (0.462).[38] In contrast, another approach is to combine citations to and "reads" of an author's articles in order to produce a longitudinal profile of their changing pattern of influence.[39]

People

Cronin et al.[40] constructed a typology of online invocations of a small group of scholars. They used a search engine to find pages containing the scholar's name and then classified the reason why the scholar was mentioned in the invoking page (if the invocation referred to the correct person). The most common type of page mentioning a professor's name was online conference proceedings. An important finding was that the contexts of invocations on the Web were different from reasons for academic citation, and so the Web gave an opportunity for tracking "modes of communication" that were previously difficult or impossible to study.

Later research hypothesized that Web mentions might be used alongside other media mentions as indicators of the fame of academics.[41,42] It is not clear yet, however, how valid this approach is.

Universities

Can the overall impact of the research of an entire university be estimated by counting the number of links to its Web site? This is perhaps a strange question to ask since impact assessments are usually applied to individual scholars, research groups or departments, but rarely to entire universities. Nevertheless, this is a logical methodological question to assess whether links can be used for impact assessment. This is because entire university Web sites are sufficiently large, at least in developed nations, to give a degree of stability to link count statistics. The World Universities' Ranking on the Web initiative (http://www.webometrics.info) is a high profile example of using links, in conjunction with other Web presence factors, to generate simple online indicators.[43]

After much research into link counts as impact indicators for universities, some clear findings have emerged, albeit from investigations mainly restricted to the United Kingdom. University Web sites attract inlinks from other universities approximately in proportion to the research productivity of the owning university.[44] University Web sites source outlinks on the same basis, and so the number of links between any pair of universities will be approximately proportional to product of their research productivities.[45] The cause of more productive universities attracting more inlinks is not the increased impact of their pages, however, it is simply that they produce more pages.[44] In the experiments deriving these results, straight link counting was found to be less effective than other forms that minimize the effect of large numbers of replicated links in Web sites.[46] Longitudinal studies of static HTML pages have shown that the results of link analyses are relatively stable over time, and suggest that academic Webs in some countries have stabilized and ceased to experience exponential growth.[47,48]

In addition to research productivity, geography is also a factor in linking: closer universities tend to interlink more.[49] On an international scale, proximity and shared languages also seem to be important, despite English being extensively used on the university Web sites of non-English-speaking nations.[50]

Research into departmental level interlinking has found results broadly consistent with those concerning university level interlinking. The outcomes of statistical tests of linking have been less significant, however, suggesting that departments have too few pages to give stable results. Nevertheless, departmental studies allow the investigation of linking by discipline, allowing comparisons to be made. As an example, U.S. departments of chemistry, history, and psychology have been compared:[51] U.S. historians were found to hardly use the Web (but some historians do operate actively online),[52] with chemists using it by far the most and extensively interlinking. Other research has investigated library and information science[53,54] and computer science,[55] and physics, sociology, and math.[56] One important (and rare) qualitative link investigation has shown how links can be valuable pointers to disciplinary differences and how qualitative interpretations can support the construction of effective frameworks for link analysis.[57]

At the lower organizational level of research groups, some studies have sought to relate inlinks to home pages with off-line factors such as gender, collaboration networks, and research productivity within the life sciences. Of these, there was some evidence that female scientists and older scientists received less inlinks than others and, counterintuitively, the same was true for those with larger collaboration networks.[58]

Link Creation Motivation

Although counts of links to university Web sites correlate significantly with university research productivity, this does not prove that a university's research causes others to link to its Web pages. Motivation studies have sought to find out if this is the case. In fact, relatively few links to university Web sites directly target research papers hosted in their general Web pages, only about 1%. There is a connection between research and link creation, but it is more indirect. About 90% of interuniversity links relate in some way to scholarly or educational activity,[59] although a smaller percentage of these links relate more directly to scholarly or educational activity.[60] This connection includes token links such as link to the home page of a collaborating researcher, or their department or university home page. Link counts, then, should be interpreted as reflecting a wide range of types of informal scholarly and educational communication. The importance of this statement is that inlink counts should not be used to assess the impact of a university's research. Nevertheless, a university that receives fewer links than should be expected for its research productivity should be concerned about whether its site is hindering its academics' online informal scholarly communication.

There is a problem with using a link classification exercise to attribute creation motivations to links in order to interpret link counts because different user groups (e.g., academic fields) can create links for different purposes.[56] Subsequent research has reinforced the complexity of link creation motivations. Bar-Ilan introduced a multifaceted framework for classifying links that included the source page, linked area, the link itself, and the target page, using it for an extensive classification of links between Israeli academic institutions.[60] The classifications included many categories and subcategories. Bar-Ilan's findings clashed to some extent with other research due to the problem of deciding which type of activities should be classed as academic-related. There is also a classification problem in differentiating between educational and research-related links.

Other Academic Studies

Some research has addressed interesting questions that do not fall into the above categories, despite being quantitative, academic-related, and Web-related. A unique and promising line of investigation is Björneborn's[61] small world analysis. He investigated the local structure of academic Web links, identifying chains of links between Web sites, particularly those that cross topic boundaries. This has the potential to give new insights into the kind of information that could be extracted from Web links, and why links are created.

Leydesdorff and Curran[62] have used AltaVista to gather time series data for connections between university, industry, and government Web sites, comparing the Netherlands to Brazil. This research exploited AltaVista's recording of the "last modified by" date on Web pages, which allowed queries for old pages: those that had not been modified since the specified date. Such facilities are now provided in the Internet Archive in a more powerful form: allowing the retrieval of old pages even if they have subsequently changed. Also focusing on university–industry–government interconnections, Stuart[63] used the case of the U.K. West Midlands Automobile Industry to show that citing practices differed greatly between the three sectors, with many collaborations not reflected on the Web in any way. A larger-scale study then found that the majority of intersector links did not reflect collaboration.[64]

Online text-based evidence of connections between universities and business has been sought through an investigation of the occurrence of the names of academic journals in business Web sites.[65] The results showed that this type of analysis was difficult because of pages that listed large numbers of journal names in the form of a list, without any real indication that individual journals were contributing knowledge to the hosting company.

Heimricks et al.[66] have compared Web link patterns to citation and collaboration patterns. This multiple data source triangulation seems to be an effective way of exploiting Web data without relying exclusively upon it. This combining of different data sources to illuminate different aspects of the same situation is a promising direction for webometrics research.

Visualization

A minority of the academic Web link analysis articles have used visualizations to display the relationships between Web sites or organizations. Diagrams are a useful way to succinctly convey large link data sets. For example Heimricks and van den Besselaar[67] used two-dimensional multidimensional scaling maps to display clusters of interlinked Web sites,[68] network diagrams to illustrate the strength of interlinking between the Web sites of various countries, and a colored hybrid cluster and link diagram to illustrate a combination of the two. A similar type of diagram has also been used to display the interlinking of national and technological sector differences within a single diagram.[69]

NONACADEMIC LINK ANALYIS

Vaughan has pioneered the application of information science link analysis to business Web sites. She has shown that colinks can be used to identify similar business organizations from the Web.[70,71] In addition, a number of studies that have elements of quantitative Web analysis have origins outside of information science but are nevertheless relevant to webometrics. Three will be discussed briefly below, all concerning sociological analyses of specific phenomena.

Garridos and Halavais[72] used hyperlinks between Web sites to illustrate and explore an online network connected to the Zapatista grass roots movement in Mexico. This gave insights into the range of different issues that were prominent amongst online activists, such as women's rights, and was also able to support a previously made assertion about the role that Zapatista support groups play in binding together a range of diverse types of nongovernmental organizations. This approach has been codified to some extent in a book of similar examples.[73]

Web Sphere Analysis[74] is an example of an integrated method for combining different information sources to study an online activity. This is described as "a 'midrange' approach to making sense of linking practices, midway between close rhetorical/ethnographic analysis of links and large-scale link mapping." Hyperlinks are used, but only as one component of a wider Web analysis. For example, in an investigation into Web sites relating to the U.S. presidential election of 2002, no strong patterns emerged, leading to the suggestion that linking was still in an experimental phase in presidential elections, and than norms of activity had yet to be established. Related research has shown that there can be connections between off-line factors and Web presences for politicians[75] and has discussed the use of a range of blog-related indicators to analyze online political campaigns.[76]

The trend to integrate link analysis into a wider theoretical framework is a positive one, which could be increasingly successful if Web practices become more standardized and stable. The need to embed a study of Web links into other phenomena is exemplified by Hine's Virtual Methodology,[77,78] which explores online activity through its organic relationship to off-line activities.

WEB 2.0

There have been many quantitative examinations of blogs and other Web 2.0 sites by computer scientists, webometricians, and the wider social science community. This section reviews those most relevant to webometrics.

A number of blog analyses have had computer science objectives but generated interesting results about the structure of blogspace. A temporal investigation into how topics are discussed within blogs showed that there were several common patterns: "mostly chatter," a steady volume of discussion; "spikey chatter," the constant discussion of a topic, like Microsoft, with occasional peaks caused by identifiable events; and "just spike," the sudden appearance of a topic and its subsequent eventual disappearance.[79] The discovery of trends within blogs has received particular attention, with the development of a variety of algorithms to identify spikes or hot topics of discussion.[80,81] In addition, there have been analyses of trends in discussion around particular events, such as the London Attacks,[82,83] using a time series of the daily number of relevant blogs containing a particular word. This technique is able to reveal the frequency with which small topics occur within larger discussions. Interestingly, simple searches in free blog search engines, such as BlogPulse, can be used to gain retrospective insights into public discussions of topics,[84] which is probably the first general-purpose source of retrospective public opinion.[85]

Folksonomy is another aspect of Web 2.0 that has attracted quantitative research. A folksonomy is a set of user-generated tags for Web pages, images, videos, or other resources. The frequency distribution of tags within such a system is of interest for information retrieval purposes because the most frequent tags are necessarily the most general and hence it is desirable for a system to encourage users to use lower-frequency, more specific tags, even though some high-frequency tags may suit some user needs better.[86] A specific study of university groups in the image sharing system Flickr found a tag distribution and types of tags which suggested that grouped images may tend to be more altruistically tagged.[87] A more systematic study of tagging behavior (one of many about the issue) included informetric-style analysis of tags created by users and showed that habit was an important factor in explaining how users tag, but was not the only factor, with others including the influence of group norms.[88]

One of the most innovative webometric studies is Voss's[89] of Wikipedia, which showed that national Wiki growth tended to begin linearly but then to become exponential. Wikipedia links exhibit a classic power law, both for inlinks and outlinks, and the number of editors per article also follows a (broken) power law. Article sizes, in contrast, follow approximately a lognormal distribution with a distinct mean, probably reflecting attempts to regulate article lengths. Another innovative approach is the History Flow visualization technique that is able to illustrate the editing history of Wikipedia articles.[90] One finding was the existence of edit wars, during which the same changes were made and removed repeatedly over a period of time.

The Facebook social networking system is interesting for the insights that statistics can give into the way in which such systems can be used.[91] Facebook started out as a college-oriented system and appears to have achieved almost universal usage amongst U.S. college students. A statistical analysis of usage patterns suggests that its use is primarily for communication between students at the same university, rather than for distant connections, and that its use was integrated into student's patterns of study rather than being a separate activity.[91]

DATA COLLECTION

Most webometric studies rely upon data from commercial search engines, such as Google. Nevertheless, there are alternatives and methods of speeding up data collection. The main alternative is to use a Web crawler to download the pages from a set of Web sites and then analyze the results. Currently available free crawlers for research purposes include SocSciBot (http://socscibot.wlv.ac.uk) and Issue Crawler (http://www.issuecrawler.net). Data collection from search engines can also be automated using the Applications Programming Interface technology,[92] and free online software for this includes LexiURL Searcher (lexiurl.wlv.ac.uk) and the Virtual Observatory for the Study of Online Networks (VOSON, voson.anu.edu.au).

EVALUATING SEARCH ENGINES

Early Web research discovered that the results returned by search engines were not reliable.[93–95] The "hit counts" reported could change by orders of magnitude from one moment to the next. A key cause of this was the probabilistic nature of reporting algorithms. To save time, a search engine may query only a fraction of its database, estimating the total hit count with a probability calculation. Rousseau[93] proposed that researchers should use the median of repeated queries in order to get more stable data. Mettrop and Nieuwenhuysen[96] also analyzed search engines from a longitudinal perspective. They planted documents on the Web where search engines could find them and analyzed the results of search engine queries that should have returned the documents. They found that search engines behaved in an unpredictable way so that changes in search engine results did not necessarily reflect real changes in the Web. Further research into the hit count estimates returned by search engines has shown that they can include systematic biases: with low hit counts

reflecting a different kind of estimate to that of high hit counts.[97] In addition, deliberate biases can be introduced into search engine results by organized groups.[98,99]

It is important to set search engine research in the context of Web coverage. Search engines have been shown to crawl and index only a minority of the publicly available Web pages.[100] Unfortunately for webometrics, however, and in addition to undesired fluctuations, this minority is biased by site age and country of origin, although not directly by language.[101,102]

WEB EVOLUTION

Longitudinal or evolutionary studies take snapshots of the Web over a period of time and compare the results, looking for important trends. There are two types: those that study the results of search engines and those that monitor the Web directly.

An example of direct monitoring is the study of Koehler,[103] who monitored a set of pages existing in 1996 on a weekly basis until February 2001, using a program to download and analyze the pages. The pages came from the random URL generator facility offered by a search engine of the time (WebCrawler). He found that pages of different types had very different longevities. For example, in commercial sites, navigational page type tended to be periodically updated, but content pages were more likely to remain unchanged for long periods of time. Interestingly, the opposite was true for academic pages: content pages were the more likely to be repeatedly updated. A trend for increasing stability over time was also found: an old collection of pages should experience less change than a young one.

Two large computing companies have combined to produce a very large scale, but short-lived, longitudinal study through direct crawling.[104] The data set was 151 million pages, which were downloaded weekly for 11 weeks from December 2002 to February 2003. The experiment produced some interesting results, including: trivial changes to documents that did not affect their contents (e.g., HTML tag changes) were very frequent; and large documents changed more frequently than small documents. Less surprisingly, the amount of change in pages was significantly affected by the page's top level domain, and pages that changed frequently were likely to continue to change frequently.

A different type of longitudinal investigation is that of Bar-Ilan and Peritz,[105] who studied the evolution of the results sets of search engines for queries for the word "Informetrics" from 1998 to 2003. They found that almost half of the pages in the results lists disappeared or changed between consecutive data gathering stages: 1998, 1999, 2002, and 2003. These results were in fact more stable than for general Web pages, which may indicate that academic information tends to fluctuate less in search engines than other kinds.

Non-webometrics research has also conducted longitudinal studies in the sense of tracking the loss of information on the Web. For example, Veronin[106] tracked the attrition-rate of health Web sites and Casserly and Byrd[107] and Lawrence and Giles et al.[108] analyzed the disappearance of URLs cited in academic papers. The latter studies touch a point that is fundamental to academia. If an article's cited resources disappear from the Web, does this undermine the credibility of its findings?

Finally, Web evolution has become an active research topic in computer science, under the name of Web dynamics.[109] This research area typically uses mathematical modeling and large-scale experiments over the Web in order to derive results that would be useful aids to algorithm design, for example to help search engine ranking algorithms.

CONCLUSION

Webometrics has been reviewed, primarily focusing on link analysis and information science approaches relating to scholarly communication. Academic link analysis has perhaps not fulfilled early expectations of being an online counterpart for citation analysis because links are not created in the systematic way that citations can be, and are often not quality-controlled in any way. It is much more of an arbitrary decision whether an author chooses to add links to their page and, if so, which kinds of resources or pages to link to. Nevertheless, links can provide useful information if either the scale of a study is large enough to average out inconsistencies in link creation (i.e., whole universities) or links are used in combination with other sources to give a more nuanced overall picture. Recently webometrics has begun to embrace the increasing trend toward user content-creation with studies of blogs and other Web 2.0 phenomena, and has also seen webometrics-style research appearing in media studies, communication science, and politics. A second recent change is the use of text analysis to identify connections between Web sites or documents, even if they do not interlink. Future webometric research is likely to continue to extend link analysis techniques to more contexts outside of the academic arena, to react to new types of Web 2.0 spaces, and to focus on developing effective methods to visualize relationships between Web sites.

REFERENCES

1. Åström, F. Changes in the LIS research front: Time-sliced cocitation analyses of LIS journal articles, 1990–2004. J. Am. Soc. Inform. Sci. Technol. **2007**, *58* (7), 947–957.

2. Björneborn, L.; Ingwersen, P. Toward a basic framework for webometrics. J. Am. Soc. Inform. Sci. Technol. **2005**, *55* (14), 1216–1227.

3. Dhyani, D.; Ng, W.K.; Bhowmick, S.S. A survey of Web metrics. ACM Comput. Surv. **2002**, *34* (4), 469–503.

4. Baldi, P.; Frasconi, P.; Smyth, P. *Modelling the Internet and the Web*; Wiley: Chichester, U.K., 2003.

5. Almind, T.C.; Ingwersen, P. Informetric analyses on the World Wide Web: Methodological approaches to "webometrics" J. Doc. **1997**, *53* (4), 404–426.

6. Brin, S.; Page, L. The anatomy of a large scale hypertextual Web search engine. Comput. Netw. ISDN Syst. **1998**, *30* (1–7), 107–117.

7. Bossy, M.J. The last of the litter: "Netometrics". Solaris **1995**, *2,* http://biblio-fr.info.unicaen.fr/bnum/jelec/Solaris/d02/2bossy.html.

8. Larson, R. Bibliometrics of the World Wide Web: An exploratory analysis of the intellectual structure of Cyberspace. In *Proceedings of the 59th Annual Meeting of the American Society for Information Science*, 1996; 71–78.

9. Rodríguez í Gairín, J.M. Valorando el impacto de la informacion en Internet: AltaVista, el "Citation Index" de la Red. Revista Espanola de Documentacion Cientifica **1997**, *20*, 175–181.

10. Rousseau, R. Sitations: An exploratory study. Cybermetrics **1997**, *1*(1), http://www.cindoc.csic.es/cybermetrics/articles/v2i1p2.html (accessed November 2003).

11. Aguillo, I.F. STM information on the Web and the development of new Internet R&D databases and indicators. In *Online Information 98: Proceedings*; Learned Information, 1998; 239–243.

12. van Raan, A.F.J. Bibliometrics and internet: Some observations and expectations. Scientometrics **2001**, *50* (1), 59–63.

13. Bar-Ilan, J. Data collection methods on the Web for informetric purposes: A review and analysis. Scientometrics **2001**, *50* (1), 7–32.

14. Björneborn, L.; Ingwersen, P. Perspectives of webometrics. Scientometrics **2001**, *50* (1), 65–82.

15. Ajiferuke, I.; Wolfram, D. Modelling the characteristics of Web page outlinks. Scientometrics **2004**, *59* (1), 43–62.

16. Ingwersen, P. The calculation of Web Impact Factors. J. Doc. **1998**, *54* (2), 236–243.

17. Cronin, B. Bibliometrics and beyond: Some thoughts on Web-based citation analysis. J. Inform. Sci. **2001**, *27* (1), 1–7.

18. Barabási, A.L. *Linked: The New Science of Networks*; Perseus: Cambridge, MA, 2002.

19. Huberman, B.A. *The Laws of the Web: Patterns in the Ecology of Information*; MIT Press: Cambridge, MA, 2001.

20. Garfield, E. Journal impact factor: A brief review. Can. Med. Assoc. J. **1999**, *161* (8), 979–980.

21. Garfield, E. The impact factor. Curent Cont. **June 20, 1994,** http://www.isinet.com/isi/hot/essays/journalcitation reports/7.html.

22. Harter, S.; Ford, C. Web-based analysis of E-journal impact: Approaches, problems, and issues. J. Am. Soc. Inform. Sci. **2000**, *51* (13), 1159–1176.

23. Smith, A.G. A tale of two Webspaces: Comparing sites using Web impact factors. J. Doc. **1999**, *55* (5), 577–592.

24. Vaughan, L.; Hysen, K. Relationship between links to journal Web sites and impact factors. Aslib Proc. New Inform. Perspect. **2002**, *54* (6), 356–361.

25. An, L.; Qiu, J.P. Research on the relationships between Chinese journal impact factors and external web link counts and web impact factors. J. Acad. Librar. **2004**, *30* (3), 199–204.

26. Vaughan, L.; Thelwall, M. Scholarly use of the Web: What are the key inducers of links to journal Web sites? J. Am. Soc. Inform. Sci. Technol. **2003**, *54* (1), 29–38.

27. Vaughan, L.; Shaw, D. Bibliographic and Web citations: What is the difference? J. Am. Soc. Inform. Sci. Technol. **2003**, *54* (4), 1313–1324.

28. Vaughan, L.; Shaw, D. Web citation data for impact assessment: A comparison of four science disciplines. J. Am. Soc. Inform. Sci. Technol. **2005**, *56* (10), 1075–1087.

29. Kousha, K.; Thelwall, M. Google Scholar citations and Google Web/URL citations: A multi-discipline exploratory analysis. J. Am. Soc. Inform. Sci. Technol. **2007**, *58* (7), 1055–1065.

30. Kousha, K.; Thelwall, M. How is science cited on the web? A classification of Google unique web citations. J. Am. Soc. Inform. Sci. Technol. **2007**, *58* (11), 1631–1644.

31. Zhao, D.; Logan, E. Citation analysis using scientific publications on the Web as data source: A case study in the XML research area. Scientometrics **2002**, *54* (3), 449–472.

32. Goodrum, A.A.; McCain, K.W.; Lawrence, S.; Giles, C.L. Scholarly publishing in the Internet age: A citation analysis of computer science literature. Inform. Process. Manag. **2001**, *37* (5), 661–676.

33. Harnad, S.; Carr, L. Integrating, navigating, and analysing open eprint archives through open citation linking (the OpCit project). Current Sci. **2000**, *79* (5), 629–638.

34. Kling, R.; Callahan, E. Electronic journals, the Internet, and scholarly communication. Annu. Rev. Inform. Sci. Technol. **2003**, *37*, 127–177.

35. Jones, S.; Cunningham, S.J.; McNab, R.J.; Boddie, S. A transaction log analysis of a digital library. Intl. J. Dig. Libr. **2000**, *3* (2), 152–169.

36. Marek, K.; Valauskas, E.J. Web logs as indices of electronic journal use: Tools for identifying a "classic" article. Libri **2002**, *52* (4), 220–230.

37. Ke, H.-R.; Kwakkelaar, R.; Tai, Y.-M.; Chen, L.-C. Exploring behavior of e-journal users in science and technology: Transaction log analysis of Elsevier's ScienceDirect OnSite in Taiwan. Libr. Inform. Sci. Res. **2002**, *24* (3), 265–291.

38. Brody, T.; Harnad, S.; Carr, L. Earlier Web usage statistics as predictors of later citation impact. J. Am. Soc. Inform. Sci. Technol. **2006**, *57* (8), 1060–1072.

39. Kurtz, M.J.; Eichhorn, G.; Accomazzi, A.; Grant, C.; Demleitner, M.; Murray, S.S. The bibliometric properties of article readership information. J. Am. Soc. Inform. Sci. Technol. **2005**, *56* (2), 111–128.

40. Cronin, B.; Snyder, H.W.; Rosenbaum, H.; Martinson, A.; Callahan, E. Invoked on the Web. J. Am. Soc. Inform. Sci. **1998**, *49* (14), 1319–1328.

41. Landes, W.M.; Posner, R.A. Citations, age, fame, and the Web. J. Legal Stud. **2000**, *29* (1), 319–344.

42. Cronin, B.; Shaw, D. Banking (on) different forms of symbolic capital. J. Am. Soc. Inform. Sci. Technol. **2002**, *53* (14), 1267–1270.

43. Aguillo, I.F.; Granadino, B.; Ortega, J.L.; Prieto, J.A. Scientific research activity and communication measured with cybermetrics indicators. J. Am. Soc. Inform. Sci. Technol. **2006**, *57* (10), 1296–1302.

44. Thelwall, M.; Harries, G. Do better scholars' Web publications have significantly higher online impact? J. Am. Soc. Inform. Sci. Technol. **2004**, *55* (2), 149–159.

45. Thelwall, M. A research and institutional size based model for national university Web site interlinking. J. Doc. **2002**, *58* (6), 683–694.

46. Thelwall, M. Conceptualizing documentation on the Web: An evaluation of different heuristic-based models for counting links between university Web sites. J. Am. Soc. Inform. Sci. Technol. **2002**, *53* (12), 995–1005.

47. Payne, N.; Thelwall, M. A longitudinal study of academic webs: Growth and stabilisation. Scientometrics **2007**, *71* (3), 523–539.

48. Payne, N.; Thelwall, M. Longitudinal trends in academic web links. J. Inform. Sci. **2008**, *34* (1), 3–14.

49. Thelwall, M. Evidence for the existence of geographic trends in university Web site interlinking. J. Doc. **2002**, *58* (5), 563–574.

50. Thelwall, M.; Tang, R.; Price, E. Linguistic patterns of academic Web use in Western Europe. Scientometrics **2003**, *56* (3), 417–432.

51. Tang, R.; Thelwall, M. Disciplinary differences in US academic departmental Web site interlinking. Libr. Inform. Sci. Res. **2003**, *25* (4), 437–458.

52. Nentwich, M. *Cyberscience: Research in the Age of the Internet*; Austrian Academy of Sciences Press: Vienna, Austria, 2003.

53. Thomas, O.; Willett, P. Webometric analysis of departments of librarianship and information science. J. Inform. Sci. **2000**, *26* (6), 421–428.

54. Chu, H.; He, S.; Thelwall, M. Library and information science schools in Canada and USA: A Webometric perspective. J. Educ. Libr. Inform. Sci. **2002**, *43* (2), 110–125.

55. Li, X.; Thelwall, M.; Musgrove, P.; Wilkinson, D. The relationship between the links/Web Impact Factors of computer science departments in U.K. and their RAE (Research Assessment Exercise) ranking in 2001. Scientometrics **2003**, *57* (2), 239–255.

56. Harries, G.; Wilkinson, D.; Price, E.; Fairclough, R.; Thelwall, M. Hyperlinks as a data source for science mapping. J. Inform. Sci. **2004**, *30* (5), 436–447.

57. Fry, J. Studying the scholarly web: How disciplinary culture shapes online representations. Cybermetrics **2006**, *10*(1), http://www.cindoc.csic.es/cybermetrics/articles/v10i1p12.html.

58. Barjak, F.; Li, X.; Thelwall, M. Which factors explain the web impact of scientists' personal home pages. J. Am. Soc. Inform. Sci. Technol. **2007**, *58* (2), 200–211.

59. Wilkinson, D.; Harries, G.; Thelwall, M.; Price, E. Motivations for academic Web site interlinking: Evidence for the Web as a novel source of information on informal scholarly communication. J. Inform. Sci. **2003**, *29* (1), 59–66.

60. Bar-Ilan, J. What do we know about links and linking? A framework for studying links in academic environments. Inform. Process. Manag. **2005**, *41* (3), 973–986.

61. Björneborn, L. 'Mini small worlds' of shortest link paths crossing domain boundaries in an academic Web space. Scientometrics **2006**, *68* (3), 395–414.

62. Leydesdorff, L.; Curran, M. Mapping university-industry-government relations on the Internet: The construction of indicators for a knowledge-based economy. Cybermetrics **2000**, *4*(1). http://www.cindoc.csic.es/cybermetrics/articles/v4i1p2.html (accessed November 2003).

63. Stuart, D.; Thelwall, M. Investigating triple helix relationships using URL citations: A case study of the U.K. West Midlands automobile industry. Res. Eval. **2006**, *15* (2), 97–106.

64. Stuart, D.; Thelwall, M.; Harries, G. U.K. academic web links and collaboration—an exploratory study. J. Inform. Sci. **2007**, *33* (2), 231–246.

65. Thelwall, M. Can the Web give useful information about commercial uses of scientific research? Online Inform. Rev. **2004**, *28* (2), 120–130.

66. Heimeriks, G.; Hörlesberger, M.; van den Besselaar, P. Mapping communication and collaboration in heterogeneous research networks. Scientometrics **2003**, *58* (2), 391–413.

67. Heimeriks, G.; van den Besselaar, P. Analyzing hyperlink networks: The meaning of hyperlink-based indicators of knowledge. Cybermetrics **2006**, *10*(1), http://www.cindoc.csic.es/cybermetrics/articles/v2010i2001p2001.html (accessed August 1, 2006).

68. Vaughan, L. Visualizing linguistic and cultural differences using Web co-link data. J. Am. Soc. Inform. Sci. Technol. **2006**, *57* (9), 1178–1193.

69. Ortega, J.L.; Aguillo, I.; Cothey, V.; Scharnhorst, A. Maps of the academic web in the European Higher Education Area: An exploration of visual web indicators. Scientometrics **2008**, *74* (2), 295–308.

70. Vaughan, L.; Wu, G. Links to commercial websites as a source of business information. Scientometrics **2004**, *60* (3), 487–496.

71. Vaughan, L.; You, J. Mapping business competitive positions using Web co-link analysis. In *Proceedings of 2005: The 10th International Conference of the International Society for Scientometrics and Informetrics*; Ingwersen, P.; Larsen, B., Eds.; Stockholm: Sweden, 2005; 534–543.

72. Garrido, M.; Halavais, A. Mapping networks of support for the Zapatista Movement: Applying social network analysis to study contemporary social movements. In *Cyberactivism: Online Activism in Theory and Practice*, McCaughey, M.; Ayers, M., Eds.; Routledge: New York, 2003; 165–184.

73. Rogers, R. *Information Politics on the Web*; MIT Press: Cambridge, MA, 2004.

74. Foot, K.; Schneider, S.; Dougherty, M.; Xenos, M.; Larsen, E. Analyzing linking practices: Candidate sites in the 2002 U.S. electoral Web sphere. J. Comput. Mediat. Commun. **2003**, *8*(4), http://www.ascusc.org/jcmc/vol8/issue4/foot.html (accessed December 2003).

75. Park, H.W.; Thelwall, M. Web linkage pattern and social structure using politicians' websites in South Korea. Qual. Quant. **2008**, *42* (6), 687–697.

76. Elmer, G.; Ryan, P.M.; Devereaux, Z.; Langlois, G.; Redden, J.; McKelvey, F. Election bloggers: Methods for determining political influence. First Monday **2007**, *12*(4), http://firstmonday.org/issues/issue2012_2004/elmer/index.html (accessed June 5, 2007).

77. Hine, C. *Virtual Ethnography*; Sage: London, U.K., 2000.

78. Beaulieu, A. Sociable hyperlinks: An ethnographic approach to connectivity. In *Virtual Methods: Issues in Social Research on the Internet*, Hine, C., Ed.; Berg: London, U.K., 2005; 182–192.

79. Gruhl, D.; Guha, R.; Liben-Nowell, D.; Tomkins, A. *Information Diffusion through Blogspace*. In *Paper presented at the WWW2004,* New York. http://www2004.org/proceedings/docs/1p491.pdf, (accessed July 10, 2006).

80. Glance, N.S.; Hurst, M.; Tomokiyo, T. *BlogPulse: Automated Trend Discovery for Weblogs;*. http://www.blogpulse.com/papers/www2004glance.pdf.

81. Thelwall, M.; Prabowo, R. Identifying and characterising public science-related concerns from RSS feeds. J. Am. Soc. Inform. Sci. Technol. **2007**, *58* (3), 379–390.

82. Thelwall, M.; Hellsten, I. The BBC, Telegraph and Wikinews timelines of the London Attacks: A comparison with contemporary discussions. Inform. Res. **2006**, *12*(1). http://informationr.net/ir/2012-2001/paper2284.html (accessed October 23, 2006).

83. Thelwall, M.; Stuart, D. RUOK? Communication technologies blogged during crises. J. Comput. Mediat. Commun. **2007**, *12*(9). http://jcmc.indiana.edu/vol2012/issue2002/thelwall.html (accessed January 16, 2007).

84. Smith, A.G. Issues in "blogmetrics"—case studies using BlogPulse to observe trends in weblogs. In *Proceedings of ISSI 2007*, http://www.vuw.ac.nz/staff/alastair_smith/publns/BlogPulseISSI07SubmShortV3.pdf (accessed September 26, 2008).

85. Thelwall, M. Blog searching: The first general-purpose source of retrospective public opinion in the social sciences? Online Inform. Rev. **2007**, *31* (3), 277–289.

86. Golder, S.A.; Huberman, B.A. The structure of collaborative tagging systems. J. Inform. Sci. **2006**, *32* (2), 198–208.

87. Angus, E.; Stuart, D.; Thelwall, M. General patterns of tag usage in Flickr image groups. Online Inform. Rev. **2008**, *32* (1), 89–101.

88. Sen, S.; Lam, S.K.; Cosley, D.; Rashid, A.M.; Frankowski, D.; Harper, F. Tagging, community, vocabulary, evolution. In *Proceedings of CSCW 2006*; ACM Press: New York, 2006; 181–190. http://www.grouplens.org/papers/pdf/sen-cscw2006.pdf (accessed June 18, 2007).

89. Voss, J. Measuring Wikipedia. In *Proceedings of the 10th International Conference of the International Society for Scientometrics and Informetrics*, 2005; 221–231.

90. Viégas, F.B.; Wattenberg, M.; Dave, K. Studying cooperation and conflict between authors with history flow visualizations. In *Proceedings of the SIGCHI Conference on Human Factors in Computing Systems*; ACM: New York, 2004; 575–582.

91. Golder, S.A.; Wilkinson, D.; Huberman, B.A. Rhythms of social interaction: Messaging within a massive online network. In *3rd International Conference on Communities and Technologies (CT2007)*, East Lansing, MI, 2007.

92. Mayr, P.; Tosques, F. Google Web APIs: An instrument for webometric analyses? 2005, http://www.ib.hu-berlin.de/%7Emayr/arbeiten/ISSI2005_Mayr_Toques.pdf (accessed January 20, 2006).

93. Rousseau, R. Daily time series of common single word searches in AltaVista and NorthernLight. Cybermetrics **1999**, *2/3*(1). http://www.cindoc.csic.es/cybermetrics/articles/v1i1p1.html (accessed November 2003).

Vietnam–Webometrics

94. Snyder, H.; Rosenbaum, H. Can search engines be used for Web-link analysis? A critical review. J. Doc. **1999**, *55* (4), 375–384.

95. Bar-Ilan, J. Search engine results over time: A case study on search engine stability. Cybermetrics **1999**, *2/3*(1). http://www.cindoc.csic.es/cybermetrics/articles/v2i1p1.html (accessed November 2003).

96. Mettrop, W.; Nieuwenhuysen, P. Internet search engines: Fluctuations in document accessibility. J. Doc. **2001**, *57* (5), 623–651.

97. Thelwall, M. Extracting accurate and complete results from search engines: Case study Windows Live. J. Am. Soc. Inform. Sci. Technol. **2008**, *59* (1), 38–50.

98. Bar-Ilan, J. Web links and search engine ranking: The case of Google and the query 'jew'. J. Am. Soc. Inform. Sci. Technol. **2006**, *57* (12), 1581–1589.

99. Bar-Ilan, J. Google bombing from a time perspective. J. Comput. Mediat. Commun. **2007**, *12*(3). http://jcmc.indiana.edu/vol2012/issue2003/bar-ilan.html (accessed May 14, 2007).

100. Lawrence, S.; Giles, C.L. Accessibility and distribution of information on the Web. Nature **1999**, *400*, 107–110.

101. Vaughan, L.; Thelwall, M. Search engine coverage bias: evidence and possible causes. Inform. Process. Manag. **2004**, *40* (4), 693–707.

102. Vaughan, L.; Zhang, Y. Equal representation by search engines? A comparison of websites across countries and domains. J. Comput. Mediat. Commun. **2007**, *12*(3). http://jcmc.indiana.edu/vol2012/issue2003/vaughan.html (accessed May 14, 2007).

103. Koehler, W. Web page change and persistence: A four-year longitudinal study. J. Am. Soc. Inform. Sci. Technol. **2002**, *53* (2), 162–171.

104. Fetterly, D.; Manasse, M.; Najork, M.; Wiener, J. A large-scale study of the evolution of Web pages. In *Proceedings of the 12th International World Wide Web Conference*, Budapest, Hungary, May, 2003, http://www2003.org/cdrom/papers/refereed/p097/P97%20sources/p97-fetterly.html (accessed April 2004).

105. Bar-Ilan, J.; Peritz, B. Evolution, continuity, and disappearance of documents on a specific topic on the Web: A longitudinal study of "informetrics" J. Am. Soc. Inform. Sci. Technol. **2004**, *55* (11), 980–990.

106. Veronin, M.A. Where are they now? A case study of health-related Web site attrition. J. Med. Internet Res. **2002**, *4* (2). e10http://www.jmir.org/2002/2/e10/index.htm.

107. Casserly, M.; Byrd, J. Web citation availability: Analysis and implications for scholarship. Coll. Res. Libr. **2003**, *64* (4), 300–317.

108. Lawrence, S.; Pennock, D.; Flake, G.; Krovetz, R.; Coetzee, F.; Glover, E. Persistence of Web references in scientific research. Computer **2001**, *34* (2), 26–31.

109. Levene, M.; Poulovassilis, A., Eds. *Web Dynamics*; Springer-Verlag: Berlin, Germany, 2004.

Word Processing: Early History *[ELIS Classic]*

Daniel Eisenberg
Florida State University, Tallahassee, Florida, U.S.A.

Abstract
This brief history of word processing hardware and software demonstrates that the ever-familiar word processing program of today had a more complicated and slowly-evolving history than might be expected.
—*ELIS Classic*, *from 1992*

DEFINITION

The term and concept of "word processing" are by now so widely used that most readers already are familiar with them. The term, created on the model of "data processing," is more vague than commonly believed. A human editor, for example, obviously processes words, but is not what is meant by a "word processor." A number of software programs process words in one way or another—a concordance or indexing program, for example—but are not understood to be word processing programs.

The term "word processor" means a facility that records keystrokes from a typewriter-like keyboard, and prints the output onto paper in a separate operation. In the meantime the words are stored, usually in memory or magnetic media. A word processor also can make improvements in the stream of words before they are printed. At their most basic these include the ability to arrange words into lines. An "editor," such as the infamous EDLINE distributed with the Microsoft Disk Operating System (MS-DOS), lacks the ability to structure lines.

Commonly a word processor is understood to be a software program, and in the 1980s and 1990s it usually meant a program written for a microcomputer. However, preceding this period and continuing through it there have been hardware word processors. These are pieces of equipment sold for the sole purpose of word processing, containing in one package a keyboard, printer, recording and playback device, and in all recent examples a video or liquid crystal display screen. These machines include word processing software permanently stored in memory and processor chips, or in the earliest examples its equivalent in relays and wiring. A great disadvantage is that their storage media are usually incompatible with those of other machines, meaning words cannot be transferred from one system to another.

PREDECESSORS

The fundamental use of a word processor is to record, edit, and play back keystrokes. The printing press, whose storage medium was lead type that had been "input" by the human or mechanical typesetter, itself carried out this function. While the press itself need not be especially bulky or expensive, the cost, weight, and complexity of the equipment and procedures needed to prepare the type for the press were great. Thus printing has rarely been found in offices, and has been relegated to a separate business, the printing shop.

Experiments in recording typewriter keystrokes, early in the twentieth century, used mechanical, air-driven mechanisms, borrowed from or inspired by the player piano. These were scarcely more than curiosities. The electric typewriter appeared in the 1930s, but despite its higher-quality output, it did not become dominant until two decades later. It seemed to offer the potential for more economical recording and reproduction of keystrokes, but it was not until the 1950s that a machine carrying out these functions was manufactured and sold in quantity: the Friden FlexoWriter. The FlexoWriter used punched paper tape as a storage medium, thus providing some compatibility with other data processing equipment.

Keystrokes could be deleted from the punched tape, which backed up as the backstroke key was pressed. The "delete" or nonprinting character consisted of all possible holes punched; this was later implemented in the ASCII character set, in which the highest character, 127, with all bits set, was a "delete" character. However, insertions could only be made by splicing the paper tape, and there was no means to turn carriage returns into spaces or vice-versa. The difficulty of revision made the noisy FlexoWriter impractical for routine office correspondence. Its main use was for what soon became known as the "form letter," in today's terminology a merge operation: a standard text with different names, addresses, or other data inserted. These were used for political purposes, fundraising, and sales.

THE MT/ST

The first true word processor, and IBM's first entry into the field, was the Magnetic Tape Selectric Typewriter or MT/

Encyclopedia of Library and Information Sciences, Fourth Edition DOI: 10.1081/E-ELIS4-120044768
Copyright © 2017 by Taylor & Francis. All rights reserved.

4993

Word–Zoological

ST, introduced about 1969. Much larger and more expensive than the FlexoWriter, the MT/ST included a model of IBM's workhorse Selectric Typewriter built into a small desk. Accompanying it was a console, about half as large as the desk, containing control relays, the tape recording and playback facility, and control buttons and dials.

As typing took place, keystrokes were recorded on 16-mm magnetic tape, using a head moved by solenoid and spring across the tape, one character per pass. The backspace key on the keyboard backed the tape up so the character could be overwritten with a new one. Cassette tapes of 100' held approximately 25K of data. A 7-bit data set was used, providing different codes for upper and lower case letters, and an increased set of control codes. In a technique borrowed from mainframe computers, the operator could mark the tape with electronic divider codes, called "Search Codes." While the concept of named files was still in the future, the machine counted the number of Search Codes on the tape and could thus search for a file. In a crude way it could thus assemble standard chunks of text into a composite output document.

The MT/ST incorporated a number of other innovations. While it had no block movement capabilities, except by very cumbersome block export and import, it did have insertion and revision capabilities. At each carriage return, one space on the tape was reserved for insertions. More important, all except the very first models incorporated two tape stations, and the ability to play from one tape while recording an updated tape on the other, incorporating insertions and deletions as desired. The two tape stations could also be played back simultaneously, typically merging a letter on one tape with a name and address list on the other.

The MT/ST also introduced what may be called word processing concepts. Within a fixed zone (1″) preceding the right margin, spaces were converted into carriage returns, and outside it returns were changed into spaces. The concept of a "soft hyphen" was used for the first time: a hyphen that would print only if it fell within the 1″ hyphenation zone, and would otherwise be ignored. An overstrike code was also implemented; this permitted underscoring.

Whereas the FlexoWriter only operated on a character basis, the MT/ST also operated on a word, line, and paragraph basis. The machine understood a word to be any string terminating with a space; a line was a string terminating with a carriage return. Two carriage returns constituted a paragraph boundary, and were not turned into spaces as single returns could be.

However, the MT/ST had no concept of a page; the division of text into pages and the numbering of pages had to be done by a human operator. While possible points of hyphenation in a word could be premarked, it had no hyphenation capability of its own. The machine did not permit operator hyphenation while playback was in process, and thus line endings were not always satisfactory. As it had no display screen, the only way to know what was on a tape was to print it out at 15 characters per second. No tape updating without printing was possible either. The operator needed to listen to the tape transport to know whether it was skipping text or awaiting keyboard input. The MT/ST required alertness and discipline from the operator.

OTHER DEDICATED WORD PROCESSORS

Subsequently, IBM introduced a number of word processors incorporating various improvements; other manufacturers followed IBM's lead. None of these achieved the success of the MT/ST. The Magnetic Card Selectric Typewriter (1969) incorporated the concept of the page into processing; one page was stored on each magnetic card. In 1971 the Lexitron (not an IBM product) added a display screen, using paper only for the final output. IBM's Magnetic Card Executive Typewriter (1972) had proportional spacing in a single type face, sacrificing the interchangeable type elements of the Selectric. Magnetic Card Selectric Typewriter II (1973) added memory, allowing text to be stored and moved in memory and only stored on media when editing was completed. It also had the double pitch available on later Selectrics.

IBM's DisplayWriter and word processors from Wang and Lanier moved closer to the word processor as we know it today. Floppy disks gradually replaced cassette tapes as storage media. Named files were introduced. On-screen menus of functions and labeled function keys made it easier to perform tasks; opening, saving, combining, printing, and deleting files; moving, centering, justifying, and underlining text; combining standard text (a letter or a financial document) with varying data; adding page numbers, headers, and footers.

WORD PROCESSING ON MULTIPURPOSE COMPUTERS

Although not customarily thought of as such, the above pieces of hardware are computers, with input and output devices and data storage and manipulation ability. However, their programming was limited to that supplied by the manufacturer, and they could not be used for other tasks. Word processing has been done on both mainframe and minicomputers, in both of which the computer simultaneously served several users, but these never achieved acceptance outside of large businesses. Besides the cost of the computer, the printers were the primary limitation. Only daisy-wheel printers could produce office-quality output in the early 1980s, and they were slow in comparison with the processor speeds. Software for mainframe and minicomputer word processing soon trailed behind, in features and ease of use, that available on microcomputers. Mainframe administrators did not consider word processing a task particularly appropriate for their computers, as it required large blocks of memory but did not need mainframe processing speed.

EARLY MICROCOMPUTERS

The microcomputer arrived on the scene in the mid-1970s. Early models used tape cassettes for data storage, with data encoded in an unreliable audio (analog) signal. There were two main families of central processing chips, the 8080 and the 6502 chip, which were later to evolve into the IBM-compatible and the Macintosh lines of computers, respectively. The commands used by the chips were the same for all machines using that chip. However, the formats by which data was stored and displayed on a screen were not standardized, meaning that each model of computer required a different version of the same program, and computers could not share data. Early dot-matrix printers, typically using a 7-pin matrix, produced a legible but low quality product, unsuitable for business correspondence. Very primitive software was written by hobbyists, or provided by hardware manufacturers.

The addition of floppy disk drives to computers in the late 1970s marked a great advance in the reliability and speed of data storage. It became practical for independent programmers to write and sell software. The only word processing program from this period to achieve recognition was Michael Shrayer's Electric Pencil, which introduced word wrap, eliminating the need to press the carriage return key at the end of each line. This was a great innovation for its day.

The advent, in the late 1970s, of the standard operating system CP/M (Control Program/Micro) brought vastly increased standardization. Formats for file and memory structure were standard across all machines of that class. By 1980 IBM Selectrics and Diablo and Qume daisy-wheel printers were coupled to computers, giving a good quality printed output and a variety of type styles, although at a high price. Changing type style meant stopping the printer and manually changing the printing element (in the case of the daisy-wheel printers this was a disk about 3 inches in diameter). The addition of memory to printers made bidirectional printing possible. This eliminated the delay caused by the return of the print head to the left margin position at the beginning of every line.

While the logical disk structure was standard, physical disk organization was unique to each computer. Standardized 8 inch disks were replaced with less standard 5.25 inch disks. The screen display codes were also not standardized. This meant that slightly different versions of a program were still required for each brand, and in some cases each model, of computer. It also meant that different brands of computers could not exchange disks, although conversion software and facilities appeared in the mid-1980s.

WORDSTAR

Throughout the CP/M period the predominant word processing program was WordStar, although there were other minor competitors, such as Select and Perfect Writer. By recent standards CP/M WordStar was very primitive, lacking features now taken for granted, such as a spelling checker, footnotes, and proportional spacing. Onscreen help was limited, and installation often required a technically knowledgeable operator. It could only support one printer at a time; multiple printers required that different versions of the program be prepared. Nevertheless, WordStar took full advantage of the features of the printers of the early 1980s. It supported super- and subscript, bold or shadow print, underscore, page numbers, and one-line headers and footers. It achieved a great success with its keyboard structure, in which cursor movement commands were arranged in a logical, one-hand design (Control-E for up, Control-S for left, Control-D for right, and Control-X for down). The MicroPro Corporation, publisher of WordStar, successfully sold its product to hardware manufacturers, such as KayPro and Morrow. It was thus "bundled" with the computer; purchase of that brand of computer featured WordStar included, at a much lower price than it would cost if purchased separately. "WordStar To Go," an abbreviated version, was stored on memory chips and sold with some of the first laptops.

MS-DOS WORD PROCESSING

In the early 1980s the CP/M computers were replaced by more powerful machines using the Microsoft Disk Operating System (MS-DOS). This system was chosen by IBM for its microcomputers, and although IBM never dominated microcomputers as it wanted to, it served to set a common technical core for a large family of "IBM-compatible" computers. Among other things, IBM's floppy disk format became standardized over a large number of brands of computers, permitting exchange of data with an ease that CP/M computers, with their manufacturer-specific formats, never achieved. A software producer needed only to prepare a single version of a program, which would then run on the machines of many manufacturers. The MS-DOS computers also vastly increased available memory, added subdirectories to their disk structures, added function keys and an "Alt" key to the keyboard, and were easily customizable without sacrificing compatibility.

This new standardization, plus the added speed of the machines, created a great hardware and software boom in the 1980s. The microcomputer software industry grew at a rapid pace; customers were eager to purchase the newly standardized machines for which abundant software was available. Prices of hardware plunged. Software gained dramatically in features and ease of use, while also declining in price.

GENERAL CHARACTERISTICS OF MS-DOS WORD PROCESSING PROGRAMS

MS-DOS word processing programs offered more of everything. The increased memory and disk storage capability meant that more extensive on-screen help could be made available. Dot-matrix printers improved the quality of their letter shapes dramatically; print quality never attained that of daisy-wheel and Selectric printers, but the dot-matrix printers were much faster and far more flexible. They offered proportional spacing (available on some daisy-wheel printers, but never successfully supported by CP/M programs), italic, a variety of type sizes, better support for foreign language characters, and the ability to print pictures. All of this kept the word processing program developers scrambling, successfully, to keep up.

New features were added to the programs yearly: footnotes; endnotes; the ability to edit more than one document; descriptive, nonprinting file headers; split screen editing; mathematical functions on data contained within the document. The features of third-party (supplementary) programs were gradually incorporated into the main programs; macros (master commands to automate repetitive operations); data exchange with other programs; spelling checkers; thesaurai; data encryption; outline processors; graphics (illustration) creation and editing; charting; file comparison; indexing; an equation editor. A word processing program actually became a package of programs, filling many disks. WordPerfect 5.0, for example, in addition to installation and setup programs came with PTR.EXE, a program to edit printer definition files; CONVERT.EXE, a file conversion program to import and export text and data; GRAPHCNV.EXE, a program to import illustrations; SPELL.EXE, to edit the spelling dictionaries; and WPINFO.EXE, a program to provide information about the user's configuration to assist in diagnosing installation problems. Available for a small additional cost was a macro editor, later incorporated into the main program.

These new features meant more complex programs, and frustration for many users. A new industry sprang up to provide training and learning aids (books and videos). Still, a significant body of users do not make efficient use of their word processors, and find them intimidating and confusing. Even experienced users often find the complexities of the programs frustrating, and to master every feature of a major program is a full-time job.

Specific Programs

WordStar failed to make the transition from CP/M to MS-DOS machines. The greatest failure in the history of word processing was WordStar 2000, an improved version of the program with many new features such as footnotes, but with a completely different command structure and user interface. It was received indifferently by the existing user base, who already had put in overtime to learn the previous commands and were not eager to repeat the process. There were never enough first-time users of WordStar 2000 to mark the program as a success and force users of the older WordStar 3 to make a switch. As a result, faced with irate users, the publisher retreated to its previous user interface, and released WordStar 4. WordStar was further damaged by a group of dissident employees who founded a new company and offered a competing program, NewWord.

WordStar 4 offered macros, improved installation, and better on-screen help, but was basically an adaptation of the older CP/M program. During the time these developments were under way, WordStar was overtaken by Microsoft Word and WordPerfect, which were first to offer such new features as laser printer support and print preview. In one of the most egregious examples of "version inflation," WordStar released versions' 5, 5.5, and 6.0, while WordPerfect more honestly released version 5.0 and 5.1. The implication is of course that the program with the higher number is better; since this view would be held only by less knowledgeable users, it is tantamount to a declaration of defeat.

Microsoft Word

In the mid-1980s, Microsoft Word was the leading word processing program, followed by WordPerfect, and very much in third place was XyWrite, a respected program for serious writers which never achieved the sales its partisans said it deserved. Word was written to take full advantage of the graphics capability of the MS-DOS computers. This allowed it to have a better display, including screen fonts for foreign language characters. It also offered superior formatting capabilities and style sheets; it was the first major program to incorporate an outline processor. Word was well-placed, by its graphics-based structure, to become the most successful program for the similarly graphics-based Macintosh, and to gain an early lead as the word processor for the IBM graphic interface Windows (also a Microsoft product). However, Word's lead, in the MS-DOS world, did not last long. Its menus were cryptic; function codes could not be searched for; and Microsoft, a controversial company which had many other software products, did not give Word as high a priority as the WordPerfect Corporation did its principal product.

Wordperfect

From the late 1980s and into the 1990s, the predominant word processing program was WordPerfect. This is only partly due to the features of the program. WordPerfect is a character-based (as opposed to graphics-based) program, its function keys are arbitrary and hard to learn, and while it has been a strong competitor, it has never held the lead in flashy features.

The triumph of WordPerfect as the predominant word processing program is due at least as much to good management and business decisions as it is to the program's features. First, the program is available for a greater variety of operating systems than any other, although the MS-DOS version is the most popular. It currently is the only word processor that has a common file format for both MS-DOS and Macintosh versions. It has also been a leader in government and international sales, providing many more foreign language versions, and more support for foreign characters and alphabets, than any competitor. It has been more successful than any other company in providing a package of programs; a spreadsheet (PlanPerfect), a database (Data-Perfect), a drawing program (DrawPerfect), and a shell providing mail, calendar, and file management functions (WordPerfect Office). A number of other characteristics, while not as easy to proclaim in advertising, have endeared it to data processing professionals, whose recommendations have had a major impact in corporate decisions to adopt it; a macro programming language and editor, a merge programming language, soft keyboards, and the broadest printer support of any program. WordPerfect also has the best documentation in the industry, a significant advantage in a field long characterized by poorly written or inaccurate documentation.

Perhaps the biggest single factor in the success of WordPerfect is quite external to the program itself: the company's liberal policy for telephone assistance. It is WordPerfect's policy to provide purchasers of its microcomputer programs unlimited telephone assistance free of charge, and indeed it subsidizes the service within the United States by supplying "800" numbers. At first the company would verify that the caller had purchased its program; subsequently it provided service even to those with stolen copies.

The contribution of this decision to WordPerfect's success cannot be exaggerated. For new users, confused or faced with installation problems, it offered reassurance and help; for the intermediate it offered help with advanced features; for advanced users faced with program bugs it offered confirmation of the bugs and indirect access to expert assistance. The telephone assistance and reduced user frustration and greatly increased loyalty to the product. A feature much commented on was the addition of "hold jockeys," similar to radio disk jockeys, to calm users on hold during busy periods by playing music, giving progress reports on their calls, and offering news about WordPerfect products. The telephone help service also provided WordPerfect with invaluable feedback on user perceptions of its programs, and the company has shown an admirable ability to assemble and use the data so generated. However, the costs of providing this service have been heavy. It remains to be seen whether WordPerfect will be able to maintain this free service indefinitely.

Simpler Word Processors

As the major word processors grew so complex, a number of smaller, cheaper, and simpler alternatives emerged in the mid-1980s. These included PC Write, Bank Street Writer, First Choice, and a number of others. While each has a number of users, none of them has achieved predominance. In 1990, WordPerfect released LetterPerfect, a simpler and smaller version of its program that retained file compatibility.

Macintosh Computers

The CP/M and IBM-compatible microcomputers all use members of a single family of processing chips: the 8080 and its descendents the Z-80, 8088, 8086, 80286, 80386, and 80486. The other main family of computer processing chip, the 6502 and its descendents, gave birth to the Apple and then to the Macintosh computer, with the short-lived Lisa as an intermediary. The Apple computer, whose color, joysticks, and oversized letters made it very successful in schools, was never used for serious word processing. Its video display was too poor to have an 80 column by 24 line screen; thus it was not possible to see at all what things would look like on the screen.

The Macintosh, introduced about 1984, quickly gained a loyal and vociferous group of followers. Its operating system, self-installation, and graphical user interface made it far easier to install and use than IBM-compatible computers, which the company emphasized in its advertising. Documents could be seen on the screen just as they would be printed, and the writer had precise control over fonts and type sizes. In contrast with the IBM microcomputers, patents and copyrights protected the Macintosh from competitors, and to date there are no Macintosh-compatible computers. This meant, however, that prices remained much higher than in the more competitive IBM-compatible environment.

The Macintosh was never much used in an office environment or for word processing. The dot-matrix printer sold with it produced an output only marginally suitable for correspondence. For some time, there was no intermediate step between that printer and an expensive PostScript laser printer. The mouse was awkward for good typists, as it required that a hand be removed from the keyboard, and the control over typeface and type size was not only unneeded but even distracting to writers.[1] The Macintosh's greatest success was in publishing and advertising, for which its graphics screen and precise preview of type, illustrations, and layout were invaluable.

WORD PROCESSING AND TYPESETTING

Reducing the cost of typesetting so that it could be incorporated in an office or small business budget has been a long-standing goal of office equipment. Traditional lead type required expensive equipment and highly trained operators; it was slow to produce and correct. Adaptations of the electric typewriter provided proportionally spaced output of typeset quality, but justification—making an even right margin—meant that each line needed to be typed twice. The first keyboarding mechanically counted the length of the line, and the repetition inserted fractional spaces between words so as to align the right margin. IBM's entry in this field was the Selectric Composer, a piece of hardware vaguely resembling but much more complex than the Selectric typewriter, with proportional spacing and with three pitches (15, 17.4, and 19.8 characters per inch). Special ribbon and paper were used to obtain a very black and crisp output, suitable for offset printing.

A model of the Selectric Composer was soon fitted to read tapes created and corrected on the MT/ST. The machine calculated interword spaces, and it was thus necessary to type only once to achieve a justified output. Hyphenation during playback, though operator assisted, was implemented for the first time. While the Magnetic Tape Selectric Composer was still out of the price range for most offices, and was limited to a maximum type size of 12 points, its input could be prepared by a secretary without the special training required of a typesetter. It marked an important first step in the marriage of word processing and typesetting.

Although from early in the computer age, typesetters had developed the hardware needed to use computer files as input, this was limited to letters, numbers, and punctuation; formatting, control of type face or size, and use of special characters were only possible if complex codes were added to the computer files. The results could not be previewed on the computer, nor could the transferred files, once processed on the target hardware, be returned for further editing on the computer. The output devices were far too expensive for office or small business use.

Production of typeset output on the microcomputer itself required an affordable output device with good resolution, speed, and print quality, the ability to handle a variety of type sizes and special characters, and the processing power to calculate microspacing needed to justify lines. The latter is the simplest; the program uses a table containing the widths of each character, calculates the total length of the letters in a line by adding the width of each, subtracts this from the desired line length (measure), and divides the remainder by the number of interword spaces. The result is then sent to the printer as fractional spacing instructions. Additionally, good typesetting requires kerning; removing space between selected pairs of letters to achieve a satisfying visual effect. This added to the previous requirement the need to look up pairs of characters in a table and send fractional spacing adjustments to the printer between letters.

Proportional spacing was partially implemented on CP/M machines, and fully adapted on both MS-DOS and Macintosh machines in the mid-1980s. Kerning was implemented with WordPerfect 5.0, in 1988. The output device of choice proved to be the laser printer. Daisy-wheel printers could handle proportional spacing, but not varying type sizes. Changes from roman to italic required that the machine be stopped twice for manual change of print wheels. Dot-matrix printers could change to different type sizes and styles without operator intervention, but were unacceptably slow when operated at their finest resolution. The blackness of their output was also unreliable.

These problems were resolved with the laser printer, which appeared on the scene in the mid-1980s. By the end of the 1980s prices had so declined that it was available to almost anyone needing to produce typeset material. Using a print engine adapted from the photocopy machine, the laser printer offered high speed and reliability together with good print quality.

All laser printers came with some typefaces built in. All but the earliest accepted and housed in memory electronic type stored in the memory chips of plug-in cartridges, or sent by the computer. The electronic type consisted of patterns of dots that would be printed on the page when the appropriate letter was sent from the computer. Any size or style of type could thus be accommodated. By the end of the 1980s and early 1990s, production of electronic type had grown into a new industry, offering the microcomputer-based typesetter virtually all the choices in type style previously available on dedicated typesetting equipment costing many times the price. Many previously unavailable fonts appeared, both ornamental (e.g., based on handwriting) and practical (exotic foreign languages; dead languages used in Biblical and historical studies).

Page design programs, sometimes described with the misleading label "Desktop Publishing," allowed microcomputer users to arrange headlines, text, and illustrations on pages with ease and precision. The leading programs were Aldus PageMaker and Ventura Publisher, and several simpler and less expensive alternatives.[2]

THE FUTURE OF WORD PROCESSING

Hardware has always set the boundaries for word processing. Hard disks and larger computer memories meant larger and more powerful programs could be stored and run. Better graphics displays meant more characters could be shown. Better printers allowed growth from letter writing to typesetting.

The huge storage capacity of the optical disk means that word processing will be linked even further with a multimedia environment including pictures and sound. At the same time, access to huge bodies of electronic text, locally or remotely stored on optical media, is rapidly becoming a reality. Reading will eventually take place primarily on a screen, and word processing software will be used for reading as well as a writing. The software offers the possibility of reading texts in new, nonlinear ways, creating links between blocks of text or between files ("hypertext") which have no parallel in the conventional, printed world.

As written communication shifts to electronic rather than paper transmission, word processors will become more closely linked with electronic mail systems. If past trends continue, functions presently carried out by separate programs from different manufacturers—grammar checking, concordance producing—will also be incorporated into the concept of word processing. Typesetting will become even less distinguishable from word processing. Users will have the option of having display screens emulate the type styles of printed books. As operating systems become more standardized—Microsoft Windows, the very successful new user interface for the IBM-compatible, resembles the Macintosh in many ways—word processors will also come to resemble each other more. They will thus become easier to learn. Voice input and output is also in the near future, as is hardware designed to place less stress on the human body (arms, fingers, back, and eyes).

REFERENCES

1. Peoples Halio, M. "Student Writing; Can the Machine Maim the Message," Acad. Comput. January **1990**, *45*, 16–19. R, Nelson, "Word Processing," Pers. Comput., August **1990**, 49–50.
2. Eisenberg, D. "In-House Typesetting on a Tight Budget," Schol. Publ., **1990**, *21*, 205–220.

World Intellectual Property Organization (WIPO)

Janice T. Pilch
Rutgers University Libraries, Rutgers University, New Brunswick, New Jersey, U.S.A.

Abstract

The World Intellectual Property Organization (WIPO) is a specialized agency of the United Nations that promotes the development of a balanced and effective international intellectual property system through cooperation among Member States and other international organizations and through the administration of international treaties. Long dedicated to the promotion and use of intellectual property as a means of stimulating innovation and creativity, the organization in recent years has directed effort toward matters relating to access to information in the public interest. Because the WIPO is responsible for international norm-setting on copyright, its decisions have an impact on the work of libraries and archives. The WIPO benefits from the participation of international and national library and archive organizations as accredited observers. This entry outlines the WIPO's activity and efforts to address international legal and policy issues that affect libraries, archives, and the public at the WIPO within the framework of advocacy.

INTRODUCTION

The World Intellectual Property Organization (WIPO) is a specialized agency of the United Nations (UN) with headquarters in Geneva, Switzerland, that promotes the international protection of intellectual property and fosters cooperation on copyrights, trademarks, industrial designs, and patents. Within the UN system, WIPO functions as an autonomous international organization established by intergovernmental (IGO) agreement. It is one of the 16 specialized agencies having wide international responsibilities in economic, social, cultural, educational, health, and related fields under Article 57 of the UN Charter and brought into relationship with the UN according to Article 63 of the charter. Others include UNESCO, the International Labour Organization, the World Health Organization, the International Monetary Fund, and the World Bank.

WIPO addresses the protection of intellectual property worldwide as a means of stimulating innovation and creativity through cooperation among Member States and in collaboration with other international organizations. In the field of copyright and related rights, WIPO administers a system of legal norms that have their origins in the invention of the printing press in the mid-fifteenth century and developed into an international copyright system in the second half of the nineteenth century. International norm-setting through treaties and other instruments provides direction for the international community and shapes national laws that have effect within the respective jurisdictions of Member States. From its origins, international copyright has been a dynamic system and this is no less true today. Copyright laws that protect literary, artistic, musical, dramatic, and other original creative works, and related rights that extend to certain groups of rightsholders such as performers, producers of phonograms, and broadcasting organizations are in a constant state of evolution as they adapt to social change and new technologies.

In the twenty-first century, WIPO faces unique political, social, and cultural challenges in the field of copyright and related rights. First, digital technology has radically transformed the copyright landscape. As the means to access and share intellectual and creative content expand and as new digital content is created at exponential rates, maintaining copyright norms that serve the interests of creators and the needs of the world's users is a central challenge. Second, the concerns of developing nations in the global information society have become more pronounced. Efforts to strengthen the voice of developing and least developed nations and to mitigate the effects of globalization in the area of information access have resulted in numerous initiatives mainstreamed across WIPO committees toward equitable participation of all nations in the global information society. Third, the organization in recent years has directed attention generally toward access to information in the public interest, following its mission to "to lead the development of a balanced and effective international intellectual property (IP) system that enables innovation and creativity for the benefit of all."[1]

WIPO benefits from the participation of international and national library and archival organizations as accredited observers. Within the framework of advocacy, they address international legal and policy issues that affect libraries, archives, and the public because of the many evolving aspects of intellectual property rights in the digital age. WIPO's engagement since 2004 on the issue of copyright limitations and exceptions to benefit blind and visually impaired persons, libraries and

Encyclopedia of Library and Information Sciences, Fourth Edition DOI: 10.1081/E-ELIS4-120050540

World–Zoological

archives, and education is a key effort toward achieving balance in international norms for the twenty-first century.

HISTORY

WIPO has its origins in the Paris Convention for the Protection of Industrial Property established in 1883 to set minimum international standards for the protection of industrial property (patents, marks, industrial designs, utility models, trade names, and geographical indications) and the Berne Convention for the Protection of Literary and Artistic Works established in 1886, the world's first international copyright treaty. These treaties were the result of an effort that began in the mid-nineteenth century to standardize protection of intellectual property among nations. The administrations of these conventions, or Unions, merged in 1892 to form the United International Bureaus for the Protection of Intellectual Property, commonly known by the French title Bureaux Internationaux Réunis pour la Protection de la Propriété Intellectuelle and the French acronym BIRPI. In 1960, BIRPI moved from Berne to Geneva. At the Intellectual Property Conference of Stockholm held from June 11 to July 14, 1967, a new treaty was adopted, the Convention Establishing the World Intellectual Property Organization (WIPO Convention), designating the International Bureau of WIPO as a successor to BIRPI.

WIPO began its work as an IGO organization in 1970 when the administrative provisions of the 1967 Stockholm Act of the Berne Convention entered into force, with the objectives of "promot[ing] the protection of intellectual property throughout the world through cooperation among States and, where appropriate, in collaboration with any other international organization" and "ensur[ing] administrative cooperation among the Unions."[2] In 1974, WIPO acquired the status of a specialized agency of the UN to promote the worldwide protection of intellectual property through cooperation of Member States and other international organizations and to administer the international treaties under its authority.

MEMBERSHIP AND GOVERNANCE

WIPO is a consensus-based organization in which Member States set the strategic direction for activities related to intellectual property and approve the organization's activities. With a constitution of 187 Member States, WIPO's reach extends to nearly all nations of the world. Delegations from Member States comprise the decision-making core of the organization. In addition, WIPO admits IGO and nongovernmental (NGO) organizations to serve as accredited observers. IGO and NGO representatives participate in the work of WIPO by making statements in

assemblies and committee meetings, providing written statements on issues under discussion, consulting with WIPO delegations, and engaging in other core WIPO activities within the framework of advocacy. There are currently 70 IGOs and 319 NGOs accredited as observers, representing the interests of libraries, archives, and museums, educational institutions, blind and reading disabled persons, indigenous peoples, consumers, members of the public, rightsholders, intellectual property industries, and other stakeholders in the intellectual property system.

ORGANIZATIONAL STRUCTURE

Various WIPO bodies are responsible for discussion, negotiation, and decision making on intellectual property issues and for administrative activity. Formal guidelines outlined in the WIPO General Rules of Procedure serve as standards for conduct of procedure and deliberation within WIPO bodies.[3]

Decision-Making Bodies

The main decision-making bodies, which meet annually, are responsible for the highest-level decisions within the organization:

- The WIPO General Assembly, described in Article 6 of the WIPO Convention, is composed of the Member States of WIPO, which are also members of any of the Unions. Its main functions are to appoint the director general upon nomination by the Coordination Committee, to review and approve reports of the director general and reports and activities of the Coordination Committee, to adopt the biennial budget of the Unions, to adopt the financial regulations of the organization, to determine the working languages of the Secretariat, to invite states to become parties to the WIPO Convention, and to accredit non-Member States and organizations as observers.
- The WIPO Conference, described in Article 7 of the WIPO Convention, consists of states that are parties to the WIPO Convention. Its main functions are to discuss intellectual property issues and adopt recommendations, to adopt the biennial budget of the Conference, to establish the biennial program of legal–technical assistance, to adopt amendments to the WIPO Convention, and to accredit non-Member States and organizations as observers.
- The WIPO Coordination Committee, described in Article 8 of the WIPO Convention, consists of States that are party to the WIPO Convention and also members of the Executive Committee of the Paris Union or the Executive Committee of the Berne Union, or both. It gives advice to the organs of the Unions, the General

Assembly, the Conference, and the director general, on financial and other matters. It prepares the draft agenda for the General Assembly and the draft agenda, draft program, and budget of the Conference. It also nominates a candidate for the position of director general for appointment by the General Assembly and appoints an acting director general if the position becomes vacant between sessions of the General Assembly.

In addition, decision-making capacity is exercised by the assemblies of the Member States of the Unions.

Activity

The organization's activity is carried out through assemblies, committees, and working groups consisting of delegations from the Member States, as well as through the work of the Secretariat that develops programs to implement strategic goals and provides expertise to Member States.

WIPO has defined nine strategic goals:

1. A balanced evolution of the international normative framework for intellectual property
2. Provision of premier global intellectual property services
3. Facilitating the use of intellectual property for development
4. Coordination and development of the global intellectual property infrastructure
5. World reference source for intellectual property information and analysis
6. International cooperation on building respect for intellectual property
7. Addressing intellectual property in relation to global policy issues
8. A responsive communications interface between WIPO, its Member States, and all stakeholders
9. An efficient administrative and financial support structure to enable WIPO to deliver its programs

WIPO bodies advance the organization's strategic goals through a broad range of activity:

- *Norm-setting*: Administration of multilateral treaties, conventions, and agreements and supporting the further evolution of the international intellectual property framework by developing laws and standards.
- *Services*: Providing global intellectual property services that offer easy and cost-effective means for obtaining international protection for patents, trademarks, designs, and appellations of origin, and for resolving disputes.
- *Development and technical assistance*: Within the framework of capacity-building, assisting governments

and organizations in developing and least developed nations to build national intellectual property infrastructures through policies and strategies that support economic development.
- *Technical infrastructure*: Providing access to free WIPO databases of intellectual property information and technical platforms for sharing of information among national intellectual property offices.
- *Promoting intellectual property*: Promoting intellectual property and understanding and respect for intellectual property norms internationally.

WIPO cooperates with other agencies of the UN in Geneva and has external offices in New York, Rio de Janeiro, Singapore, and Tokyo. On December 22, 1995, WIPO signed an agreement between the World Intellectual Property Organization and the World Trade Organization (WTO), which came into force on January 1, 1996, establishing a commitment to support and cooperate with the WTO in matters relating to intellectual property.[4]

Committees

WIPO Member States participate in a large number of committees. The committee structures evolve with the directions taken by WIPO in international norm-setting and development. Advisory committees and ad hoc committees may focus on emerging issues in intellectual property, to serve as a means for exploration, study, and scoping of issues. This often involves the creation of reports, recommendations, and proposals. Any committee or other body may establish working groups to study specific issues in more detail. Some of the most important committees include the following:

Permanent committees

- The Program and Budget Committee sets the biennial budget, closely linked to the strategic goals and priorities of the organization.
- The Committee on Development and Intellectual Property (CDIP) addresses issues related to intellectual property and development as part of the organization's commitment to the WIPO Development Agenda adopted in 2007.
- The Intergovernmental Committee on Intellectual Property and Genetic Resources, Traditional Knowledge and Folklore (IGC) works toward normative solutions for the protection of genetic resources, traditional knowledge, and traditional cultural expressions, also referred to as expressions of folklore.
- The Advisory Committee on Enforcement addresses global enforcement issues through technical assistance to Member States and coordination with private sector organizations to fight piracy and counterfeiting and

engages in education and training activity, within the framework of recommendation 45 of the WIPO Development Agenda.

Standing committees

WIPO established a system of standing committees in 1998 to facilitate the progressive development of international intellectual property law. Standing committees bring together representatives of Member States at regular intervals to discuss and reach consensus on global intellectual property norms. Norm-setting activity includes making recommendations to the General Assembly to conclude new treaties, to amend treaties, or to adopt other forms of international agreement. The adoption of new treaties requires the convening of diplomatic conferences, high-level meetings of Member States where the language of new treaties is finalized.

- The Standing Committee on the Law of Patents is a forum for discussion, coordination, and guidance on the development of patent law.
- The Standing Committee on the Law of Trademarks, Industrial Designs and Geographical Indications is a forum to discuss issues, facilitate coordination, and provide guidance on the development of international law on trademarks, industrial designs, and geographical indications, including the harmonization of national laws and procedures.
- The Standing Committee on Copyright and Related Rights (SCCR) advances international norms in copyright and related rights. Many of the issues on the committee's current agenda concern the development of copyright law that addresses new technologies and the Internet.
- The Committee on WIPO Standards was created in 2009 as a forum for discussion of standards relating to industrial property information and documentation. It grew out of the work of the Standards and Documentation Working Group of the Standing Committee on Information Technologies.

WIPO Secretariat

The Secretariat provides administrative and specialized support to all WIPO bodies. It consists of the WIPO staff of specialists in intellectual property law and practice, administration, and related fields such as economics, information technology, public policy, and translation. The WIPO Secretariat, called the International Bureau, is responsible for coordinating meetings of Member States and implementing their decisions, administering international registration systems, developing and implementing programs established to achieve the organization's goals, and providing legal–technical assistance to Members. The

Secretariat operates under the directorship of the WIPO director general and the deputy or assistant director general of each of its seven sectors: brands and designs, development, global issues, innovation and technology, administration and management, culture and creative industries, and global infrastructure.

WIPO's program of technical assistance to developing and least developed nations is one of its major activities, providing legislative advice, training and consultation programs in intellectual property, support for national policy development and national intellectual property infrastructure, human resource and institutional development, automation services, and enforcement programs.[5] It is worth noting that this activity is often criticized by civil society organizations for having an inherent bias toward the interests of rightsholders in developed nations because of the emphasis on strengthening standards of intellectual property protection and enforcement in developing nations.

TREATY ADMINISTRATION

WIPO administers 26 international treaties, of which 7 are in the area of copyright and related rights. The most recent WIPO treaty, the Marrakesh Treaty to Facilitate Access to Published Works for Persons Who Are Blind, Visually Impaired, or Otherwise Print Disabled, was adopted on June 27, 2013. The 26 treaties administered by WIPO include its foundation treaty:

- Convention Establishing the World Intellectual Property Organization (1967)

Treaties in the area of copyright and related rights include

- Berne Convention for the Protection of Literary and Artistic Works (1886)
- International Convention for the Protection of Performers, Producers of Phonograms and Broadcasting Organizations (Rome Convention) (1961)
- Convention for the Protection of Producers of Phonograms against Unauthorized Duplication of their Phonograms (Geneva Convention) (1971)
- WIPO Copyright Treaty (WCT) (1996)
- WIPO Performances and Phonograms Treaty (WPPT) (1996)
- Beijing Treaty on Audiovisual Performances (2012)
- Marrakesh Treaty to Facilitate Access to Published Works for Persons Who Are Blind, Visually Impaired or Otherwise Print Disabled (2012)

Intellectual property treaties establishing basic standards of protection in each member country in the area of patents, trademarks, industrial designs, utility models, and geographical indications include

- Paris Convention for the Protection of Industrial Property (1883)
- Madrid Agreement for the Repression of False or Deceptive Indications of Source on Goods (1891)
- The Brussels Convention Relating to the Distribution of Program-Carrying Signals Transmitted by Satellite (1974)
- Nairobi Treaty on the Protection of the Olympic Symbol (1981)
- Treaty on Intellectual Property in Respect of Integrated Circuits (Washington Treaty) (1989)
- Trademark Law Treaty (1994)
- Patent Law Treaty (2000)
- Singapore Treaty on the Law of Trademarks (2006)

Global protection system treaties providing an international registration or filing system for intellectual property to simplify the application or filing process in all countries in which protection is sought include

- Madrid Agreement Concerning the International Registration of Marks (1891)
- Hague Agreement Concerning the International Registration of Industrial Designs (1934)
- Lisbon Agreement for the Protection of Appellations of Origin and their International Registration (1958)
- Patent Cooperation Treaty (1970)
- Budapest Treaty on the International Recognition of the Deposit of Microorganisms for the Purposes of Patent Procedure (1977)
- Protocol Relating to the Madrid Agreement Concerning the International Registration of Marks (1989)

Treaties that create classification systems that index information on inventions, trademarks, and industrial designs and facilitate information retrieval include

- Nice Agreement Concerning the International Classification of Goods and Services for the Purposes of the Registration of Marks (1957)
- Locarno Agreement Establishing an International Classification for Industrial Designs (1968)
- Strasbourg Agreement Concerning the International Patent Classification (1971)
- Vienna Agreement Establishing an International Classification of the Figurative Elements of Marks (1973)

WIPO AND THE DEVELOPMENT OF INTERNATIONAL COPYRIGHT NORMS

In the global information society, international copyright norms govern access to information in all parts of the world. International copyright treaties and agreements, implemented into national legislation, form a system of interrelated laws that provide a basis for copyright protection for literary and artistic works and neighboring rights protection for performances, producers of phonograms, and broadcasting organizations.

Copyright laws are shaped by the international treaties and agreements that have developed since the late nineteenth century to provide some degree of harmonization across national jurisdictions. For more than a century, major treaties and conventions have been established to respond to needs arising from the increasing interdependence of nations. International agreements are in a constant process of change and are shaped by social and economic needs and technological advances.

The Berne Convention for the Protection of Literary and Artistic Works was adopted in 1886 as the result of an effort that began in the mid-nineteenth century, when international cooperation was needed to standardize protection of authors' rights among nations. It was amended eight times over the course of nearly a century to meet the evolving social and technological landscape. Gradually, there was a need to address specific aspects of copyright protection relating to computer technology and digital networks. The WCT and WPPT were adopted in 1996 for this purpose. Expanding on the Berne Convention, they adapted copyright to the digital age. The Beijing Treaty on Audiovisual Performances was adopted in June 2012 to protect the rights of audiovisual performers, defined as actors, singers, musicians, dancers, and other persons who act, sing, deliver, declaim, play in, interpret, or otherwise perform literary or artistic works or expressions of folklore. The treaty was designed to fill the gap in related rights protections left by the 1996 WPPT that protected audio performers but not audiovisual performers.

The adoption on June 27, 2013, of the *Marrakesh Treaty to Facilitate Access to Published Works for Persons Who Are Blind, Visually Impaired, or Otherwise Print Disabled* was the result of an effort spurred by citizens and civil society organizations to facilitate uses of new information and communication technologies to benefit persons with visual impairments or with other print disabilities through an enhanced legal framework at the international level. It is the first treaty in history dedicated to the expansion of copyright limitations and exceptions.

WIPO continues to deliberate on the adoption of a treaty for the protection on broadcasting organizations. Proponents of the treaty proposal argue that advances in technology are not adequately covered by the 1961 Rome Convention, and that a treaty covering broadcasting and cablecasting is necessary in order to prevent piracy and theft of signals. This is also an issue that was left out of the WPPT. Discussions that began at the WIPO Worldwide Symposium on Broadcasters' Rights in 1997 gradually led to treaty proposals that continue in the SCCR.

WIPO's engagement since 2004 on the issue of copyright limitations and exceptions to benefit blind and visually impaired persons, libraries and archives, and education is a key effort toward achieving balance in international norms for the twenty-first century. Following the success of the Marrakesh Treaty, the SCCR continues its discussions toward the possible adoption of treaty instruments to benefit libraries, archives, and education.

LIBRARIES, ARCHIVES, AND INTERNATIONAL COPYRIGHT

WIPO benefits from the active participation of international and national library organizations as accredited observers at committee meetings and other events. Library and archival groups contribute to the promotion of a balanced and equitable international intellectual property system and share common interests with other nongovernmental, nonprofit organizations working in the public interest, such as those dedicated to environmental and sustainable development concerns, consumer groups, charities, organizations representing the interests of blind and visually impaired persons, organizations representing indigenous peoples, and organizations representing educational institutions.

Because WIPO is responsible for international normsetting on copyright, its decisions have an impact on the work of libraries and archives. Decisions made at WIPO may result in new international treaties that are implemented into national copyright laws. They may also result in nonbinding forms of norm-setting such as recommendations, resolutions, declarations, or guidelines. Libraries share a unique social responsibility for preservation of and access to the world's intellectual heritage and have an interest in promoting copyright laws that provide the broadest possible use of information for creativity, research, and education. Library and archival associations with accreditation at WIPO actively respond to and develop proposals to influence international copyright norms at the SCCR. They have also been active at the CDIP and the IGC and in other fora. Participation of library and archival organizations at WIPO benefits the broadest possible range of social interests.

Among the accredited international NGOs are those representing libraries, archives, and museums: Electronic Information for Libraries (EIFL), the European Bureau of Library, Information and Documentation Associations, the International Council of Museums, the International Council on Archives (ICA), the International Federation of Library Associations and Institutions (IFLA), the Scholarly Publishing and Academic Resources Coalition, and the Special Libraries Association. Among the national NGOs representing libraries, archives, and museums are Corporación Latinoamericana de Investigación de la Propiedad Intelectual para el Desarrollo (Corporación Innovarte), the German Library Association, the Library Copyright Alliance (LCA), the Italian Library Association, and the Society of American Archivists.

LIBRARY ADVOCACY AT WIPO

Issues being discussed at the highest levels in international policymaking have direct implications on the work of libraries and the future of information access.

Copyright Limitations and Exceptions for Libraries and Archives

One of the key issues of library advocates at WIPO is the need to reinforce copyright limitations and exceptions by means of a new international agreement. Work on limitations and exceptions occurs at the meetings of the SCCR. In successive meetings of the SCCR and the WIPO General Assembly, with increasing involvement since 2004, library and archival groups have argued in favor of global norms for limitations and exceptions that enable uses of works without prior consent of or payment to the copyright holder for purposes such as research, scholarship and teaching, library preservation, and interlibrary loan. They take the position that limitations and exceptions are a fundamental part of the copyright system but have not expanded at an equal pace with standards of protection introduced by new WIPO treaties in the last two decades and by the 1994 WTO Agreement on Trade-Related Aspects of Intellectual Property Rights that added a new dimension of enforcement by linking intellectual property protection with international trade. Other factors that have prompted library and archival organizations to voice their concerns include extension of copyright terms, anticircumvention legislation, and an increasing culture of enforcement in many nations. Their concerns are expressed in statements, referred to as interventions, at official meetings and also in panels and discussions held as side events in the course of committee sessions.[6]

Library and archival advocates generally support the positions of developing and least developed nations in opposing higher and more rigid standards of protection that are not in the interests of developing nations and that hinder them from equitable participation in the global information society. In keeping their markets open for other types of trade, developing and least developed nations often adopt higher standards of protection than might best serve them domestically, with the effect that available limitations and exceptions are not used optimally for creativity, research, and education. Free trade agreements that incorporate high standards of intellectual property protection are considered by library advocates to hinder access to knowledge and to thwart social, cultural, and economic development. IFLA, together with ICA, EIFL, and Corporación Innovarte, is working with WIPO Member States to gain support for a binding international instrument to update copyright limitations and exceptions for libraries and archives worldwide.

To address matters of the public interest, in the last decade WIPO has initiated a series of expert studies highlighting the importance of copyright limitations and exceptions in the interest of blind and visually impaired persons, libraries and archives, and education:

- *WIPO Study on Limitations and Exceptions of Copyright and Related Rights in the Digital Environment*, prepared by Sam Ricketson[7]
- *Automated Rights Management Systems and Copyright Limitations and Exceptions*, prepared by Nic Garnett[8]
- *Study on Copyright Limitations and Exceptions for the Visually Impaired*, prepared by Judith Sullivan[9]
- *Study on Copyright Limitations and Exceptions for Libraries and Archives*, prepared by Kenneth Crews[10]
- *Study on the Limitations and Exceptions to Copyright and Related Rights for the Purposes of Educational and Research Activities in Latin America and the Caribbean*, prepared by Juan Carlos Monroy Rodríguez[11]
- *WIPO Study on Limitations and Exceptions for Copyright and Related Rights for Teaching in Africa*, prepared by Joseph Fometeu[12]
- *Study on Limitations and Exceptions for Copyright for Educational Purposes in the Arab Countries*, prepared by Victor Nabhan[13]
- *WIPO Study on the Copyright Exceptions for the Benefit of Educational Activities for Asia and Australia*, prepared by Daniel Seng[14]
- *Study on Copyright Limitations and Exceptions for Educational Activities in North America, Europe, Caucasus, Central Asia and Israel*, prepared by Raquel Xalabarder.[15]

The studies are comparative in nature, comparing levels of limitations and exceptions across national laws worldwide. The *Study on Copyright Limitations and Exceptions for Libraries and Archives* provides the first comprehensive overview of statutory provisions in national copyright laws of WIPO Member States for the benefit of libraries and archives and underlines the need for expanding the scope of copyright limitations and exceptions worldwide.

In support of increasing minimum levels of limitations and exceptions internationally, the US-based LCA, along with EIFL and IFLA, drafted a *Statement of Principles on Copyright Exceptions and Limitations for Libraries and Archives* in May 2009.[16] The statement outlines the urgency of taking action to expand limitations and exceptions to meet the needs of librarians and the public in the digital environment. The statement asks WIPO Member States to address the gaps in copyright provisions for libraries and archives in their national laws. It supports WIPO's commitment to developing nations in the WIPO Development Agenda adopted in 2007 to ensure that intellectual property law and policy continue to serve the public good in a balanced way in all parts of the world. It

respectfully requests Member States to adopt 12 principles to guide the formulation of copyright limitations and exceptions for libraries and archives in national copyright laws:

- *Preservation*: A library should be permitted to make copies of published and unpublished works in its collections for purposes of preservation, including migrating content to different formats.
- *Legal deposit*: Legal deposit laws and systems should be broadened to include works published in all formats and to allow for preservation of those works.
- *Interlibrary loan and document supply*: Libraries should be able to supply documents to the user directly or through the intermediary library irrespective of the format and the means of communication.
- *Education and classroom teaching*: It should be permissible for works that have been lawfully acquired by a library or other educational institution to be made available in support of classroom teaching or distance education in a manner that does not unreasonably prejudice the rightsholder. A library or educational institution should be permitted to make copies of a work in support of classroom teaching.
- *Reproduction for research or private purposes*: Copying individual items for or by individual users should be permitted for research and study and for other private purposes.
- *Provision for persons with disabilities*: A library should be permitted to convert material from one format to another to make it accessible to persons with disabilities. The exception should apply to all formats to accommodate user needs and technological advances. To avoid costly duplication of alternative format production, cross-border transfer should be permitted.
- *General free use exceptions applicable to libraries*: A general free use exception consistent with fair practice helps ensure the effective delivery of library services.
- *Orphan works*: An exception is needed to resolve the problem of orphan works, where the rightsholder cannot be identified or located.
- *Copyright term*: Consistent with the Berne Convention, the general term of copyright should be the life of the author plus 50 years.
- *Technological protection measures that prevent lawful uses*: It should be permissible for libraries and their users to circumvent a technological protection measure for the purpose of making a noninfringing use of a work. Implementation of anticircumvention legislation in many nations exceeds the requirements of Article 11 of the WIPO Copyright Treaty, effectively eliminating existing exceptions in copyright law.
- *Contracts and statutory exceptions*: Contracts should not be permitted to override exceptions and limitations. The goals and policies providing for exceptions

are important statements of national and international principle and should not be varied by contract.

- *Limitation on liability*: There should be a limitation on liability for libraries and library staff who act in good faith, believing or having reasonable grounds to believe, that they have acted in accordance with copyright law.

The statement is part of the sustained effort that began in 2004 to encourage WIPO to address copyright limitations and exceptions for blind and visually impaired persons, for libraries and archives, and for education. As the issue advanced at WIPO, in November 2010 the SCCR officially placed limitations and exceptions on its agenda and established a work program and a timetable for discussion over several years.

An effort by library and archival associations to prepare more formal proposals in the form of a draft treaty produced the *Treaty Proposal on Limitations and Exceptions for Libraries and Archives* by IFLA, ICA, EIFL, and Corporación Innovarte.[17] The draft treaty sets out key issues for libraries and archives in taking a global approach to copyright limitations and exceptions to secure the effective and unhindered flow of information essential for global equality of access to research, ideas, and innovation. The treaty proposal is composed of 30 articles outlining the rights and obligations of Member States in reinforcing the role of libraries and archives in the digital future. Core articles cover

- Right to Parallel Importation
- Right to Acquire Works
- Right to Library and Archive Lending and Temporary Access
- Right of Reproduction and Supply of Copies by Libraries and Archives
- Right of Preservation of Library and Archival Materials
- Right to Use of Works and Material Protected by Related Rights for the Benefit of Persons with Disabilities
- Right to Access Retracted and Withdrawn Works
- Right of Use of Orphan Works and Materials Protected by Related Rights
- Right to Cross-Border Uses
- Right to Translate Works and Materials Protected by Related Rights
- Obligation to Respect Exceptions to Copyright and Related Rights
- Obligations Concerning Technological Protection Measures
- Limitation on Liability for Libraries and Archives
- Legal Deposit
- Government Publications
- Right to Extract and Reuse Facts and Information

At the SCCR/23 meeting in November–December 2011 and in subsequent meetings, library and archive groups gained sufficient support from WIPO Member States to bring their proposals into an official working document, the *Working Document Containing Comments on and Textual Suggestions towards an Appropriate International Legal Instrument (in Whatever Form) on Exceptions and Limitations for Libraries and Archives*.[18] An extensive document, it contains proposed text and comments offered by Member States in the course of discussions on 11 cluster topics: preservation; right of reproduction and safeguarding copies; legal deposit; library lending; parallel importations; cross-border issues; orphan works, retracted and withdrawn works, and works out of commerce; limitations on liability of libraries and archives; technological measures of protection; contracts; and the right to translate works. As of January 2014, the SCCR was continuing its text-based work toward an appropriate international legal instrument or instruments—whether model law, joint recommendation, treaty, or other form—with the target to submit recommendations on limitations and exceptions for libraries and archives to the WIPO General Assembly by late 2014.

Digital Preservation and Copyright

Digital preservation has attracted attention at WIPO as an issue deserving more analysis. One of the most critical areas in which copyright limitations and exceptions have failed to maintain a balance in the digital environment is library preservation, which faces an uncertain future due to the absence in many nations of adequate copyright laws and policies. In July 2008, WIPO held its first International Workshop on Digital Preservation and Copyright at which national representatives presented preservation scenarios in their own countries, revealing variations and flaws in public policy and legal approaches to preservation of cultural heritage and memory. The workshop coincided with a study released in July 2008 by the International Digital Preservation and Copyright Initiative to survey recent developments and trends in digital preservation and copyright. The *International Study on the Impact of Copyright Law on Digital Preservation*[19] provides recommendations to improve national copyright and related rights laws and policies that concern the digital preservation of copyrighted works.

The report and the workshop emphasized the global need for more attention to limitations and exceptions for digital preservation in view of the fact that many works are physically disappearing, resulting in loss of cultural heritage and the historical record. Highlighting that this problem is likely to become more serious more in the coming years, participants in the workshop supported adoption of provisions in copyright laws to enable more robust systems of digital preservation.

Copyright Limitations and Exceptions for Persons Who Are Blind, Visually Impaired, or Otherwise Print Disabled

The World Blind Union (WBU) set a path for development of new international standards for limitations and exceptions in the public interest that culminated in the adoption of the Marrakesh Treaty in June 2013. With strong support from civil society groups, in 2003 the WBU resumed efforts dating to a 1985 report that recommended a new international instrument permitting production and distribution of special media materials and services for handicapped persons.[20] The WBU actively urged WIPO to address the needs of the visually impaired, emphasizing the need for greater harmonization in copyright limitations and exceptions globally and for provisions permitting cross-border export and import of works in accessible formats.

In October 2008, the WBU presented a proposal for a possible Treaty for Improved Access for Blind, Visually Impaired and Other Reading Disabled Persons.[21] It was formally introduced at the May 2009 SCCR meeting by Brazil, Ecuador, and Paraguay. The two main features of the proposed treaty were to provide a minimum standard for limitations and exceptions for the blind and visually impaired and reading disabled, reflecting current technological opportunities, and to allow for the import and export of works in accessible formats by eligible parties.

Library organizations strongly supported the proposal, arguing that the need for improved access to copyright-protected works in readable formats, such as Braille, large print, and audio versions is universal. National laws in some countries allow such copying and adaptation without the permission of rightsholders, but in other countries such activity could infringe copyright if undertaken without authorization. The decision of the SCCR in 2010 to include limitations and exceptions officially in its agenda led to intensive discussions of this proposal as well as those concerning libraries and archives and education in sequence. The WBU effort succeeded in the adoption of the Marrakesh Treaty at a diplomatic conference in Marrakesh on June 27, 2013, coinciding with the birthday of Helen Keller. It is the first international treaty in history dedicated to the expansion of copyright limitations and exceptions. As of January 2014, the treaty had been signed by 60 nations.[22]

Copyright Limitations and Exceptions for Education and Persons with Other Disabilities

Work on an international instrument to expand limitations and exceptions for education is also in progress at WIPO and is strongly supported by civil society organizations asserting that a binding international instrument would be particularly effective in facilitating uses for education in developing and least developed countries to bridge the knowledge gap and the digital divide. Additionally, it would include exceptions for disabilities not covered by the Marrakesh Treaty.

A compilation of proposals and comments proposed by the Member States was prepared by the WIPO Secretariat as a lengthy working document, the *Provisional Working Document towards an Appropriate International Legal Instrument (in Whatever Form) on Limitations and Exceptions for Educational, Teaching and Research Institutions and Persons with Other Disabilities Containing Comments and Textual Suggestions.*[23] It constitutes the basis for continued text-based work being undertaken by the SCCR.

Topics included in the working document cover definitions, generally applicable considerations including flexibilities; uses (educational, teaching, and research institutions; in-classroom uses; uses outside the classroom; availability on an interactive basis and communication to the public for educational purposes; anthologies and chrestomathies; distance learning; research; and reverse engineering); persons with other disabilities; broader topics with implications for education (technology; orphan works and withdrawn or out of print works; public domain; contracts; Internet service provider liability; importation and exportation; and public health or security).

WIPO Development Agenda

Library groups have been active in support of the WIPO Development Agenda, a set of 45 recommendations adopted on September 28, 2007, by the WIPO General Assembly.[24] It aims to address the interests and needs of developing and least developed countries within the international intellectual property system. This initiative originated in an effort to ensure that intellectual property law and policy continue to serve the public good by encouraging and rewarding innovation and creativity in a balanced way in all parts of the world. Upon its adoption, the WIPO Development Agenda was viewed as a major historical shift in the direction of WIPO because it addresses the knowledge gap and the digital divide that separate wealthy nations from poor nations.

The library groups at WIPO offer a critical perspective on the possibilities of social, economic, and cultural development through access to information and knowledge. Libraries have long served as the foundation for the preservation and broadest possible dissemination of knowledge in societies. Library organizations have articulated support for a copyright system that is balanced to serve all members of society in all parts of the world. In contributing to discussions that transform the 45 recommendations into concrete activities, the library community has advocated at WIPO to enable developing and least developed countries to fully benefit from the global intellectual property system through

- A fair balance between intellectual property protections and the public interest
- Minimizing levels of copyright protection in developing and least developed countries
- A robust public domain
- Adequate limitations and exceptions for the purposes of education, research, learning, creativity, and preservation of information
- Access to knowledge and technology to foster innovation, material progress, and social well-being
- The goals of information literacy
- Bridging the digital divide
- Library participation in local efforts at technical assistance and capacity building in developing and least developed countries
- Balanced IP education in developing and least developed countries
- New approaches to the licensing of copyrighted works
- The social good that results from a true balance between intellectual property protections and the public interest.[25]

The WIPO CDIP is concerned exclusively with the WIPO Development Agenda, but the work program to implement the recommendations is being mainstreamed into the activity of other WIPO bodies.

Traditional Cultural Expression

The international community has been engaged for over four decades in discussions concerning copyright and other legal protection of traditional cultural expression. Traditional and indigenous communities have long sought respect and recognition for their creative expressions ranging from stories, myths, folk tales, songs and music, to symbols, designs, paintings, sculptures, carvings, handicrafts, dances, and rituals. Existing international and national legal systems are not typically compatible with indigenous culture and law, and they do not sufficiently address the concerns of indigenous peoples for protection of their creative heritage.

There is no international mandate for protection of traditional cultural expression, and there is great variation in the level of protection for indigenous and traditional works in national laws. Some nations protect traditional cultural expression, while others do not, and still others do not specify in their laws. There is still a lack of consensus internationally about the type of protection, if any, that would best apply universally to traditional works. The issue has taken on new dimensions since WIPO established the IGC that began working in 2001 toward a solution to the protection of traditional

cultural expressions, also referred to as expressions of folklore.[26]

The Berne Convention was amended in 1967 by Article 15(4) to provide a means for protecting works of folklore. Various sets of model laws and provisions have also been drafted over the years by WIPO and UNESCO. Expert groups have addressed the issue, and indigenous groups have been active advocates at WIPO. The IGC has been working toward possible *sui generis* protection, a special kind of protection for traditional cultural expression that falls outside the framework of the existing copyright system because the copyright system is not suited for works that are traditionally unpublished, often not fixed in tangible medium, created not by one individual known author but collectively by a community, and created not on a certain date but over time.

After years of discussion that did not lead to agreement, the committee's mandate was renewed in October 2013 and it continues to work on text-based negotiations with the goal of reaching an agreement on an international legal instrument or instruments to ensure the effective protection of genetic resources, traditional knowledge, and traditional cultural expressions, if consensus can be reached on this issue.

CONCLUSION

As the governance of intellectual property evolves in the twenty-first century through norm-setting activity at WIPO and as technology further advances, decisions made by WIPO will continue to have a direct impact on libraries and archives. Participation by library and archival organizations in WIPO discussions builds the cooperation and understanding necessary for a balanced evolution of copyright law, the key to WIPO's mission. Library and archival organizations view their engagement with WIPO Member States as a way to influence the direction of copyright law and to support fair and equitable use of copyrighted works into the digital future.

ACKNOWLEDGMENTS

This entry is based in part on issue briefs I prepared as Visiting Program Officer on International Copyright for the Association of Research Libraries in 2009 and International Copyright Advocate for the Library Copyright Alliance in 2007–2011. The issue briefs on "International Copyright: Why It Matters to Libraries," "Treaty for Improved Access for Blind, Visually Impaired and Other Reading Disabled Persons," "Traditional Cultural Expression," and "The WIPO Development Agenda" are available on the website of the Library Copyright Alliance at http://www.librarycopyrightalliance.org.

REFERENCES

1. World Intellectual Property Organization. *Inside WIPO*, http://www.wipo.int/about-wipo/en/ (accessed January 2014).

2. World Intellectual Property Organization. *Convention Establishing the World Intellectual Property Organization*, http://www.wipo.int/treaties/en/convention/trtdocs_wo029. html (accessed January 2014).

3. World Intellectual Property Organization. *General Rules of Procedure*, http://www.wipo.int/edocs/pubdocs/en/general/ 399/wipo_pub_399.pdf (accessed January 2014).

4. World Intellectual Property Organization; World Trade Organization. *Agreement between the World Intellectual Property Organization and the World Trade Organization*, http://www.wipo.int/treaties/en/agreement/trtdocs_wo030. html (accessed January 2014).

5. WIPO Committee on Development and Intellectual Property, Twelfth Session. *Manual on the Delivery of WIPO Technical Assistance* (CDIP 12/7), October 8, 2013, http://www.wipo.int/meetings/en/doc_details.jsp?doc_id= 252306 (accessed January 2014).

6. Reports of WIPO SCCR sessions include summaries of the interventions given by Member States and by accredited observer organizations. World Intellectual Property Organization. *Standing Committee on Copyright and Related Rights*, http://www.wipo.int/meetings/en/topic. jsp?group_id=62 (accessed January 2014).

7. WIPO Standing Committee on Copyright and Related Rights, Ninth Session. *WIPO Study on Limitations and Exceptions of Copyright and Related Rights in the Digital Environment*, prepared by Sam Ricketson, (SCCR/9/7), April 5, 2003, http://www.wipo.int/meetings/en/doc_details. jsp?doc_id=16805 (accessed January 2014).

8. WIPO Standing Committee on Copyright and Related Rights, Fourteenth Session. *Automated Rights Management Systems and Copyright Limitations and Exceptions*, prepared by Nic Garnett (SCCR/14/5), April 27, 2006, http:// www.wipo.int/meetings/en/doc_details.jsp?doc_id=59952 (accessed January 2014).

9. WIPO Standing Committee on Copyright and Related Rights, Fifteenth Session. *Study on Copyright Limitations and Exceptions for the Visually Impaired*, prepared by Judith Sullivan (SCCR/15/7), February 20, 2007, http:// www.wipo.int/meetings/en/doc_details.jsp?doc_id=75696 (accessed January 2014).

10. WIPO Standing Committee on Copyright and Related Rights, Seventeenth Session. *Study on Copyright Limitations and Exceptions for Libraries and Archives*, prepared by Kenneth Crews (SCCR/17/2), August 26, 2008, http:// www.wipo.int/meetings/en/doc_details.jsp?doc_id=109192 (accessed January 2014).

11. WIPO Standing Committee on Copyright and Related Rights, Nineteenth Session. *Study on the Limitations and Exceptions to Copyright and Related Rights for the Purposes of Educational and Research Activities in Latin America and The Caribbean*, prepared by Juan Carlos Monroy Rodríguez (SCCR/19/4), September 30, 2009, http://www.wipo.int/meetings/en/doc_details.jsp?doc_id= 130303 (accessed January 2014).

12. WIPO Standing Committee on Copyright and Related Rights, Nineteenth Session. *Study on Limitations and Exceptions for Copyright and Related Rights for Teaching in Africa*, prepared by Joseph Fometeu (SCCR/19/5), October 26, 2009, http://www.wipo.int/meetings/en/doc_ details.jsp?doc_id=130241 (accessed January 2014).

13. WIPO Standing Committee on Copyright and Related Rights, Nineteenth Session. *Study on Limitations and Exceptions for Copyright for Educational Purposes in the Arab Countries*, prepared by Victor Nabhan (SCCR/19/6), October 7, 2009, http://www.wipo.int/meetings/en/doc_ details.jsp?doc_id=130302 (accessed January 2014).

14. WIPO Standing Committee on Copyright and Related Rights, Nineteenth Session. *WIPO Study on the Copyright Exceptions for the Benefit of Educational Activities for Asia and Australia*, prepared by Daniel Seng (SCCR/19/7), October 29, 2009, http://www.wipo.int/meetings/en/ doc_details.jsp?doc_id=130249 (accessed January 2014).

15. WIPO Standing Committee on Copyright and Related Rights, Nineteenth Session. *Study on Copyright Limitations and Exceptions for Educational Activities in North America, Europe, Caucasus, Central Asia and Israel*, prepared by Raquel Xalabarder (SCCR/19/8), November 5, 2009, http://www.wipo.int/meetings/en/doc_details.jsp?doc_id= 130393 (accessed January 2014).

16. Electronic Information for Libraries; International Federation of Library Associations and Institutions; Library Copyright Alliance. *Statement of Principles on Copyright Exceptions and Limitations for Libraries and Archives*, http://www.ifla.org/publications/statement-of-principles-on-copyright-exceptions-and-limitations-for-libraries-and (accessed January 2014).

17. International Federation of Library Associations and Institutions; International Council on Archives; Electronic Information for Libraries; Corporación Innovarte. *Treaty Proposal on Copyright Limitations and Exceptions for Libraries and Archives*, http://www.ifla.org/node/5856 (accessed January 2014).

18. WIPO Standing Committee on Copyright and Related Rights, Twenty-sixth Session. *Working Document Containing Comments on and Textual Suggestions Towards an Appropriate International Legal Instrument (in Whatever Form) on Exceptions and Limitations for Libraries and Archives* (SCCR/26/ 3), April 15, 2013, http://www.wipo.int/meetings/en/ details.jsp?meeting_id=29944 (accessed January 2014).

19. The Library of Congress National Digital Information Infrastructure and Preservation Program; The Joint Information Systems Committee; The Open Access to Knowledge (OAK) Law Project; The SURF Foundation. *International Study on the Impact of Copyright Law on Digital Preservation*, http://www.digitalpreservation. gov/documents/digital_preservation_final_report2008.pdf (accessed January 2014).

20. Executive Committee of the International Union for the Protection of Literary and Artistic Works (Berne Union), Twenty-fourth Session; Intergovernmental Committee of the Universal Copyright Convention, Sixth Ordinary Session. Copyright Problems Raised by the Access by Handicapped Persons to Protected Works (B/EC/XXIV/ 10; IGC (1971) /VI/11), March 12, 1985. Knowledge

Ecology International Website, *Wanda Noel's 1985 Report on Problems Experienced by the Handicapped in Obtaining Access to Protected Works*, http://keionline.org/node/644 (accessed January 2014).

21. World Blind Union. *Proposal for WIPO Treaty for Improved Access for Blind, Visually Impaired and Other Reading Disabled Persons*, http://www.keionline.org/content/view/210/1 (accessed January 2014).

22. World Intellectual Property Organization. *Marrakesh Treaty to Facilitate Access to Published Works for Persons Who Are Blind, Visually Impaired, or Otherwise Print Disabled*, http://www.wipo.int/treaties/en/ip/marrakesh/ (accessed January 2014).

23. WIPO Standing Committee on Copyright and Related Rights, Twenty-sixth Session. *Provisional Working Document Towards An Appropriate International Legal Instrument (in Whatever Form) on Limitations and Exceptions for Educational, Teaching and Research Institutions and Persons with Other Disabilities Containing Comments and Textual Suggestions* (SCCR/26/4), April 15, 2013, http://www.wipo.int/meetings/en/details.jsp?meeting_id=29944 (accessed January 2014).

24. World Intellectual Property Organization. *Development Agenda for WIPO*, http://www.wipo.int/ip-development/en/agenda (accessed January 2014).

25. Reports of WIPO CDIP sessions include summaries of the interventions given by Member States and by accredited observer organizations. World Intellectual Property Organization. *Committee on Development and Intellectual Property (CDIP)*, http://www.wipo.int/policy/en/cdip/ (accessed January 2014).

26. World Intellectual Property Organization. *Traditional Cultural Expressions*, http://www.wipo.int/tk/en/folklore/ (accessed January 2014).

BIBLIOGRAPHY

1. Goldstein, P.; Hugenholtz, P.B. *International Copyright: Principles, Law, and Practice*, 3rd Ed.; Oxford University Press: Oxford, U.K., 2013.

2. Lewinski, S.V. *International Copyright Law and Policy*; Oxford University Press: Oxford, U.K., 2008.

World Summit on the Information Society (WSIS)

Alex Byrne
University of Technology, Sydney, Sydney, New South Wales, Australia

Abstract
Promoted by the United Nations organizations, the World Summit on the Information Society was initiated to interrogate the global issues and challenges resulting from the widespread use of information and communication technologies and the growth of the information economy and to propose global strategies. Its first phase, held in Geneva in December 2003, was directed toward the adoption of a declaration and an action plan. The second phase, held in Tunis in November 2005, focused on reaffirming the commitment and advancing implementation of the agreed goals. Identifying the crucial role of libraries and information services as enablers for a fair and just information society, the International Federation of Library Associations and Institutions, worked successfully in concert with other civil society organizations to highlight the vital issues including freedom of access to information, information literacy, and strategies to overcome the digital divide.

INTRODUCTION

The proposal to hold a global summit meeting on the information society emerged from the growing concern about the implications of the "digital divide," the gap between communities or nations with adequate access to information and communications technologies—and the services they make possible—and those whose access is deficient. Initiated at the 1998 session of the Plenipotentiary Conference of the International Telecommunication Union (ITU) in Minneapolis, United States, the proposal for the Summit was formally adopted by the General Assembly of the United Nations (UN) on December 21, 2001.[1]

That resolution proposed that the outcomes of the World Summit on the Information Society (WSIS) should consist of a common vision and understanding of the information society, a declaration or principles, and an action plan to be implemented by Governments, international institutions, and all sectors of civil society. This signaled at the outset that this Summit process, to a greater extent than previous UN summit meetings, would recognize and involve civil society. The resolution also made particular reference to the urgency of providing effective access to information, knowledge and communication technologies for all, and especially people in developing nations. In addition, the resolution acknowledged the complexity of the issues to be addressed by endorsing the holding of WSIS in two phases, the first in Geneva from December 10 to December 12, 2003 and the second in Tunis in 2005, again unlike the singular process adopted for previous summits.

PROCESS

The framing of the Summit's purpose drew on background work by the ITU and the UN Administrative Committee on Coordination and the consensus about future global priorities expressed by nations in the UN Millennium Declaration. Responsibility for coordinating the summit was assigned to the ITU guided by a high level organizing committee of representatives of UN agencies.

The process, in which representatives of governments and intergovernmental agencies were well versed, consisted of a series of preparatory committee meetings, or PrepComs, plus regional meetings in various parts of the world.[2] A number of UN agencies, including UNESCO, organized consultative meetings and many organizations held conferences or meetings on specific questions. During the first phase, they included the "Pan-Arab Regional Conference on WSIS" on June 16–18, 2003 in Cairo (Egypt), the World Information Technology Forum, August 27–29, 2003 in Vilnius (Lithuania), the World Summit of Cities and Local Authorities on the Information Society on December 4–5, 2003 in Lyon (France), and the conference on "The Role of Science in the Information Society" which was organized by the European Organization for Nuclear Research and held in Geneva (Switzerland) on December 8–9, 2003, immediately before the first WSIS summit meeting.

In the first phase, these activities were focused on identifying the issues of concern and ways of addressing them. The issues, underlying and guiding principles, and strategies for addressing both were codified into a *Declaration of Principles*[3] and a *Plan of Action*[4] by government representatives during the extended PrepComs in order to

Encyclopedia of Library and Information Sciences, Fourth Edition DOI: 10.1081/E-ELIS4-120044325

World–Zoological

finalize agreed documents before the formal Summit meetings at which set speeches would be made by heads of government, senior ministers, or their representatives. In the second phase, similar activities aimed to develop some momentum to achieve the agreed goals by the UN Millennium deadline of 2015, again formulating an agreed plan, the *Tunis Commitment* and the *Tunis Agenda for the Information Society*,[5] through negotiation in the PrepComs.

In both phases, a number of major concerns and the intransigence of some governments threatened to derail the process. Despite the efforts of the presidents of the PrepComs and behind the scenes negotiations, both preparatory processes came down to the line, with agreement secured very late during the night preceding the opening of the summit meeting. In the first phase, the third and final PrepCom was not concluded in September 2003 as planned, and despite an Intersessional Meeting held in Paris in July, but it had to be reconvened in Geneva on November 10–14 and again December 5–6, only concluding late on December 9. In the second, a "Group of Friends of the Chair" was used to try to smooth the process, but nevertheless the third PrepCom held in Geneva on September 19–30 had to be reconvened on the eve of the summit in Tunis November 13–15.

ROLE OF CIVIL SOCIETY

The WSIS process and documents recognized the tripartite— "multistakeholder"—interests of governments, civil society, and business entities, taking the central role of the intergovernmental agencies for granted. Space was made available and some logistical and administrative support was provided to civil society and business entities. That recognition of nongovernmental stakeholders was instituted in accordance with the UN resolution but was an unprecedented innovation for a UN sponsored summit. It went well beyond the involvement permitted to business and nongovernmental organizations during previous summits such as the World Summit on Sustainable Development held in Johannesburg in 2002. But, welcome as it was, the multistakeholder approach was somewhat grudgingly accepted by many of the governmental delegations which clearly regarded themselves to be "more equal" than the other elements of the process, in keeping with their traditionally central role in international negotiations. Crucially, the capacity to intervene vigorously in the process was severely constrained because opportunities to speak in the formal PrepComs were largely limited to governments and intergovernmental organizations, especially those of the UN system but including the Bretton Woods organizations such as the World Bank. Interventions by business entities and civil society organizations were restricted to 15 min. slots once or twice a day; slots in which the myriad organizations had to vie for opportunities to make 2–3 min addresses.

Nevertheless, civil society took full advantage of the opportunities provided. "Civil society" is a misnomer: it is the term employed by the UN agencies for the broad coalition of nongovernmental organizations (NGOs), which represented the many dimensions of civil society in the WSIS process. They extended from globally active transnational social movement organizations such as Greenpeace to localized NGOs including the Computer Association of Nepal to professional peak bodies such as the International Federation of Library Associations and Institutions (IFLAs). Many very different organizations with very different agendas, structures, and capabilities were trying to influence the process and outcomes. Their concerns ranged across many domains from feminist issues, environmental concerns to broad human rights agendas. Most were concerned about redressing inequity, especially the digital divide and its consequences, and the inequalities between developed and developing countries, urban and rural populations, and mainstream and marginalized peoples.

The civil society organizations demonstrated a remarkable capacity to self organize with guidance from the Conference of NGOs in Consultative Relationship with the UN (CONGO), a vehicle for NGOs which wish to interact with the UN and its agencies. Regular meetings of participating civil society organizations were held under the aegis of the Civil Society Bureau during the PrepComs and other meetings and a number of thematic caucuses and working groups were established, such as "Education and academic," "Cultural and linguistic diversity," and "Persons with disabilities." Reflecting the level of leadership which emerged from the groupings, some appeared to work quite well, others struggled to find a common voice. Although they were a useful device to focus discussion on specific domains of concern, so that key issues and draft phrases for documents could be identified, the thematic groupings poorly served organizations with wide interests but limited resources such as IFLA.

"Business entities" participating in WSIS largely comprised peak bodies representing business interests although some powerful companies such as Microsoft were individually influential. Offered the same support and opportunities as civil society organizations, business entities showed less capacity or interest in self-organization and appeared to focus on key issues of importance to them individually with little apparent coordination. Their participation was most visible during the formal summits in Geneva and Tunis where extensive trade exhibitions, ICT4All, were held.

In contrast, civil society organizations showed remarkable unanimity, putting aside their differences and specific concerns in the shared interest of emphasizing the big issues. They achieved considerable success but were often frustrated by the attitudes of most government delegations who clearly felt that international negotiations were their province and resented the involvement of other parties. The concerns and frustrations of the civil society sector in the WSIS process were expressed in an alternative civil society declaration which was agreed and issued during the Geneva Summit.[6]

THE ISSUES

Effective access to information, knowledge and communication technologies for all, and especially people in developing nations, was the key issue identified in the UN resolution. Consequently, the desired outcomes were initially considered to fall essentially in the technological realm. For that reason and because the host organization was the ITU, responsibility for participation in the WSIS processes was assigned by most governments to ministries of communications, information technology, and similar areas. Thus, the governmental representatives who advised and worked with the nations' accredited diplomatic representatives to the UN in Geneva came mainly from such ministries and focused on the primary, largely technological, concerns of those ministries.

That technologically deterministic approach to the information society characterized early discussions. Challenging that orientation and seeking to introduce other issues—social, cultural, linguistic, gender, environmental, etc.—then became the first and major obstacle that civil society organizations, international agencies with broader priorities, and some likeminded governments had to surmount. UNESCO, for example, took an early lead by organizing four thematic meetings at its Paris headquarters in February 2002 to begin to draw up an agenda on educational, scientific, social, and cultural matters which should be raised in the WSIS processes.[7]

Setting the common vision of the information society on a firm and unqualified foundation of agreed fundamental human rights principles, as a just and fair information society for all, became the second major challenge. The crucial importance of establishing that foundation was fiercely advocated by the coalition of civil society interests and forcefully promoted by many governmental delegations, including especially those of the European Union. It was, however, opposed by some which sought to qualify such rights by asserting the supremacy of governments.

The Group of 77,[8] an alliance of developing nations which seeks to advance their economic interests through collaborative advocacy, argued strongly that a major focus on development was an essential key to creating an information society for all. The Group emphasized both the need to prioritize development and to resource it. Achievement of this third key element was vigorously supported by the civil society organizations but did not appear to be a priority for the business sector. All government delegations expressed support for development as a desirable goal but differed on the means of achieving it.

The major technological questions came fourth and were not strictly technological in nature but rather contextual factors which would condition technological developments. Primary among them was the question of governance of the Internet, a question which placed the U.S. representatives in opposition to most other governmental representatives and divided opinion among civil society organizations.

LIBRARY AND INFORMATION SECTOR INTERVENTIONS

As the peak international organization for libraries and information services, the IFLAs, strove to highlight the central role of libraries and information services "at the heart of the information society." International Federation of Library Associations and Institutions embarked on its most extensive advocacy campaign ever to try to ensure that the sector's concerns, including freedom of access to information and the digital divide, would be recognized in the WSIS outcomes. International Federation of Library Associations and Institutions representatives worked with cognate peak professional bodies such as the International Publishers' Association, participated in consultative meetings, accredited delegations to the PrepComs, and organized conferences before each summit meeting. Formal submissions, statements on key issues, and a booklet of library success stories were produced and used in lobbying in the WSIS processes and in home countries.[9]

These interventions, which extended from the UNESCO meeting in early 2002 to the Tunis summit meeting at the end of 2005, demanded an intense period of focused activity by IFLA staff, members of the Governing Board, and library representatives from many nations, including notably a team of Swiss librarians and students who provided essential logistical support and representation in Geneva. Also important was the strong support provided by a number of national delegations, especially the representatives from New Zealand, which articulated the sector's concerns in preparatory meetings in which civil society representatives, including those from IFLA, were not permitted to speak. The campaign demonstrated the need for IFLA to establish an effective advocacy capability while still drawing on the knowledge, persuasiveness, and contacts of members.

During the first phase, the *Libraries @ the Heart of the Information Society Pre Summit Conference* was crucial in providing an opportunity for librarians to gather in the General Assembly Hall of the Palais des Nations in Geneva (Fig. 1) a month before the summit meeting to highlight the centrality of library and information services to the information society and to meet with members of

Fig. 1 Libraries @ the Heart Pre Summit Conference, Geneva, December 2005.

their governments' delegations. More than 70 countries were represented at the Conference, and in many cases discussions with governments continued in national capitals. Delegates called upon the nations of the world to:[10]

> Support and extend the existing global network of library and information services to make available and preserve knowledge and cultural heritage, to provide information access points and to develop the twenty-first century literacies which are essential to the realization of the information society. High quality library and information services provide access to the information required by the communities they serve: a modest investment in them would quickly return significant dividends.

Those interventions within the WSIS processes were echoed by initiatives taken by a number of national library associations within their own countries. For example, the participation of IFLA President Kay Raseroka in a meeting organized by the Danish Library Association and other Danish NGOs lead to the inclusion of library views in the Danish government position which was presented at PrepCom3. Other library associations and national libraries sought to interact with the responsible ministries and, in some cases, were successful in gaining representation in the governmental delegations.

The library and information service sector argued that libraries and information services serve as gateways to knowledge, thought, and culture for individuals and groups and promoted the benefits of lifelong literacy, as the range of competencies necessary to engage fully with the Information Society. A broader vision was also expressed, a vision based on the right to both access and express information without restriction in which

libraries and information services contribute to the development and maintenance of intellectual freedom and help to safeguard democratic values and universal civil rights.

Advocacy continued in the same vein during the second, Tunis, phase but with increased emphasis on demonstrating practical outcomes. The success stories list was redeveloped as a database and libraries and information services were encouraged to submit local examples of good practice. Another presummit conference was held, *Libraries: the Information Society in Action*, at the Bibliotheca Alexandrina in Alexandria, Egypt on November 10–11, 2005. Highlighting the importance of information literacy, this conference was held in conjunction with a UNESCO supported to *High Level Colloquium on Information Literacy and Lifelong Learning*. Communiqués from both conferences were used at the summit meeting in Tunis the following week at which IFLA gained a rare invitation to give a plenary address.[11]

OUTCOMES

After all the negotiation and brinkmanship, a compromise *Declaration of Principles* was agreed. It has three parts: a statement of shared vision about the developing information society; a list of key principles to underpin the developing information society; and, a summary of the processes which will lead the world's peoples toward an equitable information society.

At its outset, the first part "Our Common Vision of the Information Society," places people, their rights and

Word–Zoological

inclusiveness at the heart of the information society but also highlights sustainable development and a global focus. The vision then identifies the transformative potential of information and communication technology (ICT) to promote the eradication of extreme poverty and hunger and achievement of a range of other contemporary international priorities including the empowerment of women, reduction of child mortality, elimination of diseases, promotion of environmental sustainability, and creation of global partnerships for development. This section reads as an affirmation of faith in technocratic management through the effective use of ICTs.

The Declaration then turns to human rights and fundamental freedoms, proclaiming their universality, and reaffirming without qualification the right to freedom of opinion and expression stated in Article 19 of the Universal Declaration of Human Rights. It asserts that this is "an essential foundation of the Information Society." The inclusion of this unqualified statement, despite the resistance of several nations, represented a major success for civil society and the governments which advocated the inclusion of this principle. The vision ends with recognition of its ambitious nature and introduces as new term to characterize the required commitment, "digital solidarity."

The second part identifies 11 key principles "for building an inclusive Information Society":

1. The role of governments and all stakeholders in the promotion of ICTs for development.
2. Information and communication infrastructure: an essential foundation for an inclusive information society.
3. Access to information and knowledge.
4. Capacity building.
5. Building confidence and security in the use of ICTs.
6. Enabling environment.
7. ICT applications: benefits in all aspects of life.
8. Cultural diversity and identity, linguistic diversity, and local content.
9. Media.
10. Ethical dimensions of the Information Society.
11. International and regional cooperation.

Some of these are indeed principles, others expose the compromise nature of the Declaration and some of its undercurrents, including the discomfort of governmental delegations with the recognition accorded to civil society organizations and concerns about security and control.

The *Declaration of Principles* was accompanied by a *Plan of Action* which assigned responsibilities for implementation of the agreed aims largely to governments but with some priorities in the province of intergovernmental agencies. Although earlier versions of the plan had identified a number of intermediate target dates, the final version placed the deadline at 2015, as for the UN Millennium Declaration.

The Tunis summit meeting, 23 months later, was intended to encourage the implementation and offer some early examples of success. It reaffirmed the outcomes achieved in Geneva and promoted concerted action toward 2015 in the *Tunis Commitment* and the *Tunis Agenda for the Information Society*. Major issues during this phase included the lack of progress in regard to Internet governance and recognition of the Digital Solidarity Fund and continuing concern at the reluctance of some governments to support unqualified recognition of human rights as an essential foundation for a just and fair information society. This last concern was heightened by the holding of the second summit meeting in Tunisia which, in the view of many especially from civil society organizations, had a repressive government. That view was confirmed during the summit meeting when a large police and military security force attempted to prevent the open expression at a number of events.

Despite sharing these concerns, the library and information sector and IFLA in particular was well pleased with the WSIS outcomes.[12] Although not always accorded the sector's priorities, all its principal issues were included in the declaration and action plan. And it was recognized that, for the first time at a global level, governments had devoted considerable time to discussing and agreed on the core concerns of libraries and information services.

UNFINISHED BUSINESS

The compromise agreed in Geneva and reiterated in Tunis had secured the unqualified recognition of human rights but left two major issues unresolved. A most contentious issue lay in the governance of the Internet, a question ultimately of control. To date, the successful development and growth of the Internet has been overseen by the Internet Corporation for Assigned Names and Numbers, a not-for-profit company registered with the U.S. Department of Commerce.[13] Some governments were uncomfortable at the possibility of interference by the U.S. government; many of the developing nations felt that they needed more influence; and some repressive governments wished to exert more control. Some suggested oversight by an international agency, possibly the ITU or a new agency, but the U.S. government and business representatives wished to continue to apply a market model. Civil society representatives sympathized with the developing nations' view, but largely felt that the current model had served the global community well and were consequently doubtful about the merits of change. In the event, this dilemma could not be resolved in Geneva or Tunis. It was referred to the Secretary-General of the UN who was requested to establish a working group, the Internet Governance Forum, to seek a solution.

The other main issue which provoked deep division in Geneva was a proposal by the President of Sénégal to establish a "Digital Solidarity Fund" which would help to reduce the digital divide. This proposal was soundly condemned by the richer nations, led by the European Union. They argued that there were many other international sources of funding that should be tried first and stated their absolute opposition to the creation of such a fund. Representatives from developing nations and many from civil society interpreted this position as an unwillingness to take urgent and decisive action to reduce inequality. Further discussion in the Tunis phase resulted in grudging acceptance but little commitment to the fund.

For libraries and information services, these outstanding issues and others which were somewhat blurred in the compromise are significant and will require continuing action. However, the achievement of satisfactory, albeit compromise, outcomes outweighed any deficiencies. If the WSIS processes had collapsed, as appeared possible in Geneva, the cause of recognizing the importance of promoting a just and fair information society for all and, specifically, the sector's priorities would have suffered a major setback.

CREATING THE "INFORMATION SOCIETY FOR ALL"

The UN General Assembly endorsed the outcomes of the WSIS without a vote on March 27, 2006. The resolution welcomed the strong orientation toward development and the progress achieved toward "a multistakeholder approach to building a people centered, inclusive and development-oriented information society."[14] Signaling the success of advocacy by developing countries, the Assembly also endorsed the Digital Solidarity Fund which it cast as a means of securing voluntary sources of "solidarity" financing to support the transformation of the digital divide into digital opportunities for developing countries. Responsibility for oversight of implementation was assigned to the Economic and Social Council and the Secretary-General was requested to convene the Internet Governance Forum.

CONCLUSION

By linking its outcomes to the UN Millennium Declaration, WSIS proclaimed that the creation of an equitable information society for all must be a global priority for the twenty-first century and that its attainment would require concerted action by all nations, the business sector, and civil society. A half century after the endorsement of the Universal Declaration of Human Rights, the summit affirmed that the global information society should be based on those agreed rights, especially the right to express and access information and should seek to redress inequality.

This was a watershed for organizations concerned with information and knowledge management because it placed information and knowledge—its creation, sharing, curation, and use—at the core of the desired new global society. The WSIS outcomes, agreed by all governments and endorsed unanimously by the United Nations, provide a strong foundation for the proliferation and further development of libraries and information services, but the process and outcomes also demonstrated the vital importance of effective and continuing advocacy in partnership with like-minded organizations.

REFERENCES

1. United Nations General Assembly. Resolution A/RES/56/183. 2001. http://www.itu.int/wsis/docs/background/resolutions/56_183_unga_2002.pdf (accessed January 2008).
2. World Summit on the Information Society. First Phase: Preparatory Process. http://www.itu.int/wsis/preparatory/index.html (accessed January 2008).
3. World Summit on the Information Society. *Declaration of Principles: Building the Information Society: A Global Challenge in the New Millennium [WSIS/PC-3/DT/6-E]*; WSIS: Geneva, 2003. http://www.itu.int/wsis/documents/doc_multi-en-1161|1160.asp (accessed January 2008).
4. World Summit on the Information Society. *Plan of Action [WSIS/PC-3/DT/5-E]*; WSIS: Geneva, 2003. http://www.itu.int/wsis/documents/doc_multi-en-1161|1160.asp (accessed January 2008).
5. World Summit on the Information Society. *Tunis Commitment and Tunis Agenda for the Information Society*; WSIS: Geneva, 2005. http://www.itu.int/wsis/documents/doc_multi.asp?lang=en&id=2266|2267 (accessed January 2008).
6. World Summit on the Information Society Civil Society Plenary. *Shaping Information Societies for Human Needs: Civil Society Declaration to the World Summit on the Information Society*; WSIS: Geneva, Switzerland, 2003. http://www.itu.int/wsis/docs/geneva/civil-society-declaration.pdf (accessed January 2008).
7. UNESCO Executive Board. *UNESCO's Contribution to the World Summit on the Information Society*; 2003. http://unesdoc.unesco.org/images/0012/001295/129531e.pdf (accessed January 2008).
8. The Group of 77 at the United Nations. http://www.g77.org (accessed January 2008).
9. International Federation of Library Associations and Institutions. *Submission to WSIS: PART I-Informative Text About the Role and Position of Libraries Generally; PART II-The IFLA Internet Manifesto; PART III-IFLA's Glasgow Declaration*; IFLA: The Hague, 2003. http://www.itu.int/dms_pub/itu-s/md/03/wsispc2/c/S03-WSISPC2-C-0062!!PDF-E.pdf (accessed January 2008).
10. International Federation of Library Associations and Institutions. *Libraries @ the Heart of the Information Society: Proceedings*; IFLA: Geneva, Switzerland, 2003. http://www.ifla.org/III/wsis.html#3 (accessed January 2008).
11. Byrne, A. Libraries the Information Society in Action: Invited address. In *World Summit on the Information*

Society. November 17, 2005. WSIS: Tunis, 2005. http:// www.itu.int/wsis/tunis/scripts/archive.asp? lang=en&c_num=293|294|296|297|298|299|300|301|302| 303|304|305 (accessed January 2008).

12. International Federation of Library Associations and Institutions. Byrne, A. *Promoting the Global Information Commons: A Commentary on the Library and Information Implications of the WSIS Declaration of Principles "Building the Information Society: A Global Challenge in the New Millennium" (Document WSIS/PC-3/DT/6)*; IFLA: The Hague, the Netherlands, 2004. http://www.ifla.org (accessed January 2008).

13. Internet Corporation for Assigned Names and Numbers (ICANN). http://www.icann.org/ (accessed January 2008).

14. United Nations Department of Public Information. *General Assembly Endorses Outcome of World Summit for Information Society, Welcomes Digital Solidarity Fund*; UN: New York, 2006. http://www.un.org/News/Press/docs/ 2006/ga10451.doc.htm (accessed January 2008).

World Wide Web (WWW)

Christinger Tomer
School of Information Sciences, University of Pittsburgh, Pittsburgh, Pennsylvania, U.S.A.

Abstract
The World Wide Web (WWW) is a system for creating, organizing, and linking documents so that they may be easily browsed. The Web has transformed the ways in which we communicate, learn, and socialize, and it has changed the ways in which we think about information, information seeking, and interacting with information systems. It is, moreover, one of the principal factors underlying globalization, in the process creating a vast array of connections involving individuals, groups, and institutions and providing a platform that has redefined workflow in many organizations through computer-to-computer data interchanges as well as the creation of collaborative communities. The Web has succeeded because of the following: (1) many relevant conditions were "right" and (2) it has relied from the outset on a simple, derivative architecture, consisting of the Hypertext Markup Language (HTML), the Hypertext Transfer Protocol, and the Uniform Resource Locator. The Web's stewards have managed the continuing development of the underlying technologies to ensure its openness and in ways that have lead to gradual changes and subtle transformations, rather than radical shifts. At the same time, the Web's stewards, most notably the World Wide Web Consortium, have fostered important innovations, such as the development of the Extensible Markup Language and the Cascading Style Sheets specification, the proposal to develop the "Semantic Web," and the evolution of HTML leading to the development of HTML5. In the process, the World Wide Web has had profound effects on libraries, librarians, and library users, changing the way in which librarians relate to vendors, clients, bibliographic utilities, and other libraries and giving rise to new, often highly creative approaches to serving readers.

INTRODUCTION

The World Wide Web is a system for creating, organizing, and linking documents so that they may be easily browsed. Created by Tim Berners-Lee, the World Wide Web is also one of the most remarkable developments of the last 25 years, and it is virtually certain that it will continue to be a pervasive influence on both information producers and information consumers for the foreseeable future.

The Web has transformed the ways in which we communicate, learn, and socialize. Perhaps even more to the point, the World Wide Web has changed the ways in which we think about information, information seeking, and interacting with information systems.

The World Wide Web may be an incomplete and imperfect manifestation of the ideas about hypertext that Ted Nelson set forth in the mid-1960s, but it has changed the ways in which we think about the world, and it has changed forever how ideas, information, and knowledge are shared.[1] According to Thomas Friedman, in his *The World Is Flat: A Brief History of the Twenty-First Century*, the World Wide Web is one of the principal factors underlying globalization, in the process creating a vast array of connections involving individuals, groups, and institutions and providing a platform that has redefined workflow in many organizations through computer-to-computer data interchanges as well as the creation of

collaborative communities. As Friedman has also noted, it is an environment that seems almost ideally suited to the needs of information seekers with what he calls a high "curiosity quotient"—Friedman believes that when curiosity is combined with passion in the exploration of a subject of interest, an individual of average intellectual endowment may be able to acquire knowledge comparable to that of a highly intelligent person, because of the vast amount of information resources available through the Internet—and it clearly appeals to writers in search of new and more expressive modes of communication.[2] For them, documents are, as Lisa Gitelman has observed, "instruments used in the kinds of knowing that are all wrapped up with showing, and showing wrapped up with knowing," and the Web affords both technologies and cultural milieus of greater power and scope than traditional, analog forms of information exchange.[3] The product, from the perspectives articulated by Timothy Morton, are often "hyperobjects," by which Morton means objects so massively distributed in time and space that they transcend "spatiotemporal specificity."[4]

Less flattering are the views of critics like Louis Menand, who has characterized the Web as an imaginary space—he calls it a "spatial imaginary"—in which visual change is often experienced (and confused with) as a physical change. Menand argues that the use of "real estate vocabulary," in the form of terms such as "address,"

Encyclopedia of Library and Information Sciences, Fourth Edition DOI: 10.1081/E-ELIS4-120053396

Word–Zoological

"site," and "domain," reinforces this dislocating illusion and changes how we think about information resources and use them in ways that obscure underlying realities.[5]

The emergence of Web 2.0, a new layer of activities shaped by participatory architectures based on cooperation rather than control, lightweight programming models, enriched user experiences, and a fuller realization of the Internet as a platform for computing, changed yet again the way in which we think about and use the Web and its contents. In its first phases, Web 2.0 allowed users to comment on published articles; participate in social networks; tag items such as digital photographs, images, and documents; and share Web bookmarks.[6] In the second phase of Web 2.0, software as a service came to maturity, through the integration of application programming interfaces (APIs), Ajax programming using JavaScript and the Document Object Model (DOM), and cloud-based storage, in the form of Web-based applications such as Google Docs, YouTube, and Microsoft Office 365.

More recently, Hypertext Markup Language 5 (HTML5), a synthesis of HTML and XHTML that integrates the DOM into the markup language and offers new opportunities for the incorporation of audio and video media, has further enhanced what may be conveyed through a Web page. It includes processing models designed to encourage more interoperable implementations, extends and improves the markup available for documents, and introduces markup and APIs for complex web applications.[7]

Looking to the near future, it seems likely that the ideas associated with the Semantic Web will soon begin to have more obvious effects, transforming the Web from a vast file system to an equally vast database capable of supporting various processes, including discovery and search, with perhaps unparalleled precision.

The Semantic Web has long been a controversial subject, marked by high aspirations and serious doubts. The debate began the day Berners-Lee, James Hendler, and Ora Lassila unveiled their proposal, focusing mainly on questions about its feasibility.[8] There were almost no doubts expressed about the desirability of this vision for the future of the Web, but many experts were not optimistic about the success of the initiative, owing to its complexity and its stringent requirements and, as Clay Shirky observed, because most of the data we use are not amenable to the syllogistic recombination that the Semantic Web presumes.[9] Others have noted, similarly, that the proposal "disregards the fundamental fuzziness and variability of human communication" and that the "rigid formality" that characterizes the Semantic Web cannot be enforced or ensured, resulting in an "interoperative polyglot" akin to, for example, RSS (Rich Site Summary or Really Simple Syndication).[10]

However, the vision of a near future in which semantically oriented technologies that systematically describe the content of the Web are coupled with artificial intelligence to create a new layer within the Web infrastructure has persisted.[11] More important, essential parts of this new infrastructure have been built, and the transformation, in which metadata in standardized forms pervades the network and affords the basis for a wide array of services, ranging from more precise retrieval of information to the automatic generation of documents, is well under way.

But the doubts persist. In 2010, the Pew Internet Research Center surveyed a group of experts on Web technologies in an effort to understand the prospects of the Semantic Web. Some of the experts, 41% of the survey's 895 respondents, thought that the concepts on which the Semantic Web is founded would be realized by 2020, while 47% of those surveyed expressed skepticism about its feasibility, agreeing with the notion that "[b]y 2020, the semantic web envisioned by Tim Berners-Lee will not be as fully effective as its creators hoped and average users will not have noticed much of a difference."[12]

Around the same time, Berners-Lee returned to the debate, arguing then and later that efforts to mark up and link datasets, but especially datasets derived from scientific research, would lead inexorably to a new version of the Web organized on the basis of semantic information interpreted by both humans and computers.[13]

Another aspect of Berners-Lee's vision for Web is the annotation. It is a feature that Berners-Lee had originally intended to incorporate, but in the effort to retain control over the technology and guarantee its openness in the mid-1990s, it was set aside. But when he wrote *Weaving the Web* in the late 1990s, Berners-Lee noted that "[w]e need the ability to store on one server an annotation about a Web page on another [server]."[14]

In recent years, the idea of creating a standard for annotations and integrating it into the Web infrastructure has been taken up by the World Wide Web Consortium (W3C) and others, in the form of Open Annotation Data Model. The primary aim of the Open Annotation Data Model is to create a "single, consistent model," within "an interoperable framework for creating associations between related resources, annotations, using a methodology that conforms to the [a]rchitecture of the World Wide Web," and in so doing provide "a standard description mechanism for sharing [a]nnotations between systems, with the mechanism facilitating sharing or migration of annotations between devices."[15]

There is considerable interest among developers in the annotation as a mechanism for information enhancement and exchange, manifest in a variety of projects active at this writing. But it is not clear if there is a widespread interest among users. Other projects of similar purpose, such as the W3C's Annotea Project, have met with limited success.[16] Perhaps even more to the point, there is no sufficiently simple mechanism for support of the Open Annotation Data Model that is available for deployment; so, the model and its potential remain untested at this writing.

HOW BIG IS THE WEB?

Since the World Wide Web does not operate under any central authority, the question of the Web's size is difficult to answer precisely. Domain name system (DNS) services, the Internet services that translate domain names into IP (or Internet Protocol) addresses, list the domain names that exist, but not every domain contains a website; many domains contain more than one website, and DNS registrars are not obliged to report how many domains their databases contain. So most of what is known about the size of the World Wide Web is based on survey results, which differ substantially, and/or the number of pages indexed by Web search engines, such as Google and Yahoo. However, within the limits of what can be measured, there is evidence not only that the Web continues to grow at a rapid rate but also that it is taking on increasing complexity and substance in the content it transports.

The Internet has been growing exponentially since at least 1993. Current estimates indicate that slightly more than a billion live websites have been created since 1991. Today, there are at least 760 million websites, with approximately 103 million new sites added in 2013 alone. How many of the current websites are active? The number depends on how "active" is defined. One source indicates that 67% of the current sites are active, while another suggests that about three-quarters of the active sites are "parked," or dormant.[4]

According to the findings of surveys last updated in 2014, there are 2.7 billion Web pages that have been indexed and approximately 2.6 billion Web users. Current estimates indicate that slightly more than a billion live websites have been created since 1991 and that there are roughly 672 million websites in existence, with about three-quarters of them dormant (or "parked").[4] (This finding is largely consistent with the results of a series of studies conducted by OCLC between 1997 and 2003, in which investigators discovered that perhaps as many as half of the websites on the Web had effectively been abandoned by their respective owners.[17])

Active sites present a total of 14.3 trillion pages, 48 billion of them indexed by Google, and consist of a total of 672 exabytes of accessible data. More than 2 trillion searches were conducted through the Google search engine in 2013, by an estimated 1.45 billion users.[18] (Another source indicates that the number of Web users is much larger, in excess of 2.5 million people.)[19]

In principle, the World Wide Web remains an open and egalitarian enterprise. Anyone can launch a website, but the vast majority of the top 100 websites, the most visited sites, are run by corporations, the most important (and almost only) exception being *Wikipedia*.[20]

The so-called deep Web, the part of the Web that is not indexed by search engines, which is generally restricted in its access and which may include non-HTML, unlinked, dynamic and/or scripted content, is thought to be much larger than the "surface Web." Recent estimates suggest that the "deep Web" may make up as much as 90% of the Web, but the size and continuing growth of the Web make it impossible to determine precisely how large it is or how much of it is part of the "surface Web" or the "deep Web." However, according to Bright Planet, an organization that specializes in content extraction, the "deep" or "invisible" Web contains nearly 550 billion individual documents, as compared to the one billion documents contained within the "surface Web."[21]

Almost 60% of the Web's users are employing mobile devices, that is, smartphones and tablets. The popularity of various Web browsers is a matter of constant contention, but it appears that Internet Explorer remains the most popular Web browser at this writing, with a combined market share of 49%. Google Chrome has a market share of 18%, and Mozilla's Firefox browser and Apple's Safari each have shares of approximately 11%.[22,23]

According to the HTTP Archive, the average page is currently 1890 KB in size, compared to 828 KB in May 2012, with an annual growth rate of about 50%.[24,25] Images typically make up about 55–60% of the overall payload. The use of Cascading Style Sheets (CSS) and JavaScript is increasing, whereas the number of requested pages including Adobe Flash is slightly below 30% and declining markedly.[26]

It is not entirely clear why Web pages are growing in size and complexity. It seems reasonable to assume, however, that there are several highly influential factors. The first is increasing penetration of broadband Internet services, which allow the creators of Web content to create and transfer files of substantial size with ease. Moreover, the widespread availability of broadband services, particularly in the developed world, means that many files with richer content can reach large audiences quickly and without difficulty. A second factor is competition. Competition for the attention of Web users, but particularly for consumers using the Web as a marketplace, is intense, and there is evidence that richness of content is often a necessary condition for success. Finally, there is the availability and use of authoring and site management tools that make it relatively easy to create HTML and/or XML documents of considerable complexity, and to be able to do so without detailed knowledge of the relevant coding languages.

Another major factor adding to the complexity of the Web is the use of streaming media, which has increased by more than 100% each year since 2000. Audio or video files that are transmitted continuously from a server can begin playing as they are being downloaded to a computer. This process is now enhanced by the Dynamic Adaptive Streaming over HTTP (DASH) standard, which has made video-on-demand a "standard" Internet application similar in its impact to e-mail and Web browsing.[27]

While videos account for only a small percentage of the responses from Web servers, the most popular video services, Netflix, YouTube, Amazon Video, Hulu, and iTunes, generate between 50 and 55% of the bytes transferred via the Web, with Netflix producing slightly more than 31% of the traffic in 2014 and YouTube accounting for about 12% of the overall traffic.[28]

Interest in downloading or streaming videos via the Web is likely to continue to grow in accord with broadband's market penetration and the increases in the speed of data transfer that are now an integral part of the market for Internet services and with improvements in the DASH protocol and end-to-end congestion controls. So, it seems reasonable to assume that the demand for videos will continue to grow, perhaps even sharply, and that the bandwidth required to fulfill those requests will continue to be a major factor in the use of the Internet, the management of Internet backbone resources, and the politics of the Internet.

Is the Web getting faster? Google claims that it is significantly faster today than it was only a couple of years ago, owing mainly to improvements in the core infrastructure, much faster mobile networks, and improvements in Web browser design.[29] However, there are other sources that dispute such findings, but resolution of the question is not possible at this time, because there is no consensus about the methods of measurement or analysis.[30]

A BRIEF HISTORY OF THE WORLD WIDE WEB

The development of the World Wide Web may be divided into three phases. In the first experimental phase, Berners-Lee developed a collaborative hypertext environment based on an adaptation of the TCP/IP protocol and aspects of Standard Generalized Markup Language (SGML). As noted in his original proposal, "the working structure of the organization is a multiply connected 'web' whose interconnections evolve with time."[31] Berners-Lee then made the source code available over the Internet, facilitating experiments with and improvements of the basic technologies, a process that continues to this day largely through the W3C.

According to the *Encyclopedia of Computer Science*

Hypertext is both the concept of interrelating information elements (linking pieces of information) and the name used to describe a collection or web of interrelated or linked nodes.[32]

Vannevar Bush is generally given credit for developing the idea of hypertext, as first articulated in an article entitled "As We May Think," which was published in the July 1945 issue of *The Atlantic Monthly*.[33] However, recent research indicates that the ideas set forth by Bush were not new and that the idea of a machine that would connect an individual to diverse sources of information and effectively help to synthesize such information had also been expressed previously, perhaps most notably by H.G. Wells

in his pre-WWII lectures on *World Brain*, by Paul Otlet, a Belgian bibliographer who proposed in 1934 a plan for a global network of "electric telescopes," which would allow anyone in the world to access to libraries of books, articles, photographs, audio recordings, and films, and by Emmanuel Goldberg, who patented a device called the "Statistical Machine" in 1927 that allowed a user to search and retrieve large volumes of data stored on microfilm by using a so-called search card and who later proposed a technique that would allow a user to enter a query via telephone.

Bush called his machine the "memex." Wells talked about an interactive encyclopedia controlled by subject experts that would function as a form of collective intelligence. He wrote the following:

[W]hat I am saying ... is this, that without a World Encyclopaedia to hold men's minds together in something like a common interpretation of reality, there is no hope whatever of anything but an accidental and transitory alleviation of any of our world troubles.[34]

Otlet called his knowledge network the Mundaneum. (Previously, Otlet and Henri La Fontaine had launched a project called the Universal Bibliography, or *Répertoire Bibliographique Universel*, a plan to catalog of all the world's published information. The project eventually resulted in the creation of more than 15 million entries, stored on index cards and classified under a system called the Universal Decimal Classification, an adapted version of the Dewey Decimal System.)[35]

In considering the history of hypertext, scholars tend to focus on the various mechanisms that were proposed as ways of bringing greater order to the formal communications of scholars and affording greater precision in the use of such materials, and in the process may not always pay enough attention to Bush's notion that memory is an associative process, and that we should build information storage and retrieval systems whose organizing structures mimic associative memory as closely as possible. So, in Bush's mind, the linking functions that connected chunks of text and articles to one another, what we now call hypertext links, represented the best available way to imitate this aspect of human memory. (This was not a new concept; in fact, the notion can be traced back to Aristotle, whose thoughts about memory and recollection may be viewed as the first articulation of principles of association and order. Bush's greater service was bringing these ideas into discussions about how to make information systems more effective, and by suggesting that "spatializing" ideas, or the chunks of text, data, and imagery, into more discrete units of presentation could enhance memory and recollection.[36])

Similarly, the idea of a "world brain" as set forth by Wells may sometimes be dismissed too quickly, in part because Wells was vaguer than, say, Otlet or Bush, about how his system might work at a mechanical level, but also because he used an ancient and familiar form, the encyclopedia, as the basis for his proposal. What gets lost are Wells' insights into the sociology of knowledge production; specifically, his recognition of science as a highly collaborative enterprise and his sense that technology, in the form of a distributed network, could enhance and extend the process known as "peer review," and thereby bring greater order and clarity to human knowledge.

There were a number of experiments with hypertext from the mid-1960s through the end of the 1980s, including Ted Nelson's Xanadu Project, whose goal was the creation of a computer file system based on hypertext concepts and Douglas Engelbart's NLS/Augment, the first distributed, shared-screen, collaborative hypertext system in 1968. Other prototype and commercial hypertext systems appeared in the 1970s and 1980s, including Document Examiner, gIBIS, Guide, Hypergate, HyperTIES, Intermedia, MacWeb (by LIRMM), Max, Neptune, NoteCards, PHIDIAS, StorySpace, Writing Environment, and ZOG/KMS. (In June 2014, 54 years after first announcing the Xanadu Project, Nelson finally released a prototype of his system, which may be viewed at http://xanadu.com/xanademos/MoeJusteOrigins.html. According to information on Nelson's website, he believes today that the Xanadu document format could supplant PDFs but is unlikely to displace the basic architecture of the World Wide Web.)[37]

One hypertext system, Apple's HyperCard, which was based on the idea of virtual "cards" in a stack akin to a Rolodex and a scripting language called HyperTalk, came into widespread use as part of the package of applications developed for and included with Apple's Macintosh computer. But HyperCard was never fully adapted for use in networked environments or recompiled to run under OS X, and Apple ceased work on its development during the transition to the OS X operating system, eventually dropping it altogether in 2004. It has been argued, moreover, that HyperCard was not a genuine hypertext system, because it lacked many of the navigation, annotation, and structural features that characterize "true" hypertext systems. But, true hypertext system or not, by the time the powers that be at Apple had lost interest in HyperCard, another initiative, developed by Tim Berners-Lee and eventually known as the "World Wide Web," had taken hold, changing forever the Internet and how we think about computerized text.

In 1989, Tim Berners-Lee was working as a software engineer at CERN, the European Organization for Nuclear Research. (The name CERN is derived from the acronym for the French "Conseil Européen pour la Recherche Nucléaire," or European Council for Nuclear Research, a provisional body founded in 1952 with the mandate of establishing a world-class fundamental physics research organization in Europe.) Scientists working at CERN used all sorts of operating systems and software on their computers, and as a result, one scientist often could not find or access another scientist's research, but then, Berners-Lee noticed

> All these systems looked different but in fact you're reading stuff on a screen and sometimes clicking on bits. So you could imagine a thin layer which would map all these existing systems into one virtual system. Wouldn't that be cool?[38]

Berners-Lee's supervisor at CERN thought the idea was vague but worth exploring, so he commissioned Berners-Lee to create a system for collaborative authoring and document sharing that could run over the local area network at CERN and entail a number of different types of computers and operating systems.

To make such a system operational, Berners-Lee needs to create a mechanism for the transport of textual data and a document format that could be interpreted by all of the operating systems that would be connected across the CERN network. And because he was interested incorporating ideas about hypertext into the system, he needs to establish a way of creating links within and among documents. According to Berners-Lee

> The idea of the Web was prompted by positive experience of a small "home-brew" personal hypertext system used for keeping track of personal information on a distributed project. The Web was designed so that if it was used independently for two projects, and later relationships were found between the projects, then no major or centralized changes would have to be made, but the information could smoothly re-shape to represent the new state of knowledge.[39]

Owing to the requirements of his assignment, the limited resources available for its support, and inspired by the success of the "home-brew" hypertext system, Berners-Lee elected to focus his efforts on the use of existing resources available to him under open licenses and/or technical standards. He realized almost from the beginning that the transport layer of his system could be built on top of the IPs—the so-called TCP/IP suite of rules for conveying data over the Internet—by adding a compatible layer, which he dubbed the Hypertext Transfer Protocol, or *http*.

Berners-Lee designed the HTTP to function as a request–response protocol under a client–server computing model, and he wrote the programming code for both a client and a server capable of carrying out the specified actions. In accord with this model, a client application, typically what we now know as a Web browser, submits a request message formed on the basis of the HTTP to a server that has been outfitted to recognize and respond to requests formatted in this way.

The key element of the request is the Uniform Resource Locator (URL). The URL is a specific character string that constitutes a reference to a resource. The now-familiar components of a URL are

- The scheme, which defines how the resource will be obtained
- The domain name or numeric IP address of the destination location for the URL
- The port number
- The path specifying the location of the resource requested on the server

The URL may also include

- A query string containing data to be passed to software running on the server
- A fragment identifier, which, if present, specifies a part or a position within the overall resource or document

The server, which provides resources such as HTML files and other content or performs other functions on behalf of the client, returns a response message to the client, using another URL to route the response to the client. The response contains completion status information about the request and may also contain requested content in its message body.

In addressing the question of how the documents mounted on the server and fetched by the client would be formatted, Berners-Lee confronted a thornier problem, in part because the process of standardizing the formats for electronic documents was nascent. However, Berners-Lee discovered the SGML in the early going and recognized that under the SGML grammar a document is separated into three parts: (1) an SGML declaration; (2) a prologue; and (3) an instance, with the prologue constituting a document type definition (DTD). He noted further that the SGML declaration determines the lexicon of the grammar, specifies the document character set, and establishes the code positions associated with those characters, binding the abstract syntax of SGML to a concrete syntax expressed through the DTD. The concrete syntax formulated by Berners-Lee on the basis of SGML and the ISO standard defining the 7 bit coded character set for information interchange became known as the Hypertext Markup Language, or HTML.[40,41]

So the HTML began as a subset, also referred to as a "document type definition," of the SGML.[42] As noted previously, Berners-Lee had been commissioned to create a system under which documents could be shared, edited, and annotated across a network, and the project required a way of formatting documents using a code base—ASCII (the American Standard Code for Information Interchange), as it happens—that was shared by a variety of computers and operating systems. Early on, Berners-Lee not only became aware of the SGML, but he also realized that SGML allowed for the creation of formatting subsets and related expressions rendered in ASCII.

The DTD Berners-Lee created was a simple expression, conceptually and syntactically. And that simplicity plays no small part in the success of the World Wide Web, because it is clear in retrospect that a more complicated scheme would have been much more difficult to implement or standardize. However, that same simplicity also became a curse of sorts, as it became clear that the wide variety of document types that authors sought to make available via the Web could not be supported adequately by a single DTD.

The system introduced by Berners-Lee provided a text-only interface. Acceptance of this system was slow. The text-only browser was not easy to use and the resources to which it had access were limited. However, that state of affairs changed in 1993, with the creation of a graphical Web browser for UNIX, known as Mosaic, by Marc Andreessen, an undergraduate student working at the National Center for Supercomputing Applications, and the distribution via the Internet of versions of Mosaic for Windows and the Mac OS in 1994. Mosaic's introduction was the culmination of the first stage of Web development, and its effect was transformative. From the perspective of end users, the Web became a graphical medium, with Mosaic as the lens, and while it would take another 10 years before Web content began to achieve real richness and sophistication in visual terms, Mosaic was a clear indication of what was possible.

(In the early days of the World Wide Web, as programmers worked to develop browsers and other tools, questions about how to format HTML documents for presentation arose, and those questions became particularly acute with the development of graphical Web browsers such as Mosaic. Under SGML, formatting for presentation had been treated as a separate issue, with the focus placed instead on structural tagging. As graphical Web browsers came into more general use, one of the limits of this approach became obvious—most of the formatting of Web documents was being rendered by the browsers themselves and determined in large measure by the default settings of the specific browser in use. While permitting the browser to format the Web page had advantages, it also placed sharp limits on the extent to which the author of a Web page could control how that page was presented to a user. In the short term, the solution was to incorporate formatting attributes and tags into HTML, which in many ways adulterated the original concept. The longer-term solution came in the form of a compatible but distinct language for formatting, which came to be known as the "Cascading Style Sheets," or CSS, specification.[43])

In the second phase, the infrastructure that supports the Web through the present day was established. Jim Clark and Andreessen founded Netscape and released its Web browser in late 1994, ending the experimental phase in the Web's development and initiating its commercialization. Microsoft, after ignoring the development of the Internet for a number of years, responded with the development of a Web browser called Internet Explorer and the subsequent release of other, Web-related technologies, including the Internet Information Server. The Apache Project, dedicated to building secure Web server software in an open-source environment, was established in 1995. In 1999, as the Web turned from this "buildout" phase to a period of rapid expansion predicated on increasingly stable server technologies and more and more sophisticated approaches to document rendering, IBM embraced open-source software and played a key role in establishing the Apache Foundation, which has become one of the leading organizations in the ongoing development of the software that runs the Web. In 2001, the first podcast was presented (in the form of a Grateful Dead recording), Wikipedia was founded, and Pope John Paul II sent the first papal e-mail from a laptop in his office at the Vatican. In 2003, Apple's iTunes music download service was launched. In 2004, Tim Berners-Lee was knighted, and Google became a public company.[44]

In this "buildout" phase, one of the most critical developments was the introduction of the CSS specification in 1994. The purpose of CSS was twofold: First, it was intended to separate structural markup and formatting in order to simplify both coding and interpretation, and, second, it was designed to enlarge and enrich opportunities for formatting HTML documents, ranging from the ability to define families of fonts to absolute positioning and the use of so-called floats to wrap text around images to the cascade itself, which was defined as "the process of combining several style sheets and resolving conflicts between them."[45,46]

How important has CSS been to the development of the Web? Håkon Wium Lie, who wrote and published the first CSS specification in 1994, has asserted that CSS "saved HTML," because it gave "authors a way to express their designs without adding new HTML tags." Perhaps more to the point, CSS has afforded authors an effective mechanism separate and apart from structural markup for creating visually richer and more interesting Web pages.[47]

In the third phase, which began in 2004–2005, the Web entered into a more highly interactive phase, characterized by network-resident applications, participatory architectures, the increasing use of XML-based technologies, and metadata interchanges that presaged the Semantic Web.

Under HTML5, yet another phase in the development was initiated. HTML5 provided a more coherent framework for the creation of Web pages and the development of Web applications. For example, whereas HTML 4 was imprecise in defining the structure of a document, HTML5 provides an "outline algorithm," under which all content residing with the <body> of a document is also part of a section, and sections are defined explicitly within the <body>, <section>, <article>, <aside>, <footer>, <header>, and <nav> tags.[48] In a related vein, under HTML5 headings, for example, <h1> and <h2> are defined and ranked within sections of the <body> of the

document. Relative ranking of the headings matters only within a section, with the structure of the sections determining the outline, and not the heading rank of the sections.

HTML5 supports video and audio tracks without plug-ins; provides programmatic access to a resolution-dependent bitmap canvas that is useful for rendering graphs, graphics, or other visual images and native support for scalable vector graphics (SVG) and math (MathML); and features supporting the development of and access to rich applications. (The HTML5 <canvas> element is used to draw graphics, on the fly, via scripting. The <canvas> element is a container for graphics, with the script, usually a JavaScript, which actually draws the graphics. A canvas is a rectangular area on an HTML page, with incorporated methods for drawing paths, boxes, circles, and text and adding images.)

HTML5 has been in use throughout its development. According to a 2014 survey, 42% of 10,000 developers polled are using the combination of HTML, CSS, and JavaScript for all or part of their mobile applications, and Gartner Research has identified HTML5 as one of the top 10 mobile technologies for 2015–2016, as "an essential technology for organizations delivering applications across multiple platforms."[49,50]

With the publication of the fifth version of HTML5 in late 2014, the W3C announced that HTML5 would serve as the core of the Open Web Platform, through which the W3C intends to lower the cost of developing cross-platform applications by focusing on the following issues:

- Security and privacy
- Web design and development
- Device interaction
- Media and real-time communications
- Performance and tuning
- Usability and accessibility
- Related services, including the social Web, payments, annotations, and Web of data[51,52]

WHY HAS THE WEB BEEN SUCCESSFUL?

The Web has succeeded not only because many relevant conditions were "right" but also because it has relied from the outset on a simple, derivative architecture, consisting of the HTML, the HTTP, and the URL. A URL is a URI that also specifies the location of an identified resource and the protocol for retrieving it. In popular usage and in many technical documents, it is often confused as a synonym for uniform resource identifier.[53] In the beginning, as Berners-Lee has noted, the World Wide Web represented a "basically trivial" expression of ideas, mainly about hypertext systems, that had been in circulation, in some instances for many years.[54]

Moreover, since the advent of the graphical browser in 1995, the technologies of the World Wide Web have been easy for end users to manipulate, and that aspect coupled with the increasing rich blend of text, graphics, and links has created a huge global audience. Of equal importance is the fact that the Web's stewards, including Berners-Lee in his role as director of the W3C, have managed the continuing development of the underlying technologies in ways that have led to gradual changes and subtle transformations, rather than radical shifts. (Berners-Lee established the W3C in 1994 as a means of ensuring that Web-related standards would remain open. It was founded at the Massachusetts Institute of Technology Laboratory for Computer Science, with the support from the European Commission and the Defense Advanced Research Projects Agency, and quickly expanded its membership to include many other organizations, including most of the leading companies in the computer industry. By 2014, W3C membership had increased to 385 organizations.) For example, the path from the first version of the HTML to HTML 4.01 and XHTML and HTML5 is one marked by a commitment to interoperability and spirit of accommodation, whereby "[e]ach version of HTML has attempted to reflect greater consensus among industry players so that the investment made by content providers will not be wasted and that their documents will not become unreadable in a short period of time."[55] At the same time, however, the interest in innovation that has driven the development of the Web has been manifested in other aspects of this stewardship, most notably in the development of the XML and proposal to develop what Berners-Lee and others refer to as the "Semantic Web."

In the longer term, the World Wide Web has succeeded because it is networked, but separate from the Internet. Berners-Lee has argued that this separation is of fundamental importance, because it allows the two layers of technology, the Internet and the Web, to work together while advancing independently.[56] Moreover, the value of what the Web provides has grown in proportion to data, services, and users connected through it. Positive network externalities, the so-called network effect, have been reinforced by the extensibility of the Web's underlying technologies and the availability of an increasing large and diverse set of resources, often available to both content creators and users at little or no cost.

Of at least equal importance, the World Wide Web has succeeded and will endure because of a commitment to open technical standards that was made at the outset by Berners-Lee, and which he and others have sustained over the years, through the W3C, the Apache Foundation, and a host of other efforts. The commitment to open standards has thwarted efforts to exert private control over the Web and its technologies, and it has been a key factor in the Web's remarkable growth, allowing other innovators and entrepreneurs to leverage the Web's technologies in often creative ways. In the beginning, Berners-Lee opted for

technologies based on open standards, because his sponsor required interoperability and because he could afford no other choice. In so doing, he set in motion processes that have radically altered the course of the digital document's evolution.

The W3C endorses the Modern Paradigm for Standards, which is based on "[r]espectful cooperation between standards organizations, whereby each respects the autonomy, integrity, processes, and intellectual property rules of the others." Under the Modern Paradigm, standards are developed on the basis of five principles:

1. Due process, under which decisions are made with equity and fairness among participants, where no one party dominates or guides standards development, and standards-making processes are transparent and opportunities exist to appeal decisions, as well as review and update standards
2. Broad consensus, whereby processes allow for all views to be considered and addressed in order to facilitate agreement
3. Transparency, based on easily accessible records of decisions and the materials used in reaching those decisions and public comment periods provided before final standards approval and adoption
4. Balance, ensuring that standards activities are not exclusively dominated by any particular person, company, or interest group
5. Openness, providing relevant information to all participants and interested parties equally[57]

IMPACT OF THE WORLD WIDE WEB ON LIBRARIES

The impact of the Web on libraries has been profound, changing the way libraries relate to vendors, clients, bibliographic utilities, and other libraries. What is more important is that the World Wide Web has liberated librarians and engendered new and often highly creative approaches to serving readers. The Web has had similar effects on publishers, ranging from scholarly presses to the U.S. Government Printing Office.[58]

An example of how influential the Web has been may be found in the case of electronic journals. In the early 1990s, the publisher Elsevier ran The University Licensing Program (TULIP), an experimental project aimed at establishing an infrastructure for the distribution and delivery of e-journals.[59] What is significant about TULIP in retrospect is that engineers at Elsevier assumed that the most effective and efficient means of delivering content would be to create a system under which digital subscriptions were maintained locally (meaning, in this instance, that copies of subscribed content would be maintained on servers situated with the subscriber's Internet domain) and updated regularly via the Internet. What they did not envision was an Internet that would be fast enough to support the real-time distribution of journal articles or the emergence of a hypertext environment capable of linking databases to e-journals, journal articles to other journal articles via hyperlinked citations, articles to datasets, and so on. By the end of the 2000s, research libraries had reached a "tipping" point, whereby electronic journals, almost all of them delivered to libraries by means of the World Wide Web, outnumbered print subscriptions.[60]

Integrated online library systems have been enhanced in a wide variety of ways, incorporating published and personal reviews of materials, support for bookmarking and personal account management, Web-based readers, citation formatting services, virtual reference services, etc. In recent years, access to library resources has been improved markedly, through the ongoing development of increasingly powerful discovery services and link resolvers. (The development of link resolution services is a great example of how the commitment to open standards has enhanced the functionality and efficacy of the Web as a medium for information interchange. Such services are based primarily on the OpenURL standard, which was developed by Herbert Van de Sompel and others in the late 1990s and early 2000s and then established as NISO standard in 2004.[61])

Google Scholar is another interesting and important case in point where libraries and the Web are concerned. Google Scholar is designed to access to the scholarly literature through a single portal, supplying a means to find scholarly papers, abstracts, and citations, locate papers via libraries and/or websites, and learn about key works in "any area of research."[62,63] In many research library environments, it is also being used as a discovery system. (How effective is Google Scholar? It has been a matter of controversy, with some studies suggesting that Google Scholar's coverage was substandard, but a recent study found that "as regards strict scientific impact, the analysis of GS data provides very similar results to the results obtained from traditional citation-based databases, with the advantage of being able to retrieve a larger and more varied number of citations, since they come from a wider range of document types, different geographical environments, and languages different to English."[64,65])

In addition, owing to the considerable efforts of archivists, curators, and scholars, there is a large and constantly expanding body of primary source materials available via the Web. Well-established projects like the American Memory Project at the Library of Congress continue to grow in terms of the number of collections available and the availability of collateral services.

The American Memory Project draws upon the collections of the Library of Congress and other institutions to provide "a digital record of American history and creativity."[66] In the process, materials to which access had previously been highly limited have become available to the general public, in most instances accompanied by expert commentary. An early contribution to the American Memory Project concerning poet Walt Whitman and his notebooks is a good case in point. Conceived as a "test bed" for digital preservation and making collections available via the World Wide Web, digital facsimiles of four of Whitman's notebooks, including a notebook that contains early drafts of segments of *The Leaves of Grass*, were rendered and made accessible via Web in a presentation entitled *Poet at Work: Recovered Notebooks* from the Thomas Biggs Harned Walt Whitman Collection.[67] The significance of *Poet at Work: Recovered Notebooks* may be expressed on many levels, but it may be sufficient to say that in making available a body of material that has previously been available only to credentialed Whitman scholars, the American Memory Project changed forever the relationship between the Library of Congress and library users and that the World Wide Web served not only as the medium of presentation but also as an agent of change in a process that has brought the Library of Congress substantially closer to the goal of "serving the public as a resource for education and lifelong learning."

Many newer projects are distinguished not only by their original content but also by their use of newer, interactive technologies; for example, the Georgia Virtual History Project is dedicated to recording the history of the state in digital forms and making those records available via the Web to "multiple audiences," ranging from middle school students and the general public to college students and scholars.[68] Another example is the eHistory website, as developed by the University of Georgia's Center for Virtual History. eHistory was founded in 2011 by two historians in the belief that digital technologies afford new forms of research, in which students, scholars, and members of the public may act as collaborators. Like sites that call on "citizen scientists" and to gather and analyze data, eHistory projects involve "citizen historians" in amassing and analyzing historical data. The creators of eHistory that what has been labeled "citizen history," often better reflects the way knowledge is created and consumed in the digital era.[69]

The Web, or, to be more precise, the audience that the World Wide Web brings, has been the impetus for a series of scanning/content preservation projects, ranging from the controversial Google Books project to JSTOR to the Internet Archive. And the World Wide Web is also changing the form of the journal article, as publishers move from the PDF format to composite document formats based in significant part on HTML5. What Elsevier has dubbed the "article of the future" is a good example of widespread efforts to deploy "better ways to create and deliver the formal published record" by taking advantage of the expressive possibilities manifest in the continuing improvement markup and scripting languages.[70]

GENERAL EFFECTS OF THE WORLD WIDE WEB

Technological Impact

The technological impact of the World Wide Web begins with the fact that Berners-Lee constructed a hypertext system based on open standards and capable of running in networked environments. It ends, for the time being, with the ongoing development of the Semantic Web and the emergence of compound documents within a multimodal "interaction domain." It encompasses the development of an increasingly sophisticated system for structuring and formatting digital documents within an open technical framework and the creation of languages that define, respectively, concepts and relationships within domains of knowledge—the Web Ontology Language (OWL)—and establish a functional basis for statements, in the form of triples, for example, (Subject, Predicate, Object) or (Subject, Property, Value), linking data in order to describe both concepts and objects, the Resource Description Framework (RDF).[71]

On another level, the World Wide Web has changed expectations in regard to computing and networking, to the point that with the rise of so-called cloud computing, the notion of the Web as a computing environment has taken on genuine meaning, in the form of myriad services, ranging from cloud storage services such Google Drive to productivity software like Microsoft's Office 365.

Social and Cultural Effects

The social and cultural effects of the World Wide Web are many, but perhaps the most pronounced have been observed in publishing, information retrieval, and collaborative work. Simply put, the Web has changed the meaning of the word "publish," providing new and breathtakingly broad connotations and linking traditional forms of publication, such as book, newspapers, and journals, with blogs and wikis.

According to research conducted by the Pew Research Center, 14% of the adult population in the United States used the Internet. In 2014, 81% of U.S. adults use laptop and desktop computers somewhere in their lives, 87% of the adults in the United States use the Internet, and 73% use social media, a pattern of growth that Pew's researchers attribute largely to the growth and popularity of the Web and the emergence of more interactive formats within the framework of the Web. In the so-called second generation of the Web, users have taken an increasingly active role. Almost all users are now able to "'create new content, share it, link to it, search for it, tag it, and modify it'—Wikipedia, Facebook, Twitter, and YouTube being the most significant, and now classic, examples of this Copernican revolution."[72] The social impact of an enterprise as vast as the World Wide Web is difficult to gauge in the fullest sense, but 90% of the Internet users polled by Pew believe that the Internet and the Web have been good for them personally, 76% regard the Internet and the Web as positive developments for society in general, and two-thirds of them indicated that "online communication has generally made them socially richer."[73,74]

In the realm of information retrieval, the Web has been a test bed that renewed and enlarged interest in information retrieval as a set of complex conceptual problems and procedural issues. At a practical level, the Web has facilitated the development of powerful tools, such as the Google Search Engine, it has placed those tools at the disposal of hundreds of millions of users, and it has created a competitive environment for IR services that virtually guarantees ongoing, vigorous commitments to basic research and development.

In terms of contemporary culture, the Web has altered how people inform themselves. News comes from the websites of CNN, *The New York Times*, the BBC, and tens of thousands of other outlets on the Web. Stock quotes, television program listings, restaurant menus, airline flight information, up-to-date weather information, satellite maps, and the current address of a distant relative or a long-lost friend are all types of information that hundreds of millions of people use the Web to locate and retrieve.

Even language has been altered. In the English-speaking world, "Google" has become a verb. A neologism arising from the popularity of the eponymous search engine, the American Dialect Society chose it as the "most useful word of 2002," and it was officially added to the Oxford English Dictionary on June 15, 2006, and to the 11th edition of the Merriam-Webster Collegiate Dictionary in July 2006.[75] (An interesting side note: Google has actively discouraged the use of the word as a verb, compelling some lexicographers to use a lowercase version of the word in order to avoid legal conflict with Google.)

The Web has also provided an operational as well as social environment consistent with the rapid development of systems for collaborative work, encompassing content management systems, collaborative authoring tools, learning management systems for asynchronous learning, Internet telephony, video conferencing, and resource sharing.

Scientists use the World Wide Web as an environment for providing remote access to and control of scientific instruments; they use the Web as the medium for grid-based architectures that combine entail parallel distributed computation, distributed data management and archiving, and interactive integrated visualization tools in support of their research.[76]

Today, as "cyberinfrastructures" designed for research and development emerge, the focus of development in systems for computer-supported cooperative work is shifting to knowledge sharing within collaborative frameworks and building shared work environments that incorporate the ontological schema and services of the

Semantic Web. However, to date, the most significant collaborative project to be hosted by the Web is Wikipedia.

Wikipedia has created a remarkable amount of controversy, but it also stands as witness to the equally remarkable social forces that the Web has unleashed. It may not have been Jimmy Wales's aim to stand H.G. Wells notion of the "world brain" on its head, but Wikipedia and its many allied projects have demonstrated the reach of digital volunteerism and have shattered, perhaps forever, the myth that valuable knowledge resides mainly within universities.[77] The Wikipedia model will undoubtedly undergo many modifications in the years ahead, some of them intended to bring collaborative models for building knowledge resources closer to the technocratic control that Wells envisioned, but no matter what happens in the future, the Wikipedia of the early twenty-first century will be remembered as revolutionary in nature and effect, because it has changed the way in which we think about encyclopedias and how they are made.

THE FUTURE OF THE WORLD WIDE WEB

When contemplating the future of the World Wide Web, it is necessary to consider what we actually know and understand about the system in its many dimensions and manifestations. Not long ago, it was argued that "[d]espite the Web's great success as a technology and the significant amount of computing infrastructure on which it is built, it remains, as an entity, surprisingly unstudied."[78] That state of affairs has changed markedly in recent years, to the extent that many studies have been conducted and published, resulting in a plethora of data. However, what we know or understand about the Web, and particularly in reference to the Web as a social machine, remains limited and ultimately inadequate. In *Weaving the Web*, Berners-Lee "hypothesized that the architectural design of the Web would allow developers, and thus end users, to use computer technology to help provide the management function for social systems as they were realized online."[79] In view of the fact that the success or failure of Web technologies often depends more on social factors than it does on technological issues, it may be argued that the ability to design and deploy successful applications requires a significantly better understanding of the features and functions of the social aspects of the systems.

At a technical level, the future of the World Wide Web is well defined, at least in the near term, by HTML5 and the Semantic Web. Each is an evolutionary extension of the World Wide Web.

The Semantic Web is an initiative and a broad area of work in which the semantics of information and services on the Web are defined in order to increase the precision of the results that are delivered to users in response to their queries.[80] The core idea of the Semantic Web is to create the metadata describing data, which will enable computers to process the meaning of things. Once computers are equipped with semantics, they will be capable of solving complex optimization problems.

The Semantic Web is based on Tim Berners-Lee's vision of the Web as a universal medium for data, information, and knowledge exchange and his belief that the existing Web may be so transformed through schemes based on the XML, focusing specifically on shifting the underlying structure of the Web from a vast file system into a huge, integrated database by marking up data and documents by content. From another perspective, the Semantic Web comprises a set of design principles, collaborative working groups, and a variety of enabling technologies. Some of the key elements of the Semantic Web are expressed as future possibilities that are yet to be implemented or realized. Other elements of the Semantic Web are expressed in formal specifications. These elements include RDF, a variety of data interchange formats (e.g., RDF/XML, N3, Turtle, N-Triples), and notations such as RDF Schema and the OWL, all of which are intended to provide a formal description of concepts, terms, and relationships within a given knowledge domain.

Is the Semantic Web inevitable? The answer is yes, insofar as it is the latest expression of humanity's desire to create better tools, because it is the logical next step in the development of information processing and distributed computing services, because its realization will play a major role in driving the global economy of the twenty-first century, and because it will also play a critical role in the development of the systems that are needed to ensure continuing progress in science, biomedical research, and other matters vital to humanity.[81] When will the Semantic Web arrive? The key building blocks—RDF, OWL, etc.—are here already, but it will take some time, perhaps a long time, to annotate and capture the world's information in the appropriate ways.

One of the factors that may speed or delay the arrival of the Semantic Web is the speed with which intelligent applications, software implementing concepts from artificial intelligence that facilitate machine-to-machine communications, grow in operational sophistication. Realizing Berners-Lee's vision depends on an ability to generate and assimilate metadata on a scale and at a speed beyond collective human capabilities, and that process will depend, in turn, on the skill with which software agents (or "bots") are designed and deployed.[82]

There are issues associated with HTML5, too. Owing to the rapid pace of device change and the attendant platform fragmentation—each browser and device vendor chooses what HTML5 features to implement—the deployment of HTML5 is uneven. Software tooling is regarded as inadequate, and many developers are not yet proficient in its uses.[83] Even bigger problems stem from the differences in purpose that troubled the development of

HTML5. Web developers want HTML to become a better application platform, and, even though HTML5 has been approved by W3C, there is continuing concern among developers that the W3C, the organization that made a long and probably ill-advised commitment to XHTML, is neither flexible enough nor future-oriented enough to provide the necessary stewardship.[84]

But the future of the World Wide Web will also be defined by a series of collateral developments and factors. Mobile computing is clearly one of the major factors. A rapidly growing array of smartphones and tablet computers already provides access to a large majority of the Internet's users in the United States, and because the devices themselves are growing more powerful and more sophisticated, this trend is not only expected to continue but to reshape more general patterns of computer (and Web) usage. Gaming systems will continue to play an important role in the future of the Web, as will online video, already a major force on the Web in the form of YouTube and Netflix. Software as a service will serve as a medium for more and more end-user computing, in many instances supplanting the personal computer, and evolutionary changes in the design of operating systems and applications will produce growing amounts of structured information, thus paving the way for more intelligent computing.

In education, the Semantic Web's greatest impact will be in the ways in which data integration influences how knowledge is aggregated, organized, and presented to students. As noted in a related essay

One vision of a well-developed semantic web includes a search feature that would return a multimedia report rather than a list of hits. The report would draw from many sources, including websites, articles from scientific repositories, chapters in textbooks, blog dialogue, speeches posted on YouTube, information stored on cell phones, gaming scenarios played out in virtual realities—anything appropriate that is accessible by the rules of Web 3.0. The report would consist of short sections that coalesce around knowledge areas that emerged naturally from your research, with keywords identified and listed conveniently off to one side as links.

The information in the report would be compared, contrasted, and collated in a basic way, presenting points of agreement and disagreement, and perhaps associating these with political positions or contrasting research. Because the web knows something about you, it also alerts you to local lectures on related topics, books you might want to read, TV programs available through your cable service, blog discussions you might find relevant, and even local groups you can contact that are also focused on this issue. Unlike a standard report, what you receive changes as the available information changes, and you might have wiki-like access to add to or edit it. And because you told your agent that this topic is a high priority, your cell phone will beep when a significant

development occurs. After all, the semantic web will be highly inclusive, providing a common language for many kinds of media and technologies, including cell phones. The net result, ideally, is that you spend less time searching and sifting and more time absorbing, thinking, and participating.[85]

Education will also be affected, perhaps profoundly, by the rise of "just-in-time" learning. Unlike traditional educational models, which are essentially supplier-driven systems that work efficiently for instructors, "just-in-time" learning is predicated on consumer-driven systems that are designed to work effectively for students, making learners active participants in the educational process. The new model focuses on learning rather than on teaching. More to the point, "just-in-time" models achieve their goals by moving from standardized to customized content, from discrete time and place to anytime and anyplace delivery, and from passive lecture models to interactive and applied learning, all of which can and will be supported by the technologies of the Semantic Web.

For libraries and archives, the changes are likely to be many and great, encompassing many, if not all of the trends noted earlier. The decline of the importance of the library as a place is inevitable. Competition for the attention and loyalties of digital information consumers will grow only keener, and librarians who wish to survive and flourish will necessarily adopt new approaches to serving clients. However, perhaps the most profound change before librarians and archivists may well be changes in the form of documents, as new technologies and the continuing pressure to improve formal communications in science, technology, and medicine combine to alter both the form and content of the scholarly (or professional) paper. The result will be the compound digital document, basically a framework for integrating text, multimedia, datasets, and hyperlinks, and those documents will present new, serious challenges across the spectrum of bibliothecal functions. (Librarians are certain to face major challenges in the area of client privacy. As the personalization of Web-based services increases, libraries will be challenged by consumer expectations and forced to confront the inevitable conflicts between the demand for more personalized services and the traditional guarantees of privacy that libraries and librarians in many countries have maintained zealously.)

Finally, the dominant role of the United States in the use and development of the World Wide Web will be somewhat diminished, as continuing growth in China, India, and parts of Africa changes the demographics of the Web's user population and broadens the base of developers and providers. Internet governance issues have become more important and more difficult. A new and potentially more balanced order for Internet governance is emerging, but there are myriad challenges to that new order, the most significant of them being government censorship and surveillance. In the midst of these changes, the stability of the Web will depend, as it has for the last 20 years, on the W3C, the commitments that Tim Berners-Lee has fostered with such great success, and the ability of its leadership, in the midst of change and contentiousness, to maintain a unifying sense of purpose.

REFERENCES

1. Nelson, T. Who invented hypertext, web history, 2016. Livinginternet.Com. http://www.livinginternet.com/w/wi_nelson.htm (accessed December 7, 2016).

2. Friedman, T. The World is Flat: A Brief History of the Twenty-First Century. (1st Picador ed., Further updated and expanded). New York, Picador/Farrar, Straus and Giroux, 314.

3. Owens, T. The PDF's place in a history of paper knowledge: An interview with Lisa Gitelman. The Signal: Digital Preservation. June 16, 2014. http://blogs.loc.gov/digital preservation/2014/06/the-pdfs-place-in-a-history-of-paper-knowledge-an-interview-with-lisa-gitelman/.

4. Worldwidewebsize.Com. The Size of The World Wide Web (The Internet). 2016. http://www.worldwidewebsize.com/ (accessed December 7, 2016).

5. Menand, L. Crooner in rights spat. The New Yorker, October 20, 2014; 84. Academic OneFile. http://go.galegroup.com.pitt.idm.oclc.org/ps/i.do?p=AONE&sw=w&u=upittmain&v=2.1&it=r&id=GALE%7CA387220375&sid=summon&asid=60455c0181308ccb91205f8e03e6e33e (accessed December 7, 2016).

6. O'Reilly, T. What is Web 2.0: Design patterns and business models for the next generation of software. http://www.oreillynet.com/pub/a/oreilly/tim/news/2005/09/30/what-is-web-20.html (accessed September 30, 2005).

7. "HTML5 Differences from HTML4" World Wide Web Consortium. October 19, 2010. Retrieved November 2, 2014. http://www.w3.org/TR/html5-diff/http://www.w3.org/TR/html5-diff/.

8. Berners-Lee, T.; Hendler, J.; Lassila, O. The semantic web. *Scientific American* 2001, 284 (5), 28–37.

9. Shirky, C. The Semantic Web, Syllogism, and Worldview First published November 7, 2003 on the "Networks, Economics, and Culture" mailing list. http://www.shirky.com/writings/herecomeseverybody/semantic_syllogism.htm (accessed December 7, 2016).

10. Anderson, J.; Lee, R. Prospects for the Semantic Web: Overview of responses. Pew Internet Research Project, 2010. http://www.pewinternet.org/2010/05/04/prospects-for-the-semantic-web/ (accessed December 7, 2016).

11. Markoff, J. Entrepreneurs see a web guided by common sense. *The New York Times*, November 12, 2006. http://www.nytimes.com/2006/11/12/business/12web.html?_r=0 (accessed October 2, 2014).

12. Anderson, J.; Lee, R. The fate of the semantic web. Pew Research Center: Internet, Science & Tech. 2010. http://www.pewinternet.org/2010/05/04/the-fate-of-the-semantic-web/ (accessed December 7, 2016).

13. Berners-Lee, T.; O'Hara, K. The read-write Linked Data Web. In Philosophical Transactions of the Royal Society A: Mathematical Physical and Engineering Sciences, 2013, 371. in special issue: Discussion Meeting Issue 'Web Science: a New Frontier' 1987), 20120513-[5pp]. (doi:10.1098/rsta.2012.0513).

14. Berners-Lee, T.; Fischetti, M. *Weaving the Web: The Original Design and Ultimate Destiny of the World Wide Web by Its Inventor*; Harper: San Francisco, CA, 1999; 163.

15. Markoff, J. (2006, Nov 12). Entrepreneurs see a web guided by common sense. New York Times. 12. Retrieved from http://pitt.idm.oclc.org/login?url=http://search.proquest.com/docview/433443158?accountid=14709 (accessed December 7, 2016).

16. World Wide Web Consortium. Annotea Project. http://www.w3.org/2001/Annotea/.

17. O'Neill, E.T.; Brian, L.; Rick, B. Trends in the evolution of the public web. D-Lib Mag. 2003, 9(4), 1998–2002. http://www.dlib.org/dlib/april03/lavoie/04lavoie.html.

18. http://www.factshunt.com/2014/01/total-number-of-websites-size-of.html.

19. See http://www.internetlivestats.com/total-number-of-websites/#trend.

20. See http://afrodigit.com/visited-websites-world/.

21. Boswell, W. How big is the Invisible Web? About Technology. http://websearch.about.com/od/invisibleweb/f/What-Is-The-Size-Of-The-Hidden-Web.htm (accessed October 18, 2014).

22. Total Number of Websites—Internet Live Stats, 2016. http://www.internetlivestats.com/total-number-of-websites/#trend (accessed December 7, 2016).

23. Chrome surges, Windows 8.x falls in September. Ars Technica. October 2, 2014. http://arstechnica.com/information-technology/2014/10/chrome-surges-windows–8-x-falls-in-september/.

24. Trends. HTTP Archive. October 4, 2014. http://httparchive.org/trends.php.

25. HTTP Archive. Httparchive.Org. 2016. The HTTP archive is a permanent repository of performance information, including the size and construction of pages. The HTTP Archive gathers this data from the top 1,000,000 Alexa-ranked websites twice a month. http://httparchive.org/index.php (accessed December 7, 2016).

26. The use of images on the Web constitute a persistent problem. Many images are rendered in the wrong format, many are poorly sized and/or uncompressed, few employ progressive rendering, and many are hosted in multiple locations, thus increasing the risk of additional latency and possible outages.

27. ISO/IEC 23009–1:2014 Information technology—Dynamic adaptive streaming over HTTP (DASH)—Part 1: Media presentation description and segment formats. ISO, 2016; http://www.iso.org/iso/home/store/catalogue_ics/catalogue_detail_ics.htm?csnumber=65274 (accessed December 7, 2016) and, T. Stockhammer Dynamic adaptive streaming over http—: standards and design principles. In Proceedings of the Second Annual ACM Conference on Multimedia Systems, ser. MMSys '11. New York, ACM. 2011, 133–144. [Online]. Available: http://doi.acm.org/10.1145/1943552.1943572 (accessed December 7, 2016).

28. Global Internet Phenomena Report. Sandvine, 2014. https://www.sandvine.com/trends/global-internet-phenomena/and The Broadband Report, Website Optimization, LLC. http://www.websiteoptimization.com/bw/.

29. MARCOM, Sandvine. Sandvine—Global Internet Phenomena. Sandvine.Com. 2016. https://www.sandvine.com/trends/global-internetphenomena/ (accessed December 7, 2016); The Bandwidth Report Us Broadband Penetration In Broadband Report On Internet Connection Speed Trends, Dsl, Cable And Dial Up Broadband News. 2016. http://www.websiteoptimization.com/bw/ (accessed December 7, 2016).

30. Everts, T. The average web page has almost doubled in size since 2010. Radware, June 5, 2013. http://www.webperformancetoday.com/2013/06/05/web-page-growth–2010–2013/.

31. Berners-Lee, T. Information management: A proposal. CERN, March 1989–May 1990. http://www.w3.org/History/1989/proposal.html.

32. Hypertext. Encyclopedia of Computer Science; Wiley: Hoboken, NJ, 2003. http://search.credoreference.com/content/entry/encyccs/hypertext/0 (accessed June 10, 2014.).

33. Bush, Vannevar. "As we may think." The atlantic monthly 1945; *176* (no. 1), 101–108.

34. Wells, H.G. *The World Brain*; Methuen: London, U.K., 1938; 34–5.

35. Wright, A. The secret life of hypertext. The Atlantic, May 22, 2014.

36. Barnet, B. Hypertext and association space, time and hypomnesis. Convergence: Int. J. Res. New Media Technol. **2000**, *6* (3), 76–100.

37. Barnes, S.B "Computer-user Interface". In *Encyclopedia of 20th Century Technology*; Hempstead, C., Worthington, W.E., Eds.; Routledge: London, U.K., 2005. http://search.credoreference.com/content/entry/routt/computer_user_interface/0 (accessed June 10, 2014).

38. Bort, J. How Steve Jobs Inadvertently Helped Create The World Wide Web. Business Insider. 2016. http://www.businessinsider.com/howsteve-jobs-helped-create-the-web-2014-6 (accessed December 7, 2016).

39. Berners-Lee, T.; The world-wide web. Commun. ACM August 1994: 76+.

40. RFC 1866—The 'Text/Html' Media Type. 2016. https://tools.ietf.org/html/rfc1866 (accessed December 7, 2016).

41. ISO/IEC 646:1991: Information Technology—ISO 7-Bit Coded Character Set For Information Interchange. ISO. 2009. http://www.iso.org/iso/catalogue_detail.htm?csnumber=4777 (accessed December 7, 2016).

42. SGML was developed by Charles Goldfarb, as part of a project at IBM, and was adopted as a technical standard by the International Standards Organization in 1986. See Goldfarb, C. F. The roots of SGML: A personal recollection. Technical communication. **1999**, *46* (1), 75–83.

43. The cascade in "Cascading Style Sheets" refers to the fact that under CSS elements of more than one style sheet may be invoked in order to format a document. Wium, H.; Bos, B.; Lilley, C.; Jacobs, I. Cascading style sheets. WWW Consortium (September 1996) (2005).

44. BBC News. Technology—Fifteen Years of The Web. 2016. http://news.bbc.co.uk/2/hi/technology/5243862.stm (accessed December 7, 2016).

45. Cascading HTML Style Sheets—A Proposal. 2016. https://www.w3.org/People/howcome/p/cascade.html. (accessed December 7, 2016): Cascading Style Sheets. 2016. https://www.w3.org/Style/CSS/Overview.html (accessed December 7, 2016).

46. Lie, H.W. Cascading Style Sheets; Thesis submitted for the degree of Doctor of Philosophy, Faculty of Mathematics and Natural Sciences, University of Oslo, 2005. https://people.opera.com/howcome/2006/phd/ (accessed December 7, 2016).

47. Dev.Opera—CSS: It was twenty years ago today—An Interview With Håkon Wium Lie. 2014. https://dev.opera.com/articles/css-twenty-years-hakon/ (accessed December 7, 2016).

48. Using HTML Sections And Outlines. Mozilla Developer Network. 2016. https://developer.mozilla.org/en-US/docs/Web/Guide/HTML/Using_HTML_sections_and_outlines (accessed December 7, 2016).

49. Brad, D. Q3 2014 Developer Economics Report From Vision Mobile. 2014. http://appconsultants.com.au/blog/industry-news/q3-2014-developer-economics-report-vision mobile/ (accessed December 7, 2016).

50. Research, G. Gartner identifies top 10 mobile technologies and capabilities for 2015 and 2016. February 24, 2014. http://www.gartner.com/newsroom/id/2669915.

51. The Open Web Platform refers collectively to the standards and specifications developed by the World Wide Web Consortium and its partners, especially as those standards and specifications support the development of new applications and services. For additional information, see "Standards - W3C". 2016. W3.Org. https://www.w3.org/standards/ (accessed December 7, 2016).

52. World Wide Web Consortium. Open web platform milestone achieved with HTML5 recommendation next generation web technologies build on stable foundation, October 28, 2014. http://www.w3.org/2014/10/html5-rec.html.en.

53. RFC 1738—Uniform Resource Locators (URL) (RFC1738). 2016. http://www.faqs.org/rfcs/rfc1738.html (accessed December 7, 2016).

54. Berners-Lee, T. The World Wide Web-past, present and future. J. Dig. Inform. **1996**, *1*.

55. HTML 4.01 Specification. 2016 https://www.w3.org/TR/html4/ (accessed December 7, 2016).

56. Berners-Lee, T. Long live the web. Scientific American, December 2010; 83–84.

57. The Modern Standards Paradigm—Five Key Principles | Openstand. 2016. https://open-stand.org/about-us/principles/ (accessed December 7, 2016).

58. Yambura, B.S.; Alan, B.A.; David, H.G. *Understanding the Web: Social, Political, and Economic Dimensions of the Internet*; Blackwell Publishing: Ames, IA, 2003; 36–37.

59. Mostert, P. TULIP at Elsevier Science. Library hi tech **1995**, *13* (4), 25–30.

60. Prabha, C. Shifting from print to electronic journals in ARL University Libraries. Ser. Rev. **2007**, *33* (1), 4–13. ISSN 0098–7913, doi: 10.1016/j.serrev.2006.12.001. [Taylor & Francis Online], [Web of Science ®].

61. Van de Sompel, H.; Beit-Arie, O. Open linking in the scholarly information environment: Using the openURL framework. D-Lib Magazine **March 2001**, *7*(3), http://

www.dlib.org/dlib/march01/vandesompel/03vandesompel. html.

62. About Google Scholar. 2016. https://scholar.google.com/ intl/en/scholar/about.html (accessed December 7, 2016).

63. Helms-Park, R.; Radia, P.; Stapleton, P. A preliminary assessment of Google Scholar as a source of EAP students' research materials. Internet High. Educ. **2007**, *10* (1), 65–76. [CrossRef].

64. Martín-Martín, A.; Orduña-Malea, E.; Ayllón, J.M.; Delgado López-Cózar, E. *Does Google Scholar contain all highly cited documents (1950-2013)?*; EC3 Working Papers 19: Granada, Spain, November 3, 2014.

65. Mejer, J.; Thomas, C. Google Scholar's coverage of the engineering literature: An empirical study. J. Acad. Libr. **2008**, *34* (3), 196–201; Jacso, P. Amazon, Google Book Search, and Google Scholar. Online **2008**, *32* (2), 53–54; Jacso, P. Google Scholar: The pros and cons. Online Inform. Rev. **2005**, *29* (2), 208–214.

66. Digital Collections. The Library of Congress. 1841. https:// www.loc.gov/collections/ (accessed December 8, 2016); About the American Memory Project. N.p., n.d. Web. 7 Dec. 2016. 66. http://memory.loc. gov/ammem/about/index.html.

67. The Library of Congress. Poet at Work: Recovered Notebooks from the Thomas Biggs Harned Walt Whitman Collection, 1995. http://memory.loc.gov/ammem/collec- tions/whitman/index.html (accessed December 8, 2016).

68. Terry, B. Georgia Virtual History Project. 2016. http:// www.virtualgeorgia.org/ (accessed December 7, 2016).

69. Ehistory—Center For Virtual History. 2016. http://www. ehistory.org/ (accessed December 7, 2016).

70. The Article of The Future. Elsevier Connect. 2016. https://www.elsevier.com/connect/the-article-of-the-future (accessed December 7, 2016).

71. Compound Document By Reference Framework 1.0. 2016. https://www.w3.org/TR/2007/CR-CDR-20070718/ (accessed December 7, 2016).

72. Levene, M. *An Introduction to Search Engines and Web Navigation*; John Wiley & Sons: New York, 2010; Gatto, M. *Corpus and Discourse: Web As Corpus: Theory and Practice*; Bloomsbury Academic: London, U.K., 2014; 207.

73. Faris, R.; Heacock, R. Measuring internet activity: A (Selective) review of methods and metrics. In *Berkman Center Research Publication* **2013**, *22*, 27; The Web At 25. Pew Research Center: Internet, Science & Tech. 2014. http://www.pewinternet.org/packages/the-web-at-25/ (accessed December 7, 2016).

74. Duggan, M.; Smith, A. Social media update 2013. Pew Research Center: Internet, Science & Tech. http:// www.pewinternet.org/2013/12/30/social-media-update-2013/ (accessed December 8, 2016).

75. "Google (verb)," 2016 https://en.wikipedia.org/wiki/Goo- gle(verb) (accessed December 8, 2016).

76. Ellisman, M. Cyberinfrastructure and the future of collaborative work. Issues Sci. Technol. **October 1, 2005**, 43–50.

77. Wells, H.G. *World Brain*; Methuen: London, U.K., 1938.

78. Hendler, J.; Nigel, S.; Wendy, H.; Tim, B.-L.; Daniel, W. Web science: An interdisciplinary approach to understand- ing the Web. Commun. ACM **2008**, *51* (7), 60.

79. Berners-Lee, T. *Weaving the Web: The Original Design and Ultimate Destiny of the World Wide Web*; Collins: New York, 2000.

80. Berners-Lee, T.; James, H.; Ora, L. The semantic web. Scientific American Magazine, May 2001 http://www. sciam.com/article.cfm?id=the-semantic-web.

81. Michael, D. *The Unfinished Revolution: Human-Centered Computers and What They Can Do for Us*; Harper-Collins: New York, 2001.

82. Internet Bots. http://en.wikipedia.org/wiki/Internet_bot.

83. The Evolution of HTML5. 2014. http://www.webrtcworld. com/topics/webrtc-world/articles/375637-evolution-html5. htm (accessed December 8, 2016).

84. Bright, P. HTML5 Specification Finalized, Squabbling Over Specs Continues. Ars Technica. 2014. http:// arstechnica.com/information-technology/2014/10/html5- specification-finalized-squabbling-over-who-writes-the- specscontinues/ (accessed December 8, 2016).

85. Ohler, J. The semantic web in education. EDUCAUSE Quarterly **2008**, *31* (4), 7–9.

World Wide Web Consortium (W3C)

Terrence Brooks
iSchool, University of Washington, Seattle, Washington, U.S.A.

Abstract

The World Wide Web Consortium (W3C) is the organization that leads the development of standards for the Web. Sir Tim Berners-Lee, the founder and current director of the W3C, envisions a linked network of information resources that guides Web standards development and points the way towards the creation of a Semantic Web. This entry describes the pioneering role of Berners-Lee in the development of the Web, the accomplishments and vision of the W3C, and the development of the Semantic Web.

INTRODUCTION

This entry introduces the World Wide Web Consortium (W3C) by outlining the pioneering role of Sir Tim Berners-Lee in the creation of the Web and Web browsers, the development process employed by the W3C community to construct Web standards, and the vision and development of the Semantic Web.

In 2007 the W3C was an international consortium with more than 400 members. Berners-Lee leads a team of about 60 researchers and engineers who are located primarily in three institutions: the Massachusetts Institute of Technology Computer Science and Artificial Intelligence Laboratory (MIT/CSAIL); the European Research Consortium in Informatics and Mathematics, Nice, France (ERCIM); and Keio University in Japan.

The W3C is the leading organization in the development of Web standards and general guidelines for Web development. Its general mission is the development of Web standards and protocols that maximize benefits for the greatest number of people. While the process model of the W3C is consensual agreement and cooperation, it lacks any means to coerce the adoption of its standards and protocols.

Since 1994, the W3C has published more than 90 Web standards called W3C Recommendations. By building applications that comply with W3C recommendations, a Web developer supports the community of users and software that promote the sharing of information and platform independence. Berners-Lee and the W3C can justifiably be credited with inventing the World Wide Web, pioneering the development of the Web browser, and developing the protocols that make sharing information possible.

THE VISION OF THE W3C

The ultimate motivation of the W3C springs from the vision of Berners-Lee for the Web, and has been variously expressed as the W3C motto: "To lead the World Wide Web to its full potential by developing protocols and guidelines that ensure long-term growth for the Web," or more simply "Leading the Web to its full potential..." This vision privileges the notions of interoperability and device independency, and suggests a public network where information can be easily shared among strangers, and is not confined to a specific application software suite or a particular vendor's products. The essence of the W3C vision is that a document or program that follows W3C specifications should work identically across different applications and different computers. To "work identically" in this context means that the essential information or functionality is preserved, while conceding that presentation issues such as the size of the display device, color options, accessibility accommodations, and so on, may introduce variability.

The vision of the W3C is displayed by its future of the Web document[1] which claims that the Web is for:

- *Everyone* (regardless of culture, abilities, etc.).
- *Everything* (applications and data stores, and on devices ranging from power computers with high-definition displays to mobile devices to appliances).
- *Everywhere* (from high to low bandwidth environments).
- *Diverse mode of interaction* (touch, pen, mouse, voice, assistive technologies, computer to computer).
- *Enable computers to do more useful work* (through advanced data searching and sharing).

To complement its advocacy of interoperability and device independence, the W3C also promotes accessibility. Accessibility refers to the degree that application software is sympathetic to people with disabilities, but also in a more general sense, the degree to which applications can be used in environments degraded by noise, lighting, etc.

Encyclopedia of Library and Information Sciences, Fourth Edition DOI: 10.1081/E-ELIS4-120044744

World–Zoological

THE SEMANTIC WEB

Residing behind the W3C's vision of the Web as networked personal and corporate information is the more ambitious vision of the Web as a network of semantics. An early statement of this particular vision of the Semantic Web appeared in the Scientific American.[2] This entry sketched a Web network of publicly available documents that possessed semantics structured as metadata. These metadata were to be harvested mechanically and manipulated by inference tools to solve ad hoc everyday problems such as finding the office hours of the closest doctor, the cheapest available tickets for the theater, and so on. The subtitle of the Scientific American article summarizes this vision of a Semantic Web: "A new form of web content that is meaningful to computers will unleash a revolution of new possibilities."

This original description of the Semantic Web was refined[3] by suggesting the difference between the Web of public HTML documents destined to be displayed in Web browsers, and a web of structured data that would be amenable to mechanical harvest. Theoretically, these two Webs would coexist and even overlap as HTML documents destined for display in Web browsers might also contain structured metadata. An example technology that could be used in this way would be Resource Description Framework attributes (RDFa). Examples of the data that exist on the Web and that could be harvested mechanically might be calendar data, travel arrangements, photograph descriptions, and financial transactions.

The vision of the Semantic Web as a web of linked open data has come to dominate. The result might be called a web of data, where islands of semantics exist; that is, pools of structured documents on the open Web that could be harvested mechanically. Current efforts are now focusing on linking common data points that are related but exist in different semantic islands on the Web. In summarizing the achievements and challenges of constructing the Semantic Web, Ivan Herman[4] gives a voice to the shift of the Semantic Web from a single huge, central ontology organizing all knowledge, which would be unmanageable if not impossible to construct. Instead he described the use of numerous ontologies and vocabularies, such as Friend of a Friend (FOAF) and Dublin Core (DC) that would capture local richness and encourage the discovery of new relationships among data. The challenge of such architecture is linking disparate data points together.

The Linking Open Data project[5] centralizes the increasingly common construction of resources that are available for the mechanical harvest of structured information. The following enumerates some of the structured data available on the Web, which are, in effect, islands of semantics that might be linked together:

- IgentaConnect (http://www.ingentaconnect.com/) offers bibliographic metadata storage and has more than 200 million RDF triplets available.
- RDFS/OWL Representation of WordNet (http://wordnet.princeton.edu/) has 150MD of RDF/XML available for download. WordNet facilitates the browsing of meaningfully related words and concepts.
- "Département/canton/commune" is available from the French Statistical Institute and represents statistical surveys on population, employment, wages, prices, business, economy ,and French national accounts.
- Geonames Ontology and Data has information on 6 million geographical features.
- RDF Book Mashup makes information about books, their authors, reviews, and online bookstores available on the Semantic Web. Information drawn from sources such as Amazon, Google, and Yahoo can be integrated into the Semantic Web.
- dbpedia is a community effort to extract structured information from Wikipedia and link this information to other sources of structured information.

Semantic Web Case Studies and Use Cases[6] list descriptions of systems that have been deployed in industry that use Semantic Web techniques.

HISTORICAL HIGHLIGHTS OF THE W3C

The invention of the World Wide Web in 1989 was a by-product of Berners-Lee's solution to a document sharing problem at CERN (European Organization for Nuclear Research). He proposed a global hypertext project of linked documents to help people coordinate their work during large project development. To manifest his vision he created the first World Wide Web server and the first browser/client called "World Wide Web." This early Web browser was first offered to CERN in December 1990 and then to the Internet at large in the summer of 1991.

During the period of 1991 to 1993, Berners-Lee extended the development of the Web by constructing basic technologies such as Uniform Resource Identifiers (URIs), Hypertext Transfer Protocol (HTTP), and Hypertext Markup Language (HTML). As an early model of community development, Berners-Lee's technological initiatives were modified by feedback from the nascent Web community. In 1994 Berners-Lee founded the W3C at MIT/CSAIL where he is a senior research scientist.

The beginnings of the World Wide Web can be found in the proposal "Information Management: A Proposal"[7] placed by Berners-Lee before CERN's governing board. Its ambition was to solve the information management problems of large projects by utilizing the idea of a hypertext, which had been pioneered by Nelson.[8] Such a hypertext featured human-readable information linked together in ad hoc and unconstrained ways, thus promoting the discovery of hitherto unrecognized parallels or points of convergence among disparate texts.

In September 1992 Berners-Lee gave an invited presentation to the Computing in High Energy Physics 92 conference, where he claimed that the "W3 project merges networked information retrieval and hypertext to make an easy but powerful global information system...W3 now defines the state of the art in networked information retrieval, for user support, resource discovery and collaborative work." In 1993 the CERN W3 software suite appeared in the public domain.

The first W3C recommendation, for Portable network graphics (PNG), appeared in October 1996. Within several years, major recommendations were issued that were foundational for the growth and development of the Web. These included the recommendation for HTML 4.0 in December 1997, which added tables, scripting, and style sheets. These features permitted authors to create significantly more expressive Web content. And in February 1998, the recommendation for XML 1.0 appeared. XML provided a platform for a host of following recommendations and has evolved into a universal language of the Internet.

The following enumerates some of the important historical achievements of the W3C:

- The portable network graphics recommendation in October 1996 provides a cross-platform graphics format.
- The Cascading style sheets recommendation of December 1996 laid the foundation for a uniform strategy for adding style (e.g., fonts, colors, spacing) to Web pages.
- The Web accessibility initiative of February 1997 promoted accessibility of the Web through four primary areas of work: technology, tools, education and outreach, and research and development.
- The HTML 4.0 recommendation of December 1997 added new features to Web publishing such as tables, scripting, style sheets, internationalization, and accessibility.
- The XML 1.0 recommendation of February 1998 introduce the fundamental technology that would become an influential Web standard.
- In August 2000, the scalable vector graphics recommendation introduced two-dimensional graphics and graphical applications in XML.
- XML schema recommendation of May 2001 provided a standard method of architecting XML vocabularies.
- Web services activities introduce a fundamental protocol for Web services in January 2002.
- In May 2003 the W3C adopted a royalty-free patent policy and encouraged the development of open standards.
- Two fundamental protocols of the Semantic Web, RDF and Web ontology language (OWL) were introduced in February 2004.

- In March 2004, VoiceXML promoted the use of interactive voice response applications to Web-based development and content delivery.
- The W3C mission of universal access was promoted in February 2005 with the introduction of the character model recommendation. The goal of the character model recommendation was the ease of use of the Web regardless of language, script, writing system, and cultural conventions.
- The mobile Web initiative of May 2005 set the mission of making Web access from a mobile device as simple as Web access from a desktop device.
- In November 2005, the Semantic Web for health care and life sciences interest group (HCLSIG) deployed standardized Semantic Web specifications for the medical industry.

This historical listing illustrates the foundational role of the W3C in designing specifications and protocols that foster the sharing of information. The culmination of the worldwide sharing of information is expressed in the vision of the Semantic Web.

MEMBERSHIP OF THE W3C

The W3C brings together a diverse group of stake holders to achieve its mission of developing Web standards and protocols. As of 2008 there were more than 400 members of the W3C representing more than 40 countries. Approximately 37% of these members are American and about 9% are from the United Kingdom. The stake holders of the W3C represent many different types of organizations with the largest category being consultants and systems integrators followed by the university research and development category and the general software companies category. Other categories of members include vendors of technology products and services, content providers, corporate users, research laboratories, standards bodies, and governments.

ACTIVITIES OF THE W3C

The activities of the W3C manifest themselves as various kinds of groups. Working groups focus on technical developments, interest groups focus on nontechnical issues, and coordination groups focus on the communication among related groups.

The following is an overview of some of the leading activities of the W3C:

- XML activities represent a core set of technologies around which orbit a number of working groups that are focused on development in the areas of extensible stylesheet language (XSL), efficient XML interchange, XML binary characterization, XML processing model, and XML linking, query, and schema.

- Graphics activities focus on the development of scalable vector graphics (SVG) technologies.
- The HTML activities group works on the evolution of this standard language of the Web. The current goal is to evolve HTML into an XML-based markup language and thereby ease its use with other markup languages.
- Internationalization activities work to ensure that the W3C's formats and protocols are amenable to all of the world's languages, writing systems, character codes, and local conventions.
- Math activities facilitate the use and presentation of mathematics on the Web.
- Mobile Web activities are working to overcome fundamental interoperability and usability problems associated with mobile Web access. They attempt to integrate the key players in the mobile area: authoring tool vendors, content providers, handset manufacturers, browser vendors, and mobile operators.
- Multimodal interaction activities target the ability of Web users to dynamically switch to the most appropriate mode of interaction. Ideally, a multimodal Web application would permit users to input data via speech, handwriting, and keystrokes, and receive output via displays, prerecorded and synthetic speech, audio, and various haptic displays.
- Patent policy activities alert the W3C community about developments in the legal and standards environment.
- Rich Web client activities focus on Web-based applications that extend the user experience on the Web beyond static HTML. Often these applications support compound documents that combine multiple formats such as Extensible Hypertext Mark-up Language (XHTML), SVG, Synchronized Media Integration Language (SMIL), and XForms.
- Security group activities focus on the security context of Web applications that prevent surfers on the Web from being deceived and defrauded.
- Semantic Web activities focus on the creation of a universal medium for the exchange of data. Ideally both personal information and enterprise applications would be smoothly integrated creating a global sharing of commercial, scientific, and cultural data.
- Style activities focus on style components of Web pages. This group is working to extend style to other types of documents such as XML, SVG, and SMIL.
- Synchronized multimedia activities focus on choreographing multimedia presentations where audio, video, text, and graphics are combined in real time. A Timed Text working group is working is designing formats for streaming text synchronized with other timed media.

- Ubiquitous Web applications activities focus on enabling value-added services and business models for ubiquitous networked devices.
- Voice browser activities aim at technologies for capturing and producing speech and managing the dialog between user and computer.
- Web content accessibility initiative (WAI) focuses on accessibility to the Web resources, while the WAI technical group focuses on the technical aspects in three areas: Web content, user agent, and authoring tool accessibility.
- Web services activities promote the technology of Web services as a standard means of interoperability between different software applications running on a variety of platforms and frameworks. This group is designing the infrastructure, architecture, and core technologies for Web services.
- XForms activity focuses on the use of Web forms for the collection and distribution of information.

New areas of interest and activity are incorporated into the W3C by a recommendation development process.

RECOMMENDATION DEVELOPMENT PROCESS

The W3C strives to create high-quality standards for the Web though the strategy of community consensus. The general public is encouraged to join the members of the W3C in coming to consensus of Web standards and protocols. A new development begins with expressions of interest in a topic, and perhaps a workshop that brings interested persons together for the exchange ideas and information. Next, a proposal for a new activity describes the scope and duration of the project, as well as working groups, interest groups, and coordination groups that will carry out the work. As the development work proceeds, candidate specifications and guidelines cycle in revision and review as they advance to recommendation status. This may be a long process that may ultimately lead to a success recommendation, or may result in the abandonment of the proposal. As successful proposals near completion, a W3C advisory committee finally examines the mature proposal and issues a recommendation.

CONCLUSION

The W3C has had a major influence on the creation of the World Wide Web, arguably the most important public information utility of our age. It has taken as its mission the development of the Web in the manner of consensus building with the aim of creating the greatest benefit for the greatest number. As the Web grows in size and sophistication, more and more Semantic Web applications are appearing.

REFERENCES

1. About W3C: Future, http://www.w3.org/Consortium/future (accessed December 27, 2007).
2. Berners-Lee, T.; Hendler, J.; Lassila, O. The Semantic Web. Sci. Am. May **2001**, 29–37.
3. Shadbolt, N.; Hall, W.; Berners-Lee, T. The Semantic Web revisited. IEEE Intell. Syst. May/June **2006**, *21* (3), 96–101, http://eprints.ecs.soton.ac.uk/12614/1/Semantic_Web_Revisted. pdf (accessed June 2008).
4. Herman, I. State of the Semantic Web. In 2008 Semantic Technology Conference, May 18–22, San Jose, CA, http:// www.w3.org/2008/Talks/0518-SanJose-IH/HTML/Overview. html (accessed May 2008).
5. Linking Open Data project, http://esw.w3.org/topic/ SweoIG/TaskForces/CommunityProjects/LinkingOpenData (accessed May 2008).
6. Semantic Web case studies and use cases, http://www.w3. org/2001/sw/sweo/public/UseCases/ (accessed May 2008).
7. Berners-Lee, T. Information management: A proposal, http://www.nic.funet.fi/index/FUNET/history/internet/w3c/ proposal.html (accessed December, 2007).
8. Nelson, T. *Literary Machines*; The report on, and of, Project Xanadu concerning word processing, electronic publishing, hypertext, thinkertoys, tomorrow's intellectual… including knowledge, education and freedom. Mindful Press: Sausalito, CA, 1981.

XML Information Retrieval

Mounia Lalmas
Department of Computing Science, University of Glasgow, Glasgow, U.K.

Abstract
Nowadays, increasingly, documents are marked-up using eXtensible Mark-up Language (XML), the format standard for structured documents. In contrast to HTML, which is mainly layout-oriented, XML follows the fundamental concept of separating the logical structure of a document from its layout. This document logical structure can be exploited to allow a focused access to documents, where the aim is to return the most relevant fragments within documents as answers to queries, instead of whole documents. This entry describes approaches developed to query, represent, and rank XML fragments.

INTRODUCTION

Documents can be structured or unstructured. Unstructured documents have no (or very little) fixed predefined format, whereas structured documents are usually organized according to a fixed predefined structure. An example of a structured document is a book organized into chapters, each with sections made of paragraphs and so on. Nowadays, the most common way to format structured content is with the W3C standard (http://www.w3.org/XML/) for information repositories and exchanges, the eXtensible Mark-up Language (XML).

Much of the content available on the Web is formatted in HTML. Although HTML imposes some structure on a Web content, this structure is mainly for presentation purposes and carries little meaning. In contrast, XML is used to provide meaning about the stored content. More precisely, in the context of text documents, with which this entry is concerned, XML is used to specify the logical, or tree, structure of documents, in which separate document parts (e.g., chapter, section, abstract) and their logical structure (e.g., a chapter made of sections, a section and its title, an article and its abstract) are explicitly marked-up. As an increasing number of documents are being made available in XML format, effective means to access them are needed. As for standard (unstructured) documents, this requires appropriate query languages, representation methods, and ranking algorithms.

Approaches for accessing logically structured documents were first proposed in the 1990s.[1–4] In the late 1990s, as XML was adopted as the standard document format, approaches for what became known as XML information retrieval were being developed.[5–7] Research in XML information retrieval was then further boosted with the set-up in 2002 of the Initiative for the Evaluation of XML Retrieval (INEX),[8] a yearly evaluation campaign that provides a forum for the evaluation of approaches specifically developed for XML information retrieval. INEX provides test collections and evaluation measures, which make it possible for organizations worldwide to evaluate and compare their XML information retrieval approaches.

By exploiting the logical structure of XML documents, the goal of an XML information retrieval system is to implement so-called focused retrieval strategies, which aim at returning document components, i.e., XML elements, instead of whole documents in response to a user query. These focused retrieval strategies aim to break away from the traditional retrieval unit of a document as a single large (text) block. This is believed to be of particular benefit for information repositories containing long documents, or documents covering a wide variety of topics (e.g., books, user manuals, legal documents), where the users effort to locate relevant content within a document can be reduced by directing them to the most useful parts, i.e., the most useful XML elements, in the document.

To identify the most useful XML elements to return as answers to given queries, XML information retrieval systems require:

- Query languages that allow users to specify the nature of relevant components, in particular with respect to their structure.
- Representation strategies providing a description not only of the content of XML documents, but also their structure.
- Ranking strategies that determine the most relevant elements and rank these appropriately for a given query.

In this entry, we provide an overview of "Query Languages," "Representation Strategies," and "Ranking Strategies" developed for XML information retrieval. The representation and ranking strategies presented in this entry were evaluated within the INEX evaluation campaigns.[9–14]

Encyclopedia of Library and Information Sciences, Fourth Edition DOI: 10.1081/E-ELIS4-120043691

Word–Zoological

The entry finishes with some conclusions on XML information retrieval research, and some references to early work related to XML information retrieval.

QUERY LANGUAGES

XML documents are organized into a logical structure, as provided by the XML mark-up. For example, a scientific article, such as those forming the IEEE test collection used in INEX (see Fig. 1), consists of a front matter (<fm>), a body (<bdy>), and a back matter (<bm>). The front matter contains the article's metadata, such as title, author, publication information, and abstract. Following it is the article's body, which contains the actual content of the articles, and is structured into sections (<sec>), subsections (<ss1>), and sub-sub-sections (<ss2>). These logical units start with a title, followed by a number of paragraphs. The back matter contains a bibliography and further information about the article's authors.

Users may want to specify conditions to limit the search to specific XML elements. For example, a user may want sections discussing "XML retrieval evaluation," whereas another user may look for paragraphs about

```
<article>
  <fm>
  ...
  <ti>IEEE Transactions on...</ti>
    <atl>Construction of...</atl>
    <au>
        <fnm>John</fnm>
        <snm>Smith</snm>
        <aff>University of...</aff>
    </au>
    <au>...</au>
  ...
  </fm>
  <bdy>
    <sec>
        <st>Introduction</st>
        <p>...</p>
        ...
    </sec>
    <sec>
      <st>...</st>
      ...
      <ss1>...</ss1>
      <ss1>...</ss1>
    ...
    </sec>
    ...
  </bdy>
  <bm>
    <bib>
        ...
    </bib>
  </bm>
</article>
```

Fig. 1 Sketch of the structure of a typical article in the INEX test collection.

"effectiveness measures" contained in sections about "XML retrieval evaluation." Here we have a combination of content constraints, "XML retrieval evaluation" and "effectiveness measures," typical to information retrieval, and structural constraints, "section," "paragraph," and "paragraph within section." XML query languages have been developed with the aim to express various levels of content and structural constraints. They can be classified as content-only or content-and-structure query languages.

Content-only queries make use of content constraints only, i.e., they are made of words, which is the standard form of input in information retrieval. They are suitable for XML retrieval scenarios where users do not know, or are not concerned, with the document logical structure when expressing their information needs. Although only content conditions are being specified, XML information retrieval systems must still determine what are the best fragments, i.e., the XML elements at the most appropriate level of granularity, to return to satisfy these conditions. For example, the best answer for a query "XML retrieval evaluation" may be a subsection and not a section, as the section, although relevant, may be less specific to the query than the subsection. An XML information retrieval system task is to determine this appropriate level of granularity for any given query.

Content-and-structure query languages provide a means for users to specify content and structural information needs. It is toward the development of this type of queries that most research on XML query languages lies. We can distinguish between three main categories of content-and-structure XML query languages, namely in sections "Tag-Based Languages," "Path-Based Languages," and "Clause-Based Languages." For the latter two types, we provide a brief description, mainly through examples, of current languages, namely XPath and Narrowed Extended XPath I (NEXI), and XQuery and XQuery Full-Text, respectively.

Tag-Based Queries

With tag-based queries, words in the query are annotated with a single tag name, which specifies the type of desired result elements, e.g., a section, an abstract. For example, the information need "retrieve sections about XML retrieval evaluation" would be expressed as section: XML retrieval evaluation. An example of a tag-based query language is XSEarch.[15]

Tag-based queries are intuitive, and have been used in domains outside XML information retrieval (e.g., faceted search, Web search). However they only express simple, although important and likely common, structural constraints. They cannot express, for instance, relationship (structural) constraints, e.g., "a paragraph contained in a section," which may be needed for complex retrieval scenarios.

Path-Based Queries

Path-based queries are based upon the syntax of XPath (XML Path language, http://www.w3.org/TR/xpath), which has been defined by the W3C to navigate to components of an XML document. The most important concept in XPath is the location path, which consists of a series of navigation steps characterizing movements within an XML document.

For example, `chapter/section` is a location path, where `chapter` and `section` are steps that navigate to elements of types "chapter" and "section," respectively. The fact that the steps are separated by "/" means that the location path selects section elements directly below chapter elements. Section elements are referred to as children of chapter elements. The navigation steps can be separated by "//". For example, `chapter//section` navigates to all section elements that are directly or indirectly below a chapter element. Section elements are referred to as descendants of chapter elements. Special steps include the self step denoted "." and parent step "..". For example, `.// section` returns all section elements contained directly or indirectly in the currently navigated element.

At each step, predicates can be specified between "[" and "]", which must be satisfied for elements to be navigated into. For example, the following XPath query `//article[@year=2002]/title` selects the "titles" of "articles" published in 2002, and only those.

An important function in XPath for the purpose of XML information retrieval is the function `contains ()`. For example, the query `//section [fn : contains (. /title, "XML retrieval")]` will return all section elements with a title containing the string "XML retrieval". The result of this XPath query is a set of section elements, and not a ranked list of section elements. Thus XPath is not an XML query language that can be directly used in XML information retrieval. Nonetheless, it is used by, or has inspired, other path-based query languages, some of which allowing the ranking of results, e.g., XXL,[16] XIRQL,[17] and NEXI.[18] We discuss the last one, NEXI.

The NEXI query language was developed by INEX, as a simple query language for XML information retrieval evaluation. NEXI consists of a small but enhanced subset of XPath. The enhancement comes from the introduction of a new function, named about(), which requires an element to be about some specified content criteria. It replaces the XPath contains() function, to reflect that an element can be relevant to a given query without actually containing any of the words used in the query.

A small subset of XPath was chosen because NEXI was not developed to test the expressiveness of a query language for XML information retrieval, but to evaluate XML information retrieval effectiveness. For instance, the parent/child navigation step "/" was considered particularly problematic as it was open to misinterpretation by assessors, and hence was dropped. We recall that in information retrieval evaluation, assessors are used in the process of building a test collection. Their task is to judge the relevance of the information returned to them as answers to given queries. All result elements must have at least one about() function. This is because for the purpose of evaluating retrieval effectiveness, what matters is that the relevant elements are actually returned. For instance, the following query `//section [about(., XML retrieval)]//title`, which requests titles of sections about "XML retrieval evaluation," is not allowed in NEXI; it is indeed a mechanical process to return the title of a section deemed relevant to "XML retrieval."

We finish with an example of a NEXI query:

```
//article [about(. //bdy, XML retrieval)]//
section [about(., evaluation)]
```

This query is asking for section elements about "evaluation" contained in articles that have a body that discusses "XML retrieval."

NEXI was developed by INEX for the purpose of evaluating XML information retrieval effectiveness. It remains the task of the XML information retrieval system to interpret a NEXI query, where the interpretation is with respect to the about() condition as implemented by the retrieval model, and the structural constraint as implemented by the query processing engine, used by the XML information retrieval system. Sections "Scoring Strategies" and "Combination Strategies" describe approaches used to implement the about conditions, whereas section "Processing Structural Constraints" describes approaches used to process structural constraints, for the purpose of ranking XML elements for given queries.

Clause-Based Queries

Clause-based queries for XML information retrieval can be compared to SQL, the standard query language for (relational) databases. These queries are made of nested clauses to express information needs. The most prominent clause-based query languages for XML information retrieval are XQuery (http://www.w3.org/TR/xquery/) and XQuery Full-Text (http://www.w3.org/TR/xpath-full-text-10/).

XQuery is an XML query language that includes XPath as a sublanguage, but adds the possibility to query multiple documents and combine the results into new XML fragments. The core expressions of XQuery are the FLWOR expressions, which we illustrate with an example. The following query is a FLWOR expression that lists the authors, ordered by their last name, that have written at least 100 articles:

```
for $aut in (doc ("aut.xml")//author)
   let $c:=
     count (doc("article.xml")/article
       [author=$aut])
       where $c>100
       order by $aut/lastname
       return
     <author>{$aut/lastname,$c}</author>
```

The for (F in FLWOR) clause binds the variable $aut so that it iterates over the author elements in the document "aut.xml" in the order that they appear. For every such binding, the let (L) clause binds the variable $c to the number of articles from author $aut (from the document "article.xml"). Those author elements for which the condition in the where (W) clause is true are selected, i. e., number of articles is above 100. The resulting bindings are sorted by the order by (O) clause on the author last name. Finally, the return (R) clause creates for each binding $aut and $c in the result of the preceding clause a new author element that contains the last name element of the author, and the associated number of articles.

XQuery is a powerful XML query language. However, its text search capabilities are limited and, in addition, the result is a set of (new) XML fragments; no ranking is performed. Thus its usefulness in XML information retrieval is limited. This has led to the development of XQuery Full-Text.[19]

XQuery Full-Text has been inspired by earlier query languages for searching structured text, e.g., ELIXIR,[20] JuruXML,[21] XIRQL.[17] The added text search capabilities come with the introduction of the *FTContainsExpr* expression, as shown in the following example:

```
//article[./title   ftcontains   {"XML",
  "retrieval"}
  all] // author
```

which returns the authors of articles whose title contains the words "XML" and "retrieval." XQuery Full-Text defines primitives for searching text, such as phrase, word order, word proximity, etc. For example, the following XQuery Full-Text expression:

```
//article[./title   ftcontains   {"XML",
  "retrieval"}
  all window 6 words]//author
```

restricts the proximity of the matched words to appear within a window of six words in title elements.

To support the ranking of results, *FTScoreClause* expressions have been introduced to allow for the specification of score variables. For instance, the following query:

```
for $b score $s in //article [.//sec-
  tion ftcontains
```

```
{"XML", "retrieval"} all]
  order by $s descending
  return  <article title= "{$arti-
    cle/title}"
  score= "{$s}"/>
```

iterates over all articles whose sections contain both "XML" and "retrieval", where the $b variable binds the score of each such article to the score variable $s. These variables are used to return the titles of the articles and their scores in order of decreasing relevance.

XQuery Full-Text does not implement a specific scoring method, but it allows an implementation to proceed as it wishes. In other words, each XQuery Full-Text implementation can use a scoring method of its choice. Therefore, an appropriate implementation of XQuery Full-Text can allow ranking of results. From a user perspective, XQuery Full-Text may be viewed as far too complex, which is one of the reasons the INEX community developed NEXI, a path-based query language with less expressiveness than a clause-based query language, as its query language. A second one was to keep the construction of the test collections manageable, for instance during the assessment task (see explanation on "assessors" earlier in the entry). Nevertheless, XQuery Full-Text is needed in applications involving expert users, e.g., medical domain, patent industry, law.

REPRESENTATION STRATEGIES

To retrieve documents relevant to a query, the first task of an information retrieval system is to index all documents forming the searched collection. The indexing task aims to obtain a representation of the content of documents (i.e., what each document is about), which can then be used to score each document according to how relevant it is to a given query. Classical indexing strategies in information retrieval make use of term statistics, the most common ones being the within-document term frequency, *tf*, and the inverse document frequency, *idf*. *tf* is the number of occurrences of a term in a document and reflects how well a term captures the topic of a document; a term that occurs frequently in a document can be considered a good description of the document content (apart from common words, referred to as stop words, e.g., "the," "every" in the English language). *idf* is the inverse number of documents in which a term appears and is used to reflect how well a term discriminates between relevant and non-relevant documents; a term that appears in all documents of the collection is not good at discriminating between the content of two documents, and hence their relevance or nonrelevance.

With these term statistics, an index is build, for instance in the form of an inverted file, which gives for each term in the collection its *idf*, and for each document containing that term, the corresponding *tf*. Indexing algorithms for XML information retrieval require similar terms statistics, but at element level, i.e., they require so-called within-element term frequency, *etf*, and inverse element frequency, *ief*. The indexing of a collection of documents involves other steps than calculating term statistics. These include tokenization, stop word removal, stemming, etc.[22] In XML information retrieval, the same steps are applied, and other steps such as parsing the XML format, which are not discussed in this entry. Also not discussed in this entry is that an index of the structure is build in order to record the relationships between elements.

In XML information retrieval, there are no a priori fixed retrieval units. The whole document, a part of it (e.g., one of its sections), or a part of a part (e.g., a paragraph in the section), that is, elements at all levels of granularity, all constitute potential answers to a given query. The simplest approach to allow the retrieval of elements at any level of granularity is to index all elements. Each element thus corresponds to a document, and conventional information retrieval representation techniques can be used. Term statistics (*etf* and *ief*) for each element are then calculated exactly in the same way as for *tf* and *idf* but based on the concatenation of the text of the element and that of its descendants.[23]

This is the most common approach. It however raises an issue because of the nested nature of the units forming an XML document: the *ief* value of a term will consider both the element that contains that term and all elements that do so in virtue of being ancestors of that element. For instance, for a section element composed of two paragraph elements, the fact that a term appears in the paragraph implies that it also appears in the section. This "double" occurrence may have an adverse effect with respect to using *ief* to discriminate between relevant and nonrelevant elements.

As a consequence, alternative means have been used to calculate *ief*. For instance, *ief* has been estimated across elements of the same type[24] or across documents.[25] The former greatly reduces the impact of nested elements on the *ief* value of a term, but does not eliminate it if elements of the same type are nested within each other (as it is the case with the Wikipedia test collection used at INEX[26]). The latter is the same as using inverse document frequency, which completely eliminates nested elements. Experimental results[27] indicate that estimating *ief* across documents shows slight improvement over using elements. However, other experimental results[28] show that better performance was obtained estimating *ief* across all elements than across elements of the same types. As of today, it is not yet clear what is the best way to estimate *ief*, whether the estimation strategy depends on the retrieval model and its artifacts used to rank elements, or whether the issue of nested elements actually matters. Further research is needed here.

An alternative to using the concatenated text in an element to estimate term statistics is to derive them through the aggregation of term statistics (both *etf* and *ief*) of the element's own text, and those of each of its children elements.[29,30] Aggregated-based ranking, discussed in section "Aggregation," uses the aggregated representation of elements to rank elements.

A second alternative approach is to only index leaf elements. A leaf element is one at the bottom of the document tree structure, i.e., an element with no children elements, or an element that is considered the smallest possible unit of retrieval. This implies that term statistics will only be calculated for leaf elements, which can then be used to rank the leaf elements themselves. With such strategy, the ranking of non-leaf elements requires propagation mechanisms (discussed in section "Propagation") that combine the score of their children elements into that of the element.[31] Both this and the above (aggregation) strategies overcome the issue of nested elements with respect to the calculation of *ief*.

It has also been common to discard elements smaller than a given threshold (usually expressed in terms of number of words),[23] which are often considered not meaningful retrieval units (they are too small to make much sense as results). It was however argued[32] that although the small elements should not be returned, they might still influence the scoring of enclosing elements, so they should still be indexed, in particular when a propagation mechanism for scoring non-leaf elements is used.

A final strategy,[25,33] referred to as selective indexing, is to only index those element types with the highest distribution of relevant elements in past relevance data. With this strategy, a separate index is built for each selected element type (e.g., for a collection of scientific articles, these types may include article, abstract, section, subsection, and paragraph). The statistics for each index are then calculated separately. Since each index is composed of terms contained in elements of the same type (and likely comparable size), more appropriate term statistics are generated. In addition, this approach greatly reduces the term statistics issue arising from nested elements, although it may not eliminate it. At retrieval time, the query is then run in parallel on each index, and the list results (one for each index) are merged to provide a single list of results, as discussed in section "Merging."

It is not yet clear which indexing strategy is the best, as obviously which approach to follow would depend on the collection, the types of elements (i.e., the DTD), and their relationships. In addition, the choice of the indexing strategy has an effect on the ranking strategy. An interesting research would be to investigate all indexing strategies within a uniform and controllable environment to determine those leading to the best performance, across, or depending, on the ranking strategies.

Word–Zoological

RANKING STRATEGIES

Given an indexed collection of XML documents, the next task of an XML information retrieval system is to return for each submitted query, with or without structural constraints, a list of XML elements ranked in order of their estimated relevance to that query. In information retrieval, retrieval models are used to calculate what is called a retrieval score (usually a value between 0 and 1), which is then used as a basis to rank documents. Many of the retrieval models developed for unstructured text (document) retrieval have been adapted to XML information retrieval to provide such a score at element level (section "Scoring Strategies"). These scores may be used to directly generate the ranked list of elements, or as input to combination strategies required for some indexing strategies in order to rank elements at all levels of granularity (section "Combination Strategies"). For content-and-structure queries, in the context of INEX as expressed by the path-based query language NEXI (see section "Path-Based Queries"), the structural constraints must be processed to provide results that not only satisfy the content, but also the structural criteria of such queries (section "Processing Structural Constraints"). Finally, not all relevant elements should be returned as results, as they may contain overlapping content. This is because of the nested nature of XML documents, which often means that a parent and its child element may both be estimated as relevant, although to a different extent. Some processing is needed to deal with overlapping elements in result lists (section "Removing Overlaps").

Scoring Strategies

Whatever the representation strategy, i.e., whether all elements or only a subset of them are indexed, a scoring function is used to estimate the relevance of these elements for a given query. With the propagation strategy (discussed in section "Propagation"), the scoring function is applied to leaf elements only, whereas in other cases, it is applied to all potentially retrievable elements. Scoring functions used in XML information retrieval have been based on standard information retrieval models, such as the vector space, BM25, language models, to name a few. These have been adapted to incorporate XML-specific features. As an illustration, we describe a scoring function defined upon a language modeling framework inspired by Sigurbjornsson, et al.[23]

Given a query $q = (t_1, t_2, \ldots, t_n)$ made of n terms t_i, given an element e and its corresponding element language model θ_e, the scoring function expressed by $P(e/q)$ is defined as follow:

$$P(e|q) \propto P(e)P(q|\theta_e)$$

$P(e)$ is the prior probability of relevance for element e and $P(q/\theta_e)$ is the probability of a query being generated

by the element language model θ_e, and can be calculated as:

$$P(t_1, .., t_n|\theta_e) = \prod_{i=1}^{n} \lambda P(t_i|e) + (1 - \lambda)P(t_i|C)$$

$P(t_i|e)$ is the probability of term t_i in element e, $P(t_i|C)$ is the probability of query term t_i in the collection, and λ is the smoothing parameter. $P(t_i|e)$ is the element model based on element term frequency (modeling *itf*), whereas $P(t_i|C)$ is the collection model, for example, based on inverse element frequency (modeling *ief*).

One important XML feature is the length of an element. Indeed, it was shown[34] that considering element length is necessary in XML information retrieval to cater for the wide range in element sizes. This can be incorporated by setting the prior probability $P(e)$ as follows:

$$P(e) = \frac{\text{length}(e)}{\sum_C \text{length}(e)}$$

where length(e) is the length of element e. Examples of other XML-specific features used in XML information retrieval include the path length,[35] the type of an element (its tag),[36] and the number of topics discussed in an element.[37]

The size of elements forming XML documents varies greatly. For example, compare a paragraph to a section in a 10-page scientific article. There are likely to be fewer terms indexing the paragraph than the section, leading to a higher chance of a vocabulary mismatch between a paragraph (or any small elements) and a query than between a section (or any large elements) and the same query. In addition, the fact that a paragraph element does not contain all query terms, but is contained in a section element that contains all query terms, is likely to be more relevant than if contained in a section element that does not contain all query terms.

More generally, the context of an element, i.e., the parent, all or some of its ancestors, or the entire document, can provide more evidence on what an element is or is not about. To incorporate the selected context(s) in estimating relevance, the score of an element is modified to include that of its (selected) context(s). The most common technique is to use the document containing the element as context (the document is also an element, albeit a large one, and corresponds to what is being referred to as the root element). This means combining the score of the element to that of the XML document containing that element, where the element and the document retrieval scores are estimated by an XML information retrieval model. The combination can be as simple as the average of the two scores.[38] A scaling factor can be used to emphasize the importance of one score compared to the other.[33] This technique (using element and document scores) has been shown to increase retrieval performance, in particular for long documents, and has been widely used in XML information retrieval.

Combination Strategies

Three of the representation strategies described in section "Representation Strategies" require combination strategies to provide a rank list of all potentially retrievable elements. These combination strategies are propagation (section "Propagation"), aggregation (section "Aggregation"), and merging (section "Merging").

Propagation

The propagation strategy is needed with the representation strategy that only indexes leaf elements. The relevance of the leaf elements for given queries is estimated on this indexing, resulting in retrieval scores for leaf elements. The relevance of non-leaf elements is estimated through a propagation mechanism, where the retrieval score of a non-leaf element is calculated on the basis of the retrieval scores of its descendant elements. The propagation starts from the leaf elements and moves upward in the document tree structure.

The most common propagation mechanism consists of a weighted sum of retrieval scores. For instance, the number of children elements of an element has been used as a weight[31]:

$$\text{score}(e, q) = D(m) \sum_{e_c} \text{score}(e_c, q)$$

where score(., q) is the retrieval score of an element with respect to query q, e_c is a child element of e, m is the number of retrieved children elements of e, $D(m) = 0.49$ if $m = 1$ (e has only one retrieved child element), and 0.99 otherwise. The value of $D(m)$, called the decay factor, depends on the number of retrieved children elements. If e has one retrieved child then the decay factor of 0.49 means that an element with only one retrieved child will be ranked lower than its child. If e has several retrieved children, the decay factor of 0.99 means that an element with many retrieved children will be ranked higher than its children elements. Thus, a section with a single relevant paragraph would be considered less relevant than the paragraph itself, as it is simply better to return the paragraph as returning the section does not add anything more. On the other hand, a section with several retrieved paragraphs will be ranked higher than any of the paragraphs, as it will allow users to access these several paragraphs through the returned section.

This approach, known as the GPX model, has been very successful within INEX, across test collections and retrieval scenarios. Another successful approach, implemented in the XFIRM system,[32] is to define the weight used in the propagation based on the distance between an element and its retrieved leaf elements.

Aggregation

This combination strategy is applied when the representation of an XML element is defined as the aggregation of the representation of its own content (if any) and the representations of the content of its children elements (if any). Retrieval is then based on these aggregated representations. The representation of the element's own content is generated using standard indexing techniques, whereas an aggregation function is used to generate the representation of the non-leaf elements. The aggregation function can include parameters (referred to as e.g., augmentation factor[29]) specifying how the representation of an element is influenced by that of its children elements (a measure of the contribution of, for instance, a section to its embedding chapter). Aggregation is to be contrasted to propagation; in the former, the combination is applied to representations, whereas in the latter, it is applied to retrieval scores.

To illustrate aggregation, we describe an approach based on the language modeling framework inspired from Ogilvie and Callan.[30] There, each element e is modeled by a language model $\theta_{e\text{own}}$ based on its own content. Now assume that e has several children, e_j, each with their own language model θ_{ej}. Let $P(t|\theta_{e\text{own}})$ and $P(t|\theta_{ej})$ be the probability of query term t being generated by the language models $\theta_{e\text{own}}$ and θ_{ej}, respectively. The language model, called θ_e, modeling the element e based on its own content and that of its children, is defined as a linear interpolation of language models:

$$P(t|\theta_e) = \lambda_{\text{own}} P(t|\theta_{e_{\text{own}}}) + \sum_{e_j} \lambda_j P(t|\theta_{e_j})$$

where

$$\lambda_{\text{own}} + \sum_{e_j} \lambda_j = 1$$

The λ parameters model the contribution of each language model (i.e., element) in the aggregation, here implemented as a linear combination. The ranking of the elements is then produced by estimating the probability that each element generates the query (e.g., similarly to the formulation described in section "Scoring Strategies"). The effectiveness of the aggregation, however, depends heavily on the appropriate settings of the λ parameters, whose values are usually estimated through learning methods.

Merging

The last combination strategy is that of merging, which is needed when a selective indexing strategy is used. With this indexing strategy, a separate index is created for each selected type of elements (e.g., article, abstract, section, paragraph, etc.). A query submitted to the XML information retrieval system is run against each index separately, resulting in separate ranked lists of e.g., article elements, section elements, paragraph elements, etc. These lists need to be merged to provide a single ranking, across all element types.

In Mass and Mandelbrod,[33] the vector space model is used to rank elements in each index. Let e be an element and q a query. The following scoring function is used:

$$\text{score}(e, q) = \frac{\sum_{t \in q} w(t, q) \times w(t, e) \times ief(t)}{||q|| \times ||e||}$$

where $w(.,.)$ is the term weight based on within-element (etf)/query term frequency, and $ief(.)$ is the inverse element frequency. To merge the lists, normalization is performed to take into account the variation in size of the elements in the different indices (e.g., paragraph index vs. article index). For each result list, the element scores are normalized with $\text{score}(q, q)$, which corresponds to the score of the query as if it was an element in the collection run against the corresponding index. This ensures that scores across indices are comparable. The lists are then merged based on the normalized scores.

Processing Structural Constraints

We described so far approaches that were developed and evaluated during the INEX campaigns to rank elements given the content condition of a query. Given a query consisting of terms, these approaches deliver a list of elements ranked according to how they have been estimated relevant to that query. As discussed in section "Query Languages," content-and-structure query languages have been developed to allow users to specify structural constraints, e.g., "give me a section in an article about XML technology that also discusses in one of its section book search."

Within INEX, structural constraints are viewed as hints as to where to look to find relevant information. The reasons for this view are twofold. First, it is well-known that users of information retrieval systems do not always, or simply cannot, properly express the content criterion (i.e., select the most useful query terms) of their information need. It is very likely that this also holds for the structural criterion of the information need. For instance, a user asking for paragraph components on "XML retrieval evaluation measures" may not have realized that relevant content for this query is scattered across several paragraphs, all of them contained within a single section. For that user, it may make more sense to return the whole section instead of individual paragraphs. Second—and to some extent as a consequence of the first reason above—there

is a strong belief in the XML information retrieval community that satisfying the content criterion is, in general, more important than satisfying the structural criterion. For instance, even if a user is looking for section components on a particular topic, returning to that user abstract components would still be satisfactory, as long as the content criterion is satisfied.

Two main approaches have been developed to process structural constraints in XML information retrieval following this so-called vague interpretation of the structural constraints in content-and-structure queries. A first approach is to build a dictionary of equivalent synonyms. If, for example, <p> corresponds to paragraph type and <p1>> corresponds to the first paragraph in a sequence of paragraphs, it would be quite logical to consider <p> and <p1> as equivalent tags.[39,40] The dictionary can also be built from analyzing past relevance data.[41] If in such a data set, for example, a query asked for <section> elements, then all types of elements assessed relevant for that query can be considered equivalent to the <section> tag. Thus with this approach, if the structural constraint refers to, e.g., <section>, then any element that is of type considered equivalent to <section>, will satisfy that structural constraint.

A second technique is that of structure boosting. There, the retrieval score of an element is generated ignoring the structural constraint of the query, but is then boosted according to how the structural constraint is satisfied by the element. The element structure and the query structure are compared and a structure score is generated. This structure score can be based on comparing the paths,[21,24] and/or the tags in the paths.[42] An important issue here is to determine the appropriate level of boosting, i.e., how much the initial content-based score should be boosted by the structure score.

The above techniques and their variants are mostly used to determine the relevance of an element according to the content condition and tag-based like structural constraints, e.g., "retrieve sections about XML retrieval." For more complex structural constraints, as allowed by a path-based language such as NEXI, e.g., "retrieve paragraphs about ranking algorithms contained in sections about XML retrieval," a first step is usually applied, which is to divide the query into two tag-based like subqueries, e.g., "retrieve paragraphs about ranking algorithms" and "retrieve sections about XML retrieval." Each subquery is then processed according to its content condition, and its tag-based like structural condition as described in the previous two paragraphs. Each subquery results in a ranked list of elements. To generate a ranked list for the whole query, the two ranked lists are compared, e.g., only elements returned for the "paragraph" subquery whose ancestors are contained among the elements returned for the "section" subquery are then retrieved. The final score depends on the implementation of the contain operation, e.g., a simple set containment, or using fuzzy operators.[43]

Techniques for processing structural constraints were evaluated in the context of INEX, where the relevance of an element was assessed based on content only. In other words, there was no assessment of whether, for instance, a section element was a better element type to return than another element type (if both were relevant according to their content). Also, considering the structural constraints did not usually increase retrieval performance, apart maybe at very early ranks.[44] This result may however be due to the evaluation methodology. More research is needed regarding the usefulness and the impact of structural constraints for XML information retrieval.

Removing Overlaps

We recall that the aim of an XML information retrieval system is to return the most relevant elements for a given query. Because of the nested structure of XML documents, when an element has been estimated relevant to a given query (by any of the XML ranking strategies presented in this entry), it is likely that its ancestors will also be estimated as relevant, although likely to a different extent. This is because the same text fragment can be contained in several elements along a same path (e.g., a paragraph, its enclosing subsection, the enclosing section, etc). Thus the element itself, its ancestors, and a number of its descendants may be contained in the result list, eventually leading to a considerable amount of redundant information being returned to users, which may not be acceptable to them.[45]

The outcome of any of the ranking strategies described so far in section "Ranking Strategies" is a list of elements ranked according to their estimated relevance to a given query, without looking at the overlap issue. XML information retrieval systems may have to decide which elements should be returned from a list of relevant but overlapping elements. Several approaches have been proposed to generate overlap-free result lists. Their starting point usually consists of the list of elements returned as results to a query, which they then process.

The most common approach, referred to as brute-force filtering, selects the highest ranked element from the result list and removes any ancestor and descendent elements from lower ranks. The process is applied recursively. This approach relies on the provision of ranking strategies that rank, among overlapping elements, those that should be selected at higher ranks. However, the ranking may not be appropriate for the purpose of returning the list of the most relevant non-overlapping results. This has led to a number of alternative approaches, where the tree structure of the XML documents has been considered to decide which elements to remove from a list of overlapping results.

In the first such approach,[41] a notion of the usefulness of an element is introduced to decide which elements to remove. Usefulness is modeled through a utility function defined upon the retrieval score of an element, its size, and the amount of irrelevant information contained in its children elements (implemented as the "amount" of text contained in the non-retrieved children elements). An element with an estimated utility value higher than the sum of the utility values of its children is selected and its children are removed. Otherwise, the children elements whose utility values exceed some set threshold are selected and the element is removed.

An alternative approach[46] looks at the distribution of retrieved elements in the XML document's tree structure, in addition to their score, to select the elements to retain. For instance, an element that has many of its descendants retrieved, but which are evenly distributed in the corresponding subtree structure, and in addition has a similar score to the parent element, is selected. This is because already from that selected element, all its descendants, many of which are being estimated as relevant, can be accessed. Otherwise, its descendants are selected to be themselves further processed.

A third approach[47] calculates a new score for each element on the basis of the retrieval scores of its (if any) descendent elements. This is done through a bottom-up propagation mechanism, using for instance the maximum or average operation to recalculate the scores. These scores are used to generate a new ranked list, which is then filtered by selecting the highest ranked elements, and then removing either all ancestors or all descendants of that selected element from the list (e.g., brute-force filtering). The best performances were obtained using the maximum function and removing the descendants.

Techniques that explicitly considered the document logical (tree) structure to remove overlaps usually outperformed those that did not. There is, however, the issue of speed, as the removal of overlaps is done at query time, thus requiring efficient implementations. An interesting question would be to investigate the effect of the original result list (how good it is, and how we define "goodness") on the overlap removal strategy. There are indications that a good initial result list, where good depends on the definition of relevance in the context of XML information retrieval, leads to better overlap-free result list than a less good one.[48]

DISCUSSION

XML information retrieval research is related to work on structured document retrieval. The term "structured document retrieval," which was introduced by the information retrieval community, refers to "passage retrieval" and "structured text retrieval." In passage retrieval, documents are first decomposed into passages (e.g., fixed-size text-windows of words,[49] fixed discourses such as paragraphs,[4] or topic segments through the application of a topic segmentation algorithm[50]). Passages are then retrieved as answers to a query (and have also been used to rank documents as answers to the query). Since 2007, INEX has a passage retrieval task.[51]

Structured text retrieval is concerned with the development of models for querying and retrieving from structured text,[52] where the structure is usually encoded with the use of mark-up languages, such as SGML, and now predominantly XML. Examples of pre-XML/NEX approaches include.[1,3,53] Most of the early structured text retrieval models, however, do not return a ranked list of results. Approaches that were specifically developed for XML retrieval, but still pre-INEX include.[54–57] A survey on indexing and searching XML retrieval is from Luk, et al.,[58] and two workshops on XML retrieval held at the SIGIR (http://www.sigir.org/) conference were reported.[5,7] A recent overview on XML retrieval research is from Amer-Yahia and Lalmas.[59]

Research on XML retrieval significantly flourished since the set-up of INEX, as the latter allowed the evaluation and comparison of XML information retrieval approaches. Nowadays, XML retrieval is almost a synonym for structured document retrieval, or structured text retrieval. In this entry, we described many of the strategies used for representing and ranking XML elements, which were experimented on the INEX test collections. We also described query languages that were developed to access XML documents with respect to both content and structural conditions.

It is not yet possible to state which approaches, whether for querying, representing, or ranking, or their combination, work best, since many factors are involved when deciding how relevant an element is to a given query (e.g., the size of an element, the type of element, the relevance of structurally related elements, the interpretation of the structural constraint, etc.). Indeed, XML information retrieval can be regarded as a combination problem, where the challenge is to decide which evidence to combine and how to combine it for effective retrieval. We can however postulate that considering the context of the element, the size of the element, and the element's own content (directly or using a propagation or aggregation strategy) to estimate that element relevance to a given query has been shown to be beneficial for XML information retrieval. An open research question is the processing of structural constraints, as so far, only limited improvement in retrieval performance has been observed with structure-and-content queries.

The querying, representation, and ranking strategies described in this entry have been developed with the purpose of estimating the relevance of an element for a given query, which is only one retrieval scenario. This may not necessarily be the end task in XML information retrieval. Returning overlap-free results is another retrieval scenario, one where users do not want redundant information (approaches developed for this purpose were described in section "Removing Overlaps"). Another retrieval scenario investigated at INEX is the relevant in context task.[60] This task is concerned with returning the most relevant documents for a given query, and within each document, identifying the most relevant elements. Such a retrieval scenario was identified as important, if not expected, in a user study carried out within a software company regarding the benefit of focused retrieval.[61]

In the relevant in context task, elements from the same documents are grouped together. A system could also create so-called "fictitious" documents, i.e., new documents made from some intelligent aggregation of elements coming from different documents, which is another retrieval scenario, currently receiving increasing attention in information retrieval research.[62] XQuery Full-Text would be an appropriate language for this task, as it allows the specification of new XML fragments to return as results.

Another retrieval scenario, also investigated at INEX, is the best in context task.[60] There, the aim is to identify the one and only best entry point in a document, i.e., the XML element, from where one could start reading relevant content. Such a retrieval scenario makes sense with a collection of relatively medium size documents (e.g., Wikipedia documents used at INEX since 2006[26]).

Although not discussed in this entry, two important issues in XML information retrieval are interface and interaction. Appropriate interfaces are needed to cater for the richer and likely more complex interaction between users and XML information retrieval systems, for example, with respect to expressing content-and-structure queries.[63] Since 2004, INEX runs an interactive track (iTrack) that looked at interaction issues in XML information retrieval.[64] One outcome of iTrack is that users did not like being returned (at least too much) redundant information (overlapping results). This led to the development of algorithms specifically dedicated to remove or reduce overlaps (see section "Removing Overlaps"). A second outcome was that users expected to have not only access to relevant elements, but also the context of these elements (e.g., the document containing, or the parent element of, a retrieved element). This led to the proposal of a table of a content shown in conjunction to the element being accessed[65] or the use of heatmap highlighting relevant elements within a retrieved document.[66]

Information retrieval approaches developed for querying, representing, or ranking are relevant to applications concerned with the effective access to repositories of documents annotated in XML, or similar mark-up languages. XML retrieval is becoming increasingly important in all areas of information retrieval, and in particular in the area of so-called focused retrieval.[67] Current applications of XML information retrieval technologies already exist.[68] An example is that of book search,[69] which is a research track being investigated at INEX since 2007.[70]

ACKNOWLEDGMENTS

This entry is based on two other entries on XML information retrieval cowritten by the author, a book chapter on "Structured Text Retrieval" to appear in the second edition of Baeza-Yates and Ribeiro-Neto,[71] and an entry on "XML Retrieval"[72] to appear in the Encyclopedia of Database Systems.[73] The author would like to thank Benjamin Piwowarski and Anastasio Tombros for their comments on this entry.

REFERENCES

1. Burkowski, F. Retrieval activities in a database consisting of heterogeneous collections of structured text. In 15th Annual International ACM SIGIR Conference on Research and Development in Information Retrieval, Copenhagen, Denmark, 1992; 112–125.

2. Clarke, C.A.; Cormack, G.; Burkowski, F. An algebra for structured text search and a framework for its implementation. Comput. J. **1995**, *38* (1), 43–56.

3. Navarro, G.; Baeza-Yates, R. Proximal nodes: A model to query document databases by content and structure. ACM Trans. Inform. Syst. **1997**, *15* (4), 400–435.

4. Wilkinson, R. Effective retrieval of structured documents. In *Proceedings of the 17th Annual International ACM SIGIR Conference on Research and Development in Information Retrieval*; Springer-Verlag: New York, Inc., 1994; 311–317.

5. Baeza-Yates, R.; Fuhr, N.; Maarek, Y. Second edition of the "XML and information retrieval" workshop held at SIGIR' 2002, Tampere, Finland. SIGIR Forum **2002**, *36* (2), 53–57.

6. Blanken, H.; Grabs, T.; Schek, H.-J.; Schenkel, R.; Weikum, G., Eds. *Intelligent Search on XML Data, Applications, Languages, Models, Implementations, and Benchmarks*; Springer: New York, 2003; Vol. 2818.

7. Carmel, D.; Maarek, Y.S.; Soffer, A. XML and information retrieval: A SIGIR 2000 workshop. SIGIR Forum **2000**, *34* (1), 31–36.

8. Gövert, N.; Kazai, G. Overview of the initiative for the evaluation of XML retrieval (INEX) 2002. First Workshop of the INitiative for the Evaluation of XML Retrieval (INEX), Schloss Dagstuhl, Germany, 2002; 1–17.

9. Fuhr, N.; Gövert, N.; Kazai, G.; Lalmas, M., Eds. *INitiative for the Evaluation of XML Retrieval (INEX)*. In Proceedings of the First INEX Workshop, Dagstuhl, Germany, December, 8–11, 2002, Sophia Antipolis: France, 2003. ERCIM Workshop Proceedings, ERCIM.

10. Fuhr, N.; Kamps, J.; Lalmas, M.; Malik, S.; Trotman, A., Eds. Focused Access to XML Documents, 6th International Workshop of the Initiative for the Evaluation of XML Retrieval, INEX 2007, Dagstuhl Castle, Germany, December, 17–19, 2007, Selected papers, 2008.

11. Fuhr, N.; Lalmas, M.; Malik, S., Eds. INitiative for the evaluation of XML retrieval (INEX). In *Proceedings of the Second INEX Workshop*, Dagstuhl, Germany, December, 15–17, 2003, 2004.

12. Fuhr, N.; Lalmas, M.; Malik, S.; Kazai G., Eds. Advances in XML information retrieval and evaluation. In Fourth Workshop of the INitiative for the Evaluation of XML Retrieval (INEX 2005). 2006; Vol. 3977 of Lecture Notes in Computer Science Springer-Verlag.

13. Fuhr, N.; Lalmas, M.; Malik, S.; Szlávik, Z., Eds. Advances in XML information retrieval. In Third International Workshop of the Initiative for the Evaluation of XML Retrieval, INEX 2004, Dagstuhl Castle, Germany, December, 6–8, 2004, Revised selected papers, 2005; Vol. 3493 of Lecture Notes in Computer Science, Springer.

14. Fuhr, N.; Lalmas, M.; Trotman, A., Eds. Comparative evaluation of XML information retrieval systems. In 5th International Workshop of the Initiative for the Evaluation of XML Retrieval, INEX 2006, 2007; Vol. 4518 of Lecture Notes in Computer Science, Springer-Verlag.

15. Cohen, S.; Mamou, J.; Kanza, Y.; Sagiv, Y. XSEarch: A semantic search engine for XML. In 29th International Conference on Very Large Data Bases, Berlin, Germany; 2003; 45–56.

16. Theobald, A.; Weikum, G. The index-based XXL search engine for querying XML data with relevance ranking. In EDBT, 2002; Springer-Verlag: London, U.K.; 477–495.

17. Fuhr, N.; Grossjohann, K. XIRQL: An XML query language based on information retrieval concepts. ACM Trans. Inform. Syst. **2004**, *22* (2), 313–356.

18. Trotman, A.; Sigurbjornsson, B. Narrowed extended Xpath I (NEXI). In Advances in XML Information Retrieval, Third International Workshop of the Initiative for the Evaluation of XML Retrieval, INEX 2004, Dagstuhl Castle, Germany, Revised selected papers, 2005; 16–40.

19. Amer-Yahia, S.; Botev, C.; Dörre, J.; Shanmugasundaram, J. Full-text extensions explained. IBM Syst. J. **2006**, *45* (2), 335–352.

20. Chinenyanga, T.T.; Kushmerick, N. Expressive retrieval from XML documents. In 24th Annual International ACM SIGIR Conference on Research and Development in Information Retrieval, New Orleans, LA, 2001; 163–171.

21. Carmel, D.; Maarek, Y.; Mandelbrod, M.; Mass, Y.; Soffer, A. Searching XML documents via XML fragments. In 26th Annual International ACM SIGIR Conference on Research and Development in Information Retrieval, Toronto, ON, Canada, 2003; 151–158.

22. Manning, C.; Raghavan, P.; Schutze, H., Eds. *Introduction to Information Retrieval*; Cambridge University Press: Cambridge, U.K., 2008.

23. Sigurbjornsson, B.; Kamps, J.; de Rijke, M. An element-based approach to XML retrieval. In Proceedings INEX 2003 Workshop, Schloss Dagstuhl, Germany, 2004; 19–26.

24. Theobald, M.; Schenkel, R.; Weikum, G. TopX and XXL at INEX 2005. In Advances in XML Information Retrieval and Evaluation, 4th International Workshop of the Initiative for the Evaluation of XML Retrieval, INEX 2005, Dagstuhl Castle, Germany, Revised selected papers, 2006; 282–295.

25. Clarke, C. Controlling overlap in content-oriented XML retrieval. In 28th Annual International ACM SIGIR Conference on Research and Development in Information Retrieval, Salvador, Brazil, 2005; 314–321.

26. Denoyer, L.; Gallinari, P. The Wikipedia XML corpus. SIGIR Forum **2006**, *40* (1), 64–69.

27. Ramírez, G. Structural features in XML retrieval, Ph.D. thesis, University of Amsterdam: Amsterdam, the Netherlands, 2007.

28. Broschart, A.; Schenkel, R.; Theobald, M.; Weikum, G. TopX @ INEX 2007. In Focused access to XML documents, 6th International Workshop of the Initiative for the Evaluation of XML Retrieval, INEX 2007, Dagstuhl Castle, Germany, Selected papers, 2008.

29. Gövert, N.; Abolhassani, M.; Fuhr, N.; Grossjohann, K. Content-oriented XML retrieval with HyRex. In First Workshop of the INitiative for the Evaluation of XML Retrieval (INEX), Schloss Dagstuhl, Germany, 2002; 26–32.

30. Ogilvie, P.; Callan, J. Hierarchical language models for XML component retrieval. In Advances in XML Information Retrieval, Third International Workshop of the Initiative for the Evaluation of XML Retrieval, INEX 2004, Dagstuhl Castle, Germany, Revised Selected Papers, 2005; 224–237.

31. Geva, S. GPX—gardens point XML IR at INEX 2005. In Advances in XML Information Retrieval and Evaluation, 4th International Workshop of the Initiative for the Evaluation of XML Retrieval, INEX 2005, Dagstuhl Castle, Germany, Revised selected papers, 2006; 240–253.

32. Sauvagnat, K.; Hlaoua, L.; Boughanem, M. XFIRM at INEX 2005: Ad-hoc and relevance feedback tracks. In Advances in XML Information Retrieval and Evaluation, 4th International Workshop of the Initiative for the Evaluation of XML Retrieval, INEX 2005, Dagstuhl Castle, Germany, Revised selected papers, 2006; 88–103.

33. Mass, Y.; Mandelbrod, M. Component ranking and automatic query refinement for XML retrieval. In Advances in XML Information Retrieval, Third International Workshop of the Initiative for the Evaluation of XML Retrieval, INEX 2004, Dagstuhl Castle, Germany, Revised selected papers, 2005; 73–84.

34. Kamps, J.; de Rijke, M.; Sigurbjörnsson, B. Length normalization in XML retrieval. In 27th Annual International ACM SIGIR Conference on Research and Development in Information Retrieval, Sheffield, U.K., 2004; 80–87.

35. Huang, F.; Watt, S.; Harper, D.; Clark, M. Compact representations in XML retrieval. In Comparative Evaluation of XML Information Retrieval Systems, 5th International Workshop of the Initiative for the Evaluation of XML Retrieval, INEX 2006, Dagstuhl Castle, Germany, Revised and selected papers, 2006; 64–72.

36. Gery, M.; Largeron, C.; Thollard, F. Probabilistic document model integrating XML structure. In INEX 2007 Pre-Proceedings, 2007; 139–149.

37. Ashoori, E.; Lalmas, M.; Tsikrika, T. Examining topic shifts in content-oriented XML retrieval. Int. J. Dig. Libr. 2007, 8 (1), 39–60.

38. Arvola, P.; Junkkari, M.; Kekäläinen, J. Generalized contextualization method for XML information retrieval. In ACM CIKM International Conference on Information and Knowledge Management, Bremen, Germany, 2005; 20–27.

39. Mass, Y.; Mandelbrod, M. Retrieving the most relevant XML Components. In INEX 2003 Proceedings, 2003; 53–58.

40. Sauvagnat, K.; Boughanem, M.; Chrisment, C. Answering content and structure-based queries on XML documents using relevance propagation. Inform. Sys. 2006, 31 (7), 621–635.

41. Mihajlovic, V.; Ramírez, G.; Westerveld, T.; Hiemstra, D.; Blok, H.E.; de Vries, A. TIJAH scratches INEX 2005: Vague element selection, image search, overlap, and relevance feedback. In Advances in XML Information Retrieval and Evaluation, 4th International Workshop of the Initiative for the Evaluation of XML Retrieval, INEX 2005, Dagstuhl Castle, Germany, Revised selected papers, 2006; 72–87.

42. van Zwol, R. B^3-SDR and effective use of structural hints. In Advances in XML Information Retrieval and Evaluation, 4th International Workshop of the Initiative for the Evaluation of XML Retrieval, INEX 2005, Dagstuhl Castle, Germany, Revised selected papers, 2006; 146–160.

43. Vittaut, J.-N.; Piwowarski, B.; Gallinari, P. An algebra for structured queries in Bayesian networks. In Advances in XML Information Retrieval, Third International Workshop of the Initiative for the Evaluation of XML Retrieval, INEX 2004, Dagstuhl Castle, Germany, December 6–8, 2004; Revised selected papers, 2004; 100–112.

44. Trotman, A.; Lalmas, M. Why structural hints in queries do not help XML retrieval. In 29th Annual International ACM SIGIR Conference on Research and Development in Information Retrieval, Seattle, WA, 2006; 711–712.

45. Tombros, A.; Malik, S.; Larsen, B. Report on the INEX 2004 interactive track. SIGIR Forum 2005, 39 (1), 43–49.

46. Mass, Y.; Mandelbrod, M. Using the INEX environment as a test bed for various user models for XML retrieval. In Advances in XML Information Retrieval and Evaluation, 4th International Workshop of the Initiative for the Evaluation of XML Retrieval, INEX 2005, Dagstuhl Castle, Germany, Revised Selected Papers, 2006; 187–195.

47. Popovici, E.; Ménier, G.; Marteau, P.-F. SIRIUS XML IR system at INEX 2006: Approximate matching of structure and textual content. In Comparative Evaluation of XML Information Retrieval Systems, 5th International Workshop of the Initiative for the Evaluation of XML Retrieval, INEX 2006, Dagstuhl Castle, Germany, Revised and selected papers, 2007; 185–199.

48. Ashoori, E. Using topic shifts in content-oriented XML retrieval, Ph.D. thesis; University of London: Queen Mary, 2009.

49. Callan, J. Passage-level evidence in document retrieval. In Proceedings of the 17th Annual International ACM SIGIR Conference on Research and Development in Information Retrieval; Springer-Verlag: New York, Inc., 1994; 302–310.

50. Hearst, M. TextTiling: Segmenting text into multi-paragraph subtopic passages. Comput. Linguist. 1997, 23 (1), 33–64.

51. Kamps, J.; Pehcevski, J.; Kazai, G.; Lalmas, M.; Robertson, S. INEX 2007 evaluation metrics. In Focused Access to XML Documents, 6th International Workshop of the Initiative for the Evaluation of XML Retrieval, INEX 2007, Dagstuhl Castle, Germany, Selected papers, 2008.

52. Baeza-Yates, R.A.; Navarro, G. Integrating contents and structure in text retrieval. SIGMOD Rec. 1996, 25 (1), 67–79.

53. Macleod, I. Storage and retrieval of structured documents. Inform. Process. Manage. 1990, 26 (2), 197–208.

54. Chiaramella, Y.; Mulhem, P.; Fourel, F. A model for multimedia information retrieval, Tech. rep, University of Glasgow: Glasgow, U.K., 1996.

Word–Zoological

55. Lalmas, M. Dempster-shafer's theory of evidence applied to structured documents: Modelling uncertainty. In 20th Annual International ACM SIGIR Conference on Research and Development in Information Retrieval, Philadelphia, PA, 1997; 110–118.

56. Rölleke, T.; Lalmas, M.; Kazai, G.; Ruthven, I.; Quicker, S. The accessibility dimension for structured document retrieval. In Advances in Information Retrieval, 24th BCS-IRSG European Colloquium on IR Research, Glasgow, U.K., 2002; 284–302.

57. Schlieder, T.; Meuss, M. Result ranking for structured queries against xml documents. In DELOS Workshop: Information Seeking, Searching and Querying in Digital Libraries, Zurich, Switzerland, 2000.

58. Luk, R.P.; Leong, H.V.; Dillon, T.; Chan, A.S.; Croft, W. B.; Allan, J. A survey in indexing and searching XML documents. J. Am. Soc. Inform. Sci. Technol. **2002**, *53* (6), 415–437.

59. Amer-Yahia, S.; Lalmas, M. XML search: Languages, INEX and scoring. SIGMOD Rec. **2006**, *35* (4), 16–23.

60. Malik, S.; Trotman, A.; Lalmas, M.; Fuhr, N. Overview of INEX 2006. In Comparative Evaluation of XML Information Retrieval Systems, 5th International Workshop of the Initiative for the Evaluation of XML Retrieval, INEX 2006, Dagstuhl Castle, Germany, December, 17–20, 2006; Revised and selected papers, 2007; 1–11.

61. Betsi, S.; Lalmas, M.; Tombros, A.; Tsikrika, T. User expectations from XML element retrieval. In 29th Annual International ACM SIGIR Conference on Research and Development in Information Retrieval, Seattle, WA, 2006; 611–612.

62. Lalmas, M.; Murdock, V., Eds. ACM SIGIR Workshop on Aggregated Search. Singapore, 2008.

63. Zwol, R.; Baas, J.; van Oostendorp, H.; Wiering, F. Bricks: The building blocks to tackle query formulation in structured document retrieval. In Advances in Information Retrieval, 28th European Conference on IR Research, ECIR 2006, London, U.K., 2006; 314–325.

64. Tombros, A.; Larsen, B.; Malik, S. The interactive track at INEX 2004. In Advances in XML Information Retrieval, Third International Workshop of the Initiative for the Evaluation of XML Retrieval, INEX 2004, Dagstuhl Castle, Germany, Revised selected papers, 2005; 410–423.

65. Szlávik, Z.; Tombros, A.; Lalmas, M. Feature- and query-based table of contents generation for xml documents. In Advances in Information Retrieval, 29th European Conference on IR Research, ECIR 2007, Rome, Italy, April, 2–5, 2007; 456–467.

66. Kamps, J.; Koolen, M.; Sigurbjörnsson, B. Filtering and clustering XML retrieval results. In Comparative Evaluation of XML Information Retrieval Systems, 5th International Workshop of the Initiative for the Evaluation of XML Retrieval, INEX 2006, Dagstuhl Castle, Germany, Revised and Selected Papers, 2006; 121–136.

67. Trotman, A.; Geva, S.; Kamps, J. Report on the SIGIR 2007 workshop on focused retrieval. SIGIR Forum **2007**, *41* (2), 97–103.

68. Pharo, N.; Trotman, A. The use case track at INEX 2006. SIGIR Forum **2007**, *41* (1), 64–66.

69. Kantor, P.B.; Kazai, G.; Milic-Frayling, N.; Wilkinson, R., Eds. Proceedings of the 2008 ACM Workshop on Research Advances in Large Digital Book Repositories, BooksOnline 2008, Napa Valley, CA, October, 30, 2008, 2008, ACM.

70. Kazai, G.; Doucet, A. Overview of the INEX 2007 book search track (BookSearch '07). SIGIR Forum **2008**, *42* (1), 2–15.

71. Baeza-Yates, R.A.; Ribeiro-Neto, B. *Modern Information Retrieval*; ACM Press/Addison-Wesley: New York, 1999.

72. Lalmas, M.; Trotman, A. XML retrieval. In *Encyclopedia of Database Systems*; Ozsu, M.; Liu, L., Eds. Springer, 2009. At press.

73. Ozsu, M.; Liu, L., Eds. *Encyclopedia of Database Systems*; Springer, 2009. At press.

Young Adult Library Services Association (YALSA)

Marjorie Lewis
Canaan, New York, U.S.A.

Abstract

As part of the continuum of total library service of the American Library Association, the Young Adult Library Services Association (YALSA) is a specific division which mission is to advocate, promote, and strengthen service to young adults ages 12 through 18. The Young Adult Library Services Association celebrated its 50th anniversary in 2007 with, still, a high energy that has drawn to it a wide variety of members: librarians, youth advocates, and publishers. These members participate through the division's many committees and other activities such as publishing, special initiatives, and continuing education activities. The five decades of its existence have been marked by profound alterations in attitudes toward young people in new kinds of media and technology as well as in changes in society. The division continues to note these changes and adds and subtracts where needed. It is a division proud of its abilities not only to keep up but to lead.

INTRODUCTION

As part of the continuum of and commitment to total library service by the American Library Association (ALA), the Young Adult Services Association (YALSA) is a specific division which mission is to advocate, promote, and strengthen service to young adults, ages 12 through 18. The Young Adult Library Services Association celebrated 50 years of dynamism and creativity in 2007. It is now the fourth largest division of the many ALA divisions and its membership is now more than 5600—librarians (both school and public), youth advocates, publishers, and library students. These members have opportunities to participate at all levels of YALSA activities through the division's many committees and other activities such as publishing, special initiatives, continuing education activities, and literary awards. The 50 years of YALSA's existence have been marked by profound alterations in societal attitudes toward young people as well as enormous and ever-changing technological and media advancement. The division notes these changes and adds and subtracts where needed. It is a division proud of its abilities not only to keep up but to lead.

OVERVIEW

In 1957, the Association of Young People's Librarians, which had been established in 1941, split into two divisions: Children's Library Association (CLA) and the Young Adult Services Division (YASD). Mildred Batchelder served as the first Executive Secretary of both divisions. One of the first acts of the two divisions was to defeat a proposal by ALA to absorb "Top of the News,"

the CLA/YASD publication, into is own "Bulletin." In 1961, when the American Association of School Librarians (AASL) was given the right to evaluate, select, and interpret materials for school use, YASD issued a function statement to clarify its role:

> The Young Adult Services Division is interested in the improvement and extension of services to young people in all types of libraries. YASD has a specific responsibility for the evaluation and selection of books and non-book materials and the interpretation and use of materials for young adults, except when such materials are designated for only one type of library.

In the 1950s, although the assignment of YASD committees to other divisions often occurred, the new YASD division became increasingly visible within ALA. The Young Adult Services Divisions' annual lists of recommended books were produced and reprinted in ALA publications such as "Booklist" and "Top of the News." When the National Education Association asked YASD to create a book list to serve college-bound students, a committee to fulfill the request was formed and the "Outstanding Books for the College Bound" was born. This list has gone through several revisions and is issued approximately every 5 years. The revisions reflect changing users, social climate, and add new titles and subtract titles no longer valid. In the 1950s, another popular publication was "Bookbait" edited by Elinor Walker.

In the 1960s, the division became more visible to the world outside the library world. In 1964, after a successful conference between publishers and librarians, the Publishers' Liaison committee was formed and first preconference was held in New York City called *Two Blocks Apart*. The preconference addressed the needs of

Encyclopedia of Library and Information Sciences, Fourth Edition DOI: 10.1081/E-ELIS4-120044718

Word–Zoological

disadvantaged youth. In 1966, the first attempt to provide guidelines for public library service to young people was published. A Television Committee was also established in the 1960s which created related book lists on request such as NBC's "Teachers' Guide to Television." During National Library Week, in 1968, over 40,000 copies of the book list "Happenings" was distributed published by the Free Library of Philadelphia. At the 1967 Annual conference in San Francisco, YASD sponsored a preconference called *Intellectual Freedom and the Teenager* in conjunction with the Intellectual Freedom Committee of ALA. Another example of outreach to libraries was the availability of attractive and informative slide series showing new approaches to young adult services available on loan to state libraries. The White House Conference on Youth in 1960 included a delegate from YASD, and "Youth in a Changing World" was published and distributed.

In the late 1960s, the ALA Committee on Organization asked the divisions to reexamine goals and activities. Although YASD conducted a membership survey, response was minimal and very little change ensued. They dissolved three committees and formed an Organization Committee to deal with further changes.

The most active committee during this time was the Book Selection Committee that, after several name changes, became the prestigious Best Books for Young Adults committee. The Peace Corps subcommittee prepared special paperback book lists, programs and exhibits, and the Dial-a-Book project at the 1964 World's Fair proved highly successful by promoting one-minute book reviews for young people.

In the volatile 1970s, an invigorated YASD emerged because of a new dues structure by ALA (which had previously given two free division memberships included in an annual membership). The new dues structure allowed the divisions the freedom to operate on an independent basis. In 1975, Evelyn Shaevel, who had been serving only four-fifths time as YASD Executive Secretary, became a full-time staff member. The social changes the country was undergoing were reflected in book lists such as the "Now Scene," one of several new additions to the latest revision of "Outstanding Books for the College Bound." In an effort to add multiculturalism to its list of recommended books, "Richer by Asia" was produced which was funded by the Asia Foundation, and then, with its own expertise, YASD published "African Encounter."

Recognizing the enormous impact of media on young people, a preconference in Dallas in 1971 focused on audio/visual materials, equipment and methods of integrating them into more traditional services. A pamphlet titled "Mixed-Means Programming with Young Adults" was a product of this preconference. The new AV Committee published "Film Profiles for Youth" which emphasized the interest in other media besides books shown by librarians and teenagers. The first cover drawn by teens was featured on the 1974 "Best Books for Young Adults"

list. Also, during that year, an official liaison from YASD was appointed to the Freedom to Read Foundation, and the Publishers' Liaison Committee gathered a list of young adult review sources and sent speakers to regional conventions to talk about young adult books. For the first time, *Top of the News* was available on subscription basis.

Also, in 1974, the Survival Kit Committee produced a list of helpful resources for establishing, promoting, and maintaining young adult services at the local level. In 1975, the Media Selection and Usage Committee established guidelines to create the first annual "Selected Films for Young Adults" list of recommended films. In 1977, the publication "Directions for Library Service to Young Adults" provided guidelines for library service to young adults.

Notable events of the 1970s included the publication of "Look, Listen, Explain: Developing Community Library Services for Young Adults." In 1975, "Book You" was the fourth preconference sponsored by YASD. Participants discussed the titles on the "Best Books for Young Adults" lists of the past 15 years and from them selected the "Best of the Best: Still Alive in '75." This was the beginning of a series of "Best of the Best" preconferences. In 1979, ALA Bylaws were amended to include the election of a representative from YASD to ALA Council.

Even though YASD members voted for a dues increase in 1983, which enabled YASD to establish specific reachable goals and objectives with appropriate strategies to achieve them, YASD did not become self-supporting. Efforts to increase membership continued, however. In 1986, 150 new members were registered after a direct mailing to school librarians publicizing a resolution passed in response to the Department of Education report "A Nation at Risk." The resolution emphasized the roles that librarians working in schools and public libraries play in the personal and educational growth of young adults. Because of scarce financial resources, YASD agreed to participate in an innovative shared staffing arrangement with the Association of Specialized and Cooperative Library Agencies.

To adequately reflect the concerns and interests of the membership, *Top of the News* (TON) was renamed *Journal of Youth Services in Libraries (JOYS)*, and, in 1988, the joint boards of the Association for Library Service to children (ALSC) and YASD made *JOYS* a refereed journal to increase research-related articles and submissions from academia and other scholars.

By the end of the 1980s, YASD's mission statement: "to advocate, promote and strengthen service to young adults as part of the continuum of total library service" was still in use. The division formed new committees to fulfill that mission. They included Intellectual Freedom, Legislation, Selected Films and Videos for Young Adults, Education, Organization and Bylaws, Program Planning Clearinghouse and Evaluation, Recommended Books for the Reluctant Young Adult Reader, Public Relations, Publications, Library Service to Young Adults with Special

Needs, Executive, Budget and Finance, Baker & Taylor/ YASD Conference Grant, Computer Applications, Long-Range Planning, Local Arrangements, Youth Participation, Division Promotion, *School Library Journal* (SLJ)/ YASD Author Achievement Award (Margaret A. Edwards Award), and Membership Recruitment. These new committees, besides fulfilling needs and goals of the division, offered increased opportunities for membership input and participation.

Reacting to the membership's desire to see genre book lists compiled to appeal to the young adults they served, in 1988 five genre committees were established: Horror, Mystery, Romance, Sports, and Science Fiction. Publication of these lists, for distribution to libraries and other venues, was expedited by the ALA Public Information Office and was partially funded by Baker & Taylor. In 1989, two more committees and subsequent lists were created: Fantasy and Humor. These lists were followed in 1991 by the Historical Fiction list.

Lists of publications produced from the 1980s through the 1990s attest to the vitality and active participation of a membership eager to provide the highest quality guidelines and reader's advisory services to young adults and the librarians that serve them. The publications include:

1981— "Young Adults Deserve the Best: Competencies for Librarians Serving Youth."
1981— "Cheap CE: Providing Continuing Education with Limited Resources: A Resource Guide."
1983—"Youth Participation in Libraries: A Training Manual."
1989—"Teen Pregnancy Crisis: Libraries Can Help."

In 1982, grants were established and supported by a variety of funders. The Frances Henne/YASD/VOYA Research Grant of $500 encouraged the research activities of YASD members. In 2009, this grant was increased to $1000. The Baker & Taylor Conference Grant enabled two librarians working with young adults (one in a school library and one in a public library) to attend their first ALA conference. In 1991, this grant was increased to $1000. The Econo-Clad Award (now the Sagebrush Corporation Award) for a Young Adult Reading or Literature Program for $1000 enabled the winner to attend an upcoming ALA conference. It was first awarded in 1990. Another award was established in 1994 by the Book Wholesalers, Inc. A Collection Grant of $1000 is given to two librarians to assist them in the development of the collection of resources for young adults in their library.

In 1985, the National Endowment for the Humanities (NEH) awarded the division a grant entitled "Courtly Love in the Shopping Mall" to present four regional workshops to train librarians working with young adults to design and implement humanities programs. In addition, a preconference based on the grant gave participants excellent ways to start such programs in their own

libraries. The Young Adult Services Division received a supplemental grant from the NEH to support an additional two regional workshops.

In 1986, the Allerton Institute focused on library service to young adults. This conference, although sponsored by the University of Illinois, was partially funded by an ALA/World Book Goal award and was titled "Missionaries and Managers: Library Services to Children and Young Adults in the Information Age." The goal of the conference was to assess the current status of library service to young adults and update goals and strategies for meeting the future information needs of youth. That same year the U.S. Department of Education worked with YASD to survey the accessibility of resources and services for young adults in public libraries and resulted in the first edition of "Services and Resources for Children and Young Adults in Public Libraries." The second edition was published in 1995.

In 1988, in collaboration with the Library Administration and Management Association and the ALSC, YASD developed a regional workshop, "Managing Youth Services," which was offered to library systems as a continuing education opportunity. The two presenters for each workshop were Mary Somerville and Vivian Wynn. This workshop was discontinued in 1991.

A new award was developed that would honor an author for lifetime achievement in writing that had lasting appeal to young adults. *School Library Journal* agreed to sponsor the award on a biannual basis beginning in 1988. The first winner was S. E. Hinton for *The Outsiders*. The award brunch was so well received that the YASD Board of Directors decided to make it an annual event. The award was originally called "The SLJ/YASD Author Achievement Award" but was changed to the "Margaret A. Edwards Award" in 1991 in honor of Margaret Alexander Edwards, a young adult specialist at the Enoch Pratt Library in Baltimore, Maryland, for many years and the author of the young adults services classic, The Fair Garden and the Swarm of Beasts. Information about the award and past winners can be found at http://www.ala.org/yalsa/edwards.

In 1989, the Board of Directors and the YASD Legislation Committee worked on the White House Conference on Library and Information Services II (WHCLIS) developing information packets. The Legislation Committee assisted in writing the paper "Kids Need Libraries: School and Public Libraries Preparing the Young of Today for the World of Tomorrow." This provided the conference delegates with a framework for discussion of issues relating to the improvement of library services for young people in this country. The Young Adult Services Division members and members of other youth divisions as well as other advocates lobbied intensively for the Omnibus Youth Literacy through Libraries Bill as the number one priority from WHCLIS II. When Evelyn Shaevel left YASD to take another position in ALA, the Board of Directors decided to share staffing with the AASL. Ann Carson Weeks was Executive when Susan Horiuchi resigned, Linda Waddle, a former board member, became Deputy Executive Director of YASD. Also, in 1991, the chairs of the Organization and Bylaws Committee and the Budget and Finance Committee became ex officio members of the Board of Directors. The Board of Directors adopted a proposal that the age definition for "young adults" for the purposes of research was ages 12 through 18. Student dues were also approved. In 1992, after several years of study, the YASD changed its name to the Young Adult Library Services Association, and the new name and its euphonious acronym, YALSA, led to increased recognition within and without the library community; its new identity, image, and name brought a dynamic liveliness to decades of tradition.

From 1994 until 2001, activities, publications, and programs proliferated. Presidents of the division identified themes for their terms of service and presented popular programs based on those themes. A new strategic plan was developed and reflected commitments to three areas: advocacy, coalition-building, and equity of access. The Board of Directors provided impetus and leadership to produce a remarkable array of accomplishments as a single entity and in partnership with other ALA divisions such as ALSC and AASL. New book lists were introduced and updated when needed. A speaker and consultant resource directory was created and, also, updated when needed.

During this period, coalitions with other organizations and divisions further integrated YALSA's work into the larger community of youth service. The Board of directors recommended collaboration with Friends of the Library, U.S.A. to develop a database of teen library groups that became the National Youth Participation Database. The Young Adult Library Services Association connected with other young adult advocacy groups through the National Organizations Serving Young Adults Liaison Committee. With other national entities and divisions, YALSA cosponsored events at the Midwinter and Annual meetings and served as consultants to organizations studying youth issues.

Two events marked the 1990s as a period of innovation and energy—Teen Read Week and the Great Books Giveaway, both of which continue to present day. Begun in 1998 as an initiative in collaboration with the ALA Public Information Office and ALA Graphics, Teen Read Week grew exponentially. The overall theme continues to be "Read for the Fun of It," and by its 4th year over 1400 schools, public libraries, and book stores participated. At present, it has more than 5,000 registrants and is sponsored and promoted by sponsors such as Mirrorstone Books, which has given large donations, and various publishers. In addition, World Wrestling Entertainment sponsors the WrestleMania Reading challenge project which challenges teen readers to read one book a week for the ten

weeks following Teen Read Week, with the chance to win a trip to WrestleMania. In addition, World Wrestling Entertainment Teen Tech Week, which encourages teens to use nonprint resources at the library, has joined these special events, and various publishers. The Great Book, Giveaway Competition, another creative project begun in the 1990s continues generating visibility for YALSA and much excitement among participating libraries. Libraries that apply are asked to describe their young adult program highlights and needs. They must also have a Board-approved selection or collection development policy. The latest recipient 2009 was the Lincoln County Public Libraries in Libby, Mont. which received a "ton" of books — a huge collection of materials such as children's, adult and young adult books, videos, CDs and audiocassettes, DVDs, etc. that publishers and producers submitted to YALSA for review by the division awards and selection committees, materials estimated to be worth thousands of dollars. The YALSA office received so many materials that are a second and third prize was given out in 2009. An emphasis on teen participation, so much a mark of the 1980s and 1990s led to the first-time development of teen-oriented products in collaboration with ALA Graphics. Such items as temporary tattoos, posters, bookmarks and water bottles promoted Teen Read Week, and other events. These products and other YALSA services were promoted via the Internet through the ALA Web site.

Publications proliferated through the 1990s and the 2000s with a variety of revised editions as well as new ones. The Young Adult Library Services Association now produces its own quarterly journal (*YALS*), a quarterly email newsletter (YAttitudes) and at least two books a year. In 2008 and 2009, YALSA published The Official YALSA Awards Guidebook, edited by Tina Frolund; Excellence in Library Services to Young Adults, Fifth Edition, edited by Amy Alessio; Quick and Popular Reads for Teens, edited by Pam Spencer Holley; and Cool Teen Programs for under $100, edited by Jenine Lillian.

For the first time since 1981, *Young Adults Deserve the Best: Competencies for Librarians Serving Young Adults* was revised and, in Past President of YALSA Michael Cart's words, aided in "redefining the profession for the 21st century." Book lists selected by a variety of YALSA committees continued to be revised and distributed. Long-lived annual lists such as *Best Books for Young Adults* and *Quick Picks* were joined by *Popular Paperbacks for Young Adults, The Alex Awards, Amazing Audiobooks for Young Adults, Fabulous Films for Young Adults, and Great Graphic Novels for Teens*. Books were made from these lists, including *Best Books for Young Adults* by Holly Koelling, and *Outstanding Books for the College Bound* edited by Marjorie Lewis.

Reading lists to complement the HBO six-program series "Life stories: Families in Crisis" were prepared. *Directions for Library Service to Young Adults* was revised as was *The Fair Garden and the Swarm of Beasts*, the classic by Margaret A. Edwards. Other publications were *Youth Participation in School and Public Libraries: It Works, Hit List: Frequently Challenged Books for Young Adults and Excellence in Library Service to Young Adults*. In the works are Annotated Booklists for Every Teen Reader, Multicultural Programs for Teens and Tweens, Risky Business, and Young Adults Deserve the Best.

In 2007, YALSA won an ALA World Book Goal Award to produce the program "Teens Need Libraries."

In the 1990s, 10,000 generalists and other staff members were trained in order to provide exemplary library service to young adults. The Excellence in Library Service to Young Adults project, begun in 1993, became a triennial event with grants to school and public libraries and a publication highlighting the winning entries. The Young Adult Library Services Association also participated in the ALA conference on Professional Education. Two annual awards were instituted honoring young adult literature the Edwards Award named for Margaret Alexander Edwards is given to an author whose writing for young adults exemplifies the highest quality books for young adults, and the Printz Award for Excellence given to an author whose young adult book is considered to be of outstanding literary quality each year. Other YALSA awards are the Alex Awards for adult books with teen appeal, the Morris Award for debut authors, the Odyssey Award for best audiobook production (co-administered with ALSC), and beginning in 2010, a nonfiction award. These awards have brought increased recognition to those who work with and those who write for ages 12 through 18.

New committees, offering membership greater opportunities to participate in division business were formed and committees that outlived their usefulness were sunsetted during the 1990s. Sunsetted were the Public Relations Committee, eight genre committees, the Econoclad Award Committee, the Baker & Taylor Conference Grant Committee and the Book Wholesalers Award Committee. The grant committees were made the responsibility of some other standing committees. Renamed and Reorganized committees included computer applications which became Technology for Young Adults, Long-Range Planning became Strategic Planning, and Membership was combined with Division Promotion to become Division and Membership Promotion. Recommended Books for Reluctant Young Adult Readers became Quick Picks for Reluctant Young Adult Readers and Selected Films and Videos for Young Adults became Selected Videos for Young Adults — which then became Fabulous Films for Young Adults. New committees included Popular Paperbacks for Young Adults and new award selection committees.

In 1993, *JOYS* benefitted from a new attractive format and a change in editorship. By including speeches from ALSC and YALSA programs, such as those given by

award winners and increasing the pool of referees from 33 to 50, the publication better informed membership about division news and views.

By 2007, seven book and media lists were published: the ever-popular *Best Books for Young Adults (new edition), Great Graphic Novels for Teens, Popular Paperbacks for Young Adults, Quick Picks for Reluctant Young Adult Readers, Amazing Audiobooks for Young Adults, and Selected DVDs and Videos*—newly named *Fabulous Films for Young Adults*.

The Young Adult Library Services Association now celebrates Support Teen Literature Day during National Library Week. Beginning in 2008, YALSA will host a Young Adult Literature Symposium every other years partially funded by the Morris endowment. Keeping up with new innovations, YALSA has a blog and a wiki, is known for its electronic discussion lists within ALA and has a distinctive presence on Face book as well as other social networking sites. The Young Adult Library Services Association is considered a leader in advocating safe use of the Internet.

The enormous growth of Internet users throughout the 1990s gave YALSA the opportunity to reach a wider audience of teens and librarians as well as educators and publishers. The Young Adult Library Services Association has had a Web site since 1992 at http://www.ala.org/yalsa which includes information about the division, projects in the works, mission and vision statements, publications, and graphics. In 2000, YALSA created the first ALA members-only Web site.

The increasing importance of technology in the 1990s to young adult patrons was recognized by the development of the popular Web site "Teen Hoopla," and its hits produced book reviews, discussions of issues and numerous links to other sites of interest to young adults. After criticism of "Teen Hoopla's" link with Columbia University's Web site "Go Ask Alice," YALSA united with ALA's public information office, and other ALA units to defend its action.

In 1996, mission and vision statements were composed to serve as guides for YALSA's activities, goals and priorities; the vision statement, in fact, served as a model for other ALA divisions. These statements together were the basis for a strategic plan adopted by YALSA's Board of Directors in June 1997. The plan's key concepts of advocacy, coalition and equity of access became YALSA's guiding principles directing the division's plan of action for the next 4 years until 2000 when, inspired by ALAction 2005, a new strategic plan was adopted with six key action areas:

Action
Coalitions
Twenty-first century literacy
Diversity
Equity of Access

In its strategic plan, YALSA mapped out its mission, vision, and specific strategies for action. The plan took a look at strengths and weaknesses of the division. Among its strengths, it acknowledged the high level of member participation, the diversity of its leadership and its openness to change and experimentation. Among its weaknesses it listed its aging membership, lack of research into the effectiveness of its book lists, too small a staff and lack of sufficient revenue. In describing environmental opportunities, the report mentioned the changing face of ethnic United States, a great growth in the number of high school students by 2009, a gradual banding together of services to young people and the value of the Internet for global involvement. In looking at environmental challenges, it recognized that young adult services suffer from low visibility, the unwillingness of school libraries to coordinate efforts and the lack of enough librarians to serve young adults at a time when such librarians' special training is increasingly important.

In 2001, *JOYS* stopped publication when *Young Adult Library Services*, a quarterly publication, was launched. In 2002, *YALS* began. In 2003, standards for serving teens in libraries were published. The 2000s also saw a YALSA mentoring program which paired experienced librarians with new young adult specialists.[1]

The Young Adult Library Services Association's momentum continues to rise — its 50th year sees an increased passion to serve young adults! That energy and dynamism exemplifies the resurgence of interest in teens, adolescent literacy and the importance of library service to those teens, one of the fastest-growing segments of the population. It gives training and guidance to librarians who serve young adults and has become a widely respected knowledgeable partner to other organizations and agencies who work with young adults. The division offers the members enormous opportunities to hone their leadership skills so that they can become leaders in their libraries and in the larger library world.

REFERENCES

1. Carter, B.; Holley, P.S. John, Paul, George, and YALSA. Sch. Lib. J. **2007**, *53* (2), 34–37.

Young Adult Services in Libraries

Mary K. Chelton
Graduate School of Library and Information Studies, Queens College
Flushing, New York, U.S.A.

Abstract

Highlighting the major components of young adult services, this entry discusses adolescent development, staff, collections, group programs, space, and major issues impacting the service such as censorship, mass assignments, parents doing homework, and technology.

INTRODUCTION

"Young adult (YA) services" is the term used to describe a variety of library services tailored to the adolescent clientele, primarily those young people in middle, junior high, and high school, or between the ages of 12 and 18, regardless of setting, although the term is most commonly used to describe public library services.[1] While library attention to adolescents actually dates from Caleb Bingham's gift of books to the Bingham Youth Library in Salisbury, Connecticut in 1803, a cohesive service perspective only began when Anne Carroll Moore, fearing that all her good work in the children's rooms of the New York Public Library (NYPL) was not continued in the adult departments there once children graduated from eighth grade, hired Mabel Williams to work with the high school clientele in NYPL's Office of Work with Young People. Secondary schooling was not mandatory then, but as more high schools were established, Moore saw them as a way to continue personalized service to young people through outreach and collaborative activities.[2,3]

Since YA services grew out of children's services at a time when books and reading were the predominant recorded means of learning and understanding the world, reading and reading promotion traditionally remain a large part of what the service is about. This continued emphasis can be seen both in the array of committees and in the activities surrounding Teen Read Week in the American Library Association's (ALA) Young Adult Library Services Association (YALSA) devoted to identifying and promoting books of interest to, or worthy of acclaim for adolescents, in various categories.[4] In Moore's time, there were no juvenile publishers involved in producing books specifically for adolescents, and YA services librarians spent their time identifying adult books of particular interest to teen readers. Since then, changes in publishing and in the formats available for library collections, as well as the growth and influence of mass media and the Internet on the YA audience, have extended the nature of what is included in library collections purchased for young adults.

The public library bias of young adult services not only stems from the fact that many of the pioneers in this service, such as Mabel Williams and Margaret Scoggin of the New York Public Library, Margaret Alexander Edwards of the Enoch Pratt Free Library in Baltimore, and Jean Roos of the Cleveland Public Library, were all public librarians, but also because tax-supported public libraries predate tax-supported school libraries historically in the United States.[5] The service also predates the ascendancy of the reference/information paradigm within the profession at large, with Edwards in particular being emphatic about library services doing more for adolescents than helping them in the mindless pursuit of facts, which is how she viewed reference services, a view largely discounted or ignored by contemporary YA practitioners. This bias is further exacerbated because of the pronounced differences between public and school library services that have emerged because of the influence of technology on the learning process in schools and also because of the national standards for school libraries promulgated by ALA's American Association of School Librarians (AASL). These standards downplay reading promotion at the secondary level of schooling in favor of information literacy instruction as the primary role of the school library media specialist.[6]

These institutional differences vary widely in specific circumstances though, in part because only a minority of large public libraries have librarians with the title, "young adult specialist" on staff, even though they serve the age group. Other common staffing configurations include extending the children's services staff to include young adolescents in their service clientele and renaming the department "Youth Services"; assigning the service responsibility to the adult services staff on the rationale that YA interests were more adult, or that they use more adult materials, than children's.[7]

Encyclopedia of Library and Information Sciences, Fourth Edition DOI: 10.1081/E-ELIS4-120043519

Word–Zoological

THEORETICAL FOUNDATIONS

While services for young adults share other theories that inform library practice, YA services are primarily supported by theories and research on the physical, social, cognitive, and psychological development of adolescents. Young adult services emphasize how library service can augment various internal and external assets that promote positive youth development in the categories of support, empowerment, boundaries and expectations, constructive use of time, commitment to learning, positive values, social competence, and positive identity.[8] Long before a recent Gallup poll asked U.S. young people how many of them were experiencing the five promises identified by America's Promise, young adult services were helping provide caring adults, safe places and constructive use of time, a healthy start and healthy development, effective education for marketable skills and lifelong learning, and opportunities to make a difference through helping others.[9] In many ways, YA services are the most client-centered of library services because they are grounded in the nature of their contemporary adolescent audience.

THE YOUNG ADULT SERVICES AUDIENCE

Definitions

The profession lacks an agreed-upon professional definition of "young adult" that is congruent with individual library service histories or school district divisions. In most public libraries, for example, middle school students (grades 6–8) are a shared constituency between children's and adult or young adult departments, depending on where the YAs present themselves whereas for any particular middle school, those are the only people there. ALA's Young Adult Services Association defines young adults as people between ages 12 and 18, but there are ongoing discussions within the Division about whether the audience focus needs to be expanded to include either tweens or older teens and 20-somethings or both.[10]

While the YALSA definition quantifies the intended YA service population by age, it is less helpful in terms of the social psychology of, and communication with, adolescents to explain library services for and problems with the age group for librarians. Adolescents do not easily fit the neat categories that libraries and the larger society create for them. They want a say in what happens to them, while often lacking the experience or resources to influence events. They are also a highly stigmatized group who arouse deep suspicion in adults who tend to misread their appearance and are often more interested in controlling them rather than either listening to, or serving them. Since most adults that YAs come in contact with outside their families seem to have total amnesia about or only an idealized memory of their own adolescence, current young adults cannot always count on them for any kind of residual empathy in or outside of libraries. Thanks to compulsory schooling and laws regarding the age at which one can leave school and work, plus the advanced preparation necessary for many highly paid jobs, there often seems to be no adequate social place for young adults in the United States outside schools, despite a developmental need for social and intellectual competence within a highly sexualized and commercial mass culture. This is a gap that good young adult services attempt to fill.

Adolescent Development

The following is an overview of adolescent development which is the basis for young adult services, with examples of how these characteristics relate to what young adult librarians do. It is important to remember that developmental characteristics can occur at different times even within the same or same-aged individuals. Social characteristics are mediated by culture, so the following generalizations can only be understood for individuals within actual social contexts. Except for the connections to library and information practice by the author, all of these developmental characteristics are drawn from the work of Jean Piaget, Lawrence Kohlberg, Joseph Adelson, David Elkind, Gisela Konopka and Joan Lipsitz' work at the Center for Early Adolescence. They can be found in any adolescent development textbook. A particularly useful book is *Adolescence: The Survival Guide for Parents and Teenagers*.[11] There has been research on the teenage brain, suggesting that remarkable changes occur during this period; however, there is little agreement to date on the applicability of this research to practice. A summary of this research appears at http://www.nimh.nih.gov/publicat/teenbrain.cfm.[12]

Physical

Early adolescence, roughly ages 10–15, is the second greatest time of growth velocity in human development. Height, weight, and secondary sex characteristics all grow or become obvious at this time. As one young person put it, "Adolescence is when you grow hair and smell bad." This is also the time at which young people reach reproductive maturity physically. Since physical growth is highly variable, even within the same age or grade, there is much angst among adolescents over what is normal and what is not. It is also disconcerting for many young adults to find themselves taller than their parents, for example, or for the girls to be taller than the boys of their same age cohort. It is worth noting that young adults who are "early bloomers," that is, those who mature physically earlier, are at risk in several ways. Girls can draw unwelcome attention from older boys while still lacking the social skills to cope with the attention; boys who are early developers often do not develop other aspects of their personalities. Physical "late bloomers" suffer from being regarded as childlike, when often, their cognitive abilities are superb. Science fiction conventions seem to specialize in bright adolescent late bloomers, for example.

Cognitive.   Adolescence is the time during which a move into formal operational thinking occurs, if it occurs at all. This is the ability to hypothesize about something which has not yet been experienced and is tied to the development of higher order ethical and political thinking because it helps people to understand abstractions. This thinking ability is what allows young adults to dream about and work toward possibilities. It is also the reason why speculative stories such as science fiction, fantasy, and horror are so popular with young adults. It is not inevitable that everyone will reach formal operational thinking, and many people, even when they do, do not reach this stage of cognitive development until their early twenties. Besides the link between this level of cognitive development and media interests, there is also the problem of adults expecting abstract thinking from people who may not be capable of it. This is where serious misinterpretations of behavior are likely to follow.

Psychological.   The overwhelming adolescent quest is identity—that is, figuring out who one is, while at the same time reevaluating familiar relationships with parents, siblings, and friends from new perspectives, while encountering many "first" experiences. Adolescent psychology basically takes two forms, which are related. The first is the "personal fable" in which the young adult feels that he or she is alone in the universe and is experiencing events for the first time. Only experience tempers this, but in the meantime, this can lead adolescents to feel invincible, and make it very difficult to get any cautionary information through to them to mitigate risky behaviors. This is why, for example, so many books in YA collections are written in the first person from the perspective of teenage protagonists.

The second facet of adolescent psychology is called "the imaginary audience." Young adults feel that everyone is looking at them. This makes them extremely self-conscious in many social circumstances, especially when they experience some unanticipated bodily function, such as sudden pimples or spontaneous erections or the emergence of breasts, or when they are ignored in service encounters. This is also why many adolescents have a particularly difficult time with cyber-bullying, which seems to have become a negative effect of new technologies.

Adolescents are exceptionally self-conscious, in part because of changes to their bodies, or in the case of "late bloomers," the long time it takes for the changes to start. This egocentrism is encouraged, not only by the age segregation experienced by adolescents in U.S. culture, but also by media targeted to adolescents as a consumer class.

Since many adolescents have little real work and intergenerational experience outside their families or schools, it is easy for them to feel that they are heroes in their own "personal fable," and therefore invincible in terms of various risk-taking activities. One of the more difficult information sharing activities with adolescents is figuring out how to cut through this psychological shield of invincibility to help them take risks within safe boundaries. It is hardly accidental that the Extreme Sports Games are primarily composed of adolescent competitors.

Social.   Adolescence is the time that young people move (or are thrust) outside the protective influence of the family into the interdependent relationships of the larger community to test and reconfigure their identities while moving into increasingly adult roles. Relationships are very important during this time. Besides figuring out romantic and sexual relationships with the opposite or same sex and renegotiating power relationships with parents and adult authority figures, adolescents depend on friends to help figure out what is and is not normal with all the changes going on in their lives. Librarians are often dismayed by adolescents in groups, but this behavior is developmentally normal; whereas the lone, seemingly friendless young adult who, while possibly more palatable in libraries, is also more at risk. This need to keep in touch with friends is also the developmental force behind young adult preoccupations with text messaging and Internet Web sites that promote social interaction such as MySpace and Facebook. E-mail is considered a technology for "old people" by today's teenagers. Unfortunately, dependence on friends can become exaggerated when no strong parental bond exists and also because teenagers, especially those who are racial or ethnic minorities, are highly stigmatized in U.S. culture, except for when they can be slotted as "consumers."

Structural age segregation separates young adults from both adults and younger children outside the home, through work limitation and mandatory schooling laws. As a result of this, young adults display all the characteristics of a subculture with specific symbols, such as clothing and language, to delineate that status. These subcultural symbols, often inspired by celebrities, are frequently misinterpreted by adults, including librarians, and often lead to unpleasant confrontations in retail settings or misunderstandings with the police. Age segregation has another effect, too, which is increasing lack of access to caring adults. Adolescents cannot mature by themselves, and librarians serving as caring adult role models for them is considered a normal and attractive part of young adult services. There are also many examples of intergenerational YA services that address this issue.

The social "place" designated for young adults is school. Here they are supposed to become critical thinkers and inquirers, developing both lifelong skills for navigating an increasingly complex information society, and deciding what kind of career they wish to pursue. Some actually achieve these things, but more often, they encounter "imposed queries" they are ill-prepared to negotiate. The very technology they love to play with outside school does not prepare them for the informed demands of information technology within school, hence the almost total preoccupation of the school library section of the profession with information literacy instruction.

Emotional. Mood swings are common in adolescents, partly because of hormonal changes and partly as a result of many first experiences, such as falling in love, for example. The swing from euphoria to depression can be very swift and disconcerting to adults, especially parents. Fears of imagined or real experiences are common, and only diminish as the young person acquires enough life experience to be able to distinguish among events where a likely emotional reaction is appropriate. This is why, for example, early adolescents are much more outraged at discriminatory treatment than senior high counterparts who are better able to think about alternative explanations for the behavior in question.

THE YOUNG ADULT SERVICES PROGRAM

Young adult services in public libraries usually consist of staff, a YA advisory group of some sort, collections, space, policies, group programs and outreach efforts to parents, schools, other libraries, and community youth organizations. Young adult services in schools consist of staff, collections, space, policies, an instructional program, collaboration with teachers and other librarians in the school district, and outreach to local public libraries and the school's parent association.

Staff

There are actually very few public library positions with the title "Young Adult Librarian," because only large libraries have them. Services are delivered by adult or children's librarians in smaller places. Other public libraries have amalgamated "youth services" departments where children and young adults are served by the same staff from birth through early adolescence. The specific services offered to young adults may depend on the boundaries imposed by a particular position description and also where the librarian is organizationally situated. Secondary school librarians are usually credentialed as teachers as well as librarians.[13,14] One of the myths about being a young adult librarian is that the person has to be young. This is not true; regardless of age, there is general agreement that the person must be mature, technically competent as a librarian, understand and genuinely like teenagers, have good interpersonal skills, and have a good sense of humor. For school library media specialists,

formal teaching skills are also important, but informal teaching skills are equally important for public librarians because of the various information technology learning curves encountered among users. Librarians working with young adults need to be able to have collegial relationships with other adults as well as excellent service skills with young adults, since a large part of YA services is advocating for YA needs with colleagues.[15,16]

Young Adult Advisory Groups

Since their new cognitive abilities often make them question everything, young adults want input into what libraries do for them because they want to know why these services are being offered. Also, their interests can be so fleeting that it is difficult for librarians to keep up. The response to these needs has been the almost universal establishment of YA advisory groups in public libraries, and some in schools. The groups vary in focus, but basically serve as idea-generators, communication conduits, publicity helpers, program volunteers, collection evaluators, advocates for library services, staff trainers, etc., anything needed to keep the library on track in terms of their age group. Young adult advisory groups also offer youth participation opportunities to local adolescents, and as such, are a YA service in themselves.[17]

Young Adult Collections

For personal reading

Since contemporary adolescents are, in general, the most "wired," multimedia generation ever, YA collections should be multimedia themselves. Many school library collections stay within the limitations of curriculum support, but public libraries tend only to have print collections of books and magazines for young adults, with other formats such as music, audio books, DVDs, computer games, etc. representing their interests in other sections of the library that YAs also have access to. Ideally, all items of interest to young adults, regardless of format, would be housed together, but this often proves difficult because of the overlap between YA and adult interests.

Another problem with YA collections is the public library's philosophy about separate collections. Some do not have separate YA collections at all; others interfile all juvenile materials with adult; some only interfile nonfiction, etc. There is a wide variety of YA collection locations within public libraries, but it should be noted that young adults do not necessarily limit themselves only to what collections are labeled "YA," regardless of location.[18]

It is still conventional wisdom among many YA services librarians and publishers that a "YA book" is a mass-market sized paperback, since the format is by far the most preferred by adolescents for reading in book form;

however, with the development of and subsequent inclusion of graphic novels in YA collections, it may now be equally true that a "YA book" is a graphic novel. The importance of this format for young adults was established first with a standing-room-only audience at a preconference on graphic novels sponsored by YALSA at the ALA annual conference in San Francisco, which, in turn, led to the establishment of a standing YALSA committee to determine the "best" graphic novels for young adults annually, followed by the selection of the graphic novel, *American Born Chinese*, for the 2007 Printz Award. The importance of the format is also underscored by research on boys and reading that points out that many of them love comics, making graphic novels a natural reading progression.[19,20]

Thanks to the establishment of the Printz Award for literary quality by YALSA in 1999 in memory of beloved YA librarian Mike Printz, of Topeka West High School in Kansas, books published specifically for young adults now receive new respect from publishers, authors, and librarians alike, while increasing both the literary sophistication and the range of stories available for the age group. In addition to titles published specifically for young adults, however, YA collections and reading interests extend well beyond the "YA" category of publishing, as documented by the adult titles of interest to young adults selected annually by the Alex Award Committee of YALSA, named for Margaret Alexander Edwards, the first YA Coordinator of the Enoch Pratt Free Library in Baltimore. Many of these titles are subsequently produced by audio book publishers and offer opportunities for young adults who are aural learners or reluctant readers. Young adults also form a major segment of the reading audience for adult science fiction and fantasy stories, whether in print or video formats.

For specific information-seeking

While school libraries include printed reference materials and subscribe to electronic databases of particular usefulness for curriculum-supported research by young adults, public libraries usually house such materials in the adult reference department and allow young adult use there, unless the library has a separate homework center or YA space with its own separate computer access. There is a growing research literature about YA information-seeking in conjunction with school assignments that can be summed up by saying that, without instructional intervention, many young adults may be great surfers of the Internet, but they do not how to search and evaluate what they find, nor do they respect intellectual property. In terms of personal or "everyday" information-seeking by young adults, peers are a preferred source of information with many adults often perceived as not helpful unless adolescents perceive them as both expert and accessible.[21,22]

Young Adult Spaces

An important trend in young adult services is how to create separate spaces, primarily within public libraries that respond to YA developmental, cultural, and aesthetic needs, although at least one study has also examined school libraries. As Anthony Bernier puts it, "Young adult areas need design elements to harmonize with the way teens sit, study, relax, read, and socialize."[23] Inspired by Teen'Scape in the Los Angeles Public Library and Teen Central in the Phoenix Public Library, this interest has led so far to new theories of spatial organization, an ongoing column presenting YA spaces in *Voice of Youth Advocates* (VOYA) and a book by Kimberly Bolan now in its second edition.[24] The teenager's need to lounge and eat and socialize while working is finally being recognized architecturally in libraries, although undoubtedly, not every librarian is happy over this trend.

Group Programs

While young adult services are similar to library services for other age groups in terms of offering one-on-one reference and readers' advisory service, one of the major accomplishments of young adult services is group programs, especially where the young adults themselves help plan and deliver the program. Since several hallmarks of adolescent development are learning that one is both normal and part of a particular generation, and learning how to relate to the opposite sex, any learning activity that allows teens to interact with each other or with other generations becomes an important information service, whether it is a teen talent show, a tutoring program, discussion programs, workshops, etc. The sheer range of young adult services programs is an ongoing topic on several YALSA electronic lists, highlighted annually in VOYA, summarized in five volumes of *Excellence in Library Services to Young Adults*, and summarized in a "best practices" overview.[25–30]

ISSUES IN YOUNG ADULT SERVICES

Censorship

Young adult materials and services are frequent targets of adult censors, partly as an ongoing product of the larger "culture wars" in the United States, but also because YA interests frighten or offend many adults who would prefer that young people not know or be interested in the topic or format. There are many people, including many librarians who sincerely believe that information may be harmful to youth; whereas, the profession has taken the position that getting information is a positive activity. The problem inevitably arises when young adults want information that some adults do not want them to have. Graphic novels, for example, come under scrutiny because many adults still consider comics to be "trash" and not worthy of library collections, and also because many of the imported Japanese graphic novels are published for adults in Japan and are not particularly sensitive to American notions of what should or should not be in books for minors. Just a brief perusal of ALA's most challenged lists shows a high percentage of popular titles aimed at young adults as well as the old standby, *Catcher in the Rye* by J. D. Salinger. While sex and "bad" words will still cause controversy such as Judy Blume's *Forever*, censors are also concerned about disrespect for adult authority as depicted in *Killing Mr. Griffin* by Lois Duncan, anything that presents homosexuality in a neutral or positive way, such as *Arizona Kid* by Ron Koertge, or the depiction of the rape scene in Stephen Chbosky's *Perks of Being a Wallflower*. Caroline Cooney's *Terrorist* has been challenged ever since 9/11, usually by people who have not read it but object to the title. The wildly popular Harry Potter series has been challenged for catering to the occult. A list of the reasons for all censorship challenges compiled by ALA between 2000 and 2005 include anti-ethnic, insensitivity, racism, sexism, homosexuality, nudity, sex education, sexually explicit, antifamily, offensive language, political viewpoint, religious viewpoint, unsuited to age group, abortion, drugs, occult/Satanism, suicide, violence, or inaccurate.[31]

Young adult librarians need to be prepared to defend decisions made in accordance with selection policies at any time, either orally or in writing, while at the same time respecting the free speech rights of the person disagreeing with library policy. Guidance for doing this is available in toolkits from ALA's Office for Intellectual Freedom and YALSA's *HitList* publication.[32,33]

Censorship challenges are not limited to books, however, but also to music and visual images, as well as to information gathered from the Internet on library terminals. Since many library users serve themselves on Internet terminals rather than go through librarians, adult concerns over youth viewing pornography have led many libraries to institute "acceptable use" policies where users sign an agreement not to visit such sites. This solution did not placate adults who wanted youth access controlled, so a law mandating electronic filters on all library terminals accessible to anyone under 18 in public libraries that received federal E-rate funds (raised by tax surcharges on phone lines) was approved by the U.S. Supreme Court. Prior to that ruling, many school districts already filtered terminals, which can lead to problems for young adults when using Internet connections in school libraries for research, since useful sites get filtered along with those deemed "inappropriate." The problem with many filters is that they are not able to be turned on and off easily, and they depend on language or image screening methods that are imprecise. For example, a perfectly good photograph of a breast for the purpose of illustrating breast cancer is as likely to be filtered as erotic images of the same body part.

The other problem with filters is that, since their programming is proprietary, librarians cannot always find out on what basis filtering decisions are made. Filtering companies also sell to home users, and what may be fine in a very conservative religious home is probably not appropriate in a public institution used by everyone.[34] Censors, however, usually generalize from their own worldview, assuming that everyone does or should believe exactly what they do. A good young adult librarian is one who is well-prepared to respond to challenges with good policies for selection and services, due process protections for public response and input, and also has good communication skills as well as the support of library or school administration and significant adult community members.

Young Adult Behavior

Congregating in groups

Young adults congregate in public places, libraries among them.[35] This is normal, inevitable teenage behavior that allows teens to socialize, flirt, make friends, etc., outside parental view. Most libraries, however, are constructed with solitary intellectual pursuits in mind, and normal young adult behavior winds up being labeled "disruptive" and viewed as aberrant in that setting. Adolescents talking with their friends is actively discouraged and disparaged in several ways through arbitrary restrictions on the number of people who can sit at tables at any particular time, the prohibition of chat room use on Internet terminals, the absence of group study rooms, the prohibitions on meeting room reservations by age and use, and the type of architecture and furnishings chosen when libraries are being built. Librarians seem to feel that making a library look like a study hall will make users act like they are in one.

Young adult librarians then have to enforce one-size-fits-all behavior rules with teenagers who, by definition, do not fit the rule. In one-room libraries, admittedly, group behavior can be a problem, but larger libraries often have the option of designating quiet vs. noisy areas. Both school and public libraries often have conference or meeting rooms that can be opened for groups of young adults to work together. As Thomas has observed, "This approach essentially privileges users for whom learning is understood as individual and task-oriented, and disaffirms activities which could be considered as cooperative, social, or reflective."[36,37]

Reference queries

The expressed information needs of adolescents in public libraries tend to cluster primarily around homework assignments which forces many teenagers to look for information on the same topic. This is the so-called mass assignments problem. Although this is an ubiquitous problem for public libraries, many librarians merely complain about it and scapegoat school librarians for "not doing their job," with little understanding of what school media specialists actually do. Planning for mass assignments by contacting local schools for curricula, buying multiple copies of needed items, creating temporary "reserve" shelves, creating pathfinders, and calling teachers when needed, even in the face of documented public support for the public library's taking a formal educational support role.[38]

The professional literature on information-seeking behavior until recently did not acknowledge that there is a class of questions that do not originate with the person asking them, so-called imposed queries, or that the person forced to ask may be less than interested in the topic of the query. Nearly all homework-related questions fall into this class.[39]

Adolescents inevitably present themselves at the last minute (because they are still learning how to be future-oriented using their new thinking abilities), with homework questions on topics they do not fully understand or care about, often unprepared to find the answer without more help than most busy public librarians are prepared to give them.

The idea that a public librarian should also be an information literacy instructor is just beginning to take hold in the field, because changing technology has changed the learning curve for everyone and made them all "adolescent users" in some fashion. This is why many public libraries have decided to offer homework centers or some sort of formal educational support besides one-on-one reference service which usually cannot bear the brunt of doing information literacy training in this fashion without breaking down under the numbers needing it.

The problem created by imposed queries for the reference encounter is further complicated by the lack of agreement among reference librarians on whether the librarian just gives users the desired information or whether the librarian just starts users on the path toward finding it for themselves and tries to teach users how to search for the next time they need something.[40] There is some hypocrisy in the way in which this unresolved dilemma is visited upon adolescents, though. Most librarians in public libraries automatically assume that all homework assignments presented by adolescents are intended to teach the user how to use the library, as opposed to any queries from adults, regardless of the fact that there is little evidence used to support this supposition. This causes the "just-get-them-started" method to be used almost exclusively (and punitively) with adolescents until it becomes obvious that the teenager does not know how, nor will be able to do the assignment without more instructional help in accessing and evaluating library resources.

Adolescent reference queries also come through surrogate users in the form of parents trying to help their children with their homework. These parents are often frustrated themselves over having to do it, and frustrating

to librarians because they do not fully understand what is needed, leaving the librarian never sure whether the correct question has been answered. The situation is even more frustrating when the parent and teenager appear together, and the parent does all the talking for both of them. This situation is also ubiquitous in public libraries.

Preference for and use of technology

As Elaine Meyers points out in her classic article, "The Coolness Factor," young adults love the Internet, (90.3% having access from more than one location in 2007), and they are very frustrated with the scarcity of familiar technology in libraries.[41] They hate waiting in line for computers they can only use for short periods of time, and the genders use the Internet differently. To attract this age group, a library needs to understand teenage Internet use and offer information and access using Web-based technology as a conscious part of young adult services. This might include reference service available through instant messaging, a library presence on social networking sites like MySpace or Facebook (used by 55% of teens in 2007), posting library and library-sponsored teen videos to YouTube, full text databases for research, a YA presence on the library Web site with YA input for its design and content, a computer gaming club or programs, downloadable music and book formats compatible with the most popular recording devices used by young adults, if possible, and participatory formats such as wikis and folksonomies.[42–44]

CONCLUSION

Young adult services remain an important component of overall library services because of the importance of a developmentally sound response to this stage of life. All secondary school libraries are "young adult services" by definition and many public libraries serve young adult users in multiple organizational and staffing formats. However the services are delivered, they must encompass the presence of caring and technically skilled adults who understand adolescent development and can advocate for the age group wherever needed in library bureaucracies. Young adult services include materials collections in the formats most desired by contemporary adolescents, relevant and topical group programs responsive to local teen interests, youth participation in service conceptualization and delivery, and access to information and communication technology. Young adult services are vibrant and fluid, very much like the audience served. Young adult services exist to serve the information needs of adolescents in the present with an eye toward the future adults they may become.

REFERENCES

1. Jones, P. *New Directions in Library Services to Young Adults*; American Library Association: Chicago, IL, 2002.
2. Bernier, A.; Chelton, M.K.; Jenkins, C.A.; Pierce, J.B. Two hundred years of young adult library services history: The chronology. Voice Youth Advocates **2005**, *28* (2), 106–111.
3. Campbell, P. *Two Pioneers of Young Adult Library Services, A VOYA Occasional Paper*; Scarecrow Press: Lanham, MD, 1998.
4. Celebrate Teen Read Week: LOL@Your Library. http://www.ala.org/ala/yalsa/teenreading/teenreading.htm (accessed December 9, 2008).
5. Braverman, M. *Youth, Society and the Public Library*; American Library Association: Chicago, IL, 1979.
6. Campbell, P. *Two Pioneers of Young Adult Services*; Scarecrow Press: Lanham, MD, 1998.
7. American Association of School Librarians; Association for Educational and Communication Technology, *Information Power: Building Partnerships for Learning*; American Library Association: Chicago, IL, 1998.
8. National Center for Education Statistics, *Services for Children and Young Adults in Public Libraries*, NCES 95–731; U.S. Government Printing Office: Washington, DC, 1995.
9. Toward quality and equality: Fulfilling our promises to America's children, Search Institute Insights and Evidence **2006**, 3, 1–10; 40. Developmental Assets for adolescents (ages 12–18); America's Promise Alliance. Five Promises http://www.americaspromise.org/APAPage.aspx?id=5928&ekmensel=fc8d405e_252_254_btnlink (accessed December 14, 2008); Search Institute. 40 Developmental Assets for adolescents (ages 12–18) http://www.search-institute.org/content/40-developmental-assets-adolescents-ages-12–18 (accessed December 14, 2008).
10. YALSA Vision Statement. http://www.ala.org/ala/yalsa/aboutyalsab/yalsavisionstatement.htm (accessed December 14, 2008); Personal communication with Beth Yoke, December 10, 2008.
11. Fenwick, E.; Smith, T. *Adolescence: The Survival Guide for Parents and Teenagers*; Dorling Kindersley: London, U.K., 1993.
12. The National Institute of Mental Health. http://www.nimh.nih.gov/publicat/teenbrain.cfm (accessed December 9, 2008).
13. National Center for Education Statistics. *Services for Children and Young Adults in Public Libraries*, NCES 95-731; U.S. Government Printing Office: Washington, DC, 1995.
14. American Association of School Librarians. *Roles and Responsibilities of the School Library Media Specialist*. http://www.ala.org/aaslTemplate.cfm?Section=informationpower&Template=/ContentManagement/ContentDisplay.cfm&ContentID=19930 (accessed December 14, 2008).
15. American Association of School Librarians; Association for Educational and Communication Technology. *Information Power: Building Partnerships for Learning*; American Library Association: Chicago, IL, 1998.
16. Chelton, M.K.; Rosinia, J. *Bare Bones: Young Adult Services Tips for Public Library Generalists*; American Library Association: Chicago, IL, 1993.
17. Tuccillo, D.P. *Library Teen Advisory Groups. VOYA Guides #2*; Scarecrow Press: Lanham, MD, 2004.
18. Walter, V.A. Materials use measures; Materials availability measures. In *Output Measures and More: Planning and Evaluating Services for Young Adults*; American Library Association: Chicago, IL, 1995; 52–67.
19. Young Adult Library Services Association. *Great Graphic Novels for Teens*. http://www.ala.org/ala/yalsa/booklistsawards/greatgraphicnovelsforteens/gn.htm (accessed December 10, 2008).
20. Smith, M.; Wilhelm, J.D. "I just like being good at it": The importance of competence in the literate lives of young men. J. Adolescent Adult Lit. **2004**, *47* (6), 454–461.
21. Chelton, M.K.; Cool, C., Eds. *Youth Information-Seeking: Theories, Models, and Approaches*; Scarecrow Press: Lanham, MD, 2004.
22. Chelton, M.K.; Cool, C., Eds. *Youth Information-Seeking Behaviors II: Contexts, Theories, Models, and Issues*; Scarecrow Press: Lanham, MD, 2007.
23. Bernier, A. Designing a 'geography of yes': Making space for teens in public libraries. In *Designing Modern Childhood: Landscapes, Buildings, and Material Culture, May 2002*; University of California: Berkeley, CA, 2002.
24. Bolan, K. *Teen Spaces: The Step-by-Step Library Makeover*, 2nd Ed.; American Library Association: Chicago, IL, 2008.
25. Chelton, M.K., Ed. *Excellence in Library Services for Young Adults: The Nation's Top Programs*. American Library Association: Chicago, IL, 1994.
26. Chelton, M.K., Ed. *Excellence in Library Services for Young Adults: The Nation's Top Programs*, 2nd Ed.; American Library Association: Chicago, IL, 1997.
27. Chelton, M.K., Ed. *Excellence in Library Services to Young Adults 3: The Nation's Top Programs*, 3rd Ed.; American Library Association: Chicago, IL, 2000.
28. McGrath, R.V., Ed. *Excellence in Library Services to Young Adults*, 4th Ed.; Young Adult Library Services Association: Chicago, IL, 2004.
29. Alessio, A., Ed. *Excellence in Library Services to Young Adults*, 5th Ed.; Young Adult Library Services Association: Chicago, IL, 2008.
30. Machado, J.; Lentz, B.; Wallace, R.; Honig-Bear, S. Survey of best practices in youth services around the country: A view from one library. J. Youth Serv. Libr. **2000**, *13* (2), 30–35.
31. Doyle, R.P. *Books Challenged or Banned in 2007–2008*. http://www.ila.org/pdf/2008banned.pdf (accessed December 14, 2008).
32. Office for Intellectual Freedom. *Intellectual Freedom Toolkits*. http://www.ala.org/ala/aboutala/offices/oif/iftoolkits/intellectual.cfm (accessed December 14, 2008).
33. Lesesne, T.S.; Chance, R. for the Young Adult Library Services Association. *Hit List for Young Adults 2: Frequently Challenged Books*. American Library Association: Chicago, IL, 2002.
34. Office for Intellectual Freedom, *Intellectual Freedom Issues: Filters and Filtering*. http://www.ala.org/Template.cfm?Section=ifissues&Template=/ContentManagement/ContentDisplay.cfm&ContentID=77636 (accessed December 14, 2008).
35. Scott, M.S. *Disorderly Youth in Public Places* (Problem-Oriented Guides for Police Series No. 6); U.S. Department

of Justice. http://www.cops.usdoj.gov/pdf/e05021549.pdf (accessed December 14, 2008).

36. Chelton, M.K. 'Problem Patron' public libraries created. Ref. Libr. **2002** (75/76), 23–33.

37. Thomas, N.P. Reading libraries: An interpretive study of discursive practices in library architecture and the interactional construction of personal identity. Unpublished doctoral dissertation, Rutgers University: New Brunswick, NJ, 1996.

38. D'Elia, G.D.; Rodger, E.J. Public opinion about the roles of the public library. The results of a recent Gallup poll. Pub. Libr. **1994**, *33* (1), 23–28.

39. Gross, M. Imposed query. RQ **1995**, *35* (1), 236–243.

40. Bopp, R.E.; Smith, L.C., Eds. *Reference and Information Services: An Introduction*, 3rd Ed.; Libraries Unlimited: Englewood, CO, 2001.

41. Meyers, E. Coolness factor: Ten libraries listen to youth. Am. Libr. **1999**, *30* (10), 42–46.

42. Harris, F.J. *I Found It on the Internet: Coming of Age Online*; American Library Association: Chicago, IL, 2005.

43. Lenhart, A.; Madden, M. *Teens, Privacy & Online Social Networks: How Teens Manage Their Online Identities and Personal Information in the Age of MySpace*; Pew Internet and American Life Project: Washington, DC, 2007.

44. Connaway, L.S.; Radford, M.L. *Service Sea Change: Clicking with Screenagers Through Virtual Reference*; Association of College and Research Libraries 13th National Conference, Baltimore, MD, March 29–April 1, 2007. http://www.oclc.org/research/publications/archive/2007/connaway-acrl.pdf (accessed December 14, 2008).

Youth Information: Needs and Behavior

Melissa Gross
School of Information, Florida State University, Tallahassee, Florida, U.S.A.

Abstract

The information needs and behavior of youth is a research area that continues to be ripe with research questions. Work investigating these users has been informed by theories of development from the field of psychology as well as models and theories of information behavior developed in the field of library and information science. Much of what is known about youth information needs and behavior is focused on the context of school and the use of electronic resources. While a body of work is accumulating related to information seeking in school and information seeking with electronic resources, there are significant gaps in our knowledge and methodological issues that need to be addressed to build a solid research base. Youth information seeking in information spaces outside of school, the place of various media in youth information seeking, and the information needs of very young children are particular topics that need to be addressed. Increasing use of theory and the inclusion of youth in research are two ongoing trends that will strengthen understanding of young people's information needs and behavior as well as inform the development of information services, systems, and resources that better respond to the needs of this diverse population.

INTRODUCTION

The information world of youth has long been defined by adult perceptions of youth information needs and adult prescriptions concerning how these needs are best met. In the early 2000s, this started to change as the voices and active participation of young people were increasingly included in studies focused on understanding what young users want to know and how they would like information resources, services, and systems to be configured. Youth information needs and behavior is an active area of study that still has much to achieve before it can provide a full picture of the diversity of needs, skills, and interests of youth as well as how these operate within the various contexts in which information needs and behaviors operate. Research in this area remains scattered and limited by research designs that are not generalizable. Many investigations have small sample sizes and with few replications or follow-up studies.[1–3] Furthermore, minimal differentiation between subsets of this population, based on developmental levels, is made in terms of subjects chosen to participate or in the analysis of the data. The result is that we cannot speak easily about the information behavior of youth at specific age levels. Even though interest in this research area continues to grow, there are still more questions than there are researchers to address them.[4] For these reasons, a comprehensive understanding of youth information needs and behaviors has yet to emerge.

This entry provides an overview of what current literature has to say about the information needs of youth, predominate theories and models that inform this literature, and a summary of current understanding of youth information behavior. Youth, in this discussion, includes both children (birth to age 12) and young adults (age 13–19). The definitions of information need, information seeking, and information behavior are adopted from Case.[5]

> An information need is a recognition that your knowledge is inadequate to satisfy a goal that you have. Information seeking is a conscious effort to acquire information in response to a need or gap in your knowledge. Information behavior encompasses information seeking as well as the totality of other unintentional or passive behaviors...as well as purposive behaviors that do not involve seeking, such as actively avoiding information.
>
> (p. 5)

YOUTH INFORMATION NEEDS

Youth is an extremely broad category involving the full range of human development and requires consideration of developmental level (physical, cognitive, social, etc.) as well as the attainment of a variety of skills, such as reading, writing, and increasingly, information literacy and information and communications technology (ICT) skills. In addition, competency in content areas such as math, science, health, finance, and civics is increasingly important today. Investigations of the information needs of youth have been mainly pragmatic, rather than driven by theory, and based on adult assessments of what the data mean, rather than seeking to understand information needs from the user's point of view. Where developmental

Word–Zoological

Encyclopedia of Library and Information Sciences, Fourth Edition DOI: 10.1081/E-ELIS4-120053110

theory has been brought to bear in the research area, a common approach is to incorporate understandings of cognitive development from the field of psychology, such as those provided by Jean Piaget, Erick Erickson, Abraham Maslow, and Lev Vygotsky as a structure for the investigation or as an aid to data analysis. Models of information seeking behavior are also used as frameworks in this literature and are discussed further in the following.

Due to the vast developmental differences from birth to age 19, it is clear that adults play a central role in the information worlds of youth, especially for the very young. The identification of information needs, as well as the ability to satisfy them, cannot be completely divorced from adult views of what is appropriate for youth as well as adult interest in making information accessible or inaccessible.

One approach to understanding the information needs of youth has been to categorize the kinds of information youth need. Walter,[6] based on in-depth interviews with informants such as teachers, scout leaders, ministers, and other adults interested in children, suggests that adults are not necessarily conscious of their role as information providers to youth and that much of the information children need does not get to them, including basic information that is important to their welfare. She suggests that children's information needs can be conceptualized along the same lines as Maslow's hierarchy of needs ranging from basic physiological needs to the highest level of information need, self-actualization. She describes children as information-poor and sees children's lack of status in our society as well as the low level of communication between children and adults as two of the major barriers they face in meeting their information needs.

A study of computer use at home of 7-, 9-, and 11-year-olds revealed motivations such as curiosity, a desire to play games, and school work.[7] The relationship between school work and computer use at home intensified with age. School work was a primary motivator for 11-year-olds, the second most important motivator for 9-year-olds, and least important among 7-year-olds.

A survey study of 641 fifth and sixth grade students in Taiwan,[8] focused on information use, demonstrated that almost two-thirds of the respondents would seek information to cope with daily life problems. Information seeking behavior was more likely among older children and did not vary by gender. Students who felt their problems were outside of their control perceived information seeking as difficult or as requiring too much time, tended to avoid trying to find information to solve their problems. Among students who sought information, the author summarized reasons for seeking information as to solve a problem, to escape from thinking about a problem, to calm down and work toward a future transition out of the problem, and to affect a mood change that would help them feel better. Information seeking for many of these participants is described as a process used to control emotions and as not necessarily requiring that problem itself be resolved.

Another scheme for identifying the information needs of children is offered by Shenton and Dixon[9] who used qualitative methods with youth ranging in age from 3 to 18 years of age to determine who they go to when they consult people for information and what types of information they seek. Twelve categories of information needs were identified that included both the need for content as well as affective needs. These categories include "advice, spontaneous 'life situation' information, personal information, affective support, empathetic understanding, support for skill development, school-related subject information, interest-driven information, self-development information, preparatory information, reinterpretations/supplementations, and verification information" (p. 222).

Meyers et al.[10] used a "Tween Day" methodology that included interviews and focus groups to study the information needs of children aged 9–13. They found that many of the information needs of this group were related to things that were currently going on in their lives and not long-term concerns. They wanted information to complete homework, for personal hobbies and interests, related social events, and popular culture. They also voiced a need for information about personal safety related to dealing with bullies and strangers, information about drugs and alcohol, and a strong need to share private information within a trusting relationship. These youth did not feel that they could necessarily expect that formal information would be available to help them with daily life concerns.

A study of the school and personal needs of high school students[11] demonstrated that students are most likely to seek information for school-related reasons. However, they also sought information for information needs related to health, relationships, current lifestyle, and for making future plans. This study also revealed that students may consciously decide not to seek information, preferring to figure things out on their own, especially if they feel their concerns are subjective or unimportant, feel time pressures, or do not believe that relevant resources exist for their problem. Students also pointed to procrastination and denial as reasons not to seek information.

Agosto and Hughes-Hassell,[12] using data from group interviews with urban young adults aged 14–17, developed a typology of the questions they identified as part of their everyday life information seeking (ELIS). The resulting categories support other research on youth information needs and include "schoolwork, time/date, social life/leisure activities, weather, daily life routine (e.g., meal and clothing selection), popular culture, current events, transportation, personal finances, consumer information, personal improvement (including self-help, college, and scholarship information), and job information" (p. 159).

Laplante[13] used social network analysis to study the use of social networks among 15–17-year-olds seeking help with homework. Data were collected using in-depth interviews with 19 students from public schools in Montreal, Canada. Respondents had a preference for people they had established relationships with (parents, friends) and who were convenient at the time information was being sought. Homework help was categorized as procedural help (how to perform a task), proofreading, comparing answers, factual (e.g., definitions, URLs), and executive help (described as copying someone else's work). Students who solicited help through social networking sites (SNS such as Facebook) tended to keep their help-seeking private by asking friends who were already signed on and using chat features rather than posting questions on their wall.

Special Populations

The information needs of special populations have also been the subject of investigations interested in youth. For example, Hamer's study[14] focused on the information seeking of gay males related to disclosing their sexual orientation to others. Interviews were performed with young men in their late teens and early twenties revealing information needs related to understanding and forming their own gay identity, the decision to label themselves gay, and the consequences of self-identifying as gay. Participants reported periods during which they avoided these information needs, felt the need to conceal information seeking activities, and interacted with other young gay adults in online forums.

Hersberger et al.[15] studied the information use environment of abused and neglected children aged 1–17 who had been removed from their homes. These children were found to first need information related to adjusting to their situation such as understanding what happened and why. After adjustment, children begin to grapple with the question of what is going to happen to them next. They cope with this question from the time of temporary placement until they are reunited with their family, placed with a relative, or moved into court-approved custodial care or possible adoption by a third party.

Agosto and Hughes-Hassell[16] chose to study urban teens as this is a group that has not been given much attention in the literature. Urban—or inner city—teens have special circumstances in that they live in high-density areas of low socio-economic status and may lack strong role models, and libraries are in a good position to provide the information they need. They found that ELIS for these teens was centered on issues related to achieving adulthood in order to better understand themselves and the world. The researchers conceptualized urban teen information behavior as supporting development of the social self, the emotional self, the reflective self, the physical self, the creative self, the cognitive self, and the sexual self, and related these to a typography of 28 topics the teens' identified as areas of information need that they experience.

Koo[17] investigated the information-seeking behaviors of newly arrived, high school–aged Korean immigrant youth in the United States. She wondered, given the importance of peers as an information source, how youth who had yet to establish relationships with peers compensate for this important resource. She found that during the period of social isolation their primary concern was doing well in school. They wanted information on how to improve their English in order to excel in class and better participate in school-related activities. They were also interested in developing social skills in order to make friends and to increase their comfort in American culture. These students demonstrated a strong preference for people when seeking information. However, in the absence of peers they relied on parents (mainly their mothers), teachers, and a do-it-yourself attitude.

Lilley[18] used mixed methods to study the information behavior of Māori students recruited from four secondary schools in New Zealand. A total of 139 students participated in a survey and 45 students participated in focus groups. The data reveal that these students prefer to seek information from people they personally know, such as friends, teammates, parents, siblings, extended family, and teachers. Students used opportunities in and around school to socialize and share information. Specific places where information exchanges take place were identified as school grounds, which includes restrooms, gym, organized sports practice, around the school shop (which sells food and school supplies), and the smoker's hangout. Information exchanged tended to center on social topics (e.g., music, film, gossip) and schoolwork.

INFORMATION SEEKING MODELS

Outside reference to developmental psychology, the use of theory to inform investigations of youth information seeking is limited. There are, however, three models of information seeking that have been widely referenced in this literature: Kuhlthau's information search process (ISP), Savolainen's ELIS, and Gross' imposed query model.

The ISP Model

The ISP model[19] seeks to describe the constructive process of completing a research assignment by taking into account the cognitive, affective, and physical dimensions of information seeking. The research process is broken down into six stages: task initiation, topic selection, prefocus exploration, focus formulation, information collection, and search closure. At each stage, an assessment of the feelings, thoughts, actions, strategies, and mood of the information seeker are tracked demonstrating an interesting pattern of movement in which confidence grows as the thought process becomes increasingly specific and interest grows as information-seeking actions become more specific.

The ISP has provided a useful framework for research and has informed interventions structured to help people gain information literacy skills. This model has been effective in bringing awareness of the role of affective response in information seeking and that recognition of uncertainty, confusion, and even frustration as a normal part of the process helps students deal with the uncertainty inherent in the process of refining a topic for study. It stands out in that it has been extensively tested in a variety of libraries and with a variety of users.[20]

One example of a recent study of the ISP sought to understand the metacognitive knowledge of adolescents working through the ISP and the potential relationship between metacognitive knowledge and the cognitive, affective, and behavioral dimensions of the ISP.[21] Using a think aloud protocol, Bowler was able to identify 13 metacognitive categories and to argue for teaching metacognitive strategies to students to support the development of information literacy skills.

Everyday Life Information Seeking

Everyday life information seeking[22] brings into focus the world of information seeking that exists outside of work and school. The framework of ELIS is made up of two major concepts, way of life and mastery of life, and suggests how they manifest as approaches to information seeking. Way of life refers to how an individual has organized daily activities and prioritized them. Way of life describes the personal context an individual sees as "normal" and how they strive to maintain that condition. Mastery of life describes the individual's ability to maintain an acceptable level of satisfaction with the way of life they have established. When things are going well, mastery of life may be a passive state. However, when problems arise or the way of life is threatened in some aspect, mastery of life may require an active stance to deal with whatever stimuli is being presented.

Like the ISP model, ELIS takes into account both the cognitive and affective nature of information seeking. However, the affective domain described by ELIS moves along a continuum of optimism versus pessimism concerning the prospect of being able to solve the information problem. It also points out that familiar information sources may not only be preferred, but their use may become so natural that they are not considered critically or considered in light of other resources or opportunities for information gathering.

One recent example of the application of ELIS to research on youth information seeking is the development of Agosto and Hughes-Hassel's model of the everyday life information needs of urban young adults.[16] The authors conclude that "the essence of teen ELIS is the gathering and processing of information to facilitate

the multifaceted teen-to-adulthood maturation process" (p. 1399). To demonstrate this, the model has as inputs seven variables related to a teen's self-understanding that may work as motivators for information seeking: the emotional self, the reflective self, the physical self, the creative self, the cognitive self, the sexual self, and the social self.

Imposed Query

The imposed query is another model that has contributed to understanding of the information seeking process.[23] This model differentiates between information seeking that is self-generated (the user who thought up the question also pursues the answer) and information seeking that is imposed (the user is acting as an agent by pursing a response to questions given to them by someone else). Over 14 categories of imposer/agent relationships have been identified that result in imposed information seeking. The four most common imposers found in a study of adult reference desk use are children, instructors, spouses, and employers. A study of children aged 4–12 in an elementary school setting revealed that while teachers are the main imposers in this environment, the children also impose information seeking on teachers, parents, and other children.[24]

A key point made by the imposed query is that there are many opportunities for the transaction of imposed queries to break down. Problems such as poor communication, beliefs and stereotypes about imposers, the nature of the relationship between the agent and the imposer, and the skill level of the person in the role of agent can all work against their successful resolution. To date, the imposed query model has been used to inform both research and practice in the areas of reference work, reference evaluation, investigations of youth and the Internet, information retrieval, information seeking, and the design of digital libraries.

A recent example of work that incorporates the imposed query is Bowler's[25] analysis of the development of student curiosity when working on a class assignment. Because of the specifications and time restraints that come with class assignments, students had to manage their level of personal interest, which could sometimes be a problem. While the development of personal interest helped to motivate students to complete the assignment, the assigned nature of the work can be at odds with fulfilling their developing personal interest. This put students in a position that can be both pleasurable and painful. Managing curiosity was a central concern when an imposed task begins to provoke self-generated questions.

YOUTH INFORMATION SEEKING BEHAVIOR

The research on the information seeking behaviors of youth is limited, but growing. Almost all investigations of youth information seeking behavior have taken place in the context of school and are focused on the use of electronic resources. These studies have mainly been pragmatic in nature, focused on the performance of specific children in specific contexts mainly in response to school assignments. In addition, research has been more focused on searching behaviors than on information needs.[9,26] Little is known about youth information seeking at home, in the public library, or in other information providing spaces. Likewise, little is known about the information needs and information seeking of very young children.

One issue that affects the information seeking of youth is the extent to which they have access to the resources they need to respond to their information needs. Young children may need help formulating their information needs and their access to information is often mediated, if not controlled by adults, if only to the extent that children often lack funds, transportation, and the independence to allow them the number of information options that adults enjoy. Issues of equity of access to information and services for youth in libraries are a continuing concern as challenges to materials, issues of filtering, inequities in information services for youth, and practices that discourage youth from interacting with librarians persist.[27–30]

It is clear, however, that youth access to technology and the Internet continues to increase. Use of the Internet by youth at home, in the library, and at school is growing, and mobile devices are increasingly providing access to information for young people; however, equity of access for all youth remains a concern.[31]

Resource Preferences

The resources used by youth to respond to both imposed and self-generated information needs can be summarized as people, the Internet, and books. Like other user groups, youth tend to go to the most accessible sources first, prefer people and resources available in the home, such as books they already own or computers they have access to. One characteristic of youth information seeking is a preference for the familiar. Children tend to prefer resources they have already interacted with whether these are print-based or electronic in format. The known story or website is generally preferred. Gradually, these preferences widen incorporating similar stories or subjects, books by the same author, and books of the same type or genre. Another issue, especially for children, is the high reading level at which many nonfiction texts are written and the difficulty of finding age-appropriate resources online. Children are very often required to use resources above their reading level when interacting with information resources.

People

In addition to the examples provided under the section, Youth Information Needs, Posten-Anderson and Edwards[32] investigated the information seeking of 13- and 14-year-old girls. They interviewed 28 girls and found them interested in information about relationships, school, and work. The girls revealed that factual information was the easiest to find, but that information needs that required interpretation were harder to satisfy. Likewise they felt school and work information was easier to find than information that would allow them to meet concerns about relationships. These girls did not see the school library as a place they could take their relationship concerns and preferred instead to talk to other people to try to satisfy these needs.

Agosto and Hughes-Hassell[12] also demonstrated a preference among young people, of age 14–17 for using other people as information sources. However, librarians are not preferred resources for youth, who would rather consult friends and family. Preferred people[9] include those who are convenient, such as parents and siblings; people youth recognize as having similar concerns, such as peers; and those believed to have expert knowledge, such as teachers. Stemmel and Ladd[33] demonstrated that even very young children have the ability to recognize expertise in others and bring this type of critical thinking to bear in their choice of peer informants in their information seeking.

The Internet

A recent report by the Pew Foundation found that teens are heavy users of the Internet as compared to adults.[34] Almost all youth aged 12 and over have cell phones, and about 75% of youth use mobile devices to access the Internet. Furthermore, while lower-income youth and youth from lower-education homes continue to have less access to the Internet, they "are just as likely and in some cases more likely than those living in higher income and more highly educated households to use their cell phone as a primary point of access" (p. 2). Studies are demonstrating that young adults are avid users of social media, and there is a call in the literature for further study of youth information behaviors related to virtual environments.[35]

Studies concerned with youth access to the Internet mainly look at access in the schools and indicate that young people generally are not very skilled at using the Internet to find information.[11,36–38] Vansickle[39] wondered if academic track (i.e., technical, college preparatory, and honors students) would correlate with ability and asked students to self-rate their skills. Uniformly students said they taught themselves how to search the Internet or learned from friends, and they all believed their search skills to be sufficient. No difference was found related to academic track.

Bilal has performed several studies[40–42] that look at children's use of search engines for imposed and self-generated information seeking. Her studies reveal that young people do not have the skills they need to find information easily and have a particularly hard time with questions that require them to retrieve information from more than one resource. Students were more satisfied with the process of answering self-generated questions than they were with retrieving information for imposed queries.

Recent research on the information literacy skills of first-year college students has demonstrated that while students are very confident about their ability to search, their actual skill level tends to be poor.[43] The majority of first-year college students in these studies report having taught themselves to use the Internet or having learned from peers. However, they also cite classroom teachers, school and public librarians, and parents as people who have taught them information literacy skills. It is not clear to what extent young people are being taught to find, evaluate, and use information via formal instruction in grades K-12.

Of particular concern is the ability of youth to assess the credibility of digital resources. Because they often lack the skills and training needed to evaluate sources, they tend to rely on the design of web pages and how the information is presented rather than focusing on content.[44]

Flanagin and Metzger[45] used large-scale surveys to study differences in how adults (18 years and older) and young adults (ages 11–18 years) perceive the credibility of information across three online encyclopedias: Encyclopedia Britannica, Citizendium, and Wikipedia. Their results indicate that both groups are aware of Wikipedia, but that many are unclear as to how content on Wikipedia is supplied. Both groups recognize that content on Encyclopedia Britannica is more credible than content provided on the other two sites. However, both groups report using Wikipedia "sometimes." Young adults are more questioning than adults of content presented as being from Wikipedia but rely heavily on contextual clues, such as recognition of the source, in making credibility judgments.

In a John D. and Catherine T. Macarthur foundation report[46] related to the Flanagin and Metzer study, the authors found that children "consistently overestimate their own skill levels and capacity to discern good information from bad information as compared to others" (p. 106).

Books

It has been established since the 1940s that reading for fun declines with age, and that age 12 is a pivotal point at which recreational reading drops precipitously.[24,47] However, traditional ideas of reading and of what a book is are variables that may need redefinition in reading studies to gain a full picture of what reading and writing look like for today's young people. The high level of Internet use indicates that youth are reading online as well as using print-based works to respond to school assignments and to support personal information and recreation needs.

National surveys have been criticized for defining reading in ways that do not reflect actual reading practice.[48] While there have been numerous surveys that have raised concern about the reading habits of the young, a 2009 National Endowment for the Arts survey[49] demonstrated an increase in the amount of time spent reading, and a 2010 Kaiser Family foundation report[50] demonstrated that heavy readers do better in school and that time spent "on screen" is not replacing time spent with print media.

A 2012 Pew report[51] found that 83% of young people of age 16–29 had read a book in the last year, that young people read for imposed and self-generated reasons, and that E-books were more popular with 18–24-year-olds than among high school age youth. A 2014 Pew report[52] discovered that people under the age of 30 are more likely to have read a book (includes all formats) weekly and over the course of a year, than those over age 30. Further young people are now "e-reading" at a rate similar to adults between the ages of 30 and 49.

Searching for Information

Early studies focused on children's use of library catalogs revealed many barriers to their use, including lack of key-boarding, spelling, and vocabulary skills, as well as problems with Boolean logic.[53,54] Children prefer to use natural language and need assistance formulating queries. They prefer browsing to searching and prefer searching library shelves to using the catalog to find books. Researchers have continued to be interested in assessing youth information seeking using electronic resources,[55] and though there continue to be many gaps in the research, the findings tend to be consistent across studies. Research studies indicate that children and young adults need help formulating searches and benefit from formal training in information-seeking skills. Visual images help children compensate for low-level reading skills, and children perform better on interfaces designed especially for them that take into account limitations related to maturation and skill attainment.[56,57]

While children and young adults can perform well on electronic interfaces, they tend to use them in a superficial way, often not taking advantage of advanced features, and overall their ability as information seekers tends to be low. Older children perform at a higher level than younger ones but do not necessarily attain competency in information seeking at school. The provision of formal information literacy instruction in primary and secondary schools is uneven, and studies[43] have demonstrated that many entering college freshmen have nonproficient information-seeking skills. Interestingly, gender differences in computer use have almost disappeared. While the culture of computing between boys and girls may differ, the gap in skill levels appears to be closing.[58]

Studies of children's use of systems are complicated by the wide range of skills and maturity that youth demonstrate. Early literature on children's use of information systems has limited usefulness as it often does not discriminate between developmental stages, does not assess skill with technology, and reflects use of systems that are now outdated.[57] While information systems have been developed especially for children, some authors point out that the use of such systems is not always practical, nor necessarily responsive to individual needs.[7]

Use of Reference Services

As with access to other resources, adults often mediate children's use of reference services in both the physical library and the virtual library. Adults play several roles in this respect, acting as role models, facilitating information seeking on the part of the child, and acting as agents for child users. The imposed query is common in reference work in the children's room. In fact, it is a common assumption that the majority of children's reference questions are related to schoolwork, although there is not sufficient information to know if this assumption is correct or not. Clearly, children have life situations and personal interests that can also be satisfied using library resources and that lead them to the reference desk. Because of the nature of traditional reference work, there is little documentation available to tell us what children are looking for when they seek assistance at the reference desk. Studies of children's use of computers in public libraries have demonstrated a high level of recreational use, such as for gaming.[59,60]

Although it might seem that digital reference, which often provides a transcript of the reference transaction, would be able to answer some questions about the nature of reference services with youth, little work has been done in this area. Silverstein[61] analyzed questions posed by youth (elementary through high school students) to science-oriented ASKA services and determined that 13% of these queries were not in response to school assignments but reflected self-initiated learning on the part of these users. Walter and Mediavilla[30] reviewed virtual reference transactions between public librarians and young adults as part of an assessment of a homework help program. They found that 40% of these queries were referred to Live Homework Help because students asked for tutoring help. Other queries, represented as reference questions by users, were later referred for tutoring based on the librarian's assessment of the users need. The majority (60%) of the 114 queries identified as homework were math problems and only 8% were science topics.

Luo[62] held focus groups with 36 teens aged 13–19 to learn about their use of text reference services. Only one teen was aware that the service was provided and none had used it. In projecting why they thought they would or would not use the service, participants felt they would most likely use it to satisfy an imposed query. However, they had concerns about the use of text reference related to response time, interacting with librarians using a technology they perceived as meant for personal use, and the constraints of the technology itself. Here they were mainly concerned not only with cost, but also the limited number of characters, and concern that text reference might be limited to questions that had short answers.

Determining Relevance

Another important research question that has received limited attention is the ability of youth to determine the relevance of information resources to their search. Such judgments are connected to their ability to think critically about resources as well as to the amount of formal instruction they have received concerning the research process. Students have been shown to depend on title information, graphics, and book covers, when they have the book in hand, as the primary determinants of the relevance of a source to a search. In electronic searching, their confidence is increased when system terms match terms used in school texts.

In general, elementary grade children have difficulty assessing electronic sources. In Hirsh's[63] study of fifth graders, she found not only that the students were interested in issues of authority, accessibility, and currency as well as the interest level of the material to themselves and their intended audience (their classmates), but also that students tended to stop searching as soon as they found an item that met the requirements of the assignment. Alexandersson and Limberg's[64] study of 11-year-olds completing a school assignment about the sea demonstrated that these students saw information seeking as a procedure in which they searched for and then compiled and presented facts. Little attention was given to developing personal questions or understanding related to the topic. Students did not report much difficulty finding books in the library or using computers to find information, but the researchers observed that students did not use the library classification system to find works and often reported there was nothing available on the Internet for their topic. None of these studies are generalizable; however, they are consistent with other work that has demonstrated an inability among middle and high school students to assess resources and to connect what they find to what they already know.

YOUTH AS PARTICIPANTS IN RESEARCH

In 1986, Dervin and Nilan[65] published a now classic article on information seeking that heralded a paradigm change from a system perspective to a user perspective in research and practice. While the important change in orientation documented by this article has had a widespread effect on research and professional work in libraries, it has had limited impact on youth services. The design and delivery of information services for children continue for the most part to be seen as the purview of professional librarians, school library media specialists, teachers, parents, and other adults interested in child welfare.

As Walter[6] makes clear in her research, there is an important logic to this. People do not always know what they need and children especially cannot be expected to be able to identify their own information needs in all areas. For example, they may very much need to know how to cross the street safely, but it may not occur to them without help, that this is something they need to know. Children do have their own ideas concerning what they want or need to know. They have their own interests and hobbies and can be articulate about their information needs and resource preferences.

In addition to the views of interested adults, the inclusion of youth in research, service design, and system development is increasingly recognized as important. Young adult advisory panels are increasingly used in libraries to help guide professional decisions concerning collection development and programming. Likewise, youth are increasingly participants, rather than just subjects, in research focused on their information behaviors. They are also being included as team members in the design and development of information technologies that are being created especially for them. However, these trends have yet to include very young children to a significant extent.

Perhaps, the most substantial example of the integration of youth in research and system development comes from the intergenerational design work by a research team at the University of Maryland. Using participatory design, this group has undertaken several innovative projects such as the SearchKids visual search interface and the International Children's Digital Library (ICDL).[66] The inclusion of young people as full members of the design team has resulted in tools that help children search by providing the support they need in a developmental sense as well as responding to their search preferences. For instance, in addition to the typical searching functions such as keyword searching, the ICDL allows users to search for books in ways children expressed as useful, such as by the color of the book cover or by story length. The successes of this approach have influenced others not only to design technologies with children in mind, but also to include them in the design process. Examples include Bilal's efforts at Web portal design that use children as design partners[67] and the use of intergenerational research teams described by Large et al.[68,69] to visualize and develop consensus on the design of information technologies meant for children.

In terms of information services for children in libraries, the Project CATE model, developed with the support of the IMLS at the St. Louis Public Library, describes an outcome-based planning and evaluation process in which youth and other stakeholders are central.[70] Stakeholders collaborate not only to make decisions about information and technology services, but also to agree on what the target outcomes of services will be. Potential outcomes include changes in knowledge, behavior, skills, attitude, or status.

CONCLUSION

The information needs and information-seeking behavior of youth are two areas that continue to be ripe for investigations that will inform both research and practice. While a body of work is accumulating related to information seeking in school and information seeking with electronic resources, there are significant gaps in our knowledge and methodological issues that need to be addressed to build a solid research base. Youth information seeking in information spaces outside of school, the place of various media in youth information seeking, and the information needs of very young children are particular topics that need to be addressed. Increasing use of theory and the inclusion of youth are two continuing trends that are resulting in new insights and improved information services, systems, and resources that respond to the needs of this diverse population.

REFERENCES

1. Agosto, D. Young adults' information behavior: what we know so far and where we need to go from here. J. Res. Libr. Young Adults **2011**, *2* (1), http://www.yalsa.ala.org/jrlya/.
2. Bilal, D.; Chelton, M.K.; Zhang, Y.; Cool, C. Challenges to children's research: the road ahead. In *Information, Connections, and Community, Proceedings of the 65th American Society for Information Science & Technology Annual Meeting*, Philadelphia, PA, November 18–21, 2002; Toms, E.G. Am. Soc. Inf. Sci. Technol. **2002**, *39*, 501–502.
3. Shenton, A. Research into young people's information-seeking: perspectives and methods. ASLIB Proc. New Inf. Perspect. **2004**, *56* (4), 243–254.
4. Walter, V.A. The once and future library. School Libr. J. **2001**, *47* (1), 49–53.
5. Case, D.O. *Looking for Information: A Survey of Research on Information Seeking, Needs, and Behavior*; Academic Press: New York, 2002.
6. Walter, V.A. The information needs of children. In *Advances in Librarianship*; Godden, I.P., Ed.; Academic Press: San Diego, CA, 1994; Vol. 18, 111–129.
7. Foss, E.; Druin, A.; Brewer, R.; Children's search roles at home: implications for designers, researchers, educators, and parents. J. Am. Soc. Inf. Sci. Technol. **2012**, *63* (3), 558–573.
8. Lu, Y.-L. Children's information seeking in coping with daily-life problems: an investigation of fifth-and sixth-grade students. Libr. Inf. Sci. Res. **2010**, *32* (1), 77–88.
9. Shenton, A.K.; Dixon, P. Youngster's use of other people as an information seeking method. J. Libr. Inf. Sci. **2003**, *35* (4), 219–233.

10. Meyers, E.M.; Fisher, K.E.; Marcoux, E. Studying the everyday information behavior of tweens: notes from the field. Libr. Inf. Sci. Res. **2007**, *29* (3), 310–331.

11. Fidel, R.; Davies, R.; Douglass, M. A visit to the information mall: web searching behavior of high school students. J. Am. Soc. Inf. Sci. Technol. **1999**, *50* (1), 24–37.

12. Agosto, D.E.; Hughes-Hassell, S. People, places, and questions: an investigation of the everyday life information-seeking behavior of urban young adults. Libr. Inf. Sci. Res. **2005**, *27* (2), 141–163.

13. Laplante, A. Social capital and academic help seeking: adolescent's use of people as information sources. In *New Directions in Children's and Adolescents' Information Behavior Research*; Bilal, D., Beheshti, J., Eds.; Emerald Group Publishing Limited: Bingley, U.K., 2014; Vol. 10, 67–103.

14. Hamer, J.S. Coming-out: gay males' information seeking. Sch. Libr. Worldw. **2003**, *9* (2), 73–89.

15. Hersberger, J.A.; Murray, A.; Sokoloff, S.M. The information use environment of abused and neglected children. Inf. Res. **2006**, *12* (1), paper 277, http://InformationR.net/ir/12-1/paper277.html.

16. Agosto, D.E.; Hughes-Hassell, S. Toward a model of the everyday life information needs of urban teenagers, Part 1: a theoretical model. J. Am. Soc. Inf. Sci. Technol. **2006**, *57* (10), 1394–1403.

17. Koo, J.H. Adolescents' information behavior when isolated from Peer Groups: lessons from new immigrant adolescents' everyday life information seeking; PhD dissertation, The Florida State University, Tallahassee, FL, 2013, http://www.lib.fsu.edu/find/etds.html.

18. Lilley, S.C. The social information grounds of Māori Secondary School students. In *New Directions in Children's and Adolescents' Information Behavior Research*; Bilal, D., Beheshti, J., Eds.; Emerald Group Publishing Limited: Bingley, U.K., 2014; Vol. 10, 191–213.

19. Kuhlthau, C.C. *Seeking Meaning: A Process Approach to Library and Information Services*, 2nd Ed.; Libraries Unlimited: Westport, CT, 2004.

20. Kuhlthau, C.C. Kuhlthau's information search process. In *Theories of Information Behavior*; Fisher, K., Erdelez, S., Mckechnie, L.E.F., Eds.; Information Today: Medford, NJ, 2005; 230–234.

21. Bowler, L. A taxonomy of adolescent metacognitive knowledge during the information search process. Libr. Inf. Sci. Res. **2010**, *32* (1), 27–42. doi:10.1016/j.lisr.2009.09.005.

22. Savolainen, R. Everyday life information seeking: approaching information seeking in the context of "way of life" Libr. Inf. Sci. Res. **1995**, *17* (3), 259–294.

23. Gross, M. The imposed query. Ref. Q. **1995**, *35* (2), 236–243.

24. Gross, M. *Studying Children's Questions: Information Seeking Behavior in School*; Scarecrow Press: Lanham, MD, 2006.

25. Bowler, L. The self-regulation of curiosity and interest during the information search process of adolescent students. J. Am. Soc. Inf. Sci. Technol. **2010**, *61* (7), 1332–1344. doi:10.1002/asi.21334.

26. Walter, V.A. Public library service to children and teens: a research agenda. Libr. Trends **2003**, *51* (4), 571–589.

27. Chelton, M.K. The "over-due-kid": a face-to-face library service encounter as ritual interaction. Libr. Inf. Sci. Res. **1997**, *19* (4), 387–399.

28. Meyers, E. The coolness factor. Ten libraries listen to youth. Am. Libr. **1999**, *30* (10), 42–44.

29. Winston, M. Reference and information services for young adults: a research study of public libraries in New Jersey. Ref. User Serv. Q. **2001**, *41* (1), 45–50.

30. Walter, V.A.; Mediavilla, C. Teens are from Neptune, librarians are from Pluto: an analysis of online reference transactions. Libr. Trends **2005**, *54* (2), 209–227.

31. Madden, M.; Lenhart, A.; Duggan, M. *Teens and Technology*; Pew Research Center: Washington, DC, 2013.

32. Posten-Anderson, B.; Edwards, S. The role of information in helping adolescent girls with their life concerns. Sch. Libr. Media Q. **1993**, *22*, 25–30.

33. Stemmel, A.J.; Ladd, G.W. Children's selective use of peer informants: criteria for making information-seeking decisions. J. Genet. Psychol. **1984**, *146* (4), 541–550.

34. Madden, M.; Lenhart, A.; Duggan, M. *Teens and Technology*; Pew Research Center: Washington, DC, 2013.

35. Meyers, E. Tip of the iceberg: meaning, identity, and literacy in preteen virtual worlds. J. Educ. Libr. Inf. Sci. **2009**, *50* (4), 226–236.

36. Julien, H.; Barker, S. How high-school students find and evaluate scientific information: a basis for information literacy skills development. Libr. Inf. Sci. Res. **2009**, *31* (1), 12–17. doi:10.1016/j.lisr.2008.10.008.

37. Large, A.; Beheshti, J.; Moukdad, H. Information seeking on the web: navigational skills of grade-six primary school students. In *Proceedings of the 62nd ASIS Annual Meeting*, Washington, DC, October 31–November 4, 1999.

38. Wallace, R.M.; Kupperman, J.; Krajcik, J.; Soloway, E. Science on the web: students online in a sixth-grade classroom. J. Learn. Sci. **2000**, *9* (1), 75–104.

39. Vansickle, S. Tenth graders' search knowledge and use of the web. Knowl. Quest. **2002**, *30* (4), 33–37.

40. Bilal, D. Children's use of the Yahooligans! web search engine: I. Cognitive, physical, and affective behaviors on fact-based search tasks. J. Am. Soc. Inf. Sci. **2000**, *51* (7), 646–665.

41. Bilal, D. Children's use of the Yahooligans! web search engine: II. Cognitive and physical behaviors on research tasks. J. Am. Soc. Inf. Sci. Technol. **2001**, *52* (2), 118–136.

42. Bilal, D. Children's use of Yahooligans! web search engine: III. Cognitive and physical behaviors on fully self-generated search tasks. J. Am. Soc. Inf. Sci. Technol. **2002**, *53* (13), 1170–1183.

43. Gross, M.; Latham, D. What's skill got to do with it?: information literacy skills and self-views of ability among first year college students. J. Am. Soc. Inf. Sci. Technol. **2012**, *63* (3), 574–583.

44. Harris, F.J. Challenges to teaching credibility assessment in contemporary schooling. In *Digital Media, Youth, and Credibility*; Metzer, M.J., Fanagin, A.J., Eds.; The MIT Press: Cambridge, MA, 2008; 155–180.

45. Flanagin, A.J.; Metzger, M.J. From Encyclopedia Britannica to Wikipedia. Inf. Commun. Soc. **2011**, *14* (3), 355–374.

46. Flanagin, A.J.; Metzger, M.J. *Kids and Credibility: An Empirical Examination of Youth, Digital Media Use, and Information Credibility. The John D. and Catherine T.*

MacArthur Foundation Reports on Digital Media and Learning; The MIT Press: Cambridge, MA, 2010.

47. Teran, L.T.; Mates, B.F. Learning to love reading: interviews with older children and teens. J. Adolesc. Adult Literacy **2004**, *48* (3), 188–200.

48. Moyer, J.E. Teens today don't read books anymore: a study of difference in interest and comprehension based on reading modalities: Part 1, introduction and methodology. J. Res. Libr. Young Adults **2010**, *1* (1), http://www.yalsa.ala.org/jrlya.

49. National Endowment for the Arts. *Reading on the Rise*; National Endowment for the Arts: Washington, DC, 2009.

50. Rideout, V.J.; Foehr, U.G.; Roberts, D.F. *Generation M2: Media in the Lives of 8- To 18-Year-Olds*; Henry J. Kaiser Family Foundation: Menlo Park, CA, 2010, http://kaiserfamilyfoundation.files.wordpress.com/2013/01/8010.pdf.

51. Zickuhr, K.; Rainie, L.; Purcell, K.; *Younger American's Reading and Library Habits*; Pew Research Center's Internet & American Life Project: Washington, DC, 2012, http://libraries.pewinternet.org/2012/10/23/younger-americans-reading-and-library-habits/.

52. Zickuhr, K.; Rainie, L. *Younger American's Reading and Library Habits and Technology Use*; Pew Research Center's Internet & American Life Project: Washington, DC, 2014, http://www.pewinternet.org/2014/09/10/younger-americans-reading-habits-and-technology-use/.

53. Borgman, C.L.; Hirsh, S.G.; Walter, V.A.; Gallagher, A.L. Children's searching behavior on browsing and keyword online catalogs: the science library catalog project. J. Am. Soc. Inf. Sci. **1995**, *46* (9), 663–684.

54. Solomon, P. Children's information retrieval behavior: a case analysis of an OPAC. J. Am. Soc. Inf. Sci. **1993**, *44* (5), 245–264.

55. Druin, A. Children's access and use of digital resources [special Issue]. Libr. Trends **2005**, *54* (2), 173–177.

56. Cooper, L.Z. Developmentally appropriate digital environments for young children. Libr. Trends **2005**, *54* (2), 286–302.

57. Grossen, T.; Nürnberger, A. Specifics of information retrieval for young users: a survey. Inf. Process. Manage. **2013**, *49* (4), 739–756.

58. Dresang, E.T.; Gross, M.; Holt, L.E. New perspectives: gender, net-generation children, and computers. Libr. Trends **2007**, *56*, 360–386.

59. Sandvig, C. Public internet access for young children in the inner city: evidence to inform access subsidy and content regulation. Inf. Soc. **2003**, *19* (2), 171–183.

60. Gross, M.; Dresang, E.T.; Holt, L.E. Children's in-library use of computers in an urban public library. Libr. Inf. Sci. Res. **2004**, *26* (3), 311–337.

61. Silverstein, J. Next generation children's digital reference services: a research agenda. In *Developing Digital Libraries for K-12 Education*; Mardis, M., Ed.; ERIC Clearinghouse on Information & Technology: Syracuse, NY, 2003; 141–158.

62. Luo, L.; Weak, E. Text reference service: teens' perception and use. Libr. Inf. Sci. Res. **2013**, *35* (1), 14–23.

63. Hirsh, S. Children's relevance criteria and information seeking on electronic resources. J. Am. Soc. Inf. Sci. Technol. **1999**, *50* (14), 1265–1283.

64. Alexandersson, M.; Limberg, L. Constructing meaning through information artefacts. New Rev. Inform. Behav. Res. **2003**, *4* (1), 17–30.

65. Dervin, B.; Nilan, M. Information needs and uses. In *Annual Review of Information Science and Technology*; Williams, M.E., Ed.; Knowledge Industry Publishers: New York, 1986; Vol. 21, 3–33.

66. Druin, A. What children can teach us: developing digital libraries for children with children. Libr. Q. **2005**, *75* (1), 20–41.

67. Bilal, D. Children design their interfaces for Web search engines: a participatory approach. In *Proceedings of the 30th Annual Conference of the Canadian Association for Information Science*, Toronto, Canada, May 30–June 1, 2002. 204–214.

68. Large, A.; Nesset, V.; Beheshti, J. Bonded design: a novel approach to intergenerations information technology design. Libr. Inf. Sci. Res. **2006**, *28* (2), 64–82.

69. Large, A.; Nesset, V.; Tabatabaei, N.; Beheshti, J. Bonded design revisited: involving children in information visualization. Can. J. Inf. Libr. Sci. **2008**, *43* (3/4), 107–139.

70. Dresang, E.T.; Gross, M.; Holt, L.E. Using outcome measures to assess school-age children's use of technology in urban public libraries: a collaborative research process. Libr. Inf. Sci. Res. **2004**, *25* (1), 19–42.

Zoological Park and Aquarium Libraries and Archives

Vernon N. Kisling, Jr.
Marston Science Library, University of Florida, Gainesville, Florida, U.S.A.

Abstract

Animal collections have existed since about 3000 B.C.; however, professional wildlife husbandry only began with the evolution of zoological parks in the early nineteenth century. This significantly increased during the second half of the twentieth century as the institutions, professional literature, and libraries matured together. Archives developed at a later and slower pace. Internationally, zoo and aquarium libraries and archives have progressed at varying rates in different countries depending on the profession's development in each country. Zoological park and aquarium libraries have services primarily concerned with the needs of their staffs. They have a specialized emphasis, reflecting the wildlife husbandry profession and its literature. As this body of literature grew, and the need for this literature became a essential part of the profession, libraries became increasingly important functions within zoos and aquariums. As these institutions grew older a sense of history encouraged them to establish archives and preserve their historic legacy.

INTRODUCTION

Zoological parks and aquariums have libraries primarily concerned with the academic and professional needs of their staffs. It is therefore important to understand the development of wildlife husbandry and the literature supporting this profession. Recognition of a need for libraries developed as the literature grew, became more sophisticated, and became a necessary part of learning the profession. Establishment of these libraries is viewed as an integral part of zoo and aquarium history and includes a review of the current status of libraries and library services in U.S. zoos and aquariums, along with a brief sampling of international zoo and aquarium libraries for comparison. Zoo and aquarium archives developed later and more slowly than the libraries. Establishment of these archives came out of a sense of history as the institutions grew older and reached significant anniversary milestones. The establishment of archives and their current status are discussed. The future of these libraries, archives, and their services is also considered.

ZOO AND AQUARIUM LITERATURE

Professional Development

Collections of living wild animals have been maintained since about 3000 B.C. when they first appeared in Mesopotamia, Egypt, and China. Central and South America explorers encountered New World animal collections in the early 1500s that had existed for a long time prior to their discovery. Likewise, early explorers in Asia found animal collections as well. Libraries have also existed for an equally long time in societies that maintained animal collections, but having a specialized library as part of an animal collection is a more recent combination of activities.

Captive wildlife management during ancient times, and throughout most of our history, had its roots in domestication and farm animal husbandry. Keeping and domesticating wild animals began about 10,000 B.C., but collections of wild animals were not feasible until the development of the early, urbanized civilizations, which occurred about 3000 B.C. Wildlife husbandry remained a practical matter for a very long time and did not differ to any great extent from agricultural husbandry until the animal collections (later known as menageries) developed into modern zoological parks during the early 1800s.[1,2]

Neither agricultural nor captive wildlife husbandry, despite several thousand years of activity, developed an organized body of knowledge that could be taught or systematically improved upon until the nineteenth and twentieth centuries. Difficulties existed for those who tried to establish academic and professional foundations in these professions, since it was felt that animal husbandry was a practical matter, not a scientific one, and what had to be learned could be taught verbally by word of mouth. Veterinary medicine and zoological park management suffered a similar fate.

Modern zoological park management began with the transition of European menageries into zoological parks, especially with the opening of the Zoological Society of London's zoo in 1828. Other important early European collections included Tiergarten Schonbrunn, Vienna (1752); Menagerie du Jardin des Plantes, Paris (1793); Zoologischer Garten, Berlin (1844); Natura Artis Magistra, Amsterdam (1838); and Zoologischer Garten

Encyclopedia of Library and Information Sciences, Fourth Edition DOI: 10.1081/E-ELIS4-120044775

Word–Zoological

Breslau, Germany, 1865 (now Miejski Ogrod Zoologiczny, Wroclaw, Poland). Modern aquariums are a more recent development. The first public aquarium was built at the London Zoological Gardens in 1853, and others appeared soon afterward in Europe and the United States.

Exotic wild animals have been exhibited in the United States since 1716, traveling menageries since the early 1800s, and small urban menageries since the 1860s. However, the first modern U.S. zoological park was the Philadelphia Zoological Garden, chartered in 1859 and opened in 1874. After the American Civil War, public and professional consensus favored improved collections and higher standards of animal care. Throughout the decades of the late 1800s and the 1900s, there continued to be improvements in many areas affecting zoos: in community standards for cultural institutions, in the aesthetic sensibilities of the public, in the educational level of the populace, in the level of scientific knowledge, in the conservation of wildlife, in the overall standard of living, and in the expertise of zoo and aquarium staffs. This period was also a time when many occupations, including wildlife husbandry, became professionalized.

Professional zoo associations began forming after the first association, the Verband Deutscher Zoodirektoren (Association of German Zoo Directors), was established in 1887. An American zoo and aquarium profession was formerly recognized with the founding of the American Association of Zoological Parks and Aquariums [AAZPA, now the Association of Zoos and Aquariums (AZA)] in 1924. With a professional association came a professional code of ethics, professional registration of individuals, and professional accreditation for institutions. Improvements in all aspects of administration and animal husbandry were made during the twentieth century, and these improvements intensified in the period following World War II. During the 1960s, there was a significant increase in the professional literature and the number of zoo and aquarium libraries. The decades of the 1970s and 1980s were a time when zoos and aquariums recognized the need for archives (at least in the United States; zoos and aquariums in Europe recognized this need earlier). As several U.S. zoos and aquariums reached their centenaries and the AZA reached its 75th anniversary, a sense of history began to permeate the profession, along with a better appreciation of libraries and archives. Even so, some zoos and aquariums still do not have these facilities, or they have operations that are not appropriately maintained and funded.

GROWTH IN THE PROFESSIONAL LITERATURE

Although the practice of wildlife husbandry at any point in time was appropriate for the time in which it occurred and although it steadily improved over time, there was little in

captive wildlife husbandry to inspire the development of its literature and little in the literature to promote the development of wildlife husbandry during most of its history. In so far as literature is an indication of a profession's development, it appears that the zoo and aquarium profession evolved significantly during and after the 1960s.

Prior to the 1960s, zoos and aquariums improved professionally but at a slower rate that was in keeping with the times. The first U.S. zoo research facility, the Penrose Research Laboratory, began about 1901–1905 at the Philadelphia Zoological Garden, the first zoo veterinary clinic was set up in 1916 at the New York Zoological Park, the first zoo field research station was established in 1916 by the New York Zoological Society, and the New York Zoological Society began publication of the first scientific journal for zoo-based wildlife research, *Zoologica*, in 1907.

Internationally, the Frankfurt Zoological Society began publishing the first zoo journal, *Der Zoologische Garten*, in 1859; the Director of the Calcutta Zoo wrote the first modern book on captive wildlife management, *A Handbook of the Management of Animals in Captivity in Lower Bengal*, published in India in 1892; *International Zoo News* began publication in 1954; and two regionally important zoo journals in Germany and Poland were founded in the 1950s. In addition, as Table 1 indicates, a tremendous increase in the professional literature took place after 1960, led by the all-important publication the *International Zoo Yearbook*.[3]

With continual changes and improvements in wildlife husbandry taking place, the 1960s was the decade when it became clear to many that word-of-mouth training was no longer adequate. Formal training and published information were starting to be recognized as important to the profession's improvement. In addition to commercial publications, there were publications from the institutions and their support organizations, as well as publications from the professional associations (which have now grown to 40 national, regional, and international associations according to the 1998 *International Zoo Yearbook*). In 1978, a Librarians Special Interest Group was formed within the Association of Zoos and Aquariums to coordinate efforts at improving zoo and aquarium library services and to help the association with library-related matters. One of their projects was to sift through the huge increase in professional literature that had developed by the 1980s in order to list the core literature that was considered essential to have in zoo and aquarium libraries.[4]

This large body of literature developed because there was a need for it. Wildlife husbandry information had become recognized as a necessary part of the work. Providing a boost to this recognition was the *International Zoo Yearbook*, published annually since 1960 with articles on every aspect of zoo, aquarium, and wildlife husbandry management. This publication, along with *International Zoo News*, provides a worldwide historical glimpse into

Table 1 Significant publications related to the wildlife husbandry profession.

1859–	*Der Zoologische Garten* (Frankfurt Zoological Society). This is a journal providing national and regional zoo research and news.
1892	*A Handbook of the Management of Animals in Captivity in Lower Bengal.* R.B. Sanyal (Bengal Secretariat Press; Calcutta, India). The earliest known book (in modern times) concerned with captive bird and mammal management.
1897–	*Wildlife Conservation* (Wildlife Conservation Society/formerly New York Zoological Society). Formerly *Animal Kingdom* (1942–1990), and before that the *Journal* (of the NYZS) and *Bulletin* (of the NYZS) (1897–1942). A popular magazine containing information about zoos and natural history articles.
1907– 1973	*Zoologica* (New York Zoological Society). This was a scientific journal that provided wildlife husbandry and natural history contributions from the Bronx Zoo staff. In its later years, it was intended to be a research journal for the American zoo community, but this was not accomplished.
1923	*Disease in Captive Wild Mammals and Birds.* Herbert Fox (Lippincott: Philadelphia, PA). This is the earliest known book (in modern times) on the diseases of captive wildlife. It is based on work done at the first American zoo research center, the Penrose Research Laboratory, Philadelphia Zoological Garden.
1926–	*ZooNooZ* (Zoological Society of San Diego). A popular magazine containing information about zoos and natural history articles.
1932	*Zoological Parks and Aquariums: An Annual Assemblage of Information and Facts* (American Association of Zoological Parks and Aquariums/AAZPA, now the AZA). Despite its title, only this one volume of articles and facts about zoos was published.
1950	*Wild Animals in Captivity.* Heini Hediger (1964, Dover reprint: New York). The first of three books by Hediger concerning the basic principles of wildlife husbandry.
1954–	*International Zoo News* (John Aspinall Foundation: Chichester, UK). The most significant resource for news and information on the world's zoos and aquariums.
1955	*The Psychology and Behavior of Animals in Zoos and Circuses.* Heini Hediger (1968, Dover reprint: New York).
1957–	*Przeglad Zoologiczny* [*Zoological Review*] (Polish Zoo Association: Wroclaw, Poland). This is a national scientific journal of regional and international importance.
1958–	*Zeitschrift des Kölner Zoo* [*Journal of the Cologne Zoo*] (Zoologischer Garten: Köln, Germany). This is a scientific magazine of regional and international importance.
1960–	*International Zoo Yearbook* (Zoological Society of London: London, UK). An annual serial with articles on all aspects of zoos, aquariums, and wildlife husbandry, this is the most important reference resource for the profession. It also includes statistical information on zoos, aquariums, and their wildlife collections covering 1959 to the present.
1960–	*AZA Communiqué* (American Zoo and Aquarium Association/AZA). Formerly the *AAZPA Newsletter* (1960–1991) and *AAZPA News* (1924–1960).
1964	*The Management of Wild Mammals in Captivity.* Lee S. Crandall (University of Chicago Press: Chicago, IL). This is the second known book on captive mammal management.
1964–	*Dodo* (Jersey Wildlife Preservation Trust: Jersey, Channel Islands). An annual journal with scientific articles written about the zoo's collection and its conservation programs in the wild.
1968	*Zoological Park Fundamentals.* Lawrence Curtis (AAZPA). First known book summarizing the philosophy, planning, design, and administration of zoos. A substantially revised and enlarged edition, *Zoological Park and Aquarium Fundamentals*, was published in 1982 (Karen Sausman, Ed.).
1968–	*AZA Annual Conference Proceedings* (AAZPA/AZA).
1968–	*AAZV Annual Proceedings* (American Association of Zoo Veterinarians).
1968	*Zookeeper Training: A Suggested Guide for Instructors* (AAZPA). A manual for formal institution-based zookeeper training courses.
1969	*Man and Animal in the Zoo.* Heini Hediger (Delacorte Press: New York).
1970–	*Journal of Zoo and Wildlife Medicine* (AAZV). Formerly the *Journal of Zoo Animal Medicine* (1970–1988).
1972	*General Principles of Zoo Design.* Geoffrey Schomberg (Lutra Consultants: London, UK).
1973–	*AZA Regional Conferences Proceedings* (AAZPA/AZA).
1974–	*Animal Keepers Forum* (American Association of Zoo Keepers/AAZK). The monthly magazine of the AAZK.
1974–	*National AAZK Conference Proceedings* (AAZK).
1975	*Zoo Design: International Symposium on Design and Construction* (Paignton Zoo and Botanical Gardens: Paignton, UK). Additional proceedings were published in 1976 (*Zoo Design 1*), 1980 (*Zoo Design 2*), 1982 (*Zoo Design 3*), and 1989 (*Zoo Design 4*).
1975	*Capture and Care of Wild Animals.* E. Young (Curtis Books: Hollywood, FL).
1975–	*Breeding Endangered Species in Captivity.* R.D. Martin, Ed. (Academic Press: New York). Proceedings of the first conference on captive breeding programs. Subsequent proceedings have been published in the *International Zoo Yearbook* and elsewhere.
1976	*The Chemical Capture of Animals.* Antoine Harthoorn (Bailliere, Tindall: London, UK).
1977–	*Bongo* (Zoologischen Gartens Berlin). This is a scientific magazine of regional and international importance.
1977–	*International Zoo Educators Journal* (International Association of Zoo Educators).

(Continued)

Table 1   *(Continued)*

1978	*Zoo and Wild Animal Medicine.* Murray Fowler (Saunders: Philadelphia, PA).
1978	*Restraint and Handling of Wild and Domestic Animals.* Murray Fowler (Iowa State University Press: Ames, IA).
1978	*Behavior of Captive Wild Animals.* Hal Markowitz and Victor Stevens (Nelson-Hall, Chicago, IL).
1982–	*Zoo Biology* (Wiley-Liss: New York). A scientific journal, independently published, but in cooperation with AZA, devoted to research conducted at zoos and aquariums.
1980s +	Important professional publications increased during the 1960s and 1970s, as these examples indicate. The number of publications, however, increased significantly during and after the 1980s, and there are far too many to list here. These more recent publications include both commercially published titles and professional association titles. Not included in this list are the numerous magazines and newsletters published by associations that support each zoo and aquarium.

the profession as it developed during the second half of the twentieth century, including the development of species ecology, animal behavior, reproductive physiology, genetics, small population biology, veterinary medicine, nutrition, exhibit architecture, education, conservation, public relations, fund-raising, and administration. Along with a recognized need for publishing this professional literature, there came a recognized need to access and store it.

ZOO AND AQUARIUM LIBRARIES

Recognizing the Need for Libraries

United States libraries have existed since the colonial period, and about the time of independence there were some 133 libraries in existence. By the time the first zoological park opened in 1874, there were some 5817 libraries in the United States. However, few of those were specialized and only about 123 (2%) were devoted to science and technology, and none were then found in zoos.[5] In contrast, natural history museums and botanical gardens have been established in the United States since the 1700s. With their emphasis on the scientific aspects of zoology and botany, these institutions were more dependent on the scientific literature to support their work and research. U.S. zoos, on the other hand, evolved out of popular entertainment and education; a more public-oriented, rather than a research-oriented, evolution. Early zoo work consisted of practical animal husbandry rather than taxonomic studies and scientific research. These developments delayed the need for a body of professional literature, the establishment of libraries to hold this literature, and the use of archives to preserve this literature. But all of this was to change as the profession emerged during the twentieth century.

Some zoos and aquariums did recognize the need for libraries early in their existence. Individuals, such as medical doctor R.W. Shufeldt, traveled widely and were familiar with zoological parks, and they held their own opinions on how these institutions should be organized and administered. In 1889, Shufeldt published his ideas, including the following opinion on libraries:

No well-appointed zoological building in connection with a garden would be complete without its reading room and library. In the latter should be found, in time, all the standard works that have appeared upon the various branches of natural science, and more particularly upon vertebrate zoology and morphology, including, of course, such subjects as classification and geographical distribution of animals, and the reports of other zoological gardens and societies. On the reading tables should appear the various authoritative zoological periodicals of the day, and bound volumes of the same should be upon the library shelves.[6]

Expressing the need for zoo libraries and achieving their establishment were two different matters, even for the large, better financed institutions. Shortly after the New York Zoological Park (the Bronx Zoo, now the Wildlife Conservation Park) had opened in 1899, its director William T. Hornaday complained to Andrew Carnegie about his lack of support, especially since the zoo's need for several buildings, including a library, were financially pressing matters for the zoo:

From the beginning it has been my fond hope that the 'Model Millionaire' would set the example for the other leading men of New York by giving a complete equipped building. Yes, I know that you have given us $5000—as much as anyone has given. But of our Managers, no other is giving away millions, and almost forgetting us! If you could see how our buildings are crowded with eager people every Sunday when the toilers can come, and note how eager they are to enjoy our beautiful wild creatures, surely we would fare as well at your hands as the people of Emporia and Tucson.[7]

Those libraries that did emerge at zoos and aquariums developed independent of the mainstream library profession in America. They were part of the zoo and aquarium profession and followed zoo and aquarium programs. Even the librarians' organization (the Librarians Special Interest Group) is a committee-like group within the Association of Zoos and Aquariums, whereas the botanical garden librarians have an independent organization (the Council on Botanical and Horticultural Libraries) and the natural history museum librarians (the Natural History

Caucus) are affiliated with the Special Libraries Association. The disadvantage of developing within the zoo and aquarium profession has been the competition with other programs and activities within the zoos and aquariums for recognition. However, the advantage is that there is a close working relationship between the librarians and the animal staff at zoos and aquariums.

Establishing the Early Libraries

Shortly after the Zoological Society of London was founded in 1826, it resolved to not only establish a collection of living animals (founded in 1828) but also a museum of preserved animals, and a library. The first books for the library arrived in 1827. By 1964, when many U.S. zoo and aquarium libraries were just getting started, there were 120,000 volumes in the Zoological Society of London's collection and the library needed rebuilding and modernization. Because of its collection size and maturity, the library's influences have been significant. Most specially, its resources have been used to develop the world's foremost index to the zoological literature, the *Zoological Record*.[8]

Table 2 Earliest American zoo and aquarium libraries and archives.

	Year established		
	Zoo/aq.	Library	Archives
Philadelphia Zoological Garden [1st zoo]	1859	?	?
Central Park Zoo (WCS[a])	1861	1900	?
Lincoln Park Zoo	1868	?	1979
Cincinnati Zoo	1875	?	1970
Ross Park Zoo	1875	?	1988
Baltimore Zoo	1876	?	1980
National Zoological Park	1889	1898	1898
Zoo Atlanta	1889	?	1988
Prospect Park Zoo (WCS)	1893	1900	?
Seneca Park Zoo	1894	?	1976
Denver Zoo	1896	?	1988
New York Aquarium (WCS)	1896	1900	?
Bronx/New York Zoo (WCS)	1899	1900	?
Toledo Zoological Gardens	1900	1937	?
Chaffee Zoo	1908	1950	1965
San Antonio Zoo	1914	1929	1968
San Diego Zoo	1916	1916	1916
Cheyenne Mountain Zoo	1926	1927	?
Detroit Zoo	1928	1950s	?
Tulsa Zoo	1927	?	1976
Mesker Park Zoo	1929	1945	?
Shedd Aquarium	1930	?	1985
Brookgreen Gardens Zoo	1931	1931	1931
El Paso Zoo	1941	1956	1970s
Pittsburgh Aviary	1952	1952	?
Cameron Park Zoo	1955	?	1976
Indianapolis Zoo	1964	?	1988

[a]WCS = Wildlife Conservation Society (formerly New York Zoological Society), which serves all of these zoos and aquariums with a central library and archives.

Only 15 libraries were established in U.S. zoos and aquariums prior to 1960, as Table 2 indicates. However, the establishment of a library within an institution is a difficult matter to determine and many zoo librarians (or zoo directors) simply do not know when their libraries began. As the latter decades of the 1900s progressed, accumulations of books, journals, and newsletters began filling shelves in directors' and curators' offices. These publications were often not organized, or recognized, as libraries. Many directors, curators, and keepers had their own personal libraries at work or at home, or they had access to local public and university libraries. This may have diminished the perceived need for an institutional library, but eventually, the quantity of specialized literature made it too difficult for each individual to expand their own libraries and made institutional libraries more of a necessity.

Transforming an accumulation of publications into an institutional library, however, is often a gradual process rather than one that occurs at a discernable point in time. Another problem with defining these libraries has been a lack of understanding within the zoo and aquarium community of how a professional library should be managed or that libraries are managed according to standards established by another profession. In addition, AZA accreditation standards for zoos and aquariums have not required these institutions to have in-house libraries. Nevertheless, the accreditation standards do stipulate that zoo and aquarium staff must have access to an appropriate local library. Accepting the appropriateness of the local library and its use is at the discretion of the accreditation review team.

While the decades of the 1960s and 1970s witnessed an upsurge in the establishment of zoo and aquarium libraries, the remaining decades of the twentieth century saw improvements in the professional management of the libraries. The AZA Librarians Special Interest Group was established in 1978 and began publishing a newsletter, *Library News for Zoos and Aquariums*, in 1982. A directory of zoo and aquarium libraries is published periodically, as is a core list of recommended publications, a set of guidelines for operating libraries, a procedures manual, and a union list of journals and zoo newsletters.[4,9–12] Several surveys and articles review the progress of zoo and aquarium libraries in the 1980s, including a special issue of *Science & Technology Libraries*.[13–16] The *Directory of Zoo and Aquarium Libraries* provides much of the information gathered in these surveys.[9] These data have also been reviewed in two previous *Encyclopedia of Library and Information Sciences* articles.[17,18] A 2008 online survey by the Librarians Special Interest Group brings the data up to date.[19]

Current Status and Services of the Libraries

Zoo and aquarium libraries vary greatly in size and functionality from institution to institution. Being specialized they encompass the breadth of staff activities at these institutions, including business administration, personnel administration, financing and fund-raising, public relations, legislative matters, visitor surveys and demographics, buildings and grounds maintenance, garden and landscaping, master planning, exhibit designing, labeling and graphics, education, animal management and nutrition, veterinary medicine, genetics and biotechnology, reproductive biology, conservation, small population biology, and in situ field ecology.

Professional zoo librarians with a master's degree in library science are still few in numbers. Many zoos and aquariums rely on non-MLIS librarians (some of which have other degrees), part-time librarians, office staff, or volunteers to maintain their collections. Because of a loose interpretation of what constitutes a library, survey results have differed. A 1981 survey indicated that 104 zoos had libraries; however, a 1984 survey, using the presence of a professional librarian and information services as criteria to define a library, reduced that number to only 40.[13,14] A 1988 survey, using a full-time professional librarian, circulation of the collection, and information services as criteria for defining a library, found that only 11 zoos had what could be considered full-service libraries.[15] According to the 1988 survey's total responses, 12 zoo and aquarium libraries were established prior to 1960, 14 were established during the 1960s, 27 during the 1970s, and 19 during the 1980s.

The *Directory of Zoo and Aquarium Libraries* for 2000 lists 43 U.S. libraries and 12 international libraries while a more recent 2002 edition lists 34 U.S. and 9 international libraries.[9] The U.S. libraries listed in this directory are the primary libraries among those that exist at the 218 accredited U.S. zoos and aquariums. An analysis of the information these libraries provide in the directory reveals how the more professionally active American zoo and aquarium libraries are doing. Three large library systems exist: the Steinhart Aquarium Library is a branch of the California Academy of Sciences Libraries; the National Zoological Park Library is a branch of the Smithsonian Institution Libraries; and the various libraries at New York City zoos are part of the Wildlife Conservation Society (formerly New York Zoological Society) library system. One of these libraries is not considered in the following analysis because it provided statistics for the larger system of which it is a part. The international libraries listed in the directory represent a very small random selection but will be considered nevertheless (like the various surveys, providing information for the directory is voluntary, and the directory is not meant to be a comprehensive listing of all libraries). The 2008 survey included 73 U.S. and international zoo and wildlife libraries.[19]

The 2000 directory and 2008 survey provide different kinds of data, so both will be briefly reviewed here.[9,19] Out of the 42 U.S. zoo libraries listed in the directory, 35 have a librarian (with a variety of titles) or someone who serves as a librarian (perhaps a zoologist, but more often

someone from the education department). In the survey, there are three libraries with more than one librarian and 10 have only half-time librarians. The survey also indicates that 16 librarians have professional librarians with an MLIS degree. Budgets vary (when there is one), but in 2008 tend to be in the $1000–5000 range.

Collections vary greatly in size. Based on the directory data, 7 have fewer than 1000 books in their collection, 7 have 1000–1999, 16 have 2000–3999, and 11 have more than 4000 (one did not provide this information). The larger book collections are those at Brookfield Zoo (with 15,000 books), San Diego Zoo (12,000), Shedd Aquarium (10,000), Bronx Zoo (7500), and the National Zoo (6500). Twelve subscribe to less than 30 journal titles, 6 have 30–49, 9 have 50–99, 11 have 100–200, and three have more than 200 (one did not provide this information). The larger journal collections include those at San Diego Zoo (850), Brookfield Zoo (310), and Bronx Zoo (210). The survey data indicates that most book collections are in the 1000–10,000 range and that online journal subscriptions, while few, are increasing.

Special collections listed by the libraries include zoo and aquarium newsletters, zoo and aquarium annual reports, studbooks, guidebooks, vertical files, graphic material, slides and photographs, video and DVDs, newspaper clippings, reprints, teacher resource materials, children's bookshelf, staff publications, maps, oral histories, and informational CD-ROMs. As of 2008, 18 specifically mention having archives and four libraries have rare book collections.

Library services usually include interlibrary loan (21 libraries in 2008) and online catalogs (11 libraries in 2008). Reference is always provided at those libraries with a librarian, but often it is only for the staff (limited reference is provided to the public over the phone or if the public is allowed to use the library). Other services include current awareness bulletins, new acquisitions newsletters, compiling bibliographies, providing book reviews, and routing journals or journal contents. Electronic databases provided at the libraries include Aquatic Sciences and Fisheries Abstracts, Biosis, CAB, Dialog, Fish and Fisheries Worldwide, OCLC (as a database and 11 libraries use it for cataloging), PubMed, Species Information Library, Wildlife and Ecology Worldwide, Web of Science/Knowledge, and Zoological Record. In 2008, digital projects became more commonplace (at 18 libraries) as did consortia and listserv memberships.

In 2008, there were 23 libraries open to the public. Library users always include staff, usually include society members and docents, and sometimes include the public. Of those zoos and aquariums allowing the public to use their library in 2000, all but one required appointments. Other users mentioned include researchers, interns, teachers, and students.

Although the 2000 sample of international zoo and aquarium libraries is random and small (12 libraries), it may be of interest to review their statistics. All 12 have a librarian. Two have book collections in the range of 1000–1999, 5 in the range of 2000–3999, and 5 have more than 4000. The largest book collections are at the London Zoo (with 170,000 books), Berlin Zoo (12,200), and Melbourne Zoo (10,000). Two have subscriptions to less than 30 journal titles, 4 have 50–99, 4 have 100–200, and 1 has more than 200 (one did not provide this information). The largest journal collection is at the London Zoo (with 1300 titles). Seven provide interlibrary loan service, and 5 provide online searching. Their library users include staff (at 12 libraries), society members (at 9 libraries), and the public (at 10 libraries, 8 of which require appointments).

ZOO AND AQUARIUM ARCHIVES

A Sense of History and the Need for Archives

Zoo and aquarium archives evolved over time as materials accumulated and a sense of history emerged. Just as some institutions consider an accumulation of books to be their library, some consider the storage of older material to be their archives. Of those institutions surveyed in 1989, 11 did not know when their archives were established, 5 archives began during the 1960s, 6 during the 1970s, and 6 during the 1980s.[20,21] Of the 43 libraries listed in the *Directory of Zoo and Aquarium Libraries*, only 8 mentioned having archives.[9] Of the 73 institutions surveyed in 2008, 18 indicated they had archives.[19] Among the total number of zoos and aquariums, only a relatively small number of archives exist. Primarily, this is because many institutions still do not understand what archives are, why they are needed, or their value. Zoo and aquarium librarians who do understand and appreciate the need for archives have difficulty getting and maintaining support for them.

Archives began receiving more attention within the profession during the 1990s, although it is not clear how many new institutional archives were established during this time. Archives were established for the Association of Zoos and Aquariums during this time and are located at the Smithsonian Institution Archives, which also houses the archives of the National Zoological Park and the International Union of Directors of Zoological Gardens. An introductory workshop to archives, document retention, and preservation was held at the 1999 annual AZA conference, with help from a representative of the Minnesota Historical Society, State Archives Department (which houses the archives of the Minnesota Zoo). This attention to archives at the national level was helped in part because the AZA celebrated its 75th anniversary in 1999 and in part by the efforts of the AZA History Committee, which was established in 1991. In addition, a number of U.S. zoos and aquariums have recently reached their centennials and several more will do so soon. This milestone often imparts a sense of history that in turn provides an interest in preserving historical documents.

Current Status and Services of the Archives

Although there have no doubt been changes since the 1989 in archives surveys, no newer information is available, so the analyses from these surveys will be reviewed. The archival material found at zoos and aquariums is often the same found at any other institution, including staff and administrative records, reports, correspondence, photographs, newspaper articles, and memorabilia. Also included, though, are rather unique materials, such as animal inventories, studbooks, veterinary records, animal husbandry record books, and wildlife research records.

Of the 28 archives surveyed in 1989 (which is 36% of the 78 zoos and aquariums with libraries surveyed separately in 1988 and 13% of the 218 U.S. zoos and aquariums accredited in 2008), archivists or librarians managed only eight of these facilities. Ten archives had 2 or 3 full-time individuals working with the collection, whereas 8 had only one full-time person. The other archives used part-time help or volunteers. Ten of the collections had been cataloged, 21 had material available for study, and 6 had restored their material. Most provided limited access to the archival collections. Nineteen contained material dating back to the establishment of the institution, and of these 7 were zoos established prior to 1900. To what extent these collections are housed under proper climate control is not known. Some collections are maintained on site at the institution, whereas others are housed at municipal archives or at local and regional historical society repositories. The National Zoological Park archives are housed at the Smithsonian Institution Archives because it is a branch of the Smithsonian Institution. The Minnesota Zoo archives are housed at the Minnesota Historical Society, State Archives Department, because it is a state institution. While only 18 institutions surveyed in 2008 said they had archives, this number is probably a more realistic recognition of well-managed archives (8% of the 218 zoos accredited in 2008; however, this survey also included some international zoos and wildlife conservation institutions).

CONCLUSION

Interest in archives will increase as more U.S. zoos and aquariums reach their centennials and develop a sense of history. This milestone is not as significant in Europe where, for example, the Schonbrunn Zoo (Vienna) celebrated its 250th anniversary in 2002. European zoos and aquariums, as well as other world zoos and aquariums, have extensive archives. Unfortunately, too much material from zoos and aquariums has already been lost. In addition, there are many zoos and aquariums that have closed with little or no trace of their existence. In the United States some 250 zoos and aquariums are known to have closed since the first zoo opened.[22]

Interest in the history of zoos and aquariums is increasing as well. A number of graduate research theses and

Word–Zoological

dissertations have recently been completed on the cultural history of zoos and aquariums and the Bartlett Society, an international society for the study of zoo and wild animal husbandry history, was founded in 1984. Several institutional histories have been published recently, as have two history books, essentially the first since Gustave Loisel wrote *Histoire des Menageries de l'Antiquite a nos jours* (Octave Doin et Fils and Henri Laurens, Paris) in 1912.[1,2] There is still much to be learned and documented. As Ken Kawata points out in his historical commentaries, many in the zoo profession do not even know the names of individuals who made important contributions to the profession in the past, or what those contributions were.[23,24]

There is still a need to stabilize and improve the quality and quantity of libraries as well. After some 5000 years of practical animal husbandry, the keeping of wild animals has come of age quickly. And as zoological parks and aquariums continue to evolve, their libraries and archives are destined to play a larger role within the institutions and the profession, providing the increasingly sophisticated information needed by the profession and preserving what is left of the historical records.

ACKNOWLEDGMENTS

The Librarians Special Interest Group and the Association of Zoos and Aquariums have made significant contributions to the development and professionalization of zoo and aquarium libraries and archives. They have also been responsible for gathering information about these libraries in order to benefit and improve the services these libraries provide.

REFERENCES

1. Kisling, V.N., Jr. *Zoo and Aquarium History: Ancient Animal Collections to Zoological Gardens*; CRC Press: Boca Raton, FL, 2001.
2. Hoage, R.J.; Deiss, W.A. *New Worlds, New Animals: From Traditional Menagerie to Zoological Park in the Nineteenth Century*; Johns Hopkins University Press: Baltimore, MD, 1996.
3. Kisling, V.N., Jr. Journals, professional and trade. In *Encyclopedia of the World's Zoos*; Fitzroy Dearborn: Chicago, IL, 2001.
4. Kenyon, K.A. *Recommended List of Books and Other Information Resources for Zoo and Aquarium Libraries*, 3rd Ed.; National Zoological Park Branch, Smithsonian Institution Libraries & AZA Librarians Special Interest Group: Washington, DC, 1995.
5. McMullen, H. Prevalence of libraries in the northeastern states before 1876. J. Libr. Hist. **1987**, *22*(3), 312–337.
6. Shufeldt, R.W. Zoological gardens: their uses and management. Pop. Sci. Mon. **1889**, *34*, 789.
7. Bridges, W. *Gathering of Animals: An Unconventional History of the New York Zoological Society*; Harper & Row: New York, 1974; 100–101.
8. Fish, R. The library and scientific publications of the zoological society of London. *The Zoological Society of London 1826–1976 and Beyond*; Zoological Society of London: London, U.K., 1976; 233–252.
9. Gordon, J. *Directory of Zoo and Aquarium Libraries*, 8th Ed.; Saint Louis Zoo Library & AZA Librarians Special Interest Group: St. Louis, MO, 2000 [9th Ed., 2002].
10. Gordon, J. *Journals and Newsletters Received by Zoo and Aquarium Libraries*, 3rd Ed.; Saint Louis Zoo Library & AZA Librarians Special Interest Group: St. Louis, MO, 1998.
11. Kenyon, K.A. *Suggested Guidelines for Zoo and Aquarium Libraries*; National Zoological Park Branch, Smithsonian Institution Libraries & AZA Librarians Special Interest Group: Washington, DC, 1986.
12. Kenyon, K.A.; Coates, L.; Braun, S.; Rohr, L. *Procedures Manual: Guidelines for Zoo and Aquarium Libraries*; National Zoological Park Branch, Smithsonian Institution Libraries & AZA Librarians Special Interest Group: Washington, DC, 1993.
13. Miller, G.D. *An Inquiry into the Role of Libraries in Zoos and Aquariums*, M.S. thesis; University of Chicago: Chicago, IL, 1981.
14. Kenyon, K.A. Zoo/aquarium libraries: a survey. Spec. Libr. **1984**, *75*, 329–334.
15. Kisling, V.N., Jr. American zoological park libraries and archives: historical considerations and their current status. Sci. Technol. Libr. **1988**, *8*, 49–60 (Summer).
16. Mount, E. *Sci-Tech Libraries Serving Zoological Gardens*; Haworth Press: New York, 1988 [Reprint of Sci. Technol. Libr. 1988, 8 (Summer)].
17. Kisling, V.N., Jr. Libraries and archives in American zoological parks and aquariums. In *Encyclopedia of Library and Information Science*; Kent, A., Hall, C.M., Eds.; Marcel Dekker: New York, 1996; Vol. 57, Suppl. 20.
18. Kisling, V.N., Jr. Zoological park and aquarium libraries and archives. In *Encyclopedia of Library and Information Science*, 2nd Ed.; Bates, M.J., Maack, M.N., Drake, M., Eds.; Taylor & Francis: Boca Raton, FL, 2003; DOI: 10.1081/E-ELIS-120008651.
19. Coates, L.; Means, K. *Zoo and Wildlife Library Survey*; Librarians Special Interest Group, Association of Zoos and Aquariums. Published by San Diego Zoo: San Diego, CA, 2008. Available at http://library.sandiegozoo.org/survey.htm.
20. Kisling, V.N., Jr. *Zoo and Aquarium Archives Survey*, 1989; Unpublished typescript.
21. Rohr, L. A survey of American zoo and aquarium archives. Sci. Technol. Libr. **1989**, *9*, 75–84 (Summer).
22. Kisling, V.N., Jr. In the shadows of history: extinct zoos and lost collections. AZA Regional Conference Proceedings Columbia, SC American Zoo and Aquarium Association: Silver Spring, MD, 2003.
23. Kawata, K. Hediger who? A plea for historical perspective. Int. Zoo News **1991**, *38*(4), 5–10.
24. Kawata, K. Who was Belle Benchley? The victimizing of history. Int. Zoo News **2000**, *47*(1), 4–11.

Index

A

AALL, *see* American Association of Law Libraries

AAM, *see* American Association of Museums

Aarhus Art museum, 1226

Aarhus State and University Library, 1216–1217, 1219

AASL, *see* American Association of School Librarians

AASL Hotlinks, 61

Abandoned Shipwreck Act of 1987, 1775

The Aboriginal and Torres Strait Islander Library and Information Resource Network (*ATSILIRN*) *Protocols*, 2041

Abridged WebDewey, 1259–1260

Absorption, distribution, metabolism, excretion, and toxicity (ADMET) testing, 837

Abstracts, 418–419

Academic art libraries, 251

Academic dishonesty
  definition, 3665
  faculty attitudes, 3668–3669
  individual differences, 3668–3669
  social factors, 3668

Academic e-mail messages, 2507

Academic law reviews, 2740

Academic Librarians Status Committee, 342

Academic libraries, 97, 2764, 3471–3472
  acquisitions units, organization of, 2918–2919
  administration, 9
  in Arab sector, 2548
  Armenia, 230–231
  in Australia, 384–385
  buildings, 10–11
  in China
    Peking University Library, 896
    Tsinghua University Library, 896–898
  in Croatia, 1125
  database integrators, 3472
  digital humanities (*see* Digital humanities)
  Ethiopia, 1498–1499
  external influence, 2–3
  in France, 1602–1603
  fund-raising and development
    access to donors, 2835
    annual fund, 2836–2837
    capital campaigns, 2838
    centralized *vs.* decentralized development, 2834–2835
    development activities, 2833–2834
    friends of libraries, 2836
    institutional barriers, 2834–2835
    institutionalization, 2839
    library director, role of, 2835
    literature, history of, 2832–2833
    major gifts, 2837
    planned giving, 2837–2838
    theoretical and philosophical foundations, 2839
    U.S. phenomenon, 2832
    Web communications, 2838–2839

games and gaming, 1639–1640
  in Germany, 1695–1696
  governance and hierarchy, 3–4
  Greece, 1731–1732
  history, 1–2
  Hungary, 1922
  in Israel, 2544–2545
  Japan, 2562–2564
  in Kazakhstan, 2582–2583
  Kenya, 2596
  Latinos, 2701–2702
  library anxiety, 2785
  Lithuania, 2951–2953
  Mexican libraries, 3083–3086
  mission, 1
  in Moldova, 3125
  music libraries, 3275
  New Zealand libraries, 3375–3376
  organizational structure, 4–5
  personnel, 10
  in Peru, 3608
  professional associations, 3
  resources and services
    expertise, 5–6
    public service, 7–8
    reference desk, 6–7
    technical services, 8–9
  in Saudi Arabia, 3974
  science and engineering librarians, 4009
  Senegal, 4106
  in Serbia, 4129–4131
  Slovakia, 4177–4178
  South Korea, 4310–4311
  strategic planning (*see* Strategic planning, academic libraries)
  Tunisia, 4628–4629
  in Ukraine, 4642
  in United Kingdom, 4703–4705
  user privileges, 5
  Venezuelan libraries, 4889–4890

Academic Library Advancement and Development Network (ALADN), 2834

Academic publications, 2826

Academic writing, 4548–4549

Academy of Beaux-Arts, 1594

Academy of Health Information Professionals (AHIP), 3035, 4356

Access control, *see* Authorization

Accessed information, 4236

Accessibility
  adaptive hardware and software, adults
    audiobooks and Playaways, 16
    audio description, 16
    Benetech, 16
    closed-circuit television, 15
    mouse challenges, 15
    outreach efforts, 16
    public meetings, signing for, 15–16
    screen reading software, 15
    talking books, 16
    TDDS and TTYS, 16

typing and voice recognition software, 15
    virtual reference, 17
    web conferencing platform, 17
    Web sites, 16–17
  audio/recorded books, 15
  books by mail service, 14
  Braille books, 15
  building accommodations, 14
  deposit collections, 14
  homebound book delivery, 14
  large print books, 14–15
  services, 14
  symbols, 4961, 4963

Access management, *see* Authorization

Access services, 173, 373, 895, 1910, 2912, 3472, 4735

Access to Knowledge (A2K) movement, 3386

Access-to-Own model, 1211

Accountability, 2055

Accounting in England and Scotland: 1543 to 1800, 645

Accreditation
  ALA, LIS programs
    Accreditation Process, Policies, and Procedures, 18, 20
    ALISE, 19–20
    ASPA Code of Good Practice, 18–19
    BEL, 19
    COA, 18–20
    Committee on Library Training, 19
    future prospects, 20–21
    Land Grant College Act, 19
    of postsecondary education, 19
    purpose of, 18
    standards, 18, 20
  of Canadian institutions, 19, 21
  fundamental assumptions of, 18

Accreditation Board for Engineering and Technology (ABET), 1434

Accredited Standards Committee (ASC), 413

Achenwall, Gottfried, 495

ACLU v. Reno, 2396

ACM, *see* Association for Computing Machinery

Acquisitions
  in academic libraries, 2918–2919
  approval plan vendors, 2919
  automated and integrated library systems, 2919
  bibliographic networks, development of, 2921
  definition, 2918
  EDI, 2919
  in public libraries, 2919
  purchasing decisions, 2918
  shared cataloging, 2921
  in small libraries, 2919
  in special libraries, 2918

Acquisitions Institute at Timberline Lodge
  collection development, 22
  facility, 2
  history and evolution, 22–23

Acquisitions Institute at Timberline Lodge
        (cont'd.)
    library acquisitions, 22
    planning committee, 23–24
    previous conference programs, 24–32
    technical services, 22
ACRL, *see* Association of College and Research
        Libraries
Acropolis Museum, 1741–1742
Acta Mathematica, 3024
Acta Mathematica Sinica, 3027
Act for the Protection of Copyright, 656
Active learning, 679, 4463, 4834, 4859
Activities Committee on New Directions for
        ALA (ACONDA), 71, 2393
1997 Act on Archival Material and Archives,
        1127
Act on the Right to Information Access, 1126
Actor-network theory (ACN), 2282, 2287,
        4022–4023
ADA, *see* Americans with Disabilities Act
Adaptive indexing, 1623
Addis Ababa Museum, 1503
Addis Ababa University (AAU), 1498
Additional improvement (AI) patents, 3565
Adelaide, 390, 393
Ad-hocracy, 3512
Ad hoc retrieval, 4555
Ad Hoc Task Force on Structure Revision
        (SRTF), 72–73
Administrative decisions, 149, 2735, 2738–2739
Administrative Management Society, 651
Administrative Procedure Act of 1946, 2150
Administrative rules, 2729, 2737, 4349, 4746
Adobe Connect, 2780
Adolescent development, YA services
    physical growth
        cognitive, 5060
        early bloomers, 5059
        emotional, 5061
        height, weight, and secondary sex charac-
                teristics, 5059
        late bloomers, 5060
        psychological, 5060
        social, 5060–5061
    social characteristics, 5059
ADRIANA, 4318
Advanced Research Project Agency (ARPA),
        1015, 2516
Advanced Research Project Agency Network
        (ARPANET), 2505, 2516
The Advantages of the Kingdome of England,
        1400
Adventure novels, 855, 3701
Advertisements, 639
Aesop's Fables, 852–853
Aëtius of Amida, 3044
Affective needs, 2115, 2119
Affective relevance judgments, 3944
AFLI, *see* Arab Federation for Libraries and
        Information
African Journals Online (AJOL), 38
African librarianship
    colonization, 33–34
    consortiums and networks, 39–40
    developing countries, 35–36, 38–39
    European colonization, 34

ICT, 38
    innovative outreach, 40
    LIS education, 40
    OA, 39
    open source software, 39
    pan-African responses, 37–38
    privately funded public libraries, 40
    scholarly information, 38
African Library and Information Association
        and Institutions (AfLIA), 37–38
African Newspapers Union List (AFRINUL),
        790
AgeLine database, 3407
Agency affordance, 1118
Agoge games, 1641
Agora Research Initiative, 679
Agricultural Extension Service, 1011
Agricultural libraries, Ukraine, 4646
AGRINET, 4631
A&HCI, *see Arts and Humanities Citation Index*
Ahmes Papyrus, 3019–3020
AIS, *see* Association for Information Systems
Aksum Archaeological Museum, 1501
ALA, *see* American Library Association
ALA Code of Ethics, 4365
Albert Scholarship, 81
Albucasis, 3044
ALCTS, *see* Association for Library Collections
        and Technical Services
ALCTS Honors, 332
ALCTS Outstanding Publications Award, 331
ALEPH network, 2545
Alert Services, 1880
Alexander of Tralles, 3044
Alexander's curriculum, 3218
Alexander Turnbull Library, 3373
Alexandria Digital Library (ADL), 2671
Alexandria Library, 745
Alexandros Soutsos, 1744
Algorithmic relevance judgments, 3944
ALIA, *see* Australian Library and Information
        Association
aliaNEWS, 400
Alien property custodian (APC) documents,
        3566
ALISE, *see* Association for Library and Infor-
        mation Science Education
ALIWEB, 2519
Alliance for Bibliographic Standards (ICABS),
        2456
Alliance for Nursing Informatics, 86
Alliance of Library Service Networks, 3922
Allied Professional Association (APA), 74–75,
        713
All India Educational Surveys (AIESs), 2001
Alphabetico-classed catalog, 754
Alpha-Numeric System for Classification of
        Sound Recordings (ANSCR), 3283
ALSC, *see* Association for Library Service to
        Children
ALTAFF, *see* Association of Library Trustees,
        Advocates, Friends and Foundations
AltaVista, 2522, 4048, 4983, 4986
Alte Pinakothek, 3153–3154
Altes Museum, 3153
Altmetrics, 44–46, 924
Amazon, 3734–3735

Amazon Kindle, 4054–4055
Ambiguous chemical identifiers
    chemical formulae, 823–824
    chemical names, 823
Ambrosian Ilaid, 1946
American Accounting Association, 651
American Alliance of Museums (AAM), 3233,
        3758
American Antiquities Act, 1774
American Archive of Public Broadcasting, 1579
American Archivist, Archival Issues, 137
American Association for State and Local His-
        tory (AASLH), 1782
American Association for the Advancement of
        Science (AAAS), 558
American Association of Colleges (AAC), 341
American Association of Law Libraries
        (AALL), 710, 1097, 2708, 2714–2716,
        2744, 4356–4357, 4370
    goals and objectives, 49
    legal information environment, 52–53
    member growth
        CPE, 50–51
        ethics and diversity, 51–52
        new members, 51
        scholarships and grants, 51
    NET (AALLNET), 50
    publications
        AALL Biennial Salary Survey, 55
        AALL Directory and Handbook, 55
        AALL Price Index for Legal Publications,
                55
        AALL Spectrum, 54
        Index to Foreign Legal Periodicals, 55
        LLJ, 55
    publisher relations, 53–54
    special interest sections, 49–50
    2005–2010 strategic directions, 48
    universal citation guide, 53
    valued partnerships, 54
American Association of Museums (AAM), 255,
        3146–3147, 3200, 3215–3216, 3255,
        4379, 4766, 4769; *see also* American
        Alliance of Museums
    activities and priorities, 57
    services to members, 58
    structure and governance, 56–57
American Association of School Librarians
        (AASL), 68, 2752, 3775, 3991,
        4001–4002, 5052, 5058
    affiliate assembly, 60–61
    awards, grants, and scholarships, 62–63
    board of directors, 60
    executive committee, 60
    goals, 59
    guidelines and standards
        fall forum, 63
        national guidelines and standards, 64
        school library programs, 63–64
    history, 60
    Knapp School Library Manpower Project, 64
    mission, 59
    national conference and exhibition, 63
    National Library Power Program, 64–65
    publications, 61
    regional institutes, 63
    responsibility, 59

sections, 61
special committees, 61
Standards, 4859
standing committees, 61
task forces, 61
values, 60
vision, 59
American Association of University Professors (AAUP), 341
American Association of Zoological Parks and Aquariums (AAZPA), 5078
American Astronomical Society (AAS), 3640
American Bar Association (ABA), 2711–2712, 2716
American Chemical Society (ACS), 3641–3642
American Civil Liberties Union (ACLU), 783, 2402
American Committee for Devastated France (CARD), 1600
American Cooperative School of Tunis (ACST), 4630
American Documentation Institute (ADI), 90, 311, 2770
American Economic Review (AER), 3470
American Federation of Labor (AFL), 4689
American Federation of Labor-Congress of Industrial Organizations (AFL-CIO), 4761
American Federation of State, County and Municipal Employees (AFSCME), 4690–4691
American Federation of Teachers (AFT), 3997–3998, 4689
American Film Institute (AFI), 1586
American Health Information and Management Association (AHIMA), 1854
American Historical Association (AHA), 1788, 3316, 4272, 4741
American Historical Review, 1791
American Indian Library Association, 334–335
American Institute for Certified Public Accountants (AICPA), 2918–2919
American Institute for Conservation of Historic and Artistic Works (AIC), 1072, 3729, 4953
American Institute of Accountants, 651
American Institute of Architects Awards, 2845
American Institute of Certified Public Accountants, 651
American Institute of Physics (AIP), 3639, 4763
American Journal of Mathematics, 3024, 3027
American Law Reports (ALR), 2741
American librarianship, 2890
American Library Association (ALA), 3, 60, 229, 255, 706, 757, 1336, 1846–1847, 2764, 2775, 2964–2965, 3728, 3775, 3778, 4001, 4649, 4773–4774, 4777
    accreditation of LIS programs
        Accreditation Process, Policies, and Procedures, 18, 20
        ALISE, 19–20
        ASPA Code of Good Practice, 18–19
        BEL, 19
        COA, 18–20, 709
        Committee on Library Training, 19
        future prospects, 20–21

    purpose of, 18
    standards, 18, 20
ACONDA/ANACONDA, 71
ACRL, 2752
    affiliated organizations, 77
    Allied Professional Association, 74–75, 713
    ALSC, 333
    awards and scholarships, 81
    chapters, 77
    children's literature, awards for, 852
    Code of Ethics, 3917
    conference
        change and controversy, 80–81
        growth and development, 79–80
        Midwinter Meeting, 80
    controversy, 72–73
    Council, 75
    Cresap, McCormick and Paget, 70
    divisions, 75–76
        self-study, 74
    dues schedule transition document, 73
    Executive Board, 75
    GameRT, 1637
    Holley Committee, OSSC, 71–72
    intellectual freedom (*see* Intellectual freedom)
    International connections, 77–78
    Latinos and library services, 2699
    library network, definition of, 3920
    LLAMA, 2841–2845
    membership and organizational change, 69
    membership statistics (August 2008), 83
    MIGs, 76–77
    offices, 81–82
    older adults, library services for, 3407
    operating agreements, 73–74
    organizational development
        ALA divisions and allied professional association, 73
        growth and democratization, 69–70
    organizational self-study (1992–1995), 72
    periodic scrutiny, 70
    PIALA, 3548
    publishing, 78–79
    round tables, 76
    RUSA, 3913
    Science and Technology Section, 4016
    standards and guidelines, 81
    standing committees, 76
    state library agencies, 4394
    values, priorities and missions, 67–69
    web-based networking, 78
American Library Association-Allied Professional Association (ALA-APA), 3777
American Library Association conference, 2770
American Library Association v. U.S. Department of Justice, 2396
American Library Directory, 249
American Management Association, 651
American Marketing Association, 651
American Mathematical Society, 324
American Medical Informatics Association (AMIA), 85–86
American Memory Project, 5027
American Museum of Natural History (AMNH), 3252, 4944

American museums, 3234
American National Standards Institute (ANSI), 221, 1857, 1981, 2343–2344
    conformity assessment, 88–89
    history, 87
    industry sectors and services, 87
    international standards activities, 88
    logo, 88
    NISO, 88
    process, 88
    standards panels, 89
    U.S. standardization system, 87
American National Trust for Historic Preservation, 4169
American Psychological Association, 4246
American Radio Archives, 1565
American Records Management Association (ARMA), 175, 1853–1855
American Sign Language (ASL), 1184, 1187
American Society for Engineering Education, Engineering Libraries Division (ASEE/ELD), 4016
American Society for Indexing (ASI), 441
American Society for Information Science (ASIS), 1097, 1375
American Society for Information Science and Technology (ASIST), 482
    awards, 95
    chapters and SIGs, 92
    governance, 93
    history
        documentation, beginnings (1937), 90
        human/social perspective, (1990s and 2000s), 91–92
        information explosion (1960s), 90
        modern information science transition (1950s), 90
        online information (1970s), 91
        personal computers (1980s), 91
    meetings, 94
    publications, 93–94
    purpose, 92
American Society for Quality National Accreditation Board (ANAB), 88
American Society of Information Science and Technology (ASIST), 3368
American Standard Code for Information Interchange (ASCII), 5024
Americans with Disabilities Act (ADA), 10, 377, 1530, 3575–3576, 3843
Americans with Disabilities Act Assembly, 3778
American Technology Pre-Eminence Act (ATPA) of 1991, 1552
American Theological Library Association (ATLA)
    Carver Policy Governance model, 4607
    Committee on Microphotography, 4606
    daunting problems, 4606
    Ethics index, 4607
    Executive Director, 4607–4608
    importance, 4606
    Library Development Program, 4606
    management structure, 4607
    premier professional association, 4608
    religion database, 4607
    Religion index two, 4606–4607
    Retrospective Indexing Project, 4607

America Online (AOL), 2521
Amigos, 3922, 3924
Ammonite, *see* Snake stones
Amos Tuck School of Administration and Finance, 650
Anacostia Community Museum, 4192
Analytical bibliography, 477–478
Analytico-synthetic classification, 967, 971, 4786
Anastosi I, 644
Anatolian University Library Consortium (ANKOS), 2829
Ancien Régime, 182
Ancient Greece, 999, 1460–1461, 1742, 1744, 1788, 2677, 3831
Andrew Mellon Foundation, 372, 988
Anglo-American Cataloging Rules (AACR), 449, 727, 2920–2921, 3062, 4144
Anglo-American Cataloguing Rules, 2nd ed. (AACR2), 137, 253, 453, 670, 1230–1231, 1982–1983, 2921, 2923, 3131, 3178, 3294, 3396, 4140–4141, 4144
Anglo-American Cataloguing Rules 3rd ed. (AACR3), 670
An Inquiry into the Wealth of Nations and Causes of the Wealth of Nations, 646
Annales de Mathématiques Pures et Appliquées, 3024, 3026
Annales typographici ab artis inventae origine ad annum MDCLXIV, 1968
ANNs, *see* Artificial neural networks
Annual fund, 2836–2837
Annual Meeting of the Document Academy (DOCAM), 1379
Annual Review of Information Science and Technology (*ARIST*), 312, 489
Anomalous state of knowledge (ASK), 2076, 2118–2119, 2225, 4526–4527, 4874, 4879
ANSI, *see* American National Standards Institute
ANSI/NISO Z39.50, 2983
Answer Garden (AG), 3865–3866
Anthropogeographie, 1687
Anthropological museum, Hungary, 1929–1930
Antiquarian book, 3820
Antiquarian Booksellers' Association of America (ABAA), 4344, 4576, 4578, 4585, 4588
Antiquarian Booksellers database, 4576
Antiquities Act of 1906, 4169
Antiquities Act of 1964, 4511
Antiquities of the Jews, 644
Apache Lucene IR system, 2204
Apache Project, 5025
Apollonios of Citium, 3043
Apologie, 1400
Appeal factors, 3700, 3705, 3850, 3857
Apple's HyperCard, 5023
Application ontologies, 3457
Application programming interfaces (APIs)
  FAST, 1545
  ILSs, 409
  ORCID, 3506–3508
Application Service Definition and Protocol Specification, 2983

Application service providers (ASPs), 698
Application software, 1056, 1333, 2272–2273, 3650, 4805, 5034
Appraisal and selection process, 131
Apprentices' libraries, 1842
The Apprentice's time enterteiner accomptantly: or a methodical means to obtain the equisite art of accomptantship, 645
Approval plan
  history, 96–97
  profiles, 97–98
  transformation, 97
  vendors, 98
Apriori, 2631
Aquaria, 3238
Aquariums and zoological parks, 5077
  archives, 5083
  libraries
    current status and services, 5081–5083
    early libraries, establishment of, 5081
    need for, 5080–5081
  professional development
    animal collections, 5077
    captive wildlife management, 5077
    European collections, 5077–5078
    exotic wild animals, 5078
    modern aquariums, 5078
    modern zoological park management, 5077
    professional associations, 5078
    public aquarium, 5078
  professional literature, growth in, 5078–5080
Aquisitions Section (AS), 328
Arab Federation for Libraries and Information (AFLI), 100–101, 3978
  finance, 102
  honors and awards, 103–104
  location, 102
  membership, 101
  objectives, 101
  organizational structures, 101–102
  publications, 103
  relationships and cooperation, 103
  seminars and conferences, 102–103
  training and workshops, 103
Arabian Nights Entertainment, 853
Arabic Union Catalog, 3978
Arab Libraries Association, 100
Arbetisgemeinschaft der Kunst-und Museumsbibliotheken (AKMB), 255
Arboreta, 3238
Archaeological collections, curation of, *see* Curation, archaeological artifacts
Archaeological Conservancy, 1777
Archaeological museums
  in Croatia, 1129
  Hungary, 1929–1930
  in Israel, 2551
Archaeological Resources Protection Act (ARPA), 1774
Archaeological site museum, 4167–4168
Archie, 2517
Architecture, museum
  eighteenth century
    American Museum in Philadelphia, 3153
    Baroque design, 3152
    Belvedere sculpture court, 3151–3152
    Corinthian loggia, 3151

    courtyard plan, 3151
    curiosity/art cabinets, 3150
    exhibition spaces and galleries, 3151
    Galleria degli Uffizi in Florence, 3152
    Grande Galerie, 3152
    Greek cross, pattern of, 3151
    Inscriptiones vel tituli teatri amplissimi, 3150–3151
    Louvre in Paris, 3152
    multifunctional institution, 3151
    Musei Capitolini in Rome, 3152
    Museo Nacional del Prado, 3152
    Museo Pio-Clementino, 3151–3152
    Museum Fridericianum, 3152
    neoclassical design, 3152–3153
    Newby Hall's gallery, 3151
    Pennsylvania Academy of the Fine Arts in Philadelphia, 3153
  nineteenth century
    Alte Pinakothek, 3153–3154
    Altes Museum, 3153
    Beaux-Arts method, 3153, 3156
    Belvedere statue court, 3154
    courtyard model, 3153–3154
    Dulwich Picture Gallery, 3154
    educational and training, 3155
    Glyptothek, 3153
    growth, specialization, and spatial concentration, 3154
    instructive decorations, 3155
    iron and glass structure, 3154–3155
    Neo-Gothic brick building, 3155
    Oxford University Museum, 3155
    shallow buildings, 3154
    South Kensington Museum, 3154–3155
    top lighting, 3154
    Victoria and Albert Museum, 3154–3155
  pre-eighteenth century
    arcaded perambulatories, 3149–3150
    Belvedere statue court, 3149
    centrally planned rooms, 3150
    circular and top-lit building, 3150
    curiosity/art cabinets, 3150
    galleries, 3150
    pinacotheca, 3149
    purpose-designed public museum, 3150
  twentieth century and beyond
    Akron Art Museum, 3158
    American metropolitan architecture, 3156
    Beaux-Arts inspired plan, 3156
    central foyer spaces, 3158
    historic museum buildings, 3157
    industrial buildings, 3157–3158
    Milwaukee Art Museum, 3158
    Modernism, 3156
    modernist glass box, 3156–3157
    Museo Civico di Castelvecchio, 3157
    Museo Guggenheim, Bilbao, 3158
    Museumsufer, 3157
    National Gallery of Art, 3156
    New York Museum of Modern Art, 3157
    open museum concept, 3157
    Quadracci Pavilion, 3158
    Solomon R. Guggenheim Museum, 3156
Architecture of integrated information systems (ARIS), 632

Archival and Manuscripts Control (MARC AMC), 136
Archival appraisal
  alternative approaches
    documentation strategies, 110
    documenting society, 109
    functions-based appraisal, 110–111
    macro appraisal, 110
    Minnesota method, 110
  American traditions, 107
  definition, 105–106
  digital recordkeeping, 112–113
  European traditions, 106–107
  practices, 108–109
  tools
    collecting/acquisition policies, 107
    disposal/retention schedules, 107–108
    sampling, 108
    systemic reviews, 108
  traditional appraisal methods, 111–112
Archival collection
  agencies, 195–196
  archival appraisal and, 200–201
  barriers, 202–203
  collectors and, 196–197
  complicated times, 203
  definition, 195–196
  early modern profession, 197
  institutional collections and individual collectors, 199–200
  marginalization, 198
  organizational repositories, 198
  psychology of, 200
  record-keeping technology, 198
  shifting notions of, 198
Archival description, 1425–1426
Archival documentation
  archival program
    appraisal and selection process, 131
    archival materials, 131
    description, housing and management, 130–131
    establishment, 129
    main phases, 128–129
    survey, 129–130
    transfer and accession, 130
  digital and networked technologies, 131–132
  principles, 128
  strategies, 201
Archival finding aids
  as access tool, 133
  archival journals, 137
  arrangement and description, 134
  container list, 134–135
  definition, 133–134
  front matter, 134
  2005 Greene-Meisner study, 138
  Next Generation Finding Aids project, 138
  NIDS-US, 136
  online finding aids, development of, 137–138
  sample finding aid, 135–136
  standards, 136–137
Archival information packages (AIP), 1365
Archival management and administration
  leadership, 143–145
  managing information
    planning, 145

policies and procedures, 146
project management, 146–147
managing money, facilities and relationships
  budgets, 147
  resource development and outreach, 147–148
theory and practice
  building partnerships, 143
  manager, role of, 142–143
Archival records, 1424–1425
Archival repositories
  academic repositories and digital projects
    California Digital Library, 4748
    Cornell University, 4747
    Duke University, 4748
    Making of America project, 4747–4748
    MIT and DSpace, 4748
    Stanford University, 4748
    University of Chicago, 4748–4749
    University of Michigan, 4747
    University of North Carolina (Chapel Hill), 4749
    Yale University, 4749
  audiovisual archives, 4755
  business archives
    Coca-Cola, 4752
    Ford Motor Company, 4753
    history associates, 4753
    History Factory, 4753
    Levi Strauss, 4753
  cultural heritage archives
    American Folklife Center, 4757
    American Heritage Center, 4757
    Amistad Center, 4757
    Balch Institute, 4757
    Center for Puerto Rican Studies, 4757
    Clark Atlanta University, 4757–4758
    Heard Museum Archives, 4758
    Japanese American History Archives, 4758
    Moorland-Spingarn Research Center, 4758
    Museum of Chinese in America, 4758–4759
    Schomburg Center for Black Culture, 4759
  data and electronic records archives
    Electronic and Special Media Records Services Division, NARA, 4754
    ERA, 4754
    ICPSR, 4753–4754
    Minerva/Library of Congress Web Archives, 4754
  gender and sexuality archives
    Cornell Human Sexuality Project, 4760
    GBLT historical society, 4760
    Kinsey Institute, 4760
    Lesbian Herstory Archives, 4760
    National Gay & Lesbian Archives, 4760–4761
  labor archives, 4761
  manuscript repositories and historical societies
    American Philosophical Society, 4750
    Chicago History Museum, 4750
    Library of Congress, 4749–4750
    urban archives (Temple University), 4750–4751
  military archives
    Air Force Historical Research Center, 4751
    American Jewish Archives, 4751

American Jewish Historical Society, 4751
Archdiocese of Chicago, 4751–4752
Billy Graham Center Archives, 4752
Center for Military History, 4751
Episcopal Church U.S.A., 4752
Family History Center, Church of Jesus Christ of Latter-Day Saints, 4752
Naval Historical Center, 4751
religious archives, 4751
United Methodist Church, 4752
museum archives
  Getty museum, 4755
  Smithsonian Institution, 4754–4755
  United States Holocaust museum, 4755
  Warhol Museum, 4755
NARA, 4746
performing arts archives
  Center for Black Music Research, 4755
  Folger Shakespeare Library, 4756
  New York Public Library, 4756
popular culture archives, 4756
science, technology, and health care archives
  Alan Mason Chesney Medical Archives, 4761–4762
  California Academy of Science, 4762
  California Institute of Technology, 4762
  Charles Babbage Center, 4762
  Claude Moore Library, 4762
  David Sarnoff Library, 4762
  Linda Hall Library, 4762
  National Agricultural Library, 4762–4763
  National Library of Medicine, 4763
  Niels Bohr Library and Archives and Center for History of Physics, 4763
state and local government archives
  Multnomah County (Oregon) Archives, 4746
  New Orleans Notorial Archives, 4746
  San Antonio Municipal Archives Program, 4746–4747
women's history archives
  Iowa Women's Archives, 4760
  Sallie Bingham Center for Women's History and Culture, 4760
  Schlesinger Library, 4759–4760
  Sophia Smith Collection, 4759
Archival science
  access and use, 173
  acquisition, 172
  appraisal, 171–172
  archive fever, 171
  arrangement and description, 172–173
  education and research, 176–177
  organizational activity, 171
  preservation, 172
  professional discipline, 173–174
  provenance and original order, 170–171
  western world, 174–176
Archival services
  access
    breach privacy, 1467
    exclusive access, 1466
    information security and freedom, 1463
    law protected data, 1466
    policy sealing, 1466
    privacy and confidentiality restriction, 1466

Archival services (cont'd.)
  access (cont'd.)
    private/confidential document posting,
      1467
    rare materials, research libraries, 1465
    SAA Code of Ethics, 1466
    safeguard privacy, 1467
    Scrolls, 1466
    sealing material, 1466
    selective access, 1466
    sensitive material, 1466
    sensitive/proprietary information, 1463
  acquisitions
    appraisals, 1464
    auction houses, 1465
    basic elements, 1464
    deed of deposit, 1464
    deed of gift, 1464
    donation, 1464
    ethical aspects, 1463
    gift and purchase materials, 1463
    intellectual and historical context, 1463
    legal issues, 1463
    long-term safekeeping, 1463
    manuscript dealers, 1465
    material's fair market value, 1464
    online auction sites, 1464
    open-ended deposits, 1464
    private sellers, 1465
    right to transfer, 1463
    tax deduction, 1464–1465
  terms of use, 1467–1468
Archival Studies Education, 4912–4913
Archive Museum of ERT, 1739
Archives
  in Australia
    Australian Joint Copying Project, 386
    business archives, 188
    as discipline and profession, 388
    educational and religious archives,
      188–189
    national and state archives, 386–387
    nongovernmental archives, 387–388
  avocational user groups, 152
  in China
    archive management bureaus and reposito-
      ries, 905–906
    CAC, 905
    China People's University, 908
    education courses, 907–908
    legislation, 905
    national archives, 906–907
    professional associations, 908
    provinces, 906–907
    religious archives, 907
    State Archives Bureau, 905
  closed-ended questions, 151
  copies, 160
  in Croatia
    Croatian State Archives, 1127–1128
    historical overview, 1126–1127
    legislation, 1127
    National Film Archives, 1128
    publishing and professional associations,
      1128
    specialized archives, 1128
  definition, 1792

  in Denmark
    archivists and records managers, education
      for, 1224
    college and university archives, 1223–1224
    conservation and preservation, 1225
    Danish Archives Act, 1222
    Danish Emigration Archives in Aalborg,
      1224
    digital archival collections and finding aids,
      1224
    electronic records, 1224–1225
    Map and Land Registry Agency, 1224
    national, regional, and local archives,
      1222–1223
    professional associations, 1224
    repositories, 1224
  digital surrogates/electronic records, 160–161
  direct use, 151
  Dodecanese, prefecture of, 1737
  Ethiopia, 1500
  evidential use, 150–151
  experience and preparation, 151
  in France (*see* France, archives)
  French Revolution and nineteenth century,
    182–183
  in Germany
    archival pedagogic/user education, 1703
    corporate archives, 1701
    digital archival collections and finding aids,
      1702
    education, 1702
    electronic records, 1703
    film and audiovisual archives, 1701
    legislation, 1699
    literary archives, 1701
    local archives, 1700–1701
    national archives and services, 1699–1700
    preservation and conservation, 1703
    private archives, 1701–1702
    professional associations, 1702–1703
    religious archives, 1701
    school and university archives, 1701
    state archives, 1700
  and human impulses, 168–181
  Hungary
    archivists and records managers, education
      for, 1926–1927
    college and university archives, 1925–1926
    corporate and religious, 1926
    as discipline and profession, 1926
    electronic documents, 1927
    film and audiovisual archives, 1926
    historical societies, 1926
    legislation, 1925
    manuscript repositories, 1926
    national archives and services, 1925
    preservation of documents, 1927
    professional associations, 1927
  ICA (*see* International Council on Archives)
  India (*see* India)
  indirect use, 151
  informational use, 150
  information family tree, 150
  information seeking
    electronic resources, 153, 162
    information seekers, 152–153
    in institutional archives, 154

    libraries, 153
    in organizations, 153–154
    people, 152–153
    personal collections, 153
    records, 153
  institutional form and function, 181–182
  institutions
    collecting tradition, 186–188
    North America, 184–185
    postcolonial era, twentieth century,
      183–184
    public records, Australia, 185–186
  intended use, 151
  intrinsic use, 151
  Ionian Islands, 1737
  in Israel
    archival science as discipline and profes-
      sion, 2557
    archives law and state archives, 2553
    branch archives, 2553–2554
    municipal archives, 2554
    professional associations, 2557–2558
    professional education, 2557
    public archives, 2554–2557
  in Japan, 2576
    academic societies, 2570
    associations and organizations, 2570–2571
    college and university, 2569
    corporate, 2569
    decentralized management, 2567
    education and training, 2571
    local public archives, 2568
    National Archives Law, 2569–2570
    National Archives of Japan, 2567–2569
    private sector archives, 2569
    Public Archives Law, 2569–2570
  in Kazakhstan
    access and use, 2586
    archival development plan, 2586
    as discipline and profession, 2586–2587
    history, 2584–2585
    legislation, 2585
    national archive system, 2585
    oblast and municipal archives, 2585
  Kenya (*see* Kenya National Archives and
    Documentation Service)
  legal access, 158–160
  loans, 161
  in Moldova, 3118–3120
  National Archives of Armenia, 235–236
  open-ended questions, 151
  Pacific Islands (*see* Pacific Islands Associa-
    tion of Libraries and Archives)
  parent institution, personal network develop-
    ment, 161
  people with disabilities, 3575
  physical access, 159–160
  as a place and virtual archives, 189–190
  popular illusion, 162
  primary uses, 150
  public programs, 161
  and records management
    careers and education (*see* Educators and
      trainers)
    institutional records and archives (*see*
      Institutional records and archives)
  reference services

administrative components of, 161
continuing interaction, 156
educating users, 154–155
exit interview, 156–157
facilitating research, 154
fundamental elements, 154
intellectual access, 149
legal access, 149
management of, 161–162
person, reference interactions in, 157–158
physical access, 149
query abstraction, 155
query resolution, 155–156
question negotiation, 155–156
reference function, evaluation of, 162
remote users, reference interaction with, 158
repository performance, quantitative and qualitative measures, 162
staff qualifications, 161–162
undertaking research, 154
Web, 158
remote inquiries, 162
research purpose, 151
SAA (*see* Society of American Archivists)
Samos, 1737
in Saudi Arabia, 3978–3979
Senegal, 4109–4110
in Serbia, 4132–4133
Slovakia
access to archives, 4181
education, 4182
history, 4180
legislation, 4180–4181
magazine and awards, 4183
national archives, 4181
organizations and associations, 4182–4183
specialized public archives, 4182
state archives, 4181–4182
South Korea
as discipline, 4309
legislative history, 4308–4309
NARS, 4308
Spain (*see* Spain)
television (*see* International Federation of Television Archives)
United Kingdom
archival profession, 4738
archive services, 4735–4736
business archives, 4736–4737
community archives, 4738
film and audiovisual archives, 4737
higher education organizations, 4736
legislation, 4732–4735
professional societies and organizations, 4738–4739
rare manuscript libraries, 4738
religious archives, 4737–4738
vocational user groups, 151–152
zoo and aquariums, 5083
Archives Association, 1224
Archives Leadership Institute, 3319
Archives Nationales of France, 1792
Archives of the Serbian Academy of Science and Arts, 4133
Archives, Personal Papers, and Manuscripts (APPM), 136

ArchivesSpace, 137
Archivum, 2437
Archway Publishing, 4058
Aristotle's *scala natura* concept, 1813
Aristotle University of Thessaloniki, 1731–1733, 1738, 1742
Arken Museum of Modern Art, 1226
ARL, *see* Association of Research Libraries
ArLA, *see* Armenian Library Association
ARMA International
association
and profession, 222–223
structure, 223–224
competencies and certification, 225
creation of, 222
education, 225
history
business records management, 221–222
government records management, 222
information and records management, 225–227
membership, 224
publications, 224
standards, 224–225
Armed services museums, United Kingdom, 4718–4719
Armenia, 238–239
education, 238
government, 238
information infrastructure and institutions, 238
libraries
academic libraries, 230
American University of Armenia Papazian Library, 230–231
Armenian Book Chamber, 230
Armenian Library Association, 233–235, 238
children's and school libraries, 230
in Diaspora, 235
education courses, 233
history of, 228
Khnko-Aper National Children's Library, 230–232
NAS RA, 232
National Library of Armenia, 230–231
public libraries, 230
RSML, 232
during Soviet era, 228–230
special libraries, 230
Yerevan State University Library, 230, 232–233
map of, 228–229
museums
Children's Art Gallery and Aesthetic Center, 237
Genocide Museum and Institute, 236–237
Matenadaran, 236–237
National Archives of Armenia, 235–236
people and economy, 238
World Summit on the Information Society, 238
Armenian Book Chamber, 230
Armenian Library Association (ArLA), 229
continuing education, 233–235
goals, 233
inaugural conference participants, 233

initiators, 233
international and regional cooperation, 234–235
library programs, 234
mission statement, 233
National Library Day, 234, 238
and National Library of Armenia, 234
Armenian Museum of Children's Artwork, 237
Arrangement and description
context control systems, 118–120
definitions, 117
digital and networked environments, 120–124
practices, 117–118
principles, 115–117
record group traditions, 118
ARSC *Journal*, 3278, 4302
Art & Architecture Thesaurus® (AAT), 1076, 1079, 2667, 2857, 4411–4412
ARTbibliographies Modern, 250
Artefacts Canada, 678
Art Full Text and Art Index Retrospective, 250
Art gallery(ies)
art world, 243–244
in Australia
Bendigo Art Gallery, 391
Indigenous art, international recognition of, 393
national and state galleries, 388–390
rock art in Kakadu National Park, 391–392
specialist galleries, 391
customers, 246–247
definition, 241–242
elite *vs.* commercially-oriented galleries, 243
in Germany, 1704
Hungary, 1928
international art market, 246
in Kazakhstan, 2587–2588
locations, 247
operations, 242
patronage to market, 244–245
primary, secondary, and tertiary markets, 245
professional artists, 245
resources
blogs, galleries, and auctions online, 248
directories and archives, 247–248
fairs, festivals, and biennials, 248
magazines and journals, 247
professional associations, 247
role, 242–243
in Serbia, 4133–4134
Arthur M. Sackler Museum of Art and Archaeology, 909–910
Article-level metrics (ALMs), 46–47
Artificial intelligence (AI), 2217, 4082–4083
automated reasoning, 271–272
Checkers playing program, 269–270, 273, 276
Deep Blue Chess program, 270, 276
in diverse disciplines, 270
electronic computers, 270
engineering and manufacturing applications, 276
environment protection, 276
financial applications, 276
heuristic search and problem solving, 271
intelligent information systems, 276–277
knowledge representation, 271–272
machine learning, 272–274

Artificial intelligence (AI) (cont'd.)
  machine translation, 277
  medicine and health care, 276
  natural language processing, 274–275
  objective of, 277
  online information tools, 270
  online shopping tools, 270
  robotics, 275
  signal and image processing, 275
  space science explorations, 276
  speech processing, 274
  syllogism, 269
  Turing test, 270
Artificial neural networks (ANNs), 273–274,
    3270
  backpropagation learning algorithm, 279
  as biological models, 279
  as computational systems, 279
  natural language processing (see Natural lan-
    guage processing, ANN)
Art Indemnity Australia, 389
Artists' books, 3736, 4337
Artists Rights Society (ARS), 4946
Art librarianship
  ARLIS/NA, 249, 254
  ARLIS/UK and Ireland, 249, 254
  art and art history-related journals, 250
  art library settings
    academic art libraries, 251
    museum, 251
    public libraries, 251–252
    visual resources, 252
  art-related library and affinity organizations,
    255–256
  digitization, 250
  directories, 249–250
  educational requirements, 250–251
  IFLA, 255
  OPACs, 250
  print-based art periodical indexes, 250
  professional responsibilities
    cataloging, 253
    collection development, 252
    reference, bibliographic instruction and
      research, 253
    staff, budget, and library facilities, man-
      agement of, 253–254
    publications, 249
    role of, 250
    VRA, 252–253, 255
Art Libraries Section, 249
Art Libraries Society of North America (ARLIS/
    NA), 249, 254–256, 4933–4934
Art Libraries Society United Kingdom and Ire-
    land (ARLIS/UK and Ireland), 249, 254
The Art Library as Place, 254
Art library, Japan, 2574
The Art Library Manual: A Guide to Resources
    and Practice, 249
Art market, 244–246
Art Museum Image Consortium (AMICO),
    3178, 3228
Art Museum Libraries and Librarianship, 249,
    251
Art museums, 3236–3237
  architecture, 261
  England, 265

ethics and governance, 264–265
exhibitions, 265–266
France, 264
gallery, 259
globalization, 266
Hermitage, 1818
history
  antiquity, 260
  Enlightenment, 261
  Middle Ages, 260
  modern period, 262–264
  nineteenth century, 261–262
  Renaissance, 260
  United States, 262
in Israel, 2551
modern art, 263–264
money and other measurements, 265
ownership, 266–267
politics, power, and representation, 3689,
  3692–3693
Switzerland, 4495
Arts administration, 4928
Arts and Humanities Citation Index (A&HCI),
    925, 2370, 3471
Arts and Humanities Research Council (AHRC),
    4718
Arts and Industries Building, 4192
Arts literatures
  artist occupations, 293–294
  arts, definition, 293
  information retrieval
    image retrieval, 297–298
    melodic retrieval, 298
    subject retrieval, 297
  user studies
    art historians, 295
    characteristic of, 294–295
    children, 293
    dance, film, theatre, 296
    fine artists, 296
    musicians, 296–297
    music scholars, 295–296
    national service organizations, 297
    retirees, 293
    serendipity, 295
ARTstor, 250, 297–298, 4941
Art theft, 4577
Art world, 243–244
arXiv, 3466, 4013
arXiv.org's mathematics archive, 3645
ASCLA, see Association of Specialized and
    Cooperative Library Agencies
ASCLA Exceptional Service Award, 377
ASCLA Leadership and Professional Achieve-
    ment Award, 377
ASCLA/National Organization on Disability
    Award, 377
Ashmolean Museum, 1817, 4716, 4718
Asian papermaking, 1826
as-if models, 2361
ASIST, see American Society for Information
    Science and Technology
ASIS&T, see Association for Information Sci-
    ence and Technology
AskJeeves, 2523
ASLIB, see Association of Special Libraries and
    Information Bureaux

ASLIB Cranfield Project, 3712
Asni Gallery, 1504
assignFAST service, 1544–1545
Assignment indexing, 1987
ASSO, 4631
Associate university librarians (AULs), 4
Association des Bibliothe'caires de France
    (ABF), 255
Association for College and Research Libraries
    (ACRL), 4338, 4850
Association for Computers and the Humanities,
    1288
Association for Computing Machinery (ACM),
    631–632, 701, 2178, 2276, 3863, 4115
Association for Health Information and Librar-
    ies in Africa (AHILA), 3039
Association for Information and Image Manage-
    ment (AIIM), 2342
Association for Information Management,
    308–309
Association for Information Science and Tech-
    nology (ASIS&T)
  awards, 316
  chapters and SIGS, 313–314
  governance, 314–315
  history
    digital world, boundaries in, 313
    documentation, beginnings in, 311
    human/social perspective, 312–313
    information explosion, 312
    modern information science, transition to,
      311
    online information, 312
  meetings, 315–316
  publications, 315
  purpose, 313
Association for Information Systems (AIS),
    631–632, 701, 2276
  in business schools, 318
  evolution of
    Bjorn-Andersen, Niels (1996), 320
    Davis, Gordon (1998), 321
    Ein-Dor, Phillip (2002), 321–322
    Galletta, Dennis (2007), 322–323
    Galliers, Bob (1999), 321
    Ives, Blake (2001), 321
    King, Bill (1995), 320
    Loebbecke, Claudia (2005), 322
    Myers, Michael (2006), 322
    SIGs, 319–320
    Vitale, Mike (2000), 321
    Watson, Richard (2004), 322
    Weber, Ron (1997), 321
    Wei, K.K. (2003), 322
  governance of, 319
  history of, 318–319
  objectives of, 318
Association for Library and Information Science
    Education (ALISE), 19–20, 708, 1475,
    2042, 2536, 3039
Association for Library Collections and Techni-
    cal Services (ALCTS)
  Aquisitions Section, 328
  awards
    ALCTS Honors, 332
    ALCTS Outstanding Publications Award,
      331

Edward Swanson Memorial Best of LRTS Award, 331
Esther J. Piercy Award, 331
First Step Award, Wiley Professional Development Grant, 331
George Cunha and Susan Swartzburg Award, 332
Jan Merrill-Oldham Professional Development Grant, 332
Library Acquisitions Award, 331
Margaret Mann Citation, 331
Outstanding Collaboration Citation, 332
Paul Banks and Carolyn Harris Preservation Award, 331
Presidential Citations, 332
ProQuest Coutts Award for Innovation, 332
Ross Atkinson Lifetime Achievement Award, 330–331
Ulrich's Serials Librarianship Award, 331
best practices, 325
CaMMS, 328–329
CMS, 329
continuing education, 325
CRS, 329
division
Advisory Committees, 328
operational committees, 327
Revenue Committees, 327
governance
Board of Directors, 326
bylaws, 326
history, 325
information exchange, 325
interest groups, 328
mission, 324
PARS, 329
products, services and member benefits, 324
professional development, 325
publications, 325
publishing
ALCTS News, 330
Continuing Education and Programming, 330
LRTS, 329–330
membership, 330
Monographs Collection, 330
Sudden Selector's Guides, 330
Z 687, 330
standards, 324–325
strategic plan
ALCTS strategic plan 2015, 326
financial plan, 326–327
preamble, 326
vision, 324
Association for Library Service to Children (ALSC), 880
activities
advocacy, 336
awards, 334–335
continuing education and professional development, 335–336
practice, 335
governance, 333–334
history, 333
Association for Literary and Linguistic Computing, 1288

Association for Recorded Sound Collections (ARSC), 3278, 4301–4302
Association for Supervision and Curriculum Development (ASCD), 3998
Association of American Law Schools (AALS), 2712, 2716
Association of American Library Schools (AALS), see Association for Library and Information Science Education
Association of American Medical Colleges (AAMC), 1872
Association of American Publishers (AAP), 3655
Association of Architecture School Librarians (AASL), 255
Association of Archivists of Quebec (AAQ), 667
Association of Art Museum Directors (AAMD), 259, 3201
Association of Canadian Archivists (ACA), 174, 666–667
Association of Central Libraries of Serbia, 4127
Association of College and Research Libraries (ACRL), 2–3, 81, 255, 367, 989, 2752, 4012, 4576, 4582, 4587–4588, 4691, 4775–4776
academic libraries, value of, 344
awards, 343–344
division of
ALA Council, 339, 340
chapters, 340
communities of practice, 340
discussion groups, 340
interest groups, 340
sections, 340–341
higher education associations, working with, 342
library campaign and grassroots advocacy, 347–348
origin of, 338–339
professional development and growth, 356
ACRL conferences, 349
ACRL consulting services, 352
ACRL Insider, 357
ACRL nonserial publications, 355–356
ACRL office, 339–340
ACRLog, 357
ACRL podcasts, 357–358
ACRL social media, 358
ACRL website, 357
ambassador, academic libraries and librarians, 341
annual conference programs, 352
career and job services, 352
CHOICE office, 354–355
clearinghouse, 341
CLIPP, 356
coordination and oversight, 341
e-learning, 349–350
information literacy immersion program, 351
Keeping Up With. . ., 357
knowledge and intellectual technique, 353
leadership, 350
library statistics, 356–357
mentoring and training programs, 350–351
section newsletters, 357

strategic planning, 341–342
workshops and preconferences, 351–352
professional recruitment, 348
public policy advocacy, 347
research and scholarly environment, 344–346
standards and guidelines, 342–343
student learning, 346–347
summits, 348–349
Association of Computing Machinery (ACM), 2222
Association of Computing Machinery/Special Interest Group (ACM/SIG) Proceedings Templates, 3067
Association of Danish Museums, 1227
Association of German Librarians, 1699
Association of Independent Information Professionals (AIIP), 4356
Association of Independent Museums (AIM), 4721
Association of Information and Image Management (AIIM), 715, 1854
Association of Information and Library Professionals, 1699
Association of Jewish Libraries (AJL), 4608
Association of Learned and Professional Society Publishers (ALPSP), 4897–4900
Association of Library Collections and Technical Services, 1332
Association of Library Directors, 1222
Association of Library Trustees, Advocates, Friends and Foundations (ALTAFF)
governance and structure
advocacy committees cluster, 362
ALTA AND FOLUSA, 362–363
business committees cluster, 362
education committees cluster, 362
publications committee cluster, 362
history, 361
membership, 361
mission of, 361
responsibilities, 361
Association of Local Archives, 1224
Association of Moving Image Archivists (AMIA), 1579, 1586–1587, 3131
Association of Public Library Managers (APLM), 3377
Association of Recorded Sound Collections (ARSC), 1579
Association of Records Executives and Administrators (AREA), 222, 1854
Association of Records Managers and Administrators (ARMA), 3870
Association of Research Libraries (ARL), 3, 344, 347, 355, 2903, 2963, 4449
CNI, 368, 375
collections and access
global resources, 372
resource sharing, 373–374
special collections, 372–373
constitution, 364
copyright and intellectual property policies, 369
cyberinfrastructure, 370
diversity initiatives, 370–371
establishment of, 364

Association of Research Libraries (ARL)
  (cont'd.)
  Executive Director, 364
  federal funding, 370
  federal legislation, influence on, 368
  governance, 375
  guiding principles, 364–365
  leadership development, 371–372
  membership, 375
  preservation, 367–368
  privacy, security, and civil liberties, 369–370
  public access policies, 369
  RTL, 370
  scholarly communication
    Create Change Web site, 367
    IAA, 366–367
    Institute on Scholarly Communication, 367
    open access, 365–366
    OSC, 365
    scholarly publishing market, 366
    SPARC, 367
  secretariat, 364
  statistics and measurement program
    ARL Statistics, 374
    performance measures, 374–375
  strategic directions (2005–2009), 365
  survey, 97
  vision statement, 364
  Web site, 375
Association of School Librarians (AASL), 334,
  1222
Association of Specialized and Cooperative
  Library Agencies (ASCLA), 3576
  awards and scholarships, 377
  continuing education opportunities, 377
  definition, 376
  membership, 376
  organization, 376–377
  problems and issues, 377
  publications, 377
  standards, 377
Association of Specialized and Professional
  Accreditors (ASPA), 18–19
Association of Special Libraries and Information
  Bureaus (ASLIB), 301–309, 1374,
  4707–4708, 4711
Association of State Libraries Agencies
  (ASLA), 4394
Association of Ukrainian Libraries (ABU), 4644
Association of Zoos and Aquariums (AZA),
  5078
Associations of Recorded Sound Collections
  (ARSC), 2467
Association to Support the Development of
  Archives and Libraries (ADABI), 3097
Astor, Jacob, 1845
Astor Library, 1845
Atheneum archive, 4322
ATLA, see American Theological Library
  Association
Atomic Energy Act of 1954, 3564
Attitude, definition of, 3192
Attribute granularity, 1174
Auckland Free Public Library, 3372
Auction sales catalogs and dealers' catalogs,
  3770
Audiobooks, 872

Audio indexing techniques, 1058
Audiophiles, 3280
Audiovisual archives, 4755
  Hungary, 1926
  UNESCO, 4659–4660
Audiovisual cataloging resources, 1575
Audiovisual preservation
  analog audio and videotape materials,
    1568–1572
  digital formats, 1571
  film, 1567–1568
  funding, 1578–1579
Aurora, 2630
Australasia, 3373
Australasian Digital Recordkeeping Initiative,
  388
Australasian Public Libraries and Information
  Services, 3407
Australia, 393–394
  archives and archival science
    Australian Joint Copying Project, 386
    as discipline and profession, 388
    national and state archives, 386–387
    nongovernmental archives, 387–388
  business archives, 188
  Education Acts in Victoria, 380
  educational and religious archives, 188–189
  institutions, public records, 185–186
  library and information professions, systems
    and services
    academic and research libraries, 384–385
    Australian Subscription Library and Read-
      ing Room, 380
    free circulating library, 380
    free public reference library, 380
    international influences, 386
    legislation, 381
    lending branch, 380
    librarianship as discipline and profession,
      385–386
    mechanics' institute, 380
    Munn-Pitt Report, 381
    National Library, 381–382
    school and college libraries, 383–384
    special libraries, 384–385
    state and public libraries, 382–383
    State Library of Victoria, 381
  map of, 379–380
  museums and galleries
    Bendigo Art Gallery, 391
    courses, 393
    curatorial issues, 393
    national and state museums and galleries,
      388–391
    national parks, 391–392
    professional associations, 393
    specialist museums and galleries, 391
    von Mueller, Ferdinand Jakob Heinrich,
      392–393
    zoos and aquaria, 391
Australian Academic and Research Libraries,
  400
Australian and New Zealand Institute for Infor-
  mation Literacy (ANZIIL), 2752
Australian Broadcasting Company (ABC), 1567
Australian Earth Sciences Information System
  (AESIS), 385

Australian Library and Information Association
  (ALIA), 385
  advocacy, 398
  awards and scholarships, 399
  conferences, 400
  constitution, 397
  copyright advice service, 399
  core values, 397
  education and training, 398–399
  governance and structure, 398
  history of, 396–397
  industrial relations advice service, 399
  interlibrary loan voucher scheme, 400
  membership, 399
  publications, 400
Australian Library Journal, 400
Australian National Maritime Museum,
  389–390
Australian National University (ANU), 384
Australian recordkeeping, 119
Australian Recordkeeping Metadata Research
  Project, 1415
Australian School Library Association, 385
Australian Science and Technology Heritage
  Centre, 387
Australian Science Archives Project, 387
Australian Society of Archivists (ASA), 174,
  688
Australian SPIRT Recordkeeping Metadata Pro-
  ject, 123
Australian Standards for Records Management
  (AS-4390), 3871
Australian Subscription Library and Reading
  Room, 380
Austrian National Library, 3322
Authentication
  assertion of identity, 401
  biometric method, 403
  Certificate Authorities, 404
  digital signatures, 404–405
  initialization processes, 404
  intermediary authenticating service, 405
  IP addresses, 403
  one-time passwords, 402
  PGP, 404
  public key encryption, 402
  shared secrets, 402
  smart cards, 402–403
  traditional signatures, 405
Author cocitation analysis, 2218
Authority, 1116; see also Cognitive authority
Authority file, 1076
Authorization
  access rules, categories, 405
  discretionary, 406
  goal of, 405
  mandatory, 405–406
  RBAC, 406
  trust management approach, 406
Authorized access points (AAPs), 726
Authors Guild, 1760–1761
Authorship, 1860
Author Solutions, 4058
AutoCAD, 2297
Autodesk, 1676
AutoDewey, 1262
Autograph collection, 199

Automated acquisitions systems
 components, 410–412
 e-commerce, 414
 electronic interfaces
  book and serial industry, 412–413
  external accounting systems, 412
 evolution, 408–410
 Internet, 414
 standards, 413–414
 workflows and organization, 414–415
Automated discourse generation, *see* Natural
  language generation
Automated patent system (APS), 3563
Automated reasoning, 271–272
Automated Records and Techniques Curriculum
  Project, 1415
Automated Retroactive Minimal Moderation
  (ARMM), 785
Automated testing, 4798
Automatic abstracting and summarization
 components/techniques
  coherence/coreference enforcers, 424
  cohesion-based methods, 422
  compression/paraphrasing, 423–424
  cue-phrase method, 421
  discourse-based method, 422
  importance identifiers, 420–422
  paraphrasing components, 420
  position-based method, 420–421
  sentence simplifiers/compressors, 422–423
  title-based method, 421
  word-frequency method, 421–422
 F-value metric, 419–420
 genres and types of, 418–419
 headline generation, 424
 multidoc summarization, 425–426
 nontextual information, 426
 recall and precision, 419–420
 semantics, 424–425
 SUMMAC evaluation, 420
Automatic Direct Access to information with
  Online UDC System (AUDACIOUS),
  4788
Automatic indexing, 1987–1988, 2221
Automatic Language Processing Advisory
  Committee of the National Academy of
  Science–National Research Council
  (ALPAC) report, 3348
Autonomous University of the State of Mexico
  (UAEM), 3092
Avant-Garde Masters Grants, 1588
Avery Index to Architectural Periodicals, 250
Avicenna (Prince of Physicians), 3044
Award of Merit, 95
A Way to Get Wealth, 1400
Axumite Heritage Library, 40

B

BaBar high-energy physics project, 2997
Babylonian Talmud, 3042
Back-of-the-book index, *see* Book indexing
Backstage LibraryWorks, 1545
Backward citation retrieval/footnote chasing,
  925
Badier's bindings, 544
Bahir Dar University, 1499

Baidu, 4051
"Ba," knowledge transfer, 2446
Bangemann report, 2140–2141
Bankers's Magazine, 1405
Bank Secrecy Act, 1106
Bank Street College's program, 3218
Barbara Kyle's classification, 971
Bardo National Museum, 4636
Bare-bones system, 1490
Bar journals, 2740
Barker, Dale Lockard, 497–498
Barnum, Phineas T., 1819
Bartlane system, 1308
Basadre, Jorge, 3607
Baseball Hall of Fame, 4756
Base de donnee´s des ressources gratuites sur
  Internet (BDRGI), 4629
Bash Scholarship, 81
Basic Local Alignment Search Tool (BLAST),
  826–827
Basic Multilingual Plane (BMP), 4665–4666
Baska Tablet, 1122
BATAB, 409
Bates' berry-picking approach, 2244, 4529,
  4878
Bates, Marcia J., 2057–2058
Bateson, Gregory, 2051
Bauhaus biography text, 436–437
Bayes Belief Networks, 274
Bayesian networks (BNs), 1204, 2635
Bayes' rule, 2355
Bayes theorem, 2205
Bayt al-Hikmah, 3972
Bayte and Snare of Fortune, 1400
BC, *see* Bibliographic classification
The Beginnings of Systematic Bibliography, 493
Behavioral economics, 2357
Behaviorism, 4918
Behaviorist theory, 2753
Beijing History Museum, 909
Beijing Jingcheng Olympic Education Museum,
  909
Beijing Library, 889–890
Beijing Library Association, 890
Beijing Museum of Natural History, 909
Beijing World Art Museum, 909
Beilstein Handbook of Organic Chemistry, 820
*Beit Hatefutsoth–The Nachum Goldman
  Museum of Jewish Diaspora*, 2552
Belgian binders, 547
Belgrade City Library, 4129
Belkin's episode model, 1898, 2246–2247
Bell system, 1013
Belmont Report, 3146
Belvedere Gallery, 1504
Belvedère Park, 4638–4639
Belvedere statue court, 3149, 3151–3152, 3154
Benakeios Library, 1729
Benaki Museum, 1732, 1742
Benaki Phytopathological Institute, 1732
Bench journals, 2740
Bendigo Art Gallery, 391
Bentham, Jeremy, 646
Bentley Systems, Inc., 1676
Bepress' Digital Commons, 2902
Berkeley Art Museum, 3218
Berkeley Community Memory, 1029

Berkeley Systems Distribution of Unix, 3488
Berlin Medical Papyrus, 3041
Bernan Press, 1724
Berne Convention, 1316, 5009
Berners-Lee's vision for Web, 5019–5020,
  5024–5026
Berry-picking model, 3936–3937
 Bates' berry-picking model, 2076, 2244,
  4529, 4878
 of searching, 3588
Bessarabia
 archives, 3119–3120
 history, 3117–3118
 library, 3123
 museum, 3120–3123
Betacam, 1568–1569
Bethje Wolff's library, 2799
Better Assessment Science Integrating Point
  and Nonpoint Sources (BASINS),
  2155
Beynon-Davies, Paul, 2058–2059
Bezalel National Museum, 2549
BI, *see* Business informatics
BIBFRAME Scribe, 1545
Bible Lands Museum, 2551
Bibliographical access control, 2910
Bibliographical Center for Research (BCR),
  3920, 3922
Bibliographical presses, 3743
Bibliographical Society (London)
 compositor analysis, 459
 ESTC, 458
 Gold Medal, 461
 grants and bursaries, 461
 handwritten slips, 459
 The Library, 460–461
 meagre and scrappy, 457
 meetings, 460
 membership, 460
 objectives and achievements, 456
 The Society's library, 461
 Society's objectives, 460
 STC, 457
 study and research, 456
Bibliographical Society of America (BSA)
 electronic publications, 466–467
 fellowships and prizes, 465
 founding and objectives, 463–464
 meetings, 464–465
 monograph publications, 466
 organization, 464
 periodical publications, 465–466
Bibliographic classification (BC), 4205–4207,
  4475
 adaptability, 574–575
 collocation, 573–574
 consensus, 574
 extent of use, 573
 gradation, 574
 notation, 576–578
  alternative location, 576
  alternative treatments, 576
  A-Z index, 578
  classification, 575–576
 present edition of, 579
 principles, 573
 weakness, 578–579

Bibliographic Classification of Henry Evelyn
      Bliss (BC1), 581
Bibliographic control
   AACR, 449
   Bicentennial Conference on Bibliographic
         Control for the New Millennium, 454
   book catalogs, 448
   British Museum's catalog, 448
   Callimachus, 448
   card catalog, 448
   catalogers, 454
   cataloging in source, 450
   CIP program, 450
   Dublin Core, 454
   electronic catalog records, 450
   FRAD, 453
   FRBR, 452–453
   ICABS, 451
   individuals, 447
   institutions, 447
   inventory lists, 448
   ISBDs, 451
   ISBN, 450
   libraries and collectors, 447
   MARC format, 449–450
   metadata, 453–454
   OCLC, 451–452
   OPAC, 451
   Panizzi's formulation, 91 rules, 448
   Paris Principles, 449
   PCC, 454
   The Pinakes, 448
   printed union catalogs, 448
   publishers, 447
   RDA, 453
   resources, 447
   retailers, 447
   RLG, 451–452
   RLIN, 451–452
   scrolls/tablets, 447
   shelf arrangement systems, 447
   Statement of International Cataloguing Prin-
         ciples, 449
   UBC, 451
   UBCIM Core Activity, 451
   WLN, 451
   Working Group address and conclusion, 455
Bibliographic coupling, 503–504, 946
Bibliographic Database of the Conservation
      Information Network (BCIN), 676
Bibliographic databases, 942
Bibliographic framework (BIBFRAME), 1079
   model, 2924
   project, 2938, 2941
   Transitions Initiative, 3295
Bibliographic instruction (BI), 1878
Bibliographic library knowledge organization
      classification, 960
   enumerative classification, 962
   faceted classifications, 962
   facet structure, 966–968
   hierarchical structure, 965–966
   history and foundations, 961–962
   idea, verbal, and notational plane, 961
   integrative levels, 968–969
   literary warrant, 962–963
   notation, 969–971

phenomenon-based knowledge organization,
      964–965
   precoordinated classification, 962
   scientific and educational consensus, 963–964
Bibliographic verification, 3914
Bibliography
   bibliographical searching, 477
   compilation
      annotation, 477
      citation style, 476–477
      organization, 477
      scope, 476
   definition of, 492–493
   history
      library cataloging codes, 471
      modern bibliography, rise of, 469–471
      new writings, serial bibliographies of,
            471–472
      origins of, 468–469
   national imprint bibliographies
      current national bibliographies, 473
      current online subject bibliographies, 474
      Germany and adjacent areas, 473
      Great Britain, 472
      Romance-Language Nations, 472
      United States, 472
   physical bibliography, 468, 472
      analytical bibliography, 477–478
      descriptive bibliography, 478
      historical bibliography, 478–468
      textual bibliography, 478
   reference, 468
Bibliography of the History of Art, 250
Bibliometrics, 523–524, 2367
   ARIST, 489
   bibliography, definition of, 492–493
   Bradford's law
      distribution, 2226
      of scattering, 509–514
   Bradford-Zipf phenomena, 516–519
   chronological list, 498
   citation analysis, 519–520
      citation indexes, 521–523
      clustering, 523
      half-life and obsolescence, 520–521
      practical applications of, 524
   cocitation map, 485
   data sources, 2227
   definition, 497, 499
   descriptive and evaluative, 499
   domain analysis, 485
   Google boom, 483–485
   human–literature interface, 488
   information behavior, 489
   interpersonal communication, 489
   IS, map of, 485–488
   L&IS definition
      answers properties, 482
      literature properties, 481
      mediating systems properties, 481
      questioners' properties, 481
   literature-based answering, 481–482, 488
   Lotka's law of scientific productivity,
         506–509
   mediators and automation, 483
   Pareto distributions, 2226
   science of recorded discourse, 499

seminal bibliometric papers, 506
   Bibliographic Coupling between Scientific
         Papers, 503–504
   Citation Analysis as a Tool in Journal
         Evaluation, 503
   Citation Indexes for Science, 502–503
   Co-Citation in the Scientific Literature: A
         New Measure of the Relationship
         between Two Documents, 505
   criteria, 499
   Fundamental Science and War, 501
   Fussler, Herman H., 502
   Generalization of the Theory of Epidemics:
         An Application to the Transmission of
         Ideas, 504–505
   The History of Comparative Anatomy-A
         Statistical Analysis of the Literature,
         499–500
   *Human Behavior and the Principle of Least
         Effort*, 502
   The Influence and Dependence of Psycho-
         logical Journals on Each Other,
         500–501
   Number of Journals Indexed arranged by
         Countries, 500
   Psycho-Biology of Language, 502
   Sources of Information on Specific Sub-
         jects, 501–502
   Statistics-The Frequency Distribution of
         Scientific Productivity, 501
   statistical bibliography, definition of, 492,
         496–497
   statistics
      Achenwall's concept of, 495
      descriptive statistics, 494–495
      Gaussian distribution, 494
      inductive statistics, 494–495
      meaning of, 493–494
      official statistics, 495
      science of method, 495
      scientific investigation, method of, 495
      theory of probability, 494–496
   uses, 523–524
   Zipf's law of word occurrence, 514–516
BIBLIONET, 1734
Biblioteca do Conhecimento Online (B-ON),
      2827
Biblioteca Nazionale Centrale, 3323
Bibliotheca Alexandrina, 2808
Bibliotheca Universalis, 749
Bibliothèque et Archives du Quebec, 3791
Bibliothèque et Archives nationales du Québec
      (BAnQ), 660
Bibliothèque nationale (BN), 1599, 1604–1605
Bibliothèque Nationale de France, 3327–3328
   mission and organization, 533
   new national library project, 532–533
   nineteenth and twentieth century, 531–532
   public and collections, 533–534
   royal library, 531
   twenty-first century
      library's web site, 534–535
      national and international cooperation and
            partnership, 535–536
Bibliothèque Nationale du Québec (BNQ), 535
BIBSAM, 2825
Biculturalism, 3377–3378

Big data, 1487, 2107, 2112
Big Science, 3639
Big6 Skills model, 2757
Bill and Melinda Gates Foundation, 3087
Billy Graham Evangelistic Association (BGEA), 4752
Binary image, 1309
Binary indexing, 2200
Binding(s), 3768–3769, 4147
    blind tooling, 540
    bosses, 540
    butter stamp, 540
    chains and catenati, 540
    chemises, 542
    clasps and catches, 540
    collation, 538
    Cosway bindings, 541
    cover boards, preparation of, 539
    doublure, 539
    edge marbling, 539
    edge-painting and gauffering, 539
    embroidered covers, 540
    end papers, decoration types, 539
    equipment and tools, 538
    Etruscan bindings, 541
    fore-edge painting, 539
    gold tooling, 540–541
    hand binding, history of, 542–548
    headbands, 539
    hollow backs, 539
    illuminated bindings, 541
    incised leather, 540
    intarsia (inlay), 541
    jeweled bindings, 542
    knocked-up, 539
    landscapes, 541
    leather, 539–540
    lettering, 541
    materials, 541
    nonato, 541
    preservation and restoration, 542
    rice marbling, 539
    sewing methods, 538–539
    slip cases, 542
    smooth gilding, 541
    spring backs, 539
    Sutherland tooling process, 541
    techniques, 538
    tight backs, 539
    trimming of edges, 539
Bing, 4051
Bingham Library for Youth, 1843
Bingham Youth Library, 5058
Biocomplexity thesaurus, 3311
Biofuels Standards Panel (BSP), 89
Biography(ies)
    children's books, 867–868
    definition, 1652
    index series, 1652
    World Biographical Information System, 1654
Bioinformatics, 555, 3308
Biological Informatics Program (BRD), 3307–3308
Biological information
    challenges
        access problem, 560

    data sharing, 559
        preservation and curation, 559
    collaborations, 555–556
    cyberinfrastructure, 555
    digital data, 556
    formats, 556
    information and data repositories, 556–557
    information infrastructures, development of, 555
    paper-based laboratory notebooks, 554, 556
    UNISIST model, 556
    users of
        amateurs, 559
        biologists, 557–558
        educational community, 558
        organizations and individuals, 558–559
        researchers, 558
        scholarly communities, 558
Biological taxonomy, 4471
BioMed Central journals, 3468–3469
Biometric systems, 403
BioOne®, 3924, 4014
Biosemiotics, 4096, 4102
Biržiška, Vaclovas, 2954
Bit depth, 1309–1310
Bitmap image, 1308–1309
Bit preservation, 1334
BitTorrent technology, 3653
Blackboard Unions, 4691
Black Hat SEO, 4031
Black Pine Animal Park, 3247
Blacksburg Electronic Village, 1031
Blind tooling, 540, 542
Bliss Bibliographic Classification 2nd edition (BC2)
    background and context, 581–582
    classes, internal structure of, 582
    in digital world, 588–589
    disadvantages, 588
    facet analysis and information retrieval, 582–583
    influence on other schemes, 589
    special libraries, 588
    structural principles
        citation order and combination of concepts, 585–586
        filing order and schedule inversion, 586–587
        fundamental categories, 584–585
        main class order, 583–584
        notation, 587
        order in array, 585
        organization within facets, 585
        practical classification, 587–588
    thesaurus format for, 589
    vocabulary, 582
Bliss Classification, 2669; see also Bibliographic Classification
Bliss Classification Association (BCA), 582
Blobworld approach, 4421
Blogs, 2507
Blogs, Interactive Groupware Wikis Interest Group (BIGWIG), 2778
Bloomberg Law, 2708
Board of Education for Librarianship (BEL), 19
Board of Trade Journal, 647
BOBBY program, 16

Bodleian catalog, 750, 751
Bodleian Library, 4649, 4703–4704
Boksburg Historical Association (1993), 1782
Bologna Declaration, 630, 710
Bologna process, 2951
Book and journal publishing trade
    advanced countries, 3984
    book readership, growth in, 3983
    budgetary constraints, 3987
    cultural outcomes, 3986–3987
    electronic products, explosion of, 3984–3985
    ephemeral literature, 3987
    future of, 3988–3990
    intellectual property protection, 3987
    international publishing, 3983
    Internet bookselling, 3986
    minor-language countries, government subsidies, 3987
    new book titles, growth in, 3982–3983
    niche/small publishers, 3983–3984
    out-of-print book dealers, 3986
    POD, 3986
    religious publishing, 3987
    retail bookstores, 3985–3986
    specialized publications, 3984
    STM writing/publishing, 3983–3984, 3987
    textbooks, 3986–3987
    twigging effect, 3984
    U.S. book trade, 3982
Book and record depository (BARD), 663
Bookbinding, see Binding
Book history, 1859–1864, 4269–4270
Book indexing
    The Chicago Manual of Style, 442–443, 445
    editing tasks, time for, 443–444
    elements
        cross-reference, 441–442
        headings, 441
        letter-by-letter alphabetizing, 442
        locators, 441
        word-by-word alphabetizing, 442
    genre specialties, 444–445
    history of, 440–441
    indented and run-in formats, 442–443
    index, definitions of, 441
    The Oxford Guide to Style, 443
    professional associations, 445
    professional software, 443
    standards, 443
    subject specialties, 445
    term selection, 444
    training, 445
Book Industry Standards and Communications (BISAC), 413, 1261
BookLab, Inc., 3729
Bookline Alert: Missing Books and Manuscripts (BAMBAM), 4576, 4578, 4588
Book Monitoring Unit, 1734
The Book of Marco Polo, 1684
Book of the Dead, 1945–1946
Bookplates, 3768
Books and Newspapers Act (Chapter 111), 2594, 2600
Bookselling, 1861–1862
Books for layperson, 2740
Book theft, 4579

Boolean algebra, 2221
  axiomatization, 594–595
  cxamples
    finite algebra, 592
    propositions, 592–593
    sets, 593–594
  history, 591–592
  physical phenomenon, 591–592
  switching function, 595–596
Boolean logic, 4048
Boolean model, 2202–2203
Boolean retrieval model, 1621–1622
Boolean searching, 833
Boone Library, 889
Border security, 2399
Borlund model, 4876
Born-digital works, 1335–1336
Boston Athenaeum, 1844
Boston Mercantile Library, 1843
Boston Public Library, 563
Botanical gardens, 3238, 4952
  Hungary, 1930
  Switzerland, 4495
  in United Kingdom, 4724–4725
Boullée's revolutionary library project, 2799
Bourbachique terminology, 328
Bourbaki gadgetry, 328
Bowker®, 3734
Bowman, Isaiah, 1688
Bradford, Samuel Clement, 501–502, 506
Bradford's law, 488, 501, 509–514, 944, 2371
  distribution, 2226–2227
  of scattering, 925, 2210
Braille and Audio Reading Download (BARD),
  568–569
Braille Authority of North America (BANA),
  570
Braille books, 3576
Braille library
  Japan, 2565
  in Korea, 4313
Bray, Thomas, 1840
Brazil
  distance education
    Bachelor in Library Science, 605
    Brazilian Association of Education in
      Information Science, 607
    CAPES, 604, 607–608
    communication process, 607
    course content preparation, 609
    course material development, 608–609
    graduate-level courses, 606
    implementation process, 608
    IPES, 607
    Knowledge Society, 603
    legislation, 604
    librarianship training, 605
    model classroom teaching, 605–606
    Moodle, 606
    new quality of education, 603
    pedagogical design, 607
    RFP, 607
    technical and operational support, 608
    UAB, 604–605
    undergraduate and graduate studies, 604
    undergraduate degree, 607
    virtual learning environments, 606

    graduate courses, 612
    Industrial Revolution, 597
    job market, 612–614
    scientific infrastructure, 597
    undergraduate courses, 597–599
Brazilian Association of Education for Library
    Science and Documentation (ABEBD),
    612
Brazilian Association of Education in Informa-
    tion Science, 607
Brazilian Institute of Bibliography and Docu-
    mentation (IBBD), 612
Brazilian Institute of Science and Technical
    Information (IBICT), 612
Brazilian museum, 611–615
Brenda Dervin's sense-making, 4119–4121
Brett Butler Entrepreneurship Award, 2778
Bridge/jump page, 4035
BrightSparcs, 557
Brisbane City Library, 383
Britain and the British Seas, 1687–1688
Britain-based Institute of Physics (IOP), 3639
British Board of Trade, 646–647
British Broadcasting Company (BBC), 1566
British Film Archive, 4737
British ISKO Chapter, 2497
British Library (BL), 3328–3329, 3729, 4701
  audiences, 628
  collections
    division, 628
    and services, 621–628
    storage building, 618–619
  finance division, 628
  funding, 619
  headquarters, 618
  history, 616–617
  operations division, 628
  strategy, 619–620
  two-site estates strategy, 617–618
  user communities, 620–621
  vision and mission, 619–620
British Library Act 1972, 616
British Library Research and Development
    Department (BLRDD), 4712
British Museum, 1818, 3260, 3758
British Museum Act of 1753, 616
*British Museum Catalogue of Books Printed in
    the Fifteenth Century*, 1970
British National Bibliography, 583, 1537
British Open University Library, 3438
British Technology Index, 1537
Broader term (BT), 1986
Brontë Parsonage Museum, 4166
Brookes, B.C., 2051
Brooklyn Museum, 1072–1073, 3252
Brooks–Dingell bill, 1020
Brotherton Library, 4704
Brown Popular Culture Library, 4756
Browsing strategies, 2241
Brugsch Maior Papyrus, 3041
Brunhes, Jean, 1687
Brute-force filtering, 5047
Bryant memorandum, 2890
BSA, *see* Bibliographical Society of America
Buckland, Michael, 2057
Budapest Open Access Initiative (BOAI), 365
Buildings and Equipment (BES), 2842, 2845

Bulgarian Information Consortium (BIC), 2829
Bulletin of the American Mathematical Society,
    3027
Bureaucratic culture, 3521–3522
Bureau of Canadian Archivists' Planning Com-
    mittee on Archival Descriptive Stan-
    dards, 3749
Bureau of Labor Statistics (BLS), 699
Büsching, Anton Friedrich, 1685
Busia Community Library, 40
Business archives
  Coca-Cola Company, 4752
  Ford Motor Company, 4753
  history associates, 4753
  History Factory, 4753
  Levi Strauss, 4753
  United Kingdom, 4736–4737
Business Archives Association (BAA),
    2570–2571
Business Archives Council of Australia
    (BACA), 188
Business broadcasters, 641
Business Committee for the Arts (BCA), 1087
Business directories, 640
Business e-mails, 2507
Business entities, 5013
Business finance, 3005–3006
Business informatics (BI)
  architectural framework, 632
  characteristics of, 631
  IS 2002 undergraduate model curriculum,
    631–632
  MSIS 2000 model curriculum, 631–632
  recommendation for, 631–632
  as science discipline, 631
  study framework, 632–633
  study program, 632–634
Business information users
  advertisements, 639
  business books, 641
  business broadcasters, 641
  contact information, 638
  credit reports, 639
  financial information, 638–639
  general information sources, 637
  industry information, 637–638
  informal and formal sources, 636
  information gathering, 636
  information technologies, 637
  internal and external sources, 636
  legal information, 637
  magazines and journals, 641
  market data, 637
  market research reports and data, 639
  newsletters, 641
  newspapers, 640–641
  product information, 637
  products and services, 639
  reference tools, 640
  small business owners and entrepreneurs,
    636–637
  soft external information, 636
  specialized and technical nonbusiness infor-
    mation, 639–640
Business & Intellectual Property Centre (BIPC),
    620–621
Business intelligence, 2449

Business literature
  abstracting services, 652
  accounting, 651
  banking, finance, and investments, 651
  Code of Hammurabi, 643
  on computer operations, 652–653
  cuneiform clay tablets, 643
  in Egypt, 643–644
  in England, 645–648
  foreign trade, 652
  France and Germany, publications in, 648
  in Greece, 643–644
  in late seventeenth century, 645–646
  loose-leaf services, 652
  marketing, sales management, and advertis-
    ing, 651–652
  newspaper indexes, 652
  periodicals, 653
  personnel and industrial relations, 651
  professional associations, 651
  public relations, 652
  real estate and insurance, 651
  during Romans, 644
  schools of business, 650
  scientific management studies
    in Europe and United States, 650
    list of books, 650–651
  in sixteenth and seventeenth centuries, 645
  statistics, 648–649
  trade associations, publications of, 649–650
  in United States, 647–649
  in Venice and Florence, 644–645
Business magazines, 641
Business process reengineering (BPR), 2658,
    3511
Business productivity software, 3650
Business Reference and Services Section
    (BRASS), 3909
Business Software Alliance (BSA), 3650–3651
Business Statistics, 649
Business Week, 650
Business writing, 4547–4548
Butterfly effect, 1036
Butter stamp, 540
Byzantine illumination, 1946–1947

C

Cabinets of curiosities, 1814
Cable Communications Policy Act, 1017
Cable Television Consumer Protection and
    Competition Act, 1017
Calcutta Public Library, 3326
Caldecott Committee, 334
Caldecott Medal, 334
Calendars, 133, 153, 170, 4084
California Digital Library, 1760
California Public Records Act, 1105
California's Meyers-Milias-Brown Act, 4690
California State University (CSU), 6, 9
Caliper Corporation, 1676
The Cambridge Crystallographic Data Centre,
    822
Cambridge Structural Database (CSD), 822, 834
*Cambridge Tracts in Mathematics and Mathe-
    matical Physics*, 3028
Camel library, Kenya, 2595

Cameo binding, 543
CaMMS, *see* Cataloging and Metadata Manage-
    ment Section
Campbell Collaboration, 1519
Canada
  broadcast archives, 1567
  library and archives (*see* Library and Archives
    Canada)
Canada Institute for Scientific and Technical
    Information (CISTI), 660–661
Canadiana.org, 667
Canadian Association of Research Libraries
    (CARL), 659–660, 664–665
Canadian Broadcasting Company (CBC), 1567
Canadian Committee on Archival Description
    (CCAD), 670
Canadian Council of Archives (CCA), 666
Canadian Federation of Library Associations
    (CFLA), 665
Canadian Heritage Information Network
    (CHIN)
  Artefacts Canada, 678
  BCIN, 676
  CIN, 676
  international activities, 675–676, 679
  knowledge exchange, 678
  membership, 679–680
  mission, 676–678
  NIP, 676
  online resources, 675
  research, 679
  strategies, 675
  VMC Investment Program, 676, 678–679
  Web sites, 678
Canadian Journal of Mathematics, 3027
Canadian Library Association (CLA), 19
  early history, 682
  governance, 682
  LIS community, 681
  roles and activities, 681–682
  1970s–2000, 682–683
  from 2000 On, 683
Canadian Urban Libraries Council (CULC), 666
Canberra, 186, 389, 1392–1393, 3692
Cancelbot, 785, 786
Canevari bindings, 543
Canned text systems, 431
Constantinopolitanus, *see* Vienna Dioscorides
Capen, Edward, 1844
*Capital and Finance in the Age of the Renais-
    sance: A Study of the Fuggers and their
    Connections*, 645
Capitalism, 891, 1790, 1859, 1861, 4198–4199
Caracas Declaration, 4887–4890
Card sort, 4797
Careers, 706
  ALA's Office on Human Resource Develop-
    ment and Recruitment, 711
  categorization analyst, 711
  digital services librarian (assistant professor),
    711
  knowledge systems librarian/taxonomist, law,
    711
  staff training and development coordinator,
    712
  Youth Services Department Head, 712
CARIST, 4631

CARL, *see* Canadian Association of Research
    Libraries
Carlos III University, 4321
Carnegie, Andrew, 1839, 1845–1846
Carnegie Corporation, 3216–3217
Carnegie Library, 2387, 2802–2803, 3325
Carnegie United Kingdom Trust (CUKT), 1839
Carnegie–Whitney endowment, 78
Carnivore project, 2070
Carolingian illumination, 1947–1948
Carolingian leather bindings, 542
Carpenter, Nathaniel, 1685
Carthage National Museum, 4637
Carus Mathematical Monographs, 3028
CAS, *see* Chemical Abstracts Service
Cascading style sheets (CSS) specification,
    5021, 5025
Case digests, 2741–2742
Case-study model, 3814–3815
Casinos, 1123
Cason, Hulsey, 500–501
CASREACT database, 818
CAS Registry Numbers®, 824
CASS, *see* Chinese Academy of the Social
    Sciences
Cassette tapes, 3280
Catalan consortium, 2824
Catalog cards, 3450
Cataloging
  bibliographic records, 730–731
  components, 726
  forms, 724–725
  functions, 725–726
Cataloging and Metadata Management Section
    (CaMMS), 328–329
Cataloging cultural objects (CCO), 3178, 3761,
    4935, 4937–4938
  assessment of, 740–742
  elements
    authorities, 739–740
    class element, 738
    creator information, 736
    description element, 738
    location and geography, 737–738
    object naming, 736
    physical characteristics, 737
    stylistic, cultural and chronological infor-
      mation, 737
    subject element, 738
  entity relationship diagram, 735
  general guidelines
    database design, 735
    display and indexing, 735
    related works, 735
    subjective interpretation, 735
    work and image records, 735
  historical context of, 733–734
Cataloging in Publication (CIP) program, 450,
    3395
Cataloging Rules and Principles, 2921
Catalogs and cataloging
  AACR, 2920–2921
  archaeological collections, 1149
  arrangement, 744
  audiovisual archives, 1574–1575
  authority control, 2920
  BIBFRAME model, 2924

Catalogs and cataloging (cont'd.)
  bibliographer, influence of, 744
  bibliographic records, 704–705
  Cataloging Rules and Principles, 2921
  Catalogue of Bretton Monastery Library,
    2920
  codes of cataloging rules, 774–776
  components, 700, 2920
  database maintenance, 2920
  DDC system, 2920
  definition, 743, 2918, 2920
  discovery interfaces, 2922–2923
  in eighteenth century, 751–752, 773
  ERMS, 2922
  format/physical form, 744
  forms, 698–699
  FRBR report, 2923
  functions, 699–700, 745
  inventory, age of
    fifteenth century, 748–749, 773
    fifth through eleventh centuries, 746–747
    fourteenth century, 747–748, 773
    Greeks, 745, 773
    primitive methods, 745
    Roman period, 745–746
    sixteenth century, 749–750, 773
    thirteenth century, 747, 773
    twelfth century, 747
  as inventory list, 744, 745
  LCC, 2920
  MARC, 2921, 2923
  mergers and acquisitions, 2921
  in nineteenth century, 773–774
    ALA, 757
    alphabetical author catalog, 754, 755
    alphabetico-classed catalog, 754, 757–758
    arrangements and indexes, combinations
      of, 755–756
    Bodleian Catalogue of 1674, 754
    Boston Athenaeum catalog, 757–758
    British Museum Rules, 759–760
    card catalog, 756–757
    centralized cataloging, 758
    classified catalog, 754–755
    combined catalog, 754–755
    Crestadoro, Andres, 761
    Cutter, Charles A., 761–763
    Dewey Decimal Classification, 757
    dictionary catalog, 754–757
    index-catalog, 758
    Jewett, Charles C., 760–761
    old inventory concept, 753
    photographic techniques, 758
    printed book catalog, 754
    printed card service, 758–759
    slip catalogs, 762
    supplementary alphabetical subject index,
      758–759
  official catalog, 744
  online catalog, 2922–2923
  original *vs.* copy cataloging, 2920
  periodical indexes, 744
  preparation of, 744
  process of, 744
  public catalog, 744
  purpose/objects of, 744
  RDA, 2923

Rules for a Printed Dictionary Catalog, 2920
Rules for the Compilation of the Catalogue,
  2920
serial publications, publication of, 743
in seventeenth century, 750–752, 773
subject catalog, 744
subject headings, 2920
in twentieth century, 774
  book catalog, 769–770
  card catalog, 765–766
  Cards-with-Books-Program, 768
  Cataloging-in-Source Program, 767–768
  cataloging policies, reevaluation/
    reappraisal of, 766–767
  centralized cataloging, 767–768, 772–773
  classified catalog, 764–765, 771
  commercial services, 767
  computer-produced catalog, 770–771
  cooperative cataloging, 764, 772–773
  depository catalogs, 769
  descriptive cataloging, 765–766
  dictionary catalog, 764
  divided catalogs, 765
  KWIC Index, 770
  linotype slugs method, 769
  local and regional union catalogs, 768–769
  microprint, 770
  photolithographic process, 769
  printed cards, 767
  selective and simplified cataloging, 765
  Shared Cataloging Program, 768
  shingled card technique, 769
  subject catalog, 762–763, 766, 771–773
  tabulating machine, use of, 769–770
union catalog, 744
Catalogue of Bretton Monastery Library, 2920
Catalogue of Printed Books, 755
Catastrophic terrorism, 2400
Categorical data, 4065
Categories for the Description of Works of Art
  (CDWA), 734, 3760–3761, 4413
Category membership, 4797
Cathleen Bourdon Service Award, 377
Catholicon, 1972
Catholic Primatial Archives of Esztergom, 1926
CBIR, *see* Content-based image retrieval
CCO, *see* Cataloging Cultural Objects
CCSDS, *see* Consultative Committee for Space
  Data Systems
CDNL, *see* Conference of Directors of National
  Libraries
CD-ROM, 2322–2326
CDSS, *see* Clinical decision-support systems
CDWA, *see* Categories for the Description of
  Works of Art
Cell phone technology, 4006
Celtic illumination, *see* Hiberno-Saxon
  illumination
Cemetery records, 1658
Censorship, Internet
  ccTLD system, 780
  definition, 780–781
  diffused packet-switching architecture, 780
  history
    1994 to 1997, 781–782
    1996 to 1999, 782
    from 2000, 782–783

ICANN, 780
  methods
    access control, 784–785
    filtering, 786
    passing laws, 785
    technology, 785–786
  problems
    Internet highlights, 784
    many-to-many spectrum, 784
    maximum freedom, 784
    Neo-Nazis frames, 784
    regulation process, 784
    regulatory paradigm, 784
    Relay Chat and voice-telephony, 784
    scanning GIF files, 784
    surfeit of information, 783
    Web-based newspaper, 784
  trends, 786
Censorship, published materials, 2387–2389
Census records, 1658
Center for Democracy and Technology (CDT),
  783
Center for Distance Higher Education of Rio de
  Janeiro (CEDERJ), 608
Center for Documentation and Information
  (CDI), 900–901, 1601
Center for Electronic Records, 1414
Center for European Nuclear Research (CERN),
  4468
Center for International Scholarship in School
  Librarianship (CISSL), 2752
Center for Museum Research and Conservation
  in France, 1596
Center for Networked Information Discovery
  and Retrieval (CNIDR), 3563
Center for Planning and Economic Research
  (KEPE), 1732
Center for Research Libraries (CRL), 372
  application, 793
  collections, 791
  cooperative collection development, 791–793
  global resources collaborations
    global resources programs, 790–791
    partnerships, 790
  history, 789
  resource sharing, 791
Centernet classification, 1290
Center of Legal and Economic Sciences (CCJE),
  612
Center of Research and Education (CORE) pro-
  gram, 3034
Central and East European Licensing Informa-
  tion Platform (CELIP), 2827
Central archive, 3000
Central Archives for the History of the Jewish
  People (CAHJP), 2555
Central European Research Network (CERN),
  3640
Central Information Officer (CIO), 1551
Central Lending Libraries, 1600
Central Library of the Ukrainian Association of
  the Blind, 4647
Central Library System (CLS), 3400
Central Medical Library (CML), 1125
Central Public Library
  of Sparta, 1730
  of Veroia, 1730

Central Zionist Archives (CZA), 2555
Centre de documentation nationale (CDN), 4631
Centre for Continuing Training of Librarians, 1126
Centre for Heritage Development in Africa (CHDA), 2606
Centre national de documentation agricole (CNDA), 4631
Centre national universitaire de documentation scientifique et technique (CNUDST), 4629
Century Scholarship, 377
Certain Ancient Tracts Concerning the Management of Landed Property, 1402
Certificate Authorities (CA), 404
Certified Public Library Administrator (CPLA) program, 2844, 3777, 3804
Certified Records Manager (CRM), 174, 1855
Chained data grids, 3000
Chain of preservation (COP), 2528
Chamber of Commerce of the United States of America, 649–650
Champion Award, NASIG, 3390
Changeable electric sign, 4974–4975
Change management, 717, 3523, 3526
Chapter-level indexing, 3131
Charleston Conference
    administration, 798
    ATG issues, 794
    commercial exhibits, 795
    concurrent presentation sessions, 795
    hotels and venues, 796
    legacy and publications, 798–799
    mentors, 796
    online program, 795
    plenary talks, 794
    printed program, 795
    program, 796–798
    registration, 796
    speakers, 794, 795
    values, 799
    vendor showcase, 795
Charleston Library Society, 1840–1841
Chartbook on Financial and Business Statistics, 649
Chartered Institute of Library and Information Professionals (CILIP), 681–682, 4709, 4711
    action plan, 813
    branches and groups, 808–810
    Ethical Principles and Code of Professional Practice, 812
    goals, 806
    governance, 806–807
        Council, Executive Board and Committees, 807
        Enterprise Board, 808
        policy development committee, 807
        professional development committee, 808
        professional practice committee, 808
    membership, 810
    mission, 806
    professional education and qualifications
        Chartered Membership, 810–811
        Fellowship, 811
        Framework of Qualifications, 811
        overseas qualifications, 811–812

    services
        conference management service, 813
        consultancy services, 813
        facet publishing, 813
        INFOmatch, 813
        information and advice, 812
        library and information update, 813
        LIS Jobnet, 813
        networking and further support, 812–813
        news and comment, 812
        qualifications and professional development, 812
        training and development, 813
Charter of Athens, 1070
Chat software, 1056, 3442–3443
Checkers playing program, 269–270, 273, 276
Check-in, 980, 2894, 2982, 4143
Check-out, 917, 921, 980, 1698, 2894
Checksums, 1366
CHEMCATS, 820
Chemical Abstracts Service (CAS), 817–818, 834
Chemical Abstracts Service Registry System, 830
Chemical database, 830, 832–833
Chemical information, 830
Chemical literature
    catalogs, 820
    chemistry and, 814
    handbooks, 820–822
    indexing and abstracting services, 817–820
    information retrieval
        ambiguous chemical identifiers, 823–824
        unambiguous chemical identifiers, 824–825
    primary literature, 814–815
        chemists, 814
        journal articles, 815
        patents, 815
        publication of primary data, 815
    review sources
        encyclopedias, 816
        treaties and review articles, 816–817
    secondary literature, 815–816
    specialized search techniques, 825–827
    tertiary literature, 816–817, 820–822
        handbooks, 820–822
        review sources, 816–817
Chemical similarity, 833
Chemical structure, 830–831, 837, 3570
Chemical substructure, 832–835, 837, 3570
Chemise, 542
Chemistry Preprint Server (CPS), 3643
Chemoinformatics
    computer-aided drug discovery
        ADMET prediction, 837
        molecular diversity analysis, 836–837
        QSAR, 836
    3D structures, database search of, 830
        Cambridge Structural Database, 834
        Chemical Abstracts Service, 834
        similarity searching and docking, 835–836
        structure generation programs, 834
        substructure search, 834–835
    2D structures, database search of, 830
        chemical graph, 831
        connection table, 831
        line notation, 831

    patent and reaction searching, 833–834
    similarity searching, 833
    structure diagram, 831
    structure search, 831
    substructure search, 832–833
Cheshire information retrieval system, 1251–1254
Chester Beatty Papyrus, 3041
Chetham catalog of 1791, 753
Chetham Library, 1837
The Chicago Manual of Style, 442–443, 445
Chicago Public Library, 563
Chicanos, 2699, 2701–2702
Chicano Thesaurus, 2699
"Chick lit," 3705–3706
Chief information officer (CIO), 2276
Chief Knowledge Officer (CKO), 2647
Chief Learning Officer (CLO), 2647
Chief Officers of State Library Agencies, Inc, (COSLA), 4394–4395
Child Internet Protection Act, 882, 1472
Child Online Protection Act (COPA), 2396
Children and information technology
    areas of research, 840–844
    digital media, 846–847
    Internet use, 844–846
Children, library services
    Armenia, 230–232
    children's librarians, 880
    collection development, 878–879
    history, 876–877
    at Hjoerring Public Library, 1221
    international dimensions, 882–883
    issues, 880–882
    programming, 879–880
    public library, implementation in, 877–878
    services
        children's librarians, 815
        collection development, 813–814
        history, 811–812
        international dimensions, 817–818
        issues, 815–817
        programming, 814–815
        public library, implementation in, 812–813
        reference services, 815, 880
        storytelling, 814, 879
    in Ukraine, 4645
    in United Kingdom, 4706–4707
Children Online Privacy Protection Act, 782
Children's Art Gallery and Aesthetic Center, 237
Children's Book Week, 334
Children's Internet Protection Act (CIPA), 817, 2396
Children's librarians, 333–336, 2842, 4645, 5061
Children's Library Association (CLA), 333, 5052
Children's literature
    awards, 852, 872–23
    children with disabilities, 871
    definition of, 852
    gay, lesbian/trangendered characters, 871
    history of
        adventures and domestic novels, 855
        fables and books of prayer, 852–853

Children's literature (cont'd.)
  history of (cont'd.)
    fantasy, 854–855
    fiction, 855
    folk tales and fairy tales, 853–854
    grammars, books of manners, and religious
      tracts, 853
    hornbook, 853
    illustrated books, 855–856
    imaginative literature, 853–854
    Newbery's books, 854
    orally transmitted stories, 852
  informational books and biographies,
    867–868
  international books, 868–869
  modern fantasy, 865–867
  multicultural books, 869–871
  nonprint media, 871–872
  picture books
    alphabet books, 859
    concept books, 859
    counting books, 859
    definitions, 856–857
    engineered books, 860
    graphic novels, 860
    illustration, styles of, 857–859
    text of, 857
    trends in, 860–861
    wordless picture books, 858–859
  poetry, 861–862
  realistic fiction
    contemporary fiction, 864–865
    historical fiction, 865
  research collections, 872
  traditional literature, 862–864
Children's museums, 3219, 3237
CHIN, see Canadian Heritage Information
  Network
China, 912–913
  archives and archival science
    archive management bureaus and reposito-
      ries, 905–906
    CAC, 905
    China People's University, 908
    education courses, 907–908
    legislation, 905
    national archives, 906–907
    professional associations, 908
    provinces, 906–907
    religious archives, 907
    State Archives Bureau, 905
  libraries
    academic and research libraries, 895–898
    agreements, 911
    American influence, 889–890
    CNKI, 902
    CNNIC Survey, 902
    CNSDL, 902
    cultural revolution and recovery, 892
    history of, 886–887
    legislation, 892–893
    library and information science education,
      903–904
    library science, 888–889
    Modern Library Movement, 888
    National Library of China, 892–895
    NPDLP, 902

People's Republic of China and Cold War,
      890–892
    professional associations, 904–905
    public libraries, 898–900
    Public Library Movement, 888
    PUL, 896, 903
    school libraries, 900
    special libraries (see Chinese Academy of
      the Social Sciences)
    WDL, 903
  map of, 886–887
  museums and museology, 908–911
  population, 886
China Academic Library Information System
  (CALIS), 896
China Association for Science and Technology
  (CAST), 904
China Education and Research Network
  (CERNET), 897
China. Ergebnisse eigener Reisen und darauf
  gegründeter Studien, 1687
China Internet Network Information Center
  (CNNIC) Survey, 902
China National Knowledge Infrastructure
  (CNKI), 902
China People's University, 908
China Science & Technology Museum,
  909–910
China Society for Library Science (CSLS),
  904
China Society for Scientific and Technical
  Information (CSSTI), 905
Chinese Academy of the Social Sciences
  (CASS)
  Institute of Law Library, 901–902
  IWAASL, 902
  library CDI, 900–901
Chinese American Librarians Association
  (CALA), 905
Chinese Archival Classification (CAC), 905
Chinese Archives Association (CAA), 905
Chinese Association for the Advancement of
  Education (CAAE), 890
Chinese Mathematics-Acta, 3027
Chinese Modern Library Movement, 888–889
Chinese National Museum, 909
Chinese National Science Digital Library
  (CNSDL), 902
Chinese radical-phonetic compound character
  types, 3834
Chinese Si Ku classification, 889
Chișinău Municipal Library (CML), 3124
Chomsky's theories, 3348
Choo's model, 2089, 2091
Chorography, 1684
Christchurch catalog, 747
Chromolithographs, 1868
Chronicon Rusticum-Commerciale; or, Memoirs
  of Wool, 1402
Churches and synagogues, 3416
CI, see Competitive Intelligence
CICs, see Corporate information centers
CIDOC Conceptual Resource Model (CIDOC
  CRM), 3760–3761
CILEA, 2827
CILIP, see Chartered Institute of Library and
  Information Professionals

CINAHL database, 1765
CINDEX, 443
Circulating library, 1842, 4481–4484
Circulation Interchange Protocol (NCIP), 2894
Circulation services
  borrowing cycle, 916
  definition, 916
  desk, 917
  ethics, 917
  kinds, 918–919
  stack management, 920–921
  staffing, 919–920
  technology, 921–922
  user communities, 919
Circumvention, 784, 1272, 1316–1319, 1321,
  2142, 2955
CISTI, see Canada Institute for Scientific and
  Technical Information
Citation analysis; see also Citer motivations
  Bradford-ZIPF phenomena, 519–520
  "impact factor," 505
Citation index, 521–523
  bibliographic and bibliometric database,
    940
  creation and structure of, 941
  definition, 941
  functions, cited references
    cited reference capture, 942
    cited reference linking, 942–943
    cited reference searching, 943–944
  information retrieval, 941
  standardized/unified cited reference index,
    941
Citation networks, 1041–1042
Citation order, 585–586
Citation tracking, 2214
Citators, 2741
Cited references, 940–946, 953, 3569, 3640
  searching, 926, 942–945, 948, 3640
  strings, 926
Citer motivations, 519–520
  altmetrics, 924
  bibliography rules, 952
  categories
    Chubin and Moitra, 955
    Moravcsik and Murugesan, 955
  citation content analysis, 935, 952
  citation context analysis, 935, 952
  citation counts, 925
  citation indexes, 521–523
  clustering, 523
  currency, 952–953
  Frost's citation classification, 954–955
  Garfield's taxonomy, 953
  half-life and obsolescence, 520–521
  Hodges's taxonomy, 953–954
  homonyms and allonyms, 927
  interdocumentary relations
    bibliographic coupling, 930
    cocitation, 930–931
    documents, 933–934
    historiographs, 933
    images, identities and recitation, 932–933
    intercitation, 930
    PFNET algorithm, 931–932
  Lipetz's citation relationships, science litera-
    ture, 953

measures derived from counts
  author statistics, 928–929
  journal statistics, 927–928
  organizational and national statistics, 929
microlevel data, 925–927
multivariate models, 953
Peritz's social science taxonomy, 954
persuasion hypothesis, 935
practical applications of, 524
prima facie validity, 951
reward hypothesis, 936
scientists, 952
self-citations, 935
social constructivists, 935
univariate model, 952
validation of, 955–956
verbal objects, 924–925
"CiteScore" metrics, 928
CiteSpace, 923
CITE system, 3428
Citizen science, 559, 4015
CityGML, 1677
Civil registration, 1657
Civil society, 5013–5014
Civil War Preservation Trust, 1774
CLA, see Canadian Library Association
Clandestine presses, 3741
Clarivate Analytics, 818, 925
Clasps, 540
Classification
  BC, 4475
    adaptability, 574–575
    alternative location, 576
    alternative treatments, 576
    A-Z index, 578
    classification, 575–576
    collocation, 573–574
    consensus, 574
    extent of use, 573
    gradation, 574
    notation, 576–578
    present edition of, 579
    principles, 573
    weakness, 578–579
  data streams
    Bayesian network, 2635
    CVFDT, 2635
    decision trees, 2635
    ensemble classifiers, 2635–2636
    learning models, 2635
    StreamMiner, 2636
    VFDT, 2635
  DDC, 961, 966, 969–970, 1802, 2669–2670,
    2920, 3283, 3397, 4205, 4466, 4472,
    4783, 4788
    applications and research, 1261–1263
    in China, 889
    classes, hierarchies, and relationships,
      1257–1258
    development, 1258, 1260
    editions, 1259
    electronic versions, 1259–1260
    general rules, 1258
    Manual and Relative Index, 1257
    mappings, 1261
    notational synthesis, 1258
    schedules and tables, 1257

summaries, 1256–1257
translations, 1260–1261
value of, 1256
LCC, 963, 970, 992, 1261–1262, 2669, 3283,
  3902, 4205, 4466, 4472, 4475
  in current information environment,
    2851–2852
  development, 2848–2849
  divisions, 2850
  domain-specific taxonomies, 2852
  factors for acceptance, 2847
  file partitioning, 2852
  guidelines, 2853
  history of, 2847–2848
  information retrieval function, 2847
  Internet, information databases, and
    OPACs, 2854
  and LCSH, 2852–2853
  library materials, shelf-ordering of, 2847
  main classes, 2849–2850
  multitopical works, 2853
  national bias, 2853
  notation (numbering system), 2849–2851
  obsolescence, 2853
  strengths, 2853–2854
  subclasses, 2849–2850
principles, 4474
schemes, 743, 753–754, 756, 772, 1175,
  1536–1537, 3029
social influences on
  hierarchical structure, consequences of,
    4208–4209
  structure, 4207–4208
  warrant, 4204–4205
systems, 509, 959–962, 3424, 3426
theory, 958–971
UDC, 574, 961, 970, 1261, 2669, 4466, 4471,
  4475
  automation and, 4788–4789
  auxiliary tables, 4785–4786
  BC2, influence of, 589
  citation order, 4787
  classification structure, 4784–4785
  filing order, 4787
  general classification schemes, 4783
  history, 4783–4784
  main classes, 4787–4788
  notation, 4785
  theoretical basis, 4786
Classification Act 1995, 381
Classification and Search Support Information
  System (CASSIS), 3563
Classification Research Group (CRG), 582–583
Classify prototype, 1546
Classsical libraries, 1221, 1797
Clay tablets, 643
Clear and present danger test, 1015
Click-wrap agreement, 1271
Clinical decision-support systems (CDSS)
  current best evidence, 974
  EBM, 974
  history of, 975
  medical knowledge engineering, guideline
    ontologies for
    AHRQ's National Guideline Clearing-
      house, 977
    barriers, 978–979

contextual factors, 979
  CRS, 979–980
  influential guidelines, 977
  MLM code, 977
  patient data codification, 979
  system interoperability, 979
  new generation of guideline, 975–977
Clinical informatics, 85–86
Clinical medical librarians (CML), 1884
Clinical reminder system (CRS), 979–980
Clinical Text De-identification (CTD) system,
  3342
Cloaking, 4035, 4042
CLOCKSS, 1213
CLOPE algorithm, 2634
Closed questions, reference interview, 3915
Closed-system indexing, 440
Cloud-based storage services, 4942
Cloud computing, 5028
Cluster analysis, 837
Clustering, 1040, 3294
  data streams
    challenges, 2633
    CluStream and variants, 2633–2634
    hierarchical method, 2633
    k-median, 2634–2635
    partitioning method, 2633
CluStream algorithm, 2633–2634
CMC, see Computer-mediated communication
CMSs, see Content management systems
Coalition for Networked Information (CNI),
  368, 375, 1391–1392
Coalition on Library Automation (COLA),
  2776
Cochrane, 1878
Cochrane Collaboration, 1519
Code4Lib, 2781
Code of ethics, 3197
Code of Ethics and Guidelines for Practice, 1071
Code of Federal Regulations (CFR), 640
Code of Hammurabi, 643
Codicology, 4336
CODiE Award Program, 4298
Codification, 1373
Codified knowledge, 4115
Cody Firearms Museum, 4382
Cognitive authority, 2759
  bases for, 1116–1117
  definition, 1116
  process, 1117–1118
Cognitive constructivism, 2753
Cognitive knowledge, 3535
Cognitive map, wayfinding, 4959
Cognitive model, 281
Cognitive moves, 2241
Cognitive needs, 2115, 2119
Cognitive psychology, 3854, 4542
Cognitive relevance judgments, 3943
Cognitive Task Analysis (CTA), 4116
Cognitive theory, 2753
Cognitive walkthrough, 4798
Coherence theory, 2612–2613
Cohesion-based methods, summarization, 422
Cole, F.J., 499–500, 506
Collaboration portals, 2893
Collaborative Initiative for French Language
  Collections (CIFNAL), 790

Collaborative IR (CIR), 4880
Collaborative recommender systems
    elicit preferences, 3861
    predictions, 3862
    recommendations, 3862
    schematic representation, 3861
Collaborative Web browsing, 3443
Collabra, 1062
Collection development, 2333–2335
Collection Development and Evaluation Section
    (CODES), 3909
Collection Development Policies: for Libraries
    & Visual Collections in the Arts, 252
Collection maintenance, see Stack management
Collection Management Section (CMS), 329
Collection of Letters for the Improvement of
    Husbandry and Trade, 1401
Collection of Tracts, on the Subjects of Taxing
    the British Colonies in America, and
    Regulating their Trade, 1402
Collections Australia Network (CAN), 3178
Collection-specific local vocabularies,
    1078–1079
College archives, Hungary, 1925–1926
College Art Association (CAA), 255,
    4933–4934
College Level Examination Program (CLEP),
    1847
College library
    in Australia, 384
    bibliographic instruction/information literacy,
        987–988
    challenges, 983, 985
    collection development, 985–986
    history of, 983
    information technology, development of,
        983–985
    interlibrary loan, 986–987
    management, structure, and staff changes, 990
    rare book collections, 3822
    resources for, 354–355
    standards, 988–990
    in United Kingdom, 4705
College Library Directors Mentor Program, 990
College & Research Libraries (C&RL), 353
Collexis, 1768
Colon Classification (CC), 961, 967, 1534, 1536,
    2669, 4466, 4475
Colonial Williamsburg, 3218, 4166–4167
Colon scheme, 574
Colorado Alliance of Research Libraries, 1209,
    1212
Color formats, 1177
Color histogram, 4422–4423
Color illustration, 1945
Color management, 4943
Columbia River Basin Ethnic History Archive
    (CRBEHA), 1783–1784
Comanaged libraries, 4160
COM cats, 2078–2079
COMEXAZ, 2699
Commemorative landscape, 4165
Commemorative site monuments, 4164–4165
Commercial and Financial Chronicle, 648, 1404
Commercial galleries, 243
Commercial journals, 2740
Commercial lending libraries, 4478

Commission for Accreditation of Law-Enforce-
    ment Agencies (CALEA), 4258
Commission for Science and Technology
    (COSTECH), 4508
Commission of Trade and Plantations, 646
Commission on Preservation and Access, 3725
Committee on Accreditation (COA), 18–20, 709
Committee on Archival Development (CAD),
    2438
Committee on Best Practices and Standards
    (ICA/CBPS), 2441
Committee on Copyright and Other Legal Mat-
    ters (CLM), 2457–2458
Committee on Development and Intellectual
    Property (CDIP), 5002
Committee on Freedom of Access to Informa-
    tion and Freedom of Expression
    (FAIFE), 2458
Committee on Institutional Cooperation (CIC),
    1757, 1759
Committee on Museum Professional Training
    (COMPT), 3219
Committee on Organization (COO), 76
Committee on Program Evaluation and Support
    (COPES), 72–74
Committee on Reorganization, 339
Common Business-Oriented Language
    (COBOL), 2272
Common Command Language (CML), 2345
Common communication format (CCF), 4627
Common Core State Standards (CCSS) Initia-
    tive, 4002
Common Music Notation (CMN), 3267
Commonsense epistemology, 1456
Commonsense knowledge, 272
Commonwealth Archives Office, 119
Commonwealth Government archives, 185
Commonwealth Library Association (COMLA),
    2597–2598
Commonwealth National Library, 381
Commonwealth Record Series (CRS), 3876
Commonwealth Scientific and Industrial
    Research Organisation (CSIRO), 382
Communication channels, 2297
Communication engineering, 2051
Communication policy
    administrative and judicial interpretation,
        1008
    competition, 1022–1023
    competitive environment
        cable, regulatory regime, 1016–1017
        deregulate broadcasting, 1018–1019
        hybrid technology, 1016
        telecom regime, 1017–1018
    cultural concerns
        electronic media, 1013
        radio, 1013
    decision makers, 1008
    goals
        democracy, 1009
        First Amendment, 1009–1010
        intellectual property, 1010
        policy mechanisms, 1008
        postal roads, 1010
        print technology, 1009
    market, 1023–1024
    market-oriented environment, 1007

    national integration, mass media and
        education
        agricultural extension, 1011
        land grant colleges and industrial educa-
            tion, 1011
        mass media, 1010–1011
        post-Civil War decision makers, 1010
        public school movement, 1011
    national security and defense
        free speech and free market, 1015
        limits on speech, 1015
    networked information society, 1007
    technological and socioeconomic develop-
        ments, 1007
    Telecommunications Act of 1996
        Internet vision, 1019
        legislative outcome, 1021–1022
        103rd Congress, defeat in, 1020
        104th Congress, retreat in, 1020
    transportation, 1008
    universal efficient interconnection via
        regulation
        defense technology, 1015
        industrial economy, 1011
        infrastructure, 1015
        "must carry rules," 1014
        public broadcasting, 1014
        public service company, 1012
        railroads and interstate commerce commis-
            sion, 1012
        spectrum licensing, 1014
        telegraph, 1012
        telephone, 1012–1013
        voluntary censorship, 1013–1014
Communications, 144–145, 994–995,
    2770–2771
    and communication studies
        contradictions, 1004–1005
        IAMCR, profile of, 1001, 1004
        ICA, profile of, 1001, 1003
        institutionalization, phases of, 999–1001
        mass and speech communication, 997–998
        media, 998–999
        NCA, profile of, 1001–1002
    CSCW, 1055–1056
    definitions of, 995–996
    human communication, 2354
    and mutual information, 2352–2354
    organization, 4117–4118
    PIALA, 3543
Communications Decency Act (CDA), 2396
Communicative memories, 1140
Communism, 4401
Communities of practice (COP), 1668, 2644,
    2661–2662, 2754–2755, 3529, 4256
Community Access Program (CAP), 2039
Community archives, 4738
Community-based museums, 3237–3238
Community hospital library, 1872
Community informatics
    community definitions, 1027–1028
    emergence, 1031
    Kling's definition, 1027
    new directions, 1031
    practitioners, 1027
    researchers, 1027
    roots of field

within libraries, 1029–1031
outside library, 1028–1029
Community Informatics Institute, 1031
Community museums
  AAM's Museums and Communities Initiative, 3246–3247
  Civic Engagement Initiative, 3247
  community advisory groups, 3248
  District Six Museum, 3245–3246
  early American museums, 3243–3244
  education, 3244
  El Museo Shan-Dany, 3245
  ethnic museum, 3244–3245
  ICOM, 3246
  Internet, 3248
  Lower East Side Tenement Museum, 3245
  mainstream museum, 3249
  National Park Service, 3247
  neighborhood museum, 3245–3246
  oral history, 3247–3248
  visitor-generated content, 3248–3249
Community Networking Initiative, 1030
Community Technology Centers Network, 1029
Compact disc (CD), 3280
Comparative librarianship
  actual comparisons, 2406
  basic elements, 2407
  cross-societal, 2405
  hierarchical, 2406
  methodology, 2407
  study-activity, 2406
  subject-methodology, 2406
Comparative Molecular Field Analysis (CoMFA), 836
Compendieuse Hausshaltungs Bibliotheck, 1403
Competitive intelligence (CI), 2108, 2662, 4354
Complex adaptive systems, 1034
Complexity and self-organization
  agents, 1035–1036
  attractors, 1038
  coevolution and synergy, 1037
  complex networks, 1042
    abstract mathematical network, 1039
    clustering, 1040
    features, 1039
    links, 1039
    nodes, 1039
    random network, 1039
    scale-free networks, 1040–1041
    small-world network, 1039–1040
    social network, 1039
  computer simulations, 1036–1037, 1042
  definition, 1037
  dissipative structures, 1034
  edge of chaos, 1035
  emergence, 1038–1039
  history, 1034–1035
  knowledge networks, 1041–1042
  Kolmogorov complexity, 1035
  local coordination to global organization, 1037–1038
  mean field effect, 1036
  natural selection, 1037
  nonlinearity, 1036, 1042
  openness, 1042
  in between order and disorder, 1035
  order from noise, 1038

order through fluctuations, 1038
  philosophy of, 1034
  remote agents, actions of, 1037
  traditional deterministic models, 1036
  Web possesses, 1034
Complutense University, 4321
Component-based architecture (CBA), 2154
Composite specification, 1535
Compressed histograms, 2630
Compression techniques, 1310–1311
Compulsory Education Act of 1949, 2548
Computed tomography (CT), 4429
Computer assisted instruction (CAI), 3444
  benefits, 3435
  computer-assisted demonstration, 3434
  independent learning tutorials, 3435
  live assistance and hand-on, computer-based learning, 3434–3435
Computer-assisted software engineering (CASE) tools, 2297, 2344
Computer credibility, 1115
Computer engineering, 694
Computer ethics, 3617
Computer Fraud and Abuse Act (CFAA), 1275
Computer games, 872
Computer–Human Interaction (CHI), 4115
Computer Interchange of Museum Information (CIMI), 677
Computer Matching and Privacy Protection Act, 1555
Computer-mediated communication (CMC), 2935–2936
  description of, 1044–1045
  groups
    chat systems, 1050
    electronic mailing lists, 1051
    groupware and collaboration, 1050
    multiple user dialog, 1050
    networked meeting software, 1050
    newsgroups and blogs, 1050
    real-time video, 1050
    social networking software, 1051
  interpersonal communication
    asynchronous voice and video, 1049
    E-mail, 1049
    text-based chat and messaging, 1049
    video conferencing, 1049
    voice communication, 1049
  mass communication
    audio, 1051
    text, 1051
    video, 1051
  primary functions
    computer-supported cooperative work, 1048
    conferencing and collaboration, 1046–1047
    dissemination and control of information, 1047–1048
    informatics, 1048
    teaching and learning, 1045–1046
  research, 1051–1052
Computer output microfilm (COM), 1414, 1851
Computer science and engineering (CS&E), 1249
Computer Security Act of 1987, 1555–1556
Computer-supported cooperative work (CSCW), 1048, 1064–1065, 2075, 2274, 2654, 3864

aim, 1053
challenges, 1060–1061
collaborative software development, 1062–1063
definitions, 1053–1054
design areas and features
  communication, 1055–1056
  configuration, 1056
  coordination, 1056–1057
  information access, 1057–1058
  interaction, 1058–1060
design space, key dimensions in, 1054–1055
electronic meetings, 1054
groupware, 1054
media spaces, 1054
productivity improvements, 1053
success factors, 1061–1062
team computing, 1054
technologies, 1063–1064
workflow, 1054
Computer technologies, 1472
Computing Research Association (CRA), 2537
CONACULTA museum, 3098
Concept-adapting very fast decision tree (CVFDT), 2635
Concept identifier (CUI), 4674
Conceptualist searcher, 4878
Conceptual knowledge, 2622, 3423
Conceptual model, 1606–1607, 1609–1610, 1612, 1615–1616
Conceptual moves, 2241
Conceptual Reference Model (CRM), 3178
The Conference Board Management Record, 650
The Conference Board Record, 650
Conference of African National Libraries (CANL), 38
Conference of Directors of National Libraries (CDNL), 2456, 2458–2459, 3330
Conference of Directors of National Libraries of Asia and Oceania (CDNLAO), 3330
Conference of European National Librarians (CENL), 536, 3330–3331
Conference of Heads of Irish Universities (CHIU), 2825
Conference of Italian University Rectors (CRUI), 2827
Conference on Fair Use (CONFU), 4935
Conferred credibility, 1115
CONFOTO, 4088
Congressional Documents, 1404
Congressional Record, 640
Congressional Research Services, 4361
Congress on Professional Education (COPE), 708
Congress's Cooperative Online Serials (CONSER) program, 4140
Connectedness-based method, 422
Connecticut State Library, 4397
Conner Prairie historical site, 1776
Connexion cataloging service, 1259, 3396–3397, 3400
Connotative meanings, 4097
CONSER, 2921
Conservation Information Network (CIN), 676
Conservation museums
  cultural heritage, preservation of, 1068
  development of, 1068

Conservation museums (cont'd.)
  documentation and public access, 1069,
    1071–1073
  ethics and guidelines, 1070–1071
  facilities, 1069
  laboratories, 1069–1070
  museum conservators, role of, 1068
  preparators, duties of, 1069
  restoration, 1068–1069
Conservation OnLine (CoOL), 1350
Conservation Plan for Canadian Archival
    Records (CPCAR), 666
Conservation science, 3769
Conservatory libraries, music libraries, 3276
Consortial DDA programs, 1212
Consortium for Computer Interchange of
    Museum Information (CIMI), 3227
Consortium of European Research Libraries
    (CERL), 3771
Consortium of Slovenian Electronic Collections
    (COSEC), 2828
Consortium of Swiss Academic Libraries, 2826
Consortium of the libraries in Serbia for Coop-
    erative Acquisition (KOBSON), 4128
Consortium of University Research Libraries
    (CURL), 2825, 4703
Constitution of Athens, 644
Constructivist model, 2118–2119
Consuetudo, vel, Lex Mercatoria, 1400
Consultative Committee for Space Data Systems
    (CCSDS), 3477–3480, 3485–3486
Consulting services, 1099–1100
Consumer contracts, 1272
ContactFinder, 3865
Contact information, 638
Contemporary academic library planning state-
    ments, 4451–4452
Content attributes, 2294
Content-based image retrieval (CBIR)
  affective image retrieval, 4428–4429
  content representation and objects
    composite object, 4421
    simple objects and attributes, 4420–4421
  digital imagery, 4417
  image formats and data compression
    encoding, 4418
    scalar quantization, 4419
    signal representation, 4418
    spatial domain, predictive coding, 4418
    spatial redundancy, 4418–4419
    thresholding, 4419
    transform domain, 4418
    vector quantization, 4419
    wavelet transform, 4418–4419
  image repositories and digital libraries
    medical image databases, 4429–4430
    oil industry, 4431
    remote sensed image databases, 4430–4431
  image searching, semantic level
    progressive semantic retrieval, 4427
    semantic content characterization, 4425
    semantic content extraction, 4426–4427
  metadata, 4427
  multiple abstraction levels
    color features, 4422–4423
    image searching, raw data level,
      4421–4422

    image segmentation, 4422
    searching, 4428
    semantics, multiple attributes combining,
      4427–4428
    shape features, 4425
    texture features, 4423–4425
  query specifications, 4420
Content-based recommender systems, 3862–
    3863
Content creators, 3066–3067
Content is king, 4034
Content licensing agreements, 1274
Content management (CM), 2659
Content management systems (CMSs), 716,
    2108, 3066, 4945
Content modeling, 3112–3113
Content scrambling system (CSS), 1319–1320
Content value standards, 3061
Context control systems, 118–120
Context of Small World, 1509–1510
Contextual Query Language (CQL), 2187, 2189,
    2347
Contingency theory, 3514–3515
Continuing Education Committee (CEC), 3035
Continuing education (CE) courses, 3034–3035
Continuing legal education (CLE), 2719
Continuing Professional Development and
    Workplace Learning (CPDWL), 713
Continuing professional education (CPE),
    50–51, 4257
Continuing Resources Section (CRS), 329
Continuous Acquisition and Life-Cycle Support
    (CALS) initiative, 3075
Continuum concept, 2379
Controlled LOCKSS (CLOCKSS), 4147
Controlled vocabulary, 2857
  LOD, 1079
  search
    authority control, 4467
    consistent and current terminology, 4469
    convenience of the public, 4468–4469
    direct and specific entry, 4469
    enumeration vs. faceting, 4469–4470
    lists, 4466–4467
    precoordination vs. postcoordination, 4470
    provision of cross-references, 4469
    uniform and unique headings, 4469
  uses, 1077–1078
  vocabulary tools, 1079–1080
Convention on Contracts for the International
    Sale of Goods (CCISG), 1270–1271
Convention on International Trade in Endan-
    gered Species of Wild Fauna and Flora
    (CITES), 1164
Conversation analysis, 2930
Co-occurrence matrix, 4423
Cooperative Africana Materials Project
    (CAMP), 790
Cooperative Children's Book Center (CCBC),
    870
Cooperative Information Retrieval Network for
    Scotland (CAIRNS), 250
Co-operative Online Bibliographic System and
    Services (COBISS), 2828
Cooperative Online Resource Catalog (CORC),
    1259, 1539, 3454
Cooperative Online Serials (CONSER), 3395

Coordinate indexing, 2221
Coordinating Committee on Service to the Dis-
    advantaged, 4222
Coordinating Council of Audiovisual Archives
    Associations (CCAAA), 691, 2453,
    3304, 4660
Coordination of Improvement of Higher Educa-
    tion Personnel (CAPES), 604, 608
Copenhagen hand-binding, 547
Coptic bindings, 540, 542
Copy cataloging, 2920
Copyright, 570, 4056
Copyright Act, 381, 682–683, 1271–1272, 2594,
    4681–4682
Copyright and software licenses
    national library amendment, 4683
    public policy, 4681–4683
    Virginia libraries amendment, 4683–4684
Copyright Clearance Center (CCC), 4145
Copyright infringement, 3664
Copyright Law of 1976, 1577
Copyright laws, 369
Copyright Ordinance of 1924, 4513
Copyright Society of Tanzania (COSOTA),
    4513
Copyright Term Extension Act (CTEA), 1577
Cornelius, Ian, 2054
Corporate amnesia, 2642–2643, 4199
Corporate Antipiracy Program, 4298
Corporate archives
    archival blog, 1083
    business archives, 1085
    communications placement, 1082
    compensation packages, 1085
    digital technology, 1083
    documentation, 1081
    functional leadership, 1082
    human resources function, 1083
    information gap, 1081
    information sharing, 1083
    intellectual capital, 1084
    litigation support, 1081
    marketplace, 1083
    mission/policy statement, 1082
    organizational scheme, 1084
    outreach programming, 1082
    research and reference responsibilities, 1084
Corporate Archives Forum, 1085
Corporate art collections
    alternative modes of, 1089–1090
    artwork, 1088
    challenges and concerns, 1090–1091
    collection management, 1089
    corporate sponsorship and patronage, 1091
    history, 1086–1087
    as investment, 1088–1089
    promoting culture, 1087–1088
    workplace evolution, 1091–1092
Corporate information centers (CICs)
    areas of service
      collection management, 1099
      current awareness, 1099
      document delivery, 1099
      information consulting, 1099–1100
      information resource management, 1099
      reference, 1098
      research, 1098–1099

building competitive edge
    challenges, 1102–1103
    customer intimacy, 1102
    for-profit sector, 1102
communication, 1101–1102
general services, 1100
organization, impact and strategic positioning
    budgets, 1101
    costs and productive time, 1100
    placement, 1100
professional development, 1096–1097
service specialization
    alerting (current awareness) service, 1094
    Deutsche Bank (see Deutsche Bank, CIC)
    information technology company, 1095
    law firm, 1096
    public libraries, 1094
special libraries, 1096
staff qualifications, 1096–1097
strategic planning, 1102
subject specialization
    Nike Design Library, areas of, 1094–1095
    textile company, 1094
user, 1095
Corporate libraries, 4374
Corporate mentality, 1089–1090
Corporate portals, 2893
Corporate records management programs
active records management
    components, 1107
    document management systems, 1108
    ECM systems, 1108
    electronic records management, 1108–1109
    equipment costs and use office space, 1107
    filing system, 1107
    imaging program, 1108
audits, 1111–1112
California Public Records Act, 1105
"cradle-to-grave" management, 1104–1105
elements, 1105
external requirements, 1104
FOIA, 1105
good corporate citizen, 1104
government agencies, 1105
inactive records management, 1109–1110
internal requirements, 1104
mergers, acquisitions and divestitures,
    1110–1111
records management placement, 1111
records retention
    appraisal, 1105
    legal environment and compliance,
        1106–1107
    litigation, legal holds, and discovery, 1107
    records series, 1105
    risk management, 1105–1106
standards, 1111
storage formats, 1104
vital records protection program, 1110
Corporation Credit, 1403
Corporation for Public Broadcasting (CPB),
    1014, 1579
Correspondence approach, 2612
Cosijn model, 4875
Cosine correlation, 2203–2204
Cosmographia, 494
Cosmographia universalis, 1685

Cost and benefit attributes, 2294
Cost per thousand model (CPM), 2522
Cosway bindings, 541
Cougar, 2630
Council for Higher Education Accreditation
    (CHEA), 18–19
Council of Australian University Librarians
    (CAUL), 384
Council of Provincial and Territorial Archivists
    (CPTA), 666
Council of Scientific and Industrial Research
    (CSIR), 2002–2003
Council of State Archivists (CoSA), 3319
Council on Library and Information Resources
    (CLIR), 368
Council on Library Resources (CLR), 988, 2873,
    2963–2964
COUNTER, 413
Counting Online Usage of Networked Electronic
    Resources (COUNTER) Project, 4146
Country code top level domain (ccTLD) system,
    780
County Library Authority, 1839
COUPERIN, 2826
The Course of the Exchange, 1401
Covers common foreign and security policy
    (CFSP), 2140
CPLEX, 1196
CQL, see Contextual Query Language
Cranfield model of information retrieval (IR),
    4872
Cranfield paradigm, 4554
Cranfield tests, 2222–2223
Create Change Web site, 367
Credentialed librarians, 4777
Credibility
    definition
        expertise, 1113–1114
        trustworthiness, 1113–1114
    historical development, 1114
    process, 1117–1118
    typology of, 1115
Credit reports, 639
Crelle's Journal, 3024, 3026
Crestadoro, Andres, 761
CRG, see Classification Research Group
Crime fiction, 3701–3702
Crimestat, 1676
Criminal network analysis, 2402
Critical discourse analysis (CDA), 1664–1665
Critical incidence technique, 4531
Criticas: An English Speaker's Guide to the
    Latest Spanish-Language Titles, 2699
CRL, see Center for Research Libraries
Croatia
    archives
        Croatian State Archives, 1127–1128
        historical overview, 1126–1127
        legislation, 1127
        National Film Archives, 1128
        publishing and professional associations,
            1128
        specialized archives, 1128
    historical development, 1121
    literacy, books, and libraries
        academic, research, and special libraries,
            1125

Church libraries, 1126
    diocese libraries, 1122–1123
    in fifteenth and sixteenth centuries, 1123
    Glagolitic and Cyrillic alphabets,
        1121–1122
    Latin language, 1121
    legislation, 1124
    library and information science education,
        1126
    monastery libraries, 1122
    national and university library, 1124–1125
    professional associations, 1126
    public and school libraries, 1125–1126
    reading rooms, 1123
    in seventeenth century, 1123
    in twentieth century, 1123–1124
location, 1121
map of, 1121–1122
museums
    history, 1129
    legislation and organization, 1129–1130
    publishing, staff, and professional associa-
        tion, 1130
National Programme for the Digitisation of
    Archival, Library and Museum Records,
    1130
Croatian Academic Research Network
    (CARNET), 1125, 2828
Croatian Archival Council, 1127
Croatian Archivist Association, 1128
Croatian Library Association, 1126
Croatian Library Council, 1124
Croatian Museum Association, 1130
Croatian National and University Library,
    1124–1125
Croatian National Film Archives, 1128
Croatian State Archives, 1127–1128
CrossCheck, 1137
Cross-correlation, 4421
Cross-disciplinary faculty teaching, 2771
Cross-domain linking, 3294
Cross-genre phenomenon, 3706–3707
Cross-Language Evaluation Forum (CLEF),
    3143
Cross-lingual information retrieval (CLIR),
    2222, 2402, 3140
CrossRef publisher linking network
    cited-by linking, 1137
    CrossCheck, 1137
    CrossRef metadata services, 1137
    database, 1133
    distributed integration, 1138
    DOI, 1133–1134
    endeavor, 1133
    history, 1132–1133
    impacts
        on intermediaries, 1137
        on libraries, 1136–1137
        on publishers, 1136
        on researchers, 1137
    initiative, 1133
    interlinking, 1138
    metadata, 1133
    mission, 1132
    working process
        citation submission, 1134
        DOI registration, 1134

CrossRef publisher linking network (cont'd.)
    working process (cont'd.)
        DOI resolution, end-user perspective, 1135
        journal-level and article-level metadata
            record, 1134
        metadata records, depositing, 1134
        non-XML interfaces, 1134
        reference linking workflow, 1134–1135
CrossRef registration agency, 1326, 1330
Crossref Web site, 1330
Crowdsourcing, 3294
CRS, see Clinical reminder system
CS AKTive Space, 4087–4088
CSCW, see Computer-supported cooperative
    work
Cue-phrase method, 421
Cuirbouilli, 540
Cuir cisele, 540, 542
Cultural heritage, 4168–4169, 4171
    archives
        American Folklife Center, 4757
        American Heritage Center, 4757
        Amistad Center, 4757
        Balch Institute, 4757
        Center for Puerto Rican Studies, 4757
        Clark Atlanta University, 4757–4758
        Heard Museum Archives, 4758
        Japanese American History Archives, 4758
        Moorland-Spingarn Research Center, 4758
        Museum of Chinese in America,
            4758–4759
        Schomburg Center for Black Culture, 4759
Cultural history museums, 1226
Cultural institutions
    advocacy, 1961–1962
    economic impact, 1961
    impact assessment, 1962–1963
    impact, definition of, 1960
    quantitative evidence, 1960–1961
    raw data and evidence, relationship between,
        1960
    requirements, 1959–1960
Cultural knowledge, 3535
Cultural management, 3522
Cultural memory
    criticisms of, 1143–1144
    group definition
        anti-Semitism, 1142
        depression, 1140–1141
        Holocaust consciousness, 1141–1142
        John F. Kennedy's death, 1140–1141
        public memory, 1141
        U.S. historical events, 1141
    historical context and terminology,
        1098–1140
    representations, 1142
    social relevance, 1142–1143
Cultural national libraries, 3321
Cultural Objects Name Authority® (CONA), 1079
Cultural patrimony, site museums
    historical perspective, interpretation chal-
        lenges, 4170
    Monument to the Great Fire of London, 4165
    preservation laws, 4169
    preventative preservation, 4170
    UNESCO, 4169
    war targets and cultural casualties, 4168

Cultural peoperty, 3772
Culture Information Systems, 2828
Cumulated gain (CG), 1903
Cumulated gain with discount (DCG), 1903
Cumulated Index to Nursing and Allied Health
    Literature (CINAHL), 1873, 1877
Cumulative frequency distribution, 2211
Cuneiform clay tablets, 643
Curating natural history collections
    administrative point of view
        collection manager, 1160–1161
        collectors, preparators, archivists and con-
            servators, 1161
        curator, 1160
        students, interns and volunteers, 1161
    organismal collections, 1156
    paleontological collections, 1156
    specimens
        accessioning, cataloging and installing,
            1158–1159
        collection and preparation, 1157–1158
        data and database management, 1159–1160
        ecological niche, speciation, 1162
        genetic diversity, 1162
        long-term care, 1159
        population structure, 1162
        predator, trophic level of, 1162
        symmetry and ecological stress, 1162
        use of, 1159
Curation, archaeological artifacts
    access and use, 1151
    acquisitions and accessions, 1149
    archaeological sites, 1147–1148
    cataloging, 1149
    ethical issues, 1152–1153
    interpretation, 1151–1152
    metadata standards, 1149–1150
    project design and records, 1148
    standards, 1148
    storage and care, 1150–1151
Curation crisis, 1152
Curatorial files, 3202
Currency, 1176
Current awareness services, 1099
Current Mathematical Publications (CPS), 3644
Current Population Surveys (CPS), 1280
Current Practice in Health Sciences Librarian-
    ship, 3037
Current research information systems (CRIS),
    1219
Curriculum Guidelines for Undergraduate
    Degree Programs in Information Sys-
    tems, 630
Custody and chain of custody
    archives, 1167–1168
    CITES, 1164
    history and post-custodial approaches,
        1165–1166
    museums, 1166
    provenience, 1165
    repatriation requests, 1166–1167
    replevin requests, 1168–1169
Customer capital, 2659
Customer relationship management (CRM),
    2274–2275
Customizable e-resource portals, 2893
Customized model generation approach, 1205

Cutter, Charles A., 761–763
Cutter numbers, 2849, 2851
Cyber-competence, 2306
Cyber-crimes, 2401
Cyberinfrastructures, 555, 5028–5029
Cybermetrics, 2367–2368
Cybernetics, 2050
"Cybernetic space," 2125
Cyc, 3456–3457
Cynefin, 4118
Cyrillic alphabet, 1121–1122
Czech National Library, 1261
Czeck and Slovak Library Information Network
    (CASLIN), 2828

D

Daily use software, 3066
DAISY, 1223
Dallas Museum of Art, 4945
Dana, John Cotton, 3244
DanBib, 1218–1219
Daniel Russell's (et al.) sensemaking,
    4115–4116
Danish Agency for Libraries and Media,
    1218–1219
Danish Agriculture Museum, 1226
Danish Archives Act, 1222
Danish Association of Research Librarians,
    1222
Danish Bibliographic Center, 1219
Danish bookbinding, 547
Danish Defence Museum, 1226
Danish Library Association, 1222
Danish Library Authority, 3784–3785
Danish Museum Act, 1225
Danish Museum of Hunting and Forestry, 1226
Danish National Archive in Copenhagen,
    1222–1223
Danish National Business Archives, 1223
Danish National Gallery, 1215
Danish National Library Authority, 1218
Danish Royal Library, 2791
Danish Union of Librarians, 1222
Danmarks Folkebogsamlinger, 1222
Dar al-Ilm, 3972
DARPA Agent Markup Language (DAML),
    4085
Darwin Core, 3311
Das Buch der Chroniken or Liber Chronicarum,
    1973
Das Kapital, 647
Das Magazin für Historiographie und
    Geographie, 495
Data and data quality
    accuracy, 1176
    completeness and duplication, 1176
    conceptual model
        attributes, 1173
        business rules, 1174
        composition, 1175
        content, 1174
        datum/data item, 1173
        domain, 1173
        entities, 1173
        IRS's model, 1173
        level of detail, 1174–1175

reaction to change, 1175
   scope, 1174
   semantic and structural consistency, 1175
   universe/enterprise, 1173
consistency and integrity, 1175
criteria, 1172
currency, 1176
data representation, 1174, 1177
definition, 1172–1173
first-generation
   error detection and correction, 1178–1179
   inspection and rework, 1177–1178
Internet, 1180–1181
life-cycle model, 1171–1172
management, 1177
quality and quality control, 1178–1180
second-generation
   error prevention, 1179–1180
   process quality management, 1178
third-generation, process design, 1178
Data and electronic records archives
   Electronic and Special Media Records Ser-
      vices Division, NARA, 4754
   ERA, 4754
   ICPSR, 4753–4754
   Minerva/Library of Congress Web Archives,
      4754
Data bank, 1171–1172
Database aesthetics, 2069
Database bashing, 1179
Database for Orientation and Research in the
   Archives, 1592
Database management system (DBMS), 1203,
   2272, 2629
Database of Archives of Non-Governmental
   Organizations (DANGO), 3386
Data Citation Index, 815
Data communication standards, 3061–3062
Data editing, 1179
Data elements, 3291–3292
Data grids, 2998
   data virtualization, 2998
   management virtualization, 3000–3002
   name spaces, 2999
   trust virtualization, 2999–3000
Data-information-knowledge-wisdom (DIKW),
   2049, 2059
Data Interchange Standards Association (DISA),
   88
Data management, 2108
Data Management Plan (DMP), 4015
Data mining, 2401–2403
   conventional algorithms, 2626–2627
   data stream algorithms (see Data streams)
   iterative and interactive process, 2637
Data Preservation Alliance for the Social Sciences (Data-PASS), 4753
Data recording, 1173
Data retrieval systems (DRS), 2193
Data streams
   applications, 2628
   challenges
      criteria, 2628–2629
      DBMS, 2629
      DWT, 2630
      histograms, 2629–2630
      one pass requirement concept, 2628

sampling, 2630–2631
   transactions/data instances, 2628
classification
   Bayesian network, 2635
   CVFDT, 2635
   decision trees, 2635
   ensemble classifiers, 2635–2636
   learning models, 2635
   StreamMiner, 2636
   VFDT, 2635
clustering algorithms
   challenges, 2633
   CluStream and variants, 2633–2634
   hierarchical method, 2633
   k-median, 2634–2635
   partitioning method, 2633
   vs. conventional algorithms, 2627–2628
frequent pattern mining
   Apriori, 2631
   FP-Streaming, 2632–2633
   frequent item mining, 2631–2632
   Lossy Counting algorithm, 2632
   Manku and Motwani's algorithm, 2632
Data structures, 4065
Data structure standards, 3060–3061
Data tracking, 1180
Data virtualization, 2998–2999
Date searching, 4049
David Adamany Undergraduate Library,
   4653
David Snowden's sense-making, 4118
Davis versus Freedom of Information Commis-
   sion, 2399
Davis, William Morris, 1688
Day, Ronald, 2059
DBMS, see Database management system
DC, see Dublin Core
DC-dot, 3063, 3066
DCMI, see Dublin Core Metadata Initiative
DCMI Abstract Model (DCAM), 1396–1397
DCMS, see Department for Culture, Media and
   Sport
DDA, see Demand-driven acquisition
DDC, see Dewey decimal classification
Deaccessioning, 1152–1153
Deaf and hearing impaired
   communication adaptment, 1188–1189
   communication environment, 1188
   communication modes, 1185
   communication with deaf people
      fingerspelling, 1187
      sign language, 1186–1187
      speaking and facial expression, 1186
      speechreading, 1186
   deafness and deaf people, 1184–1185
   empathy with Listener, 1189
   group communication, 1189
   initiating communication, 1188
   interactive communication, 1188
   misconceptions, 1185–1186
   NTID, 1183
   RIT reference librarians, 1183
   simultaneous communication and total
      communication
      learning sign language, 1187
      writing, 1188
   terminology, 1184

Decatur Public Library v. The District
   Attorney's Office of Wise County,
   2390
Decimal Classification, 574
Deciphering MedSpeak publications,
   3036–3037
Decision analysis, 1203–1205
Decision making
   information use for
      ecological rationality, 2361–2365
      PsycINFO, 2359–2360
      rationality perspectives, 2360–2361
Decision processing portals, 2893
Decision rule, 2363
Decision sciences
   deterministic model
      advantage of, 1193
      economic lot sizing model, 1196–1197
      IP models, 1195–1196
      LP model, 1194–1195
   game theoretic models, 1198
   MCDM, 1198
   professional associations, 1193
   quantitative modeling (OR/MS) perspective,
      1192–1193
   queuing, and simulation, 1198
   stochastic models, 1197
Decision support system (DSS), 2193–2194,
   2274, 2654
   application areas of, 1200, 1202
   architecture of, 1203
   DBMS, 1203
   decisions and decision modeling
      decision options, 1202
      decision problem, 1201–1202
      good decisions vs. outcomes, 1202
      judgmental heuristics, 1201
      preference, 1202
      types of, 1201
      uncertainty, 1202
   DGMS, 1203
   goal of, 1203
   MBMS, 1203
   normative systems, 1201
      decision analysis, 1203–1205
      ESP, 1206
      expert systems, 1203
      heuristic methods and ad hoc reasoning
         schemes, 1203
      structural equation models, 1205–1206
   user interfaces
      decision variables, choice and optimization
         of, 1206
      graphical interface, 1207
      graphical model, 1203
      model construction and analysis, 1203
      numerical calculations, 1203
Decision Tree learning algorithm, 273
Declaration of Principles, 5016
Deductive justification, 1457
Deep archives, 3000
Deep Blue Chess program, 270, 276
Deep Web, 5021
de facto phenomenon, 2144
Defence of Trade, 1400
Defence Research and Development Organiza-
   tion (DRDO), 2003

Defense Advanced Research Program Agency
   (DARPA), 2402, 2516
Delivery and Registration of Publications Act of
   Bombay Government, 1993
Delivery of Advanced Network Technology to
   Europe (DANTE), 4629
Delivery of Books (Public Libraries) Amend-
   ment Act, 1956, 1993
Delivery of Books and Newspapers (Public
   Libraries) Act, 1954, 1993
DELNET database, 2005
DeLone and McLean IT success model,
   2293–2294
Delphi approach, 3598
Demand-driven acquisition (DDA)
   collection development, 1209–1210
   consideration pool, 1212
   consortia, 1212
   ILL, 1213
   models, 1210–1211
   preservation, 1213
   print monographs, 1211–1212
   rationale, 1209
   risks, 1212–1213
   themes, 1210
   video, 1211
Demand Purchase Program, 792
Demangeon, Albert, 1687
Democratic Ideals and Reality, 1688
Demographics, 3168
*Demonstrating Results: Using Outcome Mea-
   surement in Your Library*, 3794
Denmark
   archives and archival science
      archivists and records managers, education
         for, 1224
      college and university archives, 1223–1224
      conservation and preservation, 1225
      Danish Archives Act, 1222
      Danish Emigration Archives in Aalborg,
         1224
      digital archival collections and finding aids,
         1224
      electronic records, 1224–1225
      Map and Land Registry Agency, 1224
      national, regional, and local archives,
         1222–1223
      professional associations, 1224
      repositories, 1224
   constitution, 1215
   library and information systems and services
      absolute monarchy, 1215
      associations, 1222
      cathedral schools, 1215
      digital library collections and services, 1220
      education, 1221–1222
      legislation, 1218
      in monasteries, 1215
      national library, 1218–1219
      public libraries, 1215–1218, 1220
      school libraries, 1220–1221
      special libraries, 1219–1220
      universities, 1219
   map of, 1215–1216
   museums and museology
      art museums, 1225–1226
      cultural history museums, 1226

   curatorship and museum administration,
      training for, 1227
   Danish museum sector, 1225
   digital museum exhibits and services,
      1226–1227
   education, 1227–1228
   Heritage Agency, 1225
   legal framework, 1225
   natural history museums, 1226
   preservation, 1227–1228
   professional associations, 1227
Denmark Electronic Research Library Project
   (DEF), 2825
Denmark's Electronic Research Library
   (DEFF), 1220
Denmark's National Private Archive Database
   (DANPA), 1223
Denotative meaning, 4096–4097
Denver Natural History Museum, 3254
Deontic authority, 1116
Departmental retention schedules, 3893
Department for Culture, Media and Sport
   (DCMS), 1958–1959, 4702
   advocacy, 1961–1962
   economic impact, 1961
   impact
      assessment, 1962–1963
      definition, 1960
   quantitative evidence, 1960–1961
   raw data and evidence, relationship between,
      1960
   requirements, 1959–1960
Department of Commerce and Labor, 647–648
Department of Energy (DOE), 1555
Department of Homeland Security (DHS), 2402
Department of Library and Information Science
   (DLIS), 4179
Department of Scientific and Industrial Research
   (DSIR), 301
Department of State Foreign Affairs Network
   (DOSFAN), 1556
Depository libraries, 1717–1718
Depository library programs, 2156
Deposit Systems for Electronic Publications
   (DSEP), 1333
De Re Medicina, 3043
Derr, Richard, 2052–2053
Dervin, Brenda, 2056–2057
Dervin's sense-making approach, 4114, 4226
Derwent World Patents Index (DWPI), 3643
Der Zoologische Garten, 5078
Descrezzione de Paesi Basse, 645
Describing Archives: A Content Standard
   (DACS), 137, 740, 1423
Description des arts et métiers, 1401
Descriptive bibliography, 478
Descriptive cataloging, 727–729
Descriptive markup, 3074–3075
Descriptive statistics, 494–495
Designer model, 4807
Design for Experiments, 1410
Designing for Digital, 1422
Design of Information Systems in the Social
   Sciences (DISISS) projects, 4246
Design science
   benefits, 1254
   constraints, 1246

   conversations with materials, 1246
   definition, 1242
   design research, 1242
      Cheshire information retrieval system,
         1251–1254
      computer science and engineering, 1249
      constraints, 1250
      corporation, strategic competency, 1249
      definition, 1249
      disciplinary value systems, 1249
      rigor *vs.* relevance, 1249–1250
   domain independent, 1243
   failure, 1247
   information retrieval systems, 1242
   as intellectual work, 1247–1249
   local vocabularies for image collections,
      1250–1251
   problem setting, 1245–1246
   product/service, 1243
   professions, 1243
   research and development, 1242
   as social science approach, 1242
   tools, 1246–1247
   uncertainty, 1243–1245
Desktop computing, 1289
Dessie Museum, 1503
Destructive information, 2095
Detailed retention schedule, *see* Departmental
   retention schedules
Deterministic model
   advantage of, 1193
   economic lot sizing model, 1196–1197
   IP models, 1195–1196
   LP model, 1194–1195
Deterministic-transformational approach,
   1295
Deterritorialization, 2124
Deutsche Bank, CIC, 1097
   alerting area, 1096
   book cabinets, 1094
   computer work area, 1094, 1096
   employee at work, 1098
   specially designed information cabinet, 1098
   storage units, 1096
   storage wall in Information Center, 1097
   work area, 1099
Deutsche Bibliothek, 1694
Deutsche Bücherei Leipzig, 1694
Deutsche Mathematiker-Vereinigung, 324
Developing and Implementing a Recordkeeping
   System (DIRKS) methodology, 111
Developing countries
   definition, 2130
   features of, 2130
   human information-seeking behavior
      barrier to information needs and seeking
         behaviors, 2135–2136
      inadequate information sources, 2133–
         2134
      individuals and individual information
         seeking, 2131–2132
      information and information resources,
         2132–2133
      two-step information-seeking approach,
         2134
Development Information Service Center, 1496
Development knowledge, 2275

Development Officers of Research Academic Libraries (DORAL), 2834
Dewey decimal classification (DDC), 757, 961, 966, 969–970, 1534–1535, 1802, 2499, 2669–2670, 2920, 3283, 3397, 3903, 4205, 4466, 4472, 4783, 4788
  applications and research, 1261–1263
  in China, 889
  classes, hierarchies, and relationships, 1257–1258
  development, 1260
  general rules, 1258
  history
    development, 1258
    editions, 1259
    electronic versions, 1259–1260
  mappings, 1261
  notational synthesis, 1258
  structure and notation
    DDC Summaries, 1256–1257
    Manual and Relative Index, 1257
    schedules and tables, 1257
  translations, 1260–1261
  value of, 1256
Dewey Decimal system, 1818
Dewey for Windows, 1259
Dewey Online Catalog (DOC), 1262
DH, see Digital humanities
Dialog, 2221
Dialog generation and management system (DGMS), 1203
Dialogue systems, 3353
Dial-up services, 2240
Diana V. Braddom FRFDS Scholarship, 2845
Diaries, 4531–4532
Diasporic communities, 1028
Diasporic Information Environment Model (DIEM), 2127
Diasporic populations
  immigrant information-seeking behavior research, 2125–2126
  information behavior, 2126–2127
  media studies, 2122, 2125
  research
    globalization and transnationalism, 2123
    hybridity, imagination and identity, 2123–2124
    nation-states, 2124–2125
  transnational information networks, 2123
  voluntary economic immigrants, 2122
Diasporization, 4208
Dickinson classification system, 3283
Dictionary-based techniques, 3143
Dictionnaire Universal de Commerce, 645
Die Deutsche Nationalbibliothek, see German national library
Die Erde und das Leben, 1687
Differential facet, 1536
DigiQUAL®, 374
Digital Archive, 3400
Digital asset management systems (DAMS), 4942, 4945–4946
Digital Betacam, 1568–1569
Digital books, 3472
Digital collection, 2826
Digital content, 4298

Digital content licensing
  commercial law
    choice of law and forum, 1272–1274
    contractual terms, enforceability of, 1271–1272
    electronic self-help and denial of access, 1275–1276
    UCC, 1270
    UCITA, 1270
    warranties, 1274–1275
    writing requirement and requirements of formation, 1270–1271
  copyright law, 1268
  definition, 1267
  e-rights, 1269
  moral rights, 1268–1269
  neighboring rights, 1268
Digital Cultural Content Forum (dCCF), 679
Digital divide
  Digital Inclusion Network, 1284
  educational divide, 1283–1284
  historical context, 1279–1280
  human capital development, 1284
  ICT access, 1280
  infrastructural level, programs, 1284
  international digital divide, assessments of, 1282–1283
  social support, 1284
  in United States
    age gap, 1282
    disability, 1282
    educational attainment, 1282
    gender gap, 1281
    geography, 1282
    income, 1282
    internet users, demographics of, 1281
    NTIA reports, 1280–1281
    race/ethnicity gap, 1281–1282
Digital humanities (DH), 1295–1296
  categories, 1299
  definitions, 1286–1288, 1298–1299
  history, 1288–1290
  Index Thomisticus, 1299
  institutional location, 1290–1292
  and libraries
    collections, 1303–1304
    consultation and collaboration, 1303
    instruction, 1302–1303
    intensive commitment, 1301
    low commitment, 1301
    moderate commitment, 1301
    theory, 1299–1301
  library community, perspective of, 1292–1293
  modularity, 1293
  pattern discovery and visualization, 1295
  representation, 1293–1295
Digital images
  create, display and share, 1307
  fundamentals
    binary image, 1309
    bit depth, 1309–1310
    bitmap image, 1308–1309
    digitization guidelines, 1309, 1311
    halftone printing, 1309
    interpolation, 1309
    lossless compression, 1310–1311

  lossy compression, 1310
  pixelation, 1309
  pixels, 1308–1310
  raster image, 1308
  resolution, 1309–1310
  vector graphics, 1308
  history of
    computing technologies, 1308
    digital fax, 1308
    image capture peripheral devices, 1308
    photographic images, 1307–1308
    visual imagery, 1307
    World Wide Web, 1308
  image file formats, 1311
  in library and archive sector
    crowdsourcing, 1313
    digitization, 1312
    technical digitization guidelines, 1312–1313
  memory institutions, surrogates for, 1307
  personal digital image collections and librarian, 1313–1314
  POD, 3733, 3735
  of provenance evidence, 3771
Digital imaging, 1414
Digital Inclusion Network, 1284
Digital library(ies), 1760, 2079, 2228–2229, 2240, 2766, 3727
  in Denmark, 1220
  in Germany, 1694, 1698
  Greece
    Anemi, 1732–1733
    digital collections and institutional repository, 1733
    e-fimeris, 1733
    National Documentation Center, 1733
    Psifiothiki, 1733
  Hungary, 1923–1924
  Japan, 2566
  in Kazakhstan, 2583
  Switzerland, 4489–4490
  Venezuelan libraries, 4890
Digital Library Federation, 1312
Digital Library Initiatives, 2228–2229
Digital Library of India (DLI), 2004
Digital Library of Wielkopolska project, 2828
Digital Library System (DLS), 4311
Digitally based information art projects, 2072
Digital Media Management (DiMeMa), 3400
Digital media piracy
  economic harm, 3650
  file sharing, 3650
  legislative framework
    Copyright Act, 3656
    DMCA, 3656–3657
    e-books, 3658
    Google Book Search, 3658
    intellectual property, 3656
    libraries, 3657
    NIH Public Access Policy, 3658–3659
    Pirate Bay, 3656
    Public Law 102-561, 3656
    RIAA, 3657
    SIAA, 3656
    Software Rental Amendments Act, 3656
    Sonny Bono Copyright Term Extension Act (1998), 3656
    Telefonica, 3657

Digital media piracy (cont'd.)
  means, prevalence, and costs
    audio files/music, 3651–3653
    published works, 3655–3656
    software, 3650–3651
    video sharing, 3654
  open access materials/license, 3649
  responses, 3659–3661
Digital Millennium Copyright Act (DMCA)
    of 1998, 369, 1472, 1577, 2142,
    3656–3657
  Bnetd case (*Davidson & Associates v. Jung*),
    1321
  computer maintenance and repair copyright
    exemption, 1322
  DeCSS case (*MPAA v. Corley*), 1319–1320
  DVDXCopy case (*321 Studios v. Metro-
    Goldwyn-Mayer Studios, Inc.*), 1321
  Felten case (*Felten v. RIAA*), 1320
  ISP liability, 1316
  Lexmark case (*Lexmark Int'l v. Static Control
    Components, Inc.*), 1321
  miscellaneous provisions, 1322
  online copyright infringement liability limita-
    tion, 1321–1322
  original designs, protection of, 1322
  Sklyarov case (*U.S. v. ElcomSoft*),
    1320–1321
  WIPO treaties
    access rights, 1317–1318
    anticircumvention, 1317
    civil and criminal penalties, 1316
    device trafficking, 1318
    enabling legislation, 1316
    particular class rule making, 1318
    Section 104 Report, 1318–1319
Digital museum, 3179–3180, 4495
Digital Object Identifier (DOI), 815, 943, 1365
  concepts
    content management of, 1325–1326
    interoperability, 1325
    persistence, 1325
    resolution, 1325
    scheme, 1325–1326
    specification, 1325
    string, 1325
    uniqueness, 1325
  content entities, 1326
  descriptive metadata, 1134
  digital content entity, 1133
  history, 1330
  International DOI Foundation, 1326, 1330
  metadata, 1326, 1329
  prefix and suffix, 1133
  registration, 1132, 1134, 1326
  resolution, 1327–1328
    component, 1326
    end-user perspective, 1135
  scope, 1326–1327
  social infrastructure, 1326, 1329–1330
  syntax, 1326–1327
  technical activities, 1330
Digital preservation
  born-digital works, 1335–1336
  definition, 1332
  digital curation, 1336
  digitization, 1334–1335

frameworks, 1332–1333
  methodologies, 1333–1334
Digital Preservation Management (DPM) Work-
    shop, 1333
Digital Preservation Network (DPN), 1760
Digital printing, 3733
Digital recordkeeping, 120–121
Digital Revolution, 3378
Digital rights management (DRM), 2277,
    4056–4057, 4778–4779
Digital rights management systems (DRMS),
    4945–4946
Digital services librarian, 711
Digital Solidarity Fund, 5016–5017
Digital stewardship, 1336
Digital storage, 4942
Digital video disc (DVD), 3280
Digitization, 1757, 1760–1761
DiMeMa, 3400
Dimension reduction vector space
  producing, 2691
  querying, 2691–2692
Dimensions in Advanced Computing (DIAC)
    conferences, 1031
Diplomatics
  acts, 1341
  approach and purpose of
    accuracy, 1340
    authentication, 1340
    authenticity, 1339–1340
    reliability, 1339
  archival bond, 1344
  building blocks of, 1340–1341
  criticism, 1344–1345
  documentary form
    extrinsic elements of form, 1343
    intrinsic elements of form, 1343–1344
  history of, 1338–1339
  meaning, 1338
  objects of, 1339
  persons, 1342
  procedure, 1342
  records creation, 1341
  transmission, status of, 1340
Diptychs, 542
Direct instructions, 3914
Directorate of Archives of France, 1590–1592
Directories, 640
Directory of Art Libraries, 249
*The Directory of Art Libraries and Visual
    Resource Collections in North America*,
    249–250
Directory of Open Access Journals (DOAJ),
    3645
Disability Discrimination Act 1992, 381
*The Disability Rights Movement: From Charity
    to Confrontation*, 3574
Disaster Information Management Research
    Center (DIMRC), 3343
Disaster planning and recovery, cultural
    institutions
  assessment of risks, 1350
  improvements
    civil unrest, armed conflicts, 1349–1350
    earthquakes, 1348
    fires, 1348–1349
    water damage, 1347–1348

preparation activities
    chain of command, communication and
      contact information, 1352–1353
    collections assets and setting priorities,
      1351
    finances, 1352
    floor maps, 1354
    insurance, 1352
    management issues, 1353
    pack-out instructions, 1351
    security, 1353–1354
    staff training, 1351–1352
    supplies, suppliers, service vendors and
      consultants, 1352
  prevention/mitigation, 1351
  recovery phase
    building concerns, 1356
    debriefing, revision and training, 1356
    returning collections, building, 1356
  response actions
    damage assessment, 1355
    salvage, 1355–1356
  responsibilities
    assessment and documentation, 1357
    building issues, 1358
    communications, 1357
    financial issues, 1358
    management, 1357
    personnel issues, 1357
    recovery operations, 1358
    salvage operations, 1358
    security, 1357
    supplies and equipment, 1358
    user issues, 1358
Disaster recovery test (DRT), 3359, 3362–3363
Disciplinary value systems, 1249
Discourse-based summarization systems, 422
*A Discourse of the Common Weal of Thys Realm
    of England*, 646
Discourse of Trade, 1400
Discovery services, 4980–4981
Discrete wavelet transformation (DWT), 2630
Discretionary access control (DAC), 406
Disintermediation, 483
DisplayWriter, 4994
Disposal/retention schedules, 108
Dissemination Information Package (DIP), 1365
Distance education
  CAPES, 604, 607–608
  GIS, 1674–1675
  Knowledge Society, 603
  legislation, 604
  library science
    Bachelor in Library Science, 605
    Brazilian Association of Education in
      Information Science, 607
    communication process, 607
    course content preparation, 609
    course material development, 608–609
    graduate-level courses, 606
    implementation process, 608
    IPES, 607
    librarianship training, 605
    model classroom teaching, 605–606
    Moodle, 606
    pedagogical design, 607
    RFP, 607

technical and operational support, 608
undergraduate degree, 607
virtual learning environments, 606
new quality of education, 603
UAB, 604–605
undergraduate and graduate studies, 604
Distinguished name space, 2999
Distributed data management
principles
authenticity and integrity, 2998
chain of custody, 2998
data virtualization, 2998–2999
infrastructure independence, 2998
management virtualization, 2998, 3000–3002
shared collections, 2998
trust virtualization, 2998–3000
virtualization mechanisms, 2998
technologies, 3002
Distributed Object Computation Testbed project, 1415
Distributive justice, 4219
District Information Documentation Centers (DIDCs), 2594
District Rural Development Agency (DRDA), 2000
Divinity binding, 540
DLF/CLIR + ER&L Cross-Pollinator Travel Award, 1422
DocBook, 3075
Docents, 3192
Docking search, 835–836
Docklands Campus Library and Business School, 254
DOCK program, 836
Documentary meaning, 1375
Documentary photography, 3206
Documentation Inc., 2221
Documentation strategy model, 201
Document delivery services, 1099
Document information systems
authenticity, 1363–1364
definition of, 1360
design methodology, 1371
advantages, 1367
definition, 1367
disadvantages, 1368
way of control, 1370
way of modeling, 1368
way of thinking, 1368
way of working, 1368–1370
digital longevity, 1364
document, definition of, 1360
information, 1360
interoperability, 1363
ISO standard 15489, 1362, 1370
practical cases, 1361–1362
records management software functions, 1362–1363
Sarbanes-Oxley Act, 1362, 1370
software applications, 1362
standards and standard components
checksums, 1366
content representation, 1366
data formats, 1367
metadata, 1364–1366
OAI-PMH and OAI-ORE, 1365

OAIS, 1365
ODMA, 1365
persistent identifier, 1365
query language, 1366–1367
software selection, 1364
storage media, 1364
XML syntactic data model family, 1365
Document input model, 3112
Document-like object (DLOs), 1391
Document management, 718–719, 2108
Document output model, 3110–3111
Document-role relationship table, 3113
Document surrogates, 4466
Document theory
complementary approach, 1378–1379
digital age, 1377–1378
LIS, materialistic critique of, 1376–1377
professional interest, 1373–1375
scientific interest, 1375–1376
Document type definition (DTD), 1365, 1424, 2343, 2986, 3075, 3460, 5024
advantages, 1388
attributes, 1383–1384
built-in general entities, 1384–1385
declarations, 1385–1387
disadvantages, 1388
entities, 1384–1385
limitations, 1383
parameter entities, 1385
readability, 1385
RELAX NG, 1388
syntax, 1381–1382
validating parsers, 1387
W3C XML Schema, 1387–1388
Document Understanding Conferences (DUC), 424, 426
DOI, see Digital Object Identifier
DOI-X prototype, 1132
Domain Name System (DNS), 1325, 5021
Domain ontologies, 3457
Domain precision, 1175
Domain searching, 4049
Domain-specific retrieval tasks, 4574
Domestic counterterrorism, 2399
Domiciliation, 180
Dominion Library, 657
Donkey library, Kenya, 2595
Donor-organized nongovernmental organizations (DONGO), 3380
Doorway page, 4035
Doublure, 539
Downward causation, 1039
DPN, see Digital Preservation Network
Dretske, Fred, 2053
Drivers Privacy Protection Act (DPPA), 2399
DRM, see Digital rights management
Dr. Martin Luther King, Jr., Library, 4161
Droit d'auteur, 2142
Drop dead software device, 1275–1276
Drug nomenclature, see RxNorm
Drypoint printing, 1867
Dry-preserved preparation, 1158
DSpace, 3467
DSS, see Decision support system
DTD, see Document type definition
Dual-use libraries, 4158

Dublin Core (DC), 1366, 1391, 1417, 3826, 4413, 4472–4473
bibliographic control, 454
FAST project, 1539
Dublin Core Abstract Model (DCAM), 3068–3069
Dublin Core Metadata Element Set (DCMES), 3059
Dublin Core Metadata Initiative (DCMI), 454, 3059, 3401
abstract model
FRSAD model, 1616
and interoperability, 1396–1397
Australia, 1392
conference series, 1395
data models, 1393
DC-Down Under, 1392–1393
Frankfurt, 1395
Helsinki, 1393–1394
INDECS project, 1394
OCLC-CNI workshop on image description, 1391–1392
OCLC-NCSA metadata workshop, 1390–1391
organizational structure, 1396
Ottawa, and LOM, 1395
standardization strategies, 1396
structure and procedures, 1395
voting, 1394–1395
Warwick Framework, 1391
Duke Mathematical Journal, 3026
Dumptown Game, 2155
Dun and Bradstreet Sales and Marketing Identification Service, 653
Dun & Bradstreet Reference Book, 647
Dun's Review and Modern Industry, 647
Durham Catalog of 1416, 749
Duyvis, Frits Donker, 4783–4784
Dynamed, 1878
Dynamic Adaptive Streaming over HTTP (DASH) standard, 5021–5022
Dynamic geography, 1688
Dyslexia, 3841, 3845–3846

E

EAD, see Encoded Archival Description
EAD Working Group (EADWG), 1430–1431
Eales, Nellie B., 499–500, 506
Earlham's developing program, 987–988
Early Detection and Rapid Response (EDRR), 3310
The Earth and Man, 1686
East African Library Association (EALA), 37, 4515
East African Literature Bureau (EALB), 4499–4500
East Asian Character Code (EACC), 4663
EASTICA, 688
eAuditorium™, 1057
EBLIP, see Evidence-based library and information practice
e-books, 920–921, 3472
Ebooks Library (EBL), 1210
EBSCO, 3471, 3473
Ecclesiastical binding, see Divinity binding
Ecclesiastical documents, 3303

Ecological Model of ELIS, 1510
Ecological rationality
    adaptive toolbox, 2361
    as-if optimization models, 2362
    fast and frugal decision making, 2362
    heuristics
        building blocks, 2362–2363
        two memory-based heuristics, 2363–2364
        usability, and environmental design,
            2364–2365
Ecomuseums, 1822, 3264
Economic Almanac, 650
Economic and business literature
    first period
        agriculture, books on, 1399–1400
        arithmetic, books of, 1400
        commercial law, 1400
        enterprises, 1400
        money, 1400
        retail selling, books on, 1400
        usury, treatises and tracts on, 1399
    fourth period
        bibliographical works, 1409
        business cycles, study of, 1409–1410
        business institutions, operation of, 1410–
            1411
        businessmen's biographies, 1411
        corporate research agencies, 1408
        economic bibliographies, 1410
        ephemeral literature, 1410
        financial foundations, 1408–1409
        governmental production, 1408
        individual business units, histories of, 1411
        manuscript material, publication of, 1410
        national economic and statistical associa-
            tions, 1408
        private institutions, 1408
        publishing houses, creative activities, 1408
        schools of business, 1408
        scientific management, 1410–1411
    second period, 1400–1401
        cameralistic thought, growth of, 1401
        cameralistic writings, 1403
        census of population, 1402
        commodity prices, lists of, 1401
        company ventures, documents on, 1403
        economic literature, bibliographies of,
            1402–1403
        economic systems, 1402
        financial affairs and shipping, periodicals
            on, 1401
        historical studies, 1402
        mercantile journal, 1401
        merchants' price lists, 1401
        political arithmetic, 1401–1402
        vital statistics, 1402
    third period
        agricultural journals, 1405–1406
        agricultural surveys, 1404
        businessmen's biographies and autobiogra-
            phies, 1406
        business publication, 1405
        census of population, 1404
        company histories, 1406
        economic thought, 1407
        graphic presentation of statistical data,
            1407

historical bibliographies, 1405
ideas and materials, international move-
    ment of, 1406
international congress, 1406–1407
international exhibition, 1407
political arithmetic, 1405–1406
political economy, 1407
private corporations, 1406
probability theory, 1405
professional publications, 1405
railway periodicals, 1405
statistical publications, 1404
translation, 1406
Economic and Social Council of the United
    Nations (ECOSOC), 2432
Economic Census, 637–638
Economic Commission for Africa's (ECA)
    library, 1499
Economic lot sizing model, 1196–1197
Economic model, 1754
Economic order quantity (EOQ) model, 1196
Economics of information, 2256–2257
Economics of reuse, 2652
Economic utility, 2354–2357
eCONTENT, 3399
e-democracy, 2945
Edge marbling, 539
Edinburgh University Library, 4453
Editorial Support System (ESS), 1259
Education
    for librarianship, 3376–3377
    LIS, 706–707
        from within, 707–708
        ALA's Committee on Accreditation, 708
        Bologna declaration, 710
        competency, 710
        continuing education, 712–713
        core courses, 708
        English language publications, 710
        IFLA, 710, 713
        M.L.I.S., 707, 709–710
        from profession, 707
        SIIA, 4298
Educational Clearinghouse, 3035
Educational need, 2116
Educational press, 3739
Educational Resources Information Center
    (ERIC), 91
Education collections, 3165
Educators and trainers
    archival research programs, 686
    career opportunities, 690–691
    competency standards, 687–688
    developing strategies, 685
    ICA Section, 689
    professional associations, role of, 688–689
    providers of, 689–690
    records management, 686
    RIBEAU, 686
Edwards, Edward, 1838
Edward Swanson Memorial Best of LRTS
    Award, 331
EFnet, 1049
Egalitarianism/equity, 4219
E-government, 2945, 4087
Egyptian Library Association, 100
e-Health Capacity strategy, 86

eHistory website, 5027
Eigenfactor metrics, 928
EINet Galaxy, 2520
E-journal preservation, 1335
Electrical Engineering (EE), 275
Electronic books, *see* Electronic publishing
    children's books, 872
Electronic commerce (e-commerce), 693, 1993
Electronic communication, 1108–1109
Electronic content management (ECM), 225,
    2659
Electronic Data Gathering, Analysis and
    Retrieval (EDGAR), 638, 1555
Electronic data interchange (EDI), 2273, 2919,
    4143
Electronic data processing (EDP), 2272
Electronic Dewey, 1259
Electronic document management (EDM), 3105
    analysis process, 3108–3109
    characteristics, 3106
    components, 3106
Electronic document management systems
    (EDMSs), 716
Electronic Freedom of Information Act
    (EFOIA), 1551
Electronic funds transfer (EFT) systems, 2273
Electronic government (e-gov), 2147, 2153–
    2154, 2158–2159
Electronic health record (EHR), 1889, 3339
Electronic Information Delivery Online System
    (EIDOS), 3399
Electronic Information for Libraries (eIFL),
    2827–2829
Electronic information packages, 1366
Electronic Information Service (EISZ), 2828
Electronic ink, 4058
Electronic Journals Library, 1696
Electronic licenses, 2823
    ANKOS, 2829
    Consortium of Swiss Academic Libraries,
        2826
    COSEC, 2828
    EBLIDA, 2827
    ELINET network, 2828
    FINELIB's programs, 2825
    HEAL, 2827
    Iceland Library Consortium, 2825
    NELSI, 2825
    UKB Association, 2826
Electronic mail (e-mail), 1108–1109
Electronic meetings, 1054
Electronic Meeting Systems (EMS), 1050
Electronic publishing, 415–416, 1335
    advantages, 4056–4057
    disadvantages, 4057
    forms, 4054
    future trends, 4058
    libraries and librarians, impact on, 4057–4058
    publishers and publishing services, 4056
    tasks, 4055–4056
    technologies for, 4054–4055
Electronic record keeping system (ERS), 1851
Electronic records
    archives context, 2384–2385
    collaboration, 2385
    content and context, 1413
    definition, 1413

deterioration and loss, 2384
NHPRC, 3315, 3319
obsolescence, 2384
poor records management, 2383
preservation
  administrative metadata, 1417
  backups and snapshots, 1417
  challenges of, 1415–1416
  descriptive metadata, 1417–1418
  history of, 1413–1415
  human error and vandalism, 1417
  software and document encoding issues, 1416–1417
  storage media, 1415–1416
records management context, 2384
Electronic Records and Signatures in Global and National Commerce Act of 2000, 1415
Electronic records management (ERM), 408, 1108–1109
Electronic Resources & Libraries conference (ER&L)
  awards and scholarships, 1422
  2016 conference tracks, 1421
  history and growth, 1419–1421
  mission, 1419
  planning committee, 1420
  presentation tracks, 1419
  purpose, 1419
Electronic resources management system (ERMS), 2922
Electronic resources sharing, 2823, 2829
  FINELIB's programs, 2825
  Francophone university libraries, 2826
  in Hungary, 2828
  in Iberian Peninsula, 2827
  in Italy, 2827
  legislation and copyright, 2827
  Norway, 2825
  in Romania, 2829
Electronic Scholarly Communication Forums (e-SCFs), 4022
Electronic Theses and Dissertations (ETDs), 2902
Electronic Theses Online Service (EThOS), 620
Element ordering, 3062
Elgin Marbles, 267, 3758
El Greco Museum, 4332
Eli M. Oboler Award, 2392
ELINET network, 2828
ELIS, *see* Everyday life information seeking
Elite galleries, 243
Ellis' model of information-seeking behaviors, 2226, 2243–2244
El Museo Shan-Dany, 3245
Elsevier, 3472, 5026–5027
Elsevier's Scopus, 923, 925
E-mail, 1414, 2507
Embedded information, 2058
Emergency preparedness, 89, 2153, 2400, 3343
Emergent credibility, 1115
e-Metrics, 2226
Emigration records, 1658
Empirical knowledge, 2610
Empiricism, 3625
Employee Retirement Income Security Act (ERISA), 1858
Emulation, 1334, 2072

Enacted information, 2058
Encoded Archival Context for Corporate Bodies, Persons, and Families (EAC-CPF), 137
Encoded archival description (EAD), 134, 136–137, 734, 1292, 1366, 3686, 3826, 4273
  semantics and structure
    hierarchal analysis, 1429–1430
    top level, 1427–1429
    technical foundation, 1426–1427
Encoded Archival Description Document Type Definition (EAD DTD), 1593
Encyclopedia of Reagents for Organic Synthesis (EROS), 816
Encyclopédie ou Dictionnaire des Sciences, des Arts et des Métiers, 645
End-user training, database searching, 1878
Energy facet, 1536
Engineering
  aerospace knowledge diffusion research project, 1448–1450
  Allen's study, 1445
  community, 1437–1439
  formal registration, 1434
  Herner's work, 1443, 1445
  information processors, 1446
  information-seeking behavior, engineers, 1433, 1439, 1444
  Kaufman's study, 1446
  knowledge, 1435–1437
  Kremer's study, 1445
  research, 1446–1448
  research agenda development, 1450–1451
  Rosenbloom and Wolek, 1445
  science and technology, 1439–1441
  and scientists, 1441–1442
  Shuchman's study, 1445–1446
  social systems, 1442–1443
  STI, 1433
  work, 1434–1435
Engineering librarianship, *see* Science and engineering librarianship
Engineering library, 4009–4010
English Fairy Tales, 854
English hand binding, 545–546
English Heritage, 4723
English Heritage Thesauri, 1080
English illumination
  Gothic period, 1950
  Romanesque period, 1948
English Short-Title Catalogue (ESTC), 458
Enterprise application integration (EAI) systems, 3455
Enterprise content management (ECM), 1108, 1854
Enterprise Integration Network (EINet), 2520
Enterprise resource planning (ERP), 2274, 2658
Enterprise systems, 2274–2275
Entry pages, 4035
Environmental Protection Agency (EPA), 2155
Environmental scanning, 2108, 3196
Environmental Systems Research Institute (ESRI), 1671, 1673, 1675, 1678
Environment for Strategic Planning (ESP), 1206
Epidemic theory model, 504

Episteme, 2678
Epistemetrics, 4199
Epistemic authority, 1116
Epistemic coherentism, 1458
Epistemic paternalism, 4199
Epistemic reason, 1461
Epistemology, 4918
  justification
    coherentism, 1458, 1460
    deductive, 1457
    defeasible, 1457
    fallibilism, 1457
    foundationalism, 1459–1460
    inductive, 1457
    inferential, 1457–1458
  knowledge, analysis of, 1455
  modern empiricism
    contemporary Anglo-American epistemology, 1455–1456
    pragmatic rationale, 1457
    purpose-independent correctness, 1457
    Russell's epistemology, 1456
  skepticism, 1460–1461
EPO, *see* European Patent Office
Equal Rights Amendment (ERA), 2394–2395
Equi-height histograms, 2630
Equi-width histograms, 2630
E-Rate Modernization Order, 1283
Eratosthenes, 1683–1684
E-referencer system, 3427–3429
Ergebnisse der Mathematik und ihrer Grenzbebiete, 3028
E-rights, 1269
ER&L, *see* Electronic Resources & Libraries conference
Escalation theory, 2283
E-Science, 555, 4015, 4086
eSerials Holdings Service, 3398
E-Sign, *see* Electronic Records and Signatures in Global and National Commerce Act of 2000
Espresso Book Machine (EBM), 3735
ESRI, *see* Environmental Systems Research Institute
Essay of Drapery, 1400
Essays on Husbandry, 1402
Esther J. Piercy Award, 331
Estonian State Library, 3326
Ethernet standard, 2342
Ethical actions
  individual actions
    employers/clients/system users, responsibility to, 1479
    profession, responsibility to, 1479
    society, responsibility to, 1479–1480
  organizational actions
    board and administration, 1478
    ethical awareness, 1479
    orientations, 1478
    staff development and training programs, 1479
    written ethics policy, 1478
  professional actions, 1479
Ethical issues, information systems
  access, 1491
  accuracy, 1489–1490
  individual rights, 1487

Ethical issues, information systems (cont'd.)
  privacy
    big data aggregation and analysis, 1489
    Bill of Rights, 1488
    cocreation of value, 1489
    databases, 1488
    enforcement, 1488
    harmonization, 1488
    invasion, 1489
    legislation, 1488
    loss of autonomy, 1487
    marketing and personalization, 1489
    patterns, 1489
    personal data dispersion, 1489
    PII, 1489
    Privacy Act, 1488
    records collection, storage, and dissemina-
      tion, 1488
    safeguards, 1488
    systematic monitoring and surveillance,
      1489
  property, 1490–1491
  sources, 1487
Ethics
  access issues, 1472
  administrative issues, 1472
  conflicting loyalties, 1473
  copyright issues, 1471–1472
  ethical actions
    individual actions, 1479–1480
    organizational actions, 1478–1479
    professional actions, 1479
  ethical dilemmas, 1480
  ethical dissonance, 1469
  factors
    respect for individuality, 1475
    social responsibility, 1474
    social utility, 1474
    survival, 1474
  limitations, 1470
  privacy issues, 1470–1471
  professional ethics, 1475–1476
  reference services, 1471, 3917
  selecting materials and censorship, 1470
  societal issues, 1473
  technology-related issues, 1472–1473
  values, information professions
    beauty, 1478
    individual liberty, 1477
    justice, 1477–1478
    tolerance, 1477
    truth, 1476–1477
Ethiopia
  history of, 1494–1495
  languages, 1494
  libraries
    academic libraries, 1498–1499
    education, 1499
    national library, 1495–1496
    professional association, 1499–1500
    public libraries, 1498
    school libraries, 1499
    special libraries, 1498–1499
  location, 1494
  museums and galleries, 1500–1501
    Addis Ababa Museum, 1503
    Asni Gallery, 1504

    Belvedere Gallery, 1504
    Dessie Museum, 1503
    exhibition of 1958, 1501
    Goshu Art Gallery, 1504
    Harar National and Community Museum,
      1503–1504
    Institute of Ethiopian Studies Museum,
      1501–1503
    before Italian occupation, 1501
    Jimma Museum, 1503
    Mekelle Museum, 1503
    National museum of Ethiopia, 1501–1502
    OAU, 1502
    SOFIES, 1503
    St. George Interior Decoration and Art
      Gallery, 1504
    UACC, 1501
    Wollega Museum, 1503
  National Archives, 1500
  printing and publishing, development of, 1495
Ethiopian Community Development Council
  (ECDC), 40
Ethiopian Institute of Agricultural Research
  (EIAR) Library and Documentation
  Center, 1499
Ethiopian Library Association (ELA), 1499
Ethiopian Library, Information Science and
  Archives Professional Association, 1500
Ethiopian Orthodox Library-Museum, 1499
Ethnic and Multicultural Materials Information
  Exchange Roundtable (EMIERT), 334
Ethnic museums, 3244–3245
Ethnographic museums, 1927–1928
  politics, power, and representation,
    3694–3695
  in Serbia, 4135
Ethnography, History, Archeology, and Natural
  Sciences, 4185
Ethnolinguistic gatekeepers, 2126
Ethnology museum, 1820
Ethnomethodology, 2055, 3815
Ethnoscapes, 2124
etoy, 2066, 2071
Etruscan bindings, 541
Etruscan calf, 541
EURBICA, 2441
EURONOMOS, 2441
EUROPEANA, 1708
Europeana Linked Open Data Project, 2941
European Association for Library and Informa-
  tion Education and Research (EUCLID),
  708
European Bureau of Library, Documentation
  and Information Associations
  (EBLIDA), 2827, 2956
European Classification (ECLA), 3566–3567
European Confederation of Conservator-
  Restorers' Organization (ECCO), 1071
European Conference on Digital Libraries
  (ECDL), 3367
European Digital Library (EDL), 2824, 3332,
  3684
European Directive on Data Privacy of October,
  1998, 1106
European Economic Community (EEC), 2312
The European Library, 250
European museums, 3234

European Patent Office (EPO)
  ECLA system, 3566–3567
  ESPACE EP, 3569
  esp@cenet, 3569
  Register Plus, 3569
European Space Agency (ESA), 1347
European Union (EU) information policy
  Bangemann report, 2140
  challenges, 2140
  data protection and privacy, 2143
  electronic commerce, 2142–2143
  European information society, 2140–2141
  Hernon and Relyea definition, 2139
  historical overview of, 2139–2140
  ICT, 2141–2142
  implications, 2144
  information society, 2140–2141
  intellectual property, 2142
  legal and regulatory issues, 2140
  normative ethics, 2139
  objectives, 2140
  pragmatic ethics, 2139
  utilitarian approach, 2139
  Weingarten definition, 2138
Eurostat survey, 1741
Evaluative Bibliometrics, 500
Everlasting match, 2913
Every Child Ready to Read (ECRR), 335
Everyday life information seeking (ELIS),
  842–843, 2087–2088, 2118–2119, 5070
  concept, 1506–1507
  information sources, 1507–1508
  needs, 1507
  theories and models
    ecological model, 1510
    information grounds, 1511–1512
    information practices, 1511
    sense-making methodology, 1508–1509
    small world, 1509–1510
    Way of Life, 1510–1511
  in "Way of Life," 1510–1511
Every Man His Own Broker, 1401
Evidence-based acquisition (EBA) model, 1211
Evidence-based librarianship (EBL), 1887–1888
Evidence-based library and information practice
  (EBLIP), 1516, 1520–1521
Evidence-based medicine (EBM), 1764, 1888
Evidence-based practice (EBP), 4255, 4259
  apply the results, 1519–1520
  components, 1517–1521
  effect evaluation, 1520–1521
  evidence appraisal, 1518–1519
  meta-analysis, 1519
  question formulation, 1517–1518
  search for evidence, 1518
  systematic review, 1518–1519
Evidence-based selection (EBS), 1211
Ewart, William, 1838
"ExaByte-Counter," 2102–2103
Excite, 2521
Executive information systems (EIS), 2274
Executive support systems (ESS), 2895
Exhibition design, 241
  accounting for sustainability, 1531
  content team, 1529
  design team, 1529
  elements

architectural elements, 1525
color, lighting and acoustics, 1526
construction and finishes materials, 1526
graphics, 1526
media, 1526
narrative, 1525
objects, artifacts and images, 1526
physical and cultural context, 1525
space, 1525
formative evaluation, 1528
front-end evaluations, 1528
history
contemporary vision, 1524–1525
European Roots, 1524
planned experiences, transition to, 1524
new narratives, 1531
new perspectives of interpretation, 1530
new technology, 1531
NLM, 3343–3344
process
concept, 1527
design development, 1527
fabrication and installation, 1528
fabrication documents, 1527
schematic phase, 1527
project management side, 1529–1530
prototype testing, 1528
special collections, 4339
summative evaluations, 1528
universal access, 1530
EXIT project, 3785
Ex Libris Student Writing Award, 2778
Exosomatic flow line, 2058
Exosomatic information, 2058, 2060
Expectancy theory, 3513
Expectation-Maximization (EM) algorithm, 4421
Experienced credibility, 1115
Experienced information, 2058
Experimental knowledge assets, 2622
Expertise Recommender (ER), 3866
Expert locator systems
automatic expertise finders, 3865
expert databases, 3864–3865
expertise recommenders, 3865–3866
expert referral systems, 3866–3867
research communities, 3864
Expert systems, 1203
ExPlain, 1768
Explicit knowledge, 2445, 2643
Expressed information, 2058
Extensible HyperText Markup Language
(XHTML), 3076
Extensible Markup Language (XML), 1058,
1063–1064, 1361, 1381, 1416, 1423,
2222, 2524, 2986–2987, 3459–3460,
3962–3963, 4082, 4561
document format, 3107
Document Type Definitions, 3077–3078
family of languages, 3079–3080
identification problem, 3078
logical structure, 3076–3077
markup techniques, 3076–3078
name collision problem, 3078–3079
physical structure, 3077
standardization, 3106
standardization levels, 3107–3108
Unicode Standard, 4667–4668

Extensible Stylesheet Language (XSL), 1365
Extensible stylesheet language transformations
(XSLT), 1365, 3079, 3965, 4084
EXTRACT, 2155
Extreme Programming (XP), 1370
Eye movements, in reading, 3838

F

Fabrication Laboratory (Fab Lab), 2991–2992
Facet analysis
classes, 1535
definition, 1534
differential facet, 1536
energy and matter facet, 1536
entity terms, 1535
general analysis of information, 1534
lattice system, 1538
personality facet
levels of, 1536
rounds of, 1536–1537
purpose of, 1535
space facet, 1536
subjects
education, 1536
Food Technology, 1536
occupational safety and health,
1535–1536
science and technology, 1537
thesaurus, 1537–1538
time facet, 1536
Faceted application of subject terminology
(FAST), 4468, 4472–4473
application rules, 1542–1543
authority files, 4473
authority records, 1539
development and maintenance, 1543
faceted subject heading vocabulary, 1539
facets
chronological headings, 1542
corporate names, 1541
event names, 1542
form headings, 1542
genre headings, 1542
geographic names, 1540–1541
personal names, 1541
title of work, 1541–1542
topical headings, 1540
history, 1539
implementations, 1545
influences, 1539–1540
and LCSH, 1539–1540
Linked Data, 1539, 1545–1546
name headings, 4473
research prototypes, 1546
schema, 4472–4473
tools, 1544–1545
Facets, 4470
Facsimile, 1307
Factory libraries, 1697
Factual data, 4065
Fair Credit Reporting Act, 1106, 2152
Fair Use Doctrine, 4946
Fairy tales, 853–854
FALCON, 3440–3441
Fallout (F), 3945
Family Online Safety Institute (FOSI), 783

Family Place Libraries, 878
Fantasy, 854–855, 865–867, 3702
Farmington Plan, 372
Farnese binding, 543
FAST, *see* Faceted application of subject
terminology
FASTConverter, 1544
FastTrack MLIS Web site, 3438–3439
Fax technology, 1307–1308
Fayetteville Free Library (FFL), 2992
FCC, *see* Federal Communications Commission
FDLP, *see* Federal Depository Library Program
Federal Advisory Committee Act of 1972,
2151
Federal Bureau of Investigation (FBI), 2148
Federal Communications Commission (FCC),
1013–1014, 1021
Federal Council of Education (CFE), 611
Federal Council of Library Science (CFB), 605
Federal Cylinder Project, 4299
Federal Depository Library Program (FDLP),
369, 1549, 1555–1557, 1715–1716, 2148
Federal Emergency Management Association
(FEMA), 1352, 2153
Federal Fluminense University (UFF), 612
Federal Office of Culture (OFC), 4495
Federal Property and Administrative Services
Act of 1949, 1851
Federal Records Act, 185, 1414, 1851
Federal Register, 640
Federal Reserve Bulletin, 649
Federal Reserve Open Market Committee, 3006
Federal Rules of Civil Procedure (FRCP), 1107,
1858
Federal University of Rio de Janeiro (UFRJ),
607–608, 612
Fédération Internationale de Documentation
(FID), 4783–4784
FEMA, *see* Federal Emergency Management
Association
Fiction, 855
contemporary fiction, 864–865
historical fiction, 865
Fidel's models, 4877–4878
Field (in)accuracy, 1176
Field-based ethnographic research, 3814
Field Museum of Natural History (FMNH),
3252
Field study, 4798
Fiji Library Association, 3548
File Index (FI) system, 3566–3567
FileMakerPro, 4942
File-sharing, 3650–3653
File transfer protocol (FTP), 2183, 2517, 2983
Film and audiovisual archives, 4737
Film and broadcast archives
academic collections, 1561, 1563
Australia, 1567
broadcasting stations, 1566
Canada, 1567
government, 1565–1566
issues and trends, 1576–1579
Japan, 1567
motion picture archives, 1561–1563
museums and libraries, 1563, 1565
scope of activities, 1567–1576
United Kingdom, 1566

Film archives
　AMIA, 1587
　FIAF, 1585
　Hungary, 1926
　moving image media, 1585
　NFPF, 1587–1588
　photographic raw stock, 1584
　public-sector archives, 1586, 1588
　"safety" film, 1585
　"Silent Era" Web site, 1584
　Yugoslavia, 4133
Filter blogs, 2507
Financescapes, 2124
Financial commentary, 4456
Financial information, 638–639
Fine art presses, 3743
Fine Arts Museums of San Francisco (FAMSF),
　3225–3226
FINELIB, 2825
Fingerprinting, 478
Firearms Museum, 4382
First-generation portals, 2893
FirstGov, 1553, 1557
First-impressions hypothesis, 3590
First Nations, 2032
First Nations libraries, 2038
FirstSearch Electronic Collections Online
　(ECO), 3399
Fisher Library, 384–385
Fishscale model of omniscience, 4201
Five star data model, 2940
Fixed content signs, 4973–4975
Fixity information, 1364
F. Kennedy Memorial Library, 1498
Fleet Library, 253, 4774
Flemish Research Libraries Council, 2826
Flexible querying, 1618, 1626–1628
Flexible scheduling, 111
FlexoWriter, 4993–4994
Flink, 4088
Floor maps, 1351, 1354
Floppy Disk Project, 1554
Florentin, Antonin, 4176
Florian Psalter, 3681
Floridi, Luciano, 2048–2049
Fluency with Information Technology (FIT),
　2304, 2306
Fluid-preserved preparation, 1158
Focus group, 4798
Fogerty, 202
Fogg Art Museum, 1070
Fogg's prominence-interpretation theory, 1117
FOIA, see Freedom of Information Act
FOLIO, 1711
Folksonomy, 1078, 4089, 4209, 4551, 4987
Folktales, 853–854, 858, 862–863, 866, 870,
　4440–4442
Food and Agricultural Organization (FAO), 3385
Forbes, Edward W., 1070
Fore-edge painting, 539
Foreign Corrupt Practices Act (FCPA), 1106
The Foreign Gifts and Decorations Act, 3716
Foreign librarianship, 2405
Forensics, 1334
*Forest Physiography: Physiography of the
　United States and Principles of Soils in
　Relation to Forests*, 1688

Formal usability testing, 4797
Format attributes, 2294
Formats, 1177
FORmula TRANslation (FORTRAN), 2272
Forster, Johann Georg, 1685
Forster, Johann Rheinhold, 1685
Fort Jesus Museum, 2605
Forum for Knowledge, Information, Documen-
　tation, and Archives (VIDA), 1224
Forward citation retrieval, 925
Foundational justification, 1459–1460
Fourth ages theory, 3406–3407
Fox, Christopher, 2053
FP-Streaming, 2632–2633
Fragment-screening approach, 832–833
Frame-level indexing, 3132
Framingham Heart Study, 1767
France
　archives
　　access to, 1591–1592
　　Ancien Régime, 1589–1590
　　definition, 1589
　　départemental archives, 1591
　　Directorate for Archives, role of,
　　　1590–1591
　　National Archives, 1590–1591
　　National Audiovisual Institute, 1591
　　private archives, 1592
　　Superior Archives Council, 1591
　　transformations, 1593
　libraries
　　BNF, 1599, 1604–1605
　　history of, 1599–1601
　　public libraries, 1601–1602
　　school, academic, and research libraries,
　　　1602–1603
　　space planning and interior design, 1603
　　visitors, 1603–1604
　map of, 1589–1590
　museums
　　Academy of Beaux-Arts, 1594
　　anthropology museum, 1595
　　architecture, 1596
　　Center for Museum Research and Conser-
　　　vation in France, 1596
　　City for Science and Industry, 1597
　　classified museums, 1595
　　cultural heritage, 1594
　　curieux, 1593–1594
　　Directorate, responsibility of, 1595–1596
　　fine arts museum, 1594
　　immigration, 1597
　　International Council of Museums, 1595
　　local museum, 1594
　　Louvre, 1596–1597
　　lycées, 1594
　　Ministry of Culture, 1595
　　Museum of Monuments, 1594
　　national heritage, 1594
　　national museums, 1595
　　natural history museum, 1594
　　in nineteenth century, 1594
　　Orsay Museum, 1597
　　Pompidou Center, 1597
　　princely collections, 1593–1594
　　professions, 1597–1598
　　Quai Branly museum, 1597

　　regional/local museums, 1596
　　smaller museums, 1595
　　transformations, 1593
　　in twentieth century, 1594
　　visitors, 1598–1599
France de l'Est, 1687
Franciscan Biblical Museum, 2550
Francis Joseph Campbell Award, 377
FRBR, see Functional Requirements for Biblio-
　graphic Records
Frederick G. Kilgour Award, 2778
Free and Open Source Software (FOSS), 4659
Free discovery, 1210
Freedman, Maurice J, 75, 4691
Freedom of Information Act (FOIA), 186, 1105,
　1472, 1551, 2150–2152, 2390
Freedom of information legislation, 3890
Freedom to Read Foundation, 2391–2393
"Free-floating" subdivisions, 4470
Free For All Web sites (FFAs), 4036
Free Matter for the Blind and Handicapped
　mailing, 570–571
Freenets, 1029
FreePatentsOnline, 3570
Free-text searcher, 4878
French bookbinding, 544
French ISKO Chapter, 2497
Frequency distribution, 2211
Frequently Asked Questions (FAQ), 2507
Frequent pattern mining
　Apriori, 2631
　FP-Streaming, 2632–2633
　frequent item mining, 2631–2632
　Lossy Counting algorithm, 2632
　Manku and Motwani's algorithm, 2632
Friedrich Althoff Consortium, 2826
Friedrich Rathgen Laboratory, 1069
Friend-of-a-friend (FOAF) ontology, 4089
Friends of Libraries Committee, 2842
Friends of Libraries USA (FOLUSA), 2834,
　2842
Frohmann, Bernd, 2059–2060
FRSAD, see Functional requirements for subject
　authority data
Full mesh topology, 3360
Full text indexing, 1621, 2653
Full-text searching, 297, 1758, 3468, 4467, 4476
Functional illiteracy, 4282–4283
Functional Requirements for Authority Data
　(FRAD), 3295
Functional Requirements for Bibliographic
　Records (FRBR), 726–727, 1233,
　1238–1239, 1606–1610, 1612–1616,
　2923, 3068
　Classify prototype, 1546
　conceptual model, 452
　entity-relationship database model, 452–453
　MARC 21, 2987
　RDA, 453
　user tasks, 452–453
Functional requirements for subject authority
　data (FRSAD), 1606–1616
　applications, 1615–1616
　conceptual model, 1606–1607, 1609–1610,
　　1612, 1615–1616
　development timeline, 1607–1608
　thema, 1615

Functional retention schedules, 3893
Fund-raising, academic libraries, *see* Academic
    libraries, fund-raising and development
Furner, Jonathan, 2060
Fussler, Herman H., 497–498, 502, 506
Fuzzy set theory, information retrieval
    associative retrieval mechanisms
        clustering techniques, 1622, 1633
        compatible purposes, 1631
        ontologies, 1622
        pseudothesauri, 1622, 1631–1632
        thesauri, 1631–1633
    Boolean retrieval model, 1621–1622
    cross language retrieval, 1619
    document indexing
        generalized Boolean indexing,
            1622–1623
        HTML document, weighted representation
            of, 1625–1626
        probabilistic models, 1622
        structured documents, representation of,
            1623–1624
        techniques for, 1621
        term significance, 1624–1625
        vector space model, 1622
    flexible query languages, 1618
        definition of, 1621–1622, 1627–1628
        linguistic query weights, 1629–1630
        query evaluation mechanism, 1027–1028
        query weights, 1628–1629
        selection conditions, linguistic quantifiers,
            1630–1631
    imprecision, vagueness, uncertainty, and
        inconsistency, 1619–1621
    knowledge-based models, 1621
    MCDM activity, 1618
    multicriteria decision-making activity, 1618
    multimedia document, 1619
    OCAT methodology, 1621
    relevance, concept of, 1619
    representation of documents, 1619
    research trends, 1619
    retrieval status value, 1633–1634
    semantic web, 1619
F-value, 419–420

G

Gabor-based features, 4424
Gallery of the Serbian Academy of Science and
    Arts, 4134
Gallica, 1604
Game Making Interes Group, 1641
Games and gaming
    game, definition of, 1636–1637
    in library
        academic libraries, 1639–1640
        ALA, GameRT, 1637
        benefits, 1637
        collections, 1637
        computer and console games, 1636–1637
        as cultural significance, 1637
        digital preservation, 1640
        for instructional purposes, 1641
        for outreach purposes, 1640–1641
        publc libraries, 1638
        school libraries, 1638–1639

tabletop games, 1637
video games, 1637
Games and Gaming Round Table (GameRT),
    1637
Game theory, 1198
Garfield, Eugene, 502–503, 506
Gary Klein's sensemaking, 4116–4117
Gateway page, 4035
Gaussian distribution, 494
Gay, Lesbian, Bisexual Transgender (GLBT)
    Historical Society, 4760
Gaylord Award, 2777
Gender and sexuality archives
    Cornell Human Sexuality Project, 4760
    GBLT historical society, 4760
    Kinsey Institute, 4760
    Lesbian Herstory Archives, 4760
    National Gay & Lesbian Archives, 4760–4761
Genealogical Library, 1649
Genealogical literature
    compiled sources, 1651–1652
        biographies, 1652, 1654
        family histories and genealogies, 1654,
            1656
        local histories, 1656
        pedigree chart, 1656
        Query services, 1656
        society and association resources, 1656
    definitions, 1644
    genealogical research
        classification and evaluation of, 1650–1651
        steps in, 1650
    genealogy, interest in, 1644
    history
        antiquity, 1645
        genealogical research, 1646
        historical associations, 1645
        Internet and digitization, 1646–1648
        modern genealogy, 1646
        new genealogy, characteristics of, 1646
        record keeping, 1645
        scientific genealogy, 1645–1646
    library catalogs and classification, use of,
        1649
    news and networking sources, 1657, 1660
    original sources, 1653–1654, 1656–1659
    periodical sources, 1657
        non-society periodicals, 1659
        periodical indexes, 1660
        society periodicals, 1659
    reference tools, 1655–1656, 1659
    users of, 1648–1649
Gene ontology, 4087
General Archives of the Nation (AGN), 3096
General comparative research methodology,
    2407
General Information Program (PGI), 2312,
    4656–4657
General International Standard Archival
    Description (ISAD-G), 1366, 1593
Generality (G), 3945
Generalized Markup Language (GML)
    applications, 3075
    descriptive markup, 3074–3075
Generalized Retrieval and Information
    Processing for Humanities Oriented
    Studies (GRIPHOS), 3179

Generalized systems of order in museum, 1817
General Material Disignation (GMD), 1235
General Research Library, 1697
General-specific-sparse search strategy,
    2213–2214
General State Archives (GSA), 1736
General systems theory, 3514
*The General Theory of Employment, Interest
    and Money*, 647
Generic ontologies, 3457
Generic Record Syntax (GRS), 2186
Genesis, 2068
Genetic Algorithms (GA), 274
Genetic flow line, 2058
Genetic information, 2058
Genetic programming, 274
Gennadius library, 1732
Genocide, 4400
Genocide Institute and Museum, 236–237
Genre
    definition, 1662
*Genreflecting: A Guide to Reading Interests in
    Genre Fiction*, 3856
Genre/form terms, 2856–2864
Genre repertoire, 2504, 2506
Genres
    commercial, 2504
    definition, 1662, 2503
    documents, 2509–2510
        automated classification, 2510–2512
        communication, 2504–2505
        educational genres, 2509
        genre chain, 2504
    environmental impact statements, 2503
    Internet
        business and academic e-mail messages,
            2507
        classifications, 2507–2509
        evolution of, 2506–2507
        information access, 2509
        non-textual documents, 2507
        personal home pages, 2507
        unsolicited commercial e-mail, 2507
        Web communication, 2505–2506
        Weblog/blog, 2507
        World Wide Web, 2505
    journalistic genres, 2504
    learning theories, 1669
    popular literature
        adventure, 3701
        appeal characteristics, 3700
        "chick lit," 3705–3706
        collection arrangement, 3700
        crime fiction, 3701–3702
        cross-genre phenomenon, 3706–3707
        fantasy, 3702
        historical fiction, 3702–3703
        horror, 3703
        narrative nonfiction, 3705
        reading interests, 3706
        romance, 3703–3704
        science fiction, 3704–3705
        slipstream, 3706
        street lit/urban fiction, 3706
        westerns, 3705
    recurrent communicative situations, 2503
    research in linguistics, 1664–1665

Genres (cont'd.)
    research process, 2503
    RGS
        Bakhtin communication, 1663–1664
        Bakhtin's insights, 1664
        Bitzer's notion of "exigence," 1663
        deliberative performances, 1662
        epideictic speeches, 1662
        forensic discourse, 1662
        Miller's insights, 1663
        pragmatic function, 1663
        reconceptualization, 1663
        renovation source, 1663
        speech genre, 1663–1664
        utterance, 1663–1664
    scientific genres, 2503
    social context theories
        activity system theory, 1667–1668
        Bourdieu's insights, 1666–1667
        Engeström definition, 1667–1668
        Giddens' insights, 1666
        Levi-Straussian structuralism, 1666
        linguistic habitus, 1667
        rhetorical and structuration theories, 1666
        socialized subjectivity, 1666
        structure and agency relationship,
            1665–1666
    vs. text type, 2503
"Gentleman's agreement," 90
GeoDA, 1676
Geodata Analysis and Display Systems (GADS),
    2274
GEO-DATA Explorer (GEODE), 2155
Geoexploration systems, 1677–1678
GeoFusion, 1677
Geographia Generalis, 1685
Geographica, 1683–1684
Geographic information system (GIS), 555,
    2155, 2274, 2402
    applications, 1677–1678
    bibliography and additional resources
        books, 1678–1679
        conferences, 1680–1681
        dictionaries, 1681
        GIS Day, 1678
        journals and magazines, 1679–1680
        organizations, 1680
    definitions, 1671–1672
    markup languages, 1677
    PPGIS and PGIS, 1672–1673
    professionals, certification of, 1678
    software packages
        Autodesk, 1676
        Bentley Systems, Inc., 1676
        Caliper Corporation, 1676
        ESRI, 1675
        free and open-source packages, 1676
        geoexploration systems, 1677–1678
        IDRISI, 1675–1676
        Intergraph, 1676
        Manifold, 1676
        MapInfo, 1676
    spatial autocorrelation, 1677
    spatial data, 1672, 1678
    spatial thinking
        colleges, 1674
        masters courses, 1674

        schools, 1673–1674
        universities, 1674
        virtual campuses, 1674–1675
    systems vs. science, 1671
    volunteered geographic information, 1673
    Web-based devices, 1672
Geographic resources analysis support system
    (GRASS), 1676
Geographike Syntaxis, 1684
Geographische Zeitschrift, 1687
Geography, 643–644
    definition of, 1683
    Eratosthenes, 1683–1684
    geographical serials, 1688–1689
    Hecataeus, 1683
    Herodotus, 1683
    Homer, 1683
    Mela, Pomponius, 1684
    modern geographers
        Bowman, Isaiah, 1688
        Brunhes, Jean, 1687
        Carpenter, Nathaniel, 1685
        Davis, William Morris, 1688
        Demangeon, Albert, 1687
        explorers, 1684–1685
        Guyot, Arnold Henry, 1686
        Hettner, Alfred, 1687
        Humboldt, Alexander von, 1686
        Huntington, Ellsworth, 1688
        LePlay, Pierre Guillaume Frédéric, 1687
        Mackinder, Halford John, 1687–1688
        Peschel, Oscar, 1687
        Ratzel, Friedrich, 1687
        Ritter, Karl, 1686
        Varenius, 1685
        Vidal de la Blache, Paul, 1687
        von Richthofen, Baron Ferdinand, 1687
    Polo, Marco, 1684
    Ptolemy, 1684
    as science, 1685–1686
    Strabo, 1684
    Thales of Miletus, 1683
    Theophrastes, 1683
    Travels, 1684
Geography markup language, 1677
Geography Network, 1673
Geological Museum of Vietnam, 4915
Geoponica, 1400
George Cunha and Susan Swartzburg Award,
    332
George Meany Memorial Archives, 4761
George Padmore Research Library, 3324
George Washington University (GWU)'s pro-
    gram, 3218
Georgia Archives Building, 4389
Georgia Historical Society (GHS), 1779
Georgia Library Association, 920
Georgia library learning online (GALILEO),
    1877
Georgia Public Library Service (GPLS), 4397
Georgia State University (GSU), 3655
Georgia Virtual History Project, 5027
Geospatial interoperability framework, 3311
Geostationary satellites, 4430
GeoWeb, 1677
German Association of Factory Libraries,
    1697

German, Austrian and Swiss Consortia Organi-
    zation (GASCO), 2826, 2829
German hand binding, 545
German Harvest automated Retrieval and Direc-
    tory (GERHARD), 4789
German illumination
    in fifteenth and sixteenth centuries, 1951
    Gothic period, 1950
    Romanesque period, 1948–1949
German ISKO Chapter, 2496
German Library Association, 1699
German National Library, 1262, 3329
German–North American Resources Partnership
    (GNARP), 790
German Popular Stories, 854
German Research Foundation, 1695
German Society of Information, 1699
Germany
    after World War II, 1693
    archives and archival science
        archival pedagogic/user education, 1703
        corporate archives, 1701
        digital archival collections and finding aids,
            1702
        education, 1702
        electronic records, 1703
        film and audiovisual archives, 1701
        legislation, 1699
        literary archives, 1701
        local archives, 1700–1701
        national archives and services, 1699–1700
        preservation and conservation, 1703
        private archives, 1701–1702
        professional associations, 1702–1703
        religious archives, 1701
        school and university archives, 1701
        state archives, 1700
    EUROPEANA, 1708
    libraries
        academic and research libraries,
            1695–1696
        BAM-Portal, 1708
        digital library collections and services,
            1694, 1698
        factory libraries, 1697
        legislation, 1694
        levels of service, 1694
        LIS education, 1698–1699
        national library and information services,
            1694–1695
        professional associations, 1699
        public libraries, 1696–1697
        research libraries, 1693
        school libraries, 1698
        special libraries, 1698
        special subject libraries, 1695
    map of, 1693–1694
    museums
        art museums and galleries, 1704
        digital museum exhibits and services, 1706
        education, 1707
        historical, anthropological, and
            archeological museums, 1705–1706
        museology as discipline and profession,
            1706–1707
        national museums, 1703–1704
        professional associations, 1707

science and natural history museums, 1704–1705
  standards and guidelines, 1707
  visitor research, 1707
  volunteers, 1707
  zoos and botanical gardens, 1706
poets and thinkers, 1693
political systems, 1693
population, 1693
Provenance Research, 1708
Gestalt psychology, 2679, 2685
Gettier problem, 1455
  knowledge, 2616
Getty End-User Online Searching Project, 296–298, 1911, 1914
Getty Research Institute Research Library Catalog, 250
Getty Thesaurus of Geographic Names® (TGN), 1079
Ghana Library Board, 3324
Ghetto Fighters' House-Itzhak Katzenelson Jewish Resistance Heritage Museum, 2552
Ghettoization, 2072, 4208
Giddens' structuration theory, 2506
GIF format, 1311
Gift books, 3824
Giles Scholarship, 81
g-index, 2370
Glagolitic script, 1121–1122
Glastonbury catalog, 747
Gleaning Resource Descriptions from Dialects of Languages (GRDDL), 4084
Glenerin Declaration, 2158
Global Biodiversity Information Facility (GBIF), 3308, 3313
Global Earth Observation System of Systems (GEOSS), 555
Global Open Knowledgebase (GOKb) project
  core features, 1711
  data model and elements, 1712
  founding partners, 1710
  governing body, 1710
  initial planning phases, 1710
  KB+, 1710–1711
  Kuali OLE and Jisc, 1710–1711
  method of access
    API, 1713
    co-reference service, 1713–1714
    OpenRefine, 1713
    Web application, 1712–1713
  phase 1 grant funding period, 1710
  preview period, 1710
  title record in, 1712
Global Partnership Program (GPP), 86
Global Resources Agriculture Partnership–Project Ceres, 790
Global Resources Law Partnership, 790
Global Resources Network (GRN), 372
Global Resources Program (GRP), 372
Glyphs, 4664
Glyptothek, 3153
GML, see Generalized Markup Language
Goals, Operators, Methods, and Selections model (GOMS), 1897
GOBI Library Solutions, 343
Goblin Threat, 1641
Goeldi Museum, 614

Goguen, Joseph, 2054–2055
Golden Gamers Group, 1638
Gold-tooled bindings, 544
  England, 546
  France, 546
  Italy, 543, 545
Good old-fashioned artificial intelligence (GOFAI), 4088
Google, 2368, 2523, 2854, 3471, 3655, 4047, 4050–4051, 4461, 5028
Google Books, 1760–1761
Google Library Project, 1757
Google PageRank, 4039–4040
Google Patents, 3570
"Google Rule," 2707
Google Scholar (GS), 489, 923, 925, 1878, 2368, 5027
Google SketchUp, 1678
Google Uncle Sam, 1553
Goolatilake, Susantha, 2058
Gopher, 2517
Gordon Scholarship, 81
Goshu Art Gallery, 1504
Gosnell, Charles F., 496, 498
Gothic bindings, 543
Göttliche Ordnung, 1402
Governmentally organized nongovernmental organization (GONGO), 3380
Government documents
  federal publications, 1715–1718
  international publications, 1721–1724
  local documents, 1720–1721
  state publications, 1718–1720
Government Documents Roundtable (GODORT), 1724
Government Information Locator Service (GILS), 1550, 1552
Government Information Security Reform Act, 1556
Government in the Sunshine Act of 1976, 2151
Government of Wales Act 1997, 4734
Government Paperwork Elimination Act (GPRA) of 1998, 1415, 1556
Government Performance and Results Act, 4771
Government Printing Office (GPO), 1549–1550, 2148, 2150, 2156
Government Printing Office Electronic Information Access Enhancement Act of 1993, 1551
GPX model, 5045
Grade 1-1/2 braille code, 563
Graduate Library Institute for Spanish-Speaking Americans, 2703
Graduate Library School (GLS), 2769, 2910–2913, 4280
Grammar syntax, 3062
GRAMMY Foundation, 1579
Grand Mosque's library, 4624
Grant-funded projects, 346–347
Grants
  AFI, 1587
  Carnegie and British Council, 396
  NHPRC, 3315, 3318–3319
  scholarship funds, 880
Granular computing, 2194
Graphical models, 2086–2088
Graphical networks, 2212

Graphical user interface, 1289
Graphic novels, 860
Graphics Communications Association Research Institute (GCARI), 4611
Grassroots organization (GRO), 3380
Grateful Med, 91
Graunt, John, 494
Gray Information Functional Plan, 1746–1747
Gray-level differences histogram, 4423
Great Barrier Reef Marine Park, 391
Great Depression, 3254
Greece
  archival studies, 1739
  audiovisual archives, 1738–1739
  college and university archives, 1738
  digital archival collections and electronic finding aids, 1739
  individual state archives, 1737
  libraries
    academic libraries, 1731–1732
    contemporary libraries, 1728–1729
    digital libraries and institutional repositories, 1732–1733
    history, 1728
    library and information science studies, 1734
    networks, consortia and union catalogs, 1733
    NLG, 1729
    Parliament Library, 1729–1730
    public libraries, 1730
    publishing activities and conferences, 1734
    school libraries, 1730–1731
    special libraries, 1732
  map, 1729
  museums
    from ancient to modern times, 1741–1742
    Benaki Museum, 1744–1745
    Byzantine and Christian Museum, 1744
    developments and concerns, 1742–1743
    National Archaeological Museum, 1743–1744
    National Gallery, 1744
  national archives and services
    Constitution of Greece, 1736
    primary mission, 1736–1737
    Processing of Personal Data, 1736
    protection of personal data, 1736
  professional associations, 1739
  state/provincial and local archives, 1737–1738
Greek Orthodox Patriarchate Museum, 2550
Greek society, 2677–2678
Green archiving, 3473
Grew, Nehemiah, 646
Grey literature
  access and dissemination, 1753–1754
  bibliographic control, 1752–1753
  five periods, 1748
  Gray Information Functional Plan, 1746–1747
  importance
    citation analyses, 1748–1749
    publications in LIS, 1749
  information professionals, 1747
  Luxembourg definition, 1746
  national program, 1747
  open archives, 1751–1752
  research activities, 1754–1755
  typology, 1749–1751

GreyLIT Network, 1553
Grigg Report framework, 111
Grisaille technique, 1949
Grolier's bindings, 543
Gross Domestic Product (GDP), 4497
Gross, E.M., 501, 506
Gross' imposed query model, 5070
Gross national product (GNP), 2256, 2312
Gross, Paul L.K., 501, 506
Group decision support systems (GDSS), 2274
GroupLens recommender system, 3863–3864
Group support systems, 2274
Groupthink, 2097
Grove Art Online, 250
GSLIS scholarships, 3034
Guangdong Science and Technology Museum,
    909
Guggenheim Bilbao Museum, 4332
Guided inquiry approach, 2237
Guided Inquiry Design (GID), 2237
Guide to Canadian Museums and Galleries, 676
Guide to the Study and Use of Reference Books,
    3913
Gulf of Evaluation, 4807
Gutenberg Bible, 1972
Gutenberg, Johannes, 1865–1866
Guyot, Arnold Henry, 1686
Gymnastic exercises, 4743

H

Haar wavelet, 2630
Hackerspaces, 2991–2992
Hague Convention for Choice of Court Agree-
    ments (CCCA), 1271
Hague Conventions, 1349
Haifa Art Museum, 2551
Haifa City Archives, 2554
Haim Attar Museum of Art Ein Harod, 2551
Halftone printing, 1309
Hallmark Art Collection, 1092
Hancock, 2630
Hand binding
    in America, 546–547
    Coptic binding, 542
    Danish bookbinding, 547
    in England, 543, 546
    in France, 544–546
    in Germany, 545
    Gothic styles, 543
    in Holland, 547
    in Italy, 543–545
    Norwegian bookbinders, 548
    romanesque bindings, 542–543
    Scandinavia styles, 547
    in Spain, 545
    in Sweden, 548
    Venetian style, 545
    Western European binding, 542
Handbook of Medical Library Practice, 3037
Handbooks
    Beilstein, 821
    categories, 820
    Gmelin, 821
    Reaxys, 821–822
    spectral atlases and crystallography collec-
        tions, 822

Handle System, 1328, 1330
Handmade paper, 1828, 1834
Hansch analysis, 836
Hanson, J.C.M., 2848
Haramaya University, 1499
Harar Community Museum, 1503
Harar National Museum, 1503–1504
"Hard-of-hearing," 1184
Harmonic Mean (F), 3946
Harvard curriculum, 3217
Harvard Graduate School of Business Adminis-
    tration, 650
Harvard University Library, 1, 11, 2833
Hashomer Hatzair Archive, 2556–2557
HathiTrust
    vs. Authors Guild, 1761
    content, 1758–1759
    copyright review, 1760
    DPN, 1760
    Google, 1760–1761
    government documents, 1760
    long term objectives, 1758
    membership, 1759
    mPach, 1760
    preservation and access, 1758
    print monograph, 1760
    repository certification, 1759
    research center, 1760
    short term objectives, 1758
    Zephir, 1760
HathiTrust Research Center (HTRC), 1760
Hawaii Library Association (HLA), 3548
Hazardous Substances Data Bank (HSDB®), 3343
HCI, *see* Human–computer interaction
Headbands, 539
Headline, 418–419
Health Care Financing Administration (HCFA),
    1873
Healthcare Information Technology Standards
    Panel (HITSP), 89
Health informatics, 85–86
Health information literacy, 3037
Health information seeking, 843
Health Information Technology for Economic
    and Clinical Health (HITECH) Act, 3339
Health Insurance Portability and Accountability
    Act (HIPAA), 1488, 1858, 3342
Health Sciences Librarianship, 3034
Health sciences professionals
    biomedical researchers, 1767–1768
    nurses, 1765–1766
    physicians, 1763–1765
    public health, 1766–1767
Health Services/Technology Assessment Text
    (HSTAT) database, 1767
Hearst Medical Papyrus, 3041
Hearst Museum of Anthropology, 3252
Heating, ventilation, air conditioning (HVAC)
    system, 1351
Hecataeus, 1683
HeinOnline, 2708
Heisei period, 3569
Heliopolitan Recension, 1945
Hellenic Academic Libraries (HEAL), 1733,
    2827
Hellenic Audiovisual Institute Archive,
    1738–1739

Hellenic Literary and Historical Archive, 1738
Hellenism, 1742, 1745
Helping Young People Exel (HYPE)
    Makerspace, 2992
Hembygdmuseum, 3263
Henkle, H.H., 497–498
Henriette Bathily Museum, 4110
Henry the Navigator, 1684–1685
Heraldry, 3768
Heritage Agency of Denmark, 1225
Heritage Forum, 677–678
Heritage Lottery Fund (HLF), 4727
Heritage network, 4329
Herodotus, 1683
Herzl Museum, 2552
Het Groote Tafereel der Dwaashied, 1403
Hettner, Alfred, 1687
Heuristic evaluation, 4798
Heuristic knowledge, 3535
Heuristic search, 271
Hey Diddle Diddle, 856–857
Hiberno-Saxon illumination, 1947
HIBs, *see* Human information behaviors
Hidden Markov Model (HMM), 3351
Hierarchical force, 4208
High Court of Kenya Library, 2593
Higher education, 4791, 4794
Higher Education Act, 2844
Higher Education General Information Survey
    Series, 2844
Higher Institute of Documentation in Tunisia in
    1984, 100
High Level Thesaurus (HILT) projects, 1262,
    4074
High Performance Computing Act of 1991,
    1551–1552
High-Quality Interactive Question-Answering
    (HITIQA) system, 1903
High School Art Program (HSAP), 3244
HighWire Press, 3645
Hill Order formula, 823
H-index, 928–929, 2370
Hippocratic Corpus, 3042
Hirschsprungske Collection, 1226
Hispanics, 2699
HistCite, 933
Histograms, 2629–2630
Histoire du Commerce du Levant au Moyen Age,
    645
Historia animalium, 1816
Historia Naturalis, 3043
Historic Adams House, 4166
Historical archives
    of Crete, 1737
    Epirus (Ioannina), 1737
    Macedonia, 1737
    National and Capodistrian University of Ath-
        ens, 1738
Historical bibliography, 478–468
Historical fiction, 865, 3702–3703
Historical Library, 643
Historical Manuscripts Commission, 183
Historical manuscripts tradition, 184
Historical museum
    in Israel, 2551–2552
    of Serbia, 4135
    Switzerland, 4495

Historical scholarship
  Anabasis of Xenophon (431-355 B.C.), 1787
  diversification, 1789
  Einhard (c. 775-840), 1787
  foundational questions, 1794
  Froissart (c. 1337-1405), 1787
  Herodotus (c. 484-after 424 B.C.), 1787
  Ibn al-Athir (1160-1233), 1787
  Ibn Khaldun (1332-1406), 1787
  Middle Kingdom period of Egypt (21ˢᵗ-18ᵗʰ
      century B.C.), 1787
  nineteenth century, 1786–1788
  primary and secondary sources, 1786
  publications, 1793–1794
  renaissance and enlightenment period,
      1787
  Sallust (86-34 B.C.), 1787
  sources, 1791–1794
  spread of, 1788
  Ssu-ma Chien (145-90 B.C.), 1787
  technology, 1793
  theory, 1789–1791
  Whig theory of history, 1794
Historical societies
  as digital library, 1783–1784
  nationalism, 1780–1781
  organization and mission, 1779–1780
  professionalism and librarianship, 1781–1782
  public history and institutional growth,
      1782–1783
Historical Society of Pennsylvania (HSP),
      1781–1782
Historic and archaeological sites
  buried sites, 1772
  excavation, 1772
  forensic sciences, 1771
  human behavior, 1771
  large-scale excavations, 1773
  "living history" approach, 1778
  "museum exhibit," 1778
  noninvasive tools, 1773
  prehistoric sites, 1772
  saving important sites, 1773–1775
  site preservation, 1776–1777
  tourism, 1777–1778
  underwater sites, 1775–1776
Historic house museums, 1820, 3237
Historic New Orleans Collection, 199
History flow visualization technique, 4988
History museums, 3237
A History of Art Libraries in Canada, 249
History of Libraries
  ancient world, 1796–1797
  change agent, 1808–1809
  diverse populations, 1807
  educator, 1809
  female participation, 1805
  globalization, 1808
  ideology of reading, 1809–1810
  librarianship education, 1804–1805
  medieval era, 1797–1798
  politics and society, 1801–1802
  professionalization and growth, 1802–1807
  Reformation, 1799–1800
  Renaissance, 1798–1799
  repository, 1808
  resource sharing, 1806–1807

  seventeenth and eighteenth centuries, 1800–
      1801
  twentieth century expansion, 1805–1806
History of Rome, 644
History Section (HS), 3909
HITS algorithm, 484
Hjoerring Public Library, 1221
Hobbes, Thomas, 646
Hodges Library, virtual tour, 3440–3441
Hollings–Danforth bill, 1020
Hollow backs, 539
Holon Mediatheque, 2546
Homebound delivery services, 14, 3577
Homeland Security Standards Panel (HSSP), 89
Homer, 1683
Homestead National Monument of America,
      4165
Horizontal portals, 2893
Hornbook, 853
Horror, 3703
Hospital librarians, 3415–3416
Hospital libraries
  administrative and management
    assessment, 1882–1883
      fiscal management, 1881–1882
      human resources, 1882
      marketing, 1882
      planning, 1882
  clinical decisions, 1873
  consumer health trends, 1889–1890
  digital resources, 1888
  EBL, 1887–1888
  educational services, 1878
  EHR and LATCH, 1889
  electronic resources, 1886–1887
  health care organizations
    cooperative networks, participation in,
      1885
    Loansome Doc, 1885–1886
  historical overview, 1870–1871
  information services, 1879
  knowledge management, 1889
  library clientele, 1874–1875
  library staff
    educational requirements, hospital librar-
      ians, 1875–1876
    hospital librarian, role of, 1875
  library standards, 1873–1874
  MEDLINE
    current awareness services, 1880
    interlibrary loan and document delivery,
      1880
    library collections, online access to, 1881
    outsourcing, 1881
  mission of, 1871
  organizational contributions
    CML, 1884
    customized services, 1883
    decision makers, 1883–1884
    health literacy, 1884–1885
    Internet access, 1883
  outreach, educational role in, 1888
  reference, 1879
  role of, 1871–1872
  services
    bibliographic information, access to,
      1877–1878

  circulation, 1877
  collection development, 1876–1877
  library collection, access to, 1877
  technical service, 1876
social networking technologies, 1887
types
  community hospital library, 1872
  nursing libraries, 1873
  specialty hospital library, 1872–1873
  teaching hospital library, 1872
value-added services, 1888–1889
HotBot, 2522
Hotline, 3652
House museums, 4165–4166
HTML, *see* Hypertext markup language
HTRC, *see* HathiTrust Research Center
Huang Ti Nei Ching, 3042
Hubert, Robert, 4716
Hugh C. Atkinson Memorial Award, 2777
Hulme, E. Wyndham, 496, 498, 500
*Human Behavior and the Principle of Least
    Effort*, 502
Human-Centered Design Processes for Interac-
    tive Systems, 4808
Human–computer interaction (HCI), 2079,
    2272, 4115–4116, 4804, 4851–4852
  information retrieval research
    applications, tools and techniques, 1902
    Bates's cascade of interaction model,
      1899–1900
    Belkin's episode model, 1897–1899
    conferences, 1904
    history, 1895–1897
    Ingwersen's cognitive IR theory, 1897
    institutions, 1904
    Lin's MISE model, 1900–1901
    methodologies, validity and reliability of,
      1903–1904
    non-performance measures, 1903
    organizations, 1904
    performance measures, 1902–1903
    user-centered studies, design implications,
      1901
    workshops, 1904
  sense-making, 4113–4121
Human development index (HDI), 2312
Human genome epidemiology (HuGE), 1767
Human information behaviors (HIBs), 3407,
    4114, 4121
Human intelligence, 269
Humanism libraries
  England, 3952
  Germanies, 3952–3954
  Italy, 3948–3950
Humanities
  definition, 1909–1910
  primary literature, 1910–1911
    access to, 1911–1912
    characteristics, 1911
    digital literature, 1911–1913
    extent of use, 1911
    sources, 1911
  scholar's workflow, information seeking and
    use, 1914–1915
  secondary literature
    age, 1913
    characteristics, 1913

Humanities (cont'd.)
  secondary literature (cont'd.)
    digital literature, 1914
    formats, 1913
    identification and location, 1914
    language, 1913–1914
  user studies, 1910
The Humanities, 1909
Humanities Advanced Technology and Informa-
    tion Institute (HATII), 4738
Humanities and Social Sciences Federation of
    Canada (HSSFC), 4896
Humanities computing, 1286, 1288–1291, 1293,
    4565
Human-like language processing, 3346
Human needs theory, 2115–2116
Human relations approach, 3513
Human Rights Archives and Documentation
    Program (HRADP), 790
Humboldt, Alexander von, 1686
Hunefer Papyrus, 1946
Hungarian Electronic Library, 1923
Hungarian National Bibliography, 1921
Hungary, 1931–1932
  archives and archival science
    archivists and records managers, education
        for, 1926–1927
    college and university archives, 1925–1926
    corporate and religious, 1926
    as discipline and profession, 1926
    electronic documents, 1927
    film and audiovisual archives, 1926
    historical societies, 1926
    legislation, 1925
    manuscript repositories, 1926
    national archives and services, 1925
    preservation of documents, 1927
    professional associations, 1927
  library and information professions
    academic and research libraries, 1922
    digital library collections and services,
        1923–1924
    education for LIS, 1925
    legislation, 1920–1921
    LIS as discipline and profession,
        1924–1925
    National Library, 1921–1922
    professional associations, 1925
    public libraries, 1923
    school libraries, 1923
    special libraries, 1923
  literacy, history of, 1917–1920
  Map of, 1917–1918
  museums
    art museums and galleries, 1928
    current priorities, 1931
    digital museum exhibits and services, 1930
    as discipline and profession, 1930–1931
    education, 1931
    historical, anthropological, and archaeolog-
        ical museums, 1929–1930
    laws, 1927
    National Museum, 1927–1928
    professional associations, 1931
    religiously affiliated museums, 1929
    science and natural history museums, 1929
    zoos and botanical gardens, 1930

Huntington, Ellsworth, 1688
Hunt Library Makerspace, 2992
Husbandry and Trade Improved, 1403
Hybridization, 4293–4294
Hybrid-mobile robots, 275
Hyper-book, 5068
HyperCard; *see also* Hypertext and hypercard
  accessibility levels, 1942
  advanced features, 1943
  Atkinson, Bill, 1940–1941
  basics, 1941
  graphics, 1942–1943
  hypermedia interface, 1943
  HyperTalk, 1943
  Message box, 1942
  navigational AIDS, 1941–1942
  stack, 1941
  text editing, 1942
Hyperlink-based data discovery, 2940
Hypertext and hypercard, 1290
  academic and corporate projects
    BioQUEST, 1938
    hyperties, 1938
    intermedia, 1938
    Jefferson notebook, 1938
    NoteCards, 1938
    Project Emperor-1, 1938
    Project Perseus, 1938
    SuperBook, 1939
  Apple II Software, 1939
  definition, 1935–1936
  history
    Bush, Vannevar, 1936–1937
    Engelbart, Douglas, 1937
    Kay, Alan, 1937–1938
    Nelson, Theodor Holm, 1937
    Wells, H.G., 1936
  Macintosh software, 1940
  MS-DOS Software, 1939–1940
Hypertext markup language (HTML), 1367,
    1416, 1677, 2343, 2986, 3072, 3075,
    4041–4042, 5025, 5029–5030
  Unicode Standard, 4667
HyperText Transfer Protocol (HTTP),
    2183
Hypnerotomachia Poliphili, 1973

I

IAS, *see* Interdisciplinary and area studies
iBooks, 4055
Iceland Library Consortium, 2825
Ichkeul National Park, 4638
ICONCLASS, 1079–1080
Iconclass, 4412
Icon formats, 1177
ICT Development Index (IDI), 1282
Ideal ethics, 1473
Identifiers, 3292–3293
Identity links, 2940
Identity Management Standards Panel (IDSP),
    89
I.D.F. & Defense Establishment Archives,
    2553–2554
IDRISI, 1675–1676
IFLA, *see* International Federation of Library
    Associations and institutions

IFLA-CDNL Alliance for Bibliographic Stan-
    dards (ICABS), 451
IFLA FRSAR working group, 1606–1609
IFLA/UNESCO Public Library Manifesto and
    Guidelines, 3781–3783
Iliad, 644
Illuminated bindings, 541
Illumination
  ancient Egypt
    Book of the Dead, 1945–1946
    Heliopolitan Recension, 1945
    Hunefer Papyrus, 1946
    Papyrus of Ani, 1945
  Byzantine art, 1946–1947
  Carolingian art, 1947–1948
  in color, 1945
  definition, 1945
  England
    Gothic period, 1950
    Romanesque period, 1948
  France
    in fifteenth century, 1951
    Gothic period, 1949
    Romanesque period, 1948
  Germany
    in fifteenth and sixteenth centuries, 1951
    Gothic period, 1950
    Romanesque period, 1948–1949
  Greco-Roman period, 1946
  Hiberno-Saxon art, 1947
  Islam (*see* Islamic illumination)
  Italy
    in fifteenth century, 1951
    Gothic period, 1950
    Romanesque period, 1949
  Low Countries
    in fifteenth century, 1951
    Gothic period, 1949–1950
    Romanesque period, 1948
  meaning, 1945
  Mogul miniatures (1525-1707), 1956–1957
  Ottonian, 1948
  Persian illumination (1502-1736), 1955–1956
  Spain, Romanesque period, 1948
  Turkish illumination (1451-1900), 1956
Illustrated books, 855–856
Image indexing, *see* Still image indexing
Imageline project, 250
Image processing, 275
Imaginary audience, 5060
Immediacy index, 928
Immigrant child mediators (ICMs), 2126
Immigration, 2065
  museum, 3245
  records, 1658
Impact factor (IF), 2370
ImpactStory, 45
Imperial Library Act, 1993
Imperial Museum, Campo de Santana,
    613–614
Imperial War Museum, 4719
Implicit learning, 2678
Imposed query, 5070
Improvisation, 3531
InChIs™, 824–825
Incised leather, 540
inCite, 400

Incunabula, 3820
  American libraries, collections in, 1974
  Catholicon, 1972
  *Das Buch der Chroniken or Liber
    Chronicarum*, 1973
  De evangelica praeparatione, 1973
  definition, 1966–1968
  European libraries, collections in, 1973–1974
  extant incunabula, 1971
  Gutenberg Bible, 1972
  Hypnerotomachia Poliphili, 1973
  Mainz Psalter, 1972
  The Recuyell of the Histories of Troy, 1973
  reference works
    *Annales typographici ab artis inventae
     origine ad annum MDCLXIV*, 1968
    *Appendices ad Hain-Copingeri
     Repertorium Bibliographicum*,
     1969–1970
    *British Museum Catalogue of Books
     Printed in the Fifteenth Century*, 1970
    *The Printers and Publishers of the XVth
     Century With a List of Their Works*,
     1969
    Repterorium Bibliographicum, 1968–1969
    *Supplement to Hain's Repertorium
     Bibliographicum*, 1969
    Subiaco Lactantius, 1973
  typographical detectives, 1971–1972
Independent Librarians' Exchange Section, 376
Independent Media Arts Preservation (IMAP),
  1568
Independent museums, in United Kingdom,
  4721–4722
Independent Television Authority (ITA), 1566
Index, 3470–3471, 4978–4982
*The Index-Catalogue of the Library of the Sur-
  geon-General's Office*, 758
Indexer, 2519
*The Indexer: The International Journal of
  Indexing*, 445
Indexing
  and abstracting services, 817–820
    chemical abstracts, 818
    Inspec and compendex, 819
    MEDLINE, 819–820
    Web of science, 818–819
  automatic indexing, 1987–1988
  back-of-the-book index (*see* Book indexing)
  consistency of, 1987
  cross-references, syndetic structure, 1980
  disciplines related to, 1982–1983
  elements, 1978–1979
  history of, 1983–1984
  literature, 1981
  locators, 1978–1982
  mission-oriented indexing, 1987
  occupational home economics, 1986–1987
  open *vs.* closed system, 440, 1979
  semantic web, 1988
  site indexes, 1978
  subheadings, 1979
  theory of, 1984–1985
  thesauri, 1985–1986
  vogue words, 1980
Indexing Books, 443
Index Medicus, 3471

India
  academic and research libraries
    college libraries, 1997–1998
    higher education sector, 1997
    public libraries, 1998–2001
    school libraries, 2001–2002
    special libraries, 2002–2004
    university libraries, 1998
  archives and archival science
    archival science, discipline and profession,
     2015
    Association of Indian Archivists, 2016
    documents preservation, 2016
    education, archivists and records managers,
     2015
    electronic records, archival documents,
     2016
    national archives and services, 2012–2015
    professional associations, 2015–2016
  digital library collections and services,
    2004–2006
  discipline and profession
    information science, 2006–2007
    librarianship, 2007
    museology, 2025
  education for LIS, 2007–2009
  emerging new India, 1993
  geography and population, 1992
  government, 1992
  history of, 1992–1993
  library legislation
    post-independence period (1947–2000),
     1993–1994
    pre-independence period, 1993
    twenty-first century, 1994
  museums and museology
    contemporary issues, 2027–2028
    digital museum exhibits and services, 2025
    education, curatorship and museum admin-
     istration, 2025–2027
    historical, anthropological and archaeolog-
     ical museums, 2022
    history, 2016–2017
    legislation, 2017–2018
    major art museums and galleries,
     2019–2020
    National Museums, 2018–2019
    National Parks, 2024–2025
    science and natural history museums,
     2020–2022
    strengthening and modernization of, 2019
    surveys, 2022–2023
    zoos, 2023–2024
  National Library and Information Services
    (*see* National Library and Information
    Services)
  professional associations, 2010–2011
Indian Association of Special Libraries and
  Information Centres (IASLIC), 2011
Indian Association of Teachers of Library and
  Information Science (IATLIS), 2008
Indiana University Digital Library Program,
  3285
Indian Copyright Act, 1993
Indian Council of Medical Research (ICMR),
  2002
Indian ISKO Chapter, 2498

Indian National Digital Library in Engineering
  Sciences and Technology (INDEST)
  Consortium, 2005
Indigenous cultural and intellectual property
  (ICIP), 2037
Indigenous Knowledge Centres (IKCs), 2035
Indigenous knowledge systems (IKS), 2133
Indigenous librarianship
  education, 2042
  methodology, 2031–2032
  peoples and libraries (*see* Indigenous peoples
    and libraries)
  professional associations, 2042–2043
  research, 2041–2042
  terminology, 2032
Indigenous museums, 3238
Indigenous Nations Library Program (INLP),
  2033
Indigenous peoples and libraries
  Aotearoa/New Zealand, 2036
  Australia, 2035–2036
  Canada, 2033–2035
  cultures and communities, 2032
  digital divide, 2038–2039
  equitable access, 2037
  ICIP rights, 2040–2041
  ICTs, 2038
  indigenous knowledge organization, 2040
  literacy, 2039–2040
  perennial funding challenges, 2037
  protocols, 2041
  and their intersections, 2036–2037
  United States, 2032–2033
  universal access, 2039
  virtual repatriation, 2041
Indira Gandhi National Centre for the Arts
  (IGNCA), 2015
Indirect instructions, 3914
Individuals with Disabilities Education Act
  (IDEA), 3843
Inductive justification, 1457
Inductive statistics, 494–495
Industrial Property Act (Chapter 509), 2594
Industrial Revolution, 597
Industry information, 637–638
Inferential justification, 1457–1458
Influence diagrams, 1204–1205
InfoEyes, 17
Information, 3106
  aboutness and relevance, 3613
  communicatory/semiotic definitions of
    Bateson, Gregory, 2051
    Brookes, B.C., 2051
    Losee, Robert, 2052
    Madden, A.D., 2051
    Nauta, Doede, 2051–2052
  cybernetics, 2050
  deconstruction
    Day, Ronald, 2059
    Frohmann, Bernd, 2059–2060
    Furner, Jonathan, 2060
  definitions
    epistemic family, 3613
    semiotic family, 3612–3613
    sociocognitive family, 3613
  DIKW, 2049, 2059
  as event, 2052

Information (cont'd.)
  human–information interaction, 3613–3614
  information-as-message, 3613
  kinesthetic and visual feedback, 2050
  knowledge-as-message, 3613
  multi-type definitions
    Bates, Marcia J., 2057–2058
    Beynon-Davies, Paul, 2058–2059
    Buckland, Michael, 2057
    Dervin, Brenda, 2056–2057
    Goonatilake's flow lines, 2058
    MacKay, Donald, 2056
  philosophy of, 3610
  Popper, Karl, 2055–2056
  propositional definitions
    Derr, Richard, 2052–2053
    Dretske, Fred, 2053
    Fox, Christopher, 2053
  resources, 3613
  Shannon's ideas, impact of, 2049–2051
    communication engineering, 2051
    deracinated definition, 2049
    information transmission, calculation of,
      2050–2051
    mathematical and engineering theory, 2050
    technical revolution(s), 2049
  social definitions
    Cornelius, Ian, 2054
    Goguen, Joseph, 2054–2055
    idiographic approach, 2054
    nomothetic approach, 2054
  structural definitions, 2053–2054
Information Access Alliance (IAA), 345,
  366–367
Informational books, children, 867–868
Informational occupations, 2257–2260
Informational semantics, *see* Semantic
  information
Information and communication technologies
  (ICTs), 2038, 2132–2133, 2141–2142,
  2253, 2304, 4212–4216, 4497, 5016
  diasporic information sources, 2125
  learning and information seeking, 2752,
    2759–2760
Information–and Intelligent Systems (IIS), 2217
Information and Knowledge Management Soci-
  ety (iKMS), 2449
Information and Learning Commons, 2794
Information and Library Network (INLIBNET),
  2005
Information and Misinformation, 2053
Information and referral (I&R) services,
  1029–1030
Information arts
  definition, 2064–2065
  flow diagram, 2067
  formalism *vs.* culturalism, 2071
  information society, 2065–2067
  in museums, 2071–2073
  practice and production cycle, 2067–2071
Information-as-action, 2060
Information-as-evidence, 3616
Information-as-knowledge, 2057
Information-as-particular, 2060
Information-as-process, 2057
Information-as-thing, 2057
Information-as-universal, 2060

Information behavior (IB), 842, 2162, 4848
  Choo's model of information needs, seeking
    and use, 2089, 2091
  definition, 2086, 4459
  Godbold's model, 2092
  graphical models, 2086–2087
  human models, 2086
  information search process, Kuhlthau's model
    of, 2088–2089
  information seeking, generic model, 2087–
    2088
  Ingwersen's cognitive model, 2089–2090
  Johnson's model, 2089–2091
  mathematical models, 2086
  model of trust in health care, 2090–2092
  Niedzwiedzka's model, 2092–2093
  physical models, 2086
  pseudo-mathematical models, 2086
  what happens, models of, 2088
  Wilson's expanded model, 2089–2090
  Wilson's problem-solving model, 2088–2089
Information behavior (IB) research
  history of
    five laws of librarianship, 2075
    Graduate Library School, 2075
    information practice, 2077
    information-related theories and models,
      2076–2077
    information seeking, 2075–2076
    ISIC conferences, 2077
    sensemaking, 2076–2077
    social constructivism, 2077
  information, 2074–2075
  information searching *vs.* information seek-
    ing, 2078
  technology, role of
    catalog innovation, 2078–2079
    digital libraries, 2079
    HCI research, 2079
    information retrieval, 2079
    MARC records, 2078
    online database searching, 2079
    World Wide Web, 2078–2079
  topics of
    children's information needs, 2081
    cognitive authority, 2080
    information genres, 2081
    information grounds concept, 2081
    information seeking, 2080
    information use, 2081
    personal and professional contexts, 2080
    principle of least effort, 2080
Information brokers, 3416
Information business
  advertising, 3007
  cash flow, 3005–3006
  competencies, 3004
  contracts, 3008–3009
  firing, 3008
  hiring, 3007–3008
  investments, 3006–3007
  marketing, 3007
  priorities, 3005
  selling, 3007
  time management, 3004–3005
Information Coding Classification, 2499
Information commons, 4653

Information communication technology (ICT)
  African librarianship, 38
Information crises and crisis information
  asymmetric campaigning, 2094
  auto-feeding, 2096
  destructive information, 2095
  imperfect, incomplete and unreliable inter-
    pretation, 2095
  knowledge, 2095
  machine-to-machine communications, 2094
  management, 2097–2099
  Plato perspective, 2094
  presumptions, 2096
  reductive analysis, 2095
  self-reinforcement, 2096–2097
  sense-making, 2094–2095
  spiraling, 2096
  uncertainty, 2095
Information culture, 3521–3522
Information discovery, 4978
Information dissemination, 4237
Information economy, 2256–2257
Information environments (IEs), 4848
Information ethics (infoethics), 3617, 4658
Information exchange, 2088
Information explosion
  "ExaByte-Counter," 2102
  information age, 2102
  information management and evaluation,
    2102
  information overload, 2103–2104
  information society, 2101–2103
  Lyman and Varian's report, 2101
Information extraction (IE), 3353
Information for All Programme (IFAP), 2308,
  4657
Information gateways, 4653
Information gathering, 3660
Information-generating behavior, 2096
"Information grounds," 2126
Information literacy (IL), 2757–2758, 4199,
  4859–4860
Information Literacy Competency Standards for
  Higher Education, 342
Information management (IM), 2618–2620,
  3521, 3523
  consolidated view
    Big Data, 2107, 2112
    digital convergence, 2107, 2111
    libraries content-creation role, 2107,
      2111–2112
  definition, 2106
  library perspective, 2106, 2110–2111
  organizational perspective
    information life cycle, 2106, 2109
    information resources, 2106–2108
    IT management, 2106, 2109
    organizational information processing,
      2109–2110
  personal perspective, 2106–2107, 2111
  process perspective, 2107
  subsystem, 2195
Information Management Journal, 1856
Information meta-studies, 3611
Information needs and LIS
  constructivist/cognitive view, 2118–2119
  educational need, 2116

historical evolution, 2116–2118
human needs
    Maslow's hierarchy of needs, 2115
    physiological, affective and cognitive, 2115
    political economy research, 2115–2116
information transfer model, 2118
people's personal situations, understanding of, 2116
research, 2120
social constructionist/social view, 2119
Information occupation, 2257–2260
Information policy, 1718
historical development
    Administrative Procedure Act of 1946, 2150
    Articles of Confederation, 2148
    Bill of Rights, 2148–2149, 2152
    Code of Federal Regulations, 2150
    common law rights of Englishmen, 2148
    fair information practices, 2152
    Federal Advisory Committee Act of 1972, 2151
    Federal Register, 2150
    FOI Act, 2150–2152
    Government in the Sunshine Act of 1976, 2151
    Internet and web activity, monitoring of, 2152–2153
    military secrecy directives/regulations, 2151
    National Security Act of 1947, 2151
    NSC, 2151–2152
    Philadelphia convention of 1787, 2149
    Printing Act of 1895, 2150
    printing and publication policy, 2149–2150
    Privacy Act, 2151–2152
    Progressive Movement, 2150
    security classification system, 2151
    state constitutions, 2148
    superintendent, responsibility of, 2150
    Trade Secrets Act, 2152
internal and external policies, impact of, 2148
Library Awareness Program, 2148
literature on, 2154
national information policy, 2158
policy framework, 2156–2157
stakeholders, 2157
in United States
    depository libraries, 2148
    depository library programs, 2156
    electronic government, 2147, 2153–2154, 2158–2159
    FBI's justification, 2148
    government information, public access to, 2154–2156
    government policies, 2147–2148
Information practice, 2077
    evolving conceptualizations, 2163–2164
    implementation, 2166–2167
    information science, 2164–2166
    opportunities and theoretical pathways, 2167–2168
Information producers, 2259
Information professional (IP), 4377–4378
Information Requirements of the Social Sciences (INFROSS) studies, 4246

Information resources management (IRM), 2108, 2619
Information retrieval, 843–844
Information retrieval (IR), 1242, 2239, 2243, 3926
    algorithms, 2221–2222
    Boolean model, 2202–2203
    components
        indexes and query matching, 2201
        text processing, 2200–2201
    definition, 2220
    experiment
        Boolean model, 2173
        experimental approach, 2178
        experimental design and analysis, 2177–2178
        laboratory experiment, 2172
        major information retrieval experiments, 2174–2176
        performance measures, 2173–2174
        research concerns, 2176–2177
        vector space model, 2173
    fuzzy set theory (*see* Fuzzy set theory, information retrieval)
    hybrid models, 2207
    inference network models, 2207
    IRSS (*see* Information Retrieval Support Systems (IRSS))
    language models, 2206–2207
    logistic regression algorithm, 2206
    NLP (*see* Natural language processing)
    Okapi BM-25 algorithm, 2205–2206
    probabilistic retrieval methods
        document retrieval problem, 2204
        higher-level Model 3, 2204
        lower-level Model 0, 2204–2205
        Model 1 system, 2204
        Model 2 system, 2204–2205
    protocols (*see* Information retrieval (IR) protocols)
    query expansion and relevance feedback, 2207–2208
    relevance, 2220–2221
    searching aboutness, 2220
    specification for search, 2220
    systems (*see* Information retrieval (IR) systems)
    testing, 2222–2223
    vector model, 2203–2204
Information retrieval (IR) protocols
    abstract model of, 2181–2182
    access points and indexes, 2182
    bibliographic databases, 2181–2182
    communications protocols, 2182–2183
    interoperability and intersystem, 2186
    IR system, 2181–2182
    query, 2181–2182
    result set and retrieved records, 2181–2182
    SRU
        CQL, 2189
        Editorial Board, 2187
        explain operation, 2187–2189
        HTTP GET request, 2187–2188
        projects and implementations, 2189–2190
        REST approach, 2187
        searchRetrieve operation, 2187–2189
        SOAP, 2187
        SRW and, 2187

Z39.50 protocol, 2983
    chronology of, 2183–2184
    client and server software, 2184
    Init service, 2184–2185
    present service, 2185–2186
    search service, 2185
    ZING project, 2186–2187
Information Retrieval Support Systems (IRSS)
    characteristics of, 2193–2194
    conceptual architecture, 2194–2195
    document-space granulation, 2196
    DRS, 2193
    implementation of
        computer graphics and information visualization, 2195–2196
        expert systems, 2195
        intelligent information agents, 2196
        machine learning and data mining, 2195
        related fields, 2195
    information retrieval support, 2193
    KRS, 2192
    retrieval-result-space granulation, 2196
    RSS, 2192
    term-space granulation, 2196
    user-space granulation, 2196
Information saturation model, 2213
Information scattering
    bibliometric laws, 2210
    Bradford's law of scattering, 2210
    coverage analyses, 2211–2212
    definition, 2210
    explanations for, 2212–2213
    frequency distributions, 2211
    future research challenges, 2214
    informetric laws, 2210
    Lotka's Law, 2210–2211
    network visualizations and analysis, 2212–2213
    search strategies and design, implications for, 2213–2214
    types of, 2211
    Zipf's Law, 2210
"Information school movement," 4114
Information schools (iSchools), 2230
    characteristics of, 2539
    iConference, 2539
    iField, 2538
    motivation, 2537
    origins, 2536–2537
    positioning, 2537–2538
    recognition, 2540
    as transdisciplinary domain, 2538
    vision, 2539–2540
Information science, 2770, 3612
    bibliometrics
        ARIST, 489
        Google boom, 483–485
        interpersonal communication, 489
        IS, map of, 485–488
        L&IS definition, 481–483
        mediators and automation, 483
    characteristics, 2230
    definition, 2216, 2537
    design science (*see* Design science)
    education
        i-Schools, 2230
        Salton model, 2229–2230
        Shera model, 2229

Information science (cont'd.)
 human information behavior
  definition, 2223
  information needs and use, 2223–2224
  information searching, 2225
  information seeking, 2224–2225
  models and theories, 2225–2226
  social and individual question, 2223
 information explosion, problems of,
   2217–2218
 intellectual structure
  author cocitation analysis, 2218–2219
  design question, 2218
  information theory, 2219
  knowledge domains, visualization of,
   2219
  library automation, 2219
  literature people, 2219
  OPACs, 2219
  physical question, 2218
  1959 Proceedings, 2218–2219
  retrieval people, 2219
  social question, 2218
  webometrics, 2219
 International Conference on Scientific Information, 2216
 Memex, 2217
 metric studies, 2226–2228
 National Science Foundation, 2217
 orientations, 2216
 philosophy of, 3611
 scope, 3614
 social and human function, 2218
 VINITI, 2217
Information Science and Automation Division
  (ISAD), 2776, 2966
Information searching, 2225
 vs. information seeking, 2078
 and search models
  Bates' berry-picking approach, 2244
  Belkin's episode model of interaction with
   texts, 2246–2247
  digital libraries, 2240
  domain knowledge, 2243
  Ellis' model of information-seeking behaviors, 2243–2244
  information retrieval systems, 2239, 2243
  Ingwersen and Järvelin's cognitive model,
   2245–2246
  IR knowledge, 2243
  Kuhlthau's ISP model, 2244
  multidimensional model of user-Web interaction, 2248–2249
  online bibliographic retrieval, conceptual
   framework for, 2245
  online databases, 2240
  OPACs, 2240
  Saracevic's stratified interaction model,
   2247
  search strategies, 2240–2242
  search tactics/moves, 2239–2241
  serendipitous information search,
   2244–2245
  system knowledge, 2243
  task complexity and stages, 2242–2243
  usage patterns, 2240, 2242
  Vakkari's task-based IR process, 2245

 Web search engines, 2240
 Xie's planned-situational interactive IR
  model, 2247–2248
 task-based approach (see Task-based information searching)
Information search process (ISP) model, 2076,
  2244, 4529, 5069–5070
 development of, 2232
 educaion, implication for, 2237
 information seeking
  focus formulation, 2235
  personal construct theory, 2234
  principle of uncertainty, corollaries,
   2235–2236
  uncertainty, increase in, 2235
  user's perspective, 2232–2234
  workplace, 2234
 information services and systems, 2236
 meaning, 2232
 students, 4460
Information seeking, 2075–2076, 2078, 2080,
  2224–2225
 strategies, 2241–2242
Information seeking and retrieval (IS&R),
  4880
Information Seeking in Context (ISIC), 2077,
  2163, 4118–4119
Information Seeking in Context (ISIC) conferences, 2117, 2772, 4856
Information seeking process (ISP) model,
  2783–2784
Information sharing, 2759–2760
Information society
 culture, 2262–2264
 economics, 2256–2257
 information, definition of, 2266–2267
 occupational definition, 2257–2260
 quantitative vs. qualitative measures,
   2264–2266
 spatial, 2260–2262
 technological definition
  computer cost, reduction in, 2253
  information grid, 2254
  ISDN systems, 2254
  microelectronics revolution, 2254
  neo-Schumpeterian approach, 2254
  objections, 2254–2255
  techno-economic paradigm, 2254
  telecommunications, computerization of,
   2253
 theoretical knowledge, 2267–2269
Information sources, 2088
Information systems (IS), 2619
 application knowledge, 2275
 and business informatics
  architectural framework, 632
  characteristics of, 631
  IS 2002 undergraduate model curriculum,
   631–632
  MSIS 2000 model curriculum, 631–632
  recommendation for, 631–632
  as science discipline, 631
  study framework, 632–633
  study program, 632–634
 careers
  certification, 701
  experience, 701

 job domains and titles, 699, 702
 jobs by keyword in Monster.com, 699, 703
 occupations, application areas and job title
  domains, 699, 703
Carr's "IT Doesn't Matter" hypothesis, 704
changing technology, effects of, 704
computer engineering, 694
computing science, 694
definition, 694
development knowledge, 2275
education
 M.S. model curriculum, 694–697
 Ph.D. programs, 694
 Schools of Information and Informatics,
  694
 training and continuing education, 696
 undergraduate curriculum, 694
ethical and social issues
 accountability and liability, 2277
 information rights and obligations, 2277
 property rights and obligations, 2277
 quality of life, 2278
 system quality, 2277–2278
ethics
 codes of ethics, 1484–1485
 definition, 1484
 domain scenarios, 1486
 ethical decision making, 1492
 ethical issues, 1486–1487
 ethical theories, 1485–1486
failure (see Information systems (IS) failure)
future organization, 702–703
industry, 696
 consultant organizations, 699
 equipment manufacturers, 697–698
 internal organizations, 698–699
 service providers and outsourcers, 698
 software firms, 698
IT talent challenge, 703–704
LIS, definition of, 693–694
management knowledge, 2275–2276
online library catalogs, 704
origins, 2272–2273
professional associations, 701, 2276
publications, 2276–2277
reference curricula, 630
research firms and consultancies, 2277
social softwares, 704
specialization and job categories, 699–701
strategic use of, 701–703
study programs, 630–631
technology knowledge, 2275
UCD (see User-centered design)
varieties
 decision support systems, 2274
 enterprise systems, 2274–2275
 group support systems, 2274
 management information systems,
  2273–2274
 transaction-processing systems, 2273
Wi-Fi and telecommuting, 704
Information systems (IS) failure
 cognate literatures, 2282–2283
 evolution of, 2281–2282
 interactionist approaches
  exchange perspective, 2286
  sociotechnical perspective, 2286

practitioners, 2287–2288
process approaches, 2286–2287
scale of, 2280–2281
static approaches
  organizational/cultural perspective, 2284–2285
  political perspective, 2285
  technological perspective, 2283–2284
Information technologies (IT), 2253–2255, 2678
competence
  digital literacy, 2307
  expertise, 2307
  incompetence, 2307
  social competence, 2306
  socio-technological information (cyber) competence, 2306–2307
  workplace competency, 2307
information behavior research, role in, 2078–2079
information management, role in, 2106, 2109
records management, 716–717
Information technology (IT) adoption
background
  discontinuities, role of, 2291–2292
  individual/organizational performance, 2290
  information society, 2291
categories
  individuals, 2298–2299
  organizations, 2299
  S-Curve, 2298
innovation decision, types of
  authoritative decision, 2296
  change agents' promotional efforts, 2297
  collective decision, 2296
  communication channels, 2297
  social system, nature of, 2297
  voluntary decision, 2296
perceived attributes of innovation (see Perceived attributes, IT adoption)
Information Technology and Libraries (ITAL), 2777, 2779–2780
Information Technology Association, 1641
Information technology innovation life cycle, 2291
Information technology (IT) literacy
assessment, 2310
connectivism, 2309
information culture literacy, 2308
knowledge sharing, 2309–2310
learning and inquiry, 2309
personal computer, 2303
stages and limitations of
  advanced literacies, 2304
  basic literacy, 2304
  multiliteracies, 2305–2306
  social and workplace literacies, 2305
  visual and media literacies, 2305
technology and academic literacies, 2308–2309
terminology issues, 2308
Information Technology Management Reform Act of 1996, 1551
Information technology project implementation
development, 2313–2314
HDI, 2312

management issues
communication, 2314
cultural, organizational and barriers, 2319–2320
financial resources, 2317
hardware and software options, 2317–2319
human resource concerns, 2315–2317
IFLA general conference, 2315
IT projects, 2314
planning committee, 2314
socioeconomic and political underdevelopment, 2314
operational issues
CD-ROM, 2322–2326
collection development, 2333–2335
interlibrary loan and document delivery, 2331–2333
internet access, 2328–2329
local databases, development and access, 2329–2331
network resources, 2326–2328
online searching, 2320–2322
user sensitization and training issues, 2335–2337
Information technology standards
ANSI, 2343–2344
definition
  by British Standards Institution, 2342
  by ISO, 2341
future, 2349
ISO
  harmonizing national standards, 2346
  ISO/IEC Joint Technical Committee 1, 2346
  library and information services, 2346–2347
  membership categories, 2346
  principal phases, 2346
NISO, 2341
  Architecture Committee, 2343
  current standards, 2345
  expert technical advisory group, 2344
  final approval, 2345
  formulation and implementation of standards, 2345
  Library Standards Alliance, 2345
  supporting organizations, 2345
  Topic Committee, 2343
  work item, 2343
standards-making bodies, 2344–2346
technical standards
  American National Standards Committee Z39, 2341
  benefits of, 2343–2344
  in librarianship, 2348
types
  conceptual standards, 2342
  implementation standard, 2342–2343
  process standard, 2343
  product standard, 2342
W3C, 2347–2348
Information-theoretic epistemology, 3613
Information theory
behavioral economics, 2357
communication
  human communication, 2354
  and mutual information, 2352–2354

compression of information, 2353
equally probable alternatives, 2350–2351
identification, 2357–2358
IEEE Society for Information Theory, 2353
library and information science, 2354
origin, 2350
random variables
  mutual information, 2351–2353
  unpredictability, 2350
  varying probabilities and entropy measure, 2351
scholarly and scientific organizations, 2358
string of characters, entropy of, 2351
surprise, 2357
symbolic utility, 2357
utility theory, 2354–2357
Information transfer model, 2118
Information workers, 2258–2260
Informetrics, 2057, 2210, 2226
citation analysis, 2369–2370
citation databases, 2370–2371
co-citation analysis, 2371
cybermetrics and webometrics, 2372–2373
h-index, 2370
impact factor, 2370
journals, 2369
link analysis, 2369
mapping and visualization, 2372
open access, 2371
research evaluation, 2373
terminology and definition, 2367–2368
theoretical informetrics, 2371–2372
WOS index, 2369
Infoseek, 2521–2522
Ingenta, 3471
IngentaConnect, 3471
Ingwersen–Järvelin integrated cognitive model, 2089–2090, 2245–2246, 4880–4881
INISS Project, 2117
Initiative to Recruit a Diverse Workforce, 371
Inktomi, 2522
Innovation diffusion theory, 2292
Innovation Project, 4263
Innovative culture, 3521–3522
Innovative libraries, 2766
Inorganic Crystal Structure Database (ICSD), 822
INQUERY IR system, 2207
Inquiry-based learning, 558
Inscriptions, 3768
Instant Response Order System (IROS), 409
Institut de presse et des sciences de l'information (IPSI), 4632
Institute for Conservation (ICON), 4739
Institute for Information Literacy (IIL), 346
Institute for International Affairs, 4912
Institute for Museum and Library Services (IMLS), 2033
Institute for Operations Research and Management Science (INFORMS), 2276
Institute for Scientific Information (ISI), 487, 2227
Institute for the History of Contemporary Publishing, 1592
Institute of Accountants, 651
Institute of Certified Records Managers (ICRM), 224, 688, 1855

Institute of Communication Research, 1000

Institute of Developing Economics (IDE) Library, 2565

Institute of Electrical and Electronics Engineers (IEEE), 4263

Institute of Ethiopian Studies Museum, 1501–1503

Institute of Information Scientists (IIS), 4710

Institute of Law Library (ILL), 901–902

Institute of Medicine (IOM), 559

Institute of Museum and Library Services (IMLS), 81, 250, 371, 911, 1030, 4120, 4770

Institute of Nuclear Research (INEGI), 3091

Institute of Scientific and Technical Information of Shanghai (ISTIS), 898–899

Institute of Scientific and Technological Information of China (ISTIC), 892

Institute of West Asian and African Studies Library (IWAASL), 902

Institute on Scholarly Communication, 367

Institutes for Knowledge Organization, 2500

Institut International de Bibliographie (IIB), 4783

Institutional logos, 4961, 4964

Institutional records and archives
  appraisal and selection
    archival, 2380–2381
    records management appraisal, 2380
  archival arrangement and description, 2381–2382
  broader information environment, 2383
  categories, 2378–2379
  conceptual models
    continuum concept, 2379
    life-cycle concept, 2379
  electronic records, challenges
    archives context, 2384–2385
    collaboration, 2385
    deterioration and loss, 2384
    obsolescence, 2384
    poor records management, 2383
    records management context, 2384
  in-house records vs. repositories, 2377
  institutional context, 2377–2378
  integrated management, 2377
  integration, 2382–2383
  research access, 2382
  value of, 2378

Institutional repositories, 1335–1336

Instituto Cultural Peruano Norteamericano (ICPNA), 3608

Instituto Nacional de Antropologia e Historia (INAH), 3245

Institut supérieur de documentation (ISD), 4632

Instructional systems design (ISD), 2307

Intaglio printing, 1867–1868

Intarsia, 541

Integer programming (IP) model
  Branch and Bound algorithms, 1195
  CPLEX, 1196
  product mix decision problem, 1195–1196

Integrated approaches to participatory development (IAPAD), 1672

Integrated library systems (ILS), 409, 725, 3451, 3453, 4141

Integrated library systems report, 2816

Integrated online library systems, 5027

Integrated Postsecondary Education Data Systems, 2844

Integrated services digital network (ISDN), 2254

integrate Rule-Oriented Data System (iRODS), 3000–3001, 3319

Intellectual capital, 2660

Intellectual Capital Management (ICM), 2642

Intellectual freedom
  ALA
    censorship of specific publications, 2387–2389
    challenges and issues, 2395–2396
    free access to materials, 2389–2391
    librarians, 2391–2393
    and libraries, 2393–2395
    profession's response, 2395
  myths, 2387

Intellectual Freedom Action Network, 2392

Intellectual Freedom Committee (IFC), 2387–2388, 2390–2392

Intellectual Freedom Round Table (IFRT), 2392

Intellectual property (IP), 3, 1487, 1490–1491
  SIIA, 4297–4298

Intellectual Property Digital Library (IPDL), 3569

Intellectual property rights (IPR), 1392, 1754

Intellectual technologies, 1472

Intelligence and Security Informatics (ISI)
  civil liberties, and data mining, 2402–2403
  goal of, 2400–2401
  information technology annd national security, 2399–2400
  objective, 2400
  privacy vs. information sharing, 2398–2399
  problems and challenges, 2400
  research framework
    crime types and security concerns, 2401
    KDD technologies, 2401–2402

Intelligent information systems, 276–277

Intelligent Systems, 4084

Interactive science centers, 3219

Interactivity affordance, 1118

Intercat, 3453–3454

Interdisciplinary and area studies (IAS)
  definitions, 209
  drivers, 210–211
  gray literature, 211–212
  humanities, 214–215
  informal information systems, 213–214
  knowledge domain maintenance, 214
  library services and collections, 213
  measures and artifacts, 210
  natural sciences, 215–216
  online searching, 212–213
  primary sources, 211–212
  publication formats, 211
  social sciences, 215

Interface, 4978–4982

Intergovernmental Conference on the Planning of National Documentation, Library and Archive Infrastructures, 4657

Intergovernmental Informatics Program (IIP), 4657

Intergovernmental organizations (IGOs), 1721–1723, 3380
  depositories, 1721–1722
  digital MARC records, 1723
  finding, 1724
  publications offices, 1723
  subscription databases, 1723–1724
  third-party vendors, 1724
  Web information, 1722–1723

Intergraph, 1676

Interlibrary Cooperation and Networking Section (ICAN), 376

Interlibrary loan and document delivery (ILL/DD) services, 372–373, 2331–2333

Interlibrary loans (ILL), 7, 987, 1210, 1213, 1220, 1880, 3914
  department, 416
  law firm librarians, 2718
  zoo and aquarium libraries, 5082

Intermediate medians, 2634

Internal Revenue Service (IRS), 1173, 1464–1465

International Accreditation Forum (IAF), 2344

International Archival Development Fund (FIDA)
  ICA, 2438, 2441

International Association for Professional Art Advisors (IAPAA), 1087

International Association of Law Libraries (IALL), 2716

International Association of Linguistic Sound Archive (IALSA), 2413

International Association of Media and Communication Research (IAMCR), 1001, 1004

International Association of Music Information Centres (IAMIC), 3277

International Association of Music Libraries (IAML), 2413–2414, 3277

International Association of School Librarianship (IASL), 2752, 3999, 4006

International Association of Sound and Audioviual Archives (IASA), 187, 2467, 3278, 4301, 4303
  committees, 2415–2417
  Executive Board, election of, 2414–2415
  foundation and constitution, 2413–2414
  founding meeting, 2414
  IAML/IASA joint annual conferences, 2414
  international cooperation, 2415–2417
  membership, 2417
  mid-term meeting, 2415
  as organization, 2416–2417
  presidents and terms served, list of, 2417
  publications, 2415–2416
  Record Libraries' Commission, 2414
  solo conference, 2415
  stages, qualities and problems, 2413

International Association of Technological University Libraries (IATUL)
  historical development, 2418–2419
  membership, 2419
  objective of, 2418
  organization and activities, 2419–2420
  publications, 2420

International Business Machines (IBM), 1086
The International Catalogue of Scientific Literature, 500
International Centre for the Study of the Preservation and Restoration of Cultural Property (ICCROM), 2432
International Children's Digital Library (ICDL), 4852, 5074
International Classification (IC), 2494
International Coalition of Library Consortia (ICOLC), 9, 2823, 2829
International Coalition on Newspapers (ICON), 790
International Committee for Documentation (CIDOC), 734, 1149
International Committee for Information Retrieval among Examining Offices (ICIREPAT), 3562
International Committee for the Training of Personnel (ICTOP), 3218
International Committee of the Blue Shield (ICBS), 2432, 2438, 2453
International Communication Association (ICA), 1001, 1003
  annual conferences, 2425
  awards
    Applied Research Award, 2426
    B. Aubrey Fisher Mentorship Award, 2426–2427
    ICA Fellows Book Award, 2427
    James W. Carey Urban Communication Grant, 2426
    Outstanding Article Award, 2426
    Outstanding Book Award, 2426
    Steven H. Chaffee Career Achievement Award, 2426
    Young Scholar Award, 2426
  communication associations, collaboration with, 2427
  defined, 2421
  division and interest groups, 2422–2424
  early days, 2421
  fellows, 2425
  governance and administration, 2421
  ICA journal journal citation impact factors, 2427–2428
  membership, 2422, 2425
  presidents, 2422
  publications, 2427
  purpose of, 2421
International Conference on Information Systems (ICIS), 2276
International Conference on Scientific Information, 2216, 2218
International Conference on the History of Records and Archives (I-CHORA), 1864
International Conferences of the Round Table on Archives (CITRA), 2442
International Congress of Medical Librarians (ICML), 2454
International Consumer Protection and Enforcement Network (ICPEN), 782
International Council for Scientific and Technical Information (ICSTI), 2453
International Council of African Museums (AFRICOM), 2606

International Council of Museums (ICOM), 910–911, 1164, 1595, 1821–1822, 2606–2607, 3217–3218, 3233
  activities, 2430, 2435–2436
  cooperative partnerships, 2429, 2431–2432
  core values and vision, 2430–2431
  governance, 2432–2434
  International Committees and Affiliated Organizations, 2430, 2434–2435
  International Museums Office, 2429
  membership, 2430–2431
  mission and purpose, 2430, 3246
  museum and community, 3246
  publications and media, 2436
International Council of Museums (ICOM) Code of Ethics, 4593
International Council of Museums-United States (ICOM-US), 56–57
International Council of Scientific Unions (ICSU), 2452
International Council on Archives (ICA), 222, 688–689, 1423, 1856–1857, 2453, 2467, 3746
  activities, 2442
  archives, definition of, 2440
  Archivum, 2437
  budget, 2442
  cold war (1948-1989), 2438–2439
  conferences, 2443
  Congress, 2442–2443
  cooperation, 2444
  elected officers, 2442
  FIDA, 2438, 2441
  governance, 2441–2442
  ICBS, 2438
  membership, 2440
  mission and values, 2439–2440
  origin, 2437
  project committees and working groups, 2441
  projects, 2443–2444
  publications, 2443
  regional branches and sections, 2438, 2440–2441
International Council on Knowledge Management (ICKM)
  acquisition, knowledge, 2449
  iKMS, 2449
  intellectual capital reporting, 2447–2448
  knowledge development and distribution, 2449
  knowledge identification, 2449
  knowledge measure, 2448–2449
  knowledge use, 2449
  Nonaka/Takeuchi's approach, 2446
  preservation, knowledge, 2449
  Probst/Raub/Romhardt's approach, 2446–2447
  Senge approach, 2446
  Vienna, 2449
International Council on Monuments and Sites (ICOMOS), 2432
International Council on Museums (ICOM), 1742
International Criminal Tribunal for Rwanda (ICTR), 4504
International Digital Publishing Forum, 4055
International Directory of Art Libraries, 250

International DOI Foundation (IDF), 1132, 1326, 1330
International Dunhuang Project (IDP), 627
International Economic Association, 1408
International Electrotechnical Commission (IEC), 88, 2344
International Federation for Documentation, 1535
International Federation for Information Processing (IFIP), 2276
International Federation of Film Archives (FIAF), 187, 1561, 1585
International Federation of Library Associations and Institutions (IFLA), 3, 234–235, 249, 255, 449, 817, 882, 1229–1230, 2040, 2308, 2408, 2672, 3386, 3774, 3998–3999, 4006, 4174, 4658, 5014
  advocacy, 2459
  China
    CSLS, 904
    General Conference in Beijing., 905
    LAC, 890
  conferences, venues, and presidents, 2461–2463
  core values, 2452
  corporate partners, 2452
  governance
    General Assembly, 2454–2455
    Governing Board, 2455
    president, 2454
    Professional Committee, 2455
  headquarters, 2459–2460
  IATUL, 2418
  Internet, 2460
  languages, 2459
  Library Services to People with Special Needs, 3576
  LIS education, 710, 713
  membership, 2451–2452
  mission, 2451
  organization chart, 2455
  PIALA, 3547–3548
  professional units, 2456–2457
    ALP core activities, 2457
    Committee on Copyright and Other Legal Matters, 2457–2458
    divisions, 2455–2456
    FAIFE, 2458
    IFLA-CDNL Alliance for Digital Strategies, 2458–2459
    PAC core activities, 2457
    regional activities, 2456
    sections, 2456
    special interest groups, 2456
  publications, 2460–2461
  regional offices, 2460
  relations with other bodies, 2452–2453
  Science and Technology Libraries Section, 4016
  Ukraine, public libraries in, 4644
  UNIMARC, 2459
  World Library and Information Congress, 2453–2454
International Federation of Television Archives (FIAT/IFTA)
  conferences, 2466
  cultural and academic approach, 2468–2469

International Federation of Television Archives
  (FIAT/IFTA)
(cont'd.)

  digital developments, 2468
  Documentation Commission, 2466
  foundation and constitution, 2465–2466
  international cooperation, 2467
  Media Management Commission, 2468
  menbership, 2467
  Preservation and Migration Commission,
    2468
  Programming and Production Commission,
    2467–2468
  Technical Commission, 2466–2467
  Training Commission, 2466
International Francophone Archival Portal
  (PIAF), 4635
International Health Terminology Standards
  Development Organisation, 4673
International Indigenous Librarians' Forum
  (IILF), 2042
International Indigenous Librarians' Forum
  (IILF)Aboriginal and Torres Strait
  Islander Library and Information
  Resource Network (ATSILIRN), 2043
International Institute for the Conservation of
  Historic and Artistic Works (IIC), 1072
International Institute of Bibliography (IIB),
  1373
International Institute of Documentation (IID),
  4783
International Interior Design Association
  (IIDA), 2845
Internationalized Domain Names (IDNs), 4659
International Knowledge Management Network
  (IKMN), 2645
International librarianship
  definitions, 2404–2405
  foreign librarianship, 2405
  methodology
    interviews, 2407
    literature, 2407
    observation, 2407
    questionnaire surveys, 2407
  Parker's definition, 2404
International Livestock Research Institute
  (ILRI), 1499
Internationally Agreed Numbers for the Identifi-
  cation of Data (INID) codes, 3564
International Medical Informatics Association
  (IMIA), 86
International Medical Information Center
  (IMIC), 2565
International modernism, 2804
International Museums Office, 2429
International Music Information Retrieval Sys-
  tems Evaluation Laboratory (IMIRSEL),
  3272
International Network for the Availability of
  Scientific Publications (INASP), 4505
International Office of Sociological Bibliogra-
  phy, 1373
International oral history movement, 3502
International Organization for Standardization
  (ISO), 88, 441, 443, 1111, 1857, 2452,
  3356

benefits, 2471–2472
conformity assessment, 2473
deliverables, 2475
democratic, 2471
as electronic downloads, 2472
finance, 2473–2474
functions, 2471
globally relevant, 2472
harmonizing national standards, 2346
information and document management, 2480
international consensus, 2471–2472
international partners, 2475–2476
international standardization, 2473
ISO/IEC Joint Technical Committee 1, 2346
ISO/ISO/TC 46 standards
  benefits, 2479
  information and documentation,
    2476–2477
  ISO 3166 and ISO 639, 2477
  market for, 2477–2478
  objectives, 2479
ISO 9001 vs. ISO 14001, 2472
library and information services, 2346–2347
market
  customers, 2478
  impact on, 2478–2479
  suppliers/manufacturers, 2478
market-driven, 2471
membership, 2473
membership categories, 2346
name, 2470
new standards, development of, 2474–2475
nongovernmental organization, 2470
operations, management of, 2473
origin, 2473
in paper form, 2472
principal phases, 2346
regional partners, 2476
standards, need for, 2470–2471
technical committees, 2474
Unicode Standard
  Consortium and ISO 15924, 4667
  ISO/IEC 10646, 4663
  ISO/IEC 2022 technique, 4662–4663
voluntary, 2471
work program, 2472
International organizations, 2404–2405, 2409
International Partnership Among Museums
  (IPAM) program, 3247
International Patent Classification (IPC) codes
  ECLA, 3567
  EPO, 3566–3567
  hierarchy, 3567
  JPO, 3566–3567
  utility model, 3565
International Permanent Exhibition of Publica-
  tions (ISIP), 1125
International Publishers Association (IPA),
  1209, 2453
International Records Management Council
  (IRMC), 1856
International Records Management Trust
  (IRMT), 689–690
  consultancy services, 2492–2493
  development research, 2491–2492
  education and training, 2492
  origins, 2488–2489

teamwork and capacity building, 2491
work, 2490–2491
International Research on Permanent Authentic
  Records in Electronic Systems
  (InterPARES) Project, 122, 1363, 1414
International Semantic Web Conference
  (ISWC), 4087
International Society for Informetrics and
  Scientometrics (ISSI), 2369
International Society for Knowledge Organiza-
  tion (ISKO), 959
  aims and tasks, 2495
  anage-old activity, 2499–2500
  British Chapter, 2497
  French Chapter, 2497
  German Chapter, 2496
  histroical developments, 2496
  Indian Chapter, 2498
  international conferences, 2495–2496
  Italian Chapter, 2496–2497
  knowledge representation, 2499
  logiic, 2495
  methodical knowledge, 2495
  Nordic Chapter, 2498
  North American Chapter, 2498
  organization, 2495
  Polish Chapter, 2497
  science theory, 2495
  Spain Chapter, 2497
  U.S. Chapter, 2498
  Web site, 2499
International Society for Technology in Educa-
  tion (ISTE), 64, 3998
International Standard Archival Authority
  Record (ISAAR), 3751
International Standard Archival Authority
  Record for Corporate Bodies, persons,
  and Families (ISAAR(CPF)), 7
International Standard Bibliographic Descrip-
  tion (ISBD), 451, 2971, 3062
  general structure
    general material designation, 1233–1234
    other title information, 1234
    parallel title, 1234
    statement of responsibility, 1234–1236
    title proper, 1233
  history and recent development
    bibliographic control, 1236
    consolidated ISBD, 1239
    data elements, 1236
    first general review project, 1238
    second general review project, 1238–1239
    shared cataloging projects, 1236
    UBC program, 1237
  IFLA, 1229
  objectives and principles, 1231–1232
  purpose, 1229–1231
  sources of information, 1232–1233
International Standard Book Number (ISBN),
  450, 1235–1236, 1325, 4055
International Standard For Describing Functions, 3751–3752
International Standard for Records Manage-
  ment, 2553
International Standard for the Description of
  Institutions with Archival Holdings
  (ISDIAH), 1432

International Standard Industrial Classification (ISIC), 638
International Standard Name Identifier (ISNI), 3288
International Standard on Records Management ISO 15489
    Australian standard, 2481–2482
    content of, 2482–2483
    evolution of, 2482
    impact of, 2484–2485
    ISO 23310-2006, 2485
    ISO 23081, recordkeeping metadata
        Australian standards, 2483
        content of, 2483–2484
        goal of, 2483
        in research projects, 2483
    role of, 2485
    work process, 2485
International Standard Serial Number (ISSN), 1236, 4139
International Standard Text Code (ISTC) numbering system, 1330
International Telecommunications Union (ITU), 1282, 2344
International Union of Pure and Applied Chemistry (IUPAC), 3642
International Vital Records Handbook, 1658
International Zoo News, 5078–5079
International Zoo Yearbook, 5078
Internation Association of Aquatic and Marine Science Libraries and Information Centers (IAMSLIC), 4016
Internet, 999, 1039, 1180–1181, 2094, 2516, 2627, 5021, 5071–5072
    bookselling, 3986
    cataloging services, 2922
    diasporic communities, 2125
    digital imaging, 1308
    IFLA, 2460
    LCC, 2852, 2854
    museum communities, 3248
    national libraries, 3331–3332
    older adults, 3410
    reading, impact on, 4283–4284
    search tools (see Search engines)
Internet access, 2328–2329
Internet Antipiracy Program, 4298
Internet Architecture Board (IAB), 2344
Internet Archive, 1415
Internet art, 2072
Internet Content Rating Association (ICRA), 782–783
Internet Corporation for Assigned Names and Numbers (ICANN), 780
Internet Engineering Task Force (IETF), 1394, 2344
Internet protocol (IP), 403, 1015, 2631
Internet relay chat (IRC) systems, 1049
Internet service providers (ISPs), 698, 3659–3660
InterPARES
    activities, 2527
    1–2 phase, 2530–2532
    methodology, 2526–2527
    principles, 2527
    products, 2527–2528

third phase, 2532–2533
trust, 2533–2534
Interpolation, 1309
Interstate Commerce Act, 1012
Inter-University Consortium for Political and Social Research (ICPSR), 3484, 4753–4754
Interuniversity Cooperation on Electronic Journals (CIPE), 2827
Interviews, 4530–4531, 4798
An Introduction to the Theory of Statistics, 493
Introduction to Universal Geography, 1685
Invasive Species Information Node (ISIN), 3310
Inventories, 133
Inverted index, 3142
IPC codes, see International Patent Classification codes
IP-specific page delivery, 4035
Iraqi Libraries Association, 100
IRCnet, 1049
IRMT, see International Records Management Trust
iSchools Caucus (iCaucus), 2536–2537, 2539
iSchools organization, 2773
Isidore of Seville, 3044
ISI Web of Science, 2368
ISI Web of Science database, 3906
Islamic Civilisation Museum, 4381
Islamic illumination
    Abbaside period (750-1258)
        Baghdad School, 1953–1954
        Seljuk School (1055-1256), 1954
    early Islamic period, 1952
    Fatimides (909-1171), 1953
    Kufic script, 1952
    Maghribi School, 1952–1953
    Maghribi script, 1952
    Mamelukes, 1953
    miniature painting, 1951
    Mongol period (1258-1500), 1954
    Moorish School (756-1492), 1953
    Mozarabic art, 1953
    Naskh script, 1952
    Nastaliq script, 1952
    styles, 1952
    Taliq script, 1952
    Timuride School (1386-1500)
        Herat, 1954–1955
        Shiraz, 1955
ISO 23950, 2983
ISO/IEC international standard, 2342
Israel
    archives
        archival science as discipline and profession, 2557
        archives law and state archives, 2553
        branch archives, 2553–2554
        municipal archives, 2554
        professional associations, 2557–2558
        professional education, 2557
        public archives, 2554–2557
    libraries
        academic libraries, 2544–2545
        Arab sector, 2547–2549
        historical perspective, 2542–2543
        national library, 2543–2544
        professional education, 2549

public libraries, 2545–2547
school libraries, 2547
special libraries, 2547
    map of, 2542–2543
    museums
        Arab sector, 2552
        archaeological museums, 2551
        art museums, 2551
        historical museums, 2551–2552
        historical perspective, 2549–2550
        holocaust heritage museums, 2552
        in Jerusalem, 2550–2551
        official recognition, 2552–2553
        professional education, 2553
        science and nature museums, 2552
Israel Archive Association (IAA), 2557–2558
Israel Center for Digital Information Services (MALMAD), 2545
Israeli Internet Sites Archive, 2557
Israel Museum, Jerusalem, 2550–2551
Italian binding, 543–545
Italian illumination
    in fifteenth century, 1951
    Gothic period, 1950
    Romanesque period, 1949
Italian ISKO Chapter, 2496–2497
Italian National Forum on Electronic Information Resources (INFER), 2827
ITARAT, 4631
Item-level indexing, 3131
Itinerarium, 4964
Itinerating libraries, 1837
ITN Archive, 1566
ITU-T international standard X.509 certificates, 404

J

Jabotinsky Institute in Israel, 2556
Jacksonville Public Library, 3785–3786
Jagiellonian Library, 3679
Janco-Dada Museum, 2551
JANET, 2825
Jan Merrill-Oldham Professional Development Grant, 332
Japan
    archives, 2576
        academic societies, 2570
        associations and organizations, 2570–2571
        college and university, 2569
        corporate, 2569
        decentralized management, 2567
        education and training, 2571
        local public archives, 2568
        National Archives Law, 2569–2570
        National Archives of Japan, 2567–2569
        private sector archives, 2569
        Public Archives Law, 2569–2570
    libraries
        academic and research libraries, 2562–2564
        digital library collections and services, 2566
        history of, 2560–2561
        legislation, 2562
        LIS education, 2566
        NDL and information services, 2562–2563

Japan (cont'd.)
  libraries (cont'd.)
    professional associations, 2566–2567
    public libraries, 2563–2564
    school libraries, 2564–2565
    special libraries, 2565
  map of, 2560–2561
  museums
    computerization and evaluation of management, 2575
    education and training systems, 2574–2575
    local governments, foundations, and private companies, 2572–2573
    museum law, revision of, 2575–2576
    museum libraries/art libraries, 2574
    national museums, 2571–2572
    organizing exhibitions, 2576
    professional staff, 2574
    societies and associations, 2574
    university museums, 2573–2574
Japan Art Documentation Society (JADS), 255, 2574
Japan Association of Art Museums, 2574
Japan Association of College and University Archives, 2571
Japan Association of National University Libraries (JANUL), 2567
Japan Association of Private Universities Libraries (JAPUL), 2567
Japanese Association of Museums, 2574
Japanese Association of Zoos and Aquariums, 2574
Japanese knowledge creation models, 2621–2622
Japan External Trade Organization (JETRO), 2565
Japan Foundation Information Center (JFIC), 2565
Japan Library Association (JLA), 2564, 2567
Japan Medical Library Association (JMLA), 2567
Japan Patent Office (JPO)
  FI/F-term classification search, 3570
  FI system, 3566–3567
  IPDL, 3569
  PAJ, 3569
Japan School Library Association (JSLA), 2567
Japan Society for Archival Science (JSAS), 2570
Japan Society of Archives Institutions (JSAI), 2570
Japan Special Libraries Association (JSLA), 2567
Java Specification Request (JSR), 2894
Jefferson, Thomas, 2832, 2847–2848
Jenkins Memorial Law Library, 2725–2726
Jeweled bindings, 540, 545
Jewett, Charles C., 760–761, 1844
Jewish National and University Library, 2557
The Jewish National Library, 2544
Jimma Museum, 1503
Jimma University Library, 1499
John Cotton Dana Public Relations Award, 2844–2845
John F. Kennedy University, 3218
John Philip Immroth Memorial Award for Intellectual Freedom, 2392

John Rylands Library, 3046
Johnson's information-seeking model, 2089–2091
John von Neumann Digital Library, 1924
Joint Commission on Accreditation of HealthCare Organizations (JCAHO), 1873
Joint Council of Library Associations of India (JOCLAI), 2007
Joint Information Systems Committee (JISC), 2825, 2897
Joint Technical Symposia (JTS), 4660
Joint-use libraries
  benefits and opportunities, 4159
  definition, 4158
  evaluation and assessment, 4161–4162
  management, organizational models of
    joint school/public libraries, 4160–4161
    university/public joint libraries, 4160
  operational issues, 4159–4160
  political and fiscal motivations, 4158–4159
  public policy, 4162
  replicable models, 4161
  types of, 4158
  world, 4161
Jordanian Library Association, 100
JORTAGRI, 4631
Joshua Roll, 1946
Journal Article Versions (JAV) Technical Working Group, 4897–4899
Journal blogs, 2507
Journal für die reine und angewandte Mathematik, 3026
Journal Impact Factor (IF), 44
Journalistic genres, 2504, 2506–2507
Journal of Archival Organization, 137
Journal of Communication, 2421
Journal of Differential Geometry, 3027
Journal officiel de la république tunisienne (JORT), 4629
Journal of Library Automation (JOLA), 2777
Journal of Library Science in China (JLSC), 904
Journal of Management Information Systems (JMIS), 2649
Journal of Symbolic Logic, 3027
Journal of the American Society for Information Science, 2766
Journal of the London Statistical Society, 1405
Journal of the Medical Library Association (JMLA), 3037
Journal publishing, *see* Book and journal publishing trade
JPEG format, 1311
JPO, *see* Japan Patent Office
JSTOR, 3472–3473, 3728
JSTOR: the Scholarly Journal Archive, 250
Jughead, 2518
Jumpstation, 2519
Justice-as-desert theory, 4219
Justice-as-fairness, 4219

K

Kahun Papyrus, 3041
Kakadu National Park, 391–392
Kansas City Public Library, 3726
Kant, Emmanuel, 1686

Kantian psychology, 2679
Kapenguria Museum, 2606
Karen Blixen Museum, 2605
Karlsruhe Virtual Catalog, 1695
Karl Weick's sensemaking, 4117–4118
Kasteyev Arts Museum, 2587
Kazakhstan, 2588–2589
  administrative units, 2580
  archives and archival science
    access and use, 2586
    archival development plan, 2586
    as discipline and profession, 2586–2587
    history, 2584–2585
    legislation, 2585
    national archive system, 2585
    oblast and municipal archives, 2585
  in early seventeenth century, 2578
  in fifteenth century, 2578
  languages, 2580
  library and information science
    digital library collections and services, 2583
    as discipline and profession, 2583–2584
    history, 2581
    legislation, 2581
    national library and information services, 2581
    public libraries, 2581–2582
    research libraries, 2582
    school libraries, 2583
    special libraries, 2583
    university libraries, 2582–2583
  map of, 2578–2579
  monetary unit, 2580
  museums and museology
    as discipline and profession, 2588
    galleries, zoos, and preserves, 2587–2588
    history of, 2587
    national museums, 2587–2588
  in nineteenth century, 2578–2579
  print publishing, 2580
  during twentieth century, 2579–2580
Kazakhstan Institute of Management, Economics and Strategic Research (KIMEP) Library, 2583
Keayne, Robert, 1839–1840
Keep Commission, 3316
Keeper, 3218
Kellogg-ALISE Information Professions and Education Reform (KALIPER), 708
Kenya
  KNA&DS
    composition, 2600–2601
    cooperation, 2602
    finding aids, 2601–2602
    history, 2598–2600
    legal framework, 2600
    legislation, 2600
    migrated archives, 2601
    personalities contributed to records management, 2602–2603
    repositories, 2601
    training institutions, 2602
  libraries
    academic libraries, 2596
    after independence, 2594
    in colonial period, 2593–2594

education, 2597
High Court of Kenya Library, 2593
legislation, 2594–2595
national library, 2595
in precolonial period, 2593
professional associations, 2597–2598
public libraries, 2595
research libraries, 2596
school libraries, 2597
special libraries, 2596–2597
map of, 2592–2593
NMK
access, preservation, and educational role,
2607
archeological and paleontological sites,
2605–2606
curators and museum administration, education for, 2606
as discipline and profession, 2607
Fort Jesus Museum, 2605
history of, 2603
Karen Blixen Museum, 2605
Lamu Museum, 2605
Lamu World Heritage Site, 2605
legislation, 2603–2604
Nairobi museum, 2604
outstanding personalities, 2607–2608
professional associations, 2606–2607
regional museums, 2604–2605
Kenya Library Association (KLA),
2597–2598
Kenya National Archives and Documentation
Service (KNA&DS)
composition, 2600–2601
cooperation, 2602
finding aids, 2601–2602
history, 2598–2600
legal framework, 2600
legislation, 2600
migrated archives, 2601
personalities contributed to records management, 2602–2603
repositories, 2601
training institutions, 2602
Kenya National Library Service (KNLS), 2594–
2595, 3324
Kerberos authentication service, 402
Kessler, M.M., 503–504, 506
Keyword
consistency, 4034
density, 4033–4034
jacking, 4035
loading, 4035
meta tag, 4035
placement, 4034
spamming, 4034–4035
Keyword AAA Thesaurus, 3889
Keyword and full-text search, 4467
Key Words in Context (KWIC), 2221, 4788
K'han Museum, 2552
Kheel Center, 4761
Khnko-Aper Apor National Children's Library,
230–232
Kibbutz Hadati Archive, 2557
Kibbutz Movement Archives, 2556
King Abd al-Aziz Public Library in Riyadh,
3974, 3976

King Abdulaziz City for Science and Technology (KACST), 2312–2313
King Fahd National Library, 3973–3974
Kirk-Othmer Encyclopedia of Chemical Technology, 816
Klein's sensemaking, 4113
Knapp School Library Manpower Project, 64
KNLS Board Act (Chapter 225), 2594
Knowledge, 2623–2624, 2677
abundant myths, 2683–2684
assets, 2641
behaviorists, 2684
creation and organizational information use
Ba, types of, 2619, 2622–2623
Choo's model, 2620–2623
hermeneutic phenomenology, 2623
information management, 2618–2620
information use environments, Taylor's
model of, 2620
Japanese models, 2621–2622
knowledge assets, 2622
knowledge management, 2618–2620
SECI model, 2619, 2621–2622
dissemination, 2445
economy, 2256
empirical knowledge, 2610
experiential, 2679
explicit and collective, 2679
explicit and individual, 2680
Gestalt psychology, 2685
Gettier counterexamples, 2616
Greek society, 2677–2678
and information, 2618–2619
and information, relationship between, 2051
information searching, 2243
Merleau-Ponty, 2685–2686
modes, 2682–2683
networks
citation networks, 1041–1042
heterogeneous network, 1041
information network, 1042
nonempirical knowledge, 2610
portals, 2893
production, 2256
propositional (see Propositional knowledge)
sharing, 3535–3537
society, 603, 4198
spiral model, 2644
state, 2086
structure, 2051
subject searching, 3423–3424
survival, 2684–2685
tacit and collective, 2680
tacit and individual, 2680–2681
tacit with explicit, 2681–2683
transformation, 2678–2679, 2683
types, 2681–2682
worker, 2645
Knowledge Base and Recommended Practice
(KBART) project, 413
Knowledge-based information (KBI), 1875
Knowledge-based management subsystem,
2195
Knowledge base plus (KB+), 1710–1711
Knowledge discovery from databases (KDD)
technologies, 2401–2402
Knowledge interchange format (KIF), 3458

Knowledge management (KM), 1889, 2445,
2618–2620, 2647–2649, 3521–3522
bibliometric representation, 2662–2663
core knowledge management
centralized database system, 2644
corporate amnesia, 2642–2643
organizational memory, 2643–2644
tacit and explicit knowledge, 2643
valuable knowledge and know-how, 2643
definition of, 2640–2641, 2658–2660
business perspective, 2641
cognitive science/knowledge science perspective, 2641
intellectual capital perspective, 2642
knowledge assets, attributes of, 2641
"people-oriented" definitions, 2642
process/technology perspective,
2641–2642
disciplines, 2641
history and evolution of, 2645–2646,
2657–2658
information professionals, role of, 2646–2647
knowledge processing cycle, 2644–2645
ontologies, 3463
special librarianship, 4354
stages, 2662–2663
best practices, 2660
communities of practice, 2661
content management and taxonomies, 2661
external information, 2662
human and cultural dimensions, recognition of, 2660–2661
information technology, 2660
intellectual capital, 2660
learning organization, 2661
lessons learned, 2660
organization's internal knowledge,
2661–2662
tacit knowledge, 2661
Knowledge management structures (KMS),
2659
Knowledge management systems (KMS)
challenges, 2654–2655
critique, 2650
definition, 2649, 2651
information systems (IS), 2649
librarian, 711
ontological aspects, 2654
roots, 2649–2650
theoretical foundation, 2650–2651
theory, 2651–2652
types
Alavi and Leidner's scheme, 2653–2654
codification vs. personalization, 2652
knowledge residence and level of structure,
2652–2653
umbrella construct, 2655
Knowledge organization classification, 2110
bibliographic library, 960
enumerative classification, 962
faceted classifications, 962
facet structure, 966–968
hierarchical structure, 965–966
history and foundations, 961–962
idea, verbal, and notational plane, 961
integrative levels, 968–969
literary warrant, 962–963

Knowledge organization classification (cont'd.)
bibliographic library (cont'd.)
notation, 969–971
phenomenon-based knowledge organization, 694–695
precoordinated classification, 962
scientific and educational consensus,
963–964
cultural concerns and contexts, 958
field of study, 958
groups of things, 958–959
indexing theories and methods, 960
joint exhaustivity, criterion of, 959
mutual exclusivity, criterion of, 959
organizations, 959–960
terminology, 960
Knowledge organization systems (KOS),
4066–4067
advantages, 2666
ANSI/NISO Z39.19-2005, 2672
BS 8723: structured vocabularies for information retrieval, 2672–2673
classification schemes, 2669–2670
data exchange, emerging standards for
ADL thesaurus protocol, 2670–2671
SKOS, 2671–2672
Zthes, 2671
definition, 2665
IFLA guidelines for multilingual thesauri,
2672
ISO 25964, 2673
name authority lists, 2670
need for, 2665–2666
requirements for, 2670
standards, 2673–2674
structures and services, 1615–1616
subject heading schemes, 2670
thesaurus standards
guidelines, 2666
ISO 2788 and Z39.19, differences between,
2668–2669
national and international standards, 2667
prehistory, 2666
principles, 2668
sector specific standards, 2667
successive updates, 2667–2668
weaknesses in, 2669
Knowledge Quest (KQ), 61
Knowledge representation (KR), 271–272
Knowledge retrieval systems (KRS), 2192
Know Your Copy Rights® Web site, 369
Kolhapur Public Libraries Act, 1993
Kolmogorov complexity, 1035
Kongelige Bibliotek, Copenhagen, 3332
Koninklijke Bibliotheek of the Netherlands, 3322
Konstanz University library, 1696
Korea Institute of Science and Technology
(KIST), 4311
Korean Committee for the Bookstart Movement,
4312
Korean Library Association, 4312
Korean Medical Library Association (KMLA),
3039
Korean War, 1144
Korolenko State Scientific Library in Kharkiv,
4645
Kosmos, 1686

Kovacs Consulting Web site, 3439–3440
Kuali Open Library Environment (Kuali OLE),
1710–1711
Kuhlthau information search model, 2225
Kuhlthau model of information seeking, 4880
Kuhlthau's information search process model,
5069–5070
Kuhlthau's ISP model, 1901, 2118–2119
Kulback-Leibler measure, 2357
Kunstfaggruppen (Denmark), 255
Kyiv-Mohyla Academy, 4646

L

La Asociación de Bibliotecas Nacionales de
Iberoamérica (ABINIA), 3330
Labor archives, 2556, 4761
Labor market, librarians
Fontoura notes, 613
segmentation, 613–614
studies, 613
transformations, 612
La Fontaine, Henri, 4783
La Géographie Humaine, 1687
*La Grande Industrie en France sous Règne de
Louis xiv*, 645
L. A. Mayer Museum, 2551
Lambeth Palace Library (LLP), 457
Lamont Library, 4650
Lamu Museum, 2605
Lamu World Heritage Site, 2605
Land Grant College Act, 19
Landscape bindings, 541
Language searching, 4049
Large aggregation retention schedules,
3893–3894
Large-scale digitization initiative (LSDI), 1335
Last.fm recommender system, 3860
Latent semantic indexing (LSI)
applications, 2695–2696
books titles and authors, 2692
cognitive psychology, 2696
computational challenges, 2695
educational applications, 2696
Henry Ford, 2692–2694
information retrieval and analysis, 2695–2696
issues and limitations, 2695
lexical matching, 2688
mechanics, 2689–2690
reduced dimension vector space
producing, 2691
querying, 2691–2692
semantic space, 2688–2689
term-by-document matrix, 2692–2693
term-document matrix
assembling, 2690
weighting elements, 2690–2691
two-dimensional vector space, 2692–2694
updating, 2695
VSM, 2689–2690
word order, 2695
La Terre, 1686–1687
Latin Americanist Research Resources Project
(LARRP), 791
Latinos
academic libraries, 2701–2702
identity labels, 2699

legislation, 2698
library services, 2699
LIS profession, 2702–2703
public libraries, 2700–2701
school libraries, 2701
in United States, history of, 2698–2699
"Lattice-based" access control systems, *see*
Mandatory access control
Law
characteristics, 2736–2737
librarians, 3415
sources, 2734–2735
users
lawyers, 2744–2745
public, 2746
students, 2745–2746
Law firm libraries
analog skills, 2705
collections, 2708
education, 2708
organization of
catalogers, 2706
electronic services librarians, 2706
embedded librarian, 2706
filer/shelver, 2706
legislative/regulatory librarians, 2706
library assistant, 2706
library director, 2705
research assistants, 2706
research librarians, 2705–2706
research managers, 2705
professional associations, 2708
services and users
collection and library catalog, maintenance
of, 2707–2708
document retrieval and interlibrary loan,
2707
firm intranet and knowledge management
systems, 2707
research desk/triage system, 2707
research projects, 2706–2707
training and orientation, 2707
twenty-first-century challenges, 2708–2709
Law librarianship
law firm libraries
budgeting and planning, 2720
business briefing book preparation, 2718
catalogs, 2718
challenges, 2723–2724
circulation systems, 2722
cite checking, 2719
classification, 2722
CLE provider, credit tracker, 2719
collection development policies, 2721–
2722
collections, 2721
conflict checking, 2719
continuing education, 2723
current awareness services, 2718–2719
customers, users, and owners, 2717–2718
education, 2723
experience and skills, 2723
history, 2723
impact on other units, 2719
interlibrary loan, 2718
organization's goals, 2719
physical arrangement/space, 2720–2721

recent developments, 2719–2720
seating type, 2721
serials, 2721
staffing, 2722–2723
technology, 2720
time, 2720
law school library
collections, 2712–2714
history and development, 2711–2712
librarians, 2714–2715
mission of, 2710
organization and administration, 2711
professional association, 2715–2716
standards and statistics, 2712
twenty-first century roles, 2716
public law libraries
challenges, 2729
collections, 2727–2728
connections and networking, 2729
customers, 2724–2725
facilities, 2728
governance and funding, 2725–2726
services, 2726–2727
staff and education, 2728
technology, 2728–2729
Law of Guidelines and Bases (LDB), 604
Law of Libraries, 4888
Layton, Jeanne, 2393
LC, se Library of Congress
LC/NACO certification, 3293
Leadership and Career Development Program
(LCDP), 370–371
Leaf elements, 5045
Leahy, Emmett, 1851–1853, 1855
Learned society, 4268
Learning and information seeking
behaviorist theory, 2753
cognitive authority, 2759
cognitive theory, 2753
constructivism
cognitive, 2753
Kuhlthau's model, 2753–2754
phenomenographic approach, 2754
sense-making, 2755
situated cognition and learning,
2754–2755
social, 2753–2754
sociocultural perspective, 2755
digital tools, 2759–2760
ICT, 2752, 2759–2760
information practices, 2752, 2755
information sharing, 2759–2760
interconnected dimensions, 2751–2752
language, 2752
learning from information, 2752
information use as text transport, 2758
learning outcomes, 2758
meaningful learning outcomes, 2758–2759
learning information seeking, 2751, 2757
learning tasks, 2756
pedagogical librarianship, 2760
research, 2755
school practice, 2759
social practices, 2752
stakeholders, associations, and institutions,
2752
students' information seeking, 2755–2757

teaching information seeking, 2751
constructivism, 2758
information/library skills, 2757
information literacy, 2757–2758
Learning literacy, 2305
Learning management system (LMS), 6
Learning Object Metadata (LOM), 1395
Leather, 539–540
Lectures in Applied Mathematics, 3028
Lectures on Mathematics in the Life Sciences,
3028
Legal encyclopedias, 2741
Legal Information Preservation Alliance
(LIPA), 2743
Legal newspapers, 2740–2741
Legal periodicals, 2740
Legal system
constitutions and charters, 2734
executive branch, 2735
formats, 2742–2744
judicial branch, 2734–2735
legislative branch, 2734
publishing, 2742
Legisigns, 4098
Legislation, 3372
Leningrad method, 478
LePlay, Pièrre Guillaume Frédéric, 1687
LeRoy C. Merritt Humanitarian Fund,
2392–2393
Letter-by-letter alphabetizing, 442
Lettering, 541
Levi-Straussian structuralism, 1666
Lexical chains, 422
Lexical matching, 2688
Lexical scattering, 2211
Lexicography, 1864
Lexington public library, 2790
Lexis-Nexis, 2708
Liber Chronicarum, 1978–1979
LIBINFO, 1924
LIBNET, 2828
LibQual, 9
LibQUAL+®, 374
Librarianship
education events, 2914–2916
music (*see* Music librarianship)
Librarianship education
South Korea, 4312
Librarians' Internet Index (LII), 2895
Libraries and Knowledge Centre (LKC) model,
2035
Libraries, Archives, and Museums of Pohnpei
(LAMP) Library Association, 3546
Libraries Serving Special Populations Section
(LSSPS), 376
Library 2.0, 4780
Library(ies)
in ancient times, 2762
Australia, 382
buildings, 2765
definition, 2762
functions, 2764–2765
India (*see* India)
medieval libraries, 2762–2763
modern libraries, 2764
in nineteenth century, 2763–2764
number of, 2765–2766

recent developments and twenty-first century,
2766
renaissance and early modern libraries, 2763
Spain (*see* Spain)
zoological parks and aquariums
current status and services, 5081–5083
early libraries, establishment of, 5081
need for, 5080–5081
Library Acquisitions Award, 331
Library Act of 1997, 1124
Library Administration and Management Association (LAMA), 74–75, 2844
The Library Administration Division (LAD)
Advisory Committee for the Library Technol-
ogy Project, 2842
ALA Annual Conferences, 2842
ALA Committee on Organization
recommendations, 2843
report, 2842
BES committees, 2842
Committee on Recruitment, 2842
Friends of Libraries Committee, 2842
LOMS Advisory Committee on USOE Statis-
tics, 2842
mission of, 2841
preexisting ALA groups, 2841
responsibility, 2841–2842
Library Advocacy Now! (LAN!), 683
Library and Archives Canada (LAC), 3303,
3324
Archives of Ontario, 661–662
associations and groups
ACA, 667
ASTED, 665
CARL, 664–665
CCA, 666
CFLA/FCAB, 665
CULC, 666
PTPLC, 665
SCCA, 666
BAnQ, 660
Bibliothèque de l'Université de Montréal, 662
Bibliothèque de l'Université Laval, 662
bibliothèque et archives, 658–660
British North America (1763–1867), 655–656
decentralized federations, 654
development of, 667–668
development, twenty-first century, 658
First Nations, 654–655
Hudson's Bay company (1670-1870), 655
issues and challenges
access, 670
collaboration, 672–673
convergence, 672
copyright, 671
description, 670
digital, 669
government information management,
670–671
human resources, 672
indigenous services and collections, 673
multilingual services, 673
National Planning and Coordination, 671–
672
preservation, 669–670
resource sharing, 671
services for people, disabilities, 673

Library and Archives Canada (LAC) (cont'd.)
Library of Parliament, 661
McGill University Library, 662–663
New France (1605–1763), 655
NRC-CISTI, 660–661
Toronto Public Library, 663
UBC Library, 663–664
University of Alberta Libraries, 663
University of Toronto Library, 664
VPL, 664
World War II, 656–658
Library and Information Association of New
Zealand Aotearoa (LIANZA), 2036,
3372, 3374, 3377–3378
Library and Information Research, 3406
Library and information science (LIS), 1029,
1372, 1516, 2162
definition, 693–694
domain, 2768–2769
emergence, 2771–2773
IM and KM, research on, 2618–2620
United Kingdom, 4709, 4711–4713
Library and Information Service of Western
Australia (LISWA), 2035
Library and information studies (LIS) programs
ALA accreditation, 18–21
Canadian institutions, accreditation of, 19, 21
Library and information system of the 3rd generation (KIS3G) project, 4175–4176
Library and Information Technology Association (LITA)
education, 2780
function statement, 2775
governing structure, 2775–2776
history
early years, 2776–2777
Internet Era, 2777–2778
twenty-first century, 2778–2779
membership, 2775
mission, 2775
outreach, 2780–2781
service, 2780
strategic functions and main programs,
2779–2780
vision, 2775
Library anxiety
antecedents, conceptualization of, 2784–2785
Bostick's LAS, 2784
definition, 2782
history and theoretical basis, 2782–2783
international students, in US institutions,
2784–2785
international studies, 2785
intervention strategies, 2785–2786
ISP model, 2783–2784
Jiao and Onwuegbuzie quantitative studies,
2784
Mellon's grounded theory, 2783
MLAS, 2784
Library Anxiety Scale (LAS), 2782, 2784
Library architecture
Anglo-American model, 2799–2801
and design
aesthetics, display space, and signs,
2792–2793
building program, 2792
construction, 2793

consulting with external experts, 2792
cultural changes, impact of, 2789–2791
enlightenment age, 2798–2799
globalization, 2808
grand library design, 2799
impact on
community, 2792
individual and group work space,
2793–2794
public service areas, 2793
security and building support spaces, 2795
shelving configurations, 2794
specialized collections and service areas,
2794–2795
staff spaces, 2795
teaching, training, and meeting space, 2793
technology support areas, 2795
master planning process, 2792
Open access, 2801–2802
Russian experiments, 2803–2804
Scandinavian model, 2804
spectacular buildings, 2805–2808
technology, impact of, 2788–2789
temple of knowledge, 2802–2803
Library Assistants' Association (LAA),
4709–4710
Library assistantship, 919
Library Association (LA), 4709–4711
LAC, 890, 904
LARK, 2584
LARM, 3125
LLA, 385
PIALA (see Pacific Islands Association of
Libraries and Archives)
of Serbia, 4127–4128
Library Association of Armenia, see Armenian
Library Association
Library Association of Australia (LAA), 385
Library Association of China (LAC), 890, 904
Library Association of Serbia, 4127–4128
Library Association of the Republic of Kazakh-
stan (LARK), 2584
Library Association of the Republic of Moldova
(LARM), 3125
Library automation
information services context
database services providers, 2817–2818
information resources, 2819
information retrieval, 2813
Internet, 2819
online services, 2815
information technology context
computing installation, 2814
microprocessors, 2818
Moore's law, 2815
print on demand, 2817
technological development, 2812
library technical services context
cataloging, 2813, 2815, 2819
cooperative networks, 2814
integrated library systems, 2816–2817
precursors, 2810–2811
societal context
digitized imaging, 2818
information economy, 2813–2815
OSRD report, 2811
virtual revolution, 2816

Library Awareness Program (LAP), 2148, 2390
Library Bill of Rights (LBR), 2387–2389, 3777
Library Binding Institute, 4147
Library Board of Western Australia Act 1951,
381
Library-College concept, 987
Library Company of Philadelphia, 1841,
2847–2848, 4338–4339
Library consortia, in Europe, 2823–2824
in Balkans, 2828
in Belgium, 2824
in Britain, 2825
in Bulgaria, 2829
in Denmark, 2825
in Dutch, 2826
eIFL, 2827–2829
in Estonia, 2828
in Finland, 2824–2825
Flemish language communities, 2826
in France, 2826
in Germany, 2826
in Greece, 2827
in Iberian Peninsula, 2827
in Iceland, 2825
in Ireland, 2825
in Italy, 2824, 2827
in Latvia, 2828
in Lithuania, 2828
meaning, 2822–2823
in Norway, 2825
in Poland, 2828
policies and administrative mechanisms, 2824
in Portugal, 2827
in Romania, 2829
in Slovakia, 2828
in Slovenia, 2824
in Spain, 2824, 2827
special programs, 2824
in Sweden, 2825
in Switzerland, 2824, 2826
in Turkey, 2829
Library Control System (LCS), of Ohio State
University Libraries, 3451–3452
Library cooperation, 2404, 2408
in Britain, 2825
in Denmark, 2825
in Finland, 2824–2825
in Germany, 2826
in Iceland, 2825
in Norway, 2825
in Portugal, 2827
in Slovenia, 2824
in Spain, 2827
special programs, 2824
in Sweden, 2825
in Switzerland, 2826
Library cooperatives, 3920
Library Copyright Alliance (LCA), 345, 369
Library Day, Germany, 1696
Library development, 2405, 2407–2409
Library Electronic Access Project (LEAP),
4644
Library Hi Tech Award, 2778
Library Idea Drop House, 1421
Library Journal, 2699
Library Leadership and Management (LL&M),
2844

Library Leadership and Management Association (LLAMA)
   American Institute of Architects Awards, 2845
   annual conferences, pre-conferences, and institutes, 2841, 2843–2844
   committees, 2841
   Cultural Diversity Grant, 2845
   Diana V. Braddom FRFDS Scholarship, 2845
   discussion groups, 2841
   Diversity Fund, 2845
   division presidents, 2845–2846
   division secretaries/executive directors, 2846
   IIDA Library Interior Design Award, 2845
   John Cotton Dana Public Relations Award, 2844–2845
   LLAMA/YBP Student Writing and Development Award Contest, 2845
   members, 2841
   mission of, 2841
   publications, 2844
   sections, 2841
   Swap and Shop program, 2845
Library legislation
   post-independence period (1947–2000), 1993–1994
   pre-independence period, 1993
   twenty-first century, 1994
Library management systems (LMS), 3066
Library marks and stamps, 3768
Library networks
   definition of, 3920
   U.S. regional library networks (see Regional library networks)
Library of American Broadcasting (LAB), 1563
Library of Congress (LC), 574, 1415, 1818, 2181, 2714, 2768–2769, 2981–2983, 3321, 3329–3330, 3722
   ARL Committee on Automation conference, 2963
   CLR, 2963–2964
   desirability, 2963
   development (1800–2000)
      American librarianship, 2890
      international role, 2890
      library's educational role, 2890–2891
      library's legislative and national roles, 2889–2890
   diversity, 2879
   460 languages, 2879
   legislative library, 2879
   library's mission, 2880
   MARC (see Machine-Readable Cataloging)
   national institution growth
      at 2000, 2889
      acquisition, 2881
      difficult times, 2881
      government institutions, 2881
      liberty and learning, 2881
      library as cultural institution, 2885–2886
      library's early history, developments in, 2880
      library services, 2883–2885
      national library debate, 2888
      postwar expansion, 2887
      public document distribution, 2881

   reorganization and new technology, 2888–2889
   role and functions, 2880
   rules and regulations, 2880
   Spofford, Ainsworth Rand, 2881–2883
   produced and distributed records, 2963
   structures
      Adams Building, 2879
      Jefferson Building, 2879–2880
      Madison Building, 2879
   symbol of American democracy, 2880
   13 million items, 2879
   world leader, 2879
Library of Congress (LCC), 2920
   classification, 963, 970, 992, 1261–1262, 2669, 3283, 3902, 4205, 4466, 4472, 4475
      in current information environment, 2851–2852
      development, 2848–2849
      divisions, 2850
      domain-specific taxonomies, 2852
      factors for acceptance, 2847
      file partitioning, 2852
      guidelines, 2853
      history of, 2847–2848
      information retrieval function, 2847
      Internet, information databases, and OPACs, 2854
      and LCSH, 2852–2853
      library materials, shelf-ordering of, 2847
      main classes, 2849–2850
      multitopical works, 2853
      national bias, 2853
      notation (numbering system), 2849–2851
      obsolescence, 2853
      strengths, 2853–2854
      subclasses, 2849–2850
Library of Congress Demographic Group Terms (LCDGT), 2876
Library of Congress Genre/Form Terms (LCGFT) for Library and Archival Materials, 2876
   application, 2861–2862
   associative relationships, 2860–2861
   authorized terms, 2859–2860
   developments, 2862–2863
   equivalence relationships, 2860
   hierarchical relationships, 2860
   project management, 2858–2859
   scope notes, 2861
   structure, 2860–2861
Library of Congress Medium of Performance Thesaurus for Music (LCMPT), 2863, 2876
Library of Congress Name Authority, 1080
Library of Congress/Name Authority Cooperative Program (LC/NACO), 3291
Library of Congress subject headings (LCSH), 1080, 1259, 1261, 1539–1540, 1615, 2670, 2847, 2852–2853, 2856–2858, 2860, 2862–2863, 3899, 3902, 3904, 3929, 4466, 4472–4473
   assignment of headings, 2870
   cross-references
      see also (SA) references, 2867–2868
      see references, 2867

      broader and narrower terms, 2867
      general see references, 2868
      related terms, 2867
   headings, 2866–2867
   LCMPT, 2876
   multiple subdivisions, 2877
   new/revised headings
      Airlie House recommendation, 2874–2875
      heading currency, 2871–2872
      heading syntax, 2872
      pre-Airlie House actions, 2874
      reference structure, 2872–2873
      scope, 2871
      subdivisions, 2873–2874
   RDA, 2876
   scope, 2866
   scope notes, 2868
   subdivisions
      chronological subdivisions, 2869
      free-floating subdivisions, 2869–2870
      geographic subdivisions, 2869
      multiple subdivisions, 2870
      pattern subdivisions, 2870
      topical subdivisions, 2869
Library of Congress television preservation report, 1578
Library of Congress Web Archives (LCWA), 4754
Library of Knesset, 2547
Library of the Eghishe Charents State Museum of Literature and Art, 230
Library of Tomorrow Project, 1030
Library Organization and Management (LOMS), 2842, 2844
Library portals
   features and functions, 2892
   issues, 2897–2898
   technology and standards used, 2894–2895
   types, 2892–2893
Library Publishing Coalition (LPC), 2901, 2903–2904, 2906–2907
Library publishing initiatives (North America)
   academic library publishing
      appendices and supplemental content, 2903
      business models, 2906
      conference proceedings, 2902
      core services, 2906
      and "crises," 2904–2905
      data, 2902–2903
      definition, 2901
      electronic journals, 2901–2902
      ETDs, 2902
      gray literature, 2902
      history, 2903–2904
      maturity, 2907
      missions and motivations, 2905
      monographs, 2902
      organization and staffing, 2906
      partnerships and collaboration, 2906–2907
      print on demand/digitization services for out-of-print books, 2903
      scholarly websites, 2902
      textbooks, 2903
   credibility and identity establishment
      scholarly publishing and academy, 2907
      sustainability, 2907
      university presses, relationship with, 2907

Library Publishing Unconference, 1422
Library Quarterly (*LQ*), 2167, 2910
Library questions, classification of, 1518
Library science, 2410, 2769
  American exceptionalism, 2909
  apostles of culture, 2909
  bibliothekswissenschaft, 2909
  in Brazil
    graduate courses, 612
    Industrial Revolution, 597
    job market, 612–614
    scientific infrastructure, 597
    undergraduate courses, 597–599
  C. C. Williamson report, 1923, 2910
  German influence, 2909
  Graduate Library School, 2910–2913
  institutional infrastructures, 2911
  knowledge and skills, 2910–2911
  librarianship education events, 2914–2916
  library automation, 2914
  library economy, 2910
  Library Quarterly (*LQ*), 2910
  protohistory, 2909
  scientism, 2913
  Social Gospel movement, 2909
  values, 2912–2913
A Library's Contribution to Your Community,
  3794
Library Services Act (LSA), 1847, 3775
Library Services and Construction Act (LSCA),
  1847, 3541, 3775, 4393
Library Services and Technology Act (LSTA),
  377, 4392, 4395
Library services platforms, 4982
Library Society of China (LSC), 893
Library's scribes, 2404
Library Support Staff Certification Program,
  2844
Library Trends, 249
LibraryU, 3438
Libricide, 4400–4403
Life-cycle concept, 2379
Lightweight Directory Access Protocol (LDAP),
  2894
Linda Hall Library (LHL), 790, 4009, 4361
Linear programming (LP) model
  applications, 1194
  limitation of, 1195
  objective function, 1194
  product mix decision problem
    graphical solution of, 1194–1195
    input data for, 1194
Lingua franca, 2982
Linguistic press, 3739
Linguistics
  discourse analysis, 2930
  lexicon, 2929
  morphology, 2929
  phonetics, 2928–2929
  phonology, 2928–2929
  structural subfields, 2927–2928
  syntax, 2929–2930
Linked data, 3294
  application, 2941
  benefits, 2940
  creation process, 2941
  five star data model, 2940

HTTPs, 2939
  identity links, 2940
  in libraries, 2941
  principles, 2938–2939
  relationship links, 2940
  standards, 2939
  vocabulary links, 2940
Linked Open Data (LOD), 1079
Linking, SEO
  content-inspired linking, 4037
  FFAs, 4036
  inbound links, 4036
  link building strategy, 4036
  link-weighting fundamentals, 4035–4036
  non-reciprocal links, 4036
  paid links, 4036
Link searching, 4049
Lister Hill National Center for Biomedical
  Communication (LHNCBC), 3341–3342
"List of Serials Indexed for Online Users"
  (LSIOU), 1877
"Literacy 2.0," 2305
Literal sources, 3109
Literary fund, 1839
Literary politics, 1864
Literary warrant, 992–963
Literature Attached to Chart (LATCH), 1889
The Literature of Political Economy: a Classi-
  fied Catalogue, 1405
Lithuania
  historical context, 2943–2945
  library network, 2943
  library sector, 2943
  library system
    academic and research libraries,
      2951–2953
    foundation and ownership, 2946
    functions and community, 2946
    legal foundations, 2943, 2945–2946
    Martynas Mazvydas National Library,
      2947–2948
    public library, 2948–2951
    school libraries, 2951
    special libraries, 2953
    types, 2946–2947
  map of, 2944
  professional associations and unions,
    2955–2956
  research and education, 2953–2955
Lithuanian Integrated Library Information Sys-
  tem (LIBIS), 2947–2948
Lithuanian Librarians' Association (LLA),
  2955–2956
Lithuanian Library for the Blind, 2953
Lithuanian Research Library Consortium
  (LIMBA), 2828
The Little Library of Museum Science Litera-
  ture, 4185
Little presses, 3743
A Little Pretty Pocketbook, 854
Little Women, 855
Liverpool University Centre for Archive Studies
  (LUCAS), 4738
Living history museums, 3237
Living Museum Online (LEMO), 1706
Livres d'artistes, 4337
Lloyd's List, 1401

Loansome Doc, 1885–1886
Local area networks (LANs), 2291, 3356
Local authority museums, in United Kingdom,
  4719–4721
Local databases, development and access,
  2329–2331
Local documents, 1720–1721
Local education authorities (LEAs), 4705–4706
Local Government (Wales) Act 1994, 4735
Local Government Act of 1972, 1839, 4734
Local Government and Planning (Scotland) Act
  1982, 4720
Local standardization, 3107
Lock-and-key theory, 836
Logical name space
  for files/digital entities, 2999
  for storage systems, 2999
Logical Observations Identifiers Names and
  Codes (LOINC), 4673
Logistical distribution network, 3002
Logons, 2056
London, 302–309
London and Country Brewer, 1402
London Mathematical Society, 324
London Price-Current, 1401
London Zoo, 4724
Long playing (LP) recordings, 3280
Loose-leaf services, 652, 2741
Los Angeles Times, 3254–3255
Losee, Robert, 2052
Lossy Counting algorithm, 2632
"Lossy"-type formats, 4942
Lotka, Alfred J., 501, 506
Lotkaian informetrics, 2372
Lotka's Law, 501, 506–509, 2210–2211, 2371
Lots of Copies Keeps Stuff Safe (LOCKSS),
  1335, 3002, 4147, 4748
Louisiana Museum of Modern Art, 1226
Louvre
  French Revolution, 2959–2960
  nineteenth-century developments, 2960
Louvre museum, 1596–1597
Lubotsky, Marcella, 500–501
Lubuto Project, 883
Lucas, Alfred, 1070
LUNAR, 3348
Lunder Conservation Center, 1073
Lviv Stefanyk Scientific Library, 4643,
  4645–4646
Lycos, 2521
Lyndon Baines Johnson Foundation, 3715
Lynx, 2518

M

MAC, *see* Mandatory access control
Machine Aided Indexer, 1987
Machine-Assisted Reference Section (MARS),
  3909
Machine learning, 272–274
Machine-lending agencies (MLAs), 565
Machine-Readable Bibliographic Information
  Committee (MARBI), 2875, 2966
Machine-readable cataloging (MARC), 2, 733,
  739, 1252, 2220, 2887, 2921, 2923,
  3396, 4468, 4472–4473
  background (1961–1965), 2963

bibliographic control, 449–450
bibliographic data, 3058
cataloging systems, 3450–3454
character set expansion, 2983
development period
    character encoding, 2981
    IBM 360, 2980
    pilot project, 2980–2981
distribution service, 2965–2966
FAST authority file, 1539
features, 2981–2982
format family, 2982
internationalization
    content designation, library functions, 2985
    convergence, 2985
    ISO 2709, 2984–2985
    maintenance, 2985
    national basis design, 2984
    umbrella formats, 2985
Internet and Web introduction
    electronic resources, 2984
    new interchange options, 2983–2984
    Unicode, 2984
MARC-8, 2984
MARC 21, 449–450, 3396
    convergence, 2985
    development period, 2980
    formats for Classification and Authority
        data, 1260
    FRBR model, 2987
    maintenance, 2985
    Unicode, 2984
OPAC database records, 3422
pilot project (1961–1965)
    card and book catalog production, 2964
    contents and content designators, 2965
    initial distribution, 2964
    MARC I, 2964
    MARC II, 2964–2965
    participants, 2964–2965
    planning, 2964
    roman alphabet languages, 2965
    structure, 2965
recent developments
    MARCXML, 2986–2988
    modeling, 2987
    MODS, 2987–2988
    syntax, 2986–2987
record, 2982–2983, 3283
retrospective conversion
    automatic identification, 2968
    format recognition process, 2968
    initial conversion method, 2967
    large-scale centralized conversion, 2967
    NCLIS, 2970
    pilot project, 2967–2968
    record types, 2970
    reverse chronological order, 2967
    special studies, 2969
    task force, 2967–2970
standardization
    bibliographic standards, 2970
    cataloging data availability, 2970
    content designators, 2971–2972
    expanded roman-alphabet character set,
        2972
    information interchange, 2970–2971

ISBD, 2971
    publication and language codes, 2972
system development, 2983
users
    book catalogs, 2972
    MDO, 2972
    printed cards, 2972–2973
    retriever, 2973
    subscribers, 2973–2974
Machine-repair volunteers, 569
Machine-to-machine communication,
    2182–2183
Machine translation (MT), 277, 3141–3144,
    3346–3347, 3353
Macintosh computers, 4997
MacKay, Donald, 2056
Mackinder, Halford John, 1687–1688
Macquarie University Library, 4452, 4454
Macrex, 443
Macro-appraisal approach, 2381
Macrocosmic bibliography, 4198
Macroplanning, 432
Madden, A.D., 2051
Made for ads (MFA) Web sites, 4039
Madras Public Libraries Act in 1948, 1993
Magnetic Card Executive Typewriter, 4994
Magnetic Card Selectric Typewriter, 4994
Magnetic tape, 3280
Magnetic Tape Selectric Typewriter (MT/ST),
    4993–4994
Mahieu binding, 545
Maimonides, Moses, 3044
Maine State Library, 4397–4398
Mainz Psalter, 1972
Maioli bindings, 543
Major Orchestral Librarians' Association
    (MOLA), 3277
Makerspace Playbook, 2993
Makerspaces in libraries
    core library rules, strategic allignment
        entities, 2994
        innovation and entrepreneurship, 2994
        K-12 and lifelong learning initiatives,
            2993–2994
        technology/activities, 2993
        traditional roles, 2994
        values, 2992–2993
    knowledge creation, 2990, 2994
    makers, maker movement and rise of
        makerspace
        do-it-yourself culture, 2990
        hackerspaces and Fab Lab, 2991–2992
        learning, 2991
        Maker Faires, 2990
    timeline, 2992
Making of Amercica-2 (MOA-2) project, 3068
Maksymovych Scientific Library, 4646
Management information base (MIB), 3361
Management information systems (MIS), 2273–
    2274, 2662
Management Information Systems Research
    Center (MISRC), 2276
Management knowledge, 2275–2276
Management virtualization, 2998
    authenticity and integrity, 3000
    logical name spaces, 3001
    management policy

        assessment criteria, 3000
        automation, 3000
        characterization, 3000
    metarule, 3001
    microservices, 3001
    persistent state information, 3001
    recovery operations, 3000
    rule-based systems, 3001–3002
Managing Electronic Records (MER) confer-
    ence, 1415
Manchester Museum, 4718
Mandatory access control (MAC), 405–406
Manifold, 1676
Manipulators, 275
Manne Katz Museum, 2551
Manufacturing Automation and Design Engi-
    neering (MADE) program, 2520
Manufacturing Census, 637
Manuscripts, 4344; *see also* Special collections
    collections, 202, 4791–4792
        AIP, 4763
        American Folklife Center, 4749
        American Heritage Center, 4757
        American Jewish Archives, 4751
        Brown Popular Culture Library, 4756
        California Academy of Science, 4762
        California Institute of Technology, 4762
        Cornell University Archives, 4747
        Iowa Women's Archives, 4760
        John Crerar Library, 4748
        Museum of Chinese in America, 4758–
            4759
        National Agricultural Library, 4762–4763
        Performing Arts Reading Room, 4749
        Schomburg Center for Black Culture, 4759
        Tamiment Library and Wagner Archives,
            4761
    core professional requirements, 4340–4341
    definition, 4336
Map
    of Armenia, 228–229
    of Australia, 379–380
    bird's-eye-view, 4961–4962
    of China, 886–887
    cognitive map, 4959
    of Croatia, 1121–1122
    of Denmark, 1215–1216
    of France, 1589–1590
    of Germany, 1693–1694
    of Greece, 1729
    history of, 4963–4964
    of Hungary, 1917–1918
    of Israel, 2542–2543
    of Japan, 2560–2561
    of Kazakhstan, 2578–2579
    of Kenya, 2592–2593
    librarianship responsibilities, 4013
    of Lithuania, 2944
    of Moldova, 3117–3118
    of Peru, 3606–3607
    plan view, 4961–4962
    of Poland, 3675
    of Saudi Arabia, 3970–3971
    of Senegal, 4104–4105
    of Slovakia, 4173–4174
    of South Korea, 4307–4308
    of Spain, 4315

Map (cont'd.)
  of Switzerland, 4487–4488
  of Tanzania, 4498
  three-dimensional tactile map, 4961–4962
  of Tunisia, 4625
mapFAST, 1546
MapInfo, 1676
Map-It, 2155
MARC, *see* Machine-readable cataloging
MARC Development Office (MDO), 2966
MarcEdit, 1545
Margaret Mann Citation, 331
Margaret Thatcher library, 2596
Maria's Libraries, 40
Market information centers (MIC), 2133
Market information prints (MIP), 2133
Marketing
  associations, 3015–3016
  definition, 3011
  education, 3017
  efforts, 3012–3013
Market researchers, 3416–3417
Markey–Fields bill, 1020
Marking format, 1177
Markov Networks, 274
Markov random fields (MRF), 4424
Markup languages, 1677
  computer use, 3073–3074
  Google search, 3072
  human use, 3073
  SGML, 3074–3075
  types, taxonomy of, 3073
  XML, 3076–3080
Marshall, Alfred, 647
Martel, Charles, 764, 961, 1806, 2848, 2850,
    3902–3903
Martel's seven points, 2848, 2850
Martynas Mažvydas National Library of
    Lithuania
  LIBIS, 2948
  library statistics, 2948
  national bibliography, 2947–2948
Marx, Karl, 647
Maslow's hierarchy of needs, 2115, 5068
Massachusetts Historical Society (MHS), 196,
    1780
Massachusetts Institute of Technology (MIT),
    2991, 4748
Mass communication, 997–998
Mass-market agreement, 1272
Master List of Medical Terms (MALIMET),
    2667
Master of library science (MLS) degrees, 3033
Master Reference File (MRF), 4784
Master's degree in library science (M.L.I.S.),
    707, 709–710
Master–slave data grids, 3000
Matching, 3294
Matenadaran, 236–237
Mathematical geography, 1683
Mathematical models, 2086
Mathematical Reviews (MR), 3025–3027, 3644
A Mathematical Theory of Communication,
    2770
Mathematics literature
  A.D. 400 to 1400, 3020–3021
  600 B.C. to A.D. 400, 3020

5000 B.C. to 600 B.C., 3019–3020
chronological periods, 3019
contemporary mathematics periods, 3019
current literature
  awareness needs, 3029–3030
  day-to-day needs, 3030–3031
  graduate education, 3025
  mathematical games, 3025
  popularizations, 3025
  primary literature, 3025–3028
  recreations, 3025
  retrospective needs, 3030
  secondary literature, 3028–3029
eighteenth century, 3022–3023
fifteenth and sixteenth centuries, 3021
prehistory, 3019
seventeenth century, 3021–3022
1800 to 1940
  abstract axiomatic approach, 3024
  algebra, 3023–3025
  analysis, 3023, 3025
  axiom system, Gödel, 3024–3025
  Disquisitiones Arithmeticae, 3023
  Euclid's *Elements*, 3025
  Gauss, Carl Friedrich, 3023
  geometry, 3023–3024
  Hilbert, David, 3024
  international congresses of mathematicians,
      3024
  mathematical journal, 3024
  national professional society, 3024
  non-Euclidean geometries, Boole, 3024
  phenomenal growth rate, 3024
  topology, 3025
Mathematics of the USSR-Izvestija, 3027
Mathematics Subject Classification (MSC), 3644
Mathematische Annalen, 3024
Matica Srpska Library, 4127, 4130–4131
Matrix structure, 3189–3190
Matter facet, 1536
Maxdiff (Max difference) histograms, 2630
McClain doctrine, 1153
McKinsey's KM strategy, 2652
MCN, *see* Museum Computer Network
MDA, *see* Museum Documentation Association
Mean average precision (MAP), 3946
Meaningful learning, 2758–2759
Measuring the Impact of Networked Electronic
    Services (MINES), 374
Mechanics' libraries, 1842
Mechanistic organizations, 3514
Media, 998–999, 3277
  credibility, 1114–1115
  overload, 2104
Mediascapes, 2124
MediaSentry, 3660
Medical imaging databases, 4429–4430
Medical libraries, 4010
  in Israel, 2547
  MeSH, 4363
  in Vietnam, 4908
Medical Library Assistance Act (MLAA) of
    1965, 3335
Medical Library Association (MLA), 710, 1097,
    1874, 4016, 4355–4358, 4370
  advocacy
    governmental relations, 3036

professional recognition, 3036
public relations, 3036–3037
global partners network, 3038–3039
knowledge creation and communication
  professional networking, 3038
  publications, 3037–3038
  research, 3037
lifelong learning
  AHIP, 3035
  continuing education, 3034–3035
  credentialing program, 3035–3036
not-for-profit educational association, 3033
organizational structure, 3033–3034
professional and membership recruitment,
    3033–3034
programs and services, 3034
The Medical Library Association Guide to Man-
    aging Health Care Libraries, 3037
Medical literature
  Arabic writings, School of Salerno and late
      manuscripts, 3044–3045
  Babylonian Talmud, 3042
  Berlin Museum, 3041
  bibliographic control, 3055–3057
  British Museum, 3041
  Code of Hammurabi, 3041
  early Greece, India, and China, 3042–3043
  early printed works, 3045–3046
  eighteenth century, 3049–3052
  King Assurbanipal of Assyria collection, 3041
  Latin and Greek manuscripts, 3043–3044
  nineteenth century, 3052–3054
  Old Testament, 3042
  papyrus, 3041
  seventeenth century, 3047–3049
  sixteenth century, 3046–3047
  Sumerian clay tablet, 3041
  twentieth century, 3054–3055
Medical Literature Analysis and Retrieval Sys-
    tem (MEDLARS®), 3336
Medical Research Library of Ethiopia, 1499
Medical Subject Headings (MeSH), 2667, 2857,
    3336, 3929, 4468
  cross-references, 4474
  National Library of Medicine, 3340
  qualifiers, 4474
  thesaurus, 819
  tree structures, 4474
MEDLARS program, 652
MEDLINE, 1764, 1767, 3339, 3471
  current awareness services, 1880
  database, 819–820
  interlibrary loan and document delivery, 1880
  library collections, online access to, 1881
  outsourcing, 1881
  PubMed database, 474
MedlinePlus Connect, 3339
MedPix™, 4430
Medvescak Public Library, 883
Meeting the Challenges of a Culturally Diverse
    Workforce project, 370
Mekelle Museum, 1503
Mela, Pomponius, 1684
Mel-Frequency Cepstral Coefficients (MFCCs),
    3270
Melina Project, 1742
Mellon Conservation Documentation Survey, 1072

Mellon's grounded theory, 2783
MELVYL, 3452
Members Council Executive Committee, 3393
Membership Initiative Groups (MIGs), 76–77
Meme Tags, 1059
Memex, 1057, 2217
Memorial museums
 in Hungary, 1928
 in Moldova, 3123
 Nehru Memorial Museum and Library, New
  Delhi, 2022
Memoria Slovaciae, 4176
Memory difficulties, 3842
Memory of the World Program, 4660–4661
Mendeley, 45
Mentions, altmetrics, 44
Mercantile libraries, 1842
Mercator projection, 1685
Merchants Avizo, 1410
Merchants' Magazine, 1404
Merchants Mappe of Commerce, 1400
Merck Index, 820
MeSH, see Medical Subject Headings
Mesrop Mashtots Institute of Ancient Manu-
 scripts, 236–237
Message credibility, 1115
Message Digest Algorithm 5 (MD-5), 1366
Messkataloge, 469
MESUR database, 45
Metacrawler, 2523
Metadata, 1294–1295, 1364–1366, 1390, 2524,
 3106
 content value standards, 3061
 data communication standards, 3061–3062
 data structure standards, 3060–3061
 definitions, 3059–3060
 editing tools, 1545
 etymology, 3058–3059
 FIAT/IFTA, 2468
 generation, 3063–3067
 historical reference, 3059
 models, 3067–3069
 standards, 3060–3063
 syntax standards, 3062–3063
Metadata Authority Description Schema, 731
Metadata Encoding and Transmission Standard
 (METS), 705, 1290, 1294, 1574–1575,
 3068, 4938
Metadata Encoding & Transmission Standard,
 731
Metadata Object Description Schema (MODS),
 705, 731, 1292, 1294, 2987–2988
Meta-field
 philosophy of information, 3610
 philosophy of information sciences, 3611
 philosophy of philosophy, 3611
Meta-information, 4559
Meta keyword tags, 4039
Metallurgy collection, 1744
Metamarkup, 3074
MetamorphoSys, 4678
Metaphilosophy, 3611, 3615
Meta-questions
 information sciences, 3611
 meta-fields, 3610–3611
 philosophy, 3614, 3619
 second-order questions, 3610–3611

Metasearch engine, 4053
MetaSearchers, 2523
Metatag Extractor, 3066
Metathesaurus
 attributes, 4675
 challenges, 4677–4678
 concept identifier, 4674
 concepts and concept names, 4673
 definition, 4673
 genomics vocabularies, 4673
 MetamorphoSys, 4678
 organization of, 4673–4674
 production and distribution, 4676–4677
 relationships, 4674–4676
 semantic type, 4675
 source vocabularies, 4673
 standard clinical terminologies, 4673
 synonymous terms and sources, 4674
Metcalfe's Law, 4081
Metrical information, 2056
Metrics
 bibliometrics, 2226
 data sources, 2226–2227
 e-metrics, 2226
 evaluative applications, 2227–2228
 goals of, 2226
 informetrics, 2226
 Lotka's and Bradford's laws, 2227
 relational applications, 2227
 scientometrics, 2226
 webometrics, 2226
Metrons, 2056
Metropolitan area network (MAN), 2291, 3356
Metropolitan Library, 893
Metropolitan Museum of Art, 1072, 3253
METS, see Metadata Encoding and Transmission Standard
Mexican Association of Librarians (AMBAC),
 3095
Mexican Association of Museum Professionals
 (AMProM), 3097
Mexican Social Security Institute (IMSS), 3091
Mexican Student Grant Award, NASIG, 3389
Mexico
 archives, 3096–3097
 libraries
  academic libraries, 3083–3086
  accreditation, 3093
  book publishing, 3095
  chronology, 3099–3100
  conferences, 3102
  education programs, 3092–3093
  government libraries, 3091
  history, 3082–3083
  information vendors, 3095
  library associations, 3095–3096
  national library institutions, 3091
  private libraries, 3091
  private university libraries, 3086
  public libraries, 3086–3089
  research institute libraries, 3090
  schools, 3089, 3100–3101
  science and technology libraries, 3090
  serials, 3094, 3101
  state university libraries, 3083–3084
  teacher's institutions, 3085–3086
  technological institutes, 3084–3085

 U. S. library principles, 3093–3094
 virtual/digital libraries, 3092
 museums, 3097–3099
Microfilming, 4585
Micronesia, 3541–3542
Microplanning, 432
Microsoft Academic, 923
Microsoft Access, 4942
Microsoft Disk Operating System (MS-DOS),
 4995–4996
Microtheory, 282
Microwave Communications, Inc. (MCI),
 1017
Mid-America College Art Association
 (MACAA), 255, 4934
Mid-Atlantic Information Node (MAIN), 3310
Middle East Materials Project (MEMP), 791
Migration, 1334, 2072
Mildred L. Batchelder Award, 334
Militarism, 4403
Military archives
 Air Force Historical Research Center, 4751
 American Jewish Archives, 4751
 American Jewish Historical Society, 4751
 Archdiocese of Chicago, 4751–4752
 Billy Graham Center Archives, 4752
 Center for Military History, 4751
 Episcopal Church U.S.A., 4752
 Family History Center, Church of Jesus Christ
  of Latter-Day Saints, 4752
 Naval Historical Center, 4751
 religious archives, 4751
 United Methodist Church, 4752
Military library, 1807, 4908
Military records, 1658
Millennium Declaration, 3382
Mill, John Stuart, 647
Milwaukee Public Museum, 3164
Milynes, Gerald de, 646
MINES for Libraries®, 374
Ming-Qing Archives, 906
Ming's New York Price Current, 1401
Miniature, 1945
Minimum Curriculum, 611–612
Minimum Standards for Public Library Systems,
 1966, 1846
Mining Journal and Commercial Gazette, 1405
MINISIS, 4627
Ministry of Culture, 1595
Ministry of Foreign Affairs Library, 1499
MINITEX, 3924
Minnesota method, 110
Minority Librarian Fellowship program, 3402
MIR, see Music information retrieval
MIR Evaluation eXchange (MIREX), 3272
MIS, see Management information systems
Misinformation, 2053
Misselden, Edward, 646
"Missing heritability paradox," 3846
Mission Operations and Information Manage-
 ment Services (MOIMS), 3486
Mission-oriented indexing, 1987
MITRE MII Expert Finder, 3865
Mixed Integer Programming (MIP) model,
 see Integer programming model
MLA, see Medical Library Association
MLIA, see Multilingual information access

Mobile information, 4236
Mobile museum, 1820
Mobile robots, 275–276
Mobile Web Initiative (MWI), 2348
Mob mentality/group think, 3529
Modality affordance, 1118
Model-base management system (MBMS), 1203
Model Curriculum and Guidelines for Graduate
    Degree Programs in Information Sys-
    tems, 630
Model human processor, 4806
Model requirements for management of elec-
    tronic records (MoReq), 1109,
    1361–1362, 1370
Modern bibliography
    commercial lists, 469
    library catalogs, 470–471
    recommended and forbidden books, 470
    topical lists, 469–470
    universal bibliography, 471
Modern Language Association of America
    (MLA), 3728–3729
Modern Library Movement, 888
Modified final judgement (MFJ), 1018
MODS, see Metadata Object Description
    Schema
Moffitt Library, 4650
Mogul miniatures (1525–1707), 1956–1957
Moldova
    archives, 3118–3120
    history, 3117–3118
    libraries
        academic libraries, 3125
        bibliographies and publications, 3124
        CML, 3124
        Internet, 3125
        LARM, 3125
        law, 3125
        library science education, 3125
        National Library, 3124
        NBC, 3125
        NLC, 3124
        programs, 3125–3126
        public libraries, 3123–3124
        special libraries, 3124
        users, 3124
    map of, 3117–3118
    museums, 3120–3123
Molecular diversity analysis, 836–837
MoMA, see Museum of Modern Art
Monastery libraries
    in Croatia, 1122
    in Greece, 1728
MONK Project, 1295
Monographic publishing, 2780
Monographs, 2739
Monster.com, 699
MONSTRAT Model, 4879–4880
Monteith College project, 987
Monuments Preservation Ordinance, 4511
Monument to the Great Fire of London,
    4164–4165
Moodle, 606
Moody, John, 647
Moral rights, 1268–1269, 2142
Morino Foundation, 1030
Morrill Act, 1011

Mosaic, 5024
Moscow Mathematical Society, 3024
Motion picture
    archives, 1561–1563
    picture film, 1575–1576
Motivation theory, 3513
Moving image collections (MIC), 3131
Moving image indexing
    chapter-level indexing, 3131
    frame-level indexing, 3132
    image tagging, 3136–3138
    item-level indexing, 3131
    multilingual indexing, 3134–3135
    scene-level indexing, 3131
    sequence-level indexing, 3131
    shot-level indexing, 3131–3132
    text and image, 3132–3134
    text recycling, 3134
Mozarabic illumination, 1948, 1953
mPach, 1760
MRI, 4430
MT/ST, see Magnetic Tape Selectric Typewriter
Multicriteria decision-making (MCDM) activ-
    ity, 1618
Multidimensional Library Anxiety Scale
    (MLAS), 2784
Multidimensional model of user–Web interac-
    tion, 2248–2249
Multidocument summarization, 425–426
Multilayer perceptrons (MLPs), 285
Multilingual cyberspace, 4659
Multilingual indexing, 3134–3135
Multilingual information access (MLIA)
    CLEF, 3143
    CLIR, 3141–3143
    history of, 3141
    information-seeking behavior, 3144
    language-specific process, 3144
    polyglots, 3140
    technological innovation, 3140
    translation quality, 3143
    Web search engines, 3144
Multilingual thesauri, 1984
Multimedia, 2242, 2524
MultimediaN E-Culture Demonstrator, 4088
Multiple criteria decision making (MCDM), 1198
Multiple identities, 3289–3291
Multiple USE MARC System (MUMS), 2966
Multiple user dialogs (MUD), 1050
Multipurpose community telecenters (MCT),
    2133
Multi-State Anti-Terrorism Information
    Exchange (MATRIX) system, 2402
Municipal Archives Tel-Aviv-Yafo, 2554
Municipalities Ordinance, 4500
Municipal library, 1803–1804
    in Belgrade, 4129
    in Bratislava, 4175, 4179
    CML, 3124
    in France, 1600–1601, 1603
    in Montreal, 660
    in Peru, 3608
    in Poland, 3674
    of Thessaloniki, 1730–1731
Municipal Library of Thessaloniki, 1730–1731
Municipal School Library Association, 1222
Munn-Barr report, 3372, 3375, 3378

Munn-Pitt report, 381, 384–385, 3372
Mun, Thomas, 646
Murphy's Law, 1350
Murray Pease report, 1070–1071
Musaeum Tradescantianum, 1817
Museographica, 1817
Museo Guggenheim, Bilbao, 3158
Museological Society of Japan, 2574
Museology, see Museum studies
Museum
    America (see United States, museums)
    archaeological collections, curation of
        (see Curation, archaeological artifacts)
    archives
        Getty museum, 4755
        Smithsonian Institution, 4754–4755
        United States Holocaust museum, 4755
        Warhol Museum, 4755
    of Armenia
        Children's Art Gallery, 237
        Genocide Museum and Institute, 236–237
        Matenadaran, 236–237
        National Aesthetic Education Center, 237
    in Australia
        Bendigo Art Gallery, 391
        courses, 393
        curatorial issues, 393
        national and state museums and galleries,
            388–391
        national parks, 391–392
        professional associations, 393
        specialist museums and galleries, 391
        von Mueller, Ferdinand Jakob Heinrich,
            392–393
        zoos and aquaria, 391
    Brazil, 611–615
    catalogs, 1816
    challenges
        funding, 3239–3240
        politics, 3239
    changing role of
        ecomuseums, 1822
        ethnology museum, 1820
        historic house museum, 1820
        ICOM, 1821–1822
        mobile museum, 1820
        national museums, 1821
        natural history museums, 1820
        open air museums, 1820–1821
        research and public education, 1820
        virtual museums, 1822
    in China, 908–911
    civic discourse, 3238–3239
    civic outreach, 3236
    collecting and collections
        age of collection, 3161–3162
        age of education, 3165–3166
        age of exhibition, 3162–3165
        anthropology and history museums, 3167
        archaeology, 3168
        art curator, 3167
        changing culture, 3166
        data, online access, 3166
        demographics, 3168
        ethnic and cultural diversity, 3168
        history, 3161
        natural history, 3167

psychographics, 3168–3169
research, 3167, 3234–3235
and community, relationship between (*see*
Community museums)
in Croatia
history, 1129
legislation and organization, 1129–1130
publishing, staff, and professional association, 1130
DCMS (*see* Department for Culture, Media
and Sport)
definition of, 2430, 3233
in Denmark
art museums, 1225–1226
cultural history museums, 1226
curatorship and museum administration,
training for, 1227
Danish museum sector, 1225
digital museum exhibits and services,
1226–1227
education, 1227–1228
Heritage Agency, 1225
legal framework, 1225
natural history museums, 1226
preservation, 1227–1228
professional associations, 1227
Ethiopia, 1500–1501
Addis Ababa Museum, 1503
Dessie Museum, 1503
exhibition of 1958, 1501
Harar National and Community Museum,
1503–1504
Institute of Ethiopian Studies Museum,
1501–1503
before Italian occupation, 1501
Jimma Museum, 1503
Mekelle Museum, 1503
National museum of Ethiopia, 1501–1502
OAU, 1502
SOFIES, 1503
UACC, 1501
Wollega Museum, 1503
evolution of, 1813–1814
exhibits and education, 3235
in France (*see* France, museums)
in Germany
art museums and galleries, 1704
digital museum exhibits and services, 1706
education, 1707
historical, anthropological, and
archeological museums, 1705–1706
museology as discipline and profession,
1706–1707
national museums, 1703–1704
professional associations, 1707
science and natural history museums,
1704–1705
standards and guidelines, 1707
visitor research, 1707
volunteers, 1707
zoos and botanical gardens, 1706
history, 3233–3234
Hungary
art museums and galleries, 1928
current priorities, 1931
digital museum exhibits and services, 1930
as discipline and profession, 1930–1931

education, 1931
historical, anthropological, and archaeological museums, 1929–1930
laws, 1927
national museum, 1927–1928
professional associations, 1931
religiously affiliated museums, 1929
science and natural history museums, 1929
zoos and botanical gardens, 1930
India (*see* India, museums and museology)
information arts, 2071–2073
institution, history of, 3148–3149
in Israel
Arab sector, 2552
archaeological museums, 2551
art museums, 2551
historical museums, 2551–2552
historical perspective, 2549–2550
holocaust heritage museums, 2552
in Jerusalem, 2550–2551
official recognition, 2552–2553
professional education, 2553
science and nature museums, 2552
in Japan
computerization and evaluation of management, 2575
education and training systems, 2574–2575
local governments, foundations, and private
companies, 2572–2573
museum/art libraries, 2574
museum law, revision of, 2575–2576
national museums, 2571–2572
organizing exhibitions, 2576
professional staff, 2574
societies and associations, 2574
university museums, 2573–2574
in Kazakhstan
as discipline and profession, 2588
galleries, zoos, and preserves, 2587–2588
history of, 2587
national museums, 2587–2588
Kenya (*see* National Museums of Kenya)
leisure destination, 3235–3236
modern museum
American Museum in New York, 1819
art, history, and natural history, 1818
Ashmolean Museum, 1817
classification systems, 1817–1818
collections, nature of, 1817
founding dates of, 1818–1819
Grimani collections, 1816
Musaeum Tradescantianum, 1817
Museographica, 1817
ordering system, 1817
Peale's museum, 1818
Sloane's collections, 1817
in Moldova
Church Museum, 3121
during communist period, 3122
during czarist Russian domination, 3120
early twentieth century, 3121
exhibition activities, 3122
during interwar period, 3122
legislation, 3122
memorial museums, 3123
Moorish style, 3121
national museums, 3121

political museums, 3123
public museums, 3121
scientific atheism, museums of, 3122
during Soviet regime, 3122–3123
during transitional period, 3123
objects
collection and classification of, 1812–1816
and knowledge transmission, 1816
power of, 1815–1816
preservation, 1813
provenance (*see* Provenance of museum
objects)
opportunities, 3238–3239
people with disabilities, 3575
place, 3263–3265
politics, power, and representation
architecture and position, 3689–3690
art museum, 3689, 3692–3693
cabinets of curiosities, 3688
contact zones, 3695–3696
cultural governance, 3688–3689
Enola Gay, 3693–3694
ethnographic museums, 3694–3695
Foucaultian perspective, 3689
national museum, 3690–3692
objects and exhibitions, 3690, 3697
regulation of conduct, 3690
representation, definition of, 3690
social power, 3689
status and community, 3688
professionalization, 3240
registration
history, 3199–3200
records, protection of, 3212–3213
in Saudi Arabia, 3979–3980
Senegal, 4110
in Serbia
art museums and galleries, 4134
churches and monasteries, 4133
historical and ethnographic museums, 4135
national museum, 4133–4134
professional association, 4133
science museums and galleries, 4134–4135
Slovakia
ecucation and professional associations,
4185–4186
gallery network, 4185
history, 4183
political and social life, documentation of,
4184–4185
SNM, 4183–4185
specialized museums, 4184
Spain (*see* Spain, museums and museology)
Switzerland, 4494–4495
technology, 3238
Temple of the Muses, 1813
training, 3240
types, 3236–3238
in United Kingdom
armed services, 4718–4719
botanical gardens, 4724–4725
English Heritage, 4723
financial support, 4727
history of, 4715–4717
independent, 4721–4722
local authority, 4719–4721
national museums, 4717–4718, 4727–4728

Museum (cont'd.)
  in United Kingdom (cont'd.)
    National Trust, 4722–4723
    profession, 4725–4727
    social exclusion, 4727
    university, 4718
    zoos, 4723–4724
  visitors
    American *vs.* European museums, 3251
    AMNH, 3252
    anecdotal assumptions, 3256
    anthropological collections, 3252
    art museums, 3251, 3253, 3255
    attendance, 3254
    blockbuster exhibitions, 3255
    Brooklyn Museum's annual report, 3252
    Carnegie Museum's annual report, 3252
    cultural patrimony, 3252
    cutting-edge research, 3252
    Denver Natural History Museum, 3254
    educational programs, 3255
    European human remains, 3255
    Excellence and Equity, 3255
    experience, United States *vs.* Europe, 3254
    Field Museum, 3255–3256
    FMNH, 3252
    golden age, 3251
    Goldstein's arguments, 3254
    historic visitors, 3251
    history of, 3251
    Los Angeles Times report, 3254–3255
    Lucas' remarks, 3252–3253
    mode of learning, 3253
    nonart museum visitor, 3255
    objects, 3252
    occupations, 3253
    Pennsylvania Museum's survey, 3254
    Philadelphia Museum, 3253
    professionals' speculation, 3251
    school groups and students, 3251
    sculptor, 3253
    Second World War, 3254, 3256
    Smithsonian's National Museum of American History, 3255
    "The Good Old Days," 3255
    transportation, 3253
    Victorian museum visitor, 3251
  volunteerism in, 4951–4952
  web sites
    business models, 3228
    collecting and preserving, 3226
    cultural experiments, 3223
    exhibitions, 3223–3224
    issues, 3228–3229
    outreach, 3227
    programming, 3223
    searchable collections, 3225–3226
    sectoral identity, 3226–3227
    social experiences, 3224–3225
    staffing and resource allocation, 3227–3228
    virtual experiences, 3225
Museum Accreditation Program, 3146–3147
Museum Act (1998), 1129
Museum and Library Services Act of 1996, 4770
Museum Assessment Program (MAP), 57
Museum Computer Network (MCN), 255, 3179
  communications, 3174

  conferences and collaborations, 3172, 3174
  consortium, 3171–3172
  governance, 3173
  incorporation and growth, 3171
  from institutions to individuals, 3171
  interactive and online, 3173
  origins, 3170–3171
  professional association, 3170
  publications, 3172–3173
  SIGs, 3173–3174
  strategic planning, 3173
  U.S. Congress, 3172
The Museum Directory, 4380
Museum documentation
  deaccessions
    authority to, 3208
    criteria, 3208
    deaccessioned objects, disposal of, 3209
    procedures, 3208–3209
    verification of records, 3208
  loan documentation
    correspondence, 3212
    duty to loan, 3210
    incoming condition reports, 3211
    insurance, 3212
    loan agreements, 3210–3212
    loan file creation, 3211
    loan requests, 3210
    notes, 3212
    outgoing condition reports, 3212
    publications, 3212
    shipping, 3212
  policies
    code of ethics policy, 3201–3202
    collections management policy, 3200–3201
  records, protection of, 3212–3213
  registration files
    accession numbers, 3202
    accessions file, 3202–3203
    appraisals, 3203
    bequests, 3205
    condition reports, 3203–3204
    correspondence, 3204
    deeds of gift, 3204–3205
    documentary files, 3202
    incoming and outgoing receipts, 3205–3206
    loan records, 3206
    notes, 3207
    photography, 3206–3207
    publications, 3207
    purchase information, 3205
Museum Documentation Association (MDA), 255–256, 3178
Museum Documentation Centre (MDC), 1129
Museum for Islamic Art, 2550
Museum informatics
  data sharing initiatives, 3178
  definition, 3176
  events, 3182
  information management, 3181
  information professionals, 3181
  information representation, 3177
  information technology
    digital museum, 3179–3180
    mainframe systems, 3178–3179

    personalization technologies, 3180–3181
    Web, 3180
  professional organizations, meetings, 3182
  repositories, 3176
  as research area, 3182
  resources, 3176–3177
  standards and metadata, 3177–3178
  visitors, 3176
Museum management
  administration, 3186
  authorizing agency, 3188
  budget and promulgate policies, 3188
  chief executive officer, 3186
  director/manager, 3186
  ethics, 3196–3197
  financial management, 3193–9134
  functions of, 3187
  funding sources, 3194
  institutional attitude, 3187
  leadership, 3190–3191
  mission, 3192–3193
  nonprofit and not-for-profit, 3186
  organizational management, 3186
  personnel management, 3191–3192
  philosophical policies, 3193
  planning methods, 3196
  planning process, 3194–3195
  public service and philosophical ownership, 3186
  resource development policies, 3193
  responsibilities, 3187
  self-assessment, 3195–3196
  structure
    hierarchic structure, 3189
    horizontal/flat structure, 3189–3191
    manager/director abilities, 3189
    matrix structure, 3189–3191
    organizational structure, 3189
  teamwork, 3187, 3192
  types of museums, 3188
  upper, middle and lower management, 3187
  volunteers, 3192
  working policies, 3193
Museum Network, 1129
Museum of Anthropology, Xalapa, 3098
Museum of Art in São Paulo (MASP), 614
Museum of Bad Art (MOBA), 4381
Museum of Broadcast Communications (MBC), 1563, 1565
Museum of Chinese History, 909
Museum of Croatian Archaeological Monuments, 1129
Museum of Cycladic Art, 1742
Museum of Israeli Art, 2551
Museum of Modern Art (MoMA), 263, 3224, 3249, 3692–3693
Museum of Natural History, 611–612
Museum of Online Museums (MOOM), 4382
Museums Act of 1845, 1837
Museums and Community Collaborations Abroad (MCCA), 58, 3247
Museum science, *see* Museum studies
Museum sense, 3215–3216
Museumshojskolen, 1227
Museums, Libraries and Archives Council (MLA), 4702
Museum studies

departments, 3214
history, 3215–3217
interdisciplinary, 3214
issues, 3215
master's degree/certificate, 3214
scholars, 3215
societal role, 3214
twentieth century second half, 3217–3219
Music Information Centres, 3276
Music information retrieval (MIR)
    audio techniques
        evaluation, 3272
        query type, 3270
        representations and extracted information,
            3270–3271
        specificity, 3271
        user interfaces, 3272
    query-by-example application, 3267, 3270
    query-by-humming application, 3267, 3272
    3SUM problem
        indexing, 3269
        note durations, 3269
        translation and scaling invariance, 3270
    symbolic techniques
        choosing representation, 3267–3268
        geometric framework, 3268–3269
        string matching framework, 3268
Music Instrument Digital Interface (MIDI), 3267
Music librarianship
    career in, 3278
    cataloging
        Anglo-American Cataloging Rules (AACR
            2 rev), 3281
        future of, 3282–3283
        music subject headings, 3282
        music uniform titles, 3282
        sheet music, 3282
        Western classical music, 3282
    definition, 3275
    future challenges, 3284–3285
    literature, 3275
    professional organizations
        ARSC, 3278
        IAMIC, 3277
        IAML, 3277
        IASA, 3278
        MLA, 3277
        MOLA, 3277
        MOUG, 3277–3278
Music libraries
    classifications, 3283
    developing collections
        audio and visual recordings, 3279–3281
        Basic Music Library, 3278
        Fling's Library Acquisition of Music, 3278
        indexes and abstracts, 3281
        printed music and sound recordings, 3278
        reference tools, 3281
        scores, 3279
    ethnic and world music, 3284
    preservation, 3283–3284
    professional organizations, 3277–3278
    services, 567
    types
        academic libraries, 3275
        conservatory libraries, 3276
        media and broadcast libraries, 3277

Music Information Centres, 3276
    national libraries, 3276
    performance libraries, 3276–3277
    public libraries, 3276
    research libraries, 3275–3276
Music Library Association (MLA), 2863,
    3277–3278
Music Library of Greece "Lilian Voudouri,"
    1732
Music OCLC Users Group (MOUG),
    3277–3278
Mütter Museum, Philadelphia, 4381
My Friend Rabbit, 858–859
MyiLibrary e-books, 1210–1211

N

Nacandros of Colophon in Ionia, 3042
Nachum Gutman Art Museum, 2551
NACO, 454, 1540–1543, 2921, 3291–3293,
    4669
Nairobi museum, 2604
Name authority control
    bibliographic and authority records, 3292
    crowdsourcing, 3294
    data elements, 3291–3292
    encoding and models, 3294–3295
    identifiers, 3292–3293
    linked data, 3294
    matching and clustering, 3294
    names and name variants, 3289
    organization names and hierarchies, 3291
    pseudonyms and multiple identities,
        3289–3291
    purposes, 3288
    record creation and reuse, 3293–3294
    undifferentiated names, 3291
    VIAF and ISNI, 3288–3289
Name Authority File (NAF), 1076, 1543, 2866,
    2921
Name variants, 3289
Nan Ching, 3042
Nancy DeLaurier Award, 4936
Nanjing Museum of Jiangsu Province,
    909–910
Nanotechnology Standards Panel (NSP), 89
Napster, 1322, 3654
NARA, see National Archives and Records
    Administration
NARA Electronic Records Archive, 3001
Narin, Francis, 500
Narrative nonfiction, 3705
Narrower terms (NTs), 1986
NARS, see National Archives and Records
    Service
NASIG, see North American Serials Interest
    Group
National-academic libraries, 3321
National Academy of Sciences of Armenia
    Library (NAS RA), 232
National Aeronautics and Space Administration
    (NASA), 2155, 3640
National Aesthetic Education Center, 237
National Air and Space Museum (NASM), 3693,
    4193
National and Capodistrian University of Athens,
    1731

National and State Libraries Australasia
    (NSLA), 382
National and University Library in Zagreb, 1124
National Anthropological Museum, 4333
National Archaeological Museum
    Athens, 1743–1744, 3689, 3691
    Spain, 4333
National Archival Information System
    (ARHiNET), 1128
National archives, 177, 1414, 1851, 3316,
    3716
    in China, 906
    concept, 3298
    of Ethiopia, 1500
    France, 1590–1592
    Germany, 1699–1700
    government, 3300–3301
    Greece, 1736–1737
    of Hungary, 1925
    India, 2012–2015
    issues, 3300
    of Japan, 2567–2568
    Kazakhstan, 2585–2586
    NHPRC (see National Historical Publications
        and Records Commission)
    scope of activity, 3304–3305
    scope of holdings, 3302–3304
    Senegal, 4109–4110
    Slovakia, 4181
    of Tanzania, 4508–4509
    Tunisia, 4633–4635
    of United States, 1792
National Archives Act, 4741
National Archives and Library of Ethiopia
    (NALE), 1495–1496
National Archives and Records Administration
    (NARA), 1362, 1566, 1648, 1851, 1853,
    2154, 3715, 4746, 4754
National Archives and Records Service (NARS),
    1851, 4308–4309, 4746
National Archives of Armenia, 235–236
National Archives of Scotland (NAS),
    4733–4734
National Archives of the Republic of Moldova
    (NARM), 3119
National Archives Trust Fund, 3715
National Army Museum, 4719
National Assembly Library, South Korea, 4310
National Assessment and Accreditation Council
    (NAAC), 2010
National Association of Accountants, 651
National Association of Broadcasters (NAB),
    1013–1014
National Association of Government Archivists
    and Records Administrators
    (NAGARA), 1854
National Association of Manufacturers, 649
National Association of State Libraries (NASL),
    4394
National Audio-Visual Conservation Center,
    4305
National Audiovisual Institute (INA), 1591,
    3132
National Autonomous University of Mexico,
    3323–3324
National Bank of Greece Historical Archives
    (NBG), 1738

National Biological Information Infrastructure
(NBII)
  biodiversity, 3306–3308, 3310
  biological information, 3313
  DiGIR protocols, 3313
  digital system, 3306
  ecological information, 3308
  ecology, 3306
  GBIF, 3313
  history, 3307–3308
  knowledge domains, 3308
  knowledge integration
    catalogs and collections, 3312
    collaborative platforms, 3313
    expert coordination, 3313
    harvesting partner sites, 3312
    hosting, 3313
    information suppliers, 3311
    sample NBII data and information partners,
    3312
    Web crawling, 3312–3313
  national standards and technology, 3311
  national themes, 3310–3311
  organization, 3309
  regional foci, 3310
  USGS, 3306
National Book Center of Greece, 1733–1734
National Book Chamber (NBC), 3125
National Book Coordination Act of 1957, 893
National Braille Association (NBA), 570
National Center for Biomedical Information
  (NCBI), 3341–3342
National Center for Biotechnology Information
  (NCBI), 559, 1768, 3037
National Center for Education Statistics
  (NCES), 2844
National Center for Geographic Information and
  Analysis (NCGIA), 1674
National Center for Science Information Sys-
  tems (NACSIS), 2563
National Center for Supercomputing Applica-
  tions (NSCA), 1390–1391, 3396
National Central Library (NCL), 4498
National Chamber of the Mexican Publishing
  Industry (CANIEM), 3095
National Civil Rights Museum, 4165
National Commission on Libraries and Informa-
  tion Science (NCLIS), 2033, 2158, 2970,
  3921, 4222
National Communication Association (NCA),
  1001–1002, 2354
National Council of Science and Technology
  (CONACYT), 3089–3090
National Council on Archives (NCA), 4739
National Defense Education Act (NDEA), 2832,
  4000
National Diet Library (NDL), 2561–2563
National Diet Library of Japan, 3321, 3326
National Digital Heritage Archive (NDHA),
  3378
National Digital Library (NDL), 2889, 3727
National Documentation Center, 4631
National Documentation Service (NDS), 2601
National Document Delivery System, 1923
National Drug Code (NDC), 979
National Educational Technology Standards, 64
National Education Association (NEA), 60

National Electronic Information Consortium
  (NEICON), 2823
National electronic library, 3727
National Electronic Site License Initiative
  (NELSI), 2825
National Endowment for the Arts (NEA), 293,
  1586
National Endowment for the Humanities, 293,
  1909
National Federation of Advanced Information
  Services (NFAIS), 4978
National Film and Sound Archive (NFSA), 187,
  388, 1567
National Film Preservation Foundation (NFPF),
  1587–1588
National Fire Protection Association (NFPA),
  1349, 1853
National Freedom Fund for Librarians (NFFL),
  2393
National Gallery of Art, 3217
National Gallery of Victoria (NGV), 388
National Herbarium of Tanzania (NHT), 4512
National Historical Publications and Records
  Commission (NHPRC), 1414, 4746
  advisory board, 3315
  funding categories, 3315–3316
  grants, 3315, 3318–3319
  history, 3316–3318
  National Archives and Records Administra-
    tion, 3315
National Historical Publications Commission
  (NHPC), 3317
National Historic Preservation Act of 1966,
  1774, 4169
National imprint bibliographies
  bibliographical guides, 474–475
  bio-bibliography, 475
  commercial lists, 475
  current national bibliographies, 473
  current online subject bibliographies, 474
  Germany and adjacent areas, 473
  Great Britain, 472
  incunabula, 476
  library publications, 475–476
  Romance-Language Nations, 472
  subject lists, monographic and analytic, 475
  United States, 472
National Index of Functional Literacy (INAF),
  603
National Information Infrastructure (NII), 1551
National Information Standards Organization
  (NISO), 3, 88, 441, 443, 1133, 1250,
  1396, 2183–2184, 2341, 2672
  Architecture Committee, 2343
  current standards, 2345
  expert technical advisory group, 2344
  final approval, 2345
  formulation and implementation of standards,
  2345
  Library Standards Alliance, 2345
  Open Discovery Initiative working group,
  4982
  supporting organizations, 2345
  Topic Committee, 2343
  version control, 4897–4900
  work item, 2343
National Information System (NATIS), 2312

National Information System in Science and
  Technology (NISSAT), 2003
National Initiative for a Networked Cultural
  Heritage (NINCH), 4935
National Institute for Information (NII), 1395
National Institute for the History of Art (INHA),
  1598
National Institute of Anthropology and History
  (INAH), 3097
National Institute of Child Health and Human
  Development (NICHD), 335
National Institute of Informatics (NII), 2563
National Institute of Science Communication
  and Information Resources (NISCAIR),
  2005
National Institute of Standards and Technology
  (NIST), 2344
National Institutes of Health (NIH), 369, 559,
  3658–3659, 4146
National Inventory of Documentary Sources in
  the United States (NIDS-US), 136
National Inventory Programme (NIP), 676
Nationalism, 4402–4403
National Knowledge Commission (NKC),
  1997
National Labor Relations Act, 4689
National Librarian and Archivist's Day,
  4888–4889
National libraries
  ABINIA, 3330
  in Australia, 381–382
  in Belgrade, 2829
  CDNL, 3330
  CDNLAO, 3330
  CENL, 3330–3331
  classification of, 3321
  definition, 3320
  in Denmark, 1218–1219
  desirable functions, 3320
  digital libraries, 3322, 3331–3332
  essential functions, 3320
  Guidelines for Legislation for National
    Library Services, 3321–3322
  Guidelines for National Libraries, 3321
  history and development of
    Bibliothèque nationale de France (France
      national library), 3327–3328
    British Library, 3328–3329
    Die Deutsche Nationalbibliothek (German
      national library), 3329
    Europe, 3322–3323
    Latin America, 3323–3324
    Library of Congress, 3329–3330
    postcolonial world, 3324–3326
    post-Soviet world, 3326–3327
  Hungary, 1921–1922
  inessential functions, 3320–3321
  in Israel, 2543–2544
  Japan, 2561–2563
  in Kazakhstan, 2581
  Kenya, 2595
  legislative position of, 3322
  music libraries, 3276
  National Library and Information Needs,
    3321
  in Peru, 3606–3608
  rare book collections, 3822

SCANUL-ECS, 3330
science and technology, 4009–4010
specific target audience, services to, 3322
subject libraries, 3321
Switzerland, 4488–4489
in Ukraine, 4642, 4645
in United Kingdom, 4701
National Library Act 1960, 381
National Library and Archives of Canada, 4338
National Library and Archives of Egypt, 3325
National Library and Information Services
Australia, 381–382
Denmark, 1218–1219
Germany, 1694–1695
India
Central Reference Library, Kolkata, 1995
DESIDOC, 1996
government, role of, 1994
IARI, 1996
inter-library cooperation, 1996–1997
NASSDOC, 1996
National Library, Kolkata, 1994–1995
National Medical Library, 1995
national planning, 1997
National Science Library, 1995–1996
NISCAIR, 1996
SENDOC, Hyderabad, 1996
UGC, 1994
Kazakhstan, 2581
Senegal, 4105–4106
Spain, 4316–4319
Switzerland, 4488–4489
Tunisia, 4626–4627
National Library Day, 234, 238
National Library for Children (NLC), 3124
National Library for Children and Youth (NLCU), 4310
National Library
of Algeria, 3325
of Armenia (NLA), 230–231
of Australia, 1392, 3324
of Beijing, see National Library of China
of Brazil, 597–598, 3323
of Bulgaria, 3323
of Canada, 1395
of Chile, 3323
of China (NLC), 892–895, 3325
of Colombia, 3323
Czech Republic, 3323
of Ecuador, 3323
of Ethiopia, 1495–1496, 1499
of Finland, 3323
of Germany, 1694–1695
of Greece (NLG), 1729
of India, 3326
of Indonesia, 3326
of Ireland, 3322
of Jamaica, 3325
of Korea (NLK), 4309–4310
of Latvia, 3326
of Lithuania, 3326
Mexico, 3323
New Zealand, 3324, 3372–3373
Nigeria, 3324

North Africa, 3325
Norway, 3323
of Peiping (NLP), 890, 893
Peru, 3323
Poland, 3323
Portugal, 3323
Republic of Argentina, 3323
Russia, 3326–3327
in Sarajevo, 3323
Scotland, 3322–3323, 4701
Serbia, 4127–4129
Singapore, 3326
South Africa, 3325
of Spain, 4317
of Sri Lanka, 3326
of Sweden, 1261
of Thailand, 3325
Tobago, 3325
of Tunisia, 3325
of Uganda, 3324
of Vietnam (NLV), 4904–4905
of Wales (NLW), 4701
in Warsaw, 3680
National Library of Medicine (NLM), 819, 1872, 3034, 3036, 3471, 3640, 4010, 4672
administration, 3335–3336
clinical terminologies, coordination of, 3341
collection
digital collections, 3338
historical, 3337
preservation, 3337–3338
print, 3337–3338
PubMed Central, 3338
databases
ClinicalTrials.gov, 3339–3340
MedlinePlus, 3339
MedlinePlus Connect, 3339
MEDLINE/PubMed®, 3339
DIMRC, 3343
exhibitions, 3343–3344
extramural programs, 3342
history of, 3334–3335
legislation, 3335
LHNCBC, 3341–3342
MeSH, 3340
mission and long range plans, 3336–3337
NCBI, 3341–3342
NN/LM, 3342–3343
ORCID identifiers, 3508
organizational structure, 3336
RxNorm, 3340
SNOMED CT®, 3340–3341
training, 3344
UMLS®, 3340
VSAC, 3341
National Library Power Program, 64–65
National library service (NLS)
Anglophone countries, 3324
British Council, 2408
Ghanaian model, 4500
in Japan, 3326
New Zealand, 3372–3373
National Library Service for the Blind and Physically Handicapped, 16, 563–564, 3576, 3778, 4395

National maritime and oceanography museum, 4639
National Moving Image Database (NAMID), 1586
National museum
in Belgrade, 4133–4134
Campo de Santana, 613–614
in Japan, 2571–2572
politics, power, and representation, 3690–3692
Switzerland, 4494–4495
in United Kingdom, 4717–4718, 4727–4728
National Museum of African American History (NMAAH), 3245
National Museum of African-American History and Culture, 4192
National Museum of American History, 4192
National Museum of Australia, 3692
National museum of Ethiopia, 1501–1502
National Museum of India, 3691
National Museum of Natural History, 4193–4195
National Museum of New Zealand, 3692
National Museum of Nigeria, 3691
National Museum of Pakistan, 3691
National Museum of Scotland, 3691–3692
National Museum of the American Indian (NMAI), 2041, 4193
National Museum of the Prado, 4331–4332
National Museums of Kenya (NMK)
access, preservation, and educational role, 2607
archeological and paleontological sites, 2605–2606
curators and museum administration, education for, 2606
as discipline and profession, 2607
Fort Jesus Museum, 2605
history of, 2603
Karen Blixen Museum, 2605
Lamu Museum, 2605
Lamu World Heritage Site, 2605
legislation, 2603–2604
Nairobi museum, 2604
outstanding personalities, 2607–2608
professional associations
AFRICOM, 2606
ICOM, 2606–2607
societies, 2607
regional museums, 2604–2605
National Network of Libraries of Medicine (NN/LM), 3342–3343, 4010
National parks
Australia, 391–392
India, 2024–2025
Tunisia
cultural and arts centers, 4639
natural parks and sites, 4638–4639
National Park Service (NPS), 3247, 4165, 4169
National Park Service Act of 1916, 4169
National Parliamentary Library of Ukraine (NPLU), 4644–4645
National Parliament Library, 4643
National patrimony, 611
National Pilot Digital Library Project (NPDLP), 902

National Policy on Library and Information System (NAPLIS), 2001
National Program for Acquisitions and Cataloging (NPAC), 2965
National Programme for the Digitisation of Archival, Library and Museum Records, 1130
National Public Broadcasting Archives (NPBA), 1561, 1563
National-public libraries, 3321
National Register of Historic Places (NRHP), 1774
National Research and Education Network (NREN), 1551
National Research Council (NRC), 559, 660–661, 1673
National Sample Survey Organisation (NSSO), 1993
National Science Digital Library (NSDL), 2998, 3646, 4012, 4073
National Science Education Standards (NSES), 558
National Science Foundation (NSF), 555, 1029, 1392, 2217, 2517, 2772, 3646, 4263
National Science Foundation Act of 1950, 2217
National Scientific and Documentation Center (CNDST), 4106
National security, *see* Intelligence and Security Informatics
National Security Act of 1947, 2151
National Security Agency, 2151
National Security Archive (NSA), 2390
National Security Council (NSC), 2151–2152
National Security Laws, 785
National Serials Data Program (NDSP), 4139
National Society for the Study of Communication (NSSC), 2421
National Stolen Art File (NASF), 4577
National Stolen Property Act (NSPA) of 1934, 1153
National Storytelling Festival, Jonesborough, 4443
National Study of School Evaluation (NSSE), 64
National System of Public Libraries (NSPL), 4886
National System of Scientific, Technical and Organizational Information (SINTO), 3676
National Technical Information Center and Library, 1922
National Technical Information Service (NTIS), 1552, 1554
National Technical Institute for the Deaf (NTID), 1183
National Telecommunications and Information Administration (NTIA), 1279–1281, 2038
National Television and Video Preservation Foundation (NTVPF), 1579
National Terrorism Advisory Board, 4579
National Training Center and Clearinghouse (NTCC), 3035
National Training Information Service (NTIS), 687
National Trust, 4169, 4722–4723
National Union Catalog (NUC), 448, 769, 771
National War Museum of Scotland, 4719

National Zoological Park, 4194
Nation's Business, 650
Native American Graves Protection and Repatriation Act (NAGPRA) of 1990, 267, 1153, 1165–1166, 1169, 3167, 3245
Natural History, 644
Natural history museum, 1820, 3237, 4134
    Denmark, 1226
    Germany, 1704–1705
    Hungary, 1929
    India, 2021–2022
    London, 3224
    Madrid, 3152
    Tanzania, 4510
    United States, 5080
Natural language generation (NLG)
    applications, 430–431
    biography text, 432
    components, 431–432
    computational linguistics, 430
    current developments and outlook, 437–438
    dialogue situations, 431
    formal and computational properties, 430
    functional linguistics, 430
    linguistic variation
        aggregation, 435
        characterizations, 433
        discourse deixis, 435
        ideational representations, 434
        interpersonal control, 434–42
        lexicogrammar, 434–435
        linguistic abstraction, 434
        Penman text generation system, 434
        propositional content, 434
        semantic control, 434
        semantics, 434
        Sentence Plan Language, 434
        sentences, 435
        stratification, 433
        syntactic theory, 434
        textual control, 434–435
    macroplanning, 432
    message/text personalization, 433
    nonlinguistic material, 430
    non-NLG-based text production system, 433
    syntactic description, 430
    text planning, 436–437
Natural language processing (NLP), 274–275, 2201
    ANN
        advantages, 279–280
        cognitive models, 282
        connectionist/subsymbolic paradigm, 281
        disadvantages, 280
        formalisms, 281
        language-oriented disciplines, 281
        local and distributed representational schemes, 283
        meaning representation, 287
        physical symbol system, 281
        research paradigms, 283
        Rumelhart and McClelland model, 287–288
        sequential processing, 284–287
        symbolic paradigm, 281

    applications, 3353
    approaches
        connectionist approach, 3351
        hybrid approach, 3350
        similarities and differences, 3351–3353
        statistical approach, 3351
        symbolic approach, 3350–3351
    definition, 3346
    divisions, 3347
    goal, 3346–3347
    history, 3347–3348
    human-like language processing, 3346
    introspection, 3348
    levels
        discourse, 3350
        lexical, 3349
        lower *vs.* higher levels, 3350
        morphology, 3349
        phonological analysis, 3349
        pragmatic, 3350
        semantic, 3350
        syntactic, 3349
    origins, 3347
    synchronic *vs.* sequential model, 3348
Natural Resource Monitoring Partnership (NRMP), 3312
Natural SEM, *see* Search engine marketing
Nauta, Doede, 2051–2052
Navigability affordance, 1118
Nazi memorabilia, 783
NBII, *see* National Biological Information Infrastructure
Nebraska Library Association, 920
Negative feedback, 1036
Neighboring rights, 1268
NELINET, 3922, 3924
NELLI, 2825
NEMO, *see* Network of European Museum Organisations
Neoclassicism, 1742
Neo-Schumpeterian approach, 2254
NESLI2, 2825
netLibrary e-books, 1209–1211
Netscape Collabra™, 1057
Networked European Deposit Library (NEDLIB), 1333
Networked Knowledge Organization Systems/ Services (NKOS)
    aims and participants, 3366–3367
    special journal issues, 3368–3369
    workshops and special sessions, 3367–3368
"Networked Talent Model," 143–144
Network management
    activities, 3356
    ancillary support systems, 3357
    applications, 3356
    components, 3356
    dimensions, 3356
        accounting management, 3358
        configuration management, 3357–3358
        distributed computing systems, 3357
        fault management, 3357
        performance management, 3358
        security management, 3358–3359
    information and activity, 3362–3363
    LAN, 3356
    MAN, 3356

operating parameters, 3357
SOPs, 3357, 3361–3363
vendor-provided software, 3357
WAN, 3356
work patterns
    and dimensions, 3361–3362
    distributed infrastructure management, 3361
    network design, 3360–3361
    RTSC work, 3359–3360
Network management organization (NMO)
    ancillary support systems, 3357
    design work, 3356
    formal databases, 3361
    information management tools, 3361
    MIBs, 3361
    monitoring, 3357
    real-time supervisory control work, 3356
    SOPs, 3357, 3361–3363
    waterfall software development life cycle, 3356
Network neutrality (NN), 4778
Network of European Museum Organisations (NEMO), 3365
Network organization, 3516
Network resources, 2326–2328
Network visualizations and analysis, 2212–2213
Neue Erdbeschreibung, 1685
Neural-cultural flow line, 2058
Neural-cultural information, 2058
New Amsterdam Public Library, 3792
Newbery Medal, 334, 852
The New Downtown Library: Designing with Communities, 3788
New England Journal of Medicine, 3470
New Jersey State Library, 4398
New Library Buildings of the World, 2808
New Media Consortium (NMC), 2993
New museology, 614–615
Newsletters, 641
Newspaper indexes, 652
Newspapers, 640–641, 647, 998
Newsvendor model, 1197–1198
Newtonian mechanics, 282
The New World: Problems in Political Geography, 1688
New York Free Circulating Library, 1845
New York Historical Society (NYHS), 1780
New York Mathematical Society, 324
New York Museum of Modern Art, 3157
New York Public Library (NYPL), 1845, 3722, 5058
New York Society Library, 1841
New York Times, 3470, 3472
New Zealand Law Libraries Association (NZLLA), 3377
New Zealand libraries
    academic libraries, 3375–3376
    biculturalism, 3377–3378
    digital revolution, 3378
    education for librarianship, 3376–3377
    history, 3371–3373, 3377
    legislation, 3372
    origins, 3372
    professional associations, 3377
    professional registration, 3377
    public libraries, 3373–3374

school libraries, 3374–3375
special libraries, 3376
New Zealand Library and Information Association, 3548
New Zealand Library Association (NZLA), 3376–3377
NGOs, see Nongovernmental organizations
NiagaraCQ, 2631
Nicomachean Ethics, 644
Niedzwiedzka's information behavior model, 2092–2093
Nieuwe Instructie, 1400
Nikola Tesla Museum, 4135
Niles, Hezebiah, 647–648
Niles Weekly Register, 647–648
Nippon Hoso Kyokai (NHK), 1567
Nirvana fallacy, 783
NISO, see National Information Standards Organization
NLG, see Natural language generation
NLM, see National Library of Medicine
NLP, see Natural language processing
NLS, see National library service
NLS Collection Building Policy, 566
NMK, see National Museums of Kenya
NMO, see Network management organization
No Child Left Behind (NCLB) Public Law 107–110, 3992
Noel Butlin Archives Centre, 387
Noisy-channel approach, 422–423
Noll, Roger, 1016
Nonacademic link analysis, 4987
Nonato bindings, 541
Noncredentialed librarians, 4777
Nonempirical knowledge, 2610
Nongovernmental organizations (NGOs), 1721–1723, 5013
    A2K movement, 3386
    archives and collections, 3386
    definition, 3380–3381
    development and international assistance, 3384–3385
    development of, 3381–3382
    educational NGOs, 3385
    global civil society, 3386–3387
    human rights information, 3383–3384
    ICT education, 3385
    information dissemination, 3382–3383
    information types, 3382–3383
    library professional development, 3386
    literacy education, 3385–3386
    pros and cons of, 3382
Non-patent literature (NPL), 3566
Non-propositional knowledge, 2610
Non-webometrics research, 4989
Nordic Council for Scientific Information (NORDINFO), 2825
Nordic Forum for Information Literacy (NordINFOLIT), 2752
Nordic ISKO Chapter, 2498
Normalized Discounted Cumulative Gain (NDCG), 3946
North American binding, 546
North American Graves Protection and Repatriation Act (NAGPRA), 3234
North American Industry Classification System (NAICS), 638

North American Interlibrary Loan and Document Delivery (NAILDD) Project, 372
North American ISKO Chapter, 2498
North American Serials Interest Group (NASIG)
    ad-hoc executive council, 3388
    annual conference, 3391
    awards and scholarships, 3389–3390
    continuing education, 3390
    membership, 3388–3389
    organizational structure, 3389
    partnerships and other outreach, 3390
    permanent archives, 3388
    publications, 3390–3391
    site selection committee, 3388
North Carolina State University (NSCU), 1710
Northeast Document Conservation Center (NEDCC), 1350
Northern/Baltic Union Catalogue of Serials (NOSP), 2825
Northern Ireland
    archives and archival science
        archive services, 4736
        legislation, 4734
    broadcasting collections, 1566
    museums, 3261
    National Trust, 4722
Northern Light, 2522–2523
Northwestern Online Total Integrated System (NOTIS), 3452
Notices of the American Mathematical Society, 3027
Notre Dame Journal of Formal Logic, 3026
Nouvelle Géographie Universelle, 1687
Novel-item retrieval, 4555
Nuclear Information and Records Management Association (NIMRA), 1854
Numerical taxonomy, 4539
Nuremberg Chronicle, 1973
Nursing libraries, 1873
Nyborg Public Library, 2804–2805
Nylink, 3924

O

OAICat, 3401
OAIHarvester, 3401
Oakland Museum, 3218
OASIS Search Web Services Technical Committee, 2347
Object-as-sign, 1376
Object modeling, 3112
Object-oriented programming (OOP), 4540
Observations, 1685
Observations Touching on Trade and Commerce with Holland, 645
Obsolescence, 520–521
Occupational Outlook Handbook 2007-2008, 636
Occupational Safety and Health Act (OSHA), 1857–1858
Occupation, information society, 2257–2260
Occurrence identifiability, 1175
Oceania, 3547–3548
Odyssey, 644
Oeconomicus, 644
Office Document Architecture (ODA), 1365
Office for Accreditation (OA), 18

Office for Intellectual Freedom (OIF), 2387, 2391–2392
Office for Scientific and Technical Information (OSTI), 306
Office of Information and Regulatory Affairs (OIRA), 1550–1551
Office of Management and Budget (OMB), 1550–1551, 2154
Office of Research and Development (ORD), 3562
Office of Scholarly Communication (OSC), 365
Office of Scientific and Academic Publishing (OSAP), 365
Office of Scientific and Technical Information (OSTI), 1553
Office of Scientific Research and Development (OSRD), 2811
Official Gazette, 3561–3562, 3566
The Official Museum Directory, 4379
Official statistics, 495
Off-line storage, 4942
Ohio College Library Center (OCLC), 451, 1847, 2981; *see also* Online Computer Library Center
  bibliographic network, 2981
  cataloging system, 729–730
  EMEA, 3400
  WorldShare Record Manager, 1545
OhioLink, 987
Okapi BM-25 algorithm, 2205–2206
Okapi system, 3427–3428
Older adults' information needs and behavior
  computers and Internet, 3410
  everyday life information seeking, 3408, 3411
  imperative for studying older age groups, 3407
  information literacy (Fourth Age), 3409
  information needs, 3408–3409
  information sources, 3409
  library-based research, 3407
  old, definitions of, 3406–3407
  residential communities, 3409–3410
Old Testament, 644
On2broker, 3458
OncologySTAT.com, 3472
On-demand books (ODB), 3735
One-clause-at-a time (OCAT) methodology, 1621
One Laptop Per Child (OLPC) program, 1283–1284
One-mode network, 4237
One-person librarian (OPL)
  churches and synagogues, 3416
  future, 3418–3420
  history, 3413–3414
  hospital librarians, 3415–3416
  information brokers, 3416
  law libraries, 3415
  market researchers, 3416–3417
  meaning, 3413
  nontraditional sector, 3417
  organization's goals, 3418
  prison librarians, 3415
  public librarians, 3416
  school librarians, 3416
  special libraries, 3414–3415
  tasks, categories, 3417–3418
  zoo librarians, 3416

One Thousand and One Nights, 853
One type, one printer theory, 1971
ONIX metadata upstream, 3395
Online Account Management Service, 683
Online bibliographic database, 4629
Online bibliographic retrieval, 2245
Online catalogs, 2079
Online Computer Library Center (OCLC), 2, 671, 733, 894, 984, 1390–1391, 1880, 2181, 2921, 3381, 3450–3452, 3454, 3916, 4472, 4578, 4774–4775, 4800
  advocate for libraries, 3401–3402
  Asia pacific, 3404
  Canada, 3404
  cataloging service, 3396–3397
  DDC
    Abridged WebDewey, 1259–1260
    BISAC subject headings, 1261
    Classify, 1262
    development, 1260
    Scorpion software, 1262
    Subject Headings for Children and People, Places & Things, 1261
    translations, 1260
    WebDewey, 1259
    WorldCat Collection Analysis service, 1258, 1262–1263
    XML representations, 1260
  digital collection services, 3400
  eCONTENT, 3399
  electronic books, 3399–3400
  eSerials Holdings Service, 3398
  Europe, Middle East and Africa, 3405
  finances, 3394
  Google, 3403–3404
  governance
    Board of Trustees, 3393–3394
    contribution, 3392–3393
    Global Council, 3394
    Members Council, 3392–3393
    membership, 3392
    membership participation levels, 3393
    WorldCat Principles of Cooperation, 3393
  history, 3392
  integrated library systems, 3400
  Latin American and Caribbean, 3404–3405
  outside United States, 3404
  programs and research, 3400–3401
  QuestionPoint, 3398–3399
  reference and resource sharing, 3398
  RLNs, 3921–3923
  U.S. activity, 3404
  WebJunction, 3402
  WorldCat
    bibliographic database, 3394
    collection analysis, 3398
    CONTENTdm collections, 3400
    enrichment and quality control, 3395–3396
    evolution, 3396
    FirstSearch service, 3395
    growth, 3396–3397
    and information standards, 3396
    Navigator, 3398
    Online Union Catalog, 3394
    Open WorldCat pilot program, 3402–3403
    selection, 3398
    statistics, 3395

    web services, 3403
    WorldCat Local, 3403
    WorldCat.org, 3403
Online databases, 2240–2241
Online information exchange (ONIX), 4056
Online library instruction
  assessment
    economic viability, 3444
    learner/instructor preferences, 3444
    learning outcomes, 3444
    usability, 3443
  CAI, 3444
    benefits, 3435
    computer-assisted demonstration, 3434
    independent learning tutorials, 3435
    live assistance and hand-on, computer-based learning, 3434–3435
  early days of distance education, 3434
  history
    emergence of distance education, 3432–3433
    need for teaching librarian, 3432
    online education as distance education, 3433
  instructional opportunities
    credit course, 3437–3438
    discipline-specific online library instruction, 3437
    intended audience, 3435
    librarian professional development, 3438–3440
    popular database and OPAC, 3436
    in schools of library and information studies, 3438–3439
    teaching information literacy skills, 3436–3437
    virtual tour, 3436
  internet, libraries and online learning
    assessment of, 3443–3444
    case for CAI, 3435
    instructional opportunities for online library instruction, 3435–3439
  predictors and predecessors, 3433
  technology
    chat, 3442–3443
    collaborative Web browsing, 3443
    conferencing software and courseware, 3442
    reaching online learner through electronic mail, 3440, 3442
    static Web pages, 3439
    web site interaction, 3439–3441
Online Programming for All Libraries (OPAL), 17
Online public access catalogs (OPAC), 1–2, 250, 451–452, 487, 841, 1878, 2219–2220, 2240, 2847, 2854, 2947, 3399, 3435–3436, 4159, 4467–4468, 4789, 4978–4982
  Boolean retrieval systems, 3422
  vs. card catalog, 3450
  database records, 3422
  design, improvements, 3429
    automated search heuristics, 3428
    best-match retrieval approaches, 3427–3428
    browse interface, 3426
    catalog records, enhancement of, 3427

E-referencer system, 3427–3429
  expert intermediary systems, 3428
  graphical and direct manipulation inter-
    faces, 3425–3426
  helpful and user-oriented interfaces,
    3425
  knowledge-based techniques, 3428
  query expansion and formulation support,
    3427
  relevance feedback capability, 3428
  search/decision trees, 3428–3429
  development, 3450–3452
  effective, 3453–3454
  functions, 3452–3453
  multicatalog and electronic database search,
    3429
  search strategies, 2241
  subject descriptors, 3422
  subject searching
    class number search, 3424
    initial and reformulation strategies, 3424
    knowledge, 3423–3424
    problems, 3424–3425
    proportion of, 3423
    vs. specific-item searching, 3423
    subject field, 3423–3424
  types, 3451–3452
  usage patterns, 2242
  users, 3422
  Web interfaces, 3422
Online searching, 2079, 2320–2322
Online self-publishing, *see* Self-publishing
    online
Online Service Provider Safe Harbors provision,
    3654
On Medical Experience, 3043
Ontolingua system, 3458
Ontology
  Cyc, 3456–3457
  definition, 3455
  expressiveness, 3457–3458
  formal semantics, 3455
  generality of, 3456–3457
  hierarchy, 3456
  information integration, 3455
  knowledge sharing and reuse, 3455, 3463
  languages
    KIF language, 3458
    KL-ONE, LOOM, and CLASSIC, 3458
    Ontobroker and On2broker, 3458
    OWL, 3461–3463
    problems, 3462–3463
    RDF schema, 3460–3462
    Semantic Web, 3458–3459
    XML document, 3459–3460
  metaphysics, 3616
  real-world semantics, 3455
  Semantic Web, 3456
  types of, 3456
Ontology Interference Language (OIL), 1366
OPACs, *see* Online Public Access Catalogs
Open access (OA)
  African librarianship, 39
  ARL, 365–366
  version control, 4898
"Open access advantage," 2371
Open Access publication, 2902, 2907

Open access scholarship and publishing
  advertising, 3472
  author-funded journals, 3468–3469
  books, 3472
  from conventional to digital publishing,
    3465–3466
  database integrators, 3471–3472
  from digital to open publishing, 3466
  e-print services, 3466
  frontiers, 3473–3474
  knowledge base, 3474
  long-term storage and retrieval, 3472–3473
  open journals, 3467–3469
  search and indexes, 3470–3471
  self-archiving, 3466–3467
  subscriptions, 3469–3470
  Wikipedia, 3467
Open Access Working Group (OAWG), 345
Open air museums, 1820–1821
Open Annotation Data Model, 5020
Open Archival Information System (OAIS),
    1332, 1361, 1364–1366, 1577
  content, 3481
  development process, 3478–3480
  functional model, 3482–3483
  information model, 3483–3484
  reference model, 3480–3481
Open Archive Initiative Standard (OAIS), 2480
Open Archives Initiative (OAI), 3063, 3227,
    3401, 3467, 4899
Open Archives Initiative-Object Reuse and
    Exchange (OAI-ORE) standard, 1365
Open Archives Initiative Protocol for Metadata
    Harvesting (OAI-PMH), 1362, 1365,
    2894, 2983
Open Conference Systems (OCS), 2902
Open Content Alliance, 3655
Open Directory Project (ODP), 2524,
    4031–4032
OpenDocument format (ODF), 2342–2343
Open Document Management API (ODMA),
    1361, 1365
Open Educational Resources (OERs), 2903,
    4659
Open Journal Software (OJS), 2902
Open Journal Systems (OJS), 39, 3468
Open Ontology Repository (OOR), 4074–4075
Open Polytechnic of New Zealand, 3376
Open Society Archives, 1926
Open Society Institute (OSI), 2827
Open Software Foundation (OSF), 2344
OpenSource Metadata Framework (OMF) Tem-
    plate, 3064–3065
Open source software (OSS)
  BSD Unix (*see* Berkeley Systems Distribution
    of Unix)
  consensus-based approach, 3489
  Cygnus Support, 3489
  Deming's work, 3491
  Free Software Foundation, 3489
  GNU, 3488
  IBM, 3490–3491
  origin, 3488
  Sun Microsystems, 3489
  tech-heavy disciplines, 3492
  text, 3489–3490
  World Wide Web, 3491

Open-system indexing, 440
Open Systems Interconnection model, 3356
Open systems theory, 3514–3515
Open Training Platform (OTP), 4659
Open University of Brazil (UAB), 604–605
OpenURL, 1136, 1330, 2894
OpenURL/link resolvers, 4899
Operationalist searcher, 4877–4878
Operational moves, 2241
Operational Selection Policies, 111
Operation Cathedral, 782
Operations research/management science (OR/
    MS) perspective, 1192–1193
Opinion poll, 4798
OPL, *see* One-person librarian
Optimized network topology, 3360
Oracle, 2272–2273
Oral history, 3247–3248, 4794
  associations, 3499–3450
  curating, 3497–3499
  definition, 3494
  history, 3494–3496
  methods, 3496–3497
  programs, 3500–3502
*Oram's New York Price Current and Marine
    Register*, 1401
ORCID
  an open effort, 3505
  APIs, 3506–3508
  community involvement and governance,
    3506
  data exchange standards, 3508
  data privacy and security, 3506–3507
  goal of, 3505
  mission activities, 3509
  ORCID iD, 3505
  participants, 3507
  record creation, 3506
  registry, 3505–3506
  revenues, 3507
  use cases, 3508
Ordered weighted averaging (OWA) operators,
    1624, 1630–1631
Ordrupgaard Collection, 1226
Oregon State Library, 4398
Organic organization, 3514
Organic search, *see* Search engine marketing
Organizational communication, 4117–4118
Organizational culture
  assessment of, 3522–3523
  influences on, 3520–3521
  information culture, 3521–3522
  library context, 3523
Organizational framework, 3110
Organizational learning (OL), 2650, 3515
  behavioral perspectives, 3528
  cognitive perspectives, 3528
  conceptual landscape of, 3533
  definition, 3526–3527
  deutero-learning, 3531
  double-loop learning, 3531
  history, 3527
  knowledge assets, 3526
  learning agents
    groups, 3529
    individuals, 3528–3529
    organizational level, 3529

Organizational learning (OL) (cont'd.)
  process
    institutionalization, 3530–3531
    integration, 3530
    interpretation, 3529–3530
    intuition, 3529
  single-loop learning, 3531
  social constructivist perspectives, 3528
  value of, 3531
Organizational memory (OM), 2643–2644,
    3538–3539
  and culture
    knowledge sharing, 3535–3537
    management task, 3535
    organization knowledge management pro-
      grams, 3536
  definition, 3534–3535
  knowledge-management system, 3537
  long term memory, 3534
  operational knowledge, types of, 3535
  organizational forgetting, 3537–3538
  short-and medium-term memory, 3534
  strategic forgetting, 3538
  tacit knowledge, 3534
Organizational Self-Study Committee (OSSC),
    67
Organizational sociology, 3520
Organization Danish Archives (ODA), 1224
Organization for the Advancement of Structured
    Information Standards (OASIS) Consor-
    tium, 2190
Organization life cycle models, 3515
Organization names, 3291–3292
Organization of African Unity (OAU), 1502
Organization of Juvenile and Adolescent Librar-
    ies, 1733
Organization theory
  administrative decision-making behavior,
    3513–3514
  authority and power relations, 3510–3511
  bureaucracy, 3510–3511
  business process reengineering, 3511
  classical organization theory, 3511–3512
  competing values framework, 3515
  contingency theory, 3514–3515
  cooperative contract, 3513
  cooperative participatory process, 3511
  differentiation and coordination, 3510
  Fayol's theory, 3511
  human relations approach, 3513
  leadership and group processes, 3513
  life-cycle approach, 3515
  line-staff principle, 3512
  motivation, 3513
  networked organizations, 3516–3517
  network theory, 3515
  open systems, 3514–3515
  organization, definition of, 3510
  population ecology, 3514
  public administration, 3510–3512
  public management, 3517
  resource dependence theory, 3515
  resource exchange, 3515
  scientific management approach, 3511
  span of control, 3512
  structural approach, 3512
  total quality management, 3511

Original cataloging, 703, 729
Original order, 105, 116
Orphaned collections, 1152
Orphans Film Symposium, 1577
Orsay Museum, 1597
Orthographic awareness, 3844
Ostraka, 3552–3553, 3557
Otlet, Paul, 4783
Ottonian illumination, 1948
Outdoor museum, 4166–4167
Out of vocabulary (OOV) words, 4573
Outstanding Collaboration Citation, 332
Ouvriers Européans, 1687
Overcasting, see Oversewing
Overdrive, 4058
Oversewing, 539
OWL DL, 3463
The Oxford Guide to Style, 443
Oxford University Museum, 3155

P

Pacifica Radio Archives, 1566
Pacific Islands Association of Libraries and
    Archives (PIALA)
  advocacy, 3546
  American Library Association, 3548
  board meetings, 3543
  conferences, 3545–3546, 3548
  Dakio Syne Memorial Fund, 3549
  Fiji Library Association, 3548
  financial organization, 3543
  Florence Nalezny Warpeha Memorial Books
    to Micronesian Libraries, 3549
  goals of, 3541
  governance, 3543
  Hawaii Library Association, 3548
  history of, 3541–3543
  human networks, 3549
  IFLA, 3547–3548
  lifetime achievement award, 3549
  membership, 3544
  Micronesia, 3541–3542
  PIALA Listserv, 3544
  PIALA Newsletter, 3544
  PIALA Web page, 3544
  PREL, 3548–3549
  proceedings, 3544–3545
  purpose of, 3543
  resource sharing, 3547
  Swedish Library Association, 3548
  training initiatives, 3546–3547
Pacific Islands Association of Libraries,
    Archives and Museums (PIALAM),
    3542
Pacific Northwest Information Node (PNWIN),
    3310
Pacific Press Professor of Literacy Technology,
    3468
Pacific Resources for Educational and Learning
    (PREL), 3548–3549
PageRank algorithm, 484, 1042
Palace Museum Archives, see Ming-Qing
    Archives
Palace Museum in the Forbidden City, 909
Palau Library Association, 3546
Paley Center for Media, 1577

PALINET, 3920, 3922
Palo Alto Research Campus (PARC), 4025
Palo Alto Research Center, Inc. (PARC), 4115
Pandora recommender system, 3863
Panel stamps, 543
Pan-Pacific Education and Communication
    Experiments by Satellite (PEACESAT),
    3542
Pantheologia, 4176–4177
Papazian Library of the American University of
    Armenia, 230–231
Paper
  antecedents to
    papyrus, 1824–1825
    parchment/vellum, 1825–1826
  decoration, 1832–1833
  fibers, 1829–1830
  grain of, 1831
  history, 1826
  manufacture
    Asian methods, 1826–1827
    western methods, 1827–1829
  modern hand papermaking, 1834
  modern papermaking, 1833–1834
  preservation, 1832
  sizes, 1830–1832
  watermarks, 1830
  weight, 1831
Paperwork Reduction Act (PRA), 1550–1551,
    1857
Papyri
  collections, 3553
  history
    culture, 3557
    language, 3557
    law and institutions, 3556
    political history, 3555–3556
    society and economy, 3556–3557
  literature
    greek authors, 3555
    history of book, 3554–3555
    religious literature, 3555
  and paper, 3552
  publications, 3554
  rediscovery of, 3552–3553
  research and research facilities, 3553–3554
  treatment of, 3553
Papyrology, 3552
Papyrus, 1824–1825
Papyrus Ebers, 3041
Papyrus of Ani, 1945
Paraprofessionals, 878–879, 919–920
PARBICA, 688, 2440–2441
Parchment/vellum, 1825–1826
Pareto distributions, 2226
Parish libraries
  in United Kingdom, 1837
  in United States, 1840
Paris Psalter, 1947
Parliamentary Online Information Service
    (POLIS), 4507
Parliament Library
  Greece, 1729–1730
  New Delhi, India, 2006
PARLMEDIA, 661
PARRY, 3348
Participatory GIS (PGIS), 1672–1673

Participatory three-dimensional modeling (P3DM), 1672–1673
Particle-induced X-ray emission (PIXE), 478
Partner institutions network, 535
Partnership libraries, 4160–4161
The Past as Prologue: The Evolution of Art Librarianship, 249
Patchwriting, 3664
Patent Abstracts of Japan (PAJ), 3569
Patent Act of 1790, 3560
Patent Act of 1793, 3561
Patent Act of 1836, 3561
Patent and Trademark Depository Libraries (PTDL), 3562
Patent and Trademark Depository Library Program (PTDLP), 640
Patent Application Information Retrieval (PAIR) system, 3566
Patent classification systems
    IPC, 3566–3567
    USPC, 3566–3567
Patent Cooperation Treaty (PCT), 815
Patent documents
    AI patents, 3565
    APC documents, 3566
    certificates of correction, 3566
    dedications, 3566
    defensive publications, 3565
    design/industrial designs, 3565
    disclaimers, 3566
    drawing, 3564
    front page, 3563–3564
    INID codes, 3564
    kind codes, 3564
    plant patents, 3565
    reexamination certificates, 3566
    reissue patents, 3565
    SIRs, 3565–3566
    specification, 3564
    TVPP publications, 3566
    utility models, 3565
    utility patents, 3564–3565
Patent information
    history
        1790–1870, 3560–3561
        1870–1970, 3561–3562
        1970–2008, 3562–3563
    monopoly right, 3560
    patentability search, 3560
    patent protection, 3560
    WIPO, 3560
Patent Lens, 3570–3571
Patent Map Guidance, 3570
Patent Office Fire of 1836, 3561
Patents, 639–640, 815, 833–834; *see also* Patent documents; Patent information
PatentScope, 3570
Patents Ordinance of 1924, 4513
PatFT patent database, 3566
Pathfinder Network (PFNET), 485, 931–932
PATRIOT Act, 2402–2403
Patron-driven acquisition (PDA), 415–416, 1209
Paul Banks and Carolyn Harris Preservation Award, 331
Paul of Aegina, 3044
Paulo Montenegro Institute (IPM), 603
Peale, Charles Willson, 1818, 4767

Pedigree chart, 1656
PeerEvaluation, 47
Peer review, version control, 4898–4899
Peer-to-peer data grids, 3000
Peer-to-peer networks, 3652
Peircean sign theory, 4098, 4101
Peking University Library (PUL), 896, 903
Penman text generation system, 434
Pennsylvania Academy of Fine Arts, 4767
Pension Protection Act of 2006, 639
People–place–information trichotomy, 1512
People with disabilities and libraries
    archives, 3575
    barriers, 3573
    cataloging and indexing, 3580–3581
    collection development, 3580
    disability
        categories of, 3574
        definition, 3573
    disability rights movement, 3574
    electronic resource accessibility
        assistive technology, 3579
        circulating equipment, 3579
        library websites, 3578–3579
        Tatomir Accessibility Checklist, 3578
        vendor database, 3578
        WCAG guidelines, 3578
    for-profit sector, 3575
    history, 3575–3576
    language, 3575
    legislation, 3575
    museums, 3575
    outreach, 3580
    physical resource accessibility
        physical books and media, 3577
        services and programming, 3577–3578
        space, 3576–3577
    print disabilities, 3574
    social model, 3573
    staff training, 3579–3580
Perceived attributes, IT adoption
    compatibility, 2296
    complexity, 2293, 2296
    observability, 2293, 2296
    relative advantage
        behavioral intention to use/actual usage, 2295
        information quality, 2293–2294
        IT quality, 2293
        service quality, 2294–2295
        user satisfaction, 2295
    triability, 2296
Performance libraries, 3276–3277
Performing arts; *see also* Visual and performing arts
    archives
        Center for Black Music Research, 4755
        Folger Shakespeare Library, 4756
        New York Public Library, 4756
    definition, 4925
    live and recorded elements, 4925
    live events, 4925
Performing Arts Data Service (PADS), 297
Perseus Project, 1290
Persian illumination (1502–1736), 1955–1956
Persistent uniform resource locator (PURL), 2155

Personal anticipated information need (PAIN) hypothesis, 2119
Personal construct theory, 2234
Personal health record (PHR), 86, 979, 3342
Personal information management, 2111
    analysis
        finding/refinding activities, 3588
        information item and form, 3586
        keeping activities map, 3588
        meta-level activities, 3588
        personal information collections, 3587
        PSI, 3587
    checkbox methodology, 3597
    convergence and integration, 3599
    e-mails, 3598–3599
    factors, 3598
    history, 3585–3586
    information fragmentation, 3585
    maintenance and organization, 3585
    observant participation, 3598
    PICs, 3584
    practical methodologies, 3597
    privacy, security and information, 3585, 3599
    research
        finding/refinding activity, 3588–3591
        GIM and PIM social fabric, 3596
        keeping activities, 3591–3593
        meta-level activity, 3593–3596
    search technology, 3599
    user-subjective approach, 3598
Personality facet
    levels of, 1536
    rounds of, 1536–1537
PERsonalized and Successive Information Search Tools (PERSIST), 1901
Personally identifiable information (PII), 1489
Personal space of information (PSI), 3587
Personnel Administration Section (PAS), 2844
Pertinence relevance judgments, 3943
Peru
    libraries
        academic libraries, 3608
        education and professional associations, 3608
        modern challenges, 3608–3609
        National Library, 3606–3608
        publications, 3607
        public libraries, 3606–3608
        school libraries, 3608
        during Spanish domination, 3606
    map of, 3606–3607
Pervasive information systems, 1488
Peschel, Oscar, 1687
Pests, 1150–1151
Peterborough library, 1839, 1843
Pew Global Attitudes project, 1061
Pew Research Center, 5028
Pew Research Institute's American Life Project, 841
PFNET algorithm, 485
Pharmacophore searching, 834–835
Phenomenography, 2754
Philadelphia Museum of Art, 1072, 3253
Philadelphia Peale Museum, 3243
Philosophical Transactions of the Royal Society, 646

Philosophy
  branches, 3615, 3617–3618
  definitions, 3614–3615
  of information
    epistemology, 3616–3617
    ethics, 3617
    as meta-field, 3610
    metaphysics, 3616
    meta-studies, 3611
  of information sciences
    approaches, 3618
    Becher's model, 3618–3619
    epistemological questions, 3618
    goals, 3618
    hard fields, 3618
    as meta-field, 3611
    nomothetic–idiographic spectrum, 3619
    preparadigmatic communities, 3618
    scientific–humanistic distinction, 3618
    soft fields, 3618–3619
  metaphilosophy, 3615
  meta-questions, 3614, 3619
  personal/professional, 3611–3612
  of philosophy, 3611
Philosophy of science
  library and information sciences, 3631–3632
  organization, 3624–3625
  scope, 3623
Phoenix Central Library, 2791
Phonetics, 2–3
Phonogramm-Archiv, 4299
Phonographs, 4055
Phonological awareness, 3842, 3844
Phonological processing hypothesis, 3842
Photographic images, 1307–1308
Photostat technology, 1782
Phrase headings, 2866
Phrase searching, 4048–4049
Phronesis, 2678
Phronetic leadership, 2446
Physical bibliography
  analytical bibliography, 477–478
  descriptive bibliography, 478
  historical bibliography, 478–468
  textual bibliography, 478
Physical Geography, 1686
Physical Symbol System Hypothesis (PSSH),
  283
Physical wayfinding, 4958
Physiological needs, 2115, 2119
PIALA, see Pacific Islands Association of
  Libraries and Archives
Picasso Museum, 1596, 4332
Picture Australia, 1363
Picture books
  alphabet books, 859
  concept books, 859
  counting books, 859
  definitions, 856–857
  engineered books, 860
  graphic novels, 860
  illustration, styles of, 857–859
  text of, 857
  trends in, 860–861
  wordless picture books, 858–859
Pinakes ("tablets"), 468–469
Pio Clemente Museum, 1818

Pipeline architecture, 431–432
Piracy, 4298
Pirate Bay, 3653, 3656
Pittsburgh Project, 1415
Pixelation, 1309
Pixel-level object, 4421
Pixels, 1308–1310
PLA, see Public Library Association
Place identity, 3262
Plagiarism of print and electronic resources
  academic dishonesty
    definition, 3665
    faculty attitudes, 3668–3669
    individual differences, 3668–3669
    social factors, 3668
  cheating, 3665
  coping with
    ethical reasoning, 3669–3670
    online instruction, 3670
    prevention techniques, 3670
    software detection programs, 3670
    teacher's role to translate moral ideology,
      3669
  definitions, 3664–3665
  effective pedagogical approaches, 3666
  fabrication, 3665
  hidden curriculum, 3669
  inadvertent/unconscious plagiarism, 3665
  paraphrasing plagiarism, 3665
  ProQuest Platinum database, 3665–3666
Planetarium, 3238
Planned-situational interactive IR model,
  2247–2248, 4881–4883
Planning and Budget Assembly (PBA), 72
Planning, organizing, staffing, directing, coordi-
  nating, reporting, and budgeting
  (POSDCORB), 3511
Planographic printing, 1868
Plaquette binding, 551
Platform for Internet content selection (PICS),
  783, 1393
PLATO, 1029
The Pleasant Art of Money Catching, 1400
PLOS ALM Reports, 47
Plum Analytics, 45
Pluralism, 3811–3812
PMEST
  energy, space, and time, 2135–2136
  matter, 2132–2133
  personality, 2131–2132
PNG format, 1311
POD, see Print-on-demand
Poetry, 861–862
Poland
  archives, 3685–3687
  historical background, 3674–3676
  library legislation, 3676–3677
  map of, 3675
  museums, 3685
  national bibliography
    Bibliografia Wydawnictw Ciągłych,
      3683
    Bibliografia Zawartości Czasopism,
      3683
    digital libraries, 3683–3684
    librarians and libraries, organizations sup-
      port to, 3684–3685

Polonica Zagraniczne. Bibliografia, 3683
professional education and training, librar-
  ians, 3684
Przewodnik Bibliograficzny, 3682–3683
public libraries, 3677–3678
research libraries
  National Library, 3679–3682
  NUKAT, 3679
school libraries, 3678
Policy and Standards Division (PSD),
  2858–2859
Policy on Loyalty Programs, 2392–2393
Polish ISKO Chapter, 2497
Political Arithmetic, 1402
Political ideologies, 4404–4405
Politics, 644
Politische Discurs, 1401
Politische Geographie, 1687
Polo, Marco, 1684
Polyphonic music, 3267–3268, 3272
Polysemy, 2689
Pompidou Center, 1597
Poor's Manual of Railroads, 1404
Popper, Karl, 2055–2056
Population ecology, 3514
Portable document format (PDF), 1367, 2342
Portico, 1213
Positional formats, 1177
Positive feedback, 1036
Positivism, 3628–3629
Post-cancellation access (PCA), 1335
Postcoordinate indexing, 1985
Poughkeepsie principles, 4565–4566
Power law, 1040–1041
Poznan Foundation of Scientific Libraries, 2828
Practical working ethics, 1473
Practice materials, 2739
Pragmatism, 2613
Prairienet, 1030
Pratt, Allan, 2052
Pratt–Smoot Act, 563, 3576
Precision (P), 3945
Precoordinated index, 1985
Preferential attachment, 1041
Pre-Hellenic mathematics, 3020
Preliterate society, 3831–3832
PrepComs, 5012–5013
Presentational markup, 3073
Preservation, 2468
  of audiovisual material
    analog audio and videotape materials,
      1568–1572
    digital formats, 1571
    film, 1567–1568, 2465, 2467
    funding, 1578–1579
    sound and audiovisual collections, 2413, 2416
    UNESCO, 4660–4661
Preservation and Conservation (PAC), 2457
Preservation and Reformatting Section (PARS),
  329
Preservation Description Information (PDI),
  1366
Preservation Metadata: Implementation Strate-
  gies (PREMIS), 1366, 1575
Preserved context indexing system (PRECIS),
  3137
Preserving Digital Information (PDI), 3484

Presidential libraries
    history
        Archivist report, 3715
        Claypoole, Richard, 3715
        Clinton Presidential Project, 3715
        Eisenhower Library, 3715
        George H.W. Bush Library, 3715
        Hoover, 3714
        John F. Kennedy Library, 3715
        Johnson, Lyndon B., 3715
        Lyndon Baines Johnson Foundation, 3715
        NARA, 3715
        public–private partnership, 3715
        Roosevelt, Franklin D., 3714
        Truman Grants program, 3714
    list, 3717–3718
    presidential materials
        audiovisual and photographic record, 3716
        Clinton Presidential Materials Project, 3716
        economic indicators and project, 3717
        The Foreign Gifts and Decorations Act, 3716
        library websites, 3717
        National Archives, 3716
        National Study Commission report, 3716
        Nixon Presidential Materials Staff, 3716
        personal papers and historical materials, 3716
        presidential papers, 3715
        PRMPA, 3716
        selective donation and selective destruction, 3716
    public and educational programs, 3717
Presidential Libraries Act of 1955, 3714–3715
Presidential Recordings and Materials Preservation Act (PRMPA), 3716
Presidential Records Act, 3716
Pressure ethics, 1473
Presumed credibility, 1115
Pretty Good Privacy (PGP), 404
Preventive censorship, 3676
Primary mathematics literature
    biological and behavioral sciences, 3025
    book series, 3027–3028
    journals, 3026–3027
    nonserial book, 3025
    publishers, 3026
Primary records
    card catalogs, conversions of, 3722
    definition, 3719–3721
    electronic forms, 3721
    survival and accessibility of
        artifacts, preservation of, 3728–3730
        collection-based institution, 3727
        dematerialization of information, 3726
        ownership and access, 3726
        paper facsimiles, 3727
        physical presentation of verbal texts, 3730
        primary texts, 3726
        print products, 3726
        rare books, 3726
        storage, conservation and preservation, 3727
    uses of, 3722–3725
Primos Library in Secane, Philadelphia, 1638
Principal component analysis (PCA), 3272
Principle of cumulative advantage, 4199

Print DDA programs, 1211–1212
Print disabilities, 3574
Printing
    in China, 1865
    histories, 1861
    intaglio, 1867–1868
    modern techniques, 1868
    planographic, 1868
    relief, 1865–1867
Printing Act of 1895, 2150
Printing press, 999, 3606
Print-on-demand (POD), 3736–3737, 3986, 4055–4056
    authors, opportunities for, 3736
    book publishing, impacts on, 3733–3734
        commercial and vanity publishers, 3735
        long tail, 3734
        nontraditional and traditional publishing, 3734–3735
        ODB, 3735
        suppliers, growth in, 3735
    book retailers, 3736
    digital printing
        art reproductions and artist books, 3736
        digital image, 3733, 3735
        vs. offset printing, 3733
    music publishing, 3736
Prison librarians, 3415
Pritchard, Alan, 497–499, 506
Privacy Act of 1974, 1857, 2151
Privacy Act of 1976, 1555
Privacy vs. information sharing, 2398–2399
Private bureaucracy, 2256
Private libraries, 748
    America, 1839
    Croatia, 1123
    Mexican libraries, 3091
    Peru, 3606
    Poland, 3674
    Saudi Arabia, 3973–3974
    Ukraine, 4642
Private press
    aristocratic plaything, 3739–3740
    author, 3740–3741
    bibliography, 3743
    clandestine, 3741
    educational press, 3739
    fine books, 3741–3742
    little, 3743
    origins, 3738
    quasi-official press, 3738–3739
    scholarly presses, 3739
Private presses, 4337
Probabilistic models, 422–423
Probabilistic Relational Models (PRM), 274
Probability, theory of, 494–496
Probate records, 1658
Problem, intervention, comparison, and outcome (PICO), 1517
Problem-solving model, 2088–2089
Procedural and descriptive markup, 4560
Procedural knowledge, 3535
Procedural markup, 3074
Proceedings of Symposia in Pure Mathematics, 3028
Proceedings of the American Mathematical Society, 3027

Proceedings of the National Academy of Sciences (PNAS), 3469
Proceedings of the Steklov Institute of Mathematics in the Academy of Sciences of the USSR, 3028
Process-based retention schedules, see Large aggregation retention schedules
Process knowledge, 3535
Process quality management, 1178
Producer–Archive Interface Methodology Abstract Standard (PAIMAS), 3485
Producer–Archive Interface Specification (PAIS), 3485
Product catalogs, 639
Professional associations, 303, 3377
Professional conference organizer (PCO), 2453
Professional machine bureaucracies, 3512
Professional metadata creators, 3066
Professional recognition, MLA, 3036
Professional Records and Information Management, International Association (PRISM), 1853
Professional registration, 3377
Program for Cooperative Cataloging (PCC), 454, 2871, 3395
Program for Museum Development in Africa (PMDA), see Centre for Heritage Development in Africa
Programme on Information and Communication Technologies (PICT), 2255
Progression of actions lifecycle model, 168
Prolegomena to Library Classification, 1534
PROLOG, 272
Promotion and Identification of Emerging Advanced Telecommunications Services (PISTA), 4322
Property rights, 2277
Prophetic Shrine Library, 3976
Propositional knowledge
    belief
        dispositional view, 2610
        state-object view, 2610–2611
    justification
        adequate indication, 2613
        contextualism, 2615–2616
        epistemic coherentism, 2614
        epistemic foundationalism, 2614–2615
        fallibilism, 2613
        inductive justification, 2613–2614
        inferential justification, 2614
        modest foundationalism, 2615
        radical foundationalism, 2615
    vs. non-propositional knowledge, 2610
    truth, 2611–2612
        coherence, 2612–2613
        correspondence, 2612
        pragmatic value, 2613
Propositions, 592–593
ProQuest Coutts Award for Innovation, 332
ProQuest Ebooks, 1211
Prospectus d'un nouveau dictionnaire de commerce, 1403
Protein Data Bank, 836
Prototypical task, 4555
Provenance, 116
Provenance information, 1364

Provenance of archival materials
  definition, 3746
  historic developments, 3750
  modern thinking
    archivalterity, 3753
    archivist, role of, 3752
    authority control, creation of, 3751
    computer retrieval systems, 3750–3751
    corporate and personal provenance, 3752
    creator context, 3752
    custodial context, 3752
    electronic records, 3751
    ISAAR (CPF), 3751
    original order, 3752–3753
    physical and theoretical organization of
      records, 3751
    provenance information, 3751
    record-keeping context, 3752
    secondary provenance, 3752
    societal provenance, 3752
  origins and development
    archive group, 3748
    in Australia, 3749–3750
    in Canada, 3749
    diplomatic manuals, 3747–3748
    organization and functions, 3748
    original order, 3748–3749, 3753
    record group, 3749
    respect des fonds, 3747–3749
    subject classification, 3747
    title deeds, arrangement of, 3747
Provenance of museum objects
  custodial paths
    art, 3757
    interest in provenance, 3758–3759
    ownership/possession, 3756–3757
    rightful, clear and good title, 3757–3758
  definition, 3756
  museum policies, 3759
  museum practices, 3759–3760
  museum standards, 3760–3761
  tempered sharing, 3762–3763
  time, diligence and care
    ascertaining provenance, 3761
    finding favored sources, 3761–3762
Provenance of rare books
  book history, 3772
  cataloging provenance information, 3770–
    3771
  definition, 3766–3767
  early printed books, 3767
  external evidence
    auctions and dealers' sales catalog, 3770
    inventories and library catalogs, 3769–
      3770
  internal evidence
    bindings, 3768–3769
    bookplates, 3768
    conservation science, 3769
    heraldry, 3768
    inscriptions, 3768
    library marks and stamps, 3768
    physical features and formats, 3767–3768
  legal implications, 3771–3772
  modern editions, 3767
  uses and value of, 3770
Provenance Online Project (POP), 3771

Provincial and Territorial Public Library Coun-
    cil (PTPLC), 665
Pseudonyms, 3289–3291
Psycho-Biology of Language, 502
Psychographics, 3168–3169
Ptolemy, 1684
Public Access to Court Electronic Records
    (PACER), 1554
Public Affairs Information Service (PAIS), 4370
Public Archives Act of 1965, 2594, 2600
Public Archives of Canada, 3749
Public art librarians, 251–252
Publication-quality photography, 3206
Public bureaucracy, 2256
Public Company Accounting Oversight Board
    (PCAOB), 639
Public entrepreneurs, 3517
Public institutions of higher education (IPES),
    607
Public international law, 2735
Public Knowledge Project (PKP), 2902, 3468
Public Lending Right Commission, 683
Public Lending Right Remuneration, 1218
Public librarians, 3416
Public librarianship
  certification, 3777
  community-based, 3776–3777
  education, 3777
  human rights, 3777–3778
  immigrants, 3779
  people with disabilities, 3778
  privacy, 3778–3779
  ranges, 3779
  United States, 3774–3776
  working conditions, 3777
Public libraries
  acquisitions units, organization of, 2919
  adults, 3786
  Armenia, 230
  in Australia, 382–383
  children, 3784–3785
  children, services to, 877–878
  in China
    autonomous regions/provincial libraries,
      898
    municipal public libraries, 898
    Shanghai Library, 898–900
    township and village libraries, 898
  in Croatia, 1123, 1125–1126
  in Denmark
    Aarhus State and University Library,
      1216–1217
    budget for, 1220–1221
    Danish National Gallery, 1215
    digital service, 1220
    interlibrary loans, 1220
    interwar and postwar periods, 1216
    legislation, 1218
    librarian training course, 1216
    merging, 1220
    OPAC, 1216
    outreach library service, 1220
    Royal Library in Copenhagen, 1216–1217
    State Inspectorate of Public Libraries, 1216
    twentieth century, 1216, 1218
    Web-based National Union Catalog, 1216
  diverse populations, 3787

  elements, 3784–3792
  Ethiopia, 1498
  in France, 1601–1602, 1837
  games and gaming, 1638
  in Germany, 1696–1697, 1837
  Greece, 1730
  human resources, 3788–3789
  Hungary, 1923
  Israel, 2542
    Arab sector, 2548
    budgetary allocation, 2546
    Center for Libraries, 2546–2547
    collections, 2545
    Department of Libraries, 2545
    Libraries Law, 2545
    nonbook collections, 2545–2546
    users, 2545
  Japan, 2563–2564
  Kazakhstan, 2581–2582
  Kenya, 2595
  Latinos, 2700–2701
  legal and financial framework, 3783–3784
  legislation, 3783–3784
  Lithuania, 2948–2951
  marketing, 3789–3790
  measurement and evaluation, 3792,
    3794–3795
  Mexican libraries, 3086–3089
  in Moldova, 3123–3124
  music libraries, 3276
  newcomers, 3786–3787
  performance measurement, 3792, 3794
  in Peru, 3606–3608
  Poland, 3677–3678
  in pre-Christian era, 1836
  purposes, 3781–3783
  rare book collections, 3822
  resource collections, 3787–3788
  in Rome, 1836
  in Saudi Arabia, 3974–3976
  science and engineering librarians, 4009
  Senegal, 4106–4107
  in Serbia, 4129
  service responses, 3783
  in sixth century B.C., 1836
  Slovakia, 4178–4179
  South Korea, 4311
  trends and challenges, 3795–3797
  Tunisia, 4629
  in Ukraine, 4642, 4644
  unions (see Unions)
  in United Kingdom, 4701–4703
    authorities, populations of, 1839
    Chetham Library in Manchester, 1837
    combined museums and libraries,
      1837–1838
    County Library Authority, 1839
    CUKT, 1839
    gifts of individuals, 1836
    itinerating libraries, 1837
    Local Government Act of 1972, 1839
    Museums Act of 1845, 1837
    parish libraries, 1837
    public and joint-stock contribution, 1836
    Public Library Acts, 1838
    social library, 1837
    town libraries, 1836–1837

in United States (*see* United States, public
    libraries)
urban libraries, 1848
users needs, 3784
value, 3794–3795
Venezuelan libraries, 4890
Public Libraries and Museums Act 1964, 4720
Public Library Act of 1919, 1839
Public Library Association (PLA), 74–75, 335,
    3783
    ALA, 3801
    CPLA program, 3804
    eight special-interest sections, 3801
    grant projects, 3804
    mangement, publications, 3803
    member-driven organization, 3801
    membership, 3802
    National Conference, 3804
    new clusters, 3802
    organization, 3802–3803
    preconferences and workshops, 3803
    presidents, 3805
    priority concerns, 3802
    Public Libraries magazine, 3803
    Public Library Data Service, 3803
The Public Library Inquiry, 2769–2770,
    3775–3776
Public Library Manifesto, 3774
Public Library Movement, 888
Public Library of Science (PLoS), 557,
    3468–3469
*Public Library Service: A Guide to Evaluation
    with Minimum Standards*, 1846
Public machine bureaucracies, 3512
Public metadata creators, 3067
Public museums
    Milwaukee Public Museum, 3164
    in Moldova, 3121
    purpose-designed public museum, 3150
    in United Kingdom, 4716
Public Participation GIS (PPGIS), 1672–1673
Public patent databases on Internet
    CIPO, 3568
    EPO, 3569
    FreePatentsOnline, 3570
    Google Patents, 3570
    JPO, 3569–3570
    Patent Lens, 3570–3751
    proliferation, 3567
    USPTO, 3568–3569
    WIPO, 3570
Public policy advocacy, 347
Public portals, 2893
Public Record Office (PRO), 108
Public Record Office (PRO) Act 1838,
    4732–4733
Public Record Office of Great Britain, 1792
Public Record Office of Northern Ireland
    (PRONI), 4734
Public Records Act, 183, 2012, 4733–4734
Public Relations and Marketing (PRMS), 2842
Public services, academic libraries, 4–5, 7–8
Public service special collections professionals,
    4349
Published informational content, 1274
Publishing histories, 1861
PubMed, 819, 1878

PubMed Central® (PMC), 3338
PubMed database, 1765, 1767
PubScience, 1555
Pugillares, 542
Punctuational markup, 3073
Pura Belpre Award, 334
Purdue University Research Repository
    (PURR), 2902
Pythagorean theorem, 3020
Python spatial analysis library (PySal), 1676

Q

Qayrawan Grand Mosque, 4626
Quai Branly Museum, 1596–1597
QuakeNet, 1049
Qualified Dublin Core (DCQ), 1366
Qualisigns, 4098
Qualitative research, 3807–3810
    methods and tools, 3813–3816
    principles, 3810–3813
    semiotics, 3816
Quality improvement, 568, 1179–1180, 1517,
    1874, 1889
Quality of service (QoS), 1056
Quality Oversight Organizations (QOO), 1889
Quantitative models, 1192–1193
Quantitative structure-activity relationships
    (QSAR), 836
Quarterly of Applied Mathematics, 3027
Quasi nongovernmental organization
    (QUANGO), 3380
Quasi-official press, 3738–3739
Queensland Art Gallery, 389
Queen Sofia Center of Art National Museum,
    4332
Query languages, 1366–1367, 1621–1622
Questia service, 985
Question-answering, NLP, 3353
Question-answering (QA) systems, 1903, 4574
Questionnaires, 4530–4531, 4798–4799
QuestionPoint, 3398–3399
Quetelet, Adolph, 495

R

Radio, 1572–1573
Radio broadcast libraries, 3277
Radio Corporation of America (RCA), 1015
Radio frequency identification (RFID), 921,
    2924
Radio stations, 998–999
Raisig, L. Miles, 496, 498
Rajput School of painting, 1957
Randomized controlled trials (RCTs), 1519
Random network, 1039
Random variables, information theory
    mutual information, 2351–2353
    unpredictability, 2350
    varying probabilities and entropy measure,
        2351
Ranganathan, S.R., 1534, 1536
Ranked half-life (RHL), 1902
Rapid automatized naming (RAN), 3842, 3845
Rare book collections, 3726
    access points, 3825–3826
    colleges and universities, 3822

deaccessioning, 3825
determination of, 3821–3822
digitization, 3828
donations, 3822–3823
environmental issues, 3826
exhibitions, 3828
growth of
    gifts, 3824
    purchase of materials, 3823–3824
    transfers, 3824–3825
independent rare book libraries, 3822
institutional support, 3827–3828
librarians, responsibilities of, 3823
national libraries, 3822
origins of, 3820
public libraries, 3822
public/quasi-public collections, 3823
restrictions, 3823
security, 3826–3827
Rare Books and Manuscripts Librarianship
    (RBML), 355
Rare Books and Manuscripts Section (RBMS),
    4336, 4338, 4344
Rare books, provenance of, *see* Provenance of
    rare books
Rare manuscript libraries, United Kingdom,
    4738
RASKE modeling, 3109
Raster images, 1308
Rathgen, Friedrich, 1069
Rationalism, 3625–3626
Ratzel, Friedrich, 1687
RDA, *see* Resource, Description and Access
RDF, *see* Resource Description Framework
rdfs:label property, 3964
rdfs:seeAlso property, 3964
Reaction searching, 825–826
Reactive strategies, 2241
A Reader in Art Librarianship, 249
ReaderMeter, 47
Readers' advisory, 3914
Readex United Nations Documents Collections,
    1724
Reading disorders
    adults, 3843
    causes of
        genetic factors, 3846
        language processes, 3845
        linguistic coding, 3844
        memory, 3845
        naming speed, 3845
        neurological basis, 3845–3846
        phonological coding, 3844
        semantic coding, 3844
        syntactic coding, 3844
        visual coding, 3844
        word recognition, 3844
    difficulties, 3841
    historical trends, 3842
    impairments, 3841
    intrinsic disorders, 3841
    learning disabilities, 3843–3844
    scientifically based interventions, 3846–3848
    subgroups of, 3842–3843
Reading interests
    advisory and appeal factors, 3857
    boredom, 3854–3855

Reading interests (cont'd.)
comprehension, 3854–3855
engagement, 3854–3855
genres, 3856–3857
high and low, 3855–3856
intrinsic motivation, 3851
research approaches
bestseller lists and circulation statistics, 3851
"a central core/radix," 3853
ethnographic research, 3852
formats, 3854
knowledge-based society, 3852
large scale questionnaires, 3851
marginalia, 3851–3852
popular literary genres, 3853
questionnaire/checklist, 3853
voluntary reading, 3850
Reading rooms, 1123
Reading, sociology of
bad reading, marginal readers, 4279–4280
creative activity, 4281
in developed countries, 4281–4283
dominant readers/dominated reader, 4281
emancipation, 4284
history, 4280
Internet, impact of, 4283–4284
literary canon, 4283
social issues, 4280–4281
young people, 4283
Read_Me 1.2 software art festival, 2071
Ready reference, 3914
Realistic fiction
contemporary fiction, 864–865
historical fiction, 865
Realizers, 432
Really simple syndication (RSS), 637, 1045, 2221, 2894, 3227, 3796, 4780, 5020
Real-time Observatories, Applications, and Data management Network (ROADNet), 2998
Real-time supervisory control (RTSC) work, 3359–3362
Reasonable tendency test, 1015
Reaxys database, 821
Recall and precision
cost factor, 3708–3709
estimating method, 3711
requirements, 3711–3712
scatter diagram, 3709–3710
table, 3709–3710, 3712
Recherche thematique pluridisciplinaire (RTP-doc), 1378
Recommender systems
challenges, 3863
collaborative systems, 3861–3862
content-based systems, 3862–3863
Internet, 3860–3861
research, 3863–3864
RECON, see Retrospective conversion
Record (in)accuracy, 1176
Recorded information, 2058
Record group traditions, 118
Recording Industry Association of America (RIAA), 3281
Recordkeeping metadata models, 122–124

Records
access
access management systems, 3890
electronic records, 3891
physical records, 3890–3891
security, and privacy, 3890
tracking process, 3889
attributes, 167–168
business transaction, 3887
definition, 167, 3887
filing and arrangement, 3889
lifecycle, 168–169
organization, 3888
series
classification, 3888–3889
indexing, 3889
unit, 3888
Records and Archives Management Department (RAMD), 4508
Records and Archives Management Program (RAMP), 2438, 4659
Records and information management (RIM), 221, 1857–1858
archives management, 1850
correspondence management, 1850
electronic records keeping, 1851
Federal Records Act of 1950, 1851
filing and indexing system, 1850
forms/reports management, 1850
Hoover Commission Paperwork Task Force, 1851
ICA, 1856–1857
image management, 1850
information technology, 1850
international standard, 1857
Leahy, Emmett, 1851–1853
literature, 1855–1856
microfilm, application of, 1851
NARS, 1851
NFPA, 1853
PRISM, 1853
professional organization growth, 1853–1854
professional status, 1855
promotional programs, 1853
records centers, 1850
records protection, 1850
retention scheduling, 1850
training, 1854–1855
Records compliance
accountability factors, 3870
compliance requirements, 3870
effective audit procedures, 3870
and risk management
AS-4390, 3871
cost/benefit analysis, 3872
qualitative approach, 3870
quantitative approach, 3870
records retention policy, 3871
risk analysis, 3870
Records continuum model, 169
archival framework, 3874
Australia
archival documents, 3875
authenticity and reliability issues, 3876
CRS system, 3876
evidence-based decision making and public accountability, 3876

Maclean's proto-continuum implementation model, 3876
reconstructible relationships, 3876
recordkeeping-accountability nexus, 3875
registry systems, 3877
dimensions of, 3878–3879
philosophical and sociological discourses, 3880–3881
points in, 3878–3880
research instrument, 3882
reshaping professional practice, 3882–3883
seminal model form, 3877
teaching tool, 3882
transactionality, 3877
uses of, 3881–3882
Records Disposal Act in 1962, 2600
Records inventory, 3895
Records management (RM), 715, 2108, 2490, 4792–4793
associated with risk, 716
compliance requirements, 3870
definition, 3869
diversity, 716
document/content management, 718–719
education, 719–720
historical and modern documents, 3869
history of, 720–721
information technology, 716–717
litigation, 717–718
purpose, 3869
records retention audits, 3870
titles, 719
Records Management Association of Australia (RMAA), 174, 388, 1856
Records Management Journal, 1856
Records management programs (RMP)
corporations (see Corporate records management programs)
establishment and administrative location, 4390–4391
NARA, 4746
records retention, 3892
Records Management Society, 4739
of Japan, 2570
United Kingdom, 4739
Records retention schedule
corporate culture, 3892
definition, 3892
development
data collection types, 3895
implementation, 3896
inventory process, 3895
legal research, 3895
maintenance, 3896
records inventory, 3895
review and approval, 3895
strategy, 3895
dispositioning, 3892
purpose, 3892–3893
records series, 3892
retention period, 3892, 3894–3895
types
departmental retention schedules, 3893
functional retention schedules, 3893
large aggregation retention schedules, 3893–3894
Records Review, 1856

Recurrent networks (RANN), 285–287
Recursive auto associative memories (RAAM), 284
Redarte-SP (Sao Paulo, Brazil), 256
Red de Bibliotecas Universitarias (REBIUN), 4316, 4320–4321
Red Universitaria Española de Catálogs Absys (RUECA), 4316
Redwood Library, 1841
Reference and Adult Services Division (RASD), *see* Reference and User Services Association
Reference and informational genres
    almanacs, 3898
    atlases, 3898
    bibliographies, 3898
    biological sciences, 3901
    canonical texts, 3900
    catalogs, 3898
    chronologies, 3898
    concordances, 3898
    DDC, 3903, 3905
    dictionaries, 3898
    directories, 3898–3899
    document types, 3906
    encyclopedias, 3899
    formats, 3901
    gazetteers, 3899
    handbooks and manuals, 3899
    idiosyncratic order, 3900
    "index volume" bibliographies, 3904
    LCC system, 3902, 3904–3905
    Martel's structure, 3902
    monographs, 3904
    multidisciplinary sources of information, 3901
    newsletters, 3899
    personal bibliographies, 3904
    primary literature, 3900
    publication types, 3905–3906
    secondary literature, 3900
    sourcebooks, 3899
    subject bibliographies, 3904–3905
    subject groupings, 3897
    term weighting, 3902
    tertiary literature, 3900
    union lists, 3899
    yearbooks, 3899
Reference and User Services Association (RUSA), 2699, 3913
    award, 3909–3910
    education opportunities, 3910
    guidelines, 3910
    membership, 3908
    name change, 3908
    organization, 3909
    problems and issues, 3910–3911
    publications, 3909
    reference and information professionals, 3908
    2000 ALA midwinter meeting, value statement, 3908
Reference and User Services Quarterly (RUSQ), 3909
Reference desk, 6–7, 3914
Reference information, 1364
Reference interview, 3912
    communication techniques, 3915–3916
    purpose of, 3915

Reference services, 1098
    bibliographic verification, 3914
    changing context of, 3913
    components of, 3912
    definition, 3912
    direct and indirect instruction, 3914
    evaluation, 3917
    history of, 3912–3913
    instruction and guidance, responsibilities for, 3914
    interlibrary loan, 3914
    readers' advisory, 3914
    ready reference, 3914
    reference collection development and mainte-nance, 3916–3917
    reference desk, 3914
    reference ethics, 3912, 3917
    reference interview, 3912
        communication techniques, 3915–3916
        purpose of, 3915
    reference sources, 3912, 3916
    reference transactions, definition of, 3913–3914
    reference work, definition of, 3914
    research consulting, 3914
    roving method, 3914
    virtual reference, 3915
Reference Services Section (RSS), 3909
Reference tools, 1655–1656, 1659
Reference transactions, 3913–3914
Referential markup, 3074
ReferralWeb, 3866–3867
Reflexive meta-field, 3611
REFORMA, 2699, 2701, 2703
Reformation libraries, 3954–3956
Refreezing process, 2297
Refreshing, *see* Bit preservation
Regimen Sanitatis Salernitanum, 3044
Regional Bell holding companies (RBOCs), 1018, 1020–1021
Regional Library Associations, 4328
Regional library networks (RLNs)
    Alliance of Library Service Networks, 3922
    challenges, 3924
    consortia/consortium, 3920, 3924
    definition, 3920
    educational programs, 3923
    electronic resources, 3923–3924
    federal/state agencies, 3922
    governance, 3922
    history, 3920–3921
    OCLC, 3921–3923
    services, 3923
    support/help desks, 3922
    unique projects, 3924
    web sites of, 3922
Register of Australian Archives and Manu-scripts, 388
Register Plus, 3569
Registry systems, 118–119
Rehabilitation Act, 3575
Reiter's pipeline architecture, 431–432
Related term (RT), 1986
Relational databases (RDBs), 4080–4082
Relationship links, 2940
Relative index, 1257, 1262

Relative relevance (RR), 1902
Relativism, 3811–3812
RELAX NG, 1388
Relevance assessment, 1902–1903, 2172, 2174, 3708–3709, 3711, 3944, 3946, 4876, 4880
Relevance feedback, 4420
Relevance judgments, 3941–3944
Relevance measurements, 3944–3947
Relevance theory
    "berrypicking" model of literature retrieval, 3933–3934
    and citation, 3936–3937
    cognitive effects, 3934
    definition, 3926–3927
    degrees of, 3931–3933
    evidentiary relevance, 3931
    historical precedents, 3928–3929
    intermediaries and disintermediation, 3928
    intersubjective agreement, 3935
    IR evaluation tests, 3934
    literature-based systems, 3927
    objectifying subjectivity, 3935–3936
    "objective system relevance," 3933
    question relevance, 3931
    systems evaluation, 3929–3931
    topical relevance, 3931
Relief printing, 1865–1867
Religious archives
    Australia, 188–189
    China, 907
    Germany, 1701
    United Kingdom, 4737–4738
Religious publishing, 3987
Religious storytelling, 4443
Renaissance libraries
    France, 3951–3952
    Italy, 3948–3950
    Spain, 3952
    Vatican Library, 3951
Renardus Service, 1262
Renouf Press, 1724
Repertoire Bibliographique Universel (RBU), 1373
Repository-based software engineering (RBSE) spider, 2520
Representational state transfer (REST), 2187, 2347, 2895
Repressive censorship, 3676
Repterorium Bibliographicum, 1968–1969
Republic, 644
Republican Book Museum in Almaty, 2587–2588
Republican Scientific-Medical Library (RSML), 232
Republican Scientific-Technical Library (RNTB), 230, 2582
Republic of Armenia, *see* Armenia
Reputed credibility, 1115
Request-for-proposal (RFP), 607
Research Assessment Exercise (RAE), 2373, 4712–4713
Research data services (RDS), 4015
Research Libraries Group (RLG), 451–452, 2181, 3400–3401
Research Libraries Information Network (RLIN), 450, 476, 2921

Research library
in Arab sector, 2548
in Australia, 384–385
in Germany, 1695–1696
Hungary, 1922
Japan, 2562–2563
in Kazakhstan, 2582
Kenya, 2596
Lithuania, 2951–2953
music libraries, 3275–3276
in Saudi Arabia, 3974
Senegal, 4106
Slovakia, 4178
Research methodology, 2407
Research Papers in Economics (RePEc),
3466
Research Scorecard, 47
Research services, 1098–1099
Research support system (RSS), 2192
Research Teaching and Learning (RTL), 370
Réseau national de santé (RNS), 4631
Residue, 2058
Resolution, digital images, 1309–1310
Resource Definition Framework (RDF), 1366
Resource dependence theory, 3515
Resource, Description and Access (RDA),
137, 453, 726–727, 1982–1983, 2923,
3283
Resource Description Framework (RDF), 1079,
1393, 2524, 2939–2941, 2986,
3067–3068, 3227, 3460–3462,
4082–4084
domain-neutral framework, 3961
FAST authority file, 1539
feature summary
ancillary properties, 3964
classes, 3963
containers and collections, 3963–3964
properties, 3963
reification, 3964
history, 3966
MCF, 3967
OWL, 3961
PICS, 3966–3967
semantics, 3965–3966
Semantic Web, 3961
1999 specifications, 3967
syntax, 3965
triple model, 3961–3962
vs. XML, 3962–363
Resources and Technical Services Division
(RTSD), 2966
Resource sharing
ARL, 373–374
Canada, 671
CRL, 766
hospital librarians, 1885
PIALA, 3547
Respect des fonds, 116, 170, 1425, 3301,
3746–3749, 4793
Response to intervention (RTI), 3843
Respublicae Elzeviranae, 494
Restatements, 2741
Retention period
based on event, 3894
definition, 3892
finite time period, 3894

in lower-cost storage area, 3895
Personnel Files, 3894–3895
termination, 3895
total retention time, 3895
in working environment, 3895
Retrieval status value (RSV), 1620, 1622, 1627,
1634
Retrieval subsystem, 2195
Retrieval task, 4555
Retrospective conversion (RECON)
automatic identification, 2968
format recognition process, 2968
initial conversion method, 2967
large-scale centralized conversion, 2967
NCLIS, 2970
pilot project, 2967–2968
record types, 2970
reverse chronological order, 2967
special studies, 2969
task force, 2967–2970
Return on investment (ROI), 1083, 3795
Reuther Library, 4761
Revised Braille code, 563
Revyu.com, 4088
RFID, see Radio-frequency identification
RGS, see Rhetorical genre studies
Rheingold's online/phone based communities,
1028
Rhetorical genre studies (RGS)
Bakhtin communication, 1663–1664
Bakhtin's insights, 1664
Bitzer's notion of "exigence," 1663
deliberative performances, 1662
epideictic speeches, 1662
forensic discourse, 1662
Miller's insights, 1663
pragmatic function, 1663
reconceptualization, 1663
renovation source, 1663
speech genre, 1663–1664
utterance, 1663–1664
Rhetorical Structure Theory (RST), 436–437
Rhind Papyrus, see Ahmes Papyrus
RIAA, 3649, 3651, 3652, 3657, 3660–3661
RIBEAU, 686
Ricardo, David, 647
Rice marbling, 539
Richelieu site, 532, 534
Rich-get-richer models, 2372
Rieh's Model of Judgment of Information Qual-
ity and Cognitive Authority, 1117
Riga Peace Treaty, 3675
RIM, see Records and information management
Ringo recommender system, 3864
Risk management and records compliance
AS-4390, 3871
cost/benefit analysis, 3872
qualitative approach, 3870
quantitative approach, 3870
records retention policy, 3871
risk analysis, 3870
Ritter, Karl, 1686
RLNs, see Regional library networks
Robert F. Sibert Informational Book Medal, 334
Roberts Commission, 3217
Robertson–Sparck Jones weights, 2206, 2208
Robotics, 275

Robots, 2518–2519
Robust networks, 4242
Rochester Institute of Technology (RIT), 1183
Rockefeller Family Foundations, 3216
Rockefeller Foundation, 77
Rockefeller Museum, 2550
Rocky Mountain Mathematical Journal, 3027
Rogers' S-Curve, 2292, 2298
Role-based access control (RBAC), 406
Role modeling, 3113
Romance, 3703–3704
Romanesque bindings, 542–543
Roman Virgil, 1946
Rosenberg, Gustav, 1069
Rose Robischon Scholarship Award, NASIG,
3390
Rostock Public Library, 1792
Round Table of Art Librarians, 249
R-O-U-N-D, wayfinding processes, 4959
Rousseau, Jean Jacques, 1685
Routine knowledge assets, 2622
Rowan Public Library, 1649
Royal Academy of Painting, 1594
Royal Air Force Museum, 4719
Royal Art Museum, 1215
Royal Botanic Gardens, Kew, 4333, 4725
Royal Charter, 655
Royal Library in Copenhagen, 1216–1217, 1219
Royal Library of Alexandria, 2762
Royal Library School, 1216
Royal Museum, Brazil, 612–613
Royal National Park, 391–392
Royal Ontario Museum (ROM), 3689
Rubin Museum, 2551
Rule interchange format (RIF), 4082
Rules for a Dictionary Catalog, 4468
Rules for a Printed Dictionary Catalog, 2920
Rules for Archival Description (RAD), 670
Rules for the Compilation of the Catalogue,
2920
"Rules of reading," 3855
Rural Free Delivery (RFD) Program, 1011
Rural knowledge centers (RKC), 2132–2133
RUSA, see Reference and User Services
Association
Russell's epistemology, 1456
Russell's sensemaking, 4113
Russian Geographical Society (RGS), 1780
Russian Information Library Consortium
(RILC), 2823
Russian State Library, 3326–3327
RxNorm, 4678

S
Sacred: Discover what we share, 624
Safe Harbor framework, 2143
Safety data sheets (SDS), 820
Salt Lake City new central library, 3793
Salton model, 2229–2230
Salton's SMART system, 2204
Sampson's writing systems, 3832
San Diego Supercomputer Center (SDSC), 3000
San Francisco Museum of Modern Art, 3218
San Francisco Public Library, 3729
Santa Monica's Public Electronic Network,
1028

Saracevic's stratified interaction model, 2247, 4875
Sarbanes-Oxley Act, 639, 1106, 1362, 1370, 1858
Saskatchewan Archives Act (1945), 658
Saudi Arabia
    adult literacy rate, 3970
    archives and archival institutions, 3978–3979
    average temperature and rainfall, 3970
    development plans, 3979–3980
    history of, 3970–3971
    libraries
        academic and research libraries, 3974
        AFLI, 3978
        in Arabic and Islamic culture, 3971–3972
        Arabic Union Catalog, 3978
        education and training, 3977–3978
        King Abd al-Aziz Public Library in Riyadh, 3974
        King Fahd National Library, 3973–3974
        planning/legislation, 3972–3973
        public libraries, 3974–3976
        school libraries, 3976
        special libraries, 3976–3977
        special library association, Gulf chapter of, 3978
    Makkah and Madinah, 3970
    map of, 3970–3971
    museums, 3979–3980
    religion, 3970
Saudi Arabian Center for Science and Technology (SANCST), 2312
Saussurean model, 4098, 4101
Savolainen's ELIS model, 2087–2088, 2118–2119
SavvySearch, 2523
Say, Jean-Baptiste, 647
Scaffold hopping, 835
Scale-free networks, 1040–1041
Scandinavian bookbinding, 548
Scene-level indexing, 3131
Schellenberg's seminal approach, 2380
Schlagwortnormdatei (SWD), 1261
Scholar, 3471
Scholarly and trade publishing, *see* Book and journal publishing trade
Scholarly communication
    European Commission, 2824
    webometrics
        AltaVista, 4986
        journals, 4984
        link creation motiation, 4986
        log analysis, 4984–4985
        people, 4985
        small world analysis, 4986
        universities, 4985–4986
        visualization, 4986–4987
Scholarly Communications Committee, 345
Scholarly presses, 3739, 3742
Scholarly publishing, 4512–4513
Scholarly Publishing and Academic Resources Coalition (SPARC), 345, 367, 2906, 3645, 4014
Scholarly treatises, 2739
Scholasticism, 4095
School librarianship
    functions and skills, 3994–3998
    global community, 3998–3999
    history, 3991
    preparation, 3992–3994
School libraries, 2764
    advocacy, 4003
    in Arab sector, 2548–2549
    Armenia, 230
    in Australia, 383
    in China, 900
    in Croatia, 1126
    in Denmark, 1220–1221
    education theory and practice, 4002
    effectiveness, 4004–4005
    Ethiopia, 1499
    expansion, 4000
    in France, 1601–1602
    games and gaming, 1638–1639
    in Germany, 1698
    Greece, 1730–1731
    Hungary, 1923
    international perspective, 4005–4006
    in Israel, 2543, 2547
    Japan, 2564–2565
    in Kazakhstan, 2583
    Kenya, 2597
    Latinos, 2701
    Lithuania, 2951
    OPLs, 3416
    in Peru, 3608
    Poland, 3678
    public libraries, 4003–4004
    in Saudi Arabia, 3976
    Senegal, 4107
    in Serbia, 4131–4132
    South Korea, 4311
    standards and guidelines, 4001–4002
    technology, 4003
    Tunisia, 4630–4631
    in United Kingdom, 4705–4706
    virtual school library, 4005
School Libraries Worldwide (journal), 4006
School Library Association (SLA), 4706
School Library Association of New Zealand (SLANZA), 3377
School Library Media Research, 61
School of Conservation, 1227
School of Industrial Arts, 3253
School of Information Science (SISA), 1499
School of Library, Archive, and Information Studies (SLAIS), 4738
School of Salerno, 3044–3045
School of the Louvre, 1598
Schools of business, 650
Science and engineering librarianship
    continuing education, 4011
    job requirements
        education, 4010
        skills, 4010–4011
    need for, 4008
    professional organizations, 4016–4017
    professional responsibilities
        citizen science, 4015
        collections, 4012
        conference proceedings, 4013
        data-management plans and RDS, 4015
        data sets, 4013
        e-Science, 4015
        handbooks and data sources, 4013
        instruction, 4012
        makerspaces, 4015
        management, marketing and promotion, 4013–4014
        maps, 4013
        open access, 4014–4015
        patents, 4013
        preprints and e-prints, 4013
        reference and consultation, 4011–4012
        research and writing, 4014
        scholarly communication, 4014
        technical reports, 4013
        translations, 4013
        Web technologies, 4014
    recruitment, 4011
    science and engineering library settings, 4008–4009
        academic, 4009
        corporate organizations, 4009
        government, 4009
        medical libraries, 4010
        museums, aquariums, and zoos, 4010
        national libraries, 4009–4010
        public, 4009
        solo, 4010
Science and natural history museums
    Croatia, 1129
    Germany, 1704–1705
    Hungary, 1929
    India, 2020–2022
    Switzerland, 4495
Science and Technology Act (Chapter 250), 2594
Science and Technology Museum, 4135
Science and Technology Museum Association of Serbia, 4135
Science and technology studies (STS)
    ALA, 4016
    ANT, 4022–4023
    empirical programme of relativism, 4020–4021
    gender and technology studies, 4024–4025
    heterogeneous engineering, 4021
    practice theory, 4025–4026
    SCOT, 4024
    social shaping of, 4021–4022
    technological determinism, 4021
    technology and information science theories, 4020
    workplace studies, 4026
Science centers, 3237
Science citation index (SCI), 503, 522, 925, 942, 2227, 2370, 3471, 3640, 4198
Science library, 4009–4010
Science museums
    gallery interpreters, 4952
    Hungary, 1929
    in Israel, 2552
    in Serbia, 4134–4135
Science, technology, and health care archives
    Alan Mason Chesney Medical Archives, 4761–4762
    California Academy of Science, 4762
    California Institute of Technology, 4762
    Charles Babbage Center, 4762
    Claude Moore Library, 4762
    David Sarnoff Library, 4762

Science, technology, and health care archives
(cont'd.)
Linda Hall Library, 4762
National Agricultural Library, 4762–4763
National Library of Medicine, 4763
Niels Bohr Library and Archives and Center
for History of Physics, 4763
Scientific Agricultural Library, 4647
Scientific American, 4084–4085
Scientific and technical information (STI), 1433
Scientific communication models, 3637–3638
Scientific computing, 2272
Scientific data collections, 2997–2998
Scientific Electronic Library Online (SciELO),
614
Scientific genealogy, 1645–1646
Scientific genres, 2503
Scientific information system, 1125
Scientific knowledge, 2056
Scientific Medical Library (SML), 3124
Scientific, technical, and medical (STM) pub-
lishing, 1132, 2143, 3983–3984, 3987
Scientometrics journal, 2226, 2367–2368, 4984
Sci2 toolset, 923
SCLOPE, 2634
Scope note (SN), 1986, 2868
Scopus digital service, 2368, 3471
Scorpion software, 1262
Scotland
archives and archival science
archive services, 4735
legislation, 4733–4734
CUKT, 1839
parish libraries, 1837
social library, 1837
town library, 1837
Scott, Alexander, 1069
Scottish Higher Education Funding Council
(SHEFC), 4718
Scoville Memorial Library Association, 1843
Screening search, 832–833
Scriptores Rei Rusticae, 1400
Scrittori classici italiani di economia politica,
1405
Sculptures Collection, 1744
Search aids, 944
Search and retrieval system, 4978–4982
Search and retrieve via URL (SRU) protocol,
1253, 2347, 2671, 2983
CQL, 2189
Editorial Board, 2187
explain operation, 2187–2189
HTTP GET request, 2187–2188
projects and implementations, 2189–2190
REST approach, 2187
searchRetrieve operation, 2187–2189
SOAP, 2187
SRW and, 2187
Search engine marketing (SEM), 4029
Search engine optimization (SEO)
Black Hat *vs.* White Hat, 4031
definition, 4029
higher rankings, 4029–4030
methods
automated search engines *vs.* manually created directories, 4031–4032
content-focused approach, 4033–4034

content, technical, and linking combination, 4037
keywords selection to target, 4033
links, 4035–4037
technical strategy, 4034–4035
Web analytics, 4037
web page elements to be optimized,
4032–4033
Web site and Web page structure, 4037
origins and history, 4030
practitioners
current SEO industry, 4031
early promoters and reporters, 4030–4031
software, 4031
standards and regulation
certification, 4042
government regulation, 4042
HTML, 4041–4042
search engines, 4042
SEO industry, 4042
strategic issues
broad *vs.* narrow targeting and long-tail
terms, 4038
building downwards *vs.* outwards,
4037–4038
geographic targeting, 4039
increased competition, 4039
lead time and longevity, 4038–4039
only index words, 4039
source tracking, 4039
targeting and serendipity balance, 4038
trends
current trends, 4040
fading trends, 4039–4040
mobile communications devices, 4041
new search engine presentation methods,
4040–4041
SMO, 4041
specialized searches, 4041
user behaviors
basic behaviors, 4043
Boolean syntax, 4043
hardened/fixed, 4043
popular topical searches, 4043
search engine loyalty, 4043
SERP links, 4042
variables affecting, 4042–4043
worldwide, 4043
worldwide, 4031
Search engine results page (SERP), 4029–4030,
4042
Search engines
ALIWEB, 2519
AltaVista, 2522
Archie, 2517
Bing, 4051
Boolean logic, 4048
date searching, 4049
definition, 4046
EINet Galaxy, 2520
Excite, 2521
Google, 2523, 4050–4051
Gopher, 2517
identification and gathering of material,
4046–4047
index and indexing program, 4047
indexer, 2519

Infoseek, 2521–2522
Inktomi, 2522
invisible/deep Web, 2524
Jughead, 2518
Jumpstation, 2519
language searching, 4049
link searching, 4049
Lycos, 2521
metasearch engine, 4053
MetaSearchers, 2523
non-U.S. general search engines, 4051–4052
Northern Light, 2522–2523
Open Directory Project, 2524
phrase searching, 4048–4049
portal dilemma, 4048
retrieval and ranking algorithms, 4047
robots, 2518–2519
RSBE, 2520
searching by file type, 4049
search results pages, 4050
specialty search engines, 4052
spider, 2519
students, 4461
syntax, 4048
title searching, 4049
URL, site, and domain searching, 4049
user interface, 4046
Veronica, 2517
visualization engines, 4052–4053
WAIS, 2518
Wanderer, 2519
WebCrawler, 2521
worm, 2519–2520
WWW, 2518
XML, 2524
Yahoo!, 2520–2521, 4051
SearchFAST, 1545
Search moves, 2239–2241
Search/retrieve webservice (SRW), 1253, 2187
Search rule, 2363
Search strategies, 2240–2242
Search tactics, 2239–2241
Search trails, 4878–4879
Sears List of Subject Headings, 1261
Seattle Public Library, 2792, 3791
The Seattle Public Library Central Library:
Economic Benefits Assessment 2007,
3794
Second Historical Archives of China (SHAC),
906–907
Second Life, 1050
Secretariat General of Communication and
Information, 1738
Section elements, 5043
Section of International Organizations (SIO),
2438
Section of Municipal Archives (SMA), 2438
Section of Professional Associations (SPA),
2438
Sectoral standardization, 3107
Secure Digital Music Initiative (SDMI), 1320
Secure Hash Algorithm 1360 (SHA-1360), 1366
Securities Act of 1933, 638
Securities and Exchange Commission (SEC),
638, 1106
Securities Exchange Act of 1934, 638
Sedgwick Museum, 4718

Selected Translations in Mathematical Statistics and Probability, 3028
Select Essays on Husbandry, 1402
Selective dissemination of information (SDI), 1880, 2221
Selective indexing, 5045–5046
Selective information, 2056
Self-censorship, 1014
Self-descriptive data, 2940
Self Generating Master (SELGEM), 3179
Self-organization, *see* Complexity and self-organization
Self-organized maps (SOM), 3272
Self-publishing online
  advantages, 4056–4057
  definition, 4054
  disadvantages, 4057
  future trends, 4058
  libraries and librarians, impact on, 4057–4058
  publishers and publishing services, 4056
  tasks, 4055–4056
  technologies for, 4054–4055
  World Wide Web, 4054
Self-reinforcement, 2096–2097
Semantic-based summarization systems, 424–425
Semantic consistency, 1175
Semantic grids, 3002
Semantic information, 3613
Semantic interoperability
  absolute crosswalking, 4070–4071
  conceptualizing underlying models, 4065–4066
  co-occurrence mapping, 4072
  cross-switching, 4070–4071
  crosswalking services, 4072
  definition, 4062
  different levels, 4065
  different processes, 4064–4065
  dimensions, 4063–4064
  direct mapping, 4070–4071
  HILT, 4074
  KOS, 4066–4067
  localization and expansion
    application profiles, 4068–4069
    core/intermediate ontologies, 4069–4070
    DC metadata element, 4068
    domain ontologies, 4069–4070
    KOS, 4069
    leaf nodes, 4068–4069
    satellite vocabulary development, 4069
    upper ontologies, 4069–4070
  metadata, 4067–4068
  new vocabulary derivation, 4068
  NSDL registry, 4073
  OOR, 4074–4075
  records conversion, 4071
  relative crosswalking, 4071
  semantic conflicts and agreements, 4062–4063
  terminology services, 4073–4074
  Web services, 4073
Semantic knowledge, 3423
Semantic scattering, 2211
Semantic space, 2688–2696

Semantic web (SW), 277, 2938, 4212, 5020, 5029–5030
  academic work, 4087–4088
  aim of, 4080–4082
  application areas, 4086–4087
  bootstrapping, 4083–4084
  commercial activity, 4087
  components of, 4082–4083
  controversies
    arguments for and against ontologies, 4088–4089
    folksonomies, 4089
    GOFAI, 4088
    resolving, 4089
    symbol grounding, 4090
  history
    development progress, 4085–4086
    early layered view, 4085
    Intelligent Systems, 4084
    ontology-related information, 4085
    OWL, 4085
    Scientific American, 4084–4085
    SPARQL, 4085
    W3C recommendation, 4085
    WWW, 4084
  information standard, 4080
  infrastructure, 4083
  layered view of, 4081
  ontologies, 4080–4081
  properties of system, 4086
  reasoners, 4083
  semantic theory, 4080
  social context, 4084
  Web services, 4080
Semantic Web Advanced Development (SWAD), 2671
Semantic Web Challenge, 4087–4088
Semiotics
  history, 4094–4096
  and information, 4101–4102
  meanings, 4096–4098
  opposition theory, 4100
  poststructuralism, 4100–4101
  signs, 4098
  structure, text and code
    intellectual codes, 4099
    messages, 4099
    paradigmatic, 4098–4099
    representation, 4099
    social codes, 4099
    syntagmatic, 4098–4099
Semistructured messages, 1058
Sendai Mediatheque, 2808
Senefelder, Alois, 1868
Senegal
  archives and archival science
    laws, 4109
    National Archives and Services, 4109–4110
  language, 4104
  libraries
    academic and research libraries, 4106
    digital library collections and services, 4108
    education, 4108
    laws, 4104–4105
    professional associations, 4108–4109
    public libraries, 4106–4107

  school libraries, 4107
  special libraries, 4107–4108
  literacy rate, 4104
  map of, 4104–4105
  museums and museology, 4110
Sense-making
  approaches, 2117, 2119
    Cognitive Systems Engineering, 4116–4117
    HCI, 4115–4116
    LIS, 4118–4121
    organizational communication, 4117–4118
  clarion call, 4121
  spiraling, 2096
  user studies, 4113–4114
Sense-making methodology (SMM), 1508–1509
Sentence plan language, 434
Sentence-reordering algorithms, 424
SEO, *see* Search engine optimization
Sequence-level indexing, 3131
Sequence searching, 826–827
Serbia
  archives, 4132–4133
  economy, 4125
  history, 4125–4127, 4136–13
  libraries
    academic libraries, 4129–4131
    association, 4127–4128
    central libraries, 4127
    education, 4132
    laws, 4127
    National Library of Serbia, 4127–4129
    public libraries, 4129
    school libraries, 4131–4132
    special libraries, 4131
  location, 4125–4126
  museum
    art museums and galleries, 4134
    Churches and monasteries, 4133
    historical and ethnographic museums, 4135
    national museum, 4133–4134
    professional association, 4133
    science museums and galleries, 4134–4135
  population of, 4125
  provinces, 4125
  telecommunication infrastructure, 4125
Serbian Library Consortium for Coordinated Acquisition, 2829
Serbian Lyceum, 4129–4130
Serbian Museum Association, 4133
Serendipitous information search, 2244–2245
Serials collection and management
  acquisition, 4142–4143
  cataloging, 4143–4144
  check-in, 4143
  definitions, 4139–4140
  history, 4141
  maintenance, 4146
  preservation, 4147
  selection, 4141–4142
  weeding, 4147–4148
Serials Specialist Award of NASIG, 3390
Serials vendors
  claiming, 4154–4155
  EDI, 4156
  electronic journals, 4154, 4156–4157
  five year price analysis, 4151

Serials vendors (cont'd.)
　ILS, 4153–4154
　invoicing, 4154
　ordering, 4154
　publishers, 4155
　renewals, 4155
　reports, 4155
　research library, 4152
　subscription, 4152
Series systems, 119–120
SERP, *see* Search engine results page
Service level agreements (SLAs), 2295
SERVQUAL measurement attributes, 2295
Sets, algebra of, 593–594
Severe acute respiratory syndrome (SARS), 683
Sewing, 538–539
Shadowing, 4532–4533
Shakespeare Project, 1290
Shanghai Library, 3793
　collection, 899–900
　digital reference services, 900
　and ISTIS, merger of, 898–899
　mission, 899
　services, 899
Shanghai Science and Technology Museum, 909
Shannon and Weaver's communication theory,
　　4198
Shannon, Claude, 2049–2051
Shannon's information theory, 3613
Shannon's model, 4101
Shannon theory, *see* Information theory
Shared legal capability, *see* Library copyright
　　alliance
Shared libraries, *See* Joint-use libraries
Sharing and Transforming Access to Resources
　　(STARS), 3909
Sharjah Museum of Islamic Civilisation, 4381
SHARP News, 4269–4270
Shelf browsing, 4467
Shepard's Citation Index, 925
Shera model, 2229
Shibboleth, 2894
The Ship and Supercargo Bookkeeper, 645
*Shipping and Commercial List and New York
　　Price Current*, 1401
Shneiderman's principles, 4807–4808
Shockwave, 2155
SHOE, 3458
Shojakukan Library, 2560–2561
Short-term loans (STLs), 1210–1211, 1213
Short-title catalog (STC), 457
Shot-level indexing, 3131–3132
Shrine Library, 3976
Shrine of the Book, Israel Museum, 2550–2551
Shrink-wrap agreement, 1271
SIAM-AMS Proceedings, 3028
Sichuan Provincial Archives, 906–907
SIGLE database, 1753–1754
Signage
　changeable content signs, 4974–4975
　definition, 4965
　design principals, 4965, 4972
　expected outcomes, 4965, 4972
　fixed content signs, 4973–4975
　history of, 4965, 4972–4973
　message groups, 4973–4974
　sign materials, 4965–4971

Signal detection theory (SDT), 3930
Signal processing, 275
Signed bindings, 543
Signs, 2263–2264
SIGUSE, 4118
Siloed information environment, 4979
Similarity searching
　2D chemical structures, 833
　3D chemical structures, 835–836
　paradigm, 4427
Simon's theory, 2194
Simple Knowledge Organization System
　　(SKOS), 1260
Simple Mail Transport Protocol (SMTP), 2183
Simple Object Access Protocol (SOAP), 2187
Simple Recurrent Network (SRN), 285, 287
Simplified Molecular Input Line Entry Specifi-
　　cation (SMILES), 831
Singapore National Library, 3791
Single-document summaries, 418
Singular value decomposition (SVD),
　　2688–2696
Sinsigns, 4098
Site museums and monuments
　archaeological site museum, 4167–4168
　commemorative landscape, 4165
　commemorative monuments, 4164–4165
　definition, 4164
　freezing time, 4170
　as heritage, 4168
　historical perspective, interpretation chal-
　　lenges, 4170
　historic site, 4164
　house museum, 4165–4166
　landscape freezing, 4170
　outdoor museum/living history site,
　　4166–4167
　preservation
　　cultural factor, 4171
　　private-sector groups and societies, 4169
　　restoration *vs.* original controversy,
　　　4170–4171
　　UNESCO, 4169
　　United States federal legislation, 4169
　traditional site museum, 4165
　as war targets and cultural casualties, 4168
Site usage log, 4798
Situational relevance judgments, 3943–3944
Skilled reading
　computer models, 3838–3839
　eye movements, 3838
　phonology, 3838
Skills knowledge, 3535
SKY Index, 443
Slavic and East European Materials Project
　　(SEEMP), 791
Slip cases, 542
Slipstream, 3706
Slovakia
　archives and archival science
　　access to archives, 4181
　　education, 4182
　　history, 4180
　　legislation, 4180–4181
　　magazine and awards, 4183
　　national archives, 4181
　　organizations and associations, 4182–4183

　　specialized public archives, 4182
　　state archives, 4181–4182
　digitization projects, 4186
　historical, geographic, economic and
　　sociocultiral context, 4173–4174
　library and information professions, systems
　　and service
　　academic and research libraries,
　　　4177–4178
　　education, 4179
　　history of, 4174
　　informatization and digitization, 4179–4180
　　legislation, 4174–4175
　　public libraries, 4178–4179
　　Slovak National Library, 4175–4177
　　ULB, 4177–4178
　museums and museology
　　ecucation and professional associations,
　　　4185–4186
　　gallery network, 4185
　　history, 4183
　　political and social life, documentation of,
　　　4184–4185
　　SNM, 4183–4185
　　specialized museums, 4184
Slovak Librarians' Association (SLA), 4175
Slovak National Archives (SNA), 4180
Slovak National Library (SNL), 3322,
　　4175–4177, 4186
Slovak National Museum (SNM)
　collections, 4184
　history, 4183–4184
　political and social life, documentation of,
　　4184–4185
　publishing activities, 4185
　specialized museums, 4184
Sloval open-air museum, 4184
Small Business Administration (SBA), 636–637
Small businesses, 636–637, 3005
Small, Henry, 505–506
SMART project, 2222
Smashwords, 4058
Smith, Adam, 646
Smith-Lever Act, 1011
Smithsonian Center for Museum Studies, 3218
Smithsonian Institution, 4766–4767
　art museums, 4191–4192
　Building or Castle, 4191, 4193
　history and culture museums, 4192–4193
　legislation, 4188
　science museums, 4193–4195
Smithsonian Institution Information Retrieval
　　System (SIIRS), 3178–3179
Smithsonian National Museum of American
　　History, 1072–1073, 3255
Smooth gilding, 541
Snake stones, 1815
Snapshots, 1417
SNOMED Clinical Terms® (SNOMED CT®),
　　3340–3341
Social capital, 2126, 2659–2660
Social construction of technology (SCOT), 4020
Social constructivism, 2753–2754, 3528
Social epistemology, 2769, 3616
　epistemic justice, 4200–4202
　philosophical foundations and library and
　　information science, 4197–4198

postmodernism, 4198–4200
Wikipedia, 4202
Social inclusion, 2127
Social informatics
    assumptions, 4214
    definitions, 4213
    history, 4213–4214
    ICTs, 4212
    Kling's description, 4212
    and library and information science, 4215–
        4216
    research
        approaches, 4214–4215
        key insights, 4215
    Semantic Web, 4212
Socialization, externalization, internalization
        and internationalization (SECI) model,
        2619, 2621–2622
Social justice
    Dervin's sense-making approach, 4226
    distributive justice, 4219
    egalitarianism/equity, 4219
    etymological and conceptual origin, 4219
    information behavior research, 4226–4227
    inward-looking professional trends, 4223
    justice-as-desert theory, 4219
    justice-as-fairness, 4219
    liberating roles, 4220
    Library 2.0 efforts, 4222
    library profession, 4224–4225
    library's role, 4220
    policy reports and guidelines, 4221
    priveleged classes, tax-funded library for,
        4223
    public libraries, 4221–4222
    socially-just society, 4218
    Taparelli's concept, 4218
    tensions, 4218
    two-way learning outcomes, 4227
    utilitarianism, 4219
Social learning theory, 3513
Social library
    in United Kingdom, 1837
    in United States, 1840–1842
Social literacy, 2305
Social media
    altmetrics, 44
    information searching, 2242
    VRA, 4937
Social media optimization (SMO), 4041
Social networks, 844–846, 1039
    actors, 4236
    data collection, 4237–4238
    graph theory, 4236
    information networks
        knowledge transfer, 4235
        mobilized/accessible information, 4236
    and information transfer
        innovation, 4238
        network structures, 4240–4242
        roles and positions, 4240
        small world hypothesis, 4239–4240
        strong and weak ties, 4238–4239
    knowledge, 3535
    network clusters, 4237
    personal and network outcomes, 4242
    tie, 4236–4237

Social Network Sites (SNS), 844–845
Social Science Data Archives, 187
Social science literature, 4250–4251
    academic communication, 4247–4248
    electronic journals, 4249–4250
    Ellis model, 4250–4251
    Garvey and Griffith's studies, 4247–4249
    Hogeweg-De Haart's discussion, 4246–4247
    Janes' bibliography, 4246–4247
    models, 4250–4252
    refereeing process, 4247–4248
    Rosenbaum's framework, 4246–4247
    Tenopir analysis, 4251–4252
    use, 4250–4252
Social science professions
    code of ethics, 4255
    information needs, 4259
    journalists, 4259
    librarians, 4256–4257
    police officers, 4258
    social workers, 4257–4258
    teachers, 4255–4256
Social Science Research Network (SSRN) data-
        base, 3466
Social sciences citation index (SSCI), 925, 2370,
        3471
Social shaping of technology (SST), 4020
Societe Mathematique de France, 324
Society for Industrial and Applied Mathematics
        (SIAM), 3026
Society for Information Management (SIM),
        2276
Society for Promoting Christian Knowledge
        (SPCK), 1802, 1840
Society for Scholarly Publishing (SSP),
        4266–4267
    annual budget, 4262
    committees, 4264–4265
    educational purposes, 4262
    funding, 4262
    history, 4262–4263
    logos of, 4262–4263
    meetings and seminars, 4265–4266
    mission of, 4262–4264
    organizational membership category,
        4262
    organizational structure, 4264
    publications, 4266
    scholarly communication chain, 4262
    scholarly publishers and producer, challenges
        to, 4264
    strategic plans, 4265
Society for the Distribution of Useful Knowl-
        edge (SDUK), 1802
The Society for the History of Authorship,
        Reading and Publishing (SHARP),
        4268–4269
    book history, 1860
    goal of, 4270
    history of print culture, 4268
    officers, 4268
    publications, 4269–4270
    scholarly and professional organizations,
        4268
Society for the Propagation of the Gospel in
        Foreign Parts (SPG), 1840
Society of Accountants in Edinburgh, 651

Society of American Archivists (SAA), 174,
        196, 256, 688, 1424, 1466, 4336, 4384,
        4742
    advocacy outreach and cooperation,
        4276–4277
    archival record formats, 4271
    Diversity Committee, 4275–4276
    governance and member services, 4276
    history of, 4271–4273
    membership interest groups, 4273
        activities, 4274
        roundtables, 4274–4275
        sections, 4274
    Mentoring Program, 4276
    national and international leadership, 4271
    publications, 4277
    work, 4271
Society of Architectural Historians (SAH), 256
Society of Archivists, 4738–4739
Society of College, National and University
        Libraries (SCONUL), 4448, 4703–4705
Society of Competitive Intelligence Profes-
        sionals (SCIP), 4354, 4356
Society of Friends of the Institute of Ethiopian
        Studies Museum (SOFIES), 1503
Society of Greek Archivists, 1739
Society of Indexers (SI), 445
Society periodicals, 1659
Socio-cognitive relevance judgments, 3944
Sociocultural theory, 2755
Sociology of the information disciplines
    cultural record, 4292–4293
    innovation and specialization, 4293–4294
    knowledge and power, 4287–4288
    modern university, 4289
    scope and definition, 4288–4289
Sociotechnical interaction networks (STINs),
        4022
Sociotechnical theory, 2286
SOFIA, 1223–1224
Software and Information Industry Association
        (SIIA), 3650
    CODiE Award Program, 4298
    departments, 4297–4298
    global services, 4297
    history of, 4297
    membership, 4298
    objective, 4297
Software art, 2071
Software Industry Association of America
        (SIAA), 3656
Software Publishers Association, 3650
Solander cases, 542
SOLINET, 3922, 3924
Solipsism, 2898
Solo librarians, 4352–4353
Somerset Archaeological and Natural History
        Society, 1794
Somerset Record Society, 1794
Sonny Bono Copyright Term Extension Act, 369
Sound and audio archives
    challenges, 4304–4305
    collection development policies, 4301–4302
    content-centered approach, 4300
    copyright, 4304
    cylinder recordings, 4299
    digital audio projects, 4305

Sound and audio archives (cont'd.)
  funding and support, 4304
  medium-centered archive, 4300
  music archives
    disc program, 4301
    Edison phonograph, 4300
    pulse code modulation (PCM), 4301
    rise of, 4301
  national efforts, 4305
  pay-as-you-go digital distribution, 4304
  Phonogramm-Archiv, 4299
  preservation and access, 4302–4304
  professional associations, 4302–4303
  sound recordings, 4299–4300
  supporting materials, 4302
  technical processing, 4302
  user needs, 4301
Source credibility, 1115
SourceForge, 1063
South Asia Materials Project (SAMP), 791
South Australian Literary Association, 391
South Central Region of National Network of
    Libraries of Medicine, 3034
South Dublin County Library Service, 3786
Southeast Asia Materials Project (SEAM), 791
Southeast Asia-Pacific Audiovisual Archive
    Association (SEAPAVAA), 1579
Southeastern College Art Conference (SECAC),
    4934
Southern Appalachian Information Node
    (SAIN), 3310
Southern California Earthquake Center (SCEC),
    2997
Southern European Libraries Link (SELL),
    2829
South Kensington Museum, 3154–3155
South Korea
  archives and archival science
    as discipline, 4309
    legislative history, 4308–4309
    NARS, 4308
  history, 4307–4308
  libraries
    academic libraries, 4310–4311
    administrative and legal systems,
      4309–4310
    Book Reading Seoul project, 4313
    Bookstart movement, 4312
    Children and Young Adult Services Pro-
      grams, 4312–4313
    education, 4312
    Enhancing Library Service for the Dis-
      abled, 4313
    Miracle Library project, 4312
    National Assembly Library, 4310
    NLK, 4309–4310
    One Book, One City movement, 4313
    professional association, 4312
    public libraries, 4311
    school libraries, 4311
    Small Library movement, 4313
    special libraries, 4311
    Supreme Court Library, 4310
    WLIC, 4313
  map of, 4307–4308
Soviet Mathematics-Doklady, 3027
Space facet, 1536

Spain
  archives and archival science
    administration, 4329–4330
    associations, 4330
    collections, 4330
    education, 4330
    expenditures, 4330
    representative archives profiles, 4330
    user services, 4330
  education, library and information science,
    4327–4328
  government libraries
    museum libraries, 4326
    religious libraries, 4327
    Royal Academies, 4326
  history, 4314–4315
  legislation, 4315–4316
  libraries
    in Peru, 3606
  library cooperation, 4329
  map of, 4315
  museums and museology
    administration, 4331
    associations, 4333
    collections, 4331
    education, 4333
    expenditures, 4331
    representative museum profiles, 4331–4333
    user services, 4331
  National Library
    CATMARC, 4316
    collections, 4317–4318
    cooperation, 4319
    databases and automation, 4318–4319
    digitization, 4319
    expenditures, 4317
    IBERMARC format, 4316
    LibEcon, 4316
    organization and structure, 4316–4317
    publications, 4318
    REBIUN, 4316
    RUECA, 4316
    special collections, 4318
    user services, 4319
  professional library associations, 4328
  public libraries
    administration and staff, 4322–4323
    automation, 4323–4324
    collections, 4323
    expenditures, 4323
    The Inform@tion Society for All, 4322
    Library of Catalonia, 4324
    Pedro Salinas Public Library, 4324
    PISTA Program, 4322
    user services, 4323
  school libraries
    administration, 4324
    automation, 4325
    collections, 4324
    expenditures, 4324
    staff, 4324
    user services, 4324–4325
  special libraries
    administration, 4325
    automation, 4325–4326
    collections, 4325
    expenditures, 4325

    staff, 4325
    user services, 4325
  university and research libraries
    administration and staffing, 4319–4320
    automation, 4320–4321
    collections, 4320
    CSIC libraries, 4321
    expenditures, 4320
    repesentative university library profiles, 4321
    Scientific and Literary Athenaeum of
      Madrid, 4322
    user services, 4320
  virtual and digital libraries, 4327
Spain ISKO Chapter, 2497
Spangler Library, 878
Spanish binding, 545
Spanish illumination, 1948
Spanish Spring Library, 2792
SPARQL, 2939–2941
Special auxiliaries, 4785
Special bulletins, 4937
Special collections, 3820–3821; see also Rare
    book collections
  age, 4336, 4344
  area studies collections, 4335
  care and security, 4335
  communication skills, 4348–4349
  condition, 4338, 4346
  core professional requirements, 4348–4349
  definition, 4335–4336
  definitions, 4343–4344
  digitization, 4341
  exhibitions, 4347
  foreign language skill, 4349
  format, 4345
  formats, 4335, 4337
  foundations, 4346
  fundraising, 4348
  future changes, 4349
  grant-writing, 4348
  and manuscripts
    core professional requirements, 4340–4341
    definition, 4336
  market value, 4336–4337, 4344
  modern special collections
    exhibitions and publications, 4339
    fund-raising and grant-writing, 4340
    public programs and performances, 4339
    security, preservation, and posterity, 4340
    teaching and research, 4339–4340
  noncirculating collections, 4335
  preservation, 4349
  provenance, 4337, 4345
  public programs, 4347
  rare book rooms, 4338
  scarcity, 4337–4338, 4345–4346
  securing posterity, 4349
  stand-alone research and independent librar-
    ies, 4336, 4338–4339
  subject matter, 4337, 4345
  teaching and research, 4347–4348
  treasure rooms, 4338
Special Collections in Mass Media & Culture
    (SCMMC), 1561
Special Committee to Review Program Assess-
    ment Processes and Procedures
    (SCRPAPP), 71

Special Interest Group for Classification Research (SIG/CR), 959–960
Special Interest Group on Computer–Human Interaction (SIGCHI), 1904, 4804
Special Interest Group on Information Retrieval (SIGIR), 482, 1904, 2222
Special Interest Group on Management Information Systems (SIGMIS), 2276
Special interest groups (SIGs), 91–92, 2007, 3173–3174
Special Interest Section on Aboriginal Archives (SISAA), 691
Special interest sections (SISs), 49–50
SPECIALIST lexicon, 4673
Special librarianship
    career opportunities, 4352–4353
    characteristics, 4354–4355
    competencies, 4357–4358
    education, 4358
    employability, 4358
    end user training, 4353–4354
    evolution, 4351
    global networks, 4357
    KM, 4354
    organizations, 4355–4357
    public image, 4353
    return on investment, 4353
    technology, 4353
    titles, 4355
    Web, 4351–4352
Special libraries, 301–303, 305, 307, 1096, 2764, 3414–3415
    acquisitions units, organization of, 2918
    Armenia, 230
    in Australia, 384–385
    in China, 900–902
    in Croatia, 1125
    definition, 4361–4362
    in Denmark, 1219–1220
    digital collections, 4368
    ethics, 4365
    Ethiopia, 1498–1499
    in Germany, 1698
    globalization, 4362–4363
    Greece, 1732
    Hungary, 1923
    information technology, 4367
    in Israel, 2547
    Japan, 2565
    in Kazakhstan, 2583
    Kenya, 2596–2597
    knowledge services, 4368
    learning organization, 4367
    library associations (see Special Libraries Association)
    Lithuania, 2953
    management
        marketing, 4366
        organizations, 4365–4366
        planning and budgeting, 4366
        value evaluation, 4366–4367
    in Moldova, 3124
    New Zealand libraries, 3376
    origin, 4362
    in Peru, 3608–3609
    physical and a virtual presence, 4368
    in Saudi Arabia, 3976–3977

Senegal, 4107–4108
    in Serbia, 4131
    services
        acquisitions and collection development, 4363
        competitive intelligence, 4364–4365
        knowledge management, 4365
        news updating, 4364
        organization of information, 4363
        reference and research center, 4363–4364
    South Korea, 4311
    Tunisia, 4631
    in Ukraine, 4646
    in United Kingdom, 4707–4708
    Venezuelan libraries, 4890
Special Libraries Association (SLA), 256, 652, 709–710, 1097, 2708, 4014, 4016, 4352, 4356–4357, 4362
    business and industry, advisory service to, 4374
    copyright legislation, 4374–4375
    core values, 4371
    corporate and technology libraries, 4374
    documentation, 4374
    Employment Committee, 4373
    Great Depression, challenges during, 4373
    information, knowledge and strategic learning, 4375–4376
    information/knowledge centers, 4370
    information professionals, 4377–4378
    knowledge services, 4372, 4376
    knowledge sharing, 4372–4373
    membership, growth of, 4374
    motto, 4373
    origin of, 4371–4372
    PAIS, creation of, 4373
    practical and utilitarian library services, 4373
    PREPS Commission, 4376
    professional knowledge workers, support to, 4370
    regional chapters, 4370
    research resources, analysis of, 4373
    research units, 4370
    responsibilities, 4374
    special libraries movement, 4374
    Vision Statement of 2004, 4370, 4377
Specialty hospital library, 1872–1873
Specialty Museums
    changing face, 4382
    examples, 4381–4382
    expertise, 4381
    number of, 4380
    organization, 4380
    types, 4379–4380
    United States, 4380
Spectrum scholarships, 81
Speculativism, 3628–3629
Speech communication, 997–998
Speech processing, 274
Speech recognition technology, 1058
SPICE (setting, perspective, intervention, comparison, and evaluation), 1517
Spiders, 2519
Spofford, Ainsworth, 2848
Spofford, Ainsworth Rand, 2881–2883
Spreading activation model, 3590
Spring backs, 539

SRW/U, 2894–2895
S-SRB, 3002
Stack management, 920–921
Standard citation order, 585
Standard Generalized Markup Language (SGML), 730–731
Standard generalized markup language (SGML), 1252, 1365, 1381, 1416, 2343, 2986, 3074–3075, 4560–4561, 5022
Standard industrial classification (SIC) system, 638, 653
Standardized Assessment of Information Literacy Skills (SAILS), 374
Standard operating procedures (SOPs), 3357, 3361–3363
Standards for Accreditation of Master's Programs in Library and Information Studies, 18, 20
Standards Institution of Israel, 2547
Standard Statistics Compustat Service, 652
Standing Committee of the National and University Libraries (SCONUL), 2545
Standing Conference of Eastern, Central and Southern African Library and Information Associations (SCECSAL), 37, 4515
Standing Conference of National and University Libraries of Eastern, Central and Southern Africa (SCANUL-ECS), 3330
Standish survey and analysis methodology, 2281
Stanford Graduate School of Business, 650
STARS, 1676
"Starvation policy," 4784
State and local government archives
    Multnomah County (Oregon) Archives, 4746
    New Orleans Notorial Archives, 4746
    San Antonio Municipal Archives Program, 4746–4747
State archives, 1222–1223
    in Dubrovnik, 1128
    establishment and administrative location, 4390–4391
    history, 4386–4389
    mission, 4384
    nature and functions, 4384–4386
    in Rijeka, 1128
    in Zadar, 1128
State Archives Bureau (SAB), 905
State Gold and Precious Metals Museum, 2587
State Historical Records Advisory Boards (SHRABs), 4743
State Historical Society of Wisconsin (SHSW), 1780–1781
State Historic Preservation Officer (SHPO), 1774
State Inspectorate of Public Libraries, 1216
State Library Agency Section (SLAS), 376
State library and state library agencies, 4392
    Arizona State Library, Archives and Public Records, 4397
    Connecticut State Library, 4397
    COSLA, 4394–4395
    definition, 4392–4393
    establishment dates, 4398–4399
    functions, 4394
    FY 2006, 4396
    GPLS, 4397
    history, 4393

State library and state library agencies (cont'd.)
   librarian qualifications, 4396
   Library of Virginia building, 4398
   Maine State Library, 4397–4398
   New Jersey State Library, 4398
   Oregon State Library, 4398
   personnel, education of, 4396
   professional organizations, 4394
   public library, federal aid to, 4393–4394
   state government structure, 4395–4396
   Texas State Library and Archives, 4398
   trends and issues, 4396
State Library of Queensland, 383
State modeling, 3112
State Museum of Archeology and Ethnography, 2587
State Museum of Popular Musical Instruments, 2587
State Records Act 1997, 387
State Scientific Medical Library of Ukraine, 4646
State Scientific Technical Library of Ukraine, 4647
Static domain model, 1205
Statistical bibliography, 492, 496–497, 2911
Statistical control, 1178
Statistical Methods for Research Workers, 1410
Statistical View of the Number of Sheep, 1404
Statistical Yearbook of the League of Nations, 649
Statistics of the Woollen Manufactories of the United States, 1404
StatsQUAL®, 374
STAT-USA, 1554–1555
Statutory invention registrations (SIRs), 3565–3566
Steering Committee on Canada's Archives (SCCA), 666
Stemming/morphological analysis, 2201
Steven Spielberg Jewish Film Archive, 2555
Steve project, 3067
St. George Interior Decoration and Art Gallery, 1504
Still image indexing
   collection level, 4408
   concept-based indexing
      data content tools, 4412–4413
      data structure tools, 4413
      data value tools, 4411–4412
      history, 4410
      theoretical basis, 4410–4411
   content-based indexing
      CBR, 4414–4415
      cognitive processing, 4413–4414
   context, 4409
   controlled vocabulary, 4408–4409
   Cranfield II experiments, 4408
   features/attributes selection, 4407
   image attribute, 4407–4408
   image collection, 4407
   image considerations, 4409
   image retrieval, 4408
   image tagging systems, 4415
   subject indexing, 4407
   user-centered indexing, 4408
   visual perception, 4408
Stochastic decision models, 1197

Stone representation theorem, 595
Stone-tipped spear point, 1778
Stopping rule, 2363
Stopword processing, 2201
Storage, 2072
Storage Networking Industry Association (SNIA), 715
Storage Resource Broker (SRB), 3000
Story Corps project, 1794
The Story of John Winchcombe, commonly called Jack of Newberry, 647
Story slams, 4444
Storytelling
   business, 4442
   education, 4442
   finding, 4440–4441
   healing, 4442–4443
   kinds, 4437–4438
   learning, 4441
   libraries, 4443
   origins, 4438–4439
   performing, 4441
   religious, 4443
   scope, 4437
Strabo, 1684
Strategic and Competitive Intelligence Professionals (SCIP), 2708
Strategic generation, 432
Strategic goals, 4455
Strategic long-range planning (SLRP), 68
Strategic planning, academic libraries
   benefits, 4447
   definition, 4447
   elements
      action planning, 4455–4456
      financial commentary, 4456
      goal statements, 4455
      library missions, 4452–4453
      scenario development, 4454–4455
      service values, 4453
      visioning, 4453–4454
   environmental appraisal, 4448
   functions, 4447
   historical context, 4448–4449
   planning processes, 4450–4451
   presentation, 4448
   program management, 4448
   published literature
      academic strategy, 4449
      library planning, 4449–4450
   strategic management, 4448
   strategic profiling, 4448
   strategy development, 4448
   strategy documents, 4451–4452
   terminology, 4447–4448
Strategy Hub, 2214
STREAM, 2630
StreamCluCD algorithm, 2634
StreamMiner, 2636
Street lit/urban fiction, 3706
Strengthening Public Health Research in Europe (SPHERE), 1767
Strengths, weaknesses, opportunities and threats (SWOT) analysis, 145, 1882, 3196
Stress/coping theory, 2089–2090
String formats, 1177
String indexing systems, 1985

String processing
   feedforward ANN for, 285
   RANN for, 285–287
   TDNN for, 285–286
Structural consistency, 1175
Structural engineering, 1248
Structural equation model (SEM), 1205–1206
Structural information, 2056
Structured metadata, 4427
Students' information needs and behavior
   developmental characteristics, 4459
   information literacy, 4462–4463
   information searching behavior, 4460–4461
   library use, 4461–4462
   net generation, 4460
   specific student groups, 4463
Student texts, 2739–2740
Studies in the History of Statistical Method, 493
Subiaco Lactantius, 1973
Subject authority cooperative program (SACO), 2853, 2871, 2921
Subject authority data, 1612, 1615–1616
Subject authority record, 4467
Subject cataloging
   approaches
      classification numbers, 4467
      controlled vocabulary search, 4466–4467
      keyword and full-text search, 4467
   library catalogs
      early standard subject lists, 4467–4468
      impact of automation, 4468
   major classification systems
      bibliographic classification, 4475
      Colon Classification, 4475
      DDC, 4474
      LCC, 4474–4475
      NLM classification, 4475
      UDC, 4475
   principles
      classification theory, 4470
      controlled vocabulary, 4468–4470
      design and application principles, 4471
      library classification, 4471
      modern classification theory, 4470–4471
      traditional classification theory, 4470
   subject access systems
      FAST, 4472–4473
      LCSH, 4472
      MeSH, 4474
      Sears list of Subject Headings, 4473–4474
Subject Cataloging Manual (SCM), 2874
Subject classification (SC), 961, 964, 970
Subject headings, 2857, 2862–2863
Subject Headings for Children and People, Places & Things, 1261
Subject Headings Manual (SHM), 2866
Subject Index for the Visual Arts, 1080
Subjective relevance, 3930, 3932–3933
Subject Portals Project (SPP), 2897
Subject scattering, 2211
Submission Information Package (SIP), 1365
Subscribing business, 1275
Subscription libraries, 916, 4478–4481
Substance identification for information retrieval
   ambiguous chemical identifiers
      chemical formulae, 823–824
      chemical names, 823

unumbiguous chemical identifiers
CAS Registry Numbers®, 824
chemical structures, 824
InChIs™, 824–825
sequences, 824
Substructure searching, 825
2D chemical structures, 832–833
3D chemical structures, 834–835
Subversive ethics, 1473
Summa de Arithmetica, Geometrica et Proportionalta, 645
Summarization, *see* Automatic abstracting and summarization
NLP, 3353
Summer Educational Institute (SEI), 4938
Sunderland Museum, 4716
Sunken Military Craft Act, 1776
SUNY Open Textbook Initiative, 2903
SuperCard, 1290
Supplement to Hain's Repertorium Bibliographicum, 1969
Supply chain management (SCM), 1180–1181, 2658
Supportive culture, 3521
Support vector machines (SVMs), 3270
Supralibros, 540
Supreme Court Library of Korea, 4310
Surface credibility, 1115
Surface Web, 5021
Survey of Current Business, 649
Survival ethics, 1473
Sutherland tooling process, 541
Šventupis secondary school library, 2951
Sveriges Allmanna Biblioteksförening (SAB), 1261
Swedish binding, 548
Swedish Library Association, 3548
Swiss Federal Archives (SFA), 4491
Swiss Library Association, 4490–4491
Switching function, 595–596
Switzerland
archives and archival studies
archivist education, 4494
cantonal and local archives, 4491
digital archival collections, 4493
electronic records, 4494
enterprise archives, 4493
film and audiovisual archives, 4492
international organizations, 4492
legislation, 4491
missionary societies, 4493
national institutions, 4492
preservation, 4494
professional association, 4494
SFA, 4491
specialized archives, 4492–4493
university archives, 4491–4492
virtual archives, 4493
Confederation, cantons, and communes, 4487–4488
culture, 4487, 4495–4496
economy, 4487
libraries
digital library, 4489–4490
legislation and types, 4487–4488

national library and information services, 4488–4489
professional associations, 4490–4491
map of, 4487–4488
museums and museology, 4494–4495
official languages, 4487
population of, 4487
SWOT analysis, *see* Strengths, weaknesses, opportunities and threats analysis
Sydney School, 1665
Syllogism, 269
Symbol grounding, 4090
Symbolic cultural theory, 3520
Symbolic interactionism, 3811
Symbolic learning approach, 273
Symbolic utility, 2357
Symbols, 4961, 4963–4964, 4972
Symposium on Computer Applications in Medical Care (SCAMC), 85
Synodontis acanthoperca, 1161
Synonymy, 2688–2689
Syntax
search engines, 4048
standards, 3062–3063
Systematized Nomenclature of Medicine-Clinical Terms (SNOMED-CT), 979, 4673
System for the Mechanical Analysis and Retrieval of Text (SMART), 2689
Systemic functional linguistic (SFL), 1664–1665
Systemic knowledge assets, 2622
System of Scientific and Technical Information project, 1125
Systems and Services Section (SASS), 2843
Systems knowledge, 3535

T

Tableau Geographique, 1687
Table of content services (TOC), 1880
Tabulated credibility, 1115
Tacit–explicit dichotomy, 2651–2652
Tacit knowledge
and explicit knowledge, 2643, 2650
organizational memory, 3534
Tactical generation, 432
Tagged Image File Format (TIFF), 1367
Take-the-best heuristics, 2362–2363
Taking Liberties: The struggle for Britain's freedoms and rights, 624
Talking-book machines (TBMs), 565, 567–568
Tallahassee FreeNet (TFN), 1030
Tamiment Library and Wagner Archives, 4761
Tamura's feature selection, 4423
TANIT, 4631
Tanzania
academic libraries
changing roles and challenges, 4505–4506
policy shifts and higher learning institutions expansion, 1990s, 4504–4505
UDSM and, 4504
archives and archival system
record management structures, 4508–4509
status and downside, 4509–4510
botanical gardens, 4511–4512
challenges, 4517–4518
characteristics and key ICT/development indicators, 4499

herbaria, 4512
higher learning institutions, 4521–4522
intellectual property regulations, 4513–4514
Internet users, 4498
LIS development, chronology of, 4518–4520
map of, 4498
museums
antiquities, 4511
National Museum System, 4510
private art galleries, 4511
private museums, 4510–4511
policy initiatives, 4517
professional associations, 4515–4516
professional development
post-independence challenges and remedies, 4514–4515
training institutions, 4515
public libraries
bibliographic control, 4502
cultural–educational relations and NGO libraries/ information centers, 4503–4504
early pre-independence efforts, 4499–4500
institutional structures and policies, 4502–4503
libraries and literacy education, 4501–4502
postindependence developments, 4500–4501
pre-independence synopsis, 4499
school libraries
information technology, teaching and learning, 4507
library services for children, 4506–4507
teacher–librarians associations, 4506
situation analysis, 4512–4513
special libraries
emergence of, 4507
specialized information services, 4507–4508
TLSB
functions, 4520–4521
powers of, 4521
zoos, 4512
Tanzania Library Services Board (TLSB), 4502
Tarlton Law Library, 4577
Task-based information interaction evaluation framework, 4883
Task-based information searching
anomalous state of knowledge, 4526–4527
contextual characteristics, 4526
experimental and natural settings, 4527
field studies
critical incident technique, 4531
diaries, 4531–4532
ethical concerns, 4534
interviews, 4530–4531
multimethod approach, 4530
questionnaires, 4530–4531
shadowing, 4532–4533
transaction log, 4533
triangulation, 4533–4534
information retrieval, 4527
task performer's traits, 4526
tasks
activity, 4527–4528
process nature of searching, 4529
task complexity, 4528–4529
task granularity, 4528

Tasman, Abel, 1685
Tatomir Accessibility Checklist, 3578
"Taxidermy and Plastic Art" teaching lab and course, 3216
Taximetrics, *see* Numerical taxonomy
Taxonomic Databases Working Group (TDWG), 3311
Taxonomy
  classical taxonomy, 4538–4539
  classification, 4537
  contemporary taxonomy
    AI ontology, 4540
    classificatory structures, 4539
    information access systems, 4540–4541
    object-oriented programming, 4540
  definition, 4537
  history, 4538
  methodology and practices, 4543–4544
  numerical taxonomy, 4539
  organization, 4538
  theory and principles, 4541–4543
Taxpayer Return on Investment in Florida Public Libraries study, 3795
Tax-supported public libraries, 3774
Taylor and Fayol's scientific approach, 142
Taylor & Francis Group Student Travel Grant, 1422
Taylorism, 2065
Taylor's information need model, 2118–2119
Taylor Society, 651
Teach Act, 1472
Teaching hospital library, 1872
Team computing, 1054
TeamWare, 1062
Technical Center for Agricultural and Rural Cooperation (CTA), 2312
Technical Chamber of Greece (TEE), 1732
Technical Committee 8 (TC8), 2276
Technical libraries, 4009
Technical Library of Lithuania, 2953
Technical metadata creators, 3066
Technical Report Archive and Image Library (TRAIL), 791, 4012
Technical services (TS)
  academic libraries, 4–5, 8–9
  acquisitions, 2918–2919
  cataloging, 2918, 2920–2924
  collections management, 2918, 2924
Technical Subcommittee for Encoded Archival Description (TS-EAD), 1424, 1431
Technical writing
  audience analysis, 4547
  composition, 4548
  documentation, 4547–4550
  field of study
    early history, 4549
    new millennium, 4551–4552
    twentieth century, 4549–4551
  information architecture, 4552
  information design and architecture, 4548
  nonacademic writing, 4547
  professional communication, 4547
  professional writing, 4547, 4549
  research, 4548
  rhetoric and writing programs, 4548
  technical communication, 4547–4548, 4552
  writing studies, 4548, 4552

Techniques in Electronic Resource Management (TERMS), 414
Techno-economic paradigm, 2254
Technological Educational Institutions (TEIs), 1731
Technological Institute of Higher Education Studies in Monterrey (ITESM), 3086
Technological scarcity argument, 1017
Technology, 4978
  economy, 2308
  knowledge, 2275
Technology Opportunities Program (TOP), 1028–1029
Technoscapes, 2124
Teeple Scholarship, 81
TEI P1, 4566
TEI P2, 4566
TEI P3, 4566
TEI P4, 4566
TEI P5, 4567
Telecommunications and Information Infrasture Assistance Program (TIIAP), 1028
Telecoms Package, 2141–2142
TelegraphCQ, 2631
Television, 999, 1573–1574
Television archives, *see* International Federation of Television Archives
Television Studies Commission, 2468–2469
TEMPUS program, 2827, 2954
Term frequency–inverse document frequency (TFIDF) weights, 2204
Test collections
  available, 4557
  construction, 4556–4557
Texas State Archives, 4385
Text analysis, 2930
Text encoding initiative (TEI), 3075
  character encoding, 4559
  Consortium, 4559
  ground rules
    customization files, 4564
    guidelines, 4561–4562
    modules, 4562–4564
    structural grammars, 4564
    text structure, 4562
  Guidelines, 1289–1290
  history, 4565–4567
  humanities
    data representation, 4559
    flags, 4560
    markup languages, 4560–4561
Text generation, *see* Natural language generation
Text mining, 2401–2402
Text planning, 432
TExtract, 1987
Text retrieval conference (TREC), 482, 484, 1904, 2175–2176, 2223, 3932, 4557
  historical context, 4569–4570
  test collections, 4570–4571
  tracks, 4571–4572
Text schemas, 437
Textual bibliography, 478
Thales of Miletus, 1683
Theatrum Orbis Terrarum, 1685
The European Library (TEL), 3331, 3682

Theft, vandalism and security
  ABAA, 4578
  Antiquarian Booksellers database, 4576
  archival repositories, 4580
  BAMBAM, 4578
  basic security and preservation policies, 4580
  bomb threats, 4580
  book theft, 4579
  communication among librarians, 4587–4588
  communication, book dealers, 4581–4582
  digital recordings, 4579
  electronic articles, 4579
  ideological vandalism, 4580
  library crimes, 4578
  Library Proxy Server, 4580
  lobby state legislatures, 4586
  MARC format, 4578
  missing treasures, Library of Congress, 4582–4583
  in museums
    definitions, 4593–4594
    history, 4594
    prevention, 4598–4600
  OCLC database, 4578
  paging slips, 4580
  play vandalism, 4580
  preventions
    consistent security procedures, 4584–4585
    mark materials and use colored photocopy paper, 4585–4586
    microfilming, 4585
    security systems and trust no one, 4583–4584
  replevin, 4577, 4583
  security devices, 4586–4587
  stolen/mutilated library books, replacement of, 4577
  tactical vandalism, 4580
  vindictive vandalism, 4580
The information literacy tutorial (TILT), 3440
The Joint Commission on Accreditation of Healthcare Organizations (JCAHO), 1874
Thema–nomen conceptual model, 4066
Thematic wayfinding, 4958
The National Archives (TNA), 111, 4733, 4735
Theodor Seuss Geisel Award, 335
Theological librarianship
  ATLA, 4606–4608
  European library, 4605
  international association, 4608–4609
  North American experience, 4605–4606
  origins, 4604–4605
  professional associations support, 4608
  today, 4609–4610
Theophrastes, 1683
Theoretical Economics, 3468
Theoretical knowledge, 2267–2269
Theory of action, 4806–4807
Theory of forms, 2094
Recuyell of the Histories of Troy, 1973
Thesauri, 1984–1986
Thesaurofacet, 589
Thesaurus, 1076, 1537–1538
  BC2, 589
  definition, 4673

standards
  guidelines, 2666
  ISO 2788 and Z39.19, differences between, 2668–2669
  national and international standards, 2667
  prehistory, 2666
  principles, 2668
  sector specific standards, 2667
  successive updates, 2667–2668
  weaknesses in, 2669
Thesaurus for Graphic Materials (TGM), 1080, 2857, 4411–4412
Thesaurus Linguae Graecae (TLG), 1912
Thesaurus of Engineering and Scientific Terms (TEST), 2666
Thesaurus structure
  descriptors, selection of, 3423–3424
  knowledge of, 3423
Thessaloniki Historical Archives, 1738
The University Licensing Program (TULIP), 5026
ThinkLab makerspace, 2992
Thomas Register of American Manufacturers, 653
THOMAS system, 1552–1553, 4874
Thompson, Frederick, 2054
ThoughtMesh project, 1288
Three ages lifecycle model, 168–169
Thumb cases, *see* Slip cases
Thwaites, 1781
Thyssen-Bornemisza Museum, 4332
Tianjin Natural History Museum of Hebei Province, 909
Ticknor, George, 1843–1844
TIFF format, 1311, 1367, 3568
TIGER initiative, 86
Tilden Trust, 1845
Tilloch, Andrew, 1867
Time-delay neural network (TDNN), 285–286
Time facet, 1536
Title-based method, summarization, 421
Title instance package platform (TIPP), 1712
Title searching, 4049
TMark, 2066
Tokenization, 2201
Tokyo National Museum, 2572
Tolbiac site, 532–534
Topical relevance
  judgments, 3943
  subjectivity, 3933–3936
Topic Maps
  application areas, 4621–4622
  associative graph-based model, 4620
  bibliographic records, 4619–4620
  constraint language, 4618
  digital libraries, 4621
  e-learning, 4621
  enterprise information integration, 4621
  entity–relation (ER) model, 4620
  faceted classification, 4619
  family of standards, 4617
  glossaries, 4619
  indexes, 4618–4619
  key strengths, 4622
  KM perspective, 4621
  query language, 4617–4618
  TAO model, 4614–4616

thesaurus, 4619
Web publishing, 4622
Top Management Roundtable (TMR), 4265–4266
Topography, 1684
Toronto Public Library, 3786
Toronto Virtual Enterprise (TOVE), 3458
Total Information Awareness (TIA) program, 2402
Total quality management (TQM), 3511
Tower and Stockade Museum, 2551–2552
Town library
  in England, 1836–1837
  in France, 1837
  in Germany, 1837
  in Scotland, 1837
Trace information, 2058
Trade associations
  magazines, 650
  official publications, 649–650
  SIIA, 4297–4298
Trade Marks Ordinance of 1922, 4513
Traderbot, 2631
Tradescant, John, 4715–4716
Trade Secrets Act, 2152
Traditional site museum, 4165
Transactional data streams, 2628
Transaction log, 4533
Transaction-processing systems, 2273
Transactions of the American Mathematical Society, 3027
Transactions of the Moscow Mathematical Society, 3028
Translation probability, 3142–3143
Translations of Mathematical Monographs, 3028
Translations Series I and II, 3028
Transmission–absorption model, 4918
Transmission control protocol (TCP), 1015
Transmission control protocol and Internet protocol (TCP/IP), 2516–2517
Transnationalism, 2123
Transportation security, 2399
Travels, 1684
Treaties and review articles, 816–817
Treatise of Commerce, 1400
Treaty of Waitangi, 2036
TREC, *see* Text retrieval conference
Tree calf, 541
Trial voluntary protest program (TVPP) publications, 3566
Triangulation, 4533–4534
Tribal Libraries Program (TLP), 2033
Tribal museums, 3245
Trinidad Public Library, 3325
Triptychs, 542
Tropical Pesticides Research Institute (TPRI), 4512
True Interest of Holland, 645
Truman Grants program, 3714
Trust management approach, 406
Trust virtualization, 2998–3000
Trustworthiness, 2529–2530
Trustworthy repositories, 1333
Truth and Reconciliation commission, 2034
Tsinghua University Library, 896–897
  automation and networking, 897
  collection development, 897
  subject librarian system, 898

Tübingen System of Text Processing Programs (TUSTEP), 1293
TUNAGRI, 4631
TUNIDOC, 4629
TUNIPER, 4629
Tunisia
  academic libraries, 4628–4629
  archives and archival science
    legislation, 4633
    National Archives, 4633–4635
  EUMEDCONNECT, 4629
  historic background
    independent Tunisia, 4625–4626
    preindependent Tunisia, libraries and books in, 4624–4625
  legislation, libraries
    legal deposit and copyright, 4627–4628
    statutes and legislation, 4628
  library, information science and archival education and training, 4631–4632
  map of, 4625
  museums and museology
    cultural heritage, 4636
    historic preservation, 4635–4636
    Musée archéologique de Chimtou, 4637
    Musée archéologique de Chimtou', 4637
    Musée Dar Cherait 4638
    Musée des arts et traditions populaires 4638
    Musée des arts islamiques de Rakkada, 4637
    Musée de Sidi Kasim al-Jalizi, 4637–4638
    Musée national de Carthage, 4637
    Musée national du Bardo, 4636–4637
    Musée national d'Utique, 4637
    Musée Sidi Zitouni, 4638
    National Parks, 4638–4639
  National Library and Information Services, 4626–4627
  public libraries, 4629
  school libraries, 4630–4631
  special libraries, 4631
Tunis summit meeting, 5016
Turing test, 270
Turkish illumination (1451-1900), 1956
Turock Scholarship, 81
Two-mode networks, 4237
Two-sheets-on sewing method, 539
Two-step information-seeking approach, 2134
Tycho Brahe's press, 3739
Typenrepertorium der Wiegendrucke, 1971–1972
Typographical detectives, 1971–1972
Typographic presses, 3742

U

UCD, *see* User-centered design
UCLA Film & Television Archive, 1563
UCS Transformation Format 8 (UTF-8), 2984
UDC Consortium (UDCC), 4784
UFRJ, *see* Federal University of Rio de Janeiro
UKB Association, 2826
Ukiyoe, 2561
Ukraine
  culture and history, 4642
  geopolitical location of, 4642–4643

Ukraine (cont'd.)
  libraries
    agricultural libraries, 4646
    Central Library of the Ukrainian Associa-
        tion of the Blind, 4647
    documents, 4643–4644
    goals, 4643
    history of, 4642
    information technologies, 4643
    international library society, 4644
    Korolenko State Scientific Library in Khar-
        kiv, 4645
    Lviv Stefanyk Scientific Library, 4643,
        4645–4646
    NPLU, 4644–4645
    problems, 4644
    professional associations, 4644
    professional education, 4644
    publications, 4643
    public libraries, 4644
    Scientific Agricultural Library, 4647
    special libraries, 4646
    State Library of Ukraine for Children,
        4645
    State Scientific Medical Library, 4646
    State Scientific Technical Library, 4647
    Ukrainica, 4643
    university libraries, 4646
    Vernadsky National Library, 4643, 4645
Ukrainian Library Association (UBA), 4644
Ukrainica, 4643
U.K. Research Assessment Exercise (RAE),
    2373
UK Research Reserve (UKRR), 620
Ulrich's Serials Librarianship Award, 331
Unambiguous chemical identifiers
    CAS Registry Numbers®, 824
    chemical structures, 824
    InChIs™, 824–825
    sequences, 824
UNCITRAL Model Law on Electronic Com-
    merce, 1270
Unconscionable contracts, 1272
Uncontrolled vocabularies, 1078
Undergraduate Librarians Discussion Group
    (UGLI), 4653
Undergraduate libraries
    architecture, 4650–4651
    collection development, 4651–4652
    current libraries, 4653–4654
    organizations, 4653
    vs. research libraries, 4652
Undernet, 1049
U.N. Development Program (UNDP), 2312
Undifferentiated names, 3291
Undiscovered public knowledge, 4201
U.N. Educational Scientific and Cultural Orga-
    nization (UNESCO), 2312, 3217
UNESCO Convention on the Means of
    Prohibiting and Preventing the Illicit
    Import, Export and Transfer of Owner-
    ship of Cultural Property, 3759
Unfreezing process, 2297
Unicode, 2984
Unicode Character Database (UCD), 4662
Unicode Standard
    BMP, allocation on, 4665–4666

character sets, 4662–4663
    ISO/IEC 2022 technique, 4662–4663
    MARC 21 and UNIMARC, 4663
    multilingual software applications, prob-
        lems, 4662
    codespace, 4665
    Consortium, 4667
    design principles
        characters vs. glyphs, 4663–4664
        convertibility, 4665
        dynamic composition, 4664–4665
        efficiency, 4663
        logical order, 4664
        plain text, 4664
        semantics, 4664
        stability, 4665
        unification, 4664
        universality, 4663
    goal, 4663
    ISO/IEC 10646, development of, 4663
    and libraries
        MARC 21, 4668–4669
        systems and services, 4669
        UNIMARC, 4669
        Z39.50, 4669
    UAXs, 4662
    UCD, 4662
    The Unicode Standard, 4662
    UTF-16, 4665–4667
    UTF-32, 4665–4667
    UTF-4669, 4665–4667
    versions, 4663
    World Wide Web and XML, 4667–4668
Unicode Standard Annexes (UAXs), 4662
Unified medical language system (UMLS), 979,
    3340, 4672
    Information Sources Map, 4673
    Metathesaurus
        attributes, 4675
        challenges, 4677–4678
        concept identifier, 4674
        concepts and concept names, 4673
        definition, 4673
        genomics vocabularies, 4673
        MetamorphoSys, 4678
        organization of, 4673–4674
        production and distribution, 4676–4677
        relationships, 4674–4676
        semantic type, 4675
        source vocabularies, 4673
        standard clinical terminologies, 4673
        synonymous terms and sources, 4674
    RxNorm, 4678
    semantic network, 4673
        nodes, 4675–4676
        portion of, 4675, 4677
        semantic links, 4675
        semantic types, 4676
    SPECIALIST lexicon, 4673
Uniform Computer Information Transactions
    Act (UCITA)
    concerns
        consumer protection and warranties,
            4684–4685
        copyright and software licenses,
            4681–4684
        First Amendment principles, 4685

forum/choice of law, 4685
    scope, 4681
    unreasonable standard amendment,
        4685–4686
    courts and related legislation, 4686
    history, 4680–4681
Uniform Electronic Legal Material Act
    (UELMA), 2744
Uniform Information Gateway (UIG), 2828
Uniform Resource Identifiers (URIs), 3962
Uniform resource locator (URL), 1365, 2518,
    4049, 5023–5024
    addressing scheme, 2984
    definition, 5025
UNIMARC format, 1733, 4627, 4629
Union Catalog of Greek Academic Libraries,
    1733
Union List of Artist Names® (ULAN), 1080
Unions
    academic unions
        ACRL, 4691, 4694–4697
        ALA, 4691–4692
        collective bargaining agreement, 4691
        faculty unionism, 4691
        human rights, 4692
        Web sites, 4692
    public libraries, 4689–4690, 4692–4694
UNISIST model, 556, 2326, 2408, 4657
United Kibbutz Movement, 2556
United Kingdom, 302, 306, 308
    archives and archival science
        archival profession, 4738
        archive services, 4735–4736
        business archives, 4736–4737
        community archives, 4738
        film and audiovisual archives, 4737
        higher education organizations, 4736
        legislation, 4732–4735
        professional societies and organizations,
            4738–4739
        rare manuscript libraries, 4738
        religious archives, 4737–4738
    broadcasting collections, 1566
    history of, 4699
    libraries and librarianship
        academic libraries, 4703–4705
        children's libraries, 4706–4707
        colleges, 4705
        history of, 4699–4701
        library and information professions,
            4708–4711
        LIS education, training, and research,
            4711–4713
        national libraries, 4701
        public libraries, 4701–4703
        schools, 4705–4706
        special libraries, 4707–4708
    library consortia, 2825
    museums
        armed services, 4718–4719
        botanical gardens, 4724–4725
        English Heritage, 4723
        financial support, 4727
        history of, 4715–4717
        independent, 4721–4722
        local authority, 4719–4721
        national museums, 4717–4718, 4727–4728

National Trust, 4722–4723
profession, 4725–4727
social exclusion, 4727
university, 4718
zoos, 4723–4724
National Museum of Computing, 4381
public library
authorities, populations of, 1839
Chetham Library in Manchester, 1837
combined museums and libraries,
1837–1838
County Library Authority, 1839
CUKT, 1839
gifts of individuals, 1836
itinerating libraries, 1837
Local Government Act of 1972, 1839
Museums Act of 1845, 1837
parish libraries, 1837
public and joint-stock contribution, 1836
Public Library Acts, 1838
social library, 1837
town libraries, 1836–1837
United Kingdom Serials Group (UKSG), 3390
United Nations Convention on the Rights of
Persons with Disabilities, 3575
United Nations Educational, Scientific and Cultural Organization (UNESCO), 1164,
3201, 4500
Action Plan, 4657
audiovisual archives, 4659–4660
CCAAA and SEAPAVAA, 4660
Communication and Information Sector,
4656–4657
Declaration of Principles, 4657
Department of Documentation, Libraries and
Archives, 4657
digital preservation, 4660–4661
documentary heritage program, 4659
goal, 4656
ICOM, 2429, 2431–2432
IDNs, 4659
IFAP, 4657
information accessibility, 4659
information ethics, 4658
information for development, 4658
information literacy, 4658
information portals, 4659
information preservation, 4659
Information Society Division, 4656–4658
infostructures, 4660
international directory database, 4658
Joint Technical Symposia, 4660
libraries, construction/reconstitution of, 4659
Memory of the World Programme,
4660–4661
multilingual cyberspace, 4659
national information policies and laws, formulation of, 4658
RAMP, 4659
site museums and monuments, 4169
strategic actions, 4660
United Nations Millennium Development
Goals, 4656
World Digital Library, 4661
WSIS, 4657
*United States Government Publications Monthly
Catalog*, 649

United States of America
academic libraries and librarians, 4775–4776
advocacy and marketing strategies, 4781
ALA, 4773–4774
American libraries
blogs and blogging, 4780
DRM, 4778–4779
gaming and libraries, 4779
Library 2.0 debates, 4781
network neutrality, 4778
podcasts, 4780
Web 2.0 and Library 2.0, 4779–4780
wikis, 4780–4781
archival repositories (*see* Archival
repositories)
from awareness to funding, 4774–4775
book trade, 3982
communication policy
see Communication policy
digital divide, 1280–1282
early history, 4740–4741
federal electronic information
citizen-centered electronic government,
1549
economics, 1554–1555
EFOIA, 1551
electronic government (e-gov) bills, 1549
FDLP, 1549, 1551, 1557
GILS, 1552
GPO Access Act, 1551
GPO Access system, 1552
High Performance Computing Act of 1991,
1551–1552
media and formats, variation and obsolescence of, 1554
NTIS, 1552
permanent public access, 1556
PRA, 1550–1551
principles, 1557
privacy, security, and authenticity,
1555–1556
safety net, 1555
subject portals, 1552–1553
tangible products, 1549
Title 44 of the U.S. Code, 1550
Web search engines, 1553–1554
information policy (*see* Information policy, in
United States)
librarians and library salaries, 4776–4777
library networks (*see* Regional library
networks)
modern era, 4741–4743
museums
accountability, 4771
affiliate organizations, 4769–4770
collections, stewardship of, 4770–4771
curators, responsibilities of, 4768–4769
definition, 4766
departments, 4769
director's role, 4768
educators, role of, 4769
federal funding, criteria for, 4766–4767
grant support, 4770
history of, 4767–4768
IMLS, leadership roles, 4770
nongovernmental organizations, 4766
professional association, 4769

and publics, relationships between, 4771–
4772
registrars and conservators, responsibilities
of, 4768
social value, 4772
staff positions, 4768
standards, 4769
urban institutions, 4766
professional societies and professionalism,
4743–4745
public libraries
Anthology Reading Room and Library,
1844
Astor Library, 1845
Bingham Library for Youth, 1843
in Boston, 1843–1844
Bray libraries, 1840
Charleston library, 1840
circulating library, 1842
continuing education, 1847–1848
early seventeenth century, 1839
gifts and grants, 1845–1846
Harris's criticism, 1844–1845
in Indiana, 1843
Keayne, Robert, 1839–1840
Library Service Act, 1847
Library Services and Construction Act,
1847
mechanics and apprentices, 1842
mercantile libraries, 1842
New York Public Library, 1845
OCLC, 1847
parish and provincial libraries, 1840
Peterborough library, 1839, 1843
Publick Library, 1840
Public Library Inquiry, 1846
social library, 1840–1842
standards, 1846
system concept, 1846–1847
Tilden Trust, 1845
YMCA Library, 1842–1843
recruitment and diversity, 4777–4778
State of America's Libraries, 4773–4774
Uniterms, 2221
Universal Access to Publications (UAP), 2408
Universal automatic computer, 2066
Universal Availability of Publications (UAP),
2456
Universal Bibliographic Control (UBC), 451,
1229, 1237
Universal Bibliographic Control and International MARC (UBCIM) Programme,
451, 2456–2457
Universal Dataflow and Telecommunications
(UDT), 2456
Universal decimal classification (UDC), 574,
961, 970, 1261, 1373, 1818, 2499, 2669,
4466, 4471, 4475
automation and, 4788–4789
auxiliary tables, 4785–4786
BC2, influence of, 589
citation order, 4787
classification structure, 4784–4785
filing order, 4787
general classification schemes, 4783
history, 4783–4784
main classes, 4787–4788

Universal decimal classification (UDC) (cont'd.)
  notation, 4785
  theoretical basis, 4786
Universal Declaration of Human Rights
    (UDHR), 2395, 4692
Universal Dictionary of Trade and Commerce,
    646
Universal MARC (UNIMARC), 2459
Universal Multi-Octet Coded Character Set
    (UCS), 2984
The Universal Photographic Digital Imaging
    Guidelines, 4943
Universal resource identifier (URI),
    4081–4082
Universal standardization, 3107
Universal Virtual Computer (UVC), 1364,
    1370
Universidad Nacional Mayor de San Marcos
    (UNMSM), 3606, 3608
Universidad Veracruzana Library, 3085
University archives
  archival domains, 4793
  archival holdings, 4793
  archivist's characteristics and professional
      background, 4795
  constituencies, 4795
  core functions, 4794
  definitions, 4791–4792
  emergence and development of, 4791
  environmental variables, 4792
  Hungary, 1925–1926
  nature of, 4793
  programmatic activities of, 4794–4795
  Switzerland, 4491–4492
University College of Addis Ababa (UCAA)
  library, 1498–1499
  museums and galleries, 1501
University Grants Commission (UGC), 1998,
    2007, 2010, 4704
University librarian (UL), 4–5
University libraries, 1498–1499
  in Australia, 384
  in Denmark, 1219
  in France, 1602–1603
  in Germany, 1696
  in Israel, 2544–2545
  Japan, 2562–2564
  in Kazakhstan, 2582–2583
  in Moldova, 3125
  in Peru, 3608
  rare book collections, 3822
  in Saudi Arabia, 3974
  in Ukraine, 4646
  in United Kingdom, 4703–4704
University Library in Bratislava (ULB),
    4177–4178
University Library in Warsaw, 3677
University Library, Leiden, 2798
University library Nikola Tesla, 4131
University Library of Prague, 3323
University Library Svetozar Marković, 4130
University museums
  in Japan, 2573–2574
  in United Kingdom, 4718
University of Belgrade Libraries Association,
    4131
University of Botswana, 1, 2325

University of British Columbia (UBC) Library,
    663–664
University of British Columbia (UBC) Project,
    1414
University of Copenhagen, 1215
University of Crete, 1731–1732
University of Gondar Library, 1499
University of Illinois at Urbana-Champaign
    (UIUC), 3272
University of Kragujevac Svetozar Marković,
    4131
University of Macedonia of Economics and
    Social Sciences, 1731
University of Michigan Community Networking
    Initiative (UM-CNI), 1030
University of Patras, 1732
University of Salamanca, 4321
University of Southern California (USC), 10,
    1641
University of Tasmania (UTAS), 9
University of the South Pacific, 1, 688, 3547
Unstructured information, 2108
Unstructured metadata, 4427
Up-front editorial costs, 3466
Upto-Date, 1878
Uptown, 858–859
Urban and Regional Information Systems Asso-
    ciation (URISA), 1673, 1678
Urban libraries, 1848
Urban Library Council (ULC), 1848, 4781
Usability testing, user interfaces
  vs. beta testing, 4797–4798
  definition, 4797
  materials, 4798–4799
  need, 4797
  outcomes, 4801
  participants, 4799–4800
  post-test activities, 4800–4801
  preparation, 4798
  process, 4798
  session, 4800
Usage, in altmetrics, 44
USA Patriot Act, 369, 2143
U.S. Department of Agriculture (USDA), 1553
U.S. Department of Education (USDE), 18–19
Usenet, 1059
User-agent-specific page delivery, 4035
User-based evaluations, 4554
User-centered design (UCD)
  definition, 4803
  foundations, 4803–4805
  philosophy
    conceptual foundation, 4806–4807
    design, 4805–4806
    information system, 4805
    user, 4806
  principles, 4809
  process
    context of use, 4808
    design evaluation against user require-
        ments, 4809
    human centered process plan, 4808
    potential designs, 4809
    Shneiderman's principles, 4807–4808
    user and organizational requirements,
        4808–4809
  rationale, 4803

  rules, 4809
  scope, 4803
  standards, 4809
  style guides, 4809
  use and value, 4809–4810
User-centered revolution, 4847–4865
  Boolean pitfalls, 4817–4818
  customer service, 4819–4820
  education, 4820–4821
  errors, 4815
  futures planning, 4819
  human-centered design, 4814–4815
  information traits, 4822–4823
  instructions, 4816
  legislation, 4820
  online design, 4815–4816
  reformulations, 4826
  search behavior, 4824–4825
  self-efficacy, 4817
  sense-making research, 4821–4822
  vs. system-centered approaches, 4812–4813
  technology, 4818
  user categories, 4822
  userfriendly features, 4814
User education, 4
User-generated content (UGC), 1508,
    4861–4862
User interfaces
  subsystem, 2195
  usability testing (*see* Usability testing, user
      interfaces)
User-oriented and cognitive information
    retrieval (IR)
  cognitive structures and actors, 4879–4880
  conceptual models, 4873–4874
  domain of, 4873
  generic models
    Ingwersen–Wormell model, 4874
    Wilson's model, 4874–4875
  online interaction–process models,
      4876–4879
  relevance models, 4875–4876
  task-based models, 4880–4883
User-oriented evaluation (UOE), 4820
User sensitization and training issues,
    2335–2337
Use studies, *see* Information behavior research
U.S. Geological Survey (USGS), 1671, 2155
U.S. Government Printing Office (GPO), 1725,
    4896
Usgovsearch, 1553
U.S. ISKO Chapter, 2498
U.S. National Archives and Records Adminis-
    tration (NARA), 111, 3748
U.S. News and World Report, 650
U.S. Patent and Trademark Office (USPTO),
    640, 3562
  AI patents, 3565
  APS, 3563
  assignment database, 3568
  bibliographic data, 3563
  CD-ROM-based patent search tool, 3563
  certificate of correction, 3566
  defensive publication, 3565
  International AIDS Patent Database, 3563
  patent databases, 3568
  Public PAIR, 3563

reexamination certificates, 3566
  Web site, 3568
  WEST and EAST search tools, 3563
U.S. Patent Classification (USPC), 3563,
    3566–3567
USPTO, *see* U.S. Patent and Trademark Office
U.S. Technical Advisory Groups (TAGs), 88
Usury Condemned, 1400
Utah Academic Library Consortium's Internet
    Navigator Tutorial, 3437–3438
Utah Library Association, 2393
Utilitarianism, 4219
Utility theory, 2354–2357
UWired, 4653
UX Day, 1421–1422

V

Vakkari's task-based information search model,
    2245, 4529, 4880
Vallerti Agreement, 3384
Value Set Authority Center (VSAC), 3341
Value structuring, 3062
Valun Tablet, 1121
Vancouver Public Library (VPL), 664, 3793
Vandalism in museums
  history, 4596–4597
    museum responses, 4598
    prevention, 4598–4600
Vanderbilt Television News Archive, 1563,
    1577
Varenius, 1685
Variable Media Network project, 2072
Variable Media Questionnaire tools, 2073
Vatican Library, 2763, 3046, 3951, 3956
Vatican Psalter, 1947
Vatican Virgil, 1946
Vector graphics, 1308
Vector space model (VSM), 2203–2204,
    2689–2690, 2696
Vellum bindings, 542, 545–546
Venezuela
  academic libraries, 4889–4890
  digital libraries and repositories, 4890
  financial issues, 4892–4893
  legal issues, 4894
  librarianship and professional education,
    4891–4892
  public libraries, 4890
  special libraries, 4890
Venice Charter, 1070–1071
Verbal working memory, 3842
Verband Deutscher Zoodirektoren, 5078
Vernadsky National Library of Ukraine, 3326,
    4643, 4645
Veronica tool, 2517
Version control
  copyright, 4897
  open access (OA), 4898
  OpenURL framework, 4899
  peer review, 4898–4899
  Sally Morris versions list, 4897–4898
  self-archiving, 4897, 4899
  Technical Working Group, 4899–4900
Version of record (VoR), 4898, 4900
Very fast decision tree (VDFT), 2635
Very large corpus (VLC) track, 4573–4574

Victorian Electronic Records Strategy (VERS),
    190, 3883
Victoria University of Wellington, 3376
Vidal de la Blache, Paul, 1687
Videoconferencing systems, 1062
Videotape, 1568, 2465
Vienna Dioscorides, 1946
Vienna Genesis, 1947
Vietnamese Women's Museum, 4915
Vietnam Military History Museum, 4915
Vilnius University Library, 2952
Virginia Historical Society (VHS), 1783, 3280
Virginia Institute of Technology, 1414
Virginia Tech Libraries, 4454
Virtual International Authority File (VIAF),
    3288
Virtual interviews, 3915
Virtual library, 1880, 1886, 4454
Virtual Museum of Canada (VMC), 676, 678–679
Virtual Museum of Canada Investment Program,
    679
Virtual museums, 1822
Virtual reference (VR), 17
Virtual reference desk, 3442–3443
Virtual school library, 4005
Virtual volunteerism, 4955
Visitor studies
  audience, 4917
  evaluation, 4918
  free-choice learning, 4918
  goals and objectives of, 4919–4920
  hypothesis-driven (deductive)/emergent
    (inductive) research, 4918
  identity-related motivations, 4923
  informal learning, 4918
  intrinsic motivation, 4922
  leisure-time learning, 4922
  longitudinal studies, 4922–4923
  mixed method research designs, 4921
  museum visitors, 4921
  outcomes, 4922
  profession, 4920
  qualitative research designs, 4921
  quantitative research designs, 4921
  self-determination, 4922
  self-fulfillment, 4922
  theoretical foundations of
    behaviorism, 4918
    constructivism, 4919
    epistemology, 4918
    logic/program modeling process, 4919
    positive youth development, 4919
    socioculturalism, 4919
Visual and performing arts
  archives, 4925
  archiving and managing
    copyright, intellectual property and privacy
      issues, 4930
    documentation, 4929–4930
    ethical issues, 4930
    professional associations, 4930–4931
    understanding of practice, 4929
    understanding the materials, 4929
  film, 4925
  materials
    advertising materials, 4927
    collaboration, 4926

creation process, 4926
creative and technical processes, 4926
dedicated repositories, 4928–4929
digital performances, 4926
examples, 4926
film and broadcasts, 4926
final outcome, 4926
live performances, 4926
local and international relevance, 4927
national repositories, 4927–4928
origin, 4926
painting, 4926–4927
SIBMAS Web site, 4929
theatrical production, 4927
Visual arts
  definition, 4925
  performance art, 4925 (*see also* Visual and
    performing arts)
Visual imagery, 1307
Visualization search engines, 4052–4053
Visual perception, 4408, 4410, 4414
Visual resources, 252
Visual Resources Association (VRA), 252–253,
    255, 3178, 4413
  affiliates, 4938
  annual conference, 4938
  appointments, 4937
  Core, 734
  data standards
    CCO, 4937–4938
    core categories, 4938
  foundation, 4936
  history, 4933–4936
  international membership, 4933
  organizational structure, 4936
  publications and communications, 4937
  regional chapters, 4936–4937
  SEI, 4938
  standing committees, 4937
Visual resources management, cultural
    institutions
  authorities, 4949
  building collections
    archival images, 4943–4944
    best practices, 4942–4943
    content sources, 4941–4942
    landscape, 4942
  cataloging, 4949
  collection access
    cataloging and standards, 4945
    copyright, 4946
    DAMS and DRMS, 4945–4946
    preservation and dispersal, 4944–4945
    rights and reproductions, 4946
    user services, 4944
    virtual organization, 4944
  collections, 4950
  content, 4949
  copyright status assess, 4948
  data standards and guidelines, 4949
  digital formats, 4948
  historic context, 4940–4941
  project reports and white papers, 4948–4949
  software selection, 4950
  staff
    and advocacy, 4949
    competencies, 4946–4947

Visual resources management, cultural
        institutions (cont'd.)
    staff (cont'd.)
        planning and administration, 4947–4948
        professional organizations, 4947
    vocabularies, 4949
Vital records, 1657–1658
Vladimirovas, Levas, 2954
Vocabulary links, 2940
Vocabulary switching, 1984
Voice of Youth Advocates (VOYA), 5062
Voice over Internet Providers (VoIP), 1049,
        1052, 1888, 3443
Volos Municipality archive, 1738
Voluntary product accessibility template
        (VPAT), 3578
Volunteered geographic information, 1673
Volunteerism
    adolescents, 4953–4954
    civic engagement, 4953
    community access, 4954–4955
    institutional advancement, 4952–4953
    Internet, impact of, 4955
    midlife adults, 4954
    museums and related institutions, 4951
        community service, 4952
        docents, 4952
        gallery interpreters, 4952
        historical societies, 4952
        museum professionals, 4953
    older adults, 4954
    orientation, 4951
    resources, 4955–4956
    smile desks, 4951–4952
    studies of, 4953
    volunteer management, 4955
von Mueller, Ferdinand Jakob Heinrich, 392–393
von Richthofen, Baron Ferdinand, 1687
V-optimal histograms, 2630
Vortals, 2893
VOSviewer, 923
Voyage around the world, 1685
VRA Bulletin, 4935, 4937
VRA Listserv, 4937
VRAweb.org, 4937

W

Wagner Act, 4689
Waitangi Tribunal, 2036, 3378
Walk-up kiosk, 4798
The Wanderer, 864, 1500, 2519
Wang–Soergel model, 4875–4876
Waples' graduate courses, 2910
Warez, 3650
Warhol, Andy, 2066
Warhol Museum, 4755
Warranties, 1274–1275
Washington Affairs Office, 52–53
Washington Conference on Scientific Informa-
        tion, 1534
Washington Library Network (WLN), 451
Waterfall software development life cycle,
        3356, 3360
Wathen and Burkell's model of credibility
        assessment, 1117
Watson Davis Award, 95

Watsonline, 250
Watts–Strogatz model, 4239
Wavelet transform, 4418–4419, 4423–4424
Wayfinding
    coordinated program, 4958
    devices, 4964–4965
    expected outcomes, 4965, 4972
    map, 4961–4964
    mental processes, 4958–4959
    physical elements
        content, 4961–4964
        legibility, 4959
        objects, 4961
        positive attributes of, 4959–4960
        spaces, 4960–4961
        structures, 4961
    physical wayfinding, 4958
    professionals, designing, 4961–4963
    and signage program (see Signage)
    thematic, 4958
    visitability, 4958
    visitors, needs of, 4961
W3C, see World Wide Web Consortium
Wealth of Nations, 1402–1403
Web 2.0, 4779, 5020
    designs, 4040
    features, 4780
Web Accessibility Initiative (WAI), 2348
Web Archiving Project (WARP), 2562
Web-based communities (WBCs), 214
Web-based Information Science Education
        (WISE), 707
Web-based recommender systems, 3860–3861
Webcasting, 2155
Web conferencing, 17
Web Content Accessibility Guidelines
        (WCAG), 3578
WebCrawler, 2521
Web credibility, 1115
WebDewey, 1259
Web Impact Factor (WIF), 2372
WebJunction, 3402
Weblogs, 2507
WebMeeting™, 1057
Web of data, 2938–2941
The Web of Science, 474, 489, 923, 925–926
    additional features and services, 948
    bibliographic full record, 946–949
    chemistry literature, 818–819
    cited reference searching, 944–945
    content, 944
    search results and results navigation, 945–946
    source records and searching, 944
Webometrics, 2219, 2226–2227, 2367–2368
    data collection, 4988
    definition, 4983
    evolutionary studies, 4988–4989
    nonacademic link analysis, 4983, 4987
    scholarly communication
        AltaVista, 4986
        journals, 4984
        link creation motiation, 4986
        log analysis of journal usage, 4984–4985
        people, 4985
        small world analysis, 4986
        universities, 4985–4986
        visualization, 4986–4987

search engine evaluation, 4983, 4988
    Web 2.0, 4987–4988
Web ontology language (OWL), 1366,
        3461–3463, 3961, 3965–3966,
        4082–4083, 5028
Web scale discovery services
    challenges, 4981–4982
    content, 4979–4980
    interface, 4980
    OPAC, 4978–4982
    potential development, 4982
    precedents, 4979
    technical infrastructure, 4980–4981
Web Science, 4084
Web science research initiative (WSRI), 4084
Web search engines, see Search engines
    emergemce of, 2240
    search strategies, 2241
    usage patterns, 2242
Weick's sensemaking, 4113
Weighted indexing, 2200
Weizenbaum's ELIZA, 3348
Wendell H. Ford Government Publications
        Reform Act of 1998, 1550
Western European illumination
    Carolingian, 1947–1948
    Hiberno-Saxon, 1947
    Ottonian, 1948
Western knowledge systems (WKS), 2133
Western novels, 3705
Westlaw, 2708, 2713, 2728, 2741–2743, 2748
Westport Public Library Makerspace, 2992
WGBH Media Archives and Preservation Cen-
        ter, 1566
Wharton School of Business, 650
Whipstitching, see Oversewing
White Hat SEO, 4031
White House Conference on Library and Infor-
        mation Services II (WHCLIS), 5054
Who-Knows, 3865
Wicked problems, 1244–1245
Wide area information system (WAIS), 2518
Wide area networks (WANs), 2291, 3356
Widener Library, 4650
Wiener, Norbert, 2049–2050
Wi-Fi, 704
Wikipedia, 277, 3467, 4461, 5029
Wildlife husbandry, 5077
Wilson's information need model, 2116, 2119
Winnipeg Public Library, 3792
Winograd's SHRDLU, 3348
Winsor, Justin, 1844
WIPO, see World Intellectual Property
        Organization
WIPO Copyright Treaty (WCT), 1316
WIPO Performances and Phonographs Treaty
        (WPPT), 1316
Wireless Information System for Emergency
        Responders (WISER®), 3343
Wiswesser line notation, 831
Wollega Museum, 1503
Women's history archives
    Iowa Women's Archives, 4760
    Sallie Bingham Center for Women's History
        and Culture, 4760
    Schlesinger Library, 4759–4760
    Sophia Smith Collection, 4759

Women Writers Project, 1291
Word-by-word alphabetizing, 442
Word-frequency method, 421–422
Wordless picture books, 858–859
WordNet, 3457
Word processor
  definition, 4993
  IBM, 4994
  Macintosh computers, 4997
  microcomputers, 4995
  Microsoft Word, 4996
  MS-DOS, 4995–4996
  MT/ST, 4993–4994
  multipurpose computers, 4994–4995
  predecessors, 4993
  simpler version, 4997
  typesetting, 4997–4998
  WordPerfect, 4996–4997
  WordStar, 4995
Workers' libraries
  in Israel, 2543
  in Vienna, 2804
Working Group on Internet Governance
  (WGIG), 780
Workplace literacy, 2305
Workplace studies, 4026
Works of art, 262, 1090, 4579
World bibliography, 492
World Blind Union (WBU), 5008
WorldCat, 2, 820, 924, 3067
  and FAST, 1545
  Identities, 1546
  OCLC
    bibliographic database, 3394
    collection analysis, 3398
    CONTENTdm collections, 3400
    enrichment and quality control, 3395–3396
    evolution, 3396
    FirstSearch service, 3395
    growth, 3396–3397
    and information standards, 3396
    Navigator, 3398
    Online Union Catalog, 3394
    Open WorldCat pilot program, 3402–3403
    selection, 3398
    statistics, 3395
    web services, 3403
    WorldCat Local, 3403
    WorldCat.org, 3403
WorldCat Collection Analysis service, 1258,
  1262–1263
World Cultures Gallery, 3691, 3694–3695
World Digital Library (WDL), 903, 3332,
  4661
World Economic Survey, 649
World economy, 2260
World Federation of Friends of Museums
  (WFFM), 2432
World Intellectual Property Organization
  (WIPO), 815, 2432, 2452, 3386, 3560,
  3564, 3570, 4514
  Copyright Treaty, 2142
  governance, 5001
  history, 5001
  international copyright norms, 5004–5005
  libraries, archives, and international copy-
    right, 5005

library advocates
  copyright limitations and exceptions,
    5005–5007
  development agenda, 5008–5009
  digital preservation and copyright, 5007
  traditional cultural expression, 5009
membership, 5001
organizational structure
  activity, 5002
  committees, 5002–5003
  decision-making bodies, 5001–5002
  Secretariat, 5003
treaty administration, 1472, 5003–5004
World Library and Information Conference
  (WLIC), 4313
World of Warcraft (WOW), 1050
World Summit on the Information Society
  (WSIS), 780, 3386, 4492, 4517, 4657
  civil society role, 5013–5014
  information society for all, 5017
  issues, 5014
  library and information sector interventions,
    5014–5015
  outcomes, 5015–5016
  process, 5012–5013
  resolution, 5012
  unfinished business, 5016–5017
World Trade Organization (WTO), 783, 1024,
  1722, 2409, 2452, 2475, 3381, 5002,
  5005
World Wide Web (WWW), 298, 1034, 1059,
  1061, 1290, 2367, 2372, 2505, 2516,
  2518, 2524, 2892, 2938–2939, 3075,
  3995, 4054, 4084, 4468
  digital image, 1308
  information behavior research, 2078–2079
  libraries, 5026–5027
  social and cultural effects, 5028–5029
  technological impact, 5028
  worm, 2519–2520
World Wide Web Consortium (W3C),
  1366–1367, 1393, 3060, 3072, 3076,
  3578, 4082–4083, 5020, 5026
  achievements, 2348
  activities, 2348, 5036–5037
  historical highlights, 5035–5036
  membership, 5036
  Modern Paradigm for Standards, 5026
  MWI, 2348
  nonproprietary standards, 2347
  recommendation, 5037
  Unicode Standard, 4667–4668
  vision, 5034
  Web, 5035
  Web interoperability, 2347
  WWW, 2348
  XML Schema, 1387–1388
Wove paper, 1828–1830
Writing; *see also* Technical writing
  children books, 334, 867–868
  communication, 1188
  electronic technology, 3985
  emergence, 3832–3833
Writing studies programs, 4548, 4552
Writing surfaces, 1824, 1826, 2717, 3552
Wunderkammern, 1524, 3150
Würzburg library, 1697

X

Xenocrates of Aphrodisias, 3043
XML, *see* Extensible Markup Language
XML information retrieval
  INEX, 5039
  query languages
    clause-based queries, 5041–5042
    content-only queries, 5040
    IEEE test collection, INEX, 5040
    path-based queries, 5041
    tag-based queries, 5040
  ranking strategies
    aggregation, 5045
    merging, 5045–5046
    overlaps removal, 5047
    propagation, 5045
    scoring, 5044–5045
    structural constraints, 5046–5047
  representation strategies, 5042–5043
XPath query, 1365, 5041
XQuery Full-Text, 5042, 5048
X-ray radiography, 4429
XSLT, *see* Extensible stylesheet language
  transformations

Y

Yad Vashem Archives, 2555–2556
Yad Vashem Museum, 2552
Yahoo!, 2368, 2520–2521, 4048, 4051
YALSA, *see* Young Adult Library Services
  Association
Yamaguchi City Library, 2563–2564
Yandex search engine, 4051
YBP Library Services, 342, 413, 1210
Year-round schooling, 4002
Yerevan Centralized Children's Library System,
  230
Yerevan State University Library, 230, 232–233
Young Adult Library Services Association
  (YALSA), 334, 3998, 5052–5059
Young adult (YA) services
  AASL, 5058
  adolescent development
    physical growth, 5059–5061
    social characteristics, 5059
  advisory groups, 5061
  Caleb Bingham's gift, 5058
  definitions, 5059
  group programs, 5062
  issues
    censorship, 5062–5063
    preference, 5064
    reference queries, 5063–5064
    technology usage, 5064
    YA congregate, 5063
  personal reading, 5061–5062
  public *vs.* school library services, 5058
  specific information-seeking, 5062
  staff, 5061
  Teen Read Week, 5058
  theoretical foundations, 5059
  YALSA, 5052–5054, 5058
Young Adult Services Division (YASD),
  5052–5054
Young Men's Christian Association (YMCA)
  Library, 1842–1843

...ce, 3653
...mation
...information behavior studies, 843
needs, 5067–5069
research and practice, 5073–5074
seeking behaviors
reference services, 5073
resource preferences, 5071–5072
searching for information, 5072–5073
YouTube, 3227, 3654, 3862, 4551, 5064
Yo! Yes? (art), 858
Yugoslav Film Archives, 4133

Z

Zagreb Diocese Metropolitan Library, 1122
Zambia Library Services, 3324
Załuski Library, 3675
Zaytūnah's al-Abdalīyah Library, 4625
Zentralblatt MATH (Zbl) tool, 3644
Zephir system, 1760
Zephyr, 1733
Z39.50 Implementors Group (ZIG),
    2183–2184

Zincographic printing process, 1868
Z39.50 information retrieval protocols
bibliographic information, 2895
chronology, 2183–2184
client and server software, 2184
Init service, 2184–2185
present service, 2185–2186
search service, 2185
ZING project, 2186–2187
Z39.50 International Next Generation (ZING)
    project, 2186–2187, 2347
Zipf, George Kingsley, 502, 506
Zipf's law, 502, 506, 514–516, 2210, 2371
Zoologica (publications), 5078
Zoological parks and aquariums
archives, 5083
libraries
current status and services, 5081–5083
early libraries, establishment of, 5081
need for, 5080–5081
professional development
animal collections, 5077
captive wildlife management, 5077
European collections, 5077–5078

exotic wild animals, 5078
modern aquariums, 5078
modern zoological park management, 5077
professional associations, 5078
public aquarium, 5078
professional literature, growth in, 5078–5080
Zoological research, 1705
Zoological Society of London, 4723, 5077, 5081
Zoology, 575, 1534, 4723
Zoos
Hungary, 1930
in Kazakhstan, 2588–2589
in museums, 3238
OPLs, 3416
Switzerland, 4495
in United Kingdom, 4723–4724
and botanical gardens
Germany, 1706
India, 2023–2025
Switzerland, 4495
Zoosemiotics, 4096
Zthes specifications, 2671, 4074
The Z Was Zapped: A Play in Twenty-Six Acts,
    859–860